W9-BIO-512

Webster's Dictionary Library

# Webster's Dictionary Library

## Seven Complete Dictionaries in One Volume

Webster's Dictionary
Webster's Synonyms, Antonyms, and Homonyms
Dictionary of Scientific Terms
Bible Dictionary
Legal Dictionary
Medical Dictionary
Crossword Puzzle Dictionary

BELL PUBLISHING COMPANY
New York

Printed in U.S.A.

This edition is published by Bell Publishing Company, distributed by Crown Publishers, Inc., by arrangement with Ottenheimer Publishers, Inc.
d e f g h
BELL 1980 EDITION

**Library of Congress Cataloging in Publication Data**
Main entry under title:

Webster's dictionary library.

CONTENTS: Webster's dictionary.—Webster's synonyms, antonyms, and homonyms.—Dictionary of scientific terms.—Bible dictionary. [etc.]
1. English language—Dictionaries.
PE1628.W5562 1980 423 80-17929
ISBN 0-517-32169-6

# CONTENTS

Webster's Dictionary Library

# Webster's Dictionary

# Webster's Dictionary

Edited by

John Gage Allee, Ph.D.
Professor of English Philology,
The George Washington University

1978 Edition

## KEY TO THIS DICTIONARY

The entries in this Dictionary are arranged in groups, derived and related words being placed under the main entry.

A. Each main entry, in bold-faced type, is syllabized. The part of speech, in italics, follows; then the definition.

Ex.: **cross** *a.* intersecting; interchanged. . . .

B. Sub-entries are shown in bold-faced type following the definition of the main entry.

1. If a hyphen precedes the sub-entry, the ending is added to the main entry.

   Ex.: **-ing** (crossing)

2. If a dash precedes the sub-entry, a hyphenated word is indicated.

   Ex.: **—examination** (cross-examination)

3. If a dash and a space precede the sub-entry, this indicates words that are commonly found together.

   Ex.: **— reference** (cross reference)

4. If the sub-entry is spelled out, this may indicate differences from the main entry. (In some instances, sub-entries are spelled out where confusion may otherwise develop).

Note: Irregularities of verb forms, plurals and comparisons are included as sub-entries to facilitate word usage.

# ABBREVIATIONS USED IN THIS DICTIONARY

*a.* adjective
*abbrev.* abbreviation
*ablat.* ablative; ablatival
*Aborig.* Aboriginal
*acc.* accusative
*A.D.* Anno Domini
(in the year of Our Lord)
*adv.* adverb
*Aero.* Aeronautics
*Afr.* Africa; African
*Agric.* Agriculture
*Alg.* Algebra
*alt.* alternative
*Amer.* America; American
*Anat.* Anatomy
*Anglo-Ind.* Anglo-Indian
*Anthropol.* Anthropology
*Ar.* Arabic
*Arch.* Archaic
*Archaeol.* Archaeology
*Archit.* Architecture
*Arith.* Arithmetic
*Astrol.* Astrology
*Astron.* Astronomy
*aux.* auxiliary
*Aviat.* Aviation

*Bacter.* Bacteriology
*B.C.* before Christ
*Bib.* Biblical
*Biol.* Biology
*Bot.* Botany
*Br., Brit.* British
*Braz.* Brazilian
*Bret.* Breton
*Build.* Building

*c.* about (L. = *Circa*)
*C.* Centigrade; Central
*Can.* Canada; Canadian
*Cap.* capital letter
*Carib.* Caribbean
*Carp.* Carpentry
*Celt.* Celtic
*cent.* century
*Cent.* Central
*cf.* compare (L. = *confer*)
*ch.* Chapter
*Chem.* Chemistry
*Chin.* Chinese
*Class. Myth.* Classical Mythology
*Colloq.* Colloquial; Colloquialism
*Comm.* Commerce; Commercial

*comp.* comparative
*conj.* conjunction
*conn.* connected
*contr.* contraction
*corrupt.* corruption

*Dan.* Danish
*dat.* dative
*def. art.* definite article
*demons.* demonstrative
*der.* derivation; derived
*Dial.* Dialect; Dialectal
*Dict.* Dictionary
*dim.* diminutive
*Dut.* Dutch
*Dyn.* Dynamics

*E.* East; English
*Eccl.* Ecclesiastical
*e.g.* for example (L. = *exemplia gratia*)
*E.Ind.* East Indian
*Elect.* Electricity
*Embryol.* Embryology
*Engin.* Engineering
*Entom.* Entomology
*esp.* especially
*Ethnol.* Ethnology
*etym.* etymology

*F., Fahr.* Fahrenheit
*fem.* feminine
*fig.* figuratively
*Finn.* Finnish
*Flem.* Flemish
*Fort.* Fortification
*fr.* from
*Fr.* French
*freq.* frequentative

*Gael.* Gaelic
*gen.* genitive
*Geog.* Geography
*Geol.* Geology
*Geom.* Geometry
*Ger.* German
*Gk.* Greek
*Gk. Myth.* Greek Mythology
*Gram.* Grammar

*Heb.* Hebrew
*Her.* Heraldry
*Hind.* Hindustani
*Hist.* History
*Hort.* Horticulture
*Hung.* Hungarian

*i.* intransitive
*Ice.* Icelandic
*i.e.* that is (L. = *id est*)
*imit.* imitation; imitative
*imper.* imperative
*impers.* impersonal
*Ind.* Indian
*indef. art.* indefinite article
*indic.* indicative
*infin.* infinitive
*interj.* interjection
*interrog.* interrogative
*Ir.* Irish
*It.* Italian

*Jap.* Japanese

*L.* Latin
*l.c.* lower case letter
*L.Ger.* Low German
*lit.* literally
*Lit.* Literature
*L.L.* Low (Late) Latin

*masc.* masculine
*Math.* Mathematics
*M.E.* Middle English
*Mech.* Mechanics
*Med.* Medicine
*Metal.* Metallurgy
*Meteor.* Meteorology
*Mex.* Mexican
*M.H.Ger.* Middle High German
*Mil.* Military
*Min.* Mineralogy
*Mod.* Modern
*Mus.* Music
*Myth.* Mythology

*n.* noun
*N.* North; Norse
*Nat.Hist.* Natural History
*Naut.* Nautical
*neg.* negative
*neut.* neuter
*nom.* nominative
*Norw.* Norwegian
*n.pl.* noun plural
*n.sing.* noun singular
*N.T.* New Testament

*obj.* object; objective
*obs.* obsolete
*O.E.* Old English
*O.Fr.* Old French
*O.H.Ger.* Old High German
*O.L.Ger.* Old Low German
*O.N.* Old Norse
*Onomat.* Onomatopoeic
*opp.* opposite; opposed
*Opt.* Optics
*orig.* originally
*Ornith.* Ornithology
*O.T.* Old Testament

*Paint.* Painting
*pa.p.* past participle
*pass.* passive
*pa.t.* past tense
*Path.* Pathology
*perh.* perhaps
*pers.* person
*Pers.* Persian
*pert.* pertaining
*Peruv.* Peruvian
*Pharm.* Pharmacy
*Philol.* Philology
*Philos.* Philosophy
*Phon.* Phonetics
*Photog.* Photography
*Phys.* Physics
*Physiol.* Physiology
*pl.* plural
*Poet.* Poetry; poetical
*Pol.* Polish
*Port.* Portuguese
*poss.* possessive
*pref.* prefix
*prep.* preposition
*pres.* present
*Print.* Printing
*prob.* probably
*pron.* pronoun
*Pros.* Prosody
*Prov.* Provincial
*pr.p.* present participle
*Psych.* psychology

*q.v.* which see (L. = *quod vide*)

*R.* River
*R.C.* Roman Catholic
*recip.* reciprocal
*redup.* reduplication
*ref.* reference; referring
*refl.* reflexive
*rel* related; relative
*Rhet.* Rhetoric
*Rom.* Roman
*Rom.Myth.* Roman Mythology
*Russ.* Russian

*S.* South
*S.Afr.* South African
*S.Amer.* South American

*Sans.* Sanskrit
*Scand.* Scandinavian
*Scot.* Scots; Scottish
*Sculp.* Sculpture
*sing.* singular
*Singh.* Singhalese
*Slav.* Slavonic
*Sp.* Spanish
*St.* Saint
*superl.* superlative
*Surg.* Surgery
*Sw.* Swedish
*Syn.* Synonym

*t.* transitive
*Teleg.* Telegraphy
*Teut.* Teutonic
*Theat.* Theatre
*Theol.* Theology
*Trig.* Trigonometry
*Turk.* Turkish

*U.S.(A.)* United States (of America)
*usu.* usually

*v.* verb
*var.* variant; variation
*v.i.* verb intransitive
*v.t.* verb transitive
*vulg.* vulgar

*W.* Welsh; West

*Yid.* Yiddish

*Zool.* Zoology

**a** *indef. art.* meaning *one.*
**aard•vark** *n.* animal resembling the anteater, found in parts of Africa.

**A.B.** Bachelor of Arts.
**ab-** *pref.* meaning from, away, off.
**ab•a•ca** *n.* Manila hemp, or the plant producing it.
**a•back** *adv.* backwards; *(Naut.)* against the masts, of sails pressed back by the wind.
**ab•a•cus** *n.* an instrument with parallel wires on which arithmetical calculations are made with sliding balls or beads; *(Archit.)* a tablet crowning a column and its capital.
**a•baft** *adv.* and *prep. (Naut.)* at or towards the stern; behind.
**ab•a•lo•ne** *n.* the name of several species of limpet-like mollusks or "earshells," yielding mother-of-pearl.
**a•ban•don** *v.t.* to give up wholly and finally; *n.* careless freedom. **-ed** *a.* deserted; unrestrained; given up entirely to, esp. wickedness. **-edly** *adv.* **-ment** *n.* the act of abandoning, or state of being abandoned.
**a•base** *v.t.* to bring low; to cast down; to humble.
**a•bash** *v.t.* to strike with shame or fear.
**a•bate** *v.t.* to beat down, lessen; *v.i.* to decrease, subside, decline.
**ab•at•toir** *n.* a slaughterhouse.
**ab•ba•cy** *n.* the office or dignity of an abbot; the building under the control of an abbot; an abbey. **abbey** *n.* a church establishment forming the dwelling-place of a community of monks or nuns. **abbot** *(fem.* **abbess)** *n.* the head of an abbey or monastery.
**ab•bre•vi•ate** *v.t.* to shorten, reduce by contraction or omission. **abbreviation** *n.* the act of abbreviating; a shortened form. **abbreviator** *n.* **abbreviatory** *a.*
**ab•di•cate** *v.t.* and *v.i.* formally to give up power or office. **abdication** *n.*
**ab•do•men** *n.* the lower part of the trunk of the body; the belly.
**ab•duct** *v.t.* to take away by fraud or force; to kidnap. **-ion** *n.*
**a•beam** *adv. (Naut.)* at right angles to a ship's length.
**a•bed** *adv.* in bed.
**a•bele** *n.* the white poplar tree.
**ab•er•rate** *v.i.* to deviate from the right path or normal course. **aberrant** *a.* deviating from the normal. **aberration** *n.*
**a•bet** *v.t.* to encourage or aid, esp. in doing wrong.
**a•bey•ance** *n.* a state of suspension or temporary inactivity; the condition of not being in use or action.
**ab•hor** *v.t.* to hate extremely. **-rent** *a.* detestable; abominable; repugnant. **-rer** *n.*
**a•bide** *v.i.* to stay; reside; continue firm or stable; *v.t.* to tolerate; bear. **abidance** *n.* **abiding** *a.*
**a•bil•i•ty** *n.* quality, state, or condition of being able.
**ab•i•o•gen•e•sis** *n. (Biol.)* the theory of spontaneous generation from nonliving matter.
**ab•ject** *a.* base; degraded; mean and worthless; contemptible; miserable. **-ly** *adv.* **-ion, -ness** *n.* degradation; abasement; servility.
**ab•jure** *v.t.* to renounce upon oath. **abjuration** *n.*
**ab•la•tive** *a.* (used as *n.*) the sixth case of Latin nouns and pronouns expressing *time when.*
**ab•laut** *n. (Philol.)* variation of root vowel in certain related words, as *sink, sank, sunk.*
**a•blaze** *a.* on fire; aglow; gleaming.
**a•ble** *a.* having skill, strength to perform a task; competent; talented; vigorous. **ability** *n.* being able. **-ness** *n.* **ably** *adv.*
**a•bloom** *adv.* or *a.* in bloom.
**ab•lu•tion** *n.* cleansing or washing; (usually plural) the purification of the body or of sacred vessels before certain religious ceremonies, e.g., Eucharist; the wine and water used. **-ary** *a.*
**ab•ne•gate** *v.t.* to deny; surrender; relinquish. **abnegation** *n.*
**ab•nor•mal** *a.* contrary to rule or system; deviating from a recognized standard. Also **-ity, -ism** *n.* the state of being abnormal. **-ly** *adv.*
**a•board** *adv.* and *prep. (Naut.)* on board; within a vessel; on a train.
**a•bode** *n.* residence, a dwelling place.
**a•bol•ish** *v.t.* to do away with; to repeal; to obliterate. **-ment** *n.*
**ab•o•li•tion** *n.* the act of abolishing, as of laws, taxes, etc. **-al** *a.* **-ist, -ism** *n.*
**A-bomb** *n.* atomic bomb.
**a•bom•i•nate** *v.t.* to loathe; detest extremely; abhor. **abominable** *a.* **abominableness** *n.* **abominably** *adv.* **abomination** *n.* the act or object of loathing.
**ab•o•rig•i•nes** *n.pl.* the original inhabitants of a country. **aboriginal** *a.*
**a•bort** *v.i.* to miscarry in giving birth. **-ifacient** *a.* capable of producing abortion. **-ion** *n.* **-ionist** *n.* **-ive** *a.* prematurely produced; undeveloped; imperfect; rudimentary. **-ively** *adv.*
**a•bound** *v.i.* to be in great plenty (used with preps. *with* and *in*). **-ing** *a.* plentiful.
**a•bout** *adv.* and *prep.* on every side; concerning; approximately; (before an infin.) on the point of.
**a•bove** *adv.* and *prep.* and *a.* higher than; more in number, quantity or degree.
**ab•ra•ca•dab•ra** *n.* corruption of sacred Gnostic term, derived from ancient Egyptian magical formula; a catchword; gibberish.
**a•brade** *v.t.* to rub or wear off; to scrape or grate off; to graze (as of skin). **abradant** *n.* a substance, e.g. emery powder, for polishing. **abrasion** *n.* **abrasive** *a.*
**ab•re•ac•tion** *n.* in psychoanalysis, elimination of a morbid complex by expression through conscious association with the original cause. **abreact** *v.t.*

**a•breast** *adv.* side by side; on a line with.

**a•bridge** *v.t.* to shorten; curtail; reduce; diminish; epitomize. **-ment** *n.*

**a•broad** *adv.* and *a.* at large, over a wide space; overseas.

**ab•ro•gate** *v.t.* to annul; repeal (a law); do away with; put an end to; cancel. **abrogation** *n.*

**a•brupt** *a.* broken off; steep; precipitous; curt; unceremonious; brusque. **-ly** *adv.* **-ness** *n.*

**ab•scess** *n.* gathering of pus in any infected organ or tissue of the body.

**ab•scind** *v.t.* to cut off; pare away; separate; rend apart.

**ab•scond** *v.i.* to take oneself off; to flee from justice. **-ence, -er** *n.*

**ab•sence** *n.* being absent. **absent** *a.* not present; inattentive. **absent** *v.t.* to withdraw (oneself); deliberately to fail to appear. **absentee** *n.* one who is not present. **absently** *adv.* casually; forgetfully.

**ab•sinthe, ab•sinth** *n.* a green-colored liqueur flavored with wormwood and other aromatics.

**ab•so•lute** *a.* unconditional; without restraint; *(Gram.)* not dependent; pure. **-ly** *adv.* positively; very; entirely. **-ness** *n.* **absolution** *n.* a remission of sin after confession, pronounced by the R. C. Church; formal acquittal by a judge. **absolutism** *n.* unrestricted and unlimited rule; arbitrary government. **absolutist** *n.* **absolutory, absolvatory** *a.*

**ab•solve** *v.t.* to set free from an obligation, guilt, debt, penalty; to pardon; acquit. **-r** *n.*

**ab•sorb** *v.t.* to swallow up; drink in; soak up; to engage one's whole attention. **-ability** *n.* **-able, -ing** *a.* **-ent** *a.* absorbing; *n.* anything which absorbs. **-ency** *n.*

**ab•sorp•tion** *n.* the act of absorbing. **absorptive** *a.* able to absorb.

**ab•stain** *v.i.* to forbear; to refrain. **-er** *n.*

**ab•ste•mi•ous** *a.* showing moderation in the use of food and drink. **-ly** *adv.* **-ness** *n.*

**ab•sten•tion** *n.* the act of abstaining or refraining from. **-ist** *n.*

**ab•sti•nence** *n.* voluntary forbearance from using or doing something. Also **abstinency. abstinent** *a.* temperate; refraining from. **abstinently** *adv.*

**ab•stract** *v.t.* to separate from; remove, summarize; reduce. **-ed** *a.* **-edly** *adv.* *a.* not concrete, theoretical. *n.* that which comprises in itself the essential qualities of a larger thing, or of several things; a summary. **-ion** *n.* abstracting or separating; a theoretical idea.

**ab•struse** *a.* hidden; difficult or hard to be understood. **-ly** *adv.* **-ness** *n.*

**ab•surd** *a.* contrary to reason; ridiculous; silly. **-ly** *adv.* **-ity** *n.*

**a•bun•dance** *n.* ample sufficiency; great plenty. **abundant** *a.* **abundantly** *adv.*

**a•buse** *v.t.* to make a wrong use of; to ill-treat; to violate; revile; malign; *n.* ill-usage; improper treatment; a corrupt practice; rude language. **abusive** *a.* **abusiveness** *n.*

**a•but** *v.i.* to end; to touch with one end; to border on; to adjoin. **-ting** *pr.p.* **-ted** *pa.p.* **-ment** *n.* *(Archit.)* the support at end of an arch or bridge.

**a•byss** *n.* any deep chasm; a gulf. **abysmal** *a.* bottomless; vast; profound. **abysmally** *adv.* **-al** *a.* inhabiting, or characteristic of, the depths of the ocean.

**a•ca•cia** *n.* thorny, leguminous tree or shrub, yielding gum arabic.

**a•cad•e•my** *n.* a place of education or specialized training; a society of men united for the promotion of the arts and sciences. **academic, academical** *a.* **academician** *n.* a member of an academy or society for promoting the arts and sciences.

**a•can•thus** *n.* a prickly plant, also called "bear's breech" or "brank-ursine."

**a•cat•a•lec•tic** *a.* not stopping short; complete in syllables; *n.* a verse that has the complete number of syllables.

**a•cat•a•lep•sy** *n.* incomprehensibility; **acatalepsia** *n.* **acataleptic** *a.*

**a•cat•a•pha•si•a** *n.* difficulty or inability in expressing ideas logically.

**ac•cede** *v.i.* to agree; assent; consent; to arrive at a certain state or condition; to succeed as heir. **-r** *n.*

**ac•cel•er•ate** *v.t.* and *v.i.* to cause to move faster; to become swifter. **acceleration** *n.* **accelerative** *a.* **accelerator** *n.* **acceleratory** *a.*

**ac•cent** *n.* stress on a syllable or syllables of a word; a mark to show this; inflection of the voice; manner of speech. *v.t.* to utter, pronounce, or mark with accent; to emphasize; to stress. **-ual** *a.* **-uate** *v.t.* to accent; to stress; to make more prominent. **-uation** *n.*

**ac•cept** *v.t.* to take; receive; admit; believe; to agree to. **-able** *a.* welcome; pleasing; agreeable. **-ably** *adv.* **-ability, -ance** *n.* **-ation** *n.* the usual meaning of a word, statement, etc. **-ed** *a.* **-er, -or** *n.*

**ac•cess** *n.* a coming to the means or way of approach; admission; entrance; attack; fit. **-ible** *a.* **-ibility** *n.* **-ion** *n.* increase; a coming to, esp. to a throne, office, or dignity. **-ory, -ary** *a.* aiding; contributing; additional; *n.* an additional, secondary piece of equipment.

**ac•ci•dence** *n.* the part of grammar dealing with changes in the form of words, e.g. plurals, etc.

**ac•ci•dent** *n.* chance; a mishap; a casualty; contingency; a quality not essential. **-al** *a.* **-ally** *adv.*

**ac•claim** *v.t.* and *v.i.* to receive with applause, etc.; cheer; to hail as; **acclamation** *n.* general applause. **acclamatory** *a.*

**ac•cli•ma•tize** *v.t.* to accustom to a new climate. Also **acclimate. acclimatization** *n.* Also **acclimatation, acclimation** *n.*

**ac•cliv•i•ty** *n.* an upward slope.

**ac•co•lade** *n.* a ceremony used in conferring knighthood, consisting now of a tap given on the shoulder; award, praise.

**ac•com•mo•date** *v.t.* to render fit or suitable; adapt; adjust; reconcile;

provide room for. **accommodating** *a.* **accommodation** *n.* (usually pl.) a loan of money; convenience; room or space for; lodgings. **accommodative** *a.*

**ac•com•pa•ny** *v.t.* to go with. **accompaniment** *n.* that which goes with; *(Mus.)* the instrumental parts played with a vocal or other instrumental part. **accompanist** *n.*

**ac•com•plice** *n.* a companion in evil deeds; an associate in crime.

**ac•com•plish** *v.t.* to carry out; to finish; to complete; to perform. **-ed** *a.* complete; perfect; having accomplishments; hence, talented. **-ment** *n.* completion; finish; that which makes for culture, elegant manners, etc.

**ac•cord** *n.* agreement; harmony; *v.t.* to grant; settle; compose; *v.i.* to agree; to agree in pitch and tone. **-ance** *n.* **-ant** *a.* corresponding. **-ing** *a.* in accordance; agreeing; suitable. **-ingly** *adv.*

**ac•cor•di•on** *n.* wind instrument fitted with bellows and button keyboards.

**ac•cost** *v.t.* to speak first to; to address; to approach.

**ac•count** *n.* a reckoning; a record; a report; a statement of debts and credits in money transactions; *v.t.* to reckon, judge; *v.i.* to give a reason; to give a financial reckoning. **-able** *a.* **-ably** *adv.* **-ability** *n.* **-ancy** *n.* the profession of an accountant. **-ant** *n.* **-ing** *n.* or *a.*

**ac•cou•tre** *v.t.* to furnish with dress or equipment, esp. military; to equip. **-ments** *n.pl.* dress; military dress and equipment.

**ac•cred•it** *v.t.* to give trust or confidence to; to vouch for; to recommend; to furnish with credentials, as an envoy or ambassador. **-ed** *a.* **-ation** *n.*

**ac•crete** *v.i.* to grow together; *v.t.* to add by growth. **accretion** *n.* **accretive** *a.*

**ac•crue** *v.i.* to increase; to result naturally; to come as an addition, e.g. interest, profit, etc. **accrual** *n.*

**ac•cu•mu•late** *v.t.* to heap up; to collect; *v.i.* to grow into a mass; to increase. **accumulation** *n.* **accumulative** *a.* **accumulatively** *adv.* **accumulator** *n.*

**ac•cu•rate** *a.* correct. **-ly** *adv.* **-ness** *n.*

**ac•curse** *v.t.* to doom to destruction; to curse. **-d** *a.* under a curse. **-dness** *n.*

**ac•cuse** *v.t.* to charge with a crime or fault; to blame. **-d** *a.* *n.* one so charged. **-r** *n.* **accusation** *n.* **accusative, accusatory** *a.*

**ac•cus•tom** *v.t.* to make familiar by use; to familiarize; to habituate. **-ed** *a.*

**ace** *n.* a card with only one spot; a single point; the best, highest; an outstanding fighter pilot.

**ac•er•bate** *v.t.* to make bitter; to exasperate; *a.* embittered; severe; exasperated. **acerbity** *n.* sourness of taste, with bitterness and astringency; hence bitterness, or severity in persons.

**a•ce•tic** *a.* pert. to acetic acid, the acid in vinegar. **acetate** *n.* *(Chem.)* a salt formed by acetic acid; also a rayon material. **acetify** *v.t.* and *v.i.* to turn into vinegar. **acetification** *n.* **acetous** *a.* sour.

**a•cet•y•lene** *n.* a highly inflammable gas used as an illuminant.

**ache** *n.* a continuous dull, heavy pain; *v.i.* to be in pain. **aching** *a.* and *n.*

**a•chieve** *v.t.* to bring to a successful end; to accomplish. **achievable** *a.* **-ment** *n.* performing; a performance; an exploit; a feat. **-r,** *n.*

**ach•ro•ma•si•a** *n.* *(Med.)* absence of color. **achromate** *a.*

**ach•ro•ma•tic** *a.* *(Opt.)* free from color. **-ity, achromatism** *n.* **achromatize** *v.t.* **achromatous** *a.*

**ac•id** *a.* sour; sharp to the taste; having the taste of vinegar; *n.* a sour substance; *(Chem.)* a substance which contains hydrogen replaceable by a metal. **-ify** *v.t.* and *v.i.* **-ity** *n.* **-ulate** *v.t.* to make slightly acid or sour; *(Fig.)* to embitter. **-ulated, -ulous** *a.*

**ac•knowl•edge** *v.t.* to admit as true; to give a receipt for; to give thanks for; to reward. **acknowledgment** *n.*

**ac•me** *n.* the highest point, the top; perfection.

**ac•ne** *n.* a skin disease characterized by hard, reddish pimples often appearing as blackheads.

**ac•o•lyte** *n.* a candidate for priesthood in the R. C. Church; a lesser church officer; an assistant; a novice.

**ac•o•nite** *n.* *(Bot.)* wolfsbane or monkshood.

**a•corn** *n.* the seed or fruit of the oak.

**a•cous•tic** *a.* pert. to the sense of hearing. **acoustics** *n.pl.* the science of sounds; the estimation of audibility in a theater, etc.

**ac•quaint** *v.t.* to make fully known or familiar; to inform. **-ance** *n.* familiar knowledge; a person known slightly. **-anceship** *n.* **-ed** *a.*

**ac•qui•esce** *v.i.* to agree in silence; to assent without objection. **-nce** *n.* **-nt** *a.*

**ac•quire** *v.t.* to gain; to obtain; to get. **acquirable** *a.* **-ment** *n.* **acquisition** *n.* the act of acquiring; the thing acquired. **acquisitive** *a.* grasping; greedy for gain. **acquisitiveness** *n.*

**ac•quit** *v.t.* to set free; release; declare innocent; to conduct oneself; to discharge a debt. *pr.p.* **-ting,** *pa.p.* and *pa.t.* **-ted. -tal, -tance** *n.*

**a•cre** *n.* a measure of land containing 4840 square yards. **-age** *n.*

**ac•rid** *a.* bitter; sharp; pungent; harsh; ill-tempered. **-ly** *adv.* **-ness, -ity** *n.*

**ac•ri•mo•ny** *n.* bitterness of temper or of language. **acrimonious** *a.* **acrimoniously** *adv.*

**ac•ro•bat** *n.* one skilled in gymnastic feats; a ropedancer; a tumbler. **-ic** *a.* **-ics** *n.pl.* skill of an acrobat.

**ac•ro•nym** *n.* a word formed from initials, e.g., *radar.*

**ac•ro•pho•bi•a** *n.* a morbid fear of heights.

**a•crop•o•lis** *n.* the fortified summit of a Greek city; a citadel, esp. the citadel of Athens.

**a•cross** *adv.* and *prep.* from side to side; transversely; athwart.

**a•cros•tic** *n.* a composition in verse, in which the first, and sometimes last, letters of the lines read in order form a name, a sentence, or title.

**act** *v.t.* to perform, esp. upon stage; to behave as; *v.i.* to exert energy; to fulfil a function; to operate. *n.* deed; performance; actuality; action; a decreee, law, edict, or judgment; principal division of a play. **-ing** *a.* **-or** *n.* one who performs. **-ress** *n.* a female actor.

**ac•tin•i•a** *n.* the sea anemone. *pl.* **actiniae.**

**ac•tin•ism** *n.* the radiation of light or heat; the property possessed by the sun's ray, of producing chemical changes, as in photography. **actinic, actiniform** *a.*

**ac•tin•i•um** *n.* a radioactive element.

**ac•ti•nol•o•gy** *n.* that branch of science concerned with chemical action of light.

**ac•ti•no•ther•a•py** *n.* the treatment of disease by natural or artificial light rays; often known as "sunlight treatment."

**ac•tion** *n.* a thing done; behavior; physical movement; function; a battle; the development of events in a play, etc.; legal proceedings; *(Chem.)* effect. **-able** *a.* affording grounds for legal proceedings. **-ably** *adv.*

**ac•ti•vate** *v.t.* to make active. **activation** *n.*

**ac•tive** *a.* having the power to act; agile; busy; alert. **-ly** *adv.* vigorously. **activism** *n.* policy of those who, by energetic action, seek to fulfill the promises of a political program. **activist, activity, -ness** *n.*

**ac•tu•al** *a.* existing now or as a fact; real; effectual. **-ize** *v.t.* to make real in fact or by vivid description. **-ist** *n.* a realist. **-ity** *n.* reality, existence. **-ly** *adv.*

**ac•tu•a•ry** *n.* registrar or clerk. **actuarial** *a.* **actuarially** *adv.*

**ac•tu•ate** *v.t.* to put into action; incite; motivate; influence. **actuation, actuator** *n.*

**a•cu•men** *n.* quickness of perception or discernment; sharpness; penetration. **acuminous** *a.*

**a•cute** *a.* sharp; pointed; sagacious; subtle; penetrating. **-ly** *adv.* **-ness** *n.*

**A.D.** in the year of our Lord.

**ad•age** *n.* saying or maxim that has obtained credit by long use; a proverb; a byword. **adagial** *a.*

**ad•a•mant** *n.* a stone of impenetrable hardness; the diamond; *a.* very hard; unyielding. **-ine** *a.*

**Ad•am's ap•ple** *n.* projection of cartilege at the front of one's throat.

**a•dapt** *v.t.* to make fit or suitable; to make to correspond. **-ability, -ableness** *n.* **-able** *a.* **-ation** *n.* **-er** *n.* any appliance which makes possible a union of two different parts of an apparatus. **-ive** *a.* **-ively** *adv.* **-iveness, -or** *n.*

**add** *v.t.* to join, unite to form one sum or whole; to annex; to increase; to say further. **-able, -ible** *a.* **-er** *n.* a machine which adds; a comptometer. **-ibility, -ition** *n.* **-itional** *a.* supplementary; extra. **-itionally** *adv.* **-itive** *a.*

**ad•dend** *n.* number to be added.

**ad•den•dum** *n.* a thing to be added; an appendix; *pl.* **addenda.**

**ad•der** *n.*a venomous serpent.

**ad•dict** *v.t.* to apply habitually; habituate; *n.* one addicted to evil habit, e.g. drug-taking. **-ed** *a.* **-ion** *n.*

**ad•dle** *v.t.* to corrupt; putrify; confuse; to make addled. **addle, addled** *a.*

**ad•dress** *v.t.* to direct in writing, as a letter; to apply (oneself); to make a speech; to present a congratulatory message or petition; accost; *n.* a formal speech; manner of speaking; direction of a letter; skill. **-es** *n.pl.* attentions in courtship. **-ee** *n.* person to whom a communication is sent. **-er** *n.*

**ad•duce** *v.t.* to bring forward as proof; to cite; to quote. **-nt** *a.* **-r** *n.* **adducible** *a.* **adduction** *n.* **adductive** *a.* **adductor** *n.* adducent muscle.

**ad•en (o)** a combining form. **-itis** *n.* inflammation of the lymphatic glands. **-oid, -oidal** *a.* glandular; gland-shaped. **-oids** *n.pl.* a swelling of tissue between nose and throat.

**ad•ept** *n.* one skilled in any art; an expert; *a.* well-skilled; expert.

**ad•e•quate** *a.* equal to; sufficient. **adequacy.** **-ness** *n.* **-ly** *adv.*

**ad•here** *v.i.* to stick fast; to be devoted to; to hold to (an opionion). **-nce** *n.* **-nt** *a.* and *n.* supporter of person or cause. **adhesion** *n.* act of adhering. **adhesive** *a.* sticky; tenacious; *n.* an agent which sticks things together. **adhesively** *adv.* **adhesiveness** *n.*

**ad•hib•it** *v.t.* to use or apply; to attach.

**a•dieu** *interj.* good-bye; farewell; *n.* a farewell; a leave-taking. *pl.* **adieus, adieux.**

**ad•i•pose** *a.* pert. to animal fat; fatty. **adiposity** *n.* fatness **adipic** *a.*

**ad•it** *n.* horizontal or inclined entrance into a mine.

**ad•ja•cent** *a.* lying close to; adjoining, bordering on. **-ly** *adv.* **adjacency** *n.*

**ad•jec•tive** *n.* a word used with a noun to qualify, limit, or define it; *a.* pert. to an adjective. **adjectival** *a.* **adjectivally** *adv.*

**ad•join** *v.t.* to join or unite to; to be next or contiguous to; *v.i.* to be next to. **-ing** *a.*

**ad•journ** *v.t.* to put off to another day; to postpone. **-ment** *n.*

**ad•judge** *v.t.* to settle judicially; to pronounce judgment. **adjudgment** *n.* **adjudicate.** *v.t.* to settle judicially; *v.i.* to pronounce judgment. **adjudication** *n.* **adjudicator** *n.* a judge.

**ad•junct** *n.* something joined to another thing, but not essential to it; *a.* added to; united with. **-ive, -ively** *adv.*

**ad•jure** *v.t.* to charge or bind, under oath; to entreat earnestly. **adjuration** *n.* a solemn command on oath; an earnest appeal. **adjuratory** *a.*

**ad•just** *v.t.* to adapt; to put in working order; to accommodate. **-able** *a.* **-ment, -er, -or** *n.*

**ad•ju•tant** *n.* an assistant; staff officer who helps the commanding officer issue orders. **adjutancy** *n.*

**ad•min•is•ter** *v.t.* to manage public affairs or an estate; to dispense, as justice or relief; to give, as medicine; to apply, as punishment or reproof; *v.i.* to give aid (to). **administrable** *a.* **administrant** *a.* executive; *n.* one who administers. **administration** *n.* the executive part of a government. dispensation; direction. **administrative** *a.* **administrator** *n.* (*fem.* **administratrix**) one who directs; executes affairs of any kind.

**administrator** *n.* (*fem.* **administratrix**) one who directs; executes affairs of any kind.

**ad•mi•ral** *n.* a naval officer of the highest rank. **-ty** *n.*

**ad•mi•ral** *n.* a species of butterfly, esp. the red admiral.

**ad•mire** *v.t.* to regard with wonder and approval, esteem, or affection; to prize highly; *v.i.* to wonder; to marvel. **-r** *n.* **admiring** *a.* **admiringly** *adv.* **admirable** *a.* excellent; praiseworthy. **admirably** *adv.* **admiration** *n.*

**ad•mis•si•ble** *a.* allowable. **admissibly** *adv.* **admissibility** *n.* **admission** *n.* permission to enter; the price paid for this.

**ad•mit** *v.t.* to grant entrance; to concede as true; to acknowledge. *pr.p.* **-ting.** *pa.p.* and *pa.t.* **-ted. -tance** *n.* permission to enter.

**ad•mix** *v.t.* to mingle with something else. **-ture** *n.*

**ad•mon•ish** *v.t.* to reprove gently; to instruct or direct. **-er** *n.* **admonition** *n.* rebuke. **admonitory** *a.*

**a•do** *n.* fuss; bustle; trouble.

**a•do•be** *n.* sun-dried brick.

**ad•o•les•cence** *n.* stage between childhood and manhood; youth. **adolescent** *a.* and *n.*

**a•dopt** *v.t.* to receive the child of another and treat it as one's own; to select and accept as one's own, e.g. a view. **-er** *n.* **-able** *a.* **-ion** *n.* **-ive** *a.*

**a•dore** *v.t.* to worship; to love deeply; **-r** *n.* **adorable** *a.* **adorably** *adv.* **adorableness, adoration** *n.*

**a•dorn** *v.t.* to decorate; to deck or ornament; to set off to advantage. **-ing** *a.* **-ment** *n.*

**ad•re•nal** *n.* a small, ductless gland situated close to upper end of each kidney (same as *suprarenal*). **-in** *n.* the hormone of the adrenal glands.

**a•drift** *adv.* and *a.* floating at random; at mercy of the wind and tide.

**a•droit** *a.* dexterous; skillful; ingenious; adept. **-ly** *adv.* **-ness** *n.*

**ad•sorb** *v.t.* said of solids, to condense and hold a gas on the surface. **adsorption** *n.*

**ad•u•late** *v.t.* to praise or flatter in a servile manner; to fawn; to cringe. **adulation, adulator** *n.* **adulatory** *a.*

**a•dult** *a.* grown to maturity, or to full size and strength; appropriate for a grown-up; *n.* a grown-up person. **-ness, -hood** *n.*

**a•dul•ter•ate** *v.t.* to debase by addition of inferior materials; to vitiate; to corrupt. *a.* debased; guilty of adultery. **adulteration** *n.*

**a•dul•ter•y** *n.* violation of the marriage vows. **adulterer** *n.* (*fem.* **adulteress**). **adulterous** *a.* **adulterously** *adv.*

**ad•um•brate** *v.t.* to shadow forth; to give faint outline of; to forecast; to typify. **adumbral** *a.* shady. **adumbrant, adumbrative** *a.* **adumbration** *n.*

**ad•vance** *v.t.* to bring or push forward; to raise in status, price, or value; to propose as a claim; to supply beforehand, esp. money; *v.i.* to go forward; to improve; to rise in rank, etc. *a.* before the time. *n.* a forward movement; gradual approach; a paying out of money before due; an increase in price; expansion of knowledge. **-d** *a.* **-ment, -r** *n.*

**ad•van•tage** *n.* any state or means favorable to some desired end; *v.t.* to benefit, to promote the interests of; to profit. **-able** *a.* able to be turned to advantage. **-ous** *a.* **-ously** *adv.*

**ad•vent** *n.* arrival; approach; the anticipated coming of Christ; **-ual** *adv.*

**ad•ven•ti•tious** *a.* accidental; out of the proper place; extraneous. **-ly** *adv.*

**ad•ven•ture** *n.* risk; bold undertaking; chance; *v.t.* to risk. *v.i.* to venture; to dare. **-r** *n.* (*fem.* **adventuress**). **-some** *a.* **-someness** *n.* **adventurous** *a.* **adventurously** *adv.*

**ad•verb** *n.* a word used to modify a verb, adjective, or other adverb. **-ial** *a.* **-ially** *adv.*

**ad•ver•sar•y** *n.* an opponent.

**ad•ver•sa•tive** *a.* expressing opposition; not favorable.

**ad•verse** *a.* contrary; opposite in position; unfortunate; opposed. **-ly** *adv.* **-ness, adversity** *n.*

**ad•vert** *v.i.* to turn the mind or attention to. **-ence, -ency** *n.*

**ad•ver•tise** *v.t.* and *v.i.* to give public notice of. **-ment, -r** *n.* **advertising** *n.* and *a.*

**ad•vice** *n.* opinion offered as to what one should do; counsel.

**ad•vise** *v.t.* to give advice to; to counsel; to give information to; to consult (with). *v.i.* to deliberate. **advisability, advisableness** *n.* expediency. **advisable** *a.* prudent; expedient. **advisably** *adv.* **-d** *a.* judicious. **-dly** *adv.* purposely. **-r** or **advisor** *n.* **advisory** *a.*

**ad•vo•cate** *n.* a vocal supporter of any cause; *v.t.* to recommend; to maintain by argument. **advocacy, advocator** *n.*

**adz, adze** *n.* a carpenter's tool for chipping.

adze

**ae•gis** *n.* orginally the shield of Jupiter; (*Fig.*) protection.

**ae•on, eon** *n.* an infinitely long period of time; an age.

**aer•ate** *v.t.* to charge with carbon dioxide or other gas; to supply with air. **aeration, aerator** *n.*

**aer•i•al** *a.* pert. to, consisting of, air; *n.* and *a.* (*Radio and Television*) an insulated wire or wires, generally elevated above the ground and connected to a transmitting or receiving set. **-ly** *adv.*

**aer•i•al•ist** *n.* high-wire acrobat.

**a•e•rie, a•e•ry** *n.* the nest of a bird of prey, esp. of the eagle.

**aer•o•dy•nam•ics** *n.pl.* the science that treats of gases in motion.

**aer•o•lite** *n.* a meteorite; a meteoric stone. Also **aerolith, aerolithic** *a.* **aerology** *n.* the science which treats of the air and its phenomena.

**aer•om•e•ter** *n.* an instrument for measuring the weight or density of air and other gases. **aerometry** *n.* this science.

**aer•o•naut** *n.* a balloonist. **-ic** *a.* **-ics** *n.* the science of flight.

**aer•o•sol** *n.* a smoke, suspension of insoluble particles in a gas.

**aer•o•stat** *n.* a generic term for all lighter-than-air flying machines. **-ics** *n.* the science that treats of the equilibrium of gases, or of the buoyancy of bodies sustained in them.

**aes•thet•ics** *n.* the laws and principles determining the beautiful in nature, art, taste, etc. **aesthetic, aesthetical** *a.* **aesthetically** *adv.* **aesthete** *n.* a lover of the beautiful. **aestheticism** *n.*

**a•far** *adv.* from, at, or to a distance.

**af•fa•ble** *a.* ready to converse; easy to speak to; courteous; friendly. **affably** *adv.* **affability** *n.*

**af•fair** *n.* what is to be done; a business or matter; a concern; a thing.

**af•fect** *v.t.* to act upon; to produce a change in; to put on a pretense of; to influence. **-ed** *a.* inclined or disposed; not natural. **-edly** *adv.* **-edness** *n.* **-ing** *a.* moving; pathetic. **-ingly** *adv.* **-ation** *n.* a striving after artificial appearance or manners. **-ive** *a.* **-ively** *adv.*

**af•fec•tion** *n.* disposition of mind; goodwill; tender attachment; disease. **-ate** *a.* loving. **-ately** *adv.*

**af•fer•ent** *a.* conveying to, esp. of nerves carrying sensations to the centers.

**af•fi•ance** *n.* plighted faith; bethrothal; the marriage contract; reliance; confidence; *v.t.* to betroth.

**af•fi•da•vit** *n.* *(Law)* a written statement of evidence on oath.

**af•fil•i•ate** *v.t.* to adopt as a son; to receive into fellowship; to unite a society, firm, or political party with another, but without loss of identity. **affiliation** *n.*

**af•fin•i•ty** *n.* relationship by marriage; close agreement. **affined, affinitive** *a.*

**af•firm** *v.t.* to assert positively; to confirm; to aver; **-able** *a.* **-ably** *adv.* **-ance, -ant, -er** *n.* **-ative** *a.* ratifying; *n.* positive. **-atively** *adv.*

**af•fix** *v.t.* to fasten to; to attach; to append to. *n.* addition to either end of word to modify meaning or use.

**af•fla•tus** *n.* inspiration; impelling inner force.

**af•flict** *v.t.* to give continued pain to; to cause distress or grief to. **-ed, -ing** *a.* **-ingly** *adv.* **-ion** *n.* **-ive** *a.* **-ively** *adv.*

**af•flu•ence** *n.* abundance, esp. riches. **affluent** *a.* wealthy; flowing to; *n.* tributary of river. **affluently** *adv.* **afflux, affluxion** *n.*

**af•ford** *v.t.* to yield, supply, or produce; to be able to bear expense.

**af•for•est** *v.t.* to plant trees on a big scale. **-ation** *n.*

**af•fran•chise** *v.t.* to enfranchise; to free from slavery; to liberate. **-ment** *n.*

**af•fray** *n.* a noisy quarrel or fight in public; *v.t.* to frighten; to startle.

**af•fright, af•fright•en** *v.t.* to impress with sudden and lively fear.

**af•front** *v.t.* to confront; to meet face to face; to insult one to the face; to abash. **-ed** *a.*

**a•field** *adv.* to or in the field; abroad; off the beaten track.

**a•fire** *adv.* and *a.* on fire.

**a•flame** *adv.* and *a.* flaming; on fire.

**a•float** *adv.* and *a.* borne on the water.

**a•flut•ter** *a.* fluttering.

**a•foot** *adv.* on foot; astir.

**a•fore** *adv.* and *prep.* before.

**a•foul** *adv.* in collision, in a tangle.

**a•fraid** *a.* filled with fear; frightened.

**a•fresh** *adv.* anew; over again.

**aft** *adv.* or *a.* *(Naut.)* toward, or at, the stem.

**af•ter** *prep.* behind; later; in pursuit of; in imitation of; according to; *adv.* behind; *a.* in the rear; succeeding. **-ward (s)** *adv.* later; subsequently.

**a•gain** *adv.* another time; once more; in return; moreover.

**a•gainst** *prep.* in contact with; opposite to; in opposition to; in preparation for.

**a•gape** *a.* or *adv.* open-mouthed, as in wonder, expectation, etc.; gaping.

**ag•ate** *n.* a precious stone, composed of layers of quartz of different colors.

**age** *n.* the length of time a person or thing has existed; a period of time; periods of history; maturity; *v.t.* to cause to grow old; *v.i.* to grow old; *pr.p.* **aging. -d** *a.* of the age of **-dness** *n.* **-less** *a.*

**a•gen•cy** *n.* instrumentality; a mode of exerting power.

**a•gen•da** *n.* literally, things to be done; the items of business to be discussed at a meeting.

**a•gent** *n.* a person or thing that exerts power or has the power to act; one entrusted with the business of another.

**ag•glom•er•ate** *v.t.* and *v.i.* to collect into a mass; *a.* heaped up; *n.* *(Geol.)* a mass of compacted volcanic debris. **agglomeration** *n.* **agglomerative** *a.*

**ag•glu•ti•nate** *v.t.* to unite with glue; *a.* united, as with glue. **agglutination** *n.* **agglutinative** *a.*

**ag•gran•dize** *v.t.* to make greater in size, power, rank, wealth, etc.; to promote; to increase; to exalt. **-ment** *n.*

**ag•gra•vate** *v.t.* to make more grave, worse. **aggravating** *a.* making worse; provoking. **aggravatingly** *adv.* **aggravation** *n.*

**ag•gre•gate** *v.t.* to collect into a total; to accumulate into a heap; *n.* a sum or assemblage of particulars; the sum total; *a.* collected together. **aggrevation** *n.* **aggregative** *a.*

**ag•gress** *v.i.* to attack; to start a quarrel. **-ion** *n.* a first act of hostility; an unprovoked attack. **-ive** *a.* **-ively** *adv.* **-iveness, -or** *n.*

**ag•grieve** *v.t.* to give pain or sorrow to; to bear heavily upon; to vex; to afflict. **-d** *a.*

**a•ghast** *a.* struck with amazement, horror, terror.

**ag•ile** *a.* having the power of quick motion;

nimble. **-ly** *adv.* **-ness, agility** *n.*

**ag•i•tate** *v.t.* to throw into violent motion; to stir up; *v.i.* to cause a disturbance. **-dly** *adv.* **agitation** *n.* **agitator** *n.*

**a•gleam** *adv.* and *a.* gleaming.

**a•glow** *adv.* and *a.* glowing.

**ag•nate** *n.* any male relation on the father's side. *a.* related on the father's side; akin; allied. **agnatic** *a.* **agnation** *n.*

**ag•no•men** *n.* an additional name.

**ag•nos•tic** *n.* one who believes that God, life hereafter, etc., can neither be proved nor disproved. **-ism** *n.*

**a•go, a•gone** *adv.* and *a.* past; gone; in time past.

**a•gog** *a.* and *adv.* eagerly excited.

**a•gon•ic** *a.* not forming an angle.

**ag•o•ny** *n.* extreme physical or mental pain. **agonize** *v.t.* to distress with great pain; to torture. *v.i.* to writhe in torment. **agonizing** *a.* **agonizingly** *adv.*

**ag•o•ra** *n.* forum, public square, or market of ancient Greek towns. **-phobia** *n.* fear of open spaces.

**a•gou•ti** *n.* a genus of rodents or gnawing animals, natives of S. America.

**a•grar•i•an** *a.* relating to lands, their management and distribution; *n.* one who favors an equal division of property. **-ize** *v.t.* **-ism** *n.*

**a•gree** *v.i.* to be of one mind; to acquiesce; to resemble; *(Gram.)* to correspond in gender, case, or number. **-ing** *pr.p.* **-d** *pa.p.* **-able** *a.* consenting; favorable; suitable; pleasant; congenial. **-ably** *adv.* **-ableness, -ment** *n.*

**ag•ri•cul•ture** *n.* the science and practice of the cultivation of the soil. **agricultural** *a.* **agriculturist** or **agriculturalist** *n.*

**a•gron•o•my** *n.* rural economy; husbandry. **agronomial, agronomic, agronomical** *a.* **agronomics** *n.pl.* the science of management of farms. **agronomist** *n.*

**a•ground** *adv.* and *a.* on the ground; stranded; run ashore; beached.

**a•gue** *n.* *(Med.)* intermittent malarial fever. **-d, aguish** *a.*

**a•head** *adv.* farther forward; in advance; in front; head foremost.

**aid** *v.t.* and *v.i.* to help; to relieve. *n.* help; assistance; the person or thing which aids; auxiliary; assistant. **aide** *n.*

**ai•guille** *n.* *(Geol.)* a sharp, slender rock; a drill for boring rock. **-tte, -t** *n.* the tag of a shoelace.

**ail** *v.t.* to trouble; disturb; to pain; afflict. *v.i.* to feel pain; to be ill. **-ing** *a.* **-ment** *n.* illness.

**ai•le•ron** *n.* adjustable flaps near the tips of the wings of an airplane.

**aim** *v.t.* to point at; to direct; to endeavor after; to intend; *n.* direction; end; purpose; intention. **-less** *a.* **-lessly** *adv.* **-lessness** *n.*

**air** *n.* the atmosphere; a gas; a light breeze; a tune; manner, bearing of a person; carriage; appearance; mien. *v.t.* to expose to air or heat, for drying or warming; to parade before the public. **-s** *n.pl.* an affected manner. **-ing** *n.* a ride or walk in the open air. **-y** *a.* of air; exposed to the air; lighthearted. **-ily** *adv.* gaily; merrily; lightly. **-iness** *n.* openness to the air; gaiety. **—condition** *v.t.* to provide a building, etc. with air through a filtering apparatus. **— conditioning** *n.* **-craft** *n.* all kinds of machines for flying. **-drome** *n.* an airport. **-field** *n.* tract of land, used for accommodation and maintenance of aircraft. **-foil** *n.* any surface wing, etc. to help in lifting or controlling an aircraft. **-plane** *n.* a heavier-than-air aircraft. **-port** *n.* a terminal station for passenger airplanes. **air sacs** *n.pl.* air cells in the bodies of birds. **-ship** *n.* lighter-than-air machine, developed from balloon. **-sick** *adj.* ill from air travel. **-strip** *n.* concrete runway on an airfield. **-tight** *a.* admitting no air. **-way** *n.* a prepared route for travel by airplane.

**aire•dale** *n.* a kind of large terrier, with a close, wiry coat of tan and black.

**aisle** *n.* the wing of a building; any lateral division of a church; the passageways between rows.

**aitch•bone** *n.* the rump bone of an ox; the cut of beef surrounding it.

**a•jar** *adv.* partly open, as a door.

**a•kim•bo** *adv.* with a crook; bent.

**a•kin** *a.* related by blood; allied by nature; having the same properties.

**al•a•bas•ter** *n.* gypsum; a semitransparent kind of soft marble-like mineral; *a.* made of, or white as, alabaster. **alabastrine** *a.*

**a•lac•ri•ty** *n.* cheerful readiness; eagerness; briskness.

**a•lar** *a.* winglike; pert. to wings; having wings.

**a•larm** *n.* sound giving notice of danger; a mechanical contrivance to rouse from sleep; *v.t.* to fill with apprehension; to call to arms. **-ingly** *adv.* **-ist** *n.* one given to exciting alarm, esp. needlessly.

**a•las** *interj.* an exclamation of sorrow, pity, etc.

**a•late** *a.* having wings; winged. Also **-d** *a.*

**alb** *n.* a vestment of white linen, reaching to the feet, worn by R.C. clergy.

**al•ba•core** *n.* tunny fish.

**al•ba•tross** *n.* a large web-footed seabird commonest in the South Seas.

**al•be•it** *conj.* although; even though.

**al•bi•no** *n.* a person, or animal, with an abnormal whiteness of the skin and hair, and a pink color in the eyes. **albinism** *n.*

**al•bum** *n.* a book for autographs, photographs, stamps, etc.; a book of selections.

**al•bu•men** *n.* white of egg; a similar substance found in the tissues of animals and plants. **albumin** *n.* any of a class of proteins, necessary for growth in the body. **albuminoid** *n.* **albuminous** *a.*

**al•bur•num** *n.* sapwood, part of tree under bark and outside heart up which sap rises.

**al•che•my** *n.* the forerunner of modern chemistry. Its chief aims were *(a)* transmuting the baser metals into gold, and *(b)* discovery of an elixir of life. **alchemic** *a.* **alchemist** *n.*

**al•co•hol** *n.* pure spirit; a liquid of strong pungent taste, the intoxicating element in fermented or distilled liquor. **-ism** *n.*

a morbid condition caused by overindulgence in alcoholic liquor. **-ic** *a.* *n.* one addicted to the immoderate use of alcohol.

**al•cove** *n.* a recess in a room.

**al•de•hyde** *n.* a liquid produced by the oxidation of alcohol.

**al•der** *n.* a tree of birch family, growing in marshy soil.

**al•der•man** *n.* a civic dignitary.

**ale** *n.* liquor made from malt by fermentation.

**a•lem•bic** *n.* a vessel of glass or metal formerly used in distillation.

**a•lert** *a.* watchful; vigilant; brisk; nimble; active; *n.* a signal by sirens of air attack; period of air raid. **-ly** *adv.* **-ness** *n.*

**al•ex•an•drine** *n.* a verse of six iambic feet.

**a•lex•i•a** *n.* inability to understand written language.

**al•fal•fa** *n.* plant of the pea family.

**al•fres•co** *a.* and *adv.* in the fresh air.

**al•ga** *n.* *(Bot.)* one of the **algae** *pl.* plants found in seawater, and in slow-moving fresh or stagnant water. **algal, algoid, algous** *a.* **algology** *n.* scientific study of marine plants.

**al•ge•bra** *n.* a branch of mathematics. **-ic(al)** *a.* **-ically** *adv.* **-ist** *n.*

**al•gid** *a.* cold. **-ity, -ness** *n.* **algific** *a.*

**a•li•as** *adv.* otherwise; *n.* an assumed name.

**al•i•bi** *n.* *(Law)* a plea that the prisoner was elsewhere when the crime was committed; excuse.

**al•ien** *a.* of another country; foreign; different in nature; estranged; *n.* a non-naturalized foreigner. **-able** *a.* **-ability** *n.* **-ate** *v.t.* **-ation, -ator** *n.* **-ism** *n.* study of mental diseases. **-ist** *n.*

**a•lif•er•ous** *a.* having wings.

**a•light** *adv.* or *a.* on fire; illuminated.

**a•light** *v.i.* to dismount; to finish one's journey; to fall; to descend.

**a•lign** *v.t.* to adjust by a line; to line up; to range; *v.i.* to form in a line; to fall in, as troops. Also **aline, -ment** *n.*

**a•like** *a.* having likeness; similar; *adv.* similarly; equally.

**al•i•ment** *n.* nourishment; nutriment; *(Law)* provision for maintenance. *v.t.* to maintain. **-al** *a.* **-ally** *adv.* **-ary** *a.* **-ation** *n.* the process of introducing nutriment into the body.

**al•i•mo•ny** *n.* means of living, esp. an allowance made to a wife out of her husband's income.

**al•i•quant** *a.* (of a number) not dividing without remainder.

**al•i•quot** *a.* dividing exactly, or without remainder.

**a•live** *a.* having life; existent; active; alert.

**al•ka•li** *n.* one of a class of chemical compounds which combine with acids to form salts. **alkalify, -ze** *v.t.* and *v.i.* to become alkaline; *pa.p.* **-fied. -fiable** *a.* **-metry** *n.* the quantitative estimation of the strength of alkalis. **-ne** *a.* **-nity** *n.* **alkaloid** *n.* nitrogenous organic compound; *a.* resembling an alkali in properties.

**all** *a.* the whole of; every one of; *n.* whole amount; whole duration of; *adv.* wholly; entirely.

**al•lay** *v.t.* to lighten; to make quiet; to lessen grief or pain. **-er, -ment** *n.*

**al•le•ga•tion** *n.* affirmation; that which is positively asserted. **allege** *v.t.* to bring forward with positiveness; to plea, or excuse; to declare; affirm; cite. **allegeable** *a.* **allegedly** *adv.*

**al•le•giance** *n.* the duty of a subject to his government or superior; loyalty; an oath of homage. **allegiant** *a.* loyal; *n.* one who owes allegiance.

**al•le•go•ry** *n.* a narrative in which abstract ideas are personified; a description to convey a different meaning from that which is expressed; a continued metaphor. **allegoric (-al)** *a.* **allegorically** *adv.* **allegorist** *n.*

**al•le•lu•iah** *n.* song of praise to the Almighty.

**al•ler•gy** *n.* hypersensitivity to particular substances; susceptibility to ill effects from eating some foods. **allergen** *n.* a substance which induces allergy. **allergic** *a.*

**al•le•vi•ate** *v.t.* to make light; to lighten; to ease; to afford relief; to mitigate. **alleviation** *n.* **alleviative** *a.* **alleviator** *n.*

**al•ley** *n.* a narrow passage between buildings; a garden path.

**al•li•ance** *n.* persons, parties, or states allied together for a common purpose.

**al•li•ga•tor** *n.* a reptile distinguished from crocodile by a broad flat head, depressed muzzle and unequal teeth.

**alligator**

**al•lit•er•ate** *v.i.* to begin each word with the same letter or sound. **alliteration** *n.* **alliterative** *adj.*

**al•lo•cate** *v.t.* to distribute; to assign to each his share; to place. **allocation** *n.*

**al•lo•cu•tion** *n.* a formal address, esp. of the Pope to his clergy.

**al•lot** *v.t.* to divide by lot; to distribute as shares. **-ting** *pr.p.* **-ted** *pa.p.* and *pa.t.* **-ment** *n.* what is allotted; distribution; a share.

**al•lot•ro•py** *n.* property of some chemical substances of being found in two or more different forms. **allotropic** *a.* **allotropism** *n.*

**al•low** *v.t.* to acknowledge; to permit; to give; to set apart; *v.i.* to provide. **-able** *a.* **-ance** *n.* **-edly** *adv.*

**al•loy** *v.t.* to melt together two or more metals; to reduce the purity of a metal by mixing with a less valuable one; to debase; *n.* any mixture of metals.

**all•spice** *n.* a spice.
**al•lude** *v.i.* to refer indirectly to; to hint at; to suggest.
**al•lure** *v.t.* to tempt by a lure, offer, or promise. **-ment** *n.* **alluring** *a.* **alluringly** *adv.*
**al•lu•sion** *n.* a passing or indirect reference; a hint; a suggestion. **allusive** *a.* referring to indirectly; symbolical. **allusively** *adv.*
**al•lu•vi•on** *n.* land formed by washed-up earth and sand. **alluvium** *n.* waterborne matter deposited on low-lying lands.
**al•ly** *v.t.* to join by treaty, marriage, or friendship; *pr.p.* **-ing;** *pa.p.* and *pa.t.* **allied. ally** *n.* a person, family country, etc., bound to another, esp. of nations in wartime; a partner.
**al•ma•nac** *n.* a calendar of days, weeks and months, to which astronomical and other information is added.
**al•might•y** *a.* all-powerful; omnipotent. **almightiness** *n.*
**al•mond** *n.* the kernel of the nut of the almond tree.
**al•mon•er** *n.* one who distributes alms or bounty. **almonry** *n.*
**al•most** *adv.* very nearly; all but.
**alms** *n.* gift offered to relieve the poor; a charitable donation.
**al•oe** *n.* a bitter plant used in medicine; a purgative drug, made from the juice of several species of aloe.

**aloe**

**a•loft** *adv.* on high; *(Naut.)* on the yards or rigging.
**a•lone** *a.* solitary; single; *adv.* by oneself; singly.
**a•long** *adv.* in a line with; throughout the length of; lengthwise; onward; in the company of (followed by *with*); *prep.* by the side of. **-side** *adv.* by the side of.
**a•loof** *a.* reserved in manner, almost unsociable; *adv.* at a distance; apart. **-ness** *n.*
**al•o•pe•cia** *n.* disease causing loss of hair.
**a•loud** *adv.* with a loud voice or noise; loudly; audibly.
**alp** *n.* a high mountain; mountain pastureland. **Alps** *n.pl.* the mountains of Switzerland. **alpine** *a.* pert. to the Alps; *n.* a plant that grows on high ground. **-inist** *n.*
**al•pac•a** *n.* a sheeplike animal of Peru; a thin kind of cloth made of the wool of the alpaca.
**al•pen•horn, alp•horn** *n.* a long wooden horn curving towards a wide mouthpiece, used by Swiss herds.
**alpenstock** *n.* a long, stout staff, shod with iron, used by mountaineers.
**al•pha** *n.* the first letter of Greek alphabet.
**al•pha•bet** *n.* letters of a language arranged in order; first principles. **-ic, -ical** *a.* **-ically** *adv.* **-ize** *v.*
**al•read•y** *adv.* before this; even now; even then; previously to the time specified.
**al•so** *adv.* and *conj.* in like manner; likewise; further.
**al•tar** *n.* a table or raised structure in a place of worship.
**al•ter** *v.t.* to change; *v.i.* to become different. **-ably** *a* **-ability** *n.* **-ation** *n.*
**al•ter•cate** *v.i.* to contend in words; to wrangle. **altercation** *n.* a dispute.
**al•ter•nate** *a.* occurring by turns; one following the other in succession. **-ly** *adv.* **alternate** *v.t.* to cause to follow by turns; *v.i.* to happen by turns. **alternation** *n.* **alternative** *a.* offering a choice of two things; *n.* a choice of two things. **alternatively** *adv.* **alternator** *n.* *(Elect.)* a dynamo for producing alternating current.
**al•though** *conj.* admitting that; notwithstanding that.
**al•tim•e•ter** *n.* an instrument for taking altitudes; in aviation, barometer to show height.
**al•ti•tude** *n.* height; perpendicular elevation above a given level.
**al•to** *n.* *(Mus.)* part sung by lowest female voice.
**al•to•geth•er** *adv.* wholly, entirely, quite; on the whole.
**al•tru•ism** *n.* the principle of living for the good of others (opp. to *egoism*). **altruist** *n.* **altruistic** *a.* unselfish. **altruistically** *adv.*
**al•um** *n.* a double sulfate of alumina and potash.
**a•lu•mi•num** *n.* a whitish metal produced largely from bauxite; it is strong, light, malleable. **alumina, alumine** *n.* an oxide of aluminum; the clay, loam, etc., from which alum is obtained. **aluminate** *v.t.* to impregnate with alum. **aluminic** *a.* **aluminiferous** *a.* containing alum or alumina. **aluminite** *n.* a sulfate of alumina.
**al•ve•o•lar** *a.* pert. to or resembling the sockets of the teeth. **alveolate** *a.* pitted; honeycombed. **alveolus** *n.*
**al•ways** *adv.* at all times; perpetually; invariably; regularly.
**a•lys•sum** *n.* a species of rock plant.
**am** the *first person sing. pres. indic.* of the verb **to be.**
**a. m.** before noon.
**a•mal•gam** *n.* a compound of mercury with another metal; a mixture of different substances. **-ate** *v.t.* to mix a metal with quicksilver; to compound; to consolidate; to combine (esp. of business firms); *v.i.* to coalesce; to blend; to fuse. **-ation** *n.* **-ative** *a.* **-ator** *n.*
**a•man•u•en•sis** *n.* one who writes what another dictates, or copies what another has written; a secretary. *pl.* **amanuenses.**
**am•a•ranth** *n.* an imaginary purple flower which never fades; a purplish color; also

a real flower. **amaranthine** *a.*

**am•a•ryl•lis** *n.* a plant, the belladonna lily.

**a•mass** *v.t.* to heap up; to collect; accumulate.

**am•a•teur** *n.* one who cultivates any study, art, or sport for the love of it, and not for money. **-ish** *a.* unskilled; clumsy. **-ism, -ishness** *n.*

**am•a•tive** *a.* pert. to love; amorous.

**am•a•tol** *n.* explosive of ammonium nitrate of trinitrotoluene **(T.N.T.).**

**am•a•to•ry** *a.* pert. to or causing love. **amatorial** *a.* **amatorially** *adv.*

**a•maze** *v.t.* to fill with astonishment or wonder; to confound; to perflex. **-dly** *adv.* **-ment** *n.* astonishment, surprise. **amazing** *a.* **amazingly** *adv.*

**Am•a•zon** *n.* one of a mythical race of female warriors of Scythia; a masculine woman. **Amazonian** *a.*

**am•bages** *n.pl.* circumlocution; subterfuge; evasion; used in *pl.*

**ab•bas•sa•dor** *n.* an envoy of highest rank sent to a foreign country. **ambassadress** *n. fem.* **-ial** *a.* **-ship** *n.*

**am•ber** *n.* a yellowish, brittle fossil resin of vegetable origin, used in making jewelry, etc.

**am•ber•gris** *n.* a fragrant, ash-colored, waxy substance, derived from a biliary secretion of the spermaceti whale.

**am•bi•dex•ter** *n.* one able to use either hand with equal dexterity; a double-dealer. **-ity** *n.* **ambidextrous** *a.* **ambidextrously** *adv.*

**am•bi•ent** *a.* encompassing on all sides.

**am•bi•gu•i•ty** *n.* any statement that may be interpreted in more than one way. **ambiguous** *a.* **ambiguously** *adv.* **ambiguousness** *n.*

**am•bit** *n.* circuit or compass; sphere of action; scope.

**am•bi•tion** *n.* an eager desire for the attainment of honor, fame, or power; aim; aspiration. **ambitious** *a.* **ambitiously** *adv.*

**am•biv•a•lence, am•biv•a•len•cy** *n.* in psychoanalysis, the simultaneous operation in the mind of two conflicting wishes. **ambivalent** *a.*

**am•ble** *v.i.* to move along easily and gently; *n.* a peculiar gait of a horse; a stroll. **-r** *n.* **ambling** *a.* **amblingly** *adv.*

**am•bro•sia** *n.* *(Myth.)* the food of the ancient Greek gods which conferred immortality; an exquisite dish. **-l** *a.*

**am•bu•lance** *n.* a covered vehicle for the transport of the injured or sick.

**ambulance**

**am•bu•lant** *a.* walking. **ambulate** *v.i.* to walk backwards and forwards. **ambulation** *n.* walking. **ambulatory** *a.* having power of walking; *n.* a cloister for walking exercise.

**am•bush** same as **ambuscade.** *n.* a surprise attack; the place of ambush; *v.i.* to lie in wait; *v.t.* to attack from a concealed position.

**a•me•lio•rate** *v.t.* and *v.i.* to make better; to improve. **amelioration** *n.* **ameliorative** *a.*

**a•men** *adv.* or *interj.* so be it; truly; verily.

**a•me•na•ble** *a.* liable to be brought to account; easily led; willing to yield or obey. **amenability, -ness** *n.* **amenably** *adv.*

**a•mend** *v.t.* to change for the better; to improve; *v.i.* to grow better. **-able** *a.* **-atory** *a.* **-ment** *n.* **-s** *n.pl.* reparation for loss or injury; compensation.

**a•men•i•ty** *n.* pleasantness in situation, climate, manners, or disposition.

**a•merce** *v.t.* to punish by a fine. **amerciable** *a.* liable to a fine. **-ment** *n.*

**A•mer•i•can** *n.* in, of, or characteristic of the United States or America. *n.* a native, citizen or resident of America or the United States. **-ism** *n.* **-ize** *v.t.* and *v.i.* **-ization** *n.*

**am•e•thyst** *n.* a kind of quartz; violet, purple, or blue color. **-ine** *a.*

**a•mi•a•ble** *a.* worthy of love or affection; sweet-tempered. **amiably** *adv.* **amiability** *n.* Also **-ness.**

**am•i•ca•ble** *a.* friendly; peaceable. **amicably** *adv.* **amicability** *n.* Also **-ness.**

**a•mid, a•midst** *prep.* in the middle of; among.

**am•i•no ac•ids** a group of nitrogenous organic compounds, basic constituents of proteins.

**a•miss** *a.* wrong; faulty; improper; *adv.* in a faulty manner.

**am•i•ty** *n.* friendship.

**am•me•ter** *n.* an instrument used to measure the strength of an electric current.

**am•mo•ni•a** *n.* a pungent, alkaline gas, very soluble in water; a solution of this gas in water, for household use. **-c, -cal, -d** *a.* **ammonium** *n.* hypothetical base of ammonia.

**am•mu•ni•tion** *n.* military projectiles and missiles of all kinds.

**am•ne•sia** *n.* memory loss.

**am•nes•ty** *n.* an act of oblivion; a general pardon of political offenders.

**a•moe•ba** *n.* a minute animalcule of the simplest structure constantly changing in shape. *pl.* **amoebae, amoebas. amoeboid, amoebic** *a.*

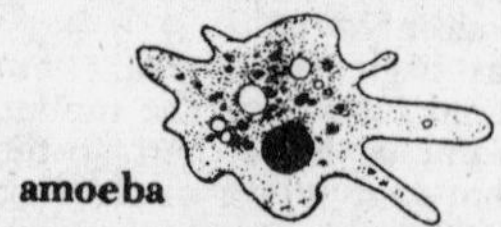

**amoeba**

**a•mok** See **amuck.**

**a•mong, a•mongst** *prep.* mixed with; making part of; amidst.

**a•mor•al** *a.* nonmoral; heedless of morals.

**am•o•rous** *a.* having a propensity for love and sexual enjoyment; in love. **-ly** *adv.* **-ness** *n.*

**a•mor•phous** *a.* without regular shape; shapeless; irregular; uncrystallized.

**am•or•tize** *v.t.* to pay off a debt, usually by periodic payments. **amortization** *n.*

**a•mount** *v.i.* to come to (in value or meaning); to be equal to; *n.* the sum total; the whole, or aggregate.

**am•pere** *n.* the unit of electric current. **amperage** *n.*

**am•per•sand** *n.* the name given to the sign &.

**am•phib•i•a** *n.pl.* animals that can live either on land or in water, as frogs, toads, newts, etc. **-n, amphibious** *a.*

**am•phi•brach** *n.* in prosody, a foot of three syllables, the middle one long, the first and last short.

**am•phi•the•a•ter** *n.* an edifice, having tiers of seats, encircling an arena, used for sports or spectacles.

**am•pho•ra** *n.* a two-handled earthenware vessel or jar, used by the ancient Greeks and Romans; 6 gallons.

**amphora**

**am•ple** *a.* of adequate size; copious. **amply** *adv.* **-ness** *n.*

**am•pli•fy** *v.t.* to extend; to enlarge; *v.i.* to dilate; to expatiate upon. **amplification, amplifier** *n.*

**am•pli•tude** *n.* largeness; extent; abundance; *Radio* (of a wave) vertical distance between its highest and lowest levels; **amplitude modulation (AM)** radio transmission by changing the amplitude of waves (contrasted with frequency modulation, FM); *(Elect.)* maximum value of an alternating current.

**am•poule** *n.* also **ampule,** a small sealed glass container holding hypodermic dose.

**am•pul•la** *n.; pl.* **ampullae;** a sacred vessel for holding oil; cruet holding wine and water for Mass.

**am•pu•tate** *v.t.* to cut off, as a limb of the body. **amputation** *n.* **amputee** *n.* one who has lost a limb through amputation.

**a•muck, a•mok** *adv.* to rush about frantically or murderously.

**am•u•let** *n.* a talisman; a charm.

**a•muse** *v.t.* to entertain agreeably; to occupy pleasantly; to divert. **-ment** *n.* **amusing** *a.*

**an** *a.* the form of the indefinite article used before a vowel sound.

**An•a•bap•tist** *n.* one who denies the validity of infant baptism and advocates rebaptism of adults.

**a•nab•o•lism** *n. (Physiol.)* the constructive form of metabolism; the building-up of tissues by plant or animal.

**a•nach•ro•nism** *n.* a chronological error. **anachronistic, anachronous** *a.*

**an•a•con•da** *n.* a gigantic, nonvenomous snake of tropical S. America.

**an•a•glyph** *n.* a figure or ornament cut in low relief; a cameo. **-ic** *a.*

**an•a•gram** *n.* a transposition of the letters of a word or phrase to form a new word or phrase. **-matic, -al** *a.* **-matically** *adv.* **-matize** *v.t.* **-matism** *n.*

**a•nal** *a.* pert. to or near the anus.

**an•a•lects, an•a•lec•ta** *n.pl.* an anthology of short literary fragments. **analectic** *a.*

**an•a•lep•sis** *n. (Med.)* restoration of strength after disease. Also **analepsy. analeptic** *a.*

**an•al•ge•sia** *n. (Med.)* absence of pain while retaining tactile sense; painlessness. **analgesic** *a.* insensible to or alleviating pain; *n.* a drug which relieves pain.

**a•nal•o•gy** *n.* resemblance in essentials between things or statements otherwise different. **analogic, analogical** *a.* **analogically** *adv.* **analogize** *v.t.* to explain by analogy. **analogism** *n.* an argument proceeding from cause to effect. **analogist** *n.* **analogous** *a.* **analogously** *adv.* **analogue** *n.* a word or thing resembling another.

**a•nal•y•sis** *n.* the resolution, separating, or breaking up of anything into its constituent elements; a synopsis. *pl.* **analyses. analyzable** *a.* **analyzation** *n.* **analyze** *v.t.* to take to pieces; to examine critically part by part. **analyst** *n.* one skilled in analysis. **analytic, analytical** *a.* **analytically** *adv.* **analytics** *n.pl.* the technique of logical analysis.

**an•a•pest, an•a•paest** *n.* in prosody, a foot of three syllables, two short or unaccented followed by one long or accented syllable. **-ic** *a.*

**an•ar•chy** *n.* want of government in society; lawless disorder in a country; a political theory, which would dispense with all laws, founding authority on the individual conscience. **anarchic, anarchically** *adv.* **anarchize** *v.t.* **anarchism, anarchist** *n.*

**a•nath•e•ma** *n.* the word used in the R.C. church as part of the formula in excommunication; something highly distasteful to one; **-tic** *a.* **-tization** *n.* **-ize** *v.t.*

**a•nat•o•my** *n., pl.* **anatomies,** art of dissecting an animal or a plant; study of form or structure of an animal; the body; a skeleton. **anatomic, anatomical** *a.* **anatomically** *adv.* **anatomize** *v.t.* **anatomist** *n.*

**an•ces•tor** *n.* forefather; forebear. **ancestral** *a.* **ancestry** *n.*

**an•chor** *n.* a heavy iron instrument by which a ship is held fast to the sea bottom; *v.t.* to weight down; **-age** *n.* a sheltered place where a ship may anchor. **-ed** *a.* **to cast anchor,** to let down anchor. **to**

**weigh anchor,** to raise anchor.
**an•chor•ite, an•chor•et** *n.* one who lives apart, renouncing the world for religious reasons; a hermit. **anchoress, -ss** *n.* **anchorage** *n.*
**an•cho•vy** *n.* small fish of the herring family.
**an•cient** *a.* very old; antique; venerable; one who lived in olden times. **-ly** *adv.* **-ness** *n.* **-ry** *n.*
**an•cil•lar•y** *a.* giving help to; attending upon.
**and** *conj.* added to; together with.
**an•dan•te** *a.* or *adv.* moving rather slowly, but in a steady, flowing manner.
**and•iron** *n.* a utensil for supporting logs in a fireplace.
**an•dro•gen** *n.* male sex hormone.
**an•drog•y•nous** *a.* having the characteristics of both sexes; hermaphrodite. Also **androgynal. androgyny** *n.*
**an•ec•dote** *n.* a brief account of any fact or happening (often amusing); **anecdotage** *n.* **anecdotal** *a.* **anecdotist** *n.*
**an•e•lec•tric** *a.* nonelectric; *n.*
**a•ne•mia** *n.* also **anaemia,** disease characterized by a deficiency of blood or of hemoglobin. **anemic** *a.*
**a•nem•o•ne** *n.* plant of crowfoot family; wind flower. **sea anemone** *n.* name given to certain plant-like marine animals.
**a•nent** *prep.* concerning; about; as to.
**an•e•roid** *a.* denoting a barometer depending for its action on the pressure of the atmosphere on a metallic box almost exhausted of air, without the use of mercury or other fluid.
**an•es•the•sia, an•aes•the•sia** *n.* absence of sensibility to external impressions, particularly touch. Also **anesthesis. anesthetic** *n.* a drug which induces insensibility to pain; *a.* producing loss of feeling and sensation. **anesthetically** *adv.* **anesthetize** *v.t.* **anesthetist** *n.*
**an•eu•rism** *n.* *(Med.)* a local widening or dilatation in the course of an artery.
**a•new** *adv.* in a new form or manner; newly; over again; afresh.
**an•gel** *n.* a heavenly messenger; a spirit who conveys God's will to man. **angelfish** *n.* a bright-colored tropical fish. **ic (al)** *a.* **-ically** *adv.*
**an•ge•lus** *n.* a short devotional service in the R.C. Church held morning, noon, and sunset.
**an•ger** *n.* a strong passion or emotion excited by injury; rage; *v.t.* to excite to wrath; to enrage. **angry** *a.* roused to anger; displeased; enraged; inflamed. **angrily** *adv.* **angriness** *n.*
**an•gi•na** *n.* *(Med.)* inflammation of the throat, e.g., quinsy. **angina pectoris,** a heart disease.
**an•gi•o•sperm** *n.* *(Bot.)* a plant whose seeds are enclosed in a seed vessel.
**an•gle** *n.* a fishhook; a rod and line for fishing; *v.i.* to fish with rod, line, and hook; **-r** *n.*
**an•gle** *n.* a corner; the point at which two lines meet.
**An•gli•can** *a.* English; of, or belonging to, Church of England; *n.* a member of Church of England. **-ism** *n.*
**an•gli•cize** *v.t.* to make or express in English idiom. **anglicism** *n.* **anglify** *v.t.*
**An•glo-** *prefix,* an angle, combining to form many compound words. **Anglophile** *a.* favoring anything English; *n.* a supporter of English customs, manners, or policy.
**An•go•ra** *n.* a Turkish province in Asia minor, famous for a breed of goats; cloth made from hair of these goats.
**an•guish** *n.* acute pain of body or of mind; grief; anxiety; moral torment. **-ment** *n.*
**an•gu•lar** *a.* having angles; sharp-cornered; (of people) not plump; gawky; irascible. **-ity** *n.* **-ly** *adv.* **angulate** *a.*
**an•hy•dride** *n.* *(Chem.)* a compound formed from an acid by evaporation of water. **anhydrous** *a.* entirely without water.
**an•il** *n.* a West Indian shrub from the leaves and stalks of which indigo is made. **-ine** *n.* a product used in the manufacture of brilliant dyes, colored inks, soaps, explosives, etc.
**an•ile** *a.* like an old woman; imbecile. **anility** *n.* senility.
**an•i•mad•vert** *v.t.* to consider disparagingly; to comment on censoriously; to reprove. **animadversion** *n.*
**an•i•mal** *n.* a living creature having sensation and power of voluntary motion; a living organism, distinct from plants; *a.* **-cule** *n.* a very minute animal (*pl.* **-cules** or **-cula). -culine** *a.* **-ism** *n.* sensuality.
**an•i•mate** *v.t.* to give natural life to; to endow with spirit or vigor; to energize; to inspire; to make alive; *a.* living or organic. **-d** *a.* **-dly** *adv.* **animating** *a.* **animation, animator** *n.*
**an•i•mism** *n.* the belief that all forms of organic life have their origin in the soul. **animist** *n.* **animistic** *a.*
**an•i•mos•i•ty** *n.* violent hatred; active enmity.
**an•i•mus** *n.* animosity; temper; grudge.
**an•ise** *n.* an herb with pungent smell and bearing aromatic seeds. **aniseed** *n.* seed of anise.
**an•kle** *n.* the joint connecting the foot with the leg. **-t** *n.* a sock which reaches just above the ankle; an ornament for the ankle.
**an•nals** *n.pl.* history of events recorded each year; a yearly chronicle. **annalize** *v.t.* **annalist** *n.*
**an•neal** *v.t.* to heat, and then cool slowly, for the purpose of rendering less brittle.
**an•nex** *v.t.* to unite at the end; to subjoin; to bind to; to take additional territory under control; *n.* something joined on. **-ation, -ion, -ment** *n.*
**an•ni•hi•late** *v.t.* to reduce to nothing; to destroy; to make null and void. **annihilable** *a.* **annihilation, annihilator** *n.*
**an•ni•ver•sa•ry** *a.* yearly; annual; *n.* day on which event is yearly celebrated.
**an•no•tate** *v.t.* to mark in writing; to write explanatory notes, esp. upon literary text. **annotation, annotator** *n.* **annotatory** *a.*
**an•nounce** *v.t.* to give first public notice of;

to proclaim; to promulgate; to publish. **-ment, -r** *n.*

**an•noy** *v.t.* disturb continually; to torment; tease. **-ance** *n.*

**an•nu•al** *a.* yearly; *n.* a periodical published once a year; a plant which completes its life cycle within a year. **-ly** *adv.*

**an•nu•i•ty** *n.* a fixed sum of money payable each year for a number of years, or for life. **annuitant** *n.*

**an•nul** *v.t.* to make void; to nullify *pr.p.* **-ling;** *pa.t.* and *pa.p.* **-led. -ment** *n.*

**an•nu•lar** *a.* ring-shaped; like a ring. **annulated** *a.* **annulet** *n.* **annularly** *adv.* **annulose** *a.* **annulation** *n.*

**an•num** *n.* year.

**an•nun•ci•ate** *v.t.* to announce; to proclaim. **annunciation, annunciator** *n.* **annunciatory** *a.*

**an•ode** *n.* positive electrode of a voltaic current; *(Radio)* plate of an electron tube.

**an•o•dyne** *n.* a drug or measures which relieve pain.

**a•noint** *v.t.* to pour oil upon; to rub over with an ointment or oil. **-ed** *a.* **-ment** *n.* **the Lord's anointed.**

**a•nom•a•ly** *n.* deviation from the common rule; irregularity. **anomalism** *n.* **anomalistic, anomalous** *a.*

**a•non** *adv.* quickly; at once. **ever and anon.**

**a•non•y•mous** *a.* applied to a writing or work of which the author is not named. **anonym** *n.* **-ly** *adv.* **anonymity** *n.*

**a•noph•e•les** *n.* the mosquito carrying the parasite which causes malaria.

**an•oth•er** *a.* not the same; one more; *pron.* anyone else.

**an•swer** *v.t.* to speak or write in return; to vindicate. **-able** *a.* **-er** *n.* **to answer for.**

**ant** *n.* a small mebranous-winged insect living in colonies in wood or the ground.

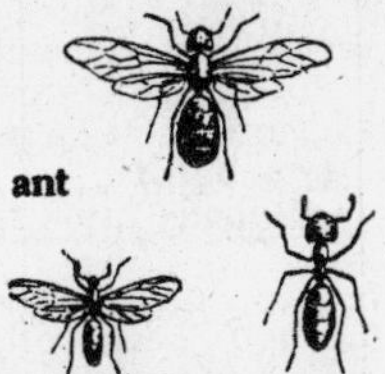

ant

**-bear** *n.* the great anteater of South America. **anteater** *n.* one of several quadrupeds. **-hill** *n.*

**ant-** *prefix* a combining form, against, used to form compounds. **antacid** *a.* counteracting acidity.

**an•tag•o•nize** *v.t.* to contend violently against; to act in opposition. **antagonism, antagonist** *n.* **antagonistic** *a.* **antagonistically** *adv.*

**ant•arc•tic** *a.* relating to southern pole or region near it.

**an•te** *n.* in poker, a player's stake.

**an•te-** *prefix* meaning *before.* **antebellum** *a.* before the war. **antecedent** *a.* going before in time, place, rank, etc. *n.* that which goes before.

**an•te•date** *v.t.* to date before the true time; to precede in time.

**an•te•di•lu•vi•an** *a.* pert. to before the Flood.

**an•te•lope** *n.* *(pl.* **-lope, -lopes)** a hoofed ruminant.

**an•te•me•rid•i•an** *a.* before noon (abbrev. a.m.)

**an•ten•na** *n.* feeler of an insect, crustacean, etc. *pl.* **antennae. antenna** *n.* *(Radio)* a wire for sending or receiving electric waves.

**an•te•pe•nult** *n.* last syllable but two of word. **-imate** *a.*

**an•te•ri•or** *a.* before; occurring earlier. **-ity** *n.*

**an•te•room** *n.* a room giving entry to another.

**an•them** *n.* a hymn sung in alternate part; church music adapted to passages from the scriptures; song of praise.

**an•ther** *n.* the little sac in a flower containing the pollen or fertilizing dust. **-al** *a.*

**an•thol•o•gy** *n.* orig. a collection of flowers; a collection of literary passages or poetry. **anthologist** *n.*

**an•thra•cene** *n.* product from distillation of coal tar, used in manufacture of dyes. **anthracite** *n.* coal, nearly pure carbon.

**an•thrax** *n.* a carbuncle; a malignant disease in cattle and sheep.

**an•thro•po-** *prefix* meaning man, combining to form derivatives. **anthropogency** *n.* science of development of man. **anthropoid** *a.* manlike.

**an•thro•pol•o•gy** *n.* study of man, including all aspects of his evolution, physical and social. **anthropological** *a.* **anthropologically** *adv.* **anthropologist** *n.*

**an•thro•pom•e•try** *n.* the scientific measurement of the human body.

**an•thro•po•mor•phism** *n.* the conception of God as a human being with human attributes. **anthropomorphist** *n.* **anthropomorphize** *v.t.* to invest with human qualities. **anthropomorphic** *a.*

**an•thro•po•mor•pho•sis** *n.* transformation into human shape.

**an•ti-** *prefix* meaning *against, opposite, instead of,* combining to form derivations; contracted to **ant-** before a vowel.

**an•ti•bi•ot•ic** *n.* substance which acts as an antibacterial agent.

**an•ti•bod•y** *n.* a substance in blood which counteracts growth and harmful action of bacteria.

**an•tic** *a.* odd; fanciful; grotesque; *n.* a comical trick or action.

**An•ti•christ** *n.* a name given in the New Testament to various incarnations of opposition to Christ.

**an•tic•i•pate** *v.t.* to be beforehand in thought or action; to forestall. **anticipant** *a.* **anticipation** *n.* **anticipative** *a.* **anticipatively, anticipatorily** *adv.* **anticipatory** *a.*

**an•ti•cli•max** *n.* a sentence or figure of speech in which ideas are arranged in descending order of importance.

**an•ti•cy•clone** *n.* an outward flow of air in a spiral movement from an atmospheric area of high pressure, tending to produce steady weather.

**an•ti•dote** *n.* a remedy which counteracts the effects of a poison. **antidotal** *a.*

**an•ti•freeze** *n.* a substance added to a liquid (as in automobile radiators) to prevent freezing.

**an•ti•gen** *n.* a substance which can produce the formation of antibodies in the bloodstream.

**an•ti•his•ta•mine** *n.* any of several drugs used to treat allergies.

**an•ti•log•a•rithm** *n.* the complement of a logarithm or of a sine, tangent, or secant.

**an•til•o•gy** *n.* a contradiction in terms, or in two separate passages of a book. **antilogous** *a.*

**an•ti•ma•cas•sar** *n.* an ornamental covering for chair backs, etc.

**an•ti•mo•ny** *n.* a whitish, brittle chemical element; a bad conductor of heat; used as an alloy in medicine and the arts. **antimonial** *a.* **antimoniate** *n.* **antimonic, antimonious** *a.* **antimonite** *n.*

**an•ti•pas•to** *n.* an appetizer course; hors d'oeuvres.

**an•tip•a•thy** *n.* opposition; aversion; dislike. **antipathetical** *a.* **antipathic** *a.* hostile to. **antipathist** *n.*

**an•ti•phon, an•tiph•o•ny** *n.* the chant, or alternate singing, in choirs. **-al** *a.*; **-ally** *adv.* **-ic, -ical** *a.*

**an•tiph•ra•sis** *n.* use of words in a sense opposite to their proper meaning. **antiphrastic, antiphrastical** *a.* **antiphrastically** *adv.*

**an•tip•o•des** *n.pl.* those living on opposite sides of globe; regions directly opposite any given point on globe.

**an•ti•pope** *n.* one who usurps the papal office; rival to pope properly elected by cardinals. **antipapal** *a.*

**an•ti•py•ret•ic** *n.* any agent which lowers temperature in fevers; *a.* counteracting fever.

**an•tique** *a.* ancient; old-fashioned; obsolete; aged; *n.* relic of bygone times. **antiquarian** *n.* student of antiquity or antiquities. *a.* pert. to old times or objects; out-of-date; obsolete. **antiquarianism** *n.* study of antiquities. **antiquary** *n.* an antiquarian. **antiquate** *v.t.* to render obsolete. **antiquated** *a.* very old; out of date. **antiquity** *n.* ancient times. **antiquities** *n.pl.* the remains and relics of ancient times.

**an•ti-Sem•i•tism** *n.* widespread outburst of hatred against members of the Hebrew race leading to persecution. **anti-Semite** *n.* **anti-Semitic** *a.*

**an•ti•sep•sis** *n.* prevention of sepsis; destruction or arresting of growth of living microorganisms which cause putrefaction. **antiseptic** *n.* a disinfectant.

**an•ti•so•cial** *a.* averse to social intercourse; opposed to social order.

**an•ti•the•ism** *n.* opposition to the belief in the existence of God. **antitheist** *n.* **antitheistic** *a.*

**an•tith•e•sis** *n.* a direct opposition of words or ideas. *pl.* **antitheses. antithetic, antithetical** *a.*

**an•ti•tox•in** *n.* a toxin which neutralizes another toxin in the blood serum. **antitoxic** *a.*

**an•ti•trust** *a.* opposed to trusts or monopolies.

**ant•ler** *n.* a horn of an animal of the deer family. **-ed** *a.*

antler

**an•to•nym** *n.* a word of contrary meaning.

**an•trum** *n.* a cavity, esp. sinus of the upper jaw. *pl.* **antra.**

**a•nus** *n.* the lower orifice of the alimentary canal.

**an•vil** *n.* an iron block, usually steel-faced, upon which blacksmith's forgings are hammered and shaped. **-led** *a.*

**anx•i•e•ty** *n.* distress of mind; disquietude; uneasiness. **anxious** *a.* **anxiously** *adv.*

**an•y** *a.* one out of many; some; *adv.* to any extent; at all. **-body** *n.* any person. **-one** *pron.* any person. **-thing** *n.* any one thing, no matter what.

**a•or•ta** *n.* the great artery leading from the left ventricle of the heart. **-l, aortic** *a.*

**a•pace** *adv.* at a quick pace; hastily; swiftly; fast.

**A•pach•e** *n.* one of a tribe of American Indians.

**a•part** *adv.* separately; aside.

**a•part•heid** *n.* racial segregation.

**a•part•ment** *n.* a room in a house; a suite of rooms; lodgings.

**ap•a•thy** *n.* indifference. **apathetic** *a.* indifferent.

**ape** *n.* a monkey, esp. one without a tail; one of the larger species, e.g. chimpanzee, gorilla, etc.; a mimic; *v.t.* to initate. **-r, -ry** *n.* **apish** *a.*

**a•pe•ri•tif** *n.* alcoholic drink taken before meals.

**ap•er•ture** *n.* an opening; a hole.

**a•pex** *n.* the top, peak, or summit of anything. *pl.* **apexes** or **apices.**

**a•pha•sia** *n.* loss of power of expressing ideas in words, often due to brain disease; loss of power of remembering words. **aphasic** *a.*

**a•phe•li•on** *n.* point of planet's orbit most distant from sun.

**aph•o•rism** *n.* a maxim. **aphoristic** *a.* **aphoristically** *adv.* **aphorize** *v.t.* and *v.i.* **aphorist** *n.*

**a•phra•sia** *n.* inability to use connected language; speechlessness.

**Aph•ro•di•te** *n.* *(Myth.)* the Greek goddess of love and beauty. **aphrodisiac** *a.* exciting sexual desire.

**a•pi•ar•y** *n.* place where bees are kept. **apiarian** *a.* **apiarist, apiculture** *n.*

**a•piece** *adv.* for each one.

**a•plomb** *n.* perpendicularity; uprightness; *(Fig.)* self-assurance; coolness.

**a•poc•a•lypse** *n.* an unveiling of hidden things; revelation; disclosure. **Apocalypse** *n. (Bib.)* the last book of the New Testament, called the Revelation of St. John. **apocalyptic** *a.*, **apocalyptically** *adv.*

**a•poc•ry•pha** *n.pl.* originally hidden or secret things not suitable to be seen by the uninitiated. **-l** *a.*

**a•pod•o•sis** *n. (Gram.)* the clause, in a conditional sentence, which expresses result as distinct from the *protasis. pl.* **apodoses.**

**ap•o•gee** *n.* that point in the orbit of a heavenly body at the greatest distance from the earth (opposed to *perigee*); the culmination; zenith. **apogeal, apogean** *a.*

**ap•o•logue** *n.* a parable; a fable.

**a•pol•o•gy** *n.* something spoken in defense; expression of regret at offense. **apologize** *v.i.* **apologist** *n.* **apologetic, apological** *a.* **apologetically** *adv.* **apologetics** *n.* the branch of theology charged with the defense of Christianity. **apologia** *n.* a defense in writing of the author's principles, etc.

**ap•o•plex•y** *n.* a sudden loss of consciousness, sensation, and voluntary motion, due generally to rupture of a blood vessel in the brain. **apoplectic** *a.*

**a•pos•ta•sy, a•pos•ta•cy** *n.* the act of renouncing one's faith, or principles, desertion of a cause. **apostate** *n.* renegade; traitor; deserter; *a.* false; traitorous. **apostatic, apostatical** *a.* **apostatize** *v.i.*

**a•pos•tle** *n.* one sent out to preach or advocate a cause; one of the twelve disciples of Christ. **apostolate** *n.* the office or dignity or mission of an apostle. **apostolic, apostolical** *a.* **apostolically** *adv.* **apostolicism** *n.*

**a•pos•tro•phe** *n.* an address delivered to the absent or the dead, as if present; a mark (') indicating possessive case, or omission of one or more letters of a word. **apostrophic** *a.* **apostrophize** *v.t.* and *i.* to address by, or to use, apostrophe.

**a•poth•e•car•y** *n.* one who prepares or sells drugs for medicines.

**ap•o•thegm** *n.* a short, pithy saying, a maxim; a proverb. **apothegmatic, apothegmatical** *a.*

**a•poth•e•o•sis** *n.* the act of raising a mortal to the rank of the gods; deification. **apotheosize** *v.t.*

**ap•pall** *v.t.* to overwhelm with sudden fear; to confound; to scare; to terrify; **-ing** a. shocking.

**ap•pa•ra•tus** *n.* things provided as a means to an end; collection of implements or utensils for effecting an experiment, or given work. *s.* and *pl.*

**ap•par•el** *n.* clothing; dress; garments; *(Naut.)* rigging, etc.; *v.t.* and *pr.p.* to dress.

**ap•par•ent** *a.* visible; evident; obvious. **-ly** *adv.*

**ap•pa•ri•tion** *n.* appearance (esp. inexplicable); ghost. **-al** *a.*

**ap•peal** *v.i.* to invoke; to call to witness; to solicit aid; *(Law)* to reopen a case before a higher court; to be pleasing to mind or senses. *n.* an urgent call for sympathy or aid; personal attraction. **-able, -ing** *a.* **-ingly** *adv.* **-ingness** *n.*

**ap•pear** *v.i.* to come in sight; to become visible; to seem. **-ance, -er** *n.*

**ap•pease** *v.t.* to quiet; to calm; to pacify; to dispel anger or hatred. **appeasable** *a.* **-ment** *n.* pacifying; **-r** *n.*

**ap•pel•lant** *n. (Law)* one who appeals to a higher court against the verdict of a lower tribunal; **appellancy** *n.* **appellation** *n.* name; title; designation. **appellational, appellative** *a.* **appellatively** *adv.*

**ap•pend** *v.t.* to hang or attach to; to add. **-age** *n.* something added. **-ant** *n.* an adjunct or unessential thing; *a.* hanging to; annexed.

**ap•pen•di•ci•tis** *n. (Path.)* inflammation of the appendix vermiformis. **appendectomy** *n.* surgical removal of appendix.

**ap•pen•di•cle** *n.* a small appendage. **appendicular** *a.*

**ap•pen•dix** *n.* thing added; an adjunct; supplement at end of book. *pl.* **-es, appendices.**

**ap•per•cep•tion** *n. (Philos.)* an act of voluntary consciousness; a mental perception of self as a conscious agent.

**ap•per•tain** *v.i.* to belong by nature; to relate. **-ing** *a.* **-ment** *n.* **appertinent** *a.*

**ap•pe•tite** *n.* desire as for food, drink, rest, etc. **appetitive** *a.* **appetize** *v.t.* to create an appetite. **appetizer** *n.* **appetizing** *a.*

**ap•plaud** *v.t.* and *v.i.* to praise by clapping; to acclaim; commend; extol. **-er, applause** *n.*

**ap•ple** *n.* fruit of the apple tree; the apple tree.

**ap•pli•cant** *n.* one who applies; a candidate; a petitioner. **applicability** *n.* the quality of being suitable. **applicable** *a.* **applicableness** *n.* **applicably** *adv.* **applicate** *a.* applied or put to some use. **application** *n.* **applicatory** *a.*

**ap•plied** *pa.p.* and *pa.t.* of **apply.**

**ap•ply** *v.t.* to place one thing upon another; to employ for a particular purpose; *v.i.* to agree with; to be relevant; to have recourse to; to become a candidate. **appliance** *n.* act of applying; thing applied; an instrument or tool.

**ap•point** *v.t.* to set apart; to assign; to ordain; to decree; to designate for an office; to fix (a date); to equip. **-ed** *a.* established, furnished. **-ee, -ment** *n.* **-ments** *n.pl.* equipment; furnishings; fittings.

**ap•por•tion** *v.t.* to divide and share in just proportion. **-ment** *n.*

**ap•po•site** *a.* appropriate; well-adapted. **-ly** *adv.* **-ness** *n.* **apposition** *n.* the act of placing beside. **appositional** *a.*

**ap•praise** *v.t.* to put a price upon; to fix the value of. **appraisal, -ment, -r** *n.* **appraising** *a.*

**ap•pre•ci•ate** *v.t.* to value justly; *v.i.* to rise in value. **appreciation** *n.* a rise in value. **appreciative, appreciatory** *a.* **appreciatively** *adv.* **appreciable** *a.* that may be estimated. **appreciably** *adv.*

**ap•pre•hend** *v.t.* to seize; to arrest; to fear.

**apprehensible** *a.* **apprehension** *n.* **apprehensive** *a.* filled with dread; suspicious. **apprehensively** *adv.*

**ap•pren•tice** *n.* one bound to another to learn a trade or art; beginner; *v.t.* **-ship** *n.*

**ap•prise** *v.t.* to inform; to give notice.

**ap•proach** *v.i.* to come near; *v.t.* to enter into negotiations with. **-es** *n.pl.* **-able** *a.* **-ability** *n.*

**ap•pro•ba•tion** *n.* approval; sanction. **approbate** *v.t.* **approbative, approbatory** *a.*

**ap•pro•pri•ate** *v.t.* to take as one's own; to set apart for a particular purpose; to claim; *a.* suitable; fitting. **-ly** *adv.* **-ness, appropriation** *n.* **appropriative** *a.* **appropriator** *n.*

**ap•prove** *v.t.* to be pleased with; to commend; to accept; to sanction officially. **approval** *n.* **approving** *a.*

**ap•prox•i•mate** *v.t.* to come near to; *a.* near to; nearly correct; not quite exact. **-ly** *adv.* **approximation** *n.* a close estimate.

**ap•pur•te•nance** *n.* that which appertains or is annexed to another thing; adjunct. **appurtenant** *a.*

**a•pri•cot** *n.* an oval, orange-yellow fruit.

**A•pril** *n.* the fourth month of the year.

**á pri•o•ri** from cause to effect.

**a•pron** *n.* a covering or protection worn in front to protect the clothes.

**a•pro•pos** *adv.* at the right time; *adj.* apt, relevant.

**apse** *n.* semicircular recess at east end of church. **apsidal** *a.*

**ap•sis** *n.* the point at which a planet is nearest to, or farthest from, the sun; *pl.* **apsides. apsidal** *a.*

**apt** *a.* fit; suitable. **-ly** *adv.* **aptitude** *n.* faculty for learning. **-ness** *n.*

**aq•ua** *n.* water.

**aq•ua•ma•rine** *n.* a semiprecious stone; *a.* of a sea-green color.

**aq•ua•plane** *n.* a plank or boat towed by a fast motorboat.

**a•quar•i•um** *n.* a glass tank in which is kept living specimens of water animals and plants; *pl.* **-s,** or **aquaria.**

**A•quar•i•us** *n.* *(Astron.)* the Water Bearer, the 11th sign of the zodiac.

**a•quat•ic** *a.* growing or living in water; practiced on, or in, water.

**aq•ua•tint** *n.* and *v.i.* an etching process.

**aq•ue•duct** *n.* a course, channel, or bridge for conveying water either under- or aboveground.

**a•que•ous** *a.* watery; made of, or from, water. **-ly** *adv.*

**aq•ui•line** *a.* belonging to the eagle; curving; hooked like the beak of an eagle.

**Ar•ab** *n.* native of Arabia; an Arab horse. **Arabian** *n.* **Arabic** *n.* the language of the Arabians.

**ar•a•besque** *n.* an ornament after the Arabian manner, with intricate interlacing of foliage, fruits, etc **-d** *a.*

**ar•a•ble** *a.* fit for plowing or tillage.

**a•rach•nid** *n.* one of the *Arachnida,* the spiders, scorpions, mites, etc. **arachnoid, arachnoidal** *a.*

**ar•bi•ter** *n.* *(fem.* **arbitress)** an umpire; a judge in a dispute. **arbitrable** *a.* **arbitrage** *n.* **arbitral** *a.* **arbitrament** *n.* decision; authoritative judgment. **arbitrary** *a.* guided by will only; high-handed; despotic; absolute. **arbitrarily** *adv.* **arbitrariness** *n.* **arbitrate** *v.t.* and *v.i.* to hear and give an authoritative decision in a dispute. **arbitration** *n.* a method of settling disputes between persons, parties and nations by an agreement on both sides to accept the findings of a third party. **arbitrator** *n.* *(fem.* **arbitratrix)** a referee; an umpire.

**ar•bor** *n.* a garden seat sheltered or enclosed by trees.

**ar•bo•re•tum** *n.* botanical garden for special planting and growing of trees; *(pl.* **arboreta). arborous** *a.*

**ar•bu•tus** *n.* evergreen shrub with scarlet berries.

**arc** *n.* a curved line or any part of a curve forming segment of a circle.

**ar•cade** *n.* a series of arches, generally supported by pillars; a walk, arched above.

**Ar•ca•di•a** *n.* region in the Peloponnesus conceived by poets to be a land of shepherds and shepherdesses. **Arcadian** *a.* **Arcady** *n.* an ideal rustic place.

**ar•ca•num** *n.* a secret; mystery. *pl.* **arcana.**

**arch** *a.* cunning; sly; mischievous; roguish. **-ness** *n.*

**arch** *prefix* used as *a.* chief; first of a class, as in *archbishop,* etc. **-angel** *n.* an angel of supreme order.

**arch** *n.* a structure for support; *v.t.* or *v.i.* to form an arch; to bend into an arch. **-ed** *a.*

**arch**

**ar•chae•ol•o•gy, archeology** *n.* the study of human antiquities. **archaeologist** *n.* **archaeological** *a.*

**ar•cha•ic** *a.* antiquated; ancient; obsolete. **-ally** *adv.* **archaism** *n.* a word, expression or idiom out of date. **archaist** *n.* an antiquary. **archaistic** *a.*

**ar•che•an** *a.* pert. to the oldest period of geological time.

**arch•er** *n.* one who shoots with a bow; a bowman. **-y** *n.* art and practice of shooting with bow and arrow.

**ar•che•type** *n.* the original pattern or model from which a thing is made or copied; prototype. **archetypal** *a.*

**ar•chi•pel•a•go** *n.* a group of islands. *pl.* **-es. archipelagic** *a.*

**ar•chi•tect** *n.* one skilled in the art of building; designer. **-ural** *a.* **-urally** *adv.* **-ure** *n.* the art of building.

**ar•chives** *n.pl.* place in which public or historical records are stored; public records. **archivist** *n.* a keeper of archives.

**arc•tic** *a.* pert. to the regions near the N. Pole.
**ar•dent** *a.* burning; passionate; eager. **-ly** *adv.* **ardency, ardor** *n.*
**ar•du•ous** *a.* high and lofty; steep; difficult to overcome; strenuous. **-ly** *adv.*
**are** present indicative plural of the verb **to be.**
**are** *n.* metric unit of land measure containing 100 square meters, about 119.6 square yards.
**a•re•a** *n.* an open space; total outside surface of a thing; superficial extent.
**a•re•na** *n.* any place of public contest. **-ceous** *a.* like sand; sandy.
**ar•e•om•e•ter** *n.* an instrument for measuring the specific gravity of fluids.
**a•rete** *n.* a sharp mountain ridge; a rocky spur.
**ar•gent** *a.* made of, or like, silver.
**ar•gil** *n.* pure clay; potter's earth.
**ar•gon** *n.* an inert gas used for filling electric light bulbs.
**ar•go•sy** *n.* a large, richly laden merchant ship.
**ar•gue** *v.t.* to prove by reasoning; to discuss; to persuade by debate; *v.i.* to prove; to offer reasons; to dispute. **arguable** *a.* **-r** *n.* **argument** *n.* a reason offered in proof for or against a thing; the subject of a speech, etc. **argumentation** *n.* **argumentative** *a.* **argumentatively** *adv.* **argumentativeness** *n.*
**a•ri•a** *n.* *(Mus.)* a melody as distinct from harmony; a solo part in a cantata, opera, oratorio, etc.
**ar•id** *a.* dry; parched; barren; *(Fig.)* uninteresting. **-ity** *n.*
**a•right** *adv.* rightly.
**a•rise** *v.t.* to come up; to stand up; to get up; to come into view; to spring up; to occur; *pr.p.* **arising.** *pa.p.* **arisen.** *pa.t.* **arose.**
**ar•is•toc•ra•cy** *n.* originally the rule of the best; later, the rule of a hereditary upper class; privileged class in a state; the nobility; upper classes. **aristocrat** *n.* a member of the aristocracy. **aristocratic** *a.* **aristocratically** *adv.*
**Ar•is•tot•le** *n.* (384-322 B.C.) a great Greek philosopher, pupil and disciple of Plato. **Aristotelian** *n.* a follower of Aristotle.
**a•rith•me•tic** *n.* the science of numbers; the art of reckoning by figures; a work on this subject. **-al** *a.* **-ally** *adv.* **-ian** *n.* one skilled in arithmetic.
**ark** *n.* the large floating vessel in which Noah lived during the Flood (Genesis 6-8); vessel of bulrushes in which the infant Moses was placed (Exodus 2).
**arm** *n.* the limb extending from shoulders to hand; anything projecting from main body, as a branch; *v.t.* to give an arm to for support. **-less** *a.* without arms. **-ful** *n.* as much as the arms can hold.
**arm** *n.* a weapon; a branch of the army, e.g. infantry, artillery, etc.; *pl.* all weapons; *v.t.* to equip with weapons; *v.i.* to take up arms. **-ed** *a.* equipped with, or supported by, arms; fortified; strengthened.
**ar•ma•da** *n.* a fleet of armed ships.
**ar•ma•dil•lo** *n.* an animal, having the body encased in armor-like covering of small, bony shell plates.
**Ar•ma•ged•don** *n.* the scene of the last battle between the powers of good and evil.
**ar•ma•ment** *n.* forces equipped for war; munitions; the process of equipping forces in time of war.
**ar•ma•ture** *n.* armor; protective covering (of plants); part of magnet or dynamo which rotates in electrical generator; coil of wire in electric motor which breaks magnetic field.
**ar•mi•stice** *n.* a temporary or lasting cessation of hostilities; a truce.
**arm•let** *n.* band worn around arm.
**ar•mor** *n.* defensive covering for the body in battle. **—bearer** *n.* **—clad** *a.*

**armor**

**ar•mor•y** *n.* place where arms are stored; building for headquarters and drill area of National Guard unit; arsenal; *(Arch.)* science of heraldry.
**ar•my** *n.* a body of men trained and equipped for war; a military force; an organized body for some special purpose; large number of people.
**a•ro•ma** *n.* fragrance. **-tic** *a.*
**a•round** *adv.* in a circle; near; *prep.* on all sides of; about.
**a•rouse** *v.t.* to excite to action; to awaken; *v.i.* to wake. **arousal** *n.*
**ar•peg•gi•o** *n.* *(Mus.)* the sounding of notes of a chord in quick succession.
**ar•que•bus** *n.* an ancient form of handgun.
**ar•raign** *v.t.* to call or set a prisoner at the bar; to call to account; to accuse publicly. **-ment** *n.*
**ar•range** *v.t.* to put into order; to settle terms; to prepare; to adapt; to adjust; *v.i.* to make agreement; to take steps. **-ment, -r** *n.* **-ly** *adv.*
**ar•rant** *a.* notorious.
**ar•ras** *n.* tapestry; large tapestries, used as wall hangings.
**ar•ray** *v.t.* to set in order; to draw up, as troops for battle; to equip; *n.* order; equipment; fine apparel.
**ar•rear** *n.* the state of being behind. **-s** *n.pl.* moneys still owing; work still to be overtaken. **-age** *n.*
**ar•rest** *v.t.* to stop; to check; to hinder; to

seize by authority of law; to engage the attention; *n.* the apprehending of a person by the authority of law. **-ation, -er, -or** *n.* **-ing** *a.* impressive; striking. **-ive** *a.* calculated to draw attention. **-ment** *n.*

**ar•rive** *v.i.* to reach a point; to come to; to attain to any aim or object. **arrival** *n.*

**ar•ro•gance** *n.* insolent pride; intolerable presumption; overbearing manner. **arrogant** *a.* **arrogantly** *adv.* **arrogate** *v.t.* to claim unduly; to take upon one's self without authority.

**ar•row** *n.* a barbed missile shot from a bow; a sign to show direction. **-y** *a.* of, like an arrow. **— grass** *n.* small, erect, grasslike plants.

**ar•row•root** *n.* a nutritious starch used in puddings, cookies, etc.

**ar•se•nal** *n.* factory for military and naval arms and stores; an armory.

**ar•se•nic** *n.* a semimetallic element; the poisonous, whitish, or steel-gray powder of white oxide of arsenic. **arsenic, -al, arsenous** *a.*

**ar•son** *n.* the crime of intentionally setting on fire houses, buildings, ships, or other property.

**art** *n.* skill; human skill as opposed to nature; skill applied to music, painting, poetry, etc.; any of the subjects of this skill; a profession or craft; cunning; trick. **-s** *n.pl.* certain branches of learning, languages, history, etc. as distinct from natural science. **-ful** *a.* exhibiting art or skill; crafty; cunning. **-fully** *adv.* **-fulness** *n.* **-less** *a.* guileless. **-lessly** *adv.* **-lessness** *n.*

**ar•ter•y** *n.* a vessel carrying blood from the heart. **arterial** *a.* **arterialize** *v.t.* to change venous blood into arterial blood by oxygenization. **arterialization** *n.* **arteriole** *n.* a small artery. **arteriosclerosis** *n.* *(Med.)* a hardening of the arteries.

**ar•te•sian well** *n.* a well bored deep enough so that water rises to the surface of the ground by internal pressure.

**ar•thri•tis** *n.* inflammation of a joint; gout. **arthritic(al)** *a.*

**ar•thro•pod** *n.* an animal with segmented body and jointed limbs, e.g. a spider, crustacean, etc. **-al** *a.*

**ar•ti•choke** *n.* a plant with thistlelike head.

**ar•ti•cle** *n.* a clause or term in a contract, treaty, etc.; a literary composition in a journal, etc.; a rule or condition; an item; a commodity or object; *(Gram.)* one of the words *a, an* and *the.*

**ar•tic•u•lar** *a.* pert. to the joints.

**ar•tic•u•late** *v.t.* to connect by a joint; to utter clearly defined sounds; *v.i.* to be connected by joints; to speak in distinct syllables or words; *a.* jointed; of speech, clear, distinct. **-ly** *adv.* **-ness, articulation** *n.*

**ar•ti•fact** *n.* object made by man.

**ar•ti•fice** *n.* an artful or skilful contrivance; a ruse; a trick; cunning. **-r** *n.* a skilled workman; an inventor. **artifical** *a.* made by art; manufactured; affected in manners. **artifically** *adv.* **artificiality** *n.*

**ar•til•lery** *n.* cannon; troops trained in the use of guns.

**ar•ti•san** *n.* a craftsman.

**art•ist** *n.* one who practices one of the fine arts; applicable to any craftsman whose work is of high standard. **-ic(al),** *a.* **-ically** *adv.* **artistry** *n.* artistic ability or effect.

**Ar•y•an** *n.* the progenitors of the Indo-European group, i.e. Celtic, Teutonic, etc.

**as** *adv.* like; in like manner; similar to; for example; *conj.* since; because; when; while; *pron.* that.

**as•bes•tos** *n.* a fibrous noninflammable mineral.

**as•cend** *v.t.* to climb, to mount; to walk up; *v.i.* to rise; to arise; to soar; to climb; to mount; to go back in time. **-able, -ible** *a.* **-ancy, -ency** *n.* superior or controlling influence; authority; domination.

**as•cent** *n.* the act of rising; the way by which one rises; a slope.

**as•cer•tain** *v.t.* to get to know; to find out for a certainty. **-able** *a.* **-ment** *n.*

**as•cet•ic** *a.* sternly self-denying; austere; strict; *n.* one who practices rigorous self-denial. **-ism** *n.* **-ally** *adv.*

**as•cot** *n.* a kind of scarf or broad tie.

**as•cribe** *v.t.* to attribute; to impute; to assign. **ascribable** *a.* **ascription** *n.*

**a•sep•sis** *n.* freeing from bacteria by use of antiseptics. **aseptic** *a.*

**a•sex•u•al** *a.* without sex; lacking sexual instinct or reproductive organs. **-ity** *n.*

**ash** *n.* a genus of trees of the olive family. **-en** *a.*

**ash** *n.* the dry white or grayish dust left after a substance has been burned. **-en** *a.* of the color of ashes; pale. **-tray** *n.* receptacle for cigarette ash. **-y** *a.*

**a•shamed** *a.* affected by shame.

**a•shore** *adv.* on or to shore.

**A•sian, A•si•at•ic** *a.* pert. to Asia or to the people of Asia.

**a•side** *n.* something said in an undertone, esp. on stage by an actor and supposed not to be heard by the other actors; *adv.* on or to one side; apart.

**as•i•nine** *a.* pert. to an ass; stupid.

**ask** *v.t.* to seek information; to interrogate; *v.i.* *(for, about)* to request.

**a•skance, a•skant** *adv.* towards one corner of the eye; awry; with disdain.

**a•skew** *adv.* askant; awry.

**a•slant** *adv.* in a slanting direction.

**a•sleep** *adv.* and *a.* in a state of sleep.

**a•slope** *a.* tilted; oblique.

**a•so•cial** *a.* not social.

**as•par•a•gus** *n.* a succulent vegetable with tender shoots.

**as•pect** *n.* look; appearance; view.

**as•pen** *n.* a tree known also as the trembling poplar.

**as•per•ate** *v.t.* to make harsh or uneven; to roughen.

**as•per•i•ty** *n.* roughness of surface, manner, or speech; harshness.

**as•perse** *v.t.* to slander; to defame; to vilify. **aspersion** *n.* slander. **aspersive, aspersory** *a.*

**as•phalt** *n.* a black, hard, tar-like substance,

used for paving, roofing, etc.; *v.t.* to cover with asphalt.

**as•phyx•i•a, as•phyx•y** *n.* suspended animation due to lack of oxygen in the blood; it is caused by obstructed breathing. **-te** *v.t.* to suffocate. **-tion** *n.*

**as•pic** *n.* the asp; *(Bot.)* the great lavender.

**as•pic** *n.* savory jelly containing pieces of fish, fowl, egg, etc.

**as•pi•rate** *v.t.* to pronounce with a full breathing sound. **aspiration** *n.*

**as•pire** *v.i.* to desire with eagerness; to strive towards something higher (usually followed by *to* or *after*). **aspirant** *a.* **aspiration, -r** *n.*

**as•pi•rin** *n.* a drug used for relief of headache, fever, etc.

**ass** *n.* a quadruped of the horse family; a donkey; *(Fig.)* a stupid person.

**as•sail** *v.t.* to leap or fall on; to attack; to ply with arguments, reproaches, etc. **-able** *a.* **-ant** *a.* and *n.*

**as•sas•sin** *n.* one who murders by secret or treacherous assault. **-ate** *v.t.* to murder by guile or by sudden violence. **-ation, -ator** *n.*

**as•sault** *n.* a violent onset or attack; *v.t.* to attack violently; to storm. **-able** *a.* **-er** *n.*

**as•say** *n.* trial; test; examination. *v.t.* to test. **-er** *n.*

**as•sem•ble** *v.t.* to bring or call together; to collect; to fit together the parts, e.g. of a machine; *v.i.* to meet together. **assemblage** *n.* a group, gathering. **assembly** *n.* a meeting; a company gathered; the putting together of parts.

**as•sent** *v.i.* to agree; to admit; to concur; *n.* acquiescence; approval. **-ation** *n.* servile assent; obsequiousness. **-er, -or** *n.* **-ient** *a.* giving assent; *n.* one who assents.

**as•sert** *v.t.* to declare strongly; to maintain or defend by argument. **-er, -or, -ion** *n.* **-ive** *a.* positive; self-confident. **-ively** *adv.* **-iveness** *n.* **-ory** *a.*

**as•sess** *v.t.* to fix the amount of a tax or fine; to tax or fine; to estimate for damage, taxation, etc.; to rate; to appraise. **-able** *a.* **-ment, -or** *n.*

**as•sets** *n.pl.* funds or property available for payment of debts, etc.; *n.sing.* an item of such property; a thing of value.

**as•sev•er•ate** *v.t.* and *v.i.* to assert positively or solemnly; to aver. **asseveration** *n.*

**as•sid•u•ous** *a.* constant in application or attention; diligent; hardworking. **-ly** *adv.* **-ness, assiduity** *n.*

**as•sign** *v.t.* to allot; to apportion; to give out; to fix; to transfer; to ascribe. **-able** *a.* **-ation** *n.* **-ment** *n.* an allotting to a particular person or use; a transfer of legal title or interest; a task assigned.

**as•sim•i•late** *v.t.* to make similar; to change into a like substance; to absorb into the system; to digest; *v.i.* to become similar; to be absorbed. **assimilation** *n.* **assimilative** *a.*

**as•sist** *v.t.* to help; to aid; to give support to; *v.i.* to lend aid; to be present. **-ance** *n.* **-ant** *a.* helping; acting under the direction of a superior; *n.* one who assists.

**as•size** *v.t.* to fix the rate of; to assess. **-ment** *n.* inspection of weights and measures. **-r** *n.*

**as•so•ci•ate** *v.t.* to join with as a friend, colleague, or partner; to class together; *v.i.* (foll. by *with*) to keep company; *n.* a companion; a coadjutor; a junior member; *a.* affiliated. **associable, associative** *a.*

**as•so•nance** *n.* a resemblance of sounds; imperfect rhyme in which vowel sounds are same, but consonants following are different, e.g. *blunder, slumber.*

**as•sort** *v.t.* to classify; to arrange; *v.i.* to suit or agree or match. **-ed** *a.* varied. **-edness, -ment** *n.*

**as•suage** *v.t.* to soften; to allay; to mitigate. **-ment, -r** *n.* **assuasive** *a.*

**as•sume** *v.t.* to take upon oneself; to take for granted; to usurp; *v.i.* to claim unduly. **assumable, -d** *a.* **-dly** *adv.* **assuming** *a.* **assumingly** *adv.* **assumption** *n.* the act of taking to or upon oneself by force or right; the act of taking for granted. **assumptive** *a.*

**as•sure** *v.t.* to make sure or certain; to affirm. **assurable** *a.* **assurance** *n.* promise; self-confidence; presumption. **-dly** *adv.*

**as•ter** *n.* a genus of plants so-called because the expanded flowers of various hues are like stars.

**as•ter•isk** *n.* the mark (*) used in printing to indicate words for reference or words omitted. **asterism** *n.* small cluster of stars.

**a•stern** *adv.* in, at, or toward the hinder part of ship.

**as•ter•oid** *n.* one of the smaller planets; *(Zool.)* starfish. **-al** *a.*

**asth•ma** *n.* a chronic disorder of the respiratory organs, marked by cough, labored breathing and feeling of suffocation. **-tic** *a.*

**a•stig•ma•tism** *n.* a defect of eye, attended with dimness of vision, due to malformation of lens of eye. **astigmatic** *a.*

**a•stir** *adv.* or *a.* on the move; alert.

**as•ton•ish** *v.t.* to impress with sudden surprise, wonder or admiration. **-ed, -ing** *a.* **-ingly** *adv.* **-ment** *n.*

**as•tound** *v.t.* to strike dumb with terror or amazement; to astonish greatly. **-ing** *a.*

**as•tra•khan** *n.* the skin of the young Persian lamb with soft, curling ringlets of wool; a cheap fabric, made in imitation.

**as•tral** *a.* pert. to the stars; star-shaped.

**a•stray** *adv.* out of the right way.

**a•strict** *v.t.* to bind fast; to confine; to restrict; to contract. **-ion** *n.* **-ive** *a.* astringent.

**a•stride** *adv.* straddling; with the legs apart; *prep.* with one foot on each side of an object.

**as•tringe** *v.t.* to bind together; to draw together. **-ncy** *n.* **-nt** *a.* binding; strengthening; *n.* a drug which causes contraction of the muscular fiber tissues. **-ntly** *adv.*

**as•tro-** *prefix* used in the construction of compound words having some reference to stars.

**as•tro•labe** *n.* instrument for finding altitude of stars, etc.

**as•trol•o•gy** *n.* science which professes to interpret the influence of heavenly bodies on human affairs. **astrologer** *n.* **astrologic, astrological** *a.*

**as•trom•e•try** *n.* the determination of the magnitudes of the fixed stars.

**as•tro•naut** *n.* a space traveler; **-ical** *a.* **-ics** *n.*

**as•tron•o•my** *n.* the science which studies the heavenly bodies. **astronomer** *n.* **astronomic, astronomical,** *a.* pert. to astronomy; boundless, countless, prodigious. **astronomize** *v.i.*

**as•tro•phys•ics** *n. (Astron.)* the study of the physical components of the stars.

**as•tute** *a.* cunning; shrewd; **-ly** *adv.* **-ness** *n.*

**a•sun•der** *adv.* apart; into different pieces; in a divided state.

**a•sy•lum** *n.* a sanctuary; refuge for criminals, debtors and others liable to be pursued; an institution for the deaf and dumb, the blind, or the insane; the protection afforded by such places.

**a•sym•me•try** *n.* want of symmetry. **asymmetric, asymmetrical** *a.*

**a•syn•chro•nism** *n.* lack of synchronism; want of correspondence in time. **asynchronous** *a.* not simultaneous.

**at** *prep.* denoting rest in a place, presence or nearness; near to, by, in; engaged on.

**at•a•vism** *n.* the recurrence in living organisms of hereditary characteristics, diseases, etc. which have skipped one or more generations. **atavistic** *n.*

**a•tax•i•a** *n. (Med.)* irregularity of bodily functions. **ataxic** *a.*

**ate** past tense of the verb **eat.**

**a•the•ism** *n.* disbelief in the existence of God. **atheist** *n.* **atheistic, atheistical** *a.* **athiestically** *adv.*

**A•the•na, A•the•ne** *n. (Myth.)* Greek goddess of wisdom, art, industries, and prudent warfare. **Athenian** *n.* native of Athens.

**a•thirst** *a.* thirsty; eager.

**ath•lete** *n.* one trained to physical exercises, feats or contests of strength, etc. **athletic** *a.* pert. to physical exercises, contests, etc.; strong; vigorous; muscular. **athletics** *n.pl.* athletic sports.

**a•thwart** *prep.* across; from side to side; *adv.* crosswise in oppositon.

**a•tin•gle** *a.* tingling.

**At•lan•tic** *a.* pert. to the ocean separating Europe and Africa from America; *n.* the ocean itself.

**At•las** *n. (Myth.)* a Titan, condemned by Zeus to carry the world on his shoulders. **atlas** *n.* a book of maps.

**at•mo•sphere** *n.* the mass of air, clouds, gases, and vapor, surrounding the earth or other heavenly body; any similar mass; atmospheric pressure; the air in any place, esp. if enclosed, e.g. in a theater. **atmospheric, atmospherical** *a.*

**a•toll** *n.* a ring-shaped coral reef.

**at•om** *n.* constituent of a chemical element; *(Fig.)* anything very small; a tiny bit. **-ic, -ical** *a.* **-ize** *v.t.* to reduce to atoms. **-izer** *n.* an instrument for reducing liquid to the form of spray.

**a•ton•al** *a. (Mus.)* without tone. **atonic** *a.* without tone; unaccented; *(Med.)* lacking tone or energy.

**a•tone** *v.t.* to appease; *v.i.* to make amends or reparation for an offense. **-ment** *n.* amends; reconciliation.

**a•top** *a., adv.* on or at the top; *prep.* on top of.

**a•tri•um** *n.* the principal room of an ancient Roman house; *(Anat.)* an auricle of the heart.

**a•tro•cious** *a.* savagely brutal; extremely cruel; very wicked. **-ly** *adv.* **-ness** *n.* **atrocity** *n.* extreme wickedness; a brutal act.

**at•ro•phy** *n.* a wasting away through lack of nutrition or use; emaciation. Also *v.t.* and *v.i.* to waste away; to cause to waste away. **atrophic, atrophied** *a.*

**at•ro•pin, at•ro•pine** *n.* a poisonous alkaloid.

**at•tach** *v.t.* to bind, fasten, or tie; to take by legal authority; to bind by affection; *v.i.* to adhere; to be ascribed to. **-able** *a.* **-ed** *a.* fixed; fond of. **-ment** *n.*

**at•tack** *v.t.* to fall on with force; to assail with hostile criticism in words or writing; to set to work on; *n.* a violent onset or assault.

**at•tain** *v.t.* to reach by exertion; to obtain by effort; to accomplish; to achieve. **-able** *a.* **-ability, -ableness, -ment** *n.*

**at•taint** *v.t.* to stain or disgrace; to accuse of; to find guilty; to deprive of civil rights for treason; *n.* a taint or disgrace. **attainder** *n.* loss of civil rights after sentence of death or outlawry for treason or felony. **-ment** *n.*

**at•tar** *n.* a fragrant oil.

**at•tempt** *v.t.* to try; to endeavor to do; to attack; *n.* trial; an effort, esp. unsuccessful; an assault.

**at•tend** *v.t.* to accompany; to be present with or at; to give medical care to; *v.i.* to be present; to pay attention; to take care of; to wait on. **-ance** *n.* **-ant** *a.* **attention** *n.* careful observation; watching; act of civility; command issued, as in a military sense, to ensure readiness to act. **attentions** *n.pl.* courtship. **attentive** *a.* **attentively** *adv.*

**at•ten•u•ate** *v.t.* to make thin or fine, to make slender; to weaken the potency of; *a.* slender; thin; *(Bot.)* tapering. **attenuant, -d** *a.* **attenuation, attenuator** *n.*

**at•test** *v.t.* and *v.i.* to bear witness to; to vouch for; to certify. **-able, -ative** *a.* **-ation** *n.*

**At•tic** *a.* pert. to *Attica* or Athens. **attic** *n.* a room under the roof of a house.

**at•tire** *v.i.* to dress; to array in splendid garments; *n.* apparel; dress. **-ment, attiring** *n.*

**at•ti•tude** *n.* posture of a person; pose (in portrait).

**at•tor•ney** *n.* one put in the *turn* or place of another; one legally authorized by another to transact business; lawyer; solicitor. **attorn** *v.t.* to transfer; *v.i.* to transfer homage; to acknowledge a new landlord. **-ship, -dom** *n.*

**at•tract** *v.t.* and *v.i.* to draw toward; to cause to approach. **-able** *a.* **-ile** *a.* attractive. **attraction** *n.* **-ive** *a.* **-ively** *adv.* **-iveness** *n.*
**at•tri•bute** *v.t.* to consider as belonging to; to ascribe to; *n.* something inherent in a person or thing.
**at•tri•tion** *n.* the act of wearing away by friction; state of being worn. **attrite** *a.* worn away by rubbing or friction; *(Theol.)* penitent through fear.
**at•tune** *v.t.* to put in tune; to make musical; *(Fig.)* to bring into spiritual harmony.
**a•typ•i•cal** *a.* not typical; abnormal. **-ly** *adv.*
**au•burn** *a.* reddish brown; *n.* rich chestnut color.
**auc•tion** *n.* a method of public sale whereby the object for sale is secured by highest bidder; *v.t.* to sell by auction. **-eer** *n.* one licensed to sell by auction; *v.i.* to sell by auction.
**auc•tion bridge** *n.* a card game in which the players bid.
**au•da•cious** *a.* bold, fearless; impudent; **-ly** *adv.* **audacity** *n.* boldness, effrontery, impudence.
**au•di•ble** *a.* capable of being heard. **audibly** *adv.* **audibility** *n.*
**au•di•ence** *n.* the act of hearing; an assembly of hearers or spectators; a ceremonial reception. **audient** *a.* listening.
**au•di•o** *a.* electronic apparatus using audible frequencies (between 15-20,000 cycles).
**au•dit** *n.* an examination, by qualified persons, of accounts of a business, public office, or undertaking; *v.t.* to test and vouch for the accuracy of accounts; listen. **-ion** *n.* the act, or sense, of hearing, hearing given to a performer as test. **-orium** *n.* the body of a concert hall or theater where the audience are seated; the nave of a church. **-ory** *a.* pert. to the sense of hearing; *n.* a lecture room; an audience.
**au•ger** *n.* a boring tool for woodwork, like a large gimlet.

auger

**aught** *n.* anything; any part; zero; *adv.* to any extent.
**aug•ment** *v.t.* to increase; to add to; *v.i.* to grow larger; *n.* an increase; a prefix added to the past tense of verbs to distinguish them from other tenses.
**au•gur** *n.* a soothsayer; a diviner; *v.t.* to foretell; to presage; to prognosticate.
**au•gust** *a.* majestic; imposing; sublime; magnificent; sacred.
**Au•gust** *n.* the eighth month of the year.
**Au•gus•tine** *n.* a member of a monastic order which follows rules framed by St. Augustine.
**auk** *n.* a marine bird, of the Arctic regions.
**aunt** *n.* a father's or a mother's sister.
**au•ra** *n.* a subtle invisible essence or fluid said to emanate from human and animal bodies, and even from things. **-l** *a.*
**au•ral** *a.* pert. to the ear, or sense of hearing. **-ly** *adv.*
**au•re•ole, au•re•o•la** *n.* a radiance around a sacred figure, in art.
**au•ric** *a.* pert. to gold. **aureate** *a.* golden.
**au•ri•cle** *n.* the external ear; each of the two upper cavities of the heart. **auricula** *n.* a part like an ear. **auricular** *a.* **auriculate, auriform** *a.* ear-shaped.
**au•rif•er•ous** *a.* yielding gold.
**Au•ro•ra** *n.* *(Myth.)* the Roman goddess of the dawn. **aurora** *n.* the dawn; the rosy tint in the sky before the sun rises; an orange-red color.
**aus•cul•ta•tion** *n.* *(Med.)* listening to the movement of heart and lungs. **ausculate** *v.t.* and *v.i.*
**aus•pice** *n.* favoring influence; an omen based on observing birds; augury; divination; *n.pl.* **-s,** protection; patronage. **auspicate** *v.t.* to predict; to inaugurate in favorable conditions. **auspicious** *a.* giving promise of success; favorable; propitious. **auspiciously** *adv.* **auspiciousness** *n.*
**aus•tere** *a.* harsh; severe; strict; simple and without luxury. **-ly** *adv.* **-ness, austerity** *n.*
**aus•tral** *a.* southern.
**au•tar•chy** *n.* absolute power; despotism; dictatorship. **autarchic** *a.*
**au•then•tic** *a.* genuine; real; not of doubtful origin; trustworthy; of attested authority. Also **-al. -ally** *adv.* **-ate** *v.t.* to prove to be genuine; to confirm. **-ation, authenticity** *n.*
**au•thor** *n.* (*fem.* **authoress**) the beginner or originator of anything; the writer of a book, article, etc. **-ial** *a.*
**au•thor•i•ty** *n.* legal power or right; accepted source of information; the writer himself; permission; a body or group of persons in control (often *pl.*). **authoritarian** *a.* advocating obedience to authority as opposed to individual liberty. **authoritative** *a.* having the weight of authority; justified. **authoritatively** *adv.*
**au•thor•ize** *v.t.* to empower; to make legal. **authorization** *n.*
**au•to** *n.* *(Colloq.)* abbrev. for automobile. **-ist** *n.* a motorist. **-mobile** *n.* a road vehicle driven by mechanical power. **-motive** *a.*
**au•to•bi•og•ra•phy** *n.* the story of a person's life, written by himself. **autobiographer** *n.* **autobiographic** *a.*
**au•to•crat** *n.* monarch who rules by his own absolute right; despot. **-ic** *a.* **-ically** *adv.* **autocracy** *n.*
**au•to•gi•ro** *n.* airplane using horizontal revolving wings for vertical ascent and descent.
**au•to•graph** *n.* a person's signature; *a.* written in one's own handwriting; *v.t.* to write with one's own hand; to write one's signature.
**au•to•mat•ic** *a.* self-acting; mechanical; not voluntary; done unconsciously; **automat** *n.* a restaurant which serves food

using automatic devices.

**au•to•mo•bile.** See **auto.**

**au•ton•o•my** *n.* the right of self-government; independence; **autonomous, autonomic** *a.*

**au•top•sy** *n.* the dissection and examination of a dead body; a postmortem examination.

**au•to•sug•ges•tion** *n.* a mental process similar to hypnotism but applied by the subject to himself.

**au•tumn** *n.* the third season of the year, generally applied to September, October, and November; fall; the season of decay; the time of declining powers. **-al** *a.*

**aux•il•ia•ry** *a.* assisting; subsidiary; *n.* a helper; a verb which helps to form moods, tenses, or voice of another verb.

**a•vail** *v.i.* to profit by; to take advantage of; *v.t.* to benefit; to profit; *n.* advantage; profit; benefit; utility. **-able** *a.* capable of being used to advantage; procurable. **-ability** *n.*

**av•a•lanche** *n.* mass of snow and ice moving down from a height and gathering momentum in its descent; *(Fig.)* tremendous downpour.

**av•a•rice** *n.* greed; miserliness. **avaricious** *a.*

**a•vast** *interj.* cease! hold! stop! enough!.

**a•ve** *interj.* hail! farewell.

**a•venge** *v.t.* and *v.i.* to take satisfaction for an injury to; to punish a wrongdoer; to seek retribution. **-ful** *a.* **-ment, -r** *n.*

**av•e•nue** *n.* a wide street with houses and trees down each side.

**a•ver** *v.t.* to declare positively; to avouch; to assert; to allege. **-ring** *pr.p.;* **-red** *pa.p.* **-ment** *n.*

**av•er•age** *a.* containing a mean proportion; ordinary; normal; *n.* a medial estimate obtained by dividing the sum of a number of quantities by the number of quantities; *v.t.* to reduce to a mean.

**a•verse** *a.* reluctant (to do) or disinclined for; unwilling; set against (foll. by *to).* **-ly** *adv.* **-ness** *n.* **aversion** *n.* a strong dislike.

**a•vert** *v.t.* to turn away from or aside; to ward off. **-ed** *a.* **-edly** *adv.* **-ible** *a.*

**a•vi•an** *a.* pert. to birds. **aviary** *n.* an enclosed space for breeding, rearing and keeping of birds.

**a•vi•a•tion** *n.* the art of flying aircraft. **aviate** *v.i.* to fly. **aviator** *n.*

**av•id** *a.* eager; greedy; desirous. **-ity** *n.* hunger.

**a•vo•ca•do** *n.* the alligator pear.

**av•o•ca•tion** *n.* a distraction; a minor plausable occupation; a hobby; a side interest; **avocative** *a.* calling off; *n.* a dissuasion.

**a•void** *v.t.* to shun; to elude; to keep clear of; to eschew; to abstain from; to escape. **-able** *a.* **-ance** *n.*

**a•vouch** *v.t.* to declare positively.

**a•vow** *v.t.* to declare openly; to own; to confess freely; to acknowledge. **-able** *a.* **-al** *n.* an open declaration or admission.

**a•wait** *v.t.* to wait for; be in store for; attend; be ready for.

**a•wake** *v.t.* to rouse from sleep; *v.i.* to cease from sleep; *pa.t.* **awoke;** *pa.p.* **awoke, -d;** *a.* not asleep; alert; vigilant; alive. **-n** *v.t.* and *v.i.* to rouse from sleep; to awake; to excite. **awak(en)ing** *n.* a revival of interest or consciousness.

**a•ward** *v.t.* to adjudge; to decide authoritatively; to assign judicially; *n.* judgment; the recorded decision of an arbitrator in a court of law; thing awarded; prize.

**a•ware** *a.* watchful; mindful; conscious of; possessing knowledge of; sensible. **-ness** *n.*

**a•wash** *adv. (Naut.)* level with the surface of the water.

**a•way** *adv.* absent; apart; be gone!.

**awe** *n.* wonder mingled with veneration and dread; *v.t.* to inspire with awe. **-some** *a.* **-struck, -stricken** *a.* **awful** *a.* full of awe; filling with fear and admiration; impressive; **awfulness** *n.*

**a•weigh** *adv. (Naut.)* when a ship's anchor is just broken out of the ground; atrip.

**aw•ful.** See **awe.**

**a•while** *adv.* for a while.

**awk•ward** *a.* ungainly; difficult to manage; inconvenient; embarrassing. **-ly** *adv.* **-ness** *n.* **awkward age,** adolescence.

**awl** *n.* a small pointed instrument for boring holes in leather.

**aw•ning** *n.* a covering of canvas, etc. to shelter from the sun's rays.

**a•woke.** See **awake.**

**a•wry** *adv.* and *a.* twisted to one side; crooked (See **wry**).

**ax, axe** *n.* a tool for cutting, chopping or hewing.

**axe**

**ax•es** plural form of **axe** and **axis.**

**ax•i•om** *n.* a necessary and self-evident proposition, requiring no proof. **-atic, -atical** *a.* self-evident. **-atically** *adv.*

**ax•is** *n.* imaginary line around which a solid body rotates. *pl.* **-s. axial** *a.* forming the axis. **axially** *adv.*

**ax•le, ax•le•tree** *n.* a bar of wood or iron rod on which a wheel, or a system of wheels, turns.

**a•za•lea** *n.* a genus of pl ants allied to the rhododendron.

**a•zo•ic** *a.* pert. to that part of geologic time before animal life existed.

**Az•tec** *n.* a member of a people dominant in Mexican Empire at the time of the Sp. conquest.

**az•ure** *n.* sky blue; *a.* sky-blue.

**Ba•al** *n.* a false deity. *pl.* **Baalim. Baalist** *n.* a worshipper of Baal.
**bab•ble** *v.t.* and *i.* to chatter senselessly; to prate; *n.* prattling; idle talk; murmuring of running water. **-r** *n.* **babbling** *n.*
**babe** *n.* an infant; a young child.
**ba•boon** *n.* a species of monkey with large body, big canine teeth and capacious cheek-pouches.

baboon

**ba•by** *n.* an infant; a young child; *a.* pert. to a baby; small, as in — **grand** (piano), etc. **-hood** *n.* the period of infancy. **-ish** *a.* infantile; behaving like a young child.
**bac•ca•lau•re•ate** *n.* the university degree of bachelor.
**Bac•chus** *n.* *(Myth.)* the god of wine.
**bach•e•lor** *n.* an unmarried man; one who has taken the first degree at a university. **-hood, -ism, -ship** *n.*
**ba•cil•lus** *n.* microscopic, rod-like organisms, capable of causing certain diseases. *pl.* **bacilli, bacillar, bacillary** *a.* **bacilliform** *a.* of a rod-like shape.
**back** *n.* the upper or hinder part of the trunk of an animal; the hinder part of an object; a football player whose position is behind the line of scrimmage; *a.* at the rear of; not current (as a magazine); reversed; *adv.* to or toward a former place, condition, or time; away from the front; in return; *v.t.* to force backward; to support; to endorse, *v.i.* to move or go back. **-bone** *n.* the spine or vertebral column; firmness; courage. **backboned** *a.* **-er** *n.* supporter; **-field** *n.* the backs as in football who play behind the line. **-fire** *n.* in internal combustion engines, premature ignition of fuel, *v.i.* to do this; to go awry; **-ground** *n.* part behind foreground of a picture or stage setting; knowledge gained by experience. **—hand** *n.* writing sloped from left to right; a stroke in tennis with the hand turned backwards. **-handed** *a.* with the back of the hand; deceitful. **-lash** *n.* the jarring reaction of a machine due to the degree of play; **-log** *n.* an accumulation, a reserve amount. **-side** *n.* back or hinder part; the buttocks. **-slide** *v.i.* to slide backwards; to lapse from a high moral standard. **-stage** *adv.* behind the stage, in the wings, etc. **—talk** *n.* insolent reply; impertinence. **-track** *v.i.* to retreat; to return over the same route. **-ward** *adv.* with the back in advance; towards, or on, the back; in a reverse direction; *a.* directed to the back or rear; dull; shy; late. **-wash** *n.* backward current. **-water** *n.* water held back by a dam; water thrown back by a paddle-wheel. **-woods** *n. pl.* outlying forest districts or remote undeveloped country. **-woodsman** *n.*
**back•gam•mon** *n.* a game played by two with 15 pieces each on a special board.
**ba•con** *n.* back and sides of hogs after being salted and smoked.
**bac•te•ri•um** *n.* group of nonspore forming bacteria. *pl.* **bacteria. bacterial** *a.* **bactericide** *n.* any agent capable of destroying bacteria. **bactericidal** *a.* **bacteriology** *n.* the study of bacteria.
**bad** *a.* ill or evil; wicked. **-ly** *adv.* **-ness** *n.* **bad blood,** ill feeling. **bad lands** *n. pl.,* badly eroded, barren land esp. in the Dakotas.
**bade** past tense of the verb **bid.**
**badge** *n.* an emblem, usually symbolic, worn to distinguish members of societies, regiments, etc.; mark; symbol.
**badg•er** *n.* a greyish-brown hibernating animal; *v.t.* to follow hotly as dogs do the badger; to tease, by persistent questioning.

badger

**bad•min•ton** *n.* a game similar to tennis with the substitution of shuttlecocks for tennis balls.
**baf•fle** *v.t.* to frustrate; to confuse. **-r** *n.* **baffling** *a.* disconcerting; confusing.
**baf•fle** *n.* a plate for regulating the flow of a liquid or gas; a metal plate used between the cylinders of an air-cooled motor engine to break up a stream of heated gases.
**bag** *n.* a sack or pouch; content of a sack; results of one's fishing or hunting; *v.t.* to put into a bag; *v.i.* to hang loosely. *pr.p.* **-ging.** *pa.p.* **-ged. -gage,** *n.* luggage. **and baggage,** with all one's belongings. **-giness** *n.* the state of being baggy (as trousers). **-gy** *a.* hanging loosely. **in the bag,** certain, assured. **to let the cat out of the bag,** to reveal a secret unwittingly.
**bag•a•telle** *n.* a thing of little worth; a game played with balls and a cue on a board.
**ba•gel** *n.* a doughnut-shaped roll.
**bag•pipe** *n.* musical reed instrument, common to Scotland. **-r** *n.*
**bail** *n.* *(Law)* security taken by the court that a person charged will attend at a future date to answer to the charge; one who furnishes this security; *v.t.* to obtain the release of a person from prison by giving security against his reappearance. **-able** *a.* **— bond** *n.* a bond given by a person who is being bailed and his surety. **bail out** *v.i.* to jump from an aircraft and descend by parachute.
**bail** *n.* a shallow vessel for clearing water out of a boat; *v.t.* to empty of water with some kind of water scoop. **-er** *n.*
**bail• iff** *n.* a minor officer of a court.

**bail•i•wick** *n.* bailiff's jurisdiction; *(Fig.)* one's special domain.

**bait** *n.* food set to entice fish or an animal; a lure; snare; *v.t.* to put food on a hook or in a trap as a lure. **-er** *n.* **-ing** *a.* and *n.*

**bake** *v.t.* to cook in an oven or over a fire; *v.i.* to work at baking. **-house** *n.* **bakery** *n.* a bakehouse. **baking** *n.* a batch of bread, etc. **a baker's dozen,** thirteen.

**Ba•ke•lite** *n.* a hard, strong synthetic resin used as a substitute for wood, bone, celluloid, etc., a trade name.

**bal•ance** *n.* an apparatus for determining the weight, or comparing the masses, of bodies; a poised beam with two opposite scales; part of a watch or clock which regulates the beats; payment still due, or cash in hand; *v.t.* to weigh, as in a balance; to render equal in proportion, etc.; to adjust, as an account; *v.i.* to be of the same weight. **— sheet** *a.* statement of the assets and liabilities of a company.

**bal•co•ny** *n.* a platform or gallery projecting from a building; a gallery in a theater or concert hall.

**bald** *a.* destitute of hair or feathers on the crown of the head; bare; without literary style. **-head, -pate** *n.* one destitute of hair. **-ly** *adv.* **-ness** *n.*

**bal•er•dash** *n.* a jargon of meaningless words jumbled together; nonsense.

**bale** *n.* that which causes sorrow or ruin. **-ful** *a.* **-fully** *adv.*

**bale** *n.* a package, compactly compressed, and wrapped in a protecting cover; *v.t.* to pack in bales. **-r** *n.* one employed in baling goods.

**balk** *n.* a crossbeam or rafter, of squared timber, stretching from wall to wall; an unploughed ridge of land; a barrier or check; a disappointment; a part of a billiard table; in *baseball,* an uncompleted pitch, entitling base runners to advance one base; *v.t.* to frustrate; to bar the way; *v.i.* to stop abruptly; refuse to move. **-y** *a.*

**ball** *n.* any round body; a sphere; the earth; bullet or shot; a delivery outside the strike zone by a pitcher; the heavy piece of a pendulum; *v.t.* and *i.* to form into a ball. **— bearings** *n.* hardened steel balls interposed in channels or 'races' between the rotating and stationary surfaces of a bearing to lessen friction. **— point pen** *n.* fountain pen with a tiny ball point leaving a fine trace of ink on the paper. **—race** *n.* the grooves in which the balls of a ball bearing run. **ball and socket,** a joint formed by a ball partly enclosed in a cup and so adjusted that it can move freely in all directions.

**ball** *n.* a social gathering for the purpose of dancing. **-room,** *n.*

**bal•lad** *n.* a story in verse, of popular origin, generally patriotic and sung orig. to the harp. **-ist** *n.* a composer or singer of ballads. **-ry** *n.* collected ballads; folk songs. **-eer** *n.*

**bal•last** *n.* heavy material taken on board ship to increase the vessel's draft and steadiness; sandy material dredged from river beds used for concrete; that which renders anything steady; *v.t.* to load with ballast; to steady.

**bal•le•ri•na** *n.* a female ballet dancer.

**bal•let** *n.* a representation, consisting of dancing and miming, aiming to express an idea or tell a story, to the accompaniment of music.

**ballistic** *a.* pert. to a projectile and its flight.

**bal•lis•tics** *n.pl.* scientific study of motion of projectiles.

**bal•lon** *n.* bag designed to float in the air and unequipped for mechanical propulsion; anything inflated. **-ing** *n.* **-ist** *n.*

**bal•lot** *n.* secret voting; slip of paper used in secret voting; *v.t.* to draw lots.

**balm** a fragrant plant; any fragrant or healing ointment; anything which soothes pain. **-iness** *n.* **-y** *a.* fragrant; bearing balm.

**bal•sa** *n.* the extremely light wood of a W. Indian tree.

**bal•sam** *n.* a name applied to many aromatic resins and oils with stimulant and tonic properties; a healing agent. **-ic** *n.* soothing, oily. **-ous** *a.* soothing. **-y** *a.*

**bal•us•ter** *n.* a stone or wooden shaft turned and molded, used to support a handrail. **-ed** *a.* provided with balusters. **balustrade** *n.* a row of balusters supporting a railing.

**bam•boo** *n.* a genus of immense grasses in the tropics.

**ban** *n.* proclamation; a sentence of outlawry; a prohibition; *v.t.* to prohibit; to curse; *pr.p.* **-ning.** *pa.t.* and *pa. p.* **-ned.**

**ba•nal** *a.* trite, trivial, petty, commonplace, **-ity** *n.*

**ba•nan•a** *n.* the edible fruit of a tropical plant.

**banana**

**band** *n.* a cord, tie or fillet; an endless belt used for driving wheels or rollers. **-box** *n.* a light cardboard box for millinery.

**band** *n.* players of musical instruments in combined performance; a company united for common purpose; *v.t.* to bind together; *v.i.* join together. **-master** *n.* director of a military or brass band. **-stand** *n.* an open-air structure suitable for musical performances.

**band•age** *n.* a strip of cloth, used for binding up wounds, etc. *v.t.* to bind with a bandage.

**ban•dan•na, ban•dan•a** a large patterned silk or cotton handkerchief.

**ban•it** *n.* robber; outlaw; *pl.* **-s, -ti. -ry** *n.*
**ban•dy** *a.* crooked; bent; *v.t.* to toss from one to another, as 'to bandy words.' **bandied** *a.* **— legged** *a.* having crooked legs, bending outwards.
**bane** *n.* any cause of ruin; mischief; poison. **-ful** *a.* **-fulness** *n.*
**bang** *v.t.* to beat, as with a club; to make a loud noise; *n.* a blow with a club or a fist; a loud noise. **-ing** *n.*
**bang** *v.t.* to cut the front hair square across; *n.* a straight fringe over the forehead.
**ban•gle** *n.* an ornamental ring worn round arm or ankle.
**ban•ish** *v.t.* to condemn to exile; to drive away; to expel; to cast from the mind. **-ment** *n.* exile.
**ban•is•ter** *n.* Same as **baluster.**
**ban•jo** *n.* a stringed musical instrument.
**bank** *n.* a ridge of earth; the edge of a stream or lake; a mass of heavy clouds or fog; *v.t.* to raise a mound; to cover a fire with small coal to procure slow combustion. **to bank on** *v.t.* to depend on.
**bank** *n.* an establishment where money is received for custody and repaid on demand; the money at stake in games of chance; *v.t.* to deposit money in a bank. **-book** *n.* a pass book in which a customer's dealings with a bank are recorded. **-er** *n.* one employed in banking. **— note** *n.* a promissory note on bank of issue promising to pay its face value to bearer on demand. **— rate** *n.* the rate of discount, fixed by a bank or banks.
**bank•rupt** *n.* insolvent person compelled to place his affairs in the hands of creditors; *v.t.* to cause to go bankrupt; *a.* insolvent, unable to pay debts. **-cy** *n.*
**ban•ner** *n.* a flag or ensign. **-ed** *a.*
**ban•quet** *n.* a feast; something specially delicious. **-ing** *n.*
**ban•shee** *n.* in Ireland and W. Highlands of Scotland, a fairy-elf who, by shrieks and wailing, foretells the approaching death of a member of a family.
**ban•tam** *n.* a variety of the small, common domestic fowl; *a.* of very light weight. **-weight** a boxer weighing less than 118 lbs.
**ban•ter** *v.i.* to make good-natured fun of someone; to joke. *n.* wit at expense of another. **-er** *n.*
**Ban•tu** *n.* an African language.
**ban•yan** *n.* the Indian fig; a tree whose branches, bending to the ground, take root and form new stocks, till they become a forest.
**bap•tize** *v.t.* to christen; give a name to. **baptism** *n.* sacrament by which a person is initiated into the membership of the Christian Church. **baptismal** *a.* **Baptist** *n.* one who insists that the rite of initiation is duly administered only by immersion upon personal profession of faith.
**bar** *n.* a long piece of any solid material, used as barrier; the bolt of a door; part of a tavern with a counter for the sale of liquor; members of the legal profession allowed to plead in court; *(Mus.)* a perpendicular line drawn across the stave immediately before the primary accent; *v.t.* to mark with a bar; to obstruct; to exclude; *prep.* except. **-maid, -man, -tender** *n.* a bar attendant. **-ring** *prep.* excepting; *n.* exclusion of any kind. *pr. p.* **-ring.** *pa. p.* **-red.**
**barb** *n.* the spike of an arrow, fish-hook, etc.; *v.t.* to furnish with barbs or prongs, as an arrow; to trim the beard. **-ed** *a.* bearded; furnished with a barb or barbs. **-ed wire** *n.* a wire armed with sharp points used for defensive purposes.
**bar•bar•i•an** *n.* an uncivilized being without culture; a cruel, brutal man; *a.* savage; rude. **barbaric** *a.* uncivilized. **barbarize** *v.t.* to render barbarous. **barbarism** *n.* want of civilization. **barbarity** *n.* cruelty; savagery. **barbarous** *a.* uncivilized or savage.
**bar•be•cue** *n.* a grid-iron on which meat is roasted over an open fire; a lavish open-air feast.
**bar•ber** *n.* one who shaves or trims and dresses the hair; a hair-dresser.
**bar•ber•ry** *n.* *(Bot.)* a shrub with clusters of red berries.
**bar•bi•tu•rates** *n.* *(Med.)* derivatives of barbituric acid, non-habit forming, hypnotic and sedative drugs.
**bare** *a.* without covering; naked; empty; *v.t.* to strip off or uncover. **-ly** *adv.* openly; scarcely. **-ness** *n.* **-facedness** *n.* sheer impudence.
**bar•gain** *n.* an agreement between parties in buying and selling; something purchased cheaply. *v.i.* to make a contract. **-er** *n.* one who haggles over the price.
**barge** *n.* flat-bottomed boat; *v.i.* to push forward roughly. **-man** *n.*
**bar•i•tone** *n.* the male human voice between tenor and bass.
**bar•i•um** *n.* metallic element (symbol *Ba*). **baric** *a.*
**bark** *n.* the outer covering of a tree; *v.t.* to strip off bark.
**bark** *v.t.* to utter a cry like a dog; to yelp.
**bar•ley** *n.* a cereal, the grain being used for malt-making, bread, and food for cattle. **-corn** *n.* a grain of barley.
**barm** *n.* the froth on fermenting malt liquors, used in making bread; yeast. **-y** *a.* light-headed, flighty, or giddy.
**barn** *n.* a covered farm-building for storing grain, hay, etc. and for stabling live stock; *v.t.* to store in a barn. **-yard** *a.* pert. to domestic fowls. *n.* open enclosure attached to barn.
**bar•na•cle** *n.* a shell-fish which attaches itself to the bottoms of ships and to rocks. **-d** *a.*
**ba•rom•e•ter** *n.* an instrument for recording the weight or pressure of the atmosphere which indicates impending weather changes. **barometric, barometrical** *a.*
**bar•on** *n.* a title of nobility, the lowest of the British peerage to sit in the House of Lords.
**ba•roque** *n.* *(Art.)* a florid style of the late Renaissance; *a.* over-lavish;

extravagantly ornamented.
**bar•o•scope** *n.* an instrument giving rough indications of variations in the atmospheric pressure.
**bar•rack** *n.* a building for the accomodation of soldiers.
**bar•ra•cuda** *n.* a large edible pike-like fish, found in the Atlantic.
**bar•rage** *n.* an artificial bar erected across a stream to regulate its flow; a screen of continuous military fire produced to protect the advance of troops or to stop hostile attacks.
**bar•rel** *n.* a cylindrical wooden container consisting of staves bound by hoops; a measure of capacity; anything cylindrical, as a gun-barrel; *v.t.* to stow in barrels. **—organ** *n.* street-organ played by rotating a wooden barrel.
**bar•ren** *a.* incapable of producing offspring or fruit; empty, lacking. **-ly** *adv.* **-ness** *n.* sterility.
**bar•rette** *n.* small bar or clasp worn to hold hair in place.
**bar•ri•cade** *n.* an obstruction which hinders free passage; *v.t.* to build this.
**bar•ri•er** *n.* a chain of military posts to protect frontiers; a railing, fence or wall; a line of separation.
**bar•row** *n.* a small kind of light frame provided with two shafts, for carrying loads.
**bar•ter** *v.t.* to exchange or give in exchange; *v.i.* to traffic by exchange of one kind of goods for another; *n.* direct exchange of commodities.
**bas•al** See **base** *n.*
**ba•salt** *n.* an igneous rock of greenish-black color. **-ic** *a.*
**bas•cule** *n.* a balancing lever. **bascule-bridge** *n.* a counterpoise bridge.
**base** *a.* morally low. **-ly** *adv.*
**base** *n.* bottom; part of a thing on which it rests; foundation; fixed point; supply point of an army; station at baseball; *(Chem.)* a substance capable of combining with an acid to form a salt; *v.t.* to put on a base; to found. **basal** *a.* situated at the base. **-less** *a.* having no foundation. **-lessness** *n.* **-ly** *adv.* **-ment** *n.* the lowest story of a building. **basic** *a.* **-board** *n.* a skirting board covering the lower part of a wall.
**base•ball** *n.* ball game, played by two teams of nine players in which a player after batting must make the complete circuit of four bases to score a run; the ball used.
**bash** *v.t. (Colloq.)* to smash in; to knock out of shape; *n.* a severe blow; a dent. **-ing** *n.* a thrashing.
**bash•ful** *a.* shy; not desiring to attract notice. **-ly** *adv.* **-ness** *n.*
**ba•sic** *a.* relating to or serving as a base; primary. **English,** simplification of English.
**bas•il** *n.* aromatic culinary plant; sweet basil.
**ba•sil•i•ca** *n.* a public building or hall of the Romans, later often converted into a church by early Christians. **basilican** *a.*
**ba•sin** *n.* a wide, hollow, bowl-shaped container; a sink; the whole tract of country drained by a river.
**ba•sis** *n.* that on which a thing rests; foundation. *pl.* **bases.**
**bask** *v.i.* to lie in warmth or sunshine.
**bas•ket** *n.* a container made of willow, cane, rushes, or other flexible materials, interwoven. **-ball** *n.* a game where a ball has to be thrown through a basket. **-ful** *n.* **-ry, -work** *n.* wickerwork.
**Basque** *n.* a native or the language of the Basque country (Western Pyrenees); *a.* relating to the Basques.
**bass** *n.* name applied to any perch-like fish.
**bass, base** *n. (Mus.)* the lowest part of harmony, whether vocal or instrumental; the deepest quality of the human voice or a stringed instrument; *a.* low. **—clef** *n.* the sign on the fourth line of the bass stave. **doublebase** *n.* the largest of the stringed instruments.
**bas•set** *n.* a hound formerly used in badger hunting; *(Geol.)* emergence of strata at the surface. **—horn** *n.* a rich-toned wind instrument.
**bas•so** *n.* a bass singer; the bass part of a harmony.
**bas•soon** *n.* a wood-wind musical instrument with a double reed mouthpiece; organ reed stop of that name. **double—**, one which sounds an octave lower. **-ist** *n.*
**bast** *n.* inner bark of a tree, used for binding purposes.
**bas•tard** *n.* a child born out of wedlock; an impure, coarse brown refuse product of sugar-refining, used to color beer; *a.* illegitimate; counterfeit; **-ize** *v.t.* to render illegitimate.
**baste** *v.t.* to sew loosely with long stitches; to moisten (meat) with butter, drippings, etc. while cooking.
**bas•tille** *n.* originally a tower or bastion. **The Bastille,** the famous state prison of Paris.
**bat** *n.* a club or stick; a shaped club used in cricket or baseball; *v.i.* to strike or hit with a bat; *pr.p.* **-ting;** *pa.p.* **-ted, -ter, -man** *n.*
**bat** *n.* nocturnal, flying mammal. **-ity** *a.*
**bat** *v.t. (Colloq.)* to wink. **never batted an eyelid,** showed no emotion whatever.
**batch** *n.* a number of articles received or dispatched at one time; a set of similar articles.
**bate** *v.t.* to lessen; to abate.
**bath** *n.* a vessel or place to bathe in; the water in which to bathe; a solution in which photographic plates are immersed; *v.t.* to wash oneself. **-s** *n.pl.* hot or mineral springs resorted to by invalids. **-house** *n.* **-room** *n.* **blood—.** *n.* a massacre. **Turkish bath,** steam bath followed by massage. **sitz bath,** a shallow bath, for bathing hips and buttocks.
**bathe** *v.t.* to wash by immersion; *v.i.* to be immersed; to swim; *pr.p.* **bathing.** **-r** *n.* **bathing** *n.* **bathingpool** *n.*
**ba•thet•ic** See under **bathos.**
**bath•i•nette** *n.* portable folding bathtub for babies.
**ba•thom•e•ter** *n.* a spring balance for

determining the depth of water.

**ba•thos** *n.* a term which indicates a ludicrous descent from the sublime to the ridiculous in speech or writing; anti-climax. **bathetic** *a.*

**ba•tiste** *n.* a fine kind of linen cloth from Flanders.

**ba•ton** *n.* a short staff or club. in music, wand used by conductor in beating time.

**batt, batting** *n.* fiber wadded into sheets.

**bat•tal•ion** *n.* a military tactical and administrative unit of command consisting of three or more companies or similar units. -s *n.pl.*

**bat•ten** *n.* a piece of wood nailed on a surface to give it strength; *v.t.* to fasten with battens.

**bat•ter** *v.t.* to strike or beat continuously; *n.* a mixture moistened to a paste and briskly beaten up. **-ing ram.** *n.* a suspended beam used to breach walls.

**bat•ter•y** *n.* a division of artillery; electric cells which store electric current; the pitcher and catcher in baseball.

**bat•tle** *n.* an encounter between enemies; *v.i.* to fight on a large scale. **— axe** *n.* primitive weapon; **— cry** *n.* a war-shout; a slogan. **-field, -ground** *n.* scene of battle. **-r** *n.* one who takes part in a battle. **-ship** *n.* the largest and most heavily armed of fast warships.

**bau•ble** *n.* a trifling piece of finery.

**baux•ite** *n.* the principal source of aluminum.

**bawd** *n.* a procurer of procuress of women for immoral purposes. **-ily** *adv.* **-iness** *n.* **-ry** *n.* **-y** *a.* unchaste. **—house,** *n.* a brothel.

**bawl** *v.t.* to proclaim; *v.i.* to shout out with a loud voice; *n.* a loud, prolonged cry. **bawl out** *(Colloq.)* reprimand.

**bay** *n.* an inlet of the sea.

**bay** *n.* the subdivision longitudinally of a building by piers, arches, girders, etc. **— window** *n.* a window projecting beyond the wall. **sick —**,. ship's hospital.

**bay** *n.* the laurel tree. **-s** *n.pl.* the victor's crown. **— rum** *n.* an aromatic liquid used as a perfume and cosmetic for the hair.

**bay** *n.* barking, esp. of hounds in pursuit of prey; *v.t.* to bark at. **at bay,** said of a hunted animal, when all escape is cut off.

**bay•ber•ry** *n.* evergreen shrub, used for making bay rum; one variety used in candle making.

**bay•o•net** *n.* a short spear-like weapon attached to the muzzle of a rifle; *v.t.* to stab with a bayonet.

**ba•zaar, bazar** *n.* a sale where articles are sold for charity.

**ba•zoo•ka** *n.* a portable light rocket-gun.

**B.C.** before Christ.

**be** *v.i.* and *aux.* *(pres. indic.* **am;** *past indic.* **was;** *past part.* **been** *),* to exist; to live; to have a state, existence, or quality; to belong.

**be-** *prefix* used in the construction of compound words, as *becalm,* etc.

**beach** *n.* the shore of the sea or of a lake, esp. where sandy or pebbly; the shore; *v.t.* to run or haul a boat up on to a beach. **-comber** *n.* a lounger who frequents beaches or seaports; scrounger. **-head** *n.* a footing gained on hostile shores by an army.

**bea•con** *n.* a fire lit on a high eminence, usually as a warning; a warning light.

**bead** *n.* any small spherical object; *v.i.* to string beads. **-s** *n.pl.* a rosary, a necklace; **-ed** *a.* in bead form. **-ing** *n.* a small rounded molding imitating beads. **-y** *a.* bead-like.

**bea•gle** *n.* the smallest hound used in hunting.

**beak** *n.* the horny bill of a bird, turtle, etc.

**beak•er** *n.* a tumbler-shaped vessel of thin glass used by chemists.

**beam** *n.* a strong, horizontal piece of timber or reinforced concrete for spanning and supporting weights; a sharply defined ray of light; the sparkle in a person's eyes manifesting extreme pleasure or interest; *v.t.* to emit beams of light; *v.i.* to send forth rays of light; to smile benignly. **-ing** *a.* radiantly happy; *n.* rays of light; manifestation of pleasure by smiling. **-less** *a.*

**bean** *n.* the flat, kidney-shaped seed of various plants, chiefly of the genus *Phaseolus;* **-bag** *n.* a toy, a small cloth bag partly filled with beans.

**bear** *v.t.* to support or to carry; to endure; to give birth to; *v.i.* to produce (as fruit); to endure; *pa.t.* **bore;** *pa.p.* **borne** or **born. -able** *a.* tolerable. **-ably** *adv.* **-er** *n.* messenger. **-ing** *n.* the manner in which a person behaves; **-ings** *n.pl.* machine surfaces carrying a moving part and bearing friction. **to bear out,** to corroborate. **to bear with,** to endure patiently. **to bring to bear,** to apply pressure. **to lose one's bearings,** to lose all sense of direction.

**bear** *n.* a carnivorous mammal of the Ursidae order; a rough, boorish person; *(Astron.)* one of two constellations in the northern hemisphere called respectively the **Great Bear** and the **Lesser Bear. -like** *a.* **skin** *n.*

**beard** *n.* the hair that grows on the chin and cheeks. **-ed** *a.* **-less** *a.*

**beast** *n.* any inferior animal as opposed to man; a four-footed animal especially if wild. **-ly** a. like a beast in nature; displeasing. **-liness** *n.*

**beat** *v.t.* to strike repeatedly; to pommel; to defeat; to mark time in music; *v.i.* to throb; *pa.t.* **beat;** *pa.p.* **-en;** *n.* a recurrent stroke; a pulse throb; *(Mus.)* the divisions in a bar, the movement of a conductor's baton; *a.* *(Colloq.)* exhausted. **-en** *a.* hammered into shape by a tool; worn by continual use. **-er** *n.* **-ing** *n.* act of giving blows. **-nik** *n.* *(Colloq.)* one who rebels against the conventions of society. **to beat about the bush,** to approach a subject in a round about way.

**be•at•i•fy** *v.t.* to render supremely blessed or happy. **beatification** *n.*

**be•at•i•tude** *n.* highest form of heavenly happiness.

**beau** *n.* suitor. *pl.* **beaux.**

**beau•ty** *n.* the inherent quality in an object

of pleasing the eye, ear, or mind; a fine specimen. **beauteous** *a.* very handsome. **beauteously** *adv.* **beauteousness** *n.* **beautician** *n.* expert in use of cosmetics. **beautifier** *n.* a cosmetic; a decorator. **beautiful** *a.* highly pleasing to eye, ear, or mind. **beautifully** *adv.* **beautifulness** *n.* **beautify** *v.t.* to make beautiful. **beautiless** *a.* lacking beauty. **—spot** *n.* a patch placed on the face to heighten beauty.

**bea•ver** *n.* an amphibious, four-footed rodent valued for its fur and for castoreum, an extract from its glands used in medicine; *a.* made of beaver fur.

**be•calm** *v.t.* to make calm or quiet.

**be•came** past tense of **become.**

**be•cause** *adv.* and *conj.* for the reason that; since.

**beck** *n.* gesture of the head or hand; a nod; *v.i.* to make such a gesture; *v.t.* to call by a nod; to beckon. **at one's beck and call,** entirely at someone's disposal.

**beck•on** *v.t.* and *v.i.* to make a sign with the hand or head.

**be•come** *v.t.* to pass from one state to another; to be suitable to; *pa.t.* **became;** *pa.p.* **become. becoming** *a.* appropriate.

**bed** *n.* a couch on which to sleep or take a rest; a plot of ground in which plants are cultivated; a layer of rock; *v.t.* to place in bed; to arrange in layers; *pr.p.* **-ding;** *pa.p.* **-ded. -bug** *n.* bloodsucking insect. **-clothes** *n.pl.* bed coverings, clothes worn to bed. **-ding** *n.* materials of a bed. **-fellow** *n.* one who sleeps in the same bed with another. **-pan** *n.* pan used as toilet. **-post** *n.* one of the upright supports of a bed. **-rid, -ridden** *a.* permanently confined to bed by age or infirmity. **-rock** *n.* the solid rock beneath loose material as sand, etc.; fundamentals. **-room** *n.* a room for sleeping. **-sore** *n.* ulcer caused by constant pressure on a part of the body of a bed-ridden patient. **-spread** *n.* a covering of fine material for a bed. **-ticking** *n.* the cloth case for holding the feathers, hair, etc. of a mattress.

**be•daub** *v.t.* to smear.

**be•daz•zle** *v.t.* to overpower by employing too strong a light or by a magnificient show.

**be•deck** *v.t.* to adorn.

**be•dev•il** *v.t.* to beat with devilish malignity; to bewitch.

**bed•lam** *n.* a scene of uproar; pandemonium.

**Bed•ou•in** *n.* Arab; nomad.

**be•rag•gle** *v.t.* to soil by trailing in the wet or mud. **-d** *a.*

**bee** *n.* highest form of insect belonging to the order Hymenoptera; gathering for amusement or mutual help, e.g. a spelling-bee. **culture** *n.* the rearing of bees, apiculture. **-hive** *n.* a case or box where the bees are housed; *a.* shaped like a bee-hive. **-keeper** *n.* **-line** *n.* the shortest route from one place to another. **-wax** *n.* the wax secreted by bees.

**bee**

**beech** *n.* a tree of the temperate and sub-frigid zones, greatly valued for its wood. **-coal** *n.* charcoal made from beechwood. **-en** *a.* made of beech. **beechnut** *n.* the triangular, edible nut of the beech.

**beef** *n.* the flesh of an ox, bull, or cow; muscular strength; *a.* consisting of beef; **beeves** *n.pl.* oxen. **-iness** *n.* tendency to put on flesh. **-steak** *n.* a thick slice of beef. **-y** *a.* stolid; stout.

**been** *pa.p.* of the verb **be.**

**beer** *n.* an alcoholic beverage made by brewing and fermentation of cereals.

**beet** *n.* a garden or field plant having a succulent tap root, the red variety being used as a vegetable, the white yielding sugar. **—sugar** *n.* crystallized sugar extracted from beetroot.

**bee•tle** *n.* name of a large order of insects, Coleoptera.

**be•fall** *v.t.* to happen to; *v.i.* to come to pass; *pr.p.* **-ing;** *pa.t.* **befell;** *pa.p.* **-en.**

**be•fit** *v.t.* to be suitable to; to become; *pr.p.* **-ting;** *pa.t., pa.p.* **-ted. -ting** *a.* **-tingly** *adv.*

**be•fog** *v.t.* to envelop in a fog; perplex. *pr.p.* **-ging.** *pa.t.* **-ged.**

**be•fore** *prep.* preceding; in the presence of; *adv.* in front of; already. *conj.* sooner than; rather than. **-hand** *adv.* previously. **-time** *adv.* of old; formerly.

**be•foul** *v.t.* to foul, dirty.

**be•friend** *v.t.* to act as a friend to; to help a stranger.

**be•fud•le** *v.t.* to confuse.

**beg** *v.t.* to ask humbly; to beseech; *pr.p.* **-ging;** *pa.t.* and *pa.p.* **-ged. -gar** *n.* one who solicits alms; *v.t.* to ruin financially. **-garliness** *n.* **-garly** *a.* like a beggar; poor; worthless; *adv.* meanly. **-gary** *n.* extreme poverty. **-ging** *n.* soliciting alms; *a.* soliciting.

**be•gan** *pa.t.* of **begin.**

**be•get** *v.t.* to generate; give rise to. *pr.p.* **-ting;** *pa.t.* **begot, begat;** *pa.p.* **begot, begotten.**

**be•gin** *v.t.* to start, to commence; *v.i.* to set about. *pr.p.* **-ning.** *pa.t.* **began;** *pa.p.* **begun. -ner** *n.* novice. **-ning** *n.* source; first part.

**be•gird** *v.t.* to bind with a girdle or band; *pa.t.* **begirt** or **-ed.**

**be•gone** *interj.* depart! **woebegon** *a.* gloomy and miserable.

**be•go•ni•a** *n.* a genus of tropical plants.

**be•got begotten** *pa. p.* of **beget.**

**be•grime** *v.t.* to soil with grime.

**be•grudge** *v.t.* to allow reluctantly. **begrudgingly** *adv.*

**be•guile** *v.t.* to cheat or deceive by trickery; to delude. **-ment** *n.* **-r** *n.* **beguilingly** *adv.*

**be•gun** *pa. p.* of **begin.**

**be•half** *n.* favor; benefit; defense.

**be•have** *v.t.* and *v.i.* to conduct oneself; to act. **behavior** *n.* deportment. **behaviorism** *n.* theory that man's actions are automatic responses to stimuli and not dictated by consciousness.

**be•head** *v.t.* to sever the head from the body. **-al, -ing** *n.*

**be•held** *pa.p.* of **behold.**

**be•hest** *n.* that which is ordered.

**be•hind** *prep.* at the back of; in the rear (of); after; *n.* rump; posterior. **-hand** *adv.* and *a.* backward; in arrears.

**be•hold** *v.t.* to fix the eyes upon; *v.i.* fix the attention. *pa.t.* and *pa.p.* **beheld. -en** *a.* owing a debt of gratitude (to). **-er** *n.* an on-looker; spectator.

**be•hoof** *n.* advantage; benefit; use. **behoove, behove** *v.t.* to be necessary, convenient for.

**beige** *n.* very light brown color of unbleached wool.

**be•ing** *n.* existence.

**be•la•bor** *v.t.* to beat soundly; to assail verbally.

**be•late** *v.t.* to cause to be late.

**be•lay** *v.t.* to make fast a rope, by winding it round a fixed pin or cleat; *n.* in mountaineering, a rock to which a climber anchors himself by a rope. **-ing-pin** *n.* a pin or cleat to which running rigging may be belayed.

**belch** *v.t.* to emit wind from the stomach by way of the mouth; *n.* eructation.

**bel•fry** *n.* a bell-tower, or a part of a steeple, where bells are hung.

**be•lie** *v.t.* to speak falsely of; to misrepresent; *pr.p.* **belying.**

**be•lieve** *v.t.* to regard as true; to trust; *v.i.* to have faith (in); to suppose. **belief** *n.* full acceptance of a thing as true; a firm persuasion of the truth of a body of religious tenets. **believable** *a.* credible. **-r** *n.* **to make believe,** to pretend.

**be•lit•tle** *v.t.* to think lightly of; to disparage. **-ment** *n.*

**bell** *n.* a hollow, cup-shaped metal vessel which gives forth a clear, musical note when struck. **bells** *n.pl.* *(Naut.)* half hours of a watch at sea, struck on a ship's bell. **-boy** *n.* page-boy in hotel. **-buoy** *n.* a buoy which by its swaying rings a bell attached.

**bell** *n.* the cry of an animal. Also **-ing;** *v.i.* to bellow; to roar.

**bel•la•don•na** *n.* deadly nightshade from which drugs, hyoscine and atropine, are obtained.

**bel•li•cose** *a.* pugnacious; quarrelsome. **-ly** *adv.* **bellicosity** *n.*

**bel•lig•er•ence** *n.* the state of being at war; warlike attitude. **belligerency** *n.* a state of war. **belligerent** *n.* a nation, party, or person taking part in war; *a.* waging war; pugnacious.

**bel•low** *v.i.* to roar like a bull; to shout loudly; to make an outcry.

**bel•lows** *n.pl.* an instrument for producing a strong blast of air (to stimulate a fire, to work an organ, etc.)

**bel•ly** *n.* part of the body which contains bowels; abdomen; *a.* abdominal; *v.i.* to bulge. **-ache** *n.* abdominal pains. **-band** *n.* a band under the belly of a horse to secure saddle. **-ful** *n.* sufficiency of food, etc.

**be•long** *v.i.* to be connected with; to be property of. **-ings** *n.pl.* possessions.

**be•loved** *a.* greatly loved; *n.* one very dear to others.

**be•low** *prep.* beneath; of inferior rank or status; *adv.* in a lower place; beneath.

**belt** *n.* a band used for encircling; a zone given over to the raising of one plant, e.g. wheat—*v.t.* to encircle, as with a belt; to thrash with a belt. **-ed** *a.* thrashed with a belt. **conveyor—***n.* an endless belt used for conveying material from one place to another. **-ing** *n.* material for skirt or bodice bands.

**be•moan** *v.t.* to express deep grief for, by moaning.

**be•muse** *v.t.* to put into a state of confusion; to daze. **-d** *a.*

**ben** *n.* a geographical term, a mountain peak, as Ben Lomond.

**bench** *n.* a long seat; a table on which wood work is done; collective name for the body of judges sitting in judgment.

**bend** *v.t.* to curve; to turn out of direct course; to subdue or make submissive; to tie, make fast—of ropes and sails *v.i.* to be moved out of a straight line; to yield; *pa.t.* **bent,** *pa.p.* **bent** or **-ed;** *n.* a curve; turn. **-er** *n.* an instrument for bending; a drinking spree. **the bends,** aenoembolism.

**be•neath** *prep.* under; lower than; unworthy of; *adv.* below.

**Ben•e•dict** *n.* the founder of Western monasticism. **Benedictine** *a.* pert. to St. Benedict or his monastic order; *n.* a Black Friar; a cordial or liqueur originally distilled by the Benedictine monks.

**ben•e•dic•tion** *n.* the blessing at the end of a religious service. **benedictory** *a.* imparting a blessing.

**ben•e•fac•tion** *n.* act of doing good; donation. **benefactor** *n.* *(fem.* **benefactress***)* one who helps others; a patron. **benefactory** *a.*

**ben•e•fice** *n.* an ecclesiastical living. **-d** *a.* in enjoyment of a benefice.

**be•nef•i•cence** *n.* habitual practice of doing good; charity. **beneficent** *a.* kindly disposed; generous **beneficently** *adv.*

**ben•e•fi•cial** *a.* advantageous; helpful. **-ly** *adv.* **-ness** *n.* **beneficiary** *n.* one who benefits from the act of another.

**ben•e•fit** *n.* an act of kindness; a favor conferred; a theatrical or other exhibition, the proceeds of which go to charity or an individual; *v.t.* to do good to; *v.i.* to gain advantage (from).

**be•nev•o•lence** *n.* disposition to do good; generosity. **benevolent** *a.* of a kindly nature.

**be•night•ed** *a.* enveloped in moral or mental darkness; unenlightened.

**be•nign** *a.* of a kindly disposition; not malignant (of disease). **-ancy** *n.* benignant quality. **-ant** *a.* kind; beneficial. **-antly** *adv.* **-ity** *n.* **-ly** *adv.* in benign fashion.

**ben•ja•min** *n.* benzoin, a kind of resin or gum used as a medicine.
**bent** *pa.t.* and *pa.p.* of **bend.**
**bent** *n.* (of mind), leaning, bias, or inclination for.
**be•numb** *v.t.* to make numb, through cold or fear; to deaden. **-ed** *a.*
**Ben•ze•drine** *n.* amphetamine, a synthetic drug.
**be•queath** *v.t.* to leave by will, said of personal property; to leave to those who follow on, as a problem, trouble, etc. **bequest** *n.* legacy.
**be•rate** *v.t.* to scold vigorously.
**be•reave** *v.t.* to deprive of; *pa.p.* **-d** or **bereft. -d** *a.* robbed by death, esp. of a relative. **-ment** *n.* loss, esp. by death.
**be•ret** *n.* a soft, round, tightfitting cap without any peak.
**berg** *n.* a large mass or mountain of ice.
**ber•i•ber•i** *n.* a nervous disease due to deficiency of vitamin B.
**ber•ry** *n.* a small, pulpy, juicy fruit; strictly a simple fruit with succulent pericarp. **-ing** *n.* **berried** *a.*
**ber•serk, ber•serk•er** *n.* a battle-frenzied Norse warrior; *a.* frenzied. **to go berserk,** to go mad with fury.
**berth** *n.* the place where a ship is anchored; a sleeping-place on a ship, etc. *v.t.* to bring to anchorage. **-age** *n.* dock or harbor dues.
**ber'yl** *n.* a group of green or bluish-green precious stones of exceptional hardness. **-lium** *n.* a rare metal of the magnesium group.
**be•seech** *v.t.* to ask or entreat earnestly; *pa.t.* and *pa.p.* **besought. -er** *n.* **-ing** *a.*
**be•seem** *v.t.* to be fit for; to become. **beseeming** *a.*
**be•set** *v.t.* to place on, in, or around; *pr.p.* **-ting.** *pa.t.* and *pa.p.* **beset, -ment** *n.* **-ter** *n.*
**be•shrew** *v.t.* to wish some slight evil to befall one.
**be•side** *prep.* and *adv.* at the side of; over and above; distinct from. **-s** *adv.* moreover; *prep.* over and above. **— oneself,** out of one's wits.
**be•siege** *v.t.* to surround with armed forces; to pay court to. **-ment** *n.* **-r** *n.* **besieging** *a.* **besiegingly** *adv.*
**be•smear** *v.t.* to smear over; to soil.
**be•spat•ter** *v.t.* to sprinkle or splash with mud, ink, etc.
**be•speak** *v.t.* to order, speak for, or engage beforehand; *pa.t.* **bespoke.** *pa.p.* **bespoke** and **bespoken. bespoke, bespoken** *a.* ordered beforehand.
**be•speck•le** *v.t.* to mark with speckles or spots.
**best** *a.* *superl.* good in the highest degree; most suitable, advantageous, or appropriate; *adv.* in the most excellent manner; *n.* perfection. **— man,** chief attendant to the groom at a wedding. **— seller,** a current popular book with an enormous sale. **to make the best of,** to resign oneself to conditions, etc.
**bes•tial** *a.* having the instincts of a beast. **-ity** *n.* beastly depravity.
**be•stir** *v.t.* to rouse into vigorous action; to stimulate. *pr.p.* **-ring.** *pa.t.* **-red.**
**be•stow** *v.t.* to lay up in store; to give ceremoniously. **-al** *n.* **-er** *n.* **-ment** *n.* what is bestowed.
**be•strew** *v.t.* to scatter over. *pa.p.* **-ed, -n.**
**be•stride** *v.t.* to stand or sit with the legs extended across. *pr.p.* **bestriding;** *pa.t.* **bestrode, bestrid;** *pa.p.* **bestrid, bestridden.**
**bet** *n.* a stake or wager on some problematical event; *v.t.* to stake money upon some contingency; *pr.p.* **-ting;** *pa.p.* **bet** or **-ted. -ter, -tor** *n.*
**be•ta** *n.* the second letter of the Greek alphabet, printed thus, β. **— particles,** fast electrons emitted when certain atoms undergo radioactive breakdown. **— rays,** streams of beta particles emanated by radioactive substances.
**be•take** *v.t.* to have recourse to; to make one's way; *pr.p.* **betaking;** *pa.t.* **betook;** *pa.p.* **-en.**
**be•think** to remind oneself; to cogitate. *pa.t.* **bethought.**
**be•tide** *v.t.* to happen to; *v.i.* to occur.
**be•took** *pa.t.* of **betake.**
**be•tray** *v.t.* to be disloyal to; to disclose (a secret); deceive. **-al** *n.* **-er** *n.* a traitor; a seducer.
**be•troth** *v.t.* to promise to give or take in marriage. **-al** *n.* an agreement with a view to marriage. **-ed** *n.* a person engaged to be married; fiancé, *(fem.)* fiancée.
**bet•ter** *a.* (compar. of *good*), showing a greater degree of excellence; improved in health; *adv.* (compar. of *well*), in a more excellent or superior manner; *v.t.* and *i.* to raise one's worldly position. **-ment** *n.* improvement. **-s** *n.pl.* one's superiors in rank or wealth. **— off,** in more prosperous circumstances.
**be•tween** *prep.* in the middle of two (of space, time, etc.); *adv.* midway. **go-between** *n.* an intermediary.
**be•twixt** *prep.* between; midway.
**bev•el** *n.* an adjustable instrument used in building, etc. for testing angles; *a.* having the form of a bevel; slanting; *v.t.* to cut to a bevel angle. **-led** *a.* **-ing, -ment** *n.*
**bev•er•age** *n.* a refreshing liquid suitable for drinking.
**bev•y** *n.* a flock of birds; a collection or group.
**be•wail** *v.t.* to express grief for; mourn over.
**be•ware** *v.i.* to be on one's guard; to take care (lest).
**be•wil•der** *v.t.* to lead astray or into confusion; puzzle. **-ed** *a.* **-ing** *a.* confusing. **-ment** *n.*
**be•witch** *v.t.* to gain power over, by sorcery; to charm. **-er** *n.* **-ery, -ment** *n.* power to bewitch; enchantment. **-ing** *a.*
**be•yond** *prep.* on the farther side of; out of reach of; past in time; *adv.* farther off; *n.* the future life.
**bi-,** *prefix* used in the construction of compound nouns, indicating two, twice, or double.
**bi•an•nu•al** *a.* happening twice a year. **-ly** *adv.*
**bi•as** *n.* prejudice; prepossession that sways the mind; a diagonal line of

direction; *v.t.* to prejudice; *pa.t.* and *pa.p.* **-sed** or **-ed.**

**bib** *n.* piece of cloth worn mainly by children over the breast when eating; part of a workman's overalls to protect chest.

**Bi•ble** *n.* the volume which contains the Scriptures of the Old and/or New Testament. **biblical** *a.* scriptural.

**bib•li•o-** *prefix* from Gk. *biblion,* a book, used in the formation of compound words referring to books. **-graphy** *n.* a list of books on a specific subject. **-grapher** *n.* one who compiles lists of books for further study of a subject; one interested in various editions of certain books. **-graphic(al)** *a.* **-logy** *n.* knowledge of the production and distribution of books. **-mania** *n.* a mania for possessing rare books. **-maniac** *n.* **-phile** *n.* a lover of books. **-pole, -polist** *n.* a dealer in books, esp. rare books. **-poly** *n.* **-theca** *n.* a library. **-thecary** *n.* a librarian.

**bi•car•bon•ate** *n.* a salt or compound containing two equivalents of carbonic acid to one of a base—usually applied loosely for 'bicarbonate of soda.'

**bi•ceps** *n.* two-headed muscle of arm or leg. **biciptial** *a.*

**bick•er** *v.i.* to wrangle; to move quickly and lightly. **-ing** *n.* **-ment** *n.*

**bi•cus•pid** *n.* a tooth with two fangs; *a.* having two cusps or fangs. Also **-ate.**

**bi•cy•cle** *n.* a vehicle with two wheels, one in front of the other, propelled by pedals; *v.i.* to cycle. **bicyclist** *n.* one who rides a bicycle. **bike** *n. (Colloq.)*

**bicycle**

**bid** *v.t.* to ask; to order or direct; to offer a price; *pr.p.* **bidding;** *pa.t.* **bid** or **bade;** *pa.p.* **bid, -den;** *n.* an offer of a price, esp. at auctions; an attempt. **-dable** *a.* compliant. **-der** *n.* **-ding** *n.* command; series of bids at cards.

**bide** *v.i.* to dwell permanently; reside. *v.t.* to endure.

**bi•en•ni•al** *a.* happening once in two years; lasting for only two years; *n.* a plant which requires two seasons to bloom. **-ly** *adv.*

**bier** *n.* a frame or carriage for conveying the dead to the grave.

**bi•fo•cal** *n.pl.* spectacles with a small lens for reading, set into a larger lens for distant vision.

**bi•fo•li•ate** *a. (Bot.)* having two leaflets springing from the same point.

**big** *a.* bulky; massive. **—hearted** *a.* **-ness** *n.* bulk; importance.

**big•a•my** *n.* the crime of having two wives or husbands at one time. **bigamist** *n.* **bigamous** *a.* **bigamously** *adv.*

**big•horn** *n.* a Rocky Mountain wild sheep.

**big•ot** *n.* one obstinately and unreasonably wedded to a particular belief or creed. **-ed** *a.* **-ry** *n.* the blind zeal of a bigot.

**bi•ki•ni** *n.* a scanty two-piece bathing suit.

**bi•lat•er•al** *a.* having two sides; affecting two parties. **-ly** *adv.*

**bile** *n.* a greenish, viscous, bitter fluid secreted by the liver; general disorder of health due to faulty secretion of bile. **biliary** *a.* pert. to the bile. **bilious** *a.* pert. to the bile; ill-humored. **biliousness** *n.* a disturbance of the digestive system associated with an excess of bile.

**bilge** *n.* the broadest part of a ship's bottom nearest the keel, acting as a sump.

**bi•lin•gual** *a.* speaking, or writing, in two languages. Also **bilinguar. bilinguist** *n.* a person who can speak fluently in two languages.

**bilk** *v.t.* to defraud, to swindle. **-er** *n.*

**bill** *n.* a kind of axle with two sharp pointed spikes mounted on a long staff.

**bill** *n.* an account of money owed; the draft of a proposed law; *v.t.* to announce by posters; to send a statement of money owed. **-board** *n.* a signboard for advertising. **-fold** *n.* a wallet. **-ing** *n.* invoicing.

**bil•let** *n.* the quarters occupied by soldiers in private houses, etc.; *v.t.* to lodge troops.

**bil•liard** *a.* pert. to billiards. **billiards,** *n.* a table game played with three balls which are hit by a cue.

**bil•lion** *n.* a thousand millions ($10^9$). **-aire** *n.* a fabulously wealthy person. **-th** *a.*

**bil•low** *n.* a great, swelling wave of the sea; a surge of flame, smoke, cloud, etc.; *v.i.* to swell or roll, as waves. **-ed, -y** *a.*

**bil•ly•goat** *n.* a he-goat.

**bi•met•al•lism** *n.* in currency, the use of both gold and silver coins at a fixed relative value.

**bi•month•ly** *a.* once in two months or twice in a month; *n.* a periodical which appears once in two months or twice a month.

**bin** *n.* a box or enclosed place with a lid, for corn, bread, etc.; *v.t.* to store in a bin. *pr.p.* **-ning** *pa.t.* **-ned.**

**bi•na•ry** *a.* composed of two; double; *n.* a double star. **binate** *a.* growing in pairs.

**bind** *v.t.* to tie together as with a band, cord, etc.; to be obligatory; to constipate; *pa.t.* and *pa.p.* **bound. -er** *n.* a person who binds; a machine for binding, as sheaves, books, etc. **-ery** *n.* a book-binding establishment. **-ing** *a.* obligatory; constipating; *n.* act of fastening.

**binge** *n.* concerted eating and especially drinking, to celebrate an occasion.

**bin•o•cle** *n.* a telescope fitted with two tubes. **binocular** *a.* adapted for the use of both eyes; *n.* a binocular telescope. **binoculars** *n.pl.* field-glasses. **binoculate** *a.* adapted for the use of two eyes.

**bi•nom•i•nal** *a. (Bot.)* having two names,

the first indicating the genus, the second indicating the species.

**bi•o-** a *prefix* used in the construction of compound terms, to express having organic life.

**bi•o•chem•is•try** *n.* physiology considered from the chemical point of view; the chemistry of living things.

**bi•o•dy•nam•ics** *n.pl.* the science which investigates the vital forces.

**bi•o•gen** *n.* a hypothetical protein molecule assumed to be the primary source of all living matter. **biogenesis** *n.* the theory that life develops only from living organisms.

**bi•og•ra•phy** *n.* the detailed story of a person's life and achievements; the section of literature devoted to the writing of the life-stories of individuals. **biographic, -al.**

**bi•ol•o•gy** *n.* the science of life, whether animal or vegetable. **biologic, biological** *a.* **biologically** *adv.* **biologist** *n.* **biological warfare,** a method of fighting in which disease bacteria would be used.

**bi•o•nom•ics** *n.* study of influence of environment on organisms; ecology.

**bi•o•phys•ics** *n.* physics of living organisms.

**bi•op•sy** *n.* the excision of a piece of living tissue for diagnosis.

**bi•ot•ic** *a.* *(Biol.)* relating to life. **biotics** *n.* the functions, properties, and activities of living things.

**bi•par•ti•san** *a.* pert. to, or composed of, members of two parties.

**bi•par•tite** *a.* consisting of two corresponding parts. **bipartition** *n.*

**bi•plane** *n.* an airplane or glider having two main wings.

**bi•pod** *n.* a two-legged stand. —cf. **tripod.**

**bi•po•lar** *a.* having two poles.

**bi•quad•rate** *n.* *(Math.)* the value of the fourth power of a number. **biquadratic** *a.; n.* the fourth power.

**birch** *n.* a tree with slim branches and silvery bark-scales; *v.t.* flog with a birch-rod. **birch, -en** *a.* of birch. **-rod** *n.* a rod of birch twigs for inflicting punishment.

**bird** *n.* a feathered animal with wings. **— cage** *n.* a cage made of wire and wood for keeping birds. **-call** *n.* the sounds made by a bird.

**bird•ie** *n.* *(Golf)* holing a ball in one stroke under par.

**birth** *n.* act of coming into life or of being born; origin. **— control** *n.* restriction of conception. **-day** *n.* the anniversary of that day. **-mark** *n.* peculiar mark on the body at birth. **-place** *n.* the place where a person is born. **— rate** *n.* the ration of births to the total population. **-right** *n.* anything to which one is entitled by birth.

**bis•cuit** *n.* a quick bread in small soft cakes.

**bi•sect** *v.t.* to divide into two equal parts. **bisection** *n.* one of two equal parts. **-or** *n.* a bisecting line. **bisegment** *n.* one of two segments of a bisected line.

**bi•sex•u•al** *a.* having the organs of both sexes.

**bish•op** *n.* a clergyman of high rank, chess man moving diagonally. **-ric** *n.* diocese, jurisdiction, or office of a bishop.

**bi•son** *n.* the large buffalo of Western N. Am.

**bisque** *n.* a thick soup made with shellfish or game.

**bi•sul•phate** *n.* a salt of sulphuric acid in which one-half of the hydrogen in the acid is replaced by a metal.

**bit** *pa.t.* of **bite.**

**bit** *n.* small piece of anything; a boring tool generally for use in brace; part of bridle

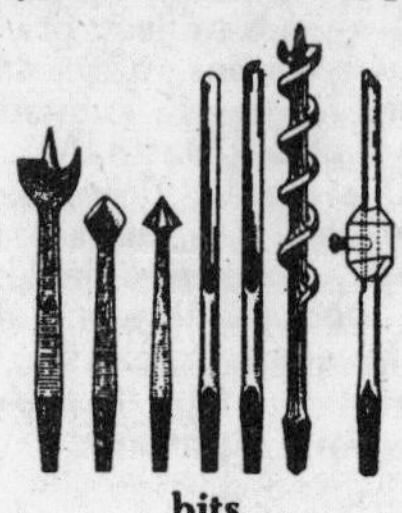

**bits**

which is placed in a horse's mouth; *v.t.* to put the bit in the mouth of a horse.

**bitch** *n.* the female of the dog, wolf, or fox.

**bite** *v.t.* to cut, seize, or wound with the teeth; to pinch with cold; *v.i.* to be given to biting; to be pungent; *pr.p.* **biting;** *pa.t.* **bit;** *pa.p.* **bit** or **bitten** *n.* act of biting; a portion bitten off; the nibble of a fish at a hook; **-r** *n.* **biting** *a.* sarcastic; caustic; chilling.

**bit•ter** *a.* biting or acrid to the taste; causing pain to the feelings; *n.* bitter beer. **-ly** *adv.* **-ness** *n.* the quality of being bitter to the taste; animosity. **-s** *n.* alcoholic liquor containing bitter flavorings. **-sweet** *n.* the woody nightshade whose root, when chewed, tastes first bitter then sweet.

**bi•valve** *a.* having two valves; *n.* an animal with a shell of two parts opening like a hinge. **bivalvous** *a.*

**biv•ou•ac** *n.* an encampment in the open air, without any cover; *v.i.* to encamp without covering. *pr.p.* **bivouacking;** *pa.t.* and *pa.p.* **bivouacked.**

**bi•week•ly** *a.* occurring once in every two weeks; occurring twice in each week; *n.* a periodical issued twice a week or once in two weeks.

**bi•zarre** *a.* eccentric; strange.

**blab** *v.t.* to imprudently reveal secrets entrusted to one; *v.i.* to tell tales; *pr.p.* **-bing;** *pa.t.* and *pa.p.* **-bed** *n.* a tell-tale. Also **-ber.**

**black** *a.* of the darkest color; nightlike; *n.* the darkest color; *v.t.* to make black. **-en** *v.t.* to make black; to defame; *v.i.* to turn black. **-ly** *adv.* **-ness** *n.* **-ball** *v.t.* to reject a candidate for admission to a club. **-berry** *n.* a fruit-bearing shrub, the bramble. **-bird** *n.* any of a number of birds which have predominantly black plumage. **-board** *n.* a slate, or any dark surface to write on with chalk. **-bread** *n.* rye bread.

**—eye** *n.* discoloration due to a blow. **-flag** *n.* flag popularly associated with pirates. **-guard** *n.* a low scoundrel; *a.* vile; *v.i.* to act in a vile manner. **-guardism** *n.* **-guardly** *a.* **-head** *n.* a small black-topped mass which plugs the mouths of the follicles of the skin. **-jack** *n.* a short, leather-covered club with a heavy head on an elastic shaft. **—lead** *n.* graphite, a form of nearly pure carbon and used in the manufacture of lead pencils. **—list** *n.* any list of undesirable persons; *v.t.* to place on such a list. **-mail** *n.* extortion of money by threats of denunciation. **—mark** *n.* a mark of failure. **—market** *n.* a clandestine market for the sale of goods whose distribution is regulated, and which are not on free sale. **—out** *n.* a total cutting off of all light.

**blad•der** *n.* a thin musculo-membranous bag, in the pelvis, serving as a reservoir for urine. **-ed** *a.* swollen like a bladder. **-y** *a.* thin and inflated.

**blade** *n.* the leaf, or flat part of the leaf, of a plant; the cutting part of a knife, or tool; a sword. **-bone** *n.* the upper bone in shoulder, scapula. **-d** *a.*

**blame** *v.t.* to express disapprobation of; *n.* fault. **-less** *a.* **-lessness** *n.*

**blanch** *v.t.* to whiten; *v.i.* to become white; to turn pale.

**bland** *a.* mild; affable. **-ly** *adv.* **-ness** *n.*

**blank** *a.* without writing or any marks; empty; *n.* an empty space. **-ly** *adv.* **—verse,** unrhymed heroic.

**blan•ket** *n.* a loosely woven woolen bedcover; a thick canopy of cloud; *v.t.* to cover with a blanket; to toss in a blanket. **-ing** *n.* thick material for blankets; tossing in a blanket. **a wet blanket,** one who depresses others.

**blare** *v.t.* and *v.i.* to sound loudly; to trumpet; *n.* a long, prolonged noise.

**blar•ney** *n.* coaxing, cajoling talk; outrageous flattery.

**bla•sé** *a.* absolutely bored; sophisticated.

**blas•pheme** *v.t.* to speak irreverently of God; *v.i.* to take God's name in vain. **-r** *n.* **blaspheming** *n.* impious talk. **blasphemous** *a.* **blasphemously** *adv.* **blasphemy** *n.* irreverence in speaking of sacred matters.

**blast** *n.* a gust or puff of air; an explosion of gunpowder in rending rocks. *v.t.* to injure, as by a noxious wind; to blight; to split as by gunpowder. **-ed** *a.* blighted; accursed; **-er** *n.* **—furnace** *n.* a smelting-furnace in which hot air is furnished by bellows or other apparatus. **-ing** *n.* a blast; explosion.

**bla•tant** *a.* offensively noisy; loud-(voiced); obtrusive. **blatancy** *n.* **-ly** *adv.*

**blaze** *n.* bright flame; outburst of activity or zeal; *v.i.* to burn brightly. **-r** *n.* sports jacket of bright color.

**blaze** *n.* white mark upon a horse's forehead; *v.t.* to mark a trail.

**bla•zon** *v.t.* to make known to everybody; *n.* art of drawing coats of arms. **-er** *n.* **-ment** *n.* **-ry** *n.* art of describing coats of arms.

**bleach** *v.t.* to whiten by exposure to sunlight and air, or by chemical action; *v.i.* to become whiter; *n.* a decolorizing, chemical agent. **-er** *n.* one who, or that which, bleaches. **bleachers** *n.pl.* outdoor, uncovered seat for a spectator in a stadium.

**bleak** *a.* without color; desolate and exposed. **-ly** *adv.* **-ness** *n.*

**blear** *a.* dim or watery, due to inflammation of the eye, or tears; *v.i.* to blur. **-y** *a.* dim.

**bleat** *v.i.* to cry as a sheep; to talk in a whining fashion; *n.* the sound made by a sheep.

**bleed** *v.t.* to draw blood surgically; *v.i.* to lose blood; *pa.t.* and *pa.p.* **bled.** **-er** *n.* a person who is afflicted by hemophilia, excessive bleeding. **-ing** *n.*

**blem•ish** *n.* any deformity, physical or moral; *v.i.* to mark with a flaw; to disfigure.

**blend** *v.t.* to mix allied articles together smoothly and inseparably; *v.i.* to mingle well; *pa.p.* **-ed** or **blent;** *n.* a mixture. **-er** *n.* **-ing** *n.*

**bless** *v.t.* to consecrate; praise; invoke happiness on. *pa.p.* **-ed** or **blest. blessed, blest** *a.* favored with blessings; hallowed. **-edness** *n.* happiness; heavenly joy. **-ing** *n.* a source of happiness or gratitude; prayer.

**blew** *pa.t.* of **blow.**

**blight** *n.* disease of plants caused by certain fungi or parasitic bacteria; *v.t.* to affect with blight.

**blimp** *n.* a small non-rigid airship.

**blind** *a.* destitute of sight; unaware of; concealed; *v.t.* to deprive sight; to deceive; *n.* a window-covering or screen. **—date** *n.* a date arranged with someone not previously known; the person involved. **-ed** *a.* rendered sightless; oblivious to all other factors. **-ers** *n.pl.* a horse's blinkers. **-fold** *a.; v.t.* to cover the eyes with something. **-ing** *a.* **—landing** *n.* grounding an aircraft by depending on radio signals. **-ly** *adv.* **-ness** *n.* lacking power of sight.

**blink** *v.i.* to wink; to look with the eyes half-shut; *v.t.* to shut out of sight, as a fact or question; *n.* a glance. **-ers** *n.pl.* pieces of leather preventing a horse from seeing to either side.

**bliss** *n.* the acme of happiness; heavenly rapture. **-ful** *a.* supremely happy. **-fully** *adv.* **-fulness** *n.* **-less** *a.*

**blis•ter** *n.* a vesicle of the skin filled with a clear or blood-stained serum.

**blithe** *a.* gay; jolly; sprightly. **-ly** *adv.* **-ness** *n.* **-some** *a.* cheerful.

**blitz** *n.* a heavy, sudden attack by enemy bombers; *v.t.* to bomb from the air. **-ed** *a.*

**bliz•zard** *n.* a blinding snowstorm.

**bloat** *v.t.* to swell or puff out; to cure fish by salting and smoking. **-ed** *a.* swollen. **-edness** *n.* **bloater** *n.* a herring—salted, smoked, and dried.

**blob** *n.* anything small and globular.

**block** *n.* a solid mass of matter; a roughly squared piece of wood, stone, etc.; a number of buildings forming one compact mass; *v.t.* to enclose; to shape (a hat). **-buster** *n.* a heavy explosive bomb.

-**head** *n.* a dullard. -**house** *n.* an improvised fort made of logs. —**letters** *n.* a form of script where the letters are printed instead of in the usual cursive style.

**block•ade** *n.* prevention of imports into countries usually during a war; *v.t.* to prevent trade with a hostile country. — **runner** *n.* a vessel employed to slip through to a blockaded country.

**blond** *n.* a person of fair complexion *a.* fair.

**blood** *n.* the red, viscid fluid which circulates in the body of men and animals; relationship, kindred; —**bank** *n.* a store of blood for use in a transfusion. — **count** *n.* the number of red and white cells in a specific quantity of blood. -**curdling** *a.* terrifying. -**hound** *n.* a hound, with keen sense and

**bloodhound**

perseverance. -**ily** *adv.* -**less** *a.* without blood; spiritless. -**lessness** *n.* -**mobile** *n.* a mobile unit for collecting blood for blood banks. — **plasma,** the fluid part of blood. — **poisoning** *n.* a condition due to circulation of bacteria in blood stream. — **pressure** *n.* the pressure exerted by the blood on the walls of the arteries. — **red** *a.* crimson. — **serum** *n.* the fluid part of the blood after the fibrin and the corpuscles have been eliminated. -**shed** *n.* the shedding of blood. -**shot** *a.* of the eyes, red or congested with blood. -**stain** *n.* the dried and darkened stain left on clothing, floors, etc. after contact with blood. -**sucker** *n.* an animal which sucks blood, esp. the leech. -**test** *n.* an examination of the blood often to determine to which of the four groups it belongs. -**thirsty** *a.* eager to shed blood. — **transfusion** *n.* the transference of blood from one person to another. — **vessel** *n.* an artery or vein through which blood flows. -**y** *a.* stained with blood.

**bloom** *n.* a blossom; state of freshness and vigor; to flow with youthful vigor; *v.t.* to cause to blossom or flourish.

**blos•som** *n.* the flower of a plant, esp. a tree; *v.i.* to flourish. -**ed** *a.* -**y** *a.* rich in blossoms.

**blot** *v.t.* to spot esp. with ink; to obliterate; to dry with blotting-paper; *pr.p.* -**ting;** *pa.p.* -**ted;** *n.* a spot or stain, as of ink; disgrace, -**ter** *n.* a blotting-pad. -**ting-paper** *n.* a kind of unsized paper for drying ink.

**blotch** *n.* an irregular, colored spot; an eruption upon the skin; *v.t.* to mark with blotches; to make spotted. -**y** *a.*

**blouse** *n.* a light, loose upper garment; *v.i.* and *v.t.* to drape loosely.

**blow** *n.* a stroke; a smack; sudden calamity.

**blow** *v.i.* to produce a current of air; to breathe hard or quickly; *v.t.* to direct a current of air on; to sound a wind instrument; *pa.t.* **blew;** *pa.p.* -**n;** *n.* a high wind. -**lamp** *n.* a portable lamp for applying intense local heat. -**n** *a.* out of breath; tainted. -**out** *n.* a burst tire. — **pipe** *n.* an instrument for concentrating the heat of a flame on some point by blowing. -**y** *a.* windy.

**blub•ber** *n.* the fat of whales and other marine animals; *v.i.* to weep unrestrainedly. -**ed** *a.* swollen by weeping. -**ing** *n.*

**bludg•eon** *v.t.* to knock out with a club.

**blue** *n.* the color of the clear sky; one of the seven primary colors; *n.pl.* a very slow jazz dance of Negro origin. **blue** *a.* of the color blue; melancholy; *v.t.* to make or dye blue. **bluish** *a.* slightly blue. -**bell** *n.* the wild hyacinth. -**berry** *n.* a shrub with edible small berries. -**bird** *n.* a migratory bird of N. Am. belonging to the thrush family. — **blood** *n.* an aristocrat. — **book** *n.* a directory of socially prominent people; a college examination book. **Blue Cross,** a system of nonprofit health insurance. -**grass** *n.* meadow grass of Kentucky which forms thick turf. -**heat,** about 550° F. -**jay** *n.* a crested bird of the eastern U.S. and Canada. —**laws** *n.* laws restricting activities on Sunday. —**pencil** *v.t.* to edit. to alter. -**print** *n.* a simple photographic reproduction of technical drawings leaving white lines of plan on a blue background. — **ribbon,** first prize.

**bluff** *a.* frank and hearty in manner; *n.* a high bank or cliff presenting a steep front. -**ness** *n.* steepness; a frank, blunt manner of speech.

**bluff** *n.* an attempt to mislead in regard to one's real purpose; *v.t.* to mislead one by giving a wrong impression. -**er** *n.* -**ing** *n.*, *a.*

**blun•der** *v.i.* to make a gross mistake; *n.* a gross mistake. -**er** *n.* -**ing** *n.* and *a.* continually making mistakes; fumbling. -**ingly** *adv.*

**blunt** *a.* having a dull edge or point; brusque in speech; *v.t.* to render less sharp. -**ly** *adv.* -**ness.**

**blur** *n.* smudge; whatever dims without effacing; *v.t.* to make indistinct. *pr.p.* -**ring;** *pa.t.* and *pa.p.* -**red.**

**blurb** *n.* an advertisement, esp. extravagant in praise.

**blurt** *n.* a sudden outburst. **to blurt out** *v.t.* to give information suddenly, indiscreetly, or tactlessly.

**blush** *v.i.* to redden in the face, from shame, modesty, or confusion; *n.* a red color suffusing the face. -**ing** *n.* a rosy glow on the face; *a.* coy; bashful. -**ingly** *adv.*

**blus•ter** *v.i.* to blow in boisterous gusts, of wind; to talk with violence and noise; *n.* fitful noise and violence. -**er** *n.* -**ous** *a.* -**y** *a.* stormy.

**bo•a** *n.* a genus of constricting, nonvenomous serpents. — **constrictor** *n.* a serpent which crushes its victims.

**boar** *n.* the male of the swine. — **hound** *n.* a large dog used in hunting boars.

**board** *n.* a long, narrow strip of timber; a table, hence food or diet; a thick paper made by pasting together several layers; *v.t.* to cover with boards; to supply with meals and lodging for payment; to embark on a ship, airplane, etc.; *v.i.* to be a lodger. **-s** *n.pl.* the covers of a book. **-er** *n.* one receiving food and lodging. **-ing** *n.* obtaining food and lodging. **-ing-house** *n.* a house in which boarders are accomodated. **-ing-school** *n.* a school in which the students are in residence.

**boast** *v.t.* to be unduly proud of; *v.i.* to praise oneself extravagantly; *n.* a statement, expressive of vain glory. **-er** *n.* **-ful** *a.* **-fully** *adv.* **-fulness, -ing** *n.* indulging in boasting. **-ingly** *adv.*

**boat** *n.* a small vessel moved by oars or sails or small motor; *v.i.* to row or sail about in a boat. **boatswain** *n.* a ship's officer.

**bob** *n.* a short, jerking motion; *v.t.* to move with a jerk; *v.i.* to dangle; to move up and down or in and out; *pr.p.* **-bing;** *pa.p.* **-bed.**

**bob•bin** *n.* a spool on which thread is wound.

**bob•o•link** *n.* a common North American songbird.

**bob•sled, bob•sleigh** *n.* two small sleds coupled together; *v.i.* to use a bobsled.

**bode** *v.t.* and *v.i.* to foretell; to be an omen of. **-ful** *a.* **-ment** *n.* an omen. **boding** *a.* ominous; *n.* an omen.

**bod•ice** *n.* that part of a woman's dress above the waist, with or without sleeves, and close-fitting.

**bod•y** *n.* the frame of a human being or of an animal; the main part of anything; a solid substance; consistency of a liquid; *v.t.* to produce in definite shape; *pa.t.* and *pa.p.* **bodied. bodied** *a.* used in compounds, e.g. able-bodied. **bodiless** *a.* possessing no body. **bodily** *a.* pert. to the body; *adv.* physically, in the body, in the flesh; in the mass. **-guard** *n.* an escort.

**bo•gey** *n. (Golf)* one over par for hole.

**bog•gle** *v.i.* to shrink back through fear; to hesitate.

**bo•gle** *n.* a fearsome apparition, imp, or hobgoblin associated with the nursery. **bogey, bogy** *n.* the devil; a goblin.

**bo•gus** *a.* sham; counterfeit.

**Bo•he•mi•an** *a.* unconventional *n.* one who leads a loose and unsettled life.

**boil** *v.t.* to bring to a seething condition, by heating; *v.i.* to be agitated by the action of heat. **-er** *n.* a vessel for boiling. **-ing point,** the temperature at which a liquid boils.

**boil** *n.* local inflammation of the skin round a hair follicle.

**bois•ter•ous** *a.* noisy; turbulent. **-ly** *adv.* **-ness** *n.*

**bold** *a.* daring; ready to meet danger; valorous. **— faced** *a.* impudent; printed with heavy thick strokes. **-ly** *adv.* **-ness** *n.*

**bo•le•ro** *n.* a short jacket, usually without sleeves, worn over a blouse.

**boll** *n.* a seed capsule of cotton, flax, etc. **-weevil, -worm,** larvae of various moths destructive of cotton crops.

**bo•lo•gna** *n.* a large smoked, seasoned type of sausage.

**Bol•she•vik** *n.* a member of the Communist Party. **bolshevism** *n.* theory and practice of Russian or other communism. **bolshevist** *n.* and *a.* **bolshevistic** *a.* **bolshevize** *v.t.*

**bol•ster** *n.* a long round bed-pillow; anything designated as a support; *v.t.* to prop. **-er** *n.* **to bolster up,** to support a weak person.

**bolt** *n.* a bar for fastening a door, window, etc.; part of a lock which engages with the keeper; a metal pin with a head at one end and screw threads at the other to receive a nut; a roll of cloth; *v.t.* to fasten with a bolt; to swallow food hurriedly; *v.i.* to rush away; to start suddenly forward.

**bomb** *n.* a cast-iron container filled with high explosives, gas, incendiary contents or smoke-producing substances exploding by percussion or by a timing mechanism. **-er** *n.* an airplane for bombs. **-proof** *a.* secure against small bomb splinters. **-shell** *n.* a bomb; something devastating. **atom(ic) bomb,** a bomb depending on the release of atomic energy. **bomb sight,** instrument for aiming bombs.

**bom•bard** *n.* an early mortar with a wide bore, using stone-shot. **bombard** *v.t.* to batter with heavy artillery fire. **-ier** *n.* a gunner in the artillery. **-ment** *n.* a sustained attack with guns, bombs, etc.

**bom•bast** *n.* inflated, high-sounding language. **-ic** *a.* **ically** *adv.*

**bo•nan•za** *n.* a profitable enterprise.

**bond** *n.* that which binds, a band, a link, a tie; an oath or promise. **-s** *n.pl.* chains; captivity. **-age** *n.* slavery.

**bond** *n.* a legal engagement in writing to fulfill certain conditions; a certificate of ownership of capital lent to a government, municipality, etc.; *v.t.* to put dutiable articles on or under bond. **-ed** *a.* mortgaged. **-ed warehouse,** a warehouse for holding goods in bond.

**bone** *n.* the hard tissue which forms the skeleton of mammals, birds, reptiles and fishes. *v.t.* to remove the bones; to filet (fish). **-s** *n.pl.* human remains. **— ash** *n.* calcined bones. **-black** *n.* finely ground animal charcoal. **— china** *n.* china in which bone ash is used. **-dry** *a.* absolutely dry. **— meal** *n.* a fertilizer for dry soils, made from ground bones. **boniness** *n.* **bony** *a.* full of bones.

**bon•fire** *n.* orig. a fire for burning bones.

**bon•net** *n.* a woman's head-gear. **-ed** *a.*

**bo•nus** *n.* something over and above that which is due.

**boo** *interj.* an exclamation of contempt, often used to startle. **-es** *n.pl.* *v.t.* and *v.i.* to show disapproval; *pr.t.* (he) **booes;** *pa.t.* **-ed.**

**book** *n.* a number of sheets of paper, etc. bound together; a literary composition written or printed; *v.t.* to obtain business order, ticket. **-s** *n.pl.* record of business transactions, especially financial. **-binder** *n.* one who binds books. **-binding** *n.*

**-case** *n.* a case with shelving for books. **— club** *n.* a club to distribute specially chosen books to subscribers. **— ends** *n.pl.* weighted props to keep books upright on a shelf. **-ing** *n.* an engagement to perform. **-ing clerk** *n.* a clerk who issues railway, etc., tickets. **-ish** *a.* found of books. **-ishness** *n.* **— jacket** *n.* an attractively printed outer paper wrapper of a book. **-keeper** *n.* **-keeping** *n.* the art of keeping a systematic account of financial transactions. **— learning, -lore** *n.* knowledge acquired by extensive reading. **-let** *n.* a pamphlet. **-maker** *n.* a professional betting-man who accepts bets. **-mark** *n.* something placed in a book to mark a particular page. **the Book of Books,** the Holy Bible. **-seller** *n.* one who sells books. **-selling** *n.* **-shelf** *n.* a shelf for displaying books. **-shop, -stall, -stand** *n.* a place for exhibiting books for sale. **-worm** *n.* one who reads intensively.

**boom** *v.i.* to make a deep hollow sound; to flourish; *n.* a hollow roar; economic prosperity. **-er** n. **-ing** *a.*

**boom•er•ang** *n.* a curved wooden missile used by the natives of Australia.

boomerang

**boor** *n.* a peasant; bumpkin. **-ish** *a.* **-ishly** *adv.* **-ishness** *n.*

**boost** *v.t.* to raise by pushing from beneath; to increase the output or power of a machine; *n.* a push up. **-er** *n.*

**boot** *n.* a covering for the foot and leg; a kick; *v.t.* to put on boots; to kick. **-black** *n.* one who polishes the shoes of passers-by. **-ee** *n.* a knitted boot. **-leg** *v.t.* to sell illicitly alcoholic liquor. **-legger** *n.* **-legging** *n.*

**booth** *n.* a temporary structure of boards or other materials; a small restaurant compartment.

**bo•rax** *n.* hydrated sodium borate, used in the manufacture of enamels and glazes, as a softener for hard water. **boracic** *a.* **boracic acid,** white powder used as an antiseptic or for checking excessive perspiration. **borate** *n.* a salt of baracic acid.

**bor•der** *n.* the outer edge of anything; a frontier; an ornamental design around the outside edge of anything; *v.t.* to adorn with a border; *v.i.* to come near. **-ing** *n.* material for a border. **-land** *n.* land contiguous to a frontier. **-line** *a.* on the verge of.

**bore** *v.t.* to make a hole in; to weary by uninteresting talk; *n.* the hole made by boring; a person that wearies one. **-dom** *n.* the state of being bored; ennui. **-r** *n.* tool for drilling.

**bore** *pa.t.* of **bear.**

**born** *pa.p.* of **bear**, to bring forth; *a.* natural. **borne** *pa.p.* of **bear,** to carry.

**bor•ough** *n.* an incorporated town.

**bor•row** *v.t.* to obtain on loan or trust. **-ed** *a.* **-er** *n.* **-ing** *n.*

**bos•om** *n.* the breast of a human being; *v.t.* to press to the bosom; *a.* intimate.

**boss** *n.* a prominent circular projection on any article; *v.t.* to emboss; to provide with bosses. **-ed** *a.* embossed.

**boss** *n.* employer; one in charge; *v.t.* to manage; **-iness** *n.* **-y** *a.* fussy and masterful. **-ism** *n.*

**bot•a•ny** *n.* that branch of biology which is concerned with the structure and growth of plants. **botanic, botanical** *a.* pert. to botany. **botanically** *adv.* **botanic garden,** a garden where plants are scientifically studied. **botanist** *n.*; **botanize** *v.i.* to study plants; to search for and collect plants for further study.

**botch** *n.* a clumsy patch of a garment; bungled work; *v.t.* to bungle; to patch clumsily; to blunder; spoil. **-er** *n.* a bungler. **-ery, -work** *n.* **-ily** *adv.* **-y** *a.*

**both** *a.* and *pron.* the one and the other.

**both•er** *v.t.* to annoy; tease; plague; *v.i.* to fuss; to be troublesome; *n.* trouble; annoyance; fuss; worry; *interj.* an exclamation of annoyance. **-ation** *n.* trouble and worry; a mild imprecation. **-some** *a.* troublesome.

**bottle** *n.* a vessel with a narrow neck for holding liquids; a thermionic valve; *v.t.* to put in bottles; to restrain; to curb. **-d** *a.* enclosed in bottles; of a bottle shape. **-d-up** *a.* confined; not allowed to speak. **— green** *a.* of a dark-green color. **bottling** *n.* and *a.* **-neck** *n.* a narrow outlet which impedes the smooth flow of traffic or production of goods. **-nose** *n.* a whale with a beaked snout. **— party** *n.* one where the guests provide the liquid refreshments. **-r** *n.*

**bot•tom** *n.* the lowest part of anything; the posterior of human body; origin; *v.t.* to put a bottom on an article; **-less** *a.*

**bot•u•lism** *n.* a rare and dangerous form of food poisoning caused by spoiled foods.

**bou•cle** *n.* a woven material with raised pile; *a.* pert. to such material.

**bou•doir** *n.* a lady's private room.

**bouf•fant** *a.* puffed out, full, as in draperies, skirts, hair.

**bough** *n.* an arm or large branch of a tree.

**bought** *pa.t.* and *pa.p.* of **buy.**

**bouil•lon** *n.* broth; stock **bouillabaisse** *n.* a Provençal fish soup or stew.

**boul•der** *n.* a rock torn from its bed, and rounded by water.

**boul•e•vard** *n.* a street or promenade planted with trees. **-ier** *n.* one who haunts the boulevards.

**bounce** *v.i.* to move with a bound and rebound; to leap or spring suddenly; *v.t.* to cause to rebound, as a ball; *n.* a sudden spring or leap; **bouncing** *a.* vigorous; big.

**bound** *pa.t.* and *pa.p.* of **bind.**

**bound** *v.i.* to leap; spring; *n.* a leap; jump.

**bound** *a.* tending to go or on the way, as in *homeward bound.*

**bound** *n.* usually in *pl.* limit or boundary;

confines; *v.t.* to restrain; to set bounds to. **-ed** *a.* restricted; cramped. **-less** *a.* without limits; infinite. **-lessness** *n.*

**bound•a•ry** *n.* a border or limit; barrier.

**boun•ty** *n.* a payment formerly made to men enlisting voluntarily in the army or navy; a premium offered by a government. **bounteous, bountiful** *a.* ample; plentiful. **bounteously, bountifully** *adv.;* **bounteousness, bountifulness** *n.*

**bou•quet** *n.* a bunch of flowers; a perfume; the aromatic flavor and aroma of wine.

**bour•bon** *n.* a whisky distilled from corn and rye.

**bour•geois** *n.* a member of middle-class society; *a.* middle-class; conventional. **bourgeoisie** *n.*

**bout** *n.* a turn; a conflict.

**bou•ton•nier** *n.* a flower or flowers worn on a lapel.

**bo•vine** *a.* pert. to cattle; ox-like; stolid.

**bow** *v.i.* to bend body in respect, assent, etc.; to submit; *v.t.* to bend downwards; *n.* an inclination of head or body; the rounded forward part of a ship. **-line** *n.* a rope used to keep the weather edge of the sail tight forward; knot used for tying a rope to a post. **-man** *n.* the one who rows the foremost oar in a boat.

**bow** *n.* anything bent or curved; weapon from which an arrow is discharged; a ribbon tied in a slip-knot. **-ed** *a.* bent like a bow. **-er** *n.* **-legged** *a.* having crooked legs. **-man** *n.* an archer. **— tie** *n.* a small bow-shaped tie.

**bow•el** *n.* an entrail; the entrails; the inside of everything. **-s** *n.pl.* the intestines.

**bow•er** *n.* *(Poetic)* a small country dwelling. **-y** *a.* shady.

**bow•ie-knife** *n.* a long hunting-knife, the point double-edged, the blade straight and single-edged at the hilt.

**bowl** *n.* a round vessel; a drinking-cup; a stadium.

**bowl** *n.* a ball rolled in certain games; *pl.* a game played on a bowling-green with bowls; *v.t.* to roll, as a bowl; *v.i.* to play with bowls; to deliver a ball. **-er** *n.* one who bowls. **-ing** *n.*

**box** *n.* a small case or chest, generally with a lid; a compartment. **— kite** *n.* a kite consisting of a square frame strength. **— office** *n.* ticket office at a theater. **— pleat** *n.* a double fold with material turned under on both sides with knife edges.

**box** *n.* a small evergreen shrub. **— berry** *n.* the wintergreen. **-en** *a.* made of or like boxwood. **-wood** *n.* a tree.

**box** *n.* a blow on the head or the ears; *v.t.* to buffet; *v.i.* to fight with the fists. **-er** *n.* a pugilist. **-ing** *n.* the sport of fighting with fists.

**boy** *n.* a male child; a lad. **-hood** *n.* **-ish** *a.* boy-like. **-ishly** *adv.* **-ishness** *n.* the natural actions of a boy.

**boy•cott** *n.* a method of coercion by refusing to deal with; *v.t.* to ostracize. **-er** *n.* **-ing** *n.*

**bra** See **brassiere.**

**brace** *n.* a rod or bar crossing a space diagonally to connect two structural parts; a support; *v.t.* to furnish with braces; to support. **-s** *n.pl.* . suspenders; wires for straightening teeth. **and bit,** small interchangeable boring tool fitted into the socket of a brace. **-r** *n.* a wrist-guard of leather used esp. by archers. **bracing** *a.* invigorating; refreshing.

**brace•let** *n.* an encircling ornament for the wrist.

**brack•en** *n.* a large coarse species of fern.

**brack•et** *n.* a projecting support fastened to a wall; one of two hooks, used to enclose explanatory words; *v.t.* to couple names together as of equal merit, etc.

**bract** *n.* a leaf in the axil of which a flower arises. **-eal** *a.* of the nature of a bract. **-eate** *a.* having bracts.

**brad** *n.* a cut nail tapering in width with a small head projecting at one end. **-awl** *n.* a small hand-boring tool.

**brag** *v.i.* to praise oneself or one's belongings; *pr.p.* **-ging** *pa.t.* and *pa.p.* **ged;** *n.* boasting. **-gart** *a.* boastful; *n.* a boaster. **-ging** *a., n.* **-gingly** *adv.*

**braid** *v.t.* to plait, or interweave; *n.* a narrow ribbon used as a dress-trimming; a tress of hair. **-ed** *a.* **-ing** *n.*

**braille** *n.* a system of printing books in relief to be read by the blind; also the letters used, consisting of raised dots in combination.

**brain** *n.* the whitish, soft mass in the skull in which are the nerve centers; mental capacity; *v.t.* to dash out the brains of. **-ed** *a.* having the brains beaten out. **-less** *a.* stupid. **— storm** *n.* *(Colloq.)* a sudden idea, inspiration. **-wash** *v.t.* *(Colloq.)* to effect a radical change in beliefs by intensive indoctrination. **-y** *a.* highly intellectual.

**braise** *v.t.* to cook meat by browning in fat and simmering in a covered dish with a small amount of liquid.

**brake** *n.* instrument for breaking flax or hemp; any device for checking speed; *v.t.* to pound or crush flax, hemp, etc., by beating; to check by applying a brake. **braking** *n.* **— shoe** *n.* the surface of a block brake.

**bram•ble** *n.* a prickly hedge-plant; the wild blackberry.

**bran** *n.* the ground husk of wheat and other grain, separated in milling from the flour.

**branch** *n.* a limb of a tree or shrub; a department of a business, etc.; an off-shoot; *a.* pert. to a subsidiary section of any business; *v.t.* to divide, as into branches; *v.i.* to spread, in branches; **-ed** *a.* **-ing** *a.* shooting out. **-y** *a.*

**bran•chi•ae** *n.pl.* the breathing organs of fishes, the gills. **branchial** *a.* pert. to gills. **branchiate** *a.* furnished with gills.

**brand** *n.* an iron used for burning marks on; a mark made by a hot iron; a trade-mark; *v.t.* to burn a mark on; to designate a commodity by a trade-mark; to reproach. **-ed** *a.* **-er** *n.* **-ing-iron** *n.*

**bran•dish** *v.t.* to wave, as a weapon.

**bran•dy** *n.* a spirit distilled from wine.

**brash** *a.* insolent; **-ness** *n.*
**brass** *n.* a yellow alloy of two parts of copper to one of zinc; *a.* brazen; made of brass. **-es** *n.pl.* the brass instruments of an orchestra. — **band** *n.* musicians who perform on brass instruments. — **hat** *n.* *(Colloq.)* staff-officer (from gold braid on hat). **-iness** *n.* bold; impudent. **-y** *a.* pert. sole. — **knuckles** *n.pl.* metal pieces fitted across the knuckles, used in fighting.
**bras•si•ere** *n.* a woman's undergarment supporting the breasts; short form, **bra.**
**brat** *n.* a child (used contemptuously).
**bra•va•do** *n.* showy bravery.
**brave** *a.* courageous; fearless; *n.* an Indian warrior; *v.t.* to encounter with courage. **-ly** *adv.* **-ry** *n.* heroism.
**bra•vo** *interj.* an expression of applause; *pl.* **-es.**
**brawl** *v.i.* to squabble noisily; *n.* a noisy quarrel. **-er** *n.*
**brawn** *n.* muscular strength esp. of the arms and legs. **-iness** *n.* **-y** *a.* muscular; robust.
**bray** *n.* the harsh noise of a donkey; *v.i.* to utter a harsh noise, like a donkey.
**bray** *v.t.* to pulverize; to grind small.
**braze** *v.t.* to make or ornament with brass. **brazing** *n.*
**bra•zen** *a.* pert. to, or made of, brass; impudent; *v.t.* to face a situation in a bold, impudent manner. **-ly** *adv.*
**bra•zier** *n.* a portable iron container to hold burning coals; a worker in brass.
**Bra•zil•i•an** *n.* a native of Brazil, in S. America; *a.* pert. to Brazil.
**breach** *n.* a break or opening, esp. in a wall; non-fulfillment of a contract. *v.t.* to make a breach in something. — **of promise,** the nonfulfillment of a promise, esp. of marriage.
**bread** *n.* form of food prepared by baking dough made from a cereal. — **winner** *n.* one who earns a living for his dependents.
**breadth** *n.* distance from side to side.
**break** *v.t.* to shatter by force; to tame; *v.i.* to divide into several parts; curl over (as waves); to crack or falter; to make the first stroke at billiards; *pa.t.* **broke;** *pa.p.* **broken.**
**break** *n.* the act of being broken; a fracture; separation; a breathing space. **-able** *a.* fragile. **-age** *n.* act of breaking; an allowance for articles broken. **-down** *n.* loss of health; an accident to machinery; suspension of negotiations; *v.t.* to divide into small categories. **-er** *n.* a long wave as it breaks into foam. **-fast** *n.* the first meal of the day. **-neck** *a.* dangerous to life and limb. **-up** *n.* disintegration; separation. **-water** *n.* a strong structure to break the force of the waves.
**breast** *n.* the external part of the thorax or chest between neck and abdomen; *v.t.* to oppose boldly. **-s** *n.pl.* the milk or mammary glands of women and female animals. **-bone** *n.* the sternum, the flat narrow bone to which the first seven ribs are attached. **-plate** *n.* a piece of armor for protecting the chest. — **stroke** *n.* a long-distance stroke in swimming.
**breath** *n.* air respired by the lungs; life; fragrance. **-less** *a.* out of breath; panting; expectant. **-lessness** *n.* **under one's breath,** in a low voice or whisper. **with bated breath,** breath held from fear or excitement.
**breathe** *v.t.* to draw in and give out air from the lungs; *v.i.* to inhale and emit air—hence to live. **breathable** *a.* **-d** *a.* *(Phon.)* uttered with breath only. **-r** *n.* a short spell of rest. **breathing** *n.* respiration; **breathing-space, breathing-time,** *n.* a pause.
**bred** *pa.t.* and *pa.p.* of **breed.**
**breech** *n.* the hinder part, esp. of a gun-barrel; *v.t.* to whip; to flog. **-es** *n.pl.* trousers, esp. those which fit tightly around knees. **-ing** *n.* that part of the harness which passes round a horse's haunches.
**breed** *v.t.* to beget; to engender; to train or bring up; *v.i.* to be produced; to increase in number; *pa.t.* and *pa.p.* **bred;** *n.* a race of animals from the same stock; sort. **-er** *n.* one who breeds cattle or other live stock. **-ing** *n.* producing; the rearing of live stock; deportment
**breeze** *n.* a wind of moderate strength. **breezy** *a.* windy; of a person, animated and brisk.
**breth•ren** *n.pl.* members of the same society or profession [See **brother**].
**breve** *n.* a mark distinguishing short vowels.
**brev•i•ty** *n.* conciseness; terseness.
**brew** *v.t.* to prepare a fermented liquor, from malt, hops, etc.; concoct; *v.i.* to be impending; *n.* something brewed. **-er** *n.* **-ery** *n.* a place where brewing is carried on.
**bribe** *n.* anything bestowed, to influence judgment and conduct; *v.t.* to influence by gifts; *v.i.* to practice bribery, **bribable** *a.* **bribery** *n.*
**bric•à•brac** *n.* ornamental articles.
**brick** *n.* a building material made from a special clay molded into a rectangular block and hardened by drying in the sun or firing in a kiln; *v.t.* to lay with bricks. **-kiln** *n.* a kiln in which bricks are baked or burnt. **-layer** *n.* one who is skilled in building with bricks. **-laying** *n.*
**bride** *n.* a woman about to be, or just, married. **bridal** *n.* wedding; *a.* pert. to a bride or a wedding; nuptial. **bridal-suite** *n.* apartments set aside for a honeymoon couple. **-groom** *n.* a man newly-married, or about to be married. **-s maid** *n.* an unmarried woman who acts as attendant on a bride.
**bridge** *n.* a structure spanning a river or a valley, etc., in order to afford passage; the bone of the nose, etc.; mounting for false teeth; *(Mus.)* connecting passage; *v.t.* to build a bridge. **-head** *n.* a footing gained by an attacking force on the far bank of a river.
**bridge** *n.* a card game for four players.
**bri•dle** *n.* the headgear of a horse; *v.t.* to put a bridle upon; control. — **path** *n.* a narrow track used by riders on

horseback.

**brief** *a.* short in duration; using few words; *n.* an abridged statement of a case; to inform personnel of the details of an impending action. **— case** *n.* a small flat case for carrying papers. **-ly** *adv.* **-ness** *n.* **-s** *n.pl.* undershorts.

**bri•er** *n.* any prickly bush; a tangled mass of them.

**brig** *n.* a sailing-ship with two masts, both square-rigged.

**brig**

**bri•gade** *n.* a sub-division of an army under the command of a general officer; a group of people organized for a specific purpose, such as a *fire brigade.* **brigadier-general** *n.*

**bright** *a.* shining; full of light or splendor; cheerful; intelligent. **-en** *v.t.* to make bright; *v.i.* to grow bright. **-ly** *adv.* **-ness** *n.*

**bril•liant** *a.* glittering; sparkling; distinguished; *n.* a polished diamond cut to a definite pattern. **-ly** *adv.* **-ness** *n.* **brilliance** *n.* **brilliancy** *a.*

**brim** *n.* rim or border; *v.i.* to be full to the brim. **-ful** *a.* **-med** *a.* **-ming** *a.*

**brine** *n.* water containing an admixture of salt; the sea. **brinish** *a.* salty, like brine. **briny** *a.*

**bring** *v.t.* to fetch, to convey from one person or place to another; to transport; *pa.t.* and *pa.p.* **brought.**

**brink** *n.* margin of a steep slope; verge.

**brisk** *a.* full of activity; *v.t.* and *i.* to enliven; to cheer up. **-ly** *adv.* **-ness** *n.*

**bris•ket** *a.* part of animal's breast which lies next to ribs.

**bris•tle** *n.* a very stiff, erect, coarse hair, as of swine; *v.t.* to erect the bristles of; *v.i.* to stand up erect, like bristles; to show anger **-d** *a.* provided with bristles.

**Brit•ish** *a.* of or pertaining to Britain; *n.* the inhabitants of Britain. **-er** *n.* a British subject.

**brit•tle** *a.* easily broken; fragile.

**broach** *n.* a tapered, hardened-steel bit for enlarging holes in metal; *v.t.* to pierce; to approach a subject.

**broad** *a.* wide, ample, open; liberal-minded; plain, unmistakable (hint); full (daylight). **broad, -ly** *adv.* **-brim** *n.* a wide-brimmed hat, much affected by Quakers, and so a Quaker. **-cloth** *n.* a finely woven woollen, cotton, or rayon cloth for clothing. **-en** *v.t.* and *v.i.* to grow broad. **— jump** *n. (Sports)* a horizontal jump from rest or from a run. **-loom** *n.* woven on a wide loom, of carpets and rugs. **— minded** *a.* tolerant. **-ness** *n.* **-side** *n.* the whole side of a ship above water-line; a volley from the gun on one side of a naval craft; violent abuse.

**broad•cast** *n.* a transmission by radio; *a.; v.t.* to disseminate by radio-telephone transmitter, news, music, etc., by receiving apparatus. **-er** *n.* a person or organization broadcasting.

**bro•cade** *n.* a fabric woven with elaborate design; *v.t.* to ornament a fabric with raised designs. **-d** *a.*

**broc•co•li** *n.* a variety of the cauliflower.

**bro•chure** *n.* a printed work of a few sheets of paper; a pamphlet.

**brogue** *n.* a mode of pronunciation peculiar to Irish speakers.

**broi•der** *v.t.* to adorn with figured needlework.

**broil** *n.* a noisy quarrel; altercation.

**broil** *v.t.* to cook under gas or electric heat in a stove; *v.i.* to be overheated.

**broke** *pa.t.* and old *pa.p.* of **break;** *a. (Colloq.)* penniless; degraded. **-n** *pa.p.* of **break;** *a.* shattered; parted; impaired; exhausted; spent. **-n English,** imperfect English, as spoken by a non-native. **-n hearted** *a.* crushed with grief; inconsolable. **-nly** *adv.* intermittently. **-nness** *n.*

**brok•er** *n.* a person employed in the negotiation of commercial transactions between other parties in the interests of one of the principals; a dealer in second-hand goods. **-age, brokerage,** *n.* the business of a broker.

**bro•mide** *n.* a compound of bromine with some other element; a sedative drug.

**bro•mine** *n.* one of the elements, related to chlorine, iodine, and fluorine. **bromic** *a.*

**bron•chi, bron•chi•a** *n.pl.* . the two tubes forming the lower end of the trachea. **-al** *a.* pert. to the bronchi. **bronchitis,** *n.* inflammation of the bronchial tubes.

**bron•chus** *n.* one of the bifurcations of the windpipe; *pl.* see **bronchi.**

**bron•co** *n.* an unbroken, or partly broken horse. **— buster** *n.*

**bronze** *n.* an alloy of copper, tin, and zinc; the color of bronze; *a.* made of or colored like bronze; *v.t.* to give the appearance of bronze to; to harden. **Bronze Age,** pre-historic period between the Stone and Iron Ages. **bronzy** *a.*

**brooch** *n.* an ornamental clasp with a pin for attaching it to a garment.

**brood** *v.t.* to sit upon, as a hen on eggs; to ponder; *v.i.* to sit upon to hatch; to meditate moodily; *n.* a family of young, esp. of birds; a race. **-er** *n.* an appliance for rearing incubator-hatched chickens by artificial heat. **— mare** *n.* a mare kept for breeding. **-y** *a.* wishing to sit, as a hen; sullen.

**brook** *n.* a small stream.

**brook** *v.t.* to bear; to support.

**broom** *n.* implement for sweeping.

**broth** *n.* water in which meat has been boiled with vegetables.

**broth•el** *n.* house of prostitution.

**broth•er** *n.* a male born of the same parents; fellow-member of a corporate body; *pl.* **-s, brethren. -hood** *n.* an association of men of the same religious order, profession, or society; the mutual regard resulting from this association. **— in-law** *n.* the brother of one's husband or wife; a sister's husband. **— like, -ly** *a.* affectionate. **-liness** *n.*

**brought** *pa.t.* and *pa.p.* of **bring.**

**brow** *n.* the ridge over the eyes; the forehead. **-beat** *v.t.* to bully a person by over-bearing speech. **-beater** *n.*

**brown** *n.* a dark color inclining to red or yellow; a mixture of black, red, and yellow; *a.* of a brown color; sunburnt; *v.t.* to sunbathe; to roast brown. **— betty** *n.* a spiced, bread and apple pudding. **-stone** *n.* a reddish-brown sandstone used in building. **— sugar,** unrefined or partly refined sugar.

**brown•ie** *n.* a member of the junior section of Girl Scouts; a chocolate cookie.

**browse** *v.t.* and *i.* to glance through a book shop, etc. **browsing** *n.*

**bruise** *v.t.* to injure by striking or crushing; to pound or pulverize; *n.* a contusion. **-r** *n.* a prize-fighter.

**brunch** *n* *(Colloq.)* breakfast and lunch combined.

**bru•nette** *n.* a woman with dark brown hair.

**brunt** *n.* the force of a blow.

**brush** *n.* an implement made of bristles, twigs, etc., bound together and used for removing dust, dressing the hair, applying paint, and the like; the smaller trees of a forest, brushwood; the bushy tail of a fox or squirrel; *v.t.* to remove dust, etc., with a brush; to touch lightly in passing; *v.i.* to touch with light contact. **-wood** *n.* thicket of small trees and shrubs. **-y** *a.* rough, shaggy.

**brusque** *a.* blunt; abrupt in speech. **-ness** *n.*

**brute** *a.* irrational; ferocious; *n.* a beast. **brutal** *a.* savage; inhuman. **brutalism** *n.* brutality. **brutality** *n.* inhumanity; savagery; **brutalize** *v.t.* to make brutal, cruel, or coarse; to treat with brutality; *v.i.* to become brutal. **brutally** *adv.* **brutish** *a.*

**bry•ol•o•gy** *n.* the science of mosses.

**bub•ble** *n.* a hollow globe of water or other liquid blown out with a globule of air or gas in liquid or solid substances; a small bladder-like excrescence on surface of paint, metals, etc.; *v.i.* to rise in bubbles; to effervesce; to gurgle; *v.t.* to cause to bubble. **bubbly** *a.*

**bu•bo** *n.* lymphatic swelling of the glands in the groin or armpit. **bubonic** *a.; pl.* **buboes, bubonic plague,** the Black Death of the 14th cent.

**buc•ca•neer** *n.* a pirate; *v.i.* to play the buccaneer.

**buck** *n.* the male of the rabbit, hare, sheep, goat, and deer; *(Colloq.)* a male Indian; *v.i.* to attempt to unseat a rider by jumping vertically with arched back and head down; to foil all attempts at improvement. **-shot** *n.* large leaden shot for killing big game. **-skin** *n.* a soft leather made of deerskin or sheepskin. **-tooth** *n.* a tooth which protrudes. **buck up!** *(Colloq.)* cheer up!

**buck•board** *n.* a four-wheeled vehicle in which a long elastic board takes the place of steel springs.

**buck•et** *n.* a vessel for carrying water. **-ful** *n.* the quantity held by a bucket.

**buck•le** *n.* a metal clasp for fastening straps, bands, etc.; a bend or kink; *v.t.* and *v.i.* to clasp with a buckle; to bend.

**buck•ram** *n.* a coarse linen or cotton cloth stiffened with sizing; *a.* made of buckram.

**buck•wheat** *n.* an herb, the seeds of which are ground into flour or fed to animals.

**bud** *n.* the sprout on a plant containing an unexpanded leaf, branch, or flower; *v.i.* to begin to grow; *v.t.* to graft by budding. **-ding** *n.* the act of inserting the bud of one tree under the bark of another, for propagation. **to nip in the bud,** to destroy at the beginning. *pr.p.* **-ding.** *pa.t.* **-ded.**

**Bud•dhism** *n.* the chief religion of E. Asia. **Buddhist** *n.* a worshipper of Buddha.

**bud•dy** *n.* a bosom friend.

**budge** *v.t.* and *i.* to move; to stir.

**budg•et** *n.* a plan for systematic spending; *v.t.* to plan one's expenditures.

**buff** *n.* a soft, yellow leather prepared from the skin of the buffalo, elk, and other animals; a revolving wooden disc covered with layers of leather used with an abrasive for polishing; a light yellow-tan color; a fan; *a.* made of buff leather; *v.t.* to polish with a buff. **-y** *a.* of a buff color.

**buf•fa•lo** *n.* a ruminating, horned animal, resembling an ox, but larger and more powerful.

**buf•fer** *n.* a resilient cushion to deaden the concussion between a moving body and one on which it strikes; a polisher. **— state,** a country lying between two powerful and rival nations.

**buf•fet** *n.* a cupboard for displaying fine china. *a.* (a meal) spread on tables from which guests serve themselves.

**buf•fet** *n.* a blow with the fist; *v.t.* to strike with the fist. **-s** *n.pl.* hardships.

**buf•foon** *n.* a person who acts the clown by his clumsy attempts at humor. **-ery** *n.* the silly antics of a buffoon. **-ish** *a.*

**bug** *n.* name applied to various insects; a concealed microphone. **-gy** *a.* swarming with bugs.

**bu•gle** *n.* a wind instrument used because of its penetrating note for conveying orders. sound a call. **-r** *n.*

**build** *v.t.* to erect a structure; to raise (hopes); *v.i.* to exercise the work of building; to depend with *on, upon; pa.t.* and *pa.p.* **built;** *n.* form; physique; style of construction. **-er** *n.* **-ing** *n.*

**bulb** *n.* a modified leaf-bud emitting roots from its base and formed of fleshy leaf scales containing a reserve supply of food; a dilated glass tube containing filament for electric lighting; *v.i.* to form bulbs; to bulge. **-aceous, -ar, -ed, -ose, -y** *a.* pert. to bulbs. **-iform** *a.* **-osity** *n.* the state of being bulbous. **-ous** *a.* having the appearance of a bulb; growing from bulbs.

**bulge** *n.* anything rounded which juts out; *v.i.* to swell out. **bulgy** *a.*

**bulk** *n.* size, the main body; the largest portion; *v.i.* to pile up; *v.i.* to be of some importance. **-age** *n.* roughage. **-iness** *n.* **-y** *a.* clumsy in shape, so difficult to handle. **in bulk,** unpackaged, in large quantity.

**bulk•head** *n.* a partition in a ship made with boards, etc., to form separate compartments; a horizontal or sloping cover to outside step leading to the cellar of a building.

**bull** *n.* the male of any bovine; the male of numerous animals as elephant, whale, seal, moose, elk, deer; *a.* to denote a male animal. **-baiting** *n.* an ancient sport of setting ferocious dogs on a bull tied to a stake. **-dog** *n.* a breed of dog formerly used for bull-baiting; **-dozer** *n.* a tractor with an attached horizontal blade in front. **-fight** *n.* the national sport of certain Latin races, esp. in Spain and consisting of a combat between men and specially bred bulls. **-finch** *n.* a bird of the thrush family with a thicker head and neck. **-frog** *n.* a large, dusky-brown frog. **-headed** *n.* headstrong. **— pen,** fenced enclosure; *(Sports)* where baseball pitchers practice. **— ring** *n.* the arena in which a bull-fight is held. **bull's-eye** *n.* a shot that hits the center of the target. **— session** *(Colloq.)* informal discussion. **— terrier** *n.* a cross between bulldog and terrier.

**bul•let** *n.* a small projectile to be discharged from a gun.

**bul•le•tin** *n.* a periodical publication; a brief statement of facts issued by authority. **-board** *n.*

**bul•lion** *n.* uncoined, refined gold or silver; the precious metals, including coined metal, when exported or imported.

**bul•ly** *n.* over-bearing person who tyrannizes the weak; *v.t.* intimidate; *v.i.* to bluster.

**bul•wark** *n.* an outwork for defense; *pl.* a railing round the deck of a ship; *v.t.* to fortify with a rampart.

**bum** *n.* an idle, dissolute person; *a.* worthless; *v.i.* to loaf.

**bum•ble-bee** *n.* a large, hairy, social bee.

**bum•bling** *a.* noisy and blundering [See **bumble-bee**].

**bump** *n.* a dull, heavy blow; a swelling resulting from a blow; one of the protuberances on the skull, said by phrenologists to give an indication of mental qualities, character, etc.; *v.t.* to strike against; *v.i.* to collide. **-y** *a.* covered with bumps.

**bump•er** *n.* *(Auto.)* a horizontal bar in front and rear of a car; *a.* very large; excellent.

**bump•kin** *n.* an awkward, stupid person; a country lout.

**bump•tious** *a.* rudely self-assertive; self-important. **-ness** *n.*

**bun** *n.* a kind of bread roll, light in texture and slightly sweetened; hair twisted into a knot at the back of a woman's head.

**bunch** *n.* a cluster of similar things, tied or growing together; a bouquet of flowers; *v.t.* to gather together; to crowd; *v.i.* to swell out like a bunch. **bunched** *a.* crowded together. **-y** *a.* growing in bunches.

**bun•dle** *n.* a number of things bound together; a definite number of things; *v.t.* to make up into a bundle or roll; *v.i.* to dress warmly.

**bun•ga•low** *n.* small detached one-storied house.

**bun•gle** *v.t.* to manage clumsily; *v.i.* to act awkwardly; *n.* a blundering performance. **-r** *n.* **bungling** *a.*

**bun•ion** *n.* an inflamed swelling occurring on the foot.

**bunk** *n.* a box-like structure used as a seat by day and a bed at night; a sleepingberth on board ship; in a camp, etc.; *v.i.* to sleep in a bunk.

**bunk•er** *n.* an underground fortification.

**bun•ny** *n.* a pet name for a rabbit.

**Bun•sen burn•er** *n.* a gas burner in which a strong current of air produces a weakly luminous, but very hot, flame.

**bunt** *v.t.* to butt with horns or head; (baseball) to bounce ball a short distance off the bat.

**buoy** *n.* any floating body of wood or iron employed to point out the particular situation of a ship's anchor, a life-buoy; *v.t.* to fix buoys. **to buoy up,** to keep afloat. **-age** *n.* a series of buoys in position; the providing of buoys. **-ancy** *n.* capacity for floating in water or air; cheerfulness. **-ant** *a.* floating lightly; hopeful.

**bur** *n.* the rough, sticky seed-case of certain plants with hooked spines to help in its distribution; a burr. See **burr.**

**bur•ble** *v.i.* to gurgle, as of running water; *(Colloq.)* to talk idly.

**bur•den** *n.* anything difficult to bear, as care, sorrow, etc.; *v.t.* to oppress; to encumber.

**bu•reau** *n.* a small chest of drawers; a government department.

**bu•reau•c•ra•cy** *n.* administration by bureaus, often excessively numerous and powerful; the officials engaged in such an administration. **bureaucrat** *n.* one who advocates such a system of government. **bureaucratic** *a.*

**bur•geon** *v.i.* to sprout; to put forth branches.

**bur•glar** *n.* one who is guilty of house-breaking. **-y** *n.* breaking and entering into a dwelling-house.

**Bur•gun•dy** *n.* name given to various wines, red or white.

**bur•i•al** *n.* interment; entombment. **— ground,** a cemetery. [See **bury**].

**burl** *n.* a knot in wood, thread or yarn. **-ed** *a.*

**bur•lap** *n.* a coarsely woven canvas of flax, hemp, or jute, used for packing and as a wall covering, etc.

**bur•lesque** *n.* exaggerating, and ridiculing a work of art; theatrical performance featuring vulgar comedy and dancing; *a.* comical; ludicrous; *v.t.* to turn into burlesque.

**bur•ly** *a.* of stout build; big and sturdy.

**burliness** *n.*
**burn** *v.t.* to consume with fire; to subject to the action of fire; to char; *v.i.* to be on fire; to flame; blaze; *pa.t.* and *pa.p.* **-ed** or **-t;** *n.* injury or damage caused by burning. **-er** *n.* part of a gas jet from which the flame issues. **-ing** *n.* act of consuming by fire; *a.* flaming; parching. **-ing-glass** *n.* a convex lens which causes intense heat by bending the rays of the sun and concentrating them upon a single point. **burning question,** a topic of universal discussion. **burnt-offering** *n.* a sacrifice of a living person or animal by burning.
**burnt** *pa.t.* and *pa.p.* of **burn.**
**burr** *n.* a tool for cutting or drilling; a rough edge left on metal by a cutting tool. Also **bur.**
**bur•ro** *n.* a donkey.
**bur•row** *n.* a hole dug in the ground by certain small animals to serve as an abode; *v.i.* to tunnel through earth.
**bur•sa** *n.* a sac or cavity, especially between joints; **-l** *a.;* **bursitis** *n.*
**bur•sar** *n.* a treasurer of a college.
**burst** *v.t.* to break into pieces; to break open violently; to break suddenly into some expression of feeling; *v.i.* to shatter; *pa.t.* and *pa.p.* **burst;** *n.* a bursting; an outbreak; spurt.
**bur•y** *v.t.* to inter in a grave; to hide by covering; *pa.p.* **buried. -ing** *n.* burial; interment. **to bury the hatchet,** to restore friendly relations.
**bus, 'bus** *n.* a vehicle for public conveyance of passengers; *pl.* **-es.**
**bush** *n.* a shrub; a thicket of small trees and shrubs; *v.i.* to grow thick or bushy; *v.t.* to plant bushes about. **— fighting** *n.* guerilla warfare where advantage is taken of trees and bushes. **-iness** *n.* the quality of being bushy. **-man** *n.* a settler in the backwoods. **-master** *n.* a large venemous snake. **-y** *a.* thick and spreading.
**bush,** *n.* the internal lining of a bearing, to form a plain bearing surface for a pin or shaft. **-ing** *n.* a removable lining to reduce friction.
**bush•el** *n.* a dry measure of 4 pecks, for corn, fruit, etc.
**busi•ness** *n.* employment; any occupation for a livelihood; firm. **-like** *a.* systematic; methodical. **-man** *n.*
**buss** *n.* a hearty kiss; *v.t.* to kiss, esp. boisterously.
**bust** *n.* sculptured representation of a person from the waist upwards; the upper part of the human body.
**bus•tle** *v.i.* to busy oneself with much movement; *n.* great stir. **-r** *n.*
**bus•tle** *n.* a stuffed pad worn by ladies to support and elevate the back of the skirt just below the waist.
**bus•y** *a.* active and earnest in work; industrious; *v.t.* to keep busy; to occupy (oneself). **busily** *adv.* **-body** *n.* a person who meddles in other people's business. **-ness** *n.* state of being busy.
**but** *conj.* yet; unless; nevertheless; *prep.* except; without; *adv.* only. **all but,** nearly.
**bu•tane** *n.* a natural gas used in refrigeration and as a fuel.
**butch•er** *n.* one who slaughters animals for food or retails the meat; *v.t.* to slaughter animals for food; to murder in cold blood. **-ing** *n.* killing for food. **-y** *n.* wanton slaughter.
**but•ler** *n.* a male servant.
**butt** *n.* the lower end of a tree-trunk providing the strongest timber; one continually subject to ridicule; *v.t.* to strike by thrusting the head downwards. *n.pl.* a mound with targets where shooting is practiced. **to butt in** *(Colloq.)* to intervene without permission.
**but•ter** *n.* the fatty ingredients of milk, emulsified by churning; *v.t.* to spread with butter. **-cup** *n.* plant with cup-shaped, yellow flowers. **-fingers** *n.* *(Colloq.)* one who drops things easily. **-milk** *n.* the fluid residue after butter has been churned from cream. **-scotch** *n.* a kind of taffy with butter as an ingredient. **-y** *a.*
**but•ter•fly** *n.* the common name of all diurnal, lepidopterous insects.
**but•tock** *n.* rounded, lower, posterior part of the body (usually in *pl.*)
**but•ton** *n.* a stud for fastening clothing; an emblem of membership; *v.t.* to fasten with buttons; *v.i.* to be fastened by a button. **-hole** *n.* the loop in which a button is fastened; **-hook** *n.* a hook for pulling a button through a buttonhole.
**but•tress** *n.* a projecting support to a wall; *v.t.* to support.
**bu•tyl** *n.* a highly elastic synthetic rubber, made from butane, a natural gas.
**bux•om** *a.* full of health; lively.
**buy** *v.t.* to obtain by payment; to purchase; *pa.t.* and *pa.p.* **bought. -er** *n.* a purchaser.
**buzz** *v.i.* to make a humming sound; *v.t.* to spread news secretly. **-er** *n.* an apparatus used for telephonic signaling. **-ingly** *adv.*
**buz•zard** *n.* a genus of birds of the hawk family.
**by** *prep.* beside; in the neighborhood of; *adv.* near; close; beyond. **by and by,** in the near future. **-name** *n.* a nick-name. **-pass** *n.* a road for the diversion of traffic from crowded centers; *v.t.* to avoid a place by going round it. **— path** *n.* a side path. **-play** *n.* action carried on apart from the main part of a play; diversion. **— product** *n.* secondary product obtained during manufacture of principal commodity. **-road** *n.* a less frequented side road. **-stander** *n.* an onlooker. **-way** *n.* a secluded road. **-word** *n.* a common saying.
**bye** *n.* having no opponent in a round of competition. **-bye** *(Colloq.)* good-bye.
**by•law, bye-law** *n.* a local law made by an association.
**Byz•an•tine** relating to *Byzantium,* the original name for Constantinople.

**cab** *n.* a taxicab; driver's accomodation on a truck. **-by** *n.* a taxi driver.

**cab•a•la, cabbala** *n.* occultism. **cabalism** *n.* **cabalist, cabalistic(al)** *a.* mysterious; occult.

**cab•a•ret** *n.* restaurant providing entertainment and space for dancing.

**cab•bage** *n.* a garden vegetable of Brassica family.

**cab•in** *n.* a small house; an apartment in a ship; the space in an airplane for the pilot and passengers; *v.t.* to confine in a cabin; *v.i.* to live in a cabin. **— boy** *n.* a boy who waits on the officers of a ship.

**cab•i•net** *n.* a council of ministers who advise the chief executive; a chest for displaying objects; **— maker** *n.* a maker of cabinets and other furniture.

**ca•ble** *n.* a large, strong chain; a stranded insulated conductor of electricity; a

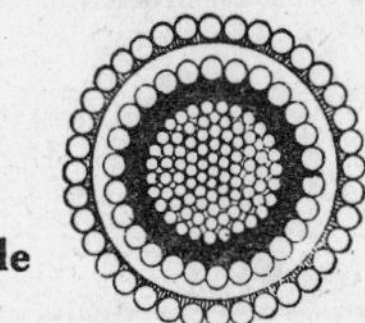

**cable**

submarine telegraph line; a message sent by such line; *v.t.* to send a message by cable. **— car** *n.* a car pulled by a moving cable. **— gram** *n.* a telegram sent by cable.

**ca•boose** *n.* a car attached to a freight train for the crew.

**ca•ca•o** *n.* a tropical tree from the seeds of which cocoa and chocolate are prepared.

**cacao**

**cache** *n.* a hole in the ground for hiding provisions, etc.; articles so hidden; *v.t.* to conceal.

**cack•le** *v.i.* to make a noise like a hen or goose; *n.*

**ca•cog•raphy** *n.* bad writing or spelling.

**ca•coph•o•ny** *n.* a harsh or disagreeable sound; a use of ill-sounding words. **cacophonous** *a.*

**cac•tus** *n.* an American desert plant with thick, fleshy, prickly stems, generally no leaves but frequently producing showy flowers. *pl.* **-es,** or **cacti.**

**cad** *n.* a mean, vulgar fellow. **-dish** *a.* ill-bred, mean.

**ca•dav•er** *n.* *(Med.)* a corpse. **-ous** *a.* corpse-like; sickly-looking.

**cad•die, cad•dy** *n.* an attendant who carries a golfer's clubs; *v.i.*

**cad•dis, cad•dice** *n.* worm-like aquatic larva of caddis-fly.

**ca•dence** *n.* a fall of the voice in speaking; the beat of any rhythmical action; *(Mus.)* the subsiding of a melody towards a close. **-d** *a.* rhythmical. **cadency** *n.*

**ca•den•za** *n.* *(Mus.)* an ornamental passage for a voice or solo instrument.

**ca•det** *n.* a youth in training for commissioned ranks in the army or air force; **-ship** *n.*

**cadge** *v.t.* and *i.* to peddle goods; to beg. **-r** *n.* a peddlar.

**cad•mi•um** *n.* *(Chem.)* a soft, bluish-white metal of zinc group. **cadmia** *n.* an oxide of zinc.

**ca•du•ce•us** *n.* the staff carried by Mercury, messenger of the gods; the emblem of the medical profession.

**cae•cum** *n.* *(Med.)* the first part of the large intestine, opening into the colon; *pl.* **caeca. caecal** *a.*

**Cae•sar** *n.* one who acts like Julius Caesar (100-44 B.C.), Roman emperor and dictator. **Caesarean. Caesarian** *a.* pert. to Julius Caesar. **Caesarian section** *(Med.)* delivery of child through an opening cut in abdominal wall.

**cae•si•um** See cesium.

**cae•su•ra, cesura** *n.* a break in a line of poetry.

**ca•fé** *n.* a restaurant, usually licensed for the sale of light refreshments only.

**caf•e•te•ri•a** *n.* a restaurant where the customers help themselves.

**caf•feine** *n.* the stimulating alkaloid in coffee and tea.

**cage** *n.* a box-like enclosure, with bars of iron or wire, for keeping animals or birds; *v.t.* to imprison. **-ling** *n.* a bird kept in a cage. **-work,** *n.* open frame-work. **-y** *a.* cautious, wary.

**cais•son** *n.* an ammunition wagon; *(Engineering)* a water-tight chamber of sheet-iron or wood, used for workmen in laying the foundations of piers or bridges, quay-walls, etc.

**ca•jole** *v.t.* to persuade by flattery; to wheedle. **-r** *n.* **-ry** *n.* the act of cajoling.

**cake** *n.* a piece of dough baked; a flattish mass of matter, esp. soap, tobacco, etc.; *v.t.* to make into a cake; *v.i.* to become a flat, doughy mass. **caky** *a.*

**cal•a•bash** *n.* the bottle-gourd tree; a species of pear.

**cal•a•mine** *n.* a silicate of zinc, used as a pigment in skin ointments.

**ca•lam•i•ty** *n.* any great misfortune. **calamitous** *a.* producing distress and misers. **calamitously** *adv.*

**cal•car•e•ous** *a.* chalky.

**cal•cif•er•ol** *n.* crystalline vitamin D used in fortifying margarine. **calciferous** *a.* containing carbonate of lime.

**cal•ci•fy** *v.t.* and *i.* to harden or petrify, by a deposit of lime. **calcification** *n.*

**cal•ci•mine** *n.* a white or tinted wash for ceiling and walls.

**cal•cine** *v.t.* to expel water and other volatile substances by heat; *v.i.* to be turned into powder. **calcinable** *a.* **calcination** *n.* **calcinatory** *n.* a vessel used in calcination.

**cal•ci•um** *n.* the metallic base of lime. **calcic** *a.* containing calcium. **calcite** *n.* native carbonate of lime.

**cal•cu•late** *v.t.* to estimate; to compute; to expect; *v.i.* to make a calculation. **calculable** *a.* **-d** *a.* intended to produce a certain effect. **calculating** *a.* shrewd in matters of self-interest. **calculation** *n.* **calculative** *a.* tending to calculate. **calculator** *n.* a machine which does automatic computations.

**cal•cu•lus** *n.* a branch of higher mathematics concerned with the properties of continuously varying quantities; *n.* a hard concretion which forms, esp. in kidney, bladder, etc. usually called stone or gravel; *pl.* **calculi. calculose, calculous** *a.* hard, like stone; gritty.

**cal•dron, cauldron** *n.* a large metal boiler.

**cal•a•fac•tion** *n.* the act of heating, the state of being heated. **calefacient** *a.* making warm; *n.* a heat-giving remedy. **calefactor** *n.* that which gives heat. **calefactory** *a.*

**cal•en•dar** *n.* a table of days, months or seasons. *v.t.* to enter in a list.

**calf** *n.* the young of the cow, and of some other mammals, such as elephant, whale, etc.; *pl.* **calves —skin** *n.* a fine, light-colored leather made from the skin of a calf. **calve** *v.i.* to bring forth a calf.

**calf** *n.* the thick, fleshy part of the leg below the knee; *pl.* **calves.**

**cal•i•ber** *n.* the diameter of the bore of a cannon, gun, etc.; *(Fig.)* quality of mind; character. **calibrate** *v.t.* to determine the caliber of a firearm tube or other cylindrical object. **calibration** *n.*

**cal•i•co** *n.* white cotton cloth, first made in *Calicut* in India; *a.* made of calico.

**cal•i•pers, callipers** *n.* a two-legged instrument for measuring diameters.

**ca•liph, ca•lif** *n.* a title given to the successors of Mohammed.

**ca•lix** See **calyx.**

**calk, caulk** *v.t.* to fill or close joints or crevices to make air- or water-tight. **-er** *n.* **-ing** *n.*

**call** *v.t.* to summon; to name, as for office; to utter in a loud voice; *v.i.* to cry out; to make a brief visit; *n.* a summons or invitation; a short visit; authorized command; the characteristic cry of a bird or animal. **-er** *n.* one who calls. **-ing** *n.* a person's usual occupation. **at call,** on demand. **on call,** of a person, ready if summoned. **-boy** *n.* a boy who calls actors to go on the stage; a bellboy. **to call down,** to rebuke. **to call up** *(Mil.)* to summon to military service.

**cal•ligra•phy** *n.* penmanship. **calligrapher, calligraphist** *n.* **calligraphic** *a.*

**cal•lis•then•ics** *n.pl.* light gymnastic exercises to promote beauty and grace of movement. **callisthenic** *a.*

**cal•lous** *a.* hardened; unfeeling. **-ly** *adv.* **-ness** *n.* **callosity** *n.* a horny hardness of the skin.

**cal•low** *a.* pert. to the condition of a young bird; unfledged; *(Fig.)* inexperienced. **-ness** *n.*

**cal•lus** *n.* a hardened part of the skin.

**calm** *a.* still; at rest; *n.* the state of being calm; *v.t.* to make calm. **-ly** *adv.* **-ness** *n.*

**ca•lor•ic** *n.* heat; *a.* heat-producing. **caloricity** *n.* the power of animals to develop heat. **calorifacient** *a.* heat-producing. **calorific** *a.* heat-producing. **calorification** *n.* the production of heat.

**cal•o•rie, calory** *n.* the unit of heat or energy produced by any food substance. **calorimeter** *n.* a scientific instrument for determining the amount of heat produced by any substance.

**ca•lum•ni•ate** *v.t.* to accuse falsely; *v.i.* to utter slanders. **calumniation** *n.* slanderous representations. **calumniator** *n.* **calumniatory, calumnious** *a.* slanderous. **calumniously** *adv.* **calumny** *n.* a flase accusation; libel.

**calve** See **calf.**

**Cal•vin•ism** *n.* the doctrines of John Calvin. **Calvinist** *n.* **Calvinistic** *a.*

**calx** *n.* the crumbly substance that remains after the calcination of a metal or mineral; *pl.* **calxes, calces.**

**ca•lyp•so** *n.* an improvised song in native rhythm from the West Indies.

**ca•lyx, ca•lix** *n.* the outer covering or leaf-like envelope of a flower.

**calyx** 

**cam** *n.* a projecting part of a wheel used to give an alternating or variable motion to another wheel or piece. **-shaft** *n.* the shaft on which cams are formed for opening the valves.

**cam**

**cam•ber** *n.* a slight convexity of an upper surface, as of a ship's deck, a bridge, a road surface.

**Cam•bri•an** *a.* pert. to Cambria or Wales; *n.* a Welshman.

**cam•bric** *n.* a fine white linen fabric first made at *Cambrai,* in N. France.

**came** *pa.t. of the verb* **come.**

**cam•el** *n.* a large ruminant animal of Asia and Africa, with one or two humps, used as a beast of burden. **-eer** *n.* a camel driver.

**ca•mel•lia** *a.* a species of Asiatic shrub with showy flowers and elegant dark-green, laurel-like leaves.

**cam•e•o** *n.* a gem stone of two layers cut in ornamental relief.

**cam•e•ra** *n.* device for taking photographs. **-man** *n.* a professional motion picture or press photographer.

**cam•ou•flage** *n.* a method of visual

deception of the enemy by disguising; *v.t.* to cover with camouflage material; to disguise.

**camp** *n.* the area of ground where soldiers are lodged in huts or tents; permanent barracks near a suitable exercise ground; *v.t.* and *i.* to pitch tents. **-er** *n.* one who lives in a camp in open country, esp. living in a tent. **-ing** *n.* the act of living in camp. **— chair** *n.* a light, portable chair with folding legs. **— meeting** *n.* a religious meeting in the open air. **— out** *v.* to live without conveniences.

**cam•paign** *n.* in politics, business, etc. an organized series of operations (meetings, canvassing, etc.); *v.i.* to conduct, or assist in political, etc. operations. **-er** *n.*

**cam•phor** *n.* a whitish substance with an aromatic taste and smell, obtained from

camphor

the camphor laurel-tree. **-aceous** *a.* resembling camphor. **-ate** *v.t.* to impregnate with camphor. **-ate, -ic** *a.* pert. to camphor.

**cam•pus** *n.* the grounds of a college or school.

**can** *pres. indic.* of a defective, intransitive verb meaning, to be able, to be allowed. *pa.p., pa.t.* **could.**

**can** *n.* a metal container for holding liquids, etc.; *v.t.* to put into a can for the purpose of preserving; *pr.p.* **-ning.** *pa.p.* and *pa.t.* **-ned. -nery** *n.* a factory where foods are preserved by canning.

**Ca•na•di•an** *n.* an inhabitant of Canada; *a.* pert. to Canada.

**ca•nal** *n.* an artificial watercourse for transport, drainage or irrigation purposes. **canalize** *v.t.* to make a canal through.

**can•a•pé** *n.* a small piece of bread, with anchovies, etc. on it served as an appetizer.

**ca•nar•y** *n.* a yellow singing bird, a species of finch; a pale-yellow color.

**ca•nas•ta** *n.* a card game played with two packs.

**can-can** *n.* a kind of dance, once popular in music-halls in France.

**can•cel** *v.t.* to blot out; to annul; *(Math.)* to strike out common factors; to offset. **-lation** *n.* the act of canceling.

**can•cer** *n. (Med.)* a malignant growth or tumor. **-ate** *v.i.* to grow into a cancer. **-ation** *n.* **-ous** *a.* pert. to cancer.

**can•de•la•brum** *n.* a branched and highly ornamented candle-stick. **candelabra** *n.sing.* and *pl.*

**can•did** *a.* fair; frank. **-ly** *adv.* **-ness** *n.* frankness; ingenuousness.

**can•di•date** *n.* one who seeks an appointment, office, honor, etc. **candidature, candidacy** *n.* the position of being a candidate.

**can•dle** *n.* a stick of tallow, wax, etc. with a wick inside, used for light. **— power,** the unit of luminosity. **-stick** *n.* an instrument for holding a candle.

**can•dor** *n.* candidness; frankness.

**can•dy** *n.* a kind of sweetmeat made of sugar; *v.t.* to form into crystals, as sugar; *v.i.* to become candied. **candied** *a.*

**cane** *n.* the stem of a small palm or long, strong reed; the sugar-cane; a walking-stick; *v.t.* to beat with a cane. **-brake** *n.* a dense growth of canes. **— sugar** *n.* sugar from the sugar-cane.

**ca•nine** *a.* of, or pert. to a dog. **— teeth,** the two pointed teeth in each jaw, between the incisors and the molars.

**can•is•ter** *n.* a small case or box for holding tea, coffee, etc.

**can•ker** *n.* ulceration of the mouth; a disease affecting horses' feet; *v.t.* to gnaw at; *v.i.* to decay, to become cankered. **-ed** *a.* corrupted; malignant. **-ous** *a.* corrupting like a canker. **-y** *a.* cankered. **-worm** *n.* a destructive caterpillar.

**can•nel-coal** *n.* a kind of coal, burning with a clear, smokeless flame, used in the manufacture of gas. Also **candle-coal.**

**can•ni•bal** *n.* one who eats human flesh; *a.* relating to this practice. **-ism** *n.* the practice of eating human flesh. **-istic** *a.* **cannibalize** *v.t.* to dismantle in the hope of getting spare parts to be used for re-conditioning.

**can•non** *n.* a large gun; *v.i.* to cannonade. **-ade** *n.* an attack with cannon; the firing of cannon; *v.t.* to bombard. **-eer, -ier** *n.* one who loads or fires cannon; an artilleryman. **— ball** *n.* an iron ball to be discharged by cannon. **— shot** *n.* a cannon ball; the range of a cannon.

**can•not** combination of *can* and *not,* therefore, = not to be able.

**ca•noe** *n.* a light, narrow boat propelled by a hand paddle. **-ist** *n.*

**can•on** *n.* the books of the Scriptures accepted by the Church as of divine authority. **-ess** *n.* a member of a religious association of women. **canonic, canonical** *a.* **canonicals** *n.pl.* official dress worn by a clergyman. **canonically** *adv.* **-ization** *n.* **-ize** *v.t.* to place in the list of saints. **-ist** *n.* one skilled in canon law. **-ry** *n.* the office of canon.

**can•o•py** *n.* a covering fixed above a bed, or a dais, or carried on poles above the head.

**cant** *n.* an inclination from the level; a tilted position; *v.t.* to tilt; *v.i.* to have, or take a leaning position.

**can•ta•loupe, can•ta•loup** *n.* a variety of muskmelon, having a furrowed rind.

**can•tan•ker•ous** *a.* quarrelsome. **-ly** *adv.*

**can•ta•ta** *n.* a short musical composition in oratorio or lyric drama form.

**can•teen** *n.* a small container for carrying water; a store and refreshment-room.

**can•ter** *v.i.* to move at an easy gallop; *n.* an easy gallop or gait.

**can•ti•lev•er** *n.* a bracket for supporting a balcony. **cantilever bridge.** a bridge built on the same principle.
**can•to** *n.* a part of a poem. **-r** *n.* the leader of the singing, esp. in a synagogue.
**can•ton** *n.* a small district administered by a separate government; *v.t.* to divide into districts, as territory. **-al** *a.* **-ment** *n.* quarters for troops.
**can•vas** *n.* a coarse cloth made of hemp, for sails, tents, etc.; a special prepared material for painting on.
**can•vass** *v.t.* to examine thoroughly; to solicit support, or votes, or contributions; *v.i.* to solicit votes; *n.* solicitation; a seeking to obtain votes. **-er** *n.*
**can•yon** *n.* a ravine; a deep gorge.
**cap** *n.* a brimless covering, for the head; a small lid used as a cover; *v.t.* to cover the top or end of; to confer a degree on; *pr.p.* **-ping.** *pa.p.* and *pa.t.* **-ped.**
**ca•pa•ble** *a.* competent; skillful. **capably** *adv.* **-ness** *n.* **capability** *n.* power.
**ca•pa•cious** *a.* roomy; spacious. **-ly** *adv.* **-ness** *n.*
**ca•pac•i•ty** *n.* power of holding or grasping; room; ability; cubic content. **capacitate** *v.t.* to render capable.
**ca•par•i•son** *n.* a covering laid over a horse; *v.t.* to cover with a decorated cloth.
**cape** *n.* a covering for the shoulders.
**cape** *n.* a point of land running out into the sea; a headland.
**ca•per** *v.i.* to leap about like a goat, in a sprightly manner.
**cap•il•lar•y** *n.* one of the microscopic blood-vessels connecting the arteries and veins. **capillarity** *n.* **capilliform** *a.* hair-shaped.
**cap•i•tal** *a.* involving the forfeiture of life; first in importance; principal; *n.* the city or town which is the seat of government in a state or nation; the estimated total value of a business. **— punishment** *n.* the death penalty; **-ize** *n.* to take advantage of. **-ization** *n.* to provide with capital letters; to supply with capital.
**cap•i•tal•ism** *n.* form of economic, industrial, and social organization of society involving ownership, control, and direction of production by privately owned business organizations. **capitalist** *n.*
**cap•i•ta•tion** *n.* a census; a tax or grant per head.
**Cap•i•tol** *n.* the building used by the U.S. Congress in Washington for its sessions; a state legislature building.
**ca•pit•u•late** *v.i.* to draw up terms of an agreement. **capitulation** *n.* **capitulator** *n.*
**ca•pon** *n.* a young castrated cock fed for the table. **caponize** *v.t.*
**ca•price** *n.* illogical change of feeling or opinion; a whim; a fancy. **capricious** *a.*
**cap•si•cum** *n.* a genus of tropical plants, whose fruits when dried and ground give Cayenne pepper.
**cap•size** *v.t.* and *i.* overturn.
**cap•stan** *n.* a heavy cable-holder revolving on an upright spindle.
**cap•sule** *n.* a small gelatinous case containing medicine; *a.* condensed.
**cap•tain** *n.* in the army, an officer commanding a company of infantry; in the navy, an officer in command of a man-of-war; the master of a merchant ship or other vessel; in sport, the leader of a team; *v.t.* to command; **-cy** *n.* the rank or commission of a captain.
**cap•tion** *n.* the heading of a newspaper, chapter, page, etc.
**cap•tious** *a.* apt to find fault; difficult to please. **-ly** *adv.* **-ness** *n.* fault-finding.
**cap•ti•vate** *v.t.* to capture the fancy of. **captivating** *a.* winning, charming. **captivation** *n.*
**cap•tive** *n.* a prisoner; one held in captivity; *a.* made prisoner. **captivity** *n.* imprisonment. **captor** *n.* one who takes a prisoner or a prize. **capture** *n.* the act of seizing by force or stratagem; arrest; the thing seized; the prize; *v.t.* to take possession of.
**car** *n.* any kind of vehicle on wheels; automobile.
**ca•rafe** *n.* a glass decanter.
**car•a•mel** *n.* burnt sugar, used for coloring and in cooking; a kind of candy.
**car•at** *n.* a measure of weight for gold and precious stones, the standard carat being 3.16 grains troy.
**car•a•van** *n.* parties of merchants or others traveling together for greater security, esp. across deserts. **-eer** *n.* the leader of a caravan.
**car•a•way** *n.* a biennial aromatic plant; its seed, used as a flavoring for bread, cakes, etc.
**car•bide** *n.* a compound of carbon with certain elements, including calcium, manganese, iron, etc.
**car•bine, carabine** *n.* a short rifle. **carbineer, carabineer** *n.* a soldier armed with a carbine.
**car•bo•hy•drate** *n.* a substance, such as sugar, starch, cellulose, etc. composed of carbon, hydrogen, and oxygen.
**car•bol•ic** *a.* derived from carbon; *n.* carbolic acid. **carbolated** *a.* treated with or containing, carbolic acid. **carbolic acid,** a poisonous acid distilled from coal tar.
**car•bon** *n.* a non-metallic element existing pure in nature as diamond, graphite, charcoal, etc. and as a compound of animal and vegetable substances; a copy made by using carbon paper. **-aceous** *a.* pert. to, or composed of, coal. **-ize** *v.t.* to make into carbon; to coat with carbon. **-ization** *n.* **— paper,** type of paper used for duplicating written work.
**car•bo•run•dum** *n.* silicon carbide, a black, crystalline substance, of exceptional hardness.
**car•bu•ret•or** *n.* an apparatus in an internal-combustion engine to convert liquid gasoline into vaporized form. **carburation** *n.* **carburize** *v.t.* cause to unite with carbon.
**car•cass, carcase** *n.* the dead body of man or animal, esp. of the latter; the framework of anything.
**car•ci•no•ma** *n.* a cancer.

**card** *n.* a small piece of pasteboard often with figures, pictures, etc. on it for playing games; a piece of pasteboard having on it a person's name and address; an ornamented piece of paper or cardboard with a greeting, such as a birthday card; **-board** *n.* finely finished pasteboard. **-sharp** *n.* one who cheats at cards.

**car•di•ac** See **cardio-**

**car•di•gan** *n.* a knitted jacketlike sweater.

**car•di•nal** *a.* of great importance; *(Color)* deep scarlet. **-ly** *adv.* **— numbers,** 1, 2, 3, 4, 5, etc.

**car•di•nal** *n.* the highest rank next to the Pope, in the Catholic Church. **-ate, -ship** *n.* the office of a cardinal.

**car•di•o-** the heart, combining to form derivatives. **cardiac** *a.* pert. to the heart; *n.* a heart stimulant. **-gram** *n.* the graphic tracing of the movements of the heart as recorded by an instrument called the **cardiograph. cardiology** *n. (Med.)* the branch of medicine which deals with the functions and diseases of the heart.

**care** *n.* concern or anxiety; caution; *v.i.* to be anxious, concerned; to be affected with solicitude. **-ful** *a.* full of solicitude; watchful; painstaking. **-fully** *adv.* **-fulness** *n.* **-less** *a.* heedless; thoughtless; regardless. **-lessly** *adv.* **-lessness** *n.* **-worn** *a.* showing the wearing effects of care. **-taker** *n.* one who takes over the care of anything or anyone.

**ca•reen** *v.t.* to turn a ship over on one side; *v.i.* to lean over.

**ca•reer** *n.* profession; conduct in life, or progress through life. **-ist** *n.* one who makes his personal advancement his one aim in life.

**ca•ress** *v.t.* to treat with affection; to fondle; *n.* a loving touch; an embrace. **-ing** *a.*

**car•et** *n.* a mark (∧) which shows where something should be inserted.

**car•go** *n.* the freight of a ship; the merchandise carried.

**car•i•bou** *n.* the N. American reindeer.

**car•i•ca•ture** *n.* a ludicrous exaggeration (usually in picture form) of peculiar personal characteristics; *v.t.* to exaggerate in words or in pictorial form. **caricaturist** *n.*

**car•il•lon** *n.* a set or peal of bells of different tones.

**car•mine** *n.* a brilliant crimson, prepared from cochineal. Also *a.*

**car•nage** *n.* massacre; bloodshed.

**car•nal** *a.* pert. to the flesh; sensual. **-ize** *v.t.* to make carnal. **carnality** *n.* fleshly lust. **-ly** *adv.* **— knowledge** sexual intercourse.

**car•na•tion** *n.* a variety of the clove-pink, noted for its beauty and sweet scent.

**car•ni•val** *n.* a traveling show with amusements such as merry-go-rounds, etc.

**car•niv•o•ra** *n.pl.* animals that feed on flesh. **carnivore** *n.* a flesh-eating animal. **carnivorous** *a.* **carnivorously** *adv.* **carnivorousness** *n.*

**car•ol** *n.* a song of joy, esp. a Christmas hymn; *v.i.* to sing a carol.

**ca•rot•id** *n.* each of the two main arteries in the neck conveying blood to the head; *a.* pert. to these.

**ca•rouse** *v.i.* to revel; to hold a drinking-party. **carousal** *n.* a noisy drinking-party. **-r** *n.*

**car•ou•sel** See **carrousel.**

**carp** *v.i.* to find fault petulantly and without reason.

**carp** *n.* a fresh-water fish.

**car•pel** *n. (Bot.)* the seed-bearing part of a plant; part of a compound ovary. **-lary** *a.*

**car•pen•ter** *n.* a worker in lumber as used in building of houses, ships, etc. **carpentry** *n.*

**car•pet** *n.* a woven covering for floors; **-ing** *n.* a covering similar to a carpet. **-bagger** *n.* a political adventurer.

**car•ra•way** See **caraway.**

**car•riage** *n.* a vehicle for passengers; a wheeled conveyor; one's posture or bearing. **-able** *a.* carriable; passable for carriages.

**car•ri•er** *n.* one who carries; one who carries goods for hire, often called a 'common carrier'; a receptacle for carrying objects; *(Med.)* one who, without showing symptoms of disease, can convey infection to others.

**car•rot** *n.* a plant cultivated for its edible root. **-y** *a.* reddish-yellow.

**car•rou•sel, car•ou•sel** *n.* a merry-go-round.

**car•ry** *v.t.* to transport; to impel; to transfer.

**cart** *n.* a two-wheeled vehicle used for the transport of heavy goods; a small four-wheeled vehicle pulled by hand; *v.t.* to convey in a cart. **-age** *n.* carting; the price paid for carting. **-er** *n.* **-wright** *n.* maker of carts.

**car•tel** *n.* an international industrial combination for regulating volume and price of output.

**car•ti•lage** *n.* a strong, transparent tissue in the body, very elastic and softer than bone. **cartilaginous** *a.*

**car•tog•ra•phy** *n.* the art of making charts or maps. **cartographer** *n.*

**car•ton** *n.* a pasteboard box.

**car•toon** *n.* a pictorial caricature; a comic strip; movie comics. **-ist** *n.*

**car•tridge** *n.* a case made of metal, cardboard, etc. to contain the charge for a gun.

**carve** *v.t.* and *i.* to fashion artistically by cutting; to cut in pieces or slices, as meat, etc.; to divide. **-r** *n.* one who carves; a large knife for carving. **carving** *n.*

**cas•cade** *n.* a waterfall; a wavy fall of lace; *v.i.* to fall in cascades.

**case** *n.* a receptacle; anything which encloses or contains; a box and its contents; *(Print.)* a frame for holding type; *v.t.* to put in a case. **casing** *n.* a case or covering. **-room** *n. (Print.)* the room in which type is set. **— shot** *n.* canister shot; small projectiles put in cases or canisters, to be shot from cannon. **-harden** *v.t.* to heat soft steel in contact with carbonaceous material, so that carbon is absorbed, and a surface of harder steel produced. **lower case** *(Print.)* denoting small letters. **upper case** *(Print.)* mew. — **burglary** a burglar who makes

**case** *n.* an event, occurrence, or circumstance; a question of facts requiring solution; *(Med.)* a patient under treatment; *(Gram.)* an inflection or terminal change in nouns, pronouns, etc. **casal** *a. (Gram.)* pert. to case.

**ca•se•in** *n.* the curd or cheesy part of milk, a protein.

**case•ment** *n.* a window, or part of a window, opening on hinges.

**cash** *n.* money, esp. ready money; *v.t.* to turn into, or exchange for, money. — **register** *n.* an automatic money-till which registers and indicates the amount paid for goods sold.

**cash•ew** *n.* a tropical American tree whose fruit, the cashew-nut, is eaten raw or roasted.

**cash•ier** *n.* one who has charge of the cash.

**cash•ier** *v.t.* to dismiss from office in disgrace; to discard.

**cash•mere** *n.* a shawl made from the hair of the Kashmir (Cashmere) goat; the material; *a.*

**ca•si•no** *n.* a public assembly-room for dancing, gambling, etc.

**cask** *n.* a large wooden vessel for holding liquor; a barrel; *v.t.* to put in a cask.

**cas•ket** *n.* a coffin; a small box.

**cas•se•role** *n.* a covered baking dish in which food is both cooked and served.

**cas•sia** *n.* a genus of plants, including senna, whose pods are used medicinally as a laxative; a cheap kind of cinnamon.

**cas•sock** *n.* a long, close-fitting black gown worn by clergymen.

**cast** *v.t.* to fling; to direct or bestow, as a glance; to shed, as a skin; to distribute the parts of a play among the actors; to throw a line in angling; to forecast (to cast a horoscope); to give (a vote); *n.* the act of casting; the distance a thing is thrown; a change of direction; that which is shed or ejected; a forecast; the actors appearing in a play; squint (of the eye). — **down** *a.* depressed. **-ing** *n.* the act of foundling and molding. **-ing-vote** *n.* the vote of a chairman, which decides a question when votes are equally divided. — **iron** *a.* indefatigable; unshakable.

**cas•ta•nets** *n.pl.* two small concave shells fastened to the thumb and clicked in time to music of a Spanish type.

**castanets**

**cast•a•way** *n.* a shipwrecked person.

**caste** *n.* an exclusive social order.

**cast•er, castor** *n.* a small bottle with perforated top; a small swivelled wheel on the foot of a chair-leg, etc.

**cas•ti•gate** *v.t.* to rebuke severly; to chastise. **castigation** *n.* severe chastisement; discipline. **castigator** *n.*

**castle** *n.* a fortified residence; a stronghold, esp. of nobleman; a piece (also called rook) in chess. **-d** *a.* having a castle; built like a castle.

**cas•tor•oil** *n.* an oil used as a cathartic.

**cas•trate** *v.t.* to deprive of the testicles; to emasculate. **castration** *n.*

**cas•u•al** *a.* incidental; occasional; offhand or careless; *n.* a casual worker, etc. **-ly** *adv.* **-ness** *n.* **-ty** *n.* an accident, mishap. **-ties** *n.pl. (Mil.)* losses caused by death, wounds, capture, etc.

**cas•u•ist** *n.* one versed in casuistry. **-ry** *n.* the science of dealing with problems of right or wrong conduct by applying principles drawn from the Scriptures. **casuistic, casuistical** *a.* **casuistically** *adv.*

**cat** *n.* a small domestic quadruped, of the family of felines; related carnivores such as the lion, tiger, leopard, lynx, etc. **-ty, -tish** *a.* spiteful. **-bird** *n.* a gray N. Am. songbird having a cry similar to a cat's mew. — **burglary** a burglar who makes his entry by climbing to windows, roofs, etc. **-call** *n.* a cat-like cry, used by audiences to express disapproval. — **eyed** *a.* able to see in the dark. — **nap** *n.* a very short, light sleep. **-'s-eye** *n.* a gem with reflections like those from a cat's eye. **cat-o-nine-tails** *n.* a whip with nine thongs or lashes. **tabby cat** a female cat; a striped cat. **tom cat** a male cat.

**cat•a-** a combining form meaning away, against, fully, used to form derivatives.

**cat•a•clysm** *n.* a social or political upheaval; a sudden and violent alteration in earth's surface. **-al** *a.* **-ic** *a.*

**cat•a•combs** *n.pl.* underground passageways with niches for tombs.

**cat•a•lec•tic** *a.* lacking a syllable at the end of a verse.

**cat•a•lep•sy** *n.(Med.)* suspension of senses and bodily powers, with muscular rigidity; a trance. **cataleptic** *a.*

**cat•a•logue** *n.* a list, usually alphabetical, of names, books, goods, etc.; a descriptive price-list; also **catalog.** *v.t.* to make such a list. **-r** *n.*

**ca•tal•y•sis** *n. (Chem.)* the chemical change effected in one substance by the aid of another which itself undergoes no change. **catalyst** *n.* a substance producing such a change. **catalytic** *a.*

**cat•a•pult** *n.* a siege engine for hurling stones, arrows, etc.; a device for launching airplanes from the deck of a ship; *v.t.*

**cat•a•ract** *n.* the flow of a large body of water over a precipice; *(Med.)* a disease of the eye, characterized by an opaque condition in the lens.

**ca•tas•tro•phe** *n.* a disaster; a calamity. **catastrophic** *a.*

**catch** *v.t.* to take hold of; to seize; to get a disease by contagion; to come upon unexpectedly; *v.i.* to seize, and keep hold; *pa.t.* and *pa.p.* **caught.** *n.* anything that holds, stops, etc.; that which is

caught. **-able** *a.* able to be caught. **-er** *n.* **-ing** *a.* **-y** *a.* containing a hidden difficulty; captivating; attractive. **-all** *n.* a receptacle for miscellaneous objects.
**catch•ment** *n.* drainage area.
**catch•pen•ny** *n.* something of little value made to sell quickly; *a.* cheap and showy.
**catch•up, catsup, ketchup** *n.* a bottled sauce made from tomatoes, vinegar, sugar and spices.
**catch•word** *n.* a word that takes the popular fancy; a slogan; the first word in the column of a dictionary, etc., repeated above the column as a reference.
**cat•e•chize** *v.t.* to instruct by question and answer, esp. in Christian doctrine. **catechism** *n.* a set form of question and answer to teach the tenets of religion. **catechist** *n.* one who catechizes. **catechetical** *a.* consisting of question and answer. **catechetically** *adv.* **catechesis** *n.* oral instruction as given to catechumens.
**cat•e•chu•men** *n.* one being instructed in the fundamentals of a subject, esp. religion. (See **catechize**).
**cat•e•go•ry** *n.* a group, division; in logic, any fundamental conception. **categorical** *a.* pert. to a category; admitting no conditions; precise. **categorically** *adv.* **categorize** *v.t.* to place in a category.
**ca•ter** *v.i.* to provide food, entertainment, etc. **-er** *n.*
**cat•er•cor•nered** *a.* diagonal.
**cat•er•pil•lar** *n.* the larva of butterflies and moths.
**ca•thar•tic** *a. (Med.)* purgative; cleansing the bowels; *n.* a purging medicine. **catharize** *v.t.* to cleanse; to purify. **catharsis** *n.* purgation, also of the emotions, through art.
**Ca•thay** *n.* an old name for China.
**ca•the•dral** *n.* the principal church in a diocese, which contains the bishop's throne; *a.* pert. to a cathedral.
**cath•ode** *n.* the negative pole of an electric cell; the conductor by which an electric current leaves an electrolyte, and passes over to the negative pole; opp. of *anode.* **— rays** negative ions or electrons.
**cath•o•lic** *a.* pert. to Roman Catholics; comprehensive in understanding; *n.* a member of the R.C. Church. **catholicism** *n.* the faith and practice of Catholic Church, or of R.C. Church; liberality of opinion; catholicity. **catholicity** *n.*
**cat•nip** *n.* an aromatic plant with blue flowers, attractive to cats.
**cat•sup** See **catchup.**
**cat•tle** *n.pl.* domestic livestock, esp. cows and bulls.
**Cau•ca•sian** *a.* Indo-European, i.e. pert. to the white race. *n.*
**cau•cus** *n.* a meeting of leaders of a political party to decide policies, etc.
**cau•dal** *a.* pert. to a tail. **caudate** *a.* having a tail.
**caught** *pa.p.* and *pa.t.* of **catch.**
**caul** *n.* the membrane covering the head of some babies at birth.
**caul•dron** See **caldron.**
**cau•li•flow•er** *n.* a variety of cabbage.
**caulk** See **calk.**
**cau•sal** *a.* relating to a cause or causes. **causality** *n.* the relation of cause and effect. **causation** *n.* agency by which an effect is produced. **causative** *a.*
**cause** *n.* that which produces a result or effect; the motive of an action; principle supported by a person or party; *v.t.* to be the occasion of; to induce. **-r** *n.* **-less** *a.* without reason or motive.
**cause•way** *n.* a raised paved road.
**caus•tic** *a. (Fig.)* biting, bitter, satirical; *n.* a substance that corrodes and destroys animal tissue. **-ally** *adv.* **causticity** *n.*
**cau•ter** *n.* a hot, searing iron. **-ize** *v.t.* to burn animal tissue in order to destroy diseased tissue, or promote healing. **-ization** *n.* **-y** *n.* the act of cauterizing; a hot iron for searing.
**cau•tion** *n.* prudence; wariness; a warning; *v.t.* to advise to take care; to admonish. **cautious** *a.* wary; discreet. **cautiously** *adv.* **-ary** *a.* containing a warning. **-er** *n.*
**cav•al•cade** *n.* procession on horseback.
**cav•a•lier** *n.* a horseman; an attendant escort to a lady; *a.* gay and offhand; supercilious. **-ly** *adv.*
**cav•al•ry** *n.* horse-soldiery.
**cave** *n.* a small chamber hollowed out of the earth horizontally, either by nature or by man. **— man** *n.* a male of primitive ways. **to cave in** (of ground) to fall in, *(Fig.)* to admit defeat.
**cav•ern** *n.* a deep, hollow place under the earth; a large dark cave. **-ed** *a.* full of caverns. **-ous** *a.* hollow; deep-set.
**cav•i•ar, caviare** *n.* a delicacy made from the roes of the sturgeon.
**cav•i•ty** *n.* a hollow place of any size.
**caw** *v.i.* to cry like a crow or raven; the sound made by the crow.
**cay•enne** *n.* a pungent red pepper.
**cease** *v.t.* to put a stop to; *v.i.* to discontinue. **-less** *a.* without stopping. **-lessly** *adv.*
**ce•dar** *n.* species of coniferous, evergreen trees yielding durable, fragrant wood. **-n, cedrine** *a.*
**cede** *v.t.* to yield; to give up, esp. of territory.
**ce•dil•la** *n.* a small sign (ç), used, principally in French, as a pronunciation mark.
**ceil•ing** *n.* the interior part of the roof of a room; the maximum height to which a particular airplane can ascend.
**cel•e•brate** *v.t.* to mark by ceremony, as an event or festival; to observe with solemn rites. **-d** *a.* famous. **celebration** *n.* the act of celebrating. **celebrant** *n.* one who celebrates. **celebrity** *n.* fame; a person of distinction.
**cel•er•y** *n.* an edible plant cultivated for eating with salads or as a cooked vegetable.
**ce•les•tial** *a.* heavenly; *n.* an inhabitant of heaven. **-ly** *adv.*
**cel•i•ba•cy** *n.* the unmarried state. **celibate** *n.* one unmarried; *a.* unmarried.
**cell** *n.* a small room, as in a prison or monastery; the simplest unit in the structure of living matter; a division of a

voltaic or galvanic battery. **-ed** *a.* furnished with, or containing, cells; contained in cells. **-ular** *a.* consisting of, or containing, cells, as cellular tissue. **-ulated** *a.* having a cellular structure.

**cel•lar** *n.* the lowest story under a building; a storeroom, esp. for wines, liquors.

**cel•lo, 'cel•lo** *n. (Mus.)* a contraction for violoncello, a stringed musical instrument. **cellist, 'cellist** *n.* a player on the violoncello.

**cel•lo•phane** *n.* a transparent, waterproof material used as wrapping tissue, etc.

**cel•lu•loid** *n.* name for a hard compound used in the manufacture of imitation ivory, coral, amber, etc.

**cel•lu•lose** *n.* a chemical substance, one of the carbohydrates, forming the chief constituent of the walls of plant cells; an essential part of wood, paper, linen, cotton, etc.

**Celt, Kelt** *n.* one of a race, including the Highlanders of Scotland, the Irish, Welsh, Bretons, Manx, and Cornish. **Celtic, Keltic** *n.* the language spoken by the Celts. *a.* pert. to the Celts.

**ce•ment** *n.* a material used in making concrete for building or paving; *v.t.* to unite by using cement; to join closely. **-ation** *n.* the act of cementing.

**cem•e•ter•y** *n.* a graveyard; a burying ground.

**cen•ser** *n.* a metal vessel in which incense is burned. **cense** *v.t.* to perfume with incense.

**cen•sor** *n.* one appointed to examine books, plays, newspaper articles, etc. before publication, and ban them if containing anything objectionable; also, in time of war or crisis, to examine letters, etc., and erase anything calculated to convey information to the enemy; one who finds fault; *v.t.* to blame or reprove; to subject to examination by the censor. **-ial** *a.* pert. to correction of morals; pert. to a censor. **-ious** *a.* apt to find fault. **-iously** *adv.* **-iousness** *n.* **-ship** *n.* the office of a censor; the act of censoring.

**cen•sure** *n.* the act of finding fault; *v.t.* to criticize adversely. **censurable** *a.*

**cen•sus** *n.* an official numbering of the inhabitants of a country. **censual** *a.*

**cent** *n.* a hundredth, as 10 per *cent;* a U.S. coin worth the hundredth part of a dollar.

**cen•taur** *n.* a fabulous being, half man and half horse.

**cen•te•nar•y** *n.* a period of a hundred years; the commemoration of a hundredth anniversary. **centenarian** *n.* a person a hundred years old.

**cen•ten•ni•al** *a.* pert. to a period of 100 years; happening once in a hundred years; *n.* a hundredth anniversary.

**cen•ter** *n.* the mid-point of anything; a point to which things are drawn; *v.t.* and *i.* to place in the center. **-piece** *n.* an ornament or cloth covering for the center of a table. **centric(al)** *a.* placed in middle. **centrically** *adv.* **centricity** *n.* the state of being centric. **center of gravity,** the point in a body about which it will balance.

**cen•ti-** a hundred, combining to form derivatives. **-grade** *a.* divided into 100 degrees, as the centigrade thermometer on which freezing-point is marked 0° and boiling-point 100°. **-meter** *n.* 100th part of a meter = .394 inch.

**cen•ti•pede** *n.* an insect, of flat and elongated shape, with a segmented body.

**cen•tral** *a.* relating to, or placed in, the center; important. **-ly** *adv.* **-ize** *v.t.* to draw to a central point; to put under one control. **-ization** *n.* **-ism** *n.* centralization, esp. of government. **centrality** *n.* the state of being central. **— heating,** heating of a building or group of buildings from one central furnace.

**cen•tri•fu•gal** *a.* tending to move away from the center of a revolving body.

**cen•trip•e•tal** *a.* tending to move towards the center.

**cen•tu•ry** *n.* a period of a hundred years.

**ce•phal•ic** *a.* pert. to the head; *n.* a medicine for headaches.

**ce•ram•ic** *a.* pert. to pottery. **ceramics** *n.pl.* the art of molding, modelling, and baking clay.

**cere** *v.t. (Obs.)* to cover with wax. **ceraceous** *a.* waxy. **cerate** *n.* an ointment of wax, oil, etc. **-cloth** *n.* a cloth smeared with melted wax in which dead bodies used to be wrapped. **-ment** *n.* (usually *pl.*) graveclothes.

**ce•re•al** *n.* any edible grain (wheat, barley, oats, etc.); a breakfast food made of such grains.

**ce•re•brum** *n.* the upper and larger division of the brain. **cerebellum** *n.* the part of the brain behind and below the cerebrum. **cerebral** *a.* pert. to the brain. **cerebral hemorrhage,** rupture of an artery of the brain with a consequent escape of blood. **cerebral palsy** *n.* paralysis from cerebral lesion, chiefly characterized by spasms. **cerebrate** *v.i.* to have the brain in action. **cerebration** *n.* cerebrospinal *a.* pert. to both brain and spinal cord.

**ce•re•mo•ny** *n.* a sacred rite; formal observance; a public or private function. **ceremonial** *a.* formal; *n.* usage followed in performing rites. **ceremonially** *adv.* **ceremonious** *a.* full of ceremony; particular in observing forms. **ceremoniously** *adv.* **ceremoniousness** *n.* **master of ceremonies** *n.* at public functions, etc. one whose business it is to see that all rules, and courtesies are observed.

**ce•rise** *n.* and *a.* light clear red; cherry-colored.

**cer•tain** *a.* sure; constant; of moderate quantity, degree, etc. **-ly** *adv.* **-ty** *n.* the quality of being certain. **certitude** *n.* freedom from doubt; certainty. **certes** *adv.* in truth.

**cer•ti•fi•cate** *n.* a written testimony to the truth of a fact; written statement of qualifications *v.i.* to attest by a certificate; to furnish with a certificate. **certify** *v.t.* to vouch for the truth of. **certifiable** *a.* able to be vouched for. **certification** *n.* the act of certifying. **certified** *a.*

**ce•ru•le•an** *a.* sky-blue; deep blue.

**ceruleous** *a.* sky-blue.

**ce•ruse** *n.* white lead. **cerussite** *n.* a carbonate of lead.

**cer•vi•cal** *a.* pert. to the neck or neck of the uterus.

**ces•sa•tion** *n.* stoppage; discontinuance.

**ces•sion** *n.* act of surrendering, as by treated; something yielded, ceded.

**cess•pool** *n.* a pit for collection of drainage water or sewage.

**chafe** *v.t.* to wear away by rubbing; to irritate; *v.i.* to be worn by friction; to fret; *n.* friction; injury caused by rubbing. *-r n.* one who chafes. **chafing dish** *n.* a dish and heating apparatus for keeping food warm on the table.

**chaff** *n.* straw cut small for cattle-feeding.

**chaff** *n.* banter; *v.t.* to make fun of (without spite).

**cha•grin** *n.* ill-humor; vexation; *v.t.* to vex deeply.

**chain** *n.* a series of metal links connected and forming a flexible cable; a succession of events; *v.t.* to fasten or connect with a chain; to restrain. **— bridge** *n.* a suspension bridge. **-drive** *n.* the transmitting of driving-power by means of chain-gear. **— gang** *n.* a number of convicts chained together. **— reaction** *n.* in nuclear physics, a self-sustaining process in which some neutrons from one splitting atom are able to split more atoms, setting free still more neutrons which carry on the reaction indefinitely.

**chair** *n.* a seat with a back, legs, and sometimes arms, usually for one person; an official seat occupied by the president of a meeting, a university professor; *v.t.* to install in a chair or office. **to take the chair,** to act as chairman of a meeting. **-man** *n.* the presiding officer of a meeting. **-manship** *n.* **-woman** *n.*

**chaise** *n.* a light, one-horse carriage. **— longue** *n.* an elongated seat with backrest at one end and support for legs.

**chal•ice** *n.* a wine-cup; a goblet.

**chalk** *n.* a soft, white, carbonate of lime; a chalk-like material used for marking; *v.t.* to mark with chalk. **-y** *a.* containing or like chalk. **-iness** *n.* **— up** *v.t.* to score.

**chal•lenge** *n.* an invitation to a contest; *v.t.* to call upon a person to settle a dispute by fighting; to summon to answer; to call in question. **-able** *a.* **-r** *n.*

**cham•ber** *n.* a room, esp. one used for lodging or study; a place where an assembly, such as a legislature meets, and the assembly itself; *v.t.* to confine, as in a chamber; *v.i.* to occupy as a chamber. **-ed** *a.* **-s** *n.pl.* rooms where a judge hears cases not requiring action in court. **-maid** *n.* a woman servant who has the care of bedrooms, esp. in hotels, etc. **— music** *n.* music suitable for performance in a house or small hall.

**cha•me•le•on** *n.* a small lizard, which changes color with its surroundings.

**cham•fer** *v.t.* to cut a groove in; to bevel; *n.* a groove; a bevel. **-ed** *a.*

**cham•ois** *n.* a goat-like species of antelope; a kind of soft leather.

**champ** *v.t.* and *i.* to bite, chew, or munch noisily. **to champ at the bit** *(Fig.)* to be impatient; *n.*

**cham•pagne** *n.* a light effervescent, white wine, made in the province of *Champagne* in N.E. France, or elsewhere.

**cham•pi•on** *n.* one who fought in single combat to defend the honor of another; one capable of defeating his competitors in any form of sport; *a.* first-class; *v.t.* to defend; to maintain or support. **-ship** *n.* the position of a champion; defense; advocacy.

**chance** *n.* an unforeseen occurrence; risk; opportunity; possibility; *a.* accidental; *v.t.* to risk; *v.i.* to happen. **by —,** accidentally.

**chan•cel•lor** *n.* the title of various high officials in the state, and in the law; the head of a university. **-ship** *n.* the office of chancellor. **chancellery** *n.* the premises of a chancellor.

**chan•cer•y** *n.* the office of a chancellor; a chancellery; a court of equity.

**chan•de•lier** *n.* a branched framework for holding lights, esp. one hanging from the ceiling.

**change** *v.t.* to alter or make different; to shift; to exchange, as money; *v.i.* to become different; to change one's clothes; *n.* alteration; that which makes for variety; money of small denomination given in exchange for money of larger; balance of money returned after payment; fresh clothing; an exchange. **-able** *a.* variable; unsteady. **-ful** *a.* **-fully** *adv.* **-fulness** *n.* **-less** *a.* unchanging; constant.

**chan•nel** *n.* a waterway; the deeper part of a river, harbor, etc.; means of access; *a.* frequency band for transmission of radio, television, etc.; *v.t.* to form a channel; to direct in a particular course.

**chant** *v.t.* and *i.* to sing; to celebrate in song; *n.* a song; sacred words recited in a singing manner. **-er** *n.*

**chant•i•cleer** *n.* a cock, rooster.

**cha•os** *n.* **chaotic** *a.*

**chap** *v.t.* to split; to crack; *v.i.* to become cracked, red, and rough (as the skin in cold weather); *pr.t.* **-ping.** *pa.t.* **-ped.** *n.* a crack in the skin.

**chap•el** *n.* a private church; a division of a church with its own altar.

**chap•e•ron** *n.* a mature person who is in attendance at social gatherings of young

**chameleon**

people; *v.t.* to escort, accompany. **-age** *n.*

**chap•lain** *n.* a clergyman. **-cy** *n.*

**chap•ter** *n.* a division of a book or treatise; an organized branch of a society, fraternity, or military order; *v.t.* to divide into chapters.

**char** *v.t.* to reduce to charcoal; to burn to a black cinder; *pr.p.* **-ring.** *pa.p.* and *pa.t.* **-red. -coal** *n.* the residue of partially burnt vegetable matter, esp. wood.

**char, chare** *n.* work done by the day; *v.i.* to work by the day; to do small jobs. **-woman** *n.*

**char•ac•ter** *n.* a mark, letter, figure, sign, stamp; any distinctive mark; the total of qualities making up an individuality; moral excellence; a personage in a play or novel; *v.t.* to characterize; to represent. **-ize** *v.t.* to depict the peculiar qualities of; to give character to. **-istic** *a.* peculiar; distinctive; *n.* that which distinguishes a person or thing from another; **-istically** *adv.* **-ization** *n.* the act or characterizing literary or dramatic portrayal of character.

**cha•rade** *n.* a game, consisting of the interpretation (usually dramatic) of a word for others to guess.

**chard** *n.* leafy vegetable.

**charge** *n.* a burden; price or cost; care or trust; accusation or allegation; the amount of powder, etc., that a gun is fitted to hold; an impetuous onset or attack, or the signal for it; electrical contents of accumulator or battery; *v.t.* to lay a task, command, trust upon; to ask as payment; to load, as a gun; *v.i.* to make an onset. **-able** *a.* **-r** *n.* a war-horse.

**char•i•ot** *n.* in ancient times, a two-wheeled cart used in warfare. **-eer** *n.*

**char•i•ty** *n.* love and goodwill to men; any act of kindness; alms; a charitable cause or institution. **charitable** *a.* liberal to the poor; generous. **charitably** *adv.*

**char•la•tan** *n.* a quack or impostor.

**charm** *n.* a magic spell; anything supposed to possess magic power; a trinket worn on a bracelet; attractiveness; *v.t.* to subjugate by magic; to attract irresistibly; *v.i.* to be fascinating. **-er** *n.* **-ing** *a.* alluring; delightful.

**chart** *n.* a map of part of the sea, showing currents, depths, islands, coasts, etc.; a graph; *v.t.* to map; to delineate. **-er** *n.*

**char•ter** *n.* a formal document confirming privileges, titles, or rights; the hiring of a vessel; *v.t.* to establish by charter; to hire, as a ship. **-ed** *a.* **— member** *n.* one of the original members.

**char•treuse** *n.* a light yellowish-green color.

**chase** *v.t.* to pursue; *v.i.* to hasten; *n.* pursuit; hunting of enemy, game, etc. **-r** *n.* one who chases; a mild beverage taken after liquor.

**chase** *v.t.* to enchase; to engrave metal. **-r** *n.*

**chase** *n.* an iron frame to hold type when set up; a wide groove.

**chasm** *n.* a deep opening in the earth; a cleft.

**chass•é** *n.* in dancing, a rapid gliding step to the right or left.

**chas•sis** *n.* the framework and undercarriage of an automobile, including the engine.

**chaste** *a.* virtuous; pure and simple in taste and style. **-ly** *adv.* **-ness** *n.* **chastity** *n.* purity.

**chas•ten** *v.t.* to correct by punishment.

**chas•tise** *v.t.* to inflict pain in order to reform; to punish. **-ment** *n.*

**chat** *v.i.* to talk idly; *n.* light, informal talk; *pr.p.* **-ting;** *pa.p.* and *pa.t.* **-ted. -ter** *v.i.* to talk rapidly. **-terbox** *n.* one who chatters excessively. **-terer** *n.* one who chatters. **-tiness** *n.* **-ty** *a.* talkative; gossipy.

**cha•teau** *n.* a castle; a mansion.

**chat•tel** *n.*, usually in *pl.* **chattels,** any kind of property, except land and buildings. **— mortgage** *n.* a mortgage on personal property.

**chat•ter** See **chat.**

**chauf•feur** *n.* the paid driver of private automobile; *v.t.* to drive.

**chau•vin•ism** *n.* absurdly exaggerated patriotism; blind enthusiasm for a cause. **chauvinist** *n.* **chauvinistic** *a.*

**chaw** *n.* *(Dia.)* See **chew.**

**cheap** *a.* low in price; of low cost, as compared with the value, or the usual cost. **-ly** *adv.* **-ness** *n.* **-en** *v.t.* to bring down the price.

**cheat** *v.t.* to defraud; to trick; *v.i.* to practice trickery; *n.* a fraud; an impostor. **-er** *n.*

**check** *n.* a restraint; control or supervision, or one employed to carry out such; a mark placed against items in a list; an order to a bank to pay money; a term in chess to indicate that opponent's king must be moved or guarded; *v.t.* to restrain; to verify; to leave articles in the custody of another; in chess, to put in check; *v.i.* to pause. **-ers** *n.pl.* a board game, for two. **-book** *n.* book of blank orders on a bank. **-mate** *n.* the final movement in chess, when the king can be neither moved or protected. **-room** *n.* a place where articles may be left under the temporary protection of others. **-up** *n.* a medical examination.

**check•er** *v.t.* to variegate with cross lines; *v.i.* to produce a checkered effect, of alternate light and shade; *n.* a pattern like a chess-board; a piece in the game of checkers. **-ed** *a.*

**Ched•dar** *n.* a kind of hard, smooth cheese.

**cheek** *n.* the fleshy side of the mouth; each side of the face below the eyes. **-bone** *n.* the bone below the outer corner of the eye. **-y** *a.*

**cheep** *v.i.* to chirp, as a small bird; *n.* a small shrill sound.

**cheer** *n.* good spirits; expression of approval, or encouragement, by shouting; *v.t.* to render cheerful; to hearten or encourage; *v.i.* to shout hurrah. **-er** *n.* **-ful** *a.* having good spirits. **-fully** *adv.* **-fulness** *n.* **-ily** *adv.* with cheerfulness. **-iness** *n.* **-less** *a.* comfortless. **-lessness** *n.* **-y** *a.* in good spirits; promoting cheerfulness.

**cheese** *n.* a curd of milk, separated from

the whey, and prepared in several ways as food. **-cloth** *n.* a thin loosely woven cotton cloth, orig. used for wrapping cheese.

**chee•tah** *n.* the hunting leopard of India and Africa.

**chef** *n.* a head cook.

**chem•i•cal** *a.* pert. to chemistry; *n.* a substance produced by chemical processes. **-ly** *adv.* according to chemical principles.

**chem•ist** *n.* a person versed in chemistry or professionally engaged in it. **-ry** *n.* the study of the various substances which compose the universe and the processes by which they act one upon another.

**chem•o•ther•a•peu•tics** *n.* the use of chemical compounds in the treatment of disease. **chemotherapy** *n.*

**che•nille** *n.* a soft plush-like cord of silk, wool, worsted, etc. used for ornamental trimmings, fringes, etc.; a soft, velvety fabric.

**cher•ish** *v.t.* to hold dear; to treat tenderly.

**cher•ry** *n.* the bright red fruit of a tree akin to the plum; *a.* pert. to a cherry; red.

**cher•ub** *n.* a winged creature with a human face; an angel; a beautiful child; *pl.* **cherubim** or **-s. cherubic** *a.*

**chess** *n.* a game of Eastern origin played by two persons on a board containing

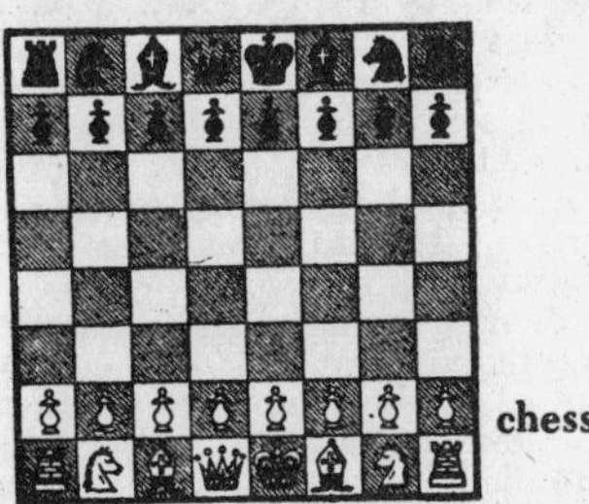

chess

sixty-four squares, with two differently colored sets of sixteen pieces or 'men.' **-man** *n.* a piece used in the game.

**chest** *n.* a large box; part of the body enclosed by ribs and breastbone; *v.t.* to place in a chest. **chest of drawers,** a piece of furniture fitted with drawers. **-y** *a.* having a large chest; conceited.

**ches•ter•field** *n.* a long overcoat, a heavily padded sofa.

**chest•nut** *n.* the nut of a forest tree; the tree itself, or its timber; a reddish-brown color; *a.* reddish-brown.

**chew** *v.t.* to bite and crush with the teeth; to masticate; *n.* action of chewing. **-ing gum** *n.* a sweet and flavored substance for chewing prepared from *chicle,* the gum of a Mexican rubber-tree.

**Chi•an•ti** *n.* an Italian red or white wine.

**chic** *n.* style and elegance; *a.* stylish; modish.

**chi•cane** *n.* trick or artifice; sharp practice, esp. in legal proceedings; *v.i.* to use trickery. **-ry** *n.* trickery. **-r** *n.*

**chick, chicken** *n.* the young of fowls, esp. of hen. **-en-hearted** *a.* cowardly; timid. **-en-pox** *n.* a mild, contagious, eruptive disease. **-weed** *n.* weed with small white blossoms.

**chic•le** *n.* a gum-like, milky juice obtained from several Central American trees.

**chic•o•ry** *n.* a plant whose taproot when roasted and ground is used to mix with

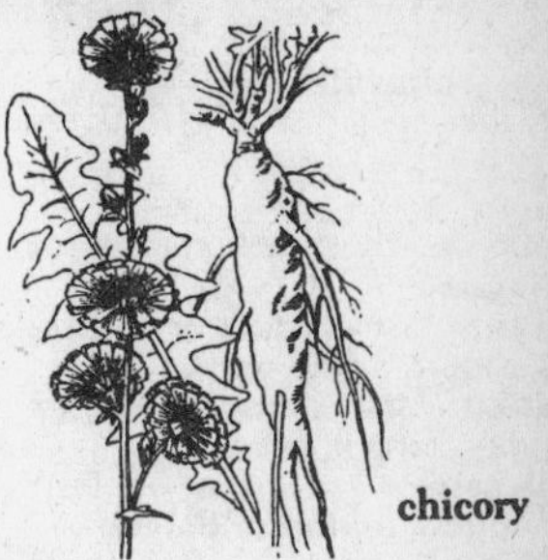

chicory

coffee and whose greens are used for salad.

**chide** *v.t.* to scold; to rebuke; *v.i.* to find fault; *pr.p.* **chiding.** *pa.p.* **chided** or **chid.** *pa.t.* **chid.**

**chief** *a.* foremost in importance; principal; at the head; *n.* a head or leader; a principal person or thing. **-ly** *adv.* principally. **-tain** *n.* the head of a clan or tribe.

**chif•fon** *n.* a thin, soft, gauzy material.

**chig•ger** *n.* a flea.

**chi•gnon** *n.* a rolled-up bun of hair at the back of a woman's head or on the nape of the neck.

**child** *n.* a very young person of either sex; offspring; *pl.* **children** offspring, descendants. **-birth** *n.* the act of bearing a child. **-bearing** *n.* producing children. **-hood** *n.* the time during which one is a child. **-ish** *a.* pert. to a child; trifling. **-ishly** *adv.* **-ishness** *n.* **-less** *a.* **-lessness** *n.* **-like** *a.* innocent; trustful.

**chil•i, chilli** *n.* the red pepper, or fruit of the capsicum, called Cayenne pepper when dried and ground.

**chill** *a.* tending to cause shivering; cool in manner or feeling; *n.* a feeling of coldness, attended with shivering; illness caused by cold; *v.t.* to cool; to cause to shiver; to dispirit; to keep cold; *v.i.* to grow cold. **-y,** cold; creating cold; ungenial. **-iness** *n.*

**chime** *n.* the musical sound of bells; a set of bells tuned to the musical scale; *v.t.* and *i.* to be in harmony.

**chim•ney** *n.* the passage through which the smoke of a fireplace is carried off. **—sweep** *n.* one who removes the soot from chimneys.

**chim•pan•zee** *n.* a large African anthropoid ape.

**chin** *n.* the part of the face below the mouth.

**Chi•na** *n.* a vast country in E. Asia; *(l.c.)* a translucent, vitreous ceramic ware. **-man** *n.* a native of China. **Chinese** *n.* the natives, or the language of China; *a.* **-ware** *n.* dishes of china.

**chin•chil•la** *n.* a small animal, with very fine, soft fur; the fur itself.

chinchilla

**chine** *n.* the backbone or spine of an animal.
**chink** *n.* a small cleft or fissure; a crack; *v.t.* to open; *v.i.* to crack.
**chink** *n.* the sound of a piece of metal when struck; *v.i.* to ring.
**Chi•nook** *n.* a tribe of N.W. American Indians; a kind of Salmon.
**chintz** *n.* a printed cotton cloth.
**chip** *v.t.* to chop off into small pieces; to break little pieces from; *v.i.* to break off in small pieces; *pr.p.* **-piping;** *pa.p.* and *pa.t.* **-ped;** *n.* a piece of wood separated from a larger body by an axe, etc.; a counter, instead of money, used in gambling. **-s** *n.pl.* fried slices of potato. **— shot** *n.* *(Golf)* a short, lofted shot onto the green. **— in,** *v.t.* to contribute.
**chipmunk** *n.* a burrowing ground-squirrel or striped gopher.
**chip•pen•dale** *n.* a style of furniture.
**chi•ro•man•cy** *n.* divination by inspection of the hand; palmistry.
**chi•rop•o•dist** *n.* one skilled in the treatment of diseases of the feet. **chiropody** *n.*
**chi•ro•prac•tic** *n.* a method of healing which relies upon the removal of nerve interference by manual adjustment of the spine. **chiropractor** *n.*
**chirp, chir•rup** *n.* a short, sharp note, as of a bird or cricket; *v.i.* to twitter; to talk gaily.
**chis•el** *n.* a tool sharpened to a cutting edge at the end, used in carpentry, sculpture, etc.; *v.i.* to carve with this tool.
**chit** *n.* a voucher; a permit or pass.
**chiv•al•ry** *n.* the qualities of a knight, viz. dignity, courtesy, bravery, gallantry. **chivalric, chivalrous** *a.* pert. to chivalry. **chivalrously** *adv.*
**chive** *n.* a small herb of the onion kind.
**chlo•rine** *n.* a heavy gas of yellowish-green color used in disinfecting, bleaching, and poison-gas warfare. **chloral** *n.* a sleep-producing drug. **chlorate** *n.* a salt of chloric acid. **chloric** *a.* pert. to chlorine. **chloride** *n.* a compound of chlorine with another element. **chlorinate** *v.t.* disinfect, bleach, or combine with chlorine. **chlorination** *n.* **chlorite** *n.* a mineral of a green color. **chloroform** *n.* a colorless, volatile liquid used as an anesthetic; *v.t.* to make insensible by using chloroform.
**chlo•ro•phyll** *n.* *(Bot.)* the green coloring matter of plants.
**chock** *n.* a wedge to steady a wheel. **-ful** *a.* packed.
**choc•o•late** *a.* a paste or hard cake made from the powdered seeds of the cacao plant, mixed with sugar, etc.; a beverage made by pouring boiling water or milk over this; candy; *a.* dark brown.
**choice** *n.* opportunity of choosing; selection; alternative; *a.* worthy of being chosen; superior.
**choir** *n.* a company of singers, belonging to a church.
**choke** *v.t.* to stop the breath by compression of the windpipe; *v.i.* to have the wind-pipe stopped; *n.* a valve regulating the proportion of gas to air in a motor. **-r** *n.* something worn closely about the neck.
**chol•er** *n.* bile; wrath. **choleric** *a.* easily angered. **cholera** *n.* deadly, epidemic, bilious disease, marked by purgings, vomiting and gripping pains.
**cho•les•ter•ol** *n.* a fatlike substance found in bile, gallstones, blood, and the brain, also in egg yolks, etc.
**choose** *v.t.* to take one thing in preference to another; *v.i.* to decide; to think fit. *pa.p.* **chosen.** *pa.t.* **chose.**
**chop** *v.t.* to cut into pieces; to mince, by striking repeatedly with a sharp instrument; *v.i.* to make strokes with a sharp instrument, as an axe; *n.* a thick slice of meat attached to a bone; a cutlet. *pr.p.* **-ping.** *pa.p.* and *pa.t.* **-ped. -per** *n.* one who chops; a large heavy knife; cleaver. **-py** *a.* of the sea, having short, broken waves.
**chop sticks** *n.* one of two small sticks of wood, ivory, etc. used by the Chinese in taking food.
**cho•ral** *a.* pert. or belonging to a choir or chorus. **-ly** *adv.* **choric** *a.* pert. to a chorus.
**chorale** *n.* a simple, dignified melody sung to religious words.
**chord** *n.* *(Mus.)* a series of tones having a harmonic relation to each other, and sounded simultaneously; *(Geom.)* a straight line between two points in the circumference of a circle.
**chore** *n.* any odd job, or occasional housework; *(pl.)* routine work.
**cho•re•og•ra•phy** *n.* the art of creating dance compositions for ballet. **choreographer** *n.* **choreographic** *a.*
**cho•rog•ra•phy** *n.* the art of making a map, or writing a description, of a region or country. **chorology** *n.* the study of the geographical distribution of plants and animals.
**chor•tle** *v.i.* to chuckle gleefully. **chortling** *n.*
**cho•rus** *n.* a combination of voices singing together; the refrain; *v.t.* to join in the refrain; to sing together. **choric** *a.* pert. to a chorus.
**chose** *pa.t.* of **choose.**
**chosen** *pa.p.* of **choose.**
**chow•der** *n.* a stew made of fish, pork, onions, etc.
**Christ** *n.* The Anointed — a name given to Jesus of Nazareth. **-like, -ly** *a.* resembling Christ.
**chris•ten** *v.t.* to give a name to. **Christendom** *n.* all Christian countries; the whole body of Christians. **-ing** *n.*

baptism.

**Chris•tian** *n.* a follower of Christ; a professed adherent of the Church of Christ; *a.* pert. to Christ or his religion. **-ize** *v.t.* to convert to Christianity. **Christianity** *n.* the religion of the followers of Christ. **—era,** the era counting from the birth of Christ. **—name,** individual name, as opposed to family name. **—Science,** a religious doctrine of faith-healing founded in America.

**Christ•mas** the annual celebration of the birth of Christ, observed on Dec. 25.

**chro•mat•ic** *a.* pert. to color; *(Mus.)* proceeding by semitones. **-s** *n.* the science of colors; *(Mus.)* chromatic notes. **-ally** *adv.*

**chrome, chro•mi•um** *n.* a metal, very resistant to corrosion, used generally for plating other metals. **chromic** *a.* pert. to, or obtained from, chrome or chromium. **chromate** *n.* a salt of chromic acid. **chromite** *n.* a mineral, the chief source of chromium.

**chro•mo•some** *n. (Biol.)* one of the gene-carrying bodies in the tissue of a cell, regarded as the transmitter of hereditary factors from parent to child.

**chron•ic** *a.* continuing for a long time; of disease, deep-seated and lasting. **-ally.**

**chron•i•cle** *n.* a register of events in order of time; *v.t.* to record in order of time. **-r** *n.*

**chro•no-** a combining form fr. Gk. *chronos,* time. **-graph** *n.* an instrument for measuring and recording time very exactly. **chronology** *n.* the science that treats of historical dates and arranges them in order; a table of events and dates. **chronologer, chronologist** *n.* one who records historical events, etc. **chronological** *a.* arranged in order of time. **chronologically** *adv.* **chronometer** *n.* a very accurate watch or time-keeper. **-metric, -metrical** *a.* **chronometry** *n.* the process of measuring time by instruments.

**chrys•an•the•mum** *n.* a mop-headed garden flower.

**chub** *n.* a fish of the carp family, small and fat. **-by** *a.* round and plump. **-biness** *n.*

**chuck** *n.* a cut of beef from the neck to the shoulder blade.

**chuck•le** *v.i.* to laugh in a suppressed manner; *n.* a short, quiet laugh.

**chug** *n.* an explosive sound made by an engine exhaust; *v.i.* to make an explosive sound. *pa.p., pa.t.* **-ged.** *pr.p.* **-ging.**

**chum** *n.* an intimate friend (with); to share a room (with). *pr.p.* **-ming.** *pa.p.* and *pa.t.* **med.** **-my** *a.* friendly; sociable.

**chump** *n.* a lump of wood.

**chunk** *n.* a short, thick piece of wood, etc. **-y** *a.*

**church** *n.* building for Christian worship; a denomination of the Christian religion; the clergy; the church service; *v.t.* to bring to church. **-goer** *n.* one who attends church regularly. **-ly** *a.* **-man** *n.* an ecclesiastic; a member of a church. **-warden** *n.* an officer entrusted with the interests of the church or parish. **-yard** *n.* the ground adjoining a church.

**church**

**churl** *n.* a countryman. **-ish** *a.* **-ishly** *adv.* **-ishness** *n.*

**churn** *n.* a vessel in which cream is violently stirred to produce butter; *v.t.* to agitate cream so as to produce butter; to stir up violently; *v.i.* to produce butter.

**chute** *n.* a rapid descent in a river; a rapid; a sloping contrivance for transferring coal, rubbish, etc. to a lower level.

**ci•ca•da, cicala** *n.* an insect, the male of which emits a shrill, chirping sound.

**ci•der** *n.* a drink made from the juice of apples.

**ci•gar** *n.* tobacco leaf made up in a roll for smoking. **-ette** *n.* finely cut tobacco rolled in thin paper.

**cil•i•a** *n.pl.* the eyelashes; *(Anat.)* hair-like, vibratile processes. **ciliary, ciliate, ciliated, ciliferous, ciliform** *a.*

**cinch** *n.* a saddle-girth; *v.t.* to fasten a cinch around; to tighten (girth).

**cin•cho•na** *n.* a genus of trees from which quinine is extracted; the bark. **-ceous** *a.*

**cinc•ture** *n.* a belt; a girdle; a zone; *v.t.* to encircle. **-d** *a.*

**cin•der** *n.* any partially burned combustible substance.

**cin•e•ma** *n.* a theater where moving pictures are shown; a motion picture; **-scope** *n.* a wide, panoramic motion picture screen. **-tography** *n.* **-tographer** *n.*

**cin•er•ar•y** *a.* pert. to ashes; made to hold ashes. **cinerarium** *n.* (*pl.* **-raria**) *n.* a place for ashes after cremation. **cineration** *n.* a reducing to ashes; incineration.

**cin•na•bar** *n.* red sulphide of mercury used as a pigment; *a.* vermillion colored.

**cin•na•mon** *n.* the inner bark of a laurel tree of Ceylon; an aromatic substance obtained from the bark, used as a spice; *n.* and *a.* a light-brown color.

**ci•pher, cy•pher** *n.* the arithmetical symbol 0; a secret writing; the key to a code; *v.i.* to work at arithmetic.

**cir•cle** *n.* a plane figure bounded by a single curved line called its circumference, every point of which is equally distant from a point within called the center; a sphere; the company associated with a person; a never-ending series; *v.t.* to revolve round; to encompass, as by a circle; *v.i.* to move in a circle.

**cir•cuit** *n.* the space enclosed within a fixed limit; *(Law)* the round made by judges holding court; path of an electric current.

**cir•cu•lar** *a.* in the form of a circle; roundabout; *n.* a notice sent out in quantities. **-ly** *adv.* **circularity** *n.* **-ize** *v.t.* to send circulars to.
**cir•cu•late** *v.t.* to cause to pass round as in a circle; to spread abroad; *v.i.* to move around and return to the same point. **circulation** *n.* the flow of blood from, and back to, the heart; the money circulating in a country. **circulative, circulatory** *a.* circulating. **circulator** *n.*
**cir•cum-** meaning *round, about,* combining to form many derivatives as in **-ambient** *a.* enclosing. **-ambiency** *n.* environment. **-ambulate** *v.t.* and *i.* to walk around or about.
**cir•cum•cise** *v.t.* to cut off the foreskin. **circumcision** *n.*
**cir•cum•fer•ence** *n.* the line that bounds a circle; the distance around; area. **circumferential** *a.*
**cir•cum•flex** *n.* an accent mark placed over a vowel to denote length, contraction, etc.
**cir•cum•flu•ent** *a.* flowing round. **circumfluence** *n.*
**cir•cum•ja•cent** *a.* bordering on every side.
**cir•cum•lo•cu•tion** *n.* a roundabout manner of speaking. **circumlocutory** *a.*
**cir•cum•nav•i•gate** *v.t.* to sail around. **circumnavigable** *a.* capable of being sailed round. **circumnavigation** *n.* **circumnavigator** *n.* one who sails around.
**cir•cum•scribe** *v.t.* to draw a circle around; to enclose within limits. **circumscription** *n.* limitation. **circumscriptive** *a.* limited in space.
**cir•cum•spect** *a.* watchful on all sides; discreet. **-ly** *adv.* **circumspection** *n.* prudence; discretion; tact. **-ive** *a.*
**cir•cum•stance** *n.* a particular fact, event, or case; *v.t.* to place in a particular situation. **-s** *n.pl.* condition as to pecuniary resources; situation; details. **circumstantial** *a.* accidental; not essential. **circumstantially** *adv.* **circumstantiality** *n.* minuteness of detail. **circumstantiate** *v.t.* to detail exactly.
**cir•cum•vent** *v.t.* to get around by stratagem. **-ion** *n.* **-ive** *a.*
**cir•cus** *n.* a travelling company of performers, animals, etc.; a circular enclosure for performances.
**cir•rho•sis** *n.* *(Med.)* hardening and enlargement of the liver. **cirrhotic** *a.*
**cir•rus** *n.* a lofty, fleecy cloud; *pl.* **cirri.**
**cis•tern** *n.* a large tank for holding water.
**cite** *v.t.* to quote; to bring forward as proof. **citation** *n.* an official notice to appear; the mention of gallantry in military orders. **citator** *n.* **citatory** *a.*
**cit•i•zen** *n.* an inhabitant of a city; a member of a state; *a.* having the character of a citizen. **-ry** *n.* citizens collectively. **-ship** *n.* the rights and duties of a citizen.
**cit•ron** *n.* the fruit of the citron tree, resembling a lemon; a yellow color. **citrate** *n.* a salt of citric acid. **citric** *a.* extracted from the citron lemon, etc. **citrus fruits,** citrons, lemons, oranges, etc.
**cit•ron•el•la** *n.* a sharp smelling oil to keep insects away (See **citron**).
**cit•y** *n.* a corporate town; the business or shopping center of a town; *a.* pert. to a city.
**civ•ic** *a.* pert. to a city or a citizen. **-s** *n.pl.* the study of civic affairs, municipal or national.
**civ•il** *a.* pert. to city, state, or citizen; polite. **-ly** *adv.* **civilian** *n.* one whose employment is non-military; *a.* pert. to civilian life (e.g. civilian dress). **civility** *n.* politeness; *pl.* acts of politeness. **civil defense,** an organization to deal with civilians during air raids, etc. **civil engineer,** one who plans bridges, roads, dams, etc. **civil service,** the government positions obtained by examination. **civil war,** war between citizens of the same country.
**civ•i•lize** *v.t.* to reclaim from a savage state; to enlighten. **-d** *a.* **civilization** *n.* the act of civilizing, or state of being civilized.
**clack** *v.i.* to make a sudden, sharp noise, as by striking; *n.* a sharp, repeated, rattling sound; continual talk.
**clad** *pa.p.* and *pa.t.* of **clothe;** *a.* clothed.
**claim** *v.t.* to demand as a right, or as due; to assert as true; *n.* the demand of a right; a title; the thing claimed. **-ant** *n.* one who claims. **— jumper** *n.* one who seizes a piece of land marked out by a settler or miner.
**clair•voy•ance** *n.* the power of seeing things not normally perceptible to the senses; second sight. **clairvoyant** *n.* one who claims the power of clairvoyance. Also *a.*
**clam** *n.* an edible bivalve shellfish.
**cla•mant** *a.* crying out; clamorous. **clamancy** *n.*
**clam•ber** *v.i.* to climb with difficulty, holding on with the hands.
**clam•my** *a.* sticky and moist; cold and damp. **clamminess** *n.*
**clam•or** *n.* loud shouting; uproar; *v.i.* to shout loudly; to utter loud complaints or demands. **-ous** *a.*
**clamp** *n.* any appliance with parts brought together by a screw for holding anything; *v.t.* to make firm.
**clan** *n.* a tribe bearing the same surname, united under a chieftain; a set of persons having a common interest. **-nish** *a.* disposed to associate only with members of the same clique. **-nishly** *adv.* **-nishness** *n.*
**clan•des•tine** *a.* secret, and contrary to law, morals, etc. **-ly** *adv.* **-ness** *n.*
**clang** *v.t.* to strike with a ringing, metallic sound; *v.i.* to give forth a ringing, metallic sound; *n.* a sharp, ringing sound. **-ing** *n.* a clang.
**clan•gor** *n.* a loud harsh, ringing sound. **-ous** *a.* **-ously** *adv.*
**clank** *n.* a brief, hard, metallic sound; *v.t.* and *i.* to produce such a sound.
**clap** *v.t.* to strike the hands together in approval; *v.i.* to strike the hands together in applause; *n.* applause; *pr.p.* **-ping.** *pa.p.* and *pa.t.* **-ped.** **-per** *n.* one who claps; the tongue of a bell. **-board** *n.* thin

board used to cover wooden houses.

**clar•i•fy** *v.t.* to make clear; to remove possibility of error; *v.i.* to become clear. **clarification** *n.* **clarity** *n.* clearness; lucidity of mind.

**clar•i•on** *n.* trumpet with shrill piercing note. **clarinet, clarionet** *n.* a wood wind instrument. **clarinettist** *n.*

**clash** *v.t.* to strike noisily together; *v.i.* to disagree; *n.* a loud noise; a conflict.

**clasp** *v.t.* to fasten together with a catch or hook; to cling to; *n.* a catch or hook for fastening; a grasping of the hands.

**class** *n.* an order or grouping of persons or things possessing the same characteristics or status; a group of students taught together; a grouping of plants or animals; rank or standing in society; *v.t.* to rank together; *v.i.* to rank. **-able, -ible** *a.*

**clas•sic** *n.* a work, writer of recognized worth; an ancient Latin or Greek writer or book; *a.* of model excellence in literature or art; conforming to standards of Greek and Roman art. **-s** *n.pl.* ancient Latin or Greek literature. **-al** *a.* **-ally** *adv.* **-ality, -alness** *n.* the quality of being classical. **classicism** *n.* classic principles in art and literature; a classical idiom. **classicist** *n.*

**clas•si•fy** *v.t.* to arrange in classes. **classifiable** *a.* **classification** *n.* the act of classifying.

**clat•ter** *v.t.* to strike and so make a rattling noise; *v.i.* to make rattling sounds; *n.* a repeated rattling noise.

**clause** *n.* *(Gram.)* a subordinate part of a sentence; *(Law)* an article or distinct portion of a document, contract.

**claus•tral** *a.* secluded. **claustration** *n.* the state of being confined in a cloister.

**claus•tro•pho•bi•a** *n.* *(Med.)* a morbid dread of confined spaces.

**clav•i•cle** *n.* the collarbone. **clavicular** *a.*

**claw** *n.* a sharp, hooked nail, as of a beast or bird; *v.t.* to pull, tear, or scratch with claws or nails.

**clay** *n.* soft earth, consisting of alumina and silica, with water used in making pottery, bricks, etc. **-ey** *a.* consisting of clay; like clay.

**clean** *a.* free from dirt, stain, or any defilement; *v.t.* to free from dirt; to purify; *adv.* so as to leave no dirt. **-er** *n.* one who, or that which, cleans. **-liness** *n.* freedom from dirt; purity. **-ly** *a.* habitually clean in persons and habits; pure. **-ly** *adv.* in a clean manner; neatly. **-ness** *n.* **—cut** *a.* well-shaped.

**clear** *a.* free from cloud; free from obstruction; without drawback; transparent; *adv.* wholly; *v.t.* to make bright or clear; to free from accusation; to pass over or through; to free from difficulty, obstruction, suspicion, etc.; *v.i.* to become clear, transparent, free. **-age** *n.* clearance. **-ance** *n.* a certificate that a ship has been cleared at the custom house. **-ing** *n.* a tract of land cleared of wood. **-ing-house** *n.* an office maintained by several banks for balancing accounts, exchanging checks, etc. **-ly** *adv.* **-ness** *n.* **—cut** *a.* sharply defined. **—eyed, —seeing, —sighted** *a.* having acuteness of sight.

**cleat** *n.* a piece of metal fastened to a shoe.

**cleave** *v.t.* to split asunder; to cut in two; *v.i.* to crack asunder; *pa.p.* **cloven** or **cleft.** *pa.t.* **clove** or **cleft. cleavage** *n.* of rocks, the quality of splitting naturally; a rupture. **-r** *n.* one who, or that which, cleaves; a butcher's chopper.

**cleave** *v.i.* to adhere closely; to stick; to be faithful to.

**clef** *n.* *(Mus.)* a sign used to indicate the pitch.

**cleft** *pa.p.* and *pa.t.* of the verb **cleave;** *n.* a fissure or split; a chink.

**clem•en•cy** *n.* leniency; mildness; mercy. **clement** *a.* compassionate.

**clench, clinch** *v.t.* to close together tightly (the hands, the teeth); *n.* a firm closing; decisive proof; a firm grip. **-er** *n.* an unanswerable argument.

**cler•gy** *n.* the body of men ordained for religious service. **-man** *n.* a minister.

**cler•ic** *n.* a clergyman; *a.* clerical. **clerical** *a.* belonging to the clergy; pert. to a clerk or copyist.

**clerk** *n.* one who is employed to do correspondence, keep accounts, etc. in an office; salesman or saleswoman; *v.i.* to act as a clerk or secretary. **-ship** *n.*

**clev•er** *a.* ingenious; intelligent. **-ly** *adv.* **-ness** *n.*

**clew, clue** *n.* a ball of thread or cord; anything that helps to solve a mystery.

**cli•ché** *n.* *(Print.)* an electrotype or stereotype plate; a stereotyped or hackneyed phrase.

**click** *n.* a slight, short sound, as a latch in a door.

**cli•ent** *n.* one who employs another professionally as his agent; a customer. **clientele** *n.* customers collectively.

**cliff** *n.* a high rock-face; the sheer side of a mountain.

**cli•mac•ter•ic** *n.* a period in human life in which a change takes place in the constitution; any critical period; *a.* critical. **-al** *a.*

**cli•mate** *n.* the general atmospherical conditions (temperature, moisture, etc.) of a region. **climatic** *a.* **climatical** *a.*

**cli•max** *n.* an arrangement of words such that they rise in rhetorical force; the point of greatest excitement or tension. **climactic** *a.*

**climb** *v.t.* and *i.* to go up, ascent (as a hill, tree, etc.); to grow upward; *n.* an ascent. **-er** *n.*

**clinch** *v.t.* and *i.* struggle at close quarters in wrestling or boxing; *n.* a close holding in wrestling or boxing. **-er** *n.*

**cling** *v.i.* to adhere to; to be attached firmly to; *pa.p.* and *pa.t.* **clung.**

**clin•ic** *n.* an institution where non-resident patients attend for treatment. **-al** *a.*

**clink** *n.* a sharp, tinkling sound.

**clip** *v.t.* to grip tightly. *pr.p.* **-ping.** *pa.t., pa.p.* **-ped.** *n.* any device for holding a thing firmly.

**clip** *v.t.* to cut with scissors or shears; *v.i.* to move quickly; *n.* act of clipping; a season's shearing of wool; a rapid pace. *pr.p.* **-ping.** *pa.p.* and *pa.t.* **-ped. -per** *n.* one who clips; a fast sailing-vessel, with a long sharp bow. **-pers** *n.* a two-bladed instrument for cutting. **-ping** *n.* an item cut from a newspaper, etc.

**clique** *n.* a circle of persons with common interests. **cliquish** *a.* **cliquishness** *n.*

**cloak** *n.* a long, loose, outer garment; something that conceals; a pretext; *v.t.* to cover with a cloak; to hide. **-room** *n.* a room where coats, hats, etc. may be temporarily left.

**clock** *n.* a device which measures time. **-wise** *adv.* in the direction of the hands of a clock. **counterclockwise** *adv.* circling in the opposite direction. **-work** *n.* the machinery of a clock; regular movement as of clock; *a.* mechanically regular. **o'clock,** by the clock.

**clod** *n.* a lump of earth or turf; a dull, stupid fellow. **-hopper** *n.* a rustic; a boor.

**clog** *n.* an impediment; an obstruction; *v.t.* to hinder; to choke up; *v.i.* to become choked, encumbered. *pr.p.* **-ging.** *pa.p.* *pa.t.* **-ged.**

**clois•ter** *n.* a monastery or nunnery; a secluded spot; *v.t.* to confine. **-al, cloistral** *a.* **-ed** *a.*

**close** *v.t.* to shut; to stop up; to conclude; to complete (a wireless circuit); *v.i.* to unite; to end. **closing** *a.* ending; *n.* the conclusion. **closure** *n.* the act of shutting; a closing; the close of a debate.

**close** *a.* confined; tight; near at hand; intimate; crowded; *adv.* in a close manner or state; tightly; *n.* an enclosed place; *(Mus.)* a cadence. **-ly** *adv.* **-ness** *n.* **— by,** near. **— call,** a very narrow escape. **— fisted** or **— handed** *a.* miserly, penurious. **— mouthed** *a.* uncommunicative. **— quarters** *n.pl.* a crowded space. **— up** *n.* a close view of anything.

**clos•et** *n.* a small room for storing things; a lavatory; *v.t.* to take into a private room for consultation.

**clot** *n.* a coagulated mass of blood; *v.t.* to form into clots; *v.i.* to coagulate. *pr.p.* **-ting.** *pa.p.* and *pa.t.* **-ted.**

**cloth** *n.* any woven fabric of wool, silk, cotton; a cover for a table. *pl.* **cloths.**

**clothe** *v.t.* to put garments on; to wrap up in. *pr.p.* **clothing.** *pa.p.* and *pa.t.* **-d** or **clad.** **-s** *n. pl.* wearing apparel. **clothier** *n.* one who makes, or sells, clothes; an outfitter. **clothing** *n.* garments in general; raiment. **clotheshorse** *n.* one who likes clothes.

**cloud** *n.* a body of visible vapor floating in the atmosphere; a mass of smoke, flying dust, etc.; a state of impending trouble; *v.t.* to overspread with clouds; to darken; to defame; v.i. to grow cloudy; to be blurred. **-y** *a.* darkened with clouds; overcast; indistinct; gloomy. **-ily** *adv.* **-iness** *n.* **-burst** *n.* a violent downpour of rain; a deluge.

**clout** *n.* a slap or blow; to strike with the open hand.

**clove** *n.* the flower-bud of the clove-tree, used as a spice.

clove

**clove** *pa.t.* of **cleave.**

**clo•ven** *pa.p.* of **cleave.** Also *a.* divided into two parts.

**clo•ver** *n.* a common field plant of the trefoil family. **-leaf** *n.* a highway intersection in the shape of a four-leaf clover.

**clown** *n.* the buffoon in a play or circus; a boor; *v.i.* to behave like a fool. **-ishly** *adv.* **-ishness** *n.*

**cloy** *v.t.* to induce a sensation of loathing by overmuch of sweetness, or flattery; to satiate. **-ing** *a.* satiating.

**club** *n.* a heavy stick, thickening towards one end, used as a weapon; a stick used in golf; an association of people united in pursuance of a common interest; *v.t.* to beat with a club; to gather into a club; *v.i.* to unite for a common end. *pr.p.* **-bing.** *pa.p.* and *pa.t.* **-bed. -foot** *n.* a congenitally deformed or crooked foot.

**clump** *n.* a shapeless mass of any substance; a cluster of trees or shrubs; a tramping sound; *v.t.* to put in a group; *v.i.* to tramp heavily.

**clumsy** *a.* awkward; ungainly. **clumsily** *adv.* **clumsiness** *n.*

**clung** *pa.p.* and *pa.t.* of **cling.**

**clus•ter** *n.* a bunch; a number of things growing together, as grapes; *v.t.* to collect into a bunch; *v.i.* to grow, or be, in clusters.

**clutch** *v.t.* and *i.* to seize or grip with the hand; *n.* a tight grip; the coupling of two working parts, used in motor vehicles to connect or disconnect engine and transmission gear. **-es** *n.pl.* the hands; power.

**clut•ter** *n.* disorder; *v.t.* to crowd together in disorder.

**coach** *n.* a tutor who prepares students; a trainer in athletics; *v.t.* to tutor or train.

**co•ac•tion** *n.* compulsion.

**co•ad•ju•tant** *a.* assisting; *n.* an assistant. **coadjutor** *n.* an associate and destined successor.

**co•ag•u•late** *v.t.* to congeal; to solidify; *v.i.* to clot. **coagulant** *n.* a substance that causes coagulation. **coagulation** *n.* **coagulative** *a.*

**coal** *n.* a black substance used for fuel, composed of mineralized vegetable matter; *v.t.* to supply with coal; *v.i.* to take in coal. **-s** *n.pl.* glowing embers. **— bin** *n.* a recess for storing coal. **— field** *n.* a district where coal abounds. **— gas** *n.* gases produced from the distillation of coal or from burning coal. **— mine, — pit** *n.* the excavation from which coal is dug. — **oil** *n.* kerosene. **— tar** *n.* a thick, sticky substance, produced during the distilling of coal.

**co•a•li•tion** *n.* a union or combination of persons, parties, or states into one body; a league. **-ist** *n.*

**coarse** *a.* rough, rude; not refined; without grace or elegance; ill-mannered; vulgar; inferior. **-ly** *adv.* **-n** *v.t.* and *i.* to make or become coarse. **-ness** *n.*

**coast** *n.* land bordering the sea; the country near the shore; *v.t.* and *i.* to run shut off, or on a bicycle without pedaling; to toboggan. **-al** *a.* pert. to the coast. **-er** *n.* a small tray placed under glasses to protect a table. **-guard** *n.* a service organized orig. to prevent smuggling; since 1925, largely a life-saving service; **-line** *n.* the outline of a coast. **-wards** *adv.* toward the coast. **-wise** *adv.* along the coast.

**coat** *n.* an outer garment; the fur or skin of an animal; a layer spread over another, as paint; *v.t.* to cover with a coat to clothe. **-ed** *a.* **-ing** *n.* a layer; cloth for making coats.

**coax** *v.t.* to win over by fond pleading. **-ingly** *adv.*

**cob** *n.* a corn-cob; a male swan.

**co•balt** *n.* a metallic element classified with iron and nickel, and used as an ingredient of many alloys. **— blue** *n.* a pigment containing an oxide of cobalt; *a.* a dark-blue color. **-ic** *a.*

**cob•ble** *v.t.* to patch coarsely; to mend boots or shoes. **-r** *n.* a mender of shoes; a deep-dish fruit pie with a biscuit crust.

**cob•ble** *n.* a stone rounded by the action of water; *v.t.* to pave with cobbles. **-stone** *n.* a rounded stone used in paving.

**co•bra** *n.* the venomous 'hooded' snake of Africa and India. **-cobric** *a.*

**cobra**

**cob•web** *n.* a spider's web.

**co•ca** *n.* a Peruvian plant or its dried leaf, which is a nerve stimulant. **cocaine** *n.* a drug made from coca leaves, used as a local anesthetic.

**coc•cyx** *n.* the triangular bone ending spinal column. *pl.* **coccyges. coccygeal** *a.*

**cock** *n.* the male of birds, esp. of the domestic fowl; the hammer of a firearm; *v.t.* to draw back the hammer of a gun; to set erect, set at an angle, as a hat. **-erel** *n.* a swaggering youth. **-scomb** *n.* the comb of a cock; a flowering plant. **-tail** *n.* a drink concocted of liquor, bitters, sugar, etc.; a mixture of fruit, or of seafood, served as an appetizer. **-y** *a.* full of self-assurance. **-ily** *adv.* **-iness** *n.*

**cock•a•too** *n.* a kind of parrot with a crested head.

**cock•a•trice** *n.* a fabulous animal represented as a cock with a dragon's tail.

**cock•er** *n.* a small variety of spaniel, used for retrieving game.

**cock•le** *n.* a weed that grows among corn: the corn rose.

**cock•le** *n.* a bivalve shell-fish, with a thick ribbed shell; *v.t.* to cause to pucker; to wrinkle. **-shell** *n.* the shell of a cockle.

**cock•pit** *n.* in aircraft, a compartment in the fuselage for the pilot and controls.

**cock•roach** *n.* a black or brown beetle infesting houses.

**cock•swain** See **coxswain.**

**co•co, co•coa** *n.* a palm tree producing the coconut. **-nut,** the fruit of the coco palm.

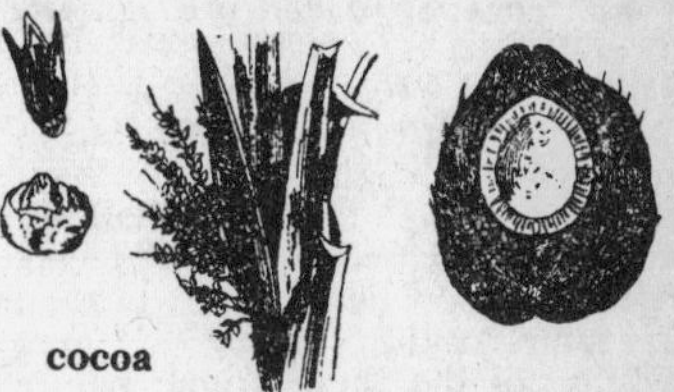

**cocoa**

**co•coa** *n.* a powder made from the kernels of the cacao plant; a beverage from this.

**co•coon** *n.* the silky envelope which larvae spin for themselves before passing into the pupa stage.

**cod, cod•fish** *n.* a large fish from northern seas, used as food.

**cod•dle** *v.t.* to pamper or spoil.

**code** *n.* an orderly collection of laws; a system of words, symbols, or numbers adopted for secrecy; **codify** *v.t.* to collect laws, into a digest. **codification** *n.* act of collecting laws.

**cod•i•cil** *n.* a supplement to a will.

**co•ed•u•ca•tion** *n.* the education of boys and girls together in mixed classes. **-al** *a.*

**co•ef•fi•cient** *a.* cooperating; combining; *n.* that which unites with something else to produce a result; *(Math.)* a number or other factor placed before another as a multiplier; *(Phys.)* a constant number or factor measuring some specified property of a substance. **coefficiency** *n.*

**co•e•qual** *a.* of the same power as another; *n.* a person having equality with another.

**co•erce** *v.t.* to compel by force; to constrain; to restrain. **coercible** *a.* **coercive** *a.* having power to compel. **coercively** *adv.* **coercion** *n.* state of being coerced; compulsory force.

**co•e•val** *a.* of same age; *n.* contemporary.

**co•ex•ist** *v.i.* to exist at the same time or together. **-ence** *n.* **-ent** *a.*

**cof•fee** *n.* an evergreen shrub, valuable for its berries; a drink from this. **-bean** *n.* the

**coffee**

seed of the berry. **-house** *n.* a restaurant where coffee and other refreshments are supplied.

**cof•fer** *n.* a chest for valuables; *v.t.* to hoard (money, etc.).

**cof•fin** *n.* a casket in which the dead are enclosed before burial; *v.t.* to place in a coffin.

**cog** *n.* one of a series of teeth on a wheel; *v.t.* to fit a wheel with cogs. *pr.p.* **-ging.** *pa.p.* and *pa.t.* **-ged.**

**co•gent** *a.* having great force; convincing. **-ly** *adv.* **cogence, cogency** *n.* convincing power.

**cog•i•tate** *v.i.* to reflect deeply; to meditate. **cogitable** *a.* **cogitation** *n.* contemplation. **cogitative** *a.*

**co•gnac** *n.* a French brandy, so called from the town of *Cognac* in S.W. France.

**cog•nate** *a.* allied by blood or birth; from the same origin, formation, etc.; *n.* anything of the same origin, nature, or effect.

**cog•ni•zance** *n.* knowledge; perception. **cognizable** *a.* capable of being known. **cognizably** *adv.* **cognizant** *a.* having knowledge of.

**cog•ni•tion** *n.* awareness; state of being able to perceive objects or ideas. **cognitive** *a.*

**co•ha•bit** *v.i.* to live together as husband and wife. **ation, -ant** *n.*

**co•here** *v.i.* to stick together; to be connected; to adhere. **-nce, -ncy** *n.* **-nt** *a.* sticking together; consistent. **-ntly** *adv.* **cohesible** *a.* capable of cohesion. **cohesion** *n.* the act of sticking together. **cohesive** *a.* having the power of cohering. **cohesiveness, cohesibility** *n.*

**co•hort** *n.* a company of persons; an associate.

**coif** *n.* a headdress in the form of a close-fitting cap, worn by nuns. **-feur** *n.* a hairdresser. **coiffure** *n.* a style of dressing the hair.

**coil** *v.t.* to twist into a spiral shape; *v.i.* to take on a spiral shape; *n.* the spiral of rings into which anything is wound.

**coin** *n.* a piece of stamped metal issued by government authority to be used as money; *v.t.* to make into money; invent or fabricate, as a word or phrase. **-age** *n.* the act of coining; money coined; currency. **-er** *n.* one who makes coins; an inventor.

**co•in•cide** *v.i.* to happen at the same time; to agree (in opinion). **coincidence** *n.* correspondence in nature, circumstances, etc. **coincident, coincidental** *a.* simultaneous. **coincidently** *adv.*

**co•i•tion** *n.* sexual intercourse; copulation. Also **coitus.**

**coke** *n.* coal half burnt, and used as fuel; *v.t.* to turn into coke.

**col•an•der** *n.* a vessel with a perforated bottom, used for draining off liquids. Also **cullender.**

**cold** *a.* wanting in heat; deficient in the emotions; *n.* absence of warmth; chilliness; a disorder of the nose, throat and chest, characterized by running at the nose, hoarseness and coughing; **-ly** *adv.* **-ish** *a.* somewhat cold. **-ness** *n.* **—blooded** *a.* having cold blood, like fish; callous or heartless. Also **—hearted. — war,** campaign carried on by means of economic pressure, press, radio, etc.

**cole** *n.* a name for plants of the cabbage family. **—slaw** *n.* a salad of finely sliced or chopped cabbage.

**Co•le•op•ter•a** *n.pl.* the order of insects, such as beetles, whose outer wings form a horny covering for the true wings.

**col•ic** *n.* severe pain in the abdomen.

**co•li•se•um** *n.* a stadium or large auditorium.

**col•lab•o•rate** *v.i.* to labor together; to act jointly. **collaboration** *n.* joint labor; willing cooperation with the enemy. **collaborator** *n.*

**col•lapse** *v.i.* to fall in; to break down; to give way under physical or mental strain; *n.* a falling in or down; a sudden and complete failure. **collapsable, collapsible** *a.*

**col•lar** *n.* something worn around the neck; the part of a garment that fits around the neck; *v.t.* to capture; to put a collar on. **-bone** *n.* the bone from the shoulders to the breast-bone; the clavicle.

**col•late** *v.t.* to arrange in order, as the sheets of a book for binding. **collation** *n.* the act of collating; a repast. **collative** *a.* **collator** *n.*

**col•lat•e•ral** *a.* running parallel; subordinately connected; additional (of a security); *n.* additional security. **-ly** *adv.* **-ness.**

**col•league** *n.* an associate or companion.

**col•lect** *v.t.* to gather; to receive payment of; *v.i.* to be assembled; to come together. **-able, -ible** *a.* **-ed** *a.* cool; self-possessed. **-edly** *adv.* **-edness** *n.* **collection** *n.* the act of collecting; a contribution or sum of money gathered at a meeting. **-ive** *a.* formed by gathering; gathered into a mass or body. **-ively** *adv.* **-ivism** *n.* a term embracing all systems on the Socialistic doctrine of the state of the economic life of the country. **-ivist** *n.* **-or** *n.* an officer appointed to receive taxes, customs, duties, tolls, etc.

**col•lege** *n.* an institution for higher education; the buildings of such an institution. **collegial** *a.* pert. to a college. **collegian** *n.* a member of a college; a student. **collegiate** *a.* pert. to or instituted like, a college.

**col•lide** *v.i.* to strike together; to clash; to come into conflict. **collision** *n.* a violent impact; a clash.

**col•lie** *n.* a breed of sheep dog.

**col•lo•cate** *v.t.* to place together; to arrange. **collocation** *n.*

**col•loid** *a.* gelatinous; *n.* a glue-like, non-crystalline substance unable to pass through animal membrances. **-al** *a.* like a colloid.

**col•lo•quy** *n.* dialogue; discussion; a debate. **colloquial** *a.* pert. to, or used in, ordinary conversation. **colloquially** *adv.* **colloquialism** *n.* an expression used in ordinary conversation, but not regarded as slang.

**col•lu•sion** *n.* a secret agreement between two or more persons for a fraudulent purpose. **collusive** *a.*

**co•logne** *n.* a perfumed toilet water.

**co•lon** *n.* a punctuation mark (:), separating parts of a sentence that are almost independent and complete in themselves; *(Anat.)* that part of the large intestine extending from the caecum to the rectum. **colonic** *a.*

**colo•nel** *n.* the officer ranking between lieutenant colonel and a brigadier general, usually commanding a regiment. **-cy, -ship** *n.* the rank of colonel.

**col•on•nade** *n.* a series of columns arranged symmetrically.

**col•o•ny** *n.* a body of people who settle in a new country but remain subject to the parent state; the country thus occupied; a group of animals or plants living and growing together. **colonial** *a.* pert. to a colony; *n.* a colonist. **colonize** *v.t.* to plant or establish a colony; *v.i.* to settle. **colonist** *n.* **colonization** *n.*

**col•o•phon** *n.* individual inscription used by publishers and printers on the title pages of books, etc.

**col•or** *n.* any hue as distinguished from white; a flush; vividness in writing; *v.t.* to tinge with color; *v.i.* to blush. **colors** *n.pl.* a flag or standard; a colored badge, device, etc. used as a distinguishing mark. **-able** *a.* capable of being colored; plausible. **-ably** *adv.* **-ful** *a.* having plenty of color. **—blind** *a.* unable to distinguish colors.

**col•or•a•tion** *n.* arrangement or disposition of colors in art. Also **coloration.**

**co•los•sus** *n.* a gigantic statue, esp. that of Apollo at Rhodes; hence any person of great stature or enormous strength. **colossal** *a.* of enormous size.

**colt** *n.* young horse, esp. a male.

**Colt** *n.* a repeating rifle; also a revolver invented by Samuel Colt.

**col•umn** *n.* a round pillar; a body of troops drawn up in deep files; a perpendicular line of figures. **-ar** *a.* having the form of columns. **-ated, -ed** *a.* furnished with, or supported on, columns. **-ist** *n.* a writer who contributes articles to a newspaper.

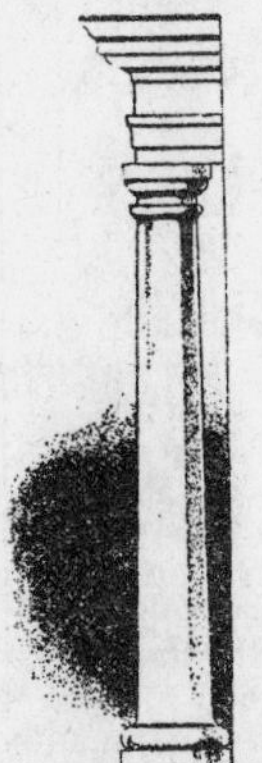

**column**

**co•ma** *n.* *(Med.)* a stupor generally resulting from injury to the brain, alcoholic or narcotic poisoning; drowsiness. **-tose** *a.* lethargic; drowsy.

**comb** *n.* a toothed instrument for separating, adjusting, or fastening hair; a decoration for a lady's hair; a cock's crest; the cell structure in which bees store their honey. **-er** *n.* one who, or that which, combs. **-ing** *n.* **-ings** *n.pl.* hair, wool, etc. removed by combing.

**com•bat** *v.t.* to oppose by force; to contend with; *v.i.* to struggle; to contend; *n.* a fight; a struggle; a contest. **-ant** *a.* contending; disposed to content; *n.* one engaged in a fight. **-ive** *a.* quarrelsome.

**com•bine** *v.t.* to join together; to unite; *v.i.* to form a union;*(Chem.)* to unite and form a new compound; *n.* an association formed to further political or commercial interests; a syndicate. **combinable** *a.* capable of combining. **combinative, combinatory** *a.* tending to combine. **combination** *n.* union; association of persons; chemical union; series of letters or numbers for operating a lock.

**com•bus•tion** *n.* the act of burning; chemical action accompanied by heat and light. **combustible** *a.* inflammable; *n.* a substance that burns readily.

**come** *v.i.* to approach; to arrive at some state or condition; to move towards; to appear. *pr.p.* **coming.** *pa.p.* **come.** *pa.t.* **came.** **-back** *n.* a return to a former activity.

**com•e•dy** *n.* a play dealing with the lighter side of life; the humorous element in life, or an incident.

**co•me•di•an** *n.* an entertainer whose songs or stories are light and humorous; a comic. **comedienne** *n. fem.*

**come•ly** *a.* good-looking; graceful. **comeliness** *n.*

**com•et** *n.* a heavenly body consisting of a diffuse, nebulous head, a nucleus, and a tail.

**com•fort** *v.t.* to allay grief or trouble; to console, cheer, gladden; *n.* solace or consolation; ease of body or mind. **-s** *n.pl.* circumstances which give greater ease to life. **-able** *a.* enjoying comfort. **-ably** *adv.* **-er** *n.* one who comforts; a quilted bedcover. **-less** *a.*

**com•ic** *a.* pert. to comedy; mirth-provoking; *n.* that which induces laughter; a comedian; *(Colloq.) (pl.)* a comic magazine or newspaper strip. **-al** *a.* ludicrous. **-ally** *adv.* **-ality.**

**com•ma** *n.* a punctuation mark (,), used to mark the shortest pauses in the division of a sentence.

**com•mand** *v.t.* to order or demand with authority; to govern or control; *v.i.* to be at the head; *n.* an order; the body of troops under an officer; a region under a commander; a word of command; mastery or facility. **-ing** *a.* fitted to control; impressive or imperious. **-ant** *n.* officer in charge of a military station or a body of troops. **-eer** *v.t.* to seize for military purposes; to take forcible possession of. **-er** *n.* a commanding officer. **-ment** *n.* a command; precept.

**-er-in-chief**, the officer in supreme command of the forces of a state.

**com•man•do** *n. (Mil.)* a selected body of men, who undergo special training for particularly dangerous enterprises against the enemy.

**com•mem•o•rate** *v.t.* to call to remembrance; to celebrate the memory of someone or something by a solemn act of devotion. **commemoration** *n.* **commemorative, commemoratory** *a.*

**com•mence** *v.t.* to begin, to start, to originate; *v.i.* to begin. **-ment** *n.* the ceremony of conferring degrees in colleges and universities.

**com•mend** *v.t.* to speak favorably of; to entrust to. **-able** *a.* **-ably** *adv.* **-ableness** *n.* **-ation** *n.* the act of commending; praise; approval. **-atory** *a.*

**com•men•su•rate** *a.* proportionate; adequate. **-ly** *adv.* **-ness** *n.* **commensuration** *n.* **commensurable** *a.* suitably proportioned. **commensurably** *adv.* **commensurability** *n.*

**com•ment** *v.t.* and *i.* to make remarks, notes, criticisms; *n.* a critical remark; an observation. **-ary** *n.* a series of notes; an exposition of a book. **-ate** *v.t.* to interpret the meaning of. **-ator** *n.* an expositor; one who speaks a commentary, either on events for braodcasting, or with a film.

**com•merce** *n.* buying and selling; trade. **commercial** *a.* pert. to commerce; broadcast program paid for by an advertiser. **commercialism** *n.* business principles, methods, or viewpoint. **commercialize** *v.t.* **commercially** *adv.*

**com•mis•er•ate** *v.t.* and *i.* to have compassion for; to sympathize. **commiseration** *n.*

**com•mis•sar•i•at** *n.* the army department which supplies food, stores, equipment, transport.

**com•mis•sa•ry** *n.* one to whom duty is assigned; *(Mil.)* a store which supplies food and equipment. **commissarial** *a.*

**com•mis•sion** *n.* something entrusted to be done; payment by a percentage for doing something; a group of people authorized to deal with specified matters; a warrant of appointment, to the rank of officer in the army, navy, etc.; *v.t.* to authorize; to appoint to the rank of officer. **-ed** *a.* **-er** *n.* one holding a commission to act; the head of a governmental department.

**com•mit** *v.t.* to entrust; to give in charge; to be guilty of; to send for trial or confinement; *pr.p.* **-ting**, *pa.p.* and *pa.t.* **-ted**. **-tal** *a.* **-ment** *n.*

**com•mit•tee** *n.* a number of persons appointed to attend any particular business by a legislative body, court, society, etc.

**com•mode** *n.* a chest of drawers.

**com•mo•di•ous** *a.* spacious. **-ly** *adv.* **-ness** *n.* **commodity** *n.* an article of trade. **commodities** *n.pl.* goods.

**com•mo•dore** *n.* rank just below rear admiral; captain of a convoy of ships.

**com•mon** *a.* shared by or belonging to all, or to several; frequent; of low social status; *n.* a tract of land belonging to a community for public use. **commons** *n.pl.* the lower House of Parliament, called the **House of Commons.** **-er** *n.* one of the common people, i.e. not a member of the nobility. **-ly** *adv.* in a common manner; jointly. **-ness** *n.* **-place** *a.* ordinary; trite; *n.* a trite remark. **— sense** *n.* sound understanding; well-balanced judgment. **— law**, unwritten law as distinguished from statute law.

**com•mon•weal** *n.* the public welfare; the common good. **commonwealth** *n.* the whole body of people.

**com•mo•tion** *n.* violent motion; public disorder.

**com•mune** *v.i.* to have spiritual intercourse *(with); (Eccl.)* to receive the communion. **communion** *n. (Christianity)* the celebration of the Lord's Supper.

**com•mune** *n.* a small administrative district. **communal** *a.* pert. to a community; for common use. **communalize** *v.t.* to make over for common use. **communalism** *n.* a system by which small local governments have large powers. **communism** *n.* the theory of a social system in which everything is held in common. **communist** *n.* **communistic** *a.*

**com•mu•ni•cate** *v.t.* to impart information; *v.i.* to have connection with; to have dealings, correspondence, with. **communicable** *a.* **communicably** *adv.* **communication** *n.* intercourse by speech, correspondence, messages, etc.; information. **communicant** *n.* one who imparts information; one who receives communion. **communicative** *a.* ready to impart information; talkative.

**com•mu•ni•ty** *n.* a locality where people reside; the public, or people in general; common possession or enjoyment.

**com•mute** *v.t.* to mitigate a sentence; travel regularly between home and work. **commutable** *a.* exchangeable. **commutability** *n.* **commutation** *n.* **commutator** *n. (Elect.)* a device for reversing the direction of an electric current. **-r** *n.*

**com•pact** *a.* closely packed; condensed; *v.t.* to press closely together; to make firm. **compact** *n.* a pocket vanity-case. **-ly** *adv.* **-ness** *n.* **-ed** *a.* firmly united.

**com•pact** *n.* a mutual bargain; covenant.

**com•pan•ion** *n.* one who is in another's company, habitually or for the moment; comrade; **-able** *a.* fitted to be a companion; sociable. **-ably** *adv.* **-ability**, **-ableness** *n.* **-ship** *n.*

**com•pa•ny** *n.* a gathering of persons; an association of persons in business, etc.; visitors; a division of a regiment.

**com•pare** *v.t.* to notice or point out the likeness and differences of two or more things; *(Gram.)* to state the comparative and superlative of an adjective or adverb; *v.i.* to be like; to compete with. **comparable** *a.* of equal regard or value. **comparably** *adv.* **comparative** *a.* estimated by comparison; not absolute; *(Gram.)* expressing 'more'. **comparatively** *adv.* **comparison** *n.* the act of comparing.

**com•part•ment** *n.* a part divided off; a division of a railway car.
**com•pass** *n.* an instrument for showing directions; a circumference; measurement around; scope; *v.t.* to go round; to surround; to accomplish. **-es** *n.pl.* a mathematical instrument for drawing circles, measuring, etc.

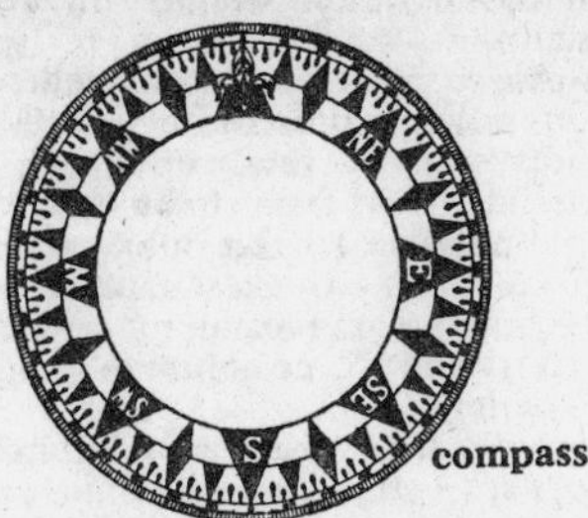

compass

**com•pas•sion** *n.* sympathy with the suffering of another; pity. **-ate** *a.* showing pity; merciful; *v.t.* to pity. **-ately** *adv.* **-ateness** *n.*
**com•pat•i•ble** *a.* agreeing with; capable of harmonious union. **-compatible** *adv.* **compatibility** *n.*
**com•pa•tri•ot** *n.* one of the same country; a fellow countryman.
**com•pel** *v.t.* to force; to overpower; to bring about by force; *pr.p.* **-ling.** *pa.p.* and *pa.t.* **-led. -lable** *a.*
**com•pen•di•um** *n.* an abridgement or summary. Also **compend.** *pl.* **-s,** or **compendia. compendious** *a.* abridged. **compendiously** *adv.*
**com•pen•sate** *v.t.* to recompense suitably; to pay; *v.i.* to make up for. **compensation** *n.* recompense; payment for some loss, injury, etc. **compensative, compensatory** *a.*
**com•pete** *v.i.* to strive against others to win something; to vie with. **competition** *n.* the act of competing; a contest. **competitive** *a.* **competitively** *adv.* **competitor** *n.* one who competes. **competitory** *a.*
**com•pe•tent** *a.* able; properly qualified; skillful. **-ly** *adv.* **competence, competency** *n.* the state of being capable.
**com•pile** *v.t.* to put together literary materials into one book or works; to collect or amass. **-r** *n.* **compilation** *n.*
**com•pla•cent** *a.* self-satisfied; gratified. **-ly** *adv.* **complacence, complacency** *n.* self-satisfaction.
**com•plain** *v.i.* to express distress, dissatisfaction; to grumble; to be ailing. **-ant** *n.* a complainer; one who beings an action against another. **complaint** *n.* the expression of distress, dissatisfaction, etc.; a malady or airment.
**com•ple•ment** *n.* that which supplies a deficiency; something completing a whole; the full number; *v.t.* to supply a deficiency. **-al, -ary** *a.* completing.
**com•plete** *a.* entire; finished; perfect, with no part lacking; *v.t.* to bring to a state of entirety; to accomplish. **-ly** *adv.* **-ness** *n.* **completion** *n.* the act of completing; conclusion.
**com•plex** *a.* consisting of two or more parts; not simple; *n.* a complicated whole; *(Psych.)* a group of repressed emotional ideas responsible for abnormal mental condition. **-ly** *adv.* **-ness, -ity** *n.*
**com•plex•ion** *n.* color of the skin, esp. of the face; appearance.
**com•pli•ance** *n.* submission; a yielding; acquiescence. **compliant** *a.* yielding; obedient; civil. **compliantly** *adv.* **compliable** *a.* inclined to comply.
**com•pli•cate** *v.t.* to twist together; to make intricate. **-d** *a.* involved. **complication** *n.*
**com•plic•i•ty** *n.* the state of being an accomplice, of having a share in the guilt.
**com•pli•ment** *n.* an expression of admiration; flattering speech; *v.t.* to congratulate; to express respect for. **-ary** *a.* expressing praise, admiration; free, a *complimentary* ticket.
**com•ply** *v.i.* to yield to; to consent; to adapt oneself to. **complier** *n.*
**com•po•nent** *a.* making up; helping to form a compound; *n.* a part helping to make a whole.
**com•pose** *v.t.* to form by uniting parts; to arrange; to calm; *v.i.* to practice composition. **-d** *a.* sedate; calm. **-dly** *adv.* **-dness** *n.* **-r** *n.* one who composes; an author. **composite** *a.* made up of distinct parts or elements. **composition** *n.* literary, musical, work; the organization of the parts of a work of art. **compositor** *n.* a typesetter. **composure** *n.* calmness.
**com•post** *n.* a fertilizing mixture.
**com•pote** *n.* fruit stewed or preserved in syrup.
**com•pound** *v.t.* to put together, as elements or parts, to form a whole.
**com•pound** *a.* composed of elements, ingredients, or parts; not simple; *n.* a mixture; a word, made up of parts; *(Chem.)* a substance composed of two or more elements, which are always present in the same fixed proportions. **— fracture,** a fracture of a bone where a portion pierces the skin, making a surface wound. **— interest,** interest paid on capital plus accumulated interest.
**com•pre•hend** *v.t.* to understand; to grasp with the mind; to take in; to comprise. **comprehensible** *a.* understandable; conceivable. **comprehensibly** *adv.* **comprehensibility, comprehensibleness** *n.* **comprehension** *n.* the capacity of the mind to perceive and understand. **comprehensive** *a.* including much within narrow limits; extensive; inclusive.
**com•press** *v.t.* to press together; to condense. **-ed** *a.* **-ible** *a.* **-ibility** *n.* **-ion** *n.* the act or effect of compressing. **-ive** *a.* tending to compress. **-or** *n.*
**com•press** *n.* *(Med.)* a pad to make pressure on a wound.
**com•prise** *v.t.* to be composed of; to consist of.
**com•pro•mise** *n.* a settling of matters by mutual adjustment, each side making some concessions; *v.t.* and *i.* to settle by making mutual concessions.

**comp•tom•e•ter** *n.* a calculating machine.
**comp•trol•ler** *n.* a form of controller.
**com•pul•sion** *n.* the act of compelling; force; violence; *(Psych.)* an irresistible impulse. **compulsive** *a.* exercising compulsion. **compulsory** *a.* compelling; obligatory.
**com•punc•tion** *n.* remorse of conscience; scruple. **compuctious** *a.* conscience-stricken; remorseful.
**com•pute** *v.t.* to calculate; to estimate. **computable** *a.* computation *n.* calculation; reckoning.
**com•rade** *n.* a close friend or companion; an associate. **-ship** *n.* close friendship; **con** *v.t.* affectionate association.
**con** *adv.* against, e.g. in the phrase **pro and con,** for and against. **the pro and con** *n.* Also *pl.* **the pros and cons,** the advantages and disadvantages.
**con•cat•e•nate** *v.i.* to unite in a series. **concatenation** to unite in a series. **concatenation** *n.* a series of things depending on each other.
**con•cave** *a.* hollow and curved inwards. **concavity** *n.* hollowness.

concave

**con•ceal** *v.t.* to hide or secrete; to disguise; to withhold from knowledge. **-ment** *n.*
**con•cede** *v.t.* to admit to be true; to surrender; *v.i.* to admit.
**con•ceit** *n.* over-estimation of self-vanity; fanciful thought. **-ed** *a.* vain. **-edly** *adv.*
**con•ceive** *v.t.* to form an idea in the mind; to imagine; *v.i.* to become pregnant; to have a notion. **conceivable** *a.* that may be believed, imagined, or understood. **conceivably** *adv.*
**con•cen•trate** *v.i.* to reduce to small space; to increase in strength; *v.i.* to come together; to devote all attention. **concentration** *n.* the act of concentrating; the fixation of the mind on something. **concentration camp,** a place of detention.
**con•cept** *n.* an abstract notion; a mental impression of an object. **conception** *n.* a mental picture; an idea; *(Med.)* the beginning of pregnancy. **conceptive** *a.* capable of conceiving. **conceptual** *a.* pert. to conception or to a concept.
**con•cern** *v.t.* to relate or belong to; to be of importance to; to make uneasy; *n.* that which relates or belongs to one; interest in, or care for, any person or thing; a business establishment. **-ed** *a.* interested; troubled; involved. **-ing** *prep.* regarding; with respect to. **-ment** *n.*
**con•cert** *v.t.* to plan together; to design. **-ed** *a.* mutually planned; (Mus.) arranged in parts. *n.* harmony; a musical entertainment. **concerto** *n.* a musical composition arranged for a solo instrument with orchestral accompaniment.
**con•ces•sion** *n.* the act of conceding; a special privilege; an admission. **-aire** *n.* one who holds a concession. **-ary** *a.*
**conch** *n.* a seashell.
**con•chol•o•gy** *n.* the scientific study of shells and shellfish. **conchologist** *n.*
**con•cil•i•ate** *v.t.* to win over to goodwill; to pacify. **conciliation** *n.* **conciliative** *a.* conciliatory. **conciliatory** *a.* tending to pacify.
**con•cise** *a.* condensed; comprehensive. **-ly** *adv.* in few words; tersely. **-ness** *n.*
**con•clave** any secret meeting.
**con•clude** *v.t.* to bring to an end; to make a final judgment of; *v.i.* to come to an end.
**con•clu•sion** *n.* the last part of anything; the final judgment; inference; result from experiment. **conclusive** *a.* final; convincing.
**con•coct** *v.t.* to make a mixture; to make up, esp. a story. **concoction** *n.*
**con•com•i•tant** *a.* accompanying; attending; *n.* an accompanying circumstance. **concomitance, concomitancy** *n.* the state of being concomitant; coexistence.
**con•cord** *n.* agreement; union between persons, as in opinions, etc.; consonance; *v.i.* to agree. **concordance** *n.* agreement; **concordant** *a.* harmonious.
**con•cor•dat** *n.* a pact; a treaty.
**con•course** *n.* a gathering together; a promenade in a park; a large space in a railroad station.
**con•crete** *a.* solid; not abstract; specific; *n.* a mixture of sand, cement, etc., used in building; anything specific; *v.t.* to form into a solid mass; *v.i.* to harden. **-ly** *adv.* **-ness** *n.* **concretion** *n.* the state of being concrete; a mass formed of parts pressed together.
**con•cu•pis•cence** *n.* violent sexual desire; lust. **concupiscent, concupiscible** *a.* lustful.
**con•cur** *v.i.* to agree; to express agreement; to coincide. *pr.p.* **-ring** *pa.p.* and *pa.t.* **-red.** **-rence** *n.* **-rent** *a.* acting in conjunction; agreeing; taking place at the same time; accompanying; *n.* a joint or contributory cause. **-rently** *adv.*
**con•cus•sion** *n.* act of shaking by sudden striking; shock; *(Med.)* a violent disturbance of the brain caused by a blow or fall.
**con•demn** *v.t.* to blame; to pronounce guilty; to sentence; to declare unfit for use. **-ation** *n.* **-atory** *a.*
**con•dense** *v.t.* to make more solid; to change a vapor or gas into liquid or solid; to pack into few words; *v.i.* to become more compact; to pass from vapor to liquid or solid. **condensation** *n.* the state of being condensed; conciseness. **-d** *a.* compressed; (of milk) evaporated and preserved in cans. **-r** *n.* one who, or that which, condenses; an apparatus for changing vapor or gas into liquid or solid.
**con•de•scend** *v.i.* to come down from one's position, rank, or dignity; to stoop; to deign; to be gracious or affable to inferiors; to patronize. **-ing** *a.* **condescension** *n.*
**con•di•ment** *n.* a relish; seasoning for food.
**con•di•tion** *n.* a thing on which a statement, happening, depends; state or circumstances of anything; a

prerequisite; *v.t.* to impose conditions on; to render fit and in good health; *v.i.* to make terms. **-al** *a.* not absolute. **-ally** *adv.* **-ed** *a.* **conditioned reflex,** in psychology, an automatic response.

**con•dole** *v.i.* to grieve with; to offer sympathy. **condolence, -ment** *n.* an expression of sympathy.

**con•done** *v.t.* to pardon; to overlook.

**con•duce** *v.i.* to lead to some result; to promote. **conducive** *a.* having a tendency to promote or forward. **conduciveness** *n.*

**con•duct** *n.* the act of guiding; behavior. **conduct** *v.t.* to lead; to manage; to behave. **-ance** *n.* *(Elect.)* the property of a body for conducting electricity. **conductible** *a.* **conduction** *n.* the transmission of heat from one body to another. **conductive** *a.* able to transmit heat, electricity, etc. **conductivity** *n.* the quality of being conductive. **conductor** *n.* the leader of a choir or orchestra; one in charge of a bus, train, who collects fares; a substance capable of transmitting heat, electricity, etc.

**cone** *n.* a solid body tapering to a point from a circular base; the fruit of the pine,

cone

fir, etc. **conic, conical** *a.* having the form of a cone. **conically** *adv.*

**con•el•rad** *n.* a system used by radio in time of war to prevent the enemy from locating cities by radio beams.

**con•fec•tion** *n.* the act of compounding different substances into one compound; candy, ice cream, etc. **-ary** *a.* **-er** *n.* one who makes or sells confections. **-er's sugar** *n.* finely powdered sugar. **-ery** *n.* a finely powdered sugar. **-ery** *n.* a shop where these are sold.

**con•fed•er•ate** *a.* bound by treaty; allied; *n.* an accomplice; *v.t.* and *i.* to unite in a league. **confederacy** *n.* an alliance. **confederation** *n.* the act of forming a confederacy; an alliance.

**con•fer** *v.t.* to bestow upon; *v.i.* to consult together; to take advice. *pr.p.* **-ring.** *pa.p.* and *pa.t.* **-red.** **-ee** *n.* recipient of an award. **conference** *n.* a meeting; a consultation.

**con•fess** *v.t.* to admit; to declare one's sins; to plead guilty. **-edly** *adv.* admittedly. **confession** *n.* avowal of sins; declaring one's sins to priest. **confessional** *n.* the stall where a priest sits to hear confessions; *a.* pert. to confession. **-or** *n.* a priest who hears confessions.

**con•fet•ti** *n.pl.* small bits of paper, for throwing at weddings.

**con•fide** *v.t.* to entrust to; to tell a secret to; *v.i.* to put faith in. **confidant** *n.* a person in whom one can confide.

**con•fi•dence** *n.* that in which faith is put; trust; feeling of security. **confident** *a.* having assurance; bold. **confidently** *adv.* **confidential** *a.* treated with confidence; secret. **confidentially** *adv.*

**con•fig•u•ra•tion** *n.* outward form, or figure; outline; aspect.

**con•fine** *v.t.* to keep within bounds; to imprison; *v.i.* to have a common boundary; **confine** *n.* usually in *pl.* **confines,** boundary; limit. **-ment** *n.* imprisonment; restraint.

**con•firm** *v.t.* to settle; to make valid by formal assent; to verify. **confirmation** *n.* the act of making valid, certain, etc. **-ative** *a.* **-atory** *a.* **-ed** *a.*

**con•fis•cate** *v.t.* to seize by authority; to take possession of without compensation; *a.* forfeited. **confiscation** *n.* **confiscator** *n.* **confiscatory** *a.*

**con•flict** *v.i.* to clash; to be at odds with; to differ. **conflict** *n.* prolonged struggle; strong disagreement. **-ing** *a.* differing; contradictory.

**con•flu•ence** *n.* a flowing together; a large assemblage. **confluent** *a.* Also **conflux.**

**con•form** *v.t.* to make like; to bring into agreement; *v.i.* to comply; *a.* in accord. **-able** *a.* corresponding in form; submissive. **-ably** *adv.* **-ation** *n.* the manner in which a body is shaped; structure. **-ist** *n.* one who complies with custom. **-ity** *n.*

**con•found** *v.t.* to bring to confusion; to bewilder. **-ed** *a.* confused; baffled.

**con•front** *v.t.* to face boldly; to bring face to face. **confrontation** *n.*

**Con•fu•cius** *n.* Chinese philosopher.

**con•fuse** *v.t.* to mix up; to mistake one thing for another. **-d** *a.* mixed up; perplexed. **confusedly** *adv.* **confusion** *n.* the state of being confused; disorder; bewilderment.

**con•fute** *v.t.* to prove to be wrong. **confutable** *a.* **confutation** *n.*

**con•geal** *v.t.* and *i.* to freeze, as a fluid; to solidify; to coagulate; *v.i.* to become stiff or solidified, from cold. **-able** *a.* **-ment** *n.* a thing congealed; a clot. **congelation** *n.*

**con•gen•ial** *a.* allied in disposition and tastes; agreeable. **-ly** *adv.* **congeniality** *n.*

**con•gen•i•tal** *a.* existing at the time of birth.

**con•gest** *v.t.* to produce a hampering accumulation; to overcrowd. **-ed** *a.* overcrowded. **congestion** *n.*

**con•glom•er•ate** *a.* gathered into a mass; *v.t.* to bring together into a mass; *n.* *(Geol.)* rock composed of fragments of rock cemented together. **conglomeration** *n.* a mixed collection.

**con•grat•u•late** *v.t.* to wish joy to; to felicitate. **congratulation** *n.* felicitation. **congratulatory** *a.*

**con•gre•gate** *v.t.* to gather into a crowd or assembly; *v.i.* to meet together; *a.* collective. **congregation** *n.* an assemblage; a gathering of persons for worship. **congregational** *a.*

**con•gress** *n.* a formal assembly, e.g. of representatives of governments. **Congress** *n.* the legislative body of the United States. **-man** *n.* a member of the U.S. House of Representatives. **congressional** *a.*

**con•gru•ent** *a.* agreeing together;

corresponding. **congruence, congruency** *n.* suitableness. **congruity** *n.* **congruous** *a.*

**con•ic** See cone.

**co•nif•e•rae** *n.pl.* an order of trees bearing a cone-shaped fruit. **coniferous** *a.*

**con•jec•ture** *n.* opinion founded on insufficient proof; *v.t.* to guess; to infer on insufficient grounds. **conjecturable** *a.* **conjectural** *a.*

**con•join** *v.t.* to join together; *a.* united; associated.

**con•ju•gal** *a.* pert. to marriage; matrimonial. **-ly** *adv.* **conjugality** *n.* the married state.

**con•ju•gate** *v.t.* *(Gram.)* to write all the different parts of a verb. **conjugation** *n.* a class of verbs inflected in the same manner; *(Biol.)* the fusion of cells for reproduction.

**con•junct** *a.* joined together. **-ly** *adv.* **conjunction** *n.* union; *(Gram.)* a word used to join clauses, etc. **conjunctive** *a.* serving to connect.

**con•junc•ti•vi•tis** *n.* inflammation of the mucous membrane lining the eyelid.

**con•jure** *v.t.* solemnly to implore. **conjure** *v.i.* to practice magic; to imagine. **conjuration** *n.* the act of calling upon by a sacred name. **conjurer, conjuror** *n.* a magician.

**con•nect** *v.t.* to fasten together; to relate; to attach; *v.i.* to unite; to have a close relation. **-ed** *a.* joined; **-edly** *adv.* **connection** *n.* a link; state of being united. **-ive** *a.* binding; *n.* a connecting word. **-or** *n.*

**con•nive** *v.i.* to pretend not to see; to co-operate secretly (with 'at'). **connivance** *n.* consent in wrong-doing. **-r** *n.*

**con•note** *v.t.* to have a meaning in addition to the primary meaning. **connotate** *v.t.* to connote. **connotation** *n.* a secondary implied meaning. **connotative** *a.*

**con•nu•bi•al** *a.* pert. to marriage. **connubiality** *n.*

**con•quer** *v.t.* to overcome; to subjugate or subdue; *v.i.* to be victorious; to prevail. **-able** *a.* **-or** *n.* **conquest** *n.* the act of conquering; that which is conquered.

**con•science** *n.* the faculty by which we know right from wrong. **conscientious** *a.* governed by dictates of conscience. **conscientiously** *adv.* **conscientiousness** *n.* **conscionable** *a.* governed by conscience. **—stricken** *a.* seized with scruples. **conscientious objector,** a man who refuses to serve in the armed forces, on moral or religious grounds.

**con•scious** *a.* having inward knowledge (of); having the use of one's faculties. **-ly** *adv.* **-ness** *n.* the state of being mentally awake to one's surroundings.

**con•script** *v.t.* to enroll compulsorily for service in the armed forces. **conscript** *n.* one compelled to serve as a soldier. **conscription** *n.*

**con•se•crate** *v.t.* to set apart for sacred uses; to dedicate. **consecration** *n.*

**con•sec•u•tive** *a.* following one another in unbroken order; successive. **-ly** *adv.* **-ness** *n.*

**con•sen•sus** *n.* a general agreement.

**con•sent** *n.* agreement; permission; *v.i.* to agree. **consentient** *a.* united in opinion. **consentience.** *n.*

**con•se•quent** *a.* following as a result; *n.* effect. **-ly** *adv.* therefore; as a result; by logical sequence. **consequence** *n.* that which naturally follows; result; importance; value. **consequential** *a.*

**con•serve** *v.t.* to keep safe; to preserve; *n.* anything conserved. **conservation** *n.* preservation; safe-guarding; the official safe-guarding of forests, rivers, etc.; the area so protected. **conservative** *a.* tending to conserve; hostile to change; *n.* one opposed to hasty innovations. **conservatory** *n.* a greenhouse for plants; a school of music.

**con•sid•er** *v.t.* to reflect upon carefully; to be of opinion; *v.i.* to deliberate seriously. **-able** *a.* worthy of attention; moderately large. **-ably** *adv.* **-ate** *a.* thoughtful for others. **-ately** *adv.* **-ateness** *n.* **-ation** *n.* deliberation; fee or recompense; thoughtful regard for others. **-ed** *a.* carefully thought out. **-ing** *prep.* in view of.

**con•sign** *v.t.* to entrust to a carrier for transport; *v.i.* to agree. **consignee** *n.* the person to whom goods are consigned. **-er, -or** *n.* the person who consigns goods. **-ment** *n.*

**con•sist** *v.i.* to be composed of; to be compatible with. **-ence, -ency** *n.* a condition of being fixed; a degree of firmness or density; harmony. **consistent** *a.* compatible; constant in adhering to principles, etc.

**con•sole** *v.t.* to comfort in distress. **consolable** *a.* able to be consoled. **consolation** *n.* the act of comforting; solace; encouragement. **consolatory** *a.*

**con•sol•i•date** *v.t.* and *i.* to make solid; to make firm; to strengthen. **consolidation** *n.* the act of making or becoming compact and firm.

**con•so•nant** *a.* agreeing with; *n.* a non-vowel. **-ly** *adv.* **consonance, consonancy** *n.* agreement; harmony.

**con•sort** *n.* a companion. **consort** *v.t.* to join; *v.i.* to keep company; to associate.

**con•sor•ti•um** *n.* an association for a common end.

**con•spec•tus** *n.* a general outline of a subject; a synopsis.

**con•spic•u•ous** *a.* very noticeable. **-ly** *adv.* **-ness, conspicuity** *n.*

**con•spire** *v.i.* to plot together. **conspiracy** *n.* a combination of persons for an evil purpose; a plot. **conspirator** *n.* **conspiratorial** *a.*

**con•sta•ble** *n.* a peace officer.

**con•stant** *a.* fixed; invariable; *n.* that which is not subject to change. **-ly** *adv.* **constancy** *n.* steadfastness; fidelity.

**con•stel•la•tion** *n.* a group of fixed stars.

**con•ster•na•tion** *n.* amazement or terror that throws the mind into confusion. **consternate** *v.t.* to fill with alarm.

**con•sti•pate** *v.t.* to clog or make sluggish. **constipation** *n.* insufficient; irregular evacuation of the bowels.

**con•sti•tute** *v.t.* to establish; to set up; to

compose. **constitution** *n.* the natural state of body or mind; the system of laws under which a state exists. **constitutional** *a.* pert. to the constitution; *n.* a walk for the benefit of health. **constitutionally** *adv.* **constitutionalist** *n.* one who upholds constitutional government. **constitutionality** *n.* **constitutive** *a.* having powers to enact or establish. **constituent** *a.* serving to compose or make up.

**con•strain** *v.t.* to force or compel; to restrain; to limit. **-t** *n.* compelling force; unnaturalness or embarrassment of manner.

**con•strict** *v.t.* to cause to shrink or contract; to squeeze. **constriction** *n.* **-ive** *a.* that which constricts; the boa-constrictor.

**con•struct** *v.t.* to fabricate; to compile. **construction** *n.* erection; structure; interpretation or meaning. **-ive** *a.* **-iveness** *n.* **-or** *n.*

**con•strue** *v.t.* to interpret; to deduce; to translate. **construable** *a.* **-r** *n.*

**con•sub•stan•ti•ate** *v.t.* and *i.* to unite in one substance or nature. **consubstantial** *a.* **consubstantiation** *n.*

**con•sul** *n.* an officer appointed by a government to represent it in a foreign country. **-ar** *a.* **-ate** *n.* the offices of a consul. **-ship** *n.*

**con•sult** *v.t.* to ask advice of; to seek the opinion of; *v.i.* to confer. **-ant** *n.* one who gives expert advice. **-ing** *a.* **-ation** *n.* a council or conference. **-ative** *a.* advisory.

**con•sume** *v.t.* to use up; to eat or drink up; *v.i.* to waste away. **consumable** *a.* **-r** *n.*

**con•sum•mate** *v.t.* to complete; to perfect; *(Law)* to complete marriage by sexual intercourse. **consummate** *a.* complete. **-ly** *adv.* **consummation** *n.*

**con•sump•tion** *n.* the act of consuming; the amount consumed; pulmonary tuberculosis. **consumptive** *a.* wasteful; affected with, or inclined to, pulmonary tuberculosis; *n.*

**con•tact** *n.* a touching; a meeting; *v.t.* to get in touch with a person. **-ual** *a.* implying contact. **— lens,** an invisible eye-glass fitting over the eyeball.

**con•ta•gion** *n.* the transmission of a disease from one person to another. **contagious** *a.* communicable.

**con•tain** *v.t.* to hold; to comprise. **-able** *a.* **-er** *n.*

**con•tam•i•nate** *v.t.* to taint; to infect. **contaminable** *a.* **contamination** *n.* pollution; *(War)* the result of coming into contact with radioactive particles.

**con•tem•plate** *v.t.* to look at with attention; to meditate on; *v.i.* to reflect. **contemplation** *n.* **contemplative** *a.* **contemplatively** *adv.*

**con•tem•po•ra•ne•ous** *a.* happening at the same time. **-ly** *adv.* **-ness** *n.* **contemporary** *a.* living at the same time; present-day; *n.* a person approximately of one's own age.

**con•tempt** *n.* scorn; disregard; open disrespect to court orders. **-ible** *a.* despicable. **-ibleness** *n.* **-ibly** *adv.* **-uous** *a.* expressing disdain; scornful. **-uously** *adv.* **-uousness** *n.*

**con•tend** *v.i.* to struggle with; to assert strongly; **-er** *n.*

**con•tent** *a.* satisfied; *v.t.* to satisfy the mind of; *n.* freedom from anxiety. **-edly** *adv.* **-edness** *n.* **-ment** *n.* satisfaction; ease of mind.

**con•tent** *n.* that which is contained; volume. **-s** *n.pl.* an index of the topics treated in a book.

**con•ten•tion** *n.* strife; subject matter of discussion. **contentious** *a.* quarrelsome.

**con•test** *v.t.* to question or resist, as a claim; to dispute; *v.i.* to contend or vie (with). **contest** *n.* conflict; dispute; strike. **-able** *a.* **-ant** *n.* a competitor.

**con•text** *n.* that which comes immediately before or after a passage and helps to explain it. **-ual** *a.* pert. to the context. **contexture** *n.* the weaving of parts into one body; structure; style of composition in writing.

**con•ti•gu•i•ty** *n.* the state of being contiguous. **contiguous** *a.* touching; adjacent.

**con•ti•nent** *n.* one of the large divisions of unbroken land. **-al** *a.* pert. to a continent.

**con•ti•nent** *a.* temperate; moderate. **continence, continency** *n.*

**con•tin•gent** *a.* possible; dependent; *n.* quota, esp. of troops. **-ly** *adv.* **contingence, contingency** *n.*

**con•tin•ue** *v.t.* to prolong or extend in duration; to resume; *v.i.* to remain in a state or place; to last. **continual** *a.* without interruption; unceasing. **continually** *adv.* **continuance** *n.* a remaining in existence; uninterrupted succession. **continuant** *a.* **continuate** *a.* uninterrupted. **continuation** *n.* the act of continuing. **continuity** *n.* uninterrupted succession; close union. **continuous** *a.* united without break; constant. **continuously** *adv.*

**con•tort** *v.t.* to twist violently; to bend out of shape. **contortion** *n.* writhing. **contortionist** *n.* one who practices contortion. **contortive** *a.*

**con•tour** *n.* outline; *v.t.* to draw the contour of.

**con•tra•band** *a.* prohibited by law or treaty; *n.* goods, the exportation or importation of which is forbidden.

**con•tra•cep•tion** *n.* birth control. **contraceptive** *a.* and *n.* a drug or appliance for preventing conception.

**con•tract** *v.t.* to draw together; to reduce to a less volume; *v.i.* to become smaller; to become involved in. **contract** *n.* an agreement. **-ed** *a.* drawn together; narrow. **-ible** *a.* **-ile** *a.* tending to contract; producing contraction. **-ility** *n.* **-ion** *n.* shortening of a word by the omission of a letter. **-or** *n.* one who undertakes to work for a fixed sum. **-ual** *a.* implying, or connected with, a contract.

**con•tra•dict** *v.t.* to deny. **contradiction** *n.* denial; discrepancy of statements. **contradictious** *a.* inclined to contradict. **-ive** *a.* containing contradiction. **-ory** *a.* diametrically opposed; inconsistent.

**con•tra•dis•tinc•tion** *n.* direct contrast.

**contradistinctive** *a.* **contradistinguish** *v.t.* to note the difference between two things by contrasting their different qualities.

**con•tral•to** *n.* the lowest of the three female voices.

**con•tra•ry** *a.* opposed; opposing; different; adverse; self-willed; *n.* something the exact opposite of. **contrariety** *n.* something contrary. **contrarily** *adv.* **contrariness** *n.* **contrariwise** *adv.* on the contrary.

**con•trast** *v.t.* to set in opposition for the purpose of comparing; *v.i.* to stand in opposition. *n.* a striking difference; a comparison to show their relative excellence.

**con•tra•vene** *v.t.* to break or infringe, as a law. **contravention** *n.*

**con•tri•bute** *v.t.* to give to a common fund; to help to a common result; *v.i.* to lend assistance. **contributable** *a.* **contribution** *n.* that which is contributed. **contributive** *a.* **contributory** *a.*

**con•trite** *a.* remorseful. **-ly** *adv.* **-ness** *n.* **contrition** *n.* remorse.

**con•trive** *v.t.* and *i.* to plan; to bring about; to invent. **contrivance** *n.* the act of planning; mechanical invention. **-r** *n.*

**con•trol** *v.t.* to have under command; to regulate; to restrain; *n.* authority or power. *pr.p.* **-ling.** *pa.p.* and *pa.t.* **-led.** **-lable** *a.* **-ler** *n.* one who controls. **-lership** *n.* **-ment** *n.*

**con•tro•vert** *v.t.* to dispute by argument; to refute. **-ible** *adv.* **controversy** *n.* disputation; debate. **controversial** *a.* leading to controversy; likely to provoke argument. **controversially** *adv.* **controversialist** *n.*

**con•tu•ma•cy** *n.* contempt of authority; stubborn disobedience. **contumacious** *a.* rebellious. **-ly** *adv.* **-ness** *n.*

**con•tu•me•ly** *n.* insult; disdainful insolence. **contumelious** *a.* haughtily disdainful.

**con•tuse** *v.t.* to injure without breaking the skin. **contusion** *n.* a bruise.

**con•va•lesce** *v.i.* to recover from illness. **convalescent** *a.* **convalescence** *n.*

**con•vec•tion** *n.* the process of transmission of heat by means of currents in liquids or gases.

**con•vene** *v.t.* to call together; *v.i.* to assemble. **-r** *n.* **convenable** *a.*

**con•ven•ient** *a.* suitable; handy or easy of access. **-ly** *adv.* **convenience** *n.* that which is convenient; any appliance which makes for comfort.

**con•vent** *n.* a community devoted to a religious life; a nunnery. **conventual** *a.*

**con•ven•tion** *n.* a formal assembly of representatives; accepted usage, custom, or rule. **-al** *a.* formed by agreement or compact; customary. **-ally** *adv.* **-alism** *n.* that which is established by usage. **-ality** *n.*

**con•verge** *v.i.* to tend to one point; to approach. **convergent** *a.* **convergence, convergency** *n.* coming together.

**con•verse** *v.i.* to talk with. **conversable** *a.* affable. **conversably** *adv.* **conversance, conversancy** *n.* the state of being acquainted with. **conversant** *a.* acquainted with by use. **conversation** *n.* talk. **conversational** *a.* **conversation(al)ist** *n.* one who excels in conversation.

**con•verse** *a.* opposite; turned around; *n.* the contrary. **-ly** *adv.*

**con•vert** *v.t.* to apply to another purpose; to cause to adopt a religion, an opinion, etc.; *v.i.* to be changed. **convert** *n.* **conversion** *n.* a change from one state to another. **-er** *n.* one who converts; *(Elect.)* a machine for changing alternating current into direct current, or altering the pressure of direct current. **-ible** *a.* capable of change; *n.* an automobile with a folding top.

**con•vex** *a.* curving outwards; bulging. **-ity, -ness** *n.*

convex

**con•vey** *v.t.* to transport; to communicate. **-able** *a.* **-ance** *n.* the act of conveying; the transference of property. **-ancing** *n.* **-er, -or** *n.*

**con•vict** *v.t.* to prove guilty; *n.* a person serving a sentence. **-ion** *n.* a verdict of guilty; a firm belief.

**con•vince** *v.t.* to persuade by argument; to satisfy by proof. **convincible** *a.* **convincing** *a.* **convincingly** *adv.*

**con•viv•i•al** *a.* jovial; merry. **-ly** *adv.* **conviviality** *n.*

**con•voke** *v.t.* to call together. **convocation** *n.* the act of calling together; an assembly.

**con•volve** *v.t.* and *i.* to wind together; to coil. **convolute, convoluted** *a.* rolled together; spiral. **convolution** *n.* the act of rolling together; a turn of a coil.

**con•voy** *v.t.* to escort for protection, by land, sea, or air. **convoy** *n.* escorting protection.

**con•vulse** *v.t.* to affect with violent and irregular spasms. **convulsion** *n.* any violent agitation; *pl. (Med.)* violent and involuntary contractions of the muscles. **convulsive** *a.* spasmodic.

**coo** *v.i.* to make a low, melodius sound like the note of a dove.

**cook** *v.t.* to prepare food by boiling, roasting, baking, etc.; *v.i.* to prepare food by the action of heat; *n.* one whose occupation is to cook food. **-ery** *n.* the process of cooking. **-er** *n.* **-out** *n.* meal cooked and eaten outdoors.

**cook•y, cook•ie** *n.* a small sweet cake made of stiff dough which is rolled, dropped, or sliced, and baked.

**cool** *a.* slightly cold; self-possessed; impudent; *n.* a moderate state of cold; *v.t.* to cause to cool; to calm; *v.i.* to become cool; to lose one's affection. **-er** *n.* a container for cooling. **-ish** *a.* fairly cool. **-ly** *adv.* **-ness** *n.* **—headed** *a.* calm; self-possessed.

**coop** *n.* pen for poultry; *v.t.* confine.

**co•op•er•ate** *v.i.* to act jointly with another;

to unite for a common effort. **co-operation** *n.* **co-operative** *a.* **co-operator** *n.* **co-operative store,** the shop of a co-operative society, where members make their purchases and share the profits.

**co•opt** *v.t.* to choose or elect into a committee by the votes of its own members. **-ion, -ation** *n.*

**co•or•di•nate** *a.* equal in degree, rank, importance, etc.; *v.t.* to bring into order as parts of a whole; *n.* a person of the same rank, importance, etc. as another. **-ly** *adv.* in the same order. **-ness** *n.* **coordination** *n.* **coordinative** *a.*

**co•part•ner** *n.* an associate. **-ship** *n.*

**cope** *v.i.* to deal successfully (with).

**Co•per•ni•can** *a.* pert. to *Copernicus* the founder of modern astronomy.

**cop•i•er** *n.* See **copy.**

**co•pi•ous** *a.* abundant; plentiful. **-ly** *adv.* **-ness** *n.*

**cop•per** *n.* a red-colored metal; *a.* copper-colored; *v.t.* to cover with copper. **-y** *a.* like copper. **-head** *n.* a poisonous N. American snake.

**cop•u•la** *n.* a connecting link; *(Gram.)* the word uniting the subject and predicate. **copulate** *v.i.* to unite sexually. **copulation** *n.* **-tive** *a.* pert. to copulation.

**cop•y** *n.* an imitation of an original; a writing like another writing; an exact reproduction; the manuscript, placed in the compositor's hands; *v.t.* to write, print, etc. in imitation of an original; to imitate. **-ist** *n.* **copier** *n.* an imitator. **-book** *n.* a book in which copies are written for learners to imitate. **-writer** *n.* a writer of advertisements. **-right** *n.* the legal exclusive right which an author, musician, or artist has to print, publish, and sell his own works, during a certain period of time; *a.* protected by the law of copyright.

**cor•al** *n.* a hard reddish yellow, white, etc. substance growing on the bottom of

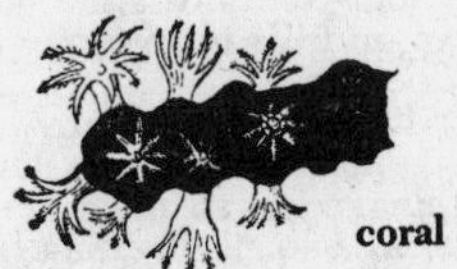

coral

tropical seas, and composed of the skeletons of zoophytes; *a.* coral-colored; made by coral.

**cord** *n.* a thick string or a thin rope of several strands; anything like a cord (e.g. spinal cord, vocal cord); a cubic measure esp. for fuel wood; *v.t.* to bind with a cord or rope. **-age** *n.* an assemblage of ropes and cords, esp. the rigging of a ship. **-ed** *a.* **-ing** *n.* ribbed surface.

**cor•dial** *a.* expressing warmth of heart; sincere; *n.* a refreshing drink or medicine. **-ly** *adv.* **-ity** *n.*

**cord•ite** *n.* a smokeless explosive.

**cor•du•roy** *n.* a thick cotton fabric, corded or ribbed on the surface. *n.pl.* trousers made of this fabric.

**core** *n.* the heart or inner part, esp. of fruit; *v.t.* to take out the core.

**co•res•pon•dent** *n.* in a divorce suit the man or woman charged along with the respondent as guilty of adultery.

**cork** *n.* a stopper for a bottle; *a.* made of cork; *v.t.* to stop up with a cork; **-screw** *n.* a tool for drawing corks from bottles; *a.* shaped like a corkscrew, with a spiral twist.

**corn** *n.* a single seed of oats, wheat, rye, barley, maize, etc.; an inclusive term for grain of all kinds; *v.t.* to preserve meat by salting. **-cob** *n.* the head in which are encased the grains of the maize plant. **-flour** *n.* a foodstuff consisting of the finely ground starch granules of Indian corn (maize). **-flower** *n.* an annual weed growing in cornfields and bearing blue flowers. **-husk** *n.* the outer leaves enclosing an ear of corn. **-starch** *n.* a starch used for thickening.

**corn** *n.* a horny growth of the skin, usually on toes and feet. **-y** *a.* pert. to a corn.

**cor•ne•a** *n.* the transparent membrane which forms part of the outer coat of the eyeball.

**cor•ner** *n.* the point where two lines meet; the part of a room where two sides meet; an embarrassing position; *v.t.* to put into a position of difficulty, leaving no escape. **-stone** *n.* a corner foundation stone laid with ceremony; something of fundamental importance; **-wise** *adv.* diagonally; with the corner in front. **to corner the market,** to obtain a monopoly.

**cor•net** *n.* a kind of trumpet with valves.

**cor•nice** *n.* an ornamental molding around the top of the walls of a room.

**cor•nu•co•pi•a** *n.* the horn of plenty, an emblem of abundance.

**cor•ol•lar•y** *n.* an inference from a preceding statement; a consequence.

**co•ro•na** *n.* the flat projecting part of a cornice; a crown; **-l** *a.* pert. to a corona;

corona

*n.* crown. **coronary** *a.* resembling a crown; pertaining to the arteries which supply the heart tissues. **coronary thrombosis** *(Med.)* a heart condition caused by a blood clot in a coronary artery. **coronate** *v.t.* to crown. **coronation** *n.* the crowning of a sovereign. **coronet** *n.* a small crown worn by nobility.

**cor•o•ner** *n.* a legal officer appointed to hold an inquest in cases of death.

**cor•po•ral** *n.* non-commissioned officer of a troop, next below a sergeant.

**cor•po•ral** *a.* belonging or relating to the body. *n.* the state of having a body. **corporate** *a.* united legally in a body; pertaining to a corporation. **corporately**

*adv.* **corporateness** *n.* **corporation** *n.* a legal, municipal, or professional association.

**corps** *n.* a division of an army forming a unit. *pl.* **corps.**

**corpse** *n.* a dead body, esp. of a human being.

**cor•pu•lence** *n.* excessive fatness; stoutness. Also **corpulency** *n.* **corpulent** *a.*

**cor•pus** *n.* the main substance of anything. *pl.* **corpora.**

**cor•pus•cle** *n.* a minute particle; *(Anat.)* an organic cell, either moving freely, as in

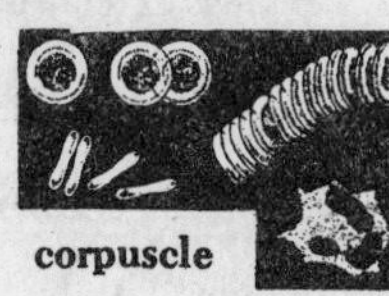
corpuscle

the blood, or intimately connected with others, as bone-corpuscles.

**cor•ral** *n.* an enclosure for cattle; *v.t.* to drive into a corral.

**cor•rect** *a.* free from faults; *v.t.* to indicate the errors in; to punish. **-ly** *adv.* **-tion** *n.* a change to remedy a fault; punishment. **-itude** *n.* **-ional** *a.* **-ive** *a.* having power to correct; *n.* that which counteracts. **-ness** *n.* **-or** *n.*

**cor•re•late** *v.i.* to be mutually related; *v.t.* to place in reciprocal relations; *n.* either of two things necessarily implying the other. **correlation** *n.* reciprocal relation. **correlative** *a.* reciprocally related; *n.* one who, or that which, is correspondingly related to another person or thing. **correlativity** *n.*

**cor•re•spond** *v.i.* to exchange letters; to agree with in some respect; to be congruous. **-ence** *n.* exchange of letters; the letters themselves; suitability. **-ent** *a.* suitable; congruous; *n.* one with whom intercourse is maintained by exchange of letters. **-ing** *a.* **-ingly** *adv.*

**cor•ri•dor** *n.* a passage in a building.

**cor•ri•gi•ble** *a.* capable of being corrected.

**cor•rob•o•rate** *v.t.* to add strength to; to support a statement. **corroborant** *a.* giving strength. **corroboration** *n.* **corroborative** *a.* confirming; strengthening.

**cor•rode** *v.t.* to eat away by degrees (by chemical action, disease, etc.); to rust. **corrodent** *a.* corrosive; *n.* a substance which eats away. **corrodible, corrosible** *a.* capable of being corroded. **corrosion** *n.* **corrosive** *a.* having the power of corroding; *n.* any corrosive sbstance.

**cor•ru•gate** *v.t.* to form into folds or alternate furrows and ridges. **corrugation** *n.* **—iron,** sheet-iron, corrugated to increase its rigidity.

**cor•rupt** *v.t.* and *i.* to make rotten; to make evil; to bribe; *a.* depraved; tainted with sin; influenced by bribery. **-er** *n.* **-ible** *a.* capable of being corrupted. **corruption** *n.* **-ive** *a.* **-ly** *adv.* **-ness** *n.*

**cor•sage** *n.* a small bouquet worn by a lady.

**cor•set** *n.* undergarment; girdle.

**cor•tex** *n.* bark; sheath of a plant. *(Anat.)* the outer covering of an organ, esp. the outer layer of gray matter of the brain; *pl.* **cortices. cortical** *a.* **corticate, corticated** *a.*

**cor•ti•sone** *n.* a substance produced in the adrenal glands.

**cor•us•cate** *v.i.* to flash; to glitter; to gleam. **coruscation** *n.*

**co•se•cant** *n.* *(Trig.)* the secant of the complement of an angle.

**co•sig•na•to•ry** *a.* signing jointly; *n.* a joint signer of a document.

**co•sine** *n.* *(Trig.)* the sine of the complement o an angle.

**cos•met•ic** *a.* making for beauty, esp. of the skin; *n.* any substance helping to enhance the appearance.

**cos•mic** *a.* See **cosmos.**

**cos•mog•o•ny** *n.* a theory of the creation of the universe and its inhabitants.

**cos•mol•o•gy** *n.* the science of the laws which control the universe. **cosmological** *a.* **cosmologist** *n.*

**cos•mo•naut** *n.* a space traveler.

**cos•mo•pol•i•tan** *a.* relating to all parts of the world; *n.* a citizen of the world. Also **cosmopolite** *n.*

**cos•mos** *n.* the ordered universe. **cosmic, cosmical** *a.* pert. to the universe, or to the earth as a part of the universe; orderly. **cosmically** *adv.* **cosmic rays,** radiations of great penetrating power, coming to the earth from outer space.

**cost** *v.i.* to entail the payment, loss, or sacrifice of; *n.* price; the amount paid, or to be paid, for anything; suffering undergone for any end. **-liness** *n.* great cost or expense; expensiveness. **-ly** *a.* very expensive. **— price,** the wholesale, as opposed to the retail, price.

**cos•tal** *a.* pert. to the ribs or to the side of the body.

**cos•tive** *a.* having sluggish motion; constipated. **-ness** *n.*

**cos•tume** *n.* dress peculiar or appropriate, as to country, period, office, or character; a person's dress or attire. **-r** *n.* one who makes or deals in costumes.

**co•sy** See **cozy.**

**cot** *n.* a light, portable bed.

**co•tan•gent** *n.* *(Trig.)* the tangent of the complement of an angle.

**cot•tage** *n.* a small dwelling house, esp. in the country or at a resort. **-r** *n.* one who inhabits a cottage. **— cheese** *n.* a soft, white cheese.

**cot•ter** *n.* a pin or wedge used for tightening or fastening.

**cot•ton** *n.* a soft, downy, substance; cloth or thread made of cotton; *a.* made of cotton;

cotton

— **gin** *n.* a machine for separating the seeds from cotton. **-mouth** *n.* the water moccasin. **-wood** *n.* a type of American poplar tree. **-y** *a.*

**couch** *v.t.* to cause to lie down, esp. on a bed; *v.i.* to lie down; to crouch; *n.* a sofa; davenport. **couchant** *a.* lying down.

**cou•gar** *n.* the puma or American panther.

cougar

**cough** *n.* noisy, violent, explosive effort to expel irritating matter from the lungs; *v.t.* to expel from the lungs by a cough.

**could** *p.at.* of the verb **can.**

**cou•lomb** *n.* the quantity transferred by a current of one ampere in one second.

**coun•cil** *n.* an assembly summoned for advice; a municipal body. **-man** *n.* **-lor** *n.*

**coun•sel** *n.* opinion; one who gives advice, esp. legal; *v.t.* admonish; recommend. **-or** *n.* an adviser; a trial lawyer. **-orship** *n.*

**count** *n.* (*fem.* **countess**) a title of nobility.

**count** *v.t.* to number; to sum up; to recite the numerals in regular succession; *v.i.* to depend or rely (with 'on'); *n.* the act of reckoning; *(Law)* a charge in an indictment. **-able** *a.* — **down** *n.* the last check before a missile is launched. **-less** *a.* innumerable. **-er** *n.* one who counts; a token used in reckoning; a table on which money is counted, goods displayed or business transacted.

**coun•te•nance** *n.* the face; aspect; support; *v.i.* to support; to approve. **to keep one's countenance,** to preserve one's composure.

**count•er** *a.* contrary; opposite; *adv.* in opposition; *n.* that which is opposite; a return blow or parry; *v.t.* and *i.* to parry; to make a counter-move. **-attack** *n.* an attack launched to stop and drive back an enemy attack. **-attraction** *n.* rival attraction. **-clockwise** *adv.* revolving in a direction opposite to the movement of the hands of a clock. **-espionage** *n.* spying directed against the enemy's system of espionage. **-tenor** *n.* a man's voice singing alto.

**coun•ter•act** *v.t.* to act in oppo[illegible].

**coun•ter•bal•ance** *v.t.* to act against with equal power or effect; *n.* a weight balancing another.

**coun•ter•charge** *n.* a charge brought in opposition to another.

**coun•ter•check** *v.t.* to check by an opposing check.

**coun•ter•feit** *v.t.* to copy without authority; to imitate with intent to deceive; *a.* forged; false; *n.* a forgery; an imposter. **-er** *n.*

**coun•ter•mand** *v.t.* to cancel an order; *n.* a contrary order.

**coun•ter•march** *v.i.* to march back; *n.* a marching back.

**coun•ter•mine** *n.* any scheme to frustrate the designs of an opponent.

**coun•ter•pane** *n.* a coverlet; a quilt.

**coun•ter•part** *n.* a duplicate; something complementary or correlative.

**coun•ter•point** *n.* *(Mus.)* the addition of a subsidiary melody to another so as to form a perfect melody.

**coun•ter•poise** *v.t.* to act against with equal weight or power; *n.* a weight sufficient to balance another.

**coun•ter•sign** *v.t.* to sign a document already signed by another; to attest authenticity; *n.* a password.

**coun•try** *n.* a region; the territory of a nation; land of birth, residence, etc.; rural districts as opposed to town; *a.* rural; rustic; pert. to territory distant from a city. **countrified** *a.* **countrify** *v.t.* to make rural. — **club** *n.* a club with grounds, a house, and facilities for outdoor sports. **-man** *n.* a rustic; a compatriot. **-side** *n.* any rural district.

**coun•ty** *n.* a division of a state for administrative purposes; the inhabitants of a county. — **seat,** the capital of a county.

**cou•ple** *n.* two things of the same kind taken together; a pair; husband and wife; *v.t.* to join together; *v.i.* to connect. **couplet** *n.* a pair of lines of verse. **coupling** *n.* a connection; that which

coupling

couples, esp. the device joining railroad cars.

**cou•pon** *n.* an interest certificate attached to a bond; a dividend warrant; a negotiable voucher.

**cour•age** *n.* fearlessness; daring. **courageous** *a.* full of courage. **courageously** *adv.* **courageousness** *n.*

**cour•i•er** *n.* a messenger; a tourist guide who accompanies travelers.

**course** *n.* the act of passing from one point to another; movement, both in space and in time; direction; the ground on which a race is run; each of the successive divisions of a meal; *v.t.* to chase; *v.i.* to run swiftly; to gallop. **-r** *n.* one who hunts.

**court** *n.* an uncovered area enclosed by buildings; a yard; a legal tribunal; the hall where justice is administered; *(Sport)* a space, usually rectangular, laid out for certain sports. **courteous** *a.* polite; well-bred. **courteously** *adv.* **courteousness** *n.* **courtier** one with the manners of a frequenter of courts. **-ly** *a.* elegant; with the manners of a courtier. **-liness** *n.* — **martial** *n.* a court of military officers for the trial of persons in the army or navy; *pl.* **-s-martial.**

**court** *v.t.* to try to gain the affections of; to seek in marriage; *v.i.* to woo; to play the lover. **-ship** *n.*

**cour•te•sy** *n.* politeness of manners; urbanity.

**cou•sin** *n.* formerly any kinsman; now, the son or daughter of an uncle or aunt.

**cove** *n.* a small bay.

**cov•e•nant** *n.* a mutual and solemn agreement; *v.t.* to agree to by covenant; *v.i.* to enter into an agreement. **-er** *n.* one who makes a covenant or agreement.

**cov•er** *v.t.* to be over the whole top of; to include; to point a revolver, gun, etc. at; to wager an equal sum of money; *n.* anything that covers; a lid; concealment; shelter. **-ing** *n.* **-let** *n.* a bedcover. **covert** *a.* covered over; concealed; veiled; *n.* a place sheltering game. **covertly** *adv.* secretly; in private. **coverture** *n.* shelter; defense.

**cov•et** *v.t.* to long to possess, esp. what belongs to another; to desire unlawfully; *v.i.* to have strong desire. **-able** *a.* that may be coveted. **-ous** *a.* very desirous; avaricious for gain. **-ously** *adv.* **-ousness** *n.*

**cow** *n.* the female of a bovine animal; **-ish** *a.* **-boy** *n.* on the western plains, a herdsman employed on a ranch to look after cattle. **-herd** *n.* one who herds cows. **-hide** *n.* leather made from the hide of a cow. **-lick** *n.* a tuft of hair not easily flattened.

**cow** *v.t.* to frighten into submission.

**cow•ard** *n.* one who lacks courage. **-ly** *a.* lacking in courage; afraid. **-ice** *n.* want of courage; fear.

**cow•er** *v.i.* to crouch down through fear, shame, cold.

**cowl** *n.* a hooded cloak; a hooded top for a chimney. **-ed** *a.*

**cox•swain, cox** *n.* the steersman of a boat. **to cox** *v.t.* and *i.* to act as coxswain.

**coy** *a.* shy; pretending to be shy. **-ly** *adv.* **-ness** *n.*

**coy•o•te** *n.* the Amer. prairie wolf.

**coz•en** *v.t.* to flatter in order to cheat; to defraud.

**co•zy** *a.* snug; comfortable; *n.* a covering to keep a teapot hot. Also **cosy, cozily** *adv.* **coziness** *n.*

**crab** *n.* an edible crustacean; a disagreeable person; *v.t.* to fish for crabs. *pr.p.* **-bing.** *pa.t.* **-bed. -biness** *n.* **-by** *a.* **— grass** *n.* rapid growing coarse grass.

**crack** *v.t.* to break with a sharp noise, either wholly or partially; to snap; *v.i.* to burst open in chinks; to give forth a sudden, sharp sound; *n.* a partial break; fissure; a break in the voice. **-ed** *a.* **-er** *n.* a thin crisp biscuit. **— up** *n.* a collision; a breakdown.

**crack•le** *v.i.* to produce slight but repeated cracking sounds; *n.* a noise composed of frequent, slight cracking sounds. **crackling** *n.* a succession of small sharp reports.

**cra•dle** *n.* a bed for infants that can be rocked; *v.t.* to place or rock in a cradle; to tend in infancy.

**craft** *n.* dexterity; a skilled trade; a vessel. **-y** *a.* cunning; artful. **-ily** *adv.* **-iness** *n.* **-sman** *n.* one engaged in a trade. **-smanship** *n.*

**crag** *n.* a steep, rugged rock or peak. **-ged** *a.* **-gy** *a.* full of crags; rugged. **-giness** *n.*

**cram** *v.t.* and *i.* to stuff; to pack tightly; *(Colloq.)* to prepare hastily for an examination. *pr.p.* **-ming.** *pa.t.* **-med.** *n.* *(Colloq.)* a crowd of people.

**cramp** *n.* a painful contraction of muscles of the body; that which restrains; *v.t.* to affect with cramp; to hamper; to hold with a cramp; *a.* narrow; cramped; restricted.

**cran•ber•ry** *n.* a red, sour, berry.

**crane** *n.* a tall wading bird with long legs, neck, and bill; a machine for lifting and

crane

lowering heavy weights; *v.t.* to stretch out the neck to look at something.

**cra•ni•um** *n.* the skull. *pl.* **crania. cranial** *a.* pert. to the skull. **craniology** *n.* the study of skulls. **craniological** *a.*

**crank** *n.* a handle attached to a shaft for turning it; the bent portion of an axis, used to change horizontal or vertical into rotatory motion, etc.; an eccentric or crotchety person; *v.t.* to shape like a crank; to operate by a crank; *v.i.* to turn the crank as in starting an automobile engine (usually with 'up'). **-case** *n.* the housing for a crankshaft. **-shaft** *n.* *(Mach.)* a shaft driven by a crank. **-y** *a.* shaky or in bad condition of machinery; bad-tempered. **-iness** *n.*

**cran•ny** *n.* an open crack; a crevice.

**crash** *n.* a violent fall accompanied by loud noise; a sudden collapse; *v.i.* to collapse; *v.t.* to break into pieces. **— helmet** *n.* a padded helmet worn by racing motorists.

**cra•sis** *n.* *(Gram.)* union of two vowels into one long vowel or diphthong.

**crass** *a.* gross; stupid. **-ly** *adv.* **-ness** *n.*

**crate** *n.* a wicker hamper, or open-work packing-case.

**cra•ter** *n.* cup-shaped mouth of a volcano; cavity resulting from the explosion of a large bomb.

**crave** *v.t.* and *i.* to have a very strong desire for; to ask with earnestness, humility. **-r** *n.* **craving** *n.* an inordinate desire.

**cra•ven** *a.* cowardly; *n.* a spiritless fellow; a coward.

**craw•fish, crayfish** *n.* a fresh-water crustacean, resembling the lobster but smaller.

**crawl** *v.i.* to move along the ground on the belly or on the hands and knees; to swim with an overarm stroke; *n.* a crawling motion; swimming stroke.

**cray•on** *n.* a coloring pencil; *v.t.* to draw with crayons.

**craze** *n.* a strong, habitual desire or passion; a general or individual mania; *v.t.* to make crazy; *(Pottery)* to crackle. **-d**

*a.* weak in mind. **craziness** *n.* **crazy** *a.* insane; extremely foolish. **crazily** *adv.*

**creak** *n.* a harsh, grating sound; *v.i.* to make a sharp, harsh, grating sound. **-y** *a.*

**cream** *n.* the fatty substance that rises to the surface of milk; the best part of anything; *v.t.* to take off the cream; *v.i.* to become covered with cream. **-y** *a.* full of cream; resembling cream. **-ery** *n.* a center to which milk is sent for distribution. **-iness** *n.* — **cheese** *n.* a soft, smooth, white cheese.

**crease** *n.* a mark made by folding anything; *v.t.* to make a crease on; *v.i.* to become creased.

**cre•ate** *v.t.* to bring into existence out of nothing; to originate. **creation** *n.* the act of creating, of bringing the world into being; any original production of the human mind. **creative** *a.* original. **creator** *n.* one who creates; a maker. **Creator** *n.* God. **creature** *n.* anything created; any living being.

**cre•dence** *n.* trust; belief. **credentials** *n.pl.* testimonials showing that a person is entitled to credit. **credible** *a.* worthy of belief. **credibility** *n.*

**cred•it** *n.* belief; trustworthiness; amount at a person's disposal in a bank; in commerce, the system of buying, borrowing and lending based on good faith; *v.t.* to put trust in. **-able** *a.* meriting credit. **-ably** *adv.* **-ableness** *n.* **-or** *n.* one to whom money is due.

**cred•u•lous** *a.* too prone to believe. **-ly** *adv.* **-ness** *n.* **credulity** *n.* gullibility.

**creed** *n.* statement of principles. **credo** *n.* a creed.

**creek** *n.* a branch or small tributary of a river.

**creep** *v.i.* to move along with the body close to the ground, like reptile; to spread, like certain plants, by clinging. *pa.t., pa.p.* **crept**. **-er** *n.* esp. a creeping plant. **-y** *a.* causing a creeping sensation on the skin.

**cre•mate** *v.t.* to consume by burning, the dead. **cremation** *n.* the act of cremating the dead. **cremator** *n.* **crematorium** *n.* an establishment for the cremation of bodies. **crematory** *a.* or *n.*

**Cre•ole** *n.* a native of Spanish America or the W. Indies, of European parentage.

**crepe** *n.* a thin crinkled fabric or paper; a kind of rough-surfaced rubber used for the soles of shoes, etc.

**crept** *pa.p.* and *pa.t.* of **creep.**

**cre•scen•do** *n.* *(Mus.)* a gradual increase in loudness; *adv.* with increase in loudness.

**cres•cent** *a.* like the young moon in shape; *n.* the moon in first quarter; a crescent-shaped object.

**cress** *n.* various salad greens.

**crest** *n.* the comb or tuft on a bird's head; the highest part of a wave; *v.t.* to reach the top of. **-fallen** *a.* dispirited; dejected.

**cre•tin•ism** *n.* condition caused by thyroid deficiency. **cretin** *n.* one suffering from cretinism. **cretinous** *a.*

**cre•vasse** *n.* a deep open chasm in a glacier; a fissure.

**crev•ice** *n.* a narrow fissure; a crack.

**crew** *n.* a group of workmen; a ship's company.

**crew•el** *n.* embroidery yarn, **-work** *n.*

**crib** *n.* a child's bed with barred sides; a key (used by students); an enclosure for storing grain.

**crib•bage** *n.* *(Cards)* a game played by two or four players.

**crick** *n.* neck or back spasm or cramp.

**crick•et** *n.* a small, brown, chirping insect.

**crick•et** *n.* a game played with bats, balls, and wickets.

**cri•er** *n.* See **cry.**

**crime** *n.* a violation of the law (usually of a serious nature). **criminal** *a.* guilty of, or pert. to, crime; wicked; *n.* one guilty of a crime. **criminality** *n.* guiltiness. **criminally** *adv.* **criminate** *v.t.* to charge with a crime. **crimination** *n.* **criminative, criminatory** *a.* accusing. **criminologist** *n.* **criminology** *n.* science dealing with the cause and treatment of crime.

**crimp** *v.t.* to form into curls or pleats; *n.* small waves, as in hair.

**crim•son** *a.* of a rich deep red color; *n.* the color itself.

**cringe** *v.t.* to shrink; to behave obsequiously.

**crin•kle** *v.t.* to make a series of twists in a surface; to rustle. **crinkly** *adv.*

**crin•o•line** *n.* a stiff, fabric petticoat.

**crip•ple** *n.* a person without the use of a limb or limbs; *a.* lame; *v.t.* to lame.

**cri•sis** *n.* the decisive moment; the turning point, esp. in an illness; *pl.* **crises.**

**crisp** *a.* brittle; breaking with a short snap; *v.t.* to make crisp; **-ly** *adv.* **-ness** *n.*

**criss•cross** *a.* arranged in crossing lines; *adv.* crossing in different directions; *v.t.* and *i.* to be marked with cross lines.

**cri•te•ri•on** *n.* a standard of judging; a rule by which opinions may be judged. *pl.* **criteria.**

**crit•ic** *n.* one who expressed a reasoned judgment on art or literature; one whose profession it is to write reviews; one given to finding fault. **-al** *a.* pert. to criticism; fault-finding; decisive. **-ally** *adv.* **criticism** *n.* the art of making a reasoned judgment. **criticize** *v.t.* and *i.* to pass judgment. **critique** *n.* review.

**croak** *v.t.* and *i.* to make a low, hoarse noise in the throat; *n.* the hoarse, harsh sound made by a frog. **-y** *a.*

**cro•chet** *n.* a kind of needlework consisting of loops; *v.t.* and *i.* to work in crochet.

**crock** *n.* an earthenware pot; a piece of broken earthenware. **-ery** *n.* dishes of all kinds, made of earthenware.

**croc•o•dile** *n.* a large, amphibious reptile of the lizard kind. — **tears,** sham grief.

**crocodile**

**cro•cus** *n.* a bulbous plant; saffon.
**cro•ny** *n.* an intimate friend.
**crook** *n.* any bend, or sharp turn; a thief; *v.t.* to curve; *v.i.* to be bent or curved. **-ed** *a.* bent; *(Fig.)* not straightforward. **-edly** *adv.* **-edness** *n.*
**croon** *v.t.* and *i.* to sing in a sentimental manner. **-er** *n.* **-ing** *n.*
**crop** *n.* the cultivated produce of any plants, in a farm, field, etc.; a harvest; closely-cut head of hair; *v.t.* to reap the produce of a field. *pr.p.* **-ping.** *pa.p.* and *pa.t.* **-ped.** **—eared** *a.* with hair cut close to head. -per *n.* one who, or that which, crops. **to crop up**, to appear unexpectedly.
**cro•quet** *n.* an outdoor game played with balls, mallets and hoops.
**cro•quette** *n.* *(Cookery)* a ball of finely minced meat, fish, etc. seasoned and fried.
**cross** *n.* a stake used for crucifixion; a misfortune; *v.t.* to mark with a cross; to make the sign of the cross. **-wise** *adv.* in the form of a cross.

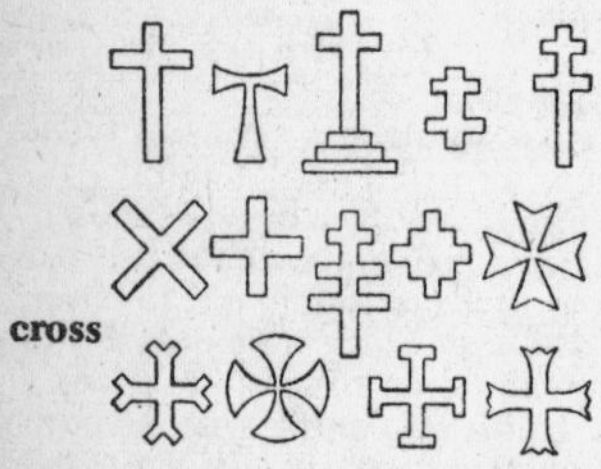
cross

**cross** *a.* transverse; intersecting; out of temper; *n.* an intermixture of breeds in cattle-breeding; *v.t.* to place so as to intersect; to pass over; to modify the breed of animals, plants, etc. by intermixture; *v.i.* to intersect; to move or pass from one side to the other; *adv.* across. **-ing** *n.* the act of passing across; an intersection; the intermixture of breeds. **-ly** *adv.* **—action** *n.* *(Law)* an action brought by a defendant against a plaintiff on points pert. to the same case. **-bones** *n.pl.* two thigh bones crossed and surmounted by a skull, used as symbol of death, a sign of deadly danger, or the flag of a pirate ship. **-breed** *n.* a hybrid. **—examination** *n.* the examination of a witness by counsel on the other side. **—eyed** *a.* with eyes turned in toward the nose. **— reference** *n.* in a dictionary, the directing of the reader to another part for related information.
**cross•bill** *n.* a bird of the Finch family, whose mandibles cross.
**cross•bow** *n.* a medieval weapon. **-man** *n.*
**crotch** *n.* the angle where the legs branch off from the human body. **-ed** *a.*
**crouch** *v.i.* to huddle down close to the ground.
**croup** *n.* *(Med.)* acute inflammation of the windpipe, accompanied by a hoarse cough. **-y** *a.*
**crou•ton** *n.* a small cube of toasted bread used in soups, etc.
**crow** *n.* a large bird, wholly black, of the

crow

genus Corvus; *v.i.* to give the shrill cry of the cock; to utter a sound of pleasure. **crow's-foot** *n.* a wrinkle about the outer corners of the eyes in adults. **crow's-nest** *n.* a perch for the lookout man near the top of the mast.
**crowd** *v.t.* to press together; to fill or occupy by crushing together; *v.i.* to be numerous; *n.* a number of persons collected into a close body.
**crown** *n.* the state headdress worn by a sovereign; royalty; the topmost part of the head; the summit; *v.t.* to bestow as a mark of honor; to surmount. **— prince** *n.* the heir apparent to the throne.
**cru•cial** *a.* decisive; critical.
**cru•ci•ble** *n.* vessel capable of withstanding great heat, used for melting metals.
**cru•ci•fy** *v.t.* to put to death by nailing to a cross; to mortify. **crucifier** *n.* **crucifix** *n.* an image of Christ on the Cross. **crucifixion** *n.* **cruciform** *a.* cross-shaped.
**crude** *a.* in the natural or raw state; unfinished. **-ly** *adv.* **-ness** *n.* **crudity** *n.*
**cru•el** *a.* hard-hearted. **-ly** *adv.* **-ty** *n.* the quality of being cruel (See **crude**). **cru•et** *n.* a small stoppered bottle for holding vinegar, oil.
**cruise** *v.i.* to sail about without precise destination; in motoring to go at a normal operating speed; *n.* an organized pleasure-sail. **-r** *n.*
**crumb** *n.* a small particle; *v.t.* to reduce to crumbs; to cover with crumbs. **-y** *a.*
**crum•ble** *v.t.* to break into fragments; *v.i.* to fall into crumbs. **crumbly** *a.*
**crum•ple** *v.t.* to wrinkle; to rumple; *v.i.* to become creased; to collapse.
**crunch** *n.* the sound made by chewing crisp food, treading on gravel, hard snow; *v.t.* and *i.* to chew, tread, with this sound.
**cru•sade** *n.* a medieval Christian war to recover the Holy Land from the Saracens; a campaign against any evil or vice; *v.i.* to join in a crusade. **-r** *n.*
**crush** *v.t.* to press between two hard bodies to break; to squeeze out by pressure; to defeat utterly; *v.i.* to be compressed by force; *n.* violent pressure.
**crust** *n.* the hard outer covering of anything; the outer part of baked bread; pastry, forming the covering of a pie; *v.t.* to cover with a crust; *v.i.* to form a crust. **-ated** *a.* incrusted. **-ation** *n.* **-ily** *adv.* in a crusty manner; morosely. **-iness** *n.* **-y** *a.* like a crust; hard; surly.
**Crus•ta•ce•a** *n.pl.* *(Zool.)* a class of mainly aquatic animals including lobsters, crabs, shrimps, etc. **-n** *a.* and *n.* pert. to the crustacea. **crustaceous** *a.* having a hard shell.
**crutch** *n.* a staff with a cross-piece to go

under the armpit for the use of cripples. *v.t.* to aid.

**crux** *n.* a perplexing problem; the real issue.

**cry** *v.t. v.i.* to exclaim vehemently; to weep; *n.* a loud utterance; the shedding of tears. **crier** *n.* one who cries. **-ing** *a.*

**crypt** *n.* a cell underground, used for burial. **crytic(al)** *a.* hidden; mysterious. **cryptically** *adv.*

**cryp•to•gram** *n.* a writing in secret characters. Also **cryptograph** *n.* **cryptology** *n.* a secret language.

**crys•tal** *n.* a transparent, colorless quartz; a superior sort of glass; *(Chem.)* a mineral body which has assumed a regular geometrical form; *a.* consisting of crystal; transparent. **-line** *a.* **-lize** *v.t.* to cause to assume a definite shape; *v.i.* to be formed into crystals. **-lizable** *a.* **-lization** *n.*

**cub** *n.* the young of the bear, fox, wolf; a junior Boy Scout.

**cub•by hole** *n.* a small place for storing things, or for hiding in.

**cube** *n. (Geom.)* a solid body with six equal sides; *(Math.)* the product of a number multiplied twice by itself; *v.t.* to raise to the third power. **cubic(al)** *a.* having the form of a cube. **cubic foot, cuboid** *a.* resembling a cube in shape. **— root** *n.* the number which gives the stated number if raised to the third power.

**cu•bi•cle** *n.* a small partitioned compartment.

**cub•ism** *n.* modern art based on geometrical forms. **cubist** *n.*

**cu•bit** *n.* a measure of length, about 18 inches. **-al** *a.*

**cuck•old** *n.* a man whose wife is unfaithful to him; *v.t.* to be unfaithful to a husband.

**cuck•oo** *n.* a migratory bird named from its call; the call of the bird.

**cuckoo**

**cu•cum•ber** *n.* plant of the gourd family and its fruit.

**cud** *n.* food brought up by ruminating animals, from their first stomach, and chewed a second time.

**cud•dle** *v.t.* to hug; to fondle; *v.i.* to lie close or snug; *n.* a close embrace. **-some** *a.*

**cudg•el** *n.* a short thick stick; *v.t.* to beat with a cudgel.

**cue** n. the last words of an actor's speech as a signal to the next actor to speak.

**cue** *n.* a long tapering rod used in billiards.

**cuff** *n.* a blow with the open hand; *v.t.* to strike with the open hand.

**cuff** *n.* the ending of a sleeve; the turned-up end of a trouser leg.

**cu•li•nar•y** *a.* pert. to the kitchen or cookery.

**cull** *v.t.* to select, or pick out.

**cul•mi•nate** *v.i.* to reach a climax. **culmination** *n.* the attainment of the highest point; climax.

**cu•lottes** *n.pl.* knee length trousers resembling a skirt.

**cul•pa•ble** *a.* deserving blame or censure. **culpably** *adv.* **culpability, -ness** *n.*

**cul•prit** *n.* one accused of a crime; an offender.

**cult** *n.* a system of religious worship, and ceremonies.

**cul•ti•vate** *v.t.* to prepare for the raising of crops; to produce by tillage, labor. **-d** *a.*

**cul•ture** *n.* tillage or cultivation; mental development; refinement; the propagation of bacteria in artificial media; *v.t.* to cultivate. **cultural** *a.* pert. to culture. **-d** *a.* educated and refined.

**cul•vert** *n.* an arched drain for the passage of water under a road.

**cum•ber** *v.t.* to burden with a useless load. **-some** *a.* burdensome. **cumbrous** *a.*

**cum•mer•bund** *n.* a broad sash worn as a belt.

**cu•mu•late** *v.t.* to heap together; *a.* heaped up. **cumulation** *n.* **cumulative** *a.* becoming greater by successive additions. **cumulatively** *adv.*

**cu•mu•lus** *n.* a piled-up cloud mass with rounded outlines. *pl.* **cumuli.**

**cu•ne•i•form, cuniform** *a.* wedge-shaped.

**cuneiform**

**cun•ning** *a.* wily; sly; *n.* craft; guile; deceit. **-ly** *adv.*

**cup** *n.* a drinking vessel; an ornamental vessel given as a prize; *v.t.* to hold, as in a cup; to form into a cup shape. *pr.p.* **-ping.** *pa.t.* **-ped. -ful** *n.* the quantity that a cup holds, 8 fluid oz. **cupboard** *n.* a small closet with shelves for cups, plates, etc. **loving cup** *n.* trophy, given as a prize.

**cu•pid•i•ty** *n.* an eager desire for possession.

**cu•pre•ous** *a.* pert. to, or containing copper.

**cur** *n.* a dog of mixed breed; a mongrel.

**cu•ra•tor** *n.* a superintendent, as of a museum, library; a guardian. **-ship** *n.*

**curb** *n.* any means of restraint; an edging to a pavement or sidewalk; *v.t.* to restrain; to confine. **-ing** *n.*

**curd** *n.* the cheesy part of milk; coagulated milk. **-le** *v.t.* and *i.* to turn into curd; to coagulate.

**cure** *v.t.* to heal; to restore to health; to preserve fish, skins, by salting; *n.* the act of healing; remedy. **curable** *a.* **curative** *a.* **cure-all** *n.* a panacea.

**cu•rette** *n.* instrument for scraping body tissue. **-ment** *n.*

**cur•few** *n.* the time after which persons may not be out of doors.

**cur•ie** *n. (Chem.)* the standard unit of emanation from one gram of radium. **curium** *n.* a radioactive, inert, gaseous element.

**cu•ri•o** *n.* a rare or curious object.

**cu•ri•ous** *a.* eager to know; inquisitive;

strange. **-ly** *adv.* **curiosity** *n.* inquisitiveness; a novelty.

**curl** *v.t.* to twist into ringlets; to bend into spiral or curved shape; *v.i.* to take a spiral or curved shape or path; to turn into ringlets; to ripple; to play at the game of curling; *n.* a ringlet of hair; anything of a similar shape. **-y** *a.* having curls; tending to curl; full of ripples. **-icue** *n.* a lock of hair; a fancy curve in writing. **-iness** *n.* **-ing** *n.* a game like bowls played on ice with large, rounded stones. **-er** *n.* a pin used as a fastener to retain a curl.

**cur•rant** *n.* the fruit of various plants allied to the gooseberry.

**cur•rent** *a.* belonging to the present time; *n.* a flowing body of water or air in motion; transmission of electricity through a conductor. **-ly** *adv.* commonly. **currency** *n.* money in circulation.

**cur•ric•u•lum** *n.* a specified course of study at a school. *pl.* **curricula.**

**cur•ry** *n.* *(Cookery)* a highly-flavored condiment much used in the East. **— powder** *n.*

**cur•ry** *v.t.* to dress leather; to beat or thrash. **currier** *n.* one who dresses tanned leather. **to curry favor,** to try to win favor by flattery.

**curse** *v.t.* to utter a wish of evil against; to swear at; *v.i.* to utter blasphemous words; the invocation of evil upon a person; oaths. **cursed** *a.* hateful. **cursedly** *adv.*

**cur•sive** *a.* written with all the letters joined. **-ly** *adv.* cursory *a.* characterized by haste; superficial.

**curt** *a.* concise to the point of rudeness; terse. *n.*

**cur•tail** *v.t.* to abridge; to diminish. **-ment** *n.*

**cur•tain** *n.* a drapery; a screen in front of stage of a theater; anything that conceals; *v.t.* to enclose with curtains. **iron curtain** *(Fig.)* any hindrance to obtaining information about conditions in a country.

**curt•sy, curtsey** *n.* a gesture of respect.

**curve** *n.* a bending without angles; an arch; *a.* bent; *v.t.* and *i.* to bend. **curvate** *a.* curved. **curvature** *n.*

**cush•ion** *n.* any padded surface used as a rest or protector; *v.t.* to protect with a cushion.

**cusp** *n.* a prominence on a molar tooth; the point at which the two branches of a curve have a common tangent. **-id** *n.* a canine tooth. **-idal** *n.* ending in a point.

**cus•tard** *n.* a sweet dish made with milk and eggs.

**cus•to•dy** *n.* guardianship; imprisonment. **custodial** *a.* **custodian, custodier** *n.* a caretaker.

**cus•tom** *n.* fashion; business patronage; toll, tax, or tribute; **-s** *n.pl.* duties levied on imports. **-able** *a.* liable to duty. **-ary** *a.* established by common usage; habitual. **-arily** *adv.* **-er** *n.* one who enters a shop to buy. **-house** *n.* office where customs are paid.

**cut** *v.t.* to sever, penetrate, or wound with an edged instrument; to intersect; to mow; to reduce; to abridge; *(Sports)* to hit the ball obliquely in order to impart spin to it. *pr.p.* **-ting.** *pa.p.* and *pa.t.* **cut** *n.* opening made with an edged instrument; a gash. **-ter** *n.* he who, or that which, cuts. **-ting** *n.* a small branch, cut from a plant, bush, etc.; *a.* sarcastic. **— glass** *n.* glass ornamented with cut designs. **-off** *n.* a device to shut off. **—rate** *a.* below usual price. **-throat** *n.* a murderer; *a.* merciless.

**cu•ta•ne•ous** *a.* belonging to, or affecting, the skin.

**cute** *a.* *(Colloq.)* attractive.

**cu•ti•cle** *n.* the epidermis around the fingernails and toenails.

**cut•ler** *n.* one who repairs, or deals in knives and cutting implements. **-y** *n.* cutting instruments, esp. tableware.

**cut•let** *n.* a piece of meat from the rib bones.

**cy•a•nide** *n.* a poisonous compound.

**cy•an•o•gen** *n.* *(Chem.)* a colorless, poisonous gas. **cyanic** *a.* blue.

**cy•ber•net•ics** *n.* the study of the mechanical brain.

**cyc•la•men** *n.* a tuberous plant of the Primrose family.

**cy•cle** *n.* a regularly recurring succession of events, or the time occupied by such a succession; a bicycle or tricycle; *v.i.* to pass through a cycle of changes. **cyclist** *n.* one who rides a bicycle or tricycle. **cycloid** *n.* *(Geom.)* a curve traced by a point in a circle when the circle revolves along a straight line.

**cy•clone** *n.* a violent storm characterized by strong winds. **cyclonic.**

**cy•clo•pe•di•a** See **encyclopedia.**

**cy•clo•ram•a** *n.* circular panorama.

**cy•clo•tron** *n.* a radio oscillator developed to disintegrate atoms, in order to study their internal structure.

**cyl•in•der** *n.* a roller-like body with straight sides, the ends being equal, parallel circles. **cylindric, cylindrical** *a.* **cylindriform** *a.*

**cym•bal** *n.* musical percussion instrument.

**cyn•ic** *n.* one who believes man's conduct is based on self-interest. **cynic(al)** *a.* distrustful of people's motives. **cynically** *adv.* **cynicalness** *n.* **cynicism** *n.* disbelief in goodness; misanthropy.

**cy•no•sure** *n.* *(Astron.)* the constellation of the Lesser Bear, containing the Pole-star; a guiding star.

**cy•press** *n.* a slender coniferous tree with evergreen foliage.

**cyst** *n.* *(Med.)* a membranous sac containing liquid secretion. **-ic** *a.* pert. to cysts.

**Czar** *n.* a title used by various Slavonic rulers, esp. by the Emperors of Russia. **Czarina** *n.* the wife of a Czar.

**Czech** *n.* a member of the Slavonic race of people inhabiting the western region of Czechoslovakia; *a.* pert. to the people or their language. **Czechoslovak, Czechoslovakian** *a.* pert. to the country, the people, or the language of Czechoslovakia; *n.* a native of the country; the language.

**dab** *n.* Eur. flatfish.

**dab** *v.t.* to pat gently and intermittently, **-bing.** *pa.p.* and *pa.t.* **-bed.** *n.* a gentle blow with a soft substance; a small lump of anything soft, as butter.

**dab•ble** *v.t.* to wet by little dips; to moisten; *v.i.* to play in water; to pursue a subject superficially.

**dach•shund** *n.* dog with long body, short legs, and drooping ears.

**dac•tyl** *n.* a metrical foot in poetry, consisting of one accented syllable followed by two unaccented syllables. **-ic** *a.* **-iography** *n.* the history of gem engraving. **-ogram** *n.* a finger print. **-ography** *n.* the science of finger prints. **-ology** *n.* the finger language of the deaf and dumb.

**da•da•ism** *n.* a school of art and literature which aims at suppressing all relation between thought and expression.

**dad•dy-long-legs** *n.* a flying insect; a harvestman.

**da•do** *n.* the part of a pedestal between the base and cornice; the lower part or wide skirting of the walls of a room.

**dae•mon** *n.* an inspiring influence; a divinity; genius. **-ic** *a.* more than human; supernatural.

**daf•fo•dil** *n.* a spring plant of the genus Narcissus; the yellow color of the daffodil.

**daft** *a.* insane; foolish. **-ness** *n.*

**dag•ger** *n.* a short, two-edged sword used in close combat; a mark of reference in typography (†) or (‡).

**dag•gle** *v.t.* to trail through mud; to bedraggle.

**da•guerre•o•type** *n.* in photography, an early method of taking pictures on plates of silver or silvered copper.

**dahl•ia** *n.* a genus of plants with large, brightly colored flowers.

**dai•ly** *a.* or *adv.* happening each day; *n.* a newspaper published each day or each weekday.

**dain•ty** *a.* pleasing to the taste; refined; pretty and delicate; scrupulous; *n.* a delicacy. **daintily** *adv.*

**dair•y** *n.* the shop where milk and its products are processed and sold; a dairy farm. **-ing** *n.* the business of conducting a dairy. **-maid, -man** n.

**da•is** *n.* the raised platform at the end of a room, esp. of dining hall.

**dai•sy** *n.* a common wild flower.

**dale** *n.* a low place between hills; a valley or vale; a glen.

**dal•ly** *v.i.* to waste time; to trifle. **dalliance** *n.*

**Dal•ma•tian** *n.* a breed of large white dogs with black or liver-colored spots.

**dam** *n.* a female parent — used of animals.

**dam** *n.* a barrier of earth, stones, etc. to obstruct the flow of water; *v.t.* to confine water by a dam; to block up.

**dam•age** *n.* any injury or harm to person, property, or reputation; *v.t.* to harm; to hurt. **-s** *n.pl.* legal compensation paid to injured party. **-able** *a.*

**dam•ask** *n.* a figured silk or linen fabric; a rose-pink color, like that of damask rose; *a.*

**dame** *n.* a noble lady; **Dame** *n.* *(Br.)* title of the wife of a knight or baronet.

**damn** *v.t.* to consign to everlasting punishment; to destroy the reputation of; *n.* an oath; a curse. **-able** *a.* **-ably** *adv.* **-ation** *n.* **-ed** *a.*

**damp** *n.* moist air; humidity; fog; noxious gases in coal mines; *a.* slightly moist; *v.t.* to retard combustion. **-en** *v.t.* **-er** *n.* a contrivance in a flue to regulate the draft; a device to minimize vibration. **-ish** *a.*

**dam•sel** *n.* a young unmarried woman.

**dam•son** *n.* a small dark plum.

**dance** *v.t.* and *v.i.* to move with measured steps; to move rhythmically; to caper; *n.* a social gathering for the purpose of dancing. **-r** *n.* **St. Vitus's dance** nervous disorder accompanied by twitching of muscles.

**dan•de•li•on** *n.* a plant with large yellow flowers, and tooth-edged leaves.

**dan•der** *n.* anger; passion; temper.

**dan•dle** *v.t.* to move up and down in affectionate play, as an infant; to pet; to caress.

**dan•druff, dandriff** *n.* a disease affecting the scalp and producing scurf or small scales of skin under the hair.

**dan•dy** *n.* one who affects special finery in dress; *a.* fine; first-rate. **dandify** *v.t.* **dandified** *a.*

**Dane** *n.* a native of Denmark; a breed of dog, large and smooth coated, usually *great Dane.* **Danish** *a.; n.* the language of the Danes.

**dan•ger** *n.* exposure to injury or evil; peril; jeopardy. **-ous** *a.* **-ously** *adv.* **dangerousness** *n.*

**dan•gle** *v.t.* to swing loosely or carelessly; *(Fig.)* to use as a bait; *v.i.*

**dank** *a.* unpleasantly damp or moist. **-ness** *n.*

**dap•per** *a.* neat; trim; smart.

**dap•ple** *n.* a spot; *a.* spotted, applied to horses and deer. **-d** *a.*

**dare** *v.i.* to have courage for; to venture (to); *v.i.* to defy; to challenge. **daring** *n.* a bold action; *a.* courageous; audacious. **daringly** *adv.* **—devil** *n.* a foolhardy, reckless fellow.

**dark** *n.* lacking light; black; somber; evil; unenlightened; *n.* absence of light; gloom; obscurity; evil. **-en** *v.t.* to obstruct light; to render dim, to cloud; to sully; *v.i.* **-ish** *a.* rather dark. **darkly** *adv.* **-ness** *n.* **-y, -ey** *n.* a Negro — **horse** *n.* one unexpectedly nominated for an office.

**dar•ling** *n.* a beloved or lovable one; *a.* cherished.

**darn** *v.t.* to mend; to repair a hole by weaving threads at right angles to one another; *n.* **-ing-needle** *n.*

**dart** *n.* a pointed arrow-like weapon; anything similar which pierces or wounds; a small seam or intake in garment to make it fit more closely; a sharp, forward movement; *v.t.* to send forward quickly. *v.i.* to run forward swiftly. **-s** *n.pl.* a popular game using darts and dartboard.

**Dar•win•i•an** *a.* pert. to Charles *Darwin* or

to his Theory of Evolution. *n.*

**dash** *v.t.* to throw violently; to cast down; to shatter; *v.i.* to rush forward or move violently. *n.* a rapid movement; a mark of punctuation (—); a small amount. **-ing** *a.* daring; spirited; showy. **-y** *a.* showy.

**das•tard** *n.* mean or cowardly fellow; *a.* cowardly. **-ly** *a.* -liness *n.*

**da•ta** *n.pl.* things known and from which inferences may be deduced.

**date** *n.* period of time of an event; epoch; duration. *v.t.* to note or fix the time of. *v.i.* to reckon back to a given time. **—line** *n.* approximately the 180° parallel of longitude on each side of which the date of the day differs.

**date** *n.* the stone fruit of the Eastern date palm.

**da•tum** *n.* a fact given; *pl.* **data.**

**daub** *v.t.* to smear with mud or plaster; to soil. *n.* a crude painting; a smudge. **-er** *n.* one who daubs.

**daugh•ter** *n.* a female child; *a.* like a daughter. **—in-law** *n.* the wife of one's son.

**daunt** *v.t.* to subdue the courage of; to dismay; to dishearten. **-less** *a.* fearless; intrepid.

**dau•phin** *n.* (*fem.* **dauphiness**) the French Crown prince.

**da•ven•port** *n.* a sofa.

**dav•its** *n.* uprights fitted with tackle for lowering life-boats over side of ship.

davits

**Da•vy Jones** *n.* a sailor's name for the Devil.

**daw** *n.* a bird of the crow family.

**daw•dle** *v.i.* to loiter; to move very slowly.

**dawn** *v.i.* to grow towards daylight; to begin to be visible; to come to the mind; *n.* daybreak; morning half-light; beginning.

**day** *n.* the period from sunrise to sunset; 24 hrs. **— bed** *n.* a divan. **-book** *n.* a book kept to record daily transactions. **-break** *n.* dawn. **-dream** *n.* a reverie; *v.i.*

**daze** *v.t.* to confuse; to bewilder; *n.* the state of being bewildered. **dazzle** *v.t.* to daze with sudden light; to confuse mentally; *n.* **dazzling** *a.*

**dea•con** *n.* an assistant to a priest or minister; a layman elected to certain duties in the church. **-ess** *n.* **-hood** *n.* **-ry** *n.* **-ship** *n.*

**dead** *a.* without life; *adv.* wholly; *n.* **-en** *v.t.* to benumb. **-ness** *n.* **—beat** *a.* without oscillation. **—end** *n.* a street with only one entrance. **-fall** *n.* a trap, esp. for large animals. **— heat** *n.* a race where two or more competitors reach the winning post at exactly the same time. **— language,** a language no longer spoken. **— letter** *n.* an undeliverable letter. **-liness** *n.* **-lock** *n.* an impasse. **-ly** *a.* causing death; *adv.* completely. **— pan** *n.* an immobile face. **— reckoning** *n.* the steering of a vessel by, compass and not by the stars. **— weight** *n.* the unrelieved weight of inert objects.

**deaf** *a.* lacking partially or wholly the sense of hearing; heedless. **-en** *v.t.* **-ening** *a.* very loud. **-ly** *adv.* **—mute** *n.* one who is deaf and dumb. **—mutism** *n.* **-ness** *n.*

**deal** *v.t.* to divide; to dole out. *v.i.* to traffic. *n.* distribution of playing cards; a business transaction. *pa.p.* **dealt. -er** *n.* **-ing** *n.pl.* relations with others. **a raw deal,** iniquitously unfair treatment. **a square deal,** fair treatment.

**dean** *n.* a dignitary in cathedral or collegiate churches; an official of a college with disciplinary authority.

**dear** *a.* precious; highly esteemed or valued; costly. **-ly** *adv.*

**dearth** *n.* scarcity; lack.

**death** *n.* extinction of life; decease; dissolution. **— blow** *n.* a fatal stroke. **-less** *a.* immortal. **-lessness** *n.* **-like** *a.* **-ly** *adv.; a.* **— mask** *n.* a plaster cast of a person's face taken immediately after death. **— rate** *n.* **—throes** *n.pl.* last struggle before death. **— warrant** *n.* an official document authorizing execution of a criminal. **-watch** *n.* a vigil.

**de•ba•cle** *n.* a sudden collapse; the breaking up of ice in a river.

**de•bar** *v.t.* to cut off from entrance; to prohibit; to exclude; *pr.p.* **-ring.** *pa.t. pa.p.* **-red. -ment** *n.*

**de•bark** *v.t.* and *v.i.* to disembark, oppos. of *embark.* **-ation, -ment** *n.*

**de•base** *v.t.* to reduce to a lower state; to disagree; to degrade; to adulterate. **-ment** *n.* **debasing** *a.* corrupting, esp. in moral sense.

**de•bate** *n.* controversy; argument. *v.t.* to discuss; to argue in detail; *v.i.* to reflect. **debatable** *a.* **-r** *n.*

**de•bauch** *v.t.* to corrupt; to seduce; to pervert. *n.* excess in eating and drinking. **-ed** *a.* **-ee** *n.* a dissipated person. **-ery** *n.* moral corruption. **-ment** *n.*

**de•ben•ture** *n.* a certificate acknowledging a debt and guaranteeing repayment of loan with interest.

**de•bil•i•tate** *v.t.* to weaken; to make infirm; to enervate. **debilitation, debility** *n.*

**deb•it** *n.* an item entered on debtor side of an account (oppos. of *credit*); *v.t.*

**deb•o•nair** *a.* bearing oneself cheerfully and well; sprightly.

**de•bris, dé•bris** *n.* rubble; ruins.

**debt** *n.* something owed to another; an obligation. **-or** *n.*

**de•but, dé•but** *n.* a first appearance in public. **debutante** *n.* one, esp. a girl, making her first appearance in society; abbrev. **deb.**

**dec•a-** *prefix,* ten.

**dec•ade** *n.* a period of ten years.

**de•ca•dence; decadency** *n.* deterioration; degeneration; decay.

**dec•a•dent** *a.* deteriorating.

**dec•a•gon** *n.* a plane figure of ten sides and ten angles.
**dec•a•gram(me)** *n.* in the metric system, a weight of 10 grams, i.e. 0.353 oz.
**dec•a•he•dron** *n.* a solid figure of a body having ten sides. **decahedral** *a.*
**de•cal•ci•fy** *v.t.* to deprive bones of lime.
**de•cal•i•ter** *n.* a measure of capacity equal to 10 liters — about 2.64 imperial gallons.
**Dec•a•logue** *n.* the Ten Commandments.
**dec•a•me•ter** *n.* in the metric system a measure of ten meters, or 32.8 ft.
**de•camp** *v.i.* to move away from a camping ground; to move off suddenly or secretly.
**de•cant** *v.t.* to pour off liquid without disturbing sediment, esp. used of wines. **-er** *n.* a slender necked glass bottle into which wine is decanted.
**de•cap•i•tate** *v.t.* to cut off the head; to behead. **decapitation** *n.*
**dec•a•pod** *n.* a shellfish of the crab family having five pairs of legs; *a.* having ten legs. **-al, -ous** *a.*
**de•car•bon•ize** *v.t.* to deprive of carbon; to remove a deposit of carbon, as from a motor cylinder. Also **decarbonate, decarburize. decarbonization, decarburization** *n.*
**dec•a•syl•lab•ic** *a.* having ten syllables. **decasyllable** *n.*
**de•cath•lon** *n.* a group of ten different contests at Olympic games.
**de•cay** *v.i.* to rot away; to become decomposed; to deteriorate; *v.t.* to impair; *n.* gradual decline. **-ed** *a.*
**de•cease** *n.* death; *v.i.* to die. **-d** *a.* dead *n.* a dead person.
**de•ceit** *n.* fraud. **-ful** *a.* crafty; fraudulent. **-fulness** *n.* **deceive** *v.t.* to delude; to cheat. **deceivable** *a.* **deceivably** *adv.* **deceiver.** *n.*
**de•cel•er•ate** *v.t.* and *v.i.* to reduce speed.
**De•cem•ber** *n.* orig. the tenth month of the Roman calendar; the twelfth month of the year.
**de•cen•nial** *a.* lasting for ten years or happening every ten years. **decennary** *n.*
**de•cent** *a.* fitting or becoming; modest; suitable. **decency** *n.* **-ly** *adv.*
**de•cen•tral•ize** *v.t.* to remove from the center or point of concentration and distribute among small areas. **decentralization** *n.*
**de•cep•tion** *n.* the act of deceiving; fraud; illusion. **deceptible** *a.* **deceptibility** *n.* **deceptive** *a.* causing a false impression. **deceptively** *adv.*
**dec•i•bel** *n.* one transmission unit; the smallest variation in sound that the human ear can detect.
**de•cide** *v.t.* to determine the result of; to make up one's mind about; *v.t.* to come to a conclusion. **-d** *a.* not ambiguous; determined. **decidedly** *adv.* **decision** *n.* determination; settlement; judgement. **decisive** *a.* conclusive; resolute. **decisively** *adv.* **decisiveness** *n.*
**de•cid•u•ous** *a.* shedding leaves in autumn, oppos. of coniferous or evergreen; not lasting; liable to fall.
**dec•i•mal** *a.* pert. to tens. *n.* some power of 10. **-ization** *n.* **-ize** *v.t.* to reduce to the decimal system. — **fraction,** a fraction the (unexpressed) denominator of which is 10 or a power of 10.
**dec•i•mate** *v.t.* to kill every tenth man, chosen by lot, as punishment; to reduce the numbers of, very considerably. **decimation** *n.*
**de•ci•pher** *v.t.* to make out what is illegible, unintelligible or written in strange symbols.
**de•ci•sion** See **decide.**
**deck** *v.t.* to adorn; to dress up. *n.* a covering; the horizontal platform extending from one side of ship to the other; a pack of cards, or part of pack remaining after dealing. **—chair** *n.* a light-weight, collapsible chair, made partly of canvas. — **hand** *n.* a person employed on deck of ship. **-ing** *n.* **hurricane-deck** *n.* a half-deck. **main-deck** *n.* deck below the upper deck. **quarter-deck** *n.* part of the deck abaft the main mast. **double-decker** *n.* a vehicle with upper and lower passenger-decks.
**deck•le** *n.* the gauge on a paper-making machine. **—edge** *n.* untrimmed edge of paper. **—edged** *a.*
**de•claim** *v.t.* to recite; *v.i.* to make a formal speech. **declamation** *n.* a set speech; **declamatory** *a.* ostentatiously rhetorical.
**de•clare** *v.t.* to proclaim; to make clear; to state publicly; *v.i.* (at Customs) to admit possession of dutiable goods. **declarable** *a.* **declaration** *n.* a solemn statement. **declaratory** *a.* explanatory.
**de•clen•sion** *n.* the act of falling away; deterioration; the inflection of nouns, pronouns, adjectives; **-al** *a.*
**de•cline** *v.t.* to bend downward; to refuse; to avoid; *v.i.* to slope; to fall in value or quantity; to pine away; to languish; *n.* a downward slope; a falling off. **declinable** *a.* **declination** *n.* a sloping away.
**de•cliv•i•ty** *n.* a downward slope; a gradual descent. **declivitous, declivous** *a.*
**de•code** *v.t.* to translate a message in code into ordinary language.
**de•col•le•tage** *n.* the line of a woman's low cut evening dress. **décollete** *a.* low-necked.
**de•com•pose** *v.t.* to break up into elements; to separate the constituent parts of; *v.i.* to decay; to rot. **decomposition** *n.*
**de•con•tam•i•nate** *v.t.* to cleanse from effects of poison gas, etc. **decontamination** *n.*
**de•con•trol** *v.t.* to release from government or state control.
**de•cor** *n.* the decoration, or setting of a theater, stage, or room.
**dec•o•rate** *v.t.* to beautify; to honor a person by giving a medal or badge of honor. **-d** *a.* **decoration** *n.* an ornament; a badge of honor. **decorative** *a.* **decorativeness** *n.* **decorator** *n.*
**dec•o•rous** *a.* seemly; decent; staid. **-ly** *adv.* **-ness** *n.* **decorum** *n.* behavior, etc. in keeping with social conventions.
**de•coy** *v.t.* to lead into a snare; *n.* a device for leading wild birds into a snare; an

enticement.

**de•crease** *v.t.* to lessen; to make smaller; to reduce gradually; *v.i.* to become less. *n.* gradual diminution; a lessening.

**de•cree** *n.* an order made by a competent authority; an edict; decision in a law court; an established law. *v.t.* to determine judicially. *v.i.* to decide authoritatively. **decretal** *a.* **decretive** *a.*

**de•cre•ment** *n.* the quantity lost by decrease.

**de•crep•it** *a.* worn out or enfeebled by old age; infirm; broken down; ramshackle. **-ude, -ness** *n.*

**de•cres•cent** *a.* becoming gradually less.

**de•cry** *v.t.* to bring into disrepute; to abuse. **decrial** *n.*

**ded•i•cate** *v.t.* to give oneself wholly to a worthy purpose; to inscribe a book or other object to someone as mark of appreciation or admiration. **-d** *a.* devoted. **dedication** *n.* **dedicatory** *a.* complimentary.

**de•duce** *v.t.* to reach a conclusion by deductive reasoning. **deducible** *a.* inferred. **deduct** *v.t.* to remove; to subtract. **deductible** *a.* **deduction** *n.;* the amount subtracted; the inference arrived at. **deductive** *a.* **deductively** *adv.*

**deed** *n.* an act; exploit; achievement; a legal document or contract; *v.t.* to convey by deed.

**deem** *v.t.* to believe on consideration.

**deep** *a.* extending far below the surface; dark; intense; low in pitch; *adv.* to a great depth; *n.* the sea. **-en** *v.t. v.i.* to become deeper. **-most** *a.* deepest. **-ness** *n.* depth. **—rooted** *a.* firmly established. **—seated** *a.* not superficial. **depth** *n.* the quality of being deep.

**deer** *n.* any of the ruminant quadrupeds.

**deer**

**de•face** *v.t.* to destroy or mar the external appearance of; to disfigure. **-able** *a.* **-ment** *n.*

**de•fal•cate** *v.t.* to misappropriate money; to embezzle. **defalcation** *n.* **defalcator** *n.*

**de•fame** *v.t.* to harm or destroy the good name or reputation of; to slander. **defamation** *n.* **defamatory** *a.*

**de•fault** *n.* failure to appear in a law court when summoned; failure to account for money held in trust; *v.i.* to fail to meet an obligation. **-er** *n.*

**de•fea•sance** *n.* defeat; a rendering null and void. **defeasible** *a.* capable of being annulled.

**de•feat** *v.t.* to overcome; to subdue; to conquer; *n.* conquest. **-ism** *n.* the attitude of mind of those who accept defeat as inevitable. **-ist** *n.; a.*

**def•e•cate** *v.t.* to clear or strain impurities from; *v.i.* to void excrement from the bowels. **defecation** *n.*

**de•fect** *n.* a want; an imperfection; absence of something necessary for completeness. **defection** *n.* the act of abandoning allegiance to a cause. **-ive** *a.* incomplete; imperfect; faulty. **-ively** *adv.* **-iveness** *n.*

**de•fend** *v.t.* to protect; to ward off attack; to maintain; to justify. **-able** *a.* **-ant** *n.* one who defends; the accused in a criminal case; the one prosecuted in a civil case. **-er** *n.*

**de•fense** *n.* that which shields or protects; *(Law)* a plea or reply to a charge. **-less** *a.* open to attack. **-lessly** *adv.* **-lessness** *n.* **Civil Defense,** an organization in World War 2 and since, for protection of civilians. **defensible** *a.* **defensibility** *n.* **defensive** *a.* resisting attack. **defensively** *adv.*

**de•fer** *v.i.* to submit; to yield or bow to the opinion of another. **deference** *n.* **deferential** *a.*

**de•fer** *v.t.* to put off; to postpone; *v.i.* **-ring;** *pa.p.* **-red. -able, -rable** *a.* **-ment** *n.*

**de•fi•ance** *n.* a challenge to combat; contempt; opposition. **defiant** *a.* aggressively hostile; insolent. **defiantly** *adv.*

**de•fi•cient** *a.* wanting; failing; lacking a full supply; incomplete. **deficiency, deficience** *n.* **-ly** *adv.* **deficit** *n.* excess of expenditure over income.

**de•file** *v.t.* to dirty; to desecrate. **-ment** *n.*

**de•fine** *v.t.* to determine the boundaries of; to state the exact meaning of; to circumscribe; to designate; to specify. **definable** *a.* **definite** *a.* **definitely** *adv.* **definiteness** *n.* **definition** *n.* description of a thing by its properties; explanation of the exact meaning of a word or term. **definitive** *a.* limiting; determining.

**de•flate** *v.t.* to empty of air or gas; to reduce inflated currency. **deflation** *n.*

**de•flect** *v.t.* to turn aside; to divert from the right direction; *v.i.* to swerve. **-ed** *a.* **deflection** *n.* **-or** *n.*

**de•flow•er** *v.t.* to deprive of flowers.

**de•fo•li•a•tion** *n.* the shedding of leaves. **defoliate** *v.t.* **defoliate, defoliated** *a.*

**de•for•est** *v.t.* to deprive of forests. **-ation** *n.*

**de•form** *v.t.* to mar or alter the form of; to make misshapen; to disfigure. **-ed** *a.* **-ation** *n.* **-ity** *n.*

**de•fraud** *v.t.* to deprive of; cheat.

**de•fray** *v.t.* to bear the cost of; to provide the money for. **-al** *n.*

**de•frock** *v.t.* to unfrock, as of a priest deprived of ecclesiastical status.

**deft** *a.* dexterous; handy. **-ly** *adv.* **-ness** *n.*

**de•funct** *a.* dead; deceased; obsolete; *n.*

**de•fy** *v.t.* to challenge; to resist authority.

**de•gen•er•ate** *v.i.* to decline; *n.* a person of low moral standards; *a.* having become less than one's kind. **degeneracy** *n.* **-ly** *adv.* **-ness** *n.* **degeneration** *n.* **degenerative** *a.*

**de•grade** *v.t.* to reduce in status; to lower the moral reputation of; to disgrace. **degradation** *n.*

**de•gree** *n.* a step upward or downward;

station or status; extent; rank to which one is admitted by a university; the 360th part of a revolution; a measured space on a thermometer, **third degree** *(U.S.)* a long, searching cross-examination by police of a suspect.

**de•gres•sion** *n.* a going down; a lowering of rate of taxation on certain wage levels.

**de•hy•drate** *v.t.* to remove water from; *v.i.* to lose water; **dehydration** *n.*

**de•i•cide** *n.* the killing of a god.

**de•i•fy** *v.t.* to make a god of; to exalt to the rank of divinity; to worship. **deific, -al** *a.* **deification** *n.* **deiform** *a.*

**deign** *v.i.* to condescend; to stoop; *v.t.*

**de•ism** *n.* belief, on purely rational grounds, in the existence of God without accepting the revelation implied in religious dogma. **deist** *n.* **deistic, -al** *a.* **deity** *n.* God, the Supreme Being; a pagan god or goddess.

**de•ject** *v.t.* to cast down; to dishearten; to depress. **-ed** *a.* downcast; moody; in low spirits. **-edly** *adv.* **-edness** *n.* **-ion** *n.*

**de•lay** *v.t.* to put off; to postpone; to stop temporarily; *v.i.* to dawdle; to procrastinate; *n.* tardiness. **-er** *n.*

**de•lec•ta•ble** *a.* highly pleasing; delightful; enjoyable. **-ness** *n.* **delectably** *adv.* **delectation** *n.*

**del•e•gate** *v.t.* to entrust authority to a deputy. *n.* a deputy; a representative. **delegation** *n.* body of delegates. **delegacy** *n.*

**de•lete** *v.t.* to erase; to strike out. **delenda** *n.pl.* things to be blotted out. **deletion** *n.*

**del•e•te•ri•ous** *a.* capable of harming or destroying health. **-ly** *adv.* **-ness** *n.*

**delft** *n.* glazed earthenware, orig. made at *Delft* in Holland. Also **delf, delft-ware.**

**de•lib•er•ate** *v.t.* to weigh in the mind; to discuss; *v.i.* to consider carefully; *a.* carefully considered; slow. **-ly** *adv.* **-ness** *n.* **deliberation** *n.* **deliberative** *a.*

**del•i•cate** *a.* dainty; frail; exquisitely wrought; nicely adjusted; highly sensitive or perceptive. **delicacy** *n.* **-ly** *adv.* **-ness** *n.*

**del•i•ca•tes•sen** *n.pl.* a shop selling cold cooked meats and other foods requiring little or no preparation.

**de•li•cious** *a.* extremely pleasing to the taste or sense of smell; delightful. **-ly** *adv.*

**de•light** *v.t.* to give great pleasure to; to charm; *v.i.* to take delight; *n.* the source of pleasure. **-ed** *a.* **-edly** *adv.* **-ful** *a.*

**de•lim•it** *v.t.* to fix the limit or boundaries of. **-ation** *n.*

**de•lin•e•ate** *v.t.* to draw an outline; to sketch; to portray; to describe clearly in words. **delineation** *n.* **delineator** *n.*

**de•lin•quent** *n.* one who fails in duty; an offender or criminal, esp. of a young person; *a.* failing in duty. **delinquency** *n.*

**del•i•quesce** *v.i.* to liquefy by absorbing moisture from the air. **deliquescence** *n.* **deliquescent** *a.*

**de•lir•i•ous** *a.* wandering in the mind; light-headed. **deliration** *n.* madness. **-ly** *adv.* **-ness** *n.* **delirium** *n.* mental disturbance caused by grave physical illness or nervous shock. **delirium tremens** (*abbrev.* **D.T.**) violent delirium resulting from excessive alcoholism.

**de•liv•er** *v.t.* to liberate from danger, captivity, restraint; to save; to distribute; to pronounce (as a speech); to give birth to a child (used passively). **-able** *a.* **-ance** *n.* **-er** *n.* **-y** *n.*

**dell** *n.* a small, deep valley; a hollow.

**Del•phic, Del•phian** *a.* pert. to the town of *Delphia* in Ancient Greece, to the oracle of Apollo in that town; oracular.

**del•phin•i•um** *n.* a genus of flowering plants.

**del•ta** *n.* the fourth letter of the Greek alphabet, $\Delta$ (small letter = $\delta$ ); a triangular tract of alluvium at the mouth of a large river. **delta rays,** rays from radioactive metals.

**de•lude** *v.t.* to lead into error; to mislead; to deceive. **deludable** *a.* **-r** *n.* **delusion** *n.* a mistaken belief. **delusive** a. **delusory** *a.*

**de•luge** *n.* a great flow of water; torrential rain; a flood; *v.t.* to flood; to inundate.

**de•luxe** *a.* sumptuous; of superlative quality.

**delve** *v.t.* and *v.i.* to carry on intensive research.

**dem•a•gogue** *n.* an unprincipled agitator. **demagogic, -al** *n.* **demagogy** *n.*

**de•mand** *v.t.* to ask authoritatively or peremptorily; to question; to require; *n.* earnest inquiry. **-ant** *n.* a plaintiff.

**de•mar•ca•tion, demarkation** *n.* the act of marking a line or boundary; a boundary. **demarcate** *v.t.*

**de•mean** *v.t.* to conduct or comport oneself. **demeanor** *n.* behavior; conduct.

**de•mean** *v.t.* to make mean; to debase; to degrade.

**de•ment•ed** *a.* insane; crazy; **dement** *v.t.* to drive mad. **dementia** *n.* incipient loss of reason; insanity marked by complete mental deterioration. **dementia praecox,** insanity in adolescence.

**de•mer•it** *n.* a fault; a mark against one's record.

**de•mesne** *n.* a manor house and the estate adjacent to it; private ownership of land.

**dem•i-** *prefix* signifying *half.*

**dem•i•god** *n.* a classical hero half human, half divine.

**dem•i•john** *n.* a glass bottle with large body, slender neck, and enclosed in wicker work.

**dem•i•monde** *n.* a class of women of doubtful reputation; prostitutes.

**de•mise** *n.* death; transmission by will to a successor; *v.t.* to bequeath.

**dem•i•tasse** *n.* a small-sized cup, esp. for after-dinner coffee.

**de•mo•bi•lize** *v.t.* to dismiss (troops); to disband. **demobilization** *n.*

**de•moc•ra•cy** *n.* a form of government for the people, by the will of the majority of the people; a state having this form of government. **democrat** *n.* one who adheres to democracy; member of Democratic party. **democratic, democratical** *a.*

**de•mog•ra•phy** *n.* science of vital and social statistics.

**de•mol•ish** *v.t.* to destroy; to pull down; to ruin. **-er** *n.* **demolition** *n.*
**de•mon** *n.* a spirit; a devil; **demoniac** *a.* devilish — also **demoniacal;** *n.* a human being possessed of an evil spirit. **-olatry, -ism** *n.* **-olater** *n.*
**de•mon•e•ti•za•tion** *n.* **demonetize** *v.t.* to diminish or deprive of monetary value.
**dem•on•strate** *v.t.* to prove by pointing out; to exhibit; to explain by specimens or experiment. **demonstrable** *a.* **demonstrably** *adv.* **demonstration** *n.* **demonstrative** *a.* **demonstrator** *n.*
**de•mor•al•ize** *v.t.* to injure the morale of; to corrupt.
**de•mos** *n.* the people.
**de•mur** *v.i.* to object. *pr.p.* **-ring;** *pa.p.* **-red;** *n.* **-rable** *a.* **-rage** *n.* undue detention of a ship, railroad car, etc.; compensation paid for such detention. **-rer** *n.* *(Law)* a plea that a case has insufficient evidence to justify its being pursued further.
**de•mure** *a.* grave; staid; shy; seemingly modest. **-ly** *adv.* **-ness** *n.*
**den** *n.* a cave or hollow place; lair or cage of a wild beast; a private sanctum.
**de•nar•i•us** *n.* a Roman silver coin; *pl.* **denarii. denary** *a.* containing ten.
**de•na•ture** *v.t.* to make unfit for eating or drinking by adulteration. **denaturant** *n.* **denaturation** *n.*
**den•dri-, dendro-** *prefix* from Gk. *dendron*, a tree, as in **-form** *a.* having the shape or appearance of a tree. **-tic, -tical** *a.* **dendroid, dendroidal** *a.*
**de•ni•al** *n.* a flat contradiction; a refusal.
**den•i•gra•tion** *n.* a blackening of; defamation of a person's character. **denigrate** *v.t.*
**den•im** *n.* a stout cotton twill cloth.
**den•i•zen** *n.* a dweller; anything successfully naturalized; *v.t.*
**de•nom•i•nate** *v.t.* to give a name to; to designate. **denominable** *a.* **denomination** *n.* a title; a religious sect; unit of measure. **denominational** *a.* **denominative** *a.* **denominatively** *adv.* **denominator** *n.* the number below the line in a fraction.
**de•note** *v.t.* to signify or imply; to be the symbol of. **denotable** *a.* **denotation** *n.*
**dé•noue•ment** *n.* the unraveling of the complication of a dramatic plot; the issue or outcome of a situation.
**de•nounce** *v.t.* to inform against; to accuse in public. **-ment** *n.* **-er** *n.*
**dense** *a.* compact; thick, crowded; *(Fig.)* stupid. **-ly** *adv.* **-ness** *n.* **density** *n.*
**dent** *n.* a small depression made (by a blow) in a surface; *v.t.*
**den•tal** *a.* pert. to the teeth or to dentistry; *n.* and *a.* a consonant sound (e.g. *d* or *t*) made by tip of tongue behind the upper front teeth. **dentate** *a.* toothed; sharply notched. **dentiform** *a.* **dentrifrice** *n.* powder, paste, or liquid used to clean and whiten teeth. **dentist** *n.* a medically trained specialist in the care of the teeth. **dentistry** *n.* **dentition** *n.* arrangement of teeth. **dentoid** *a.* **denture** *n.* set or part set of teeth, esp. artificial teeth.
**den•ti•cle** *n.* a small tooth or projection. **denticular, denticulate, denticulated** *a.* having notches or sharp projections.
**de•nude** *v.t.* to lay bare; to strip. **denudation** *n.*
**de•nun•ci•ate** *v.t.* Same as **denounce. denunciation** *n.* **denunciator** *n.*
**de•ny** *v.t.* to declare to be untrue; to refuse a request; to disavow; to disown.
**de•o•dor•ize** *v.t.* to deprive of odor. **deodorant, deodorizer** *n.*
**de•ox•i•dize** *v.t.* to remove oxygen from.
**de•part** *v.i.* to go away; to leave; to die; to deviate; *v.t.* to leave. **-ed** *n.* the dead. **-ment** *n.* a section of a business or administration; a special branch of the arts or science. **-mental** *a.* affecting only a section of a business, etc. **-ure** *n.*
**de•pend** *v.i.* to rely on; to be sustained by; to be contingent on. **-able** *a.* trustworthy. **-ably** *adv.* **-ant, -ent** *n.* one who is supported, esp. financially by another; *a.* hanging down; varying according to; **-ence** *n.* **-ency** *n.* **-ently, -antly** *adv.*
**de•pict** *v.t.* to portray; to present a visual image of; to describe in words. **-tion** *n.* **-ive** *a.*
**dep•i•late** *v.t.* to remove hair from. **depilation** *n.* **depilatory** *n.* agent for removing superfluous hair from body; *a.*
**de•plete** *v.t.* to empty; to diminish; to reduce. **depletion** *n.* **depletive, depletory** *a.*
**de•plore** *v.t.* to suffer remorse for; to regret. **deplorable** *a.* **deplorably** *adv.*
**de•ploy** *v.t.* to spread out; to extend troops in line; *v.i.* **-ment** *n.*
**de•po•lar•ize** *v.t.* to deprive of polarity.
**de•pone** *v.t.* to give evidence under oath, in a law court. **deponent** *n.*
**de•port** *v.t.* to carry away; to expel; to banish into exile; (reflex.) to behave; to bear oneself. **-ation** *n.* the compulsory removal of people from one country to another. **-ment** *n.* conduct of a person.
**de•pose** *v.t.* to remove from a throne; to oust from a high position; to degrade; *(Law)* to state upon oath. **deposable** *a.* **deposal** *n.* **deposition** *n.* removal of someone from a high position; *(Law)* a written declaration by a witness.
**de•po•sit** *v.t.* to lay down; to entrust; *n.* that which is deposited or laid down; sediment falling to the bottom of a fluid; money placed in safe-keeping of a bank; partial payment. **-ary** *n.* **-or** *n.* **-ory** *n.*
**de•pot** *n.* a railway station; a storage center for supplies and materials.
**de•prave** *v.t.* to make bad or worse; to corrupt; to pervert. **depravation** *n.* **-d** *a.* immoral. **depravity** *n.*
**dep•re•cate** *v.t.* to express disapproval of. **deprecatingly** *adv.* **deprecation** *n.* **deprecative, deprecatory** *a.* **deprecator** *n.*
**de•pre•ci•ate** *v.t.* to lower in value; *v.i.* to lose quality; to diminish in market value. **depreciation** *n.* **depreciative, depreciatory** *a.* **depreciator** *n.*
**dep•re•date** *v.t.* to plunder; to lay waste. **depredation** *n.*
**de•press** *v.t.* to deject or cast a gloom over; to press down; to lower; to diminish the vigor of. **-ed** *a.* **-ible** *a.* **depression** *n.* a

hollow; despondency; in meteorology, an area of low barometric pressure. **-or** *n.*

**de•prive** *v.t.* to take away; to dispossess; **deprivation** *n.* **deprivable** *a.* **depriver** *n.*

**depth** *n.* deepness; distance measured downwards from surface; distance from front to back.

**de•pute** *v.t.* to send with commission to act for another; to delegate duties to another. **deputation** *n.* **deputize** *v.i.* **deputy** *n.*

**de•range** *v.t.* to put out of order or place; to upset; to make insane. **-d** *a.* **-ment** *n.*

**der•by** *n.* a man's felt hat, with stiff rounded crown and narrow brim.

**der•e•lict** *a.* forsaken; abandoned and disclaimed by owner; *n.* a ship abandoned by captain and crew; a person abandoned by society. **dereliction** *n.*

**de•ride** *v.t.* to ridicule; to mock; to laugh at with scorn. **-r** *n.* **deridingly** *adv.* **derision** *n.* **derisive** *a.* **derisively** *adv.* **derisiveness** *n.* **derisory** *a.*

**de•rive** *v.t.* to obtain or draw from a source; to trace the descent or origin; *v.i.* to have as an origin; to proceed. **derivable** *a.* **derivation** *n.* etymology. **derivative** *n.* a word derived from another; *a.*

**der•ma, der•mis** *n.* the true skin below epidermis. **dermal** *a.* **dermatic** *a.* **-titis** *n.* inflammation of the skin. **-tology** *n.* branch of medical science concerned with the skin and skin diseases. **-tologist** *n.*

**der•o•gate** *v.i.* to lessen. **derogation** *n.* **derogatory** *a.* tending to impair the value of; detracting. **derogatorily** *adv.*

**der•rick** *n.* an apparatus like a crane for hoisting heavy weights.

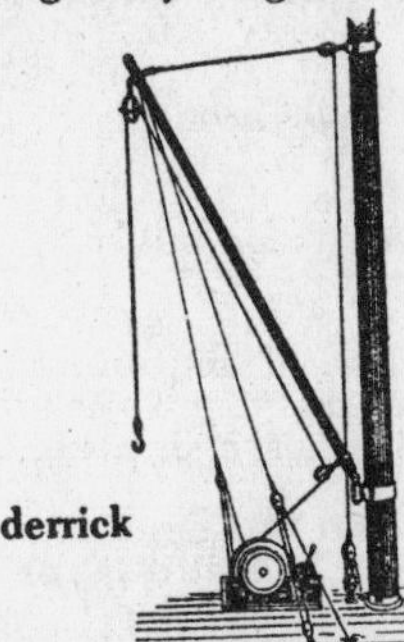
derrick

**der•rin•ger** *n.* a short-barrelled pistol with a large bore.

**der•vish** *n.* a member of one of the mendicant orders among the Mohammedans.

**des•cant** *n.* a melody harmonizing with and sung or played as accompaniment to a musical theme; a discourse on a theme; *v.i.* to sing. **-er** *n.*

**de•scend** *v.t.* to go down; *v.i.* to sink; to lower oneself or stoop to something. **-ant** *n.* offspring. **-ent** *a.* **descending** *a.* **descent** *n.* act of coming down; lineage.

**de•scribe** *v.t.* to represent the features of; to portray in speech or writing. **describable** *a.* **description** *n.* **descriptive** *a.* **descriptively** *adv.*

**de•scry** *v.t.* to discover by the eye; to perceive from a distance. **descrier** *n.*

**des•e•crate** *v.t.* to violate the sanctity of; to profane. **-r, -or** *n.* **desecration** *n.*

**de•sert** *n.* that which is deserved.

**des•ert** *n.* a wide, sandy waste region; *a.* uncultivated; solitary.

**de•sert** *v.t.* to abandon; to leave; *v.i.* to quit the armed forces without authorization. **-ed** *a.* **-er** *n.* **desertion** *n.*

**de•serve** *v.t.* to earn by service; to be entitled to; *v.i.* to be worthy of reward. **deservedly** *adv.* **deserving** *a.*

**des•ic•cate** *v.t.* to extract all moisture from; to dehydrate. **desiccant** *a. n.* substance capable of absorbing moisture. **desiccation** *n.*

**de•sign** *v.t.* to draw the outline of; to plan; *v.i.* to purpose; *n.* sketch in outline; a pattern. **-able** *a.* **designate** *v.t.* **designation** *n.* **designative** *a.* **-edly** *adv.* intentionally. **-er** *n.* **-ful** *a.* **-ing** *a.*

**de•sire** *v.t.* to yearn for the possession of; to request; *n.* anything desired; a longing. **desirable** *a.* **desirably** *adv.* **desirableness, desirability** *n.* **desirous** *a.*

**de•sist** *v.t.* to cease; to discontinue. **-ance, -ence** *n.*

**desk** *n.* a table for reading or writing; a lectern.

**des•o•late** *v.t.* to devastate; to make lonely or forlorn; *a.* waste; deserted. **-ly** *adv.* **-ness** *n.* **-r** *n.* **desolation** *n.* **desolatory** *a.*

**de•spair** *v.i.* to be without hope; *n.* despondency; hopelessness. **-ing** *a.* **-ingly** *adv.*

**des•patch** See **dispatch.**

**des•pi•ca•ble** *a.* contemptible; deserving to be despised. **despicably** *adv.* **despicability** *n.*

**de•spise** *v.t.* to look down upon; to hold in contempt. **despisable** *a.*

**de•spite** *n.* contemptuous treatment; *prep.* notwithstanding. **-ful** *a.* **-fully** *adv.*

**de•spoil** *v.t.* to take away by force; to rob. **-er** *n.* a plunderer. **-ment, despoliation** *n.*

**de•spond** *v.i.* to be cast down in spirit. **-ence, -ency** *n.* depression. **-ent** *a.* **-ently** *adv.* **-ingly** *adv.*

**des•pot** *n.* one who rules with absolute power; a tyrant. **-ic** *a.* **-ically** *adv.* **-ism** *n.*

**des•sert** *n.* a course served at end of a dinner.

**des•tine** *v.t.* to predetermine. **destination** *n.* the place to which one is traveling. **destiny** *n.* fate.

**des•ti•tute** *a.* in want; needy. **destitution** *n.*

**de•stroy** *v.t.* to turn to rubble; to put an end to. *pa.p.* **-ed. -able** *a.* **-er** *n.* a type of fast warship armed with guns and torpedoes.

**de•struc•tion** *n.* the act of destroying; state of being destroyed; ruin. **destructible** *a.* **destructibleness, destructibility** *n.* **destructive** *a.*

**des•ue•tude** *n.* discontinuance of a custom or practice.

**de•sul•tor•y** *a.* leaping from one thing to another; unmethodical. **desultorily** *adv.* **desultoriness** *n.*

**de•tach** *v.t.* to separate; to disunite; to detail for special service. **-able** *a.* **-ed** *a.*

standing alone; impersonal; disinterested. **-edly** *adv.* **-edness**, **-ment** *n.*

**de•tail** *v.t.* to relate minutely; to record every item; to appoint for a special duty. **detail** *n.* a minute part. **-ed** *a.*

**de•tain** *v.t.* to keep back or from; to prevent someone proceeding. **-er** *n.* **-ment** *n.* **detention** *n.*

**de•tect** *v.t.* to uncover; to discover. **-able, -ible** *a.* **-or** *n.* **-ion** *n.* **-ive** *a., n.* a member of the police force, not in uniform, who apprehends criminals and investigates cases.

**de•ter** *v.t.* to frighten from; to discourage; to restrain. *pr.p.* **-ring;** *pa.p.* **-red. -ment** *n.* **-rent** *a., n.* **deterrence** *n.*

**de•terge** *v.t.* to cleanse; to wipe off. **detergence, detergency** *n.* **detergent** *a.* cleansing *n.* cleansing substance.

**de•te•ri•o•rate** *v.t.* to make worse; to cause to depreciate; *v.i.* to degenerate. **deterioration** *n.*

**de•ter•mine** *v.t.* to fix the limits of; to define; to decide; *v.i.* to make a decision or resolution. **determinable** *a.* **determinant** *a.* serving to fix, or limit; *n.* **determinate** *a.* having fixed limits. **determinately** *adv.* **determination** *n.* resolution. **-d** *a.* unwavering. **-dly** *adv.* **determinism** *n.* the doctrine that man is not a free agent, and that his actions and mental activity are governed by causes or motives outside his own will.

**de•test** *v.t.* to dislike intensely; to hate. **-able** *a.* **-ableness, -ability** *n.* **-ation** *n.*

**de•throne** *v.t.* to remove from a throne; to depose. **-ment** *n.*

**de•to•nate** *v.t.* to cause to explode; *v.i.;* **detonation** *n.* **detonator** *n.* device to make another substance explode.

**de•tour** *n.* a roundabout way; a digression.

**de•tract** *v.t.* to take away a part from; to defame; *v.i.* **-or** *n.* **-ingly** *adv.* **detraction** *n.* depreciation; slander.

**de•tri•ment** *n.* injury; harm; loss. **-al** *a.*

**de•trun•cate** *v.t.* to lop off from the trunk; to shorten. **detruncation** *n.*

**deuce** *n.* a card or die with two spots; *(Tennis)* score of 40 all.

**deuce** *n.* the devil; bad luck.

**deu•te•ri•um** *n.* a form of hydrogen twice as heavy as the normal gas.

**deu•ter•on•o•my** *n.* the fifth book of the Pentateuch.

**de•val•u•ate, devalue** *v.t.* to reduce the value of. **devaluation** *n.*

**dev•as•tate** *v.t.* to lay waste. **devastation** *n.* destruction.

**de•vel•op** *v.t.* to cause to grow; to increase the resources of; to produce image on photographic plate or film by chemical application; *v.i.* to evolve by natural processes. **-er** *n.* a chemical for producing image on plate or film. **-ment** *n.* a gradual unfolding or growth.

**de•vi•ate** *v.i.* to diverge; to turn away from the direct line; *v.t.* **deviation** *n.*

**de•vice** *n.* that which is planned out or designed; contrivance; emblem on a shield.

**dev•il** *n.* the spirit of evil; Satan; *v.t.* to torment; to prepare with hot or savory seasoning. **-ish** *a.* **-ishly** *adv.* **—may-care** *a.* happy-go-lucky. **-ment** *n.* mischief. **-ry; -try** *n.* **-'s advocate,** one appointed by papal court to oppose a proposed canonization; one who maintains an argument with which he really disagrees. **give the devil his due,** give even the worst person credit for something.

**de•vi•ous** *a.* not direct; erring. **-ly, -ness** *n.*

**de•vise** *v.t.* to invent; to contrive; to scheme; to plan; *v.i.* to consider; *n.* *(Law)* the act of bequeathing. **devisable** *a.* **devisal,** *n.* **-r** *n.* **devisor** *n.* one who bequeaths by will.

**de•vi•tal•ize** *v.t.* to deprive of life or vitality. **devitalization** *n.*

**de•void** *a.* empty; free from; without.

**dev•o•lu•tion** *n.* delegation of powers to subsidiary or local bodies; opposite of evolution. [See **devolve**].

**de•volve** *v.t.* to transmit; to transfer; *v.i.* *(Law)* to pass, by inheritance, from one to another.

**de•vote** *v.t.* to give oneself wholly to; to dedicate. **-d** *a.* **-dly** *adv.* **devotedness** *n.* **devotee** *n.* a zealous supporter. **devotion** *n.* **devotions** *n.pl.* worship and prayer. **devotional** *a.*

**de•vour** *v.t.* to consume completely and wantonly; to destroy. **-ing** *a.*

**de•vout** *a.* -ious; passionately religious. **-ly** *adv.*

**dew** *n.* moisture in the atmosphere or in the soil itself, condensed on exposed surfaces, esp. at night; *v.t.* to moisten. **-fall** *n.* **-iness** *n.* **-y** *a.*

**dex•ter** *a.* pert. to the right hand. **dexterity** *n.* manual skill; cleverness. **-ous, dextrous** *a.* **-ously** *adv.* **-ousness** *n.* **dextral** *a.* right as opposed to left. **dextrality** *n.* right-handedness. **dextrally** *adv.*

**dex•trin, dextrine** *n.* a soluble gummy substance used for stiffening fabrics, sizing paper.

**di•a•be•tes** *n.* a disease marked by excessive flow of sugar-urine due to failure of pancreas to produce insulin.

**di•a•bol•ic, diabolical** *a.* devilish; fiendish. **-ally** *adv.*

**di•ac•o•nal** *a.* pert. to a deacon.

**di•a•dem** *n.* a headdress or crown significant of royalty. **-ed** *a.*

**di•ag•no•sis** *n.* a scientific discrimination of any kind; the identification of a disease from its signs and symptoms; *pl.* **diagnoses. diagnose** *v.t.* **diagnostic** *a.* symptomatic; *n.* a clue. **diagnostician** *n.*

**di•ag•o•nal** *n.* a straight line joining two opposite angles in a rectilineal figure; *a.* from corner to opposite corner; oblique. **-ly** *adv.*

**di•a•gram** *n.* a figure drawn to demonstrate a theorem; a drawing or plan in outline. **-matically** *adv.*

**di•al** *n.* any plate or face on which a pointer moves; *v.t.* to measure on a dial; to call a number on automatic telephone; *pr.p.* **-ling.** *pa.p.* **-led.**

**di•a•lect** *n.* a mode of speech peculiar to a district or social group; vernacular.

**di•a•lec•tic, -al** *a.* pert. to dialectics; *n.* the science of reasoning. **-ally** *adv.* **dialectician** *n.*
**di•a•logue** *n.* a conversation between two (or more) persons. **dialogistic** *a.* **dialogize** *v.i.*
**di•al•y•sis** *n.* separation of colloid (non-crystalline) from crystalline substances in solution, by filtration through a membrane; *pl.* **dialyses. dialytic** *a.*
**di•am•e•ter** *n.* a line passing through the center of a circle and terminated by the circumference; transverse measurement; unit of magnifying power of a lens. **diametric (-al)** *a.* directly opposite.
**di•a•mond** *n.* one of the crystalline forms of carbon and the hardest substance

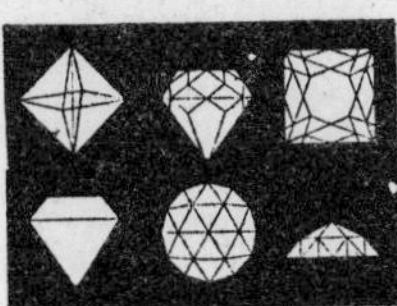
**diamonds**

known; a popular gem stone; a four-sided figure with two acute and two obtuse angles; one of the four suits of playing-cards; playing field for baseball. *a.* **—wedding,** the sixtieth anniversary of a marriage. **black diamonds,** coal.
**di•a•pa•son** *n.* correct pitch; harmony; the two foundation stops of an organ.
**di•a•per** *n.* a baby's breechcloth; *v.t.* to change a baby's diaper.
**di•aph•a•nous** *a.* having the power to transmit light; transparent; translucent.
**di•a•pho•ret•ic** *n.* a medicine which induces perspiration; *a.*
**di•a•phragm** *n.* a dividing membrane; a dome-shaped muscular partition between chest and abdomen; vibrating disc in telephone or microphone; a disc with a circular hole used in telescope or camera to cut off part of a ray of light. **-atic, -al** *a.*
**di•ar•chy** *n.* a system of government in which power is held jointly by two authorities.
**di•ar•rhe•a, diarrhoea** *n.* an excessive and frequent looseness of the bowels. **diarrhetic** *a.*
**di•a•ry** *n.* a daily record; personal record of thoughts, actions, etc. **diarist** *n.*
**di•a•stase** *n.* an enzyme capable of converting starch into sugar, **diastasic** *a.*
**di•as•to•le** *n.* a rhythmical dilatation of the heart and arteries; the lengthening of a syllable usually short, before a pause.
**di•a•ther•mal** *a.* permeable by heat. **diathermanous, diathermous, diathermic** *a.* **diathermy** *n.*
**di•a•tom** *n.* one of an order of microscopic unicellular marine or vegetable organisms.
**di•a•tom•ic** *a.* consisting of two atoms.
**di•a•ton•ic** *a.* pert. to major or minor scales.
**di•a•tribe** *n.* a wordy denunciation. **diatribist** *n.*
**dib•ble** *n.* a pointed instrument used in gardening for making holes. Also **dibber.** *v.t.; v.i.* to make holes. **-r** *n.*
**dice** *n.pl.* small cubes on each of the six faces of which are spots representing numbers 1-6; *Sing.* form **die**; *v.t.* to cut into small squares; *v.i.* to play with dice. **dicer** *n.*
**di•ceph•a•lous** *a.* having two heads.
**di•chot•o•my** *n.* *(Logic)* division of ideas into two classes. **dichotomize** *v.t.* and *v.i.* **dichotomous** *a.*
**dick•er** *v.t.* and *v.i.* to barter; to haggle; to quibble; *n.* a bargain; a deal.
**dick•ey, dicky** *n.* detachable shirt front; seat for servants at back of old-fashioned carriage.
**dic•tate** *v.t.* to read aloud a passage for another to transcribe; to give orders; *v.i.* to speak with authority; *n.* direction that must be obeyed. **dictation** *n.* that which is read aloud for another to write down. **dictator** *n.* one who holds absolute power. **dictatorial** *a.* tending to force one's opinions on another. **dictatorially** *adv.* **dictatorship** *n.*
**dic•tion** *n.* verbal style; enunciation.
**dic•tion•ar•y** *n.* a book containing, alphabetically arranged, the words of a language, their meanings and etymology.
**dic•to•graph** *n.* sound-recording telephonic instrument.
**dic•tum** *n.* a positive assertion; an authoritative statement or opinion; *pl.* **dicta.**
**did** *pa.t.* of verb **do.**
**di•dac•tic** *a.* designed to instruct; containing precepts or doctrines. **-ally** *adv.* **-s** *n.* the science of teaching.
**did•y•mous** *a.* twin.
**die** *n.* a small cube used in games of chance; *pl.* **dice. the die is cast,** one's fate is irrevocably settled.
**die** *v.i.* to cease to live; to become extinct; to wither. *pr.p.* **dying.** *pa.p.* **-d. dying** *a.* **to die for** to want desperately. **to die hard,** to resist stubbornly.
**die** *n.* a device for cutting in a press; an engraved metal block used for stamping a design; the cubical part of a pedestal; *pl.* **dies. — casting** *n.* method of making castings in permanent molds.
**di•e•lec•tric** *a.* non-conducting; *n.* name for a substance through or across which electric induction takes place.
**di•er•e•sis, diaeresis** *n.* a mark ( ¨ ) placed over the second of two consecutive vowels to indicate that each is to be pronounced separately, as in coöperate. *pl.* **diereses, diaereses.**
**Die•sel en•gine** *n.* an internal combustion engine.
**di•e•sis** *n.* *(Print.)* a mark of reference, the double dagger (‡); *pl.* **dieses.**
**di•et** *n.* what one habitually eats and drinks; a regulated allowance of provisions; *v.i.* to slim. **-ary** *n.; a.* **-etic** *a.* **-etics** *n.* the science and study of food values, and their effect on health. **-ician, -itian** *n.*
**di•et** *n.* a legislative assembly in certain countries; an international conference.
**dif•fer** *v.i.* to be unlike; to have distinctive

characteristics. **-ence** *n.* unlikeness; the amount by which one thing exceeds another in weight or number. **-ent** *a.* distinct; **-entia** *n.* the essential quality or characteristic distinguishing any one species from another in a genus; *pl.* **-entiae. -ential** *a.* characteristic; proceeding by increments infinitely small. **-entially** *adv.* **-entiate** *v.t.* to distinguish; *v.i.* to acquire different characteristics. **-entiation** *n.* **-ently** *adv.* **-ential gear,** a mechanism by which two sets of wheels are made to rotate at different speeds.

**dif•fi•cult** *a.* hard to do or understand; not easy. **-ly** *adv.* **-y** *n.* **-ies** *n.pl.* financial embarrassment.

**dif•fi•dent** *a.* timid; shy. **diffidence** *n.* lack of confidence. **-ly** *adv.*

**dif•fract** *v.t.* to break or separate into parts, esp. of rays of light and sound waves. **diffraction** *n.* the phenomenon caused by light passing through a narrow slit.

**dif•fuse** *v.t.* to spread; to scatter; *v.i.* to mix. **diffuse** *a.* widely spread. **diffusely** *adv.* **-ness** *n.* **diffusible** *a.* **diffusion** *n.* term applied to the intermixture of two gases or fluids without chemical combination. **diffusive** *a.* spreading. **diffusively** *adv.* **diffusiveness** *n.*

**dig** *v.t.* to break and turn up earth; to excavate; to delve; to poke or nudge someone; *v.i.* to till the soil; *pr.p.* **-ging.** *pa.p., pa.t.* **dug.** *n.* **-ger** *n.* **-gings** *n.pl.* areas where mining or other digging is carried on.

**di•gest** *v.t.* to convert into a substance which can be readily absorbed into the blood; to think over; *v.i.* **digest** *n.* a magazine containing condensed version of articles already published elsewhere. **-er** *n.* **-ible** *a.* **-ibility** *n.* **digestion** *n.* **digestive** *a.; n.* any medicine that aids digestion.

**dig•it** *n.* a finger; integer under 10. **-al** *a.* pert. to the fingers; *n.* one of the keys of piano or organ. **-alin** *n.* the drug obtained from leaves of digitalis. **-alis** *n.* a strong drug obtained from foxglove, and used medicinally as sedative, narcotic and as cardiac stimulant. **-ate, -ated** *a.* **-igrade** *n.* an animal which walks on its toes; *a.* walking on the toes.

**di•glot** *a.* speaking two languages.

**dig•ni•fy** *v.t.* to invest with dignity or honor; to exalt; to ennoble. **dignified** *a.*

**dig•ni•ty** *n.* state of being dignified; loftiness. **dignitary** *n.* one who holds a high position.

**di•graph** *n.* two vowels or two consonants combined to express one sound as *ea* in head.

**di•gress** *v.i.* to wander from the main theme, topic, or argument; to be diffuse. **digression** *n.* **digressional, -ive** *a.*

**di•he•dral** *a.* having two plane faces. **dihedron** *n.*

**dike, dyke** *n.* an artificial embankment to prevent inundation of low lying ground; igneous rock, once molten, which has filled up fissures of stratified rocks.

**di•lap•i•date** *v.t.* to pull stone from stone; to suffer to fall into ruin; *v.i.* to be in a condition of disrepair. **-d** *a.* **dilapidation** *n.*

**di•late** *v.t.* to swell out; to expand in all directions; *v.i.* to widen. **dilatable** *a.* elastic. **dilatancy, dilatation, dilation** *n.* **dilatant** *a.* **dilator, -r** *n.*

**dil•a•tory** *a.* tardy; inclined to procrastination. **dilatorily** *adv.* **dilatoriness** *n.*

**di•lem•ma** *n.* choice between alternatives equally undesirable; a predicament.

**dil•et•tante** *n.* a lover of the fine arts, esp. in a superficial way; a dabbler. *pl.* **dilettantes, -ti. dilettantish** *a.* **dilettantism, dilettanteism** *n.*

**dil•i•gent** *a.* steady and constant in application; industrious. **diligence** *n.* **-ly** *adv.*

**dill** *n.* a perennial yellow-flowered herb used in medicines and flavoring.

**dil•ly-dal•ly** *v.i.* to loiter; to delay.

**di•lute** *v.t.* to make thinner or more liquid; to reduce the strength of by addition of something; *v.i.* to become thin; *a.* reduced in strength; **diluent** *a.; n.* that which thins or weakens the strength, color, etc. **-ness** *n.* **dilution** *n.*

**di•lu•vi•um** *n.* a surface deposit of sand, gravel, etc. regarded as glacial drift. **diluvial, diluvian** *a.* pert. to or produced by a flood.

**dim** *a.* not bright or distinct; faint; shadowy; vague; *v.t.* to cloud; *v.i.* to become dull or indistinct. *pr.p.* **-ming.** *pa.p., pa.t.* **-med. -ly** *adv.* **-mer** *n.* in motoring, a device to dimish power of headlights. **-ness** *n.*

**dime** *n.* U.S. silver coin equal to 10 cents.

**di•men•sion** *n.* a measurement of extent in a single direction; usually *pl.* measurement in three directions; capacity; importance. **-al** *a.*

**dim•e•ter** *n.* a verse with two measures or accents.

**di•min•ish** *v.t.* to weaken; to reduce; *v.i.* to become smaller. **-ed** *a.* lessened; *(Mus.)* lowered by a semi-tone.

**di•min•u•en•do** *n.* *(Mus.)* a gradual decrease in volume of sound and marked >.

**dim•i•nu•tion** *n.* state of being reduced in size, quality, or amount. **diminutive** *a.* of small size; applied to a suffix expressing smallness; *n.*

**dim•i•ty** *n.* a thin cotton cloth ribbed or figured.

**di•morph•ic** *a.* existing in two forms; capable of crystallizing in two forms under different degrees of temperature. **dimorphism** *n.* **dimorphous** *a.*

**dim•ple** *n.* a slight indentation in any surface; *v.t.; v.i.*

**din** *n.* a loud, continuous noise; racket; clamor; *v.t.* to harass with insistent repetition. *pr.p.* **-ning.** *pa.p., pa.t.* **-ned.**

**dine** *v.t.* to entertain at dinner; *v.i.* to take dinner. **-r** *n.* a compartment on a railway train for serving meals to passengers. Also **dining car. dinette** *n.* a small dining room. **dinner** *n.* the principal meal of the day. **dinner jacket,** a black coat (without

tails) worn as informal evening dress.
**ding** *v.t.* to ring. **—dong** *n.* the sound of bells continuously rung; *a.* monotonous.
**din•ghy, dingy, dingey** *n.* a small boat.
**din•gy** *a.* soiled; of a darkish color. **dinginess** *n.*
**di•no•saur** *n.* a gigantic extinct four-footed reptile of the Mesozoic age.
**dint** *n.* a mark or depression made by a blow; force or energy exerted; *v.t.* **by dint of,** by means of.
**di•o•cese** *n.* the district in which a bishop exercises ecclesiastical jurisdiction. **diocesan** *a.; n.*
**di•oe•cious, diecious** *a. (Bot.)* having the stamens and pistils borne by separate plants of the same species; *(Zool.)* having the male and female reproductive organs separate.
**di•op•ter, dioptre** *n.* the unit for measuring power of a lens.
**di•o•ram•a** *n.* a miniature, three-dimensional scene; varied effects of reality being realized by manipulation of lights.
**di•ox•ide** *n.* a substance the molecules of which comprise one part metal, two parts oxygen.
**dip** *v.t.* to immerse momentarily in a liquid; to dye; to lower and raise again; to wash; *v.i.* to sink below at a certain level; *pr.p.* **-ping.** *pa.p., pa.t.* **-ped.** *n.* a liquid into which something is dipped; immersion; inclination downward of rock strata. **-per** *n.* a semi-aquatic diving bird; *(Astron.)* the Great Bear; the Little Bear. **-py** *a.*
**diph•the•ri•a** *n.* epidemic disease affecting mainly throat and air passages. **-l, diphtheric, diphtheritic,** *a.*
**diph•thong** *n.* a union of two vowel sounds pronounced as one. **-al** *a.* **-ally** *adv.* **-ize** *v.t.* **diphthongization** *n.*
**di•plex** *a. (Radio)* pert. to the reception or transmission of two messages simultaneously.
**dip•lo•car•di•ac** *a.* having a double or divided heart.
**di•plo•ma** *n.* a document or certificate conferring some honor, privilege, or degree; *v.t.*
**di•plo•ma•cy** *n.* the art of conducting international negotiations; tact in dealing with people. **diplomat, diplomatist** *n.* **diplomatic, -al** *a.* **diplomatically** *adv.* **diplomatic corps,** the body of accredited foreign diplomatists resident in any capital.
**di•po•lar** *a.* having two poles. **dipolarize** *v.t.* to magnetize.
**dip•so•ma•ni•a** *n.* an uncontrollable craving for alcoholic stimulants. **dipsomaniac** *n.* **dipsomaniacal** *a.*
**Dip•ter•a** *n.* an order of insects which have only two wings. **dipteral** *a.* **dipteran** *n.* **dipterous** *a.*
**dip•tych** *n.* an ancient writing tablet hinged in the middle and folding together like a book; a pair of carvings or pictures similarly hinged.
**dire** *a.* dreadful; calamitous; disastrous. Also **-ful. -ly, -fully** *adv.*
**di•rect** *a.* straightforward; in line of descent; sincere; unambiguous; *v.t.* to manage; to prescribe a course or line of procedure; *v.i.* to act as a guide; *adv.* in a straight line. **direction** *n.* instruction; guidance; management; line taken by a moving body. **directional, -ing, -ive** *a.* **-ive** *n.* orders from a supreme authority. **-ly** *adv.* in a straight line; immediately after. **-ness** *n.* the quality of being unimpeded by extraneous details. **-or** *n.* (*fem.* **-ress**) one who directs. **-orate** *n.* a board of directors. **-orial** *a.* **-ory** *a.* containing directions; *n.* a book containing the alphabetically arranged names and addresses of the residents of a town or district. **— current** a current flowing in one direction. **direction finder** an aerial which determines direction of incoming radio signals.
**dirge** *n.* a funeral chant; a lament. **-ful** *a.*
**dir•i•gi•ble** *a.* capable of being directed or steered; *n.* a navigable balloon elongated in shape and propelled by engine-driven propellers.
**dirk** *n.* a short dagger; *v.t.*
**dirn•dl** *n.* a type of skirt.
**dirt** *n.* any filthy substance; loose soil; obscenity. **—cheap** *a.* uncommonly cheap. **-ily** *adv.* **-iness** *n.* **-y** *a.; v.t.* to befoul.
**dis-** *pref.* implying *separation,* as in *dis*miss; *negation,* as in *dis*band; *deprivation,* as in *dis*animate; *thoroughness,* as in *dis*annul.
**dis•a•ble** *v.t.* to make incapable or physically unfit; to disqualify. **-ment** *n.* **disability** *n.* incapacity.
**dis•a•buse** *v.t.* to free from misapprehension or error; to undeceive.
**dis•ad•van•tage** *n.* a drawback; a hindrance; a handicap; detriment; hurt. **disadvantageous** *a.* **disadvantageously** *adv.*
**dis•af•fect** *v.t.* to alienate the affection of; to fill with discontent. **-ed** *a.* **-edly** *adv.* **-edness, disaffection** *n.*
**dis•af•firm** *v.t.* to annul; to invalidate; to reverse a decision. **disaffirmation** *n.*
**dis•a•gree** *v.i.* to be at variance; to differ in opinion. **-able** *a.* **-ably** *adv.* **-ment** *n.*
**dis•al•low** *v.t.* to refuse to allow; to reject as untrue or invalid. **-able** *a.* **-ance** *n.*
**dis•ap•pear** *v.i.* to vanish; to become invisible; to cease to exist. **disappearance** *n.*
**dis•ap•point** *v.t.* to fail to realize the hopes of; to frustrate. **-ed** *a.* **-ing** *a.* **-ment** *n.*
**dis•ap•pro•bation** *n.* act of disapproving; censure.
**dis•ap•prove** *v.t.* to form an unfavorable judgment of; to dislike; *v.i.* **disapproval** *n.* **disapprovingly** *adv.*
**dis•arm** *v.t.* to deprive of arms; to render unable to attack; to conciliate; *v.i.* **-ament** *n.* **-ing** *a.* ingenuous.
**dis•ar•range** *v.t.* to disturb the order or arrangement of; to throw into confusion. **-ment** *n.*
**dis•ar•ray** *v.t.* to throw into disorder; to undress; *n.* disorder; confusion.
**dis•as•so•ci•ate** *v.t.* to disunite.

**dis•as•ter** *n.* an adverse happening; sudden misfortune; catastrophe. **disastrous** *a.*
**dis•a•vow** *v.t.* to refuse to acknowledge; to repudiate. **-al, -ment** *n.*
**dis•band** *v.t.* to break up an organization; to dismiss; *v.i.* **-ment** *n.*
**dis•bar** *v.t.* to expel a lawyer from the legal profession. *pr.p.* **-ring.** *pa.p., pa.t.* **-red. -ment** *n.*
**dis•be•lieve** *v.t.* to maintain to be untrue; to refuse to believe; *v.i.* **disbelief** *n.* **disbeliever** *n.*
**dis•burse** *v.t.* to pay out money. **-ment** *n.* **-r** *n.*
**disc** See **disk.**
**dis•card** *v.t.* and *v.i.* to put aside; to cast off; *n.* anything thrown out as useless.
**dis•car•nate** *a.* having no physical body.
**dis•cern** *v.t.* to distinguish clearly; to behold as separate. **-er** *n.* **-ible** *a.* **-ing** *a.* discriminating. **-ment** *n.* power or faculty of judging.
**dis•charge** *v.t.* to unload a cargo; to fire off the charge with which gun is loaded; to emit smoke; to perform a duty; to pay a debt; to demobilize soldiers; to dismiss; *n.* performance; matter which exudes, as from an abscess; the rate of flow of a liquid or waste matter through a pipe.
**dis•ci•ple** *n.* one who receives instruction from another; one who adheres to a particular school of philosophy, religious thought, or art. **-ship** *n.*
**dis•ci•pline** *n.* instruction; subjection to authority; self-control; *v.t.* to improve behavior by judicious penal methods. **disciplinarian** *n.* **disciplinary** *a.* **-r** *n.*
**dis•claim** *v.t.* to renounce claim to, or responsibility for; to disown; *v.i.* **-ant** *n.* **-er** *n.* denial; disavowal.
**dis•close** *v.t.* to reveal; to divulge. **-r** *n.* **disclosure** *n.*
**dis•col•or** *v.t.* to spoil the color of; to stain; *v.i.* **-ation, -ment** *n.* **-ed** *a.*
**dis•com•fit** *v.t.* to defeat; to foil. **-ure** *n.*
**dis•com•fort** *n.* uneasiness; pain; *v.t.* to make uneasy.
**dis•com•mode** *v.t.* to put to inconvenience; to disturb.
**dis•com•pose** *v.t.* to upset the self-possession of; to disturb. **discomposure** *n.*
**dis•con•cert** *v.t.* to embarrass. **-ment** *n.* state of disagreement.
**dis•con•nect** *v.t.* to sever. **-ed** *a.* separated.
**dis•con•so•late** *a.* forlorn; utterly dejected. **-ly** *adv.* **-ness, disconsolation** *n.*
**dis•con•tent** *a.* dissatisfied; *n.* dissatisfaction; *v.t.* to dissatisfy. **-ed** *a.* **-edly** *adv.* **-edness, -ment** *n.*
**dis•con•tin•ue** *v.t.* to interrupt; to break off; *v.i.* to cease. **discontinuance, discontinuation** *n.* **discontinuity** *n.* **discontinuous** *a.*
**dis•cord** *n.* want of agreement; lack of harmony; strife. **discord** *v.i.* to be out of tune. **discordance, discordancy** *n.* **discordant** *a.* dissonant. **discordantly** *adv.*
**dis•count** *v.t.* to deduct a sum or rate per cent from; to disregard; *v.i.* to lend money with discount. **discount** *n.* a deduction.
**dis•coun•te•nance** *v.t.* to refuse to give approval to.
**dis•cour•age** *v.t.* to dishearten; to deter. **-ment** *n.* dejection. **discouraging** *a.*
**dis•course** *n.* a formal speech; a sermon; a dissertation; conversation. **discourse** *v.t.* to utter; *v.i.* to converse.
**dis•cour•te•ous** *a.* lacking in courtesy; rude. **-ly** *adv.* **discourtesy** *n.*
**dis•cov•er** *v.t.* to find out; to bring to light. **-able** *a.* **-er** *n.* **-y** *n.*
**dis•cred•it** *v.t.* to bring into disrepute; *n.* loss of credit or of reputation. **-able** *a.*
**dis•creet** *a.* prudent; judicious; cautious. **-ly** *adv.*
**dis•crep•an•cy** *n.* inconsistency; variance; difference. **discrepant** *a.*
**dis•crete** *a.* separate; distinct. **-ly** *adv.* **-ness** *n.*
**dis•cre•tion** *n.* the quality of being discreet; prudence; discernment. **-al, -ary** *a.* **ally** *adv.*
**dis•crim•i•nate** *v.t.* to detect as different; *v.i.* to make a distinction in. **-ly** *adv.* **discriminating** *a.* able to observe subtle differences. **discriminatingly** *adv.* **discrimination** *n.* **discriminative** *a.*
**dis•cur•sive** *a.* passing from one topic to another; rambling. **-ly** *adv.* **-ness** *n.* **discursory** *a.*
**dis•cus** *n.* a circular plate of stone or metal, used in athletic contests.
**dis•cuss** *v.t.* to examine critically; to exchange ideas on; **-able** (or **-ible**) *a.* **discussion** *n.*
**dis•dain** *v.t.* to look down upon; to scorn; *n.* contempt. **-ful** *a.* **-fully** *adv.* **-fulness** *n.*
**dis•ease** *n.* an unhealthy condition of mind or body; malady; **-d** *a.*
**dis•em•bark** *v.t.* to put on shore; *v.i.* to land. **-ation, -ment** *n.*
**dis•em•bod•y** *v.t.* to free from the body or flesh. **disembodiment** *n.*
**dis•em•bowel** *v.t.* to gut; to eviscerate.
**dis•en•chant** *v.t.* to disillusion.
**dis•en•fran•chise** *v.t.* to deprive of the right to vote. **-ment** *n.*
**dis•en•gage** *v.t.* to unfasten. **-d** *a.* unattached. **-ment** *n.*
**dis•en•tan•gle** *v.t.* to unravel; to untwist.
**dis•es•tab•lish** *v.t.* to deprive of established position. **-ment** *n.*
**dis•fa•vor** *n.* disapproval; *v.t.* to regard unfavorably.
**dis•fig•ure** *v.t.* to mar the appearance of; to deface; to deform. **-ment** *n.*
**dis•frock** *v.t.* to unfrock; to deprive of the right to wear clerical garb.
**dis•gorge** *v.t.* to eject from the throat; to hand over. **-ment** *n.*
**dis•grace** *n.* dishonor; discredit; shameful conduct; *v.t.* to bring dishonor to. **-ful** *a.*
**dis•grun•tled** *a.* vexed; sulky.
**dis•guise** *v.t.* to change the outward appearance of; to misrepresent; *n.*
**dis•gust** *n.* loathing; nausea; aversion; repugnance; *v.t.* **-edly** *adv.* **-ing** *a.*
**dish** *n.* a plate or shallow concave vessel for serving food; the food in such a vessel. *v.t.*
**dis•ha•bille** *n.* partial undress. Also **deshabille.**

**dis•har•mo•ny** *n.* lact of harmony; discord.
**dis•heart•en** *v.t.* to deprive of courage, confidence, or hope; to depress.
**di•shevel** *v.t.* to cause the hair or clothes to be untidy or unkempt; *v.i.* to spread in disorder. **-ment** *n.*
**dis•hon•est** *a.* lacking in honesty. **-ly** *adv.* **-ty** *n.*
**dis•hon•or** *n.* loss of honor; shame; indignity; *v.t.* to disgrace; **-able** *a.* **-ableness** *n.* **-ably** *adv.*
**dis•il•lu•sion** *v.t.* to make the truth apparent; *n.* **-ment** *n.*
**dis•in•cline** *v.t.* to excite dislike or aversion. **disinclination** *n.* unwillingness.
**dis•in•fect** *v.t.* to destroy disease germs. **-ant** *n.* **disinfection** *n.* **-or** *n.*
**dis•in•her•it** *v.t.* to deprive of rights and privileges of an heir. **-ance** *n.*
**dis•in•te•grate** *v.t.* to break up; *v.i.* to crumble to pieces. **disintegration** *n.*
**dis•in•ter** *v.t.* to disentomb; to unearth.
**dis•in•ter•est•ed** *a.* free from self-interest; unprejudiced. **-ness** *n.*
**dis•join** *v.t.* to sever; to disunite. **-t** *v.t.* to separate at the joints; *v.i.* to fall to pieces. **-ted** *a.* incoherent.
**dis•junct** *a.* disjoined. **disjunction** *n.* disconnection; **-ive** *a.*
**disk, disc** *n.* a flat circular plate or surface. **-al** *a.* — **jockey** *n.* announcer of a radio program of recorded music.
**dis•like** *v.t.* to have an aversion to; *n.* distaste; antipathy.
**dis•lo•cate** *v.t.* to put out of place or out of joint. **dislocatedly** *adv.* **dislocation** *n.*
**dis•lodge** *v.t.* to remove from a position of rest; *v.i.* **dislodg(e)ment** *n.*
**dis•loy•al** *a.* failing in duty or allegiance; faithless; treacherous. **-ly** *adv.* **-ty** *n.*
**dis•mal** *a.* gloomy; dreary; depressing; bleak. **-ly** *adv.* **-ness, -ity** *n.*
**dis•man•tle** *v.t.* to strip of furnishings; to take apart.
**dis•may** *v.t.* to alarm; *n.* loss of courage.
**dis•mem•ber** *v.t.* to tear limb from limb; to mutilate. **-ment** *n.*
**dis•miss** *v.t.* to send away; to disperse. **-al** *n.*
**dis•mount** *v.i.; v.t.* to bring down from a place of elevation.
**dis•o•bey** *v.t.* to refuse to do what is commanded. **disobedient** *a.* **disobediently** *adv.* **disobedience** *n.*
**dis•o•blige** *v.t.* to refuse to grant a request to. **disobliging** *a.* ungracious.
**dis•or•der** *n.* muddle; confusion; discomposure; *v.t.* to upset. **-ed** *a.* **-ly** *a.*
**dis•or•gan•ize** *v.t.* to upset the structure or regular system of; **disorganic** *a.* **disorganization.**
**dis•own** *v.t.* to repudiate ownership.
**dis•par•age** *v.t.* to belittle; to lower in rank or reputation. **-ment** *n.* unjust comparison.
**dis•pa•rate** *a.* essentially different. **-ness** *n.*
**dis•par•i•ty** *n.* difference in form, character, or degree; incongruity.
**dis•pas•sion** *n.* lack of feeling; serenity. **-ate** *a.* impartial.
**dis•patch, despatch** *v.t.* to send away; to execute promptly; to dispose of; *n.* speed; the sending out of mails, etc. **-er** *n.*
**dis•pel** *v.t.* to drive away; to scatter; to cause to disappear. *pr.p.* **-ling.** *pa.p., pa.t.* **-led.**
**dis•pense** *v.t.* to divide out in parts; *v.i.* to excuse from; **dispensable** *a.* **dispensary** *n.* a place where medicines are made up and distributed. **dispensation** *n.* the act of distributing; a license to do what is normally prohibited. **-r** *n.* **to dispense with,** to do without.
**dis•perse** *v.t.* to scatter here and there; to spread; to distribute; *v.i.* to separate. **dispersal** *n.* **dispersedly** *adv.* **dispersedness** *n.* **dispersion** *n.* **dispersive** *a.*
**dis•pir•it** *v.t.* to deject; to depress; to discourage. **-ed** *a.*
**dis•place** *v.t.* to put out of position; to oust from situation or office. **-able** *a.* **Displaced Persons,** homeless war victims. **-ment** *n.* the weight of water displaced by a floating ship.
**dis•play** *v.t.* to unfold; to set out conspicuously; *n.* exhibition; exaggerated expression of feeling.
**dis•please** *v.t.* and *v.i.* to offend; to cause dissatisfaction to. **displeasure** *n.* slight anger; dislike.
**dis•pose** *v.t.* to arrange; to regulate; to adjust; *v.i.* to settle; to determine. **disposable** *a.* free to be disposed of. **disposal** *n.* control; regulation. **disposed** *a.* inclined; arranged. **disposedly** *adv.* **disposition** *n.* arrangement. **to dispose of,** to get rid of.
**dis•pos•sess** *v.t.* to put out of possession; to deprive of property; to eject. **-ion** *n.* **-or** *n.*
**dis•proof** *n.* the act of disproving; refutation; a proving to be erroneous.
**dis•pro•por•tion** *n.* want of proportion, symmetry, proper quantity; *v.t.* to mismatch. **-able, -al, -ate, -ed** *a.*
**dis•prove** *v.t.* to prove to be false; to refute; to prove the opposite of.
**dis•pute** *v.t.* to debate; to argue; to discuss; *n.* an argument; a debate. **disputable** *a.* **disputably** *adv.* **disputability** *n.* **disputant** *n.* one who takes part in a dispute. **disputation** *n.* a controversy in words. **disputatious, disputative** *a.*
**dis•qual•i•fy** *v.t.* to make unfit for some special purpose; to make ineligible. **disqualification** *n.*
**dis•qui•et** *v.t.* to disturb; to make restless; *n.* apprehensiveness; **-ment, -ude** *n.* uneasiness.
**dis•qui•si•tion** *n.* a formal enquiry into a subject by argument or discussion. **-al, -ary** *a.*
**dis•re•gard** *v.t.* to take no notice of; to ignore; *n.* indifference.
**dis•re•pair** *n.* state of being out of repair; delapidation.
**dis•re•pute** *n.* discredit; state of being unpopular. **disreputable** *a.* **disreputableness** *n.*
**dis•re•spect** *n.* want of respect or deference; rudeness. **-ful** *a.* **-fully** *adv.*
**dis•robe** *v.t.* to undress.
**dis•rupt** *v.t.* to break; to create a schism.

**disruption** *n.* breach. **disruptive** *a.* **disrupture** *n.* a bursting asunder.

**dis•sat•is•fy** *v.t.* to fail to satisfy; to make discontented. **dissatisfaction** *n.*

**dis•sect** *v.t.* to cut up; to divide for minute examination of its parts. **dissection** *n.* **-or** *n.*

**dis•sem•ble** *v.t.* to disguise; to ignore; *v.i.* to give an erroneous impression; to be hypocritical. **-r** *n.*

**dis•sem•i•nate** *v.t.* to scatter abroad; to broadcast; **dissemination** *n.* scattering; circulation. **disseminative** *a.* **disseminator** *n.*

**dis•sent** *v.i.* to differ in opinion; to disagree; *n.* disagreement; nonconformity. **dissension** *n.* quarrelling; discord. **-er** *n.*

**dis•ser•tate** *v.i.* to discourse. **dissertation** *n.* a formal treatise or discourse.

**dis•serve** *v.i.* to serve badly another's interests. **disservice** *n.* injury; harm.

**dis•sev•er** *v.t.* to separate; to disunite. **-ance, -ation, -ment** *n.*

**dis•si•dent** *a.* differing; disagreeing; *n.* a dissenter. **dissidence** *n.*

**dis•sim•i•lar** *a.* unlike. **dissimilarity, dissimilitude** *n.; difference.* **-ly** *adv.*

**dis•sim•u•late** *v.t.* to feign; *v.i.* to conceal one's true feelings; to be hypocritical. **dissimulation** *n.* the act of pretending.

**dis•si•pate** *v.t.* to scatter; to squander; to dispel; *v.t.* to disappear. **-d** *a.* dissolute. **dissipation** *n.* **dissipative** *a.*

**dis•so•ci•ate** *v.t.* to separate; to disunite; to disclaim connection with. **dissociability** *n.* **dissociable** *a.* incongruous. **dissocial** *a.* anti-social. **dissociation** *n.* separation. **dissociative** *a.*

**dis•sol•u•ble** *a.* capable of being dissolved, liquefied, melted, or decomposed.

**dis•so•lute** *a.* lax in morals; dissipated. **-ly** *adv.* **-ness** *n.* **dissolution** *n.* act of dissolving or passing into solution; disintegration; termination.

**dis•solve** *v.t.* to break up, esp. a solid by the action of a liquid; to terminate; to annul; *v.i.* to melt; to waste away. **dissolvability, dissolvableness** *n.* **dissolvable** *a.* **dissolvent** *a.*

**dis•so•nant** *a.* discordant; harsh; unharmonious. **dissonance** *n.* Also **dissonancy.**

**dis•suade** *v.t.* to persuade not to; to advise against. **-r** *n.* dissuasion *n.* **dissuasive** *a.*

**dis•taff** *n.* a cleft stick for holding the fiber from which thread is made in the process of hand spinning. **the distaff side,** the female line.

**dis•tance** *n.* the space between two objects; the interval between two events; remoteness; *v.t.* to outstrip; to surpass. **distant** *a.* far off; aloof. **distantly** *adv.*

**dis•taste** *n.* dislike; aversion. **-ful** *a.* unpleasant.

**dis•tem•per** *n.* a method of painting (also called *tempera*) with pigments, in powder form, mixed with any glutinous substance soluble in water; *v.t.* to paint in distemper.

**dis•tem•per** *n.* a disordered state of mind or body; a highly infectious inflammatory disease in young dogs.

**dis•tend** *v.t.* to stretch out; to swell; to inflate. *v.i.* to become swollen or puffed out. **distensible** *a.* **distention, distension** *n.*

**dis•till** *v.t.* to vaporize and recondense a liquid; to cause to fall in drops; to cause to trickle; *v.i.* to undergo distillation. **-ate** *n.* the essence produced by distilling. **-ation** *n.* **-atory** *a.* used in distilling. **-er** *n.* **-ery** *n.* a place where distilling is carried on.

**dis•tinct** *a.* of marked difference; separate; clear; well-defined; precise. **distinction** *n.* that which indicates individuality. **-ive** *a.* marking distinction. **-ively** *adv.* **-iveness** *n.* **-ness** *n.*

**dis•tin•guish** *v.t.* to observe the difference between; to keep apart; to give individuality to; *v.i.* to make distinctions. **-ed** *a.* eminent; dignified. **-ing** *a.* characteristic.

**dis•tort** *v.t.* to twist out of shape; to misrepresent. **-ed** *a.* **-edly** *adv.* **distortion** *n.* a twisting awry; misrepresentation.

**dis•tract** *v.t.* to divert; to bewilder; to disturb mentally. **-ed** *a.* **-edly** *adv.* **-edness** *n.* **distraction** *n.* **-ive** *a.* **distraught** *a.* perplexed; bewildered; frantic.

**dis•train** *v.t.* to seize goods, esp. to enforce payment of debt. **-ment, -t** *n.* **-or, -er** *n.*

**dis•tress** *n.* extreme pain; misfortune; extreme poverty; *v.t.* to cause pain or anguish to. **-ful** *a.* **-fully** *adv.* **distressed area,** a part of the country where unemployment is rife.

**dis•tri•bute** *v.t.* to divide among several; to allot or hand out. **distributable** *a.* **distribution** *n.* **distributive** *a.* **distributor(-er)** *n.*

**dis•trict** *n.* an administrative division of a country; *a.* local; *v.t.* to divide into specified areas.

**dis•trust** *v.t.* to have no faith in; to suspect; *n.* doubt.

**dis•turb** *v.t.* to upset the normal condition of; to disquiet; to agitate. **-ance** *n.* confusion.

**dis•un•ion** *n.* discord; dissension. **disunite** *v.t.* to cause a breach between. **disunity** *n.*

**dis•use** *n.* cessation of use or practice.

**di•syl•la•ble** *n.* a word of two syllables. Also **dissyllable.**

**ditch** *n.* a trench dug esp. for drainage or defense; a natural waterway; *v.t.* to cut a ditch in; *v.i.* to make a forced 'landing' on the sea.

**dith•er** *n.* a state of nervous agitation or confusion.

**dit•to** *n.* that which has been said; the same; — **symbol:**", placed below thing to be repeated; *adv.* as aforesaid; *v.t.* to copy.

**dit•ty** *n.* a song; a short poem to be sung.

**dit•ty bag** *n.* a small bag used by soldiers and sailors for holding needles, thread, etc. **ditty box** *n.*

**di•u•ret•ic** *a.* exciting the discharge of urine; *n.* a medicine which tends to increase the flow of urine. **diuresis** *n.* excessive urinary excretion.

**di•ur•nal** *a.* belonging to the day; daily. **-ly** *adv.*
**di•va** *n.* a popular female singer.
**di•va•lent** *a.* *(Chem.)* capable of combining with two radicals; bivalent.
**di•van** *n.* a long cushioned seat; a council room; a smoking room.
**dive** *v.i.* to plunge into water head first; to remain under water; to penetrate deeply into; *n.* a plunge head-first. **diving bell** *n.* an apparatus by which deep-sea divers can work under water.
**di•verge** *v.i.* to turn in different directions; to differ. **-ment, -nce, -ncy** *n.* **-nt** *a.* branching off. **-ntly** *adv.*
**di•vers** *a.* several; sundry. **diverse** *a.* of different kinds. **diversely** *adv.* **diversity** *n.*
**di•ver•si•fy** *v.t.* to give variety to.
**di•vert** *v.t.* to turn aside; to alter the direction of; to amuse or entertain. **diversion** *n.* **-ing** *a.* **divertissement** *n.* a diversion; a short ballet or interlude between the acts of a play.
**di•vest** *v.t.* to strip; to dispossess. **-iture, -ment** *n.*
**di•vide** *v.t.* to separate into parts; to share; to keep apart; to find how many times one number is contained in another; *v.i.* to be separated. *n.* a watershed. **-rs** *n.pl.* compasses for measuring or dividing lines.
**div•i•dend** *n.* the sum to be divided by the divisor to obtain the quotient; interest payable on loans; the share of profits paid to holders of stocks, insurance, etc.
**di•vine** *a.* belonging to or having the nature of God, or a god; holy; sacred; heavenly; *n.* a clergyman; *v.t.* and *v.i.* to forecast by supernatural means. **divination** *n.* the art or act of foretelling the future by non-rational methods. **divinator, diviner** *n.* **-ly** *adv.* **-ness** *n.* **divining rod,** a forked twig used to locate underground water. **divinity** *n.* God; the study of theology.
**di•vi•sion** *n.* part of a whole; a section; difference in opinion. **divisibility** *n.* **divisible** *a.* **-al, divisionary** *a.* pert. to or belonging to a division. **divisor** *n.* the number by which another is divided.
**di•vorce** *n.* the legal dissolution of a marriage contract; *v.t.* to separate; to sever. **divorcee** *n.* a divorced person. **-ment** *n.*
**div•ot** *n.* *(Golf)* a piece of turf cut out accidentally by golfer.
**di•vulge** *v.t.* to disclose something secret or unknown; **divulgate** *v.t.* to publish. **-ment, -nce** *n.*
**Dixie** *n.* the Southern States of the U.S.
**diz•zy** *a.* giddy; light-headed; stupid; *v.t.* to make dizzy. **dizzily** *adv.* **dizziness** *n.* vertigo.
**do** *(Mus.)* the first tone of the major diatonic scale.
**do** *v.t.* to perform; to execute; to finish; to prepare; *v.i.* to act. *pr.p.* **-ing.** *pa.t.* **did.** *pa.p.* **done.** *n.* **to do away with,** to destroy. **-er** *n.* an agent. **to do in,** to murder. **-ings** *n.pl.* things done; activities. **done-out** *a.* exhausted.
**dob•bin** *n.* a name for patient, quiet workhorse.
**do•cent** *n.* a teacher in a university below professorial rank.
**doc•ile** *a.* easily instructed or managed. **-ly** *adv.*
**dock** *v.t.* to cut short; to deduct; *n.* the part of tail left after clipping.
**dock** *n.* wharf, or row of piers where ships are berthed; enclosed space in a law court where accused stands. **-age** *n.* space available in docks for ships; charge made for use of docks. **-er** *n.* one who works at the docks. **-yard,** *n.* **dry dock,** *n.*
**dock•et** *n.* a list of cases for trial; a memorandum; a bill or label affixed to goods giving instructions; *v.t.* to summarize.
**doc•tor** *n.* one who holds the highest degree granted by any faculty of a university; a medical practitioner; *v.t.* to falsify; *v.i.* to practice medicine; to take medicine. **-ate** *n.* **-ship** *n.* **-ial** *a.*
**doc•trine** *n.* principle of belief; instruction. **doctrinal** *a.* **doctrinally** *adv.* **doctrinaire** *n.* a theorist who tends to urge the application of a doctrine beyond all practical considerations; *a.* impracticable.
**doc•u•ment** *n.* an official paper containing information, giving instructions, or establishing facts; *v.t.* to furnish with written evidence of. **-al, documentary** *a.* **-ation** *n.* **-ed** *a.*
**dod•der** *v.t.* or *v.i.* to totter or tremble, as with age. **-ing** *a.*
**do•dec•a•gon** *n.* a plane figure with twelve sides and twelve angles. **-al** *a.*
**dodge** *v.t.* to evade or escape by a sudden turning; *v.i.* to twist aside; *n.* a quick, evasive movement; a trick; **-r** *n.*
**do•do** *n.* an extinct flightless bird. *pl.* **-(e)s.**
**doe** *n.* the female of the fallow deer; antelope, rabbit, goat, rat, mouse. **-skin** *n.* a fine close-woven cloth.
**does** *3rd pers. sing. pr. ind.* of verb **do.**
**doff** *v.t.* to take off; to rid oneself of.
**dog** *n.* a common, carnivorous quadruped of the same genus as the wolf, mainly domesticated; a worthless fellow; one of the two constellations of stars *(Canis Major, Canis Minor);* a metal bar for holding logs of wood or supporting fire-irons; *v.t.* to pursue relentlessly. *pr.p.* **-ging.** *pa.p.* **-ged. —collar. —** days *n.pl.* the hottest period of the northern summer. **—eared** *a.* having the corners of the pages turned down. **-ged** *a.* stubborn; persistent. **-gedly** *adv.* **-gedness** *n.* **-gish** *a.* surly. **-gy** *a.* **-house** *n.* **-like** *a.* faithful. **—tired,** *a.* completely exhausted. **-tooth,** *n.* a canine tooth. **-watch** *n.* one of the two-hour watches on board ship from 4-6 or 6-8 p.m. **a dog in the manger,** a spoil-sport. **a hot dog, a hot** sausage inside a roll. **in the doghouse,** in disfavor. **to go to the dogs,** to be ruined. **to let sleeping dogs lie,** not to stir up trouble unnecessarily.
**dog•ger•el** *n.* unpoetical burlesque verse; *a.*
**dog•ma** *n.* a philosophical tenet; a

principle or belief. **dogmatic, -al,** *a.* opinionated; authoritative. **dogmatically** *adv.* **dogmatics** *n.* doctrinal theology. **-tize** *v.i.* to express an opinion positively or arrogantly. **-tism** *n.* positive assertion. **-tist** *n.*

**doi•ly** *n.* a small table mat placed under dishes or put on plate.

**dol•ce** *a.* sweet; soft.

**dol•drums** *n.pl.* a belt of calms at the Equator; a state of depression.

**dole** *v.t.* to distribute in small portions; *n.* something given or paid out.

**dole•ful** *a.* grievous; melancholic. **-ly** *adv.* **-ness** *n.*

**doll** *n.* a puppet; a toy baby as a child's plaything; a pretty, rather brainless girl. **to doll up** to dress up smartly.

**dol•lar** *n.* a silver coin or paper note, the monetary unit of U.S.A. and Canada.

**dol•lop** *n.* a lump, a shapeless mass.

**doll•y** *n.* a mobile platform; a small locomotive used in quarries, etc. **dollied** *a.*

**dol•man** *n.* a long, loose Turkish garment; Hussar's coat worn like a cape.

**dol•men** *n.* a prehistoric tomb formed by a large unhewn stone resting on two or

**dolmen**

more unhewn uprights.

**dol•or•ous** *a.* full of, expressing, or causing grief. **-ly** *adv.*

**dol•phin** *n.* a sea mammal; a mooring buoy.

**dolphin**

**dolt** *n.* a dull, stupid fellow. **-ish** *a.* **-ishly** *adv.*

**do•main** *n.* that which one has dominion over; property; the scope or sphere of any branch of human knowledge. **-al, dominial** *a.*

**dome** *n.* a hemispherical vault reared above the roof of a building; a large cupola. **-d, domical** *a.*

**do•mes•tic** *a.* pert. to a house or home; tame (of animals); not foreign (of a country's policy); *n.* a household servant. **-ally** *adv.* **-ate** *v.t.* **domesticity** *n.* life in a household. **— science,** science of home management, etc.

**dom•i•cile** *n.* an abode; a person's permanent residence; *v.t.* to establish in a fixed residence. **domiciliary** *a.*

**dom•i•nant** *a.* ruling; prevailing; *n.* the fifth note of the diatonic scale. **dominance** *n.* authority. **dominancy** *n.* **-ly** *adv.* **dominate** *v.t.* and *v.i.* to influence strongly. **domination** *n.* **dominative** *a.* **dominator** *n.* **domineer** *v.i.* to rule with arbitrary sway. **domineering** *a.* arrogant. **dominion** *n.* territory under one government.

**do•min•i•cal** *a.* belonging to the Lord's Day.

**Do•min•i•can** *a.* belonging to *St. Dominic,* or to the order of preaching friars, founded by him. *n.*

**dom•i•no** *n.* a long cloak of black silk with a hood, worn at masquerades; a mask; one of the 28 oblong pieces marked each with a certain number of spots used in the game of *dominoes.*

**don** *v.t.* to put on; to assume. *pr.p.* **-ning** *pa.p., pa.t.* **-ned.**

**do•na•tion** *n.* act of giving; a gift; a contribution. **donate** *v.t.* **donative** *n.* **donor** *n.*

**done** *pa.p.* of the verb **do. done!** agreed.

**don•key** *n.* an ass; a foolish person. **— engine** *n.* a small auxiliary steam engine.

**don't** contr. of **do not.**

**doo•dle** *v.i.* to scribble aimlessly.

**doom** *n.* fate; evil destiny; judgment; ruin; *v.t.* to destine; to pass sentence on; to condemn. **-ed** *a.* under sentence. **-ful** *a.* **-sday** *n.* the Day of Judgment. **Doomsday or Domesday Book,** the census compiled by order of William the Conqueror, for purposes of taxation.

**door** *n.* the wooden or metal structure, hinged or sliding, giving access to house, room, passage, or cupboard. **dead as a door nail** quite dead. **-post** *n.* the jamb. **-step** *n.* the step outside a door. **-way** *n.* the entrance to a house, room, etc. **to darken one's door,** to enter one's house.

**dope** *n.* any thick liquid, or semi-liquid lubricant; a varnish; any narcotic; a stupid person; inside information; *v.t.* to administer dope to. **dopey** *a.* stupefied with drugs; slow-witted.

**Do•ri•an** *a.* pert. to *Doris,* in ancient Greece, or to its inhabitants. **Doric,** *a.* pert. to the simple style of architecture of the Dorians; (of dialect) unpolished; *n.* a mode of Greek music.

**dor•mant** *a.* sleeping; hibernating; not in action. **dormancy** *n.* **dormer-window** *n.* a small vertical window projecting from a roof slope. **dormitory** *n.* a building primarily containing sleeping rooms. **dormouse** *n.* a small, hibernating rodent.

**dor•sal** *a.* pert. to, near, or belonging to, the back.

**do•ry** *n.* a flat-bottomed boat.

**dose** *n.* the prescribed quantity of medicine to be taken at one time; anything disagreeable that must be taken or done; *v.t.* **dosage** *n.* the amount of a dose. **dosimeter** *n.* an instrument for measuring minute doses accurately.

**dos•si•er** *n.* a set of documents.

**dot** *n.* a small point or spot made with a pencil, or sharp instrument; a speck; *v.t.* to mark with dots; *v.i. pr.p.* **-ting.** *pa.p.* **-ted. -ty** *a.* **dot and dash,** in Morse code, the short and long symbols.

**dot** *n.* a dowry. **dotal** *a.*

**dote** *v.i.* to be foolishly sentimental; to be over-fond of. **dotage** *n.* childishness of old people; senility. **dotard** *n.* one whose intellect is impaired by old age.

**dou•ble** *a.* denoting two things of the same

kind; existing in pairs; serving for two; deceitful; ambiguous; *adv.* twice; *v.t.* to fold in two; *v.i.* to increase to twice as much; *n.* a duplicate; an actor's substitute or understudy. — **bass** *n.* the largest and lowest pitched of the stringed instruments. —**breasted** *a.* able to fasten over on either side. — **cross** *v.t.* to cheat a swindler. —**dealing** *n.* —**decker** *n.* a ship or bus with two decks. —**edged** *a.* having two edges; effective for and against. — **entry** *n.* in bookkeeping, a system by which every entry is made both on debit and credit side of an account. —**faced** *a.* hypocritical. **-r** *n.* **doublet** *n.* one of a pair; a close-fitting garment for the upper part of body. — **time** *n.* the fastest marching pace next to a run.

**doubt** *v.t.* to disbelieve; *v.i.* to be in a state of uncertainty; to hesitate; *n.* uncertainty of mind; distrust of others. **-able** *a.* **-er** *n.* **-ful** *a.* dubious; uncertain. **-fully** *adv.* **-fulness** *n.* **-ing** *a.* **-ingly** *adv.* **-less** *adv.* without doubt; probably. **-lessly** *adv.*

**douche** *n.* a jet of water directed upon or into the body; an apparatus for douching.

**dough** *n.* a mass of flour moistened and kneaded, to be baked afterwards; money. **-boy** *n.* an infantryman. **-nuts** *n.* sweetened dough in shape of balls or rings, fried in fat and finally dipped in sugar. **-y** *a.*

**dough•ty** *a.* brave; valiant. **doughtily** *adv.*

**dour** *a.* sullen; gloomy; obstinate. **-ly** *adv.*

**douse, dowse** *v.t.* to dip or plunge into water; to lower a sail; to put out.

**dove** *n.* a pigeon; a symbol of peace or of the Holy Ghost. —**colored** *a.* soft pinkish grey. **-cot(e)** *n.* nesting box of pigeons. **-tail** *n.* a joint made by fitting

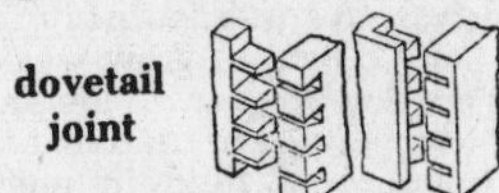

**dovetail joint**

one piece toothed with wedge like projections into cavities of corresponding shape; *v.t.* to link together.

**dow•a•ger** *n.* widow with property or title left by her husband; a dignified elderly lady.

**dow•dy** *a.* untidy; lacking style. **dowdily** *adv.* **dowdiness** *n.*

**dow•el** *n.* a wooden or iron pin for joining two adjacent boards or stones.

**dow•er** *n.* a widow's share of her husband's property; gift; talent. **-ed** *a.* **-less** *a.* **dowry** *n.* goods given to the husband by the bride or her family at marriage.

**down** *n.* the fine, soft feathers of birds. **-y** *a.* resembling or covered with down.

**down** *n.* a hillock of sand by the sea; treeless land.

**down** *prep.* along a descent; towards a lower place; towards the mouth of a river; passing from the past to less remote times; *adv.* in a downward direction; to the bottom; *v.t.* to knock down; *n.* a reversal of fortune. **-cast** *a.* depressed. **-fall** *n.* ruin; a heavy fall of rain. **-fallen** *a.* **-hearted** *a.* despondent. **-hill** *a.; adv.* **-pour** *n.* a heavy fall of water. **-right** *adv.* completely; *a.* unqualified. **-stairs** *adv.; n.* the ground floor. **-stream** *adv.* with the current. **-trodden** *a.* oppressed. **-ward** *a.* **-wards** *adv.* —**town**; towards the center of the town.

**dowse** *v.t.* and *v.i.* to find subterranean water supply by means of a divining rod. **-r** *n.*

**dox•ol•o•gy** *n.* a short hymn of praise to God.

**doze** *v.i.* to sleep lightly; *n.* a nap.

**doz•en** *n.; a.* twelve. **baker's dozen, devil's dozen,** thirteen.

**drab** *n.* a dingy, brownish-grey color; *a.* dull; monotonous.

**drach•ma** *n.* a Greek coin.

**draft** *n.* a sketch or rough copy; a current of air; an order directing payment of money by a bank; a drink. *v.t.* to compose and write; to take for military service. **-sman** *n.* **-smanship** *n.* **-y** *a.* **-iness** *n.*

**drag** *v.t.* to draw with main force; to trawl with a drag or net; *v.i.* to move heavily or slowly. *pr.p.* **-ging.** *pa.p.* **-ged.** *n.* a net or hook to bring up submerged things; anything that slows progress. **-ger** *n.* **-net** *n.* a fishing net for dragging along the sea floor.

**drag•gle** *v.t.* and *v.i.* to make or become wet and dirty by trailing on the ground.

**dra•gon** *n.* a fabulous winged reptile represented as breathing out fire and smoke. **-et** *n.* a little dragon. **-fly** *n.* an insect. **-'s blood,** a carmine fruit resin used for coloring varnishes and lacquers.

**dra•goon** *n.* a cavalryman; *v.t.* to oppress.

**drain** *v.t.* to filter; to make dry; to swallow down; to exhaust; *v.i.* to flow off or drip away gradually; *n.* a pipe, sewer or ditch; **-able** *a.* **-age** *n.* system of carrying away surplus water from an area. **-er** *n.* a kitchen utensil on which plates, etc. are placed to dry; a colander or sieve.

**drake** *n.* the male of the duck.

**dram** *n.* a unit of weight; ⅛ of an ounce.

**dra•ma** *n.* a composition to be acted on the stage; the branch of literature dealing with plays; a series of real emotional events. **dramatic** *a.* tense. **dramatically** *adv.* **dramatization** *n.* **dramatize** *v.t.* **dramatist** *n.* a writer of plays. **-turge** *n.* **-turgy** *n.* the art of writing or producing plays. **dramatis personae** characters of a drama.

**drank** *pa.t.* of **drink.**

**drape** *v.t.* to hang something loosely in folds; to adorn with drapery. **drapery** *n.*

**dras•tic** *a.* very powerful; harsh; thorough.

**drat** *interj.* a mild expletive expressing annoyance.

**draught** *n.* **-s** *n.pl.* the game of checkers; *a.* drawn from a barrel, as beer. **-(s)man** *n.* See **draft.**

**draw** *v.t.* to pull along; to haul towards oneself; to deduce; to receive (as money, salary, etc.); to inhale; to sketch; *v.i.* to attract; to pull out a weapon for action; to be equal in a match; to cast lots; to have a free passage of air (as a chimney). *pr.p.* **-ing.** *pa.t.* **drew.** *pa.p.* **-n.** *n.* a game ending with same score for both sides. **-able** *a.* **-back** *n.* a disadvantage. **-bridge** *n.* a bridge that can be raised or let down. **-er** *n.* one who or that which draws; a lidless, sliding box in a table, chest, etc. **-ers** *n.pl.* close fitting undergarment for lower limbs. **-ing** *n.* a lottery; the art of representing objects by line or color on paper, canvas, etc. **-ing-room** *n.* a room in which guests are entertained. **to draw a blank,** to fail to find what one is seeking. **to draw the line,** to stop. **drawn and quartered** quartered and disemboweled.

**drawl** *v.i.* to speak with slow and lengthened tone; *v.t.; n.* a manner of speech.

**dray** *n.* a low cart for heavy goods.

**dread** *n.* overwhelming apprehension; awe; terror; *a.* dreadful; *v.t.* and *v.i.* to regard with fear; **-ed** *a.* **-ful** *a.* terrifying; **-fully** *adv.* **-fulness** *n.* **-nought** *n.* a large-sized battleship mounting heavy guns; a thick woolen overcoat.

**dream** *n.* a series of images or thoughts in the mind of a person asleep; a vision; an aspiration; *v.i.* to have yearnings; *v.t.* to see in a dream; *pa.t.* and *p.p.* **-ed** or **-t.** **-er** *n.* **-ily** *adv.* **-iness** *n.* **-land** *n.* an imaginary land seen in dreams. **-less** *a.* **-like** *a.* **-y** *a.*

**drear•y** *a.* dismal; gloomy; bleak. **drearily** *adv.* **dreariness** *n.* *(Poetic)* **drear** *a.*

**dredge** *v.t.* to sprinkle. **-r** *n.* a flour can with perforated lid.

**dredge** *n.* a machine like a large scoop for taking up mud from a river bed; a dragnet for oysters or zoological specimens.

**dregs** *n.pl.* sediment in a liquid that falls to the bottom; the most worthless class.

**drench** *v.t.* to wet thoroughly; to soak.

**dress** *v.t.* and *v.i.* to put clothes on; to adorn; *n.* clothes. **-er** *n.* a dressing table or bureau. **-ing** *n-* a sterile substance for a wound; manure; substance used to stiffen fabrics; a sauce; stuffing for a fowl. **-ing-down** *n.* a scolding. **-ing gown** *n.* a robe worn while dressing. **-ing table** *n.* **-maker** *n.* **-making** *n.* **-y** *a.* fashionable.

**drew** *pa.t.* of **draw.**

**drib•ble** *v.i.* to trickle down, esp. of saliva; to bounce the ball repeatedly. **driblet** *n.* a small drop.

**dried** *pa.t.* and *pa.p.* of verb **dry.**

**drift** *n.* the state or process of being driven; the accumulation of substance driven by the wind; a slow surface current in the sea caused usually by the prevailing wind; tendency; *v.t.* to drive into heaps; to cause to float in a certain direction; *v.i.* to follow unconsciously. **-age** *n.* deviation of a ship from its course. **— anchor** *n.* an anchor for keeping a ship's head to the wind during a storm. **-er** *n.* an aimless wanderer. **-wood** *n.* wood cast on shore by tide.

**drill** *v.t.* to pierce; to bore a hole through; to instruct thoroughly; *n.* revolving tool for boring holes; an implement for making holes for seed; instruction. **drilling** *n.*

**drink** *v.t.* to swallow; to empty as a glass; to breathe in. *pa.t., pa.p.* **drunk.** *n.* intoxicating liquor. **-able** *a.* **-er** *n.* a tippler. **to drink in,** to absorb through the senses.

**drip** *v.t.; v.i.* to ooze; to trickle. *pr.p.* **-ping.** *pa.t., pa.p.* **-ped.** *n.* a drop; the sound made by water dripping. **-ping** *a.* thoroughly wet; *n.* that which falls in drops; *pl.* fat, from meat while roasting. **-stone** *n.* a projecting molding over doors to deflect rain water.

**drive** *v.t.* to urge on; to guide the course of; to cause to work; to strike in, as a nail; to hit a ball with force; *v.i.* to be forced along. *pr.p.* **driving.** *pa.t.* **drove.** *pa.p.* **driven.** *n.* the capacity for getting things done. **-r** *n.* a golf club for hitting ball from the tee. **to drive at,** to hint at.

**driv•el** *v.i.* to dribble like a child; to talk nonsense; *n.* nonsense. **-er** *n.*

**driz•zle** *v.t.* and *v.i.* to rain gently; *n.* fine rain.

**droit** *n.* legal right.

**droll** *a.* laughable; funny; queer; *n.* a buffoon; a jester; an odd character. **-ery** *n.*

**drom•e•dar•y** *n.* a one-humped camel.

**dromedary**

**drone** *n.* the male of the honey-bee; an idler who lives on the work of others; a deep, humming sound; the largest pipe of the bagpipes; *v.t.* and *v.i.* to speak or sing in a monotone.

**drool** *v.i.* to drivel; to speak foolishly.

**droop** *v.i.* to hang down; to grow weak; to sag; to wilt (as flowers); *v.t.* to lower.

**drop** *n.* a globular particle of fluid that falls; a minute quantity of fluid in medical dose; *v.t.* to let fall; to dismiss or break off; (of animals) to give birth to prematurely; *v.i.* to sink to a lower level. *pr.p.* **-ping.** *pa.t.* and *pa.p.* **-ped.** **— curtain** *n.* a painted curtain lowered in front of theater stage between scenes in a play. **—kick** *n.* a kick effected by letting the ball fall from the hands to the ground to be kicked immediately on the rebound. **-let** *n.* a tiny drop. **-per** *n.* a small glass tube from which liquid is measured out in drops. **-pings** *n.pl.* dung. **to drop in,** to make an informal visit. **a drop in the bucket,** a small amount.

**drop•sy** *n.* a morbid collection of fluid in any part of body. **dropsical** *a.*

**dross** *n.* the scum of metals thrown off in smelting; refuse.

**drought, drouth** *n.* dryness; absence of rain over a prolonged period. **-iness** *n.* **-y** *a.*

**drove** *n.* a herd or flock, esp. on the move. **-r** *n.* one who drives cattle or sheep.

**drown** *v.t.* to suffocate by submerging in water; to deluge; to render inaudible; *v.i.*

**drowse** *v.t.* to make sleepy; *v.i.* be heavy with sleep; *n.* a doze. **drowsy** *a.* **drowsily**

*adv.* **drowsiness** *n.*
**drub** *v.t.* to beat; *v.i.* to defeat. *pr.p.* **-bing.** *pa.p., pa.t.* **-bed.** **-bing** *n.* a thrashing.
**drudge** *v.i.* to labor at menial tasks; *n.* one who must do menial work. **drudgery** *n.* hard, monotonous, toil. **drudgingly** *adv.*
**drug** *n.* any substance used in the composition of a medicine; a narcotic; *v.t.; v.i.* to take drugs habitually and in excess. *pr.p.* **-ging.** *pr.p.* **-ged.** **-gist** *n.* a pharmaceutical chemist.
**drum** *n.* a percussion instrument comprising a hollow, parchment-covered cylinder beaten with a drumstick; the middle portion of ear; *v.t.* to teach by constant repetition; *v.i.* to beat rhythmically. *pr.p.* **-ming.** *pa.p., pa.t.* **-med.** **— major** *n.* the leader of a marching drum corps or band. **-mer** *n.* **-stick** *n.* lower part of leg of cooked fowl.
**drunk** *pa.p.* of **drink;** *a.* intoxicated; *n.* a drunk person. **-ard** *n.* one who habitually drinks to excess. **-en** *a.* given to excessive drinking. **-enness** *n.*
**drupe** *n.* a fleshy fruit, such as peach, with a stone or kernel containing the seed.
**dry** *a.* free from moisture; not giving milk, as a cow; thirsty; unsweetened, as wines; uninteresting; sarcastic; plain; pert. to a district subject to prohibition laws; *v.t.* to drain; *v.i.* to evaporate; to become void of ideas. **drier** *n.* **— battery** *n.* a battery composed of *dry cells* sealed in a container to prevent leakage. **to dry clean,** to clean garments with chemicals. **— goods** *n.pl.* textile fabrics. **-ly, drily** *adv.* **— measure,** a measure of bulk, used for grain, etc. **-ness** *n.* **— rot** *n.* a decay caused by fungous disease. **—shod** *a.* with dry feet.
**dry•ad** *n.* in Greek mythology a spirit of the trees.
**du•al** *a.* consisting of two; *n.* the dual number. **duad** *n.* pair of things regarded as one. **-ism** *n.* the belief in the existence of good and evil as separate entities. **-ist** *n.* **-ity** *n.* state of being double.
**dub** *v.t.* to knight; to give a nickname to; to make smooth; to provide a film with a sound track not in the original language. *pr.p.* **-bing.** *pa.p. and pa.t.* **-bed.**
**du•bi•ous** *a.* doubtful; liable to turn out well or ill; shady. **-ly** *adv.* **-ness** *n.* **dubiety** *n.* hesitancy; uncertainty. **dubitable** *a.* doubtful. **dubitancy, dubitation** *n.*
**du•cal** *a.* pert. to a duke. **-ly** *adv.* in a ducal manner. **ducat** *n.* a coin. **duce** *n.* leader, **duchess** *n.* the wife or widow of a duke. **duchy** *n.* dominions of dukes.
**duch•ess** *n.* See **ducal.**
**duck** *n.* a coarse cloth or light canvas. **-s** *n.pl.* trousers made of this.
**duck** *n.* any broad-beaked, web-footed, short-legged water bird; female duck; a sudden lowering of head; *v.i.* to cringe; *v.i.* to dodge. **-board** *n.* planking to cross swampy areas. **duckling** *n.* a young duck. **-pins,** small bowling pins. **-weed** *n.* minute, floating, green plants growing on all standing waters.
**duct** *n.* a canal or tube for conveying fluids. **-less glands** endocrine glands which discharge their secretions directly into the blood.
**duc•tile** *a.* (of metals) capable of being drawn out in fine threads or hammered thin; easily influenced. **ductility** *n.*
**dud** *n.* anything defective or worthless; *n.pl.* clothes, esp. old and sloppy.
**dudg•eon** *n.* anger; resentment.
**due** *a.* fitting to be paid or done to another; appointed to arrive; attributable; *adv.* directly; *n.* that which is owed. **duly** *adv.* properly.
**du•el** *n.* any two-sided contest; *v.i.* to fight a duel. **-ist** *n.*
**du•et** *n.* a musical composition for two performers. **-ist** *n.*
**duff** *v.t.* to make old things look like new; to fake. **-er** *n.* a poor player.
**duf•fel, duffle** *n.* a coarse woolen cloth with a thick nap. **— bag** *n.* a canvas bag used for carrying clothes, etc.
**dug** *n.* a teat, esp. of an animal.
**dug** *pa.t.* and *pa.p.* of **dig.** **-out** *n.* a canoe hollowed out of a tree trunk; covered shelter for players not on field.
**duke** *n.* (*fem.* **duchess**) the highest order of nobility in the British peerage. **-dom** *n.* possessions of a duke. See **ducal.**
**dul•cet** *a.* sweet to the ear; melodious.
**dul•ci•mer** *n.* an old musical instrument probably like a small harp; a modern instrument related to the guitar.
**dull** *a.* stupid; slow of hearing or seeing; tedious; uninspired; dim or cloudy; blunt; *v.t.* to stupefy; to mitigate; *v.i.* to become dull. **-ard** *n.* a slow-witted person. **-ness** *n.*
**dulse** *n.* an edible reddish-brown seaweed.
**du•ly** See **due.**
**dumb** *a.* lacking permanently the power of speech; mute; *v.t.* to silence. **-bell** *n.* two heavy iron balls connected by a bar for a handle, used in gymnastic exercises; moron. **-ly** *adv.* in silence. **-ness** *n.* **—waiter** *n.* a hand-operated elevator. **dum(b)found** *v.t.* to amaze; **-ed** *a.* **dummy** *a.* sham; *n.* a tailor's mannequin.
**dum-dum** *n.* a soft nosed bullet.
**dump** *v.t.* to deposit; to unload; *n.* refuse or scrap heap; a poorly kept up place. **-ling** *n.* a ball of dough boiled in water. **-y** *a.* short; thick; squat. **-iness** *n.* **— truck** *n.* a truck whose body tilts and end opens for unloading.
**dun** *a.* greyish-brown color; dark; *n.*
**dun** *v.t.* to importune for payment of a debt. *pr.p.* **-ning.** *pa.p.* **-ned.**
**dunce** *n.* one who is slow at learning.
**dune** *n.* a low hill of sand in desert areas or on the seacoast.
**dung** *n.* the excrement of animals; *v.t.* to treat with manure; *v.i.* **-hill** *n.* a mound of dung.
**dun•ga•ree** *n.* a coarse hard-wearing cotton cloth. **-s** *n.pl.* trousers of this material.
**dun•geon** *n.* orig. the principal tower or 'keep' of a castle; a damp subterranean prison cell; *v.t.* to confine in a dungeon.
**dunk** *v.t.* to dip into tea, coffee, soup, etc.
**du•o** *n.* a duet; a pair of stage artists.
**du•o•de•cen•ni•al** *a.* occurring every

twelve years. **duodenary** *a.* pert. to 12.

**du•o•dec•i•mo** *n.* a 12 mo. book. **duodecimal** *a.* proceeding by twelves; *n.* **duodecimals** *n.pl.* a method of computation by denominations of 12 instead of 10. **duodecimally** *adv.*

**du•o•de•num** *n.* upper part of intestines; *pl.* **duodena. duodenal** *a.*

**dupe** *n.* one who is easily cheated; *v.t.* to cheat; to mislead. **-ry** *n.*

**du•plex** *a.* twofold; *n.* a house consisting of two family units. **duple** *a.* double.

**du•pli•cate** *a.* double; *n.* an exact copy; facsimile; *v.t.* to make a copy. **duplication** *n.* **duplicator** *n.* a machine for making copies of written matter. **duplicity** *n.* deception.

**du•ra•ble** *a.* lasting; able to resist wear and tear. **-ness, durability** *n.* **durably** *adv.* **durance** *n.* confinement. **duration** *n.* continuance in time.

**du•ress** *n.* compulsion; coercion.

**dur•ing** *prep.* in the time of; in course of.

**dusk** *a.* tending to darkness; *n.* twilight. **-y** *a.* partially dark; dim; dark-skinned.

**dust** *n.* very fine particles of matter; *v.t.* to remove dust from. **— jacket** *n.* a book cover. **-er** *n.* a tin with perforated lid for sprinkling; a light garment used as a robe. **-ily** *adv.* **-iness** *n.* **-ing** *n.*

**Dutch** *a.* pert. to Holland; *n.* the language, people of Holland. **-man** *n.* **— treat,** an entertainment for which each person pays his own share.

**du•ty** *n.* that which is due; military service; a period of work set down for each person on a roster. **duteous** *a.* obedient. **duteously** *adv.* **dutiable** *a.* subject to customs duties. Also **dutied. dutiful** *a.* attentive to duty; submissive. **dutifully** *adv.* **dutifulness** *n.* **—free** *a.* exempt from customs duty.

**dwarf** *n.* abnormally small in size; *v.t.* to hinder the growth of. **dwarf, -ish** *a.* undersized.

**dwell** *v.i.* to abide; to be domiciled; to deal with in detail. **-er** *n.* **-ing** *n.*

**dwin•dle** *v.i.* to shrink; *v.t.* to lessen.

**dye** *v.t.* to give a new color to; to stain; *v.i.* to undergo change of color. *pr.p.* **-ing.** *pa.p.* **-d** *n.* **-r** *n.* **-stuff** *n.* substance used for dyeing.

**dy•ing** *pr.p.* of **die.**

**dyke** *n.* See **dike.**

**dy•nam•ic** *a.* possessing energy and forcefulness. Also **-al.** **-s** *n.* branch of mechanics which deals with *force in motion.* **dynamism** *n.* a school of scientific thought which explains phenomena of universe as resulting from action of natural forces. **dynamist** *n.* **dynamite** *n.* a powerful high explosive, with great disruptive force; *v.t.* **dynamiter** *n.* one who uses dynamite. **dynamo** *n.* a generator for transforming mechanical energy into electrical energy; *pl.* **dynamos. dynamo-graph** *n.* **dynamometer** *n.* an instrument for measuring force.

**dy•nas•ty** *n.* a line of kings of the same family; the period of a family's rule. **dynast** *n.* a ruler. **dynastic** *a.*

**dyne** *n.* a centimeter-gram-second unit of force.

**dys-** *prefix* fr. Gk. meaning bad, ill, difficult.

**dys•en•ter•y** *n.* inflammation of the mucous membrane of the large intestine. **dysenteric, -al** *a.*

**dys•pep•sia** *n.* indigestion. **dyspeptic** *a.; n.*

**each** *a.* and *pron.* denoting every one of a number, separately considered. Abbrev. **ea.**

**ea•ger** *a.* yearning; earnest. **-ly** *adv.* **-ness** *n.*

**ea•gle** *n.* large bird of prey; *(Golf)* a hole played in two under par. **—eyed** *a.* sharp-sighted. **-t** *n.* a young eagle.

**ear** *n.* the organ of hearing, esp. external part of it; sensitiveness to musical sounds. **-ache** *n.* acute pain in ear. **-drum** *n.* the middle ear or tympanum. **-ed** *a.* **-lobe** *n.* **-mark** *v.t.* to reserve for a particular purpose. **-shot** *n.* distance at which sounds can be heard. **-splitting** *a.* exceedingly loud and piercing. **-wax** *n.* cerumen, a waxy secretion of glands of ear.

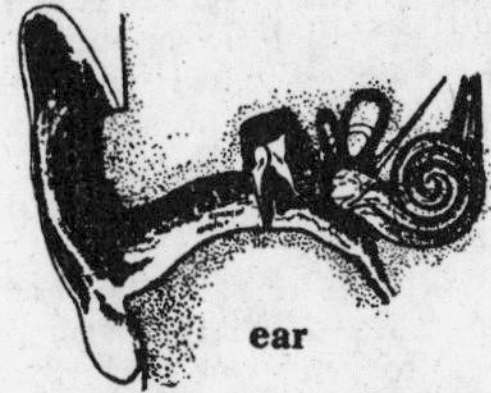
ear

**earl** *n.* a nobleman ranking between a marquis and a viscount. **-dom** *n.* territory of an earl.

**ear•ly** *a.* and *adv.* in the beginning of a period of time; belonging far back in time. **earliness** *n.*

**earn** *v.t.* to gain money by labor; to merit by service; to get. **-ings** *n.pl.* wages; savings.

**ear•nest** *a.* sincere; zealous; *n.* seriousness. **-ly** *adv.* **-ness** *n.*

**ear•nest** *n.* a pledge.

**earth** *n.* the planet on which we live; the soil, dry land, on the surface of the earth. **-bound** *a.* worldly. **-en** *a.* **-enware** *n.* crockery made of earth. **-iness** *n.* **-ling** *n.* a dweller on the earth. **-ly** *a.* terrestrial. **-quake** *n.* disturbance of the earth's surface due to contraction of a section of the crust of the earth. **-worm** *n.* the common worm. **-y** *a.*

**ease** *n.* leisure; freedom from anxiety, bodily effort; facility; natural grace of manner; *v.t.* to free from pain. **-ful** *a.* **-ment** *n.(Law)* right of way. **easily** *adv.* **easiness, easing** *n.* **easy** *a.* moderate; comfortable. **stand at ease!** military term to relax. **easy chair** *n.* an armchair. **easygoing** *a.*

**ea•sel** *n.* a wooden frame to support pictures.

**east** *n.* one of the four cardinal points; the part of the horizon where the sun rises; **-ern** *a.* toward, in, or from the east; oriental. **-ing** *n.* distance eastward from a given meridian. **-ward** *adv.* or *a.* **-wards** *adv.* **Far East,** China, Japan, etc. **Middle East,** Iran, Iraq, etc. **Near East,** Turkey, Syria, Palestine, etc.

**Eas•ter** *n.* a festival commemorating Christ's resurrection.

**eas•y** See **ease.**

**eat** *v.t.* to chew and swallow; gnaw; corrode; wear away; *v.i.* to take food. **ate** *pa.t.* **-en** *pa.p.* **-able** *a.* or *n.*

**eaves** *n.pl.* the lower edges of a sloping roof overhanging the walls of a building. **-drop** *v.i.* to listen furtively to a conversation. **-dropper** *n.*

**ebb** *n.* a decline; growing less; *v.i.* to flow back; to sink. **— tide** *n.* the retiring tide.

**eb•on** *a.* black as ebony. **-y** *n.* a cabinet wood which is jet black. **-ite** *n.* hard rubber or form of a vulcanite.

**e•bul•lient** *a.* overflowing; exuberant; enthusiastic. **ebullience** *n.* **ebullition** *n.* act of boiling; outburst of feeling; agitation.

**ec•cen•tric** *a.* departing from the center; irregular; odd; *n.* a whimsical person; one who defies the social conventions. **-ally** *adv.* **-ity** *n.* departure from normal way of conducting oneself.

**ec•cle•si•a** *n.* a church; a religious assembly. **-stic** *n.* a clergyman. **-stical** *a.* **-sticism** *n.* **ecclesiology** *n.* the science and study of church architecture and decoration. **ecclesiologist** *n.*

**ech•e•lon** *n.* a level of command; formation of airplanes in which each plane flies slightly above and to the right or left of the one in front.

**e•chi•nus** *n.* a sea urchin; a rounded molding.

**ech•o** *n.* repetition of sound produced by sound waves reflected from an obstructing object; close imitation of another's remarks or ideas; repetition; *pl.* **-es.** **-ism** *n.* forming words to imitate natural sounds.

**é•clair** *n.* a pastry filled with cream and frosted with chocolate.

**é•clat** *n.* splendor; renown; acclamation.

**e•clec•tic** *a.* and *n.* a thinker who selects and reconciles principles, opinions, belonging to different schools of thought. **-ally** *adv.*

**e•clipse** *n.* an interception of the light of one heavenly body by another; *v.t.* to obscure or hide; to surpass.

**e•clip•tic** *n.* the great circle on the celestial sphere which lies in the plane of the sun's apparent orbit around the Earth. Also **-al** *a.*

**ec•logue** *n.* a short poem of a pastoral nature.

**e•col•o•gy** *n.* a study of relations between animals, plants, people and their environment.

**e•con•o•my** *n.* wise expenditure of money; careful use of materials. **economic(al)** *a.* **economically** *adv.* **economics** *n.pl.* **political economy** *n.* the science which deals with the production, distribution, and consumption of the world's resources and the management of state income and expenditure. **economize** *v.i.* **economist** *n.*

**ec•ru** *n.* beige.

**ec•sta•sy** *n.;* a sense of uplift and joyfulness and increased well-being; excessive joy. **ecstatic** *a.* to be in a state of rapture; overjoyed. **-ally** *adv.*

**ec•to-, ect-** *pref.* implying *outside, without.*

**ec•to•plasm** *n.* *(Zool.)* exterior protoplasm of a cell. **-ic** *a.*

**ec•u•men•ic, ecumenical** *a.* universal; representative of the Church. Also **oecumenic.**

**ec•ze•ma** *n.* disease of the skin, characterized by itchiness and inflammatory eruption.

**ed•del•weiss** *n.* a small white flowering plant found in the Swiss Alps.

**ed•dy** *n.* a current of air, smoke, or water, swirling back contrary to the main current; a vortex; *v.i.* to move in a circle.

**E•den** *n.* the garden where Adam and Eve lived: (lc.) a place of delight; a paradise.

**e•den•tate** *a.* lacking teeth.

**edge** *n.* the thin cutting side of the blade of an instrument; rim; keenness; *v.t.* to sharpen; to move almost imperceptibly; *v.i.* to move sideways. **-d** *a.* sharp. **-less** *a.* **-ways, -wise** *adv.* in the direction of the edge. **edging** *n.* border or fringe; narrow lace. **edgy** *a.* irritable.

**ed•i•ble** *a.* fit for eating. **edibility** *n.*

**e•dict** *n.* a law or decree.

**ed•i•fy** *v.t.* to instruct in moral and religious knowledge. **edified** *pa.t.* and *pa.p.* **edification** *n.* improvement of the mind or morals. **edifice** *n.* a fine building. **edifier** *n.* **-ing** *a.*

**ed•it** *v.t.* to prepare for publication; to revise and alter or omit. **-ion** *n.* the form in which a book is published. **-or** *n.* **-orial** *n.* an article in a newspaper presenting the newspaper's point of view.

**ed•u•cate** *v.t.* to cultivate and discipline the mind and other faculties by teaching. **educable** *a.* able to absorb education. **educability** *n.* **education** *n.* process of training. **educational** *a.* **educationally** *adv.* **educative** *a.* **educator** *n.*

**e•duce** *v.t.* to draw or bring out that which is latent; to elicit; to extract. **educible** *a.* **educt** *n.* that which is educed. **eduction** *n.*

**eel** *n.* a group of fish with elongated bodies.

**ee•rie, eery** *a.* weird, superstitiously timid; frightening. **eerily** *adv.* **eeriness** *n.*

**ef•face** *v.t.* to erase or scratch out. **-ment** *n.*

**ef•fect** *n.* that which is produced by an agent or cause; result; *v.t.* to bring about. **-s** *n.pl.* property. **-ive** *a.* in a condition to produce desired result; powerful. **-ively** *adv.* **-iveness** *n.* **-ual** *a.* **-uality** *n.* **-ually** *adv.* **-uate** *v.t.* to achieve. **in effect,** for practical purposes. **to take effect,** to become operative.

**ef•fem•i•nate** *a.* unmanly; womanish.

**ef•fer•ent** *a.* conveying away from the center.

**ef•fer•vesce** *v.i.* to bubble, to seethe; to be in a state of excitement. **-nce** *n.* **-nt** *a.* bubbling; lively; sparkling.

**ef•fete** *a.* no longer capable of bearing young; sterile; unfruitful; worn-out; spent.

**ef•fi•ca•cious** *a.* producing the desired effect. **-ly** *adv.* **-ness, efficacity, efficacy** *n.*

**ef•fi•cient** *a.* producing results; capable; able; effective. **efficiency** *n.* competency. **-ly** *adv.*

**ef•fi•gy** *n.* an image or representation of a person. **hang in effigy,** to hang an image of a person as a public expression of hatred.

**ef•flo•resce** *v.i.* to burst into bloom; to blossom. **-nce, -ncy** *n.* **-nt** *a.*

**ef•flu•ent** *a.* flowing out; *n.* a stream which flows out from another river or lake. **effluence** *n.* issue; emanation.

**ef•flu•vi•um** *n.* an exhalation with a disagreeable smell; *pl.* **effluvia. effuvial** *a.*

**ef•flux** *n.* that which flows out.

**ef•fort** *n.* putting forth an exertion of strength or power, bodily or mental; attempt. **-less** *a.*

**ef•fron•ter•y** *n.* brazen impudence; audacity.

**ef•fulge** *v.i.* to shine brightly. **-nce** *n.* **-nt** *a.* diffusing a flood of light; radiant.

**ef•fuse** *v.t.* to pour out or forth. *effusion* *n.* that which is poured out. **effusive** *a.* gushing.

**e•gad** *interj.* a mild imprecation.

**egg** *v.t.* to urge on; to encourage one to take action.

**egg** *n.* an oval body laid by birds and a few animals in which the embryo continues development apart from parent body; matured female germ cell or ovum; anything egg-shaped. **—cell** *n.* the ovum. **-nog** *n.* a drink made of egg, milk, sugar, and alcoholic liquor. **-shell** *n.* **-plant** *n.* an edible plant with somewhat egg-shaped purple fruit.

**e•gis** See **aegis.**

**eg•lan•tine** *n.* the sweetbrier; honeysuckle.

**e•go** *n.* I; self; the personal identity. **-centric** *a.* self-centered. **-centricism, -centricity** *n.* **-ism** *n.* theory that bases morality on self-interest. **-ist** *n.* **-istical** *a.* **-mania** *n.* abnormal self-esteem. **-tism** *n.* selfishness. **-tist** *n.* **-tistical** *a.* **-tistically** *adv.*

**e•gre•gious** *a.* remarkably flagrant. **-ly** *adv.*

**e•gress** *n.* act of leaving an enclosed place; exit; the right of departure. **-ion** *n.*

**e•gret** *n.* several species of heron.

**E•gyp•tian** *a.* pert. to Egypt. **Egyptology, Egyptologist** *n.*

**ei•der** *n.* a species of sea ducks. **-down** *n.* the breast down of the eider.

**eight** *n.* and *a.* one more than seven; written as 8 or VIII. **-een** *n.* and *a.* eight more than ten; written 18 or XVIII. **-eenth** *n.* and *a.* written 18th. **-fold** *a.* eight times quantity **-h** *n.* one of eight equal parts; 8th; the interval of an octave. **-ieth** *a.* written 80th; *n.* written 1/80. **-y** *n.* and *a.* fourscore.

**ei•ther** *a.* or *pron.* one or the other; one of two.

**e•jac•u•late** *v.t.* to utter suddenly and briefly; to eject. **ejaculation** *n.* a sudden emission. **ejaculatory** *a.*

**e•ject** *v.t.* to throw out; to cast forth; to turn out. **-a** *n.* waste matter. **-ion** *n.* **-ment** *n.* explusion; *(Law)* the forcible removal of a defaulting tenant by legal process from land or house. **-or** *n.*

**eke** *v.t.* to add or augment. **—out,** to supplement; to use makeshifts.

**e•lab•o•rate** *v.t.* to work out in detail; to

take pains with; *v.i.* to give fuller treatment; *a.* highly finished; complicated. **-ly** *adv.* **-ness, elaboration** *n.*

**é•lan** *n.* dash; impetuosity.

**e•land** *n.* the largest of the antelopes, found in Africa.

**e•lapse** *v.i.* of time, to pass by; to slip away.

**e•las•tic** *a.* possessing the property of recovering the original form when a distorting or constraining force has been removed; springy; *n.* a fabric whose threads are interwoven with strands of rubber; a rubber band. **-ity** *n.*

**e•late** *v.t.* to raise or exalt the spirit of; make proud. **-d** *a.* **elation** *n.* exultation.

**el•bow** *n.* the joint between the arm and forearm; any sharp bend or turn; *v.t.* and *v.i.* to jostle. **—grease** *n.* hard work. **-room** *n.* ample room for free movement.

**el•der** *a.* older; senior; prior; *n.* one who is older. **-liness** *n.* **-ly** *a.* up in years. **eldest** *a.*

**el•der** *n.* a flowering shrub which yields berries.

**e•lect** *v.t.;* to choose by vote; to select; *v.i.* to determine on a course of action; *a.* chosen; *n.* those predestined to eternal life. **-ion** *n.* the act of electing. **-ioneer** *v.i.* to work for the election of a candidate. **-ive** *a.* appointed by. **-ively** *adv.* **-or** *n.* one with right to vote at election. **-oral** *a.* **-oral college** *n.* a body of electors chosen by voters in the states to elect the president and vice-president of the U.S. **-orate** *n.* the whole body of electors.

**e•lec•tric** *a.* pertaining to, worked by, producing electricity; thrilling. **— chair** *n.* **—eel** *n.* a freshwater fish of S. America which is capable of inflicting powerful shocks. **-al** *a.* **-ally** *adv.* **-ity** *n.* a form of energy generated by friction, induction, or chemical change.

**e•lec•tri•cian** *n.* a mechanic who makes or repairs electrical apparatus.

**e•lec•tri•fy** *v.t.* to charge with electricity; to thrill, startle, excite by an unexpected statement or action.

**e•lec•tro-** *pref.* referring to some phase of electricity. **-analysis** *n.* chemical analysis by electrolysis. **-cardiogram** *n.* a tracing of electrical changes of contractions of heart. **-cardiograph** *n.* machine which makes the tracing.

**e•lec•tro•cute** *v.t.* to cause death by electric shock. **electrocution.** *n.*

**e•lec•trode** *n.* a metallic conductor of an open electric circuit in contact with some other kind of conductor.

**e•lec•tro•dy•nam•ics** *n.* a branch of the science of electricity which treats of the laws of electricity in motion or of electric currents and their effects. Also **electrokinetics.**

**e•lec•trol•y•sis** *n.* the resolution of dissolved or fused chemical compounds into elements by passing a current of electricity through them; destruction of hair roots, tumors, by an electric current. **electrolyze** *v.t.* **electrolyte** *n.* the liquid which carries the electric current between two electrodes.

**e•lec•tro•mag•net** *n.* a mass of soft iron temporarily magnetized by a current of electricity. **-ic** *a.* **-ism** *n.* branch of electrical science which deals with the relation of magnetism and electricity.

**electromagnet**

**e•lec•trom•e•ter** *n.* an instrument for measuring electricity.

**e•lec•tro•mo•tion** *n.* the flow of an electric current in a voltaic circuit. **electromotive** *a.* producing motion by means of electricity.

**e•lec•tron** *n.* the lightest known particle, a constituent of all atoms. **-ics** *n.* the branch of physics which deals with the behavior of free electrons. **— microscope,** and instrument of immense magnifying power in which controlled rays of electrons are used instead of light rays.

**e•lec•tro•neg•a•tive** *a.* carrying a negative charge of electricity.

**e•lec•trop•a•thy** *n.* treatment of disease by means of electricity. Also **electrotherapy. electrotherapeutics** *n.*

**e•lec•tro•plate** *v.t.* to cover with a coating of metal by means of electrolysis.

**e•lec•tro•pos•i•tive** *a.* carrying a positive charge of electricity.

**e•lec•tro•type** *n.* a facsimile printing plate of type or illustrations.

**e•lec•trum** *n.* an alloy of gold and silver.

**el•ee•mos•y•nar•y** *a.* given in charity.

**el•e•gant** *a.* graceful; refined; luxurious. **-ly** *adv.* **elegance** *n.* grace; beauty.

**el•e•gy** *n.* a poem of mourning. **elegiac** *a.* **elegiacs** *n.pl.* **elegiacal** *a.* **elegiast, elegist** *n.* a writer of elegies.

**e•lek•tron** *n.* a magnesium alloy of unusual lightness.

**el•e•ment** *n.* the first principle or rule; a component part; the habitation most suited to a person or animal; a substance which cannot be separated into two or more substances. **-s** *n.pl.* the physical forces of nature which determine the state of the weather. **-al** *a.* of the powers of nature; basic; fundamental. **-ary** *a.* rudimentary; simple.

**el•e•phant** *n.* the largest four-footed animal, having a long flexible trunk, two ivory tusks, and exceedingly thick skin. **-ine** *a.* huge; unwieldy. **-oid** *a.* like an elephant.

**el•e•phan•ti•a•sis** *a.* disease in which there is gross enlargement of the affected parts.

**el•e•vate** *v.t.* to lift up; to raise to a higher rank or station. **-d** *n.* a railroad on elevated tracks. **elevation** *n.* elevated place, a hill, a height. **elevator** *n.* a lift or hoist. **elevatory** *a.* tending or having power to elevate.

**e•lev•en** *n.* and *a.* one more than ten,

written as 11 or XI. **-th** *n.* one of 11 equal parts of a whole.

**elf** *n.* a supernatural, diminutive being of folklore with mischievous traits; a dwarf; *pl.* **elves. -in** *n.* a little elf. **-ish** *a.*

**e•lic•it** *v.t.* to draw out; to extract; to bring to light facts by questioning or reasoning.

**el•i•gi•ble** *a.* legally qualified; fit and worthy to be chosen; desirable. **eligibility** *n.*

**e•lim•i•nate** *v.t.* to remove; get rid of; leave out of consideration. **elimination, eliminator** *n.*

**e•lite** *n.* a choice or select body.

**e•lix•ir** *n.* a cure-all; a medicine.

**E•liz•a•be•than** *a.* pert. to Queen Elizabeth I or her times; *n.* a writer or distinguished person of her reign.

**elk** *n.* the largest member of the deer family in the N. of Europe.

**elk**

**el•lipse** *n.* a regular oval; the plane section across a cone not taken at right angles to the axis. **ellipsoid** *n.* a closed solid figure of which every plane section is an ellipse. **elliptic(al)** *a.* oval. See **ellipsis.**

**el•lip•sis** *n.* in English syntax a term denoting the omission of a word or words from a sentence whereby the complete meaning is obtained by inference. **elliptic(al)** *a.*

**elm** *n.* a genus of trees.

**el•o•cu•tion** *n.* art of effective public speaking from the point of view of enunciation, voice-production, delivery. **-ary** *a.* **-ist** *n.*

**e•lon•gate** *v.t.* to lengthen; to extend. **elongation** *n.* the act of stretching out.

**e•lope** *v.i.* to run away with a lover; to marry secretly; to bolt unexpectedly. **-ment** *n.*

**el•o•quence** *n.* oratory; rhetoric; fluency. **eloquent** *a.* **eloquently** *adv.*

**else** *adv.* besides; other; otherwise; instead. **-where** *adv.* in or to some other place.

**e•lu•ci•date** *v.t.* to make clear; to throw light upon; to explain. **elucidation** *n.* **elucidative, elucidatory** *a.* **elucidator** *n.*

**e•lude** *v.t.* to keep out of sight; to evade; to baffle. **elusion** *n.* evasion. **elusive, elusory** *a.*

**el•van, elves, elvish** See **elf.**

**E•ly•si•um** *n.* any place of perfect happiness. **Elysian** *a.* like a paradise.

**em-** *pref.* in or with; or adding a transitive or casual force in the composition of verbs.

**em** *n.* typographical unit of width (approx. 1/6th of an in.) used for measuring the length of a line of type.

**e•ma•ci•ate** *v.t.* to reduce one to flesh and bones; *v.i.* to waste away; to become extremely thin. **-d** *a.* **emaciation** *n.*

**em•a•nate** *v.i.* to issue from; to originate; to proceed from. **emanant** *a.* flowing from. **emanation** *n.* a flowing out from. **emanative, emanatory** *a.*

**e•man•ci•pate** *v.t.* to set free from any restraint or restriction. **emancipation, emancipator** *n.*

**e•mas•cu•late** *v.t.* to castrate; to render effeminate. **emasculation** *n.* **emasculatory** *a.*

**em•balm** *v.t.* to preserve a corpse from decay by means of antiseptic agents, balm, aromatic oils and spices. **-er, -ing, -ment** *n.*

**em•bank** *v.t.* to enclose or defend with a bank, mound, or earthwork. **-ment** *n.*

**em•ar•go** *n.* in international law, an order by which a government prevents a foreign ship from entering or leaving port; a general prohibition; *pl.* **-es.**

**em•bark** *v.t. or v.i.* to put on board a ship; to enter on some business or enterprise. **-ation** *n.*

**em•bar•rass** *v.t.* to perplex; to impede; to involve one in difficulties. **-ed, -ing** *a.* **-ment** *n.*

**em•bas•sy** *n.* the person sent abroad as an ambassador along with his staff; the residence of an ambassador.

**em•bat•tle** *v.t.* to furnish with battlements. **-ment** *n.*

**em•bed** *v.t.* to lay as in a bed; to bed in soil. Also **imbed.**

**em•bel•lish** *v.t.* to make beautiful or elegant with ornaments; to add fanciful details to a report or story. **-er** *n.* **-ingly** *adv.* **-ment** *n.*

**em•ber** *n.* a live piece of coal or wood; *pl.* red-hot ashes.

**em•bez•zle** *v.t.* to misappropriate fraudulently. **-ment, -r** *n.*

**em•bit•ter** *v.t.* to make bitter. **-ed** *a.*

**em•bla•zon** *v.t.* to adorn with heraldic figures; to deck in blazing colors. **-ment, -ry** *n.*

**em•blem** *n.* sign; badge; symbol; device. **-atical** *a.* **-atically** *adv.* **-atize** *v.t.* to represent by an emblem.

**em•bod•y, imbody** *v.t.* to form into a body; to incorporate; to represent. **embodiment** *n.*

**em•bold•en** *v.t.* to give boldness or courage to; to encourage.

**em•bo•lism** *n.* the insertion of days between other days to adjust the reckoning of time; *(Med.)* the result of the presence in the bloodstream of a solid foreign substance, as a clot. **-al** *a.*

**em•bos•om, imbosom** *v.t.* to clasp or receive into the bosom; to enclose; to shelter; to foster.

**em•boss** *v.t.* to raise or form a design above the surrounding surface. **-ed** *a.* **-ment** *n.*

**em•bow•el** *v.t.* to disembowel.

**em•bow•er** *v.t.* to surround (with flowers).

**em•brace** *v.t.* to press to the bosom; to accept; to encircle; *n.* a hug.

**em•bro•cate** *v.t.* to moisten and rub with lotion, etc. **embrocation** *n.*

**em•broi•der** *v.t.* to ornament fabrics with threads of silk, linen, etc. to form a design. **-er** *n.* **-y** *n.* ornamental needlework.
**em•broil** *v.t.* to involve in a quarrel or strife; to entangle; to confound. **-ment** *n.*
**em•bry•o, embryon** *n.* fetus during first months of gestation; a plant in rudimentary stage of development within seed; *a.* rudimentary. **-logical** *a.* **-logist** *n.* **-logy** *n.* science which deals with the growth and structure of the embryo. **-nic** *a.* at an early stage of development.
**e•mend** *v.t.* to remove faults or blemishes from; to alter for the better. **-ate** *v.t.* **-ation** *n.* correction of errors or blemishes. **-ator** *n.* **-atory** *a.*
**em•er•ald** *n.* precious stone of beryl species, transparent and bright green in color.
**e•merge** *v.i.* to come forth; **-nce** *n.* coming into view; an outgrowth from a plant. **-ncy** *n.* state of pressing necessity; difficult situation; urgent need. **-nt** *a.* rising into view.
**e•mer•i•tus** *n.* and *a.* one who has honorably resigned or retired from a position of trust or responsibility but is retained on the rolls.
**e•mer•sion** *n.* an emerging.
**em•er•y** *n.* a naturally occurring mixture of corundum and iron oxide, used as an abrasive for polishing; *v.t.* to rub with emery.
**e•met•ic** *a.* and *n.* any agent which causes vomiting.
**em•i•grate** *v.i.* to leave one's country to settle in another. **emigrant** *a.* and *n.* one who emigrates. **emigration.** *n.*
**em•i•nent** *a.* exalted in rank, office, or public estimation; prominent. **eminence** *n.* elevation; official dignity; fame.
**em•is•sar•y** *n.* agent sent on a mission.
**e•mit** *v.t.* to send forth; to utter (a declaration). **-ting** *pr.p.* **-ted** *pa.p.* and *pa.t.* **emission** *n.* **emissive** *a.*
**e•mol•lient** *a.* softening; relaxing; a soothing agent or medicine.
**e•mol•u•ment** *n.* profit arising from office or employment; gain; pay; salary; fee.
**e•mo•tion** *n.* strong, generalized feeling. **-al** *a.* easily excited or upset. **-alism** *n.* **-ally** *adv.* **-less** *a.* **emotive** *a.* causing emotion.
**em•pa•thy** *n.* intellectual identification of oneself with another.
**em•per•or** *n.* the title assumed by the ruler of an empire.
**em•pha•sis** *n.* stress on anything. *pl.* **emphases. emphasize** *v.t.* to stress. **emphatical** *n.*
**em•pire** *n.* a country with its satellite states under the rule of an emperor or some other supreme control.
**em•pir•ic, em•pir•i•cal** *a.* having reference to actual facts. **empiric** *n.* one who depends for his knowledge entirely on experience. **-ally** *adv.* **empiricism** *n.* the formulation of scientific laws by the process of observation and experiment. **empiricist** *n.*
**em•place•ment** *n.* the place or site of a building; placing in position.
**em•ploy** *v.t.* to make use of; to hire or engage; to exercise; to occupy; *n.* paid service. **-able** *a.* **-ce** *n.* one who is employed at a wage or salary. **-er, -ment** *n.*
**em•po•ri•um** *n.* a place of extensive commerce or trade; a big shop. *pl.* **-s, emporia.**
**em•pow•er** *v.t.* to authorize.
**em•press** *n.* the wife of an emperor; a female who exercises similar supreme power to that of an emperor.
**emp•ty** *a.* containing nothing; void; vacant; hollow; senseless; *v.t.* to drain; *v.i.* to discharge. **emptiness** *n.*
**em•py•e•ma** *n.* a collection of pus in body cavity, esp. in pleura.
**em•py•re•al** *a.* of pure fire or light; pert. to highest and purest regions of heaven. **empyream** *a.* and *n.* the firmament.
**e•mu, emeu** *a.* a large flightless bird.
**em•u•late** *v.t.* to strive to equal or surpass; to imitate. **emulation** *n.* **emulative** *a.* **emulator** *n.* **emulous** *a.* anxious to outdo another.
**e•mul•sion** *n.* a liquid mixture in which a fatty or oily substance is suspended in water and by aid of a mucilaginous medium forms a smooth milky white fluid; the coating of silver salts on a photographic film or plate. **emulsic** *a.* **emulsification** *n.* **emulsify** *v.t.* **emulsive** *a.* yielding a milklike substance.
**en-** *pref.* in; with; or adding transitive or causal force in verb composition.
**en•a•ble** *v.t.* to make able; to authorize to empower; to fit; to qualify.
**en•act** *v.t.* to make into a law; to act the part of. **-ing, -ive** *a.* **-ment** *n.*
**e•nam•el** *n.* a vitreous compound fused into surface of metal, pottery, or glass for utility and ornament; the hard, glossy surface of teeth; paint with glossy finish; *v.t.* to enamel.
**en•am•or** *v.t.* to inflame with love; to charm.
**en•camp** *v.t.* to form into a camp; *v.i.* to settle down temporarily. **-ment** *n.* campsite.
**en•caus•tic** *a.* pertaining to the fixing of colors by burning; *n.* an ancient style of decorative art, consisting in painting on heated wax.
**en•ceinte** *a.* pregnant; *n.* the precincts within the walls of a fort.
**en•ceph•a•lon** *n.* the brain. **encephalic** *a.* cerebral. **encephalitis** *n.* inflammation of the brain.
**en•chain** *v.t.* to fasten with a chain. **-ment** *n.*
**en•chant** *v.t.* to charm by sorcery. **-ed** *a.* held by a spell. **-er** *n.* (*fem.* **-ress**). **-ingly** *adv.* **-ment** *n.* magic; delight.
**en•chase** *v.t.* to set with jewels. **-d** *a.*
**en•cir•cle** *v.t.* to enclose in a circle; to surround. **-ment** *n.*
**en•clave** *n.* a country entirely surrounded by territories of another power; anything entirely enclosed into something else.
**en•close, inclose** *v.t.* to shut in; to

surround; to envelop; to contain. **enclosure** *n.*

**en•co•mi•um** *n.* high commendation; formal praise. *pl.* **-s, encomia. encomiast** *n.* eulogist. **encomiastic(al)** *a.* **encomiastically** *adv.*

**en•com•pass** *v.t.* to include; to encircle. **-ment** *n.*

**en•core** *n.* a recall awarded by an audience;

**en•coun•ter** *v.t.* to meet face to face; to confront; *n.* an unexpected meeting; a fight or combat.

**en•cour•age** *v.t.* to give courage to; to inspire with hope. **-ment** *n.* **encouraging** *a.*

**en•croach** *v.i.* to invade the rights or possessions of another. **-er** *n.* **-ingly** *adv.* **-ment** *n.*

**en•cum•ber** *v.t.* to load; to burden. **encumbrance** *n.* a burden; a dependent person.

**en•cyc•li•cal** *a.* intended to circulate among many people and in many places. Also **encyclic.**

**en•cy•clo•pe•di•a, encyclopaedia** *n.* works which give detailed account, in alphabetical order, of field of human knowledge. **-n** *a.* embracing all forms of knowledge. **encyclopedia** *a.* having universal knowledge; full of information. **encyclopedist** *n.*

**en•cyst** *v.t.* or *v.i.* to enclose or become enclosed in a sac or cyst.

**end** *n.* termination; conclusion; limit; extremity; final condition; result; purpose; *v.t.* to bring to conclusion; to destroy, to put to death; *v.i.* to finish; to cease. **-ed** *a.* **-ing** *n.* **-less** *a.* **-lessly** *adv.* **-lessness** *n.* **to make both ends meet,** to keep out of debt.

**en•dan•ger** *v.t.* to place in jeopardy; to expose to loss or injury.

**en•dear** *v.t.* to render more beloved. **-ed, -ing** *a.* **-ingly** *adv.* **-ment** *n.* tender affection; loving word; a caress.

**en•deav•or** *v.i.* to attempt; to strive; *n.* effort; struggle.

**en•dem•ic, endemical** *a.* terms applied to recurring diseases confined to certain people or localities and which arise from local causes.

**en•dive** *n.* an annual plant of the family *Compositae,* used for salads.

**en•do-** *pref.* indicating *within.*

**en•do•car•di•tis** *n.* inflammation of the lining membrane of the heart.

**en•do•car•di•um** *n.* the lining membrane of the heart. **endocardiacal** *a.*

**en•do•crine** *a.* describing the tissues and organs giving rise to an internal secretion; *n.* any such secretion. **endocrinology** *n.* study of internal secretions of ductless glands.

**en•dog•a•my** *n.* the custom of compulsory marriage within the limits of a tribe or between members of the same race. **endogamous** *a.*

**en•do•plasm** *n.* inner portion of cytoplasm of a cell.

**en•dorse, indorse** *v.t.* to sign one's name on back of a check; to sanction; to confirm; to vouch for **endorsable** *a.* **endorsee** *n.* the person to whom a bill of exchange is assigned by endorsement. **-ment, -r** *n.*

**en•do•sperm** *n.* the nutritive starchy tissue which surrounds the embryo in many seeds. **-ic** *a.*

**en•dow** *v.t.* to enrich or furnish. **-er** *n.* **-ment** *n.* grant; bequest; natural capacity.

**en•dure** *v.t.* to remain firm under; to bear with patience; to put up with; to sustain; to suffer; to tolerate; *v.i.* to continue; to last. **endurable** *a.* can be endured. **endurableness** *n.* **endurably** *adv.* **endurance** *n.* patience; fortitude; stamina. **-r** *n.* **enduring** *a.* and *n.* **enduringly** *adv.*

**en•e•ma** *n.* a liquid solution injected into intestine through rectum; device for this.

**en•e•my** *n.* an armed foe; opposing state; something harmful; *a.* due to an enemy.

**en•er•gy** *n.* vigor; force; activity; the power of doing mechanical work. **energetic(al)** *a.* active; forcible. **energetically** *adv.* **energize** *v.t.* to give energy to.

**en•er•vate** *v.t.* to deprive of nerve, strength, or courage; *a.* spiritless. **enervating, enervative** *a.* **enervation** *n.*

**en•fee•ble** *v.t.* to render feeble.

**en•fi•lade** *n.* a line or straight passage; fire from either flank along a line.

**en•force** *v.t.* to give strength to; to put in force; to compel; to urge on; to execute. **-able** *a.* **enforcedly** *adv.* under threat or compulsion. **-ment** *n.*

**en•fran•chise** *v.t.* to set free from slavery; to extend political rights to; to grant the privilege of voting. **-ment** *n.*

**en•gage** *v.t.* to bind by contract, pledge, or promise; to hire; to order; to attract; to interlock; *v.i.* to begin to fight; to employ oneself. **-d** *a.* **-ment** *n.* obligation by contract or agreement; pledge; betrothal; occupation; affair of business or pleasure. **engaging** *a.* attractive; pleasing.

**en•gen•der** *v.t.* to beget; to cause to exist; to sow the seeds of; to breed.

**en•gine** *n.* any mechanical contrivance for producing and conveying motive power; a machine. **-er** *n.* one who constructs, designs, or is in charge of engines, military works, or works of public utility; *v.t.* to direct or design work as a skilled engineer; to bring about. **-ering** *n.* the art of constructing and using machines or engines.

**En•glish** *a.* belonging to England or its inhabitants; *n.* the people or the language of England; *v.t.* to anglicize. **-man** *n.*

**en•gorge** *v.t.* to swallow greedily and in large quantities; *v.i.* to devour. **-ment** *n.*

**en•graft, ingraft** *v.t.* to graft on; to incorporate; to add to. **-ation, -ment** *n.*

**en•grave** *v.t.* to imprint; to make a deep impression; *v.i.* to practice the art of engraving. **-r** *n.* **engraving** *n.* the art of cutting designs, etc. on wood, metal, or stone; a print. See **grave.**

**en•gross** *v.t.* to occupy wholly; to absorb; to copy in legal form; to monopolize. **-er,**

-ing, -ment *n.*
**en•gulf, ingulf** *v.t.* to swallow up or absorb as in a gulf; to encompass wholly.
**en•hance** *v.t.* to intensify; to increase in value or worth; to add to the effect. **-ment** *n.*
**en•har•mon•ic, enharmonical** *a.* having the same pitch but written in different notation, as G# and A♭.
**e•nig•ma** *n.* an obscure question or saying difficult of explanation; anything or anybody puzzling; a riddle. **-tic(al)** *a.* **-tically** *adv.*
**en•jamb•ment** *n.* in verse, continuation of a sentence from one line into the next.
**en•join** *v.t.* to direct with authority; to order; to prohibit by judicial order; **-ment** *n.*
**en•joy** *v.t.* to delight in; to have the use or benefit of. **-able** *a.* pleasurable. **-ably** *adv.* **-ment** *n.*
**en•large** *v.t.* and *v.i.* to make or become larger; to broaden. **-d** *a.* **-ment** *n.*
**en•light•en** *v.t.* to give information to; to instruct; to make clear; to free from superstition, etc. **-ment** *n.*
**en•list** *v.t.* to enter on a list; to enroll; to secure support of; *v.i.* to enter heartily into a cause. **-ment** *n.*
**en•liv•en** *v.t.* to give life, action, or motion to; to quicken; to make merry. **-er** *n.*
**en masse** *adv.* in a group.
**en•mesh, immesh, inmesh** *v.t.* to catch in a mesh or net; to entangle; to trap.
**en•mi•ty** *n.* the quality of being an enemy; hatred; rancor; hostility.
**en•noble** *v.t.* to exalt; to dignify. **-ment** *n.*
**en•nui** *n.* boredom; listlessness due to satiety or lack of interest.
**e•nor•mous** *a.* huge; vast; immense. **enormity** *n.* **-ly** *adv.* **ness** *n.*
**e•nough** *a.* as much or as many as need be; sufficient; adequate. *n.* a sufficiency; *adv.* sufficiently; fully.
**e•nounce** *v.t.* to state; to declare; to pronounce; to proclaim. **-ment** *n.*
**en•rage** *v.t.* to fill with rage; to provoke to frenzy or madness. **-d** *a.*
**en•rap•ture** *v.t.* to transport with pleasure, to delight excessively. **-d, enrapt** *a.*
**en•rich** *v.t.* to make rich; to add to; to enhance; to embellish. **-ment** *n.*
**en•robe** *v.t.* to dress; to clothe.
**en•roll** *v.t.* to enter a name in a roll or register; to enlist; to record. **-ment** *n.*
**en•sconce** *v.t.* to shelter; to hide securely.
**en•sem•ble** *n.* all the parts taken together; general effect; an entire costume.
**en•shrine** *v.t.* to enclose in a shrine; to treasure with affection. **-ment** *n.*
**en•shroud** *v.t.* to hide from view.
**en•sign** *n.* a badge of rank or insignia of office; a flag or banner; an emblem.

**ensign**

**en•si•lage** *n.* a process of storing crops to serve as winter food for cattle.
**en•slave** *v.t.* to reduce to slavery or bondage. **-ed** *a.* **-ment** *n.*
**en•snare, insnare** *v.t.* to entrap; to entangle.
**en•sue** *v.i.* to follow; to happen after; to be the consequence of. **ensuing** *a.*
**en•sure** *v.t.* to make sure, safe, or certain.
**en•tail** *n.* a predetermined order of succession; an estate; *v.t.* to involve as a result; to bring about or cause. **-ment** *n.*
**en•tan•gle** *v.t.* to twist or interweave so as not to be easily separated; to ensnare. **-ment** *n.*
**en•tente** *n.* cordial agreement or understanding.
**en•ter** *v.t.* to go or come into; to invade; to join; *v.i.* to make a beginning; to take a part or interest in. **to enter on, upon,** to begin.
**en•ter-** Gk. *pref.* used in the construction of compound words relating to the intestine. **-a** *n.pl.* **-ic** *a.* **-itis** *n.* inflammation of the intestines.
**en•ter•prise** *n.* that which is undertaken or attempted; daring spirit. **enterprising** *a.* adventurous; energetic. **enterprisingly** *adv.*
**en•ter•tain** *v.t.* to show hospitality to; to amuse; to consider favorably. **-er** *n.* **-ing** *a.* **-ment** *n.*
**en•thrall** *v.t.* to thrill; to hold spellbound.
**en•throne** *v.t.* to place on a throne; to raise to sovereignty; to exalt. **-ment** *n.*
**en•thu•si•asm** *n.* passionate zeal; keen interest. **enthusiast** *n.* **enthusiastic(al)** *a.* **enthusiastically** *adv.*
**en•tice** *v.t.* to draw on by exciting hope or desire; to lead astray. **-able** *a.* **-ment** *n.* allurement. **enticing** *a.* **enticingly** *adv.*
**en•tire** *a.* whole; unimpaired; not castrated. **-ly** *adv.* **-ness, -ty** *n.* completeness.
**en•ti•tle** *v.t.* to give a title to; to name; to qualify; to fit for; to give claim to.
**en•ti•ty** *n.* a real being; reality; existence.
**en•tomb** *v.t.* to deposit in a tomb; to inter; to bury. **-ment** *n.*
**en•to•mol•o•gy** *n.* scientific study, classification, and collection of insects. **entomological** *a.* **entomologically** *adv.* **entomologize** *v.t.* **entomologist** *n.*
**en•tou•rage** *n.* one's habitual associates.
**en•trails** *n.pl.* the internal parts of anything.
**en•trance** *n.* the act of entering; a door, gateway, or passage to enter by; the beginning. **entrant** *n.* one who enters; a competitor.
**en•trance** *v.t.* to ravish with delight and wonder. **-ment** *n.* **entrancing** *a.*
**en•trap** *v.t.* to catch; to ensnare. **-ment** *n.*
**en•treat** *v.t.* to ask earnestly; to implore; *v.i.* to make an earnest request. **-y** *n.* supplication.
**en•tree** *n.* right of access; a dish served as a main course, or between main courses.
**en•trench, intrench** *v.t.* to dig a trench; to surround; *v.i.* to encroach. **-ment** *n.* any fortification or defense.
**en•tre•pre•neur** *n.* a contractor; an organizer.
**en•trust, intrust** *v.t.* to charge with a

responsibility; to confide to the care of.
**en•try** *n.* the act of entering; a place to enter by; an item noted down in a ledger.
**en•twine, intwine** *v.t.* to twist together; to plait; to encircle.
**e•nu•mer•ate** *v.t.* to count, one by one; to give in detail. **enumeration, enumerator** *n.*
**e•nun•ci•ate** *v.t.* to state clearly; to announce; to pronounce each syllable distinctly. **enunciable** *a.* **enunciation** *n.* articulation or pronunciation. **enunciator** *n.*
**en•vel•op** *v.t.* to cover by folding or wrapping; to surround. **-e** *n.* a cover or wrapper. **-ment** *n.*
**en•ven•om** *v.t.* to impregnate with venom; to poison; to embitter.
**en•vi•a•ble, envious** See **envy.**
**en•vi•ron** *v.t.* to surround; to encompass. **-ment** *n.* external conditions. **-s** *n.pl.* neighborhood; suburbs.
**en•vis•age** *v.t.* to face; to imagine; to visualize.
**en•voy** *n.* a diplomatic agent of a country below the rank of ambassador; messenger.
**en•vy** *v.t.* to grudge another person's good fortune; to feel jealous of. **-ing** *pr.p.* **envied** *pa.p.* **eviable, envious** *a.* **enviously** *adv.*
**en•wrap, inwrap** *v.t.* to wrap up; to envelop.
**en•zyme, enzym** *n.* a complex organic substance which in solution produces fermentation and chemical change in other substances apparently without undergoing any change itself; a form of catalyst. **enzymatic** *a.*
**e•o•lith** *n.* the oldest known stone implement used by prehistoric men. **-ic** *a.* pertaining to the earliest stage of human culture.
**e•pact** *n.* the excess of a solar over a lunar month or year in number of days.
**ep•au•let, epaulette** *n.* an ornamental shoulder-piece or badge of rank.
**é•pée** *n.* a dueling sword with a sharp point but no cutting edge, used in fencing.
**e•pergne** *n.* an ornamental table centerpiece.
**ep•ex•a•ge•sis** *n.* a further explanation of a previous statement. **epexegetical** *a.*
**e•phed•rine** *n.* an alkaloid drug, derived from plants of the genus *Ephedra.*
**e•phem•er•a** *n.* anything of temporary interest and value; a genus of insects, which as adults, live only for one day; *pl.* **ephemerae. -l** *a.* transitory.
**e•phem•er•is** *n.* a table or calendar giving for successive days the positions of heavenly bodies; *pl.* **ephemerides.**
**epi-** Gk. *pref.* meaning upon, at, in addition to, etc., used in the construction of compound terms.
**ep•ic** *n.* a long narrative poem in the grand style, usually dealing with the adventures of great soldiers or heroes whose deeds are part of the history of a nation; *a.* in the grand style; lofty in conception; memorable; heroic.
**ep•i•car•di•um** *n.* the serous membrane of the pericardium, the sac which envelops the heart. **epicardial** *a.*
**ep•i•cene** *a.* common to both sexes; *n.* a person having characteristics of both sexes; a hermaphrodite.
**ep•i•cen•ter** *n.* the point on the upper crust of the earth below which an earthquake has originated.
**ep•i•crit•ic** *a.* pert. to fine sensitivity, e.g. to the slightest sensation of heat or touch.
**Ep•i•cu•rus** *n.* a Greek philosopher. **epicure** *n.* one with a refined taste in food and drink. **epicurean** *a.* and *n.* a sensualist. **epicureanism** *n.* the doctrine that the chief end of man was physical and mental happiness.
**ep•i•cy•cle** *n.* a circle whose center moves around in the circumference of a greater circle.
**ep•i•dem•ic, epidemical** *a.* common to or affecting a whole people or community; prevalent. **epidemic** *n.* the temporary appearance of infectious disease attacking whole communities.
**ep•i•der•mis** *n.* the outer protective layer of skin; a sheath which forms a layer over surface of leaves. **epidermatoid, epidermic, epidermal, epidermidal** *a.*
**ep•i•glot•tis** *n.* a covering of tissue which closes the opening leading into the larynx during the act of swallowing. **epiglottic** *a.*
**ep•i•gram** *n.* a neat, witty, pointed saying. **-matical** *a.* **-matically** *adv.* **-matize** *v.t.* **-matist** *n.*
**ep•i•graph** *n.* an inscription, esp. on a building, statue, etc.; an appropriate motto or saying at the beginning of a book or chapter.
**ep•i•lep•sy** *n.* a nervous disease characterized by sudden convulsions and unconsciousness. **epileptic** *n.* one subject to epilepsy.
**ep•i•logue** *n.* conclusion of a literary work.
**E•piph•a•ny** *n.* a church festival held on the twelfth day after Christmas.
**ep•i•phyte** *n.* a plant which grows on but does not draw nourishment from another plant.
**e•pis•co•pa•cy** *n.* the government of the church by bishops; the office of a bishop; prelacy. **episcopal** *a.* governed by bishops. **Episcopalian** *a.* or *n.* a member or adherent of an episcopal church. **Episcopalianism** *n.* **episcopally** *adv.* **episcopate** *n.* the office or order of bishop.
**ep•i•sode** *n.* an incident; a digression, only remotely relevant to the plot. **episodal, episodical** *a.* **episodically** *adv.*
**e•pis•tle** *n.* a letter, written for effect or for instruction. **epistolary** *a.*
**ep•i•taph** *n.* an inscription placed on a tombstone in commemoration of the dead.
**ep•i•tha•la•mi•um** *n.* a nuptial song.
**ep•i•the•li•um** *n.* cellular tissue covering cutaneous, mucous, and serous surfaces.
**ep•i•thet** *n.* phrase or word used adjectivally to express some quality or

attribute of its object; a designation; title. **epithetical** *a.*

**e•pit•o•me** *n.* a brief summary; synopsis; digest. **epitomize** *v.t.* to make or be a short abstract of.

**ep•och** *n.* a fixed point or duration of time from which succeeding years are reckoned; era; date; period; age. **-al** *a.*

**eq•ua•ble** *a.* uniform in action or intensity; not variable. **equability, -ness** *n.* **equably** *adv.*

**e•qual** *a.* having the same magnitude, dimensions, value, degree, or the like; identical; *n.* a person of the same rank, age, etc. **-ization** *n.* **-ize** *v.t.* **-itarian** *n.* one who holds that all men are equal in status. **-ity** *n.* **-ly** *adv.*

**e•qua•nim•i•ty** *n.* evenness of mind or temper; composure; calmness.

**e•quate** *v.t.* to make or treat as equal. **equation** *n.* the act of making equal; allowance for any inaccuracies; the sign of equality (=). **equational** *a.* **equationally** *adv.*

**e•qua•tor** *n.* a great circle supposed to be drawn around the earth 90° from each pole and dividing the globe into the N. & S. hemispheres. **-ial** *a.* of or pertaining to the equator; *n.* an astronomical telescope. **ially** *adv.*

**eq•uer•ry** *n.* one charged with the care of horses.

**e•ques•tri•an** *a.* pertaining to horses or horsemanship; mounted on a horse (*fem.* **equestrienne**). **-ism** *n.*

**e•qui-** *pref.* denoting equal, used in the construction of compound words.

**e•qui•an•gu•lar** *a.* having equal angles.

**e•qui•dis•tance** *n.* an equal distance from some point. **equidistant.** *a.*

**e•qui•lat•er•al** *a.* having all the sides equal.

**e•quil•i•brate** *v.t.* to balance exactly. **equilibrant, equilibration** *n.* **equilibrator** *n.* in aviation the stabilizing fin which controls the balance of an airplane.

**e•qui•lib•ri•um** *n.* *(Mech.)* the state of rest of a body produced by action and reaction of a system of forces; a state of balance.

**e•quine, equinal** *a.* pert. to a horse; *n.* a horse.

**e•qui•noc•tial** *a.* pert. to the equinoxes; *n.* a great circle in the heavens corresponding to the plane of the equator when extended.

**e•qui•nox** *n.* the time at which the sun crosses the plane of the equator. Approx. March 21 and Sept. 22, when day and night are equal.

**e•quip** *v.t.* to supply with all requisites for service; to furnish. **-ping** *pr.p.* **-ped** *pa.p.* and *pa.t.* **-age** *n.* furniture, accoutrements. **-ment** *n.* outfit; apparatus.

**e•qui•poise** *n.* the state of equality of weight or force; even balance.

**eq•ui•ta•ble** *a.* giving each his due; just. **-ness** *n.* **equitably** *adv.* fairly; justly.

**eq•ui•ta•tion** *n.* skill in horsemanship.

**eq•ui•ty** *n.* fairness; equal adjustment or distribution.

**e•quiv•a•lent** *a* and *n.* equal in value, power, import, etc. **equivalence** *n.* identical value. **equivalency** *n.*

**e•quiv•o•cal** *a.* of double or doubtful meaning; questionable; ambiguous. **-ly** *adv.* **-ness** *n.* **equivocate** *v.i.* to use words of doubtful signification to mislead. **equivocation, equivocator** *n.*

**e•ra** *n.* a fixed point of time from which a series of years is reckoned; epoch; time; age; a memorable date or period.

**e•rad•i•cate** *v.t.* to pull up by the roots; to destroy. **eradicable** *a.* **eradication** *n.*

**e•rase** *v.t.* to rub or scrape out; to efface. **erasable, -d** *a.* **-r, -ment, erasure** *n.*

**ere** *adv.* before; sooner; *prep.* before; *conj.* sooner than.

**e•rect** *v.t.* to set upright; to elevate; to construct; *a.* upright. **-ion, -or** *n.*

**erg** *n.* the absolute unit of measurement of work and energy in the metric system.

**er•go** *adv.* therefore; consequently.

**er•got** *n.* a dried fungus used as a drug to stop bleeding and contract muscles.

**Er•in** *n.* Ireland.

**er•mine** *n.* a member of weasel family the white winter coat of which is highly prized as a fur; the robe of a judge in England.

**ermine**

**e•rode** *v.t.* to eat into; to wear away. **-nt** *n.* a caustic drug. **erose** *a.* appearing as if gnawed or worn irregularly. **erosion** *n.* act or operation of eating away; corrosion. **erosive** *a.*

**E•ros** *n.* the Greek god of love. **erotic** *a.* pertaining to love; *n.* a love poem; **erotics** *n.pl.* science and art of love. **erotica** *n.* literature dealing with sexual love. **eroticism, erotism** *n.*

**err** *v.i.* to commit a mistake; to go astray; to sin. **-atic(al)** *a.* wandering; eccentric; changeable; not dependable. **-atic** *n.* a wanderer. **-atically** *adv.* **-atum** *n.* an error in writing or printing; *pl.* **-ata.**

**er•rand** *n.* commission; message.

**er•rant** *a.* roving; wild; abandoned. **-ly** *adv.* **-ry** *n.* a state of wandering about, esp. of a knight-errant in search of adventures.

**er•ror** *n.* a deviation from right or truth; a mistake. **erroneous** *a.* wrong; incorrect; false. **erroneously** *adv.* **erroneousness** *n.*

**er•satz** *a.* substituted for articles in everyday use; artificial; makeshift.

**erst** *adv.* formerly; of old. **while** *adv.* former.

**e•ruct, e•ruc•tate** *v.t.* to belch. **eructation** *n.* belching.

**er•u•dite** *a.* learned; deeply read; scholarly. **-ly** *adv.* **erudition** *n.* learning; scholarship.

**e•rupt** *v.i.* to throw out; to break through. **-ion** *n.* outburst of lava, ashes, gas, etc. from the crater of a volcano; a rash on the skin. -ive *a.*

**er•y•sip•e•las** *n.* contagious disease causing acute inflammation of the skin.

**es•ca•lade** *n.* mounting the walls of a fortress by means of ladders; *v.t.* to scale.

**es•ca•la•tor** *n.* continuous, moving stairway.

**es•cape** *v.t.* to gain freedom; to evade; to pass unnoticed; *v.i.* to hasten away; to avoid capture; *n.* flight from danger; evasion. **escapable** *a.* **escapade** *n.* a wild prank or exploit. **-ment** *n.* the act or means of escaping. **escapism** *n.* morbid desire to escape from the realities of life by concentrating on some other interest. **escapist** *n.*

**es•carp** *v.t.* to make into a steep slope. **-ment** *n.* a steep, sloping bank.

**es•cha•tol•o•gy** *n.* the department of theology which treats of the last things, such as death, the return of Christ, the resurrection, the end of the world, etc.

**es•cheat** *n.* the legal process of property reverting to the crown or government on the tenant's death without heirs; *v.t.* to forfeit; to confiscate.

**es•chew** *v.t.* to shun; to abstain from.

**es•cort** *n.* a person or persons accompanying another on a journey for protection or as an act of courtesy; *v.t.* to accompany.

**es•cri•toire** *n.* a writing desk with drawers.

**Es•cu•la•pi•an** *a.* pertaining to the art of healing.

**es•cu•lent** *a.* suitable as a food for man; edible.

**es•cutch•eon** *n.* that part of a vessel's stern on which her name is inscribed; an ornamental plate or shield placed around a keyhole opening. **-ed** *a.*

**Es•ki•mo, Esquimau** *n.* and *a.* one of an aboriginal people thinly scattered along the northern seaboard of America and Asia and in many of the Arctic islands; *pl.* **-s, -x.**

**e•soph•a•gus** *n.* the gullet.

**es•o•ter•ic** *a.* secret; profound.

**es•pe•cial** *a.* distinguished; preeminent; more than ordinary; particular. **-ly** *adv.*

**Es•pe•ran•to** *n.* a universal auxiliary language.

**es•pi•o•nage** *n.* the practice of employing secret agents; spying.

**es•pla•nade** *n.* a level space, esp. for a promenade.

**es•pouse** *v.t.* to marry; to support. **espousal** *n.* **espousals** *n.pl.* nuptials. **-r** *n.*

**es•prit** *n.* spirit; wit; liveliness. **— de corps** *n.* loyalty and attachment to the group of which one is a member.

**es•py** *v.t.* to catch sight of.

**-esque** *suff.* in the manner or style of.

**es•quire** *n.* originally, a 'squire or shield bearer, one of two attendants on a knight; now a courtesy title.

**es•say** *n.* a literary composition; a trial; *v.t.* to try; to attempt. **-ist** *n.* a writer of essays.

**es•sence** *n.* the very being or power of a thing; the formal cause of being; essential part; a perfume. **essential** *a.* necessary to the existence of a thing; inherent; *n.* something indispensable; a chief point; a leading principle. **essentiality** *n.* **essentially** *adv.* **essentialness** *n.*

**es•tab•lish** *v.t.* to make stable or firm; to set up; to prove; to substantiate. **-ed** *a.* fixed; settled.. **-er** *n.* **-ment** *n.* an institution; settlement; place of business, residence, etc. **-mentarian** *a.* and *n.* supporting church establishment.

**es•tate** *n.* a piece of landed property; rank; position; quality. **the Fourth Estate** *n.* a satirical term for the press. **real estate** *n.* property in land.

**es•teem** *v.t.* to regard with respect or affection; to set a value on; *n.* high regard; favorable opinion.

**es•thet•ic** See **aesthetic.**

**es•ti•ma•ble** *a.* able to be estimated; worthy of regard. **estimably** *adv.*

**es•ti•mate** *v.t.* to calculate; *v.i.* to offer to complete certain work at a stated cost; *n.* appraisement. **estimator** *n.*

**es•ti•va•tion, aestivation** *n.* a state of torpor, affecting some insects, during the dry summer months. **estival** *a.* pertaining to the summer aestival. **estivate** *v.i.*

**Es•to•ni•an, Esthonian** *a.* pert. to Est(h)onia, a country on the Baltic; the Finnish-Ugrian language.

**es•top** *v.t.* to impede; to bar by one's own act.

**es•trange** *v.t.* to alienate; to divert from its original use. **-d** *a.* **-ment** *n.*

**es•tu•ar•y** *n.* a narrow arm of the sea at the mouth of a river. **estuarine** *a.*

**e•su•ri•ent** *a.* hungry; voracious; gluttonous.

**et cet•er•a** *n.* phrase meaning "and the others"; and so on; *(abbrev.)* **etc.**

**etch** *v.t.* to make an engraving by eating away the surface of a metal plate with acid; *v.i.* to practice this art. **-er** *n.* **-ing** *n.* the printed impression taken from an etched plate.

**e•ter•nal** *a.* without beginning or end in relation to time; everlasting. **-ize, eternize** *v.t.* to perpetuate. **-ly** *adv.* **eternity** *n.* the infinity of time; the future state after death.

**eth•ane** *n.* a colorless, odorless, inflammable gas.

**e•ther** *n.* the higher regions beyond the earth. **-eal** *a.* celestial; airy; delicate. **-ealization** *n.* **-alize** *v.t.* to render ethereal or spiritual. **-eality** *n.* **-eally** *adv.*

**e•ther** *n.* a volatile liquid, prepared by the action of sulfuric acid on alcohol, used as a solvent and as an anesthetic.

**eth•ic, eth•i•cal** *a.* relating to morals or moral principles. **-ally** *adv.* **-s** *n.pl.* philosophy which treats of human character and conduct, of distinction between right and wrong, and moral duty and obligations to the community.

**E•thi•o•pi•a** *n.* a kingdom in E. Africa; Abyssinia. **-n** *a.* pertaining to Ethiopia.

**eth•nic, eth•ni•cal** *a.* pert. to races or peoples; heathen; pagan. **ethnography** *n.* detailed study of the physical characteristics and social customs of racial groups. **ethnographer** *n.*

**ethnographic** *a.* **ethnology** *n.* the science which traces the origin and distribution of races, their peculiarities and differences. **ethnological** *a.* **ethnologist** *n.*
**e•thos** *n.* the character, customs, and habits which distinguish a people or community from another.
**eth•yl** *n.* the univalent radical $C_2H_5$; an antiknock fluid. **—alcohol** *n.* common alcohol.
**e•ti•o•late** *v.t.* to render pale or unhealthy by denying light and fresh air. **etiolation** *n.*
**e•ti•ol•o•gy** *n.* the study of the causes of diseases. Also **aetiology.**
**et•i•quette** *n.* the conventional code of good manners which governs behavior in society.
**e•tude** *n.* a short musical composition.
**et•y•mol•o•gy** *n.* the investigation of the origins and meanings of words and word forms. **etymological** *a.* **etymologically** *adv.* **etymologist** *n.*
**eu•caine** *n.* a synthetic drug, resembling cocaine, used as a local anesthetic.
**eu•ca•lypt** *n.* any member of the genus Eucalyptus. **-us** *n.* the gum tree of Australia with tough and durable wood. **-ol** *n.* eucalyptus oil.

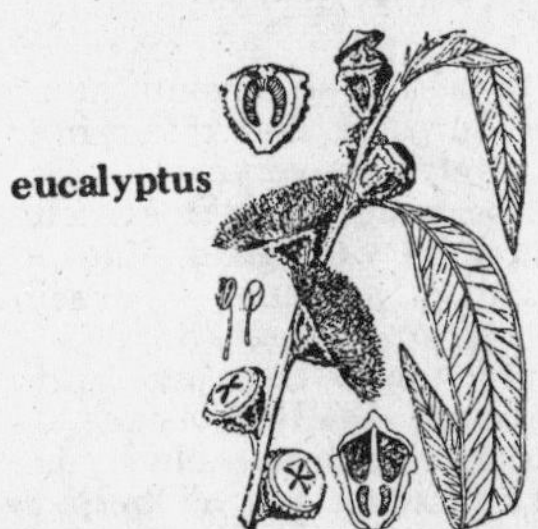
eucalyptus

**Eu•cha•rist** *n.* Holy Communion; the consecrated elements at the sacrament of the Lord's Supper. **-ic(al)** *a.*
**eu•chre** *v.t.* to outwit; to get the best of.
**Eu•clid•e•an** *a.* pert. to Euclid of Alexandria; geometric; three-dimensional.
**eu•de•mo•nism, eudaemonism** *n.* the doctrine that the attainment of personal happiness, power and honor is the chief end and good of man. **eudemonist** *n.*
**eu•gen•ic** *a.* relating to the production of fine offspring. **-s** *n.pl.* the scientific application of the findings of the study of heredity to human beings with the object of perpetuating those inherent and hereditary qualities which aid in the development of the human race. **eugenist** *n.*
**eu•ge•nol** *n.* an aromatic acid, obtained from the oil of cloves.
**eu•lo•gy, eu•lo•gi•um** *n.* a speech or writing in praise, especially a speech praising a dead person. **eulogic(al)** *a.* commendatory. **eulogize** *v.t.* to speak in flattering terms. **eulogist** *n.* **eulogistic** *a.* **eulogistically** *adv.*
**eu•nuch** *n.* a castrated male.
**eu•pep•sia** *n.* healthy normal digestion — opposed to *dyspepsia.* **eupeptic** *a.*
**eu•phe•mism** *n.* a figure of speech where a less disagreeable word or phrase is substituted for a more accurate but more offensive one. **euphemize** *v.t.* or *v.i.* **euphemistic** *a.*
**eu•pho•ny** *n.* pleasantness or smoothness of sound; assimilation of the sounds of syllables to facilitate pronunciation and to please the ear. **euphonic, euphonious** *a.* **euphoniously** *adv.*
**eu•pho•ri•a** *n.* a sense of health and well-being which may, however, be misleading; state of irrational happiness. **euphoric** *a.*
**eu•phu•ism** *n.* an affected, elaborate, bombastic prose style; a stilted expression. **euphuist** *n.* **euphuistic** *a.*
**Eur•a•sian** *n.* offspring of mixed European and Asiatic parentage.
**eu•rhyth•mics** *n.pl.* an art of rhythmical free movement to music.
**Eu•rope** *n.* the continent which extends from the Atlantic Ocean to Asia. **European** *n.* a native or inhabitant of Europe.
**eu•tec•tic** *a.* easily melted or fused; *n.* alloy of metals whose melting point is lower than other mixtures of the same ingredients.
**eu•tha•na•sia** *n.* an easy, painless death; the putting of a person to death painlessly. Also **euthanasy.**
**e•vac•u•ate** *v.t.* to make empty; to withdraw from; to excrete; *v.i.* to quit. **evacuant** *n.* **evacuation** *n.* the act of emptying out. **evacuative** *a.* **evacuator** *n.* **evacuee** *n.* a person temporarily removed from dangerous area.
**e•vade** *v.t.* to avoid by dexterity, artifice, or stratagem; to elude; to avoid. **evadable** *a.*
**e•val•u•ate** *v.t.* to appraise or determine the value of. **evaluation** *n.* estimation of worth.
**ev•a•nesce** *v.i.* to vanish; to fade or melt away. **-nce** *n.* **-nt** *a.* vanishing; fleeting; transitory; scarcely perceptible. **-ntly** *adv.*
**e•van•gel** *n.* good tidings; one of the first four books of the New Testament. **-ic(al)** *a.* consonant with the Gospel; orthodox; *n.* one who holds the views of the evangelical school. **-ically** *adv.* **-ical, -ness, -icism, -icalism, -ism** *n.* **-ization** *n.* conversion. **-ize** *v.t.* and *v.i.* to convert, by preaching the Gospel. **-ist** *n.* **-istic** *a.*
**e•vap•o•rate** *v.t.* and *v.i.* to pass off in vapor; to disperse; to disappear. **evaporable, evaporative** *a.* **evaporation** *n.*
**e•va•sion** *n.* the act of eluding; excuse; dodge. **evasible** *a.* **evasive** *a.* not straightforward. **evasively** *adv.*
**eve** *n.* evening; the period immediately preceding an event or important occasion. **evensong** *n.* evening prayer. **eventide** *n.*
**e•ven** *a.* level; equal in surface; uniform in quality; balanced; equable; unruffled; impartial; exactly divisible by two; *v.t.* to smooth; to equalize; *adv.* just; still. **-handed** *a.* fair, impartial, just. **-ly** *adv.* **-ness** *n.* **— tempered** *a.*

**eve•ning** *n.* the close of day. **—dress** *n.* formal dress worn at evening functions.

**e•vent** *n.* that which happens; a notable occurrence. **-ful** *a.* momentous. **-ual** *a.* happening as a consequence; ultimate. **-uality** *n.* force of circumstances. **-ually** *adv.* **-uate** *v.i.* to happen.

**ev•er** *adv.* at any time; constantly; unceasingly. **-glade** *n.* a swampy, grassy tract. **-green** *a.* always green; *n.* nondeciduous tree or shrub which remains green throughout the year. **-more** *adv.* eternally. **for ever and a day,** always.

**ev•er•last•ing** *a.* enduring forever; eternal; *n.* eternity; a flower which does not lose shape or color when dried.

**e•vert** *v.t.* to turn inside out. **eversible** *a.* **eversion** *n.*

**ev•er•y** *a.* each of all; all possible. **-body** *n.* every person. **-day** *a.* ordinary. **-where** *adv.* universally. **—other,** alternately.

**e•vict** *v.t.* to dispossess by a judicial process; to turn out. **-ion** *n.* ejectment. **-or** *n.*

**ev•i•dent** *a.* visible; obvious. **evidence** *n.* ground for belief; testimony; proof; *v.t.* to render evident. **-ial, -iary** *a.* proving conclusively. **-ly** *adv.* apparently; plainly. **to turn State's evidence,** to give evidence, on the part of one accused, against an accomplice.

**e•vil** *a.* having bad natural qualities; harmful; disagreeable; vicious; corrupt; wicked; unfortunate; *n.* harm; misfortune; wickedness; sinfulness; wrong; *adv.* in an evil manner. **—eye** *n.* the power of bewitching others by the glance of the eyes. **-ly** *adv.* **-ness** *n.*

**e•vince** *v.t.* to prove beyond any reasonable doubt; to show clearly. **evincible** *a.* **evincibly** *adv.* **evincive** *a.* tending to prove.

**e•vis•cer•ate** *v.t.* to disembowel; to take out the entrails or viscera. **evisceration** *n.*

**e•voke** *v.t.* to call up; to summon forth; to draw out; to bring to pass. **evocation** *n.*

**ev•o•lu•tion** *n.* gradual unfolding or growth; the scientific theory according to which the higher forms of life have gradually developed from simple and rudimentary forms. **-al, -ary** *a.* **-ism, -ist** *n.*

**e•volve** *v.t.* to develop gradually; to unfold; *v.i.* to open out.

**ewe** *n.* a female sheep.

**ew•er** *n.* a large jug with a wide spout.

**ex-** *pref.* used in the construction of compound terms, signifying *out of, from, former.*

**ex•ac•er•bate** *v.t.* to render more bitter; to increase the violence of; to exasperate; to irritate; to aggravate. **exacerbation** *n.*

**ex•act** *a.* accurate; correct; precise; *v.t.* to insist upon. **-ing** *a.* making severe demands on. **-ion** *n.* **-itude** *n.* extreme accuracy. **-ly** *adv.* precisely.

**ex•ag•ger•ate** *v.t.* to magnify in the telling. **-dly** *adv.* **exaggeration** *n.* a statement going beyond the facts. **exaggerative** *a.* **exaggerator** *n.* **exaggeratory** *a.*

**ex•alt** *v.t.* to elevate as in rank; to praise; to elate with joy. **-ation** *n.* **-ed** *a.*

**ex•am•ine** *v.t.* to inquire into and determine; to try to assay by the appropriate tests; to inspect; to investigate. **exam** *n.* examination. **-e** *n.* one who undergoes an examination test. **examination** *n.* interrogation; a scholastic test of knowledge, written or oral. **-r** *n.*

**ex•am•ple** *n.* a thing illustrating a general rule; a specimen; sample.

**ex•as•per•ate** *v.t.* to rouse angry feelings; to provoke beyond endurance. **exasperating** *a.* extremely trying. **exasperation** *n.* **-r** *n.*

**ex•ca•vate** *v.t.* to form a cavity or hole in; to dig out. **excavation, excavator** *n.*

excavator

**ex•ceed** *v.t.* to pass or go beyond the limit of; *v.i.* to surpass; to excel. **-ing** *a.* excessive. **-ingly** *adv.* very.

**ex•cel** *v.t.* to be better than; to exceed; to outdo; *v.i.* to be very good **-ling** *pr.p.* **-led** *pa.t.* and *pa.p.* **-lence** *n.* **-lency** *n.* complimentary title borne by ambassadors, etc. **-lent** *a.* worthy; remarkably good. **-lently** *adv.*

**ex•cept** *v.t.* to leave out; to exclude; *v.i.* to object; *prep.* leaving out; all but; *conj.* with the exception (that). **-ing** *prep.* excluding. **-ion** *n.* that which is not included in a rule. **-ionable** *a.* objectionable. **-ionably** *adv.* **-ional** *a.* outstanding; superior. **-ionally** *adv.*

**ex•cerpt** *v.t.* to extract; *n.* a passage quoted or culled from a book, speech, etc.

**ex•cess** *n.* that which goes beyond a definite limit; extravagance. **-ive** *a.* more than enough.

**ex•change** *v.t.* to give or take in return for; to barter; *n.* the act of giving or taking one thing in return for another; the transfer of goods between countries. **-able** *a.*

**ex•cheq•uer** *n.* the public treasury.

**ex•cise** *n.* a tax or duty upon certain articles of home production and consumption; *v.t.* to impose an excise duty on. **excisable** *a.* liable to excise duty.

**ex•cise** *v.t.* to cut out; to cut off. **excision** *n.* act of cutting; surgical operation.

**ex•cite** *v.t.* to rouse; to call into action; to stir up; to stimulate. **excitability** *n.* **excitable** *a.* capable of being easily excited. **excitant** *n.* a stimulant. **excitation** *n.* the act of exciting; the excitement produced. **excitative, excitatory, -d** *a.* **-dly** *adv.* **-ment** *n.* agitation; commotion. **exciting** *a.* rousing to action; thrilling. **excitingly** *adv.*

**ex•claim** *v.i.* and *v.t.* to utter loudly and vehemently; to declare suddenly. **exclamation** *n.* vehement utterance. **exclamation mark,** the mark (!) used to suggest sudden emotion. **exclamatory** *a.*

**ex•clude** *v.t.* to shut out; to eject. **exclusion** *n.* **exclusive** *a.* limited to a special favored few. **exclusively** *adv.* **exclusiveness** *n.*

**ex•cog•i•tate** *v.t.* to find out by thinking; to think out. **excogitation** *n.*

**ex•com•mu•ni•cate** *v.t.* to expel from the communion and membership of the church by an ecclesiastical sentence; to deprive of spiritual privileges. **excommunication** *n.*

**ex•co•ri•ate** *v.t.* to strip, wear, or rub the skin off; to flay. **excoriation** *n.*

**ex•cre•ment** *n.* matter excreted; feces. **-al** *a.* **-itious** *a.* resembling feces.

**ex•cres•cence** *n.* an abnormal protuberance which grows out of anything, as a wart or tumor; a normal outgrowth, such as hair. **excrescent** *a.* growing out unnaturally.

**ex•crete** *v.t.* to eject waste matter. **excreta** *n.pl.* the normal discharges from the animal body as urine, feces, and sweat. **excretion** *n.* **excretive, excretory** *a.*

**ex•cru•ci•ate** *v.t.* to inflict the severest pain on; to torture. **excruciating** *a.*

**ex•cul•pate** *v.t.* to clear from a charge or imputation of fault or guilt. **exculpation** *n.* vindication. **exculpatory** *a.*

**ex•cur•sion** *n.* a short trip for a special purpose; deviation. **-ist** *n.* one who makes a journey for pleasure. **excursive** *a.* prone to wander; rambling. **excursus** *n.* a dissertation appended to a book and containing a fuller exposition of some relevant point.

**ex•cuse** *v.t.* to free from fault or blame; to pardon; *n.* a pretext; an apology. **excusable** *a.*

**ex•e•crate** *v.t.* to feel or express hatred for; to curse; to loathe. **execrable** *a.* **execrably** *adv.* **execration** *n.* a curse; imprecation.

**ex•e•cute** *v.t.* to accomplish; to perform; to complete; to enforce a judgment of a court of law; to put to death by sentence of a court. **executable** *a.* **executant** *n.* a performer, esp. of music. **execution** *n.* death penalty inflicted by law; performance. **executioner** *n.* hangman. **executive** *a.* administrative; *n.* a body appointed to administer the affairs of a corporation, a company, etc.; a high official of such a body. **executively** *adv.* **executor** *n.* (*fem.* **executrix, executress**) a person appointed under a will to fulfill its terms and administer the estate **executorial** *a.*

**ex•e•ge•sis** *n.* literary commentary. **exegete, exegetist** *n.* one versed in interpreting the text of the Scriptures. **exegetic, exegetical** *a.*

**ex•em•plar** *n.* a person or thing to be imitated; model. **-ily** *adv.* in a manner to be imitated. **-iness** *n.* **-y** *a.* commendable.

**ex•em•pli•fy** *v.t.* to show by example; to illustrate. **-ing** *pr.p.* **exemplified** *pa.t.* and *pa.p.* **exemplification** *n.*

**ex•empt** *v.t.* to free from; to grant immunity from; *a.* not included; freed from; not affected by. **-ible** *a.* **-ion** *n.* immunity.

**ex•er•cise** *n.* use of limbs for health; practice for the sake of training; *pl.* a ceremony; *v.t.* to exert; to apply; to practice; *v.i.* to take exercise.

**ex•ert** *v.t.* to put forth; to exercise; to strive; to labor. **-ion** *n.* **-ive** *a.*

**ex•hale** *v.t.* to breathe out; to discharge; *v.i.* to rise or be given off as vapor. **exhalable, exhalant** *a.* **exhalation** *n.*

**ex•haust** *v.t.* to empty; to weaken; to tire; to use up; *n.* conduit through which steam, waste gases and the like, pass to the outer air; the steam or gases themselves. **-ed** *a.* tired out; emptied; consumed. **-ible** *a.* **-ion** *n.* state of being completely deprived of strength or vitality. **-ive** *a.* comprehensive; thorough. **-ively** *adv.*

**ex•hib•it** *v.t.* to show; to display; to express; *n.* anything displayed at an exhibition. **-er, -or** *n.* one who sends articles to an exhibition for display. **-ion** *n.* display; a public show. **-ionism** *n.* a tendency to show off before people. **-ionist** *n.* **-ory** *a.*

**ex•hil•a•rate** *v.t.* to make cheerful; to animate. **exhilarant** *a.* exciting joy, mirth, or pleasure; *n.* **exhilarating** *a.* **exhilaration** *n.*

**ex•hort** *v.t.* to advise strongly; to admonish earnestly. **-ation** *n.* **-ative, -atory** *a.*

**ex•hume** *v.t.* to dig up; to unearth; to disinter. **exhumation, -r** *n.*

**ex•i•gent** *a.* calling for immediate action or aid; pressing; urgent. **exigence, exigency** *n.* emergency. **exigible** *a.*

**ex•i•gu•i•ty** *n.* smallness; slenderness. **exiguous** *a.*

**ex•ile** *n.* separation or enforced banishment; one living away from his native country; *v.t.* to banish or expel.

**ex•ist** *v.t.* to be; to live; to subsist; to occur. **-ence** *n.* state of being actual; life; **-ential** *a.* consisting in existence. **-entialism** *n.* a school which describes, analyzes and classifies the experiences of an individual mind. **-ibility** *n.*

**ex•it** *n.* a departure; a way out of a place. **exeunt,** stage direction.

**ex•o-** *pref.* outside, without.

**ex•o•dus** *n.* a departure. **Exodus** *n.* the second book of the Old Testament.

**ex•og•a•my** *n.* a custom compelling a man to marry outside his tribe or clan. **exogamous** *a.*

**ex•on•er•ate** *v.i.* to declare free from blame or responsibility; to relieve of a charge or obligation. **exoneration, exonerator** *n.*

**ex•o•ra•ble** *a.* capable of being moved by entreaty.

**ex•or•bi•tant** *a.* very excessive; extravagant. **exorbitance, exorbitancy** *n.* **-ly** *adv.*

**ex•or•cise** *v.t.* to free a person of evil spirits. **exorcism** *n.*

**ex•or•di•um** *n.* a beginning; the introduction part of a discourse or treatise. **exordial** *a.*

**ex•o•skel•e•ton** *n.* external hard supporting structure such as scales, nails, feathers. **exoskeletal** *a.*
**ex•o•ter•ic, extrical** *a.* capable of being understood by many; not secret; the opposite to *esoteric.*
**ex•ot•ic** *a.* introduced from a foreign country; unusual or colorful. **-ism** *n.*
**ex•pand** *v.t.* to enlarge; to increase in volume or bulk; to stretch. **expanse** *n.* a wide extent of surface. **-able, expansible** *a.* **expansibly** *adv.* **expansion** *n.* spreading; distension. **expansive** *a.* widely extended; communicative. **expansively** *adv.* **expansiveness** *n.*
**ex•pa•ti•ate** *v.i.* to speak or write at great length. **expatiation** *n.* **expatiative** *a.*
**ex•pa•tri•ate** *v.t.* to banish from one's native land; to exile. **expatriation** *n.*
**ex•pect** *v.t.* to look forward to; to anticipate; to suppose. **-ance, -ancy** *n.* that which is expected. **-ant** *a.* waiting; hopeful. **-antly** *adv.* **-ation** *n.* **-ations** *n.pl.* prospects in life.
**ex•pec•to•rate** *v.t.* or *v.i.* to spit; to cough up. **expectorant** *a.* aiding expectoration. **expectoration** *n.* sputum; spittle.
**ex•pe•di•ent** *a.* suitable; fitting; advisable; desirable; useful; *n.* suitable means to accomplish an end. **expediency** *n.* **-ly** *adv.*
**ex•pe•dite** *v.t.* to free from hindrance or obstacle; to hurry forward; *a.* quick; ready. **expedition** *n.* a journey for a specific purpose. **expeditionary** *a.* **expeditious** *a.* prompt; speedy. **expeditiously** *adv.*
**ex•pel** *v.t.* to drive or force out; to eject. **-ling** *pr.p.* **-led** *pa.t.* and *pa.p.*
**ex•pend** *v.t.* to use up; to exhaust. **-able** *a.* **-iture** *n.* expense; cost. **expense** *n.* cost. **expensive** *a.* costly; dear.
**ex•pe•ri•ence** *n.* practical knowledge gained by trial or practice; personal proof; continuous practice; an event in one's life; *v.t.* to undergo; to feel. **-d** *a.* skilled; expert; wise; capable. **experiential** *a.* empirical.
**ex•per•i•ment** *n.* the action of trying anything; practical test; *v.i.* to make an experiment. **-al** *a.* founded on or known by experiment. **-alist** *n.* **-ally** *adv.* **-ation** *n.* **-ative** *a.* **-er, -ist** *n.*
**ex•pert** *a.* adroit; dexterous; skillful. *n.* an authority; a specialist. **-ly** *adv.* **-ness** *n.*
**ex•pi•ate** *v.t.* to atone for; to make amends for. **expiable** *a.* **expiation** *n.*
**ex•pire** *v.t.* to exhale; *v.i.* to die; to come to an end. **expirant** *n.* one who is dying. **expiration** *n.* the exhalation of air from the lungs; termination. **expiratory, expiring** *a.* **expiry** *n.* conclusion.
**ex•plain** *v.t.* to elucidate; to define. **-able** *a.* **explanation** *n.* the meaning of or reason given for anything. **explanative, explanatory** *a.*
**ex•ple•tive** *a.* serving only to fill out a sentence; *n.* a word inserted to fill up or to add force to a phrase; an exclamation.
**ex•pli•cate** *v.t.* to unfold the meaning of; to explain; to interpret. **explicable** *a.* **explication** *n.* **explicative, explicatory** *a.*
**ex•plic•it** *a.* stated in detail; unambiguous; clear; unequivocal. **-ly** *adv.* **-ness** *n.*
**ex•plode** *v.t.* to cause to blow up; *v.i.* to become furious with rage. **-d** *a.* rejected; debunked. **explosion** *n.* sudden release of gases, accompanied by noise and voilence; a manifestation of rage. **explosive** *a.* liable to explode; *n.* a chemical intended to explode.
**ex•ploit** *n.* a brilliant feat; a heroic deed; *v.t.* to utilize for personal gain. **-able** *a.* **-age, -ation** *n.* **-er** *n.*
**ex•plore** *v.t.* to search through with the view of making discovery; to investigate; to examine. **exploration** *n.* **exploratory** *a.* **-r** *n.*
**ex•po•nent** *n.* one who expounds, demonstrates, or explains; in algebra, index number or quantity, written to the right of and above another to show how often the latter is to be multiplied by itself, e.g. $a^3 = a \times a \times a$.
**ex•port** *v.t.* to send goods or produce out of a country. **-able** *a.* **-ation, -er** *n.*
**ex•pose** *v.t.* to leave unprotected; to exhibit; to disclose. **exposé** *n.* an exposure or disclosure of discreditable facts. **exposition** *n.* exhibition; display. **expositor** *n.* **expository** *a.* **exposure** *n.* the state of being laid bare.
**ex•post•u•late** *v.i.* to remonstrate with; to reason earnestly. **expostulation** *n.* **expostulative, expostulatory** *a.*
**ex•pound** *v.t.* to explain; to interpret.
**ex•press** *v.t.* to make known one's opinions or feelings; to put into words; to represent by pictorial art; *a.* explicit; clear; plain; speedy; *adv.* posthaste; by express messenger or train; *n.* a messenger sent on a special errand; a fast train making few stops en route. **-ible** *a.* **-ion** *n.* utterance; declaration; phrase; term; remark; aspect; look; a quantity denoted by algebraic symbols. **-ionism** *n.* an antirealistic art theory that all art depends on the expression of the artist's creative self. **-ionist** *n.* **-ionless** *a.* **-ive** *a.* full of expression. **-ively** *adv.* **-iveness** *n.* **-ly** *adv.* plainly; explicitly; specially.
**ex•pro•pri•ate** *v.t.* to dispossess; to take out of the owner's hand. **expropriation** *n.*
**ex•pul•sion** *n.* the act of expelling or casting out; banishment. **expulsive** *a.*
**ex•punge** *v.t.* to erase; to obliterate; to cancel.
**ex•pur•gate** *v.t.* to cleanse; to purify; to purge. **expurgation** *n.* **expurgator** *n.*
**ex•qui•site** *a.* of extreme beauty or delicacy; of surpassing excellence. **-ly.**
**ex•sic•cate** *v.t.* to dry up; to evaporate. **exsiccation** *n.*
**ex•tant** *a.* still existing.
**ex•tem•po•re** *a.* or *adv.* without previous study or meditation; on the spur of the moment. **extemporal, extemporaneous, extemporary** *a.* impromptu. **extemporization** *n.* **extemporize** *v.i.*
**ex•tend** *v.t.* to prolong in duration; to offer; to enlarge; *v.i.* to be continued in length or breadth; to stretch. **-ible, extensible, extensile** *a.* capable of being stretched, expanded, or enlarged. **extensibility,**

**extension** *n.* **extensional** *a.* **extensive** *a.* large; spacious. **extensively** *adv.* **extensiveness** *n.* **extensor** *n.* a muscle which straightens or extends a limb. **extent** *n.* size; scope; area; degree; volume; length; expanse.

**ex•ten•u•ate** *v.t.* to mitigate; to make less blameworthy. **extenuating** *a.* **extenuation** *n.*

**ex•te•ri•or** *a.* outer; external; *n.* outer surface; outward appearance.

**ex•ter•mi•nate** *v.t.* to root out; to destroy utterly. **extermination, exterminator** *n.*

**ex•ter•nal** *a.* not inherent or essential; outward; exterior; superficial; apparent. **-s** *n.pl.* outward appearances. **-ly** *adv.*

**ex•tinct** *a.* no longer existing. **-ion** *n.*

**ex•tin•guish** *v.t.* to put out; to quench; to destroy. **-able** *a.* **-er** *n.*

**ex•tir•pate** *v.t.* to pull or pluck up by the roots; to destroy utterly. **extirpative** *a.* **extirpation, extirpator** *n.*

**ex•tol** *v.t.* to praise highly. **-ling** *pr.p.* **-led** *pa.t.* and *pa.p.*

**ex•tort** *v.t.* to obtain by force or threats; to extract. **-ive** *a.* **-ion** *n.* illegal compulsion; unjust exaction. **-ionary, -ionate** *a.* **-ioner, -ionist** *n.*

**ex•tra-** *pref.* meaning *beyond, on the other side of, on the outside of;* denoting *excess. a.* extraordinary; additional; *adv.* unusually; *n.* additional item. **-curricular** *a.* pert. to the studies or activities which are not included in the curriculum. **-judicial** *a.* out of the proper court or the ordinary legal procedure. **-mural** *a.* beyond the walls, as outside a university. **-sensory** *a.* beyond the senses. **-sensory perception** *(abbrev. E.S.P.),* an awareness of events not presented to the physical senses. **-territorial** *a.* outside the limits of a country or its jurisdiction.

**ex•tract** *v.t.* to take out, esp. by force; to obtain against a person's will; to quote; to calculate; *n.* matter obtained by distillation; a passage from a book, speech, etc. **-able, -ible** *a.* **-ion** *n.* parentage; ancestry; lineage; descent. **-ive** *a.* **-or** *n.*

**ex•tra•dite** *v.t.* to deliver up a fugitive to another nation or authority. **extradition** *n.*

**ex•tra•ne•ous** *a.* not naturally belonging to; not essential; foreign. **-ly** *adv.*

**ex•traor•di•nar•y** *a.* beyond or out of the common order or method. **extraordinarily** *adv.* **extraordinariness** *n.*

**ex•trav•a•gant** *a.* profuse in expense; excessive; wasteful. **extravagance** *n.* **extravagate** *v.i.* to wander beyond proper limits.

**ex•trav•a•gan•za** *n.* an extravagant, farcical, or fantastic composition, literary or musical.

**ex•trav•a•sate** *v.t.* to let out of the proper vessels, as blood; *a.* let out of its proper vessel.

**ex•treme** *a.* at the utmost point, edge, or border; outermost; severe; excessive; most urgent; *n.* the utmost point or degree; the first and last of a series. **-ly** *adv.* **extremism** *n.* holding extreme views or doctrines. **extremist** *n.* **extremity** *n.* the most distant point or side. **extremities** *n.pl.* hands and feet; arms and legs.

**ex•tri•cate** *v.t.* to free from difficulties or perplexities. **extricable** *a.* **extrication** *n.*

**ex•trin•sic, extrinsical** *a.* developing or having its origin from outside the body; not inherent.

**ex•tro•vert** *n.* in psychology, a person whose emotions express themselves readily in external actions and events, as opposed to an *introvert.* **extroversion** *n.*

**ex•trude** *v.t.* to thrust out; to press out. **extrusion** *n.*

**ex•u•ber•ant** *a.* effusive; vivacious; **exuberance, exuberancy** *n.* **-ly** *adv.*

**ex•ude** *v.t.* to discharge through the pores, as sweat; *v.i.* to ooze out; to escape slowly.

**ex•ult** *v.i.* to rejoice exceedingly; to triumph. **-ance, -ancy** *n.* **-ant** *a.* **-tation** *n.*

**ex•u•vi•ae** *n.pl.* cast off skin, teeth, shells, etc. of animals. **exuvial** *a.* **exuviate** *v.i.*

**eye** *n.* the organ of sight or vision; sight; bud; shoot; view; keen sense of value; a small staple or ring to receive a door hook; an aperture for observing; *v.t.* to look at; to view. **-eying** or **-ing** *pr.p.* **-d** *pa.t.* and *pa.p.* **-ball** *n.* the globe of the eye. **-brow** *n.* the arch of hairs above the eyes. **-d** *a.* having eyes. **-glass** *n.* the eyepiece of an optical instrument; *pl.* spectacles. **-lash** *n.* one of the hairs which edge the eyelid. **-let** *n.* a small eye or hole for a lace or cord, as in garments, sails, etc.; *v.i.* to make eyelets. **-lid** *n.* folds of skin which may be drawn at will over the eye. **—opener** *n.* revealing statement. **-piece** *n.* lens in an optical instrument by means of which the observer views the image of the object formed in the focus of the other lenses. **-sight** *n.* power of vision. **-sore** *n.* an object offensive to the eye. **-tooth** *n.* either of the two canine teeth of the upper jaw. **-wash** *n.* eye lotion. **-witness** *n.* one who gives testimony as to what he actually saw. **to see eye to eye,** to agree; to think alike.

**ey•rie** *n.* the nest of a bird of prey.

**fa•ble** *n.* a short tale or prolonged personification, often with animal characters, intended to convey a moral truth; a myth; legendary.

**fab•ric** *n.* structure; woven, knitted or felted cloth. **-ate** *v.t.* to frame; to fake; to concoct. **-ation, -ator** *n.*

**fab•u•lous** *a.* amazing; exaggerated.

**fa•cade** *n.* the front view of a building.

**face** *n.* the front of the head; the outer appearance; the outer or upper surface of anything; the dial of a clock, etc.; the front; *v.t.* to confront; to stand opposite to; to admit the existence of (as facts); to put a layer of different material on to, or to trim an outer surface; *v.i.* to turn. **— value** *n.* apparent worth. **facial** *a.* pert. to the face; *n.* a beauty treatment for the face. **facing** *n.* material applied to the edge of a garment.

**fac•et** *n.* a small surface, as of a crystal or precious stone; aspect. *a.* having facets.

**fa•ce•tious** *a.* witty; jocular.

**fac•ile** *a.* easy. **-ly** *adv.* **-ness** *n.* **facilitate** *v.t.* to make easy; to expedite. **facilitation** *n.* **facility** *n.* ease; deftness; aptitude; easiness of access.

**fac•sim•i•le** *n.* an exact copy; *a.* identical; *v.t.* to make a facsimile.

**fact** *n.* anything done; anything actually true; that which has happened. **-ual** *a.* pert. to facts; actual. **matter-of-fact** *a.* prosaic; unimaginative.

**fac•tion** *n.* a group of people working together, esp. for subversive purposes; dissension; party clique. **factious** *a.* **factiously** *adv.*

**fac•ti•tious** *a.* oppos. of *natural;* artificial; manufactured.

**fac•tor** *n.* one of numbers which, multiplied together, give a given number; a contributory element or determining cause; *v.t.* to express as a product of two or more quantities. **-ial** *a.* pert. to a factor. *v.t.* to find the factors of a given number. **-ship** *n.* **-y** *n.* a building where things are manufactured.

**fac•ul•ty** *n.* ability or power to act; mental aptitude; talent; natural physical function; the teaching body. **facultative** *a.* optional.

**fad** *n.* a pet whim; a fancy or notion.

**fade** *v.i.* to lose freshness, brightness, or strength gradually; to disappear slowly. **-less** *a.* not liable to fade; fast (of dye).

**Fahr•en•heit** *n.* a type of thermometer graduated so that freezing point of water is fixed at 32° and boiling point at 212°.

**fail** *v.i.* to be lacking; to diminish; to deteriorate; to miss; to be unsuccessful in; *v.t.* to disappoint or desert; to omit; **-ing** *pr.p.* **-ed** *pa.p.* **-ing** *n.* a fault; a weakness; a shortcoming; *prep.* in default of. **-ure** *n.* bankruptcy; lack of success.

**faint** *a.* lacking strength; indistinct; giddy; timorous; *v.i.* to become weak; to grow discouraged; to swoon; *n.* a swoon.

**fair** *a.* clear; light-colored; blond; not cloudy; hopeful; just; plausible; middling; *adv.* in a fair or courteous manner; according to what is just. **-ly** *adv.* justly; tolerably; wholly. **-ness** *n.* **— play** *n.* straightforward justice. **-way** *n.* a navigable channel on a river. **fair and square**, honest; honestly.

**fair** *n.* periodic competitive exhibition for showing produce of a district; a sale of fancy articles to raise money for charitable purposes.

**fair•y** *n.* an imaginary creature in the form of a diminutive human being, supposed to meddle with the affairs of men; *a.* fairylike. **-land** *n.* land of the fairies; wonderland. **— tale** *n.* a story about fairies and magic.

**faith** *n.* belief, esp. in a revealed religion; trust or reliance; a system of religious doctrines believed in; loyalty; pledged word. **-ful** *a.* loyal; reliable; honorable; exact. **-fully** *adv.* **-fulness** *n.*

**fake** *v.t.* to conceal the defects of, by artifice; to copy, as an antique, and pass it off as genuine; *v.i.* to pretend; *n.* a fraud; a deception; a forgery; a faker. **-r** *n.*

**fal•con** *n.* a subfamily of birds of prey, allied to the hawk, with strong curved beaks and long sickle-shaped claws. **-er** *n.* one who breeds and trains falcons or hawks for hunting wildfowl. **-ry** *n.* the sport of flying hawks in pursuit of game.

**fal•de•ral** See **folderol.**

**fall** *v.i.* to drop; to collapse; to decline in value; to become degraded; to be captured; *n.* the act of falling; a drop; the amount (of rain, snow, etc.) deposited in a specified time; a cascade; a wrestling bout; diminution in value, amount, or volume; the autumn. **-ing** *pr.p.* **fell** *pa.t.* **-en** *pa.p.* **-en** *a.* prostrate; degraded; of loose morals. **-ing star** *n.* a meteor. **-out** *n.* radioactive particles which descend to earth after a nuclear explosion.

**fal•la•cy** *n.* deceptive appearance; a delusion; an apparently forcible argument which is really illogical. **fallacious** *a.* misleading; illogical.

**fal•li•ble** *a.* liable to error; not reliable.

**fal•low** *a.* left untilled for a season; untrained; *n.* land which has lain untilled and unsown for a year or more; *v.t.* to plow without sowing.

**false** *a.* untrue; inaccurate; dishonest; deceptive; artificial. **— face** *n.* a mask. **-hood** *n.* an untruth; a lie. **-ly** *adv.* **-ness** *n.* **falsifiable** *a.* capable of being falsified. **falsification** *n.* **falsifier** *n.* one who falsifies. **falsify** *v.t.* to distort the truth; to forge; to tamper with; to prove to be untrue.

**fal•set•to** *n.* forced high notes esp. of a male voice.

**fal•ter** *v.i.* to stumble; to hesitate.

**fame** *n.* good repute. **-d** *a.* celebrated. **famous** *a.* celebrated; noted. **famously** *adv.*

**fa•mil•iar** *a.* intimate; well-known; *n.* a close acquaintance. **-ize** *v.t.* to make familiar; to get to know thoroughly. **-ity** *n.* intimacy; forwardness. **-ly** *adv.*

**fam•i•ly** *n.* parents and their children; the children of the same parents; descendants of one common ancestor. **— tree**, a diagram representing the genealogy of a family.

**fam•ine** *n.* large-scale scarcity of food. **famish** *v.t.* to starve; *v.i.* to feel acute hunger.

**fan** *n.* an instrument to produce currents of air or assist ventilation; a decorative folding object, made of paper, silk, etc. used to cool face; *v.t.* to cool with a fan; to ventilate; to cause to flame (as a fire); to excite; to spread out like a fan. **-ning** *pr.p.* **-ned** *pa.p.*

**fa•nat•ic** *n.* a person inspired with excessive and bigoted enthusiasm, esp. a religious zealot; *a.* over-enthusiastic. **-al** *a.* **-ally** *adv.* **-ism** *n.* violent enthusiasm.

**fan•cy** *n.* a whim; a notion; partiality; *a.* pleasing to the taste; guided by whim; elaborate; *v.t.* to imagine; to have a liking for; to desire.

**fan•fare** *n.* a flourish of trumpets; a showy display.

**fang** *n.* the canine tooth of a carnivorous animal.

**fan•ta•sy** *n.* mental image; hallucination. Also **phantasy. fantasia** *n.* a composition not conforming to the usual rules of music. **fantasied** *a.* fanciful. **fantastic, fantastical** *a.* fanciful; wild. **fantastically** *adv.*

**far** *a.* distant; remote; more distant of two; *adv.* to a great extent or distance; *n.* a distant place. **-ther** *a. (comp.).* **-thest** *a. (superl.)* and *adv.* **Far East,** that part of Asia including India, China, Japan. **-sighted** *a.* seeing to a great distance; taking a long view; prudent.

**far•ad** *n.* the unit of electrostatic capacity — the capacity of a condenser which requires one coulomb to raise its potential by one volt. **-ay,** *n.* the quantity of electricity required to liberate 1 gram-equivalent of an ion. **-aic, -ic** *a.* pert. to induced electrical currents.

**farce** *n.* a style of comedy marked by boisterous humor and extravagant gesture; absurd or empty show; a pretense.

**fare** *n.* the sum paid by a passenger on a vehicle; a passenger; food and drink at table. **-well** *interj.* good-bye; *n.* a parting wish for someone's welfare; *a.* parting.

**fa•ri•na** *n.* flour or meal of cereal grains, used for cereal and puddings; starch.

**farm** *n.* a tract of land set apart for cultivation or for other industries, as dairy farm, etc.; the buildings on this land; *v.t.* cultivate land for agricultural purposes; *v.i.* and *v.t.* to cultivate; to operate a farm. **-er** *n.* **-ing** *n.* the occupation of cultivating the soil. **-yard** *n.* enclosure surrounded by farm buildings.

**far•row** *n.* a litter of pigs; *v.t.* to give birth to (pigs).

**far•ther** *a.* more far; more remote; *adv.* to a greater distance. **-most** *a.*

**fas•ci•nate** *v.t.* to enchant; to deprive of the power of movement, by a look. **fascinating** *a.* **fascination** *n.* enchantment; irresistible attraction. **fascinator** *n.*

**fas•cism** *n.* a centralized autocratic national regime with extremely nationalistic policies with an economic system based on state-controlled capitalism. **Fascist** *n.*

**fash•ion** *n.* the style in which a thing is made or done; pattern; *v.t.* to form; to shape. **-able** *a.* **-ably** *adv.*

**fast** *v.i.* to abstain from food; to deny oneself certain foods as a form of religious discipline; *n.* abstinence from food; a day of fasting.

**fast** *a.* rapid; securely fixed; firm; permanent, as a dye; in advance of the correct time, as a clock; *adv.* firmly; soundly; securely; rapidly. **-ness** *n.* security; a stronghold.

**fas•ten** *v.t.* to fix firmly; to hold together; *v.i.* to fix itself; to catch (of a lock). **-er** *n.* a contrivance for fixing things firmly together. **-ing** *n.* that by which anything fastens, as a lock, bolt, nut, screw.

**fas•tid•i•ous** *a.* difficult to please; discriminating. **-ly** *adv.* **-ness** *n.*

**fat** *a.* **-ter** *(comp.).* **-test** *(superl.).* fleshy; plump; oily; yielding a rich supply; *n.* an oily substance found in animal bodies; solid animal or vegetable oil; the best or richest part of anything; *v.t.* to make fat; *v.i.* to grow fat. **-ting** *pr.p.* **-ted** *pa.p.* **-ten** *v.t.* to make fat; to make fertile; *v.i.* to grow fat. **-tener, -tiness** *n.* **-ty** *a.* resembling or containing fat; greasy.

**fate** *n.* an inevitable and irresistible power supposedly controlling human destiny; appointed lot; death; doom. **fatal** *a.* causing death. **fatalism** *n.* the doctrine that all events are predetermined and unavoidable. **fatalist** *n.* **fatalistic** *a.* **fatality** *n.* accident causing death; the state of being fatal. **-d** *a.* destined; preordained; doomed. **-ful** *a.* momentous; irrevocable. **-fully** *adv.* **-fulness** *n.*

**fa•ther** *n.* a male parent; *v.t.* to make oneself the father of; to adopt; to assume or admit responsibility for. **-hood** *n.* the state of being a father; paternity. **—in-law** *n.* (*pl.* **-s-in-law**) the father of one's wife or husband. **-less** *a.* without a father living. **-liness** *n.* **-ly** *a.* and *adv.* like a father in affection and care; paternal; benevolent.

**fath•om** *n.* a nautical measure of depth, 6 ft.; *v.t.* to ascertain the depth of; to sound; to understand.

**fa•tigue** *n.* weariness from bodily or mental exertion; *v.t.* to weary by toil; to exhaust the strength of; to tire out. **-ing** *pr.p.* **-d** *pa.p.*

**fau•cet** *n.* a fixture for controlling the flow of liquid from a pipe, etc.; a tap.

**fault** *n.* a failing; blunder; mistake; defect; flaw; responsibility for error; a dislocation of rock strata; a defect in electrical apparatus. **-ed** *a.* broken by one or more faults. **-ily** *adv.* **-iness** *n.* **-less** *a.* without flaws; perfect. **-lessly** *adv.* **-lessness** *n.* perfection. **-y** *a.* imperfect.

**fa•vor** *n.* a gracious act; kind regard; goodwill; partiality; token of generosity or esteem; a gift; *v.t.* to regard with kindness; to show bias towards; to resemble in feature. **-able** *a.* friendly; propitious; advantageous; suitable; satisfactory. **-ableness** *n.* **-ably** *adv.* **-ed** *a.*

fortunate; **-ite** *n.* a person or thing regarded with special favor; the likely winner; *a.* regarded with particular affection; most esteemed. **-itism** *n.* undue partiality.

**fawn** *n.* a young deer; its color; *a.* delicate yellowish-brown; *v.i.* to give birth to a fawn.

**fawn** *v.i.* to flatter unctuously; to curry favor. **-er** *n.* **-ing** *n.* servile flattery; *a.* over-demonstrative. **-ingly** *adv.* **-ingness** *n.*

**fear** *n.* alarm; dread; anxiety; reverence towards God; *v.t.* to regard with dread or apprehension; to anticipate (as a disaster); to hold in awe; *v.i.* to be afraid; to be anxious. **-ful** *adv.* **-fulness** *n.* **-less** *a.* without fear; intrepid; dauntless. **-lessly** *adv.* **-lessness** *n.* courage; intrepidity. **-some** *a.* causing fear; terrifying.

**fea•si•ble** *a.* capable of being done; suitable. **-ness, feasibility** *n.* **feasibly** *adv.*

**feast** *n.* a day of joyful or solemn commemoration; a banquet; *v.t.* to feed sumptuously; *v.i.* to eat sumptuously; to be highly gratified or delighted. **-er** *n.*

**feat** *n.* an exploit or action of extraordinary strength, courage, skill, or endurance.

**feath•er** *n.* one of the epidermal growths forming the body covering of a bird; a

**feather**

plume. **-weight,** the lightest weight that may be carried by a racehorse; a boxer weighing not more than 126 lbs. **-y** *a.* pert. to, covered with, or resembling feathers.

**fea•ture** *n.* any part of the face; distinctive characteristic; main attraction; *v.t.* to portray; to outline; to present as the leading attraction. **-less** *a.* void of striking features. **-s** *pl.* the face.

**Feb•ru•ar•y** *n.* the second month of the year.

**fe•ces, fae•ces** *n.pl.* dregs; the solid waste matter from the bowels. **fecal** *a.*

**fe•cund** *a.* prolific; fruitful; fertile. **-ate** *v.t.* to make fruitful; to impregnate.

**fed** *pa.t.* and *pa.p.* of the verb **feed.**

**fed•er•al** *a.* pert. to a league or treaty, esp. between states; of an association of states which, autonomous in home affairs, combine for matters of wider national and international policy. **federacy** *n.* **-ize** *v.t.* to form a union under a federal government. **-ism** *n.* **-ist** *n.* a supporter of such a union. **federate** *v.t.* to unite states into a federation. *a.* united; allied. **federation** *n.* a federal union. **federative** *a.*

**fee** *n.* orig. land held from a lord on condition of certain feudal services; remuneration for professional services; *v.t.* to pay a fee to.

**fee•ble** *a.* weak; deficient in strength; frail; faint. **—minded** *a.* mentally subnormal. **-ness** *n.* **feebly** *adv.*

**feed** *v.t.* to give food to; to supply with nourishment; *v.i.* to eat; to subsist; *n.* that which is consumed, esp. by animals; **-ing** *n.* act of eating; that which is consumed; grazing. **fed** *pa.p.* and *pa.t.*

**feel** *v.t.* to perceive by the touch; to be sensitive to; to experience emotionally; *v.i.* to know by the touch; *n.* the sensation of touch; the quality of anything touched. **-er** *n.* one of the tactile organs (antennae, tentacles, etc.) of certain insects and animals; a tentative remark. **-ing** *n.* sense of touch; intuition; sensibility; sympathy. **-ings** *n.pl.* emotions; *a.* kindly; responsive. **-ingly** *adv.* **felt** *pa.p.* and *pa.t.*

**feet** *n.pl.* of **foot.**

**feign** *v.t.* to invent; to pretend; to counterfeit. **-ed** *a.* pretended; disguised. **-edly** *adv.* **-edness** *n.* **-ing** *n.* pretense; invention. **feint** *n.* an assumed appearance; *v.i.* to make a deceptive move.

**feld•spar** *n.* a constituent of granite and other igneous rocks.

**fe•lic•i•ty** *n.* happiness. **felicitate** *v.t.* to express joy or pleasure to; to congratulate. **felicitation** *n.* congratulation; the act of expressing good wishes. **felicitous** *a.* happy; appropriate; aptly expressed.

**fe•line** *a.* pert. to cats; catlike.

**fell** *a.* cruel; ruthless; deadly.

**fell** *n.* an animal's skin or hide.

**fell** *pa.t.* of the verb **fall.**

**fell** *v.t.* to cause to fall; to cut down. **-er** *n.*

**fel•low** *n.* a man; boy; a person; **-ship** *n.* companionship.

**fel•on** *n.* one who has committed felony; *a.* fierce; traitorous. **-ious** *a.* **-iously** *adv.* **-iousness** *n.* **-y** *n.* a crime more serious than a misdemeanor (as murder, manslaughter, etc.).

**felt** *pa.t.* and *pa.p.* of **feel.**

**felt** *n.* a closely matted fabric of wool, hair, etc.: *v.t.* to make into felt; to cover with felt; *v.i.* to become matted like felt. **-ing** *n.* the art or process of making felt; the felt itself.

**fe•male** *n.* one of the sex that bears young; a plant which produces fruit; *a.* feminine. **feminine** *a.* pert. to or associated with women; womanly; tender. **femininely** *adv.* **feminineness, femininity** *n.* the nature of the female sex; womanliness. **feminism** *n.* the doctrine that maintains the equality of the sexes; advocacy of women's rights. **feminist** *n.*

**fe•mur** *n.* the thighbone. **femoral** *a.*

**fence** *n.* a wall or hedge for enclosing; the art of fencing; *v.t.* to enclose with a fence; to guard; *v.i.* to practice the art of swordplay; to evade a direct answer to an opponent's challenge. **-r** *n.* one who is skilled in fencing. **fencing** *n.* the art or practice of self-defense with the sword, foil, etc.; the act of enclosing by a fence; the materials of which a fence is made.

**fend** *v.t.* to ward off; *v.i.* to resist; to provide. **-er** *n.* that which acts as a protection; the metal part over wheels of an automobile.

**fen•nel** *n.* a perennial umbelliferous plant with yellow flowers.

**fer•al** *a.* wild; not domesticated; run wild (of plants). **ferine** *a.*

**fer•ment** *n.* a substance which causes fermentation, as yeast; fermentation; *v.t.* to induce fermentation in; *v.i.* to undergo fermentation; to work (of wine). **-ability** *n.* **-able** *a.* **-ation** *n.* the decomposition of organic substances produced by the action of a living organism, or of certain chemical agents. **-ative** *a.*

**fern** *n.* plant characterized by fibrous roots, and leaves called fronds. **-y** *a.*

**fe•roc•i•ty** *n.* cruelty; savage fierceness of disposition. **ferocious** *a.* fierce; violent; wild. **ferociously** *adv.* **ferociousness** *n.*

**fer•ric** *a.* pert. to or extracted from iron; applied to compounds of trivalent iron. **— acid,** an acid containing iron and oxygen.

**fer•ro-** containing or made of iron, occurring in compound words. **ferroconcrete** *n.* reinforced concrete; concrete with inner skeleton of iron or steel. **ferromagnetic** *a.* reacting like iron in a magnetic field. **-us** *a.* pert. to iron.

**fer•ry** *v.t.* to transport over stretch of water by boat; *n.* a place where one is conveyed across a river, etc. by boat; the ferryboat.

**fer•tile** *a.* producing or bearing abundantly; prolific; fruitful. **-ly** *adv.* **-ness,** *n.* **fertilization** *n.* the act of fertilizing; enrichment of soil, by natural or artificial means; union of the female and male cells. **fertilize** *v.t.* to make fruitful; to fecundate; to pollinate. **fertilizer** *n.* one who, or that which, fertilizes; material to enrich soil. **fertility** *n.*

**fer•vent** *a.* glowing; ardent; zealous, enthusiastic. **fervency** *n.* ardor; intensity of devotion. **-ly** *adv.* **fervid** *a.* burning; vehement; intense. **fervidity** *n.* **fervidly** *adv.* **fervidness** *n.* zeal; enthusiasm. **fervor** *n.* heat; ardor; passion.

**fes•ter** *v.t.* to cause to putrefy; *v.i.* to become inflamed; to rot; *n.* an ulcer; a sore.

**fes•tive** *a.* joyous, convivial. **festival** *n.* a feast or celebration; an annual competition- or periodic gathering of musical or dramatic societies. **-ly** *adv.* **festivity** *n.* merriment; merrymaking; festival.

**fetch** *v.t.* to go for and bring; to summon; *v.i.* to go and bring things; *n.* the act of bringing; a trick or artifice. **-ing** *a.* attractive; alluring.

**fete** *n.* a festival; a holiday; *v.t.* to honor with celebrations. **-d** *a.* honored.

**fe•tish, fetich, fetiche** *n.* anything regarded with exaggerated reverence. **-ism,** *n.* fetish worship. **-istic,** *a.*

**fe•tus, foetus** *n.* the young of vertebrate animals between the embryonic and independent states. **fetal, foetal** *a.* **fetation, foetation** *n.* pregnancy. **feticide, foeticide** *n.* destroying of the fetus; abortion.

**feud** *n.* a lasting hereditary strife between families or clans.

**feud** *n.* an estate or land held on condition of service; a fief. **-al** *a.* pert. to feuds or to feudalism. **-alism** *n.* a system which prevailed in Europe in the Middle Ages, by which vassals held land from the king and the tenants-in-chief in return for military service. Also **feudal system. -ary, -atory** *a.* holding land by feudal tenure; *n.* a vassal holding land in fee.

**fe•ver** *n.* bodily disease marked by unusual rise of temperature and usually a quickening of pulse; *v.t.* to put into a fever; *v.i.* to become fevered. **-ed** *a.* affected with fever; frenzied. **-ish** *a.* slightly fevered. **-ishly** *adv.*

**few** *a.* not many; *n.* and *pron.* a small number. **-ness** *n.*

**fi•an•cé** *n.* a betrothed man.

**fi•as•co** *n.* any spectacular failure.

**fib** *n.* a falsehood; a mild lie; *v.i.* to tell a petty lie. **-bing** *pr.p.* **-bed** *pa.p.* and *pa.t.*

**fi•ber** *n.* one of the bundles of threadlike tissue constituting muscles, etc.; any threadlike substance used for weaving fabric. **-ed, -less, fibriform** *a.* **fibril** *n.* a very small fiber. **fibrillose** *a.* covered with fibers. **fibrillous** *a.* composed of small fibers. **fibrin** *n.* a protein formed in coagulation of blood. **fibroid** *a.* of a fibrous nature; *n.* a fibrous tumor. **fibrous** *a.* composed of fibers. **fibrousness** *n.*

**fib•u•la** *n.* the slender outer bone of the leg between knee and ankle. **-r** *a.*

**fick•le** *a.* inconstant; capricious; unreliable. **-ness** *n.*

**fic•tion** *n.* literature dealing with imaginary characters and situations; something invented, or imagined. **-al** *a.* **fictitious** *a.* imaginary; feigned; false. **fictitiously** *adv.*

**fid•dle** *n.* a stringed musical instrument; a violin; *v.t.* and *v.i.* to play on a fiddle. **— bow** *n.* the bow used in playing a violin. **—dee-dee** *n.* nonsense. **—faddle** *v.i.* to trifle; to dawdle; *n.* triviality; *interj.* rubbish. **-sticks** nonsense. **fiddling** *a.* trifling.

**fi•del•i•ty** *n.* faithfulness; loyalty; devotion to duty; adherence to marriage vows.

**fid•get** *v.i.* to move restlessly; to be uneasy; *n.* uneasiness. **-s** *n.pl.* nervous restlessness. **-y** *a.*

**fi•du•ciar•y** *a.* holding or held in trust; *n.* a trustee. **fiducial** *a.* having faith or confidence.

**field** *n.* cleared land; a division of farmland; scene of a battle; any wide expanse; sphere of influence within which magnetic, electrostatic, or gravitational forces are perceptible; the background of a flag, coin, etc. on which a design is drawn; area of ground used for sports; *v.t.* to catch the ball; *v.i.* to act as fielder. **— artillery** *n.* light guns for active operations. **— battery** *n.* battery of field guns. **— book** *n.* book used for notes by land surveyor or naturalist. **— day** *n.* a day for athletic contests; a gala day. **-er** *n.* one who fields at cricket, baseball, etc.

**fiend** *n.* a demon; the devil; a malicious

foe; one who is crazy about something, as, *a fresh-air fiend*. **-ish** *a.*
**fierce** *a.* ferocious; violent; savage; intense. **-ly** *adv.* **-ness** *n.* ferocity; rage.
**fi•er•y** *a.* flaming; hot; ardent; fierce; vehement; irritable. **fierily** *adv.* **fieriness** *n.*
**fife** *n.* a high-pitched flute. **-r** *n.* one who plays the fife.
**fif•teen** *a.* and *n.* five and ten; the symbol, 15 or XV.
**fifth** *a.* next after the fourth; *n.* one of five equal parts of a whole.
**fif•ty** *a.* and *n.* five times ten; the symbol 50 or L. **fifieth** *a.* next in a series of forty-nine others; *n.* a fifieth part. **to go fifty-fifty**, share and share alike.
**fig** *n.* a Mediterranean tree or its fruit.
**fight** *v.t.* to wage war against; to contend against; to oppose; *v.i.* to take part in single combat or battle; to resist; *n.* a combat; a battle; a struggle. **fought** *pa.p.* **-er** *n.* one who fights; an aircraft designed for fighting. **-ing** *a.* able to, or inclined to, fight; pert. to a fight.
**fig•ment** *n.* an invention, fiction, or fabrication.
**fig•ure** *n.* outward form of anything; the form of a person; a diagram, drawing, etc.; the sign of a numeral, as 1, 2, 3; *v.t.* to note by numeral characters; to calculate; to symbolize; to image in the mind; *v.i.* to make a figure. **figurative** *a.* not literal. **figuratively** *adv.* **figurativeness** *n.* **-head** *n.* the nominal head of an organization, without real authority; ornamental figure under the bowsprit of a ship. **figurine** *n.* a statuette. **figure of speech,** an unusual use of words to produce a desired effect, such as metaphor, simile, etc.
**fil•a•ment** *n.* a slender thread; a fiber, the stalk of a stamen. **-ous** *a.* threadlike.
**fil•bert** *n.* the nut of the hazel tree.
**file** *n.* an orderly line; a cabinet, wire, or portfolio for keeping papers in order; the papers or cards thus kept; *v.t.* to set in order in a public record office; *v.i.* to march in a file; to make application. **Indian** or **single file,** a single line of men marching one behind the other. **rank and file,** noncommissioned soldiers; the general mass of people as distinct from well-known figures.
**file** *n.* a steel instrument for smoothing rough surfaces or cutting through metal; *v.t.* to cut or abrade with a file. **filing** *pr.p.* **-d** *pa.p.* **filing** *n.* a particle of metal rubbed off by a file; *v.t.* the action of abrading stone or cutting metal.
**fil•i•al** *a.* pert. to or befitting a son or daughter. **-ly** *adv.*
**fil•i•bus•ter** *n.* one who deliberately obstructs legislation, esp. by making long speeches; *v.i.* to act as a filibuster.
**Fil•i•pi•no** *n.* a native of the Philippine Islands.
**fill** *v.t.* to make full; to replenish; to occupy as a position; to stop up (a tooth); *v.i.* to become full; *n.* a full supply. **-er** *n.* one who, or that which, fills. **-ing** *n.* that which fills up a space, as gold, etc. used by dentists; a mixture put into sandwiches, cakes, etc.; *a.* satisfying; ample.
**fil•let** *n.* piece of meat cut from the thigh; a piece of meat boned and rolled; fish after bones are removed; *v.t.* to bone.
**fil•ly** *n.* a young mare.
**film** *n.* a thin coating or membrane; a delicate filament; a roll of flexible, sensitized material used for photography; pictures taken on this roll; *pl.* a movie show; *v.t.* to cover with a film; to take a moving picture of; to reproduce on a film. **-iness** *n.* **-y** *a.* composed of or covered with film; membranous; sheer.
**fil•ter** *n.* a device for separating liquids from solids, or for straining impurities from liquids; a device for removing dust from the air; a piece of colored glass placed in front of the lens, passing certain rays only; *v.t.* to purify by passing through a filter; to filtrate; *v.i.* to pass through a filter. **filtrate** *v.t.* to filter; *n.* the liquid which has been strained through a filter. **filtration** *n.*
**filth** *n.* foul matter; dirt; pollution; immorality; obscenity. **-ily** *adv.* **-iness** *n.* **-y** *a.*
**fin** *n.* a paddle-like organ of fishes and other aquatic forms serving to balance and propel; a vertical surface, fixed usually on the tail of an aircraft to aid lateral and directional stability.
**fi•nal** *a.* pert. to the end; last; *n.* the last stage of anything; *pl.* the last examination or contest in a series. **-ist** *n.* a competitor who reaches the finals of a contest. **-ity** *n.* the state of being final; conclusiveness. **-ize** *v.t.* to give a final form to. **-ly** *adv.*
**fi•na•le** *n.* the end; the last movement of a musical composition; final scene.
**fi•nance** *n.* the management of money affairs; *pl.* the income of a state or person; resources; funds; *v.t.* to provide funds for; to supply capital. **financial** *a.* pert. to finance; fiscal. **financially** *adv.* **financier** *n.* one who deals in large-scale money transactions.
**finch** *n.* the name applied to various species of small, seed-eating birds, including the *chaffinch, bullfinch*.
**find** *v.t.* to come to by searching; to meet with; to discover; *n.* a discovery, esp. of unexpected value. **found** *pa.t.* and *pa.p.* **-er** *n.* **-ing** *n.* the act of one who finds; a legal decision arrived at by a jury after deliberation; a discovery.
**fine** *a.* excellent; thin; refined; *v.t.* to make fine; to refine or purify; *v.i.* to become fine, pure, or slender; delicately thin (of wire). **-ly** *adv.* **-ness** *n.* the state of being fine; the amount of gold in an alloy. **-r** *n.* refiner. **-ry** *n.* ornament; gay clothes; a furnace for making wrought iron. **finesse** *n.* subtlety of contrivance to gain a point; *v.i.* and *v.t.* to use artifice; to try to take a trick by finesse.
**fine** *n.* a sum of money imposed as a penalty for an offense; *v.t.* to impose a fine on.
**fi•nesse** See **fine.**
**fin•ger** *n.* any one of the extremities of the

hand, excluding thumb; *v.t.* to touch with fingers; to handle; to perform with fingers; *v.i.* to use the fingers. **-ing** *n.* the act of touching or handling lightly with fingers; the manner of manipulating the fingers in playing an instrument.

**fin•i•cal** *a.* affectedly fine; overfastidious. **-ly** *adv.* **finicking, finicky,** *a.* overparticular.

**fin•ish** *v.t.* to bring to an end; to terminate; *v.i.* to conclude; *n.* that which finishes, or perfects; last stage; the final coat of paint, etc. **-ed** *a.* terminated. **-er** *n.* one who or that which finishes or gives the final touches. **-ing school,** a school for completing the education of young women.

**fi•nite** *a.* limited in quantity, degree, or capacity. **-ly** *adv.* **-ness, finitude** *n.*

**Finn** *n.* a native of Finland. **-ic, -ish** *a.* **Finlander** *n.* a Finn.

**fir** *n.* cone-bearing evergreen tree, yielding valuable timber. **— cone** *n.* fruit of the fir.

**fire** *n.* heat and light caused by combustion; burning; flame; *v.t.* to set on fire; to kindle; to supply with fuel; *v.i.* to be ignited. **— alarm** *n.* an alarm giving warning of an outbreak of fire. **— brigade** *n.* men specially trained to deal with fire. **— escape** *n.* iron stair used as emergency exit from burning building. **-fly** *n.* a type of beetle which has light-producing organs. **-man** *n.* a member of a fire-fighting unit. **-place** *n.* hearth or grate. **-plug** *n.* a hydrant for drawing water by hose to extinguish a fire. **-proof** *a.* **-r** *n.* **— screen** *n.* a movable protective screen in front of a fire. **-side** *n.* the hearth. **-wood** *n.* wood for fuel; kindling. **-work** *n.* a preparation containing gunpowder, sulfur, etc. for making spectacular explosions. **firing line** *n.* the area of a battle zone within firing range of the enemy. **firing party** or **squad,** soldiers detailed to fire the final salute at a military funeral, or to shoot a condemned person.

**firm** *a.* fixed; solid; compact; rigid; steady; unwavering; stern; inflexible. **-ly** *adv.* **-ness** *n.*

**firm** *n.* the name, title, or style under which a company transacts business.

**fir•ma•ment** *n.* the expanse of the sky; the heavens.

**first** *a.* preceding all others in a series or in kind; foremost (in place); earliest (in time); *adv.* before anything else in time, place, degree, or preference; *n.* beginning. **— aid** *n.* preliminary treatment given to injured person before the arrival of a doctor. **-born** *n.* eldest child. **— class** *a.* first-rate; of highest worth; of superior accommodation; *adv.* in the firstclass. **-hand** *a.* obtained direct from the source. **-ly** *adv.* **—rate** *a.* of highest excellence.

**fis•cal** *a.* pert. to the public treasury or revenue; pert. to financial matters generally.

**fish** *n.* a cold-blooded, aquatic vertebrate animal, with limbs represented by fins, and breathing through its gills; *pl.* **fish, -es;** *v.t.* to catch by fishing; *v.i.* to follow the occupation of a fisherman, for business or pleasure. **-er** *n.* one who fishes. **-erman** *n.* one whose employment is to catch fish; one who fishes for pleasure; an angler. **-ery** *n.* the business of fishing; a fishing ground; the legal right to fish in a certain area. **-hook** *n.* a barbed hook for catching fish by line. **-ily** *adv.* **-iness** *n.* **-ing** *n.* the act of fishing. **-ing rod** *n.* a long supple rod with line attached, used by anglers. **-ing tackle** *n.* an angler's gear comprising, rod, lines, hooks, etc. **-y** *a.* abounding in fish; pert. to fish; expressionless; dubious.

fish

**fis•sion** *n.* the process of splitting or breaking up into parts; cell cleavage; *v.t.* and *v.i.* to split into two parts. **-able** *a.*

**fis•sure** *n.* a cleft, crack, or slit.

**fist** *n.* the hand clenched with fingers doubled into the palm.

**fis•tu•la** *n.* a narrow duct; an infected channel in the body leading from an internal abscess to the surface. **-r, fistulous** *a.* hollowed like a pipe.

**fit** *a.* **-ter. -test.** suitable; qualified; proper; vigorous; *v.t.* to make suitable; to qualify; to adapt; to adjust; to fashion to the appropriate size; *v.i.* to be proper or becoming. **-ting** *pr.p.* **-ted** *pa.t.* **-ly** *adv.* **-ness** *n.* the state of being fit; appropriateness; sound bodily health. **-ter** *n.* one who or that which makes fit; a tailor or dressmaker who fits clothes on a person. **-ting** *a.* appropriate; suitable; *n.* a trial of a garment to see that it fits. **-tings** *n.pl.* fixtures; equipment. **-tingly** *adv.*

**fit** *n.* a sudden and violent attack of a disorder; a seizure. **-ful** *a.* spasmodic; intermittent. **-fully** *adv.*

**five** *n.* four and one; the symbol 5 or V; *a.* one more than four. **-fold** *a.* five times repeated; quintuple. **-r** *n.* a five-dollar bill.

**fix** *v.t.* to make firm; to establish; to secure; to immobilize; to gaze at; to repair; to put in order; *v.i.* to settle permanently; to become hard; *n.* dilemma; predicament. **-ation** *n.* the act of fixing; steadiness; in psychoanalysis, an emotional arrest of part of the psychosexual development. **-ative** *n.* a fixing agent; a chemical which preserves specimens in a lifelike condition. **-ed** *a.* settled, permanent, not apt to change; steady. **-edly** *adv.* **-edness** *n.* **-er** *n.* one who, or that which, fixes. **-ity** *n.* fixedness; immobility. **-ings** *n.pl.* apparatus, trimmings. **-ture** *n.* that which is fixed or attached; anything of an accessory nature considered a part of the real property.

**fizz** *v.i.* to effervesce; *n.* a hissing sound; any effervescent liquid. **-le** *v.i.* to fizz or splutter.

**flab•ber•gast** *v.t.* to overcome with

amazement.

**flab•by** *a.* soft; yielding to the touch; drooping; weak. **flabbily** *adv.* **flabbiness** *n.*

**flag** *v.i.* to hang loosely; to grow spiritless or dejected; to become languid; to lose vigor. **-ging** *pr.p.* **-ged** *pa.p.*

**flag** *n.* a flat paving stone; a type of sandstone which splits easily into large slabs. Also **-stone.**

**flag** *n.* an ensign or colors; a standard; a banner as a mark of distinction, rank, or nationality; *v.t.* to decorate with flags or

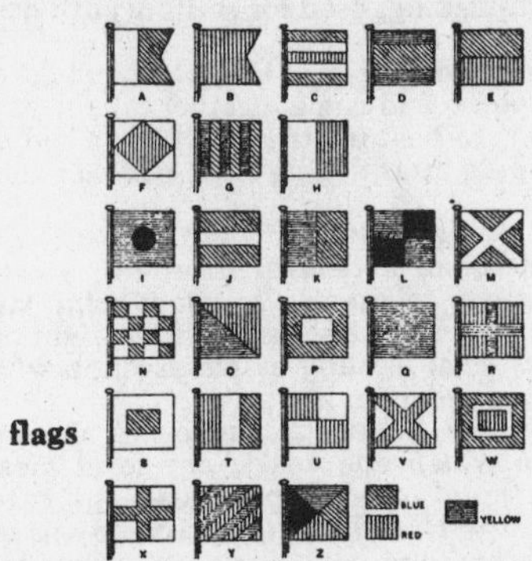


**flags**

bunting; to convey a message by flag signals. **-ship** *n.* the ship flying the admiral's flag. **white flag,** the symbol of truce or surrender. **yellow flag,** a flag indicating that a ship is in quarantine. **to fly a flag half-mast,** to hoist flag halfway as token of mourning.

**fla•grant** *a.* glaring; notorious; scandalous. **flagrance, flagrancy** *n.* **-ly** *adv.*

**flair** *n.* instinctive discernment; a keen scent.

**flake** *n.* a scalelike particle; *v.t.* to form into flakes, to cover with flakes; *v.i.* to scale; to fall in flakes. **flaky** *a.* consisting of flakes.

**flam•boy•ant** *a.* florid; showy; ornate. **flamboyance, flamboyancy** *n.*

**flame** *n.* a mass of burning vapor or gas; a blaze of light; fire in general; *v.i.* to blaze; to blush; to become violently excited, fervent, or angry. **flaming** *a.* blazing; gaudy; fervent. **flamingly** *adv.* **flammability** *n.* **flammable** *a.*

**fla•min•go** *n.* tropical wading bird.

**flan** *n.* a pastry shell or cake filled with fruit filling.

**flange** *n.* a projecting edge, as of a railway-car wheel to keep it on the rails, or of castings to fasten them together.

**flank** *n.* the fleshy part of side of animal between ribs and hip; *v.t.* to stand at the side of; to protect the flank of an army, etc.; to border.

**flan•nel** *n.* a soft-textured, loosely woven woolen cloth; *a.* made of flannel; *v.t.* to cover or rub with flannel. **-s** *n.pl.* clothes made of this, esp. sports garments; woolen undergarments. **-ette** *n.* a cotton material like flannel.

**flap** *n.* a piece of flexible material attached on one side only and usually covering an opening, as of envelope; anything hinged and hanging loose; *v.t.* to cause to sway or flutter; *v.i.* to flutter; to fall like a flap; to move, as wings. **-ping** *pr.p.* **-ped** *pa.p.* **-jack** *n.* a broad, flat pancake.

**flare** *v.i.* to burn with a glaring, unsteady or fitful flame; to burst out with flame, anger, etc.; *n.* an unsteady, blazing light; a brilliant, often colored, light used as a signal; a sudden burst of flame, passion, etc. **-d** *a.* (of a skirt) spreading gradually out toward the bottom. **flaring** *a.*

**flash** *n.* a sudden brief burst of light; an instant or moment; a news story; *a.* showy; tawdry; *v.i.* to blaze suddenly and die out; to pass swiftly; *v.t.* to cause to flash; to transmit instantaneously, as news by radio, telephone, etc. **-back** *n.* momentary turning back to an episode in a story. **-bulb** *n.* *(Photog.)* an electric bulb giving brilliant flash for night picture. **-ily** *adv.* **-iness** *n.* **-light** *n.* a portable light powered by batteries or a small generator. **-y** *a.* showy; tawdry; cheap.

**flask** *n.* a narrow-necked, usually flat bottle easily carried in the pocket.

**flat** *a.* **-ter.** **-test.** level; even; tasteless; monotonous; dull; below the true pitch; *n.* a level surface; low-lying sometimes flooded, tract of land; a note, a semitone below the natural; the symbol for this; *adv.* prone; in a manner below true pitch. **— finish** *n.* a flat surface in paint work. **—footed** *a.* having fallen arches in the feet. **-ly** *adv.* peremptorily. **-ness** *n.* **— rate,** uniform rate. **-ten** *v.t.* to make flat; to lower the true musical pitch of. **-ware** *n.* silver knives, forks, etc.

**flat•ter** *v.t.* to praise unduly and insincerely; to pay fulsome compliments to. **-er** *n.* **-ing** *a.* **ingly** *adv.* **-y** *n.* the act of flattering; undue praise.

**flaunt** *v.t.* to display ostentatiously or impudently; *v.i.* to wave or move in the wind; to parade showily; *n.* a vulgar display.

**fla•vor** *n.* savor; quality affecting taste or smell; distinctive quality of a thing; *v.t.* to season; to give zest to. **-ous** *a.* **-ing** *n.* substance to add flavor to a dish, e.g. spice, essence.

**flaw** *n.* a crack; a defect; a weak point as in an argument; *v.t.* to break; to crack. **-less** *a.* perfect.

**flax** *n.* the fibers of an annual blue-flowered plant, used for making linen; the plant itself. **-en** *a.* pert. to or resembling flax; loose or flowing; of the color of unbleached flax, hence yellowish or golden.

**flea** *n.* a small, wingless, very agile insect with irritating bite. **—bitten** *a.* bitten by a flea; mean; worthless.

**fleck** *n.* a spot; a streak; *v.t.* to spot; to dapple.

**fled** *pa.t.* and *pa.p.* of **flee.**

**flee** *v.i.* to fly or retreat from danger; *v.t.* to hasten from. **-ing** *pr.p.* **fled** *pa.p.* and *pa.t.*

**fleece** *n.* the coat of wool covering a sheep or shorn from it; anything resembling wool; *v.t.* to shear wool. **fleecy** *a.* woolly;

resembing wool.

**fleet** *n.* a group of ships; a force of naval vessels under one command.

**fleet** *a.* swift; nimble; *v.t.* to pass swiftly; *v.t.* to make to pass quickly. **-ing** *a.* transient; ephemeral; passing. **-ingly** *adv.* **-ness** *n.* swiftness. **—footed** *a.* swift of foot.

**Flem•ing** *n.* a native of Flanders. **Flemish** *a.* pert. to Flanders.

**flesh** *n.* the body tissue; kindred; the pulpy part of fruit; *v.t.* to incite to hunt, as a hound, by feeding it on flesh; to remove flesh from the underside of hides preparatory to tanning process. **— color** *n.* the pale pink color of the human skin (of white races). **-iness** *n.* state of being fleshy; plumpness. **-less** *a.* **-liness** *n.* **-ly** *a.* corporeal; worldly; sensual. **— wound** *n.* **-y** *a.* pert. to flesh; corpulent; gross; thick and soft.

**fleur-de-lis** *n.* a design based on the shape of an iris; the royal insignia of France.

**flew** *pa.t.* of verb **fly**.

**flex** *v.t.* and *v.i.* to bend. **-ibility** *n.* quality of being pliable; adaptability; versatility. **-ible** *a.* **-ibly** *adv.* **-ile** *a.* bendable. **-ion, flection** *n.* a bend; a fold; an inflection. **-or** *n.* a muscle. **-uose, -uous** *a.* bending; tortuous. **-ure** *n.* act of bending; a bend.

**flick** *v.t.* to strike lightly, as with whip; *n.* light, smart stroke.

**flick•er** *v.i.* to flutter; to waver; to quiver; to burn unsteadily; *n.* act of wavering; quivering.

**flight** *n.* the act or power of flying; the distance covered in flying; a journey by airplane; a flock of birds. **— deck,** *n.* the deck of an aircraft carrier for planes to land or take off. **-y** *a.* capricious; giddy; volatile.

**flight** *n.* the act of fleeing; retreat. **to put to flight,** to rout.

**flim•sy** *a.* thin; fragile; unsubstantial; *n.* thin, transfer paper. **flimsily** *adv.* **flimsiness** *n.*

**flinch** *v.i.* to shrink from pain or difficulty; to wince. **-ing** *n.* the act of flinching.

**fling** *v.t.* to throw from the hand; *v.i.* to flounce; to throw oneself violently; *n.* a cast or throw; a gibe; abandonment to pleasure; lively dance. **flung** *pa.t.* and *pa.p.* **-er** *n.*

**flint** *n.* quartz, which readily produces fire when struck with steel; a prehistoric stone weapon; *a.* made of flint. **-lock** *n.* a gunlock with a flint fixed on the hammer for firing the priming. **-y** *a.* made of, or resembling, flint; hardhearted; cruel.

**flip** *v.t.* to flick; to jerk; *n.* a flick; a snap. **-ping** *pr.p.* **-ped** *pa.t.* and *pa.p.* **-per** *n.* the limb of an animal which facilitates swimming.

**flip•pant** *a.* smart or pert in speech. **flippancy** *n.* **-ly** *adv.*

**flirt** *v.t.* to jerk, as a bird's tail; to move playfully to and fro, as a fan; *v.i.* to move about briskly; *n.* a jerk; a philanderer; a flighty girl. **-ation** *n.* **-atious** *a.*

**flit•ter** *v.i.* to flutter.

**float** *v.i.* to flutter.

**float** *v.i.* to rest or drift on the surface of a liquid; to be buoyed up; to be suspended in air; to wander aimlessly; *v.t.* to cause to stay on the surface of a liquid; *n.* anything which is buoyant; a raft; cork or quill on a fishing line, or net; a hollow floating ball of metal indicating depth of liquid in tank or cistern. **-able** *a.* **-age** *n.* See **flotage. -ation** *n.* See **flotation. -er** *n.* **-ing** *a.* buoyant on surface of the water or in air; movable; fluctuating; in circulation. **-ing dock,** a floating dry dock. **-ingly** *adv.*

**flock** *n.* a small tuft of wool; refuse of wool in cloth-making, used for stuffing cushions, etc.

**flock** *n.* a collection of animals; a crowd of people; *v.i.* to come together in crowds.

**flog** *v.t.* to beat or strike, as with a rod or whip; to thrash. **-ging** *pr.p.* **-ged** *pa.t.* and *pa.p.*

**flood** *n.* an overflow of water; an inundation; a deluge; a torrent; *v.t.* to overflow; to drench; to overwhelm; *v.i.* to spill over; to rise (as the tide). **-lighting** *n.* artificial lighting by lamps fitted with special reflectors.

**floor** *n.* the horizontal surface of a room upon which one walks; any level area; minimum level, esp. of prices; *v.t.* to cover with a floor; to strike down; to perplex; to stump. **-ing** *n.* materials for floors. **— show** *n.* a show at a nightclub.

**flop** *v.t.* to flap; to set down heavily; *v.i.* to drop down suddenly or clumsily; *n.* a fall, as of a soft, outspread body. **-ping** *pr.p.* **-ped** *pa.t.* and *pa.p.* **-py** *a.* slack.

**flo•ra** *n.* the plants native to a certain geographical region or geological period; a classified list of such plants. **-l** *a.* **-lly** *adv.* adorned with flowers. **floriated,** *a.* **floret** *n.* a single flower in a cluster of flowers; a small compact flower head. **florist** *n.* a grower or seller of flowers.

**flo•res•cence** *n.* a bursting into flower. **florescent** *a.*

**floss** *n.* untwisted threads of very fine silk. **— silk** *n.* very soft silk thread. **-y** *a.*

**flo•tage** *n.* state or act of floating; the floating capacity of anything.

**flo•ta•tion** *n.* the act of floating; act of launching, esp. a business venture, loan, etc. Also **floatation.**

**flo•til•la** *n.* a fleet of small vessels.

**flounce** *v.i.* to turn abruptly; to flounder about; *n.* a sudden, jerky movement.

**floun•der** *n.* a small, edible flatfish.

**floun•der** *v.i.* to struggle helplessly, as in marshy ground; to tumble about; to stumble hesitatingly, as in a speech.

**flour** *n.* the finely ground meal of wheat, etc.; *v.t.* to turn into flour; to sprinkle with flour. **-y** *a.*

**flour•ish** *v.t.* to decorate with flowery ornament or with florid diction; *v.i.* to grow luxuriantly; to prosper; *n.* ornament; a fanciful stroke of the pen. **-ing** *a.* thriving; vigorous.

**flout** *v.t.* to mock; *v.i.* to jeer; *n.* a gibe; an insult.

**flow** *v.i.* to run, as a liquid; to rise, as the tide; to circulate, as the blood; to glide along; *v.t.* to overflow; *n.* a stream; a current; the rise of the tide; any easy expression of thought, diction, etc.; output. **-ing** *a.* moving; running; fluent; curving gracefully, as lines; falling in folds, as drapery. **-ingly** *adv.*

**flow•er** *n.* the reproductive organ in plants; a blossom. **-s** *n.pl.* a substance in the form of a powder, as *flowers of sulfur; v.t.* to adorn with flowers or flowerlike shapes; *v.i.* to produce flowers; to bloom;

**flower**

to come to prime condition. **-ed** *a.* decorated with a flower pattern, as fabric. **-et** *n.* a small flower; a floret. **-ing** *a.* having flowers. **-y** *a.* abounding in or decorated with flowers; highly ornate; euphuistic.

**flown** *pa.p. of* **fly.**

**flu** *n.* influenza.

**fluc•tu•ate** *v.i.* to move up and down, as a wave; to be unstable; to be irresolute. **fluctuant** *a.* **fluctuation** *n.* a vacillation.

**flue** *n.* a shaft or duct in a chimney.

**flu•ent** *a.* flowing; ready in the use of words. **fluency** *n.*

**fluff** *n.* light, floating down; *v.t.* to give a fluffy surface to; *v.i.* to become downy; **-y** *a.*

**fluid** *n.* a substance which flows; a nonsolid; *a.* capable of flowing; liquid; gaseous; shifting. **-ify** *v.t.* to make fluid. **-ity, -ness** *n.* the state or quality of being a nonsolid; **-ly** *adv.*

**fluke** *n.* the flounder; a parasitic worm.

**fluke** *n.* any lucky chance.

**flung** *pa.t.* and *pa.p.* of **fling.**

**flunk** *v.i.* to fail as in an examination or course; *v.t.* to fail in.

**flu•or** *n.* a mineral, fluoride of source of fluorine. **-esce** *v.i.* to exhibit calcium, usually called *fluorite;* principle fluorescence. **-escense** *n.* the property of some substances which emit surface reflections of light different in color from the mass of the material upon exposure to external radiation. **-escent** *a.* **-ide** *n.* a compound of fluorine with another element. **-ine** *n.* a pale yellow very active gaseous element. **-escent lighting,** *a.* form of artificial diffused lighting, giving the effect of permanent daylight.

**flur•ry** *n.* a sudden, brief gust of wind; bustle; commotion; *v.t.* to agitate; to fluster.

**flush** *v.i.* to turn red in the face; to blush; to cause to blush or turn red; to cleanse with a rush of water; *n.* a flow of water; a rush of blood to the face.

**flush** *n.* a run of cards of the same suit.

**flush** *v.t.* to level up; *a.* being in the same plane; well-supplied, as with money; full; even with margins.

**flus•ter** *v.t.* to make agitated; to flurry; *v.i.* to be confused and flurried; *n.* confusion; nervous agitation. **-ed** *a.*

**flute** *n.* a musical tubular wind instrument; a stop in the pipe organ; a vertical groove in the shaft of a column; *v.i.* to play the flute; *v.t.* to play (tune) on the flute; to make flutes or grooves in. **-d** *a.* ornamented with grooves, channels, etc. **fluting** *n.* action of playing a flute; the ornamental vertical grooving on a pillar, on glass. **flutist** *n.* one who plays a flute. Also **flautist. fluty** *a.*

**flut•ter** *v.t.* to throw into confusion; *v.i.* to flap the wings; *n.* quick and irregular motion; nervous hurry; confusion.

**flux** *n.* the act of flowing; fluidity; *v.t.* to fuse; to melt; *v.i.* to flow. **-ion** *n.* a flow or flux.

**fly** *v.t.* to cause to fly; to flee from; *v.i.* to move through the air, as a bird or an aircraft; to become airborne; to travel by airplane; to move rapidly; to flee; *n.* a winged insect, esp. of the order *Diptera;* a housefly; a fishhook in imitation of a fly; a flap on a garment covering a row of buttons or other fastener; a ball sent high in the air (*pa.t.* and *pa.p.* in baseball, **flied). -ing** *pr.p.* **flew** *pa.t.* **flown** *pa.p.* **-ing** *n.* moving through the air; air navigation; *a.* capable of flight; streaming; swift. **-ing saucer** *n.* name given to a saucerlike object reputedly seen flying at tremendous speeds and high altitudes. **-paper** *n.* a paper smeared with sticky substance to trap flies. **-wheel** *n.* a heavy-rimmed wheel attached to the crankshaft of an engine to regulate its speed or accumulate power.

**flywheel**

**foal** *n.* the young of a mare, a colt or a filly; *v.t.* and *v.i.* to bring forth a foal.

**foam** *n.* froth; the bubbles of air on surface of effervescent liquid; *v.i.* to froth; to bubble; to gather foam. **-ing** *a.* **ingly** *adv.* **— rubber** *n.* latex made into a soft, elastic, and porous substance, resembling a spong. **-y** *a.* frothy.

**fo•cus** *n.* the point at which rays of light meet after reflection or refraction; one of two points connected linearly to any point on a curve; any point of concentration; *v.t.* to bring to a focus; to adjust; to concentrate; *v.i.* to converge. **-es, foci** *pl.* **-ing** *pr.p.* **-ed** *pa.p.* **focal** *a.* pert. to a focus. **focalize** *v.t.* to bring into focus; to cause to converge; to concentrate. **focalization** *n.* **in focus,** clearly outlined; well-defined. **out of**

focus, distorted.
**foe** *n.* an enemy.
**foe•tus** See **fetus.**
**fog** *n.* thick mist; mental confusion; *v.t.* to shroud in fog; to perplex the mind. *v.i.* to become cloudy or obscured. **-bank** *n.* a mass of fog. **-gily** *adv.* **-giness** *n.* **-gy** *a.* **-horn** *n.* a loud siren used during fog for warnings.
**fo•gy, fogey** *n.* dull, old fellow; an elderly person whose ideas are behind the times.
**foi•ble** *n.* weakness of character; a failing.
**foil** *v.t.* to frustrate; to baffle.
**foil** *n.* a thin leaf of metal, as *tinfoil.*
**foist** *v.t.* to palm off. **-er** *n.*
**fold** *n.* a doubling over of a flexible material; a pleat; a crease or a line made by folding; a dip in rock strata caused originally by pressure; *v.t.* to double over; to enclose within folds or layers; to embrace; *v.i.* to be pleated or doubled. **-er** *n.* the one who or that which folds; a folded, printed paper; a file for holding papers, etc.
**fold** *n.* an enclosure for sheep; a flock of sheep; *v.t.* to confine in a fold.
**fol•der•ol** *n.* the refrain to a song.
**fo•liage** *n.* leaves of a plant in general; leafage. **-d** *a.* having leaves.
**fo•li•o** *n.* the two opposite pages of a ledger used for one account and numbered the same; page number in a book; *a.* pert. to or formed of sheets folded so as to make two leaves; *v.t.* to number the pages of a book on one side only.
**folk** *n.* people in general, or as a specified class; *a.* originating among the common people. **-s** *n.pl.* one's own family and near relations. **— dance** *n.* a traditional country dance. **-lore** *n.* popular superstitions or legends.
**fol•li•cle** *n.* a one-celled seed vessel; a small sac; a gland, as in *hair follicle.* **follicular** *a.* pert. to a follicle.
**fol•low** *v.t.* to go after; to move behind; to succeed (in a post); to adhere to (a belief); to watch carefully; to keep in touch with; *v.i.* to come after; to pursue; to occur as a consequence; *n.* the act of following. **-er** *n.* one who comes after; adherents; vocation; *a.* coming next after.
**fol•ly** *n.* weakness of mind; a foolish action; *(pl.)* a theatrical revue.
**fond** *a.* loving; doting; very affectionate. **fond of,** much attached to. **-le** *v.t.* to caress; to stroke tenderly. **-ly** *adv.* **-ness** *n.*
**fon•dant** *n.* a thick, creamy sugar candy.
**font** *n.* a stone basin for holding baptismal water.
**food** *n.* matter which one feeds on; solid nourishment as contrasted with liquids; mental or spiritual nourishment. **-stuff** *n.* edible commodity with nutritional value.
**fool** *n.* one who behaves stupidly; one devoid of common sense; *v.t.* to make a fool of, to impose on; to trick; *v.i.* to behave like a fool; to trifle. **-ery** *n.* silly behavior; foolish act. **-hardily** *adv.* **-hardiness** *n.* **-hardy** *a.* recklessly daring; venturesome. **-ish** *a.* weak in intellect. **-ishly** *adv.* **-ishness** *n.* **-ing** *n.* foolery. **-proof** *a.* (of machines) so devised that mishandling cannot cause damage to machine or personnel.
**foot** *n.* the extreme end of the lower limbs, below the ankle; a base or support, like a foot; the end of a bed, couch, etc. where the feet would normally lie; a measure of length = 12 inches; *v.t.* to traverse by walking; *v.i.* to dance; to walk. *pl.* **feet** **-age** *n.* the length expressed in feet. **-ball** *n.* a game played by two teams of eleven each trying to carry or pass the ball over the opponents' goal line; the elongated inflated leather ball used in the game. **-ed** *a.* having feet or a foot. **-ing** *n.* ground to stand on; the part of a construction contacting the ground; status. **-lights** *n.pl.* a row of screened lights along the front of the stage. **-note** *n.* a note of reference or explanation at foot of a page.
**for** *prep.* in place of; instead of; because of; during; as being; considering; in return for; on behalf of; in spite of; in respect to; intended to belong to; suited to; with the purpose of; *conj.* because. **as for,** regarding.
**for•as•much as** *conj.* seeing that; because; since.
**for•ay** *n.* a raid to get plunder; *v.t.* to pillage.
**for•bade** *pa.t.* of **forbid.**
**for•bear** *v.t.* to abstain from; to avoid; to bear with; *v.i.* to refrain from; to control one's feelings. **forbore** *pa.t.* **forborne** *pa.p.* **-ing.** *a.* long-suffering.
**for•bid** *v.t.* to prohibit. **forbade** or **forbad** *pa.t.* **-den** *pa.p.* **-den** *a.* prohibited. **-ding** *a.* repellent; menacing; sinister. **-dingly** *adv.*
**force** *n.* strength; energy; coercion; power; body of soldiers, police, etc.; *v.t.* to compel; to strain. **-s** *n.pl.* Army, Navy and Air Force. **-d** *a.* achieved by great effort, or under compulsion; lacking spontaneity, as *forced laugh.* **-ful** *a.* full of energy; vigorous. **-fully** *adv.* **-less** *a.* weak; inert. **-r** *n.* **forcible** *a.* having force; compelling; cogent; effective. **forcibly** *adv.* **forcing** *n.* the action of using force or applying pressure.
**for•ceps** *n.* a surgical instrument like tongs.
**ford** *n.* a shallow part of a stream, etc. where a crossing can be made on foot; *v.t.* to cross by a ford. **-able** *a.*
**fore** *a.* in front; forward; prior; *adv.* in front, as opp. to *aft; n.* the front. *interj.* a warning cry to person in the way.
**fore-** *prefix* meaning in front or beforehand.
**fore•arm** *n.* the part of the arm between the elbow and the wrist.
**fore•arm** *v.t.* to take defensive precautions.
**fore•bear, forbear** *n.* an ancestor.
**fore•bode** *v.t.* to predict; to prognosticate. **-ment** *n.* **foreboding** *n.* an intuitive sense of impending evil or danger.
**fore•cast** *n.* a prediction; *v.t.* and *v.i.* to conjecture beforehand; to predict.
**fore•close** *v.t.* to prevent; to exclude; to deprive of the right to redeem a mortgage or property. **foreclosure** *n.*
**fore•fa•ther** *n.* an ancestor.

**fore•fin•ger** *n.* the finger next to the thumb; the index finger.

**fore•front** *n.* the foremost place.

**fore•go** *v.t.* to precede. **-ing** *a.* preceding; just mentioned. **-ne** *a.* predetermined or inevitable, as in a *foregone conclusion.*

**fore•ground** *n.* the part of a picture which seems nearest the observer.

**fore•hand** *n.* *(Tennis)* used of a stroke played *forward* on the right or natural side, as opp. to *backhand.* **-ed** *a.*

**fore•head** *n.* the upper part of the face above the eyes; the brow.

**for•eign** *a.* situated outside a place or country; alien; irrelevant. **-er** *n.* a native of another country; an alien. **-ism** *n.*

**fore•man** *n.* the principal member and spokesman of a jury; the overseer of a group of workmen.

**fore•mast** *n.* the mast in the forepart of a vessel, nearest the bow.

**fore•most** *a.* first in place or time; first in dignity or rank.

**fo•ren•sic** *a.* pert. to the law courts, public discussion, or debate. **-ally** *adv.*

**fore•see** *v.t.* to see beforehand; to foreknow. **foresaw** *pa.t.* **-n** *pa.p.* **foresight** *n.* wise forethought; prudence; front sight on gun.

**fore•shad•ow** *v.t.* to shadow or indicate beforehand; to suggest in advance.

**fore•skin** *n.* the skin covering the glans penis.

**for•est** *n.* a tract of wooded, uncultivated land; the trees alone; *v.t.* to cover with trees. **-er** *n.* one who practices forestry; one who has forestland, game etc. under supervision. **-ry** *n.* the science of growing timber.

**fore•stall** *v.t.* to thwart by advance action; to buy up goods before they reach the market, so as to resell at maximum price; to get in ahead of someone else. **-er, -ment** *n.*

**fore•tell** *v.t.* to predict; to prophesy. **-ing** *pr.p.* **foretold** *pa.t.* and *pa.p.*

**fore•thought** *n.* anticipation; provident care; a thinking beforehand.

**for•ev•er** *adv.* always; *n.* eternity. **-more** *adv.*

**fore•warn** *v.t.* to warn or caution in advance.

**fore•word** *n.* a preface; an introductory note to a book.

**for•feit** *v.t.* to be deprived of, as a punishment; *n.* that which is forfeited; a fine or penalty. **-able** *a.* **-ure** *n.* the act of forfeiting; the state of being deprived of something as a punishment; the thing confiscated.

**for•gave** *pa.t.* of verb **forgive.**

**forge** *v.t.* to fabricate; to counterfeit; *v.i.* to work with metals; to commit forgery. **-r** *n.* **-ry** *n.* the making of an imitation of money, work of art, etc., and representing it as genuine; the act of falsifying a document, or illegally using another's signature; that which is forged.

**forge** *v.i.* to move forward steadily.

**for•get** *v.t.* to lose remembrance of; to neglect inadvertently; to disregard. **-ting** *pr.p.* **forgot** *pa.t.* **forgot** or **forgotten** *pa.p.* **-table** *a.* **-ful** *a.* apt to forget; heedless; oblivious. **-fully** *adv.* **-fulness** *n.*

**for•give** *v.t.* to pardon; to exercise clemency; to grant pardon. **forgave** *pa.t.* **-n** *pa.p.* **forgivable** *a.* **-ness** *n.* **forgiving** *a.* ready to pardon.

**for•go** *v.t.* to renounce; to abstain from possession or enjoyment. **forewent** *pa.t.* **-ne** *pa.p.*

**fork** *n.* a table utensil of silver, etc. usually with four prongs; each part into which anything divides, as a road, river, etc.; *v.i.* to divide into branches; *v.t.* to pitch with a fork, as hay; to lift with a fork (as food); to form a fork. **-ed, -y** *a.* shaped like a fork; cleft.

**for•lorn** *a.* deserted; forsaken. **-ly** *adv.* **-ness** *n.*

**form** *n.* shape or appearance; a mold; style; *v.t.* to give shape to; to construct; to devise; to arrange to conceive; *v.i.* to assume position; to develop. **-al** *a.* according to form; conventional; ceremonious. **-alization** *n.* **-alize** *v.t.* and *v.i.* to give form to; to make formal. **-alism** *n.* the quality of being formal. **-alist** *n.* quality of being conventional or pedantically precise; propriety. **-ally** *adv.* **-ation** *n.* structure; an arrangement, of troops, aircraft, etc. **-ative** *a.* giving form; conducive to growth. **-less** *a.*

**form•al•de•hyde** *n.* a colorless, pungent gas, soluble in water, used as a disinfectant and preservative.

**for•mat** *n.* the general makeup of a book, its size, shape, style of binding, quality of paper, etc.

**for•mer** *a.* preceding in time; long past; first mentioned. **-ly** *adv.*

**for•mi•da•ble** *a.* exciting fear or apprehension; overwhelming. **formidability, -ness** *n.* **formidably** *adv.*

**for•mu•la** *n.* a prescribed form; a general rule or principle expressed in algebraic symbols; the series of symbols denoting the component parts of a substance. *pl.* **-s, -e. -te, formulize** *v.t.* to reduce to a formula; to express in definite form.

**for•ni•cate** *v.i.* to indulge in unlawful sexual intercourse. **fornication** *n.* sexual intercourse between unmarried persons. **fornicator** *n.*

**for•sake** *v.t.* to abandon. **forsaking** *pr.p.* **forsook** *pa.t.* **-n** *pa.p.* **-n** *a.* deserted.

**for•syth•i•a** *n.* a spring-flowering shrub with bright yellow blossoms.

**fort** *n.* a stronghold; a small fortress; outpost.

**forte** *a.* and *adv.* loud; loudly; *n.* a loud passage. **fortissimo** *adv.* very loudly.

**forth** *adv.* forwards, in place of time; into view; away. **-coming** *a.* ready to come forth or appear; available.

**for•ti•fy** *v.t.* to strengthen, as by forts, batteries, etc. **-ing** *pr.p.* **fortified** *pa.t.* and *pa.p.* **fortification** *n.* the art or act of strengthening; a defensive wall; a fortress.

**for•ti•tude** *n.* power to endure pain or confront danger; resolute endurance; **fortitudinous** *a.* courageous.

**for•tress** *n.* a fortified place; a stronghold.

**for·tu·i·tous** *a.* happening by chance; accidental. **-ness, fortuity** *n.*
**for·tune** *n.* chance; good luck or ill luck; possessions, esp. money or property. **fortunate** *a.* lucky; propitious. **fortunately** *adv.* **fortunateness** *n.* **—teller** *n.* one who reveals the future by palmistry, crystal-gazing, etc.
**for·ty** *a.* and *n.* four times ten; a symbol expressing this, as 40 or XL. **fortieth** *a.* fortieth part.
**fo·rum** *n.* the marketplace of ancient Rome where legal as well as commercial business was conducted; a public discussion of questions of common interest.
**for·ward** *adv.* towards a place in front; onwards in time; *a.* toward or at the forepart, as in a ship; eager; progressive; bold; *n.* a player in the front line; *v.t.* to promote; to redirect (letter, parcel) to new address; to send out or dispatch. **-ness** *n.* the state of being advanced; precocity; presumption.
**fos·sil** *n.* any portion of an animal or vegetable organism or imprint of such, which has undergone a process of petrifaction and lies embedded in the rock strata. **-iferous** *a.* bearing or containing fossils. **-ize** *v.t.* to turn into a fossil; to petrify; *v.t.* to become a fossil.
**fos·ter** v.t. to rear; to promote; to cherish. **— child** *n.* a child reared by one who is not the parent.
**fought** *pa.t.* and *pa.p.* of verb **fight.**
**foul** *a.* filthy; obscene; wicked; stormy of weather; *n.* the breaking of a rule (in sports); *v.t.* to make foul; to obstruct deliberately; to clog or jam; *v.i.* to become foul, clogged, or jammed; to come into collision. **-ly** *adv.*
**found** *pa.t.* and *pa.p.* of verb **find. -ling** *n.* a small child who has been found abandoned.
**found** *v.t.* to lay the basis or foundation of; to establish; to endow; *v.i.* to rely; to depend. **-ation** *n.* the base or substructure of a building; groundwork; underlying principle; an endowment; an endowed institution. **-er** *n.*
**found** *v.t.* to melt and pour into a mold; to cast. **-er** *n.* **-ing** *n.* metal casting. **-ry** *n.* works for casting metals; the process of metal-casting.
**foun·tain** *n.* a natural spring; an artificial jet of water. **-head** *n.* source of a stream.
**four** *a.* one more than three; twice two; *n.* the sum of four units; the symbol representing this sum, 4 or IV. **-fold** *a.* quadruple; folded or multiplied four times. **—in-hand** *n.* a necktie. **-some** *n.* a group of four persons. **-teen** *n.* the sum of four and ten; the symbol representing this, 14 or XIV; *a.* four and ten. **-teenth** *a.* making one of fourteen equal parts. **-th** *a.* next after third; *n.* one of four equal parts. **-thly** *adv.*
**fowl** *n.* barnyard cock or hen; a similar game bird; *v.i.* to catch or kill wild fowl. *pl.* **-s, fowl. -er** *n.* one who traps wild fowl.
**fox** *n.* an animal of the canine family, genus *Vulpes,* reddish-brown or gray in color, with large, bushy tail and erect ears; a wily person; *v.t.* to trick; to mislead. **-hole** *n.* a small trench; a dugout for one or more men. **-iness** *n.* the quality of being foxy. **— terrier** *n.* a popular breed of dog sometimes trained for unearthing foxes.

**fox terrier**

**—trot** *n.* a social dance. **-y** *a.* pert. to foxes; cunning; reddish-brown in color. **-ily** *adv.* slyly.
**foy·er** *n.* an entrance hall.
**fra·cas** *n.* a noisy quarrel; a disturbance; a brawl.
**frac·tion** *n.* a small portion; a fragment; a division of a unit. **decimal fraction,** a fraction expressed with numerator above and denominator below the line. **-al** *a.* **fractious** *a.* quarrelsome; peevish. **fractiously** *adv.* **fracture** *n.* the act of breaking; the breaking of a bone; *v.t.* to break; to crack; *v.i.* to become broken. **compound fracture,** a fracture of a bone, the jagged edge of which protrudes through the skin. **simple fracture,** a fracture where the bone is broken, but surrounding tissues and skin are undamaged.
**frag·ile** *a.* easily broken; frail; brittle. **fragility** *n.*
**frag·ment** *n.* a part; an unfinished portion, as of a literary composition. **-al** *a.* composed of fragments of different rocks. **-ary** *a.* broken.
**fra·grant** *a.* sweet-smelling. **fragrance, fragrancy** *n.* sweet scent; perfume; pleasant odor. **-ly** *adv.*
**frail** *a.* fragile; infirm; morally weak. **-ly** *adv.* **-ness, -ty** *n.* quality of being weak.
**frame** *v.t.* to construct; to contrive; to provide with a frame; to bring a false charge against; *v.i.* to take shape; *n.* anything made of parts fitted together; the skeleton of anything; a structure; the case or border around a picture; a mood of the mind; a structure upon which anything is stretched. **-work** *n.* the fabric which supports anything. **framing** *n.*
**franc** *n.* a coin and monetary unit of France, Belgium and Switzerland.
**fran·chise** *n.* the right to vote; permission by a manufacturer to sell his products.
**Fran·cis·can** *n.* one of the order of friars founded by St. Francis of Assisi.
**frank** *a.* open; candid; unreserved; *v.t.* to exempt from charge, esp. postage; *n.* a signature on outside of a letter authorizing its free delivery. **-ly** *adv.* candidly. **-ness** *n.* openness; honesty; candor.
**Frank·en·stein** *n.* any creation which brings disaster or torment to its author.
**frank·furter** *n.* a smoked sausage.
**Frank·lin** *n.* a type of open iron stove.

**fran•tic** *a.* frenzied; wild. **-ally** *adv.*

**fra•ter•nal** *adv.* brotherly. **fraternization** *n.* **fraternize** *v.i.* to associate with others in a friendly way. **fraternizer** *n.* **fraternity** *n.* a student society, designated by letters of the Greek alphabet; brotherhood; a group of men associated for a common purpose.

**fraud** *n.* deception deliberately practiced; trickery; a cheat; imposter. **-ulence, -ulency** *n.* trickery, deceitfulness. **-ulent** *a.* pert. to or practicing fraud; dishonest. **-ulently** *adv.*

**fraught** *a.* loaded; charged.

**fray** *n.* a brawl; a contest.

**fray** *v.t.* to wear through by friction; to ravel the edge of cloth; to irritate, as the nerves, or temper; *v.i.* to become frayed.

**fraz•zle** *v.t.* to fray; to exhaust; *n.* exhaustion.

**freak** *n.* a sudden whim; a prank; capricious conduct; something or someone abnormal; *a.* odd; unusual. **-ish** *a.* **-ishly** *adv.* **-ishness** *n.*

**freck•le** *n.* a small brownish spot on the skin; any small spot; *v.t.* to color with freckles; *v.i.* to become covered with freckles. **freckly,** *a.*

**free** *a.* having political liberty; unrestricted; loose; independent; open; liberal; spontaneous; exempt from impositions, duties, or fees; *adv.* without hindrance; *v.t.* to set at liberty; to emancipate; to clear; to disentangle. **-ing** *pr.p.* **-d** *pa.p.* **-man** *n.* one who has been freed from slavery. **-dom** *n.* liberty; immunity; indecorous familiarity. **-hand** *a.* unrestricted authority; drawn by hand without instruments, etc. **-handed** *a.* generous; liberal. **—lance** *n.* orig. a mercenary soldier who sold his services to any country, esp. said of a journalist, not attached to a particular staff. **— love** *n.* doctrine that sexual relations should be unhampered by marriage, etc. **-ly** *adv.* **-thinker** *n.* one who professes to be independent of all religious authority; a rationalist. **-thinking, — thought** *n.* **— will** *n.* the power of the human will to choose without restraint; *a.* voluntary.

**freeze** *v.t.* to harden into ice; become congealed or stiff with cold; *n.* frost. **freezing** *pr.p.* **froze** *pa.t.* **frozen** *pa.p.* **freezing point** *n.* the temperature at which a liquid turns solid, esp. that at which water freezes, marked 32°F. or 0° C.

**freight** *n.* the cargo of a ship, etc; charge for conveyance of goods; *v.t.* to load a ship, etc. **-age** *n.* charge for transport of goods; freight. **-er** *n.* cargo boat.

**French** *a.* pert. to France or its inhabitants; *n.* the inhabitants or the language of France. **— horn** *n.* a musical wind instrument with mellow note like a hunting horn. **-man** *n.* a native of France.

**fren•zy** *n.* violent agitation of the mind; madness; *v.t.* to render frantic. **frenzied** *a.* **frenetic** *a.* mad; frenzied.

**fre•on** *n.* gas used in refrigeration and for air-conditioning.

**fre•quent** *a.* happening at short intervals; constantly recurring; repeated.

**fre•quent** *v.t.* to visit often. **frequency** *n.* the state of occurring repeatedly; periodicity; number of vibrations per second of a recurring phenomenon. **-ation** *n.* the practice of visiting repeatedly. **-ative** *a.* denoting the repetition of an action; *n.* a word, usually a verb, expressing frequency of an action. **-er** *n.* **-ly** *adv.* **-ness** *n.*

**fres•co** *n.* a method of mural decoration on walls of fresh, still damp, plaster; *v.t.* to paint in fresco.

**fresh** *a.* vigorous; unimpaired; new; not stale; *n.* a stream of fresh water. **-en** *v.t.* to make fresh; *v.i.* to grow fresh; to become vigorous. **-ness** *n.* **-water** *a.* pert. to or living in water which is not salty.

**fret** *v.t.* to wear away by friction; to eat away; to ruffle; to irritate; *v.i.* to wear away; to be corroded; to be vexed or peevish; *n.* irritation; erosion. **-ting** *pr.p.* **-ted** *pa.t.* and *pa.p.* **-ful** *a.* querulous. **-fully** *adv.* **-fulness** *n.*

**fret** *n.* a small piece of wood or wire fixed on the fingerboard, as of a guitar, under the strings.

**Freud•i•an** *a.* pert. to *Sigmund Freud* (1856-1939), the Austrian psychoanalyst, or to his theories.

**fric•as•see** *n.* a dish of fowl, rabbit, etc. stewed with rich gravy sauce; *v.t.* to make a fricassee.

**fric•tion** *n.* the act of rubbing one thing against another; unpleasantness. **fricative** *a.* produced by friction. **-al** *a.* caused by friction. **-ally** *adv.*

**Fri•day** *n.* the sixth day of the week.

**fried** *pa.t.* and *pa.p.* of verb **fry.**

**friend** *n.* one attached to another by esteem and affection; an intimate associate; a supporter. **Friend** *n.* a member of the Quakers. **-less** *a.* without friends. **-liness** *n.* **-ly** *a.* having the disposition of a friend; kind; propitious. **-ship** *n.* attachment; comradeship. **Society of Friends,** the Quaker sect.

**frieze** *n.* decoration on the upper part of the wall, around a mantel, etc.

frieze

**frig•ate** *n.* a fast 2-decked sailing ship of war of the 18th and 19th centuries.

frigate

**fright** *n.* sudden and violent fear; extreme terror; alarm; an ugly or grotesque person or object; *v.t.* to make afraid. **-en** *v.t.* to terrify; to scare. **-ened** *a.* **-ful** *a.* terrible; calamitous; shocking. **-fully** *adv.* terribly. **-fulness** *n.* **-some** *a.* frightful.

**frig•id** *a.* very cold; unfeeling; passionless. **-ity** *n.* coldness. **-ly** *adv.* **-ness** *n.*

**Frigidaire** *n.* a brand of refrigerator.

**frill** *n.* a gathered cloth or paper edging; a ruffle; excessive ornament; *v.t.* to ornament with a frill; *v.i.* to become crinkled like a frill.

**fringe** *n.* loose threads as ornamental edging of cloth; *v.t.* to adorn with fringe; to border.

**frisk** *v.i.* to leap; to skip; *n.* a frolic. **-ily** *adv.* playfully. **-iness** *n.* **-y** *a.* lively.

**frit•ter** *n.* a slice of fruit, vegetable or meat dipped in batter and fried to form a cake.

**frit•ter** *v.t.* to waste in a futile way. **-er** *n.*

**friv•ol** *v.t.* and *v.i.* to squander, esp. time or energy; to fritter away. **-ity** *n.* the act or habit of idly wasting time; lack of seriousness. **-ous** *a.* **-ously** *adv.* **-ousness** *n.*

**frizz** *v.t.* to curl; to crisp; *n.* a row of small curls. **-le** *v.t.* to curl; *n.* curled hair.

**fro** *adv.* from; back, as in *to and fro.*

**frock** *n.* a woman's dress; a monk's long, wide-sleeved garment.

**frog** *n.* an amphibious, tailless animal (developed from a tadpole); hoarseness caused by mucus in the throat; ornamental braiding on uniform, or ornamental fastening of loop and button; *v.t.* to ornament with frogs.

**frol•ic** *n.* a merrymaking; *a.* full of pranks; merry; *v.i.* to play merry pranks; to have fun. **-king** *pr.p.* **-ked** *pa.t.* and *pa.p.* **-some** *a.*

**from** *prep.* away; forth; out of; on account of; at a distance.

**frond** *n.* an organ of certain flowerless plants, such as ferns, in which leaf and stem are combined and bear reproductive cells.

**front** *n.* the forepart, the forehead; firing line; battle zone; outward appearance; *a.* pert. to, or at the front of, anything; *adv.* to the front; *v.t.* and *v.i.* to have the face or front towards any point. **-age** *n.* the front part of general exposure of a building; land abutting on street, river, or sea. **-al** *a.* pert. to the forehead or foremost part; direct, as an attack, without flanking movement; *n.* a bone of the forehead; an ornamental cloth for altar front.

**fron•tier** *n.* border of a country; the undeveloped areas of a country; *a.* bordering; pioneering. **-sman** *n.* one who settles on a frontier.

**frost** *n.* condition when water turns to ice, i.e. when temperature falls below 32° F.; severe cold; *v.t.* to ice a cake. **-bite** *n.* freezing of the skin and tissues due to exposure to extreme cold. **-bitten** *a.* **-ed** *a.* covered with frost. **-ily** *adv.* **-iness** *n.* **-y** *a.* accompanied with frost; chilly; white.

**froth** *n.* foam; trivial things or ideas; *v.t.* to cause to froth; *v.i.* to bubble. **-iness** *n.* **-y** *a.*

**frown** *v.i.* to wrinkle the brow; *v.t.* to rebuke by a stern look; *n.* a wrinkling of the brow to express disapproval.

**fro•zen** *pa.p.* of the verb **freeze.**

**fru•gal** *a.* sparing; thrifty; economical. **-ly** *adv.* **-ity** *n.*

**fruit** *n.* the produce of the earth used for man's needs; the edible produce or seed of a plant; offspring; *v.i.* to produce fruit. **-er** *n.* fruit-grower. **-ful** *a.* producing fruit; abundant; profitable. **-fully** *adv.* **-fulness** *n.* **-ing** *n.* the process of bearing fruit. **-less** *a.* having no fruit; profitless; empty. **-lessly** *adv.* **-lessness** *n.* **-y** a. resembling fruit; mellow.

**frus•trate** *v.t.* to bring to nothing; to balk; to thwart; to circumvent. **frustration** *n.* disappointment; defeat. **frustrative** *a.*

**fry** *v.t.* to cook with fat in a pan over the fire; *v.i.* to be cooked in a frying pan; to sizzle. **-ing** *pr.p.* **fried** *pa.t.* and *pa.p.* **-er, frier** *n.*

**fry** n. young fish just spawned; young children.

**fuch•sia** *n.* a genus of flowering plants, with drooping bright purplish-red flowers.

**fud•dle** *v.t.* to make confused.

**fudge** *interj.* stuff; nonsense; *n.* a soft chocolate candy; space reserved in a newspaper for last-minute news.

**fuel** *n.* anything combustible to feed a fire, as wood, coal; *v.t.* to provide with fuel.

**fu•gi•tive** *a.* escaping; fleeing; fleeting; wandering; *n.* a refugee; one who flees from justice.

**ful•crum** *n.* the pivot of a lever. *pl.* **-s, fulcra.**

**ful•fill** *v.t.* to carry into effect; to execute; to discharge; to satisfy. **-er** *n.* **-ment** *n.* accomplishment; completion.

**full** *a.* filled to capacity; replete; crowded; complete; plump; abundant; showing the whole surface (as the moon); ample (of garments, etc.); clear and resonant (of sounds); *n.* the utmost extent; highest degree; *adv.* quite; completely; exactly. **—blooded** *a.* of pure race; vigorous. **—blown** *a.* fully developed, as a flower. **— dress** *n.* dress worn on ceremonial occasions. **— dress** *a.* formal. **-y** *adv.* completely.

**ful•some** *a.* excessive; insincere. **-ly** *adv.* **-ness** *n.*

**ful•vous** *a.* tawny; dull yellow.

**fu•ma•role** *n.* a small fissure in volcano.

**fum•ble** *v.i.* to grope blindly or awkwardly; *v.t.* to handle clumsily.

**fume** *n.* pungent vapor from combustion or exhalation; rage; *v.i.* to smoke; to be in a rage; *v.t.* to send forth as fumes.

**fu•mi•gate** *v.t.* to expose to poisonous gas or smoke, esp. for the purpose of destroying germs. **fumigator** *n.* apparatus or substance used in fumigation.

**fun** *n.* merriment; hilarity; sport. **-nies** *n.pl.* comic strips. **-nily** *adv.* **-niness** *n.* **-ny** *a.* full of fun.

**func•tion** *n.* performance; the special work done by an organ or structure; a quantity the value of which varies with that of another quantity; a social entertainment;

*v.i.* to operate; to fulfill a set task. **-al** *a.* having a special purpose; pert. to a duty or office. **-ally** *adv.* **-ary** *n.* an official.

**fund** *n.* permanent stock or capital; an invested sum, the income of which is used for a set purpose; ample supply; *pl.* money in hand; *v.t.* to establish a fund for the payment of interest or principal. **-ed** *a.*

**fun•da•men•tal** *a.* pert. to the foundations; basic; essential; original; *n.* a primary principle. **-ism** *n.* belief in literal truth of the Bible. **-ist** *n.* **-ly** *-adv.*

**fu•ner•al** *n.* the ceremony of burying the dead; *a.* pert. to or used at burial. **funerary, funereal** *a.* gloomy.

**fun•gus** *n.* any of a group of thallophytes (molds, mushrooms, mildews, puffballs, etc.). *pl.* **fungi, -es. fungicide** *n.* any preparation which destroys molds or fungoid growths. **fungoid, fungous** *a.* pert. to or caused by fungus.

**fungi**

**fun•nel** *n.* an inverted hollow metal cone with tube, used for filling vessels with narrow inlet; the smokestack of a steamship.

**fur** *n.* the short, fine, soft hair of certain animals; animal pelts used for coats; *v.t.* to line, face, or cover with fur. **-ring** *pr.p.* **-red** *pa.p.* **-rier** *n.* a dealer in furs. **-ry** *a*

**fur•bish** *v.t.* to polish; to burnish; to renovate.

**fu•ri•ous** *a.* raging; violent; savage. **-ly** *adv.*

**furl** *v.t.* to roll, as a sail.

**fur•long** *n.* eighth of mile; 220 yards.

**fur•lough** *n.* leave of absence; *v.t.* to grant leave.

**fur•nace** *n.* an enclosed structure for the generating of heat required for smelting ores, warming houses, etc.

**fur•nish** *v.t.* to supply; to equip; to fit out. **-er** *n.* **-ings** *n.pl.* fittings, of a house, esp. furniture, curtains, carpets, etc.

**fur•ni•ture** *n.* equipment; that which is put into a house, office, etc. for use or ornament.

**fu•ror** *n.* wild excitement; enthusiasm.

**fur•row** *n.* a trench made by a plow; channel; groove; deep wrinkle; *v.t.* to plow; to mark with wrinkles. **-y** *a.*

**fur•ther** *a.* more remote; additional; *adv.* to a greater distance; moreover. **-more** *adv.* moreover; besides. **-most** *a.* most remote. **furthest** *adv.* and *a.* most remote. (**farther, farthest** are preferred as *comp.* and *superl.* of **far.**)

**fur•ther** *v.t.* to help forward; to promote. **-ance** *n.* the act of furthering.

**fu•ry** *n.* rage; passion; frenzy.

**fuse** *v.t.* to melt by heat; to amalgamate; *v.i.* to become liquid; *n.* a tube filled with combustible matter, used in blasting or discharge of bombs, etc.; a device used as a safety measure in electric lighting and heating systems. **fusibility** *n.* **fusible** *a.* **fusion** *n.* the act or process of melting; the state of being melted or blended; coalition.

**fu•se•lage** *n.* the body of an airplane.

**fuss** *n.* bustle; unnecessary ado; needless activity; *v.i.* to become nervously agitated; *v.t.* to bother another with excessive attentions. **-budget** *n.* a fussy person. **-ily** *adv.* **-iness** *n.* **-y** *a.*

**fu•tile** *a.* ineffectual, unavailing, useless. **-ly** *adv.* **futility** *n.* uselessness; fruitlessness.

**fu•ture** *a.* about to happen; that is to come hereafter; *n.* time to come. **futurism** *n.* a modern aesthetic movement marked by complete departure from tradition. **futurist** *n.* **futuristic** *a.* **futurity** *n.* time to come.

**fuzz** *n.* fine, light particles; fluff. **-iness** *n.* **-y** *a.*

**gab** *n.* trifling talk; *v.i.* to chatter. *pr.p.* **-bing.** *pa.t.* **-bed. -by** *a.* **-ble** *n., v.i.*

**gab•ar•dine** *n.* a firm, woven twilled fabric of cotton, rayon or wool. Also **gaberdine.**

**gad** *v.i.* to go about idly; to ramble. *pr.p.* **-ding.** *pa.p.* and *pa.t.* **-ded. -about** *v.i.* to wander idly; *n.* a pleasure seeker.

**gadg•et** *n.* a general term for any small mechanical contrivance or device.

**Gael** *n.* a Scottish Highlander of Celtic origin. **-ic** *a. n.* the language of the Gaels.

**gaff** *n.* a barbed fishing spear; a stick with an iron hook for landing fish; *v.t.* to seize with a gaff.

**gag** *n.* something thrust into or over the mouth to prevent speech; *v.t.* to apply a gag to; to silence by force; *v.i.* to heave with nausea. *pr.p.* **-ging.** *pa.t., pa.p.* **-ged.**

**gag** *n.* a joke.

**gag•gle** *v.i.* to crackle like geese; *n.* a flock of geese.

**gai•e•ty** *n.* mirth; merriment; glee; jollity. **gaily** *adv.* merrily.

**gain** *v.t.* to attain to, or reach; to get by effort; to get profit; to earn; to win; *v.i.* to have advantage or profit; to increase; to improve; to make an advance; *n.* profit; advantage; incease. **-ful** *a.* profitable; lucrative. **-fully** *adv.* **-fulness** *n.*

**gait** *n.* manner of walking or running; pace.

**ga•la** *n.* a show or festivity; *a.* festive.

**gal•ax•y** *n.* a band of stars encircling the heavens; the Milky Way. **galactic** *a.*

**gale** *n.* a wind between a stiff breeze and a hurricane.

**gall** *n.* bile secreted in the liver; anything bitter; bitterness; rancor. **—bladder** *n.* a small sac on the under side of the liver, in which the bile is stored. **-stone** *n.* a concretion formed in the gall bladder.

**gall** *v.t.* to fret and wear away by rubbing; to vex, irritate, or harass; *n.* a skin wound caused by rubbing. **-ing** *a.* irritating.

**gal•lant** *a.* splendid or magnificent; brave; chivalrous; courteous to women; amorous. *n.* a brave, high-spirited man; **-ly** *adv.* **-ry** *n.* bravery; chivalry.

**gal•ler•y** *n.* a long corridor, hall, or room; a room or series of rooms in which works of art are exhibited; a balcony; the uppermost tier of seats, esp. in theater; audience or spectators.

**gal•ley** *n.* a low, one-decked vessel, navigated both with oars and sails; a large rowboat; the kitchen of a ship.

**galley**

**Gal•lic** *a.* pert. to ancient Gaul, or France; French. **gallicize** *v.t.* to make French in opinions, manners.

**gal•li•um** *n.* a soft grey metal of extreme fusibility.

**gal•li•vant** *v.i.* to gad about.

**gal•lon** *n.* a measure of capacity both for liquid and dry commodities, containing four quarts.

**gal•lop** *n.* fastest gait of horse, when it lifts forefeet together, and hind feet together; a ride at a gallop; *v.i.* to ride at a gallop; to go at full speed; *v.t.* to cause to gallop. **-ing** *a.* speedy; swift.

**gal•lows** *n.* a frame from which criminals are hanged.

**gal•lore** *adv.* abundantly; in plenty.

**ga•losh, golosh** *n.* a rubber overshoe.

**gal•va•nism** *n.* the branch of science which treats of the production of electricity by chemical action. **galvanic** *a.* **galvanize** *v.t.* to apply galvanic action to; to stimulate by an electric current; to coat metal with zinc. **galvanization** *n.* **galvanizing** *n.* coating with zinc. **galvanized iron,** iron coated with zinc to prevent rust.

**gam•bit** *n.* in chess, opening move involving sacrifice of pawn.

**gam•ble** *v.i.* to play for money; to risk esp. by financial speculation; *v.t.* to lose or squander in speculative ventures; *n.* a risky undertaking; a reckless speculation. **-r** *n.*

**game** *n.* any sport; a pastime; a contest for amusement; a trial of strength, skill, or chance; animals and birds protected by law and hunted by sportsmen; *a.* pert. to animals hunted as game; brave; plucky; *v.i.* to gamble. *n.pl.* athletic contests. **-ly** *adv.* **-ness** *n.* **-ster** *n.* a gambler. **gamy** *a.* having the flavor of dead game which has been kept uncooked for a long time. **— preserve,** land stocked with game for hunting or shooting. **— warden** *n.* an official who enforces game laws. **big game,** all large animals hunted for sport. **to play the game,** to act in a sportsmanlike way.

**gam•ete** *n.* a protoplasmic body, ovum, or sperm, which unites with one of opposite sex for conception.

**gam•ma** *n.* the third letter of the Greek alphabet. **— rays,** electro-magnetic radiations, of great penetrative powers, given off by radioactive substances, e.g. radium.

**gam•ut** *n.* the whole series of musical notes; a scale; the compass of a voice; the entire range.

**gan•der** *n.* a male goose.

**gang** *n.* people banded together for some purpose, usually bad; body of laborers working together. *v.i.* to act as a gang **-ster** *n.* one of a gang of criminals.

**gan•gli•on** *n.* a globular, hard tumor, situated on a tendon. *pl.* **-s, ganglia. gangliate** *a.* furnished with ganglia. **-ic** *a.*

**gang plank** *n.* a moveable plank bridge between a ship and the shore.

**gan•grene** *n.* the first stage of mortification or death of tissue in the body; *v.t.* and *v.i.* to affect with, or be affected with, gangrene. **gangrenous** *a.* mortified; putrefying.

**gang•way** *n.* a passageway; a platform and ladder slung over the side of a ship; *interj.* make way, please!

**gap** *n.* an opening.

**gape** *v.i.* to open wide, esp. the mouth; to stare with open mouth; to yawn. *n.* a wide opening; the act of gaping.

**ga•rage** *n.* a covered enclosure for motor vehicles; a fuel and repair station for motor vehicles; *v.t.* to place in a garage.

**garb** *n.* clothing; mode or style of dress; *v.t.* to dress.

**gar•bage** *n.* kitchen refuse; anything worthless.

**gar•ble** *v.t.* to pervert or mutilate, as a story, a quotation, an account, etc. by picking out only certain parts.

**gar•den** *n.* ground for cultivation of flowers, vegetables, etc. generally attached to a house; *v.i.* to cultivate, or work in, a garden. **-er** *n.* **-ing** *n.* the act of tending a garden.

**gar•den•nia** *n.* a genus of tropical trees and shrubs with sweet-scented, beautiful white flowers.

**gar•gan•tu•an** *a.* immense, enormous, esp. of appetite.

**gar•gle** *v.t.* to rinse; *v.i.* to make a sound of gargling; to use a gargle; *n.* a throat wash.

**gar•goyle** *n.* a projecting spout, often in the form of a grotesque carving, found on old

**gargoyle**

buildings and intended to carry off the water.

**gar•ish** *a.* gaudy; showy; glaring; dazzling. **-ly** *adv.*

**gar•land** *n.* a wreath of flowers; *v.t.* to ornament with a garland.

**gar•lic** *n.* a plant having a bulbous root, a strong smell like onion, and a pungent taste. **-ky** *a.*

**gar•ment** *n.* any article of clothing.

**gar•net** *n.* a semi-precious stone, usually of a dark-red color and resembling a ruby; a dark-red color.

**gar•nish** *v.t.* to adorn; to embellish; to ornament; to make food attractive or appetizing; *n.* ornament; decoration; **-ment** *n.* **garniture** *n.* that which garnishes.

**gar•ri•son** *n.* a body of troops stationed in a fort, town, etc.; the fort or town itself; *v.t.* to occupy with a garrison.

**gar•ru•lous** *a.* talkative; loquacious. **-ly** *adv.* **-ness** *n.* **garrulity** *n.*

**gar•ter** *n.* a string or band worn near the knee to keep a stocking up; *v.t.* to support with a garter.

**gas** *n.* an elastic fluid such as air, esp. one not liquid or solid at ordinary temperatures; mixture of gases, used for heating or lighting; an anesthetic; a chemical substance used to poison or incapacitate the enemy; *v.t.* to poison with gas; *v.i.* *pr.p.* **-sing.** *pa.p.* and *pa.t.* **-sed.** **-eous** *a.* like, or in the form of gas. **-ification** *n.* **-fy** *v.t.* to convert into gas, as by the action of heat, or by chemical processes. **-sy** *a.* full of gas. **— burner** *n.* a gas jet or stove. **— jet** *n.* a nozzle or burner of a gas burner; the burner itself. **—mask** *n.* a respirator worn to protect against poisonous gases. **—meter** *n.* a metal box used to measure the amount of gas consumed. **-ometer** *n.* an apparatus for measuring or storing gas. **—range** *n.* a gas cooking stove.

**gash** *v.t.* to make a long, deep cut in; *n.* a deep cut.

**gas•ket** *n.* washer between parts such as the cylinder head and cylinder block.

**gas•o•line, gasolene,** *n.* a volatile, inflammable, liquid mixture produced by the distillation of petroleum, used as a fuel solvent, etc.

**gasp** *v.i.* to struggle for breath with open mouth; to pant; *v.t.* to utter with gasps; *n.* the act of gasping; a painful catching of the breath.

**gas•tric** *a.* pert. to the stomach. **gastritis** *n.* inflammation of the stomach. **gastro-enteritis** *n.* inflammation of the stomach and intestines. **gastrology** *n.*

**gas•tro•pod** *n.* a class of molluscs, e.g. snails and whelks, having a fleshy, ventral disk, which takes the place of feet.

**gate** *n.* an opening into an enclosure, through a fence, wall, etc.; **-way** *n.* an entrance.

**gath•er** *v.t.* to bring together; to collect; to pick; in sewing, to draw into puckers; to infer or deduce; to harvest; *v.i.* to come together; to congregate; to increase; *n.* a pucker or fold in cloth. **-ing** *n.* an assemblage; a crowd.

**Gat•ling•gun** *n.* machine gun invented by R. J. *Gatling.*

**gauche** *a.* awkward; clumsy; tactless. **gaucherie.**

**gau•cho** *n.* a cowboy of the S. American pampas.

**gaud** *n.* a piece of worthless finery; a trinket. **-ily** *adv.* **-y** *a.*

**gauge** *v.t.* to ascertain the capacity of; to measure the ability of; to estimate; *n.* an instrument for determining dimensions or capacity; a standard of measure; test; criterion; **-r** *n.* one who gauges.

**Gaul** *n.* an old name for France; a Frenchman.

**gaunt** *a.* lean and haggard; pinched and grim; desolate. **-ly** *adv.* **-ness** *n.*

**gauss** *n.* the unit of density of a magnetic field.

**gauze** *n.* a thin, transparent fabric. **gauziness** *n.* **gauzy** *a.*

**gave** *pa.t.* of **give.**

**gav•el** *n.* a mallet; a small wooden hammer used by a chairman or auctioneer.

**gawk** *n.* an awkward person; a simpleton; *v.i.* to stare stupidly. **-y** *a.*

**gay** *a.* lively; merry; light-hearted. **-ly, gaily** *adv.* **-ety, gaiety** *n.*

**gaze** *v.i.* to look fixedly; to stare; *n.* a fixed, earnest look; a long, intent look. **-r** *n.* one who gazes.

**ga•ze•bo** *n.* a summerhouse commanding a wide view.

**ga•zelle** *n.* a small, swift, graceful antelope.

gazelle

**ga•zette** *n.* a newspaper. **gazetteer** *n.* formerly a writer for a gazette; now, a geographical dictionary.

**gear** *n.* apparatus; equipment; tackle; utensils; a set of toothed wheels working together, esp. by engaging cogs; *v.t.* to provide with gear; to put in gear; *v.i.* to be in gear. **-ing** *n.* the series of toothed wheels for transmitting power, changing speed, etc.

**gee** *interj.* exclamation of surprise.

**geese** *n.* plural of **goose.**

**Gei•ger counter** *n.* a hypersensitive instrument for detecting radio-activity, cosmic radiation, etc.

**gei•sha** *n.* a Japanese dancing girl.

**gel** *n.* a colloidal solution which has set into a jelly; *v.i.* to become a gel. **-ling.** *pa.t., pa.p.* **-led. -ation** *n.* a solidifying by means of cold.

**gel•a•tin, gelatine** *n.* a glutinous substance gotten by boiling parts of animals (bones, hoofs, etc.) which is soluble in hot water and sets into a tremulous jelly. **-ous** *a.* of the nature of consistency of gelatin; like jelly. **-age, ize** *v.t.* to convert into gelatine. **-ation** *n.*

**gem** *n.* a precious stone of any kind; a jewel; anything of great value; *v.t.* to adorn with gems. *pr.p.* **-ming.** *pa.p., pa.t.* **-med.**

**gem•i•nate** *a.* doubled; existing in pairs; *v.i.* and *t.* to make or become paired or doubled. **gemination** *n.*

**Gem•i•ni** *n.pl.* the third sign of the Zodiac; a constellation containing the two bright stars Castor and Pollux, twin heroes of Greek legend.

**gen•der** *n.* sex, male or female; the classification of nouns according to sex or animateness.

**gene** *n.* the hereditary factor which is transmitted by each parent to offspring and which determines hereditary characteristics.

**ge•ne•al•o•gy** *n.* a record of the descent of a person or family from an ancestor; lineage. **genealogist** *n.* one who traces the descent of persons or families. **genealogical** *a.*

**gen•er•a** *n.* See **genus.**

**gen•er•al** *a.* pert. to a whole class or order; not precise, particular, or detailed; usual, embracing the whole, not local or partial; *n.* **-ly** *adv.* as a whole; for the most part; commonly; extensively. **generality** *n.* indefiniteness; vagueness; a vague statement; the main body. **-issimo** *n.* the chief commander of all the country's forces in China and the U.S.S.R. **in general,** in most respects. **general practitioner,** a doctor whose work embraces all types of cases.

**gen•er•al•ize** *v.t.* to make universal in application; *v.i.* to draw general conclusions from particular instances; to speak vaguely. **generalization** *n.* a general conclusion from particular instances.

**gen•er•ate** *v.t.* to bring into being; to produce; **generation** *n.* a bringing into being; the act of begetting; the act of producing; all persons born about the same time; family. **generative** *a.* having the power of generating or producing; prolific. **generator** *n.* one who, or that which, generates; an apparatus for producing steam, etc.; a machine for converting mechanical into electrical energy.

**ge•ner•ic** *a.* pert. to a genus; of a general nature in regard to all members of a genus. **-ally** *adv.*

**gen•er•ous** *a.* liberal, free in giving; **-ly** *adv.* **generosity** *n.* magnanimity; liberality in giving.

**gen•e•sis** *n.* origin; creation; production; birth. *pl.* **geneses. Genesis** *n.* the first book of the Old Testament.

**ge•net•ic** *a.* pert. to origin, creation, or reproduction. **-s** *n.* the scientific study of the heredity of individuals, esp. of inherited characteristics. **geneticist** *n.*

**Ge•ne•van** *a.* pert. to *Geneva,* in Switzerland. **Geneva Conventions,** international agreements, signed at Geneva in 1864, 1868, 1906 and 1949, to lessen sufferings of the wounded in war by providing for the neutrality of hospitals, amubulances, etc.

**gen•ial** *a.* kindly; sympathetic; cordial. **geniality** *n.* the quality of being genial; friendliness; sympathetic cheerfulness. **-ly** *adv.*

**gen•i•tal** *a.* pert. to generation, or to the organs of generation. **-s** *n.pl.* the external sexual organs. Also **genitalia.**

**gen•i•tive** *a.* pert. to, or indicating, source, origin, possession, etc.; *n.* the case used to indicate source, origin, possession and the like.

**gen•ius** *n.* one's mental endowment or individual talent; a person endowed with the highest mental gifts.

**gen•o•cide** *n.* race murder. **genocidal** *a.*

**gen•re** *n.* a kind; sort; style.

**gen•teel** *a.* possessing the qualities belonging to high birth and breeding; well-bred; stylish; refined. **-y** *adv.* **-ness** *n.* **gentility** *n.*

**gen•tian** *n.* the common name of Gentiana, plants whose root is used medicinally as a tonic and stomachic; its flower is usually of a deep, bright blue.

**gen•tile** *n.* one who is not a Jew.

**gen•tle** *a.* kind and amiable; mild and

refined in manner; *v.t.* to tame; to make docile. **gently** *adv.* **-ness** *n.* **gentry** *n.* people of birth and good breeding.

**gen•tle•man** *n.* a man of good breeding and refined manners; *pl.* **gentlemen. -ly** *a.* **-like** *a.* **-'s agreement,** one binding in honor but not legally.

**gen•u•flect** *v.i.* to bend the knee, esp. in worship. **genuflection, genuflexion** *n.* **-or** *n.* **-ory** *a.*

**gen•u•ine** *a.* real; true; pure.

**ge•nus** *n.* a class; an order; a subdivision ranking next above species, and containing a number of species having like characteristics. *pl.* **genera.**

**ge•o-, ge-** combining forms from Gk. *ge,* meaning earth, ground, soil. **geocentric** *a.* having reference to the earth as center.

**ge•ode** *n.* in mineralogy, a rounded nodule of stone, containing a cavity, usually lined with crystals.

**ge•og•ra•phy** *n.* the science of the earth's form, its physical divisions into seas, rivers, mountains, plains, etc.; a book on this. **geographer** *n.* one versed in geography. **geographic, geographical** *a.* pert. to geography. **geographically** *adv.*

**ge•ol•o•gy** *n.* the science of the earth's crust, the rocks, their strata, etc. **geological** *a.* **geologically** *adv.* **geologist** *n.*

**ge•om•e•try** *n.* the mathematical study of the properties of lines, angles, surfaces, and solids. **geometric(al)** *a.* pert. to geometry. **geometrically** *adv.* **geometric progression** a series of quantities in which each quantity is obtained by multiplying the preceding term by a constant factor, e.g. 2, 6, 18, 54, etc.

**ge•ot•ro•pism** *n.* the tendency of a growing plant to direct its roots downwards. **geotropic** *a.*

**ge•ra•ni•um** *n.* plant having showy flowers.

**ger•i•at•rics** *n.* science of the diseases and care of the old.

**germ** *n.* the rudimentary form of a living things, whether animal or plant; a microbe; **-icide** *n.* a substance for destroying disease-germs. **germicidal** *a.* **— warfare** waged with bacteria for weapons.

**Ger•man** *a.* belonging to *Germany;* *n.* a native of Germany; the German language. **Germanic** *a.* pert. to Germany; Teutonic. **Germanize** *v.t.* to make German. **German measles,** a disease like measles, but less severe.

**ger•ma•ni•um** *n.* a rare metallic element.

**ger•mi•nate** *v.i.* to sprout; to bud; to shoot; to begin to grow; *v.t.* to cause to grow. **germinative** *a.* pert. to germination. **g tion** *n.*

**ger•on•tol•o•gy** *n.* the science that studies the decline of life of man.

**ger•ry•man•der** *v.t.* to arrange or redistribute electoral districts to private advantage.

**ger•und** *n.* part of the Latin verb used as a verbal noun; used to **ger•und** *n.* part of the Latin verb used as a verbal noun; used to express **ger•und** *n.* part of the Latin verb used as a verbal noun; used to express purpose. **gerundial** *a.* of the nature of a gerund. **gerundive** *n.* the future passive participle of a Latin verb expressing the action of having to be done.

**Ge•sta•po** *n.* the secret police of the German Nazi party.

**ges•ta•tion** *n.* carrying young in womb; pregnancy.

**ges•tic•u•late** *v.i.* to make violent gestures or motions, esp. with hands and arms, when speaking. **gesticulation** *n.* a gesture.

**ges•ture** *n.* a motion of the head, hands, etc. as a mode of expression; an act indicating attitude of mind; *v.i.* to make gestures.

**get** *v.t.* to procure; to obtain; to gain possession of; to come by; to receive; to earn; to induce or persuade; to understand; *v.i.* to become; to reach or attain; to bring one's self into a condition. *pr.p.* **-ting.** *pa.t.* **got.** *pa.p.* **got, gotten. -away** *n.* escape. **get-up** *n.* equipment; dress; energy.

**gey•ser** *n.* a hot spring which spouts water intermittently.

**ghast•ly** *a.* horrible; shocking. Also *adv.* **ghastliness** *n.*

**gher•kin** *n.* a small species of cucumber used for pickling.

**ghet•to** *n.* a section to which Jews were restricted; a section of a city in which members of a national or racial group live or are restricted.

**ghost** *n.* the apparition of a dead person; semblance or shadow; a person who does literary or artistic work for another, who takes the credit for it. **-ly** *a.* **-liness** *n.* **-like** *a.* **Holy Ghost,** the Holy Spirit; the third element in the Trinity.

**ghoul** *n.* imaginary evil being. **-ish** *a.*

**gi•ant** *n.* a man of extraordinary bulk and stature; a person of unusual powers, bodily or intellectual; *a.* like a giant. **-ism** *n.* abnormal development.

**gib•ber** *v.i.* and *t.* to speak rapidly and inarticulately; to chatter. **-ish** *n.* meaningless speech; nonsense.

**gibe, jibe** *v.i.* to taunt; to sneer at; to scoff at; *n.* an expression of contempt; a taunt.

**gib•lets** *n. pl.* the internal edible parts of poultry, e.g. heart, liver, gizzard, etc.

**gid•dy** *a.* dizzy; feeling a swimming sensation in the head; liable to cause this sensation; whirling; flighty; frivolous. **giddily** *adv.* **giddiness** *n.*

**gift** *n.* a present; a thing given; a donation; natural talent; faculty; power; *v.t.* to endow; to present with; to bestow. **-ed** *a.* possessing natural talent. **-edness** *n.*

**gi•gan•tic** *a.* like a giant; of extraordinary size; huge. **-ally** *adv.*

**gig•gle** *v.i.* to laugh in a silly way, *n.* such a laugh. **-r** *n.* **giggling** *n.*

**gild** *v.t.* to overlay with gold-leaf or gold-dust; to make gold in color; to brighten; to give a fair appearance to; to embellish.

**gill** *n.* a measure of capacity containing one fourth of a pint.

**gill** *n.* the organ of respiration in fishes and other water animals.
**gilt** *n.* a thin layer of gold, or something resembling gold; *a.* yellow like gold; gilded. **-edged** *a.* having the edges gilded; of the best quality.
**gim•mick** *n.* a gadget.
**gimp** *n.* a narrow fabric or braid used as an edging or trimming.
**gin** *n.* a distilled alcoholic beverage, flavored with juniper berries, orange peel, etc.
**gin** *n.* a machine for separating the seeds from cotton; *v.t.* to clear cotton of seeds by a gin; *pr.p.* **-ning.** *pa.p.* and pa.t. **-ned.**
**gin•ger** *n.* a plant of the Indies with a hot-tasting spicy root; *v.t.* to flavor with ginger. **—ale** *n.* an effervescent beverage. **-bread** *n.* a. cake, flavored with ginger and molasses; showy ornamentation. **-y** *a.* hot and spicy.
**gin•ger•ly** *adv.* cautiously; carefully.
**ging•ham** a kind of cotton cloth, usually checked or striped.
**gin rum•my** *n.* a card game for two or more players.
**gip•sy** See **Gypsy.**
**gi•raffe** *n.* an African animal with spotted coat and very long neck and legs.
**gird -er** *n.* an iron or steel beam used as a support in constructional engineering.
**gir•dle** *n.* a tight-fitting undergarment worn for support of the lower part of the body; *v.t.*
**girl** *n.* a female child; **-hood** *n.* the state, or time, of being a girl. **-ish** *a.* like a girl. **-ishly** *adv.* **-ishness** *n.*
**girth** *n.* band to hold a saddle, blanket, etc. in place on a horse; a girdle; the measurement around a thing.
**gist** *n.* the main point of a question; the substance or essential point of any matter.
**give** *v.t.* to bestow; to make a present of; to grant; to deliver; to pledge, as one's word; *v.i.* to yield; to give away; to move; *n.* elasticity; a yielding to pressure. *pr.p.* **giving.** *pa.p.* **given.** *pa.t.* **gave. -n** *a.* granted; admitted; supposed; certain; particular; addicted to; inclined to. **-r** *n.*
**giz•zard** *n.* a bird's strong muscular second stomach.
**gla•cé** *a.* of a cake, iced; of a kind of leather, polished or glossy; of fruits, candied.
**gla•cier** *n.* a mass of ice, formed by accumulated snow in high cold regions, which moves very slowly down a mountain. **glacial** pert. to ice or its action; pert. to glaciers; icy; frozen; crystallized. **glaciate** *v.t.* to cover with ice; to turn to ice. **glaciology** *n.* the scientific study of the formation and action of glaciers.
**glad** *a.* pleased; happy; joyous. **-den** *v.t.* to make glad; to cheer; to please. **-ly** *adv.* with pleasure; joyfully; cheerfully. **-ness** *n.*
**glad•i•a•tor** *n.* a combatant who fought in the arena.
**glad•i•o•lus** *n.* a plant of the iris family, with long sword-shaped leaves.
**glam•our** *n.* deceptive or alluring charm; **-ous** *a.* Also **glamor.**
**glance** *n.* a quick look; a glimpse; *v.t.* to cast a glance; *v.i.* to give a swift, cursory look. **glancing** *a.*
**gland** *n.* an organ or collection of cells secreting and abstracting certain substances from the blood and transforming them into new compounds. **-ular, -ulous** *a.* consisting of or pert. to glands.
**glare** *n.* a strong, dazzling light; an overwhelming glitter; a fierce, hostile look or stare; *v.i.* to shine with a strong dazzling light; to stare in a fierce and hostile manner. **glaring, glary** *a.* brilliant; open and bold.
**glass** *n.* a hard, brittle, generally transparent substance formed by fusing silica with fixed alkalis; articles made of glass; *a.* made of glass; *v.t.* to cover with glass; to glaze. **-es** *n.pl.* spectacles. **-y** *a.* made of glass; vitreous; like glass; dull or lifeless. **-ily** *adv.* **-iness** *n.* **-ful** *n.* the contents of a glass. **—blowing** *n.* the art of shaping and fashioning glass by inflating it through a tube, after heating. **—blower** *n.* **-ware** *n.* articles made of glass.
**glau•co•ma** *n.* a serious eye disease causing tension and hardening of the eyeball with progressive loss of vision.
**glaze** *n.* the vitreous, transparent coating of pottery or porcelain; any glossy coating; *v.t.* to furnish with glass, as a window; to overlay with a thin, transparent surface, as earthenware; to make glossy. **-r** *n.* a workman who glazes pottery, cloth, etc. **glazier** *n.* one who sets glass in windows, etc.
**gleam** *n.* a faint or transient ray of light; brightness; glow *v.i.* to shoot or dart, as rays of light; to flash; to shine faintly.
**glee** *n.* mirth; merriment; joy; a part song for three or more voices. **-ful** *a.* **-fully** *adv.* **-fulness** *n.* **—club** *n.* a group of singers.
**glen** *n.* a valley, usually wooded and with a stream.
**glib** *a.* smooth; fluent. **-ly** *adv.* **-ness** *n.*
**glide** *v.i.* to move gently or smoothly; of an airplane, to move, or descend, usually with engines shut off; *n.* 'a sliding movement. **-r** *n.* one who or that which, glides; a plane capable of flight without motive power, by utilizing air currents.
**glim•mer** *v.i.* to shine faintly and unsteadily; to flicker; *n.* a faint, unsteady light; a faint glimpse; an inkling. Also **-ing** *n.* and *a.*
**glimpse** *n.* a momentary view; a passing appearance; *v.t.* to catch a glimpse of; *v.i.* to look briefly.
**glis•ten** *v.i.* to glitter; to sparkle; to shine; *n.*
**glit•ter** *v.i.* to shine with a bright; quivering light; to sparkle; to be showy and attractive; *n.* a bright, sparkling light; brilliance.
**gloat** *v.i.* to gaze with adulation; to think about with evil satisfaction. **-ing** *a.*
**globe** *n.* a sphere; a sphere with a map of

the earth or the stars; anything approximately of this shape, e.g. a fish bowl, a lamp shade, etc. **global** *a.* taking in the whole world. **globate, globated** *a.* spherical. **globoid** *a.* globe-shaped. **globose, globous** *a.* round, spherical (or nearly so). **globosity** *n.* **globular** *a.* globe-shaped (or nearly so). **-trotter** *n.* traveler; tourist.

**glob•u•lin** *n.* one of the proteins of the blood.

**glock•en•spiel** *n.* a musical instrument consisting of a row of bells suspended from a rod, or of a series of flat bars, which when struck with a mallet give forth a bell-like sound; a carillon.

**gloom** *n.* thick shade; partial or almost total darkness; melancholy; *v.i.* to become dark or threatening; to be dejected. **-y** *a.* dark and dreary; melancholy. **-ily** *adv.* **-iness** *n.*

**glo•ry** *n.* renown; whatever brings honor; praise and adoration; splendor or brilliance; *v.i.* to be proud; boast; to exult triumphantly. **glorious** *a.* illustrious; conferring renown; splendid; noble. **gloriously** *adv.* **gloriousness** *n.* **glorify** *v.t.* to exalt; to praise esp. in worship; to make eternally blessed; to shed radiance on; to magnify. **glorifier** *n.* **glorification** *n.*

**gloss** *n.* luster from a smooth surface; polish; *v.t.* to make smooth and shining; **-y** *a.* smooth and shining.

**glos•sa•ry** *n.* a vocabulary of obscure or technical words; vocabulary to a book. **glossarial** *a.*

**glove** *n.* a cover for the hand and wrist with a sheath for each finger; *v.t.* to cover with a glove. **-r** *n.* one who makes or sells gloves.

**glow** *v.i.* to shine with an intense heat; to feel hot, as the skin; to burn; to rage; *n.* incandescence; warmth or redness; sensation of warmth; ador. **-ing** *a.* bright; warm; excited; enthusiastic. **-ingly** *adv.*

**glu•cose** *n.* a white crystalline sugar obtained from fruits and honey.

**glue** *n.* an adhesive, gelatinous substance made by boiling skins, hoofs, etc. of animals; *v.t.* to join with glue; to cause to stick as with glue. **-y** *a.*

**glum** *a.* sullen; moody; morose. **-ness** *n.* **-ly** *adv.*

**glut** *v.t.* overindulge; to fill to excess. *pr.p.* **-ting.** *pa.p., pa.t.* **-ted** *n.* an oversupply.

**glut•ton** *n.* one who eats too much; **-ize** *v.i.* to eat to excess. **-ous** *a.* **-ously** *adv.* **-y** *n.*

**glyc•er•ine** *n.* a sweet, colorless, odorless, syrupy liquid. Also **glycerol.**

**gly•co•gen** *n.* the form in which the body stores carbohydrates.

**gly•col** *n.* an artificial compound linking glycerine and alcohol used as an antifreeze.

**gnarl** *n.* a knot in wood or on the trunk of a tree. **-ed, -y** *a.* knotty; knobby.

**gnat** *n.* a kind of small biting insect.

**gnaw** *v.t.* to wear away by scraping with the teeth; to bite steadily, as a dog a bone; to fret; to corrode; *v.i.* to use the teeth in biting; to cause steady pain. **-er** *n.* **-ing** *a., n.*

**go** *v.i.* to pass from one place or condition to another; to move along; to be in motion; to proceed; to depart; to be able to be put; to result; to contribute to a result; to tend to; to pass away; to become; *pr.p.* **-ing** *pa.p.* **gone.** *pa.t.* **went** *n.* a going; **-ings on** usually in a bad sense, behavior; conduct. **gone** *a.* lost; beyond recovery; weak and faint. **-between** *n.* an intermediary. **to go in for,** to indulge in. **to go off,** to depart; to explode.

**goad** *n.* a sharp, pointed stick for driving cattle; anything that urges to action; *v.t.* to drive with a goad; to urge on; to irritate.

**goal** *n.* an object of effort; an end or aim; in a race, the winning post; in football, hockey, etc., the space marked by two upright posts and a cross-bar; the act of kicking or driving the ball between these posts.

**goat** *n.* a long-haired, ruminant quadruped with cloven hoofs and curving horns; the 10th sign of the Zodiac, Capricorn.

**gob** *n.* a lump or mass.

**gob•ble** *v.t.* to eat hurriedly or greedily. **-r** *n.* a greedy eater.

**gob•ble** *n.* the throaty, gurgling cry of the turkey cock; *v.i.* to make such a noise. **-r** *n.* a turkey.

**gob•let** *n.* a drinking glass with a stem and foot.

**gob•lin** *n.* an evil or mischievous sprite or elf.

**god** *n.* a being of more than human powers; a divinity; an idol; *n.pl.* false deities; the Supreme Being; Jehovah. **-dess** *n.* a female god or idol. **godly** *a.* reverencing God; pious; devout. **godliness** *n.* holiness; righteousness. **-less** *a.* wicked; impious; acknowledging no God. **godsend** *n.* an unexpected piece of good fortune. **-forsaken** *a.* dreary; dismal.

**god•child** *n.* one for whom a person become sponsor, guaranteeing his religious education. Also. **-daughter; -son, -parent, -mother, -father,** the sponsor.

**god•wit** *n.* a long-billed wading bird.

**gog•gle** *v.i.* to roll the eyes; to stare; *n.* a rolling of the eyes; *a.* rolling; bulging; **-s** *n.pl.* spectacles to protect the eyes.

**gold** *n.* a precious metal of a bright yellow color; money; riches; a bright yellow color; *a.* made of gold; of color of gold. **-en** *a.* made of gold; having the color of gold; precious. **-finch** *n.* a beautiful bird, so named from its color. **-fish** *n.* a small fish of the carp family named from its color. **-smith** *n.* one who manufactures vessels and ornaments of gold. **-dust** *n.* gold in very fine particles. **-mine** *n.* a mine from which gold is due; a source of wealth. **-rush** *n.* the mad scramble to reach a new goldfield. **—standard,** a currency system under which banknotes are exchanged for gold at any time. **-en age,** the most flourishing period in the history of a nation. **-enrod,** a plant with branching clusters of small yellow flowers. **-en rule,** the rule of doing as you would be done by.

**golf** *n.* out door game played with set of clubs and a ball, in which the ball is driven with the fewest possible strokes, into a succession of holes. *v.i.* to play this game. **-er** *n.* **—course,** tract of land for playing golf.

**gol•ly** *interj.* to express joy, sorrow, surprise, etc.

**go•losh** See **galosh.**

**gon•ad** *n.* a gland that produces reproductive cells; ovary or testis. **-al** *a.*

**gon•do•la** *n.* a long, narrow, flat-bottomed boat, used in the canals of Venice. **gondolier** *n.* the boatman.

**gone** *pa.p.* of the verb **go. -r** *n.*

**gong** *n.* a circular metal plate which gives out a deep note when struck with a soft mallet; anything used in this way.

**gon•o•coc•cus** *n.* microbe of gonorrhea. **gonorrhea** *n.*

**good** *a.* commendable; right; proper; suitable; virtuous; honest; just; kind; adequate; *comp.* **better.** *superl.* **best** *n.* that which is good; welfare; well-being; profit; advantage; *n.pl.* property; wares; commodities; merchandise; textiles; *interj.* well! right! so be it! **-ly** *a.* pleasant; of considerable size. **-liness** *n.* **-ness** *n.* the quality of being good; *interj.* used for emphasis; *pl.* **-ies** candy; sweets. **— turn,** a kindly action. **— will** *n.* benevolence; kindly disposition; the right, on transfer or sale of a business, to the reputation, trade, and custom of that business.

**goose** *n.* a web-footed bird like a duck but larger; *pl.* **geese. gosling** *n.* a young goose. **— flesh** *n.* a bristling state of the skin due to cold or fright.

**go•pher** *n.* in N. America, the ground squirrel; a kind of rat with pouched cheeks.

gopher

**gore** *n.* thick or clotted blood; blood. **gory** *a.* bloody.

**gore** *v.t.* to pierce with a spear, horns, or tusks.

**gore** *n.* a tapering piece of material inserted in a garment or a sail, to widen it; *v.t.* to cut into a wedge shape.

**gorge** *n.* a narrow pass between mountains; *v.t.* to swallow with greediness; *v.i.* to feed greedily and to excess.

**gor•geous** *a.* splendid; showy; magnificent; **-ly** *adv.*

**go•ril•la** *n.* an ape inhabiting W. Africa, of great size and strength.

**gor•y** See **gore.**

**gosh** *interj.* a minced and very mild oath.

**gos•pel** *n.* glad tidings; the revelation of the Christian faith; story of Christ's life as found in first four books of New Testament; doctrine; belief accepted as infallibly true; *a.* pert. to, or in accordance with, the gospel.

**gos•sa•mer** *n.* a filmy substance, like cobwebs; think gauzy material; *a.* light, thin and filmy.

**gos•sip** *n.* idle talk about others, regardless of fact; idle talk or writing; one who talks thus; *v.i.* to talk gossip; to chat.

**got** *pa.pa.* and *pa.t. of* **get.**

**Goth** *n.* a member of ancient Teutonic tribe; a barbarian. **-ic** *a.* pert. to Goths; barbarous; pert. to pointed-arch style of architecture; *n.* the language of Goths; a printing type Gothic.

**got•ten** *pa.p.* of **get.**

**Gou•da** *n.* a well-known Dutch cheese.

**gouge** *n.* a chisel with a curved cutting edge, for cutting grooves or holes; *v.t.* to cut or scoop out with a gouge; to hollow out; to force out, as the eye of a person, with the thumb or finger.

**gou•lash** *n.* a Hungarian stew.

**gourd** *n.* trailing or climbing plant: pumpkin, squash, etc.; large fleshy fruit of this plant.

**gour•mand** *n.* one fond of eating; a judge of fine foods. Also **gormand, gourmet.**

**gout** *n.* a disease characterized by acute inflammation and swelling of the smaller joints. **-iness** *n.* **-y** *a.*

**gov•ern** *v.t.* to rule; to direct; to guide; to control; to regulate by authority; *v.i.* to exercise authority; to administer the laws. **-able** *a.* **-ance** *n.* directions; control; management. **-ess** *n.* woman with authority to control and direct; a lady, usually resident in a family, in charge of children's education. **-ment** *n.* act of governing; the system of governing in a state or community; the administrative council or body; **-mental** *a.* **-or** *n.* the executive head of a state; regulating mechanical device for velocity, pressure, etc.

**gown** *n.* a losse, flowing garment; outer dress of a woman; *v.t.* to dress in a gown; *v.i.* to put on a gown.

**grab** *v.t.* to grasp suddenly; to snatch; to clutch; to seize. *pr.p.* **-bing.** *pa.p.* and *pa.t.* **-bed.** *n.* a sudden clutch; unscrupulous seizure.

**grace** *n.* charm; attractiveness; easy and refined motion, a short prayer of thanksgiving before or after a meal; a period of delay granted as a favor; *v.t.* to adorn; to honor; to add grace to. **-ful** *a.* displaying grace or charm in form or action; elegant; easy. **-fully** *adv.* **-fulness** *n.* **-less** *a.* lacking grace. **gracious** *a.* favorable; kind; friendly; merciful; pleasing; proceeding from divine grace; **graciously** *adv.* **graciousness** *n.*

**gra•da•tion** *n.* successive stage in progress; degree; a step, or series of steps. **gradate** *v.t.* to cause to change by imperceptable degrees, as from one color to another.

**grade** *n.* a step or degree in rank, merit, quality, etc.; a mark or rating of a student's work; a gradient; *v.t.* to arrange in order, degree, or class; to gradate.

**gra•di•ent** *n.* an incline.

**grad•u•al** *a.* proceeding by steps or degrees; progressive; **-ly** *adv.*

**grad•u•ate** *v.t.* to grant a diploma or university degree; *v.i.* to receive a diploma or university degree; *n.* one who has received a diploma or degree upon completing a course of study. **graduation** *n.*

**graft, graff** *v.t.* to insert a bud or small branch of a tree into another; to transplant living tissue, from one part of the body to another; *n.* a bud, etc. so inserted, or a piece of tissue so transplanted.

**gra•ham** *a.* made of whole-wheat flour.

**grail** *n.* a cup. **The Holy Grail,** in medieval legend, the cup or vessel used by Jesus at the Last Supper.

**grain** *n.* a kernel, esp. of corn, wheat, etc.; any small, hard particle; that arrangement of the particles of any body which determines its roughness, markings or texture; *v.t.* to paint in imitation of the grain of wood; to form into grains, as sugar, powder, etc. **-ed** *a.* **against the grain,** *i.e.* against the fiber of the wood.

**gram** *n.* unit of weight in metric system = 15.432 grains. Also gramme.

**gram•mar** *n.* a system of general principles for speaking and writing according to the forms and usage of a language; *n.* a philologist; **grammatical** *a.* pert to grammar; according to the rules of grammar.

**gramme** See **gram.**

**gram•o•phone** *n.* a phonograph.

**gran•a•ry** *n.* a storehouse for threshed grain; a barn.

**grand** *a.* great; high in power and dignity; eminent; distinguished; superior; splendid; lofty; noble; dignified; majestic; indicating family relationship of the second degree; *n.* **-child** *n.* a son's or daughter's child. **-daughter, -son** *n.* a son's or daughter's daughter. **-eur** *n.* nobility of action; majesty; splendor; magnificence. **-father (-mother)** *n.* a father's or mother's father (mother). **-iosely** *adv.* **-iosity** *n.* **-ly** *adv.* in a grand manner, splendidly. **- ness** *n.* greatness; magnifence. **-stand** *n.* main seating structure for spectators at a sporting event.

**grange** *n.* a farm; an association of farmers.

**gran•ite** *n.* a hard igneous rock, consisting of quartz, feldspar, and mica; gray or pink in color.

**grant** *v.t.* to allow; to yield; to concede; to bestow; to confer; to admit as true; *n.* a bestowing; a gift; an allowance. **-er, -or** *n.* the person who transfers property.

**gran•ule** *n.* a little grain; a small particle. **granular** *a.* consisting of grains or granules. **granulate** *v.t.* to form into grains; to make rough on the surface; *v.i.* to be formed into grains. **granulated** *a.* **granulation** *n.* the process of forming into grains; the development of new tissue in a wound, characterized by the formation of grain-like cells.

**grape** *n.* the fruit of the vine. **-ry** *n.* a place for the cultivation of grapes.

**graph** *n.* a diagram of curve representing the variation in value of some phenomenon or relationship of two or more things, according to stated conditions; *v.t.* to show variation by

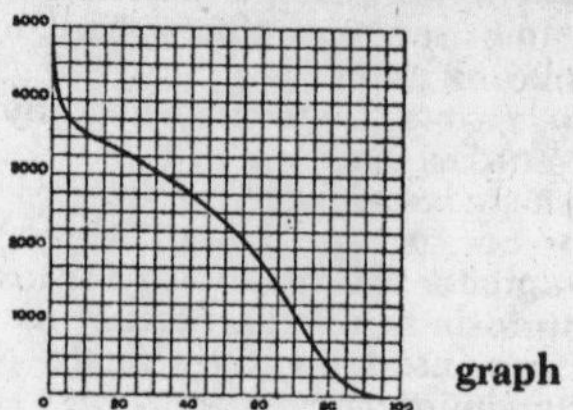

**graph**

means of a diagram. **-ic(al)** *a.* pert. to writing or delineating; truly descriptive; vivid. **-ically** *adv.* **ic arts,** drawing, engraving, and painting. **-ics** *n.* the art of drawing, esp. mechanical drawing. **-ite** *n.* a natural form of carbon used in the making of the 'lead' of pencils.

**grasp** *v.t.* to seize firmly; to clutch; to take possession of; to understand. *v.i.* to endeavor to seize; to catch at; *n.* a firm grip of the hand; the power of seizing and holding; reach of the arms; mental power or capacity. **-ing** *a.* seizing; greedy of gain.

**grass** *n.* ground covered with grass; *v.t.* to cover with grass; to feed with grass. **-y** *a.* **-hopper** *n.* a jumping, chirping insect, allied to the locust family. **—roots** *a.* close to, or from, the people.

**grate** *n.* a framework of crossed bars. **grating** *n.* a partition of parallel or cross bars.

**grate** *v.t.* to rub or scrape into small bits; *v.i.* sound harshly; to irritate. **-r** *n.* an instrument with a rough surface for rubbing off small particles.

**grate•ful** *a.* thankful; pleasant.

**gra•ti•fy** *v.t.* to give pleasure to; to satisfy. **-ing** *a.* **gratifier** *n.* one who gratifies. **gratification** *n.* the act of pleasing; satisfaction.

**grat•in** *n.* a dish prepared with a covering of bread crumbs or cheese. **au gratin** *a.* food so cooked.

**gra•tis** *adv.* free.

**grat•i•tude** *n.* thankfulness.

**gra•tu•i•ty** *n.* a gift of money for services rendered; a tip. **gratuitous** *a.* free; voluntary; granted without obligation; asserted without cause or proof. **gratuitously** *adv.*

**grave** *n.* a hole dug for a dead body; a place of burial; **-stone** *n.* a memorial stone set at a grave. **-yard** *n.* a burial ground.

**grave** *a.* solemn; serious; weighty; important. **grave** *n.* the 'grave' accent in French or its sign (`). **-ly** *adv.*

**grave** *v.t.* to engrave; to impress deeply. **-n image,** an idol.

**grav•el** *n.* small stones; *v.t.* to cover with gravel; to puzzle. **-ly** *a.*

**grav•i•tate** *v.i.* to obey the law of gravitation; to tend towards a center of attraction; **gravitation** *n.* the act of gravitating; the tendency of all bodies to attract each other. **gravitational,**

**gravitative** *a.*
**grav•i•ty** *n.* weight; seriousness; the force of attraction of one body for another, esp. of objects to the earth.
**gra•vy** *n.* the juices from meat in cooking; sauce made with this. **—boat** *n.* a dish for holding gravy.
**gray, grey** *a.* between black and white in color, as ashes or lead; clouded; dismal; *v.t.* to cause to become gray; *v.i.* to become gray. **-ish** *a.* somewhat gray. **—matter** the gray nerve tissue of the brain and spinal cord; **-ness** *n.*
**graze** *v.t.* to touch lightly in passing; *n.* a light touch in passing; a grazing.
**graze** *v.t.* to feed, as cattle, with grass; *v.i.* to eat grass or herbage.
**grease** *n.* soft melted fat of animals; thick oil as a lubricant; *v.t.* to apply grease to; **greasy** *a.* like grease; oily; fat; **-r** *n.* **greasiness** *n.*
**great** *a.* large in size or number; admirable; eminent; uncommonly gifted; **-ly** *adv.* **-ness** *n.* **great-grandchild** *n.* the child of a grandchild. **Great Britain** England, Wales and Scotland.
**Gre•cian** *a.* Greek; pert. to Greece; *n.* a native of Greece.
**greed** *n.* an eager and selfish desire; **-y** *a.* having a keen desire for food, drink, wealth, etc.; ravenous. **-ily** *adv.* **-iness** *n.*
**Greek** *a.* pert. to Greece; Grecian; *n.* a native of Greece; the language of Greece.
**green** *a.* of color between blue and yellow; grass-colored; emerald-colored; unripe; easily deceived; *n.* the color; *n.pl.* fresh leaves or branches; wreaths; green leafy vegetables. **-ery** *n.* a place where plants are cultivated; vegetation. **-ish** a somewhat green. **-ness** *n.* the quality of being green; freshness. **-house** *n.* a glass building for keeping or growing plants. **— light** traffic signal to go; **— thumb** apparent skill in growing plants.
**Greenwich time,** the basis for calculating standard time everywhere.
**greet** *v.t.* to welcome; to receive. **-ing** *n.* a salutation; expression of good wishes.
**gre•gar•i•ous** *a.* living in flocks or herds; fond of company. **-ly** *adv.* **-ness** *n.*
**gre•nade** *n.* an explosive shell or bomb, thrown by hand or shot from a rifle; **grenadier** *n.* formerly, a soldier trained to throw grenades.
**gren•a•dine** *n.* a syrup for flavoring drinks.
**grew** *pa.t.* of **grow**
**grey** See **gray.**
**grey•hound** *n.* a swift, slender dog, used in racing.
**grid** *n.* a frame of bars; a grating.
**grid•dle** *n.* flat utensil for cooking over direct heat; *v.t.* to cook on a griddle.
**grid•i•ron** *n.* a framework of metal bars, for broiling meats, fish, etc.; a football field.
**grief** *n.* deep sorrow.
**grieve** *v.t.* to cause grief; to afflict; *v.i.* to feel grief; to be distressed; to lament. **grievance** *n.* a real or imaginary complaint; a cause of grief or uneasiness. **-r** *n.* **grievous** *a.* causing sadness; atrocious. **grievously** *adv.*
**grill** *v.t.* to broil on a gridiron; to question relentlessly; *n.* a cooking utensil for broiling meat, fish, etc.
**grille** *n.* a metal grating screening a window, doorway, etc. **grillwork** *n.*
**grim** *a.* stern; severe; of forbidding aspect; fierce; surly. **-ly** *adv.* **-ness** *n.*
**gri•mace** *n.* a distortion of the face to express contempt, dislike, etc.; a wry face; *v.i.* to make a grimace.
**grime** *n.* ingrained dirt; soot; *v.t.* to soil deeply; to dirty. **grimy** *a.* dirty.
**grin** *v.i.* to show the teeth as in laughter derision, or pain. *pr.p.* **-ning.** *pa.t., pa.p.* **-ned.** *n.* a wide smile.
**grind** *v.t.* to crush to powder between hard surfaces; to sharpen by friction; *v.i.* to grind; to work hard. *pa.p.* and *pa.t.* **ground.** *n.* the action of grinding.
**grip** *n.* a firm hold; a grasp or pressure of the hand; a clutch; mastery of a subject, etc. a handle; a suitcase; *v.t.* to grasp or hold tightly; **-ping.** *pa.p., pa.t.* **-ped. -per** *n.*
**gripe** *v.t.* to grip; to oppress; to afflict with sharp pains; *v.i.* to grasp at gain; to suffer griping pains; to complain constantly; *n.* grasp; clutch; severe intestinal pain. **griping** *a.*
**grippe** *n.* influenza.
**gris•ly** *a.* grim; horrible. **grisliness** *n.*
**gris•tle** *n.* a smooth, solid, elastic substance in animal bodies; cartilage.
**grit** *n.* the coarse part of meal; particles of sand; coarse sandstone; *pl.* grain coarsely ground; *v.t.* to grind; to grate; *v.i.* to cover with grit. *pr.p.* **-ting.** *pa.t., pa.p.* **-ted. -ty** *a.*
**griz•zle** *n.* gray hair. **-d** *a.* gray; grayhaired. **grizzly** *a.* gray; *n.* a large ferocious bear of N. Amer.
**groan** *v.i.* to make a low deep sound of grief or pain; *n.* the sound. **-er** *n.* **-ing** *n.*
**gro•cer** *n.* storekeeper. **-y** *n.* a store. **groceries** *n.pl.* goods sold by a grocer.
**grog** *n.* a mixture of spirits, esp. rum and cold water. **-gy** *a.* drunk; unsteady; shaky.
**groin** *n.* the depression where the abdomen joins the thigh.
**groom** *n.* a bridegroom; *v.t.* to dress with neatness and care; to tend a horse.
**groove** *n.* a channel or hollow, esp. one cut by a tool; a rut; a routine; *v.t.* to cut a groove in.
**grope** *v.t.* to feel about; to search blindly as if in the dark.
**gros•grain** *n.* corded ribbon or cloth.
**gross** *a.* coarse; indecent; crude; thick; not net; *n.* twelve dozen; mass; bulk; *v.t.* to earn a total of. **-ly** *adv.* **-ness** *n.*
**gro•tesque** *a.* wildly formed; irregular in design or form; *n.* a whimsical figure; a caricature. **-ness.**
**ground** *pa.p.* and *pa.t.* of **grind.**
**ground** *n.* the surface of the earth; dry land; territory; reason; motive; basis; a conducting line between electrical equipment and the ground; *v.t.* to establish; to place on the ground; to run ashore; *v.i.* to come to the ground. **-s** *n.pl.* dregs; sediment; lands around a house.

-**less** *a.* without reason. -**ed** *a.* of aircraft, unable to fly because of weather conditions. -**ing** *n.* the background; thorough knowledge of the essentials of a subject. -**work** *n.* foundation; basis; —**rent** *n.* rent paid to a landlord for the privilege of building on his ground.

**group** *n.* a number of persons or things near, placed, or classified together; *v.t.* to arrange in groups; *v.i.* to fall into groups. -**ing** *n.*

**grout** *n.* coarse meal; thin mortar to fill cracks; plaster; *v.t.* to fill with grout.

**grow** *v.t.* to produce by cultivation; to raise; *v.i.* to develop naturally; to increase in size, height, etc.; *pa.p.* -**n.** *pa.t.* **grew.** -**er** *n.* -**th** *n.* the process of growing; something already grown; a morbid formation; a tumor. **grown-up** *n.* an adult.

**growl** *v.i.* to make a low guttural sound, of anger or menacing like an animal; to grumble; *n.* such a sound. -**er** *n.*

**grub** *v.t.* to dig superficially; to root up; *v.i.* to dig; to rummage; that which is dug up for food; *pr.p.* -**bing.** *pa.p., pa.t.* -**bed.** -**ber** *n.* -**biness** *n.* the state of being grubby. -**by** *a.* unclean; dirty; grimy.

**grudge** *v.t.* to be reluctant to give or allow; to envy; *n.* a feeling of ill will; resentment. **grudging** *a.*

**gru•el -ing** *a.* exhausting.

**grue•some** *a.* causing horror, fear or loathing.

**grum•ble** *v.i.* to murmur with discontent; to complain; to make growling sounds; *n.* grumbling; a complaint.

**grump•y** *a.* surly; irritable; gruff. **grumpily** *adv.* **grumpiness** *n.*

**grunt** *v.i.* of a pig, to make its characteristic sound; to utter a sound like this; *n.* a deep, guttural sound; a pig's sound. -**er** *n.* -**ing** *a.*

**Gru•yère** *n.* a whole-milk cheese.

**guar•an•tee** *n.* formal assurance given by way of security; an assurance of the truth, genuineness, permanence, etc. of something, the one who receives such promise or assurance; guaranty; *v.t.* to promise; to answer for. **guaranty** *n.* a pledge of commitment; security; basis of security. **guarantor** *n.*

**guard** *v.t.* to protect from danger; to accompany for protection; *v.i.* to keep watch; to take precautions; *n.* he who, or that which, guards; a protective device. -**ed** *a.* cautious; wary. -**edly** *adv.* -**ian** *n.* a keeper; a protector; one who has custody of a minor. -**ianship** *n.*

**gu•ber•na•to•ri•al** *a.* pert. to a governor.

**guer•ril•la guerilla** *n.* a member of a band of irregular troops taking part in a war independently of the principal combatants; *a.* pert. to this kind of warfare.

**guess** *v.t.* and *i.* to estimate without calculation or measurement; to judge at random; to suppose; *n.* a rough estimate; a random judgment.

**guest** *n.* a visitor received or entertained.

**guide** *n.* one who shows the way; a sign, mark, or device to indicate direction; *v.t.* to lead; to direct; to influence; to act as a guide to. **guidance** *n.* direction. **guided missile,** powered rocket or other projectile which can be directed by remote control.

**guild** *n.* a society for mutual help, or with a common object.

**guil•lo•tine** *n.* a machine for beheading by the descending stroke of a heavy blade; *v.t.* to use a guillotine upon.

**guilt** *n.* the fact or state of having offended; criminality and consequent liability to punishment. -**y** *a.* judged to have committed a crime. -**ily** *adv.* -**iness** *n.* -**less** *a.* innocent.

**guin•ea** *n.* a former Brit. gold coin. —**pig** *n.* a small rodent, used frequently in scientific experiments; a person used as a subject for experimentation.

**guise** *n.* external appearance, semblance; pretense.

**gui•tar** *n.* a six-stringed musical instrument resembling the lute. -**ist** *n.* a player of the guitar.

guitar

**gulch** *n.* a ravine; a deep-walled valley.

**gulf** *n.* a large bay; a sea extending into the land; *v.t.* to swallow up.

**gull** *n.* a long-winged, web-footed seabird.

**gull** *n.* a dupe; *v.t.* to deceive; to trick; to defraud. -**ible** *a.* easily imposed on; credulous. -**ibility** *n.*

**gul•let** *n.* the tube from mouth to stomach; the throat.

**gul•ly** *n.* a channel or ravine worn by water; a ravine; a ditch.

**gulp** *v.t.* to swallow eagerly; to swallow in large amounts; *v.t.* to gasp; to choke; *n.* an act of gulping; an effort to swallow; a large mouthful.

**gum** *n.* the firm flesh in which the teeth are set.

**gum** *n.* a sticky substance issuing from certain trees; this substance used for stiffening or adhesive purposes; resin; an adhesive; chewing gum; *v.t.* to coat with gum; *v.i.* to exude gum; to become clogged. *pr.p.* -**ming.** *pa.p., pa.t.* -**med.** -**miness** *n.* -**my** *a.* consisting of gum; sticky.

**gum•bo** *n.* okra; soup thickened with this.

**gump•tion** *n.* resourcefulness; courage; common sense; courage.

**gun** *n.* a weapon consisting of a metal tube from which missiles are thrown by explosion; *v.i.* to shoot with a gun. *pr.p.* -**ning.** *pa.pa., pa.t.* -**ned.** -**ner** *n.* one who works a gun. -**nery** *n.* the firing of guns;

the science of artillery. **-powder** *n.* an explosive. *n.* the range of a gun; a shot fired from a gun. **-smith** *n.* one who makes, repairs, deals in guns.

**gup•py** *n.* tiny fresh-water fish.

**gur•gi•ta•tion** *n.* a surging rise and fall.

**gur•gle** *n.* a bubbling noise; *v.i.* to make a gurgle.

**gush** *v.i.* to flow out suddenly and copiously; to display exaggerated and effusive affection; *n.* a sudden copious flow; **-er** *n.* a gushing person; an oil-well with a natural flow. **-iness** *n.* **-ing, -y** *a.* effusive.

**gus•set** *n.* a triangular piece of material inserted in a garment to strengthen or enlarge it.

**gust** *n.* a sudden blast of wind; an outburst of passion. **-y** *a.*

**gus•to** *n.* keen enjoyment; zest; artistic style.

**gut** *n.* a material made from animal intestines, as violin strings, etc.; *n.pl.* entrails; intestines; courage; pluck; determination; *v.t.* to remove the entrails from; to destroy the interior as by fire. *pr.p.* **-ting.** *pa.p.* and *pa.t.* **-ted.**

**gut•ter** *n.* a passage for water; a trough or pipe for conveying rain from the eaves of a building; a channel at the side of a road for carrying water; *v.t.* to make channels in; *v.i.* to flow in streams.

**gut•tur•al** *a.* pert. to or produced in the throat; *n.* a guttural sound.

**guz•zle** *v.t.* and *i.* to drink greedily. **-r** *n.*

**gym•kha•na** *n.* a place for athletic games; a sports meet.

**gym•na•sium** *n.* a building or room equipped for physical training or sports; *pl.* **gymnasia** or **-s. gymnast** *n.* an expert in gymnastics. **gymnastic** *a.* **gymnastics** *n.pl.* muscular and bodily exercises. **gym** *n.* a gymnasium; a school athletic course.

**gy•ne•col•o•gy** *n.* the science which deals with the diseases and disorders of women, esp. the organs of generation. **gynecologist** *n.*

**gyp•sum** *n.* a mineral, consisting mostly of sulfate of lime, used for making plaster of Paris.

**Gyp•sy** *n.* one of a nomadic tribe of Indian origin; a person who resembles or lives like a Gypsy; *a.* of or like a Gypsy.

**gy•rate** *v.i.* to revolve around a central point; to move in a circle; to move spirally. **gyratory** *a.* **gyration** *n.* a circular or spiral motion.

**gy•ro•scope** *n.* a wheel so mounted that its axis can turn freely in any direction when set rotating and left undisturbed, it will maintain the same direction in space, independently of its relation to the earth.

**gyroscope**

**ha** *interj.* denoting surprise, joy, or grief.
**ha•be•as cor•pus** *n.* writ requiring that a prisoner be brought to court to determine legality of confinement.
**ha•ber•dash•er** *n.* a dealer in men's furnishings. **-y** *n.*
**ha•bil•i•ment** *n.* (usually in *pl.*) dress.
**hab•it** *n.* custom; usage; tendency to repeat an action in the same way; *v.t.* to dress; to clothe. **-ual** *a.* formed by habit. **-ually** *adv.* **habituate** *v.t.* to accustom to a practice or usage; to familiarize; *(Colloq.)* to frequent. **-uation** *n.* **-ude** *n.* customary manner of action; confirmed practice. **-ué** *n.* a frequenter (of a place).
**hab•it•a•ble** *n.* fit to live in. **-ness, habitability** *n.* **habitably** *adv.* **habitant** *n.* an inhabitant. **habitat** *n.* the natural home of an animal or plant; place of residence. **habitation** *n.*
**hack** *v.t.* to cut irregularly; to notch; *v.i.* to make cuts or notches; to give harsh dry coughs; *n.* a cut; a notch; an ax, a pick; a short cough.
**hack** *n.* a horse for ordinary riding; a horse worn out by over work; a drudge, esp. literary; *a.* hackneyed; hired; a hired carriage.
**hack•ney** *n.* a horse for riding or driving; a horse (and carriage) kept for hire; *a.* to let out for hire; *v.i.* to use often; to make trite or commonplace. **-ed** a.
**had** *pa.p.* and *pa.t.* of **have.**
**had•dock** *n.* a fish of the cod family.
**Ha•des** *(Myth.)* the underworld.
**haft** *n.* a handle, esp. of a knife; a hilt; *v.t.* to set in a handle.
**hag** *n.* an ugly old woman; a witch. **-gish** *a.* **-gishly** *adv.* **-ridden** troubled with nightmares.
**hag•gard** *a.* wild-looking; lean and gaunt; *n.* untrained hawk. **-ly** *adv.*
**hag•gle** *v.t* to hack; to mangle; *v.i.* to dispute terms; to be difficult in bargaining; *n.* act of haggling. **-r** *n.*
**Hag•i•og•ra•pha** *n.pl.* the last of the three divisions of the Old Testament.
**hag•i•ol•o•gy** *n.* a history of the lives of saints. **hagiologist** *n.* **hagiography** *n.*
**hail** *n.* frozen rain falling in pellets; *v.i.* to rain hail; *v.t.* to pour down like hail. **-stone** *n.* frozen raindrops.
**hail** *v.t.* to greet, salute or call; *n.* an exclamation of respectful saluation.
**hair** *n.* a filament growing from the skin of an animal; such filaments collectively, esp. covering the head; bristles; anything small or fine. **-ed** *a.* having hair. **-iness** *n.* **-y** *a.* covered with, made of, resembling hair. **-brush** *n.* a brush for the hair. **-cloth** *n.* cloth made wholly or partly of hair. **-dresser** *n.* one who dresses or cuts hair; a barber. **-pin** *n.* a special two-legged pin for controlling hair.
**hal•cy•on** *n.* the kingfisher; *a.* calm. **— days,** peaceful, tranquil days; calm weather just before and after the winter solstice.
**hale** *a.* robust; sound; healthy, esp. in old age. **-ness** *n.*
**hale** *v.t.* to haul.
**half** *v.t.* either of two equal parts of a thing. *pl.* **halves** *a.* forming a half; *adv.* to the extent of half. **-back** *n.* *(Football)* a player, or position, behind the forward line. **—breed** *n.* one whose parents are of different races. **— brother** *n.* a brother by one parent only. **—caste** *n.* a half-breed. **— mast** *n.* the position of a flag lowered halfway down the staff, as a signal of distress, or as a sign of mourning. **— measure** *n.* inadequate means to achieve an end. **— moon** *n.* the moon when half its disk appears illuminated; a semicircle. **— title** *n.* the name of a book, or subdivision of a book, occupying a full page. **—tone** *n.* an illustration printed from a relief plate, showing light and shade by minute dots.

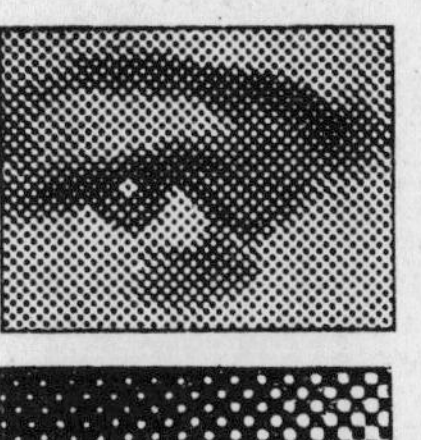

**half-tone**

**halve** *v.t.* to divide into two equal portions; to reduce to half the previous amount.
**hal•i•but** *n.* a large, flat sea fish.
**hal•i•to•sis** *n.* foul or offensive breath.
**hall** *n.* a corridor in a building; a place of public assembly; a room at the entrance of a house; a building belonging to a collegaite institution, guild, etc. **-mark** *n.* the mark used to indicate the standard of tested gold and silver; any mark of quality.
**Hal•le•lu•jah, Halleluiah** *n.* and *interj.* used in songs of praise to God.
**hal•liard** See **halyard.**
**hal•low** *v.t.* to make holy; to consecrate; to treat as sacred; to reverence. **-ed** *a.* **Hallowe'en** *n.* the evening before All Hallows' or All Saints' day.
**hal•lu•ci•nate** *n.* to produce illusion in the mind of. **hallucination** *n.* **hallucinative, hallucinatory** *a.*
**ha•lo** *n.* a circle of light around the moon, sun, etc.; a ring of light around a saint's head in a picture. *pl.* **-s, -es.**
**hal•o•gen** *n.* *(Chem.)* one of the elements chlorine, bromine, iodine, and fluorine.
**halt** *n.* a stoppage on a march or journey; *v.t.* to cause to stop; *v.i.* to make a stop.
**halt** *v.i.* to falter in speech or walk; to hesitate; *n.* cripple. **-ing.**
**hal•ter** *n.* a rope or strap with headstall to fasten or lead horses or cattle.
**halve** *v.t.* to divide into two equal parts.
**hal•yard, halliard** *n.* *(Naut.)* a rope for hoisting or lowering yards or sails.
**ham** *n.* the thigh of any animal, esp. a hog's thigh cured by salting and smoking. **-string** *n.* a tendon at the back of the

knee; *v.t.* to cripple by cutting this.
**ham•burg•er** *n.* ground beef, seasoned and formed into cakes.
**ham•let** *n.* a small village.
**ham•mer** *n.* a tool, usually with a heavy head at the end of a handle, for beating metal, driving nails, etc.; a contrivance for exploding the charge of a gun; *v.t.* and *i.* to beat with, or as with, a hammer; to work hard at. **-head** *n.* a rapacious kind of shark.
**ham•mock** *n.* a kind of hanging bed, consisting of a piece of canvas, and suspended by cords from hooks.
**ham•per** *n.* a large covered basket for conveying goods.
**ham•per** *n.* *(Naut.)* cumbrous equipment; *v.t.* to impede.
**ham•shack•le** *v.t.* to fasten the head of an animal to one of the forelegs.
**ham•ster** *n.* a species of rodent.
**ham•string** See **ham.**
**hand** *n.* the extremity of the arm beyond the wrist; a pointer on a dial, e.g. on a watch; a measure of the hand's breadth, four inches; a style of handwriting; cards dealth to a player; a manual worker; *a.* belonging to, worn on, carried in, the hand; *v.t.* to give with the hand; to deliver; to pass; to hold out. **-y** *a.* convenient. **-ily** *adv.* **-iness** *n.* **-bag** *n.* bag for carrying in the hand. **-bill** *n.* printed sheet for circulation by hand. **-book** *n.* a short treatise; a manual. **-breath** *n.* the breadth of a hand (about four inches). **-cart** *n.* a small cart drawn or pushed by hand. **-cuff** *n.* shackle around wrist connected

**handcuff**

by a chain with one on other wrist; a manacle; *v.t.* to manacle. **-ful** *n.* as much as the hand will grasp or contain. **-maid(en)** *n.* female servant.
**hand•i•cap** *n.* a race or contest in which competitors' chances are equalized by starts given, weights carried, etc.; a condition so imposed; *v.t.* to hinder or impede.
**hand•i•craft** *n.* manual occupation or skill.
**hand•ker•chief** *n.* a small square of fabric carried in the pocket for wiping the nose, etc.
**han•dle** *v.t.* to touch or feel with the hand; to manage; to wield; to deal with. *n.* the part of a thing by which it is held.
**hand•some** *a.* of fine appearance; generous. **-ly** *adv.* **-ness** *n.*
**hang** *v.t.* to suspend; to put to death by suspending from gallows; to cover with, as wallpaper, curtains, pictures, etc.; to display; *v.i.* to be suspended; to incline; to be in suspense; to linger; to cling to. *pa.p.* and *p.t.* **-ed** or **hung.** *n.* **-er** *n.* that by which a thing is suspended. **-man** *n.* one who hangs another; a public executioner. **-nail** *n.* piece of skin hanging from root of fingernail. **-over** *n.* depressing after-effects of drinking.
**han•gar** *n.* a shed for aircraft.
**hank** *n.* a coil, esp. as a measure of yarn.
**han•ker** *v.i.* to long for; to crave. **-ering** *n.* an uneasy longing for; a craving.
**han•som** *n.* a light two-wheeled cab with the driver's seat at the back.
**hap•haz•ard** *n.* chance; accident; *a.* ransom; without design. **-ly** *adv.* **-ness** *n.*
**hap•less** *a.* unlucky. **-ly** *adv.*
**hap•pen** *v.i.* to come by chance; to occur; to take place. **-ing** *n.* occurrence; event.
**hap•py** *a.* glad; content; lucky; fortunate; apt; fitting. **happily** *adv.* **happiness** *n.*
**ha•rangue** *n.* a loud, passionate speech; *v.i.* to deliver a harangue; *v.t.* to speak vehemently to. **-r** *n.*
**har•ass** *v.t.* to attack repeatedly; to worry; to trouble. **-ed** *a.* **-er** *n.* **-ing** *a.* **-ment** *n.*
**har•bing•ger** *n.* one who announces another's approach; a forerunner.
**har•bor** *n.* shelter for ships; a port; any shelter; *v.t.* to give shelter to; to protect; *v.i.* to take shelter.
**hard** *a.* firm; solid; resisting pressure; difficult; harsh; unfeeling; difficult to bear; strenuous; bitter, as winter; keen, as frost; of water, not making lather well with soap; strong; said of alcoholic liquors; *adv.* vigorously; intently; solidly. **-en** *v.t.* to make hard or more hard; to strengthen; to confirm in wickedness or obstinacy; to make less sympathetic; *v.i.* to become hard. **-ly** *adv.* with difficulty; not quite; scarcely; severly. **-ness** *n.* **ship** *n.* severe toil or suffering; ill-luck; privation; suffering. **-ware** *n.* articles made of metal, e.g. tools, locks, fixtures, etc.
**har•dy** *a.* robust; vigorous; bold; brave; daring; able to bear exposure. **-ily** *adv.* **-ihood** *n.* **-iness** *n.*
**hare** *n.* a rodent with long hind legs, long ears, short tail, and divided upper lip, noted for its speed. **-lip** *n.* *(Med.)* a congenital fissure in the upper lip. **-lipped** *a.*
**har•em** *n.* apartment for females in a Mohammedan household; the occupants.
**hark** *v.i.* to listen; *interj.* listen! hear!
**har•lot** *n.* a prostitute. **-ry** *n.*
**harm** *n.* injury; hurt; misfortune; *v.t.* **-ful** *a.* **-fully** *adv.* **-fulness** *n.* **-less** *a.* **-lessly** *adv.* **-lessness** *n.*
**har•mo•ny** *n.* agreement; concord; friendliness; peace; the science that treats of musical sounds in their combination and progression. **harmonic, harmonical** *a.* **harmonically** *adv.* **harmonica** *n.* a mouth organ. **harmonicon** *n.* **harmonics** *n.* sounds. **harmonious** *a.* **harmoniously** *adv.* **harmoniousness** *n.* **harmonize** *v.t.* **harmonizer** *n.* **harmonist** *n.* **harmonium** *n.* a small reed organ. **harmonic progression,** a series of numbers whose reciprocals are in arithmetical progression.
**har•ness** *n.* the working gear, straps, bands, etc. of a draft horse; *v.t.* to put harness on.
**harp** *n.* a stringed musical instrument played by hand; *v.i.* to dwell persistently upon a particular subject. **-ist** *n.* **-sichord** *n.* a forerunner of the piano.
**har•poon** *n.* a barbed spear with a rope attached for catching whales, etc.; *v.t.* to

strike with a harpoon. **-er** *n.*

**Har•py** *n. (Myth.)* ravenous monster, with head and breast of woman and wings and claws of vulture; *(l.c.)* a rapacious woman.

**har•ri•dan** *n.* a haggard old woman.

**har•row** *n.* a toothed agricultural implement to break clods or cover seed

when sown; *v.t.* to draw harrow over; *(Fig.)* to distress greatly. **-er** *n.* **-ing** *a.*

**har•ry** *v.t.* to ravage; to torment.

**harsh** *a.* rough; unpleasing to the touch or taste; severe. **-ly** *adv.* **-ness** *n.*

**hart** *n.* a male deer or stag.

**harte•beest** *n.* a large S. African antelope.

**har•um-scar•um** *a.* reckless; wild; *n.* a rash person.

**har•vest** *n.* (season for) gathering crops; the crop itself; *v.t.* to gather in. **-er** *n.* **— moon** *n.* the full moon nearest the autumn equinox.

**has** 3rd sing. pres. indic. of the verb **have.**

**hash** (hash) *v.t.* to chop into small pieces; to mince; *n.* a dish of hashed meat and potatoes.

**hasp** *n.* a clasp passing over a staple for fastening a door, etc.; *v.t.* to fasten with a hasp.

**has•sock** *n.* a padded cushion for kneeling.

**haste** *n.* speed; quickness. **hasten** *v.t.* **hastener** *n.* **hasty** *a.* **hastily** *adv.*

**hat** *n.* covering for head, usually with brim. **-ter** *n.* one who makes hats. **top hat,** a silk hat with a high crown. **to pass (round) the hat,** to make a collection.

**hatch** *v.t.* to bring forth; to plot; *v.i.* to come forth; *n.* the act of hatching; the brood hatched. **-er** *n.* **-ery** *n.* a place for hatching eggs.

**hatch** *n.* the lower half of a divided door; an opening in a floor or roof; the hatchway itself. **-way** *n.* a square opening in a ship's deck.

**hatch** (hach) *v.t.* to shade with lines.

**hatch•et** *n.* a small ax. **— faced** *a.* having a face with sharp features. **to bury the hatchet,** to make peace.

**hate** *v.t.* to dislike strongly; to detest; *n.* strong dislike; hatred. **-ful** *a.* **-fully** *adv.* **-fulness** *n.* **-r** *n.* **hatred** *n.*

**haugh•ty** *a.* proud. **haughtily** *adv.* **haughtiness** *n.*

**haul** *v.t.* to pull with force; to steer a ship closer to the wind; *v.i.* to pull; *n.* a catch; good profit, gain. **-age** *n.* **-er** *n.* **close-hauled** *a.*

**haunch** *n.* the part of the body between the ribs and thighs; the hop.

**haunt** *v.t.* to frequent; of ghosts, to visit regularly; *v.i.* to loiter about a place. *n.* a place of frequent resort. **-ed** *a.* frequently visited by ghosts.

**haut•boy** *n.* an older form of the oboe.

**hau•teur** *n.* haughtiness.

**Ha•van•a** *n.* a fine brand of cigar [named from *Havana,* the capital of Cuba].

**have** *v.t.* to hold or possess; to be possessed or affected with; *pr.p.* **having.** *pa.p.* and *pa.t.* **had.**

**ha•ven** *n.* a bay or inlet giving shelter for ships; any place of shelter.

**hav•er•sack** *n.* a soldier's canvas ration-bag; a similar bag for travelers.

**hav•oc** *n.* devastation; ruin.

**haw** *n.* a hesitation in speech.

**hawk** *n.* a bird of prey. *v.t.* and *i.* to hunt with hawks. **hawker** *n.* **-ing** *n.* falconry.

**hawk** *v.i.* to clear the throat noisily; *n.* an audible clearing of the throat.

**hawk** *v.i.* to carry about wares for sale; to peddle. **-er** *n.* an itinerant dealer.

**hawk** *n.* a plaster's tool for holding.

**hawse** *n.* the part of a ship's bows.

**haw•ser** *n.* a large rope or small cable.

**hay** *n.* grass mown and dried for fodder. **— fever** *n.* irritation of the mucous membrane of the nose. **-rick** *n.* **-stack** *n.* a large pile of hay with ridged or pointed top.

**haz•ard** *n.* chance; a chance; risk; danger; *v.t.* to expose to risk; to run the risk of. **-ous** *a.*

**haze** *n.* a misty appearance in the air; mental obscurity. **hazy** *a.* **hazily** *adv.*

**haze** *v.t.* to torment or punish.

**ha•zel** *n.* a nut-bearing bush or small tree; the reddish-brown color of the nuts; *a.* of this color. **-nut** *n.* the nut of the hazel tree.

**he** *pron.* the 3rd pers. sing. masc. pronoun.

**head** *n.* the upper part of a man's or animal's body; the brain; intellectual capacity; upper part of anything; the top; the chief part, a chief; something the shape of a head; progress; a section of a chapter; the source of a stream; a cape or headland; a crisis; freedom to go on; *a.* chief; principal; of wind, contrary; *v.t.* to lead; to be at the head of; to direct; to go in front, so as to hinder. *v.i.* to originate; to form a head; to make for. **-y** *a.* impetuous; apt to intoxicate. **-ily** *adv.* **-iness** *n.* **-ache** *n.* a nerve-pain in the head. **-achy** *a.* **-gear** *n.* a hat; the harness about an animal's head. **-ing** *n.* **-land** *n.* a cape; a promontory. **-light** *n.* a strong light carried on the front of a locomotive, motor vehicle, etc. **—line** *n.* a summary of news in large print in a newspaper; a caption. **-quarters** *n.pl. (Mil.)* a center of operations. **-sman** *n.* an executioner. **-stone** *n.* a memorial stone placed at the head of a grave. **-strong** *a.* obstinate; stubborn; self-willed. **-way** *n.* progress.

**heal** *v.t.* to make whole; to restore to health; to make well; *v.i.* to become sound. **-er** *n.* **-ing** *a.*

**health** *n.* soundness of body; general condition of the body; a toast drunk in a person's honor. **-y** *a.* **-ily** *adv.* **-iness** *n.* **-ful** *a.*

**heap** *n.* a number of things lying one on

another; a pile; a mass; *v.t.* to throw or lay in a heap; to amass.

**hear** *v.t.* to perceive with the ear; to listen to; to heed; *(Law)* to try (a case); *v.i.* to perceive sound; to learn by report. *pr.p.* **-ing.** *pa.p.* and *pa.t.* **heard.** **-er** *n.* **-ing** *n.* **-say** *n.* rumor; common talk.

**hearse** *n.* a vehicle to carry a coffin to the place of burial.

**heart** *n.* the hollow, muscular organ which makes the blood circulate; the seat or

**heart**

source of life; the seat of emotions and affections; the inner part of anything; courage; warmth or affection; a playing-card marked with a figure of a heart. -y *a.* cordial; friendly; vigorous; in good health; of a meal, satisfying the appetite. **-ily** *adv.* **-iness** *n.* **-less** *a.* unfeeling. **-en** *v.t.* to encourage; to stimulate. **-blood** *n.* life; essence. **-break** *n.* overpowering sorrow. **-burn** *n.* a form of dyspepsia.

**hearth** *n.* the fireside; the house itself.

**heat** *n.* hotness; a sensation of this; hot weather or climate; warmth of feeling; anger; excitement; sexual excitement in animals, esp. female; *v.t.* to make hot; to excite; *v.i.* to become hot. **-ed** *a.* **-edly** *adv.* **-er** *n.*

**heath** *n.* waste land; moor; shrub of genus Erica. -y *a.*

**hea•then** *n.* one who is not an adherent of a religious system; and infidel.

**heath•er** *n.* a small plant of the genus Erica.

**heave** *v.t.* to lift with effort; to utter (a sigh); to pull on a rope, etc.; to haul; *v.i.* to rise and fall in alternate motions; *n.* a heaving; an effort to lift something; a rise and fall. *pr.p.* **heaving.** *pa.p.* and *pa.t.* **heaved** or **hove.**

**heav•en** *n.* the sky; the upper air; the abode of God; God Himself; a place of bliss; supreme happiness. **-ly** *a.* **-liness** *n.* **-ward, -wards** *adv.* toward heaven.

**Heav•i•side lay•er** *n.* the upper part of the atmosphere, which reflects radio waves.

**heav•y** *a.* weighty; striking or falling with force; large in amount, as a debt. **heavily** *adv.* **heaviness** *n.*

**heb•do•mad** *n.* a group of seven things; a week.

**He•brew** *n.* one of the ancient inhabitants of Palestine; an Israelite; a Jew; the language. **Hebraic** *a.*

**hec•a•tomb** *n.* any large number of victims.

**heck•le** *n.* a comb for cleaning flax; *v.t.* to comb flax; to ask awkward questions of a speaker at a public meeting.

**hec•to-** *prefix* combining to form derivatives used in the metric system. **-gram, -gramme** *n.* a weight of 1-0 grammes. **-liter** *n.* a unit of capacity, containing 100 liters. **-meter** *n.* a unit of length.

**hec•tic** *a.* exciting; wild.

**hec•to•graph** *n.* an apparatus for multiplying copies of writings.

**Hec•tor** *n.* the chief hero of Troy in war with Greeks.

**hedge** *n.* a fence of bushes; a protecting barrier; *v.t.* to enclose with a hedge; to obstruct; to hem in; *v.i.* to bet on both sides so as to guard against loss: to shift; to shuffle; to skulk. **hedging** *n.* **hedgy** *a.* **-hog** *n.* a small quadruped.

**hedgehog**

**he•don•ism** *n.* the doctrine that pleasure is the chief good. **hedonist** *n.*

**heed** *v.t.* to take notice of; to care for; to mind; to observe; *n.* attention; notice; care; caution. **-ful** *a.* **-fully** *adv.* **-fulness** *n.* **-less** *a.*

**heel** *n.* back part of foot, shoe, boot, or stocking; *v.t.* to add a heel to, as in knitting; to touch ground, or a ball, with the heel.

**heel** *v.i.* of a ship; to lean to one side; to incline; *v.t.* to cause to do this.

**heft** *v.t.* to try the weight by lifting; -y *a.* heavy; vigorous.

**he•gem•o•ny** *n.* leadership; predominance. **hegemonic** *a.*

**He•gi•ra, hejira** *n.* Mohammed's flight from Mecca to Medina, A.D. 622.

**heif•er** *n.* a young cow.

**height** *n.* measurement from base to top; quality of being high; a high position; a hill; eminence. **-en** *v.t.*

**hei•nous** *a.* extremely wicked; atrocious; odious.

**heir** *n.* *(fem.* **-ess***)* a person legally entitled to succeed to property or rank. **— apparent** *n.* the person who is first in the line of succession to an estate, crown, etc. **-loom** *n.* article of personal property which descends to heir along with inheritance.

**held** *pa.p.* and *pa.t.* of **hold.**

**hel•i•cal** *a.* pert. to a helix; spiral. **helicopter** *n.* an airplane which can rise or descend vertically.

**he•li•o•graph** *n.* signaling apparatus employing a mirror to reflect the sun's rays; *v.t.* to signal by means of a heliograph. **-ic** *a.* **heliography** *n.*

**he•li•o•trope** *n.* a plant with fragrant purple flowers. **heliotropism** *n.* *(Bot.)* the tendency of plants to direct their growth towards light.

**he•li•um** *n.* *(Chem.)* an inert non-inflammable, light gas.

**he•lix** *n.* a spiral. **helical** *a.* spiral.

**hell** *n.* the abode of the damned; the lower regions; a place or state of vice, misery, or torture. **-ish** *a.* **-ishly** *adv.* **-ishness**

*n.* **-ion** *n.* troublemaker.
**Hel•lene** *n.* ancient Greek; a subject of modern Greece. **Hellenic** *a.* **Hellenism** *n.* Grecian culture; a Greek idiom. **Hellenist** *n.* Greek scholar. **Hellenistic** *a.*
**hel•lo** *interj.* a greeting or call to attract attention.
**helm** *n.* *(Naut.)* a tiller or wheel for turning the rudder of a ship; *v.t.* to steer; to control.
**hel•minth** *n.* an intestinal worm.
**help** *v.t.* to aid; to succor; to relieve; to prevent; *v.i.* to lend aid; to be useful; *n.* one who, or that which, helps; aid; assistance; support; a domestic servant. **-er** *n.* **-ful** *a.* **-fulness** *n.* **-ing** *n.* a portion of food. **-less** *a.* not able to take care of oneself; weak; dependent. **-lessly** *adv.* **-lessness** *n.* **-mate** *n.* an assistant; a partner; a wife or husband.
**hel•ter-skel•ter** *adv.* in disorder; in hurry and confusion.
**Hel•ve•tia** *n.* the Latin, and political, name for Switzerland.
**hem** *n.* border, esp. one made by sewing; *v.t.* to fold over and sew down. *pr.p.* **-ming.** *pa.p.* and *pa.t.* **-med.**
**he•ma-, hemo-** a word element meaning "blood."
**he•mal, haemal** *a.* of the blood.
**hem•a•tin, haematin** *n.* the constituent of hemoglobin containing iron.
**hem•i-** *prefix* meaning half.
**hem•i•sphere** *n.* a half sphere; half of the celestial sphere; half of the earth. **hemispheric, hemispherical** *a.*
**hem•i•stich** *n.* half a line of verse.
**hem•lock** *n.* a poisonous umbelliferous plant; a coniferous spruce.
**he•mo•glo•bin, haemoglobin** *n.* the coloring matter of the red blood corpuscles.
**he•mo•phil•i•a, haemophilia** *n* *(Med.)* tendency to excessive bleeding due to a deficiency in clotting power of blood; *n.* a bleeder.
**hem•or•rhage, haemorrhage** *n.* *(Med.)* a flow of blood. **hemorrhagic** *a.*
**hem•or•rhoids, haemorrhoids** *n.pl.* dilated veins around anus; piles.
**he•mo•stat•ic, haemostatic** *n.* an agent which stops bleeding; a styptic. Also *a.*
**hemp** *n.* a plant whose fiber is used in the manufacture of coarse cloth, ropes,

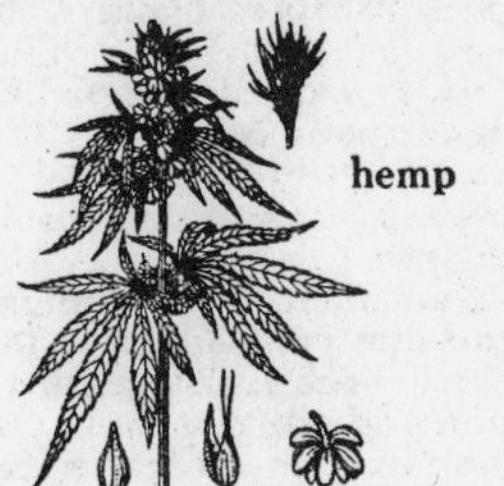
hemp

cables, etc. **-en** *a.*
**hen** *n.* the female of any bird, esp. the domestic fowl.
**hence** *adv.* from this point; for this reason; *interj.* go away! begone! **-forth, -forward** *adv.* from now.
**hench•man** *n.* a servant; a loyal supporter.
**hen•dec•a•gon** *n.* a plane figure having eleven sides.
**hen•na** *n.* a shrub or small tree of the Near East; a dye made from it.
**he•pat•ic** *a.* pert. to the liver. **hepatitis** *n.*
**hep•ta-** *prefix* meaning seven. **-l** *n.* a group of seven. **-gon** *n.* a plane figure with seven sides. **-gonal** *a.* **-meter** *n.* a line of verse of seven feet.
**hep•tar•chy** *n.* government by seven persons.
**her** *pron.* the objective case of the pronoun she; also, the possessive case used adjectivally. **hers** *pron.* the absolute possessive case. **herself** *pron.* emphatic and reflexive form.
**her•ald** *n.* an officer who makes royal proclamations; a messenger; an envoy; a forerunner. **heraldic** *a.* **-ry** *n.* the science of recording genealogies and blazoning armorial bearings.

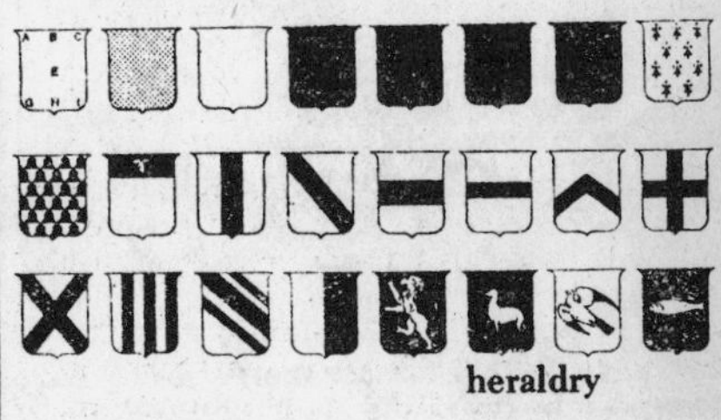
heraldry

**herb** *n.* a plant of which parts are used for medicine, food, or scent. **-aceous** *a.* **-age** *n.* herbs; nonwoody vegetation.
**Her•cu•les** *n.* *(Myth.)* Latin name of Greek hero Heracles distinguished for his prodigious strength; hence any person of extraordinary strength and size. **Herculean** *a.*
**herd** *n.* a number of animals feeding or traveling together; *v.i.* to go in a herd; *v.t.* to tend (a herd); to drive together. **-er** *n.* **-sman** *n.* one who tends cattle.
**here** *adv.* in this place; at or to this point (opposed to *there*). **-about,-abouts** *adv.* about this place. **-after** *adv.* after this; *n.* a future existence. **-by** *adv.* by means of this; by this. **-in** *adv.* in this. **-on** *adv.* hereupon. **-to** *adv.* to this. **-tofore** *adv.* up to the present; formerly. **-with** *adv.* with this.
**he•red•i•ty** *n.* the transmission of characteristic traits and qualities from parents to offspring. **herditable** *a.* **hereditament** *n.* *(Law)* property that may be inherited. **hereditary** *a.*
**her•e•sy** *n.* opinion contrary to orthodox opinion, teaching, or belief. **heresiarch** *n.* the originator or leader of a heresy. **heretic** *n.* one holding opinions contrary to orthodox faith. **heretical** *a.*
**her•it•a•ble** *a.* that can be inherited; attached to the property or house, as opposed to movable. **heritage** *n.* **heritor** *n.*
**her•maph•ro•dite** *n.* and *a.* animal or

flower with the characteristics of both sexes. **hermaphroditic, hermaphroditical** *a.* **hermaphrodism, hermaphroditism** *n.*

**her•met•ic** *a.* pert. to alchemy; magical. sealed. — **sealing,** the airtight closing of a vessel by fusion.

**her•mit** *n.* a person living in seclusion. **-age** *n.* the abode of a hermit.

**her•ni•a** *n. (Med.)* the external protrusion of any internal part through the enclosing membrane; rupture.

**he•ro** *n. (fem.* **heroine***)* one greatly regarded for his achievements or qualities; the chief man in a poem, play, or story; an illustrious warrior. *pl.* **-es. heroic** *a.* **heroical** *a.* **heroically** *adv.* **heroics** *n.pl.* high-flown language; bombastic talk. **heroism** *n.* courage; valor; bravery.

**her•o•in** *n. (Med.)* habit-forming drug used as a sedative.

**her•on** *n.* a long-legged wading bird.

**heron**

**her•pes** *n.* a skin disease. **herpetic** *a.*

**her•pe•tol•o•gy** *n.* the study of reptiles.

**her•ring** *n.* a familiar sea-fish, moving in shoals, much used as a food. **-bone** *n.* a zig-zag pattern.

**hers** See **her.**

**hes•i•tate** *v.i.* to feel or show indecision; to hold back; to stammer. **hesitant** *a.* **hesitance, hesitancy** *n.* **hesitation** *n.* **hesitantly, hesitatingly** *adv.*

**Hes•per•us** *n.* the planet Venus as the evening star. **Hesperian** *a.* western.

**he•ter•o•dox** *a.* contrary to accepted opinion. **-y** *n.*

**he•ter•o•ge•ne•ous** *a.* composed of diverse elements. **heterogeneity, -ness** *n.*

**het•er•o•gen•e•sis** *n. (Biol.)* spontaneous generation. **heterogenetic** *a.*

**he•ter•o•sex•u•al** *a.* directed towards the opposite sex.

**hew** *v.t.* to chop or cut with an ax or sword; to cut in pieces; to shape or form. *pa.p.* **-ed** *or* **-n. -er** *n.*

**hex** *n.* a witch.

**hex•a-** *prefix* meaning six **-gon** *n.* a plane figure having six sides and six angles. **-gonal** *a.* **-hedron** *n.* solid figures having six faces. e.g. a cube.

**hex•ad** *n.* a group of six.

**hex•am•e•ter** *n.* a verse of six feet.

**hex•a•pod** *n.* a six-footed insect.

**hey** *interj.* used to call attention, or to express joy, wonder, or interrogation. **-day** *n.* the time of fullest strength and greatest vigor.

**hi•a•tus** *n.* a gap in a series; an opening; a lacuna.

**hi•ber•nate** *v.i.* to winter; to pass the winter, esp. in a torpid state. **hibernation** *n.*

**Hi•bis•cus** *n. (Bot.)* a genus of shrubs or tree with large flowers.

**hic•cup** *n.* a spasm of the breathing organs with an abrupt cough-like sound; the sound itself; *v.i.* to have this. *pr.p.* **-ping.** *pa.p.* and *pa.t.* **-ped.**

**hick•ory** *n.* a nut-bearing tree.

**hide** *v.t.* to put or keep out of sight; to keep secret; *v.i.* to lie concealed. *pa.p.* **hidden, hid.** *pa.t.* **hid. hidden** *a.* **hiddenly** *adv.* **hiding** *n.*

**hide** *n.* skin of an animal; the dressed skin of an animal.

**hid•e•ous** *a.* repulsive; revolting; horrible; frightful. ly *adv.*

**hie** *v.i.* and *refl.* to go quickly; to hurry on; to urge on.

**hi•er•arch** *n.* one who has authority in sacred things; a chief priest. **-al, -ical** *a.* **-ically** *adv.* **-y** *n.* a graded system of people or things.

**hi•er•at•ic** *a.* priestly; pert. to a cursive style of ancient Egyptian writing.

**hi•er•o-** *prefix* meaning holy. **hierograph** *n.* a sacred inscription. **hierology** *n.* the science or study of sacred things.

**hi•er•o•glyph•ic** (usually *pl.*) *n.* ancient Egyptian characters or symbols used in place of letters; picture-writing. Also **hieroglyph. hieroglyphic, hieroglyphical** *a.*

**hig•gle** *v.i.* to dispute about terms.

**high** *a.* elevated; tall; elevated in rank, etc.; chief; eminent; proud; loud; strongly marked, as color; dear; costly; extreme; sharp, as tone or voice; *adv.* far up; strongly; to a great extent. **-ly** *adv.* **-ball** *n.* mixed whisky and soda. **—born** *a.* of noble birth. **-bred** *a.* of superior breeding, thoroughbred. **—flown** *a.* elevated; extravagant. **—lands** *n.pl.* a mountainous region. **-lights** *n.pl. (Art.)* the brightest parts of a painting; *(Fig.)* moments of crisis; persons of importance. **-ness** *n.* the quality of being high; a title of honor to princes and princesses. **— school,** a school following grammar school. **— seas,** the sea or ocean beyond the three-mile belt of coastal waters. **-spirited** *a.* bold; daring. **—strung** *a.* in a state of tension. **— water** *n.* tide at its highest elevation. **-way** *n.* a main road. **-wayman** *n.* a robber on a public road.

**hike** *v.i.* to walk; to tramp; *v.t.* to hoist or carry on one's back; *n.* a journey on foot. **-r** *n.*

**hi•lar•i•ous** *a.* mirthful; joyous. **-ly** *adv.* **hilarity.**

**hill** *n.* a natural elevation of land; a small mountain; a mound; *v.t.* to heap up. **-y** *a.* **-iness** *n.* **-ock** *n.* a small hill.

**hilt** *n.* the handle of a sword, dagger, etc.

**him** *pron.* the objective case of the pronoun **he. -self** *pron.* emphatic and reflexive form of **he** and **him.**

**hind** *n.* the female of the deer.

**hind, hind•er** *a.* at the back; placed at the back.

**hin•der** *v.t.* to prevent from progressing; to

stop. **-er** *n.* **hindrance** *n.*

**Hin•du•stan** *n.* *(Geog.)* the name applied to the country of the upper valley of the R. Ganges, India. **Hindi, Hindes** *n.* an Indo-Germanic language spoken in N. India. **Hindu, Hindoo** *n.* a native of Hindustan. **Hindustani, Hindoostanee** *n.* chief language of Hindu India.

**hinge** *n.* a movable joint; point on which thing depends; *v.t.* to turn on; to depend on.

**hint** *n.* a slight allusion; an indirect suggestion; *v.t.* and *i.* to allude to indirectly.

**hin•ter•land** *n.* the district inland from the coast or a river.

**hip** *n.* the upper part of the thigh.

**hip** *n.* the fruit of the rose.

**Hip•poc•ra•tes** *n.* a Greek physician, the 'Father of Medicine,' born about 460 B.C. **Hippocratic** *a.*

**hip•po•drome** *n.* in ancient Greece and Rome, a stadium for horse and chariot races; an arena.

**hip•po•pot•a•mus** *n.* a very large pachydermatous African quadruped frequenting rivers. *pl.* **-es** or **hippopotami.**

**hir•cine** *a.* pert to a goat; strong-smelling.

**hire** *n.* payment for the use of a thing; a hiring or being hired; *v.t.* to pay for the use of a thing; to contract with for wages; to take care or give on hire. **-r** *n.* **-ling** *n.* one who serves for wages.

**hir•sute** *a.* hairy; *(Bot.)* set with bristles.

**his** *pron.* and *a.* the possessive case of the pronoun **he,** belonging to him.

**his•pid** *a.* *(Bot.)* bristly; having rough hairs.

**hiss** *v.i.* to make a sound like that of *ss* to express strong dislike or disapproval; *n.* the sound. **-ing** *n.*

**hist** *interj.* a word used to command attention or silence.

**his•ta•mine** *n.* substance released by the tissues in allergic reactions.

**his•to-** *prefix* meaning a web or tissue. — **histology** *n.* the science that treats of the minute structure of the tissues of animals, plants, etc.

**his•to•ry** *n.* the study of past events; a record of events in the life of a nation, state, institution, epoch, etc.; a description of animals, plants, minerals, etc. existing on the earth, called **natural history. historian** *n.* **historic** *a.* **historically** *adv.* **historicity** *n.* the historical character of an event; the genuineness of it.

**his•tri•on•ic** *a.* theatrical; affected. **-al** *a.* **-ally** *adv.* **-s** *n.pl.* theatrical representation.

**hit** *v.t.* to strike with a blow or missile; *v.i.* to strike; to light (upon). *pr.p.* **-ting.** *pa.p.* and *pa.t.* **hit.** *n.* a blow; a stroke; a success.

**hitch** *v.t.* to raise or move with a jerk; to fasten with a loop, etc.; to harness; *v.i.* to be caught or fastened; *n.* a jerk; a fastening, loop, or knot; a difficulty; **-er** *n.* **to -hike,** to travel by begging rides from motorists, etc.

**hith•er** *adv.* to or toward this place; *a.* situated on this side. **-most** *a.* nearest in this direction. **-to** *adv.* up to now.

**hive** *n.* a place where bees live; place of great activity; *v.t.* to gather or place bees in a hive.

hive

**hives** *n.* an eruptive skin disease.

**hoar** *a.* gray with age; grayish-white. **-y** *a.* **-frost** *n.* white frost.

**hoard** *n.* a stock or store, esp. if hidden away; *v.t.* to store secretly; *v.i.* to lay up a store. **-er** *n.*

**hoarse** *a.* rough and harsh sounding; husky. **-ly** *adv.* **-ness** *n.*

**hoax** *v.t.* to deceive by an amusing or mischievous story; *n.* a practical joke. **-er** *n.*

**hob** *n.* the flat-topped casing of a fireplace where things are placed to be kept warm. **-nail** *n.* a large-headed nail for boot soles.

**hob** *n.* an elf.

**hob•ble** *v.i.* to walk lamely; to limp; *v.t.* to tie the legs together of a horse, etc.; to impede; *n.* a limping gait; a fetter; a rope for hobbling.

**hob•by** *n.* formerly a small horse; a favorite pursuit or pastime.

**hob•nail** See **hob.**

**hob•nob** *v.i.* to drink together; to be very friendly with.

**ho•bo** *n.* a vagrant; a tramp.

**hock** *n.* the joint of a quadruped's hind leg between the knee and the fetlock.

**hock** *v.t., n.* pawn.

**hock•ey** *n.* a game played with a ball or disk and curved sticks.

**ho•cus** *v.i.* to hoax; to stupefy with drugs.

**hod** *n.* a small trough on a staff used by builders.

**hodge-podge** *n.* a medley or mixture.

**hoe** *n.* a tool for breaking ground, scraping out weeds, etc.; *v.t.* to break up or weed with a hoe. **-r** *n.*

**hog** *n.* a swine; a pig, esp. if reared for fattening; *(Colloq.)* a greedy or dirty fellow; *v.i.* to arch the back. **-gish** *a.* **-back, -s-back** *n.* a crested hill-ridge.

**hogs-head** *n.* a large cask; a liquid measure.

**hoist** *v.t.* to raise aloft, esp. of flags; to raise with tackle, etc.; *n.* a hoisting; an elevator.

**hold** *v.t.* to keep fast; to grasp; to support in or with the hands, etc.; to own; to occupy; to detain; to celebrate; to believe; to contain; *v.i.* to cling; not to give way; to abide (by); to keep (to); to proceed; to be in force. *pa.p.* and *pa.t.* **held.** *n.* a grasp;grip; handle; binding power and influence; a prison. **-er** *n.* **-ing** *n.* land, farm, etc. rented from another;

stocks held.

**hold** *n.* the space below the deck of a ship, for cargo.

**hole** *n.* a hollow; cavity; pit; den; lair; burrow; opening; a perforation; mean habitation; *v.t.* to make a hole in; to perforate; to put into a hole; *v.i.* to go into a hole.

**hol•i•day** *n.* a day of rest from work esp. in memory of an event or a person.

**hol•low** *n.* a cavity; a hole; a depression; a valley; *a.* having a cavity; not solid; empty; *v.t.* to make a hollow in. **—toned** *a.* deep toned. **-ware** *n.* silver serving dishes.

**hol•ly** *n.* an evergreen shrub.

**hol•ly•hock** *n.* a tall garden plant.

**hol•o-** a combining form meaning whole, used in many derivatives. **-caust** *n.* a burnt offering; destruction, or slaughter. **-graph** *n.* and *a.* any writing, as a letter, deed, will, etc. wholly in the handwriting of the signer of it. **-graphic** *a.*

**hol•ster** *n.* a leather case for a pistol.

**ho•ly** *a.* belonging to, or devoted to, God; morally perfect; divine; sacred; pious; religious. **holily** *adv.* **holiness** *n.*

**hom•age** *n.* in feudal times, service due by a vassal to his over-lord; tribute; respect paid.

**hom•burg** *n.* a type of men's soft, felt hat.

**home** *n.* one's fixed residence; a dwelling-place; a native place or country; an institution for the infirm, sick, poor, etc.; *a.* pert. to, or connected with, home; not foreign; domestic; *adv.* to or at one's home; to the point aimed at; close. **-ly** *a.* belonging to home; plain; ugly. **-liness** *n.* **-land** *n.* **-sick** *a.* depressed in spirits through absence from home. **-sickness** *n.* **-spun** *a.* spun or made at home; anything plain or homely. **-stead** *n.* a house with land and buildings. **-work** *n.* schoolwork to be done outside of class.

**home** *v.i.* of a pigeon, to fly home; *v.t.* in naval warfare, to guide by radio to the attack of a target.

**ho•me•op•a•thy** *n.* the treatment of disease by the administration of very small doses of drugs which would produce in a healthy person effects similar to the symptoms of the disease. Also **homeotherapy, homeopath, homeopathist** *n.* **homeopathic** *a.*

**hom•i•cide** *n.* manslaughter; the one who kills. **homicidal** *a.*

**hom•i•ly** *n.* a discourse on a religious or moral subject; a sermon. **homilist** *n.*

**hom•i•ny** *n.* maize porridge.

**ho•mo-** a combining form meaning same, used in derivatives. **-centric** *a.* having the same center.

**ho•mog•e•ne•ous** *a.* of the same kind or nature; similar; uniform. **-ness, homogeneity** *n.* sameness; uniformity. **homogenize** *v.*

**hom•o•graph** *n.* a word having the same spelling as another, but different meaning and origin.

**ho•mol•o•gate** *v.t.* to approve; to confirm. **homologous** *a.* having the same relative value, position, etc. **homologation** *n.*

**hom•o•nym** *n.* a word having the same pronunciation as another but a different meaning, e.g. *air* and *heir*. Also **homophone.**

**ho•mo•sex•u•al•ity** *n.* attraction between individuals of the same sex. **homosexual** *n.*

**hone** *n.* a stone for sharpening knives, etc. *v.t.* to sharpen on one.

**hon•est** *a.* upright; dealing fairly; just; faithful; free from fraud; unadulterated. **-ly** *adv.* **-y** *n.* *(Bot.)* a small flowering plant.

**hon•ey** *n.* the sweet, thick fluid collected by bees from flowers; anything very sweet; sweetness; *(Colloq.)* sweetheart; darling; *a.* sweet; luscious; *v.t.* to sweeten. *pa.p.* and *a.* **-ed.** Also **honied** *a.* sweet; *(Fig.)* flattering. **-bee** *n.* the common hive-bee. **-comb** *n.* the structure of wax in hexagonal cells in which bees place honey, eggs, etc.; *v.t.* to fill with cells or perforations. **-combed** *a.* **-dew** *n.* a sweet sticky substance found on plants; a melon. **-moon** *n.* the holiday taken by a newlywed couple. Also, *v.i.* **-suckle** *n.* a climbing plant with yellow flowers.

**honk** *n.* the cry of the wild goose; any sound resembling this.

**hon•or** *n.* high respect; renown; glory; reputation; sense of what is right or due; *v.t.* to respect highly; to confer a mark of distinction on; to accept or pay (a bill, etc.) when due. **-s** *n.pl.* public marks of respect or distinction. **-able** *a.* **-ably** *adv.* **-ableness** *n.*

**hon•or•ary** *a.* conferred for the sake of honor only. **honorarium** *n.* a sum of money granted voluntarily to a person for services rendered. **honorific** *a.* conferring honor; *n.* term of respect.

**hood** *n.* covering for the head and neck; the cover of an automobile engine; *v.t.* to cover with a hood. **-wink** *v.t.* to blindfold; to deceive.

**hood•lum** *n.* a hooligan.

**hoof** *n.* the horny casing of the foot of a horse, ox, sheep, etc.; *pl.* **-s, hooves.**

**hook** *n.* a bent piece of metal, etc. for catching hold, hanging up, etc.; anything curved or bent like a hook; *v.t.* and *i.* to fasten, draw, catch, etc. with a hook.

**hook•ah, hoo•ka** *n.* a tobacco pipe in which the smoke is drawn through water.

**hook•worm** *n.* *(Med.)* a parasitic worm.

**hoo•li•gan** *n.* one of a gang of street roughs.

**hoop** *n.* a band for holding together the staves of casks, etc.; a circle of wood or metal.

**hoot** *n.* the cry of an owl; a cry of disapproval; *v.t.* to assail with hoots; *v.i.* to cry as an owl; to cry out in disapproval. **-er** *n.*

**hooves** *pl.* of **hoof.**

**hop** *v.i.* of persons, to spring on one foot; of animals or birds, to leap or skip on all feet at once. *pr.p.* **-ping.** *pa.p.* and *pa.t.* **-ped.** *n.* an act or the action of hopping. **-per** *n.* a device for feeding material into a mill or machine; a railroad car with dumping device for coal, sand, etc.

**hop** *n.* a climbing plant with bitter cones used to flavor beer, etc.; *v.t.* to flavor with hops. **-s** *n.pl.* the cones of the hop plant.

**hope** *n.* a desire combined with expectation; *v.t.* to desire, with belief in possibility of obtaining; *v.i.* to feel hope. **-ful** *a.* **-fully** *adv.* **-fulness** *n.* **-less** *a.* **-lessly** *adv.*

**hop•scotch** *n.* a child's game.

**ho•ral** *a.* of or pert. to an hour.

**horde** *n.* a great multitude; a troop of nomads or tent-dwellers.

**hore•hound** *n.* a plant with bitter juice. Also **hoarhound.**

**ho•ri•zon** *n.* the boundary of the part of the earth seen from any given point; the line where earth (or sea) and sky seem to meet. **horizontal** *a.* parallel to the horizon; level. **horizontally** *adv.*

**hor•mone** *n.* a substance secreted by certain glands.

**horn** *n.* a hard projecting organ growing from heads of cows, deer, etc.; substance forming this organ; a wind instrument of music; a drinking cup; a utensil for holding gunpowder; a sounding contrivance on motors as warning; either of the extremities of the crescent moon; *v.t.* to furnish with horns; to gore. **-y** *a.* of, or made of, horn; hard or callous. **-beam** *n.* a small tree or shrub. **-book** *n.* a primer

**hornbook**

for children, formerly covered with horn to protect it. **-pipe** *n.* an old musical instrument; a vigorous dance; the lively tune for such a dance.

**hor•net** *n.* a large insect.

**ho•ro-** time; used as a combining form, e.g. —**horologe** *n.* an instrument of any kind for telling the time. **horologer, horologist** *n.* **horology** *n.*

**hor•o•scope** *n.* a chart of the heavens which predicts character as well as future events. **horoscopic** *a.*

**hor•ri•ble** *a.* tending to excite horror, fear, dread. **horribly** *adv.* **-ness** *n.* **horrid** *a.* frightful; shocking; abominable. **horrify** *v.t.* **horrific** *a.*

**hor•ror** *n.* painful emotion of fear, dread and repulsion.

**horse** *n.* a large hoofed quadruped used for riding, drawing vehicles, etc.; *v.t.* to

**horse**

provide with a horse, or horses; to carry or support on the back; *v.i.* to mount on a

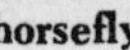

**horsefly**

horse. **-fly** *n.* a stinging fly troublesome to horses. **-hair** *n.* hair from the tail or mane of a horse, haircloth. **-man** *n.* a man on horseback; a skilled rider. **-manship** *n.* the art of riding or of training horses. **-pistol** *n.* an old kind of large pistol, **-play** *n.* rough and boisterous play. **-power** *n.* (abbrev. **h.p.**), the power a horse is capable of exerting. **-radish** *n.* a cultivated plant used for sauces, salads, etc. **-shoe** *n.* a curved, narrow band of iron for nailing to the underpart of the hoof.

**hor•ta•tive, hor•ta•tory** *a.* tending or serving to exhort; advisory.

**hor•ti•cul•ture** *n.* gardening; the art of cultivating a garden.

**ho•san•na** *n.* a cry of praise to God.

**hose** *n.* stockings; socks; tight-fitting breeches or pants; a flexible tube or pipe for conveying water; *v.t.* to water with a hose. **hosier** *n.* dealer in hosiery. **hosiery** *n.* a collective word for stockings and similar garments.

**hos•pice** *n.* a traveler's house of rest kept by a religious order.

**hosp•i•ta•ble** *a.* receiving and entertaining guests in a friendly and liberal fashion. **hospitality** *n.*

**hos•pi•tal** *n.* an institution for the care of the sick. **-ization** *n.* being in the hospital. **-ize** *v.t.*

**host** *n.* one who lodges or entertains another; an animal or plant which has parasites living on it. **-ess** *n.* a woman who entertains guests. **hostel** *n.* a lodging place for young people who are hiking or traveling by bicycle; *(Arch.)* an inn.

**host** *n.* a large number; a multitude; a crowd.

**Host** *n.* the bread consecrated in the Eucharist.

**hos•tage** *n.* one handed over to the enemy as security.

**hos•tel** See **host.**

**hos•tile** *a.* of, or pert. to, an enemy; unfriendly; opposed. **-ly** *adv.* **hostility** *n.*

**hot** *a.* of high temperature; very warm; of quick temper; ardent or passionate. **-ly** *adv.* **-ness** *n.*

**ho•tel** *n.* a large and superior kind of inn. **-keeper** *n.*

**Hot•ten•tot** *n.* a member of a native race of S. Africa.

**hound** *n.* a dog used in hunting, esp. in hunting by scent; *v.t.* to chase with, or as with, hounds; (with 'on') to urge or incite; to pursue, to nag.

**hound**

**hour** *n.* the twenty-fourth part of a day, or 60 minutes; the time of the day; an appointed time or occasion; *pl.* the fixed times of work, prayers, etc. **-glass** *n.* a sand-glass running for an hour. **-ly** *adv.*
**hou•ri** *n.* a nymph of the Mohammedan paradise.
**house** *n.* a dwelling-place; a legislative or other assembly; a family; a business firm; audience at theater, etc.; dynasty; *v.t.* to shelter; to receive; to store; *v.i.* to dwell. **housing** *n.* shelter; the providing of houses; a support for part of a machine, etc. **-ful** *n.* **-less** *a.*
**hous•ing** *n.* a saddle-cloth; *pl.* the trappings of a horse.
**hove** *pa.p.* of **heave.**
**hov•el** *n.* a small, mean house; *v.t.* to put in a hovel.
**hov•er** *v.i.* to hang fluttering in the air, or on the wing; to loiter; to waver.
**how** *adv.* in what manner; by what means; to what degree or extent; in what condition. **-beit** *adv.* nevertheless. **-ever** *adv.* in whatever manner or degree; *conj.* in spite of how.
**how•itz•er** *n.* a form of gun.

**howitzer**

**howl** *v.i.* to utter a prolonged, wailing cry such as that of a wolf or dog; to cry; *v.i.* to utter with howling; *n.* a wail or cry. **-er** *n.* one who howls.
**hoy•den, hoiden** *n.* a rude, bold girl; a tomboy. **-ish** *a.* romping; bold; boisterous.
**hub** *n.* the central part, or nave, of a wheel; center of activity.
**hub•bub** *n.* a commotion.
**huck•a•back** *n.* a kind of coarse linen with an uneven surface, much used for towels. Also **huck.**
**huck•le•ber•ry** *n.* an American shrub.
**huck•le•bone** *n.* the hopbone; the anklebone.
**huck•ster** *n.* retailer of small articles; a street peddler; a mean, mercenary fellow; *(Colloq.)* an advertising man; *v.i.* to peddle.
**hud•dle** *v.t.* to crowd together; to heap together confusedly; *v.i.* to press together.
**hue** *n.* color; tint. **-d** *a.* having a color.
**huff** *n.* a fit of petulance or anger; *v.t.* to bully; *v.i.* to take offense. **-y** *a.*
**hug** *v.t.* to clasp tightly in the arms; to embrace; to cling to. *pr.p.* **-ging.** *pa.t., pa.p.* **-ged.** *n.*
**huge** *a.* very large; immense; enormous. **-ly** *adv.* **-ness** *n.*
**Hu•gue•not** *n.* a 16th cent. French Protestant.
**hu•la** *n.* native Hawaiian dance.
**hulk** *n.* the body of a ship, esp. dismantled ship; anything big and unwieldy; *v.i.* to be bulky. **-ing, -y** *a.*
**hull** *n.* husk of any fruit, seed, or grain; frame or body of a vessel; *v.t.* to remove shell or husk.
**hul•la•ba•loo** *n.* uproar; outcry.
**hum** *v.t.* to sing with the lips closed; *v.i.* to make droning sound, as bee. *n.* the noise of bees or the like. *pr.p.* **-ming.** *pa.p.* and *pa.t.* **-med.**
**hu•man** *a.* belonging to, or having the qualities of, man or mankind. **-ly** *adv.* **-ness** *n.* **humane** *a.* having the moral qualities of man; kind; benevolent. **-ness** *n.* **-ism** *n.* a philosophic mode of thought devoted to human interests; literary culture. **-ist** *n.* **-istic** *a.* **-ize** *v.t.* **humanity** *n.* the quality of being human; human nature; the human race; kindss or benevolence. **humanities** *n.pl.* language, literature, art, philosophy, etc. **humanitarian** *n.* one who denies the divinity of Jesus; a philanthropist. **-kind** *n.* the whole race of man.
**hum•ble** *a.* lowly; meek; *v.t.* to bring low; to make meek. **humbly** *adv.* **-ness** *n.*
**hum•bug** *n.* a hoax; sham; nonsense; an imposter; *v.t.* to hoax; to deceive.
**hum•drum** *a.* commonplace.
**hu•mer•al** *a.* belonging to the shoulder. **humerus** *n.* the long bone of the upper arm.
**hu•mid** *a.* damp; moist. **-ly** *adv.* **humidify** *v.t.* **humidity, -ness** *n.* **humidor** *n.* a device for keeping the air moist in a jar, case, etc.
**hu•mil•i•ate** *v.t.* to humble; to lower the dignity of. **humilating** *a.* **humiliation** *n.* **humility** *n.*
**hum•mock** *n.* a hillock.
**hu•mor** *n.* quality of imagination quick to perceive the ludicrous or to express itself in an amusing way; disposition; mood; the fluids of animal bodies; *v.t.* to indulge; to comply with mood or whim of. **-ous** *a.* **-ously** *adv.*
**hump** *n.* the protuberance or hunch formed by a crooked back; a hillock; *v.t.* to bend into a hump shape.
**hu•mus** *n.* a brown or black constituent of the soil, composed of decayed vegetable or animal matter.
**Hun** *n.* a barbarian.
**hunch** *n.* a hump; *v.t.* to bend or arch into a hump; *v.i.* to move forward in jerks.
**hun•dred** *n.* a cardinal number, the product of ten times ten. **-th** *a.* last, or one, of a hundred; *n.* one of a hundred equal parts. **-weight** *n.*
**hung** *pa.p.* and *pa.t.* of **hang.**
**hun•ger** *n.* discomfort or exhaustion caused by lack of food; a craving for food; any strong desire; *v.i.* to feel hunger; to long for; *v.t.* to starve. **hungry** *a.* feeling hunger. **hungrily** *adv.*
**hunk** *n.* a lump.
**hunt** *v.t.* to pursue and prey on (as animals on other animals); to pursue animals or game for food or sport; to search diligently after; *v.i.* to go out in pursuit of game; to search; *n.* the act of hunting; chase; search; an association of huntsmen. **-er** *n.*
**hur•dle** *n.* a barrier in a race course; an

obstacle; *v.t.* to enclose with hurdles.
**hur•dy-gur•dy** *n.* an old-fashioned musical instrument.
**hurl** *v.t.* to send whirling; to throw with violence; *n.* a violent throw.
**hur•ly-bur•ly** *n.* tumult; bustle; confusion.
**hur•ri•cane** *n.* a wind of 60 m.p.h. or over; a violent cyclonic storm of wind and rain.
**hur•ry** *v.t.* to hasten; to impel to greater speed; to urge on; *v.i.* to move or act with haste; *n.* the act of pressing forward in haste; quick motion. **hurried** *a.* **hurriedly** *adv.*
**hurt** *v.i.* to cause pain; to wound or bruise; to impair or damage. *v.i.* to give pain; *n.* wound, injury, or harm. **-ful** *a.*
**hur•tle** *v.t.* to fling, to dash against; *v.i.* to move rapidly; to rush violently.
**hus•band** *n.* a married man; *v.t.* to manage with economy. **-ry** *n.* farming; thrift.
**hush** *interj.* or *imper.* be quiet! silence! *n.* silence or stillness; *v.t.* to make quiet.
**husk** *n.* the dry, external covering of certain seeds and fruits; *v.t.* to remove the outer covering. **-y** *a.* rough in tone; hoarse; *(Colloq.)* big and strong. **-ily** *adv.* **-iness** *n.*
**husk•y** *n.* an Eskimo sled-dog.
**hus•sar** *n.* one of the light cavalry of European armies.
**hus•sy** *n.* an ill-behaved woman.
**hus•tings** *n.* any platform from which political campaign speeches are made.
**hus•tle** *v.t.* to push about; to jostle; *v.i.* to hurry; to bustle; *n.* speed; jostling. **-r** *n.*
**hut** *n.* a small house or cabin.
**hutch** *n.* a chest or box; a grain-bin; a pen for rabbits, etc.
**hy•a•cinth** *n.* a bulbous plant; a purplish-blue color.
**hy•a•line** *a.* glassy; transparent.
**hy•brid** *n.* the offspring of two animals or plants of different species; a mongrel.
**hy•dra** *n.* *(Myth.)* a monstrous water-serpent with many heads, slain by Hercules; *(Zool.)* a small fresh-water polyp.
**hy•dran•gea** *n.* a genus of shrubs.
**hy•drant** *n.* a water-pipe with a nozzle to which a hose can be attached.
**hy•drate** *n.* *(Chem.)* a compound of water with another compound or an element; *v.t.* to combine with water. **hydrated** *a.* **hydration** *n.*
**hy•drau•lic** *a.* relating to the conveyance of water.
**hy•dro-** *prefix* meaning water, combining to form derivatives; in many compounds used to indicate hydrogen. **-carbon** *n.* a compound of hydrogen and carbon. **-cephalus** *n.* *(Med.)* an excess of cerebrospinal fluid in the brain. **-cephalic, -cephalous** *a.* **-chloric** *a.* containing hydrogen and chlorine.
**hy•dro•dy•nam•ics** *n.pl.* the branch of physics which deals with the flow of fluids.
**hy•dro•e•lec•tric** *a.* pert. to the generation of electricity by utilizing water power.
**hy•dro•gen** *n.* an inflammable, colorless, and odorless gas, the lightest of all known substances. **hydrogenous** *a.* **— bomb** *n.* atom bomb of enormous power.
**hy•drol•o•gy** *n.* the science of the properties, laws, etc. of water. **hydrolysis** *a.* **hydrolytic** *a.*
**hy•drom•e•ter** *n.* a graduated instrument for finding the specific gravity, and thence the strength of liquids.

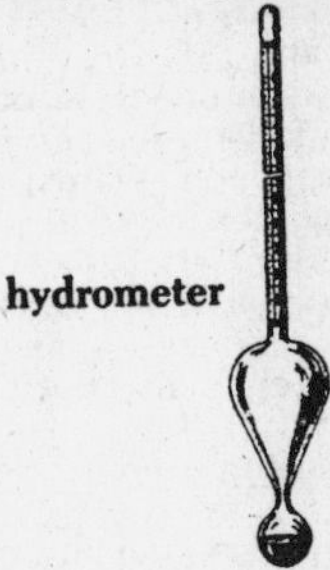
hydrometer

**hy•drop•a•thy** *n.* the treatment of diseases with water. Also **hydrotherapy.**
**hy•dro•pho•bi•a** *n.* an acute infectious disease in man caused by the bite of a mad dog; rabies; an extreme dread of water.
**hy•dro•plane** *n.* an airplane designed to land on and take off from water; a kind of flat-bottomed boat.
**hy•drous** *a.* containing water; containing hydrogen.
**hy•e•na** *n.* a carnivorous mammal of Asia and Africa, allied to the dog.
**hy•giene** *n.* medical science which deals with the preservation of health. **hygienic, hygienist** *n.*
**hy•gro-** *prefix* meaning moist, combining to form derivatives.
**hy•gro•scope** *n.* an instrument which indicates variations of humidity.

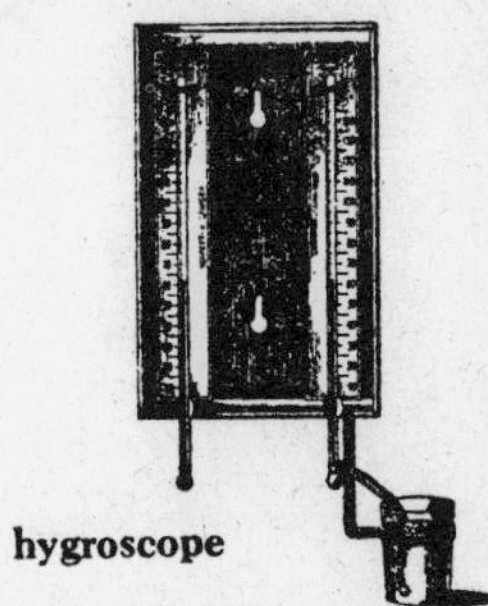
hygroscope

**Hy•men** *n.* *(Myth.)* the god of marriage; *(l.c.)* membrane fold at entrance to female sex organs. **hymeneal** *a.* pert. to marriage.
**hy•me•nop•ter•ous** *a.* belonging or pert. to an order of insects as the bee, the wasp, etc.
**hymn** *n.* an ode or song of praise, esp. a religious one; *v.t.* to praise in song; *v.i.* to sing in worship. **-al** *n.* a hymn book.
**hy•per•bo•la** *n.* *(Geom.)* a curve. **hyperbolic** *a.*
**hy•per•bo•le** *n.* *(Gram.)* a figure of speech

which expresses much more or much less than the truth, for the sake of effect; exaggeration. **hyperbolic, hyperbolical** *a.* **hyperbolically** *adv.*

**hy•per•crit•ic** *n.* one who is critical beyond measure or reason. **-al** *a.* **-ally** *adv.*

**hy•per•phys•i•cal** *a.* supernatural.

**hy•per•sen•si•tive** *a.* abnormally sensitive. **-ness, hypersensitivity** *n.*

**hy•per•tro•phy** *n.* *(Med.)* abnormal enlargement of organ or part of body.

**hy•phen** *n.* a mark (-) used to connect syllables or compound words; *v.t.* to connect with a hyphen. **-ated** *a.*

**hyp•no•sis** *n.* the state of being hypnotized; abnormal sleep. **hypnotic** *a.* **hypnotize** *v.t.* to produce a mental state resembling sleep. **hypnotism** *n.* **hypnotist** *n.*

**hy•po-** *prefix* meaning under, beneath, below.

**hy•po•chon•dri•a** *n.* a mental disorder, in which one is tormented by melancholy and gloomy views, especially about one's own health. **hypochondriac** *a.* and *n.*

**hy•poc•ri•sy** *n.* stimulation or pretense of goodness; feigning to be what one is not; insincerity. **hypocrite** *n.* **hypocritical** *a.*

**hy•po•der•mic** *a.* pert. to parts underlying the skin; *n.* the injection of a drug beneath the skin by means of a needle and small syringe. **-ally** *adv.*

**hy•pos•ta•sis** *n.* essential nature of anything; the substance of each of the three divisions of the Godhead; *(Med.)* a deposit of blood in an organ; *pl.* **hypostases.**

**hy•pot•e•nuse** *n.* *(Geom.)* the side of a right-angled triangle which is opposite the right angle.

**hy•poth•e•cate** *v.t.* to give in security; to mortgage.

**hy•poth•e•sis** *n.pl.* **hypotheses,** a supposition used as a basis from which to draw conclusions; a theory. **hypothesize** *v.i.* and *v.t.* **hypothetic, hypothetical** *a.*

**hys•te•ri•a, hysterics** *n.* an affection of the nervous system, characterized by excitability and lack of emotional control. **hysteric, hysterical** *a.* **hysterically** *adv.*

**I** *pron.* the pronoun of the first person singular.
**i•am•bus** *n.* a metrical foot of two syllables, the first unaccented, and the second accented. **iamb** *n.* **iambic** *a.*
**i•at•ric, iatrical** *a.* pert. to physicians, medicine.
**I•ber•ri•an** *a.* pert. to Iberia, viz. Spain and Portugal.
**i•bex** *n.* variety of wild goat.
**i•bis** *n.* a stork-like wading bird.

**ibis**

**I•car•i•an** *a.* adventurous in flight; rash.
**ice** *n.* frozen water; a frozen dessert made with fruit juices and water; *v.t.* to freeze; to chill with ice; to frost a cake; *pr. p.* **icing. icily** *adv.* coldly. **iciness** *n.* **icing** *n.* a covering of sugar on cakes, etc. **icy** *a.*
**Ice•land•er** *n.* a native of Iceland. **Icelandic** *a.*
**ich•nol•o•gy** *n.* the classification of fossil footprints.
**i•chor** *n.* *(Gk. Myth)* the fluid which flowed in the veins of the Gods; the colorless, watery discharge from ulcers. **-ous** *a.*
**ich•thy•ol•o•gy** *n.* the branch of zoology which treats of fishes. **ichthyological** *a.* **ichthyologist** *n.* **ichthyic** *a.* **ichthyoid** *a.*
**i•ci•cle** *n.* a pendent conical mass of ice.
**i•con** *n.* any sign which resembles the thing it represents; a venerated representation of Christ, an angel, or a saint, found in Greek and Orthodox Eastern Churches. **-ic, -ical** *a.* **-oclasm** *n.* act of breaking images; an attack on the cherished beliefs or enthusiasms of others. **-oclast** *n.* **-ography** *n.* **-olator** *n.* an image worshipper. **-olatry** *n.* image worship.
**ic•ter•us** *n.* jaundice. **icteric, icterical** *a.*
**id** *n.* in psycho-analysis, the primary source in individuals of instinctive energy.
**i•de•a** *n.* a product of intellectual action; way of thinking; a thought; belief; plan; aim; principle at the back of one's mind. **ideal** *a.* existing in fancy only; perfect; satisfying desires; *n.* an imaginary type or norm of perfection to be aimed at. **idealization** *n.* **idealize** *v.t.* **idealizer** *n.* an idealist. **idealism** *n.* tendency to seek the highest spiritual perfection; imaginative treatment in comparative disregard of the real. **-list** *n.* **-listic** *a.*
**i•den•ti•cal** *a.* the very same; not different. **-ly** *adv.* **-ness** *n.*
**i•den•ti•fy** *v.t.* to establish the identity of; to recognize; to associate (oneself) in interest, purpose, use, etc. **identifiable** *a.* **identification** *n.*
**i•den•ti•ty** *n.* state of having the same nature or character with; absolute sameness, as opposed to mere similarity; individuality.
**id•e•o•graph** *n.* a picture, symbol, diagram, etc., suggesting an idea or object without specifically naming it. **ideogram** *n.* an ideograph. **-ic, -ical** *a.* **ideography** *n.*
**i•de•ol•o•gy** *n.* the body of beliefs of any group. **ideologic, ideological** *a.* **ideologist** *n.* a theorist.
**ides** *n. pl.* in the Roman calendar, the 15th day of March, May, July, and October, and the 13th day of the other months.
**id•i•o•cy** *n.* See **idiot.**
**id•i•om** *n.* a peculiar mode of expression; the genius or peculiar cast of a language. **-atic, -atical** *a.* **-atically** *adv.*
**id•i•o•syn•cra•sy** *n.* a peculiarity in a person; peculiar view. **idiosyncratic, idiosyncratical** *a.*
**id•i•ot** *n.* one mentally deficient; a born fool. **idiocy** *n.* extreme and permanent mental deficiency. **-ic, -ical** *a.* **-ically** *adv.* **-ism** *n.* natural imbecility.
**i•dle** *a.* doing nothing; inactive; *v.t.* to spend in idleness; *v.i.* to be idle or unoccupied. **-ness** *n.* **-r** *n.* **idly** *adv.*
**i•dol** *n.* an image of a diety as an object of worship. **-ater** *n.* *(fem.* **idolatress** *)* a worshipper of idols. **-atrize** *v.t.* to worship as an idol. **-atrous** *a.* **-atrously** *adv.* **-atry** *n.* worship of idols. **-ization -ize** *v.t.* **-izer** *n.*
**i•dyl, idyll** *n.* a short pastoral poem; a picture of simple perfection and loveliness. **-lic** *a.* of a perfect setting; blissful.
**if** *conj.* on the condition or supposition that; whether; in case that.
**ig•loo** *n.* a dome-shaped house built of blocks of hard snow by Eskimos.
**ig•ne•ous** *a.* resembling fire.
**ig•nite** *v.t.* to set on fire; to kindle; *v.i.* to catch fire. **ignitible** *a.* **ignition** *n.*
**ig•no•ble** *a.* of humble birth or family; mean; base; inferior. **ignobility, -ness** *n.* **ignobly** *adv.*
**ig•no•min•y** *n.* public disgrace of dishonor; infamous conduct. **ignominious** *a.* **ignominiously** *adv.* **ignominiousness** *n.*
**ig•no•ra•mus** *n.* an ignorant person.
**ig•no•rant** *a.* uninstructed; uninformed; unlearned. **ignorance** *n.* **-ly** *adv.*
**ig•nore** *v.t.* to refuse to take notice of.
**i•gua•na** *n.* a family of lizards, found in tropical America.

**iguana**

**ilk** *a.* the same.
**ill** *a.* bad or evil in any respect; sick; *n.* evil of any kind; misfortune; misery; pain, *adv.* not well; faultily; unfavorably. **-ness** *n.* sickness.
**ill-** *prefix,* used in the construction of

compound words, implying badness in some form or other.

**il•le•gal** *a.* unlawful. **-ize** *v.t.* to render unlawful. **-ity** *n.* unlawful act. **-ly** *adv.*

**il•leg•i•ble** *a.* incapable of being read or deciphered. **-ness, illegibility** *n.* **illegibly** *adv.*

**il•le•git•i•mate** *a.* unlawful; not authorized by good usage; born out of wedlock. **illegitimacy** *n.* **-ly** *adv.*

**il•lib•eral** *a.* not liberal; niggardly; narrow-minded; intolerant. **illiberality** *n.*

**il•lic•it** *a.* not permitted; unlawful. **-ly** *adv.* **-ness** *n.*

**il•lim•it•a•ble** *a.* incapable of being limited or bounded.

**il•lit•er•ate** *a.* unable to read or write; *n.* a person unable to read or write; *adv.* **-ness, illiteracy** *n.*

**il•log•i•cal** *a.* not according to the rules of logic; unsound; fallacious. **-ly** *adv.* **-ness, illogicality** *n.*

**il•lu•mi•nate** *v.t.* to enlighten literally and figuratively; to light up; to embellish, as a book or manuscript with gold and colors. **illuminable** *a.* **illuminant** *a.* and *n.* **illumination** *n.* act of giving light; instructions; enlightenment; decoration on manuscripts and books. **illuminative** *a.* **illuminator** *n.* **illumine** *v.t.* and *v.i.*

**il•lu•sion** *n.* an erroneous interpretation or unreal image. **illusionist** *n.* a professional entertainer who produces illusions. **illusive, illusory** *a.* **illusively** *adv.* **illusiveness** *n.*

**il•lus•trate** *v.t.* to make clear or bright; to exemplify, esp. by means of figures, diagrams, etc.; to adorn with pictures. **illustration** *n.* **illustrative, illustratory** *a.* **illustratively** *adv.* **illustrator** *n.*

**il•lus•tri•ous** *a.* conferring honor; possessing honor or dignity. **-ness** *n.*

**im•age** *n.* a mental picture of any object; a representation of a person or object; a symbol; idol; figure of speech; *v.t.* to form an image of; to reflect; to imagine; *n.* images regarded collectively; figures of speech.

**im•ag•ine** *v.t.* to form in the mind an idea or image; to conjecture; to picture; to believe; to suppose; *v.i.* to form an image of; to picture in the mind. **imaginable** *a.* **imaginableness** *n.* **imaginably** *adv.* **imaginary** *a.* existing only in imagination or fancy; fanciful; unreal. **imaginative** *a.* gifted with the creative faculty; fanciful. **imagination** *n.* the mental faculty which apprehends and forms ideas of external objects, the poetical faculty. **imaginatively** *adv.* **imaginativeness** *n.*

**i•mam, imaum** *n.* a Moslem priest.

**im•be•cile** *a.* mentally feeble; silly; idiotic; *n.* one of feeble mentality. **imbecility** *n.*

**im•bed** *v.t.* See **embed.**

**im•bibe** *v.t.* to drink in; to absorb; to receive into the mind; *v.t.* to drink. **imbiber** *n.*

**im•brue** *v.t.* to wet, to drench.

**im•bro•glio** *n.* an intricate, complicated plot.

**im•bue** *v.t.* to inspire; to tinge deeply; to saturate.

**im•i•tate** *v.t.* to follow, as a pattern, model, or example; to copy. **imitable** *a.* **imitation** *n.* **imitative** *a.* inclined to imitate; not original. **imitatively** *adv.* **imitativeness** *n.* **imitator** *n.*

**im•mac•u•late** *a.* without blemish; spotless; unsullied; pure; undefiled. **-ly** *adv.* **-ness** *n.*

**im•ma•nent** *a.* abiding in; inherent; intrinsic; innate. **immanence, immanency** *n.*

**im•ma•te•ri•al** *a.* not consisting of matter; incorporeal; of no essential consequence; unimportant. **-ize** *v.t.* to separate from matter. **-ism** *n.* **-ist** *n.*

**im•ma•ture** *a.* not mature or ripe; raw; unformed; undeveloped; untimely. **-ness, immaturity** *n.*

**im•meas•ur•a•ble** *a.* incapable of being measured. **immeasurably** *adv.*

**im•me•di•ate** *a.* occuring at once; present; not separated by others. **immediacy** *n.* **-ly** *adv.* **-ness** *n.*

**im•me•mo•ri•al** *a.* beyond the range of memory. **immemorable** *a.* **-ly** *adv.*

**im•mense** *a.* unlimited; immeasureable; very great; vast. **-ly** *adv.* **-ness, immensity** *n.*

**im•merge** *v.t.* to plunge into.

**im•merse** *v.t.* to plunge into anything, esp. a fluid; to dip. **immersable, immersible** *a.* **-d** *a.* **immersion** *n.*

**im•mi•grate** *v.i.* to migrate into a country. **immigrant** *n.* **immigration** *n.*

**im•mi•nent** *a.* threatening immediately to fall or occur. **imminence** *n.* **-ly** *adv.*

**im•mis•ci•ble** *a.* not capable of being mixed. **immiscibility** *n.*

**im•mit•i•ga•ble** *a.* incapable of being mitigated or appeased; relentless.

**im•mo•bile** *a.* incapable of being moved. **immobilize** *v.t.*

**im•mod•er•ate** *a.* exceeding just bounds; excessive. **-ness** *n.* **-ly** *adv.* **immoderation** *n.*

**im•mod•est** *a.* wanting in modesty or delicacy. **-ly** *adv.* **-y** *n.*

**im•mo•late** *v.t.* to sacrifice; to offer as a sacrifice. **immolation** *n.* immolator *n.*

**im•mor•al** *a.* uninfluenced by moral principle; wicked. **-ity** *n.* **-ly** *adv.*

**im•mor•tal** *a.* not mortal; undying; deathless; *n.* one exempt from death or decay; a divine being. **immortalize** *v.t.* to make famous for all time. **immortality** *n.*

**im•mov•a•ble** *a.* incapable of being moved. **-ness, immovability** *n.* **immovably** *adv.*

**im•mune** *a.* exempt; protected against any particular infection; *n.* one who is so protected. **immunization** *n.* **immunize** *v.t.* **immunity** *n.*

**im•mure** *v.t.* to enclose within walls; to imprison.

**im•mu•ta•ble** *a.* not susceptible to any alteration; invariable; unalterable. **immutability, immutableness** *n.*

**imp** *n.* a little demon; a mischievous child. **-ish** *a.*

**im•pact** *v.t.* to press or drive forcibly together. **impact** *n.* impulse communicated by one object striking another.

**im•pair** *v.t.* to diminish in quantity, value, excellence, or strength.

**im•pale** *v.t.* to fix on a sharpened stake; to put to death by fixing on an upright sharp stake. **-ment** *n.*

**im•pal•pa•ble** *a.* not capable of being felt or perceived by the senses, esp. by touch. **impalpability** *n.* **impalpably** *adv.*

**im•pan•el** *v.t.* to place a name on a panel or list. **-ment** *n.*

**im•part** *v.t.* to bestow a share or portion or.

**im•par•tial** *a.* not partial; without prejudice. **impartiality, impartialness** *n.*

**im•pas•sa•ble** *a.* incapable of being passed; impervious. **impassability, impassableness** *n.*

**im•passe** *n.* deadlock; dilemma.

**im•pas•sion** *v.t.* to move or affect strongly with passion. **-ed** *a.*

**im•pas•sive** *a.* not susceptible of pain or suffering; showing no emotion; calm. **-ly** *adv.* **-ness, impassivity** *n.*

**im•pa•tient** *a.* uneasy or fretful under trial or suffering; averse to waiting; restless. **impatience** *n.* **-ly** *adv.*

**im•pav•id** *a.* fearless.

**im•peach** *v.t.* to charge with a crime or misdemeanor; to call to account; to denounce; to challenge. **-able** *a.* **-er** *n.* **-ment** *n.*

**im•pec•ca•ble** *a.* not liable to sin or error; perfect. **impeccability, impeccancy** *n.*

**im•pe•cu•ni•ous** *a.* having no money; poor; hard up. **impecuniosity** *n.*

**im•pede** *v.t.* to stop the progress of; to hinder; to obstruct. **impedance** *n.* **impedible** *a.* **impediment** *n.* **impedimenta** *n.pl.* baggage, esp. military; encumbrances. **impedimental** *a.*

**im•pel** *v.t.* to drive or urge forward; to induce; to incite. *pr. p.* **-ling.** *pa. t.* and *pa. p.* **-led. -lent** *a.*

**im•pend** *v.i.* to hang over; to threaten; to be imminent. **-ence, -ency** *n.* **-ent** *a.*

**im•pen•e•tra•ble** *a.* incapable of being penetrated or pierced; obscure. **impenetrability** *n.*

**im•pen•i•tent** *a.* not repenting of sin; not contrite; obdurate.

**im•per•a•tive** *a.* expressive of command; authoritative. **-ly** *adv.*

**im•per•cep•ti•ble** *a.* not discernible by the senses; minute. **-ness, imperceptibility** *n.* **imperceptibly** *adv.* **imperceptive** *a.*

**im•per•fect** *a.* wanting some part or parts; defective; faulty; *n.* **-ly** *adv.* **imperfection** *n.*

**im•per•fo•rate, imperforated** *a.* not perforated or pierced.

**im•pe•ri•al** *a.* pertaining to an empire or to an emperor. **-ism** *n.* **-istic** *a.*

**im•per•il** *v.t.* to bring into peril; to endanger.

**im•pe•ri•ous** *a.* commanding; domineering; dictatorial. **-ly** *adv.* **-ness** *n.*

**im•per•ish•a•ble** *a.* not liable to decay. **-ness** *n.* imperishability *n.*

**im•per•ma•nence** *n.* want of permanence or stability.

**im•per•me•a•ble** *a.* not permitting passage. **impermeability** *n.* **-ness** *n.* **impermeably** *adv.*

**im•per•son•al** *a.* having no personal reference; objective. **-ly** *adv.*

**im•per•son•ate** *v.t.* to represent in character or form. **impersonation** *n.* **impersonator** *n.*

**im•per•ti•nent** *a.* having no bearing on the subject; irrelevant; impudent. **impertinence** *n.*

**im•per•turb•a•ble** *a.* incapable of being disturbed or agitated. **imperturbability** *n.* **imperturbably** *adv.* **imperturbation** *n.*

**im•per•vi•a•ble, im•per•vi•ous** *a.* not admitting of entrance or passage through; impenetrable; impassable. **-ness, imperviability** *n.* **imperviously** *adv.*

**im•pe•ti•go** *n.* *(med.)* a pustulous skin disease.

**im•pet•u•ous** *a.* rushing with force and violence; vehement; hasty. **-ly** *adv.* **-ness, impetuosity** *n.*

**im•pe•tus** *n.* the force with which a body moves; momentum.

**im•pi•e•ty** *n.* lack of reverence.

**im•pinge** *v.i.* to fall or dash against; to touch on; to infringe.

**im•pi•ous** *a.* not pious; proceeding from or manifesting a want of reverence. **-ly** *adv.* **-ness, impiety** *n.*

**im•pla•ca•ble** *a.* inexorable; not to be appeased; urelenting. **-ness, implacability** *n.*

**im•plant** *v.i.* to set in; to insert; to sow (seed).

**im•plead** *v.t.* to sue at law.

**im•ple•ment** *n.* a weapon, tool, or instrument; a utensil; *v.t.* to fulfill an obligation or contract which has been entered into. **-al** *a.* **-ation** *n.*

**im•pli•cate** *v.t.* to involve; to include; to entangle; to imply. **implication** *n.* the implied meaning. **implicative** *a.* **implicatively** *adv.* **implicit** *a.* implied; without questioning. **implicity** *adv.*

**im•plore** *v.t.* to entreat earnestly; to beseech. **imploration** *n.* **-r** *n.* **imploringly** *adv.*

**im•ply** *v.t.* to contain by implication; to signify; to insinuate.

**im•po•lite** *a.* rude; discourteous. **-ly** *adv.* **-ness** *n.*

**im•pol•i•tic** *a.* ill-advised; not in the best interests of; inexpedient. **impolicy** *n.* injudicious action. **-ly** *adv.*

**im•pon•der•a•ble** *a.* without perceptible weight; not able to be weighed. **-ness, imponderability** *n.*

**im•port** *v.t.* to bring in from abroad; to convey a meaning; to be of consequence. **-ance** *n.* consequence; moment. *a.* **-antly** *adv.* **-ation** *n.* act of bringing from another country.

**im•por•tune** *v.t.* to request with urgency; to entreat; to solicit. **importunacy, importunateness** *n.* **importunate** *a.* earnestly solicitous; troublesome. **importunately** *adv.*

**im•pose** *v.t.* to lay on; to levy; to lay, as a charge or tax; to force oneself upon others; *v.i.* (with *upon*) to deceive; to take undue advantage of a person's good-nature; to impress. **imposable**. *a.* **imposing** *a.* adapted to impress considerably; commanding; grand. **imposition** *n.*

**im•pos•si•ble** *a.* that which cannot be done. **impossibility** *n.*

**im•post** *n.* tax duty.

**im•pos•tor** *n.* one who assumes a false character. **imposture** *n.* deception.

**im•po•tent** *a.* powerless; wanting natural strength. **impotence, impotency** *n.*

**im•pound** *v.t.* to confine cattle in a pound or pen; to restrain within limits.

**im•pov•er•ish** *v.t.* to reduce to poverty; to exhaust the strength, richness, or fertility of land. **-er** *a.* **-ment** *n.*

**im•prac•ti•ca•ble** *a.* not able to be accomplished; unfeasible. **impracticability, impracticableness** *n.* **impractical** *a.*

**im•pre•cate** *v.t.* to invoke by prayer (evil) upon; to curse. **imprecation** *n.* **imprecatory** *a.*

**im•preg•na•ble** *a.* not to be stormed or taken by assault; not to be moved, impressed, or shaken. **impregnability** *n.* **impregnably** *adv.*

**im•preg•nate** *v.t.* to make pregnant; to render fertile; to saturate; to imbue. **impregnable** *a.* **impregnation** *n.*

**im•pre•sa•ri•o** *n.* an organizer of public entertainments.

**im•press** *v.t.* to take forcibly, persons or goods, for public service; to commandeer. **-ment** *n.*

**im•press** *v.t.* to press in or upon; to make a mark or figure upon; to fix deeply in the mind; to stamp. *n.* a mark made by pressure. **-ibility** *n.* susceptibility. **-ible** *a.* **-ibly** *adv.* **impression** *n.* **impressionable** *a.* **-ive** *a.* **-ively** *adv.* **-iveness** *n.*

**im•pres•sion•ism** *n.* a revolutionary modern movement, originating in France, in art, literature and music, aiming at reproducing the *impression* which eye and mind gather, rather than representing actual fact. **impressionist** *n.*

**im•pri•ma•tur** *n.* a license to print a book.

**im•print** *v.t.* to mark by pressure; to fix indelibly *n.* an impression.

**im•prob•a•ble** *a.* unlikely. **improbability** *n.* **improbably** *adv.*

**im•pro•bi•ty** *n.* want of integrity or rectitude; dishonesty.

**im•promp•tu** *adv.* or *a.* offhand.

**im•prop•er** *a.* unsuitable to the end or design; unfit; indecent; inaccurate. **-ly** *adv.* **impropriety** *n.*

**im•prove** *v.t.* to make better; *v.i.* to grow better. **improvability, improvableness** *n.* **improvable** *a.* **improvably** *adv.* **-ment** *n.* **improvingly** *adv.*

**im•prov•i•dent** *a.* not prudent or foreseeing. **improvidence** *n.*

**im•pro•vise** *v.t.* to extemporize; to make the best of materials at hand; to compose, speak or perform without preparation. **improvisation** *n.* **-r** *n.*

**im•pru•dent** *a.* lacking in discretion. **imprudence** *n.* **-ly** *adv.*

**im•pu•dent** *a.* brazen; boldfaced; rude. **impudence** *n.* **-ly** *adv.*

**im•pugn** *v.t.* to call in question; to contradict. **-able** *a.* **-er** *n.* **-ment** *n.*

**im•pulse** *n.* the motion or effect produced by a sudden action or applied force. **impulsion** *n.* **impulsive** *a.* **impulsively** *adv.* **impulsiveness** *n.*

**im•pu•ni•ty** *n.* exemption from punishment.

**im•pure** *a.* not pure; mixed; adulterated; foul; unchaste. **-ly** *adv.* **impurity, impureness** *n.*

**im•pute** *v.t.* to ascribe to (in a bad sense); to attribute to. **imputable** *a.* **imputableness, imputability** *n.* **imputation** *n.* **imputative** *a.* **imputatively** *adv.*

**in** *prep.* within; inside of; indicating a present relation to time, space, or condition; *adv.* inside; closely.

**in•a•bil•i•ty** *n.* want of strength, means, or power.

**in•ac•cu•rate** *a.* not correct; not according to truth or reality; erroneous. **inaccuracy** *n.* **-ly** *adv.*

**in•ac•tive** *a.* not disposed to action or effort; idle. **inaction** *n.* **inactivate** *v.t.* to make inactive. **inactivation** *n.* **-ly** *adv.* **inactivity** *n.*

**in•ad•e•quate** *a.* insufficient. **inadequacy** *n.* **-ly** *adv.* **-ness** *n.*

**in•ad•mis•si•ble** *a.* not allowable; improper. **inadmissibly** *adv.*

**in•ad•vert•ent** *a.* not turning the mind to a matter; inattentive; thoughtless; careless. **inadvertence, inadvertency** *n.* **-ly** *adv.*

**in•al•ien•a•ble** *a.* incapable of being separated or transferred.

**in•ane** *a.* empty; void; foolish; silly. **inanition** *n.* **inanity** *n.*

**in•an•i•mate** *a.* destitute of life or spirit. **inanimation** *n.* **-ness** *n.*

**in•ap•pli•ca•ble** *a.* unsuitable; irrelevant.

**in•ap•pre•ci•a•ble** *a.* not worth reckoning.

**in•ap•pro•pri•ate** *a.* unsuitable; at the wrong time. **-ly** *adv.* **-ness** *n.*

**in•apt** *a.* inappropriate; unsuitable; awkward. **-itude** *n.* **-ly** *adv.*

**in•ar•tic•u•late** *a.* unable to put one's ideas in words; not uttered distinctly. **-ly** *adv.* **-ness** *n.* **-inarticulation** *n.*

**in•au•di•ble** *a.* not able to be heard. **inaudibility, inaudibleness** *n.* **inaudibly** *adv.*

**in•au•gu•rate** *v.t.* to induct into an office in a formal manner. **inaugural, inauguratory** *a.* **inauguration** *n.* **inaugurator** *n.*

**in•aus•pi•cious** *a.* ill-omened. **-ly** *adv.* **-ness** *n.*

**in•born** *a.* born in or with; innate; natural; inherent.

**in•bred** *a.* bred within; innate. **inbreed** *v.t.* to mate animals of the same blood stock; to marry within the family or tribe. **inbreeding** *n.*

**in•cal•cu•la•ble** *a.* countless; beyond calculation; uncertain. **incalculability, -ness** *n.*

**in•can•des•cent** *a.* glowing with white heat and providing light. **incandescense** *n.*

**in•can•ta•tion** *n.* a formula or charm-words used to produce magical or supernatural effect. **incantatory** *a.*

**in•ca•pa•ble** *a.* wanting ability or capacity. **incapability** *n.*

**in•ca•pa•ci•tate** *v.t.* to render incapable. **incapacitation** *n.* **incapacity** *n.*

**in•car•cer•ate** *v.t.* to confine; to imprison. **incarcerator, incarceration** *n.*

**in•car•na•dine** *a.* flesh-colored; of a carnation color; crimson; *v.t.* to dye crimson.

**in•car•nate** *v.t.* to put into concrete form; to embody in flesh; *a.* embodied in flesh; typified. **incarnation** *n.*

**in•cen•di•ar•y** *n.* one who maliciously sets fire to property; an agitator who inflames passions. **incendiarism** *n.*

**in•cense** *v.t.* to inflame to violent anger.

**in•cense** *n.* a mixture of aromatic gums and spices which, when burned produces a sweet-smelling smoke.

**in•cen•tive** *a.* inciting; provoking; *n.* motive; stimulus.

**in•cep•tion** *n.* beginning; start; origin. **inceptive** *a.* **inceptively** *adv.*

**in•ces•sant** *a.* continuing or following without interruption. **incessancy** *n.* **-ly** *adv.*

**in•cest** *n.* sexual intercourse of kindred within the forbidden degrees. **-uous** *a.*

**inch** *n.* twlefth part of a linear foot; *v.i.* to push forward by slow degrees.

**in•cho•ate** *a.* just begun; rudimentary; incipient. **-ly** *adv.* **inchoation** *n.* **inchoative** *a.*

**in•ci•dent** *a.* liable to happen; subordinate to; *n.* that which takes place; event. **incidence** *n.* **-al** *a.* and *n.* **-ally** *adv.* **-alness** *n.*

**in•cin•er•ate** *v.t.* to consume by fire. **incineration** *n.* **incinerator** *n.* furnace for consuming refuse.

**in•cip•i•ent** *a.* beginning; originating. **incipience, incipiency** *n.*

**in•cise** *v.t.* to cut into. **incision** *n.* the act of cutting with a sharp instrument; a cut; gash. **incisive** *a.* having the quality of cutting or penetrating; sharp; biting. **incisively** *adv.* **incisiveness** *n.* **incisor** *n.* one of the eight front cutting teeth.

**in•cite** *v.t.* to move the mind to action. **incitant** *n.* and *a.* **incitation** *n.* **-ment** *n.*

**in•clem•ent** *a.* severe; harsh; stormy. **inclemency** *n.*

**in•cline** *v.t.* to cause to deviate from a line or direction; to give a tendency to, as to to the will or affections; to bend; *v.i.* to deviate from the vertical; to be disposed; *n.* an ascent or descent; a slope. **inclination** *n.*

**in•clude** *v.t.* to confine within; to comprise. **inclusion** *n.* **inclusive** *a.* **inclusively** *adv.*

**in•cog•ni•to** *a.* and *adv.* in a disguise; *n.* *(fem* **incognita***)* the state of being unknown; a person who conceals his identity.

**in•co•her•ent** *a.* not connected or clear; confused. **incoherence** *n.* **-ly** *adv.* **incoherency** *n.*

**in•com•bus•ti•ble** *a.* not capable of being burned. **incombustibility, incombustibleness** *n.* **incombustibily** *adv.*

**in•come** *n.* the gain or reward from one's labors or investments. **incoming** *n.* and *a.*

**in•com•men•su•ra•ble** *a.* having no common measure or standard of comparison. **-ness** *n.* **incommensurably** *adv.* **incommensurate** *a.* **incommensurately** *adv.*

**in•com•mode** *v.t.* to put to inconvenience or discomfort; to hinder. **incommodious** *a.* **incommodiously** *adv.* **incommodity** *n.*

**in•com•mu•ni•ca•ble** *a.* incapable of being communicated or shared. **incommunicability** *n.* **-ness** *n.* **incommunicably** *adv.* **incommunicative** *a.* reserved.

**in•com•pa•ra•ble** *a.* not admitting any degree of comparison; unequaled. **incomparability** *n.* **-ness** *n.* **incomparably** *adv.*

**in•com•pat•i•ble** *a.* incapable of existing side by side. **incompatibility, incompatibleness** *n.* **incompatibly** *adv.*

**in•com•pe•tent** *a.* not efficient in the performance of function. **incompetence** *n.*

**in•com•plete** *a.* defective; unfinished; imperfect. **-ly** *adv.*

**in•com•pre•hen•si•ble** *a.* incapable of being comprehended or understood. **-ness, incomprehensibility, incomprehension** *n.* **incomprehensibly** *adv.* **incomprehensive** *a.* limited; not extensive.

**in•com•pres•si•ble** *a.* cannot be compressed or reduced in bulk.

**in•con•ceiv•a•ble** *a.* not capable of being conceived in the mind; unthinkable. **inconceivability, inconceivableness** *n.* **inconceivably** *adv.*

**in•con•clu•sive** *a.* not decisive or conclusive. **-ly** *adv.*

**in•con•gru•ous** *a.* inappropriate; not reciprocally agreeing; *(Math.)* not coinciding. **incongruent** *a.* **incongruity, incongruousness** *n.*

**in•con•se•quent** *a.* not following from the premises; illogical. **inconsequence** *n.* **inconsequential** *a.* not to the point; illogical; of no import; trivial. **inconsequentially** *adv.*

**in•con•sid•er•a•ble** *a.* unworthy of consideration; unimportant.

**in•con•sid•er•ate** *a.* thoughtless; careless of others' feelings.

**in•con•sis•tent** *a.* liable to sudden and unexpected change. **inconsistency** *n.* **-ly** *adv.*

**in•con•spic•u•ous** *a.* scarcely noticeable.

**in•con•stant** *a.* not constant or consistent; subject to change. **inconstancy** *n.* **-ly** *adv.*

**in•con•ti•nent** *a.* morally incapable of restraint. **incontinence, incontinency** *n.* **-ly** *adv.*

**in•con•tro•vert•i•ble** *a.* too clear or certain to admit of dispute; unquestionable. **incontrovertibly** *adv.*

**in•con•ven•ient** *a.* awkward; unsuitable. **inconvenience** *v.t.* **inconvenience, inconveniency** *n.* **-ly** *adv.*

**in•con•vert•i•ble** *a.* cannot be changed or exchanged. **inconvertibility** *n.*

**in•co•or•di•nate** *a.* not in orderly relation with one another.

**in•cor•po•rate** *v.t.* and *v.i.* to combine, as different ingredients, into one body or

mass. **incorporation** *n.* **incorporative** *a.* **incorporeal** *a.* not possessed of a body. **incorporeality** *n.*
**in•cor•rect** *a.* not in accordance with the truth; improper -**ly** *adv.* -**ness** *n.*
**in•cor•ri•gi•ble** *a.* beyond any hope of reform.
**in•cor•rupt** *a.* morally pure. -**ible** *a.* -**ibility** *n.* -**ly** *adv.* -**ness** *n.*
**in•crease** *v.t.* to make greater; to extend; to lengthen; *v.t.* to become greater; *n.* growth; produce; interest; progeny. **increasable** *a.* **increasingly** *adv.*
**in•cred•i•ble** *a.* impossible to be believed. **incredibility, -ness** *n.* **incredibly** *adv.*
**in•cred•u•lous** *a.* not disposed to believe; showing unbelief. **incredulity** *n.* -**ness** *n.* -**ly** *adv.*
**in•cre•ment** *n.* increase; matter added; growth. -**al** *a.*
**in•crim•i•nate** *v.t.* to charge with a crime; to involve one in a criminal action. **incriminatory** *a.*
**in•crust, encrust** *v.t.* to charge with a crime; to involve one in a criminal action. **incriminatory** *a.*
**in•cu•bate** *v.i.* to sit, as on eggs, for hatching; of disease germs, to pass through the stage between infection and appearance of symptoms; *v.t.* to hatch; to ponder over. **incubation** *n.* **incubative, incubatory** *a.* **incubator** *n.* a cabinet used

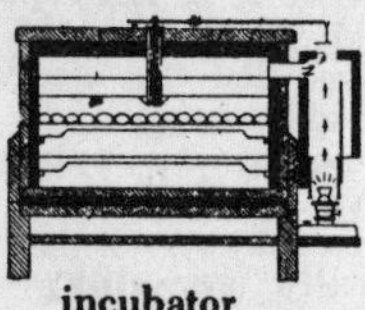
**incubator**

to hatch eggs; similar devices for premature infants or bacterial cultures.
**in•cu•bus** *n.* a nightmare; any burdensome or depressing influence.
**in•cul•cate** *v.t.* to urge forcibly and repreatedly; to impress by admonition. **inculcation** *n.* **inculcator** *n.*
**in•cum•bent** *a.* lying or resting upon; *n.* holder of an office. **incumbency** *n.*
**in•cur** *v.t.* to become liable to. *pr. p.* -**ring.** *pa. t.* and *pa. p.* -**red.**
**in•cur•a•ble** *a.* not able to be cured; *n.* one beyond cure. **incurability** *n.*
**in•cu•ri•ous** *a.* not inquisitive. -**ly** *adv.*
**in•cur•sion** *n.* a raid into a territory with hostile intention. **incursive** *a.*
**in•curve** *v.t.* to bend into a curve; *v.i.* to bend inward. **incurvate** *v.t.* to bend inward or upward; *a.* curved in.
**in•debt•ed** *a.* placed under an obligation. -**ness** *n.*
**in•de•cent** *a.* unbecoming; immodest; obscene. **indecency** *n.* -**ly** *adv.*
**in•de•ci•pher•a•ble** *a.* incapable of being deciphered; illegible.
**in•de•ci•sion** *n.* irresoluteness. **indecisive** *a.* **indecisively** *adv.* **indecisiveness** *n.*
**in•de•clin•a•ble** *a.* *(Gram.)* having no inflections or cases.
**in•dec•o•rous** *a.* contrary to good manners. -**ly** *adv.* -**ness, indecorum** *n.*
**in•deed** *adv.* in reality; in truth; in fact; certainly. *interj.* denotes surprise.
**in•de•fat•i•ga•ble** *a.* incapable of being fatigued; unwearied; untiring. -**ness, indefatigability** *n.* **indefatigably** *adv.*
**in•de•fea•si•ble** *a.* not to be defeated. **indefeasibility** *n.* **indefeasibly** *adv.*
**in•de•fen•si•ble** *a.* incapable of being maintained, vindicated, or justified; untenable.
**in•de•fin•a•ble** *a.* not able to be defined. **indefinably** *adv.*
**in•def•i•nite** *a.* having no known limits. -**ly** *adv.* -**ness, indefinitude** *n.*
**in•del•i•ble** *a.* not to be blotted out or erased; ineffaceable; ingrained. **indelibility, -ness** *n.* **indelibly** *adv.*
**in•del•i•cate** *a.* offensive to good manners or to purity of mind; indecorous. **indelicacy** *n.* -**ly** *adv.*
**in•dem•ni•fy** *v.t.* to reimburse; to free one from the consequences of a technically illegal act. **indemnification** *n.* **indemnitor** *n.* **indemnity** *n.* an agreement to render a person immune from a contingent liability.
**in•de•mon•stra•ble** *a.* cannot be demonstrated or proved.
**in•dent** *v.t.* to cut into points or inequalities; to make notches or holes in; *(Print.)* to begin the first line of a paragraph farther away from the margin than the remaining lines; *v.i.* to wind back and forth; to make an agreement; to make an order in duplicate. -**ation** *n.* a notch; a depression. -**ure** *n.* a contract of apprenticeship.
**in•de•pen•dent** *a.* not dependent; not subject to the control of others. **independence, independency** *n.* -**ly** *adv.*
**in•de•scrib•a•ble** *a.* incapable of being described.
**in•de•struct•i•ble** *a.* not able to be destroyed; imperishable. **indestructibility** *n.* **indestructibly** *adv.*
**in•de•ter•mi•na•ble** *a.* cannot be determined, classified, or fixed. -**ness** *n.* **indeterminably** *adv.* **indeterminate** *a.* **indeterminately** *adv.* **indeterminateness, indetermination** *n.* an unsettled or wavering state of mind.
**in•dex** *n.* any table for facilitating reference in a book; a directing sign; that which points out, shows, indicates, or manifests; a pointer or hand which directs to anything; the forefinger or pointing finger; *pl.* -**es, indices.** *v.t.* to provide with an index or table references.
**In•di•a** *n.* a country in Asia, named from river *Indus.*
**In•di•an** *a.* pert. to India in Asia, to the East Indies, or to the aborigines of America; *n.* a native of India in Asia, of the East Indies, or one of the aboriginal inhabitants of America. *n.*
**in•di•cate** *v.t.* to point out; to be a sign of; to denote. **indication** *n.* **indicative** *a.* and *n.* **indicatively** *adv.* **indicator** *n.* **indicatory** *a.*
**in•dict** *v.t.* to charge with a crime; to accuse; to arraign. -**able** *a.* -**ment** *n.*

**in•dif•fer•ent** *a.* uninterested; without concern; not making a difference; neither good not bad. **indifference** *n.* **-ly** *adv.*

**in•di•gene** *n.* an aborigine; a native animal or plant. Also **indigen. indigenous** *a.* born or originating in a country; native. **indigenously** *adv.*

**in•di•gent** *a.* destitute of property or means of subsistence. **indigence** *n.*

**in•di•ges•ted** *a.* not digested; lacking order or system. **indigestibility** *n.* **indigestible** *a.* **indigestibly** *adv.* **indigestion** *n.* dyspepsia. **indigestive** *a.*

**in•dig•nant** *a.* moved by a feeling of wrath, mingled with scorn or contempt; roused. **-ly** *adv.* **indignation** *n.* **indignity** *n.* affront; contemptuous treatment.

**in•di•go** *n.* a blue dye-stuff; *a.* of a deep-blue color.

**in•di•rect** *a.* not direct or straight; crooked; dishonest. **-ion** *n.* roundabout way; trickery. **-ly** *adv.* **-ness** *n.*

**in•dis•creet** *a.* imprudent; injudicious; reckless. **-ly** *adv.* **indiscretion** *n.*

**ind•dis•crim•i•nate** *a.* not making any distinction. **-ly** *adv.* **indiscriminating, indiscriminative** *a.* **indiscrimination** *n.*

**in•dis•pen•sa•ble** *a.* absolutely necessary. **indispensability, -ness** *n.* **indispensably** *adv.*

**in•dis•pose** *v.t.* to render unfit or unsuited; to render averse or disinclined (toward). **-d** *a.* averse; ill. **indisposition** *n.*

**in•dis•put•a•ble** *a.* too obvious to be disputed.

**in•dis•sol•u•ble** *a.* perpetually binding or obligatory; inviolable. **-ness. indissolubility** *n.* **indissolubly** *adv.*

**in•dis•tinct** *a.* not distinct or distinguishable. **-ive** *a.* **-ly** *adv.*

**in•dis•tin•guish•a•ble** *a.* may not be distinguished. **-ness** *n.* **indistinguishably** *adv.*

**in•dite** *v.t.* to compose; to write. **-ment** *n.*

**in•di•vid•u•al** *a.* not divided; peculiar to single person or thing; *n.* a single being, or thing. **-ization** *n.* **-ize, individuate** *v.t.* **-ism** *n.* theory which asserts the rights of the individual as against those of the community. **-ist** *n.* **-istic** *a.* **-ity** *n.* **-ly** *adv.*

**in•di•vis•i•ble** *a.* not divisible; not separate. **indivisibility, -ness** *n.* **indivisibly** *adv.*

**in•doc•tri•nate** *v.t.* to instruct; to imbue with political or religious principles and dogmas. **indoctrination** *n.*

**in•do•lent** *a.* habitually idle or lazy. **indolence, indolency** *n.* **-ly** *adv.*

**in•dom•i•ta•ble** *a.* not to be subdued. **indomitably** *adv.*

**In•do•ne•sia** *n.* Republic of S.E. Asia (since 1945). **-n** *a.*

**in•door** *a.* being within doors. **indoors** *adv.*

**in•dorse, in•dorse•ment** See **en•dorse.**

**in•du•bi•ta•ble** *a.* too obvious to admit of doubt. **indubitably** *adv.*

**in•duce** *v.t.* to overcome by persuasion or argument; to produce or cause (as electricity). **-ment** *n.* **-r** *n.* **inducible** *a.*

**in•duct** *v.t.* to bring in or introduce; to install or put formally into office. **-ion** *n.* **-ional** *a.* **-ive** *a.* **-ively** *adv.* **-or** *n.*

**in•dulge** *v.t.* to give freedom or scope to; to allow one his own way; to gratify; to give oneself to the habit or practice of. **-nce** *n.* **-nt** *a.* yielding; compliant; very forbearing. **-ntly** *adv.*

**in•du•rate** *v.t.* to make hard; to deprive of sensibility; *v.i.* grow hard.

**in•dus•try** *n.* habitual diligence in any employment, bodily or mental; a particular branch of trade or manufacture. **industrial** *a.* pert. to industry or manufacture. **industrialism** *n.* **industrially** *adv.* **industrious** *a.* diligent. **industriously** *adv.* **industriousness** *n.*

**in•e•bri•ate** *v.t.* to make drunk; to exhilarate; *a.* intoxicated; *n.* a habitual drunkard. **inebriation, inebriety** *n.* **inebrious** *a.*

**in•ed•i•ble** *a.* not eatable. **inedibility** *n.*

**in•ef•fa•ble** *a.* incapable of being expressed in words. **-ness, ineffability** *n.* **ineffably** *adv.*

**in•ef•face•a•ble** *a.* incapable of being rubbed out. **ineffaceably** *adv.*

**in•ef•fec•tive** *a.* incapable of producing any effect or the effect intended. **-ly** *adv.* **ineffectual** *a.* **ineffectuality, ineffectualness** *n.* **ineffectually** *adv.*

**in•ef•fi•ca•cy** *n.* want of power to produce the proper effect. **inefficacious** *a.* **inefficaciously** *adv.*

**in•ef•fi•ci•ent** *a.* not fitted to perform work in a capable, economical way. **inefficiency** *n.* **-ly** *adv.*

**in•e•las•tic** *a.* not elastic. **inelasticity** *n.*

**in•el•e•gant** *a.* lacking in form or beauty **inelegance, inelegancy** *n.* **-ly** *adv.*

**in•el•i•gi•ble** *a.* unsuitable; legally disqualified. **ineligibility** *n.*

**in•e•luc•ta•ble** *a.* inevitable. **ineluctability** *n.*

**in•ept** *a.* not apt or fit; inexpert. **-itude, -ness** *n.* **-ly** *adv.*

**in•e•qual•i•ty** *n.* want of equaltiy; disparity.

**in•eq•ui•ta•ble** *a.* not fair or just.

**in•e•rad•i•ca•ble** *a.* incapable of being rooted out; deep-seated.

**in•ert** *a.* without the power of action or resistance; sluggish. **inertia** *n.* **-ly** *adv.* **-ness** *n.*

**in•es•cap•a•ble** *a.* inevitable.

**in•es•sen•tial** *a.* not necessary.

**in•es•ti•ma•ble** *a.* not possible to be estimated. **inestimably** *adv.*

**in•ev•i•ta•ble** *a.* unavoidable. **-ness, inevitability** *n.* **inevitably** *adv.*

**in•ex•act** *a.* not exact; not strictly true. **-itude, -ness** *n.*

**in•ex•cus•a•ble** *a.* not admitting excuse of justification; unpardonable.

**in•ex•haust•i•ble** *a.* incapable of being exhausted, emptied, or spent; unfailing. **inexhaustibility** *n.* **inexhaustibly** *adv.* **inexhaustive** *a.*

**in•ex•o•ra•ble** *a.* not to be persuaded or moved by entreaty; unyielding. **-ness, inexorability** *n.* **inexorably** *adv.*

**in•ex•pe•di•ent** *a.* not advisable; impolitic; undesirable at the moment. **inexpedience, inexpediency** *n.*

**in•ex•pen•sive** *a.* cheap.
**in•ex•pe•ri•ence** *n.* absense or want or experience. **-d** *a.*
**in•ex•pert** *a.* unskilled; clumsy. **-ness** *n.*
**in•ex•pi•a•ble** *a.* admitting of no atonement; implacable; inexorable.
**in•ex•pli•ca•ble** *a.* incapable of being explained. **inexplicability** *n.* **inexplicably** *adv.*
**in•ex•plic•it** *a.* not explicit; not clearly stated; equivocal.
**in•ex•press•i•ble** *a.* cannot be expressed; indescribable. **inexpressibly** *adv.*
**in•ex•pres•sive** *a.* not expressive; lacking emphasis; insignificant.
**in•ex•ten•si•ble** *a.* not capable of extension. **inextensibility** *n.*
**in•ex•tin•guish•a•ble** *a.* cannot be extinguished; unquenchable.
**in•ex•tri•ca•ble** *a.* not to be extricated or disentangled. **inextricably** *adv.*
**in•fal•li•ble** *a.* incapable of error. **infallibilism, infallibility** *n.* **infallibly** *adv.*
**in•fa•my** *n.* total loss of reputation; public disgrace; ill-fame. **infamous** *a.* **infamously** *adv.*
**in•fant** *n.* a young baby. **infancy** *n.* **infanticide** *n.* the killing of a newly-born child. **-ile** *a.* pert. to infants; extremely childish.
**in•fan•try** *n.* foot-soldiers.
**in•fat•u•ate** *v.t.* to render foolish; to inspire with a foolish passion. **-d** *a.* **infatuation** *n.* excessive and foolish love.
**in•fea•si•ble** *a.* not capable of being done or accomplished; impracticable.
**in•fect** *v.t.* to affect (with disease); to make noxious; to corrupt. **-ion** *n.* **-ious. -ive. -iously** *adv.*
**in•fe•li•i•ty** *n.* unhappiness; anything not appropriate. **infelicitous** *a.*
**in•fer** *v.t.* to draw as a conclusion; to deduce. *pr. p.* **-ring.** *pa. t.* and *pa. p.* **-red. -able** *a.* **-ence** *n.* **-ential** *a.* deduced or deducible by inference. **-entially** *adv.*
**in•fe•ri•or** *a.* lower in rank, order, or excellence; *n.* a person of a lower rank or station. **-ity** *n.* **-ly** adv.
**in•fer•nal** *a.* pert. to the lower regions; hellish. **-ity** *n.* **-ly** *adv.* **inferno** *n.* hell.
**in•fest** *v.t.* to inhabit; to swarm in such numbers as to be a source of annoyance. **-ed** *a.* **-ation** *n.*
**in•fi•del** *a.* unbelieving; *n.* one who is without religious faith; unbeliever. **-ity** *n.* unfaithfulness to the marriage contract.
**in•field** *n.* *(Baseball)* the three basemen and the short stop, or the diamond; a field in close proximity to a farmhouse. **-er** *n.*
**in•fil•trate** *v.t.* and *v.i.* to filter into; to enter gradually. **infiltration** *n.*
**in•fi•nite** *a.* unlimited in time or space; *n.* the boundlessness and immeasurableness of the universe. **-ly** *adv.* **-ness** *n.* **infinitesimal** *a.* **infinitesimally** *adv.* **infinitude** *n.* boundlessness. **infinity** *n.* unlimited and endless extent.
**in•fin•i•tive** *n.* the simple form of the verb which can be preceded by *to (to be); a.* not defined or limited.
**in•firm** *a.* not strong; feeble. **-ary** *n.* a hospital. **-ity** disease; failing. **-ly** *adv.*
**in•flame** *v.t.* to set on fire; to arouse, as desire. **imflammable** *a.* combustible. **inflammability, inflammableness** *n.* **inflammably** *adv.* **inflammation** *n.* inflaming; disease condition characterized by heat, redness and pain. **inflammatory** *a.* tending to arouse passions.
**in•flate** *v.t.* to swell with air or gas; to raise (price) artificially. **-d** *a.* swollen; bloated; bombastic. **inflatable** *a.* **inflation** *n.* swelling; increase in the amount of fiduciary money issued, beyond what is justified by the country's tangible resources; a rise in prices. **inflationary** *a.*
**in•flect** *v.t.* to bend; to modulate the voice. **-ion** *n.* a bending inwards or deviation; a variation in the tone of the voice. **-ional** *a.* **-ive** *a.* **inflexibility** *n.* **inflexible** *a.* incapable of being bent; unyielding to influence of entreaty. **inflexibly** *adv.*
**in•flict** *v.t.* to lay on; to afflict with something painful. **-ion** *n.* pain; burden. **-ive** *a.*
**in•flu•ence** *n.* power over men or things; effect on the mind; *v.t.* to act on the mind; to induce. **influential** *a.* **influentially** *adv.*
**in•flu•en•za** *n.* *(Med.)* an acute, infectious epidemic catarrhal fever.
**in•flux** *n.* act of flowing in; the mouth of a stream.
**in•fold, enfold** *v.t.* to wrap up; to enclose; to encircle.
**in•form** *v.t.* and *v.i.* to give information.
**in•form** *a.* without form. **-al** *a.* without formality, unceremonious. **ation** *n.* knowledge; intelligence; news. **-ative, -atory** *a.* educational. **-ed** *a.* **-er** *n.* one who gives information.
**in•frac•tion** *n.* breach; violation.
**in•fran•gi•ble** *a.* not capable of being broken; not to be violated. **infrangibility** *n.*
**in•fra•red** *a.* of the longer invisible heat rays below the red end of the visible spectrum.
**in•fre•quent** *a.* seldom happening. **infrequence, infrequency** *n.* **-ly** *adv.*
**in•fringe** *v.t.* to violate; to transgress. **-ment** *n.*
**in•fu•ri•ate** *v.t.* to enrage; to madden. **infuriation** *n.*
**in•fuse** *v.t.* to pour into; to instill; to inspire; to steep in order to extract soluble properties. **infusible** *a.* **infusibility** *n.* **infusion** *n.* act of infusing, instilling, or inspiring; aqueous solution containing the soluble parts of a substance.
**in•gen•ious** *a.* skilled in inventing new ideas; curious or clever in design. **-ly** *adv.* **-ness, ingenuity** *n.*
**in•ge•nue** *n.* an artless, naive, girl; *a.* frank; artless; innocent. **-ly** *adv.* **-ness** *n.*
**in•got** *n.* a metal casting, esp. of unwrought silver or gold.
**in•grain, engrain** *v.t.* to fix firmly in the mind; *a.* firmly fixed; dyed, before manufacture into articles. **-ed** *a.*

**in•grate** *n.* an ungrateful person. **ingratitude** *n.*
**in•gra•ti•ate** *v.t.* to work oneself into favor with another. **ingratiation** *n.*
**in•gre•di•ent** *n.* a component part of any mixture.
**in•gress** *n.* entrance.
**in•grow•ing** *a.* growing inwards, esp. of a toenail. **ingrowth** *n.* **ingrown** *a.*
**in•gur•gi•tate** *v.t.* to swallow up greedily or hastily; to engulf. **ingurgitation** *n.*
**in•hab•it** *v.t.* to live or dwell in; to occupy. **-able** *a.* **-ant** *n.* **-ation** *n.*
**in•hale** *v.t.* to breath in. **inhalation** *n.*
**in•here** *v.i.* (usu. followed by *in*) to exist in. **-nce, -ncy** *n.* **-nt** *a.* **-ntly** *adv.*
**in•her•it** *v.t.* to receive by descent, or by will; to fall heir to; *v.i.* to succeed as heir. **-able** *a.* **-ance** *n.* **-or** *n* (*fem.* **-ress, -rix**).
**in•hib•it** *v.t.* to hold back; to restrain. **inhibition** *n.* a subconscious repressed emotion which controls attitude or behavior. **-ory** *a.*
**in•hos•pi•ta•ble** *a.* averse to showing kindness to guests; discourteous. **-ness, inhospitality** *n.* **inhospitably** *adv.*
**in•hu•man** *a.* not human or humane; without feeling or pity. **inhumane** *a.* cruel. **-ity** *n.*
**in•hume** *v.t.* to put into the ground; to bury. **inhumation** *n.*
**in•im•i•cal** *a.* like an enemy. **-ly** *adv.*
**in•im•i•ta•ble** *a.* defying imitation; incomparable. **inimitably** *adv.*
**in•iq•ui•ty** *n.* gross injustice. **iniquitous** *a.* **iniquitously** *adv.*
**in•i•tial** *a.* occurring at the beginning; *v.t.* to put one's initials to; *n.* the first letter of a word. **initiate** *v.t.* to begin; to instruct in the rudiments of; to admit into a society, etc., with formal rites; *n.* one who is initiated. **initiation** *n.* **initiative** *a.* serving to initiate; *n.* the first step; the quality of being able to set things going. **initiator** *n.* **initiatory** *a.*
**in•ject** *v.t.* to throw in; to force in; to introduce (a fluid) under the skin by means of a hollow needle. **-ion** *n.* **-or** *n.*
**in•ju•di•cious** *a.* ill-advised; inprudent; lacking in judgment. **injudicial** *a.* not according to the form of law. **-ly** *adv.*
**in•junc•tion** *n.* an order of command; an exhortation.
**in•jure** *v.t.* to do wrong, injury, damage, or injustice to. **injurious** *a.* **injuriously** *adv.* **injury** *n.*
**in•jus•tice** *n.* an unjust act.
**ink** *n.* a fluid for writing, printing and sketching. **-iness** *n.* **-y** *a.*
**ink•ling** *n.* a hint or whisper.
**in•land** *a.* remote from the sea; *n.* the interior part of a country. **-er** *n.*
**in•lay** *v.t.* to ornament, by cutting out part of a surface and inserting pieces of pearl, ivory, wood, etc., to form a pattern. *pa. p.* **inlaid.** *n.*
**in•let** *n.* an entrance; a small bay or creek.
**in•mate** *n.* a dweller in a house or institution; a fellow-lodger.
**inn** *n.* a house which provides lodging accomodation for travelers.
**in•nate** *a.* inborn; native; natural. **-ly** *adv.*
**in•ner** *a.* farther in; interior; private; not obvious; **-most, inmost** *a.* farthest in.
**in•ner•vate** Also **innerve,** *v.t.* to give nervous strength to; to stimulate. **innervation** *n.*
**in•ning** *n.* in games, a side's turn of batting; the ingathering of grain.
**in•no•cent** *a.* free from guilt; *n.* an innocent person, exp. a child. **innocence, innocency** *n.* **-ly** *adv.*
**in•noc•u•ous** *a.* producing no ill effects; harmless. **-ly** *adv.* **-ness.**
**in•no•vate** *v.t.* to make changes by introducing something new. **innovation** *n.*
**in•nox•ious** *a.* innocuous.
**in•nu•en•do** *n.* an allusive remark (usually deprecatory).
**in•nu•mer•a•ble** *a.* not able to be numbered. **innumerability** *n.* **innumerably** *adv.*
**in•nu•tri•tion** *n.* want of nutrition. **innutritious** *a.*
**in•ob•serv•ant** *a.* not observant; heedless. **inobservance** *n.*
**in•oc•u•late** *v.t.* (*Med.*) to introduce into the body pathogenic bacteria or living virus to secure immunity. **inoculation** *n.*
**in•op•er•a•ble** *a.* (*Surgery*) not in a condition for operating on. **inoperative** *a.* not operating; without effect.
**in•op•por•tune** *a.* unseasonable in time; untimely. **-ly** *adv.* **inopportunity** *n.*
**in•or•di•nate** *a.* not limited; disordered. **-ness** *n.* **-ly** *adv.* excessively.
**in•or•gan•ic** *a.* devoid of an organized structure; not derived from animal or vegatable life. **-ally** *adv.*
**in•os•cu•late** *v.t.* and *v.i.* to join by openings (arteries, etc.).
**in•pa•tient** *n.* a patient who is lodged and fed in a hospital.
**in•put** *n.* (*Elect.*) the power supplied to batter, condenser, etc.
**in•quest** *n.* a judicial inquiry.
**in•qui•e•tude** *n.* uneasiness either of body or of mind; restlessness.
**in•quire, enquire** *v.i.* to ask questions; to seek information; *v.t.* to ask about. **-r** *n.* **inquiring** *a.* **inquiringly** *adv.* **inquiry** *n.* investigation; a question.
**in•qui•si•tion** *n.* a strict investigation; official inquiry. **-al** *a.* **inquisitive** *a.* apt to ask questions; prying. **inquisitively** *adv.* **inquisitiveness** *n.* **inquisitor** *n.* **inquisitorial** *a.* **inquisitorially** *adv.*
**in•road** *n.* a sudden incursion into enemy territory.
**in•sane** *a.* unsound in mind; mentally diseased; lunatic. **-ly** *adv.* **-ness, insanity** *n.*
**in•sa•tia•ble** *a.* incapable of being satisfied; voracious; rapacious. **-ness, insatiability** *n.* **insatiably** *adv.*
**in•sa•ti•ate** *a.* not to be satisfied. **-ly** *adv.* **-ness** *n.*
**in•scribe** *v.t.* to write upon; to engrave; to address or dedicate. **inscribable** *a.* **-r** *n.* **inscription** *n.* **inscriptional, inscriptive** *a.*
**in•scru•ta•ble** *a.* incapable of being searched into and understood by inquiry or study; mysterious. **inscrutability, -ness**

*n.* **inscrutably** *adv.*

**in•sect** *n.* one of a class of invertebrate animals called the *Insecta.* **insecticide** *n.* killing insect pests. **-ivorous** *a.* living on insects.

**in•se•cure** *a.* not securely fixed; unguarded; having doubts and fears. **insecurity** *n.*

**in•sem•i•nate** *v.t.* to sow; to impregnate. **insemination** *n.*

**in•sen•sate** *a.* destitute of sense; without power of feeling. **-ly** *adv.*

**in•sen•si•ble** *a.* without bodily sensation; not perceived by the senses; unconscious; callous; imperceptible. **-ness** *n.* **insensibility, insensibly** *adv.*

**in•sen•si•tive** *a.* not sensitive; callous. **-ness, insensitivity** *n.*

**in•sen•ti•ent** *a.* not having perception; inanimate.

**in•sep•a•ra•ble** *a.* not divisible or separable. **inseparably** *adv.*

**in•sert** *v.t.* to put in; to place among; to introduce. *n.* anything inserted. **-ion** *n.*

**in•side** *prep.* or *adv.* within the sides of; in the interior; *a.* internal; interior; *n.* the part within.

**in•sid•i•ous** *a.* lying in wait; treacherous. **-ly** *adv.* **-ness** *n.*

**in•sight** *n.* view of the interior of anything; mental penetration.

**in•sig•ni•a** *n. pl.* symbols of authority, dignity, or office.

**in•sig•ni•fi•cant** *a.* having little importance, use or value; trifling. **insignificance, insignificancy** *n.* **-ly** *adv.*

**in•sin•cere** *a.* not sincere; dissembling; hypocritical. **-ly** *adv.* **insincerity** *n.*

**in•sin•u•ate** *v.t.* to introduce gently and adroitly; to suggest by remote allusion; to work oneself into favor; *v.i.* to ingratiate oneself. **insinuating** *a.* **insinuatory** *a.*

**in•sip•id** *a.* destitute of taste; deficient in spirit, life, or animation. **-ly** *adv.* **-ness, -ity** *n.*

**in•sip•i•ent** *a.* not wise; foolish. **insipience** *n.*

**in•sist** *v.i.* to dwell upon as a matter of special moment; to be urgent or pressing. **-ence** *n.* **-ency** *n.* **-ent** *a.*

**in•so•bri•e•ty** *n.* drunkeness.

**in•so•lent** *a.* proud and haughty. **insolence** *n.* contemptuous rudeness or arrogance. **-ly** *adv.*

**in•sol•u•ble** *a.* incapable of being dissolved; inexplicable. **insolubility, -ness** *n.* **insolvable** *a.*

**in•sol•vent** *a.* not able to pay one's debts; bankrupt. **insolvency** *n.*

**in•som•ni•a** *n.* chronic sleeplessness.

**in•so•much** *adv.* so that; to such a degree; in such wise that.

**in•sou•ci•ance** *n.* carelessness of feeling or manner. **insouciant** *a.*

**in•spect** *v.t.* to view narrowly and critically; to examine officially. **-ingly** *adv.* **inspection** *n.* **inspectional, -ive** *a.* **-or** *n.* official examiner. **-orate** *n.* **-orial** *a.*

**in•spire** *v.t.* to breathe in; to infuse thought or feeling into; to arouse; *v.i.* to give inspiration; to inhale. **inspirable** *a.* **inspiration** *n.* **inspirational** *a.* **inspiratory** *a.* **inspired** *a.*

**in•sta•bil•i•ty** *n.* want of stability or firmness.

**in•stall** *v.t.* to place in position; to induct, with ceremony, a person into an office. **installation** *n.* complete equipment of a building for hearing, lighting, etc.; generally, placing in position for use. **-ment** *n.* act of installing; a periodical payment.

**in•stance** *n.* case in point; example; *v.t.* to mention as an example; to cite. **instant** *a.* urgent; pressing; immediate; *n.* a particular point of time; moment. **instantaneity** *n.* **instantaneous** *a.* **instantaneously** *adv.* **instantaneousness** *n.* **instantly** *adv.* at once.

**in•stead** *adv.* in the stead, place, or room.

**in•step** *n.* the arched upper part of the human foot; that part of a shoe.

**in•sti•gate** *v.t.* to goad or urge forward; to incite, esp. to evil; to bring about. **instigation** *n.* **instigator** *n.*

**in•still** *v.t.* to put in by drops; to infuse slowly. **-ed. -ation, -ment** *n.*

**in•stinct** *n.* intuition; an innate train of reflexes; inborn impulse or propensity. **instinctively, instinctly** *adv.* **instinctivity** *n.*

**in•sti•tute** *v.t.* to establish; to set going; to originate; *n.* a society or organization established for promoting some particular work, scientific, educational, etc. **institution** *n.* the act of instituting or establishing; an established law, custom, or public occasion; an institute; **institutional** *a.* **institutionally** *adv.* **institutive** *a.* **institutively** *adv.* **institutor, -r** *n.*

**in•struct** *v.t.* to teach; to inform; to order or command. **-ible** *a.* **-ion** *n.* **-ional** *a.* **-ive** *a.* **-ively** *adv.* **-iveness** *n.* **-or** *n.*

**in•stru•ment** *n.* a tool or implement; a person or thing made use of; a means of producing musical sounds; *(Law)* a formal or written document. **-al** *a.* **-alist** *n.* one skilled in playing upon a musical instrument. **-ality** *n.* **-ally** *adv.* **-ation** *n.*

**in•sub•or•di•nate** *a.* disobedient; unruly. **insubordination** *n.*

**in•suf•fer•a•ble** *a.* not able to be endured; intolerable. **insufferably** *adv.*

**in•suf•fi•cient** *a.* not enough; deficient. **insufficiency** *n.* **-ly** *adv.*

**in•su•lar** *a.* pert. to or like an island. **-ism, -ity** *n.* **-ly** *adv.*

**in•su•late** *v.t.* to keep rigidly apart from contact with other people; to bar the passage of electricity, heat, sound, light, dampness, or vibration by the use of nonconducting materials. **insulation** *n.*

**in•su•lin** *n.* a hormone; organic drug for the treatment of diabetes.

**in•sult** *v.t.* to treat with insolence or contempt; *n.* gross abuse.

**in•su•per•a•ble** *a.* not able to be overcome or surmounted. **insuperability** *n.* **insuperably** *adv.*

**in•sup•port•a•ble** *a.* incapable of being borne or endured. **-ness** *n.*

**in•sure** *v.t.* to make sure or certain; to secure the payment of a sum in event of loss. **insurable** *a.* **insurance** *n.*

**in•sur•gent** *a.* rising in opposition to lawful authority; rebellious; *n.* one in revolt; a rebel. **insurgency** *n.* Also **insurgence.**

**in•sur•mount•a•ble** *a.* not able to be surmounted or overcome. **insurmountability** *n.* **insurmountably** *adv.*

**in•sur•rec•tion** *n.* a rising against civil or political authority. **-al, -ary** *a.* **-ist** *n.*

**in•sus•cep•ti•ble** *a.* not susceptible. **insusceptibility** *n.*

**in•take** *n.* that which is taken in; inlet of a tube or cylinder.

**in•tan•gi•ble** *a.* not perceptible to the touch; not clear to the mind. **-ness, intangibility** *n.* **intangibly** *adv.*

**in•te•ger** *n.* the whole of anything; whole number. **integral** *a.* constituting an essential part of a whole. **integrally** *adv.* **integrate** *v.t.* to make entire. **integration** *n.* **integrator** *n.* **integrity** *n.* the state of being entire; wholeness; probity; honesty.

**in•teg•u•ment** *n.* the outer protective layer of tissue which covers a plant or animal. **integumentary** *a.*

**in•tel•lect** *n.* the faculty of reasoning and thinking. **ive** *a.*

**in•tel•lect•u•al** *a.* of high mental capacity; *n.* one well endowed with intellect. **-ism** *n.* **-ly** *adv.*

**in•tel•li•gent** *a.* having or showing good intellect; quick at understanding. **intelligence** *n.* **-ly** *adv.* **-sia** *n.* the intellectual or cultured classes. **intelligible** *a.* that can be readily understood; rational. **intelligibleness, intelligibility** *n.* **intelligibly** *adv.*

**in•tem•per•ate** *a.* immoderate; indulging to excess any appetite or passion; extreme in climate. **intemperance** *n.* **-ly** *adv.*

**in•tend** *v.t.* and *v.i.* to design; to purpose; to mean; to have in mind. **-ant** *n.* one who has the charge of some public business. **-ancy** *n.* **-ed** *a.* and *n.*

**in•tense** *a.* to an extreme degree; very strong or acute; emotional. **-ly** *adv.* **-ness, intensity** *n.* **intensification** *n.* **intensify** *v.t.* and *v.i.* *pa. t.* and *pa. p.* **intensified.** **intensive** *a.* giving emphasis; unrelaxed; increasing in force. **intensively** *adv.*

**in•tent** *a.* havint the mind bent on an object; absorbed; *n.* intention. **-ion** *n.* design; aim; purpose. **-ional, -ioned** *a.* done purposely. **-ionally** *adv.* **-ly** *adv.* **-ness** *n.*

**in•ter-** *prefix,* between, among, with, amid.

**in•ter•act** *v.i.* to act mutually on each other. **-ion** *n.*

**in•ter•cede** *v.i.* to act as peacemaker; to plead in favor of one; to mediate. **-r** *n.* **intercession** *n.* **intercessor** *n.* **intercessorial, intercessory** *a.*

**in•ter•cept** *v.t.* to stop or obstruct passage. **-er, -or** *n.* **-ion** *n.* **-ive** *a.*

**in•ter•ces•sion, intercessor** See **intercede.**

**in•ter•change** *v.t.* to exchange; to reciprocate; *v.i.* to succeed alternately; to exchange places; *n.* access to a freeway; a mutual exchange. **-able** *a.* **-ability, -ableness** *n.*

**in•ter•communicate** *v.t.* to exchange conversations or messages. **intercommunication** *a., n.* **intercommunicative** *a.*

**in•ter•con•nect** *v.t.* and *v.i.* to connect mutually and intimately.

**in•ter•cos•tal** *a.* *(Anat.)* between the rigs.

**in•ter•course** *n.* communication between individuals; exchange of goods; coition.

**in•ter•cur•rent** *a.* running between or among; occurring during the course of another (disease).

**in•ter•de•pend** *v.i.* to depend mutually. **-ence** *n.* **-ent** *a.* **-ently** *adv.*

**in•ter•dict** *v.t.* to forbid; to prohibit; *n.* prohibition. **-ion** *n.* **-ive, -ory** *a.*

**in•ter•est** *v.t.* to engage and keep the attention of; *n.* special attention; regard to personal profit or advantage; curiosity; the profit per cent derived from money lent. **-ed** *a.* having a share in; feeling an interest in. **-edly** *adv.* **-edness** *n.* **-ing** *a.* appealing to or exciting one's interest or curiosity. **-ingly** *adv.*

**in•ter•fere** *v.i.* to be in or come into, opposition; to enter into or take part in the concerns of others; to intervene. **-nce** *n.* meddling with other people's business; uncalled-for intervention. **-r** *n.* **interferingly** *adv.*

**in•ter•im** *n.* the time between; the meantime; *a.* for the time being; temporary.

**in•te•ri•or** *a.* innter; internal; inland, away from coast or frontiers; *n.* the inside part or portion. **-ly** *adv.*

**in•ter•ject** *v.t.* to throw between; to insert; to exclaim abruptly. **-ion** *n.* act of throwing between; a word which expresses strong emotion or passion when suddenly uttered. **-ional, -ionary, -ory** *a.* **-ionally** *adv.*

**in•ter•lace** *v.t.* to lace together; to entwine.

**in•ter•lard** *v.t.* to diversify by mixture (of words, etc.).

**in•ter•line** *v.t.* to write or mark between the lines; to put an inner lining in a garment. **-al, -ar** *a.* **-ate** *v.t.*

**in•ter•lock** *v.t.* to unite by locking together; to fasten together so that one part cannot move without the other; *v.i.* to be locked or jammed together.

**in•ter•lo•cu•tion** *n.* dialogue; a conference; speaking in turn.

**in•ter•lope** *v.i.* to traffic without a proper license; to intrude into other people's affairs. **-r** *n.*

**in•ter•lude** *n.* a dramatic or musical performance given between parts of an independent play; an interval.

**in•ter•mar•ry** *v.i.* to connect families or races by a marriage between two of their members. **intermarriage** *n.*

**in•term•me•di•ate** *a.* lying or being between two extremes; intervening; *n.* anything in between; *v.i.* to mediate; to intervene. **intermediacy** *n.* **intermediary** *a.* and *n.* **intermedium** *n.* **intermediation** *n.*

**in•ter•ment** See **inter.**

**in•ter•mez•zo** *n.* a light dramatic entertainment between the acts; *(Mus.)* a short movement connecting more important ones.

**in•ter•mi•na•ble** *a.* endless; unlimited. **-ness** *n.* **interminably** *adv.*

**in•ter•min•gle** *v.t.* to mingle or mix together.

**in•ter•mit** *v.t.* to give up or forbear for a time; to interrupt; *v.i.* to cease for a time. *pr. p.* **-ting.** *pa. t., pa. p.* **-ted.** **intermission** *n.* intervening period of time. **intermissive.** *a.* coming after temporary cessations. **-tence, -tency** *n.* **-tent** *a.* occurring at intervals. **-tently** *adv.*

**in•ter•mix** *v.t.* and *v.i.* to mix together. **-ture** *n.*

**in•tern** *v.t.* to confine, esp. aliens or suspects in time of war; *n.* a resident doctor in a hospital. Also **interne.** **internee** *n.* one who is confined to a certain place. **-ment** *n.* **-ship** *n.*

**in•ter•nal** *a.* interior; inward; domestic, as opposed to foreign. **-ly** *adv.*

**in•ter•na•tion•al** *a.* pert. to the relations between nations. **-ist** *n.* **-ly** *adv.*

**in•ter•ne•cine** *a.* mutually destructive; deadly.

**in•ter•nee** See **intern.**

**in•ter•nist** *n.* a specialist in internal medicine.

**in•ter•pel•late** *v.t.* to interrupt a speaker in a legislative assembly by demanding an explanation. **interpellation** *n.* **interpellator** *n.*

**in•ter•pen•e•trate** *v.t.* to grow through one another; to penetrate thoroughly. **interpenetration** *n.*

**in•ter•plan•e•tar•y** *a.* situated between the planets.

**in•ter•play** *n.* reciprocal action of two things.

**in•ter•po•late** *v.t.* to insert new (esp. misleading) matter into a text; to interpose with some remark. **interpolation** *n.* **interpolator** *n.*

**in•ter•pose** *v.t.* and *i.* to place or come between; to offer, as aid or service; to interrupt. **interposal** *n.* **-r** *n.* **interposition** *n.*

**in•ter•pret** *v.t.* to explain the meaning of; to translate orally for the benefit of others. **-able** *a.* **-ation** *n.* **-ative** *a.* **-er** *n.*

**in•ter•reg•num** *a.* the time a throne is vacant between the death or abdication of a king and the accession of his successor; any interruption in continuity.

**in•ter•re•la•tion** *n.* reciprocal or mutual relation. **-ship** *n.*

**in•ter•ro•gate** *v.t.* to question. **interrogation** *n.* **interrogative** *a.* **interrogatory** *a.*

**in•ter•rupt** *v.t.* to break in upon; to break continuity of. **-edly** *adv.* **-er** *n.* **-ion** *n.* **-ive** *a.*

**in•ter•sect** *v.t.* to cut into or between; to divide into parts; to cross on another. **-ion** *n.* **-ional** *a.*

**in•ter•sperse** *v.t.* to scatter or place here and there. **interspersion** *n.*

**in•ter•stel•lar** *a.* passing between, or situated among, the stars. **-y.**

**in•ter•stice** *a.* a small gap or chink; a crevice. **interstitial** *a.*

**in•ter•twine** *v.t.* to twine or twist together.

**in•ter•val** *n.* time or distance between; a pause; a break.

**in•ter•vene** *v.i.* to come or be between; to interfere. **-r** *n.* **intervention** *n.* **interventionist** *n.* or *a.*

**in•ter•view** *n.* a meeting or conference; *v.t.* to have an interview with. **-er** *n.*

**in•tes•tate** *a.* not having made a valid will; *n.* a person who dies intestate. **intestacy** *n.*

**in•tes•tine** *a.* internal; domestic; *n. pl.* the bowels; the entrails. **intestinal** *a.*

**in•ti•mate** *a.* innermost; familiar; closely-related; *n.* an intimate friend; *v.t.* **intimate** to hint; to imply. **intimacy** *n.*

**in•tim•i•date** *v.t.* to force or deter by threatsl to inspire with fear. **intimidation** *n.* **intimidator** *n.*

**in•to** *prep.* expresses motion to a point within, or a change from one state to another.

**in•tol•er•a•ble** *a.* insufferable; unbearable. **-ness** *n.* **intolerably** *adv.* **intolerance** *n.* **intolerant** *a.* **intolerantly** *adv.*

**in•tone** *v.t.* to tuter or recite with a long drawn out musical note or tone; to chant; *v.i.* to modulate the voice; to give forth a deep protracted sound. **intonate** *v.t.* **intonation** *n.*

**in•tox•i•cate** *v.t.* to make drunk; to excite beyond self-control. **intoxicating** *a.* **intoxicant** *n.* **intoxication** *n.*

**in•tra-** *prefix,* within, inside of, used in the construction of many compound terms.

**in•trac•ta•ble** *a.* not to be managed or governed. **intractability, intractably** *adv.*

**in•tra•mu•ral** *a.* pert. to a single college or its students; within the walls or limits.

**in•tran•si•gent** *a.* refusing in any way to compromise; *n.* one who adopts this attitude. **intransigence,** *n.* **-ly** *adv.*

**in•tran•si•tive** *a. (Gram.)* denoting such verbs as express an action or state which is limited to the agent.

**in•trep•id** *a.* free from fear or trepidation. **-ity** *n.* undaunted courage. **-ly** *adv.*

**in•tri•cate** *a. involved; entangled; complicated; difficult.* **intricacy, -ness** *n.* **-ly** *adv.*

**in•trigue** *n.* a plot to effect some purpose by secret artifices; *v.i.* to scheme secretly; *v.t.* to fascinate; to arouse interest in. *pr. p.* **intriguing. intrigant, -r** *n.* **intriguing** *a.* **intriguingly** *adv.*

**in•trin•sic** *a.* from within; having internal value; inherent. **-ality** *n.* **-ally** *adv.*

**in•tro-** *prefix,* inwards, used in compound terms.

**in•tro•duce** *v.t.* to lead or bring in; to make known formally (one person to another); **introduction** *n.* **introductory, introductive** *a.* **introductively, inductorily** *adv.*

**in•tro•spect** *v.t.* to look within; to inspect; *v.i.* to pre-occupy oneself with one's own thoughts, emotions and feelings. **-ion** *n.* **-ive** *a.* **-ively** *adv.*

**in•tro•vert** *v.t.* to turn inward; *n.* a self-centered, introspective individual. **introversion** *n.* **introversive, -ive** *a.*

**in•trude** *v.i.* to thrust oneself in; to enter unwelcome or uninvited; *v.t.* to force in. **-r** *n.* **intrusion** *n.* **intrusive** *a.* **intrusively**

*adv.* **intrusiveness** *n.*
**in•trust** See **entrust.**
**in•tu•i•tion** *n.* immediate and instinctive perception of a truth; direct understanding without reasoning. **intuit** *v.t.* and *v.i.* to know intuitively. **-al** *a.* **-alism, -ism** *n.* the doctrine that the perception of good and evil is by intuition. **-alist** *n.* **intuitive** *a.* **intuitively** *adv.*
**in•tu•mesce** *v.i.* to swell; to enlarge or expand, owing to heat. **-nce** *n.*
**in•twine** See **entwine.**
**in•un•date** *v.t.* to overflow; to flood; to overwhelm. **inundation** *n.*
**in•ure** *v.t.* to accustom (to); to habituate by use; to harden (the body) by toil, etc. **-ment** *n.*
**in•vade** *v.t.* to attack; to enter with hostile intentions; to encroach upon. **-r** *n.* **invasion** *n.* **invasive** *a.*
**in•val•id** *a.* not valid; void; *v.t.* to render invalid. **-ate** *v.* **-ation** *n.* **-ity, -ness** *n.*
**in•va•lid** *n.* a person enfeebled by sickness or injury; *a.* ill; sickly; weak; *v.t.* and *v.i.* to make invalid.
**in•val•u•a•ble** *a.* incapable of being valued; priceless.
**in•var•i•able** *a.* not displaying change. **-ness, invariability** *n.* **invariably** *adv.* **invariant** *n.*
**in•va•sion** *n.* See **invade.**
**in•vec•tive** *n.* violent outburst of censure; abuse; *a.* abusive.
**in•veigh** *v.i.* to exclaim or rail against. **-er** *n.*
**in•vei•gle** *v.t.* to entice by deception or flattery. **-ment** *n.* **-r** *n.*
**in•vent** *v.t.* to devise something new or an improvement; to originate; to think out something untrue. **-ion** *n.* **-ive** *a.* **-ively** *adv.* **-or** *n.*
**in•ven•to•ry** *n.* a detailed list of articles comprising the effects of a house, etc.; *v.t.* to make a list.
**in•verse** *a.* inverted; opposite in order or relation. **-ly** *adv.* **inversion** *n.* **inversive** *a.*
**in•vert** *v.t.* to turn over; to put upside down; to place in a contrary order. **-edly** *adv.*
**in•ver•te•brate** *a.* not having a vertebral column or backbone; *n.* animal with no spinal column.
**in•vest** *v.t.* to lay out capital with a view to profit; to clothe, as with office or authority; *v.t.* to make a purchase or an investment. **-iture** *n.* ceremony of installing anyone in office. **-ment** *n.* **-or** *n.*
**in•ves•ti•gate** *v.t.* to inquire into; to examine thoroughly. **investigable** *a.* **investigation** *n.* **investigator** *n.* **investigatory** *a.*
**in•vet•er•ate** *a.* firmly established by long continuance. **-ly** *adv.* **-ness, inveteracy,** *n.*
**in•vid•i•ous** *a.* likely to provoke envy, ill-will or hatred; offensive. **-ly** *adv.* **-ness** *n.*
**in•vig•or•ate** *v.t.* to animate with life and energy. **invigoration** *n.* **-d** *a.*
**in•vin•ci•ble** *a.* unconquerable; insuperable. **-ness, invincibility** *n.* **invincibly.**
**in•vi•o•la•ble** *n.* not to be violated; sacred. **inviolably** *adv.* **inviolate** *a.* **inviolately** *adv.* **inviolateness** *n.*
**in•vis•i•ble** *a.* incapable of being seen. **invisibility, -ness** *n.* **invisibly** *adv.*
**in•vite** *v.t.* to ask by invitation; to attract. **invitation** *n.* act of inviting; the spoken or written form with which a request for a person's company is extended. **-r** *n.* **inviting** *a.* **invitingly** *adv.*
**in•vo•ca•tion** *n.* act of addressing in prayer. **invocatory** *a.* [See **invoke.**].
**in•voice** *n.* a detailed list of goods, with prices, sold or consigned to a purchaser: *v.t.* to make such a list.
**in•voke** *v.t.* to address (esp. God) earnestly or solemnly in prayer.
**in•vol•un•ta•ry** *a.* outside the control of the will; unintentional; instinctive. **involuntarily** *adv.* **involuntariness** *n.*
**in•vo•lute** *a.* *(Bot.)* rolled inwardly or spirally; *n.* the locus of the far end of a flexible thread unwound from a circle. **involution** *n.* that in which anything is involved; entanglement; complication. [See **involve**].
**in•volve** *v.t.* to envelop; to wrap up; to include; to comprise; to embrace; to implicate (a person); to complicate (a thing). **-ment** *n.*
**in•vul•ner•a•ble** *a.* incapable of being wounded or injured. **invulnerability** *n.* **invulnerably** *adv.*
**in•ward** *a.* placed within; towards the inside; interior; internal; seated in the mind or soul; *adv.* toward the inside; into the mind. Also **inwards. -ly** *adv.*
**i•o•dine** *n.* a non-metallic chemical element belonging to the halogen group. **iodiferous** *a.* yielding iodine. **iodize** *v.t.* to treat with compounds of iodine.
**i•on** *n.* electrically charged atom. **ionic** *a.* **-ization** *n.* **-ize** *v.t.* **ionosphere** *n.* the layer of ionized molecules in the upper atmosphere.
**i•on•ic** *a.* pert. to section of Greece; *(Archit.)* denoting type of column with fluted molding and ram's horn design.

**i•o•ta** *n.* a very small quantity or degree.
**ir-** *prefix* for *in;* not, before 'r.'
**i•ras•ci•ble** *a.* easily provoked; hot-tempered, **irascibility** *n.* **irascibly** *adv.*
**i•rate** *a.* angry; incensed.
**ire** *n.* anger; wrath. **-ful** *a.* **-fully** *adv.* **-fully** *adv.* **-fulness** *n.*
**irid-, irido-,** *prefix* used in the construction of compound terms, pertaining to the iris of the eye or to the genus of plants, as **iridescence** *n.* rainbow-like display of colors. **iridescent** *a.*

**iris** *n.* (*Anat.*) the thin colored membrane between the cornea and the lens of the eye; (Bot.) a genus of flowering plants; an appearance resembling the rainbow.

**I•rish** *a.* pert. to Ireland; *n.* the early language spoken in Ireland. **-ism** *n.*

**irk** *v.t.* to weary; to trouble; to distress. **-some** *a.* **-somely** *adv.*

**i•ron** *n.* the most common and useful of the metallic elements; something hard and unyielding; an instrument or utensil made of iron; an instrument used, when heated, to press and smooth cloth; in golf, an ironheaded club. **-s** *n. pl.* fetters; mannacles; *a.* made of iron; inflexible; *v.t.* to smooth with a heated flat iron; *v.i.* to furnish or arm with iron; to fetter.

**i•ro•ny** *n.* a mode of speech in which the meaning is the opposite of that actually expressed. **ironic, ironical** *a.* **ironacally** *adv.*

**ir•ra•di•ate** *v.t.* to shine upon, throw light upon; *v.t.* to emit rays; to give forth light; *a.* illumined with beams of light. **irradiance, irradiancy** *n.* **irradiant** *a.* **irradiation** *n.* exposure to X-rays, ultra-violet rays, solar rays, etc.; illumination; enlightenment. **irradiative** *a.* **irradiator** *n.*

**ir•ra•tion•al** *a.* incompatible with or contrary to reason. **-ity** *n.* **-ly** *adv.*

**ir•re•claim•a•ble** *a.* incapable of being reclaimed. **irreclaimably** *adv.*

**ir•rec•on•cil•a•ble** *a.* incapable of being reconciled. **-ness, irreconcilability** *n.* **irreconcilably** *adv.*

**ir•re•cov•er•a•ble** *a.* cannot be recovered; irreparable; irretrievable. **-ness** *n.* **irrecoverably** *adv.*

**ir•re•deem•a•ble** *a.* not redeemable; incorrigible. **-ness, irredeemability** *n.* **irredeemably** *adv.*

**ir•re•duc•i•ble** *a.* that which cannot be reduced or lessened. **-ness, irreducibility** *n.* **irreducibly** *adv.*

**ir•ref•u•ta•ble** *a.* that cannot be refuted. **irrefutability** *n.* **irrefutably** *adv.*

**ir•reg•u•lar** *a.* not regular; deviating from the moral standard. **-ity** *n.* **-ly** *adv.*

**ir•rel•a•tive** *a.* not relative; unconnected. **-ly** *adv.*

**ir•re•li•gion** *n.* state of indifference of opposition to religious beliefs. **irreligious** *a.* **irreligiously** *adv.* **irreligiousness** *n.*

**ir•re•me•di•a•ble** *a.* not to be remedied or redressed. **-ness** *n.* **irremediably** *adv.*

**ir•re•place•able** *a.* that cannot be passed by or forgiven; unpardonable.

**ir•rep•a•ra•ble** *a.* that cannot be repaired or rectified. **-ness** *n.* **irreparability** *n.* **irreparably** *adv.*

**ir•re•place•able** *a.* that cannot be replaced.

**ir•re•press•i•ble** *a.* not able to be kept under control. **irrepressibility** *n.* **-ness** *n.* **irrepressibly** *adv.*

**ir•re•proach•a•ble** *a.* free from blame; faultless. **irreproachably** *adv.*

**ir•re•sist•i•ble** *a.* incapable of being resisted. **-ness, irresistibility** *n.* **irresistibly** *adv.*

**ir•res•o•lute** *a.* infirm or inconstant in purpose; vacillating. **-ly** *adv.* **-ness, irresolution** *n.*

**ir•re•spec•tive** *a.* and *adv.* without regard to; apart from. **-ly** *adv.*

**ir•re•spon•si•ble** *a.* not liable to answer (for consequences); without a due sense of responsibility. **irresponsibility** *n.* **irresponsibly** *adv.*

**ir•re•spon•sive** *a.* not responsive (to); unanswering; taciturn. **-ness** *n.*

**ir•re•triev•a•ble** *a.* incapable of recovery or repair. **-ness** *n.* **irretrievability** *n.* **irretrievably** *adv.*

**ir•rev•er•ent** *a.* not reverent; disrespectful. **irreverence** *n.* **-ly** *adv.*

**ir•re•vers•i•ble** *a.* that cannot be reversed. **irreversibly** *adv.*

**ir•rev•o•ca•ble** *a.* incapable of being recalled or revoked. **-ness, irrevocability** *n.* **irrevocably** *adv.*

**ir•ri•gate** *v.t.* to water (by artificial channels). **irrigable, irrigative** *a.* **irrigation** *n.* **irrigator** *n.*

**ir•ri•tate** *v.t.* to excite to anger; to annoy; to excite heat and redness in the skin by friction. **irritability** *n.* **irritable** *a.* easily provoked or annoyed; able to be acted upon by stimuli. **irritableness** *n.* **irritably** *adv.* **irritant** *a.* and *n.* **irritation** *n.* **irritative** *a.*

**ir•rup•tion** *n.* a sudden invasion; a violent incursion into a place. **irruptive** *a.* **irruptively** *adv.*

**is** *v.* the *third pers. sing. pres. idic.* of the verb **to be.**

**is•land** *n.* a piece of land surrounded by water. **-er** *n.*

**isle** *n.* an island. **islet** *n.* a tiny island.

**i•so-** *prefix,* equal, used in the construction of compound terms.

**i•so•dy•nam•ic** *a.* having equal force or power.

**i•so•gon** *n.* a plane figure having equal angles. **isogonal** *a.* **-ic** *a.*

**i•so•late** *v.t.* to place in a detached position. **isolation** *n.* **isolationist** *n.*

**i•so•met•ric** *a.* of equal measurement.

**i•sos•ce•les** *a.* having two sides which are equal (said of a triangle).

**i•so•topes** *n. pl.* (*physics*) of most of the elements, atoms with nuclei of slightly different weights.

**Is•ra•el** *n.* since 1948, the name of the Jewish State in Palestine. **Israeli** *n.* an inhabitant of Israel. **-ite** *n.* (*Bib.*) a descendant of Israel or Jacob; a Jew. **-itic, -itish,** *a.*

**is•sue** *n.* act of passing or flowing out; the act of sending out; a topic of discussion or controversy; a morbid discharge from the body; outlet; edition; consequence; progeny; *v.t.* to send out (a book, etc.); to put into circulation; to proclaim or set forth with authority; to supply with equipment, etc.; *v.i.* to pass or flow out; to come out; to proceed; to be born or spring from. **-less** *a.* **-er** *n.*

**isth•mus** *n.* a narrow neck of land connecting two larger portions. **isthmian** *a.*

**it** *pron.* the neuter pronoun of the third person.

**I•tal•ian** *a.* pert. to Italy, its inhabitants or

their language.

**i•tal•ics** *n. pl.* a printing type having the type sloping from the right downwards, *as these letters.* **italicization** *n.* **italicize** *v.t.*

**itch** *n.* an irritation in the skin; *v.i.* to feel uneasiness or irritation in the skin. **-iness** *n.* **-y** *a.*

**i•tem** *n.* a piece of news, as in a newspaper; a detail. **itemize** *v.t.* to list.

**it•er•ate** *v.t.* to repeat; to do again. **iteration** *n.* **iterative, iterant** *a.*

**i•tin•er•ant** *a.* traveling from place to place; of notsettled abode. *n.* one who goes from place to place, esp. on business. **itineracy, itinerancy** *n.* **-ly** *adv.* **itinerary** *n.* a record of travel; a guide-book for travelers. **itinerate** *v.i.* to travel up and down a country, exp. in a regular circuit. **itineration** *n.*

**its** the *possessive case of pron. it.* **itself** *pron.* the neuter reciprocal pronoun applied to things; the reflexive form of it.

**i•vo•ry** *n.* the hard, white, opaque, dentine constituting tusks of elephant, walrus, etc.; as carving of ivory; creamy white color; *a.* made of or like ivory.

**i•vy** *n.* a climbing evergreen plant. **ivied** *a.*

**jab** *v.t.* to poke sharply; *n.* a sharp poke, stab, or thrust. **-bing** *pr.p.* **-bed.** *pa.t.* and *pa.p.*

**jab•ber** *v.i.* to speak quickly and indistinctly; *vt.* to utter indistinctly; *n.* rapid, incoherent talk. **-er** *n.* **-ingly** *adv.*

**Jack** *n.* a popular nickname and diminutive of *John. lc* the knave in a pack of cards; a device to facilitate removal of boots, as a *bootjack;* a portable apparatus for raising heavy weights, esp. for raising a motor vehicle to change a tire; the male of certain animals, as *jackass; v.t.* to raise with a jack. Also **jack up. —in-the-box** *n.* a child's toy comprising a small figure which springs out of a box when the lid is lifted. **-knife** *n.* a strong clasp knife. **—o'-lantern,** a latern made from hollowed-out pumpkin, with holes cut to make a face. **—of-all-trades** *n.* one who can turn his hand to anything. **-pot** *n.* a pool, in poker, which cannot be opened except by player holding two jacks or better. **-rabbit** *n.* a hare with very long ears. **yellow jack** *n.* yellow fever.

**jack•al** *n.* bushy-tailed carnivorous animal of Asia and Africa; wild dog.

**jack•ass** *n.* a male ass; a stupid fellow.

**jack-daw** *n.* a glossy, black bird of the crow family.

**jack•et** *n.* a short, sleeved coat; outer covering or skin (as of potatoes); an outer casing; a loose dustcover for a book; *v.t.* to cover with a jacket.

**Ja•cob's lad•der** *n.* a rope ladder with wooden rungs.

**jac•quard** *n.* a pattern woven into fabrics.

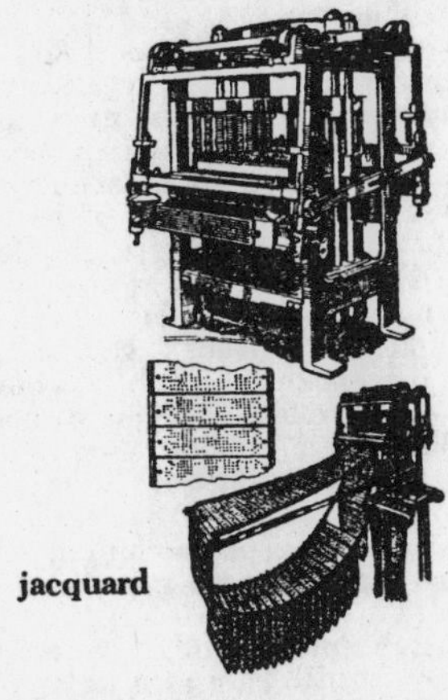
jacquard

**jade** *n.* an overworked, worn-out horse; *v.t.* to wear out. **jading** *pr.p.* **-d** *pa.p.* **-d** *a.* tired; sated.

**jade** *n.* a very hard, compact silicate of lime and magnesia, of various colors, carved for ornaments.

**jag** *n.* a ragged protuberance; *(Bot.)* cleft or division; *v.t.* to slash. **-ging** *pr.p.* **-ged** *pa.p.* **-ged, -gy** *a.* notched; rough-edged; sharp. **-gedness** *n.*

**jag•uar** *n.* a large spotted yellowish beast of prey.

**jail** *n.* a prison; *v.t.* to take into custody. **-bird** *n.* a prisoner; a criminal. **-er, -or** *n.* one who has charge of prisoners in the cells.

**jal•ou•sie** *n.* a blind or shutter with slats at an angle. **-d** *a.*

**jam** *n.* preserve made from fruit, boiled with sugar. **-my** *a.*

**jam** *v.t.* to wedge in; to block up; *v.i.* to cease to function because of obstruction; *n.* a crush; a holdup (as of traffic); a tight corner. **-ming** *pr.p.* **-med** *pa.p.* **-ming** *n.* *(Radio)* to interfere with signals by sending out others of like frequency.

**jamb** *n.* the sidepiece of a door, fireplace, etc.

**jam•bo•ree** *n.* a large, usually international, rally of Boy Scouts.

**jan•gle** *v.t.* to ring with a discordant sound; *v.i.* to sound out of tune; *n.* a discordant sound; a dispute. **jangling** *n.*

**jan•i•tor** *n.* a caretaker of a building; a porter.

**Jan•u•ar•y** *n.* the first month, dedicated by Romans to *Janus,* the god with two faces.

**Ja•pan** *n.* a N.E. Asiatic insular country. **-ese** *n.* a native of Japan; *a.* pert. to Japan, the people or language.

**japan** *v.t.* to lacquer with black varnish. *n.* the black laquer japanned. **-ning** *pr.p.* **-ned** *pa.p.*

**jar** *n.* vessel narrower at top than at base, with or without handles.

**jar** to give forth a discordant sound; to affect the nerves, feelings, etc. unpleasantly; *v.t.* to cause to vibrate by sudden impact; to shake physically or mentally; *n.* a jolting movement. **-ring** *pr.p.* **-red** *pa.p.* **-ringly** *adv.*

**jar•gon** *n.* confused speech; slang; technical phraseology.

**jas•mine** *n.* a shrub with fragrant white, yellow or pink flowers. Also **jessamine.**

**jas•per** *n.* an opague form of quartz, often highly colored.

**jaun•dice** *n.* a disease, characterized by yellowness of skin and eyes; *v.t.* to affect with jaundice. **-d** *a.* affected with jaundice.

**jaunt** *v.i.* to make an excursion; *n.* an outing; a ramble. **-ing** *a.* rambling.

**jaun•ty** *a.* sprightly; trim. **jauntily** *adv.*

**jav•e•lin** *n.* a light hand-thrown spear.

**jaw** *n.* one of the two bones forming framework of mouth and containing the teeth; part of any device which grips object held by it, as a vise; *v.t.* bone of the mouth in which teeth are set.

**jay** *n.* a chattering bird with gay plumage. **-walker** *n.* a careless pedestrian who disregards traffic rules.

common jay

**jazz** *n.* syncopated music played as accompaniment to dancing; *a.* pert. to jazz; *v.t.* and *v.i.* to dance to or play jazz music. **-y** *a.*

**jeal·ous** *a.* envious; apprehensively watchful; zealously careful. **-y** *n.*

**jean** *n.* a strong, twilled cotton cloth; *n.pl.* trousers.

**jeep** *n.* light motor utility truck designed in World War II.

**jeer** *v.i.* to mock; *v.t.* to treat scoffingly; *n.* a railing remark. **-er** *n.*

**Je·ho·vah** *n.* Hebrew name of the supreme God.

**jel·ly** *n.* gelatinous substance; juice of fruit boiled with sugar. **jell** *v.i.* to stiffen. **jellied** *a.* of the consistency of jelly. **jellify** *v.t.* to make into jelly; *v.i.* to become set like a jelly. **-fish** *n.* name given certain marine animals of gelatinous structure.

**jen·ny** *n.* a spinning machine; a female ass; a female bird, the wren.

**jeop·ar·dy** *n.* danger; risk. **jeopardize** *v.t.* to imperil.

**Jer·e·mi·ah** *n.* a Hebrew prophet and author of the Book of Lamentations.

**jerk** *v.t.* to give a sudden pull, twist, or push; *n.* a short, sudden thrust, pull, etc.; a twitching. **-er** *n.* **-ily** *adv.* **-iness** *n.* **-y** *a.* fitful; spasmodic; lacking rhythm.

**jerk** *v.t.* to cure (meat) by cutting in long slices and drying in the sun. **-ed** *a.*

**jer·kin** *n.* a close-fitting jacket.

**Jer·sey** *n.* the largest of the Channel Islands; *a.* pert. to State of New Jersey. **jersey** *n.* a close-fitting, knitted vest, or pullover.

**jest** *n.* a joke; an object of ridicule; *v.i.* to joke; to scoff. **-er** *n.* one who jests; a professional fool, originally attached to the court. **-ful** *a.* **-ingly** *adv.*

**Je·su·it** *n.* one of a religious order founded by Ignatius Loyola in 1534 under the title of The Society of Jesus.

**jet** *n.* a variety of very hard, black lignite, capable of a brilliant polish and used for ornaments; *a.* having the glossy blackness of jet. **— black** *a.* black like jet. **-tiness** *n.* **-ty** *a.*

**jet** *n.* a sudden rush, as of water or flame, from a pipe; the spout emitting water, gas, etc.; a jet airplane; *v.t.* to spout; *v.i.* to shoot forth. **— propulsion** *n.* propulsion of a machine by the force of a jet of fluid or of heated gases, expelled backwards from the machine. **-ting** *pr.p.* **-ted** *pa.t.*

**jet·sam** *n.* goods washed ashore from a wrecked ship. **jettison** *n.* act of throwing overboard; *v.t.* to throw overboard, as cargo.

**jet·ty** *n.* a structure of piles, stones, built to protect a harbor; a landing pier.

**Jew** *n.* a Hebrew or an Israelite. **-ish** *a.* of or belonging to Jews. **-ishness** *n.* **-ry** *n.* the Jewish people.

**jew·el** *n.* a precious stone; an ornament set with gem(s); *v.t.* to adorn with jewels; to fit (as a watch) with a jewel for pivot bearings. **-er** *n.* one who makes or deals in jewels. **-ery** *n.* jewels collectively.

**jib** *n.* *(Naut.)* a triangular staysail in front of forward mast.

**jibe** *v.t.* to swing (the sail) from one side of the ship to the other; *v.i.* to alter the course so that the sail shifts; *n.* a jeer.

**jig** *n.* a lively dance; a tool used to guide cutting tools in the making of duplicate parts; *v.t.* to jerk up and down; *v.i.* to bob up and down. **-ging** *pr.p.* **-ged** *pa.p.* **-saw** *n.* a narrow saw in a frame for cutting curves, etc. **-saw puzzle,** a picture cut into irregular pieces for putting together again.

**jig·ger** *n.* one who or that which jigs; any mechanical device which operates with jerky movement, esp. an apparatus for washing and separating ores by shaking in sieves under water; a bridge for a billiard cue; *(Naut.)* a sail nearest the stern; a 1½ oz. measure for liquor.

**jig·ger** *n.* a flea, the female of which burrows under the human flesh to lay its eggs. Also **chigger.**

**jig·gle** *v.i.* and *v.t.* to move with repeated short, quick jerks; *n.* a short, quick movement.

**jilt** *n.* one who capriciously disappoints a lover; *v.t.* to disappoint in love; to break an engagement to marry.

**jim·my** *n.* a small crowbar, as used by burglars; *v.t.* to force open.

**jin·gle** *v.t.* to cause to give a sharp, tinkling sound; *v.i.* to tinkle; to give this effect in poetry; *n.* correspondence of sounds, rhymes, etc., in verse to catch the ear.

**jin·rik·i·sha** *n.* a small, two-wheeled hooded carriage pulled by one or more men, commonly used in Japan.

**jinx** *n.* a person or thing of ill omen.

**jit·ney** *n.* public bus traveling a regular route.

**jiu·jit·su** See **jujitsu.**

**job** *n.* a piece of work; labor undertaken at a stated price; *a.* lumped together (of miscellaneous articles); *v.i.* to do odd jobs; to use influence unscrupulously; *v.t.* to buy and sell as a jobber; to let out work in portions. **-bing** *pr.p.* **-bed** *pa.p.* **-ber** *n.* a wholesale dealer who sells to retailers; one who transacts public business to his own advantage; one who does odd jobs. **-bery** *n.* underhand means to gain private profit at the expense of public money. **-bing** *a.* **— lot** *n.* a large amount of goods. as handled by a jobber. **— printing, — work,** the printing of handbills, circulars, etc.

**Job** *n.* *(Bib.)* a Hebrew patriarch of the Old Testament regarded as a monument of patience.

**jock·ey** *n.* a professional rider in horse races; *v.t.* to ride as a jockey; to maneuver for one's own advantage; *v.i.* to cheat. **-ism, -ship** *n.*

**jo·cose** *a.* given to jesting; waggish. **-ly** *adv.* **-ness, jocosity** *n.* the quality of being jocose. **jocular** *a.* given to jesting; facetious.

**jo·cund** *a.* merry; genial. **-ity, -ness** *n.* **-ly** *adv.*

**jodh·purs** *n.pl.* long riding breeches, close-fitting from knee to ankle.

**jog** *v.t.* to push with the elbow or hand; to stimulate (as the memory); *v.i.* to move on at a slow jolting pace; to plod on; *n.* a nudge; a slow walk, trot, etc. **-ging** *pr.p.*

**-ged** *pa.p.*
**jog** *n.* a projecting part.
**jog·gle** *v.t.* to shake slightly; to join by notches to prevent sliding apart; *v.i.* to shake; *n.* a jolt; a joint of two bodies so

**joggle-joints**

constructed that sliding apart is prevented.
**John** *n.* a proper name; a familiar appellation. **— Doe** *n.* fictitious plaintiff in a law case. **johnnycake** *n.* corn bread.
**join** *v.t.* to bring together; to unite; to become a member of; to become united in marriage, partnership; *n.* a junction; a fastening. **-er** *n.* one who or that which joins; a carpenter. **-ery** *n.* the trade of a joiner. **to join battle,** to begin fighting. **to join issue,** to take different sides on a point in debate.
**joint** *n.* the place where two things are joined; the articulation of two or more bones in the body; a hinge; *v.t.* to unite; to provide with joints; *v.i.* to fit like joints; *a.* jointed; held in common. **-ed** *a.* having joints. **-ly** *adv.* cooperatively. **— stock company,** a mercantile, banking, or cooperative association with capital made up of transferable shares. **out of joint,** dislocated; disordered.
**joist** *n.* a beam to which the boards of a floor or the laths of a ceiling are nailed.
**joke** *n.* something said or done to provoke laughter; a witticism; *v.t.* to make merry with; *v.i.* to make sport; to be merry. **-r** *n.* one who plays pranks; *(Cards)* an extra card in the pack, used in some games. **jokingly** *adv.*
**jol·ly** *a.* jovial; cheerful; *v.t.* *(Colloq.)* to humor a person with pleasant talk; to tease. **jollification** *n.* a celebration; a noisy party. **jolliness, jollity** *n.* mirth.
**jol·ly boat** *n.* a ship's small boat.
**jolt** *v.t.* to shake with a sudden jerk; *v.i.* to shake, as a vehicle on rough ground; *n.* a sudden jerk.
**Jo·nah** *n.* *(Bib.)* a Hebrew prophet.
**Jon·a·than** *n.* a variety of eating apple.
**jon·quil** *n.* variety of narcissus.
**josh** *v.t. and v.i.* to make fun of, to tease.
**jos·tle** *v.t.* to push against, esp. with the elbow; *v.i.* to push; *n.* a pushing against.
**jot** *n.* an iota; something negligible; *v.t.* to make a memorandum of. **-ting** *pr.p.* **-ted** *pa.p.*
**joule** *n.* *(Elect.)* the energy expended in 1 sec. by 1 ampere flowing through a resistance of 1 ohm.
**jour·nal** *n.* a book recording daily transactions of a business firm; a daily newspaper; a periodical. **-ize** *v.i.* to write for a journal; to keep a daily record of events. **-ism** *n.* **-ist** *n.* one who writes professionally for a newspaper or periodical. **-istic** *a.*
**jour·ney** *n.* travel from one place to another; *v.i.* to travel. **-ing** *pr.p.* **-ed** *pa.p.* **-man** *n.* a skilled mechanic or artisan who has completed his apprenticeship.
**joust** *n.* a tournament; *v.i.* to tilt.
**Jove** *n.* Jupiter. **Jovial** *a.* orig. born under the influence of the planet Jupiter; *lc* convivial. **joviality, jovialness** *n.* **jovially** *adv.*
**jowl** *n.* the cheek; the dewlap, of cattle.
**joy** *n.* exhilaration of spirits; *v.i.* to rejoice; to exult. **-ing** *pr.p.* **-ed** *pa.p.* **-ful** *a.* **-fully** *adv.* **-fulness** *n.* **-less** *a.* dismal. **-lessly** *adv.* **-lessness** *n.* **-ous** *a.* full of joy. **-ously** *adv.* **-ousness** *n.*
**ju·bi·lant** *a.* rejoicing. **-ly** *adv.* **jubilate** *v.i.* to rejoice; to exult. **jubilation** *n.* rejoicing; exultation.
**ju·bi·lee** *n.* the fiftieth anniversary of any outstanding event; a time of rejoicing. **silver jubilee,** the twenty-fifth anniversary. **diamond jubilee,** the sixtieth anniversary.
**Ju·da·ism** *n.* the religious doctrines of the Jewish people. **Judaical** *a.* pert. to the Jews. **Judaically** *adv.*
**Ju·das** *n.* *(Bib.)* the disciple of Christ who betrayed him; a traitor.
**judge** *n.* officer authorized to hear and determine civil or criminal cases, and to administer justice; an arbitrator; *v.t.* to hear and try a case in a court of law; to give a final opinion or decision; *v.i.* to act as a judge; to come to a conclusion. **-ship** *n.* the office of a judge. **judgment** *n.* a legal decision arrived at by a judge in a court of law; discernment; an opinion.
**ju·di·ca·ture** *n.* the power of justice; a judge's period of office. **judicable** *a.* capable of being judged. **judicative** *a.* having the power to judge. **judicatory** *a.* dispensing justice. **judicial** *a.* pert. to a court or to a judge; impartial. **judicially** *adv.* **judiciary** *n.* judicial branch of government; *a.* pert. to the courts of law; passing judgment. **judicious** *a.* prudent; showing discrimination.
**ju·do** *n.* a form of jujitsu.
**jug** *n.* a vessel of earthenware, with handle and narrow neck; vessels for holding liquids; *v.t.* to put in a jug. **-ging** *pr.p.* **-ged** *pa.p.*
**jug·ger·naut** *n.* any fanatical idea for which people are prepared to sacrifice their lives.
**jug·gle** *v.t.* to toss up and keep in motion; *v.i.* to perform tricks with the hands; to use trickery; *n.* a trick by sleight of hand. **-r** *n.* one who juggles. **-ry** *n.*
**jug·u·lar** *a.* pert. to the neck or throat; *n.* one of the large veins of the neck.
**juice** *n.* the liquid constituent of fruits or vegetables. **juiciness** *n.* **juicy** *a.*
**ju·jit·su** *n.* a form of wrestling, originating in Japan.
**juke·box** *n.* a coin-operated phonograph.
**ju·li·enne** *n.* a clear soup containing vegetables finely shredded; *a.* of vegetables in thin strips.
**Ju·ly** *n.* the seventh month of the year.
**jum·ble** *v.t.* to mix in a confused mass; *v.i.* to be in a muddle; *n.* a chaotic muddle.
**jum·bo** *n.* a huge person, animal, or thing.
**jump** *v.t.* to spring over; to skip (as page of a book); *v.i.* to lift feet from ground and alight again; *n.* a leap; a sudden, nervous

start. **-er** *n.* **-iness** *n.* nervous twitching. **-y** *a.* **-ing bean** *n.* the seed of a Mexican plant containing larva which make it appear to jump.

**jum•per** *n.* a one-piece sleeveless dress.

**junc•tion** *n.* the act of joining; a connection. **juncture** *n.* a joint; an exigency.

**June** *n.* the sixth month of the year.

**jun•gle** *n.* land covered with trees, tangled undergrowth, esp. the dense forests of equatorial latitudes. **— fever** *n.* a severe form of malaria.

**ju•nior** *a.* younger, esp. of a son with the same name as his father; *n.* a young person; one in a subordinate position; a student in the next to last year of study.

**ju•ni•per** *n.* a genus of evergreen coniferous shrub.

**junk** *n.* useless, discarded articles; *v.t.* to turn into junk. **— dealer, -man** *n.* one who buys and sells junk.

**jun•ket** *n.* a dessert of milk curded with flavored rennet; a pleasure excursion; *v.i.* to feast; to go on a pleasure trip; *v.t.* to entertain.

**jun•ta** *n.* a meeting; a council of state in Spain or Italy.

**jun•to** *n.* a group of conspirators.

**Ju•pi•ter** *n.* in Roman mythology, the superme ruler of heaven; the brightest of the outer planets. Also **Jove.**

**ju•rid•i•cal** *a.* the administration of justice. **-ly** *adv.*

**ju•ris•dic•tion** *n.* the administration of justice; legal authority; extent within which this authority may be exercised. **jurisdictive** *a.*

**ju•ris•pru•dence** *n.* study of the fundamental principles underlying any legal system.

**ju•rist** *n.* one versed in the law.

**ju•ry** *n.* a body of citizens selected and sworn to give a verdict from the evidence produced in court. **juror** *n.* one who serves on a jury.

**jus•sive** *a.* expressing a command; *n.* a grammatical form expressing a command.

**just** *a.* founded on fact; fair; *adv.* exactly; scarcely. **-ly** *adv.* deservedly. **-ness** *n.* fairness.

**jus•tice** *n.* equity; merited reward or punishment; administration of the law. **-ship** *n.* the office of a judge. **justiciary** *a.* pert. to the administration of the law.

**justice of the peace** (J.P.), a local officer authorized to try minor cases, administer oaths, perform marriages, etc.

**jus•ti•fy** *v.t.* to prove the justice of; to excuse. **-ing** *pr.p.* **justified** *pa.p.* **justifiable** *a.* defensible; excusable. **justifiableness** *n.* **justifiably** *adv.* **justification** *n.* vindication.

**jut** *v.i.* to project. **-ting** *pr.p.* **-ted** *pa.t.* and *pa.p.*

**jute** *n.* fiber of an Indian plant.

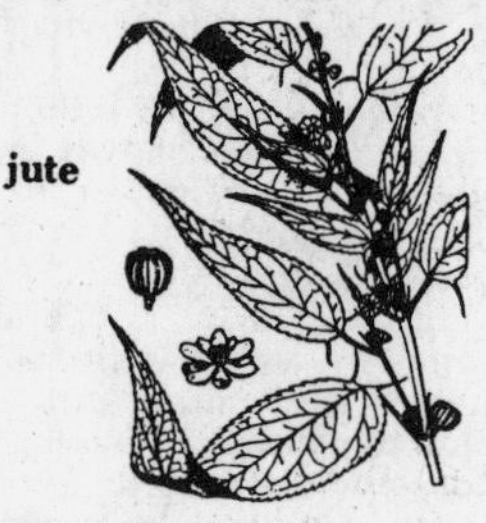

jute

**ju•ve•nes•cent** *a.* becoming young. **juvenescence** *n.*

**ju•ve•nile** *a.* young; youthful; *n.* a young person; a book written for children. **-ness, juvenility** *n.* **juvenilia** *n.pl.* works of author produced in childhood.

**jux•ta•pose** *v.t.* to place side by side. **juxtaposition** *n.* the act of placing side by side; contiguity.

**kai•nite** *n.* hydrated compound of the chlorides and sulfates of magnesium and potassium.

**kale** *n.* a hardy member of the mustard family with curled leaves.

**ka•lei•do•scope** *n.* an optical instrument, varying symmetrical, colorful patterns being displayed on rotation. **kaleidoscopic** *a.* ever-changing in beauty and form.

**kame** *n.* a high narrow ridge of gravel and sand left by a glacier.

**ka•mi•ka•ze** *n.* a suicide attack by Jap. pilot.

**kam•pong** *n.* a native of any South Sea island.

**kan•ga•roo** *n.* a ruminating marsupial found in Australia.

**kangaroo**

**ka•o•lin** *n.* fine porcelain clay chiefly produced from feldspar.

**kar•at** *n.* in fineness of gold, a twenty-fourth part (pure gold being 24 karats fine). also **carat.**

**kath•ode** See **cathode.**

**kat•i•on, cation** *n.* an electropositive ion which, in electrolysis, travels towards the cathode.

**ka•ty•did** *n.* a green insect of the grasshopper family.

**ka•va** *n.* an intoxicating Polynesian beverage.

**kay•ak** *n.* Eskimo sealskin canoe.

**keck** *v.i.* to show disgust.

**keck•le** *v.t.* to protect a cable from damage by fraying, by wrapping old rope around the length.

**kedge** *n.* a small anchor; *v.t.* to move a ship by means of small anchors.

**keel** *n.* the lengthwise beam of a ship on which the frames of the ship rest; *v.i.* to turn up the keel; to provide with a keel. **-haul** *v.t.* to haul under the keel of a ship by ropes attached to the yardarms. **to keel over,** *(Colloq.)* to fall over; to capsize.

**keen** *a.* sharp; penetrating; intense; shrewd; discerning. **-ly** *adv.*

**keep** *v.t.* to retain possession of; to detain; to have the care of; to cause to continue; *v.i.* to remain (in good condition); *n.* guardianship; maintenance; a stronghold. **kept** *pa.p.* and *pa.t.* **-er** *n.* one who guards; an attendant; a gamekeeper. **-ing** *n.* care; support; harmony. **-sake** *n.* anything given to recall the memory of the giver.

**keg** *n.* a small barrel.

**kelp** *n.* the calcined ash of certain seaweeds, used as a source of iodine.

**Kelt, Keltic** Same as **Celt, Celtic.**

**kelt** *n.* a salmon which has just spawned.

**kemps** *n.pl.* coarse rough hairs in wool.

**ken** *n.* range of sight.

**ken•nel** *n.* a shelter for dogs; an establishment where dogs are bred or lodged; *v.t.* to confine in a kennel; *v.i.* to live in a kennel. **-ling** *pr.p.*

**kent•ledge** *n.* pig iron placed in a ship's hold for permanent ballast.

**kept** *pa.t.* and *pa.p.* of **keep.**

**ker•at(o)-,** a horn, used in the formation of compound terms. **keratin** *n.* an essential constituent of horny tissue. **keratoid** *a.* horny. **keratosis** *n. (Med.)* a skin disease characterized by abnormal thickening.

**ker•chief** *n.* any cloth used in dress, esp. on the head or around the neck. **-ed** *a.*

**ker•mis, kermess** *n.* affair, usually for charitable purposes; originally a dedication service at the opening of a new church.

**kern** *n. (Print.)* a part of the face of a type projecting beyond the body, as an italic *f.*

**ker•nel** *n.* edible part of a nut; the body of a seed; central part.

**ker•o•sene** *n.* an illuminating or burning oil.

**ker•sey** *n.* coarse woolen cloth, usually ribbed.

**ketch** *n.* a small two-masted vessel.

**ketch•up, catch•up, cat•sup** *n.* a sauce made from mushrooms, tomatoes or walnuts.

**ket•tle** *n.* a metal vessel, with spout and handle, used for heating and boiling water or other liquids. **-drum** *n.* a musical percussion instrument made of a hemispherical copper shell covered with vellum. **-drummer** *n.*

**key** *n.* a low-lying island or reef near the coast, used esp. of Spain's former possessions off the coast of Florida.

**key** *n.* an instrument which shuts or opens a lock; a spanner; a lever in a musical instrument, depressed by the fingers in playing; a lever on a typewriter for actuating the mechanism; a switch adapted for making and breaking contact in an electric circuit; *(Mus.)* the keynote of a scale, or tonality, the pitch of a voice; explanation; a translation of a book, or solutions to questions set; *a.* critical; of vital importance; controlling. **-board** *n.* the whole range of keys on a keyed instrument. **-hole** *n.* a hole in a door or lock for receiving a key. **— industry** *n.* an industry on which vital interests of the country or other industries depend. **-man** *n.* an indispensable employee. **-note** *n. (Mus.)* the first tone of the scale in which a passage is written; the essential spirit of speech, thought, etc. **— ring** *n.* a ring for keeping a number of keys together. **— signature** *n. (Mus.)* the essential sharps and flats placed at the beginning of a piece after the clef to indicate the tonality. **all keyed up,** agog with excitement and expectation.

**kha•ki** *a.* dust-colored or buff; *n.* a cloth of this color, used for the uniforms of soldiers.

**khan** *n.* a title of respect in various Mohammedan countries among Mongol

races. **-ate** *n.* the dominion of a Khan.
**khe•dive** *n.* the title of the Turkish ruler of Egypt.
**kick** *v.t.* to strike or hit with the foot; *v.i.* to strike out with the foot; to recoil violently (of a rifle, etc.); *n.* a blow with the foot; the recoil of a gun. **-er** *n.* **-off** *n.* the commencement of a game of football. **to kick over the traces,** to throw off all restraint; to rebel openly. **dropkick** *n.* *(football)* a kick made as the ball, just dropped from the hand, rebounds from the ground. **placekick** *n.* kicking a football placed on the ground.
**kid** *n.* a young goat; leather made from the skin of a goat; *pl.* gloves of smooth kid leather; *a.* made of kid leather.
**kid** *v.t.* and *v.i.* to fool; **-ded** *n.* teasing. **-ding** *pr.p.* **-ded** *pa.p.* and *pa.t.* **-der** *n.*
**kid•nap** *v.t.* to carry off, abduct, or forcibly secrete a person (esp. a child). **-per** *n.* **-ping** *n.*
**kid•ney** *n.* one of two glandular organs in the lumbar region of the abdominal

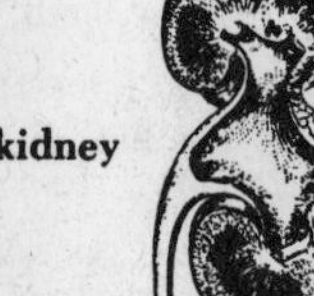
**kidney**

cavity which excrete urine. **— bean,** the kidney-shaped seed of a bean plant.
**kill** *v.t.* to deprive of life; to put to death; to destroy; to weaken or dilute; *n.* the act of killing; animal killed. **-er** *n.* **-er whale** *n.* the grampus, a whale capable of swallowing seals, porpoises, whole. **-ing** *a.* depriving of life; *n.* the act of destroying life; game killed on a hunt; a profitable business deal. **-ingly** *adv.*
**kiln** *n.* furnace for burning, baking or drying something.
**ki•lo-** in the metric system denoting a thousand. **kilocycle** *n.* unit for measuring vibrations, esp. the frequency of electromagnetic waves, 1,000 oscillations per second. **kilogram** *n.* 1,000 grams, equal to 2.2046 lb. avoirdupois. **kiloliter** *n.* 1,000 liters. **kilometer** *n.* 1,000 meters, 3280.899 feet or nearly ⅝ of a mile. **kilowatt** *n.* an electric unit of power equal to 1,000 watts. **kilowatt-hour** *n.* one kilowatt expended for one hour.
**kilt** *n.* a short skirt usually of tartan cloth, deeply pleated.
**ki•mo•no** *n.* a flowered overgarment with short wide sleeves, worn in Japan by men and women.
**kin** *n.* family relations; relationship; *a.* of the same kind. **next of kin,** the person closest in relationship to a deceased person.
**kind** *n.* genus; variety; *a.* having a sympathetic nature; obliging. **-hearted** *a.* **-heartedness** *n.* **-liness** *n.* benevolence. **-ly** *a.* and *adv.* **-ness** *n.* kind feeling or action.
**kin•der•gar•ten** *n.* a school for young children.
**kin•dle** *v.t.* to set on fire; to excite (the passions); *v.i.* to catch fire; to become bright or glowing. **kindling** *n.* the act of starting a fire; the material for starting a fire.
**kin•dred** *n.* relatives by blood or marriage; *a.* related; of like nature; congenial.
**ki•ne•mat•ic, ki•ne•mat•i•cal** *a.* relating to pure motion. **-s** *n.pl.* branch of mechanics dealing with problems of motion.
**kin•es•the•sia** *n.* the perception of muscular effort. **kinesthetic** *a.* Also **kinaesthesia, kinesthesis.**
**ki•net•ic, kinetical** *a.* imparting or growing out of motion. **-s** *n.* the science which treats of changes in movements of matter produced by forces.
**king** *n.* *(fem.* **queen***)* supreme ruler of a country; a playing card in each suit with a picture of a king; the chief piece in the game of chess; in checkers, a man which is crowned. **-craft** *n.* **-dom** *n.* domain; one of the great divisions (animal, vegetable, and mineral) of natural history. **-fisher** *n.* a stout-billed bird, with brilliant plumage. **-hood** *n.* kingship. **-like, -ly** *a.* **-pin** *n.* *(Fig.)* in bowling, the pin at the front apex when the pins are set up.
**kink** *n.* a short twist, accidentally formed, in a rope, wire, chain, etc; in the neck, a crick; a whim; *v.i.* and *v.t.* to twist spontaneously; to form a kink (in).
**kins•folk** *n.* blood relations; members of the same family; also **kinfolk. kinship** *n.* state of being related by birth. **kinsman, kinswoman** *n.*
**kip** *n.* the untanned hide of young cattle.
**kip•per** *n.* herring, salmon, etc. split, then smoked; *v.t.* to cure fish by splitting, salting, smoking, or drying.
**kis•met** *n.* fate or destiny
**kiss** *v.t.* and *v.i.* to touch with the lips, in affection or reverence; *n.* a salute by touching with lips. **-able** *a.* **-er** *n.* one who kisses.
**kit** *n.* a set of tools or implements.
**kitch•en** *n.* a room in which food is prepared and cooked. **-ette** *n.* a small kitchen. **— garden** *n.* a garden for raising vegetables for the table. **— police** (abbrev. **(K.P.)** *n.* soldiers on kitchen duty. **-ware** *n.* cooking utensils.
**kite** *n.* a sheet of paper, silk, etc., stretched over a light frame and flown by a cord attached and held from ground.
**kith** *n.* in phrase **kith and kin,** friends and acquaintances.
**kit•ten** *n.* a young cat; *v.i.* to bring forth young cats. **-ish** *a.* like a kitten; playful. **kitty** *n.* a pet name for a cat.
**kit•ty** *n.* the pool in card games.
**Klax•on** *n.* electric horn on automobiles.
**klep•to•ma•ni•a** *n.* an uncontrollable impulse to steal things. **-c** *n.*
**klick** See **click.**
**knack** *n.* inborn dexterity; adroitness; habit.
**knag** *n.* a knot in wood; *a.* knotty; rough.
**knap•sack** *n.* a bag for food and clothing, borne on the back.
**knave** *n.* a dishonest person; *(Cards)* a jack.

-ry *n.* trickery; sharp practice. **knavish** *a.* fraudulent; roguish. **knavishly** *adv.*

**knead** *v.t.* to work dough by pressing with the heel of the hands, and folding over; to massage. **-er** *n.*

**knee** *n.* the joint formed by the articulation of the femur and the tibia, the two principal bones of the leg; *v.t.* to touch with the knees. **—breeches** *n.pl.* breeches fastened just below the knee. **-cap** *n.* the patella, a flattened bone in front of knee joint.

**kneel** *v.i.* to bend a knee to the floor; to rest on the knees as in prayer. **-ed** *or* **knelt** *pa.t.* and *pa.p.* **-ing** *n.*

**knell** *n.* the stroke of a bell rung at a death; a portent of doom; *v.i.* to toll; *v.t.* to summon by tolling bell.

**knew** *pa.t.* of **know.**

**knick•er•bock•ers** *n.pl.* loose breeches gathered in at the knees. Also **knickers.**

**knick•knack** *n.* a trifle or trinket. **-ery** *n.* knickknacks collectively.

**knife** *n.* a cutting instrument; *pl.* **knives;** *v.t.* to stab with a knife. **—edge** *n.* anything with a thin, sharp edge.

**knight** *n.* in feudal times, a young man admitted to the privilege of bearing arms; a minor piece in chess bearing a horse's head; *v.t.* to dub a knight. **-hood** *n.* the order of knights. **-liness** *n.* **-ly** *a.* and *adv.*

**knit** *v.t.* to form fabrie by interlooping yarn by means of needles or a machine; to cause to grow together, as a fractured bone; *v.i.* to be united closely. **-ting** *pr.p.* **-ted** *pa.t.* and *pa.p.* **-ter, -ting** *n.* **-wear** *n.* knitted garments.

**knives** *pl.* of **knife.**

**knob** *n.* a rounded lump; a hard protuberance or swelling; small round handle of a door. **-bed** *a.* set with knobs. **-biness** *n.* **-by** *a.* full of knobs; lumpy.

**knock** *v.t.* and *v.i.* to strike with something hard or heavy; to make a periodic noise, due to a faulty bearing in a reciprocating engine or too much ignition advance in a gasoline engine; to criticize adversely; *n.* a stroke with something heavy; a rap on a door; the noise of a faulty engine. **-er** *n.* an ornamental metal attachment on a door. **— kneed** *a.* having the knees bent inward.

**knoll** *n.* the top of a hill; a mound.

**knot** *n.* a complication of threads, cords, or ropes, formed by entangling; in cordage, a method of fastening a rope to an object or to another rope; a hard lump, esp. of wood where a branch has sprung from the stem; *(Naut.)* a measure of speed of ships, equal to one nautical mile (6,080 ft.) per hour; *v.t.* to form a knot in; *v.i.* to form knots. **-ting** *pr.p.* **-ted** *pa.t.* and *pa.p.* **-hole** *n.* a hole in a board where a piece of a knot has fallen out. **-tiness** *n.* **-ty** *a.* full of knots; puzzling.

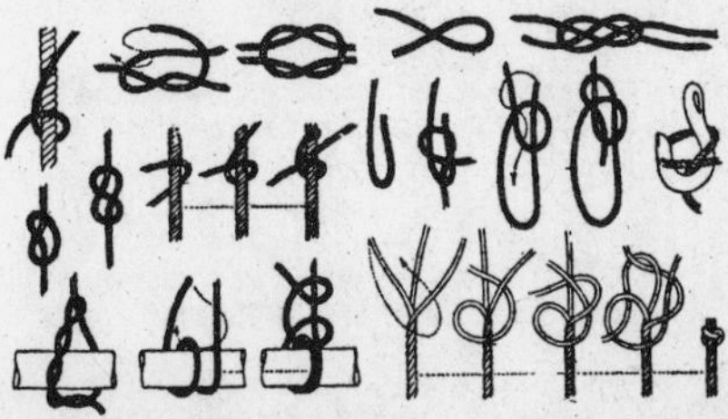

knot

**know** *v.t.* to be aware of; to have information about; to have experience; *v.i.* to have information or understanding. **knew** *pa.t.* **-n** *pa.p.* **-ing** *a.* professing to know; clever. **-ingly** *adv.* **to know the ropes,** to know from experience what to do.

**knowl•edge** *n.* direct perception; acquaintance with; learning. **-able** *a.* well-informed.

**knuck•le** *n.* the joint of a finger; *v.t.* to strike with the knuckles; *v.i.* to hold the knuckles close to the ground in the game of marbles. **brass knuckles** *n.pl.* iron or brass rings fitting across the knuckles, used to deliver murderous blows. **to knuckle down,** to tackle a job vigorously. **to knuckle down** or **under,** to submit.

**knurl** *n.* a series of rough indentations on the edge of a thumbscrew, coin, etc.; *v.t.* to roughen edges of a circular object; to indent. **-ed.** *a.*

**ko•a•la** *n.* a small marsupial of arboreal habit, native to Australia.

koala

**Ko•dak** *n.* a trademark for photographic film, apparatus and supplies.

**kohl** *n.* powdered lead sulfide used in the East for darkening eyebrows and eyelashes.

**kohl•ra•bi** *n.* a cabbage with an edible turnip-shaped stem.

**ko•la** *n.* an African tree whose seeds contain a large quantity of caffeine and are used as a stimulant.

**kook•a•bur•ra** *n.* the great kingfisher with a laugh-like cry.

**Ko•ran** *n.* sacred book of Islam, containing revelations received by Mohammed.

**ko•sher** *a.* (of food) pure, clean, esp. meat, made ceremonially clean according to Jewish ordinances.

**krem•lin** *n.* the citadel of a Russian city; *(cap.)* the citadel of Moscow, seat of Soviet government.

**kreut•zer** *n.* an Austrian monetary unit. Also **kreuzer.**

**kro•ne** *n.* a silver coin of Denmark and Norway; *pl.* **kroner.**

**kryp•ton** *n.* a nonmetallic chemical element belonging to the group of rare gases.

**ku•dos** *n.* fame; credit.

**Ku Klux Klan** *n.* a lawless secret society, founded c. 1865, to oppose granting of privileges to the freed Negroes.

**ku•lak** *n.* a prosperous landholder in Russia who resisted the efforts of the Soviet to nationalize agriculture.
**küm•mel** *n.* a liqueur flavored with cumin and caraway seeds.
**kum•quat** *n.* a shrub, native to China and Japan, produces a small orange-like fruit.
**ky•pho•sis** *n.* humpback, angular deformity of the spine.
**ky•ir•e** *n.* the words and music of part of the service in the R.C. Church; the response in the Anglican communion service after each of the Ten Commandments.

**la** *n.* syllable for sixth tone of scale in tonic sol-fa notation.
**lab•da•num** *n.* a fragrant resin used in perfumes, etc.
**la•bel** *n.* paper, card, etc., affixed to anything, denoting its contents, nature, ownership, destination, etc.
**la•bel•lum** *n.* the posterior petal of a flower of the orchid type.
**la•bi•al** *a.* pert. to the lips; formed by the lips, as certain speech sounds such as *p, b, w, o; n.* a sound formed by the lips. **labiate, -d** *n.* with calyx or corolla formed in two parts, resembling lips.
**la•bi•o•den•tal** *a.* pert. to the lips and teeth; *n.* a sound made with the lips and teeth, as *f* and *v.* **labium** *n.* a lip or lip-like structure.
**la•bor** *n.* exertion of body or mind; toil; work demanding patience and endurance; manual workers collectively or politically; *(Med.)* the pains of childbirth; *v.i.* to work strenuously; to take pains; to move with difficulty. **— union** *n.* an organization of workers for mutual aid and protection and for collective bargaining.
**lab•o•ra•to•ry** *n.* a place used for experiments or research in science, pharmacy, etc.
**la•bret** *n.* an ornament inserted into a hole pierced in the lip, worn by some primitive tribes. **labral** *a.* **labrose** *a.* having thick lips.
**la•bur•num** *n.* a small, hardy deciduous tree.
**lab•y•rinth** *n.* a system of intricate winding passages; a maze.
**lac, lakh** *n.* one hundred thousand, as a *lac of rupees.*
**lac** *n.* a deep-red, resinous substance, the excretion of an insect, found especially on trees in southern Asia, and used as a dye, in varnishes, sealing wax, etc.
**lace** *n.* a string or cord used for fastening dress, shoes, etc.; a net-like fabric of linen, cotton or silk with ornamental design interwoven by hand or machine. **lacing** *n.* a fastening formed by a lace threaded through eyeholes.
**lac•er•ate** *v.t.* to tear; to rend; to injure; to afflict sorely.
**lach•ry•mal** *a.* pert. to or producing tears, as *lachrymal* duct, the tear duct.
**lack** *v.t.* and *v.i.* to be destitute of; to want; *n.* deficiency; shortage; need; want. **-luster** *a.* dim; wanting in brightness.
**lack•a•dai•si•cal** *a.* affectedly pensive or languid.
**lack•ey** *n.* a liveried manservant; a footman; a follower.
**la•con•ic** *a.* brief; concise; expressing maximum meaning in the minimum of words.
**lac•quer, lacker** *n.* a varnish consisting of a solution of shellac in alcohol.
**la•crosse** *n.* an outdoor ball game played with a *crosse* or stick which has a net at the end.
**lac•te•al** *a.* pert. to milk; milky; resembling chyle. **lactate** *n.* a salt of lactic acid; *v.i.* to produce milk. **lactation** *n.* the act of giving or secreting milk. **lacteous** *a.* resembling milk. **lactic** *a.* pert. to milk; procured from milk or whey, as *lactic acid.* **lactose** *n.* milk-sugar.
**la•cu•na** *n.* a hollow; a hiatus; an omission.
**lad** *n.* a young man; a boy.
**lad•der** *n.* a frame of wood, steel, ropes, etc., consisting of two sides connected by rungs for climbing.
**lade** *v.t.* to load; to burden; to draw by means of a ladle.
**la•dle** *n.* a long-handled spoon.
**la•dy** *n.* a well-bred woman; orig. a woman having authority over a household or estate; a woman of social distinction, position.
**lag** *v.t.* to bind round, as pipes, boiler, etc., with non-conducting material to prevent loss of heat.
**lag** *n.* time lapse; retardation; *v.i.* to move slowly; to fall behind.
**la•ger-beer** *n.* a light German beer.
**la•goon** *n.* a shallow pond or lake.
**la•ic** *a.* lay; secular; *n.* a layman.
**laid** *pa.t.* and *pa.p.* of the verb **lay**; *a.* put down; (of paper) having a slightly ribbed surface showing the marks of the close parallel wires on which pulp was laid.
**lain** *pa.p.* of verb **lie.**
**lair** *n.* a den or bed of a wild animal; a place to rest.
**lais•sez-faire** *n.* a policy of non-interference.
**la•i•ty** *n.* the people, as distinct from those specially skilled; lay.
**lake** *n.* a large sheet of water within land.
**lake** *n.* a deep-red coloring matter.
**lakh** Same as **lac.**
**la•ma** *n.* a Buddhist priest in Tibet. **Lamaism** *n.* form of Buddhist religion practiced in Tibet.
**lamb** *n.* the young of a sheep; the flesh of lamb as food; a young and innocent person.
**lam•bent** *a.* playing on the surface; gleaming; flickering.
**lame** *a.* crippled in a limb; hobbling; *(Fig.)* unsatisfactory, as an excuse; imperfect; *v.t.* to cripple.
**lam•é** *n.* a textile containing metal threads giving a gold or silver effect.
**la•mel•la** *n.* a thin, plate-like structure or scale.
**la•ment** *v.i.* to utter cries of sorrow; to bemoan; to mourn for; *v.t.* to deplore; *n.* a heartfelt expression of sorrow; an elegy or dirge. **lamentable** *a.* grievous; sad. **Book of Lamentations** *(Bib.)* one of the poetical books of the Old Testament.
**lam•i•na** *n.* a thin plate or scale lying over another; *(Bot.)* the blade of a leaf. *pl.* **laminae, laminable, laminar, laminary** *a.* consisting of, or resembling, thin plates. **laminate** *v.t.* to cause to split into thin plates; to make into thin layers (as metal).
**lamp** *n.* a vessel containing combustible oil to be burned by a wick, or inflammable gas from a jet; any light-giving contrivance.
**lam•poon** *n.* a bitter personal satire, usually in verse; abusive or scurrilous

publication.

**la•nate** *a.* wooly; *(Bot.)* covered with fine hairs resembling wool.

**lance** *n.* a former war weapon consisting of a spearhead on a long wooden shaft. *v.t.* to pierce with a lance; to open with a lancet. **lancet** *n.* a small two-edged surgical knife. **lancet arch** *n.* narrow, pointed arch. **a free lance,** one who acts on his own initiative; a journalist not attached to the staff of any particular newspaper.

**lan•ci•nate** *v.t.* to tear; to lacerate.

**land** *n.* earth; the solid matter of surface of globe; any area of the earth; ground; soil; the inhabitants of a country; real estate. **-fall** *n.* sighting of land by a ship at sea. **— grant** *n.* a grant of land from the government esp. for colleges, railroads, etc. **-holder** *n.* a proprietor of land. **-ing** *n.* the act of coming to land; disembarkation; the level part of a staircase between two flights of steps. **-ing gear** *n.* the wheeled under-carriage of an airplane on which it rests when landing or taking off. **-lady** *n.* the owner of property who leases land, buildings, etc. to tenants. **-locked** *a.* enclosed by land. **-lord** *n.* the owner of houses rented to tenants; the proprietor of an inn, etc. **-mark** *n.* a mark to indicate a boundary; any outstanding or elevated object indicating general direction or distinguishing a particular locality. **— mine** *n.* military high-explosive bomb. **-scape** *n.* that portion of land which the eye can comprehend in a single view. **-scape architecture** *n.* art of aesthetically arranging or changing features of the landscape. **-scape gardener,** one who is employed professionally to lay out gardens, etc. **-scapist** *n.* a painter of landscape. **-slide** *n.* a fall of rock from a hillside or cliff.

**lan•dau** *n.* a carriage, the top of which may be opened and thrown back. **landaulet, landaulette** *n.* an automobile with folding hood.

**land•grave** *n.* a German nobleman.

**lane** *n.* a narrow track between hedges or across fields; a narrow street or road; a specified route followed by ships or airplanes; part of a street or highway for one line of traffic.

**lan•guage** *n.* speech; expression of ideas by words or written symbols; mode of speech peculiar to a nation, a class, profession, etc.; communication of animals, etc.

**lan•guid** *a.* indifferent; listless; flagging from exhaustion. **languish** *v.i.* to become languid; to droop with weariness; to pine or suffer; to become wistful. **languor** *n.* lassitude; sentimental softness.

**lan•gur** *n.* a long-tailed Indian monkey.

**lank** *a.* drooping; gaunt and thin; long and straight, as hair. **-y** *a.* tall and slender.

**lan•o•lin, lanoline** *n.* an oily substance obtained from wool.

**lan•tern** *n.* something portable or fixed, enclosing a light and protecting it from wind, rain, etc.

**lan•yard, laniard** *n.* a short rope or line for fastening; a cord, with knife attached, worn round the neck.

**La•od•i•ce•an** *a.* like the Christians of *Laodicea;* lukewarm in religion; lacking strong feeling on any subject.

**lap** *n.* that part of the clothing between waist and knees of a person who is sitting; the part of the body thus covered; an overlying part of any substance or fixture; a course or circuit, as in bicycle-racing, etc. **-el** *n.* that part of a coat or dress which laps over the facing. **-pet** *n.* a part of a garment which hangs loose; a fold of flesh.

**lap** *v.i.* to take up food or drink by licking; to make a sound like an animal lapping its food.

**lap•i•dar•y** *a.* pert. to stones or to the art of cutting stones. **lapidate** *v.t.* to stone (to death). **lapillus** *n.* a small, rounded fragment of lava. *pl.* **lapilli, lapis lazuli** *n.* an opaque mineral, sapphire-blue in color, much used in jewelry, ornaments, mosaics, etc.

**Lapp** *n.* a native of Lapland.

**lapse** *v.i.* to slip or fall; to fail to maintain a standard of conduct; to pass from one proprietor to another because of negligence; to pass slowly or by degrees. **lapsable** *a.* **-d** *a.* no longer valid or operative.

**lar•ce•ny** *n.* theft. **larcenist** *n.* a thief. **larcenous** *a.* thieving; pilfering.

**larch** *n.* a genus of cone-bearing, deciduous trees.

**lard** *n.* the clarified fat of swine; *v.t.* to smear with fat; to stuff, as meat or fowl, with bacon or pork.

**lard•er** *n.* a pantry where meat and food stuffs are kept; supply of provisions.

**large** *a.* of great size; spacious; extensive; liberal; numerous; extravagant.

**lar•gess** *n.* a generous gift; a donation.

**lar•ghet•to** *a.* *(Mus.)* rather slow; less slow than *largo.* **largo** *(Mus.)* *a.* and *adv.* slow and stately.

**lar•i•at** *n.* a lasso; a rope or thong of leather, with a noose for catching wild horses, etc.

**lark** *n.* a frolic; a prank; *v.i.* to play practical jokes.

**lark** *n.* a small songbird.

**lar•rup** *v.t.* to thrash.

**lar•va** *n.* an insect in the caterpillar, grub, or maggot stage.

**lar•ynx** *n.* the upper part of the trachea or windpipe; a cartilaginous cavity

larynx

containing the vocal cords. **laryngitis** *n.* inflammation of the larynx.

**las•civ•i•ous** *a.* loose; lustful; wanton.

**lash** *n.* the thong of a whip; a cord; a stroke with a whip; a satirical or sarcastic reproof; an eyelash.

**lass** *n.* a young woman; a girl; a sweetheart. **lassie** *n.* a little girl.

**las•si•tude** *n.* exhaustion of body or mind; languor.

**las•so** *n.* a long rope with a noose, used for catching wild horses.

**last** *a.* following all the rest; most recent; most unlikely; final; supreme. **the Last Supper,** the memorial supper celebrated by Jesus on the eve of his betrayal.

**last** *n.* a model of the human foot in wood on which shoes are made or repaired.

**last** *v.i.* to continue in time; to endure; to remain unimpaired in strength or quality; to suffice.

**las•tex** *n.* a fine rubber thread wound with cotton, rayon, or silk and woven into cloth or knitted into fabrics.

**lat•a•ki•a** *n.* a superior quality of Turkish tobacco from *Latakia* in Syria.

**latch** *n.* a small piece of iron or wood used to fasten a door; a catch.

**late** *a.* behindhand; coming after; delayed; earlier than the present time; occurring at the close of a period of time; no longer in office; deceased. **latter** *a.* later or more recent; the second of two just mentioned; modern. **latterly** *adv.* **of late,** recently.

**la•tent** *a.* not visible or apparent; dormant; hid; concealed. **— heat,** heat which is absorbed in changing a body from solid to liquid, or liquid to gas, without increasing its temperature.

**lat•er•al** *a.* relating to the side.

**Lat•er•an** *n.* the Pope's cathedral Church in Rome.

**la•tex** *n.* the milky sap of trees, plants; the milky juice of the rubber tree.

**lath** *n.* a thin, narrow slip of wood to support plaster, slates, etc. **-er** *n.* **-ing** *n.* the process of constructing with laths; the work done.

**lathe** *n.* a machine-tool for turning articles of wood, metal, etc.

**lath•er** *n.* foam or froth made with soap and water; froth from sweat.

**Lat•in** *a.* pert. to *Latium,* a part of ancient Italy with Rome as its chief center, or its inhabitants; written or spoken in Latin. **— America,** parts of Central and South America where Romance languages are spoken. **— Church,** the Roman Catholic Church using Latin as its official language.

**lat•i•tude** *n.* distance, measured in degrees, north or south of the equator; any region defined according to latitude; the angular distance of a heavenly body from the ecliptic. **latitudinarian** *a.* broad; liberal, esp. in religious principles; *n.* one who departs from, or is indifferent to, strictly orthodox religious principles.

**la•trine** *n.* a toilet, esp. in barracks, hospitals, etc.

**lat•ten** *n.* a metallic alloy of copper and zinc, with appearance of brass; metal in thin sheets.

**lat•tice** *n.* framework of wood, metal, etc., formed by strips, laths, or bars crossing each other; a gate, trellis, or window thus formed.

**Lat•vi•an** *a.* pert. to the Baltic state of Latvia; Lettish.

**laud** *v.t.* to praise in words or singing; to extol; *n.* a eulogy; praises.

**laugh** *v.i.* to express mirth spontaneously; to make an involuntary explosive sound of amusement; to be merry or gay. **-ing gas** *n.* nitrous oxide gas used as anesthetic in dental operations. **-ing hyena** *n.* the spotted hyena with a peculiar cry like a human laugh. **-ing stock** *n.* object of ridicule.

**launch, lanch** *v.t.* to throw as a lance; to let fly; to cause to slide into the water for the first time, as a ship. **— vehicle** *n.* a rocket used to place a satellite or space vehicle in orbit. **-ing pad** *n.* platform from which a missile is fired by remote control.

**launch** *n.* the largest boat carried on a warship; an open boat driven by steam, gasoline, or electricity.

**laun•dry** *n.* a place where clothes are washed, dried, and ironed; the process of washing clothes, etc. **launder** *v.t.* to wash clothes; *n.* *(Mining)* a long hollow trough for conveying powdered ore from the box where it is bruised.

**lau•rel** *n.* evergreen shrub, much used formerly to make wreaths symbolic of honor. **laureate** *a.* crowned with laurel.

**la•va** *n.* the molten rock, ejected by a volcano, hardening as it cools.

**la•va•bo** *n.* ceremonial washing of a celebrant's hands after the offertory and before the eucharist.

**lave** *v.t.* *(Poetic)* to wash; to bathe; *v.i.* to bathe; to wash oneself. **lavatory** *n.* a place for washing.

**lav•en•der** *n.* an aromatic plant of mint family, yielding an essential oil; pale-lilac color of lavender flowers; dried flowers used as a sachet.

**lav•ish** *a.* over-generous; extravagant; ample.

**law** *n.* a rule established by authority; a body of rules the practice of which is authorized by a community or state; legal science; established usage; a rule, principle, or maxim of science, art, etc. **—abiding** *a.* well-behaved; conforming to the law. **— court** *n.* a court in which lawcases are heard and judged. **-ful** *a.* allowed by law. **— officer** *n.* a policeman. **-suit** *n.* a process in law for recovery of a supposed right. **-yer** *n.* a practitioner of law. **common law,** body of laws established more by custom than by definite legislation. **written law,** statute law, codified and written down, as distinct from *Common law.*

**lawn** *n.* a stretch of closely-cut, carefully-tended grass. **— mower** *n.* a machine for cutting grass.

**lawn** *n.* a fine linen or cambric.

**lax** *a.* slack; flabby; loose, esp. in moral sense; careless; not constipated. **-ative** *a.* having purgative effect.

**lay** *v.t.* to place or put down; to apply; to beat down, as corn; to cause to subside; to exorcise, as an evil spirit; to spread on a surface; to wager; to produce, to prepare; to station, as an ambush; to form, as a plot; to set out dishes, etc. (on a table). **laid.** *n.* a situation; disposition. **-erage** *n.* the artificial propagation of plants by layers.

**lay** *pa.t.* of **lie** (to recline).

**lay** *n.* a song; a narrative poem such as was recited by minstrels.

**lay** *a.* pert. to the laity, as distinct from the clergy; unprofessional. **laicize** *v.t.* to deprive of clerical character.

**lay•ette** *n.* a complete outfit for a new-born baby.

**laz•ar** *n.* a person afflicted with a loathsome disease, like *Lazarus,* the beggar.

**laze** *v.i.* to be lazy; to lounge.

**la•zy** *a.* disinclined to exertion; slothful.

**lea** *n.* a meadow; land left untilled; pasturage.

**leach** *v.t.* to wash by causing water to pass through; *(Bot.)* to remove salts from soil by percolation.

**lead** *n.* a well-known malleable bluish-grey metal, ductile and heavy, used for roofing, pipes, etc.; a plummet for sounding ocean depths; a thin strip of type metal to separate lines of print; graphite for pencils; bullets. **— poisoning** *n.* a form of poisoning called plumbism caused by lead being absorbed into the blood and tissues.

**lead** *v.t.* to show the way; to guide; to direct; to persuade; to precede. **-er** *n.* a guide; a conductor; a commander. **-ership** *n.* the state or function of a leader. **-ing** *n.* direction; the act of guiding. **-ing-article** *n.* a leader or editorial in a newspaper. **-ing-lady, -man** *n.* the actress (or actor) playing the principal role. **-ing-question** *n.* *(Law)* a question so phrased as to suggest the answer expected. **to lead astray,** to tempt from virtue.

**leaf** *n.* thin deciduous shoot from the stem or branch of a plant; one of the sections

of a dropleaf or extension table; a hinged flap; a very thinly beaten plate, as of gold. **-age** *n.* leaves collectively; foliage. **-iness** *n.* **-less** *a.* devoid of leaves. **-let** *n.* a tiny leaf; a printed sheet advertisement, notice of meeting, etc. **— mold** *n.* leaves decayed and reduced to mold, used as manure.

**league** *n.* an old nautical measure equal to three geographical miles.

**league** *n.* a compact made between nations or individuals for mutual aid and the promoting of common interests.

**lea•guer** *n.* a military camp, esp. a siege camp.

**leak** *n.* a crack, crevice, fissure, or hole in a vessel; the oozing of liquid from such; *(Elect.)* an escape of electrical current from a faulty conductor.

**lean** *v.t.* to incline; to cause to rest against; *v.i.* to deviate from the perpendicular; to incline. **-ing** *n.* inclination (of body or mind). **— to** *n.* a shed built against a wall or side of a house or supported at one end by posts or trees.

**lean** *a.* thin; wanting in flesh or fat; *(Fig.)* empty; impoverished.

**leap** *v.i.* to spring; to jump up or forward; to vault. **-frog** *n.* a game, in which one stoops down, and another vaults over his head. **— year** *n.* a year of 366 days.

**learn** *v.t.* to acquire knowledge; to get to know; to gain skill by practice.

**lease** *n.* a contract renting lands, houses, farms, etc., for a specified time; time covered by lease; any tenure. **— hold** *a.* held on lease.

**leash** *n.* a line by which a hawk, dog, or other animal is held.

**least** *a.* (*superl.* of **little**) smallest; faintest; most minute. **at least,** at any rate.

**leath•er** *n.* the skin of an animal dressed and prepared for use. **-back** *n.* a large sea turtle. **— bound** *a.* (of a book) bound in calf, morocco, or other leather. **patent leather,** leather with shiny, varnished surface.

**leave** *n.* liberty granted; formal good-bye; furlough; permission to be temporarily absent from duty.

**leave** *v.t.* to quit; to forsake; to omit; to remove; to allow to remain unaltered; to bequeath; to permit; to entrust; to refer.

**leav•en** *n.* a substance due to fermentation which causes bread dough to rise.

**lech•er** *n.* a man given to lewdness; a fornicator. **-ous** *a.* lascivious; lustful.

**lec•tern** *n.* a reading desk in a church.

**lec•tion** *n.* a variation in copies of a manuscript; a portion of scripture read during a church service. **lector** *n.* a reader; a minor ecclesiastic in the early church; a lecturer in a college or university.

**lec•ture** *n.* a discourse on any subject; a formal reproof. **-r** *n.* one who lectures; an assistant to a professor in a university department.

**led** *pa.t.* and *pa.p.* of verb **lead.**

**ledge** *n.* a projection, as from a wall or cliff; a shelf; a ridge of rock near the surface of the sea.

**ledg•er** *n.* a book in which a business firm enters all debit and credit items in summary form; a cash book; a flat stone lying horizontally as on a grave. **— line** *n.* a line with hook and sinker to keep it stationary.

**lee** *n.* a place protected from the wind; shelter. **-board** *n.* a plank lowered on the side of a boat to diminish its drifting to leeward. **-gage** *n.* the sheltered side. **-ward** *a.* pert. to, or in, the direction towards which the wind is blowing. **-way** *n.* the side movement of a vessel to the leeward of her course; loss of progress.

**leech** *n.* a blood-sucking worm used for bloodletting.

**leek** *n.* a biennial bulbous plant allied to the onion; also, the national emblem of Wales.

**leer** *n.* a sly or furtive look expressive of malignity, lasciviousness, or triumph.

**leer•y** *a.* wary; suspicious.
**lees** *n.pl.* the sediment which settles at the bottom of a wine-cask; dregs.
**left** *a.* on the side of the body which is westward when one is facing north. **—handed** *a.* using the left hand more easily than the right; awkward. **— wing** *n.* a political group with extremist views.
**leg** *n.* the limb of an animal used in supporting the body and in walking, esp. that part of the limb between the knee and the foot. **-ging** *n.* a garment to cover the legs.
**leg•a•cy** *n.* a bequest; a gift of personal property by will. **legatee** *n.* one who receives a legacy.
**le•gal** *a.* pert. to, or according to, the law; defined by law; statutory; binding; consitutional. **— tender,** the form of money, coin, or notes, which may be lawfully used in paying a debt.
**leg•ate** *n.* Pope's highest diplomatic envoy; a diplomatic minister below ambassadorial rank. **legation** *n.* a minister and his staff.
**le•ga•to** *adv. (Mus.)* in a smooth, gliding manner.
**leg•end** *n.* orig. a chronicle of the lives of the saints; any traditional story of ancient times; an inscription on a coin, medal, etc.
**le•ger•de•main** *n.* a sleight of hand; trickery.
**Leg•horn** *n.* a plaited straw, from Leghorn in Italy; a hat made of this straw; a breed of domestic fowl.
**leg•i•ble** *a.* capable of being read.
**le•gion** *n.* in ancient Rome, a body of infantry of from three to six thousand; a military force; a great number.
**leg•is•late** *v.i.* to make or enact laws. **legislation** *n.* act of legislating; laws made. **legislative** *a.* having power to make laws; constitutional. **legislature** *n.* the body empowered to make and repeal laws.
**le•git•i•mate** *a.* lawful; in accordance with the law; born in lawful wedlock; justifiable; reasonable; genuine. **legitimation** *n.* the act of investing with the rights and privileges of lawful birth.
**leg•ume** *n.* a seed pod with two valves and having the seeds attached at one suture, as the pea; a plant bearing seed-pods.
**lei** *n.* a garland of flowers worn around the neck.
**lei•sure** *n.* freedom from occupation; spare time; *a.* unoccupied.
**leit•mo•tif** *n. (Mus.)* a theme associated with a person or idea, constantly recurring in a composition.
**lem•ma** *n. (Math.)* a subsidiary proposition; *(Logic)* a premise taken for granted; a theme; a heading of an entry.
**lem•on** *n.* an oval-shaped fruit with rind pale yellow in color and containing very acid pulp and juice.
**le•mur** *n.* one of a family of nocturnal monkey-like mammals found in Madagascar.
**lend** *v.t.* to grant the temporary use of, to give in general; to let out money at interest.
**lend-lease** *v.t.* to grant (material aid) to a foreign country in accordance with the Lend-Lease Act of March 11, 1941.
**length** *n.* the measurement of anything from end to end; extension; duration of time.
**le•ni•ent** *a.* clement; acting without severity.
**lens** *n. (Optics)* a piece of glass or other transparent substance ground with one or both sides curved so as to refract rays

lens 

of light, and thereby modify vision; the crystalline biconvex tissue between the cornea and retina of the eye.
**Lent** *n.* the season of 40 days from Ash Wednesday until Easter Day.
**len•tic•u•lar** *a.* shaped like a lens or lentil; resembling a double-convex lens.
**len•til** *n.* a Mediterranean plant allied to the bean.
**l'en•voi** *n.* a kind of postscript to a poem; a short, final stanza.
**Le•o** *n.* the lion, the fifth sign of the Zodiac which the sun enters about July 22nd.
**leo•pard** *n.* a large carnivorous member of the cat family, of a yellow or fawn color with black spots.
**le•o•tard** *n.* a one-piece, tight-fitting garment worn by dancers.
**lep•er** *n.* a person afflicted with leprosy; *(Fig.)* an outcast. **leprosy** *n.* a chronic contagious disease affecting skin, tissues and nerves.
**Lep•i•dop•ter•a** *n.pl.* an order of insects having four wings covered with gossamer scales, as moths, butterflies, etc.
**lep•re•chaun** *n.* a sprite; a brownie commonly referred to in Irish folk-stories.
**Les•bi•an** *a.* pert. to the island of *Lesbos* (Mytilene) in the Aegean Sea, or to the ancient school of lyric poets there; amatory; *n.* a woman who is sexually attracted to another woman; a homosexual woman.
**lese maj•es•ty** *n. (Law)* a crime committed against the sovereign, or sovereign power of a state; high treason.
**le•sion** *n. (Med.)* any morbid change in the structure or functioning of the living tissues of the body; injury.
**less** *a.* smaller in size; not equal to in number; lower; inferior.
**les•see** *n.* one to whom a lease is granted.
**les•son** *n.* a reading; a piece of instruction; something to be learned by pupils.
**let** *v.t.* to allow; to give permission.
**le•thal** *a.* deadly; mortal.
**leth•ar•gy** *n.* unnaturally heavy drowsiness; overpowering lassitude; inertia.
**le•the** *n.* oblivion.
**let•ter** *n.* a mark or symbol used to represent an articulate, elementary sound; a written or printed

communication. — **file** *n.* a device for holding letters for reference. **-head** *n.* printed heading on business stationery. **-press** *n.* printed matter as distinct from illustrations, diagrams, etc.; print. **letter of credit**, a letter authorizing money to be paid by a bank to the bearer. **letters patent**, a document under seal of the state, granting some property privileges or authority, or conferring the exclusive right to use an invention or design.

**Let•tic** *a.* pert. to the Letts or to their language. **Letts** *n.pl.* the inhabitants of Lithuania and Latvia.

**let•tuce** *n.* a common garden plant, used in salads.

**leu•co•cyte** *n.* one of the white corpuscles of the blood, destroying bacteria.

**leu•ke•mi•a, leukaemia** *n.* a disease characterized by an excessive number of white corpuscles in the blood.

**Le•vant** *n.* Eastern Mediterranean countries.

**le•va•tor** *n.* a muscle in the body which raises any part, as the eyelid, lips, etc.

**lev•ee** *n.* a reception; orig. a reception held by royal personage on rising from bed.

**lev•ee** *n.* a river embankment to prevent flooding.

**lev•el** *n.* a line or plane which is everywhere parallel to the horizon; the horizontal plane on which a thing rests; a state of equality; an instrument for finding or drawing a true horizontal line. **-ing rod** *n.* a graduated rod used in surveying.

**lev•er** *n.* a bar used to exert pressure or sustain a weight at one point of its length by receiving a force or power at a second, and turning at a third on a fixed point called a fulcrum; a crowbar for forcing open.

**le•vi•a•than** *n.* a huge aquatic animal; a whale; a sea-monster; anything of colossal size.

**lev•i•ta•tion** *n.* the act of making buoyant or light; the phenomenon of heavy bodies being made to float in air by spiritual agencies.

**Le•vite** *n.* one of the tribe of Levi; lesser priest in ancient Jewish synagogue. **Leviticus** *n. (Bib.)* third book of Old Testament.

**lev•i•ty** *n.* lightness; buoyancy; lack of seriousness.

**le•vo•ro•ta•tion** *n.* counterclockwise or left-hand rotation.

**lev•u•lose** *n.* fruit sugar found in honey and certain fruits.

**lev•y** *v.t.* to raise by assessment, as taxes; to enlist or collect, as troops; to impose, as a fine.

**lewd** *a.* obscene; indecent; given to unlawful indulgence.

**lew•is** *n.* an iron clamp dove-tailed into a stone block to raise it.

**lex•i•con** *n.* a dictionary, esp. of Greek, Latin, or Hebrew. **lexicographer** *n.* one who compiles a dictionary.

**li•a•ble** *a.* obliged in law or equity; subject; answerable; responsible. **liability** *n.* the state of being liable; responsibility; obligation.

**li•ai•son** *n.* a union; connection; illicit intimacy between a man and a woman.

**li•a•na** *n.* a climbing tropical plant.

**li•ar** *n.* one who tells lies.

**li•ba•tion** *n.* the ceremonial pouring of wine in honor of some deity.

**li•bel** *n.* a defamatory writing or printed picture; *(Law)* a written statement by the plaintiff of his allegations in a law case.

**lib•er•al** *a.* open-minded; generous; catholic; unbiased; (in politics) favoring democratic or progressive ideals, and freedom of religion. **liberate** *v.t.* to set free. **liberator** *n.* one who sets others free, esp. from tyranny.

**lib•er•ty** *n.* freedom from bondage or restraint; power to act according to one's natural rights as an individual; privilege; undue freedom of act or speech. **libertine** *n.* one who leads a dissolute life.

**li•bi•do** *n.* in psychology, the emotional craving behind all human impulse; esp. used by Freud to denote the sex-urge.

**Li•bra** *n.* the balance, the 7th sign of the Zodiac.

**li•brar•y** *n.* a collection of books; the room or building which contains it. **librarian** *n.* the person in charge of a library. — **science** *n.* the knowledge and skills required for library service.

**li•brate** *v.i.* to be poised; to oscillate. **libration** *n.* balancing; a quivering motion.

**li•bret•to** *n.* the words of an opera or oratorio.

**Lib•y•an** *a.* pert. to *Libya* in N. Africa or to the language of the district.

**li•cense** *n.* authority granted to do any act; a legal permit; excess of liberty; *v.t.* to permit by grant of authority. **licentiate** *n.* one who has a license to practice a profession.

**li•chen** *n.* one of an order of cellular flowerless plants; *(Med.)* a skin eruption.

**lic•it** *a.* lawful; allowable.

**lick** *v.t.* to pass or draw the tongue over; to lap; to take in by the tongue; to touch lightly. **-ing** *n.* a lapping with tongue; a flogging; a beating.

**lic•o•rice, liquorice** *n.* a Mediterranean plant, the root of which contains a sweet juice; the brittle, black substance extracted from the roots of this plant, and used medicinally and in candy.

**lic•tor** *n.* an officer who attended a Roman magistrate, bearing the fasces.

**lid** *n.* a cover of a vessel or box; the covering of the eye.

**lie** *v.i.* to utter untruth; to misrepresent; to deceive; to make false statement.

**lie** *v.i.* to be recumbent; to be in a horizontal position or nearly so.

**lie•der** *n.pl.* German lyrics set to music; *sing.*

**lief** *adv.* gladly; willingly.

**li•en** *n. (Law)* a legal claim upon real or personal property for the satisfaction of some debt or duty.

**lieu** *n.* place; stead, as in phrase 'in *lieu of*'.

**lieu•ten•ant** *n.* a deputy; an officer who takes the place of a superior in his absence. — **governor** *n.* state official ranking below a governor.

**life** *n.* existence; vitality; condition of plants, animals, etc. in which they exercise functional powers; the span between birth and death; mode of living; narrative of a person's history; animation. — **assurance** or **insurance** *n.* insurance of a person's life. — **belt** *n.* a belt either inflated, or made buoyant with cork, for keeping person afloat in case of shipwreck. **-boat** *n.* a special type of boat, designed for stability in stormy seas, for

**lifeboat**

saving of human lives — **expectancy** *n.* probable life span. **-guard** *n.* someone employed at a swimming pool, etc. to prevent accidents. — **history** *n.* the cycle of life of a person, organism, etc. — **interest** *n.* interest in an estate or business which continues during one's life, but which cannot be bequeathed by will. — **jacket** *n.* a life belt. **-less** *a.* inanimate; dead; inert. **-like** *a.* like a living creature; resembling closely. **-long** *a.* lasting a lifetime. — **preserver** *n.* any apparatus (as life belt, -buoy, -line) for preserving or rescuing life. **-saver** *n.* someone who rescues a person, esp. from drowning. **-size** *a.* resembling in proportions the living model. **-time** *n.* the duration of person's life. **-work** *n.* any task, usually creative, demanding a lifetime's work.

**lift** *v.t.* to raise; to take up and remove; to elevate socially; to exalt spiritually.

**lig•a•ment** *n.* anything which binds one thing to another; *(Anat.)* strong fibrous tissue bands connecting the bones of the body; a bond.

**light** *v.i.* to come to by chance; to alight; to settle.

**light** *a.* having little weight; not heavy; easy; active; nimble. **-en** *v.t.* to make less heavy; to jettison; to enliven. **—fingered** *a.* dexterous, esp. in picking pockets. **—footed** *a.* agile. **—handed** *a.* delicate of touch; empty-handed. **—headed** *a.* delirious; frivolous. **—hearted** *a.* carefree; gay. **—minded** *a.* frivolous. **—s** *n.pl.* the lungs of a slaughtered animal. **-some** *a.* lively; cheerful.

**light** *n.* that form of radiant energy which stimulates visual perception; anything which has luminosity; day; illumination; a source of illumination. **-er** *n.* a mechanical device for producing a flame, as a cigarette-lighter. **-house** *n.* a tower-like structure built at danger points on seacoast and provided with very powerful light to serve as warning to ships. — **year** *n.* *(Astron.)* the distance in a year (calculated at 5,878,000,000,000 miles) light travels. **Northern Lights,** aurora borealis.

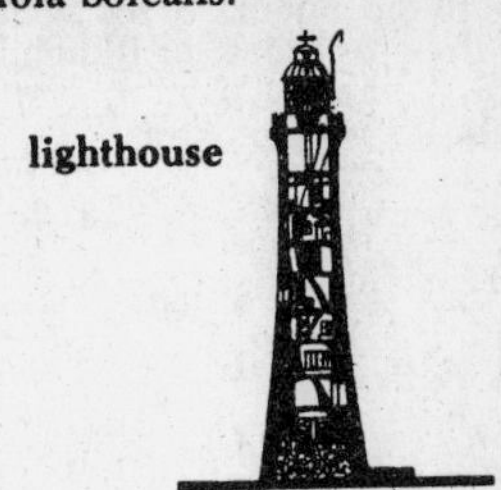

**lighthouse**

**light•ning** *n.* a flash produced by an electrical discharge between two clouds, or between cloud and ground. — **bug** *n.* a firefly. — **rod** *n.* a rod serving, by a connected wire called a **lightning-conductor,** to carry electric current into the earth or water.

**lig•ne•ous** *a.* woody; resembling wood. **lignify** *v.t.* to convert into wood. **lignin** *n.* an organic substance formed in the woody tissues of plants. **lignite** *n.* coal of recent origin still showing ligneous texture; brown coal.

**lig•ure** *n.* a precious stone.

**like** *a.* equal; similar; *n.* an equal; a person or thing resembling another; an exact resemblance. **-lihood** *n.* probability. **-ly** *a.* probable; credible; of excellent qualities; *adv.* probably.

**like** *v.t.* to be pleased with or attracted by; to enjoy; to approve.

**li•lac** *n.* a shrub, with delicately perfumed flower clusters, purple, pale mauve, or white in color.

**lilt** *n.* a light or rhythmic tune; *v.t.* and *v.i.* to sing.

**li•ly** *n.* a bulbous plant, with fragrant and showy bell-shaped flowers; *a.* resembling a lily; pure; pale; delicate. **—livered** *a.* cowardly. **—white** *a.* pure white; unsullied.

**limb** *n.* an extremity of the human body, as an arm or leg; a branch of a tree.

**limb** *n.* an edge or border.

**lim•ber** *a.* easily bent; pliant; supple.

**lim•bo** *n.* a region intermediate between heaven and hell in which the souls of unbaptized children etc., are confined after death.

**lime** *n.* a tree which produces a small sour kind of lemon; the fruit of this tree.

**lime** *n.* birdlime; oxide of calcium; white, caustic substance obtained from limestone, shells, marble, etc.; a calcium compound to enrich soil. **-kiln** *n.* a furnace in which limestone is heated to produce lime. **-light** *n.* a powerful light, as on a stage; the public view. **-stone** *n.* a rock consisting chiefly of carbonate of lime.

**li•men** *n.* the threshold of consciousness.

**lim•er•ick** *n.* a five-lined nonsense verse.

**lim•it** *n.* boundary; edge; utmost extent. **-able** *a.* that may be bounded or restricted. **-ary** *a.* of, pert. to, or serving as a limit; restricted. **limited liability,** said of a joint stock company in which liability of the shareholder is in proportion to the amount of his stock.

**limn** *v.t.* to draw or paint; to illuminate a manuscript. **limner** *n.* painter; one who decorates books with pictures.

**lim•ou•sine** *a.* pert. to a type of closed automobile with roof over the driver's head; *n.* a closed car.

**limp** *v.i.* to walk lamely; *n.* lameness.

**limp** *a.* wanting in stiffness, as covers of a book; flaccid; flexible.

**lim•pet** *n.* a small, univalve conical shaped shellfish which clings firmly to rocks.

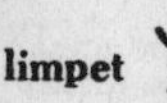
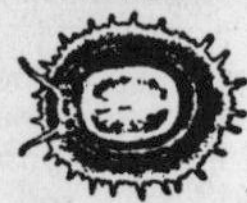

limpet

**lim•pid** *a.* clear; translucent; crystal.

**linch•pin** *n.* a pin used to prevent a wheel from sliding off the axle tree.

**lin•den** *n.* a tree with yellowish flowers and heart-shaped leaves.

**line** *n.* a rope, wire or string; a slender cord; a thread-like mark; an extended stroke. a boundary; a row or continued series; progeny; a verse; a short letter or note; a course of conduct, thought, or policy; a trend; a department; a trade, business or profession. **lineage** *n.* descendants in a line from common progenitor; pedigree. **lineation** *n.* the act of marking with lines; the lines marked or engraved. **-d** *a.* marked with lines; ruled. **— engraving** *n.* a process of engraving lines on a copper plate. **-r** *n.* a steamship or passenger aircraft belonging to a regular transport line. **linesman** *n.* one who installs and repairs telephone and electric lines, etc.; an official (at football or tennis match) who determines whether ball has crossed the outside line or not.

**line** *v.t.* to cover on the inside, as a garment, pan, etc. **lining** *n.* the material used.

**lin•en** *n.* thread or cloth made from flax; underclothing; napery; *a.* made of flax or linen.

**lin•ger** *v.i.* to delay; to dally; to loiter.

**lin•ge•rie** *n.* orig. linen goods; women's underclothing.

**lin•go** *n.* language; a dialect.

**lin•gual** *a.* pert. to the tongue; *n.* a sound or letter made by the tongue, as *d, l, n.* **-ly** *adv.* **linguiform** *a.* shaped like a tongue. **linguist** *n.* fluent speaker of several languages; an expert in linguistics. **linguistic** *a.* **linguistically** *adv.* **linguistics** *n.* study of human speech including its sounds, history, nature, structure, etc.; comparative philology.

**lin•i•ment** *n.* a lotion or soft ointment.

**link** *n.* a single ring of a chain; anything doubled and closed like a link. **-age** *n.* a system of connections. **missing link,** a connection without which a chain of argument is incomplete.

**links** *n.pl.* a golf course.

**lin•net** *n.* a small song bird of the finch family.

**li•no•le•um** *n.* a hard floor covering of burlap impregnated with a cement of linseed oil, cork, etc.

**lin•o•type** *n.* a type-setting machine in which the matter is cast in solid lines of type.

**lin•seed** *n.* flaxseed. **— cake,** compressed mass of husks of linseed, after oil has been pressed out, much used for cattle feeding.

**lin•sey-wool•sey** *a.* made of wool and linen mixed.

**lint** *n.* a linen material, one side with a soft, wooly surface formerly used for dressing wounds; scraps of thread; fluff from cloth.

**lin•tel** *n.* a horizontal beam or stone over a doorway or window.

**li•on** *n.* (*fem.* **-ess**) the largest of the cat tribe, tawny-colored, with powerful, tufted tail, the male having a shaggy mane.

**lip** *n.* one of the two fleshy, outer edges of the mouth; a liplike part; the edge of anything; brim. **— reading** *n.* the art of 'hearing' by reading the motions of a speaker's lips; this system as taught to the deaf. **-stick,** a salve, in the form of a small stick, used by women to redden the lips.

**li•quate** *v.t.* to melt; to separate or purify solids or gases by liquefying.

**liq•ue•fy** *v.t.* to transform a liquid; to melt.

**li•queur** *n.* a preparation of distilled liquors flavored with fruits or aromatic substances.

**liq•uid** *a.* fluid; in a state intermediate between a solid and a gas; flowing smoothly; (of sounds) pleasing to the ear. **-ate** *v.t.* to settle a debt; to wind up the affairs of business, etc.; to convert into cash; to destroy; *v.i.* (of business) to be wound up.

**liq•uor** *n.* any liquid or fluid, esp. alcoholic.

**li•ra** *n.* the monetary unit and a silver coin of Italy; a monetary unit and gold coin of Turkey.

**lisle** *n.* a fine hard-twisted cotton or linen thread.

**lisp** *v.i.* to speak imperfectly, esp. to substitute the sound *th* for *s.*

**lis•some** *a.* supple; flexible; lithe.

**list** *n.* the outer edge or selvage of woven cloth; a row or stripe; a roll; a catalogue; a register; a boundary line enclosing a field of combat at a tournament.

**list** *v.i.* *(Naut.)* to lean or incline (of a ship).

**lis•ten** *v.i.* to attend closely; to yield to advice.

**list•less** *a.* indifferent; languid; apathetic.

**lit** *pa.t.* and *pa.p.* of verb **light.**

**lit•a•ny** *n.* an earnest prayer of supplication.

**li•ter** *n.* a unit of volume in the metric system, equal to 1.0567 quarts. Also **litre.**

**li•te•ral** *a.* according to the letter; real; not figurative; word for word, as a translation.

**lit•er•ar•y** *a.* pert. to letters or literature; versed in literature. **literate** *a.* versed in learning and science; educated.

**lit•er•a•ture** *n.* the body of writings of a language, period, subject, etc.

**lithe** *a.* capable of being easily bent; supple; pliant.

**li•thog•e•nous** *a.* rock-producing, as certain corals.

**lith•o•glyph** *n.* an engraving on a precious stone.

**lith•o•graph** *v.t.* to trace on stone, zinc, or aluminium, and transfer to paper by special printing process. **lithography** *n.* the art of tracing designs on stone or other media, and taking impressions of these designs.

**lith•oid, -al** *a.* resembling a stone.

**li•thol•o•gy** *n.* the science which treats of the characteristics of rocks.

**lith•o•tint** *n.* the lithographic production of a tinted picture; the picture itself.

**lith•o•tome** *n.* a stone resembling an artificially cut gem; *(Surg.)* an instrument for performing a lithotomy. **lithotomy** *n.* *(Surg.)* the operation by which stones are removed from the bladder.

**lith•o•type** *n.* a stereotype plate; print from this plate.

**Lith•u•a•ni•an** *n.* a native of Lithuania; the language. Also **Lett.**

**lit•i•gate** *v.t.* to contest in law. *a.* **litigant** *n.* a person engaged in a lawsuit.

**lit•mus** *n.* a bluish purple vegetable dye (obtained from lichens) which turns red with an acid, and blue with an alkali. **— paper,** used to test solutions.

**li•to•tes** *n.* a figure of speech which expresses a strong affirmative.

**lit•ter** *n.* a heap of straw as bedding for animals; a vehicle containing bed carried on men's shoulders; a stretcher; odds and ends left lying about; state of disorder.

**lit•tle** *a.* small in size, extent, or quantity; brief; slight; mean.

**lit•to•ral** *a.* pert. to a lake or seashore.

**lit•ur•gy** *n.* the established ritual for public worship in a church, esp. the Mass. **liturge** *n.* a leader in public worship.

**live** *v.i.* to have life; to subsist; to be conscious; to dwell; to enjoy life; to keep oneself (as on one's income). **livable** *a.* habitable.

**live** *a.* having life; quick; active; vital; unexploded, as a mine; burning, as coal; full of zest; dynamite. **—circuit** *n.* a circuit through which an electric current is passing. **— wire** *n.* a wire carrying an electric current.

**live•li•hood** *n.* a means of living; sustenance.

**live•ly** *a.* animated; active; gay; exciting; light; *adv.* briskly.

**liv•er** *n.* *(Anat.)* glandular organ in body secreting bile; the flesh of this organ in animals or fowls used as food. **-wort** *n.* a moss-like plant with liver-shaped leaves. **-wurst** *n.* a sausage with a large amount of liver.

**liv•er•y** *n.* orig. the special dress or food *delivered* by a lord to his household retinue. **— stable** *n.* a stable where horses and vehicles are kept for hire.

**liv•id** *a.* black and blue; discolored, as flesh, by bruising.

**liv•ing** *a.* having life; active; flowing (of water); resembling closely; contemporary; *n.* livelihood.

**liz•ard** *n.* an order of four-footed scale-clad reptiles.

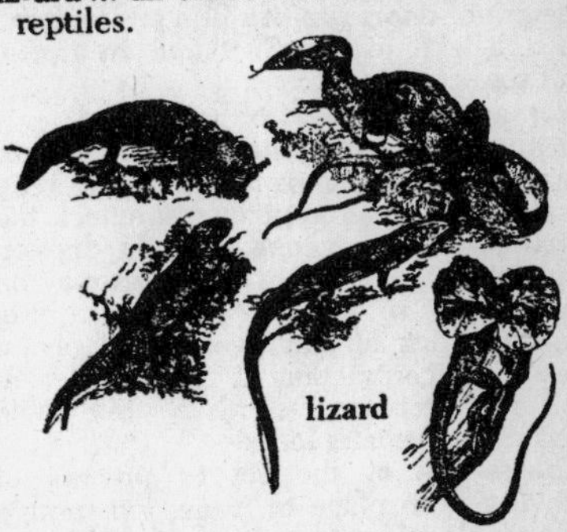

lizard

**lla•ma** *n.* a S. America two-toed ruminant, used as a beast of burden.

**loach** a small river fish.

**load** *n.* a burden; the amount normally carried at one time; any heavy weight; a cargo. to charge (a gun); to weight (as dice); to insert a spool into (as a camera). **— line** *n.* a line painted on the side of a vessel to indicate maximum immersion when loaded. **-stone** *n.* a metal which attracts other metals.

**loaf** *n.* shaped portion of dough baked in the oven; a lump of sugar.

**loaf** *v.i.* to spend (time) idly; to lounge. **-er** *n.* one who loafs; a moccasin style of shoe.

**loam** *n.* a rich, fertile soil of clay, sand, oxide of iron, and carbonate of lime.

**loan** *n.* the act of lending; that which is lent, esp. money for interest. **— office** *n.* a pawnbroker's shop.

**loath, loth** *a.* unwilling; reluctant; disinclined.

**loathe** *v.t.* to detest; to abominate; to be nauseated by. **loathing** *n.* disgust; repulsion. **loathly** *a.* **loathsome** *a.* detestable; repugnant.

**lob** *n.* *(Tennis)* a ball rising high in air over opponent's head; *v.t.* to bowl underhand; to hit (tennis ball, shuttle-cock) high into air.

**lob•by** *n.* a passage, or hall, forming the entrance to a public building or private dwelling; a waiting-room; a pressure group seeking to influence members of a legislature.

**lobe** *n.* a rounded division of an organ; the lower, fleshy, rounded part of human ear; a division of the lung.

**lo•bel•ia** *n.* a genus of herbaceous plants (including the blue dwarf variety).

**lob•lol•ly** *n.* a pine tree of the southern U.S.

**lob•ster** *n.* an edible, marine, long-tailed crustacean, with pincer-claws.

**lo•cal** *a.* pert. to a particular place; confined to a definite spot, district, or part. **locale** *n.* the scene of an occurrence; the scene of a film-shot.

**localize** *v.t.* to assign to a definite place; to decentralize. **locality** *n.* position of a thing; site; neighborhood. **-ly** *adv.* **locate** *v.t.* to set in a particular place; to find the exact position of. **location** *n.* act of locating; situation; geographical position; the out-of-doors site of a film production.

**loch** *n.* a lake, esp. in Scotland; an arm of the sea.

**lock** *n.* a strand or tress of hair.

**lock** *n.* a device for fastening a door, box, case, etc.; a mechanism on a gun to keep it from firing; an appliance to check the revolution of a wheel. **-er** *n.* a drawer, small chest, etc. where valuables may be locked. **-et** *n.* a small case containing portrait, lock of hair, worn on a chain. **-jaw** *n.* a contraction of the muscles of the jaw; tetanus. **-smith** *n.* one who makes and repairs locks.

**lo•co•mo•tion** *n.* the act or process of moving from place to place. **locomotive** *a.* capable of moving from one place to another.

**lo•cus** *n.* the exact position of anything; *(Math.)* the path traced out by a point moving in accordance with some mathematical law.

**lo•cust** *n.* a winged insect, allied to the grasshopper and found in N. Africa, Asia, and the U.S.; a thorny-branched N. American tree with very durable wood.

**locust**

**lo•cu•tion** *n.* speech; mode or style of speaking.

**lode** *n.* a metallic vein; a body of ore. **-star, loadstar** *n.* a star by which one steers, esp. the Pole-star.

**lodge** *n.* a small country-house; a cottage at the entrance to an estate; a branch of a society, as of Freemasons, or the building where such a society meets. **lodg(e)ment** *n.* lodgings; accumulation of something deposited. **lodging(s)** *n.* room(s) let temporarily.

**loft** *n.* an upper room; an attic in space between top story and roof; the gallery in a church, as the *organ-loft; v.t. (Golf)* to strike a ball high.

**log** *n.* an unhewn piece of timber; an apparatus to measure the speed of a ship and distance covered; the tabulated record of a ship's voyage. **-ger** *n.* a lumberjack. **-ging** *n.* the process of cutting trees and getting the logs to a sawmill to be cut for lumber.

**lo•gan•ber•ry** *n.* a shrub, a cross between raspberry and blackberry.

**log•a•rithm** *n.* the index of the power to which a fixed number or base must be raised to produce the number; a method of reducing arithmetical calculations to a minimum by substituting addition and subtraction for multiplication and division.

**log•ger•head** *n.* a blockhead; a dunce; a kind of turtle.

**log•gia** *n.* a kind of open elevated gallery with pillars, common in Italian buildings.

**log•ic** *n.* the science of reasoning; the science of pure and formal thought; *(Colloq.)* commonsense. **-al** *a.* pert. to formal thought; skilled in logic; reasonable.

**lo•gis•tic, -al** *a.* pert. to calculating. **-s** *n.pl.* (used as *sing.*); *(Mil.)* branch of military science which deals with the moving of and providing for troops.

**log•o•gram** *n.* a symbol representing a whole word or phrase.

**lo•go•gra•pher** *n.* a speech-writer in ancient Greek times. **logography** *n.* a method of printing in which words cast in a single type are used instead of single letters.

**loin** *n.* part of animal or man above hips and on either side of spinal column.

**loi•ter** *v.i.* to linger; to be slow in moving; to spend time idly.

**loll** *v.i.* to lounge about lazily; to hang out.

**lol•li•pop lollipop** *n.* a piece of flavored toffee or hard candy on a stick.

**lone** *a.* solitary; standing by itself.

**long** *a.* extended in distance or time; drawn out in a line; protracted; slow in coming; continued at great length; *v.i.* to be filled with a yearning to desire. **-boat** *n.* the largest boat carried by a sailing ship. **-bow** *n.* a bow drawn by hand, and usually 5½-6 feet long—so called to distinguish it from the *Cross*-bow. **longevity** *n.* length of life. **-hand** *n.* ordinary handwriting. **-horn** *n.* a kind of cattle of Mexico and U.S. **— house** *n.* a long communal dwelling of the Iroquois Indians. **-ing** a yearning; a craving. **-ingly** *adv.* **-ish** *a.* rather long. **longitude** *n.* angular distance east or west of a given meridian, measured in degrees. **— measure** *n.* linear measure. **-shore** *a.* existing or employed on the shore. **-shoreman** *n.* a dock laborer. **-sightedness** *n. (Med.)* hypermetropia, an abnormal eye condition whereby the rays of light are focused *beyond* and not on the retina. **-wise, -ways** *a.* lengthwise.

**loo** *n.* a card-game.

**look** *v.i.* to turn one's eyes upon; to seem to be; to consider; to seem; to face. **-ing glass** *n.* a mirror. **-out** *n.* a watch; a place from which a careful watch is kept; person stationed to keep watch.

**loom** *n.* a machine for weaving cloth from thread.

**loom** *v.i.* to emerge indistinctly and larger than the real dimensions; to appear over the horizon.

**loom** *n.* a kind of guillemot; a puffin; a loon.

**loon** *n.* a large fish-eating diving bird of the

**loon**

northern regions.

**loop** *n.* a doubling of string or rope, through which another string may run; anything with a similar shape.

**loop•hole** *n.* a narrow slit or opening as in the walls of a fortification; *(Fig.)* a way out of a difficult situation.

**loose** *v.t.* to free from constraint; to untie; to disconnect; to relax; to discharge. **—jointed** *a.* loosely built. **—leaf** *a.* having sheets of paper which can be removed and rearranged.

**loot** *n.* plunder; the act of plundering.

**lop** *v.t.* to cut off, esp. top of anything; to cut away superfluous parts.

**lop** *v.i.* to hand down loosely. **—eared** *a.* having drooping ears. **—sided** *a.* heavier on one side than the other.

**lope** *v.i.* to run with a long, leisurely gait.

**lo•qua•cious** *a.* talkative; babbling; garrulous.

**lo•quat** *n.* a low-growing Japanese plum tree; the fruit itself.

**lo•ran** *n.* *(Flying)* a navigational device which locates the position of an airplane.

**lord** *n.* a master; a ruler; a king; *(Cap.)* the Supreme Being; Jehovah; God; Christ. **-ship** *n.* the state of being a lord; authority; estate owned by a lord.

**lore** *n.* learning; erudition; traditional knowledge.

**lor•gnette** *n.* a pair of eyeglasses attached to a long handle; an opera glass.

**lo•ri•ca** *n.* a cuirass; *(Zool.)* a protective covering of bony plates, scales, etc., like a cuirass.

**lorn** *a.* *(Arch.)* lost; forsaken; desolate.

**lor•ry** *n.* *(esp. Brit.)* a wagon for transporting heavy loads; a car on rails, used in factories, mines, etc.; *(Brit.)* a truck.

**lose** *v.t.* to be deprived of; to mislay; to forfeit; to fail to win; to miss; to waste, as time; to destroy.

**lot** *n.* what happens by chance; destiny; object used to determine something by chance; the choice thus determined; a separate part; a large number of articles such as at an auction sale. **-tery** *n.* a scheme by which prizes are given to people, not on merit, but by drawing lots.

**Lo•thar•i•o** *n.* libertine, rake.

**lo•tion** *n.* a fluid with healing, antiseptic properties esp. for the skin.

**lot•to** *n.* a game of chance.

**lo•tus** *n.* the Egyptian water lily; a decorative representation, as in Egyptian

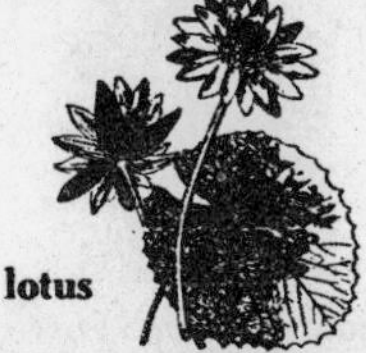
**lotus**

and Hindu art; a genus of plants including the British bird'sfoot trefoil.

**loud** *a.* making a great sound; noisy; flashy; obtrusive; vulgar. **-speaker** *n.* a device which makes speech, music, etc. audible at a distance.

**lou•is** *n.* an obsolete French gold coin worth 20 francs. Also **—d'or. —quatorze, —quinze, —seize,** applied to architecture, furniture, style of interior decoration characteristic of the reigns of the French Kings Louis XIV, VX, XVI [Fr.].

**lounge** *v.i.* to recline at ease; to loll; to spend time idly; *n.* the act of lounging; a room in which people may relax; a kind of sofa.

**louse** *n.* a small wingless parasitic insect infesting hair and skin of human beings; a sucking parasite found on mammals or plants.

**lout** *n.* a clumsy fellow; a bumpkin.

**lou•ver** *n.* an opening in the roof of ancient buildings for the escape of smoke or for ventilation.

**love** *n.* affection; strong liking; goodwill; benevolence; charity; devoted attachment to one of the opposite sex; passion. **— affair** *n.* a passionate attachment between two members of the opposite sex. **— apple** *n.* the tomato. **-bird** *n.* a small parrot with bright-colored plumage. **/ knot** *n.* bow of ribbon tied in a special way, as a token of love. **—lies-bleeding** *n.* a garden flower with reddish-purple spike flowers. **-liness** *n.* **-lock** *n.* a curl worn on the forehead or over the temple. **— match** *n.* a marriage founded on true love. **— philter** *or* **— potion** *n.* a drink supposed to induce the emotion of love towards a chosen person. **— seat** *n.* a seat for two. **-sick** *a.* pining because of love. **—song** *n.* lyric inspired by love. **—token** *n.* an object, as a ring, given as a symbol of love. **loving** *a.* affectionate; loyal.

**low** *a.* not high; lying near the ground; depressed below the adjacent surface; near the horizon; shallow; not loud, as a voice; moderate, as prices. **-boy** *n.* a chest about three feet high usu. with two tiers of drawers and on slender legs. **-brow** *n.* a non-intellectual. **Low Countries,** the Netherlands, Belgium, and Luxemburg. **-down** *a.* mean; underhand. **-land** *n.* country which is relatively flat in comparison with surrounding hilly district. **—pressure,** having only a small expansive force (less than 50 lbs. to the square inch) said of steam and steam engines.

**low** *v.i.* to bellow as an ox or cow.

**low•er** *v.i.* to frown; to look gloomy or threatening, as the sky.

**lox** *n.* liquid oxygen. *n.* salty smoked salmon.

**loy•al** *a.* faithful to the lawful government, the sovereign, a cause, or a friend.

**loz•enge** *n.* a figure with two acute and two obtuse angles; small (often medicated) confection orig. lozenge-shaped.

**lub•ber** *n.* a heavy, clumsy fellow.

**lu•bri•cate** *v.t.* to make smooth or slippery; to smear with oil, grease, etc., to reduce friction.

**luce** *n.* a fresh-water fish, the pike when full grown.
**lu•cent** *a.* shining; bright.
**lu•cid** *a.* shining; clear; easily understood, as of style; normally sane.
**Lu•ci•fer** *n.* the planet Venus, when appearing as the morning star; Satan.
**lu•cite** *n.* a very clear plastic compound.
**luck** *n.* accidental fortune, good or bad; fate; chance.
**lu•cre** *n.* material gain; profit, esp. ill-gotten.
**lu•cu•brate** *v.i.* to study by lamp or candlelight, or at night.
**lu•cu•lent** *a.* clear; self-evident.
**lu•di•crous** *a.* provoking laughter; ridiculous; droll.
**luff** *v.i.* to turn the head of a ship towards the wind; to sail nearer the wind.
**Luft•waf•fe** *n.* the German Air Force.
**lug** *v.t.* to pull with force; to tug; to haul.
**lug** *n.* a projecting piece by which an object may be grasped, supported, etc.
**lu•gu•bri•ous** *a.* mournful; woeful; dismal.
**lug•worm** a large earthworm.
**luke•warm** *a.* moderately warm; tepid; indifferent.
**lull** *v.t.* to soothe to sleep; to quiet.
**lum•ba•go** *n.* a painful rheumatic affection of the lumbar muscles. **lumbaginous, lumbar, lumbral** *a.* pert. to the lower part of the back.
**lum•ber** *n.* anything useless and cumbersome; odds and ends hoarded; timber cut and split for market.
**lum•ber** *v.i.* to move heavily.
**lu•mi•nar•y** *n.* any body which gives light, esp. one of the heavenly bodies.
**lump** *n.* a small mass of matter of indefinite shape; a swelling; the gross.
**lu•nar** *a.* pert. to the moon; measured by revolutions of the moon. Also **lunary. lunacy** *n.* madness, formerly supposed to be influenced by changes of moon. **lunatic** *a.* insane; *n.* a mad person. **lunation** *n.* the period from one new moon to the next. **lunar month,** period of the moon's revolution, about 29½ days. **lunar year,** period of twelve synodic lunar months (354⅓ days).
**lunch** *n.* a light meal taken between breakfast and dinner.
**lune** *n.* anything in the shape of a half-moon.
**lung** *n.* one of the two main organs of respiration in a breathing animal.
**lunge** *n.* in fencing, a sudden thrust.
**lu•pine** *n.* a genus of leguminous plants, some cultivated for their flowers, others for cattle fodder.
**lu•pus** *n.* a spreading tubercular condition affecting the skin.
**lurch** *n.* a sudden roll of a ship to one side; a staggering movement; *v.i.* to stagger.
**lurch** *n.* a critical move in the game of cribbage.
**lure** *n.* a decoy used by the falconer to recall the hawk; an artificial bait.
**lu•rid** *a.* extravagantly colored.
**lurk** *v.i.* to lie hidden; to lie in wait.
**lus•cious** *a.* excessively sweet.
**lush** *a.* luxuriant; juicy.
**lust** *n.* longing desire; sexual appetite; craving.
**lus•ter** *n.* clearness; glitter; gloss; renown; radiance; chandelier with drops or pendants of cut glass; a cotton dress fabric with glossy, silky surface; a pottery glaze.
**lus•trine** *n.* a glossy silk fabric.
**lus•trum** *n.* a period of five years; purification. **lustration** *n.* the act of purifying; the sacrifice or ceremony by which cities, fields, armies, or people were purified.
**lute** *n.* a stringed instrument with a pear-shaped body. **lutanist, luter, lutist** *n.* a lute-player.
**Lu•ther•an** *n.* a follower of Martin Luther; a member of the Lutheran Church. **-ism, Lutherism.**
**lu•thern** *n.* a dormer-window.
**lux•ate** *v.t.* to put out of joint; to dislocate.
**lux•u•ry** *n.* indulgence in the pleasures which wealth can procure; that which is not a necessity of life.
**Ly•ce•um** *n.* orig. a place in Athens where Aristotle taught his pupils.
**lydd•ite** *n.* picric acid; a powerful explosive used in shells.
**lye** *n.* alkaline solution of wood ashes and water; used in soap making.
**ly•ing** *a.* untruthful; *n.* habit of being untruthful. **-ly** *adv.*
**lymph** *n.* an alkaline fluid, watery in appearance, contained in the tissues and organs of the body.
**lynch** *v.t.* to inflict capital punishment (on an accused) illegally.
**lynx** *n.* an animal of the cat tribe with abnormally keen sight.

lynx

**ly•on•naise** *a.* prepared with onions.
**lyre** *n.* a stringed, musical instrument in use among ancient Greeks, esp. to accompany minstrels. **lyrate** *a.* shaped like a lyre. **-bird** *n.* an Australian bird

lyrebird

with tail feathers which curve upward in the shape of a lyre. **lyric.** *n.* orig. a poem sung to music; a short, subjective poem expressing emotions of poet. **lyricism** *n.* lyrical quality of a poem; emotional expression.

**ma'am** *n.* contr. of **madam.**
**ma•ca•bre** *a.* gruesome; ghastly; grim.
**mac•a•dam** *n.* a road-surface material of crushed stones.
**ma•caque** *n.* a genus of Asian monkeys.
**mac•a•ro•ni** *n.* a paste of wheat flour made in long slender tubes; a dandy of the 18th cent. **-c** *a.* affected; burlesque verse in modern words with Latinized endings.
**mac•a•roon** *n.* a small cookie made of white of egg, ground almonds or coconut, and sugar.
**ma•caw** *n.* a long-tailed S. Amer. parrot.
**mace** *n.* a heavy club of metal; a staff carried as an emblem of authority; a billiard cue.
**mace** *n.* a spice made from nutmeg.
**mac•er•ate** *v.t.* to soften by soaking; to cause to grow thin.
**ma•chet•e** *n.* a heavy knife or cleaver used to cut down sugar canes, and as a weapon.
**Ma•chi•a•vel•lian** *a.* pert. to Machiavelli; unscrupulous; crafty.
**mach•i•nate** *v.t.* to contrive, usually with evil or ulterior motive. **machinator** *n.* one who plots.
**ma•chine** *n.* *(Mech.)* any contrivance for the conversion and direction of motion; an apparatus for doing some kind of work; an engine; a vehicle. **— gun** *n.* an automatic small-arms weapon capable of continuous firing. **-ry** *n.* machines collectively; the parts of a machine. **machinist** *n.* one who makes machinery; one who works at a machine.
**mack•er•el** *n.* an edible sea fish with blue and black stripes above and silver color below.
**mack•i•naw** *n.* a short woolen coat, usually plaid.
**mack•in•tosh** *n.* a waterproof coat.
**mac•ra•me** *n.* a coarse fringe.
**mac•ro•bi•ot•ic** *a.* long-lived. **macrobiosis** *n.* long life.
**mac•ro•cosm** *n.* the great universe.
**ma•cron** *n.* short line put over vowel to show it is long in quantity or quality, as *fate.*
**mac•ro•scop•ic** *a.* visible to the naked eye; opp. of *microscopic.*
**mac•u•la** *n.* a spot; *pl.* **-e. -te** *v.t.* to spot.
**mad** *a.* *(comp.* **-der;** *superl.* **-dest)** deranged in mind; insane; crazy; frenzied; angry; infatuated; irrational, as a scheme. **-den** *v.t.* to enrage; to drive mad; to annoy.
**mad•am** *n.* a formal mode of address in speaking to a married or elderly woman. **madame** *n.* French form.
**Ma•dei•ra** *n.* a rich amber-colored wine from *Madeira;* port.
**ma•de•moi•selle** *n.* French mode of addressing unmarried lady.
**Ma•don•na** *n.* the Virgin Mary; a statue of the Virgin.
**mad•ras** *n.* a fine cotton cloth, usu. striped or plaid.
**mad•re•pore** *n.* white perforate coral.
**mad•ri•gal** *n.* a short love poem; an unaccompanied part-song.
**mael•strom** *n.* a whirlpool.
**mae•sto•so** *a.* and *adv.* *(Mus.)* with dignity.
**mae•stro** *n.* master, esp. an eminent composer, conductor, or teacher of music.
**Mae West** *n.* an inflatable life jacket.
**ma•fi•a** *n.* a criminal Sicilian secret society; hostility to the law.
**mag•a•zine** *n.* a military storehouse; part of a ship where ammunition is stored; a periodical containing miscellaneous articles.
**ma•gen•ta** *n.* a purplish dye from coal tar.
**mag•got** *n.* a grub; larva of a housefly.
**ma•gi** *n.pl.* a class of priests among the ancient Persians. **Magi** *n.* in the N.T. the Wise Men who came to visit the infant Jesus.
**mag•ic** *n.* the feigned art of influencing nature or future events by occult means; sorcery; charm. **-ian** *n.* one skilled in magic; a conjurer.
**mag•is•te•ri•al** *a.* pert. to or conducted by a magistrate; authoritative; judicial; overbearing.
**mag•is•trate** *n.* a person vested with public judicial authority; a justice of the peace.
**mag•ma** *n.* a paste of mineral or organic matter; *(Geol.)* the molten rock beneath the earth's crust; *(Pharm.)* a salve.
**Mag•na Car•ta (Charta)** *n.* great charter of English public and private liberties signed by King John in 1215.
**mag•na•nim•i•ty** *n.* greatness of mind; generosity of heart, esp. in forgiveness.
**mag•nate** *n.* an eminent person, esp. a wealthy businessman.
**mag•ne•si•um** *n.* the silvery-white metallic base of magnesia, burning with an intensely brilliant white light and used for fireworks, flashbulbs, etc.
**mag•net** *n.* the loadstone; a bar of iron having property of attracting iron or steel and, when suspended, of pointing N. and S.; a person or thing with powers of attraction. **-ize** *v.t.* to give magnetic properties to; to attract. **-ism** *n.* the natural cause of magnetic force; the science of the phenomena of magnetic force; attraction. **-o** *n.* a magnetoelectric machine, esp. used to generate ignition spark in internal-combustion engine. **-ic field** *n.* the sphere of influence of magnetic forces.
**mag•ni•fy** *v.t.* to make greater; to cause to appear greater. **Magnificat** *n.* the song of the Virgin Mary. **magnificent** *a.* splendid; brilliant.
**mag•nil•o•quent** *a.* speaking pompously; boastful.
**mag•ni•tude** *n.* greatness; size; importance.
**mag•no•lia** *n.* a species of tree bearing large perfumed flowers.
**mag•num** *n.* a wine bottle holding two quarts. **— opus** *n.* one's best artistic or literary work.
**mag•pie** *n.* a bird of the crow family, with a harsh chattering cry.
**Mag•yar** *n.* dominant people of Hungary; the language of Hungary.
**ma•ha•ra•jah** *n.* *(fem.* **maharani** or

maharanee) the title of an Indian prince.

**ma•hat•ma** *n.* a man of saintly life with supernatural powers derived from purity of soul.

**ma•hog•a•ny** *n.* a tree of hard, reddish wood used for furniture; the red-brown color of mahogany.

**maid** *n.* a girl or unmarried woman; a female domestic servant. **-en name** *n.* surname of a woman before marriage.

**mail** *n.* defensive armor composed of steel rings or plates.

**mail** *n.* letters, packages, etc., carried by post; the person or means of conveyance for transit of letters, parcels, etc.

**maim** *v.t.* to deprive of the use of a limb; to disable; to disfigure.

**main** *a.* principal; first in size, importance, etc.; sheer; *n.* the principal pipe or line in water, gas, or electricity system. **-land** *n.* a continent, as distinct from islands.

**main•tain** *v.t.* and *v.i.* to hold or keep in any state; to sustain; to preserve; to defend, as an argument; to support.

**maize** *n.* Indian corn, a cereal; yellow.

**maj•es•ty** *n.* grandeur; exalted dignity; royal state; the title of a sovereign.

**ma•jol•i•ca** *n.* a decorative, enameled pottery.

**ma•jor** *a.* greater in number, quality, quantity, or extent; *(Mus.)* greater by a semitone; pert. to a field of study; *n.* an officer in the army ranking below a lieutenant colonel. **— general** *n.* an army officer in rank below a lieutenant-general. **-ity** *n.* the greater part; more than half; full legal age (21).

**make** *v.t.* to cause to be or do; to create; to constitute; to compel; to appoint; to secure; to arrive at; to reckon; to perform; *n.* structure; texture; form; style; brand.

**mal•a•chite** *n.* a green carbonate of copper, used for inlaid work.

**mal•ad•just•ment** *n.* faulty adjustment; inability to adjust to one's environment.

**mal•ad•min•is•tra•tion** *n.* faulty administration, esp. of public affairs.

**mal•a•droit** *a.* clumsy, awkward.

**mal•a•dy** *n.* a disease; ailment.

**Mal•a•gas•y** *n.* a native of, or the language of, Madagascar.

**mal•aise** *n.* a physical discomfort.

**mal•a•prop(ism)** *n.* the ludicrous misuse of a word.

**ma•lar•i•a** *n.* a febrile disease transmitted by the bite of mosquito.

**Ma•lay** *n.* a native of the Malay Peninsula.

**mal•con•tent** *a.* discontented; rebellious.

**male** *a.* pert. to the sex which begets young; masculine; *(Bot.)* having stamens; *n.* a male animal.

**mal•e•dic•tion** *n.* evil-speaking; a curse.

**mal•e•fac•tor** *n.* an evil-doer; a criminal.

**ma•lev•o•lent** *a.* evilly disposed; malicious.

**mal•fea•sance** *n.* misconduct, esp. in public affairs.

**mal•for•ma•tion** *n.* irregular formation. **malformed** *a.* deformed.

**mal•func•tion** *v.i.* to fail to operate correctly or normally.

**ma•lic** *a.* from the apple.

**mal•ice** *n.* ill will; spite; desire to injure others; *(Law)* criminal intention. **malicious** *a.* spiteful; showing malice.

**ma•lign** *a.* malicious; evil; spiteful. **-ant** *a.* being evilly disposed; harmful; (of disease) virulent; likely to prove fatal.

**ma•lin•ger** *v.i.* to feign illness in order to avoid duty. **-er** *n.* a shirker.

**mall** *n.* a level, shaded walk; a heavy mallet used in game of pall-mall.

**mal•lard** *n.* a wild drake or duck.

**mal•le•a•ble** *a.* capable of being hammered or extended by beating; amenable; tractable.

**mal•let** *n.* any of various types of wooden hammer.

**mal•low** *n.* plant with downy leaves, and having emollient properties.

**mal•nu•tri•tion** *n.* the state of being undernourished.

**mal•od•or•ous** *a.* having an offensive odor.

**mal•prac•tice** *n.* professional impropriety or negligence.

**malt** *n.* barley or other grain steeped in water until it germinates, then dried in a kiln for use in brewing.

**Mal•tese** *n.* native of Malta; its dialect and people.

**mal•treat** *v.t.* to ill-treat; to abuse; to handle roughly.

**mal•ver•sa•tion** *n.* corruption in office; fraudulent handling of public funds.

**mam•bo** *n.* rhythmic music and dance of Sp. Amer. origin.

**mam•ma** *n.* child's name for mother.

**mam•ma** *n.* milk-secreting gland in females; *pl.* **-e. mammary** *a.*

**Mam•ma•li•a** *n.pl.* *(Zool.)* the class of mammals or animals which suckle their young.

**mam•mon** *n.* wealth personified and worshipped.

**mam•moth** *n.* a huge extinct elephant; *a.* colossal.

**mam•my** *n.* a Negro woman who took care of white children, esp. in the South.

**man** *n.* a human being; an adult male; a manly person. **— hour** *n.* work performed by one man in one hour. **-kind** *n.* human beings. **— of-war** *n.* a warship. **— power** *n.* a unit of power equal to one-eighth of a horsepower; the total number of people in industry, the armed forces, etc. **-slaughter** *n.* culpable homicide without malice aforethought.

**man•a•cle** *n.* a handcuff.

**man•age** *v.t.* to direct; to control; to carry on; to cope with. **-ment** *n.* the act of managing; administration; body of directors controlling a business.

**Man•chu** *n.* one of the original inhabitants of Manchuria.

**man•ci•ple** *n.* a steward; a caterer.

**man•da•mus** *n.* a written order.

**man•da•rin** *n.* a European name for a Chinese provincial governor; the language used in Chinese official circles; a small orange; a long brocade coat with loose sleeves.

**man•date** *n.* an official order; a precept; a prescript of the Pope; a commission to act as representative of a body of people. **mandatory** *a.* containing a mandate; obligatory.

**man•di•ble** *n.* a jaw; in vertebrates, the lower jaw; in birds, the upper or lower beak.

**man•do•lin** *n.* a musical instrument with a rounded pear-shaped body.

**man•drake** *n.* a narcotic plant, the root thought to resemble human form.

**man•drel** *n.* a shaft on which objects may be fixed for turning, milling, etc.; the spindle of a lathe.

**man•drill** *n.* a large African baboon.

**mandrill**

**mane** *n.* long hair on the neck of an animal.

**ma•nege** *n.* the art of horsemanship; a riding school.

**ma•neu•ver** *n.* a controlled strategic movement; scheme; artifice.

**man•ga•nese** *n.* a grayish, hard, brittle metal which oxidizes rapidly in humid atmosphere.

**mange** *n.* a parasitic disease affecting the skin of animals, causing hair to fall out.

**man•ger** *n.* a trough for holding fodder for cattle.

**man•gle** *n.* a machine for pressing linen between rollers.

**man•gle** *v.t.* to hack; to mutilate; to spoil the beauty of.

**man•go** *n.* a tropical tree, the unripe fruit used in making chutney.

**mango**

**man•grove** *n.* a tropical tree the bark of which is used in tanning.

**man•hat•tan** *n.* a cocktail containing whiskey, vermouth, bitters.

**ma•ni•a** *n.* madness; a violent excitement; extravagant enthusiasm; an obsession. **-c** *n.* a madman; *a.* raving; frenzied.

**man•i•cure** *n.* the care of the hands and nails.

**man•i•fest** *a.* clearly visible; apparent to the mind or senses. **-ation** *n.* the act of revealing; the state of being revealed; display; disclosure. **-o** *n.* a public declaration of the principles or policy of a leader or party.

**man•i•fold** *a.* many and varied; numerous; *v.t.* to make many copies of, as letters, by a machine, such as a duplicator; *n.* *(Mech.)* a pipe fitted with several lateral outlets.

**man•i•kin** *n.* a little man; a dwarf; a model of the human body used in medical schools; a mannequin.

**ma•nil•a** *n.* a cigar made in Manila, capital of the Philippine Islands. **—paper** *n.* a stout buff-colored paper.

**man•i•ple** *n.* part of a Roman legion; a scarf worn by celebrant at mass.

**ma•nip•u•late** *v.t.* to operate with the hands; to manage (a person) in a skillful, esp. unscrupulous, way; to falsify.

**man•na** *n.* the food supplied miraculously to the Israelites in the wilderness; sweetish juice of the ash; spiritual nourishment.

**man•ne•quin** *n.* one employed to model new fashions; figure for a similar purpose.

**man•ner** *n.* way of doing anything; custom; style; a person's habitual bearing; *pl.* social behavior; customs.

**man•or** *n.* the land belonging to a lord; a unit of land in feudal times over which the owner had full jurisdiction.

**man•sard roof** *n.* roof in which lower slope is nearly vertical and upper much inclined.

**manse** *n.* a minister's residence.

**man•sion** *n.* a large, imposing house; a manor house.

**man•sue•tude** *n.* gentleness; tameness.

**man•tel** *n.* the shelf above a fireplace; the framework around a fireplace.

**man•til•la** *n.* a veil covering head and shoulders, worn esp. by Spanish women.

**man•tis** *n.* a genus of insects holding the forelegs folded as if praying.

**mantis**

**man•tis•sa** *n.* the decimal part of a logarithm.

**man•tle** *n.* a loose outer garment; a cloak; a covering. **-t** *n.* a bulletproof shelter.

**man•tu•a** *n.* a woman's loose gown.

**man•u•al** *a.* pert. to, made by or done with the hand; *n.* a handbook or small textbook; a keyboard of a pipe organ.

**man•u•fac•ture** *n.* making goods either by hand or by machine.

**man•u•mit** *v.t.* to give freedom to a slave; to emancipate.

**ma•nure** *v.t.* to enrich soil with fertilizer; *n.* animal excrement used as fertilizer.

**man•u•script** *a.* written, or typed, by hand; *n.* a book written by hand; an author's script or typewritten copy for perusal by publisher.

**man•y** *a.* comprising a great number *n.* and *pron.* a number of people or things.

**map** *n.* a representation, esp. on a plane surface, of the features of the earth, or of part of it.

**ma•ple** *n.* a deciduous tree, valuable for its timber and the sap from which sugar is extracted.

**mar•a•bou** *n.* a kind of stork; the feathers of this bird used as trimming.

**ma•ra•ca** *n.* gourd-shaped rattle.

**mar•a•schi•no** *n.* a sweet liqueur distilled from cherries.

**mar•a•thon** *n.* a foot race (approx. 26 miles); endurance contest.

**ma•raud** *v.i.* to rove in quest of plunder; to loot.

**mar•ble** *n.* hard limestone which takes on a brilliant polish and is used for ornaments, statuary, etc.

**mar•ca•site** *n.* white iron pyrite used in jewelry because of its brilliance.

**mar•cel** *n.* an artificial hair wave.

**March** *n.* third month of year, named after *Mars,* Roman god of war.

**march** *v.i.* to move in order, as soldiers; to proceed at a steady pace.

**mar•chio•ness** *n.* the wife of a marquis; lady, holding in her own right, the rank of marquis.

**mare** *n.* the female of the horse, mule, donkey, etc.

**mar•ga•rine** *n.* pearly waxlike substance obtained from animal fat; a fatty extract of certain vegetable oils.

**mar•gin** *n.* a border; a blank space at top, bottom and sides, of a written or printed page; allowance made for contingencies.

**mar•gue•rite** *n.* a large oxeye daisy.

**mar•i•gold** *n.* name applied to a plant bearing yellow or orange flowers.

**ma•ri•jua•na** *n.* a type of hemp dried and used as tobacco, having a narcotic effect.

**ma•rim•ba** *n.* a jazz-band instrument resembling the xylophone.

**ma•ri•na** *n.* a small harbor or boat basin.

**mar•i•nade** *n.* a seasoned vinegar or wine used for steeping meat, fish, vegetables.

**ma•rine** *a.* pert. to the sea; found in, or near, the sea.

**mar•i•o•nette** *n.* a puppet worked by strings.

**mar•i•tal** *a.* pert. to a husband or to marriage.

**mar•i•time** *a.* pert. to the sea; bordering on the sea; living near the sea; pert. to overseas trade or navigation.

**mar•jo•ram** *n.* an aromatic plant of the mint family used in cookery.

**mark** *n.* a visible sign; a cross; a character made by one who cannot write; a stamp; a proof; a target; a point. **-sman** *n.* one who is expert at hitting a target. **trademark** *n.* a special symbol marked on commodities to indicate the maker.

**mark** *n.* unit of exchange of various countries.

**mar•ket** *n.* a public meeting place for the purchase and sale of commodities; a trading center.

**marl** *n.* a crumbly soil used for fertilizer and in brickmaking.

**mar•lin** *n.* a large slender deep-sea fish.

**mar•line** *n.* a small rope used to secure a splicing. **-spike** *n.* a pointed tool used to separate strands of a rope in splicing.

**mar•ma•lade** *n.* a preserve made of the pulp and peel of fruit.

**mar•mo•set** *n.* a small monkey of S. America.

**marmoset**

**mar•mot** *n.* a bushy-tailed rodent; the prairie dog.

**ma•roon** *n.* orig. a fugitive slave of the W. Indies; a marooned person; *v.t.* to put ashore on a desolate island; to isolate, cut off.

**ma•roon** *a.* a brownish-crimson.

**marque** *n.* seizure by way of retaliation.

**mar•quee** *n.* a roof-like structure or awning outside a public building.

**mar•que•try** *n.* decorative, inlaid wood; the process of inlaying wood with designs.

**mar•quis** *n.* noble ranking next below a duke; pointed oval diamond.

**mar•qui•sette** *n.* thin, lightweight fabric.

**mar•row** *n.* the soft substance in the cavities of bones; the essence of anything.

**mar•ry** *v.t.* to unite, take, or give in wedlock. **marriage** *n.* the legal union of husband and wife; the ceremony, civil or religious, by which two people become husband and wife.

**Mars** *n.* the Roman god of war; the planet nearest to the earth.

**Mar•seil•laise** *n.* the French national anthem.

**marsh** *n.* a tract of low, swampy land. **— gas** *n.* a gaseous product of decomposing organic matter. **-mallow** *n.* a red-flowered plant growing in marshes; a confection made from the root of this, or from gelatin.

**mar•shal** *n.* a civil officer of a district with powers of a sheriff; a person in charge of arrangements for ceremonies, etc.

**mar•su•pi•al** *a.* having an external pouch, to carry the young.

**mart** *n.* a market.

**mar•ten** *n.* a kind of weasel, valued for its fur.

**mar•tial** *a.* pert. to war or to the armed services; warlike; military. **— law** *n.* law enforced by military authorities and

superseding civil law.
**mar•tin** *n.* a bird of the swallow family.

martin

**mar•ti•net** *n.* a strict disciplinarian.
**mar•tin•gale** *n.* a strap fastened to a horse's girth to keep its head down.
**mar•ti•ni** *n.* a cocktail of dry vermouth and gin.
**mar•tyr** *n.* one who suffers punishment or the sacrifice of his life for adherence to principles or beliefs.
**mar•vel** *n.* anything wonderful; *v.i.* to wonder exceedingly. **-ous** *a.* wonderful; astonishing.
**Marx•ism** *n.* the doctrines of Karl Marx, which profoundly influenced socialists and communists of Europe in latter part of 19th cent.
**mar•zi•pan** *n.* a paste of ground almonds, sugar and egg white made into confections.
**mas•car•a** *n.* a cosmetic preparation for eyelashes.
**mas•cot** *n.* a person or thing reputed to bring good luck.
**mas•cu•line** *a.* male; strong; virile; (of a woman) mannish.
**mash** *v.t.* to beat to a pulp or soft mass; to mix malt with hot water.
**mash•ie** *n.* a golf club with short iron head.
**mask** *n.* a covering for the face; an impression of a human face, as a *death mask;* a respirator to be worn as protection against poison gas; a false face, as worn by children at Halloween.
**mas•och•ism** *n.* a form of sex gratification by endurance of physical or mental pain.
**ma•son** *n.* a builder in stone, brick, etc.; a Freemason. **-ry** *n.* the work of a mason; stonework; freemasonry.
**ma•son•ite** *n.* a fiberboard made from pressed wood fibers used in building.
**mas•quer•ade** *n.* an assembly of masked persons; disguise.
**mass** *n.* the quantity of matter in a body; a shapeless lump; magnitude; crowd; chief portion. **-ive** *a.* forming a mass; bulky; weighty. **— production** *n.* cheap production in great quantities.
**Mass** *n.* the communion service in the R.C. Church; the music to accompany High Mass. **High Mass** *n.* Mass celebrated with music. **Low Mass** *n.* a simple celebration of Mass without music.
**mas•sa•cre** *n.* general, ruthless slaughter; carnage.
**mas•sage** *n.* a treatment of physical disorders by kneading, rubbing, carried out by specialists. **massagist, masseur** *n.* specialist in massage.
**mast** *n.* upright pole supporting rigging and sails of a ship.
**mast** *n.* fruit of oak, beech, esp. as food for swine.
**mas•ter** *n.* one who directs and controls; an employer of labor; male head of a household; a ship captain; a graduate degree in arts, or science *(abbrevs.* M.A., M.Sc.). **-ful** *a.* compelling; domineering. **— key** *n.* a key which opens several locks. **— switch** *n.* an electric switch which must be turned on before other switches will function.
**mas•ti•cate** *v.t.* to chew; to reduce to a pulp.
**mas•tiff** *n.* a powerful breed of dog.

mastiff

**mas•ti•tis** *n. (Med.)* inflammation of the breast.
**mas•to•don** *n.* an extinct mammal resembling an elephant.
**mas•toid** *a.* nipple-shaped; *n.* the prominence on the temporal bone behind the human ear.
**mas•tur•bate** *v.i.* to practice self-excitation; autoeroticism.
**mat** *n.* a coarse fabric of twine, rope, or rushes for wiping the shoes on; a rug; a border or frame for a picture.
**mat, matte** *a.* having a dull finish; not shiny.
**mat•a•dor, matadore** *n.* the man who kills the bull in a bullfight.
**match** *n.* splint of wood or taper tipped with a substance capable of ignition by friction with a rough surface; a piece of rope for firing a gun; a fuse.
**match** *n.* a person or thing equal to or resembling another; a sporting contest; a marriage; a mate. **-less** *a.* having no match; peerless; unique.
**mate** *n.* a companion; a spouse; one of a pair; an assistant.
**mate** *v.t.* to checkmate (chess).
**ma•te•ri•al** *a.* consisting of matter corporeal; (of persons) not spiritually minded; the substance out of which something is fashioned; fabric. **-ize** *v.t.* to render material; to give bodily form to. **-ism** *n.* the theory that matter, and matter only, exists in the universe.
**ma•te•ri•a med•i•ca** *n. (Med.)* the substances used in the making of medicines, drugs, etc.
**ma•ter•nal** pert. to a mother; motherly; related on the mother's side.
**math•e•mat•ics** *n.* the science of quantity and space, including arithmetic, algebra, trigonometry, geometry.
**mat•in** *n.* a morning song; a morning service.
**ma•tri•cide** *n.* the murder of a mother.
**ma•tric•u•late** *v.t.* and *v.i.* to enroll as a student, esp. of a college.
**mat•ri•mo•ny** *n.* marriage; wedlock.
**ma•trix** *n.* the womb; the cavity where anything is formed; a mold, esp. for casting printer's type; rock where minerals are embedded.

**ma•tron** *n.* a married woman; a woman in charge of domestic affairs of an institution.

**mat•ter** *n.* that which occupies space and is the object of the senses; substance.

**mat•ting** *n.* mat work; coarse material used as floor covering.

**mat•tock** *n.* a kind of pickaxe with only one end pointed.

**mat•tress** *n.* a casing of strong fabric filled with hair, foam rubber, cotton, etc.

**mat•u•rate** *v.i.* to mature.

**ma•ture** *a.* ripe; fully developed; *(Med.)* come to suppuration; resulting from adult experience; due for payment, as a bill.

**ma•tu•ti•nal** *a.* morning; early.

**maud•lin** *a.* over-sentimental; tearful.

**maul** *n.* a heavy wooden hammer; *v.t.* to maltreat; to handle roughly.

**maun•der** *v.i.* to mutter; to talk or to wander aimlessly.

**mau•so•le•um** *n.* a large imposing tomb.

**mauve** *n.* a delicate purple color.

**mav•er•ick** *n.* an unbranded calf; an independent.

**maw** *n.* the stomach of an animal; in birds, the craw.

**mawk•ish** *a.* loathsome; sickly sweet; maudlin.

**max•il•lar•y** *a.* pert. to the upper jawbone or jaw.

**max•im** *n.* an accepted principle; an axiom; a proverb or precept.

**max•i•mum** *a.* greatest; *n.* the greatest number, quantity or degree.

**may** *v.i.* expressing possibility, permission, contingency; uncertainty; hope.

**May** *n.* the fifth month of the year; *(Fig.)* youthful prime. **-pole** *n.* a pole with streamers, around which people dance on May Day.

**may•hem** *n.* *(Law)* the offense of maiming by violence.

**may•on•naise** *n.* a sauce or dressing for salads.

**may•or** *n.* the chief official of a city or town.

**maze** *n.* a network of intricate paths; a labyrinth; confused condition; mental perplexity.

**me** *pron.* the objective case of first pers. pronoun, "*I*".

**mead** *n.* a fermented drink made of honey, yeast and water.

**mead•ow** *n.* a low, level tract of grassland; pasture. **-lark** *n.* a yellow-breasted Amer. songbird.

**mea•ger** *a.* scanty; having little flesh; gaunt.

**meal** *n.* the food served at one time; a repast.

**meal** *n.* edible grain coarsely ground. **-worm** *n.* an insect found in meal.

**mean** *a.* humble in rank or birth; sordid; lacking dignity; stingy; malicious.

**mean** *a.* in a middle position; average; *n.* the middle point of quantity, rate, position, or degree.

**mean** *v.t.* to have in view; to intend; to signify. **-t, -ing** *n.* that which is meant; sense; signification; *a.* expressive.

**me•an•der** *v.i.* to flow with a winding course; to saunter aimlessly.

**mea•sles** *n.* *(Med.)* a highly contagious disease, characterized by rash of bright red spots. **German measles,** a disease resembling measles but less severe.

**mea•sure** *n.* dimension reckoned by some standard; an instrument for measuring; a vessel of predetermined capacity; *(Mus.)* tempo; the notes between two bars in staff notation. **-ment** *n.* dimension, quantity, etc., ascertained by measuring with fixed unit.

**meat** *n.* flesh used as food; food of any kind.

**Mec•ca** *n.* the reputed birthplace of Mohammed; a holy city.

**me•chan•i•cal** *a.* pert. to machines, mechanism, or mechanics; produced or operated by machinery; automatic. **mechanic** *n.* one who works with or repairs machines or instruments. **mechanics** *n.* that branch of applied mathematics which deals with force and motion; the science of machines. **mechanism** *n.* the structure of a machine; machinery; a piece of machinery.

**med•al** *n.* a piece of metal, struck like a coin, as a memento or reward. **-lion** *n.* a large medal; a metal disk, usually round, with portrait in bas-relief. **-ist** *n.* a maker of medals; one who has been awarded a medal.

**med•dle** *v.i.* to interfere officiously; to tamper with.

**me•di•al** *a.* in, or through, the middle; pert. to a mean or average. **median** *a.* situated in the middle; *n.* *(Geom.)* a line drawn from vertex of a triangle to the middle point of the opposite side.

**me•di•ate** *a.* being between two extremes; intervening; depending on an intermediary; not direct. **mediation** *n.* the act of mediating; the steps taken to effect a reconciliation. **mediatize** *v.t.* to annex a small state, still leaving the ruler his title.

**med•ic** *n.* a leguminous plant with leaves like clover, used as fodder.

**med•i•cal** *a.* pert. to medicine or the art of healing; medicinal. **medicate** *v.t.* to treat with medicine.

**med•i•cine** *n.* any substance used in the treatment of disease; the science of healing and prevention of disease. **medicinal** *a.* pert. to medicine; remedial.

**me•di•e•val, mediaeval** *a.* pert. to or characteristic of the Middle Ages. **-ist** *n.* one who makes a special study of the Middle Ages.

**me•di•o•cre** *a.* middling; neither good nor bad; second-rate.

**med•i•tate** *v.t.* to consider thoughtfully; to intend; *v.i.* to ponder, esp. on religious matters. **meditative** *a.* given to reflection.

**med•i•ter•ra•ne•an** *a.* (of water) encircled by land. **Mediterranean** *a.* pert. to the almost landlocked water between S. Europe and N. Africa. **Mediterranean climate,** a climate of warm wet winters, hot dry summers.

**me•di•um** *n.* that which is in the middle; a

means; an agency; *pl.* **-s** or **media;** *a.* middle; average; middling.
**med•ley** *n.* a miscellaneous collection of things.
**me•dul•la** *n.* marrow in a bone; inner tissue of a gland; pith of hair or plants.
**me•du•sa** *n.* a kind of jellyfish, with tentacles.
**meed** *n.* reward; recompense.
**meek** *a.* submissive; humble; mild.
**meer•schaum** *n.* a fine, white clay used for the bowl of tobacco pipes.
**meet** *a.* fit; suitable.
**meet** *v.t.* to encounter; to join; to find; to satisfy; to pay, as a debt; to await arrival.
**me•ga-** *Gk. pref.* meaning great, mighty.
**meg•a•cy•cle** *n.* *(Elect.)* one million cycles.
**meg•a•lith** *n.* a huge stone.
**meg•a•lo•ma•ni•a** *n.* a form of insanity in which the patient has grandiose ideas of his own importance; lust for power.
**meg•a•phone** *n.* a large funnel-shaped device to increase the volume of sounds.
**meg•a•ton** *n.* a unit for measuring the power of thermonuclear weapons.
**meg•ohm** *n.* one million ohms.
**me•grim** *n.* a severe headache, usu. on one side.
**mei•o•sis** *n.* *(Rhet.)* a figure of speech which makes a deliberate understatement to achieve emphasis; a form of litotes.
**mel•an•chol•y** *n.* depression of spirits; morbidity; *a.* gloomy; depressed; pensive. **melancholia** *n.* morbid state of depression; abnormal introspectiveness bordering on insanity.
**Mel•a•ne•sian** *a.* pert. to *Melanesia,* a S. Pacific dark-skinned island group; *n.* a native.
**mé•lange** *n.* a mixture; a medley.
**mel•a•nin** *n.* a black pigment found in the eye, hair and skin. **melanism** *n.* an excess of coloring matter in the skin
**mel•ba toast** *n.* thin slice of toast.
**meld** *v.t.* and *v.i.* to blend; merge; a combination of cards melded.
**me•lee** *n.* a confused, hand-to-hand fight.
**me•lio•rate** *v.t.* to improve; *v.i.* to become better.
**mel•lif•er•ous** *a.* producing honey. **mellifluence** *n.* a flowing sweetly or smoothly.
**mel•low** *a.* soft and ripe; well-matured; genial; jovial; resonant, as a voice.
**me•lo•de•on** *n.* a small hand keyboard organ; a kind of accordion.
**mel•o•dra•ma** *n.* a dramatic entertainment, sensational and emotional; a play of romantic sentiment and situation.
**mel•o•dy** *n.* a rhythmical succession of single sounds forming an agreeable musical air; a tune.
**mel•on** *n.* a kind of gourd with a sweet, juicy pulp, and a center full of seeds.
**melt** *v.t.* to reduce to a liquid state; to dissolve; to soften; to make tender.
**mem•ber** *n.* a limb, esp. of an animal body; a constituent part of a complex whole; one of a society, group, etc. **-ship** *n.* the state of being a member, or one of a group; members collectively.
**mem•brane** *n.* *(Anat.)* a thin, flexible tissue forming or lining an organ of the body; a sheet of parchment.
**me•mem•to** *n.* anything which serves as a reminder of a person or event; a souvenir.
**mem•oir** *n.* a short, biographical sketch; a scientific record of personal investigations on a subject.
**mem•o•ry** *n.* the faculty of retaining and recalling knowledge; recollection; remembrance. **memorial** *a.* serving as a reminder; contained in the memory. **memorialize** *v.t.* to commemorate; to present a memorial. **memorize** *v.t.* to commit to memory.
**men** *n.pl.* of **man.**
**men•ace** *n.* a threat or threatening; potential danger; *v.t.* to threaten.
**mé•nage** *n.* a household; housekeeping.
**me•nag•er•ie** *n.* a collection of caged wild animals for exhibition.
**mend** *v.t.* to repair; to set right; to improve.
**men•da•cious** *a.* given to telling lies; untruthful.
**men•di•cant** *a.* begging; living as a beggar; *n.* a beggar.
**me•ni•al** *a.* pert. to domestic service; servile; *n.* a servant; a servile person.
**me•nin•ges** *n.pl.* the three membranes enveloping the brain and spinal cord.
**me•nis•cus** *n.* a lens convex on one side and concave on the other; the curved surface of a liquid in a vessel; *(Math.)* a crescent.
**Men•non•ite** *n.* a member of or pert. to a Protestant sect favoring plain dress and plain living.
**men•o•pause** *n.* female change of life.
**men•sal** *a.* monthly.
**men•ses** *n.pl.* the monthly discharge from the uterus of the female. **menstrual** *a.* monthly; pert. to the menses. **menstruate** *v.i.* to discharge the menses.
**men•stru•um** *n.* a solvent.
**men•su•ra•ble** *a.* capable of being measured.
**men•tal** *a.* pert. to, or of, the mind; performed in the mind. **-ity** *n.* intellectual power; mental attitude.
**men•thol** *n.* a camphor obtained from oil of peppermint. **-ated** *a.* treated or flavored with menthol.
**men•tion** *n.* a brief notice; a casual comment; *v.t.* to notice; to name.
**men•tor** *n.* an experienced and prudent adviser.
**men•u** *n.* a bill of fare; the food served.
**me•phi•tis** *n.* noxious exhalation, esp. from the ground or from decaying matter.
**mer•can•tile** *a.* pert. to commerce. **mercantilism** *n.* the mercantile system. **— system,** the economic theory that money alone is wealth and that a nation's exports should far exceed its imports.
**mer•ce•nar•y** *a.* working merely for money or gain; hired; greedy; *n.* a hired soldier.
**mer•cer•ize** *v.t.* to treat cotton fabrics with caustic lye to impart a silky finish.
**mer•chant** *n.* one who engages in trade; a storekeeper. **merchandise** *n.*

commodities bought and sold. **— marine** *n.* the ships and men engaged in commerce.

**Mer•cu•ry** *n.* the planet of the solar system nearest to the sun. **mercury** *n.* a metallic chemical element, silvery-white in color, with very low melting point, used in barometers, thermometers, etc.

**mer•cy** *n.* forbearance; clemency; leniency shown to a guilty person; compassion. **merciful** *a.* full of mercy; compassionate.

**mere** *a.* nothing but; simple. **-ly** *adv.* simply; solely.

**mer•e•tri•cious** *a.* tawdry; cheap.

**mer•gan•ser** *n.* a diving fish-eating bird.

**merganser**

**merge** *v.t.* to cause to be swallowed up; to plunge or sink. **-r** *n.* a combine of commercial or industrial firms.

**me•rid•i•an** *n.* an imaginary line passing through the poles at right angles to the equator.

**me•ringue** *n.* a mixture of sugar and white of egg whipped until stiff, and baked in a cool oven.

**me•ri•no** *n.* a breed of sheep with very fine, thick fleece, orig. from Spain; a dress fabric of this wool.

**mer•it** *n.* quality of deserving reward; excellence; worth.

**mer•lin** *n.* a species of falcon.

**mer•maid** *n.* an imaginary sea creature with the upper body and head of a woman, and the tail of a fish. **merman** *n.* the male equivalent.

**mer•ry** *a.* gay; hilarious; lively. **—go-round** *n.* a revolving platform with horses, cars, etc.

**mer•thi•o•late** *n.* an antiseptic and germicide.

**me•sa** *n.* a high plateau.

**mes•dames** *n.pl.* of madam, Mrs.

**mes•en•te•ry** *n.* a fold of abdominal tissue keeping the intestines in place.

**mesh** *n.* the space between the threads of a net; network; *v.i.* to become interlocked, as gears of a machine.

**mes•mer•ism** *n.* exercising an influence over will and actions of another; hypnotism.

**mesne** *a.* middle; *(Law)* intermediate.

**mes•o•lith•ic** *a.* of period between paleolithic and neolithic ages.

**me•son** *n.* a particle equal in charge to, but having greater mass than, an electron or positron, and less mass than a neutron or proton.

**Mes•o•po•ta•mi•a** *n.* the land between Euphrates and Tigris; now Iraq.

**Mes•o•zo•ic** *a.* pert. to the second geological period.

**mess** *n.* unpleasant mixture; disorder; a muddle.

**mess** *n.* a dish of food served at one time; the meal; a number of people who eat together, esp. in army, navy, etc. **— kit** *n.* a soldier's portable eating equipment.

**mes•sage** *n.* a communication, verbal or written, sent by one person to another; an inspired utterance. **messenger** *n.* one who delivers a communication; one employed to deliver goods.

**mes•si•ah** *n.* an expected savior or liberator.

**mes•suage** *n. (Law)* a dwelling house with lands and outbuildings.

**mes•ti•zo** *n.* a half-caste, esp. the offspring of a Spaniard and an Amer. Indian.

**met** *pa.t.* and *pa.p.* of the verb **meet.**

**me•tab•o•lism** *n.* the name given to the chemical changes continually going on in the cells of living matter.

**me•ta•car•pus** *n.* the hand between the wrist and fingers; the bones of this part.

**met•age** *n.* official weighing, as of coal; the price paid for this.

**met•al** *n.* a mineral substance, opaque, fusible and malleable, capable of conducting heat and electricity; molten glass. **-lic** *a.* pert. to, like, or consisting of, metal. **-loid** *n.* an element with both metallic and nonmetallic properties, as arsenic; *a.* pert. to a metal.

**met•al•lur•gy** *n.* the art of working metals or of obtaining metals from ores.

**met•a•mor•pho•sis** *n.* a change of form or structure; evolution.

**met•a•phor** *n.* a figure of speech which makes an *implied* comparison between things which are not *literally* alike. **-ically** *adv.* **-ist** *n.* **mixed metaphor** *n.* a combination of metaphors drawn from different sources.

**met•a•phrase** *n.* literal, word for word translation from foreign language.

**met•a•phys•ics** *n.* the science which investigates first causes of all existence and knowledge; speculative philosophy.

**me•tas•ta•sis** *n.* change of position, state, or form; shift of malignant cells from one part of the body to another.

**met•a•tar•sus** *n.* the front part of the foot excluding the toes.

**me•tath•e•sis** *n.* the transposition of a letter or letters in a word, as in *curl,* orig. *crul.*

**met•a•zo•a** *n.pl.* multicellular organisms.

**mete** *v.t.* to distribute by measure; to allot, as punishment.

**me•te•or** *n.* any rapidly passing, luminous body seen in the atmosphere; a shooting star. **-ite** *n.* a mass of stone or metal from outer space which lands on earth. **-ograph** *n.* an instrument for automatically recording weather conditions. **-ological** *a.* **-ologist** *n.* **-ology** *n.* the science which treats of atmospheric phenomena, esp. in relation to weather forecasts.

**me•ter** *n.* a unit of length in the metric system, 39.37 U.S. inches. **metric** *a.* **metric system** *n.* a decimal system based on the French meter. **metrology** *n.* the science of weights and measures.

**me•ter** *n.* an instrument for recording the consumption of gas, electricity, water, etc.

**me•ter** *n.* in poetry, the rhythmical arrangement of syllables, these groups being termed *feet;* verse; stanza form; *(Music)* rhythmical structure indicated by measures; time or beat.

**meth•ane** *n.* an inflammable, hydrocarbon gas.

**meth•od** *n.* manner of proceeding, esp. in scientific research; orderliness; system; technique.

**Meth•od•ist** *n.* a member of Protestant sect founded in 18th century by Charles and John Wesley.

**meth•yl** *n.* the chemical basis of wood.

**me•tic•u•lous** *a.* orig. afraid to make a mistake; overscrupulous as to detail; over-exact.

**me•ton•y•my** *n.* a figure of speech in which the name of one thing is put for another associated with it.

**met•ro•nym•ic** *a.* a name derived from a female ancestor.

**me•trop•o•lis** *n.* the chief city of an area; a large city; a diocese.

**met•tle** *n.* spirit; courage. **-some** *a.*

**mew** *v.t.* to shed or cast; to confine, as in a cage; *n.pl.* stables around a court or alley.

**mewl** *v.i.* to whimper or whine.

**Mex•i•can** *n.* a native or inhabitant of Mexico.

**mez•za•nine** *n.* *(Archit.)* a low story between two main ones; in a theater usu. the first few rows in the balcony.

**mez•zo** *a.* middle; moderately.

**mi•as•ma** *n.* noxious exhalations from decomposing matter.

**mi•ca** *n.* a group of mineral silicates capable of cleavage into very thin, flexible, and often transparent laminae.

**mi•crobe** *n.* a minute organism; a bacterium or disease germ.

**mi•cro•ceph•a•lous** *a.* *(Med.)* having a very small head.

**mi•cro•coc•cus** *n.* a spherical or oval organism or bacterium.

**mi•cro•cosm** *n.* miniature universe; man, regarded as the epitome of the universe.

**mi•cro•film** *n.* film used to make reduced photographic copies of books, etc.

**mi•cro•graph** *n.* an instrument for producing microscopic engraving; a microphotograph. **micrographer** *n.* **micrography** *n.* the study of microscopic objects; the art of writing or engraving on a minute scale.

**mi•crol•o•gy** *n.* the science which deals with microscopic objects.

**mi•crom•e•ter** *n.* an instrument for measuring very small distances or angles.

**mi•cron** *n.* the millionth part of a meter.

**mi•cro•or•gan•ism** *n.* a microscopic organism.

**mi•cro•phone** *n.* an instrument for turning sound waves into electrical waves, so enabling them to be transmitted.

**mi•cro•pho•tog•ra•phy** *n.* the art of producing minute photographs.

**mi•cro•scope** *n.* an optical instrument for magnifying minute objects. **microscopic, -al** *a.* visible only with a microscope; very minute.

**mi•cro•zo•a** *n.pl.* microscopic animals.

**mic•tu•ri•tion** *n.* *(Med.)* the passing of urine.

**mid** *a.* situated between extremes; middle, as in *midair, mid-Atlantic.* **-shipman** *n.* rank in U.S. Navy and Coast Guard held by young men attending service academies.

**mid•dle** *a.* equidistant from the extremes; intermediate; *n.* middle point. **-man** *n.* an agent acting between producer and consumer; a go-between. **-weight** *n.* *(Boxing)* a boxer of a weight not more than 160 lbs. **—class** *n.* that section of the community between the very wealthy higher social classes and the laboring classes; the bourgeoisie.

**midge** *n.* a gnat; a very small person. **-t** *n.* a dwarf; *a.* miniature.

**mid•riff** *n.* the diaphragm; body part between chest and abdomen.

**midst** *n.* the middle; *prep.* amidst.

**mid•wife** *n.* a woman who assists another at childbirth.

**mien** *n.* manner; bearing; general appearance.

**miff** *v.t.* and *v.i.* to offend or take offense.

**might** *pa.t.* of verb **may.**

**might** *n.* power; strength; energy. **-iness** *n.* the state of being powerful; greatness.

**mi•gnon•ette** *n.* a sweet-scented, greenish-gray flowered plant.

**mi•graine** *n.* severe headache often accompanied by nausea.

**mi•grate** *v.i.* to remove one's residence from one place to another; (of birds) to fly to another place in search of warmer climate. **migrant** *n.* a person or creature who migrates.

**mil** *n.* .001 in., a unit of measurement in calculating the diameter of wire.

**milch** *a.* giving milk.

**mild** *a.* gentle; kind; placid; calm, or temperate, as weather.

**mil•dew** *n.* whitish coating of minute fungi on plants; a mold on paper, cloth, leather caused by dampness.

**mile** *n.* a measure of length equal to 5,280 ft. **geographical** or **nautical mile** *n.* 1/60 of 1 degree of the earth's equator, 6,080.2 ft. **-age** *n.* distance in miles; rate of travel calculated in miles; traveling expenses calculated on the number of miles traveled.

**mil•i•ar•y** *a.* like millet seeds. **miliaria** *n.* *(Med.)* a fever, accompanied by a rash resembling millet seeds (heat rash).

**mi•lieu** *n.* environment.

**mil•i•tant** *a.* aggressive; serving as a soldier. **militancy** *n.* warlike, fighting spirit. **militarist** *n.* one who upholds the doctrine of militarism; a student of military science. **military** *a.* pert. to soldiers, arms, or war; warlike; *n.* the army.

**mi•li•tia** *n.* a citizen army, liable to be called out in an emergency.

**milk** *n.* a white fluid secreted by female mammals for nourishment of their young and in some cases used for humans; the juice of certain plants. **Milky Way** *n.* the galaxy, an irregular, luminous belt in the heavens, from the light of innumerable stars. **condensed milk** *n.* milk with sugar added and evaporated to the consistency of syrup. **evaporated milk** *n.* unsweetened condensed milk.

**mill** *n.* a building equipped with machinery to grind grain into flour; an apparatus for grinding, as *coffee mill;* a factory or machinery used in manufacture. **-board** *n.* stout pasteboard used in bookbinding. **-dam** *n.* a dam built to provide water for turning a mill wheel. **-race** *n.* the current of water which turns mill wheel. **-stone** *n.* one of the flat stones used in grinding grain; a burden.

**mill** *n.* one-thousandth of a dollar; one-tenth of a cent.

**mil•len•ni•um** *n.* a thousand years; a future time or perfect peace on earth. **millennarian** *n.* one who believes in the millennium. **millennary** *a.* comprising a thousand; *n.* a period of a thousand years.

**mil•li-** *pref.* one-thousandth of. **-gram** *n.* one-thousandth of a gram. **-meter** *n.* one-thousandth of a meter.

**mil•liard** *n.* a thousand millions; a billion.

**mil•li•ner** *n.* one who makes or sells ladies' hats.

**mil•lion** *n.* a thousand thousands (1,000,000); **-aire** *n.* one whose wealth amounts to a million (or more) dollars.

**mil•li•pede** *n.* an insect with many legs.

**milt** *n.* the spleen; the reproductive glands or secretion of the male fish; *v.t.* to impregnate the female roe.

**mime** *n.* a farce in which scenes of real life are expressed by gesture only; an actor in such a farce. **-tic(al)** *a.* imitative. **mimic** *v.t.* to imitate; to burlesque; to ridicule by imitating another.

**mim•e•o•graph** *n.* a form of duplicating machine.

**mi•mo•sa** *n.* any of a genus of leguminous plants, shrubs, or trees, with small, fluffy flowers.

**min•a•ret** *n.* a turret on a Mohammedan mosque.

**mi•na•to•ry** *a.* threatening; menacing.

**mince** *v.t.* to cut or chop into very small pieces. **-meat** *n.* currants, raisins, spices, apple, suet and sugar, chopped and mixed together, used as pie filling; *(Fig.)* anything chopped up.

**mind** *n.* the intellectual faculty; the understanding; memory; opinion; inclination. purpose; a person regarded as an intellect. **— reader** *n.* one who can sense another's thoughts.

**mine** *n.* a pit in the earth from which minerals are excavated; a hidden explosive to blow up a wall, vessel, etc.; a profitable source. **-field** *n.* an area of land or stretch of the sea where mines have been placed.

**mine** *poss. pron.* belonging to me.

**min•er•al** *n.* any substance, generally inorganic, taken from the earth by mining; a chemical element or compound occurring in nature. **-ization** *n.* **-ize** *v.t.* to convert into or impregnate with minerals. **-ogy** *n.* the science of minerals and their classification.

**min•e•stro•ne** *n.* thick vegetable soup.

**min•gle** *v.t.* to mix; to blend; to join in.

**min•i•a•ture** *n.* a small-sized painting done on ivory, vellum, etc.; anything on a small scale; *a.* minute.

**min•i•fy** *v.t.* to lessen; to minimize.

**min•im** *n.* anything very minute; *(Med.)* 1/60 of a fluid dram; a drop; *(Mus.)* a half note. **-al** *a.* smallest possible. **-um** *n.* the least to which anything may be reduced.

**min•ion** *n.* a favorite; a servile flatterer; *(Print.)* a small type.

**min•is•ter** *n.* an agent or instrument; a clergyman; *(Brit.)* one entrusted with a govt. department; to serve. **ministration** *n.* the act of performing a service.

**min•i•ver** *n.* fine white fur.

**mink** *n.* a semiaquatic animal of the weasel tribe; its fur.

**mink**

**min•now** *n.* a small freshwater fish.

**mi•nor** *a.* lesser; inferior in bulk, degree, importance, etc.; *n.* a person under 21.

**mi•nor•ca** *n.* a breed of fowl.

**min•ster** *n.* church cathedral.

**min•strel** *n.* a medieval poet or wandering singer; an entertainer in a minstrel show.

**mint** *n.* the place where money is coined; a great amount of money.

**mint** *n.* an aromatic plant used for medicinal and culinary purposes.

**min•u•end** *n.* the number from which another is to be subtracted.

**min•u•et** *n.* a slow, stately dance.

**mi•nus** *prep.* less by; *a.* showing subtraction; negative; *n.* the sign (−) of subtraction; an amount less than nothing. **-cule** *a.* small; *n.* a lowercase letter.

**mi•nute** *a.* very small; slight; particular; exact.

**min•ute** *n.* the 60th part of an hour or degree; a moment; *pl.* the official record of a meeting.

**minx** *n.* a pert, saucy girl.

**mir•a•cle** *n.* a wonder; a supernatural happening; a prodigy. **miraculous** *a.* supernatural; extraordinary.

**mi•rage** *n.* an optical illusion; a delusion.

**mire** *n.* slimy soil; mud; defilement.

**mir•ror** *n.* a looking glass; a brilliantly polished reflecting surface.

**mirth** *n.* gaiety; merriment; joyousness; laughter.

**mis-** *pref.* wrong; ill.

**mis•ad•ven•ture** *n.* an unlucky adventure; a mishap.

**mis•ad•vise** *v.t.* to advise wrongly.

**mis•al•li•ance** *n.* an unfortunate alliance, esp. in marriage.

**mis•an•thrope** *n.* a hater of mankind.

**mis•ap•ply** *v.t.* to apply wrongly or dishonestly.
**mis•ap•pre•hend** *v.t.* to apprehend wrongly; to misconceive.
**mis•ap•pro•pri•ate** *v.t.* to use wrongly, esp. to embezzle money.
**mis•be•got•ten** *a.* unlawfully conceived; illegitimate.
**mis•be•have** *v.i.* to behave badly, improperly or dishonestly.
**mis•be•lieve** *v.t.* to believe wrongly.
**mis•cal•cu•late** *v.t.* to calculate wrongly.
**mis•car•riage** *n.* failure; premature birth.
**mis•ce•ge•na•tion** *n.* a mixture of races by interbreeding.
**mis•cel•la•ne•ous** *a.* mixed; heterogenous.
**mis•chance** *n.* a mishap; ill luck.
**mis•chief** *n.* harm; damage; conduct intended to annoy. **mischievous** *a.* tending to stir up trouble; playfully annoying.
**mis•ci•ble** *a.* capable of being mixed.
**mis•con•ceive** *v.t.* to misunderstand.
**mis•con•duct** *n.* bad management; dishonest conduct.
**mis•con•strue** *v.i.* to interpret wrongly; misunderstand.
**mis•count** *v.t.* to count wrongly; to miscalculate.
**mis•cre•ant** *n.* unprincipled person.
**mis•cue** *n.* *(Billiards)* a stroke spoiled by the cue slipping; a mistake.
**mis•date** *v.t.* to put a wrong date on; *n.* a wrong date.
**mis•deal** *v.t.* and *v.i.* to deal cards wrong; *n.* wrong deal. **-t** *pa.t.*
**mis•deed** *n.* an evil deed, a crime.
**mis•de•mean•or** *n.* dishonest conduct; *(Law)* a crime less than felony.
**mis•di•rect** *v.t.* to direct or advise wrongly.
**mi•ser** *n.* one who hoards money and lives in wretched surroundings.
**mis•er•a•ble** *a.* unhappy; causing misery; worthless; deplorable.
**mis•er•y** *n.* great unhappiness; extreme pain of body or mind.
**mis•fire** *n.* (of internal combustion engine, gun, etc.) failure to start or go off.
**mis•for•tune** *n.* ill luck.
**mis•give** *v.t.* to fill with doubt; to cause to hesitate; *v.i.* to fail.
**mis•guide** *v.t.* to lead astray; to advise wrongly.
**mis•han•dle** *v.t.* to maltreat; to bungle.
**mis•in•form** *v.t.* to give wrong information to.
**mis•in•ter•pret** *v.t.* to interpret or explain wrongly.
**mis•join•der** *n.* *(Law)* introduction into court of parties or causes not belonging.
**mis•judge** *v.t.* to judge wrongly.
**mis•lay** to lay down something in a place which cannot later be recollected.
**mis•lead** *v.t.* to lead astray.
**mis•man•age** *v.t.* to manage incompetently.
**mis•no•mer** *n.* a wrong name; incorrect designation.
**mi•sog•a•my** *n.* hatred of marriage.
**mi•sog•y•ny** *n.* hatred of women.
**mis•place** *v.t.* to place wrongly; to mislay.
**mis•print** *v.t.* to make an error in printing.
**mis•pro•nounce** *v.t.* to pronounce incorrectly.
**mis•quote** *v.t.* to quote incorrectly.
**mis•reck•on** *v.t.* to estimate or reckon incorrectly.
**mis•rep•re•sent** *v.i.* to represent falsely; to report inaccurately.
**mis•rule** *n.* disorder; misgovernment.
**Miss** *n.* title of unmarried women; girl.
**miss** *v.t.* to fail to hit, reach, find, catch, notice; to be without; to feel the want of.
**mis•sal** *n.* a book containing the R.C. service of the mass for a year.
**mis•sel** *n.* the large European thrush, supposed to eat mistletoe berries.
**mis•shape** *v.t.* to shape badly; to deform. **-en** *a.*
**mis•sile** *n.* that which is thrown or shot. **guided missile** *n.* a projected unmanned object which travels above the earth and performs some specific function, such as communication.
**mis•sion** *n.* the act of sending; the duty on which one is sent. **-ary** *a.* pert. to missions or missionaries; *n.* one sent to preach religion.
**mis•sive** *n.* a letter or message.
**mis•spell** *v.t.* to spell incorrectly.
**mis•spend** *v.t.* to spend foolishly; to squander.
**mist** *n.* visible vapor in the lower atmosphere; droplets of rain; a cloudiness or film.
**mis•take** *v.t.* to misunderstand; to take one person for another; *v.i.* to err.
**mis•ter** *n.* sir; title of courtesy to a man (abbrev. **Mr.**).
**mis•tle•toe** *n.* a parasitic, evergreen plant with white berries.
**mis•tral** *n.* a cold, often violent, N.W. wind which blows over S. France.
**mis•tress** *n.* *(fem.*of **master**) a woman in authority (as over a household, animal, institution); a kept woman.
**mis•tri•al** *n.* a trial made invalid by an error in proceedings.
**mis•trust** *n.* lack of confidence; *v.t.* to suspect; to lack faith in.
**mis•un•der•stand** *v.t.* to interpret incorrectly; to form a wrong judgment.
**mis•use** *v.t.* to use improperly; to maltreat.
**mite** *n.* any very small thing or person; a kind of arachnid, as *cheese mite*.
**mi•ter** *n.* a bishop's headdress, a tall cap; in carpentry, a joint made by two pieces of wood fitting into each other at an angle of 45°.
**mit•i•gate** *v.t.* to relieve; to alleviate; to temper. **mitigable** *a.* capable of being lessened. **mitigation** *n.* alleviation.
**mi•to•sis** *n.* *(Biol.)* method of cell division in which chromatin divides into chromosomes.
**mitt** *n.* a covering for wrist and hand leaving fingers exposed; a baseball glove, with palm heavily padded.
**mix** *v.t.* to unite into a mass; to blend; to combine a mixture; to associate. **-ed marriage** *n.* a marriage between two people of different religions or different races.

**miz•zen, mizen** *n.* fore-and-aft sail of a vessel.

**mne•mon•ic -al** *a.* assisting the memory.

**moan** *n.* a low cry of grief or pain; *v.i.* to utter a low, wailing cry.

**moat** *n.* a deep trench around a castle, usu. filled with water.

**mob** *n.* a disorderly crowd of people; a rabble; the populace; *v.t.* to attack in a disorderly crowd; to jostle.

**mob•cap** *n.* a frilled cap, tied under the chin, worn by women in the 18th cent.

**mo•bile** *a.* easily moved; changing; facile; (of troops) mechanized; capable of moving rapidly from place to place; *n.* an artistic arrangement of wires, etc., easily set in motion. **mobilization** *n.* the wartime act of calling up men and women for active service.

**moc•ca•sin** *a.* shoe of soft leather worn by N. American Indians, trappers, etc.; a bedroom slipper of similar shape; a poisonous water snake.

**mo•cha** *n.* a coffee orig. from *Mocha* in Yemen; *a.* flavored with coffee.

**mock** *v.t.* to laugh at; to ridicule; to make a fool of; to defy; to mimic; substitute. **-ing bird** *n.* a N. Amer. bird which imitates

mock

other birds. **—orange** *n.* shrub with fragrant white flowers. **—turtle** *n.* a soup made of calf's head and spices to imitate turtle soup.

**mode** *n.* manner, form, or method; custom; fashion; *(Mus.)* one of the two classes of keys (major or minor); *(Gram.)* the *mood* of the verb. **modal** *a.* relating to mode or form. **modality** *n.* **modish** *a.* fashionable. **modishly** *adv.*

**mod•el** *n.* an exact, three-dimensional representation of an object, in miniature; a pattern or standard to copy; one who poses for an artist; a mannequin; *a.* serving as a model or criterion.

**mod•er•ate** *a.* restrained; temperate; average; not extreme; *v.t.* to restrain; to control; to decrease the intensity or pressure of; *v.i.* to become less violent or intense; to act as moderator; *n.* a person of moderate opinions in politics, etc.

**mod•ern** *a.* pert. to present or recent time; up-to-date.

**mod•est** *a.* unassuming; restrained; decent; retiring in manner; not excessive, as *modest* means.

**mod•i•cum** *n.* a small amount.

**mod•i•fy** *v.t.* to moderate; to alter the form or intensity of. **modifiable** *a.* **modification** *n.* the act of modifying; the state of being modified; a change of form, manner, or intensity.

**mod•u•late** *v.t.* to regulate, esp. the pitch of the voice; to adapt; *(Mus.)* to change the key of; *v.i. (Mus.)* to pass from one key to another. **modular** *a.* of a mode, modulation, or module. **modulation** *n.* the act of modulating; the changing of the pitch or key; *(Elect.)* the variation of the amplitude or frequency of continuous waves, usu. by a lower frequency. **module** *n.* a unit of measurement; *(Archit.)* the radius of a shaft at its base.

**mo•gul** *n.* a powerful or important person.

**mo•hair** *n.* the silky hair of the Angora goat.

**Mo•ham•me•dan** *a.* of Mohammed or the Moslem religion.

**Mo•ha•ve** *n.* a tribe of Amer. Indians.

**Mo•hawk** *n.* the name of a N. Amer. Indian tribe.

**Mo•hi•can** *n.* a N. Amer. Indian tribe of Algonquin stock.

**moire** *n.* watered fabric; *a.* having a wavy pattern.

**moist** *a.* damp; humid; rather wet.

**mo•lar** *a.* grinding or able to grind, as back teeth; a back double-tooth.

**mo•las•ses** *n. sing.* a dark-colored syrup obtained from sugar; treacle.

**mold** *n.* a pattern, form or matrix for giving shape to something in a plastic or molten state.

**mold** *n.* fine, soft soil; the upper layer of the earth.

**mold** *n.* a downy fungus which grows on leather, cheese, bread, etc.

**mole** *n.* a slightly raised, dark spot on the skin.

**mole** *n.* a small burrowing animal.

mole

**mole** *n.* a breakwater.

**mol•e•cule** *n.* the smallest portion of a substance which can retain the characteristics of that substance. **molecular** *a.* **molecular weight** *n.* the weight of a molecule of a substance in relation to the weight of a hydrogen atom.

**mo•lest** *v.t.* to trouble; to accost with sinister intention.

**mol•i•fy** *v.t.* to appease; to placate; to soften.

**mol•lusk, mol•lusc** *n.* an invertebrate animal with soft, pulpy body and a hard outer shell (oyster, snail, etc.).

**molt** *v.t.* and *v.i.* to shed feathers, as of birds, or skins, as of snakes; *n.* the act of shedding.

**mol•ten** *a.* melted; of metals, liquified.

**mo•lyb•de•num** *n.* a rare metal, used in alloys.

**mo•ment** *n.* a short space of time; interval; importance; the measure of a force by its effect in causing rotation. **-ous** *a.* very important. **-um** *n.* the impetus in a body; increasing force.

**mo•nad** *n. (Biol.)* a single-celled organism; *(Chem.)* an atom with the valence of one;

(*Philos.*) an individual thought of as a microcosm.

**mon•arch** *n.* a hereditary sovereign; the supreme ruler of a state. **-y** *n.* government by a single ruler; a kingdom or empire.

**mon•as•ter•y** *n.* a settlement of monks.

**mon•au•ral** *a.* of sound reproduction from one source only.

**Mon•day** *n.* the second day of the week.

**mon•e•tary** *a.* concerning money or coinage.

**mon•ey** *n.* any form of token, as coin, banknote, used as medium of exchange, and stamped by state authority; currency; wealth.

**mon•ger** *n.* (*Brit.*) a dealer, usu. in compound words, as *fishmonger, ironmonger*.

**Mon•gol** *n.* a native of Mongolia (Asia); *a.* also **Mongolian. -ism** *n.* arrest of physical and mental development with Asiatic features.

**mon•goose** *n.* a small weasel-like animal, a snake-killer.

mongoose

**mon•grel** *a.* and *n.* impure; hybrid of mixed breed.

**mo•nism** *n.* the philosophical doctrine which seeks to explain varied phenomena by a single principle.

**mo•ni•tion** *n.* cautionary advice; admonition; notice; (*Law*) a summons. **monitive** *a.* expressing warning.

**monk** *n.* a hermit; a member of a religious community living in a monastery.

**mon•key** *n.* a long-tailed mammal of the order of Primates resembling man in organization; mischievous child; the weighted head of a pile driver; a hammer for driving home bolts.

**mon•o•bloc** *n.* the cylinders of the internal-combustion engine in one casting.

**mon•o•car•pous** *a.* bearing fruit only once.

**mon•o•chord** *n.* a one-stringed instrument; a one-stringed device for measuring musical intervals.

**mon•o•chrome** *n.* a painting in different tones of the same color. **monochromatic, monochromic** *a.* **monochromatism** *n.* color-blindness.

**mon•o•cle** *n.* a single eyeglass.

**mo•noc•ra•cy** *n.* government by a single person.

**mon•o•dy** *n.* an elegy expressive of mourning; a monotonous tone.

**mo•nog•a•my** *n.* the state of being married to one person at a time.

**mon•o•gen•e•sis** *n.* the descent of an organism or all living things, from a single cell.

**mon•o•gram** *n.* two or more letters, as initials of a person's name.

**mon•o•graph** *n.* a specialized treatise on a single subject.

**mo•nog•y•nous** *a.* (*Bot.*) having single pistil; (*Zool.*) mating with a single female. **monogyny** *n.* the custom of having only one female mate.

**mon•o•lith** *n.* a monument or column fashioned from a single block of stone.

**mon•o•logue** *n.* a dramatic scene in which an actor soliloquizes; a dramatic entertainment by a solo performer.

**mon•o•ma•ni•a** *n.* a form of mental derangement in which sufferer is irrational on one subject only, or is obsessed by one idea.

**mo•no•mi•al** *a.* (*Math.*) comprising a single term or expression; *n.* an algebraic expression containing a single term.

**mon•o•nym** *n.* a name comprising a single term.

**mon•o•pho•bi•a** *n.* (*Path.*) a morbid fear of being alone.

**mon•o•plane** *n.* an aircraft with only one set of wings.

**mo•nop•o•ly** *n.* the sole right to trade in certain commodities; exclusive possession or control; a commodity so controlled; a controlling company.

**mon•o•syl•la•ble** *n.* a word of one syllable.

**mon•o•the•ism** *n.* the doctrine which admits of one God only.

**mon•o•tint** *n.* a sketch or painting in one tint.

**mon•o•tone** *n.* a single, unvaried tone or sound. **monotonous** *a.* uttered or recited in one tone; dull; unvaried.

**mon•o•type** *n.* (*Biol.*) a genus with one species; (*Print.*) a two-part machine for setting and casting type in individual letters, as distinct from *linotype*.

**mon•ox•ide** *n.* oxide containing one oxygen atom in a molecule.

**Mon•sei•gneur** *n.* my lord; a title given in France to princes, bishops, etc. *pl.* **Messeigneurs. Monsignor** *n.* an Italian title given to prelates.

**mon•soon** *n.* a seasonal wind of S. Asia; the very heavy rainfall season in summer, esp. in India.

**mon•ster** *n.* a creature of unnatural shape; a person of abnormal callousness, cruelty, or wickedness. **monstrosity** *n.* an unnatural production; an abnormal creature; a freak.

**mon•strance** *n.* a shrine for the consecrated host in R.C. services.

**mon•tage** *n.* (*Motion pictures*) assembling various shots of a film into one well-arranged series; a picture made by superimposing various elements from several sources.

**Mon•tes•so•ri Sys•tem** *n.* educational system to give free scope to child's individuality and creative powers.

**month** *n.* one of the twelve divisions of the year. **lunar month** *n.* about 29 days; a period of 28 days, or four complete weeks. **-ly** *a.* lasting, performed in, a month.

**mon•u•ment** *n.* any structure, as a tombstone, building tablet, erected to the memory of person, or event.

**mooch** *v.t.* and *v.i.* (*Colloq.*) to loiter; to sponge from another.

**mood** *n.* (*Gram.*) the inflection of a verb expressing its function, as *indicative*, *imperative, subjunctive, infinitive.*

**mood** *n.* disposition; frame of mind; temper.

**moon** *n.* the satellite which revolves around the earth in the period of a lunar month; any secondary planet; a month; anything crescent-shaped or shining like the moon. **-stone** *n.* an almost pellucid form of feldspar. **-struck** *a.* dazed.

**Moor** *n.* a native of the Barbary States; one of the conquerors of Spain in the 8th cent.

**moor** *n. (Brit.)* marshy wasteland.

**moor** *v.t.* to secure by cables and anchors, as a vessel.

**moose** *n.* largest species of deer; elk.

**moot** *v.t.* to debate; to discuss. **— court** *n.* a mock court.

**mope** *v.i.* to be dull or depressed; to sulk.

**mo•raine** *n.* rock debris which accumulates along the sides or at the end of a glacier.

**mor•al** *a.* pert. to right conduct or duties of man; ethical; virtuous; chaste; *n.* the underlying meaning implied in a fable, allegory, etc. **-istic** *a.* **-ity** *n.* the practice of moral duties; virtue; ethics; an early form of drama, in which the characters were the virtues and vices of men personified. **-ly** *adv.* **— victory** *n.* a defeat, which in a deeper sense, is a victory.

**mo•rale** *n.* the disposition or mental state which causes a man or body of people to face an emergency with spirit.

**mo•rass** *n.* marshy ground; difficult state of affairs.

**mor•a•to•ri•um** *n.* a law to delay payment of debts for a given period of time.

**mo•ray** *n.* a sharp-toothed marine eel.

**mor•bid** *a.* diseased; unhealthy; (of the mind) excessively gloomy.

**mor•dant** *n.* any substance, metallic or vegetable, which fixes dyes; a corrosive acid used in etching; *a.* biting; corrosive; sarcastic.

**more** *a.* greater in amount, degree, quality, etc.; in greater number; additional.

**mo•rel** *n.* an edible mushroom.

**mo•rel** *n.* the common and deadly nightshade.

**mo•rel•lo** *n.* a variety of dark-red cherry used in manufacture of brandy.

**more•o•ver** *adv.* besides; also; further.

**mo•res** *n.pl.* customs.

**mor•ga•nat•ic** *a.* applied to a marriage between a man of high, esp. royal rank, and a woman of lower station, the issue having no claim to his rank or property.

**morgue** *n.* a place where bodies of people killed in accidents, etc., are taken to await identification.

**mor•i•bund** *a.* at the point of death.

**Mor•mom** *n.* a member of The Church of Jesus Christ of Latter-day Saints founded by Joseph Smith in 1830 in Utah and professing theocracy and, formerly, polygamy.

**morn•ing** *n.* the first part of the day between dawn and midday. **— glory** *n.* a twining vine with flowers. **— coat** *n.* a tailcoat with cutaway front. **— star** *n.* a planet visible before sunrise.

**mo•ron** *n.* an adult with the mental development of an 8- to 12-yr.-old child.

**mo•rose** *a.* sullen; gloomy; soured in nature.

**mor•pheme** *n. (Gram.)* the smallest meaningful linguistic unit.

**mor•phine** *n.* an alkaloid of opium; a drug used to induce sleep and to deaden pain.

**Morse** *n.* a system of telegraphic signals in which the alphabet is represented by combinations of dots and dashes.

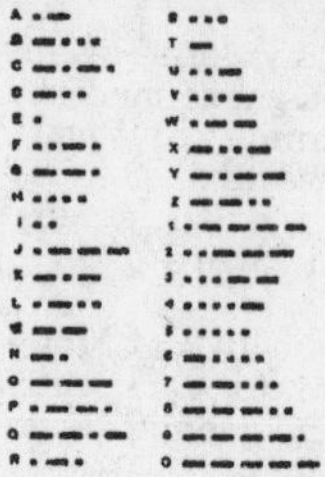

**Morse**

**mor•sel** *n.* a mouthful; a small piece.

**mor•tal** *a.* subject to death; fatal; meriting damnation, as sin.

**mor•tar** *n.* a thick bowl of porcelain, glass, etc., in which substances are pounded with a pestle; a mill for pulverizing ores; *(Mil.)* a short-barreled cannon for short-distance firing of heavy shells; a cement made of lime, sand and water, used in building.

**mort•gage** *n. (Law)* a conveyance of property in security of a loan; the deed effecting this; *v.t.* to pledge as security.

**mor•ti•cian** *n.* an undertaker.

**mor•ti•fy** *v.t.* to discipline the flesh; to humiliate; to vex; *v.i. (Med.)* to become gangrenous.

**mor•tise** *n.* a hole in a piece of wood to receive the projection or tenon of another piece, made to fit it.

**mort•main** *n.* an inalienable bequest; the holding of land by a corporation, which cannot be transferred.

**mor•tu•ar•y** *n.* a place for the temporary reception of dead bodies.

**mo•sa•ic** *a.* pert. to or made of mosaic; *n.* inlaid work of colored glass or marble.

**Mo•selle** *n.* a light wine.

**Mos•lem** *n.* a Mohammedan; *a.* pert. to the Mohammedans or their religion.

**mosque** *n.* a Mohammedan temple.

**mos•qui•to** *n.* an insect which draws blood, leaving a raised, itchy spot.

**moss** *n.* a small, thickly growing plant which thrives on moist surfaces.

**most** *a.* the greatest number or quantity; greatest; *adv.* in the greatest degree; *n.* the greatest quantity, number, etc.

**mot** *n.* pithy, witty saying.

**mote** *n.* a small particle; a speck of dust.

**mo•tel** *n.* lodging for travelers.

**mo•tet** *n.* a musical composition for (usu. unaccompanied) voices.

**moth** *n.* a nocturnal winged insect; larva of this insect which feeds on cloth, esp. woolens.

**moth•er** *n.* a female parent; the head of a

convent; the origin of anything; *a.* characteristic of a mother; native; original —**of-pearl** *n.* the iridescent lining of several kinds of shells. **Mother Superior** *n.* the head of a convent.

**mo•tif** *n.* the dominant theme in a literary or musical composition.

**mo•tion** *n.* the act of moving; movement; a gesture; a proposal made in an assembly. **-less** *a.* still; immobile.

**mo•tive** *n.* that which incites to action; inner impulse; motif; *a.* causing movement or motion; *v.t.* to impel; to motivate. **motivate** *v.t.* to incite. **motivation** *n.* **-less** *a.* without purpose or direction.

**mot•ley** *a.* varicolored; diversified.

**mo•tor** *n.* that which imparts motion; a machine which imparts motive power, esp. the internal-combustion engine; *a.* causing motion. **-cade** *n.* procession of automobiles.

**mot•tle** *v.t.* to mark with spots of different colors; to dapple.

**mot•to** *n.* a maxim or principle of behavior.

**moue** *n.* a pout.

**mou•lage** *n.* the making of molds.

**mound** *n.* an artificial elevation of earth; a knoll; an earthwork for defensive purposes; a heap.

**mount** *n.* a mountain or hill; that on which anything is mounted for exhibition; a horse for riding; *v.t.* to raise up; to ascend; to get on a horse or bicycle; to frame (a picture); to set (gemstones).

**moun•tain** *n.* a high hill; *a.* pert. to a mountain —**ash** *n.* any of a variety of small trees. **-eer** *n.* one who lives on or climbs high mountains. —**range** *n.* a series or system of mountains.

**moun•te•bank** *n.* a quack doctor; a charlatan.

**Mount•ie** *n.* a member of the Canadian N.W. Mounted Police.

**mourn** *v.t.* to grieve over; to lament; *v.i.* to express grief; to wear mourning.

**mouse** *n.* a small rodent found in fields, or houses; a timid person.

**mousse** *n.* a lightly frozen dessert.

**mouth** *n.* an opening between lips of men and animals through which food is taken; lips, as a feature; the cavity behind the lips containing teeth, tongue, palate, and vocal organs; an opening as of a bottle, cave, etc.; the estuary of a river; a wry face. —**organ** *n.* harmonica. **-piece** *n.* the part of a musical instrument, pipe, etc., held in mouth.

**move** *v.t.* to set in motion; to stir emotions of; to prevail on; to incite; to propose for consideration; *v.i.* to change one's position, posture, residence, etc.; to march; to make a proposal or recommendation; *n.* the act of moving; a change of residence; a movement, as in game of checkers. **moving** *a.* causing motion; affecting the emotions; pathetic.

**mow** *v.t.* to cut down with a scythe or machine; to cut down in great numbers.

**mow** *n.* a heap of hay, or corn, in a barn.

**much** *a.* great in quantity or amount; abundant; *n.* a great quantity.

**mu•cid** *a.* moldy, musty.

**mu•ci•lage** *n.* a gummy substance extracted from plants and animals; an adhesive.

**muck** *n.* moist manure; anything vile or filthy.

**muck•rake** *n.* one, esp. a reporter, who searches for corruption, scandal.

**mu•cus** *n.* a viscid fluid secreted by the mucous membranes; slimy.

**mud** *n.* soft, wet dirt. —**flat** *n.* a stretch of mud below high water. **-guard** *n.* a shield to protect from mud splashes.

**mud•dle** *v.t.* to make muddy; to confuse; to bewilder; to mix up.

**muff** *n.* a warm covering for both hands, usu. of fur, shaped like a cylinder and open at both ends.

**muf•fin** *n.* a small cup-shaped bread.

**muf•fle** *v.t.* to wrap up for warmth or to hide something; to deaden (sound of); *n.* something used to deaden sound or provide warmth.

**mug** *n.* a straight-sided earthenware or metal cup with or without a handle; the contents of this.

**mug•gins** *n.* *(Brit.)* a simpleton; a game of dominoes.

**mug•gy** *a.* warm and humid, as weather; close; enervating.

**mug•wump** *n.* one who holds independent political views.

**mu•lat•to** *n.* offspring of white person and Negro.

**mul•ber•ry** *n.* a deciduous tree on the leaves of which the silkworm feeds.

**mulch** *n.* a protective covering of straw, manure, etc., for plants.

**mulct** *n.* a fine imposed as a penalty; *v.t.* to punish with a fine; to deprive of.

**mule** *n.* the hybrid offspring of a donkey or horse; a small tractor for hauling, in mines, along canals, etc.; a heelless bedroom slipper; an obstinate person.

**mull** *v.t.* to heat, sweeten and spice.

**mull** *v.i.* to muse upon; to cogitate.

**mul•let** *n.* an edible fish.

**mullet**

**mul•li•gan** *n.* a stew made from leftover meat and vegetables.

**mul•li•ga•taw•ny** *n.* a rich soup flavored with curry.

**mul•lion** *n.* a dividing upright between the lights of windows, panels.

**mul•ti•col•or** *a.* having many colors. **-ed** *a.*

**mul•ti•far•i•ous** *a.* manifold; made up of many parts.

**mul•ti•form** *a.* having many forms. **-ity** *n.*

**mul•ti•lat•er•al** *a.* having many sides. **-ly** *adv.*

**mul•ti•par•tite** *a.* having many parts.

**mul•ti•ped** *n.* and *a.* (animal) with many feet. Also **multipede.**

**mul•ti•ple** *a.* manifold; of many parts; repeated many times; *n.* *(Math.)* a quantity containing another an exact number of times. —**fission** *n.* repeated division.

**mul•ti•ply** *v.t.* to increase in number; to add a number to itself a given number of times. **multipliable, multiplicable** *a.* **multiplicand** *n.* the number to be multiplied. **multiplication** *n.* the act of multiplying. **multiplicative** *a.* **multiplicator** *n.* a multiplier. **multiplier** *n.* a number by which another, the **multiplicand,** is multiplied.

**mul•ti•tude** *n.* a great number; numerousness; a crowd; an assemblage.

**mul•ti•va•lent** *a. (Chem.)* having a valency of more than two.

**mum** *a.* silent; *n.* silence.

**mum•ble** *v.t., v.i.* to utter, speak indistinctly; *n.* an indistinct utterance.

**mum•my** *n.* a dead body preserved by embalming.

**mumps** *n.* a highly infectious disease causing painful swelling of face and neck glands.

**munch** *v.t.* and *v.i.* to chew noisily.

**mu•nic•i•pal** *a.* pert. to local government or to internal affairs (not international). **-ity** *a.* town or district with its own local self-government.

**mu•nif•i•cence** *n.* liberality; generosity.

**mu•ni•ment** *n.* means of protection; *pl.* title deeds; charter.

**mu•ni•tion** *v.t.* to equip with the weapons of war.

**mu•ral** *n.* a wall painting.

**mur•der** *n.* homicide with premeditated and malicious intent; *v.t.* to commit a murder; to kill.

**mu•ri•ate** *n.* a chloride. **-d** *a.* briny. **muriatic acid** *n.* hydrochloric acid.

**murk** *a.* dark; *n.* darkness; gloom.

**mur•mur** *n.* a low, unbroken sound, as of wind, water, etc.; a complaint expressed in subdued tones; softly uttered speech.

**mur•rain** *n.* a disease affecting cattle, foot-and-mouth disease.

**mus•cat** *n.* a sweet grape.

**mus•cle** *n.* a band of contractile fibrous tissue which produces movement in an animal body; strength. **muscular** *a.* pert. to muscle; brawny; strong.

**mus•coid** *a. (Bot.)* like moss. **muscology** *n.* the study of mosses.

**Mus•co•vite** *n.* a native or inhabitant of Moscow or of Russia.

**muse** *v.i.* to think over dreamily; to ponder; to consider meditatively.

**mu•sette** *n.* a small bagpipe; a melody for this instrument; a reed stop on an organ; a country dance.

**mu•se•um** *n.* a building or room housing a collection of works of art, antiques, objects of natural history, the sciences, etc.

**mush** *n.* a pulp; (U.S.) porridge of cornmeal; a soft mass.

**mush** *v.t.* to journey on foot with dogs over snowy wastes.

**mush•room** *n.* an edible fungus of very quick growth; *(Fig.)* an upstart; *a.* of rapid growth; shaped like a mushroom.

**mu•sic** *n.* the art of combining sounds or sequences of notes into harmonious patterns pleasing to the ear and satisfying to the emotions. —**box** *n.* a box which when wound up plays a tune. **-al comedy** *n.* a form of light entertainment in which songs, dialogue, dancing, humor are combined. **-ian** *n.* a composer or skilled performer of musical compositions.

**musk** *n.* a fragrant substance obtained from a gland of the musk deer. —**ox** *n.* a sheeplike ox with brown, long-haired

**muskox**

shaggy coat. **-rat** *n.* a large N. Amer. water rat with musk gland, valued for its fur. —**rose** *n.* a climbing rose with white blossoms faintly perfumed with musk.

**mus•ket** *n.* (formerly) a handgun or matchlock.

**mus•lin** *n.* a thin cotton cloth of open weave; *a.* made of muslin.

**mus•quash** *n.* the muskrat.

**mus•sel** *n.* a class of marine bivalve shellfish.

**mussel**

**must** *v.i.* to be obliged, by physical or moral necessity.

**must** *n.* wine newly pressed from grapes but not fermented.

**mus•tache** *n.* the hair on the upper lip.

**mus•tang** *n.* a wild horse of the Amer. prairies; a bronco.

**mus•tard** *n.* a plant with yellow flowers and pungent seeds; a powder or paste made from the seeds, used as a condiment.

**mus•ter** *v.t.* to assemble, as troops for a parade; to gather together.

**mus•ty** *a.* moldy; stale.

**mu•ta•ble** *a.* subject to change; inconstant. **mutation** *n.* change; the process of vowel change; *(Biol.)* a complete divergence from racial type which may ultimately give rise to a new species.

**mute** *a.* dumb; silent; unexpressed in words; not sounded, as *e* of *cave; n.* a person who cannot speak.

**mu•ti•late** *v.t.* to maim; to cut off.

**mu•ti•ny** *n.* insurrection against lawful authority, esp. military or naval.

**mut•ter** *v.t.* to speak indistinctly or in a low voice; to grumble.

**mut•ton** *n.* the flesh of sheep.

**mu•tu•al** *a.* reciprocally acting or related; interchanged.

**mu•zhik** *n.* a Russian peasant.
**muz•zle** *v.t.* the snout; the mouth and nose of an animal; a cage-like fastening for the mouth to prevent biting; the open end of a gun.
**my** *poss. a.* belonging to **me.**
**my•col•o•gy** *n.* the science of fungi.
**my•e•lin** *n.* *(Zool.)* the fatty substance forming the sheath of nerve fibers. **myelitis** *n.* inflammation of the spinal cord or bone marrow.
**my•na(h)** *n.* a tropical starling.
**my•o•car•di•tis** *n.* *(Med.)* inflammation of the heart muscle.
**my•o•ma** *n.* tumor of muscle tissue.
**my•o•pi•a** *n.* nearsightedness.
**my•o•sis** *n.* prolonged contraction of the pupil of the eye.
**my•o•so•tis** *n.* a genus of herbs including the forget-me-not.
**myr•i•ad** *n.* an indefinitely large number.
**myr•i•a•pod** *n.* *(Zool.)* an animal with great number of legs, as centipede.
**myr•me•col•o•gy** *n.* the scientific study of ants and ant life.
**myrrh** *n.* a transparent yellow-brown aromatic gum resin formerly used as incense, now used in antiseptics.
**myr•tle** *n.* an evergreen plant with fragrant flowers and glossy leaves.
**my•self** *pron.* I or me, used emphatically, or reflexively.
**mys•ter•y** *n.* anything strange and inexplicable; a puzzle; a religious truth beyond human understanding; secrecy; a medieval drama based on Scripture.
**mys•tic** *a.* pert. to a mystery, to secret religious rites, or to mysticism. **mystification** *n.* **mystify** *v.t.* to perplex; to puzzle.
**myth** *n.* a fable; a legend embodying primitive faith in the supernatural. **-iologist** *n.* one who has studied myths of various countries; a writer of fables. **-ology** *n.* a collection of myths.
**myx•e•de•ma** *n.* *(Med.)* a disease caused by deficiency of secretion from thyroid gland.

**nag** *n.* a small horse; an old horse; any horse.

**nag** *v.t.* and *v.i.* to worry by constant faultfinding. *pr.p.* **-ging.** *pa.t.* and *pa.p.* **-ged. -ger** *n.*

**nai•ad** *n.* a nymph of the streams.

**nail** *n.* the horny shield covering the ends of the fingers or toes; a strip of pointed metal provided with a head, for fastening

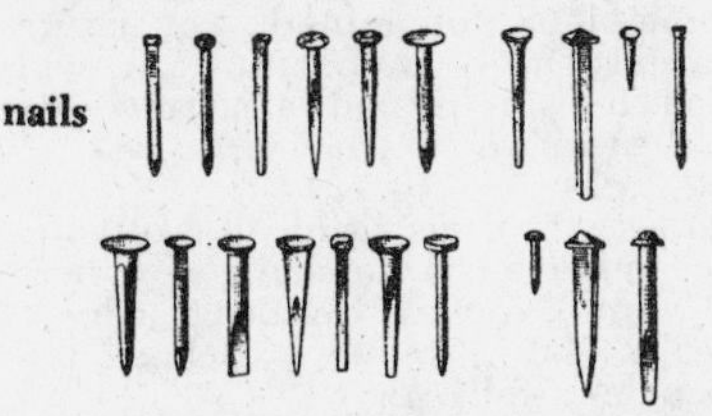
nails

wood, etc.; *v.t.* to fasten with a nail; to fix or secure.

**na•ive** *a.* having native or unaffected simplicity; childishly frank. **-ly** *adv.* **naïveté** *n.* childlike ingenuousness. Also **naivety.**

**na•ked** *a.* having no clothes; exposed; bare; nude; uncovered. **-ly** *adv.* **-ness** *n.*

**name** *n.* the term by which any person or thing is known; *v.t.* to give a name to; to call or mention by name; to nominate; **-less** *a.* without a name. **-lessly** *adv.* **-ly** *adv.* by name; that is to say. **-sake** *n.* a person who bears the same name as another.

**nan•ny** *n.* a child's nurse. **— goat** *n.* a she-goat.

**nap** *n.* a short sleep; a doze; *v.i.* to indulge in a short sleep. *pr.p.* **-ping** *pa.t., pa.p.* **-ped.**

**nap** *n.* the pile of velvet.

**na•palm** *n.* jellied gasoline used in flame throwers.

**nape** *n.* the back part of the neck.

**nap•kin** *n.* a cloth used for wiping the hands or lips at table.

**na•po•le•on** *n.* a pastry of several cream-filled layers. **-ic** *a.* pert. to Napoleon I or III.

**Nar•cis•sus** *n.* bulbous plant genus including the daffodil, jonquil, narcisus; **narcissim** *n.* in psychoanalysis, an abnormal love and admiration for oneself. **narcissist** *n.*

**nar•cot•ic** *n.* a substance which relieves pain and induces sleep, and in large doses, insensibility and stupor; one addicted to the habitual use of narcotics. **narcosis** *n.* a state of unconsciousness or stupor with deadening of sensibility to pain, produced by narcotics.

**nar•rate** *v.t.* to relate; to tell (story) in detail; to give an account of; to describe. **narration** *n.* an account. **narrative** *n.* a tale; a detailed account of events; *a.* pert. to, containing, narration. **narratively** *adv.* **narrator** *n.*

**nar•row** *a.* of little breadth; not wide or broad; limited; bigoted; *n.pl.* straits. **-ly** *adv.* **—minded** *a.* bigoted; prejudiced.

**nar•whal** *n.* a cetaceous mammal, closely related to the white whale, with one large protruding tusk.

**na•sal** *a.* pert. to the nose; *n.* a nasal sound or letter, such as *m* or *n.*

**na•stur•tium** *n.* a common trailing garden plant of the genus Tropaeolum.

**nas•ty** *a.* very dirty; filthy; disgusting; offensive; repulsive; unpropitious (of the weather, etc.); ill-natured; indecent. **nastily** *adv.* **nastiness** *n.*

**na•tal** *a.* pert. to one's place of birth or date of birth; **-ity** *n.* birth rate.

**na•tion** *n.* a people inhabiting a country under the same government; an aggregation of persons of the same origin and language.

**na•tion•al** *a.* belonging to or pertaining to a nation; public; general; **-ization** *n.* **-ize** *v.t.* to make national; to acquire and manage by the state; to make a nation of. **-ism** *n.* devotion to the interests of one's nation, often to the detriment of common interests of all nations. **-ity** *n.* the quality of being a nation or belonging to a nation; one's nation; patriotism. **-ly** *adv.* **— anthem,** a hymn or song expressive of patriotism, praise, or thanksgiving, commonly sung by people of a nation at public gatherings. **— debt,** the debt due from a nation to individual creditors. **National Guard,** State military force which can be called to active duty.

**na•tive** *a.* pert. to one's birth; belonging by birth; innate; indigenous; natural; *n.* a person born in a place; **-ly** *adv.* **nativity** *n.* the time or circumstances of birth; in astrology, the position of the stars at a person's birth.

**nat•u•ral** *a.* in accordance with, belonging to, or derived from, nature; inborn; unconstrained; unaffected; unassuming; true to life. **-ization** *n.* **-ize** *v.t.* to give to an alien the rights of a native subject; **-ism,** *n.* natural condition or quality; theory of art, etc. which holds that any artistic creation must be a reproduction of nature or reality. **-ist** *n.* one versed or interested in natural history. **-istic** *a.* in accordance with nature. **-istically** *adv.* **-ly** *adv.* **-ness** *n.* **— gas,** an inflammable product, usually methane, occurring in association with mineral oil deposits. **— history,** the science which deals with the earth's crust and its productions, but applies more especially to biology or zoology. **— science,** the science of nature as distinguished from mental and moral science and mathematics.

**na•ture** *n.* the world, the universe, known and unknown; the innate or essential qualities of a thing; the environment of man; **good-, bad-natured** *a.* showing one's innate disposition.

**naught** *n.* nothing; figure 0; zero. Also **nought.** **-y** *a.* not behaving well; mischievous; bad. **-ily** *adv.* **naughtiness** *n.*

**nau•se•a** *n.* any sickness of the stomach accompanied with a propensity to vomit. **-te** *v.i.* to feel nausea; *v.t.* to fill with disgust. **nauseous** *a.* loathsome; disgusting; producing nausea. **nauseously** *adv.*

**nau·ti·cal** *a.* pert. to ships, seamen, or to navigation. **-ly** *adv.* — **mile, 6,080.2 ft.**

**na·val** *a.* pert. to ships, esp. warships; belonging to or serving with the navy.

**nave** *n.* the middle or body, of a church.

**na·vel** *n.* the umbilicus, place of attachment of the umbilical cord to the body of the embryo, marked by a rounded depression in the center of the lower part of the abdomen.

**nav·i·gate** *v.t.* and *v.i.* to steer or manage a ship or aircraft; **navigable** *a.* may be sailed over or upon; seaworthy; **navigability, navigableness** *n.* **navigably** *adv.* **navigation** *n.* the science of directing course of seagoing vessel and of ascertaining its position at any given time; the control and direction of aircraft in flight; **navigator** *n.*

**na·vy** *n.* a fleet; the warships of a country with their crews and organization. — **blue** *n.* and *a.* dark blue.

**Naz·a·rene** *n.* a native of *Nazareth;* name given to Jesus; *pl.* an early Christian sect.

**Na·zi** *n.* and *a.* a member of the National Socialist Party of Germany (1922-1945). **-sm, -ism** *n.*

**Ne·an·der·thal** *a.* denoting a man of the earliest long-headed race in Europe which became extinct at least 20,000 years ago.

**neap** *a.* low; *n.* neap tide. — **tide** *n.* the tide whose rise and fall is least marked.

**Ne·a·pol·i·tan** *a.* and *n.* pert. to Naples or its inhabitants.

**near** *adv.* at or to a short distance; *prep.* close to; *a.* close; closely related; *v.t.* and *v.i.* to approach. **-by** *a.* in close proximity; adjacent. — **East,** part of Asia nearest Europe, from Asia Minor to Persia. **-ly** *adv.* closely; intimately; almost. **-ness** *n.* **-sighted** *a.* myopic; short-sighted. **-sightedness** *n.*

**neat** *a.* orderly; clean; trim; in good taste; **-ly** *adv.* **-ness** *n.*

**nec·es·sar·y** *a.* needful; requisite indispensable; that must be done; *n.* a needful thing; essential need. **necessarily** *adv.*

**ne·ces·si·ty** *n.* pressing need; indispensability; compulsion; urgency; a requisite; an essential. **necessitate** *v.t.* to make necessary or indispensable. **necessitous** *a.* needy; destitute.

**neck** *n.* the part of the body joining the head to the trunk; the narrower part of a bottle, etc. **-erchief** *n.* a band of cloth or kerchief worn round the neck. **-lace** *n.* a string of beads or precious stones worn round neck. **neck and neck,** just even.

**nec·tar** *n.* the fabled drink of the gods; honey-like secretion of the nectary gland of flowers. **-ine** *n.* a smooth-skinned variety of peach.

**need** *n.* a constitutional or acquired craving or want, appeased by recurrent satisfactions; necessity; poverty; urgency; *v.t.* to be in want of; to require; *v.i.* to be under a necessity. **-ful** *a.* necessary; requisite **-fully** *adv.* **-fulness** *n.* **-ily** *adv.* **-iness** *n.* condition of need. **-less** *a.* unnecessary; not needed. **-lessly** *adv.* **-lessness** *n.* **-y** *a.* in need; indigent.

**nee·dle** *n.* a slender pointed instrument with an eye, for passing thread through cloth, etc.; a slender rod for knitting; **-point** *n.* canvas with a design worked in yarn. **-work** *n.* **-ly** *a.* thorny.

**ne·gate** *v.t.* to deny; to prove the contrary. **negation** *n.* the act of denying; negative statement; disavowal; contradiction.

**neg·a·tive** *a.* expressing denial, prohibition, or refusal; not positive; minus; *n.* a proposition in which something is denied; a negative word; *v.t.* to refuse to sanction; to reject. **-ly** *adv.* **-ness** *n.*

**neg·lect** *v.t.* to disregard; to take no care of; to fail to do; to slight; *n.* omission; disregard; careless treatment. **-edness** *n.* **-er** *n.* **-ful** *a.* careless; inclined to be heedless. **-fully** *adv.*

**neg·li·gee** *n.* a woman's loose dressing gown.

**neg·li·gence** *n.* carelessness; habitual neglect. **negligent** *a.* careless; inattentive; untidy. **negligently** *adv.* **negligible** *a.* hardly worth noticing.

**ne·go·ti·ate** *v.t.* to settle by bargaining; to arrange; to transfer; *v.i.* to discuss with a view to finding terms of agreement; to bargain. **negotiable** *a.* capable of being negotiated; transferable. **negotiability** *n.* **negotiation** *n.* **negotiant, negotiator** *n.*

**Ne·gro** *n.* member of one main ethnological group of human race, with dark skin. *a.* pert. to black African race. **Negress** *n.* Negro woman.

**neigh** *v.i.* to whinny, like horse; *n.* cry of horse.

**neigh·bor** *n.* a person who lives, works, near another; *a.* neighboring; *v.t.* to adjoin; to be near. **-hood** *n.* adjoining district and its people; proximity; vicinity. **-ing** *a.* close by. **-ly** *a.* friendly; sociable. **-liness** *n.*

**nei·ther** *a.* and *pron.* not the one or the other; *adv.* not on the one hand; not either; *conj.* nor yet; not either.

**nem·e·sis** *n.* inevitable retributive justice.

**ne·o·dym·i·um** *n.* a metallic element belonging to the group of rare earth metals.

**ne·o·lith·ic** *a.* pert. to the late Stone Age.

**ne·on** *n.* a non-metallic chemical element belonging to the group of the rare gases. — **light,** — **sign,** or — **tube,** one containing neon gas and glowing with a characteristic reddish-orange light.

**ne·o·pho·bi·a** *n.* a dread of the unknown.

**ne·o·phyte** *n.* a novice; a convert.

**neph·ew** *n.* a brother's or sister's son.

**nephr-** (or **nephro-**) prefix used in the construction of compound terms, from Greek *nephros,* a kidney. **-algia, -algy** *n.* pain in the kidney. **-ic** *a.* pert. to the kidneys. **-itic(al)** *a.* pert. to (diseases of) the kidneys. **-itis** *n.* Bright's disease, non-infective inflammation of the kidney.

**nep·o·tism** *n.* undue favoritism in awarding public appointments to one's relations.

**Nep·tune** *n.* the Roman god of the sea;

second most remote planet of solar system.

**nerve** *n.* one of the bundles of fibers which convey impulses either *from* brain (motor nerves) to muscles, etc., producing motion, or *to* brain (sensory nerves) from skin, eyes, nose, etc., producing sensation; courage; *pl.* irritability; unusual sensitivity to fear, annoyance, etc.; *v.t.* to give courage or strength to. **-d** *a.* **-less** *a.* lacking in strength or will; **-lessness** *n.*

**nerv•ous** *a.* pert. to, containing, or affecting nerves; uneasy; apprehensive. **-ly** *adv.* **-ness** *n.* **— breakdown** *n.* a condition of mental depression.

**nest** *n.* the place in which a bird or other animal lays and hatches its eggs; *v.t.* to form to place in a nest; *v.i.* to occupy or build a nest. **-ling** *n.* a bird too young to leave the nest. **— egg** *n.* an egg left in a nest to induce a bird to lay; a small sum of money put aside for some later purpose.

**nes•tle** *v.i.* to settle comfortably and close to one another; to lie snugly, as in a nest.

**net** *n.* an open-work fabric of meshes of cord, etc.; sections of this used to catch fish, protect fruit, etc.; lace formed by netting; a snare. *a.* made of netting; caught in a net; *v.t.* to cover with, or catch in, a net; to veil; *pr.p.* **-ting.** *pa.t.* and *pa.p.* **-ted. -ted** *a.* **-ting** *n.* the act or process of forming network; net like fabric; snaring by means of a net. **-work** *n.* anything made like, or resembling, a net.

**net** *a.* left after all deductions; *v.t.* to gain or produce as clear profit; *pr.p.* **-ting.** *pa.p.* **-ted. — price,** net price without discount.

**neth•er** *a.* lower; low-lying; lying below; belonging to the lower regions. **-most** *a.* lowest.

**net•tle** *n.* a common weed covered with fine stinging hairs; *v.t.* to irritate; to provoke; to make angry; to rouse to action.

**neu•ral** *a.* pert. to the nerves or nervous system.

**neu•ral•gia** *n.* a spasmodic or continuous pain occurring along the course of one or more distinct nerves. **neuralgic** *a.*

**neu•rax•is** *n.* the cerebrospinal axis, or central nervous system, including the brain and spinal cord.

**neu•ri•tis** *n.* an inflammatory condition of a nerve.

**neu•rol•o•gy** *n.* the study of the structure, function and diseases of the nervous system. **neurological** *a.* **neurologist** *n.*

**neu•ron** *n.* a nerve cell and all its processes.

**neu•ro•sis** *n.* a psychic or mental disorder resulting in partial personality disorganization. *pl.* **neuroses. neurotic** *a.* pert. to the nerves; *n.* a highly strung person.

**neu•ter** *a.* neither masculine nor feminine; *n.* the neuter gender.

**neu•tral** *a.* taking neither side in a war, dispute, etc.; indifferent; without bias; grey; intermediate (shade of color); neither acid nor alkaline; asexual; *n.* nation, person, not taking sides in a dispute; **-ize** *v.t.* to render neutral; to make ineffective; to counterbalance. **-izer** *n.* nonintervention by a state or third-party in a dispute; the state of being neutral. **-ly** *adv.* **-ity** *n.*

**neu•tron** *n.* one of the minute particles composing the nucleus of an atom.

**nev•er** *adv.* at no time; not ever; in no degree; **-more** *adv.* **-theless** *conj.* none the less; in spite of that; notwithstanding.

**new** *a.* not existing before; lately discovered or invented; *adv.* recently; freshly; **-ly** *adv.* **-ness** *n.* **-born** *a.* recently born. **New Deal,** a campaign initiated in 1933 by President Franklin Roosevelt involving social reforms. **— moon,** the period when the first faint crescent of the moon becomes visible. **New Testament,** later of the two main divisions of Bible. **New World,** N. and S. America.

**news** *n.sing.* report of recent happenings; fresh information; **— bulletin** *n.* the latest news, esp. as disseminated by radio or television. **-paper** *n.* a regular publication giving latest news. **-print** *n.* cheap paper for newspapers. **-reel** *n.* a short film depicting items of news and topical features.

**next** *a.* nearest; immediately following in place or time; *adv.* nearest or immediately after; on the first future occasion; *prep.* nearest to. **— of kin,** *n.* nearest blood relative. **-door** *a.*

**nib•ble** *v.t.* to bite a little at a time; *v.i.* to catch at (as a fish); to bite gently; *n.* a tiny bite.

**nice** agreeable; attractive; kind; **-ly** *adv.* **-ness** *n.* **-ty** *n.* precision; delicacy; exactness; refinement.

**niche** *n.* one's ordained position in life or public estimation; *v.t.* to place in a niche. **-d** *a.*

**nick** *v.t.* to make a notch in; to indent; *n.* a notch; a slit; the opportune moment as *in the nick of time.*

**nick•el** *n.* a silver white metallic element, malleable and ductile, and much used in alloys and plating; a five-cent piece; *v.t.* to plate with nickel.

**nick•el•o•de•an** *n.* a player phonograph operated by the insertion of a nickel.

**nick•nack** See **knickknack.**

**nick•name** *n.* a name given in contempt, derision, or familiarity to some person, nation, or object.

**nic•o•tine** *n.* a colorless, highly poisonous alkaloid present in the tobacco plant.

**niece** *n.* the daughter of a brother or sister or of one's husband's or wife's brother or sister.

**nif•ty** *a.* fine; smart.

**nigh** *a.* near; direct. *adv.* near.

**night** *n.* the time of darkness from sunset to sunrise; end of daylight; **-ly** *a.* happening or done every night; of the night; *adv.* every night; by night. **— club** *n.* establishment for dancing and entertainment remaining open until early morning. **-dress, -gown** *n.* a loose gown worn in bed. **-fall** *n.* the close of day. **-light** *n.* bulb of low wattage kept burning all night. **-mare** *n.* a frightening dream. **—owl** *n.* one who habitually keeps late hours.

**night•in•gale** *n.* a bird of the thrush family, the male being renowned for its beautiful song at night.

**ni•hil, nil** *n.* nothing; zero. **nihilism** *n.* the rejection of all religious and moral principles as the only means of obtaining social progress; the denial of all reality in phenomena. **nihilist** *n.* **nihilistic** *a.*

**nim•ble** *a.* light and quick in motion. **-ness** *n.* **nimbly** *adv.*

**nin•com•poop** *n.* a foolish person.

**nine** *a.* and *n.* one more than eight; the symbol 9 or IX. **-teen** *a.* and *n.* nine and ten. **-teenth** *a.* and *n.* **ninetieth** *a.* the tenth after the eightieth. **-ty** *a.* and *n.* **ninth** *a.* the first after the eighth; *n.* **ninthly** *adv.* **the Nine,** the Muses.

**nip** *v.t.* to pinch sharply; to detach by pinching; to check growth (as by frost); *pr.p.* **-ping.** *pa.t.* and *pa.p.* **-ped.** *n.* a pinch; sharp touch of frost; a sip. **-piness** *n.* **-pingly** *adv.* **-py** *a.* sharp in taste; curt; smarting.

**nip•ple** *n.* the protuberance in the center of a breast by which milk is obtained from the female during breast-feeding; the mouthpiece of a nursing bottle.

**Nip•pon** *n.* Japan. **-ese** *n., a.*

**Nir•va•na** *n.* in Buddhism, that state of blissful repose or absolute existence reached by one in whom all craving is extinguished.

**ni•ter** *n.* potassium nitrate; saltpeter, a white crystalline solid used in the manufacture of gunpowder, acids, etc. **nitrate** *n.* a salt of nitric acid; a fertilizer. **nitrated** *a.* combined with nitric acid. **nitration** *n.* the conversion of nitrites into nitrates by the action of bacteria; the introduction of a nitro-group ( $NO_2$ ) into an organic substance. **nitric** *a.* containing nitrogen. **nitric acid,** a powerful, corrosive acid. **nitride** *n.* a compound of a metal with nitrogen. **nitrify** *v.t.* to treat a metal with nitric acid; to oxidize to nitrates or nitrites, esp. by action of bacteria. **nitrite** *n.* a salt of nitrous acid. **nitrous oxide,** laughing gas, used as an anaesthetic in dentristry.

**ni•tro•gen** *n.* a non-metallic gaseous chemical element, colorless, odorless and tasteless, forming nearly four-fifths of the atmosphere. **nitrogenous** *a.*

**nit•wit** *n.* a fool. **-ted** *a.*

**no** *a.* not any; *adv.* expresses a negative reply to a question or request; not at all; *n.* a refusal; a denial; a negative vote. **-es** *n.pl.* term used in parliamentary proceedings, *the noes have it.*

**No•bel Prize** *n.* one of a series of five prizes awarded annually to persons who have distinguished themselves in physics, chemistry, medicine, literature, or the promotion of peace.

**no•bil•i•ty** *n.* the class holding special rank, usually hereditary, in a state.

**no•ble** *a.* distinguished by deeds, character, rank, or birth; of lofty character; titled; *n.* a nobleman; **-man** *n.* (*fem.* **-woman**). **-ness** *n.* **nobly** *adv.*

**no•bod•y** *n.* no one; a person of no importance.

**nock** *n.* notch, esp. of bow or arrow; upper end of fore-and-aft sail.

**noc•turn** *n.* a service held during the night. **-al** *a.* pertaining to night; happening or active by night. **-ally** *adv.*

**noc•u•ous** *a.* hurtful; noxious. **-ly** *adv.*

**nod** *v.t.* and *v.i.* to incline the head forward by a quick motion, signifying assent or drowsiness; *pr.p.* **-ding.** *pa.t.* and *pa.p.* **-ded.** *n.* an act of nodding. **-der** *n.*

**nod•al** See **node.**

**node** *n.* a knot or knob; the part of a stem to which a leaf is attached; an articulation. **nodal, nodical** *a.* pert. to nodes. **nodated** *a.* knotted. **nodation** *n.* the knots. **nodular** *a.* like a nodule. **nodulated** *a.* having nodules. **nodule** *n.* a small node or act of making knots. **nodiferous** *a.* having nodes. **nodose, nodous** *a.* full of swelling.

**No•ël** *n.* Christmas.

**nog** *n.* a wooden peg or block.

**nog** *n.* a beverage made with eggs and usually liquor; eggnog; a kind of strong ale.

**no•how** *adv.* in no way; not at all; ability.

**noise** *n.* sound; din; loud outcry; *v.t.* to spread by rumor; *v.i.* to sound loud. **-less** *a.* making no noise; silent. **-lessly** *adv.* **-lessness** *n.* **noisy** *a.* making much noise; **noisily** *adv.* **noisiness** *n.*

**no•mad** *a.* roaming from pasture to pasture; *n.* a wanderer; a member of a wandering tribe. **nomadic** *a.* pert. to nomads; having no fixed dwelling place. **nomadically** *adv.* **-ism** *n.*

**no•men•cla•tor** *n.* one who gives names to things. **nomenclatural** *a.* **nomenclature** *n.* a system of naming; the vocabulary of a science, etc.

**nom•i•nal** *a.* pert. to a name; existing only in name; pert. to a noun. **-istic** *a.* **-ly** *adv.* in name only; not really.

**nom•i•nate** *v.t.* to put forward the name of, as a candidate; to propose; to designate. **nomination** *n.* act of nominating; power or privilege of nominating. **nominative** *a.* *(Gram.)* denoting the subject; *n.* a noun or pronoun which is the subject of a verb. **nominator** *n.* one who nominates. **nominee** *n.* one who is nominated.

**non-** *prefix* from L. *non* = not, used in the formation of compound terms signifying absence or omission.

**non•a•ge•nar•i•an** *n.* one who is ninety years old or upwards; *a.* relating to ninety.

**non•cha•lance** *n.* unconcern; coolness; indifference; nonchalant *a.* **nonchalantly** *adv.*

**non•con•form•ist** *n.* one who refuses to comply with the usages and rites of an established church, etc. **nonconforming** *a.* **nonconformity** *n.*

**non•de•script** *a.* lacking in distinction; hard to classify; *n.*

**none** *a.* and *pron.* no one; not anything. **-such, nonsuch** *n.* a person or thing without a rival or equal. **nonetheless,** nevertheless; all the same.

**nones** *n.pl.* one the canonical hours of the R.C. Breviary, the *ninth* hour after sunrise at the equinox, viz. 3 p.m., or the appropriate mass celebrated at this time.

**non•en•ti•ty** *n.* a thing not existing; nonexistence.

**non•pa•reil** *n.* a person or thing without an equal; *a.* unrivalled; peerless; matchless.

**non•sense** *n.* lack of sense; language without meaning; silly conduct. **nonsensical** *a.* **nonsensically** *adv.*

**non•such** See **none.**

**noo•dle** *n.* a strip of dough, made of flour and eggs, baked and served in soups.

**nook** *n.* a corner; a recess; a secluded retreat.

**noon** *n.* midday; twelve o'clock by day; the exact instant when, at any given place, the sun crosses the meridian. **-day, -tide** *n.* and *a.* midday.

**noose** *n.* a running loop with a slip knot which binds closer the more it is drawn; tight knot; *v.t.* to tie, catch in noose.

**nor** a particle introducing the second clause of a negative proposition; and not.

**Nor•dic** *a.* of or pert. to peoples of Germanic, esp. Scandinavian, stock.

**norm** *n.* a rule or authoritative standard; a unit for comparison; a class-average test score. **-a** *n.* a rule, pattern, or standard; **-al** *a.* conforming to type or natural law; the standard; the average. **-alcy** *n.* normality. **normality** *n.* normal state or quality. **-ly** *adv.* **-ative** *a.* setting up a norm; regulative.

**Nor•man** *n.* a native of Normandy; *a.* pert. to Normandy or the Normans. **— architecture,** a style of medieval architecture characterized by rounded arch and massive simplicity.

**Norse** *a.* pert. to ancient Scandinavia, esp. Norway, its language, or its people; *n.* Norwegians or ancient Scandinavians; the old Scandinavian language.

**north** *n.* the region or cardinal point in the plane of the meridian to the left of a person facing the rising sun; the part of the world, of a country, etc., towards this point; *adv.* towards or in the north; *a.* to, from, or in the north. **northerly** *a.* towards the north; of winds, coming from the north. **northern** *a.* pert. to the north; in or of the north. **northerner** *n.* an inhabitant of the northern parts of a country. **northernly** *adv.* in a northern direction. **northernmost** *a.* situated at the most northerly point. **-ward, -wardly** *a.* situated towards the north; *adv.* in a northerly direction. **-wards** *adv.* **northern lights,** aurora borealis. **North Pole,** northern extremity of earth's axis. **North Star** *n.* polar star, the only star which does not change its apparent position.

**Nor•we•gian** *a.* pert. to Norway; *n.* a native or language of Norway.

**nose** *n.* the organ for breathing and smelling; *v.t.* to detect by smell; to nuzzle; to sniff; to move forward; *v.i.* to smell; to pry; to push forward. **— dive** *n.* in aviation, a sudden steep plunge directly towards an objective, usually from a great height; *v.i.* to perform this evolution. **-gay** *n.* a bunch of sweet-smelling flowers; a bouquet. **nosy** *a.* inquisitive.

**nos•tal•gia** *n.* honesickness; a phase of melancholia due to the unsatisfied desire to return home. **nostalgic** *a.*

**nos•tril** *n.* one of the external openings of the nose.

**not** *adv.* a word expressing denial, negation, or refusal.

**no•ta•ble** *a.* worthy of notice; remarkable; *n.* a person of distinction. **notabilia** *n.pl.* things worth noting; famous remarks. **notability** *n.* an eminent person. **-ness** *n.* **notably** *adv.*

**no•ta•ry** *n.* a *notary-public,* a person authorized to record statements, to certify deeds, to take affidavits, etc., on oath.

**no•ta•tion** *n.* any system of figures, signs and symbols which conveys information; a note.

**notch** *n.* a V-shaped cut or indentation; nick; a groove formed in a piece of timber to receive another piece; *v.t.* to make notches in; to indent.

**note** *n.* a brief comment; *pl.* a record of a lecture, speech, etc.; a memorandum; a short letter; a written or printed promise of payment; a musical tone; a character to indicate a musical tone; notice; *v.t.* to observe; to set down in writing; to attend to; to heed. **-book** *n.* a book for jotting down notes, memoranda, etc. **-d** *a.* well-known by reputation or report; celebrated; **-dly** *adv.* **-dness** *n.* **— paper** *n.* a small size of writing paper. **-worthy** *a.* worthy of notice; remarkable.

**noth•ing** *n.* not anything of account, value, note, or the like; non-existence; nonentity; zero; *adv.* in no degree; not at all. **-ness** *n.*

**no•tice** *n.* act of noting; remarking, or observing; note; consideration; news; a notification; *v.t.* to observe; to remark upon; to treat with regard. **-able** *a.* **-ably** *adv.* **to give notice,** to warn beforehand.

**no•ti•fy** *v.t.* to report; to give notice of or to; to announce; to inform. **notifiable** *n.* **notification** *n.* act of making known or giving notice; official notice or announcement.

**no•tion** *n.* apprehension; idea; conception; opinion; belief; sentiment; fancy; *pl.* small articles such as sewing supplies, etc.

**no•to•ri•e•ty** *n.* the state of being generally known, esp. in a disreputable way. **notorious** *a.* infamous. **notoriously** *adv.* **notoriousness** *n.*

**not•with•stand•ing** *adv.* nevertheless; however; yet; *prep.* in spite of; despite; *conj.* although.

**nou•gat** *n.* a confection of almonds, pistachio-nuts, or other nuts, in a sugar and honey paste.

**noun** *n.* a word used as a name of a person, quality, or thing; a substantive.

**nour•ish** *v.t.* to supply with food; to feed and cause to grow. **-ing** *a.* nutritious.

**-ment** *n.* food; nutriment.

**nov•el** *a.* new; unusual; *n.* a fictitious prose tale dealing with the adventures or feelings of imaginary persons so as to portray, by the description of action and thought, the varieties of human life and character. **-ette** *n.* a shorter form of novel. **-ist** *n.* a writer of novels. **-ty** *n.* newness; something new or unusual.

**No•vem•ber** *n.* the eleventh month of the year.

**no•ve•na** *n.* devotions on nine consecutive days.

**nov•ice** *n.* a candidate for admission to a religious order; one new to anything.

**no•vo•caine** *n.* a nonirritant drug which has replaced cocaine as a local anesthetic.

**now** *adv.* at the present time; *conj.* this being the case; *n.* the present time. **-adays** *adv.* in these days.

**no•where** *adv.* not in any place.

**nox•a** *n.* anything harmful to the body; *pl.* **-e. noxal** *a.* **noxious** *a.* hurtful; pernicious; unwholesome. **noxiously** *adv.* **noxiousness** *n.*

**noz•zle** *n.* a projecting spout or vent; the outlet end of a pipe, hose, etc.

**nu•ance** *n.* a shade or subtle variation in color, tone of voice, etc.

**nub** *n.* a knob; lump; protuberance.

**nu•cle•us** *n.* a central part of anything; the inner essential part of a living cell; the core of the atom, composed of protons and neutrons. *pl.* **nuclei. nuclear** *a.* **nuclear energy,** a more exact term for atomic energy; energy freed or absorbed during reactions taking place in atomic nuclei. **nuclear fission,** a process of disintegration which breaks up into chemically different atoms. **nucleolus** *n.* a minute body of condensed chromatin inside a nucleus.

**nude** *a.* bare; naked; *n.* a picture or piece of sculpture in the nude. **-ly** *adv.* **-ness, nudity,** *n.* nakedness. **nudism** *n.* cult emphasizing practice of nudity for health. **nudist** *n.*

**nudge** *v.t.* to touch slightly with the elbow; *n.* a gentle push.

**nug•get** *n.* rough lump or mass, esp. of native gold.

**nui•sance** *n.* something harmful, offensive, or annoying; a troublesome person; a pest; an inconvenience.

**null** *a.* of no legal validity; void; non-existent; of no importance; *v.t.* to annul; to render void. **-ify** *v.t.* to render useless; to invalidate; **-fication** *n.* **-ifier** *n.* **-ity** *n.* state of being null and void.

**numb** *a.* insensible; insensitive; chilled; *v.t.* to benumb; to paralyze. **-ness** *n.*

**num•ber** *n.* a word used to indicate how great any quantity is when compared with the unit quantity, one; a sum or aggregate of quantities; *v.t.* to give a number to; to count; *v.i.* to amount to. **-s** *n.pl.* fourth book of Pentateuch. **-er** *n.* **-less** *a.* innumerable. **numerability, numerableness** *n.* **numerable** *a.* may be numbered or counted.

**nu•mer•al** *a.* designating a number; *n.* a sign or word denoting a number. **numerable** *a.* able to be counted. **numerably** *adv.* **-ly** *adv.* according to number. **numerate** *v.t.* to count; to read figures according to their notation. **numeration** *n.* **numerator** *n.* top part of a fraction, figure showing how many of the fractional units are taken. **numerically** *adv.* **numerous** *a.* many. **numerously** *adv.* **numerousness** *n.*

**nu•mis•mat•ic** *a.* pert. to coins and medals, esp. as an aid to study of archaeology. **numismatist** *n.*

**nun** *n.* a female member of a religious order, vowed to celibacy, and dedicated to active or contemplative life. **-nery** *n.* convent of nuns.

**nup•tial** *a.* pert. to or constituting ceremony of marriage; *pl.* wedding ceremony; marriage.

**nurse** *n.* a person trained for the care of the sick or injured; *v.t.* to tend, as a nurse; **nursery** *n.* a room set aside for children; a place for the rearing of plants. **nursery rhymes,** jingling rhymes written to amuse young children. **nursery school,** a school for children of 2-5 years of age.

**nur•ture** *n.* rearing; breeding; nourishment; *v.t.* to nourish; to cherish; to tend; to train; to rear; to bring up. **-r** *n.*

**nut** *n.* a fruit consisting of a hard shell enclosing a kernel; *v.i.* to gather nuts; *pr.p.* **-ting.** *pa.t.* and *pa.p.* **-ted. -cracker** *n.* an instrument for cracking nuts; **-shell** *n.* the hard shell enclosing the kernel of a nut. **-ting** *n.* **-ty** *a.* abounding in nuts; having a nut-flavor.

**nu•tant** *a.* hanging with the apex of the flower downwards; nodding. **nutation** *n.* nodding.

**nut•meg** *n.* an aromatic flavoring spice.

**nu•tri•ent** *a.* nourishing; *n.* something nutritious. **nutriment** *n.* that which nourishes; food; sustenance. **nutrition** *n.* the act of nourishing. **nutritional, nutritious, nutritive, nutritory** *a.* nourishing; promoting growth.

**nuz•zle** *v.t.* and *v.i.* to rub with the nose; to nestle.

**nyc•ta•lo•pi•a** *n.* night blindness.

**ny•lon** *n.* an artificial fabric the yarn of which is produced synthetically; *n.pl.* stockings made of nylon yarn.

**nymph** *n.* a lesser goddess inhabiting a mountain, grove, fountain, river, etc.; **-al, -ean, -ic, -ical** *a.* **-like** *a.* **-omania** *n.* a morbid and uncontrollable sexual desire in women. **-omaniac** *n.*

**O, oh** *interj.* an exclamation of address, surprise, sorrow, wonder, entreaty.

**oaf** *n.* a changeling; simpleton. *pl.* **oafs** or **oaves.**

**oak** *n.* a familiar forest tree yielding a hard, durable timber and acorns as fruit.

**oar** *n.* a wooden lever with a broad blade worked by the hands to propel a boat; *v.t.* and *v.i.* to row. **-ed** *a.* having oars.

**o•a•sis** *n.* a fertile spot in the desert. *pl.* **oases.**

**oat** *n.* but usually in *pl.* **oats,** the grain of a common cereal plant, used as food. **-meal** *n.* meal made from oats.

**oath** *n.* confirmation of the truth by naming something sacred, esp. God; *pl.* **oaths.**

**ob•du•rate** *a.* hard-hearted; stubborn; unyielding. **-ly** *adv.* **obduracy** *n.*

**o•be•di•ent** *a.* willing to obey. **-ly** *adv.* **obedience** *n.* submission to authority; doing what one is told.

**ob•e•lisk** *n.* a tall, four-sided, tapering pillar, ending in a small pyramid; in

**obelisk**

printing, a reference mark (†) also called 'dagger'; an **obelus,** the marks – or ÷.

**o•bese** *a.* fat. **obesity** *n.* excessive fatness.

**o•bey** *v.i.* to be obedient; *v.t.* to comply with the orders of; to yield submission to; to be ruled by.

**o•bit•u•ar•y** *a.* pert. to death of person; *n.* a notice, often with a biographical sketch, of the death of a person.

**ob•ject** *n.* a material thing; an end or aim; *(Gram.)* a noun, pronoun, or clause governed by, and dependent on, a transitive verb or a preposition. **-less** *a.* having no aim or purpose.

**ob•ject** *v.t.* to offer in opposition; to put forward as reason against; *v.i.* to make verbal opposition; to protest against; to feel dislike or reluctance. **objection** *n.* act of objecting; adverse reason; argument against. **objectionable** *a.* **objectionably** *adv.* **-or** *n.*

**ob•jec•tive** *a.* pert. to the object; relating to that which is external to the mind; unbiased. **-ly** *adv.* **objectivity** *n.* the quality of being objective.

**ob•li•gate** *v.t.* to bind, esp. by legal contract. **obligation** *n.* the binding power of a promise or contract; indebtedness for a favor of kindness; a duty. **obligatory** *a.* binding legally or morally; compulsory. **obligatorily** *adv.*

**o•blige** *v.t.* to constrain by physical, moral, or legal force; to do a favor to; to compel. **-d** *a.* grateful; indebted. **-ment** *n.* a favor. **obliging** *a.* helpful; courteous. **obligingly** *adv.* **obligingness** *n.*

**ob•lique** *a.* slanting; inclined; indirect; obscure; not straightforward. **-ly** *adv.* **-ness, obliguity** *n.* slant or inclination; deviation from moral uprightness; dishonesty.

**ob•lit•er•ate** *v.t.* to blot out; to efface or destroy. **obliteration** *n.* the act of blotting out; destruction; extinction. **obliterative** *a.*

**ob•liv•i•on** *n.* a forgetting, or being forgotten; forgetfulness; heedlessness. **oblivious** *a.* forgetful; causing to forget; heedless. **obliviously** *adv.* **obliviousness** *n.*

**ob•long** *a.* longer than broad; *n.* a rectangular figure with adjacent sides unequal.

**ob•nox•ious** *a.* offensive; objectionable. **-ly** *adv.* **-ness** *n.*

**o•boe** *n.* a woodwind instrument, long and slender, with tone produced by a double reed. **oboist** *n.*

**ob•scene** *a.* indecent; filthy. **-ly** *adv.* **-ness** *n.* **obscenity** *n.* lewdness; indecency.

**ob•scure** *a.* dark; hidden; dim; uncertain; *v.t.* to dim; to conceal; to make less intelligible; to make doubtful. **-ly** *adv.* **-ness** *n.* **obscurity** *n.* absence of light; lack of clear expression or meaning.

**ob•serve** *v.t.* to watch; to perform or keep religiously; *v.i.* to take notice; to make a remark; to comment. **observable** *a.* **observance** *n.* a paying attention; the keeping of a law, custom, religious rite; a religious rite; a rule or practice. **observant** *a.* quick to notice; alert; carefully attentive; obedient to. **observantly** *adv.* **observation** *n.* the action or habit of observing; the result of watching, examining, and noting; a comment; a remark. **observatory** *n.* a building for the observation and study of astronomical, meteorological, etc., phenomena. **-r** *n.*

**ob•sess** *v.t.* to haunt; to fill the mind completely; to preoccupy. **-ion** *n.* complete domination of the mind by one idea; a fixed idea.

**ob•sid•i•an** *n.* vitreous lava or glassy volcanic rock.

**ob•so•lete** *a.* no longer in use; out of date. **-ly** *adv.* **-ness** *n.* **obsolescent** *a.* becoming obsolete; going out of use. **obsolescence** *n.*

**ob•sta•cle** *n.* anything that stands in the way; an obstruction; a hindrance.

**ob•stet•rics** *n.* *(Med.)* the science dealing with the care of pregnant women. **obstetric, obstetrical** *a.* **obstetrician** *n.*

**ob•sti•nate** *a.* stubborn. **-ly** *adv.* **-ness** *n.* **obstinacy** *n.* unreasonable firmness; stubbornness.

**ob•strep•er•ous** *a.* noisy; clamorous; vociferous; unruly; *adv.* **-ness** *n.*

**ob•struct** *v.t.* to block up; to impede; to hinder the passage of; **-er, -or** *n.* **-ion** *n.* the act of obstructing; that which obstructs or hinders. **-ive** *a.* **-ively** *adv.*

**ob•tain** *v.t.* to gain; to acquire; to procure;

*v.i.* to be customary or prevalent. **-able** *a.* procurable. **-ment** *n.* Also **obtention.**

**ob•trude** *v.t.* to thrust forward unsolicited; to push out; *v.i.* to intrude. **-r** *n.* **obtrusion** *n.* the act of obtruding. **obtrusive** *a.* **obtrusively** *adv.*

**ob•tuse** *a.* blunt; dull of perception; greater than a right angle, but less than 180°. **-ly** *adv.* **-ness** *n.*

**ob•vi•ous** *a.* easily seen or understood; evident; apparent. **-ly** *adv.* **-ness** *n.*

**oc•ca•sion** *n.* opportunity; a time of important occurrence; *v.t.* to cause; to bring about. **-al** *a.* occurring now and then; incidental; meant for a special occasion. **-ally** *adv.* from time to time.

**oc•ci•dent** *n.* part of the horizon where the sun sets, the west. **occidental** *a.* western; *n.* native of Europe or America.

**oc•cult** *a.* secret; mysterious; magical; supernatural; **-ly** *adv.* **-ism** *n.* the doctrine or study of the supernatural, magical, etc.

**oc•cu•py** *v.t.* to take possession of; to inhabit; to fill; to employ. **occupancy** *n.* the act of having or holding possession; tenure. **occupant** *n.* one who occupies or is in possession. **occupation** *n.* occupancy; possession; employment; trade; calling; business, profession. **occupational** *a.*

**oc•cur** *v.i.* to happen; to be met with. *pr.p.* **-ring.** *pa.p.* and *pa.t.* **-red.** **-rence** *n.* a happening; an event.

**o•cean** *n.* great body of salt water surrounding land of globe; *a.* pert. to the great sea. **oceanic** *a.* pert. to, found, or formed in the ocean. **-ography** *n.* the scientific description of ocean phenomena. **-ographer** *n.* **-ographic, -ographical** *a.* **-ology** *n.* science which relates to the ocean.

**o•ce•lot** *n.* a S. Amer. quadruped of the leopard family.

ocelot

**o'clock** *adv.* by the clock.

**oct-, octa-, octo-** *prefix* fr. Gk. *okto,* eight, combining to form derivatives. **-agon** *n.* a plane figure with 8 sides and 8 angles. **-agonal** *a.* **-ahedron** *n.* a solid figure with 8 plane faces. **-ahedral** *a.* **-ane** *n.* a hydrocarbon of the paraffin series, obtained from petroleum and used as a fuel, esp. for airplanes.

**oc•tave** *n.* a stanza of 8 lines.

**oc•tet** *n.* a group of 8 musicians or singers; a composition for such a group; a group of 8 lines, esp. the first 8 lines of a sonnet. Also **octette.**

**Oc•to•ber** *n.* tenth month.

**oc•to•ge•nar•i•an** *a.* and *n.* between 80 and 90 years of age.

**oc•to•pus** *n.* a mollusk with 8 arms or tentacles covered with suckers.

**oc•u•lar** *a.* pert. to the eye, or to sight; visual; *n.* the eyepiece of an optical instrument. **oculist** *n.* a specialist in the defects and diseases of the eye.

**odd** *a.* not even; not divisible by two; extra; surplus; out-of-the-way; strange. **-ity** *n.* quality of being odd; peculiarity; **-ly** *adv.* **-ness** *n.* **odds** *n.pl.* the difference in favor of one as against another; advantage or superiority; the ratio by which one person's bet exceeds another's; likelihood or probability.

**ode** *n.* a lyric poem of exalted tone.

**o•dont-** *prefix* from the Gk. *odous, odontos,* a tooth. **odontalgia** *n.* toothache. **odontology** *n.* the science of the teeth.

**o•dor** *n.* smell; fragrance; perfume; repute or estimation.

**O•dys•seus** *n.* hero of Homer's **Odyssey** *n.* a Greek epic poem glorifying the adventures and wanderings of Odysseus; hence, any long, adventurous journey.

**Oed•i•pus** *n.* a king of Thebes who unwittingly slew his father and married Jocasta, his mother. **Oedipus complex,** in psychoanalysis, a complex involving an abnormal love by a person for the parent of opposite sex.

**of** *prep.* belonging to; from; proceeding from; relating to; concerning.

**off** *adv.* away; in general, denotes removal or separation, also completion, as in *to finish off; prep.* not on; away from; *a.* distant; on the farther side; *interj.* begone! depart! **-hand** *a.* without preparation; free and easy; curt; *adv.* without hesitation; impromptu. **-shoot** *n.* that which shoots off or separates from a main branch or channel; a descendant. **— side** *a.* of a player, being illegally ahead of the ball, etc. **-spring** *n.* children; **off and on,** intermittently.

**of•fend** *v.t.* to displease; to make angry; to wound the feelings of; *v.i.* to cause displeasure; to do wrong; to sin. **-er** *n.*

**of•fense** *n.* transgression; sin; insult; wrong; resentment; displeasure; **offensive** *a.* causing or giving offense; insulting; unpleasant; *n.* attack; onset; aggressive action. **offensively** *adv.* **offensiveness** *n.*

**of•fer** *v.t.* to present for acceptance or refusal; to tender; to bid, as a price; to propose; to attempt; to express readiness to do; *v.i.* to present itself or to occur; *n.* an act of offering; a presentation; a price bid; a proposal, esp. of marriage. **-ing** *n.* that which is offered, as a contribution through the church; a sacrifice; a gift. **-er** *n.*

**of•fer•to•ry** *n.* a part of the mass during which the elements are offered up.

**of•fice** *n.* a place for doing business; an official position; **-r** *n.* a person who holds an official position; one who holds commissioned rank in the navy, army, air force, etc.

**of•fi•cial** *a.* pert. to an office; vouched for by one holding office; authorized; *n.* one holding an office, esp. in a public body. **-ly** *adv.*

**of•fi•ci•ate** *v.i.* to perform the duties of an officer; to perform a divine service.

**of•ten** *adv.* frequently; many times.

**o•gle** *v.i.* to make eyes; *v.t.* to make eyes

at; to cast amorous glances at; *n.* an amorous glance. **-r** *n.*

**oh** *interj.* an exclamation of surprise, sorrow, pain, etc.

**ohm** *n.* the standard unit of electrical resistance. **-meter** *n.* an instrument for measuring electrical current and resistance.

**oil** *n.* one of several kinds of light viscous liquids, obtained from various plants, animal substances, and minerals, used as lubricants, illuminants, fuel, medicines, etc.; *v.t.* to apply oil to; *v.i.* to take oil aboard as fuel. **-y** *a.* consisting of, or resembling, oil; greasy; **-ily** *adv.* **-iness** *n.* **-s** *n.pl. (Paint.)* short for 'oil-colors'; **-cloth** *n.* coarse canvas cloth coated with oil and pigment to make waterproof, used for table coverings, etc. **— colors** *n.pl.* colors made by grinding pigments in oil. **— painting** *n.* one done in oil colors. **— well** *n.* boring made in district yielding petroleum.

**oint•ment** *n.* an unguent.

**o•kay** *a.* and *adv.* abbrev. to **O.K.,** an expression signifying approval.

**old** *a.* advanced in age; having lived or existed long; not new or fresh. **-en** *a.* old; ancient; pert. to the past. **—fashioned** *a.* out of date; not modern. **— school** *a.* old-fashioned. **Old Testament,** the first division of Bible. **Old World,** the Eastern hemisphere.

**o•le•o•mar•ga•rine** *n.* a butter substitute. *Abbrev.* oleo.

**ol•fac•tion** *n.* smelling; sense of smell. **olfactory** *a.* pert. to smelling.

**ol•i•gar•chy** *n.* government in which supreme power rests with a few; those who constitute the ruling few. **oligarch** *n.* a member of an oligarchy. **oligarchal** *a.* Also **oligarchic(al).**

**ol•i•go•cene** *a.* pert. to a geological period between the eocene and miocene.

**ol•ive** *n.* an evergreen tree, long cultivated in the Mediterranean countries for its

olive

fruit; its oval, oil-yielding fruit; *a.* of the color of an unripe olive, or of the foliage.

**O•lym•pi•a** a plain in ancient Greece, the scene of the Olympic Games. **Olympiad** *n.* the name given to period of four years between each celebration of Olympic Games. **Olympic** *a.* pert. to Olympia, or to the games. **Olympics** *n.pl.* the Olympic Games.

**om•e•let, omelette** *n.* a dish of eggs beaten with milk and seasonings and cooked in a frying pan.

**o•men** *n.* a sign of future events; a foreboding; *v.t.* to foreshadow by means of signs.

**o•mit** *v.t.* to leave out; to neglect; to fail to perform. *pr.p.* **-ting** *pa.p., pa.t.* **-ted. omission** *n.* the act of omitting; neglect; failure to do; that which is omitted or left undone. **omissible** *a.* that may be omitted. **omissive** *a.*

**om•ni•po•tent** *a.* all-powerful, esp. of God; almighty. **-ly** *adv.* **omnipotence** *n.* unlimited power.

**om•ni•pres•ent** *a.* present in all places at the same time. **omnipresence** *n.*

**om•nis•cience** *n.* infinite knowledge. **omniscient** *a.* all-knowing.

**om•niv•o•rous** *a.* all-devouring; eating every kind of food. **-ly** *adv.*

**on** *prep.* above and touching; in addition to; following from; referring to; at; near; towards, etc.; *adv.* so as to be on; forwards; continuously.

**once** *adv.* at one time; on one occasion; formerly; ever; *n.* one time. **at once,** immediately.

**on•com•ing** *a.* approaching; *n.* approach.

**one** *a.* single; only; *n.* the number or figure 1, I; the lowest cardinal number; unity; a single specimen; *pron.* a particular but not stated person; any person. **-ness** *n.* unity; uniformity; singleness. **-self** *pron.* one's own self or person. **—sided** *a.* esp. of a contest, game, etc., limited to one side; considering one side only; partial; unfair. **—way** *a.* denoting a system of traffic circulation in one direction only.

**on•go•ing** *n.* a going on; advance; procedure; *a.* continuing.

**on•ion** *n.* an edible, bulbous plant with pungent odor. **— skin** *n.* thin, glazed paper.

**on•ly** *a.* being the one specimen; single; sole; *adv.* solely; singly; merely; exclusively; *conj.* but then; except that.

**on•o•mat•o•poe•ia** *n.* the formation of a word by using sounds that resemble or suggest the object to be named; e.g. *hiss, ping-pong.* **onomatopoeic, onomatopoetic** *a.*

**on•shore** *a.* towards the land, esp. of a wind.

**on•slaught** *n.* attack; an onset; an assault.

**on•to** *prep.* upon; on the top; to.

**on•tol•o•gy** *n.* the science that treats of reality of being; metaphysics. **ontological** *a.* **ontologist** *n.*

**o•nus** *n.* burden; responsibility.

**on•ward** *a.* and *adv.* advancing; going on; forward. **-s** *adv.* in a forward direction; ahead.

**on•yx** *n.* a variety of quartz.

**ooze** *n.* soft mud or slime; a gentle flow; *v.i.* to flow gently as if through pores; to leak or percolate; *v.t.* to exude or give out slowly. **oozy** *a.*

**o•pal** *n.* a mineral much used as a gem owing to its beautiful and varying hues of green, yellow and red.

**o•paque** *a.* not transparent; impenetrable to light; not lucid; dull-witted. **-ly** *adv.* **-ness** *n.* **opacity** *n.*

**o•pen** *a.* not shut or blocked up; allowing passage in or out; without restrictions; available; exposed; frank and sincere; *n.*

clear, unobstructed space; *v.t.* to set open; to uncover; to give access to; to cut or break into; *v.i.* to become open; to begin. **-er** *n.* one who or that which opens. **-ing** *a.* first in order; initial; *n.* a hole or gap; an open or cleared space; an opportunity; a beginning. **-ly** *adv.* publicly; frankly. **-ness** *n.*

**op•er•a** *n.* a musical drama; the theater where opera is performed. **operatic** *a.* pert. to opera. **operetta** *n.* a short light opera. **grand opera,** opera in which no spoken dialogue is permitted.

**op•er•ate** *v.t.* to cause to function; to effect; *v.i.* to work; to perform an act of surgery; **operation** *n.* the act of operating; a method or mode of action; treatment involving surgical skill. **operational** *a.* **operative** *a.* having the power of acting; exerting force; producing the desired effect; efficacious; **operator** *n.*

**o•phid•i•an** *n.* a snake; *a.* snake-like.

**oph•thal•mi•a** *n.* inflammation of the eye. **ophthalmic** *a.* of the eye. **ophthalmologist** *n.* a physician skilled in the study and treatment of the eye. **ophthalmology** *n.* the science dealing with the structure, functions, and diseases of the eye. **ophthalmoscope** *n.* an instrument for viewing the interior of the eye.

**o•pi•ate** *n.* any preparation of opium; a narcotic; *a.* containing opium; inducing sleep. **opiatic** *a.*

**o•pin•ion** *n.* judgment or belief; formal statement by an expert. **-ated** *a.* dogmatic.

**o•pi•um** *n.* narcotic used to induce sleep or allay pain.

**o•pos•sum** *n.* a small marsupial animal. Also **possum.**

**opossum**

**op•po•nent** *a.* opposite; opposing; antagonistic; *n.* one who opposes.

**op•por•tune** *a.* well-timed; convenient. **-ly** *adv.* **-ness** *n.* **opportunism** *n.* the policy of doing what is expedient at the time regardless of principle. **opportunist** *n.* **opportunity** *n.* a fit or convenient time; a good chance.

**op•pose** *v.t.* to set against; to resist; to compete with. **opposable** *a.* **-r** *n.*

**op•po•site** *a.* contrary; *n.* the contrary; *prep.* and *adv.* in front of; on the other side; across from; **-ly** *adv.* facing each other. **-ness** *n.* **opposition** *n.* the state of being opposite; resistance; contradiction; a party opposed to that in power.

**op•press** *v.t.* to govern with tyranny; to treat severely; to lie heavily on. **-ion** *n.* harshness; tyranny; dejection. **-ive** *a.* unreasonably burdensome; hard to bear. **-ively** *adv.* **-iveness** *n.* **-or** *n.*

**opt** *v.i.* to make a choice; to choose. **-ative** *a.* expressing wish or desire.

**op•tic** *a.* pert. to the eye or to sight; pert. to optics; *n.* the eye. **-s** *n.* the science which deals with light and its relation to sight. **-al** *a.* pert. to vision; visual. **-ally** *adv.* **optician** *n.* a maker of, or dealer in, optical instruments, esp. spectacles.

**op•ti•mism** *n.* belief that everything is ordered for the best; disposition to look on bright side. **optimist** *n.* believer in optimism; one who takes hopeful view. **optimistical** *a.*

**op•tion** *n.* the power or right of choosing; choice. *a.* left to one's free choice. **-ally** *adv.*

**or** *conj.* introducing an alternative; if not.

**or•a•cle** *n.* shrine where ancient Greeks consulted deity; response given, often obscure; a person of outstanding wisdom.

**o•ral** *a.* spoken; pert. to the mouth. **-ly** *adv.*

**or•ange** *n.* a juicy, gold-colored citrus fruit; tree bearing it; reddish yellow color like an orange; *a.* reddish yellow in color. **-ade** *n.* drink of orange juice, sugar, and water.

**o•rang•u•tan, o•rang•ou•tang** *n.* a large long-armed ape.

**o•rate** *v.i.* to talk loftily; **oration** *n.* a formal and dignified public speech. **orator** *n.* one who delivers an oration; one distinguished for gift of public speaking. **oratorical** *a.* pert. to orator(y); rhetorical. **oratorically** *adv.* **oratorio** *n.* a religious musical composition for voices and orchestra. **oratory** *n.* the art or exercise of speaking in public; eloquence.

**orb** *n.* a sphere or globe. **-it** *n.* path traced by one heavenly body in its revolution round another; range of influence or action. **-ital** *a.*

**or•chard** *n.* a garden or enclosure containing fruit trees.

**or•ches•tra** *n.* the space in a theater occupied by musicians; the main floor of a theater; a group of performers on various musical instruments. **orchestral** *a.* **orchestrate** *v.t.* to arrange music for performance by an orchestra. **-tion** *n.*

**or•chid, orchis** *n.* a genus of plants with fantastically-shaped flowers of varied and brilliant colors.

**orchid**

**or•dain** *v.t.* to decree; to destine; to appoint; **ordination** *n.* the act of ordaining admission to the ministry.

**or•deal** *n.* a trying experience; a test of endurance.

**or•der** *n.* rank; class; group; regular arrangement; sequence; succession; method; regulation; a command or direction; one of the five styles of architecture; a subdivision of a class of plants or animals, made up of genera. *v.t.* to arrange; to command; to require; to regulate; to systematize; to give an order for. **-ly** *a.* methodical; tidy; well regulated; *n.* a soldier following an officer to carry orders; in a hospital, an attendant; *adv.* in right order. **-liness** *n.* **in order to,** for the purpose of.

**or•di•nal** *a.* and *n.* showing order or position in a series, e.g. *first, second,* etc.; pert. to an order, of plants, animals, etc.

**or•di•nance** *n.* an established rule, religious rite, or ceremony; a decree.

**or•di•nar•y** *a.* usual; regular; normal, commonplace; plain; *n.* something customary; **ordinarily** *adv.*

**or•di•na•tion** See **ordain.**

**ore** *n.* a native mineral from which metal is extracted.

**or•gan** *n.* a musical instrument of pipes worked by bellows and played by keys; a member of an animal or plant exercising a special function. **organic** *a.* pert. to or affecting bodily organs; having either animal or vegetable life; derived from living organisms; **organically** *adv.* **-ism** *n.* an organized body or system; a living body. **-ist** *n.* a player on the organ. **organic chemistry,** the branch of chemistry dealing with the compounds of carbon.

**or•gan•dy** *n.* a muslin of great transparency and lightness. Also **organdie.**

**or•gan•ize** *v.t.* to give a definite structure; to get up, arrange, or put into working order; **organizable** *a.* **organization** *n.* act of organizing; the manner in which the branches of a service, etc., are arranged; individuals systematically united for some work; a society. **-r** *n.*

**or•gasm** *n.* immoderate action or excitement, esp. sexual. **orgastic** *a.*

**o•ri•ent** *a.* rising, as the sun; lustrous; *n.* the east; Eastern countries; *v.t.* to place so as to face the east; to determine the position of, with respect to the east; to take one's bearings. **oriental** *a.* eastern; pert. to, coming from, of, the east; *n.* an Asiatic. **orientate** *v.t.* and *i.* to orient; to bring into clearly understood relations. **orientation** *n.* the act of turning to, or determining, the east; sense of direction.

**or•i•fice** *n.* a mouth or opening.

**or•i•gin** *n.* beginning; starting point; a source. **original** *a.* earliest; first; new, not copied or derived; thinking or acting for oneself; *n.* origin; model; a pattern. **originally** *adv.* **originality** *n.* the quality of being original; initiative. **originate** *v.t.* to bring into being; to initiate; *v.i.* to begin; to arise. **originative** *a.* **origination** *n.* **originator** *n.*

**o•ri•ole** *n.* bird of the thrush family.

**oriole**

**or•na•ment** *n.* decoration; any object to adorn or decorate; *v.t.* to adorn; to beautify; to embellish. **ornamental** *a.* serving to decorate. **ornamentally** *adv.* **ornamentation** *n.* decoration. **ornate** *a.* richly decorated. **ornately** *adv.* **ornateness** *n.*

**or•ni•tho-** *prefix* fr. Gk. *ornis, ornithos,* a bird, used in derivatives. **ornithology,** the scientific study of birds. **ornithological** *a.* **ornithologist** *n.*

**or•phan** *n.* and *a.* a child bereft of one or both parents; *v.t.* to make an orphan. **-age** *n.* a home or institution for orphans.

**or•ris** *n.* a kind of iris. **-root** *n.* the dried root, used as a powder in perfumery and medicine.

**or•tho•dox** *a.* having the correct faith; sound in opinions or doctrine; conventional. **-ly** *adv.* **-y** *n.* soundness of faith, esp. in religion. **-ness** *n.*

**or•thog•ra•phy** *n.* correct spelling. **orthographer** *n.* **orthographic, orthographical** *a.* **orthographically** *adv.*

**or•tho•pe•dics, orthopaedics** *n.* treatment and cure of bodily deformities, esp. in children. Also **orthop(a)edia, orthop(a)edy. orthopedic** *a.* **orthopedist** *n.*

**os•cil•late** *v.i.* to swing to and fro; to vibrate; **oscillation** *n.* a pendulum-like motion; variation between extremes. **oscillator** *n.* **oscillatory** *n.*

**os•cu•late** *v.t.* and *i.* to kiss; *a.* of species sharing characteristics. **osculant, osculation** *n.* kissing; contact. **osculatory** *a.*

**os•mo•sis** *n.* the tendency of fluid substances, if separated by a porous membrane, to filter through it and become equally diffused. **osmotic** *a.*

**os•ten•si•ble** *a.* professed; apparent. **ostensibly** *adv.* **ostensibility** *n.*

**os•ten•ta•tion** *n.* vain-glorious display; showing off. **ostentatious** *a.* fond of display; characterized by display. **ostentatiously** *adv.* **ostentatiousness** *n.*

**os•te•o-** *prefix* fr. Gk *osteon,* bone, used in derivatives mainly medical. **-arthritis** *n.* chronic inflammation of a joint. **osteoid** *a.* resembling bone. **osteology** *n.* that branch of anatomy dealing with bones, their structure, etc. **osteologist** *n.*

**os•te•op•a•thy** *n.* a system of healing, based on the belief that the human body can effect its own cure with the aid of manipulative treatment of the spinal column, joints, etc. **osteopath** *n.* a practitioner of this system. **osteopathic** *a.*

**os•tra•cise** *v.t.* to exclude from society; to exile; **ostracism** *n.* exclusion from society; social boycotting.

**os•trich** *n.* a large flightless bird, native of Africa.

**oth•er** *a.* and *pron.* not this; not the same; different; opposite; additional; *adv.* otherwise. **-wise** *adv.* differently; in another way; *conj.* else; if not. **every other,** every second (one); each alternate.

**o•ti•ose** *a.* at ease; at leisure; superfluous; futile.

**o•ti•tis** *n.* inflammation of the ear. **otology** *n.*

**ot•ter** *n.* an aquatic, fish-eating animal of the weasel family.
**Ot•to•man** *a.* pert. to the Turks; *n.* a cushioned seat without back or arms.
**ought** *auxil. v.* to be bound by moral obligation or duty.
**oui•ja** *n.* board with letters, used at seances to answer questions.
**ounce** *n.* a unit of weight, abbrev. oz.; in avoirdupois weight = 1/16 of a pound; in troy weight 1/12 of a pound; a fluid measurement.
**our** *n.* belonging to us. **-s** *poss. pron.* used with a noun. **-self** *pron.* myself. **-selves** *pron. pl.* we, i.e. not others.
**oust** *v.t.* to put out; to expel; to dispossess, esp. by unfair means.
**out** *adv.* on, at, or to, the outside; from within; from among; away; in bloom; on strike; unemployed; *a.* outlying; remote; *prep.* outside; out of; *interj.* away! begone! *v.t.* to put out; to knock out; **-er** *a.* being on the outside; away from the inside. **-ermost, -most** *a.*
**out•board** *a.* projecting beyond and outside the hull of a ship, e.g. of a ladder; also, of a detachable motor.
**out•break** *n.* a sudden breaking out; a burst, esp. of anger; the beginning, esp. of an epidemic of disease, of war, etc.
**out•burst** *n.* a bursting out, esp. of anger, laughter, cheering, etc.
**out•cast** *a.* cast out as useless; *n.* one rejected by society.
**out•come** *n.* issue; result.
**out•do** *v.t.* to excel; surpass.
**out•door** *a.* out of doors; in the open air. **-s** *adv.* outside.
**out•field** *n.* the part of the field beyond the diamond or infield; the players there.
**out•fit** *n.* a supply of things, esp. clothes, tools, etc., required for any purpose; equipment; kit; *v.t.* to supply with equipment, etc. **-ter** *n.* one who supplies equipment.
**out•go** *v.t.* to go beyond; *n.* expenditure; outlay. **-ing** *a.* sociable; departing; going out.
**out•grow** *v.t.* to surpass in growth; to become too large or old for; to grow out of. **-th** *n.* what growth out of anything.
**out•ing** *n.* a going out; an excursion; a trip.
**out•land•ish** *a.* remote; barbarous; not according to custom.
**out•law** *n.* one placed beyond the protection of the law; a bandit; *v.t.* to declare to be an outlaw. **-ry** *n.* defiance of the law.
**out•lay** *n.* expenditure; expenses.
**out•let** *n.* a passage or way out; an exit; a vent; an opening.
**out•line** *n.* the lines that bound a figure; a boundary; a sketch without details; a rough draft; a general plan; *v.t.* to draw in outline; to give a general plan of.
**out•look** *n.* a looking out; a prospect; a person's point of view; prospects.
**out•ly•ing** *a.* remote; isolated; detached.
**out•mod•ed** *a.* out of fashion.
**out•pa•tient** *n.* a patient who comes to a hospital, infirmary, etc., for treatment but is non-resident.
**out•put** *n.* production; the amount of goods produced in a given time.
**out•rage** *n.* excessive violence; gross insult or indignity; *v.t.* to do grievous wrong or violence to; to insult grossly. **outrageous** *a.* violent; atrocious. **outrageously** *adv.*
**out•set** *n.* a beginning; start.
**out•side** *n.* the outer surface; the exterior; *a.* pert. to the outer part; exterior; external; outdoor; *adv.* not inside; out of doors; in the open air; *prep.* on the outer part of. **-r** *n.* one not belonging to a particular party, set, circle, etc.
**out•skirt** *n.* generally in *pl.* the border; the suburbs of a town.
**out•spo•ken** *a.* not afraid to speak aloud one's opinions; bold of speech.
**out•stand•ing** *a.* standing out; prominent; conspicuous; of debts, unpaid; of work, etc., still to be done.
**out•ward** *a.* pert. to the outside; external; exterior; *adv.* towards the outside. **-s** *adv.* outward; toward the outside. **-ly** *adv.*
**out•wit** *v.t.* to defeat by cunning, stratagem, etc.; to get the better of.
**o•va** *n.pl.* eggs; the female germ cells; *sing.* **ovum. ovary** *n.* one of two reproductive organs in female animal in which the ova are formed and developed. **ovarial, ovarian** *a.* pert. to the ovary.
**o•val** *a.* egg-shaped; elliptical; *n.* an oval figure. **-ly** *adv.*
**o•va•tion** *n.* an enthusiastic burst of applause; a triumphant reception.
**ov•en** *n.* an enclosed chamber in a stove, for baking or heating.
**o•ver** *prep.* above; on; upon; more than; in excess of; across; from side to side of; throughout; etc.; *adv.* above; above and beyond; going beyond; in excess; too much; past; finished; across; *a.* upper; outer; covering; *n.* **-all** *a.* inclusive.
**o•ver•act** *v.t.* and *i.* to play a part in an exaggerated manner.
**o•ver•all** *n.* loose trousers worn over the ordinary clothing as a protection against dirt, etc. Also *n.pl.*
**o•ver•arm** *a.* and *adv.* in swimming, ball, etc., with the hand and arm raised.
**o•ver•bear** *v.t.* to bear down; to repress; to overpower. **-ing** *a.* domineering.
**o•ver•board** *adv.* over the side of a ship; out of a ship into the water.
**o•ver•cast** *v.t.* to cast over; to cloud; to darken. **overcast** *a.* cloudy; dull.
**o•ver•coat** *n.* an outdoor garment for men worn over ordinary clothing.
**o•ver•do** *v.t.* to do too much; to fatigue; to exaggerate. *pa.t.* **overdid.** *pa.p.* **overdone** *a.* exaggerated; over-acted; over-cooked.
**o•ver•dose** *v.t.* to give an excessive dose; *n.* to take too great a dose.
**o•ver•draw** *v.t.* and *i.* to exaggerate; to draw money in excess of one's credit. **overdraft** *n.* act of overdrawing; amount drawn from bank in excess of credit.
**o•ver•due** *a.* unpaid at right time; not having arrived at right time.
**o•ver•flow** *v.t.* to flow over; to flood; to fill too full; *v.i.* to flow over the edge, bank, etc.; to abound. *n.* what flows over; flood; excess; superabundance; surplus.

**o•ver•hand** *a.* and *adv.* with the hand raised.
**o•ver•haul** *v.t.* to examine thoroughly and set in order; **overhaul** *n.* a thorough examination, esp. for repairs; repair.
**o•ver•head** *a.* and *adv.* over the head; above; aloft; in the sky; the permanent expenses of running a business.
**o•ver•hear** *v.t.* to hear by accident. *pa.p.* and *pa.t.* **overheard.**
**o•ver•lay** *v.t.* to spread over, to cover completely; to span. *n.* a covering, as a transparent sheet, superimposed on another.
**o•ver•load** *v.t.* to place too heavy a load on. *n.* an excessive load.
**o•ver•look** *v.t.* to look over; to inspect; to superintend; to fail to notice by carelessness; to excuse; to pardon.
**o•ver•night** *adv.* through and during the night.
**o•ver•ride** *v.t.* to ride over; to ride too much; to set aside; to cancel. *n.* a gear; larger than usual payment.
**o•ver•run** *v.t.* to run over; to grow over, e.g. as weeds; to take possession by spreading over, e.g. as an invading army.
**o•ver•seas** *a.* and *adv.* from or to a country or place over the sea; foreign.
**o•ver•see** *v.t.* to superintend; to supervise. **overseer** *n.* a supervisor.
**o•ver•shoe** *n.* a shoe made of rubber, felt, etc., worn over the ordinary shoe.
**o•ver•sight** *n.* failure to notice; unintentional neglect; management.
**o•ver•state** *v.t.* to exaggerate, **-ment** *n.* exaggeration.
**o•vert** *a.* open to view. **-ly** *adv.*
**o•ver•take** *v.t.* to come up with; to catch; to take by surprise.
**o•ver•throw** *v.t.* to throw over or down; to upset; to defeat. *pa.t.* **overthrew;** *pa.p.* **overthrown. overthrow** *n.* the act of throwing over; defeat; ruin; fall.
**o•ver•time** *n.* time at work beyond the regular hours; the extra wages paid for such work.
**o•ver•ture** *n.* an orchestral introduction.
**o•ver•turn** *v.t.* and *i.* to throw down or over; to upset; to turn over.
**o•ver•weight** *n.* excess weight; extra weight beyond the just weight.
**o•ver•whelm** *v.t.* to crush; to submerge; to overpower. **-ing** *a.* decisive; irresistible. **-ingly** *adv.*
**o•vi-** *prefix* fr. L. *ovum,* an egg, used in derivatives. **oviduct** *n.* a passage for the egg, from the ovary. **oviferous** *a.* egg-bearing. **oviform** *a.* egg-shaped. **oviparous** *a.* producing eggs.
**o•vo-** *prefix* fr. L. *ovum,* an egg, used in derivatives. **ovoid** *a.* egg-shaped; oval.
**o•vum** See **ova.**
**owe** *v.t.* to be bound to repay; to be indebted for. **owing** *a.* requiring to be paid.
**owl** *n.* a night bird of prey. **-et** *n.* a young owl; a small owl. **-ish** *a.* owl like in appearance.
**own** *a.* is used to emphasize possession, e.g. my *own* money; *v.t.* to possess; to acknowledge; to admit; *v.i.* to confess. **-er** *n.* the rightful possessor. **-ership** *n.* right of possession.
**ox** *n.* a large cloven-footed and usually horned farm animal; a male cow. *pl.* **-en.**
**ox•ford** *n.* a low shoe laced over the instep.
**ox•ide** *n.* a compound of oxygen and one other element. **oxidize, oxidate** *v.t.* and *i.* to combine with oxygen to form an oxide; of metals, to rust, to become rusty. **oxidization** *n.*
**ox•y-** *prefix* fr. Gk. *oxus* sharp, used in derivatives. **-acetylene** *a.* denoting a very hot blowpipe flame, produced by a mixture of oxygen and acetylene, and used in cutting steel plates, etc.
**ox•y•gen** *n.* a colorless, odorless, and tasteless gas, forming about ½ by volume of the atmosphere, and essential to life, combustion, etc. **-ate, -ize** *v.t.* to combine or treat with oxygen. **-ation** *n.* **-ous** *a.* pert. to or obtained from, oxygen.
**oys•ter** *n.* an edible, bivalve shellfish.
**o•zone** *n.* a condensed and very active form of oxygen with a pungent odor.

**pace** *n.* a step; the length of a step in walking (about 30 inches); gait; rate of movement; *v.t.* to measure by steps; to set the speed for; *v.t.* to walk with measured fashion. **-d** *a.* having a certain gait. **-r** *n.* one who sets the pace for another.

**pach•y; -derm** *n.* a thick-skinned, nonruminant quadruped, e.g. the elephant. **-dermatous** *a.* thick-skinned; insenitive.

**pac•i•fy** *v.t.* to appease; to tranquilize. **pacifism** *n.* a doctrine which advocates abolition of war. **pacifist** *n.* **pacific** *a.* peaceful; calm or tranquil. **pacification.** *n.* **pacificatory** *a.* tending to make peace. **pacifier** *n.*

**pack** *n.* bundle for carrying, esp. on back; a band (of animals); a set of playing cards; *v.t.* to arrange closely in a bundle, box or bag; to fill, press together; to carry; to load. **-age** *n.* a bundle or parcel. **-er** *n.* **-et** *n.* a small package. **— horse** *n.* a horse for carrying burdens, in packs. **-ing** *n.* any material used to pack, fill up, or make close.

**pact** *n.* an agreement; a compact.

**pad** *n.* anything stuffed with soft material, to fill out or protect; a cushion; sheets of paper fastened together in a block; the foot or sole of certain animals; *v.t.* to furnish with a pad; to stuff; *pr.p.* **-ding.** *pa.p.* and *pa.t.* **-ded.** **-ding** *n.* the material used in stuffing; unnecessary matter inserted in a book, speech, etc., to expand it.

**pad• dle** *n.* a short oar with a broad blade at one or each end; a balance or float of a paddle wheel, a flipper; *v.t.* and *i.* to propel by paddles.

**pad• dock** *n.* a small grass field or enclosure where horses are saddled before race.

**pad• dy** *n.* rice in the husk.

**pad• lock** *n.* a detachable lock with a hinged hoop to go through a staple or ring.

**pa• dre** *n.* priest; chaplain.

**pa• gan** *n.* a heathen; *a.* heathenish.

**page** *n.* one side of a leaf of a book or manuscript; *v.t.* to number the pages of.

**page** *n.* formerly a boy in service of a person of rank; a uniformed boy attendant esp. in a hotel; *v.t.* to summon by sending a page to call.

**pag• eant** *n.* a show of persons in costume in procession, dramatic scenes, etc. a spectacle. **-ry** *n.* a brilliant display; pomp.

**pa• go• da** *n.* a temple or sacred tower in India, Burma, etc.

**paid** *pa.p.* and *pa.t.* of the verb **pay.**

**pail** *n.* a round, open vessel of wood, tin, etc., for carrying liquids; a bucket.

**pain** *n.* bodily or mental suffering; distress; *pl.* trouble; exertion; *v.t.* to inflict bodily or mental suffering upon. **-ful** *a.* full of pain; causing pain; difficult; **-fully** *adv.* **-fulness** *n.* **-less** *a.* **-lessly** *adv.* **-lessness** *n.* **-staking** *a.* carefully laborious.

**paint** *n.* coloring matter for putting on surface with brush, etc.; *v.t.* to cover or besmear with paint; to make a picture with paint; to adorn with, or as with, paint.

**paint• er** *n.* a rope at the bow of a boat used to fasten it to any other object.

**pair** *n.* two things of a kind; a single article composed of two similar pieces, e.g. a pair of scissors; a courting, engaged, or married couple; a mated couple of animals or birds; *v.t.* to unite in couples.

**pa• ja• mas** *n.pl.* loose trousers, worn by Mohammedans; a sleeping suit.

**pal** *n.* a close friend.

**pal• ace** *n.* the house in which a great personage resides; any magnificent house.

**pal• ate** *n.* the roof of the mouth; sense of taste; relish; liking. **palatable** *a.* agreeable to the taste or mind. **palatably** *adv.* **palatal** *a.* of a sound, produced by placing tongue against palate.

**pal• a• tine** *a.* having royal privileges; *n.* one who possesses royal privileges. **palatinate** *n.* the office or dignity of a palatine; the territory under his jurisdiction.

**pa• lav• er** *n.* idle talk.

**pale-, palae-, paleo-, palaeo-** *prefix* ancient. **-ography** *n.* ancient writings. **-ographic** *a.* **-ographer** *n.* **-olith** *n.* an unpolished stone implement of the earlier stone age. **-olithic** *a.* **-ology** *n.* study of antiquities; archaeology. **-ologist** *n.* **ontology** *n.* a study of fossils. **-ontologist** *n.* **-ontological** *a.* **-ozoic** *a.* denoting the lowest fossiliferous strata and the earliest forms of life.

**pale** *a.* faint in color; whitish; dim; *v.t.* to make pale; *v.i.* to become pale. **-ly** *adv.* **-ness** *n.* **palish** *a.* somewhat pale.

**pal• ette** *n.* a thin oval board on which a painter mixes his colors.

**Pa• li** *n.* the sacred language of the Buddhists.

**pal• in• drome** *n.* a word or sentence that is the same when read backward or forward, e.g. *level.*

**pal• i• sade** *n.* fence of pales or stakes; *(pl.)* an expanse of high cliffs; *v.t.* to enclose with palisades.

**pall** *n.* a large, ususally black cloth laid over the coffin at a funeral.

**pall** *v.t.* to make tedious or insipid.

**Pal• la• di• an** *a.* denoting a classical style of architecture.

**pal• la• di• um** *n.* a rare metal of the platinum group.

**pal• la• di• um** *n.* a safeguard; *pl.* **paladia.**

**pal• let** *n.* a tool with a flat blade used by potters, etc.

**pal• li• ate** *v.t.* to lessen or abate without curing; to excuse or extenuate. **palliation** *n.* **palliative** *a.* to mitigate. *n.* that which mitigates, alleviates.

**pal• lid** *a.* pale; wan, **-ly** *adv.* **-ness** *n.* **pallor** *n.* paleness.

**palm** *n.* the inner, slightly concave surface of hand, between wrist and fingers; flat, expanding end of any arm-like projection, esp. blade of oar; *v.t.* to conceal in the palm. **palmate** *a.* having shape of hand; *(Zool.)* web-footed. **-ist** *n.* one who claims to tell fortunes by the lines on the palm of the hand. **-istry** *n.*

**palm** *n.* a branchless, tropical tree; a branch or leaf of this tree used as a symbol of victory; prize or honor. **-er** *n.* in the Middle Ages, one who visited the Holy Land, and bore a branch of palm in token thereof; an itinerant monk. **-etto** *n.* a species of palm tree. *(Cap.)* **— Sunday,** Sunday before Easter.

**pal•my•ra** *n.* a tall E. Indian palm.

**pal•pa•ble** *a.* capable of being touched or felt; certain; obvious. **palpably** *adv.* **-ness** *n.* **palpate** *v.t.* to examine with the hand. **palpation** *n.*

**pal•pi•tate** *v.i.* to throb; to pulsate. **palpitation** *n.*

**pal•sy** *n.* paralysis; *v.t.* to paralyze. **palsied** *a.*

**pal•ter** *v.i.* to deal evasively; to use trickery; to dodge. **-er** *n.* **paltry** *a.* mean; worthless. **paltriness** *n.*

**pam•per** *v.t.* to gratify unduly; to over-indulge; to coddle. **-er** *n.*

**pam•phlet** *n.* a thin, paper-covered, unbound book; a short treatise or essay on a current topic. **-eer** *n.* a writer of pamphlets.

**pan** *n.* a broad, shallow metal vessel for house hold use; of an old type of gun, part of the flintlock that held the priming; *v.t.* and *i.* to wash gold-bearing soil in a pan in order to separate earth and gold.

**pan-** *prefix,* all, used in such words as **Pan-American** *a.* pert. to movement of the American republics to foster collaboration between N. and S. America.

**pan•a•ce•a** *n.* a cure for all diseases; a universal remedy.

**pa•nache** *n.* plume of feathers used as an ornament on a cap, etc.

**Pan•a•ma** *n.* a hat made of fine, pliant strawlike material.

**pan•cake** *n.* a thin cake of batter fried in a pan.

**pan•cre•as** *n.* *(Anat.)* digestive gland behind stomach; in animals, the sweetbread. **pancreatic** *a.*

**pan•da** *n.* a racoon-like animal; the bearcat.

**panda**

**pan•dem•ic** *a.* of a disease, universal; widely distributed; affecting a nation.

**pan•de•mo•ni•um** *n.* the abode of evil spirits; any disorderly, noisy place or gathering; a riotous uproar.

**pan•der** *n.* a go-between in base love intrigues; *v.i.* to act as a pander; to help to satisfy any unworthy desires.

**pane** *n.* a sheet of glass in a window; a square in a pattern. **-d** *a.*

**pan•e•gyr•ic** *n.* a speech or writing of praise; a eulogy. **-al** *a.* **panegyrist** *n.* one who writes or pronounces a eulogy. **panegyrize** *v.t.* to praise highly.

**pan•el** *n.* a rectangular piece of cloth, parchment, or wood; a sunken portion of a door, etc.; a list of jurors; a group of speakers, etc. *v.t.* to divide into, or decorate with panels. **-ing** *n.* paneled work. **-ist** *n.* member of a panel.

**pang** *n.* a sudden pain, physical or mental.

**pan•ic** *n.* sudden terror, often unreasoning; infectious fear; *v.i.* to be seized with sudden, uncontrollable fright. *pr.p.* **panicking.** *pa.p.* and *pa.t.* **panicked. panicky** *a.* affected by panic. **— stricken, — struck** *a.* seized with paralyzing fear.

**pan•ier** *n.* one of a pair of baskets carried on each side of a pack animal; a puffing-out round hips of a lady's skirt.

**pan•o•ply** *n.* a complete suit of armor; anything that covers or envelopes completely. **panoplied** *a.* fully armed.

**pan•o•ram•a** *n.* a complete view in every direction; a picture exhibited by being unrolled and made to pass continuously before the spector. **panoramic** *a.*

**pan•sy** *n.* a cultivated species of violet with richly colored flowers.

**pant** *v.i.* to breathe quickly and in a labored manner; to gasp for breath; *v.i.* to utter gaspingly; *n.* a gasp.

**pan•ta•loon** *n.(pl.)* tight trousers.

**pan•the•ism** *n.* the doctrine that identifies God with the universe, everything being considered as part of or a manifestation of Him. **pantheist** *n.* **pantheistic (al)** *a.* **pantheology** *n.* a system which embraces all religions and all gods.

**pan•ther** *n.* *(fem.* **-ess)** a variety of leopard.

**pan•to-** *prefix,* all, used in derivatives. **-graph** *n.* an instrument for copying drawings, maps, etc.

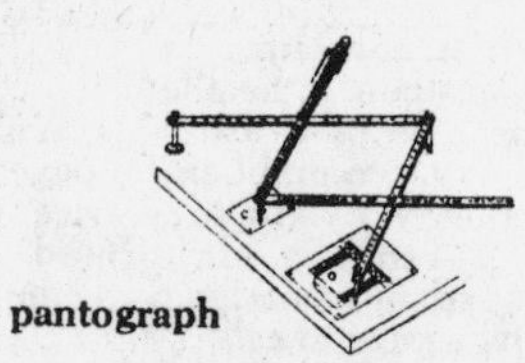

**pantograph**

**pan•to•mime** *n.* a gesture without speech; *v.t.* and *i.* to act or express by gestures only. **pantomimic** *a.* **pantomimist** *n.*

**pan•try** *n.* a small room for storing food or kitchen utensils.

**pants** *n.pl.* trousers.

**pa•pa•cy** *n.* the office and dignity of the Pope; Popes collectively. **papal** *a.*

**pa•per** *n.* a material made by pressing pulp of rags, straw, wood, etc., into thin flat sheets; a newspaper; an article or essay; a document; wall covering; a set of examination questions; *n.pl.* document(s) establishing one's identity; *a.* consisting of paper; *v.t.* to cover with paper. **— clip** *n.* a device for holding together sheets of paper. **— hanger** *n.* one who hangs paper on walls. — **money** *n.* official pieces of paper issued by a government or bank for circulation. **-weight** *n.* small, heavy object to prevent loose sheets of paper from being displaced.

**pa•pier•mâ•ché** *n.* paper pulp, mixed with glue, etc., shaped or molded into articles.

**pa•pil•la** *n.* a small nipple-shaped protuberance in a part of the body, e.g. on surface of tongue.

**pa•pist** *n.* a supporter of the papal system; a Roman Catholic. **papistic(al)** *a.* **-ry** *n.*

**pa•poose** *n.* a N. Amer. Indian baby.

**pap•pus** *n.* down, as on the seeds of the thistle, dandelion, etc. **pappose** *a.* downy.

**pa•py•rus** *n.* a species of reed, the pith of which was used by the ancients for making paper; a manuscript on papyrus. *pl.* **papyri.**

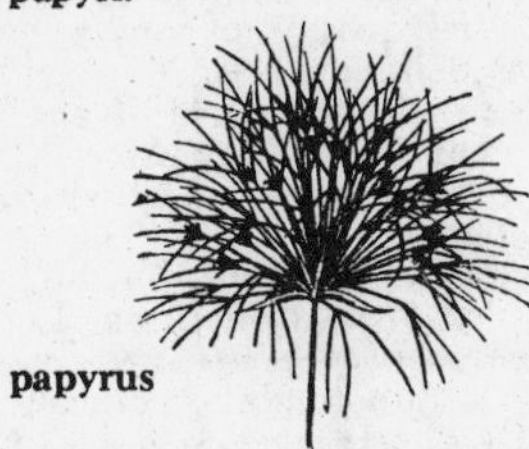

**papyrus**

**par** *n.* equality of value or circumstances; face value (of stocks and shares); *(Golf)* the number of strokes for hole or course in perfect play.

**par•a•ble** *n.* a story or allegory with a moral. **parabolical** *a.* **parabolically** *adv.*

**pa•rab•o•la** *n.* *(Geom.)* a conic section made by a plane parallel to side of cone. **parabolic** *a.* **paraboloid** *n.* solid formed when parabola is revolved round its axis.

**par•a•chute** *n.* a collapsible umbrellalike device used to retard the descent of a falling body. **parachutist** *n.*

**par•a•clete** *n.* *(Bib.)* the name given to the Holy Spirit; one called to aid or support; an advocate.

**pa•rade** *n.* a public procession; a muster of troops for drill or inspection; show; *v.t.* to make a display or spectacle of; to marshal in military order.

**par•a•digm** *n.* an example; a model. **-atic** *a.* **-atically** *adv.*

**par•a•dise** *n.* the garden of Eden; Heaven; a state of bliss. **paradisaic, paradisaical** *a.*

**par•a•dox** *n.* a statement seemingly absurd or self-contradictory, but really founded on truth. **-ical** *a.* **-ically** *adv.*

**par•af•fin** *n.* a white wax-like substance obtained from crude petroleum, shale, coal tar, wood, etc.

**par•a•gon** *n.* a pattern of excellence.

**par•a•graph** *n.* a section or subdivision of a passage, indicated by the sign ¶, or begun on a new line.

**par•a•keet** *n.* a small long-tailed parrot.

**par•al•de•hyde** *n.* a powerful hypnotic.

**par•al•lel** *a.* continuously at equal distance apart; similar; *n.* a line equidistant from another at all points; a thing exactly like another; a line of latitude; **-ism** *n.* the state of being parallel; comparison, resemblance. — **bars,** horizontal bars for gymnastic exercises.

**par•al•lel•o•gram** *n.* a four-sided plane figure with both pairs of opposite sides parallel.

**pa•ral•y•sis** *n.* *(Med.)* loss of power of movement or sensation. **paralyze** *v.t.* to affect with paralysis; to make useless; to cripple. **paralytic** *n.* one affected with paralysis. **infantile paralysis,** inflammation of grey matter in spinal cord, usually in children; poliomyelitis.

**par•a•mount** *a.* superior; of highest importance; **-cy** *n.* **-ly** *adv.*

**par•a•noi•a, paranoea** *n.* *(Med.)* a form of chronic insanity, often characterized by delusions of grandeur, persecution, etc. **paranoiac** *a.* and *n.*

**par•a•pher•na•li•a** *n.pl.* personal belongings; furnishings or accessories.

**par•a•phrase** *n.* a restatement of a passage; a free translation into the same or another language.

**par•a•site** *n.* formerly, one who habitually ate at the table of another, repaying with flattery; a plant or animal that lives on another. **parasitic** *a.* **parasitically** *adv.* **parasitology** *n.* the study of parasites, esp. as causes of disease. **parasitological** *a.* **parasitologist** *n.*

**par•a•sol** *n.* a small, light sun umbrella.

**par•a•troops** *n.pl.* *(World War 2)* troops organized to descend by parachute with their equipment from airplanes and gliders. **paratrooper** *n.*

**par•boil** *v.t.* to boil partially.

**par•cel** *n.* *(Arch.)* a part or portion, a bundle or package (wrapped in paper); a number of things forming a group or lot; a piece of land; *v.t.* to divide into portions; to distribute; to wrap up.

**parch** *v.t.* to search; to shrivel with heat.

**parch•ment** *n.* the skin of a sheep or goat, etc., prepared for writing on; a document written on this.

**par•don** *v.t.* to forgive; to free from punishment; to excuse; *n.* forgiveness; remission of a penalty. **-able** *a.* excusable.

**pare** *v.t.* to remove the outer skin; to peel. **-er** *n.* **paring** *n.* the action of peeling; that which is pared off.

**par•e•gor•ic** *a.* soothing; assuaging pain; *n.* a soothing medicine.

**par•ent** *n.* a father or mother; one who, or that which, brings forth or produces. **-age** *n.* descent from parents; birth. **parental** *a.* pert. to, or becoming, parents; tender; affectionate. **parentally** *adv.*

**pa•ren•the•sis** *n.* a word or sentence inserted in a passage independently of the grammatical sequence and usually marked off by brackets, dashes, or commas; **parentheses** *n.pl.* round brackets ( ), used for this. **parenthetic, parenthetical** *a.*

**pa•ri•e•tal** *a.* pert. to a wall; pert. to the wall of the body or its cavities.

**par•ish** *n.* an ecclesiastical district under a priest or clergyman; a local church and its area of activity. **parishioner** *n.* an inhabitant of a parish; a member of a parish church.

**par•i•ty** *n.* equality; analogy; close correspondence.

**park** *n.* a large piece of ground, usually with grass and trees for public use and recreation; a sports' ground; grounds around a country house; *v.t.* to enclose in a park; to leave an automobile in a certain place.

**par•ka** *n.* an Eskimo garment of undressed skin; a hooded outer garment.

**par•lance** *n.* a way of speaking; **parley** *n.* a meeting between leaders of opposing forces to discuss terms.

**par•lia•ment** *n. (usually cap.)* the supreme legislature of the United Kingdom, composed of the House of Lords and House of Commons; any similar assembly. **-ary** *a.* pert. to, enacted by, or according to, the established rules of parliament; of language, admissible in parliamentary debate, hence, decorous and non-abusive. **-arian** *n.* a skilled debater in parliament.

**par•lor, parlour** *n.* living room; a semi-private room in an inn.

**pa•ro•chi•al** *a.* pert. to a parish; provincial; narrow-minded **-ly** *adv.* **-ism** *n.*

**par•o•dy** *n.* an imitation of a poem, song, etc., where the style is the same but the theme ludicrously different; a feeble imitation; *v.t.* to write a parody of; to burlesque in verse. **parodist** *n.*

**pa•role** *n.* release of a prisoner on condition of good behavior; word of honor, esp. a promise given by a prisoner of war not to attempt to escape.

**par•o•no•ma•si•a** *n.* a play on words; a pun. **paronym** *n.* a word similar to another in having the same derivation or root. **paronymous** *a.*

**pa•rot•id** *a.* near the ear; *n.* a large salivary gland, in front of and below the ear.

**par•ox•ysm** *n.* sudden, violent attack of pain, rage, laughter; fit; convulsion.

**par•quet** *n.* flooring of wooden blocks; *v.t.* to lay such a floor. **-ry** *n.*

**parr** *n.* a young salmon.

**parr**

**par•ri•cide** *n.* one who murders his parent, a near relative, or a person who is venerated; the crime itself.

**par•rot** *n.* tropical bird; one who repeats words, actions, ideas, etc. of another.

**par•ry** *v.t.* to ward off; to turn aside; to avoid.

**parse** *v.t.* to classify a word or analyze a sentence in terms of grammar. **parsing** *n.*

**par•si•mo•ny** *n.* stinginess; undue economy. **parsimonious** *a.* **parsimoniously** *adv.* **parsimoniousness** *n.*

**pars•ley** *n.* a garden herb, used as a flavoring or garnish in cookery.

**pars•nip** *n.* a root vegetable, carrot-like in shape.

**par•son** *n.* a clergyman; the incumbent of a parish. **-age** *n.* the residence of a parson.

**part** *n.* a portion, fragment, or section of a whole; a share or lot; a division; an actor's role; duty; interest; a melody in a harmonic piece; *pl.* accomplishments or talents; region; *v.t.* to divide; to separate; to share; *v.i.* to separate; to take leave; to part with or give up. **-ing** *n.* the act of separating; leave-taking; division; dividing line; *a.* given on taking leave. **-ly** *adv.* in part; in some measure or degree. **-ible** *a.* divisible. **-ibility** *n.*

**par•take** *v.t.* and *i.* to have or take a share in; to take food or drink. *pr.p.* **partaking.** *pa.p.* **-n** *pa.t.* **partook. -r** *n.*

**Par•the•no•gen•e•sis** *n.* reproduction without sexual union.

**Par•the•non** *n.* famous Doric temple of Athena.

**par•tial** *a.* affecting only a part; not total; inclined to favor unreasonably. **-ly** *adv.* **partiality** *n.* quality of being partial; favoritism; fondness for.

**par•tic•i•pate** *v.t.* and *i.* to share in; to partake (foll. by 'in'). **participant** *n.* a partaker; *a.* sharing. **participator** *n.* **participation** *n.*

**par•ti•ci•ple** *n. (Gram.)* an adjective formed by inflection from a verb. **participial** *a.*

**par•ti•cle** *n.* a minute portion of matter.

**par•tic•u•lar** *a.* relating to a single person or thing, not general; considered apart from others; minute in details; fastidious in taste; *n.* a single point or circumstance; a detail or item. **-ly** *adv.* especially; with great attention. **particularity** *n.* quality or state of being particular; individual characteristic. **-ize** *v.t.* and *i.* to mention one by one; to give in detail; to specify. **-ization** *n.*

**par•ti•san, partizan** *n.* adherent, often prejudiced, of a party or cause; a member of irregular troops engaged in risky enterprises; *a.* adhering to a faction. **-ship** *n.*

**par•ti•tion** *n.* division or separation; any of the parts into which a thing is divided; that which divides or separates, as a wall, etc.; *v.t.* to divide into shares; to divide by walls. **partitive** *n.* a word expressing partition; a distributive; *a.* denoting a part. **partitively** *adv.*

**part•ner** *n.* a partaker; a sharer; an associate, esp. in business; a husband or wife; one who dances with another; in golf, tennis, etc., one who plays with another; *v.t.* in games, to play with another against opponents. **-ship** *n.* the state of being a partner; the association of two or more persons for business.

**par•tridge** *n.* a small game bird of the grouse family.

**partridge**

**par•ty** *n.* a number of persons united in opinion; a political group; a social assembly; a participator; an accessory; a litigant; *a.* pert. to a party or faction.

**pas•quin** *n.* a writer of lampoons or satires; a lampoon or satire. **-ade** *n.* a lampoon.

**pass** *v.t.* to go by, beyond, through etc.; to spend; to exceed; to approve; to disregard; to circulate; to send through; to move; *v.i.* to go; to elapse; to undergo examination successfully; to happen; to die; to circulate. *pa.p.* **-ed, past.** *pa.t.* **-ed.** *n.* a passage or way, esp. a narrow and difficult one; a permit; success in an examination, test, etc.; in football, hockey, etc., the passing of the ball from one player to another. **-able** *a.* that may be passed or crossed; fairly good; admissible. **-ably** *adv.* **-book** *n.* a bankbook. **-key** *n.* a masterkey. **-port** *n.* an official document, issued by a State Department, granting permission to travel abroad.

**pas•sage** *n.* the act, time, or right of passing; movement from one place to another; a voyage across the sea; fare for a voyage; an entrance or exit; part of a book, etc.; the passing of a law.

**pas•sé** *a.* past one's best; faded; rather out of date; antiquated.

**pas•sen•ger** *n.* a traveller, esp. by some conveyance; *a.* adapted for carrying passengers.

**pas•sion** *n.* intense emotion, as of grief, rage, love; eager desire; *(Cap.)* the story of Christ's suffering and last agony. **-ate** *a.* moved by strong emotions; vehement. **-agely** *adv.* **-ateness** *n.* **-less** *a.* **— play** *n.* a theatrical representation of Christ's passion.

**pas•sive** *a.* inactive; submissive; acted upon, not acting; *n.* *(Gram.)* (or passive voice) the form of the verb which expresses that the subject is acted upon. **-ly** *adv.* **-ness** *n.*

**Pass•o•ver** *n.* a feast of the Jews to commemorate the time when God, smiting the first-born of the Egyptians, passed over the houses of Israelites.

**past** *a.* pert. to former time; gone by; elapsed; ended; *n.* former state; bygone times; one's earlier life; *prep.* beyond; after; exceeding; beyond the scope of; *adv.* by; beyond.

**paste** *n.* a soft composition, as of flour and water; dough prepared for pies, etc.; any soft plastic mixture or adhesive; *v.t.* to fasten with paste. **pastry** *n.* the crust of pies and tarts; articles of food made of paste or dough. **pastry-cook** *n.* one who makes and sells pastry. **-board** *n.* a stiff, thick paper; flimsy or unsubstantial.

**pas•tel** *n.* a colored chalky crayon; a drawing made with such crayons. **— shades,** delicate and subdued colors.

**Pas•teur** *n.* a French chemist and biologist. **pasteurization** *n.* the sterilization of milk, etc. by heating to 140° F. or over and then cooling. **pasteurize** *v.t.*

**pas•time** *n.* that which amuses and makes time pass agreeably; recreation; diversion.

**pas•tor** *n.* a minister of the gospel. **-al** *a.* pert. to shepherds or rural life; relating to a pastor and his duties. **-ally** *adv.* **-ate** *n.* the office or jurisdiction of a spiritual pastor. **-ship** *n.*

**pas•ture** *n.* grass for food of cattle; ground on which cattle graze. **pasturable** *a.* **pasturage** *n.* pasture land; the business of grazing cattle.

**pat** *n.* a light, quick blow, esp. with hand or fingers; a small lump, esp. of butter; *pr.p.* **-ting.** *pa.p.* and *pa.t.* **-ted.**

**patch** *n.* a piece of material used to mend a hole, rent, etc.; a covering for a wound. **-y** *a.* full of patches; unequal. **-work** *n.* work made by sewing together pieces of cloth of different material and color.

**pa•tel•la** *n.* the kneecap.

**pat•ent** *a.* open; evident; protected by a patent; *n.* short for *letters patent,* an official document granting a right or privilege, or securing the exclusive right to invention; the invention itself. *v.t.* to secure or protect by a patent. **-ee** *n.* one who has secured a patent. **— leather,** leather with a varnished or lacquered surface.

**pa•ter•nal** *a.* pert. to a father; fatherly; hereditary. **-ly** *adv.* **paternity** *n.* the relation of a father to his offspring.

**path** *n.* a way, course, or track of action, conduct, or procedure. **-finder** *n.* a pioneer. **-way** *n.* a narrow footway.

**pa•thet•ic** *a.* affecting or moving the tender emotions; causing pity; touching.

**path•o-** *prefix,* suffering, feeling, used in derivatives. **-genesis, pathogeny** *n.* the origin and development of disease. **-genetic, -genic** *a.* causing disease. **-logy** *n.* the science and study of diseases, their causes, nature, cures, etc. **-logic, -logical** *a.* **-logically** *adv.* **-logist** *n.*

**pa•thos** *n.* the power of exciting tender emotions; deep feeling.

**pa•tient** *a.* not easily made angry; calm; not hasty; *n.* a person under medical treatment. **-ly** *adv.* **patience** *n.* the quality of enduring with calmness; quiet perseverance.

**pa•tri•arch** *n.* the father and ruler of a family, esp. in Biblical history; the highest dignitary in the Eastern church; a venerable old man. **-al** *a.* **-ate** *n.* dignity or jurisdiction of a patriarch. **-y** *n.* government by the head or father of a tribe.

**pa•tri•ot** *n.* one who loves his country and upholds its interests. **-ic** *a.* filled with patriotism. **-ically** *adv.* **-ism** *n.* love for, and loyalty to, one's country.

**pa•trol** *v.t.* and *i.* to go or walk around a camp, garrison, etc. in order to protect it. *pr.p.* **-ling.** *pa.p.* and *pa.t.* **-led.** *n.* a going of the rounds by a guard; the man or men who go to the rounds.

**pa•tron** *n.* a man who protects or supports a person, cause, entertainment, artistic production, etc.; a guardian saint. a regular customer. **-age** *n.* countenance, support, or encouragement given to a person or cause; condescending manner; in trade, regular customer. **-ize**

*v.t.* to act as a patron to; to assume the air of a superior towards; to frequent, as a customer. **patronizing** *a.* **patronizingly** *adv.* — **saint,** a saint who is regarded as the special protector of a person, city, trade, etc.

**pat•ter** *v.i.* to make a quick succession of small taps or sounds, like those of rain falling.

**pat•tern** *n.* a model, example, or guide; a decorative design; *v.t.* to design from a pattern; to imitate.

**pat•ty** *n.* a little pie.

**pau•ci•ty** *n.* fewness; scarcity; smallness of quantity.

**paunch** *n.* the belly. **-iness** *n.* **-y** *a.*

**pau•per** *n.* *(fem.* **-ess)** a very poor person, esp. one supported by the public. **-ize** *v.t.* to reduce to pauperism.

**pause** *n.* a temporary stop or rest; cessation; hesitation; a break in speaking, reading, or writing; in music, a sign or placed under or over a note to indicate the prolongation of a note or rest.

**pave** *v.t.* to form a level surface with stone, brick, etc.; to make smooth and even; **-ment** *n.* a paved floor, road, or sidewalk; material used.

**pa•vil•ion** *n.* orig. a tent; hence, anything like a tent, e.g. a garden summerhouse.

**paw** *n.* the foot of an animal having claws; *v.t.* and *i.* to scrape with the paws.

**pawn** *n.* something deposited as security for money borrowed; a pledge; the state of being pledged; *v.t.* to deposit as security for a loan; to pledge. **-broker** *n.* one who lends money on something deposited with him.

**pawn** *n.* a piece of the lowest rank in the game of chess.

**pay** *v.t.* to discharge one's obligations to; to give money, etc., for goods received or services rendered. *pa.p.* and *pa.t.* **paid** *n.* reward; compensation; wages; salary. **-able** *a.* justly due; profitable. **-ment** *n.* the act of paying; discharge of a debt; recompense.

**pea** *n.* the fruit, growing in pods, of a leguminous plant; the plant itself. **-nut** *n.* the earth nut. — **soup** *n.* soup made of dried peas.

**peace** *n.* calm; repose; freedom from disturbance, war, or hostilities. **-able** *a.* in a state of peace; disposed to peace; not quarrelsome. **-ably** *adv.* **-ableness** *n.* **-ful** *a.* free from war, tumult, or commotion; mild; undisturbed. **-fully** *adv.* **-fulness** *n.* **-maker** *n.* one who makes peace.

**peach** *n.* a juicy fruit with light orange flesh, and a velvety skin; the tree which bears this fruit; a pale orange-pink color. **-y** *a.* peach-like.

**pea•cock** *n.* *(fem.* **peahen)** *a.* bird remarkable for the beauty of its plumage, and for its large tail.

**peak** *n.* the sharp top of a hill; the pointed top of anything; the projecting part of a cap brim.

**peal** *n.* a loud sound, or succession of loud sounds, as of thunder, bells, laughter, etc.; a set of bells attuned to each other.

**pear** *n.* a sweet, juicy fruit of oval shape; tree on which it grows.

**pearl** *n.* a hard, smooth, lustrous substance, found in several mollusks, particularly pearl oyster, and used as a gem; something very precious; a creamy grey; a. made of pearls; pert. to pearls; *v.t:* to adorn with pearls; to take a round form like pearls. **-y** *a.* of the color of pearls; like pearls; abounding in pearls; clear; pure. **-iness** *n.*

**peas•ant** *n.* a rural laborer; a rustic; *a.* rural. **-ry** *n.* peasants collectively.

**peat** *n.* a brown, fibrous turf, formed of decayed vegetable matter, which is used as fuel. **-y** *a.* like peat, in texture or color.

**peb•ble** *n.* a small, roundish stone; transparent and colorless rock crystal used pebbles.

**pe•can** *n.* **-d, pebbly** *a.* full of oval nut with edible kernel; the tree on which it grows.

**pec•ca•ble** *a.* liable to sin. **peccability** *n.* liability to sin. **peccant** *a.* sinful; offensive; causing trouble.

**pec•ca•dil•lo** *n.* a trifling offense; an indiscreet action.

**peck** *n.* a measure of capacity for dry goods =2 gallons, or the fourth part of a bushel.

**peck** *v.t.* and *i.* to strike with the beak; to dab; to eat little quantities at a time. *n.*

**pec•tin** *n.* a carbohydrate from fruits which yields a gel.

**pec•to•ral** *a.* pert. to the breast or chest.

**pe•cul•iar** *a.* belonging solely to; appropriate; particular; singular; strange. **-ly** *adv.* **peculiarity** *n.* something that belongs to only one person, thing, class, people; a distinguishing feature; characteristic.

**pe•cu•ni•ar•y** *a.* pert. to or consisting of, money. **pecunniarily** *adv.*

**ped•a•gogue** *n.* a schoolteacher; a pedantic person. **pedagogic, pedagogical** *a.* **pedagogy, pedagogics** *n.* science of teaching.

**pe•dal** *a.* pert. to the foot; *n.* a mechanical contrivance to transmit power by using foot as a lever, e.g. on bicycle, sewing-machine.

**ped•dle** *v.t.* to travel from place to place selling small articles; *v.t.* to sell or hawk goods thus. **-r; pedlar** *n.* one who peddles goods.

**ped•es•tal** *n.* anything that serves as a support or foundation; the base of a column, statue, etc.

**pe•des•tri•an** *a.* going on, performed on, foot; of walking; commonplace; *n.* a walker; one who journeys on foot.

**pe•di•at•rics** *n.* *(Med.)* the branch dealing with the diseases and disorders of children. **pediatric** *a.* **pediatrician** *n.*

**pe•dic•u•lar** *pert.* to lice.

**ped•i•cure** *n.* treatment of the feet.

**ped•i•gree** *n.* a line of ancestors; genealogy; *a.* having a line of ancestors.

**ped•i•ment** *n.* *(Archit.)* the triangular ornamental facing of a portico door, or window, etc. **pedimental** *a.*

**pe•dom•e•ter** *n.* an instrument which measures the distance walked by recording the number of steps.

**pe•dun•cle** *n.* a flower stalk; *(Zool.)* a stalk or stalklike process in an animal body, **peduncular** *a.*

**peek** *v.i.* to peep; to peer; *n.* a glance.

**peel** *v.t.* to strip off the skin, bark, or rind; to free from a covering; *n.* the outside skin of a fruit; rind or bark.

**peep** *v.i.* to look through a crevice; to look furtively or slyly; to emerge slowly; *n.* a furtive or sly glance. **— show** *n.* a small exhibit, viewed through an aperture containing a magnifying glass.

**peep** *v.i.* to cry, as a chick.

**peer** *n.* *(fem.* **-ess***)* an equal in any respect; a nobleman; an associate. **-less** *a.* having no equal. **-lessly** *adv.* **-lessness** *n.*

**peer** *v.i.* to look closely and intently; to peer.

**pee•vish** *a.* fretful; irritable; hard to please; childish. **-ly** *adv.* **-ness** *n.* **peeve** *v.t.* to annoy.

**peg** *n.* a nail or pin of wood or other material. *v.t.* to fix or mark with a peg; *pr.p.* **-ging** *pa.t., pa.p.* **-ged.**

**Pe•king•esé** *n.* a breed of Chinese lap-dog.

**pe•koe** *n.* a black tea of superior quality.

**pel•i•can** *n.* a large water fowl.

pelican

**pel•let** *n.* a little ball; a pill; small shot.

**pelt** *n.* raw hide; undressed skin of furbearing animal.

**pel•vis** *n.* *(Anat.)* the bony basin-shaped cavity at the base of the human trunk. **pelvic** *a.*

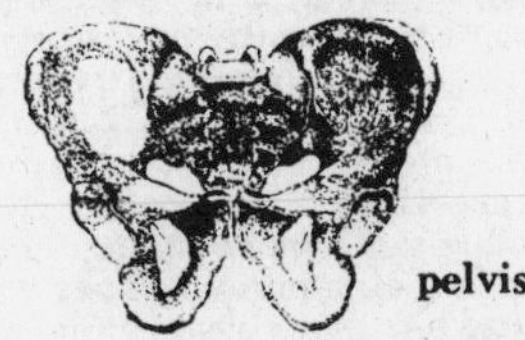

pelvis

**pen** *n.* an instrument for writing with ink; a large wing feather (a quill) used for writing. *pr.p.* **-ning.** *pa.p.* and *pa.t.* **-ned. -knife** *n.* a pocketknife. **-man** *n.* one who writes a good hand; an author. **-manship** *n.* **— name** *n.* an assumed name of author.

**pen** *n.* a small enclosure, as for sheep; a coop. *v.t.* to confine in a pen; to shut in. *pr.p.* **-ning** *pa.p., pa.t.* **-ned.**

**pe•nal** *a.* pert. to, prescribing, incurring, inflicting, punishment. **-ize** *v.t.* to make penal; to impose a penalty upon; to handicap. **-ly** *adv.* **penalty** *n.* punishment for a crime or offense; in games, a handicap imposed for infringement of rule, etc.; **penology** *n.* study and arrangement of prisons and prisoners.

**pen•ance** *n.* suffering submitted to in penitence; act of atonement.

**pen•cil** *n.* a stick of graphite encased in wood, used for writing or drawing; *v.t.* to draw, write with pencil. **-ed** *a.* marked, as with pencil; having pencils or rays. **-ing** *n.* the work of a pencil.

**pend•ant** *n.* a hanging ornament, esp. a locket or earring; a lamp or chandelier hanging from the ceiling. **pendent** *a.* suspended; hanging; projecting. pendently *adv.* **pending** *a.* awaiting settlement; in suspense; undebted; prep. during; until.

**pen•du•lous** *a.* hanging loosely; swinging. **-ly** *adv.* **-ness** *n.* **pendulum** *n.* a body suspended from a fixed point, and swinging freely; the swinging rod with weighted end which regulates movements of a clock, etc.

**pen•e•trate** *v.t.* to enter into; to pierce; to pervade or spread through; to touch with feeling; to arrive at the meaning of; *a.* **penetrable** *a.* capable of being entered or pierced.

**pen•guin** *n.* a flightless sea bird inhabiting the S. temperate and Antarctic regions.

penguin

**pen•i•cil•lin** *n.* an antibacterial agent produced from the fungus *penicillium.*

**pen•in•su•la** *n.* a portion of land nearly surrounded by water, and connected with the mainland by an isthmus **-r** *a.*

**pe•nis** *n.* the male organ of generation. **penial** *a.*

**pen•i•tent** *a.* deeply affected by sense of guilt; contrite; repentant; *n.* one who repents of sin. **-ly** *adv.* **penitence** *n.* sorrow for having sinned; repentance. **penitential** *a.* pert. to or expressing penitence; *n.* among R.C.s, a book containing rules of penance. **penitentially** *adv.* **penitentiary** *a.* pert. to punish by confinement; *n.* a prison.

**pen•nant** *n.* a very long, narrow flag tapering to a point.

**pen•ny** *n.* the U.S. and Canadian cent; an English coin (about 2 U.S. cents); a small sum. *pl.* **pennies. pennilesss** *a.* without money; poor.

**pen•sion** *n.* an annual grant of money for past services; an annuity paid to retired officers, soldiers, etc.; *v.t.* to grant a pension to.

**pen•sive** *a.* thoughtful; deep in thought; somewhat melancholy **-ly** *adv.* **-ness** *n.*

**pent** *a.* closely confined; shut up.

**pen•ta-** *prefix,* five, used in derivatives. **-gon, -gram** *n.*

**pen•tane** *n.* a paraffin hydrocarbon, a very inflammable liquid.

**Pen•ta•teuch** *n.* the first five books of the Old Testament.

**Pen•te•cost** *n.* a Jewish festival, celebrated on the 50th day after the Passover; a Christian festival (Whitsunday) commemorating the descent of the Holy Ghost on the Apostles. **Pentecostal** *a.*

**pent•house** *n.* an apartment, or structure, on the roof of a building; a shed attached to a main building, its roof sloping down from the wall.

**pen•to•thal** *n.* sometimes called the 'truth' drug; an anesthetic.

**pe•nult** *n.* the next to last syllable of a word.

**pe•num•bra** *n.* in an eclipse, the partially shadowed region which surrounds the full shadow.

**pe•on** *n.* in Mexico, a day laborer or serf; in India, a foot soldier, or messenger. **-age** *n.*

**pe•o•ny** *n.* plant having beautiful showy flowers.

**peo•ple** *n.* the body of persons that compose a community, tribe, nation, or race; the populace as distinct from rulers.

**pep•per** *n.* a pungent, spicy condiment obtained from an E. Indian plant; *v.t.* to sprinkle with pepper; to pelt with missiles. **—corn** *n.* the berry or fruit of the pepper-plant. **-mint** *n.* a pungent plant which yields a volatile oil; essence gotten from this oil; a lozenge flavored with this essence.

**pep•sin, pepsine** *n.* a ferment formed in gastric juice of man and animals, and serving as an aid to digestion. **peptic** *a.* pert. to pepsin and to digestion; *n.pl.* medicines that promote digestion. **peptone** *n.* one of the soluble compounds due to the action of pepsin, etc. on proteins.

**per an•num** L. by the year; annually.

**per•cale** *n.* closely woven cotton cloth.

**per•ceive** *v.t.* to obtain knowledge of through the senses; to see, hear, or feel; to understand. **perceivable** *a.* **perceivably** *adv.* **-r** *n.* **perceptible** *a.* capable of being perceived; discernible. **perceptibly** *adv.* **perceptibility** *n.* **perception** *n.* the faculty of perceiving; intuitive judgment. **perceptive** *a.* having perception; used in perception. **perceptual** *a.* involving perception.

**per•cent•age** *n.* proportion or rate per hundred. **per centum** *(abbrev.* **per cent***)* by, in, or for, each hundred; portion.

**perch** *n.* an edible fresh-water fish.

**perch** *n.* roosting bar for birds; high place; lineal measure (also 'pole' or 'rod') = 5½ yards; a measure of area = 30¼ square yards; *v.t.* to place on a perch; *v.i.* to alight or settle on a perch.

**per•chance** *adv.* perhaps; by chance.

**per•cip•i•ent** *a.* having the faculty of perception; perceiving; *n.* one who has the power of perceiving. **percipience, percipiency** *n.*

**per•co•late** *v.t.* and *i.* to pass slowly through small openings, as a liquid; to filter. **percolation** *n.* **percolator** *n.* a coffee pot fitted with a filter.

**per•cuss** *v.t.* to strike sharply. **percussion** *n.* a collision; an impact; *(Med.)* tapping the body to determine condition of internal organ. **-ive** *a.*

**per di•em** L. daily.

**per•emp•to•ry** *a.* authoritative; dictatorial; non-debatable; decisive; absolute. **peremptorily** *adv.* **peremptoriness** *n.*

**per•en•ni•al** *a.* lasting through the year; lasting; everlasting; lasting more than two years; *n.* a plant lasting for such a time. **-ly** *adv.*

**per•fect** *a.* complete; faultless; correct; excellent; of the highest quality; *(Gram.)* a tense denoting completed action; **perfect** *v.t.* to finish or complete; to make perfect; to improve; to make skillful. **-ly** *adv.* **perfectible** *a.* capable of becoming perfect. **perfectibility** *n.* **perfection** *n.* state of being perfect. **perfectionist** *n.* one who believes that moral perfection is attainable, or that he has attained it.

**per•fo•rate** *v.t.* to pierce; to make a hole or holes in. **perforation** *n.* act of perforating; a hole, or series of holes.

**per•form** *v.t.* to do; to accomplish; to fulfill; to represent on the stage; *v.i.* to do; to play, as on a musical instrument. **-ing** *a.* trained to act a part or do tricks. **-er** *n.* **-ance** *n.* act of performing; execution or carrying out.

**per•fume** *n.* a sweet scent or fragrance; a substance which emits an agreeable scent. *v.t.* to fill or imbue with an agreeable odor; to scent.

**per•func•to•ry** *a.* done as a duty, carelessly and without interest; indifferent; superficial. **perfunctorily** *adv.*

**per•haps** *adv.* it may be; possibly; perchance.

**per•i•car•di•um** (Anat.) the double membranous sac which encloses the heart. **pericardiac, pericardial** *a.*

**per•i•gee** *n.* that point in the moon's orbit nearest to the earth. opp. to *apogee.*

**per•il** *n.* danger; hazard; exposure to injury or loss; *v.t.* to expose to dangers, etc. **-ous** *a.* full of peril. **-ously** *adv.* **-ousness** *n.*

**per•im•e•ter** *n.* *(Geom.)* the outer boundary of a plane figure; the sum of all its sides; circumference. **perimetrical** *a.*

**pe•ri•od** *n.* a particular portion of time; the time in which a heavenly body makes a revolution; a series of years; a cycle; conclusion; a punctuation mark (.), at the end of a sentence; menstruation; *a.* of furniture, dress, a play, etc., belonging to a particular period in history. **periodic** *a.* recurring at regular intervals. **periodical** *a.* periodic; pert. to a periodical; *n.* a publication, esp. a magazine issued at regular intervals.

**pe•riph•er•y** *n.* circumference; perimeter; the outside. **peripheral** *a.*

**per•i•scope** *n.* an optical instrument which enables an observer to view surrounding objects from a lower level.

**per•ish** *v.t.* and *i.* to die; to waste away; to decay; to be destroyed. **-able** *a.* liable to perish, decay, etc., e.g. fish, fruit, etc.

**per•i•to•ne•um** *n.* membrane which lines abdominal cavity, and surrounds intestines, etc. **peritonitis** *n.* inflammation of peritoneum.

**per•i•wig** *n.* a wig; a peruke. **-ged** *a.*

**per•i•win•kle** *n.* an edible shellfish.

**per•i•win•kle** *n.* a trailing shrub with blue flowers; myrtle.

**per•jure** *v.t.* to violate one's oath (used reflex.). **-d** *a.* guilty of perjury. **perjury** *n.* false testimony; the crime of violating one's oath. **-r** *n.*

**per•ma•nent** *a.* remaining unaltered; lasting. *n.* a wave put into the hair to last several months. **-ly** *adv.* **permanence** *n.*

**per•man•ga•nate** *n.* a salt of an acid of manganese, which, dissolved in water, forms a disinfectant and antiseptic.

**per•me•ate** *v.t.* to penetrate and pass through; to diffuse itself through; to saturate. **permeable** *a.* admitting of passage of fluids. **permeably** *adv.* **permeability** *a.* capable of permeating.

**per•mit** *v.t.* to allow; to give leave or liberty to; *v.t.* to give leave. **permit** *n.* written permission. *pr.p.* **-ting.** *pa.p.* and *pa.t.* **-ted. permission** *n.* authorization; leave or license granted. **permissible** *a.* allowable. **permissibly** *adv.* **permissive** *a.* allowing. **permissively** *adv.*

**per•mute** *v.t.* to change the order of **permutable** *a.* **permutably** *adv.* **permutableness, permutability** *n.* **permutation** *n.* *(Math.)* the arrangement of a number of quantities in every possible order.

**per•ni•cious** *a.* having the quality of destroying or injuring; wicked. **-ly** *adv.* **-ness** *n.*

**per•o•ra•tion** *n.* the concluding part of an oration. **perorate** *v.i.* to deliver a speech.

**per•ox•ide** *(Chem.)* oxide containing more oxygen than the normal oxide of an element.

**per•pen•dic•u•lar** *a.* exactly upright or vertical; at right angles to the plane of the horizon; at right angles to a given line or surface; *n.* a line at right angles to the plane of the horizon or to any line or plane.

**per•pe•trate** *v.t.* to commit (something bad, esp. a crime). **perpetration** *n.* **perpetrator** *n.*

**per•pet•u•al** *a.* continuing indefinitely; everlasting. **-ly** *adv.* **perpetuate** *v.t.* to make perpetual; not to allow to be forgotten. **perpetuation** *n.* **perpetuity** *n.* the state or quality of being perpetual.

**per•plex** *v.t.* to make intricate, or difficult; to puzzle; to bewilder. **-ed** *a.* puzzled; bewildered. **-ing** *a.* **-ity** *n.* bewilderment; a confused state of mind.

**per•se•cute** *v.t.* to oppress unjustly for the holding of an opinion; to subject to persistent ill-treatment; to harass. **persecution** *n.* **persecutor** *n.*

**per•se•vere** *v.i.* to persist; to maintain an effort; not to give in. **persevering** *a.* **perseveringly** *adv.* **perseverance** *n.*

**per•sian** *a.* pert. to Persia (now Iran) its people, or the language. **— cat,** a breed of cat with long, silky fur.

**per•sim•mon** *n.* an American tree with plumlike fruit.

**per•sist** *v.i.* to continue firmly in a state or action in spite of obstacles or objections. **-ent** *a.* persisting; steady; persevering; lasting. **-ently** *adv.* **-ence, -ency** *a.*

**per•sim•mon** *n.* an American tree with plumlike fruit.

**per•sist** *v.i.* to continue firmly in a state or action in spite of obstacles or objections. **-ent** *a.* persisting; steady; persevering; lasting. **-ently** *adv.* **-ence, -ency** *a.*

**per•son** *n.* a human being; an individual; the body of a human being; a character in a play; *(Gram.)* one of the three classes of personal pronouns (first, second, or third) showing the relation of the subject to a verb, as speaking, spoken to, or spoken of. **-able** *a.* attractive in appearance. **-age** *n.* a person, esp. of rank or social position. **-al** *a.* pert. to, peculiar to, or done by, a person; pert. to bodily appearance; directed against a person; *(Gram)* denoting the pronouns, I, you, he, she, it, we, you, and they. **-ally** *adv.* in person; individually. **-ality** *n.* individuality; distinctive personal qualities. **personalty** *n.* *(Law)* personal effects; movable possessions. **-ate** *v.t.* to assume character of; to pretend to be. **-ator** *n.* **-ation** *n.*

**per•son•i•fy** *v.t.* to endow inanimate objects or abstract ideas with human attributes; to be an outstanding example of **personification** *n.*

**per•son•nel** *n.* the persons employed in a public service, business, office, etc.; staff.

**per•spec•tive** *n.* the art of drawing objects on a plane surface to give impression of the relative distance of objects, indicated by the convergence of their receding lines; relation of parts of a problem, etc. in the mind.

**per•spire** *v.t.* to emit through the pores of the skin; *v.i.* to evacuate the moisture of the body through the pores of the skin; to sweat. **perspiration** *n.* the process of perspiring; the moisture emitted.

**per•suade** *v.t.* to influence by argument, entreaty, etc.; to win over. **persuasive** *a.* having the power of persuading. **persuasively** *adv.* **persuasiveness** *n.* **persuasion** *n.* the act of persuading; the quality of persuading; conviction; belief; sect. **persuasible** *a.*

**per•tain** *v.i.* to belong; to concern.

**per•ti•na•cious** *a.* adhering to an opinion, etc. with obstinacy; persevering; resolute. **-ly** *adv.* **-ness** *n.* **pertinacity** *n.*

**per•ti•nent** *a.* related to the subject or matter in hand. **-ly** *adv.* **pertinence, pertinency** *n.*

**per•turb** *v.t.* to disturb; to trouble greatly. **-ation** *n.* mental uneasiness or disquiet; disorder.

**Pe•ru** *n.* a republic on the west coast of S. America. **-vian** *n.* a native of Peru; *a.* pert. to Peru.

**pe•ruse** *v.t.* to read through, esp. with care. **perusal** *n.* the act of perusing.

**per•vade** *v.t.* to spread through the whole

of; to be diffused through all parts of. **pervasion** *n.* **pervasive** *a.*

**per•verse** *a.* obstinately or unreasonably wrong; refusing to do the right, or to admit error; self-willed. **-ness, perversity** *n.*

**per•ver•sion** *n.* a turning from the true purpose, use, or meaning; corruption; unnatural manifestation of sexual desire. **perversive** *a.* tending to pervert.

**per•vert** *v.t.* to turn from its proper purpose; to misinterpret; to lead astray; to corrupt. **pervert** *n.* one who has deviated from the normal, esp. from right to wrong.

**per•vi•ous** *a.* giving passage to; penetrable. **-ness** *n.*

**pes•si•mism** *n.* the doctrine that the world is fundamentally evil; the tendency to look on the dark side of things; melancholy. **pessimist** *n.* **pessimistic** *a.* **pessimistically** *adv.*

**pest** *n.* a plague or pestilence; a troublesome or harmful thing or person; nuisance. **-iferous** *a.* pestilential; carrying disease.

**pes•ter** *v.t.* to trouble or vex persistently; to annoy.

**pest•i•cide** *n.* a pest killer.

**pes•ti•lence** *n.* any infectious or contagious, deadly disease. **pestilent** *a.* producing disease; noxious; harmful to morals.

**pes•tle** *n.* an instrument for pounding substances in a mortar.

**pet** *n.* an animal or person kept or regarded with affection; a favorite; *a.* favorite; *v.t.* to make a pet of; to indulge. *pr.p.* **-ting.** *pa.p.* and *pa.t.* **-ted.**

**pet** *n.* a sudden fit of peevishness.

**pet•al** *n.* a colored flower-leaf. **-ed, -led** *a.* having petals.

**pet•it** *(Law)* small; minor. *fem.* **petite** small, dainty, trim of figure. **— Point** *a.* slanting stitch used in embroidery and tapestry.

**pe•ti•tion** *n.* a formal request or earnest prayer; *v.t.* and *i.* to present a petition to; to entreat. **-ary** *a.* **-er** *n.*

**pet•ri•fy** *v.t.* to turn into stone; to make hard like stone; to make motionless with fear. **petrified, pertifactive** *a.*

**pe•tro•le•um** *n.* a mineral oil drawn from the earth by means of wells.

**pet•ti•coat** *n.* a woman's underskirt.

**pet•tish** *a.* petulant; easily annoyed. **-ly** *adv.* **-ness** *n.*

**pet•ty** *a.* small; unimportant; trivial; small-minded; of lower rank. **pettily** *adv.* **pettiness** *n.* **— cash,** small items of expenditure, esp. in an office. **— officer,** a non-commissioned officer in the Navy.

**pet•u•lant** *a.* given to small fits of temper; irritable. **-ly** *adv.* **petulance, petulancy** *n.* peevishness; crossness; fretfulness.

**pe•tu•ni•a** *n.* a common garden plant with showy flowers.

**pew** *n.* a long, fixed bench in a church.

**pe•wee** *n.* a small bird, the phoebe.

**pew•ter** *n.* an alloy of tin and lead or some other metal, esp. copper; ware made of this; *a.* made of pewter.

**pha•lanx** *n.* in ancient Greece, a company of soldiers in close array; hence, any compact body of people; *(Anat.)* a small bone of a toe or finger. *pl.* **-es, phalanges.**

**phal•lus** *n.* sexual organs. *pl.* **phalli. phallic** *a.*

**phan•tasm** *n.* an imaginary vision; a phantom; a specter. **-al, -ic** *a.* **phantasmagoria** *n.* an exhibition of optical illusions; a shifting scene of dim or unreal figures. **phantasmagoric** *a.* **phantasy** *n.*

**Phar•aoh** *n.* 'The Great House' a title of the kings of ancient Egypt.

**phar•ma•ceu•ti•cal** *a.* pert. to pharmacy. **pharmaceutics** *n.pl.* the science of pharmacy. **pharmaceutist** *n.*

**phar•ma•cy** *n.* the science of preparing, compounding, and dispensing drugs and medicines; a drugstore. **pharmacist** *n.* one skilled in pharmacy. **pharmacology** *n.* the study of drugs and their action. **pharmacologist** *n.* one skilled in pharmacy. **pharmacopoeia** *n.* an authoritative book containing information on medicinal drugs.

**phar•ynx** *n.* the cavity at back of mouth, opening into the gullet. *pl.* **pharynges. pharyngeal** *a.* Also **pharyngal. pharyngitis** *n.* *(Med.)* inflammation of pharynx. **pharyngoscope** *n.* instrument for examing throat.

**phase** *n.* *(Astron.)* an aspect of moon or a planet; a stage in development; an aspect of a subject or question. **phasic** *a.*

**pheas•ant** *n.* a gamebird with brilliant plumage.

pheasant

**phe•nom•e•non** *n.* anything appearing or observed, esp. if having scientific interest; a remarkable person or thing; *(Philos.)* sense appearance as opposed to real existence. *pl.* **phenomena. phenomenal** *a.* pert. to a phenomenon; remarkable; extraordinary. **phenomenally** *adv.*

**phi•al** *n.* a small glass bottle; a vial.

**phi•lan•der** *v.i.* to flirt. **-er** *n.*

**phi•lan•thro•py** *n.* love of mankind, esp. as shown in acts of charity; an act of charity. **philanthropic, philanthropical** *a.* **philanthropically** *adv.* **philanthropist** *n.* one who loves and seeks to do good to his fellowmen. Also **philanthrope.**

**phi•lat•e•ly** *n.* stamp collecting. **philatelic** *a.* **philatelist** *n.*

**phil•har•mon•ic** *a.* loving harmony or music; musical.

**Phi•lis•tine** *n.* one with no love of music, painting, etc.; an uncultured person.

**phi•lol•o•gy** *n.* scientific study of origin, development, etc. of languages. **philological** *a.* **philogian philologist** *n.* one versed in philology.

**phi•los•o•phy** *n.* originally, any branch of investigation of natural phenomena; now, the study of beliefs regarding God, existence, conduct, etc. and of man's relation with the universe; a calmness of mind; composure. **philosopher** *n.* a student of philosophy. **philosophic, philosophical** *a.* pert. to philosophy; wise; calm. **philosophically** *adv.* **philosophize** *v.i.* to reason like a philosopher; to theorize; to moralize.

**phle•bi•tis** *n. (Med.)* inflammation of a vein. **phlebitic** *a.* **phlebotomy** *n. (Surg.)* blood-letting.

**phlegm** *n.* a secretion of thick mucous substance discharged from throat by expectoration; calmness; apathy; sluggishness. **phlegmatic** *a.* cool and collected; unemotional.

**phlox** *n.* a genus of garden plants.

**pho•bi•a** *n.* a morbid dread of anything; used esp. as a suffix, *e.g.* claustro*phobia*, hydro*phobia*, etc.

**phone** *n.* a sound made in speaking. **phonic** *a.* pert. to sound, esp. to speech sounds. **phonics** *n.* method of teaching reading, etc. on basis of speech sounds.

**pho•net•ic** *a.* pert. to the voice; pert. to, or representing, vocal sounds. Also **-al** *a.* **-ally** *adv.* **-s** *n.* the branch of the study of language which deals with speech sounds, and their production. **-ize** *v.t.* to represent phonetically. **— spelling,** a simplified system of spelling in which same letter or symbol is always used for same sound, e.g. cat = kat.

**pho•no-** *prefix,* sound, used in many derivatives. **-gram** *n.* a character or symbol, esp. in shorthand, used to represent a speech sound. **-graph** *n.* an instrument for reproducing sounds from records. **phonography** *n.* a system of shorthand. **phonology** *n.* study of speech sounds; phonetics. **-logic(al)** *a.*

**phos•phate** *n.* a salt of phosphoric acid. **phosphatic** *a.* **— of lime,** commercially, bone-ash. **phosphide** *n.* a compound of phosphorus with another element, e.g. copper.

**phos•pho•rus** *n.* a non-metallic element, a yellowish waxlike substance giving out a pale light in the dark. **phosphorous** *a.* pert. to phosphorus.

**pho•to** *prefix,* light, used in derivatives. **-chemistry** *n.* the branch of chemistry which treats of the chemical action of light. **-electron** *n.* an electron liberated from a metallic surface by the action of a beam of ultraviolet light. **— finish,** in racing, a photo taken at the finish to show correct placing of contestants. **-genic** *a.* producing light; of a person, having features, etc. that photograph well.

**pho•tog•ra•phy** *n.* the art of producing pictures by the chemical action of light on a sensitive plate or film. **photograph** *n.* a picture so made; *v.i.* to take a photograph of. **photographer** *n.* **photographic(al)** *a.* pert. to resembling, or produced by, photography. **photographically** *adv.*

**pho•tol•o•gy** *n.* the science of light. **photometer** *n.* an instrument for measuring the intensity of light.

**pho•ton** *n.* the unit of measurement of light intensity.

**pho•to•stat** *n.* a photographic apparatus for making copies of documents, etc. directly on paper; *v.t.* to copy thus. **photostatic** *a.*

**pho•to•syn•the•sis** *n.* the process by which a plant, under the influence of sunlight, can build up, in its chlorophyll-containing cells, carbohydrates from the carbon dioxide of the atmosphere and from the hydrogen of the water in the soil.

**phrase** *n.* a small group of words forming part of a sentence; a short pithy expression; a characteristic mode of expression; *(Mus.)* a short, distinct part of a longer passage; *v.t.* to express suitably in words.

**phre•net•ic** *a.* having the mind disordered; frenzied; frantic.

**phre•nol•o•gy** *n.* character reading from the shape of the head. **phrenologic(al)** *a.* **phrenologically** *adv.* **phrenologist** *n.*

**phthi•sis** *n. (Med.)* a wasting away of the lungs; consumption.

**phy•log•e•ny** *n. (Bot.)* the evolution of an animal or plant type. **phylum** *n.* one of the primary divisions of the animal or plant kingdoms. *pl.* **phyla.**

**phys•i•cal** *a.* pert. to physics; pert. to nature; bodily, as opposed to mental or moral; material. **-ly** *adv.*

**phys•ics** *n.* sciences (excluding chemistry and biology) which deal with natural phenomena, e.g. motion, force, light, sound, electricity, etc. **physicist** *n.*

**phys•i•og•no•my** *n.* art of judging character from contours of face; face itself; expression of the face. **physiognomic, physiognomical** *a.* **physiognomist** *n.*

**phys•i•og•ra•phy** *n.* the study and description of natural phenomena; physical geography. **physiographer** *n.*

**phys•i•ol•o•gy** *n.* science which deals with functions and life processes of plants, animals, and human beings. **physiological** *a.* **physiologist** *n.*

**phys•i•o•ther•a•py** *n.* the application of massage, manipulation, light, heat, electricity, etc., for treatment of certain disabilities.

**phy•sique** *n.* bodily structure and development.

**phy•to** *prefix,* a plant. **phytogenesis, phytogeny** *n.* the evolution of plants.

**pi** *n.* the Greek letter $\pi$, esp. as a mathematical symbol for the ratio of the circumference of a circle to its diameter, approx. 3 1/7, or 3.14159.

**pi•a•no** *adv. (Mus.)* softly. **pianissimo** *adv.* very softly.

**pi•a•no** *n. abbrev.* of **pianoforte** *n.* a musical instrument having wires of graduated tension, struck by hammers moved by notes on a keyboard. **pianist** *n.* one who plays the piano.

**pi•az•za** *n.* a porch of a house; a public

square.

**pi•ca** *n.* *(Print.)* a size of type, having 6 lines to the inch.

**pic•a•dor** *n.* a mounted bullfighter armed with a lance to prod the bull.

**pic•co•lo** *n.* *(Mus.)* a small flute, sounding an octave higher than the ordinary flute.

**pick** *v.t.* to peck at, like birds with their bills; to pierce with a pointed instrument; to open with a pointed instrument, as a lock; to pluck, or cull, as flowers, etc.; to raise or lift (with 'up'); to choose or select; to rob; to pluck the strings of a musical instrument; *n.* a sharp-pointed tool; the choicest or best of anything. **-ax** *n.* an instrument for digging. **-pocket** *n.* one who steals from pockets.

**pick•a•nin•ny** a small child; a Negro baby.

**pick•et** *n.* a sharpened stake (used in fortifications, etc.); a peg or pale; a guard posted in front of an army; a party sent out by trade unions to dissuade men from working during a strike; *v.t.* to fence with pickets.

**pick•le** *n.* brine or vinegar in which fish, meat, or vegetables are preserved; any food preserved in brine or vinegar; *v.t.* to preserve with salt or vinegar. *n.pl.* vegetables in vinegar and spices.

**pic•nic** *n.* pleasure excursion with meal out of doors; agreeable situation; *v.i.* to go on a picnic. *pr.p.* **-king.** *pa.p.* and *pa.t.* **-ked.**

**pic•to•graph** *n.* a picture representing an idea.

**pic•to•ri•al** *a.* pert. to pictures; expressed by pictures; illustrated. **-ly** *adv.*

**pic•ture** *n.* a representation of objects or scenes on paper, canvas, etc., by drawing, painting, photography, etc.; a mental image; a likeness or copy; an illustration; picturesque object; a graphic or vivid description in words; *v.t.* to draw or paint an image or representation of; to describe graphically; to recall vividly. **picturesque** *a.* making effective picture; vivid in description. **-squely** *adv.* **-squeness** *n.* **— gallery** *n.* a hall containing a collection of pictures for exhibition.

**pid•dle** *v.i.* to trifle. **piddling** *a.* trifling.

**pie** *n.* *(Cookery)* a dish of meat or fruit covered with upper or lower pastry crust or both; *(Print.)* a confused mass of type.

**piece** *n.* a part of anything; a bit; a portion; a single object; a separate example; a coin; a counter in chess, checkers, etc.; a literary work; a musical composition; a gun; a plot of land; *v.t.* to mend; to put together. **— goods** *n.pl.* textile fabrics sold by measured lengths of the material. **— meal** *adv.* little by little; gradually. **— work** *n.* work paid for by the amount done, and not by the hour, day, etc.

**pier** *n.* a piece of solid, upright masonry, as a support or pillar for an arch, bridge, or beam; a structure built out over the water as a landing.

**pierce** *v.t.* to thrust into, esp. with a pointed instrument; to make a hole in; to penetrate; *v.i.* to enter; to penetrate. **piercing** *a.* penetrating; sharp; keen. **piercingly** *adv.*

**pi•e•ty** *n.* the quality of being pious; devotion to religion; affectionate respect for one's parents. **pietist** *n.* an ultrapious person; a sanctimonious person. **pietistic** *a.* **pietism** *n.*

**pig** *n.* a hoofed domestic animal, reared for its flesh; oblong mass of smelted metal, as pig iron; **-gish** *a.* pert. to, or like, pigs; dirty; greedy; stubborn. **-tail** *n.* the tail of a pig; a braid of hair hanging from the back of the head; a roll of twisted tobacco. **-headed** *a.* obstinate; stupidly perverse. **—iron, —lead,** iron, lead, cast in rough oblong bars. **-skin** *n.* strong leather made from the pig's skin, and used for saddles, etc. **-sty** *n.* a covered enclosure for keeping pigs; a dirty house or room.

**pi•geon** *n.* any bird of the dove family, both wild and domesticated; a simpleton or dupe. **—hearted** *a.* timid. **-hole** *n.* a little division in a desk or case, for holding papers, etc.; *v.t.* to place in the pigeonhole of a desk, etc.; to shelve for future reference; to classify. **—toed** *a.* having turned-in toes.

**pig•ment** *n.* paint; coloring matter; coloring matter in animal tissues and cells. **-ation** *n.* *(Biol.)* coloring matter.

**pile** n. a mass or collection of things; a heap; a large building or mass of buildings; to throw into a pile or heap; to accumulate.

**pile** *n.* fur or hair; nap of a fabric; esp. if thick and close-set, as in velvet.

**piles** *n.pl.* a disease of the rectum; hemorrhoids.

**pil•fer** *v.t.* and *i.* to steal in small quantities.

**pil•grim** *n.* a traveler, esp. one who journeys to visit a holy place. **-age** *n.* journey to a holy place; any long journey.

**pill** *n.* a small ball of medicine, to be swallowed whole; anything disagreeable that has to be endured.

**pil•lar** *n.* a slender upright structure of stone, iron, etc.; a column; a support. **-ed** *a.*

**pil•low** *n.* a cushion, esp. for the head of a person in bed; *v.t.* to place on a pillow. **-case, -slip** *n.* a removable covering for a pillow.

**pi•lot** *n.* a person qualified to take charge of a ship entering or leaving a harbor, or where knowledge of local waters is needed; one qualified to operate an aircraft; a steersman; a guide; a small jet of gas kept burning in order to light a stove, etc.; *v.t.* to direct the course of; to guide through dangers or difficulties. **— engine** *n.* a locomotive sent on ahead to clear the way for a train.

**pi•men•to** *n.* allspice; pimiento, a reddish pepper.

**pimp** *n.* a procurer; a pander; *v.i.* to pander.

**pim•per•nel** *n.* an annual plant of the primrose family.

**pim•ple** *n.* a small, red, pustular spot on the skin. **-d, pimply** *a.*

**pin** *n.* a short, thin piece of stiff wire with a

point and head for fastening soft materials together; a wooden or metal peg or rivet; an ornament that fastens on cloth; *(Golf)* a thin metal or wooden stick (with a flag) to mark the position of the hole; a rolling pin; a clothespin; a trifle; *pl. v.t.* to fasten with pins; to seize and hold fast. *pr.p.* **-ning.** *pa.p.* and *pa.t.* **-ned. -cushion** *n.* a small pad in which pins are stuck. **— money** *n.* an allowance for incidental or personal expenses. **-point** *v.t.* to locate (a target) with great accuracy.

**pin•a•fore** *n.* an apron for a child or young girl.

**pin•cers** *n.pl.* a tool for gripping, composed of two limbs crossed and pivoted; nippers; pliers; the claw of a lobster, crab, etc.

**pinch** *v.t.* to nip or squeeze, e.g. between the thumb and finger; to stint; to make thin, e.g. by hunger; *v.i.* to press hard; to be miserly; *n.* as much as can be taken up between the thumb and finger; a nip; an emergency. **-ed** *a. (Fig.)* thin and hungry looking.

**pine** *n.* a coniferous tree with evergreen, needlelike leaves; wood of this tree; **-y, piny** *a.* **-apple** *n.* tropical plant and its fruit resembling a pine cone; the ananas; **— cone** *n.* fruit of the pine.

**pine** *v.t.* to waste away from grief, anxiety, want, etc.; to languish; to wither; to desire eagerly.

**ping** *n.* the sound that a bullet makes **—pong** *n.* table tennis.

**pink** *n.* a carnation, a garden flower of various colors; a light crimson color; that which is supremely excellent; *a.* of a pale crimson color.

**pink** *v.t.* to pierce with small holes; to pierce with a sword, etc.; to ornament the edge with notches, etc.

**pin•na•cle** *n.* a slender turret elevated above the main building; a rocky mountain peak; a summit; *(Fig.)* the climax.

**pinnacle**

**pint** *n.* a liquid and a dry measure equal to ½ quart.

**pin•to** *n.* a piebald horse.

**pi•o•neer** *n.* one who originates anything or prepares the way for others; *v.i.* to open a way or originate; an explorer; *(Mil.)* one of an advance body clearing or repairing a road for troops.

**pi•ous** *a.* having reverence and love for God; marked by pretended or mistaken devotion; **-ly** *adv.*

**pipe** *n.* a tubular instrument of music; any long tube; a tube of clay, wood, etc. with a bowl for smoking; a bird's note; a pipeful of tobacco; a pipe-like vein of ore; *pl.* bagpipes; *v.t.* to perform on a pipe; to utter in a shrill tone; to convey by means of pipes; to ornament with a piping or fancy edging; *v.i.* to play on a pipe, esp. the bagpipes; to whistle. **piped** *a.* furnished with a pipe; tubular; conveyed by pipes. **piping** *a.* giving forth a shrill sound; *n.* the act of playing on a pipe; a system of pipes (for gas, water, etc.); a kind of cord trimming for ladies' dresses; ornamentation made on cakes **— clay** *n.* a fine, whitish clay used in the manufacture of tobacco pipes; *v.t.* to whiten with pipe clay. **— line** *n.* a long line of piping for conveying water, oil, etc.

**pi•pette** *n.* a thin, glass tube used for withdrawing small quantities of a liquid from a vessel.

**pi•quant** *a.* agreeably pungent to the taste; arousing interest. **-ly** *adv.* **piquancy.**

**pique** *v.t.* to irritate; to hurt the pride of; to displease; to stimulate; to pride oneself. *pr.p.* **piquing.** *pa.p.* and *pa.t.* **piqued,** *n.* annoyance from a slight; vexation.

**pi•qué** *n.* a ribbed cotton fabric.

**pi•rate** *n.* a sea robber; a vessel manned by sea robbers; a publisher, etc. who infringes copyright; *v.t.* and *v.i.* to act as a pirate; to plunder; to publish or reproduce regardless of copyright. **piratical** *a.* **piratically** *adv.* **piracy** *n.*

**pir•ou•ette** *n.* a spinning round on the toes of one foot.

**Pis•ces** *n.pl. (Astron.)* the Fishes, the twelfth sign of the zodiac.

**pis•ta•chi•o** *n.* the nut of an Asiatic tree, whose kernel is used for flavoring.

**pis•til** *n.* the seed-bearing organ of a flower, consisting of the stigma, style, and ovary. **-late** *a.* having a pistil but sometimes no stamen.

**pis•tol** *n.* a small handgun; *v.t.* to shoot with a pistol.

**pistol**

**pis•ton** *n.* a closely fitting metal disk moving to and fro in a hollow cylinder, e.g. as in a steam engine, automobile, etc. **— rod** *n.* a rod which connects the piston with another part of the machinery.

**pit** *n.* a deep hole in the ground, esp. one from which coal etc. is dug or quarried; the abyss of hell; a hollow or depression; an area for cock-fighting, etc.; in the theater, the section for musicians in front of stage; in motor racing, the base where cars are refilled, etc.; *pr.p.* **-ting.** *pa.p.* and *pa.t.* **-ted;** *a.* marked with small hollows. **-fall** *n.* a pit lightly covered, intended to entrap animals; any hidden danger.

**pitch** *n.* a thick, black, sticky substance obtained by boiling down tar; *v.t.* to cover over, smear with pitch. **-iness** *n.* **—black, —dark** *a.* very dark.

**pitch** *v.t.* to throw, toss, fling; to set up (a tent, camp, wickets, etc.); *(Music)* to set the keynote of; to plunge or fall forward; to slope down; of a ship, to plunge. *n.* the act of tossing or throwing; a throw or toss; steepness of a roof; downward slope; the highest point; the plunging motion of a vessel lengthwise; degree of acuteness of musical note. **-ed** *a.* **-er** *n.* **-fork** *n.* a fork for tossing hay, etc.

**pitch•er** *n.* a jug; a vessel for pouring liquids, usually with a handle and a lip or spout.

**pith** *n.* the soft, spongy substance in the center of plant stems; the essential substance; force or vigor. **-y** *a.* consisting of pith; terse and forceful; energetic. **-ily** *adv.* **-iness** *n.* **-less** *a.*

**pi•tu•i•tar•y** *a.* pert. to the pituitary gland. **— gland,** a ductless gland at base of the brain, secreting an endocrine influencing growth.

**pit•y** *n.* sympathy or sorrow for others' suffering; a cause of grief or regret; *v.t.* to feel grief or sympathy for. **-ing** *a.* expressing pity. **-ingly** *adv.* **pitiable** *a.* deserving pity. **pitiably** *adv.* **pitiful** a. full of pity; tender; woeful; exciting pity. **pitifully** *adv.* **pitifulness** *n.* **pitiless** *a.* feeling no pity; hardhearted. **pitilessly** *adv.* **pitilessness** *n.* **piteous** *a.* fitted to excite pity; sad or sorrowful.

**piv•ot** *n.* a pin or shaft on which a wheel or other body turns; that on which important results depend.

**pla•ca•ble** *a.* readily appeased or pacified; willing to forgive. **-ness, placability** *n.* **placate** *v.t.* to appease, conciliate. **placatory** *a.*

**place** *n.* a particular part of space; a spot; a locality; a building; rank; position; priority of position; stead; duty; office or employment; *(Sport)* a position among the first three competitors to finish; *v.t.* to put in a particular spot; to find a position for; to appoint; to fix; to put; to identify. **-d** *a.* in a race, etc., to be first, second, or third at the finish. **— kick** *n.* *(Football)* one made by kicking the ball after it has been placed on the ground for the purpose.

**pla•cen•ta** *n.* *(Med.)* the soft, spongy substance (expelled from the womb after birth) through which the mother's blood nourishes the fetus.

**plac•id** *a.* calm; peaceful. **-ly** *adv.* **-ity** *n.* mildness; sweetness; serenity.

**pla•gi•a•rize** *v.t.* to steal the words, ideas, etc. of another and use them as one's own. **plagiarism** *n.* the act of plagiarizing; literary theft. **plagiarist** *n.* **plagiary** *n.*

**plague** *n.* a deadly, epidemic, and infectious disease; a pestilence; a nuisance.

**plaid** *n.* a long, woolen garment, usually with a tartan pattern, worn as a wrap by Scottish Highlanders; *a.* marked with strips. **-ed** *a.*

**plain** *a.* evident; clear; unobstructed; not intricate; simple; ordinary; without decoration; not beautiful; level; flat; even; *adv.* clearly; *n.* a tract of level country. **-ly** *adv.* **-ness** *n.*

**plaint** *n.* *(Poet.)* a lamentation; *(Law)* a statement in writing of the complaint, accusation, etc. **-iff** *n.* the one who sues in a court of law.

**plan** *n.* a drawing representing a thing's horizontal section; a diagram; a map; a project; a design; a scheme; *v.t.* to make a plan of; to arrange beforehand. *pr.p.* **-ning** *pa.p.* and *pa.t.* **-ned.**

**plane** *n.* a flat, level surface; *(Geom.)* a surface such that, if any two points on it be joined by a straight line, that line will lie wholly on the surface; *a.* perfectly level; pert. to, or lying in, a plane.

**— geometry,** branch of geometry which deals with plane, not solid, figures.

**plan•et** *n.* a celestial body revolving round the sun (e.g. Venus, Mars, etc.) as distinct from the fixed stars. **-arium** *n.* a working model of the planetary system; a projected representation of the heavens on a dome. **-ary** *a.* pert. to planets; of the nature of a planet; erratic; wandering.

**plank** *n.* a thick, heavy board; an article of policy in a political program; *v.t.* to lay with planks. **-ing** *n.* planks collectively.

**plank•ton** *n.* *(Biol.)* the minute animal and vegetable organisms floating in the ocean.

**plant** *n.* a living organism belonging to the vegetable kingdom, generally excluding trees and shrubs; a slip or cutting; machinery, tools, etc., used in an industrial undertaking; *v.t.* to set in ground for growth; to implant (ideas, etc.). **-ation** *n.* large estate for growing a certain crop. **-er** *n.* one who plants; the owner of a plantation.

**plaque** *n.* a thin, flat, ornamental tablet hung on a wall or inserted into a wall or furniture.

**plas•ma** *n.* *(Biol.)* protoplasm; the fluid part of the blood, as opposed to the corpuscles. Also **plasm. -tic, plasmic** *a.*

**plas•ter** *n.* a composition of lime, water, and sand, for coating walls; gypsum, for making ornaments, molds, etc.; *(Med.)* an adhesive, curative application; *(Surg.)* a composition used to hold a limb, etc. rigid; *v.t.* to cover with plaster; to smooth over or conceal. **-er** *n.*

**plas•tic** *a.* capable of molding or of being

molded; pliable; capable of change; *n.* a substance capable of being molded; a group of synthetic products derived from casein, cellulose, etc. which may be molded into any form. — **surgery,** the art of restoring lost or damaged parts of the body by grafting on sound tissue.

**plat** *n.* map.

**plate** *n.* a shallow, round dish from which food is eaten; a plateful; a flat; thin sheet of metal, glass, etc.; *(Dentistry)* a thin sheet of vulcanic, or metal, to hold artificial teeth; *(Photog.)* short for 'photographic plate'; a separate page of illustrations in a book; *v.t.* to cover with a thin coating of gold, silver, or other metal; to protect with steel plates, *e.g.* as a ship. **-r** *n.* — **glass** *n.* thick glass, rolled in sheets and used for windows, mirrors, etc.

**pla•teau** *n.* a tract of level, high ground. *pl.* **plateaus, plateaux.**

**plat•form** *n.* a wooden structure raised above the level of the floor, as a stand for speakers; a landing area at a railway-station; *(Mil.)* a stage on which a gun is mounted; policy of a political party.

**plat•i•num** *n.* a hard, silvery-white, malleable metal. **platinic, platinous.**

**Pla•to** *n.* a famous Greek philosopher (427-347 B.C.). **Platonic, -nical** *a.* pert. to Plato or to his philosophy. **-nism** *n.* the doctrines of Plato. **-nist** *n.* **Platonic love,** spiritual affection between man and woman without sexual desire.

**pla•toon** *n. (Mil.)* a small body of soldiers employed as a unit.

**plat•ter** *n.* a large shallow plate or dish.

**plat•y•pus** *n.* a small, acquatic, furred animal of Australia; the duckbill.

**plau•si•ble** *a.* having the appearance of being true; apparently right; fairspoken. **plausibly** *adv.* **plausibility** *n.*

**play** *v.t.* and *i.* to move with light or irregular motion; to frolic; to flutter; to amuse oneself; to take part in a game; to gamble; to act a part on the stage; to perform on a musical instrument; to operate; to trifle with; *n.* a brisk or free movement; activity; action; amusement; fun; frolic; sport gambling; a dramatic piece or performance. **-er** *n.* **-able** *a.* **-ful** *a.* fond of play or fun; lively. **-fully** *adv.* **-bill** *n.* a bill or poster to advertise a play. **-boy** *n.* a habitual pleasure-seeker. **-ground** *n.* an open space or courtyard for recreation. **-house** *n.* a theater. **-mate** *n.* a companion in play. **-pen** *n.* a portable enclosure for small children to play in. **-thing** *n.* a toy. **playwright** *n.* a writer of plays; a dramatist. **-ing card** *n.* one of a set of cards, usually 52 in number, used in card games.

**plea** *n. (Law)* the defendant's answer to the plaintiff's declaration; an excuse; entreaty.

**plead** *v.t.* to allege in proof or vindication; *(Law)* to argue at the bar; to urge reasons in support of or against; to beg or implore. *pa.p.* and *pa.t.* **-ed.**

**please** *v.t.* to excite agreeable sensations or emotions in; to gratify; to delight; to satisfy; *v.i.* to give pleasure. **pleasant** *a.* fitted to please; cheerful; lively; merry; agreeable. **pleasantly** *adv.* **pleasantness** *n.* **pleasantry** *n.* playfulness in conversation; a joke; a humorous act; *pl.* **pleasantries. pleasing** *a.* agreeable; gratifying. **pleasingly** *adv.* **pleasingness** *n.* **pleasure** *n.* agreeable sensation or emotion; gratification of the senses or mind; amusement, diversion, or self-indulgence; choice; a source of gratification. **pleasurable** *a.* **pleasurably** *adv.*

**pleat** *n.* a flattened fold fastened in position.

**ple•be•ian** *a.* pert. or belonging to the common people; vulgar; uncultured; *n.* a common person.

**pleb•i•scite** *n.* a vote of the whole community or nation.

**pledge** *n.* something deposited as a security; a sign or token of anything; a drinking to the health of; a solemn promise; *v.t.* to deposit in pawn; to leave as security; to engage for, by promise or declaration; to drink to the health of.

**plen•ty** *n.* a full supply; abundance; quite enough; sufficiency.

**pleth•o•ra** *n.* an excess of red corpuscles in the blood; superabundance. **plethoric** *a.*

**pleu•ra** *n. (Med.)* the membrane lining the chest and covering the lungs. *pl.* **-e. -l** *a.* **pleurisy** *n. (Med.)* inflammation of the pleura.

**plex•us** *n.* a network, esp. of nerves, blood vessels, fibers, etc. **plexal** *a.*

**pli•a•ble** *a.* easily bent; easily influenced. Also **pliant pliably, pliantly** *adv.* **pliability, pliancy** *n.*

**pli•ers** *n.pl.* small pincers with a flat grip.

**plight** *n.* a state or condition of a distressing kind; predicament.

**plight** *v.t.* to pledge, as one's word of honor; to betroth.

**plod** *v.t.* to tread with a heavy step; *v.i.* to walk or work laboriously; to toil or drudge *pr.p.* **-ding** *pa.t., pa.p.* **-ded.**

**plot** *n.* a small patch of ground; a plan of a field, farm, etc. drawn to scale; the plan of a play, novel, etc.; a secret scheme; a conspiracy. *v.t.* to draw a graph or plan of; to plan or scheme. *v.i.* to conspire. *pr.p.* **-ting** *pa.t., pa.p.* **-ted.**

**plow** *n.* an implement with a heavy cutting blade for turning up the soil; *v.t.* to turn up with the plow; to furrow; to advance laboriously; *v.i.* to till the soil with a plow. **-share** *n.* the heavy iron blade of a plow.

**pluck** *v.t.* to pull off; to pick as flowers; to strip off feathers, as a fowl; to snatch, or pull with sudden force; *n.* a pull or jerk; the act of plucking; courage or spirit.

**plug** *n.* anything used to stop a hole; a cake of compressed tobacco; *(Elect.)* a device for connecting and disconnecting of a circuit; *abbrev.* for spark plug; *v.t.* to stop with a plug; to insert a plug in.

**plum** *n.* a round or oval fruit; the tree that bears it; a particularly good appointment or position; a dark purplish color.

**plum•age** *n.* a bird's feathers, collectively.

**plumb** *n.* a weight of lead attached to a line, and used to determine perpendicularity; the perpendicular position; *a.* perpendicular; *adv.* perpendicularly; *v.t.* to adjust by a plumb line; to sound or take the depth of water with a plummet. **-er** *n.* one who installs or repairs water and sewage systems. **-ing** *n.* the trade of a plumber; the system of water and sewage pipes in a building. **— line** *n.* a weighted string for testing the perpendicular.

**plume** *n.* a feather or tuft of feathers; a crest on a helmet; a token of honor; *v.t.* to furnish with plumes.

**plump** *a.* of rounded form; moderately fat. **-ness** *n.*

**plun•der** *v.t.* to rob systematically; to take by force; *n.* the act of robbing by force; property so obtained.

**plunge** to immerse suddenly in a liquid; *n.* the act of plunging; a dive; a sudden rush. **-r** *n.* one who plunges; a solid, cylindrical rod used as a piston in pumps.

**plu•ral** *a.* more than one; *(Gram.)* denoting more than one person or thing; *n.* *(Gram.)* a word in its plural form. **-ly** *adv.* **-ism** *n.* *(Philos.)* doctrine that existence has more than one ultimate principle. **-ist** *n.* **-istic** *a.* **-ity** *n.* large number; a majority of votes; state of being plural.

**plus** *n.* symbol of addition ( +); positive quantity; extra quantity; *a.* to be added; *(Math., Elect.,* etc.) positive; *prep.* with the addition of.

**plush** *n.* a fabric with a long, velvet-like nap.

**Plu•to** *n.* *(Myth.)* god of the lower world; the planet farthest from the sun. **-nic rocks** *(Geol.)* name given to igneous rocks formed by action of intense subterranean heat. **-nium** *n.* a metal of high atomic weight made by bombarding atoms of uranium with neutrons.

**ply** *v.t.* to wield; to work at steadily; to use or practice with diligence; to urge.

**ply** *n.* a fold; a strand of yarn; thickness. *pl.* **plies. -wood** *n.* board made of two or more thin layers of wood cemented together.

**pneu•mat•ic** *a.* pert. to air or gas; inflated with wind or air; operated by compressed air. **-s** *n.pl.* the branch of physics dealing with the mechanical properties of gases.

**pneu•mo•nia** *n.* acute inflammation of a lung.

**poach** *v.t.* to cook eggs, by breaking them into a pan of boiling water.

**pock** *n.* pustule on skin, as in smallpox. **— mark** *n.* pit left in skin by pock.

**pock•et** *n.* a small pouch or bag inserted into a garment; a cavity or hollow; *(Mil.)* isolated area held by the enemy. to accept without resentment, as an insult. **-book** *n.* a small bag or case for holding money or papers. **— money** *n.* money for small, personal expenses, e.g. allowance to child.

**pod** *n.* a seed vessel of a plant, esp. a legume, as peas, beans, etc.

**po•em** *n.* a composition in verse; any composition written in elevated and imaginative language; opp. to 'prose.' **poesy** *n.* poetry. **poetically** *adv.* **poetics** *n.* principles of art of poetry; criticism of poetry. **poetry** *n.* language of imagination expressed in verse; metrical composition. **poetic justice,** ideal justice, in which crime is punished and virtue rewarded. **poetic license,** latitude in grammar or facts, allowed to poets. **poet laureate,** official poet.

**poign•ant** *a.* acutely painful; strongly appealing; pungent. **-ly** *adv.* **poignancy** *n.*

**point** *n.* sharp or tapering end of anything; dot or mark; dot in decimal system; punctuation mark; full stop; *(Geom.)* that which has position but no magnitude; item or detail; gist of argument; striking or effective part of a speech, story, etc.; moment of time; purpose; a fine lace made with a needle; of a dog, to indicate the position of game by standing facing it. **-ed** *a.* having a sharp point; direct; telling; aimed; **-edly** *adv.* **-edness** *n.* **-less** *a.* having no point; blunt; irrelevant; insipid.

**poise** *v.t.* to place or hold in a balanced or steady position; *n.* equilibrium; carriage of the head, body, etc.; self-possession.

**poi•son** *n.* any substance which kills or injures when introduced into a living organism; that which has an evil influence on health or moral purity; **-er** *n.* **-ous** *a.* having a deadly or injurious quality; corrupting. **-ously** *adv.* **— ivy** *n.* a vine which, if touched, causes a skin rash.

**poke** *v.t.* to push or thrust against with a pointed object, e.g. with a finger, stick, etc.; to thrust in; to tease.

**pok•er** *n.* a card game in which the players bet on the value of their hands. **—faced** *a.* having an expressionless face.

**po•lar** *a.* pert. to, or situated near, the North or South Poles; pert. to the magnetic poles (points on the earth's surface where a magnetic needle dips vertically); pert. to either pole of a magnet; directly opposed; having polarity. **— bear,** a large, white bear, found in the Arctic regions.

**po•lar•ize** *v.t.* to give polarity to; *(Elect.)* to reduce the electromotive force (E.M.F.) of a primary cell by the accumulation of certain electrolytic products on the plates; *(Chem.)* to separate the positive and negative charges on a molecule; *(Light)* to confine the vibrations of light waves to certain directions, e.g. to a plane. **polarization** *n.* **polaroid** *n.*

**pole** *n.* a long, rounded piece of wood or metal.

**pole** *n.* either of the ends of the axis of a sphere, esp. of the earth (in the latter case called the North Pole and South Pole); either of the opposite ends or terminals of a magnet, electric battery, etc.

**Pole** *n.* a native of Poland. **Polish** *a.* pert. to

Poland or the Poles.

**pole•cat** *n.* a small, carnivorous animal, resembling the weasel; a skunk.

**po•lice** *n.* the civil force which maintains public order; the members of the force; *v.t.* to control with police; to keep in order. **-man, — officer** *n.* (*fem.* **-woman)** member of a police force. **— court** *n.* a court for the trial of minor offenses. **— station** *n.* the headquarters of the police.

**pol•i•cy** *n.* a course of action adopted, esp. in state affairs; prudent procedure.

**pol•i•cy** *n.* a document containing a contract of insurance.

**pol•i•o•my•e•li•tis** *n.* (*Med.*) inflammation of the grey matter of the spinal cord; infantile paralysis. *abbrev.* **polio.**

**pol•ish** *v.t.* to make smooth and glossy; to make polite and cultured; *n.* the act of polishing; a smooth, glassy surface; a substance used in polishing; refinement; elegance of manners. **-er** *n.*

**po•lite** *a.* elegant in manners; well-bred; courteous; refined. **-ly** *adv.* **-ness** *n.*

**pol•i•tic** *a.* prudent; wise; shrewd; cunning; advisable. **-s** *n.pl.* the art of government; political affairs, life, or principles. **-ly** *adv.* **-al** *a.* pert. to the state or its affairs; pert. to politics. **-ally** *adv.* **politician** *n.* a holder of a political position; a statesman; a member of a political party. **political economy,** the science dealing with the nature, production, distribution, and consumption of wealth.

**pol•ka** *n.* a lively dance of Bohemian origin; music for it.

**poll** *n.* a register of persons; a list of persons entitled to vote; (the place) of voting; number of votes recorded; *v.t.* to cut off the top of, e.g. tree; to canvass; to receive (votes); to cast a vote.

**pol•len** *n.* the fertilizing dust of a flower. **pollinate** *v.t.* to fertilize a flower by conveying pollen to the pistil.

**pol•lute** *v.t.* to make foul or unclean; to defile; to desecrate. **pollution** *n.*

**po•lo** *n.* a game like hockey played on horseback.

**po•lo•ni•um** *n.* a metallic, radio active chemical.

**pol•troon** *n.* a coward. **-ery** *n.*

**pol•y-** *prefix,* many words used in derivatives. **-chrome** *n.* a picture, statue, etc. in several colors. **-chromatic, -chromic, -chromous** *a.* many-colored.

**po•lyg•a•my** *n.* the practice of having more than one wife at the same time. **polygamous** *a.* **polygamist** *n.*

**pol•y•gon** *n.* a plane figure with more than four sides or angles. **polygonal** *a.*

**pol•y•he•dron** *n.* (*Geom.*) a solid figure with many faces, usually more than six.

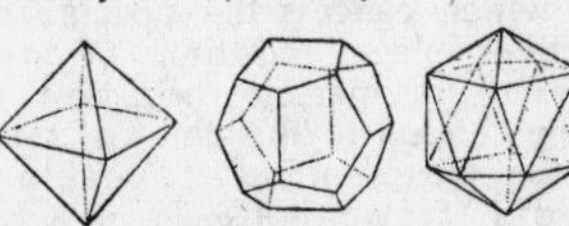

polyhedra

**pol•y•mor•phous** *a.* assuming many forms. Also **polymorphic. polymorphism** *n.*

**Pol•y•ne•sia** *n.* (*Geog.*) a group of islands in the S. Pacific, east of Australia. **-n** *a.*

**pol•y•no•mi•al** *n.* (*Alg.*) a quantity having many terms.

**pol•y•syl•a•ble** *n.* a word of three or more syllables. **polysyllabic** *a.*

**pol•y•tech•nic** *a.* pert. to many arts and sciences; *n.* a school or college of applied arts and sciences.

**pol•y•the•ism** *n.* belief in the existence of many gods, or in more than one. **polytheist** *n.* **polytheistic** *a.*

**po•made** *n.* scented ointment for the hair. Also **pomatum. pomander** *n.* ball of or case for mixture of perfumes.

**pome•gran•ate** *n.* a large fruit containing many seeds in a red pulp.

**pom•er•a•ni•an** *n.* a small breed of dog with bushy tail, sharp pointed muzzle, pointed ears and long silky hair.

**pomp** *n.* splendid display or ceremony; magnificence. **-ous** *n.* showy with grandeur; of a person, self-important; of language, inflated. **-ously** *adv.* **-ousness** *n.* **-osity** *n.*

**pom•pa•dour** *n.* woman's high swept hairstyle; man's hair style with hair brushed up from forehead.

**pond** *n.* a pool of water, either naturally or artificially enclosed.

**pon•der** *v.t.* to weigh in the mind; to consider attentively; *v.i.* to mediate. **-er** *n.* **-ing** *a.*

**pon•der•ous** *a.* very heavy; weighty; massive; unwieldy; dull or lacking in spirit. **-ly** *adv.* **-ness** *n.* **ponderosity** *n.*

**pon•tiff** *n.* the Pope; a bishop; a high priest. **pontifical** *a.* belonging to a high priest; popish; pompous and dogmatic; *n.pl.* the garb of a priest, bishop, or pope. **pontifically** *adv.* **pontificate** *n.* the state, dignity, or term of office of a priest, bishop, or pope.

**po•ny** *n.* a small breed of horse.

**poo•dle** *n.* one of a breed of dogs with thick, curly hair, often clipped into ornamental tufts.

poodle

**pool** *n.* a small body of still water; a deep place in a river.

**pool** *n.* the collective stakes in various games; the place where the stakes are put; a variety of billiards; a combination of capitalists to fix prices and divide into a common fund.

**poop** *n.* the stern of a ship; raised deck at the stern.

**poor** *a.* having little or no money; without means; needy; miserable; wretched; unfortunate; feeble; deserving of pity; unproductive; of inferior quality. **-ly** *adv.*

inadequately; with little or no success; without spirit.

**pop** *n.* an abrupt, small explosive sound; a shot; an effervescing drink; *v.i.* to make a sharp, quick sound; to go or come unexpectedly or suddenly; to dart; *v.t.* to put or place suddenly; *adv. pr.p.* **-ping** *pa.p.* and *pa.t.* **-ped. -corn** *n.* Indian corn exposed to heat causing it to burst open.

**Pope** *n.* the Bishop of Rome and head of the R.C. Church. **popish** *a.* **pert. to the** Pope or the papacy. **-dom** *n.* the office, dignity, or jurisdiction of the Pope.

**pop•lar** *n.* a tree noted for its slender tallness.

**pop•py** *n.* a bright flowered plant, one species of which yields opium.

**pop•u•lace** *n.* the common people; the masses. **populate** *v.t.* to people. **population** *n.* the total number of people in a country, town, etc. **populous** *a.* thickly inhabited.

**pop•u•lar** *a.* pert. to the common people; finding general favor; **-ly** *adv.* **-ize** *v.t.* to make popular; to make familiar, plain, easy, etc. to all. **-ization** *n.* **-ity** *n.* public favor.

**por•ce•lain** *n.* the finest kind of earthenware—white, glazed and semi-transparent; china.

**porch** *n.* a covered entrance to a doorway.

**por•cu•pine** *n.* a large quadruped of the rodent family, covered with spines.

**pore** *n.* a minute opening in the skin for the passage of perspiration. **porous** *a.* full of pores.

**pork** *n.* the flesh of swine used for food.

**por•nog•ra•phy** *n.* obscene literature or pictures. **pornographer** *n.* **pornographic** *a.*

**por•poise** *n.* a blunt-nosed cetacean mammal 5 to 8 feet long, frequenting the northern seas.

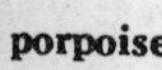
porpoise

**por•ridge** *n. (Brit.)* a soft breakfast food.

**port** *n.* a harbor; a town with a harbor.

**port** *n.* the way in which a person carries himself.

**port** *n.* a strong, sweet, dark-red wine.

**port** *n.* the left side of a ship, looking towards the bow.

**port•a•ble** *a.* capable of being easily carried.

**por•tal** *n.* a gate or entrance.

**por•tend** *v.t.* to foretell; to give warning in advance; to be an omen of. **portent** *n.* an omen, esp. of evil.

**por•ter** *n.* a door- or gatekeeper; railway sleeping-car attendant.

**por•ter** *n.* one employed to carry baggage esp. at stations or hotels.

**por•ter•house** *n.* place where beer (porter) was served. **— steak** choice cut of beef next to the sirloin.

**port•fo•li•o** *n.* case for holding loose documents, drawings, etc.

**port•hole** *n.* window in side of ship.

**por•ti•co** *n. (Archit.)* a row of columns in front of the entrance to a building; a covered walk.

**por•tion** *n.* a piece; a part; a share; a helping of food; *v.t.* to divide into shares.

**por•tray** *v.t.* to represent by drawing, painting, acting, or imitating; to describe vividly in words. **-al** *n.* the act of portraying; the representation. **-er** *n.* **portrait** *n.* picture of a person, esp. of the face; a graphic description of a person in words.

**Por•tu•guese** *a.* pert. to Portugal, its inhabitants, or language.

**pose** *n.* attitude or posture of a person, natural or assumed; a mental attitude or affectation; *v.t.* to place in a position for the sake of effect; to lay down or assert.

**po•si•tion** *n.* place; situation; the manner in which anything is arranged; posture; social rank or standing; employment.

**pos•i•tive** *a.* formally laid down; clearly stated; absolute; dogmatic; of real value; confident; not negative; plus; *(Math.)* pert. to a quantity greater than zero; *n.* the positive degree of an adjective or adverb, i.e. without comparison; in photography, a print in which the lights and shadows are not reversed (as in the negative). **-ly** *adv.* **-ness** *n.* **positivism** *n.* the philosophical system which recognizes only matters of fact and experience. **positivist** *n.* a believer in this doctrine. **— pole,** of a magnet, the northseeking-pole. **— sign,** the sign (+ read *plus)* of addition.

**pos•i•tron** *n.* particle differing from an electron in that it has positive electrical charge.

**pos•se** *n.* a company or force, usually with legal authority; men under orders of the sheriff, maintaining law and order.

**pos•sess** *v.t.* to own or hold as property; to have as an attribute; to enter into and influence, as an evil spirit or passions. **-ed** *a.* influenced, as by an evil spirit; demented. **-ion** *n.* the act of possessing; ownership; actual occupancy; the state of being possessed; the thing possessed. -ive *a.* denoting possession.

**pos•si•ble** *a.* capable of being or of coming into being; feasible.

**post** *n.* a piece of timber or metal, set upright as a support; a prop or pillar; **-er** *n.* one who posts bills; a large placard for posting.

**post** *n.* a fixed place; a military station or the soldiers occupying it; an office or position of trust, service, or emolument; a trading settlement; **-age** *n.* the cost of conveyance by mail. **-al** *a.* pert. to the post office or mail service. **-man** *n.* one who delivers mail. **-mark** *n.* a post office mark which cancels the postage stamp and gives place and time of mailing. **-master** *n.* the manager of a post office. **-master general** *n.* the chief of the post office department of a government. **— card** *n.* a stamped card on which a message may be sent through the mail. **— office** *n.* an office where letters and parcels are received for distribution; the government postal department. **-age stamp** *n.* an adhesive stamp, affixed to mail to indicate payment.

**post-** *adv.* and *prefix* after, behind, used in many compound words. **-date** *v.t.* to put on a document, letter, etc., a date later than the actual one. **-graduate** *a.* of academic study, research, etc., undertaken after taking a university degree. **—mortem** *a. n.* the dissection of a body after death; an autopsy.

**pos•te•ri•or** *a.* coming after; *n.* the rump. **-ly** *adv.* **-ity** *n.* **posterity** future generations.

**post•hu•mous** *a.* born after the death of the father; published after the death of the author.

**post•pone** *v.t.* to put off till a future time; to defer; to delay. **-ment** *n.* **-r** *n.*

**post•script** *n.* something added to a letter after the signature; *abbrev.* **P.S.**

**pos•tu•late** *v.t.* to assume without proof; to lay down as self-evident; to stipulate; *n.* a prerequisite; a proposition assumed without proof.

**pos•ture** *n.* the position of a body, figure, etc. or of its several members; attitude; *v.i.* to assume an artificial or affected attitude.

**po•sy** *n.* a bouquet; a flower.

**pot** *n.* a rounded vessel of metal, earthenware, etc., used for cooking, holding fluids. plants, etc.; the contents of a pot; *v.t.* to plant in pots; **-hole** *n.* cavity formed in rock by action of stones in the eddy of a stream; a hole in the roadway. **-luck** *n.* whatever may happen to have been provided for a meal.

**po•ta•ble** *a.* drinkable. **potation** *n.* a drinking; a draft.

**pot•ash** *n.* a powerful alkali obtained from wood ashes. **potassium** *n.* metallic base of potash.

**po•ta•to** *n.* an edible tuber widely grown for food. *pl.* **-es.**

**po•tent** *a.* having great authority or influence; powerful; mighty; procreative. **-ly** *adv.* **potency** *n.* moral or physical power; influence; energy; efficacy. *a.* latent; existing in possibility but not in actuality; *n.* inherent capability of doing anything; *(Elect.)* the level of electric pressure. **-ially** *adv.* **-iality** *n.* possibility as distinct from actuality. **-ial difference** *(Elect.)* the difference of pressure between two points; voltage.

**po•tion** *n.* a dose, esp. of liquid, medicine, or poison.

**pot•pour•ri** *n.* a mixture of dried rose petals, spices, etc.; a musical or literary medley.

**pot•tage** *n.* soup or stew; *(Bib.)* a dish of lentils.

**pot•ter** *n.* a maker of earthenware vessels. **-y** *n.* pots, vessels, etc. made of earthenware; the place where it is made; the art of making it.

**pouch** *n.* a small bag or sack; a baglike receptacle in which certain animals; e.g. the kangaroo, carry their young.

**poult** *n.* a young fowl. **poultry** *n.* domestic fowls. **-erer** *n.* a dealer in poultry.

**pounce** *v.i.* to spring upon suddenly; to swoop; *n.* a swoop or sudden descent.

**pound** *n.* a measure of weight *(abbrev.* **lb.**), 16 ounces avoirdupois, or 12 ounces troy; a unit of British money *(abbrev.* **£**), **-age** *n.* charge of so much per pound. **-al** *n.* a unit of force.

**pound** *v.t.* and *i.* to beat or strike; to crush to pieces or to powder; to walk, run, etc., heavily.

**pound** *n.* an enclosure for animals; *v.t.* to shut up in one.

**pour** *v.i.* to come out in a stream, crowd, etc.; to flow freely; to rain heavily; *v.t.* to cause to flow, as a liquid from a vessel; to shed; to utter.

**pout** *v.i.* to thrust out the lips, as in displeasure, etc.; to look sullen or sulky; *n.* the act of pouting; a protrusion of the lips. **-er** *n.* one who pouts.

**pov•er•ty** *n.* the state of being poor; poorness; lack of means.

**pow•der** *n.* dust; a solid matter in fine dry particles; a medicine in this form; short for gunpowder, face powder, etc.; *v.t.* to reduce to powder; to pulverize; to sprinkle with powder.

**pow•er** *n.* a capacity for action, physical, mental, or moral; energy; might; agency or motive force; authority; one in authority; influence or ascendancy; a nation; mechanical energy; *(Math.)* the product arising from the continued multiplication of a number by itself. **-ful** *a.* having great power; capable of producing great effect. **-fully** *adv.* **-fulness** *n.* **-less** *a.* **-lessly** *adv.* **-lessness.**

**pox** *n.* a disease attended with pustules on the skin, as smallpox, chickenpox, etc.; syphilis.

**prac•tice** *n.* performance or execution, as opposed to theory; custom or habit; systematic exercise for instruction; training; exercise of a profession. **practicable** *a.* capable of being accomplished or put into practice; capable of being used, e.g. a weapon, a road, etc. *n.* **practitioner** *n.* one engaged in a profession, esp. law or medicine.

**prag•mat•ic, pragmatical** *a.* pert. to state affairs; concerned with practical consequences; matter-of-fact. **-ally** *adv.* **-alness** *n.* **pragmatize** *v.t.* to represent an imaginary thing as real. **pragmatism** *n.* a philosophy based on the conception that the truth of a doctrine is to be judged by its practical consequences. **pragmatist** *n.*

**prai•rie** *n.* a large tract of grassland, destitute of trees.

**praise** *v.t.* to express approval or admiration; to glorify; *n.* approval of merit; commendation; worship. **—worthy** *a.* deserving of praise.

**prance** *v.i.* to spring or bound like a high-spirited horse; to swagger; to caper, esp. of children; *n.* a prancing movement.

**prank** *n.* a mischievous trick; a practical joke.

**prawn** *n.* an edible crustacean of the shrimp family.

**pray** *v.i.* to ask earnestly; to entreat; to petition; *v.i.* to make a request or confession, esp. to God; to commune with God. **-er** *n.* one who prays; the act of praying; an earnest entreaty; the words used; the thing asked for; a petition.

**pre-** *prefix,* before, beforehand, used with many nouns and verbs.

**preach** *v.i.* and *t.* to deliver a sermon; to speak publicly on a religious subject, esp. as a clergyman; to advocate.

**pre•am•ble** *n.* the introductory part of a discourse, story, document, etc.; a preface.

**pre•ar•range** *v.t.* to arrange beforehand. **-ment** *n.*

**pre•car•i•ous** *a.* depending on the will or pleasure of another; depending on circumstances; uncertain; dangerous; perilous. **-ly** *adv.* **-ness** *n.*

**pre•cau•tion** *n.* care taken beforehand; *v.t.* to forewarn. **-ary** *a.* characterized by precaution.

**pre•cede** *v.t.* to go before in place, time, rank, or importance. **-nt** *a.* preceding; **-nt** *n.* something done, or said, that may serve as an example in similar cases. **-ntly** *adv.* **-nce** *n.* the act of preceding; priority in position, rank, or time. **preceding** *a.*

**pre•cept** *n.* an instruction intended as a rule of conduct, esp. moral conduct; *(Law)* a written warrant or mandate given to an administrative officer. **-ive** *a.*

**pre•ces•sion** *n.* a going before. **-al** *a.*

**pre•cinct** *n.* a division of a city for police protection, voting, etc.; a boundary or limit; a minor territorial division.

**pre•cious** *a.* of great value or price; costly; highly esteemed; over-refined; fastidious; *adv.*

**pre•cip•i•tate** *v.i.* to throw headlong; to urge on eagerly; to hasten the occurrence of; *(Chem.)* to cause to separate and fall to the bottom, as a substance in solution; of vapor, to condense. **precipitant** *n.* falling headlong; too hasty; unexpectedly hastened. **precipitation** *n.* the act of precipitating; rash haste; a falling headlong; condensation of vapor, rain, snow, etc.

**pre•cise** *a.* exact; definite; distinct; prim. **-ly** *adv.* **-ness** *n.* **precision** *n.* accuracy; definiteness; *a.* done with great accuracy.

**pre•clude** *v.t.* to shut out; to hinder; to prevent from happening **preclusion** *n.* **preclusive** *a.*

**pre•co•cious** *a.* having the mental powers or bodily growth developed at an early age; premature; forward. **-ly** *adv.* **-ness, precocity** *n.*

**pre•con•ceive** *v.t.* to form an opinion or idea of beforehand. **preconception** *n.* a prejudice.

**pre•cur•sor** *n.* a person or thing going before; a forerunner; a harbinger. **-y, precursive** *a.*

**pre•da•cious** *a.* living on prey; predatory. **predatory** *a.* living by preying on others; plundering; pillaging.

**pre•date** *v.t.* to date earlier than the true date.

**pred•e•ces•sor** *n.* one who has preceded another in an office, position, etc.

**pre•des•tine** *v.t.* to destine beforehand; to foreordain. **predestinate** *v.t.* to determine beforehand; to foreordain. **predestination** *n. (Theol.)* the doctrine that the salvation or damnation of individuals has been foreordained by God; the determination beforehand of future events; destiny; fate.

**pre•de•ter•mine** *v.t.* to determine beforehand. **predeterminate** *a.* determined beforehand. **predetermination** *n.*

**pre•dic•a•ment** *n.* an awkward plight; a trying situation.

**pred•i•cate** *v.t.* to affirm; to assert; to declare; *n.* that which is predicated; *(Gram.)* a statement made about the subject of the sentence. **predication** *n.* **predicative** *a.* **predicatively** *adv.*

**pre•dict** *v.t.* to tell beforehand; to foretell; to prophesy. **-able** *a.* **-ion** *n.* the act of foretelling; prophecy. **-ive** *a.* **-or** *n.*

**pre•di•lec•tion** *n.* a prepossession of mind in favor of something; partiality.

**pre•dis•pose** *v.t.* to incline beforehand; to give a tendency or bias to; to render susceptible to. **predisposition** *n.*

**pre•dom•i•nate** *v.i.* to surpass in strength, influence, or authority; to rule; to have ascendancy; to prevail. **predominance, predominancy** *n.* ascendancy; superiority. **predominant** *a.* superior in influence, authority, etc.; having ascendancy. **predominantly** *adv.*

**pre•em•i•nent** *a.* distinguished above others; outstanding. **-ly** *adv.*

**pre•emp•tion** *n.* the act or right of purchasing before others. **pre-empt** *v.t.* to appropriate beforehand.

**pre•ex•ist** *v.i.* to exist beforehand, or before something else. **-ence** *n.* **-ent** *a.*

**pre•fab** *n.* a prefabricated house.

**pre•fab•ri•cate** *v.t.* to build houses and ships in standardized units in factories for rapid assembly. **prefabrication** *n.*

**pref•ace** *n.* introductory remarks at beginning of book, or spoken before a discourse; foreword; *v.t.* to furnish with a preface. **prefatory** *a.* introductory.

**pre•fer** *v.t.* to like better; to choose rather; to promote to an office or dignity. **-able** *a.* worthy of preference; more desirable. **-ably** *adv.* **-ence** *n.* what is preferred; choice. **-ential** *a.* giving or receiving a preference.

**pre•fix** *n.* a letter, syllable, or word put at the beginning of another word to modify its meaning, e.g. *pre*digest, *under*ground.

**preg•na•ble** *a.* able to be taken by assault or force.

**preg•nant** *a.* being with child. **pregnancy.**

**pre•hen•sile** *a. (Zool.)* capable of grasping.

**pre•his•to•ry** *n.* the period before written records were kept; **prehistoric** *a.*

**prej•u•dice** *n.* an opinion, favorable or unfavorable, formed without fair examination of facts; bias; **prejudicial** *a.* injurious.

**prel•ate** *n.* a bishop, or other church

dignitary of equal or higher rank.

**pre•lect** *v.t.* to deliver a lecture or discourse in public. **prelection** *n.* a lecture.

**pre•lim•i•nary** *a.* introductory; preparatory; *n.* an introduction.

**prel•ude** *n.* an introductory performance or event; a musical introduction; *v.t.* to serve as a prelude or forerunner to. **prelusive, prelusory** *a.* introductory.

**pre•ma•ture** *a.* ripe before the natural or proper time; untimely. **-ly** *adv.* **-ness, prematurity** *n.*

**pre•med•i•tate** *v.t.* to consider, or revolve in the mind beforehand.

**pre•mier** *a.* first; chief or principal; *n.* the prime minister. **-ship** *n.*

**pre•miere** *n.* a first public performance of a play.

**prem•ise** *v.t.* to set forth beforehand, or as introductory to the main subject. **premise** *n.* Also **premiss,** a proposition previously supposed or proved; *n.pl.* a building with its adjuncts.

**pre•mi•um** *n.* a prize; money paid for insurance; the amount exceeding the par value of shares of stock. **at a premium,** in great demand.

**pre•mo•ni•tion** *n.* previous warning. **premonitory** *a.* **premonitorily** *adv.*

**pre•na•tal** *a.* previous to birth.

**pre•oc•cu•py** *v.t.* to take possession of before another. **preoccupied** *a.* occupied previously; engrossed in thought. **preoccupancy** *n.* **preoccupation** *n.*

**pre•or•dain** *v.t.* to ordain beforehand. **preordination** *n.*

**pre•paid** *a.* paid in advance.

**pre•pare** *v.t.* to make ready for use; to fit for a particular purpose; to provide; to fit out; *v.i.* to make things ready; to make oneself ready. **preparation** *n.* the act of making ready for use; readiness; a substance, esp. medicine or food, made up for use. **preparatory** *a.* preparing the way; preliminary; introductory. **preparedness** *n.*

**pre•pay** *v.t.* to pay beforehand.

**pre•pon•der•ate** *v.i.* to exceed in power, influence, numbers, etc.; to outweigh. **preponderance** *n.* superiority of power, numbers, etc. **preponderant** *a.* **preponderantly** *adv.*

**prep•o•si•tion** *n.* *(Gram.)* a word, e.g. *with, by, for,* etc., used before a noun or pronoun to show the relation to some other word in the sentence. **-al** *a.*

**pre•pos•sess** *v.t.* to possess beforehand; to influence a person's mind, heart, etc. beforehand; to prejudice favorably. **-ing** *a.* tending to win a favorable opinion; attractive. **-ingly** *adv.* **prepossession** *n.*

**pre•pos•ter•ous** *a.* contrary to nature, truth, reason, or common sense; utterly absurd. **-ly** *adv.* **-ness** *n.*

**pre•rog•a•tive** *n.* an exclusive right or privilege by reason of rank, position, etc.

**Pres•by•te•ri•an** *n.* one belonging to Presbyterian Church. **-ism** *n.* **presbytery** *n.* a body of elders; court of pastors.

**pre•sci•ence** *n.* knowledge of events before they take place. **prescient** *a.*

**pre•scribe** *v.t.* to lay down authoritatively for direction; to set out rules for; *(Med.)* to order or advise the use of. **-r** *n.* **prescript** *n.* direction; ordinance. **prescription** *n.* the act of prescribing or directing; a doctor's direction for use of medicine. **prescriptive** *a.*

**pres•ent** *a.* being in a certain place; here or at hand; now existing; *(Gram.)* pert. to time that now is; *n.* present time; *(Gram.)* the present tense. **presence** *n.* the state of being present; nearness or proximity; the person of a superior; mien or appearance; apparition. **-ly** *adv.* at once; soon; by and by.

**pre•sent** *v.t.* to introduce into the presence of; to exhibit or offer to the notice; to offer as a gift; to bestow; to aim, as a weapon; *n.* a gift. **-able** *a.* fit to be presented. **-ation** *n.* the act of presenting; the state of being presented; that which is presented.

**pre•sen•ti•ment** *n.* a previous notion or opinion.

**pre•serve** *v.t.* to keep from injury or destruction; *n.* that which is preserved, as fruit, etc. a place for the preservation of game, fish, etc. **-r** *n.* **preservable** *a.* **preservation** *n.* the act of keeping safe. **preservative** *n.* that which preserves. **preservatory** *a.*

**pre•side** *v.i.* to be chairman of a meeting; to direct. **president** *n.* the head of a society, company, association, etc.; the elected head of a republic. **presidency** *n.* the office, or term of office, of a president. **presidential** *a.* pert. to a president.

**press** *v.t.* to push or squeese; to crush; to smooth by pressure; *n.* an instrument or machine for squeezing; a printing machine; newspapers collectively; **-ing** *a.* urgent; persistent. **—agent** *n.* one employed to advertise and secure publicity for any person or organization. **to go to press,** of a newspaper, to start printing.

**press** *v.t.* to force to serve in the navy or army.

**pres•sure** *n.* the act of pressing.

**pres•su•ri•za•tion** *n.* maintenance of pressure inside aircraft at great altitudes. **pressurize** *v.t.*

**pres•ti•dig•i•ta•tion** *n.* conjuring; sleight of hand. **prestidigitator** *n.* a conjurer, a magician.

**pres•tige** *n.* influence resulting from past achievement, character, reputation, etc.

**pres•to** *adv.* *(Mus.)* quickly.

**pre•sume** *v.t.* to take for granted; to suppose to be true without proof. **presumable** *a.* probable. **presumably** *adv.* **presumption** that which is taken for granted; **presumptive** *a.* based on probability; **presumptively** *adv.* **presumptuous** *a.* forward; taking liberties.

**pre•sup•pose** *v.t.* to assume or take for granted beforehand.

**pre•tend** *v.t.* to assert falsely; to make believe; *n.* one who simulates or feigns; **pretense** *n.* simulation; the act of laying claim; **pretentious** *a.* given to outward show; **pretentiously** *adv.* **pretentiousness** *n.*

**pre•ter-** *prefix* meaning beyond, above, more than, etc., used in combining forms. **-natural** *a.* beyond or different from what is natural.

**pre•text** *n.* ostensible reason or motive which cloaks the real reason; pretense.

**pret•ty** *a.* of a beauty that is charming and attractive, but not striking or imposing; neat and tasteful; pleasing; fine or excellent in an ironical sense; *adv.* in some degree; moderately; fairly; rather.

**pre•vail** *v.i.* to gain the upper hand or mastery; to succeed; to be current; to be in force; to persuade or induce (with 'on' or 'upon'). **-ing** *a.* **prevalent** *a.* most generally; extensively existing; rife. **prevalently** *adv.* **prevalence** *n.*

**pre•vent** *v.t.* to keep from happening; to stop. **-able** *a.* **-ion** *n.* obstruction; hinderance; preventive. **-ive** *a.* tending to prevent or ward off; *n.* that which prevents; antidote to keep off disease.

**pre•view** *n.* a private showing of works of art, films, etc. before being exhibited.

**pre•vi•ous** *a.* preceding; happening before.

**prey** *n.* any animal hunted and killed for food by another animal; a victim; to seize and devour; to weigh heavily; to pillage.

**price** *n.* the amount at which a thing is valued, bought, or sold; value; cost; *v.t.* to fix the price of; to ask the cost of. **-less** *a.* beyond any price.

**prick** *n.* a sharp-pointed instrument; a puncture made by a sharp point; the act of pricking; a sharp, stinging pain; *v.t.* to pierce slightly with a sharp point; to incite; to affect with sharp pain; to sting.

**prick•le** *n.* a small sharp point; a thorn; a spike; a bristle; *v.t.* to prick slightly; *v.i.* to feel a tingling sensation. **prickly** *a.* full of prickles; stinging; tingling.

**pride** *n.* the state or quality of being proud; too high an opinion of oneself; worthy self-esteem.

**priest** *n.* *(fem.* **-ess***)* a clergyman; in R.C. and Episcopal churches; in pagan times, one who officiated at the altar, or performed the rites of sacrifice. **-like, -ly** *a.* **-liness** *n.* **-hood** *n.*

**prim** *a.* formal and precise; affectedly nice; prudish. **-ly** *adv.* **-ness** *n.*

**pri•ma** *a.* first. **— donna,** the principal female singer in an opera.

**pri•mal** *a.* first, original; chief. **primary** *a.* first in order of time, elementary; *n.* that which stands highest in rank or importance; a preliminary election (often *pl.);* **primarily** *adv.* in the first place. **primary colors,** red, yellow and blue.

**pri•mate** *n.* *(Brit.)* the chief dignitary in a church; an archbishop. **primacy** *n.* the chief dignitary in a national church.

**prime** *a.* first in time; original; of highest quality; *(Math.)* that cannot be separated into factors; *n.* the best portion; *v.t.* to prepare a firearm by charging with powder; to prepare wood with a protective coating before painting it; to fill with water, etc., as a pump, to make it start working; **-r** *n.* one who, or that which, primes; a small elementary book used in teaching. **-ly** *adv.* **-ness** *n.* **priming** *n.* **— minister,** the first minister of state in some countries. **— number,** a number divisible without remainder only by itself or one.

**pri•me•val** *a.* original; primitive; **-ly** *adv.*

**prim•i•tive** *a.* pert. to the beginning or origin; *(Biol.)* rudimentary; undeveloped; **-ly** *adv.* **-ness** *n.*

**pri•mo•gen•i•ture** *n.* the state of being the first-born child. **primogenital, primogenitary** *a.* **primogenitor** *n.* the earliest ancestor.

**pri•mor•di•al** *a.* existing from the beginning.

**prim•rose** *n.* a plant bearing pale-yellow and other colored flowers in spring.

**prince** *n.* *(fem.* **princess***)* a ruler or chief; the son of a king or emperor. **-dom** *n.* the jurisdiction. **-ly** *a.* stately. **-liness** *n.* **Prince Consort,** the husband of a reigning queen.

**prin•ci•pal** *a.* chief in importance; first in rank; *n.* the chief person in authority; the head of certain institutions, esp. a school; the chief actor in a crime; a chief debtor; a sum of money lent and yielding interest. **-ly** *adv.* **-ship** *n.* **principality** *n.* the territory of a prince; sovereignty.

**prin•cip•i•a** *n. pl.* first principles; beginnings.

**prin•ci•ple** *n.* a fundamental truth or law; a moral rule.

**print** *v.t.* to reproduce words, pictures, etc. by pressing inked types on paper, etc.; to write in imitation of this; to publish; *n.* a photograph. **-er** *n.* one engaged in the setting of type for, and the printing of books, newspapers, etc. **-ing press** *n.* a machine for reproducing on paper, etc. impressions made by inked type.

**pri•or** *a.* previous; former; earlier; preceding in time; *n.* the state of being antecedent in time; precedence; preference in regard to privilege.

**prism** *n.* *(Geom.)* a solid whose bases or ends are any similar, equal, and parallel plane figures, and whose sides are parallelograms; *(Optics)* a transparent figure of this nature, ususally with triangular ends. **colors,** the seven colors, red, orange, yellow, green, blue indigo, violet, into which a ray of light is separated by a prism.

**pris•on** *n.* building for confinement of criminals; jail; any place of confinement or restraint.

**private** *a.* not public; belonging to or concerning an individual; peculiar to oneself; personal; secluded; secret; of a soldier, not holding any rank; *n.* a common soldier. **-ly** *adv.* **-ness** *n.* **privacy** *n.* the state of being in retirement from company; solitude; seclusion; secrecy.

**pri•va•teer** *n.* an armed private vessel commissioned by a government to attack enemy ships.

**pri•va•tion** *n.* the state of being deprived, esp. of something required; destitution;

want.

**priv•i•lege** *n.* a special right or advantage; *v.t.* to grant some special favor to. **-d** *a.* enjoying a special right or immunity.

**priv•y** *a.* private; admitted to knowledge of a secret; *n.* a person having an interest in a law suit; a latrine.

**prize** *n.* a reward given for success in competition; a reward given for merit; a thing striven for; a thing won by chance, e.g. in a lottery. *v.t.* to value highly; to esteem. **— fight** *n.* a professional boxing match.

**pro-** *prefix* meaning for; instead of; on behalf of; in front of; before; forward; according to.

**prob•a•ble** *a.* likely; to be expected; having more evidence for than against. **probably** *adv.* **probability** *n.* likelihood.

**pro•bate** *n.* the process by which a last will and testament is legally authenticated after the testator's death; an official copy of a will.

**pro•ba•tion** *n.* a trial or test of a person's character, conduct, ability, etc.; the testing of a candidate before admission to full membership of a body, esp. a religious sect or order; a system of releasing offenders, esp. juveniles, and placing them under supervision of.

**probe** *n. (Med.)* instrument for examining a wound, ulcer, cavity, etc.; an investigation; *v.t.* to explore a wound, etc. with a probe; to examine thoroughly.

**prob•lem** *n.* a matter proposed for solution; a question difficult of solution; a puzzle. **-atical** *a.* questionable; uncertain.

**pro•ceed** *v.i.* to move onward; to advance; to renew progress; to pass from one point or topic to another; to come forth; to carry on a series of acts; to take legal proceedings. **-ing** *n.* going forward; movement or process; *pl. (Law)* the several steps of prosecuting a charge, claim, etc. **proceeds** *n.pl.* yield; sum realized by a sale. **procedure** *n.* act, method of proceeding.

**pro•cess** *n.* continued forward movement; lapse of time; a series of actions or measures; a method of operation; *(Anat.)* a projecting part or growth; *(Law)* procedure; *v.t.* to subject to some process, as food or material. **procession** *n.* a moving line of people, cars, animals, etc.; regular progress. *n.* **-ional** a hymn sung during a church procession.

**pro•claim** *v.t.* to make known by public announcement; to declare. **proclamation** *n.* the act of announcing publicly; an official public announcement.

**pro•cras•ti•nate** *v.i.* to put off till some future time. **procrastination** *n.* **procrastinator** *n.*

**pro•cre•ate** *v.t.* to bring into being; to beget; to generate. **procreation** *n.* **procreative** *a.* having the power to beget; productive.

**proc•tor** *n. (Law)* one who manages the affairs of another in a court; one who supervises students in an examination.

**proc•u•ra•tion** *n.* management of another's affairs; power of attorney.

**pro•cure** *v.t.* to acquire; to obtain; to get; to bring about; *v.i.* to act as a procurer. **procurable** *a.* obtainable. **-ment** *n.* **-r** *n.*

**prod** *v.t.* to poke with something pointed; to goad; *n.* a pointed instrument; a poke.

**prod•i•gal** *a.* wasteful; spending recklessly; *n.* one who spends recklessly; a spendthrift.

**prod•i•gy** *n.* a person or thing causing wonder; a marvel; a very gifted person; a monster; a portent.

**pro•duce** *v.t.* to bring forth; to exhibit; to give birth to; to yield; to make; to cause; of a play, to present it on the state. **produce** *n.* that which is produced; product; agricultural products; crops. **-r** *n.*

**prod•uct** *n.* that which is produced; *(Arith.)* a number resulting from the multiplying of two or more numbers.

**pro•fane** *a.* not sacred; irreverent; blasphemous; vulgar; *v.t.* to treat with irreverence; to put to a wrong or unworthy use; to desecrate. **-ly** *adv.* **-ness** *n.* **-r** *n.* **profanity** *n.* profaneness; irreverence; the use of bad language.

**pro•fess** *v.t.* to make open declaration of; to confess publicly; to affirm belief in; to pretend to knowledge or skill in. **-ed** *a.* openly acknowledged. **-ion** *n.* occupation or calling, esp. one requiring learning. **-ional** *a.* engaged in for money, as opposed to *amateur;* *n.* one who makes a livelihood in sport or games.

**pro•fes•sor** *n.* a teacher of the highest rank in a university. **professorial** *a.* **-ially** *adv.* **professoriate** *n.* the office of a professor; his period of office; body of professors. **-ship** *n.*

**pro•fi•cient** *a.* thoroughly versed or qualified in any art or occupation; skilled; *n.* an expert. **-ly** *adv.* **proficience, proficiency** *n.*

**pro•file** *n.* an outline or contour; a portrait in a side view; the side face; short biographical sketch; *v.t.* to draw the outline of.

**prof•it** *n.* advantage or benefit; the excess of returns over expenditure; pecuniary gain in any transaction or occupation. **-able** *a.* yielding profit or gain; advantageous; helpful. **-ably** *adv.* **-ableness** *n.* **profiteer** *n.* one who makes excessive profits.

**prof•li•gate** *a.* abandoned to vice; dissolute; extravagant; *n.* a depraved person. **-ly** *adv.* **-ness** *n.*

**pro•found** *a.* deep; intellectually deep; learned; deeply felt. **-ly** *adv.* **profundity** *n.* depth of place, knowledge, skill, feeling.

**pro•fuse** *a.* giving or given generously; lavish; extravagant. **-ly** *adv.* **-ness, profusion** *n.* great, abundance.

**prog•e•ny** *n.* descendants; offspring; children.

**prog•no•sis** *n.* a forecast; *(Med.)* foretelling the course of a disease.

**pro•gram, programme** *n.* a plan or detailed notes of intended proceedings at a public entertainment, ceremony, etc.; a party policy at election time.

**prog•ress** *n.* a moving forward; advancement; development. **progress** *n.* the act of moving forward; onward movement; progress. **-ively** *adv.* **-iveness** *n.* **arithmetical progression,** a series of numbers increasing or decreasing by the same amount, e.g. 3, 6, 9, 12, 15, etc. **geometrical progression,** a series of numbers increasing or decreasing by a common ratio, e.g. 3, 9, 27, 81, etc.

**pro•hib•it** *v.t.* to forbid; to prevent; to hinder. **-er, -or** *n.* **-ion** *n.* the act of forbidding; interdict; the forbidding by law of manufacture, importation, sale, or purchase of alcoholic liquors. **-ionist** *n.* one in favor of prohibition. **-ive, -ory** *a.* tending to forbid, prevent, or exclude; exclusive. **-ively** *adv.*

**pro•ject** *v.t.* to throw or cast forward; to plan; to contrive; to throw a photographic image on a screen; *n.* a plan; a scheme; a task. **-ile** *a.* capable of being thrown; *n.* a heavy missile, esp. a shell or cannon ball. **-ion** *n.* the act of projecting; something that juts out; a plan; delineation; the representation on a plane of a curved surface or sphere; in psychology, mistaking for reality something which is only an image in the mind. **-ive** *a.* **-or** *n.* an apparatus for throwing photographic images, esp. films, on a screen.

**pro•lapse** *n.* *(Med.)* the falling down on a part of the body from its normal position, esp. womb or rectum.

**pro•le•tar•i•an** *a.* pert. to the proletariat; belonging to the working class; *n.* one of the proletariat. **proletariat** *n.* propertyless wage-earners who live by sale of their labor.

**pro•lif•er•ous** *a.* *(Biol.)* reproducing freely by cell division; developing anthers. **-ly** *adv.* **proliferate** *v.t.* to bear.

**pro•lif•ic** *a.* bringing forth offspring; fruitful, abundantly productive; bringing about results. **-ally** *adv.*

**pro•lix** *a.* long drawn out; diffuse; wordy. **-ly** *adv.* **-ity** *n.*

**pro•loc•u•tor** *n.* a chairman of an assembly.

**pro•logue** *n.* the preface or introduction to a discourse, poem, book, or performance, esp. the address spoken before a dramatic performance.

**pro•long** *v.t.* to lengthen out; to extend the duration of.

**prom•e•nade** *n.* a leisurely walk, generally in a public place; a place adapted for such a walk; a march of dancers.

**prom•i•nent** *a.* sticking out; projecting; conspicuous; distinguished. **-ly** *adv.* **prominence, prominency** *n.*

**pro•mis•cu•ous** *a.* mixed without order or distinction; indiscriminate. **-ly** *adv.*

**prom•ise** *n.* an undertaking to do or not to do something; cause or grounds for hope; *v.t.* to give one's word to do or not to do something; to give cause for expectation; to agree to give. **promising** *a.* likely to turn out well or to succeed; hopeful.

**prom•is•so•ry** *a.* containing a promise. **— note,** written agreement to pay sum to named person at specified date.

**pro•mote** *v.t.* to move forward; to move up to a higher rank or position; to encourage the growth or development of; to help organize a new business venture or company. **-r** *n.* a supporter; an initiator. **promotion** *n.* advancement; preferment; a higher rank, station, or position.

**prompt** *a.* ready and quick to act; done at once; punctual; *v.t.* to excite to action; to suggest; to help out (actor or speaker) by reading, suggesting next words. **-ly** *adv.*

**pro•mul•gate** *v.t.* to proclaim; to publish; to make known officially. **promulgation** *n.*

**prone** *a.* lying face downward; sloping; inclined; naturally disposed. **-ly** *adv.* **-ness** *n.* inclination; tendency.

**prong** *n.* one of the pointed ends of a fork; a spike.

**pro•noun** *n.* *(Gram.)* a word used instead of a noun.

**pro•nounce** *v.t.* to speak with the correct sound and accent; to speak distinctly; to utter formally or officially; to declare or affirm. **-d** *a.* strongly marked; very definite or decided. **-able** *a.* **-ment** *n.* a formal declaration. **-r** *n.* **pronouncing** *a.* teaching or indicating pronounciation. **pronunciation.**

**proof** *n.* something which proves; a test or trial; demonstration; evidence that convinces the mind and produces belief; argument; standard strength of alcoholic spirits; *(Print.)* a trial impression from type, on which corrections may be made; *a.* firm in resisting; impenetrable; serving as proof or designating a certain standard or quality. **-reader** *n.* one who corrects printer's proofs.

**prop** *v.t.* to support by placing something under or against; to sustain.

**prop•a•gan•da** *n.* the propagating of doctrines or principles. **propagandize** *v.t.* and *i.* to spread propaganda. **propagandist** *n.*

**prop•a•gate** *v.t.* to cause to multiply or reproduce by generation; to breed; to spread the knowledge of; to transmit or carry forward; *v.i.* to have young; to breed. **propagator** *n.* **propagation** *n.*

**pro•pel** *v.t.* to drive forward; to press onward by force; to push. *pr.p.* **-ling.** *pa.p.* **-led.** **-ler** *n.* one who, or that which, propels; a revolving shaft with blades for driving a ship or airplane.

**pro•pen•si•ty** *n.* bent of mind; leaning or inclination.

**prop•er** *a.* fit; suitable; correct or according to usage. **-ly** *adv.* **— fraction** *(Arith.)* one in which the numerator is less than the denominator.

**prop•er•ty** *n.* an inherent or essential quality or peculiarity; ownership; the thing owned; possessions; land; *pl.* theatrical requisites, as scenery, costumes, etc.

**proph•e•cy** *n.* the foretelling of future events; prediction; revelation of God's will. **prophesy** *v.t.* to predict; to utter by divine inspiration; **prophet** *n.* one who foretells future events; an inspired teacher or revealer of the Divine Will.

**pro•phy•lac•tic** *a.* *(Med.)* tending to prevent disease, preventive; *n.* medicine or treatment tending to prevent disease. **prophylaxis** *n.* preventive treatment of disease.

**pro•pi•ti•ate** *v.t.* to appease; to conciliate; to gain the favor of.

**pro•po•nent** *n.* one who supports or makes a proposal.

**pro•por•tion** *n.* relative size, number, or degree; comparison; relation between connected things or parts; *(Arith.)* equality of ratios; the rule of three; *n.pl.* dimensions; **-al** *a. n.* a number of quantity in arithmetical or mathematical proportion. **-ally** *adv.* **-ality** *n.* **-ate** *a.* **-ed** *a.* **-ment** *n.*

**pro•pose** *v.t.* to offer for consideration; to suggest; to nominate; *v.i.* to form a plan; to intend; to offer oneself in marriage. **proposal** an offer, esp. of marriage. **-r** *n.* **proposition** *n.* a proposal; a statement or assertion. **propositional** *a.*

**pro•pri•e•tor** *n.* one who is the owner of property, a business, restaurant, etc. made and sold by an individual or firm having the exclusive rights of manufacture and sale.

**pro•pri•e•ty** *n.* properness; correct conduct.

**pro•pul•sion** *n.* the act of driving forward. **propulsive, propulsory** *a.* tending, or having power, to propel.

**pro•rate** *v.t.* and *i.* to divide or distribute proportionally.

**pro•scribe** *v.t.* to put outside the protection of the law; to outlaw; to prohibit. **-r** *n.* **proscription** *n.* **proscriptive** *a.*

**prose** *n.* ordinary language in speech and writing; language not in verse; *a.* pert. to prose; not poetical; *v.i.* to write prose; to speak or write in a dull, tedious manner.

**pros•e•cute** *v.t.* to follow or pursue with a view to reaching or accomplishing something; *(Law)* to proceed against judicially; *v.i.* to carry on a legal suit. **prosecution** *n.* *(Law)* the institution and carrying on of a suit in a court of law; the party by which legal proceedings are instituted, as opposed to the *defense*.

**pros•pect** *n.* a wide view; anticipation; reasonable hope; promise of future good. *v.t.* and *i.* to search or explore (a region), esp. for precious metals, oil, etc. **-ive** *a.* looking forward; relating to the future. **-ively** *adv.* **-or** *n.* **-us** *n.* a preliminary statement of an enterprise.

**pros•per** *v.t.* to cause to succeed; *v.i.* to succeed; to do well. **-ity** *n.* **-ous** *a.* **-ously** *adv.*

**pros•tate** *n.* a small gland at the neck of the bladder in males.

**pros•ti•tute** *n.* a harlot; *v.t.* to make a prostitute of; to put to base, infamous, or unworthy use. **prostitution** *n.*

**pros•trate** *a.* lying on the ground, esp. face downwards; mentally or physically exhausted; *v.t.* to lay flat, as on the ground; to bow down in adoration; to overcome. **prostration** *n.*

**pro•tag•o•nist** *n.* the principal actor in a drama; a leading character.

**pro•tect** *v.t.* to defend; to guard; to put a tariff on imports to encourage home industry. **-ion** *n.* defending from injury or harm; state of being defended; that which defends. **-ive** *a.* affording protection; sheltering. **-ively** *adv.* **-or** *n.* one who defends.

**pro•te•in** *n.* a nitrogenous compound required for all animal life processes.

**pro•test** *v.i.* to assert formally; to make a declaration against; *v.t.* to affirm solemnly; to object to. **protest** *n.* a declaration of objection. **-ant** *n.* one who holds an opposite opinion.

**Protestant** *a.* pert. or belonging to any branch of the Western Church outside the Roman communion; *n.* a member of such a church. **Protestantism** *n.* **protestation** *n.* a solemn declaration, esp. of dissent.

**pro•to-** *prefix* first; hence, original; primitive. **-plasm** *n.* a semi-fluid substance forming the basis of the primitive tissue of animal and vegetable life; living matter. **-plasmatic, -plasmic** *a.* **-type** *n.* original or model from which anything is copied; a pattern. *a.* **Protozoa** *n.pl.* first or lowest division of animal kingdom, consisting of microscopic, unicellular organisms. **-zoon** *n.* a member of this division. **-zoal, -zoan, -zoic** *a.*

**pro•to•col** *n.* an original copy; a rough draft, esp. a draft of terms signed by negotiating parties as the basis of a formal treaty or agreement; rules of diplomatic etiquette.

**pro•ton** *n.* in physics, the unit of positive electricity, found in the nuclei of all atoms.

**pro•tract** *v.t.* to lengthen; to draw out; to prolong; to draw to scale. **-ed** *a.* prolonged; long drawn out; tedious. **-ion** *n.* **-ive** *a.* **-or** *n.* a mathematical instrument for measuring angles; *(Anat.)* a muscle which draws forward or extends a limb.

**pro•trude** *v.t.* and *i.* to stick out; to project; to thrust forward. **protrusion** *n.* **protrusive** *a.*

**pro•tu•ber•ant** *a.* bulging; swelling out; prominent. **-ly** *adv.* **protuberance** *n.*

**proud** *a.* haughty; self-respecting. **-ly** *adv.*

**prove** *v.t.* to try by experiment; to ascertain as fact, by evidence; to demonstrate; to show; to establish the validity of; to be found by trial. *pr.p.* **proving.** *pa.p.* **-d** or **-n.** *pa.t.* **provable** *a.* able to be proved.

**prov•e•nance** *n.* source or place of origin.

**proverb** *n.* a short pithy saying to express a truth or point a moral; an adage. **Proverbs** *n.pl.* *(Bib.)* book of Old Testament. **-ial** *a.* well-known. **-ially** *adv.*

**pro•vide** *v.t.* to supply; to furnish; to get or make ready for future use. **providence** *n.* prudence; wise economy; God's care; an event regarded as an act of God. **Providence** *n.* God Himself. **provident** *a.* prudent; thrifty. **providently** *adv.*

**prov•ince** *n.* a division of a country or empire; an administrative district; a district under the jurisdiction of an archbishop; a department of knowledge; *n.* an inhabitant of a province.

**pro•vi•sion** *n.* the act of providing; measures taken beforehand; store esp. of food (generally in *pl.*); a condition or proviso; **-al** *a.* temporary; adopted for the time being. **-ally** *adv.*

**pro•vi•so** *n.* a condition or stipulation in a deed or contract. *pl.* **-s** or **-es.** **-ry** *a.* containing a proviso or condition.

**pro•voke** *v.t.* to excite or stimulate to action, esp. to arouse to anger or passion; to bring about or call forth. **provoking** *a.* **provocation** *n.* the act of provoking. **provocative** *a.* serving or tending to provoke. **provocatively** *adv.* **provocativeness** *n.*

**prow•ess** *n.* bravery, esp. in war; valor.

**prowl** *v.i.* to roam about stealthily.

**prox•i•mate** *a.* next or nearest; closest; immediately following or preceding. **-ly** *adv.* **proximity** *n.* being next in time, place, etc.

**prox•y** *n.* an authorized agent or substitute; one deputed to act for another; a writing empowering one person to vote for another.

**prude** *n.* a woman of affected or over-sensitive modesty or reserve. **prudish** *a.*

**pru•dent** *a.* cautious and judicious; careful; not extravagant. **-ly** *adv.* **prudence** *n.* **prudential** *a.* **-ially** *adv.*

**prune** *n.* a dried plum.

**prune** *v.t.* to cut off dead parts, excessive branches.

**Prus•sia** *n.* *(Geog.)* formerly the leading state of Germany, and the recognized home of German militarism. **-n** *n./a.* **-n blue,** a deep blue salt of potassium and iron, used as a pigment.

**pry** *v.i.* to look curiously; to peer; to nose about.

**psalm** *n.* a sacred song or hymn. **the Psalms** *(Bib.)* a book of the Old Testament. **psalmnist** *n.* a writer of psalms.

**pseu•d(o)-** *prefix* false, used in many derivatives to signify, false; pretended; sham; not real; wrongly held to be, etc. **-nym** *n.* a fictitious name; a pen name.

**pso•ri•a•sis** *n.* *(Med.)* chronic skin disease.

**psy•che** *n.* the soul personified; the principle of life.

**psy•chi•a•try** *n.* study and treatment of mental disorders. **psychiatrist** *n.* a specialist in mental disorders.

**psy•chic(al)** *a.* pert. to soul, spirit, or mind; spiritualistic.

**psy•cho•a•nal•y•sis** *n.* process of studying the unconscious mind; **psychoanalyze** *v.t.* **psychoanalyst** *n.* **psychoanalytic(al).**

**psy•chol•o•gy** *n.* the scientific study of the mind, its activities, and human and animal behavior. **psychological** *a.* **psychologically** *adv.* **psychologist** *n.*

**psy•cho•pa•thol•o•gy** *n.* the science or study of mental diseases. **psychopathy** *n.* mental affliction. **psychopath** *n.* one so afflicted. **psychopathic** *a.*

**psy•cho•sis** *n.* a general term for any disorder of the mind. *pl.* **psychoses.**

**psy•cho•so•mat•ic** *a.* of mind and body as a unit; treatment of physical diseases as having a mental origin.

**psy•cho•ther•a•py** *n.* the treatment of disease through the mind, e.g. by hypnotism, auto-suggestion, etc. **psychotherapeutic (-al)** *a.*

**pto•maine** *n.* substance, usually poisonous, found in putrefying organic matter.

**pu•ber•ty** *n.* the earliest age at which an individual is capable of reproduction. **pubescence** *n.* the period of sexual development; puberty. **pubescent** *a.*

**pub•lic** *a.* of, or pert. to, the people; not private or secret; open to general use; accessible to all; serving the people; *n.* community or its members; a section of community. **-ly** *adv.* **ation** *n.* making known to the public; proclamation; printing a book, etc. for sale or distribution; a book, periodical, magazine, etc. **publicize** *v.t.* to make widely known; to advertize. **publicist** *n.* one versed in, or who writes on, international law, or matters of political or economic interest. **publicity** *n.* the state of being generally known; notoriety; advertisement. **—prosecutor,** the legal officer appointed to prosecute criminals in serious cases on behalf of the state. **—school,** one of a system of schools, maintained at public expense.

**pub•lish** *v.t.* to make general known; to proclaim; to print and issue for sale (books, music, etc.); to put into circulation. **-er** *n.*

**puck** *n.* a rubber disk used in ice hockey.

**puck•er** *v.t.* and *i.* to gather into small folds or wrinkles; *n.* a wrinkle; a fold; **-y** *a.*

**pud•ding** *n.* name of various forms of cooked foods, usually in a soft mass, served as a dessert.

**pud•dle** *n.* a small pool of dirty water; a mixture of clay and water used as rough cement.

**puff** *n.* a short blast of breath or wind; its sound; a small quantity of smoke, etc.; a swelling; a light pastry; a soft pad for applying powder; *v.i.* to send out smoke, etc. in puffs; to breathe hard; to pant; to swell up; *v.t.* to send out in a puff; to blow out; to smoke hard; to cause to swell.

**pug** *n.* a small, snub-nosed dog; *a.* **— nose** *n.* a turned-up nose.

**pu•gil•ism** *n.* the art of fighting with the fists; boxing. **pugilist** *n.* a boxer. **pugilistic** *a.*

**pug•na•cious** *a.* given to fighting; quarrelsome. **-ly** *adv.*

**pull** *v.t.* to draw towards one; to drag; to haul; to tug at; to pluck; to row a boat; *v.i.* to draw with force; to tug; *n.* act of pulling; force exerted by it; a tug; a means of pulling; effort.

**pul•ley** *n.* a small wheel with a grooved rim on which runs a rope, used for

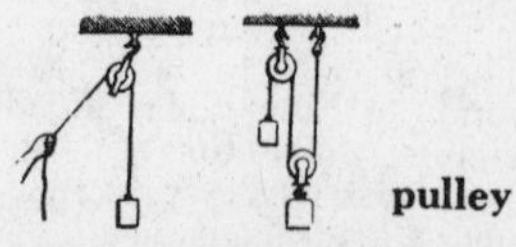

pulley

hauling or lifting weights.

**Pull•man•car** *n.* a railway car.

**pul•mo-** *prefix,* the lung. **-nary** *a.* pert. to or affecting the lungs.

**pulp** *n.* a soft, moist, cohering mass of animal or vegetable matter; the soft, succulent part of fruit; the material of which paper is made.

**pul•pit** *n.* elevated place in a church for preacher.

**pul•sate** *v.t.* to beat or throb, as the heart; to vibrate; to quiver. **pulsation** *n.*

**pulse** *n.* the beating or throbbing of the heart or blood vessels, esp. of the arteries; the place, esp. on the wrist, where this rhythmical beat is felt; any measured or regular beat. *v.i.* to throb or pulsate.

**pul•ver•i•ze** *v.t.* to reduce to a fine powder; to smash or demolish; *v.i.* to fall down into dust. **pulverization** *n.* **-r** *n.*

**pu•ma** *n.* a large American carnivorous animal of the cat family; cougar.

**pum•ice** *n.* Also — **stone,** a light, porous variety of lava, used for cleaning, polishing, etc.

**pump** *n.* an appliance used for raising water, putting in or taking out air or liquid, etc.; *v.t.* to raise with a pump, as water; to free from water by means of a pump; to extract information by artful questioning.

**pump** *n.* a low, thin-soled shoe.

**pump•kin** *n.* a plant of the gourd family; its fruit, used as food.

**pun** *n.* a play on words similar in sound but different in sense; *v.i.* to use puns. *pr.p.*

**punch** *n.* a drink made of fruit juices, sugar, and water, sometimes carbonated or with liquor.

**punch** *n.* a tool used for making holes or dents; a machine for perforating or stamping; *v.t.* to perforate, dent, or stamp with a punch.

**punch** *v.t.* to strike with the fist; to beat; to bruise.

**punc•tu•al** *a.* arriving at the proper or fixed time; prompt; not late.

**punc•tu•ate** *v.t.* to separate into sentences, clauses, etc. by periods, commas, colons, etc.; to emphasize in some significant manner; to interrupt at intervals. **punctuation** *n.* the act or system separating by the use of **punctuation marks** (the period, comma, colon, semi-colon, etc.).

**punc•ture** *n.* an act of pricking; a small hole made by a sharp point; a perforation; *v.t.* to make a hole with a sharp point.

**pun•gent** *a.* sharply affecting the taste or smell; stinging; sarcastic; caustic. **-ly** *adv.* **pungency** *n.*

**pun•ish** *v.t.* to inflict a penalty for an offense; to chastise. **-able** *a.* **-ment** *n.* **punitive** *a.* pert. to or inflicting punishment.

**punt** *v.t.* and *i.* to kick a football, when dropped from the hands, before it touches the ground; *n.* such a kick.

**pu•ny** *a.* small and feeble; petty. **puniness** *n.*

**pup** *n.* a puppy or young dog; a young seal; *v.i.* to bring forth puppies or whelps. *pr.p.* **-ping.** *pa.p., pa.t.* **-ped.**

**pu•pil** *n.* a student; a boy or girl under the care of a guardian; the small circular opening in the center of the iris of the eye.

**pup•pet** *n.* a marionette; a person whose actions are completely controlled by another. **-ry** *n.* a puppet show.

**pur•chase** *v.t.* to buy; to obtain by any outlay of labor, time, sacrifice, etc.; *(Law)* to obtain by any means other than inheritance; *n.* acquisition of anything for a price or equivalent; a thing bought.

**pure** *a.* free from all extraneous matter; untainted; spotless; blameless; unsullied; chaste; innocent; absolute; theoretical, not applied. **-ly** *adv.* entirely; solely. **-ness** *n.* **purity** *n.* freedom from all extraneous matter; freedom from sin or evil.

**pu•rée** *n.* a thick soup.

**purge** *v.t.* to purify; to cleanse; to clear out; to clear from guilt, accusation, or the charge of a crime, etc.; to cleanse the bowels by taking a cathartic medicine; *n.* a cleansing, esp. of the bowels; a purgative. **purgative** *a.* having the power of purging; *n.* any medicine which will cause evacuation of bowels. **purgatory** *a.* tending to cleanse; purifying; expiatory; *n.* in R.C. faith, place where souls of dead are purified by suffering; *(Fig.)* a place or state of torment.

**pu•ri•fy** *v.t.* to make pure, clear, or clean; to free form impurities; to free from guilt or defilement. **purification** *n.* **purificative** *a.* **purifier** *n.*

**pur•ist** *n.* an advocate of extreme care or precision in choice of words, etc.; a stickler for correctness.

**Pu•ri•tan** *n.* a member of the extreme Protestant party, who desired further *purification* of the Church after the Elizabethan reformation; *(l.c.)* a person of extreme strictness in morals or religion. **-ically** *adv.* **-ism** *n.* doctrine and practice of Puritans; narrow-mindedness.

**purl** *n.* an embroidered border; a knitting stitch that is reverse of plain stitch.

**pur•loin** *v.i.* to steal; to pilfer.

**pur•ple** *n.* a color between crimson and violet; robe of this color, formerly reserved for royalty; royal dignity; *a.* purple-colored; dark red; *v.i.* to make or dye a purple color; *v.i.* to become purple. **born to the purple,** of princely rank.

**pur•port** *n.* meaning; apparent meaning; import; aim.

**pur•pose** *n.* object in view; aim; end; plan; intention; effect; purport; *v.t.* to intend; to mean to. **-ly** *adv.* intentionally; expressly. **-ful** *a.* determined resolute. **-fully** *adv.* **-less** *a.* aimless. **-lessly** *adv.* **purposive** *a.* done with a purpose.

**pur•pu•ra** *n.* *(Med.)* the appearance of purple patches under the skin, caused by hemorrhage; shellfish, yielding purplish fluid.

**purr** *n.* a low, murmuring sound made by a cat; *v.i.* to utter such a sound.

**purse** *n.* a small bag or pouch to carry money in; money offered as a prize, or collected as a present; money.

**pur•sue** *v.t.* to follow with the aim of overtaking; to run after; to chase; to aim at; to seek; to continue; *v.i.* to go on; to proceed; **-r** *n.* **pursuance** *n.* the act of pursuing. **pursuant** *a.* done in consequence, or performance, of anything. **pursuit** *n.* the act of pursuing; a running after; chase; profession occupation. **pursuivant** *n.* an attendant.

**pur•vey** *v.t. (Brit.)* to furnish or provide; to supply, esp. provisions. **-ance** *n.* act of purveying; supplies; former royal prerogative of requisitioning supplies, or enforcing personal service. **-or** *n.*

**pus** *n.* the yellowish-white matter produced by suppuration.

**push** *v.t.* to move or try to move away by pressure; to drive or impel; to press hard; to press or urge forward; to shove; *v.i.* to make a thrust; to press hard in order to move; *n.* a thrust; any pressure or force applied; emergency; enterprise; *(Mil.)* an advance or attack on a large scale. **-er** *n.* **-ing** *a.* given to pushing oneself or one's claims; self-assertive. **-ingly** *adv.*

**pus•tule** *n.* a small swelling or pimple containing pus. **pustular, pustulous** *a.*

**put** *v.t.* to place; to set; to lay; to apply; to state; to propose; to throw; *v.i.* to go. *pr.p.* **-ting.** *pa.p.* and *pa.t.* **put.** *n.* a throw, esp. of a heavy weight. **to put about** *(Naut.)* to alter a ship's course.

**pu•ta•tive** *a.* commonly thought; supposed; reputed. **-ly** *adv.* **putation** *n.*

**pu•tre•fy** *v.t.* and *i.* to make or become rotten; to decompose; to rot. **putrefaction** *n.* the rotting of animal or vegetable matter; rottenness; decomposition. **putrefactive** *a.*

**putt** *v.t.* and *i.* (Golf) to hit a ball in the direction of the hole; *n.* the stroke so made in golf; the throw of the weight. **-er** *n.* one who putts; a short golf club.

**put•ter** *v.i.* to work or act in a feeble, unsystematic way; to dawdle.

**put•ty** *n.* a kind of paste or cement, used by plasterers; *v.t.* to fix, fill up, etc. with putty.

**puz•zle** *n.* a bewildering or perplexing question; a problem, etc. requiring clever thinking to solve it; a conundrum; *v.t.* to perplex; to bewilder; (with 'out') to solve after hard thinking; (with 'over') to think hard over; **-r** *n.* **puzzling** *a.* bewildering, perplexing.

**Pyg•my, Pigmy** *n.* one of a race of dwarf Negroes of C. Africa. *(l.c.)* a very small person or thing; a dwarf; *a.* diminutive.

**py•or•rhe•a** *n. (Med.)* a dental discharge of pus from the gums. Also **pyorrhoea.**

**pyr•a•mid** *n.* a solid figure on a triangular, square, or polygonal base, and with sloping sides meeting at an apex; a structure of this shape. **-al** *a.* pert. to, or having the form of a pyramid. **-ally** *adv.*

**pyre** n. a pile of wood for burning a dead body; funeral pile.

**py•ret•ic** *a. (Med.)* pert. to producing, or relieving, fever; feverish. **pyrexia** *n.* fever.

**py•rite** *n.* a yellow mineral formed of sulphur and iron; iron pyrites. **pyrites** *n.pl.* a name for many compounds of metals with sulphur, esp. iron pyrites, or copper pyrites. **pyritic, pyritiferous, pyritous** *a.* pert. to, or yielding, pyrites.

**py•ro-** *prefix,* fire, used in many derivatives. **— electricity** *n.* the property possessed by some crystals, of becoming electrically polar when they are heated.

**py•ro•ma•ni•a** *n.* a mania for setting things on fire. **pyromaniac** *n.*

**py•ro•tech•nics** *n.pl.* the art of making fireworks; the art of displaying them. Also **pyrotechny. pyrotechnic, pyrotechnical** *a.*

**Py•thag•o•ras** *n.* a Greek philosopher and mathematician (582-507 B.C.).

**py•thon** *n.* a large, non-poisonous snake that kills its prey by crushing it; a spirit.

**quack** *v.i.* to cry like a duck; *n.* cry of duck or like sound; one who pretends to skill in medicine; a charlatan; *a.* pert. to quackery. **-ery** *n.* **-salver** *n.* a quack doctor.

**quad•ran•gle** *n.* in geometry, a plane figure having four sides and angles; a square surrounded by buildings. **quadrangular** *a.*

**quad•rant** *n.* the fourth part of the area of a circle; an arc of 90°; in gunnery, an instrument to mark the degrees of a gun's elevation.

**quad•rate** *a.* having four sides and four right angles; divisible by four (used in antaomical names); *n.* square; *v.i.* to suit. **quadratic** *a.* pert. to, or resembling, a square; *(Alg.)* involving the second power of the unknown quantity, esp. in **quadratic equation. quadrature** *n.* the act of squaring or reducing to a square.

**quad•ri•cen•ten•ni•al** *a.* pert. to a period of four hundred years; *n.* the four-hundredth anniversary.

**quad•ri•lat•er•al** *a.* having four sides; *n.* *(Geom.)* a plane figure having four sides.

**qua•dril•lion** *n.* a number represented in the Fr. and U.S. notation by one with 15 ciphers annexed.

**quad•ri•no•mi•al** *a.* *(Alg.)* consisting of four terms.

**quad•ri•par•tite** *a.* divided into four parts.

**quad•ru•mane** *n.* an animal which has all four feet formed like hands. **quadrumanous** *a.* four-handed.

**quad•ru•ped** *n.* an animal having four feet; *a.* having four feet.

**qua•dru•ple** *a.* fourfold; *n.* a sum four times as great as another; *v.t.* to multiply by four; *v.i.* to be multiplied by four. **-t** *n.* one of four children born at a birth. **quadruplicate** *v.t.* to multiply by four; *n.* one of four things corresponding exactly; *a.* fourfold. **quadruplication** *n.*

**quaff** *v.t.* and *v.i.* to swallow in large drafts; *n.* a drink.

**quag•mire** *n.* soft, wet land, yielding under feet. **quaggy** *a.* boggy.

**quail** *v.i.* to lose spirit; to flinch.

**quail** *n.* a game bird.

**quaint** *a.* interestingly old-fashioned or odd; whimsical. **-ly** *adv.* **-ness** *n.*

**quake** *v.i.* to shake with emotion; to quiver or vibrate; *n.* a trembling.

**Quak•er** *n.* a member of a religious sect founded in the 17th cent. **-ism** *n.*

**qual•i•fy** *v.t.* to describe (as); to prepare by requisite training for special duty; to furnish with the legal title to; *v.i.* to show oneself fit for. **qualifier** *n.* **qualifiable** *a.* **qualification** *n.* condition of being qualified; any acquirement that fits a person for an office or employment; restriction.

**qual•i•ty** *n.* a particular property inherent in a substance; an essential attribute, distinguishing feature, or characteristic; superiority of sound, tonal color. **qualitative** *a.* relating to quality; concerned with quality.

**qualm** *n.* a sudden attack of illness, distress; a scruple of conscience.

**quan•da•ry** *n.* a state of perplexity; a dilemma.

**quan•ti•fy** *v.t.* to measure. **quantification** *n.*

**quan•ti•ty** *n.* property of things ascertained by measuring; number; *pl.* profusion. **quantitative** *a.* relating to quantity.

**quan•tum** *n.* amount; a specified or required amount. *pl.* **quanta.**

**quar•an•tine** *n.* isolation of infected persons to prevent spread of serious disease; *v.t.* to put under quarantine.

**quar•rel** *n.* rupture of friendly relations; an angry altercation; *v.i.* to dispute; to disagree. **-er** *pr.p.* and *n.* **-some** *a.* contentious.

**quar•ry** *n.* an excavation whence stone is dug for building; *v.t.* to dig from a quarry. **quarried** *pa.p.* and *pa.t.*

**quar•ry** *n.* prey; victim.

**quart** *n.* the fourth part of a gallon.

**quar•ter** *n.* fourth part; *(U.S. and Canada)* one fourth of a dollar, or the coin valued at this amount; one of the four cardinal points of the compass; a territory; *pl.* assigned position; lodgings, esp. for soldiers; *v.t.* to divide into four equal parts; to furnish with shelter; *v.i.* to have temporary residence. **-ing** *n.* an assignment of quarters for soldiers. **-ly** *a.* occurring every quarter of a year; *n.* a magazine published four times a year; *adv.* by quarters; once in a quarter of a year. **-deck** *n.* a part of deck of a ship which extends from stern to mainmast. **-master** *n.* *(Mil.)* an officer in charge of quarters, clothing. **-master -sergeant** *n.* the N.C.O. assistant to the quartermaster.

**quar•tet, quartette** *n.* *(Mus.)* a composition of four parts, each performed by a single voice or instrument; *a.* denoting the size of a book in which the paper is folded to give four leaves to the sheet.

**quartz** *n.* kinds of mineral, consisting of pure silica or silicon dioxide.

**quash** *v.t.* to quell; *(Law)* to annul, or make void.

**qua•si** as if; as it were; in a certain sense or degree.

**qua•train** *n.* *(Pros.)* a stanza of four lines.

**qua•ver** *v.i.* to tremble, or vibrate; to sing with tremulous modulations; *n.* a trembling, esp. of the voice.

**quay** *n.* a landing place for loading and unloading of ships. **-age** *n.* payment for use of a quay.

**quea•sy** *a.* affected with nausea; fastidious. **queasily** *adv.* **queasiness** *n.*

**queen** *n.* woman who is the sovereign of a kingdom; the sovereign of a swarm of bees, ants, etc.; one of the chief pieces in a game of chess; *v.i.* to act the part of a queen. **-ly** *a.* majestic. **-liness** *n.* **-hood** *n.* position of a queen. **— dowager** *n.* the widow of a king. **— mother** *n.* a queen dowager who is also mother of reigning monarch. **— regent** *n.* a queen reigning in her own right.

**queer** *a.* odd; of a questionable character. **-ly** *adv.* **-ish** *a.* somewhat queer. **-ness** *n.*

**quell** *v.t.* to subdue; to suppress forcibly. **-er** *n.*

**quench** *v.t.* to put out, as fire or light; to

slake (thirst). **-able, -less** *a.* **-er** *n.*
**quer•u•lous** *a.* peevish; fretful. **-ly** *adv.* **-ness** *n.*
**que•ry** *n.* an inquiry; a mark of interrogation; *v.t.* to inquire into.
**quest** *n.* search; the thing sought; *v.i.* to search; to seek.
**ques•tion** *n.* interrogation; inquiry; that which is asked; subject of debate; a problem; *v.t.* to inquire of by asking questions; to take objection to. **-able** *a.* suspicious. **-ably** *adv.* **-ableness, -er** *n.* **— mark** *n.* a mark of interrogation (?). **out of the question,** not to be thought of.
**ques•tion•naire** *n.* a list of questions.
**queue** *n.* a pigtail.
**quib•ble** *n.* an evasion of the point in question by a play upon words; equivocation; *v.i.* to use quibbles. **-r** *n.*
**quick** *a.* prompt; rapid; hasty; impatient; *n.* sensitive flesh under nails; *(Fig.)*one's tenderest susceptibilities. **-ly** *adv.* rapidly; promptly. **-ness** *n.* **-en** *v.t.* to make sprightly; to hasten; to stimulate; *v.i.* to move with greater rapidity. **-ener** *n.* **-ening** *n.* becoming quick. **-sand** *n.* sand, readily yielding to pressure, esp. if loose and mixed with water. **-silver** *n.* mercury. **-step** *n.* a lively dance step.
**quid** *n.* a portion suitable for chewing, esp. of tobacco; a cud.
**quid•di•ty** *n.* a trifling nicety; the essence of anything.
**qui•es•cent** *a.* motionless; at rest. **-ly** *adv.* **quiescence, quiescency** *n.*
**qui•et** *a.* peaceful; not agitated; of gentle disposition; *n.* calm; tranquillity; *v.t.* to reduce to a state of rest; to calm; to allay or appease; *v.i.* to become quiet. **-en** *(Dial.) v.t.* and *v.i.* to quiet. **-ly** *adv.* **-ness** *n.* **-ude** *n.* freedom from noise, alarm; tranquillity; repose. **-us** *n.* final acquittance, of debt.
**quill** *n.* a large, hollow feather used as a pen; a prickle, as of a porcupine; an implement for striking the strings of certain instruments.
**quilt** *n.* any thick, warm coverlet; *v.t.* to stitch together, like a quilt, with a soft filling; to pad. **-ed.** *a.*
**qui•na•ry** *a.* consisting of, or arranged in, fives.
**quince** *n.* a hard, yellow, acid fruit, somewhat like an apple.
**qui•nine** *n.* a bitter alkaloid obtained from various species of cinchona bark; a tonic and febrifuge. **quinic** *a.*
**Quin•qua•ge•si•ma** *n.* the Sunday before Ash Wednesday, so-called because fifty days before Easter.
**quin•sy** *n.* a severe inflammation of the throat and tonsils.
**quin•tes•sence** *n.* the perfect embodiment of a thing. **quintessential** *a.*
**quin•tet, quintette** *n. (Mus.)* a composition for five voices or instruments; a set of five.
**quin•til•lion** *n. (U.S. and France)* a number represented by one with 18 ciphers following.
**quin•tu•ple** *a.* multiplied by five; to multiply by five. **-ts** *n.pl.* five children at a birth *(Colloq.* **quints***).*
**quip** *n.* a sarcastic turn of phrase; a witty saying. **-ster** *n.*
**quire** *n.* 24 sheets of paper of the same size, the twentieth part of a ream.
**quirk** *n.* sudden twist; a quibble; a peculiarity. **-y** *a.*
**quit** *v.t.* to cease from; to give up; *v.i.* to stop doing a thing; *a.* released from obligation. **-ting** *pr.p.* **quit** or **-ted** *pa.p.* and *pa.t.* **-tance** *n.* discharge from a debt or obligation. **-ter** *n.* a person easily discouraged.
**quite** *adv.* completely; entirely.
**quiv•er** *n.* a sheath for holding arrows.
**quiv•er** *v.i.* to shake with a tremulous motion; *n.* the act of quivering; a tremor.
**Qui•xo•te** *n.* the hero of the great romance of Miguel Cervantes. **quixotic** *a.* like Don Quixote; ideally and extravagantly romantic. **quixotically** *adv.* **quixotism, quixotry** *n.*
**quiz** *n.* a test or examination; a hoax; *v.t.* to question. **-zing** *pr.p.* **-zed** *pa.p.* and *pa.t.* **-zer** *n.* **-zical** *a.* odd; teasing.
**quoin** *n.* a cornerstone; *(Gun.)* a metallic wedge inserted under the breech of a gun to raise it; *(Print.)* a small wooden wedge used to lock the types in the galley etc.
**quoit** *n.* a flat, iron ring to be pitched at a fixed object in play; *pl.* game of throwing these onto a peg; *v.i.* to play at quoits.
**quon•dam** *a.* that was once; sometime.
**quo•rum** *n.* number of members present at a meeting to make its transactions valid.
**quo•ta** *n.* a proportional share.
**quote** *v.t.* to repeat a passage from; to state a price for; *pl.* quotation marks. **quotation** *n.* **— marks** *n.pl.* marks ("—") to indicate beginning and end of a quotation.
**quo•tid•i•an** *a.* daily; *n.* thing returning daily, esp. fever.
**quo•tient** *n.* number resulting from division of one number by another.

**rab•bet** *n.* a groove made to form, with a corresponding edge, a close joint; *v.t.* to cut such an edge.

**rab•bi** *n.* a Jewish teacher of the Law. **-nic (al)** *a.*

**rab•bit** *n.* a small, burrowing rodent mammal, like the hare, but smaller. **— hutch** *n.* an enclosure for rearing tame rabbits.

**rab•ble** *n.* a noisy, disorderly crowd; *v.t.* to mob.

**ra•bid** *a.* affected with rabies. **-ly** *adv.* **-ness, -ity** *n.*

**ra•bies** *n.* canine madness; hydrophobia.

**rac•coon, racoon** *n.* one of a genus of plantigrade carnivorous mammals of N. America.

**raccoon**

**race** *n.* distinct variety of human species; a peculiar breed, as of horses, etc.; lineage; descent. **racial** *a.* pert. to race or lineage. **racially** *adv.* **racialism, racism** *n.* animosity shown to peoples of different race.

**race** *n.* rapid motion; a contest involving speed; *v.t.* to cause to run rapidly; *v.i.* to run swiftly; of an engine, pedal, to move rapidly without control. **-r** *n.* one who races; a racehorse, yacht, car, etc. used for racing. **—horse** *n.* a horse bred to run for a price. **—track** *n.* a track used for horse-racing, etc. **racing** *n.*

**ra•chis** *n.* an axial structure, such as vertebral column in animals; *pl.* **rachides. rachitic** *a.* having rickets. **rachitis** *n.* rickets.

**rack** *n.* an instrument for stretching; an open framework for displaying; a straight cogged bar to gear with a toothed wheel to produce linear motion from rotary motion, or vice versa; *v.t.* to stretch almost to breaking point; to overstrain; to place in a rack. **-ed** *a.* **-ing** *a.* agonizing (pain). **— and ruin,** destruction.

**rack•et, racquet** *n.* bat used in tennis, etc.; *pl.* a ball game played in a paved court with walls.

**rack•et** *n.* a confused, clattering din; *v.i.* to make clatter.

**ra•cy** *a.* lively; pungent. **racily** *adv.* **raciness** *n.*

**ra•dar** *n.* radiolocation or apparatus used in it.

**ra•di•al** *a.* pert. to a ray; branching out like spokes of a wheel.

**ra•di•an** *n.* angle subtended by an arc of a circle equal in length to the radius.

**ra•di•ant** *a.* emitting rays; beaming; *n.* *(Astron.)* point in sky from which a shower of meteors appears to come. **radiance, radiancy** *n.* brilliancy; splendor. **-ly** *adv.*

**ra•di•ate** *v.i.* to shine; *v.t.* to emit rays, as heat, etc.; *a.* with rays diverging from a center. **radiation** *n.* emission and diffusion of rays from central point. **radiator** *n.* any device which emits rays of heat or light; in motoring, apparatus to split up and cool circulating water in water-cooling system.

**rad•i•cal** *a.* pert. to the root; thorough; of extreme or advanced liberal views; *n.* *(Gram.)* a root; a politician who advocates thorough reforms; *(Bot.)* a radicle; *(Math.)* a quantity expressed as the root of another. **-ly** *adv.* **-ness** *n.*

**rad•i•cle** *n.* *(Med.)* the initial fibril of a nerve; *(Bot.)* primary root of an embryo plant.

**ra•di•o-** used in forming compound terms with the meaning of "rays", as in **radioactive** *a.* emitting from an atomic nucleus invisible rays which penetrate matter. **radioactivity** *n.* **radioelement** *n.* metallic chemical element having radioactive properties. **radiograph** *n.* an instrument for measuring and recording the intensity of the heat given off by the sun. **radiographer, radiography** *n.* **radiology** *n.* the science of radioactivity in medicine. **radiologist** *n.* **radioscopy** *n.* examination by X rays. **radiotherapy, radiotherapeutics** *n.* treatment of disease by X rays.

**ra•di•o** *n.* wireless telegraphy; apparatus for reception of broadcast. **-gram** *n.* a telegram transmitted by radio.

**rad•ish** *n.* an herb with pungent edible root.

**ra•di•um** *n.* a metallic, radioactive element.

**ra•di•us** *n.* a straight line from center of circle to circumference; distance from any one place; *pl.* **-es, radii.**

**ra•dix** *n.* a root; *(Anat.)* the point of origin of a structure, as the root of a tooth; *(Math.)* fundamental base of a system of logarithms; *pl.* **-es, radices.**

**ra•don** *n.* a gaseous, radioactive element.

**raf•fi•a** *n.* fiber from a cultivated palm used for baskets.

**raf•fle** *n.* a lottery; *v.t.* to sell by raffle. **-r** *n.*

**raft** *n.* a mass of logs chained together for transportation down a river; *v.i.* to proceed by raft.

**raf•ter** *n.* a sloping beam, from the ridge to the eaves, to which the roof covering is attached; *v.t.* to provide with rafters.

**rag** *n.* a fragment of cloth; *pl.* tattered attire; *a.* made of rags. **-man** *n.* one who collects rags. **-time** *n.* dance music marked by strong syncopation. **-weed** *n.* a widespread weed, common cause of hay fever.

**rag** *v.t.* to tease. **-ging** *pr.p.* **-ged** *pa.t.* and *pa.p.*

**rage** *n.* extreme anger; fashion; *v.i.* to be furious with anger; to proceed violently and without check. **raging** *a.* **ragingly** *adv.*

**rag•ged** *a.* worn to tatters; imperfectly performed. **-ly** *adv.* **-ness** *n.*

**rag•lan** *n.* wide sleeves running up to the neck, not to the shoulders.

**raid** *n.* a hostile incursion depending on surprise and rapidity; *v.t.* to make a sudden attack upon. **-er** *n.*

**rail** *n.* bars of steel on which the flanged

wheels of vehicles run; a horizontal bar for support; *v.t.* to enclose with rails; to send by railway. **-ing** *n.* material for rails; a construction of rails. **-road** *n.* a road on which steel rails are laid for wheels to run on; a system of such rails and all equipment.
**rail** *n.* wading bird.
**rail** *v.i.* to use insolent language; to utter abuse. **-er** *n.* **-lery** *n.* good-humored banter; ridicule.
**rain** *n.* condensed moisture, falling in drops from clouds; *v.t.* and *v.i.* to pour down like rain. **-bow** *n.* arch showing seven prismatic colors and formed by refraction and reflection of sun's rays in falling rain. **— check** *n.* a ticket for a future performance, when one is stopped by rain. **-coat** *n.* a light, rainproof overcoat. **-fall** *n.* the amount of rain, in inches, which falls in a particular place. **-iness** *n.* **-less** *n.* **-proof** *a.* impervious to rain. **-y** *a.*
**raise** *v.t.* to cause to rise; to elevate; to produce by cultivation; to rear; to heighten (voice). **-d** *a.* elevated. **raising** *n.*
**rai•sin** *n.* a dried grape.
**rake** *n.* a long-handled garden implement; *v.t.* and *v.i.* to scrape with a toothed implement; sweep over.
**rake** *n.* a dissolute man of fashion. **rakish** *a.* **rakishly** *adv.*
**rake** *n.* inclination of masts from the perpendicular; *v.i.* to incline from perpendicular. **rakish** *a.* having a backward inclination of the masts. **rakishly** *adv.*
**ral•ly** *v.t.* and *v.i.* to reassemble; to collect and restore order; to recover (health); to return a ball (in tennis); *n.* outdoor demonstration; lively exchange of strokes in tennis.
**ram** *n.* male sheep; a swinging beam with a metal head for battering; *(Astron.)* Aries, one of the signs of zodiac; *v.t.* to drive against with violence. **-ming** *pr.p.* **-med** *pa.t.* and *pa.p.* **-er** *n.*
**ram•ble** *v.i.* to walk without definite route; to talk or write incoherently; *n.* a short walk. **-r** *n.* one who rambles. **rambling** *a.* wandering.
**ram•i•fy** *v.t.* and *v.i.* to branch out in various directions. **ramification** *n.* subdivision proceeding from a main structure.
**ramp** *v.i.* to rear up on hind legs; *n.* a gradual slope.
**ram•page** *n.* a state of excitement, as **on the rampage**; *v.i.* to rush about, in a rage; to act violently. **-ous** *a.*
**ram•pant** *a.* rearing; violent; rank. **rampancy** *n.*
**ram•part** *n.* mound of earth around fortified place; *v.t.* to strengthen with ramparts.
**ram•rod** *n.* a rod for cleaning barrel of a rifle, etc.
**ram•shack•le** *a.* tumbledown; beyond repair.
**ran** *pa.t.* of run.
**ranch** *n.* prairie land for sheep- and cattle-rearing; *v.i.* to keep a ranch. **-er** *n.* man who owns or works on a ranch.
**ran•cid** *a.* having a rank smell. **-ly** *adv.* **-ness, -ity** *n.*
**ran•cor** *n.* bitter and inveterate ill-feeling. **-ous** *a.* evincing intense hatred; malignant. **-ously** *adv.*
**ran•dom** *a.* done haphazardly; *n.* in phrase, **at random,** haphazard.
**rang** *pa.t.* of ring.
**range** *v.t.* to set in a row; to rove over; *v.i.* to roam; to fluctuate between, as prices, etc.; *n.* limits, within which something is possible; a large kitchen stove; line of mountains; place for practice shooting; pastureland. **-er** *n.* keeper of park or forest. **rangy** *a.* roaming; long-limbed.
**rank** *n.* soldiers standing side by side; grade in armed services; relative position; *pl.* enlisted soldiers; *v.t.* to arrange in order, or division; to place abreast; *v.i.* to be placed in a class; to possess social distinction. **-er** *n.* **-ing** *n.* arrangement.
**rank** *a.* offensively strong of smell; rancid. **-le** *v.i.* to remain a sore point with. **-ly** *adv.* **-ness** *n.*
**ran•sack** *v.t.* to search thoroughly.
**ran•som** *n.* a price paid for release of prisoner; *v.t.* to redeem from captivity.
**rant** *v.i.* to talk wildly and noisily; *n.* noisy and meaningless declamation. **-er** *n.*
**rap** *n.* a smart, light blow; *v.t.* and *v.i.* to deliver a smart blow. **-ping** *pr.p.* **-ped** *pa.t.* and *pa.p.*
**ra•pa•cious** *a.* subsisting on prey; grasping. **-ly** *adv.* **-ness, rapacity** *n.*
**rape** *n.* carnal knowledge of a female against her will; *v.t.* to ravish or violate.
**rape** *n.* an annual of the cabbage family.
**rap•id** *a.* very quick; hurried; descending steeply. **-s** *n.pl.* part of a river where current rushes over rocks. **-ity** *n.* **-ly** *adv.* **-ness** *n.*
**ra•pi•er** *n.* a light, slender, pointed sword, for thrusting only.
**rap•ine** *n.* act of plundering; pillage; plunder.
**rap•port** *n.* harmony; agreement.
**rapt** *a.* intent; in a state of rapture. **-ure** *n.* extreme joy; exultation. **-urous** *a.* exulting. **-urously** *adv.*
**rare** *a.* underdone (of meat).
**rare** *a.* uncommon; thin, not dense, as air; extremely valuable. **-faction** *n.* decrease of quantity of a gas in fixed volume. **-fy** *v.t.* to make less dense; *v.i.* to become less dense. **-ly** *adv.* **-ness** *n.* **rarity** *n.* state of being rare; something seldom seen.
**ras•cal** *n.* a rogue; *a.* dishonest; low. **-ity** *n.* base villainy. **-ly** *a.*
**rash** *a.* without reflection; precipitate. **-ly** *adv.* **-ness** *n.*
**rash** *n.* a temporary eruption of the skin.
**rash•er** *n.* a thin slice of bacon.
**rasp** *v.t.* to file; to scrape (skin) roughly; to speak in grating manner; a rough, grating sound. **-ing** *a.* irritating. **-ingly** *adv.*
**rasp•ber•ry** *n.* a plant, cultivated for its fruit; a small drupe, the fruit of the plant.
**rat** *n.* large rodent; *v.i.* to hunt rats; to abandon associates in times of difficulty. **-ting** *pr.p.* **-ted** *pa.t.* and *pa.p.* **-ter** *n.* a terrier which kills rats. **-ting** *n.*
**ratch•et** *n.* a piece of mechanism turning at

one end upon a pivot, while the other end falls into teeth of wheel, allowing the latter to move in one direction only.

ratchet

**rate** *n.* established measure; proportion; value; movement, as fast or slow; *v.t.* to estimate value; to settle relative rank, price or position of; *v.i.* to be set in a class; to have rank. **-able, ratable** *a.* **ratability** *n.* **rating** *n.* assessment; amount set as a rate.

**rate** *v.i.* to take to task; to chide.

**rath•er** *adv.* preferably; on the other hand; somewhat.

**rat•i•fy** *v.t.* to sanction officially; to make valid. **ratification** *n.*

**rat•ing** See **rate.**

**ra•tio** *n.* relation one quantity has to another; proportion.

**ra•ti•oc•i•nate** *v.i.* to reason logically. **ratiocination** *n.* deductive reasoning. **ratiocinative** *a.*

**ra•tion** *n.* fixed allotted portion; *pl.* provisions; *v.t.* to limit to fixed amount.

**ra•tio•nal** *a.* reasonable; *(Math.)* a quantity expressed in finite terms. **-e** *n.* logical basis; exposition of principles. **-ization** *n.* in psychology, the attempt to square one's conscience by inventing reasons for one's own conduct. **-ize** *v.t.* **-ism** *n.* philosophy which makes reason the sole guide. **-ist, -istic(al)** *a.* **-istically** *adv.* **-ity** *n.* the faculty of reasoning; soundness of mind. **-ly** *adv.*

**rat•tan, ratan** *n.* a species of palm found in India and the Malay Peninsula; the stems used for wickerwork, etc.

**rat•tle** *v.i.* to clatter; to move along, quickly and noisily; *v.t.* to shake briskly; *n.* a rapid succession of clattering sounds; a toy for making a noise; rings at the end of a rattlesnake's tail. **-brained, -headed, -pated** *a.* empty-headed; lacking stability. **-snake** *n.* an American poisonous snake. **rattling** *n.* clattering; *a.* brisk; *adv.* extremely.

**rau•cous** *a.* hoarse; rough. **-ly** *adv.*

**rav•age** *v.t.* to lay waste; to plunder; *n.* destruction.

**rave** *v.i.* to talk in delirium. **-r** *n.* **raving** *n.* incoherent talk; *a.* delirious; exceptional. **ravingly** *adv.*

**rav•el** *v.t.* to entangle; to fray out; *v.i.* to become twisted and involved; *n.* complication.

**ra•ven** *n.* crow with glossy black plumage, predatory in habit; *a.* glossy black.

**rav•en, ravin** *v.t.* and *v.i.* to prowl for prey; *n.* rapine; spoil. **-er** *n.* a plunderer. **-ous** *a.* famished; eager for prey. **-ously** *adv.*

**ra•vine** *n.* a deep, narrow gorge.

**rav•ish** *v.t.* to seize and carry away by violence. **-er** *n.* **-ing** *a.* entrancing; captivating. **-ingly** *adv.* **-ment** *n.*

**raw** *a.* not cooked; not covered with skin; not manufactured; *n.* naked state. **-boned** *a.* having little flesh; gaunt. **-hide** *n.* compressed untanned leather. **-ly** *adv.* **-ness** *n.* — **deal,** unfair and undeserved treatment.

**ray** *n.* beam of light; the path along which light and electromagnetic waves travel in space; a gleam (of hope, truth, etc.); *v.t.* and *v.i.* to radiate; to send forth rays. **-ed** *a.* having rays.

**ray•on** *n.* a synthetic fibrous material in imitation of silk.

**raze, rase** *v.t.* to level to the ground; to demolish.

**ra•zor** *n.* a keen-edged cutting appliance for shaving.

**razz** *v.t.* to ridicule.

**reach** *v.t.* to stretch; to touch by extending hand; to come to; *v.i.* to stretch out the hand; to arrive; *n.* easy distance; scope; grasp. **-able** *a.*

**re•act** *v.i.* to respond to stimulus; to exercise a reciprocal effect on each other; *(Chem.)* to undergo a chemical or physical change when brought in contact with another substance. **-ance** *n.* *(Elect.)* resistance in a coil to an alternating current due to capacity in the circuit. **-ion** *n.* response to stimulus, events, etc. **-ionary** *a.* tendency to reaction; *n.* one opposed to progressive ideas in politics, thought, etc. **-ionist** *n.* -ivation *n.* restoration to an activated state. **-ive** *a.*

**re•act** *v.t.* to act again.

**re•ac•tor** *n.* apparatus for generating heat by nuclear fission.

**read** *v.t.* to peruse and understand printed matter; to understand any indicating instrument (as a gas meter); *v.i.* to perform the act of reading; to find mentioned in print; to surmise. **read** *pa.t.* and *pa.p.; a.* versed in books; learned. **-able** *a.* informative; interesting; legible. **-ably** *adv.* **-er** *n.* one who reads; one who determines suitability for publication of manuscripts offered to publisher; corrector of printer's proofs. **-ing** *a.* pert. to reading; *n.* a public recital of passages from books.

**read•i•ly, readiness** *See* **ready.**

**re•ad•just** *v.t.* to put in order again. **-ment** *n.*

**read•y** *a.* prepared; fitted for use; willing; *v.t.* to prepare. *n.* position of fighting unit. **readily** *adv.* **readiness** *n.*

**re•a•gent** *n.* substance to bring about a characteristic reaction in chemical analysis. **reagency** *n.*

**re•al** *a.* actual; not fictitious or imaginary; denoting property not movable or personal, as lands and tenements. **-ity** *n.* actuality; truth. **-ly** *adv.* actually; *interj.* is that so? **-ty** *n.* real estate. — **estate,** — **property** *n.* immovable property.

**re•al•i•ty, re•al•al•ty** See **real.**

**re•al•ize** *v.t.* to make real; to yield (profit); to apprehend the significance of. **realization** *n.* **realism** *n.* interest in things as they are; practical outlook on life. **realist** *n.* **realistic** *a.* factual; true to life. **realistically** *adv.*

**realm** *n.* kingdom.

**ream** *n.* a paper measure containing usually 500 sheets.

**ream** *v.t.* to enlarge a tapered or conical hole with a reamer. **-er** *n.* a machine tool for enlarging a hole.

**reap** *v.t.* to cut down ripe grain for harvesting; to receive as fruits of one's labor. **-er** *n.* a harvester; a reaping machine.

**rear** *n.* back of hindmost part. **-most** *a.* at the very back.

**rear** *v.t.* to bring to maturity, as young; *v.i.* to rise up on the hind legs, as a horse.

**re•arm** *v.t.* to equip the fighting services with new weapons. **-ament** *n.*

**re•ar•range** *v.t.* to set in a different order. **-ment** *n.*

**rea•son** *n.* a faculty of thinking; power of understanding; cause; purpose; *v.i.* to exercise rational faculty; to deduce from premises; *v.t.* to discuss by arguments. **-able** *a.* rational; fair. **-ableness** *n.* **-ably** *adv.* **-er, -ing** *n.*

**re•as•sure** *v.t.* to allay anxiety; to restore confidence. **reassurance** *n.* **reassuring** *a.*

**re•bate** *v.t.* to allow as discount; *n.* deduction.

**re•bate** See **rabbet.**

**reb•el** *n.* one who resists the lawful authority; revolutionist; one who is defiant; *a.* rebellious; *v.i.* to revolt. **-ling** *pr.p.* **-led** *pa.t.* and *pa.p.* **-lion** *n.* organized resistance to authority; mutiny. **-lious** *a.*

**re•birth** *n.* state of being born again, spiritually; renaissance.

**re•bound** *v.i.* to leap back; *v.t.* to cause to fly back; *n.* rebounding; recoil.

**re•buff** *n.* a blunt contemptuous refusal; *v.t.* to beat back.

**re•buke** *v.t.* to censure; to reprove; *n.* reprimand; reproof.

**re•but** *v.t.* to disprove. **-ting** *pr.p.* **-ted** *pa.t.* and *pa.p.* **-table** *a.* **-tal** *n.* refutation of an argument.

**re•cal•ci•trate** *v.i.* to be refractory. **recalcitrant** *n.* one who defies authority; *a.* willfully disobedient. **recalcitrance, recalcitration** *n.*

**re•call** *v.t.* to take back (a gift, etc.); to revoke; to remember; *n.* a summons to return.

**re•cant** *v.t.* to take back, words or opinions. **-ation** *n.*

**re•ca•pit•u•late** *v.t.* to relate in brief the matter of a previous discourse; *v.i.* to sum up what has been previously said. **recapitulation** *n.*

**re•cap•ture** *v.t.* to capture back; *n.* act of retaking.

**re•cast** *v.t.* to remodel; to throw back.

**re•cede** *v.i.* to retreat; to ebb. **receding** *a.*

**re•ceipt** *n.* a written acknowledgment of money received; *pl.* money received; *v.t.* to give a receipt for.

**re•ceive** *v.t.* to accept; to get (an offer, etc.); to welcome. **receivable** *a.* **-r** *n.* one who receives; receptacle, place of storage, etc.; earpiece of a telephone. **receiving** *n.*

**re•cent** *a.* that has lately happened. **-ly** *adv.* **-ness** *n.*

**re•cep•ta•cle** *n.* a vessel—that which receives, or into which anything is received and held.

**re•cep•tion** *n.* receiving; ceremonial occasion when guests are personally announced; the quality of signals received in broadcasting. **receptible** *a.* receivable. **-ist** *n.* person in hotel, office, who receives guests or clients. **receptive** *a.* able to grasp ideas quickly. **receptiveness, receptivity** *n.*

**re•cess** *n.* a withdrawing from usual activity; vacation, as of legislative body or school; a niche in a wall; *(Zool.)* a small indentation in an organ; *v.i.* to go on a recess. **-ed** *a.* fitted with recess. **-ion** *n.* act of withdrawing; a period of reduced business; a procession at the close of a service. **-ional** *a.* pert. to recession; *n.* hymn sung as clergyman leaves chancel. **-ive** *a.* **iveness** *n.*

**rec•i•pe** *n.* a prescription; a cookery receipt.

**re•cip•i•ent** *a.* receptive; *n.* one who receives.

**re•cip•ro•cal** *a.* moving backwards and forwards; mutual; *n.* idea alternating with another by contrast. **-ly** *adv.* **-ness** *n.* **reciprocate** *v.t.* to interchange; *v.i.* to move backwards and forwards; to alternate. **reciprocating, reciprocatory** *a.* **reciprocation** *n.* mutual giving and receiving. **reciprocative** *a.* **reciprocity** *n.* action and reaction; in international trade, equal advantages gained by abolition of protective duties.

**re•ci•sion** *n.* the act of cutting.

**re•cite** *v.t.* and *v.i.* to repeat aloud before an audience. **recital** *n.* detailed narration; a musical or dramatic performance by one person. **recitation** *n.* repetition of something from memory. **recitative** *n.* declamation to musical accompaniment, as in opera; *a.* in the style of recitative. **-r** *n.*

**reck** *v.t.* and *v.i.* *(Arch.)* to heed. **-less** *a.* rashly negligent. **-lessly** *adv.* **-lessness** *n.*

**reck•on** *v.t.* and *v.i.* to calculate; to estimate; to be of opinion. **-er** *n.* table of calculations. **-ing** *n.* computing; a bill.

**re•claim** *v.t.* to win back from error or sin. **-able** *a.* able to be reformed. **reclamation** *n.*

**re•claim** *v.t.* to demand the return of.

**re•cline** *v.t.* to lean back; *v.i.* to rest. **-r** *n.*

**re•cluse** *a.* secluded from the world; *n.* a hermit.

**rec•og•nize** *v.t.* to identify; to acknowledge. **recognizable** *a.* **recognizably** *adv.* **recognizance** *n.* acknowledgment of a person or thing; sum pledged as surety. **recognition** *n.* acknowledgment. **recognitive, recognitory** *a.*

**re•coil** *v.i.* to roll, bound, fall back; *n.* return motion.

**rec•ol•lect** *v.t.* to recall; to remember. **-ion** *n.* power of recalling ideas to the mind; things remembered.

**rec•om•mend** *v.t.* to speak well of; to advise. **-able** *a.* worthy of recommendation. **-ation** *n.* statement that one is worthy of favor.

**rec•om•pense** *v.t.* to reward, to make an equivalent return for service; *n.* repayment; requital.
**rec•on•cile** *v.t.* to conciliate; to make agree; to adjust or compose. **reconcilable** *a.* **-ment, reconciliation** *n.* harmonizing of apparently opposed ideas. **reconciliatory** *a.*
**re•con•dite** *a.* hidden from view or mental perception. **-ness** *n.*
**re•con•di•tion** *v.t.* to restore to sound condition; to repair.
**re•con•nais•sance** *n.* an examination by land or air, for military operations.
**re•con•sid•er** *v.t.* to take up for renewed discussion.
**re•con•sti•tute** *v.t.* to constitute anew; to reconstruct.
**re•con•struct** *v.t.* to rebuild. **reconstruction** *n.*
**re•cord** *v.t.* to commit to writing; to make a note of; to inscribe; to make a sound record; *v.i.* to speak, sing, etc. for reproduction on a record; *n.* register; authentic copy of any writing; finest performance or highest amount ever known; a disk, cylinder, for mechanical reproduction of sound; *pl.* public documents. **-er** *n.* one who registers transactions; instrument which transforms sounds into disk impressions. **-ing** *n.* reproduction of sound by mechanical means. **off the record,** unofficial.
**re•count** *v.t.* to relate; to enumerate; *n.* a second enumeration.
**re•coup** *v.t.* to recover equivalent for what has been lost.
**re•course** *n.* application made to another in distress; person or thing resorted to.
**re•cov•er** *v.t.* to get back; to reclaim; *v.i.* to regain health or a former state. **-able** *a.* **-y** *n.* regaining, or obtaining possession; restoration to health.
**re•cov•er** *v.t.* to cover again.
**rec•re•ant** *a.* cowardly; *n.* a craven; an apostate. **recreancy** *n.*
**re•cre•ate** *v.t.* to give fresh life to; to refresh from weariness. **recreation** *n.* any pleasurable interest; amusement. **recreational** *a.*
**re•crim•i•nate** *v.t.* and *v.i.* to charge an accuser with a similar crime. **recrimination** *n.* a countercharge brought by the accused against the accuser. **recriminative, recriminatory** *a.*
**re•cruit** *v.t.* to enlist persons for army, navy, etc.; *v.i.* to gain health, spirits, etc.; *n.* a newly enlisted soldier. **-ing, -ment** *n.*
**rect•an•gle** *n.* a four-sided figure with four right angles. **rectangular** *a.*
**rec•ti•fy** *v.t.* to correct; to convert an alternating current of electricity into a direct current. **rectifiable** *a.* **rectification** *n.* **rectifier** *n.* one who corrects; a device which rectifies.
**rec•ti•lin•e•al, rectilinear** *a.* bounded by straight lines.
**rec•ti•tude** *n.* honesty of purpose.
**rec•to** *n.* the right-hand page of an open book.
**rec•tor** *n.* clergyman (as of Episcopal Church) who has charge of a parish. **-y** *n.* house of a rector.
**rec•tum** *n.* lower end of the large intestine; *pl.* **recta. rectal** *a.*
**re•cum•bent** *a.* reclining; lying on back.
**re•cu•per•ate** *v.i.* to win back health and strength. **recuperation** *n.* convalescence. **recuperative** *a.*
**re•cur** *v.i.* to happen again. **-ring** *pr.p.* **-red** *pa.t.* and *pa.p.* **-rence, -rency** *n.* **-rent** *a.* returning periodically.
**re•curve** *v.t.* to bend backwards.
**red** *a.* (*comp.* **-der**; *superl.* **-dest**) of the color of arterial blood, rubies, glowing fire, etc.; connected with bloodshed, revolution, left-wing politics, etc.; *n.* color of blood; a danger signal. **-den** *v.t.* to make red; *v.t.* to become red; to blush. **-ness** *n.* quality of being red. **—blooded** *a.* vigorous; manly. **-breast** *n.* the robin. **-coat** *n.* a British soldier, because of the bright scarlet tunic. **— corpuscle** *n.* a colored blood corpuscle, containing hemoglobin and carrying oxygen. **Red Cross** *n.* international emblem of organization for relief of sick and wounded in wartime and for helping distressed persons in emergencies, as floods. **— hat** *n.* cardinal's hat. **— heat** *n.* temperature of a body emitting red rays, about 700-800° C. **— herring** *n.* the common herring, cured by drying, smoking and salting. **— hot** *a.* heated to redness; enthusiastic. **— pepper** *n.* seasoning, such as cayenne. **— tape** *n.* adherence to official regulations, fr. red tape used for tying up government documents. **-wing** *n.* a blackbird with a red patch on wings. **-wood** *n.* the sequoia tree of California, a gigantic evergreen coniferous tree.
**re•dact** *v.t.* to digest or reduce to order, literary, or scientific materials. **-ion** *n.* **-or** *n.* an editor.
**re•deem** *v.t.* to regain, as mortgaged property, by paying principal, interest and costs of mortgage; to deliver from sin; to recover. **-able** *a.* **-ableness** *n.* **-er** *n.*
**re•demp•tion** *n.* buying back; salvation. **-er** *n.* one who has redeemed himself. **redemptive** *a.* redeeming. **redemptory** *a.*
**red•in•te•grate** *v.t.* to make whole again. **redintegration** *n.*
**re•di•rect** *v.t.* to readdress a communication. **-ion** *n.*
**re•dis•trib•ute** *v.t.* to apportion again. **redistribution** *n.*
**red•o•lent** *a.* diffusing a strong or fragrant odor. **redolence** *n.*
**re•doubt** *n.* a central part within fortifications for a final stand by the defenders.
**re•doubt•able** *a.* dreaded; valiant.
**re•dound** *v.i.* to turn to; to conduce (to); to recoil.
**re•draft** *v.t.* to draw up a second time; *n.* a new bill of exchange.
**re•dress** *v.t.* to make amends for; *n.* reparation; remedy. **-er** *n.* **-ible** *a.*
**re•duce** *v.t.* to diminish in number, length, quantity, value, price, etc.; (*Chem.*) to remove oxygen or add hydrogen; to

decrease valency number. **-d** *a.* **reducible** *a.* **reduction** *n.* subjugation; diminution; amount by which something is reduced. **reductive** *a.* having the power of reducing. **reductively** *adv.* **reducing agent** *n.* a reagent for abstracting oxygen or adding hydrogen.

**re•dun•dant** *a.* superfluous; using more words than necessary for complete meaning. **redundance, redundancy** *n.* **-ly** *adv.*

**re•ech•o** *v.t.* to echo back.

**reed** *n.* a tall hollow-stemmed grass growing in marshes; in certain wind instruments, a thin strip of metal which vibrates and produces a musical sound; a musical instrument made of the hollow joint of some plant; *pl.* a molding; *v.t.* to fit with a reed. **-ed** *a.* covered with reeds; molded like reeds. **-iness** *n.* **— instrument** *n.* *(Mus.)* a wind instrument played by means of a reed. **— pipe** *n.* organ pipe whose tone is produced by vibration of metal tongue. **— stop** *n.* organ stop owing its tone to vibration of little metal tongues. **-y** *a.*

**reef** *n.* a portion of square sail which can be rolled up and made fast to the boom; *v.t.* to reduce the area of sail by taking in a reef. **-er** *n.* a sailor's close-fitting jacket.

**reef** *n.* a ridge of rock near the surface of the sea.

**reek** *n.* fume; *v.i.* to smell strongly unpleasant. **-ing, -y** *a.*

**reel** *n.* bobbin on which yarn is wound; in motion pictures, a flanged spool on which film is wound; a portion of film; *v.t.* to draw (in) by means of a reel.

**reel** *v.i.* to stagger; to be dizzy.

**re•fec•tion** *n.* a simple repast. **refectory** *n.* a hall in a monastery, convent, or college where meals are served.

**re•fer** *v.t.* and *v.i.* to have relation to; to offer, as testimony in evidence of character; to allude (to). **-ring** *pr.p.* **-red** *pa.t.* and *pa.p.* **-able, -rable** *a.* may be assigned to. **-ee** *n.* a neutral judge in various sports. **-ence** *n.* appeal to the judgment of another; a passage in a book to which reader is referred; a testimonial. **-endum** *n.* vote for ascertaining the public will on a single definite issue. **-ential** *a.* used for reference.

**re•fine** *v.t.* to reduce crude metals to a finer state; to improve; to free from coarseness; *v.i.* to improve in accuracy, or good taste. **-d** *a.* clarified; well-bred. **-dly** *adv.* **-ment** *n.* **-ry** *n.* place where process of refining sugar, oil, is effected.

**re•flect** *v.t.* to throw back rays of light, heat or sound, from surfaces; to mirror; *v.i.* to consider attentively; to disparage. **-ed** *a.* **-ing** *a.* thoughtful; throwing back rays of light, etc. **-ingly** *adv.* **-ion** *n.* return of rays of heat or light, or waves of sound, from a surface; image given back from mirror or other reflecting surface; contemplation. **-ive** *a.* meditative; reciprocal. **-ively** *adv.* **-iveness** *n.* **-or** *n.* a reflecting surface.

**re•flex** *a.* turned, bent, or directed backwards; produced by reaction; *(Anat.)* denoting the involuntary action of the motor nerves under a stimulus from the sensory nerves; involuntary; *n.* a reflex action; *v.t.* to bend back; to reflect. **-ible** *a.* **-ibility** *n.* **-ive** *a.* bending or turned backwards. **-ively, -ly** *adv.* **conditioned reflex,** reflex action due to power of association and suggestion.

**re•flux** *n.* a flowing back; ebbing.

**re•form** *v.t.* to amend; to improve; *v.i.* to amend one's ways; to improve; *n.* improvement; correction. **-able** *a.* **-ation** *n.* reforming; change for the better. **-ative** *a.* aiming at reform. **-atory** *a.* tending to reform; *n.* institution for reforming young lawbreakers. **-ed** *a.* amended; reclaimed. **-er** *n.* an advocate of reform.

**re•fract** *v.t.* to cause to deviate from a direct course, as rays of light on passing from one medium to another. **-able, -ed** *a.* **-ing** *a.* serving to refract; refractive. **-ion** *n.* **-tive** *a.* **-or** *n.*

**re•frac•to•ry** *a.* suitable for lining furnaces because of resistance to fusion at very high temperatures; *(Med.)* resistant to treatment. **refractorily** *adv.*

**re•frain** *v.i.* to abstain. **-ment** *n.*

**re•frain** *n.* chorus recurring at end of each verse of song.

**re•fran•gi•ble** *a.* able to be refracted.

**re•fresh** *v.t.* to revive; to freshen up. **-er** *n.* one who, or that which, refreshes. **-ing** *a.* invigorating. **-ment** *n.* that which adds fresh vigor, as rest, drink, or food—hence, *pl.* food and drink.

**re•frig•er•ate** *v.t.* to preserve food by cooling; *v.i.* to become cold. **refrigerant** *a.* **refrigeration** *n.* **refrigerative, refrigeratory** *a.* cooling. **refrigerator** *n.* apparatus and plant for the manufacture of ice; chamber for preserving food by mechanical production of low temperatures.

**ref•uge** *n.* shelter; retreat. **-e** *n.* one who flees to a place of safety.

**re•ful•gent** *a.* shining. **refulgence** *n.* splendor. Also **refulgency.**

**re•fund** *v.t.* to return compensation for; to repay. **refund** *n.* repayment.

**re•fur•bish** *v.t.* to furbish up again; to renovate.

**re•fuse** *v.t.* to deny or reject; *v.i.* not to comply. **refusal** *n.* act of refusing; the first chance of accepting or declining an offer.

**ref•use** *a.* worthless; *n.* waste matter.

**re•fuse** *v.t.* of metals, to fuse again. **refusion** *n.*

**re•fute** *v.t.* to prove to be false. **refutable** *a.* capable of being refuted. **refutably** *adv.* **refutation** *n.*

**re•gain** *v.t.* to retrieve; to reach again.

**re•gal** *a.* pert. to a king; royal. **-ia** *n.pl.* insignia of royalty. **-ity** *n.* sovereignty **-ly** *adv.*

**re•gale** *v.t.* to entertain in sumptuous manner; *v.i.* to feast.

**re•gard** *v.t.* to consider; to pay respect to; *n.* aspect; esteem; concern; *pl.* good wishes. **-able** *a.* **-ful** *a.* heedful. **-fully** *adv.* **-ing** *prep.* concerning—also **in,**

**with, regard to, as regards. -less** *a.* without regard; neglectful. **-lessly** *adv.*
**re•gat•ta** *n.* boat races.
**re•gen•cy** See **regent.**
**re•gen•er•ate** *v.t.* and *v.i.* to give fresh life or vigor to; to cause to be born again; *a.* born anew; changed from a natural to a spiritual state; regenerated. **regeneracy, regeneration** *n.* **regenerative** *a.*
**re•gent** *a.* holding the office of regent; *n.* one who governs a kingdom during the minority, absence, or disability of sovereign. **regency** *n.* office of a regent.
**reg•i•cide** *n.* one who kills, or the killing of, a king. **regicidal** *a.*
**re•gime** *n.* style of rule or management.
**reg•i•men** *n.* orderly government; systematic method of dieting, exercising.
**reg•i•ment** *n.* a body of soldiers commanded by a senior officer; *v.t.* to systematize. **-al** *a.* **-ation** *n.* thorough systemization.
**re•gion** *n.* territory of indefinite extent; part of body. **-al** *a.* **-ally** *adv.*
**reg•is•ter** *n.* an official record; book in which a record is kept; an alphabetical index; a metal damper to close a heating duct; *v.t.* to record; to indicate, by cash register, scales, etc., by facial expression. **registrable, -ed** *a.* **registrant** *n.* one who registers. **registrar** *n.* an official who keeps a record. **registration** *n.* record; total entries registered. **registry** *n.* office for registering births, deaths and marriages. **-ed mail,** a method of postal delivery by which mail is insured against loss or damage in transit.
**reg•nal** *a.* pert. to reign of monarch. **regnancy** *n.* reign.
**re•gress** *n.* the power of passing back; reentry; *v.i.* to fall back; to return to a former state. **-ion** *n.* returning; retrogression. **-ive** *a.*
**re•gret** *v.t.* to grieve over; *n.* grief; sorrow; remorse. **-ting** *pr.p.* **-ted** *pa.t.* and *pa.p.* **-ful** *a.* **-fully** *adv.* **-table** *a.* lamentable. **-tably** *adv.* **-ter** *n.*
**reg•u•lar** *a.* conforming to, governed by rule; periodical; habitual. **-ization** *n.* **-ity** *n.* uniformity. **-ly** *adv.*
**reg•u•late** *v.t.* to adjust by rule, method, etc.; to control. **regulation** *n.* state of being reduced to order; a law. **regulator** *n.*
**re•gur•gi•tate** *v.t.* to throw, flow, or pour back in great quantity; *v.i.* to be thrown back. **regurgitation** *n.*
**re•ha•bil•i•tate** *v.t.* to restore to former position; to recondition. **rehabilitation** *n.*
**re•hash** *v.t.* to mix together and use a second time.
**re•hearse** *v.t.* and *v.i.* to repeat aloud; to recite; to narrate. **rehearsal** *n.* trial performance of a play, opera, etc.
**re•i•fy** *v.t.* to make concrete. **reification** *n.*
**reign** *n.* the period during which a sovereign occupies throne; *v.i.* to possess sovereign power.
**re•im•burse** *v.t.* to refund; to give the equivalent of. **-ment** *n.* **-r** *n.*
**rein** *n.* strap of bridle to govern a horse; restraint; *pl.* means of exercising power.
**re•in•car•nate** *v.t.* to embody again in the flesh. **reincarnation** *n.*
**rein•deer** *n.* large deer of colder regions.

reindeer

**re•in•force** *v.t.* to strengthen with new force; to increase. **-ment** *n.*
**re•in•state** *v.t.* to restore to former position. **-ment** *n.*
**re•is•sue** *v.t.* to republish; *n.* a reprint.
**re•it•er•ate** *v.t.* to repeat again and again. **reiterant** *a.* **reiteration** *n.*
**re•ject** *v.t.* to throw away; to refuse; *n.* a person or thing rejected as not up to standard. **-ion** *n.*
**re•joice** *v.t.* to give joy to; to cheer; *v.i.* to triumph. **rejoicing** *n.* act of expressing joy; *pl.* festivities.
**re•join** *v.t.* to unite again; to meet again; *v.i.* to become united again; to reply. **-der** *n.* an answer to a reply.
**re•ju•ve•nate** *v.t.* to make young again. **rejuvenation, rejuvenator** *n.* **rejuvenesce** *v.i.* to grow young again. **rejuvenescence** *n.* **rejuvenescent** *a.*
**re•lapse** *v.i.* to slide back, esp. into state of ill health, evil ways; *n.* a falling back.
**re•late** *v.t.* to establish relation between; *v.i.* to refer (to). **-d** *a.* connected by blood or marriage; akin. **relation** *n.* telling; *pl.* dealings between persons or nations; connection between things; a relative. **relational** *a.* indicating some relation. **relationship** *n.*
**rel•a•tive** *a.* dependent on relation to something else, not absolute; *n.* a person connected by blood. **-ly** *adv.* comparatively. **-ness** *n.* **relativity** *n.* doctrine that all observable motion, and time, are relative.
**re•lax** *v.t.* to make less stern; to loosen; *v.i.* to unbend; to ease up. **-ation** *n.* recreation. **-ing** *a.*
**re•lay** *n.* supplies conveniently stored at successive stages of a route; a device for making or breaking a local electrical circuit; a low-powered broadcasting station which broadcasts programs originating in another station; *v.t.* to pass on, as a message, broadcast, etc. **— race,** a race between teams of which each runner does a part of the distance.
**re•lease** *v.t.* to set free; to exempt from obligation; *n.* liberation; exemption; a catch for controlling mechanical parts of a machine; *(Law)* a surrender of a claim. **releasable** *a.*
**rel•e•gate** *v.t.* to send away; to demote. **relegation** *n.*
**re•lent** *v.i.* to give up harsh intention. **-less** *a.* showing no sympathy. **-lessly** *adv.* **-lessness** *n.*
**rel•e•vant** *a.* pertinent. **relevance,**

**relevancy** *n.* **-ly** *adv.*
**re•li•a•ble** *a.* trustworthy; creditable. **-ness, reliability** *n.* **reliably** *adv.* **reliance** *n.* trust; dependence. **reliant** *a.*
**rel•ic** *n.* something surviving from the past.
**re•lief** *n.* alleviation of pain, distress; one who relieves another at his post. — **map** *n.* a map showing the elevations and depressions of a country in relief.
**re•lieve** *v.t.* to alleviate; to remedy. **relieving** *a.* serving to relieve.
**re•li•gion** *n.* recognition of God as object of worship; any system of faith and worship. **-ist, -ary, -er** *n.* one who makes inordinate professions of religion. **religiosity** *n.* sense of, or tendency towards, religiousness. **religious** *a.* pert. to religion; pious. **religiously** *adv.*
**re•lin•quish** *v.t.* to give up; to yield. **-er, -ment** *n.*
**rel•i•quar•y** *n.* a shrine.
**rel•ish** *v.t.* to taste with pleasure; *v.t.* to have a pleasing taste; *n.* savor; what is used to make food more palatable, as sauce.
**re•luc•tant** *a.* unwilling; disinclined. **reluctance** *n.* **reluctancy** *n.* **-ly** *adv.*
**re•ly** *v.i.* to trust; to depend; **relier** *n.*
**re•main** *v.i.* to stay; to continue or endure; *n.pl.* a corpse. **-der** *n.* what remains; remnant.
**re•mand** *v.t.* to send back; *n.* such a recommital.
**re•mark** *v.t.* to take notice of; to express in words or writing; to comment. **-able** *a.* extraordinary. **-ableness** *n.* **-ably** *adv.*
**rem•e•dy** *n.* a means of curing or relieving a disease; legal means to recover a right; antidote; *v.t.* to restore to health; to put right; *a.* curable. **remedial** *a.* affording a remedy.
**re•mem•ber** *v.t.* to retain in the memory; *v.i.* to have in mind. **-able** *a.* **remembrance** *n.* act of remembering; recollection; keepsake.
**re•mind** *v.t.* to cause to remember. **-er** *n.* that which reminds.
**rem•i•nis•cence** *n.* a recollection of past events; *pl.* memoirs. **reminiscent** *a.*
**re•mise** *v.t.* to remit; to surrender (property, etc.) by deed; *n.* *(Law)* a surrender.
**re•miss** *a.* not exact in duty; careless. **-ful** *a.* **-ible** *a.* able to be remitted. **-ion** *n.* act of remitting; abatement; period of moderation of intensity of a disease; pardon. **-ive** *a.* **-ly** *adv.* **-ness** *n.*
**re•mit** *v.t.* to send back; to transmit to a distance, as money bills; to slacken (efforts); *v.i.* to slacken off. **-ting** *pa.p.* **-ted** *pa.t.* and *pa.p.* **-tal** *n.* act of remitting to another court. **-tance** *n.* transmitting money, bills, to a distant place; the money sent. **-tent** *a.* increasing and decreasing at periodic intervals.
**rem•nant** *n.* fragment of cloth; remainder.
**re•mon•strate** *v.t.* to make evident by strong protestations; *v.i.* to speak strongly against. **remonstrance** *n.* protest. **remonstrant** *n.* one who remonstrates; *a.* expostulatory. **remonstration** *n.* **remonstrative, remonstratory** *a.*
**re•morse** *n.* self-reproach excited by sense of guilt; repentance. **-ful** *a.* repentant. **-fully** *adv.* **-less** *a.* relentless.
**re•mote** *a.* far back in time or space; **-ly** *adv.* **-ness** *n.* — **control,** control of apparatus from a distance.
**re•move** *v.t.* to take or put away; to extract; *v.i.* to change residence; *n.* removal; a step in any scale of gradation. **removable** *a.* not permanently fixed. **removal** *n.* dismissal from a post. **-d** *a.* denoting distance of relationship. **-r** *n.*
**re•mu•ner•ate** *v.t.* to reward for services; to compensate. **remunerable** *a.* that may, or should be, remunerated. **remuneration** *n.* recompense; salary. **remunerative** *a.*
**ren•ais•sance** *(Cap.)* *n.* a rebirth; a period of intellectual revival; *a.* pert. to renaissance. Also **renascence.**
**re•nal** *a.* pert. to kidneys.
**re•nas•cent** *a.* regaining lost vigor. **renascence** *n.* See **renaissance.**
**rend** *v.t.* to pull to pieces; to lacerate. **rent** *pa.t.* and *pa.p.*
**ren•der** *v.t.* to give in return; to deliver up; to portray; to extract animal fats by heating. **-able** *a.* **-er, -ing** *n.* **rendition** *n.* rendering.
**ren•dez•vous** *n.* an appointed place for meeting.
**ren•di•tion** See **render.**
**ren•e•gade** *n.* one faithless to principle or party; *a.* false. **renege** *v.t.* and *v.i.* to break a promise.
**re•new** *v.t.* and *v.i.* to restore; to renovate. **-able** *a.* **-al** *n.* restoration.
**ren•net** *n.* preparation used for curdling milk and in preparation of cheese; junket, etc.
**re•nounce** *v.t.* to disavow; to give up. **-ment, renunciation** *n.*
**ren•o•vate** *v.t.* to make as good as new; to overhaul and repair. **renovation** *n.*
**re•nown** *n.* great reputation. **-ed** *a.* eminent.
**rent** *n.* *pa.t.* and *pa.p.* of **rend;** *n.* an opening made by rending; a split; a rift.
**rent** *n.* a periodical payment at an agreed rate for use of something; *v.t.* to lease; *v.i.* to be leased. **-able** *a.* **-al** *n.* the amount of rent; *a.* pert. to rent. **-er** *n.* one who rents.
**re•nun•ci•a•tion** *n.* a surrender of claim or interest; repudiation. Also **renunciance. renunciative, renunciatory** *a.*
**re•or•ga•nize** *v.t.* to organize anew.
**re•pair** *v.t.* to restore to a sound state after injury; *n.* mending. **-able** *a.* **-er** *n.*
**rep•a•ra•ble** *a.* that can be made good. **reparably** *adv.* **reparation** *n.* making amends; compensation. **reparative** *a.*
**rep•ar•tee** *n.* apt, witty reply.
**re•past** *n.* a meal.
**re•pa•tri•ate** *v.t.* to restore to one's own country. **repatriation** *n.*
**re•pay** *v.t.* to pay back; to make return for; to require. **repaid** *pa.t.* and *pa.p.* **-able** *a.* **-ment** *n.*
**re•peal** *v.t.* to revoke, rescind, annul, as a law, or statute; to abrogate; *n.* revocation; abrogation. **-able** *a.*
**re•peat** *v.t.* to say or do again; to reiterate; frequent; recurring. **-edly** *adv.* **-er** *n.* one

*n.* repetition; encore. **-able** *a.* **-ed** *a.* who, or that which, repeats; fire alarm which may be discharged many times. **ing** *n.*

**re•pel** *v.t.* to drive back; to repulse; *v.i.* to cause repugnance. **-ling** *pr.p.* **-led** *pa.t.* and *pa.p.* **-lence, -lency** *n.* **-lent** *a.* driving back; *n.* that which repels. **-ler** *n.*

**re•pent** *v.t.* and *v.i.* to desire to change one's life as a result of sorrow for one's sins. **-ance** *n.* sorrow for a deed; penitence. **-ant** *a.*

**re•per•cus•sion** *n.* reverberation; indirect effect.

**rep•er•toire** *n.* list of musical works, dramatic roles, within sphere of an individual. **repertory** *n.* a repertoire; *a.* pert. to the stock plays of a resident company.

**rep•e•ti•tion** *n.* act of repeating; a copy. **repetitious** *a.* full of repetitions. **repetitive** *a.* involving much repetition.

**re•pine** *v.i.* to fret. **repining** *n.*

**re•place** *v.t.* to put back into place; to substitute for. **-able** *a.* **-ment** *n.* substitution.

**re•plen•ish** *v.t.* to fill up again; to supply. **-ment** *n.*

**re•plete** *a.* completely filled; surfeited. **-ness, repletion** *n.* satiety.

**rep•li•ca** *n.* exact copy of work of art by the artist of the original; facsimile. **-te** *v.t.* to duplicate. **-tion** *n.* an answer; a copy.

**re•ply** *v.t.* and *v.i.* to return an answer; to respond; *n.* answer; response.

**re•port** *v.t.* to take down in writing; to give an account of; *v.i.* to make official statement; to present oneself as to superior officer; *n.* an official statement of facts; reputation. **-er** *n.* one who reports, for newspapers.

**re•pose** *v.t.* to put trust (in). **reposit** *v.t.* to lodge, in a place of safety. **repository** *n.* place where valuables are deposited for safety.

**re•pose** *v.i.* to sleep; to recline; *v.t.* to lay at rest; *n.* sleep; relaxation. **reposal** *n.* **-ful** *a.* **-fully** *adv.*

**rep•re•hend** *v.t.* to find fault with; to rebuke. **reprehensible** *a.* blameworthy. **reprehensibly** *adv.* **reprehension** *n.* reproof.

**rep•re•sent** *v.t.* to express the image of; to be the agent for; to personate; to be the member for. **-able** *a.* **-ation** *n.* that which represents, as a picture; the act of representing. **-ational** *a.* **-ative** *a.* typical; exhibiting a likeness; *n.* an agent, delegate, or substitute.

**re•press** *v.t.* to keep under control; to quell. **-er, -or** *n.* **-ible** *a.* **-ibly** *adv.* **-ion** *n.* restraint; in psychoanalysis, the rejection from consciousness of anything unpleasant. **-ive** *a.*

**re•prieve** *v.t.* to commute a sentence; to grant temporary relief; *n.* temporary suspension of execution of sentence; relief.

**rep•ri•mand** *v.t.* to reprove severely; *n.* a sharp rebuke.

**re•print** *v.t.* to print again; *n.* new edition of any printed work.

**rep•pri•sal** *n.* an act of retaliation.

**re•proach** *v.t.* to rebuke; *n.* reproof; an object of scorn. **-ful** *a.* expressing censure. **-fully** *adv.* **-fulness** *n.*

**rep•ro•bate** *v.t.* to disapprove with signs of extreme dislike; cast off by God; *n.* scoundrel. **reprobation** *n.* condemnation; censure.

**re•pro•duce** *v.t.* to produce over again; *v.i.* to propagate; to generate. **reproducible** *a.* **reproduction** *n.* a facsimile; process of multiplication of living individuals whereby the species is perpetuated. **reproductive** *a.* pert. to reproduction; yielding profits.

**re•proof** *n.* reprimand; admonition. **reprove** *v.t.* to charge with a fault; to rebuke. **reprovable** *a.* deserving censure. **reproval** *n.*

**rep•tile** *n.* animal of class Reptilia, cold-blooded, air-breathing vertebrates which move on their bellies or by means of small, short legs.

**re•pub•lic** *n.* a state, in which supremacy of the people or its elected representatives is formally acknowledged; commonwealth. **-an** *a.* pert. to republic; *(Cap.)* one of the two traditional political parties of the U.S.A. **-anism** *n.*

**re•pu•di•ate** *v.t.* to reject; to disown. **repudiation** *n.*

**re•pug•nance** *n.* condition of being repugnant. **repugnancy** *n.* habitual feeling of aversion. **repugnant** *a.* distasteful in a high degree; adverse.

**re•pulse** *v.t.* to drive back; to repel decisively; *n.* act of driving off; rejection. **repulsion** *n.* act of driving back. **repulsive** *a.* loathsome. **repulsively** *adv.*

**re•pute** *v.t.* to account or consider; to reckon; *n.* good character; reputation; esteem. **reputation** *n.* estimation in which a person is held; reported character; good name; renown. **reputable** *a.* held in esteem; respectable; creditable. **reputably** *adv.* **reputedly** *adv.* generally believed.

**re•quest** *v.t.* to ask for earnestly; to petition; *n.* expression of desire for; demand. **-er** *n.*

**re•qui•em** *n.* (R.C.) celebration of the mass for soul of a dead person.

**re•quire** *v.t.* to claim as by right; to need. **-ment** *n.* what is required; an essential condition.

**req•ui•site** *a.* necessary; essential; *n.* something indispensable. **requisition** *n.* a written order for supplies; *v.t.* to demand certain supplies; to request formally; to seize. **requisitionist** *n.* one who makes a requisition.

**re•quite** *v.t.* to return an equivalent in good or evil; to make retaliation. **requital** *n.* that which repays; compensation.

**re•scind** *v.t.* to annul; to cancel; to abrogate. **-able** *a.* **recission** *n.* act of rescinding. **rescissory** *a.*

**re•script** *n.* an edict or decree.

**res•cue** *v.t.* to free from danger, or restraint; to deliver; *n.* deliverance. **-r** *n.*

**re•search** *n.* diligent inquiry; scientific investigation and study to discover facts;

*a.* pert. to research; *v.i.* to examine with care. **-er** *n.*

**re•seat** *v.t.* to provide with a new seat; to patch (trousers, etc.).

**re•sem•ble** *v.t.* similar to. **resemblance** *n.* similarity. **resembling** *a.*

**re•sent** *v.t.* to consider as an affront; to be angry at. **-er** *n.* **-ful** *a.* full of resentment. **-fully** *adv.* **-ment** *n.* deep sense of affront.

**re•serve** *v.t.* to set apart; to keep for future use; *a.* acting as a reserve; *n.* what is reserved; troops, held back from line of battle to assist when necessary. **reservation** *n.* booking of a hotel room, etc.; a condition; land reserved for some public use. **-d** *a.* booked; self-restrained; uncommunicative. **-dly** *adv.* **-dness** *n.* **reservist** *n.* a member of the armed forces belonging to reserves.

**res•er•voir** *n.* area for storage and filtering of water; a large supply.

**reservoir**

**re•set** *v.t.* to set again. **-ting** *pr.p.* **reset** *pa.p.* and *pa.t.*

**re•side** *v.i.* to dwell permanently; to be inherent in. **-nce** *n.* place where one resides; house. **-ncy** *n.* a residence. **-nt** *a.* dwelling; *n.* one who resides in a place. **-ntial** *a.* pert. to a part of a town consisting mainly of dwelling houses.

**res•i•due** *n.* balance. **residual** *a.* remaining after a part is taken away. **residuary** *a.* pert. to part remaining. **residuum** *n.* what is left after any process of separation.

**re•sign** *v.t.* and *v.i.* to relinquish formally (office, etc.); to give up. **-ation** *n.* giving up, as a claim, office, or place; endurance. **-ed** *a.* relinquished; patient. **-edly** *adv.*

**re•sile** *v.i.* to draw back from a previous offer; to recoil. **resilience, resiliency** *n.* elasticity, esp. of mind. **resilient** *a.* possessing power of quick recovery.

**res•in** *n.* term for brittle, thickened juices exuded by certain plants; *v.t.* to coat with resin.

**re•sist** *v.t.* and *v.i.* to oppose; to withstand; to strive against. **-ance** *n.* hindrance; power possessed by an individual to resist disease. **-ant** *n.* one who, or that which, resists; *a.* offering resistance. **-er** *n.* **-ibility, -ibleness** *n.* the quality of being resistible. **-ible** *a.* **-ibly, -ingly** *adv.* **-less** *a.* irresistible; unable to resist. **-lessly** *adv.* **-lessness** *n.* **-or** *n.* apparatus possessing resistance to electrical current. **-ance movement**, the organized, underground movement.

**res•o•lute** *a.* having a decided purpose; determined; *n.* a determined person. **-ly** *adv.* **-ness** *n.* determination. **resolution** *n.* intention; motion or declaration.

**re•solve** *v.t.* to solve and reduce to a different form; to make clear; to unravel; *v.i.* to purpose; to determine unanimously; *n.* act of resolving; firm determination. **resolvable** *a.* **-d** *a.* determined; resolute. **-dly** *adv.* **-dness** *n.*

**res•o•nant** *a.* resounding; ringing. **resonance** *n.*

**re•sort** *v.i.* to have recourse; *n.* a frequented place; vacation spot; aid.

**re•sound** *v.i.* to send back sound; *v.i.* to reverberate.

**re•source** *n.* that on which one depends, for supply or support; skill in improvising; *pl.* wealth. **-ful** *a.* clever in devising fresh expedients. **-fully** *adv.* **-fulness** *n.*

**re•spect** *v.t.* to esteem; to relate to; *n.* consideration; *pl.* expression of esteem. **-able** *a.* worthy of respect; reputable. **-ability, -ableness** *n.* **-ably** *adv.* **-ful** *a.* polite. **-fully** *adv.* **-fulness** *n.* **-ing** *prep.* concerning. **-ive** *a.* relative; not absolute. **-ively** *adv.* each.

**re•spire** *v.t.* and *v.i.* to breathe. **respirable** *a.* fit to be breathed. **respiration** *n.* process of breathing. **respirational** *a.* respiratory. **respirator** *n.* a device to produce artificial respiration. **respiratory** *a.* serving for, pert. to, respiration.

**re•spite** *n.* a temporary intermission; *v.t.* to reprieve.

**re•splen•dent** *a.* shining with brilliant luster. **resplendence, resplendency** *n.* **-ly** *adv.*

**re•spond** *v.i.* to reply; to correspond to; to react. **-ent** *a.* giving response; *n.* one who refutes in a debate.

**re•sponse** *n.* answer or reply. **responsibility** *n.* state of being responsible; duty; an obligation. **responsible** *a.* accountable; rational. **responsibly** *adv.* **responsive** *a.* able, ready, or inclined, to respond. **responsively** *adv.* **responsiveness** *n.*

**rest** *n.* repose; a cessation from motion or labor; a pause; *v.t.* to lay at rest; *v.i.* to cease from action; to repose; to be undisturbed. **-ful** *a.* soothing; quiet. **-fully** *adv.* **-fulness** *n.* **-less** *a.* continually on the move; uneasy. **-lessly** *adv.* **-lessness** *n.*

**rest** *v.i.* to continue to be; *n.* that which is left over or remainder.

**res•tau•rant** *n.* a place where customers are provided with meals on payment.

**res•ti•tu•tion** *n.* reparation; compensation. **restitutive** *a.* **restitutor** *n.*

**res•tive** *a.* impatient; stubborn. **-ly** *adv.* **-ness** *n.*

**re•store** *v.t.* to give back or return; to recover from decay; to reinstate; to cure. **restorable** *a.* **restoration** *n.* reconstruction; reestablishment. **restorative** *a.* having power to renew strength; *n.* a remedy for restoring health and vigor.

**re•strain** *v.t.* to hinder; to check. **-able** *a.* **-edly** *adv.* with restraint. **-ment** *n.* **-t** *n.* curb; imprisonment.

**re•strict** *v.t.* to restrain within bounds; to limit. **-ed** *a.* limited. **-edly** *adv.* **-ion** *n.*

state of being restricted; restraint. **-ive** *a.* **-ively** *adv.*

**re•sult** *v.i.* to follow, as a consequence; *n.* issue; outcome; *a.* following as a result.

**re•sume** *v.t.* to renew; to take again. **resumable** *a.* **resumption** *n.* act of taking back or taking again; a fresh start. **resumptive** *a.* resuming.

**re•surge** *v.i.* to rise again. **-nce** *n.* **-nt** *a.* rising again (from the dead).

**res•ur•rect** *v.t.* to restore to life; to use again. **-ion** *n.* rising of the body after death; a revival. **-ion, -ionary** *a.* **-ionist** *n.* a believer in resurrection.

**re•sus•ci•tate** *v.t.* to restore to life one apparently dead; to revive; *v.i.* to come to life again. **resuscitable** *a.* **resuscitation** *n.* **resuscitative** *a.* tending to reanimate. **resuscitator** *n.*

**re•tail** *v.t.* to sell to consumer, in small quantities; *a.* denoting sale to consumer, as opposed to wholesale; *n.* sale in small quantities. **-er, -ment** *n.*

**re•tain** *v.t.* to continue to keep in possession; to engage services of. **-able** *a.* **-er** *n.* follower; a fee paid to secure services of, esp. lawyer. **-ment** *n.*

**re•tal•i•ate** *v.t.* and *v.i.* to repay in kind; to requite. **retaliation** *n.* **retaliative, retaliatory** *a.* **retaliator** *n.*

**re•tard** *v.t.* to hinder progress; to impede, **-ation** *n.* delaying; delayed mental development in children. **-ment** *n.*

**retch** *v.i.* to strain at vomiting. **-ing** *n.*

**re•ten•tion** *n.* power of retaining; memory. **retentive** *a.* **retentively** *adv.* **retentiveness** *n.*

**ret•i•cent** *a.* uncommunicative. **reticence** *n.;* also **reticency.** **-ly** *adv.*

**ret•i•cle** *n.* a group of lines in the focus of an optical instrument. **reticule** *n.* a little bag. **reticular, reticulary** *a.* intricate. **reticulate** *v.t.* to cover with netlike lines. **reticulated** *a.* **reticulation** *n.*

**ret•i•na** *n.* innermost, semitransparent, sensory layer of the eye.

**re•tire** *v.t.* to withdraw from circulation notes or bills; *v.i.* to give up one's work or office; to go to bed. **retiral** *n.* occasion when one retires from office, etc. **-d** *a.* secluded; withdrawn permanently from work. **-dly** *adv.* **-ment, -dness** *n.* state of being retired. **retiring** *a.* reserved; modest.

**re•tort** *v.t.* to repay in kind; *v.i.* to make a smart reply; *n.* vigorous reply.

**re•trace** *v.t.* to go back the same way. **-able** *a.*

**re•tract** *v.t.* and *v.i.* to take back, as a statement. **-able** *a.* **-ation** *n.* recalling of opinion; recantation. **-ile** *a.* *(Zool.)* capable of being drawn back or inwards, as claws, etc. **-ion** *n.* retractile power. **-ive** *a.* **-ively** *adv.*

**re•tread** *v.t.* to replace a worn tread on the outer cover of a rubber tire with a new tread.

**re•treat** *n.* withdrawing; a military signal for retiring; *v.i.* to move back; to retire before an enemy. **-ing** *a.* sloping backward, as forehead or chin.

**re•trench** *v.t.* to curtail; *v.i.* to economize. **-ment** *n.* dimunition of expenditure; economy.

**ret•ri•bu•tion** *n.* just or suitable return; repayment. **retributive, retributory** *a.*

**re•trieve** *v.t.* to gain back. **retrievable** *a.* **retrievably** *adv.* **-ment, retrieval** *n.* **-r** *n.* dog trained to find and bring back game.

retriever

**ret•ro•act** *v.i.* to act backwards; to react. **-ion** *n.* **-ive** *a.* acting in regard to past events; retrospective. **-ively** *adv.*

**ret•ro•cede** *v.t.* to go or move back. **retrocession** *n.* going back.

**ret•ro•grade** *v.i.* to move backward; to deteriorate; *a.* deteriorating. **retrogradation** *n.* **retrogress** *v.i.* to deteriorate. **retrogression** *n.* a decline into an inferior state of development. **retrogressive** *a.* degenerating; assuming baser characteristics. **retrogressively** *adv.*

**re•trorse** *a.* pointing backwards, as feathers of birds. Also **retroverse.** **-ly** *adv.*

**ret•ro•spect** *n.* survey of past events; a review. **-ion** *n.* **-ive** *a.* applicable to past events; of laws, rules, having force as if authorized at earlier date. **-ively** *adv.*

**ret•ro•verse** *a.* bent backwards; retrorse. **retroversion** *n.* **retrovert** *v.t.* to turn back.

**re•turn** *v.t.* to bring, give, or send back; to restore; to yield (a profit); *v.i.* to go or come back; *n.* coming back to the same place; profit; restitution. **-able** *a.* **— match** *n.* second game played by same opponents. **— ticket** *n.* ticket for journey, there and back.

**re•u•nion** *n.* union formed anew after separation; a social gathering. **reunite** *v.t.* and *v.i.* to join after separation.

**re•veal** *v.t.* to disclose; to show. **-able** *a.* **-er** *n.* **-ment** *n.* revelation.

**rev•eil•le** *n.* the bugle call or roll of drums sounded in military establishments at daybreak to rouse inmates.

**rev•el** *v.i.* to carouse; to delight in; *pr.p., pa.t., pa.p.* and *n.* noisy celebration; *pl.* entertainment, with music and dancing. **-er, -ment, -ry** *n.*

**rev•e•la•tion** *n.* act of revealing; God's disclosure of himself to man; *(Cap.)* last book of New Testament. **-al, revelatory** *a.*

**re•venge** *v.t.* to make retaliation for; to avenge; *n.* infliction of injury in return for injury; passion for vengeance. **-ful** *a.* **-fully** *adv.* **-fulness** *n.*

**rev•e•nue** *n.* income derived from any source, esp. annual income of a state or institution; profits.

**re•ver•ber•ate** *v.t.* and *v.i.* to send back, as sound; to reflect, as light or heat; to resound. **reverberant** *a.* beating back. **reverberation** *n.* **reverberative** *a.* tending to reverberate. **reverberator** *n.*

**reverberatory** *a.* producing reverberation.

**re•vere** *v.t.* to regard with mingled fear, respect and affection. **-nce** *n.* awe mingled with respect and esteem; *(Cap.)* a title applied to a clergyman; *v.t.* to venerate. **-nd** *a.* worthy of reverence; a title of respect given to clergy. **-nt** *a.* showing, behaving with, reverence. **-ntial** *a.* respectful. **-ntially, -ntly** *adv.*

**rev•er•ie, revery** *n.* state of mind, akin to dreaming.

**re•verse** *v.t.* to turn in an opposite direction; to give a contrary decision; to invert; *v.i.* to change direction; *n.* side which appears when object is turned around; contrary; gear to drive a car backward; *a.* turned backward; opposite. **reversal** *n.* changing, annulling. **-d** *a.* turned in opposite direction; annulled. **-ly** *adv.* **reversibility** *n.* property of being reversible. **reversible** *a.* capable of being used on both sides or in either direction. **reversibly** *adv.* **reversion** *n.* returning or reverting; a deferred annuity; right or hope of future possession; atavism. **reversional, reversionary** *a.* involving a reversion. **reversive** *a.*

**re•vert** *v.i.* to return to former state or rank; to come back to subject; *v.t.* to turn back or reverse. **-ible** *a.*

**re•view** *v.t.* to reexamine; to consider critically (book); to inspect troops, etc.; *n.* revision; survey; inspection, esp. of massed military forces; a critical notice of a book. **-er** *n.* one who writes critical reviews; inspector.

**re•vile** *v.t.* to abuse with opprobrious language; to defame. **-ment, -r** *n.*

**re•vise** *v.t.* to review, alter and amend; *n.* a revised form. **revisal** *n.* reexamination. **revision** *n.* revisal; revised copy of book or document. **-r** *n.* **revisional, revisionary** *a.* pert. to revision. **revisory** *a.* having power to revise.

**re•vive** *v.i.* to come back to life; to awaken; *v.t.* to resuscitate; to recover from neglect; to refresh (memory). **revivability** *n.* **revivable** *a.* capable of being revived. **revivably** *adv.* **revival** *n.* reviving or being revived; renewed activity, of trade; reappearance of old, neglected play, etc. **revivalism** *n.* religious fervor of a revival. **revivalist** *n.* one who promotes religious revivals. **-r** *n.* one who, or that which, revives; a stimulant. **revivification** *n.* renewal of life and energy. **revivify** *v.t.* to reinvigorate.

**re•voke** *v.t.* to annul; to reverse (a decision); *v.i.* at cards, to fail to follow suit; *n.* neglect to follow suit at cards. **-r** *n.* **revocable** *a.* able to be revoked. **revocableness, revocability** *n.* **revocably** *adv.* **revocation** *n.* reversal. **revocatory** *a.*

**re•volt** *v.i.* to renounce allegiance; to rise in rebellion; *v.t.* to rebel; *n.* rebellion; loathing. **-er** *n.* **-ing** *a.* disgusting. **-ingly** *adv.*

**rev•o•lu•tion** *n.* motion of body around its orbit or focus; a radical change in constitution of a country after revolt. **-ary** *a.* marked by great and violent changes; *n.* one who participates in a revolution. **-ize** *v.t.* to change completely.

**re•volve** *v.i.* to turn around on an axis; to rotate; *v.t.* to cause to turn; to reflect upon. **revolvable** *a.* **-r** *n.* pistol.

**re•vue** *n.* theatrical entertainment, partly musical comedy, with little continuity of structure or plot.

**re•vul•sion** *n.* sudden, violent change of feeling; abhorrence. **revulsive** *a.*

**re•ward** *v.t.* to give in return for; to recompense; *n.* what is given in return; assistance in any form. **-er** *n.* **-ing** *a.*

**rhap•so•dy** *n.* collection of verses. **rhapsodic(al)** *a.* in extravagant, irregular style. **rhapsodically** *adv.* **rhapsodize** *v.t.* and *v.i.* to recite, as a rhapsody; to be ecstatic over.

**rhe•o-** used in the formation of scientific compound terms. **rheometer** *n.* instrument for measuring force of flow of fluids. **rheostat** *n.* instrument for controlling and varying within limits value of resistance in electrical circuit. **rheostatic** *a.*

**rhe•sus** *n.* small Indian monkey. **rhesian** *a.* **— factor** *(Med.)* *n.* Rh factor; a peculiarity of red cells of blood of most individuals, the so-called **rhesus positive**, rendering transfusion of their blood unsuitable for rhesus negative minority of patients.

**rhet•o•ric** *n.* art of persuasive speech or writing; exaggerated oratory. **-al** *a.* concerning style or effect; of the nature of rhetoric. **-al question** *n.* statement in the form of question to which no answer is expected. **-ally** *adv.* **-ian** *n.* one versed in principles of rhetoric.

**rheum** *n.* thin, serous fluid secreted by mucous glands and discharged from nostrils or eyes during a common cold. **-atic(al)** *a.* suffering from rheumatism. **-atism** *n.* a disease with symptoms of sharp pains and swelling in muscles and larger joints. **-atoid** *a.* resembling rheumatism. **-y** *a.* damp. **-atoid arthritis** *n.* severe chronic inflammation of joints, esp. knees and fingers.

**rhi•nal** *a.* pert. to the nose.

**rhine•stone** *n.* paste imitation of diamonds.

**rhi•noc•er•os** *n.* thick-skinned mammal allied to elephant, hippopotamus, with strong horn on nose.

**rhinoceros**

**rhod-, rhodo-** used in the formation of compound terms, signifying rose-colored. **rhodocyte** *n.* red blood corpuscle. **rhododendron** *n.* evergreen shrub with magnificent red blossoms.

**rhom•bus** *n.* *(Geom.)* parallelogram whose sides are all equal but whose angles are not right angles. **rhomb** *n.* diamond-shaped figure. **rhombic, rhombiform, rhomboid(al)** *a.*

**rhomboid** *n.* parrallelogram like rhombus, but having only opposite sides and angles equal.
**rhu•barb** *n.* two species of cultivated plants, rhubarb of kitchen garden, and an eastern variety whose roots are used as a purgative.
**rhyme** *n.* identity of sound in word endings of verses; *v.t.* to put into rhyme; *v.i.* to make verses. **-r, -ster** *n.* one who makes rhymes.
**rhythm** *n.* regular flow of sound, as in music and poetry, or of action, as in dancing; measured, periodic movement, as in heart pulsations. **-ic(al)** *a.* **-ically** *adv.* **-ics** *n.* science of rhythm.
**ri•ant** *a.* laughing; genial. **-ly** *adv.*
**rib** *n.* one of arched and very elastic bones springing from vertebral column; *v.t.* to furnish with ribs. **-bing** *pr.p.* **-bed** *pa.t.* and *pa.p.* **-bing** *n.* an arrangement of ribs.
**rib•ald** *a.* vulgar; indecent. **-ry** *n.* obscenity. **-ish** *a.*
**rib•bon** *n.* woven strip of material such as silk or satin, as trimming for a dress; inked tape in a typewriter. **blue ribbon** *n.* first-prize award.
**ri•bo•fla•vin** *n.* chemical substance present in vitamin $B_2$ complex, with growth-promoting properties.
**rice** *n.* annual grass plant, cultivated in Asia, the principal food of one-third of world. **— paper** *n.* very thin and delicate paper used in China and Japan for drawing and painting.
**rich** *a.* wealthy; abounding in possessions; abounding in nutritive qualities; *n.* the wealthy classes. **-es** *n.pl.* wealth. **-ly** *adv.* **-ness** *n.*
**rick•ets** *n.* rachitis, infantile disease marked by defective development of bones. **rickety** *a.* affected with rickets; insecure.
**ric•o•chet** *n.* glancing rebound of object after striking flat surface at oblique angle; *v.t.* and *v.i.* to rebound.
**rid** *v.t.* to free of; to disencumber. **-ding** *pr.p.* **rid** or **-ded** *pa.t.* and *pa.p.* **-dance** *n.* removal.
**rid•den** *pa.p.* of **ride.**
**rid•dle** *n.* large sieve for sifting gravel; *v.t.* to separate, as grain from chaff, with a riddle.
**rid•dle** *n.* puzzling fact, thing, person; *v.i.* to speak in riddles.
**ride** *v.t.* to be mounted on horse, bicycle; to cover distance; *v.i.* to be carried on back of animal; *n.* act of riding; journey on horseback, in a vehicle. **riding** *pr.p.* **rode** *pa.t.* **ridden** *pa.p.* **-r** *n.* one who rides; addition to a document; supplement to original motion or verdict. **riding** *a.* used for riding on; used by a rider; *n.* act of riding.
**ridge** *n.* line of meeting of two sloping surfaces; long narrow hill; highest part of roof; *v.t.* to form into ridges; *v.i.* to wrinkle. **-d** *a.* having ridges on its surface.
**rid•i•cule** *n.* mockery; *v.t.* to make fun of. **-r** *n.* **ridiculous** *a.* exciting ridicule; laughable.
**ri•fle** *v.t.* to search and rob. **-r** *n.* **rifling** *n.* pillaging.
**ri•fle** *v.t.* to make spiral grooves in; *n.* artillery piece whose barrel is grooved. **rifling** *n.* arrangement of grooves in a gun barrel or rifle tube. **-man** *n.* a man armed with rifle.
**rift** *n.* fissure; *v.t.* and *v.i.* to crack.
**rig** *v.t.* to provide (ship) with spars, ropes; to equip; to clothe; *n.* manner in which masts and sails of vessel are rigged; equipment used in installing machinery. **-ging** *pr.p.* **-ged** *pa.t.* and *pa.p.* **-ger** *n.* **-ging** *n.* system of ropes and tackle, esp. for supporting mast or controlling sails; adjustment of components of an aircraft.
**right** *a.* proper; in accordance with truth and duty; in politics, implying preservation of established order or of former institutions; *(Geom.)* applied to regular figures rising perpendicularly; *adv.* in a right manner; according to truth and justice; exactly; *n.* that which is correct; a just claim; that which is opposite to left; political party inclined towards conservatism and preservation of status quo; *v.t.* to do justice to; *v.i.* to recover natural position; to become upright. **-ful** *a.* legitimate; fair. **-fully** *adv.* **-fulness** *n.* **-ly** *adv.* in accordance with justice; correctly. **-ness** *n.* justice. **—about** *n.* the opposite direction. **—angled** *a.* having a **right angle,** one of ninety degrees.
**righ•teous** *a.* doing what is right; just. **-ly** *adv.* **-ness** *n.*
**rig•id** *a.* not easily bent; rigorous. **-ness, -ity** *n.* **-ly** *adv.*
**rig•or** *n.* strictness, stiffness; *(Med.)* a chill with fever. **-ism** *n.* austerity. **-ist** *n.* a person of strict principles. **-ous** *a.* **-ously** *adv.* **-ousness** *n.* **—mortis** *n.* stiffening of body after death.
**rile** *v.t.* to irritate.
**rim** *n.* border; metal ring forming outer part of a car wheel and carrying the tire; *v.t.* to furnish with a rim. **-ming** *pr.p.* **-med** *pa.t.* and *pa.p.* **-less** *a.*
**ri•mose** *a.* having surface covered with cracks.
**rind** *n.* external covering of trees, fruits, cheese, bacon; *v.t.* to strip off rind.
**ring** *n.* small circle of gold, esp. on finger; band, coil, rim; circle formed for dance or sports; *v.t.* to encircle; to cut a ring around trunk of a tree. **-ed** *a.* wearing, marked with, or surrounded by, a ring or rings. **-ing** *n.* **-leader** *n.* the leader of people associated together for a common object. **-less** *a.* **-master** *n.* one who directs performance in circus ring. **-worm** *n.* contagious disease of skin, scalp, leaving circular bare patches.
**ring** *v.t.* to cause to sound, by striking; *v.i.* to give out a clear resonant sound, as a bell; to chime; *n.* a resonant note; chime (of church bells); a telephone call. **rang** *pa.t.* **rung** *pa.p.*
**rink** *n.* place for skating or ice hockey; floor for roller skating, etc.
**rinse** *v.t.* to wash out, by filling with water,

etc. and emptying. **rinsing** *n.*

**ri•ot** *n.* tumultuous disturbance of peace; noisy festivity; profusion, as of color; *v.i.* to make, or engage in, riot; to disturb peace. **-er** *n.* **-ing** *n.* **-ous** *a.* boisterous. **-ously** *adv.* **-ousness** *n.* **-ry** *n.* riotous conduct.

**rip** *v.t.* to rend; to tear off or out; *v.i.* to tear; to move quickly and freely; *n.* tear. **-ping** *pr.p.* **-ped** *pa.t.* and *pa.p.* **-per** *n.* **-ping** *a.* **— cord** *n.* cord to withdraw parachute from pack so that ascending air forces it open. **-saw** *n.* saw with large teeth for cutting timber in direction of grain.

**rip** *n.* a stretch of broken water in river. **— current, -tide** *n.*

**ri•par•i•an** *a.* pert. to, or situated on, banks of a river.

**ripe** *a.* ready for reaping; fully developed. **-ly** *adv.* **-n** *v.t.* to mature; *v.i.* to grow ripe. **-ness** *n.*

**rip•ple** *n.* dimpling of surface of water; a little wave; subdued murmur or sound; *v.t.* to cause ripple in; *v.i.* to flow into little waves.

**rise** *v.i.* to ascend; to get up; to increase in value, price, power; *n.* that which rises or seems to rise; increase, as of price, wages, etc.; elevation. **rising** *pr.p.* **rose** *pa.t.* **-n** *pa.p.* **-r** *n.* one who, or that which, rises; vertical part of a step. **rising** *n.* insurrection; *a.* advancing.

**ris•i•ble** *a.* very prone to laugh. **-ness, risibility** *n.* **risibly** *adv.*

**risk** *n.* danger; peril; amount covered by insurance; *v.t.* to expose to danger or possible loss. **-er** *n.* **-y** *a.*

**rite** *n.* formal custom, esp. religious; ceremonial. **ritual** *a.* ceremonial; *n.* prescribed book of rites. **ritualism** *n.* fondness for ceremonial customs in public worship. **ritualist** *n.* **ritualistic** *a.* **ritually** *adv.*

**ri•val** *n.* opponent; *a.* having same claims; competing; *v.t.* to strive to equal or excel. **-ry** *n.* emulation.

**rive** *v.t.* to split; *v.i.* to be rent asunder. **-d, -n** *pa.p.*

**riv•er** *n.* natural stream of water flowing in a channel; abundance. **— basin** *n.* area drained by a river and its tributaries. **-bed** *n.* channel of a river. **-side** *n.* the bank of a river.

**riv•et** *n.* cylindrical iron or steel pin with strong flat head at one end, used for uniting two overlapping plates, by hammering down the stub end; *v.t.* to fasten with rivets; to fasten firmly.

**riv•u•let** *n.* a little river.

**roach** *n.* freshwater fish.

**roach** See **cockroach.**

**road** *n.* a track prepared for passengers, vehicles; direction; route. **-block** *n.* an obstruction placed across a road to stop someone. **-side** *n.* strip of ground along edge of road. **-way** *n.* a road.

**roam** *v.t.* and *v.i.* to wander; *n.* a ramble; a walk. **-er** *n.*

**roan** *a.* having coat in which the main color is thickly interspersed with another, esp. chestnut mixed with white or grey; *n.* a roan horse.

**roar** *v.t.* and *v.i.* to shout; to make loud, confused sound, as winds, waves, traffic, etc.; to laugh loudly; *n.* sound of roaring, deep cry. **-ing** *n.* sound of roaring. **-ingly** *adv.*

**roast** *v.t.* to cook by exposure to open fire or in oven; to expose to heat (as coffee, etc.); *v.i.* to become overheated; *n.* what is roasted, as joint of meat; *a.* roasted. **-ing** *n.* **-er** *n.*

**rob** *v.t.* to take by force or stealth; to steal. **-bing** *pr.p.* **-bed** *pa.t.* and *pa.p.* **-ber** *n.* **-bery** *n.* forcibly depriving a person of money or of goods.

**robe** *n.* a long outer garment, esp. of flowing style; ceremonial dress denoting state, office; *v.t.* to array; to dress. **robing** *n.*

**rob•in** *n.* brown red-breasted bird of thrush family. Also **— redbreast.**

**ro•bot** *n.* automaton; mechanical man.

**ro•bust** *a.* strong; muscular, vigorous. **-ly** *adv.* **-ness** *n.*

**rock** *n.* *(Geol.)* any natural deposit of sand, earth, or clay when in natural beds. **-ery** *n.* small artificial mound of stones planted with flowers, ferns, etc. **-iness** *n.* **-y** *a.* full of rocks; resembling rocks. **— crystal** *n.* transparent quartz used in making certain lenses. **— garden** *n.* a garden laid out with rocks and plants. **— salt** *n.* unrefined sodium chloride found in great natural deposits.

**rock** *v.t.* to sway to and fro; to put to sleep by rocking; *v.i.* to be moved, backward and forward; to totter. **-er** *n.* curving piece of wood on which cradle or chair rocks. **-y** *a.* shaky. **-ing** *n.* **-ing chair** *n.* chair mounted on rockers. **-ing horse** *n.* hobbyhorse.

**rock•et** *n.* cylindrical tube filled with a mixture of sulfur, niter, and charcoal, which, on ignition, hurls forward by action of liberated gases; firework; *v.i.* to soar up.

**ro•co•co** *n.* style of architecture, overlaid with ornamentation.

rococo

**rod** *n.* slender, straight stick, or switch; lightning conductor; linear measure equal to 5½ yards or 16½ feet.

**rode** *pa.t.* of **ride.**

**ro•dent** *a.* gnawing; *n.* gnawing animal, as rabbit, rat.

**ro•de•o** *n.* exhibition in steer wrestling and bronco busting by cowboys.

**roe** *n.* small deer; female hart. **-buck** *n.* male of roe.

**roe** *n.* the eggs or spawn of fish.

**roent•gen** *n.* *(Nuclear Phys.)* measuring unit of radiation dose. **— rays** *n.pl.* X rays. **-ize** *v.t.* to submit to action of X rays.

**ro•ga•tion** *n.* in ancient Rome demand, by tribunes, of a law to be passed by people; supplication. **Rogation Days,** three days preceding Ascension Day, on which special litanies are recited by R.C.

clergy invoking a blessing on crops. **rogatory** *a.* commissioned to gather information.

**rogue** *n.* rascal; mischievous person. **roguery** *n.* cheating; waggery. **roguishly** *adv.* **roguishness** *n.*

**rogue** *v.t.* and *v.i.* to remove plant from crop (potatoes, cereals, etc.) when that plant falls short of standard; to keep strain pure; *n.* plant that falls short of a standard or has reverted to original type.

**rois•ter** *v.i.* to bully; to swagger. **-er** *n.* **-ous** *a.*

**role** *n.* a part played by an actor in a drama — hence, any conspicuous part or task in public life.

**roll** *v.t.* to turn over and over; to move by turning on an axis; to level with a roller; *v.i.* to move forward by turning; to revolve upon an axis; to keep falling over and over; to rock from side to side, as a ship; *n.* a piece of paper, etc., rolled up; bread baked into small oval or rounded shapes; official list of members; a full corkscrew revolution of an airplane about its longitudinal fore and aft. **-able** *a.* **— call** *n.* calling over list of names to check absentees. **-er** *n.* a cylinder which distributes ink over type in printing; long, broad bandage; small, insectivorous bird which tumbles about in the air. **-er skate** *n.* skate with wheels or rollers instead of steel runner. **-ing** *a.* moving on wheels; turning over and over; *n.* *(Naut.)* reeling of a ship from side to side. **-ing pin** *n.* cylindrical device for rolling out dough.

**rol•lick** *v.i.* to move about in a boisterous, careless manner; *n.* frolicsome gaiety. **-ing** *a.* jovial; high-spirited.

**ro•ly-po•ly** *a.* plump and rounded.

**Ro•man** *a.* pert. to Rome or Roman people; in printing, upright letters as distinguished from *italic* characters; expressed in letters, not in figures, as I, IV. **-ic** *a.* **-ize** *v.t.* to introduce many idioms derived from Latin; *v.i.* to use Latin expressions. **— candle** *n.* a firework which throws out differently colored stars. **— Catholic,** a member of section of Christian Church which acknowledges supremacy of Pope.

**Ro•mance** *n.* languages; *a.* pert. to these languages. **romance** *n.* historical novel; story depending mainly on love interest; romantic quality; *(Mus.)* composition sentimental and expressive in character; *v.i.* to write or tell romances; embroider one's description with extravagances. **romantic** *a.* fanciful; sentimental; imaginative. **romantically** *adv.* **romanticism** *n.* the reactionary movement in literature and art against formalism and classicism. **romanticist** *n.*

**romp** *v.i.* to leap and frisk about in play; a boisterous form of play. **-ers** *n.pl.* a child's overall, with leg openings. **-ish** *a.*

**ron•deau** *n.* poem, thirteen lines with only two rhymes, the opening words recurring additionally, after eighth and thirteenth lines. **rondel** *n.* poem of thirteen or fourteen iambic lines, first two lines of which are repeated in middle and at close. **rondo** *n.* sonata movement in music in which a principal theme is repeated two or three times.

**roof** *n.* outside structure covering building; framework supporting this covering; ceiling; *v.t.* to cover with a roof; to shelter. **— garden** *n.* miniature garden on flat roof. **-tree** *n.* the ridgepole or roof itself.

**rook** *n.* in chess, one of the four pieces placed on corner squares of the board; also known as a castle.

**rook** *n.* blue-black, hoarse-voiced bird of crow family; swindler; *v.t.* to swindle. **-ery** *n.* colony of rooks and their nests.

**room** *n.* (enough) space; apartment or chamber; *pl.* lodgings; *v.i.* to lodge. **-ful** *a.* **-ily** *adv.* **-iness** *n.* spaciousness. **-y** *a.*

**roost** *n.* pole on which birds rest at night; perch; *v.i.* to settle down to sleep, as birds on a perch; to perch. **-er** *n.* a cock.

**root** *n.* part of plant which grows down into soil seeking nourishment for whole plant; origin; vital part; basis; *v.t.* to plant and fix in earth; to establish firmly; to pull out by roots; *v.i.* to enter earth, as roots; to be firmly established. **-ed** *a.* firmly established. **-stock** *n.* a rhizome.

**root** *v.t.* and *v.i.* to turn up with the snout, as swine; to uncover (with *up*).

**rope** *v.t.* stout cord of several twisted strands of fiber or metal wire; *v.t.* to mark off a rack track, with ropes; to lasso. **— ladder, — bridge,** etc. *n.* one made of ropes.

**Roque•fort** *n.* a cheese of ewe's milk.

**Ro•sa•ceae** *n.pl.* order of plants including rose, strawberry, blackberry, spiraea. **rosaceous** *a.* belonging to rose family. **rosarium** *n.* rose garden.

**ro•sa•ry** *n.* string of prayer beads.

**rose** *pa.t.* of **rise.**

**rose** *n.* genus of plant family of Rosaceae; shade of pink. **-ate** *a.* blooming; optimistic. **-bud** *n.* the bud of the rose; **-water** *n.* water tinctured with roses by distillation. **— window** *n.* circular window with a series of mullions diverging from center. **-wood** *n.* rich, dark-red hardwood from S. America, used for furniture-making. **rosily** *adv.* **rosiness** *n.* **rosy** *a.* blooming; red; favorable.

**rose•mar•y** *n.* a small fragrant evergreen shrub.

**ro•sette** *n.* something fashioned to resemble a rose, as ribbon; a rose-shaped architectural ornament.

**ros•in** *n.* resin in solid state; *v.t.* to cover with rosin. **-y** *a.*

**ros•ter** *n.* a list showing turns of duty; register of names.

**ros•trum** *n.* beak of a ship; raised platform; pulpit. **rostral** *a.* pert. to a rostrum. **rostrate, rostrated** *a.* beaked.

**ros•y** See **rose.**

**rot** *v.t.* and *v.i.* to decompose naturally; to become morally corrupt; to molder away; *n.* decomposition; decay. **-ting** *pr.p.* **-ted** *pa.t.* and *pa.p.*

**ro•ta•ry** *a.* turning, as a wheel; rotatory; *n.*

(*Cap.*) international association of businessmen's clubs. **Rotarian** *n.* member of Rotary Club. **— engine** *n.* (*Aero.*) engine in which cylinder and crankcase rotate with propeller.

**ro•tate** *v.t.* to cause to revolve; *v.i.* to move around pivot; *a.* (*Bot.*) wheel-shaped, as a calyx. **rotation** *n.* turning, as a wheel or solid body on its axis; serial change, as **rotation of crops. rotational** *a.* **rotator** *n.* **rotatory** *a.* turning on an axis, as a wheel; following in succession.

**rote** *n.* mechanical repetition.

**ro•tis•ser•ie** *n.* grill with a turning spit.

**ro•tor** *n.* revolving portion of dynamo, motor, or turbine.

**rot•ten** *a.* putrefied; decayed; corrupt. **-ly** *adv.* **-ness** *n.*

**ro•tund** *a.* round; plump. **-a** *n.* circular building or hall, covered by dome. **-ity, -ness** *n.* globular form; roundness.

**rouge** *n.* cosmetic for tinting cheeks; *v.t.* and *v.i.* to tint (face) with rouge.

**rough** *a.* not smooth; uneven; uncut; unpolished; stormy; *adv.* in rough manner; *n.* crude, unfashioned state; *v.t.* to make rough; to roughen; to shape out in rough-and-ready way. **-age** *n.* fibrous, unassimilated portions of food which promote intestinal movement. **— diamond** *n.* uncut diamond; a person of ability and worth, but uncouth. **-en** *v.t.* to make rough; *v.i.* to become rough. **—hew** *v.t.* to give first form to a thing. **-ly** *adv.*

**rou•lette** *n.* game of chance, played with a revolving disk and a ball.

**round** *a.* circular; spherical; not fractional, as a number; plump; *n.* circle; circuit; cycle; series; a course of action performed by persons in turn; beat of policeman, milkman, etc.; one of successive stages in competition; 3-minute period in boxing match; circular dance; *adv.* on all sides; circularly; back to the starting point; *v.t.* to make circular, spherical, or cylindrical; to finish; *v.i.* to become round or full in form. **-about** *a.* indirect; circuitous. **-er** *n.* a tool for rounding off objects. **-house** *n.* circular building for locomotives. **-ly** *adv.* vigorously; open. **-ness** *n.* **—table conference** *n.* one where all participants are on equal footing. **-up** *n.* collecting cattle into herds; *v.t.* to collect and bring into confined space.

**rouse** *v.t.* to wake from sleep; to startle or surprise; *v.i.* to awake from repose. **-r** *n.* **rousing** *a.*

**rout** *n.* tumultous crowd; confusion of troops in flight; *v.t.* to defeat and throw into confusion.

**rout** *v.i.* to roar; to snore.

**rout** *v.t.* to turn up with the snout; to cut grooves by gouging; *v.i.* to poke about.

**route** *n.* course which is traveled or to be followed.

**rou•tine** *n.* regular course of action adhered to by habit; *a.* in ordinary way of business; according to rule.

**rove** *v.t.* to wander over; *v.i.* to wander about; to ramble. **-r** *n.* wanderer; roving machine. **roving** *n.* and *a.*

**row** *n.* persons or things in straight line; a file; a line.

**row** *v.t.* to impel (a boat) with oars; *v.t.* to labor with oars; *n.* spell of rowing; a trip in a rowboat. **-boat** *n.* boat impelled solely by oars.

**row** *n.* riotous, noisy disturbance. **-dy** *a.* noisy. **-dyism, -diness** *n.*

**row•el** *n.* wheel of a spur, furnished with sharp points.

**roy•al** *a.* pert. to the crown; worthy of, patronized by, a king or queen; *n.* a size of paper. **-ism** *n.* principles of government by king. **-ist** *n.* adherent to sovereign, or one attached to kingly government. **-ly** *adv.* **-ty** *n.* kingly office; person of king or sovereign; members of royal family; payment to inventor for use of his invention, or to author depending on sales of his book.

**rub** *v.t.* to subject to friction; to chafe; to wipe; *v.i.* to come into contact accompanied by friction; *n.* difficulty, impediment; a sore spot from rubbing. **-bing** *pr.p.* **-bed** *pa.t.* and *pa.p.* **-ber** *n.* **-bing** *n.* applying friction to a surface.

**rub•ber** *n.* coagulated sap of certain tropical trees; *pl.* overshoes; galoshes; *a.* made of rubber. **-ized** *a.* mixed with rubber, as rubberized fabrics.

**rub•bish** *n.* anything worthless; refuse; nonsense.

**rub•ble** *n.* upper fragmentary decomposed mass of stone overlying a solid stratum of rock; rough stones used to fill up spaces between walls, etc. **-rubbly** *a.*

**ru•bi•cund** *a.* ruddy; florid; reddish. **-ity** *n.*

**ru•bid•i•um** *n.* rare silvery metallic element, one of the alkali metals.

**ru•ble** *n.* Russian monetary unit.

**ru•bric** *n.* medieval manuscript or printed book in which initial letter was illumined in red; heading or portion of such a work, printed in red — hence, the title of a chapter, statute, etc. originally in red; *v.t.* to illumine with red. **-al** *a.* colored in red; to formulate as a rubric. **-ian** *n.* one versed in the rubrics. **-ist** *n.* a strict adherent to rubrics; a formalist.

**ru•by** *n.* a red variety of corundum valued as a gem; *a.* having the dark-red color of a ruby.

**ruck** *v.t.* to wrinkle; *v.i.* to be drawn into folds; *n.* fold; wrinkle.

**ruck** *n.* rank and file; common herd.

**ruck•sack** *n.* pack carried on back by climbers, etc.

**rudd** *n.* British freshwater fish allied to the roach.

**rud•der** *n.* flat frame fastened vertically to stern of ship, which controls direction; anything which guides, as a bird's tail feathers.

**rud•dle** red ocher, used for marking sheep; *v.t.* to mark (sheep) with ruddle.

**rud•dy** *a.* of a red color; of healthy flesh color. **ruddiness** *n.*

**rude** *a.* uncivil; roughly made. **-ly** *adv.* **-ness** *n.*

**ru•di•ment** *n.* beginning; vestige; (*Biol.*) imperfectly developed or formed organ;

*pl.* elements, first principles, beginning. **-al, -ary** *a.* **-arily** *adv.*

**rue** *v.t.* and *v.i.* to grieve for; to repent of. **-ing** *pr.p.* **-ful** *a.* woeful; sorrowful. **-fully** *adv.*

**rue** *n.* aromatic, bushy, evergreen shrub.

**ruff** *n.* broad, circular collar, plaited, or fluted; light-brown mottled bird, the male being ringed with ruff of long, black, red-barred feathers during breeding season; *(fem.)* **reeve**; neck fringe of long hair or feathers on animal or bird. **-ed** *a.*

**ruf•fi•an** *n.* a rough, lawless fellow; *a.* brutal. **-ism** *n.* conduct of a ruffian. **-ly** *a.*

**ruf•fle** *v.t.* to draw into wrinkles, open plaits, or folds; to roughen surface of; to put out (of temper); *v.i.* to be at variance; *n.* a strip of gathered cloth, attached to a garment, a frill; commotion.

**rug** *n.* piece of carpeting.

**rug•by** *n.* English form of football, played with teams of 15 players each.

**rug•ged** *a.* rough; uneven; unpolished; vigorous. **-ly** *adv.* **-ness** *n.*

**ru•gose** *a.* wrinkled; ridged. **-ly** *adv.* **rugosity** *n.*

**ru•in** *n.* downfall; remains of demolished city, work of art, etc.; state of being decayed; *v.t.* to bring to ruin; to spoil; to cause loss of livelihood to. **-s** *n.pl.* ruined buildings, etc. **-ation** *n.* state of being ruined. **-er** *n.* **-ous** *a.* dilapidated; destructive. **-ously** *adv.*

**rule** *n.* act, power, or mode of directing; authority; prescribed law; established principle or mode of action; *v.t.* to govern; to decide authoritatively; to mark with straight lines, using ruler; *v.i.* to have command. **-r** *n.* sovereign; instrument with straight edges for drawing lines. **ruling** *a.* governing; predominant; *n.* an authoritative decision; a point of law settled by a court of law.

**rum** *n.* spirit distilled from sugarcane skimmings or molasses.

**rum•ba** *n.* Cuban dance.

**rum•ble** *v.i.* to make a low, vibrant, continuous sound; to reverberate; *n.* vibrant, confused noise, as of thunder; seat for footmen at back of carriage. **-r** *n.*

**ru•mi•nant** *n.* animal which chews cud, as sheep, cow; *a.* chewing cud. **ruminate** *v.t.* to chew over again; *v.i.* to chew cud; to meditate. **ruminatingly** *adv.* **rumination** *n.* **ruminative** *a.* **ruminator** *n.*

**rum•mage** *v.t.* to search thoroughly into or through; to ransack; *v.i.* to make a search; *n.* careful search; odds and ends. **-r** *n.*

**rum•my** *n.* a simple card game for any number of players.

**ru•mor** *n.* current but unproved report; *v.t.* to spread as a rumor.

**rump** *n.* end of backbone of animal with the parts adjacent; buttocks.

**rum•ple** *v.t.* to muss; crumple; *n.* an irregular fold.

**run** *v.i.* to move rapidly on legs; to hurry; to contend in a race; to stand as candidate for; to flee; to continue in operation; to be worded; *v.t.* to cause to run; to drive, push, or thrust; to manage; to maintain regularly, as bus service; to incur (risk); *n.* flow; act of running; course run; regular, scheduled journey; pleasure trip by car; unconstrained liberty; point gained in baseball; a great demand. **-ning** *pr.p.* **ran** *pa.t.* **run** *pa.p.* **-about** *n.* motorboat. **-away** *n.* fugitive; horse which has bolted. **-ner** *n.* one taking part in a race; messenger; one of curved pieces on which sleigh, skate, slides; device for facilitating movement of sliding doors, etc.; smuggler. **-ner-up** *n.* one who gains second place. **-ning** *a.* flowing; entered for a race, as a horse; successive (numbers); *n.* flowing quickly; chance of winning; operation of machine, business, etc. **-ning board** *n.* narrow, horizontal platform running along locomotive, car, to provide step for entering or leaving. **-ning commentary** *n.* broadcast description of event by eyewitness. **-ning knot** *n.* knot made so as to tighten when rope is pulled. **-way** *n.* prepared track on airfields for landing and taking off.

**run•dle** *n.* a step of a ladder; something which rotates like a wheel.

**rung** *pa.p.* of **ring.**

**rung** *n.* rounded step of a ladder; spoke.

**run•nel** *n.* small brook.

**runt** *n.* small, weak specimen of any animal, person or thing.

**rup•ture** *n.* breaking or bursting; state of being violently parted; hernia; *v.t.* to part by violence; to burst.

**ru•ral** *a.* pert. to the country; pert. to agriculture; pastoral. **-ize** *v.t.* to make rural; *v.i.* to live in the country; to become rural. **-ism** *n.* **-ly** *adv.*

**ruse** *n.* trick; strategem.

**rush** *v.t.* to carry along violently and rapidly; to hasten forward; *v.i.* to speed; *n.* heavy current of water, air, etc.; haste. **-er** *n.*

**rush** *n.* name of plants of genus Juncus, found in marshy places; straw. **—bottomed** *a.* of chair with seat made of rushes. **-y** *a.*

**rus•set** *a.* of reddish-brown color; *n.* apple of russet color.

**Rus•sian** *a.* pert. to Russia; *n.* inhabitant of Russia; Russian language.

**rust** *n.* coating formed on iron or various other metals by corrosion; reddish fungus disease on plants; *v.t.* to corrode with rust; *v.i.* to dissipate one's potential powers by inaction. **-ily** *adv.* **-iness** *n.* **-proof** *a.* not liable to rust. **-y** *a.*

**rus•tic** *a.* pert. to the country; rural; *n.* a simple country person. **-ally** *adv.* **-ate** *v.t.* to make rustic; *v.i.* to live in the country. **-ation, -ity** *n.*

**rus•tle** *v.i.* to make soft, swishing sounds, like rubbing of dry leaves; *v.t.* *(U.S.)* to steal, esp. cattle; *n.* a soft whispering sound. **-r** *n.* one who, or that, which rustles. **rustling** *n.*

**rut** *n.* furrow made by wheel; settled way of living; *v.t.* to form ruts in. **-ting** *pr.p.* **-ted** *pa.t.* and *pa.p.*

**ruth•less** *a.* pitiless; cruel. **-ly** *adv.* **-ness** *n.*

**rye** *n.* a kind of grass allied to wheat; whiskey made from rye.

**Sab•bath** *n.* seventh day of week; Sunday; Lord's Day.

**sa•ber** *n.* sword with broad and heavy blade; *v.t.* to wound or cut down with saber.

**Sa•bine** *n.* one of an ancient tribe of Italy who became merged with the Romans; *a.* pert. to the Sabines.

**sa•ble** *n.* small carnivorous mammal of weasel tribe; sable fur; *pl.* mourning garments; *a.* black.

**sable**

**sab•ot** *n.* a wooden shoe.

**sab•o•tage** *n.* willful damage or destruction of property perpetrated for political or economic reasons. **saboteur** *n.*

**sac** *n.* pouch-like structure or receptacle.

**sac•cha•rin, saccharine** *n.* a white crystalline solid substance, with an intensely sweet taste. **saccharine** *a.* pert. to sugar; cloying; sickly sentimental. **saccharify** *v.t.* to convert into sugar. **saccharinity** *n.* **saccharize** *v.t.* to convert into sugar. **saccharoid, -al** *a.* having granular texture resembling that of loaf sugar.

**sac•cule** *n.* a small sac. **saccular** *a.*

**sac•er•do•tal** *a.* pert. to priests, or to the order of priests. **-ism** *n.* **-ist** *n.* **-ly** *adv.*

**sa•chet** *n.* a small scent bag.

**sack** *n.* a large bag, usually of coarse material; contents of sack; also **sacque,** loose garment or cloak; any bag; *v.t.* to put into sacks. **-ing** *n.* coarse cloth or canvas.

**sack** *n.* old name for various kinds of dry wines.

**sack** *v.t.* to plunder or pillage; to lay waste; *n.* pillage of town. **-ing** *n.*

**sac•ra•ment** *n.* one of the ceremonial observances in Christian Church. **-al** *n.* **-ally** *adv.* **-arian** *n.* **-arianism** *n.*

**sac•ri•fice** *v.t.* to consecrate ceremonially offering of victim by way of expiation or propitiation to deity; to surrender for sake of obtaining some other advantage; *v.i.* to make offerings to God of things consumed on the altar; *n.* anything consecrated and offered to divinity; anything given up for sake of others. **-r** *n.* **sacrificial** *a.* **sacrificially** *adv.*

**sac•ri•lege** *n.* profanation of sacred place or thing; church robbery. **sacrilegious** *a.* violating sacred things; profane; desecrating. **sacrilegiously** *adv.* **sacrilegiousness** *n.*

**sac•ris•tan** *n.* officer in church entrusted with care of sacristy or vestry; sexton. **sacristy** *n.* vestry.

**sac•ro•sanct** *a.* inviolable and sacred in the highest degree. **-ity** *n.*

**sa•crum** *n.* a composite bone at the base of the spinal column. *pl.* **sacra.**

**sad** *a.* sorrowful; affected with grief; deplorably bad; somber-colored. **-den** *v.t.* to make sad or sorrowful; *v.i.* to become sorrowful and downcast. **-ly** *adv.* **-ness** *n.*

**sad•dle** *n.* rider's seat to fasten on horse, or form part of a cycle, etc.; part of a shaft; joint of mutton or venison containing part of backbone with ribs on each side; ridge of hill between higher hills; *v.t.* to put a saddle upon; to burden with; to encumber. **-r** *n.* one who makes saddles and harness for horses. **saddlery** *n.*

**sad•ism** *n.* insatiate love of inflicting pain for its own sake. **sadist** *n.* **sadistic** *a.*

**sa•fa•ri** *n.* hunting expedition.

**safe** *a.* free from harm; sound; protected; sure; *n.* a fireproof chest for protection of money and valuables; case with wire gauze panels to keep meat, etc. fresh. **-guard** *n.* protection; precaution; convoy; escort; passport; *v.t.* to make safe; to protect. **-ly** *adv.* **-ness** *n.* **-ty** *n.*

**saf•fron** *n.* plant of iris family, used in medicine and as a flavoring and coloring in cookery; *a.* deep yellow.

**sag** *v.i.* to sink in middle; to hang sideways or curve downwards under pressure; to give way; to tire. *pr.p.* **-ging.** *pa.p.* **-ged.** *n.* a droop.

**sa•ga** *n.* a prose narrative, written in Iceland in the 12th and 13th centuries, concerning legendary and historic people and actions of Iceland and Norway; novels describing life of a family.

**sa•ga•cious** *a.* quick of thought; acute; shrewd. **-ly** *adv.* **-ness, sagacity** *n.*

**sage** *n.* dwarf shrub of mint family.

**sage** *a.* wise; discerning; solemn; *n.* wise man. **-ly** *adv.* **-ness** *n.*

**sage-brush** *n.* a shrub smelling like sage and found chiefly on western plains of U.S.

**Sa•git•ta** *n.* a constellation north of Aquila—the Arrow. **sagittal, sagittate** *a.* shaped like an arrow or arrowhead. **sagittally** *adv.* **Saggitarius** *n.* the Archer, 9th sign of zodiac; constellation in Milky Way.

**sa•go** *n.* dry, granulated starch.

**said** *pa.t.* and *pa.p.* of say; the before-mentioned; already specified; aforesaid.

**sail** *n.* sheet of canvas to catch wind for propelling ship; sailing vessel; a journey upon the water; arm of windmill; *v.t.* to navigate; to pass in a ship; to fly through; *v.i.* to travel by water; to glide in stately fashion. **-able** *a.* navigable. **-boat** *n.* a boat propelled by sails. **-less** *a.* **-or** *n.* mariner; seaman; tar.

**saint** *n.* outstandingly devout and virtuous person; one of the blessed in heaven; one formally canonized by R.C. Church; *v.t.* to canonize. **-ed** *a.* pious; hallowed; sacred; dead. **-hood** *n.* **—like, -ly** *a.* **-liness** *n.*

**sake** *n.* cause; behalf; purpose; account; regard.

**sal** *n.* salt (much used in compound words pert. esp. to pharmacy).

**sa•la•cious** *a.* lustful; lewd; lecherous. **-ly** *adv.* **-ness, salacity** *n.*

**sal•ad** *n.* green vegetables raw or cooked, meat, fish, fruit, dressed with various seasonings or dressings.

**sal•a•man•der** *n.* small, tailed amphibian, allied to newt. **salamandriform,**

common salamander

**salamandrine** *a.* pert. to or shaped like a salamander; fire-resisting.

**sa•la•mi** *n.* Italian salted sausage.

**sal•a•ry** *n.* fixed remuneration, usually monthly, for services rendered; stipend. **salaried** *a.*

**sale** *n.* exchange of anything for money; demand (for article); public exposition of goods; a special disposal of stock at reduced prices. **-able, salable** *a.* capable of being sold. **-ableness** *n.* **-ably** *adv.* **-sman** *n.* **-smanship** *n.*

**sal•i•cin** *n.* a bitter white crystalline glucocide used as drug. **salicylate** *n.* any salt of salicylic acid. **salicylic** *a.*

**sa•li•ent** *a.* moving by leaps; projecting angle in line of fortifications, etc. **-ly** *adv.*

**sa•lif•er•ous** *a.* bearing or producing salt.

**sal•i•fy** *v.t.* to form a salt by combining an acid with a base; to combine with a salt. **salifiable** *a.*

**sa•line** *a.* of or containing salt; salty; *n.* a saline medicine. **salina** *n.* salt marsh; saltworks. **saliniferous** *a.* **salinity** *n.*

**sa•li•va** *n.* digestive fluid or spittle. **-ry** *a.* **-te** *v.t.* to produce abnormal secretion of saliva.

**sal•low** *a.* of sickly yellow color. **-ish** *a.* **-ness** *n.*

**sal•ly** *n.* sudden eruption; sortie; witticism; *v.i.* to issue suddenly.

**salm•on** *n.* silver-scaled fish with orange-pink flesh.

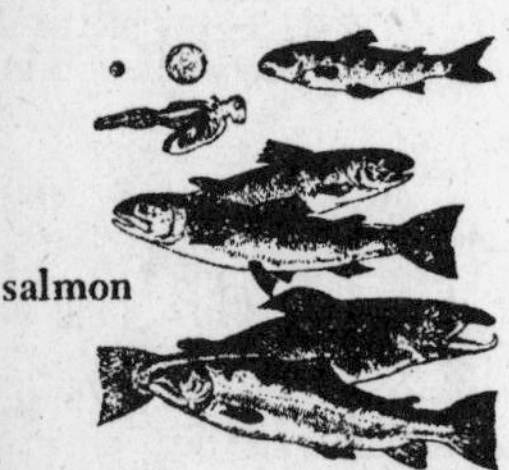
salmon

**sa•lon** *n.* spacious apartment for reception of company.

**sa•loon** *n.* public dining room; principal cabin in steamer; a place where liquor is sold and drunk.

**sal•si•fy, salsafy** *n.* hardy, biennial, composite herb with edible root.

**salt** *n.* sodium chloride or common salt; compound resulting from reaction between acid and a base; savor; piquancy; wit; *a.* containing or tasting of salt; preserved with salt; pungent; *v.t.* to season or treat with salt. **-er** *n.* **-ern** *n.* saltworks. **-ing** *n.* land covered regularly by tide. **-less** *a.* **-ness** *n.* **-y** *a.*

**sal•tant** *a.* leaping; jumping; dancing. **saltation** *n.*

**sal•tire, saltier** *n.* cross in the shape of an X, or St. Andrew's cross.

**salt•pe•ter** *n.* common name for niter or potassium nitrate.

**sa•lu•bri•ous** *a.* wholesome; healthy. **-ly** *adv.* **-ness, salubrity** *n.*

**sal•u•tar•y** *a.* wholesome; healthful; beneficial. **salutarily** *adv.* **salutariness** *n.*

**sa•lute** *v.t.* to address with expressions of kind wishes; to recognize one of superior rank by a sign; to honor by a discharge of cannon or small arms, by striking colors, etc.; to greet; *n.* greeting showing respect. **salutation** *n.* **salutatory** *a.* welcoming. **salutatorian** *n.*

**salvage** See **salve.**

**sal•va•tion** *n.* preservation from destruction; redemption; deliverance.

**salve** *v.t.* to save or retrieve property from danger or destruction. **salvability** *n.* **salvable** *a.* **salvage** *n.* compensation allowed to persons who assist in saving ship or cargo, or property in general, from destruction; property, so saved; *v.t.* to save from ruins, shipwreck, etc. **-r, salvor** *n.*

**salve** *n.* healing ointment applied to wounds or sores; *v.t.* to anoint with such; to heal; to soothe.

**sal•ver** *n.* a tray for visiting cards.

**sal•vo** *n.* guns fired simultaneously, or in succession as salute; sustained applause or welcome from large crowd. *pl.* **salvo(e)s.**

**Sa•mar•i•tan** *a.* pert. to Samaria in Palestine; *n.* native or inhabitant of Samaria; kind-hearted, charitable person.

**sam•ba** *n.* a dance of S. American origin.

**sam•bo** *n.* offspring of black person and mulatto.

**Sam Browne** *n.* military belt.

**same** *a.* identical; not different; of like kind; unchanged; uniform; aforesaid. **-ly** *adv.* **-ness** *n.*

**sam•ite** *n.* rich silk material; any lustrous silk stuff.

**sam•o•var** *n.* Russian tea urn.

**Sam•o•yed** *n.* Mongolian race inhabiting N. shores of Russia and Siberia; breed of dog, orig. a sledge dog.

**sam•pan** *n.* a Chinese light river vessel. Also **sanpan.**

**sam•phire** *n.* European herb found on rocks and cliffs, St. Peter's wort.

**sam•ple** *n.* specimen; example; *v.t.* to take or give a sample of; to try; to test; to taste. **-r** *n.*

**san•a•tive** *a.* having power to cure or heal. **-ness** *n.* **sanatorium** *n.* (*pl.* **sanatoria**) institution for open air treatment of tuberculosis; institution for convalescent patients. Also **sanitarium.** See **sanitary.** **sanatory** *a.*

**sanc•ti•fy** *v.t.* to set apart as sacred or holy; to consecrate; to purify. **sanctification** *n.* **sanctified** *a.* **sanctifiedly** *adv.* **sanctimonious** *a.* hypocritically pious. **sanctimoniously** *adv.* **sanctimoniousness, sanctimony** *n.* affected piety. **sanctitude** *n.* saintliness; holiness. **sanctity** *n.*

**sanc•tion** *n.* solemn ratification; express permission; legal use of force to secure obedience to law; *v.t.* and *v.i.* to confirm; to authorize; to countenance. **sanctions** *n.pl.* measures to enforce fulfillment of international treaty obligations.

**sanc•tu•ar•y** *n.* holy place; shrine; the chancel; a church or other place of protection for fugitives. **sanctum** *n.* sacred place; private room or study. **sanctum sanctorum,** holy of holies in Jewish temple.

**sand** *n.* fine, loose grains of quartz or other mineral matter formed by disintegration of rocks; *n.pl.* sandy beach; desert region; moments of time; *v.t.* to sprinkle or cover with sand; to smooth with sandpaper. **-iness** *n.* **-piper** *n.* small wading bird of plover family. **-y** *a.*

**sand-piper**

**san•dal** *n.* a shoe consisting of flat sole, bound to foot by straps or thongs. **-led** *a.*

**san•dal•wood** *n.* fragrant heartwood of santalum.

**sand•er•ling** *n.* a wading bird.

**sand•wich** *n.* two thin pieces of bread with slice of meat, etc., between them. *v.t.* to make into sandwich; to form of alternating layers of different nature; to insert or squeeze in between, making a tight fit.

**sane** *a.* of sound mind; not deranged; rational; reasonable; lucid. **-ly** *adv.* **-ness** *n.*

**sang** *pa.t.* of **sing.**

**san•guine** *a.* hopeful; confident; cheerful; deep red; florid; *n.* a crayon; blood-red color. **sanguinarily** *adv.* **sanguinariness** *n.* **sanguinary** *a.* bloody; blood-thirsty; murderous. **-ly** *adv.* **-ness** *n.* **-ous** *a.* bloody; blood-red; containing blood.

**San•he•drin** *n.* supreme court of Ancient Jerusalem. Also **Sanhedrim.**

**san•i•tar•y** *a.* pert. to health; hygienic; clean; free from dirt, germs, etc. **sanitarian** *n.* one interested in the promotion of hygienic reforms. **sanitarily** *adv.* **sanitation** *n.* **sanitarium,** *n.* private hospital for treatment of special or chronic diseases.

**san•i•ty** *n.* state of being sane.

**sank** *pa.t.* of the verb **sink.**

**sans•cu•lotte** *n.* ragged fellow.

**San•skrit, Sanscrit** *n.* classic literary language of ancient India.

**San•ta Claus** *n.* traditional 'Father Christmas' of children.

**sap** *n.* watery juice of plants. **-less** *a.* **-ling** *n.* young tree. **-py** *a.* **-wood** *n.* alburnum, exterior part of wood of tree next to bark.

**sap** *n.* tunnel driven under enemy positions for purpose of attack; *v.t.* and *v.i.* to undermine. *pr.p.* **-ping.** *pa.t.* and *pa.p.* **-ped.**

**sap•id** *a.* savory; palatable; tasty. **-ity** *n.*

**sa•pi•ent** *a.* discerning; wise; sage. **sapience** *n.* **-ly** *adv.*

**sap•o•na•ceous** *a.* resembling soap; slippery, as if soaped. **saponify** *v.t.*

**sa•por** *n.* taste; savor; flavor. **-oific** *a.* **-osity** *n.*

**Sap•phic** *a.* pert. to Sappho, lyric poetess of Greece of 7th cent. B.C.; denoting verse in which three lines of five feet each are followed by line of two feet; *n.* Sapphic verse. **sapphism** *n.* unnatural sexual relations between women.

**sap•phire** *n.* translucent precious stone of various shades of blue; *a.* deep, pure blue.

**sar•a•band** *n.* slow, stately dance.

**Sar•a•cen** *n.* Arab or Mohammedan who invaded Europe and Africa; an infidel. **-ic, -ical** *a.*

**sar•casm** *n.* taunt; scoffing gibe; veiled sneer; irony; use of such expressions. **sarcastic, -al** *a.* **sarcastically** *adv.*

**sar•coph•a•gus** *n.* kind of limestone used by Greeks for coffins and believed to consume flesh of bodies deposited in it; stone coffin; monumental chest or case of stone, erected over graves. *pl.* **sarcophagi.**

**sar•dine** *n.* small fish of herring family.

**sar•don•ic** *a.* (of laugh, smile) bitter, scornful, derisive, mocking. **-ally** *adv.*

**sar•do•nyx** *n.* semiprecious stone.

**sar•gas•sum** *n.* genus of seaweeds. **sargasso** *n.* gulfweed.

**sargasso**

**sa•ri** *n.* long outer garment of Hindu women. Also **saree.**

**sa•rong** *n.* garment draped round waist by Malayans.

**sar•sa•pa•ril•la** *n.* several plants of genus Smilax, with roots yielding a mild diuretic; a soft drink flavored with the extract.

**sar•to•ri•al** *a.* pert. to tailor, tailoring.

**sash** *n.* silken band; belt or band, usually decorative.

**sash** *n.* frame of window which carries panes of glass.

**sas•sa•fras** *n.* a tree of the laurel family.

**sat** *pa.t.* and *pa.p.* of **sit.**

**Sa•tan** *n.* the devil. **-ic, -al** *a.* devilish; infernal; diabolical. **-ically** *adv.*

**satch•el** *n.* small bag for books, etc.

**sate** *v.t.* to satisfy appetite of; to glut.

**sa•teen** *n.* glossy cloth for linings.

**sat•el•lite** *n.* one constantly in attendance upon important personage; an obsequious follower; *(Astron.)* a secondary body which revolves round planets of solar system; a moon. **satellitic** *a.*

**sa•ti•ate** *v.t.* to satisfy appetite of; to surfeit; to sate. **satiability** *n.* **satiable** *a.* capable of being satisfied. **satiation** *n.* state of being satiated. **satiety** *n.*

**sat•in** *n.* soft, rich, usually silk fabric with smooth, lustrous surface; *a.* made of satin; smooth; glossy. **-et** *n.* thin kind of satin. **-wood** *n.* beautiful hard yellow wood. **-y** *a.*

**sat•ire** *n.* literary composition holding up to ridicule vice or folly of the times. **satiric, -al** *a.* **satirically** *adv.* **satiricalness** *n.* **satirize** *v.t.* **satirist** *n.*

**sat•is•fy** *v.t.* to gratify fully; to convince; to content; to answer; to free from doubt; *v.i.* to give content; to supply to the full; to make payment. **satisfaction** *n.* **satisfactorily** *adv.* **satisfactoriness** *n.* **satisfactory** *a.* **-ing** *a.* **-ingly** *adv.*

**sa•trap** *n.* governor of province under ancient Persian monarchy; petty, despotic governor. **-al** *a.* **-y** *n.*

**sat•u•rate** *v.t.* to soak thoroughly; to steep; to drench. **-d** *a.* **saturation** *n.* **saturator** *n.* contrivance for saturating air with water-vapor.

**Sat•ur•day** *n.* seventh day of week.

**Sat•urn** *n.* old deity, father of Jupiter; sixth of major planets in order of distance from sun. **saturnalian** *a.* **Saturnian** *a.* pert. to epoch of Saturn; golden; distinguished for prosperity and peacefulness. **saturnine** *a.* gloomy, sluggish in temperament.

**sat•yr** *n.* woodland deity in Greek mythology, part human and part goat, fond of sensual enjoyment; lecherous person. **satyriasis** *n.* excessive and morbid desire for sexual intercourse exhibited by men. **-omaniac** *n.* **-ical** *a.*

**sauce** *n.* liquid or soft seasoning for food; condiment; relish; *v.t.* to season with sauce; to give flavor or interest to; *(Colloq.)* to be rude in speech or manner. **saucy** *a.* bold; pert; cheeky. **saucily** *adv.* **sauciness** *n.*

**sau•cer** *n.* small plate put under cup.

**sauer•kraut** *n.* cabbage cut fine and allowed to ferment in brine.

**saun•ter** *v.i.* to stroll. *n.* leisurely walk or stroll. **-er** *n.* **-ing** *n.*

**sau•ri•an** *n.* lizard-like reptile.

**sau•sage** *n.* meat-minced and seasoned and enclosed in thin membranous casing obtained from small entrails of pig or sheep.

**sau•terne** *n.* a well-known white wine.

**sav•age** *a.* remote from human habitation; wild; uncivilized; primitive; cruel; *n.* man in native state of primitiveness; a barbarian. **-ly** *adv.* **-ry** *n.*

**sa•vant** *n.* a man of learning.

**save** *v.t.* to rescue, preserve from danger, evil, etc.; to redeem; to protect; to lay by; to spare; to except; *v.i.* to lay by money; to economize; *prep.* except; *conj.* but. **savable** *a.* **-r** *n.* **savingly** *adv.*

**sav•ior** *n.* one who saves or delivers from destruction or danger; *(Cap.)* the Redeemer, Jesus Christ. Also **saviour.**

**sa•voir•faire** *n.* the knack of knowing the right thing to do at the right time; tact.

**sa•vor** *n.* taste; flavor; relish; odor; *v.t.* to like; to taste or smell with pleasure; to relish; *v.i.* to have a particular smell or taste; to resemble; to indicate the presence of. **-ily** *adv.* **-less** *a.* **-y** *a.*

**sa•vor•y** *n.* genus of aromatic plants.

**saw** *pa.t.* of the verb **see.**

**saw** *n.* old saying; maxim; proverb; aphorism; adage.

**saw** *n.* hand or mechanical tool with thin blade, band, or circular disk with

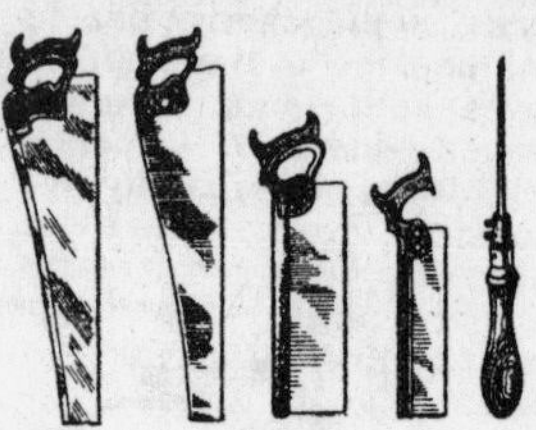

saws

serrated edge, used for cutting; *v.t.* and *v.i.* to cut with a saw; *pa.t.* **sawed.** *pa.p.* **sawed** or **sawn. -er** *n.* **-yer** *n.*

**sax•horn** *n.* brass wind instrument.

**sax•i•frage** *n.* popular name of various plants, most of them true rock plants.

**Sax•on** *n.* one of the people who formerly dwelt in N. Germany and who invaded England in the 5th and 6th cents.; a person of English race; native of Saxony; language of Saxons.

**Sax•o•ny** *n.* very fine quality of wool; flannel.

**sax•o•phone** *n.* brass wind instrument.

**say** *v.t.* to utter with speaking voice; to state; to express; to allege; to recite; to take as near enough. *pa.t.* and *pa.p.* **said** *n.* something said; what one has to say; share in a decision. **-er** *n.* **-ing** *n.* proverbial expression; adage.

**scab** *n.* crust forming over open wound or sore; *v.i.* to heal over; to form a scab. *pa.t.* and *pa.p.* **-bed.** *pr.p.* **-bing. -bed** *a.* covered with scabs. **-bedness** *n.* **-by** *a.*

**scab•bard** *n.* sheath for sword or dagger; *v.t.*

**sca•bies** *n.* skin disease caused by parasite; the itch; the scab.

**sca•bi•ous** *a.* consisting of scabs; scabby; itchy.

**sca•brous** *a.* rough; scaly; harsh; full of difficulties; indelicate. **-ly** *adv.* **-ness** *n.*

**scad** *n.* a species of mackerel.

**scaf•fold** *n.* temporary structure for support of workmen; framework; stage; platform, esp. for execution of criminal; *v.t.* to furnish with a scaffold; to prop up. **-ing** *n.*

**scal•a•wag, scallawag** *n.* *(Colloq.)* scamp; worthless fellow.

**scald** *v.t.* to burn with moist heat or hot liquid; to cleanse by rinsing with boiling water; to heat to point approaching boiling point; *n.* injury by scalding.

**scald** See **skald.**

**scale** *n.* dish of a balance; balance itself;

machine for weighing, chiefly in *pl.;* Libra, one of signs of zodiac; *v.t.* to weigh, as in scales.

**scale** *n.* horny or bony plate-like outgrowth from skin of certain mammals, reptiles, and fishes; *v.t.* to deprive of scales; *v.i.* to come off or peel in thin layers. **-d** *a.* having scales. **-less** *a.* **scaliness** *n.* **scaly** *a.* covered with scales.

**scale** *n.* series of steps or gradations; ratio between dimensions as shown on map, etc. to actual distance, or length; basis for a numerical system, as *binary scale;* instrument for measuring, weighing, etc. *(Mus.)* succession of notes arranged in order of pitch between given note and its octave; gamut; *v.t.* to climb as by a ladder; to measure; *v.i.* to mount.

**sca•lene** *a.* uneven; *(Geom.)* having all three sides unequal; *n.* a scalene triangle.

**scal•lion** *n.* a variety of shallot.

**scal•lop, scollop** *n.* bivale mollusk; ornamental edge of rounded projections; *v.t.* to cut edge of material into scallops.

**scalp** *n.* covering dome of cranium consisting of skin and hair; skin and hair torn off by Indian warriors as token of victory; *v.t.* to deprive of integument of head; to make quick profits in buying and prompt reselling.

**scal•pel** *n.* small, straight surgical knife.

**scamp** *n.* scoundrel; rascal; rogue.

**scam•per** *v.i.* to run about; to run away in haste and trepidation; *n.* a hasty, impulsive flight.

**scan** *v.t.* to examine closely; to scrutinize; *v.i.* to be metrically correct. *pr.p.* **-ning.** *pa.t.* and *pa.p.* **-ned. -ning** *n.*

**scan•dal** *n.* malicious gossip; disgraceful action; disgrace; injury to a person's character. **-ize** *v.t.* to shock by disgraceful actions. **-ous** *a.* **-ously** *adv.* **-ousness** *n.*

**Scan•di•na•vi•a** *n.* peninsula of Norway, Sweden, and Finland. **-n** *a.*

**scansion.** See **scan.**

**scant** *a.* barely sufficient; inadequate; *v.t.* to put on short allowance; to fail to give full measure. **-ily** *adv.* **-iness** *n.* **-ly** *adv.* sparingly; scarcely; barely. **-ness** *n.* scantiness; insufficiency. **-y** *a.*

**scant•ling** *n.* a small amount.

**scape•goat** *n.* one who has to shoulder blame due to another. **scapegrace** *n.* graceless, good-for-nothing fellow.

**scaph•oid** *a.* boat-shaped.

**scap•u•la** *n.* shoulder blade. *pl.* **scapulae. -r** *a.* Also **-ry.**

**scar** *n.* permanent mark left on skin after healing of a wound, burn; *v.t.* to mark with scar; *v.i.* to heal with a scar.

**scar•ab** *n.* beetle regarded by ancient Egyptians as emblematic of solar power; gem cut in shape of this beetle.

scarab

**scarce** *a.* not plentiful; deficient; scanty. **-ly** *adv.* hardly; not quite. **-ness, scarcity** *n.*

**scare** *v.t.* to terrify suddenly; to alarm; to drive away by frightening; *n.* sudden alarm (esp. causeless).

**scarf** *n.* long, narrow, light article of dress worn loosely over shoulders or about neck; a muffler. *pl.* **-s, scarves.**

**scarf** *v.t.* to unite lengthways to pieces of timber; *n.* joint for connecting timbers lengthwise.

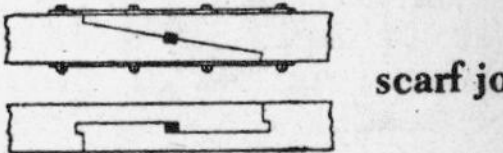
scarf joint

**scar•i•fy** *v.t.* to scratch or slightly cut the skin; to stir the surface soil of; to lacerate; to criticize unmercifully. **scarification** *n.* **scarifier** *n.*

**scar•la•ti•na** *n.* scarlet fever.

**scar•let** *n.* bright red color of many shades; cloth of scarlet color; *a.* of this color. **— fever** *n.* childhood disease characterized by a scarlet rash.

**scarp** *n.* steep inside slope of ditch in fortifications; *v.t.* to make steep. **-ed** *a.*

**scar•y** *a.* *(Colloq.)* producing fright or alarm; exceedingly timid.

**scathe** *v.t.* to criticize harshly. **scathing** *a.* damaging; cutting; biting. **scathingly** *adv.*

**sca•tol•o•gy** *n.* scientific study of fossilized excrement of animals; interest in obscene literature. **scatological** *a.*

**scat•ter** *v.t.* to strew about; to sprinkle around; to put to rout; to disperse; *v.i.* to take to flight; to disperse. **-er** *n.* **-ingly** *adv.*

**scav•en•ger** *n.* one employed in cleaning streets, removing refuse, etc.; animal which feeds on carrion; *v.i.* to scavenge. **scavenge** *v.t.* to cleanse streets, etc.

**sce•nar•i•o** *n.* script or written version of play to be produced by motion picture; plot of a play. **scenarist** *n.*

**scene** *n.* place, time of action of novel, play, etc.; a division of a play; spectacle, show, or view. **-ry** *n.* stage settings; natural features of landscape which please eye. **scenic** *a.* **scenographic, -al** *a.* drawn in perspective. **scenographically** *adv.* **scenography** *n.*

**scent** *v.t.* to discern or track by sense of smell; to give a perfume to; to detect; to become suspicious of; *v.i.* to smell; *n.* odor or perfume; trail left by odor. **-ed** *a.* perfumed.

**sceptic.** See **skeptic.**

**scep•ter** *n.* ornamental staff or baton, as symbol of royal power; royal or imperial dignity. **-ed** *a.* Also **sceptre.**

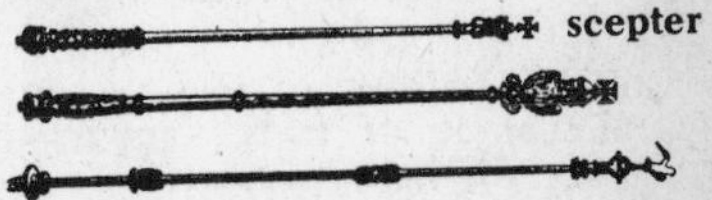
scepter

**sched•ule** *n.* document containing list of details forming part of principal document, deed, etc.; order of events; *v.t.* to note and enter in a schedule.

**sche•ma** *n.* plan or diagram; outline; scheme; *pl.* **-ta. -tic** *a.* **-tically** *adv.* **-tize** *v.t.*

**scheme** *n.* plan; design; system; plot; diagram; *v.t.* to plan; to contrive; to frame; *v.i.* to intrigue; to plot. *pr.p.* **scheming. -r** *n.* **scheming** *n.* and *a.* **schemist** *n.*

**scher•zo** *n.* *(Mus.)* composition of a lively, playful character.

**schism** *n.* split of a community into factions; crime of promoting this. **schismatic** *a.* —*n.* one who separates from a church. **-atical** *a.* schismatic. **-atically** *adv.*

**schiz•o-** *prefix* to cleave, used in the construction of compound terms. **schizoid** *a.* exhibiting slight symptoms of schizophrenia. **-phrenia** *n.* mental disorder known as 'split personality.' **-phrenic** *a.*

**schnapps, schnaps** *n.* kind of Holland gin.

**schol•ar** *n.* learned person; holder of scholarship. **-ly** *a.* **-ship** *n.* learning; erudition; a grant to aid a student. **scholastic** *a.* pert. to schools, scholars, or education. **scholastically** *adv.* **Scholasticism** *n.* system of philosophy during Middle Ages.

**scho•li•ast** *n.* ancient commentator or annotator of classical texts. **scholiastic** *a.* **scholium** *n.* — *pl.* **scholia,** marginal note or comments.

**school** *n.* a shoal (of fish, whales, etc.).

**school** *n.* institution for teaching or giving instruction in any subject; group of writers, artists, thinkers, etc. with principles or methods in common; branch of study, in a university; *v.t.* to educate; to discipline; to instruct; to train. **-room** *n.* **-teacher** *n.*

**schoon•er** *n.* small sharp-built vessel, having two masts, fore-and-aft rigged.

three-masted schooner

**schot•tische, shottish** *n.* round dance resembling polka; music in 2/4 time for this dance. **Highland schottische,** lively dance to strathspey tunes, Highland fling.

**sci•at•i•ca** *n.* neuralgia of sciatic nerve, with pains in region of hip. **sciatic, -al** *a.* situated in, or pert. to, hip region. **-lly** *adv.*

**sci•ence** *n.* systematic knowledge of natural or physical phenomena; ordered arrangement of facts known under classes or heads; **scientific, -al** *a.* **scientifically** *adv.* **scientism** *n.* **scientist** *n.* **natural science, physical science,** science which investigates nature and properties of material bodies and natural phenomena. **pure science,** science based on self-evident truths, as mathematics, logic, etc.

**scim•i•tar** *n.* short saber with curved, sharp-edged blade.

**scin•til•la** *n.* spark; least particle. **-nt** *a.* emitting sparks; sparkling. **-te** *v.i.* to emit sparks; to sparkle; to glisten. **-tion** *n.*

**sci•o•lism** *n.* superficial knowledge used to impress other. **sciolist** *n.* **sciolistic** *a.*

**sci•on** *n.* slip for grafting; offshoot; a descendant; heir.

**scis•sile** *a.* *(Bot.)* capable of being cut, split, or divided. **scission** *n.* act of cutting; division.

**scis•sors** *n.pl.* instrument of two sharp-edged blades pivoted together for cutting; small shears. **scissor** *v.t.* to cut with scissors.

**scle•ro-** *prefix* hard, used in the construction of compound terms, implying hardness or dryness. **sclera** *n.* strong, opaque fibrous membrane forming outer coat of eyeball. **scleral** *a.* hard, bony. **scleritis** *n.* inflammation of sclera of eye. **sclerodermatous** *a.* *(Zool.)* possessing a hard, bony, external structure for protection. **scleroid** *a.* of hard texture. **scleroma** *n.* hardening of tissues. **sclerosal** *a.* pert. to sclerosis. **sclerosis** *n.* hardening of organ as a result of excessive growth of connective tissue; induration.

**scoff** *v.i.* to treat with derision; to mock; to jeer; *n.* expression of scorn; an object of derision. **-er** *n.* **-ingly** *adv.*

**scold** *v.t.* and *v.i.* to find fault (with); to chide; to reprove angrily; *n.* one who scolds. **-er** *n.* **-ing** *n.* rebuke. **-ingly** *adv.*

**sconce** *n.* ornamental bracket fixed to wall, for carrying a light.

**scone** *n.* a thin, flat cake.

**scoop** *n.* article for ladling; kind of shovel; hollow place; *v.t.* to ladle out, shovel, lift, dig or hollow out with scoop.

**scoot** *v.i.* to move off quickly; to dart away suddenly; to scamper off.

**scope** *n.* range of activity or application; space for action; room; play; outlet.

**scor•bu•tic** *a.* affected with, or relating to, scurvy.

**scorch** *v.t.* to burn the surface of; to parch; to char; *v.i.* to be burnt on surface; to dry up; to parch. **-er** *n.* **-ing** *a.*

**score** *n.* a cut, notch, line, stroke; tally mark; reckoning, bill, account; number twenty; reason; sake; *v.t.* to mark with lines, scratches, furrows; to cut; to enter in account book, to record; to make (points, etc.) in game; *v.i.* to add a point, run, goal, etc. in a game; to make a telling remark; to achieve a success. **-r** *n.* **scoring** *n.* **-book, -card, -sheet** *n.*

**sco•ri•a** *n.* dross or slag resulting from smelting of metal ores. *pl.* **scoriae. scorify** *v.t.* to reduce to dross or slag.

**scorn** *n.* extreme disdain or contempt; *v.t.* to contemn. **-ful** *a.* **-fully** *adv.*

**Scor•pi•o** *n.* Scorpion, 8th sign of zodiac; scorpion. **-n** *n.* insect allied to spiders having slender tail which ends in very acute sting.

**scot** *n.* formerly, tax, contribution, fine. **—free** *a.* unhurt; exempt from payment.

**Scot** *n.* native of Scotland.
**Scotch** *a.* pert. to Scotland or its inhabitants; *n.* Scots; Scots dialect; Scotch whiskey.
**scotch** *v.t.* to support, as a wheel, by placing some object to prevent its rolling; *n.* prop, wedge, strut.
**scotch** *v.* to wound slightly; to cut; *n.* scratch; mark or score.
**Scots** *n.* dialect of English spoken in lowland Scotland; *a.* pert. to Scotland. **-man, -woman** *n.*
**Scot•tish** *a.* pert. to Scotland or its people.
**scoun•drel** *n.* rascal; villain. **-ly** *a.*
**scour** *v.t.* to clean or polish the surface of, by hard rubbing; to purge violently; to flush out; *v.i.* to clean by rubbing; *n.* act or material used in scouring. **-er** *n.*
**scour** *v.t.* to pass rapidly along or over in search of something; to range; *v.i.* to scamper; to rove over; to scurry along. **-er** *n.*
**scourge** *n.* whip made of leather thongs; lash; punishment; *v.t.* to flog; to lash; to chastise;
**scout** *n.* one sent out to reconnoiter; lookout; *v.t.* to reconnoiter; to spy out.
**scout** *v.t.* to reject with contempt.
**scow** *n.* large flat-bottomed barge.
**scowl** *v.i.* to wrinkle brows in displeasure; *n.* an angry frown.
**scrab•ble** *v.t.* to scribble; to scrawl; *v.i.* to scratch with hands.
**scrag** *n.* anything thin, lean, gaunt, or shrivelled. **-ged** *a.* **-gedness, -giness** *n.* **-gily** *adv.* **-gly** *a.* rough and unkempt. **-gy** *a.*
**scram•ble** *v.t.* to move by crawling, climbing, etc. on all fours; to struggle with others for; *v.t.* to collect together hurriedly and confusedly; *n.* scrambling; disorderly proceeding. **scrambling** *a.*
**scrap** *n.* small detached piece or fragment; material left over which can be used as raw material again; *pl.* odds and ends; *v.t.* to make into scraps; to discard; *pa.t.* and pa.p. **-ped.** *pr.p.* **-ping.** **-py** *a.*
**scrape** *v.t.* to abrade; to grate; to scratch; *v.i.* to produce grating noise; to live parsimoniously; to bow awkwardly with drawing back of foot; to scratch in earth, as fowls; *n.* act or sound of scraping; scratch; predicament; embarrassing situation. **-r** *n.*
**scratch** *v.t.* to score or mark a narrow surface wound with claws, nails, or anything pointed; to erase; to scrape; to rub an itchy spot; *v.i.* to use claws or nails in tearing, abrading, or shallow digging; *n.* slight wound, mark, or sound made by sharp instrument; *a.* taken at random, brought together in a hurry, as *a scratch team.* **-er** *n.* **-y** *a.*
**scrawl** *v.t.* to write or draw untidily; to scribble; *v.i.* to write unskillfully; *n.* hasty, careless writing; **-er** *n.*
**scraw•ny** *a.* lean; scraggy; rawboned. **scrawniness** *n.*
**scream** *v.t.* and *v.i.* to utter a piercing cry; *n.* a shrill, piercing cry; a person who excites much laughter; laughter-provoking incident. **-ing** *a.*
**scree** *n.* pile of débris at base of cliff or hill; a talus.
**screech** *v.i.* to utter a harsh, shrill cry; *n.* a shrill and sudden, harsh cry. **—owl** *n.* owl with persistent harsh call.
**screed** *n.* long letter or passage; long boring speech.
**screen** *n.* covered frame to shelter from heat, light, draft, or observation; coarse, rectangular sieve for grading coal, pulverized material, etc.; white surface on which image is projected by optical means; *v.t.* to provide with shelter or concealment; to protect from blame or censure; to sift; to film; to project film, lantern slide, etc. on a screen; to subject a person to political scrutiny. **-ing** *n.*
**screw** *n.* in mechanics, a machine consisting of an inclined plane wound round a cylinder; cylinder with a spiral ridge running round it, used as holding

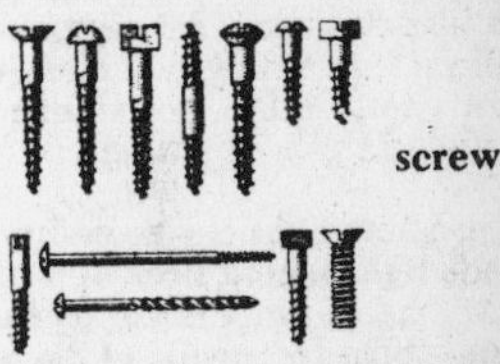
screw

agent or as mechanical power; turn of screw; twist to one side; a screw propeller; *v.t.* to fasten with screw; to press or stretch with screw; to work by turning; to twist round; to obtain by pressure; to extort; *v.i.* to assume a spiral motion; to move like a screw. **-ed** *a.* **-er** *n.* **-ing** *a.* **-y** *a.*
**scrib•ble** *v.t.* and *v.i.* to write carelessly; to draw meaningless lines; *n.* something scribbled. **-r** *n.* **scribbling** *a.* used for scribbling; *n.* careless writing.
**scribe** *n.* a writer; official or public writer; clerk; copyist; *v.t.* to incise wood, metal, etc. with a sharp point as a guide to cutting. **scribal** *a.*
**scrim•mage** *n.* a confused struggle.
**scrimp** *v.t.* to make too short or small; to stint. **-ed** *a.* **-ily** *adv.* **-iness** *n.* **-y** *a.*
**scrim•shaw** *(Naut.)* *v.t.* and *v.i.* to make decorative article out of bone, whale's tooth, shell, etc.; *n.* such work.
**scrip** *n.* a writing; interim certificate of holding bonds, stock, or shares.
**script** *n.* kind of type, used to imitate handwriting; handwriting; text of words of play, or of scenes and word of film.
**scrip•ture** *n.* anything written; sacred writing; passage from Bible. **scriptural, scripture** *a.*
**scrive•ner** *n.* rotary.
**scrof•u•la** *n.* a tuberculous condition most common in childhood. **scrofulitic, scrofulous** *a.*
**scroll** *n.* roll of paper or parchment; a list; flourish at end of signature; ornament consisting of spiral volutes. **-ed** *a.*
**scro•tum** *n.* external muscular sac which lodges testicles of the male.
**scrub** *v.t.* to clean with a hard brush, etc. and water; *v.i.* to clean by rubbing; *pa.t.*

and *pa.p.* **-bed** *pr.p.* **-bing** *n.*
**scrub** *n.* stunted growth of trees and shrubs; an animal of unknown or inferior breeding; *a.* stunted; inferior. **-by** *a.*
**scruff** *n.* the back of the neck; nape. Also **skruff.**
**scrunch** *v.t.* to crush with the teeth; to crunch; to crush.
**scru•ple** *n.* very small quantity; feeling of doubt; conscientious objection; qualm; *v.i.* to hesitate from doubt; to have compunction. **scrupulous** *a.* extremely conscientious; attentive to small points. **scrupulously** *adv.* **scrupulousness, scrupulosity** *n.*
**scru•ti•ny** *n.* close search; critical examination. **scrutator** *n.* **scrutinate, scrutinize** *v.t.*
**scud** *v.i.* to move quickly; to run before a gale; *pr.p.* **-ding.** *pa.t.* and *pa.p.* **-ded.**
**scuff** *v.t.* to graze against; *v.i.* to shuffle along without raising the feet; *n.* a mark left by scuffing; a flat slipper.
**scuf•fle** *v.i.* to struggle at close quarters; to fight confusedly; to shuffle along; *n.* confused fight, or struggle; a shuffling. **-r** *n.*
**scull** *n.* short light oar pulled with the one hand; light racing boat of a long, narrow build; *v.t.* to propel boat by two sculls; to propel boat by means of oar placed over stern.
**sculp•ture** *n.* art of reproducing objects in relief or in the round out of hard material by means of chisel; carved work; art of modeling in clay or other plastic material; *v.t.* to represent by sculpture. **sculptor** *n.* (*fem.* **sculptress**). **sculptural** *a.*
**scum** *n.* impurities which rise to surface of liquids; vile person or thing, riffraff; *v.t.* to take scum off; to skim; *v.i.* to form scum. *pr.p.* **-ming.** *pa.t.* and *pa.p.* **-med, -my** *a.*
**scup•per** *n.* channel alongside bulwarks of ship to drain away water from deck.
**scurf** *n.* dry scales or flakes formed on skin. **-y** *a.*
**scur•ril•ous** *a.* indecent; abusive; vile. **-ness, scurrility** *n.* **-ly** *adv.*
**scur•ry** *v.i.* to hurry along; to run hastily. **-ing** *n.*
**scur•vy** *n.* deficiency disease due to lack of vitamin C; *(Med.)* scorbutus; *a.* afflicted with the disease; mean; low; vile. **scurvily** *adv.* **scurviness** *n.*
**scut** *n.* a short tail, as that of a hare.
**scu•tate** *a.* *(Bot.)* shield-shaped; *(Zool.)* protected by scales.
**scutch•eon** See **escutcheon.**
**scu•tel•lum** *n.* horny plate or scale. **scutellate, -d** *a.* **scutelliform** *a.* scutellate. **scutiform** *a.* *(Bot.)* shield-shaped.
**scut•tle** *n.* wide-mouthed vessel for holding coal.
**scut•tle** *n.* hole with a cover, for light and air, cut in ship's deck or hatchway; *v.t.* to make holes in ship, esp. to sink it.
**scut•tle** *v.i.* to rush away.
**scythe** *n.* mowing implement; *v.t.* to cut with scythe.
**sea** *n.* mass of salt water covering greater part of earth's surface; certain large expanses of inland water, when salt; vast expanse; flood; large quantity.
**seal** *n.* an aquatic carnivorous animal with flippers as limbs; *v.i.* to hunt for seals. **-er**

seal

*n.* ship, or person, engaged in seal fishing. **-ery** *n.* seal fishing station.
**seal** *n.* piece of metal or stone engraved with a device, cipher, or motto for impression on wax, lead, etc.; that which closes or secures; symbol, token, or

seal

indication; *v.t.* to affix a seal to; to confirm; to ratify; to shut up; to close up joints, cracks, etc. **-ed** *a.*
**seam** *n.* line of junction of two edges, e.g. of two pieces of cloth, or of two planks; thin layer or stratum, esp. of coal; *v.t.* to join by sewing together; to mark with furrows or wrinkles; to scar. **-less** *a.* **-ster** *n.* (*fem.* **-stress, seamstress**) one who sews by profession. **-y** *a.* showing seams; sordid.
**sé•ance** *n.* assembly; meeting of spiritualists for consulting spirits and communicating with 'the other world.'
**sear** *v.t.* to scorch or brand with a hot iron; to dry up; to wither; to brown meat quickly *a.* *(Poetic.)* dry; withered.
**search** *v.t.* to look over or through in order to find; to probe into; *v.i.* to look for; to explore; *n.* searching; quest; investigation. **-ing** *a.* thorough; penetrating; keen; minute. **-ingly** *adv.* **-ingness** *n.*
**sea•son** *n.* one of four divisions of year—spring, summer, autumn, winter; time of the year for certain activities, foods, etc.; convenient time; period; time; *v.t.* to render suitable; to spice; to mature; *v.i.* to grow fit for use. **-able** *a.* suitable or appropriate for the season. **-ableness** *n.* **-ably** *adv.* **-al** *a.* depending on, or varying with seasons. **-ally** *adv.* **-ing** *n.* flavoring.
**seat** *n.* thing made or used for sitting; right to sit (e.g. in council, etc.); sitting part of body; part of trousers which covers buttocks; locality of disease, trouble, etc.; country house; place from which a country is governed; *v.t.* to place on a seat; to fit up with seats; to establish. **-ed** *a.*
**se•ba•ceous** *a.* made of, or pert. to tallow or fat.
**se•cant** *a.* cutting; dividing into two parts; *n.* any straight line which cuts another line, curve, or figure.
**se•cede** *v.t.* to withdraw formally from

federation, alliance, etc. **-er** *n.* **secession** *n.*

**se•clude** *v.t.* to shut up apart. **-d** *a.* **-dly** *adv.* **seclusion** *n.* **seclusive** *a.*

**sec•ond** *a.* next to first; another; inferior; *n.* one who, or that which, follows the first; one next and inferior; sixtieth part of a minute; *n.pl.* inferior quality of commodity or article; *v.t.* to support, esp. a motion before a meeting or council; to back; to encourage. **-ly** *adv.* in the second place.

**sec•ond•ar•y** *a.* succeeding next in order to the first; of second place, origin, rank; second-rate; inferior; unimportant; *n.* one who occupies a subordinate place. **secondarily** *adv.*

**se•cret** *a.* kept from general knowledge; concealed; unseen; private; *n.* something kept secret or concealed; a mystery. **secrecy** *n.* **-ly** *adv.* **-ness** *n.* secrecy. **secretive** *a.* uncommunicative; reticent; underhand. **-ively** *adv.* **-iveness** *n.*

**sec•re•tar•y** *n.* one employed to deal with papers and correspondence, keep records, prepare business, etc.; official in charge of a particular department of government; a desk with bookshelves on top. **secretarial** *a.* **secretariat** *n.* administrative office or officials controlled by secretary.

**se•crete** to hide or conceal; of gland, etc. to collect and supply particular substance in body; *a.* separate; distinct. **secreta** *n.pl.* products of secretion. **secretion** *n.* **secretional** *a.* **secretive** *a.* **secretor** *n.* **secretory** *a.*

**sect** *n.* followers of philosopher or religious leader; faction. **-arian** *a.* pert. to a sect; *n.* one of a sect; a bigot; a partisan. **-arianism** *n.* **-ary** *n.* one of a sect.

**sec•tion** *n.* cutting or separating by cutting; part separated from the rest; *(Bot.* and *Zool.)* thin, translucent slice of organic or inorganic matter mounted on slide for detailed microscopic examination. **-al** *a.* **-alism** *n.* partial regard for limited interests of one particular class at expense of others. **-ally** *adv.* **-ize** *v.t.*

**sec•tor** *n.* portion of circle enclosed by two radii and the arc which they intercept; mathematical instrument; *(Mil.)* a subdivision of the combat area. **-al** *a.*

**sec•u•lar** *a.* worldly; temporal, as opposed to spiritual; lay; lasting for, occurring once in, a century or age; *n.* layman; clergyman, not bound by vow of poverty and not belonging to religious order. **-ization** *n.* **secularize** *v.t.* **secularism** *n.* ethical doctrine which advocates a moral code independent of all religious considerations or practices. **-ist** *n.* **-ity** *n.* worldliness; secularism. **-ly** *adv.*

**se•cure** *a.* free from care, anxiety, fear; safe; in close custody; certain; confident; *v.t.* to make safe, certain, fast; to close, or confine, effectually; to gain possession of; to obtain; to assure. **securable** *a.* **securance** *n.* **-ly** *adv.* **-ness** *n.* **-r** *n.* **security** *n.* being secure; protection; anything given as bond, caution, or pledge. **securities** *n.pl.* general term for shares, bonds, stocks, debentures, etc.

**se•dan** *n.* old-time closed conveyance for one, carried on two poles; a closed automobile with two full seats.

**se•date** *a.* staid; not excitable, composed; calm. **-ly** *adv.* **-ness** *n.* **sedative** *a.* and *n.*

**sed•en•tar•y** *a.* sitting much; requiring sitting posture; inactive. **sedentariness** *n.*

**sedge** *n.* any marshgrass. **sedgy** *a.*

**sed•i•ment** *n.* matter which settles to bottom of liquid; lees; dregs. **-ary** *a.* **-ation** *n.*

**se•di•tion** *n.* any act aimed at disturbing peace of realm or producing insurrection. **-ary** *n.* **seditious** *a.* **seditiously** *adv.* **seditiousness** *n.*

**se•duce** *v.t.* to lead astray; to draw aside from path of rectitude and duty; to induce woman to surrender chastity; to allure. **-ment** *n.* **-r** *n.* **seducible** *a.* **seduction** *n.* **seductive** *a.* **seductively** *adv.* **seductiveness** *n.*

**sed•u•lous** *a.* diligent; steady; industrious; persevering. **sedulity** *n.* **-ness** *n.* **-ly** *adv.*

**see** *n.* diocese or jurisdiction of bishop; province of archbishop.

**see** *v.t.* to perceive by eye; to form an idea; to have interview with; *v.i.* to have the power of sight; to pay regard; to consider; to understand. *pa.t.* **saw.** *pa.p.* **seen. -ing** *conj.* considering; since; *n.* act of perceiving.

**seed** *n.* ovule, which gives origin to new plant; that from which anything springs; origin; offspring; sperm; first principle; *v.t.* to sow with seed; to remove seeds from; to arrange draw for sports tournament. *v.i.* to produce seed. **-ed** *a.* **-ily** *adv.* in seedy manner. **-iness** *n.* being seedy; shabbiness. **-less** *a.* **-ling** *n.* young plant or tree, grown from seed. **-y** *a.* abounding with seeds; run to seed; shabby; worn out; miserable looking.

**seek** *v.t.* to make search or enquiry for; *v.i.* to make search. *pa.t.* and *pa.p.* **sought. -er** *n.*

**seem** *v.i.* to appear (to be or to do). **-ing** *a.* *n.* appearance; apparent likeness. **-ingly** *adv.* **-liness** *n.* **-ly** *a.* **fit; becoming;** *adv.* in a decent or proper manner.

**seen** *pa.p.* of **see.**

**seep** *v.i.* to ooze; to trickle. **-age** *n.*

**se•er** *n.* a prophet.

**seer•suck•er** *n.* a cotton fabric of alternating plain and crinkled stripes.

**see•saw** *n.* game in which two children sit at opposite ends of plank supported in middle and swing up and down; plank for this; *a.* moving up and down or to and fro; reciprocal; *v.i.* to move up and down.

**seethe** *v.t.* to soak; *v.i.* to be in a state of ebullition; to be violently agitated.

**seg•ment** *n.* part cut off from a figure by a line; section; portion; part; *v.t.* and *v.i.* to separate into segments. **-al** *a.* **-ary, -ate** *a.* **-ation** *n.* **-ed** *a.*

**seg•re•gate** *v.t.* and *v.i.* to set or go apart from the rest; *a.* set apart. **segregation** *n.*

**seine** *n.* open net for sea fishing. *v.t.* to catch fish by dragging a seine.

**seism** *n.* earthquake. **-al, -ic** *a.* **-ogram** *n.* record of earthquake made by seismograph. **-ograph** *n.* instrument which records distance and intensity of slightest earth tremors. **-ologic, -al** *a.* **-ologist** *n.* one versed in seismology. **-ology** *n.* the study of earthquakes.

**seize** *v.t.* to grasp; to take hold of; to take possession of by force or legal authority; to comprehend; *v.i.* to take hold. **seizable** *a.* **seizure** *n.* thing or property seized; sudden attack, as apopletic stroke.

**sel•dom** *adv.* rarely.

**se•lect** *v.t.* to choose; to cull; to prefer; *a.* of choice quality; exclusive; *n.* the best people. **-ed** *a.* **-edly** *adv.* **-ion** *n.* selecting; things selected; variety of articles from which to select. **-ive** *a.* having power of selection; discriminating. **-ively** *adv.* **-ivity** *n.* **-or** *n.*

**sel•e•nite** *n.* a colorless and translucent crystalline form of gypsum.

**self** *n.* one's individual person; one's personal interest; ego. *pl.* **selves.** *pron. affix* used to express emphasis or a reflexive usage; *prefix* used in innumerable compounds. **-ish** *a.* concerned unduly over personal profit or pleasure; lacking consideration for others; mercenary; greedy. **-less** *a.* unselfish.

**sell** *v.i.* to dispose of for an equivalent, usually money; to betray for money or a consideration; *v.t.* to fetch a price; to be in demand; *pa.t.* and *pa.p.* **sold.** *n.* deception; hoax. **-er** *n.*

**Selt•zer** *n.* a carbonated mineral water.

**sel•vage, selvedge** *n.* edge of cloth finished to prevent raveling.

**selves** *n.pl.* of **self.**

**se•man•tic** *a.* pert. to meaning of words. **-s** *n.pl.* branch of linguistic research concerned with studying meaning and changes in meaning of words.

**sem•a•phore** *n.* a post with movable arms used for signaling.

**se•ma•si•ol•o•gy** *n.* the science of the development of the meanings of words, semantics. **semasiological** *a.*

**sem•blance** *n.* real or seeming likeness; appearance.

**se•men** *n.* male secretion containing sperm.

**se•mes•ter** *n.* one of two or three divisions of the school year.

**sem•i-** *prefix* with the meaning of half, partly, imperfectly, etc., used in the construction of compound terms, the meaning being usually obvious. *a.* **-colon** *n.* punctuation mark (;) used to separate clauses of a sentence requiring a more marked separation than is indicated by a comma.

**sem•i•nal** *a.* pert. to seed of plants or semen of animals; reproductive, **semination** *n.* act of sowing or disseminating; seeding. **seminiferous, seminific** *a.*

**sem•i•nar** *n.* group of advanced students pursuing research.

**sem•i•nar•y** *n.* academy; secondary school for girls; a training college for priesthood or ministry; *a.* trained in seminary. **seminarist** *n.*

**Sem•i•nole** one of a nomadic tribe of American Indians.

**se•mi•ol•o•gy** *n.* *(Med.)* study of signs and symptoms of disease; symptomatology. **semiotics** *n.* science or language of signs.

**Sem•ite** *n.* member of a speech family comprising Hebrews, Arabs, Assyrians, etc. **Semitic** *a.*

**sem•o•li•na** *n.* hard grains of wheat used in production of spaghetti, macaroni, etc. Also **semola.**

**sen** *n.* Japanese copper coin.

**sen•ate** *n.* supreme legislative and administrative assembly in ancient Rome; upper house of legislature. **senator** *n.* **senatorial** *a.*

**send** *v.t.* to cause to go; to transmit; to forward; *v.i.* to despatch messenger; to transmit message. *pa.t.* and *pa.p.* **sent.**

**se•nes•cence** *n.* the state of growing old; decay; old age. **senescent** *a.*

**se•nile** *a.* pert. to old age; aged; doting. **senility** *n.*

**sen•ior** *a.* older; superior in rank or standing; *n.* a person older, or of higher rank, or of longer service, than another. **-ity** *n.* state of being older; precedence in rank, or longer in service.

**sen•na** *n.* a valuable purgative drug.

**sen•sa•tion** *n.* what we learn through senses; effect produced on a sense organ by external stimulus; exciting event; strong impression. **sensate** *a.* perceived by the senses. **-al** *a.* **-alist** *n.* **-ally** *adv.*

**sen•sa•tion•al•ism** *n.* matter, language or style designed to excite and please vulgar taste; sensualism.

**sense** *n.* any of the bodily faculties of perception or feeling; ability to perceive; meaning; coherence; wisdom; prudence. *pl.* wits; faculties; *v.t.* to perceive; to suspect; *(Colloq.)* to understand. **-less** *a.* **-lessly** *adv.* **-lessness** *n.*

**sen•si•ble** *a.* capable of being perceived by the senses; characterized by good sense; reasonable. **sensibility** *n.* **sensibly** *adv.*

**sen•si•tive** *a.* open to, or acutely affected by, external stimuli or impressions; easily upset by criticism. **-ly** *adv.* **-ness** *n.* **sensitivity** *n.*

**sen•si•tize** *v.t.* to render sensitive. **sensitizer** *n.*

**sen•so•ry** *a.* pert. to, or serving, senses; conveying sensations.

**sen•su•al** *a.* pert. to the senses; given to pursuit of pleasures of sense; self-indulgent; voluptuous; lewd. **-ization** *n.* **-ize** *v.t.* **-ism** *n.* fleshly indulgence. **-ist** *n.* one given to lewd or loose mode of life. **-istic** *a.* **-ity** *n.* **-ly** *adv.* **sensuous** *a.* stimulating, or apprehended by, senses. **sensuously** *adv.* **sensuousness** *n.*

**sent** *pa.t.* and *pa.p.* of **send.**

**sen•tence** *n.* combination of words, which is complete as expressing a thought; judgment passed on criminal by court or judge; decision; *v.t.* to pass sentence upon; to condemn. **sententious** *a.* abounding with axioms and maxims.

**sen•tient** *a.* feeling or capable of feeling; perceiving by senses; sensitive. **sentience, sentiency** *n.* consciousness at

a sensory level. **-ly** *adv.*
**sen•ti•ment** *n.* abstract emotion; tendency to be moved by feeling rather than idea; opinion. **sentimental** *a.* **-alism, -ality** *n.* **-alist** *n.*
**sen•ti•nel** *n.* guard; sentry; *a.* acting as sentinel.
**sen•try** *n.* soldier on guard; sentinel.
**se•pal** *n. (Bot.)* leaf-like member of outer covering, or calyx, of flower. **-ous** *a.*
**sep•a•rate** *v.t.* to part in any manner; to divide; *a.* disconnected; distinct; individual. **separability** *n.* **separable** *a.* **-ly** *adv.* **-ness** *n.* **separation** *n.* **separationist** *n.* **separatist** *n.*
**se•pi•a** *n.* brown pigment.
**sep•sis** *n. (Med.)* state of having bodily tissue infected by bacteria. **septic** *a.*
**sept** *n.* clan, race, or family, proceeding from common progenitor.
**Sep•tem•ber** *n.* ninth month of year.
**sep•te•nar•y** *a.* crossing of seven; lasting seven years; occurring once in seven years.
**sep•tet, septette** *n. (Mus.)* composition for seven voices or instruments.
**sep•tic** *a.* pert. to sepsis; infected. **-emia, -aemia** *n.* blood poisoning. **-ally** *adv.*
**sep•tu•a•ge•nar•i•an** *n.* person between seventy and eighty years of age. **septuagenary** *a.* and *n.*
**Sep•tu•a•ges•i•ma** *n.* third Sunday before Lent.
**Sep•tu•a•gint** *n.* the first and only complete version in Greek of the Old Testament. **-al** *a.*
**sep•tu•ple** *a.* sevenfold; *v.t.* to multiply by seven.
**sep•ul•cher** *n.* tomb; grave; burial vault; *v.t.* to place in a sepulcher. **sepulchral** *a.* **sepulture** *n.* act of burying dead.
**se•qua•cious** *a.* following; attendant; easily led. **-ness, sequacity** *n.*
**se•quel** *n.* that which follows; continuation, complete in itself, of a novel or narrative previously published.
**se•quence** *n.* connected series; succession. **sequent** *a.* following; succeeding; *n.* sequence. **sequential** *a.* **sequentially** *adv.*
**se•ques•ter** *v.t.* to put aside; to separate; to seclude.
**se•quin** *n.* small, ornamental metal disk on dresses, etc.
**Se•quoi•a** *n.* genus of gigantic coniferous evergreen trees native to California.

sequoia

**ser•aph** *n.* member of the highest order of angels. **-s, -im** *n.pl.* **-ic, -ical** *a.*
**Serb, Serbian** *a.* pert. to Serbia; *n.* native or inhabitant of Serbia, the chief constituent state of Yugoslavia.
**sere** *a.* dry; withered.
**ser•e•nade** *n.* music sung or played at night below person's window, esp. by lover; *v.t.* to entertian with serenade. **-r** *n.* **serenata** *n.* instrumental work, between suite and symphony.
**ser•en•dip•ity** *n.* knack of stumbling upon interesting discoveries in a casual manner.
**se•rene** *a.* clear and calm; fair; placid. **-ly** *adv.* **-ness, serenity** *n.*
**serf** *n.* under feudalism, vassal. **-age, -dom, -hood** *n.*
**serge** *n.* hard-wearing worsted fabric.
**ser•geant, sergeant** *n.* noncommissioned officer in army, ranking above corporal; police officer ranking above constable; officer of a law court. **-ship, sergeancy** *n.*
**se•ri•al** *a.* consisting of a series; appearing in successive parts or installments; *n.* a periodical publication. **-ize** *v.t.* to publish as a serial. **-ly, seriately** *adv.* in a regular series or order. **seriatim** *adv.* point by point.
**se•ries** *n.s.* and *pl.* succession of related objects or matters; sequence.
**ser•if** *n. (Printing)* a fine line at the end of the stems and arms of unconnected Roman type letters, as M, y, etc.
**se•ri•ous** *a.* grave in manner or disposition; earnest; important. **-ly** *adv.* **-ness** *n.*
**ser•jeant.** See **sergeant.**
**ser•mon** *n.* discourse for purpose of religious instruction. **-ic, -al** *a.* **-ize** *v.t.* to preach earnestly; to compose a sermon. **-izer** *n.*
**se•rous** *a.* pert. to, containing, or producing serum; watery; thin. **serosity** *n.*
**ser•pent** *n.* snake; treacherous or malicious person; kind of firework; *(Cap.)* constellation in northern hemisphere; *a.* deceitful treacherous. **-ine** *a.; n.* skin; *v.i.* to wind in and out like a serpent. **-inely** *adv.*
**ser•rate, serrated** *a.* notched or cut like saw, as a leaf edge. **serration** *n.* **serrature** *n.* **serriform** *a.*
**ser•ried** *a.* in close order; pressed shoulder to shoulder.
**se•rum** *n.* watery secretion; whey; thin straw-colored fluid, residue of plasma or liquid part of the blood.
**serv•ant** *n.* personal or domestic attendant.
**serve** *v.t.* to work for; to be a servant to; to distribute, as rations, stores, etc.; to deliver formally; *v.i.* to work under another; to be a member of a military, naval, etc. unit; to be useful, or suitable, or enough. **servable** *a.* **-r** *n.*
**serv•ice** *n.* state of being a servant; work done for and benefit conferred on another; act of kindness; military, naval, or air force duty; advantage; use; form of divine worship; regular supply, as water, bus, electricity, etc.; a set of dishes, etc.; *v.t.* to perform service for, e.g., automobiles, etc. **-able** *a.*
**serv•ice** *n.* a small fruit tree.
**ser•vi•ette** *n.* a table napkin.
**ser•vile** *a.* pert. to or befitting a servant or slave; submissive; dependent; menial. **-ly** *adv.* **servility** *n.*

**ser•vi•tor** *n.* attendant; follower or adherent. **servitude** *n.*
**ses•a•me** *n.* annual berbaceous plant cultivated in India and Asia Minor for seeds.
**ses•qui-** *prefix* denoting a proportion of 3:2. **-alteral, -alterate, -alterous** *a.* one and a half more. **-centennial** *a.* pert. to a century and a half; *n.* the 150th anniversary. **-pedalian** *a.* measuring a foot and a half long; applied humorously to any long cumbersome technical word or to one given to using unnecessarily long words. **-pedalianism** *n.*
**ses•sile** *a.* attached by the base, as a leaf; fixed and stationary.
**ses•sion** *n.* actual sitting of a court, council, etc. for transaction of business; a period of time at school or college when a definite course of instruction is given. **-al** *a.*
**ses•tet, seste** *n. (Mus.)* composition for six instruments or voices; last six lines of a sonnet.
**set** *v.t.* to put; to cause to sit; to seat; to place; to plant; to make ready; to adjust; to crouch or point, as dog, to game; *v.i.* to pass below horizon; to go down; to strike root; to become fixed or rigid; to put forth an effort; to begin. *pr.p.* **-ting.** *pa.t.* and *pa.p.* **set.**
**set** *n.* a number of things or persons associated as being similar or complementary or used together, etc.; the manner in which a thing is set, hangs, or fits, as a dress; an attitude or posture; young plant, cutting, or slip for planting out; group or clique; setting of sun; equipment to form the ensemble of a scene for stage or film representation; *a.* fixed; firm; prescribed; regular; established; arranged; appointed; obstinate; determined. **-back** *n.* check to progress.
**se•ta** *n.* bristle or bristlelike structure. **setaceous, setose** *a.*
**set•tee** *n.* couch or sofa.
**set•ter** *n.* hunting dog trained to crouch or set when game is perceived.

english setter

**set•ting** *n.* fixing, adjusting, or putting in place; descending below horizon, as of sun; bezel which holds a precious stone, etc. in position; mounting of scene in play or film; background or surroundings.
**set•tle** *v.t.* to put in place, order, arrangement, etc.; to decide upon; to bring (dispute) to an end; to pay; to take up residence in; to colonize; *v.i.* to become fixed or stationary; to arrange; to (cause to) sink to bottom; to subside; to take up residence in; to dwell; to become calm; to become clear (of liquid). **-d** *a.* **-ment** *n.* **-r** *n.* one who makes his home in a new country; colonist. **settling** *n.*
**set•tle** *n.* long high-backed bench; settee.
**sev•en** *a.* one more than six; *n.* number greater by one than six, symbol 7 or VII.
**sev•en•teen** *a.* one more than sixteen; *n.* sum of ten and seven; symbol 17, or XVII *a.* and *n.* the seventh after the tenth.
**sev•enth** *a.* constituting one of seven equal parts; *n.* one of seven equal parts.
**sev•en•ty** *a.* seven times ten; *n.* sum of seven times ten; the symbol 70 or LXX. **seventieth** *a.* constituting one of seventy equal parts.
**sev•er** *v.t.* to part or divide by violence; to sunder; to cut or break off; *v.i.* to divide. **-able** *a.* **-ance** *n.*
**sev•er•al** *a.* more than two; some; separate; *pron.* several persons or things. **-ly** *adv.*
**se•vere** *a.* serious; rigidly methodical; harsh; not flowery, as style. **-ly** *adv.* **-ness, severity** *n.*
**sew** *v.t.* to fasten together with needle and thread; *v.i.* to practice sewing. **-er** *n.* **-ing** *n.* and *a.*
**sew•age** *n.* drainage; organic refuse carried off by a regular system of underground pipes.
**sew•er** *n.* underground drain or conduit to remove waste water and organic refuse. **-age** *n.*
**sex** *n.* state of being male or female; sum total of characteristics which distinguish male and female organisms; function by which most animal and plant species are perpetuated; males or females collectively. **-ual** *a.* **-uality** *n.* **-ually** *adv.*
**sex-**, comb. form, six.
**sex•ag•e•nar•y** *a.* pert. to the number sixty; proceeding by sixties. **sexagenarian** *n.* person of age of sixty.
**Sex•a•ges•i•ma** *n.* second Sunday before Lent. **sexagesimal** *a.*
**sex•en•ni•al** *a.* continuing for six years; happening once every six years. Also **sextennial. -ly, sextennially** *adv.*
**sex•tant** *n.* an astronomical instrument used in measuring angular distances.

sextant

**sex•ten•nial.** See **sexennial.**
**sex•tet, sex•tette** *n.* musical composition for six voices or instruments.
**sex•ton** *n.* church lay officer acting as caretaker.
**sex•tu•ple** *a.* sixfold; *v.t.* to multiply by six.
**shab•by** *a.* torn or worn to rags; poorly dressed; faded; worn; mean. **shabbily** *adv.* **shabbiness** *n.*
**shack** *n.* roughly built wooden hut.
**shack•le** *n.* metal loop or staple; *pl.* fetters; manacles; anything which hampers; restraints; *v.t.* to fetter; to hamper.
**shad** *n.* name of several species of herring family.

**shade** *n.* partial darkness, due to interception of light; screen; darker part of anything; depth of color; tint; hue; a very minute difference. *pl. invisible world or region of the dead; Hades; v.t.* to shelter or screen, from light or a source of heat; to darken; to pass almost imperceptibly from one form or color to another. **-d** *a.* shadily *adv.* **shadiness** *n.* **shading** *n.* interception of light; slight variation; light and color values in a painting or drawing. **shady** *a.* providing shade; in shade; *(Colloq.)* disreputable.

**shad•ow** *n.* patch of shade; dark figure projected by anything which intercepts rays of light; inseparable companion; ghost; gloom; *v.t.* to cast a shadow over; to follow and watch closely. **-er** *n.* **-iness** *n.* **-ing** *n.* gradation of light and color; shading. **-y** *a.* full of shadow; faint; obscure.

**shaft** *n.* straight rod, stem, or handle; shank; anything long and slender.

**shag** *n.* coarse, matted wool or hair; strong mixture of tobacco leaves cut and shredded for smoking; *a.* rough; shaggy. **-gedness, -giness** *n.* **-gy** *a.* covered with rough hair or wool; rough; unkempt.

**shah** *n. abbrev.* of Shah-in-Shah (King of Kings), the title given to the monarchs of Iran, Persia.

**shake** *v.t.* to cause to move with quick vibrations; to weaken stability of; *v.i.* to tremble; to totter. *pa.t.* **shook.** *pa.p.* **-n.** *n.* shaking; vibration; jolt; severe shock to system; friendly grasping of hands by two individuals. **-n** *a.* **shakily** *adv.* **shakiness** *n.* **shaky** *a.*

**shak•o** *n.* military peaked headdress.

**shale** *n.* *(Geol.)* clay or mud become hardened.

**shall** *v.i.* and *aux.* used to make compound tenses or moods to express futurity, obligation, command, condition or intention.

**shal•low** *a.* having little depth of water; having little knowledge; superficial; *n.* place where water is of little depth. **-ly** *adv.* **-ness** *n.*

**sham** *n.* any trick, fraud, or device which deludes; *a.* counterfeit; false; pretended; *v.t.* to counterfeit; to feign, to pretend; *v.i.* to make false pretenses. *pr.p.* **-ming.** *pa.t.* and *pa.p.* **-med.**

**sham•ble** *v.i.* to walk unsteadily with shuffling gait.

**shame** *n.* emotion caused by consciousness of something wrong or dishonoring in one's conduct or state; cause of disgrace; ignominy; *v.t.* to cause to feel shame; **-ful** *a.* disgraceful. **-fully** *adv.* **-fulness** *n.* **-less** *a.* destitute of shame; brazen-faced; immodest. **-lessly** *adv.* **-lessness** *n.*

**sham•my.** See **chamois.**

**sham•poo** *v.t.* to wash (scalp); *n.* act of shampooing; preparation used. **-er** *n.*

**sham•rock** *n.* small trefoil plant; national emblem of Ireland.

**shang•hai** *v.t.* to drug or render a man unconscious by violence so that he may be shipped as member of a crew; to bring by deceit and force; *pa.t.* and *pa.p.* **shanghaied.**

**shank** *n.* lower part of leg, from knee to ankle; long connecting part of an appliance.

**shan•tung** *n.* silk cloth with rough, knotted surface.

**shan•ty** *n.* crude wooden building.

**shan•ty** *n.* sailor's song. Also **chanty, chantey.**

**shape** *v.t.* to mold or make into a particular form; to figure; to devise; *v.i.* to assume a form or definite pattern; *n.* form; figure; appearance; outline. **-able, shapable** *a.* **-less** *a.* without regular shape or form; deformed; ugly. **-lessness** *n.* **-liness** *n.* beauty of shape or outline. **-ly** *a.*

**shard** *n.* broken fragment, esp. of earthenware; hard wing-case of beetle. Also **sherd.**

**share** *n.* pointed, wedge-shaped, cutting blade of plough.

**share** *n.* part allotted; unit of ownership; *v.t.* to give or allot a share; to enjoy with others; to apportion; *v.i.* to take a share; to participate. **-r** *n.*

**shark** *n.* general name applied to certain voracious marine fishes; swindler; rapacious fellow.

shark

**sharp** *a.* having keen, cutting edge or fine point; abrupt; having ready perception; acid; acrid; pungent; sarcastic; harsh; strongly marked, esp. in outline; shrill; *(Mus.)* raised a semitone in pitch; *n.* acute sound, esp. note raised semitone above its proper pitch; *v.t.* and *v.i.* to raise or sound a half tone above a given tone; *adv.* punctually. **-en** *v.t.* **-ener** *n.* one who, or that which, sharpens. **-er** *n.* swindler. **-ly** *adv.* **-ness** *n.*

**shat•ter** *v.t.* to break into many pieces; to smash; to disorder; *v.i.* to fly in pieces.

**shave** *v.t.* to pare away; to cut close, esp. hair of face or head with razor; to miss narrowly; to graze; *v.i.* to shave oneself; *pa.p.* **-d** or **-n.** **-r** *n.* **shaving** *n.*

**shawl** *n.* cloth used as loose covering for neck and shoulders; *v.t.* to wrap in a shawl.

**shay** *n.* an obsolete one-horse carriage.

**she** *pron.* this or that female; feminine pronoun of the third person.

**sheaf** *n.* bundle of stalks of wheat, rye, oats, or other grain; a sheave; *pl.* **sheaves.** *v.t.* and *v.i.* to make sheaves.

**shear** *v.t.* to clip or cut through with shears or scissors; to deprive. *v.i.* to divide by action of shears; to reap with a sickle. *pa.t.* **-ed.** *pa.p.* **-ed, shorn** *n.; pl.* a cutting instrument, consisting of two blades movable on a pin. **-er** *n.* **-ing** *n.*

**sheath** *n.* close-fitting cover, esp. for knife or sword; scabbard; thin protective covering. **-e** *v.t.* to put into a sheath; to envelop; to encase. **-ing** *n.*

**sheave** *n.* grooved wheel in block, etc. on which a rope works.
**sheave** *v.t.* to bind into sheaves.
**shed** *n.* shelter used for storage or workshop.
**shed** *v.t.* to cause to emanate, proceed, or flow out; to cast off, as hair, feathers, shell; to radiate; *v.i.* to come off. *pr.p.* **-ding.** *pa.t.* and *pa.p.* **shed.**
**sheen** *n.* gloss; glitter; brightness. **-y** *a.*
**sheep** *n. sing.* and *pl.* ruminant mammal, valued for its flesh and its soft fleecy wool; simple, bashful person; *pl.* pastor's church congregation. **-ish** *a.* like a sheep; bashful; awkwardly timid and diffident. **-ishly** *adv.* **-ishness** *n.* **-shank** *n.* knot or hitch for temporarily shortening rope, halyard, etc.
**sheer** *a.* pure; unmixed; absolute; perpendicular; of linen or silk, very thin; *adv.* quite; completely.
**sheer** *v.i.* to deviate from the right course; to swerve.
**sheet** *n.* any broad expanse; a broad piece of cloth spread on bed; broad piece of paper; *v.t.* to cover, as with a sheet. **— metal,** etc. *n.* metal in broad, thin sheets. **-ing** *a.*
**sheik, sheikh** *n.* Arab chief; a title of respect to Moslem ecclesiasts.
**shel•drake** *n.* (*fem.* **shelduck**) genus of wild duck.
**shelf** *n.* board fixed horizontally on frame, or to wall, for holding things; ledge of rocks; sandbank in sea, rendering water shallow. *pl.* **shelves.**
**shell** *n.* hard, rigid, outer, protective covering of many animals, particularly mollusks; outer covering of eggs of birds; protective covering of certain seeds; hollow steel container, filled with high explosive; outer part of structure left when interior is removed; frail racing boat or skiff; group of electrons in atom all having same energy. **-ed** *a.* **-fish** *n.* aquatic animal with external covering of shell.
**shel•lac** *n.* refined, melted form of seed lac used as varnish. *v.t.* to cover with shellac.
**shel•ter** *n.* place or structure giving protection; *v.t.* to give protection to; *v.i.* to take shelter. **-er** *n.*
**shelve** *v.t.* to furnish with shelves; to place on a shelf; to put aside, as unfit for use; to defer consideration of; *v.i.* to slope gradually; to incline. **shelving** *n.*
**shep•herd** *n.* (*fem.* **shepherdess**) one who tends sheep; pastor of church; *v.t.* to tend sheep; to watch over and guide.
**Sher•a•ton** *n.* style of furniture design distinguished for grace and beauty.
**sher•bet** *n.* a frozen dessert.
**sherd.** See **shard.**
**she•rif, shereef** *n.* a descendant of Mohammed.
**sher•iff** *n.* chief law enforcement officer.
**sher•ry** *n.* Spanish wine of deep amber color.
**Shet•land** *(Geog.)* group of islands off N. coast of Scotland. **-er** *n.*
**shib•bo•leth** *n.* testword or password; a distinctive custom.
**shield** *n.* broad piece of armor carried on arm; buckler; anything which protects or defends; *v.t.* to protect; to screen; to forfend.
**shift** *v.t.* to change position (of); to change gears in an automobile; *v.i.* to move; to change in opinion; *n.* change; evasion; expedient. **-er** *n.* **-iness** *n.* trickiness of character or behavior. **-ing** *a.* **-less** *a.* lacking in resource or character. **-lessness** *n.* **-y** *a.* not to be trusted; unreliable.
**shil•le•lagh, shillelah** *n.* a club or cudgel.
**shil•ling** *n.* formerly, a British silver coin.
**shil•ly-shal•ly** *n.* vacillation; indecision; *v.i.* to hesitate or trifle; to waver. **shilly-shallier** *n.*
**shim•mer** *v.i.* to shine with faint, tremulous light; *n.* faint, quivering light or gleam. **-ing** *n.* **-y** *a.*
**shim•my** *n.* dance characterized by exaggerated wriggling; wobbling, as in wheel of a car; *v.i.* to wobble.
**shin** *n.* forepart of leg, between ankle and knee; shank; *v.i.* to climb (up) with aid of one's arms and legs. Also **-ny.**
**shine** *v.i.* to give out or reflect light; to perform in brilliant fashion. *pa.t.* and *pa.p.* **shone.** *v.t.* to cause to shine; to polish, shoes, etc. *pa.t.* and *pa.p.* **shined.** *n.* brightness; gloss. **shining** *a.* **shininess** *n.* **shiny** *a.*
**shin•gle** *n.* rounded water-worn pebbles. **shingly** *a.*
**shin•gle** *n.* thin, rectangular slat for roofing and house siding; small signboard (esp. of physician, lawyer); *v.t.* to cover with shingles.
**shin•gles** *n.pl.* *(Med.)* *herpes zoster,* viral infection of nerve ganglia, accompanied by severe pain and a vesicular eruption along the nerve course.
**Shin•to** *n.* native religion of Japan. **-ism** *n.*
**ship** *n.* a vessel for carriage of passengers and goods by sea; *v.t.* to engage for service on board a ship; to place object in position as oar; to take in water (over the side); *v.i.* to transport. *pr.p.* **-ping.** *pa.t.* and *pa.p.* **-ped.** **-board** *n.* deck or side of ship. **-ment** *n.* process of shipping; cargo. **-per** *n.* **-ping** *n.* **-shape** *a.* orderly, trim; *adv.* properly. **-wright** *n.* one engaged in building or repairing ships. **-yard** *n.* place where ships are built or repaired.

ship

**shire** *n.* territorial division in Great Britain.
**shirk** *v.t.* to evade; to try to avoid (duty, etc.) **-er** *n.*

**shirr** *n.* in needlework, row of puckering or gathering; *v.t.* to gather with parallel threads; to bake eggs.
**shirt** *n.* garment for upper part of body.
**shiv•er** *v.t.* to quiver or shake from cold or fear; *v.t.* to cause to shake; *n.* shaking or shuddering. **-y** *a.*
**shiv•er** *n.* small piece or splinter; *v.t.* and *v.i.* to break into many small pieces or splinters.
**shoal** *n.* large number of fish swimming together; a crowd; *v.i.* to crowd together.
**shoal** *n.* a sandbank or bar; shallow water; *a.* shallow; *v.i.* to become shallow. **-y** *a.*
**shoat** *n.* a young pig.
**shock** *n.* violent impact or concussion when bodies collide; sudden depression of the system due to violent injury or strong mental emotion; paralytic stroke; effect of electric discharge through body; *v.t.* to strike against suddenly; to strike with surprise, horror, or disgust. **-er** *n.* **-ing** *a.* appalling; terrifying; frightful; repulsive; offensive. **-ingly** *adv.*
**shock** *n.* disordered mass of hair; *a.* shaggy; bushy.
**shock** *n.* group of sheaves of grain; *v.t.* to make into shocks.
**shod** *pa.t.* and *pa.p.* of verb **shoe.**
**shod•dy** *n.* inferior textile material; *a.* inferior; of poor quality.
**shoe** *n.* covering for foot, but not enclosing ankle; various protective plates or undercoverings; *v.t.* to furnish with shoes; to put shoes on. *pr.p.* **-ing.** *pa.t., pa.p.* **-less** *a.*
**shone** *pa.t.* and *pa.p.* of **shine.**
**shoo** *interj.* begone; *v.t.* to scare or drive away.
**shook** *pa.t.* of **shake.**
**shoot** *v.t.* to discharge missile from gun, etc.; to kill or wound with such a missile; to propel quickly; to thrust out; to pass swiftly over (rapids) or through (arch of bridge); to photograph episode or sequence of motion picture; *v.i.* to move swiftly and suddenly; to let off a gun, etc.; to sprout; to advance; to kick towards goal. *pa.t.* and *pa.p.* **shot.** *n.* shooting; young branch or stem. **-er** *n.* **-ing** *n.*
**shop** *n.* building where goods are made, or sold; workshop; store *v.i.* to visit shops to purchase articles. *pr.p.* **-ping** *pa.t.* and *pa.p.* **-ped. -lifter** *n.* one who makes petty thefts from shop counter. **-ping** *n.* **-worn** *a.* soiled or tarnished by long exposure in shop.
**shore** *n.* land adjoining sea or large lake; *v.t.* to put ashore.
**shore** *n.* strong beam set obliquely against wall of building or ship to prevent movement during alterations; *v.t.* to support by post or buttress; to prop. **shoring** *n.*
**shorn** *pa.p.* of **shear;** *a.* cut off; having the hair or wool cut off.
**short** *a.* having little length; not long in space; low; not extended in time; limited or lacking in quantity; hasty of temper; pronounced with less prolonged accent; concise; abrupt; *adv.* suddenly; abruptly; without reaching the end; *pl.* short trousers reaching down to above knees. **-age** *n.* **-coming** *n.* failing; fault; defect. **-cut** *n.* quicker but unorthodox way of reaching a place or of accomplishing a task, etc. **-en** *v.t.* to make shorter; *v.t.* to contract; to lessen. **-ening** *n.* lard, butter, or other fat used when baking pastry, etc. **-hand** *n.* system of rapid reporting by means of signs or symbols. **—handed** *a.* not having the full complement of staff on duty. **-ly** *adv.* in a brief time; soon; in a few words; curtly. **-ness** *n.* **— shrift,** summary treatment.
**shot** *pa.t.* and *pa.p.* of **shoot.**
**shot** *a.* pert. to fabrics woven with warp and weft of contrasting tints or colors.
**shot** *n.* act of shooting; one of small pellets, contained in cartridge fired from sporting rifle; charge of blasting powder; stroke in billiards, tennis, etc.; a photograph; a try to attempt; *v.t.* to load or weight with shot. *pr.p.* **-ting.** *pa.t.* and *pa.p.* **-ted. -gun** *n.* smoothbore gun for shooting small game or birds.
**should** *v.* and *aux.* used in Future-in-the-Past tenses of verbs with pronouns I or we; auxiliary used after words expressing opinion, intention, desire, probability, obligation, etc.
**shoul•der** *n.* ball and socket joint formed by humerus with scapula; upper joint of foreleg of animal; anything resembling human shoulder, as prominent part of hill; *v.t.* to push forward with shoulders; to bear (burden, etc.); to accept (responsibility); *v.i.* to push forward through crowd.
**shout** *n.* loud, piercing cry; *v.t.* and *v.i.* to utter loud sudden cry.
**shove** *v.t.* to push; to press against; to jostle; *v.i.* to push forward; *n.* act of pushing.
**shov•el** *n.* spade with broad blade slightly hollowed; scoop; machine for scooping and lifting; *v.t.* to lift or move with a shovel; *v.i.* to use shovel. **-ler** *n.*
**show** *v.t.* to present to view; to disclose; to explain; to prove; to conduct; to guide; *v.i.* to appear; to be visible; to come into sight. *pa.p.* **-n** or **-ed** *n.* that which is shown; spectacle; exhibition; display; **-er** *n.* **-ily** *n.* **-man** *n.* one who presents a show; one who is skilled at presenting things. **-manship** *n.* **-y** *a.* gaudy; attracting attention; ostentatious.
**show•er** *n.* a brief fall of rain or hail; anything coming down like rain; great number; *v.t.* to wet with rain; to give abundantly; *v.i.* to rain; to pour down. **-y** *a.* raining intermittently.
**shrank** *pa.t.* of **shrink.**
**shrap•nel** *n.* shell timed to explode over, and shower bullets and splinters on, personnel; shell splinters.
**shred** *n.* long, narrow piece cut or torn off; strip; *v.t.* to cut or tear to shreds. *pr.p.* **-ding.** *pa.t.* and *pa.p.* **-ded.**
**shrew** *n.* noisy, quarrelsome woman; a termagant; mammal resembling, but unrelated to, mouse. **-ish** *a.* **-ishly** *adv.* **-ishness** *n.*

shrew

**shrewd** *a.* intelligent; discerning; cunning. **-ly** *adv.* **-ness** *n.*
**shriek** *v.t.* and *v.i.* to scream; to screech; *n.* a loud, shrill cry.
**shrift** *n.* confession made to a priest.
**shrike** *n.* bird which preys on birds, frogs, and insects.
**shrill** *a.* uttering an acute sound; piercing; high-pitched; *v.i.* to sound in a shrill tone. **-y** *adv.*
**shrimp** *n.* small edible crustacean allied to prawns; small person; *v.i.* to catch shrimps with net. **-er** *n.*
**shrine** *n.* case in which sacred relics are deposited; tomb of saint; place of worship; any sacred place.
**shrink** *v.i.* to contract; to dwindle; to recoil; to draw back; *v.t.* to cause to contract. *pa.t.* **shrank, shrunk.** *pa.p.* **shrunk. -age** *n.* **shrunken** *a.*
**shrive** *v.t.* to give absolution to; to confess (used reflexively); *v.i.* to receive or make confession. **-d** or **shrove.** *pa.p.* **shriven.**
**shriv•el** *v.t.* and *v.i.* to cause to contract and wrinkle; to wither.
**shroud** *n.* that which clothes or covers; sheet for a corpse; winding sheet; *v.t.* to enclose in winding sheet; to cover with shroud; to conceal.
**shrove** *pa.t.* of the verb **shrive. Shrovetide** *n.* period immediately before Lent.
**shrub** *n.* any hard-wooded plant of smaller and thicker growth than tree; bush; low, dwarf tree. **-bery** *n.* collection of shrubs. **-by** *a.*
**shrug** *v.i.* to raise and narrow shoulders in disdain, etc. *v.t.* to move (shoulders) thus. *pr.p.* **-ging.** *pa.t.* and *pa.p.* **-ged.** *n.* drawing up of shoulders.
**shrunk, shrunken** See **shrink.**
**shuck** *n.* husk or pod; shell of nut; *v.t.* to remove husk, pod, or shell from.
**shud•der** *v.i.* to tremble violently; *n.* trembling or shaking. **-ing** *n.* and *a.* trembling; shivering.
**shuf•fle** *v.t.* to shove one way and the other; to throw into disorder; to mix (cards); to scrape (feet) along ground; *v.i.* to change position of cards in pack; to prevaricate; to move in a slovenly manner; to scrape floor with foot in dancing or walking; *n.* act of throwing into confusion by change of places; artifice or pretext; scraping movement of foot in dancing.
**shun** *v.t.* to keep clear of; to avoid. *pr.p.* **-ning.** *pa.t.* and *pa.p.* **-ned.**
**shunt** *v.t.* to move or turn off to one side; *v.i.* to go aside; to turn off. *n.* act of shunting. **-er** *n.*
**shut** *v.t.* to close to hinder ingress or egress; to forbid entrance to; *v.i.* to close itself; to become closed. *pr.p.* **-ting.** *pa.t.* and *pa.p.* **shut.** *a.* closed; made fast. **-ter** *n.* one who, or that which, shuts; movable protective screen for window.
**shut•tle** *n.* instrument used in weaving for shooting thread of woof between threads of warp; *v.t.* and *v.i.* to move backwards

shuttle

and forwards. **-cock** *n.* cork with fan of feathers for use with battledore or in badminton.
**shy** *a.* sensitively timid; reserved; easily frightened; cautious; falling short; *v.i.* to start suddenly aside. *pa.t.* and *pa.p.* **shied. -ly** *adv.* **-ness** *n.* **-ster** *n.* unscrupulous lawyer or person.
**shy** *v.t.* to throw; to fling. *pa.t.* and *pa.p.* **shied.** *n.* throw; cast.
**Si•a•mese** *a.* pert. to Siam, the people, or language; *n.* native of Siam; the language.
**sib** *a.* having kinship; related by blood; *n.* a blood relation.
**Si•be•ri•an** *a.* pert. to Siberia, part of the Soviet Union.
**sib•i•lance** *n.* hissing sound; quality of being sibilant. Also **sibilancy. sibilant** *a.* *n.* letter uttered with hissing of voice, as *s*, *x*, etc. **sibilate** *v.t.*
**sib•yl** *n.* a name applied to certain votaresses of Apollo. **-lic, -line** *a.*
**sic** *adv.* abbreviated form of *sic in originail* printed in brackets as guarantee that passage has been quoted correctly; so; thus.
**sic•ca•tion** *n.* act or process of drying. **siccative** *a.* and *n.*
**Si•cil•i•an** *a.* pert. to island of Sicily; *n.* native of Sicily.
**sick** *a.* affected with physical or mental disorder; tired of. **-en** *v.t.* to make sick; to disgust; *v.i.* to become sick; to be filled with abhorrence. **-ening** *a.* causing sickness or disgust; nauseating. **-eningly** *adv.* **-ly** *a.* **-ness** *n.*
**sick•le** *n.* reaping hook.
**side** *n.* one of surfaces of object, esp. upright inner or outer surface; one of the edges of plane figure; margin; border; part of body from hip to shoulder; slope, as of a hill; one of two parties, teams, or sets of opponents; line of descent traced through one parent; *a.* being on the side; lateral; indirect; incidental; *v.i.* (with) to hold or embrace the opinions of another. **-board** *n.* piece of furniture designed to hold dining utensils, etc. in dining room. **-car** *n.* small box-shaped body attached to motorcycle. **— light** *n.* any source of light situated at side of room, door, etc.; lantern, showing red or green, on side of a vessel; incidental information or illustration. **—long** *a.* lateral; oblique; not directly forward; *adv.* obliquely; on the side. **-r** *n.* **-show** *n.* minor entertainment or attraction; subordinate affair. **-slip** *n.* involuntary skid or slide sideways; *v.i.* to skid. **-stroke** *n.* style of swimming where body is turned on one side. **-track** *v.t.* to shunt into siding; to

postpone indefinitely; to shelve; *n.* a railway siding. **siding** *n.* **sidle** *v.i.* to move sideways; to edge.
**si•de•re•al** *a.* relating to constellations and fixed stars.
**sid•er•ite** *n.* brown ironstone.
**siege** *n.* the surrounding of a town or fortified place by hostile troops in order to induce it to surrender; continuous effort to gain (affection, influence, etc.); *v.t.* to besiege.
**si•en•na** *n.* natural yellow earth which provides pigment. **burnt sienna,** pigment giving reddish-brown tint. **raw sienna,** pigment giving a yellowish-brown tint.
**si•er•ra** *n.* chain of mountains with saw-like ridge.
**sieve** *n.* utensil with wire netting or small holes for separating fine part of any pulverized substance from the coarse; *v.t.* to sift.
**sift** *v.t.* to separate coarser portion from finer; to sieve; to scrutinize.
**sigh** *v.i.* to make a deep, single respiration, as expression of exhaustion or sorrow; *v.t.* to utter sighs over; *n.* long, deep breath.
**sight** *n.* one of the five senses; act of seeing; that which is seen; anything novel or remarkable; exhibition; spectacle; any guide for eye to assist direction; *v.t.* to catch sight of; to see; *v.i.* to take aim by means of a sight. **-less** *a.* blind; invisible. **-lessly** *adv.* **-lessness** *n.* **-liness** *n.* comeliness. **-ly** *a.* pleasing to the eye; graceful; handsome.
**sig•il** *n.* seal; signet; occult sign. **sigillary** *a.*
**sign** *n.* movement, mark, or indication to convey some meaning; token; symbol; omen; signboard; password; *(Math.)* character indicating relation of quantities or operation to be performed; *(Mus.)* any character, as flat, sharp, dot, etc.; *v.t.* to represent by sign; to affix signature to; to ratify; *v.i.* to make a signal or gesture; to append one's signature.
**sig•nal** *n.* sign to give notice at a distance; that which in the first place impels any action; *v.t.* to communicate by signals; *v.i.* to make signals. *pr.p.* **-ing.** *pa.t.* and *pa.p.* **-ed** *a.* pert. to a signal; remarkable; conspicuous. **-ize** *v.t.* to make notable, distinguished, or remarkable; to point out. **-er** *n.* **-ly** *adv.* eminently; remarkably.
**sig•na•to•ry** *a.* and *n.* (one) bound by signature to terms of agreement.
**sig•na•ture** *n.* a sign, stamp, or mark impressed; a person's name written by himself; act of writing it.
**sig•net** *n.* seal used for authenticating documents.
**sig•ni•fy** *v.t.* to make known by a sign; to convey notion of; to indicate; *v.i.* to express meaning; *pa.t.* and *pa.p.* **signified. significance** *n.* **significant** *a.* fitted or designed to signify or make known something; important. **significantly** *adv.* **signification** *n.* **significative** *a.* **significatory** *a.*
**si•lage** *n.* compressed, acid-fermented fodder.
**si•lence** *n.* stillness; quietness; calm; refraining from speed; oblivion; *interj.* be quiet!; *v.t.* to cause to be still; to forbid to speak; to refute; to kill. **-r** *n.* **silent** *a.* **silently** *adv.* **silentness** *n.*
**si•lex** *n.* silica.
**sil•hou•ette** *n.* portrait or picture done in black upon a light ground; outline of object seen against the light; *v.t.* to represent in outline.
**sil•i•ca** *n.* silicon dioxide, main component of most rocks, occurring in nature as sand, flint, quartz, etc. **silicate** *n.* salt of silicic acid. **silicated** *a.* **siliceous** *a.* Also **silicious. silicic** *a.*
**sil•i•cones** *n.pl.* new family of materials—petroleum, brine, ordinary sand.
**silk** *n.* fine, soft, lustrous thread; fabric made from this; *a.* made of silk. **-en** *a.* made of, or resembling, silk; soft; smooth; silky. **-iness** *n.* **-screen** *a.* and *n.* (pert. to) the reproduction of a design by means of a pattern made on a screen of nylon or silk. **-worm** *n.* caterpillar of any moth which produces silk.
**sill** *n.* base or foundation; horizontal member at the bottom of window frame, door, or opening.
**sil•ly** *a.* weak in intellect; foolish; senseless; stupid; *n.* silly person. **sillily** *adv.* **silliness** *n.*
**si•lo** *n.* large, airtight tower, elevator, or pit in which green crops are preserved; *v.t.* to preserve in a silo.
**silt** *n.* fine, alluvial, soil, particles, mud; sediment; *v.t.* and *v.i.* to choke or obstruct with silt.
**sil•ver** *n.* soft, white, metallic element, very malleable and ductile; silverware; silver coins; anything resembling silver; *a.* made of, or resembling, silver; white or gray, as hair; bright, silvery; *v.t.* to coat or plate with silver; to tinge with white or gray; to render smooth and bright; *v.i.* to become gradually white, as hair. **-ize** *v.t.* **-plating** *n.* **-ware** *n.* articles made of silver. **-ry** *a.* like silver; lustrous; (of sound) soft and clear.
**sim•i•an** *a.* pert. to or like an ape generally; *n.* a monkey or ape.
**sim•i•lar** *a.* like; resembling; exactly corresponding. **-ity** *n.* quality or state of being similar. **-ly** *adv.*
**sim•i•le** *n.* figure of speech using some point of resemblance observed to exist between two things which differ in other respects.
**si•mil•i•tude** *n.* state of being similar or like; parable.
**sim•mer** *v.t.* to cause to boil gently; *v.i.* to be just bubbling or just below boiling-point; to be in a state of suppressed anger or laughter; *n.* gentle, gradual heating.
**si•mo•ni•ac** *n.* one guilty of simony. **-al** *a.* **-ally** *adv.* **simonist** *n.*
**si•mo•ny** *n.* the offense of offering or accepting money or other reward for nomination or appointment.
**sim•per** *v.i.* to smile in a silly, affected manner; *n.* smile with air of silliness or

affectation. **-er** *n.*

**sim•ple** *a.* single; not complex; entire; mere; plain, sincere; clear; intelligible; simple-minded; *(Chem.)* composed of a single element; *n.* something not compounded. **—minded** *a.* ingenuous; open; frank; mentally weak. **-ness** *n.* **-ton** *n.* foolish person; person of weak intellect. **-simplicity** *n.* **simplification** *n.* **simplificative** *a.* **simplify** *v.t.* to make or render simple, plain, or easy. *pa.t.* and *pa.p.* **simplified. simply** *adv.*

**sim•u•la•crum** *n.* image; representation. *pl.* **simulacra.**

**sim•u•lant** *a.* simulating; having the appearance of; *n.* one simulating something. **simular** *a.* and *n.*

**sim•u•late** *v.t.* to assume the mere appearance of, without the reality; to feign. **simulation** *n.* **simulator** *n.*

**si•mul•ta•ne•ous** *a.* existing or occurring at same time. **-ness, simultaneity** *n.* **-ly** *adv.*

**sin** *n.* transgression against divine or moral law, esp. when committed consciously; iniquity; evil; *v.i.* to depart from path of duty prescribed by God; to do wrong. *pr.p.* **-ning.** *pa.t.* and *pa.p.* **-ned. -ful** *a.* **-fully** *adv.* **-fulness** *n.* **-ner** *n.*

**since** *adv.* from then till now; subsequently; ago; *prep.* at some time subsequent to; after; *conj.* from the time that; seeing that; because.

**sin•cere** *a.* not assumed or merely professed; straightforward. **-ly** *adv.* **-ness, sincerity** *n.*

**sine** *n.* (*abbrev.* sin) *(Math.)* perpendicular drawn from one extremity of an arc to diameter drawn through other extremity; function of one of the two acute angles in a right angle triangle, ratio of line subtending this angle to hypotenuse.

**si•ne•cure** *n.* office, position, etc. with salary but with few duties. **sinecurist** *n.*

**sin•ew** *n.* ligament or tendon which joins muscle to bone; source of strength or vigor. **-ed** *a.* **-y** *a.* well braced; muscular.

**sing** *v.t.* to utter with musical modulations of voice; to celebrate in song; *v.i.* to utter sounds with melodious modulations of voice; to pipe, twitter, chirp, as birds; to hum; to reverberate. *pa.t.* **sang** or **sung.** *pa.p.* **sung. -er** *n.* one who sings; vocalist. **-ing** *n.*

**singe** *v.t.* to burn the surface slightly; to burn loose fluff from yarns, etc. *pr.p.* **-ing.** *n.* superficial burn.

**Sin•gha•lese** *a.* pert. to Ceylon, its people, or language. *n.* a native of Ceylon.

**sin•gle** *a.* sole; not double; unmarried; sincere; whole-hearted; straightforward; upright; *n.* unit; *v.t.* (with *out*) to select from a number; to pick; to choose. **-ness** *n.* **singly** *adv.* one by one; by oneself.

**sin•gle•ton** *n.* *(Cards)* hand containing only one card of some suit.

**sing•song** *n.* rhythmical, monotonous fashion of uttering. *a.* monotonous; droning.

**sin•gu•lar** *a.* existing by itself; individual; unique; outstanding; *n.* single instance; word in the singular number. **-ize** *v.t.* **-ity** *n.* state of being singular; anything unusual or remarkable; oddity. **-ly** *adv.*

**Sin•ic** *a.* Chinese. **-ism** *n.*

**sin•is•ter** *a.* on left hand; evil-looking. **sinistral** *a.* to the left; reversed.

**sink** *v.t.* to cause to descend; to submerge; to dig; to excavate; to ruin; to suppress; to invest; *v.i.* to subside; to descend; to penetrate (into); to become submerged. *pa.t.* **sank** or **sunk.** *pa.p.* **sunk.** *n.* a receptacle for washing up; place notoriously associated with evildoing. **-er** *n.* **-ing** *n.* operation of excavating; subsidence; settling; ebb; part sunk below surrounding surface.

**Si•no-**, in compounds, meaning Chinese.

**Si•nol•o•gy** *n.* that branch of knowledge which deals with the Chinese.

**sin•u•ate** *v.i.* to bend in and out; *a.* *(Bot.)* wavy; tortuous; curved on the margin, as a leaf. Also **-d. sinuation** *n.* **sinuose, sinuous** *a.* bending in and out; morally crooked; supple. **sinuously** *adv.*

**si•nus** *n.* *(Anat.)* opening; hollow; cavity. **-itis** *n.* inflammation of sinus.

**Sioux** *n.* member of great Siouan division of N. American aborigines; their language. *pl.* **Sioux.**

**sip** *v.t.* and *v.i.* to drink or imbibe in very small quantities; to taste. *pr.p.* **-ping.** *pa.t.* and *pa.p.* **-ped.** *n.* a small portion of liquid sipped with the lips.

**si•phon, syphon** *n.* a bent tube or pipe by which a liquid can be transferred by atmospheric pressure from one receptacle to another; bottle provided with internal tube and lever top, for holding and delivering aerated water; projecting tube in mantle of shell of bivalve; *v.t.* to draw off by means of a siphon. *n.* action of a siphon.

**sir** *n.* a title or respect to any man of position.

**sire** *n.* title of respect to a king or emperor; male parent of an animal (applied esp. to horses); *pl.* *(Poetic)* ancestors; *v.t.* to beget (of animals).

**si•ren** *n.* *(Myth.)* one of several nymphs said to sing with such sweetness that sailors were lured to death; seductive alluring woman; form of horn which emits series of loud, piercing notes used as warning signal; steam whistle; *a.* pert. to, or resembling a siren.

**Sir•i•us** *n.* *(Astron.)* a star of the first magnitude known as the Dog Star.

**sir•loin** *n.* the upper part of a loin of beef.

**si•roc•co** *n.* a hot, southerly, dust-laden wind from Africa.

**si•sal** *n.* fiber plant, native to Florida and Yucatan.

**sis•sy** *n.* *(Colloq.)* ineffective effeminate man or boy; *a.* effeminate.

**sis•ter** *n.* female whose parents are same as those of another person; woman of the same faith; nun; *a.* related; of a similar nature to, as institute, college, etc. **-hood** *n.* state of being a sister; society of women united in one faith or order. **-like, -ly** *a.*

**Sis•tine** *a.* pert. to any Pope named Sixtus. **— Chapel,** the Pope's private chapel in the Vatican at Rome.

**sit** *v.i.* to rest upon haunches, a seat, etc.; to remain; to rest; to perch, as birds; to be in session; to be representative in legislative for constituency; to fit (of clothes); *v.t.* to keep good seat, upon, as on horseback; to place upon seat; *pr.p.* **-ting.** *pa.t.* and *pa.p.* **sat.** *n.* position assumed by an object after being placed. **-ter** *n.* **-ting** *n.* and *a.*

**site** *n.* situation; plot of ground for, or with, building; locality; place where anything is fixed; *v.t.* to place in position; to locate.

**si•tol•o•gy** *n.* dietetics.

**sit•u•ate** *v.t.* to give a site to; to place in a particular state or set of circumstances to locate; **-d** *a.* **situation** *n.* location; place or position; site; condition; job; post; plight.

**six** *a.* one more than five; *n.* sum of three and three; symbol 6 or VI. **-teen** *n.* and *a.* six and ten, symbol 16 or XVI. **-teenth** *a.* sixth after the tenth; being one of sixteen equal parts into which anything is divided; *n.* one of sixteen equal parts. **-th** *a.* next in order after the fifth; one of six equal parts. **-ty** *a.* six times ten; three score; *n.* symbol 60 or LX. **-tieth** *a.* next in order after the fifty-ninth; one of sixty equal parts.

**size** *n.* bulk; bigness; comparative magnitude; dimensions; *v.t.* to arrange according to size. **-able, sizable** *a.* of considerate size or bulk.

**size** *n.* substance of a gelatinous nature, like weak glue; *v.t.* to treat or cover with size.

**siz•zle** *v.i.* to make hissing or sputtering noise; *n.* hissing, sputtering noise. **sizzling** *n.*

**skald** *n.* ancient Scandinavian poet. **-ic** *a.* Also **scald.**

**skate** *n.* steel blade attached to boot, used for gliding over ice; *v.i.* to travel over ice on skates. **-r** *n.* **skating** *n.* **skating-rink** *n.* stretch of ice or flat expanse for skating.

**skate** *n.* a large, edible, flat fish of the ray family.

**skean** *n.* Highland dagger or dirk.

**skeet** *n.* trapshooting with clay targets.

**skein** *n.* small hank, of fixed length, of thread, silk, or yarn.

**skel•e•ton** *n.* body framework providing support for human or animal body; any framework; *a.* pert. to skeleton; containing mere outlines. Also **skeletal.**

**skel•ter.** See **helter-skelter.**

**skep** *n.* beehive made of straw; light basket.

**skep•tic** *n.* one who doubts, esp. existence of God, or accepted doctrines. **-al** *a.* **-ally** *adv.* **-alness** *n.* **skepticize** *v.i.* **skepticism** *n.*

**sker•ry** *n.* rocky isle; reef.

**sketch** *n.* first rough draft or plan of any design; drawing in pen, pencil, or similar medium; descriptive essay or account, in light vein; *v.t.* to make rough draft of; *v.i.* to draw. **-er** *n.* **-ily** *adv.* **-iness** *n.* lack of detail. **-y** *a.*

**skew** *a.* awry; askew; turned aside; *n.* a deviation; *v.t.* to put askew; to skid.

**skew•er** *n.* pointed rod for fastening meat to a spit; *v.t.* to fasten with skewers.

**ski** *n.* long wooden runner strapped to foot, for running, sliding and jumping over snow; *v.i.* to run, slide, or jump on skis. **-er** *n.*

**ski•a•graph** *n.* an X-ray photograph. Also **skiagram.** **-er** *n.* **-ic** *a.*

**skid** *n.* a piece of timber to protect side of vessel from injury; inclined plane down which logs, etc. slide; low, wooden platform for holding and moving loads; *v.i.* to slide or slip sideways; *v.t.* to slide a log down a skid; to place on skids. *pr.p.* **-ding** *pa.p., pa.t.* **-ded.**

**skiff** *n.* a small rowboat or sailboat.

**skill** *n.* practical ability and dexterity; knowledge; expertness; aptitude. **-ful** *a.* **-fully** *adv.* **-fulness** *n.* **-ed** *a.*

**skil•let** *n.* a frying pan.

**skim** *v.t.* to remove from surface of liquid; to glide over lightly and rapidly; to glance over in superficial way; to graze; *v.i.* to pass lightly over. *pr.p.* **-ming.** *pa.t.* and *pa.p.* **-med.** *n.* skimming; matter skimmed off. **-mer** *n.*

**skimp** *v.t.* to stint; *v.i.* to be mean or parsimonious. **-y** *a.*

**skin** *n.* external protective covering of animal bodies; coat of fruits and plants; thick scum; *v.t.* to strip off skin or hide of. **-ner** *n.* dealer in hides; furrier. **-niness** *n.* leanness. **-ny** *a.* of skin; very lean or thin.

**skip** *v.t.* to leap over lightly; to omit without noticing; *v.i.* to leap lightly, esp. in frolic; to pass from one thing to another. *pr.p.* **-ping.** *pa.t.* and *pa.p.* **-ped.** *n.* **-ping** *a.*

**skip•per** *n.* captain of ship or team.

**skirl** *v.i.* to sound shrilly. *n.* shrill, high-pitched sound of bagpipe.

**skir•mish** *n.* irregular, minor engagement between two parties of soldiers; *v.i.*

**skirt** *n.* lower part of coat, gown; outer garment of a woman fitted to and hanging from waist; margin; edge; rim; *v.t.* to be on border; to go around.

**skit** *n.* short, usually humorous, play; *v.i.* to leap aside. **-tish** *a.* frisky; frivolous; fickle; apt to shy, of a horse. **-tishly** *adv.* **-tishness** *n.*

**skit•tle** *n.* game of ninepins.

**skive** *v.t.* in shoe-making, to pare away edges of leather.

**skoal** *interj.* salutation, hail!

**skulk** *v.i.* to lurk or keep out of sight in a furtive manner; to act sullenly; *n.* one who skulks.

**skull** *n.* body framework which encloses brain; cranium along with bones of face.

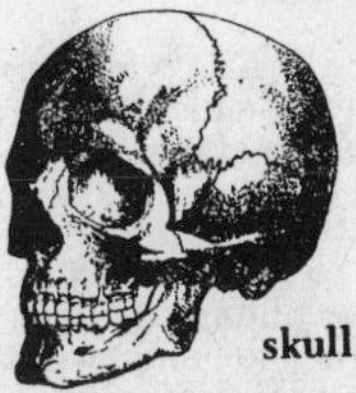

skull

**skunk** *n.* small N. American burrowing animal, allied to weasel, which defends itself by emitting evil-smelling fluid; *(Colloq.)* a base, mean person.

**sky** *n.* the apparent vault of heaven; heavens; firmament; climate. *v.t.*

**Skye** *n.* or **Skyeterrier**, breed of Scotch terrier, with long hair.

**slab** *n.* thickish, flat, rectangular piece of anything.

**slack** *a.* not taut; not holding fast; remiss about one's duties; easygoing; *n.* part of a rope which hangs loose; quiet time. **-en** *v.t.* and *v.i.* **-er** *n.* **-ly** *adv.* **-ness** *n.* **-s** *n.pl.* loose trousers worn by men or women.

**slack** *n.* the finer screenings of coal.

**slag** *n.* silicate formed during smelting of ores; *v.i.*

**slain** *pa.p.* of the verb **slay.**

**slake** *v.t.* to quench; to extinguish; to combine quicklime with water; to slacken; *v.i.* to become mixed with water.

**slam** *v.t.* to shut violently and noisily; to bang; to hit; to dash down. *pr.p.* **-ming.** *pa.t.* and *pa.p.* **-med.** *n.* act of slamming; bang.

**slan•der** *n.* false or malicious statement about person; calumny; *v.t.* to injure by maliciously uttering false report; to defame. **-er** *n.* **-ous** *a.*

**slang** *n.* word or expression in common colloquial use but not regarded as standard English.

**slant** *v.t.* to turn from a direct line; to give a sloping direction to; *v.i.* to lie obliquely; *n.* slanting direction or position; point of view or illuminating remark (on); *a.* sloping; oblique. **-ingly** *adv.* **-ly, -wise** *adv.*

**slap** *n.* blow with open hand or flat instrument; insulting remark; *v.t.* to strike with open hand or something flat. *pr.p.* **-ping.** *pa.t.* and *pa.p.* **-ped.** **-stick** *n.* boisterous farce of pantomime or low comedy.

**slash** *v.t.* to cut by striking violently and haphazardly; *v.i.* to strike violently and at random with edged weapon; *n.* long cut; gash. **-er** *n.*

**slat** *n.* narrow strip of wood, metal, etc. **-ted** *a.*

**slate** *n.* a form of shale which splits readily into thin leaves; dark blue-gray color; list of candidates for offices; *a.* made of slate; bluish-gray; *v.t.* to cover with slates; to put on a list for nomination, etc. **slating** *n.* act of covering with slates; roof covering thus put on. **slaty** *n.*

**slat•tern** *n.* slut; slovenly woman or girl. **-liness** *n.* **-ly** *a.* and *adv.* like a slattern.

**slaugh•ter** *n.* carnage; massacre; butchery; killing of animals to provide food; *v.t.* to kill; to slay in battle; to butcher. **-er** *n.* **-ous** *a.* **-ously** *adv.*

**Slav** *n.* a member of a group of peoples in E. and S.E. Europe, comprising Russians, Ukrainians, White Russians, Poles, Czechs, Slovaks, Serbians, Croats, Slovenes and Bulgarians; *a.* relating to the Slavs; Slavic; Slavonic. **-ic** *a.* **-onic** *a.*

**slave** *n.* person held legally in bondage to another; *v.i.* to work like a slave, to toil unremittingly. **-r** *n.* person or ship engaged in slave traffic. **-ry** *n.* **slavish** *a.* **slavishly** *adv.* **slavishness** *n.*

**slav•er** *n.* saliva running from mouth; sentimental nonsense; *v.t.* to smear with saliva issuing from mouth; *v.i.* to slobber; to talk in a weakly sentimental fashion. **-er** *n.*

**slaw** *n.* sliced cabbage served cooked, or uncooked, as a salad.

**slay** *v.t.* to kill. *pa.t.* **slew** *pa.p.* **slain.** **-er** *n.*

**sleave** *n.* knotted or entangled part of silk or thread; a fine wisp of silk made by separating a thread; *v.t.* to separate and divide as into threads.

**slea•zy** *a.* thin or poor in texture.

**sled, sledge** *n.* a vehicle on runners, for conveying loads over hard snow or ice; a sleigh; a small flat sled for coasting; *v.t.* to convey on a sled; *v.i.* to ride on a sled.

**sledge** *n.* large, heavy hammer.

**sleek** *a.* having a smooth surface; ingratiating; *v.t.* to make smooth; to calm; to soothe; *adv.* **-ly** *adv.* **-ness** *n.*

**sleep** *v.i.* to rest by suspension of exercise of powers of body and mind; to become numb (of limb). *pa.t.* and *pa.p.* **slept.** *n.* slumber; repose; rest; death. **-er** *n.* **-ily** *adv.* **-iness** *n.* **-ing** *a.* and *n.* **-less** *a.* wakeful; restless; alert; vigilant; unremitting. **-lessly** *adv.* **-lessness** *n.* **-y** *a.* inclined to sleep; drowsy.

**sleet** *n.* rain that is partly frozen; *v.i.* to fall as fine pellets of ice. **-iness** *n.* **-y** *a.*

**sleeve** *n.* part of garment which covers arm.

**sleigh** *n.* a sled; an open carriage on runners, usually horse-drawn; *v.i.* to drive in a sleigh.

**sleight** *n.* artful trick; skill.

**slen•der** *a.* thin or narrow; weak; feeble; not strong. **-ly** *adv.* **-ness** *n.*

**slept** *pa.t.* and *pa.p.* of **sleep.**

**sleuth** *n.* bloodhound; a relentless tracker; *(Colloq.)* detective.

**slew** *pa.t.* of **slay.**

**slew, slue** *v.t.* and *v.i.* to turn about.

**slice** *v.t.* and *v.i.* to cut off thin flat pieces; *n.* thin, flat piece cut off; share or portion. **-r** *n.*

**slick** *a.* smooth; sleek; smooth-tongued; smart; clever; slippery; *adv.* deftly; cleverly; *v.t.* to sleek; to make glossy. *n.* a smooth spot. See **sleek.**

**slick•er** *n.* waterproof coat.

**slid, slidden** See **slide.**

**slide** *v.i.* to slip smoothly along; to pass imperceptibly; to deteriorate morally; *v.t.* to move something into position by pushing along the surface of another body. *pr.p.* **sliding.** *pa.t.* **slid.** *pa.p.* **slid** or **slidden.** *n.* sliding; track on ice made by sliding; anything which moves freely in or out; photographic film holder for projecting; chute. **-r** *n.* **— rule** *n.*

**slight** *a.* trifling; slim; slender; *n.* contempt by ignoring another; *v.t.* to ignore; to insult. **-ing** *n.* and *a.* **-ingly** *adv.* **-ly** *adv.* to slight extent; not seriously. **-ness** *n.*

**slim** *a.* of small diameter or thickness; slender; unsubstantial; *v.t.* and *v.i.* to make or become slim. *pa.t., pa.p.* **-med.** *pr.p.* **-ming. -ly** *adv.*

**slime** *n.* soft, sticky, moist earth or clay; viscous secretion of snails, etc.; **slimily** *adv.* **sliminess** *n.* **slimy** *a.*

**sling** *n.* pocket of leather, etc., with a string attached at each end for hurling a stone; hanging bandage, for supporting an arm or hand; rope, chain, belt, etc. for hoisting weights; *v.t.* to throw by means of sling or swinging motion of arm; to suspend. *pa.t.* and *pa.p.* **slung. -er** *n.*

**sling** *n.* American iced drink.

**slink** *v.i.* to move in a stealthy, furtive manner. *pa.t.* and *pa.p.* **slunk.**

**slip** *v.t.* to move an object smoothly, secretly, or furtively into another position; to escape (memory); *v.i.* to lose one's foothold; to move smoothly along surface of; to withdraw quietly; to make a mistake; to lose one's chance; to pass without notice. *pr.p.* **-ping.** *pa.t.* and *pa.p.* **-ped.** *n.* act of slipping; unintentional error; loose garment worn under woman's dress; covering for a pillow; skid; inclined plane from which ships are launched. **-per** *n.* light shoe for indoor use; dancing-shoe. **-perily** *adv.* **-periness** *n.* **-pery** *a.* so smooth as to cause slipping or to be difficult to hold or catch; unstable; untrustworthy; changeable.

**slit** *v.t.* to cut lengthwise; to cut open; *v.i.* to be slit. *pr.p.* **-ting.** *pa.t.* and *pa.p.* **slit.** *n.* straight, narrow cut or incision; narrow opening. **-ter** *n.*

**slith•er** *v.i.* to slide and bump (down a slope, etc.); to move in a sliding, snakelike fashion; *n.*

**sliv•er** *v.t.* to divide into long, thin strips; *v.i.* to split; to become split off; *n.* thin piece cut lengthwise; splinter.

**slob•ber** *v.i.* to let saliva drool from mouth; dribble; *v.t.* to cover with saliva. *n.* saliva coming from mouth; sentimental drivel. Also **slabber. -er** *n.*

**sloe** *n.* blackthorn; small dark fruit of blackthorn.

**slog** *v.t.* to hit wildly and vigorously; *v.i.* to work or study with dogged determination. *pr.p.* **-ging.** *pa.t.* and *pa.p.* **-ged, -ger** *n.*

**slo•gan** *n.* war cry of Highland clan in Scotland; catchword for focusing public interest, etc.

**sloop** *n.* one-masted sailing vessel.

**slop** *n.* liquid carelessly spilled; puddle; *v.t.* to spill; to soil by spilling over; *v.i.* to overthrow or be spilled. *pr.p.* **-ping.** *pa.t.* and *pa.p.* **-ped. -pily** *adv.* **-piness** *n.* **-py** *a.*

**slope** *n.* upward or downward inclination; *v.t.* to form with slope; *v.i.* to assume oblique direction. **sloping** *a.*

**slosh** *n.* soft mud; *v.t.* to stir in liquid; *v.i.* to splash.

**slot** *n.* slit cut out for reception of object or part of machine; *v.t.* to make a slot in. *pr.p.* **-ting.** *pa.t.* and *pa.p.* **-ted.**

**sloth** *n.* lethargy; indolence. **-ful** *a.* **-fully** *adv.* **-fulness** *n.*

**sloth** *n.* group of edentate mammals of S. America.

**sloth**

**slouch** *n.* ungraceful, stooping manner of walking or standing; shambling gait; *v.i.* to sit or stand in a drooping position; *v.t.* to depress; to cause to hang down loosely. **-y** *a.*

**slough** *n.* bog; swamp.

**slough** *n.* cast-off outer skin; *v.t.* to cast off, or shed, as a slough; *v.i.* to separate as dead matter which forms over sore.

**Slo•vak** *n.* member of Slav people in northern Carpathians; language spoken in Slovakia; *a.* pert. to Slovaks. Also **Slovakian.**

**slov•en** *n.* person careless of dress, or negligent of cleanliness. **-liness** *n.* **-ly** *a.* *adv.*

**slow** *a.* not swift; indicating time earlier than true time; mentally sluggish; dull; *adv.* slowly; *v.t.* to render slow; to retard; *v.i.* to slacken speed. **-ly** *adv.* **-ness** *n.*

**sludge** *n.* mud which settles at bottom of waterways, of vessel containing water, or a shaft when drilling. **sludgy** *a.*

**slug** *n.* one of land snails without a shell. **-gard** *n.* person habitually lazy and idle; *a.* disinclined to exert oneself. **-gishly** *adv.* **-ishness** *n.*

**slug** *n.* small thick disk of metal.

**slug** *(Colloq.) v.i.* to strike heavily; to slog; *n.* heavy blow.

**sluice** *n.* valve or shutter for regulating flow; artificial channel along which stream flows; *v.t.* to drain through a sluice; *v.i.* to run through a sluice.

**slum** *n.* squalid street, or quarter of town, characterized by gross over-crowding, dilapidation, poverty, vice and dirt; *v.i.* to visit slums. *pr.p.* **-ming** *pa.t.* and *pa.p.* **-med.**

**slum•ber** *v.i.* to sleep lightly; *n.* light sleep; doze. **-er** *n.* **-ous, slumbrous** *a.* inducing slumber; drowsy.

**slump** *n.* act of slumping; sudden, sharp fall in prices or volume of business done; *v.i.* to drop suddenly.

**slung** *pa.t.* and *pa.p.* of **sling.**

**slunk** *pa.t.* and *pa.p.* of **slink.**

**slur** *v.t.* to pass over lightly; to deprecate; to insult; to pronounce indistinctly; *(Mus.)* to sing or play in a smooth, gliding style. *pr.p.* **-ring.** *pa.t.* and *pa.p.* **-red.** *n.* stigma; reproach; implied insult; indistinct sound.

**slush** *n.* half-melted snow; any greasy, pasty mass; overly sentimental talk or writings; *v.t.* to splash or cover with slush. **-y** *a.*

**slut** *n.* dirty, untidy woman; slattern. **-tish** *a.*

**sly** *a.* artfully cunning; mischievous. **-ly** *adv.* **-ness** *n.*

**smack** *v.t.* to make a loud, quick noise; to slap loudly; to strike; *v.i.* to make sharp, quick noise with lips; *n.* quick, sharp noise, esp. with lips.

**smack** *v.i.* to have a taste or flavor; to give a suggestion (of); *n.* a slight taste.

**smack** *n.* small sailing vessel.

**small** *a.* little in size, number, degree, etc.; unimportant; slender; mean; *n.* small or slender part, esp. of back. **-ish** *a.* **-ness** *n.*

**small•pox** *n.* infectious disease, characterized into pustules.

**smart** *n.* sharp, stinging pain; *v.i.* to feel such a pain; *a.* causing a sharp, stinging pain; clever; active; well-dressed. **-ly** *adv.* **-ness** *n.* **smarten** *v.t.* and *v.i.* to make more spruce.

**smash** *v.t.* to break into pieces to shatter; to hit hard; to ruin; *v.i.* to break into pieces; *n.* crash; accident, wrecking vehicles; utter ruin. **-ing** *a.*

**smat•ter** *v.i.* to talk superficially. **-ing** *n.* slight, superficial knowledge.

**smear** *v.t.* to rub over with a greasy, oily, or sticky substance; to daub; to impute disgrace to. **-iness** *n.* **-y** *a.*

**smell** *n.* sense of perceiving odors by nose; (unpleasant) odor; scent; perfume; *v.t.* to perceive by nose; to detect; *v.i.* to use nose; to give out odor. *pr.p.* **-ing.** *pa.p.* and *pa.t.* **-ed** or **smelt. -ing** *n.* **-y** *a.* having unpleasant smell.

**smelt** *n.* small, silvery fish of salmon family.

**smelt** *v.t.* to melt or fuse ore in order to extract metal. **-ing** *n.*

**smi•lax** *n.* genus of evergreen climbing shrubs.

**smile** *v.i.* to express pleasure, approval, amusement, contempt, irony, etc. by curving lips; to look happy; *v.t.* to express by smile; *n.* act of smiling. **smiling** *a.* cheerful; gay; joyous.

**smirch** *v.t.* to dirty; to stain; to bring disgrace upon; *n.* stain.

**smirk** *v.i.* to smile in an affected or conceited manner; *n.*

**smite** *v.t.* to hit hard; to defeat; to afflict; *v.i.* to strike. *pa.p.* **smitten.** *pa.t.* **smote. -r** *n.*

**smith** *n.* one who shapes metal, esp. with hammer and anvil; blacksmith. **-y** *n.* smith's workshop.

**smith•er•eens** *n.pl.* *(Colloq.)* small bits. Also **smithers.**

**smit•ten** *pa.p.* of **smite.**

**smock** *n.* a loose garment worn over other clothing. **-ing** *n.* embroidered gathering of dress, etc.

**smog** *n.* mixture of smoke and fog.

**smoke** *n.* cloudy mass of suspended particles that rises from fire; *v.t.* to consume by smoking; to expose to smoke (esp. in curing fish, etc.); *v.i.* to inhale and expel smoke of burning tobacco; to give off smoke. **-r** *n.* **smoking** *n.* **smokiness** *n.* **smoky** *a.*

**smol•der** *v.i.* to burn slowly without flame.

**smolt** *n.* young salmon.

**smooth** *a.* not rough; calm; steady in motion; pleasant; easy; *v.t.* to make smooth; *adv.* in a smooth manner. **-ly** *adv.*

**smor•gas•bord** *n.* meal of appetizers served buffet style.

**smote** *pa.p.* and *pa.t.* of **smite.**

**smoth•er** *v.t.* to destroy by depriving of air; *v.i.* to be stifled; to be without air; *n.* thick smoke or dust.

**smudge** *n.* smear; stain; smoky fire to drive off insects; *v.t.* to smear; to make a dirty mark; *v.i.* to become dirty or blurred.

**smug** *a.* very neat and prim; self-satisfied; complacent. **-ly** *adv.* **-ness** *n.*

**smug•gle** *v.t.* to import or export goods secretly to evade customs duties. **-r** *n.* **smuggling** *n.*

**smut** *n.* black particle of dirt; lewd or obscene talk or writing; *v.t.* to blacken; to smudge. *pr.p.* **-ting.** *pa.p.* and *pa.t.* **-ted. -ty** *a.* **-tily** *adv.* **-tiness** *n.*

**smutch** *v.t.* to blacken, as with soot, etc.; *n.* dirty spot; stain; smudge.

**snack** *n.* share; slight, hasty meal.

**snaf•fle** *n.* horse's bridle bit jointed in middle but without curb; *v.t.*

**snag** *n.* stump projecting from tree-trunk; any obstacle, drawback, or catch; *v.t.* to catch on a snag. *pr.p.* **-ging.** *pa.p., pa.t.*

**snail** *n.* slow-moving mollusk with spiral shell; slow person.

**snake** *n.* long, scaly, limbless reptile; serpent; treacherous person; *v.i.* to move like a snail. **snaky** *a.*

**snap** *v.t.* to break abruptly; to seize suddenly; to snatch; to bite; to shut with click; *v.i.* to break short; to try to bite; to utter sharp, cross words; to make a quick, sharp sound; to sparkle. *pr.p.* **-ping.** *pa.p.* and *pa.t.* **-ped.** *n.; a.* unprepared; without warning. **-per** *n.* one who snaps; kind of fresh-water turtle. **-py** *a.* lively; brisk.

**snare** *n.* running noose of cord or wire, used to trap animals or birds; a trap; *v.t.* to catch with snare; to entangle.

**snarl** *v.i.* to growl like an angry dog; *n.* growling sound; surly tone of voice. **-er** *n.*

**snarl** *n.* tangle or knot of hair, wool, etc.; complication; *v.t.* and *v.i.*

**snatch** *v.t.* to seize hastily or without permission.

**sneak** *v.i.* to creep or steal away; to slink; *n.* furtive, cowardly fellow. **-ing** *a.* **-ingly** *adv.* **-iness, -ingness** *n.* **-y** *a.*

**sneer** *v.i.* to show contempt; *n.* look of contempt or ridicule; scornful utterance. **-er** *n.* **-ing** *a.*

**sneeze** *v.i.* to expel air through nose and mouth with sudden convulsive spasm and noise; *n.* a sneezing.

**snick** *n.* small cut; notch; nick; *v.t.* to cut; to notch.

**snick•er** *v.i.* to laugh with small, audible catches of voice; to giggle; *n.* half-suppressed laugh.
**sniff** *v.i.* to draw in breath through nose with sharp hiss; to snuff; *v.t.* to take up through nose, to smell; *n.* **-le** *v.i.* to sniff noisily through nose; to snuffle. **-ler** *n.*
**snip** *v.t.* to clip off with scissors; to cut; *n.* a single, quick stroke, as with scissors; a bit cut off. *pr.p.* **-ping.** *pa.p.* and *pa.t.* **-ped.** **-per** *n.* **-pet** *n.* a fragment.
**snipe** *n.* long-billed gamebird; a shot; *v.i.* to shoot snipe; *(Mil.)* to shoot from cover; *v.t.* to hit by so shooting. **-r** *n.*

**snipe**

**sniv•el** *n.* running at the nose; sham emotion; whining, as a child. *v.i.* to run at the nose; to show real or sham sorrow; to cry or whine.
**snob** *n.* one who judges by social rank or wealth rather than merit. **-bery** *n.* **-bish** *a.* **-bishly** *adv.* **-bishness** *n.*
**snood** *n.* ribbon formerly worn to hold back hair; fillet.
**snoot** *n.* snout; nose; contemptuous. **-ily** *adv.* arrogantly. **-iness** *n.* **-y** *a.*
**snooze** *n.* *(Colloq.)* short sleep; nap; *v.i.* to take a snooze.
**snore** *v.i.* to breathe heavily and noisily during sleep; *n.* such noisy breathing. **-r** *n.*
**snor•kel** *n.* device for submarines and divers for air intake.
**snort** *v.i.* to force air with violence through nose, as horses; *v.t.* to express by snort; *n.* snorting sound.
**snout** *n.* projecting nose and jaws of animal, esp. of pig.
**snow** *n.* frozen vapor which falls in flakes; *v.t.* to let fall like snow; to cover with snow; *v.i.* to fall as or like snow. **-y** *a.* **-ily** *adv.* **-iness** *n.* **-fall** *n.* **-flake** *n.*
**snub** *v.t.* to check or rebuke with rudeness or indifference. *pr.p.* **-bing.** *pa.p.* and *pa.t.* **-bed.** *n.* intentional slight; rebuff; check; *a.* of nose, short and slightly turned up.
**snuff** *n.* charred part of wick of candle or lamp; *v.t.* to nip this off; to extinguish.
**snuff** *v.t.* to draw up or through nostrils; to smell; to inhale; *v.i.* to draw air or snuff into nose; *n.* powdered tobacco for inhaling through nose; sniff. **-er** *n.*
**snuf•fle** *v.i.* to breathe noisily through nose; to speak through nose; *n.* act of snuffling; a nasal twang. **-r** *n.*
**snug** *a.* cosy; trim; comfortable; sheltered; close fitting. **-ly** *adv.* **-ness** *n.* **-gle** *v.i.* to lie close to, for warmth or from affection.
**so** *adv.* in this manner or degree; very; the case being such; accordingly; *conj.* therefore; in case that; *interj.* well.
**soak** *v.t.* to steep; to wet thoroughly; *v.i.* to lie steeped in water or other fluid; *n.* a soaking; the act of soaking; heavy rain. **-er** *n.* **-ing** *a.*
**soap** *n.* compound of oil or fat with alkali, used in washing; *v.t.* and *v.i.* to apply soap to. **-y** *a.* **-iness** *n.*
**soar** *v.i.* to fly high; to glide; to rise far above normal or to a great height.
**sob** *v.i.* to catch breath, esp. in weeping. *pr.p.* **-bing.** *pa.p.* and *pa.t.* **-bed.** *n.* convulsive catching of breath, esp. in weeping or sighing.
**so•ber** *a.* temperate; not intoxicated; subdued; *v.t.* and *v.i.* to make or become sober. **-ly** *adv.* **-ness** *n.* **sobriety** *n.*
**soc•cer** *n.* association football.
**so•cia•ble** *a.* inclined to be friendly; fond of company. **sociably** *adv.* **-iness** *n.* **sociability** *n.*
**so•cial** *a.* pert. to society; affecting public interest; living in communities, as ants; sociable; companionable; convivial; *n.* social meeting. **sociably** *adv.* **-ite** *n.* member of fashionable society.
**so•cial•ism** *n.* economic and political system, aiming at public or government ownership of means of production, etc. **socialize** *v.t.* **socialization** *n.* **socialist** *a.* **socialistic** *a.* **socialistically** *adv.*
**so•ci•e•ty** *n.* people in general; people of culture and good breeding in any community; the world of fashion; fellowship; wealthy; a company; an association; a club.
**so•ci•ol•o•gy** *n.* science of problems confronting society; social science. **sociological** *a.* **sociologist** *n.*
**sock** *n.* a short stocking.
**sock•et** *n.* opening or hollow into which anything is fitted; *v.t.* to provide with, or place in, socket.
**sock•eye** *n.* a red salmon.
**sod** *n.* flat piece of earth with grass; turf; *v.t.* to cover with turf. *pr.p.* **-ding** *pa.p.*, *pa.t.* **-ded.**
**so•da** *n.* name applied to various compounds of sodium, *e.g.* baking soda, caustic soda, washing soda. (See **sodium**); *(Colloq.)* soda water.
**so•dal•i•ty** *n.* fellowship; an association.
**sod•den** *a.* soaked; soft with moisture; dull and heavy; stupid.
**so•di•um** *n.* silvery-white metallic alkaline element, the base of soda.
**sod•o•my** *n.* unnatural sexual intercourse, esp. between males or with an animal.
**so•fa** *n.* an upholstered couch.
**soft** *a.* yielding easily to pressure; not hard; smooth; gentle; melodious; quiet; susceptible; sentimental; weak; not astringent; containing no alcohol; in phonetics, esp. of consonants 'c' and 'g,' pronounced with a sibilant sound; *adv.* softly; quietly. **-ish** *a.* **-ly** *adv.* **-ness** *n.* **-headed** *a.* weak in intellect. **-hearted** *a.* kind; gentle.
**soft•ball** *n.* variant of the game of baseball.
**soft•en** *v.t.* to make soft or softer; to lighten; to mitigate; to tone down; to make less loud; *v.t.* to become soft or softer. **-ing** *n.* act, process, or result of becoming soft or softer.
**sog•gy** *a.* soaked with water.
**soil** *v.t.* to make dirty; to defile; dirty

marks; filth; manure; top layer of earth's surface; earth, as food for plants.

**so•journ** to dwell for a time; *n.* short stay.

**sol•ace** *n.* comfort in grief; consolation; *v.t.* to console.

**so•lan** *n.* large sea bird like a goose; a gannet.

**so•lar** *a.* pert. to, caused by, measured by sun. **-ize** *v.t.* and *v.i.* to expose to sun's rays. **solarium** *n.* a sun room or porch. *pl.* **solaria.**

**sold** *pa.p.* and *pa.t.* of **sell.**

**sol•der** *n.* easily melted alloy for joining metals; *v.t.* to join or mend with solder.

**sol•dier** *n.* man engaged in military service; an enlisted man as distinguished from commissioned officer. **-y** *n.* soldiers collectively; troops.

**sole** *n.* flat of the foot; lower part of anything, or that on which anything rests; small flatfish, used for food; *v.t.* to supply with a sole.

**sole** *a.* being, or acting, without another; alone; only. **-ly** *adv.*

**sol•e•cism** *n.* breach of grammar; a breach of etiquette. **solecist** *n.*

**sol•emn** *a.* marked, or performed, with religious ceremony; inspiring awe or dread. **-ly** *adv.* **-ness** *n.* **-ize** *v.t.* to perform with ceremony. **-ity** *n.* sacred rite; gravity; seriousness.

**so•len** *n.* genus of bivalve molluscs.

**sol•fa** *v.i.* to sing notes of scale.

**so•lic•it** *v.t.* to ask with earnestness; to entreat; *v.i.* to try to obtain, as trade, etc.; to accost. **-ant** *n.* **-ation** *n.* **-or** *n.* **-ous** *a.* anxious; eager; earnest. **-ously** *adv.* **-ousness, -ude** *n.* being solicitous; uneasiness; anxiety.

**sol•id** *a.* not in a liquid or gaseous state; not hollow; dependable; sound; *n.* a firm, compact body. **-ly** *adv.* **-arity** *n.* state of being solidly united in support of common interests, rights, etc. **-ity** *n.*

**so•lid•i•fy** *v.t.* to make solid or firm; to harden; *v.i.* to become solid.

**sol•i•dus** *n.* oblique stroke (/) in fractions, dates, etc. *pl.* **solidi.**

**so•lil•o•quy** *n.* talking to oneself; monologue, esp. by actor alone on stage. **soliloquize** *v.i.*

**sol•i•taire** *a.* living alone; done or spent alone; *n.* hermit; a single gem set by itself. **solitarily** *adv.* **solitariness** *n.* **solitude** *n.*

**so•lo** *n.* musical composition played or sung by one person; *a.* done or performed by one person; unaccompanied; alone. **soloist** *n.*

**sol•stice** *n.* either of two points in sun's path at which sun is farthest N. or S. from equator, about June 21 and December 22 respectively. **solstitial.**

**sol•u•ble** *a.* capable of being dissolved in a liquid; able to be solved or explained. **solubility** *n.*

**so•lus** *a.* as a stage direction, alone. *fem.* **sola.**

**so•lu•tion** *n.* process of finding answer to problem; answer itself; dissolving gas, liquid, or solid, esp. in liquid; mixture so obtained; *v.t.* to coat with solution.

**solve** *v.t.* to find the answer to; to explain; to make clear. **solvable** *a.* **-r** *n.* **solvent** *a.* having the power to dissolve another substance; able to pay all one's debts; *n.* substance, able to dissolve another's substance. **-ncy** *n.* state of being able to pay one's debts.

**so•mat•ic** *a.* pert. to the body; corporeal; physical. Also **-al.**

**som•ber** *a.* dark; gloomy; melancholy. **-ly** *adv.* **-ness** *n.* **sombrous** *a.* *(Poet.)* somber **sombrously** *adv.*

**som•bre•ro** *n.* broad-brimmed felt hat.

**some** *a.* denoting an indefinite number, amount, or extent; amount of; one or other; approximately; *(pron.)* portion; particular persons not named; *adv.* approximately. **-body** *n.* person not definitely known. **-how** *adv.* in one way or another; by any means. **-one** *pron.* **-such** *a.* denoting person or thing of the kind specified. **-thing** *n.* **-time** *adv.* **-times** *adv.* at times; now and then; occasionally. **-what** *n.* indefinite amount or degree; *adv.* to some extent; rather. **-where** *adv.*

**som•er•sault** *n.* a movement in which one turns heels over head; *v.i.*

**som•nam•bu•late** *v.i.* to walk in one's sleep. **somnambulation** *n.* **somnambulism** *n.* **somnambulist** *n.* **somnambulistic** *a.*

**som•ni•fa•cient** *a.* inducing sleep; *n.* soporific. **somniferous** *a.* **somnific** *a.*

**som•no•lent** *a.* sleepy; drowsy. **-ly** *adv.* **somnolence** *n.* Also **somnolency. somnolescent** *a.*

**son** *n.* male child; term of affection; native of a place; disciple.

**so•nant** *a.* pert. to sound; *n.* a syllabic sound. **sonance** *n.*

**so•na•ta** *n.* a musical composition in three or four movements. **sonatina** *n.* a short sonata.

**song** *n.* singing; poem, or piece of poetry, esp. if set to music; musical sounds made by birds; *(Colloq.)* a mere trifle. **-ster** *n.* *(fem.* **songstress)** one who sings.

**son•ic** *a.* pertaining to sound.

**son•net** *n.* poem of fourteen lines. **soneteer** *n.* a writer of sonnets.

**so•no•rous** *a.* giving out a deep, loud sound when struck; resonant; high-sounding. *adv.* **-ness, sonority** *n.*

**soon** *adv.* in a short time; shortly; without delay; willingly.

**soot** *n.* a black powdery substance formed by burning coal, etc.; *v.t.* to cover with soot. **-y** *a.*

**sooth** *n.* *(Arch.)* truth; reality. **-sayer** *n.* one who claims to be able to foretell future. **-saying** *n.*

**soothe** *v.t.* to please with soft words or kind actions; to calm; to allay, as pain. **soothing** *a.* **soothingly** *adv.*

**sop** *n.* piece of bread, etc., dipped in a liquid; *v.t.* to steep in liquid. *pr.p.* **-ping.** *pa.p.* and *pa.t.* **-ped. -ping** *a.* **-py** *a.* soaked; rainy.

**soph•ism** *n.* specious argument; clever but fallacious reasoning. **sophist** *n.* **sophistry** *n.* **sophistic, sophistical** *a.* **sophistically**

adv. **sophisticate** *v.t.* to deceive by using sophisms; to make artificial; to make wise in the ways of the world. **sophisticated** *a.* **sophistication** *n.*

**soph•o•more** *n.* second year student.

**so•por** *n.* unnaturally deep sleep. **-ific** *a.* causing or inducing sleep; *n.* drug, which induces deep sleep. **-iferous, soporose** *a.*

**so•pran•o** *n.* highest type of female or boy's voice; soprano singer; *pl.* **-s, soprani.**

**sor•cer•y** *n.* witchcraft; magic; enchantment. **sorcerer** *n.; fem.* **sorceress.**

**sor•did** *a.* filthy; squalid; meanly avaricious. **-ly** *adv.* **-ness** *n.*

**sore** *a.* painful when touched; distressed; grieved; *n.* diseased, injured, or bruised spot on body. **-ly** *adv.* **-ness** *n.*

**sor•ghum** *n.* cereal grasses of several varieties.

**so•ror•i•ty** *n.* a girls' or women's society.

**so•ro•sis** *n.* compound fleshy fruit; women's club.

**sor•rel** *n.* meadow plant.

**sor•rel** *a.* reddish-brown; *n.* (horse of) reddish-brown color.

**sor•row** *n.* grief; sadness; distress; cause of grief, etc.; *v.i.* to feel pain of mind; to grieve. **-er** *n.* **-ful** *a.* **-fully** *adv.* **-fulness** *n.*

**sor•ry** *a.* feeling regret; mean; shabby; wretched; worthless. **sorriness** *n.*

**sort** *n.* kind or class; quality; character; order or rank; *v.t.* to classify; to put in order. **-er** *n.*

**sor•tie** *n.* sally by besieged forces to attack besiegers.

**sot** *n.* confirmed drunkard. **-tish** *a.*

**sou** *n.* former French coin.

**soubriquet** See **sobriquet.**

**souf•flé** *n.* a delicate dish made of eggs.

**sough** *n.* low murmuring, sighing sound; *v.i.*

**sought** *pa.p.* and *pa.t.* of **seek.**

**soul** *n.* spiritual and immortal part of human being; seat of emotion, sentiment, and aspiration; spirit. **-ful** *a.* **-fully** *adv.* **-less** *a.* without a soul; not inspired; prosaic.

**sound** *a.* healthy; in good condition; profound; free from error; reliable; *adv.* soundly; completely. **-ly** *adv.* **-ness** *n.*

**sound** *n.* long, narrow stretch of water.

**sound** *v.t.* to find depth of water, by means of line and lead; *(Fig.)* to try to discover the opinions of; *v.i.* to find depth of water; of a whale, to dive suddenly. **-ing** *n.*

**sound** *n.* that which is heard; noise; *v.t.* to cause to make a sound; to utter; to play on; *v.i.* to make a noise; to be conveyed by sound; to seem. **-ing** *a.*

**soup** *n.* liquid food made by boiling meat, vegetables, etc.

**sour** *a.* acid; having a sharp taste; pungent; rancid; cross; *v.t.* and *v.i.* to make or become sour. **-ed** *a.* **-ly** *adv.* **-ness** *n.*

**source** *n.* spring; origin (of stream, information, etc.).

**sour•dough** *n.* fermented batter of flour and water used to leaven fresh dough.

**souse** *v.t.* to steep in brine; to pickle; to soak; *n.* a pickle made with salt; brine; a drenching.

**sou•tane** *n.* gown worn by R.C. priests.

**south** *n.* cardinal point of compass opposite north; region lying to that side; *a.; adv.* toward or in the south; *v.i.* to move towards the south. **southerly** *a.* **-ern** *a.* **-erner** *n.* **-ernly** *adv.* towards the south. **-ernmost** (also **-ermost, —most**) *a.* lying farthest towards the south. **—ward** *a.* and *adv.*

**sou•ve•nir** *n.* a keepsake.

**sov•er•eign** *n.* ruler; British gold coin; *a.* supreme in power. **-ty** *n.* supreme power.

**so•vi•et** *n.* council. **Soviet** *n.* political body elected to local municipalities, regional councils, etc. and sending delegates to higher congresses. *a.* **Soviet Union,** short for the Union of Soviet Socialist Republics,' i.e. Russia; *abbrev.* **U.S.S.R.**

**sow** *n.* female pig.

**sow** *v.t.* to scatter or deposit (seed); to spread abroad; *v.i.* to scatter seed. *pa.p.* **sown** or **sowed** *pa.t.* **-ed. -er** *n.*

**soy** *n.* sauce made from soybean **-bean** *n.* seed of leguminous plant of Far East.

**Spa** *n.* inland watering place in Belgium. **spa** *n.* any place with mineral spring.

**space** *n.* expanse of universe; area; extent; empty place; *v.t.* to place at intervals. **spacious** *a.* roomy; capacious; extensive. **spaciously** *adv.*

**spade** *n.* digging tool; *v.t.* to dig with spade.

**spade** *n. (Cards)* one of two black suits, marked by figure like a pointed spade.

**spa•ghet•ti** *n.* foodstuff resembling macaroni.

**spake** *pa.t. (Arch.)* of **speak.**

**span** *pa.t. (Arch.)* of **spin.**

**span** *n.* distance between thumb and little finger, when fingers are fully extended; this distance as measure = 9 in; short distance or period of time; *v.t.* to reach from one side of to the other; to extend across. *pr.p.* **-ning** *pa.p.* and *pa.t.* **-ned. -ner** *n.*

**span•drel** *n. (Archit.)* the space between outer curves of arch and square head over it; ornamental design in corner of postage stamp.

**span•gle** *n.* a small piece of glittering metal, used to ornament dresses; *v.t.* to adorn with spangles; *v.i.* to glitter.

**Span•iard** *n.* native of Spain. **Spanish** *a.; n.* language of Spain.

**span•iel** *n.* breed of dogs, with long, drooping ears; fawning person.

spaniel

**spank** *v.i.* to move with vigor or spirit. **-ing** *a.* **-er** *n.*

**spank** *v.t.* to strike with flat of hand, esp. on buttocks as punishment; *n.* slap.

**spar** *v.i.* to fight with the fists; to fight with spurs, as in cock fighting; to dispute, bandy words. *pr.p.* **-ring.** *pa.p.* and *pa.t.* **-red.**

**spar** *n.* pole or beam, esp. as part of ship's rigging.
**spar** *n.* crystalling mineral.
**spare** *v.t.* and *v.i.* to use frugally; to do without; to save; to leave unhurt; *a.* frugal; scanty; parsimonious; lean; in reserve; *n.* that which is held in reserve; a duplicate part. **-ly** *adv.* **-ness** *n.* thinness; leanness. **sparing** *a.* **sparingly** *adv.*
**spark** *n.* small glowing or burning particle; flash of light; *v.i.* to send out sparks.
**spar•kle** *n.* small spark; a glitter; vivacity; *v.i.* to emit small flashes of light. **-r** *n.* **sparkling** *a.*
**spar•row** *n.* small brown bird of finch family.
**sparse** *a.* thinly scattered; scanty; rare. **-ly** *adv.* **-ness** *n.* scantiness.
**Spar•ta** *n.* ancient Greek city-state. **Spartan** *n.* citizen of this town; one who is frugal and faces danger, etc. without flinching; *a.*
**spasm** *n.* sudden, involuntary contraction of muscle(s); fitful effort. **spasmodic(al)** *a.* **spasmodically** *adv.* by fits and starts. **spastic** *a.*
**spat** *pa.t.* of **spit.**
**spat** *n.* kind of cloth gaiter. Usually in *pl.* **spats.**
**spat** *n.* spawn of shellfish or oyster; *v.i.* to spawn, of oysters.
**spate** *n.* flood in a river, exp. after heavy rain.
**spathe** *n.* leaflike sheath enveloping flower cluster. **spathed, spathose** *a.*
**spa•tial** *a.* pert. to space. **-ly** *adv.*
**spat•ter** *v.t.* to cast drops of water, mud, etc. over; to splash; *v.i.* to fall in drops; *n.* the act of spattering.
**spat•u•la** *n.* broad-bladed implement. **spatular, spatulate** *a.*
**spav•in** *n.* swelling on horse's leg, causing lameness. **-ed** *a.*
**spawn** *n.* eggs of fish, frogs; offspring; *v.t.* and *v.i.* of fish, frogs, to cast eggs; to produce offspring.
**speak** *v.i.* to utter words; to deliver a discourse; *v.t.* to utter; to express in words; to express silently or by signs; *pr.p.* **-ing.** *pa.p.* **spoken.** *pa.t.* **spoke.** **-er** *n.* **-ing** *n.* having power to utter words.
**spear** *n.* long, pointed weapon, used in fighting, hunting, etc.; lance; pike; *v.t.* to pierce or kell with spear.
**spe•cial** *a.* pert. to a species or sort; beyond the usual; distinct; intimate. **-ly** *adv.* **-ize** *v.t.* and *v.i.* **-ization** *n.* **-ist** *n.* one trained and skilled in a special branch. **-istic** *a.* **-ty** *n.* a special characteristic of a person or thing; a special product; that in which a person is highly skilled.
**spe•cie** *n.* coined money.
**spe•cies** *n.* kind; sort; subdivision of a more general class or genus.
**spe•cif•ic** *a.* pert. to, or characteristic of, a species; peculiar to; well defined; *n.* a specific statement, etc. **-ally** *adv.*
**spec•i•fi•ca•tion** *n.* act of specifying. **specify** *v.t.* to state definitely; to give details of; to indicate precisely. **specifiable** *a.*
**spec•i•men** *n.* part of anything, or one of a number of things, used to show nature and quality of the whole.
**spe•cious** *a.* having a fair appearance; apparently acceptable, esp. at first sight. **-ly** *adv.* **-ness speciosity** *n.*
**speck** *n.* small spot; very small thing; *v.t.* to mark with specks. **-le** *n.* a small speck or spot; *v.t.* **speckled** *a.* **-less** *a.*
**spec•ta•cle** *n.* sight; thing exhibited. **spectacles** *n.pl.* eyeglasses. **-ed** *a.* wearing spectacles. **spectacular** *a.* showy; making great display. **spectacularly** *adv.*
**spec•ta•tor** *n.* an onlooker; specter is ghost or apparition not spectator ghost; apparition. **spectral** *a.* **spectrally** *adv.* **spectrum** *n.* the colored band into which a ray of light can be separated; *pl.* **spectra.**
**spec•tro-** *prefix* an image, used in many derivatives.
**spec•u•late** *v.i.* to make theories of; guesses; to meditate; to engage in risky commercial transactions. **speculation** *n.* **speculative** *a.* **speculatively** *adv.* **speculator** *n.* **speculatory** *a.*
**spec•u•lum** *n.* mirror. *pl.* **specula.**
**sped** *pa.p.* and *pa.t.* of **speed.**
**speech** *n.* power of speaking; what is spoken; faculty of expressing thoughts in words; language; formal address. **-less** *a.* without power of speech. **-lessly** *adv.* **-lessness** *n.*
**speed** *n.* swiftness of motion; velocity; *v.t.* to cause to move faster; to aid; to bid farewell to; *v.i.* to move quickly *pa.p.* and *pa.t.* **sped.** **-y** *a.* **-ily** *adv.* **-ometer** *n.* instrument indicating speed.

**speedometer**

**spell** *n.* word or words supposed to have magical power; fascination. **-bind** *v.t.* to hold as if by spell; to enchant; to fascinate. *pa.p., pa.t.* **-bound** *a.*
**spell** *n.* a brief period of time.
**spell** *v.t.* to read letter by letter; to mean; *v.i.* to form words with proper letters. *pa.p.* and *pa.t.* **-ed** or **spelt.**
**spe•lun•ker** one who explores caves.
**spend** *v.t.* and *v.i.* to pay out; to disburse; to pass, as time; to employ; to waste; to exhaust. *pa.p., pa.t.,* **spent** *a.* exhausted; worn out; of a fish, having deposited spawn. **-er** *n.*
**sperm** *n.* fertilizing fluid of male animals; the male cell. **— whale** *n.* cachalot, large

**sperm whale**

whale, valuable for its oil and for spermaceti. **spermaceti** *n.* waxlike substance obtained from head of sperm whale. **-atic** *a.*

**sperm•a•to-** *prefix* seed. **spermatoid** *a.* resembling sperm. **spermatozoon** *n.* male generative cell, found in semen. *pl.* **-zoa, -zoal, -zoan** *a.*

**spew, spue** *v.t.* and *v.i.* to eject from the stomach; to vomit.

**sphere** *n.* round, solid body, ball; globe; celestial body; range of knowledge, influence, etc.; *v.t.* to put in a sphere; to encircle. **spheral** *a.* **spheric** *a.* pert. to heavenly bodies. **spherical** *a.* **spherically** *adv.* **sphericity** *n.* **spheroid** *n.* body almost, but not quite, spherical, e.g. orange, earth, etc. **spheroidal** *a.* Also **spheroidic. spherule** *n.* a small sphere. **spherular, spherulate** *a.*

**sphinc•ter** *n. (Anat.)* circular muscle which contracts or expands orifice of an organ.

**sphinx** *n. (Myth.)* fabulous monster, with winged body of lion and head of woman, which proposed riddles.

sphinx

**sphyg•mus** *n. (Med.)* pulse. **sphygmic** *a.*

**spice** *n.* aromatic substance, used for seasoning; *(Fig.)* anything that adds flavor, zest, etc. *v.t.* to season with spice. **spicery** *n.* **spicy** *a.* **spicily** *adv.*

**spi•der** *n.* small eight-legged insect-like animal; an evil person. *a.* like a spider.

**spied** *pa.p.* and *pa.t.* of **spy.**

**spig•ot** *n.* peg for stopping hole in cask; a faucet.

**spike** *n.* sharp-pointed piece of metal or wood; *(Bot.)* flower cluster growing from central stem; *v.t.* **spiky** *a.*

**spill** *v.t.* to cause to flow out; to shed (blood); to throw off, as from horse, etc.; to upset; *v.i.* to flow over; to be shed; *pa.p.* and *pa.t.* **-ed** or **spilt. -er** *n.*

**spill** *n.* thin strip of wood or twist of paper, for lighting a fire, pipe, etc.

**spin** *v.t.* to twist into threads; to cause to revolve rapidly; to draw out tediously, as a story; to prolong; *n.* rapid whirling motion; short, quick run or drive. *pr.p.* **-ning** *pa.p.* and *pa.t.* **spun** or *(Arch.)* **span. -ner** *n.* **-ning jenny** *n.* machine for spinning several threads simultaneously.

**spin•ach** *n.* leafy vegetable. **spinaceous** *a.*

**spin•dle** *n.* long, slender rod, used in spinning; measure of yarn, thread, or silk; shaft; axis; *v.i.* to grow long and slender. **spindly** *a.* **spindling** *a.*

**spine** *n.* thorne; quill; backbone; back of book. **spinal** *a.* **-less** *a.* having no spine; weak of character. **spiny** *a.* **spinule** *n.* small spine.

**spin•it** *n.* musical instrument.

**spin•na•ker** *n.* a large triangular sail.

**spin•ster** *n.* unmarried woman. **-hood** *n.* **spinstress** *n.* woman who spins.

**spi•ra•cle** *n.* breathing-hole; blowhole of whale. **spiracular, spiraculate** *a.*

**Spi•rae•a** *n.* a genus of herbaceous plants.

**spi•rant** *n.* consonant pronounced with perceptible emission of breath.

**spire** *n.* winding line like threads of screw; burl; coil. **spiral** *a.* winding; coiled; *n.* spiral curve; *v.i.* to follow spiral line.

**spire** *n.* blade of grass; anything tall and tapering to point; steeple; *v.i.* to rise high, like spire. **spiral** *a.* **spiry** *a.*

**spir•it** *n.* vital force; immortal part of man; ghost; frame of mind; disposition; eager desire; courage; essential character; *(Cap.)* Holy Spirit; liquid got by distillation, esp. alcoholic; *v.t.* to carry away mysteriously; to put energy into. **spirits** *n.pl.* a state of mind; mood; distilled alcoholic liquor. **-ed** *a.* **-edly** *adv.* **-edness** *n.* **-ism** *n.* See **spiritualism. -less** *a.* without spirit or life; lacking energy; listless. **-essly** *adv.* **-uous** *a.* containing alcohol.

**spir•it•u•al** *a.* pert. to spirit or soul; not material; holy; *n.* Negro sacred song or hymn. **-ly** *adv.* **-ize** *v.t.* **-ism, spiritism** *n.* belief that spirits of dead can communicate with living people. **-ist** *n.*

**spit** *n.* pointed rod put through meat for roasting; narrow point of land projecting into sea; *pr.p.* **-ting.** *pa.p.* and *pa.t.* **-ted.**

**spit** *v.t.* to eject from mouth; *v.i.* to eject saliva from mouth; to expectorate; *pr.p.* **-ting.** *pa.p. pa.t.* **spat** *n.* **-ter** *n.* **-tle** *n.* saliva ejected from mouth; **-toon** *n.* a vessel for spittle.

**spite** *n.* malice; ill will; *v.t.* to treat maliciously; to annoy. **-ful** *a.* **-fully** *adv.* **-fulness** *n.*

**spit•fire** *n.* hot tempered person.

**spitz** *n.* kind of Pomeranian dog.

**splash** *v.t.* to spatter water, mud, etc. over; to soil thus; *v.i.* to dash or scatter, of liquids; to fall in drops; *n.* sound of object falling into liquid.

**splat•ter** *v.t.* and *v.i.* to splash; to spatter.

**splay** *v.t.* to slope; to slant; to spread outwards; *a.* turned outwards.

**spleen** *n.* organ lying to left of stomach; ill humor.

**splen•did** *a.* magnificent; gorgeous; *(Colloq.)* excellent. **-ly** *adv.* **splendor** *n.* **splendorous** *a.*

**sple•net•ic** *a.* pert. to spleen; morose; irritable.

**splice** *v.t.* to join together; to join, as wood, etc. by overlapping and binding.

**splint** *n.* rigid piece of material for holding broken limb in position; *v.t.* to bind with splints. **-er** *n.* thin piece of wood, metal, etc. split off; *v.t.* and *v.i.* to make or break into thin pieces. **-ery** *a.*

**split** *v.t.* to cut lengthwise; to cleave; to separate; *v.i.* to break asunder; to dash to pieces; to spearate; *n.* crack; fissure; a breach; a share. *pr.p.* **-ting.** *pa.p.* and *pa.t.* **split. -ing** *n.* cleaving or rending; *a.* severe; distressing.

**splut•ter** *v.t.* to utter incoherently with spitting sounds; *v.t.* to emit such sounds; *n.* such sounds or speech. **-er** *n.*

**Spode** *n.* highly decorated porcelain.

**spoil** *v.t.* to damage; to cause to decay; *v.i.* to decay; *n.* booty; prey; plunder. *pa.p.* and *pa.t.* **-ed** or **-spoilt.**

**spoke** *pa.t.* of the verb **speak.** *pa.p.* **spoken. -s-man** *n.* one deputed to speak for others.

**spoke** *n.* one of small bars connecting hub of wheel with rim.

**spo•li•ate** *v.t.* to rob; to plunder; *v.i.* to practice plundering. **spoliative** *a.* **spoliation** *n.* **spoliator** *n.*

**spon•dee** *n.* in poetry a foot of two long syllables. **spondaic** *a.*

**sponge** *n.* marine animal of cellular structure, outer coating of whose body is perforated to allow entrance of water; skeleton of this animal; *v.t.* to wipe, cleanse, with sponge; *v.i.* to live at expense of others. **-r** *n.* **spongy** *a.* **sponginess** *n.* **-cake** *n.* light, sweet cake.

**spon•sor** *n.* one who is responsible for another; surety; a patron; *v.t.* to support; to act as guarantor or patron of; **-ial** *a.* **-ship** *n.*

**spon•ta•ne•ous** *a.* of one's own free will; natural; produced by some internal cause. **-ly** *adv.* **-ness, spontaneity** *n.*

**spook** *n. (Colloq.)* ghost; apparition. **-ish, -y** *a.*

**spool** *n.* small cylinder for winding thread, wire, etc.; *v.t.* to wind on spool.

**spoon** *n.* implement with bowl at end of handle; *v.t.* and *v.i.* to use a spoon. **-bill** *n.* long-legged wading bird.

**spoon•er•ism** *n.* transposition of letters of spoken words, causing a humorous effect.

**spoor** *n.* track or trail of wild animal.

**spo•rad•ic** *a.* occurring singly here and there; occasional. Also **-al. -ally** *adv.*

**spore** *n.* in flowerless plants, minute cell with reproductive powers; germ; seed. **sporangium** *n.* spore case. *pl.* **sporangia. sporangial** *a.* **sporoid** *a.*

**spor•ran** *n.* large pouch worn in front of the kilt.

**sport** *n.* that which amuses; pastime; object of jest; outdoor game or recreation esp. of athletic nature; *v.i.* to play; to take part in outdoor recreation. **-s** *n.pl.* games; athletic meetings. **-ing** *a.* **-ive** *a.* pert. to sport; playful.

**spot** *n.* speck; blemish, esp. on reputation; place; *v.t.* to cover with spots; *(Colloq.)* to detect; to recognize; *v.i.* to become marked. *pr.p.* **-ting** *pa.p.* and *pa.t.* **-ted. -less** *a.* **-lessly** *adv.* **-lessness** *n.* **-ted, -ty** *a.* marked with spots or stains; irregular. **-tedness, tiness** *n.* **-ter** *n.*

**spouse** *n.* married person, husband or wife. **spousal** *a.*

**spout** *v.t.* to shoot out, as liquid through a pipe; *v.i.* to gush out in jet; *n.* projecting tube, pipe, etc., for pouring liquid.

**sprag** *n.* piece of wood or metal used to lock wheel of vehicle.

**sprain** *v.t.* to wrench or twist muscles *n.* such an injury.

**sprang** *pa.t.* of the verb **spring.**

**sprat** *n.* small sea fish.

**sprawl** *v.i.* to sit or lie with legs out-stretched or in ungainly position; to move about awkwardly; to write carelessly and irregularly; *n.*

**spray** *n.* twigs; small, graceful branch with leaves and blossoms; sprig.

**spray** *n.* fine droplets of water; atomizer; *v.t.* to sprinkle. **-er** *n.*

**spread** *v.t.* to stretch out; to extend; to cover surface with; to circulate, as news, etc.; *v.i.* to extend in all directions; *n.* extension; expanse; covering for bed, etc. *pa.p.* and *pa.t.* **spread. -ing** *n.; v.t.* to lie with outstretched limbs.

**spree** *n.* lively frolic; drinking bout.

**sprig** *n.* small shoot or twig; ornament in form of spray; scion; youth; small, headless nail. *pr.p.* **-ging.** *pa.p., pa.t.* **-ged.**

**spright•ly** *a.* lively; airy; vivacious. **sprightliness** *n.*

**spring** *v.i.* to leap; to shoot up, out, or forth; to appear; to recoil; to result, as from a cause; *v.t.* to cause to spring up; to bend so as to weaken; to release, as catch of trap; *n.* a leap; recoil; a contrivance of coiled or bent metal with much resilience; resilience; flow of water from earth; fountain; season of year; upward curve of arch. *pa.p.* **sprung.** *pa.t.* **sprang** or **sprung. -er** *n.* **-y** *a.* elastic; light in tread or gait. **-iness** *n.* **-board** *n.* springy board used in jumping and diving.

**springe** *n.* snare with a spring noose; *v.t.* to catch in a springe.

**sprin•kle** *v.t.* to scatter small drops of water, sand, etc.; *v.i.* to scatter (a liquid or any fine substance); *n.* small quantity scattered; occasional drops of rain. **-d** *a.* **-r** *n.* **sprinkling** *n.*

**sprint** *v.i./n.* short run at full speed. **-er** *n.*

**sprit** *n. (Naut.)* small spar set diagonally across fore-and-aft sail to extend it.

**sprite** *n.* elf; a fairy; a goblin.

**sprock•et** *n.* toothlike projection on outer rim of wheel.

**sprout** *v.i.* to begin to grow; to put forth shoots; *n.* shoot; bud.

**spruce** *a.* neat in dress; *v.t.* and *v.i.* to dress smartly. **-ly** *adv.* **-ness** *n.*

**spruce** *n.* common name of some coniferous trees.

**sprung** *pa.p.* and *pa.t.* of **spring.**

**spry** *a.* nimble; agile.

**spud** *n.* small spadelike implement.

**spue.** See **spew.**

**spume** *n. / v.i.* froth; foam; scum. **spumous** *a.* **spumy** *a.*

**spun** *pa.p.* and *pa.t.* of verb **spin.**

**spunk** *n.* wood that readily takes fire; *(Colloq.)* spirit **-y** *a. (Colloq.)* plucky.

**spur** *n.* pricking instrument worn on horseman's heels, used as goad; anything that incites to action; mountain projecting from range; projection; *v.t.* to apply spurs to; to urge to action; *pr.p.* **-ring** *pa.p.* and *pa.t.* also *a.* **-red.**

**spurge** *n.* plant of several species, having milky juice.

**spu•ri•ous** *a.* not genuine or authentic; false. **-ly** *adv.*

**spurn** *v.t.* to reject with disdain; to scorn; *n.* disdainful rejection.

**spurt** *v.t.* to force out suddenly in a stream; *v.i.* to gush out with force; *n.* a sudden, strong flow or effort. Also **spirt.**

**sput•ter** *v.t.* to throw out in small particles

with haste and noise; *v.i.* to scatter drops of saliva, as in excited speech; to fly off with crackling noise; *n.* act of sputtering; sound made. **-er** *n.*

**spu•tum** *n.* spittle; saliva. *pl.* **sputa.**

**spy** *n.* one who enters enemy territory secretly, to gain information; one who keeps watch on others. *v.t.* to catch sight of; *v.i.* to act as a spy. **-glass** *n.* small telescope.

**squab** *a.* fat and short; *n.* nestling pigeon used for food.

**squab•ble** *v.i.* to wrangle; to dispute noisily; *n.* petty, noisy quarrel.

**squad** *n.* *(Mil.)* smallest unit of soldiers, etc.

**squad•ron** *n.* a military tactical unit; an athletic team.

**squal•id** *a.* mean and dirty, esp. through neglect; filthy; foul. *adv.* **-ity, -ness, squalor** *n.* filth; foulness.

**squall** *v.t.* and *v.i.* to scream or cry out violently; *n.* loud scream; sudden gust of wind. **-y** *a.*

**squa•ma** *n.* scale; scalelike part *pl.* **squamae.**

**squan•der** *v.t.* to waste; to dissipate. **-er** *n.* spendthrift.

**square** *n.* plane figure with four equal sides and four right angles; in town, open space of this shape; *(Math.)* product of a number or quantity multiplied by itself; *a.* square shaped; at right angles; giving equal justice; balanced or settled, as account or bill; *adv.* squarely; directly; *v.t.* to make like a square; to place at right angles; *(Math.)* to multiply by itself; to balance; to settle; *v.i.* to agree exactly; **-ly** *adv.* **-ness** *n.* **squarish** *a.*

**squash** *v.t.* to beat or crush flat; to suppress; *v.i.* to fall into a soft, flat mass; *n.* anything soft and easily crushed; packed crowd; game played with rackets. **-iness** *n.* **-y** *a.*

**squash** *n.* gourdlike fruit.

**squat** *v.i.* to sit on heels; to settle on land without having title to it, or in order to acquire title; *a.* short and thick *pr.p.* **-ting.** *pa.p.* and *pa.t.* **-ted. -ter** *n.*

**squaw** *n.* N. American Indian woman.

**squeak** *n.* short, sharp, shrill sound; sharp, unpleasant, grating sound; *v.i.* to utter, or make, such sound. **-y** *a.*

**squeal** *n.* long, shrill cry; *v.i.* to utter long, shrill cry. **-er** *n.*

**squeam•ish** *a.* easily made sick; easily shocked. **-ly** *adv.* **-ness** *n.*

**squee•gee** *n.* implement with rubber edge for clearing water from deck of ship, etc. Also **squilgee.**

**squeeze** *v.t.* to press or crush; to extract by pressure; to force into; *v.i.* to force one's way; to press; *n.* pressure; close hug or embrace. **squeezable** *a.*

**squelch** *n.* crushing blow; suppression; sound made when withdrawing feet from sodden ground; *v.t.* to crush down; *v.i.* to make sound of a squelch.

**squid** *n.* kind of sea mollusc.

**squil•gee** *n.* Same as **squeegee.**

**squill** *n.* plant of lily family. **-s** *n.pl.* drug from bulb of squill.

**squint** *a.* looking obliquely; having eyes turned in; *v.i.* to look with eyes partly closed; *n.* act, habit of squinting.

**squire** *n.* *(Brit.)* rural landowner; lady's escort; *v.t.* to escort.

**squirm** *v.i.* to move like a snake, eel, worm, etc.; to wriggle. **-iness** *n.* **-y** *a.*

**squir•rel** *n.* small graceful animal with bushy tail.

**squirt** *v.t.* and *v.i.* to eject, or be ejected, in a jet; *n.* instrument for squirting; thin jet of liquid. **-er** *n.*

**stab** *v.t.* to pierce or wound with pointed instrument; to hurt feelings of; *v.i.* to strike with pointed weapon; *n.* blow or wound so inflicted; sudden pain. *pr.p.* **-bing.** *pa.p.* and *pa.t.* **-bed. -ber** *n.*

**sta•bi•lize** *v.t.* to make stable, fixed, etc. **stabilization** *n.* **stabilizer** *n.* **stability** *n.*

**sta•ble** *a.* firmly fixed, established; steady; resolute. **stably** *adv.* Also **stabile.**

**sta•ble** *n.* building for horses; *v.t.* and *v.i.*

**stac•ca•to** *a.* and *adv.* *(Mus.)* short, sharp, and distinct.

**stack** *n.* large heap or pile; a chimney; *(Colloq.)* a great number; *pl.* book shelves; *v.t.* to heap or pile up; to arrange cards for cheating.

**sta•di•um** *n.* arena for sports events, entertainments, etc.

**staff** *n.pl.* **-s** or **staves:** pole or stick used in walking, climbing, etc. or for support or defense; flagpole; body of persons working in office, school, etc.; *v.t.* to provide with staff.

**stag** *n.* male of red or other large deer; man who attends party without a woman.

**stage** *n.* raised floor or platform esp. of theater, etc.; dramatic art of literature; scene of action; degree of progress; *v.t.* to put (a play) on stage. **staging** *n.* scaffolding.

**stag•ger** *v.i.* to walk or stand unsteadily; to hesitate; *v.t.* to cause to reel; to shock; to distribute in overlapping periods; to arrange in zigzag fashion; *n.* **-ing** *a.* amazing.

**stag•nate** *v.i.* to be motionless; to be dull. **stagnant** *a.* of water, not flowing; hence, foul; impure. **stagnantly** *adv.* **stagnation** *n.*

**staid** *a.* of sober and quiet character. **-ly** *adv.* **-ness** *n.*

**stain** *v.t.* and *v.i.* to discolor; to spot; to dye; to mark with guilt; *n.* discoloration; dye; taint of guilt; disgrace. **-less** *a.* not liable to stain or rust, esp. of a kind of steel.

**stair** *n.* steps one above the other for connecting different levels. **-s** *n.pl.* flight of steps. **-case** *n.* flight of steps with railings, etc. Also **-way.**

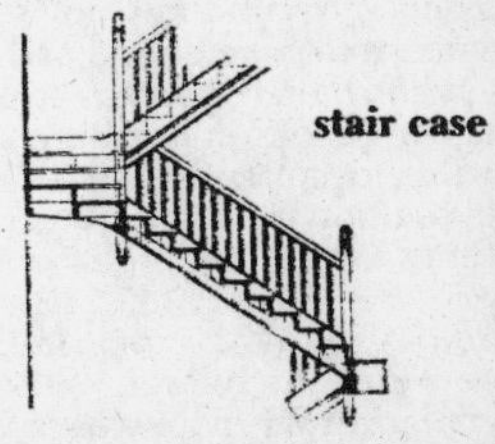
**stair case**

**stake** *n.* sharpened stick or post; post to which one condemned to be burned, was tied; interest in result of enterprise; *pl.* money in contention; *v.t.* to mark out with stakes.

**sta•lac•tite** *n.* deposit of carbonate of lime, hanging like icicle from roof of cave. **stalactic, stalactitic** *a.* **stalactical** *a.*

**sta•lag•mite** *n.* deposit of carbonate of lime from floor of cave. **stalagmitic(al).**

**stale** *a.* not fresh; tasteless; musty; trite; common; *v.i.* to lose freshness. **-ly** *adv.* **-ness** *n.*

**stale** *v.i.* of horses, to make water.

**stale•mate** *n. (Chess)* position, resulting in drawn game; standstill.

**stalk** *n.* stem of plant, leaf, etc.

**stalk** *v.i., v.t.* to steal up to game cautiously; to walk in stiff and stately manner; *n.* act of stealing up to game; stiff and stately gait. **-er** *n.*

**stall** *n.* compartment for animal in stable; erection for display and sale of goods; *v.t.* and *v.i.* to place or keep in stall; to come to a standstill; of engine or automobile, to stop running unintentionally.

**stal•lion** *n.* an uncastrated male horse kept for breeding.

**stal•wart** *a.* sturdy; brave; steadfast; *n.* strong, muscular person; staunch supporter. **-ly** *adv.*

**sta•men** *n. (Bot.)* male organ of flowering plant, pollen-bearing part. **staminal** *a.*

**stam•i•na** *n.* power of endurance.

**stam•mer** *v.i.* to speak with repetition of syllables or hesitatingly; to stutter; *n.* halting enunciation; stutter. **-er** *n.* **-ing** *n.*

**stamp** *v.i.* to put down a foot with force; *v.t.* to set down (a foot) heavily or with force; to make an official mark on; to affix postage stamp; to brand; *n.* act of stamping; instrument for making imprinted mark; mark imprinted; piece of gummed paper printed with device. **-er** *n.*

**stam•pede** *n.* sudden, frightened rush, esp. of herd of cattle, crowd, etc.; *v.t.* to put into a state of panic; *v.i.* to take part in a stampede.

**stance** *n.* position of feet in certain games.

**stanch** *v.t.* to stop or check flow (of blood). *a.* firm; loyal; trustworthy. **-ly** *adv.* **-ness** *n.* Also **staunch.**

**stan•chion** *n.* upright support; iron bar, used as prop.

**stand** *v.i.* to remain at rest in upright position; to become or remain stationary; to endure; to adhere to principles; to have a position, order, or rank; to place oneself; to persist; to be of certain height; *v.t.* to endure; to sustain; to withstand; to set. *pa.p.* and *pa.t.* **stood.** *n.* place where one stands; structure for spectators; piece of furniture on which things may be placed; stall for display of goods; position on some question. **-by** *n.* something in reserve. **-point** *n.* a point of view.

**stand•ard** *n.* weight, measure, model, quality, etc. to which others must conform; criterion; pole with a flag; royal banner; *a.* serving as established rule, model, etc.; standing upright. **-ize** *v.t.* **-ization** *n.*

**stand•ing** *a.* established by law, custom, etc.; settled; permanent; not flowing; erect; *n.* duration; existence; reputation.

**stank** *pa.t.* of the verb **stink.**

**stan•za** *n.* group of lines or verses of poetry having definite pattern. **stanzaic** *a.*

**sta•ple** *n.* chief product of a country or district; unmanufactured material; *a.* established in commerce; principal; chief; *v.t.* of textiles, to grade according to length and quality of fiber. **-r** *n.*

**sta•ple** *n.* U-shaped piece of metal with pointed ends; piece of wire to hold sheets of paper together. **-r** *n.* mechanical device for fastening papers together.

**star** *n.* shining celestial body, seen as twinkling point of light; five or six-pointed figure asterisk; *v.t.* to set or adorn with stars; *v.i.* to shine, as star. *pr.p.* **-ring.** *pa.p., pa.t.* **-red. -let** *n.* small star; **-lit** *a.* **-red** *a.* **-ry** *a.* **-riness** *n.* **-fish** *n.* marine animal shaped like a star.

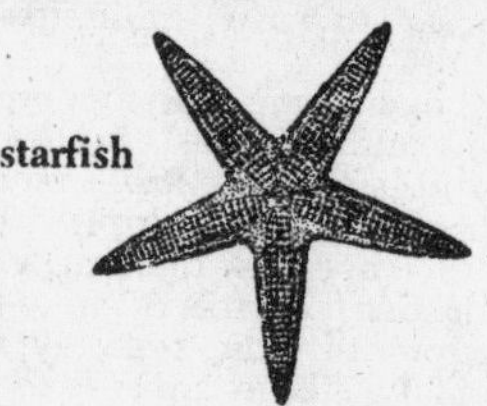
**starfish**

**star•board** *n.* and *a.* right-hand side of a ship, looking forward; *v.t.* to put (the helm) to starboard.

**starch** *n.* substance forming main food element in bread, potatoes, etc. and used, mixed with water, for stiffening linen, etc.; formality; primness; *v.t.* to stiffen with starch. **-y** *a.* **-ily** *adv.* **-iness** *n.*

**stare** *v.i.* to look fixedly; to gaze; *v.t.* to abash by staring at; *n.* fixed, steady look. **-r** *n.* **staring** *n. a.*

**stark** *a.* stiff; desolate; naked; downright; *adv.* completely. **-ly** *adv.*

**star•ling** *n.* bird, bluish-black and speckled.

**start** *v.i.* to make sudden movement; to spring; to begin, esp. journey; *v.t.* to cause to move suddenly; to begin; to loosen; *n.* sudden involuntary movement, spring or leap; act of setting out. **-er** *n.*

**star•tle** *v.t.* to cause to start; to give a fright to; *v.i.* to move abruptly, esp. from fright, apprehension, etc. **startling** *a.* **startlingly** *adv.*

**starve** *v.i.* to suffer from hunger; to be short of something necessary; *v.t.* to cause to suffer or die from lack of food, etc. **starvation** *n.*

**state** *n.* condition of person or thing; formal dignity; politically organized community; *a.* pert. to state; governmental; ceremonial; *v.t.* to express in words; to specify. **-d** *a.* fixed; regular; settled. **-ly** *a.* dignified; imposing; majestic. **-liness** *n.* **-ment** *n.*

**stat•ic** *a.* pert. to bodies at rest, or in equilibrium; motionless; *n.* *(Radio)* crackling noises during reception. **-al** *a.*
**sta•tion** *n.* place where thing or person stands; situation; rank; regular stopping place for trains, etc.; local or district office for police force, fire-brigade, etc.; *v.t.* to put in a position; to appoint to place of duty. **-ary** *a.* not moving; fixed.
**sta•tion•er** *n.* one who deals in writing materials. **-ery** *n.*
**sta•tis•tics** *n.pl.* numerical data collected systematically. **statistic(al)** *a.* **statistically** *adv.* **statistician** *n.*
**stat•ue** *n.* image carved out of solid substance or cast in metal. **statuary** *n.* collection of statues. **statuesque** *a.* **statuette** *n.*
**stat•ure** *n.* the height of a person or animal.
**sta•tus** *n.* position; rank.
**stat•ute** *n.* law passed by legislature. **statutory** *a.*
**staunch.** See **stanch.**
**stave** *n.* one of curved strips of wood forming cask; rung of ladder; staff; *v.t.* to fit with staves; to ward off; to deter. *pa.p.* and *pa.t.* **-d** or **stove.**
**staves** *n.pl.* See **staff** and **stave.**
**stay** *v.t.* to restrain; to check; to support; to last; *v.i.* to remain; to dwell.
**stead** *n.* place which another had; use; service; frame of bed.
**stead•fast** *a.* firmly fixed; steady; constant. **-ly** *adv.* **-ness** *n.*
**stead•y** *a.* firm; uniform; temperate; reliable; *v.t.* to make steady; to support; *v.i.* to become steady. **steadily** *adv.* **steadiness** *n.*
**steak** *n.* slice of meat, esp. beef.
**steal** *v.t.* to take by theft; to win gradually by skill, affection, etc.; *v.i.* to move silently, or secretly. *pa.p.* **stolen.** *pa.t.* **stole. stealth** *n.* secret means used to accomplish anything. **stealthy** *a.* **stealthiness** *n.*
**steam** *n.* vapor rising from boiling water; any exhalation of heated bodies; *a.* worked by steam; *v.t.* to apply steam; to; *v.i.* to give off steam; to move under power of steam. **-y** *a.* **-iness** *n.* **-er** *n.* steamship; vessel for cooking or washing by steam; something operated by steam. **-roller** *n.* heavy roller, driven by steam.
**ste•a•rin** *n.* hard, waxy solid used in manufacture of candles. Also **stearine. stearic** *a.*
**steed** *n.* horse.
**steel** *n.* hard and malleable metal; tool or weapon of steel; *a.* made of steel; inflexible; unfeeling; *v.t.* to harden; to make obdurate. **-y** *a.* **-iness** *n.*
**steel•yard** *n.* balance with unequal arms and movable weight.

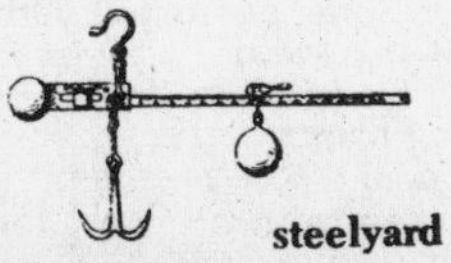
steelyard

**steep** *a.* having abrupt or decided slope; *n.* steep place; precipice. **-ly** *adv.* **-en** *v.t.* and *v.i.* to make, or become, steep.
**steep** *v.t.* to soak in a liquid; to saturate; *n.* act or process of steeping.
**stee•ple** *n.* a church tower with a spire. **-chase** *n.* a cross-country horse race.
**steer** *n.* a young male ox.
**steer** *v.t.* to guide or direct the course of (a ship, car, etc.) by means of a rudder, wheel, etc. **-age** *n.* the part of a ship allotted to passengers paying the lowest fare. **-er, -sman** *n.*
**stel•lar** *a.* pert. to, or like, stars. **stellate, stellated** *a.* arranged in the form of a star; star-shaped; radiating. **stelliform** *a.* **stellular** *a.*
**stem** *n.* the principal stalk of a tree or plant; any slender shaft resembling a stalk; part of word to which inflectional endings are added; *v.t.* to remove the stem of; *v.i.* to originate. *pr.p.* **-ming** *pa.p.* and *pa.t.* **-med.**
**stem** *v.t.* to check; to stop; to dam up. *pr.p.* **-ming.** *pa.p.* and *pa.t.* **-med.**
**stench** *n.* strong, offensive odor.
**sten•cil** *n.* thin sheet of metal, paper, etc. pierced with pattern or letters; *v.t.* to mark or paint with a stencil. *pr.p.* **-ing.** *pa.p.* and *pa.t.* **-ed.**
**ste•nog•ra•phy** *n.* shorthand writing. **stenograph** *n.* character used in stenography; stenographic machine; *v.i.* to write in shorthand. **stenographer, stenographist** *n.* **stenotype** *n.* a machine for writing shorthand. **stenographic, stenographical** *a.*
**step** *v.i.* to move and set down the foot; *n.* act of stepping; complete movement of foot in walking, dancing, etc.; manner of walking; tread of stair; degree of progress. *pr.p.* **-ping.** *pa.p.* and *pa.t.* **-ped. -per** *n.*
**step-** *prefix*, showing relation acquired by remarriage. **-father** *n.* second, or later, husband of one's mother. Similarly **-mother, -brother, -sister.**
**steppe** *n.* vast, treeless plain.
**ster•e•o-** solid, used in referring to hardness solidity, three-dimensionality. **-phonic** *a.*, of or denoting a system of placing microphone to impart greater realism of sound.
**ster•e•o•scope** *n.* optical instrument. **-scopic(al)** *a.* **-scopically** *adv.* **-scopy** *n.*
**ster•e•o•type** *n.* in printing, plate made by pouring metal into mold of plaster or papier maché made from original type; fixed form. *a.* pert. to stereotypes; *v.t.* to make a stereotype from; to make always the same. **-d** *a.* **-r, stereotypist** *n.*
**ster•ile** *a.* barren; not fertile; *(Med.)* entirely free from germs of all kinds. **sterilize** *v.t.* **sterilization** *n.* **sterilizer** *n.* **sterility** *n.* barrenness.
**ster•ling** *a.* pert. to standard value, weight, or purity of silver 922/ pure; of solid worth.
**stern** *a.* severe; strict; rigorous. **-ly** *adv.* **-ness** *n.*
**stern** *n.* after part of ship.
**ster•num** *n.* breastbone. *pl.* **sterna. sternal** *a.*

**ster•nu•ta•tion** *n.* act of sneezing.

**ster•tor** *n.* heavy, sonorous breathing. **-ous** *a.* **-ously** *adv.*

**stet** *v.i.* word used by proofreaders as instruction to printer to cancel previous correction. *pr.p.* **-ting.** *pa.p., pa.t.* **-ted.**

**steth•o•scope** *n.* instrument for listening to action of lungs or heart.

**ste•ve•dore** *n.* one who loads and unloads ships.

**stew** *v.t.* to cook slowly in a closed vessel; *v.i.* to be cooked slowly; *n.* stewed meat, etc. **-ed** *a.*

**stew•ard** *n.* one who manages another's property; on ship, attendant on passengers. **-ess** *n.* **-ship** *n.*

**stib•i•um** *n.* antimony **stibial** *a.*

**stich** *n.* verse or line of poetry. **-ic** *a.* **-ometry** *n.* measurement of manuscript by number of lines it contains. **-ometric, -ometrical** *a.*

**stick** *n.* small branch cut off tree or shrub; staff; rod.

**stick** *v.t.* to stab; to puncture; to cause to adhere; to thrust; *v.i.* to pierce; to adhere closely; to hesitate. *pa.p.* and *pa.t.* **stuck.** **-er** *n.* **-y** *a.* adhesive; viscous. **-iness** *n.*

**stick•le** *v.i.* to hold out stubbornly. **-r** *n.*

**stick•pin** *n.* necktie pin.

**stiff** *a.* not easily bent; moved with difficulty. **-ly** *adv.* **-ness** *n.* **-en** *v.t.* and *v.i.* to make or become stiff or stiffer. **-ener** *n.*

**sti•fle** *v.t.* and *v.i.* to smother. **stifling** *a.*

**stig•ma** *n.* brand; mark of disgrace; *(Bot.)* top of pistil of a flower. *pl.* **-s** or **-ta.** **stigmata** *n.pl.* marks resembling five wounds of Christ, said to have been miraculously impressed on bodies of certain saints. **-tic(al)** *a.* **-tization** *n.* **-tizer** *n.*

**stile** *n.* arrangement of steps for climbing fence or wall.

**sti•let•to** *n.* small dagger; pointed instrument.

**still** *a.* motionless; quiet; of wine, not sparkling; *n.* stillness; *v.t.* to quiet; *adv.* to this time; yet; even; *conj.* yet; however. **-ness** *n.* **-birth** *n.* state of being dead at time of birth. **-born** *a.*

**still** *n.* apparatus for distilling.

**stilt** *n.* pole with footrest for walking raised from ground; *v.i.* to walk on stilts. **-ed** *a.* formal; pretentious.

**stim•u•lus** *n.* goad; incentive. *pl.* **stimuli.** **stimulate** *v.t.* to rouse to activity. **stimulater** *n.* **stimulant** *a.* and *n.* *(Med.)* any agent which temporarily increases action of any organ of body. **stimulation** *n.* **stimulative** *a., n.*

**sting** *n.* pointed organ often poisonous, of certain animals, insects, or plants; thrust, wound, or pain of one; *v.t.* to thrust sting into; *v.i.* to use a sting. *pa.p.* and *pa.t.* **stung.** **-er** *n.* **-ing** *a.* **-ingly** *adv.*

**stin•gy** *a.* meanly avaricious; miserly. **stinginess** *n.*

**stink** *v.i.* to give out strongly offensive smell. *pa.p.* **stunk** *pa.t.* **stank.** *n.* stench. **-er** *n.* **-ing** *a.*

**stint** *v.t.* to limit; to skimp; *v.i.* to be frugal; *n.* limitation of supply or effort; allotted task. **-ed** *a.*

**sti•pend** *n.* money paid for a person's services; regular payment. **-iary** *a.*

**stip•ple** *v.t.* and *v.i.* to engrave, draw, or paint by using dots instead of lines; *n.* this process. **-r** *n.* **stippling** *n.*

**stip•u•late** *v.i.* to arrange; to settle definitely. **stipulation** *n.* **stipulator** *n.*

**stir** *v.t.* to set or keep in motion; to mix up ingredients, materials, etc.; to incite; *v.i.* to begin to move; to be emotionally moved. *pr.p.* **-ring.** *pa.p.* and *pa.t.* **-red.** *n.* act of stirring; commotion. **-rer** *n.* **-ring** *a.*

**stir•rup** *n.* metal loop hung from strap, for foot of rider on horse.

**stitch** *n.* in sewing, a single pass of needle; bit of clothing; sharp, sudden pain in the side; *v.t.* and *v.i.* to form stitches; to sew. **-er** *n.* **-ing** *n.*

**stith•y** *n.* anvil; forge.

**stoat** *n.* ermine or weasel.

**stock** *n.* stump or post; stem or trunk of tree or plant; piece of wood to which the barrel, lock, etc. of firearm are secured; ancestry; domestic animals on farm; supply of goods merchant has on hand; capital of company or corporation; quantity; juices of meat, etc. to form a liquid used as foundation of soup; *v.t.* to lay in supply for future use; *a.* used, or available, for constant supply; commonplace; pert. to stock. **-breeder** *n.* one who raises cattle, horses, etc. **-broker** *n.* one who buys and sells stocks or shares for others. **-broking** *n.* **-still** *a.* still as stock or post; motionless.

**stock•ade** *n.* enclosure or pen made with posts and stakes; *v.t.* to surround by erecting line of stakes.

**stock•fish** *n.* codfish, hake, etc., split and dried in open air.

**stock•ing** *n.* woven or knitted covering for foot and leg.

**stock•y** *a.* short and stout; thickset. **stockily** *adv.*

**stodge** *v.i.* to stuff; to cram. **stodgy** *a.* heavy; lumpy; indigestible; *(Fig.)* dull and uninteresting. **stodginess** *n.*

**sto•ic** *n.* disciple of Greek philosopher Zeno; one who suffers without complaint; one indifferent to pleasure or pain. **-al** *a.* **-ally** *adv.* **-ism** *n.*

**stoke** *v.t.* and *v.i.* to stir up, feed, or tend (fire). **-r** *n.*

**stole** *pa.t.* of **steal.**

**stole** *n.* long, narrow scarf.

**stol•en** *pa.p.* of **steal.**

**stol•id** *a.* dull or stupid. **-ly** *adv.* **-ness, -ity** *n.*

**stom•ach** *n.* chief digestive organ in any animal; appetite; desire; *v.t.* to put up with; to endure.

**stone** *n.* hard, earthy matter of which rock is made; hard center of certain fruits; gem; concretion in kidneys or bladder; *a.* made of stone; *v.t.* to pelt with stones; to remove stones from, as from fruits. **stony** *a.* **stonily** *adv.* **stoniness** *n.* **-crop** *n.* creeping plant.

**stood** *pa.p.* and *pa.t.* of **stand.**

**stool** *n.* chair with no back; low backless seat for resting feet on; discharge from bowels.

**stoop** *v.i.* to bend body; to lean forward; to condescend; *n.* act of stooping; stooping carriage of head and shoulders.

**stoop** *n.* raised entrance landing in front of doorway.

**stop** *v.t.* to fill up opening; to keep from going forward; to obstruct; to impede; to desist from; to bring to an end; *v.i.* to cease; to halt. *pr.p.* **-ping.** *pa.p.* and *pa.t.* **-ped;** *n.* act of stopping; halt; halting place; any device for checking movement, e.g. peg, pin, plug, etc. **-page** *n.* **-per** *n.* **-cock** *n.* valve for regulating flow of liquid.

**store** *n.* great quantity; reserve supply; shop; *pl.* supplies; *v.t.* to collect; to place in a warehouse. **storage** *n.* act of placing goods in a warehouse.

**stork** *n.* large wading bird.

**common stork**

**storm** *n.* violent wind or disturbance of atmosphere with rain, snow, etc.; assault on fortified place; outburst of emotion; *v.t.* to take by storm; to assault; *v.i.* to raise tempest; to scold violently. **-y** *a.* **-ily** *adv.* **-iness.** *n.*

**sto•ry** *n.* history or narrative of facts or events. **storied** *a.* **-teller** *n.*

**sto•ry** *n.* horizontal division of building. **storied** *a.*

**stoup** *n.* holy water basin.

**stout** *a.* strong; vigorous; thickset; *n.* strong, dark-colored beer; porter. **-ly** *adv.* **-ness** *n.* **-hearted** *a.* brave.

**stove** *n.* apparatus for cooking, warming room, etc.; oven of blast furnace. **-pipe** *n.* metal pipe for carrying off smoke.

**stove** *pa.p.* and *pa.t.* of **stave.**

**stow** *v.t.* to fill by packing closely. **-age** *n.* act of packing closely; space for stowing goods. **-away** *n.* one who hides on ship to obtain free passage.

**strad•dle** *v.i.* to spread legs wide; *v.t.* to bestride something; *n.* act of straddling; **astraddle** *adv.*

**Strad•i•var•i•us** *n.* a violin, usually of great value, made at Cremona, Italy, by Antonio *Stradivari.*

**strag•gle** *v.i.* to wander from direct course; to lag behind. **-r** *n.* **straggling** *a.*

**straight** *a.* passing from one point to another by nearest course; without a bend; honest; frank; *adv.* in a direct line or manner; without ambiguity; at once. **-ly** *adv.* **-en** *v.t.* to make straight. **-ener** *n.* **-away** *a.* straight forward. **-forward** *a.* proceeding in a straight course; honest; frank; simple.

**strain** *n.* race; inherited quality.

**strain** *v.t.* to stretch to the full or to excess; to exert to the utmost; to injure by overexertion, as muscle; to wrench; to pass through sieve; *v.i.* to make great effort; to filter; *n.* stretching force; violent effort; injury caused by over-exertion; tune; manner; tone of speaking or writing. **-ed** *a.* **-er** *n.* filter; sieve.

**strait** *n.* narrow channel of water connecting two larger areas; financial embarrassment. **-en** *v.t.* to narrow; to put into position of difficulty or distress.

**strand** *n.* *(Poetic)* edge of sea or lake; the shore; *v.t.* to cause to run aground; to leave in helpless position; *v.i.* to run aground. **-ed** *a.*

**strand** *n.* single string or wire of rope; any string, e.g. of hair, pearls, etc.

**strange** *a.* unaccustomed; uncommon; extraordinary. **-ly** *adv.* **-ness** *n.* **-r** *n.* unknown person; newcomer; one unaccustomed (to).

**stran•gle** *v.t.* to kill by squeezing throat; to stifle; **strangulate** *v.t.* to constrict so that circulation of blood is impeded. **strangulation** *n.*

**strap** *n.* long, narrow strip of leather, cloth, or metal; strop; *v.t.* to fasten, bind, chastize with strap. *pr.p.* **-ping.** *pa.p.* and *pa.t.* **-ped.** **-ping** *n.*

**stra•ta** *n.pl.* See **stratum.**

**strat•a•gem** *n.* artifice in war; scheme for deceiving enemy.

**strat•e•gy** *n.* skillful management in getting the better of an adversary. **strategic** *a.* pert. to, based on, strategy. **strategics** *n.pl.* strategy. **strategical** *a.* **strategically** *adv.* **strategist** *n.*

**strat•i•fy** *v.t.* to form or deposit in strata or layers. **stratification** *n.*

**strat•o•sphere** *n.* upper part of atmosphere.

**stra•tum** *n.* bed of earth, rock, coal, etc. in series of layers; class in society. *pl.* **strata.** **stratus** *n.* cloud form, in low, horizontal layers or bands. *pl.* **strati.**

**straw** *n.* stalk of wheat, rye, etc. after grain has been thrashed out; hollow tube for sipping beverage; *a.* made of straw.

**straw•ber•ry** *n.* a red berry.

**stray** *v.i.* to wander from path; *a., n.* stray animal.

**streak** *n.* stripe; flash of lightning; trait; strain; *v.t.* to mark with streaks. **-ed, -y** *a.*

**stream** *n.* flowing body of water, or other liquid; river, brook, etc.; steady flow of air or light, or people; *v.i.* to issue in stream; to float or wave in air. **-y** *a.* **-er** *n.* **-let** *n.* little stream. **-line** *n.* shape of a body calculated to offer least resistance to air or water when passing through it; *v.t.* to design body of this shape.

**street** *n.* road in town or village, usually with houses or buildings at the side.

**strength** *n.* quality of being strong; ability to endure; physical, mental, or moral force; potency of liquid, esp. of distilled or malted liquors; vigor of style; security. **-en** *v.t.* and *v.i.* **-ener** *n.*

**stren•u•ous** *a.* eagerly pressing; full of, requiring effort. **-ly** *adv.* **-ness** *n.* **strenuosity** *n.*

**strep•to•coc•cus** *n.* *(Med.)* bacterium of chain formation, the organism responsible for serious infections. *pl.* **streptococci.**

**strep•to•my•cin** *n.* *(Med.)* antibiotic drug.

**stress** *n.* force; strain; emphasis; accent; *v.t.* to lay stress on.

**stretch** *v.t.* to pull out; to reach out; to exaggerate; *v.i.* to be drawn out; to spread; *n.* extension; effort; expanse. **-er** *n.* one who, or that which, stretches; a frame or litter for carrying sick or wounded.

**strew** *v.t.* to scatter over surface; to spread loosely. *pa.p.* **-ed** or **-n**, *pa.t.* **-ed.**

**stri•a** *n.* line or small groove. *pl.* **-e** thread-like lines. **-te, -ted** *a.* **-tion** *n.*

**strick•en** *a.* struck; smitten; afflicted.

**strict** *a.* stern; exacting; rigid; without exception; accurate. **-ly** *adv.* **-ness** *n.* **-ure** *n.* severe criticism; *(Med.)* morbid contraction of any passage of body.

**stride** *n.* long step, or its length; *v.i.* to walk, with long steps. *pa.p.* **stridden** *pa.t.* **strode.**

**stri•dent** *a.* harsh in tone. **stridence, stridency** *n.* **-ly** *adv.*

**strife** *n.* conflict; struggle.

**strike** *v.t.* to hit; to collide; to sound; to occur to; to afflict; to stamp; to cancel; *v.i.* to hit; to stop work for increase of wages, etc.; to take root, of a plant; *n.* a stoppage of work to enforce demand; find, esp. in prospecting for gold; stroke of luck. *pa.p.* **struck,** or **-n** *pa.t.* **struck. striking** *a.* affecting with strong emotions; impressive. **strikingly** *adv.*

**string** *n.* cord; thick thread; chain; succession; stretched cord of gut or wire for musical instrument; *pl.* stringed musical instruments collectively; *v.t.* to furnish with strings; to put on string, as beads, pearls, etc. *pa.p.* and *pa.t.* **strung. -ed** *a.* **-y** *a.* fibrous; of person, long and thin. **-iness** *n.*

**strin•gent** *a.* binding strongly; severe. **-ly** *adv.* **-ness, stringency** *n.*

**strip** *v.t.* to pull or tear off; to peel; to lay bare; to rob; *v.i.* to take off one's clothes; *n.* long, narrow piece of anything. *pr.p.* **-ping.** *pa.p.* and *pa.t.* **-ped. -ling** *n.* youth.

**stripe** *n.* narrow line, band, or mark; *v.t.* to mark with stripes. **-d** *a.*

**strive** *v.i.* to make an effort; to struggle. *pa.p.* **-n.** *pa.t.* **strove.** *n.*

**strode** *pa.t.* of **stride.**

**stroke** *n.* blow; paralytic fit; sound of bell or clock; mark made by pen, pencil, brush, etc.; completed movement of club, stick, racquet, etc.; in swimming, completed movement of arm; in rowing, sweep of an oar; single, sudden effort, esp. if successful, in business, diplomacy, etc.; piece of luck.

**stroke** *v.t.* to pass hand gently over; *n.*

**stroll** *v.i.* to walk leisurely from place to place; *n.* a leisurely walk. **-er** *n.*

**strong** *a.* having physical force; muscular; healthy; violent; intense; not easily broken; positive. **-ly** *adv.*

**stron•ti•um** *n.* *(Chem.)* a yellowish, reactive, metallic element.

**strop** *n.* strip of leather for sharpening razor; *v.t.* to sharpen on strop. *pr.p.* **-ping.** *pa.p.* and *pa.t.* **-ped.**

**stro•phe** *n.* in ancient Greek drama, song sung by chorus while dancing from right to left of orchestra; stanza. **strophic** *a.*

**strove** *pa.t.* of **strive.**

**struck** *pa.p.* and *pa.t.* of **strike.**

**struc•ture** *n.* that which is built; organization. **structural** *a.* **structurally** *adv.*

**stru•del** *n.* type of Ger. pastry.

**strug•gle** *v.i.* to put forth great efforts, esp. accompanied by violent twistings of body; *n.* violent physical effort; any kind of work in face of difficulties; strife. *n.*

**strum** *v.t.* and *v.i.* to play badly and noisily on (stringed instrument). *pr.p.* **-ming.** *pa.p.* and *pa.t.* **-med.**

**strum•pet** *n.* prostitute; harlot.

**strung** *pa.p.* and *pa.t.* of **string.**

**strut** *v.i.* to walk pompously; *n.* stiff, proud and affected walk. *pa.p.* **-ting.** *pa.p.* and *pa.t.* **-ted.**

**strut** *n.* rigid support, usually set obliquely; *v.t.* to brace.

**strych•nine** *n.* highly poisonous alkaloid; stimulant. Also **strychnin.**

**stub** *n.* stump of a tree; short, remaining part of pencil, cigarette, etc.; *v.t.* to strike toe against fixed object. *pr.p.* **-bing.** *pa.p.* and *pa.t.* **-bed. -bed** *a.* short and blunt like stump; obtuse. **-by** *a.* **-biness** *n.*

**stub•ble** *n.* short ends of cornstalks left after reaping; short growth of beard. **-d** *a.* **stubbly** *a.*

**stub•born** *a.* fixed in opinion; obstinate. *adv.* **-ness** *n.*

**stuc•co** *n.* plaster of lime, sand, etc. used on walls; *v.t.* to make stucco.

**stud** *n.* a movable, double-headed flat-headed nail; upright wooden support, as in wall; *v.t.* to furnish with studs; to set thickly in, or scatter over. *pr.p.* **-ding.** *pa.p.* and *pa.t.* **-ded.**

**stud** *n.* collection of horses, kept for breeding, or racing.

**stu•dent** *n.* one who studies.

**stu•di•o** *n.* workroom of artist, sculptor, or professional photographer.

**stu•di•ous** *a.* given to, or fond of, study; contemplative. **-ly** *adv.*

**stud•y** *n.* application of the mind to books, etc. to gain knowledge; subject of such application; meditation; room for study; *v.t.* to set the mind to; to ponder over; *v.i.* to read books closely in order to gain knowledge. **studies** also *a.* examined closely; carefully considered.

**stuff** *n.* essential part; material; goods; worthless things, trash, esp. in stuff and nonsense; *v.t.* to fill by pressing closely. **-ing** *n.* material used to stuff or fill.

**stuff•y** *a.* badly ventilated; conceited. **stuffiness** *n.*

**stul•ti•fy** *v.t.* to make to look ridiculous; to make ineffectual.

**stum•ble** *v.i.* to trip in walking and nearly fall; to fall into error; *n.* **stumblingly** *adv.*

**stump** *n.* part of tree left after trunk is cut down; part of limb, tooth, etc. after main part has been removed; remnant; *v.t.* to reduce to a stump; to puzzle or perplex; *v.i.* to walk noisily or heavily. **-y** *a.*

**stun** *v.t.* to knock senseless; to amaze. *pr.p.* **-ning.** *pa.p.* and *pa.t.* **-ned. -ner** *n.* **-ning** *a.*

**stung** *pa.p.* and *pa.t.* of **sting.**

**stunk** *pa.p.* and *pa.t.* of **stink.**

**stunt** *v.t.* to check the growth of. **-ed** *a.*

**stunt** *n.* *(Colloq.)* any spectacular feat of skill or daring.

**stu•pe•fy** *v.t.* to deprive of full consciousness; to amaze. **stupefier** *n.* **stupefaction** *n.* **stupefactive** *a.* **stupefacient** *a.* and *n.*

**stu•pen•dous** *a.* astonishing, esp. because of size, power, etc.; amazing. **-ly** *adv.* **-ness** *n.*

**stu•pid** *a.* unintelligent; foolish; dull. **-ly** *adv.* **-ness, -ity** *n.*

**stu•por** *n.* complete or partial loss of consciousness. **-ous** *a.*

**stur•dy** *a.* hard; vigorous; strongly built; firm. **sturdily** *adv.* **sturdiness** *n.*

**stur•geon** *n.* large fish, whose roe is made into caviar.

**sturgeon**

**stut•ter** *v.i.* and *v.t.* to stammer; *n.* the act or habit of stuttering. **-er** *n.* **-ing** *a.*

**sty** *n.* place to keep pigs; hence, any filthy place.

**sty, stye** *n.* small abscess on edge of eyelid.

**styg•i•an** *a.* pert. to river *Styx* in Hades; gloomy; dismal.

**style** *n.* engraving tool; manner of expressing thought in writing, speaking, acting, painting, etc.; mode of dress; fine appearance; title; sort, kind, make, shape, etc. of anything; *(Bot.)* stem-like part of pistil of flower, supporting stigma. **-t** *n.* stiletto; probe. **stylize** *v.t.* to make conform to convention. **stylish** *a.* fashionable; elegant. **stylishly** *adv.* **stylishness** *n.* **stylist** *n.* writer, who is attentive to form and style. **stylistic** *a.* **stylistically** *adv.* **stylus** *n.* style.

**sty•mie** *n.* to thwart.

**styp•tic** *a.* contracting; astringent; *n.* *(Med.)* any substance used to arrest bleeding.

**sua•sion** *n.* persuasion.

**suave** *a.* smoothly polite. **-ly** *adv.* **suavity** *n.*

**sub-** *prefix*, meaning under, lower, inferior, about, slightly, moderately.

**sub•al•tern** *(Mil.)* *a.* of lower rank.

**sub•a•que•ous** *a.* living, lying, or formed under water. **subaquatic** *a.*

**sub•arc•tic** *a.* pert. to region immediately next to the Arctic.

**sub•con•scious** *a.;* *n.* subconscious mind. **-ly** *adv.*

**sub•cu•ta•ne•ous** *a.* under the skin. **-ly** *adv.*

**sub•di•vide** *v.t.* to divide again; *v.i.* to be subdivided. **subdivision** *n.*

**sub•duc•tion** *n.* withdrawal; deduction.

**sub•due** *v.t.* to bring under one's power; to bring under control; to soften. **-d** *a.* **-r** *n.* **subdual** *n.*

**sub•head•ing** *n.* division of main heading.

**sub•hu•man** *a.* less than human.

**sub•ject** *a.* under power or control of another; subordinate; liable to; exposed; *n.* one owing allegiance to a sovereign, state, government, etc.; topic; theme. **subject** *v.t.* to bring under power or control of; to cause to undergo. **ion** *n.* act of bringing under power or control. **-ive** *a.* existing in the mind; relating to, or reflecting, thoughts and feelings of person. **-ively** *adv.* **-iveness** *n.* **-ivity** *n.*

**sub•join** *v.t.* to append; to annex. **-der** *n.* something added at end.

**sub•ju•gate** *v.t.* to force to submit. **subjugation** *n.* **subjugator** *n.*

**sub•junc•tive** *a.* mood of verb implying condition, doubt, or wish.

**sub•lease** *n.* lease granted to another tenant by one who is himself a tenant; *v.t.* to grant or hold a sublease.

**sub•let** *v.t.* to let to another tenant property of which one is a tenant; *pr.p.* **-ting.** *pa.t.*, *pa.p.* **sublet.**

**sub•li•mate** *v.t.* to direct repressed impulses, esp. sexual, towards new aims and activities. **sublimation** *n.*

**sub•lime** *a.* exalted; eminent; majestic; grandiose; *n.* that which is sublime; *v.t.* to sublimate; to purify; to exalt; to ennoble. **-ly** *adv.* **-ness, sublimity** *n.*

**sub•lim•i•nal** *a.* in psychology, below level of consciousness.

**sub-ma•chine gun** *n.* *(Mil.)* light, portable machine gun.

**sub•ma•rine** *a.* situated, living, or able to travel under surface of sea; *n.* submersible boat.

**sub•merge** *v.t.* to put under water; *v.i.* to go under water. **-nce** *n.*

**sub•merse** *v.t.* to submerge; to put under water. **submersible** *a.* **submersion** *n.*

**sub•mit** *v.t.* to put forward for consideration; to surrender; *v.i.* to yield oneself to another. *pr.p.* **-ting.** *pa.p.* and *pa.t.* **-ted. submission** *n.* **submissive** *a.* **submissively** *adv.* **submissiveness** *n.*

**sub•mul•ti•ple** *n.* number or quantity that divides into another exactly.

**sub•nor•mal** *a.* below normal.

**sub•or•di•nate** *a.* lower in rank, importance, power, etc.; *n.* one of lower rank, importance, etc. than another; *v.t.* to make or treat as subordinate; to make subject. **-ly** *adv.* **-ness, subordinacy** *n.* **subordination** *n.*

**sub•orn** *v.t.* to induce (person) to commit perjury; to bribe to do evil. **-ation** *n.* **-er** *n.*

**sub•poe•na** *n.* *(Law)* writ summoning person to appear in court; *v.t.* to issue such an order.

**sub•rep•tion** *n.* concealment or misrepresentation of truth. **subreptitious** *a.*

**sub•scribe** *v.t.* to write underneath; to sign at end of paper or document; to contribute; *v.i.* (with *to*) to pay in advance for regular supply of issues of newspaper, magazine, etc.; to agree with or support. **-r** *n.* **subscript** *a.* written underneath. **subscription** *n.*

**sub•se•quent** *a.* following or coming after

in time; happening later. **-ly** *adv.*

**sub•serve** *v.t.* to serve in small way; to promote. **subservient** *a.* submissive; servile. **subserviently** *adv.* **subservience, subserviency** *n.*

**sub•side** *v.i.* to sink or fall to the bottom; to abate. **subsidence, subsidency** *n.*

**sub•sid•i•ar•y** *a.* aiding, helping, supplementary, secondary; auxiliary; *n.* one who, or that which, helps; auxiliary.

**sub•si•dy** *n.* financial aid; government grant for various purposes, e.g. to encourage certain industries, to keep cost of living steady, etc. **subsidize** *v.t.*

**sub•sist** *v.i.* to continue to be; *v.t.* to support with food; to feed. **-ent** *a.* having real being; existing. **-ence** *n.*

**sub•soil** *n.* the layer of earth lying just below the top layer.

**sub•son•ic** *a.* pert. to speeds less than that of sound; below 700-750 m.p.h.

**sub•stance** *n.* essence; material, etc. of which anything is made; property. **substantial** *a.* **substantiation** *n.* **substantive** *a.* having independent existence; real; fixed. **substantively** *adv.*

**sub•sti•tute** *v.t.* to put in place of another; to exchange. *v.i.* to take place of another; *n.* **substitution** *n.* **substitutional, substitutionary** *a.* **substitutionally** *adv.*

**sub•stra•tum** *n.* underlying stratum or layer of soil, rock, etc.; a basic element. *pl.* **substrata. substrative** *a.*

**sub•sume** *v.t.* to include under a class as belonging to it. e.g. 'all sparrows are birds.' **subsumption** *n.* **subsumptive** *a.*

**sub•ten•ant** *n.* tenant who rents house, farm, etc. from one who is himself a tenant. **subtenancy** *n.*

**sub•tend** *v.t. (Geom.)* of line, to extend under or be opposite to, e.g. angle.

**sub•ter•fuge** *n.* that to which a person resorts in order to escape from a difficult situation.

**sub•ter•ra•ne•an** *a.* being or lying under surface of earth. Also **subterraneous, subterrene, subterrestrial.**

**sub•ti•tle** *n.* additional title of book.

**sub•tle** *a.* delicate; discerning; clever; making fine distinctions. **subtly** *adv.* **-ness, -ty** *n.* quality of being subtle.

**sub•tract** *v.t.* to take away (part) from rest; to deduct one number from another. **-ion** *n.* **-ive** *a.* **subtrahend** *n.* quantity or number to be subtracted from another.

**sub•trop•i•cal** *a.* designating zone just outside region of the tropics.

**sub•urb** *n.* residential district on outskirts of town; *pl.* outskirts. **suburban** *a.* and *n.* **-ia** *n.*

**sub•ven•tion** *n.* act of coming to the help of; subsidy.

**sub•vert** *v.t.* to overthrow, esp. government; to destroy. **-er** *n.* **subversion** *n.* **subversive** *a.*

**sub•way** *n.* underground passage; underground railway.

**suc•ceed** *v.t.* to come immediately after; to take place of, esp. of one who has left or died; *v.i.* to come next in order; to become heir (to); to achieve one's aim to prosper. **-er** *n.* **success** *n.* favorable accomplishment; prosperity; **successful** *a.* **successfully** *adv.* **successfulness** *n.* **succession** *n.* sequence; act or right of entering into possession of property, place, office, title, etc., of another, esp. of one near of kin. **successional** *a.* **successionally** *adv.* **successive** *a.* **successively** *adv.* **successor** *n.*

**suc•cinct** *a.* expressed in few words; concise. **-ly** *adv.* **-ness** *n.*

**suc•cor** *v.t.* to help esp. in great difficulty or distress; *n.* aid; support. **-er** *n.*

**suc•cu•lent** *a.* full of juice; juicy. **-ly** *adv.* **succulence** *n.*

**suc•cumb** *v.i.* to yield; to submit; to die.

**such** *a.* of like kind; of degree, quality, etc. mentioned; *pron.* used to denote a certain person or thing; these or those. **-like** *a.* similar; *pron.* similar things.

**suck** *v.t.* to draw into mouth (by using lips and tongue); to absorb; *v.i.* to draw in with mouth; *n.* act of drawing with the mouth; milk drawn from mother's breast. **-er** *n.* shoot of plant from roots or lower part of stem. **-ing** *a.* **-le** *v.t.* to give suck to; to feed at mother's breast. **-ling** *n.* young child or animal not yet weaned.

**su•crose** *n.* cane sugar, beet sugar, etc.

**suc•tion** *n.* act of sucking or drawing in; 'force' that causes one object to adhere to another when air between them is exhausted.

**sud•den** *a.* happening without notice or warning. **-ly** *adv.* **-ness** *n.*

**suds** *n.pl.* water in which soap has been dissolved.

**sue** *v.t. (Law)* to seek justice by taking legal proceedings; *v.i.* to begin legal proceedings.

**suede** *n.* soft, undressed kid leather; *a.* made of undressed kid.

**su•et** *n.* hard animal fat around kidneys and loins. **-y** *a.*

**suf•fer** *v.t.* to endure; to tolerate; *v.i.* to undergo pain, punishment, etc. **-able** *a.* **-ableness** *n.* **-ably** *adv.* **-ance** *n.*

**suf•fice** *v.t.* to satisfy; *v.i.* to be enough; to meet the needs of. **sufficient** *a.* enough; satisfying the needs of. **sufficiently** *adv.* **sufficiency** *n.*

**suf•fix** *n.* letter or syllable added to end of word; affix. *v.t.* to add to end of. **-al** *a.* **-ion** *n.*

**suf•fo•cate** *v.t.* to kill by choking; to stifle; *v.i.* to be choked, stifled, or smothered. **suffocating** *a.* **suffocatingly** *adv.* **suffocation** *n.*

**suf•frage** *n.* vote; right to vote. **-tte** *n.*

**suf•fuse** *v.t.* to spread over, as fluid. **suffusion** *n.* **suffusive** *a.*

**sug•ar** *n.* sweet, crystalline substance; *(Fig.)* sweet words; *v.t.* to sweeten with sugar; *v.i.* to turn into sugar; *a.* made of, tasting of, or containing sugar; sweet; flattering. **-iness** *n.*

**sug•gest** *v.t.* to bring forward; to propose; to insinuate. **-er** *n.* **-ion** *n.* **-ive** *a.* **-ively** *adv.* **-iveness** *n.*

**su•i•cide** *n.* one who kills himself intentionally; act of doing this. **suicidal** *a.* *(Fig.)* disastrous; ruinous. **suicidally** *adv.*

**suit** *n.* act of suing; request; courtship;

series or set of things of same kind or material; set of clothes; *v.t.* to fit; to appropriate; to meet desires of; *v.i.* to agree; to be convenient. **-able** *a.* **-ably** *adv.* **-ability, -ableness** *n.* **-or** *n.*

**suite** *n.* a number of things used together, e.g. set of apartments, furniture; *(Mus.)* series of dances.

**sul•cus** *n.* groove; a furrow. **sulcate, sulcated** *a.* **sulcation** *n.*

**sul•fa** *n.* abbrev. for sulfa drugs, a group of antibacterial compounds.

**sul•fate** *n.* salt of sulfuric acid. **sulfide** *n.* compound of sulfur with metal or other element. **sulfite** *n.* salt of sulfurous acid.

**sul•fur** *n.* yellow, nonmetallic element. **-ous** *a.* **-y** *a.* **-ic acid,** colorless acid.

**sulk** *v.i.* to be silent owing to ill humor, etc.; *n.* sullen fit or mood. **-y** *a.; n.* light two-wheeled carriage for one person. **-ily** *adv.* **-iness** *n.*

**sul•len** *a.* gloomily ill-humored. **-ly** *adv.* **-ness** *n.*

**sul•ly** *v.t.* to soil; to disgrace; *v.i.* to be sullied.

**sul•tan** *n.* Mohammedan prince or ruler. **-a** *n.* wife, mother, or daughter of sultan; kind of raisin.

**sul•try** *a.* hot, close, and oppressive; sweltering. **sultrily** *adv.* **sultriness** *n.*

**sum** *n.* result obtained by adding together two or more things, quantities, etc.; quantity of money; *v.t.* (generally with up) to add up; to make summary of main parts. *pr.p.* **-ming.** *pa.p.* and *pa.t.* **-med. -mation** *n.*

**sum•ma•ry** *a.* expressed in few words; *n.* abridgment or statement of chief points of longer document, speech; etc.; epitome. **summarily** *adv.* **summarize** *v.t.* **summarist** *n.* **summarization** *n.* **summarizer** *n.*

**sum•mer** *n.* warmest of four seasons of year, season between spring and autumn; *a.* pert. to period of summer. **-y** *a.*

**sum•mit** *n.* highest point.

**sum•mon** *v.t.* to demand appearance of, esp. in court of law; to gather up (energy, etc.). **-er** *n.*

**sump** *n.* lowest part of excavation; well in crankcase of motor vehicle for oil.

**sump•tu•ar•y** *a.* pert. to, or regulating, expenditure. **sumptuous** *a.* costly; lavish; magnificent. **sumptuously** *adv.* sumptuousness *n.*

**sun** *n.* luminous body round which earth and other planets revolve; its rays; any other heavenly body forming the center of system of planets; *v.t.* to expose to sun's rays; to bask. *pr.p.* **-ning.** *pa.p.* and *pa.t.* **-ned. -ny** *a.* **-niness** *n.* **-bathe** *v.i.* to expose body to sun. **-beam** *n.* **-burn** *n.* darkening of skin, due to exposure to sun; *v.t.* and *v.i.* to darken by exposure to sun. **-burned, burnt** *a.* **-down** *n.* sunset. **-flower** *n.* tall plant with yellow-rayed flowers. **-light** *n.* **-lit** *a.* lighted by sun. **-rise** *n.* dawn. **-set** *n.* descent of sun below horizon. **-shine** *a.* **-spot** *n.* dark, irregular patch on surface of sun. **-stroke** *n.* feverish prostration caused by undue exposure to strong sunlight.

**sun•dae** *n.* ice-cream served with topping.

**Sun•day** *n.* first day of week.

**sun•der** *v.t.* to separate; *v.i.* to come apart. **sundry** *a.* separate; various. **sundries** *n.pl.* sundry things; odd items.

**sung** *pa.p.* of **sing.**

**sunk** *pa.p.* and alt. *pa.t.* of **sink.**

**sunk•en** alt. *pa.p.* of **sink.**

**sup** *v.t.* to take in sips; *v.i.* to have supper; to sip; *n.* small mouthful; sip. *pr.p.* **-ping.** *pa.p.* and *pa.t.* **-ped.**

**su•per** *n.* *(Colloq.)* short for superfine, super-excellent, etc.

**su•per-** *prefix,* above, over, higher, superior, to extra, etc.

**su•per•a•ble** *a.* capable of being overcome.

**su•per•a•bound** *v.i.* to be exceedingly abundant. **superabundant** *a.* **superabundantly** *adv.* **superabundance** *n.*

**su•per•an•nu•ate** *v.t.* to pension off because of age or infirmity. **superannuation** *n.* pension.

**su•perb** *a.* grand; splendid. **-ly** *adv.* **-ness** *n.*

**su•per•car•go** *n.* ship's officer who takes charge of cargo.

**su•per•charge** *v.t.* to charge or fill to excess.

**su•per•cil•i•ar•y** *a.* pert. to eyebrow. **supercilious** *a.* lofty with pride; haughty and indifferent. **superciliously** *adv.*

**su•per•cool** *v.t.* *(Chem.)* to cool (liquid) below its freezing point without solidifying it. **-ing** *n.*

**su•per•e•go** *n.* in psychoanalysis, that unconscious morality which directs action of censor.

**su•per•er•o•ga•tion** *n.* doing more than duty or necessity requires.

**su•per•fi•cial** *a.* on surface; understanding only what is obvious. **-ly** *adv.* **-ity.**

**su•per•fine** *a.* fine above others.

**su•per•flu•ous** *a.* more than is required or desired; useless. **-ly** *adv.* **superfluity** *n.* **-ness** *n.*

**su•per•heat** *v.t.* to heat (steam) above boiling point of water.

**su•per•het•er•o•dyne** *n.* *(Radio)* receiving set of great power and selectivity. *abbrev.* **superhet.**

**su•per•hu•man** *a.* more than human; divine; excessively powerful.

**su•per•im•pose** *v.t.* to lay upon another thing. **superimposition** *n.*

**su•per•in•tend** *v.t.* to manage; to supervise; *v.i.* to supervise. **-ence, -ency** *n.* **-ent** *a.* and *n.*

**su•pe•ri•or** *a.* higher in place, position, rank, quality, etc.; *n.* one who is above another, esp. in rank or office. **superiority** *n.*

**su•per•la•tive** *a.* of or in the highest degree; *n.* superlative degree of adjective or adverb. **-ly** *adv.*

**su•per•man** *n.* one endowed with powers beyond those of the ordinary man.

**su•per•nal** *a.* pert. to things above; celestial; heavenly.

**su•per•nat•u•ral** *a.* beyond powers or laws of nature; miraculous.

**su•per•nu•mer•ar•y** over and above; *n.*

person or thing in excess of what is necessary or usual.

**su•per•scribe** *v.t.* to write or engrave on outside or top of. **superscription** *n.*

**su•per•sede** *v.t.* to set aside; to replace by another person or thing. **supersession** *n.*

**su•per•son•ic** *a.* pert. to soundwaves of too high a frequency to be audible.

**su•per•sti•tion** *n.* belief in, or fear of, what is unknown or supernatural. **superstitious** *a.* **superstitiously** *adv.*

**su•per•struc•ture** *n.* structure built on top of another. **superstructive, superstructural** *a.*

**su•per•vene** *v.i.* to happen in addition, or unexpectedly; to follow closely upon. **supervenient** *a.* **supervenience, supervention** *n.*

**su•per•vise** *v.t.* to oversee; to direct and control. **supervision** *n.* Also **supervisal** *n.* **supervisor** *n.* **supervisory** *a.*

**su•pine** *a.* lying on one's back; indolent; inactive.

**sup•per** *n.* the last meal of the day.

**sup•plant** *v.t.* to displace (person) esp. by unfair means. **-er** *n.*

**sup•ple** *a.* easily bent; limber; obsequious; *v.t.* and *v.i.* to make or become supple. **-ly** *adv.* **-ness** *n.*

**sup•ple•ment** *n.* something added to fill up or supply deficiency. **supplement** *v.t.* **-al** *a.* **-ary** *a.*

**sup•pli•ant** *a.* asking humbly and submissively; *n.* one who supplicates. **-ly** *adv.* **supplicant** *a.* and *n.* **supplicate** *v.t.* and *v.i.* **supplication** *n.*

**sup•ply** *v.t.* to provide what is needed; *n.* act of supplying; what is supplied; stock; store. **supplies** *n.pl.* food or money. **supplier** *n.*

**sup•port** *v.t.* to keep from falling; to bear or tolerate; to furnish with means of living; *n.* act of sustaining; maintenance or subsistence; one who, or that which, supports. **-er** *n.*

**sup•pose** *v.t.* to assume as true without proof; to imagine. **-d** *a.* **supposedly** *adv.* **supposable** *a.*

**sup•po•si•tion** *n.* act of supposing; assumption; that which is supposed; **-ally** *adv.* **supposititious** *a.*

**sup•pos•i•to•ry** *n.* medicinal substance, cone-shaped, introduced into a body canal.

**sup•press** *v.t.* to put down or subdue. **suppression** *n.* **-ive** *a.* **-or** *n.*

**sup•pu•rate** *v.i.* to form pus; to fester. **suppurative** *a.* **suppuration** *n.*

**su•pra-** *prefix*, meaning above.

**su•preme** *a.* holding highest authority; greatest possible. **-ly** *adv.* **-ness** *n.* **supremacy** *n.*

**sur-** *prefix*, meaning over, above, upon, in addition.

**sur•cease** *v.t.* *(Arch.)* to cause to cease; *v.i.* to cease; *n.* cessation.

**sur•charge** *v.t.* to make additional charge; to overload or overburden. **surcharge** *n.* excessive charge, load, or burden.

**sur•cin•gle** *n.* girth for holding something on a horse's back.

**sur•coat** *n.* long and flowing cloak worn by knights over armor.

**surd** *a.* *(Math.)* not capable of being expressed in rational numbers.

**sure** *a.* certain; admitting of no doubt; firmly established; strong or secure. **-ly** *adv.* certainly; undoubtedly; securely. **-ness** *n.* **-ty** *n.* certainty; that which makes sure.

**surf** *n.* foam or water of sea breaking on shore or reefs, etc.

**sur•face** *n.* external layer or outer face of anything; *a.* involving the surface only; *v.t.* to cover with special surface; *v.i.* to come to the surface.

**sur•feit** *v.t.* to overfeed; to fill to satiety; *n.* excess in eating and drinking. **-er** *n.* **-ing** *n.*

**surge** *n.* rolling swell of water, smoke, people; *v.i.* to swell. **surging** *a.*

**sur•geon** *n.* medical man qualified to perform operations. **surgery** *n.* branch of medicine dealing with cure of disease or injury by manual operation. **surgical** *a.* **surgically** *adv.*

**sur•ly** *a.* of unfriendly temper. **surlily** *adv.* **surliness** *n.*

**sur•mise** *v.t.* to imagine or infer something without proper grounds; *n.* supposition; a guess or conjecture.

**sur•mount** *v.t.* to rise above; to conquer or overcome. **-able** *a.*

**sur•name** *n.* family name.

**sur•pass** *v.t.* to go beyond; to outstrip. **-ing** *a.*

**sur•plice** *n.* white linen vestment worn over cassock by clergy.

**sur•plus** *n.* excess beyond what is wanted; excess of income over expenditure; *a.* more than enough.

**sur•prise** *v.t.* to fall or come upon unawares; to strike with astonishment; *n.* astonishment; unexpected event, piece of news, gift, etc. **surprisal** *n.* **surprising** *a.* **surprisingly** *adv.*

**sur•re•al•ism** *n.* 20th cent. phase in art and literature of expressing subconscious in images without order or coherence, as in dream. **surrealist** *n.* **surrealistic** *a.*

**sur•ren•der** *v.t.* to yield or hand over to power of another; to yield to emotion, etc.; *v.i.* to cease resistance; to capitulate; *n.* act of surrendering. **-er** *n.*

**sur•rep•ti•tious** *a.* done by stealth. **-ly** *adv.*

**sur•rey** *n.* lightly built, four-wheeled carriage.

**sur•ro•gate** *n.* deputy who acts for bishop or chancellor of diocese. **-ship** *n.*

**sur•round** *v.t.* to be on all sides of. **-ings** *n.* that which surrounds; *pl.* things which environ.

**sur•tax** *n.* additional tax; *v.t.* to impose extra tax on.

**sur•veil•lance** *n.* close watch; supervision.

**sur•vey** *v.t.* to look over; to view as from high place. **survey** *n.* general view, as from high place; measured plan or chart of any tract of country. **-or** *n.* one who surveys.

**sur•vive** *v.t.* to live longer than; *v.i.* to remain alive. **survival** *n.* **survivor** *n.* **surviving** *a.*

**sus•cep•ti•ble** *a.* capable of; readily

impressed; sensitive. **susceptibly** *adv.* **-ness** *n.* **susceptibility** *n.* **susceptive** *a.* receptive. **susceptivity, susceptiveness** *n.*

**sus•pect** *v.t.* to imagine existence or presence of; to imagine to be guilty; to mistrust. **suspect** *n.* suspected person; *a.* inspiring distrust. **-er** *n.*

**sus•pend** *v.t.* to cause to hang; to bring to a stop temporarily; to debar from an office or privilege; to defer or keep undecided. **-er** *n.* one who suspends; *pl.* pair of straps for holding up trousers, skirt, etc. **suspense** *n.* state of uncertainty or anxiety; indecision. **suspension** *n.* **suspensive** *a.* **suspensively** *adv.* **suspensor** *n.* **suspensory** *a.*

**sus•pi•cion** *n.* act of suspecting; imagining of something being wrong, on little evidence; doubt; mistrust; slight trace or hint. **suspicious** *a.* **suspiciously** *adv.*

**sus•tain** *v.t.* to keep from falling or sinking; to nourish or keep alive; to endure or undergo. **-able** *a.* **-er** *n.* **sustenance** *n.* that which sustains (life); food, nourishment. **sustentation** *n.* **sustentative** *a.* **sustention** *n.*

**su•ture** *n.* sewing up of wound; connection or seam, between bones of skull; *v.t.* to join by stitching. **sutural** *a.*

**su•ze•rain** *n.* feudal lord; paramount ruler. **-ty** *n.* authority or dominion of **suzerain.**

**svelte** *a.* supple; lithe; slender.

**swab** *n.* mop; bit of cotton on stick for applying medicine; *v.t.* to clean with mop or swab. *pr.p.* **-bing.** *pa.t.* and *pa.p.* **-bed. -ber** *n.*

**swad•dle** *v.t.* to bind or wrap as with bandages; *n.* the cloth wrapping.

**swage** *n.* tool for bending, marking, or shaping metal. *v.t.*

**swag•ger** *v.i.* to walk with a conceited or defiant strut; to boast or brag; *n.* defiant or conceited bearing. **-er** *n.* **-ing** *a.*

**Swa•hi•li** *n.* people of mixed Bantu and Arab stock, occupying Zanzibar and adjoining territory; their language. *(Poetic)* **-an** *a.*

**swain** *n.* *(Poetic)* country lad; rustic lover.

**swal•low** *n.* small migratory, passerine, insectivorous bird. **-tail** *n.* forked tail.

swallow

**swal•low** *v.t.* to receive into stomach through mouth and throat; *(Colloq.)* to accept without criticism or scruple; *v.i.* to perform act of swallowing; *n.* act of swallowing; amount taken down at one gulp. **-er** *n.*

**swam** *pa.t.* of **swim.**

**swamp** *n.* tract of wet, low-lying ground; marsh; *v.t.* to cause to fill with water, as boat; *v.i.* to overwhelm; to sink. **-y** *a.*

**swan** *n.* large, web-footed bird of goose family. **-nery** *n.* place where swans are bred.

**swap** *v.t.* and *v.i.* to exchange; to barter; *n.* exchange. *pr.p.* **-ping.** *pa.p.* and *pa.t.* **-ped.** Also **swop.**

**sward** *n.* land covered with short green grass; turf; *v.t.* to cover with sward. **-ed** *a.*

**swarm** *n.* large number of insects esp. in motion; crowd; *v.i.* to collect in large numbers.

**swarm** *v.i.* to climb with arms and legs.

**swarth•y** *a.* dark in hue; of dark complexion.

**swash•buck•ler** *n.* swaggering bully. **swashbuckling** *a.*

**swas•ti•ka** *n.* symbol in form of Greek cross with ends of arms bent thus 卐

**swat** *v.t.* *(Colloq.)* to hit smartly; to kill, esp. insects. *pr.p.* **-ting.** *pa.t., pa.p.* **-ted.**

**swatch** *n.* piece of cloth, cut as a sample of quality.

**swath** *n.* line of hay or grain cut by scythe or mowing machine. Also **swathe.**

**swathe** *v.t.* to bind with bandage; *n.* bandage; folded or draped band.

**sway** *v.t.* to cause to incline to one side or the other; *v.i.* to incline to one side or the other; to totter; *n.* swaying or swinging movement; control. **-er** *n.* **-back** *a.* having inward curve of the spine.

**swear** *v.t.* to utter, affirm or declare on oath; *v.i.* to utter solemn declaration with appeal to God for truth of what is affirmed; to curse. *pa.p.* **sworn.** *pa.t.* **swore. -er** *n.* **-ing** *n.*

**sweat** *n.* perspiration; moisture exuding from any substance; *v.t.* to cause to excrete moisture from skin; *v.i.* to excrete moisture; *(Colloq.)* to toil or drudge at. **-er** *n.* warm knitted jersey or jacket. **-y** *a.* damp with sweat. **-ily** *adv.* **-iness** *n.*

**Swede** *n.* native of Sweden. **Swedish** *a.* pert. to Sweden; *n.* language of Swedes.

**sweep** *v.t.* to pass brush or broom over to remove loose dirt; to scan rapidly; *v.i.* to pass with swiftness or violence; to move with dignity; to extend in a curve; to effect cleaning with a broom; *n.* act of sweeping. *pa.p.* and *pa.t.* **swept. -er** *n.* **-ing** *a.* of great scope; comprehensive. **-ingly** *adv.*

**sweet** *a.* tasting like sugar; having agreeable taste; melodious; gentle; dear or beloved; likeable; *n.* sweetness; darling; *pl.* confections. **-en** *v.t.* **-ening** *n.* **-ly** *adv.* **-ness** *n.* **-bread** *n.* pancreas or thymus of animal, as food. **-pea** *n.* climbing plant with fragrant flowers. **-potato** *n.* sweet, starchy tuber.

**swell** *v.t.* to increase size, sound, etc.; *v.i.* to grow larger; to rise in waves; to be filled to bursting point with some emotion. *n.* act of swelling. *pa.p.* **swollen** or **swelled.** *pa.t.* **-ed. -ing** *n.*

**swel•ter** *v.i.* to be oppressive, or oppressed, with heat; *n.* heated or sweaty state. **-ing** *a.* **sweltry** *a.*

**swept** *pa.t.* and *pa.p.* of **sweep.**

**swerve** *v.i.* to depart from straight line; *v.t.* to cause to bend or turn aside; *n.* act of swerving.

**swift** *a.* quick; prompt. **-ly** *adv.* **-ness** *n.*

**swig** *v.t.* and *v.i.* *(Colloq.)* to gulp down; to drink in long drafts; *n.* long draft. *pr.p.* **-ging.** *pa.p., pa.t.* **-ged.**
**swill** *v.t.* and *v.i.* to drink greedily; *n.* act of swilling; pig food; hogwash slops. **-er** *n.*
**swim** *v.i.* to propel oneself in water by means of hands, feet, or fins, etc.; to float on surface; *v.t.* to cross or pass over by swimming; *n.* act of swimming. *pr.p.* **-ming.** *pa.p.* **swum.** *pa.t.* **swam.** **-mer** *n.* **-mingly** *adv.* easily, successfully.
**swim** *v.i.* to be dizzy or giddy; *n.* dizziness or unconsciousness. *pr.p.* **-ming.** *pa.p.* **swum.** *pa.t.* **swam.**
**swin•dle** *v.t.* and *v.i.* to cheat or defraud; *n.* act of defrauding.
**swine** *n.sing.* and *pl.* thick-skinned domestic animal, fed for its flesh; pig; hog. **—herd** *n.* one who tends swine. **swinish** *a.*
**swing** *v.i.* to move to and fro, esp. as suspended body; *v.t.* to attach so as to hang freely; to move to and fro; to brandish; *n.* act of swinging or causing to swing. *pa.p.* and *pa.t.* **swung.** **-er** *n.* **-ing** *a.* **-ingly** *adv.*
**swing** *n.* *(Mus.)* kind of jazz music.
**swipe** *v.t.* and *v.i.* to strike with a wide, sweeping blow, as with a bat, racket, etc.
**swirl** *n.* eddy of wind or water; whirling motion; *v.i.* to whirl; *v.t.* to carry along with whirling motion.
**swish** *n.* *v.i.* to move with hissing or rustling sound.
**Swiss** *n.sing.* and *pl.* native of Switzerland; *a.* pert. to Switzerland or the Swiss.
**switch** *n.* flexible twig or rod; tress of false hair; *(Elect.)* device for making, breaking, or transferring, electric current; act of switching; *v.t.* to strike with switch; to wisk; *(Elect.)* to turn electric current off or on with switch; to transfer one's thoughts to another subject; to transfer. **-er** *n.* **—like** *a.* **-back** *n.* zigzag method of ascending slopes. **-board** *n.* set of switches at telephone exchange.
**swiv•el** *n.* ring turning on pivot, forming connection between two pieces of mechanism and enabling one to rotate independently of the other; *v.i.* to swing on pivot; *v.t.* to turn as on pivot.
**swol•len** *a.* swelled. *pa.p.* of **swell.**
**swoon** *v.i.* to faint; *n.* fainting fit.
**swoop** *v.t.* to catch up with sweeping motion (with 'up'); *v.i.* to sweep down swiftly upon prey, as hawk or eagle; *n.*
**swop.** See **swap.**
**sword** *n.* **-fish** *n.* large fish with sword-like

sword-fish

upper jaw. **-play** *n.* fencing. **-sman** *n.* one skillful with sword. **—smanship** *n.*
**swore** *pa.t.* of **swear.**
**sworn** *pa.p.* of **swear.**
**swum** *pa.p.* of **swim.**
**swung** *pa.p.* and *pa.t.* of **swing.**
**syb•a•rite** *n.* person devoted to luxury and pleasure. **sybaritic, sybaritical** *a.*
**syc•a•more** *n.* tree with broad leaves.
**syc•o•phant** *n.* flatterer, or one who fawns on rich or famous; parasite; *a.* servile; obsequious. **sychophancy, -ism** *n.* **-ic, -ical, -ically** *adv.* **-ish** *a.*
**syl•la•ble** *n.* sound uttered at single effort of voice, and constituting word, or part of word; *v.t.* to utter in syllables; to articulate. **syllabic, syllabical** *a.* **syllabically** *adv.* **syllabicate, syllabify, syllabize,** *v.t.* to divide into syllables.
**syl•la•bus** *n.* outline or program of main points in a course of lectures, etc.
**syl•lo•gism** *n.* formal statement of argument, consisting of three parts, major premise, minor premise, and conclusion. **syllogize** *v.t.* and *v.i.* **syllogization** *n.* **syllogizer** *n.* **syllogistic, syllogistical** *a.*
**sylph** *n.* elemental spirit of the air; fairy or sprite; graceful girl. **-id** *n.* little sylph. **-like** *a.*
**syl•van** *a.* forest-like; pert. to or inhabiting the woods.
**sym•bi•o•sis** *n.* *(Biol.)* living together of different organisms for mutual benefit. **symbiotic** *a.* **symbiont** *n.*
**sym•bol** *n.* something that represents something else; emblem, type character or sign used to indicate relation or operation in mathematics. **-ic, -ical** *a.* **-ically** *adv.* **-ize** *v.t.* to stand for, or represent. **-ism** *n.* representation by symbols; system of symbols. **-ist** *n.* one who uses symbols.
**sym•me•try** *n.* due proportion between several parts of object. **symmetric, symmetrical** *a.* **symmetricalness** *n.* **symmetrize** *v.t.*
**sym•pa•thy** *n.* fellow feeling, esp. feeling for another person in pain or grief; compassion or pity. **sympathetic(al)** *a.* **sympathetically** *adv.* **sympathize** *v.i.* **sympathizer** *n.*
**sym•pho•ny** *n.* *(Mus.)* composition for full orchestra. **symphonic** *a.* **symphonist** *n.* composer of symphonies.
**sym•po•si•um** *n.* gathering, esp. one at which interchange or discussion of ideas takes place. *pl.* **symposia.**
**symp•tom** *n.* *(Med.)* perceptible change in body or its functions, which indicates disease. **-atic, -atical** *a.*
**syn-** *prefix,* meaning with, together, at the same time; becomes *sym-,* before *p, b,* and *m,* and *syl-* before *l.*
**syn•a•gogue** *n.* congregation of Jews meet for worship. **synagogical** *a.*
**syn•chro•nize** *v.i.* to agree in time; to be simultaneous; *v.t.* to cause to occur at the same time. **synchronization** *n.* **synchronism** *n.* **synchronal** *a.* **synchronous** *a.*
**syn•chro•tron** *n.* scientific machine for accelerating electrons to very high speeds.
**syn•co•pate** *v.t.* *(Gram.)* to contract, as a word, by taking one or more sounds or syllables from middle; in music, to alter rhythm by accenting a usually unaccented note. **syncopation** *n.*
**syn•cope** *n.* the omission of one or more letters from the middle of a word; *(Med.)* a fainting or swooning. **syncopal,**

syncopic *a.* (See **syncopate**).

**syn•dic** *n.* legal representative chosen to act as agent for corporation or company. **-ate** *n.* council of syndics; body of persons associated to carry out enterprise; *v.t.* to control by a syndicate; to publish news, etc. simultaneously in several periodicals owned by one syndicate.

**syn•ed•do•che** *n.* *(Rhet.)* figure of speech by which the whole is put for the part, or a part for the whole. **synecdochic, synecdochical** *a.*

**syn•od** *n.* an assembly of ecclesiatus; convention or council. **-al, -ic, -ical,** *a.* **-ically** *adv.*

**syn•o•nym** *n.* **-ous** *a.* **-ously** *adv.*

**syn•op•sis** *n.* general outlook, view; summary. *pl.* **synopses. synoptic, synoptical** *a.* **synoptically** *adv.*

**syn•tax** *n.* rules governing sentence construction. **syntactic, syntactical** *a.* **syntactically** *adv.*

**syn•the•sis** *n.* combination or putting together; *(Chem.)* uniting of elements to form compound. *pl.* **syntheses. synthetic, synthetical** *a.* not derived from nature; artificial. **synthetically** *adv.*, **synthesize, synthetize** *v.t.* **synthesist, synthetist** *n.*

**syph•i•lis** *n.* contagious venereal disease. **syphilitic** *a.*

**sy•phon.** See **siphon.**

**Syr•i•a** *n.* country in W. Asia. **-c** *n.* language of Syria. **-n** *n.* and *a.*

**syr•inge** *n.* tube and piston serving to draw in and then expel fluid; *v.t.* to inject by means of syringe Panpipe.

**syr•inx** *n.* *(Mus.)* *(Anat.)* the Eustachian tube; vocal organ of birds. *pl.* **-ed, syringes. syringeal** *a.*

**syr•up, sirup** *n.* fluid separated from sugar in process of refining. **-y** *a.*

**sys•tem** *n.* assemblage of objects arranged after some distinct method, usually logical or scientific; universe; organization; classification; set of doctrines or principles; the body as functional unity. **-atic, -atical** *a.* **-atically** *adv.* **-atize, -ize** *v.t.* to reduce to system; to arrange methodically. **-atization, -ization** *n.*

**sys•to•le** *n.* contraction of heart and arteries for expelling blood and carrying on circulation. **systolic** *a.*

**tab** *n.* small flap; a label.
**tab•by** *n.* stout kind of watered silk; striped cat, esp. female; *a.* striped; *v.t.* to give watered finish to, as silk.
**tab•er•nac•le** *n.* movable shelter for religious worship by Israelites; place for worship.
**tab•la•ture** *n.* painting on ceiling or wall; mental picture.
**ta•ble** *n.* smooth flat surface of wood, etc. supported by legs, as furniture for working at, or serving meals; systematic arrangement of figures, facts, as *multiplication table;* index, schedule; *a.* pert. to a table; *v.t.* to form into a catalog; to postpone for subsequent consideration. **-spoon** *n.* a large spoon for serving, measuring, holding ½ fluid ounce. **— tennis** *n.* game of indoor tennis played on a table; Ping-Pong. **-ware** *n.* utensils (incl. china, glass and silver) for table use.
**tab•leau** *n.* vivid representation of scene in history, literature, art, by group of persons appropriately dressed and posed.
**tab•let** *n.* anything flat on which to write; slab of stone with inscription; small, compressed solid piece of medication.
**tab•loid** *n.* illustrated newspaper, giving topical and sensational events in compressed form.
**ta•boo** *n.* system by which certain objects and persons are set aside as accursed; political, social, or religious prohibition; *a.* prohibited; *v.t.* to forbid the use of; to ostracize.
**ta•bor** *n.* small drum, like a tambourine. **-et** *n.* small tabor; low cushioned stool.
**tab•u•lar** *a.* having a broad, flat top; arranged systematically in rows or columns. **-ize** *v.t.* to tabulate. **-ly** *adv.* **tabulate** *v.t.* to form into a table, scheme or synopsis.
**ta•chom•e•ter** *n.* instrument for measurement of speed.
**tac•it** *a.* implied, but not expressed; silent. **-ly** *adv.* **-urn** *a.* reserved of speech. **-urnity** *n.* **-urnly** *adv.*
**tack** *n.* small sharp-pointed nail; long stitch; course of action; *v.t.* to fasten with long, loose stitches; to nail with; *v.t.* to change policy. **-er** *n.* **-iness** *n.* stickiness. **-y** *a.* sticky; viscous.
**tack** *n.* food; fore.
**tack•le** *n.* mechanism of ropes and pulleys for raising heavy weights; gear; *(Football)* move by player to grasp and stop opponent; *v.t.* to undertake; *(Football)* to seize and stop. **tackling** *n.* rigging of a ship. **— block** *n.* pulley.
**tact** *n.* awareness of right thing to say to avoid giving offense. **-ful** *a.* **-fully** *adv.* **-ile** *a.* capable of being felt; tangible. **-less** *a.* wanting in tact. **-ual** *a.* pert. to sense of touch.
**tac•tics** *n. sing.* adroit management of situation. **tactical** *a.* **tactically** *adv.* **tactician** *n.*
**tad•pole** *n.* young of frog in its first state before gills and tail are absorbed.
**taf•fe•ta** *n.* lightweight glossy silk of plain weave.
**tag** *n.* tie-on label; appendage; game in which one player chases and tries to touch another; *v.t.* to fit with tags; to add on. **-ging** *pr.p.* **-ged** *pa.t.* and *pa.p.*
**tail** *n.* flexible prolongation of animal's spine; back, inferior part of anything; *(Aero.)* group of stabilizing fins at rear of airplane; *v.t.* to furnish with tail; to extend in line; to trail. **-ed** *a.* **-less** *a.* **-light** *n.* red rear light of vehicle. **— plane** *n. (Aero.)* stabilizing surface at rear of aircraft.
**tai•lor** *n.* one who makes clothes; *v.t.* and *v.i.* to make men's suits, women's costumes, etc. **-ing** *n.* work of a tailor. **-less** *a.* **— made** *a.* plain in style and fitting perfectly.
**taint** *v.t.* to contaminate; *v.i.* to be infected with incipient putrefaction; *n.* touch of corruption.
**take** *v.t.* to grasp; to capture; to win; to photograph; *v.i.* to be effective; to please; to direct course of; to resort to; *n.* quantity of fish caught at one time; one of several movie shots of same scene; receipts. **taking** *pr.p.* **took** *pa.t.* **-n** *pa.p.* **taking** *n.* act of gaining possession; *pl.* cash receipts of shop, theater, etc.; *a.* infectious. **takingly** *adv.* **takingness** *n.* quality of being attractive.
**talc** *n.* fine, slightly perfumed powder. **-ose** *a.* composed of talc. **-um** *n.* powdered talc, as toilet powder.
**tale** *n.* narrative; false report. **-bearer** *n.* one who spitefully informs against another.
**tal•ent** *n.* special or outstanding ability. **-ed** *a.* gifted.
**tal•is•man** *n.* object endowed with magical power of protecting the wearer from harm. **-ic, -al** *a.*
**talk** *v.t.* and *v.i.* to converse; to speak; *n.* short dissertation; gossip. **-ative** *a.* chatty. **-atively** *adv.* **-ativeness, -er** *n.* **-ing** *a.* capable of speaking.
**tall** *a.* high in stature; lofty. **-ness** *n.*
**tal•low** *n.* animal fat melted down and used in manufacture of candles, etc.; *v.t.* to smear with tallow. **-ish** *a.* pasty; greasy. **-like, -y,** *a.*
**tal•ly** *n.* something on which a score is kept; identity label; *v.t.* to score; *v.i.* to agree. **tallied** *pa.t.* and *pa.p.*
**Tal•mud** *n.* collection of texts on Jewish religious law. **-ic(al)** *a.* **-ist** *n.* student of the Talmud. **-istic** *a.*
**tal•on** *n.* hooked claw of bird of prey. **-ed** *a.* having talons.
**tam•bour** *n.* small flat drum; piece of embroidery worked in metal threads on tambour.
**tam•bou•rine** *n.* round, shallow, single-sided drum with jingling metal disks, used to accompany Spanish dances.
**tame** *a.* domesticated; subdued; *v.t.* to domesticate. **-ability, tamability, -ableness** *n.* **able** *a.* **-ly** *adv.* **-ness, -r** *n.*
**tam•per** *v.i.* to meddle; to alter with malicious intent. **-er** *n.*
**tan** *n.* bark of oak, etc. bruised to extract tannic acid for tanning leather; yellowish-brown color; *v.t.* to convert

skins into leather by soaking in tannic acid; *v.i.* to become sunburned. **-ning** *pr.p.* **-ned** *pa.t.* and *pa.p.* **-nate** *n.* *(Chem.)* salt of tannic acid. **-ner** *n.* one who works in tannery. **-nery** *n.* place where leather is made. **-nic** *a.* pert. to tannin. **-nin** *n.* now called **tannic acid. -ning** *n.*

**tan•dem** *adv.* one behind the other; *n.* a bicycle for two people.

**tang** *n.* a prong (of a tool) which connects with the handle; a pungent smell or taste; *v.t.* to furnish (a tool) with a tang. **-ed, -y** *a.*

**tan•gent** *n.* *(Geom.)* line which touches curve but, when produced, does not cut it; *a.* touching but not intersecting. **tangency, tangence** *n.* state of touching. **tangential** *a.* digressing. **tangentially** *adv.*

**tan•ger•ine** *n.* small sweet orange originally grown near Tangiers.

**tan•gi•ble** *a.* perceptible by the touch; concrete. **tangibility** *n.* **tangibly** *adv.*

**tan•gle** *n.* knot of raveled threads, hair; *v.t.* to form into a confused mass; to muddle.

**tan•go** *n.* dance of Spanish origin in two-four time.

**tank** *n.* large basin or reservoir for storing liquids or gas; a mechanically propelled bulletproof armored vehicle with

tank

caterpillar treads; *v.t.* to store in a tank. **-age** *n.* storage of water, oil, gas, in a tank. **-er** *n.* vessel designed to carry liquid cargo.

**tan•kard** *n.* large drinking vessel, with lid and handle.

**tan•nin** See **tan.**

**tan•sy** *n.* common perennial plant used in medicine.

**tan•ta•lize** *v.t.* to tease. **tantalizing** *a.* provocative.

**tan•ta•lum** *n.* *(Chem.)* rare metallic element, symbol **Ta**, used for filaments of electric lamps, chemical apparatus, and surgical instruments.

**tan•ta•mount** *a.* equivalent in significance.

**tan•trum** *n.* fit of bad temper.

**tap** *v.t.* to strike lightly; *v.i.* to strike gentle blow; *n.* a rap; *pl.* military signal for lights out; leather patch on shoe sole. **-ping** *pr.p.* **-ped** *pa.p.* **— dance** *n.* a dance step audibly tapped out with the feet. **— dance** *v.i.*

**tap** *n.* hole, pipe, or screw device with valve, through which liquid is drawn; *v.t.* to pierce to let fluid flow out, as from a cask, tree, etc.; *(Surg.)* to draw off fluid from body, as from lung, abdomen, etc. **-ping** *pr.p.* **-ped** *pa.p.* **-per** *n.* one who taps. **-root** *n.* the root of a plant which goes straight down into earth without dividing.

**tape** *n.* narrow piece of woven material used for tying, fastening clothes, etc.; strip of paper used in a printing telegraph instrument; strip of paper marked off in units used for measuring; *v.t.* to fasten with tape; to measure. **— measure** *n.* strip marked in units for measuring. **-worm** *n.* parasite found in alimentary canal of vertebrates.

**ta•per** *n.* long wick for lighting candles; *v.i.* to narrow gradually toward one end; *v.t.* to cause to narrow. **-ing** *a.* narrowing gradually.

**tap•es•try** *n.* fabric covering for furniture, walls, woven by needles, not in shuttles.

**tap•i•oc•ca** *n.* starchy granular substance used for desserts, thickening, etc.

**ta•pir** *n.* ungulate mammal with piglike body and flexible proboscis.

tapir

**ta•pis** *n.* carpeting.

**tar** *n.* black viscid liquid, used for waterproofing, road-laying; *v.t.* to cover, or treat with tar. **-ring** *pr.p.* **-red** *pa.t.* and *pa.p.* **-ry** *a.* pert. to, or smelling of, tar.

**ta•ran•tu•la** *n.* large, hairy, venomous spider.

**tar•dy** *a.* slow; late. **tardily** *adv.* **tardiness** *n.*

**tare** *n.* plant grown for fodder; a weed.

**tar•get** *n.* mark to aim at in shooting, esp. flat circular board with series of concentric circles; object of attack.

**tar•iff** *n.* list of goods (imports and exports) on which duty is payable; the duty imposed.

**tar•nish** *v.t.* to lessen luster of; to sully, as one's reputation; *v.i.* to become dull.

**ta•ro** *n.* plant of Pacific islands, cultivated for edible leaves and root.

**tar•pau•lin** *n.* canvas sheet treated with tar to make it waterproof.

**tar•pon** *n.* large edible fish of herring family.

**tar•ra•gon** *n.* perennial herb cultivated for its aromatic leaves.

**tar•ry** *v.i.* to linger; to stay behind.

**tar•sus** *n.* ankle. *pl.* **tarsi. tarsal** *a.*

**tart** *a.* sour to taste; acid. **-ish** *a.* rather sour. **-ly** *adv.* **-ness** *n.*

**tart** *n.* small pastry cup containing fruit.

**tar•tan** *n.* woolen cloth of colored plaids, each genuine Scottish clan possessing its own pattern; *a.* made of tartan.

**tar•tar** *n.* crust deposited in wine cask during fermentation; acid incrustation on teeth. **-ous** *a.* containing tartar. **-ic** *a.* pert. to, or obtained from, tartar. **tartrate** *n.* a salt of tartaric acid. **cream of tartar,** purified form of tartar used medicinally and as raising agent in baking.

**task** *n.* specific amount of work apportioned and imposed by another; *v.t.* to impose task on; to exact. **-er** *n.* **— force** *n.* body of soldiers sent to do specific operation. **-master** *n.* overseer.

**Tass** *n.* official news agency of the U.S.S.R.

**tas•sel** *n.* ornamental fringed knot of silk,

wool. **-ed** *a.*

**taste** *v.t.* to perceive by tongue or palate; *v.i.* to eat or drink very small quantity; to have specific flavor; *n.* one of five senses; aesthetic appreciation; small amount. **-ful** *a.* having or showing good taste. **-fully** *adv.* **-fulness** *n.* **-less** *a.* insipid. **-lessly** *adv.* **-lessness** *n.* **-r** *n.* one whose palate is trained to discern subtle differences in flavor. **tastily** *adv.* with good taste. **tasty** *a.* savory.

**tat•ter** *n.* rag; shred of cloth hanging loosely; *v.t.* and *v.i.* to hang in tatters. **-demalion** *n.* ragged fellow. **-ed, -y** *a.*

**tat•tle** *v.i.* to tell a secret; *n.* chatter. **-r** *n.*

**tat•too** *v.t.* to prick colored designs, initials, into skin with indelible inks; *n.* such design. **-er** *n.*

**taught** *pa.t.* and *pa.p.* of verb **teach.**

**taunt** *v.t.* to reproach with insulting words; *n.* sarcastic remark. **-er** *n.* **-ing** *a.*

**Tau•rus** *n.* bull, 2nd sign of zodiac, which sun enters about April 21st. **taurian** *a.* pert. to a bull. **taurine** *a.* bovine.

**taut** *a.* fully stretched. **-en** *v.t.* to make tight or tense. **-ness** *n.*

**tau•tol•o•gy** *n.* repetition of same idea in different words in same sentence. **tautological** *a.* **tautologically** *adv.* **tautologism** *n.* superfluous use of words.

**tav•ern** *n.* licensed house for sale of liquor; inn.

**taw** *n.* large marble for children's game.

**taw•dry** *a.* showy but cheap. **tawdrily** *adv.* **tawdriness** *n.*

**taw•ny** *a.* of yellow-brown color. **tawniness** *n.*

**tax** *n.* levy imposed by state on income, property; *v.t.* to impose tax on; to subject to strain. **-able** *a.* **-ness, -ability** *n.* **-ably** *adv.* **-ation** *n.* act of levying taxes; assessing of bill of costs.

**tax•i** *n.* (*abbrev. of* **taximeter cab**) automobile for hire, fitted with a taximeter; *v.i.* to travel by taxi. **-ing** *pr.p.* **-ed** *pa.p.* **-cab** *n.* automobile for public hire. **— driver, -man** *n.* **-meter** *n.* instrument which automatically registers mileage and corresponding fare of journey by taxi.

**tax•i•der•my** *n.* art of preserving pelts of animals and stuffing them for exhibition. **taxidermist** *n.* **taxidermal, taxidermic** *a.*

**tea** *n.* dried and prepared leaves of tea plant, native to China and Japan; infusion of dry tea in boiling water. **-spoon** *n.* small spoon used with teacup. **-spoonful** *n.* ⅓ tablespoon.

**teach** *v.t.* to impart knowledge of; *v.i.* to follow profession of a teacher. **taught** *pa.t.* and *pa.p.* **-ability** *n.* **-able** *a.* capable of being taught; willing to learn. **-ableness** *n.* **-er** *n.* one who instructs.

**teak** *n.* tree of E. Indies yielding very durable timber.

**team** *n.* people working together for common purpose; side of players in game, as *football team.* **-ster** *n.* one who drives a truck as an occupation. **-work** *n.* cooperation among members of a group.

**tear** *n.* small drop of fluid appearing in and flowing from eyes, due to emotion; *pl.* sorrow. **-drop** *n.* tear. **-ful** *a.* weeping. **-fully** *adv.* **-fulness** *n.* **— gas** *n.* irritant gas causing abnormal watering of eyes and temporary blindness. **-less** *a.* dry-eyed.

**tear** *v.t.* to pull apart forcibly; *v.i.* to become ragged; *n.* fissure. **-ing** *pr.p.* **tore** *pa.t.* **torn** *pa.p.* **-er** *n.*

**tease** *v.t.* to annoy in fun; to chaff. **-r** *n.* **teasing** *a.*

**teat** *n.* nipple of female breast.

**tech•ni•cal** *a.* pert. to mechanical arts; connected with particular science; accurately defined. **-ity** *n.* term peculiar to specific art; point of procedure. **-ly** *adv.* **-ness** *n.* **technician** *n.* expert in particular branch of knowledge. **technics** *n.pl.* industrial arts. **technique** *n.* skill acquired by thorough mastery of subject. **technological** *a.* pert. to technology. **technologically** *adv.* **technologist** *n.* **technology** *n.* science of mechanical and industrial arts, as contrasted with fine arts.

**te•di•ous** *a.* wearisome; irksome. **-ness** *n.* **-ly** *adv.* **tedium** *n.* wearisomeness.

**tee** *n.* wooden peg, etc. on which golf ball is placed for first drive of each hole; *v.t.* to place (ball) on tee.

**teem** *v.i.* to bring forth, as animal; to be stocked to overflowing. **-ing** *a.* prolific.

**teens** *n.pl.* the years of one's age, thir*teen* through nine*teen*. **-ager** *n.* a young person of this age.

**teeth.** See **tooth.**

**teeth•ing** *n.* the process, in babyhood, of cutting the first teeth. **teethe** *v.i.* to cut the first teeth.

**tee•to•tal** *a.* pert. to teetotalism; abstemious. **-er** *n.* one who abstains from intoxicating liquors. **-ism** *n.*

**teg•u•ment** *n.* covering, esp. of living body. **-al, -ary** *a.*

**tel•e•cast** *v.i.* to transmit program by television.

**tel•e•gram** *n.* message sent by telegraph. **-mic** *a.*

**tel•e•graph** *n.* electrical apparatus for transmitting messages by code to a distance; a message so sent; *v.i.* to send a message by telegraph. **-er, -ist** *n.* one who operates telegraph. **-ic(al)** *a.* **-ically** *adv.* **-y** *n.* electrical transmission of messages to a distance.

**tel•e•ol•o•gy** *n.* science of final causes. **teleological** *a.* **teleologically** *adv.* **teleologist** *n.*

**te•lep•a•thy** *n.* occult communication of facts, feelings, impressions between mind and mind at a distance. **telepathic** *a.*

**tel•e•phone** *n.* electrical instrument by which sound is transmitted and reproduced at a distance; *v.t.* and *v.i.* to communicate by telephone. **telephonic** *a.* **telephonically** *adv.* **telephony** *n.* process of operating telephone.

**tel•e•pho•to** *a.* pert. to a camera lens which makes distant objects appear close.

**Tel•e•Promp•Ter** *n.* in television, a device to enable the speaker to refer to his script out of sight of the cameras, giving viewers the impression of a talk without script.

**tel•e•scope** *n.* optical instrument for magnifying distant objects; *v.i.* to be impacted violently, as cars in railway collision. **telescopical** *a.* pert. to a telescope.

**Tel•e•type** *n.* automatically printed telegram.

**tel•e•vi•sion** *n.* transmission of scenes, persons, etc. at a distance by means of electromagnetic radio waves. **televise** *v.t.*

**tell** *v.t.* to recount or narrate; *v.i.* to produce marked effect; to report. **told** *pa.t.* and *pa.p.* **-er** *n.* bank clerk who pays out money; enumerator. **-ing** *a.* striking. **-ingly** *adv.* **-tale** *n.* one who betrays confidence; *a.* warning.

**te•mer•i•ty** *n.* rashness; audacity.

**tem•per** *v.t.* to mingle in due proportion; to moderate; *n.* consistency required and achieved by tempering; attitude of mind; irritation. **-ed** *a.* having a certain consistency, as clay, or degree of toughness, as steel; having a certain disposition. **-edly** *adv.* **-ing** *n.* **-er** *n.*

**tem•per•a** *n.* process of painting using pigments mixed with size, casein, or egg instead of oil.

**tem•per•a•ment** *n.* physical, moral and mental constitution peculiar to individuals. **-al** *a.* liable to moods. **-ally** *adv.*

**tem•per•ance** *n.* moderation; sobriety.

**tem•per•ate** *a.* moderate; not extreme. **-ly** *adv.* **-ness** *n.* **temperative** *a.* **temperature** *n.* degree of heat or cold of atmosphere or of a human or living body; fevered condition. **— zones** *n.* areas of earth between polar circles and tropics.

**tem•pest** *n.* violent commotion. **-uous** *a.* violent. **-uously** *adv.* **-uousness** *n.*

**tem•ple** *n.* place of worship.

**tem•ple** *n.* part of forehead between outer end of eye and hair. **temporal** *a.*

**tem•po** *n.* degree of speed at which passage should be played or sung.

**tem•po•ral** *a.* pert. to time or to this life; secular. **-ity** *n.* concept of time; *pl.* material possessions, esp. ecclesiastical revenues. **-ly** *adv.* **temporariness** *n.* **temporarily** *adv.* only for a time. **temporary** *a.* fleeting. **temporization** *n.* **temporize** *v.i.* to hedge; to compromise. **temporizer** *n.* **temporizing** *n.*

**tempt** *v.t.* to entice. **-ation** *n.* inducement to do evil. **-er** *n.* one who tempts, esp. Satan. **-ing** *a.* seductive. **-ingly** *adv.* **-ingness** *n.*

**ten** *a.* one more than nine; *n.* the number nine and one; the symbol representing this, as 10 or X. **-fold** *a.* ten times repeated; *adv.* ten times as much. **-th** *a.* being one of ten equal divisions of anything; *n.* tenth part of anything; tithe. **-thly** *adv.*

**ten•a•ble** *a.* capable of being held, logically maintained. **-ness, tenability** *n.*

**te•na•cious** *a.* holding fast; pertinacious. **-ly** *adv.* **-ness, tenacity** *n.*

**ten•ant** *n.* one who occupies property for which he pays rent; *v.i.* to occupy as tenant. **tenancy** *n.* act of holding property as tenant; property held by tenant. **-able** *a.* fit for occupation. **-ry** *n.* tenants collectively on estate.

**tend** *v.i.* to hold a course; to have a bias. **-ency** *n.* inclination. **-entious** *a.* (of writings) having a biased outlook.

**tend** *v.t.* to minster to. **-er** *n.* one who tends; small vessel supplying larger one with stores, or landing passengers.

**ten•der** *v.t.* to offer for acceptance; *n.* an offer, esp. contract to undertake specific work, or to supply goods at fixed rate.

**ten•der** *a.* expressive of gentler passions; considerate; not tough (of meat).

**ten•der•loin** *n.* choice cut of meat between loin and ribs.

**ten•don** *n.* a tough fibrous cord attaching muscle to bone. **tendinous** *a.*

**ten•dril** *n.* spiral shoot of climbing plant by which it clings to another body for support; curl, as of hair. **-lar, -ous** *a.*

**ten•e•brous** *a.* dark; obscure. **tenebrosity** *n.*

**ten•e•ment** *n.* building divided into separate apartments, of very poor quality, and let to different tenants. **-al, -ary** *a.*

**te•net** *n.* any opinion or principle which a person holds as true.

**ten•nis** *n.* game for two or four players, played on a court by striking a ball with rackets, across a net. **— court** *n.* specially marked enclosed court for tennis.

**ten•or** *n.* *(Mus.)* highest male adult voice; one who sings tenor; *a.* pert. to tenor voice.

**tense** *n..* *(Gram.)* form of verb which indicates *time* of action, as *present, past* or *future tense.*

**tense** *a.* strained almost to breaking point; unrelaxed. **-ly** *adv.* **-ness** *n.* **tensibility, -ness** *n.* the quality of being **tensile. tensible, tensile** *a.* capable of being subjected to stress. **tension** *n.* strain; a state of being nervously excited or overwrought.

**tent** *n.* portable canvas shelter stretched and supported by poles and firmly pegged ropes; *v.i.* to pitch tent. **-ed** *a.* covered with tents.

**ten•ta•cle** *n.* long flexible appendage of head or mouth in many lower animals for exploring, touching, grasping; feeler. **tentacular** *a.* **—like** *a.*

**ten•ta•tive** *a.* experimental; done as a trial. **-ly** *adv.*

**ten•ter** *n.* machine for stretching cloth by means of hooks; *v.t.* to stretch on hooks. **-hook** *n.* one of the sharp hooks stretched on a tenter.

**te•nu•i•ty** *n.* thinness. **tenuous** *a.* slender; unsubstanial. **tenuously** *adv.* **tenuousness** *n.*

**ten•ure** *n.* holding of office, property.

**te•pee** *n.* Indian wigwam.

**tep•e•fy** *v.t.* to make moderately warm. **tepefaction** *n.*

**tep•id** *a.* moderately warm; lukewarm. **-ity, -ness** *n.*

**ter•cen•te•na•ry** *n.* the 300th anniversary of an event; *a.* pert. to a period of 300 years.

**ter•cet** *n.* *(Mus.)* triplet; *(Pros.)* group of three lines or verses.

**ter•gi•ver•sate** *v.i.* to make use of subterfuges; to be vacillating. **tergiversation, tergiversator** *n.*

**term** *n.* limit, esp. of time; expression with specific meaning; *(Math.)* member of compound quantity; *pl.* stipulation; *v.t.* to call. **-inological** *a.* pert. to terminology. **-inologically** *adv.* **-inologist** *n.* **-inology** *n.* technical words; nomenclature.

**ter•mi•nate** *v.t.* to set limit to; to end; *v.i.* to finish. **terminable** *a.* liable to cease. **terminal** *n.* extremity; *a.* pert. to end; occurring in, or, at end of, a term; *(Bot.)* growing at tip. **terminally** *adv.* **termination** *n.* conclusion; ending of word. **terminational** *a.* **terminative** *a.* **terminatively** *adv.* **terminus** *n.* farthest limit; railway station, airport, at end of line; *pl.* **termini, -es.**

**ter•mite** *n.* insect, very destructive to wood.

**tern** *n.* seabird allied to gull.

**tern** *n.* that which consists of three; *a.* threefold. **-al, -ary** *a.* consisting of three; *(Chem.)* comprising three elements, etc. **-ate** *a.* *(Bot.)* having three leaflets. **-ion** *n.* group of three.

**Terp•sich•o•re** *n.* *(Myth.)* Muse of choral song and dancing. **terpsichorean** *a.* pert. to dancing.

**ter•ra** *n.* earth as in various Latin phrases. **— cotta** *n.* reddish, brick-like earthenware, porous and unglazed. **-nean** *a.* belonging to surface of earth. **-neous** *a.* growing on land. **-queous** *a.* comprising both land and water, as the globe.

**ter•race** *n.* level shelf of earth, natural or artificial; flat roof used for open-air activities; *v.t.* to form into terraces.

**ter•rain** *n.* tract of land, considered for suitability for various purposes.

**ter•ra•pin** *n.* edible tortoise found in eastern U.S.

**ter•res•tri•al** *a.* pert. to earth; earthly, as opp. to *celestial*; *n.* inhabitant of earth.

**ter•ri•ble** *a.* frightful; formidable. **-ness** *n.* **terribly** *adv.*

**ter•ri•er** *n.* breed of small or medium-sized dog, originally trained for hunting foxes, badgers, etc.

**ter•ri•fy** *v.t.* to frighten greatly; to inspire with terror. **terrified** *pa.t.* **terrific** *a.* causing alarm. **terrifically** *adv.*

**ter•ri•to•ry** *n.* part of country which has not yet attained political independence. **territorial** *a.* limited to certain district. **territoriality** *n.*

**ter•ror** *n.* extreme fear; one who causes terror. **-ization** *n.* **-ize** *v.t.* to rule by intimidation. **-izer** *n.* **-ism** *n.* mass-organized ruthlessness. **-ist** *n.* one who rules by terror.

**ter•ry cloth** *n.* cotton fabric with pile of uncut loops on both sides.

**terse** *a.* (of speech, writing) concise; brief. **-ly** *adv.* **-ness** *n.*

**ter•tian** *a.* *(Med.)* occurring every other day; *n.* fever, with paroxysms occurring at intervals of forty-eight hours.

**ter•ti•ar•y** *a.* of third formation or rank; *(Geol.)* *(Cap.)* pert. to era of rock formation following Mezozoic; *n.* *(Geol.)* *(Cap.)* the Tertiary era.

**test** *n.* critical examination; substance used to analyze compound into its several constituents; *v.i.* to make critical examination of; *(Chem.)* to analyze properties of a compound. **— case** *n.* *(Law)* case tried for purpose of establishing a precedent. **-er** *n.* **-ing** *n.* and *a.* demanding endurance. **— paper** *n.* examination paper; litmus paper used to test acid or alkaline content of chemical solution. **— tube** *n.* glass tube rounded and closed at one end, used in chemical tests.

**tes•ta•ment** *n.* solemn declaration of one's will; one of the two great divisions of the Bible, as the *Old Testament*, or the *New Testament*. **-al -ary** *a.* pert. to testament or will; bestowed by will.

**tes•tate** *a.* having left a valid will. **testacy** *n.* state of being testate. **testator** *n.* one who leaves a will.

**tes•ti•cle** *n.* one of the two male reproductive glands. **testicular** *a.* **testiculate, -d** *a.* having testicles; resembling testicle in shape. **testis** *n.* a testicle; *pl.* **testes**

**tes•ti•fy** *v.i.* to bear witness; to give evidence upon oath; *v.t.* to manifest. **testifier** *n.*

**tes•ti•mo•ny** *n.* solemn affirmation; proof of some fact; in Scripture, the two tables of the law; divine revelation as a whole. **testimonial** *a.* containing testimony; *n.* written declaration testifying to character and qualities of person, esp. of applicant for a position.

**tes•ty** *a.* fretful; irascible.

**tet•a•nus** *n.* a disease in which a virus causes spasms of violent muscular contraction; lockjaw. **tetanic** *a.*

**tetch•y** *a.* peevish; fretful. **techily** *adv.* Also **techy.**

**teth•er** *n.* rope fastened to grazing animal to keep it from straying; *v.t.* to restrict movements of.

**tet•rad** *n.* group of four things.

**tet•ra•gon** *n.* a plane figure, having four angles. **-al** *a.*

**tet•ra•gram** *n.* *(Geom.)* figure formed by four right angles.

**tet•ra•he•dron** *n.* solid figure enclosed by four traingles. **tetrahedral** *a.*

**te•tral•o•gy** *n.* group of four dramas, connected by some central character.

**tet•ter** *n.* skin disease; ringworm; *v.t.* to affect with this. **-ous** *a.*

**Teu•ton** *n.* member of one of Germanic tribes. **-ic** *a.* pert. to Teutons or their language.

**text** *n.* original words of author, orator; passage of Scripture chosen as theme of sermon. **-book** *n.* manual of instruction. **-ual** *a.* based on actual wording; literal. **-ually** *adv.*

**tex•tile** *a.* capable of being woven; *n.* fabric made on loom.

**tex•ture** *n.* quality of surface of a woven material; that which is woven.

**tha•las•sic** *a.* pert. to the sea; living in the sea.
**thal•lus** simple plant organism which shows little or no differentiation into leaves, stem, or root as in *fungi, algae,* etc. *pl.* **thalli.**
**than** *conj.* introducing adverbial clause of comparison and occurring after comparative form of an adjective or adverb.
**thank** *v.t.* to express gratitude to; *n.* expression of gratitude (usually in *pl.*). **-fulness** *n.* **-less** *a.* unappreciated by others. **-lessly** *adv.* **-lessness** *n.* **-sgiving** *n.* service held as expression of thanks for Divine goodness.
**that** *demons. pron.* or *a.* (*pl.* **those**) pointing out a person or thing, or referring to something already mentioned; *rel. pron.* who or which; *conj.* introducing a noun clause, adjective clause, or adverbial clause of purpose, result, reason.
**thatch** *n.* straw, rushes, used to roof cottage; *v.t.* to roof with thatch. **-er, -ing** *n.*
**thaw** *v.t.* to cause to melt by increasing temperature; *n.* melting of ice or snow.
**the** *a.* or *def. ar.,* placed before nouns, and used to specify general conception, or to denote particular person or thing; *adv.* by that amount.
**the•ar•chy** *n.* government by gods. **thearchic** *a.*
**the•a•ter** *n.* building for plays or motion pictures; field of military, naval operations. **theatrical** *a.* **theatrically** *adv.* **theatricals** *n.pl.* dramatic performances, esp. by amateurs.
**theft** *n.* act of stealing.
**their** *a.* and *pron.* of **them**; *poss. case* of **they.** **-s** *poss. pron.* form of **their** used absolutely.
**the•ism** *n.* belief in existence of personal God who actively manifests Himself in world. **theist** *n.* **theistical** *a.*
**them** *pron.* ob. and dat. case of **they.**
**theme** *n.* subject of writing, or discussion; *(Mus.)* groundwork melody recurring at intervals and with variations. **thematic** *a.* **thematically** *adv.* **— song** *n.* recurring melody in play, film.
**them•selves** *pron. pl.* of **himself, herself,** and **itself;** emphatic form of **them** or **they;** reflexive form of **them.**
**then** *adv.* at that time (past or future); immediately afterwards; in consequence of; *conj.* moreover; *a.* acting at particular time.
**thence** *adv.* from that place; from that time; for that reason. **-forth** *adv.* from that time on.
**the•oc•ra•cy** *n.* government professedly in the name of God; government by priests. **theocrat, theocratist** *n.* ruler under this system. **theocratical** *a.* **theocratically** *adv.*
**the•od•o•lite** *n.* instrument for measuring angles, used in surveying.
**the•ol•o•gy** *n.* science of facts and phenomena of religion, relations between God and man. **theologian** *n.* one learned in theology. **theological** *a.* pert. to theology. **theologically** *adv.* **theologize** *v.t.* to theorize upon theological matters. **theologist** *n.*
**the•oph•a•ny** *n.* manifestation of God to men, in human form. **theophanic** *a.*
**the•o•rem** *n.* established principle; *(Math.)* propostion to be proved by logical reasoning. **-atic, -atical** *a.*
**the•o•ry** *n.* supposition put forward to explain something; speculation. **theoretical** *a.* speculative as opp. to *practical.* **theoretics** *n.pl.* speculative side of science. **theorize** *v.t.* to speculate. **theorizer, theorist** *n.* **theorization** *n.*
**ther•a•peu•tic** *a.* pert. to healing. **-ally** *adv.* **-s** *n.* branch of medicine concerned with treatment and cure of diseases. **therapeutist** *n.*
**ther•a•py** *n.* remedial treatment.
**there** *adv.* in that place; an introductory adverb; *interj.* expressing surprise. **-after** *adv.* after that time. **-by** *adv.* in consequence. **-fore** *conj.* and *adv.* accordingly. **-of** *adv.* of that or this. **-to** *adv.* to that or this. **-upon** *adv.* upon that or this; immediately.
**therm** *n.* a unit of heat; unit of 1.000 large calories. **-al** *a.* pert. to heat. **-ic** *a.* caused by heat.
**therm•i•on** *n.* positively or negatively charged particle emitted from incandescent substance. **-ic** *a.* pert. to thermions. **-ics** *n.* branch of science dealing with thermions.
**ther•mo•chem•is•try** *n.* branch of science which deals with heat in relation to chemical processes.
**ther•mo•dy•nam•ics** *n.* branch of science which deals with the conversion of heat into mechanical energy.
**ther•mo•e•lec•tric•i•ty** *n.* electricity developed by action of heat alone on two different metals. **thermoelectrical** *a.*
**ther•mo•gen•e•sis** *n.* production of heat, esp. in body. **thermogenetic, thermogenic** *a.*
**ther•mom•e•ter** *n.* instrument for measuring temperature, usually consisting of graduated and sealed glass tube with bulb containing mercury. **thermometrical** *a.* **thermometrically** *adv.* **thermometry** *n.*
**ther•mo•pile** *n.* instrument for measuring minute variations in temperature.
**Ther•mos** *n.* double-walled bottle which substantially retains temperature of liquids by the device of surrounding interior vessel with a vacuum jacket.
**ther•mo•scope** *n.* instrument for detecting fluctuations in temperature without actual measurement.
**ther•mo•stat** *n.* instrument which controls temperature automatically. **-ic** *a.* **-ics** *n.* science dealing with equilibrium of heat.
**ther•mot•ic** *a.* pert. to heat. Also **-al** *n.* the science of heat.
**the•sau•rus** *n.* treasury of knowledge; lexicon.
**these** *demons. a.* and *pron. pl.* of **this.**
**the•sis** *n.* dissertation. *pl.* **theses. thetic** *a.* dogmatic.
**the•ur•gy** *n.* art of working so-called miracles by supernatural agency.

**theurgical** *a.* **theurgically** *adv.* **theurgist** *n.*

**they** *pers. pron. pl.* of **he, she, it;** indefinitely, for a number of persons.

**thi•a•mine** *n.* Vitamin B, complex compound, deficiency of which causes beriberi.

**thick** *a.* dense; not thin; packed; *n.* thickest part; *adv.* to a considerable depth. **-en** *v.t.* to make thick; *v.i.* to become thick. **-ening** *n.* something added to thicken. **-et** *n.* dense growth of shrubs, trees, etc. **-ly** *adv.* **-ness** *n.* measurement of depth between opposite surfaces; layer.

**thief** *n.* *(pl.* **thieves)** one who steals the goods of another. **thieve** *v.i.* to steal. **thievery** *n.* **thievish** *a.* addicted to stealing. **thievishness** *n.*

**thigh** *n.* fleshy part of leg between knee and trunk.

**thim•ble** *n.* metal cap for tip of middle finger, in sewing. **-ful** *n.* very small amount.

**thin** *a. (comp.)* **-ner.** *(superl.)* **-nest.** having little thickness; slim; *adv.* sparsely; *v.t.* to make thin; *v.i.* to grow or become thin. **-ning** *pr.p.* **-ned** *pa.p.* and *pa.t.* **-ly** *adv.* **-ness, -ning** *n.*

**thing** *n.* entity; specimen; commodity; *pl.* belongings; clothes, furniture.

**think** *v.t.* to conceive; to surmise; to believe; *v.i.* to reason; to deliberate; to recollect. **thought** *pa.t.* and *pa.p.* **-able** *a.* **-ing** *a.* reflective; rational.

**thi•o-** word element used in chemistry to illustrate the replacement by sulfur of part or all of the oxygen atoms in a compound.

**third** *a.* forming one of three equal divisions; *n.* one of three equal parts; *(Mus.)* interval of three diatonic degrees of the scale. **— class** *a.* accommodation for passengers not traveling first or second class. **-ly** *adv.* **—rate** *a.* inferior.

**thirst** *n.* desire to drink; craving; *v.i.* to wish for earnestly. **-er** *n.* **-ily** *adv.* **-iness** *n.* **-y** *a.* having a desire to drink; parched; eager for.

**thir•teen** *a.* ten and three; *n.* symbol representing thirteen units, as 13 or XIII, **-th** *a.* being one of thirteen equal parts; *n.* one of these parts.

**thir•ty** *a.* three times ten; *n.* symbol representing this, as 30 or XXX. **thirtieth** *a.* being one of thirty equal parts; *n.* thirtieth part.

**this** *demons. pron.* and *a.* denoting a person or thing near at hand, just mentioned, or about to be mentioned.

**this•tle** *n.* one of the numerous prickly plants of the genus *Carduus,* with yellow or purple flowers. **thistly** *a.*

**thith•er** *adv.* to that place; to that point, result.

**thole** *v.t.* pin in gunwale of boat to keep oar in oarlock. Also **-pin.**

**thong** *n.* narrow strap of leather used for reins, whiplash, etc.

**tho•rax** *n.* chest cavity containing heart, lungs, etc. **thoracic** *a.*

**thorn** *n.* sharp, woody shoot on stem of tree or shrub; prickle; *(Fig.)* anything which causes trouble. **-y** *a.* prickly; beset with difficulties.

**thor•ough** *a.* absolute. **-bred** *a.* (of animals) purebred from pedigree stock; (of people) aristocratic; *n.* animal of pure breed. **-fare** *n.* highway. **-ly** *adv.* **-ness** *n.*

**those** *a.* and *pron. pl.* of **that.**

**though** admitting; even if; however.

**thought** *pa.t.* and *pa.p.* of **think.**

**thought** *n.* act of thinking; that which one thinks; reflection; opinion; serious consideration. **-ful** *a.* contemplative; considerate. **-fully** *adv.* **-fulness** *n.* **-less** *a.* without thought; inconsiderate. **-lessly** *adv.* **-lessness** *n.*

**thou•sand** *a.* consisting of ten hundred; *n.* symbol for this, 1,000 or M. **-fold** *a.* multiplied by a thousand. **-th** *a.* constituting one of thousand equal parts; *n.* thousandth part.

**thrall** *n.* slave; servitude. **-dom, thraldom** *n.* bondage.

**thrash** *v.t.* to flog; to defeat soundly. **-er** *n.* **-ing** *n.* flogging.

**thra•son•i•cal** *a.* bragging. **-ly** *adv.*

**thread** *n.* very thin twist of wool, cotton, linen, silk, etc.; filament as of gold, silver; consecutive train of thought; *v.t.* to pass thread through eye of needle. **-bare** *a.* worn away with wear; shabby. **-worm** *n.* threadlike parasitic worm often found in intestines of children. **-y** *a.*

**threat** *n.* declaration of determination to harm another; menace. **-en** *v.t.* to menace; to portend. **-ener** *n.* **-ening** *a.* menacing; portending.

**three** *a.* two and one; *n.* symbol of this sum, 3 or III. **-fold** *a.* triple. **— ply** *a.* having three layers or thicknesses; **-score** *a.* and *n.* sixty. **-some** *n.* group of three people.

**thren•o•dy** *n.* song of lamentation; dirge. Also **threnode. threnodial, threnodic** *a.* funereal.

**thresh** *v.t.* to separate grain from chaff by use of machine; to beat. **-er** *n.*

**thresh•old** *n.* doorsill; point of beginning.

**threw** *pa.t.* of **throw.**

**thrice** *adv.* three times; repeatedly.

**thrift** *n.* economical management. **-ily** *adv.* **-iness** *n.* frugality. **-less** *a.* extravagant; wasteful. **-lessly** *adv.* **-y** *a.*

**thrill** *n.* emotional excitement; *v.t.* to arouse tingling emotional response; *v.i.* to feel a glow of enthusiasm. **-ing** *a.* **-ingly** *adv.*

**thrive** *v.i.* to prosper; to develop healthily. **throve** and **-d** *pa.t.* **thriven, -d** *pa.p.* **thriving** *a.* **thrivingly** *adv.*

**throat** *n.* passage connecting back of mouth with lungs, stomach. **-iness** *n.* quality of having throaty voice. **-y** *a.* guttural.

**throb** *v.i.* to pulsate; *n.* pulsation; palpitation (of heart, etc.); beat. **-bing** *pr.p.* **-bed** *pa.t.* and *pa.p.*

**throe** *n.* suffering; pains of childbirth.

**throm•bo•sis** *n.* formation of blood clot in vein or artery.

**throne** *n.* royal seat; sovereign power and dignity; *v.t.* to place on royal seat; to exalt. **throning** *pr.p.* **-d** *pa.p.*

**throng** *n.* multitude; crowd; *v.t.* to press in crowds.

**throt•tle** *n.* windpipe; valve controlling

amount of vaporized fuel delivered to cylinders in internal-combustion engine; *v.i.* to choke by external pressure on windpipe; to silence; *v.i.* to pant for breath, as if suffocated.

**through** *prep.* from end to end of; along; by means of; as consequence of; *adv.* from one side to the other; from beginning to end; *a.* passing from one to another without stops; unobstructed. **through and through** *adv.* completely. **-ly** *(Arch.) adv.* thoroughly. **-out** *adv.* and *prep.* wholly; during entire time of.

**throve** *pa.t.* of **thrive.**

**throw** *v.t.* to fling, cast, or hurl; to send; to unseat, as of a horseman; to spread carelessly; *v.i.* to hurl; *n.* distance something can be thrown; light blanket. **-ing** *pr.p.* **threw** *pa.t.* **-n** *pa.p.* **-er** *n.* **-n** *a.*

**thrum** *n.* fringe of threads left on loom after web is cut off.

**thrum** *v.t.* to strum on instrument; to drum with fingers. **-ming** *pr.p.* **-med** *pa.p.* and *pa.t.*

**thrush** *n.* songbird.

**thrush** *n.* *(Med.)* inflammatory disease affecting mouth, tongue and lips, commonly found in young children.

**thrust** *v.t.* to drive with sudden force; *v.i.* to make a push; to attack with a pointed weapon; *n.* assault; stress acting horizontally, as in machinery. **thrust** *pa.t.* and *pa.p.* **-er** *n.*

**thud** *n.* dull sound made by heavy fall; *v.i.* to make sound of thud.

**thug** *n.* ruffian; gangster. **-gery** *n.*

**thumb** *n.* short, thick finger of human hand; *v.t.* to manipulate awkwardly. **-ed** *a.* having thumbs; soiled with thumb marks. **-less** *a.* **-like** *a.* **-nail** *n.* nail on human thumb. **-nail sketch,** miniature; succinct description.

**thump** *n.* sudden fall of heavy weight; *v.t.* to beat with something heavy; *v.i.* to fall with a thud. **-er** *n.* **-ing** *a.* very large.

**thun•der** *n.* rumbling sound which follows lightning flash; *v.t.* to rage with loud voice; *v.i.* to roar. **-bolt** *n.* flash of lightning followed by peal of thunder. **-clap** *n.* a peal of thunder. **-ing** *n.* thunder; booming, as of guns; *a.* making a loud noise. **-ous** *a.* **-ously** *adv.* **-storm** *n.* storm of thunder and lightning with torrential rain. **-struck** *a.* speechless with amazement. **-y** *a.*

**thu•ri•ble** *n.* a metal censer.

**Thurs•day** *n.* fifth day of week, after *Thor,* Scandinavian god of thunder.

**thus** *adv.* in this or that manner; to this extent; so; in this wise. **— far,** so far.

**thwack** *v.t.* to flog; *n.* a hard slap.

**thwart** *a.* lying across; *v.t.* to hinder; to frustrate; *n.* seat athwart a rowboat; *adv.* and *prep.* across. **-er** *n.* **-ing** *a.*

**thyme** *n.* small flowering shrub cultivated for its aromatic leaves for flavoring in cookery.

**thy•mus** *n.* small ductless gland in upper part of the chest.

**thy•roid** *a* signifying cartilage of a gland of trachea. **— gland,** ductless gland situated in neck on either side of trachea, secreting hormone which profoundly affects physique and temperament of human beings.

**ti•ar•a** *n.* gem-studded coronet worn by ladies.

**tib•i•a** *n.* shinbone; inner, larger of two bones of leg, between knee and ankle. *pl.* **-s, tibiae. -l** *a.*

**tic** *n.* spasmodic twitching of muscle, esp. of face.

**tick** *n.* a parasitic bloodsucking insect.

**tick** *n.* cover of mattress, pillow, etc. **-ing** *n.* specially strong material used for mattress covers.

**tick** *v.i.* to make small, recurring, clicking sound; *n.* sound made by watch. **-er** *n.* anything which ticks regularly.

**tick** *v.t.* to dot lightly; *n.* small mark placed after word, entry.

**tick•et** *n.* piece of paper entitling admission to anything, to travel by public transport; *(U.S.)* list of candidates in an election; *v.t.* to mark with ticket. **season ticket** *n.* ticket entitling holder to attend a series of concerts, lectures, etc.

**tick•le** *v.t.* to touch skin lightly to excite nerves and cause laughter; *v.i.* to feel sensation of tickling; to be gratified. **-r** *n.* **ticklish** *a.* easily tickled; requiring skillful handling. **ticklishly** *adv.* **ticklishness** *n.*

**tid•bit** *n.* choice morsel.

**tid•dly•winks** *n.pl.* game in which players try to snap small disks into cup.

**tide** *n.* time; periodical rise and fall of ocean due to attraction of moon and sun; *(Fig.)* trend. **tidal** *a.* pert. to tide. **tidal basin** *n.* harbor which is affected by tides. **tidal wave** *n.* mountainous wave as caused by earthquake, atom bomb explosion, etc. **-less** *a.* having no tides. **ebb** or **low tide** *n.* the falling level of the sea. **flood** or **high tide** *n.* the rising level of the sea.

**tid•ings** *n.pl.* news; information.

**ti•dy** *a.* neat; orderly; *n.* chair-back cover; *v.t.* to put in order.

**tie** *v.t.* to fasten by rope, string, etc.; to fashion into knot; to bind together, by connecting piece of wood or metal; *v.t.* *(Sport)* to make equal score, etc.; *n.* knot; necktie; connecting link; equality of score; traverse supports for railroad tracks. **tying** *pr.p.* **tied** *pa.t.* and *pa.p.* **— beam** *n.* horizontal timber connecting two rafters. **-r** *n.*

**tier** *n.* row when two or more rows are arranged behind and above the other.

**tierce** *n.* cask containing third of pipe or 42 wine gallons; in fencing, particular thrust (third position).

**tiff** *n.* slight quarrel; *v.i.* to quarrel.

**ti•ger** *n.* fierce carnivorous quadruped of cat tribe, with tawny black-striped coat. **— cat** *n.* wildcat; ocelot or margay.

**tight** *a.* compressed; not leaky; fitting close to body; *adv.* firmly. **-en** *v.t.* to make tighter; to make taut; *v.i.* to become tight. **-ener** *n.* **-ly** *adv.* **-ness** *n.* **-rope** *n.* a strong, taut rope, or steel wire on which acrobats perform. **-s** *n.pl.* close-fitting woven hose and trunks worn by acrobats, dancers, etc.

**tile** *n.* a thin piece of slate, plastic, asphalt, used for roofs, walls, floors, drains; *v.t.* to cover with tiles. **-r** *n.* **tiling** *n.*

**till** *n.* a cash register.

**till** *prep.* until; *conj.* to the time when.

**till** *v.t.* to plow the soil, sow seeds, etc. **-age** *n.* the act of preparing soil for cultivation; the cultivated land. **-er** *n.*

**til•ler** *n.* a bar used as a lever, for turning a rudder.

**tilt** *v.t.* to raise one end of; *v.i.* to slant; *n.* inclination. **-er** *n.* — **hammer** *n.* a heavy hammer used in ironworks and tilted by a lever.

**tilt** *n.* canvas covering of a cart; *v.t.* to cover with a tilt.

**tim•bal** *n.* kettledrum.

**tim•ber** *n.* trees or wood suitable for building purposes; *v.t.* to furnish with timber. **-ed** *a.* **-line** *n.* tree line, above which altitude trees will not grow.

**tim•bre** *n.* special tone quality in sound of human voice or instrument.

**tim•brel** *n.* kind of drum.

**time** *n.* particular moment; period of duration; conception of past, present, and future, as sequence; opportunity; *(Mus.)* rhythmical arrangement of beats within measures or bars; *pl.* period characterized by certain marked tendencies; term indicating multiplication; *v.t.* to ascertain time taken, as by racing competetitor; *(Mus.)* to measure; *v.i.* to keep time. — **bomb** *n.* delayed-action bomb. **-keeper** *n.* one who keeps a record of men's hours of work; clock. **-less** *a.* eternal; unending. **-lessly** *adv.* **-liness** *n.* **-ly** *a.* opportune. **-piece** *n.* clock. **-r** *n.* a stopwatch. **timing** *n.* control of speed of an action or actions for greatest effect.

**tim•id** *a.* lacking self-confidence; shy. **-ness, -ity** *n.* **-ly** *adv.*

**ti•moc•ra•cy** *n.* government in which possession of property is qualification for holders of offices.

**tim•pa•num** *n.* kettledrum, part of percussion section of orchestra. *pl.* **timpani. timpanist, tympanist** *n.*

**tin** *n.* soft, whitish-gray metal, used for plating, as consituent of alloys and for food containers in canning industry; *a.* made of tin; *v.t.* to plate with tin **-ning** *pr.p.* **-ned** *pa.p.* and *pa.t.* **-foil** *n.* wafer-thin sheets of tin. **-ned** *a.* preserved in a tin. **-ning** *n.* **-ny** *a.* making a sound like tin when struck. **-type** *n.* *(Photog.)* ferrotype; positive on varnished tinplate. **-ware** *n.* utensils, etc. made of tinplate.

**tinc•ture** *n.* tinge of color; *(Pharm.)* solution of a substance in alcohol; *v.t.* to affect to a small degree.

**tin•der** *n.* anything inflammable used for kindling fire from a spark.

**tine** *n.* prong of fork; branch of deer's antler.

**ting** *n.* sharp, ringing sound, as of bell; *v.t.* and *v.i.* to tinkle.

**tinge** *v.t.* to color or flavor slightly; *n.* a faint touch.

**tin•gle** *v.i.* to feel faint prickling sensation; *n.* pricking sensation.

**tin•ker** *n.* mender of pots, kettles, who travels around countryside; jack-of-all trades; *v.i.* to attempt to mend.

**tin•kle** *v.t.* to cause to make small, quick, metallic sounds; *v.i.* to jingle; *n.* small, sharp, ringing sound. **tinkling** *n.* **tinkly** *a.*

**tin•sel** *n.* very thin, glittering, metallic strips for decorations; *a.* showy and cheap; *v.t.* to decorate with tinsel; to make gaudy. **-ly** *a.*

**tint** *n.* hue or dye; color with admixture of white; *v.t.* to give faint coloring to; to tinge. **-er** *n.*

**ti•ny** *a.* very small; diminutive.

**tip** *n.* point of anything slender; end; *v.t.* to form a point on. **-ping** *pr.p.* **-ped** *pa.p.* **-toe** *adv.* on tips of toes; *v.t.* to walk stealthily.

**tip** *v.t.* to tilt; to weigh down, as scales; to recompense with small gratuity; *n.* light stroke; advice; gratuity. **-ping** *n.*

**tip•ple** *v.i.* to drink small quantities of intoxicating liquor frequently; *n.* strong drink. **-r** *n.*

**tip•sy** *a.* intoxicated; staggering. **-tipsily** *adv.* **tipsiness** *n.*

**ti•rade** *n.* long denunciatory speech; volley of abuse.

**tire** *v.t.* to fatigue; *v.i.* to become wearied, impatient. **-d** *a.* wearied; bored. **-dness** *n.* **-less** *a.* **-lessly** *adv.* **-some** *a.*

**tire** *n.* hoop of iron, rubber, or rubber tube, placed around a wheel.

**tis•sue** *n.* *(Biol.)* cellular structures which make up various organs of plant or animal body; fine cloth interwoven with gold or silver; *a.* made of tissue. **-d** *a.* made of tissue. — **paper** *n.* very thin, white or colored semi-transparent paper.

**tit** *n.* teat.

**tithe** *n.* orig. tenth part of produce of land and cattle given to the church, later paid in form of tax; small portion; *v.t.* to levy a tithe; *v.i.* to give a tithe. **-r** *n.* **-less** *a.*

**ti•tian** *a.* rich auburn; color of hair in many portraits by Titian, Italian painter.

**tit•il•late** *v.t.* to tickle, usually in sense of stimulating mind, palate, etc. — **titillation** *n.* any pleasurable sensation. **titillative** *a.*

**ti•tle** *n.* designation; appellation denoting rank or office; just claim or right; title deed. **-d** *a.* having title, esp. aristocratic title. — **deed** *n.* document giving proof of legal ownership of property. — **page** *n.* page of book on which is inscribed name of book, author and publication data. — **role** *n.* part in play from which it takes its name.

**tit•mouse** *n.* small bird which builds in holes of trees. *pl.* **titmice.**

**titmouse**

**ti•trate** *v.t.* to determine amount of ingredient in solution by adding quantities of standard solution until required chemical reaction is observed. **titration** *n.*

**tit•ter** *v.i.* to give smothered laugh; *n.* such a laugh. **-er** *n.*

**tit•tle** *n.* minute particle; jot.

**tit•u•lar** *a.* pert. to a title; ruling in name but not in deed. **-ity** *n.* **-y** *a.* titular; *n.* nominal holder of title.

**to** *prep.* expressing motion towards; as far as; compared with; preceding infinitive mood of the verb; *adv.* forward.

**toad** *n.* amphibian resembling frog, but brownish with dry warty skin and short legs. **-stool** *n.* fungus resembling mushroom, but poisonous. **-y** *n.* obsequious flatterer; *v.i.* to fawn on. **-ying** *pr.p.* **-ied** *pa.t.* and *pa.p.* **-yish** *a.* **-yism** *n.* sycophancy.

**toast** *v.t.* to warm by exposure to fire; to crisp and brown (as bread) before fire, under grill; to drink in honor of; *v.i.* to drink a toast; *n.* slice of bread crisped and browned by heat; person in whose honor toast is drunk; the drink itself. **-er** *n.* **-master** *n.* one who presides at luncheon or dinner, proposes toasts, introduces speakers, etc.

**to•bac•co** *n.* plant, dried leaves of which are used for chewing, smoking, or as snuff. *pl.* **-s, -es**

**to•bog•gan** *n.* flat-bottomed sled used for coasting down snow-clad hill slopes; *v.i.* to slide down hills on toboggan. **-ing** *n.*

**to•by** *n.* small jug in shape of an old man wearing a three-cornered hat.

**to•day** *n.* this day; present time; *adv.* on this day; at the present time.

**tod•dle** *v.i.* to walk with short, hesitating steps; *n.* unsteady gait. **-r** *n.* child just learning to walk.

**tod•dy** *n.* drink of whisky, sugar, and hot water.

**toe** *n.* one of five small digits of foot; part of boot, shoe, or stocking covering toes; *v.t.* to reach with toe; *v.i.* to tap with toes. **-d** *a.* having toes.

**tof•fee, tof•fy** *n.* hard candy made of sugar, butter, flavoring, etc. boiled together. Also **taffy.**

**to•geth•er** *adv.* in company; in or into union; simultaneously.

**toil** *v.i.* to labor; *n.* exhausting labor; task. **-er** *n.* **-ful, -some** *a.* laborious. **-somely** *adv.* **-someness** *n.*

**toi•let** *n.* process of dressing; a lavatory. **— articles** *n.pl.* objects used in dressing, as comb, brush, mirror, toothbrush, etc. **— paper** *n.* thin paper for lavatory use. **— powder** *n.* talcum powder.

**to•ken** *n.* symbol; concrete expression of esteem; coin-like piece of metal for special use, as *bus token, etc.* **— payment** *n.* deposit paid as token of later payment of full debt.

**told** *pa.t.* and *pa.p.* of verb **tell.**

**tol•er•ate** *v.t.* to put up with. **tolerable** *a.* endurable; passably good. **tolerability, tolerableness** *n.* **tolerably** *adv.* **tolerance** *n.* forbearance. **tolerant** *a.* broad-minded. **tolerantly** *adv.* **toleration** *n.* practice of allowing people to worship as they please; granting to minorities political liberty. **tolerationist** *n.* **tolerator** *n.*

**toll** *n.* tax, esp. for right to use bridge, ferry, public road, etc.; charge for long-distance telephone call. *v.i.* to exact toll.

**toll** *v.t.* to cause to ring slowly, as bell, esp. to signify death; *v.i.* to peal with slow, sonorous sounds; *n.* sound of such bell.

**tom** *n.* used to denote male animal, as tomcat. **-boy** *n.* girl of boyish behavior; romping, mischievous girl.

**tom•a•hawk** *n.* war hatchet used by N. Amer. Indians; *v.t.* to wound or kill with tomahawk.

**tomahawk**

**to•ma•to** *n. pl.* **-es.** plant with red or yellow fruit much-used in salads.

**tomb** *n.* a grave; underground vault; any structure for a dead body. **-stone** *n.* stone erected over grave.

**to•mor•row** *n.* day after today; *adv.* on the following day.

**tom-tom** *n.* small drum used by Indian and African natives.

**ton** *n.* weight consisting of 2,000 lb.; measure of capacity varying according to article being measured. **-nage** *n.* cubical content (100 cu. ft.) of ship in tons; shipping collectively assessed in tons.

**tone** *n.* quality or pitch of musical sound; modulation of speaking or singing voice; color values of picture; *(Med.)* natural healthy functioning of bodily organs; *v.t.* to give tone or quality to; to modify color or general effect of, as in photograph; to tune (instrument); *v.i.* to blend (with). **tonal** *a.* **tonality** *n.* quality of tone or pitch; system of variation of keys in musical composition. **tonally** *adv.* **—deaf** *a.* unable to distinguish musical intervals.

**tongs** *n.pl.* implement consisting of pair of pivoted levers, for grasping.

**tongue** *n.* flexible muscular organ in mouth used in tasting, swallowing, and for speech; facility of utterance; language; clapper of bell; *v.t.* to modulate with tongue as notes of flute; to chide. **-d** *a.* having a tongue. **—tied** *n.* having tongue defect causing speech impediment.

**ton•ic** *a.* pert. to tones or sounds; having an invigorating effect bodily or mentally; *n.* a medicine which tones up the system; *(Mus.)* a keynote. **-ally** *adv.* **-ity** *n.*

**to•night** *n.* this night; night following this present day; *adv.* on this night.

**ton•nage** *n.* See **ton.**

**ton•sil** *n.* one of two oval-shaped lymphoid organs on either side of pharynx. **-litis** *n.* inflammation of the tonsils.

**ton•sure** *n.* act of shaving part of head as

token of religious dedication; shaved crown of priest's head. **tonsor** *n.* barber.

**too** *adv.* in addition; more than enough.

**took** *pa.t.* of **take.**

**tool** *n.* implement operated by hand, or by machinery; cutting or shaping part of a machine; *v.t.* to cut, shape, or mark with a tool. **-ing** *n.*

**toot** *v.t.* to cause to sound, as an automobile horn or wind instrument; *n.* sound of horn; hoot.

**tooth** *n.* hard projection in gums of upper and lower jaws of vertebrates, used in mastication; prong of comb, rake. *pl.* **teeth.** *v.t.* to provide with teeth; *v.i.* to interlock. **-ache** *n.* pain in tooth. **-brush** *n.* small brush for cleaning teeth. **-ed** *a.* **-some** *a.* pleasant to taste. **-y** *a.* having prominent teeth; toothed.

teeth

**top** *n.* highest part of anything; highest rank; first in merit; *a.* highest; most eminent; best; *v.t.* to cover on the top; to rise above; to surpass; *v.i.* to be outstanding. **— heavy** *a.* having top too heavy for base. **-per** *n.* something placed on the top; topcoat. **-ping** *n.* act of lopping off top of something; something put on top of a thing as decoration. **-pingly** *adv.* **-soil** *n.* surface layer of soil.

**to•paz** *n.* gem stone, translucent and of varied colors.

**tope** *v.i.* to drink to excess. **-r** *n.*

**to•pi•a** *n.* mural decoration comprising landscapes. **-ry** *a.* cut into ornamental shapes, as trees, hedges, etc.; *n.* topiary work or art; a garden or single shrub so trimmed. **-rist** *n.*

**top•ic** *n.* subject of essay, discourse, or conversation; branch of general subject. **-al** *a.* pert. to a place; concerning local matters. **-ally** *adv.*

**to•pog•ra•phy** *n.* description of a place; physical features of region. **topographer** *n.* **topographical** *a.*

**top•ple** *v.t.* to overturn; *v.i.* to overbalance.

**top•sy-tur•vy** *adv.* upside down; *a.* turned upside down; *n.* disorder; chaos.

**torch** *n.* piece of wood with some substance at the end soaked in inflammable liquid, and used as portable light. **-bearer** *n.*

**tore** *pa.t.* of **tear.**

**to•re•a•dor** *n.* bullfighter.

**tor•ment** *n.* extreme pain of body; anguish of mind; *v.t.* to inflict pain upon; to tease. **-ing** *a.* **-ingly** *adv.* **-or, -er** *n.*

**torn** *pa.p.* of **tear.**

**tor•na•do** *n.* whirling progressive windstorm causing widespread devastation.

**tor•pe•do** *n.* cigar-shaped underwater projectile with high explosive charge; *pl.* **-es;** *v.t.* to attack, sink with torpedoes. **-ist** *n.* expert in handling and firing torpedoes.

**tor•pid** *a.* dormant, as hibernating animal; physically or mentally inert. **-ity** *n.* lethargy. **-ly** *adv.* **-ness** *n.* **torpor** *n.* inertia. **torporific** *a.*

**tor•re•fy** *v.t.* to roast, as metals. **torrefaction** *n.*

**tor•rent** *n.* downpour; rapid flow, as of words. **-ial** *a.* pert. to, resembling torrent; overwhelming.

**tor•rid** *a.* extremely hot, dry or burning; passionate. **-ness, -ity** *n.* **-ly** *adv.* **—zone,** broad belt lying between Tropics of Cancer and Capricorn.

**tor•sion** *n.* act of turning or twisting; *(Mech.)* force with which twisted wire tends to return to original position. **-al** *a.* **— balance,** scientific instrument for measuring minute forces by small bar suspended horizontally at end of very fine wire.

**tor•so** *n.* trunk of human body.

**tort** *n.* *(Law)* private injury to person or property for which damages may be claimed in court of law. **-ious** *a.* **-iously** *adv.*

**tor•toise** *n.* land reptile or turtle. **-shell** *n.* mottled brown outer shell of tortoise used for combs; *a.* mottled like tortoiseshell.

tortoise

**tor•tu•ous** *a.* full of twists; deceitful. **tortuosity** *n.* **-ly** *adv.* **-ness** *n.*

**tor•ture** *n.* act of deliberately inflicting extreme pain as punishment or reprisal; *v.t.* to inflict agony. **torturing** *a.* **torturous** *a.*

**To•ry** *n.* and *a.* supporter of Britain in the American Revolution. **-ism** *n.*

**toss** *v.t.* to throw upwards with a jerk; *v.i.* to roll and tumble; *n.* fling; distance anything is tossed. **-er, -ing** *n.* **— up,** *n.* tossing of coin to decide issue.

**tot** *n.* anything small, esp. a child.

**to•tal** *a.* complete; *n.* the whole; sum; *v.t.* to add; *v.i.* to amount to. **-izator,** *n.* machine which registers totals. **-ity** *n.* entirety. **-ly** *adv.* **-ness** *n.*

**to•tal•i•tar•i•an** *a.* open-party dictatorial form of government. **-ism** *n.*

**tote** *v.t.* *(Colloq.)* to carry; to transport.

**to•tem** *n.* natural object, taken by primitive tribe as emblem of hereditary relationship with that object; image of this. **-ic** *a.* **-ism** *n.* **-ist** *n.* member of tribe. **-istic** *a.* **— pole** *n.* pole with totems carved on it, one above the other.

**tot•ter** *v.i.* to walk with faltering steps; to reel. **-er** *n.* **-ing** *a.* **-ingly** *adv.* **-y** *a.* unsteady.

**tou•can** *n.* bird of tropical Amer.

**touch** *v.t.* to come in contact with; to

finger; to move deeply; *v.i.* to be in contact; to take effect on; *n.* contact; sense of feeling; unique quality; tinge; mild attack. **-able** *a.* **-ableness** *(Football)* scoring by having ball behind goal line. **-er** *n.* **-ily** *adv.* **-iness** *n.* **-ing** *a.* emotionally moving; *prep.* referring to. **-ingly** *adv.* **-ingness** *n.* **-y** *a.* hypersensitive.

**tough** *a.* flexible but not brittle; not easily broken; difficult to chew; difficult to solve; *n.* a bully; a ruffian. **-en** *v.t.* to make hardy; *v.i.* to become tough. **-ly** *adv.* **-ness** *n.*

**tou•pee** *n.* artificial lock of hair.

**tour** *n.* journey from place to place in a country; *v.t.* to travel around; to visit as part of tour. **-ism** *n.* **-ist** *n.* sightseer.

**tour•na•ment** *n.* any sports competition or championship. **tourney** *n.* a tournament.

**tour•ni•quet** *n.* surgical device for arresting hemorrhage by compression of a blood vessel, as a bandage tightened by twisting.

**tous•le** *v.t.* to make untidy by pulling, as hair; *a.* untidy.

**tout** *v.i.* and *v.t.* to solicit business; to praise highly; *n.* one who pesters people to be customers. **-er** *n.*

**tow** *v.t.* to drag by rope or chain; *n.* act of pulling; rope or chain used for towing. **-age** *n.* act of or charge for towing.

**to•ward(s)** *prep.* in direction of; regarding.

**tow•el** *n.* cloth or paper for drying skin, or for domestic purposes. **-ing** *n.* soft fabric for making towels.

**tow•er** *n.* lofty round or square structure; *v.i.* to soar. **-ed** *a.* having towers. **-ing** *a.* lofty; violent.

**town** *n.* collection of houses, etc., larger than village; *a.* pert. to town. **— clerk** *n.* official of administrative side of a town's affairs.

**tox•i•col•o•gy** *n.* science of poisons, their effects. **toxemia,** *n.* blood poisoning. **toxemic** *a.* **toxical** *a.* poisonous. **toxically** *adv.* **toxicant** *a.* poisonous; *n.* poison. **toxicological** *a.* **toxicologist** *n.* **toxin** *n.* poison of bacterial origin.

**tox•oph•i•lite** *n.* student of, or expert in, archery. **toxophilitic** *a.*

**toy** *n.* child's plaything; *v.i.* to trifle.

**trace** *n.* mark; outline; barely perceptible sign; *v.t.* to draw exactly on a superimposed sheet; to follow track of; to work out step by step; *v.i.* to move. **-able** *a.* capable of being detected. **-ableness** *n.* **-ably** *adv.* **-r** *n.* **tracing** *n.* traced copy of drawing. **tracing paper** *n.* transparent paper for tracing design.

**trace** *n.* strap, rope, by which horse pulls vehicle.

**tra•che•a** *n.* windpipe between lungs and back of throat. *pl.* **tracheae.** **-l** *a.* **tracheotomy** *n.* *(Surg.)* operation by which opening is made in windpipe.

**track** *n.* mark left by something; footprint; laid-out course for racing; (railway) metal rails forming a permanent way; *(Fig.)* evidence; *v.t.* to make a track of footprints on; *v.i.* to follow a trail; to be in alignment. **-er** *n.* **—meet,** athletic contest held on a track.

**tract** *n.* region of indefinite extent; continuous period of time. **-ability** *n.* state of being tractable. **-able** *a.* amenable to reason. **-ableness** *n.* **-ably** *adv.* **-ile** *a.* capable of being drawn out. **-ility** *n.* **-ion** *n.* gripping power, as of a wheel on a road. **-ional** *a.* **-ion engine** *n.* locomotive, steam-driven, for haulage. **-ive** *a.* pulling. **-or** *n.* motor vehicle for drawing agricultural machinery.

**trade** *n.* the business of buying and selling; occupation, esp. in industry, shopkeeping, etc.; employees collectively in a particular trade; *v.t.* to engage in commerce; *v.i.* to exchange. **-mark** *n.* registered name on maker's goods. **— name** *n.* name given by manufacturer to proprietary article. **-r** *n.* merchant (wholesale or retail). **— union** *n.* legally recognized association of workmen. **— unionist** *n.* member of trade union. **trading** *n.*

**tra•di•tion** *n.* belief, custom, transmitted by word of mouth from age to age. **-al, -ary** *a.* **-alism, -alist** *n.* **-alistic** *a.*

**tra•duce** *v.t.* to defame the character of; to calumniate. **-r** *n.* a slanderer.

**traf•fic** *n.* business dealings; movement of people, vehicles, to and fro, in streets; coming and going of ships, trains, aircraft; *v.i.* to carry on trade. **-king** *pr.p.* **-ked** *pa.t.* and *pa.p.* **-ker** *n.*

**trag•e•dy** *n.* serious and dignified dramatic composition in prose or verse with unhappy ending; sad or calamitous event. **tragedian** *n.* actor in or writer of tragedy. **tragical** *a.* pert. to tragedy; calamitous. **tragically** *adv.* **tragicalness** *n.*

**trail** *v.t.* to draw along ground or through water; to follow track of; to carry rifle in hand with butt close to the ground; *v.i.* to drag one foot wearily after other; *n.* visible trace left by anything; scent of hunted animal. **-er** *n.* vehicle towed by another. **-less** *a.*

**train** *v.t.* to instruct or educate; to submit person to arduous physical exercise, for athletics; to cause plant to grow in certain way; *v.i.* to exercise body or mind to achieve high standard of efficiency; *n.* retinue; line of cars drawn by locomotive on railway track; sequence of events, ideas. **-ed** *a.* **-ee** *n.* one who is training. **-er, -ing** *n.*

**traipse** *v.i.* *(Colloq.)* to walk aimlessly.

**trait** *n.* distinguishing feature, esp. in character.

**trai•tor** *n.* one who betrays person, country, or cause. **-ous** *a.* guilty of treachery; pert. to treason or to traitors. **-ously** *adv.*

**tra•jec•to•ry** *n.* curve of projectile in its flight through space.

**tram•mel** *n.* long net for catching birds or fish; anything which impedes movement; *v.t.* to confine. **-er,** *n.*

**tramp** *v.t.* to hike over or through; *v.i.* to plod; *n.* homeless vagrant; cargo boat with no regular route. **-er** *n.*

**tram•ple** *v.t.* to tread heavily underfoot; *n.* act of trampling. **-r** *n.*

**tram•po•line** *n.* canvas springboard.

**trampolinist** *n.*
**trance** *n.* a fit of complete mental absorption; semiconscious condition.
**tran•quil** *a.* serene; undisturbed. **-ly** *adv.* **tranquillity, -ness** *n.*
**trans-** *pref.* meaning across, beyond, on the other side of.
**trans•act** *v.t.* to negotiate; *v.i.* to do (business). **-or** *n.* **-ion** *n.* act of transacting business; *pl.* records of a society. **-ional** *a.*
**trans•at•lan•tic** *a.* across the Atlantic.
**tran•scend** *v.t.* to go beyond; to surpass. **-ence, -ency** *n.* *(Theol.)* supremacy of God above all human limitations. **-ent** *a.* surpassing all; beyond all human knowledge. **-ently** *adv.* **-entness** *n.* **-ental** *a.* supernatural; intuitive. **-entalism, -entalist** *n.* **-entally** *adv.*
**trans•con•ti•nen•tal** *a.* crossing a continent.
**tran•scribe** *v.t.* to write over again; to reproduce in longhand notes taken in shorthand. **-r** *n,* **transcript** *n.* written copy. **transcription** *n.* act of copying; transcript.
**tran•sect** *v.t.* to cut transversely.
**trans•fer** *v.t.* to move from one place to another; to pass an impression from one surface to another; to convey, as property, legally to another; *n.* ticket allowing change of vehicle during single trip without further charge; design to be, or which has been transferred. **-ring** *pr.p.* **-red** *pa.t.* and *pa.p.* **-ability** *n.* **-able** *a.* capable of being transferred; valid for use by another. **-ence** *n.* the act of transferring.
**trans•fig•ure** *v.t.* to change outward appearance of. **-ment** *n.* **transfiguration** *n.* change of appearance.
**trans•fix** *v.t.* to pierce through; to stun. **-ion** *n.*
**trans•form** *v.t.* to change form, nature, or disposition of; *v.i.* to be changed. **-able** *a.* **-ation** *n.* change of outward appearance of inner nature. **-ative** *a.* **-er** *n.* an electrical device for changing voltage up or down. **-ing** *a.*
**trans•fuse** *v.t.* to pour, as liquid, from one receptacle into another; *(Med.)* to transfer blood from one person to vein of another. **-r** *n.* **transfusible, transfusive** *a.* **transfusion** *n.*
**trans•gress** *v.t.* to violate law; *v.i.* to sin. **-ion** *n.* act of violating civil or moral law. **-ive** *a.* **ively** *adv.* **-or** *n.*
**tran•sient** *a.* momentary; not permanent. **transience, transiency** *n.* **-ly** *adv.* **-ness** *n.*
**tran•sit** *n.* the act of conveying. **-ion** *n.* change from one condition to another. **-ional, -ionary** *a.* **-ionally** *adv.* **-ive** *a.* having power of passing across. **-ively** *adv.* **-iveness** *n.* **-orily** *adv.* **-oriness** *n.* state of being transitory. **-ory** *a.*
**trans•late** *v.t.* to turn from one language into another; to change from one medium to another; *v.i.* to be capable of translation. **translatable** *a.* **translation, translator** *n.*
**trans•lit•er•ate** *v.t.* to write words of language in alphabetic symbols of another. **transliteration, transliterator** *n.*
**trans•lu•cent** *a.* diffusing light but not revealing definite contours of object. **translucence, translucency** *n.* **-ly** *adv.* **translucid** *a.* translucent.
**trans•mi•grate** *v.i.* to pass from one country to another as permanent residence. **transmigration, transmigrator** *n.* **transmigratory** *a.*
**trans•mit** *v.t.* to send from one person to another; to communicate. **-ting** *pr.p.* **-ted** *pa.t.* and *pa.p.* **transmissibility** *n.* **transmissible, -tible** *a.* capable of being transmitted. **transmission** *n.* in motoring, gear by which power is transmitted from engine to axle. **-tal** *n.* transmission. **-tance** *n.* **-ter** *n.* apparatus for transmitting radio waves through space.
**trans•mute** *v.t.* to change from one nature, species, form, or substance into another. **transmutable** *a.* **transmutableness, transmutability** *n.* **transmutably** *adv.* **transmutant** *a.* **transmutation** *n.* alteration, esp. biological transformation of one species into another; in alchemy, supposed change of baser metals into gold. **transmutative** *a.* **-r** *n.*
**tran•som** *n.* window over a doorway; horizontal crossbar in window.
**trans•par•ent** *a.* that may be distinctly seen through; pervious to light. **transparence, transparency** *n.* **-ly** *adv.* **-ness** *n.*
**tran•spire** *v.t.* to emit through pores of skin; *v.i.* to exhale; *(Bot.)* to lose water by evaporation. **transpiration** *n.* **transpiratory** *a.*
**trans•plant** *v.t.* to remove and plant elsewhere; *(Surg.)* to graft live tissue from one part of body to another. **-able** *a.* **-ation, -er** *n.*
**trans•port** *v.t.* to convey from one place to another; to overwhelm emotionally; *n.* vehicles collectively used in conveyance of passengers. **-able** *a.* **-ability, -er** *n.* **-ation** *n.* act or means of transporting from place to place. **-ed** *a.*
**trans•pose** *v.t.* to change respective place or order of two things. **transposable** *a.* **transposal** *n.* change of order. **transposition** *n.* **transpositional** *a.*
**tran•sub•stan•ti•ate** *v.t.* to change into another substance.
**tran•sude** *v.i* to pass through pores of substance.
**trans•verse** *a.* lying in crosswise direction. **transversal** *n.* line which cuts across two or more parallel lines. **-ly** *adv.*
**trap** *n.* device for catching animals, vermin; U-shaped bend in pipe which, by being always full of water, prevents foul air or gas from escaping; plot to catch person unawares; *v.t.* to catch in a trap, or by stratagem. **-ping** *pr.p.* **-ped** *pa.p.* and *pa.t.* **-door** *n.* hinged door in floor. **-per** *n.*
**tra•pe•zi•um** *n.* quadrilateral with no parallel sides; *(Anat.)* one of wrist bones *pl.* **-s, trapezia. trapeze** *n.* apparatus comprising horizontal crossbar swing for gymnastics, acrobatic exhibitions, etc. **trapezoid** *n.* quadrilateral with only two of its sides parallel. **trapezoidal** *a.*
**trash** *v.t.* to lop off, as branches, leaves.

etc.; *n.* worthless refuse; rubbish. **-ily** *adv.* **-iness** *n.* **-y** *a.* worthless; shoddy.

**trass** *n.* volcanic material used in making cement.

**trau•ma** *n. (Med.)* bodily injury caused by violence; emotional shock (psychic trauma) with a lasting effect. *pl.* **-ta. -tic** *a.*

**tra•vail** *n.* painful, arduous labor; *v.i.* to labor with difficulty.

**trave** *n.* beam.

**trav•el** *v.t.* to journey over; *v.i.* to journey on foot or in a vehicle; *n.* act of traveling; journey; touring, esp. abroad; *pl.* prolonged journey, esp. abroad. **-ed** *a.* **-er** *n.* **-ing** *a.* **-ogue** *n.* travel lecture illustrated by slides, film.

**tra•verse** *a.* lying across; built crosswise; anything set across; lateral movement; *v.t.* to cross; to obstruct; to survey across a plot of ground; to discuss, as topic, from every angle; *v.i.* to move sideways. **traversable** *a.* **-r** *n.*

**trav•es•ty** *n.* parody; *v.t.* to caricature.

**trawl** *v.t.* to catch fish with a trawl; *v.i.* to drag with a trawl; *n.* a strong fishing net, shaped like a large bag with one end open. **-er** *n.* one who fishes with a trawl; fishing vessel. **-ing** *n.*

**tray** *n.* flat, shallow, rimmed vessel used for carrying dishes, food, etc.

**treach•er•y** *n.* violation of faith; treason; perfidy. **treacherous** *a.* **treacherously** *adv.*

**tread** *v.i.* to walk; to move with measured step; to crush; *v.t.* to crush with foot; to operate with foot, as treadle; *n.* that which one steps on, as surface of horizontal step of flight of stairs; part of a rubber tire in contact with ground. **trod** *pa.t.* and *pa.p.* **trodden** *pa.p.* **-ing** *n.* **-le** *n.* part of machine operated by foot pressure, as sewing machine, etc.; *v.i.* to work treadle. **-ler** *n.*

**trea•son** *n.* act of betrayal. **-able** *a.* treason. **-ableness** *n.* **-ably** *adv.* **-ous** *a.*

**trea•sure** *n.* hoard of valuables; that which has great worth; *v.t.* to hoard; to value; to cherish, as friendship. **— chest** *n.* box for storing valuables. **-r** *n.* person appointed to take charge of funds of church, club, etc. **-ship** *n.* **treasury** *n.* place where treasure or public funds are deposited; anthology. **Treasury** *n.* government department which controls management of public revenues.

**treat** *v.t.* to entertain with food or drink; to pay for another's entertainment or refreshment; to apply a remedy to; *v.i.* to come to terms of agreement; to give entertainment; *n.* entertainment given as a celebration or expression of regard; one's turn to pay for another's entertainment. **-er, -ing** *n.* **-ise** *n.* dissertation on particular theme. **-ment** *n.* mode of treating person, subject, artistic work; method of counteracting disease or injury. **-y** *n.* a negotiated agreement between states.

**tre•ble** *a.* triple; *(Mus.)* singing highest part; *n.* highest part; soprano part or voice; *v.i.* to become three times as much. **trebly** *adv.*

**tree** perennial plant, having trunk, bole, or woody stem with branches; *v.t.* to chase up a tree; to corner. **-less** *a.* **-lessness** *n.* **-top** *n.* uppermost branches of tree.

**tre•foil** *n.* plant of genus *Trifolium,* with leaves comprising three leaflets; clover.

**trek** *v.i.* to migrate; *n.* mass migration. **-king** *pr.p.* **-ked** *pa.p.* and *pa.t.* **-ker** *n.*

**trel•lis** *n.* lightweight lattice structure esp. as frame for climbing plants. **-ed** *a.* **-work** *n.* latticework.

**trem•ble** *v.i.* to shake involuntarily; to quake; *n.* tremor. **-r** *n.* **trembling** *n.* and *adv.* **trembly** *a.* shaky. **tremulant, tremulous** *a.* fearful. **tremulously** *adv.* **tremulousness** *n.*

**tre•men•dous** *a.* awe-inspiring; *(Colloq.)* great. **-ly** *adv.* **-ness** *n.*

**trem•o•lan•do** *a. (Mus.)* tremulous. **tremolo** *n.* quivering of singing voice.

**trem•or** *n.* involuntary quiver; shaking, as caused by earthquake. **-less** *a.* steady.

**trem•u•lous** *a.* See **tremble.**

**trench** *v.t.* to dig, as a ditch; to fortify with ditch, using earth dug out for rampart; *v.i.* to encroach; *n.* deep ditch to protect soldiers from enemy fire. **-ancy** *n.* quality of being trenchant. **-ant** *a.* penetrating. **— coat** *n.* waterproof coat. **-ing** *n.*

**trend** *v.i.* to stretch in a certain direction; *n.* inclination; tendency; general direction.

**tre•pan** *n.* heavy tool for boring shafts.

**trep•id** *a.* quaking. **-ation** *n.* involuntary trembling; fluster.

**tres•pass** *v.i.* to cross boundary line of another's property unlawfully; to intrude. **-er** *n.*

**tress** *n.* long lock, curl, braid or strand of hair; ringlet. **-ed** *a.*

**tres•tle** *n.* frame consisting of two pairs of braced legs fixed underneath horizontal bar, used as support; similar construction supporting a bridge.

**tri-** *pref.* meaning three.

**tri•ad** *n.* union of three; *(Mus.)* the common chord, one of three notes. **-ic** *a.* **-ist** *n.* writer of triads.

**tri•al** *n.* act of trying, testing, or proving properties of anything; judicial examination in law court of accused person.

**tri•an•gle** *n. (Math.)* figure bounded by three lines and containing three angles; *(Mus.)* small percussion instrument consisting of a bar of steel bent in shape of triangle and struck with small steel rod. **-d, triangular** *a.* **triangularity** *n.* **triangularly** *adv.*

**tri•ar•chy** *n.* government by three persons.

**tri•a•tom•ic** *a.* consisting of three atoms; having valency of three.

**tribe** *n.* family, race, or succession of generations descending from same progenitor. **tribal** *a.* **tribalism** *n.* tribal feeling; tribal life. **tribally** *adv.* **-sman** *n.* one of a tribe.

**trib•u•la•tion** *n.* severe affliction; prolonged suffering, esp. of mind.

**tri•bune** *n.* in ancient Rome, magistrate chosen by the people to defend their rights. **tribunal** *n.* court of justice. **tribunate, -ship** *n;* office of tribune.

**trib•ute** *n.* personal testimony to achievements or qualities of another;

prearranged payment made at stated times by one state to another. **tributarily** *adv.* **tributary** *a.* paying tribute; subordinate; (of river) flowing into main river; *n.* one who pays tribute; stream flowing into larger river.

**trice** *n.* moment; a very short time.

**tri•ceps** *a.* three-headed; *n.* three-headed muscle as at back of upper arm.

**trich•i•no•sis** *n.* disease due to the presence of the nematode worm, trichina, in the intestines and muscular tissue.

**tri•chol•o•gy** *n.* study of hair and diseases affecting it.

**tri•cho•sis** *n.* any disease affecting the hair.

**tri•chot•o•mous** *a.* divided into three or threes. **trichotomy** *n.*

**trick** *n.* stratagem designed to deceive; conjurer's sleight of hand; dexterity; *v.t.* to deceive; to mystify; to dress, decorate. **-er** *n.* **-ery** *n.* practice of playing tricks; fraud. **-ily** *adv.* **-iness** *n.* **-sy** *a.* ingenious; neat. **-ster,** *n.* swindler. **-y** *a.* full of tricks; crafty; intricate.

**trick•le** *v.i.* to flow gently in a slow, thin stream; *n.* slow movement of anything.

**tri•col•or** *n.* national flag of three colors, esp. French national flag. **-ed** *a.*

**tri•corn** *a.* having three horns, or points; *n.* three-cornered hat.

**tri•cot** *n.* machine-made knitwear fabric. **-tine** *n.* a ribbed, fine woolen fabric, machine-made.

**tri•cus•pid** *a.* having three cusps or points, as certain teeth; a valve of the right ventricle of the heart.

**tri•cy•cle** *n.* three-wheeled cycle, esp. for children's use; *v.t.* to ride a tricycle. **tricyclist** *n.*

**tri•dent** *n.* any three-pronged instrument, such as fish spear. **-ate,** *a.* having three prongs.

**tried** See **try.**

**tri•en•ni•al** *a.* lasting for three years; happening once every three years. **-ly** *adv.*

**tri•fle** *n.* anything of little value or importance; *v.i.* to speak or act lightly; to toy, or waste time. **-r** *n.* **trifling** *a.* trivial. **triflingly** *adv.*

**tri•form** *a.* having a triple form. Also **-ed. -ity** *n.*

**tri•fur•cate** *a.* having three branches. **trifurcation** *n.*

**trig•ger** *n.* catch of firearm which, when pulled, releases hammer of lock.

**trig•o•nom•e•try** *n.* branch of mathematics which deals with relations between sides and angles of triangle. **trigonometer** *n.* instrument for solving plane right-angled triangles by inspection. **trigonometrical** *a.* **trigonometrically** *adv.*

**tri•lat•er•al** *a.* having three sides. **-ly** *adv.*

**tri•lin•e•ar** *a.* consisting of three lines.

**tri•lin•gual** *a.* expressed in three languages; speaking three languages.

**trill** *v.t.* and *v.i.* to sing or play (instrument) with vibratory quality; *n.* vibration of voice, in singing.

**tril•lion** *n.* a million million (U.S.), i.e. 1 with 12 ciphers.

**tril•o•gy** *n.* group of three plays, novels, with common theme, or common central character.

**trim** *a.* *(comp.)* **-mer.** *(superl.)* **-est.** neat; in good order; to decorate, as hat; to clip shorter; *(Naut.)* to arrange sails according to wind direction; *v.i.* to balance; *n.* dress; decoration; anything trimmed off. **-ming** *pr.p.* **-med** *pa.t.* and *pa.p.* **-ly** *adv.* **-mer** *n.* one who trims; instrument for clipping. **-ming** *n.* that which trims, edges, or decorates. **-ness** *n.* neatness; readiness for use.

**trim•e•ter** *n.* verse containing three measures. **trimetrical** *a.*

**tri•nal** *a.* threefold; three in one. **trinary** *a.* ternary. **trine** *a.* threefold; *n.* group of three; aspect of two planets distant from each other 120°, or one-third of the zodiac.

**tri•ni•tro•tol•u•ene** *n.* *(abbrev.* **T.N.T.)** high explosive.

**Trin•i•ty** *n.* union of one Godhead of Father, Son, and Holy Ghost; *(l.c.)* combination of three people or things as one. **Trinitarian** *a.* pert. to doctrine of the Trinity; *n.* one who believes in this doctrine. **Trinitarianism** *n.*

**trin•ket** *n.* small ornament of little value. **-ry** *n.*

**tri•no•mi•al** *a.* *(Bot. Zool.)* having three names as of *order, species* and *subspecies; (Math.)* consisting of three terms connected by sign + or −; *n.* a trinomial quantity.

**tri•o** *n.* group of three persons or things; *(Mus.)* composition arranged for three voices or instruments.

**tri•ox•ide** *n.* *(Chem.)* compound comprising three atoms of oxygen with other element.

**trip** *v.t.* to cause to stumble; to start up, as machine, by releasing clutch; *v.i.* to walk lightly; to stumble over an obstacle; *n.* a journey; false step; indiscretion in speech or conduct. **-ping** *pr.p.* **-ped** *pa.p.* **-per** *n.* device to start a mechanism. **-ping** *a.* light-footed. **-pingly** *adv.*

**tri•par•tite** *a.* having three corresponding parts; arranged or agreed to, by three nations. **tripartition** *n.*

**tripe** *n.* large stomach of ruminating animal, prepared for food.

**triph•thong** *n.* a syllable containing three vowels together.

**tri•ple** *a.* three times repeated; *v.t.* to make three times as many; *v.i.* to become trebled. **-t** *n.* three of a kind; *(Mus.)* three notes played in the time of two; one of three children born at a birth. **-x** *a.* threefold; *n.* *(Mus.)* triple time. **triplicate** *a.* threefold; *n.* third copy corresponding exactly to two others; *v.t.* to make three copies of. **triplication** *n.*

**tri•pod** *n.* three-legged, folding stand for a camera; *a.* having three legs. **-al, -ic** *a.*

**trip•o•li** *n.* mineral substance used for polishing metals, originally from *Tripoli.*

**trip•tych** *n.* picture in three panels.

**tri•sect** *v.t.* to divide into three equal parts, as a line or angle. **-ion** *n.*

**tri•sul•fide** *n.* *(Chem.)* chemical compound containing three sulfur atoms.

**tri•syl•la•ble** *n.* word of three syllables.

**trisyllabical** *a.* **trisyllabically** *adv.*

**trite** *a.* made stale by use; banal. **-ly** *adv.* **-ness** *n.*

**Tri•ton** *n.* *(Gk. Myth.)* god of the sea.

**trit•u•rate** *v.t.* to grind to a very fine powder. **triturable** *a.* **trituration** *n.*

**tri•umph** *n.* victory; great achievement; *v.i.* to celebrate victory with great ceremony; to exult. **-al** *a.* expressing joy for success. **-antly** *adv.*

**tri•um•vir** *n.* one of three men sharing governing power in ancient Rome. *pl.* **-i, -s. -al** *a.* **-ate** *n.* coalition of three men in authority.

**tri•une** *a.* three in one. **triunity** *n.*

**tri•va•lent** *a.* *(Chem.)* having valency of three; capable of combining with three atoms of hydrogen. **trivalence** *n.*

**triv•et** *n.* three-legged support; short-legged metal rack to put under a hot platter, etc.

**triv•i•al** *a.* of little consequence. **-ism** *n.* **triviality** *n.pl.* insignificant matters. **-ly** *adv.* **-ness** *n.*

**trod, trodden** *pa.t.* and *pa.p.* of **tread.**

**trog•lo•dyte** *n.* cave dweller; a hermit.

**Tro•jan** *a.* pert. to ancient Troy; *n.* inhabitant of Troy.

**troll** *n.* mischievous humpbacked cave-dwelling dwarf.

**troll** *v.t.* and *v.i.* to roll; to sing in succession the parts of a round; to fish with baited line trailing behind boat; *n.* a round or catch; act of trolling. **-er** *n.*

**trol•ley** *n.* form of truck, body of which can be tilted over; device to connect electric streetcar with wires. **-bus,** passengar bus not operating on rails but drawing power from overhead wires. **— car** *n.* electric streetcar.

**trom•bone** *n.* deep-toned brass musical instrument. **trombonist** *n.*

**troop** *n.* assembly of people; body of cavalry; *pl.* soldiers collectively; *v.i.* to gather in a crowd. **-er** *n.* policeman; horse cavalryman. **-ship** *n.* vessel for transporting soldiers.

**trope** *n.* phrase used metaphorically. **tropical** *a.* figurative. **tropically** *adv.* **tropist** *n.* one who uses figurative language. **tropological** *a.* containing figures of speech. **tropology** *n.* figurative language; metaphorical interpretation of the Bible.

**tro•phical** *a.* pert. to nutrition. **trophi** *n.pl.* masticating organs of insect. **trophology** *n.* study of nutrition.

**tro•phy** *n.* memorial of victory; prize, esp. for sports, etc.

**trop•ic** *n.* one of the two circles of celestial sphere, situated 23½° N. *(Tropic of Cancer)* and 23½° S. *(Tropic of Capricorn)* of equator. *pl.* region *(torrid zone)* between tropics of Cancer and Capricorn. **tropical** *a.* pert. to or within tropics; very hot. **-ally** *adv.*

**tro•po•sphere** *n.* lower layer of atmosphere below stratosphere.

**trot** *v.i.* to move at sharp pace; *v.t.* to cause to trot; *n.* quick walk. **-ting** *pr.p.* **-ted** *pa.p.* and *pa.t.* **-ter** *n.* one who trots.

**troth** *n.* fidelity. **to plight one's troth,** to become engaged to be married.

**trou•ble** *v.t.* to stir up; to distress; *v.i.* to feel anxiety; *n.* disturbance; agitation of mind; inconvenience. **-r** *n.* **-some** *a.* difficult; irksome. **-somely** *adv.* **-someness** *n.*

**trough** *n.* long, open vessel for water or fodder for animals.

**trounce** *v.t.* to beat severely; *(Colloq.)* to defeat completely.

**troupe** *n.* company, esp. of actors, acrobats, etc. **-r** *n.* member of a theatrical troupe.

**trou•sers** *n.pl.* garment extending from waist to ankles; slacks. **trousered** *a.* wearing trousers. **trouserless** *a.*

**trous•seau** *n.* bride's outfit of clothes, etc.

**trout** *n.* fish resembling salmon.

**trout**

**trow•el** *n.* mason's tool for spreading mortar; garden tool for scooping out earth, plants; *v.t.* to smooth with trowel.

**troy weight** *n.* system of weight for precious metals and gems.

**tru•ant** *n.* one who shirks his duty; pupil who absents himself from school; *a.* idle; *v.i.* to play truant. **truancy** *n.*

**truce** *n.* temporary cessation of hostilities; lull.

**truck** *v.t.* to exchange; *v.i.* to deal with by exchange; *n.* exchange of commodities; garden produce. **-er** *n.* **— farm** *n.* a small farm on which vegetables are grown for market.

**truck** *n.* horse-drawn or automotive vehicle for hauling; barrow for heavy luggage. **-age** *n.* transport by trucks. **-le** *n.* small caster. **— bed** *n.* low bed on casters which may be pushed beneath another.

**truc•u•lent** *a.* aggressive; ruthless. **truculence, truculency** *n.* **-ly** *adv.*

**trudge** *v.t.* to plod along; *n.* wearisome walk.

**trud•gen** *n.* fast racing stroke in swimming.

**true** *a.* conformable with fact; genuine; loyal; *v.t.* to adjust accurately, as machine; *adv.* truly conforming to type. **-ness** *n.* **truism** *n.* self-evident truth. **truly** *adv.*

**tru•ism** See **true.**

**trump** *n.* *(Arch.)* trumpet; its sound. **-et** *n.* wind instrument of brass, consisting of long tube bent twice on itself, ending in wide bell-shaped mouth, and having finger stops; *v.t.* to proclaim by trumpet; *v.i.* (of elephant) to utter characteristic cry trough trunk. **-eter** *n.* one who plays on trumpet; wild swan of N. Amer. **-eting** *n.*

**trump** *n.* one of the suit of cards, declared by dealing, bidding of which takes any card of another suit; *v.t.* and *v.i.* to play trump card; to take a trick with trump.

**trump** *v.t.* to deceive. **-ery** *n.* anything showy but of little value.

**trun•cate** *v.t.* to cut off; to maim. **truncated, truncation** *a.* appearing as if cut off at tip; blunt.

**trun•dle** *n.* anything capable of being

rolled; a small caster; *v.t.* to roll on little wheels; *v.i.* to roll.

**trunk** *n.* stem of tree, as distinct from branches and roots; torso; main part of anything; main lines of railway, bus, or telephone system; proboscis of elephant; *pl.* short pants, esp. for swimming.

**truss** *n.* bundle; framework of beams constructed to bear heavy loads; *(Med.)* appliance to keep hernia in place; *v.t.* to bind or pack close; to support, as a roof, with truss.

**trust** *n.* confidence; implicit faith; moral responsibility; *v.t.* to have implicit faith in; to give credit; *v.i.* to be confident or to confide in; *a.* held in trust. **-ee** *n.* person or group which manages the business affairs of another. **—eeship, -er** *n.* **-ful** *a.* **-fully** *adv.* **-fulness** *n.* **-ily** *adv.* **-iness** *n.* quality of being trusty. **-ing** *a.* confiding. **-ingly** *adv.* **-worthiness** *n.* **-worthy** *a.* **-y** *a.* reliable; *n.* reliable prisoner given special privileges.

**truth** *n.* conformity to reality; true statement; undisputed fact. **-ful** *a.* **-fully** *adv.* **-fulness** *n.* **-less** *a.*

**try** *v.t.* to test; *(Law)* to examine judicially; *v.i.* to make effort; *n.* effort; attempt. **tried** *a., pa.t.* and *pa.p.* **trier** *n.*

**tryst** *n.* appointment to meet. **-er** *n.*

**tset•se** *n.* African fly, its bite causing sleeping sickness.

**T square** *n.* ruler with crossbar at one end for drawing parallel lines.

**tub** *n.* vessel to bathe in; small cask. **-by** *a.* (of persons) squat and portly.

**tu•ba** *n.* *(Mus.)* largest brass instrument of orchestra.

**tube** *n.* long hollow cylinder for conveyance of liquids, gas; inner rubber tire of bicycle or automobile wheel. **tubing** *n.* **tubular, tubulated, tubulous, tubulose** *a.* **tubule** *n.* a small tube.

**tu•ber** *n.* fleshy, rounded underground stem or root, containing buds for new plant; *(Med.)* a swelling. **-ous, -ose** *a.*

**tu•ber•cle** *n.* small swelling; *(Med.)* morbid growth, esp. on lung causing *tuberculosis; a.* having tubercules. **tubercular, tuberculated, tuberculose, tuberculous** *a.* affected with tuberculosis. **tuberculin** *n.* liquid extract from tubercle bacillus used as injection in testing for, in treatment of, tuberculosis. **tuberculosis** *n.* phthisis, disease caused by infection with the tubercle bacillus. **tuberculum** *n.* tubercle.

**tuck** *v.t.* to make fold(s) in cloth before stitching down; to enclose snugly in bedclothes; *n.* flat fold in garment to shorten it.

**Tues•day** *n.* third day of week.

**tuft** *n.* bunch of something soft, as hair, feathers; *v.t.* to adorn with, arrange in tufts. **-ed, -y** *a.*

**tug** *v.t.* to pull with effort; *v.i.* to comb, as hair, with difficulty; *n.* strong pull. **-ging** *pr.p.* **-ged** *pa.t.* and *pa.p.* **-boat** *n.* a small but powerful boat used for towing larger vessel.

**tu•i•tion** *n.* the price for instruction. **-al, -ary** *a.*

**tu•lip** *n.* bulbous plant popular in Holland.

**tulle** *n.* fine silk net used for dresses.

**tum•ble** *v.i.* to fall heavily; to turn head over heels; to perform acrobatic tricks; *v.t.* to overturn; to toss about; *n.* act of tumbling; confusion. **-er** *n.* acrobat; glass drinking vessel; spring catch of a lock. **tumbling** *n.* act of turning somersault

**tum•brel, tumbril** *n.* low open cart in which victims of French Revolutionists were conveyed to guillotine.

**tu•me•fy** *v.t.* to cause to swell; *v.i.* to develop into a tumor. **tumefaction** *n.* a tumor.

**tu•mid** *a.* swollen; pompous. **tumescence** *n.* **tumescent** *a.* **-ness, -ity** *n.* **-ly** *adv.*

**tu•mor** *n.* *(Med.)* morbid overgrowth of tissue, sometimes accompanied by swelling. **-ous** *a.*

**tu•mult** *n.* commotion of a crowd; disturbance. **-uary, -uous** *a.* uproarious; disturbing. **-uously** *adv.* **-uousness** *n.*

**tu•mu•lus** *n.* artificial burial mound, erected by primitive peoples. *pl.* **-es, tumuli. tumulous** *a.*

**tun** *n.* measure of liquid, for wine, equivalent to 252 gallons; *v.t.* to store in casks.

**tu•na** *n.* large oceanic food and game fish.

**tun•dra** *n.* one of vast treeless plains of Arctic Circle.

**tune** *n.* melody; unison; harmony; *v.t.* to adjust to proper pitch; to make efficient, esp. part of machine; *(Radio)* to adjust circuit to give resonance at desired frequency. **tunable** *a.* **tunableness** *n.* **tunably** *adv.* **-ful** *a.* melodious; harmonious. **-fully** *adv.* **-fulness** *n.* **-less** *a.* without melody; discordant; silent. **-r** *n.* **tuning fork** *n.* steel two-pronged instrument giving specified note when struck.

**tung•sten** *n.* hard gray metallic element used in alloys, special forms of steel, and for filaments in electric lamps.

**tu•nic** *n.* short-sleeved knee-length garment worn by women and boys in ancient Greece and Rome.

**tun•nel** *n.* subterranean passage; *v.t.* and *v.i.* to excavate. **-er** *n.*

**tun•ny** *n.* edible fish of mackerel family; tuna fish.

**tur•ban** *n.* headdress comprising long strip of cloth swathed around head or cap. **-ed, -like** *a.*

**tur•bid** *a.* muddy; dense. **-ly** *adv.* **-ness, -ity** *n.*

**tur•bine** *n.* rotary engine driven by steam, hot air, or water striking on curved vans of wheel, or drum; high-speed prime

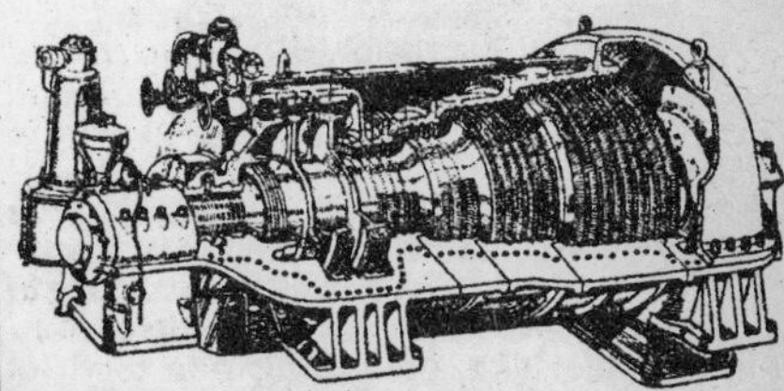

steam turbine

mover used for generating electrical energy. **turbinal, turbinate** *a.* coiled like a spiral. **turbojet** *n.* jet-propelled gas turbine. **turboprop** *n.* jet engine in which turbine is coupled to propeller.

**tur•bot** *n.* large flat sea fish.

**tur•bu•lent** *a.* disturbed; refractory. **-ly** *adv.* **turbulence, turbulency** *n.*

**tu•reen** *n.* large, deep dish with removable cover, for serving soup.

**turf** *n.* surface soil containing matted roots, grass; a racecourse; *v.t.* to cover with turf, as lawn. **-like** *a.* **-y** *a.* covered with turf.

**turgent** *a.* *(obs.)* puffing up like a tumor; bombastic. **-ly** *adv.* **turgescence, turgescency** *n.* swelling caused by congestion; **turgid** *a.* distended abnormally; bombastic. **turgidity, turgidness** *n.* **-ly** *adv.*

**Turk** *n.* native of Turkey; Ottoman. **-ish** *a.* pert. to Turks or Turkey. **-ish bath** *n.* steam bath after which person is massaged, etc. **-ish towel** *n.* an absorbent towel.

**tur•key** *n.* large bird, bred for food. **— trot** *n.* ragtime dance.

**tur•moil** *n.* commotion; tumult.

**turn** *v.t.* to cause to revolve; to change direction of; to convert; *v.i.* to rotate; to move as on a hinge; (of tides) to change from ebb to flow or the reverse; to become sour, as milk; *n.* act of turning; change of bend; an action, as *good turn;* action done in rotation with others; short walk; a subtle quality of expression; crisis. **-about** *n.* reversal of opinion. **-ing** *n.* deflection; winding. **-ing point** *n.* decisive moment; crisis. **-over** *n.* rate at which employees are replaced by others; tart of pastry folded over a filling of fruit. **-pike** *n.* **-pike road,** main highway with tollgate. **-stile** *n.* revolving gate for controlling admission of people. **-table** *n.* revolving circular platform. **to turn down,** to decline, as offer; to reject, as application.

**tur•nip** *n.* plant of mustard family.

**tur•pen•tine** *n.* oily liquid extracted by distillation of resin exuded by pine and other coniferous trees.

**tur•pi•tude** *n.* revolting baseness; infamy.

**tur•quoise** *n.* bluish-green gem stone.

**tur•ret** *n.* revolving gun tower on ship, tank, or aircraft. **-ed** *a.* having turrets.

**tur•tle** *n.* marine tortoise with hard shell and limbs like paddles.

**turtle**

**tur•tle•dove** kind of pigeon, noted for its soft cooing and its affection for its mate.

**Tus•can** *a.* *(Archit.)* denoting the simplest of the five classical styles in architecture.

**tusk** *n.* the long, protruding side tooth of certain animals such as elephant, wild boar, walrus. **-ed** *a.* **-er** *n.* animal with fully developed tusks. **-y** *a.* **-less** *a.* **-like** *a.*

**tus•sle** *n.* and *v.t.* struggle; scuffle.

**tut** *interj.* exclamation of irritation.

**tu•te•lage** *n.* guardianship; state or period of being under this. **tutelar, tutelary** *a.* protective.

**tu•tor** *n.* private teacher; *v.t.* to prepare another for special examination by private coaching. **-ial** *a.* pert. to tutor. **-ially** *adv.* **-ing, -ship** *n.*

**tut•ti•frut•ti** *n.* preserve of fruits; ice cream made with mixed fruits.

**tu•tu** *n.* ballet dancer's skirt.

**tux•e•do** *n.* semiformal dinner jacket.

**twad•dle** *n.* inane conversation; *v.i.* to talk inanely. **-r** *n.* **twaddling** *n.* twaddle. **twaddly** *a.* silly.

**twang** *n.* sharp, rather harsh sound made by tense string sharply plucked; nasalized speech; *v.t.* to pluck tense string of instrument; *v.i.* to speak with a twang.

**tweak** *v.t.* to twist and pull with sudden jerk; *n.* sharp pinch.

**tweed** *n.* heavy woolen fabric esp. for coats, suits; *a.* of tweed.

**tweez•ers** *n.sing.* small pair of pincers, esp. for pulling superfluous hairs.

**twelve** *a.* one more than eleven; dozen; *n.* symbol representing twelve units, as 12 **twelfth** *a.* constituting one of twelve or XII. equal parts; *n.* one of twelve equal parts. **Twelfth Day,** January 6th, twelfth day after Christmas; Feast of Epiphany. **twelfthly** *adv.*

**twen•ty** *a.* twice ten; *n.* score; symbol representing twenty units, as 20 or XX. **twentieth** *a.* and *n.* one of twenty equal parts. **-fold** *adv.* twenty times as many.

**twice** *adv.* two times; doubly.

**twid•dle** *v.t.* to play with; *v.i.* to trifle with. **-r** *n.*

**twig** *n.* small branch of tree. **-gy** *a.* covered with twigs.

**twi•light** *n.* half-light immediately after sunset; *a.* pert. to or like twilight.

**twill** *n.* fabric woven with diagonal ribbing; *v.t.* to weave with twill.

**twin** *n.* one of two born at birth; exact counterpart; *a.* being one of two born at birth; growing in pairs. **-ned** *a.* **— beds** *n.pl.* two single beds of identical size. **-born** *a.* born at the same birth. **— brother, sister** *n.*

**twine** *n.* cord composed of two or more strands twisted together; *v.t.* to twist together; *v.i.* to coil spirally, as tendrils of plant; to follow circuitous route. **twining** *a.*

**twinge** *n.* acute spasm of pain; *v.t.* to affect momentarily with sudden pain.

**twin•kle** *v.i.* to sparkle; to light up; *n.* gleam of amusement in eyes; quick movement of feet, in dancing; sparkle. **twinkling** *n.* an instant.

**twirl** *v.t.* to whirl around; to flourish; *v.i.* to turn around rapidly; *n.* a rapid, rotary motion; convolution. **-er** *n.* one who or that which twirls.

**twist** *v.t.* to contort; to form, as cord, from

several fibers wound together; *v.i.* to become tangled or distorted; to wriggle; to follow a roundabout course; *n.* turning movement; a turn in meaning; a heavy silk thread; **-ed** *a.* **-er** *n.* one who, or that which, twists. **-ability** *n.* **-able** *a.* **-ingly** *adv.*

**twit** *v.t.* to reproach; to tease; *n.* taunt. **-ting** *pr.p.* **-ted** *pa.t.* and *pa.p.*

**twitch** *v.t.* to pull suddenly with a jerk; *v.i.* to contract with sudden spasm, as a muscle; *n.* sudden spasmodic contraction of muscle. **-ing** *n.*

**twit•ter** *n.* chirping sound; slight trembling of nerves; *v.i.* to make succession of small light sounds; to talk rapidly. **-ing** *n.* **-y** *a.*

**two** *a.* one and one; *n.* symbol representing two units, as 2 or II; a pair. **—edged** *a.* having two sharp edges; **-faced** *a.* hypocritical; double-dealing. **-fold** *a.* doubly. **—handed** *a.* requiring two hands or players. **—ply** *a.* having two strands twisted together. **—sided** *a.* having two aspects; reversible.

**ty•coon** *n.* head of great business combine; a magnate.

**tym•pa•num** *n.* a drum *(Anat.)* cavity of the middle ear. *pl.* **-s, tympana. tympanal, tympanic** *a.* like a drum; pert. to middle ear. **tympanist** *n.* one who plays percussion instrument.

**type** *n.* model; class or group; person or thing representative of certain quality; *(Biol.)* individual specimen representative of species; *(Print.)* metal block on one end of which is raised letter; *v.t.* to represent in type; to reproduce by typewriter; to classify; *v.i.* to use a typewriter. **typal** *a.* **— cutter** *n.* one who engraves blocks for printing types. **-founder** *n.* one who casts type for printing. **— metal** *n.* alloy of lead, antimony, and tin used for casting type. **-script** *n.* a typewritten document. **-setting** *n.* process of preparing type for printing. **-writer** *n.* machine with

typewriter

keyboard operated by fingers, which produces printed characters on paper; typist. **-writing** *n.* **-written** *a.* **typical** *a.* symbolic. **typing** *n.* script typed. **typist** *n.* one who operates typewriter. **typographer** *n.* printer. **typographical** *a.* pert. to printing. **typography** *n.* style of printing.

**ty•phoid** *a.* resembling typhus; pert. to typhoid fever. **— fever** *n.* infectious disease characterized by severe diarrhea, profound weakness, and rash. **-al** *a.*

**ty•phoon** *n.* cyclonic hurricane. **typhonic** *a.*

**ty•phus** *n.* highly contagious disease caused by virus and characterized by purplish rash, prostration, and abnormally high temperature. **typhous** *a.*

**ty•rant** *n.* harsh, despotic ruler. **tyrannical, tyrannous** *a.* **tyrannically, tyrannously** *adv.* **tyrannicalness** *n.* **tyrannize** *v.i.* to exert authority ruthlessly; *v.t.* to subject to tyrannical authority. **tyrannizer** *n.* **tyrannizingly** *adv.* **tyranny** *n.* harsh enforcement of authority.

**ty•ro** *n.* novice.

**u•biq•ui•ty** *n.* existing in all places at same time; omnipresence. **ubiquitous, ubiquitary** *a.* existing or being everywhere.
**U-boat** *n.* German submarine.
**ud•der** *n.* milk gland of certain animals, as cow.
**u•dom•e•ter** *n.* instrument for measuring rainfall.
**ug•ly** *a.* offensive to the sight; of disagreeable aspect; dangerous, of situation.
**U•krain•i•an** *n.* citizen of Ukraine in S.W. Russia; Slavic language related to Russian. *a.* pert. to Ukraine.
**u•ku•le•le** *n.* small four-stringed instrument like guitar.
**ul•cer** *n.* superficial sore discharging pus.
**ul•lage** *n.* amount which cask lacks of being full; loss of wine, grain, etc. by leakage.
**ul•na** *n.* the larger of two bones of forearm.
**ul•ster** *n.* long loose overcoat originally made in *Ulster*, Ireland. **-ed** *a.*
**ul•te•ri•or** *a.* situated on the farther side; beyond; (of motives) undisclosed; not frankly stated.
**ul•ti•mate** *a.* farthest; final; primary; conclusive. **-ly** *adv.* **-ness** *n.* **ultimatum** *n.* final proposition; final terms offered as basis of treaty.
**ul•tra** *a.* beyond; extreme; in combination words with or without hyphen, as **ultra modern.**
**ul•tra•ma•rine** *a.* situated beyond the sea; *n.* bright blue pigment obtained from powdered lapis lazuli, or produced synthetically.
**ul•tra•mon•tane** *a.* being beyond the mountains, esp. the Alps; pert. to absolute temporal and spiritual power of Papacy or to party upholding this claim; *n.* advocate of extreme or ultra-papal views.
**ul•tra•vi•o•let** *a.* beyond limit of visibility at violet end of the spectrum.
**ul•u•lant** *a.* howling. **ululate** *v.i.* to howl; to lament.
**um•bel** *n.* *(Bot.)* flower clusters, the stalks of which rise from a common center on main stem, forming a convexed surface above.

**umbel**

**um•ber** *n.* natural earth pigment, yellowish-brown in color when raw, reddish-brown when calcined or burnt.
**um•bil•i•cal** *a.* pert. to umbilicus or umbilical cord. **—cord** *(Anat.)* fibrous cord joining fetus to placenta.
**um•bra** *n.* shadow; *(Astron.)* complete shadow cast by earth or moon in eclipse, as opposed to *penumbra*, partial shadow in eclipse.
**um•brage** *n.* *(Poetic)* shadow; feeling of resentment. **umbrageous** *a.* shady.
**um•brel•la** *n.* light-weight circular covering of silk or other material on folding framework of spokes, carried as protection against rain (or sun).
**um•laut** *n.* term used to denote mutation, e.g., caused by influence of vowel *i* (earlier *j*) on preceeding vowel such as a, o, u.
**um•pire** *n.* person chosen to arbitrate in dispute; impartial person chosen to see that rules of game are properly enforced; referee.
**un-** *prefix* before nouns, adjectives, and adverbs adding negative force; before verbs, expressing reversal of the action, separation, etc.
**un•a•bashed** *a.* **(abash)**
**un•a•bat•ed** *a.* **(abate)**
**un•a•bridged** *a.* **(abridge)**
**un•ac•cept•a•ble** *a.* **(accept)**
**un•ac•com•mo•dat•ing** *a.* **(accommodate)**
**un•ac•com•pa•nied** *a.* not accompanied; sung or played on instrument without piano, organ, or orchestral accompaniment.
**un•ac•cus•tomed** *a.* **(accustom)**
**un•ac•quaint•ed** *a.* **(acquaint)**
**un•a•dul•ter•at•ed** *a.* **(adulterate)**
**un•af•fect•ed** *a.* not affected; unmoved; straightforward; sincere.
**un•al•ter•a•ble** *a.* not capable of alteration; fixed; permanent.
**un•am•bi•tious** *a.* **(ambition)**
**u•nan•i•mous** *a.* all of one mind; agreed to by all parties.
**un•an•nealed** *a.* **(anneal)**
**un•ap•pre•ci•at•ed** *a.* **unappreciative** *a.* **(appreciate)**
**un•arm** *v.t.* to disarm; to render harmless.
**un•as•sail•a•ble** *a.* not assailable; irrefutable; invincible. **unassailed** *a.*
**un•as•sist•ed** *a.* **(assist)**
**un•as•sum•ing** *a.* not assuming; modest; not overbearing.
**un•at•tached** *a.* not attached; dangling; not posted to a particular regiment; not married or engaged.
**un•at•trac•tive** *a.* not attractive; repellent; plain; not prepossessing.
**un•au•thor•ized** *a.* **unauthoritative** *a.* **(authorize)**
**un•a•vail•ing** *a.* not availing; fruitless; having no result. **unavailability** *n.* **unavailable** *a.* not procurable; not at one's disposal.
**un•a•ware** *a.* having no knowledge of; *adv.* unawares.
**un•bal•ance** *v.t.* to upset. **-d** *a.* not balanced; lacking equipoise, or mental stability; not adjusted or equal on credit and debit sides (of ledger). **unbalance** *n.*
**un•bear•able** *a.* not bearable; intolerable; (of pain) excruciating.
**un•be•com•ing** *a.* not becoming; not suited to the wearer; (of behavior) immodest; indecorous.
**un•be•fit•ting** *a.* **(befit)**
**un•be•known** *a.* not known. **-st** *adv.* without the knowledge of.
**un•be•lief** *n.* **unbelievability** *n.* **unbelievable** *a.* **unbelieving** *a.* **unbelievingly** *adv.* **(believe)**
**un•bend** *v.t.* to free from bend position; to

straighten; to relax; to loose, as anchor. **unbent** *a.* straight.
**un•bi•ased** *v.t.* **(bias)**
**un•bleached** *a.* **(bleach)**
**un•blem•ished** *a.* not blemished; faultness; (of character) pure; perfect.
**un•bod•ied** *a.* free from the body; incorporeal.
**un•bolt•ed** *a.* (of grain) unsifted; not fastened with a bolt. **unbolt** *v.t.*
**un•born** *a.* not yet born; future, as *unborn generations.*
**un•bos•om** *v.t.* to disclose freely; to reveal one's intimate longings.
**un•bound** *a.* not bound; free; without outer binding, as a book; *pa.p., pa.t.* of **unbind. -ed** *a.* illimitable; abundant; irrepressible. **-edly** *adv.*
**un•break•a•ble** *a.* **(break)**
**un•bri•dle** *v.t.* to remove the bridle from, as a horse. **-d** *a.* unrestrained; violently passionate.
**un•bro•ken** *a.* complete; whole; (of horse) untamed; inviolate; continuous.
**un•bur•den** *v.t.* to relieve of a burden; *(Fig.)* to relieve the mind of anxiety.
**un•busi•ness•like** *a.* **(business)**
**un•cal•cu•la•ted** *v.t.* **(calculate)**
**un•called** *a.* not summoned. **uncalled for,** unnecessary or without cause.
**un•can•ny** *a.* weird; unearthly.
**un•ceas•ing** *a.* **-ly** *adv.* **(cease)**
**un•cer•e•mo•ni•ous** *a.* not ceremonious; informal; abrupt.
**un•cer•tain** *a.* not certain; not positively known; unreliable; insecure. **-ty** *n.* state of being or that which is uncertain; lack of assurance.
**un•change•a•ble** *a.* **unchangeability, -ness** *n.* **unchangeably** *adv.* **unchanged** *a.* **unchanging** *a.* **unchangingly** *adv.* **(change)**
**un•char•i•ta•ble** *a.* **-ness** *n.* **uncharitably** *adv.* **(charity)**
**un•chart•ed** *a.* not shown on a map; unexplored.
**un•church** *v.t.* to excommunicate; to deprive of name and status of a church.
**un•ci•al** *a.* pert. to a type of rounded script, found in ancient MSS from 4th-9th

CENTESIMO:

uncial letters

cents.; *n.* uncial letter or manuscript.
**un•ci•form** *a.* shaped like a hook. **uncinal, uncinate** *a.* hooked; having hook-like prickles.
**un•claimed** *a.* **(claim)**
**un•cle** *n.* brother of one's father or mother; any elderly man.
**un•clean** *a.* not clean; filthy; ceremonially unsanctified; obscene.
**un•cock** *v.t.* to let down hammer of gun without exploding charge.
**un•come•ly** *a.* not comely; unprepossessing; ugly; obscene.
**un•com•fort•a•ble** *a.* **-ness** *n.* **uncomfortably** *adv.* **uncomforted** *a.* **(comfort)**
**un•com•mer•cial** *a.* **(commerce)**
**un•com•mu•ni•ca•tive** *a.* not communicative; discreet; taciturn. **-ly** *adv.* **-ness** *n.* **uncommunicable** *a.* not capable of being shared or communicated.
**un•com•plain•ing** *a.* not complaining; resigned.
**un•com•pro•mis•ing** *a.* not compromising; making no concession; rigid.
**un•con•cern** *n.* lack of concern; apathy. **-ed** *a.* not concerned; disinterested; apathetic; not involved.
**un•con•di•tioned** *a.* not subjected to conditions; absolute; instinctive. **unconditional** *a.* complete; absolute; without reservation. **— reflexes,** the instinctive responses of an animal to external stimuli.
**un•con•firmed** *a.* **(confirm)**
**un•con•gen•i•al** *a.* **(congenial)**
**un•con•scion•a•ble** *a.* beyond reason; unscrupulous; excessive.
**un•con•scious** *a.* not conscious; unaware; deprived of consciousness; involuntary.
**un•con•sti•tu•tion•al** *a.* not constitutional; contrary to the constitution, as of a society or state.
**un•con•tro bdla•ble** *a.* not capable of being controlled; unmanageable; irrepressible.
**uncontrolled** *a.* not controlled; (of prices) not restricted by government regulations.
**un•con•ven•tion•al** *a.* **-ity** *n.* **-ly** *adv.* not conforming to convention, rule or precedent.
**un•con•vert•ed** *a.* not converted; unchanged in heart; heathen; not changed in opinion. **unconversion** *n.* **unconvertible** *a.* not convertible.
**un•count•ed** *a.* not counted; innumerable.
**un•cou•ple** *v.t.* to loose, as a dog from a leash; to disjoin, as railway carriages.
**un•couth** *a.* awkward in manner; strange; unpolished; unseemly.
**un•cov•a•nant•ed** *a.* not agreed to by covenant.
**unc•tion** *n.* act of anointing with oil, as in ceremony of consecration or coronation; *(Med.)* ointment; act of applying ointment; that which soothes; insincere fervor. **extreme unction,** R.C. rite of anointing the dying.
**un•cul•ti•va•ble** *a.* not capable of being cultivated; waste. **uncultivated** *a.* not cultivated; not tilled. **uncultured** *a.* not cultured; not educated; crude.
**un•damped** *a.* not damped; dry.
**un•daunt•ed** *a.* **-ly** *adv.* **(daunt)**
**un•de•ceive** *v.t.* to free from deception. **-d** *a.*
**un•de•c-d•ed** *a.* not settled; irresolute; vacillating. **undecidable** *a.* not capable of being settled.
**un•de•ci•pher•a•ble** *a.* **(decipher)**
**un•de•clared** *a.* not declared; (of taxable goods at customs) not admitted as being in one's possession during customs examination.
**un•de•filed** *a.* **(defile** *v.***)**
**un•dem•o•crat•ic** *a.* not according to the principles of democracy. **undemocratize** *v.t.* to make undemocratic.
**un•de•mon•stra•tive** *a.* **-ly** *adv.* **-ness** *n.* **(demonstrate)**
**un•der** *prep.* below; beneath; subjected

to; less than; liable to; included in; in the care of; during the period of; bound by.

**un•der•act** *v.t.* or *v.i.* to act a part in a play in a colorless, ineffective way.

**un•der•arm** *a.n.* under the arm; armpit; *adv.* from below the shoulder (as a throw).

**un•der•bid** *v.t.* to bid lower than another for a contract, etc.; to make lower bid at bridge than one's cards justify.

**un•der•bred** *a.* of inferior manners; not thoroughbred.

**un•der•brush** *n.* undergrowth of shrubs and bushes.

**un•der•car•riage** *n. (Aero.)* landing gear of aircraft.

**un•der•charge** *v.t.* to charge less than true price; *n.* price below the real value.

**un•der•clothes** *n.pl.* garments worn below the outer clothing, esp. next to the skin; underclothing; lingerie.

**un•der•cov•er** *a. (Colloq.)* secret; used esp. of secret service agents.

**un•der•cur•rent** *n.* current under surface of main stream, sometimes flowing in a contrary direction; hidden tendency.

**un•der•cut** *v.t.* to cut away from below, as coal seam; to strike from beneath; to sell goods cheaply in order to capture a market or monopoly; *(Golf)* to hit ball so it backspins.

**un•der•de•vel•op** *v.t. (Photog.)* to develop insufficiently so that the photographic print is indistinct.

**un•der•es•ti•mate** *v.t.* to miscalculate the value of; to rate at too low a figure; *n.* an inadequate valuation.

**un•der•ex•posed** *a. (Photog.)* insufficiently exposed to the light to impress details on a sensitive surface with clarity of outline.

**un•der•feed** *v.t.* to feed insufficiently; to undernourish. **underfed** *a.*

**un•der•foot** *adv.* beneath the feet; *a.* lying under the foot; in subjection.

**un•der•gar•ment** *n.* a garment worn underneath the outer clothes.

**un•der•grad•u•ate** *n.* student attending classes for his first degree at a university or college.

**un•der•ground** *a.* under the ground; subterranean; secret; *n. (chiefly Brit.)* a subway; *(Fig.)* secret organization or resistance movement.

**un•der•growth** *n.* small trees, shrubs, or plants growing beside taller trees.

**un•der•hand** *adv.* by secret means; fraudulently; *a. (Sports)* served or thrown, as a ball, with hand underneath and an upward swing of the arm from below the waist; sly and dishonorable.

**un•der•hung** *a.* projecting beyond upper jaw, as lower jaw.

**un•der•lay** *v.t.* to lay underneath; to support by something put below.

**un•der•lie** *v.t.* to lie underneath; to be the basis of. **underlying** *a.* basic; placed beneath; obscure.

**un•der•line** *v.t.* to mark with line below, for emphasis.

**un•der•ling** *n.* one who holds inferior position.

**un•der•manned** *a.* supplied (as a ship) with too small a crew; having too small a staff.

**un•der•mine** *v.t.* to excavate for the purpose of mining, blasting, etc.; to erode; to sap, as one's energy; to weaken insidiously.

**un•der•neath** *adv.* and *prep.* beneath; below; in a lower place.

**un•der•nour•ished** *a.* insufficiently nourished.

**un•der•pass** *n.* road or passage (for cars, pedestrians) under a highway or railroad.

**un•der•pay** *v.t.* to pay inadequately for the work done; to exploit.

**un•der•priv•i•leged** *a.* deficient in the necessities of life because of poverty, discrimination, etc.

**un•der•proof** *a.* containing less alcohol than proof spirit.

**un•der•rate** *v.t.* to rate too low; to underestimate.

**un•der•score** *v.t.* to underline for emphasis.

**un•der•sec•re•tar•y** *n.* secretary who ranks below the principal secretary., esp. of government department.

**un•der•sell** *v.t.* to sell more cheaply than another.

**un•der•set** *n. (Naut.)* an ocean undercurrent.

**un•der•side** *n.* the surface underneath.

**un•der•sign** *v.t.* to write one's name at the foot of or underneath.

**un•der•skirt** *n.* petticoat; skirt worn or placed under another.

**un•der•stand** *v.t.* to comprehend; to grasp the significance of.

**un•der•state** *v.t.* to state less strongly than truth warrants; to minimize deliberately.

**un•der•stud•y** *n.* one ready to substitute for principal actor (or actress) at a moment's notice.

**un•der•take** *v.t.* to take upon oneself as a special duty; to agree (to do).

**un•der•tone** *n.* low, subdued tone of voice or color.

**un•der•tow** *n.* undercurrent or backwash of a wave after it has reached the shore.

**un•der•wear** *n.* underclothes.

**un•der•wood** *n.* small trees growing among larger trees.

**un•der•world** *n.* the nether regions; Hades; the antipodes; section of community which lives by vice and crime.

**un•der•write** *v.t.* to write under something else; to subscribe; to append one's signature, as to insurance policy; to undertake to buy shares not bought by the public.

**un•de•sir•a•ble** *a.* not desirable; having no appreciable virtues; *n.* person of ill-repute.

**un•de•vi•at•ing** *a.* not deviating; resolute in pursuing a straight course.

**un•dine** *n.* water sprite.

**un•do** *v.t.* to reverse what has been done; to annul; to loose; to unfasten; to damage character of. **-ing** *n.* act of reversing what has been done; ruin, esp. of reputation. **undone** *a.* ruined; not done; not completed.

**un•dress** *n.* informal dress; off-duty

military uniform.

**un•due** *a.* not yet payable; unjust; immoderate; not befitting the occasion.

**un•du•late** *v.t.* to move up and down like waves; to cause to vibrate; *v.i.* to move up and down; to vibrate; to have wavy edge; *a.* wavy. **undulant** *a.* undulating; wavy. **-ly** *adv.* **undulating** *a.* wavy; having series of rounded ridges and depressions, as surface of landscape. **undulatingly** *adv.* **undulation** *n.* wave; fluctuating motion, as of waves; wave-like contour of stretch of land; series of wavy lines; vibratory motion. **undulatory** *a.* pert. to undulation; moving like a wave; pert. to theory of light which argues that light is transmitted through ether by wave motions.

**un•du•ly** *adv.* unjustly; improperly; excessively.

**un•dy•ing** *a.* not dying; immortal; everlasting.

**un•earned** *a.* not earned by personal labor. **— income,** income derived from sources other than salary, fees, etc. **— increment,** increased value of property, land, etc. due to circumstances other than owner's expenditure on its upkeep.

**un•earth** *v.t.* to dig up; to drive as a fox, rabbit, etc. from its burrow; to bring to light.

**un•eas•y** *a.* anxious; awkward; uncomfortable

**un•em•ploy•ment** *n.* state of being unemployed. **— benefit,** money received by unemployed workers according to conditions laid down by insurance regulations. **— insurance,** insurance against periods of unemployment contributed to by workers, employers, etc.

**U•nes•co** *n.* coined word from initial letters of *U*nited *N*ations *E*ducational, *S*cientific and *C*ultural *O*rganization, established in November, 1945.

**un•ex•pect•ed** *a.* not expected; sudden; without warning.

**un•fail•ing** *a.* not liable to fall; ever loyal; inexhaustible.

**un•fair** *a.* not fair; unjust; prejudiced; contrary to the rules of the game.

**un•feel•ing** *a.* void of feeling; callous; unsympathetic.

**un•fin•ished** *a.* not finished; roughly executed; not published.

**un•fledged** *a.* not yet covered with feathers; immature.

**un•fleshed** *a.* (of sword) not yet used in fighting; not having tasted blood. **unfleshly** *a.* uncorporeal. **unfleshy** *a.* having no flesh.

**un•fold** *v.t.* to open the folds of; to spread out; to disclose; *v.i.* to expand.

**un•fore•seen** *a.* unexpected. **unforeseeable** *a.* not capable of being foreseen; unpredictable.

**un•formed** *a.* not formed; amorphous; immature.

**un•found•ed** *a.* not based on truth; not established.

**un•frock** *v.t.* to deprive of a frock, esp. to deprive of the status of a monk or priest.

**un•fruit•ful** *a.* not productive; not profitable.

**un•furl** *v.t.* and *i.* to open or spread out.

**un•gain•ly** *a.* clumsy; awkward; *adv.* in a clumsy manner.

**un•god•ly** *a.* not religious; sinful.

**un•ground•ed** *a.* having no foundation; false.

**un•gual** *a.* having nails, hooves, or claws. **ungulate** *a.* having hoofs, *n.* one of the hoofed mammals.

**un•guent** *n.* ointment. **-ary** *a.* pert. to unguents. **unguinous** *a.* oily.

**un•hal•lowed** *n.* unholy; not consecrated; wicked. **unhallowing** *n.*

**un•hand** *v.t.* to let go. **-ily** *adv.* awkwardly. **-iness** *n.* **-led** *a.* not handled. **-y** *a.* not handy; inconvenient; lacking skill.

**un•heard** *a.* not heard; not given hearing. **unheard of,** unprecedented.

**un•hes•i•tat•ing** *a.* not hesitating; spontaneous; resolute. **-ly** *adv.* without hesitation.

**un•hinge** *v.t.* to take from the hinges; *(Fig.)* to cause mental instability. **-d** *a.* (of the mind) unstable; distraught.

**un•ho•ly** *a.* not sacred.

**un•horse** *v.t.* to throw from a horse; to cause to fall from a horse.

**un•hy•gi•en•ic** *a.* not hygienic; unsanitary; unhealthy.

**u•ni-**, *prefix* denoting one or single.

**u•ni•ax•i•al** *a.* having a single axis; having one direction along which ray of light can travel without bifurcation. **-ly** *adv.*

**u•ni•cam•er•al** having one legislative chamber.

**u•ni•cel•lu•lar** *a.* having a single cell; monocellular.

**u•ni•corn** *n.* *(Myth.)* horselike animal with a single horn protruding from forehead.

**un•i•de•al** *a.* realistic; prosaic.

**u•ni•form** *a.* having always same form; conforming to one pattern; regular; consistent; not varying, as temperature; *n.* official dress, as a livery, etc. **-ed** *a.* wearing uniform. **-ity** *n.* conformity to pattern or standard. **-ly** *adv.* **-ness** *n.*

**u•ni•fy** *v.t.* to make into one; to make uniform. **unifiable** *a.* capable of being made one. **unification** *n.* act of unifying; state of being made one; welding together of separate parts. **unifier** *n.*

**u•ni•lat•er•al** *a.* one-sided; binding one side only, as in party agreement.

**u•ni•loc•u•lar** *a.* having single chamber or cavity.

**un•im•ag•i•n•ble** *a.* not imaginable; inconceivable.

**un•im•peach•a•ble** *a.* not impeachable; irreproachable; blameless.

**un•in•formed** *a.* having no accurate information; ignorant; not expert.

**un•ion** *n.* act of joining two or more things into one; federation; marriage; harmony; combination of administrative bodies for a common purpose; trade union; **-ed** *a.* joined. **-ist** *n.* one who supports union.

**union flag**

**Union Jack,** national flag of United Kingdom.
**u•nip•a•rous** *a.* producing normally just one at a birth; *(Bot.)* having single stem.
**u•nique** *a.* single in kind; having no like or equal; unusual; different.
**u•ni•sex•u•al** *a.* of one sex only, as a plant; not hermaphrodite or bisexual.
**u•ni•son** *n.* harmony; concord; *(Mus.)* identity of pitch. **in unison** with all voices singing the same note at the same time; sounding together; in agreement.
**u•nit** *n.* single thing or person; group regarded as one; standard of measurement; *(Math.)* the least whole number.
**U•ni•tar•i•an** *n.* one who rejects doctrine of the Trinity and asserts the oneness of God and the teachings of Jesus.
**u•nite** *v.t.* to join; to make into one; to form a whole; to associate; to cause to adhere. *(Math.)* any quantity taken as one. **unitive** *a.* **United Nations,** international organization, formed 1942. **United Nations Organization,** international organization set up after *World War 2* with Security Council as chief executive body.
**u•ni•va•lent** *a. (Chem.)* having a valence of one; *(Bot.)* unpaired.
**u•ni•valve** *a.* having only one valve; *n.* a single-shelled mollusk.
**u•ni•verse** *n.* all created things regarded as a system or whole; the world. **universal** *a.* pert. to universe; embracing all created things; world-wide. **Universalism** *n.* theological doctrine of the ultimate salvation of all mankind. **Universalist** *n.* **universalistic** *a.* **-ity** *n.* **—joint** (in motoring) device whereby one part of machine has perfect freedom of motion in relation to another.
**u•ni•ver•si•ty** *n.* institution for educating students in higher branches of learning, and having authority to confer degrees.
**un•kempt** *a.* dishevelled; rough.
**un•kind** *a.* not kind, considerate, or sympathetic; cruel.
**un•know•a•ble** *a.* not capable of being known; *n.* that which is beyond man's power to understand; the absolute.
**un•leav•ened** *a.* not leavened; made without yeast, as *unleavened bread.*
**un•less** *conj.* except; if not; supposing that; *prep.* except.
**un•let•tered** *a.* illiterate.
**un•like** *a.* not like; dissimilar; *prep.* different from; *adv.* in a different way from.
**un•load** *v.t.* to remove load from; to remove charge from, as gun; to sell out quickly, as stocks, shares, etc. before slump.
**un•looked-for** *a.* unexpected, unforeseen.
**un•loose** *v.t.* to set free.
**un•make** *v.t.* to destroy what has been made; to annul; to ruin, destroy; to depose.
**un•marked** *a.* without a mark.
**un•mean•ing** *a.* without meaning; unintentional; insignificant. **-ly** *adv.* **unmeant** *a.* not intended; accidental.
**un•men•tion•a•ble** *a.* not worthy of mention; not fit to be mentioned. **-ness** *n.* **-s** *n.pl.* facetious synonym for undergarments.
**un•mer•ci•ful** *a.* having or showing no mercy; cruel. **-ly** *adv.*
**un•mind•ed** *a.* not remembered. **unmindful** *a.* forgetful; regardless.
**un•mis•tak•a•ble** *a.* clear; plain; evident.
**un•mit•i•gat•ed** *a.* not softened or lessened; absolute; unmodified.
**un•mor•al** *a.* not concerned with morality or ethics. **-izing** *a.* not given to reflecting on ethical values.
**un•nerve** to deprive of courage, strength; cause to feel weak.
**un•num•bered** *a.* not counted; innumerable.
**un•oc•cu•pied** *a.* not occupied; untenanted; not engaged in work; not under control of troops.
**un•or•gan•ized** *a.* without organic structure; having no system or order; not belonging to a labor union.
**un•pack** *v.t.* to remove from a pack or trunk; to open by removing packing; *v.i.* to empty contents of.
**un•par•al•leled** *a.* having no equal; unprecendented.
**un•par•lia•men•ta•ry** *a.* contrary to parliamentary law or usage.
**un•prec•e•dent•ed** *a.* without precedent; having no earlier example; novel. **-ly** *adv.*
**un•print•a•ble** *a.* not printable; too shocking to be set down in print.
**un•pro•fes•sion•al** *a.* not professional; contrary to professional ethics.
**un•qual•i•fied** *a.* not qualified; not having proper qualifications; not modified; absolute. **unqualifying** *a.*
**un•quote** *v.t.* and *i.* to end a quotation.
**un•read** *a.* (of a book) not read; not having gained knowledge by reading. **-able** *a.* not readable — illegible, uninteresting or unsuitable.
**un•real** *a.* not real; insubstantial; illusive. **-izable** *a.* not realizable. **-izableness** *n.* **-ized** *a.* not realized; unfulfilled. **unreality** *n.* want of reality. **-ly** *adv.* **-ity** *n.*
**un•rea•son** *n.* lack of reason; irrationality. **-able** *a.* immoderate; impulsive; exorbitant (of prices). **-ableness** *n.* **-ably** *adv.* **-ed** *a.* not logical. **ing** *a.* irrational.
**un•re•lat•ed** *a.* not related; having no apparent connection; diverse.
**un•re•mit•ting** *a.* not relaxing; incessant; persistent. **unremitted** *a.* not remitted. **unremittedly, -ly** *adv.*
**un•rest** *n.* want of rest; disquiet; political or social agitation. **-ful** *a.* **-fulness** *n.* **-ing** *a.* not resting. **-ingly** *adv.*
**un•ruf•fled** *a.* not ruffled; placid. **unruffle** *v.i.* to become placid.
**un•ruled** *a.* not ruled; ungoverned; (of paper) blank; unrestrained. **unruliness** *n.* state of being unruly. **unruly** *a.* lawless; disobedient.
**un•say** *v.t.* to retract (what has been said).
**un•scathed** *a.* unharmed; without injury.
**un•scram•ble** *v.t.* to decode a secret message; to straighten out.

**un•scru•pu•lous** *a.* not scrupulous; ruthless; having no moral principles.

**un•sea•son•a•ble** *a.* untimely; out of season.

**un•seat** *v.t.* to throw from a horse; to deprive of official seat.

**un•self•con•scious** *a.* not self-conscious; natural.

**un•set•tle** *v.t.* to move or loosen from a fixed position; to disturb mind; to make restless or discontented. **-d** *a.* not settled; changeable, as weather; unpaid, as bills; not allocated; not inhabited.

**un•shod** *a.* barefoot.

**un•sight•ed** *a.* not sighted; not observed; (of gun) without sights; (of shot) aimed blindly. **unsightable** *a.* invisible. **unsightliness** *n.* ugliness. **unsightly** *a.* ugly; revolting to the sight.

**un•sling** *v.t. (Naut.)* to remove slings from, as from cargo; to take down something which is hanging by sling, as a rifle.

**un•so•lic•i•ted** *a.* not solicited; gratuitous. **unsolicitous** *a.* unconcerned.

**un•so•phis•ti•cat•ed** *a.* not sophisticated; ingenuous; simple.

**un•sound** *a.* imperfect; damaged; decayed; (of the mind) insane; not based on reasoning; fallacious.

**un•speak•a•ble** *a.* beyond utterance or description (in good or bad sense); ineffable.

**un•sport•ing** *a. (Colloq.)* not like sportsman; unfair. **unsportsmanlike** *a.* not in accordance with the rules of fair play.

**un•sprung** *a.* not fitted with springs, as a vehicle, chair, etc.

**un•sta•ble** *a.* unsteady; wavering; not firm; unreliable; *(Chem.)* applied to compounds which readily decompose or change into other compounds.

**un•stop** *v.t.* to open by removing a stopper, as a bottle; to clear away an obstruction; to open organ stops. *pr.p.* **-ping.** *pa.p., pa.t.* **-ped.** *a.* not stopped; having no cork or stopper.

**un•strained** *a.* not strained, as through a filter; *(Fig.)* relaxed; friendly.

**un•stuck** *a.* not glued together.

**un•suc•cess•ful** *a.* not succeeding; unfortunate; incomplete.

**un•sung** *a.* not sung or spoken; not celebrated.

**un•sup•port•ed** *a.* not supported; without backing. **unsupportable** *a.* not supportable; intolerable.

**un•taught** *a. pa.p., pa.t.* of **unteach**; uneducated; ignorant; natural, without teaching.

**un•thank•ful** *a.* ungrateful.

**un•think•ing** *a.* thoughtless; heedless.

**un•til** *prep.* till; to; as far as; as late as; *conj.* up to the time that; to the degree that.

**un•time•ly** *a.* not timely; premature; inopportune.

**un•to** *prep. (Poet.)* to; until.

**un•touch•a•ble** *a.* incapable of being touched; unfit to be touched; out of reach; belonging to non-caste masses of India; *n.* non-caste Indian whose touch or even shadow was regarded as defiling.

**un•to•ward** *a.* unlucky; inconvenient; hard to manage.

**un•trav•eled** *a.* not having traveled; unexplored.

**un•tried** *pa.p., pa.t.* of **try**; not proven, attempted or tested, not tried in court.

**un•true** *a.* not true; false; disloyal; not conforming to a requisite standard. **-ness** *n.* **untruly** *adv.* falsely. **untruth** *n.* **untruthful** *a.* dishonest; lying.

**un•used** *a.* not used; not accustomed. **unusual** *a.* not usual; uncommon; strange. **unusually** *adv.* **unusualness** *n.*

**un•ut•ter•a•ble** *a.* unspeakable beyond utterance. **utterability** *n.*

**un•war•rant•a•ble** *a.* unjustifiable; improper.

**un•washed** *a.* not washed; dirty; not reached by the sea.

**un•well** *a.* ill; ailing.

**un•wept** *a.* not mourned or regretted.

**un•will•ing** *a.* loathe; reluctant.

**un•wind** *v.t.* to wind off; to loose what has been wound; to roll into a ball from a skein, as wool, silk, etc.; *v.i.* to become unwound.

**un•wit•ting** *a.* unawares; not knowing.

**un•wont•ed** *a.* unaccustomed; unusual.

**un•writ•ten** *a.* not written; oral; not expressed in writing. **unwritten Law,** law originating in custom, usage.

**un•yield•ing** *a.* not yielding; stubborn; implacable; not flexible.

**up** *adv. prep.* to or toward a higher place or degree; on high; on one's legs; out of bed; above horizon; in progress; in revolt; as far as; of equal merit or degree; thoroughly well versed in; competent.

**u•pas** *n.* tree of E. Indian islands, yielding sap of deadly poison.

**up•braid** *v.t.* to reprove severely; to chide; *v.i.* to voice a reproach.

**up•bring•ing** *n.* the process of rearing and training a child; education.

**up•coun•try** *adv.* inland; *a.* away from the sea.

**up•grade** *a., adv.* uphill; *n.* incline; *v.t.* to raise to a higher level.

**up•heave** *v.t.* to lift up, as heavy weight. **upheaval** *n.* raising up, as of earth's surface, by volcanic force.

**up•hill** *a.* going up; laborious; difficult; *adv.* towards higher level.

**up•hold** *v.t.* to hold up; to sustain; to approve; to amaintain, as verdict in law court.

**up•hol•ster** *v.t.* to stuff and cover furniture.

**up•keep** *n.* maintenance; money required for maintenance, as of a home.

**up•land** *n.* high land or region. *a.* pert. to or situated in higher elevations.

**up•lift** *v.t.* to lift up; to improve conditions of, morally, socially etc.; to exalt.

**up•per** *a.* higher in place, rank, or dignity; superior; more recent; *n.* the part above. **—hand** *n.* superiority; advantage over another.

**up•right** *a.* standing, pointed straight up; honest; *adv.* in such a position.

**up•rise** *v.i.* to rise up; to revolt. *pa.p.*

**up•roar** *n.* tumult; violent, noisy disturbance.

**up•root** *v.t.* to tear up by the roots.
**up•set** *v.t.* to turn upside down; to knock over; to defeat; to disturb or distress.
**up•shot** *n.* final issue; conclusion.
**up•side** *n.* the upper side. **—down** *adv.* with the upper side underneath; inverted; in disorder.
**up•stage** *a.*, *adv.* of or toward rear of stage; *v.t.* to act on stage so as to minimize another actor.
**up•stairs** *adv.* in the upper story; on the stairs; *a.* pert. to upper story.
**up•stand•ing** *a.* erect; honorable.
**up•start** *n.* one who has suddenly risen to wealth, power, or honor; parvenu.
**up•stream** *adv.* in direction of source (of stream).
**up•stroke** *n.* the upward line in handwriting; upward stroke.
**up•surge** *v.t.* to surge upwards. *n.* welling, as of emotion.
**up•sweep** *n.* a curve upward.
**up•swing** *n.* a trend upward.
**up•thrust** *n.* upward thrust.
**up•to•date** *a.* modern; most recent; extending up to, pert. to, the present time.
**up•town** *a.* pert. to, or in upper part of, town; *adv.*
**up•turn** *v.t.* to turn up. *n.* an upward turn for the better.
**up•ward** *a.* directed towards a higher place; *adv.* upwards.
**u•ra•nite** *n.* an almost transparent ore of uranium.
**u•ra•ni•um** *n.* radio-active metallic element (symbol U), used as an alloy in steel manufacture and in the production of atom bomb.
**u•ra•nog•ra•phy** *n.* descriptive astronomy.
**ur•ban** *a.* pert. to, or living in, city or town. **urbane** *a.* refined; suave; courteous.
**ur•chin** *n.* sea urchin.
**u•re•a** *n.* crystalline solid, the principle organic constituent of urine.
**u•re•ter** *n.* one of two ducts of kidney conveying urine to bladder. **urethra** *n.* duct by which urine passes from bladder.
**urge** *v.t.* to press; to drive; to exhort; to simulate; to solicit earnestly; *v.i.* to press onward; to make allegations, entreaties, etc. *n.* act of urging; incentive; irresistible impulse. **-ncy** *n.* quality of being urgent; compelling necessity; importunity.
**u•rine** *n.* yellowish fluid secreted by kidneys, passed through ureters to bladder from which it is discharged through urethra. **uremia** *n.* toxic condition of the blood caused by insufficient secretion of urine. **urology** *n.* branch of Med. dealing with urinogenital system.
**urn** *n.* vase-shaped vessel of pottery or metal with pedestal, and narrow neck, as used for ashes of dead after cremation.
**ur•sine** *a.* pert. to or resembling a bear.
**use** *v.t.* to make use of; to employ; to consume or expend. **use** *n.* act of using or employing for specific purpose; utility; custom. **usable** *a.* fit for use. **usability** *n.* **usage** *n.* mode of using; treatment; long-established custom. **usance** *n.* usual time allowed for payment of foreign bills of exchange.
**ush•er** *n.* doorkeeper; one who conducts people to seats in church, theater, etc.
**us•que•baugh** *n.* whiskey.
**u•su•al** *a.* customary; ordinary.
**u•su•fruct** *n.* right of using and enjoying produce benefit, or profits of another's property provided that the property remains undamaged.
**u•surp** *v.t.* to take possession of unlawfully or by force.
**u•su•ry** *n.* charging of exorbitant interest on money lent. **usurer** *n.* money lender who charges exorbitant rates of interest.
**u•ten•sil** *n.* vessel of any kind which forms part of domestic, esp. kitchen, equipment.
**u•ter•ine** *a.* pert. to uterus or womb; born of the same mother but by a different father.
**u•til•i•tar•i•an** *n.* one who accepts doctrines of utilitarianism. **-ism** *n.* ethical doctrine, the ultimate aim and criterion of all human actions must be 'the greatest happiness for the greatest number.'
**u•ti•lize** *v.t.* to put to use; to turn to profit.
**ut•most** *a.* situated at farthest point or extremity; to highest degree; *n.* most that can be; greatest possible effort.
**u•to•pi•a** *n.* any ideal state, constitution, system, or way of life.
**u•tri•cle** *n.* *(Bot.)* little bag or bladder, esp. of aquatic plant; *(Anat.)* a sac in inner ear influencing equilibrium.
**ut•ter** *a.* total; unconditional.
**ut•ter** *v.t.* to speak; to disclose; to put into circulation.
**ut•ter•most** *a.* farthest out; utmost; *n.* the highest degree.
**u•vu•la** *n.* fleshy tag suspended from middle of lower border of soft palate.
**ux•o•ri•ous** *a.* foolishly or excessively fond of one's wife.

**va•cant** *a.* empty; void; not occupied; unintelligent. **-ly** *adv.* **vacancy** *n.* emptiness; opening; lack of thought; place or post; unfilled. **vacate** *v.t.* to leave empty or unoccupied; to quit possession of; to make void. **vacation** *n.* act of vacating; intermission of stated employment; recess; holiidays.

**vac•cine** *a.* pert. to, or obtained from cows; *n.* virus of cowpox, used in vaccination; any substance used for inoculation against disease. **vaccinate** *v.t.* to inoculate with cowpox, to ward off smallpox or lessen severity of its attack. **vaccination** *n.* act or practice of vaccinating; the inoculation.

**vac•il•late** *v.i.* to move to and fro; to waver; to be unsteady; to fluctuate in opinion.

**vac•u•um** *n.* space devoid of all matter; space from which air, or other gas, has been almost wholly removed, as by air pump. **—cleaner** *n.* apparatus for removing dust from carpets, etc. by suction. **—tube** used in radio, TV, and electronic equipment; a sealed tube containing metallic electrodes but (almost) no air or gas.

**va•de•me•cum** *n.* small handbook or manual for ready reference.

**vag•a•bond** *a.* moving from place to place without settled habitation; wandering; *n.* wanderer or vagrant, having no settled habitation; idle scamp; rascal.

**va•gar•y** *n.* whimsical or freakish notion; unexpected action; caprice.

**va•gi•na** *n.* *(Anat.)* canal which leads from uterus to external orifice.

**va•grant** *a.* wandering from place to place; moving without certain direction; roving.

**vague** *a.* uncertain; indefinite; indistinct; not clearly expressed.

**vain** *a.* useless; unavailing; fruitless; empty; worthless; conceited. **-ly** *adv.* **-ness** *n.* **vanity** *n.* conceit; something one is conceited about; worthlessness; dressing table.

**vain•glo•ry** *n.* excessive vanity; boastfulness.

**val•ance** *n.* short drapery across the top of a window, bed, etc.

**vale** *n.* valley.

**val•e•dic•tion** *n.* farewell; a bidding farewell. **valedictory** *a.* bidding farewell. **valedictorian** *n.* student in a graduating class with the highest scholastic standing who gives the valedictory at graduation exercises.

**va•lence, va•len•cy** *n.* *(Chem.)* the combining power of an element or atom as compared with a hydrogen atom.

**va•len•tine** *n.* sweetheart chosen on *St, Valentine's* day; card containing profession of love, sent on *St. Valentine's* day, Feb. 14th.

**va•le•ri•an** *n.* flowering herb with strong odor; its root, used as sedative drug.

**val•et** *n.* manservant who cares for clothing, etc. of his employer.

**val•e•tu•di•nar•i•an** *a.* sickly; infirm; solicitous about one's own health.

**val•iant** *a.* brave; heroic; courageous; intrepid.

**val•id** *a.* sound or well-grounded; capable of being justified; *(Law)* legally sound; executed with proper formalities.

**va•lise** *n.* suitcase.

**val•ley** *n.* low ground between hills; river basin.

**val•or** *n.* bravery; prowess in war; courage.

**valse** *n.* waltz, esp. one played as concert piece.

**val•ue** *n.* worth; utility; importance; estimated worth or valuation; precise significance; equivalent. **valuation** *n.* value estimated or set upon a thing; appraisal.

**valve** *n.* device for closing aperture (as in pipe) in order to control flow of fluid, gas, etc.

**vamp** *n.* upper leather of shoe or boot; new patch put on old article.

**vam•pire** *n.* reanimated body of dead person who cannot rest quietly in grave. **— bat** *n.* of several species of bat of S. America which sucks blood of animals.

**van** *n.* covered wagon or motor truck for goods.

**van** *n.* leaders of a movement. **-guard** *n.* detachment of troops who march ahead of army.

**va•na•di•um** *n.* a metallic element (the hardest known) used in manufacture of hard steel.

**van•dal** *n.* one who wantonly damages or destroys property of beauty or value.

**van•dyke** *n.* one of the points forming an edge, as of lace, ribbon, etc.

**vane** *n.* a device on a windmill, spire, etc. to show the direction of the wind; a weathercock; the blade of a propeller, of a windmill, etc.

**va•nil•la** *n.* tropical American plant of orchid family; long pod of plant, used as flavoring.

**van•ish** *v.i.* to pass away; to be lost to view; to disappear; *(Math.)* to become zero.

**van•quish** *v.t.* to conquer in battle; to defeat in any contest; to get the better of.

**van•tage** *n.* better situation or opportunity; advantage; in tennis, same as 'advantage.'

**vap•id** *a.* having lost its life and spirit; flat; insipid; dull.

**va•por** *n.* any light, cloudy substance which impairs clearness of atmosphere, as mist, fog, smoke, etc.; a substance converted into gaseous state; anything unsubstantial. **-ize** *v.t.* to convert into vapor; *v.i.* to pass off in vapor.

**var•i•a•ble** *a.* changeable; capable of being adapted; unsteady or fickle; *n.* that which is subject to change. **variant** *a.* different; diverse; *n.* different form or reading. **variation** *n.* act of varying; alteration; modification; extent to which thing varies; *(Gram.)* change of termination; in magnetism, deviation of magnetic needle from true north.

**var•i•col•ored** *a.* having various colors.

**var•i•cose** *a.* enlarged or dilated, as veins, esp. in legs.

**var•i•e•gate** *v.t.* to diversify by patches of different colors; to streak, spot, dapple, etc.

**va•ri•e•ty** *n.* state of being varied; diversity; collection of different things; many-sidedness; different form of something; subdivision of a species.

**var•i•o•rum** *n.* an edition of a work with notes by various commentators.

**var•i•ous** *a.* different; diverse; manifold; separate; diversified.

**var•let** *n.* *(Arch.)* page or attendant; scoundrel.

**var•nish** *n.* clear, resinous liquid laid on work to give it gloss and protection.

**var•si•ty** *n.* team, usu. athletic, representing a university, school, etc. in competition; *a.* designating such a team.

**var•y** *v.t.* to change; to make different or modify; to diversify; *v.i.* to alter, or be altered; to be different. **varied** *a.* various; diverse; diversified.

**vas** *n.* *(Anat.)* vessel or duct. **-cular** *a.* pert. to vessels or ducts for conveying blood, lymph, sap, etc.

**vase** *n.* vessel for flowers or merely for decoration; large sculptured vessel, used as ornament, in gardens, on gateposts, etc.

**vas•e•line** *n.* brand of petroleum used in ointments, pomades, as lubricant, etc.

**vas•sal** *n.* one who holds land from superior, and vows fealty and homage to him; dependant; retainer. **-age** *n.* state of being a vassal.

**vast** *a.* of great extent; very spacious; very great in numbers or quantity.

**vat** *n.* large vessel, tub, for holding liquids.

**vat•ic** *a.* prophetic; oracular.

**Vat•i•can** *n.* palace and official residence of Pope on Vatican Hill.

**vaude•ville** *n.* stage show with mixed specialty acts; variety show.

**vault** *n.* arched roof; room or passage covered with vault, esp. subterranean; cellar; sky; anything resembling a vault.

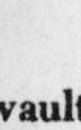

vault

**vault** *v.i.* to spring or jump with hands resting on something; to leap or spring, as horse.

**vaunt** *v.t.* to boast of; to make vain display of; *n.* boast; vainglorious display.

**veal** *n.* flesh of a calf killed for the table.

**vec•tor** *n.* *(Math.)* any quantity requiring direction to be stated as well as magnitude in order to define it properly; disease-carrying insect.

**Ve•da** *n.* most ancient sacred literature of Hindus.

**ve•dette** *n.* mounted sentinel placed in advance of outposts to give notice of danger.

**veer** *v.t.* and *v.i.* to turn; of wind, to change direction, esp. clockwise; *(Naut.)* to change ship's course; *(Fig.)* to change one's opinion or point of view.

**veg•e•ta•ble** *a.* belonging to plants; having nature of plants; *n.* plant, esp. plant used as food. **vegetal** *a.* **vegetarian** *n.* one who abstains from animal flesh and lives on vegetables, eggs, milk, etc. **vegetation** *n.* process of vegetating; vegetable growth; plants in general.

**ve•he•ment** *a.* acting with great force; impetuous; vigorous; passionate.

**ve•hi•cle** *n.* any means of conveyance (esp. on land) as carriage, etc.; liquid medium in which drugs are taken, or pigments applied; means or medium of expression or communication.

**veil** *n.* piece of thin, gauzy material worn by women to hide or protect face; covering; curtain; disguise.

**vein** *n.* each of the vessels or tubes which receive blood from capillaries and return it to heart; layer of mineral intersecting a stratum of rock; streak or wave of different color appearing in wood, marble, etc.

**veld, veldt** *n.* in S. Africa, open grass country.

**vel•lum** *n.* fine parchment made of skin; paper of similar texture.

**ve•loc•i•pede** *n.* a vehicle propelled by the rider, early form of bicycle or tricycle.

**ve•loc•i•ty** *n.* rate of motion; swiftness; speed; distance traversed in unit time in a given direction.

**ve•lours** *n.sing.* and *pl.* fabric resembling velvet or plush.

**vel•vet** *n.* soft material of silk with thick short pile on one side. **-een** *n.* a pile fabric made of cotton, or of silk and cotton mixed.

**ve•nal** *a.* to be obtained for money; prepared to take bribes; mercenary. **venality** *n.* quality of being purchaseable.

**ve•nat•ic, ve•nat•i•cal** *a.* relating to hunting.

**vend** *v.t.* to sell; to dispose of by sale. **-or** *n.* person who sells.

**ven•det•ta** *n.* blood feud, in which it was the duty of the relative of murdered man to avenge his death by killing murderer or relative of murderer.

**ve•neer** *n.* thin layer of valuable wood glued to surface of inferior wood.

**ven•er•ate** *v.t.* to regard with respect and reverence. **venerable** *a.* worthy of veneration; deserving respect by reason of age, character, etc.

**ve•ne•re•al** *a.* pert. to sexual intercourse; arising from sexual intercourse with infected persons.

**ver•er•y** *n.* *(Arch.)* hunting; sports of the chase.

**Ve•ne•tian** *a.* pert. to city of Venice, Italy; *n.* native, inhabitant of Venice. **— blind,** blind made of thin, horizontal slats, so hung as to overlap each other when closed.

**venge•ance** *n.* infliction of pain or loss on another in return for injury or offense. **vengeful** *a.* disposed to revenge; vindictive.

**ve•ni•al** *a.* capable of being forgiven; excusable.

**ven•i•son** *n.* flesh of the deer.

**ven•om** *n.* poison, esp. that secreted by serpents, bees, etc.; spite; malice. **-ous** *a.* poisonous; spiteful; malicious.
**ve•nous, ve•nose** *a.* pert. to veins or the blood in veins.
**vent** *n.* small opening; outlet; flue or funnel of fireplace; touch hole of gun; utterance; emission; voice; escape. **-age, -er** *n.* **-less** *a.* **to give vent to,** to pour forth.
**ven•ti•late** *v.t.* to remove foul air from and supply with fresh air; to expose to discussion; to make public. **ventilation** *n.* replacement of stale air by fresh air; free exposure to air; open discussion.
**ven•tral** *a.* belonging to belly; abdominal; opp. of *dorsal; n.* one of the pair of fins on belly of fish. **ventricle** *n.* *(Anat.* or *Zool.)* small cavity in certain organs, esp. one of chambers of heart.
**ven•tril•o•quism** *n.* art of speaking in such a way that words or sounds seem to come from some source other than speaker.
**ven•ture** *n.* undertaking of chance or danger; business speculation. **-r** *n.* **venturous** *a.* daring; risky.
**ven•ue** *n.* *(Law)* district in which case is tried; scene of an event.
**ven•ule** *n.* small vein.
**Ve•nus** *n.* *(Myth.)* Roman goddess of love and beauty; brightest planet of solar system; beautiful woman.
**ve•ra•cious** *a.* truthful; true. **veracity** *n.* quality of being truthful; truth; correctness.
**ve•ran•da, verandah** *n.* open porch or gallery, along side of house, often with roof.
**verb** *n.* *(Gram.)* part of speech which expresses action or state of being. **-less** *a.* **-al** *a.* pert. to words; expressed in words, esp. spoken words; literal or word for word.
**ver•be•na** *n.* genus of plants of family Verbenaceae, used in ornamental flower beds. Also called **vervain.**
**ver•bi•age** *n.* excess of words; use of many more words than are necessary; wordiness. **verbose** *a.* prolix; tedious because of excess of words.
**ver•dant** *a.* green or fresh; flourishing; ignorant or unsophisticated. **verdure** *n.* greenness or freshness; green vegetation.
**ver•dict** *n.* decision of jury in a trial; decision or judgment.
**ver•di•gris** *n.* green rust on copper, bronze, etc.; basic acetate of copper, used as pigment, etc.
**verge** *n.* border, or edge; brink; a rod of office; mace of bishop, etc.
**verge** *v.i.* to tend; to slope; to border upon.
**ver•i•fy** *v.t.* to prove to be true; to confirm truth of.
**ver•i•ly** *adv.* *(Arch.)* truly; certainly.
**ver•i•ta•ble** *a.* actual; genuine.
**ver•i•ty** *n.* quality of being true; truth; reality.
**ver•juice** *n.* sour juice of crab-apples, unripe grapes, etc.
**ver•mi-** *prefix.* worm. **-an** *a.* worm-like; pert. to worms. **-celli** *n.* paste made from same ingredients as macaroni, and formed into slender worm-like threads.
**ver•mil•ion** *n.* prepared red sulfide of mercury; brilliant red color.
**ver•min** *n.* collectively noxious or troublesome small animals or insects, e.g. squirrels, rats, worms, lice, etc.; low contemptible persons. **-ous** *a.* infested by vermin; caused by vermin; tending to breed vermin.
**ver•mouth, vermuth** *n.* cordial of white wine flavored with wormwood, used as aperitif.
**ver•nac•u•lar** *a.* belonging to country of one's birth.
**ver•nal** *a.* belonging to, or appearing on, spring; youthful.
**ver•ni•er** *n.* short, graduated-scale instrument, for measuring fractional parts.
**Ver•o•nal** *n.* hypnotic or sedative drug.
**ve•ron•i•ca** *n.* genus of plants, including speedwell.
**ver•ru•ca** *n.* **ver•sa•tile** *a.* having aptitude in many subjects; liable to change; capable of moving freely in all directions.
**verse** *n.* metrical line containing certain number of feet; metrical arrangement of language; short division of any literary composition; stanza; piece of poetry.
**ver•sion** *n.* translation; account from particular point of view.
**ver•so** *n.* left-hand page; reverse side of coin or medal.
**ver•sus** *prep.* *(Law, Games)* against; contrasted with.
**ver•te•bra** *n.* one of the small bony segments of spinal column. **vertebrate** *a.* having backbone; *n.* vertebrate animal.
**ver•tex** *n.* highest point; summit; top of head. **vertical** *a.* situated at vertex; directly overhead or in the zenith; upright or perpendicular. **vertiginous** *a.* revolving; giddy; causing giddiness.
**verve** *n.* enthusiasm or vigor; energy; spirit.
**ver•y** *a.* true; real; actual; genuine; now used chiefly to emphasize word following.
**ves•i•cal** *a.* *(Med.)* pert. to bladder. **vesicant** *a.* tending to raise blisters; *n.* blistering application.
**Ves•per** *n.* the evening star, Venus; *(l.c.)* evening; *a.* *(l.c.)* pert. to evening or vespers. **-s** *n.pl.* an evening prayer; evensong; late afternoon or evening service.
**ves•sel** *n.* utensil for holding either liquids or solids; large ship; *(Anat.)* tube or canal; recipient or means of conveying something.
**vest** *n.* short, sleeveless garment worn under a man's suit coat; undergarment. **-ment** *n.* ceremonial or official garment.
**ves•tal** *a.* chaste; pure. *n.* nun; chaste woman.
**ves•ti•bule** *n.* small room or hall between outer and inner doors at entrance to house or building.
**ves•tige** *n.* trace or sign; mark of something that has been; remains; *(Biol.)* trace of some part or organ formerly present in

body.

**ves•try** *n.* room attached to church for holding ecclesiastical vestments, prayer meetings, etc.

**vetch** *n.* plant of bean family used for fodder.

**vet•er•an** *n.* person who has served a long time; *a.* long practiced.

**vet•er•i•nar•y** *a.* pert. to healing diseases and surgical treatment of domestic animals. **veterinarian** *n.* one skilled in medical and surgical treatment of animals.

**ve•to** *n.* power or right of forbidding.

**vex** *v.t.* to make angry; to irritate; to distress.

**vi•a•ble** *a.* born alive and sufficiently developed to be able to live; capable of living or growth.

**vi•a•duct** *n.* high bridge or series of arches for carrying road or railway over valley, etc.

**vi•al** *n.* small glass bottle; phial.

**vi•and** *n.* article of food; chiefly *pl.* food, victuals, provisions.

**vi•at•i•cum** *n.* supplies for a journey; Communion or Eucharist given to dying person.

**vi•brate** *v.t.* to move to and fro; to cause to quiver; to measure by vibrations or oscillations. **vibrant** *a.* vibrating; thrilling or throbbing; powerful.

**vi•bur•num** *n.* any of a group of shrubs of honeysuckle family.

**vic•ar** *n.* a deputy; clergyman. **-age** *n.* residence of vicar.

**vi•car•i•ous** *a.* delegated; substituted; done or suffered for another.

**vice** *n.* depravity or immortal conduct; blemish or defect in character, etc. **vicious** *a.* depraved; wicked; spiteful; not well broken, as horse.

**vice-** *prefix* in words signifying persons, denoting one who acts in place of another, or one who is second in authority.

**vice•ge•rent** *a.* exercising delegated power; *n.* holder of delegated authority.

**vice•roy** *n.* governor of country or province who rules as representative of his king.

**vi•ce ver•sa** *adv.* the order being reversed; the other way round.

**vi•chy•ssoise** *n.* thick cream soup of potatoes.

**vi•cin•i•ty** *n.* neighborhood; nearness or proximity.

**vi•cis•si•tude** *n.* regular change or succession; alteration.

**vic•tim** *n.* living creature sacrificed in performance of religious ceremony; person, or thing, destroyed or sacrificed; person who suffers; dupe or prey.

**vic•tor** *n.* one who defeats enemy in battle; conqueror; winner in contest. **-y** *n.* defeat of enemy in battle, or of antagonist in contest; conquest; triumph.

**vic•to•ri•a** *n.* low four-wheeled carriage with folding top.

**Vic•to•ri•an** *a.* of or characteristic of time of Queen *Victoria;* prudish; easily shocked; (of style) ornate, flowery.

**vic•tro•la** *n.* a phonograph.

**vict•ual** *v.t.* to supply with provisions.

**vid•e•o** *n.* television; *a.* of picture phase of television.

**vie** *v.i.* to strive for superiority; to contend.

**view** *n.* sight; inspection by eye or mind; power of seeing; range of sight; what is seen; pictured representation of scene. **— finder** *n.* device in camera for showing limits of picture. **-point** *n.* attitude or standpoint.

**vig•il** *n.* staying awake at night, either for religious exercises, or to keep watch. **-ante** *n.* a member of an unlawful group which sets itself up to control and punish crime.

**vi•gnette** *n.* orig. running ornament of leaves or tendrils; small designs used as headings or tail pieces in books; any engraving, woodcut, etc. not enclosed within border.

**vig•or** *n.* active strength; capacity for exertion; energy; vitality; forcefulness of style, in writing.

**vi•king** *n.* Scand. sea rover or pirate who ravaged the northwest coast of Europe (8th-10th cent.).

**vile** *a.* mean; worthless; base; depraved. **vilify** *v.t.* to speak ill of; to try to degrade by slander; to defame or traduce.

**vil•la** *n.* country seat; large suburban residence.

**vil•lage** *n.* assemblage of houses, smaller than town and larger than hamlet.

**vil•lain** *n.* wicked, depraved or criminal person.

**vil•la•nelle** *n.* poem of 19 lines on 2 rhymes having 5 three-lined stanzas, followed by one of four lines.

**vil•lein** *n.* serf who was slave to his lord but free with respect to others.

**vil•lus** *n.* one of the small, fine, hair-like processes which cover certain membranes; any of the fine soft hairs covering certain fruits, flowers, or plants.

**vin•ai•grette** *n.* small box, containing sponge saturated with aromatic vinegar salts, etc.; a savory sauce.

**vin•ci•ble** *a.* that may be conquered.

**vin•cu•lum** *n.* bond of union; *(Alg.)* straight, horizontal mark placed over several members of compound quantity to be treated as one quantity.

**vin•di•cate** *v.t.* to justify; to maintain as true and correct.

**vin•dic•tive** *a.* given to revenge; revengeful.

**vine** *n.* woody, climbing plant that produces grapes; any plant which trails or climbs. **vinery** *n.* greenhouse for rearing vines. **-yard** *n.* plantation of grapevines.

**vin•e•gar** *n.* acid liquor obtained from malt, wine, cider, etc. by fermentation, and used as condiment or in pickling.

**vin•tage** *n.* gathering of grapes; season's yield of grapes or wine; wine of particular year. **— wine,** wine made from grapes of particularly good year.

**vi•nyl** *n.* man-made plastic material.

**vi•o•la** *n.* instrument larger than violin, but smaller than violoncello.

**vi•o•la** *n.* *(Bot.)* genus of plants including

violet and pansy.

**vi•o•late** *v.t.* to infringe or break a promise; to treat with disrespect; to outrage or rape.

**vi•o•lence** *n.* force; vehemence; intensity; assault or outrage. **violent** *a.* characterized by physical force.

**vi•o•let** *n.* flower of genus Viola, generally of bluish-purple color.

**vi•o•lin** *n.* modern musical instrument of viol family, with four strings, played with bow.

**vi•o•lon•cel•lo** *n.* bass violin, much larger than violin, held between player's knees.

**vi•per** *n.* a venomous snake; malicious person.

**vi•res•cent** *a.* turning green.

**vir•gin** *n.* girl or woman who has not had sexual intercourse; maiden. **the Virgin,** mother of Christ.

**Vir•gin•ia creep•er** climbing vine whose leaves turn bright red in autumn.

**Vir•go** *n. (Astron.)* the Virgin, one of the signs of Zodiac.

**vir•gule** *n.* short diagonal line (/) between two words indicating either may be used.

**vir•ile** *a.* pert. to man; masculine; strong; having vigor.

**vir•tu** *n.* objects of art or antiquity, collectively.

**vir•tu•al** *a.* being in essence or effect, though not in fact; potential. **-ly** *adv.* to all intents and purposes.

**vir•tue** *n.* moral excellence; merit; good quality; female chastity.

**vir•tu•o•so** *n.* one with great knowledge of fine arts.

**vir•u•lent** *a.* extremely poisonous; bitter in enmity; malignant; deadly. **virus** *n.* organism causing disease; corrupting influence.

**vi•sa** *n.* official endorsement, as on passport, in proof that document has been examined and found correct.

**vis•age** *n.* face; countenance; look or appearance.

**vis•a•vis** *adv.* face to face; *n.* person facing another.

**vis•cer•a** *n.pl.* internal organs of body; intestines; entrails.

**vis•cid** *a.* glutinous; sticky; tenacious. **-ity** *n.* **viscose** *n.* viscid solution of cellulose, drawn into fibers and used in making rayon, cellophane.

**vis•count** *n.* a degree or title of nobility next in rank below earl.

**vise** *n.* device with two jaws that can be brought together with screw, for holding steady anything which needs filing.

**vis•i•ble** *a.* that can be seen; perceptible; in view. **visibly** *adv.* **visibility** *n.* degree of clarity of atmosphere.

**vi•sion** *n.* act or faculty of seeing external objects; sight; thing seen; imaginary sight; phantom; imaginative insight or foresight.

**vis•it** *v.t.* to go, or come, to see; to punish; *v.i.* to be a guest.

**vi•sor** *n.* front part of helmet which can be lifted to show face.

**vis•ta** *n.* view, esp. distant view, as through avenue of trees.

**vis•u•al** *a.* relating to sight; used in seeing; visible.

**vi•tal** *a.* necessary to or containing life; very necessary. **—statistics** data concerning births, deaths, etc.

**vi•ta•min** *n.* any of a group of chemical substances present in various foods and indispensable to health and growth.

**vi•ti•ate** *v.t.* to make faulty or impure; to corrupt; to impair; to invalidate.

**vit•i•cul•ture** *n.* cultivation of grapevines.

**vit•re•ous** *a.* pert. to, or resembling, glass; glassy; derived from glass.

**vit•ri•fy** *v.t.* to convert into glass or glassy substance; *v.i.* to be converted into glass.

**vit•ri•ol** *n.* sulfuric acid. **-ic** *a.* pert. to, resembling, derived from, vitriol; sarcastic, caustic; bitter.

**vi•tu•per•ate** *v.t.* to abuse in words; to revile; to berate.

**vi•va** *interj.* long live.

**vi•va•cious** *a.* lively; sprightly; animated; having great vitality.

**vi•var•i•um** *n.* place for keeping or raising living animals or plants.

**vi•va vo•ce** *adv.* orally; *a.* oral.

**viv•id** *a.* animated; lively; clear; evoking brilliant images.

**viv•i•fy** *v.t.* to endue with life; to animate; to make vivid.

**vi•vip•a•rous** *a.* producing young in living state, instead of eggs.

**viv•i•sec•tion** *n.* dissection of, or experimenting on, living animals for purpose of physiological investigations.

**vix•en** *n.* she-fox; cross bad-tempered woman.

**vi•zier, vi•zir** *n.* high executive officer in Turkey and other Oriental countries.

**vo•ca•ble** *n.* a word esp. with ref. to sound rather than meaning; term.

**vo•cab•u•lar•y** *n.* list of words, usu. arranged in alphabetical order and explained; wordbook; stock of words used by language, class, or individual.

**vo•cal** *a.* pert. to voice or speech; having voice; uttered by voice.

**vo•ca•tion** *n.* divine call to religious career; profession, or occupation.

**voc•a•tive** *a.* relating to, used in, calling or address; *n. (Gram.)* case used in direct address.

**vo•cif•er•ate** *v.t.* to utter noisily or violently; to bawl; *v.i.* to cry with loud voice.

**vod•ka** *n.* in Russia and Poland alcoholic liquor distilled from cereals or potatoes.

**vogue** *n.* prevailing fashion; mode; style; current usage.

**voice** *n.* faculty of uttering audible sounds; sound produced by organs of respiration. **-d** *a.* furnished with voice or with expression.

**void** *a.* empty; being without; not legally binding; *n.* an empty space. **-ance** *n.* act of voiding; state of being void.

**voile** *n.* thin cotton, woolen, or silk material.

**vo•lant** *a.* borne through the air; capable of flying.

**Vo•la•puk** *n.* artificial language invented in 1879.

**vol•a•tile** *a.* evaporating quickly; easily passing into a vapor state; fickle; changeable.
**vol•ca•no** *n.* opening in crust of earth, from which heated solid, liquid, and gaseous matters are ejected.
**vole** *n.* mouse-like rodent living out-of-doors.
**vol•i•tant** *a.* volant; flying; having power of flight.
**vo•li•tion** *n.* act of willing or choosing; exercise of will.
**vol•ley** *n.* discharge of many shots or missiles at one time; missiles so discharged; rapid utterance; *(Tennis)* return of ball before it touches ground. **-ball** *n.* team game played with ball and net.
**volt** *n.* practical unit of electro-motive force, being the pressure which causes current of one ampere to flow through resistance of one ohm. **-age** *n.* electro-motive force reckoned in volts.
**volt, volte** *n.* in fencing, sudden turn or movement to avoid thrust; gait, or track, made by horse going sideways round center; circle so made.
**volte•face** *n.* turning round; sudden reversal of opinion or direction.
**vol•u•ble** *a.* having flowing and rapid utterance; fluent in speech; glib.
**vol•ume** *n.* formerly, roll or scroll; book; part of a work which is bound; bulk or compass; cubical content; power, fullness of voice or musical tone. **voluminal** *a.* pert. to cubical content. **voluminous** *a.* consisting of many volumes; bulky.
**vol•un•tar•y** *a.* proceeding from choice or free will; unconstrained; spontaneous; subject to the will.
**vol•un•teer** *n.* one who enters service, esp. military, of his own free will; *a.* serving as a volunteer; composed.
**vo•lup•tu•ar•y** *n.* one addicted to luxurious living or sensual gratification; sensualist; *a.* concerned with, or promoting, sensual pleasure.
**vo•lute** *n.* *(Archit.)* spiral scroll used in Ionic, Corinthian, and Composite capitals; *(Zool.)* tropical spiral shell; *a.* rolled up spiraled.

volute

**vom•it** *v.t.* to eject from stomach by mouth; to spew or disgorge; *v.i.* to eject contents of stomach by mouth.
**voo•doo** *n.* body of primitive rites and practices; one who practices such rites; evil spirit; *a.* belonging to, or connected with, system of voodoo.
**vo•ra•cious** *a.* greedy in eating; eager to devour; ravenous.
**vor•tex** *n.* whirling motion of any fluid, forming depression in center of circle; whirlpool; whirling mass of air, fire, etc. which draws with irresistable power.
**vo•ta•ry** *a.* consecrated by vow or promise; devoted to any service, study, etc. **votaress** *n. (fem.).*
**vote** *n.* formal expression of wish, choice, or opinion, of individual, or a body of persons; expression of will by a majority; right to vote; suffrage; what is given or allowed by vote.
**vo•tive** *a.* offered or consecrated by vow; given in fulfillment of vow.
**vouch** *v.t.* to warrant; to attest; to affirm; *v.i.* to bear witness.
**vouch•safe** *v.t.* to condescend to grant or do something; *v.i.* to deign.
**vow** *n.* solemn promise made esp. to deity; *v.t.* to consecrate or dedicate by solemn promise.
**vow•el** *n.* any vocal sound (such as *a, e, i, o, u*) produced with least possible friction or hindrance from any organ of speech.
**voy•age** *n.* journey esp. by sea; *v.i.* to sail or traverse by water.
**Vul•can** *n.* *(Myth.)* Roman god of fire and of metal working. **vulcanize** *v.t.* to treat rubber with sulfur at high temperature to increase durability and elasticity.
**vul•gar** *a.* of common people; in common use; coarse or offensive; rude; boorish. **-ness, vulgarity** *n.* commonness; lack of refinement in manners; coarseness of ideas or language.
**vul•ner•a•ble** *a.* capable of being wounded; offering open to criticism; assailable; in contract bridge, denoting side which has won first game in rubber and is subject to increased honors and penalties.
**vul•pine** *a.* pert. to fox; cunning; crafty.
**vul•ture** *n.* large, rapacious bird of prey; rapacious person.

vulture

**vul•va** *n.* fissure in external organ of generation in female.

**wad** *n.* little tuft or bundle; soft mass of loose, fibrous substance, for stuffing, etc.; *v.t.* to form into wad; to line with wadding; to pad; *pr.p.* **-ding.** *pa.t.* and *pa.p.* **-ded. -ding** *n.* soft material for wads.

**wad•dle** *v.i.* to walk like duck, with short swaying steps; *n.* slow, rocking gait.

**wade** *v.i.* to walk through something which hampers movement, as water, mud, etc.; *v.t.* to cross (stream) by wading; *n.* a wading.

**wa•fer** *n.* very thin biscuit; *v.t.* to seal or close with wafer. **-y** *a.*

**waf•fle** *n.* a thin cake of batter with criss-cross pattern. **— iron** *n.* hinged metal utensil for baking both sides of waffle at once.

**waft** *v.t.* to impel lightly through water or air; *v.i.* to float gently; *n.* breath or slight current of air or odor; puff. **-ure** *n.*

**wag** *v.t.* to cause to move to and fro; *v.i.* to shake; to swing; to vibrate. *pr.p.* **-ging.** *pa.p., pa.t.* **-ged** *n.* swinging motion, to and fro.

**wage** *v.t.* to carry on; *n.* payment paid for labor or work done.

**wa•ger** *n.* something staked on issue of future event or of some disputed point; bet; stake; *v.t.* to bet; to lay wager. **-er** *n.*

**wag•gle** *v.t.* and *v.i.* to move one way and the other; to wag.

**wag•on** *n.* four-wheeled vehicle or truck, for carrying heavy freight. **-less** *a.* **-load** *n.*

**waif** *n.* homeless person, esp. neglected child; stray article or animal.

**wail** *v.t.* and *v.i.* to lament (over); to express sorrow audibly; to weep; *n.* loud weeping; great mourning; doleful cry. **-er** *n.* **-ing** *n.* **-ingly** *adv.*

**waist** *n.* part of human body immediately below ribs and above hips. **-band** *n.* part of dress or trousers which fits round waist.

**wait** *v.t.* to stay for; *v.i.* to stop until arrival of some person or event; to be temporarily postponed; to be expecting; to serve at table; to attend (on); *n.* act, period of waiting. **-er** *n.* one who waits; a man who waits on table. **-ing** *n.* and *a.* **-ing-list** *n.* list of names of those wishing some article, etc. in short supply. **-ing room** *n.* room set aside for use of people waiting in public place, office, etc. **-ress** *n.* female waiter.

**waive** *v.t.* to give up claim to; to forgo; to relinquish a right, etc. **-r** *n.* relinquishment, or statement of such.

**wake** *v.t.* to rouse from sleep; to waken; to excite; to kindle; to provoke; *v.i.* to awaken. *pa.t.* and *pa.p.* **-d** or **woke.** *pr.p.* **waking.** *n.* vigil; act of sitting up overnight with corpse. **-ful** *a.* indisposed to sleep; sleepless. **-fully** *adv.* **-n** *v.t., i.* **-ner** *n.* **waking** *a.* as in *waking hours,* period when one is not asleep.

**wale** *n.* mark left on flesh by rod or whip; ridge in the weave of a fabric; *v.t.* to mark with wales. **waling** *n,* wale, piece of heavy timber fastened horizontally to tie together boards supporting sides of trench or vertical pieces of jetty.

**walk** *v.t.* to pass through, along, upon; to lead, drive, or ride (horse) at a slow pace; *v.i.* to go on foot; *n.* act of walking; characteristic gait or style of walking; path for pedestrians; avenue set with trees; stroll; distance walked over; sphere of life; conduct. **-er** *n.* **-ie-talkie** *n.* portable wireless combined transmitting and receiving set. **-out** *n.* a strike.

**wall** *n.* structure of brick, stone, etc. serving as fence, side of building, etc.; *pl.* fortifications; works for defense; *v.t.* to enclose with wall; to block up with wall. **—board** *n.* lining of various materials for applying to or making walls. **-ed** *a.* provided with walls; fortified. **-flower** *n.* garden plant, with sweet-scented flowers; lady left sitting at dance for lack of partners. **-less** *a.* **-like** *a.*

**wal•la•by** *n.* a small kangaroo.

**wal•la•roo** *n.* large kangaroo.

**wal•let** *n.* folding pocketbook for paper money identification, cards, etc.

**wal•lop** *v.t.* to beat soundly; to strike hard; *n.* stroke or blow. **-ing** *n.* a thrashing; *a.* tremendous; big.

**wal•nut** *n.* large tree producing rich, dark-brown wood of fine texture; fruit of tree, large nut with crinkled shell.

**wal•rus** *n.* mammal closely related to seal but with down-turned tusks.

**walrus**

**waltz** *n.* ballroom dance in three-four time; music for this dance; *v.i.* to dance a waltz. **-er** *n.* **-ing** *n.*

**wan** *a.* having a sickly hue; pale; pallid; ashy; gloomy. **-ly** *adv.* **-ness** *n.*

**wand** *n.* long, slender, straight rod.

**wan•der** *v.i.* to ramble; to go astray; to depart from subject. **-er** *n.* **-ing** *a.* rambling; unsettled; *n.* journeying here and there, usually in *pl.*

**wane** *v.i.* to decrease; to fail; *n.* decrease of illuminated part of moon; decline; diminution.

**wan•gle** *v.t.* to obtain by deception or trickery; *v.i.* to manage with difficulty. **-r** *n.* trickery; artifice.

**want** *n.* scarcity of what is needed; poverty; *v.t.* to be without; lack; *v.t.* to be without; to lack; to need; to crave; *v.i.* to be lacking; to have need. **-ed** *a.* desired; required; sought after; searched for (by police). **-er** *n.* **-less** *a.* **-ing** *a.* lacking; deficient. *prep.* without; minus. **-s** *n.pl.* requirements.

**wan•ton** *a.* dissolute; unrestrained; recklessly arrogant, malicious; *n.; v.i.* **-ly** *adv.* **-ness** *n.*

**war** *n.* armed conflict between two (groups of) states; state of opposition or hostility; *v.i.* to make war; to carry on hostilities; to contend. *pr.p.* **-ring.** *pa.t.* and *pa.p.* **-red.** **-fare** *n.* hostilities. **-ship** *n.* vessel equipped for war. Also **-man-of-war. civil war,** war between citizens of same country. **cold war,** state of international hostility short of actual warfare.

**ward** *v.t.* to repel; to turn aside; *n.* division of city; room for patients in hospital; guardianship; minor legally in the care of a guardian; divisions of a prison; custody. **-en** *n.* civil defense officer; keeper; supervisor of prison. **-robe** *n.* cupboard for holding clothes; wearing apparel in general. **-ship** *n.* office of guardian; state of being under guardian.

**ware** *n.* article of merchandise; pottery; usually in combinations as, *earthenware, hardware,* etc.; *pl.* goods for sale; commodities; merchandise. **-house** *n.* storehouse for goods; *v.t.* to store in warehouse.

**warm** *a.* having heat in moderate degree; not cold; hearty; lively; of colors, suggesting heat, as red, orange, yellow; excited; passionate; affectionate; *v.t.* to communicate moderate degree of heat to; to excite interest or zeal in; *v.i.* to become moderately heated; to become animated. **—blooded** *a.* of animals with fairly high and constant body-temperature; passionate; generous. **—hearted** *a.* affectionate; kindly disposed; sympathetic. **-ly** *adv.* **-ness, -th** *n.* slight heat; cordiality; heartiness; enthusiasm.

**warn** *v.t.* to notify by authority; to caution; to admonish; to put on guard. **-ing** *n.* advance notice of anything; admonition; caution; *a.* cautioning.

**warp** *v.t.* to twist permanently out of shape; to bend; to pervert; *v.i.* to turn, twist, or be twisted; *n.* distortion of wood due to unequal shrinkage in drying. **-ed** *a.* twisted by unequal shrinkage; perverted; depraved. **-er** *n.* one who, or that which, warps. **-ing** *n.*

**war•rant** *v.t.* to give justification for; to authorize or sanction with assurance of safety; to guarantee to be as represented; to assure; to indemnify against loss; *n.* instrument which warrants or justifies act otherwise not permissible or legal; instrument giving power to arrest offender; authorization; guarantee. **-able** *a.* **-ably** *adv.* **-ableness** *n.* **-ed** *a.* guaranteed. **-er, -or** *n.* **-y** *n.* security; guarantee.

**war•ren** *n.* enclosure for breeding rabbits and other game.

**war•ri•or** *n.* soldier.

**wart** *n.* small hard conical excrescence on skin; hard, glandular protuberance on plants and trees.

**war•y** *a.* cautious; heedful; careful; prudent. **warily** *adv.* **wariness** *n.*

**was** *pa.t.* of verb **to be.**

**wash** *v.t.* to free from dirt with water and soap; *v.i.* to perform act of ablution; to cleanse clothes in water; to be washable; *n.* clothes, etc. washed at one time; liquid applied to surface as lotion or coat of paint. **-able** *a.* **-er** *n.* one who washes; flat ring of metal, rubber, etc. to make a tight joint, distribute pressure from nut or head of bolt, prevent leakage, etc. **-ing** *n.* act of one who washes; ablution; clothes washed at one time; *a.* used in, or intended for, washing. **-ed out,** exhausted; faded.

**wasp** *n.* stinging insect like bee with longer body and narrow waist.

**waste** *v.t.* to expend uselessly; to use extravagantly; to squander; to neglect; to lay waste; to spoil; *v.i.* to wear away by degrees; to become worn and emaciated; to decrease; to wither; *a.* lying unused; of no worth; desolate; *n.* act of wasting; that which is wasted; refuse; uncultivated country; loss; squandering. **wastage** *n.* loss by use, leakage, or decay. **-basket** *n.* container for waste materials. **-ful** *a.* full of waste; destructive; prodigal; extravagant. **-fully** *adv.* **-fulness** *n.* **-land** *n.* barrenland. **-r** *n.*

**watch** *n.* state of being on the look-out; close observation; vigil; one who watches; watchman; sentry; portable timekeeper for pocket, wrist, etc.; to keep in view; to guard; to observe closely; *v.i.* to be vigilant; to be on watch; to keep guard; to be wakeful; to look out (for); to wait (for). **-dog** *n.* guard dog; any watchful guardian. **-er** *n.* **-ful** *a.* vigilant; attentive; cautious. **-fully** *adv.* **-fulness** *n.* **-maker, -making** *n.* **—man** *n.* man who guards property. **—word** *n.* password; a slogan; rallying cry.

**wa•ter** *n.* transparent, tasteless liquid, substance of rain, rivers, etc.; body of water; *v.t.* to wet or soak with water; to cause animal to drink; to irrigate; *v.i.* to shed water; to take in or obtain water. **—color** *n.* artist's color ground up with water; painting in this medium. **-ed** *a.* diluted with water. **-fall** *n.* fall or perpendicular descent of water of river; cascade; cataract. **-fowl** *n.* any aquatic bird with webbed feet and coat of closely packed feathers or down. **— gauge** *n.* instrument for measuring height of water in boiler, etc. **-less** *a.* **— level** *n.* level formed by surface of still water; leveling instrument in which water is employed. **-lily** *n.* aquatic plant with fragrant flowers and large floating leaves. **—line** *n.* line on hull of ship to which water reaches. **—main** *n.* large pipe running under streets, for conveying water. **—mark** *n.* in paper making, faint translucent design stamped in substance of sheet of paper and serving as trademark. **-melon** *n.* large fruit with smooth, dark-green rind and red pulp. **— power** *n.* power of water used as prime mover. **-proof** *a.* impervious to water; *v.t.* to make impervious to water. **-shed** *n.* area drained by a river. **-spout** *n.* drain carrying rain water down side of building. **-tight** *a.* so fitted as to prevent water escaping or entering. **— tower** *n.* raised tank for water storage. **-way** *n.* fairway for vessels; navigable channel. **-works** *n.pl.* reservoirs, etc. for the purification, supply and distribution of water; **-y** *a.* resembling water; thin or transparent, as a liquid. **above water,**

financially sound; solvent. **mineral water,** water impregnated with mineral matter and possessing specific medicinal properties; artificially aerated water.

**watt** *n.* unit of power represented by current of one ampere produced by electromotive force of one volt.

**wat•tle** *n.* fleshy excrescence, usually red, under throat of cock or turkey. **-d** *a.*

**wave** *n.* waving movement or gesture of hand; advancing ridge or swell on surface of liquid; wavelike style of hair dressing; passage of sound or light through space; *pl.* the sea; *v.t.* to raise into inequalities of surface; to move to and fro; to give the shape of waves; to brandish; to beckon; *v.i.* to wave one way and the other; to flap; to undulate; to signal. **—band** *n.* range of wave lengths allotted for broadcasting, morse signals, etc. **-d** *a.* undulating. **wavily** *adv.* **— length** *n.* distance between maximum positive points of two successive waves; velocity of wave divided by frequency of oscillations. **—like** *a.* **waviness** *n.* **waving** *a.* moving to and fro. **wavy** *a.*

**wa•ver** *v.i.* to move to and fro; to fluctuate; to vacillate; to tremble; to totter. **-er** *n.* **-ing** *n.* and *a.* **-ingly** *adv.*

**wax** *n.* a fatty acid ester of a monohydric alcohol; an amorphous, yellowish, sticky substance derived from animal and vegetable substances; beeswax; sealing wax; *v.t.* to smear, rub, or polish with wax. **-en** *a.* made of or resembling wax; plastic; impressionable. **-er** *n.* **-iness** *n.* **-ing** *n.* **—paper** *n.* paper coated with wax, used for airtight packing. **-y** *a.* made of or like wax.

**way** *n.* street; passage; path; lane; route; progress; distance; method; mode; custom; usage; habit; means; plan; desire; momentum. **-ward** *a.* liking one's way; perverse; refractory. **-wardly** *adv.* **-wardness** *n.* **ways and means,** methods; resources. **by the way,** as we proceed; incidentally. **right-of-way** *n.* right to use path through private property; such a path.

**we** *pron.* plural form of **I;** another person, or others, and I.

**weak** *a.* feeble; frail; delicate; fragile; watery; diluted; inconclusive. **-en** *v.t.* to make weak; *v.i.* to become weak or less resolute. **-liness** *n.* **-ling** *n.* feeble person, physically or mentally. **-ly** *adv.* **-ness** *n.*

**weal** *n.* streak left on flesh by blow of stick or whip; wale.

**wealth** *n.* riches; affluence; opulence; abundance. **-iness** *n.* **-y** *a.*

**wean** *v.t.* to discontinue breast-feeding of infant gradually. **-ling** *n.* newly-weaned infant.

**weap•on** *n.* instrument to fight with.

**wear** *v.t.* to carry clothes, decorations and the like, upon the person; to consume or impair by use; to deteriorate by rubbing; *v.i.* to last or hold out; to be impaired gradually by use or exposure. *pa.t.* **wore.** *pa.p.* **worn.** *n.* act of wearing; impairment from use. **-able** *a.* **-er** *n.* **-ing** *a.* intended for wearing; exhausting; exhausting to mind and body. **wear and tear,** loss or deterioration due to usage. **to wear off,** to disappear slowly.

**wear•y** *a.* fatigued; tired; bored; exhausted; tiresome; *v.t.* to exhaust one's strength or patience; to make weary; *v.i.* to become weary; to become dissatisfied with. **wearily** *adv.* **weariless** *a.* tireless. **weariness** *n.* **wearisome** *a.* tedious; causing annoyance or fatigue. **wearisomely** *adv.* **wearisomeness** *n.*

**wea•sel** *n.* small, long-bodied, short-legged bloodthirsty carnivore.

weasel

**weath•er** *n.* combination of all atmospheric phenomena existing at one time in any particular place; *v.t.* to expose to the air; to season by exposure to air; to endure; *v.i.* to decompose or disintegrate, owing to atmospheric conditions. **Weather Bureau** *n.* meterorological office directed by U.S. Department of Commerce. **— forecast** *n.* prediction of probable future weather conditions based on scientific data collected by meteorological office. **-ing** *n.* process of decomposing of rocks, wood, etc. exposed to elements. **—report,** daily report of meteorological conditions. **-vane** *n.* weather cock.

**weave** *v.t.* to interlace threads, etc.; to interlace threads, etc.; to construct, to fabricate, as a tale; *v.i.* to practice weaving; to move from side to side. *pa.t.* **wove.** *pa.p.* **woven.** *n.* style of weaving. **-r** *n.*

**web** *n.* that which is woven; membrane which unities toes of waterfowl; network spun by spider. **-bing** *n.* strong, hemp fabric woven in narrow strips, used for chairs, etc. **—footed** *a.*

**wed** *v.t.* to marry; *v.i.* to contract matrimony. *pr.p.* **-ding.** *pa.t.* and *pa.p.* **-ded** or **wed. -ded** *a.* married; wholly devoted (to art, etc.) **-ding** *n.* nuptial ceremony; nuptials; marriage.

**wedge** *n.* piece of wood or metal, tapering to thin edge at fore end, used for splitting, lifting heavy weights, or rendering rigid two parts of structure; anything shaped like wedge; *v.t.* to jam; to compress; to force (in); to squeeze (in); to fasten with wedge. **-d** *a.* cuneiform or wedge-shaped; jammed tight.

**Wedg•wood** *n.* and *a.* fine Eng. pottery.

**Wednes•day** *n.* fourth day of week.

**wee** *n.* small; tiny.

**weed** *n.* plant growing where it is not desired; *v.t.* to free from weeds. **-y** *a.* full of weeds.

**week** *n.* seven successive days, usually Sunday to Sunday. **—day** *n.* any day of week except Sunday. **—end** *n.* Friday or

Saturday to Monday. **-ly** *a.* pert. to a week; happening once a week; *n.* publication issued weekly; *adv.* once a week.

**weep** *v.i.* to grieve for by shedding tears; to cry; to drip; *v.t.* to lament; to bewail. *pa.t.* and *pa.p.* **wept.** **-er** *n.* one who weeps. **-ing** *a.* of trees whose branches droop, as *weeping willow.* **-y** *a.*

**wee•vil** *n.* common name given to thousands of different kinds of small beetles, all distinguished by heads lengthened out to resemble beaks—larvae attack plants and stored grain.

**weigh** *v.t.* to find weight of; to deliberate or consider carefully; *v.i.* to have weight; to be considered as important. **-er** *n.* **-t** *n.* gravity as property of bodies; heavy mass; object of known mass for weighing; importance; power and influence; *v.t.* to make more heavy. **-tily** *adv.* **-tiness** *n.* **-ty** *a.* having great weight; important; momentous; forcible. **dead weight** *n.* heavy burden.

**weird** *a.* unearthly; uncanny; odd. **-ly** *adv.* **-ness** *n.*

**wel•come** *a.* received gladly; free to enjoy or use; *n.* kind or hearty reception; *v.t.* to greet with kindness and pleasure.

**weld** *v.t.* to join pieces of heated, plastic metal by fusion without soldering materials, etc. **-er** *n.*

**wel•fare** *n.* well-doing or well-being; prosperity.

**well** *n.* shaft or tube sunk deep in ground to obtain water, oil, etc.; spring; fountain; *v.i.* to issue forth in volume, as water.

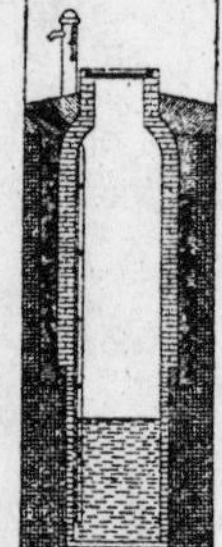

well

**well** *a. comp.* **better.** *superl.* **best.** in good health; fortunate; comfortable; satisfactory; *adv.* agreeably; favorably; skillfully; intimately; satisfactorily; soundly; *interj.* exclamation of surprise, interrogation, resignation, etc. **—being** *n.* welfare. **—meaning** *a.* having good intentions. **—spoken** *a.* cultured in speech; favorably commented on; speaking easily, fluently, graciously.

**Welsh, Welch** *a.* relating to Wales or its inhabitants; *n.* language or people of Wales. **—man, —woman** *n.* **— rabbit,** or **rarebit,** savory dish consisting of melted cheese on toast.

**welt** *n.* cord around border or seamline of upholstery, etc.; a flat, overlapping seam; ridge on flesh from whiplash, etc. *v.t.* to furnish with welt; beat soundly. **-ed** *a.* **-ing** *n.*

**wel•ter•weight** *n.* in boxing or wrestling, class of contestants weighing between 135 lb. and 147 lb.; boxer or wrestler of this weight.

**wench** *n.* girl; maid.

**went** *pa.t.* of **go.**

**wept** *pa.t.* and *pa.p.* of **weep.**

**were** *pa.t.* plural, and subjunctive singular and plural, of **be.**

**were•wolf, wer•wolf** *n.* human being who, at will, could take form of wolf while retaining human intelligence.

**Wes•ley•an** *n.* pert. to Wesley or Wesleyanism. **-ism** *n.* Wesleyan Methodism, i.e. religion practiced in methodical manner.

**west** *n.* point in heavens where sun sets; one of four cardinal points of compass; region of country lying to the west; *a.* situated in, facing, coming from the west; *adv.* to the west. **-erly** *a.* situated in west; of wind, blowing from west; *adv.* in west direction; *n.* wind blowing from west. **-ern** *a.* situated in west; coming from west; *n.* inhabitant of western country or district; film featuring cowboys in western states of U.S. **-erner** *n.* native of the west.

**wet** *a. comp.* **-ter.** *superl.* **-test.** containing water; full of moisture; humid; damp; rainy; *n.* water; moisture; rain; *v.t.* to make wet; to moisten; *pr.p.* **-ting.** *pa.p.* **wet** or **ted.** **-ness** *n.* **-tish** *a.* humid; damp.

**whack** *v.t.* to hit, esp. with stick; to beat; *v.i.* to strike with smart blow; *n.* blow. **-y** *a.*

**whale** *n.* large fishlike mammal; *v.i.* to hunt for whales. **-bone** *n.* baleen, an elastic, flexible, horny product of jaws of baleen whale. **— oil** *n.* lubricating oil extracted from blubber of sperm whale.

whale

**wharf** *n.* structure on bank of navigable waters at which vessels can be loaded or unloaded. *pl.* **-s, wharves.** *v.t.* to moor at, or place on, wharf. **-age** *n.* charge for use of wharf; wharf accomodation.

**what** *pron.* interrogative pronoun; relative pronoun, meaning that which; *a.* which; which kind; *conj.* that; *interj.* denoting surprise, anger, confusion, etc.; *adv.* to what degree? **-ever** *pron.* anything that; all that. **-soever** *pron.* whatever.

**what•not** *n.* piece of furniture, having shelves for books, bric-a-brac, etc.; indescribable thing.

**wheat** *n.* edible portion of annual cereal grass providing most important bread food of the world.

**whee•dle** *v.t.* to cajole; to coax.

**wheel** *n.* solid disk or circular frame with spokes; steering wheel; *v.t.* to convey on wheels; to furnish with wheels; *v.i.* to turn on, or as on, axis; to change direction by pivoting about an end unit, as in marching; to roll forward; to revolve. **-barrow** *n.* conveyance with a single wheel and two shafts for pushing.

**wheeze** *v.i.* to breathe audibly and with difficulty; *n.* the sound or act of wheezing. **-r** *n.* **wheezingly** *adv.* **wheezy** *a.* **wheezily** *adv.* **wheeziness** *n.*

**whelm** *v.t.* to cover completely; to submerge; to overpower.

**when** *adv.* and *conj.* at what time? at the time that; whereas; at which time. **-ever** *adv.* and *conj.* at whatever time. **-soever** *adv.* and *conj.* whenever.

**where** *adv.* and *conj.* at what place?; in what circumstances?; at or to the place in which. **-abouts** *adv.* and *conj.* about where; near what or which place? *n.* place where one is. **-as** *conj.* considering that; when in fact. **-by** *adv.* and *conj.* by which; how. **-in** *adv.* in which; in which, or what, respect, etc.; in what. **-of** *adv.* of which; of what. **-on** *adv.* on which; on what. **-to** *adv.* to which; to what; to what end. **-upon** *adv.* upon which; in consequence of which. **-'er, -ver** *adv.* at whatever place. **-with** *adv.* with what. **the wherewithal,** the money; the means.

**whet** *v.t.* to sharpen by rubbing; to make sharp, keen, or eager; *n.* act of sharpening. *pr.p.* **-ting.** *pa.t.* and *pa.p.* **-ted.** **-stone** *n.* fine-grained stone used for sharpening cutlery and tools; sharpener. **-ter** *n.*

**wheth•er** *conj.* used to introduce the first of two or more alternative clauses, the other(s) being connected by *or.*

**whew** *n.* or *interj.* whistling sound, expressing astonishment, dismay, or pain.

**which** *pron.* as interrogative, signifying *who,* or *what one,* of a number; as relative, used of things; a thing or fact that; whatever. **-ever, -soever** *pron., a.* whether one or the other.

**whiff** *n.* puff of air, smoke, etc.; an odor; *v.t.* to throw out in whiffs; to blow; *v.i.* to emit whiffs, as of smoke.

**Whig** *n.* supporter of American Revolution; member of early political party (1834-1955).

**while** *n.* space of time; *conj.* during time when; as long as; whereas; *adv.* during which. **to while away,** to pass time.

**whim** *n.* passing fancy; caprice; fad. **-sical** *a.* capricious; freakish; fanciful; quaint. **-sicality** *n.* fanciful idea; whim. **-sically** *adv.* **-sicalness** *n.* **-sy** *n.* caprice; fancy.

**whim•per** *v.i.* and *v.t.* to cry, or utter, with low, fretful, broken voice; *n.* low peevish, or plaintive cry. **-er** *n.* **-ing** *n.*

**whine** *n.* drawing, peevish wail; unmanly complaint; *v.i.* to utter peevish cry; to complain in childish way. *n.* **whining** *n.* **whiningly** *adv.* **whiny** *a.*

**whin•ny** *v.i.* to neigh; *n.* sound made by horse.

**whip** *v.t.* to strike with lash; to flog; to overcast edges of seam, etc.; to beat into froth, as cream or eggs; to defeat decisively; *v.i.* to start suddenly. *pr.p.* **-ping.** *pa.t.* and *pa.p.* **-ped.** *n.* lash attached to handle for urging on or correction; legislative manager appointed to ensure fullest possible attendance of members of his party at important debates, etc.**-ping** *n.* flogging.

**whip•poor•will** *n.* nocturnal American bird.

**whir** *v.i.* to dart, fly, or revolve with buzzing or whizzing noise. *pr.p.* **-ring.** *pa.t.* and *pa.p.* **-red.** *n.* buzzing or whizzing sound.

**whirl** *v.t.* to turn round rapidly; to cause to rotate; *v.i.* to rotate rapidly; to spin; to gyrate; *n.* rapid rotation; anything which whirls; bewilderment. **-ing** *n.* and *a.* **-pool** *n.* vortex or circular eddy of water.

**whish** *v.i.* to move with soft, rustling sound; *n.* such a sound.

**whisk** *n.* rapid, sweeping motion; small bunch of feathers, straw, etc. used for brush; instrument for beating eggs, etc.; *v.t.* to sweep with light, rapid motion or with a whisk. **-er** *n.* thing that whisks; *pl.* hair on a man's face; long stiff hairs at side of mouth of cat or other animal. **-ered** *a.*

**whis•key** *n.* distilled alcoholic liquor made from various grains. Also **whisky.**

**whis•per** *v.t.* to utter in low, sibilant tone; to suggest secretly or furtively; *v.i.* to speak in whispers, under breath; to rustle; *n.* low, soft, sibilant remark. **-er** *n.* **-ing** *n.* **-ingly** *adv.*

**whis•tle** *n.* sound made by forcing breath through rounded and nearly closed lips; instrument or device for making a similar sound; form of horn; *v.i.* to make such sound; *v.i.* and *v.t.* to render tune by whistling; to signal, by whistling. **-r** *n.* one who whistles. **whistling** *n.*

**white** *a.* of the color of snow; light in color; pure; clean; bright; spotless; *n.* color of pure snow; albuminous part of an egg; white part of eyeball surrounding iris. **-cap** *n.* wave with crest of white foam. **—collar** *a.* of clerical or professional workers. **— elephant,** sacred elephant of Siam; gift entailing bother and expense; object valueless to the owners. **— fish** *n.* non-oily food fish. **— flag,** sign of truce or surrender. **— gold,** alloyed gold with platinum appearance. **— lie,** harmless fib. **-n** *v.t.* and *v.i.* to make or turn white. **-ner** *n.* **-ening** *n.* making white. **-ness** *n.* **-wash** *n.* mixture of whiting, water, and size, for coating walls; *v.t.* to cover with whitewash; to clear reputation of; to conceal errors, faults, etc. **whitish** *a.* somewhat white.

**whith•er** *adv.* to which, or what, place?

**whit•ing** *n.* edible seafish; pulverized chalk, for making putty and whitewash.

**whit•tle** *v.t.* and *v.i.* to cut off thin slices or shavings with knife; to pare away.

**whiz, whizz** *v.i.* to make hissing sound, as arrow flying through air. *pr.p.* **-zing.** *pa.t.* and *pa.p.* **-zed.** *n.* violent hissing and humming sound; person or thing regarded as excellent. **-zingly** *adv.*

**who** *pron.* relative or interrogative, referring to persons. **-ever** *pron.* whatever person; any one, without exception. **-m** *pron.* objective case of *who.* **-msoever** *pron.* objective of **-soever** *pron.* any person, without exception. **-se** *pron.* possessive case of *who* or *which.*

**whoa** *interj.* stop!

**whole** *a.* entire; complete; not defective or imperfect; unimpaired; *n.* entire thing; complete system; aggregate; gross; sum; totality. **-hearted** *a.* earnest; sincere. **-heartedly** *adv.* **-heartedness** *n.* **-ness** *n.* **-sale** *n.* sale of goods in bulk to retailers; *a.* selling or buying in large quantities; extensive; indiscriminate. **-saler** *n.* **-some** *a.* tending to promote health; healthy; nourishing; beneficial. **-someness** *n.* **wholly** *adv.* completely.

**whom** See **who.**

**whoop** *n.* loud cry or yell; hoot, as of owl; convulsive intake of air after cough; *v.i.* to utter loud cry; to hoot; to make the sound characteristic of whooping cough. **-ee** *interj.* exclamation of joy or abandonment. **-er** *n.* one who whoops; bird with a loud harsh note. **-ing cough** *n.* infectious disease marked by fits of convulsive coughing, followed by characteristic loud whoop or indrawing of breath.

**whore** *n.* harlot; prostitute.

**whose** *poss.* of *who, which.* **whosoever, whomsoever.** See **who.**

**why** *adv.* and *conj.* for what reason? on which account? wherefore? *interj.* expletive to show surprise, indignation, protest; *n.* reason; cause; motive.

**wick** *n.* cotton cord which draws up oil or wax, as in lamp or candle, to be burned. **-less** *a.*

**wick•ed** *a.* addicted to vice; evil; immoral; mischievous. **-ly** *adv.* **-ness** *n.*

**wick•er** *n.* small flexible twig; wickerwork; *a.* made of pliant twigs.

**wide** *a.* broad; spacious; comprehensive; *adv.* to a distance; far. **—awake** *a.* fully awake. **-ly** *adv.* **-n** *v.t.* to make wide or wider; *v.i.* to grow wide or wider; to expand. **-ness** *n.* width. **-spread** *a.* extending on all sides; diffused; circulating among numerous people. **width** *n.* wideness; breadth. **widthwise** *adv.*

**wid•ow** *n.* woman who has lost husband by death; *v.t.* to bereave of husband; to be a widow to. **-er** *n.* man whose wife is dead. **-hood** *n.*

**width** See **wide.**

**wield** *v.t.* to use with full command or power; to swing; to handle; to manage; to control. **-able** *a.* **-er** *n.* **-iness** *n.* **-y** *a.* manageable; controllable.

**wie•ner** *n.* smoked sausage in casing; frankfurter. Also **weenie.**

**wife** *n.* married woman; spouse; *pl.* **wives. -hood** *n.* **-less** *a.* **-lessness** *n.* without wife; unmarried. **-ly** *a.* as befits a wife.

**wig** *n.* artificial covering for head which imitates natural hair. **-ged** *a.*

**wig•gle** *v.i.* to waggle; to wriggle; *n.* a wriggling motion. **-r** *n.* wiggling thing.

**wig•wam** *n.* Amer. Ind. conical shelter.

**wild** *a.* living in state of nature; not domesticated or cultivated; native; savage; turbulent; *n.* uncultivated, uninhabited region. **-cat** *n.* medium-sized, undomesticated feline; *a.* reckless; financially unsound; highly speculative. **-fire** *n.* anything which burns rapidly or spreads fast; sheet lightning; **— goosechase** *n.* foolish, futile pursuit or enterprise. **-ly** *adv.* **-ness** *n.*

**wil•der•ness** *n.* tract of land uncultivated and uninhabited by human beings; waste; desert.

**will** *n.* power of choosing what one will do; volition; determination; wish; desire; declaration in writing showing how property is to be disposed of after death; *v.t.* to determine by choice; to decree; to bequeath; to devise; *v.i.* to exercise act of colition; to choose; to elect; *v.* used as an auxiliary, to denote futurity dependent on subject of verb, intention, or insistence. *pa.t.* **would. -able** *a.* **-er** *n.* **-ing** *a.* favorably inclined; minded; disposed; ready. **-ingly** *adv.* readily; gladly. **-ingness** *n.*

**wil•low** *n.* name of number of trees of genus Salix, having flexible twigs used in weaving. **-er** *n.* **— pattern,** design used in decorating chinaware, blue on white ground. **-y** *a.* abounding in willows; pliant; supple and slender. **weeping willow** *n.* tree with pendent branches.

**wilt** *v.i.* to fade; to droop; to wither; *v.t.* to depress; *n.* weakness; plant disease.

**win** *v.t.* to gain by success in competition or contest; to earn; to obtain; to reach, after difficulty; *v.i.* to be victorious; *pr.p.* **-ning.** *pa.p., pa.t.* **won.** *n.* victory. **-ningly** *adv.*

**wince** *v.i.* to shrink or flinch, as from blow or pain; *n.* act of wincing. **-r** *n.*

**wind** *n.* air in motion; current of air; gale; breath; power of respiration; point of compass; *pl.* wind instruments of orchestra; *v.t.* to follow by scent; to run, ride, or drive till breathless; to expose to wind; *v.t.* to sound by blowing. *pa.p.* **-ed. -breaker** *n.* a warm sports jacket. **-ed** *a.* breathless. **-ily** *adv.* **-iness** *n.* **— instrument** *n.* musical instrument played by blowing or air pressure. **-less** *a.* calm; out of breath. **-mill** *n.* mill worked by action of wind on vanes or sails. **-pipe** *n.* trachea; cartilaginous pipe admitting air to lungs. **-storm** *n.* **-y** *a.* consisting of, exposed to wind; tempestuous; flatulent; empty.

**wind** *v.t.* to twist around; to coil; *v.i.* to twine; to vary from direct course. *pa.t.* and *pa.p.* **wound. -er** *n.* one who, or that which, winds; step, wider at one end than the other. **-ing** *a.* twisting or bending from direct line; sinuous; meandering; *n.* turning; twist. **-up** *n.* conclusion; closing stages; baseball pitcher's preliminary swing of arm before delivery. **wound-up** *a.* highly excited.

**win•dow** *n.* opening in wall to admit air and light, usually covered with glass.

**wine** *n.* fermented juice of grape; similar liquor made from other fruits; *v.t.* to entertain by serving wine; *v.i.* to drink much wine at a sitting. — **cellar,** stock of wine. **-ry** place where wine is made.

**wing** *n.* organ of flight; one of two feathered fore limbs of bird; flight; main lifting surface of airplane; extension or section of a building; *pl.* the side parts of a stage; *v.t.* to furnish with wings; to enable to fly or hasten; *v.i.* to soar on the wing. **-ed** *a.* furnished with wings. **-less** *a.*

**wink** *v.t.* and *v.i.* to close and open eyelids; to blink; to convey hint by flick of eyelid; to twinkle; *n.* act of winking; hint conveyed by winking.

**win•ner, win•ning** See **win.**

**win•ter** *n.* fourth season; in northern latitudes, period between winter solstice and vernal equinox (22nd Dec.— 20th-21st March); *a.* wintry; pert. to winter; *v.t.* to keep and feed throughout winter; *v.i.* to pass the winter. **-er** *n.* **-green** *n.* aromatic evergreen plant from which is obtained oil of wintergreen, used in medicine and flavoring. **-ize** *v.t.* ready for winter. **-ly** *adv.* **wintriness** *n.* **wintry** *a.* of or like winter.

**wipe** *v.t.* to rub lightly, so as to clean or dry; to remove gently; to clear away; to efface; *n.* act of wiping. **-r** *n.* one who, or that which, wipes; in motoring, automatically operated arm to keep part of windshield free from rain or dust. **wiping** *n.* act of wiping. **to wipe out,** to erase; to destroy utterly.

**wire** *n.* metal drawn into form of a thread or cord; a length of this; a telegram; *v.t.* to bind or stiffen with wire; to pierce with wire; to fence with wire; to install (building) with wires for electric circuit; *a.* formed of wire. **-d** *a.* **—haired** *a.* having short, wiry hair. **-less** *a.* without wires; pert. to several devices operated by electromagnetic waves. *n.* wireless telegraphy or telephony; *v.t.* and *v.i.* to communicate by wireless. — **tapping,** act of tapping telephone wires to get information. **wirily** *adv.* **wiriness** *n.* **wiring** *n.* system of electric wires forming circuit. **wiry** *n.* stiff (as hair); lean, sinewy and strong.

**wis•dom** *n.* quality of being wise; knowledge and the capacity to make use of it; judgment. — **tooth** *n.* posterior molar tooth, cut about twentieth year.

**wise** *a.* enlightened; sagacious; learned; dictated by wisdom. **-crack** *n.* concise flippant statement; *v.i.* to utter one. **-ly** *adv.* **-ness** *n.*

**wise** *adv. suffix.* in the way or manner of, arranged like, as in *clockwise, likewise, crosswise, etc.*

**wish** *v.t.* to desire; to long for; to request; *v.i.* to have a desire; to yearn; *n.* expression or object of desire; longing; request. **(ing)-bone** *n.* forked bone of fowl's breast. **-er** *n.* **-ful** *a.* desirous; anxious; longing; wistful. **-fully.** *adv.* **-fulness** *n.*

**wisp** *n.* twisted handful, usually of hay; whisk or small broom; stray lock of hair. **-like** *a.* **-y** *a.*

**wist•ful** *a.* pensive; sadly contemplative; earnestly longing. **-ly** *adv.* **-ness** *n.*

**wit** *n.* intellect; understanding; humor; pleasantry; *pl.* mental faculties. **-ticism** *n.* witty remark. **-tily** *adv.* **-tiness** *n.* **-tingly** *adv.* with foreknowledge or design; knowingly; of set purpose. **-ty** *a.* possessed of wit; amusing.

**witch** *n.* woman who was supposed to practice sorcery; *v.t.* to bewitch; to enchant. **-craft** *n.* black art; sorcery. — **doctor** *n.* medicine man of a savage tribe. **-ery** *n.* arts of a witch; sorcery. **-ing** *a.* fascinating. **-ingly** *adv.*

**witch haz•el** *n.* shrub with yellow flowers and edible seeds; of dried bark and leaves of the tree used, in distilled form, as astringent drug.

**with** *prep.* in company or possession of; in relation to; against; by means of; denoting association, cause, agency, comparison, immediate sequence, etc.

**with•draw** *v.t.* to take away; to recall; to retract; *v.i.* to go away; to retire; to retreat; to recede. *pa.t.* **withdrew.** *pa.p.* **-n, -al** *n.* **-ment** *n.*

**with•er** *v.t.* to cause to fade and become dry; to blight; to rebuff; *v.i.* to fade; to decay; to languish. **-ing** *a.* **-ingly** *adv.* scathingly; contemptuously.

**with•hold** *v.t.* to hold or keep back. *pa.p., pa.t.* **withheld.**

**with•in** *prep.* in the inner or interior part of; in the compass of; *adv.* in the inner part; inwardly; at home.

**with•out** *prep.* on or at the outside of; out of; not within; beyond the limits of; exempt from; all but; *adv.* on the outside.

**with•stand** *v.t.* to oppose; to stand against; to resist. *pa.t.* and *pa.p.* **withstood. -er** *n.*

**wit•ness** *n.* testimony; one who, or that which, furnishes evidence or proof; one who has seen or has knowledge of incident; one who attests another person's signature to document; *v.t.* to be witness of or to; *v.i.* to give evidence; to testify. — **stand** *n.* place where witness gives testimony in court of law. **-er** *n.*

**wit•ti•cism, wit•ty,** etc. See **wit.**

**wives** *pl.* of **wife.**

**wiz•ard** *n.* one devoted to black art; sorcerer; magician; *a.* with magical powers. **-like** *a.* **-ly** *a.* **-ry** *n.* magic.

**wob•ble, wabble** *v.i.* to rock from side to side; to be hesitant; *n.* rocking; unequal motion. **-r,** *n.* **wobbly, wabbly** *a.* shaky; unsteady.

**woe, wo** *n.* grief; heavy calamity; affliction; sorrow. **-ful** *a.* sorrowful; pitiful; paltry. **-fully** *adv.*

**woke.** alt. *pa.t. of* **wake.**

**wolf** *n.* carnivorous wild animal, allied to dog; rapacious, cruel person. *pl.* **wolves.** *v.t.* to devour ravenously. **-ish** *a.* rapacious, like wolf; voracious; fierce and greedy. **-ishly** *adv.* **-ishness** *n.*

**wolves** *pl.* of **wolf.**

**wo•man** *n.* adult human female; the quality of being a woman. *pl.* **women. -hood** *n.* adult stage of women; the qualities of women. **-ish** *a.* like a woman; effeminate. **-ishness** *n.* **-liness** *n.* **-ly** *a.* befitting a mature woman; essentially feminine;

*adv.* in manner of a woman.
**womb** *n.* female organ of conception and gestation; uterus.
**wo•men** *pl.* of **woman.**
**won** *pa.t.* and *pa.p.* of **win.**
**won•der** *n.* astonishment; surprise; amazement; admiration; *v.i.* to feel wonder; to marvel; to speculate. **-er** *n.* **-ful** *a.* very fine; remarkable; amazing. **-fully** *adv.* **-fulness** *n.* **-ing** *a.* **-ingly** *adv.* in a wondering and expectant manner. **-land** *n.* land of marvels; fairyland. **wondrous** *a.* wonderful. **wondrously** *adv.* **wondrousness** *n.*
**wont** *a.* accustomed; used; *n.* habit; custom; use; *v.i.* to be accustomed. **-ed** *a.* accustomed; habitual; usual. **-edness.**
**won't** *v.i.* a contr. of **will not.**
**woo** *v.t.* to make love to; to court. **-er** *n.* **-ing** *n.*
**wood** *n.* land with trees growing close together; grove; forest; hard, stiffening tissue in stem and branches of tree; timber; wood-wind instrument; *v.t.* to supply with wood; to plant with trees. **— alcohol** *n.* methyl alcohol, product of dry distillation of wood, esp. beech and birch. **-cut** *n.* engraving on wood; impression from such engravings. **-ed** *a.* covered with trees. **-en** *a.* made of wood. **— engraver** *n.* **— engraving** *n.* art or process of cutting design on wood for printing; impression from this; woodcut. **-land** *n.* and *a.* wooded country. **-pecker** *n.* bird which taps and bores with bill the bark of trees in search of insects. **— pulp** *n.* wood crushed and pulped for paper making. **-sman** *n.* forest dweller; forester; woodcutter. **-shed** *n.* firewood storage place. **-sy** *a.* like the woods. **—wind** *n.* wooden musical instrument, as flute, oboe, clarinet, bassoon, etc. **-work** *n.* fittings made of wood, esp. interior moldings of a house. **-y** *a.* abounding with trees or wooded growth.
**woof•er** *n.* large loud-speaker that reproduces low frequency sound waves.
**wool** *n.* soft, curled hair of sheep, goat, etc.; yarn or cloth of this. **-(l)en** *n.* cloth made of wool; *pl.* woolen goods; *a.* made of, pert. to, wool. **-liness** *n.* **-ly** *a.* of, or like wool; muddled and confused.
**word** *n.* spoken or written sign of idea; term; oral expression; message; order; *pl.* speech; language, esp. contentious; wordy quarrel; *v.t.* to express in words; to phrase. **-ed** *a.* phrased; expressed. **-ily** *adv.* verbosely; pedantically. **-iness** *n.* verbosity. **ing** *n.* precise words used; phrasing; phraseology. **-less** *a.* **-ly** *a.* verbose; prolix. **word for word,** literally; verbatim. **by word of mouth,** orally.
**wore** *pa.t.* of **wear.**
**work** *n.* exertion of strength; effort directed to an end; employment; toil; labor; occupation; production; achievement; manufacture; that which is produced; result of force overcoming resistance over definite distance; *pl.* structures in engineering; manufacturing establishment; good deeds; artistic productions; mechanism of a watch, etc.; fortifications; *v.i.* to exert oneself; to labor; to be employed; *v.t.* to produce or form by labor; to operate; to perform; to effect. **-able** *a.* **-aday** *a.* commonplace. **-er** *n.* **-ing** *n.* act of laboring or doing something useful; mode of operation; *pl.* a mine as a whole, or a part of it where work is being carried on, e.g. level, etc.; *a.* laboring. **-man** *n.* one actually engaged in manual labor; craftsman. **-manship** *n.* skill. **-shop** *n.* place where things are made or repaired; people meeting for intensive study in some field. **to work off,** to get rid of gradually. **to work out,** to solve (problem); to plan in detail; to exhaust (mine, etc.)
**world** *n.* earth and its inhabitants; universe; this life; human race; mankind. **-liness** *n.* state of being worldly. **-ling** *n.* one who is absorbed in the affairs, interests, or pleasures of this world. **-ly** *a.* relating to the world; earthly; mundane; carnal; not spiritual. **-ly-wise** *a.* experienced in the ways of people. **—wide** *a.* extending to every corner of the globe. **the New World,** N. and S. America. **the Old World.** Europe, Africa, and Asia.
**worm** *n.* small, limbless, invertebrate animal with soft, long, and jointed body; *pl.* disease of digestive organs or intestines of humans and animals due to parasite worms; *v.i.* to work (oneself) in insidiously; to move along like a worm; *v.t.* to work slowly and secretly; to free from worms. **-y** *a.* worm-like; abounding with worms.
**worn** *pa.p.* of **wear. —out** *a.* no longer serviceable; exhausted; tired.
**wor•ry** *v.t.* to cause anxiety; to torment; to vex; to plague; *v.i.* to feel undue care and anxiety; *n.* mental disturbance due to care and anxiety; trouble; vexation. **worrier** *n.* **worrisome** *a.* causing trouble, anxiety, or worry. **-ing** *a.*
**worse** *a. comp.* of **bad, ill;** more unsatisfactory; of less value; in poorer health; *adv.* in a manner more evil or bad. **worsen** *v.t.* to make worse; to impair; *v.t.* and *i.* to make or become worse; to deteriorate. **worsening** *n.*
**wor•ship** *n.* religious reverence and homage; act or ceremony of showing reverence; *v.t.* to adore; to pay divine honors to; *v.i.* to perform religious service; to attend church. **-ful** *a.* **-fully** *adv.* **-fulness** *n.* **-er** *n.*
**worst** *a. superl.* of **bad, ill;** most evil; of least value or worth; *adv.* in most inferior manner or degree; *n.* that which is most bad or evil; *v.t.* to get the better of; to defeat.
**wor•sted** *n.* yarn spun from long-fibred wools which are combed, not carded; cloth of this yarn; *a.* made of worsted.
**worth** *n.* quality of thing which renders it valuable or useful; value, in terms of money; merit; excellence; *a.* equal in value to; meriting; having wealth or estate to the value of. **-ily** *adv.* **-iness** *n.* **-less** *a.* of no worth or value; useless. **-while** *a.* **-lessly** *adv.* **-lessness** *n.* **-y** *a.*

having worth or excellence; deserving; meritorious; *n.* man of eminent worth; local celebrity. *pl.* **worthies.**

**would** *pa.t.* of **will**; expresses condition, futurity, desire. **—be** *a.* desiring or intending to be.

**wound** *pa.t.* and *pa.p.* of **wind.**

**wound** *n.* injury; cut, stab, bruise, etc.; hurt; *v.t.* to hurt by violence; to hurt feelings of; to injure. **-er** *n.* **-less** *a.*

**wove** *pa.t.* of **weave. -n** *pa.p.* of **weave.**

**wow** *interj.* exclamation of astonishment.

**wraith** *n.* apparition of person seen shortly before or after death; specter; ghost.

**wrap** *v.t.* to cover by winding or folding something around; to roll, wind, or fold together. *pr.p.* **-ping.** *pa.t., pa.p.* **-ped** (or **-t**). *n.* a loose garment; a covering. **-per** *n.* one who, or that which, wraps. **-ping** *n.* wrapping material.

**wrath** *n.* violent anger; indignation; rage; fury. **-ful** *a.* **-fully** *adv.* **-fulness** *n.*

**wreath** *n.* circular garland or crown of flowers, leaves, etc. entwined together. **wreathe** *v.t.* to surround; to form into a wreath; to wind round; to encircle; *v.i.* to be interwoven or entwined.

**wreck** *n.* destruction of vessel; hulk of wrecked ship; remains of anything destroyed or ruined; *v.t.* to destroy, as vessel; to bring ruin upon; to upset completely. **-age** *n.* remains of something wrecked. **-er** *n.* one who wrecks; one employed in tearing down buildings, salvaging or recovering cargo from wreck.

**wren** *n.* tiny song-bird about 4 in. long, with reddish-brown plumage.

**wrench** *v.t.* to wrest, twist, or force by violence; to distort; *n.* sudden, violent twist; tool with fixed or adjustable jaws for holding or adjusting nuts, bolts, etc.

**wres•tle** *v.i.* to contend by grappling and trying to throw another down; to struggle. **-r** *n.* **wrestling** *n.* sport in which contestants endeavor to throw each other to the ground in accordance with rules.

**wrig•gle** *v.i.* to move sinously, like a worm; to squirm; *v.t.* to cause to wriggle; *n.* act of wriggling; wriggling motion. **-r** *n.* **wriggling** *n.* **wriggly** *a.*

**wring** *v.t.* to twist and compress; to turn and strain with violence; to squeeze or press out; *v.i.* to turn or twist, as with pain. *pa.t.* and *pa.p.* **wrung. -er** *n.* one who wrings; machine for pressing out water from wet clothes, etc. **-ing wet,** absolutely soaking.

**wrin•kle** *n.* ridge or furrow on surface due to twisting, shrinking, or puckering; crease in skin; fold; corrugation; *v.i.* to make ridges, creases, etc.; *v.i.* to shrink into wrinkles. **-ling** *n.* **wrinkly** *a.*

**wrist** *n.* joint connecting the forearm and hand; the carpus.

**writ** *n.* that which is written; in law, mandatory precept issued by a court; **Holy Writ,** the Scriptures.

**write** *v.t.* to set down or express in letters or words on paper, etc.; to compose, as book, song, etc.; *v.i.* to form characters representing sounds or ideas; to be occupied in writing; to express ideas in writing. *pr.p.* **writing.** *p.t.* **wrote.** *pa.p.* **written. -r** *n.* one who writes; scribe; clerk; author. **writing** *n.* mechanical act of forming characters on paper or any other material; anything written; style of execution or content of what works; official papers, etc. **written** *a.* expressed in writing. **to write off,** to cancel, as bad debts.

**wrong** *a.* not right; incorrect; mistaken; immoral; injurious; unjust; illegal; unsuitable; improper; *n.* harm; evil; injustice; trespass; transgression; error; *adv.* not rightly; erroneously; *v.t.* to treat with injustice; to injure; to impute evil to unjustly. **-doer** *n.* one who injures another; one who breaks law; offender; sinner. **-ful** *a.* **-fully** *adv.* **-fulness** *n.* **wrong,** at fault; blameworthy.

**wrought** *pa.t.* and *pa.p.* of **work.** *a.* hammered into shape, as metal products. **—iron** *n.* purest form of commercial iron, fibrous, ductile, and malleable, prepared by puddling.

**wrung** *pa.t.* and *pa.p.* of **wring.**

**X chro•mo•some** *n.* chromosome which determines the sex of the future organism.

**xe•nog•a•my** *n.* cross-fertilization. **xenogamous** *a.*

**xen•o•gen•e•sis** *n.* fancied generation of organism totally unlike parent. **xenogenetic** *a.*

**xe•non** *n.* non-metallic element belonging to group of rare or inactive gases.

**xen•o•pho•bi•a** *n.* fear or hatred of strangers or aliens.

**xe•rog•ra•phy** *n.* a process similar to photography, but not requiring specifically sensitized paper or plates, using instead a special photoconductive plate.

**X rays** *n.pl.* Röntgen rays —electromagnetic rays of very short wave length, capable of penetrating matter opaque to light rays and imprinting on sensitive photographic plate picture of objects; the picture so made. *v.t.* to treat, examine, or photograph with X-rays.

**xy•lo•graph** *n.* a wood engraving; impression from wood block. **-er** *n.* **-ic** *a.* **-ical** *a.* **-y** *n.* the art of wood engraving.

**xy•lo•phone** *n.* musical instrument consisting of blocks of resonant wood, notes being produced by striking blocks of resonant wood, notes being produced by striking blocks with two small hammers. **xylophonist** *n.*

**xy•lo•py•rog•ra•phy** *n.* production of designs in wood by charring with hot iron.

**yacht** *n.* light sailing or power-driven vessel, for pleasure or racing; *v.i.* to sail in a yacht. **-ing** *n.* art or act of sailing a yacht; *a.* pert. to yacht. **-sman** *n.* **-smanship** *n.*

**yak** *n.* species of ox found in C. Asia, with a hump and long hair.

**yam** *n.* tuber of tropical climbing-plant; sweet potato.

**Yan•kee** *n.* (in U.S.A.) citizen of New England, or of Northern States; (outside U.S.A.) an American; *a.* American. **-dom** *n.*

**yap** *v.i.* to yelp; *n.* yelp.

**yard** *n.* standard measure of length, equal to three feet of thirty-six inches; *(Naut.)* spar set crosswise to mast, for supporting a sail. **-age** *n.* measurement in yards. **-arm** *n.* either half of a ship's yard. **-stick** *n.* measuring stick 36 inches long.

**yard** *n.* grounds surrounding a building; enclosed space used for specific purpose as *brickyard,* a *railroad yard,* etc.

**yarn** *n.* spun thread, esp. for knitting or weaving; thread of rope.

**yar•row** *n.* plant having strong odor and pungent taste.

**yaw** *v.i.* of ship or aircraft, to fail to keep steady course; *n.* act of yawing; temporary deviation from a straight course.

**yawl** *n.* small, two-masted sailing boat, with smaller mast at stern; ship's small boat.

**yawn** *v.i.* to open mouth involuntarily through sleepiness, etc.

**yaws** *n.* tropical contagious disease of the skin, usually chronic.

**yean** *v.t.* and *v.i.* to bring forth young; as sheep or goat. **-ling** *n.* a lamb; kid.

**year** *n.* time taken by one revolution of earth round sun, i.e. about 365¼ days; twelve months; scholastic session in school, university, etc.; *pl.* age; old age. **-ly** *a.* and *adv.* happening every year; annual. **-ling** *n.* young animal, esp. horse, in second year; *a.* being a year old. **-long** *a.* **-book** *n.* reference book of facts and statistics published yearly. **leap year,** year of 366 days, occurring every fourth year.

**yearn** *v.i.* to seek earnestly: to feel longing or desire; to long for. **-ing** *n.* earnest desire; longing; *a.* desirous.

**yeast** *n.* froth that rises on malt liquors during fermentation; frothy yellow fungus growth causing this fermentation, used also in bread making, as leavening agent to raise dough. **-y** *a.* frothy; fermenting. **-cake** *n.* yeast mixed with meal and formed into small cakes for use in baking.

**yell** *v.i.* to cry out in a loud, shrill tone; *n.* a loud, shrill cry.

**yel•low** *n.* primary color; color of gold, lemons, buttercups, etc. **— fever** *n.* infectious, tropical disease, characterized by a yellow skin, vomiting, etc. **— jacket** *n.* a bright yellow wasp.

**yelp** *n.* sharp, shrill bark or cry.

**yeo•man** *n.* *(Arch.)* officer of royal household; *(Navy)* petty officer. *pl.* **yeomen.**

**yes** *interj.* word expressing affirmation or consent.

**yes•ter** *a.* *(Arch.)* pert. to yesterday; denoting period of time just past, esp. in compounds, e.g. 'yester-eve.' **-day** *n.* day before today. **-year** *n.* last year.

**yet** *adv.* in addition; at the same time; still; *conj.* nevertheless; notwithstanding.

**yew** *n.* cone-bearing evergreen tree; its fine-grained wood, formerly used for making bows for archers.

**Yid•dish** *n.* a mixture of dialectal German, Hebrew and Slavic, spoken by Jews.

**yield** *v.t.* to produce; to give in return, esp. for labor, investment, etc.; to bring forth; to give way; to bear; *n.* amount produced; return for labor, investment, etc; profit; crop.

**yo•del, yo•dle** *v.t.* and *v.i.* to sing or warble, with frequent changes from the natural voice to falsetto tone.

**yo•ga** *n.* system of Hindu philosophy; strict spiritual discipline practiced to gain control over forces of one's own being, to gain occult powers, but chiefly to attain union with the Deity or Universal Spirit.

**yo•gurt** *n.* a thick liquid food made from fermented milk.

**yoke** *n.* wooden framework fastened over necks of two oxen, etc. to hold them together, and to which a plough, etc. is attached; separately cut piece of material in garment, fitting closely over shoulders.

**yo•kel** *n.* rustic; country bumpkin.

**yolk** *n.* yellow part of egg.

**yore** *n.* the past; old times.

**York•shire** *n.* country in north of England. **— pudding,** batter baked in roasting tin along with meat. **— terrier,** small, shaggy terrier, resembling Skye terrier.

**you** *pron. sing., pl.* of second person in nominative or objective case, indicating person or persons addressed; also used indefinitely meaning, one, they, people in general. **your, yours** *a.* possessive form of *you,* meaning belonging to you, of you, pert. to you.

**young** *a.* not far advanced in growth, life, or existence; not yet old; vigorous; immature; *n.* offspring of animals. **-ster** *n.* young person or animal; child.

**youth** *n.* state of being young; life from childhood to manhood; young persons collectively.

**yowl** *v.i.* to howl; *n.* cry of a dog.

**yo-yo** *n.* toy consisting of flat spool with string wound round in the deep groove in its edge, which when released from hand spins up and down on a string.

**yuc•ca** *n.* genus of lilaceous plants, having tall, handsome flowers.

**Yu•go•slav** *a.* pert. to *Yugoslavia,* the country of the Serbs, Croats, and Slovenes, in the N.W. of the Balkan Peninsula.

**yule** *n.* feast of Christmas. **-tide** *n.* season of Christmas.

**za•ny** *n.* formerly, buffoon who mimicked principal clown; simpleton. *a.* comical. **-ism** *n.*

**zeal** *n.* intense enthusiasm for cause or person; passionate ardor. **zealot** *n.* fanatic; enthusiast. **zealotry** *n.* fanaticism. **zealous** *a.* ardent; enthusiastic; earnest. **zealously** *adv.* **zealousness** *n.*

**ze•bra** *n.* genus of African quadrupeds of horse family, with tawny coat striped with black.

**ze•brass** *n.* offspring of male zebra and she-ass.

**Zend** *n.* interpretation of the *Avesta,* sacred writings of Zoroastrians; Iranian language in which Zend-Avesta is written. **—Avesta** *n.* sacred writings and commentary thereon (Zend) of Zoroastrians.

**ze•nith** *n.* point of heavens directly above observer's head; summit; height of success; acme; climax. **-al** *a.*

**zeph•yr** *n.* west wind; gentle breeze; fine soft woolen fabric.

**zep•pe•lin** *n.* cigar-shaped long-range dirigible.

**ze•ro** *n.* nought; cipher; symbol, 0; neutral fixed point from which graduated scale is measured, as on thermometer, barometer, etc.; lowest point. **— hour,** precise moment at which military offensive, etc. is timed to begin; crucial moment. **— in,** *v.i.* to adjust gun fire to a specific point.

**zest** *n.* relish; fillip; stimulus; keen pleasure.

**Zeus** *n.* in Greek mythology, chief deity and father of gods and men, his seat being Mt. Olympus.

**zig•zag** *n.* line, with short sharp turns; *a.* forming zigzag; *v.t.* and *v.i.* to form, or move with, short sharp turns.

**zinc** *n.* hard bluish-metal used in alloys, esp. brass, and because of its resistance to corrosion, for galvanizing iron; *v.t.* to coat with zinc, to galvanize. **— alloys** *(Met.)* alloys containing percentage of zinc, as brass, etc.

**zing** *n.* the high-pitched sound of something moving at great speed; pep.

**zin•ni•a** *n.* plant with bright-colored flowers.

**Zi•on** *n.* hill in Jerusalem; town of Jerusalem; the Jewish people; Church of God; heaven. **-ism** *n.* movement among Jews to further the Jewish national state in Palestine. **-ist** *n.* advocate of Zionism.

**zip** *n.* whizzing sound, as of bullet in air; *v.t.* to shut with a zipper; *v.i.* to move with great speed. *pr.p.* **-ping.** *pa.p., pa.t.* **-ped, -per** *n.* device of interlocking flexible teeth opened and shut by sliding clip.

**zir•con** *n.* silicate of zirconium occurring in crystals; transparent ones used as gems. **zirconium** *n.* metal obtained from zircon, and resembling titanium **-ic** *a.*

**zith•er** *n.* flat, stringed instrument comprising resonance box with strings.

**zo•di•ac** *n.* *(Astron.)* imaginary belt in heavens following path of sun, and divided into twelve equal areas containing twelve constellations, each represented by appropriate symbols, called the *signs of the zodiac;* namely Aries *(Ram),* Taurus *(Bull),* Gemini *(Twins),* Cancer *(Crab),* Leo *(Lion),* Virgo *(Virgin),* Libra *(Balance),* Scorpio *(Scorpion),* Sagittarius *(Archer),* Capricornus *(Goat),* Aquarius *(Water-bearer),* Pisces *(Fishes);* a circular chart representing these signs **-al** *a.*

**zom•bi, zom•bie** *n.* orig. in Africa, deity of the python; in West Indies, corpse alleged to have been revived by black magic; the power which enters such a body; human being without will or speech but capable of automatic movement; intoxicating drink made with rum.

**zone** *n.* girdle; climatic or vegetation belt; one of five belts into which earth is divided by latitude lines, as *frigid zone* of Arctic and Antarctic, *torrid zone* between Tropics of Cancer and Capricorn, *temperate zone* north of Tropic of Cancer and south of Tropic of Capricorn; division of a city, etc., for building or other purposes; *v.t.* to enclose; to divide into zones; to divide country into regional areas.

**zoo** *n.* zoological garden; place where wild animals are kept for showing.

**zo•o•chem•is•try** *n.* chemistry of constituents of animal body.

**zo•o•ge•og•ra•phy** *n.* science which treats the regional distribution of animals in the world.

**zo•oid** *a.* resembling an animal; *n.* organism capable of relatively independent existence; a compound organism.

**zo•ol•o•gy** *n.* natural history of animals, part of science of biology. **zoological** *a.* **zoologically** *adv.* **zoologist** *n.* one versed in zoology, **zoological gardens, zoo,** park where wild animals are kept for exhibition.

**zoom** *n. v.t.* (of prices) to become inflated; (of aircraft) to turn suddenly upward at sharp angle; to move camera rapidly toward or away from an object which thus appears to move similarly.

**zo•o•phyte** *n.* plant-like animal, such as sponge.

**zoot suit** *n.* flashy type of man's suit, generally with padded shoulders, fitted waist, knee-length jacket and tight trousers.

**zuc•chi•ni** *n.* a long green-skinned squash.

**Zu•lu** *n.* member of Bantu tribe of S. Africa; *a.* pert. to Zulus.

**zwie•back** *n.* a dry crisp bread, usually sweetened, that has been baked, sliced and then toasted.

**zyme** *n.* ferment; disease germ. **zymic** *a.* **zymogen** *n.* any substance producing an enzyme. **zymotic disease,** infectious or contagious disease caused by germs introduced into body from without.

**zy•mur•gy** *n.* branch of chemistry dealing with fermentation process.

# RULES OF SPELLING

*The rules listed below are meant to guide you in spelling; but there are exceptions to these rules. The most common exceptions are noted.*

**Drop the silent "e"** at the end of a word when adding a termination that begins with a vowel (*Ex: shade, shading; move, movable*). Exceptions: words ending in *ce* or *ge* before terminations beginning with *a* or *o* (*Ex: change, changeable; notice, noticeable*); where confusion would result (*Ex: dye, dyeing* [*dying*]).

**Keep the silent "e"** at the end of a word when adding a termination that begins with a consonant (*Ex: bare, bareness; hate, hateful*). Exceptions: *acknowledge, acknowledgment; whole, wholly.*

**Repeat the final consonant** at the end of a single syllable or last syllable accented word if it is preceded by a single vowel when adding a terminal beginning with a vowel (*Ex: hit, hitting; begin, beginning*).

**Do not repeat the final consonant** at the end of a word if it is preceded by a consonant, two vowels, or if the last syllable is unaccented when adding a terminal beginning with a vowel (*Ex: art, artful; troop, trooping; profit, profiting*).

**Keep the double consonant** at the end of a word when adding a terminal (*Ex: fall, falling; stiff, stiffen*). Exception: where the terminal begins with the same letter as the double consonant (*Ex: full, fully*).

**Add "k" to words ending in "c"** when adding a terminal beginning with *e, i,* or *y* (*Ex: picnic, picnicked; shellac, shellacking; panic, panicky*).

**Drop one "e" of an "ee" ending** when adding a terminal beginning with *e* (*Ex: agree, agreed*).

**Change "ie" to "y"** before adding the terminal *-ing* (*Ex: die, dying*).

**Change "y" to "i"** before adding a terminal other than *-ing* (*Ex: racy, raciest; twenty, twentieth*). Exceptions: where a vowel precedes the *y* (*Ex: gay, gayest*).

## USE OF CAPITALS

**Capitals** (denotes capitalization of the first letter of the word) are used: (1) at the beginning of each sentence; (2) for proper names and adjectives derived from these names; (3) for words referring to the Deity; (4) for official and honorary titles; (5) at the beginning of every line of poetry; (6) for each important word in a title (book, magazine, etc.); (7) for the pronoun "I" and the exclamation "O"; (8) for the days of the week and the months of the year; (9) at the beginning of each quotation; (10) for special words.

## USE OF PUNCTUATION MARKS

**Period** (.) Used: (1) at the end of a sentence that is not a question or explanation; (2) after abbreviations; and (3) to mark off decimals.

**Question Mark** (?) Used: (1) at the end of a sentence that asks a question; and (2) to denote something questionable.

**Exclamation Mark** (!) Used at the end of a strong exclamatory word, phrase, or sentence.

**Comma** (,) Used: (1) to separate words, phrases and clauses of a series; (2) to set off parenthetical expressions, non-restrictive clauses, transitional words or phrases, appositives, and nouns of direct address from the rest of the sentence; (3) to separate words in a date or address; (4) before a quotation; (5) to separate independent clauses, containing no commas, that are joined by a simple conjunction; (6) denote the omission of a word; and (7) after the salutation of an informal letter.

**Semi-colon** (;) Used: (1) to separate parts of a complex series; (2) to separate independent clauses not connected by co-ordinating conjunction, or which already contain one or more commas; and (3) where a comma would not afford the proper clarity.

**Colon** (:) Used: (1) to introduce a formal direct quotation; (2) after the salutation of a business letter; and (3) to introduce a long series.

**Dash** (—) Used: (1) to show an interruption or change of thought or sense; (2) to denote omission of a word or part of a word; and (3) to introduce a repetitious phrase.

**Hyphen** (-) Used: (1) to break a word between syllables when the word must be divided between the end of one line and the beginning of another; (2) to divide certain compound words; (3) to divide words which would be otherwise confusing; and (4) after a prefix that is before a proper noun.

**Parentheses** (( )) Used to set off words, phrases, clauses, or sentences which are in the text as comment or explanation.

**Brackets** ([ ]) Used: (1) to show editorial comment; and (2) as parentheses containing parentheses.

**Apostrophe** (') Used: (1) to indicate possession; and (2) to replace the missing letters in a contraction.

**Quotation marks** (" ") Used: (1) to enclose direct quotations [quotations within quotations are enclosed by single quotation marks (' ')]; (2) to indicate titles of plays, books, etc.; and (3) to indicate the opposite meaning of the word used.

## WORDBREAK RULES

1. Division of words should be minimized in leaded matter and avoided in double-leaded matter.

2. Except in narrow measures, wordbreaks should be avoided at the ends of more than two lines. Similarly, no more than two consecutive lines should end with the same word, symbol, group of numbers, etc.

3. In two-line centerheads, the first line should be centered and set as full as possible, but it is not set to fill the measure by unduly wide spacing. Wordbreaks should be avoided. Flush sideheads are set full measure and wordbreaks are permitted if unavoidable. They are not set ragged unless so indicated on copy.

4. The final word of a paragraph should not be divided.

5. Words should preferably be divided according to pronunciation; and to avoid mispronunciation, they should be divided so that the part of the word left at the end of the line will suggest the whole word: *capac-ity*, not *capa-city; extraor-dinary*, not *extra-ordinary; Wednes-day*, not *Wed-nesday; physi-cal*, not *phys-ical; service-man*, not *serv-iceman*.

6. Although WORD DIVISION lists beginning and ending one-letter syllables for pronunciation purposes, under no circumstances are words to be divided on a single letter (e.g., *usu-al-ly*, not *u-su-al-ly; imag-i-nary*, not *i-mag-i-nar-y*).

7. Division of short words (of five or fewer letters) should be avoided; two-letter divisions, including the carry-over of two-letter endings (*ed*, *el*, *en*, *er*, *es*, *et*, *fy*, *ic*, *in*, *le*, *ly*, *or*, and *ty*); should also be avoided. In narrow measure, however, a sounded suffix (e.g., paint-*ed;* not rained) or syllable of two letters may be carried over—only if unavoidable. (See rule 10.)

8. Words of two syllables are split at the end of the first syllable: *dis-pelled, con-quered;* words of three or more syllables, with a choice of division possible, divide preferably on the vowel: *particu-lar*, *sepa-rate*.

9. In words with short prefixes, divide on the prefix; e.g., *ac, co, de, dis, ex, in, non, on, pre, pro, re, un,* etc. (e.g., *non-essential,* not *nonessential; pre-selected,* not *prese-lected*).

If possible, prefixes and combining forms of more than one syllable are preserved intact: *anti, infra, macro, micro, multi, over, retro, semi,* etc. (e.g., *anti-monopoly,* not *antimo-nopoly; over-optimistic,* not *overop-timistic*). (For chemical prefixes, see rule 30.)

10. *Words ending in* -er.—Although two-letter carryovers are to be avoided (rule 7), many *-er* words which are derived from comparatives (*coarse, coarser; sharp, sharper*) have been listed to prevent a wrong wordbreak; e.g., *coars-er,* not *coar-ser.*

Nouns ending in *-er* (*adviser, bracer, keeper, perceiver, reader*) derived from action verbs are also listed to prevent a wrong division; e.g., *perceiv-er,* not *percei-ver.*

Except in narrow measure and if unavoidable, the above *-er* words are not divided unless division can be made on a prefix; e.g., *per-ceiver.*

11. *Words ending in* -or.—Generally, *-or* words with a consonant preceding are divided before the preceding consonant; e.g., *advi-sor* (legal), *fabrica-tor, guaran-tor, interve-nor, simula-tor,*

*tai-lor;* but *bail-or, bargain-or, consign-or, grant-or.*

12. The following suffixes are not divided: *ceous, cial, cient, cion, cious, scious, geous, gion, gious, sial, tial, tion, tious,* and *sion.*

13. The suffixes *-able* and *-ible* are usually carried over intact; but when the stem word loses its original form, these suffixes are divided according to pronunciation: *comfort-able, corrupt-ible, manage-able;* but *dura-ble, audi-ble.*

14. Words ending in *-ing,* with stress on the primary syllable, are preferably divided on the base word; e.g., *appoint-ing, combat-ing, danc-ing, engineer-ing, process-ing, program-ing, stencil-ing, trac-ing,* etc. However, present participles, such as *control-ling, forbid-ding, refer-ring,* with stress placed on the second syllable, divide between the doubled consonants (see also rule 16).

15. When the final consonant sound of a word belongs to a syllable ending with a silent vowel, the final consonant or consonants become part of the added suffix: *chuck-ling, han-dler, han-dling, crum-bling, twin-kled, twin-kling;* but *rollick-ing.*

16. When the addition of *-ed, -er, -est,* or of a similar ending, causes the doubling of a final consonant, the

added consonant is carried over: *pit-ted, rob-ber, thin-nest, glad-den, control-lable, transmit-table;* but *bless-ed* (adj.), *dwell-er, gross-est.*

17. Words with doubled consonants are usually divided between these consonants: *clas-sic, ruf-fian, neces-sary, rebel-lion;* but *call-ing, mass-ing.*

18. If formation of a plural adds a syllable ending in an *s* sound, the plural ending should not be carried over by itself: *hor-ses, voi-ces;* but *church-es, cross-es,* thus not breaking the base word (see also rule 7).

19. The digraphs *ai, ck, dg, gh, gn, ng, oa, ph, sh, tch,* and *th* are not split.

20. Do not divide contractions: *doesn't. haven't.*

21. Solid compounds are divided preferably between the members: *bar-keeper, hand-kerchief, proof-reader, humming-bird.*

22. Avoid a division which adds another hyphen to a hyphened compound: *court-martial,* not *court-mar-tial; tax-supported,* not *tax-sup-ported.*

23. A word of one syllable is not split: *tanned, shipped, quenched, through, chasm, prism.*

24. Two consonants preceded and followed by a vowel are divided on the first consonant: *abun-dant, advan-tage, struc-ture;* but *attend-ant, accept-ance, depend-ence.*

25. When two adjoining vowels are sounded separately, divide between them: *cre-ation, gene-alogy.*

26. In breaking homonyms, distinction should be given to their relative functions: *pro-ject* (v.), *proj-ect* (n.); *pro-duce* (v.), *prod-uce* (n.); *stran-ger* (n.), *strang-er* (comparative adjective); *rec-ollect* (recall), *re-collect* (collect again); but *proc-ess* (n., v.); *pro-test* (n., v.).

27. *Words ending in* -meter.—In the large group of words ending in *-meter,* distinction should be made between metric system terms and terms indicating a measuring instrument. When it is necessary to divide metric terms, preserve the combining form *-meter;* e.g., *centi-meter, deca-meter, hecto-meter, kilo-meter.* But measuring instruments divide after the *m: al-tim-e-ter, ba-rom-e-ter, mi-crom-e-ter, mul-tim-e-ter,* etc. Derivatives of these *-meter* terms follow the same form; e.g., *mul-tim-e-ter, mul-tim-e-try.*

For orthographic reasons, however, several measuring instruments do not lend themselves to the general rule; e.g., *flow-meter, flux-meter, gauss-meter, taxi-meter, torque-meter, volt-meter, water-meter, watt-meter,* etc.

28. *Foreign languages.*—Rules for word division in foreign languages, by

language, are printed in the 1967 GPO Style Manual (unabridged), pages 387–492.

29. *Chemical formulas.*—In chemical formulas, the hyphen has an important function. If a break is unavoidable in a formula, division is preferably made after an original hyphen to avoid the introduction of a misleading hyphen. If impractical to break on a hyphen, division may be made after an original comma, and no hyphen is added to indicate a runover. The following formula shows original hyphens and commas where division may be made. No letterspacing is used in a chemical formula, but to fill a line, a space is permitted on both sides of a hyphen.

1-(2,6,6-trimethylcyclohex-1- en -1- yl)-
3,7,12,16

30. *Chemical combining forms, prefixes, and suffixes.*—If possible, and subject to rules of good spacing, it is desirable to preserve as a unit such combining forms as follows:

*aceto, anhydro, benzo, bromo, chloro, chromo, cincho, cyclo, dehydro, diazo, flavo, fluoro, glyco, hydroxy, iso, keto, methyl, naphtho, phospho, poly, silico, tetra, triazo.*

The following suffixes are used in chemical printing. For patent and narrow measure composition, two-letter suffixes may be carried over.

*al, an, ane, ase, ate, ene, ic, id, ide, in, ine, ite, ol, ole, on, one, ose, ous oyl, yl, yne.*

31. *Mineral elements.*—When it is necessary to break mineral constituents, division should preferably be made before a center period and beginning parenthesis, and after inferior figures following a closing parenthesis; but elements within parentheses are not separated. In cases of unavoidable breaks, a hyphen is not added to indicate a runover.

$$Mg(UO_2)_2(SiO_3)_2(OH)_2 \cdot 6H_2O$$

32. The em dash is not used at the beginning of any line of type, unless it is required before a credit line or signature, or in lieu of opening quotation marks in foreign languages. (See rules 9.52, 9.53, p. 142, 1967 GPO Style Manual.)

33. Neither periods nor asterisks used as an ellipsis are overrun alone at the end of a paragraph. If necessary, run over enough preceding lines to provide a short word or part of a word to accompany the ellipsis. If a runback is possible, subject to rules of good spacing and word division, this method may be adopted.

34. Abbreviations and symbols

should not be broken at the end of a line: *A.F. of L.*, *A.T. & T.*, *C. Cls. R.*, *f.o.b.*, *n.o.i.b.n.*, *R. & D.*, *r.p.m.*, *WMAL*. Where unavoidable in narrow measures and AGO's, long symbols may be broken after letters denoting a complete word. Use no hyphens. COM SUB A C LANT (Commander Submarine Allied Command Atlantic).

35. Figures of less than six digits, decimals, and closely connected combinations of figures and abbreviations should not be broken at the end of a line: *$15,000, 34,575, 31.416, £8 4s. 7d., $10.25, 5,000 kw.-hr., A.D. 1952, 9 p.m., 18° F., NW¼*. If a break in six digits or over is unavoidable, divide on the comma or period, retain it, and use a hyphen.

36. Closely related abbreviations and initials in proper names and accompanying titles should not be separated, nor should titles, such as *Rev., Mr., Esq., Jr., 2d*, be separated from surnames.

37. Avoid dividing proper names, but if inescapable, follow general rules for word division.

38. Divisional and subdivisional paragraph reference signs and figures, such as *§ 18, section (a)(1), page 363(b)*, should not be divided, nor should such references be separated from the matter to which they pertain.

In case of an unavoidable break in a lengthy reference (e.g., *7*(*B*)(*1*)(*a*)(*i*)), division will be made after elements in parentheses, and no hyphen is used.

39. In dates, do not divide the month and day, but the year may be carried over.

40. In case of an unavoidable break in a land-description symbol group at the end of a line, use no hyphen and break after a fraction.

41. Avoid breaking longitude and latitude figures at the end of a line; space out the line instead. In case of an unavoidable break at end of line, use hyphen.

# PRESIDENTS OF THE UNITED STATES

| *Name (and party)* | *State of Birth* | *Born* | | *Died* |
|---|---|---|---|---|
| George Washington (F) | Va. | 1732 | 1789-97 | 1799 |
| John Adams (F) | Mass. | 1735 | 1797-1801 | 1826 |
| Thomas Jefferson (D-R) | Va. | 1743 | 1801-09 | 1826 |
| James Madison (D-R) | Va. | 1751 | 1809-17 | 1836 |
| James Monroe (D-R) | Va. | 1758 | 1817-25 | 1831 |
| John Quincy Adams (D-R) | Mass. | 1767 | 1825-29 | 1848 |
| Andrew Jackson (D) | S.C. | 1767 | 1829-37 | 1845 |
| Martin Van Buren (D) | N.Y. | 1782 | 1837-41 | 1862 |
| William Henry Harrison (W) | Va. | 1773 | 1841 | 1841 |
| John Tyler (W) | Va. | 1790 | 1841-45 | 1862 |
| James Knox Polk (D) | N.C. | 1795 | 1845-49 | 1849 |
| Zachary Taylor (W) | Va. | 1784 | 1849-50 | 1850 |
| Millard Fillmore (W) | N.Y. | 1800 | 1850-53 | 1874 |
| Franklin Pierce (D) | N.H. | 1804 | 1853-57 | 1869 |
| James Buchanan (D) | Pa. | 1791 | 1857-61 | 1868 |
| Abraham Lincoln (R) | Ky. | 1809 | 1861-65 | 1865 |
| Andrew Johnson (R) | N.C. | 1808 | 1865-69 | 1875 |
| Ulysses Simpson Grant (R) | Ohio | 1822 | 1869-77 | 1885 |
| Rutherford Birchard Hayes (R) | Ohio | 1822 | 1877-81 | 1893 |
| James Abram Garfield (R) | Ohio | 1831 | 1881 | 1881 |
| Chester Alan Arthur (R) | Vt. | 1830 | 1881-85 | 1886 |
| Grover Cleveland (D) | N.J. | 1837 | 1885-89 | 1908 |
| Benjamin Harrison (R) | Ohio | 1833 | 1889-93 | 1901 |
| Grover Cleveland (D) | N.J. | 1837 | 1893-97 | 1908 |
| William McKinley (R) | Ohio | 1843 | 1897-1901 | 1901 |
| Theodore Roosevelt (R) | N.Y. | 1858 | 1901-1909 | 1919 |
| William Howard Taft (R) | Ohio | 1857 | 1909-13 | 1930 |
| Woodrow Wilson (D) | Va. | 1856 | 1913-21 | 1924 |
| Warren Gamaliel Harding (R) | Ohio | 1865 | 1921-23 | 1923 |
| Calvin Coolidge (R) | Vt. | 1872 | 1923-29 | 1933 |
| Herbert Clark Hoover (R) | Iowa | 1874 | 1923-33 | 1965 |
| Franklin Delano Roosevelt (D) | N.Y. | 1882 | 1933-45 | 1945 |
| Harry S. Truman (D) | Mo. | 1884 | 1945-53 | 1972 |
| Dwight David Eisenhower (R) | Tex. | 1890 | 1953-61 | 1969 |
| John F. Kennedy (D) | Mass. | 1917 | 1961-63 | 1963 |
| Lyndon B. Johnson (D) | Tex. | 1908 | 1963-69 | 1973 |
| Richard M. Nixon (R) | Calif. | 1913 | 1969-74 (r) | |
| Gerald R. Ford (R) | Nebr. | 1913 | 1974-77 | |
| James Earl Carter, Jr. (D) | Ga. | 1924 | 1977- | |

# VICE-PRESIDENTS OF THE UNITED STATES

| *Name (and party)* | *State of Birth* | *Born* | *Term* | *Died* |
|---|---|---|---|---|
| John Adams (F) | Mass. | 1735 | 1789-97 | 1826 |
| Thomas Jefferson (D-R) | Va. | 1743 | 1797-1801 | 1826 |
| Aaron Burr (R) | N.J. | 1756 | 1801-05 | 1836 |
| George Clinton (R) | N.Y. | 1739 | 1805-12 | 1812 |
| Elbridge Gerry (R) | Mass. | 1744 | 1813-14 | 1814 |
| Daniel D. Tompkins (R) | N.Y. | 1774 | 1817-25 | 1825 |
| John U. Calhoun (R) | S.C. | 1782 | 1825-32 | 1850 |
| Martin Van Buren (D) | N.Y. | 1782 | 1833-37 | 1862 |
| Richard M. Johnson (D) | Ky. | 1780 | 1837-41 | 1850 |
| John Tyler (W) | Va. | 1790 | 1841 | 1862 |
| George M. Dallas (D) | Pa. | 1792 | 1845-49 | 1864 |
| Millard Fillmore (W) | N.Y. | 1800 | 1849-50 | 1874 |
| William R. King (D) | N.C. | 1786 | 1853 | 1853 |
| John C. Breckinridge (D) | Ky. | 1821 | 1857-61 | 1875 |
| Hannibal Hamlin (R) | Me. | 1809 | 1861-65 | 1891 |
| Andrew Johnson (R) | N.C. | 1808 | 1865 | 1875 |
| Schuyler Colfax (R) | N.Y. | 1823 | 1869-73 | 1885 |
| Henry Wilson (R) | N.H. | 1812 | 1873-75 | 1875 |
| William A. Wheeler (R) | N.Y. | 1819 | 1877-81 | 1887 |
| Chester A. Arthur (R) | Vt. | 1830 | 1881 | 1886 |
| Thomas A. Hendricks (D) | Ohio | 1819 | 1885 | 1885 |
| Levi P. Morton (R) | Vt. | 1824 | 1889-93 | 1920 |
| Adlai E. Stevenson (D) | Ky. | 1835 | 1893-97 | 1914 |
| Garrett A. Hobart (R) | N.J. | 1844 | 1897-99 | 1899 |
| Theodore Roosevelt (R) | N.Y. | 1858 | 1901 | 1919 |
| Charles W. Fairbanks (R) | Ohio | 1852 | 1905-09 | 1918 |
| James S. Sherman (R) | N.Y. | 1855 | 1909-12 | 1912 |
| Thomas R. Marshall (D) | Ind. | 1854 | 1913-21 | 1925 |
| Calvin Coolidge (R) | Vt. | 1872 | 1921-23 | 1933 |
| Charles G. Dawes (R) | Ohio | 1865 | 1925-29 | 1951 |
| Charles Curtis (R) | Kan. | 1860 | 1929-33 | 1936 |
| John N. Garner (D) | Tex. | 1869 | 1933-41 | 1967 |
| Henry A. Wallace (D) | Ia. | 1888 | 1941-45 | 1965 |
| Harry S. Truman (D) | Mo. | 1884 | 1945 | 1972 |
| Alben W. Barkley (D) | Ky. | 1877 | 1949-53 | 1956 |
| Richard M. Nixon (R) | Calif. | 1913 | 1953-61 | |
| Lyndon B. Johnson (D) | Tex. | 1908 | 1961-63 | 1973 |
| Hubert H. Humphrey (D) | S.D. | 1911 | 1965-69 | |
| Spiro T. Agnew (R) | Md. | 1918 | 1969-73 (r) | |
| Gerald R. Ford (R) | Nebr. | 1913 | 1973-1974 | |
| Nelson A. Rockefeller (R) | Me. | 1908 | 1974-77 | |
| Walter F. Mondale (D) | Minn. | 1928 | 1977- | |

F—Federalist; D—Democratic; R—Republican; W—Whig; (r)—resigned

# Webster's Synonyms, Antonyms, and Homonyms

# Webster's Synonyms, Antonyms, and Homonyms

## DEFINITIONS

**Synonyms**—Words that have the same meaning.

*Example:* big, large.

**Homonyms**—Words that sound alike, but are spelled differently and have different meanings.

*Example: one, won.*

**Antonyms**—Words that have opposite meanings.

*Example: large, small.*

*Note:* Antonyms appear in parentheses ( ) following the synonyms.

A

**abandon**—leave, forsake, desert, renounce, cease, relinquish, discontinue, cast off, resign, retire, quit, forgo, forswear, depart from, vacate, surrender, abjure, repudiate. (*pursue, prosecute, undertake*)

**abandoned**—profligate, wicked, vicious, unprincipled, reprobate, incorrigible, sinful, graceless, demoralized, dissolute, depraved, bad, licentious, corrupt. (*virtuous, conscientious, correct, upright*)

**abbreviate**—shorten, reduce, abridge, contract, curtail, epitomize, condense, prune, compress. (*lengthen, prolong, extend, enlarge, produce, elongate*)

**abdicate**—abandon, relinquish, resign, surrender, vacate. (*retain, maintain, claim, occupy, assert*)

**abet**—aid, support, promote, countenance, uphold, assist, instigate, encourage, incite, advocate, sanction, subsidize, embolden. (*thwart, contradict, obstruct, oppose, baffle, confound, discourage, disapprove, disconcert, counteract, deter, dissuade, frustrate*)

**abeyance**—suspension, reservation, dormancy, expectation, intermission. (*revival, renewal, operation, resuscitation, action, enjoyment, possession*)

**abhor**—hate, abominate, detest, loathe, despise, dislike, eschew, nauseate. (*love, admire, enjoy*)

**abide**—dwell, stay, inhabit, continue, rest, tarry, lodge, reside, live, wait, sojourn, remain, expect, endure, tolerate, anticipate, confront, await, bear, face, watch. (*deport, migrate, move, journey, proceed, resist, mislike, forfend, avoid, shun, reject, abandon, forfeit*)

**ability**—power, cleverness, faculty, skill, capacity, talent, expertness, aptitude, dexterity, efficiency, competency, qualification. (*weakness, incapacity, imbecility, inability, unreadiness, maladroitness*)

**abject**—degraded, outcast, miserable, vile, pitiable, worthless, despicable, groveling, fawning, squalid, base-minded, slavish, beggarly, servile, cringing, low, wretched, sordid. (*honorable, dignified, eminent, exalted, esteemed, worthy, venerable, noble, princely, illustrious, independent, self-assertive, self-reliant, vain, arrogant, insolent, haughty*)

**abjure**—renounce, deny, apostatize, discard, recant, disclaim, disavow, repudiate, revoke, retract, disown. (*profess, assert, demand, vindicate, claim, cherish, advocate, retain, acknowledge, appropriate, hug*)

**able**—strong, powerful, clever, skillful, talented, capable, fitted, efficient, effective, learned, gifted, masterly, telling, nervous, vigorous. (*weak, inefficient, unskillful, incapable, ineffective, unqualified*)

**abnormal**—irregular, erratic, peculiar, unusual, exceptional, monstrous, aberrant, devious, divergent, eccentric, strange. (*typical, normal, regular, ordinary, usual, natural, customary, illustrative*)

**abode**—home, stay, place, residence, domicile, habitation, lodgings, berth, quarters. (*halt, perch, tent, bivouac, caravansary: with the idea of transience*)

**abolish**—destroy, eradicate, invalidate, make void, obliterate, extirpate, abrogate, annul, subvert, cancel, revoke, quash, nullify, overthrow, annihilate, supersede, suppress, expunge. (*support, sustain, cherish, promote, continue, confirm, restore, repair, revive, reinstate, enact, institute, re-enact*)

**abominable**—abhorrent, foul, accursed, detestable, hateful, horrible, loathsome, odious, offensive, execrable, nauseous, impure. (*delectable, desirable, admirable, enjoyable, lovable, charming, delightful, grateful, pure*)

**abortion**—failure, miscarriage, misadventure, downfall, mishap, misproduction, defect, frustration, blunder, mess. (*success, consummation, completion, achievement, realization, perfection, exploit, feat, development*)

**abound**—stream, swell, flow, increase, overflow, superabound, luxuriate, teem, swarm, flourish, prevail, be plentiful, wanton, revel, multiply. (*fall, waste, dry, lack, wane, evaporate, drain, die, decay, vanish, lessen, decrease*)

**about**—almost, with respect to, near, nearly, touching, concerning, surrounding, relative to, relating to, in relation to, approximately, touching, roughly, generally. (*afar, away from, precisely, exactly*)

**above**—over, beyond, exceeding. (*below, within, beneath*)

**abridge**—abbreviate, diminish, shorten, lessen, curtail, restrict, contract, condense, epitomize, compress. (*amplify, expand, spread out*)

**abrupt**—sudden, steep, precipitous, craggy, coarse, curt, blunt, violent, harsh, unceremonious, rugged, rough. (*undulating, easy, gliding, polished, smooth, blending, courteous*)

**absent**—*a.* not present, gone away, elsewhere, inattentive, thoughtless, listless, preoccupied. (*present, in this place, here, attentive*)

**absent**—*v.* keep away, depart, withdraw. (*be present, stay, remain*)

**absolute**—perfect, complete, unconditional, irrelative, irrespective, supreme, despotic, autocratic, certain, authoritative, unqualified, unequivocal, irresponsible, arbitrary. (*imperfect, incomplete, conditional, conditioned, contingent, relative, dependent, constitutional, dubious, accountable, responsible*)

**absorb**—swallow, drown, consume, imbibe, engross, drink in, suck up, engulf, monopolize, exhaust. (*eject, emit, exude, disgorge, dissipate, distract, distil, disperse*)

**abstain**—refrain, forbear, refuse, demur, avoid, cease, stop, keep back, desist, discontinue, withhold, scruple. (*indulge, exceed, reveal, wanton*)

**abstemious**—abstinent, moderate, self-denying, sober, temperate, sparing, frugal. (*sensual, self-indulgent, gluttonous, greedy, intemperate*)

**abstract**—separate, detach, part, eliminate, draw away, remove, take away, appropriate, purloin, steal, thieve, draw from. (*add, unite, conjoin, adduce, impose, restore, surrender, return*)

**absurd**—irrational, ridiculous, monstrous, senseless, asinine, stupid, chimerical, unreasonable, preposterous, silly, nonsensical, foolish. (*sensible, rational, reasonable, consistent, sound, substantial, logical, wise, sagacious, reflective, philosophical*)

**abundant**—plentiful, copious, plenteous, large, ample, overflowing, teeming, full, lavish, luxuriant, liberal, rich. (*rare, scarce, scant, deficient, short, insufficient, niggardly, sparing, dry, drained, exhausted, impoverished*)

**abuse**—*v.* injure, damage, spoil, maltreat, treat ill, ill-use, ill-treat, revile, scandalize, disparage, reproach, upbraid, asperse, malign, slander, vituperate, prostitute, defame, pervert, misuse, misemploy, vilify. (*tend, protect, conserve, consider, regard, shield, cherish, praise, extol, laud, vindicate, panegyrize, respect*)

**abuse**—*n.* mistreatment, invective, ill-treatment, opprobium, scurrility, vituperation, ribaldry, obloquy, reproach, insolence, misusage, ill usage. (*good usage, good treatment, kindness, praise, deference, respect*)

**accelerate**—hasten, urge, expedite, quicken, speed, urge on, press forward, hurry, promote, dispatch, facilitate. (*delay, obstruct, impede, clog, retard, hinder, shackle, drag*)

**accent**—stress, rhythm, pulsation, beat, emphasis. (*smoothness, inaccentuation, monotony, equableness, babble, flow*)

**accept**—welcome, hail, admit, recognize, avow, acknowledge, take, accede to, receive, assent to. (*refuse, decline, reject, disown, disavow, ignore, repudiate*)

**acceptable**—grateful, pleasant, welcome, agreeable, pleasurable, seasonable, gratifying.

**accessory**—assistant, additive, additional, auxiliary, supplementary, conducive, accomplice, ally, associate, abettor, colleague, confederate, helper. (*essential, inherent, immanent, incorporate, superfluous, irrelevant, malapropos, obstructive, cumbersome*)

**accident**—chance, fortuity, disaster, incident, adventure, casualty, hazard, contingency, calamity, misadventure, mishap. (*law, purpose, appointment*)

**accommodate**—convenience, oblige, adapt, supply, reconcile, suit, fit, adjust, furnish, serve, harmonize. (*inconvenience, disoblige, disturb, misfit*)

**accommodating**—kind, unselfish, obliging, polite, considerate, yielding, conciliatory. (*disobliging, selfish, churlish, rude, imperious, dictatorial, exacting*)

**accomplice**—abettor, confederate, accessory, ally, associate, partner, colleague, coadjutor, assistant, *particeps criminis*. (*rival, foe, adversary, antagonist*)

**accomplish**—execute, perfect, perform, fulfil, do, carry out, attain, realize, consummate, achieve, finish, complete. (*fail of, frustrate, defeat, disconcert, destroy, baffle, mar, spoil*)

**accord**—agree, consent, harmonize, tally, answer, comport, consist, conform, grant, concede, surrender, allow. (*disagree, differ, misfit, miscomport*)

**accordingly**—agreeably, suitably, conformably, hence, consequently.

**account**—*n.* narration, report, rehearsal, story, statement, narrative, recital, relation, description, motive, value, importance, advantage, ground, reason, profit. (*silence, suppression, disadvantage, concealment*)

**account**—*v.* deem, esteem, consider, regard, hold, judge, rate, estimate, value, reckon, explain, solve. (*disesteem, misestimate, mystify, underrate, undervalue, perplex, darken*)

**accountable**—responsible, liable, amenable, punishable, answerable, accredited, delegated, subordinate. (*autocratic, independent, irresponsible*)

**accredit**—believe, trust, entrust, delegate, depute, commission, authorize. (*disbelieve, distrust*)

**accumulate**—collect, garner, grow, mass, heap, store, bring together, hoard, gather, agglomerate, husband, augment, amass, increase. (*dissipate, disperse, diminish, scatter, expend, waste*)

**accumulation**—heap, collection, store, mass, aggregation, hoard, pile. (*segregation, separation*)

**accurate**—careful, exact, faithful, precise, correct, close, truthful, strict, just, actual, nice. (*careless, inexact, faulty, incorrect, inaccurate, loose, defective*)

**accuse**—charge, incriminate, impeach, arraign, tax, taunt, censure, cite, summon, criminate. (*defend, vindicate, discharge, acquit, absolve, condone*)

**accustom**—habituate, familiarize, form, inure, train, reconcile. (*disaccustom, dishabituate, estrange, wean, alienate*)

**achieve**—accomplish, do, gain, perform, execute, effect, fulfil, finish, attain, win. (*fail, lose, miss*)

**achievement**—exploit, feat, attainment, accomplishment, performance. (*failure, lack in completion*)

**acknowledge**—avow, admit, recognize, own, accept, profess, endorse, grant, concede, concern. (*disavow, disclaim, disown, repudiate, ignore, deny*)

**acme**—summit, zenith, climax, apex, pitch, culmination, meridian. (*base, floor, ground, foundation, nadir, depth, depression, foot, root*)

**acquaint**—advertise, inform, impart, make known, divulge, teach, notify, apprize, advise, tell. (*misinform, deceive, delude, mislead, misguide*)

**acquaintance**—knowledge, intimacy, familiarity, experience, companionship. (*ignorance, unfamiliarity, inexperience*)

**acquiesce**—assent, concur, repose, agree, yield, be resigned, comply. (*dissent, demur, object*)

**acquit**—discharge, exonerate, absolve, exculpate, release, dismiss, liberate, pardon. (*charge, accuse, impeach, constrain, implicate, bind, compel, condemn*)

**acquittance**—release, receipt, discharge. (*bond, claim, charge, obligation*)

**across**—athwart, against, transversely, opposed. (*lengthwise, along, concurrently, parallel*)

**act**—deed, performance, action, movement, proceeding, exercise, operation, play. (*inaction, rest, repose, cessation, suspension, quiet, immobility*)

**active**—nimble, agile, lively, sprightly, brisk, quick, expert, dexterous, supple, wide-awake, prompt, busy, industrious, diligent. (*slow, inactive, indolent, sluggish, heavy*)

**actual**—developed, positive, unquestionable, demonstrable, certain, real, authentic. (*potential, undeveloped, hypothetical, supposititious, possible, virtual*)

**acute**—pointed, penetrating, sagacious, perspicacious, keen, astute, piercing, sharp, shrewd, keen-sighted, severe, distressing. (*dull, blunt, obtuse*)

**adapt**—fit, accommodate, suit, adjust, conform, admeasure, harmonize, attune. (*misfit, misconform, misapply*)

**add**—adduce, adjoin, increase, extend, enlarge, sum up, cast up, subjoin, amplify, annex. (*deduct, subtract, dissever, abstract*)

**addicted**—given, accustomed, prone, inclined, disposed, habituated. (*unaddicted, disinclined, unaccustomed, indisposed, averse, free*)

**addition**—accession, enlargement, increase, extension, accretion, appendage. (*deduction, detraction, drawback, decrement, deterioration*)

**address**—*n.* tact, manners, speech, abode. (*awkwardness, unmannerliness*)

**address**—*v.* accost, greet, salute, approach, apostrophize, appeal, hail, woo, court. (*elude, avoid, shun, ignore, pass*)

**adept**—expert, adroit, handy, master, performer, professor, artist. (*awkward, clumsy, inexpert, tyro*)

**adequate**—equal, sufficient, fit, satisfactory, full, competent, capable, able. (*unequal, insufficient*)

**adherence**—adhesion, attachment, devotion, fidelity, cleaving to, constancy, endearment. (*separation, disunion, unfaithfulness, desertion, treachery*)

**adherent**—follower, supporter, ally, disciple, admirer, backer, aid, partisan. (*opponent, deserter, adversary, renegade, antagonist*)

**adieu**—good-bye, farewell, leavetaking, parting, valediction. (*greeting, welcome, recognition, salutation*)

**adipose**—obese, corpulent, sebaceous, oleaginous. (*leathery, skinny, bony, thin*)

**adjacent**—near, neighboring, contiguous, close, bordering, conterminous. (*remote, distant*)

**adjoin**—annex, add, connect, append, supplement, attach, unite, border, neighbor, touch, abut, approximate, verge, trench. (*disjoin, dismember, disconnect, detach, disintegrate, disunite, part, separate, recede, return, diverge, be distant, removed*)

**adjourn**—postpone, suspend, defer, prorogue, delay, protract, put off. (*expedite, dispatch, urge*)

**adjunct**—addition, additament, attachment, appendage, auxiliary, appurtenance, aid, acquisition, advantage, help. (*essence, substance, body, clog*)

**adjust**—harmonize, collocate, arrange, localize, adapt, affix, right, suit, classify, set in order, reconcile, accommodate, compose. (*dislocate, disarrange, disturb, confound, dismember, disorder*)

**administer**—distribute, award, accord, dole, give, impart, afford, discharge, dispense, execute, perform, furnish, contribute, conduct. (*withdraw, withhold, refuse, retain, assume, resume, resign, deny*)

**admirable**—wonderful, excellent, surprising, astonishing, praiseworthy, pleasing. (*commonplace, mediocre, ridiculous, abominable, displeasing*)

**admissible**—allowable, permissible, probable, reasonable, just, proper, fair, right, qualified. (*unallowable, inadmissible, improper, unreasonable*)

**admit**—receive, pass, permit, accept, grant, concede, allow, acknowledge, confess, own, avow, suffer. (*exclude, debar, disallow, reject, deny, discharge, dismiss, eject, extrude, repudiate, disavow*)

**admonish**—remind, forewarn, advise, warn, dissuade, caution, counsel, reprove, censure, rebuke. (*encourage, instigate, abet, incite, urge, applaud*)

**adopt**—assume, select, affiliate, take, elect, arrogate, choose, endorse, avow, appropriate. (*reject, decline, repudiate, disavow, discard, renounce*)

**adore**—admire, hallow, glorify, praise, venerate, reverence, worship, idolize. (*abhor, despise, disesteem, abominate, execrate, blaspheme*)

**adulation**—flattery, compliment, sycophancy, courtship, incense, praise, blandishment, fawning, cringing. (*detraction, obloquy, defamation, calumny, traducement, sarcasm, ridicule, satire, bespatterment*)

**advance**—propel, elevate, promote, further, lend, propagate, progress, increase, prosper, rise. (*retard, hinder, withhold, withdraw, recall, depress, degrade*)

**advantage**—gain, success, superiority, help, assistance, benefit, good, avail, interest, utility, service, profit, acquisition. (*loss, disappointment, defeat, frustration, inferiority, obstacle, obstruction*)

**adventurous**—bold, brave, daring, enterprising, courageous, gallant, fearless, venturesome, rash, chivalrous, hazardous. (*timid, unenterprising, inadventurous, cowardly, nervous, hesitating, cautious*)

**adversary**—antagonist, foe, enemy, rival, assailant. (*accessory, abettor, aider, friend, helper, assistant, ally, accomplice*)

**adversity**—ill luck, misfortune, misery, calamity, disaster, distress, unsuccess, failure, ruin, trouble, affliction, sorrow. (*good luck, prosperity, happiness*)

**advertent**—attentive, regardful, mindful, watchful, thoughtful, observant, considerate. (*inattentive, inadvertent, casual, thoughtless, heedless, inobservant, inconsiderate*)

**advertise**—publish, inform, advise, circulate, announce, notify, proclaim, promulge. (*suppress, hush, conceal, ignore, hoodwink, misguide, mislead*)

**advise**—admonish, warn, deliberate, counsel, persuade, urge, prompt, instigate, incite, instruct, acquaint, inform. (*dissuade, deter, expostulate, remonstrate, prohibit, inhibit, restrain, curb, mislead, misadvise, hoodwink, deceive, delude, misinform*)

**advocate**—pleader, counselor, upholder, propagator, promoter, supporter, countenancer, defender, maintainer. (*opponent, adversary, discountenancer*)

**affable**—courteous, accessible, condescending, conversable, gracious, sociable, gentle, complaisant, urbane, polite, easy, approachable. (*exclusive, discourteous, distant, inaccessible, unapproachable, inconversable, haughty, contemptuous, supercilious*)

**affect**—like, desire, favor, seek, assume, move, influence, concern, interest, feign, pretend. (*dislike, eschew, shun, repel, repudiate*)

**affectation**—pretense, artifice, hypocrisy, assumption, simulation, mannerism, euphuism, airs. (*genuineness, naturalness, unaffectedness, simplicity, artlessness*)

**affection**—influence, condition, state, inclination, bent, mood, humor, feeling, love, desire, propensity. (*insensibility, indifference, repugnance, disaffection*)

**affinity**—relationship, relation, kindred, conformity, connection, alliance, similarity, analogy, homogeneity, harmony, correlativeness, sympathy, interdependence, interconnection, intercommunity. (*dissimilarity, discordance, disconnection, independence, antagonism, antipathy, repugnance, interrepulsiveness*)

**affirm**—assert, swear, testify, tell, aver, propound, asseverate, depose, state, declare, endorse, maintain. (*deny, dispute, doubt, demur, negative*)

**affliction**—trouble, trial, grief, pain, disease, misery, hardship, sorrow. (*consolation, relief, alleviation, assuagement, boon, blessing, gratification, pleasure*)

**afford**—produce, supply, give, yield, grant, confer, bestow, impart, administer, extend. (*withhold, deny, withdraw, retain, stint, grudge*)

**affront**—outrage, provocation, insult, ill-treatment, abuse, wrong, offense, indignity. (*homage, salutation, courtesy, apology, amends, compliment*)

**afloat**—adrift, abroad, at sea, abroach, loose, distracted, dazed. (*ashore, snug, tight, close, fast, collected, concentrated*)

**afoot**—working, launched, afloat, agoing, inaugurated, started, instituted, established. (*uncommenced, incomplete, projected, proposed, contemplated, designed*)

**afraid**—fearful, apprehensive, timid, timorous, cowardly, fainthearted, cautious, careful, frightened, alarmed, terrified, suspicious, distrustful, anxious. (*fearless, inapprehensive, unsolicitous*)

**afresh**—anew, again, frequently, repeatedly, intermittently. (*continuously, uniformly, uninterruptedly, unintermittently, connectedly*)

**after**—behind, following, succeeding. (*before, afore, introducing, preceding*)

**again**—anew, afresh, repeatedly, frequently. (*continuously, uniformly, uninterruptedly, unintermittently, once*)

**against**—over, opposite, abutting, opposing, resisting, despite, across, athwart, counter. (*with, for, accompanying, aiding, suiting, promoting*)

**age**—period, generation, era, epoch, date, century, antiquity, senility, eldership, seniority. (*youth, infancy, boyhood, childhood, moment, instant*)

**agent**—doer, performer, actor, force, means, instrument, influence, cause, promoter, operator. (*counteragent, counteractor, counteraction, opponent*)

**aggravate**—exasperate, provoke, wound, heighten, intensify, irritate, make worse, increase, enhance, embitter, magnify. (*soothe, conciliate, assuage, diminish, palliate, neutralize, soften, lessen*)

**agile**—nimble, active, fleet, brisk, alert, featly, lithe, prompt, ready, quick, supple, swift, sprightly. (*slow, heavy, awkward, inert, clumsy, bulky, ponderous, elephantine*)

**agitate**—disturb, trouble, excite, ruffle, stir, fluster, oscillate, instigate, convulse, shake. (*calm, compose, allay, pacify, smooth*)

**agony**—pain, torture, torment, distress, woe, throe, suffering, pang, excruciation. (*assuagement, comfort, peace, ease, relief, gratification, enjoyment*)

**agree**—suit, tally, accord, fit, harmonize, combine, assent, concur, acquiesce, admit, consent, conform, consort, comport, coincide. (*differ, disagree, revolt, protest, decline, refuse, dissent, demur*)

**agreeable**—obliging, pleasant, accommodating, grateful, acceptable, welcome, suitable, consistent, consonant, amiable, gratifying, pleasing, good-natured, complaisant. (*disobliging, unpleasant, un-*

*accommodating, disagreeable, obnoxious, ungrateful)*

**agreement**—contract, compact, bond, concord, concurrence, conformity, harmony, unison, consonance, bargain, covenant, obligation, undertaking, treaty. (*disagreement, informal understanding or promise, parole*)

**aid**—help, assist, succor, support, befriend, cooperate, contribute, favor, foster, protect, abet, encourage, instigate, subsidize. (*oppose, resist*)

**ailment**—complaint, sickness, illness, disease. (*recovery, convalescence, sanity, health, robustness*)

**aim**—*n.* tendency, intent, aspiration, bent, drift, object, scope, goal, purpose, mark, end, design, intention. (*shunning, disregarding, disaffecting*)

**aim**—*v.* seek, level, propose, design, affect, intend, mean, purpose. (*shun, disregard, disaffect, ignore*)

**akin**—related, agnate, cognate, homogeneous, similar, consanguineous, congenial, allied, sympathetic. (*unrelated, unconnected, foreign, alien, heterogeneous, uncongenial, hostile, unallied, antagonistic*)

**alacrity**—quickness, readiness, briskness, activity, cheerfulness, compliance, willingness, promptitude. (*slowness, reluctance, repugnance*)

**alarming**—terrible, fearful, frightful, portentous, ominous, threatening. (*soothing, assuring, encouraging, inviting, propitious, hopeful, alluring*)

**alert**—active, brisk, nimble, prepared, prompt, vigilant, ready, wakeful, watchful, on the watch, lively. (*slow, sleepy, lazy, absent, unready, oblivious*)

**alien**—foreign, strange, undomesticated, inappropriate, irrelevant, impertinent. (*pertinent, essential, proper, appropriate, relevant, germane, akin*)

**alike**—resembling, similar, together, twin-fellow, analogous, identical, equal, equivalent, same, homogeneous, akin, equally. (*unlike, heterogeneous*)

**alive**—quick, living, breathing, warm, lively, vivacious, alert, existing, existent, safe, subsisting, active, brisk, animated. (*dead, departed, cold, lifeless, defunct, inanimate, dispirited, dull*)

**allege**—declare, affirm, assert, asseverate, depose, plead, cite, quote, assign, advance, maintain, say. (*contradict, gainsay, refute, deny, disprove, neutralize*)

**allegiance**—subjection, obedience, loyalty, fealty, homage. (*disloyalty, rebellion, resistance, disaffection, malcontentment, treason*)

**alleviate**—lighten, lessen, assuage, mitigate, soothe, moderate, relieve, remit, diminish. (*aggravate, enhance, increase, embitter, augment*)

**alliance**—compact, treaty, cooperation, union, connection, partnership, league, combination, coalition, confederation, friendship, relation, relationship. (*disunion, enmity, divorce, discord, disruption*)

**allot**—assign, grant, award, give, apportion, deal, dispense, parcel, distribute, divide, mete out, portion out. (*refuse, withhold, retain, appropriate*)

**allow**—concede, apportion, allot, assign, afford, tolerate, authorize, grant, remit, recognize, acknowledge, avow, confess, admit, permit, suffer, sanction, yield. (*withhold, withdraw, resume, refuse*)

**alloy**—admixture, deterioration, adulteration, drawback, diminution, decrement, impairment, debasement, depreciation, disparagement. (*purity, genuineness, enhancement, integrity*)

**allude**—point, indicate, suggest, hint, signify, insinuate, refer, imply, intimate. (*specify, demonstrate, declare, mention, state*)

**ally**—friend, companion, supporter, aider, abettor, accomplice, assistant, confederate, helper, associate, accessory, colleague, coadjutor. (*foe, enemy, opponent, adversary, baffler, counteractor*)

**aloud**—audibly, loudly, clamorously, sonorously, vociferously, obstreperously. (*softly, silently, inaudibly, suppressedly*)

**alter**—substitute, change, vary, modify, exchange, diversify, remodel. (*retain, perpetuate, conserve, stereotype, arrest, solidify, stabilitate*)

**alternative**—choice, resource, opinion. (*compulsion, quandary, necessity, fix*)

**altogether**—collectively, combined, in one, totally, entirely, wholly, fully, completely, utterly, thoroughly. (*separately, individually, partially*)

**amass**—collect, accumulate, aggregate, heap, gather, store up, hoard, pile up. (*divide, dissipate, waste, scatter, disperse, parcel, portion, spend*)

**amazement**—astonishment, awe, wonder, bewilderment, surprise, stupefaction, marvel. (*expectation, preparation, anticipation, familiarity*)

**ambiguous**—equivocal, vague, doubtful, enigmatical, uncertain, obscure, unintelligible, perplexing, indistinct, dubious. (*univocal, obvious*)

**ameliorate**—improve, raise, better, advantage, promote, advance, amend, rectify, meliorate. (*debase, depress, deteriorate, injure, impair, vitiate*)

**amend**—improve, mend, repair, correct, rectify, better, ameliorate, reform. (*deteriorate, degenerate, neglect, aggravate, tarnish, blemish, spoil, corrupt*)

**amiable**—lovable, good, kind, benevolent, charitable, delectable, engaging, fascinating, agreeable, lovely, pleasing, charming, attractive. (*churlish, disagreeable, hateful, abominable, ill-natured, ill-conditioned, unamiable*)

**amiss**—wrong, untrue, wide, bad, false, defective, short, inappropriate, inopportune, injudicious, untimely, abortive. (*right, true, good, complete, effective, successful, satisfactory, consummate, expedient, appropriate, opportune*)

**amnesty**—pardon, acquittal, remission, condonation, oblivion, dispensation, absolution. (*penalty, retaliation, punishment, retribution, requital, visitation, infliction, exaction, trial, account*)

**ample**—large, bountiful, liberal, copious, spacious, roomy, diffusive, full, complete, sufficient, plentiful, abundant. (*narrow, niggardly, insufficient, stingy, scant, mean, stint, bare*)

**amplify**—enrich, enlarge, increase, augment, multiply, dilate, develop, swell, expatiate, expand, discuss, unfold, extend. (*retrench, amputate, curtail, condense, abbreviate, epitomize, gather, collect*)

**analogy**—relation, resemblance, proportion, similarity, similitude, coincidence, affinity, comparison, parity. (*disproportion, dissimilarity, disharmony*)

**analysis**—dissection, separation, anatomy, segregation, decomposition, resolution, partition. (*composition, synthesis, aggregation, combination, coalition, amalgamation, coherence*)

**anarchy**—disorder, tumult, rebellion, riot, misgovernment, insubordination. (*order, subjection*)

**anatomy**—dissection, division, segregation, analysis, resolution, dismemberment. (*synthesis, collocation, organization, union, construction, structure*)

**ancient**—old, antiquated, old-fashioned, antique, obsolete, old-time, aged, primeval, primordial, immemorial, time-honored. (*new, young, modern*)

**anger**—*n.* ire, incensement, vexation, grudge, pique, exasperation, indignation, enmity, displeasure, irritation, passion, spleen, gall, resentment, rage, animosity, fury, choler, wrath. (*peace, peacefulness, peaceableness, appeasement, forgiveness*)

**anger**—*v.* enrage, vex, kindle, fret, ruffle, chafe, infuriate, exasperate, provoke, irritate, incense, wound, inflame, embitter. (*appease, compose, forbear, allay, soothe, calm, conciliate, heal*)

**animosity**—hatred, antipathy, dissension, aversion, acrimony, feud, strife, rancor, antagonism, bitterness, acerbity, hostility, enmity, malice, anger, malevolence, ill will, malignity, feeling against. (*congeniality, companionship, friendship*)

**annex**—add, attach, fasten, affix, subjoin, append, connect, unite. (*withdraw, detach, disconnect*)

**annihilate**—abolish, destroy, bring to naught, uproot, eradicate, nullify, exterminate, end, extinguish, demolish, obliterate, efface. (*keep, conserve, preserve, foster, tend, protect, cherish, develop*)

**announce**—declare, propound, give notice, enunciate, advertise, publish, report, notify, make known, give out, reveal, herald, proclaim, intimate, promulge. (*conceal, suppress, hush, stifle, withhold*)

**annoy**—tease, vex, irritate, disturb, affront, molest, pain, disquiet, incommode, tantalize, bother, weary, inconvenience, plague, discommode, harass, chafe. trouble. (*soothe, conciliate, appease, regard*)

**anomaly**—irregularity, abnormity, exception, informality, peculiarity, eccentricity. (*conformity, regularity, illustration, conformance, exemplification*)

**anonymous**—nameless, unattested, authorless, unidentified, unauthenticated. (*authenticated, attested, identified, authorized, verified, signed*)

**answer**—reply, response, counterargument, confutation, acceptance (as of a challenge), tally counterpart, solution, vindication, apology, exculpation, defense, rejoinder, repartee, retort. (*challenge, question, defiance, summons, interrogation*)

**antecedent**—prior, foregoing, previous, precursive, precedent, earlier, introductory, preliminary, former. (*posterior, later, subsequent, consequent*)

**anticipate**—forestall, prejudge, expect, foretaste, apprehend, prevent, prearrange, prepare, meet, obviate, intercept, forecast. (*remember, recollect, remedy, recall, undo, cure, misapprehend*)

**anticipation**—expectation, awaiting, preoccupation, preconception, foresight, forethought, foretaste, prevention, forestallment, contemplation, hope, trust, prospect, forecast, provision. (*surprise, unpreparedness, unexpectedness*)

**anxiety**—care, trouble, eagerness, disquiet, apprehension, carefulness, diffidence, solicitude, misgiving. (*carelessness, ease, confidence, contentment*)

**anxious**—solicitous, careful, uneasy, concerned, restless, watchful, disturbed, unquiet. (*without care, careless, inert, ease, unconcerned, calm, composed*)

**apathy**—indifference, insensibility, unfeelingness in company, insusceptibility, unconcern, sluggishness, hebetude. (*anxiety, care, eagerness, interestedness, sensibility, susceptibility, sensitiveness, irritability, curiosity*)

**ape**—mimic, imitate, simulate, personate, represent. (*not to imitate, vary, modify, change*)

**apiece**—distributively, individually, separately, severally, analytically. (*collectively, together, accumulatively, indiscriminately, confusedly, synthetically*)

**apology**—defense, justification, plea, exculpation, excuse, vindication, acknowledgment, confession. (*charge, imputation, impeachment, offense, incrimination, injury. accusation, wrong, insult*)

**appall**—affright, alarm terrify, scare, daunt, cow, shock, frighten, discourage, dishearten, horrify, dismay, astound. (*encourage, rally, assure, embolden*)

**apparel**—clothes, robes, vesture, vestments, raiment, garniture, habiliments, habit, dress, clothing, caparison, trappings, housings. (*nudity, divestiture, dishabille, tatters, rags*)

**apparent**—obvious, plain, conspicuous, manifest, appearing, unmistakable, clear, probable, seeming, presumable, likely, patent, ostensible, visible, evident, indubitable, notorious, certain. (*uncertain, dubious, inapparent, minute, unobservable, improbable, insupposable, hidden, real*)

**appeal**—accost, address, apostrophize, invite, cite, invoke, urge, refer, call upon, entreat, request, resort. (*deprecate, repudiate, protest, disavow, disclaim, defy, abjure*)

**appearance**—advent, coming, arrival, presence, apparition, aspect, manifestation, probability, likeness, exhibition, mien, manner, semblance, air, show, look, pretense, likelihood, presumption. (*departure, disappearance, unlikelihood, nonappearance, concealment, evanition*)

**append**—affix, supplement, subjoin, attach. (*separate, disengage, disconnect, detach*)

**appetite**—passion, desire, propensity, proclivity, inclination, propension, appetency, want, craving, disposition, tendency, proneness. (*repugnance, aversion, antipathy, loathing, indifference, apathy*)

**applause**—praise, plaudit, laudation, encomium, commendation, approbation, acclamation, approval, eulogy, acclaim. (*obloquy, condemnation, denunciation, dissatisfaction, contempt, censure, blame*)

**applicable**—available, ancillary, convenient, useful, pertinent, conducive, appropriate. (*useless, unavailable, inconducive, inapplicable, irrelevant*)

**appoint**—fix, determine, install, allot, order, prescribe, institute, employ, apportion, apply, designate, assign, intrust, invest, ordain, arrange. (*reverse, cancel, recall, withdraw, reserve, withhold*)

**apportion**—assign, deal, allot, grant, share, divide, dispense, administer, distribute, appoint. (*reserve, retain, refuse, withhold, assume, resume*)

**appreciate**—esteem, recognize, acknowledge, respect, value, prize, regard, reckon, estimate. (*undervalue, misconceive, misjudge, ignore, misappreciate*)

**apprehend**—comprehend, understand, take, expect, seize, conceive, arrest, fancy, dread, imagine, presume, anticipate, fear, conjecture. (*ignore, miss, lose, misconjecture, misconceive, misapprehend*)

**approach**—access, avenue, entrance, adit, vestibule, arrival, approximation, advent, nearing, admission, appropinquation, admittance, mode, path, way, advance, similarity. (*exit, egress, debouchure, outlet, departure, recession, distance*)

**approve**—like, comment, sanction, praise, support, second, promote, encourage, authorize. (*disapprove, dislike, censure, blame, disown, disavow*)

**approximate**—approach, resemble, border, abut, near, trench. (*separate, differ, vary, recede, diverge*)

**apt**—fit, apposite, clever, meet, liable, becoming, appropriate, ready, fitting, suitable, pertinent, qualified, prompt, adapted, likely. (*unfitted, illtimed, awkward, unlikely, inapt*)

**arbitrary**—tyrannical, despotic, harsh, dictatorial, imperious, unforbearing, overbearing, selfish, absolute, irresponsible, tyrannous, domineering, peremptory. (*mild, modest, lenient, considerate*)

**arbitrate**—settle, adjust, compose, decide, determine, accommodate, adjudicate. (*dispute, claim*)

**ardent**—longing, passionate, aspiring, warm, eager, fervent, excited, fiery, glowing, zealous, fervid, fierce, keen, vehement, hot, affectionate, impassioned, burning, heated. (*cool, cold, indifferent, dispassioned, apathetic, passionless, unimpassioned, phlegmatic, platonic*)

**argue**—discuss, debate, prove, question, evidence, establish, imply, sift, dispute, persuade, controvert, contend, demonstrate, reason. (*dictate, assert, propound, command*)

**argument**—reasoning, controversy, evidence, discussion, topic, dispute. (*assertion, assumption*)

**arid**—dry, parched, sterile, unproductive. (*moist, dewy, watered, fertile, luxuriant, exuberant, verdant*)

**aright**—right, well, rightly, correctly, truly, properly, uprightly, unexceptionably, justly, suitably, appropriately. (*wrongly, awry, incorrectly, improperly, defectively, erroneously*)

**arouse**—stir, excite, disturb, animate, wake up, stimulate, alarm, provoke, cheer. (*allay, assuage*)

**arraign**—summon, accuse, censure, indict, charge, impeach. (*acquit, condone, discharge, release*)

**arrange**—order, put in order, group, array, place, adjust, range, locate, dispose, assort, deal, sort, parcel, classify. (*derange, disarrange, confuse, disturb, disperse, jumble, disorder*)

**array**—*v.* vest, deck, equip, decorate, rank, adorn, dress, accoutre, invest, attire, place, arrange, draw up, marshal, set in order, dispose. (*disarray, disarrange, confuse, jumble, divest, denude, strip*)

**array**—*n.* arrangement, order, disposition, sight, exhibition, show, parade. (*disarray, disorder, confusion, confusedness, jumble*)

**arrest**—seize, take, stop, capture, withhold, restrain, hold, detain, apprehend. (*release, dismiss*)

**arrive**—reach, attain, come to, enter, get to, land. (*embark, depart, start*)

**arrogance**—haughtiness, overbearingness, contemptuousness, hauteur, browbeating, loftiness, self-conceit, stateliness, vainglory, insolence, self-importance, assumption, discourtesy. (*bashfulness, servility, considerateness, deference, courtesy, modesty, shyness, diffidence, politeness*)

**artful**—cunning, designing, maneuvering, sharp, knowing, subtle, sly, crafty, wily, shrewd. (*simple, undesigning, artless, open, innocent, unsophisticated*)

**artificial**—invented, fabricated, fictitious, constructed, manufactured, pretended, simulated, false, assumed, concocted, contrived, deceptive, artful, affected, unnatural, constrained. (*natural,* *inartificial, genuine, spontaneous, transparent, artless, unaffected)*

**ascertain**—prove, verify, find out, discover, confirm, detect, determine, learn, discern. (*guess, conjecture, surmise, suppose, presume)*

**ascribe**—assign, attribute, impute, refer, render, allege, charge. (*deny, refuse, exclude, dissociate)*

**aspiration**—longing, desire, aim, wish, craving, ambition, endeavor, hope, effort, eagerness. (*apathy, indifference, aimlessness, dullness, inertia, callousness, carelessness, aversion, avoidance)*

**assembly**—meeting, concourse, assemblage, multitude, group, synod, conclave, conference, convocation, unison, company, congregation, collection, crowd, gathering, convention, aggregate. (*dispersion, dissipation, disunion, disruption)*

**assent**—coincidence, agreement, concert, acknowledgment, consent, acquiescence, approval, concurrence, approbation, compliance. (*dissent, disagreement, difference, disavowal, repudiation)*

**assign**—attribute, apportion, allege, refer, specify, consign, entrust, commit, point out, allot to, adduce, advance, appoint, convey. (*withhold, withdraw, resume, retain, refuse, disconnect, dissociate)*

**assist**—help, succor, aid, support, relieve, befriend, second, cooperate with, back, benefit, further. (*hinder, resist, oppose, antagonize, counteract, clog, prevent)*

**assistant**—helper, aider, attendant, coadjutor, auxiliary, ally, associate, contributor, partner, confederate. (*hinderer, opposer, rival, foe, antagonist)*

**association**—union, connection, conjunction, consortment, companionship, alliance, familiarity, community, membership, society, company, denomination, partnership, fellowship, fraternity, friendship. (*disunion, disconnection, estrangement)*

**assortment**—collection, disposition, distribution, class, quantity, selection, stock, miscellany, lot, variety. (*misarrangement, disarrangement, displacement, misplacement)*

**assume**—take, appropriate, arrogate, wear, exhibit, postulate, suppose, presume, usurp, claim, pretend, feign, affect. (*waive, allow, doff, render, surrender, concede, grant, demonstrate, abandon)*

**assure**—advise, advertise, promise, inform, rally, console, encourage, countenance, aid, support, convince, uphold, certify. (*misinform, misadvise)*

**astonish**—startle, surprise, confound, amaze, astound, fill with wonder, stupefy, alarm, terrify, electrify, scare, dumfound. (*rally, encourage)*

**astray**—loose, abroad, missing, about, at large, wrong, erring, wandering. (*right, close, at home)*

**athletic**—strong, vigorous, powerful, stalwart, brawny, muscular, ablebodied, lusty, sinewy, robust. (*weak, puny, effeminate, nerveless, strengthless, unbraced)*

**atrocious**—monstrous, nefarious, wicked, outrageous, villainous, enormous, shameful, heinous, cruel, flagrant, facinorous, flagitious. (*laudable, noble, honorable, generous, humane, admirable)*

**attach**—fasten, apply, append, add, fix, subjoin, annex, unite, conciliate, tie, connect, conjoin, attract, win, bind. (*unfasten, loose, disunite, untie)*

**attack**—*v.* assail, assault, invade, encounter, charge, besiege, impugn, contravene. (*defend, resist, repel, protest, withstand on one's own part or for another, support, aid, shield, uphold, vindicate)*

**attack**—*n.* invasion, assault, onset, aggression, onslaught. (*defense, resistance, repulse, protection)*

**attain**—reach, extend, master, arrive at, earn, win, achieve, accomplish, get, obtain, acquire, gain, secure. (*lose, fail, forfeit, miss, abandon, resign)*

**attempt**—try, endeavor, strive, undertake, seek, essay, attack, violate, force. (*disregard, abandon, pretermit, dismiss, neglect, shun, drop)*

**attend**—listen, heed, notice, observe, wait on, serve, mind, watch, accompany, consort, follow, imply, involve. (*wander, disregard, leave, forsake)*

**attention**—observation, notice, regard, watchfulness, heed, consideration, circumspection, study, vigilance, care. (*disregard, inadvertence, remission, indifference, carelessness, abstraction, distraction)*

**attest**—vouch, aver, assert, certify, witness, vouch for, affirm, testify, evidence, support, confirm, suggest, prove, involve, demonstrate, establish, imply, bespeak. (*deny, controvert, contradict, contravene, disprove, disestablish, exclude, neutralize)*

**attire**—robes, garment, clothing, vestments, habiliment, habit, raiment, clothes, garb, apparel, accoutrements, livery, uniform, costume. (*nudity, divestment, exposure, denudation, bareness, disarray)*

**attract**—influence, induce, dispose, incline, tempt, prompt, allure, charm, fascinate, invite, entice. (*repel, deter, indispose, disincline, estrange, alienate)*

**attractive**—winning, alluring, tempting, inviting, engaging, captivating, fascinating, enticing, interesting, charming, pleasant, beautiful, agreeable. (*unattractive, repugnant, repulsive, uninteresting, disagreeable, unpleasant, deformed, ugly, deterrent)*

**attribute**—*v.* refer, assign, associate, apply, ascribe, charge, impute, connect. (*divorce, disconnect, dissociate, dissever)*

**attribute**—*n.* property, quality, characteristic, attainment, sign, mark, indication, manifestation, symbol.

**attrition**—sorrow, repentance, affliction, penitence, compunction, remorse, self-reproach. (*impenitence, callousness, obduracy, reprobation, relentlessness)*

**audacious**—insolent, adventurous, presumptuous, valiant, rash, bold, daring, reckless, enterprising. (*timid, cowardly, cautious, inadventurous, unventuresome, unenterprising)*

**audacity**—boldness, rashness, temerity, recklessness, hardihood. (*caution, self-preservation, timidity, calculation, forethought, foresight, diffidence, inadventurousness)*

**augment**—increase, enlargement, amplification, enrichment, supply, enhancement, addition, acquisition, improvement. (*deduction, detraction, diminution, contraction, withdrawal, reservation, expenditure, loss, waste, detriment, deterioration, impoverishment, reduction, curtailment)*

**augury**—prophecy, prediction, divination, conjecture, omen, prognostication. (*experience, science)*

**august**—majestic, dignified, stately, noble, pompous, imposing, grand, solemn, exalted. (*mean, undignified, unimposing, common, vulgar, despicable, paltry, unnoticeable, beggarly, commonplace)*

**auspicious**—propitious, lucky, favorable, encouraging, satisfactory, successful, hopeful, promising, happy, golden, fortunate, opportune, prosperous. (*unpropitious, unfavorable, discouraging, unsatisfactory, inauspicious, unpromising, abortive)*

**austere**—hard, rigid, stern, severe, morose, unrelenting, unyielding, strict, rigorous, harsh, sour, relentless. (*mild, affable, kindly, tender feeling)*

**authentic**—genuine, veritable, reliable, real, original, trustworthy, not spurious, true, legitimate, certain, accepted, current, received. (*unreliable, spurious, false, apocryphal, disputed, exploded, rejected, counterfeit, unfounded, unauthorized, baseless)*

**authoritative**—decisive, sure, conclusive, authentic, powerful, firm, potent, dictatorial, imperious, arbitrary, arrogant, imperative, dogmatic, commanding. (*weak, inconclusive, vague, indeterminate, indefinite, vacillating, undecisive, bland, conciliatory)*

**authority**—ground, justification, authenticity, genuineness, conclusiveness, decisiveness, control, direction, jurisdiction, government, regulation, power, right, rule, sway, sufferance, supremacy, dominion. (*groundlessness, spuriousness, indecision, inconclusiveness, inoperativeness, incompetency, weakness, usurpation, wrong)*

**autocratic**—independent, arbitrary, despotic, irresponsible, absolute. (*dependent, subordinate, responsible, constitutional, limited)*

**auxiliary**—helpful, abetting, aiding, accessory, promotive, conducive, assistant, ancillary, assisting, subsidiary, helping. (*unassisting, unconducive, unpromotive, redundant, superfluous, obstructive)*

**avail**—suffice, hold, stand, endure, answer, tell,

profit, help, benefit, advantage, service, use, utility. (*fail, fall, disappoint, betray*)

**available**—useful, appropriate, convertible, attainable, handy, conducive, applicable, procurable, advantageous, helpful, profitable, suitable, serviceable. (*useless, inappropriate, inapplicable, unprocurable, inconducive, irrelevant, inoperative, unavailable*)

**avarice**—greed, cupidity, rapacity, penuriousness, niggardliness, miserliness, stinginess, covetousness, acquisitiveness, griping, greediness. (*largeheartedness, unselfishness, liberality, bountifulness*)

**aver**—assert, asseverate, affirm, depose, avouch, protest, oblige, declare. (*deny, contradict, contravene, disavow, disclaim, repudiate, gainsay, oppugn*)

**avidity**—cupidity, avarice, desire, greed, longing, rapacity, eagerness. (*coldness, indifference, apathy, insensibility, antipathy, nausea, aversion, repugnance, loathing*)

**avoid**—quit, shun, abandon, desert, forsake, relinquish, fly, eschew, elude, dodge, escape, shirk. (*seek, court, approach, accost, address, affect*)

**award**—assign, apportion, attribute, accord, grant, distribute, divide, allot, give, determine, decree, order, adjudge. (*refuse, withhold, withdraw*)

**aware**—conscious, sensible, informed, certified, assured, known, apprized, cognizant. (*unconscious, insensible, ignorant, unaware, uninformed*)

**awful**—fearful, direful, appalling, terrible, alarming, dreadful, horrible, solemn, portentous, horrific. (*inocuous, informidable, unimposing, unastonishing*)

**awkward**—ungainly, clownish, clumsy, maladroit, unhandy, uncouth, rough, boorish, bungling, gawky. (*neat, clever, dexterous, skillful, adroit*)

**axiom**—self-evident truth, aphorism, truism, apophthegm, maxim. (*nonsense, absurdity, stultiloquy, absurdness*)

## B

**babble**—prate, prattle, dribble, chatter, gabble, twaddle, blab, cackle. (*enunciate, vociferate, hush*)

**babel**—hubbub, confusion, clamor, jargon, din, discord, clang. (*elocution, articulation, monotony, distinctness, consecutiveness, intonation, enunciation*)

**baffle**—frustrate, counteract, estop, disconcert, elude, mock, thwart, confound, defeat, perplex, restrain, upset, foil, mar, balk, neutralize, dodge, counterfoil. (*point, aid, abet, enforce, promote*)

**bait**—morsel, snare, decoy, enticement, allurement, inducement. (*warning, scarecrow, dissuasive, deterrent, prohibition, intimidation, threat*)

**balance**—weigh, poise, pit, set, counterpoise, counteract, neutralize, equalize, estimate, redress, adjust. (*upset, tilt, cant, subvert, mispoise, overbalance*)

**balderdash**—gasconade, flummery, rhodomontade, bombast, fustian, froth. (*sense, wisdom*)

**balk**—estop, bar, thwart, frustrate, foil, stop, prevent, hinder, neutralize, nullify, mar, counteract, disappoint, defeat, baffle. (*aid, abet, promote*)

**banish**—expel, abandon, dispel, eject, extrude, exclude, relegate, expatriate, repudiate, disclaim. (*cherish, foster, protect, consider, encourage, locate*)

**banquet**—feast, festivity, treat, entertainment, festival, carousal, carouse, regalement, cheer. (*fast, abstinence, starvation*)

**banter**—badinage, chaff, mockery, derision, ridicule, irony, jeering, raillery. (*discussion, discourse*)

**bargain**—transaction, negotiation, business, profit, speculation, higgling, gain, hawking, chaffer, haggling. (*loss, misprofit*)

**base**—vile, dishonorable, low, sordid, ignoble, worthless, mean, infamous, shameful, groveling, disingenuous, disesteemed, cheap, corrupt, deep. (*lofty, exalted, refined, noble, esteemed, honored*)

**bashful**—modest, diffident, shy, retiring, reserved. (*bold, impudent, forward, unreserved, pert, conceited, ostentatious, egotistic*)

**battle**—fight, conflict, contest, combat, engagement, encounter, action. (*peace, truce, pacification, arbitrament, council, mediation*)

**bawl**—shout, vociferate, halloo, roar, bellow. (*whisper, mutter, babble, mumble*)

**beach**—shore, coast, strand, seacoast, seaboard, seashore. (*sea, ocean, deep, main*)

**beaming**—shining, gleaming, bright, radiant, beautiful, transparent, translucid. (*dull, opaque, dingy, beamless, wan*)

**bear**—carry, lift, transport, convey, maintain, uphold, suffer, undergo, support, tolerate, waft, yield, sustain, hold, harbor, entertain, fill, enact, endure, admit, produce, generate. (*drop, refuse*)

**beat**—strike, pound, batter, surpass, thrash, cudgel, overcome, defeat, conquer, worst, whack, belabor, vanquish. (*defend, protect, shield, fall*)

**beauty**—loveliness, grace, fairness, seemliness, comeliness, picturesqueness, exquisiteness, adornment, embellishment. (*foulness, ugliness, deformity, hideousness, bareness, unattractiveness*)

**because**—owing, consequently, accordingly. (*irrespectively, independently, inconsequently, unconnectedly*)

**beck**—nod, sign, signal, symbol, token, indication, authority, orders, instruction, subserviency, influence, call, command, control, mandate. (*independence, unsubservience*)

**becoming**—beseeming, neat, fit, proper, decorous, comely, seemly, befitting, graceful, decent, suitable, improving. (*unbeseeming, unseemly, uncomely, unbecoming, unbefitting, ungraceful, indecent*)

**befitting**—fitting, decent, becoming, suitable, appropriate, proper, consistent, expedient, desirable. (*obligatory, compulsory, unbefitting, indecent*)

**before**—precedently, anteriorly, antecedently. (*after, afterward, subsequently, posteriorly, later*)

**beg**—ask, request, entreat, supplicate, beseech, implore, pray, petition, crave. (*insist, exact, extort, require, demand*)

**beggarly**—miserable, poor, stinted, wretched, niggardly, stingy, scant, illiberal. (*noble, princely, stately, prodigal, sumptuous, liberal, profuse, gorgeous, magnificent*)

**begin**—initiate, commence, prepare, start, originate, arise, inaugurate. (*achieve, complete, terminate, conclude, consummate, finish, close, end*)

**beginning**—commencement, start, origin, rise, initiation, preparation, preface, prelude, inauguration, inception, threshold, opening, source, outset, foundation. (*end, close, termination, conclusion, consummation, completion*)

**behavior**—conduct, bearing, demeanor, proceeding, comportment, action, manner, deportment. (*misdemeanor, misbehavior, misconduct*)

**belief**—assent, faith, trust, credence, avowal, assurance, admission, conviction, opinion, permission, creed, reliance, concession, confidence. (*dissent, unbelief, distrust, denial, misgiving, disavowal*)

**belonging**—related, connected, appertaining, cognate, congenial, obligatory, accompanying. (*unrelated, unconnected, irrelevant, impertinent, alien*)

**bend**—curve, deviate, incline, tend, swerve, diverge, mold, persuade, influence, bias, dispose, direct, lower, subordinate to, lean, deflect, bow, condescend, yield, stoop, submit. (*proceed, continue, extend, advance, stand, stiffen, break, crush*)

**benediction**—blessing, commendation, approval, benison, gratitude, thankfulness, thanksgiving. (*curse, malediction, disapproval, censure, obloquy*)

**benefactor**—friend, supporter, contributor, upholder, well-wisher, favorer, well-doer, patron. (*foe, opponent, disfavor, antagonist, rival, backfriend, oppressor*)

**beneficial**—profitable, salutary, advantageous, wholesome, salubrious. (*prejudicial, noxious, hurtful, unprofitable, detrimental*)

**benefit**—boon, behoof, service, utility, avail, use, good, advantage, profit, favor, blessing. (*evil, loss, disadvantage, detriment, damage, calamity*)

**bequeath**—give, grant, will to, bestow, impart, leave to. (*withhold, alienate, transfer, disinherit, dispossess*)

**bereavement**—destitution, affliction, deprivation, loss. (*gift, blessing, donation, benefaction,* *compensation, reparation, restoration, reinstatement)*

**besotted**—intoxicated, steeped, stupefied, drunk, drenched, doltish, gross, prejudiced. (*sober, temperate, clear, unbiased, unprejudiced, enlightened*)

**bespeak**—betoken, foreorder, forestall, provide, prearrange, indicate, evidence. (*belie, resign*)

**betimes**—early, beforehand, prepared, readily. (*behindhand, slowly, sluggishly, belatedly*)

**betray**—deceive, delude, dupe, circumvent, ensnare, dishonor, manifest, indicate, reveal. (*protect, preserve, guard, conserve, foster, cherish, fence*)

**better**—meliorate, improve, amend, emend, ameliorate, rectify, reform. (*make worse*)

**beware**—care, refrain, consider, heed, look, fear, avoid. (*ignore, overlook, neglect, incur, brave, dare*)

**bewilder**—daze, dazzle, confound, mystify, puzzle, embarrass, astonish, perplex, confuse, mislead. (*guide, inform, lead, instruct, enlighten*)

**bewitch**—enchant, fascinate, charm, captivate, entrance. (*exorcise, disillusionize, disenchant*)

**bid**—tell, request, instruct, direct, order, proffer, charge, command, propose, offer. (*forbid, deter*)

**bide**—wait, remain, tarry, stay, await, expect, anticipate, continue, bear, abide, endure. (*quit, depart, migrate, move, resist, resent, repel, abjure*)

**big**—large, great, wide, huge, bulky, proud, arrogant, pompous, fat, massive, gross. (*little, small, narrow, minute, slight, lean, affable, easy*)

**binding**—restrictive, obligatory, restraining, stringent, styptic, costive, astringent. (*loosening, opening, enlarging, distending*)

**birth**—parentage, extraction, nativity, family, race, origin, source, rise, lineage, nobility. (*death, extinction, plebeianism*)

**bitter**—harsh, sour, sharp, tart, acrimonious, sarcastic, severe, sad, afflictive, intense, stinging, pungent, acrid, cutting. (*sweet, mellow, pleasant*)

**blacken**—bespatter, befoul, bedaub, defame, decry, calumniate, dishonor, asperse, traduce, vilify, slander, malign. (*vindicate, clear, eulogize*)

**blackguard**—scoundrel, rascal, rapscallion, blackleg, villain. (*gentleman*)

**blame**—censure, chide, rebuke, reproach, vituperate, dispraise, disapprove, condemn, reprehend, reprobate, reprove. (*acquit, exculpate, exonerate, encourage, praise, approve*)

**bland**—soft, mild, gentle, complaisant, courteous, affable, gracious, tender, benign. (*harsh, abrupt*)

**blast**—*n.* breeze, efflation, explosion, blight, burst, blaze, frustration, destruction, squall, gale, tempest, hurricane. (*zephyr, gentle breeze*)

**blast**—*v.* blight, shrivel, destroy, wither. (*restore, expand, swell*)

**bleak**—blank, bare, open, cold, exposed, stormy, nipping. (*warm, sheltered, verdant, luxuriant*)

**blemish**—spot, blur, blot, flaw, speck, fault, imperfection, stain, daub, tarnish, defacement, discoloration, disfigurement, disgrace, dishonor, defect. (*purity, unsulliedness, honor, intactness*)

**blend**—mix, harmonize, unite, combine, fuse, merge, amalgamate, mingle, commingle, coalesce. (*run, separate, divide, dissociate, confound*)

**bless**—felicitate, endow, enrich, gladden, rejoice, cheer, thank. (*deprive, sadden, impoverish, ignore*)

**blind**—sightless, unseeing, eyeless, depraved, undiscerning, ignorant, prejudiced, uninformed, unconscious, unaware. (*farsighted, penetrating, sensitive, keen, discriminating, clear-sighted, pure-minded, aware, conscious*)

**blink**—wink, ignore, connive, overlook. (*notice, visit, note, mark*)

**bliss**—blessedness, joy, ecstasy, rapture. (*condemnation, accursedness, suffering, misery, woe*)

**blithe**—light, merry, joyous, happy, bright, elastic, gladsome, bonny, vivacious, lively, cheerful, blithesome, gay. (*heavy, dull, dejected, sullen*)

**blockhead**—dolt, dunderhead, jolterhead, dunce ninny, numskull, dullard, simpleton, booby, loggerhead, ignoramus. (*sage, adept, luminary, schoolman, philosopher, savant*)

**blooming**—flourishing, fair, flowering, blossoming, young, beautiful. (*fading, waning, blighted*)

**blot**—obscure, tarnish, spoil, sully, spot, discolor, pollute, obliterate, erase, blur, stain, blotch, smear, smutch. (*elucidate, clear, absterge, perpetuate*)

**blow**—puff, blast, breath, stroke, infliction, wound, disappointment, affliction, knock, shock, calamity, misfortune. (*assuagement, consolation, relief, comfort, blessing, sparing*)

**bluff**—bare, open, bold, abrupt, frank, plain-spoken, blunt, surly, rude, blustering, swaggering, brusque, hectoring, coarse, discourteous, rough, bullying. (*undulating, inclined, inabrupt, courteous*)

**blunder**—error, mistake, misunderstanding, fault, oversight, inaccuracy, delusion, slip. (*accuracy, truthfulness, exactness, correctness, faultlessness*)

**blush**—bloom, color, carnation, complexion, aspect, shame, confusion, guiltiness, self-reproach. (*innocence, purity, guiltlessness, unconsciousness*)

**boast**—vaunt, brag, swagger, swell, bluster, vapor, triumph, glory.

**body**—substance, mass, whole, substantiality, collectiveness, assemblage, collection, matter, association, organization. (*spirit, soul, individual*)

**boggle**—halt, hesitate, dubitate, falter, blunder, blotch, botch, spoil, mar. (*encounter, face, advance*)

**bold**—courageous, fearless, adventurous, brave, self-confident, forward, intrepid, dauntless, valiant, daring, audacious, lionhearted, doughty. (*timid, fearful, inadventurous, shy, bashful, retiring*)

**bombast**—bluster, inflatedness, pomposity, boastfulness, exaggeration, fustian. (*truthfulness, moderation, restraint, modesty, humility*)

**bond**—tie, fastening, chain, association, manacle, fetter, compact, obligation, security. (*freedom, option, discretion, honor, parole*)

**bondsman**—slave, serf, prisoner, captive, vassal. (*freeman, yeoman, gentleman, lord, master*)

**bonny**—fair, pretty, pleasant, lively, cheerful, shapely, buxom. (*dull, unseemly, ill-favored*)

**border**—limit, boundary, brink, rim, verge, brim, edge, edging, band, hem, enclosure, confine. (*land, tract, interior, substance, space, center*)

**border on**—be contiguous to, be adjacent to, conterminous with, adjoin, adjacent to. (*remote from, away from*)

**botch**—patch, cobble, blunder, clump, disconcert, spoil, jumble, mess, bungle, mar, blacksmith. (*finedraw, trim, harmonize, mend, beautify, embroider*)

**bother**—fuss, worry, pester, excitement, stir, plague, vex, annoy, tease, confusion, vexation, flurry, trouble. (*calm, composure, orderliness*)

**boundless**—unbounded, immeasurable, infinite, unlimited, illimitable, unmeasurable. (*narrow, restricted, limited, confined, circumscribed*)

**bounty**—liberality, bounteousness, benevolence, munificence, donation, gift, generosity, charity, benignity. (*illiberality, closeness, hardness, churlishness, stinginess, niggardliness*)

**brag**—boast, vaunt, swagger, bully. (*cringe, whine, whimper*)

**branch**—member, bifurcation, bough, limb, offspring, shoot, spray, sprig, twig, ramification, offshoot, relative, scion. (*trunk, stock, stem, race*)

**break**—fracture, rupture, shatter, shiver, destroy, tame, curb, demolish, tear asunder, rend, burst, sever, smash, split, subdue, violate, infringe. (*heal, piece, conjoin, protect, conserve, encourage*)

**breath**—respiration, inspiration, expiration, inhalation, exhalation. (*cessation, passing, departure*)

**breeding**—nurture, education, training, discipline, instruction, manners, air, demeanor, decorum. (*ill manners, ill training, ill behavior, ignorance*)

**brevity**—shortness, closeness, conciseness, succinctness, terseness, compendiousness, pointedness, abbreviation, abridgment. (*length, protraction, elongation, extension, prolixity, diffuseness, interminableness, tediousness*)

**bright**—shining, brilliant, burnished, luminous, lucid, sparkling, limpid, clever, happy, witty, joyous, cheerful, radiant. (*opaque, dull, dead, muddy*)

**brilliant**—flashing, radiant, shining, lustrous, highly intelligent, sparkling. (*dull, stupid*)

**bring**—fetch, procure, convey, carry, bear, adduce, import, produce, cause, induce. (*export, remove, abstract, subtract, prevent, exclude, debar*)

**brisk**—quick, lively, vivacious, active, alert, nimble, sprightly, spirited, animated, prompt, effervescent. (*slow, heavy, dull, inactive, indolent*)

**broad**—wide, extensive, expansive, ample, liberal, comprehensive, unreserved, indelicate, coarse, generic. (*narrow, restricted, confined, limited*)

**brotherhood**—fraternity, association, fellowship, society. (*division, disunity, individual*)

**brutal**—savage, inhuman, rude, unfeeling, merciless, ruthless, brutish, barbarous, sensual, beastly, ignorant, stolid, dense, cruel, violent, vindictive, bloodthirsty, intemperate. (*humane, civilized, generous, intelligent, polished, chivalrous, conscientious*)

**bubble**—trifle, toy, fancy, conceit, vision, dream, froth, trash. (*acquisition, prize, treasure, reality*)

**bugbear**—hobgoblin, goblin, gorgon, ghoul, spirit, spook, specter, ogre, scarecrow.

**building**—edifice, architecture, construction, erection, fabric, structure. (*ruin, dilapidation, dismantlement, demolition*)

**bulk**—mass, whole, entirety, integrity, majority, size, magnitude, extension, body, volume, bigness, largeness, massiveness, dimension. (*tenuity, minority, dismemberment, disintegration, diminution, portion, contraction, section, atom, particle*)

**bungler**—botcher, clown, lubber, fumbler, novice. (*adept, adroit, master, artist, workman, proficient, professor*)

**buoyant**—sprightly, spirited, vivacious, lively, light, floating, hopeful, cheerful, elastic, joyous. (*heavy, depressed, cheerless, joyless, dejected, moody*)

**burden**—load, weight, incubus, obstruction, oppression, grief, difficulty, affliction. (*ease, lightness, airiness, expedition, facility, acceleration, abjugation, liberation, lightheartedness, alleviation*)

**burn**—ignite, kindle, brand, consume, cauterize, rage, glow, smoulder, blaze, flash, cremate, incinerate. (*extinguish, stifle, cool, wane, subside*)

**bury**—inter, inhume, conceal, repress, suppress, obliterate, cancel, entomb, compose, hush. (*disinter, exhume, bruit, excavate, expose, resuscitate*)

**business**—occupation, profession, vocation, transaction, trade, calling, office, employment, interest, duty, affair, matter, concern. (*stagnation, leisure, inactivity*)

**bustle**—business, activity, stir, commotion, energy, excitement, haste, hurry, eagerness, flurry. (*idleness, vacation, inactivity, indolence, indifference*)

**busy**—industrious, diligent, assiduous, engaged, occupied. (*idle, slothful, lazy, indolent, unoccupied*)

**but**—save, except, barring, yet, beside, excluding, still, excepting, notwithstanding. (*with, including, inclusive, nevertheless, however, notwithstanding*)

## C

**calamity**—disaster, misfortune, mishap, catastrophe, misadventure, trouble, visitation, affliction, reverse, blight. (*godsend, blessing, boon*)

**calculate**—estimate, consider, weigh, number, count, apportion, proportion, investigate, reckon, rate, compute. (*guess, conjecture, hit, chance, risk*)

**calculation**—estimation, consideration, balance, apportionment, investigation, reckoning, computation, anticipation, forethought, regard, circumspection, watchfulness, vigilance, caution, care. (*inconsiderateness, inconsideration, incaution, indiscretion, miscalculation, misconception, exclusion, exception, omission, carelessness, supposition*)

**caliber**—gauge, diameter, ability, capacity, force, quality, character. (*weakness, incapacity*)

**called**—named, designated, denominated, yclept, termed. (*unnamed, undesignated, misnamed, misdesignated*)

**calm**—smooth, pacify, compose, allay, still, soothe, appease, assuage, quiet, tranquilize. (*stir, excite, agitate, disconcert, ruffle, lash, heat, discompose*)

**calumny**—slander, defamation, detraction, libel, traducement, backbiting, opprobrium, aspersion. (*vindication, clearance, eulogy, panegyric*)

**cancel**—efface, blot out, annul, expunge, nullify, quash, rescind, repeal, revoke, abrogate, obliterate, discharge, erase, abolish, countervail. (*enforce, enact, re-enact, confirm, perpetuate, contract*)

**candid**—fair, honest, open, sincere, frank, artless, impartial, plain, straightforward, aboveboard, transparent, unreserved, ingenious. (*unfair, close*)

**candidate**—aspirant, petitioner, canvasser, applicant, claimant, solicitor. (*waiver, decliner, abandoner, resigner, abjurer, noncompetitor*)

**canvass**—question, investigate, challenge, test, dispute, solicit, sift, examine, discuss, apply for, request. (*pretermit, allow, ignore, disregard, admit*)

**capacity**—space, size, volume, tonnage, caliber, ability, faculty, capability, cleverness, talents, magnitude, parts, competency, comprehensiveness, accommodation. (*narrowness, restriction, incapacity, coarctation, contractedness*)

**capital**—chief, excellent, important, cardinal, principal, consummate, high. (*inferior, unimportant, subordinate, minor, defective, mean*)

**capricious**—wayward, uncertain, fanciful, freakish, fitful, fickle, changeful, whimsical, humorsome, inconstant, crotchety. (*firm, unchanging, inflexible, decided, unswerving, constant*)

**captivated**—taken, charmed, smitten, fascinated, enslaved, captured, enthralled. (*free, unaffected, uninfluenced, unscathed, insensible, insensitive*)

**care**—attention, pains, anxiety, concern, trouble, circumspection, regard, solicitude, caution, prevention, custody, preservation, thrift, heed, foresight, wariness, economy, prudence. (*inattention, neglect*)

**career**—course, success, walk, line, progress, history, way of life, passage, race. (*misproceeding, misdeportment, unsuccess, miscarriage*)

**caress**—endearment, blandishment, wheedling, fondling, stroking. (*vexation, irritation, annoyance*)

**caricature**—mimicry, parody, travesty, burlesque, extravagance, exaggeration, hyperbole, monstrosity, farce. (*portraiture, representation, resemblance, justice, fidelity, truthfulness*)

**carnival**—revel, rout, festivity, masquerade. (*fast, mortification, lent, retirement*)

**carpet**—table, board, consideration, consultation. (*shelf, rejection, disposal, oblivion*)

**carriage**—transportation, conveyance, bearing, manner, conduct, demeanor, walk, gait, mien, behavior, deportment, vehicle. (*misconveyance, miscarriage, misconduct, misconsignment*)

**case**—occurrence, circumstance, contingency, event, plight, predicament, fact, subject, condition, instance. (*hypothesis, supposition, fancy, theory*)

**cast**—*v.* hurl, send down, throw, fling, pitch, impel, project, construct, mold, frame. (*raise, elevate*)

**cast**—*n.* mold, stamp, kind, figure, form, aspect, mien, air, style, manner, character. (*malformation, deformity, abnormity*)

**caste**—order, class, rank, lineage, race, blood, dignity, respect. (*degradation, taboo, disrepute*)

**casual**—accidental, occasional, incidental, contingent, unforeseen, fortuitous. (*regular, ordinary*)

**catastrophe**—revolution, disaster, calamity, misfortune, misadventure, reverse, blow, visitation. (*blessing, victory, triumph, felicitation, achievement*)

**cause**—source, origin, producer, agent, creator, purpose, inducement, reason, account, principle, motive, object, suit, action. (*effect, result, accomplishment, end, production, issue, preventive*)

**cease**—intermit, stop, desist, abstain, discontinue, quit, refrain, end, pause, leave off. (*ceaseless, never-ending, everlasting, constant, incessant*)

**celebrated**—famed, renowned, illustrious, eminent, glorious, famous, noted, distinguished, notable, exalted. (*unrenowned, obscure, undistinguished*)

**celebrity**—fame, honor, glory, star, reputation, distinction, renown, notability, eminence, notoriety. (*obscurity, meanness, ingloriousness, ignominy, disgrace, contempt, cipher, nobody*)

**celestial**—heavenly, ethereal, atmospheric, supernal, angelic, radiant, eternal, immortal, seraphic, divine, godlike, elysian. (*earthly, terrestrial, terrene*)

**censure**—blame, stricture, reproach, reprobate, inculpate, reprove, condemn, reprehend, chide, berate, scold, upbraid, disapproval, remonstrance, rebuke, reprimand, dispraise. (*praise, eulogy, approbation, encouragement, commendation*)

**ceremonial**—official, ministerial, functional, pompous, imposing, sumptuous, scenic. (*ordinary, private, unimposing, unostentatious, undramatic*)

**certain**—true, fixed, regular, established, incontrovertible, undoubtful, indubitable, infallible, unmistakable, sure, unfailing, real, actual, undeniable, positive, convinced, assured. (*uncertain, dubious, exceptional, irregular, casual, occasional*)

**certify**—acknowledge, aver, attest, vouch, avow, avouch, testify, protest, declare, demonstrate, prove, evidence, inform, assure. (*disprove, disavow, misinform, misadvise*)

**challenge**—defy, summon, dare, question, investigate, brave, canvass. (*pass, allow, grant, concede*)

**chance**—accident, fortuity, hazard, haphazard, fortune, random, casualty, befallment, luck. (*law, rule, sequence, consequence, causation, effectuation*)

**changeless**—regular, settled, steady, firm, stationary, consistent, resolute, reliable, undeviating, uniform, immutable, immovable. (*irregular, unsettled, unsteady, wavering, fluctuating, capricious*)

**character**—symbol, letter, nature, type, disposition, genius, temperament, cast, estimation, repute, office, reputation, part, capacity, class, order, sort, stamp, kind, quality, species, sign, tone, mark, figure, record. (*vagueness, anonymousness, nondescription, disrepute*)

**characteristic**—distinction, peculiarity, diagnosis, idiosyncrasy, specialty, individuality, personality, singularity. (*nondescription, abstractedness, generality, miscellany*)

**charitable**—kind, benign, benevolent, beneficent, liberal, considerate, forgiving, compassionate, placable, inexacting, inextreme. (*uncharitable, unkind, harsh, selfish, churlish, illiberal, censorious*)

**charm**—*v.* bewitch, enchant, fascinate, lay, soothe, mesmerize, delight, enrapture, transport, entice, allure, entrance, captivate, subdue. (*disenchant, rouse, disturb, annoy, irritate*)

**charm**—*n.* spell, incantation, enchantment, fascination, attraction, allurement. (*disenchantment, repulsion, fear*)

**chaste**—pure, modest, uncontaminated, spotless, immaculate, undefiled, virtuous, incorrupt, simple, unaffected, nice. (*impure, corrupt, meretricious*)

**cheap**—common, inexpensive, uncostly, mean, vile, worthless, low-priced. (*rare, costly, worthy*)

**cheat**—*v.* overreach, fleece, silence, trick, gull, cozen, juggle, defraud, swindle, dupe, beguile, deceive, deprive, hoodwink, prevaricate, dissemble, shuffle, inveigle. (*enlighten, guide, remunerate*)

**cheat**—*n.* deception, fraud, imposition, trick, artifice, illusion, impostor, swindle, finesse, deceit, lie, fiction. (*truth, reality, verity, fact, certainty*)

**cheer**—hope, happiness, comfort, hospitality, plenty, conviviality. (*dejection, sullenness, gloom, starvation, niggardliness, dearth, inhospitableness*)

**cheerful**—lively, gay, bright, happy, bonny, merry, joyful, pleasant, buoyant, sunny, enlivening, in good spirits, sprightly, blithe, joyous. (*lifeless, dull, gloomy, unhappy, dejected, depressed, sullen*)

**childish**—weak, silly, puerile, infantile, imbecile, foolish, trifling, paltry, trivial. (*strong, resolute, manly, wise, judicious, sagacious, chivalrous*)

**chivalrous**—courageous, generous, knightly, gallant, heroic, adventurous, valiant, spirited, handsome, high-minded. (*unhandsome, dirty, sneaking*)

**choice**—option, adoption, selection, election, preference, alternative. (*compulsion, necessity, rejection, refusal, unimportance, indifference, refuse*)

**chuckle**—grin, crow, cackle. (*cry, wail, grumble, whimper, whine*)

**cipher**—nonentity, dot, nothing, trifle, button (*fig.*), straw, pin, rush, molehill. (*somebody, bigwig, something, notability, celebrity, triton, colossus*)

**circumstance**—detail, feature, point, event, occurrence, incident, situation, position, fact, topic, condition, particular, specialty. (*deed, case, transaction*)

**civil**—well-mannered, political, courteous, well-bred, complaisant, affable, urbane, polite, obliging, accommodating, respectful. (*disobliging, unaccommodating, disrespectful, boorish, clownish, churlish*)

**claim**—*v.* demand, ask, require, insist, pretend, request, maintain. (*forgo, waive, disclaim, abjure, disavow, abandon*)

**claim**—*n.* assertion, vindication, pretension, title, right, privilege, arrogation, demand. (*waiver, abjuration, disclaimer, surrender*)

**claimant**—assertor, vindicator, appellant, litigant. (*relinquisher, resigner, conceder, waiver*)

**classification**—order, species, nature, character, cast, stamp, group, kind, section, sect, category, assortment, designation, description, genus. (*individuality, specialty, isolation, alienation, division*)

**clause**—portion, paragraph, stipulation, provision, article, condition, chapter, section, passage. (*document, instrument, muniment*)

**clear**—*v.* clarify, disencumber, disentangle, disembarrass, vindicate, liberate, set free, release, exonerate, exculpate, justify, retrieve, acquit, absolve, whitewash, extricate, eliminate. (*befoul, contaminate, pollute, clog, encumber, embarrass*)

**clear**—*a.* open, pure, bright, transparent, free, disencumbered, disentangled, disengaged, absolved, acquitted, serene, unclouded, evident, apparent, distinct, manifest, conspicuous, unobstructed, plain, obvious, intelligible, lucid. (*thick, muddy*)

**clever**—able, ready, talented, quick, ingenious, dexterous, adroit, expert, gifted, quick-witted, skillful, well-contrived. (*weak, dull, stupid, slow*)

**cling**—fasten, hold, adhere, embrace, stick, cleave, hang, twine, hug. (*drop, recede, secede, apostatize, abandon, relax, forgo, swerve, surrender*)

**cloak**—conceal, disguise, mask, veil, hide, cover, palliate, screen, mitigate, extenuate. (*exhibit, propound, promulge, portray, aggravate, expose, demonstrate, reveal*)

**close**—narrow, limited, restricted, condensed, packed, secret, compressed, solid, firm, compact, reserved, niggardly, shut, fast, dense. (*wide, open*)

**clownish**—rustic, boorish, bucolic, foolish, awkward, clumsy, cloddish, untutored, rude. (*polite, civil, urbane, affable, graceful, polished, refined*)

**clumsy**—awkward, inexpert, uncouth, maladroit, botching, bungling, unskillful, unwieldy, unhandy, ill-shaped. (*neat, workmanlike, artistic, handy*)

**coarse**—common, ordinary, indelicate, vulgar, gross, unrefined, immodest, rough, rude, unpolished. (*fine, refined, gentle, polished, delicate, choice*)

**cognizance**—notice, observation, recognition, knowledge, experience. (*inadvertence, neglect, ignorance, inexperience, oversight, connivance*)

**coherent**—consecutive, consistent, complete, sensible, compact, logical, close. (*inconsecutive, rambling, disunited, inconsistent, discursive, loose*)

**coincidence**—chance, fortuity, casualty, concurrence, correspondence, contemporaneousness, commensurateness, harmony, agreement, consent. (*design, purpose, adaptation, asynchronism, anachronism, disharmony, incommensurateness, discordance, variation, difference*)

**colleague**—helper, companion, associate, ally, confederate, coadjutor, partner, assistant, adjutant, assessor. (*co-opponent, corival, counteragent, coantagonist, competitor*)

**collect**—collate, gather, glean, sum, infer, learn, congregate, assemble, convoke, convene, muster, amass, garner, accumulate. (*classify, arrange, distribute, dispose, dispense, divide, sort, deal*)

**collection**—assembly, assemblage, store, gathering, collation. (*dispersion, distribution, dispensation, division, arrangement, disposal, classification*)

**color**—hue, tint, complexion, pretense, speciousness, tinge, garbling, falsification, distortion, perversion, varnish. (*achromatism, paleness, nakedness, openness, genuineness, transparency, truthfulness*)

**combination**—union, association, consortment, concert, confederacy, alliance, league, coalition, cabal, synthesis, cooperation. (*division, disunion*)

**comfortable**—snug, satisfied, pleasant, agreeable, cozy, commodious, convenient, consoled. (*uncomfortable, dissatisfied, troubled, miserable, wretched*)

**commerce**—trade, traffic, merchandise, barter, exchange, business, communication, dealing, intercourse. (*stagnation, exclusion, inactivity, interdict*)

**commodious**—ample, easy, convenient, spacious, suitable, comfortable. (*inconvenient, incommodious, narrow, ill-contrived, incommensurate, discommodious*)

**common**—ordinary, familiar, habitual, everyday, frequent, coarse, vulgar, low, mean, universal. (*unusual, exceptional, scarce, rare, uncommon, refined, partial, infrequent, sporadic, egregious, excellent*)

**community**—aggregation, association, commonwealth, coordination, society, sympathy, order, class, brotherhood, fraternity, polity, unity, nationality, similarity, homogeneity. (*segregation, secession, independence, dissociation, disconnection*)

**company**—aggregation, association, union, sodality, order, fraternity, guild, corporation, society, community, assemblage, assembly, crew, posse, gang, troop, audience, congregation, concourse. (*rivalry, opposition, disqualification, antagonism*)

**compass**—encompass, surround, enclose, environ, circumscribe, embrace, achieve, effect, effectuate, consummate, complete, circumvent. (*expand, dispand, unfold, amplify, display, dismiss, liberate, discard, fail, bungle, botch, misconceive, mismanage*)

**compatible**—consistent, consentaneous, harmonious, coexistent, correspondent, congruous, accordant, agreeable, congenial, consonant. (*incompatible, impossible, insupposable, inconsistent, discordant, hostile, adverse, antagonistic, incongruous*)

**compel**—force, oblige, drive, constrain, necessitate, make, coerce, bind. (*persuade, convince, coax*)

**compensation**—remunerative, equivalent, wages, pay, allowance, restoration, restitution, satisfaction, atonement, expiation, indemnification, amercement, damages. (*deprivation, injury, nonpayment, gratuity, donation, fraudulence, damage*)

**competition**—rivalry, emulation, race, two of a trade. (*association, colleagueship, alliance, jointstock, copartnership, confederation*)

**complacent**—pleased, satisfied, content, pleasant, affable, kind, mannerly, acquiescent, amiable. (*dissatisfied, irritated, churlish, unmannerly, morose*)

**complaint**—murmur, discontent, repining, grievance, annoyance, remonstrance, expostulation, lamentation, sickness, disease. (*congratulation, rejoicing, approbation, complacency, boon, benefit*)

**complement**—completion, fulfilment, totality, supply, counterpart, correlative. (*deficiency, deficit, insufficiency, abatement, detraction, defalcation*)

**complete**—full, perfect, finished, adequate, entire, consummate, total, exhaustive, thorough, accomplished. (*incomplete, partial, imperfect, unfinished, inadequate*)

**complexion**—face, aspect, color, look, feature, appearance, character, hue, interpretation, indication. (*unindicativeness, concealment, reticence, inexpression, heart, core*)

**complicated**—confused, intricate, involved, perplexed, entangled. (*clear, simple, uninvolved, lucid*)

**compliment**—homage, courtesy, flattery, praise. (*insult, discourtesy, contempt*)

**complimentary**—commendatory, laudatory, panegyrical, eulogistic, encomiastic, lavish of praise. (*disparaging, condemnatory, damnatory, denunciatory, reproachful, abusive, objurgatory, vituperative*)

**composition**—compound, conformation, structure, mixture, combination, compromise, adjustment, settlement, commutation. (*analysis, segregation, examination, criticism, discussion, disturbance, aggravation, perpetuation*)

**comprehend**—comprise, embody, grasp, understand, conceive, apprehend, enclose, include, involve, embrace. (*exclude, except, misunderstand*)

**comprehensive**—wide, ample, general, extensive, large, broad, all-embracing, generic, significant, capacious, inclusive, compendious, pregnant. (*narrow, restricted, shallow, exclusive, adversative*)

**compromise**—arbitrate, adjust, compose, settle, endanger, implicate, involve. (*aggravate, excite, foster, perpetuate, exempt, enfranchise, disengage*)

**conceal**—hide, secrete, disguise, keep secret, dissemble, screen, suppress. (*reveal, manifest, exhibit, avow, confess, expose, promulgate, publish*)

**concentrate**—assemble, converge, muster, congregate, convene, draw, conglomerate, condense, localize, centralize. (*disperse, scatter, dismiss, decentralize*)

**concerning**—about, of, relating, regarding, touching, in relation to, respecting, with respect to, with regard to, with reference to, relative to. (*omitting*)

**concert**—union, combination, concord, harmony, agreement, association, cooperation. (*dissociation, counteraction, opposition*)

**condescension**—affability, graciousness, favor, stooping. (*haughtiness, arrogance, pride, superciliousness, disdain, scorn*)

**condition**—state, case, mood, term, mode, qualification, requisite, stipulation, predicament, proviso, situation, circumstances, plight. (*relation*)

**conditionally**—provisionally, relatively, provided, hypothetically, contingently. (*absolutely, unconditionally, categorically, positively*)

**conducive**—contributive, promotive, subsidiary, causative, effective, productive. (*preventive, counteractive, contrariant, repugnant, destructive*)

**conduct**—lead, bring, carry, transfer, direct, guide, control, manage, administer. (*mislead, miscarry, mismanage, misconduct, misadminister*)

**confer**—compare, collate, discuss, deliberate, converse, consult, give, present. (*dissociate, contrast, hazard, conjecture, withhold, withdraw*)

**confession**—creed, catechism, articles, doctrine, tenets, profession, declaration, subscription. (*heresy, apostasy, protest, condemnation, refutation*)

**confidant**—confessor, adviser, confederate. (*traitor, betrayer, rival*)

**confident**—positive, assured, sure, certain, impudent, bold, sanguine. (*unsure, afraid, timid*)

**confidential**—private, secret, trustworthy, intimate. (*public, open, patent, official, treacherous*)

**confirm**—strengthen, stabilitate, establish, substantiate, settle, prove, fix, perpetuate, sanction, corroborate, ratify. (*weaken, shake, upset, cancel*)

**confront**—oppose, face, encounter, resist, intimidate, menace. (*rally, encourage, abet, countenance*)

**confused**—abashed, embarrassed, perplexed, disconcerted, disorganized, promiscuous, chaotic, complex, involved, disarranged, disordered. (*unabashed, unembarrassed, systematic, unconfused*)

**congress**—parliament, council, conclave, assembly, synod, legislature, convention. (*cabal, conclave, mob*)

**conjecture**—guess, divination, hypothesis, theory, notion, surmise, supposition. (*computation, calculation, inference, reckoning, proof, deduction*)

**connection**—junction, conjunction, union, association, concatenation, relation, affinity, relevance, intercourse, communication, kinsman, relationship, kindred. (*disconnection, disjunction, dissociation*)

**conquer**—subdue, vanquish, surmount, overcome, overpower, overthrow, defeat, crush, master, subjugate, prevail over. (*fail, fall, retreat, succumb, fly, submit, surrender, lose, forfeit, sacrifice*)

**conscious**—aware, cognizant, sensible. (*unaware, unconscious, insensible*)

**consecutive**—orderly, arranged, coherent, continuous. (*disordered, undigested, incoherent*)

**consent**—submit, agree, acquiesce. (*resist, disagree, dissent, decline, refuse*)

**consequence**—effect, issue, result, inference, coherence, deduction, conclusion, outcome, importance, note, moment, dignity. (*cause, causation, antecedence, premise, origin, datum, postulate*)

**consider**—attend, revolve, meditate, think, reflect, investigate, regard, observe, judge, opine, infer, deduce, weigh, cogitate, deliberate, ponder, deem. (*disregard, ignore, pretermit, despise, guess*)

**considerate**—thoughtful, attentive, forbearing, unselfish, judicious, serious, prudent, circumspect, reflective, careful, cautious. (*thoughtless, inconsiderate, inattentive, rude, overbearing, selfish, injudicious, rash, careless*)

**consistency**—consistence, congruity, composition, substance, material, amalgamation, compound, mass, density, solidity, closeness, compactness, coherence, uniformity, harmony, analogy, proportion. (*volatility, vaporousness, subtility, tenuity, sublimation, incoherence, inconsistency, incongruity, disproportion, contrariety, contradiction*)

**consistent**—congruous, accordant, consonant, agreeing, compatible, harmonious. (*incongruous, at variance with, not agreeing with, incompatible*)

**conspicuous**—visible, easily seen, prominent, distinguished, manifest, eminent, famous, noted, salient, observable, noticeable, magnified. (*invisible, inconspicuous, inobservable, noticeable, microscopic*)

**constant**—uniform, regular, invariable, perpetual, continuous, firm, fixed, steady, immutable, faithful, true, trustworthy. (*irregular, exceptional*)

**constitution**—temperament, frame, temper, character, habit, nature, government, polity, state, consistence, composition, substance, organization, structure, regulation, law. (*accident, habituation, modification, interference, anarchy, despotism, tyranny, rebellion, revolution, dissipation, disorganization, demolition, destruction*)

**construction**—composition, fabrication, explanation, rendering, erection, fabric, edifice, reading, understanding, interpretation, view. (*dislocation, dismemberment, demolition, displacement, misplacement, misconstruction, misunderstanding, misconception, misinterpretation*)

**consult**—interrogate, canvass, question, deliberate, confer, advise with, regard, consider, ask advice of, care for, promote. (*resolve, explain, expound, direct, instruct, dictate, counteract, contravene*)

**consumption**—decline, decay, expenditure, waste, decrement, lessening, decrease. (*growth, development, enlargement, augmentation*)

**contact**—touch, contiguity, continuity, apposition, adjunction. (*proximity, adjacence, interruption, disconnection, separation, distance, isolation*)

**contagious**—catching, epidemic, infectious, pestilential, communicated, transferred, transmitted, infectious. (*sporadic, endemic, preventive, antipathetic*)

**contaminate**—defile, taint, corrupt, sully, befoul, soil. (*purify, cleanse, lave, clarify, sanctify, chasten*)

**contemplate**—meditate, behold, observe, ponder, study, purpose, design, intend, project. (*ignore, overlook, waive, abandon*)

**contemptible**—despicable, mean, vile, pitiful, disreputable, paltry, trifling, trivial. (*important, grave, weighty, honorable, respectable, venerable*)

**content**—full, satisfied, pleased, gratified, contented, willing, resigned. (*unsatisfied, dissatisfied*)

**contentious**—litigious, perverse, wayward, splenetic, cantankerous, exceptious. (*pacific, obliging*)

**contingent**—dependent, incidental, resultant, coefficient, hypothetical, uncertain, conditional. (*positive, absolute, independent, unmodified, unaffected, uncontrolled, irrespective*)

**continually**—constantly, persistently, always, ever, perpetually, unceasingly, repeatedly, frequently, continuously. (*casually, occasionally, contingently, sometimes, rarely, fitfully, intermittently*)

**contract**—*n.* covenant, agreement, compact, bond, pact, stipulation, bargain. (*promise, assurance, parole*)

**contract**—*v.* abridge, abbreviate, narrow, lessen, reduce, compress, decrease, retrench, curtail, form, agree. (*expand, amplify, dilate, elongate*)

**contradict**—oppose, dissent, negative, controvert, deny, disprove, confute, refute, gainsay, contravene. (*state, propound, maintain, argue, confirm, affirm*)

**contrary**—opposed, opposite, repugnant, antagonistic, adverse, incompatible, inconsistent. (*agreeing, consentaneous, compatible, kindred, coincident*)

**contribute**—conduce, add, subscribe, give, cooperate, assist, tend, supply. (*refuse, withhold*)

**contrive**—plan, design, arrange, fabricate, adapt, manage, scheme, devise, concert, adjust. (*hit, hazard, run, chance, venture, bungle, over-vault*)

**control**—check, curb, moderate, repress, guide, regulate, restrain, coerce, manage, administer, govern. (*neglect, abandon, license, liberate, mismanage, misconduct*)

**convenient**—handy, apt, adapted, fitted, suitable, helpful, commodious, useful, timely, seasonable, opportune. (*inconvenient, awkward, obstructive, useless, superfluous, unseasonable, untimely*)

**conventional**—customary, usual, ordinary, stipulated, prevalent, social. (*unusual, unsocial, legal*)

**conversant**—familiar, acquainted, proficient, experienced, versed, learned. (*unfamiliar, unacquainted, ignorant, unversed, unlearned, strange*)

**convertible**—identical, commensurate, conterminous, equivalent, equipollent. (*variant, incommensurate, unequivalent, contrary, contradictory*)

**conviction**—assurance, persuasion, belief. (*doubt, misgiving, disbelief*)

**cooperate**—assist, abet, contribute, concur, work together, help, conspire. (*thwart, oppose*)

**copy**—imitation, portraiture, facsimile, counterfeit, duplicate, image, likeness, transcript. (*original, prototype, model, example, pattern*)

**cordial**—warm, earnest, sincere, reviving, invigorating, affectionate, hearty. (*cold, distant, formal*)

**corner**—cavity, hole, nook, recess, retreat. (*coin, abutment, prominence, salience, angle, protrusion, elbow, protection, convexity*)

**corpulent**—stout, burly, fat, portly, gross, lusty, plethoric, fleshy. (*lean, thin, attenuated, slight*)

**correct**—*a.* true, exact, faultless, accurate, proper, decorous, right. (*false, untrue, incorrect*)

**correct**—*v.* chasten, punish, rectify, amend, reform, emend, redress, set right, improve. (*spare, falsify, corrupt*)

**correction**—amendment, discipline, emendation, chastisement, punishment. (*deterioration, debasement, retrogradation, reward, recompense*)

**correspond**—match, tally, fit, answer, agree, suit, harmonize. (*vary, differ, disagree, jar, clash*)

**correspondence**—fitness, agreement, adaptation, congruity, answerableness, match, congeniality, communication, letter, writing, dispatches. (*conversation, colloquy, confabulation, reservation, withdrawal, withholding, nonintercourse, difference*)

**corrupt**—defiled, polluted, vitiated, decayed, depraved, putrid, rotten, infected, tainted, profligate, contaminated. (*pure, uncorrupt, undefiled*)

**corruption**—decomposition, decay, putrescence, adulteration, depravity, rottenness, defilement, deterioration, perversion, debasement, taint, contamination, putrefaction. (*vitality, organization*)

**cost**—*v.* require, consume, absorb. (*bring, produce, yield, afford, fetch, return*)

**cost**—*n.* expenditure, outlay, disbursement, payment, compensation, price, worth, expense, charge, outgoings. (*receipt, income, emolument*)

**costly**—valuable, expensive, high-priced, rich, precious, sumptuous. (*valueless, cheap, low-priced, mean, worthless, beggarly, paltry*)

**council**—cabinet, bureau, chamber, consultation, conclave, parliament, congress, synod, company, assembly, meeting, conference, convention, convocation. (*league, conspiracy, cabal, intrigue, mob*)

**counsel**—advice, instruction, monition, admonition, warning, recommendation. (*misguidance, misinstruction, betrayal*)

**count**—compute, reckon, enumerate, estimate, number, sum, calculate. (*hazard, conjecture, guess*)

**countenance**—*v.* help, aid, abet, favor, sanction, patronize, support, encourage. (*oppose, confront, discourage, discountenance, browbeat*)

**countenance**—*n.* aid, abet, encourage, support. (*discountenance*)

**counteract**—counterinfluence, counterfoil, foil,

baffle, neutralize, oppose, rival, thwart, hinder. (*aid, help, abet, promote, conserve, cooperate, subserve*)

**counterpart**—match, fellow, tally, brother, twin, copy, correlative, complement, supplement. (*opponent, counteragent, reverse, obverse, opposite, antithesis, contrast, contradiction*)

**countryman**—rustic, clown, boor, compatriot, swain, yeoman, husbandman, farmer, agriculturist, laborer, peasant, fellow countryman, fellow subject, fellow citizen, subject, citizen, inhabitant, native. (*oppidan, townsman, cockney, foreigner, alien*)

**couple**—bracket, link, conjoin, unite, splice, buckle, button, clasp, pair, yoke, connect, tie, brace. (*loose, part, isolate, separate, detach, divorce, uncouple*)

**courage**—bravery, boldness, valor, pluck, fortitude, resolution, gallantry, fearlessness, intrepidity. (*timidity, cowardice, pusillanimity, poltroonery, dastardliness*)

**course**—order, sequence, continuity, direction, progress, line, way, mode, race, career, road, route, series, passage, succession, round, manner, plain, conduct, method. (*disorder, discursion, solution, interruption, deviation, hindrance, error, conjecture*)

**courtly**—dignified, polished, refined, aristocratic, high-bred, mannerly. (*undignified, rough, unpolished, coarse, unrefined, plebeian, awkward, boorish, rustic, unmannerly*)

**covetous**—acquisitive, avaricious, greedy, grasping, rapacious. (*unselfish, liberal, self-sacrificing*)

**coward**—craven, dastard, recreant, poltroon, renegade. (*champion, hero, daredevil, desperado*)

**coxcomb**—fop, dandy, puppy, prig, pedant. (*genius, savant, authority, celebrity, philosopher, sage*)

**coy**—shy, reserved, bashful, shrinking, retreating, modest. (*bold, forward, rompish, hoydenish*)

**crabbed**—sour, morose, cross-grained, petulant, churlish, irritable, crusty. (*pleasant, open, easy, genial, conversable, warm, cordial, hearty*)

**craft**—art, artifice, cunning, guile, stratagem, maneuver, wiliness, trickery, duplicity, chicanery, intrigue, underhandedness, dodge. (*openness, fairness, candor, honesty, frankness, sincerity, artlessness*)

**cram**—stuff, choke, squeeze, ram, pack, gorge. (*disgorge, vent, discharge, unload, unpack, eviscerate*)

**crash**—jar, clang, clash, resonance. (*murmur, whisper, babble, rumbling, reverberation, din*)

**cream**—marrow, pith, gist, acme. (*refuse, offal, dregs, dross, garbage*)

**credential**, or **credentials**—missive, diploma, title, testament, seal, warrant, letter, vouchers, certificates, testimonials. (*self-license, self-constitution, self-appointment, autocracy*)

**credit**—relief, trustworthiness, reputation, security, honor, praise, merit, confidence, faith. (*disbelief, distrust, untrustworthiness, shame, insecurity*)

**creed**—belief, catechism, articles, confession, subscription. (*protest, abjuration, recantation, retractation, disbelief, nonsubscription*)

**criminal**—illegal, felonious, vicious, culpable, wrong, iniquitous, sinful, immoral, guilty, nefarious, flagitious. (*lawful, virtuous, right, just, innocent*)

**critical**—nice, delicate, exact, fastidious, discriminating, censorious, accurate, dubious, precarious, ticklish, crucial, important, momentous, hazardous. (*inexact, popular, loose, easy, undiscriminating, safe, determined, decided, settled, retrieved, redressed*)

**criticism**—stricture, censure, animadversion. (*approval, praise*)

**cross-grained**—perverse, wayward, peevish, morose, cantankerous, ill-conditioned. (*genial, pleasant, agreeable, jolly, obliging, accommodating*)

**crude**—raw, undigested, unconsidered, half-studied, harsh, unshaped, unchastened, unfinished, unrefined, ill-prepared. (*well-prepared, well-digested, well-considered, well-studied, ripe, well-adapted, well-proportioned, well-expressed, classical*)

**cruel**—savage, barbarous, pitiless, inexorable, unrelenting, ruthless, truculent, hardhearted, harsh, unmerciful, brutal, inhuman, maleficent, malignant. (*humane, forbearing, generous, merciful, forgiving, benevolent, beneficent*)

**crush**—pulverize, triturate, pound, bray, crumble, overpower, demolish. (*consolidate, compact*)

**cuff**—slap, box, smack, punch, pummel, hustle buffet. (*cudgel, flagellate, thrash, cane, strap, lash*)

**cultivate**—promote, foster, study, improve, fertilize, till, advance, refine, improve, civilize, nourish, cherish. (*neglect, desert, abandon, stifle, prevent*)

**cupidity**—avarice, acquisitiveness, covetousness, stinginess. (*prodigality, extravagance, liberality*)

**cure**—remedy, alleviation, restorative, heal-all, amelioration, reinstatement, restoration, renovation, convalescence. (*aggravation, confirmation*)

**curiosity**—inquisitiveness, interest, wonder, marvel, interrogativeness, rarity, phenomenon, celebrity, oddity, lion. (*indifference, heedlessness, disregard, abstraction, absence, weed, drug, dirt, cipher*)

**curious**—inquiring, inquisitive, scrutinizing, prying, meddling, singular, searching, interrogative, peeping, peering, rare, unique, odd, recondite. (*indifferent, uninquiring, incurious, uninterested*)

**current**—running, prevalent, ordinary, present, popular, general, floating, exoteric, vulgar. (*rejected, obsolete, exploded, confined, private, secret*)

**custody**—keeping, guardianship, conservation, care. (*neglect, betrayal, exposure, abandonment*)

**cynical**—sarcastic, snarling, snappish, sneering, cross-grained, currish, carping. (*genial, lenient*)

## D

**daft**—silly, innocent, idiotic, lunatic, light-headed, cracked. (*sane, sound, sensible, practical*)

**dainty**—choice, rare, refined, tasty, exquisite, luxurious, epicurean. (*common, coarse, unrelishing, nasty, dirty, omnivorous, greedy, gluttonous*)

**damp**—cool, blunt, dishearten, quench, slack, moderate, humid, wet, moist, discourage, discountenance, repress. (*urge, inflame, incite, fan*)

**dapper**—spruce, neat, natty, smart. (*slovenly, awkward, unwieldy, untidy*)

**daring**—adventurous, dashing, bold, courageous, venturesome, dauntless, foolhardy, fearless, brave, intrepid, valorous. (*cautious, timid, inadventurous*)

**dark**—black, dusky, sable, swarthy, opaque, obscure, enigmatical, recondite, abstruse, unintelligible, blind, ignorant, besotted, benighted, dim, shadowy, inexplicable, secret, mysterious, hidden, murky, nebulous, cheerless, dismal, dim, gloomy, somber, joyless, sorrowful. (*white, fair, cheerful*)

**dash**—hurl, cast, throw, subvert, detrude, drive, rush, send, fly, speed, dart, scatter, strike, course. (*raise, reinstate, erect, creep, crawl, lag, hobble*)

**daunt**—terrify, scare, frighten, cow, dishearten, appall, intimidate, confront. (*countenance, encourage, rally, inspirit*)

**dawdle**—lag, dally, idle. (*haste, speed, dash*)

**dead**—defunct, deceased, departed, gone, inanimate, lifeless, insensible, heavy, unconscious, dull, spiritless, cheerless, deserted, torpid, still. (*vital, living, animate, vivacious, susceptible, alive, joyous*)

**deadly**—mortal, fatal, malignant, baleful, pernicious, noxious, venomous, destructive, baneful, implacable. (*vital, life-giving, healthful, wholesome*)

**deaf**—surd, hard of hearing, disinclined, averse, inexorable, insensible, rumbling, inaudible, heedless, dead. (*acute, listening, disposed, interested*)

**dear**—high-priced, costly, expensive, beloved, precious, loved. (*cheap, inexpensive, misliked, vile*)

**death**—departure, demise, decease, dissolution, mortality, fall, failure, termination, cessation, expiration, release, exit. (*birth, rise, life, growth*)

**debatable**—dubious, doubtful, inestimable, uncertain, problematical, floating, unsettled, disputable. (*certain, sure, unquestionable, indisputable*)

**debauchery**—riot, revel, excess, orgies, gluttony. (*moderation, frugality, asceticism*)

**debt**—debit, liability, default, obligation, claim, score, something due. (*liquidation, assets, credit, trust, grace, favor, obligation, accommodation, gift*)

**decay**—*v.* decline, wane, sink, dwindle, rot, wither, perish, waste, ebb, decrease. (*rise, grow, increase*)

**decay**—*n.* declension, waning, sinking, wasting, decrease, corruption, decadence, putrefaction, rottenness, dry rot, consumption, decline. (*rise, growth, birth, increase, fertility, exuberance, luxuriance, prosperity*)

**deceit**—cheat, imposition, trick, fraud, deception, double dealing, delusion, circumvention, guile, beguilement, treachery, sham, insidiousness, indirection, duplicity, cunning, artifice. (*enlightenment, instruction, guidance, reality, verity, fair dealing, honesty, openness*)

**deceitful**—deceptive, delusive, fraudulent, fallacious. (*open, fair, honest, truthful, veracious*)

**deceive**—trick, cheat, beguile, delude, gull, dupe, take in, overreach, mislead, betray, ensnare, entrap, circumvent. (*enlighten, advise, illumine, guide, disabuse, undeceive, deliver*)

**decide**—determine, fix, settle, adjudicate, terminate, resolve. (*waver, raise, moot, drop, doubt*)

**decipher**—read, spell, interpret, solve, unravel, explain, unfold. (*cipher, symbolize, mystify*)

**declaration**—avowal, exhibition, manifestation, statement, ordinance, assertion, affirmation, profession. (*denial, concealment, suppression*)

**decompose**—analyze, segregate, individualize, resolve, dissolve. (*compound, concoct, mix, organize*)

**decorum**—seemliness, propriety, dignity, order, decency, good manners, good behavior, modesty. (*impropriety, bad manners or behavior*)

**decrease**—diminish, lessen, subside, abate, lower, decline, retrench, curtail, reduce, wane. (*increase, grow, amplify, expand, augment, extend*)

**decrepit**—infirm, weak, crippled, superannuated, effete, broken down, enfeebled, tottering, aged. (*strong, straight, young*)

**dedicate**—devote, consecrate, offer, set, apportion, assign, apply, separate, hallow, set apart. (*alienate, misapply, desecrate, misconvert, misuse*)

**deed**—act, action, commission, achievement, perpetration, instrument, document, muniment, exploit, feat. (*omission, failure, abortion, false witness, innocent, canceling, disproof, invalidation*)

**deep**—profound, subterranean, submerged, designing, abstruse, recondite, learned, low, sagacious penetrating, thick, obscure, mysterious, occult, intense, heartfelt. (*shallow, superficial, artless*)

**deface**—mar, spoil, injure, disfigure, deform, damage, mutilate, destroy. (*decorate, adorn*)

**default**—lapse, forfeit, omission, defect, delinquency, absence, want, failure. (*maintenance, appearance, plea, satisfaction, forthcoming, supply*)

**defeat**—*n.* frustration, overthrow, discomfiture. (*victory, triumph, success*)

**defeat**—*v.* conquer, overcome, worst, beat, baffle, rout, overthrow, vanquish, frustrate, foil. (*secure, promote, insure, speed, advance, establish*)

**defect**—shortcoming, omission, fault, imperfection, flaw, blemish, want. (*supply, sufficiency*)

**defective**—faulty, imperfect, insufficient, deficient, wanting, short. (*correct, complete, sufficient*)

**defense**—resistance, protection, vindication, plea, justification, excuse, rampart, bulwark, apology, shelter, excuse. (*abandonment, surrender*)

**defer**—delay, postpone, waive, adjourn, prorogue, put off, retard, procrastinate, protract, hinder, prolong. (*expedite, hasten, quicken, press*)

**deference**—respect, consideration, condescension, contention, regard, honor, veneration, submission, reverence, obedience, homage, allegiance. (*disrespect, contumely, contumacy, disregard, slight*)

**definite**—clear, specified, determined, definitive, restricted, specific, certain, ascertained, precise, exact, fixed, limited, bounded, positive. (*vague, unspecified, undetermined, indefinite, obscure, confused, intermingled*)

**definition**—determination, limitation, specification, restriction. (*confusion, vagueness, acceptation*)

**defray**—meet, liquidate, pay, settle, bear, discharge, quit. (*dishonor, repudiate, dissatisfy, misappropriate, embezzle*)

**defy**—scorn, challenge, provoke, oppose, brave. (*accept, give in, concede*)

**degree**—grade, rank, stage, step, extent, measure, mark, rate, position, quality, class, station, range, quantity, amount, limit, order. (*space, mass, magnitude, size, numbers*)

**deliberate**—*v.* consider, meditate, consult, weigh, reflect, ponder, debate, perpend. (*shelve, burke, discard, hazard, chance, risk*)

**deliberate**—*a.* grave, purposed, intentional, designed, determined, resolute, earnest, unbiased, unprejudiced. (*playful, jocose, facetious, irresolute*)

**delicious**—exquisite, luxurious, delightful, dainty, choice. (*coarse, common, unsavory, unpalatable, nauseous, loathsome*)

**delight**—enjoyment, pleasure, happiness, transport, ecstasy, joy, gratification, gladness, rapture, bliss. (*pain, suffering, sorrow, trouble, misery, displeasure, dissatisfaction, disappointment, discomfort*)

**delinquent**—criminal, culprit, offender. (*worthy, paragon, pattern*)

**deliver**—liberate, free, save, utter, set free, surrender, yield, transmit, concede, give up, rescue, pronounce, hand, give, entrust, consign. (*confine, capture, suppress, retain, betray, withdraw, assume*)

**democratic**—popular, leveling, radical, subversive, unlicensed, anarchical, destructive, republican. (*regal, imperial, aristocratic, oligarchical, constitutional, conservative, tyrannical, despotic, autocratic*)

**demonstrate**—prove, show, exhibit, manifest, evince, illustrate. (*disprove, conceal, misdemonstrate, misexemplify*)

**demure**—sedate, staid, grave, modest, downcast, sober, dispassionate, prudish, discreet. (*lively, vivacious, facetious, wanton, wild, noisy, boisterous*)

**denomination**—name, designation, description, kind, class, order. (*nondescription, misnomer*)

**dense**—slow, thick, stupid, stolid, solid, stout, compact, consolidated, condensed, close, thickset. (*quick, clever, intelligent, rare, rarefied, sparse*)

**deny**—refuse, reject, withhold, negative, contradict, gainsay, disclaim, disavow, disown, oppose. (*grant, accept, concede, admit, affirm, confirm, afford*)

**department**—section, division, portion, function, office, branch, province, line. (*institution, establishment, art, science, literature, service, state, whole*)

**dependent**—hanging, resting, contingent, trusting, relying, subject, relative. (*independent, irrelative, irrespective, absolute, free*)

**depression**—lowering, degradation, debasement, dejection, discouragement, hollow, valley, dip. (*raising, elevation, exaltation, promotion, preferment*)

**deprive**—strip, bereave, despoil, rob, divest, dispossess, abridge, depose, prevent, hinder. (*invest, endow, compensate, enrich, supply, present, reinstate*)

**derision**—scorn, contempt, mockery, irony, sarcasm, contumely, disrespect. (*respect, regard, admiration, reverence*)

**descendant**—offspring, progeny, stock, scion, seed, branch, issue, house, family, lineage. (*author, founder, parent, ancestor, progenitor, stock, root*)

**describe**—draw, delineate, portray, explain, illustrate, define, picture, depict, represent, relate, narrate, recount. (*confound, confuse, mystify, misrepresent, caricature, distort*)

**desert**—wild, waste, wilderness, solitude, void. (*inclosure, field, pasture, garden, oasis*)

**design**—*v.* contemplate, purpose, intend, plan, prepare, project. (*hit, risk, guess, conjecture*)

**design**—*n.* contemplation, purpose, intention, plan, preparation, draft, delineation, sketch, drawing, artifice, cunning, artfulness, guile, contrivance, intent, project, scheme. (*execution, performance, result, issue, construction, structure, candor, fairness*)

**desirable**—expedient, advisable, valuable, acceptable, proper, judicious, beneficial, profitable, good, enviable, delightful. (*undesirable, inadvisable, inexpedient, objectionable, improper, injudicious, unprofitable, evil*)

**desire**—longing, affection, propension, craving, concupiscence, appetency. (*loathing, hate, repugnance, disgust, aversion, abomination, horror*)

**despair**—hopelessness, despondency, desperation.

(*hopefulness, elation, anticipation, hilarity, confidence, sanguineness, expectation*)

**desperate**—wild, daring, audacious, determined, reckless, abandoned, rash, furious, frantic, despairing, regardless, mad, desponding, hopeless, inextricable, irremediable. (*cool, calm, cautious*)

**despotic**—autocratic, domineering, arbitrary, arrogant, imperious, self-willed, irresponsible, absolute, cruel, tyrannical. (*limited, constitutional*)

**destination**—purpose, intention, design, consignment, object, end, fate, doom, arrival, application, use, scope, appointment, point, location, goal, aim. (*operation, tendency, exercise, action, movement, design, initiation, project, effort*)

**destiny**—fate, decree, lot, fortune, predestination, necessity, doom, end. (*will, volition, choice, deliberation, freedom, free will*)

**destroy**—demolish, annihilate, subvert, ruin, overthrow, undo, waste, consume. (*restore, reinstate, repair, fabricate, make, construct, create*)

**destructive**—detrimental hurtful, noxious, injurious, deleterious, baleful, baneful, ruinous, subversive. (*wholesome, conservative, preservative, beneficial, reparatory, subsidiary, restorative*)

**detraction**—diminution, deterioration, depreciation, slander, backbiting, derogation. (*augmentation, improvement, enhancement, eulogy, compliment*)

**detriment**—loss, harm, hurt, injury, deterioration, impairment, disadvantage, prejudice, damage, inconvenience. (*enhancement, improvement, remedy, reinstatement, repair, augmentation*)

**detrimental**—injurious, hurtful, pernicious. (*beneficial, profitable, augmentative*)

**develop**—educe, enucleate, eliminate, enunciate, lay open, disclose, unravel, unfold, clear, amplify, expand, enlarge. (*envelop, wrap, obscure, mystify*)

**device**—artifice, expedient, design, plan, stratagem, project, symbol, emblem, show, invention, contrivance, cognizance. (*fair dealing, openness*)

**devil**—satan, lucifer, fiend, arch-fiend, foul fiend, demon. (*archangel, angel, seraph, cherub*)

**devise**—contrive, plan, maneuver, concert, manage. (*miscontrive, mismanage*)

**devoid**—void, wanting, destitute, unendowed, unprovided. (*furnished, supplied, replete, provided*)

**devotion**—piety, devoutness, religiousness, dedication, self-abandonment, consecration, ardor, self-surrender, self-sacrifice, love, attachment. (*impiety, profanity, selfishness, aversion, alienation*)

**devour**—eat, consume, swallow, gorge, gobble, bolt, absorb. (*disgorge, vomit*)

**dictate**—prompt, suggest, enjoin, order, direct, prescribe, decree, instruct, propose, command. (*follow, repeat, obey, echo, answer*)

**dictation**—imperative, imperious, domineering, arbitrary. (*condescending, affable, indulgent, modest, unassuming, suppliant, supplicatory, precatory*)

**die**—expire, depart, perish, decline, decease, disappear, wither, languish, wane, sink, fade, decay, cease. (*begin, originate, rise, live, develop*)

**difference**—separation, destruction, dissimilarity, unlikeness, disagreement, dissonance, discord, contrariety, dissent, distinction, dissimilitude, estrangement, variety. (*community, consociation*)

**difficult**—hard, intricate, involved, perplexing, enigmatical, obscure, trying, arduous, troublesome, uphill, unmanageable, unamenable, reserved, opposed. (*easy, plain, straight, simple, lucid, categorical, tractable, amenable, unreserved, favorable*)

**digest**—sort, arrange, dispose, order, classify, study, ponder, consider, prepare, assimilate, incorporate, convert, methodize, tabulate. (*displace, confound, complicate, derange, disorder, discompose*)

**dilemma**—fix, hobble, quandary, doubt, difficulty, scrape. (*extrication, rebutment, freedom, advantage, superiority, escape, solution, retort*)

**diligence**—care, assiduity, attention, appiication, heed, industry. (*indifference, carelessness, neglect*)

**dingy**—dull, dusky, rusty, bedimmed, soiled, tarnished, dirty, dim, colorless, obscure, dead, somber. (*bright, burnished, glossy, high-colored*)

**diplomacy**—embassage, ministry, ambassadorship, representation, tact, contrivance, management, negotiation, outwitting, circumvention. (*cancel, recall, conge, miscontrivance, mismanagement*)

**diplomatic**—judicious, knowing, wise, prudent, well-contrived, clever, astute, politic, discreet, well-planned, well-conceived, sagacious, well-managed. (*injudicious, bungling, stultifying, ill-managed, undiplomatic*)

**direction**—course, tendency, inclination, line, control, command, bearing, superscription, order, address. (*misdirection, deviation, miscontrol, misinstruction, aberration*)

**directly**—straightly, straightaway, immediately, undeviatingly, at once, promptly, quickly, instantly. (*indirectly, by-and-by, interveniently*)

**disability**—disqualification, impotency, unfitness, incapacity, forfeiture, incompetency. (*qualification, recommendation, fitness, deserving, merit*)

**disappoint**—betray, deceive, frustrate, baffle, delude, vex, mortify, defeat, foil. (*realize, justify*)

**discernible**—visible, conspicuous, manifest, palpable, apparent, plain, perceptible, evident. (*invisible, inconspicuous, obscure, indiscernible, impalpable, microscopic, minute*)

**discipline**—order, strictness, training, government, instruction, drilling, control, coercion, punishment, organization. (*disorder, confusion, rebellion, mutiny, encouragement, reward, disorganization*)

**discomfort**—disquiet, vexation, annoyance, trouble, unpleasantness, disagreeableness. (*comfort, ease, pleasantness, agreeableness*)

**disconcert**—abash, confuse, confound, upset, baffle, derange, discompose, thwart, disturb, defeat, fret, interrupt, vex, ruffle, disorder, unsettle, frustrate, discomfit. (*encourage, rally, countenance*)

**discreet**—discerning, wise, prudent, circumspect, cautious, wary, regulative, sensible, judicious. (*undiscerning, blind, foolish, imprudent, indiscreet, unrestrained, reckless*)

**discrimination**—penetration, sagacity, acuteness, nicety, shrewdness, judgment, discernment, insight, distinction. (*dullness, confusedness, indiscriminateness, shortsightedness, hebetude, indiscernment*)

**disease**—complaint, disorder, illness, indisposition, distemper, ailment, malady, sickness. (*health, convalescence, sanity, salubrity*)

**disgust**—nausea, loathing, abomination, aversion, dislike, repugnance, abhorrence, distaste. (*desire, liking, partiality, predilection, relish, fondness, longing, avidity*)

**dismal**—dreary, ominous, foreboding, lonesome, cheerless, gloomy, sad, depressed, lugubrious, funereal, sorrowful, melancholy, tragic, blank. (*gay, propitious, promising, cheerful, lively, elated*)

**dispatch**—expedite, send, accelerate, hasten, execute, conclude, get rid of. (*retard, detain, obstruct, impede, retain*)

**dispel**—disperse, scatter, dissipate, drive away, dismiss. (*collect, recall, summon, convene, congregate, conglomerate, mass, accumulate*)

**disperse**—dispel, scatter, disseminate, separate, break up, spread abroad, deal out, distribute, dissipate. (*collect, summon, recall, gather, concentrate*)

**dispute**—argue, question, canvass, contest, contend, challenge, debate, controvert, controversy. difference, gainsay, impugn, quarrel, altercation, (*waive, concede, allow, forgo*)

**dissemble**—disguise, conceal, repress, smother, restrain, cloak. (*exhibit, manifest, protrude, vaunt*)

**disseminate**—spread, propagate, preach, proclaim, publish, promulgate, scatter, circulate. (*repress, suppress, stifle, discountenance, extirpate*)

**dissolute**—abandoned, profligate, loose, licentious, wanton, vicious. (*upright, conscientious*)

**distance**—interval, removal, separation, interspace, remoteness, absence, space, length. (*proximity, nearness, adjacency, contiguity, neighborhood*)

**distinct**—separate, independent, unconnected, detached, disjoined, unlike, definite, obvious, different, dissimilar, clear, conspicuous, plain, perspicuous. (*united, consolidated, conjoined, one*)

**distinction**—difference, separation, dignity, eminence. (*unity, identity, debasement, insignificance*)

**distinguish**—discern, descry, perceive, characterize, make famous, know, discriminate, see, discover, separate, divide, dissimilate, differentiate. (*miss, overlook, confound, confuse*)

**distinguished**—illustrious, noted, celebrated, conspicuous, eminent, marked, famous. (*obscure, inconspicuous, hidden, not famous*)

**distress**—harass, embarrass, trouble, grieve, annoy, vex, mortify, pain, disturb, afflict, worry. (*soothe, compose, please, gratify, gladden, console*)

**disturb**—derange, discompose, disorder, discommode, plague, confuse, rouse, agitate, annoy, trouble, interrupt, incommode, worry, vex, molest, disquiet. (*order, collocate, arrange, pacify, soothe*)

**diversion**—detour, divergence, deviation, recreation, amusement, pastime, sport, enjoyment. (*continuity, directness, procedure, business, task*)

**divide**—separate, dissect, bisect, portion, part, divorce, segregate, sever, sunder, deal out, disunite, keep apart, part among, allot, distribute, multiply. (*unite, collocate, classify, convene, congregate, conglomerate, conglutinate, commingle, join, consociate*)

**divorce**—separate, disconnect, dissever, divert, alienate. (*conjoin, unite, connect, apply, reconcile*)

**do**—work, act, accomplish, execute, achieve, transact, finish, enact, perform, produce, complete. (*undo, mar, neglect, omit*)

**docile**—compliant, amenable, easily managed, yielding, gentle, quiet, pliant, tractable, teachable, tame. (*intractable, stubborn, obstinate, self-willed*)

**dogmatic**—doctrinal, theological, imperious, dictatorial, authoritative, arrogant, magisterial, self-opinionated, positive. (*practical, active, moderate*)

**doleful**—dolorous, rueful, melancholy, piteous, somber, sorrowful, woebegone, dismal. (*merry, joyful, gay, blithe, beaming*)

**dominion**—power, authority, rule, tyranny, despotism, government, control, empire, sway, realm, territory, jurisdiction. (*weakness, submission, subjugation, inferiority, servitude*)

**dormant**—sleeping, slumbering, latent, undeveloped, quiescent, inert. (*vigilant, wakeful, active*)

**doubt**—dubiousness, dubitation, scruple, hesitation, suspense, distrust, suspicion, perplexity, uncertainty, ambiguity, difficulty, indecision. (*certainty, clearness, precision, determination, decision*)

**drain**—draw, strain, drip, percolate, drop, exhaust, empty, dry. (*replenish, fill, supply, pour*)

**draw**—drag, pull, attract, induce, haul, entice, inhale, sketch, delineate, describe. (*push, carry, propel, throw, repel, drive, compel, impel, thrust*)

**dreadful**—fearful, shocking, monstrous, dire, terrible, frightful, terrific, horrible, alarming, awful. (*encouraging, inspiriting, assuring, promising*)

**dreamy**—fanciful, visionary, speculative, abstracted, absent, foggy. (*collected, earnest, attentive, awake, active, energetic, practical*)

**dregs**—refuse, sediment, offal, lees, off-scouring, dross, trash. (*cream, flower, pink, pickings, bouquet*)

**dress**—garniture, preparation, arrangement, clothing, habiliments, accoutrements, vestments, uniform, raiment, apparel, attire, clothes, array, garments, livery, costume, garb, investiture. (*nudity, disorder, disarrangement, undress, deshabille*)

**drift**—tendency, direction, motion, tenor, meaning, purport, object, intention, purpose, scope, aim, result, issue, inference, conclusion, end, course. (*aimlessness, pointlessness, vagueness, unmeaningness, indefiniteness, confusedness, aberrancy*)

**drink**—imbibe, swallow, quaff, absorb, drain, draught. (*disgorge, replenish, pour, exude, water*)

**drivel**—fatuity, nonsense, trifling, snivel, babble. (*soundness, coherence, substance, solidity*)

**droll**—whimsical, comical, odd, queer, amusing, laughable, funny, comic, fantastic, farcical. (*sad, lamentable, tragic, lugubrious, funereal*)

**drop**—ooze, emanate, distill, percolate, fall, decline, descend, faint, droop. (*evaporate, rally, rise*)

**drown**—sink, immerse, swamp, overwhelm, engulf, deluge, inundate, submerge. (*dry, drain*)

**dry**—arid, parched, moistureless, juiceless, barren, tame, sarcastic, vapid, lifeless, dull, tedious, uninteresting, monotonous. (*moist, fresh, juicy*)

**dull**—stupid, stolid, doltish, insensible, callous, heavy, gloomy, dismal, cloudy, turbid, opaque, dowdy, sluggish, sad, tiresome, commonplace, dead. (*sharp, clever, lively, animated, sensible, cheerful*)

**durable**—lasting, permanent, stable, persistent, abiding, constant, continuing. (*evanescent, transient, impermanent, unstable*)

**duty**—obligation, part, business, responsibility, allegiance, function, office, province, calling, trust, commission, service. (*freedom, exemption, immunity, license, dispensation, desertion, dereliction*)

**dwindle**—pine, waste, diminish, decrease, fall off, decline, melt. (*expand, enlarge, increase, grow*)

## E

**early**—soon, betimes, forward, shortly, quickly, erelong, anon, matutinal, beforehand. (*late, tardily, backward, vespertinal, belated*)

**earn**—merit, acquire, achieve, obtain, win, gain, deserve. (*forfeit, forgo, waste, lose, spend, squander*)

**earnest**—eager, serious, intent, determined, strenuous, solemn, grave, warm, fervent, intense, ardent. (*indifferent, idle, playful, desultory, irresolute, unearnest, sportive, jesting, flippant*)

**easy**—quiet, comfortable, manageable, indulgent, facile, lenient, unconstrained, gentle, not difficult, unconcerned, self-possessed. (*uneasy, disturbed, uncomfortable, difficult, unmanageable, hard, exacting*)

**economy**—administration, dispensation, management, rule, arrangement, distribution, husbanding. (*maladministration, waste, misrule, mismanagement*)

**ecstasy**—rapture, inspiration, fervor, frenzy, transport, emotion, joy, delight, enthusiasm, happiness. (*indifference, coolness, dullness, weariness*)

**edifice**—structure, building, tenement, fabric. (*ruin, heap, demolition, dismantlement*)

**educate**—instruct, nurture, discipline, train, teach, develop, ground, school, initiate. (*miseducate, misinstruct, misnurture*)

**effective**—powerful, conducive, operative, cogent, telling, able, potent, talented, efficacious, efficient, serviceable, effectual. (*weak, ineffective*)

**effort**—trial, attempt, endeavor, exertion. (*failure, misadventure, unsuccess, frustration, futility*)

**egotism**—conceit, vanity, self-assertion, self-conceit, self-praise, self-exaltation, conceitedness. (*considerateness, deference, self-abnegation*)

**ejaculation**—exclamation, utterance, cry. (*silence, speechlessness*)

**elastic**—ductile, extensile, alterable, resilient, modifiable, flexible, buoyant, springy. (*tough, unchangeable, rigid, unflexible, inelastic, crystallized*)

**elated**—cheered, joyed, inspirited, overjoyed, proud, inflated. (*depressed, dispirited, disappointed*)

**elegance**—beauty, grace, refinement, symmetry, gracefulness, taste. (*deformity, awkwardness, inelegance, disproportion, ungracefulness, coarseness*)

**elegant**—graceful, lovely, well formed, well made, symmetrical, accomplished, polished, refined, handsome. (*inelegant, deformed, unsymmetrical, ill-proportioned, ungraceful, coarse, rude*)

**elementary**—physical, material, natural, primary, rudimentary, simple, inchoate, component, constituent, ultimate. (*immaterial, incorporeal, impalpable, compound, collective, aggregate*)

**eligible**—capable, suitable, worthy, desirable, preferable, choice, prime. (*undesirable, worthless*)

**elude**—escape, avoid, baffle, shun, eschew, evade, parry, fence, mock, frustrate. (*encounter, meet, confront, court, dare, defy*)

**embalm**—conserve, preserve, treasure, store, enshrine, consecrate. (*expose, desecrate, abandon*)

**embarrass**—entangle, disconcert, trouble, perplex, confuse, hamper, clog, distress, puzzle, encumber. (*extricate, liberate, expedite, facilitate*)

**embezzle**—appropriate, confuse, falsify, peculate, misappropriate. (*square, balance, clear*)

**embody**—express, methodize, systematize, codify, incorporate, aggregate, integrate, compact, introduce, enlist, combine. (*eliminate, segregate*)

**embrace**—clasp, comprehend, include, hug, comprise, contain, close, embody, incorporate. (*exclude, reject, except*)

**emergency**—crisis, conjuncture, pitch, embarrassment, strait, necessity, exigency, casualty, difficulty. (*rescue, deliverance, solution, subsidence*)

**emotion**—passion, feeling, excitement, agitation, perturbation, trepidation, tremor. (*indifference, lack of feeling*)

**emphatic**—earnest, forcible, strong, energetic, impressive, positive, important, special, egregious, consummate. (*mild, unemphatic, cool, unimpassioned, unimportant, ordinary, unnoticeable*)

**employ**—use, apply, economize, occupy, engage, engross. (*discard, dismiss, misuse, misemploy*)

**empower**—enable, commission, encourage, qualify, delegate, warrant, sanction, direct, authorize. (*hinder, prevent, discourage, disable, disqualify*)

**empty**—vacant, void, unencumbered, unobstructed, unoccupied, waste, uninhabited, unfrequented, devoid, vacuous, destitute, unfilled, unfurnished, untenanted, evacuated, deficient, weak, silly, idle, senseless. (*full, occupied, encumbered, obstructed, cultivated, colonized, inhabited, informed, well-instructed, experienced, sensible, significant, forcible, important, substantial*)

**enamor**—captivate, fascinate, enslave, charm, endear, bewitch, enchain. (*repel, disgust, estrange*)

**enclose**—shut, encircle, environ, include, circumscribe, envelop, wrap, afforest. (*open, disclose, exclude, bare, disencircle, expose, develop, disafforest*)

**encourage**—embolden, rally, enhearten, cheer, incite, stimulate, foster, cherish, promote, urge, impel, advance, countenance, forward, reassure, animate, inspirit, prompt, abet. (*deter, discourage*)

**endanger**—imperil, expose, peril, jeopardize, hazard, risk. (*cover, defend, protect, shield, screen*)

**endear**—attach, conciliate, gain. (*estrange, alienate, embitter*)

**endless**—interminable, illimitable, unending, unceasing, boundless, deathless, imperishable, everlasting, perpetual, eternal, infinite. (*terminable*)

**endorse**—sanction, approve, subscribe, accept. (*protest, repudiate, cancel, abjure, renounce*)

**endowment**—gift, provision, benefit, benefaction, capacity, attainment, qualification. (*impoverishment, spoliation, disendowment, incapacity*)

**enforce**—urge, compel, require, exact, exert, strain. (*relax, waive, forgo, remit, abandon*)

**engage**—promise, undertake, vouch, employ, occupy, hire, gain, attract, enlist, stipulate, pledge, agree, buy, adopt, involve. (*decline, refuse, withdraw, dismiss, discard, extricate, disengage*)

**enigmatical**—puzzling, perplexing, obscure, mystic. (*lucid, explanatory, plain, self-evident*)

**enlarge**—amplify, expand, augment, broaden, swell, stretch out, extend, stretch, dilate, increase. (*narrow, lessen, contract, restrict, diminish, curtail*)

**enlighten**—illumine, edify, instruct, illuminate, inform, teach. (*mislead, darken, confound, obscure*)

**enlist**—enter, register, enroll, incorporate, embody. (*withdraw, erase, expunge, dismiss, disband*)

**enmity**—discord, hate, hostility, malevolence, maliciousness, aversion, malignity, ill-feeling, animosity, opposition, bitterness, acrimony, asperity. (*friendship, love, affection, esteem, friendliness, cordiality*)

**enormous**—huge, immense, gigantic, colossal, elephantine, vast, gross, monstrous, prodigious. (*diminutive, insignificant, trivial, venial, average*)

**enough**—sufficient, ample, plenty, abundance. (*bare, scant, insufficient, inadequate, short*)

**ensue**—follow, accrue, supervene, befall. (*precede, threaten, premonish, forewarn*)

**ensure**—fix, determine, secure, seal. (*imperil, hazard, jeopardize, forfeit*)

**enterprising**—active, bold, daring, adventurous, speculative, dashing, venturesome. (*inactive, timid, inadventurous, cautious*)

**entertain**—harbor, maintain, conceive, foster, receive, recreate, amuse. (*eject, exclude, deny, debar, annoy, weary, bore, tire.*)

**enthusiasm**—excitement, frenzy, sensation, inspiration, transport, rapture, warmth, fervor, fervency, zeal, ardor, vehemence, passion, devotion. (*coldness, callousness, indifference, disaffection, repugnance, alienation, contempt*)

**entire**—whole, complete, unimpaired, total, perfect, all, full, solid, integral, undiminished. (*partial*)

**entitle**—qualify, empower, fit, enable, name, style, denominate, designate, characterize. (*disqualify, disentitle, disable, not designate, not characterize*)

**entreat**—implore, obsecrate, beg, beseech, importune, crave, solicit, supplicate, pray, ask, urge. petition. (*command, insist, bid, enjoin*)

**enumerate**—specify, name, number, recount, detail, reckon, compute, calculate, call over. (*confound, miscount, misreckon*)

**ephemeral**—transient, evanescent, fleeting, fugacious, fugitive, momentary. (*abiding, persistent*)

**equable**—uniform, regular, proportionate, even, smooth, easy. (*irregular, desultory, variable, fitful,*

**equal**—uniform, commensurate, coordinate, adequate, alike, equivalent, even, equable, sufficient, impartial, coextensive, smooth. (*unequal, incommensurate, incoordinate, inadequate, disparate*)

**equitable**—fair, just, proportionate, impartial, upright, proper, reasonable, evenhanded, honest. (*unfair, unjust, disproportionate, partial*)

**erase**—obliterate, efface, expunge, blot, cancel. (*mark, write, delineate*)

**erect**—elevate, raise, establish, plant, uplift, construct, build, found, institute, set up. (*lower, supplant, subvert, depress, remove, destroy, demolish*)

**erratic**—desultory, aberrant, abnormal, flighty, changeful, capricious. (*regular, normal, methodical, calculable, unalterable, steady, undeviating*)

**error**—fault, mistake, blunder, falsity, deception, fallacy, untruth, hallucination. (*correction, correctness, truth, accuracy, soundness, rectification*)

**escape**—elude, decamp, abscond, fly, flee, evade, avoid. (*incur, confront, encounter, meet, suffer*)

**essential**—innate, inherent, requisite, necessary, vital, immanent, indispensable, leading. (*accidental, qualitative, quantitative, promotive, regulative, induced, imported, adventitious*)

**establish**—plant, fix, settle, found, demonstrate, organize, confirm, institute, prove, substantiate. (*supplant, unsettle, break up, disestablish*)

**esteem**—price, value, consider, deem, judge, believe, estimate, think, regard, affect, appreciate, revere, honor, respect, admire, venerate, prize, love, like. (*disregard, disconsider, disaffect, dislike, undervalue, underrate, decry, deprecate*)

**eternal**—infinite, endless, everlasting, deathless, imperishable, never-dying, ceaseless, ever-living, perpetual, undying, unceasing. (*ephemeral, transient, temporal, fleeting, evanescent, sublunary*)

**etiquette**—manners, breeding, fashion, conventionality. (*boorishness, rudeness, misobservance*)

**evaporate**—melt, colliquate, liquefy, vaporize, disappear, dissolve, exhale, distill. (*consolidate, compact, solidify, indurate, crystallize*)

**event**—occurrence, circumstance, episode, adventure, issue, accident, result, fact, incident. (*cause, antecedent, operation, inducement, contribution, convergence, predisposition, tendency*)

**eventful**—remarkable, memorable, signal, important, marked, noted, critical, stirring, notable. (*ordinary, unmarked, unimportant, eventless, uninteresting, characterless, trivial*)

**evidence**—manifestation, attraction, averment, testimony, disposition, declaration, appearance, sign, token, proof, indication, exemplification, illustration. (*surmise, conjecture, counterevidence, disproof, refutation, concealment, suppression, misindication, fallacy*)

**evident**—plain, visible, conspicuous, manifest, indisputable, obvious, clear, palpable, incontrovertible. (*doubtful, obscure, questionable, uncertain, dubious*)

**evil**—ill, noxious, deleterious, wrong, bad, mischievous, hurtful, sinful, unhappy, adverse, unpropitious, wicked, corrupt, harmful, unfair, notorious, miserable, sorrowful. (*wholesome, beneficial, right, virtuous, holy, pure, happy, fortunate*)

**exactly**—precisely, accurately, correspondently. (*loosely, inadequately, incorrectly, differently, otherwise*)

**exaggerate**—amplify, enlarge, heighten, magnify, overstate, overdraw, strain, overpaint, overestimate. (*disparage, attenuate, palliate, understate*)

**examine**—weigh, ponder, investigate, perpend, test, scrutinize, criticize, prove, study, discuss, inquire, search, overhaul, explore, inspect. (*discard, conjecture, guess, slur, misconsider, misinvestigate*)

**example**—sample, specimen, pattern, model, copy, illustration, instance, issue, development. (*stock, material, substance, law, rule, character*)

**except**—exclude, save, bar, segregate, negative. (*count, include, reckon, state, classify, propound*)

**exceptional**—rare, peculiar, uncommon, irregular, unusual, abnormal. (*common, regular, normal, usual, ordinary*)

**excessive**—enormous, undue, exorbitant, overmuch, superabundant, superfluous, unreasonable, immoderate, inordinate, extravagant. (*insufficient, scant, inadequate*)

**excuse**—exculpate, absolve, pardon, forgive, overlook, condone, remit, indulge, justify, vindicate, defend, acquit, mitigate, extenuate, release, exempt, exonerate. (*charge, inculpate, condemn*)

**execrable**—detestable, loathsome, accursed, cursed, villainous, diabolical, hateful, abominable, damnable. (*desirable, eligible, respectable, laudable*)

**exemplary**—laudable, praiseworthy, conspicuous, honorable, wary, meritorious, worthy, excellent. (*detestable, objectionable, exceptionable*)

**exempt**—free, irresponsible, unamenable, clear, liberated, privileged, absolved. (*subject, responsible, liable, amenable*)

**exercise**—exertion, use, practice, application, training, employment, drill. (*rest, ease, relaxation*)

**exhaust**—empty, spend, consume, debilitate, waste, void, drain, weaken, weary. (*fill, replenish*)

**existence**—being, entity, creature. (*nonentity, nonexistence, chimera*)

**expand**—swell, dilate, spread, extend, open, diffuse, develop, unfold, enlarge, amplify. (*contract, curtail, attenuate, restrict, condense*)

**expect**—anticipate, await, forecast, forebode, wait for, rely on, look for, foresee. (*welcome, hail, recognize, greet, realize*)

**expediency**—utility, advantage, interest. (*inexpediency, disadvantage, inutility, detriment*)

**expend**—spend, disburse, lay out, waste, consume, use. (*save, husband, economize*)

**expense**—price, cost, charge, payment, expenditure, outlay. (*income, profit, receipt*)

**experience**—*n.* experiment, trial, test, proof, habit, knowledge. (*ignorance, inexperience*)

**experience**—*v.* try, feel, undergo, encounter, endure. (*evade, escape, miss, lose*)

**explain**—expound, teach, illustrate, clear up, interpret, elucidate, decipher. (*mystify, obscure*)

**explanation**—exposition, explication, interpretation, sense, description. (*mystification, obscuration, confusion, misinterpretation*)

**explicit**—plain, detailed, inobscure, declaratory, categorical, stated, distinctly stated, express, definite, determinate. (*implicit, implied, hinted*)

**expression**—countenance, look, indication, phrase, term, face, feature, lineament. (*falsification, misstatement, solecism, enigma, suppression*)

**exquisite**—choice, rare, refined, delicate, perfect, matchless, intense, consummate, delicious. (*common, coarse, ordinary*)

**extend**—prolong, stretch, expand, enlarge, increase, augment, reach, spread, amplify, avail, apply. (*curtail, contract, restrict, narrow, limit*)

**extent**—degree, distance, quantity, space, size. (*diminution, restriction, limitation*)

**extinguish**—abolish, destroy, extirpate, eradicate, kill, quench, annihilate, put out. (*implant, replenish, cherish, promote, invigorate, propagate, establish, confirm, secure*)

**extortionate**—hard, closefisted, severe, rigorous, exorbitant, preposterous, monstrous, exacting. (*liberal, indulgent, bountiful, reasonable, fair, moderate*)

**extraordinary**—unwonted, uncommon, peculiar, unusual, unprecedented, wonderful, marvelous, prodigious, monstrous, remarkable, strange, preposterous. (*wonted, common, usual, ordinary*)

**extravagant**—wild, monstrous, preposterous, absurd, prodigal, wasteful, reckless, excessive, lavish, profuse, abnormal. (*sound, sober, consistent, rational, fair, economical, frugal, careful*)

**extreme**—terminal, final, remote, utmost, farthest, last, extravagant, immoderate, most violent, distant, ultimate. (*initial, primal, moderate, judicious*)

## F

**fable**—apologue, fiction, parable, allegory, romance, invention, fabrication, untruth, novel, falsehood. (*history, narrative, fact*)

**facetious**—witty, funny, humorous, jocular, waggish, playful, droll, jocose. (*heavy, matter-of-fact, dull, grave, serious, lugubrious, somber, saturnine*)

**facile**—docile, tractable, manageable, indulgent, weak, irresolute, easy, affable, flexible, characterless, pliable. (*sturdy, obstinate, determined, resolute, pigheaded, crusty, inflexible, self-willed, independent, self-reliant*)

**facility**—ease, address, readiness, quickness, adroitness, dexterity, pliancy. (*labor, awkwardness, difficulty*)

**fact**—truth, deed, occurrence, certainty, circumstance, event, reality. (*fiction, supposition, falsehood, unreality, lie, delusion, chimera, invention, romance*)

**fade**—fall, fail, decline, sink, droop, dwindle, vanish, change, pale, bleach, set, etiolate. (*rise, increase, grow, bloom, flourish, abide, stand, last*)

**fag**—work, toil, slave, drudge. (*bask, idle, lounge, dawdle, strike*)

**faint**—weak, languid, fatigued, unenergetic, timid, irresolute, feeble, exhausted, halfhearted, obscure, dim, pale, faded, inconspicuous. (*strong, vigorous, energetic, fresh, daring, resolute, prominent*)

**fair**—open, clear, spotless, unspotted, untarnished, reasonable, unblemished, serene, beautiful, just, honorable, equitable, impartial. (*lowering, dull, foul, disfigured, ugly, unfair, dishonorable*)

**faithful**—true, firm, attached, loyal, accurate, close, consistent, correspondent, exact, equivalent, staunch, incorruptible. (*false, fickle, capricious*)

**fallacy**—sophistry, error, blunder, misconception, bugbear, fiction, delusion, chimera. (*truth, verity*)

**false**—untrue, erroneous, fallacious, sophistical, spurious, deceptive, fabrication, counterfeit, mendacious, sham, mock, bogus, unfaithful, fib, falsity, fiction, dishonorable, faithless. (*true, correct*)

**falsify**—mistake, misinterpret, misrepresent, belie, betray, garble, cook. (*verify, correct, rectify*)

**falter**—halt, hesitate, hobble, slip, dubitate, stammer, demur, waver, flinch, vacillate. (*proceed, run, speed, flow, discourse, determine, persevere, resolve, career*)

**familiar**—household, common, free, frank, affable, everyday, well-acquainted, accustomed, conversant, intimate. (*uncommon, rare, strange*)

**famous**—renowned, glorious, celebrated, illustrious, far-famed. (*unknown, obscure, unsung, inglorious*)

**fanciful**—grotesque, chimerical, unreal, imaginary, quaint, eccentric, freakish, humorous, erroneous, capricious, whimsical, erratic, absurd, fitful. (*natural, literal, regular, real, sober, ordinary, truthful, accurate, correct, orderly, calculable*)

**fancy**—thought, belief, idea, supposition, imagination, caprice, notion, conceit, vagary, inclination, whim, humor, predilection, desire. (*object, subject, fact, reality, order, law, truth, system, verity*)

**fashion**—form, shape, guise, style, appearance, character, figure, mold, mode, custom, practice, usage, manner, way, ceremony. (*person, work, dress, speech, formlessness, shapelessness, derangement, eccentricity, strangeness, outlandishness*)

**fast**—firm, secure, fixed, constant, steadfast, stable, unyielding, unswerving, rapid, accelerated, wild, reckless, dissipated, gay. (*loose, insecure*)

**fastidious**—critical, overnice, overrefined censorious, punctilious, particular, squeamish, dainty. (*easy, indulgent, uncritical, coarse, omnivorous*)

**fat**—corpulent, fleshy, brawny, pursy, rich, luxuriant, portly, stout, fertile, unctuous, obese, oleaginous. (*lean, slender, attenuated, emaciated*)

**fatal**—calamitous, deadly, destructive, mortal, lethal. (*beneficial, wholesome, nutritious, vitalizing, salubrious, restorative, slight, superficial, harmless.*)

**fate**—necessity, destiny, lot, end, fortune, doom. (*will, choice, decision, freedom, independence*)

**fault**—defect, error, imperfection, flaw, misdeed, failure, omission, want, drawback. (*sufficiency, correctness, completeness, perfection*)

**favor**—permission, grace, concession, predilection, gift, civility, benefit, kindness, good will, regard, condescension, preference, boon, countenance, patronage. (*refusal, denial, prohibition*)

**favorable**—permissive, indulgent, propitious, concessive, partial, fond, liberal, advantageous, auspicious, friendly. (*reluctant, unpropitious, unfavorable, impartial*)

**fear**—apprehension, solicitude, alarm, fright, dread, terror, trepidation, dismay, consternation, misgiving, horror, timidity, awe. (*assurance, confidence, courage, fearlessness, trust, boldness*)

**feeble**—wretched, weak, poor, frail, debilitated, dull, forceless, puny, nerveless, enfeebled, enervated, faint, infirm, incomplete, vain, fruitless, scanty, pitiable. (*strong, robust, active, effective*)

**feeling**—touch, sensation, contact, pathos, tenderness, impression, consciousness, sensibility, emotion, sentiment, passion, sensitiveness. (*insensibility, callousness, imperturbability, inexcitability, coldness, insensateness*)

**felicitous**—happy, timely, successful, opportune, joyous. (*unfortunate, unhappy, untimely, unsuccessful, disastrous, inopportune, sad*)

**feminine**—delicate, womanly, tender, modest, soft. (*robust, manly, indelicate, rude, rough, unfeminine*)

**fertile**—rich, luxuriant, teeming, productive, exuberant, causative, conducive, pregnant, fraught, prolific, fecund, fruitful, ingenious, inventive. (*poor, sterile, barren, unproductive, ineffective, inconducive, fruitless, inoperative, uninventive, unimaginative*)

**fickle**—fanciful, fitful, capricious, irresolute, changeable, vacillating, mutable, unreliable, veering, shifting, variable, restless, inconstant, unstable. (*sober, orderly, reliable, well-regulated, calculable, trustworthy, steady, uniform*)

**fiction**—invention, fabrication, creation, figment, fable, falsehood, romance, myth. (*fact, truth*)

**fidelity**—fealty, attachment, truthfulness, allegiance, accuracy, closeness, exactness, faithfulness, integrity, loyalty, honesty. (*treachery, disloyalty*)

**fiery**—hot, vehement, ardent, fervent, fierce, passionate, irascible, choleric, excited, enkindled, glowing, fervid, impassioned, irritable, hot-brained, (*cold, icy, indifferent, phlegmatic, passionless, unimpassioned, mild, quenched, extinguished, tame*)

**fight**—battle, contention, struggle, conflict, combat, contest, action, engagement, encounter, (*pacification, reconciliation*)

**figure**—aspect, shape, emblem, type, image, condition, appearance, form, symbol, metaphor, likeness, delineation, illustration. (*misrepresentation, deformity, disfigurement*)

**fill**—replenish, content, supply, satisfy, gorge, glut, occupy, appoint, stuff, store, rise, swell, glow, expand, increase. (*exhaust, deprive, drain, dissatisfy, stint, vacate, misappoint, subside, shrink*)

**final**—terminal, last, latest, conclusive, definite, developed, ultimate, decisive. (*initiative, open*)

**find**—meet, confront, ascertain, experience, perceive, discover, furnish, invent. (*miss, elude, overlook, lose, withhold, withdraw, miscontrive*)

**fine**—thin, minute, slender, delicate, pure, smooth, filmy, gauzy, keen, artistic, choice, finished, high, grand, noble, sensitive, refined, generous, honorable, excellent, superior, pretentious, handsome, pretty, beautiful, showy, elegant, ostentatious, presumptuous, nice, casuistical, subtle, (*coarse, large, rough, blunt, rude, unfinished, mean*)

**finical**—affected, overnice, dandyish, dallying, foppish, spruce, factitious, euphuistic. (*unaffected, effective, practical, energetic, real, genuine, natural*)

**finish**—complete, perfect, accomplish, conclude, achieve, end, shape, terminate. (*begin, commence, start, undertake, fail, miscontrive, mismanage, botch*)

**first**—leading, primary, pristine, original, foremost, primitive, principal, primeval, highest, chief, earliest, onmost. (*subsequent, secondary*)

**fit**—decent, befitting, meet, apt, fitting, adapted, seemly, appropriate, becoming, decorous, qualified, congruous, peculiar, particular, suitable, prepared, adequate, calculated, contrived, expedient, proper, ripe. (*awkward, ungainly, misfitting, ill-suited*)

**fix**—place, settle, fasten, link, locate, attach, consolidate, tie, plant, root, establish, secure, determine, decide. (*displace, unsettle, disarrange, remove, uproot, transfer, transplant, disestablish*)

**flat**—dull, tame, insipid, vapid, spiritless, level, horizontal, absolute, even, downright, mawkish, tasteless, lifeless. (*exciting, animated, interesting*)

**flexible**—pliant, lithe, supple, elastic, easy, indulgent, ductile, flexible, yielding, pliable. (*tough, rigid, inelastic, inflexible, hard, inexorable*)

**flimsy**—gauzy, poor, thin, transparent, trifling, trivial, puerile, insane, slight, superficial, weak, shallow. (*solid, sound, irrefragable, substantial*)

**flippant**—pert, forward, superficial, thoughtless, saucy, malapert. (*flattering, servile, obsequious*)

**flock**—herd, congregate, throng, assemble, crowd. (*disperse, scatter, separate, segregate*)

**flood**—deluge, inundation, abundance. (*drought, drain, ebb, scarcity, subsidence*)

**florid**—rubicund, flowery, sanguine, ornate, overwrought, meretricious. (*pallid, exsanguineous, bare, unadorned, nude, sober, chaste*)

**flounder**—roll, blunder, bungle, boggle, wallow, tumble. (*emerge, flow, course, career, speed, rise*)

**flourish**—prosper, thrive, speed, triumph, brandish, wave. (*fail, fade, decline, miscarry, founder*)

**flow**—stream, issue, progress, glide, course, career, run. (*halt, stick, stickle, stop, hesitate, fail*)

**flurry**—agitate, excite, worry, ruffle, fluster. (*soothe, compose, quiet, calm, mesmerize*)

**foible**—peccadillo, failing, fault, weakness, infirmity. (*crime, atrocity, enormity, sin*)

**follow**—pursue, chase, accompany, obey, imitate, succeed, result, ensue, attend, shadow, observe, copy. (*avoid, elude, quit, disobey, precede*)

**folly**—madness, nonsense, misconduct, imprudence, silliness, foolishness, weakness, absurdity, imbecility. (*sense, wisdom, sanity, judgment, prudence, sobriety*)

**foment**—excite, cherish, fan, propagate, encourage. (*allay, extinguish, discourage, extirpate*)

**fond**—loving, attached, affectionate, foolish, silly, weak, doting, empty, enamored, devoted. (*unloving, averse, unaffectionate, strong-minded*)

**foolish**—senseless, idiotic, crazed, shallow, weak, silly, injudicious, irrational, absurd, contemptible, objectionable, witless, brainless, imbecile, preposterous, ridiculous, nonsensical, simple. (*sensible, sane, deep, clearsighted, sound, sagacious*)

**forbidding**—repulsive, deterrent, prohibitory, offensive. (*attractive, encouraging, alluring, seductive, permissive*)

**force**—power, strength, agency, instrumentality, compulsion, cogency, vigor, might, dint, vehemence, pressure, host, army, coercion, validity, violent. (*feebleness, weakness, counteraction, neutralization*)

**foreign**—strange, exotic, outlandish, alien, irrelevant, extraneous. (*domestic, native, congenial, pertinent, germane*)

**forfeit**—fine, penalty, mulct, amercement, damages, loss. (*premium, bribe, douceur, remuneration, compensation, reward, gratuity*)

**forge**—work, frame, produce, elaborate, fabricate, counterfeit, feign, falsify, form, shape, make falsely. (*shatter, batter, shiver, blast, fuse, detect*)

**forget**—lose, pretermit, unlearn, obliviate, overlook. (*acquire, learn, remember, recollect, mind*)

**form**—shape, mold, fashion, constitute, arrange, frame, construct, contrive, make, produce, create, devise. (*deform, dislocate, distort, dissipate*)

**formal**—regular, complete, shapely, sufficient, correct, stately, dignified, ceremonious, pompous, stiff, precise. explicit, exact, affected, methodical. (*irregular, incomplete, informal, inadequate, incorrect, easy, unassuming, unceremonious*)

**formality**—ceremony, parade, affectation, stateliness, punctiliousness, etiquette. (*informality, casualness, simplicity*)

**former**—preceding, antecedent, previous, prior, earlier, ancient, bygone, anterior, first-mentioned, foregoing. (*succeeding, subsequent, posterior, latter, modern, coming, future*)

**fortunate**—lucky, propitious, happy, felicitous, prosperous, auspicious, providential, successful. (*unlucky, unfortunate, unhappy, infelicitous*)

**forward**—advanced, ready, eager, anxious, obtrusive, self-assertive, impertinent, progressive, onward, confident, bold, presumptuous. (*tardy, backward, reluctant, indifferent, slow, modest*)

**found**—establish, institute, fix, set, build, set up, base, endow, rest, ground, plant, root. (*disestablish, subvert, supplant, uproot*)

**foundation**—institution, establishment, footing, base, basis, origin, ground, groundwork, rudiments, substratum, underlying principle. (*disestablishment, superstructure*)

**fragrant**—odorous, scented, perfumed, balmy, sweet-smelling, aromatic, sweet-scented, odoriferous, spicy. (*inodorous, scentless, fetid*)

**frail**—irresolute, erring, mutable. (*resolute, virtuous, lasting*)

**frank**—ingenuous, candid, open, unreserved, artless, free, familiar, honest, easy, sincere, outspoken, plain. (*disingenuous, close, reserved*)

**freakish**—sportful, frisky, whimsical, fanciful, capricious, erratic. (*steady, sober, demure, unwhimsical, unfanciful, reliable, consistent, uniform*)

**free**—detached, playing, operating, open, unoccupied, unobstructed, unimpeded, permitted, unhindered, exempt, gratuitous, unconditional, at liberty, clear, liberal, untrammeled, unconfined, careless, loose, easy, munificent, unreserved, frank, bountiful, generous, bounteous. (*subservient*)

**frequent**—many, repeated, numerous, recurrent, general, continual, usual, common. (*few, solitary, rare, scanty, casual*)

**fresh**—new, young, vigorous, cool, recent, renewed, unimpaired, untarnished, unfaded, blooming, ruddy, novel, untried, modern, unskilled. (*old, stale, jaded, weary, former, stagnant, ordinary*)

**fretful**—irritable, fractious, peevish, impatient, petulant, waspish. (*patient, forbearing, contented*)

**friction**—rubbing, grating, attrition, abrasion, contact. (*lubrication, detachment, isolation*)

**friend**—associate, companion, acquaintance, familiar, ally, chum, messmate, coadjutor, confidant, adherent. (*opponent, foe, adversary, antagonist, enemy*)

**friendly**—well-inclined, well-disposed, amicable, kindly, social, neighborly, sociable, affectionate, favorable, cordial. (*ill-inclined, ill-disposed, hostile, inimical, adverse, antagonistic*)

**frightful**—terrible, horrible, alarming, ugly, hideous, monstrous, dreadful, direful, awful, shocking, horrid, terrific. (*pleasing, attractive, beautiful*)

**frivolous**—trifling, silly, trivial, petty, worthless. (*serious, earnest, important, grave*)

**frolic**—play, game, sport, festivity, entertainment, gambol, gaiety, lark, spree, merrymaking, prank. (*study, undertaking, purpose, engagement*)

**frugal**—sparing, economical, parsimonious, abstinent, abstemious, temperate, saving, thrifty, provident. (*profuse, luxurious, extravagant, prodigal, self-indulgent, intemperate*)

**fruitful**—productive, prolific, pregnant, fraught, causative, effectual, useful, successful, fertile, abundant, plenteous, fecund, plentiful. (*unproductive, sterile, barren, fruitless, ineffectual, useless*)

**fulfill**—fill, complete, discharge, verify, accomplish, achieve, execute, effect. (*neglect, ignore*)

**fulsome**—excessive, gross, loathsome, nauseous, sickening, fawning, offensive. (*chaste, sober, nice*)

**function**—office, part, character, capacity, business, administration, discharge, operation, exercise, power, duty, employment. (*usurpation, maladministration, misconduct, misdemeanor*)

**fundamental**—primary, important, indispensable, essential. (*secondary, unimportant, adventitious, ascititious, nonessential*)

**funny**—sportive, droll, comical, laughable, humorous, jocose, ridiculous, ludicrous, diverting. (*dull, tedious, mournful, lugubrious, dismal, grave*)

**furnish**—supply, provide, equip, afford, yield, bestow, purvey, give. (*withhold, withdraw, dismantle*)

**fuss**—stir, excitement, tumult, worry, ado, bustle, flurry, fidget. (*quiet, peace, sedateness, tranquillity*)

**future**—forthcoming, coming, advenient. (*gone, bygone, past*)

## G

**gabble**—prate, jabber, jargon, stuff, babble, rattle, twaddle, gibber, chatter, gibberish. (*conversation, speech, eloquence, reticence, taciturnity*)

**gain**—acquire, get, win, procure, obtain, profit, benefit, earn, attain, realize, achieve, reap, reach. (*lose, forfeit, suffer*)

**gallant**—brave, chivalrous, intrepid, courteous, heroic, fearless, courageous, valiant, bold, splendid, showy, gay. (*cowardly, churlish, discourteous*)

**game**—sport, recreation, pastime, amusement, frolic, diversion, play. (*study, toil, labor, business*)

**garble**—misrepresent, misquote, mutilate, cook, dress, color, falsify, pervert, distort. (*quote, cite*)

**gaudy**—tawdry, fine, meretricious, bespangled, glittering, showy, gay, garish. (*rich, simple*)

**gauge**—measure, fathom, probe. (*survey, conjecture, view, scan, guess, observe, mismeasure*)

**gawky**—awkward, ungainly, uncouth, clumsy, clownish. (*neat, handy, graceful, handsome*)

**gay**—merry, blithe, lively, jolly, sportive, sprightly, smart, festive, gladsome, pleasuresome, cheerful. (*heavy, melancholy, grave, sad, somber*)

**generous**—noble, chivalrous, liberal, disinterested, bountiful, magnanimous, openhearted, munificent, honorable. (*mean, ignoble, illiberal*)

**genial**—warm, cordial, balmy, cheering, merry, festive, joyous, hearty, revivifying, restorative. (*cold, cutting, harsh, deleterious, noxious, deadly*)

**genteel**—polite, well-bred, refined, courteous, fashionable, elegant, aristocratic, polished, graceful. (*rude, boorish, ill-bred, clownish, unfashionable, unpolished, inelegant, plebeian*)

**gentle**—courteous, polite, high-bred, mild, bland, tame, docile, amiable, meek, soft, placid, tender. (*rough, rude, coarse, fierce, savage*)

**genuine**—authentic, true, real, pure, unalloyed, natural, unaffected, sincere, unadulterated, veritable, sound. (*spurious, fictitious, adulterated*)

**get**—gain, procure, acquire, earn, obtain, attain, secure, achieve. (*lose, forfeit, surrender, forgo*)

**ghastly**—deathlike, wan, grim, cadaverous, spectral, pallid, hideous, shocking. (*blooming, fresh*)

**giddy**—whirling, vertiginous, thoughtless, inconstant, unsteady, lofty, beetling, dizzy, harebrained, flighty. (*stationary, slow, ponderous, thoughtful*)

**gift**—donation, present, grant, boon, gratuity, benefaction, endowment, talent, faculty, alms, douceur. (*reservation, refusal, wages, purchase*)

**gist**—essence, pith, marrow, substance, kernel, force, main point. (*surplusage, redundancy, additament, environment, accessories, garb, clothing*)

**give**—bestow, grant, confer, impart, yield, produce, surrender, concede, present, afford, communicate, furnish. (*withhold, withdraw, refuse*)

**glad**—happy, joyous, pleased, gratified, blithesome, gleeful, gladsome, delighted, cheerful, elated, joyful. (*unhappy, sorrowful, disastrous*)

**glare**—beam, shine, gleam, ray, radiate, glow. (*shimmer, scintillate, glitter, smolder, glimmer*)

**glassy**—vitreous, smooth, polished, glacial, glabrous, brittle, transparent, crystalline, pellucid, limpid, glossy, silken. (*rough, uneven, rugged*)

**glory**—brightness, radiance, effulgence, honor, fame, celebrity, pomp, luster, magnificence, splendor, renown. (*obscurity, ignominy, cloud, dishonor*)

**glut**—*v.* gorge, fill, stuff, cram, satiate, cloy, surfeit. (*disgorge, empty, void*)

**glut**—*n.* surplus, redundancy, superfluity, overstock. (*scarcity, drainage, exhaustion, dearth*)

**go**—move, depart, pass, travel, vanish, reach, extend, proceed, stir, set out, budge. (*stand, stay*)

**good**—*a.* right, complete, virtuous, sound, pious, benevolent, propitious, serviceable, suitable, efficient, sufficient, competent, valid, real, actual, considerable, honorable, reputable, righteous, proper, true, upright, just, excellent. (*wrong, imperfect, unsound, vicious, profane, niggardly*)

**good**—*n.* boon, benefit, advantage, gain, blessing, mercy, virtue, prosperity, weal, profit, interest, welfare. (*hurt, injury, loss, detriment*)

**goodly**—pleasant, desirable, excellent, fair, comely, considerable, graceful, fine. (*unpleasant*)

**gorgeous**—magnificent, splendid, costly, rich, superb, grand, strong. (*poor, naked, bare, cheap*)

**govern**—rule, direct, control, moderate, guide sway, supervise, manage, command, conduct (*misrule, misdirect, miscontrol*)

**grace**—favor, beauty, condescension, kindness, elegance, charm, excellence, pardon, mercy. (*disfavor, deformity, unkindness, pride, inelegance*)

**gracious**—affable, courteous, benignant, kind, civil, condescending, merciful, friendly, tender, gentle, beneficent. (*haughty, discourteous, ill-disposed, ungracious, churlish*)

**gradual**—slow, continuous, unintermittent, gradational, regular, step by step, progressive. (*sudden, momentary, instantaneous, periodic, recurrent*)

**grand**—large, dignified, imposing, important, eventful, magnificent, grandly, majestic, august, exalted, stately, splendid, lofty, elevated, pompous, gorgeous, sublime, superb. (*little, undignified*)

**graphic**—picturesque, illustrative, descriptive, pictorial, forcible, vivid, feeling, described, picturesquely. (*unpicturesque, unillustrative, undescriptive*)

**grateful**—pleasant, acceptable, agreeable, thankful, obliged, welcome. (*unpleasant, disagreeable*)

**gratify**—please, satisfy, indulge, humor. (*displease, dissatisfy, disappoint, stint, discipline, inure*)

**gratitude**—thankfulness, gratefulness. (*unthankfulness, ingratitude, thanklessness, oblivion*)

**grave**—sad, serious, momentous, weighty, pressing, sedate, demure, thoughtful, sober, somber, solemn, important, aggravated, heavy, cogent. (*joyous, merry, facetious, unimportant, ridiculous*)

**great**—big, wide, huge, numerous, protracted, excellent, large, immense, bulky, majestic, gigantic, vast, grand, sublime, august, eminent, magnanimous, noble, powerful, exalted, noticeable. (*little, narrow, puny, scanty, few, short, mean, ignoble, weak, unimportant*)

**greedy**—gluttonous, voracious, hungry, desirous, avaricious. (*abstemious, abstinent, indifferent, contented*)

**grief**—trouble, tribulation, woe, mourning, regret, affliction, sorrow, sadness. (*joy, exultation*)

**grieve**—trouble, burden, annoy, distress, bewail, wound, pain, sorrow, hurt, afflict, mourn, lament, complain, deplore. (*ease, console, soothe, please*)

**grim**—fierce, ferocious, terrible, hideous, ugly, ghastly, sullen, stern. (*mild, docile, attractive*)

**groan**—moan, whine, growl, grumble. (*giggle*)

**groundless**—vain, supposititious, unfounded, baseless, fanciful, gratuitous, chimerical, false. (*well-founded, substantial, authoritative, actual, authentic*)

**group**—cluster, bunch, knot, assemblage, collocation, class, collection, clump, order, assembly. (*isolation, individual, crowd, confusion, medley*)

**grudge**—*v.* spare, retain, covet, envy, withhold. (*spend, impart, welcome, satisfy, gratify*)

**grudge**—*n.* spite, grievance, aversion, rancor, hatred, pique, dissatisfaction, discontent, refusal. (*welcome, satisfaction, approval, contentment, complacency, bestowal, benefaction*)

**gruff**—rough, surly, bearish, harsh, rude, blunt. (*smooth, mild, affable, courteous*)

**guess**—conjecture, surmise, divine, suppose, suspect, fancy, imagine. (*examine, prove, investigate, establish, demonstrate, elaborate, deduce*)

**guide**—lead, direct, conduct, pilot, regulate, superintend, influence, train, manage. (*mislead*)

**gush**—burst, stream, flow, gush, spout, rush, pour out, flow out. (*drip, drop, dribble, trickle*)

## H

**habit**—habituation, custom, familiarity, association, inurement, usage, practice, way, manner. (*dishabituation, inexperience, inconversance, desuetude*)

**habitual**—regular, ordinary, perpetual, customary, usual, familiar, accustomed, wonted. (*irregular, extraordinary, occasional, unusual, exceptional, rare*)

**half**—moiety, bisection, dimidiation. (*integrity, entirety, totality, whole*)

**halt**—stop, rest, limp, falter, hammer, stammer, demur, dubitate, pause, hold, stand still, hesitate. (*advance, decide, determine, speed, flow, career*)

**handsome**—comely, good-looking, generous, liberal, beautiful, ample, pretty, graceful, lovely, elegant. (*uncomely, ill-looking, ungenerous, illiberal, unhandsome*)

**handy**—near, convenient, useful, helpful, manageable, dexterous, ready, expert. (*remote, inconvenient, awkward, useless, cumbrous, unwieldy*)

**happy**—lucky, fortunate, felicitous, successful, delighted, joyous, merry, blithesome, prosperous, glad, blissful. (*unlucky, unfortunate, infelicitous*)

**hard**—firm, dense, solid, compact, unyielding, impenetrable, arduous, difficult, grievous, distressing, rigorous, oppressive, exacting, unfeeling, stubborn, harsh, forced, constrained, inexplicable, flinty, severe, cruel, obdurate, hardened, callous. (*soft, fluid, liquid, elastic, brittle, penetrable, easy*)

**hardship**—trouble, burden, annoyance, grievance, calamity, infliction, endurance, affliction. (*pleasure, amusement, alleviation, recreation, gratification, relief, assuagement, facilitation, boon*)

**hardy**—inured, robust, strong, resolute, stout-hearted, vigorous, intrepid, brave, manly, valiant. (*weak, uninured, delicate, irresolute, enervated, debilitated, tender, fragile*)

**harm**—hurt, mischief, injury, detriment, damage, evil, wrong, misfortune, ill, mishap. (*benefit, boon, amelioration, improvement, reparation*)

**harmonious**—congruous, accordant, proportioned, uniform, melodious, musical, dulcet, tuneful, consistent, peaceful, agreeable, amicable, friendly, concordant. (*incongruous, discordant*)

**hasty**—speedy, rapid, superficial, hurried, irascible, impetuous, reckless, headlong, crude, incomplete, undeveloped, immature, swift, precipitate, fiery, passionate, slight, quick, excitable, rash, cursory. (*slow, leisurely, careful, close, reflective, developed, matured, complete, elaborate*)

**hateful**—abominable, detestable, vile, odious, heinous, execrable, loathsome, repulsive. (*lovable*)

**have**—own, possess, feel, entertain, accept, bear,

enjoy, keep. (*want, need, lose, forgo, discard, reject, miss, desiderate, covet, desire*)

**hazard**—peril, risk, jeopardy, danger, chance, imperil, dare. (*safety, security, protection, warrant, certainty, calculation, law*)

**hazy**—foggy, nebulous, misty, filmy, gauzy, cloudy, murky, caliginous. (*diaphanous, clear*)

**head**—top, crown, chief, leader, ruler, mind, source, section, division, topic, gathering, culmination, crisis, leadership, guide, commander, acme, summit. (*tail, bottom, follower, servant, retainer*)

**heart**—core, nucleus, kernel, interior, center, character, disposition, courage, hardihood, nature, life, feeling, benevolence. (*exterior, hand, action*)

**hearty**—healthy, robust, cordial, sound, warm, honest, earnest, genuine, well, sincere, heartfelt, hale. (*unhealthy, delicate, infirm, cold, insincere*)

**heat**—warmth, ardor, passion, excitement, fever, ebullition, intensity. (*coolness, indifference, subsidence, calmness, composure, reflection*)

**heavy**—weighty, ponderous, inert, slow, stupid, dull, impenetrable, stolid, cumbrous, grievous, afflictive, oppressive, burdensome, sluggish, laborious, depressed. (*light, trifling, trivial, agile, active, quick, joyous, alleviative, consolatory, inspiriting, animating, buoyant*)

**heighten**—exalt, increase, enhance, intensify, color, vivify, aggravate, raise, exaggerate, lift up, amplify. (*lower, depress, diminish, deteriorate*)

**heinous**—hateful, flagrant, detestable, flagitious, atrocious, odious, abominable, execrable, enormous. (*excellent, laudable, meritorious, praiseworthy, distinguished, justifiable, excusable, palliable*)

**help**—aid, succor, remedy, prevent, avoid, assist, promote, cooperate, relieve, second. (*oppose*)

**hereditary**—inherited, ancestral, lineal. (*conferred, acquired, won*)

**hesitate**—dubitate, waver, demur, scruple, falter, stammer, pause, doubt. (*decide, determine*)

**hide**—conceal, secrete, mask, dissemble, store, protect, disguise, ensconce, screen, cover, burrow. (*expose, discover, exhibit, manifest, betray, strip*)

**hideous**—frightful, unshapely, monstrous, horrid, horrible, ugly, grisly, grim, ghastly. (*graceful*)

**high**—elevated, lofty, tall, eminent, excellent, noble, haughty, violent, proud, exalted. (*depressed, low, stunted, ignoble, mean, base, affable*)

**hinder**—prevent, interrupt, obstruct, retard, debar, embarrass, impede, thwart, block, stop. (*accelerate, expedite, enable, promote, facilitate*)

**hoarse**—harsh, grating, husky, raucous, rough, gruff. (*mellifluous, mellow, rich, sweet, melodious*)

**hold**—keep, grasp, retain, support, restrain, defend, maintain, occupy, possess, sustain, regard, consider, cohere, continue, have. (*drop, abandon*)

**hollow**—empty, concave, foolish, weak, faithless, insincere, artificial, unsubstantial, void, flimsy, transparent, senseless vacant, unsound, false. (*full, solid, well-stored, strong, firm, sincere, true*)

**homely**—plain, coarse, uncomely. (*handsome, beautiful, refined, courtly*)

**honest**—honorable, upright, virtuous, proper, right, sincere, conscientious. (*dishonest, dishonorable, vicious, improper, wrong, insincere*)

**honor**—respect, reverence, nobility, dignity, eminence, reputation, fame, high-mindedness, spirit, self-respect, renown, grandeur, esteem. (*disrespect, contempt, irreverence, slight, obscurity*)

**honorary**—gratuitous, unofficial, unremunerative, nominal, titular. (*official, remunerative, professional, jurisdictional*)

**hope**—anticipation, prospect, vision, longing, confidence, desire, expectation, trust. (*despair, despondency, distrust, disbelief, abandonment, abjuration*)

**horrible**—abominable, detestable, dreadful, fearful, hideous, ghastly, terrific, hateful, direful, horrid, awful, frightful. (*lovely, desirable, enjoyable*)

**huge**—enormous, monstrous, colossal, vast, bulky, large, great, prodigious, immense, stupendous, gigantic. (*petty, undersized, pigmy, puny*)

**humane**—benign, kind, tender, merciful, benevolent, compassionate. (*unkind, cruel, unmerciful*)

**humble**—low, lowly, obscure, meek, modest, unassuming, unpretending, submissive. (*high, lofty, eminent, proud, boastful, arrogant, assuming, pretentious*)

**humor**—disposition, temper, mood, caprice, jocoseness, pleasantry, frame, drollery, fun. (*nature, personality, mind, will, purpose, seriousness*)

**hurt**—*v.* wound, bruise, harm, injure, damage, pain, grieve. (*heal, soothe, console, repair, reinstate, compensate, benefit*)

**hurt**—*n.* harm, injury, damage, wound, detriment, mischief. (*benefit, pleasure*)

**hurtful**—mischievous, injurious, pernicious, baleful, deleterious, baneful, noxious, detrimental, prejudicial. (*helpful, remedial*)

**hypocritical**—pharisaical, sanctimonious, smug, smooth, mealy, unctuous, mincing. (*plain-spoken, candid, truthful, sincere, genuine, transparent*)

## I

**idea**—image, notion, conception, belief, doctrine, supposition, understanding, fiction, fancy, thought, opinion, impression, sentiment. (*object*)

**ideal**—mental, notional, conception, intellectual, creative, spiritual, poetical, supposititious, fictitious, unreal, imaginary, chimerical, fanciful, imaginative. (*physical, visible, material, tangible*)

**idle**—void, unoccupied, waste, vain, empty, unemployed, useless, inactive, lazy, indolent. (*tilled, occupied, populated, filled, employed, assiduous, industrious*)

**ignoble**—mean, base, dishonorable, humble, plebeian, lowly. (*honorable, noble, eminent, exalted, lordly, grand, notable, illustrious*)

**ignominious**—shameful, scandalous, dishonorable, infamous. (*honorable, reputable, creditable*)

**ignorant**—untaught, uneducated, uninformed, unlearned, illiterate, unlettered. (*wise, learned*)

**illusion**—dream, mockery, deception, delusion, hallucination, phantasm, vision, myth, false show, error, fallacy. (*form, reality, body, substance*)

**illustrious**—renowned, glorious, brilliant, deathless, eminent, distinguished, celebrated, conspicuous, noble, famous. (*ignominious, disgraceful*)

**ill will**—antipathy, hatred, malevolence, dislike, aversion. (*good will, beneficence*)

**imaginative**—creative, conceptive, ideal, poetical, romantic, inventive, original. (*unimaginative, unpoetical, unromantic, prosaic, matter-of-fact*)

**imagine**—conceive, suppose, surmise, understand, fancy, fabricate, deem, presume, think, apprehend. (*represent, exhibit, demonstrate, prove*)

**imitate**—represent, copy, resemble, follow, portray, depict, repeat, pattern after, mock, ape, counterfeit, mimic. (*misrepresent, caricature, alter*)

**immediate**—proximate, contiguous, present, direct, instant, next. (*distant, remote, future, mediate*)

**impair**—deteriorate, injure, reduce, damage, enfeeble, vitiate, diminish, lessen. (*enhance, improve, augment, repair*)

**impassible**—immaterial, immortal. (*passible*)

**impediment**—hindrance, obstacle, obstruction, stumbling block. (*aid, aidance, help, assistance*)

**imperative**—urgent, irresistible, dictatorial, inexorable, peremptorily, compulsory, obligatory. (*indulgent, lenient, mild, entreative, supplicatory*)

**imperious**—arrogant, exacting, dictatorial, authoritative, domineering, haughty, lordly. (*yielding, submissive, compliant, docile, ductile, lenient*)

**implement**—instrument, utensil, tool, appliance. (*labor, work, science, art, manufacture, agriculture*)

**implicate**—connect, associate, charge, criminate, involve, entangle, infold, compromise. (*disconnect, dissociate, acquit, extricate*)

**imply**—involve, mean, indicate, suggest, hint,

import, denote, include. (*express, declare, state*)

**importance**—weight, moment, consequence, significance, signification, avail, concern. (*unimportance, insignificance, nothingness, immateriality*)

**important**—significant, expressive, relevant, main, leading, considerable, great, dignified, influential, weighty, momentous, material, grave, essential. (*insignificant, trivial, inexpressive, irrelevant, inconsiderable, petty, mean, uninfluential*)

**impotent**—weak, powerless, useless, feeble, helpless, nerveless, enfeebled. (*strong, vigorous, powerful, virile*)

**impressive**—forcible, solemn, affecting, imposing, important. (*weak, unimpressive, feeble, tame, jejune, dry, vapid, unimportant, insignificant*)

**improvement**—advancement, amendment, progress, increase, correction, proficiency. (*degeneracy, deterioration, debasement, retrogression*)

**impudent**—impertinent, insolent, saucy, shameless, brazenfaced, rude, bold, immodest. (*servile*)

**impulse**—incentive, push, incitement, force, influence, instigation, feeling, sudden thought, motive. (*rebuff, premeditation, deliberation*)

**inadvertence**—oversight, negligence, inattention, carelessness, blunder. (*carefulness, exactness, meticulousness*)

**inaudible**—low, inarticulate, suppressed, muttering, mumbling, stifled, muffled. (*audible, outspoken, sonorous, articulate, clear, ringing, loud*)

**incapable**—unqualified, unable, unfitted, weak, incompetent, feeble, disqualified, insufficient. (*qualified, able, fitted, strong, clever*)

**incidental**—casual, occasional, appertinent, concomitant, concurrent, accidental, fortuitous. (*systematic, regular, independent, disconnected*)

**incivility**—discourtesy, ill-breeding, ill-manners, uncourteousness. (*civility, urbanity, good manners*)

**inclement**—harsh, tyrannical, cruel, unmerciful, severe, stormy, rough, rigorous. (*mild, benign*)

**inclination**—leaning, slope, tendency, disposition, proneness, aptness, predilection, bias, bent, attachment, affection, liking, wish. (*inaptitude*)

**incoherent**—unconnected, incongruous, inconsequential, loose. (*coherent, connected*)

**incomparable**—matchless, unique, consummate, transcendent. (*common, ordinary, average*)

**inconsolable**—cheerless, joyless, spiritless, melancholy, gloomy, disconsolate, comfortless, forlorn, heartsick, in despair. (*cheerful, hopeful, consolable*)

**inconstant**—fickle, mutable, variable, fitful, unstable, undependable, changeable, capricious. (*stable, steadfast, dependable*)

**incontestable**—indisputable, unquestionable, unassailable, impregnable. (*dubious, questionable*)

**inconvenience**—incommode, discommode, distrust, molest. (*suit, aid, benefit, subserve, assist*)

**increase**—advance, heighten, dilate, enhance, aggregate, pile up, raise, magnify, spread. (*lessen*)

**incredible**—surpassing belief, fabulous, marvelous. (*credible, believable*)

**inculcate**—impress, urge, enforce, infuse, instill, implant, press, teach. (*insinuate, suggest, disavow, abjure, denounce*)

**incumbent**—pressing, binding, coercive, indispensable, urgent, devolvent, obligatory. (*optional, discretional*)

**incurable**—irremediable, irredeemable, terminal. (*tractable, removable, remediable*)

**indecent**—indelicate, immodest, improper.

**indelible**—indestructible, indefeasible, ineffaceable, persistent, irreversible. (*mutable, evanescent, transient, effaceable*)

**indescribable**—unaccountable, inexpressible, ineffable, unutterable. (*familiar, ordinary*)

**indestructible**—imperishable, indiscerptible. (*perishable, destructible, dissoluble*)

**indicate**—show, evidence, betray, evince, manifest, declare, specify, denote, point out, betoken, designate, mark. (*conceal, contradict, negative*)

**indifference**—triviality, unimportance, insignificance, coolness, carelessness, apathy, insensibility, composure. (*importance, significance, weight, gravity, eagerness, interest, affection, ardor*)

**indiscriminate**—mixed, confused, medley, promiscuous, ill-assorted, undiscerning, undistinguishing, undiscriminating. (*careful, sorted, select*)

**indispensable**—necessary, essential, requisite, needful, expedient. (*unnecessary, unessential, inexpedient, dispensable*)

**individual**—personal, specific, peculiar, indivisible, identical, singular, idiosyncratic, special, single, separate, particular. (*general, common*)

**indivisible**—minute, atomic, ultimate. (*divisible*)

**induce**—produce, cause, prompt, persuade, instigate, impel, actuate, urge, influence, move, prevail on. (*slave, prevent, disincline, dissuade*)

**indulge**—spoil, pamper, humor, gratify, cherish, bask, revel, grovel, foster, favor, allow. (*thwart*)

**indulgent**—compliant, tender, tolerant. (*harsh*)

**industrious**—diligent, laborious, busy, assiduous, active, hardworking. (*lazy, shiftless, idle*)

**ineffable**—inexpressible, inconceivable, insurpassable, indeclarable, indescribable, exquisite, perfect. (*common, trivial, superficial, vulgar, conversational, colloquial, obvious, commonplace*)

**ineffectual**—fruitless, useless, vain, idle, unavailing, abortive, inoperative, ineffective. (*effective, effectual, successful*)

**inexcusable**—unmitigated, unpardonable, indefensible, unjustifiable. (*mitigable, pliable, justifiable, vindicable, defensible, pardonable*)

**inexhaustible**—incessant, unwearied, indefatigable, perennial, illimitable. (*limited, scant, poor*)

**inexpedient**—undesirable, inadvisable, disadvantageous. (*advisable, profitable, expedient*)

**infamy**—despair, degradation, disgrace, ignominy, obloquy, extreme vileness, dishonor. (*honor*)

**infatuation**—fatuity, hallucination, madness, self-deception. (*clear-sightedness, sagacity, wisdom*)

**inference**—deduction, corollary, conclusion, consequence. (*statement, proposition, enunciation*)

**inferiority**—subordination, minority, poverty, mediocrity, subjection, servitude, depression. (*superiority, majority, excellence, eminence, independence, mastery, exaltation, elevation*)

**infidel**—skeptic, unbeliever, heretic, freethinker. (*believer, Christian, devotee, pietist*)

**inflame**—fire, kindle, excite, rouse, fan, incense, madden, infuriate, exasperate, irritate, embitter, anger, enrage. (*quench, extinguish, allay, cool*)

**influence**—effect, control, causation, affection, impulse, power, credit, character, sway, weight, ascendancy, prestige, authority. (*inefficiency, ineffectiveness, inoperativeness, nullity, neutrality*)

**influential**—potent, powerful, efficacious, forcible, persuasive, controlling, guiding, considerable. (*weak, ineffective, inoperative, unpersuasive*)

**information**—instruction, advice, counsel, notice, notification, knowledge. (*concealment, hiding, occultation, mystification, ignorance*)

**infringe**—break, violate, transgress, contravene. (*observe, conserve, preserve, keep within bounds*)

**ingenious**—skillful, adept, clever, inventive, ready, frank, sincere. (*unskillful, slow, uninventive, unready*)

**ingenuous**—noble, candid, generous, frank, sincere, straightforward, honorable, open, artless, honest. (*mean, reserved, sly, disingenuous*)

**ingredient**—element, component, constituent. (*noningredient, refuse, residuum, counteragent*)

**inherent**—innate, congenial, immanent, ingrained, inborn, intrinsic, natural, inbred. (*foreign, ascititious, temporary, separable, extraneous*)

**initiative**—start, leadership, commencement, example. (*wake, rear, prosecution, termination*)

**injunction**—mandate, order, command, exhortation, precept. (*disobedience, insubordination*)

**injurious**—hurtful, deleterious, prejudicial, noxious, detrimental, baleful, pernicious, wrongful, mischievous, damaging, baneful. (*helpful, beneficial, advantageous*)

**innocence**—innocuousness, inoffensiveness, guilelessness, guiltlessness, simplicity, purity, sinlessness. (*hurtfulness, offensiveness, guile, guilt, contamination, corruption, impurity, sinfulness*)

**innocuous**—inoffensive, harmless, wholesome. (*obnoxious, hurtful, deleterious, insidious*)

**inquiry**—interrogation, question, asking, investigation, search, examination, research, scrutiny, exploration. (*conjecture, guess, intuition, hypothesis, assumption, supposition*)

**insatiable**—voracious, unappeasable, omnivorous, ravenous, rapacious, greedy. (*moderate, delicate, fastidious, dainty, squeamish*)

**insidious**—wily, treacherous, designing, dangerous, deceitful, sly, crafty, artful. (*straightforward*)

**insinuate**—introduce, insert, worm, ingratiate, intimate, suggest, infuse, hint. (*withdraw, retract*)

**insipid**—tasteless, vapid, uninteresting, characterless, flavorless, flat, insulse, lifeless, prosy, stupid. (*tasty, sapid, relishing, racy, interesting*)

**insist**—stand, demand, maintain, contend, persist, persevere, urge. (*abandon, waive, concede*)

**insolent**—haughty, overbearing, contemptuous, abusive, saucy, impertinent, opprobrious, offensive. (*meek, polite, well-mannered*)

**insolvent**—bankrupt, ruined, penniless, beggared. (*flush, flourishing, monied, thriving*)

**inspire**—animate, inspirit, inflame, imbue, impel, encourage, inhale, enliven, cheer, breathe in, infuse, exhilarate. (*depress, dispirit, discourage, deter*)

**instance**—entreaty, request, prompting, persuasion, example, solicitation, case, illustration, exemplification, occurrence, point, precedence. (*dissuasion, depreciation, warning, rule, statement*)

**instill**—pour, infuse, introduce, import, implant, insinuate, inculcate. (*drain, strain, extract, eradicate, eliminate, remove, extirpate*)

**instinctive**—natural, voluntary, spontaneous, intuitive, impulsive. (*cultivated, forced, reasoning*)

**instruction**—teaching, education, information, counsel, advice, direction, order, command. (*misteaching, misinformation, misguidance*)

**insufferable**—intolerable, unpermissible, unallowable, unendurable, unbearable. (*tolerable, allowable, endurable, supportable*)

**insupportable**—unbearable, intolerable, insufferable, unendurable. (*endurable, comfortable*)

**integrity**—uprightness, honor, honesty, probity, truthfulness, candor, single-mindedness, conscientiousness, entireness, rectitude, completeness, parity. (*unfairness, sleight, underhandedness, meanness, chicanery, duplicity, fraud, roguery, rascality*)

**intellectual**—mental, metaphysical, psychological, inventive, learned, cultured. (*unintellectual*)

**intelligence**—understanding, apprehension, comprehension, conception, announcement, report, rumor, tidings, news, information, publication, intellectual capacity, mind, knowledge, advice, notice, instruction, intellect. (*misunderstanding, misinformation, misconception, stupidity, dullness*)

**intensity**—tension, force, concentration, strain, attention, eagerness, ardor, energy. (*laxity, debility, relaxation, languor, indifference, coolness, hebetude, diminution*)

**intentional**—purposed, designed, deliberate, intended, done on purpose, contemplated, premeditated, studied. (*undesigned, casual, unintentional*)

**intercourse**—correspondence, dealing, intercommunication, intimacy, connection, commerce. (*reticence, suspension, cessation, disconnection, interception, interpellation*)

**interest**—concern, business advantage, profit, attention, curiosity, behalf, cause, share. (*unconcern, disconnection, repudiation, disadvantage, loss*)

**intermediate**—intervening, included, interposed, comprised, middle, moderate, interjacent. (*circumjacent, surrounding, enclosing, embracing, outside, extreme, excluded, exclusive*)

**interpret**—translate, render, construe, explain, expound, expone, represent, declare, understand, elucidate, decipher, solve. (*misinterpret, misunderstand, mistake, misconceive, falsify, distort, misdeclare, misrepresent*)

**interrupt**—break, disconnect, discontinue, intersect, disturb, stop, hinder. (*continue, prosecute*)

**interval**—interim, meantime, period, gap, intermission, interspace, cessation, space between, season. (*continuity, simultaneousness, uninterruptedness*)

**intimate**—impart, communicate, announce, declare, tell, suggest, hint, insinuate, mention briefly. (*reserve, repress, withhold, conceal*)

**intoxication**—venom, poison, obfuscation, bewilderment, delirium, hallucination, ravishment, ecstasy, inebriation, drunkenness, inebriety. (*antidote, clarification, sobriety, sanity, ebriety, melancholy, depression*)

**intricate**—complicated, involved, mazy, labyrinthine, entangled, tortuous. (*simple, uninvolved*)

**introduction**—induction, importation, leading, taking, presentation, insertion, commencement, preliminary, preface, initiative, portico, vestibule, entrance, gate, preamble, prelude. (*eduction, extraction, exportation, elimination, ejection, estrangement, conclusion, completion, end, egress*)

**introductory**—prefatory, initiatory, commendatory, precursory, preliminary, preparatory. (*completive, final, conclusive, alienative, supplemental*)

**intuition**—instinct, apprehension, recognition, insight. (*information, learning, instruction, elaboration, acquirement, induction, experience*)

**invalid**—infirm, sick, weak, frail, feeble. (*strong, vigorous, healthy, well*)

**invent**—discover, contrive, concoct, imagine, elaborate, conceive, design, devise, fabricate, originate, find out, frame, forge, feign. (*imitate*)

**invincible**—impregnable, immovable, inexpugnable, unsubduable, irresistible, indomitable, unconquerable, insuperable, insurmountable. (*weak, spiritless, powerless, puny, effortless*)

**involve**—implicate, confound, mingle, envelop, compromise, include, complicate, entangle. (*separate, extricate, disconnect*)

**irreligious**—undevout, ungodly, godless, profane, impious. (*religious, godly, reverent, reverential, pious, devout*)

**irrepressible**—unrepressible, ungovernable, uncontrollable, insuppressible, free, unconfined, excitable. (*repressible, governable, controllable, calm*)

**irresponsible**—unbound, unencumbered, unaccountable, not answerable, excusable, lawless.

## J

**jealous**—envious, self-anxious, covetous, invidious, suspicious. (*unenvious, liberal, genial*)

**jingle**—rhyme, chime, tinkle, tingle. (*euphony*)

**join**—unite, adhere, adjoin, add, couple, connect, associate, annex, append, combine, link, accompany, confederate. (*separate, disjoin, subtract, disconnect*)

**jollification**—revelry, festivity, conviviality, fun, carnival, merrymaking. (*weariness, tediousness*)

**jolly**—gay, joyful, gladsome, mirthful, genial, jovial, jubilant, robust, lively, plump, merry. (*sad*)

**jostle**—hustle, push, thrust, jog, jolt, incommode. (*clear, lead, extricate, convoy, escort, precede, pilot, attend*)

**joy**—gladness, pleasure, delight, happiness, exultation, transport, felicity, ecstasy, rapture, bliss, gaiety, mirth, merriment, festivity, hilarity, charm, blessedness. (*sorrow, pain, trouble, misery*)

**jubilant**—joyous, triumphant, festive, congratulatory, exultant. (*doleful, mournful, sorrowful, wailing, penitent, penitential, lugubrious, remorseful*)

**judgment**—decision, determination, adjudication, sagacity, penetration, judiciousness, sense, intellect, belief, estimation, opinion, verdict, sentence, discernment, discrimination, intelligence, prudence, award, condemnation. (*argument, consideration, inquiry, speculation, proposition*)

**judicious**—wise, sagacious, expedient, sensible, prudent, discreet, well-judged, well-advised, polite, discerning, thoughtful. (*foolish, unwise, silly*)

**juggle**—conjure, cheat, bamboozle, shuffle, trick, beguile, circumvent, swindle, overreach, mystify, mislead. (*expose, correct, enlighten, guide, lead, undeceive, disillusionize, detect*)

**just**—exact, fitting, true, fair, proportioned, harmonious, honest, reasonable, sound, honorable, normal, impartial, equitable, upright, regular, orderly, lawful, right, righteous, proper. (*inexact*)

**justice**—equity, impartiality, fairness, right, reasonableness, propreity, uprightness, desert, integrity. (*injustice, wrong, partiality, unfairness*)

**juvenile**—youthful, young, infantile, boyish, girlish, early, immature, adolescent, pubescent, childish, puerile. (*mature, later, manly, womanly*)

## K

**keen**—eager, vehement, sharp, piercing, penetrating, acute, cutting, biting, severe, sarcastic, satirical, ardent, prompt, shrewd. (*indifferent*)

**keep**—hold, restrain, retain, detain, guard, preserve, suppress, repress, conceal, tend, support, maintain, conduct, continue, obey, haunt, observe, frequent, celebrate, protect, adhere to, practice, hinder, sustain. (*release, acquit, liberate, send, dismiss*)

**kind**—*n.* style, character, description, designation, denomination, genus, species, sort, class, nature, set, breed. (*dissimilarity*)

**kind**—*a.* benevolent, benign, tender, indulgent, humane, clement, lenient, compassionate, gentle, good, gracious, forbearing, kindhearted. (*unkind, harsh, severe, cruel, hard, illiberal*)

**knot**—tie, bond, intricacy, difficulty, perplexity, cluster, collection, band, group, protuberance, joint. (*loosening, unfastening, dissolution, solution, explication, unraveling, dispersion, multitude*)

**knowing**—shrewd, astute, discerning, sharp, acute, sagacious, penetrating, proficient, skillful, intelligent, experienced, well-informed, accomplished. (*simple, dull, innocent, gullible, undiscerning, stolid, silly*)

**knowledge**—apprehension, comprehension, recognition, understanding, conversance, experience, acquaintance, familiarity, cognizance, notice, information, instruction, learning, enlightenment, scholarship, attainments, acquirements. (*misapprehension, inobservance, incomprehension, misunderstanding, misconception, inconversance, inexperience, ignorance, unfamiliarity, incognizance*)

## L

**laborious**—assiduous, diligent, painstaking, indefatigable, arduous, burdensome, toilsome, wearisome, industrious, hard-working, active, difficult, tedious. (*idle, indiligent, lazy, indolent, easy*)

**laconic**—terse, curt, epigrammatic. (*prolix*)

**lame**—weak, faltering, hobbling, hesitating, ineffective, impotent, crippled, halt, defective, imperfect. (*robust, agile, potent, efficient, satisfactory*)

**language**—speech, talk, conversation, dialect, discourse, tongue, diction, phraseology, articulation, accents, vernacular, expression. (*jargon, jabber, gibberish, babel, gabble, cry, whine, bark, howl*)

**languid**—faint, weary, feeble, unnerved, unbraced, pining, drooping, enervated, exhausted, flagging, spiritless. (*strong, healthy, robust, vigorous, active, braced*)

**large**—big, bulky, extensive, abundant, capacious, ample, liberal, comprehensive, enlightened, catholic, great, vast, wide. (*small, mean, narrow*)

**last**—*v.* continue, remain, hold, endure, abide, live. (*cease, fail, fade, fly, wane, depart, disappear*)

**last**—*a.* latest, ending, final, concluding, hindmost, past, extreme, lowest, remotest, ultimate. (*first, introductory, initiatory, opening, foremost*)

**laughter**—merriment, glee, derision, ridicule, cachinnation, contempt. (*weeping, tears, mourning, sorrow, admiration, veneration, respect*)

**law**—rule, edict, regulation, decree, command, order, statute, enactment, mode, method, sequence, principle, code, legislation, adjudication, jurisdiction, jurisprudence. (*misrule, disorder, anarchy*)

**lawful**—legal, permissible, orderly, right, allowable, fair, constitutional, rightful, legitimate. (*illegal, impermissible, unlawful, wrong, lawless, unfair*)

**lay**—place, establish, deposit, allay, prostrate, arrange, dispose, put, spread, set down. (*erect*)

**lead**—*v.* conduct, guide, precede, induce, spend, pass, commence, inaugurate, convoy, persuade, direct, influence. (*misconduct, mislead, follow*)

**lead**—*n.* priority, pre-eminence, initiative, guidance, control. (*subordination, inferiority, submission*)

**lean**—*a.* meager, lank, tabid, emaciated, shriveled, bony, thin, scraggy, skinny, slender, scanty. (*fat, brawny, plump, well-conditioned*)

**lean**—*v.* incline, rest, support, tend, bend, depend, hang, repose, confide, slope. (*stabilitate*)

**learned**—conversant, erudite, read, skilled, scholarly, literary, knowing, well-informed, versed. (*inconversant, illiterate, ignorant, unlearned, unscholarly*)

**learning**—knowledge, erudition, literature, lore, letters, acquirements, attainments, scholarship, education, tuition, culture. (*ignorance, boorishness, illiterateness, emptiness, sciolism, intuition*)

**leave**—liberty, permission, license, concession. (*restriction, prohibition, prevention, inhibition, refusal*)

**legend**—myth, fable, marvelous story, fiction. (*history, fact, actual occurrence*)

**lengthy**—diffuse, prolix, tedious, long-drawn, verbose. (*concise, compendious, curt, short, brief*)

**lesson**—precept, warning, instruction, lecture, homily, information. (*misinstruction, misguidance, misinformation*)

**level**—*n.* plane, surface, floor, equality, aim, platform, ground, coordinateness, horizontalness. (*unevenness, acclivity, declivity, inequality, incoordinateness, verticality*)

**level**—*v.* plane, smooth, roll, flatten, equalize, raze. (*roughen, furrow, disequalize, graduate*)

**level**—*a.* horizontal, plain, flat, even, smooth. (*rough, uneven, broken, rolling*)

**libel**—defamation, detraction, traducement, calumny, slander, defamatory publication, lampoon. (*retraction, vindication, apology, eulogy, panegyric*)

**liberal**—free, gentle, refined, polished, generous, bountiful, catholic, enlarged, copious, ample, profuse, large, handsome, munificent, abundant, noble-minded, bounteous, tolerant, plentiful. (*churlish*)

**liberty**—freedom, leave, independence, permission, privilege, license, franchise, immunity, insult, impropriety, volition, voluntariness, exemption, (*slavery, servitude, restraint, constraint, submission*)

**licentious**—voluptuous, dissolute, rakish, debauched, self-indulgent, lax, profligate, loose, unbridled. (*temperate, strict, sober, self-controlled*)

**lie**—*n.* falsehood, untruth, fabrication, subterfuge, evasion, fib, fiction, falsity. (*truth, fact, veracity*).

**lie**—*v.* rest, repose, be, remain. (*rise, move, stir*)

**life**—vitality, duration, existence, condition, conduct, animation, vivacity, personality, state, society, morals, spirit, activity, history, career. (*mortality, decease, death, nonexistence, dullness*)

**lift**—raise, elevate, upraise, upheave, exalt, hoist, elate, erect. (*lower, sink, depress, crush, overwhelm*)

**light**—*n.* luminosity, radiance, beam, gleam, phosphorescence, scintillation, coruscation, flash, brightness, brilliancy, effulgence, splendor, blaze, candle, lamp, lantern, explanation, instruction, illumination, understanding, interpretation, day, life. (*darkness, dimness, obscurity, shade, duskiness, gloom, extinction, misinterpretation, ignorance*)

**light**—*a.* imponderous, portable, unweighty, buoyant, volatile, easy, digestible, scanty, active, unencumbered, empty, slight, gentle, unsteady, capricious, vain, frivolous, characterless, thoughtless, unthoughtful, unconsidered, inadequate, incompact, unsubstantial, inconsiderable, not difficult, bright, whitish, trifling. (*heavy, ponderous*)

**likeness**—similarity, resemblance, correspondence, similitude, parity, copy, imitation, portrait, representation, image, effigy, carte de visite, picture. (*dissimilarity, dissimilitude, disparity, inequality, unlikeness, original*)

**line**—cord, thread, length, outline, row, direction,

verse, course, method, succession, sequence, continuity. (*breadth, contents, space, divergency*)

**liquid**—fluid, liquescent, melting, running, watery, fluent, soft, mellifluous, limpid, flowing, clear, smooth. (*solid, solidified, concrete, congealed*)

**listen**—hear, attend, hearken, incline, give ear, heed. (*disregard, ignore, refuse, repudiate*)

**literal**—exact, grammatical, verbal, close, real, positive, actual, plain. (*general, substantial, metaphorical, free, spiritual*)

**literary**—erudite, scholarly, studious. (*illiterate*)

**literature**—lore, erudition, reading, study, learning, attainment, scholarship, literary works. (*genius, intuition, inspiration*)

**little**—small, tiny, pigmy, diminutive, short, brief, scanty, unimportant, insignificant, slight, weak, inconsiderable, trivial, illiberal, mean, petty, paltry, dirty, shabby, dwarf. (*big, bulky, large*)

**live**—*v.* vegetate, grow, survive, continue, abide, dwell, last, subsist, behave, act, breathe, exist. (*die, perish, wither, demise, migrate, vanish, fade*)

**live**—*a.* animate. (*inanimate, defunct*)

**load**—*n.* weight, lading, cargo, oppression, incubus, drag, burden. (*refreshment, support, solace*)

**load**—*v.* burden, charge, lade, cargo, cumber, oppress. (*disburden, unload, disencumber, lighten*)

**loan**—advance, mortgage, hypothecation. (*recall, resumption, foreclosure*)

**locate**—place, establish, settle, fix, dispose, lodge. (*displace, disestablish, dislodge, remove*)

**lofty**—elevated, towering, high, dignified, eminent, stately, haughty, majestic, airy, tall. (*depressed, low, stunted, undignified, ordinary, unstately, mean, unimposing, unassuming, affable*)

**logical**—close, argumentative, sound. (*inconclusive, illogical, fallacious*)

**lonesome**—forlorn, dreary, forsaken, wild, solitary, desolate, lonely. (*cheerful, befriended, festive*)

**long**—protracted, produced, dilatory, lengthy, tedious, prolix, extensive, diffuse, far-reaching. (*short, curt, curtailed, brief, speedy, quick, concise*)

**loose**—*v.* untie, unfasten, let go. (*tie, fasten, hold*)

**loose**—*a.* unbound, detached, flowing, scattered, sparse, incompact, vague, inexact, rambling, dissoluted, licentious. (*bound, tied, fastened, tight*)

**lose**—miss, drop, mislay, forfeit. (*keep, retain*)

**loss**—mislaying, dropping forfeiture, missing, privation, waste, detriment, damage. (*preservation, recovery, earning, satisfaction, restoration, economy, augmentation, advantage, gain*)

**lot**—chance, fortune, fate, hazard, ballot, doom. (*law, provision, arrangement, disposal, design, purpose, plan, portion, allotment*)

**loud**—sounding, sonorous, resonant, noisy, audible, vociferous, clamorous, obstreperous. (*soft*)

**love**—affection, attachment, passion, devotion, benevolence, charity, kindness. (*hatred, dislike*)

**lovely**—amiable, lovable, enchanting, beautiful, pleasing, delightful, charming. (*unamiable, unlovable, hateful, hideous, plain, homely, unattractive*)

**lover**—suitor, wooer, sweetheart, swain, beau. (*husband, wife, mate*)

**low**—abated, sunk, depressed, stunted, declining, deep, subsided, inaudible, cheap, gentle, dejected, degraded, mean, abject, base, unworthy, lowly, feeble, moderate, frugal, repressed, subdued, reduced, poor, humble. (*elevated, lofty, tall*)

**lower**—*v.* depress, decrease, reduce, bate, abate, drop, humiliate, sink, debase, humble, diminish. (*hoist, raise, heighten, exalt, increase, aggrandize*)

**lower**—*a.* inferior. (*higher, superior*)

**loyal**—submissive, obedient, faithful, allegiant, true, constant. (*insubmissive, insurgent, malcontent, rebellious, disobedient, unfaithful, unallegiant*)

**lucky**—fortunate, auspicious, prosperous, successful, favorable. (*unlucky, unfortunate, inauspicious*)

**ludicrous**—ridiculous, farcical, laughable, comic, droll, funny, comical. (*serious, momentous, grave*)

**lunatic**—mad, maniacal, crazy, wild, unthinking. (*sane, levelheaded, intelligent*)

**lurid**—murky, lowering, wan, dismal, gloomy. (*bright, luminous*)

**luscious**—sweet, delicious, sugary, honied, delightful, toothsome, delightsome. (*sour, sharp*)

**luxurious**—voluptuous, self-indulgent, pleasurable, sensual, pampered. (*hard, painful, self-denying, ascetic, hardy*)

**luxury**—effeminacy, epicurism, voluptuousness, wantonness, self-indulgence, softness, animalism, delicacy, dainty, profuseness. (*hardness, asceticism, stoicism, self-denial, hardship*)

**lying**—mendacious, false, untrue, untruthful. (*true, veracious*)

## M

**mad**—insane, demented, furious, lunatic, infuriated, crazy, maniacal, frantic, rabid, wild, distracted. (*sane, sound, sensible, quiet, composed*)

**madden**—infuriate, enrage, exasperate, inflame. (*calm, pacify, assuage, mesmerize, lay*)

**magnanimous**—noble, high-minded, exalted, high-souled, great-souled, lofty, honorable. (*mean*)

**magnificent**—grand, magnanimous, noble, splendid, superb, august, imposing, gorgeous, stately, majestic, dignified, sublime, pompous. (*petty*)

**maid**—maiden, girl, damsel, lass, virgin. (*matron, married woman*)

**main**—bulk, majority, body, principal, trunk, chief, leading, most important, first. (*portion, section, minority, branch, limb, tributary, member*)

**majority**—superiority, eldership, priority, bulk, preponderance, seniority. (*inferiority, juniority*)

**make**—create, produce, fashion, frame, fabricate, construct, effect, do, perform, execute, find, gain, compel, establish, constitute, reach, mold, shape, form, bring about. (*annihilate, unmake, undo, dismember, disintegrate, destroy, defeat, miss, lose, mar*)

**manage**—handle, manipulate, control, conduct, administer, mold, regulate, contrive, train, husband, direct, wield. (*mismanage, misconduct, upset, derange, misuse*)

**manageable**—easy, feasible, possible, docile, tractable, practicable. (*difficult, impracticable, impossible, unmanageable, intractable, refractory*)

**management**—treatment, conduct, administration, government, address, skill, superintendence, skillful treatment. (*maltreatment, misconduct, maladministration, misgovernment, maladroitness*)

**manifest**—visible, obvious, distinct, conspicuous, indubitable, clear, plain, patent, apparent, evident, open. (*invisible, dubious, inconspicuous, indistinct*)

**manly**—bold, courageous, generous, open, chivalrous, frank, firm, noble, stately, fine, mature, masculine, brave, fearless, hardy, vigorous, manlike, manful, dignified. (*womanish, childish, timid, unmanly, dastardly, weak, puny, ungrown, boyish*)

**manner**—mode, method, style, form, fashion, carriage, behavior, deportment, habit, sort, kind. (*work, project, design, performance, life, action, proceeding, appearance, being*)

**manners**—deportment, behavior, carriage, courtesy, politeness, intercourse, demeanor. (*misdemeanor, misbehavior, unmannerliness*)

**manufacture**—make, production, fabrication, composition, construction, manipulation, molding. (*use, employment, consumption, wear*)

**many**—numerous, abundant, frequent, manifold, divers, sundry, multifarious. (*few, scarce, rare*)

**mark**—*n.* trace, token, sign, symptom, impression, vestige, indication, note. (*erasure, obliteration, effacement, unindicativeness, plainness*)

**mark**—*v.* stamp, label, sign, indicate, decorate, brand, stigmatize, signalize, note, observe, regard, heed, specify, specialize. (*ignore, overlook, omit*)

**martial**—military, brave, warlike. (*unmartial, unmilitary, peaceful*)

**marvel**—wonder, prodigy, admiration, portent, miracle, astonishment, amazement, phenomenon. (*incuriosity, unconcern, joke, trifle, farce, bagatelle*)

**masculine**—male, manly, manful, hardy, courageous, virile. (*female, feminine, womanish, womanly, effeminate*)

**mask**—*n.* pretext, screen, pretense, ruse, cover, hypocrisy. (*truth, nakedness, detection, exposure*)

**mask**—*v.* hide, screen, blink, cloak, disguise. (*expose, unmask, detect*)

**master**—*n.* lord, ruler, governor, owner, possessor, proprietor, teacher, professor, adept, chief. (*servant, slave, subject, property, learner, pupil, tyro*)

**master**—*v.* conquer, overcome, subdue, overpower. (*yield, fail, surrender, succumb*)

**masterly**—finished, artistic, consummate, skillful, clear, dexterous, expert. (*clumsy, rude, bungling, unskilled, botchy, maladroit*)

**match**—*n.* equal, mate, companion, contest, competition, tally, equality, pair. (*superior, inferior*)

**match**—*v.* equal, compare, oppose, pit, adapt, sort, suit, mate. (*fail, exceed, predominate, surpass, mismatch, dissociate, separate, misfit, misadapt, missort*)

**matchless**—consummate, incomparable, peerless, surpassing, inimitable. (*common, ordinary*)

**matter**—substance, stuff, subject, body, importance, (or, prefixing the definite article) the visible, tangible, substantial, corporal, physical, ponderable. (*immateriality, spirituality, mind, intellect*)

**meager**—thin, lean, lank, scanty, barren, dry, tame. (*stout, fat, brawny, abundant, fertile, copious*)

**mean**—*a.* common, low, base, spiritless, dishonorable, contemptible, despicable, beggarly, sordid, vulgar, niggardly, vile, middle, intermediate, average. (*high, exalted, eminent, spirited, honorable*)

**mean**—*n.* medium, moderation, balance, average. (*extreme, excess, preponderance, disproportion*)

**mean**—*v.* intend, purpose, design, signify, denote, indicate, hint, suggest. (*say, state, enunciate*)

**meanness**—penuriousness, littleness, selfishness, baseness, smallness, illiberality, ungenerousness, sordidness. (*nobleness, unselfishness, liberality*)

**means**—resources, instrument, media. (*end, purpose, object*)

**mechanical**—habitual, automatic, unreflective, spontaneous, effortless, unimpassioned. (*labored, self-conscious, feeling, forced, spirited, appreciative*)

**meddlesome**—officious, obtrusive, intrusive, interfering. (*unofficious, inobtrusive, unmeddlesome*)

**mediocrity**—mean, commonplace, medium, average, sufficiency. (*excellence, superiority, rarity*)

**meek**—mild, gentle, submissive, modest, yielding, unassuming. (*bold, arrogant, self-asserting*)

**melancholy**—gloomy, sad, dejected, disconsolate, dismal, moody, hypochondriacal, cast down. (*lively, sprightly, gladsome, gleesome, blithesome*)

**mellow**—ripe, rich, full-flavored, jovial, mature, soft. (*unripe, harsh, sour, acid, acrid, crabbed*)

**memorable**—great, striking, remarkable, conspicuous, prominent, noticeable, illustrious, extraordinary, famous, distinguished. (*petty, trifling*)

**memory**—remembrance, reminiscence, perpetuation, recollection, retention, retrospect, fame. (*forgetfulness, oblivion*)

**mend**—repair, restore, correct, promote, improve, rectify, reform, amend, ameliorate, better. (*damage, impair, pervert, retard, deteriorate, falsify*)

**menial**—domestic, attendant, dependent, servile, drudge. (*paramount, sovereign, supreme, lordly*)

**mental**—intellectual, subjective, metaphysical, psychical, psychological. (*corporal, objective, physical, bodily*)

**mention**—declaration, notice, announcement, observation, remark, hint, communication. (*silence, suppression, forgetfulness, omission*)

**mercantile**—commercial, interchangeable, wholesale, retail, marketable. (*stagnant, unmarketable*)

**merchant**—trader, dealer, importer, tradesman, trafficker. (*shopman, salesman, hawker, huckster*)

**merciful**—compassionate, kindhearted, clement, gracious, kind. (*pitiless, unrelenting, remorseless*)

**mere**—pure, unmixed, absolute, uninfluenced, unadulterated, unaffected, simple. (*mixed, compound, impure, biased*)

**merit**—goodness, worth, worthiness, desert, excellence. (*badness, demerit, unworthiness, worthlessness, weakness, imperfection, error, defect, fault*)

**meteoric**—momentary, flashing, displosive, phosphorescent, pyrotechnic, coruscant, volcanic. (*permanent, beaming, burning, steady, persistent, enduring*)

**method**—order, system, rule, way, manner, mode, course, process, regularity, arrangement. (*disorder, conjecture, quackery, empiricism, experimentation, assumption, guesswork*)

**methodical**—methodic, orderly, systematical, systematic, regular. (*disorderly, unmethodical, unsystematical, irregular*)

**middling**—ordinary, average, pretty well, not bad, well enough.

**midst**—middle, center, thick, throng, heart. (*outskirt, confine, edge, limit, extreme, purlieu, margin*)

**might**—strength, force, power, ability. (*weakness, infirmity, feebleness*)

**mild**—moderate, lenient, calm, gentle, genial, tempered, soft, meek, tender, placid. (*violent, wild, fierce, savage, strong, severe, merciless, harsh*)

**mind**—soul, spirit, intellect, understanding, opinion, sentiment, judgment, belief, choice, inclination, desire, will, liking, purpose, spirit, impetus, memory, remembrance, recollection. (*body, limbs, organization, action, proceeding, conduct*)

**mindful**—regardful, attentive, thoughtful, careful, recollective. (*regardless, inattentive, mindless*)

**mingle**—mix, compound, blend, confound, confuse, intermingle, associate, amalgamate. (*separate, segregate, sift, sort, analyze, discompound, eliminate, classify, unravel, avoid*)

**minister**—servant, officer, delegate, official, ambassador, subordinate, ecclesiastic, clergyman, priest, parson, divine, preacher, pastor, shepherd, reverend, curate, vicar. (*monarch, government, master, superior, principal, head, layman, fold, flock*)

**minute**—diminutive, microscopic, tiny, exact, searching, specific, detailed. (*monstrous, enormous, huge, inexact, superficial, general, broad, comprehensive*)

**mischief**—damage, hurt, detriment, disservice, annoyance, injury, ill turn, damage, harm. (*compensation, good turn, benefit, gratification*)

**mischievous**—detrimental, injurious, spiteful, wanton. (*beneficial, advantageous, reparatory, conservative, careful, protective*)

**miser**—niggard, churl, skinflint, curmudgeon, screw, scrimp, hunks. (*prodigal, spendthrift, rake*)

**miserable**—abject, forlorn, pitiable, wretched, worthless, despicable, disconsolate. (*respectable, worthy, happy, contented, comfortable*)

**misery**—wretchedness, heartache, woe, unhappiness. (*happiness, glee*)

**mock**—jeer, ridicule, flout, mimic, insult, ape, deride, deceive, imitate. (*salute, welcome, respect, admire, compliment*)

**model**—standard, pattern, example, type, mold, design, kind. (*imitation, copy, production, execution, work*)

**moderate**—*v.* control, soften, allay, regulate, repress, govern, temper. (*disturb, disorganize, excite, misconduct*)

**moderate**—*a.* limited, temperate, calm, dispassionate, sober, abstinent, sparing, steady, ordinary. (*extravagant, intemperate, rigorous, excessive, violent, extraordinary*)

**modern**—present, existent, new, newfangled, new-fashioned, recent, late, novel, later. (*past, bygone, former, older, ancient, old-fashioned, antiquated, obsolete*)

**modesty**—sobriety, diffidence, bashfulness, humility, pure-mindedness. (*vanity, conceit, self-sufficiency, self-admiration, foppery, coxcombry, wantonness, shamelessness, effrontery*)

**moment**—instant, second, importance, twinkling, trice, weight, force, gravity, consequence, avail. (*age, period, century, generation, triviality, insignificance, worthlessness, unimportance, inefficacy*)

**monopoly**—privilege, engrossment, appropriation, exclusiveness, preoccupancy, impropriation. (*participation, partnership, community, competition*)

**monotonous**—uniform, unvaried, dull, humdrum, undiversified, tedious. (*varying, changing*)

**monstrous**—prodigious, portentous, marvelous, deformed, abnormal, hideous, preposterous, intolerable. (*ordinary, familiar, unnoticeable, fair, comely, shapely, regular, natural, reasonable, just*)

**moral**—mental, ideal, intellectual, spiritual, ethical, probable, inferential, presumptive, analogous, virtuous, well-conducted. (*physical, material, practical, demonstrative, mathematical, immoral, vicious*)

**mortal**—human, ephemeral, sublunary, short-lived, deadly, fatal, perishable, destructive. (*immortal, divine, celestial, life-giving, venial, superficial*)

**motive**—inducement, purpose, design, prompting, stimulus, reason, impulse, incitement. (*execution, action, effort, deed, attempt, project, preventive*)

**move**—change, go, progress, stir, affect, agitate, actuate, impel, propose, advance, propel, instigate, provoke. (*stand, stop, lie, rest, stay, allay, deter*)

**movement**—motion, move, change of place. (*stop, rest, pause, stillness, quietness*)

**much**—abundant, plenteous, greatly, abundantly, far, considerable, ample. (*little, scant, slightly, shortly, short, near*)

**muddle**—fail, waste, fritter away, confuse, derange, misarrange. (*clarify, manage, economize*)

**muggy**—foggy, misty, dank, damp, murky, dim, vaporous, cloudy. (*clear, bright, vaporless*)

**multitude**—crowd, swarm, accumulation, throng, concourse, number, host, mob, rabble. (*paucity, scantiness, sprinkling*)

**munificent**—liberal, princely, bounteous, generous. (*niggardly, beggarly*)

**murmur**—undertone, whisper, mutter, grumble, complaint, repining. (*clamor, vociferation, bawling*)

**muscular**—powerful, brawny, robust, sinewy, strong, stalwart, athletic, lusty, sturdy. (*debile, flabby, feeble, lanky*)

**musical**—melodious, harmonious, dulcet, concordant, rhythmical, tuneful, mellifluous. (*unmelodious, inharmonious, harsh, discordant*)

**musty**—fusty, rank, moldy, frowzy, stale, sour, fetid, mildewed. (*fragrant, fresh, balmy, aromatic*)

**mutter**—murmur, mumble. (*enunciate, exclaim, pronounce, vociferate*)

**mysterious**—dim, obscure, unrevealed, unexplained, unaccountable. reserved, veiled, hidden, secret, incomprehensible, mystic, inexplicable. (*clear, plain, obvious, explained, understood, easy*)

**mystery**—enigma, puzzle, obscurity, secrecy, veil, shroud, arcanum. (*publication, solution, commonplace, truism, matter of fact*)

**mystify**—confuse, bamboozle, hoodwink, puzzle, confound, mislead, obfuscate. (*illumine, enlighten, inform, guide*)

## N

**naked**—nude, bare, unclothed, denuded, undraped, defenseless, destitute, unqualified, uncolored, unvarnished, mere. simple. (*dressed, robed, draped, muffled, protected, qualified, veiled, shrouded*)

**name**—*n.* designation, cognomenation, appellation, title, fame, reputation, authority, appointment, stead, representation. (*namelessness, anonymity, misnomer, pseudonym, obscurity, ingloriousness, disrepute, individuality, person*)

**name**—*v.* specify, designate, call, indicate. (*misname, miscall, misdesignate, misindicate, hint, suggest, shadow, adumbrate*)

**narrow**—straight, straightened, slender, thin, spare, contracted, limited, cramped, pinched, scant, close, scrutinizing, near, bigoted, niggardly, tight. (*wide, broad, ample, thick, expanded, easy, liberal*)

**nasty**—foul, offensive, odious, disagreeable, indelicate, impure, gross, unclean, obscene. (*nice, pleasant, sweet, savory, agreeable, pure*)

**natural**—intrinsic, essential, regular, normal, cosmical, true, probable, consistent, spontaneous, artless, original. (*ascititious, adventitious, abnormal*)

**nature**—essence, creation, constitution, structure, disposition, truth, regularity, kind, sort, character, species, affection, naturalness. (*thing, object, subject, man, being, creature, monstrosity, unnaturalness, art, fiction, romance, invention*)

**near**—nigh, close, adjacent, neighboring. (*far away, distant, remote*)

**necessary**—certain, inevitable, indispensable, requisite, essential, compulsory, needful, expedient. (*contingent, casual, optional, discretional, unnecessary, unessential, free*)

**necessity**—indispensableness, inevitableness, need, indigence, requirement, want, fate, destiny. (*dispensableness, uncertainty, superfluity, uselessness, competence, affluence, casualty, contingency*)

**neglect**—*v.* slight, overlook, omit, disregard, disesteem, despise, contemn. (*consider, respect, notice, observe, regard, esteem, tend, attend, foster, study*)

**neglect**—*n.* negligence, disregard, omission, failure, default, slight, carelessness, remissness. (*attention, consideration, respect, notice, regard, esteem*)

**nerve**—strength, firmness, resolution. (*nerveless, forceless, feeble, weak, enfeebled, impotent, palsied*)

**new**—novel, recent, fresh, modern. (*old, ancient, antique, antiquated, obsolete*)

**nice**—fastidious, scrupulous, accurate, neat, discerning, dainty, pleasant, agreeable, exact, fine, finished, particular. (*coarse, unscrupulous, inaccurate, rude, rough, undiscriminating, nasty, nauseous, disagreeable*)

**nobility**—distinction, dignity, rank, peerage, lordship, loftiness, generosity, rank, aristocracy. (*obscurity, meanness, commonalty, serfdom, paltriness, contemptibleness, plebeianism*)

**noble**—grand, aristocratic, generous, illustrious, exalted, worthy, magnanimous, dignified, excellent, lofty-minded, honorable, fine. (*mean, plebeian, ignoble, paltry*)

**noisome**—hurtful, harmful, nocuous, pestilential. (*wholesome, salutary, salubrious, beneficial*)

**noisy**—loud, clamorous, stunning. (*still, soft, inaudible, whispering, soothing, musical, melodious*)

**nominal**—trifling, suppositious, ostensible, professed, pretended, formal. (*real, deep, serious, important, grave, substantial, actual, intrinsic, veritable*)

**nonsense**—absurdity, trash, folly, pretense, jest, balderdash. (*sense, wisdom, truth, fact, gravity*)

**notice**—observation, cognizance, heed, advice, news, consideration, visitation, mark, note. (*oversight, disregard, misinformation, mistidings, neglect*)

**notion**—apprehension, idea, conception, judgment, opinion, belief, expectation, sentiment. (*misapprehension, falsification, misbelief, misjudgment, frustration, misconception*)

**notorious**—known, undisputed, recognized, allowed. (*suspected, reported, reputed*)

**nuisance**—offense, annoyance, plague, pest, trouble. (*gratification, blessing, pleasure, delight*)

## O

**obedience**—submission, compliance, subservience. (*resistance, rebellion, violation, transgression*)

**obesity**—fatness, fleshiness, corpulence, plumpness, corpulency, embonpoint. (*leanness, thinness*)

**obey**—submit, comply, yield. (*resist, disobey*)

**object**—appearance, sight, design, end, aim, motive, intent, view, goal. (*idea, notion, conception, fancy, subject, proposal, purpose, effect*)

**object to**—oppose, contravene, obstruct, demur to, except to, gainsay, disapprove. (*approve, approve of*)

**oblige**—compel, coerce, necessitate, force, benefit, favor, accommodate, gratify, bind, constrain. (*release, acquit, induce, persuade, annoy, disoblige*)

**obliging**—kind, considerate, compliant, complaisant, accommodating. (*discourteous, rude, cross-grained, perverse, unaccommodating, disobliging*)

**obscene**—impure, immodest, indecent, lewd, foul, indelicate, filthy, disgusting, foulmouthed. (*pure, modest, decent*)

**obscure**—dark, dim, lowering, indistinct, enigmatical, uncertain, doubtful, unascertained, humble, unintelligible, mean. (*bright, luminous, distinct, lucid, plain, plain-spoken, intelligible, unambiguous, ascertained, eminent, prominent*)

**observance**—attention, fulfillment, respect, celebration, performance, ceremony, custom, form, rule, practice. (*inobservance, inattention, breach, disrespect, disregard, desuetude, disuse, nonperformance, informality, unceremoniousness, omission*)

**observant**—regardful, attentive, mindful, obedient, watchful, heedful. (*disregardful, neglectful*)

**observation**—contemplation, study, remark, attention, notice, comment. (*disregard, oversight*)

**obstacle**—impediment, obstruction, hindrance, objection, bar, difficulty, check. (*course, proceeding, career, advancement*)

**obstinate**—headstrong, stubborn, refractory, self-willed, pertinacious, obdurate, perverse, intractable. (*amenable, complaisant, yielding, docile, ductile, characterless, irresolute, wavering*)

**obvious**—plain, self-evident, manifest, explicit, apparent, open, patent. (*remote, obscure, far-fetched, involved, latent*)

**occasion**—conjuncture, opportunity, occurrence, cause, need, event, reason, necessity, opening, ground. (*untimeliness, unseasonableness, frustration*)

**occult**—latent, hidden, unrevealed, mysterious, secret, dark, unknown. (*developed, plain, patent*)

**occupation**—employment, avocation, possession, usurpation, encroachment, tenure, calling, pursuit, trade, business, holding. (*idleness, vacancy, leisure*)

**odd**—alone, sole, unmatched, remaining, over, fragmentary, uneven, singular, peculiar, queer, quaint, fantastical, uncommon, nondescript. (*aggregate, consociate, matched, balanced, squared, integrant, even, common, usual, regular, normal*)

**odious**—hateful, offensive, detestable, abominable, hated. (*delectable, grateful, acceptable*)

**offense**—attack, sin, crime, umbrage, transgression, misdeed, injury, wrong, affront, outrage, insult, trespass, indignity, misdemeanor. (*defense, innocence, guiltlessness*)

**offensive**—aggressive, obnoxious, distasteful, displeasing, foul, fetid, unsavory. (*defensive, grateful, pleasant, savory*)

**offer**—propose, exhibit, proffer, present, tender, extend, adduce, volunteer. (*withhold, withdraw*)

**office**—service, duty, appointment, function, employment, station, business, post. (*leisure, vacancy*)

**officious**—meddling, interfering, pushing, forward, intrusive, intermeddling. (*backward, negligent, remiss, unofficious, retiring, modest, backward*)

**often**—frequently, repeatedly. (*infrequently*)

**old**—aged, pristine, long-standing, ancient, preceding, antiquated, obsolete, senile, antique. (*youthful, young, recent, fresh, modern, subsequent*)

**ominous**—portentous, suggestive, threatening, foreboding, premonitory, unpropitious. (*auspicious, propitious, encouraging*)

**open**—*v.* unclose, lay open, lay bare, expose, explain, disclose, initiate, begin, commence. (*close, shut up, conceal, enclose, mystify, misinterpret, conclude, cover*)

**open**—*a.* accessible, free, available, unshut, unfolded, public, free, unrestricted, unreserved, unaffected, genuine, barefaced, undisguised, above-board, liberal, unclosed, candid, frank, ingenuous, unsettled, undetermined. (*inaccessible, closed, barred, unavailable, shut, close, secretive, reserved*)

**opening**—aperture, gap, opportunity, space, commencement, initiation, start, inauguration, hole, fissure, chink, beginning. (*occlusion, obstruction, stopgap, unreasonableness, contretemps, inopportuneness, enclosure, termination, close, end, conclusion*)

**operation**—agency, action, exercise, production, influence, performance. (*cessation, inaction, rest*)

**opinion**—conviction, view, judgment, notion, idea, impression, estimation, theory.

**opportunity**—occasion, turn, opening, convenience. (*inopportuneness, unseasonableness, lapse*)

**opposite**—facing, adverse, repugnant, inconsistent, irreconcilable, contrary, antagonistic, counter, contradictory. (*agreeing, coincident, consentaneous*)

**opposition**—resistance, hostility, obstacle, obstruction.

**oppressive**—heavy, overpowering, unjust, galling, extortionate, grinding. (*light, just, compassionate*)

**order**—*n.* arrangement, condition, sequence, direction, rank, grade, class, decree, succession, series, method, injunction, precept, command. (*disarrangement, confusion, disorder*)

**order**—*v.* arrange, dispose, regulate, adjust, direct, command, classify, ordain, enjoin, prescribe, appoint, manage. (*disarrange, confuse, unsettle, disorganize*)

**ordinary**—settled, wonted, conventional, plain, inferior, commonplace, humdrum, matter of fact. (*extraordinary, unusual, uncommon, superior*)

**organization**—structure, form, construction. (*disorganization*)

**origin**—source, commencement, spring, cause, derivation, rise, beginning. (*termination, conclusion, extinction*)

**original**—primary, initiatory, primordial, peculiar, pristine, ancient, former, first. (*subsequent, terminal, modern, later, derivative*)

**oust**—eject, dispossess, deprive, evict, eject, dislodge, remove. (*install, reinstate, readmit, restore*)

**outcast**—castaway, reprobate, vagrant, vagabond, exiled.

**outlandish**—strange, queer, grotesque, foreign, rustic, barbarous, rude. (*fashionable, modish*)

**outline**—delineation, sketch, contour, draft, plan. (*form, substance, figure, object, subject, field*)

**outrage**—outbreak, offense, wantonness, mischief, abuse, ebullition, violence, indignity, affront, insult. (*moderation, self-control, self-restraint, subsidence, coolness, calmness*)

**outrageous**—excessive, unwarrantable, unjustifiable, wanton, flagrant, nefarious, atrocious, violent. (*moderate, justifiable, reasonable*)

**outset**—opening, start, commencement, exordium, beginning, inauguration, preface. (*close, termination, conclusion, peroration*)

**outward**—external, apparent, visible, sensible, superficial, ostensible, forthcoming, extrinsic, extraneous. (*internal, intrinsic, withdrawn, inapparent, inward*)

**overcome**—vanquish, conquer, surmount, exhaust, defeat.

**overflow**—redundancy, exuberance, superabundance, deluge, inundation. (*deficiency, exhaustion*)

**overlook**—condone, connive, disregard, oversee, supervise, inspect, survey, review, excuse, pardon, forgive, neglect. (*visit, scrutinize, investigate, mark*)

**oversight**—error, omission, mistake, neglect, slip, inadvertence, inspection, superintendence. (*scrutiny, correction, emendation, attention, mark*)

**overthrow**—destroy, subvert, upset, overturn, ruin, demolish, defeat, rout, overcome, discomfit, invert, overset, reverse. (*restore, reinstate, construct, regenerate, redintegrate, revive, re-edify*)

**overwhelm**—crush, quell, extinguish, drown, subdue, swamp. (*raise, reinvigorate, reinstate*)

**owing**—due, imputable, ascribable, attributable. (*casually, perchance, by chance, by accident*)

**own**—possess, hold, have, acknowledge, avow, admit, confess. (*alienate, forfeit, lose, disclaim*)

## P

**pacify**—appease, conciliate, calm, still, soothe, quiet, tranquilize. (*exasperate, agitate, excite, irritate, rouse, provoke*)

**pack**—*n.* burden, bundle, package, lot, parcel, load.

**pack**—*v.* stow, compact, compress, cook. (*unpack, unsettle, jumble, displace, misarrange, dissipate, neutralize*)

**pain**—*n.* penalty, suffering, distress, uneasiness, grief, labor, effort, anguish, torture, agony. (*reward, remuneration, ease, gratification, joy, pleasure*)

**pain**—*v.* hurt, grieve, afflict, torment, rack, agonize, trouble, torture, aggrieve, annoy, distress. (*gratify, please, delight, rejoice, charm, relieve, ease*)

**painful**—afflicting, distressful, grieving, grievous, excruciating, hurting.

**painstaking**—careful, attentive, diligent, laborious. (*careless, negligent*)

**palatable**—tasteful, savory, appetizing, delicious, toothsome.

**pale**—pallid, wan, faint, dim, undefined, etiolated, sallow, cadaverous. (*ruddy, high-colored*)

**palmy**—prosperous, glorious, distinguished, victorious, flourishing. (*depressed, inglorious, undistinguished, unflourishing*)

**paltry**—mean, shabby, shuffling, trifling, prevaricating, shifty, contemptible, pitiable, vile, worthless, beggarly, trashy. (*noble, honorable, candid, conscientious, determined, straightforward*)

**pang**—paroxysm, throe, agony, convulsion, smart, anguish, pain, twinge. (*pleasure, enjoyment, gratification, delight, delectation, fascination*)

**paradox**—contradiction, enigma, mystery, absurdity, ambiguity. (*precept, proposition, axiom*)

**parallel**—correspondent, congruous, correlative, analogous, concurrent, equidistant. (*different, opposed, incongruous, irrelative, unanalogous, divergent*)

**paralyze**—deaden, benumb, prostrate, enervate, debilitate, enfeeble. (*give life, strengthen, nerve*)

**pardon**—forgive, condone, absolve, acquit, remit, excuse, overlook. (*condemn, punish, visit*)

**pardonable**—venial, excusable. (*inexcusable, unpardonable*)

**parsimonious**—sparing, close, penurious, frugal, niggardly, illiberal, stingy. (*liberal, unsparing, profuse, extravagant*)

**part**—portion, piece, fragment, fraction, division, member, constituent, element, ingredient, share, lot, concern, interest, participation, side, party, interest, faction, behalf, duty. (*whole, completeness, entirety, integrity, totality, mass, bulk, body*)

**partake**—share, participate, accept, derive. (*forfeit, relinquish, forego, cede, yield, afford*)

**partial**—restricted, local, peculiar, specific, favoring, inequitable, unfair, biased, particular. (*unrestricted, total, universal, general, impartial, equitable, just, fair, unbiased*)

**particular**—local, specific, subordinate, detailed, partial, special, fastidious, minute, scrupulous, careful, accurate, exact, circumstantial, precise, delicate, nice. (*universal, general, unspecial, comprehensive, unscrupulous, uncareful, inaccurate, inexact, rough, coarse, indiscriminate, undiscriminating*)

**partisan**—adherent, follower, party man, henchman, clansman, supporter, disciple

**partition**—barrier, division, enclosure, compartment, interspace, separation, distribution, allotment, screen. (*nonpartition, nondistinction, nonseparation, inclusion, comprehension, combination*)

**partner**—associate, sharer, participator, colleague, coadjutor, confederate, accomplice, partaker, companion, spouse. (*rival, alien, competitor*)

**passable**—traversable, navigable, penetrable, admissible, tolerable, ordinary. (*impassable, impervious, impenetrable, inadmissible, excellent*)

**passage**—journey, thoroughfare, road, course, avenue, route, channel, clause, phrase, sentence, paragraph.

**passive**—inactive, inert, quiescent, unresisting, unquestioning, negative, enduring, patient. (*active, alert, resistant, positive, unsubmissive, malcontent, vehement, impatient*)

**pastime**—recreation, entertainment, amusement, diversion, play, sport. (*business, study, labor, task*)

**patent**—obvious, evident, indisputable, plain. (*dubious, ambiguous, questionable*)

**pathetic**—affecting, moving, emotional, tender, melting. (*ludicrous, unimpassioned, farcical, unaffecting*)

**patience**—endurance, resignation, submission, perseverance. (*resistance, unsubmissiveness, repining, rebellion, inconsistency, impatience*)

**pattern**—model, sample, archetype, exemplar, specimen, shape, precedent, mold, design, shape. (*monstrosity, caricature, perversion, misrepresentation*)

**pause**—*n.* stop, cessation, suspension, halt, intermission, rest. (*continuance, advancement, perseverance*)

**pause**—*v.* cease, suspend, intermit, forbear, stay, wait, hesitate, demur, stop, desist. (*continue, proceed, advance, persist, persevere*)

**peace**—quiet, tranquility, calm, repose, pacification, order, calmness, reconciliation, harmony, concord. (*noise, disturbance, tumult, agitation, hostility*)

**peaceable**—unwarlike, inoffensive, quiet, peaceful, innocuous, mild, unquarrelsome, serene, placid. (*pugnacious, warlike, litigious, quarrelsome, savage*)

**peculiar**—private, personal, characteristic, exceptional, exclusive, special, specific, particular, unusual, singular, uncommon, strange, rare, odd. (*public, common, general, universal, unspecial, ordinary*)

**peculiarity**—speciality, individuality, distinctiveness, idiosyncrasy. (*generality, universality, community, uniformity, homology, homogeneity*)

**people**—nation, community, populace, mob, crowd, vulgar, herd, mass, persons, inhabitants, commonalty, fellow creatures, tribe, race, group. (*aristocracy, nobility, government, ruler, oligarchy*)

**perceive**—discern, distinguish, descry, observe, feel, touch, see, recognize, understand, know. (*miss, misobserve, overlook, misunderstand, misconceive, misperceive*)

**perception**—cognizance, apprehension, sight, understanding, discernment. (*incognizance, ignorance, imperception, misapprehension, misunderstanding*)

**peremptory**—decisive, express, absolute, authoritative, dictatorial, dogmatic, imperious, despotic, positive. (*suggestive, entreative, mild, postulatory*)

**perfect**—consummate, complete, full, indeficient, immaculate, absolute, faultless, impeccable, infallible, unblemished, blameless, unexceptionable, mature, ripe, pure. (*incomplete, meager, faulty, scant, short, deficient, defective, imperfect, peccable*)

**perfectly**—fully, wholly, entirely, completely, totally, exactly, accurately. (*imperfectly, incompletely, partially, inaccurately*)

**perform**—accomplish, do, act, transact, achieve, execute, discharge, fulfill, effect, complete, consummate, enact. (*miss, mar, misperform, misexecute*)

**perhaps**—possibly, peradventure, perchance, maybe. (*certainly, inevitably*)

**perilous**—hazardous, dangerous. (*safe, secure*)

**period**—time, date, epoch, era, age, duration, continuance, limit, bound, end, conclusion, determination. (*eternity, datelessness, immemoriality, infinity, perpetuity, illimitability, endlessness, indefiniteness, indeterminateness*)

**periodic**—stated, recurrent, regular, systematic, calculable. (*indeterminate, eccentric, irregular, incalculable, spasmodic, fitful*)

**permeable**—penetrating, pervading. (*impenetrable, ineffective*)

**perpetual**—constant, unceasing, endless, eternal, everlasting, unfailing, perennial, continual, enduring, incessant, uninterrupted. (*inconstant, periodic, recurrent, temporary, transient, falling, exhaustible*)

**perplex**—embarrass, puzzle, entangle, involve, encumber, complicate, confuse, bewilder, mystify, harass, entangle. (*clear, enlighten, explicate, disentangle, simplify, elucidate, disencumber*)

**perseverance**—persistence, steadfastness, constancy, indefatigability, resolution, tenacity. (*inconstancy, unsteadfastness, fitfulness, caprice, irresoluteness, vacillation, wavering, indecision, variableness, levity, volatility*)

**persuade**—induce, influence, incline, convince, dispose, urge, allure, incite. (*deter, disincline, indispose, mispersuade, misinduce, coerce, compel*)

**perverse**—forward, untoward, stubborn, fractious, wayward, unmanageable, intractable, crochety. (*docile, ductile, amenable, governable, complacent, accommodating, pleasant, obliging*)

**pet**—darling, fondling, favorite, cosset, jewel, minion, idol. (*horrow, bugbear, aversion, scarecrow*)

**petition**—supplication, entreaty, craving, application, appeal, salutation, prayer, request, instance. (*deprecation, expostulation, protest, command, injunction, claim, demand, requirement*)

**petty**—small, mean, paltry, ignoble, trifling, narrow, trivial, contemptible. (*large, bighearted, noble, generous, chivalrous, magnificent, liberal*)

**philanthropy**—humanity, love of mankind, generosity, charity, benevolence. (*misanthropy, hatred of men. selfishness, stinginess*)

**philosopher**—doctor, savant, teacher, master, schoolman. (*ignoramus, sciolist, freshman, tyro, greenhorn, fool, booby, dunce*)

**philosophical**—wise, sound, conclusive, scientific, accurate, enlightened, rational, calm, unprejudiced. (*unsound, crude, vague, loose, inaccurate, popular*)

**physical**—natural, material, visible, tangible, substantial, corporeal. (*mental, moral, intellectual, spiritual, immaterial, invisible, intangible, unsubstantial, supernatural, hyperphysical*)

**picture**—likeness, resemblance, drawing, painting, representation, image, engraving. (*original*)

**picturesque**—comely, seemly, graceful, scenic, artistic, pictorial, graphic. (*unseemly, uncouth, rude, unpicturesque, ugly, flat, tame, monotonous*)

**pinch**—squeeze, grip, press, compress, nip, distress.

**piquant**—pungent, sharp, lively, racy, severe, biting, cutting, smart, stimulating, keen, stinging, tart. (*tame, dull, flat, characterless, insipid*)

**pithy**—terse, forceful, laconic, expressive, concise. spongy. (*weak, characterless, diluted, pointless*)

**pity**—mercy, compassion, tenderness, commiseration, ruth, sympathy, condolence. (*cruelty, hardheartedness, relentlessness, pitilessness, ruthlessness*)

**place**—locate, assign, fix, establish, settle, attribute, situate, put, set. (*disturb, remove, unsettle, disarrange, disestablish, misplace, misattribute, misassign, uproot, transplant, extirpate, eradicate, transport*)

**plain**—level, even, flat, smooth, open, clear, unencumbered, unobstructed, uninterrupted, manifest, evident, obvious, unmistakable, simple, easy, natural, unaffected, homely, unsophisticated, open, unvarnished, unembellished, unreserved, artless. (*uneven, undulating, rugged, rough, abrupt, broken, confused, encumbered, obstructed, interrupted, questionable, uncertain, dubious, ambiguous, enigmatical*)

**plan**—*n.* design, drawing, sketch, draft, scheme, project, contrivance, stratagem, device.

**plan**—*v.* contrive, devise, sketch out, design, hatch.

**platonic**—cold, intellectual, unsensual, mental, philosophical. (*ardent, animal, sensual, passionate*)

**plausible**—specious, superficial, passable, unctuous, fair-spoken, pretentious, ostensible, right, apparent, colorable, feasible, probable. (*genuine, sterling, unmistakable, profound*)

**playful**—lively, sportive, jocund, frolicsome, gay, vivacious, sprightly. (*somber, dull*)

**plea**—excuse, vindication, justification, ground, defense, apology, entreaty, request. (*charge, accusation, impeachment, action*)

**pleasant**—grateful, agreeable, acceptable, pleasurable, desirable, gratifying, cheerful, enlivening, sportive, delicious, delectable, jocular, satisfactory, exquisite, merry. (*unpleasant, ungrateful, disagreeable, obnoxious, unacceptable, offensive, unlively*)

**pleasure**—enjoyment, gratification, sensuality, self-indulgence, voluptuousness, choice, preference, will, inclination, purpose, determination, favor, satisfaction, indulgence. (*pain, suffering, affliction, trouble, asceticism, self-denial, abstinence, disinclination, aversion, indisposition, denial, refusal*)

**plebeian**—low, vulgar, low-born, low-bred, coarse, ignoble. (*patrician, noble, aristocratic, refined, high-born, high-bred*)

**plodding**—painstaking, industrious, persevering, laborious, studious. (*indiligent, unindustrious, distracted, inattentive, impatient, unpersevering, flighty, fitful*)

**plot**—*n.* scheme, plan, stratagem, conspiracy, machination.

**plot**—*v.* devise, concoct, conspire, contrive, frame, hatch, plan, scheme.

**plump**—well-conditioned, well-rounded, chubby, strapping, bouncing, fleshy, brawny, full, fat, round, massive, portly. (*ill-conditioned, lean, emaciated, scraggy, weazen, macilent, lank, rawboned, shriveled, flaccid, tabid*)

**plunge**—dip, dive, douse, duck, submerge, immerse, precipitate, sink, overwhelm, thrust under, pitch headlong. (*emerge, issue, soar, raise, extricate*)

**poetical**—metrical, rhythmic, versified, lyric, rhyming, imaginative, creative, romantic, fictitious, dreamy, flighty. (*unmetrical, unrhythmical, prosaic, unpoetical, unversified, unimaginative, commonplace, historical, mathematical, logical, matter-of-fact, veracious, sober*)

**poisonous**—venomous, infectant, vicious, corruptive, vitiative, noxious, baneful, malignant, morbific, virulent, pestiferous, deleterious. (*wholesome, genial, beneficial, sanative, invigorative, healthful, innoxious, restorative, remedial, hygienic*)

**polite**—elegant, refined, well-bred, courteous, obliging, complaisant, civil, courtly, polished, genteel, accomplished. (*awkward, rude, uncouth, ill-bred, discourteous, boorish, clownish, disobliging*)

**politic**—prudent, wise, sagacious, provident, diplomatic, judicious, cunning, wary, well-devised, discreet. (*imprudent, unwise, improvident, undiplomatic, impolitic*)

**pompous**—magnificent, gorgeous, splendid, showy, sumptuous, ostentatious, stately, lofty, grand, bombastic, turgid, stiff, inflated, pretentious, coxcombical, assuming. (*unpretending, unobtrusive, modest, unassuming, plain-mannered, humbleminded*)

**ponder**—think over, meditate on, weigh, consider, cogitate, deliberate, ruminate, reflect, amuse, study, resolve.

**poor**—indigent, moneyless, impecunious, penniless, weak, meager, insufficient, deficient, faulty, unsatisfactory, inconsiderable, thin, scanty, bald, (*rich, wealthy, copious, affluent, abundant, liberal*)

**popular**—common, current, vulgar, public, general, received, favorite, beloved, prevailing, approved, widespread, liked. (*exclusive, restricted, scientific, esoteric, unpopular, odious, detested*)

**positive**—real, actual, substantial, absolute, independent, unconditional, unequivocal, explicit, fixed, settled, definitive, indisputable, decisive, express, enacted, assured, confident, direct, dogmatic, overbearing, dogmatical. (*negative, insubstantial, unreal, fictitious, imaginary, relative, contingent, dependent, conditional, implied, dubious, questionable*)

**possess**—occupy, enjoy, have, hold, entertain, own. (*abandon, renounce, abjure, surrender, lose, forfeit, resign*)

**possible**—practicable, feasible, likely, potential, (*impracticable, impossible*)

**postpone**—defer, delay, prorogue, procrastinate, (*expedite, dispatch, accelerate*)

**poverty**—want, need, indigence, destitution. (*abundance, wealth, affluence*)

**power**—faculty, capacity, capability, potentiality, ability, strength, force, might, energy, susceptibility, influence, dominion, sway, command, government, agency, authority, rule, jurisdiction, effectiveness. (*incapacity, incapability, impotence, inability, weakness, imbecility, inertness, insusceptibility, subjection, powerlessness, obedience, subservience, ineffectiveness*)

**powerful**—strong, potent, puissant, masterful, mighty. (*weak, poor*)

**practice**—*n.* usage, habit, exercise, experience, exercitation, action, custom, manner, performance. (*disuse, dishabituation, inexperience, theory, speculation, nonperformance*)

**practice**—*v.* perform, exercise, deal in, carry on.

**praise**—eulogize, laud, commend, honor, glorify, compliment, celebrate, puff, extol, applaud, panegyrize. (*blame, censure, discommend, reprove*)

**pray**—beg, beseech, entreat, implore, solicit, supplicate, adjure, invoke, crave.

**prayer**—petition, supplication, entreaty, orison, benediction, suit, request.

**precaution**—forethought, provision, premonition, anticipation, prearrangement, care, providence. (*carelessness, thoughtlessness, improvidence*)

**preceding**—precedent, former, forgoing, prior, previous, antecedent, anterior. (*following, subsequent, posterior*)

**precious**—dear, valuable, costly, cherished, treasured, beloved, estimable, of great value. (*cheap, valueless, worthless, unvalued, disesteemed*)

**precise**—definite, exact, nice, pointed, accurate, correct, particular, formal, explicit, scrupulous, terse, punctilious, ceremonious, formal. (*indefinite, vague, inexact, rough, inaccurate, loose, circumlocutory, ambagious, tortuous, informal, unceremonious*)

**predict**—prophesy, foretell, forecast, prognosticate, forebode, foreshadow.

**prediction**—prophecy, prognostication, vaticination, foreannouncement, premonstration, foretelling, forebodement, presage, augury, foreshowing. (*narration, relation, history, account, report*)

**preface**—introduction, proem, prelude, prologue, preamble, premiss. (*peroration, sequel, appendix, epilogue, postscript*)

**prefer**—choose, elect, select, fancy, promote, advance, further. (*reject, postpone, defer, withhold*)

**prejudice**—prepossession, prejudgment, predisposition, bias, unfairness, injury, harm, impairment, detriment, partiality, disadvantage, damage. (*judgment, fairness, impartiality, advantage*)

**premature**—hasty, crude, unauthenticated, untimely, precocious, precipitate, too early, rash, unseasonable. (*ripe, timely, seasonable, opportune*)

**premium**—reward, guerdon, encouragement, douceur, enhancement, bribe, recompense, bonus, prize, bounty. (*penalty, fine, amercement, mulct, forfeit, depreciation*)

**preparation**—provision, readiness. (*unpreparedness, without provision*)

**prepare**—fit, adapt, qualify, adjust, provide, arrange, order, lay, plan, equip, furnish, ready. (*misfit, misadapt, misprovide, derange, disarrange*)

**prepossessing**—attractive, alluring, charming, winning, taking, engaging. (*repulsive, unattractive*)

**preposterous**—monstrous, exorbitant, unreasonable, absurd, irrational, foolish, ridiculous. (*just, due, fair, reasonable, moderate, right, judicious*)

**presence**—nearness, influence, intercourse, closeness. (*remoteness, absence, separation, distance*)

**preserve**—defend, guard, save, keep safe, uphold, protect, maintain, rescue, spare. (*ruin, destroy*)

**president**—chairman, moderator, principal, superintendent. (*member, subordinate, constituent, corporation, society, ward, institution*)

**press**—urge, crowd, compel, force, squeeze, crush, compress, express, constrain, hurry, instigate, inculcate, impress, throng, encroach, lean, weigh, harass. (*relax, inhibit, persuade, entice, allure, solicit, touch, skim, graze, free, liberate, ease*)

**presume**—suppose, anticipate, apprehend, venture, take for granted, conjecture, believe, deem, assume. (*infer, deduce, prove, argue, retire, withdraw, hesitate, distrust*)

**pretend**—feign, simulate, offer, allege, exhibit, propound, affect, profess. (*verify, unmask, detect*)

**pretense**—excuse, pretext, fabrication, simulation, cloak, mask, color, show, garb, plea, assumption, make-believe, outside show, pretension. (*verity, reality, truth, simplicity, candor, guilelessness, openness, veritableness, actuality, fact*)

**pretty**—handsome, attractive, neat, trim, tasteful, pleasing, beautiful, fine, comely. (*ugly, grotesque*)

**prevailing**—controlling, ruling, influential, operative, predominant, prevalent, rife, ascendant, most general, most common. (*mitigated, diminishing, subordinate, powerless*)

**prevent**—hinder, obstruct, bar, neutralize, nullify, thwart, intercept, anticipate, forefend, frustrate, obviate, checkmate. (*promote, aid, facilitate, expedite, encourage, advance, accelerate, induce*)

**price**—cost, figure, charge, expense, compensation, value, appraisement, worth. (*donation, discount, allowance, remittance, abatement*)

**pride**—loftiness, haughtiness, lordliness, self-exaltation, arrogance, conceit, vainglory. (*lowliness, meekness, modesty, self-distrust*)

**priggish**—coxcombical, dandified, foppish, affected, prim, conceited. (*plain, sensible, unaffected, simple-minded, simple-mannered*)

**prim**—formal, precise, demure, starched, stiff, self-conscious, unbending, priggish. (*unformal, easy, genial, unaffected, natural, free, naive*)

**primary**—first, original, earliest, elementary, main, chief, principal, important, leading, primitive, pristine. (*secondary, subordinate, posterior, unimportant, inferior, subsequent, later*)

**primitive**—old-fashioned, primeval, quaint, simple, unsophisticated, archaic, pristine. (*modern, newfangled, sophisticated, modish*)

**princely**—imperial, munificent, magnificent, superb, august, regal, royal, supreme. (*beggarly, mean, niggardly, poverty-stricken*)

**principal**—highest, first, main, leading, chief, primary, foremost, pre-eminent, prominent. (*inferior, subordinate, secondary, supplemental, subject, auxiliary, minor*)

**principle**—source, origin, motive, cause, energy, substance, element, power, faculty, truth, tenet, law, doctrine, axiom, maxim, postulate, rule. (*exhibition, manifestation, application, development*)

**private**—special, peculiar, individual, secret, not public, retired, privy. (*general, public, open, unconcealed*)

**privilege**—prerogative, immunity, franchise, right, liberty, advantage, claim, exemption. (*disfranchisement, disqualification, exclusion, prohibition, inhibition*)

**prize**—booty, spoil, plunder, prey, forage, trophy, laurels, guerdon, premium, honors, ovation, palm. (*loss, forfeiture, fine, penalty, amercement, sacrifice, disappointment, failure, brand, stigma*)

**probability**—likelihood, presumption, verisimilitude, chance, appearance. (*unlikelihood, improbability, impossibility, inconceivableness*)

**probable**—likely, presumable, credible, reasonable. (*unlikely, unreasonable, incredible*)

**proceed**—move, pass, advance, progress, continue, issue, emanate, flow, arise. (*recede, deviate, retreat, stand, stop, stay, desist, discontinue, ebb, retire*)

**procession**—train, march, caravan, file, cortege, cavalcade, retinue. (*rabble, herd, rush, disorder, mob, confusion, rout*)

**prodigal**—lavish, profuse, extravagant, reckless, wasteful, squandering, improvident. (*frugal, saving, hoarding, economical, niggardly, miserly, close*)

**prodigious**—marvelous, portentous, wonderful, astounding, enormous, monstrous, amazing, surprising, remarkable, extraordinary, huge, vast. (*ordinary, commonplace, everyday, usual, familiar, moderate*)

**produce**—*v.* exhibit, bear, furbish, afford, cause, create, originate, yield, extend, prolong, lengthen. (*withdraw, retain, stifle, withhold, neutralize, destroy, annihilate, curtail, shorten, contract, reduce*)

**produce**—*n.* product, yield, fruit, profit, effect, consequence, result, amount.

**product**—fruit, result, issue, consequence, effect, emanation, work. (*cause, principle, power, motive, energy, operation, action, tendency, law*)

**production**—origination, evolution, formation, genesis, manufacture.

**profane**—unconsecrated, secular, temporal, unsanctified, unholy, irreligious, irreverent, ungodly, wicked, godless, impious, blasphemous. (*holy, consecrated, sacred, spiritual, sanctified, reverent*)

**profess**—declare, avow, acknowledge, own, confess, pretend, proclaim, lay claim to. (*conceal, suppress, disown, disavow, repudiate, renounce, abjure*)

**profit**—gain, emolument, advantage, avail, acquisition, benefit, service, use, improvement. (*loss, detriment, damage, disadvantage, waste*)

**profitable**—gainful, advantageous, desirable,

beneficial, useful, productive, remunerative, lucrative. (*unprofitable, disadvantageous, undesirable, detrimental, unbeneficial, unprofitable, useless, vain, fruitless, unproductive, unremunerative*)

**program**—advertisement, notice, plan, catalogue, schedule, performance. (*review, rehearsal, repetition, resume, analysis, précis*)

**progress**—advancement, advance, movement, proceeding, way, journey, proficiency, speed, growth. (*delay, stoppage, retreat, stay, retrogression, failure, relapse*)

**project**—plan, purpose, design, scheme, contrivance, device, venture. (*hazard, chance*)

**prominent**—jutting out, protuberant, embossed, extended, manifest, conspicuous, eminent, distinguished, main, important, leading, characteristic, distinctive. (*receding, concave, rebated, indented, hollowed, engraved, entailed, withdrawn*)

**promiscuous**—mingled, confused, undistinguished, unselected, unarranged, undistributed, unassorted, common, unreserved, casual, disorderly, unordered. (*sorted, select, orderly, arranged, distributed, reserved, assorted, exclusive, nice*)

**promise**—*v.* pledge, engage, assure, covenant, pledge, stipulate.

**promise**—*n.* engagement, assurance, word, pledge, oath, covenant.

**promote**—aid, further, advance, excite, exalt, raise, elevate, prefer. (*discourage, repress, hinder, check, allay, depress, degrade, dishonor*)

**prompt**—ready, alert, responsive, active, quick, brisk, apt, unhesitating. (*unready, sluggish, irresponsive, inactive*)

**pronounce**—articulate, utter, declare, propound, deliver, assert, affirm, enunciate, express. (*mispronounce, mispropound, misaffirm, suppress, stifle, silence, choke, swallow, gabble, mumble*)

**proof**—test, trial, examination, criterion, essay, establishment, comprobation, demonstration, evidence, testimony, scrutiny. (*disproof, failure, invalidity, shortcoming, fallacy, undemonstrativeness, reprobation*)

**proper**—peculiar, appertinent, personal, own, constitutional, special, befitting, adapted, suited, suitable, appropriate, just, fair, equitable, right, decent, becoming, fit. (*common, inappertinent, alien, universal, nonspecial, unbefitting, unadapted*)

**property**—quality, attribute, peculiarity, nature, characteristic, possessions, goods, wealth, estate, gear, resources, ownership.

**proportion**—adaptation, relation, rate, distribution, adjustment, symmetry, interrelationship, uniformity, correlation. (*misproportion, misadjustment, incongruity, disparity, disharmony, disorder, irrelation, disproportion*)

**propose**—offer, tender, proffer, bring forward, purpose, intend, mean, propound, move, design.

**prosaic**—dull, matter-of-fact, tedious, prolix. (*poetic, animated, interesting, lively, fervid, eloquent*)

**prospect**—view, vision, field, landscape, hope, anticipation, probability. (*viewlessness, dimness, obscurity, darkness, cloud, veiling, occultation, hopelessness, improbability*)

**prospectus**—program, plan, catalogue, announcement, bill, scheme, compendium, brochure. (*subject, transaction, proceeding*)

**prosperity**—success, wealth, welfare, good fortune, well-being, good luck. (*unsuccess, woe, adversity, failure, reverse*)

**protect**—defend, fortify, guard, shield, preserve, cover, secure, save, vindicate. (*betray, endanger, imperil, abandon, expose*)

**proud**—arrogant, haughty, imperious, supercilious, presumptuous, boastful, vainglorious, vain, ostentatious, elated, self-satisfied, lofty, imposing, magnificent, self-conscious. (*deferential, humble, affable, unpresuming, meek, lowly, ashamed, unimposing, mean*)

**prove**—try, assay, test, establish, demonstrate, ascertain, argue, show, confirm, examine, substantiate, make trial of, verify, ascertain. (*pass, pretermit, misdemonstrate, misindicate, refute, disprove, contradict, disestablish, neutralize*)

**proverbial**—notorious, current, acknowledged, unquestioned. (*dubious, unfounded, suspicious, suspected, questionable*)

**provide**—prepare, arrange, procure, afford, supply, contribute, yield, cater, furnish, get, agree, produce, collect, stipulate. (*misprovide, neglect, overlook, withhold, retain, appropriate, refuse, deny*)

**province**—tract, region, department, section, sphere, domain, territory. (*metropolis, center, capital*)

**provision, provisions**—preparation, arrangement, produce, supply, anticipation, food, supplies, victuals, edibles, eatables. (*neglect, misprovision, forgetfulness, thoughtlessness, oversight, destitution*)

**provoke**—educe, summon, rouse, irritate, excite, challenge, vex, impel, offend, exasperate, anger, tantalize. (*allay, relegate, pacify, soothe, conciliate*)

**proxy**—agency, substitution, representation, agent, substitute, representative, deputy, commissioner, lieutenant, delegate. (*principalship, personality, principal, person, authority, deputer*)

**prudent**—wise, wary, cautious, circumspect, discreet, careful, judicious. (*foolish, unwary, incautious, uncircumspect, indiscreet, rash, imprudent*)

**prudish**—coy, overmodest, overnice, squeamish, reserved, demure. (*promiscuous*)

**public**—open, notorious, common, social, national, exoteric, general, generally known. (*close, secret, private, domestic, secluded, solitary, personal*)

**pull**—draw, drag, adduce, extract, tug, haul, pluck. (*push, eject, extrude, propel*)

**punch**—perforate, poke, pierce, puncture, terebrate, bore. (*stop, plug, seal, bung*)

**punish**—chastise, castigate, chasten, correct, whip, scourge, discipline. (*reward, recompense, remunerate, indemnify*)

**pupil**—scholar, learner, student, tyro, novice, ward. (*teacher, master, proficient, adept, guardian*)

**puppy**—youth, fop, coxcomb, prig. (*boor, clown, lout*)

**pure**—clear, unmixed, simple, genuine, sheer, mere, absolute, unadulterated, uncorrupted, unsullied, unblemished, chaste, real, clean, spotless, immaculate, undefiled, unspotted, guileless, innocent, guiltless. (*foul, turbid, impure, adulterated, corrupt, sullied, stained, tarnished, defiled, mixed*)

**purpose**—*v.* intend, determine, design, resolve, mean, propose. (*chance, risk, hazard, revoke, miscalculate. venture. stake*)

**purpose**—*n.* intention, design, mind, meaning, view, object, aim, end, scope, point, resolve. (*chance, fortune, fate, accident, hazard, lot, casualty, lottery, hit*)

**push**—press, drive, impel, shove, press against, propel, butt, thrust, urge, expedite, accelerate, reduce. (*pull, draw, drag, adduce*)

**put**—place, lay, set, propose. (*remove, raise, displace, transfer, withdraw*)

**puzzle**—*v.* pose, perplex, embarrass, bewilder, confound, mystify, confuse. (*enlighten, instruct*)

**puzzle**—*n.* embarrassment, bewilderment, enigma, confusion, conundrum, intricacy, labyrinth. (*disentanglement, solution, explanation, extrication*)

## Q

**quack**—empiric, mountebank, charlatan, impostor, pretender, humbug. (*dupe, gull, victim*)

**quaint**—curious, recondite, abstruse, elegant, nice, affected, whimsical, odd, antique, archaic, fanciful, singular, old-fashioned. (*commonplace, ordinary, usual, coarse, common, modern, modish, fashionable, dowdy*)

**qualified**—fitted, adapted, competent, suitable. (*unsuited, inappropriate, ineligible*)

**quality**—condition, character, property, attribute, peculiarity, disposition, temper, sort, kind, description, capacity, power, virtue, nature, tendency. (*anomalousness, heterogeneousness, nondescript, incapacity, weakness, indistinctiveness, in-*

*effectiveness, disqualification, negation, disability)*

**quantity**—measure, amount, bulk, size, sum, portion, aggregate, muchness, part, share, division. (*margin, deficiency, deduction, want, inadequacy, scantiness, insufficiency, loss, deterioration, diminution, waste, wear, leakage*)

**quarrel**—brawl, altercation, affray, squabble, feud, tumult, dispute, wrangle, variance, disagreement, misunderstanding, hostility, quarreling, embroilment, bickering, broil. (*confabulation, conversation, pleasantry, conciliation, friendliness*)

**quarrelsome**—choleric, irascible, petulant, litigious, pugnacious, brawling, fiery, hot-tempered, contentious, irritable. (*peaceable, amenable, genial, unquarrelsome, inoffensive, mild, meek, conciliatory*)

**quarter**—region, district, locality, territory, mercy, forbearance, pity. (*extermination, mercilessness, unsparingness, pitilessness, ruthlessness*)

**queer**—odd, whimsical, quaint, cross, strange, crochety, singular, eccentric. (*ordinary, common, usual, familiar, customary*)

**question**—*v.* ask, inquire, interrogate, doubt, investigate, dubitate, controvert, dispute. (*dictate, state, assert, pronounce, enunciate, concede, endorse*)

**question**—*n.* inquiry, interrogation, doubt, scrutiny, investigation, topic. (*reply, response, solution, answer, explanation, admission, concession*)

**questionable**—doubtful, dubious, problematical, disputable, debatable, uncertain, suspicious. (*certain, evident, self-evident, obvious, indisputable*)

**quick**—fast, rapid, speedy, expeditious, swift, hasty, prompt, ready, clever, sharp, shrewd, adroit, keen, fleet, active, brisk, nimble, lively, agile, alert, sprightly, transient, intelligent, irascible. (*slow, tardy, sluggish, inert, inactive, dull, insensitive*)

**quiet**—*n.* rest, repose, stillness, calm, appeasement, pacification, silence, peace. (*unrest, motion, noise, agitation, excitement, disturbance, turmoil*)

**quiet**—*v.* allay, appease, still, pacify, hush, lull, tranquilize, soothe, calm. (*rouse, excite, disturb, agitate, stir, urge, goad*)

**quit**—leave, resign, abandon, relinquish, discharge, release, surrender, give up, depart from, forsake. (*seek, occupy, invade, bind, enforce, haunt*)

**quite**—perfectly, entirely, completely, wholly, truly, altogether, totally. (*partially, imperfectly, barely, insufficiently, hardly*)

**quote**—cite, name, adduce, plead, allege, note, repeat. (*disprove, refute, retort, oppose, contradict*)

## R

**racy**—fine-flavored, fresh, rich, pungent, piquant, spirited, smart, lively, vivacious, spicy. (*flavorless, dull, stupid*)

**radical**—original, fundamental, thoroughgoing, unsparing, extreme, entire, innate, natural, essential, immanent, ingrained, underived, deep-seated. (*derived, ascititious, adventitious, superficial, extraneous, partial, moderate, conservative, acquired*)

**rage**—*n.* fury, rabidity, choler, indignation, frenzy, anger, ire, dudgeon, mania, passion, madness, ferocity. (*reason, moderation, gentleness, temperateness, calmness, quiescence, mitigation, assuagement, tranquillity, mildness, softness*)

**rage**—*v.* rave, storm, fume, be furious, be violent. (*be calm, be composed, be peaceful*)

**raise**—lift, heave, elevate, exalt, advance, promote, heighten, enhance, awaken, rouse, excite, call forth, cultivate, rear, produce, collect, summon, erect, originate, propagate. (*lay, cast, depress, degrade, retard, dishonor, lower, depreciate, lull, compose, quiet, calm, blight, destroy, disperse, disband*)

**range**—rank, dispose, class, place, order, collocate, file, concatenate, ramble, stroll, rove. (*disturb, disconnect, disorder, derange, intermit, disconnect, remain, be stationary*)

**rank**—*a.* luxuriant, exuberant, extreme, excessive, rampant. (*meager, sparse, thin*)

**rank**—*n.* row, line, tier, order, degree, grade, dignity. (*disconnection, disorder, incontinuity, intermission, hiatus, plebeianism, meanness*)

**rankle**—fester, smolder, burn, irritate, gall, disquiet. (*heal, cool, close, calm, quiet, compose*)

**rapid**—quick, swift, speedy, accelerated, flying (*slow, tardy, retarded, cumbrous, lazy*)

**rare**—scarce, choice, infrequent, excellent, few, exceptional, sparse, unusual, singular, uncommon, incomparable, extraordinary, unique, dispersed, valuable, precious, thin, volatile. (*common, frequent, abundant, numerous, mean, ordinary, usual, regular, crowded, dense, vulgar, worthless, cheap*)

**rash**—headstrong, audacious, hasty, precipitate, reckless, foolhardy, careless, adventurous, thoughtless, indiscreet, venturesome, overventuresome, incautious, unwary, heedless. (*wary, cautious, calculating, discreet, unventuresome, dubitating, hesitating, reluctant, timid*)

**rashness**—hastiness, precipitancy, recklessness, venturesomeness, temerity, indiscretion. (*slowness, carefulness, cautiousness, discretion*)

**rate**—*n.* tax, impost, assessment, duty, standard, allowance, ratio, quota, worth, price, value.

**rate**—*v.* compute, calculate, estimate, value, scold, abuse, appraise.

**rational**—sane, sound, intelligent, reasoning, reasonable, judicious, sober, sensible, probable, equitable, moderate, fair. (*insane, unsound, weak, silly, unintelligent, absurd, injudicious, fanciful, extravagant, preposterous, unreasoning, unreasonable*)

**ravel**—separate, undo, untwist, unwind, disentangle. (*entangle, complicate, confuse*)

**ravish**—entrance, transport, enchant, enrapture, charm, violate, outrage, debauch.

**raw**—uncooked, unprepared, unfinished, unripe, crude, unseasoned, inexperienced, fresh, green, unpracticed, untried, bare, bald, exposed, galled, chill, bleak, piercing. (*cooked, dressed, prepared, finished, ripe, mature, mellow, seasoned, experienced, expert, adept, habituated, familiar, practiced, trained, tried*)

**reach**—extend, thrust, stretch, obtain, arrive at, attain, gain, grasp, penetrate, strain, aim. (*fail, stop, cease, revert, rebate, miss, drop*)

**read**—peruse, interpret, decipher, unravel, discover, recognize, learn. (*misread, misinterpret, overlook, misobserve*)

**ready**—prompt, alert, expeditious, speedy, unhesitating, dexterous, apt, skillful, handy, expert, facile, easy, opportune, fitted, prepared, disposed, willing, free, cheerful, compliant, responsive, quick. (*unready, tardy, slow, hesitating, reluctant, dubitating, awkward, unhandy, clumsy, remote, inaccessible, unavailable, inopportune, unsuited, unfitted, unprepared, indisposed, unwilling, constrained, grudging*)

**real**—actual, veritable, existent, authentic, legitimate, true, genuine, developed. (*fictitious, imaginary, unreal, nonexistent, untrue, false, artificial, adulterated, assumed, pretended, potential, possible*)

**really**—veritably, truly, indeed, unquestionably, (*questionably, possibly, perhaps, falsely, untruly*)

**reason**—*n.* ground, account, cause, explanation, motive, proof, apology, understanding, reasoning, rationality, right, propriety, justice, order, object, sake, purpose. (*pretext, pretense, misinterpretation, falsification, misconception, disproof, unreasonableness, absurdity, fallacy, irrationality, wrong, unreason, impropriety, unfairness, folly, aimlessness*)

**reason**—*v.* debate, discuss, argue, infer, deduce, conclude.

**reassure**—rally, restore, encourage, inspirit, animate, countenance. (*discourage, cow, browbeat, intimidate, discountenance*)

**rebuff**—*n.* rebuke, discouragement, repulsion, check. (*welcome, acceptance, encouragement*)

**rebuff**—*v.* rebuke, repel, repulse, check, snub, oppose.

**rebuke**—reprove, chide, rebuff, reprimand, censure. (*approve, encourage, eulogize, applaud, incite*)

**receipt**—acknowledgment, reception, voucher.

**receive**—take, accept, admit, hold, entertain, assent to. (*give, impart, afford, reject, discharge*)

**reception**—admission, admittance, acceptance, acceptation, entertainment. (*denial, protest, repudiation, rejection, nonacceptance, dismissal, discardment, renunciation, abjuration*)

**recess**—cavity, nook, withdrawal, retirement, retreat, seclusion, privacy, vacation, holiday. (*promontory, protrusion, projection, publicity, work-time*)

**reckless**—careless, heedless, incautious, foolhardy, thoughtless, rash, overventuresome, regardless, inconsiderate, improvident. (*careful, heedful, cautious, timid, chary, thoughtful, calculating, provident, considerate, wary, circumspect*)

**reckon**—compute, calculate, count, regard, estimate, value, account, consider, argue, infer, judge. (*miscompute, miscalculate, misestimate, misreckon*)

**recognize**—identify, acknowledge, concede, know again, avow, own, allow. (*ignore, overlook, misobserve, repudiate, disavow, disown, disallow*)

**recollect**—recover, recall, remember, bethink, bring to mind, call up, think of. (*forget, lose*)

**recommend**—commend, confide, praise, applaud, approve, advise. (*discommend, disapprove, warn*)

**recompense**—*n.* reward, indemnification, satisfaction, remuneration, amends.

**recompense**—*v.* requite, remunerate, reward, indemnify, satisfy, repay, reimburse, compensate. (*damnify, injure, misrequite, dissatisfy*)

**reconcile**—unite, conciliate, propitiate, pacify, harmonize, adjust, adapt, suit, reunite. (*separate, sever, dissever, estrange, disharmonize, derange*)

**record**—registry, entry, enrollment, list, index, catalogue, register, schedule, roll, scroll, enumeration, inventory, muniment, instrument, archive, memorandum, rememberance. (*obliteration, oblivion, nonregistration, desuetude, obsolescence*)

**recover**—regain, repossess, resume, retrieve, recruit, heal, cure, revive, restore, reanimate, save. (*lose, forfeit, miss, sacrifice, deteriorate, impair, decay, decline, relapse*)

**recovery**—repossession, regaining, reinstatement, vindication, renovation, restitution, re-establishment, retrieval, rectification, replacement, reanimation, resuscitation, revival, redemption. (*loss, forfeiture, privation, deprival, sacrifice, abandonment, relapse, retrogression, decay, declension, incurableness, ruin*)

**recreation**—refreshment, cheer, reanimation, amusement, diversion, revival, holiday, sport, pastime, relaxation. (*weariness, toil, lassitude, labor, fatigue, employment, assiduity, work*)

**redeem**—repurchase, regain, retrieve, make amends for, recompense, ransom, liberate, rescue, recover, satisfy, fulfill, discharge. (*pledge, lose, forfeit, abandon, betray, surrender, sacrifice*)

**reduce**—lessen, diminish, curtail, attenuate, impoverish, narrow, contract, weaken, impair, subdue, subjugate, bring, refer, subject, classify, convert. (*enlarge, magnify, increase, augment, produce, extend, amplify, broaden, expand, renovate, invigorate, restore, repair, liberate, free, except, dissociate, transform*)

**refer**—attribute, associate, assign, advert, connect, relate, point, belong, allude, apply, appeal, (*disconnect, dissociate, misapply, misappertain, alienate, misbeseem, disresemble*)

**reference**—relation, regard, intimation, allusion.

**refinement**—clarification, purification, filtration, sublimation, polish, elegance, cultivation, civilization, subtility, finesse, sophistry. (*turbidity, grossness, foulness, coarseness, impurity, unrefinement, rudeness, inelegance, boorishness, broadness, bluntness, unsophisticatedness*)

**reflect**—return, image, mirror, exhibit, consider, think, cogitate, meditate, contemplate, ponder, muse, ruminate, heed, advert, animadvert. (*divert, dissipate, idle, dream, wander, rove, stargaze, woolgather, connive, disregard, overlook*)

**reform**—amend, ameliorate, correct, rectify, better, reclaim, regenerate, remodel, reconstitute, reorganize, improve. (*corrupt, vitiate, worsen, deteriorate, perpetuate, stabilitate, confirm, impair, deform*)

**refresh**—cool, refrigerate, invigorate, revive, reanimate, renovate, recreate, renew, restore, cheer, freshen, brace. (*heat, oppress, weary, burden, afflict, annoy, tire, fatigue, exhaust, debilitate, enervate*)

**refuse**—*v.* deny, withhold, reject, decline, repudiate. (*grant, afford, yield, concede, acquiesce*)

**refuse**—*n.* offal, scum, dregs, sediment, recrement, sweepings, trash, offscourings, debris, remains, dross. (*cream, pickings, first fruits, flower*)

**regard**—behold, view, contemplate, esteem, consider, deem, affect, respect, reverence, revere, value, conceive, heed, notice, mind. (*miss, overlook, disregard, despise, dislike, contemn, hate, loathe, misconsider, misconceive, misestimate, misjudge*)

**regardless**—heedless, inconsiderate, careless, unmindful, inattentive, unobservant, disregarding, indifferent, despising. (*careful, considerate, regardful, attentive, prudent, cautious, circumspect, scrupulous*)

**regret**—*n.* sorrow, grief, concern, remorse, lamentation, repentance. (*see* **grief**)

**regret**—*v.* grieve, lament, repent, miss, desiderate, deplore. (*welcome, hail, approve, abandon, abjure, forget, disregard*)

**regular**—customary, normal, ordinary, orderly, stated, recurrent, periodical, systematic, methodic, established, recognized, formal, symmetrical, certain. (*unusual, exceptional, abnormal, capricious, rare, irregular, disordered, fitful, unsymmetrical, variable, eccentric, erratic, uncertain*)

**regulation**—rule, law, adjustment, disposal, method, government, order, control, arrangement. (*misrule, disorder, anarchy, misgovernment, maladministration, disarrangement, nonregulation, caprice, license, insubjection, uncontrol*)

**reject**—repel, renounce, throw by, cast away, repudiate, decline, discard, refuse, exclude. (*hail, welcome, accept, appropriate, choose, select, admit*)

**rejoice**—delight, glory, exult, joy, triumph, gladden, delight, revel, be glad, cheer, please, enliven, gratify. (*mourn, grieve, lament, weep, sorrow, repent, trouble, afflict, oppress, weary, depress, disappoint, burden, darken, distress, pain, sadden, vex, annoy*)

**relation**—reference, aspect, connection, narration, proportion, bearing, affinity, homogeneity, association, relevancy, pertinency, fitness, harmony, ratio, relative, agreement, kinsman, kindred, appurtenancy. (*irrelation, disconnection, dissociation, irrelevancy, impertinency, disproportion, misproportion, unfitness, unsuitableness, heterogeneity, disharmony, disagreement, alien*)

**release**—free, loose, liberate, discharge, quit, acquit, exempt, extricate, disengage, indemnify. (*bind, constrain, confine, shackle, fetter, yoke*)

**reliance**—confidence, trust, dependence, assurance. (*distrust, misgiving, suspicion, diffidence*)

**relief**—succor, support, release, extrication, alleviation, mitigation, aid, help, assistance, remedy, redress, exemption, deliverance, refreshment, comfort. (*oppression, aggravation, intensification, burdensomeness, trouble, exhaustion, weariness, discomfort*)

**religion**—faith, creed, theology, belief, profession, piety, sanctity, godliness, holiness. (*unbelief, irreligion, godlessness, atheism, impiety, sacrilege, scoffing, blasphemy, skepticism, profanity, hypocrisy, sanctimoniousness, pharisaism*)

**religious**—pious, godly, devout, devotional, divine, holy, sacred. (*impious, ungodly, undevout, sacrilegious, blasphemous, skeptical, profane*)

**relish**—zest, recommendation, enhancement, flavor, savor, gusto, taste, appetite, piquancy sapidity. (*drawback, disflavor, disrecommendation nauseousness, disrelish, insipidity, unsavoriness*)

**remain**—stay, continue, wait, stop, tarry, halt, sojourn, rest, dwell, abide, last, endure, accrue, survive. (*fly, vanish, remove, depart, speed, hasten press, flit, disappear, pass*)

**remarkable**—observable, noticeable, extraordinary, unusual, rare, striking, noteworthy, notable, distinguished, famous, peculiar, prominent, singular. (*unremarkable, unnoticeable, ordinary, mean, commonplace, everyday, undistinguished*)

**remedy**—cure, restorative, counteraction, reparation, redress, relief, help, specific. (*evil, disease, hurt, infection, plague, ill, impairment, deterioration, aggravation, provocation*)

**remember**—recollect, recall, retain, bear in mind, mind. (*forget, obliviate, disregard, overlook*)

**remembrance**—recollection, memory, memorial, token, souvenir, memento, reminiscence, (*forgetfulness, oblivion*)

**remiss**—slack, careless, negligent, inattentive, wanting, slow, slothful, idle, lax, dilatory, tardy, remissful. (*energetic, careful, attentive, active, assiduous, alert, painstaking, diligent, strict*)

**remit**—relax, pardon, absolve, forgo, discontinue, surrender, forgive, resign. (*increase, intensity, enforce, exact*)

**remorse**—compunction, anguish, self-condemnation, penitence, sting of conscience. (*complacency, self-approval, self-congratulation*)

**remote**—distant, indirect, unconnected, unrelated, foreign, alien, heterogeneous, separate, contingent. (*near, close, direct, connected, related, homogeneous, immediate, proximate, essential, present, pressing, urgent, actual*)

**remove**—displace, separate, abstract, transport, carry, transfer, eject, oust, dislodge, suppress, migrate, depart. (*restore, conserve, stabilitate, perpetuate, establish, reinstate, reinstall, install, fix*)

**render**—give, present, return, restore, give up, apportion, assign, surrender, pay, requite, deliver. (*keep, retain, withhold, appropriate, alienate, misapportion, misappropriate, misrequite*)

**renew**—recreate, restore, refresh, renovate, rejuvenate, furbish, recommence, repeat, reiterate, reissue, regenerate, reform, transform. (*impair, wear, deteriorate, vitiate, exhaust, discontinue, corrupt, weaken, defile, deprave*)

**renounce**—reject, abjure, disclaim, disown, forgo, disavow, deny, quit, resign, abandon, recant, relinquish, repudiate. (*acknowledge, recognize, claim, maintain, assert, propound, own, vindicate, avow, profess, hold, retain, defend*)

**renowned**—famous, celebrated, wonderful, illustrious.

**repay**—remunerate, reimburse, recompense, reward, retaliate, requite, refund. (*defraud, misappropriate, embezzle, waste, alienate, extort, confiscate*)

**repeal**—*v.* abolish, revoke, rescind, cancel, annul, recall, abrogate, reverse, discontinue, make void. (*continue, establish, pass, institute, sanction, enact, perpetuate, confirm*)

**repeal**—*n.* abrogation, rescisson, revocation, annulment. (*continuance, establishment, perpetuation*)

**repeat**—reiterate, iterate, renew, cite, quote, relate, rehearse, recapitulate, reproduce. (*discontinue, drop, discard, abandon, ignore, suppress, misrepeat, misquote, misrecite, misrepresent, misinterpret, misconvey*)

**repeatedly**—frequently, again and agian, often. (*seldom, rarely*)

**repentance**—penitence, contrition, compunction, regret, remorse, sorrow, self-reproach, self-condemnation. (*impenitence, obduracy, recusancy, hardness, reprobation, self-approval*)

**repetition**—iteration, reiteration, dwelling upon, diffuseness, verbosity, relation.

**replace**—restore, supply, substitute, reinstate, rearrange, re-establish. (*move, abstract, withdraw, remove, damage, deprive*)

**reply**—*n.* answer, rejoinder, response, replication. (*passing by, ignoring*)

**reply**—*v.* replicate, answer, respond, rejoin. (*ignore, drop, pretermit, pass, disregard*)

**report**—*v.* announce, relate, tell, circulate, notify, narrate, recite, describe, detail, communicate, declare. (*silence, hush, suppress, misreport, misrepresent, misrelate, falsify*)

**report**—*n.* tidings, announcement, relation, narration, recital, description, communication, declaration, news, rumor, fame, repute, noise, reverberation. (*silence, suppression, misannouncement, fabrication, noiselessness*)

**represent**—portray, delineate, reproduce, exhibit, personate, state, describe, indicate, embody, enact, illustrate, denote, play, dramatize, resemble. (*misportray, misdelineate, distort, falsify, caricature*)

**representative**—agent, commissioner, proxy, deputy, substitute, embodiment, personation, delegate, vicar, vicegerent, principal, sovereign. (*autocrat, dictator*)

**reproach**—blame, censure, taunt, rebuke, upbraid, reprobate, reprove. (*laud, praise, approve, commend*)

**reprobate**—castaway, villain, ruffian, miscreant, scapegrace, scalawag. (*example, pattern, mirror, model, paragon*)

**repudiate**—disavow, disown, discard, cast off, abjure, renounce, disclaim, divorce. (*avow, own, vindicate, assert, retain, vaunt, claim, profess, recognize, acknowledge, accept*)

**repulsive**—forbidding, deterrent, ungenial, odious, ugly, unattractive, disagreeable, revolting. (*charming, agreeable, attractive, winning, captivating, fascinating, alluring, seductive, pleasant*)

**reputable**—respectable, creditable, honorable, estimate. (*unrespectable, discreditable, dishonorable, disgraceful, disreputable*)

**rescue**—retake, recover, recapture, liberate, extricate, save, deliver, preserve. (*endanger, imperil, betray, surrender, abandon, expose*)

**resemblance**—likeness, similarity, similitude, semblance, representation, portrait, reflection, image. (*unlikeness, dissimilarity, disresemblance, difference, contrariety*)

**resent**—repel, resist, rebel, recalcitrate, take ill. (*acquiesce, submit, condone, pardon, overlook*)

**reserve**—reservation, retention, limitation, backwardness, coldness, shyness, coyness, modesty. (*boldness, rashness, recklessness, immodesty*)

**residence**—sojourn, stay, abode, home, habitation, domicile, mansion.

**resist**—withstand, oppose, hinder, check, thwart, baffle, disappoint. (*weaken, yield, give up, surrender*)

**resolute**—determined, decided, fixed, steadfast, steady, constant, persevering, bold, firm, unshaken, (*weak, infirm, shy, cowardly, inconstant*)

**resource**—material, means, supplies, expedients, wealth, riches. (*destitution, exhaustion, lack, drain, nonplus, poverty*)

**respect**—regard, esteem, honor, revere, venerate.

**respond**—answer, reply, rejoin.

**rest**—remainder, overplus, remnant, residue, others.

**restless**—unquiet, uneasy, disturbed, disquieted, sleepless, agitated, anxious, unsettled, roving, wandering. (*steady, quiet, settled*)

**restrain**—check, hinder, stop, withhold, repress, curb, suppress, coerce, restrict, abridge, limit, confine. (*give full rein to, let go, release, free*)

**result**—effect, consequence, conclusion, inference, issue, event.

**retain**—keep, hold, restrain. (*yield, give up*)

**retire**—withdraw, leave, depart, secede, recede.

**retort**—repartee, answer.

**retreat**—retirement, departure, withdrawment, seclusion, solitude, privacy, asylum, shelter, refuge. (*advance, forward march*)

**return**—restore, requite, repay, recompense, render, remit, report.

**reveal**—communicate, disclose, divulge, unveil, uncover, open, discover, impart, show. (*keep secret, withhold, cover, conceal, hide*)

**revengeful**—vindictive, resentful, spiteful, malicious. (*open, ingenuous, frank, hearty, generous, kind, cordial*)

**revenue**—receipts, returns, income, proceeds, wealth, result. (*expense, outgo*)

**reverence**—awe, honor, veneration, adoration.

**review**—re-examination, resurvey, retrospect, survey, reconsideration, revise, revision

**reward**—recompense, compensation, remuneration, pay, requital, retribution, punishment.

**rich**—wealthy, affluent, opulent, ample, copious, abundant, fruitful, costly, sumptuous, precious, generous, luscious. (*poor, weak, straitened, cheap, scanty, sordid*)

**ridicule**—derision, twit, banter, raillery, burlesque, mockery, sarcasm, gibe, jeer, sneer.

**ripe**—mature, mellow, complete, finished. (*green, young, incomplete, unfinished*)

**rise**—arise, mount, ascend, climb, scale.

**risk**—danger, hazard, peril, jeopardy, exposure.

**rival**—competitor, emulator, antagonist.

**road**—way, highway, street, lane, pathway, route, passage, course.

**robbery**—theft, depredation, spoliation, despoilation, despoilment, plunder, pillage, freebooting, piracy.

**romance**—fable, novel, fiction, tale.

**romantic**—sentimental, fanciful, fictitious, extravagant, wild, chimerical.

**room**—space, compass, scope, latitude.

**round**—circular, spherical, globular, globose, orbicular, orbed, cylindrical, full, plump, rotund. (*square, oblong, angular, lean, thin*)

**rout**—defeat, smite, conquer. (*victory*)

**route**—roadway, path, track.

**royal**—kingly, regal, monarchical, imperial, kinglike, princely, august, majestic, superb, splendid, illustrious, noble, magnanimous.

**ruin**—destruction, downfall, perdition, fall, overthrow, subversion, defeat, bane, pest, mischief.

**rule**—regulation, law, precept, maxim, guide, canon, order, method, direction, control, government, sway, empire.

**rustic**—rural, rude, unpolished, inelegant, untaught, awkward, rough, coarse, plain, unadorned, simple, artless, honest.

## S

**sacred**—holy, divine, hallowed, consecrated, dedicated, devoted, religious, venerable, reverend.

**sad**—sorrowful, mournful, gloomy, dejected, dedepressed, cheerless, downcast, sedate, serious, grave, grievous, afflictive, calamitous. (*gay, lively, happy, spirited, sprightly, jolly, fortunate, seductive*)

**safe**—secure, unendangered, sure. (*in danger, dangerous, exposed, risky*)

**sagacity**—penetration, shrewdness, judiciousness. (*stupidity, thickheadedness, dullness, foolishness*)

**salutary**—wholesome, healthful, salubrious, beneficial, useful, advantageous, profitable. (*unhealthy, infectious, tainted*)

**sample**—specimen, example, illustration.

**sanction**—ratify, support, endorse.

**satire**—lampoon, sarcasm, irony, ridicule, burlesque, wit, humor.

**satisfaction**—contentment, content, gratification, pleasure, recompense, compensation, amends, remuneration, indemnification, atonement.

**satisfy**—satiate, content, please, gratify, recompense, compensate, remunerate, indemnify.

**saucy**—impertinent, insolent, rude, impudent.

**savage**—ferocious, wild, uncultivated, untaught, uncivilized, unpolished, rude, brutish, brutal, heathenish, barbarous, cruel, inhuman, fierce, pitiless, merciless, unmerciful, murderous. (*cultured, refined, kind, gentle, merciful, humane, human, tame*)

**save**—preserve, rescue, deliver, protect, spare, reserve, prevent. (*abandon, expose, give up, throw away*)

**saying**—declaration, speech, adage, maxim, aphorism, apothegm, saw, proverb, byword.

**scandal**—defamation, detraction, slander, calumny, opprobrium, reproach, shame, disgrace. (*honor, glory, respect*)

**scanty**—deficient, gaunt, meager, scarce. (*full, ample, plenty*)

**scarce**—rare, infrequent, deficient, uncommon. (*common, general, usual, frequent*)

**scatter**—disperse, dissipate, spread, strew, sprinkle. (*gather, keep together, collect, preserve*)

**scheme**—plan, project, design, contrivance, purpose, device, plot.

**scholar**—pupil, learner, disciple, learned man, sage.

**science**—literature, art, knowledge.

**scorn**—contempt, disdain, derision, contumely, despite, slight, dishonor, contempt. (*love, respect, honor, admiration, flattery*)

**scrupulous**—cautious, careful, conscientious, hesitating. (*unscrupulous, careless, scatterbrained, reckless, daring, dishonest*)

**scurrilous**—opprobrious, abusive, reproachful, insulting, insolent, offensive, gross, vile, vulgar, low, foul, foul-mouthed, indecent, mean.

**seasonable**—opportune, timely, fit convenient.

**secret**—hidden, concealed, secluded, unseen, unknown, private, obscure, recondite, latent, covert, clandestine, privy. (*open, free, known, public*)

**sectarian**—heretic, partisan, schismatic.

**section**—part, division, portion.

**security**—protection, defense, guard, shelter, safety, certainty, ease, assurance, carelessness, confidence, surety, pledge. (*danger, exposure, doubt, uncertainty*)

**sedate**—sober, demure, serious, calm, grave, settled, serene, passive, quiet. (*flighty, frolicsome, indiscreet, ruffled, agitated, disturbed*)

**seem**—appear, look.

**seemly**—becomingly, fit, suitable, proper, appropriate, congruous, meet, decent, decorous. (*improper, immodest, unconventional, gross, rude*)

**seize**—catch, grasp, clutch, snatch, append, arrest, take, capture.

**sense**—understanding, reason, perception, sensation, feeling, meaning, import, signification, notion, opinion, judgment.

**sensible**—intelligent, wise, cognizant, satisfied, persuaded. (*scatterbrained, foolish, ignorant of*)

**sentiment**—thought, opinion, sensibility, feeling.

**serious**—grave, solemn, important, weighty. (*gay, lively, happy, light, unimportant*)

**serve**—obey, minister to, subserve, promote, aid, help, assist, benefit, succor.

**set**—*v.* sink, settle, subside, decline, compose, consolidate, harden. (*rise, ascend, soar, mount, stir, agitate, loosen, run, soften, melt, mollify, fuse, flow*)

**set**—*a.* fixed, established, firm, determined, regular, formal.

**settle**—fix, establish, regulate, arrange, compose, adjust, determine, decide, adjudicate, quiet, allay, still, sink, fall, subside, lower, calm, acquiesce, abate, agree. (*remove, disestablish, misregulate, derange, discompose, aggravate, disorder, disturb, confuse, misdetermine, misarrange, misplace, unsettle, rise, ascend, move, disagree, increase, heighten*)

**settlement**—subsidence, dregs, residuum, precipitation, colonization, location, colony. (*excitement, perturbation, turbidity, fluctuation*)

**several**—separate, distinct, diverse, sundry, divers, various, different. (*one, same, identical, indistinguishable, inseparable, united, total, integral*)

**severe**—serious, austere, stern, grave, strict, harsh, rigid, rigorous, sharp, afflictive, distressing, violent, extreme, exact, critical, censorious, caustic, sarcastic, cutting, keen, better, cruel. (*gay, smiling, cheerful, relaxed, jocose, jocund, joyous, mild, genial, indulgent, light, trivial, trifling, inconsiderable, inexact, loose, uncritical, lenient, inextreme, moderate, kind, considerate, feeling, tender, gentle*)

**shabby**—ragged, threadbare, contemptible, beggarly, paltry.

**shadowy**—dim, cloudy, obscure, dark, murky, gloomy, mysterious.

**shallow**—shoal, slight, flimsy, trifling, simple, superficial, unprofound. (*deep, profound*)

**sham**—phantom, ghost, delusion, illusion, mockery, shadow, pretense, counterfeit, unreality. (*substance, reality, verity, substantiality, truth*)

**shame**—abashment, humiliation, modesty, shamefacedness, decency, decorum, reproach, dishonor, ignominy, contempt, degradation, discredit, dispraise. (*shamelessness, barefacedness, immodesty, impudence, indecency, indecorum, impropriety, honor, glory, exaltation, renown, credit*)

**shameful**—disgraceful, degrading, scandalous, outrageous, dishonorable, indecent, unbecoming.

**shape**—*v.* form, mold, figure, adapt, delineate, adjust, contrive, create, execute, make. (*pervert,* *distort, misadapt, misdelineate, derange, discompose, miscontrive, misproduce, caricature)*

**shape**—*n.* figure, form, outline, mold, fashion, pattern, cast, model.

**share**—portion, apportionment, lot, division, participation, allowance, quota, contingent, allotment. (*whole, mass, aggregate, entirety*)

**sharp**—thin, fine, keen, shrewd, discerning, clever, sarcastic, acute, pointed, aculeated, penetrating, pungent, acid, shrill, piercing, afflictive, distressing, harsh, severe, cutting, eager, active, ardent, sore, hard, animated, spirited. (*thick, blunt, dull, obtuse, knobbed, rounded, bluff, mellow, bass, hollow, deep, light, trifling, trivial, mild, gentle, soft, tender, lenient, sluggish, inactive, indifferent, careless, spiritless, tame*)

**shatter**—split, dissipate, disrupt, derange, break in pieces, rend, demolish, shiver, dismember, disintegrate. (*construct, organize, collocate, fabricate, compose, rear, constitute*)

**sheer**—pure, mere, unmixed, unqualified, unmitigated, absolute, simple, unadulterated. (*mixed, qualified, adulterated, modified, partial*)

**shelve**—dismiss, discard, swamp, stifle, shift. (*start, prosecute, pursue, revive, agitate*)

**shift**—*v.* change, alter, transfer, shelve, displace, remove. (*fix, fasten, locate, insert, pitch, plant, place*)

**shift**—*n.* contrivance, expedient, substitute, pretext, motive, change, evasion, device, artifice, resource, transference. (*miscontrivance, fixity, steadiness, retention, location, permanence*)

**shocking**—sad, horrible, disgraceful, hateful, revolting, abominable, loathsome, foul. (*pleasing, honorable, charming, delightful, creditable, edifying, exemplary, attractive, alluring, enticing*)

**short**—brief, limited, scanty, inadequate, insufficient, lacking, deficient, defective, imperfect, incomplete, soon, near, narrow, weak, incomprehensive, inextensive, less, abrupt, blunt, concise, condensed. (*long, protracted, extended, unlimited, plentiful, ample, abundant, adequate, sufficient. exuberant, liberal, large, copious, complete, distant, deferred, wide, strong, comprehensive, extensive, exceeding, bland, courteous, inabrupt, expanded, diffuse*)

**show**—*n.* appearance, exhibition, demonstration, parade, pomp, semblance, likeness, pretext, profession, pretense, illusion. (*nonappearance, disappearance, concealment, suppression, secrecy, disguise, dissimilarity, unlikeness, ungenuineness, reality, sincerity, substance*)

**show**—*v.* exhibit, present, demonstrate, unfold, reveal, teach, inform, conduct, manifest, evince, evidence, prove, explain. (*conceal, suppress, hide, withhold, obscure, mystify, wrap, misdemonstrate, misdeclare, contradict, refute, deny, disprove, misinterpret, falsify, misexplain*)

**showy**—gay, gaudy, high-colored, gorgeous, flashy, tinsel. (*inconspicuous, unnoticeable, quiet, subdued*)

**shrewd**—sagacious, penetrating, astute, discriminating, intelligent, discerning, acute. (*stolid, undiscerning, unsagacious, stupid, dull*)

**shrink**—contract, shrivel, withdraw, retire, recoil, revolt. (*stretch, expand, dilate, venture, dare*)

**shrivel**—contract, dry up, wither, wrinkle, corrugate, decrease. (*expand, flatten, develop, unfold, spread, dilate*)

**shuffle**—confuse, interchange, shift, intershift, intermix, derange, agitate, evade, prevaricate, equivocate, quibble, cavil, sophisticate, mystify, palter, dissemble. (*deal, distribute, order, arrange, compose, confess, propound, declare, explain, elucidate, reveal*)

**shy**—timid, reserved, modest, bashful, suspicious, shrinking, chary. (*bold, brazenfaced, impudent, audacious, reckless*)

**sick**—diseased, ill, disordered, distempered, indisposed, weak, ailing, feeble, morbid, nauseated, disgusted, corrupt, impaired, valetudinarian. (*whole, well, healthy, sound, robust, strong, well conditioned, salubrious*)

**sickly**—weak, diseased, disordered, ailing, feeble, pining, drooping, morbid, unhealthy, vitiated, delicate, tainted, valetudinary. (*strong, healthy, vigorous, flourishing, salubrious, sound, robust*)

**side**—margin, edge, verge, border, laterality, face, aspect, plane, party, interest, cause, policy, behalf. (*center, body, core, interior, essence, neutrality, disconnection, severance, secession, opposition*)

**sight**—seeing, perception, view, vision, visibility, spectacle, show, inspection, examination, representation, appearance. (*nonperception, invisibility, blindness, obscuration, disappearance, oversight, nonappearance, undiscernment*)

**sign**—token, indication, proof, memorial, expression, symbol, emblem, prefiguration, badge, type, premonition, symptom, prognostic, mark, wonder, presage, signal. (*misindication, misrepresentation, misleader*)

**signal**—eminent, conspicuous, remarkable, extraordinary, notable, memorable, illustrious, important, salient, distinguished. (*ordinary, common, unnoticeable, mediocre, unmemorable, unimportant*)

**signify**—portend, purport, prognosticate, mean, represent, indicate, communicate, denote, betoken, declare, utter, forebode, presage. (*conceal, suppress, misindicate, misdenote, nullify, refute, neutralize, preclude*)

**silence**—taciturnity, stillness, calm, peace, hush, muteness, secrecy, oblivion. (*garrulity, loquacity, talkativeness, chatter, noise, brawl, clamor, clatter, din, babel, tumult, agitation, restlessness, storm, unrest, roar, bruit, reverberation, resonance, commotion, cackling, proclamation, publicity, fame, rumor, remembrance, repute, celebrity*)

**silly**—simple, foolish, weak, shallow, witless, unwise, indiscreet, imprudent, absurd. (*sagacious, intelligent, astute, wise, deep, discreet, prudent, sound, rational*)

**similar**—correspondent, resembling, alike, common, homogeneous, concordant, harmonious, congruous. (*different, unlike, dissimilar, alien, heterogeneous, discordant, incongruous*)

**simple**—single, incomplex, uncompounded, unblended, isolated, pure, unmixed, mere, absolute, plain, unadorned, unartificial, artless, sincere, undesigning, single-minded, unaffected, silly, weak, unsophisticated, humble, homely, lowly, elementary, ultimate, primal, rudimentary. (*double, complex, compounded, blended, mixed, fused, multiform, multigenerous, various, compound, articulated, subdivided, organized, connected, modified, complicated, elaborate, artificial, artful, designing, insincere, double-minded, affected, self-conscious, sagacious, sophisticated, great, eminent, illustrous, complete, developed, perfect*)

**simultaneous**—synchronous, concomitant, concurrent. (*separate, apart, intermittent, periodic*)

**sin**—transgression, iniquity, unrighteousness, ungodliness, wickedness, evil, impurity, crime, wrongdoing. (*sinlessness, obedience, holiness, righteousness, purity, godliness, goodness*)

**sincere**—pure, unmixed, genuine, unadulterated, hearty, honest, unaffected, unvarnished, candid, cordial, frank, unfeigned, true. (*impure, adulterated, dishonest, insincere, hypocritical, feigned, false*)

**single**—one, unique, only, individual, sole, solitary, separate, uncombined, unmarried, uncompounded. (*plural, many, collective, united, numerous, frequent, married*)

**singular**—single, individual, unique, eminent, extraordinary, conspicuous, consummate, unusual, uncommon, odd, whimsical quaint, peculiar, unexampled, unprecedented, solitary, sole, eccentric, fantastic, exceptional, particular, remarkable, curious, queer. (*common, frequent, numerous, ordinary, usual, unnoticeable, everyday, customary, general, regular*)

**situation**—locality, position, topography, state, seat, post, place, condition, residence, aspect, footing, office, birth, plight, predicament, standing. (*nonsituation, nonlocation, absence, nonassignment, unfixedness, displacement, dislodgement*)

**slender**—thin, narrow, slight, slim, small, trivial,

spare, inadequate, fragile, feeble, flimsy, meager, inconsiderable, superficial. (*stout, thick, broad, robust, massive, considerable, ample, deep*)

**slow**—sluggish, inactive, inert, lazy, unready, tardy, late, gradual, tedious, dull, dilatory, lingering, slack. (*active, quick, fast, rapid, alert, ready, prompt, early, sudden, immediate*)

**sly**—cunning, subtle, crafty, artful, wily, underhanded, astute, stealthy. (*open, frank, artless, undesigning*)

**small**—little, diminutive, slight, minute, feeble, trivial, insignificant, paltry, narrow, mean, weak, slender, fine, inferior. (*great, large, big, considerable, bulky, extensive, ample, spacious, stout, strong, important, broad, liberal*)

**smart**—keen, pungent, piercing, quick, vigorous, sharp, severe, active, clever, brilliant, vivacious, witty, ready, spruce, brisk, fresh, dressy, showy. (*dull, heavy, aching, slow, inactive, stupid, sluggish, unready, slow-minded, unwitty, dowdy, shabby, clownish*)

**smooth**—even, plain, level, flat, polished, glossy, sleek, soft, unruffled, unobstructed, bland, oily, suave. (*uneven, rough, rugged, abrupt, precipitous, unpolished, harsh, blunt*)

**smother**—suffocate, stifle, repress, gag, conceal, suppress, choke, strangle, allay, swallow. (*fan, ventilate, foster, cherish, nurture, publish, promulgate, divulge, spread, excite, vent*)

**sneer**—scoff, gibe, jeer, taunt, disparagement, contempt, scorn, superciliousness, disdain. (*compliment, eulogy, commendation, deference*)

**snub**—mortify, check, rebuke, reprimand.

**snug**—close, housed, compressed, compact, comfortable, sheltered. (*exposed, loose, disordered, incompact, uncomfortable, bare, shivering*)

**sober**—temperate, unintoxicated, cool, dispassionate, reasonable, calm, self-possessed, sound, unexcited, serious, grave, sedate, steady, abstemious, moderate. (*intemperate, drunk, intoxicated, heated, excited, impassioned, unreasonable, agitated, furious, passionate, extravagant, extreme, exorbitant, immoderate, flighty, erratic, eccentric*)

**society**—community, polity, association, collection, companionship, fellowship, connection, participation, company, sociality, communion, intercourse, sodality. (*individuality, personality, segregation, separation, solitariness, unsociality, privacy, dissociation, disconnection*)

**soft**—yielding, pressible, impressible, smooth, delicate, fine, sleek, glossy, mild, gentle, balmy, kind, feeling, flexible, effeminate, luxurious, unmanly, tender, irresolute, undecided. (*hard, tough, stubborn, unyielding, rigid, unimpressible, rough, coarse, harsh, abrupt, ungentle, rigorous, cutting, severe, unkind, unfeeling, sharp, inflexible, stern, austere, ascetic, self-denying, resolute, determined*)

**soften**—mollify, palliate, compose, mitigate, assuage, dulcify, lenify, yield, macerate, humanize, abate, moderate. (*harden, indurate, aggravate, excite, infuriate, consolidate*)

**solemn**—sacred, formal, devotional, reverential, ritual, ceremonial, impressive, religious, grave, serious. (*profane, undevotional, secular, light, gay, trivial, unceremonial, informal, unsolemn*)

**solid**—hard, firm, compact, resistant, dense, substantial, weighty, strong, valid, just, sound, impenetrable, stable, cubic. (*soft, hollow, yielding, frail, brittle, flimsy, elastic, resilient, malleable, impressible, fluid, liquid, frivolous, light, trifling, weak, invalid, unsound, fallacious, weakly*)

**solitude**—loneliness, remoteness, seclusion, retirement, isolation, wildness, desertion, barrenness, wilderness, privacy. (*publicity, populousness, society, frequentedness, intercourse, resort, meeting, reunion, throng, crowd*)

**solution**—separation, discerption, disruption, breach, discontinuance, disconnection, disentanglement, elucidation, explanation, key, answer, resolution, disintegration. (*union, combination, amalgamation, continuity, connection, conjunction, entanglement, complication, confusion, mystification, obscurity, integration*)

**sore**—painful, irritated, susceptible, excoriated, raw, scarified, ulcerous, grievous, afflictive, heavy, burdensome. (*painless, sound, whole, healthful, healed, unbroken, unscarified, light, trivial, unburdensome, pleasant, untroublesome, grateful*)

**sorry**—grieved, pained, hurt, afflicted, woebegone, doleful, downhearted, mortified, vexed, dejected, poor, mean, vile, shabby, worthless. (*glad, rejoiced, delighted, pleased, gratified, fine, choice, handsome*)

**sort**—kind, species, nature, class, order, character, rank, manner, quality, condition, description, designation, genus. (*nondescription, solitariness, uniqueness, nonclassification, heterogeneity*)

**sound**—entire, unbroken, whole, perfect, unhurt, well-grounded, uninjured, unimpaired, healthy, firm, strong, vigorous, weighty, solid, irrefragable, irrefutable, thorough, valid, wholesome, correct, substantial. (*partial, broken, injured, impaired, unhealthy, unsound, weak, frail, fragile, light, trivial, unfounded, hollow, fallacious, imperfect, unwholesome, incorrect, unsubstantial, invalid*)

**sour**—tart, rancid, coagulated, turned, harsh, crabbed, austere, morose, pungent, crusty, acid, churlish, bitter, acetous, acrimonious, peevish. (*sweet, wholesome, untainted, mellow, genial, kindly*)

**spacious**—ample, extensive, broad, vast, capacious, large, wide, roomy, expansive. (*narrow, restricted, limited, cramped, confined, inextensive*)

**spare**—*a.* scanty, unplentiful, inabundant, meager, economical, frugal, stinted, restricted, parsimonious, niggardly, chary, superfluous, disposable, available, lean, thin, ill-conditioned. (*ample, plentiful, abundant, profuse, liberal, unrestricted, generous, bountiful, unsparing, unstinted, unbounded, available, well-conditioned*)

**spare**—*v.* save, afford, grant, reserve, do without, husband, economize, retain, store, grudge, discard, omit, forbear, withhold, refrain, abstain. (*spend, squander, waste, lavish, scatter, expend, indulge, vent*)

**special**—particular, specific, peculiar, appropriate, proper, distinctive, extraordinary, especial, exceptional. (*general, universal, common, generic*)

**speculation**—contemplation, consideration, view, weighing, thought, theory, scheme, hypothesis, conjecture. (*realization, proof, fact, verification, certainty*)

**speed**—dispatch, expedite, accelerate, urge, hasten, hurry, press. (*retard, delay, postpone, obstruct, drag, loiter, dawdle, linger, lag, stay*)

**spend**—bestow, waste, exhaust, squander, expend, lay out, consume, disburse, lavish. (*retain, save, hoard, accumulate, husband, economize*)

**spirit**—air, breath, life, soul, vital, force, essential quality, essence, immateriality, intelligence, disembodiment, specter, apparition, ghost, energy, ardor, enthusiasm, activity, earnestness, courage, zeal, disposition, temper, principle, motive, distillation. (*substance, body, corporeity, materiality, flesh, organization, frame, embodiment, spiritlessness, listlessness, soullessness, lifelessness, torpor, deadness, timidity, dejection, slowness, sluggishness*)

**spirited**—animated, lively, vivacious, ardent, buoyant, sprightly, courageous. (*dull, dispirited, depressed, cowardly*)

**spiritual**—divine, religious, holy, ghostly, ethical, immaterial, incorporeal, intellectual. (*carnal, fleshy, unspiritual, gross, material, sensuous*)

**spite**—malice, malevolence, grudge, pique, hatred, ill will, vindictiveness, rancor, spleen. (*good will, benevolence, kindness*)

**splendid**—brilliant, showy, magnificent, sumptuous, gorgeous, glorious, pompous, imposing, illustrious, superb, famous, heroic, grand, signal. (*dull, obscure, tame, somber, poor, beggarly, unimposing, ordinary, ineffective, inglorious*)

**split**—divide, separate, rive, cleave, crack, splinter, burst, rend, sunder, disagree, secede, disunite. (*cohere, unite, amalgamate, coalesce, conform, agree, splice, consolidate, integrate*)

**spoil**—plunder, strip, rob, devastate, pillage, denude, corrupt, vitiate, mar, deteriorate. (*invest, enrich, endow, replenish, renovate, improve, better, ameliorate, rectify, preserve*)

**spontaneous**—voluntary, self-generated, self-originated, willing, unbidden, gratuitous. (*involuntary, imposed, compulsory, unwilling, necessitated*)

**sport**—play, frolic, wantonness, joke, diversion, merriment, gaiety, fun, amusement, recreation, game, pastime. (*work, seriousness, business, earnestness*)

**spread**—extend, stretch, expand, open, unfurl, divulge, propagate, publish, disperse, diffuse, overlay, distribute, scatter, circulate, disseminate, ramify. (*contract, furl, gather, fold, close, shut, secrete, suppress, confine, restrict, repress, hush, conceal, recall, collect, stagnate, concentrate, localize*)

**spring**—leap, bound, jump, start, emerge, issue, proceed, orginate, rise, emanate, germinate, burst, flow. (*settle, alight, land, drop, arrive, issue, eventuate, end, terminate, debouch, disembogue*)

**staid**—grave, demure, steady, sober, sedate. (*unsteady, flighty, indiscreet, wanton, insedate, erratic, eccentric, agitated, discomposed, ruffled*)

**stammer**—stutter, hesitate, falter. (*speak clearly, speak unhesitatingly*)

**stamp**—genus, kind, description, make, mark, impression, imprint, print, brand, cast, mold, character, type. (*heterogeneity, nondescription, formlessness*)

**stand**—rest, remain, stop, be, exist, keep one's ground, insist, depend, await, consist, hold, continue, endure, pause, halt. (*progress, move, proceed, advance, fall, fail, yield, succumb, drop, lie, vanish, fade, run, depart*)

**standard**—measure, gauge, criterion, test, rule, exemplar, banner, flag, type, model, scale, plummet, touchstone. (*mismeasurement, misrule, misadjustment, miscomparison, inconformity, misfit, incommensurateness, noncriterion*)

**state**—*n.* position, condition, situation, circumstances, plight, predicament, case, province.

**state**—*v.* say, declare, propound, aver, set forth, narrate, specify, avow, recite. (*suppress, repress, suppose, imply, deny, contradict, retract*)

**stately**—dignified, imposing, lofty, elevated, lordly, proud, majestic, pompous, magnificent, grand. (*undignified, unimposing, unstately, commonplace, mean*)

**stay**—hold, stop, restrain, withhold, arrest, hinder, delay, obstruct, support, rest, repose, remain, continue, dwell, await, halt, abide, wait, tarry, confide, trust, lean. (*loose, liberate, send, expedite, speed, free, accelerate, hasten, oppress, depress, burden, fail, fall, proceed, move, depart, overthrow, mistrust*)

**steady**—firm, fixed, constant, uniform, consistent, equable, regular, undeviating, well-regulated. (*infirm, variable, unsteady, inconstant, changeable, wavering, ill-regulated*)

**step**—advance, pace, space, grade, remove, degree, gradation, progression, track, trace, vestige, walk, gait, proceeding, action, measure. (*retreat, recession, halting, station, standing, nongraduation, nonprogression, standstill, stop, tracklessness, untraceableness, nonimpression, desinence, desistance, inaction*)

**stern**—severe, austere, rigid, harsh, strict, rigorous, unrelenting, unyielding, forbidding. (*lenient, genial, kindly, easy, flexible, encouraging*)

**stiff**—unbending, inflexible, rigid, unyielding, unpliant, strong, stubborn, obstinate, pertinacious, constrained, affected, starched, formal, ceremonious, difficult. (*pliant, flexible, flaccid, yielding, easy, unaffected, genial, affable, unceremonious*)

**still**—quiet, calm, noiseless, hushed, silent, pacific, serene, motionless, stagnant, peaceful, quiescent, tranquil, stationary. (*unquiet, disturbed, agitated, moved, noisy, resonant, turbulent, moving, transitional*)

**stingy**—close, avaricious, mean, niggardly, close-fisted, hidebound, parsimonious, sparing, sordid, penurious. (*liberal, generous, large, handsome, lavish, bountiful, unsparing*)

**stop**—close, obstruct, plug, cork, bar, seal, arrest, suspend, end, rest, halt, hinder, suppress, delay, cease, terminate. (*open, expedite, clear, broach, unseal, promote, advance, further, continue, proceed, speed, hasten*)

**stout**—strong, lusty, vigorous, robust, sturdy, brawny, corpulent, resolute, brave, valiant, redoubtable. (*weak, debile, frail, attenuated, thin, slender, lean, irresolute, feeble, cowardly, timid*)

**straight**—direct, rectilinear, undeviating, unswerving, right, nearest. (*indirect, winding, incurved, tortuous, sinuous, serpentine, circuitous, waving, crooked*)

**strange**—foreign, alien, exotic, unfamiliar, unusual, odd, irregular, abnormal, exceptional, surprising, wonderful, marvelous, astonishing, uncommon, peculiar. (*home, domestic, familiar, usual, ordinary, common, regular, customary, commonplace, unsurprising, universal, general*)

**strength**—force, vigor, power, security, validity, vehemence, intensity, hardness, soundness, nerve, fiber, sinew. (*weakness, imbecility, feebleness, insolidity, insecurity, invalidity, frailty, delicacy, softness, flimsiness, hollowness*)

**strenuous**—strong, resolute, determined, earnest, vigorous, ardent, bold, energetic, vehement. (*weak, irresolute, undetermined, unearnest, debile, feeble, emasculate*)

**strict**—close, exact, accurate, rigorous, severe, stringent, nice, precise. (*loose, inexact, inaccurate, lenient, mild, indulgent, lax*)

**striking**—impressive, affecting, admirable, wonderful, surprising.

**strong**—powerful, vigorous, solid, secure, fortified, forcible, impetuous, hale, hearty, brawny, sinewy, sound, robust, cogent, influential, zealous, potent, pungent, muscular, hardy, stanch, tenacious. (*powerless, weak, frail, insecure, defenseless, feeble, mild, calm, gentle, delicate, sickly, inefficacious, unsatisfactory, unconvincing, unimpressive, vapid, impotent, unavailing, lukewarm, debile, flaccid, nerveless, tender, moderate, indifferent*)

**stubborn**—tough, unbending, unyielding, hard, obstinate, intractable, obdurate, stiff, harsh, inflexible, headstrong, refractory, heady, contumacious, pigheaded. (*docile, tractable, manageable, pliant, pliable, malleable, flexible*)

**studious**—literary, diligent, desirous, attentive, careful, thoughtful, assiduous, reflective. (*unliterary, illiterate, idle, indulgent, careless, regardless, indifferent, inattentive, negligent, thoughtless*)

**stupid**—dull, senseless, stolid, doltish, besotted, insensate, obtuse, prosy, addlepated, dull-witted. (*quick, sharp, bright, sensible, sagacious, penetrating, clever*)

**subdue**—conquer, reduce, overpower, break, tame, quell, vanquish, master, subjugate. (*aggrandize, exalt, fortify, strengthen, empower, liberate, enfranchise*)

**subject**—subordinate, subservient, exposed, liable, prone, disposed, obnoxious, amenable. (*superior, independent, exempt, indisposed, unliable, unamenable*)

**submissive**—obedient, compliant, yielding, obsequious, humble, docile, modest, passive, acquiescent, subservient. (*disobedient, incompliant, unyielding, inobsequious, recalcitrant, refractory, proud, resistant, renitent, malcontent, recusant*)

**substantial**—existing, real, solid, true, corporeal, material, strong, stout, massive, bulky, tangible. (*imaginary, unreal, insubstantial, fictitious, suppositious, incorporeal, chimerical, visionary, immaterial, weak, frail, airy, disembodied, spiritual*)

**subtle**—sly, artful, cunning, insinuating, wily, astute, nice, discriminating, crafty, fine, shrewd, sophistical, jesuitical. (*open, frank, honest, artless, undiscriminating, rough, blunt, undiscerning, unsophisticated, simple*)

**success**—achievement, luck, consummation, prosperity, victory, good fortune. (*failure, defeat, disaster, ruin*)

**succession**—following, supervention, consecutive, sequence, order, series, rotation, continuity, supply, suite. (*precedence, anticipation, prevention, antecedence, irregularity, disorder, nonsequence, solution, failure, intermission, break, gap, inconsecutiveness*)

**suffer**—bear, endure, sustain, undergo, let, permit, allow, admit, tolerate, experience, support. (*resist, repel, expel, reject, disallow, repudiate, forbid, ignore*)

**sufficient**—adequate, equal, competent, satisfactory, fit, qualified, adapted, suited, enough, ample. (*inadequate, unequal, incompetent, unqualified, unadapted, insufficient, unsuited, meager, bare, scanty, short, deficient*)

**suit**—fit, adapt, match, adjust, harmonize, apportion, befit, beseem, tally, correspond, answer, comport, please, serve, agree, become, accord. (*misfit, misadapt, mismatch, misapportion, unbeseem, vary, differ, disagree, miscomport*)

**summary**—analysis, tabulation, abridgment, résumé, compendium, digest, epitome, abstract. (*dilatation, expansion, dilution*)

**superb**—grand, magnificent, elegant, princely, splendid, showy, proud, august, stately, gorgeous. (*mean, common, commonplace, unimposing, shabby*)

**supercilious**—haughty, contemptuous, disdainful, arrogant, insolent. (*affable, courteous, respectful, modest, bashful*)

**superficial**—light, slight, imperfect, showy, external, flimsy, surface, shallow, smattering, skin-deep. (*deep, profound, abstruse, recondite, accurate, exact, deep-seated*)

**superior**—higher, upper, better, preferable, surpassing, loftier, excellent, remarkable, eminent, conspicuous. (*inferior, lower, worse, subordinate, ordinary, common, unremarkable, average, mean, mediocre*)

**supple**—pliant, bending, yielding, flexible, elastic, servile, fawning, cringing, adulatory, sycophantic, lithe, limber, compliant. (*firm, unbending, unyielding, stiff, stubborn, inflexible, inelastic, independent, self-assertive, supercilious*)

**supply**—furnish, afford, provide, accouter, give, minister, yield, contribute. (*expend, use, consume, waste, exhaust, absorb, demand, withhold, withdraw, retain*)

**support**—*n.* prop, stay, foundation, buttress, help, aid, assistance, influence, maintenance, living, patronage, subsistence, livelihood, food.

**support**—*v.* bear, uphold, sustain, underlie, befriend, assist, second, promote, further, suffer, defend, foster, nurture, nourish, cherish, endorse, maintain, continue, countenance, patronize, subsidize, help, back, stay, favor, prop. (*drop, betray, surrender, abandon, discontinue, oppose, discourage, weaken, exhaust, thwart, discountenance, disfavor, subvert, suppress*)

**suppose**—assume, presume, believe, divine, deem, fancy, think, regard, conceive, imagine, imply, presuppose, conjecture, guess, conclude, judge, consider. (*prove, demonstrate, substantiate, realize, disbelieve, negative, deny*)

**sure**—certain, secure, safe, assured, unmistakable, stable, firm, knowing, believing, confident, trusting, unquestioning, positive, unfailing, strong, permanent, abiding, enduring, infallible, indisputable, fast. (*uncertain, ignorant, dubious, doubtful, hesitating, distrustful, questioning, vacillating, weak, untrustworthy, precarious, insecure, impermanent, transient, evanescent, fallible, disputable, loose*)

**susceptible**—capable, impressible, tender, sensitive. (*incapable, unimpressible, insensitive, insusceptible, impassible*)

**suspense**—protraction, uncertainty, doubt, solicitude, cessation, pause, waiting, intermission, discontinuance, abeyance, stoppage, indetermination, incertitude, indecision. (*determination, settlement, execution, continuance, uninterruption, revival, decision, finality*)

**sway**—*n.* wield, influence, rule, authority, government, superiority, bias, dominion, control, preponderance, domination, supremacy, mastery, ascendancy, weight, force, power. (*weakness, inferiority, subordination, irresistance, obedience, subservience, subjection*)

**sway**—*v.* influence, govern, rule, bias, wave, swing, wield

**sweet**—saccharine, luscious, fragrant, dulcet, melodious, harmonious, musical, beautiful, lovely, wholesome, pleasing, pure, mild, winning, agreeable, fresh, gentle, amiable. (*sour, bitter, unsweet, fetid, offensive, nauseous, olid, stinking, nasty, inharmonious, discordant, unlovely, repulsive, unwholesome, putrid, tainted, ungentle, unamiable*)

**swell**—dilate, extend, enlarge, heighten, heave, enhance, rise, expand, increase, augment, protuberate, aggravate, amplify, distend. (*contract, curtail, shrivel, diminish, lessen, retrench, reduce, collapse, fold, narrow, condense, concentrate*)

**sympathy**—fellow feeling, congeniality, commiseration, compassion, pity, concert, tenderness, agreement, condolence. (*antipathy, antagonism, incongeniality, pitilessness, mercilessness, compassionlessness, unkindness, harshness, unkindliness*)

**system**—method, scheme, order, regularity, classification, arrangement, rule, plan. (*disorder, derangement, confusion, fortuity, chance, medley, haphazard, incongruity, nonarrangement, nonclassification*)

## T

**take**—seize, grasp, catch, capture, siege, use, obtain, pursue, employ, follow, assume, procure, captivate, engage, interest, charm, choose, select, admit, accept, receive, conduct, transfer. (*drop, reject, abandon, surrender, lose, miss, repel*)

**tall**—high, lofty, towering, elevated. (*low*)

**tame**—domesticated, reclaimed, tamed, subjugated, broken, gentle, mild, docile, meek, spiritless, tedious, dull, flat. (*undomesticated, unreclaimed, untamed, unbroken, savage, wild, fierce, spirited, animated, ferine, interesting, exciting, stirring, lively*)

**task**—work, function, labor, job, operation, business, undertaking, drudgery, toil, lesson. (*relaxation, leisure, amusement, hobby*)

**taste**—gustation, savor, flavor, sapidity, relish, perception, judgment, discernment, nicety, critique, sensibility, choice, zest, predilection, delicacy, elegancy, refinement. (*nongustation, illsavor, insipidity, disrelish, nonpreception, indiscrimination, indiscernment, indelicacy, coarseness, inelegancy*)

**tasteful**—sapid, relishing, savory, agreeable, tasty, toothsome, palatable, elegant, refined. (*insipid, unrelishing, unsavory, unpalatable, nauseous, inelegant, tasteless, unrefined, vapid*)

**teach**—impart, tell, direct, instruct, inform, counsel, admonish, educate, inculcate, enlighten, advise, indoctrinate, train. (*withhold, misteach, misdirect, misinstruct, misinform, misguide, mislead*)

**teacher**—instructor, schoolmaster, preceptor, tutor, professor, pedagogue, educationist, educator, schoolmistress. (*pupil, scholar, disciple, learner*)

**tedious**—wearisome, tiresome, monotonous, dilatory, dreary, sluggish, irksome, dull, flat, prolix. (*interesting, exciting, stirring, charming, fascinating, delightful, amusing*)

**tell**—mention, number, enumerate, count, recount, utter, recite, state, narrate, disclose, publish, betray, divulge, promulgate, acquaint, teach, inform, explain, communicate, report, rehearse, discern, judge, discriminate, ascertain, decide, describe. (*repress, suppress, misrecount, misnarrate, miscommunicate, misdeclare, misrecite, misjudge, misdescribe*)

**temporary**—present, immediate, partial, limited, transient, impermanent. (*perpetual, lasting, confirmed, complete, final, perfect, permanent, entire*)

**tendency**—vergency, proneness, bias, gravitation, drift, scope, aim, disposition, predisposition, proclivity, leaning, inclination, attraction, conduciveness, course. (*disinclination, aversion, repulsion, contravention, deviation, divergency, tangency, divarication, opposition, renitency, reluctance, prevention, neutralization, termination*)

**tender**—*v.* offer, proffer, propose, bid, produce, present. (*withhold, withdraw, retain, appropriate*)

**tender**—*a.* delicate, frail, impressible, susceptible, yielding, soft, effeminate, weak, feeble, compassionate, affectionate, careful, jealous, gentle, mild, meek, pitiful, merciful, pathetic. (*strong, sturdy, hardy, robust, tough, iron, pitiless, unmerciful, cruel, hard-hearted, careless, liberal, lavish, unchary, ungentle, rough, rude, coarse, unsentimental, unmoving, unfeeling, unimpressive, unimpassioned, unimpressed, vigorous, tenacious*)

**term**—limit, boundary, condition, time, season, period, expression, designation, word, name, article, proviso, stipulation.

**terrible**—awful, fearful, dreadful, formidable, terrific, frightful, tremendous, horrible, shocking. (*unimpressive, not startling or astonishing*)

**terror**—fear, dread, alarm, fright, consternation, horror, dismay. (*confidence, fearlessness, boldness, reassurance*)

**test**—cupel, trial, examination, proof, criterion, standard, experiment, touchstone, experience, ordeal. (*misindication, misjudgment, misproof*)

**testimony**—witness, evidence, attestation, affirmation, corroboration, confirmation, proof. (*refutation, contradiction, disproof, confutation, contravention, invalidation*)

**theatrical**—dramatic, scenic, melodramatic, showy, ceremonious, gesticulatory, pompous, meretricious, tinsel. (*chaste, genuine, simple, unaffected, quiet, subdued, mannerless, plain*)

**thick**—dense, condensed, inspissated, close, compact, turbid, luteous, coagulated, muddy, dull, misty, foggy, vaporous, crowded, numerous, solid, bulky, deep, confused, inarticulate. (*race, fine, thin, sparse, strained, pure, percolated, limpid, crystalline, scanty, incompact, slight, shallow, laminated, clear, articulate, distinct*)

**thicken**—condense, inspissate, incrassate, compact, solidify, befoul, obscure, bemire, becloud, increase, coagulate, amalgamate, commingle, intermix, crowd, multiply, enlarge, expand, extend, broaden, deepen, obstruct, confuse. (*rarify, dissipate, refine, attenuate, clear, purify, strain, percolate, clarify, defecate, depurate, brighten, lighten, open, filtrate, diminish, separate, reduce, narrow, contract, liberate, free, extricate, unravel, disentangle, loosen*)

**thin**—slim, slender, flimsy, attenuated, diluted, watery, meager, unsubstantial, lean.

**think**—ponder, meditate, consider, reflect, contemplate, conceive, imagine, apprehend, fancy, hold, regard, believe, deem, opine, purpose, judge, reckon.

**thought**—reflection, reasoning, cogitation, supposition, view, sentiment, meditation, conception, idea, opinion, judgment, conceit, fancy, design, purpose, intention, deliberation, care, provision. (*vacuity, incogitation, thoughtlessness, dream, hallucination, aberration, misconception, incogitancy, carelessness, improvidence, unreflectiveness*)

**threatening**—menacing, intimidating, minatory, comminatory, minacious, foreboding, unpromising, imminent, impending. (*encouraging, promising, reassuring, enticing, passed, overpast, withdrawn*)

**tide**—flow, course, current, rush, inundation, influx, stream, movement, flood. (*stagnation, arrestation, stoppage, cessation, motionlessness, subsidence*)

**tight**—firm, compact, fast, close, tidy, neat, smart, natty, tense, stretched. (*loose, incompact, open, flowing, loose-fitting, large, untidy, lax, relaxed*)

**time**—period, duration, season, interval, date, opportunity, age, era, occasion, term, space, span, spell. (*neverness, eternity, nonduration, indetermination, indeterminableness*)

**timid**—fearful, pusillanimous, shy, diffident, coy, timorous, afraid, cowardly, fainthearted, inadventurous. (*bold, confident, venturesome, courageous, overventuresome, rash, audacious*)

**tint**—color, hue, tinge, dye, complexion. (*achromatism, decoloration, paleness, pallor, bleaching, etiolation, colorlessness, sallowness, wanness, cadaverousness, exsanguineousness*)

**title**—inscription, heading, denomination, style, designation, appellation, distinction, address, epithet, name. (*nondesignation, indistinction, nondescript, namelessness, indenomination*)

**together**—unitedly, conjointly, contemporaneously, concertedly, simultaneously, coincidently, concomitantly, concurrently. (*separately, disconnectedly, independently, variously, incoincident, inconcurrently*)

**tolerable**—endurable, bearable, supportable, sufferable, allowable, permissible, sufficient, passable. (*unendurable, unbearable, insupportable, insufferable, unallowable, impermissible, insufficient, intolerable*)

**tongue**—discourse, speech, language, dialect idiom.

**tool**—utensil, implement, machine, instrument, dupe, cat's-paw, hireling.

**topic**—question, theme, subject, subject matter.

**tough**—resistant, stubborn, lentous, fibrous, difficult, refractory, hard, unmanageable, tenacious, firm, strong. (*yielding, tender, soft, brittle, fragile, frangible, friable*)

**tragedy**—disaster, calamity, affliction, adversity, catastrophe, grief. (*joy, delight, boon, prosperity, comedy*)

**train**—*n.* suite, procession, retinue, cortege, course, series.

**train**—*v.* lead, rear, accustom, habituate, inure, drill, exercise, practice, discipline, instruct, bend, educate. (*force, break, trail, disaccustom, dishabituate, miseducate, disqualify*)

**transfer**—convey, transport, remove, sell, assign, remand, make over, transplant, give, alienate, translate, transmit, forward, exchange. (*retain, withhold, fix, appropriate, keep*)

**transient**—fleeting, fugitive, transitory, temporary, passing, evanescent, ephemeral, momentary, brief. (*abiding, permanent, perpetual, persistent, lasting, enduring*)

**transparent**—pellucid, crystalline, translucent, limpid, diaphanous, obvious, clear, indisputable, self-evident. (*thick, turbid, opaque, intransparent, mysterious, dubious, questionable*)

**travel**—journey, wandering, migration, pilgrimage, excursion, tramp, expedition, trip, ramble, voyage, tour, peregrination. (*rest, settlement, domestication*)

**treatise**—tract, essay, paper, pamphlet, disquisition, brochure, dissertation, monograph, article. (*jottings, notes, adversaria, memoranda, effusion, ephemera*)

**treaty**—contract, agreement, league, covenant, alliance, negotiation, convention. (*neutrality, noninterference, nonalliance, nonagreement, nonconvention*)

**tremble**—shake, quake, quiver, totter, shiver) shudder, vibrate, jar. (*stand, steady, settle, still, calm,*

**tremendous**—terrible, dreadful, awful, fearful, appalling. (*unimposing, unappalling, inconsiderable*)

**trial**—test, gauge, experiment, temptation, trouble, affliction, grief, burden, suffering, attempt, endeavor, proof, essay, criterion, ordeal, tribulation, verification. (*nontrial, nonprobation, mismeasurement, miscalculation, misestimate, trifle, triviality, alleviation, relief, disburdenment, refreshment, nonattempt, pretermission, oversight, disregard, nonverification*)

**trick**—artifice, contrivance, machination, guile, stratagem, wile, fraud, cheat, juggle, antic, vagary, finesse, sleight, deception, imposition, delusion, legerdemain. (*blunder, exposure, bungling, mishap, botch, fumbling, inexpertness, maladroitness, genuineness, openhandedness, artlessness*)

**trifle**—bauble, bagatelle, toy, straw, nothing, triviality, levity, joke, cipher, bubble, gewgaw, kickshaw, rush. (*treasure, portent, phenomenon, crisis, conjuncture, importance, urgency, weight, necessity, seriousness*)

**triumph**—victory, success, ovation, achievement, conquest, exultation, trophy. (*defeat, discomfiture, failure, unsuccess, abortion, baffling, disappointment*)

**trivial**—trifling, trite, common, unimportant, useless, nugatory, paltry, inconsiderable. (*important, weighty, critical, original, novel*)

**trouble**—*v.* disturb, vex, agitate, confuse, perplex, distress, annoy, harass, tease, molest, grieve, mortify, oppress. (*compose, calm, allay, appease, please, soothe, delight, gratify, recreate, entertain, relieve, refresh*)

**trouble**—*n.* affliction, disturbance, annoyance, perplexity, molestation, vexation, inconvenience, calamity, distress, uneasiness, tribulation, disaster, torment, misfortune, adversity, anxiety, embarrassment, sorrow, misery, grief, depression, difficulty, labor, toil, effort. (*alleviation, composure, pleasure, appeasement, delight, assuagement, happiness, gratification, boon, blessing, exultation, joy, gladness, ease, facility, luck, recreation, amusement, carelessness, indifference, indolence, inertia, indiligence*)

**troublesome**—tiresome, irksome, difficult, tedious, arduous, laborious, grievous, importunate, vexatious. (*easy, pleasant, amusing, facile, light, unlaborious, untroublesome*)

**true**—veritable, veracious, exact, precise, accurate, faithful, actual, loyal, genuine, pure, real. (*fictitious, unreliable, unhistorical, untrustworthy, inveracious, false, inaccurate, unfaithful, faithless, fickle, treacherous, erroneous, spurious, perfidious, counterfeit, adulterated*)

**trust**—*v.* confide, rely, credit, believe, charge, deposit, entrust, repose, hope. (*distrust, suspect, discredit, doubt, disbelieve, withdraw, despair*)

**trust**—*n.* faith, confidence, reliance, belief, hope, expectation, credit, duty, commission, charge.

**try**—attempt, endeavor, strive, aim, examine, test, sound, gauge, probe, fathom. (*ignore, pretermit, reject, abandon, discard, misexamine, misinvestigate*)

**turn**—*n.* revolution, rotation, recurrence, change, alteration, vicissitude, winding, bend, deflection, curve, alternation, opportunity, occasion, time, deed, office, act, treatment, purpose, requirement, convenience, talent, gift, tendency, character, exigence, crisis, form, cast, shape, manner, mold, fashion, cut. (*stability, fixity, immobility, stationariness, unchangeableness, uniformity, rectilinearity, indeflection, continuity, untimeliness, incognizance, oversight, independence, nonrequirement, malformation, shapelessness*)

**turn**—*v.* round, shape, mold, adapt, spin, reverse, deflect, alter, transform, convert, metamorphose, revolve, rotate, hinge, depend, deviate, incline, diverge, decline, change. (*misshape, perpetuate, stabilitate, stereotype, fix, arrest, continue, proceed*)

**turncoat**—trimmer, deserter, renegade.

**tutor**—guardian, governor, instructor, teacher, preceptor, professor, master, savant. (*ward, pupil, scholar, student, disciple, learner, tyro*)

**twine**—twist, wind, embrace, entwine, wreath, bind, unite, braid, bend, meander. (*untwist, unwind, separate, disunite, detach, unwreath, unravel, disentwine, continue, straighten*)

**twist**—contort, convolve, complicate, pervert, distort, wrest, wreath, wind, encircle, form, weave, insinuate, unite, interpenetrate. (*straighten, untwist, rectify, verify, represent, reflect, render, preserve, express, substantiate, unwreath, unwind, detach, disengage, separate, disunite, disentangle, disincorporate, unravel*)

**type**—mark, stamp, emblem, kind, character, sign, symbol, pattern, archetype, form, model, idea, image, likeness, expression, cast, mold, fashion. (*nondescription, nonclassification, inexpression, misrepresentation, misindication, falsification, abnormity, deviation, caricature, monstrosity*)

## U

**ugly**—loathesome, hideous, hateful, frightful, uncouth, ill-favored, unsightly, ill-looking, plain, homely, deformed, monstrous, ungainly. (*attractive, fair, seemly, shapely, beautiful, handsome*)

**ultimate**—last, final, extreme, conclusive, remotest, farthest. (*prior, intermediate, proximate, preliminary*)

**unanimous**—of one mind, agreeing, like-minded. (*discordant, disagreeing*)

**unanswerable**—unquestionable, indisputable, undeniable, incontrovertible.

**uncertain**—doubtful, dubious, questionable, fitful, equivocal, ambiguous, indistinct, variable, fluctuating.

**undeniable**—incontestable, indisputable, unquestionable, incontrovertible.

**undergo**—bear, suffer, endure, sustain, experience. (*evade, shun, elude*)

**underhand**—clandestine, furtive, dishonest, unfair, fraudulent, surreptitious. (*openhanded, straightforward, fair, honest, undisguised*)

**understand**—apprehend, comprehend, know, perceive, discern, conceive, learn, recognize, interpret, imply. (*misapprehend, miscomprehend, ignore, misinterpret, declare, state, enunciate, express*)

**understanding**—knowledge, discernment, interpretation, construction, agreement, intellect, intelligence, mind, sense, conception, reason, brains, (*ignorance, misapprehension, misunderstanding, misinterpretation, misconstruction, mindlessness, irrationality*)

**unfit**—*a.* improper, unsuitable, inconsistent, untimely, incompetent.

**unfit**—*v.* disable, incapacitate, disqualify, render unfit.

**unfortunate**—calamitous, ill-fated, unlucky, wretched, unhappy, miserable.

**uniform**—unvarying, invariable, conformable, homogeneous, consistent, equal, even, alike, unvaried, regular, symmetrical, equable. (*varying, variable, inconformable, incongruous, diverse, heterogeneous, inconsistent, irregular, unsymmetrical, multifarious, multigenous, polymorphic, bizarre, eccentric, erratic*)

**union**—junction, coalition, combination, agreement, harmony, conjunction, concert, league, connection, alliance, confederacy, concord, confederation, consolidation. (*disjunction, separation, severance, divorce, disagreement, discord, disharmony, secession, disruption, multiplication, diversification, division*)

**unit**—ace, item, part, individual. (*total, aggregate, collection, sum, mass*)

**unite**—join, combine, link, attach, amalgamate, associate, coalesce, embody, merge, be mixed, conjoin, connect, couple, add, incorporate with, cohere, concatenate, integrate, converge. (*disjoin, sever, dissociate, separate, disamalgamate, resolve, disconnect, disintegrate, disunite, disrupt, divide, multiply, part, sunder, diverge*)

**unity**—oneness, singleness, individuality, concord, conjunction, agreement, uniformity, indivisibility. (*plurality, multitude, complexity, multiplicity, discord, disjunction, separation, severance, variety, heterogeneity, diversity, incongruity, divisibility*)

**universal**—all-embracing, total, unlimited, boundless, comprehensive, entire, general, whole, exhaustive, complete. (*partial, local, limited, incomplete, exclusive, particular, inexhaustive, exceptional, narrow, special, only*)

**unreasonable**—foolish, silly, absurd, preposterous, immoderate, exorbitant, ridiculous.

**upright**—vertical, erect, perpendicular, honest, honorable, pure, principled, conscientious, just, fair, equitable. (*inverted, inclined, dishonest, dishonorable, corrupt, unprincipled, unconscientious*)

**urge**—press, push, drive, impel, propel, force, importune, solicit, animate, incite, instigate, stimulate, hasten, expedite, accelerate, dispatch. (*repress, hold, retain, inhibit, coerce, restrain, cohibit,* *hinder, retard, discourage, damp, obstruct)*

**urgent**—pressing, imperative, immediate, importunate, forcible, strenuous, serious, grave, momentous, indeferrable. *(unimportant, insignificant, trifling, trivial, deferrable)*

**use**—*n.* advantage, custom, habit, practice, service, utility, usage.

**use**—*v.* employ, exercise, treat, practice, accustom, habituate, inure. *(discard, suspend, ignore, avoid, dishabituate, disinure)*

**useful**—advantageous, profitable, helpful, serviceable, beneficial, available, adapted, suited, conducive. *(disadvantageous, unprofitable, obstructive, retardative, preventative, antagonistic, hostile, cumbersome, burdensome, unbeneficial, unavailable, inconducive, useless, fruitless, ineffectual)*

**usual**—common, customary, ordinary, normal, regular, habitual, wonted, accustomed, general. *(uncommon, rare, exceptional, uncustomary, extraordinary, abnormal, irregular, unusual)*

**utter**—*a.* extreme, perfect, complete, unqualified, absolute, thorough, consummate, entire, sheer, pure. *(imperfect, incomplete, impure)*

**utter**—*v.* circulate, issue, promulgate, express, articulate, pronounce, speak. *(recall, suppress, repress, hush, stifle, check, swallow)*

**utterly**—totally, completely, wholly, quite, altogether, entirely.

## V

**vacant**—empty, leisure, unemployed, unencumbered, unoccupied, void, unfilled, mindless, exhausted. *(full, replenished, business, employed, engaged, occupied, filled, thoughtful)*

**vague**—general, lax, indefinite, undetermined, popular, intangible, equivocal, unsettled, uncertain, ill-defined, pointless. *(strict, definite, determined, limited, scientific, pointed, specific)*

**vain**—empty, worthless, fruitless, unsatisfying, unavailing, idle, ineffectual, egotistic, showy, unreal, conceited, arrogant. *(solid, substantial, sound, worthy, efficient, effectual, cogent, potent, unconceited, modest, real)*

**valid**—strong, powerful, cogent, weighty, sound, substantial, available, efficient, sufficient, operative, conclusive. *(weak, invalid, powerless, unsound, unsubstantial, unavailable, inefficient, insufficient, inoperative, obsolete, effete, superseded, inconclusive)*

**value**—appreciate, compute, rate, estimate, esteem, treasure, appraise, prize. *(miscompute, misestimate, disesteem, disregard, vilipend, underrate)*

**vanity**—emptiness, unsubstantiality, unreality, falsity, conceit, self-sufficiency, ostentation, pride, worthlessness, triviality. *(substance, solidity, substantiality, reality, truth, modesty, self-distrust, simplicity, unostentatiousness, humility)*

**variable**—changeable, mutable, fickle, capricious, wavering, unsteady, inconstant, shifting. *(unchanging, unchangeable, immutable, constant, firm)*

**variation**—deviation, alteration, mutation, diversity, departure, change, abnormity, exception, discrepancy. *(continuance, fixity, indivergency)*

**variety**—difference, diversity, medley, miscellany, multiplicity, multiformity, abnormity. *(uniformity, species, type, specimen)*

**various**—different, diverse, multiform, multitudinous, several, sundry, uncertain, manifold, diversified. *(one, same, identical, uniform, few)*

**vast**—waste, wild, desolate, extensive, spacious, widespread, gigantic, wide, boundless, measureless, enormous, mighty, huge, immense, colossal, prodigious, far-reaching. *(narrow, close, confined, frequented, populated, cultivated, tended, tilled, limited)*

**vehement**—violent, impetuous, ardent, burning, fervent, raging, furious, passionate, fervid, urgent, forcible, eager. *(mild, feeble, inanimate, subdued*

**vengeance**—retribution, retaliation, revenge. *(forgiveness, pardon, condonation, amnesty, grace, remission, absolution, oblivion, indulgence, reprieve)*

**venture**—speculation, risk, chance, hazard, stake, undertaking, luck experiment, throw. *(nonspeculation, caution, reservation, calculation, certainty, law)*

**veracity**—truth, truthfulness, credibility, exactness, accuracy.

**verdict**—finding, judgment, answer, opinion, decision, sentence. *(nondeclaration, indecision, indetermination)*

**verge**—tend, bend, slope, incline, approach, approximate, trend, bear. *(decline, deviate, revert, depart, recede, return, back, retrocede)*

**verify**—establish, confirm, fulfill, authenticate, substantiate, identify, realize, test, warrant, demonstrate. *(disestablish, subvert, fail, falsify, mistake)*

**versed**—skilled, practiced, conversant, acquainted, initiated, indoctrinated, clever, familiar, thoroughly acquainted, proficient. *(unskilled, ill-versed, unpracticed, inconversant, unfamiliar, uninitiated, ignorant, awkward, strange, unversed, untaught)*

**vex**—tease, irritate, provoke, plague, torment, tantalize, bother, worry, pester, trouble, disquiet, afflict, harass, annoy. *(soothe, appease, gratify, quiet)*

**vice**—corruption, fault, defect, evil, crime, immorality, sin, badness. *(purity, faultlessness, perfection, virtue, immaculateness, goodness, soundness)*

**vicious**—corrupt, faulty, defective, bad, morbid, peccant, debased, profligate, unruly, impure, depraved. *(pure, sound, perfect, virtuous, healthy)*

**victory**—conquest, triumph, ovation, success. *(failure, defeat, frustration, disappointment, abortion)*

**view**—*v.* behold, examine, inspect, explore, survey, consider, contemplate, reconnoiter, observe, regard, estimate, judge. *(ignore, overlook, disregard)*

**view**—*n.* sight, vision, survey, examination, inspection, judgment, estimate, scene, representation, apprehension, sentiment, conception, opinion, object, aim, intention, purpose, design, end, light, aspect. *(blindness, occultation, obscuration, darkness)*

**vile**—cheap, worthless, valueless, low, base, mean, despicable, hateful, bad, impure, vicious, abandoned, abject, sinful, sordid, ignoble, wicked, villainous, degraded, wretched. *(costly, rare, precious, valuable, high, exalted, noble, honorable, lofty)*

**villain**—scoundrel, ruffian, wretch.

**villainous**—base, knavish, depraved, infamous.

**vindicate**—assert, maintain, uphold, clear, support, defend, claim, substantiate, justify, establish. *(waive, abandon, surrender, forgo, disprove, disestablish, neutralize, nullify, destroy, subvert, annul)*

**violate**—ravish, injure, abuse, disturb, hurt, rape, outrage, debauch, break, infringe, profane, transgress, disobey. *(respect, foster, observe, regard)*

**violence**—vehemence, impetuosity, force, rape, outrage, rage, profanation, injustice, fury, infringement, fierceness, oppression. *(lenity, mildness, self-restraint, feebleness, gentleness, respect, forbearance)*

**virtue**—power, capacity, strength, force, efficacy, excellence, value, morality, goodness, uprightness, purity, chastity, salubrity. *(weakness, incapacity)*

**visible**—perceptible, apparent, clear, plain, obvious, conspicuous, observable, discernible, palpable, manifest, distinguishable, evident. *(imperceptible)*

**visionary**—fanciful, dreamy, chimerical, baseless, shadowy, imaginary, unreal, fabulous, romantic. *(actual, real, truthful, sound, substantial, palpable)*

**vivid**—bright, brilliant, luminous, resplendent, lustrous, radiant, graphic, clear, lively, animated, stirring, striking, glowing, sunny, bright, scintillant. *(dull, opaque, nonluminous, obscure, rayless, lurid)*

**volume**—size, body, bulk, dimensions, book, work, tome, capacity, magnitude, compass, quantity. *(diminutiveness, tenuity, minuteness, smallness)*

**voluntary**—deliberate, spontaneous, free, intentional, optional, discretional, unconstrained, willing. *(compulsory, coercive, necessitated, involuntary)*

**volunteer**—offer, proffer, tend, originate. *(withhold, refuse, suppress)*

**voluptuous**—sensual, luxurious, self-indulgent, licentious, highly pleasant. *(unsensual, abstinent)*

**vulgar**—popular, general, loose, ordinary, public, vernacular, plebeian, uncultivated, unrefined, low, mean, coarse, underbred. *(strict, scientific, philosophical, restricted, technical, accurate, patrician, se-*

*lect, choice, cultivated, refined, polite, high-bred, stylish, aristocratic)*

## W

**wages**—remuneration, hire, compensation, stipend, salary, allowance. (*gratuity, douceur, premium, bonus, grace)*

**wander**—ramble, range, stroll, rove, expatiate, roam, deviate, stray, depart, err, swerve, straggle, saunter, navigate, circumnavigate, travel. (*rest, stop, perch, bivouac, halt, lie, anchor, alight, settle)*

**want**—deficiency, lack, failure, insufficiency, scantiness, shortness, omission, neglect, nonproduction, absence. (*supply, sufficiency, provision)*

**wanton**—wandering, roving, sportive, playful, frolicsome, loose, unbridled, uncurbed, reckless, unrestrained, irregular, licentious, dissolute, inconsiderate, heedless, gratuitous. (*stationary, unroving, unsportive, unplayful, unfrolicsome, joyless, thoughtful, demure, sedate, discreet, staid, self-controlled)*

**warm**—blood-warm, thermal, genial, irascible, hot, ardent, affectionate, fervid, fiery, glowing, enthusiastic, zealous, eager, excited, interested, animated. (*frigid, cold, tepid, starved, indifferent)*

**warmth**—ardor, glow, fervor, zeal, heat, excitement, intensity, earnestness, cordiality, animation, eagerness, vehemence, geniality, sincerity, passion, irascibility, emotion, life. (*frigidity, frost, congelation, iciness, coldness, calmness, coolness, indifference, torpidity, insensitiveness, apathy, slowness, ungeniality, insincerity, passionlessness, hypocrisy)*

**waste**—ruin, destroy, devastate, impair, consume, squander, dissipate, throw away, diminish, lavish, desolate, pine, decay, attenuate, dwindle, shrivel, wither, wane. (*restore, repair, conserve, preserve, perpetuate, protect, husband, economize, utilize, hoard, treasure, enrich)*

**watchful**—vigilant, expectant, wakeful, heedful, careful, observant, attentive, circumspect, wary, cautious. (*unwatchful, invigilant, unwakeful, slumbrous, drowsy, heedless, careless, inobservant, inattentive, uncircumspect, unwary, incautious, distracted)*

**weak**—feeble, infirm, enfeebled, powerless, debile, fragile, incompact, inadhesive, pliant, frail, soft, tender, milk and water, flabby, flimsy, wishy-washy, destructible, watery, diluted, imbecile, inefficient, spiritless, foolish, injudicious, unsound, undecided, unconfirmed, impressible, wavering, ductile, easy, malleable, unconvincing, inconclusive, vapid, pointless. (*strong, vigorous, robust, muscular, nervous, powerful, sturdy, hard)*

**weaken**—debilitate, enfeeble, enervate, dilute, impair, paralyze, attenuate, sap. (*strengthen, invigorate, empower, corroborate, confirm)*

**wealth**—influence, riches, mammon, lucre, plenty, affluence, abundance, opulence. (*indigence, poverty, scarcity, impecuniosity)*

**wear**—carry, bear, exhibit, sport, consume, don, waste, impair, rub, channel, groove, excavate, hollow, diminish. (*doff, abandon, repair, renovate, renew, increase, swell, augment)*

**weary**—fatigued, tired, exhausted, worn, jaded, debilitated, spent, toil-worn, faint. (*fresh, vigorous, recruited, renovated, hearty)*

**weave**—interlace. braid. intertwine, intermix, plait, complicate, intersect. (*unravel, untwist, disunite, disentangle, extricate, simplify, enucleate)*

**weight**—gravity, ponderosity, heaviness, pressure, burden, importance, power, influence, efficacy, consequence, moment, impressiveness. (*lightness, levity, portableness, alleviation, unimportance, insignificance, weakness, inefficacy, unimpressiveness)*

**well**—rightly, thoroughly, properly, hale, sound, healthy, hearty. (*wrongly, imperfectly, improperly)*

**white**—colorless, pure, snowy, umblemished, unspotted, stainless, innocent, clear. (*black, impure)*

**whole**—total, entire, all, well, complete, sound, healthy, perfect, unimpaired, undiminished, integral, undivided, gross. (*partial, imperfect, incomplete, unsound, sick, impaired, diminished, fractional)*

**wholesome**—healthful, salubrious, salutary, salutiferous, beneficial, nutritious, healing. (*unhealthy, unhealthful, insalubrious, insalutary, prejudicial, unwholesome, deleterious, detrimental, morbific)*

**wicked**—evil, bad, godless, sinful, immoral, iniquitous, criminal, unjust, unrighteous, irreligious, profane, ungodly, vicious, atrocious, black, dark, foul, unhallowed, nefarious, naughty, heinous, flagitious, abandoned, corrupt. (*good, virtuous, just, moral, honest, pure)*

**wild**—untamed, undomesticated, uncultivated, uninhabited, desert, savage, uncivilized, unrefined, rude, ferocious, untrained, violent, ferine, loose, disorderly, turbulent, ungoverned, inordinate, disorderly, chimerical, visionary, incoherent, raving, distracted, haggard. (*tame, domesticated, cultivated coherent, mild, orderly, sane, calm)*

**willful**—purposed, deliberate, designed, intentional, prepense, premeditated, preconcerted, wayward, refractory, stubborn, self-willed, headstrong. (*undesigned, accidental, unintentional, unpremeditated, docile, obedient, amenable, manageable, deferential, considerate, thoughtful)*

**wisdom**—knowledge, erudition, learning, enlightenment, attainment, information, discernment, judgment, sagacity, prudence, light. (*ignorance, illiterateness, sciolism, indiscernment, injudiciousness, folly, imprudence, darkness, empiricism, smattering, inacquaintance)*

**wit**—mind, intellect, sense, reason, understanding, humor, ingenuity, imagination. (*mindlessness, senselessness, irrationality, dullness, stolidity, stupidity, inanity, doltishness, wash, vapidity, platitude)*

**withhold**—retain, keep, inhibit, cohibit, stay, restrain, refuse, stint, forbear, detain. (*grant, afford, furnish, provide, allow, permit, encourage, incite)*

**withstand**—oppose, resist, confront, thwart, face. (*yield, surrender, submit, acquiesce, countenance, support, encourage, aid, abet, back)*

**witness**—attestation, testimony, evidence, corroboration, cognizance, corroborator, eyewitness, spectator, auditor, testifier, voucher, earwitness. (*invalidation, incognizance, refutation, ignorance)*

**wonder**—amazement, astonishment, surprise, admiration, phenomenon, prodigy, portent, miracle, sign, marvel. (*inastonishment, indifference, apathy, unamazement, anticipation, expectation, familiarity, triviality)*

**wonderful**—amazing, astonishing, wondrous, admirable, strange, striking, surprising, awful, prodigious, portentous, marvelous, miraculous, supernatural, unprecedented, startling. (*unamazing, unastonishing, unsurprising, common, everyday, regular, normal, customary, usual, expected, anticipated, calculated, current, natural, unwonderful, unmarvelous)*

**word**—term, expression, message, account, tidings, order, vocable, signal, engagement, promise. (*idea, conception)*

**work**—exertion, effort, toil, labor, employment, performance, production, product, effect, result, composition, achievement, operation, issue, fruit, (*effortlessness, inertia, rest, inoperativeness, nonemployment, nonperformance, nonproduction, abortion, miscarriage, frustration, neutralization, fruitlessness)*

**worldly**—terrestrial, mundane, temporal, secular, earthly, carnal. (*heavenly, spiritual)*

**worry**—harass, irritate, tantalize, importune, vex, molest, annoy, tease, torment, disquiet, plague, fret. (*soothe, calm, gratify, please, amuse, quiet)*

**worth**—value, rate, estimate, cost, price, merit, desert, excellent, rate. (*inappreciableness, cheapness, worthlessness, demerit)*

**worthless**—cheap, vile, valueless, useless, base, contemptible, despicable, reprobate, vicious. (*costly, rich, rare, valuable, worthy, useful, honorable, estimable, excellent, noble, precious, admirable, virtuous)*

**wrench**—wrest, twist, distort, strain, extort, wring.

**wretched**—miserable, debased, humiliated, fallen, ruined, pitiable, mean, paltry, worthless, vile, despicable, contemptible, sorrowful, afflicted, melancholy, dejected. (*flourishing, prosperous,* *happy, unfallen, admirable, noble, honorable, worthy, valuable, enviable, joyous, felicitous, elated)*

**wrong**—unfit, unsuitable, improper, mistaken, incorrect, erroneous, unjust, illegal, inequitable, immoral, injurious, awry. (*fit, suitable, proper, correct, accurate, right, just, legal, equitable, fair, moral, beneficial, straight*)

Y

**yearn**—long, hanker, crave, covet, desire. (*loathe, revolt, recoil, shudder*)

**yet**—besides, nevertheless, notwithstanding, however, still, eventually, ultimately, at last, so far, thus far

**yield**—furnish, produce, afford, bear, render, relinquish, give in, let go, forgo, accede, acquiesce, resign, surrender, concede, allow, grant, submit, succumb, comply, consent, agree. (*withdraw, withhold, retain, deny, refuse, vindicate, assert, claim, disallow, appropiate, resist, dissent, protest, recalcitrate, struggle, strive*)

**yielding**—conceding, producing, surrendering, supple, pliant, submissive, accommodating, unresisting. (*firm, defiant, stiff, hard, unyielding, resisting, unfruitful*)

**yoke**—couple, conjoin, connect, link, enslave, subjugate. (*dissever, divorce, disconnect, liberate, release, manumit, enfranchise*)

**youth**—youngster, young, person, boy, lad, minority, adolescence, juvenility.

**youthful**—juvenile, young, early, fresh, childish, unripe, puerile, callow, immature, beardless. (*aged, senile, mature, decrepit, decayed, venerable, antiquated, superannuated*)

Z

**zeal**—ardor, interest, energy, eagerness, engagedness, heartiness, earnestness, fervor, enthusiasm. (*apathy, indifference, torpor, coldness, carelessness, sluggishness, incordiality*)

**zenith**—height, highest point, pinnacle, acme, summit, culmination, maximum. (*nadir, lowest point, depth, minimum*)

**zest**—flavor, appetizer, gusto, gust, pleasure, enjoyment, relish, sharpener, recommendation, enhancement. (*distaste, disrelish, detriment*)

# HOMONYMS

A

**able**, strong, skillful. **Abel**, a name.
**accidence**, rudiments. **accidents**, events.
**acclamation**, applause. **acclimation**, used to climate.
**acts**, deeds. **ax** or **axe**, a tool.
**ad**, advertisement. **add**, to increase.
**adds**, increases. **adze** or **adz**, a tool.
**adherence**, constancy. **adherents**, followers.
**ail**, pain, trouble. **ale**, a liquor.
**air**, atmosphere. **ere**, before. **heir**, inheritor.
**aisle**, passage. **isle**, island. **I'll**, I will.
**ait**, an island. **ate**, devoured. **eight**, a number.
**ale**, liquor. **ail**, pain, trouble.
**all**, everyone. **awl**, a tool.
**allegation**, affirmation. **allegation**, uniting.
**aloud**, with noise. **allowed**, permitted.
**altar**, for worship. **alter**, to change.
**amend**, to make better. **amende**, retraction.
**anker**, a measure. **anchor**, of a vessel.
**Ann**, a name. **an**, one.
**annalist**, historian. **analyst**, analyzer.
**annalize**, to record. **analyze**, to separate.
**ant**, insect. **aunt**, relative.
**ante**, before. **anti**, opposed to.
**arc**, part of a circle. **ark**, chest, boat.
**arrant**, bad. **errant**, wandering.
**ascent**, act of rising. **assent**, consent.
**asperate**, make rough. **aspirate**, give sound of "h."
**asperation**, making rough. **aspiration**, ambition.
**assistance**, help, aid. **assistants**, helpers.
**ate**, consumed or devoured. **ait**, an island. **eight**, a number.
**Ate**, a goddess. **eighty**, a number.
**attendance**, waiting on. **attendants**, those who attend, are in attendance.
**aught**, anything. **ought**, should.
**augur**, to predict. **auger**, a tool.
**aune**, a cloth measure. **own**, belonging to oneself.
**aunt**, relative. **ant**, insect.
**auricle**, external ear. **oracle**, counsel.
**awl**, a tool. **all**, everyone.
**axe**, a tool. **acts**, deeds.
**axes**, tools. **axis**, turning line.
**aye**, yes. **eye**, organ of sight. **I**, myself.

B

**bacon**, pork. **baken**, baked.
**bad**, wicked. **bade**, past tense of the verb TO BID.
**bail**, security. **bale**, a bundle.
**bait**, food to allure. **bate**, to lessen.
**baize**, cloth. **bays**, water, garland, horses.
**bald**, hairless. **bawled**, cried aloud.
**balks**, frustrates, refuses to proceed. **box**, case tree.
**ball**, round body, dance. **bawl**, to cry aloud.
**bare**, naked. **bear**, animal, to carry.
**bard**, poet. **barred**, fastened with a bar.
**bark**, cry of dog, rind of tree. **barque**, vessel.
**baron**, nobleman. **barren**, unfruitful.
**baroness**, baron's wife. **barrenness**, sterility.
**base**, mean. **bass**, musical term.
**bask**, to lie in warmth. **basque**, fitted tunic.
**bass**, musical term. **base**, mean.
**batten**, a board, to fatten. **baton**, a staff, a rod
**bay**, water, color, tree. **bey**, governor.
**beach**, seashore. **beech**, a tree.
**bear**, an animal, to carry. **bare**, naked.
**beat**, to strike. **beet**, vegetable.
**beau**, man of dress. **bow**, archery term.
**bee**, insect. **be**, to exist.
**been**, past participle of the verb TO BE. **bin**, container for grain.
**beer**, malt liquor. **bier**, carriage for the dead.
**berry**, fruit. **bury**, to inter.
**berth**, sleeping place. **birth**, act of being born.
**better**, superior. **bettor**, one who bets.
**bey**, governor. **bay**, sea, color, tree.
**bier**, carriage for the dead. **beer**, malt liquor.
**bight**, of a rope. **bite**, with the teeth.
**billed**, furnished with a bill. **build**, to erect.
**bin**, for grain. **been**, of the verb TO BE.
**binocle**, telescope. **binnacle**, compass box.
**birth**, being born. **berth**, sleeping place.
**blew**, did blow. **blue**, a color.
**bloat**, to swell. **blote**, to dry by smoke.
**boar**, swine. **bore**, to make a hole.
**board**, timber. **bored**, pierced, worried.
**bold**, courageous. **bowled**, rolled balls.
**boll**, a pod, a ball. **bowl**, basin. **bole**, earth, trunk of tree.
**border**, outer edge. **boarder**, lodger.

bourn, a limit, stream. **borne**, carried.
**borough**, a town. **burrow**, hole for rabbits.
**bow**, in archery. **beau**, a man of dress.
**bow**, to salute, part of ship. **bough**, branch of tree.
**bowl**, basin. **bole**, earth, trunk of tree. **boll**, a pod, a ball.
**boy**, male child. **buoy**, floating signal.
**braid**, to plait. **brayed**, did bray.
**brake**, device for retarding motion, a thicket. **break**, opening, to part.
**bray**, harsh sound. **brae**, broken ground.
**breach**, a gap, a break. **breech**, part of a gun.
**bread**, food. **bred**, brought up.
**brewed**, fermented. **brood**, offspring.
**brews**, to make malt liquor. **bruise**, to crush.
**bridal**, belonging to a wedding. **bridle**, a curb.
**Briton**, native of Briton. **Britain**, England, Scotland, Wales, Northern Ireland.
**broach**, to utter. **brooch**, a jewel.
**brows**, edges. **browse**, to feed.
**bruit**, noise, report. **brute**, a beast.
**build**, to erect. **billed**, furnished with a bill.
**bun**, small cake or bread. **bonne**, a nurse.
**buoy**, floating signal. **boy**, male child.
**burrow**, hole for rabbit. **borough**, a town.
**bury**, to cover with earth. **berry**, a fruit.
**but**, except, yet. **butt**, a cask, to push with head.
**by**, at, near. **buy**, to purchase.

C

**cache**, hole for hiding goods. **cash**, money.
**caddy**, a box. **cadi**, a Turkish judge.
**Cain**, man's name. **cane**, walking stick.
**calendar**, almanac. **calender**, to polish.
**calk**, to stop leaks. **cauk** or **cawk**, mineral.
**call**, to name. **caul**, a membrane.
**can**, could, tin vessel. **Cannes**, French city.
**cannon**, large gun. **canon**, a law, a rule.
**canvas**, cloth. **canvass**, to solicit, to examine.
**capital**, upper part, principal. **capitol**, statehouse.
**carat**, weight. **caret**, mark. **carrot**, vegetable.
**carol**, song of joy. **Carroll**, a name.
**carrot**, vegetable. **carat**, weight. **caret**, mark.
**cash**, money. **cache**, hole for hiding goods.
**cask**, wooden vessel. **casque**, a helmet.
**cast**, to throw, to mold. **caste**, rank.
**castor**, a beaver. **caster**, frame for bottles, roller.
**caudal**, tail. **caudle**, drink.
**cause**, that which produces. **caws**, cries of crows.
**cede**, to give up. **seed**, germ of plants.
**ceiling**, of a room. **sealing**, fastening.
**cell**, small room. **sell**, to part for price.
**cellar**, a room under house. **seller**, one who sells.
**censor**, critic. **censer**, vessel.
**cent**, coin. **sent**, caused to go. **scent**, odor.
**cerate**, a salve. **serrate**, shaped like a saw.
**cere**, to cover with wax. **sear**, dry. **seer**, a prophet.
**cession**, yielding. **session**, a sitting.
**cetaceous**, whale species. **setaceous**, bristly.
**chagrin**, ill-humor. **shagreen**, fish skin.
**chance**, accident. **chants**, melodies.
**champaign**, open country. **champagne**, a wine.
**chaste**, pure. **chased**, pursued.
**cheap**, inexpensive. **cheep**, a bird's chirp.
**chews**, masticates. **choose**, to select.
**choir**, singers. **quire**, of paper.
**choler**, anger. **collar**, neckwear.
**chord**, musical sound. **cord**, string. **cored**, taken from center.
**chronical**, a long duration. **chronicle**, history.
**chuff**, a clown. **chough**, a sea bird.
**cilicious**, made of hair. **silicious**, flinty.
**cingle**, a girth. **single**, alone, only one.
**cion** or **scion**, a sprout. **sion** or **zion**, mountain.
**circle**, round figure. **sercle**, a twig.
**cit**, a citizen. **sit**, to rest.
**cite**, to summon, to quote, to enumerate. **site**, situation. **sight**, view.
**clause**, part of a sentence. **claws**, talons.
**climb**, to ascend. **clime**, climate.
**coal**, fuel. **cole**, cabbage.
**coaled**, supplied with coal. **cold**, frigid, not hot.
**coarse**, rough. **course**, route. **corse** or **corpse**, dead body.
**coat**, garment. **cote**, sheepfold.
**coddle**, to fondle. see **caudal.**
**codling**, apples. **coddling**, parboiling.
**coffer**, money chest. **cougher**, one who coughs.
**coin**, money. **quoin**, wedge.
**colation**, straining. **collation**, a repast.
**collar**, neckwear. see **choler.**
**colonel**, officer. **kernel**, seed in a nut.
**color**, tint. **culler**, a chooser.
**complacence**, satisfaction. **complaisance**, affability, compliance.
**complacent**, civil. **complaisant**, seeking to please.
**compliment**, flattery. **complement**, the full number.
**confidant**, one trusted with secrets. **confident**, having full belief.
**consonance**, concord. **consonants**, letters which are not vowels.
**consequence**, that which follows. **consequents**, deduction.
**consession**, a sitting together. **concession**, a yielding.
**coolly**, without heat, calmly. **coolie**, East Indian laborer.
**coom**, soot. **coomb**, a measure.
**coquet**, to deceive in love. **coquette**, vain girl.
**coral**, from the ocean. **corol**, a corolla.
**cord**, string. **chord**, musical sound. **cored**, taken from center.
**cores**, inner parts. **corps**, soldiers.
**correspondence**, interchange of letters. **correspondents**, those who correspond.
**council**, assembly. **counsel**, advice.
**cousin**, relative. **cozen**, to cheat
**coward**, one without courage. **cowered**, frightened.
**creak**, harsh noise. **creek**, stream.
**crewel**, yarn. **cruel**, savage.
**crews**, seamen. **cruise**, voyage. **cruse**, a cruet.
**cue**, hint, rod, tail. **queue**, pigtail, waiting line.
**culler**, a selecter. **color**, a tint.
**currant**, fruit. **current**, flowing stream.
**cygnet**, a swan. **signet**, a seal.
**cymbal**, musical instrument. **symbol**, sign.
**cypress**, a tree. **Cyprus**, an island.

D

**dam**, wall for stream. **damn**, to doom or curse.
**dammed**, confined by banks. **damned**, doomed.
**Dane**, a native of Denmark. **deign**, condescend.
**day**, time. **dey**, a governor.
**days**, plural of day. **daze**, to dazzle.
**dear**, beloved, costly. **deer**, an animal.
**deformity**, defect. **difformity**, diversity of form.
**deign**, to condescend. **Dane**, native of Denmark.
**demean**, to behave. **demesne**, land.
**dents**, marks. **dense**, close, compact.
**dependents**, subordinates. **dependence**, reliance.
**depravation**, corruption. **deprivation**, loss.
**descent**, downward. **dissent**, disagreement.
**descendent**, falling. **descendant**, offspring.
**desert**, to abandon. **dessert**, last course of a meal.
**deviser**, contriver. **divisor**, a term in arithmetic.
**dew**, moisture. **do**, to perform. **due**, owed.
**die**, to expire, a stamp. **dye**, to color.
**dire**, dreadful. **dyer**, one who dyes.
**discous**, flat. **discus**, quoit.
**discreet**, prudent. **discrete**, separate.
**doe**, female deer. **dough**, unbaked bread.
**does**, female deer. **doze**, to slumber.
**done**, performed. **dun**, a color.
**dost**, from verb TO BE. **dust**, powdered earth.
**drachm**, weight. **dram**, small quantity.
**draft**, bill. **draught**, a drink, a potion.
**dual**, two. **duel**, combat.
**due**, owed. **dew**, moisture. **do**, to perform.
**dun**, color, ask for debt. **done**, finished.
**dust**, powdered earth. **dost**, from verb TO BE.
**dye**, to color. **die**, to expire, a stamp.

**dyeing**, staining. **dying**, expiring.
**dyer**, one who dyes. **dire**, dreadful.

E

**earn**, to gain by labor. **urn**, a vase.
**eight**, a number. **ate**, consumed or devoured.
**eighty**, a number. **Ate**, a goddess.
**ere**, before. **air**, atmosphere. **heir**, inheritor.
**errant**, wandering. **arrant**, bad.
**ewe**, female sheep. **yew**, tree. **you**, *pronoun*.
**ewes**, sheep. **yews**, trees. **use**, employ.
**eye**, organ of sight. **I**, myself. **aye**, yes.

F

**fain**, pleased. **fane**, temple. **feign**, pretend.
**faint**, languid. **feint**, pretense.
**fair**, beautiful, just. **fare**, price, food.
**falter**, to hesitate. **faulter**, one who commits a fault.
**fane**, temple. **fain**, pleased. **feign**, to pretend.
**fare**, price, food. **fair**, beautiful, just.
**fate**, destiny. **fete**, a festival.
**faulter**, one who commits a fault. **falter**, to hesitate.
**fawn**, young deer. **faun**, woodland deity.
**feat**, deed. **feet**, plural of foot.
**feign**, pretend. **fain**, pleased. **fane**, temple.
**feint**, pretense. **faint**, languid.
**felloe**, rim of wheel. **fellow**, companion.
**feod**, tenure. **feud**, quarrel.
**ferrule**, metallic band. **ferule**, wooden pallet.
**feted**, honored. **fated**, destined.
**feud**, quarrel. **feod**, tenure.
**fillip**, jerk of finger. **Philip**, man's name.
**filter**, to strain. **philter**, love charm.
**find**, to discover. **fined**, punished.
**fir**, tree. **fur**, animal hair.
**fissure**, a crack. **fisher**, fisherman.
**fizz**, hissing noise. **phiz**, the face.
**flea**, insect. **flee**, to run away.
**flew**, did fly. **flue**, chimney. **flu**, influenza.
**flour**, ground grain. **flower**, a blossom.
**flue**, chimney. **flu**, influenza. **flew**, did fly.
**for**, because of. **fore**, preceding. **four**, cardinal number.
**fort**, fortified place. **forte**, peculiar talent.
**forth**, forward. **fourth**, ordinal number.
**foul**, unclean. **fowl**, a bird.
**four**, cardinal number. **for**, because of. **fore**, preceding.
**fourth**, ordinal number. **forth**, forward.
**franc**, French coin. **Frank**, a name, generous.
**frays**, quarrels. **phrase**, parts of a sentence.
**freeze**, to congeal with cold. **frieze**, cloth. **frees**, to set at liberty.
**fungus**, spongy excresence. **fungous**, as fungus.
**fur**, hairy coat of animals. **fir**, a tree.
**furs**, skins of beasts. **furze**, a shrub.

G

**gage**, a pledge, a fruit. **gauge**, a measure.
**gait**, manner of walking. **gate**, a door.
**gall**, bile. **Gaul**, a Frenchman.
**gamble**, to wager. **gambol**, to skip.
**gantlet**, punishment. **gauntlet**, a glove.
**gate**, a door. **gait**, manner of walking.
**gauge**, a measure. **gage**, a pledge, a fruit.
**Gaul**, a Frenchman. **gall**, bile.
**gild**, to overflow with gold. **guild**, a corporation.
**gilt**, gold on surface. **guilt**, crime.
**glare**, splendor. **glair**, white of an egg.
**gneiss**, rock similar to granite. **nice**, fine.
**gnu**, animal. **new**, not old. **knew**, understood.
**gourd**, a plant. **gored**, pierced.
**grate**, iron frame. **great**, large.
**grater**, a rough instrument. **greater**, larger.
**great**, large. **grate**, iron frame.
**greater**, larger. **grater**, a rough instrument.
**Greece**, country in Europe. **grease**, fat.
**grisly**, frightful. **grizzly**, an animal, gray.
**groan**, deep sigh. **grown**, increased.
**grocer**, merchant. **grosser**, coarser.
**grown**, increased. **groan**, deep sigh.
**guessed**, conjectured. **guest**, visitor.
**guild**, a corporation. **gild**, to overflow with gold.
**guilt**, crime. **gilt**, gold on surface.
**guise**, appearance. **guys**, ropes.

H

**hail**, ice, to salute. **hale**, healthy.
**hair**, of the head. **hare**, a rabbit.
**hale**, healthy. **hail**, ice, to salute.
**hall**, large room, a passage. **haul**, to pull.
**hare**, a rabbit. **hair**, of the head.
**hart**, an animal. **heart**, seat of life.
**haul**, to pull. **hall**, a large room, a passage.
**hay**, dried grass. **hey**, an expression.
**heal**, to cure. **heel**, part of foot or shoe, the end of a loaf of bread, a scoundrel.
**hear**, to hearken. **here**, in this place.
**heard**, did hear. **herd**, a drove.
**heart**, seat of life. **hart**, an animal.
**heel**, part of foot or shoe, the end of a loaf of bread, a scoundrel. **heal**, to cure.
**heir**, inheritor. **air**, atmosphere. **ere**, before.
**herd**, a drove. **heard**, did hear.
**here**, in this place. **hear**, to hearken.
**hew**, to cut down. see **hue.**
**hey**, an expression. **hay**, dried grass.
**hide**, skin, to conceal. **hied**, hastened.
**hie**, to hasten. **high**, lofty, tall.
**hied**, hastened. **hide**, skin, to conceal.
**higher**, more lofty. **hire**, to employ.
**him**, that man. **hymn**, sacred song.
**hire**, to employ. **higher**, more lofty.
**hoa**, exclamation. **ho**, cry, stop. **hoe**, tool.
**hoard**, to lay up. **horde**, tribe.
**hoarse**, rough voice. **horse**, animal.
**hoe**, tool. **ho**, cry, stop. **hoa**, exclamation.
**hoes**, tools. **hose**, stockings, tubing.
**hole**, cavity. **whole**, all, entire.
**holm**, evergreen oak. **home**, dwelling.
**holy**, pure sacred. **wholly**, completely.
**home**, dwelling. **holm**, evergreen oak.
**horde**, tribe. **hoard**, to lay up.
**horse**, animal. **hoarse**, rough voice.
**hose**, stockings, tubing. **hoes**, tools.
**hour**, sixty minutes. **our**, belonging to us.
**hue**, color. **hew**, to cut down. **Hugh**, man's name.
**hymn**, sacred song. **him**, that man.

I

**idol**, image. **idle**, unemployed. **idyl**, poem.
**I'll**, I will. **isle**, island. **aisle**, passage.
**in**, within. **inn**, a tavern.
**indict**, to accuse. **indite**, to dictate, write, compose.
**indiscreet**, imprudent. **indiscrete**, not separated.
**indite**, to dictate. **indict**, to accuse.
**inn**, a tavern. **in**, within.
**innocence**, purity. **innocents**, harmless things.
**instants**, moments. **instance**, example.
**intense**, extreme. **intents**, designs.
**intention**, purpose. **intension**, energetic use or exercise.
**intents**, designs. **intense**, extreme.
**invade**, to infringe. **inveighed**, censured.
**irruption**, invasion. **eruption**, bursting forth.
**isle**, island. **I'll**, I will. **aisle**, passage.

J

**jail**, prison. **gaol**, prison.
**jam**, preserves. **jamb**, side of door.

K

**kernel**, seed in nut. **colonel**, officer.
**key**, for a lock. **quay**, wharf.
**knag**, knot in wood. **nag**, small horse.
**knap**, protuberance, noise. **nap**, short sleep.
**knave**, rogue. **nave**, center, hub.
**knead**, work dough. **need**, want. **kneed**, having knees.
**kneel**, to rest on knee. **neal**, to temper.
**knew**, understood. **gnu**, animal. **new**, not old.
**knight**, title of honor. **night**, darkness.
**knit**, unite, weave, frown. **nit**, insect's egg.
**knot**, tied. **not**, word of refusal.
**know**, understand. **no**, not so.
**knows**, understands. **nose**, organ of smell.

L

**lack**, to want. **lac**, gum.
**lacks**, wants, needs. **lax**, loose, slack.
**lade**, to load. **laid**, placed, produced eggs.
**lane**, a road. **lain**, rested.
**Latin**, language. **latten**, brass.
**lax**, loose, slack. **lacks**, wants, needs.
**lea**, meadow. **lee**, shelter place.
**leach**, to filtrate. **leech**, a worm.
**lead**, metal. **led**, guided.
**leaf**, part of a plant. **lief**, willingly.
**leak**, a hole. **leek**, a plant.
**lean**, not fat, to rest, to slant. **lien**, mortgage.
**leased**, rented. **least**, smallest.
**led**, guided. **lead**, metal.
**lee**, shelter, place. **lea**, meadow.
**leech**, a worm. **leach**, to filtrate.
**leek**, a plant. **leak**, a hole.
**lesson**, task. **lessen**, to diminish.
**levee**, bank, visit. **levy**, to collect.
**liar**, falsifier. **lyre**, musical instrument. **lier**, one who lies down.
**lie**, falsehood. **lye**, liquid.
**lief**, willingly. **leaf**, part of a plant.
**lien**, legal claim. **lean**, not fat, to rest, to slant.
**lightning**, electricity. **lightening**, unloading.
**limb**, branch. **limn**, to draw.
**links**, connecting rings. **lynx**, an animal.
**lo**, look, see. **low**, not high, mean.
**loan**, to lend. **lone**, solitary.
**lock**, hair, fastening. **loch** or **lough**, lake.
**lone**, solitary. **loan**, to lend.
**low**, not high, mean. **lo**, look, see.
**lusern**, a lynx. **lucerne**, clover.
**lye**, liquid. **lie**, falsehood.
**lynx**, animal. **links**, connecting rings.
**lyre**, musical instrument. **liar**, falsifier. **lier**, one who lies down.

M

**made**, created. **maid**, unmarried woman.
**mail**, armor, post bag. **male**, masculine.
**main**, principal. **mane**, hair. **Maine**, a state.
**maize**, corn. **maze**, intricate.
**male**, masculine. **mail**, armor, post bag.
**mall**, hammer, walk. **maul**, to beat.
**manner**, method. **manor**, landed estate.
**mantel**, chimney piece. **mantle**, a cloak.
**mark**, visible line. **marque**, a pledge.
**marshall**, officer. **martial**, warlike.
**marten**, an animal. **martin**, a bird.
**martial**, warlike. **marshall**, officer.
**maul**, to beat. **mall**, hammer, walk.
**mead**, drink. **meed**, reward. **Mede**, native of Media.
**mean**, low. **mien**, aspect.
**meat**, food. **meet**, to encounter, a match, suitable.
**Mede**, native of Media. **mead**, drink. **meed**, reward.
**meddle**, interfere. **medal**, a token.
**meddler**, one who meddles. **medlar**, a tree.
**meed**, reward. **mead**, drink. **Mede**, native of Media.
**meet**, to encounter a match, suitable. **meat**, food.
**mettle**, spirit, courage. **metal**, mineral.
**mew** or **mue**, to melt. **mew**, fowl enclosure.
**mewl**, to cry. **mule**, an animal.
**mews**, cat cries. **muse**, deep thought.
**mien**, look aspect. **mean**, low.
**might**, power. **mite**, insect.
**mighty**, powerful. **mity**, having mites.
**mince**, to cut. **mints**, coining places.
**miner**, worker in mines. **minor**, one underage.
**mints**, coining places. **mince**, to cut.
**missal**, book. **missel**, bird. **missile**, weapon
**mite**, insect, small. **might**, power.
**mity**, having mites. **mighty**, powerful.
**moan**, lament. **mown**, cut down.
**moat**, ditch. **mote**, small particle.
**mode**, manner. **mowed**, cut down.
**morning**, before noon. **mourning**, grief.
**mote**, small particle. **moat**, ditch.
**mowed**, cut down. **mode**, manner.
**mucous**, slimy. **mucus**, a fluid.
**mue**, to molt. **mew**, fowl enclosure.
**mule**, an animal. **mewl**, to cry.
**muscat**, grape. **musket**, gun.
**muse**, deep thought. **mews**, cat cries.
**mustard**, plant. **mustered**, assembled.

N

**nag**, small horse. **knag**, knot in wood.
**nap**, short sleep. **knap**, protuberance, noise.
**naval**, nautical. **navel**, center of abdomen.
**nave**, center, hub. **knave**, rogue.
**navel**, center of abdomen. **naval**, nautical.
**nay**, no. **neigh**, whinny of a horse.
**neal**, to temper. **kneel**, to rest on knee.
**need**, necessity, want. **knead**, work dough. **kneed**, having knees.
**neigh**, whinny of a horse. **nay**, no.
**new**, not old. **gnu**, animal. **knew**, understood.
**nice**, fine. **kneiss**, rock similar to granite.
**night**, darkness. **knight**, title of honor.
**nit**, insect's egg. **knit**, to unite, to form.
**no**, not so. **know**, to understand.
**none**, no one. **nun**, female devotee.
**nose**, organ of smell. **knows**, understands.
**not**, word of refusal. **knot**, a tie.
**nun**, female devotee. **none**, no one.

O

**oar**, rowing blade. **o'er**, over. **ore**, mineral.
**ode**, poem. **owed**, under obligation.
**o'er**, over. **oar**, paddle. **ore**, mineral.
**oh**, denoting pain. **O!** surprise. **owe**, indebted.
**one**, single unit. **won**, gained.
**onerary**, fit for burdens. **honorary**, conferring honor.
**oracle**, counsel. **auricle**, external ear.
**ordinance**, a law. **ordnance**, military supplies.
**ore**, mineral. **o'er**, over. **oar**, paddle.
**ottar**, oil of roses. **otter**, an animal.
**ought**, should. **aught**, anything.
**our**, belonging to us. **hour**, sixty minutes.
**owe**, to be indebted. **oh**, denoting surprise. **O!** surprise.
**owed**, under obligation. **ode**, poem.

P

**paced**, moved slowly. **paste**, flour and water mixed.
**packed**, bound in a bundle. **pact**, contract.
**pail**, bucket. **pale**, whitish.
**pain**, agony. **pane**, a square of glass.
**pair**, a couple, two. **pare**, to peel. **pear**, a fruit.
**palace**, princely home. **Pallas**, heathen deity.
**palate**, organ of taste. **pallette**, artist's board. **pallet**, a bed.
**pale**, whitish. **pail**, bucket.
**pall**, covering for the dead. **Paul**, man's name.
**pare**, to peel. **pair**, a couple, two. **pear**, a fruit.

**passable**, tolerable. **passible**, with feeling.
**paste**, flour and water mixed. **paced**, moved slowly.
**patience**, calmness. **patients**, sick persons.
**paw**, foot of a beast. **pa**, papa.
**paws**, beasts' feet. **pause**, stop.
**peace**, quiet. **piece**, a part.
**peak**, the top. **pique**, grudge. **peek**, to peep.
**peal**, loud sound. **peel**, to pare.
**pealing**, sounding loudly. **peeling**, rinds.
**pear**, a fruit. **pair**, a couple, two. **pare**, to peel.
**pearl**, a precious substance. **purl**, a knitting stitch.
**pedal**, for the feet. **peddle**, to sell.
**peek**, to peep. **peak**, the top. **pique**, grudge.
**peer**, nobleman. **pier**, column, wharf.
**pencil**, writing instrument. **pensile**, suspended.
**pendant**, an ornament. **pendent**, hanging.
**philter**, love charm. **filter**, to strain.
**phiz**, the face. **phizz**, hissing noise.
**phrase**, expression. **frays**, quarrels.
**piece**, a part. **peace**, quiet.
**pier**, a column, wharf. **peer**, nobleman.
**pique**, grudge. **peak**, the top. **peek**, to peep.
**pistil**, part of a flower. **pistol**, firearm.
**place**, situation. **plaice**, a fish.
**plain**, clear, simple. **plane**, flat surface, tool.
**pleas**, arguments. **please**, to delight.
**plum**, a fruit. **plumb**, perpendicular, leaden weight.
**pole**, stick. **poll**, the head.
**pool**, water. **poule** or **pool**, stakes played for.
**pore**, opening. **pour**, cause to flow.
**poring**, looking intently. **pouring**, raining, flowing.
**port**, harbor. **porte**, Turkish court.
**praise**, commendation. **prays**, entreats, petitions. **preys**, feeds by violence, plunders.
**pray**, to supplicate. **prey**, plunder.
**presence**, being present. **presents**, gifts.
**pride**, self-esteem. **pried**, moved by a lever.
**prier**, inquirer. **prior**, previous.
**pries**, looks into. **prize**, reward.
**prints**, impressions. **prince**, king's son.
**principal**, chief. **principle**, an element.
**prior**, previous. **prier**, inquirer.
**prize**, reward. **pries**, looks into.
**profit**, gain. **prophet**, a foreteller.
**purl**, a knitting stitch. **pearl**, precious substance.

## Q

**quarts**, measure. **quartz**, rock crystal.
**quay**, wharf. **key**, lock fastener.
**queen**, king's wife. **quean**, worthless woman.
**queue**, pigtail, waiting line. **cue**, hint, rod.
**quire**, package of paper. **choir**, church singers.
**quoin**, a wedge. **coin**, money.

## R

**rabbet**, a joint. **rabbit**, small animal.
**radical**, of first principles. **radicle**, a root.
**rain**, water. **reign**, rule. **rein**, bridle.
**raise**, to lift. **rays**, sunbeams. **raze**, to demolish.
**raised**, lifted. **razed**, demolished.
**raiser**, one who raises. **razor**, shaving blade.
**rancor**, spite. **ranker**, stronger, more immoderate.
**rap**, to strike. **wrap**, to fold.
**rapped**, quick blows. **wrapped**, enclosed.
**rapping**, striking. **wrapping**, a cover.
**rays**, sunbeams. **raise**, to lift. **raze**, to demolish.
**raze**, to demolish. **raise**, to lift. **rays**, sunbeams.
**razed**, demolished. **raised**, lifted.
**razor**, shaving blade. **raiser**, one who raises.
**read**, to peruse. **reed**, a plant.
**real**, true. **reel**, winding machine, to stagger.
**receipt**, acknowledgment. **reseat**, to sit again.
**reck**, to heed. **wreck**, destruction.
**red**, color. **read**, perused.
**reek**, to emit vapor. **wreak**, to inflict.
**reel**, winding machine, to stagger. **real**, true.
**reign**, rule. **rein**, bridle. **rain**, water.
**reseat**, to seat again. **receipt**, acknowledgment.
**residence**, place of abode. **residents**, citizens.
**rest**, quiet. **wrest**, to twist.
**retch**, to vomit. **wretch**, miserable person.
**rheum**, thin, water matter. **room**, space.
**Rhodes**, name of an island. **roads**, highways.
**rhumb**, point of a compass. **rum**, liquor.
**rhyme**, harmonical sound. **rime**, hoar frost.
**rigger**, rope fixer. **rigor**, severity.
**right**, correct. **rite**, ceremony. **write**, to form letters.
**rime**, hoar frost. **rhyme**, harmonical sound.
**ring**, circle, sound. **wring**, to twist.
**road**, way. **rode**, did ride. **rowed**, did row.
**roads**, highways. **Rhodes**, name of an island.
**roan**, color. **rown**, impelled by oars. **Rhone**, river.
**roe**, deer. **row**, to impel with oars, a line.
**roes**, eggs, deer. **rows**, uses oars. **rose**, a flower.
**Rome**, city in Italy. **roam**, to wander.
**rood**, a measure. **rude**, rough.
**rote**, memory of words. **wrote**, did write.
**rough**, not smooth. **ruff**, plaited collar.
**rouse**, stir up, provoke. **rows**, disturbances.
**rout**, rabble, disperse. **route**, road.
**row**, to impel with oars, a line. **roe**, a deer.
**rowed**, did row. **road**, way. **rode**, did ride.
**rows**, uses oars. **roes**, deer. **rose**, a flower.
**rude**, rough. **rood**, measure.
**ruff**, collar. **rough**, not smooth.
**rum**, liquor. **rhumb**, point of a compass.
**rung**, sounded, a step. **wrung**, twisted.
**rye**, grain. **wry**, crooked.

## S

**sail**, canvas of a ship. **sale**, traffic.
**sailer**, vessel. **sailor**, seaman.
**sale**, traffic. **sail**, canvas of a ship.
**sane**, sound, in mind. **seine**, fish net.
**saver**, one who saves. **savor**, taste, scent.
**scene**, a view. **seen**, viewed.
**scent**, odor. **sent**, caused to go. **cent**, coin.
**scion** or **cion**. sprout. **sion** or **zion**, a mountain.
**scull**, oar, boat. **skull**, bone of the head.
**sea**, ocean. **see**, to perceive.
**seal**, stamp, an animal. **seel**, to keel over, to close the eyes.
**sealing**, fastening. **ceiling**, top of a room.
**seam**, a juncture. **seem**, to appear.
**seamed**, joined together. **seemed**, appeared.
**sear**, to burn. **cere**, wax.
**seas**, water. **sees**, looks. **seize**, take hold of.
**seed**, germ of a plant. **cede**, to give up.
**seen**, viewed. **scene**, a view.
**seine**, a net. **sane**, sound in mind.
**sell**, to part for price. **cell**, small room.
**seller**, one who sells. **cellar**, room.
**senior**, elder. **seignoir**, a title.
**sense**, feeling. **scents**, odors. **cents**, coins. **cense**, tax.
**sent**, caused to go. **scent**, odor. **cent**, coin.
**serf**, a slave. **surf**, of the sea.
**serge**, a cloth. **surge**, a billow.
**serrate**, notched, like a saw. **cerate**, salve.
**session**, a sitting. **cession**, a yielding.
**setaceous**, bristly. **cetaceous**, whale species
**sew**, to stitch. **sow**, to scatter seed. **so**, in this manner.
**sewer**, one who uses a needle. **sower**, one who scatters seed.
**sewer**, a drain. **suer**, one who entreats.
**shear**, to clip. **sheer**, to deviate, pure.
**shoe**, covering for foot. **shoo**, begone.
**shone**, did shine. **shown**, exhibited.
**shoo**, begone. **shoe**, covering for foot.
**shoot**, to let fly, to kill. **chute**, a fall.
**shown**. exhibited. **shone**, did shine.
**side**, edge, margin. **sighed**, did sigh.
**sigher**. one who sighs. **sire**, father.
**sighs**, deep breathings. **size**, bulk.
**sight**, view. **site**, situation. **cite**, to summon.
**sign**, token, mark. **sine**, geometrical term.
**signet**, a seal. **cygnet**, a swan.
**silicious**, flinty. **cilicious**, made of hair.
**silly**, foolish. **Scilly**, name of islands.

**single**, alone. **cingle**, a girth.
**sit**, to rest. **cit**, a citizen.
**skull**, bone of the head. **scull**, oar, boat.
**slay**, to kill. **sley**, weaver's reed. **sleigh**, vehicle.
**sleeve**, cover for arm. **sleave**, untwisted silk.
**slew**, killed. **slue**, to turn about. **slough**, bog.
**slight**, neglect, small. **sleight**, artful trick.
**sloe**, fruit, animal. **slow**, not swift.
**soar**, to rise high. **sore**, painful.
**soared**, ascended. **sword**, a weapon.
**sold**, did sell. **soled**, furnished with soles. **souled**, instinct with soul or feeling.
**sole**, part of foot, only. **soul**, spirit of man.
**some**, a part. **sum**, the whole.
**son**, a male child. **sun**, luminous orb.
**sow**, to scatter seed. **sew**, to stitch.
**sower**, one who scatters seed. **sewer**, one who uses a needle.
**staid**, sober, remained. **stayed**, supported.
**stair**, steps. **stare**, to gaze.
**stake**, a post, a wager. **steak**, meat.
**stare**, to gaze. **stair**, steps.
**stationary**, motionless. **stationery**, paper, etc.
**steel**, metal. **steal**, to thieve.
**sticks**, pieces of wood. **Styx**, a fabulous river.
**stile**, stairway. **style**, manner.
**straight**, not crooked. **strait**, narrow pass.
**style**, manner. **stile**, stairway.
**Styx**, a fabulous river. **sticks**, pieces of wood.
**subtle**, cunning. **suttle**, net weight.
**subtler**, more cunning. **sutler**, trader.
**succor**, aid. **sucker**, a shoot of a plant, a fish.
**suer**, one who entreats. **sewer**, a drain.
**suite**, train of followers. **sweet**, having a pleasant taste, dear.
**sum**, the whole. **some**, a part.
**sun**, luminous orb. **son**, a male child.
**surcle**, a twig. **circle**, a round figure.
**surf**, dashing waves. **serf**, a slave.
**surge**, a billow. **serge**, cloth.
**sutler**, trader. **subtler**, more cunning.
**suttle**, net weight. **subtle**, cunning.
**swap**, to barter. **swop**, a blow.
**symbol**, emblem, representative. **cymbal**, musical instrument.

### T

**tacked**, changed course of ship. **tact**, skill.
**tacks**, small nails. **tax**, a tribute.
**tale**, story. **tail**, the hinder part.
**taper**, a wax candle. **tapir**, an animal.
**tare**, a week, allowance. **tear**, to pull to pieces.
**taught**, instructed. **taut**, tight.
**teal**, a water fowl. **teil**, a tree.
**team**, two or more horses. **teem**, to be full.
**tear**, moisture from eyes. **tier**, a rank, a row.
**tear**, to pull to pieces. **tare**, weed, allowance.
**teas**, different kinds of tea. **tease**, to torment.
**tense**, rigid, form of a verb. **tents**, canvas houses.
**the**, adjective. **thee**, thyself.
**their**, belonging to them. **there**, in that place. **they're**, they are.
**threw**, did throw. **through**, from end to end.
**throne**, seat of a king. **thrown**, hurled.
**throw**, to hurl. **throe**, extreme pain.
**thrown**, hurled. **throne**, seat of a king.
**thyme**, a plant. **time**, duration.
**tide**, stream, current. **tied**, fastened.
**tier**, a rank, a row. **tear**, moisture from eyes.
**timber**, wood. **timbre**, crest, quality.
**time**, duration. **thyme**, a plant.
**tire**, part of a wheel, weary. **Tyre**, city. **tier**, one who ties.
**toad**, reptile. **toed**, having toes. **towed**, drawn.
**toe**, part of foot. **tow**, hemp, to drag.
**told**, related. **tolled**, rang. **toled**, allured.
**tole**, to allure. **toll**, a tax.
**ton**, a weight. **tun**, a large cask.
**too**, denoting excess. **to**, toward. **two**, couple.
**tracked**, followed. **tract**, region.
**tray**, shallow vessel. **trey**, three of cards.
**tun**, a large cask. **ton**, a weight.
**two**, a couple. **to**, toward. **too**, denoting excess.

### U

**urn**, a vase. **earn**, to gain by labor.
**use**, to employ. **yews**, trees. **ewes**, sheep.

### V

**vain**, proud, delusive. **vane**, weathercock. **vein**, blood vessel.
**vale**, valley. **vail**, a fee. **veil**, to cover.
**vane**, weathercock. **vein**, blood vessel. **vain**, proud, delusive.
**veil**, a covering for face. **veil**, to cover. **vail**, a fee.
**vein**, blood vessel. **vane**, weathercock. **vain**, proud, delusive.
**Venus**, planet. **venous**, relating to the veins.
**vial**, a bottle. **viol**, violin. **vile**, wicked.
**vice**, sin. **vise**, a press.

### W

**wade**, to ford. **weighed** balanced.
**wail**, to moan. **wale**, a mark. **whale**, a sea animal.
**waist**, part of the body. **waste**, destruction.
**wait**, to stay for. **weight**, heaviness.
**waive**, to relinquish. **wave**, a billow.
**wall**, a fence. **wawl**, wail, bowl.
**wane**, to decrease. **wain**, a wagon.
**want**, desire. **wont**, custom, habit.
**ware**, merchandise. see **wear**.
**wart**, hard, excrescence. **wort**, beer.
**way**, road, manner. **whey**, curdled milk. **weigh**, to balance.
**weak**, not strong. **week**, seven days.
**weal**, happiness. **wheal**, a pustule. **wheel**, circular body.
**wear**, to impair by use. **ware**, merchandise.
**weasel**, an animal. **weazel**, thin, weasen.
**ween**, to think. **wean**, to alienate.
**weigh**, to balance. **way**, road. **whey** of milk.
**weighed**, balanced. **wade**, to ford.
**weight**, heaviness. **wait**, to stay for.
**wen**, a tumor. **when**, at what time.
**wether**, a ram. **weather**, state of air.
**what**, that which. **wot**, to know.
**wheel**, circular body. **wheal**, a pustule.
**whey**, thin part of milk. **way**, road, manner. **weigh**, to balance.
**Whig**, name of a party. **wig**, false hair.
**whist**, a game of cards. **wist**, thought, knew.
**whole**, all, entire. **hole**, a cavity.
**wholly**, completely. **holy**, sacred, pure.
**wig**, false hair. **Whig**, name of a party.
**wight**, a person. **wite**, blame.
**wist**, thought, knew. **whist**, a game of cards.
**won**, gained. **one**, single, unit.
**wont**, custom, habit. **want**, desire.
**wood**, substance of trees. **would**, was willing.
**wort**, beer, herb. **wart**, hard excrescence.
**wot**, to know. **what**, that which.
**wrap**, to fold. **rap**, to strike.
**wrapped**, covered. **rapped**, struck with quick blows.
**wrapping**, a cover. **rapping**, striking.
**wreak**, to inflict. **reek**, to emit vapor.
**wrest**, to twist. **rest**, quiet.
**wretch**, miserable person. **retch**, to vomit.
**wring**, to twist. **ring**, a circle, a sound.
**write**, to form letters. **wright**, workman. **right**, correct.
**wrote**, did write. **rote**, a memory of words.
**wrung**, twisted. **rung**, sounded.
**wry**, crooked. **rye**, a grain.

### Y

**yew**, a tree. **you**, person spoken to. **ewe**, a sheep.
**yews**, trees. **use**, employ. **ewes**, sheep.
**yolk**, yellow of egg. **yoke**, collar for oxen.
**your**, belonging to you. **you're**, you are.

# Dictionary of Scientific Terms

# Dictionary of Scientific Terms

## ABBREVIATIONS

Aero.—Aeronautics
Acous.—Acoustics
Anat.—Anatomy
Arch.—Architecture
Astron.—Astronomy
Bacteriol.—Bacteriology
Biol.—Biology
Bot.—Botany
Build.—Building
Carp.—Carpentry
Chem. Eng.—Chemical Engineering
Chem.—Chemistry
Civ. Eng.—Civil Engineering
Crystal.—Crystallography
Cyt.—Cytology
Ecol.—Ecology
Elec. Eng.—Electrical Engineering
Elec.—Electricity
Embryol.—Embryology
Eng.—Engineering
Entomol.—Entomology
Gen.—Genetics
Geol.—Geology
Geom.—Geometry
Histol.—Histology
Maths.—Mathematics
Mech.—Mechanics
Med.—Medicine
Met.—Metallurgy
Meteor.—Meteorology
Micros.—Microscopy
Min.—Mineralogy
Nuclear Eng.—Nuclear Engineering
Ocean.—Oceanography
Phys.—Physics
Physiol.—Physiology
Psychiatry
Psycho-an.—Psycho-analysis
Psychol.—Psychology
Psycho-path.—Psycho-pathology
Radiology
Surg.—Surgery
Surv.—Surveying
Zool.—Zoology

### A

**ab'acus**: A term applied to various early forms of an instrument used for mechanically performing addition and subtraction.

**abamu'rus** (Build.): A supporting wall or buttress built to add strength to another wall.

**aba'picul** (Zool.): Situated at, or pertaining to, the lower pole: remote from the apex.

**abatjour, ab-a-joor'** (Build.): An opening to admit light, generally deflecting it downwards as a skylight.

**abatvoix, ab-a-vwa'** (Acous.): A sounding board over a rostrum or pulpit, to deflect speech downwards and in the direction of the listeners.

**abaxial** (Bot.): The side of a leaf, petal etc. which is farthest from the axis. (Zool.): Remote from the axis.

**Abbe refractometer** (Chem.): An instrument for measuring directly the refractive index of oils, etc.

**abbreviated** (Bot.): Shortened suddenly.

**A. B. C. process** (Sewage): A process of sewage treatment in which charcoal, blood, clay and alum are used as precipitants.

**abdo'men** (Zool.): In mammals, the region of the body, lying between the diaphragm and the pelvis, which contains the urinogenital and digestive organs.

**abduction** (Zool.): The action of pulling a limb or part away from the main axis.

**abductor** (Zool.): Any muscle that draws a limb or part away from the median axis.

**aber'rant** (Bot., Zool.): Showing some unusual difference of structure.

**aberration** (Astron.): An apparent change of position of a heavenly body, due to the velocity of light having a finite ratio to the relative velocity of the source and the observer. (Bot.): Some peculiarity of an individual plant not capable of transmission to offspring, and usually due to some special environmental condition.

**abjection** (Bot.): The forcible projection of spores from the sporophore.

**ablation** (Surg.): Removal of body tissue by surgical methods.

**abnormal** (Psychol.): Said of a person who is maladjusted to himself and/or to the outside world.

**aboma'sum** (Zool.): The true or fourth stomach in ruminant mammals. Also called rennet, reed.

**abo'ral** (Zool.): Leading away from or distant from the mouth.

**abortifa'cient** (Med.): Anything which causes artificial abortion.

**abortion** (Med.): Expulsion of the foetus from the uterus during the first three months of pregnancy. May be induced or spontaneous. (Bot.): A state of incomplete development, or the product of such defective development. (Zool.): Cessation of development in a foetus or in an organ.

**abran'chiate** (Zool.): Lacking gills.

**abrasion**: A rubbing away.

**abrasive** (Chem.): A substance used for the removal of matter by grinding and scratching.

**Abney level** (Surv.): A particular form of reflecting level, devised for the measurement of vertical angles.

**abreac'tion** (Psycho-an.): A release of blocked psychic energy attached to repressed and forgotten memories and phantasies; effected by living through these in action or feeling.

**abscess** (Med.): Pus localised in infected tissue and separated from healthy tissue by an abscess wall.

**absciss layer** (Bot.): A layer of parenchymatous cells across the base of a petiole or a branch, or embedded in bark, through which the scale of bark, the branch or leaf, separates off.

**absolute potential** (Chem.): The true potential difference between a metal and a solution.

**absolute pressure** (Phys.): Pressure measured with respect to zero pressure, in units of force per unit of area.

**absolute transpirations** (Bot.): The rate of loss of water from a plant, as determined by experiment.

**absolute weight** (Chem.): The weight of a body in a vacuum.

**absorber** (Nucleonics): Material for capturing neutrons without generating more neutrons.

**absorptiom'eter** (Chem.): An apparatus for determining the solubilities of gases in liquids.

**abutment** (Eng.): A surface or point provided to withstand thrust; e.g. the end supports of a bridge or an arch.

**abys'sal, abys'mal** (Ocean.): Relating to the greatest depths of the ocean.

**A. C.** (Elec. Eng.): Abbreviations for alternating current.

**acana'ceous** (Bot.): A general term for prickly.

**acan'tha** (Bot.): A spine or prickle.

**acantho'sis ni'gricans** (Med.): A condition in which warty pigmented growths appear on the surface of the body.

**acap'nia** (Med.): Excessive diminution of carbon dioxide in the blood.

**ac'arus** (Biol.): A mite.

**a'cauline, a'caulose** (Bot.): Stemless or nearly so.

**acceleration** (Mech.): The rate of change of velocity, expressed in feet or centimetres per second.

**accelerator** (Nucleonics): Any device for accelerating to high kinetic energy protons, electrons, deuterons and helium ions.

**accelerator** (Bot.): Any substance which increases the efficient action of an enzyme. (Chem.): A substance which increases the speed of a chemical reaction. (Automobiles): A pedal connected to the carburetor throttle valve of a motor vehicle, or to the fuel injection control where oil engines are used. (Zool.): Any nerve or muscle which increases rate of action.

**accelerom'eter** (Aero.): An instrument carried in aircraft for measuring acceleration in a specific direction.

**accentuation** (Photog.): High-lights or high contrasts in the composition of a photographic picture.

**acceptor** (Chem.): (1) The reactant in an induced reaction which does not react directly with the inductor. (2) The atom which contributes no electrons to a semi-polar bond.

**accesso'rius** (Zool.): A muscle which supplements the action of another muscle: in Vertebrates, the eleventh cranial nerve or spinal accessory.

**acclimatisation** (Chem.): The change produced in a colloidal sol by the addition of a precipitating agent in small quantities, resulting in less complete precipitation for the addition of a given total amount of precipitant.

**accommodation** (Bot.): The capacity possessed by a plant to adjust itself to new conditions of life, provided the changed conditions come gradually into operation. (Physiol.): The ability of the eye to change its effective focal length in order to see objects distinctly at varying distances.

**accouplement** (Carp.): A tie or brace of timber.

**accres'cent** (Bot.): Enlarged; usually applied to a calyx which increases in size as the fruit ripens.

**accretion** (Zool.): External addition of new matter: growth by such external addition.

**accuracy**: Implies exactitude in measurement.

**A.C.E. mixture** (Med.): A common general anaesthetic, containing 1 part of alcohol ° parts of chloroform and 3 parts of ether.

**aceph'alous** (Bot.): Said of a style which does not terminate in a well-marked stigma.

**acerose, acerous** (Bot.): Needle-shaped.

**acetates** (Chem.): The salts of acetic acid; e.g. sodium acetate.

**acetic acid** (Chem.): $CH_3$ • COOH, an important raw material of the chemical industry, synthesised from acetylene; also obtained by the oxidation of alcohol and by the destructive distillation of wood.

**achala'sia** (Med.): Failure to relax.

**achene, akene, achae'nocarp** (Bot.): A small, dry, one-seeded fruit which ripens without bursting its thin outer sheath or pericarp.

**achlorhy'dria** (Med.): Absence of hydrochloric acid from the gastric juice.

**achon'drite** (Geol.): A type of stony meteorite which compares with some basic igneous rocks; e.g. eucrite.

**achon'dropla'sia** (Med.): A condition of dwarfism characterised by shortness of the legs and the arms and by a big head.

**achondroplas'tic** (Zool.): Having a normal body with stunted limbs or appendages.

**achro'matin** (Cyt.): That part of the nucleus which does not stain with basic dyes.

**acic'ular** (Bot., Zool.): Stiff, pointed and slender, like a pine needle.

**acic'ulate** (Bot.): Marked on the surface by fine scratches.

**acid** (Chem.): (1) A substance which tends to lose a proton. (2) A substance containing hydrogen which may be replaced by metals with the formation of salts. (3) A substance which dissolves in water with the formation of hydrogen ions.

**acid solution** (Chem.): An aqueous solution containing more hydrogen ions than hydroxye ions; one which turns blue litmus red.

**acid'ophil** (Zool.): Said of structures which stain intensely with acid dyes.

**acina'ceous** (Bot.): Full of pips.

**acinaciform** (Bot.): Scimitar-shaped.

**ac'me** (Biol.): The period of maximum vigor of an individual, race or species.

**ac'ne** (Med.): Inflammation of a sebaceous gland. Pimples in adolescents are commonly due to infection with the acne bacillus.

**acoustics**: The science of sounds.

**acre** (Surv.): A unit of area equal to 4,840 square yards.

**acrocar'pons** (Bot.): Having fruit at the end of the stem or branch.

**acrodro'mous** (Bot.): Said of venation when the main veins, after running parallel along most of the leaf, unite at the leaf apex.

**ac'ron** (Zool.): In insects, the region in front of the mouth.

**acti'noid** (Zool.): Star-shaped.

**acti'nomere** (Zool.): A radial segment.

**action** (Acous.): The mechanism for selecting notes in musical instruments.

**activity** (Nucleonics): Rate of breakdown of atoms through radioactivity.

**acu'leate** (Bot.): Bearing prickles, or covered with needle-like outgrowths.

**acute** (Bot.): Bearing a sharp and abrupt point; said usually of a leaf-tip. (Med.): Said of a disease which rapidly develops to a crisis.

**acy'clic** (Bot.): Having the parts of the flower arranged in spirals.

**adaptation** (Bot.): Any morphological or physiological characteristic which may be supported to help in adjusting the organism to the conditions under which it lives. (Zool.): The process by which an animal becomes fitted to its environment.

**adapter** (Elec. Eng.): An accessory used in electrical installations for connecting a piece of apparatus fitted with one type of terminals to a supply-point fitted with another size.

**addict** (Med.): One who is unable to resist taking harmful drugs.

**adductor** (Zool.): A muscle that draws a limb or part inwards, or towards another part.

**adelomor'phic** (Zool.): Of indefinite form.

**adeni'tis** (Med.): Inflammation of a gland.

**adhesion** (Elec.): The mutual force which tends to hold two electrified non-conducting bodies together. (Med.): Abnormal union of two parts which have been inflamed.

**a'biabat'ic** (Bot.): Not capable of translocation. (Phys.): Without gain or loss of heat.

**adit** (Civ. Eng.): An access tunnel, that is usually nearly horizontal, leading to a main tunnel.

**adjustor** (Zool.): An organ or faculty determining the behavior of an organism in response to stimuli received.

**adj'utage** (Hyd.): A tube or nozzle through which water is discharged.

**adj'uvant** (Med.): A remedy which assists the action of other remedies.

**adnexa** (Anat.): Appendages; usually refers to Fallopian tubes and ovaries.

**ado'ral** (Zool.): Adjacent to the mouth.

**adpressed, appressed** (Bot.): Pressed closely together but not joined.

**adre'nal** (Zool.): Adjacent to the kidney.

**adsorption** (Chem.): The taking up of one substance at the surface of another.

**adulares'cence** (Min.): A milky or bluish sheen in gemstones.

**advection** (Meteor.): The transference of heat by horizontal motion of the air.

**adven'tive** (Bot.): Denotes a plant which has not secured a permanent foothold in a given locality.

**aeolotro'pic** (Phys.): Having physical properties which vary according to the position or direction in which they are measured.

**aerial** (Radio): Any exposed wire capable of radiating or receiving the energy to or from an electromagnetic wave.

**aer'obe, aerobi'ont** (Bot.): A plant which requires elementary oxygen for respiration.

**aerodynam'ics** (Aero.): That part of the mechanics of fluids that deals with the dynamics of gases. Primarily, the study of forces acting upon bodies in motion in air.

**aero-engine** (Aero.): The power unit of an aircraft.

**aer'olites** (Geol.): A general name for stony as distinct from iron meteorites.

**aerol'ogy** (Aero.): The study of the upper air, that part of the atmosphere removed from the effect of surface conditions.

**aeronautical engineering**: That branch of engineering concerned with the design, production and maintenance of aircraft structures and power units.

**aeronautics**: All activities concerned with aerial locomotion.

**aeroph'agy** (Med.): The swallowing of air, with consequent inflation of the stomach.

**aeroplane** (Aero.): Any power-driven heavier-than-air flying machine with fixed wings.

**aer'ostat** (Aero.): Any form of aircraft deriving support in the air primarily from its buoyancy.

**aes'tival** (Bot., Zool.): Occurring in summer.

**aestivation** (Bot.): The arrangement of the sepals and petals.

**aetiology, etiol'ogy** (Med.): The medical study of the causation of disease.

**afeb'rile** (Med.): Without symptoms or signs of fever.

**af'fect** (Psychol.): The degree of pleasantness or unpleasantness accompanying any emotional state.

**affinity** (Bot.): Likeness, especially in relationships.

**agalac'tia, agala'cia** (Med.): Failure of the breast to secrete milk.

**agamic** (Bot.): Said of reproduction without the cooperation of a male gamete.

**agam'ogen'esis** (Bot., Zool.): Asexual reproduction.

**agamotro'pic** (Bot.): Said of a flower which does not shut after having once opened.
**agar'ic** (Bot.): A mushroom or toadstool.
**agene'sia, agen'esis** (Med.): Imperfect development or failure to develop of any part of the body.
**age'otro'pism** (Bot.): The condition of not reacting to gravity.
**agglomerate** (Bot.): Crowded or heaped into a cluster.
**agglutinate** (Bot.): Cemented together by sticky material.
**aggregate** (Bot.): Closely packed but not confluent. (Zool.): Massed or clustered. (Geol., Min.): A mass consisting of rock or mineral fragments.
**aggressiveness** (Bot.): The capacity of a parasite to attack its host.
**aglos'sate, aglos'sal** (Zool.): Lacking a tongue.
**agno'sia** (Med.): Loss of the ability to recognize the nature of an object through the senses of the body.
**ag'orapho'bia** (Psychol.): The fear of being alone in an open space.
**agraph'ia** (Med.): Loss of the power to express thought in writing, as a result of a lesion in the brain.
**agres'tal** (Bot.): Growing in cultivated ground, but not itself cultivated; e.g. a weed.
**agrostol'ogy** (Bot.): The study of grasses.
**air-cooling** (Eng.): The cooling of hot bodies by means of a stream of cold air, as distinct from water-cooling.
**air brake** (Aero.): An extendable device to increase the drag of an aircraft.
**air-drain** (Build.): A cavity in the external walls of a building, designed to prevent damp from getting through to the interior.
**aircraft** (Aero.): All air-supported vehicles.
**air ducts** (Eng.): Pipes or channels through which air is distributed throughout buildings for heating and ventilation.
**airflow meter** (Aero.): An instrument for measuring the airflow in ducts.
**air gate** (Eng.): A passage from the interior of a mold to allow the escape of air and gases as the metal is poured in.
**air log** (Aero.): An instrument for registering the distance travelled by an aircraft relative to the air.
**air pocket** (Aero.): A colloquialism for a localized region of low air density, a rising or descending air current.
**air speed** (Aero.): Speed measured relative to the air in which the aircraft is moving, as distinct from speed relative to the ground.
**akine'sia** (Med.): A disinclination to move, as a result of a brain lesion.
**a'lar** (Zool.): Pertaining to wings.
**al'binism** (Bot.): An abnormal condition due to the absence of chlorophyll or other pigments. (Zool.): Absence of pigmentation especially marked in the skin, epidermal outgrowths and the eyes.
**albu'men** (Zool.): White of an egg.
**alex'ia** (Med.): Loss of the ability to interpret written language, due to a brain lesion.
**Algae** (Bot.): A large group of simple organisms, mostly aquatic. They contain chlorophyll and/or other photosynthetic pigments and have simple organized reproductive organs.
**algebra** (Maths.): The abstract investigation of the properties of numbers by means of symbols; e.g. x, y, etc.
**algesim'eter** (Med.): An instrument for measuring sensitivity to pain.
**alignment** (Civ. Eng.): A setting in line, usually straight.
**alimentary**: Pertaining to the nutritive functions or organs.
**alinentary canal** (Zool.): The digestive tract.
**al'kali** (Chem.): A substance which dissolves in water to form an alkaline solution, especially the sodium and potassium hydroxides.
**alkaline solution** (Chem.): An aqueous solution containing more hydroxyl ions than hydrogen ions; one which turns red litmus blue.
**aller'gy** (Med.): A state in which the cells of the body are supersensitive to substances.
**allette** (Build.): A wing of a building or a buttress.
**allocar'py** (Bot.): Fruiting after cross-fertilization.
**allom'eric** (Chem.): Having the same crystalline form but a different chemical composition.
**allomor'phous** (Chem.): Having the same chemical composition but a different crystalline form.
**allotro'pous flower** (Bot.): A flower in which the nectar is readily accessible to all kinds of visiting insects.
**alloy** (Chem.): Any metal other than a pure metallic element. (Met.): Metal prepared by adding other metals or non-metals to a basic metal to obtain desirable properties.
**alopecia** (Med.): Baldness.
**alternate** (Bot.): Said of leaves and branches which are placed singly on the parent axis; not opposite.
**alternating current** (Elec. Eng.): An electric current the direction of flow of which alternates in direction.
**altri'ces** (Zool.): Birds whose young are hatched in a very immature condition.
**alu'minum** (Met.): Light ductile metal with high electrical conductivity and good resistance to corrosion.
**amal'gam** (Chem.): The solution of a metal in mercury.
**amaweo'sis** (Med.): Blindness due to a lesion of the optic nerve, the retina, or optic tracts, or to hysteria.
**ama'zia** (Med.): Non-development of the female mammary glands.
**am'bergris** (Zool.): A grayish fatty substance obtained from the intestines of diseased sperm whales; used as a fixative in perfumery.
**am'bient** (Biol.): Environmental.
**ambiva'lence** (Psychol.): The co-existence, in one person, of opposing emotional attitudes, as love and hate, towards the same object.
**ambula'tory** (Zool.): Having the power of walking.
**amelification** (Zool.): The formation of enamel.
**amenorrhoe'a** (Med.): Suppression or absence of menstruation.
**amenta'ceous** (Bot.): Bearing catkins.
**am'ntia** (Med.): Mental deficiency.
**amito'sis, amitot'ic division** (Cyt.): Direct nuclear division.
**am'meter** (Elec. Eng.): An indicating instrument for measuring the current in an electric circuit.
**am'modyte** (Bot.): A plant living in sandy places.
**amne'sia** (Med.): Loss of memory.
**amoe'ba** (Zool.): A form of primitive Protozoon of indeterminate shape.
**ampere** (Elec. Eng.): The most frequently used unit of current.
**amphibian** (Aero.): Aeroplane capable of taking off and landing on land or water.
**amphibious** (Zool.): Adapted for life on land or in the water.
**amphicar'pic** (Bot.): Having two kinds of fruits.
**amphig'ony** (Zool.): Reproduction by fertilization.
**amphilep'sis** (Gen.): Inheritance such that the off-spring has characteristics derived from both parents.
**amphitheatre** (Build.): An oval or circular building in which the spectators' seats surround the arena in which the spectacle is presented, the seats rising away from the arena.
**amphoter'ic** (Chem.): Having both basic and acidic properties.
**amplitude** (Phys.): The maximum value of a periodically varying quantity during a cycle.
**ampoule** (Med.): A small, sealed glass capsule for holding measured quantities of serums, drugs, vaccines etc., ready for use.
**amyg'dale, amyg'dule** (Geol.): An almond-shaped infilling by secondary minerals of elongated steam cavities in igneous rocks.
**amyla'ceous** (Bot.): Starchy.
**anabat'ic** (Meteor.): A term applied to winds caused by the upward convection of heated air.
**anae'mia, ane'mia** (Med.): Diminution of the amount of hemoglobin in the blood, from lowering of the quality or the quantity of the red blood cells.
**anesthe'sia** (Med.): Loss of sensibility to touch.
**anesthet'ic** (Med.): A drug which produces insensibility to touch, temperature and pain, with or without loss of consciousness.
**anesthetist**: One skilled in the administration of an anesthetic drug.
**analep'tic** (Med.): A drug or medicine that strengthens.
**analge'sia** (Med.): Loss of sensibility to pain.
**analogy** (Bot., Zool.): Likeness in function but not in origin.
**analysis** (Struct.): The process of reducing a problem to its primary parts.
**anamne'sis** (Med.): The past history of all matters relating to a patients' health.
**anamor'pha** (Zool.): Larvae which do not possess the full number of segments at the time of hatching.
**anas'tral** (Cyt.): Without asters.
**anatomy** (Bot., Zool., etc.): The study of the form and structure of animals and plants.
**anax'ial** (Zool.): Asymmetrical.
**an'con** (Arch.): A console built on each side of a door-opening to carry a cornice.
**anconeal** (Zool.): Pertaining to, or situated near, the elbow.
**andiron** (Build.): A metal support for wood in an open fire.
**an'drocyte** (Bot.): A sperm mother-cell.
**androdiviecious** (Bot.): Said of a species in which some of the plants bear staminate flowers, other hermaphrodite flowers.
**androgen'esis** (Bot., Zool.): Development from a male cell.
**androl'ogy** (Med.): That branch of medical science which deals with the functions and diseases peculiar to the male sex.
**anemom'eter** (Meteor.): An instrument for measuring the velocity of the wind.

**ane'mophily** (Bot.): Pollination by means of the wind.
**an'emotro'pism** (Biol.): Active response to the stimulus of an air current.
**anenceph'aly** (Med.): Developmental defect of the skull and absence of the brain.
**anen'terous** (Zool.): Without a gut.
**an'er** (Zool.): A male ant.
**aneroid barometer** (Meteor., Surv.): A portable instrument for the recording of changes in atmospheric pressure and for the approximate determination of altitude.
**Angiosper'mae** (Bot.): A major group of flowering plants in which the seeds develop and ripen inside a closed ovary.
**angle**: The inclination of one line to another, measured in degrees, of which there are 360 to one complete revolution.
**angle bar, angle iron, angle steel** (Eng.): Mild steel bar rolled to the cross-section of the letter L, much used for light structural work.
**angle-bead** (Build.): A small round molding placed at an external angle formed by plastered surfaces in order to preserve the corner from accidental fracture.
**angle block** (Carp.): A small wooden block used in woodwork to make joints more rigid, especially right angle joints.
**angle-board** (Carp.): One used as a gauge by which to plane boards to a required angle between two faces.
**angle brace** (Carp.): (1) Any bar fixed across the inside of an angle in a framework in order to make the latter more rigid. (2) A special tool for drilling in corners where there is not room to use the cranked handle of an ordinary brace.
**angle-closer** (Build.): A portion of a whole brick, used to close up the bond of brickwork at corners.
**angle of contact** (Phys.): The angle made by the surface separating two fluids (one of them usually air) with the wall of the containing vessel or with any other solid surface cutting the fluid surface.
**angle of depression** (Surv.): The vertical angle measured below the horizontal from the surveyors's instrument to the point observed.
**angle of elevation** (Surv.): The vertical angle measured above the horizontal, from the surveyor's instrument to the point observed.
**angle of incidence, angle of reflection** (Acous.): Respectively, the angle with which a beam of sound arrives at a surface, and the angle with which it leaves after reflection, the angle being measured with respect to the normal at the point of incidence.
**angle plate** (Eng.): A bracket used to support work on a lathe faceplate or other machine-tool.
**anglesite** (Min.): A common lead ore.
**Angström unit** (Phys.): The unit employed for expressing wave lengths of light, X-rays, and ultraviolet radiations.
**angular diameter** (Astron.): The angle which the apparent diameter of a heavenly body subtends at the observer's eye.
**angular velocity** (Phys.): The rate of change of angular displacement, usually expressed in radians per second.
**anhidro'sis** (Med.): Diminution of the secretion of sweat.
**anhy'drides** (Chem.): Substances which either combine with water to form acids, or which may be obtained from the latter by the elimination of water.
**an'ima** (Analytical Psychol.): Term used in Jungian psychology to denote the unconscious feminine component of a male personality.
**animal charcoal** (Chem.): The carbon residue obtained from the carbonization of organic matter as flesh, blood, etc.
**an'imus** (Analytical Psychol.): A Jungian term denoting the unconscious masculine component of a female personality.
**annealing**: General term denoting heating followed by slow cooling.
**annoyance** (Acous.): The psychological effect arising from excessive noise.
**annual** (Bot.): A plant which, in the same season that it develops from a seed, flowers, fruits, and dies.
**annual equation** (Astron.): One of the four principal periodic terms in the mathematical expression of the moon's orbital motion.
**annual ring** (Bot.): One of the circular bands seen when a branch or trunk is cut across; the band is a section of the cylinder of secondary wood added in one season of growth.
**annular** (Bot.): Having the form of a ring.
**annular eclipse** (Astron.): A central eclipse of the sun, in which the moon's disc does not completely cover the sun's disc at the moment of greatest eclipse but leaves a ring of the solar surface visible.
**an'ode** (Elec.): The positive electrode of an electrolytic cell.
**anodon'tia**: Absence of teeth.
**an'olyte** (Elec. Eng.): That part of the electrolyte of an electrolytic cell which is near the anode.
**anomaly**: Any departure from the strict characteristics of the type.
**anorex'ia** (Med.): Loss of appetite.
**anosmat'ic** (Zool.): Lacking the sense of smell.
**anox'ia, anoxe'mia** (Med., Zool.): Deficiency of oxygen in the blood.
**antagonist** (Physiol.): A muscle which opposes the action of another muscle.
**antenna** (Radio): An elevated or extended system of conductors used for the transmission and/or reception of electromagnetic waves. (Zool.): One of a pair of anterior appendages, usually many jointed and of sensory function.
**ante-sola'rium** (Build.): A balcony which faces the sun.
**anther** (Bot.): The fertile part of a stamen.
**an'thophore** (Bot.): An elongation of the floral receptacle between the calyx and the corolla.
**anthoxanthin** (Bot.): Yellow pigment in flowers.
**anthacite coals** (Fuels): Slow burning coals, yielding little ash, moisture and volatiles.
**anthraco'sis** (Med.): "Coal-miners' lung," produced by inhalation of coal dust.
**an'tibody** (Bacteriol.): Specific substances liberated into the plasma in response to the presence of bacteria and their toxins, and antagonistic to them.
**anticathode** (Phys., Radiol.): The anode target of an X-ray tube on which the cathode rays are focused, and from which the X-rays are emitted.
**anticline** (Geol.): A type of fold, the strata dipping outwards, away from the fold-axis.
**anticy'clone** (Meteor.): A distribution of atmospheric pressure in which the pressure increases towards the center.
**an'tigen** (Med.): Any bacterium, toxin or other vegetable or animal substance which, introduced into the body, gives rise to an antibody.
**an'timony** (Met.): A white metallic element with a bluish tinge.
**antinode** (Phys.): A point of maximum amplitude in a system of stationary waves.
**anti-neutron** (Nucleonics): Recently discovered particle which can mutually annihilate a neutron, with the evolution of vast energy.
**antisep'sis** (Med.): The inhibition of growth, or the destruction, of bacteria in the field of operation by chemical agents.
**antiseptic** (Med.): An agent which destroys bacteria or prevents their growth.
**antithrom'bin** (Chem.): An anti-enzyme, produced by the liver, preventing the intravascular clotting of the blood.
**antitox'ins** (Path.): Substances, produced by the organism, which, by uniting with toxins, prevent their poisonous action.
**antler** (Zool.): In deer, the annual outgrowth of bony material from the frontal bone.
**antrorse** (Zool.): Directed or bent forwards.
**anu'ral** (Zool.): Without a tail.
**anu'ria** (Med.): Suppression of the secretion of urine.
**a'nus** (Zool.): The opening of the alimentary canal by which indigestible residues are voided, generally posterior.
**anvil** (Anat.): One of the three small bones which transmit mechanical vibrations between the outer ear drum and the inner ear. (Eng.): A block of iron on which work is supported during forging.
**anvil cloud** (Meteor.): A common feature of a thunder-cloud, consisting of a wedge-shaped projection of cloud suggesting the point of an anvil.
**anxiety** (Psychol.): A state of mental apprehension and tension.
**aor'ta** (Zool.): The main arterial vessel or vessels by which blood leaves the heart and passes to the body.
**ap'atite** (Min.): Naturally occurring phosphate of calcium, widely distributed in igneous rock.
**aperiodic** (Acous., Elec.): Said of any potentially vibrating system which, because of sufficient damping, does not vibrate when impulsed.
**apeture** (Build.): An opening provided in a wall for ventilation purposes.
**apex**: The top or pointed end of anything.
**apha'sia** (Med.): Loss of, or defect in, the faculty of expressing thought in words.
**aphonia** (Med.): Loss of voice in hysteria, laryngitis, or in paralysis of the vocal cords.
**apho'tic** (Bot.): Able to grow with little or no light.
**Apjohn's formula** (Phys.): A formula which may be used for determining the pressure of water vapor in the air from readings of the dry and wet bulb hygrometer.
**apla'sia** (Med.): Defective structural development.
**apneu'sis** (Physiol.): Want of oxygen.
**apo'dal, apo'dous** (Zool.): Without feet.
**ap'ogee** (Astron.): The point farthest from the earth on the apse line of a central orbit having the earth as a focus.
**ap'ogeny** (Bot.): Sterility.

**apomecom'eter** (Surv.): An instrument which may be used to measure the height of trees, buildings, etc.
**apopet'alous** (Bot.): Lacking petals.
**ap'oplexy** (Med.): Sudden loss of consciousness and paralysis as a result of thrombosis of a cerebral artery or of hemorrhage into the brain.
**appendage:** A general term for any external outgrowth; as fins, limbs, etc.
**appendix** (Zool.): An outgrowth.
**applaus'eograph** (Acous.): A recording noise-meter, suitable for recording applause in a theatre.
**approach** (Civ. Eng.): The access road leading to a tunnel or bridge.
**apron** (Aero.): A firm surface laid down adjacent to aerodrome buildings to facilitate the movements, loading and unloading, of airplanes.
**apt'erous** (Zool.): Without wings.
**apty'alism** (Med.): Deficiency or absence of salivary secretion.
**apyrex'ia** (Med.): Absence of fever.
**aquamarine** (Min.): A variety of beryl, of blue-green color, used as a gemstone.
**aqueduct** (Civ. Eng.): An artificial conduit used to convey water.
**aqueous:** Made of, or pertaining to, water.
**arachnid'ium** (Zool.): The spinnerets and silk glands in spiders.
**arach'noid** (Bot., Zool.): Cobweb-like.
**arc:** A portion of a circle. (Elec.): A luminous discharge of electricity through an ionised gas.
**arch** (Civ. Eng.): A form of structure having a curved shape, used to support loads or to resist pressure.
**Archimedes' principle** (Phys.): When a body is wholly or partly immersed in a fluid, it suffers a loss in weight equal to the weight of fluid which it displaces.
**architectural acoustics** (Acous.): The study of the propagation of sound-waves in interiors.
**ar'chitype** (Zool.): A primitive type from which others may be derived.
**archoplasmic apparatus** (Cyt.): In cell-division, the asters, and the spindle-shaped bundle of fibers between them.
**arc'uate** (Bot., Zool.): Bent like a bow.
**are** (Surv.): The metric unit of area. 1 are = 119.6 sq. yds.
**arena'ceous** (Bot.): Growing best in sandy soil.
**a'reopyknom'eter** (Chem.): An instrument for the measurement of the specific gravity of viscous liquids.
**ar'gentite** (Min.): An important silver ore.
**argilla'ceous rocks** (Geol.): Sedimentary rocks of the clay grade.
**argument** (Maths.): The angle between a vector and its reference axis.
**ar'istate** (Bot.): Bearing a beard or awn.
**arithmetic:** The science of numbers.
**armature** (Elec.): A moving part in a magnetic circuit to indicate the presence of electric current as the agent of actuation.
**arrhi'zal** (Bot.): Lacking roots.
**arrhyth'mia** (Med.): Abnormal rhythm of the heart beat.
**arrow** (Surv.): The steel pin, looped at one end and pointed at the other, used to mark in the field the end of a chain.
**arrowroot:** Starch derived from the roots of plants of the maranta genus.
**ar'senic** (Chem.): An element which occurs in a large number of minerals. Symbol As.
**ar'tefact:** A man-made stone implement.
**arte'riosclero'sis** (Med.): Hardening or stiffening of the arteries.
**artery** (Zool.): One of the vessels of the vascular system, that conveys the blood from the heart to the body.
**arthri'tis** (Med.): Inflammation of a joint.
**arthro'dia** (Zool.): A joint.
**article** (Bot.): A joint of a stem or fruit, breaking apart at maturity.
**articulation** (Eng.): The connection of two parts in such a way as to permit the same relative movements. (Zool.): The movable or immovable connection between two or more bones.
**artiodac'tyl** (Zool.): Possessing an even number of digits.
**asexual** (Bot., Zool.): Without sex.
**asphalt:** The name given to various bituminous substances.
**asphyxia** (Med.): State of suspended animation as a result of deficiency of oxygen in the blood.
**aspirator** (Chem.): A device for draining a stream of liquids or air through an apparatus by suction.
**assimilation** (Zool.): The conversion of food material into protoplasm.
**aster** (Cyt.): A group of radiating fibrils formed of cytoplasmic granules surrounding the centrosome, seen immediately prior to and during cell-division.
**asteroid** (Astron.): A small planetary body.
**asthe'nic type** (Psychol.): One of Kretschmer's three types of individuals, characterized by tall thin men, with hands long in proportion to the trunk.
**asthma** (Med.): A disorder in which there occur attacks of difficult breathing due to spasm of the bronchial muscles.
**ast'roid** (Cyt.): In cell division, the star-shaped figure formed by the looped chromosomes aggregated around the equator of the nuclear spindle.
**as'trolabe** (Astron.): In ancient Greece, a circular instrument for stellar observation.
**astrology:** The pseudo science which treats of the influences of the stars upon human affairs, and of foretelling terrestrial events by their aspects and positions.
**astronomy:** The science of the heavens in all its branches.
**astrophysics:** That branch of astronomy which applies the laws of physics to the study of interstellar matter and the stars.
**astyl'len** (Civ. Eng.): A small dam built across an adit to restrict the flow of water.
**asymmetric:** Irregular in form; not divisible into halves.
**at'avism** (Gen.): The recurrence, in a descendant, of characters of a remote ancestor, as a great-grandparent.
**ataxia** (Med.): Inco-ordination of muscles.
**a'telomit'ic** (Cyt.): Said of a chromosome having the spindle fibre attached somewhere along the side.
**athletic type** (Psychol.): One of Kretschmer's three types of individual, characterized by a well-developed skeletal musculature, in which the relation of limbs to trunk is well-proportioned.
**atmosphere, pressure of** (Phys.): The pressure exerted by the atmosphere at the surface of the earth is due to the weight of the air.
**atmospheric** electricity (Meteor.): The electric charges which exist in the atmosphere.
**at'olls:** Coral reefs.
**atom** (Chem.): The smallest particle of an element which can take part in a chemical reaction.
**atom'ic** (Chem.): Pertaining to an atom or atoms.
**atomic mass** (Phys.): The mass of an atom.
**atomic number** (Phys.): The number of an element when arranged with others in order of increasing atomic weight.
**atomic weight** (Chem.): The relative weight of an atom of an element when the weight of an atom of oxygen is taken as 16.000.
**atomicity** (Chem.): The number of atoms contained in a molecule of an element.
**at'omiser** (Eng.): A nozzle through which oil fuel is sprayed into the combustion chamber of an oil engine or boiler furnace.
**at'rophy** (Med.): Wasting of a cell or of an organ of the body.
**attenuate** (Bot.): Narrowing gradually to a point.
**attenuation** (Bot.): A weakening by parasitic bacteria and fungi in culture.
**attracted-disc electrometer** (Elec. Eng.): An instrument in which potential is measured by the attraction between two oppositely charged discs.
**attrition test** (Civ. Eng.): A test for the determination of the wear-resisting properties of stone.
**audibility** (Acous.): Ability to be heard.
**audiom'eter** (Acous.): An electrical apparatus for measuring the minimum intensities of sounds perceivable by an ear, for specified frequencies.
**auditory, aural** (Zool.): Pertaining to the sense of hearing.
**aug'er** (Carp., Civ. Eng.): A tool used for boring holes.
**aur'eole** (Meteor.): (1) The clear transparent space between the sun or moon and a halo or corona. (2) The bright indefinite ring around the sun in the absence of clouds.
**Auro'ra Borea'lis** (Astron.): The Northern Lights, a phenomenon consisting of luminous arcs.
**Australasian region** (Zool.): One of the primary faunal regions into which the land surface of the globe is divided.
**aut'ocarp** (Bot.): A fruit resulting from self-fertilization.
**autoclave** (Chem.): A vessel for carrying out chemical reactions under pressure and at high temperatures.
**autog'amy** (Bot., Zool.): Self-fertilization.
**auto-infection** (Zool.): Re-infection of a host by its own parasites.
**auto-intoxication** (Med.): Poisoning of the body by toxins produced in it.
**automatic digital computer** (Maths.): Electronic calculating machine using conventional arithmetical digits.
**automatic pilot** (Aero.): A device for guiding and controlling an aircraft on a given path.
**automation:** Industrial technique in which the whole of a manufacturing process is performed automatically under electronic control.
**autonomic, auton'omous** (Bot., Zool.): Self-regulating, independent.
**autoph'agous** (Zool.): Capable of self-feeding from birth.

**aut'ophyte** (Bot.): A plant which builds up its food substances from simple compounds.
**auxe'tic** (Zool.): Stimulating cell-division.
**awl** (Carp.): A small pointed tool for making holes which are to receive screws or nails.
**awn** (Bot.): A long bristle borne on some cereals and grasses.
**axil** (Bot.): The solid angle between a stem and the upper surface of a leaf base growing from it.
**axis** (Aero.): The three axes of an aircraft are the straight lines through the center of gravity about which change of altitude occurs.
**axis**: A line, usually imaginary, which has a peculiar importance in relation to a particular set of circumstances.
**axle** (Eng.): The cross-shaft or beam which carries the wheel of a vehicle.

## B

**bacil'lus** (Bacteriol.): A rod-shaped member of bacteria.
**backlash** (Eng.): The lost motion between two elements of a mechanism.
**backing** (Meteor.): The changing of a wind into a counter-clockwise direction.
**bacteria** (Bacteriol.): A large group of unicellular or filamentous microscopic organisms, lacking chlorophyll and well-defined nuclei, multiplying rapidly by simple fissure.
**bacteriology**: The scientific study of bacteria.
**bacte'rium** (Bacteriol.): A rod-shaped member of bacteria.
**badger** (Build.): An implement used to clear mortar from a drain after it has been laid.
**baffle** (Acous.): A rigid structure for regulating the distribution of sound-waves from a reproducer.
**baffle plate** (Eng.): A plate used to prevent the movement of a fluid in the direction in which it would normally flow, and to direct it into the desired path.
**baffle tube**: A pipe of sufficient length to lower the temperature of hot gases before they enter a furnace.
**balance**: Equilibrium of the body.
**balcony** (Build.): A projecting platform, either inside or outside a building.
**baleen'** (Zool.): In certain whales, horny plates arising from the mucous membrane of the palate, and acting as a food strainer.
**ball-pane hammer** (Eng.): A hammer, the head of which has a flat face at one end, and a smaller hemispherical face at the other.
**ballis'tics** (Mech.): The science of projectiles.
**balloon** (Aero.): A general term for aircraft supported by buoyancy and not driven mechanically.
**balsa wood** (Acous.): A highly porous wood valued for its lightness.
**baluster** (Build.): A small pillar supporting the hand-rail of a staircase.
**band**: A transverse marking broader than a line.
**banker** (Build.): A bench upon which bricklayers and stonemasons shape their material.
**banking** (Aero.): Angular displacement of the wings of an airplane about the longitudinal axis, to cause turning.
**bar** (Civ Eng.): A deposit of sand or gravel in a river or across the mouth of a river. (Eng.): Material of uniform cross-section which may be extruded or rolled.
**barb** (Bot.): A hooked hair-like bristle. (Zool.): One of delicate thread-like structures extending obliquily from a feather rachis, and forming the vane.
**barbate** (Zool.): Bearded.
**barbel** (Zool.): A tactile process arising from the head of various fishes.
**bark** (Bot.): The external group of tissues, from the cambrium outwards, of a woody stem.
**bar'nacle** (Zool.): A crustacean.
**barometer** (Meteor.): An instrument used for the measurement of atmospheric pressure.
**barophore'sis** (Chem.): Diffusion of suspended particles at a speed dependent on extraneous forces.
**baroscope** (Meteor.): An instrument giving rough indications of changes in atmospheric pressure.
**barren** (Bot.): Infertile.
**barysphere**: The solid heavy interior core of the earth inside the lithosphere.
**bas relief** (Arch.): Sculpture in which the figures project their true proportions from the surface on which they are carved.
**basal** (Bot.): At, or near the base.
**basal metabolic rate** (Zool.): The rate of oxygen consumption in a resting organism or organ.
**bas'alt** (Geol.): A fine-grained, dark colored igneous rock.
**base** (Bot.): That end of a plant member nearest to the point of attachment to another member. (Chem.): A substance which tends to gain a proton.
**base bullion** (Met.): Impure lead.
**base line** (Surv.): A survey line the length of which is accurately measured.
**ba'seost** (Zool.): One of the distal elements of a fin-ray in fish.
**basichro'matin** (Cyt.): A form of chromatin which stains relatively deeply.
**basicity** (Chem.): The number of hydrogen atoms of an acid replaceable by a metal atom.
**basid'ium** (Bot.): A special cell or rom of cells, of certain fungi, forming spores by abstriction.
**basin** (Geol.): A geological formation in which the strata dip towards the center.
**bass frequencies** (Acous.): Those frequencies towards the lower end of the audible scale.
**bathom'eter** (Ocean.): An instrument used for deep-sea soundings.
**bathoph'ilous** (Zool.): Adapted to an aquatic life at great depths.
**bathotonic** (Chem.): Tending to diminish surface tension.
**bath'yal zone** (Geol.): The sea-floor between 600 & 3,000 ft. below sea-level.
**bath'ybic** (Biol.): Relating to the deep sea.
**bath'ysphere** (Ocean.): A spherical diving apparatus capable of resisting tremendous pressure.
**batter** (Build.): Slope of the face of a structure from the vertical.
**batter pile** (Civ. Eng.): A pile which is driven in at an angle to the vertical.
**battery** (Elec.): A group of two or more primary cells electrically connected in series or in parallel.
**bauxite** (Min.): A residual clay formed by the chemical weathering of basic igneous rocks.
**bead** (Carp.): A small convex molding formed on wood or other material.
**beaked** (Bot.): Bearing a pointed prolongation.
**bearing** (Build.): The part of a girder which rests on the supports.
**bearing** (Surv.): The horizontal angle between any survey line and a given reference direction.
**Beaufort notation** (Meteor.): A code of letters used for indicating the state of the weather.
**Beckmann apparatus** (Chem.): Apparatus used for measuring the boiling and freezing points.
**bed** (Geol.): A term used for stratum.
**beha'viourism** (Psychol.): A school of thought that bases its doctrine on objective observation and experiment.
**bell**: A sound-emitting metal device, operated by striking.
**belt** (Eng.): An endless strip of leather used to transmit rotary motion from one shaft to another by running over pulleys.
**benthos** (Ecol.): The animal and plant life on the sea bottom.
**benzine** (Chem.): Petroleum hydrocarbons.
**ber'iber'i** (Med.): A disease resulting from thiamine deficiency.
**berm** (Civ. Eng.): A horizontal ledge on the side of an embankment to intercept earth rolling down the slopes.
**berry** (Bot.): A simple fleshy fruit.
**beryllium** (Met.): Used in nuclear reactors, as it reflects neutrons.
**betatron** (Phys.): An apparatus for imparting high velocities to electrons.
**Bethell's process** (Build.): A process for preserving timber.
**bevel** (Carp.): The sloping surface formed when two surfaces meet at an angle which is not a right angle.
**bicar'bonates** (Chem.): The acid salts of carbonic acid.
**bi'ceps** (Zool.): A muscle with two parts at one end.
**bicon'jugate** (Bot.): Said of a compound leaf when each of the two main ribs bears a pair of leaflets.
**bicus'pid** (Bot.): Having two short horn-like points.
**bien'nial** (Bot.): A plant which completes its life cycle within two years and then dies.
**bifa'cial** (Bot.): Flattened, and having the upper and lower faces of different structure.
**bifa'rious** (Bot.): Arranged in two rows, one on each side of an axis.
**bi'fid** (Bot., Zool.): Forked.
**bigem'inate** (Bot.): In two pairs.
**bigener'ic** (Zool.): Hybrids produced by crossing two distinct genera.
**bight**: A loop formed in a rope or chain.
**bila'biate** (Bot.): With two lips.
**bilat'eral** (Med.): Pertaining to, or having, two sides.
**bilateral symmetry** (Biol.): The arrangement of body parts so that the right and left halves are mirror images of each other.
**bile** (Physiol.): A viscous liquid produced by the liver.
**bile ducts** (Zool.): The excretory ducts of the liver and gall bladder.
**bilge**: The space above the double bottom of a ship, into which waste water from the engine-room and holds is drained.
**bill** (Zool.): In birds, the beak.
**biloc'ular** (Bot.): Consisting of two chambers.
**bilo'phodent** (Zool.): Having the two anterior and the

two posterior cusps of the grinding teeth joined by ridges.
**bi'manous** (Zool.): Having two hands.
**biman'ual** (Med.): Performed with both hands.
**bimolec'ular reaction** (Chem.): A reaction in which two molecules interact.
**bi'nary** (Astron.): A double star in which the two components revolve about their common center of mass under the influence of gravitational attraction. (Chem.): Consisting of two components.
**binary fission** (Biol.): The type of asexual reproduction in which division in two parts is approximately equal.
**bi'nate** (Bot.): Occurring in pairs.
**binaur'al** (Acous.): Pertaining to the use of two ears.
**binding energy** (Nucleonics): Total energy required to separate the protons and neutrons in a nucleus.
**binding screw** (Eng.): The general name for a set-screw used for clamping two parts together.
**Binet's test** (Psychol.): A method of testing a child's intelligence.
**binomial nomenclature** (Biol.): The system of denoting an organism by two Latin words, the first the name of the genus and the second the specific name.
**biochemistry**: The chemistry of living things.
**biocoenosis** (Ecol.): The association of plants and animals together, especially in relation to a feeding area.
**biocoenotic** (Ecol.): Pertaining to the inter-relationship between the organisms of a community.
**bi'ogen** (Bot.): A hypothetical protein molecule of instable nature which is assumed to be primarily responsible for life.
**biogen'esis** (Biol.): The doctrine that life comes only from pre-existing life.
**biology**: The science of plant and animal life.
**biolumines'cence** (Biol.): The production of light by living organisms.
**biom'eter** (Biol.): An instrument for measuring the amount of life by assessing the respiration.
**bi'on** (Bot.): An individual plant.
**bi'ophore** (Bot.): A hypothetical particle of minute size, assumed to be capable of growth and reproduction.
**bi'opsy** (Med.): Diagnostic examination of tissue removed from the living body.
**bi'os** (Chem.): A group of substances which act as a growth promoter for yeast.
**biot'is** (Biol.): Relating to life.
**bi'otite** (Min.): A form of black mica distributed in igneous rocks as shiny black crystals.
**bi'otype** (Biol.): One individual of a population composed of organisms which are alike in their inheritable characters.
**bip'arous** (Zool.): Giving birth to two young at a time.
**biped** (Zool.): A two-footed animal.
**bipen'niform** (Zool.): Feather-shaped, with the sides of the vane of equal size.
**bipolar** (Zool.): Having two poles.
**bipyramid (Crystal.): A crystal form consisting of two pyramids on a common base, the one being the mirror-image of the other.**
**bird's-eye grain** (Bot.): The appearance when worked timber shows large numbers of small circular areas dotted about the wood.
**bi'refrin'gence** (Min.): The double-bending of light by crystalline minerals.
**bi'sac'cate** (Bot.): Having two sepals each with a small pouch at the base.
**bise'riate** (Bot.): (1) In two rows. (2) A vascular ray two cells wide.
**bisex'ual** (Bot., Zool.): Possessing both male and female sexual organs.
**bismuth** (Chem.): A gray-white metallic element.
**bis'toury** (Med.): A long, narrow surgical knife for cutting abscesses, etc.
**bisul'cate** (Bot.): Marked by two furrows.
**bisymmet'ric** (Bot.): Symmetrical in two planes at right-angles to one another.
**bit** (Carp.): A boring tool.
**bittern** (Chem.): The residual liquid remaining from the evaporation of sea water
**biva'lent** (Cyt.): Paired homologous chromosomes.
**bi'valve** (Zool.): Having the shell in the form of two plates.
**biva'riant** (Chem.): Having two degrees of freedom.
**bivol'tine** (Zool.): Having two broods in each year.
**bladder** (Bot.): A device which catches small aquatic animals. (Zool.): Any membranous sac containing fluid or gas.
**blade** (Bot.): The flattened part of a leaf, sepal or petal.
**blast**: The ignition of an explosive charge. (Met.): Air under pressure, blown into a furnace.
**blaste'ma** (Bot.): The axial part of an embryo (Zool.): The protoplasmic part of an egg.
**blasting** (Civ. Eng.): The operation of disintegrating rock, etc.
**blast'ocyst** (Zool.): The germinal vesicle.
**blast'oderm**: The germinal disc.
**blastogen'esis** (Gen.): Transmission of inherited characters by means of germ-plasm only.
**blast'okine'sis** (Zool.): Migration of embryo in insect eggs.
**blast'omere** (Zool.): One of the cells formed during the early stages of cleavage of the ovum.
**Blavier's text** (Elec. Eng.): A method of locating a fault on an electric cable.
**bleb** (Med.): A small blister containing clear fluid.
**bleeder** (Med.): One afflicted with hemophilia.
**bleeding** (Bot.): The exudation of sap from wounds.
**blinding** (Civ. Eng.): The process of sprinkling small stone chips over a tár-dressed road surface.
**blink microscope** (Astron.): An instrument in which two photographic plates of the same region are viewed simultaneously.
**blister** (Med.): A subcutaneous bubble filled with fluid.
**block time** (Aero.): The time elapsed from the moment an aircraft starts to leave to the moment it comes to rest.
**blood** (Zool.): The fluid circulating in the vascular system of animals, distributing food material and oxygen and collecting waste products.
**blood corpuscle** (Physiol.): A cell normally contained in suspension in the blood.
**blood count** (Med.): The number of red or white corpuscles in the blood.
**blood dust** (Physiol.): Neutral fats carried by the blood-plasma in the form of very fine globules.
**blood groups**: A classification of human bloods based on their mutual agglutination reactions.
**blood plasma** (Physiol.): The fluid part of the blood, under normal conditions.
**blood serum** (Physiol.): The fluid part of the blood remaining after the corpuscles and the fibrin have been removed.
**blood-vessel** (Physiol.): An enclosed space with well-defined walls, through which blood passes.
**blow-holes** (Met.): Gas-filled cavities in solid metals.
**blowpipe** (Chem.): An apparatus using a mixture of air under pressure and coal gas in order to give a hot localized flame.
**blower** (Eng.): A rotary air-compressor for supplying a large volume of air at low pressure.
**blub** (Build.): A swelling on the surface of newly plastered work.
**blubber** (Zool.): In marine mammals, a thick fatty layer on the dermis.
**blur** (Acous.): The introduction of alien frequencies into reproduced sounds, making the sounds indistinct.
**board** (Build.): Timber cut to a thickness of less than 2 in., and to any width from 4 in. upwards.
**board-foot** (Build.): The unit of measurement in the board-measure system, being a piece of lumber of 1 in. thickness by 12 in. square.
**bobbin** (Elec. Eng.): A flanged structure used for the winding of a coil. Also called a spool.
**body cell** (Zool.): Somatic cell.
**body wall** (Zool.): The wall of the perivisceral cavity, comprising the skin and muscle layers.
**Bohr magneton** (Nucleonics): Unit for expressing magnetic moments of electrons or nuclei.
**boiler** (Eng.): A steam-generator consisting of tubes and water-drums, exposed to the heat of a furnace and arranged so as to promote rapid circulation.
**boiling**: The rapid conversion of a liquid into vapor by the violent evolution of bubbles; it occurs when the temperature reaches such a value that the saturated vapor pressure of the liquid equals the pressure of the atmosphere.
**boiling point**: The temperature at which a liquid boils when exposed to the atmosphere.
**bole** (Bot.): A tree trunk.
**bo'lide** (Astron.): A large meteor, generally one that explodes.
**boll** (Bot.): The fruit of a cotton plant.
**bollard**: On a vessel or quay, a short upright post round which ropes are secured for mooring purposes.
**bolom'eter** (Elec. Eng.): An instrument for measuring radiant energy.
**bolt** (Eng.): A cylindrical, screwed metal bar with a nut, it is the most common means of fastening two parts together.
**bomb**: A high-explosive, incendiary, smoke or gas projectile. (Geol.): A spherical or ovoid mass of lava formed by explosions in an active volcano vent.
**bone** (Zool.): Connective tissue in which the ground substance contains salts of lime.
**bone beds** (Geol.): Strata characterized by a high content of fossil remains.
**boning-in** (Surv.): The process of locating and driving in pegs so that they are in line.
**booking** (Surv.): A surveyor's term to describe the operation of recording field observations.
**boom** (Eng.): Any long beam.
**boost control** (Aero.): **A capsule device regulating reciprocating-engine manifold pressure so that supercharged engines are not over-stressed at low altitude.**

**booster transformer** (Elec. Eng.): A transformer connected in series with a circuit in order to raise or lower the voltage of that circuit.

**booted** (Zool.): Having the feet protected by horny scales.

**bora** (Meteor.): A squally winter wind blowing on the shores of the Adriatic and Aegean seas.

**borax** (Min.): A mineral deposited by evaporation of the waters of alkaline lakes.

**boring** (Civ. Eng.): The process of drilling holes into ground or rock.

**bornite** (Min.): A copper ore.

**bo'ron** (Chem.): A non-metallic element.

**botany**: The branch of science that deals with plant life.

**botryoi'dal** (Zool.): Shaped like a bunch of grapes.

**bottoming** (Civ. Eng.): The lowest layer of foundation material for a road.

**boulder** (Geol.): The unit of largest size occurring in rocks.

**bow** (Elec. Eng.): A sliding type of current collector, used on electric vehicles to collect the current from an overhead contact-wire.

**Boyle's law** (Phys.): The volume of a given mass of gas kept at a uniform temperature varies inversely as the pressure.

**braccate** (Zool.): Feathered legs or feet; said of birds.

**brace** (Carp., Eng.): A tool used to hold a bit and give it rotary motion.

**bra'chial** (Zool.): Pertaining to the ar of a vertebrate.

**bra'chiate** (Bot., Zool.): Branched; bearing arms.

**brachycerous** (Zool.): Having short antennae.

**brach'ycla'dous** (Bot.): Having very short branches.

**brach'ymeio'sis** (Cyt.): A simplified form of meiosis, completed in one division.

**brachypterous** (Zool.): With short wings that do not cover the abdomen.

**bracing** (Civ. Eng.): The supporting ties or rods which are used in the strengthening of a structure.

**bracket** (Build.): A projecting support for a shelf.

**bract** (Bot.): A modified leaf from the axil of which arises [illegible] r or an inflorescence.

**brad**: A [illegible] ith a small head.

**bradyar'thria** (Med.): Abnormally slow delivery of speech.

**bradycar'dia** (Med.): Slowness of the heart beat.

**bradykine'sia** (Med.): Abnormal slowness of the movements of the body.

**brad'yspore** (Bot.): A plant from which the seeds are liberated slowly.

**Bragg method** (Min.): A method of investigating crystal structure by X-rays.

**brain** (Zool.): Center of nervous system; mass of nervous matter in vertebrates at the anterior end of the spinal cord, lying in the cranium; in invertebrates, the pre-oral ganglia.

**brake** (Eng.): A device for applying resistance to the motion of a body.

**bran'chin** (Zool.): Gills.

**brass** (Met.): Primarily an alloy of zinc and copper.

**brazing** (Eng.): The process of joining two pieces of metal by fusing a layer of brass between the adjoining surfaces.

**break** (Elec. Eng.): The shortest distance between the contacts of a switch or similar apparatus, when the contacts are in an open position.

**breakwater** (Civ. Eng.): A natural or artificial coastal barrier to break the force of the waves.

**breast** (Anat.): An accessory gland of the generative system, rudimentary in the male and secreting milk in the female.

**brick**: A shaped and hardened block of special clay, used for building purposes.

**bridge** (Civ. Eng.): A structure built over or under a road or railway, or over a body of water, to provide a continuous roadway from one side to the other for transportation.

**bristle** (Bot.): A very stiff, erect hair.

**brittleness** (Met.): The tendency to fracture without appreciable deformation and under low stress.

**brochone'ma** (Cyt.): In cell division, the spireme thread when it has become arranged in the form of loops.

**bromides** (Chem.): Salts of hydrobromic acid.

**bromine** (Chem.): A non-metallic element.

**bronchi'tis** (Med.): Inflammation of the bronchi.

**bron'choscope** (Med.): An instrument consisting of a hollow tube with light and mirrors arranged for inspecting the interior of the bronchi.

**bronchus** (Zool.): One of the two branches into which the trachea divides, and which leads to the lungs.

**bronze** (Met.): Primarily an alloy of copper and tin.

**brood** (Zool.): A set of offsprings produced at the same birth or from the same batch of eggs.

**Brückner cycle** (Meteor.): A recurrence of periods of cold and damp alternating with warm and dry years, the period of a cycle being about 35 years.

**bruise** (Med.): Rupture of blood-vessels in a tissue.

**brush** (Elec. Eng.): A conductor arranged to make electrical contact between a stationary and a moving surface.

**Bry'ophy'ta** (Bot.): One of the main divisions of the plant kingdom; the liverworts and masses.

**bubble** (Surv.): The bubble of air and spirit vapor within a level tube; sometimes the level tube itself.

**buc'cal** (Zool.): Pertaining to the cheek or the mouth.

**buckle** (Eng.): To twist or bend out of shape.

**bud** (Bot.): The undeveloped stage of a branch.

**budding** (Bot.): (1) The production of daughter cells in the form of rounded outgrowths, characteristic of yeasts. (2) The production of buds. (3) A means of artificial propogation.

**buff** (Eng.): A revolving disc composed of layers of cloth charged with abrasive powder; used for polishing metals.

**building line** (Build.): The line beyond which a building may not be erected on any given plot.

**bulb** (Bot.): A large underground bud consisting of swollen leaf bases containing reserved food material, arranged on a short conical stem. (Illum.): The glass container holding the filament of an electric filament lamp or the electrodes of an electric discharge lamp.

**bulbous** (Bot.): Having underground bulbs. Swollen like a bulb.

**bulkhead** (Civ. Eng.): A timber or masonry partition to retain earth.

**bullate** (Bot.): Having a blistered surface.

**bulldozer** (Civ. Eng.): A power-operated machine provided with a blade for spreading and levelling material.

**bulling** (Civ. Eng.): The operation of detaching a piece of loosened rock by exploding blasting charges inserted in the surrounding fissures.

**bullion** (Met.): Gold or silver in bulk.

**bulwark** (Civ. Eng.): A sea-wall built to withstand the force of the waves.

**bundle** (Anat.): Fibers collected into a band in the nervous system or in the heart.

**bunker** (Eng.): A storage room for coal or oil fuel for use in steam boilers.

**Bunsen burner** (Chem.): A gas burner consisting of a tube with a small gas jet at the lower end, and an adjustable air inlet which controls the heat of the flame.

**buoy** (Hyd. Eng.): A floating vessel moored in ship-canals to mark the position of minor shoals and to show the limits of the navigable channel.

**buoyancy** (Phys.): The loss in weight of a body when immersed in a fluid.

**buran** (Meteor.): A frequent winter north-easterly wind in Russia and Central Asia.

**burden** (Elec. Eng.): A term used to signify the load on an instrument transformer.

**burette** (Chem.): A long glass tube with a ground-glass tap at one end and open at the other end; used in volumetric analysis.

**burial** (Nuclear Eng.): Place for the safe deposition of the highly radioactive products of the operation of nuclear reactors.

**bu'rin** (Engraving): A tool of tempered steel used in engraving and for retouching etched plates.

**burnisher** (Engraving): A polished steel tool used to soften or remove lines on engraved plates.

**burr** (Acous.): The rough edge which a victrola record has when it is removed from the press. (Eng.): (1) A rough edge left on metal by a cutting tool. (2) A blank punched from sheet-metal. (Engraving): A ridge raised on an engraved plate by a cutting tool.

**bursa** (Zool.): Any sac-like cavity.

**bush** (Bot.): A low woody plant forming a number of branches at ground level.

**butt joint** (Carp.): A joint formed between the squared ends of the two jointing pieces, which come together but do not overlap.

**butte** (Geol.): A steep-sided flat-topped hill.

**buttress** (Civ. Eng.): A supporting pier built on the exterior of a wall to enable it to resist outward thrust.

**Buys Bal'lot's law** (Meteor.): The law giving the direction of rotation of cyclones and anticyclones.

**buzzer** (Elec. Comm.): A vibrating reed used to generate a note to indicate the presence of actuating current.

**bys'malith** (Geol.): A form of igneous intrusion bounded by a circular fault and having a dome-shaped top.

**byssa'ceous** (Bot.): Consisting of a mass of fine threads; delicate, filamentous structure.

## C

**cab** (Eng.): The covered shelter for the driver of a locomotive or road-transport vehicle.

**cabin altitude** (Aero.): The nominal pressure altitude maintained in the cabin of a pressurized airplane.

**cable** (Eng.): A general term for rope or chain used for engineering purposes. (Elec. Comm.): An electrical circuit suitable for laying on the bed of the ocean for carrying telegraphic signals.

**cable code** (Teleg.): The modification of the Morse

code in which a dash becomes a dot reserved in polarity; used for telegraph transmission in submarine cables.
**cable-length**: One-tenth of a nautical mile (6080 feet).
**cabling** (Arch.): A round molding used to decorate the lower parts of the flutes of a column. (Elec. Comm.): The collection of cables required for distributing the power supplies in a telephone exchange.
**caboose** (Rail.): A separate car at the end of a freight train for the guide and brakemen.
**cada'ver** (Anat.): A dead human body.
**cadmium** (Nucleonics): Metal element characterized by high absorption of neutrons, and hence used for controlling nuclear reactors.
**cadmium** (Met.): A white metallic element.
**cadu'cous** (Bot.): Lasting for a short time only.
**Caesa'rean section** (Med.): Artificial delivery of a foetus through the incised abdomen and uterus.
**cae'sions** (Bot.): Bearing a bluish-gray waxy bloom.
**cae'spitose** (Bot.): Growing from the root in tufts.
**cage** (Civ. Eng.): The platform on which goods are hoisted up or down a vertical shaft.
**Cainozo'ic** (Geol.): The word signifies "recent life" and is applied to the fourth of the great geological eras.
**caisson** (Civ. Eng.): A water-tight box used to surround the works involved in laying the foundations of a bridge.
**calamif'erous** (Bot.): Having a hollow stem.
**cal'amus** (Zool.): A quill.
**calca'reous** (Bot.): Coated with or containing lime.
**cal'cicole** (Bot.): Flourishing on soils or rocks rich in calcium carbonate.
**calcico'sis** (Med.): Lung disease caused by the inhalation of marble dust.
**calcifica'tion** (Bot.): The accumulation of calcium carbonate on or in cell walls. (Zool.): The deposition of lime salts.
**calcination** (Chem.): The process of subjecting a material to the effect of prolonged heating at fairly high temperatures.
**calcium** (Met.): A silvery-white metallic element.
**caldera** (Geol.): A volcanic crater of large size.
**calibration** (Phys.): The process of determining experimentally the absolute values corresponding to the graduations on an arbitrary or inaccurate scale on an instrument.
**caliber**: The internal diameter or bore of a pipe.
**caliduct** (Build.): A hot water or steam pipe used for heating purposes.
**callipers**: An instrument, consisting of a pair of hinged legs, used to measure external and internal dimensions.
**callous** (Bot., Med.): Hardened, usually thickened.
**cal'lus** (Bot.): A mass of parenchymatous cells formed by plants over a wound. (Med.): Newly formed bony tissue between the broken end of a fractured bone.
**cal'orie** (Physics.): (1) Used as a unit in expressing the heat or energy producing value of food. (2) The unit quantity of heat.
**calor'ifier** (Heat): An apparatus for heating water in a tank.
**calorim'etry** (Heat): The measurement of thermal constants.
**calvities** (Med.): Baldness.
**ca'lyx** (Bot.): The outer whorl of the flower, consisting of sepals. (Zool.): A pouch of an oviduct, in which eggs may be stored.
**cam** (Eng.): A projection on a revolving shaft.
**cambium** (Bot.): A soft meristematic tissue which gives rise to new tissue (wood, bark).
**campanile** (Build.): A bell-tower.
**canal** (Bot.): An elongated intercellular space. (Hyd. Eng.): An artificial water channel used for irrigational or navigational purposes.
**can'cellate** (Bot.): Lattice-like.
**Cancer** (Astron.): Crab. Fourth sign of the Zodiac.
**candle** (Illum.): The unit of luminous intensity.
**candle-power** (Illum.): The luminous flux emitted by a source of light per unit solid angle in a given direction.
**canes'cent** (Bot.): Having a somewhat hoary appearance.
**canine** (Zool.): Pertaining to a dog. In mammals, a pointed tooth with a single cusp.
**canker** (Bot.): A name applied to various diseases of trees, caused by fungi.
**cañon** (Geol.): A deep, narrow, steep-sided valley.
**canopy** (Aero.): The fabric body of a parachute. (Build.): An enriched roof-like part projecting from a wall or supported on pillars.
**cant**: To tilt. (Build.): A molding having plane surfaces and angles instead of curves. (Surv.): The transverse slope given to the surface of the rails on a railway curve or to the road surface on a highway curve.
**cantilever** (Struct.): A beam or girder fixed at one extremity and free at the other.
**canyon** (Nuclear Eng.): Long narrow space with heavy shielding for essential processing of wastes from reactors.
**capacitor** (Elec. Eng.): A piece of electrical apparatus consisting of two conducting plates separated by a layer of insulating material.
**capacity** (Elec. Eng.): A term commonly used to denote the output of a piece of electrical apparatus.
**capilla'ceous** (Bot.): Hair-like.
**capillarity** (Phys.): A phenomenon associated with surface tension and angle of contact.
**capil'lary** (Bot., Zool.): Of very small diameter; slender, hair-like.
**capillit'ium** (Bot.): A mass of threads.
**cap'itate** (Bot.): (1) Resembling a pin-head in appearance. (2) Bearing a rounded swelling at the apex. (3) Having flowers grouped in a head.
**cap'reolate** (Bot.): Having tendrils.
**capricornus** (Astron.): Goat. Tenth sign of the Zodiac.
**capsule** (Med.): A soluble case of gelatine in which a dose of medicine may be enclosed.
**carat**: A standard of weight for precious stones.
**carbohy'drates** (Chem.): Any of a group of neutral compounds composed of carbon, hydrogen, and oxygen, and including the sugars, starches, etc.
**carbon** (Chem.): A non-metallic element.
**carbon compounds** (Chem.): Compounds containing one or more carbon atoms in the molecule.
**carbon dioxide** (Chem.): A colorless gas with a slight smell.
**carbon disulphide** (Chem.): Sulphur vapor passed over heated charcoal combines with the carbon to form carbon disulphide.
**carbona'ceous** (Bot.): Hard, blackened and appearing as if charred.
**carbonaceous rocks** (Geol.): Sedimentary deposits of which the chief constituent is carbon, derived from plant residues.
**carbonated** (Chem.): Said of a liquid saturated with carbon dioxide under pressure.
**carbonic acid** (Chem.): A weak acid formed when carbon dioxide is dissolved in water.
**carburetor** (Eng.): A device for mixing air and a volatile fuel in correct proportions, in order to form a combustible mixture.
**carceru'lus** (Bot.): A fruit which splits at maturity into several one-seeded portions.
**car'cinogen'esis** (Med.): The production and development of cancer.
**carcinogen** (Chem.): A substance which induces cancer in a living organism.
**car'cinomato'sis** (Med.): Cancer widely spread throughout the body.
**card** (Surv.): The graduated dial or face of a magnetic compass in which the card and needle are firmly connected.
**cardiac**: Pertaining to the heart.
**car'diograph** (Med.): A recording device to exhibit a wave-form determined by heart electromotive forces.
**cardinal points** (Astron.): The name given to the four principal points of the horizon—north, south, east, and west.
**cardiol'ogy** (Med.): Medical science concerned with the function and diseases of the heart.
**cardiovas'cular** (Med.): Pertaining to the heart and the blood vessels.
**cardo** (Zool.): The hinge of a bivalve shell.
**car'et** (Typog.): A symbol (Λ) used in proof correcting to indicate that something is to be inserted at that point.
**ca'ries** (Med.): (1) Pathological absorption of bone infected by the tubercle bacillus. (2) Decay of teeth.
**ca'riose** (Bot., Med.): Appearing as if decayed.
**car'neous** (Bot.): Flesh-colored.
**Carniv'ora** (Zool.): An order of carnivorous mammals.
**carniv'orous**: Flesh-eating.
**car'nose** (Bot.): Fleshy in texture.
**car'notite** (Min.): An important source of radium.
**carotene** (Chem.): A ruby-red crystalline hydrocarbon, found in various plants and used as a pigment.
**carpel** (Bot.): The ovule-bearing structure of a plant.
**carpet strip** (Carp.): A strip of wood secured to the floor below a door.
**carpus** (Zool.): The wrist.
**carrar'a marble** (Geol.): A well-known, pure-white, statuary marble quarried at Carrara, Italy.
**carrier** (Med.): One who carries pathogenic bacteria without having the disease caused by the bacteria, but does infect other people.
**cartilage** (Histol.): A form of connective tissue in which the cells are embedded in a stiff matrix of chondrin.
**cartog'raphy** (Surv.): The preparation and drawing of maps.
**caruncle** (Zool.): Any fleshy outgrowth.
**cascade** (Elec. Comm.): A number of devices con-

nected in such a way that each operates the next one in turn.

**casein** (Chem.): The principal albuminous constituent of milk, in which it is present as a calcium salt.

**casement** (Build.): A window hinged to open about one of its vertical edges.

**cast-iron** (Met.): An iron-carbon alloy.

**cast-steel** (Met.): Steel as cast; not shaped by mechanical working.

**casta'neous** (Bot.): Chestnut brown.

**casting** (Met.): The operation of pouring molten metals into sand or metal molds in which they solidify.

**catgut** (Surg.): Sterilized strands of sheep's intestines used as ligatures.

**catal'ysis** (Chem.): The acceleration or retardation of a chemical reaction by a substance which itself undergoes no permanent chemical change.

**cat'alyst** (Chem.): A substance which catalyses a chemical reaction.

**cataract** (Med.): Opacity of the lens of the eye as a result of degenerative changes in it.

**catch** (Carp.): A spring bolt for securing doors when shut.

**catch-net** (Elec. Eng.): A wire netting placed under high-voltage transmission lines.

**catenation** (Cyt.): The arrangement of chromosomes in chains.

**caterpillar** (Eng.): A device for increasing the tractive effort of a road vehicle. (Zool.): A type of larva.

**cathar'sis** (Psycho-an.): The purging of the effects of a pent-up emotion by bringing them to the surface of consciousness.

**cathetom'eter** (Phys.): An instrument for measuring vertical distances not exceeding a few centimeters.

**cathode** (Elec.): The electrode through which a current leaves an electrolytic cell.

**cathode rays** (Phys.): Streams of electrons emitted from the cathode during an electrical discharge in a rarefied gas.

**cat'olyte** (Elec.): The part of the electrolyte of an electrolytic cell which is near the cathode.

**caud'a** (Zool.): Any tail-like appendage.

**caules'cent** (Bot.): Having a stem.

**cauline** (Bot.): Growing from the stem.

**caulking** (Civ. Eng.): Making a joint tight to withstand pressure.

**causeway** (Civ. Eng.): A road carried by an embankment across water or marshy land.

**caustic** (Med.): Corrosive or destructive to living tissue.

**cavern** (Geol.): A chamber in a rock.

**cavernic'olous** (Ecol.): Cave-living.

**cavetto** (Arch.): A hollow molding, quarter round.

**cavitation** (Eng.): The formation of a cavity between the downstream surface of a moving body and a liquid normally in contact with it.

**ceiling** (Aero.): The maximum height attainable under standard conditions by an airplane.

**celestial equator** (Astron.): The great circle in which the plane of the earth's equator cuts the celestial sphere.

**celestial poles** (Astron.): The two points in which the earth's axis cuts the celestial sphere.

**celestial sphere** (Astron.): An imaginary sphere, of indeterminate radius of which the observor is the center.

**cell** (Biol.): One of the specialized units, consisting of nucleus and protoplasm, which compose the bodies of animals and plants.

**cell division** (Cyt.): The splitting of a cell into daughter cells.

**cell inclusion** (Cyt.): Any non-living material present in the cytoplasm.

**cell sap** (Cyt.): The fluid constituents of a cell.

**cell tissue** (Bot.): A group of cells formed by division of one or a few original cells, remaining associated and functioning as a whole.

**cell wall** (Cyt.): The membrane confining the contents of a cell.

**cell** (Elec.): The unit of a battery, in which chemical action takes place between two electrodes.

**cellulation** (Zool.): The reformation of cells in injured tissue.

**cement** (Build., Civ. Eng., etc.): A material for uniting other materials.

**cement gun** (Civ. Eng.): An apparatus for spraying cement mortar by pneumatic pressure.

**Centigrade scale:** The most widely used method for graduating a thermometer; the temperature interval between the freezing and boiling points of water is divided into 100 equal parts, each of which is a centigrade degree.

**central heating** (Build.): A system of heating a building, in which water is heated by a central boiler, and hot water or steam is circulated throughout the building through pipes and radiators.

**central nervous system** (Zool.): The main ganglia of the nervous system with their associated nerve cords.

**center** (Civ. Eng.): A timber frame built as a temporary support during the construction of a dome or an arch. (Surv.): To set up a surveying instrument vertically above a station point.

**center of action** (Meteor.): A position occupied by an anticyclone or a depression, which largely determines the weather conditions over a wide area.

**center of buoyancy** (Hyd.): The center of gravity of the liquid displaced by a floating body.

**center of curvature:** The point of intersection of normals drawn to a curve at two consecutive points.

**center of gravity** (Mech.): That point in a body at which the body may be supported in neutral equilibrium.

**center square** (Eng.): A device for marking the centers of bars and circular objects.

**centrifugal force** (Mech.): A body constrained to move along a curved path reacts against the constraint with a force directed away from the center of curvature of its path.

**cen'trifuge:** Apparatus rotating at very high speed, designed to separate solids from liquids, or liquids from other liquids dispersed therein.

**cen'triole** (Cyt.): A central granule within the centrosome.

**centrip'etal force** (Mech.): It is equal and opposite to the force directed towards the center of curvature which is deviating the body from a straight path.

**centrodes'mose** (Cyt.): A delicate thread of stainable material connecting the centrosomes at the time of nuclear division.

**cen'trosome** (Cyt.): A minute protoplasmic cell-inclusion associated with the nucleus and dividing with it.

**cephal'ic** (Zool.): Pertaining to, or situated on or in the head region.

**cer'anoid** (Bot.): Bearing branches shaped like horns.

**cerebel'lum** (Zool.): A dorsal thickening of the hind-brain in vertebrates.

**cere'bral** (Zool.): Pertaining to the brain.

**cer'nuous** (Bot.). Drooping.

**cer'vix u'teri** (Med.): The neck of the uterus.

**chain** (Chem.): A series of atoms linked together, generally in an organic molecule. (Eng.): A series of interconnected metal links forming a flexible cable. (Surv.): An instrument used for the measurement of length.

**chain reaction** (Chem.): A reaction in which a large number of molecules or atoms take part in succession.

**chalced'ony** (Min.): A cryptocrystalline variety of silica.

**chalcopy'rite** (or copper pyrite) (Min.): Sulphide of copper and iron.

**chalk** (Geol.): A fine-grained and relatively soft limestone.

**character** (Biol.): Any well-marked feature which helps to distinguish one species from another. (Psychol.): The quality of the whole organized self.

**character trait** (Psycho-an.): A distinguishing behavior pattern of an individual.

**charcoal** (Chem.): The residue from the destructive distillation of animal matter or wood with exclusion of air.

**charge** (Elec. Eng.): The quantity of electricity on a body.

**charta'ceous** (Bot.): Papery in texture.

**chase** (Build.): A trench dug to accommodate a drain pipe.

**chaser** (Eng.): A lathe tool the cutting edge of which is serrated to the profile of a screw thread.

**chas'mogam'ous** (Bot.): Having large conspicuous flowers which open and are pollinated by insects or wind.

**chas'mophyte** (Bot.): A plant inhabiting rocky places and rooting in a crevice containing mineral and organic debris.

**chatter** (Eng.): Vibration of a cutting tool or of a machine.

**check-lock** (Carp.): A device for locking in position the bolt of a door lock.

**check valve** (Eng.): A non return valve, closed automatically by fluid pressure.

**cheek** (Build.): One of the sides of an opening.

**chemical affinity** (Chem.): The force which binds atoms together in molecules.

**chemical analysis** (Chem.): The splitting up of a material into its component parts or constituents by chemical methods.

**chemical bond** (Chem.): The unit of force joining two atoms together in a molecule.

**chemical change** (Chem.): A change involving the formation of a new substance.

**chemical compound** (Chem.): A substance composed of two or more elements in definite proportion by weight, which are independent of its mode of preparation.

**chemical constitution** (Chem.): The [illegible]mber and arrangement of the atoms present in a molecule.

**chemical energy** (Chem.): The energy liberated in a chemical reaction.

**chemical engineering:** Design, construction and opera-

tion of plant and works in which matter undergoes change of state and composition.
**chemical equation** (Chem.): A symbolic representation of the changes occurring in a chemical reaction.
**chemical kinetics** (Chem.): The study of the velocities of chemical reactions.
**chemical reaction** (Chem.): A process in which one substance is changed into another.
**chemical symbol** (Chem.): A single capital letter, or a capital and small letter combined, which are used to represent either an atom or a gram-atom of a chemical element.
**chemilumines'cence** (Chem.): The production of light without heat in certain chemical reactions.
**chemistry** (Chem.): The study of the composition of substances and the changes of composition which they undergo.
**chemotherapy**: Treatment of disease by a chemical compound having a specific bacteriostatic effect against the micro-organism involved.
**chest saw** (Carp.): A small handsaw without a bark; with 6 to 12 teeth to the inch.
**chias'ma** (Cyt.): The exchange of material between paired chromosomes during nuclear division.
**chimera** (Bot.): A plant in which there are at least two kinds of tissue differing in their genetic constitutions.
**chili** (Meteor.): A sirocco-type hot and dry southerly wind blowing in Tunis.
**chimney jambs** (Build.): The upright sides of a fireplace opening.
**chimney lining** (Build.): The tile within a chimney space.
**chimney shaft** (Build.): The part of a chimney projecting above a roof.
**chimney stack** (Build.): The unit containing a number of flues grouped together.
**chim'onophi'lous** (Bot.): Growing primarily during the winter.
**chinook'** (Meteor.): A föhn-like west wind blowing on the eastern side of the Rocky Mountains.
**chipping** (Met.): The removing of surface defects from semi-finished metal produces by using pneumatic chisels.
**chirop'ody**: The care and treatment of minor ailments of the feet.
**chirop'tera** (Zool.): An order of aerial mammals. Bats.
**chisel** (Build.): A steel tool for cutting wood, stone or metal.
**chlorates** (Chem.): Salts of chloric acid; powerful oxidizing agents.
**chlorides** (Chem.): Salts of hydrochloric acid obtained by the action of an acid on many metals.
**chlorination** (Chem.): The substitution or addition of chlorine in organic compounds; the sterilization of water with chlorine.
**chlorine** (Chem.): A greenish-yellow gas.
**chlor'oform** (Chem.): A colorless liquid of a peculiar odor; used as an important anesthetic.
**chlor'ophyll** (Bot.): The mixture of two green and two yellow pigments, present in the chloroplasts of all plants, essential for photosynthesis.
**chlo'roplast**: Specialized cytoplasmic body containing chlorophyll.
**choke** (Eng.): (1) The throat in the air passage of a carburetor. (2) A valve in a curburetor intake.
**chol'era** (Med.): An acute bacterial infection in Eastern countries.
**chon'drin** (Histol.): A firm, elastic, translucent substance of a gelatinous nature, which forms the ground substance of cartilage.
**chop** (Carp.): The movable wooden jaw of a carpenter's bench vice.
**chord**: A straight line drawn between two points on a curve.
**chords** (Zool.): Any string-like structure.
**chre'sard** (Bot.): The total amount of water in the soil which can be drawn up by plants.
**chro'matin** (Cyt.): The deeply staining portion of the nucleoplasm.
**chro'miole** (Cyt.): One of the deeply staining granules of which chromatin is composed.
**chromium** (Met.): A metallic element.
**chromium plating** (Met.): A thin layer of chromium on the surface of another metal by electrodeposition, to protect it against corrosion.
**chro'momeres** (Cyt.): One of the many linearly arranged bead-like structures found on a chromosome.
**chro'moplast** (Bot.): Specialized protoplasmic body containing orange or yellow pigments.
**chro'mosome** (Cyt.): Deeply staining rod-shaped bodies within the nucleus and conspicuously visible during cell division; it contains the genes.
**chro'mule** (Bot.): A general term for plant pigments.
**chronic** (Med.): Said of a disease which is long-continued.
**chrys'alis** (Zool.): The pupa of some insects.
**cic'atrix** (Bot.): A scar left on a plant where a member has been shed.
**cil'lia** (Zool.): Microscopic hair-like projections from certain cells which vibrate, causing fluid movement; eyelashes.
**cincture** (Arch.): A plain ring around a column, generally placed at the top and the bottom to separate the shaft from its capital and its base.
**cip'olin** (Build.): A white marble with green streaks.
**circle** (Geom.): A plane curve which is the locus of a point which moves so that it is at a constant distance (the radius) from a fixed point (the center).
**circuit** (Elec. Comm.): The whole or part of the path of transmitted electrical energy in a communication channel.
**circulating pumps** (Eng.): A pump used to circulate cooling water through the condenser of a steam plant.
**circulation** (Bot.): A rotary movement of the protoplasm inside a cell. (Physiol.): The continuous movement of the blood through the heart, arteries, capillaries and veins.
**circumpolar stars** (Astroan.): Those stars which for a given locality on the earth revolve about the elevated celestial pole, always above the horizon.
**cirrho'sis** (Med.): A disease of the liver.
**cirro-cumulus** (Meteor.): Small white flakes of cloud without shadows, arranged in groups or in lines.
**cirro-stratus** (Meteor.): A thin sheet of whitish cloud.
**cir'rose** (Bot., Zool.): Curly.
**cistern** (Build.): A tank for storing up water which may later be used.
**citrine, citron** (Bot.): Lemon-colored.
**civil engineering**: The design and construction of roads, railways, bridges, aqueducts, canals, docks, ports, breakwaters, lighthouses and drainage works.
**clamp** (Build.): A wooden frame consisting of two parallel bars connected by two tightening screws; used to secure work.
**class** (Bot., Zool.): Principal sub-division of a phylum in the animal kingdom and one of the larger subdivisions in the plant kingdom.
**clastic rocks** (Geol.): Rocks formed of fragments of pre-existing rocks.
**claustrophobia** (Med.): Abnormal fear of being in a confined space.
**clav'icle** (Zool.): The collar-bone, in vertebrates.
**claw** (Bot.): The narrow, elongated, lower portion of a petal in some plants. (Carp.): A tool with a bent and split end, used for extracting tacks. (Zool).: A curved, sharp-pointed process at the distal extremity of a limb.
**clay** (Geol.): A fine-textured, sedimentary or residual deposit.
**cleavage** (Bot., Zool.): Divisions of the fertilized egg. (Chem.): (1) The splitting of a crystal along certain planes. (2) The splitting up of a complex protein molecule into simpler molecules. (Geol.): A property of rocks, whereby they can be split into thin sheets.
**cleis'togam'y** (Bot.): The production of small flowers, which do not open and are self-pollinated.
**climate** (Meteor.): The average weather conditions of a place.
**climatology** (Mèteor.): The study of climate and its causes in relation to a particular region.
**climom'eter** (Surv.): A hand instrument for the measurement of angles of slope.
**cloaca** (Zool.): A common receptacle for digestive and excretory wastes and the reproductive cells of lower vertebrates.
**clone** (Zool.): A group of organisms produced by asexual reproduction from a single individual.
**closed circuit** (Elec. Eng.): An electrical circuit in which there is a complete path for the current to flow.
**clot** (Med.): The semi-solid state of blood or of lymph when they coagulate.
**cloud** (Meteor.): A mass of water droplets remaining more or less at a constant altitude.
**cloud-burst** (Meteor.): An extremely heavy downpour of rain.
**club** (Zool.): The distal joints of the antenna, when they are enlarged in insects.
**cluster** (Bot.): A general term for an inflorescence of small flowers closely crowded together.
**clutch** (Eng.): A device by which two shafts or rotating members may be connected or disconnected, either at rest or in motion.
**coagulation** (Biol.): The irreversible setting of protoplasm on exposure to heat or to poisons. (Chem.): The process of changing a sol into gel. (Med.): The process of clotting of blood.
**coal** (Geol.): A general name for firm, brittle carbonaceous rocks.
**coal-tar** (Chem.): The distillation products of the high or low temperature carbonization of coal.
**coales'cent** (Bot., Zool.): Grown together, especially by union of the walls.
**coating** (Elec. Eng.): The metallic sheets forming the plates of a condenser.
**cob** (Build.): An unburnt brick.
**cobalt** (Met.): A metallie element.
**cobalt 60**: Radioactive isotope of cobalt, used in cancer treatment.

**cocaine** (Chem.): Used as a local anesthetic.
**coccin'eous** (Bot.): Bright red.
**coccus** (Bot.): (1) A one-seeded portion formed by the break-up of a dry fruit. (2) A minute spherical bacterium.
**coccyx** (Zool.): A bony structure in primates and amphibia, formed by the fusion of the caudal vertebrae.
**cochleate** (Bot., Zool.): Spirally twisted, like a snail shell.
**cockpit** (Aero.): The compartment in which the pilot of an aircraft is seated.
**cockscomb** (Min.): Aggregate of pyrite.
**coconut oil** (Chem.): Oil obtained from the fruit of a coconut palm.
**cocoon** (Zool.): In insects, a special envelope constructed by the larva for protection during the pupal stage.
**cod liver oil** (Chem.): Oil obtained from fresh livers of cod fish; very rich in vitamins.
**co'deine** (Chem.): An alkaloid of the morphine group.
**coefficient** (Phys.): A numerical constant prefixed as a multiplier to a variable quantity, in calculating the magnitude of a physical property.
**coel'iac** (Zool.): In vertebrates, pertaining to the abdomen or belly.
**coe'lom** (Zool.): The body cavity lined with tissue of mesodermal origin in which the digestive and other organs lie.
**co-enzyme** (Chem.): A relatively simple substance which is involved in the transfer of hydrogen atoms during oxidative reactions in protoplasm.
**coercive force** (Elec. Eng.): The magnetizing force necessary to annul the residual magnetism of a substance.
**coffering** (Civ. Eng.): The operation involved in the construction of dams for impounding water.
**coffin** (Phys.): Heavy box of absorbing material, for the safe transportation of highly radioactive materials.
**cogs** (Eng.): Separate wooden teeth.
**cognition** (Psychol.): Intellectual perception; ideas and reasons.
**cohesion** (Phys.): The attraction between the molecules of a liquid which enables drops and thin films to be formed.
**cohort** (Bot.): A group of related families.
**coil** (Elec. Comm.): Any winding of conducting wire, with a core of air or of magnetic material for providing inductance.
**coke** (Min.): The solid residue from the carbonization of coal after the volatile matter of the coal has been distilled off.
**cold bend** (Eng.): A test of the ductility of a metal.
**cold-blooded** (Zool.): Of animals having a body temperature which is dependent on the environmental temperature.
**cold chisel** (Eng.): A chisel for chipping away surplus metal.
**cold front** (Meteor.): The leading edge of an advancing mass of cold air.
**cold-saw** (Eng.): A metal-cutting circular saw for cutting steel bars to length.
**cold short** (Met.): Brittle at atmospheric temperature.
**cold wave** (Meteor.): The fall of temperature following the passage of a depression.
**Coleop'tera** (Zool.): An order of insects; beetles.
**coleop'tile** (Bot.): The first leaf to appear above the ground in a seedling of grass.
**colic** (Med.): Severe spasmodic pain in the belly due to affections of abdominal organs.
**collapse** (Med.): Extreme prostration and depression of vital functions.
**collateral** (Zool.): Running parallel.
**collimation**: The process of aligning the various parts of the optical system.
**colloid** (Chem.): A system in which particles larger than molecules of one substance are suspended throughout the second substance.
**collum** (Zool.): Any collar-like structure.
**colon** (Zool.): The wide posterior part of the hind-gut in insects. The large intestine in vertebrates.
**colonnade** (Arch.): A row of columns supporting an entablature.
**colony** (Bot.): A group of individuals of one species which are invading new ground. (Zool.): A collection of individuals living together and in some degree interdependent.
**column** (Civ. Eng.): A vertical shaft supporting an axial load. (Zool.): In vertebrates, a bundle of nerve fibers running longitudinally in the spinal cord.
**coma** (Bot.): A tuft of hairs attached to the testa of a seed. (Med.): A state of complete unconsciousness.
**combination** (Chem.): Formation of a compound.
**combinations** (Maths.): The different groups that can be formed from a given number of items.
**combustion chamber** (Eng.): In a boiler furnace, the space in which combustion of gaseous products from the fuel takes place.
**co'mes** (Zool.): A blood-vessel which runs parallel and close to a nerve.
**comet** (Astron.): A member of the solar system that revolves elliptically around the sun.
**common bricks** (Build.): A class of bricks used in ordinary construction.
**combustion** (Chem.): Chemical union of oxygen with gas, accompanied by the evolution of light and rapid production of heat.
**compass** (Surv.): An instrument for indicating the directions.
**compass brick** (Build.): A brick which tapers so as to be especially useful for curved work.
**compass saw** (Carp.): A handsaw with tapering blade, used for cutting curves.
**compasses**: An instrument for describing arcs, taking or marking distances, etc.
**compatible** (Bot.): Capable of self-fertilization.
**competition** (Biol.): The struggle between organisms for the necessities of life.
**complement** (Cyt.): A group of chromosomes derived from one nucleus, and consisting of one, two or more sets.
**complete flower** (Bot.): A flower which has both calyx and corolla.
**complic'ant** (Zool.): Folding one over another, as wings of some insects.
**composition** (Chem.): The nature of the elements present in a substance and the proportions in which they occur.
**compound fruit** (Bot.): A fruit formed from several closely associated flowers.
**compressed** (Bot.): Pressed together.
**compressor** (Eng.): Any kind of reciprocating rotary, or centrifugal pump for raising the pressure of gas.
**computing scale** (Surv.): A special scale fitted with a sliding cursor, used for the computation of area on maps, etc.
**concentration** (Chem.): Number of molecules or ions of a substance in a given volume.
**concentric arch** (Build.): An arch laid in several courses whose curves have a common center.
**conception** (Physiol.): The fertilization of an ovum with a spermatozoon.
**concha** (Arch.): The smooth concave surface of a vault. (Zool.): In vertebrates, the outer ear.
**con'chate** (Bot.): Shaped like a sea-shell.
**concres'cence** (Bot.): Growing together to form a single structure.
**concrete** (Bot.): Grown together to form a solid body. (Build.): A mixture of cement, sand and gravel with water.
**concrete blocks** (Civ. Eng., Build.): Solid or hollow pre-cast blocks of concrete used in construction.
**concussion** (Med.): A violent blow to the head, or the condition resulting from it.
**condensation** (Chem.): The linking together of two or more molecules, resulting in the formation of long chain compounds. (Meteor.): The process of forming a liquid from its vapor.
**condenser** (Chem.): Apparatus used for condensing vapors obtained during distillation. (Eng.): A chamber into which the exhaust steam from a steam engine or turbine is delivered to be condensed by cooling water.
**conditioned reflex** (Zool.): A reflex response to a stimulus which depends upon the former experience of an individual.
**conductance** (Elec. Eng.): The property of a material by which it allows current to flow through it when a potential difference is applied.
**conductor** (Elec. Eng.): (1) A material which offers a low resistance to the passage of an electrical current. (2) That part of a wiring system which actually carries the current.
**conduit** (Elec. Eng.): A pipe for containing electric wires in order to protect them against damage from external causes. (Hyd. Eng.): A pipe for the conveyance of water.
**confluent** (Bot.): Said of two or more structures which, as they enlarge, grow together and unite.
**congenital** (Zool.): Dating from birth.
**congested** (Bot.): Packed into a tight mass.
**congestion** (Med.): Pathological accumulation of blood in a part of the body.
**conglomerate** (Bot.): Clustered. (Geol.): A cemented clastic rock containing rounded small fragments.
**conglu'tinate** (Bot.): United onto a mass by a sticky substance.
**conic section** (Geom.): A curve obtained by the intersection of a right circular cone by a plane.
**conif'erae** (Bot.): The chief class of the Gymnospermae; primarily large evergreen trees.
**conif'erous** (Bot.): Cone-bearing.
**conjugate** (Bot.): Occurring in pairs.
**conjunction** (Astron.): Term signifying that two heavenly bodies have the same apparent geocentric longitude or right ascension.
**connecting-rod** (Eng.): In a reciprocating engine or pump, the rod connecting the piston or cross-head to the crank.
**connective** (Zool.): A bundle of nerve fibers uniting two nerve centers.
**conni'vent** (Bot.): Converging and muting at the tips.
**consciousness** (Psychol.): A comprehensive state of

awareness of the mind to stimuli from the outside world and to emotions and thoughts from within the individual.
**consen'sual** (Zool.): Said of response to stimuli in which voluntary action and involuntary action are correlated.
**conservatory** (Build.): A glazed building in which plants may be grown under controlled atmospheric conditions.
**consistom'eter** (Chem.): An instrument for determining the consistency or hardness of semi-fluid and brittle materials.
**constellation** (Astron.): A group of stars to which have been given a pictorial configuration and a name, although of no scientific significance.
**constituent** (Met.): A component of a solid alloy.
**constituents** (Chem.): All the substances present in a system.
**constricted** (Bot., Zool.): Narrowed suddenly.
**consumption** (Med.): Wasting of the body.
**contact-breaker** (Elec. Eng.): A device for repeatedly breaking and making an electric circuit.
**conta'gion** (Med.): The communication of disease by direct contact between two persons or between an infected object and a person.
**contiguous** (Bot.): In contact but not in organic union.
**continuous** (Bot.): With a smooth surface of even uninterrupted outline.
**contorted** (Bot.): Twisted together.
**contortion** (Geol.): Of strata the deformation of rocks by directed pressure.
**contour** (Build.): The profile of the face of a molding. (Surv.): The imaginary intersection line between the ground surface and any given level surface.
**contour gradient** (Surv.): A line on the ground surface having a constant inclination to the horizontal.
**contraceptive** (Med.): Any agent which prevents the fertilization of the ovum with a spermatozoon.
**contractility** (Zool.): The power of changing shape.
**control** (Acous.): The regulation of the contrast between the highest and lowest power levels in a sound-reproducing system.
**controller** (Elec. Eng.): An assembly of equipment for controlling the operation of electric apparatus.
**co'nus** (Zool.): Any cone-shaped organ or structure.
**convergence:** (Meteor.): An accumulation of air over a region caused by lack of uniformity of the winds.
**converging** (Bot.): Having the tips gradually approaching.
**conveyor** (Eng.): A device for the continuous transport of articles over a distance.
**con'volute** (Bot.): Coiled, folded or rolled, so that one half is covered by the other.
**convulsion** (Med.): Generalized involuntary spasm of the muscles normally under control of the will.
**coping** (Build., Civ. Eng.): A stone or brick covering to the top of wall exposed to the weather.
**copper** (Met.): A metallic element.
**core** (Civ. Eng.): A watertight wall built within a dam as an absolute barrier to water. (Elec. Eng.): That part of a magnetic circuit around which the winding is placed.
**cork** (Bot.): A layer of dead cells on the outside of a stem or root.
**corm** (Bot.) A rounded, swollen, underground, solid stem, resembling a bulb in appearance.
**corne'a** (Zool.): In vertebrates, the transparent part of the outer coat of the eyeball in front of the eye.
**cornice** (Build.): A projecting molding decorating the top of a window, building etc.
**corol'la** (Bot.) The general name for the whole of the petals of a flower.
**coron'ary** (Zool.): Crown shaped.
**coronary thrombosis** (Med.): The formation of a clot in one of the arteries of the heart.
**corpus:** Latin for body. Plural-corpora.
**corpuscle** (Zool.): A cell which lies freely in a fluid or solid matrix and is not in continuous contact with other cells.
**correlation** (Biol.): Mutual relationship. (Bot.): The conditions of balance existing between the various organs of a plant. (Maths.): The mathematical statements respecting the degree to which one variable is dependent on another variable.
**corrosion** (Chem.): The slow wearing away of solids by chemical attack.
**cor'rugated** (Bot.): Having a ridged surface.
**cortical** (Bot., Zool.): Relating to bark.
**corundum** (Min.): Oxide of aluminum; next to diamond in hardness.
**cosmog'ony** (Astron.): The science of the origins of stars, planets and satellites.
**cosmog'raphy:** The science of the constitution of the universe.
**cosmology** (Astron.): The branch of theoretical astronomy that deals with the known universe as a systematised whole.
**cosmotron** (Phys.): Machine for liberating nuclear energy.
**Cotyle'don** (Bot.): One of the leaves of the embryo in flowering plants.
**counterbalancing** (Eng.): The system of neutralizing the effect of a force by a counter-weight which provides an opposite effect.
**coupling** (Gen.): The tendency for dominant characters to remain in association. (Elec. Comm.): An arrangement for transferring electric energy from one circuit to another.
**co-valency** (Chem.): The union of two atoms by the sharing of a pair of electrons.
**cramp** (Carp.): A contrivance for holding parts of a frame in place during construction. (Med.): Painful spasm of muscle.
**crane** (Eng.): A machine for hoisting and lowering heavy weights.
**cranium** (Zool.): That part of the skull which encloses and protects the brain.
**crater** (Geol.): The orifice of a volcano through which the lavas and gases are emitted.
**creep** (Eng.): A slow relative movement between two parts of a structure. (Met.): Continuous deformation of metals under steady load.
**cren'ate** (Bot.): Having a margin bearing rounded teeth.
**crevasse'** (Geol.): A fissure in a glacier.
**cris'pate** (Bot.): Having a frizzled appearance.
**cross** (Gen.): An individual whose parents belong to different breeds or races.
**cross-fertilization** (Biol.): The fertilization of the female gametes of one individual by the male gametes of another individual.
**cross pollination** (Bot.): The conveyance of pollen from an anther of one flower to the stigma of another, either on the same or on a different plant of the same species.
**cross section:** A drawing showing the section of a body at right-angles to its length.
**cross staff** (Surv.): An instrument for setting out right-angles in the field.
**crown** (Bot.): A very short knotstock.
**crown** (Build., Civ. Eng.): The highest part of an arch.
**croy** (Civ. Eng.): A protective barrier built out into a stream to prevent erosion of the bank.
**cruciate** (Bot.): Having the form of a cross.
**crucible** (Chem., Met.): A refractory vessel in which metals are melted.
**crustaceous** (Bot.): Forming a crust on the surface of anything.
**cryoplank'ton** (Bot.): Algae which live on the surface of snow and ice in polar regions and on high mountains.
**cryptocrystalline** (Crystal.): Consisting of very minute crystals.
**cryptozo'ic** (Zool.): Living in dark places.
**crystal:** A body whose atoms are arranged in a definite pattern, the crystal faces being an outward expression of the regular arrangement of the atoms.
**crystal nuclei** (Chem.): The minute crystals whose formation is the beginning of crystallization.
**crystal systems** (Crystal.): A classification of crystals based on the intercepts made on the crystallographic axes by certain planes.
**cryst'alline:** Clear, transparent. (Bot.): Having a shining appearance.
**crystalline form** (Crystal.): The external geometrical shape of a crystal.
**crystalline schists** (Geol.): A group of rocks which have resulted from heat and pressure.
**crystallization** (Chem.): The preparation of a solid, especially from solution, in the form of crystals.
**cryst'allites** (Chem.): Very small ,imperfectly formed crystals.
**crystallogram** (Chem.): A photograph of the X-ray diffraction pattern produced by a crystal.
**crystallog'raphy:** The study of the forms, properties and structures of crystals.
**cubic system** (Crystal.): The crystal system which has the highest degree of symmetry.
**cul-de-sac** (Civ. Eng.): A road which is stopped at one end.
**culture** (Bot., etc.): An experimental preparation containing a micro-organism growing on a medium.
**cu'mulo-nimbus** (Meteor.): Great masses of clouds, generally having a screen of fibrous texture at the top and a cloud mass similar to nimbus at the bottom; usually associated with thunderstorms.
**cu'mulus** (Meteor.): Thick cloud with a well defined, dome-shaped upper surface, while the base is generally horizontal.
**cuprite** (Min.): Oxide of copper.
**curing** (Chem.): A term applied to a fermentation process of natural products. (Civ. Eng.): A method of reducing the cracking on concrete on setting.
**current:** A flow.
**cursorial** (Zool.): Adapted for running.
**curvature** (Maths.): A measure of the departure of a

line from the straight, or a surface from the plane. (Surv.): The difference in height at any point between the horizontal and the level lines through some other point on the earth's surface.

**cu'ticle** (Bot.): A deposit of waterproof, waxy material forming the external layer of the outer walls of epidermal cells. (Zool.): The epidermis.

**cy'anides** (Chem.): Salts of hydrocyanic acid.

**cycle**: A series of occurrences in which conditions at the end of the series are the same as they were at the beginning.

**cyclic** (Bot.): Having the parts arrayed in whorls not in spirals.

**cycloid**: The curved path traced out by a point on the circumference of a circle which rolls along a straight line.

**cyclom'eter**: A revolution counter calibrated in miles or kilometers.

**cyclone** (Meteor.): A depress of small area but considerable pressure gradient, in which the winds attain hurricane force.

**cyclo'sis** (Biol.): The circulation of protoplasm within a cell.

**cylinder**: A solid of uniform cross-section which may be generated by a straight line moving round a clo ed curve and remaining parallel to a given direction.

**cy'ma** (Arch.): A molding showing a reverse curve in profile. Also called an ogee.

**cypress knee** (Bot.): A vertical upgrowth from the roots of the swamp cypress.

**cyst** (Zool.): A non-living membrane enclosing a cell.

**cy'tode** (Biol.): A mass of protoplasm without a nucleus.

**cytol'ogy** (Biol.): The study of the structure, functions and reproduction of cells.

**cy'toplasm** (Cyt.): The protoplasm of a cell, apart from that of the nucleus.

## D

**dactyl** (Zool.): A digit.

**dac'tyline, dac'tyloid** (Bot.): Spreading like outstretched fingers.

**da'do** (Arch.): One of the faces of the solid block forming the body of a pedestal.

**da'is** (Build.): A raised platform at one end of a room.

**dam'askeen**: Inlay of ivory, metal or mother-of-pearl on metal.

**damper** (Acous.): A vibration-absorbing pad for reduction of the transmission of vibrational energy from a disturbing source.

**damper** (Aero.): Widely used term applied to devices for the suppression of unfavorable characteristics or behavior.

**dasypae'des** (Zool.): Birds which when hatched have a complete covering of down.

**dasyphyl'lons** (Bot.): Having crowded leaves or thick leaves or merely hair on leaves.

**date line** (Geog.): An imaginary line on the Earth's surface for the purpose of fixing the change of date; it runs approximately along the meridian of longitude 180° from Greenwich, deviating around certain islands for convenience.

**da'tum** (Surv.): An assumed level surface used as a reference surface for the measurement of reduced levels.

**daughter** (Biol.): Offspring belonging to the first generation, whether male or female.

**day** (Astron.): Apparent solar day-the interval, not constant due to the earth's elliptic orbit, between two successive transits of the true sun over the meridian. Mean solar day—the interval, perfectly constant, between two successive transits of the mean sun across the meridian.

**deactivation** (Chem.): The return of an activated atom, molecule or substance to the normal state.

**dead** (Elec. Eng.): Said of electric circuits which are not connected to any source of supply.

**deafness** (Acous.): Lack of sensitivity of hearing in one or both ears.

**deammimila'tion** (Bot.): The utilization of food by the plant.

**death** (Biol.): In a cell or an organism, complete and permanent cessation of the characteristic activities of living matter.

**debacle** (Meteor.): The breaking up of the surface ice of great rivers in spring.

**debridement** (Surg.): The removal of foreign matter and excision of infected and lacerated tissue from a wound.

**decade**: The time period of ten years.

**decalcification** (Med.): The process of absorption of lime salts from bone.

**dec'androus** (Bot.): Having ten stamens.

**dec'aploid** (Cyt.): Having ten times the haploid number of chromosomes.

**dec'astyle** (Arch.): A portico having ten columns.

**deceleration** (Mech.): The rate of diminution in the speed of a vehicle or moving part.

**decid'uous** (Bot.): Falling off, generally before cold or drought sets in.

**decimal**: The name for a system of units of which each unit is ten times the next smaller one.

**decimal fraction**: A fraction having a power of ten as denominator.

**dec'linate** (Bot.): Descending in the form of a curve.

**declining** (Bot.): Straight and pointing downwards.

**declinom'eter** (Elec Eng.): An instrument for making accurate measurements of the angle between the magnetic and geographic meridians.

**decomposition** (Chem.): The more or less permanent breakdown of a molecule into simpler molecules or atoms.

**decomposition voltage** (Elec. Eng.): The minimum voltage which will cause continuous electrolysis in an electrolytic cell.

**decompound** (Bot.): A term applied to a compound leaf having leaflets made up of several distinct parts.

**decompression** (Surg.): Any procedure for the relief of pressure.

**deconjugation** (Cyt.): The separation of the chromosomes before the end of the prophase of meiosis.

**decor'ticated** (Bot.): Having no bark.

**decrepitation** (Chem.): The crackling sound made when crystals are heated.

**decumbent** (Bot.): Lying flat, except for the tip, which ascends.

**decurved** (Bot.): Bent downwards.

**deductive reasoning**: The mental process whereby an unobserved fact is inferred from relevant observations of other facts.

**deep therapy** (Radiology): Treatment of diseases by deep X-rays.

**deficiency** (Cyt.): The loss of a portion of a chromosome.

**definition** (Acous.): The clarity of perception of speech sounds.

**definitive** (Zool.): Fully developed.

**def'lagrating spoon** (Chem.): A small spoon-shaped instrument used in chemical laboratories for handling materials which are liable to take fire when exposed to air.

**deflagra'tion** (Chem.): Sudden combustion.

**deflection** (Eng.): (1) The amount of bending or twisting of a structure. (2) The movement of the hand of any recording instrument.

**deflection angle** (Surv.): The angle between one survey line and the prolongation of another survey line which meets it.

**deflectom'eter** (Eng.): A device for measuring the amount of bending suffered by a beam during a transverse test.

**deflexed** (Bot.): Bent outwards and downwards.

**degaussing** (Elec. Eng.): Neutralization of the magnetization of a mass of magnetic material.

**degeneration** (Bot.): The loss of morphological or physiological characters by a fungus kept in culture for a long time. (Biol.): Evolutionary retrogression.

**deglutit'ion** (Zool.): The act of swallowing.

**degradation** (Chem.): The conversion of a complex alkaloid molecule into simpler fragments.

**degree of a curve** (Surv.): The angle subtended at the center of a curve by a standard chord length of 100 ft.

**degressive** (Bot.): A change towards simplification or degeneration.

**dehis'cence** (Bot.): The spontaneous opening at maturity of a fruit or any other reproductive body. (Zool.): The act of splitting open.

**dehydration** (Chem.): (1) The splitting off of $H_2O$ from a molecule by the action of heat or by a dehydrating agent. (2) The removal of water from tars, oils, crystals etc. by heating, distillation, or by chemical action. (Med.): Excessive loss of water from the body tissues.

**deionization** (Au. Eng.): The process whereby an ionized gas returns to its normal neutral condition.

**de-ionization** (Phys.): Disappearance of ions in an ionized gas.

**dekad'**: The interval of ten days.

**delamination** (Zool.): The division of cells in a tissue, leading to the formation of layers.

**delay** (Elec. Comm.): The time taken for a signal to travel from one end of an electrical communication system to the other.

**delayed opening** (Aero.): Delaying the opening of a parachute by an automatic device.

**deletion** (Cyt.): The loss of a portion of a chromosome.

**delinquent** (Psychol.): An individual, generally a child or adolescent, who shows definite lack of moral and social sense.

**deliquescence** (Chem.): The change undergone by certain substances which become damp and finally liquefy when exposed to the air.

**delivery** (Eng.): (1) The discharge from a compressor or pump. (2) The withdrawal of a pattern from a mold. (Med.): The birth of a child.

**delta** (Geol.): A more or less triangular area of river-borne sediment deposited at the mouths of rivers.

**deltoid** (Bot., Zool.): Any triangular structure.

**delusion** (Psychiatry): A belief in events for which there is no objective evidence.

**demagnetization** (Elec. Eng.): The process whereby a magnetized body has its degree of magnetization reduced.
**dementia** (Psychol.): Any form of insanity characterized by the failure of mental powers.
**demer'sal** (Zool.): Found on the sea bottom.
**demography**: The study of population statistics and the estimation of their variation with time.
**demul'cent** (Med.): Soothing.
**dena'tured alcohol** (Chem.): Alcohol which according to law has been made unfit for human consumption by the admixture of poisonous substances.
**dendrite** (Crystal.): A tree-like crystal formation.
**dendrit'ic** (Bot.): Much branched.
**den'drograph** (Bot.): An instrument which is used to measure the periodical swelling and shrinkage of tree trunks.
**dendroid** (Bot.): Freely branched.
**dener'vated** (Med.): Deprived of nerve supply.
**denig'rate** (Bot.): Blackened.
**denizen** (Bot.): A specimen which maintains its footing as a mild plant, though probably introduced by man.
**densi-tensim'eter** (Chem.): An apparatus for determining the pressure and density of a vapor.
**density** (Phys.): The mass of unit volume of a substance.
**density bottle** (Chem.): A thin, glass, calibrated bottle used for the determination of the density of a liquid.
**density function** (Astron.): A formula expressing the total number of stars per unit volume chosen.
**dental**: Pertaining to the teeth.
**dentate** (Bot.): Having a toothed margin.
**denticles** (Zool.): Any small tooth-like structures.
**dentine** (Zool.): A hard calcareous substance of which teeth and placoid scales are mainly composed.
**dentistry**: The treatment of diseases and irregularities of the teeth.
**denu'date** (Bot.): Having a worn or stripped appearance.
**deoxidation** (Met.): The process of elemination of oxygen from molten metal before casting.
**departure** (Surv.): The projected length of a survey line upon a line at right angles to the reference meridian.
**depaup'erate** (Bot.): Having a starved, undeveloped appearance.
**dephosphorization** (Met.): Elimination of phosphorous from steel.
**dep'ilate** (Med.): To remove the hair from.
**depil'atories** (Chem.): Compounds for removing or destroying hair.
**deplan'ate** (Bot.): Flattened.
**deposit** (Elec. Eng.): The coating of metal deposited electrolytically upon any material.
**deposition** (Geol.): The placing into position of sheets of sediment or of mineral veins and lodes.
**depressed** (Med.): Lowering functional activity.
**depressed** (Bot.): Flattened.
**depression** (Meteor.): The name for that distribution of atmospheric pressure in which the pressure decreases to a minimum at the center. (Psychol.): A state of dejection.
**depth gauge** (Eng.): A gauge used for measuring the depth of a hole.
**derivative hybrid** (Gen.): A hybrid obtained by crossing two hybrids or by crossing a hybrid with one of its parents.
**dermal** (Bot.): Appertaining to the epidermis. (Zool.): Pertaining to the skin.
**dermati'tis** (Med.): Inflamation of the skin surface.
**dermatol'ogy** (Med.): That branch of medical science which deals with the skin and its diseases.
**derrick** (Civ. Eng.): An arrangement for hoisting material.
**dertrum** (Zool.): In birds, the horny casing of the beak.
**descending** (Bot.): Growing or hanging downwards in a gradual curve.
**desert** (Geol): A barren and uninhabited tract of large extent.
**des'iccants** (Chem.): Substances capable of absorbing moisture and used as drying agents.
**dessication**: The process of drying.
**des'iccator** (Chem.): Laboratory apparatus for drying substances.
**desynap'sis** (Cyt.): Abnormally early breaking up of synapsis in meiosis.
**detailer** (Civ. Eng.): A draughtsman who designs the details involved in steelwork construction.
**detector** (Elec. Eng.): A simple form of galvanometer used for detecting the presence of cu rent in a circuit.
**deter'gents** (Chem.): Cleansing agents.
**determinate** (Bot.): With a well-marked edge.
**det'onator**: A substance which initiates an explosion.
**detrition** (Geol.): The natural process of rubbing or wearing down strata by blown wind or running water.
**development** (Bot., Zool.): The succession of stages in the life growth.
**deviation** (Matho.): The amount by which one of a set of observed values differs from the mean value.
**dew** (Meteor.): The deposit of moisture on exposed surfaces which accumulates during clear, calm nights.
**dew claw** (Zool.): The useless claw which represents the rudimentary first digit.
**dew-point** (Meteor., Phys.): The temperature at which a given sample of moist air will become saturated and deposit dew.
**diagnosis** (Med.): The identification of a diseased state.
**diagonal**: A straight line drawn between two non-adjacent angles of a polygon.
**diagram** (Geom., etc.): An outline figure to represent an object or area, to indicate the relation between parts, or to show the value of forces or quantities.
**dial**: The observable functional part of an indicating instrument.
**diameter** (Geom.): (1) A straight line passing through the center of a figure and terminated by its boundaries. (2) A straight line bisecting a system of parallel chords in a curve.
**diamond** (Min.): One of the crystalline form of carbon.
**dian'drous** (Bot.): Having two anthers or two stamens.
**diaphragm** (Zool.): Generally, a transverse partition subdividing a cavity.
**diarrhea** (Med.): The frequent evacuation of liquid faeces.
**di'astase** (Chem.): Enzymes capable of converting starch into sugar.
**diather'manous** (Phys.): Capable of transmitting radiant heat.
**diather'my** (Med.): The generation of heat in body tissues by the passage of electric current.
**dibasic acids** (Chem.): Acids containing two replaceable hydrogen atoms in the molecule.
**dicar'yon** (Cyt.): A pair of closely associated nuclei which divide at the same time.
**dichotomy** (Astron.): The half-illuminated phase of a planet.
**didac'tyl** (Zool.): Having two digits.
**die** (Eng.): A metal block used in stamping operations.
**diecasting** (Met.): A process by which castings of various alloys and cast-iron are produced in permanent molds.
**differential calculus** (Maths.): A branch of mathematics dealing with continuously varying quantities.
**differentiation** (Bot.): The organization of mature tissues or members from generalized rudiments.
**dif'fluent** (Bot.): Readily becoming fluid.
**difformed** (Bot.): of unusual form.
**digestion** (Zool.): The process by which food material ingested by an organism is made soluble and assimilable by enzyme action.
**digit** (Zool.): A finger or toe.
**dilated** (Bot.): Expanded and flattened.
**dilution** (Chem.): Decrease of concentration.
**dimonoecious** (Bot.): Having perfect flowers as well as staminate, pistillate and neuter flowers.
**dimor'phic** (Bot., Zool.): Existing in two forms.
**dioecious** (Bot.): Having the male and female organs on separate plants of the same species, each plant being unisexual.
**di'orite** (Geol.): A coarse-grained igneous rock.
**dip** (Elec. Eng.): The angle between the earth's magnetic field at any point and the horizontal. (Geol.): A term implying inclination of strata, measured by the horizontal.
**dip stick** (Eng.): A rod inserted in a tank to measure the depth of oil or other liquids.
**diphylet'ic** (Biol.): Of dual origin.
**diph'yodont** (Zool.): Having two sets of teeth.
**diploid** (Cyt.): Having the somatic number of chromosomes characteristic of the species.
**diplo'sis** (Cyt.): The doubling of the chromosome number.
**dip'lotene** (Cyt.): The fourth stage of meiotic prophase.
**diplozo'ic** (Zool.): Bilaterally symmetrical.
**di'pole** (Chem.): A molecule in which the effective centers of the positive and negative charges are separated.
**dipping** (Eng.): The immersion of pieces of material in a liquid bath for surface treatment.
**direct current** (Elec. Eng.): A current which flows in one direction only.
**direct heating** (Build.): A system of heating by radiation.
**direct sounds** (Acous.): The sound intensity arising from the direct radiation from a source to a listener.
**disc valve** (Eng.): A form of suction and delivery valve used in pumps and compressors.
**disc wheel** (Eng.): A wheel in which hub and rim are connected by a solid disc of metal instead of by separate spokes.
**discharge** (Elec. Eng.): The process of taking energy from a charged accumulator.
**discriminator** (Elec. Eng.): A device used in connection with the metering of an electrical supply.
**disinfectant** (Chem.): Any compound for destroying germs and microbes.
**disintegration** (Phys.): Radioactive breakdown in natural isotopes or radioelements.
**disjunction** (Cyt.): The separation during meiosis of

the two members of each pair of homologous chromosomes.
**dislocation** (Surg.): The displacement of one part from another; especially two bones at a joint.
**disorientation** (Psychol.): A mental state in which there is inability to judge the proper relations between events in time and space.
**dispensary** (Med.): (1) A place where drugs are dispensed. (2) A clinic for the treatment of out-patients.
**dispersal** (Biol.): The establishment of individuals in a new area.
**dispersed phase** (Chem.): A substance in the colloidal state.
**displacement** (Aero.): The mass of the air displaced by the volume of gas in any lighter-than-air craft. (Eng.): The volume of fluid displaced by a pump plunger per stroke or per unit time. (Psychol.): A mechanism commonly observed in dreams, whereby a hidden element may be replaced by something more remote.
**disposition** (Psychol.): The mental constitution of an individual, as formed by his reactions to environment and experience.
**dissected** (Bot.): Cut deeply into many narrow leaflets or lobes.
**disseminate** (Bot.): Scattered.
**dissociation** (Chem.): The reversible or temporary breaking-down of a molecule into simpler molecules or atoms. (Psycho-path.): A state of temporary loosening of control over consciousness.
**dissolution** (Chem.): The taking up of a substance by a liquid, with the formation of a homogeneous solution.
**distal** (Biol.): Widely spaced.
**disti'chorus** (Bot.): Arranged in two opposite vertical rows.
**distillation** (Chem.): A process of evaporation and recondensation used for separating liquids into various fractions according to their boiling points.
**distinct** (Bot.): Said of a species which has strongly marked characters.
**distortion** (Elec. Comm.): Any departure from the initial wave-form of a signal during transmission.
**distributor** (Elec. Eng.): The cable forming that part of the electric distribution system to which the consumers' circuits are connected.
**ditch** (Civ. Eng.): A channel cut in the surface of the ground for drainage purposes.
**ditching** (Aero.): Emergency alighting of a land plane on water.
**diurnal**: During a day.
**diva'lent** (Chem.): Capable of combining with two atoms of hydrogen or their equivalent.
**dive** (Aero.): A steep descent, the nose of the aircraft being down.
**divergent** (Bot.): Said of two or more organs which gradually spread so that they are farther apart at their tips than at their bases.
**diving-bell** (Civ. Eng.): A water-tight working chamber, open at the bottom, which is lowered into water beneath which excavation or other works are to proceed.
**doldrums** (Meteor.): Regions of calm in equatorial oceans.
**dol'erite** (Geol.): The general name for basic igneous rocks of medium-grain size.
**dol'omite** (Min.): An important gangue mineral.
**dome** (Bot.): The growing point of the receptacle of a flower. (Geol.): A form of igneous intrusion the roof of which has a dome-like shape.
**donor** (Med.): One who gives his blood for transfusion to another.
**door case** (Carp.): The frame into which a door fits to shut an opening.
**door frame** (Carp.): The framework of stiles, rails and mountings into which the panels are fitted.
**door strip** (Carp.): A strip attached to a door to cover the space between the bottom of the door and the floor.
**dormancy** (Bot.): In seeds and other structures, a condition of inactivity.
**dormer** (Build.): A small window projecting from a roof slope.
**dorsal** (Anat.): Said of the back of any part.
**dorsal or dorse** (Arch.): A canopy.
**dorsif'erous** (Zool.): Said of animals which bear their young on their back.
**dose** (Med.): The prescribed quantity of a medicine.
**double-acting engine** (Eng.): Any reciprocating engine in which the working fluid acts on each side of the piston alternately.
**double-acting pump** (Eng.): A reciprocating pump in which both sides of the piston act alternately.
**double-beat valve** (Eng.): A hollow cylindrical valve for controlling high-pressure fluids.
**double-hung window** (Build.): A window having top and bottom sashes.
**double-pole** (Elec. Eng.): Said of switches, circuit-breakers etc. which can make or break a circuit on two poles simultaneously.
**double-wire system** (Elec. Eng.): It employs separate wire for the go and return conductors.
**dowel** (Eng.): A pin fixed in one part which, by accurately fitting in a hole in another attached part, locates the two, thus facilitating accurate re-assembly.
**down** (Bot.): A fine soft coating of hairs on the surface of a plant member.
**downpipe** (Build.): A pipe for conveying rain water from the gutter to the drain. Also called downspout.
**drag** (Aero.): Resistance to motion through a fluid.
**drain** (Civ. Eng.): A pipe to carry away wastes and liquid sewage. (Surg.): Any piece of material used in directing away the discharges of a wound.
**drain tiles** (Civ. Eng.): Hollow tiles laid end to end without joints to carry off surface or excess water.
**drainage** (Geol.): The removal of surface meteoric waters by rivers and streams.
**draught** (Eng.): The flow of air through a boiler furnace.
**draw-bridge** (Civ. Eng.): A general name for any type of bridge of which the span is capable of being moved bodily to allow the passage of large vessels.
**dredge** (Civ. Eng.): Any apparatus used for excavating under water.
**dresser** (Eng.): (1) An iron block used in forging bent work on an anvil. (2) A mallet for flattening sheet-lead.
**dressing** (Surg.): The application of sterile material to a wound or infected part.
**drift** (Aero.): The motion of an aircraft in a horizontal plane, under the influence of an air current. (Civ. Eng.): The direction in which a tunnel is driven. (Geol.): A general name for the superficial formations of the Earth's crust.
**drift currents** (Meteor.): Ocean currents produced by prevailing winds.
**drill** (Eng.): A revolving tool used for making cylindrical holes in metal.
**drizzle** (Meteor.): A very fine rain.
**drone** (Aero.): Pilotless aircraft, electronically controlled by radio, which serves as a target for anti-aircraft weapons.
**drone** (Zool.): In social bees, a male.
**dross** (Met.): Similar to slag somewhat.
**drought** (Meteor.): Lack of rain.
**drug**: Any substance which has a physiological action on a living body.
**drum** (Eng.): Any hollow cylindrical barrel.
**drupe** (Bot.): A succulent fruit formed from a superior ovary.
**dry cell** (Elec. Eng.): A primary cell in which the contents are in the form of a paste.
**dry dock** (Civ. Eng.): A dock in which ships are repaired.
**dry ice** (Chem.): Solid (frozen) carbon dioxide, used in refrigeration and engineering.
**dry rot** (Build.): A decay of timber due to a fungus attack.
**duct** (Elect. Eng.): (1) A pipe for containing electric cables. (2) An air passage in the core of an electric machine along which cooling air may pass.
**dust counter** (meteor.): An instrument for counting dust particles in a known volume of air.
**dyke** (Geol.): A form of minor intrusion injected into the crust during its subjection to tension.
**dy'namo** (Elec. Eng.): A term used to denote any electromagnetic generator, but commonly used only for a direct-current generator.
**dyspep'sia** (Med.): Indigestion.
**dyspha'sia** (Med.): Disturbed utterance of speech, due to a lesion in the brain.
**dyspho'ria** (Med.): Unease.

## E

**ear** (Zool.): The sense-organ which receives auditory impressions.
**earth** (Astron.): The third planet in the solar system, counting from the sun outwards.
**earth pressure** (Civ. Eng.): The pressure exerted on a wall by earth which is retained.
**earthquake** (Geol.): A shaking of the earth's crust, usually by displacement along a fault.
**earthshine** (Astron.): The reflected sunlight from the surface of the earth.
**earth thermometer** (Meteor.): A thermometer used for measuring the temperature of the earth at depths up to a few feet.
**easing** (Build., Civ. Eng.): The shaping of a curve so that there is no abrupt change of curvature in it.
**eave** (Build.): The lower part of a roof which projects beyond the face of the walls.
**ecdem'ic** (Zool.): Foreign.
**echard** (Bot.): Water present in the soil which cannot be used by plants.
**echo** (Acous.): A delayed sound-wave which arrives at the recipient at a later time than the directly radiated sound-wave from a source.
**echo sounder** (Ocean.): A sounding apparatus for determining automatically the depth of sea beneath a ship.

**eclipse** (Astron.): A name applicable to cases where a non-luminous body passes into the shadow of another.
**eclipse seasons** (Astron.): The two periods, approximately six months apart, in which solar and lunar eclipses can occur.
**ecology**: The study of organisms in relation to their environment.
**ec'togen'y** (Bot.): The effect of pollen on the tissues of the female organs of the plant.
**ec'tophyte** (Bot.): A parasite growing on the surface of its host.
**ec'toplasm** (Cyt.): A layer of clear non-granular cytoplasm at the periphory of a cell.
**eddy**: An interruption in the steady flow of a fluid.
**effervescence** (Chem.): The vigorous escape of small gas bubbles from a liquid.
**efficiency**: The performance of a machine.
**efflores'cence** (Bot.): Production of flowers. (Chem.): The loss of water from a crystalline hydrate on exposure to air.
**effluent** (Nuclear Eng.): Radioactive waste from atomic plants.
**efflux** (Aero.): The mixture of combustion products and cooling air which forms the propulsive medium of any jet or rocket engine.
**e'gest** (Zool.): To expel.
**egg albumen** (Chem.): A simple protein from the white of the egg.
**e'go** (Psycho-an.): That part of the self formed originally from the instinctual life forces.
**eidograph** (Surv.): An instrument for reducing and enlarging plans.
**ejector** (Eng.): A device for exhausting a fluid by entraining it by a high-velocity steam or air jet.
**ejection capsule** (Aero.): A cockpit or cabin, in a high altitude and/or high speed military airplane which can be fired clear in emergency and which, after being slowed down, descends by parachute.
**elasticity** (Phys.): The tendency of a body to return to its original size or shape, after having been compressed, stretched or deformed.
**elbow**: A bend.
**electric field** (Elec. Eng.): A region in which forces are exerted on any electric charge present in the region.
**electric furnace** (Elec. Eng.): A furnace for industrial purposes in which the heat is produced electrically.
**electric generator** (Elec. Eng.): A machine for converting mechanical energy into electrical energy.
**electric shock**: The sudden pain or convulsion which results from the passage of an electric current through the body of a human being or animal.
**electric storm** (Meteor.): A condition of high electric field within a cloud.
**electrical engineering**: That branch of engineering chiefly concerned in the design and construction of all electrical machinery, communications, etc.
**electrician**: A person engaged in the construction or maintenance of electrical apparatus or installations.
**electricity**: The manifestation of a form of energy believed to be due to the separation or movement of certain constituent parts of an atom known as electrons.
**electrocar'diograph** (Med.): An instrument used for making graphic records of the electrical changes during contraction of the muscle of the heart.
**electrochemistry** (Chem.): The study of the relation between electricity and chemical changes.
**electrocrat'ic** (Chem.): Owing its stability to an electric charge.
**electro-culture** (Bot.): The stimulation of the growth of plants by electrical means.
**electrocution** (Elec. Eng.): The causing of death by electric shock.
**electrode** (Elec. Eng.): A conductor whereby an electric current is led into a liquid or into a gas.
**elec'trolyte** (Chem.): An electrolytic conductor.
**electrolytic conduction** (Chem.): The conduction of electricity accompanied by the actual transfer of matter, which is shown by the occurrence of chemical changes at the electrodes.
**electromagnet** (Elec. Eng.): A core of iron or steel which is magnetized when a current is passed through a coil surrounding the core and behaves as a magnet.
**electrom'eter** (Elec. Eng.): An electrical measuring instrument for measuring potential difference.
**electromotive force** (Elec. Eng.): The force which tends to cause a movement of electricity around an electric circuit.
**electron** (Phys.): An electrically charged particle.
**electronegative** (Chem.): (1) Carrying a negative charge of electricity. (2) Tending to form negative ions.
**electronics**: The science which deals with the behavior of free electrons. Now defined as the science and technology of conduction of electricity in vacuum, in a gas, and in semi-conductors, and the utilization of devices based on these phenomena.
**electro-physiology** (Biol.): The science of electrical phenomena associated with living organisms.
**electroplating**: The production of a thin coating of one metal on another by electrodeposition.
**electropositive** (Chem.): (1) Carrying a positive charge of electricity. (4) Tending to form positive ions.
**elec'troscope** (Elec. Eng.): An apparatus which indicates the presence of a charge or a potential difference.
**electrostatics** (Elec. Eng.): The science which deals with the behavior of electric charges and potentials.
**electro-therapy** (Med.): The treatment of disease by electric currents or by electrically produced radiations.
**electrova'lence** (Chem.): A chemical bond in which an electron is transferred from one atom to another, the resulting ions being held together by electrostatic attraction.
**element** (Chem.): A substance which cannot be decomposed by chemical means into simpler substances.
**elements** (Meteor.): Those components, as temperature, humidity, wind, rainfall, etc., which determine the state of the weather.
**elevation** (Build.): The facade of a building.
**elimination** (Chem.): The removal of a simple molecule from different parts of the same molecule, or from two or more different molecules.
**elix'ir** (Med.): A strong extract or tincture.
**ellipse** (Geom.): A plane curve, the path of a point the sum of whose distances from two fixed points is constant; a conic section, the closed intersection of a right circular cone.
**elongation** (Astron.): The angular distance between the moon on planets and the sun. (Met.): The total extension produced in a tensile test.
**emasculation** (Med.): The removal of testes, or of testes and penis.
**embankment** (Civ. Eng.): A ridge of earth, stones, etc., especially constructed to carry a highway or railroad at a higher level than the surrounding ground; or as a protective bank to prevent water encroachment.
**em'bolism** (Med.): The blocking of a blood vessel by a mass carried, to the point of obstruction, from a remote part of the circulation.
**embossed** (Build.): A term applied to any form of ornamentation surface which is raised from the general surface which it is decorating.
**embryo** (Bot.): A young plant in a rudimentary state of development. (Zool.): An immature organism in the early stages of its development, before it emerges from the egg or the uterus.
**embryol'ogy** (Biol.): The study of the formation and development of embryos.
**emerald** (Met.): The brilliant green gemstone, a form of beryl.
**emergence** (Biol.): An epidermal outgrowth in insects, the appearance of the imajo from the cocoon or pupa-case.
**emersed** (Bot.): (1) Protruding upwards. (2) Amphibious.
**emersion** (Astron.): The exit of the moon, or other body, from the shadow which causes its eclipse.
**emery** (Min.): A finely granular admixture of corundum and magnetite or hematite; used as an abrasive.
**emet'ic** (Med.): Having the power to cause vomiting.
**emotion** (Psychol.): A mental state characterized by a strong degree of feeling.
**empirical**: Said of a rule or generalization which is induced solely from observation, without correlation, without scientific law.
**emulsion** (Chem.): A colloidal suspension of one liquid in another.
**ena'tion** (Bot.): A general term for an outgrowth.
**encephali'tis** (Med.): Inflammation of the brain substance.
**enceph'alogram** (Med.): An X-ray photograph of the skull and the brain.
**enchyle'ma** (Cyt.): The more fluid constituents of cytoplasm.
**endem'ic** (Med.): Prevalent in, and confined to, a particular country or area; said of disease.
**endolith'ic** (Bot.): Growing within the substance of rocks or stones.
**endoplasm** (Cyt.): The granular central portion of the cytoplasm of a cell.
**en'doscope** (Med.): A tubular instrument for inspecting the cavities of internal organs.
**en'dosperm** (Bot.): A multicellular tissue formed inside a developing seed.
**en'dospore** (Bot.): The innermost layer of the wall of a spore.
**endurance** (Aero.): The maximum time, or distance, that an aircraft can continue to fly without refueling.
**energetics** (Chem.): The abstract study of the energy relations to physical and chemical changes.
**energy** (Phys.): The capacity of a body for doing work.
**engine** (Eng.): Generally, a machine in which power is applied to do work.
**engine speed** (Aero.): In a turbine engine, the revolutions per minute of the main rotor assembly.
**engineer**: One engaged in the science and art of engineering practice.

**enlargement** (Bot.): Primary growth in thickness before secondary thickening begins.
**enrich** (Nuclear Eng.): To increase the proportion of fissile material in a fuel for a nuclear reactor.
**entab'lature** (Arch.): The whole of the parts immediately supported upon columns, consisting of an architrave, a frieze and a cornice.
**entel'echy** (Zool.): The vital element that controls and directs response to stimuli.
**enter'ic** (Med.): Pertaining to the intestines.
**enthal'py** (Phys.): The heat content of a substance per unit mass.
**entomol'ogy**: The branch of zoology which deals with the study of insects.
**entomoph'agous** (Zool.): Feeding on insects.
**en'tomophi'ly** (Zool.): Pollination by insects.
**entozo'ic** (Bot.): Living inside an animal.
**entozo'on** (Zool.): An animal parasite living within the body of the host.
**entrain** (Eng.): In a moving fluid, a suspension of bubbles or particles.
**entrainment** (Chem.): Transport of small liquid particles in vapor.
**entrance lock** (Eng.): A lock through which vessels must pass in entering or leaving a dock.
**environment** (Biol.): The sum total of the external and internal conditions which influence existence, growth, development and activity.
**en'zymes** (Chem.): Catalysts produced by living cells.
**e'olith** (Geol.): A term applied to the oldest-known stone implements used by early man.
**Eolith'ic** (Geol.): The time of the primitive men who manufactured and used eoliths.
**ephe'bic** (Zool.): Adult; mature.
**ephemeral** (Bot.): A plant which completes its whole life-history in a very short time.
**ephemeral movement** (Bot.): A movement of a plant member which cannot be repeated; as the opening of a bud.
**ephem'eris** (Astron.): A compilation, published at regular intervals, in which are tabulated the daily positions of the sun, moon, planets and certain stars with other data necessary for the astronomer and navigator.
**epicenter**: That point on the surface of the earth lying immediately above the focus of an earthquake.
**epidem'ic** (Med.): An outbreak of an infectuous disease spreading widely among people at the same time in any region.
**epide'miol'ogy** (Med.): That branch of medical science concerned with the study of epidemics.
**epider'mis** (Bot.): A sheath of closely united cells forming a layer over the surface of the leaves and young stems of a plant. (Zool.): Those layers of the integument which are ectodermal in origin.
**ep'ilepsy** (Med.): A general term for a sudden disturbance of cerebral function accompanied by loss of consciousness with or without convulsion.
**ep'isperm** (Bot.): The outer part of a seed coat.
**equal** (Bot.): Not lop-sided.
**equilibrium** (Chem.): The state reached in a reversible reaction when the reaction velocities in the two opposing directions are equal. (Mech.): The state of a body which is at rest or is moving with uniform velocity.
**equinoctial** (Bot.): Said of plants bearing flowers which open and close at definite times.
**equinox** (Astron.): The instant at which the sun in its apparent annual motion crosses the celestial equator.
**eq'uivalve** (Zool.): Said of bivalves which have the two halves of the shell of equal size.
**erect** (Bot.): Set at right angles to the part from which it grows.
**erg** (Mech.): A unit of work or energy.
**eroded** (Bot.): Appearing as if gnawed or worn irregularly.
**erosion** (Geol.): The lowering of the land surface by weathering.
**error**: Term for any small difference from the correct value.
**eruption** (Med.): A rash.
**escapement**: A device for converting circular motion into reciprocating motion.
**escarpment** (Geol.): A long cliff-like ridge. Generally consists of a short steep rise and a long gentle slope.
**establishment** (Bot.): The successful germination and subsequent growth of a plant.
**ester** (Chem.): Derivatives of acids.
**estuary** (Geol.): An inlet of the sea at the mouth of a river.
**etching** (Met.): The process of revealing the structure of metals and alloys.
**ete'sian winds** (Meteor.): In the Mediterranean, winds which blow from the north-west for about 40 days in the summer.
**e'theogen'esis** (Zool.): Parthenogenesis of male individuals.
**e'thers** (Chem.): Compounds derived from two molecules of an alcohol by elimination of one molecule of water.
**et'iola'tion** (Bot.): The condition of a green plant which has not received sufficient light.
**eudiom'eter** (Chem.): An apparatus for determining the composition of gases.
**eugam'ic** (Zool.): Pertaining to the period of maturity.
**eumito'sis** (Cyt.): Typical normal mitosis.
**eupep'tic** (Med.): Possessing a good digestion.
**eupot'amous** (Ecol.): Normally living in rivers and streams.
**euryha'line** (Ecol.): Normally inhabiting salt water.
**eurythe'rmous** (Ecol.): Tolerant of a wide range of temperature.
**eustatic movements** (Geol.): Changes of sea level.
**eutec'tic** (Chem.): Relative to a mixture of two or more substances having a minimum melting-point.
**euthana'sia** (Med.): Easy or painless death.
**eu'tropy** (Chem.): The regular variation of the crystalline form of a series of compounds with the atomic number of the element.
**evaporation** (Phys.): The conversion of a liquid into vapor, at temperatures below the boiling point.
**evaporation, natural** (Meteor.): The evaporation that takes place at the surface of rivers, ponds, etc., which are exposed to the weather.
**evaporim'eter** (Meteor.): An instrument used for measuring the rate of natural evaporation.
**even** (Bot.): Having a smooth surface.
**evening star** (Astron.): The name given in popular language to a planet, generally Mercury or Venus, seen in the western sky at or just after sunset.
**e'volute** (Biol.): Having the margins rolled outwards.
**evolution** (Biol.): The gradual development of more complex organisms from simpler forms.
**evulsion** (Surg.): Plucking out by force.
**exacerba'tion** (Med.): An increase in the severity of a disease.
**excavation** (Civ. Eng.): The operation of digging material out from the solid mass and depositing it elsewhere.
**excavator** (Civ. Eng.): A power-driven machine for excavating earth.
**excision** (Surg.): The action of cutting a part out or off.
**excitation** (Bot.): The action of a stimulus on a plant organ. (Zool.): The setting of a metabolic process into activity or acceleration.
**excited** (Nucleonics): Said of an atom when, by absorption of photons or by collision, its energy rises above that of the ground state.
**excres'cence** (Med.): Any abnormal outgrowth of tissue.
**excre'ta** (Zool.): Poisonous or waste substances eliminated from a cell, tissue or organism.
**exfoliation**: The process of falling away in flakes, layers or scales.
**exha'lant** (Zool.): Emitting or carrying outwards a fluid or gas.
**exhaust** (Eng.): The working fluid discharged from an engine cylinder after expansion.
**exhaust fan** (Eng.): A fan used in artificial draught systems.
**exhaust pipe** (Eng.): The pipe through which the exhaust products of an engine are discharged.
**ex'oderm** (Zool.): The outer cell layer.
**ex'ogan'ete** (Zool.): A gamete which unites with one from another parent.
**ex'ogam'y** (Bot., Zool.): Union between gametes which are not closely related.
**ex'ospore** (Bot.): The outer layer of the wall of a spore.
**exotoxin** (Bacteriol.): The toxin produced by a bacterium in the medium in which it grows.
**expanded**: Of cellular structure and therefore light in weight.
**expansion**: Increase in one or more of the dimensions of a body.
**expiration** (Zool., etc.): The expulsion of air or water from the respiratory organs.
**exploring cell** (Elec. Eng.): A small coil used for measuring the flux in a magnetic field.
**explosion** (Chem.): A rapid increase of pressure in a confined space.
**exposure** (Meteor.): The method by which an instrument is exposed to the elements.
**exser'ted**: Stretched out.
**extensom'eter** (Met.): An instrument used, in the testing of metals, for measuring small values of strain.
**exten'sor** (Zool.): A muscle which by its contraction straightens a limb, or a part of the body.
**extraction** (Met.): The processes used in obtaining metals from their ores.
**extravert** (Psychol.): An individual well adapted to the outside world and to other people.
**extrusive rocks** (Geol.): Rocks formed by the consolidation of magma on the surface of the ground.

**exudation** (Bot.): The liberation of liquid water or sap from special pores in the plant.

**eye** (Eng.): A loop formed at the end of a steel wire or bolt. (Meteor.): The central calm area of a cyclone or hurricane. (Zool.): The sense organ which receives visual impressions.

**eyepiece** (Phys.): In an optical instrument, the lens to which the observer applies his eye in using the instrument.

## F

**facade** (Build.): The front elevation of a building.

**face**: The outer, upper or more important surface of any object. (Eng.): The working surface of any part.

**face lathe** (Eng.): A lathe designed for work of large diameter but short length.

**facette** (Arch.): A projecting flat surface between adjacent flutes in a column.

**facia** (Arch.): A flat banded projection from the face of a member.

**fa'cial** (Zool.): Pertaining to or situated on the face.

**facies** (Bot.): The general form and appearance of a plant.

**facing** (Civ. Eng.): An outer covering applied to the exposed face of sea-walls, embankments, etc. (Eng.): (1) The operation of turning a flat face on a piece of work in the lathe. (2) A raised machine surface to which another part is to be attached.

**fac'ulae** (Astron.): The name given to large bright areas of the photosphere of the sun.

**fac'ultative** (Zool.): Optional; able to live under different conditions.

**fadom'eter** (Chem.): An instrument used to determine the resistance of a dye or pigment to fading.

**faeces** (Zool.): The indigestible residues remaining in the alimentary canal after digestion and absorption of food-materials.

**Fahrenheit scale**: The method of graduating a thermometer with the fixed points marked 32° F and 212° F.

**fairing** (Aero.): A secondary structure added to any part of an aircraft to reduce drag by improving the streamlining.

**falcu'la** (Zool.): A sharp curved claw.

**fall** (Civ. Eng., etc.): The inclination of rivers, streams, etc.

**Fallo'pian tube** (Zool.): In mammals, the oviduct.

**fall-out** (Nuclear Warfare): Deposition of highly radioactive particles down-wind, after being vaporized and sucked up by the heat of a nuclear explosion on or near the ground.

**false ceiling** (Build.): A lower dummy ceiling formed to provide covered accommodation for wires, conduits, etc.

**family** (Biol.): A group of individuals within an order or suborder.

**fan** (Eng.): A device for delivering or exhausting large volumes of air or gas.

**fascia** (Arch., Build.): (1) A wide flat member in an entablature. (2) A board carrying a gutter around the leaves of a building. (3) The broad flat surface below a cornice.

**fas'cicle** (Bot.): A tuft of leaves crowded on a short stem.

**fastener** (Build.): A device such as a nail, screw, dowel, etc. for securing two parts together.

**fats** (Chem.): An important group of naturally occurring substances consisting of the glycerides of higher fatty acids.

**fathom**: A unit of measurement; generally, a nautical measurement of depth = 6 ft.

**fatigue** (Zool.): The condition of an excitable cell or tissue which, as a result of activity, is less ready to further stimulation until it has had time to recover.

**fatigue test** (Eng., Met.): A test made on a material to determine the range of alternating stress.

**fault**: A defect in a mechanism in which normal function is impaired.

**fault** (Geol.): A fracture in rocks along which some displacement has taken place.

**fauna** (Zool.): A collective term denoting the animals occurring in a particular region or period.

**fauton** (Build.): A metal rod embedded in concrete.

**fa'veolate** (Bot., Zool.): Resembling a honeycomb in appearance.

**feathers** (Zool.): Epidermal outgrowths forming the body-covering of birds.

**feb'rile** (Med.): Pertaining to, produced by, or affected with fever.

**feed** (Eng.): (1) The rate at which the cutting tool of a machine is advanced. (2) Fluid pumped into a vessel. (3) Mechanism for advancing material into a machine for processing.

**feeling** (Psychol.): An affective experience.

**feldspar** (Min.): A group of rock-forming silicates.

**female** (Bot.): A flower having carpels and no stamens. (Zool.): An individual the gonads of which produce ova.

**fen**: Low marshy land.

**fence** (Eng.): (1) A guard or stop to limit motion. (2) A guide for material, as in a circular saw.

**fenes'tra** (Build.): A window or other opening in the outer walls of a building. (Zool.): An aperture in a bone or cartilage or between two or more bones.

**fenestral** (Build.): A window-opening covered with oiled paper or cloth.

**fe'ral** (Bot., Zool.): Wild.

**fermentation** (Chem.): A slow decomposition process of organic substances induced by micro-organisms.

**ferritin** (Chem.): Protein containing iron.

**ferro-electric** (Phys.): Said of non-magnetic material exhibiting spontaneous and substantially permanent electric polarization.

**ferrous oxide** (Chem.): An oxide of iron.

**ferru'genous** (Bot.): Reddish-brown.

**ferrugenous deposits** (Geol.): Sedimentary rocks containing sufficient iron to justify exploitation as iron ore.

**ferrule** (Eng.): A short length of tube.

**fertile** (Bot.): Able to produce spores or seeds.

**fertile flower** (Bot.): A pistillate flower.

**fertilization** (Biol.): The union of two sexually differentiated gametes to form a zygote.

**fever** (Med.): The complex reaction of the body to infection, associated with a rise in temperature.

**fibre** (Bot.): (1) A very narrow, elongated, thick-walled cell, tapering to a sharp point at both ends. (2) A very delicate root. (Met.): Any arrangement of the constituents of metals parallel to the direction of working.

**fi'bril** (Bot.): A small fibre. (Zool.): Any minute thread-like structure.

**fibrin** (Chem., Zool.): An insoluble protoid substance which is precipitated in the form of a meshwork of fibres when blood coagulates.

**fibrinogen** (Chem., Zool.): A protein contained in the plasma of blood.

**fibroid** (Med.): Resembling fibrous tissue.

**fibrous tissue** (Zool.): Any tissue containing a large number of fibres.

**fidelity** (Elec. Comm.): The measure of the performance of a reproducing system.

**fidu'cial** (Surv.): Said of a line or point assumed as a fixed basis of reference.

**field** (Phys.): The region in which the forces being considered are visible. (Surv.): The term denoting the scene of operation of the surveyor.

**field coil** (Elec. Eng.): The coil which carries the current for producing the magnetomotive force to set up the flux in an electric machine.

**filament** (Bot.): (1) A chain of cells set end to end. (2) The stalk of a stamen. (Elec. Eng.): A fine wire of high resistance. (Zool.): Any fine thread-like structure.

**file** (Eng.): A hand metal-cutting tool.

**filial generation** (Gen.): The offspring of a cross-mating.

**filicin'ean** (Bot.): Relating to ferns.

**filing block** (Eng.): A wooden block which is held in the vice, and to which light flat work is secured for filing.

**fillet** (Arch.): A flat and narrow surface separating or strengthening curved moldings.

**film** (Chem.): A thin layer of a substance, generally differing in properties from other layers in contact with it.

**filter** (Chem.): An apparatus used for the separation of liquids from solids.

**filter paper** (Chem.): Paper, consisting of pure cellulose, which is used for separating solids from liquids by filtration.

**filtrate** (Chem.): The liquid freed from solid matter after having passed through a filter.

**fin** (Aero.): In an airplane, a fixed vertical surface giving lateral stability of motion.

**fineness** (Chem.): The state of subdivision of a substance. (Met.): The purity of a gold or silver alloy.

**fin'ial** (Build.): A term applied to an ornament placed at the summit of a gable, spire or pillar.

**fiords or fjords** (Geol.): Narrow winding inlets of the sea bounded by mountain slopes.

**fire escape** (Build.): A special means of exit from a building, for use in event of fire.

**fire extinguishers**: Generally portable with a range up to 40 ft.

**fireplace** (Build.): The place where a chimney opens into a room.

**fire plug**: A hydrant for service in extinguishing fires.

**fire-stone** (Geol.): A stone or rock capable of withstanding a considerable amount of heat without injury.

**fire stop** (Build.): An obstruction across an air passage in a building to prevent flames from spreading further.

**firing** (Eng.): (1) The process of adding fuel to a boiler furnace. (2) The ignition of an explosive mixture.

**fissile** (Bot., Zool.): Split.

**fissile** (Nuclear Eng.): Said of isotopes which can, in a reactor, maintain a chain reaction of neutrons.

**fission** (Astron.): The breaking-up of a single gaseous body into two unequal masses, to form a binary star. (Phys.): The splitting of an atomic nucleus, as the result of bombardment by neutrons, into two other atomic nuclei.

**fission** (Phys.): Breakdown of atomic nuclei into approximately equal parts, identifiable as isotopes of lower-number elements, yet yielding neutrons and gamma-rays with much energy.

**fissure** (Geol.): A cleft in rock determined in the first instance by a fracture, a joint plane or fault, subsequently widened by erosion or solution. (Med.): Any normal cleft in organs of the body.

**fis'tular** (Bot.): Hollow like a pipe.

**fitter** (Eng.): A mechanic who assembles finished parts in an engineering workshop.

**fittings** (Eng.): (1) Small auxiliary parts of an engine or machine. (2) Boiler accessories.

**fix** (Aero.): The exact geographical position of an aircraft.

**fixation** (Zool.): The action of certain muscles which prevent disturbance of the equilibrium of the body or limbs.

**fixative** (Bot., Zool.): A reagent which will permanently fix the structure of a specimen in a life-like condition.

**fixture** (Build.): An attachment to a building.

**flaccid** (Bot.): Limp and flabby.

**flagstone** (Civ. Eng.): A flat thin stone used as a paving material.

**flagellate** (Bot., Zool.): Bearing a long thread-like appendage.

**flakes** (Met.): Minute transverse internal fissures which appear as bright scales on fractured surfaces of steel forgings.

**flame** (Chem.): A region in which chemical interaction between gases occur, accompanied by the evolution of light and heat.

**flame test** (Chem.): The detection of the presence of an element in a substance by the coloration imparted to a Busen flame.

**flame** (Eng.): A projecting rim.

**flap** (Aero.): Any surface attached to the wing which can be adjusted in flight to alter the lift as a whole.

**flare**: A bright light used as a signal.

**flash test** (Elec. Eng.): A test applied to electrical equipment for testing its insulation strength.

**flats** (Eng.): Steel or iron bars of rectangular section.

**flat roof** (Build.): A roof surface laid nearly horizontal.

**flight engineer** (Aero.): A member of the flying crew of an aircraft responsible for engineering duties as management of the engineers, etc.

**flocculation** (Chem.): The coalescence of a finely divided precipitate into larger particles.

**floccus** (Zool.): A tuft.

**floor plan** (Build.): A separate plan drawn for each floor of a building showing dimensions of the rooms and the thicknesses of walls.

**flora** (Bot.): The plant population of any area under consideration.

**floral envelope** (Bot.): The calyx and corolla.

**floret** (Bot.): An individual flower in a crowded inflorescence.

**flow** (Eng.): A pipe by which water leaves a boiler or pressure cistern.

**flow lines** (Met.): Lines which appear in the surface of iron and steel when stressed to the yield points.

**flower** (Bot.): A group of closely crowded specialized leaves at the end of a short branch, including one or more of the following members: sepals, petals, carpels, stamens.

**flower bud** (Bot.): A bud enclosing one or more young flowers but no foliage leaves.

**fluctuating variation** (Gen.): Variation as shown by the differences between the individuals of one progeny.

**fluctuation** (Bot.): A change in a plant due to the effect of its environment on it. (Med.): The palpable undulation of fluid in any cavity or abnormal swelling of the body.

**flue** (Build.): A smoke-duct in a chimney.

**fluid**: A substance which flows and offers no permanent resistance to change of shape.

**fluidization**: The handling of solids as if they were liquids.

**fluores'cence**: The absorption of radiation of a particular wave length by a substance and its reemission as light of greater wave length.

**fluorescope**: Screen coated with fluorescent material for observing images excited by X-rays.

**fluorine** (Chem.): A non-metallic element. The presence of small quantities in water supplies has been found to promote strong resitsance to dental decay.

**fluorophore** (Chem.): A group of atoms which give a molecule fluorescent properties.

**flush** (Bot.): (1) A period of renewed growth in a woody plant. (2) A limited area watered by a spring, or by the run off from rainfall.

**flush** (Build.): In the same plane.

**flute** (Build.): A long vertical groove.

**flying buttress** (Build.): An arched buttress giving support to the foot of another arch.

**foam** (Chem.): A suspension, often colloidal, of a gas in a liquid.

**focus** (Maths.): The point of contact of the focal sphere.

**foetus** (Zool.): A young animal within the egg or the uterus of the mother.

**fog** (Meteor.): A condition of obscurity in which visibility is less than 1 kilometer; fog may consist of a cloud of water droplets, dust or smoke particles.

**Fogbow** (Meteor.): A bow seen opposite the sun in fog.

**folding** (Geol.): The bending of strata.

**fo'liose** (Bot.): Bearing leaving.

**foliage leaf** (Bot.): The ordinary green leaf of a plant.

**foliation** (Geol.): The arrangement of minerals normally possessing a platy habit in leaves.

**fol'licle** (Bot.): A fruit formed from a single carpel and containing several seeds. (Zool.): Any small saclike structure.

**foot** (Zool.): A locomotor appendage.

**footing** (Build, Civ. Eng.): The lower part of a column or wall. (Elec. Eng.): The foundation which is set in the ground to support a tower of an overhead transmission line.

**forb** (Bot.): Any herb other than a grass.

**force** (Mech.): That which, when acting on a body which is free to move, produces an acceleration in the motion of the body.

**force pump** (Eng.): Any pump which delivers liquid under a pressure greater than its suction pressure.

**forceps** (Med.): A pincer-like instrument with two blades, for holding or extracting objects.

**forcing**: The process of hastening growth by artificial means.

**forecast** (Meteor.): A statement of the anticipated weather conditions in a given region.

**forging** (Eng.): The operation of shaping that metal by means of pressure or hammers.

**fork lift truck**: A vehicle with power operated prongs, which can be raised or lowered, for loading and unloading goods.

**forked** (Bot.): Dividing into two or more distinct branches which diverge as they elongate.

**formal'dehyde** (Chem.): A gas of pungent odor, readily soluble in water and usually used in aqueous solution.

**formative stage of growth** (Bot.): The stage in development when a cell is formed from a pre-existing cell.

**formula**: A fixed rule or set form.

**fossette** (Zool.): In general, a small pit.

**fossil** (Geol.): A relic of some former living thing—plant or animal—embedded in, or dug out of, the superficial deposits of past geological periods.

**fosso'rial** (Zool.): Adopted for digging.

**fouling** (Eng.): Coming into accidental contact with.

**foundation** (Build., Civ. Eng.): The formation upon which a building or construction rests.

**foundry** (Eng.): A workshop in which metal objects are made by casting in sand or loam molds.

**fo'vea** (Zool.): A small depression.

**fovil'la** (Bot.): The material inside a pollen grain.

**fractional crystallization** (Chem): The separation of substances by the repeated partial crystallization of a solution.

**fractional distillation** (Chem.): Distillation process for the separation of the various components of liquid mixtures.

**fracture** (Min.): The broken surface of a mineral as distinct from its cleavage. (Surg.): Breaking of a bone.

**fragmentation** (Cyt.): The separation of a portion from the main body of a chromosome.

**frames** (Civ. Eng.): The centring used in concrete construction.

**framework**: The supporting skeleton of a structure.

**framed** (Carp.): Said of work assembled with mortise and tenon joints.

**free** (Bot.): Not joined laterally to another member of the same kind.

**free association** (Psycho-an.): The method used for making unconscious processes conscious.

**free cell formation** (Bot.): The formation of daughter cells which do not remain united.

**free end** (Build.): The end of a cantilever which is not built in or fixed.

**free nuclear division** (Cyt.): Nuclear division unaccompanied by the formation of cell walls.

**free pole** (Elec. Eng.): A magnet pole which is imagined, for theoretical purposes, to exist separately from its corresponding opposite pole.

**free radical** (Chem.): A group of atoms which normally exists only in combination with other atoms, brought into independent existence by special conditions.

**freezing**: The conversion of a liquid into a solid form.

**freezing-point**: The temperature at which a liquid solidifies.

**French window** (Buildg.): A glazed casement, serving as both window and door.

**frequency** (Phys.): The number of vibrations, waves or cycles of any periodic phenomenon per second. (Ecol.): The relative number of any given species in a given place. (Elec.): The frequency at which an electric current alternates.
**friction** (Mech.): The resistance to motion when it is attempted to slide one surface over another.
**frieze** (Arch., Build.): (1) The middle part of an entablature between the architrave and the cornice. (2) The decorated upper part of a wall, below the cornice.
**frigidity** (Psychol.): In women, decrease or absence of the normal sexual response.
**frond** (Bot.): A general term for the leaf of a fern.
**front** (Carp.): The sole face of a plane. (Meteor.): The line of separation between masses of air at different temperatures.
**frost** (Meteor.): A frost is said to occur when the air temperature falls below the freezing point of water.
**fructification** (Bot.): A general term for the body which develops after fertilization and containing spores or seeds.
**fruit** (Bot.): The structure which develops from the ovary of an angiosperm after fertilization.
**fuel** (Nuclear Eng.): Fissile material inserted through a reactor, the source of the chain reaction of neutrons, and so of the energy released.
**fuel cell** (Chem.): A galvanic cell in which the oxidation of a fuel is utilized to produce electricity.
**fulcrum** (Mech.): The point of support or pivot of a lever.
**function** (Biol.): The normal vital activity of a cell, tissue or organ.
**Fungi** (Bot.): One of the main groups of the Thallophyta, distinguished from the algae chiefly by the absence of chlorophyll.
**fun'gicide** (Bot.): A substance which kills fungi.
**fuse** (Elec. Eng.): A device used for protecting electrical apparatus against the effect of excess current.
**fu'selage** (Aero.): The name generally applied to the main structural body of a heavier-than-air craft, other than the hull of a flying-boat or amphibian.
**fusion** (Nucleonics) Atomic condensation.

## G

**gabbro** (Geol.): The name of a specific igneous rock type.
**gable** (Build.): A triangular part of an outside wall, between the sides of the roof and the line of the eaves.
**gadget**: A small mechanical device.
**galactic plane** (Astron.): The plane passing as nearly as possible through the center of the belt known as the Milky Way or Galaxy.
**Gal'axy** (Astron.): (1) The name given to the belt of faint stars which encircles the heavens and which is known as the Milky Way. (2) The name is also used for the entire system of dust, gases and stars within which the sun moves.
**gale** (Meteor.): A wind having a velocity of about 40 miles per hour or more, at a height of 32 ft. above the ground.
**gale'na** (Min.): Lead sulphide.
**gall** (Bot.): An abnormal growth formed on a plant following attack by a parasite.
**gall-bladder** (Zool.): A lateral diverticulum of the bile-duct in which the bile is stored.
**gall-stones** (Med.): Pathological concretions in the gall-bladder and bile passages.
**gallery** (Build.): An elevated floor projecting beyond the walls of a building so as to command a view upon the main floor.
**galvanizing** (Met.): The coating of steel or iron with zinc.
**galvanom'eter** (Elec. Eng.): An electrical instrument for measuring small electric currents.
**gal'vanotro'pism** (Biol., Bot.): Response of an organism to an electric stimulus.
**gam'etes** (Biol.): Reproductive cells which will unite in pairs to produce zygotes.
**gamma rays** (Phys.): Short, highly penetrating X-rays emitted by radioactive substances during their spontaneous disintegration.
**gan'grene** (Med.): Death of a part of the body, associated with putrefaction.
**gangue** (Met.): The portion of an ore which contains no metal.
**gangway** (Build.): Rough planks laid to provide a footway for the passage of workmen on a site.
**gape** (Zool.): The width of the mouth when the jaws are open.
**gargoyle** (Build.): A grotesquely shaped spout projecting from the upper part of a building, to carry away the rain water.
**gas**: A state of matter in which a substance completely fills the region in which it is contained, no matter how small its amount.
**gas-turbine engine** (Aero. and Eng.): The generic term of an engine deriving its energy from internal combustion gases expanded through a turbine.
**gas mill** (Geol.): A deep boring which yields natural gas rather than oil.
**gas'oline** (Chem.): Low-boiling petroleum distillates.
**gas'tric** (Zool.): Pertaining to the stomach.
**gate** (Eng.): (1) A valve controlling the supply of water in a conduit. (2) A frame in which saws are stretched to prevent buckling.
**gauge**: An object or instrument for the measurement of dimensions, volume, pressure, etc.
**gaze'bo** (Build.): A summerhouse resembling a temple in form and commanding a wide open view.
**gear** (Eng.): A moving part that transmits motion.
**gel** (Chem.): The apparently solid, often jelly-like, material formed from a colloidal solution on standing.
**gel'atine** (Chem.): A colorless, ordorless and tasteless glue prepared from albuminous substances.
**geminate** (Bot.): Paired.
**Gemine** (Astron.): Twins. Third sign of the Zodiac.
**gem'ini** (Bot.): Bivalent chromosomes.
**gemma** (Bot.): A small multicellular body produced by vegetative means, and able to separate from the parent plant and from a new individual. (Zool.): A bud that will give rise to a new individual.
**gemmology**: The science and study of gemstones.
**genes** (Cyt., Gem.): In the modern chromosome theory, hypothetical units supposed to be arranged in linear fashion on the chromosomes, each representing a unit character.
**gene-mutation** (Gen.): A heritable variation caused by spontaneous change at single points in the chromosomes.
**gene string** (Cyt., Gen.): A hypothetical component of a chromosome, consisting of a series of genes arranged like a string of beads.
**generating plant** (Elec. Eng.): The equipment necessary for the generation of electrical energy.
**generation** (Biol.): Origin; the individuals of a species which are separated from a common ancestor by the same number of broods in the direct line of descent.
**genesis** (Biol.): The origin, formation or development of a group, a species, an individual, an organ, a tissue or a cell.
**genet'ics** (Biol.): The study of variation and heredity.
**genetic complex** (Gen.): The sum-total of the hereditary factors contained in the chromosomes and in the cytoplasm.
**genetic variation** (Gen.): Variation due to differences in the gametes.
**genial** (Zool.): Pertaining to the chin.
**genic'ular** (Zool.): Pertaining to the region of the knee.
**genita'lia** (Zool.): The gonads and their ducts and all associated accessory organs.
**genom** (Cyt., Gen.): The total chromosome content of the nucleus of a gamete.
**genotyp'ic** (Gen.): Determined by the genes.
**ge'nus** (Biol.): A taxonomic category of closely related forms.
**ge'obiot'ic** (Zool.): Terrestrial.
**geocen'tric** (Astron.): The term applied to any system or mathematical construction which has as its point of reference the center of the earth.
**ge'ochem'istry** (Chem.): The study of the chemical composition of the earth's crust.
**ge'odes** (Geol.): Large cavities in rocks, lined with crystals that were free to grow inwards.
**geodesic** (Maths.): The shortest path between two points on any surface.
**ge'oid** (Surv.): The figure of the mean sea-level surface assumed to be continued across the land.
**geological time** (Geol.): The time extending from the end of the Formative Period of earth history to the beginning of the Historical Period.
**geology**: The science which investigates the history of the earth's crust, from the earliest times to the beginning of the Historical Period.
**geophys'ics**: The science concerned with the physical characteristics and properties of the earth.
**geotax'y** (Biol.): The response of an organism to the stimulus of gravity.
**ge'otome** (Bot.): An instrument used for taking soil samples without disturbing the surrounding soil.
**germ** (Zool.): The primitive rudiment which will develop into a complete individual.
**germ cells** (Zool.): Special reproductive cells which are liberated by the organism and in which the qualities of the organism are inherent.
**germination** (Bot.): The beginnings of growth in a seed or spore.
**gerontol'ogy** (Med.): The scientific study of old age and of diseases peculiar to this period of life.
**gestalt** (Psychol.): German, 'form," 'pattern;" an organized whole. A school of psychology based on the gestalt theory.
**gestation** (Zool.): Pregnancy.
**geyser** (Geol.): A volcano in miniature, from which hot water and steam are erupted periodically.
**gibbous** (Astron.): The word applied to the phase of the moon or of a planet, when it appears less than a circular disc but greater than a half disc.
**gill** (Zool.): A membranous respiratory outgrowth of aquatic animals.

**gimlet** (Carp.): A small hand tool for boring holes in wood.
**gimped** (Bot.): Crenate.
**gin'gival** (Zool.): Pertaining to the gums, in mammals.
**girder** (Eng.): A beam, usually steel, to bridge an open space.
**glabres'cent** (Bot.): Almost but not quite without hairs.
**glab'rous** (Bot.): Hairless.
**glacial denudation** (Geol.): Disintegration of rocks consequent upon glacial conditions.
**glaciation** (Geol.): The subjection of an area to glacial conditions, with the development of an ice-sheet on its surface.
**glacier** (Geol.): A field or body of ice.
**gla'cis** (Civ. Eng.): An inclined bank.
**glad'iate** (Bot.): Shaped like a sword blade.
**gland** (Bot.): A cell or group of cells, inside or on the surface of the plant, secreting an oily or resinous substance, sometimes containing digestive enzymes. (Zool.): A single epithelial cell or an aggregation of them, specialized for the elaboration of a secretion useful to the organism, or of an excretory product.
**glans** (Bot.): A dry, hard indehiscent fruit, containing one or a few seeds, derived from an inferior ovary and surrounded partly by a cupule; an acorn is an example.
**glass**: An amorphous substance, usually transparent, consisting ordinarily of a mixture of silicates.
**glass-cutter** (Build.): A tool for cutting glass to sizes.
**glauco'ma** (Med.): An eye condition causing partial or complete loss of sight.
**glau'cous** (Bot.): Covered with a dull greenish-gray waxy bloom.
**glaze** (Build.): A glass-like surface given to tiles, bricks, etc.
**glazier** (Build.): A workman who cuts panes of glass to size and fits them in position.
**glider** (Aero.): A heavier-than-air craft driven within itself.
**glob'ular, glob'ose** (Bot.): Almost spherical.
**glob'ulites** (Geol.): Minute crystallites of spherical shape occurring in natural glasses.
**glom'erule** (Bot.): A small ball-like cluster of spores.
**glossa** (Zool.): In vertebrates, the tongue.
**glu'cophore** (Chem.): A group of atoms which causes sweetness of taste.
**glue** (Carp., etc.): A substance used as an adhesive; obtained from bones, gelatine, starch, etc.
**gluma'ceous** (Bot.): Brownish, thin and papery in texture.
**glu'tinous** (Chem.): Covered by a sticky exudation.
**gneiss** (Geol.): A metamorphic rock.
**godroon'** (Arch.): An ornamentation taking the form of a bead or cable.
**going** (Build.): The horizontal interval between consecutive risers in a stairs.
**gold** (Met.): A heavy, yellow, metallic element.
**gonad** (Zool.): A sex gland; ovary or testis.
**gones** (Cyt.): The groups of four nuclei or of four cells which are the immediate results of meiosis.
**goniom'eter** (Min.): An instrument for measuring the angles between crystal faces.
**gonorrhe'a** (Med.): A contagious infection of the mucous membrane of the genital tract with the gonococcus.
**gore** (Aero.): One of the sector-like sections of the canopy of a parachute.
**gouge** (Carp.): A tool having a curved blade and a cutting edge capable of forming a rounded groove.
**gout** (Med.): A disorder of metabolism in which there is an excess of uric acid in the blood.
**governor** (Eng.): A device for controlling the fuel or steam supply to an engine in accordance with the power demand.
**grade** (Civ. Eng.): The degree of slope.
**grade pegs** (Surv.): Pegs driven into the ground as references in construction work
**grader** (Civ. Eng.): A power-operated machine for shaping excavated surfaces to the desired slope or shape.
**gradient** (Phys.): The rate of change of a quantity with distance. (Surv.): The ratio of the difference in elevation between two given points and the horizontal distance between them, or the distance for unit rise or fall.
**gradine** (Arch.): A tier of seats rising above one another in an amphitheater.
**grading** (Build.): The proportions of the different sizes of stone used in mixing concrete. (Civ. Eng.): The operation of preparing a surface to follow a given gradient.
**gradiom'eter** (Surv.): An instrument for setting out long uniform gradients.
**graduated circle** (Surv.): A circular plate, marked off in degrees, used on surveying instruments as a basis for the measurement of horizontal or vertical angles
**graduated vessels** (Chem.): Vessels which are used for measuring liquids and are adapted to measure definite volumes of liquid.
**graft** (Bot.): A plant consisting of a rooted part (the stock) into which another part (the scion) has been inserted so as to make organic union. (Surg.): A piece of skin, bone or tissue taken from one part of the body and grafted to another.
**grain** (Bot.): The pattern on the surface of wood due to variations of the cells forming the wood.
**gram**: The unit of mass in the metric system.
**gram-atom** (Chem.): The quantity of an element whose mass in grams is equal to its atomic weight.
**gram-equivalent** (Chem.): The quantity of a substance or radical whose mass in grams is equal to its equivalent weight.
**gram-molecule** (Chem.): The quantity of a substance whose mass in grams is equal to its molecular weight.
**graminiv'orous** (Zool.): Grass-eating.
**granite** (Geol.): A coarse-grained igneous rock.
**granulated sugar** (Chem.): A term for loose sugar crystals of grain-like appearance.
**gran'ulization** (Geol.): The process in regional metamorphism of reducing the components of a solid rock to grains.
**graphic formula** (Chem.): A formula in which every atom is represented by the appropriate symbol, valency bonds being indicated by dashes.
**graphic instrument** (Elec. Eng.): An electrical instrument in which the pointer consists of a pen moving over a paper chart so that a graphic record of the quantity measured is obtained.
**graphical methods**: The name given to those methods in which items, such as forces in structures, are determined by drawing diagrams to scale.
**graphic** (Min.): One of the two naturally occurring forms of crystalline carbon, the other being diamond.
**grate** (Build.): The cast-iron fire bars and frame of a fireplace. (Eng.): That part of a furnace which supports the fuel.
**grating** (Build.): A perforated cover across a drain, gulley, etc.
**gravel** (Build.): A natural mixture of sand, loam and flints. (Geol.): The name of an aggregate consisting of pebbles and a considerable amount of sand.
**gravitation** (Phys.): The name given to that force of nature which manifests itself as a mutual attraction between masses.
**gravitational astronomy** (Astron.): That branch of astronomy that deals with the motions of the heavenly bodies under the forces of gravitation.
**gravity cell** (Elec. Eng.): A two-fluid cell in which the electrolytes lie in separate layers because of their difference in specific gravity.
**gravity water system**: A system in which flow occurs under the natural pressure due to gravity.
**grease gun**: A device for forcing grease into bearings under high pressure.
**great circle** (Maths.): The intersection of a sphere by a plane passing through its center.
**green** (Civ. Eng.): A colloquial term for concrete in the hardening stage.
**gregale** (Meteor.): A north-easterly winter wind blowing in the central Mediterranean.
**grega'rious** (Bot.): Growing in close companies, but not matted together.
**grey matter** (Zool.): An area of the central nervous system, mainly composed of cell bodies.
**grid** (Civ. Eng.): A timber framework so built that a vessel may be floated in at high water and repairs undertaken as the tide falls. (Surv.): A network of lines super-imposed upon a map and forming squares for referencing.
**grille** (Build.): A plain or ornamented openwork of metal or wood, used as a protecting screen or grating.
**grinding teeth** (Zool.): The molars and premolars of mammals.
**grinding wheel** (Eng.): An abrasive wheel for cutting and finishing metal.
**grit** (Geol.): Siliceous sediment, the component grains being angular.
**grit cell** (Bot.): A stone cell occurring in the flesh of a fruit.
**grooving** (Eng.): Cracking of the plates of steam boilers at points where stresses are set up by the differential expansion of hot and colder parts.
**ground engineer** (Aero.): An individual, selected by the licensing authorities, who has power to certify the safety for flight of an aircraft.
**ground loop** (Aero.): An uncontrollable and violent turn by an airplane while taxying, landing or taking-off.
**ground noise** (Acous.): Extraneous noise accompanying reproduced sound.
**ground plan** (Build., Civ. Eng.): A drawing showing a plan view of the foundations for a building or of the layout of rooms etc., on the ground floor.
**ground-postion indicator** (Aero.): An instrument which continuously displays the dead-reckoning position of an aircraft.

**ground speed** (Aero.): The speed of an aircraft relative to a point on the earth's surface.
**ground state** (Nucleonics): State of a molecule when its energy is the minimum possible.
**groundwork** (Civ. Eng.): The work involved in preparing a site for a foundation.
**ground-zero** (Nuclear Warfare): Point on the ground directly under an air-burst of a nuclear weapon.
**group** (Chem.): (1) A vertical column of the periodic system, containing elements of similar properties. (2) A number of atoms which occur together in several compounds.
**growth** (Biol.): A change in the body of an organism and in the cells composing it, accompanied by all division and nearly always, by increase in the size and weight of the organism or of the part under consideration. (Met.): Applied to cast-iron, the tendency to increase in volume when repeatedly heated and cooled.
**growth ring** (Bot.): The cylinder of secondary wood added during one season of growth, as seen in cross-section.
**gudgeon** (Build.): A metal pin used for joining adjacent stones.
**guide** (Civ. Eng.): A pile driven to indicate a site.
**guided weapon** (Aero.): Any missile which is guided to its target; propulsion is usually by rocket, ramjet or simplified turbojet.
**gums** (Zool.): In higher vertebrates, the thick tissue masses surrounding the bases of the teeth.
**gus'tatory** (Zool.): Pertaining to the sense of taste.
**gut** (Zool.): The alimentary canal.
**guttate** (Bot.): Containing little drops of material.
**gutter** (Build., Civ. Eng.): A channel along the side of a road, or around the eaves of a building, to collect and carry away surface waters.
**guy-rope** (Civ. Eng.): A rope holding a structure in a desired position.
**Gym'nosperm'ae** (Bot.): One of the two main divisions of seed plants.
**gynan'drous** (Bot.): Having the stamens and styles united to form a column, as in the flowers of orchids.
**gyroscope**: A small heavy wheel or top rotated at high speed in anti-friction bearings.

## H

**haar** (Meteor.): A wet set-fog advancing in summer from the North Sea upon the shores of Scotland and England.
**habit** (Cryst.): A term used to cover the varying development of the crystal forms possessed by any one mineral. (Zool.): The established normal behavior of an animal species.
**habit spasm** (Med.): Tic.
**habitat** (Biol.): The normal locality or place of living of an organism.
**habitat form** (Bot.): A plant showing features which can be related to the place where it is growing.
**habitat group** (Bot.): A set of unrelated plants which inhabit the same kind of situation.
**haboob'** (Meteor.): A line-square, with dust storms, blowing in the Sudan during the rainy season.
**hack-saw** (Eng.): A hand-saw for cutting metal.
**hacking** (Build.): The process of making surface rough.
**hade** (Geol.): The angle of inclination of a fault-plane, measured from the vertical.
**had'romal** (Bot.): An enzyme present in some fungi which enables them to decompose wood.
**hae'mal, haemic** (Zool.): Pertaining to the blood-vessels or to the blood.
**hae'mapoi'esis** (Zool.): The formation of blood.
**hae'matite** (Min.): An oxide of iron.
**haematol'ogist** (Med.): One who specializes in the study of the blood and its diseases.
**haemat'ozo'on** (Zool.): An animal living parasitically on the blood.
**haemoglo'bin** (Zool.): The respiratory pigment in the red corpuscles of vertebrates, a compound of hematin and globin.
**haemophil'ia** (Med.): A hereditary disorder in which bleeding after injury persists, owing to delayed coagulation of the blood.
**haem'orrhage** (Med.): Bleeding.
**haemostat'ic** (Med.): Arresting bleeding.
**hail** (Meteor.): Precipitation in the form of hard pellets of ice.
**hair** (Anat., Zool.): Any thread-like outgrowth of the epidermis.
**half-pace** (Build.): A landing at the end of a flight of steps.
**half-rip saw** (Carp.): A hand-saw designed for cutting timber along the grain.
**halides** (Chem.): Fluorides, bromides, iodides and chlorides.
**holite** (Min.): Common or rock salt.
**halito'sis** (Med.): Offensively smelling breath.
**Hall effect** (Elec. Eng.): A change in the distribution of current in a strip of metal, due to a magnetic field.
**hallucination** (Psychol.): A perception of sensation for which there is no objective reality.
**hallux** (Zool.): In land vertebrates, the first digit of the hind-limb.
**halo** (Meteor.): A bright ring or system of rings seen surrounding the sun or moon.
**ha'lobion'tic** (Ecol.): Strictly confined to salt water.
**ha'logens** (Chem.): A group consisting of the non-metallic elements, fluorine, bromine, chlorine and iodine.
**haloid acids** (Chem.): A group consisting of hydrogen fluoride, hydrogen bromide, hydrogen chloride and hydrogen iodide.
**ha'lophile** (Ecol.): A fresh-water species capable of surviving in salt water.
**ha'lophole** (Bot.): A plant which will not grow in a soil containing an appreciable amount of salt.
**ha'lophyte** (Bot.): A plant which will live in a soil containing an appreciable amount of common salt or other inorganic salts.
**hamiros'trate** (Zool.): Having a hooked beak, as vultures.
**handle**: The part of a tool by which it is grasped.
**hangar** (Aero.): A special construction for the accommodation of aircraft.
**hapan'thous** (Bot.): Flowering once and then dying.
**hap'loid** (Cyt.): Having the basic chromosomes number half the number in somatic cells.
**haplo'sis** (Cyt.): The halving in the number of the chromosomes at meiosis.
**harbor** (Civ. Eng.): A sheltered area of water giving safe anchorage to ships.
**hardpan** (Civ. Eng.): A layer of hardened subsoil.
**hard water** (Chem.): Water having calcium and magnesium salts in solution and offering difficulty in making a soap lather.
**hardening** (Met.): The process of making steel hard.
**hardness** (Met.): In general, signifies resistance to deformation.
**harelip** (Med.): A congenital cleft in the upper lip.
**harmattan'** (Meteor.): A dusty, dry north-easterly wind blowing over West Africa during the dry season.
**hatch** (Build.): A door closing only the lower half of a door opening.
**hatchet** (Carp.): A small axe used for splitting timber.
**hay-fever** (Med.): Paroxysmal attacks of running at the nose, congestion and irritation of the nasal mucous membrane and of the eyes, due to sensitivity to grass pollens.
**head**: A generic term for the essential part of an apparatus. (Arch.): The capital of a column. (Bot.): A dense inflorescence of small crowded flowers.
**hearing** (Acous.): The subjective appreciation of externally applied sounds.
**heart** (Zool.): A hollow organ, with muscular walls, which by its rhythmic contractions pumps the blood through the vessels and cavities of the circulatory system.
**heart wood**: The dense wood which lies in the inner part of a trunk or branch.
**hearth** (Build.): The floor of the fireplace.
**heat** (Phys.): That which when given to a body raises its temperature, and when removed lowers the temperature. Heat is also a form of energy into which mechanical energy may be converted. (Zool.): The period of sexual desire.
**heat index** (Astron.): An indication of the proportion of heat to light received from a star.
**heat insulation** (Build.): The property of impeding the transmission of heat.
**heater** (Build.): Appliance for heating a building.
**heating-element** (Elec. Eng.): The heating resistor, together with its former in any device in which heat is produced by the passage of an electric current through a resistance.
**height** (Build., Civ. Eng.): The rise of an arch.
**heliacal rising and setting** (Astron.): The rising or setting of a star or planet, simultaneously with the rising or setting of the sun.
**helicopter** (Aero.): A rotorcraft capable of vertical take-off and landing.
**helio**: A prefix meaning sun.
**heliom'eter** (Astron.): An instrument for determining the sun's diameter and for measuring the angular distance between two celestial objects in close proximity.
**he'liophyte** (Bot.): A plant able to live with full exposure to the sun.
**he'liostat** (Astron.): An instrument used for photographic and spectroscopic study of the sun. (Surv.): An instrument used to reflect the sun's rays in a continuous beam.
**heliotro'pism** (Biaol.): Reaction of an organism to the stimulus of the sun's rays.
**helium** (Chem.): An inert element; the lightest of the rare gases.
**helix** (Zool.): A spirally coiled structure.
**hemi**: A prefix meaning half.
**Hemip'tera** (Zool.): An order of insects usually with the characteristic of having two pairs of wings.
**hemisphere**: The half of a sphere.
**henry** (Elec. Eng.): The practical unit of inductance.

**hepat**: A prefix meaning liver.
**hepatic** (Med.): Pertaining to the liver.
**hepati'tis** (Med.): Inflammation of the liver.
**hept**: A prefix meaning seven.
**heptam'erous** (Bot.): Having parts in sevens.
**heptava'lent** (Chem.): Capable of combining with seven hydrogen atoms or their equivalent.
**herb** (Bot.): A small flowering plant, of which the aerial shoots last only as long as it is necessary to develop the flowers and the fruits.
**herba'ceous** (Bot.): Soft and green, containing little woody tissue.
**herba'rium** (Bot.): A collection of dried plants; also the place where such a collection is kept.
**hereditary** (Biol.): Inherited.
**heredity** (Biol.): That factor in evolution which causes the persistence of characters in successive generations.
**hermaph'rodite** (Zool.): Having both male and female reproductive organs in one individual.
**hernia** (Med.): Protrusion of a viscus through a defective area in the cavity containing it.
**heroin** (Chem.): An alkaloid prepared by the acetylation of morphine.
**hertz** (Elec. Comm.): The unit of frequency, one cycle per second.
**hesperid'ium** (Bot.): A fruit like an orange; a fleshy fruit covered by a firm rind.
**heter-, hetero**: A prefix meaning other or different.
**het'erobares** (Chem.): Atoms having different atomic weights.
**heteroblastic** (Zool.): Showing indirect development.
**heterocar'pous** (Bot.): Having more than one kind of fruit.
**heterochro'mosome** (Cyt.): A differentiated chromosome, determining sex.
**heterochro'sis** (Zool.): Abnormal coloration.
**heterodynam'ic** (Biol.): Of unequal potentiality.
**heterog'eneous** (Chem.): Said of a system consisting of more than one phase.
**heteromorpho'sis** (Zool.): The regeneration of a part in a different form from the original part; the production of an abnormal structure.
**heteromor'phous** (Bot.): Existing in more than one form.
**het'eroploid** (Cyt.): Possessing an additional chromosome.
**hetero'sis** (Zool.): Cross-fertilization.
**het'erospo'ry** (Bot.): The formation of more than one kind of spore.
**heterosynap'sis** (Cyt.): Pairing of two dissimilar chromosomes.
**het'erotopes** (Chem.): Atoms having different atomic numbers.
**heterotyp'ic** (Zool.): Differing from the normal condition.
**hex**: A prefix meaning six.
**hexam'erous** (Bot.): Having parts in sixes.
**hex'apod** (Zool.): Having six legs.
**hexap'terous** (Zool.): Having six wing-like processes.
**hex'astyle** (Arch.): A portico formed of six columns in front.
**hex'ava'lent** (Chem.): Capable of combining with six hydrogen atoms or their equivalent.
**hia'tus** (Zool.): A large opening.
**hibernation** (Zool.): The condition of partial or complete torpor into which some animals relapse during the winter season.
**hiccup** (Med.): Sudden spasm of the diaphragm followed immediately by clossure of the glottis.
**hidro'sis** (Zool.): Formation and excretion of sweat.
**highs** (Acous.): The same as top.
**high-fidelity** (Acous.): An inexact term generally meaning sound reproduction of a superior quality.
**high-voltage** (Elec. Eng.): Legally, any voltage above 650 volts.
**hinge** (Carp.): A means of connecting two members, such as a door to its frame, as that one may swing in relation to the other.
**hipped roof** (Build.): A pitched roof having sloping ends instead of gable ends.
**hirsute** (Bot.): Hairy.
**his'tocyte** (Zool.): A tissue cell as opposed to a germ cell.
**his'togen** (Bot.): An area within a plant where tissues undergo differentiation.
**histogen'esis** (Zool.): Formation of new tissues.
**histol'ogy** (Zool.): The study of the minute structure of tissues and organs.
**histol'ysis** (Bot.): The breakdown of a cell or tissue.
**hoar-frost** (Meteor.): A deposit of ice crystals formed on objects, especially during cold clear nights when the dew-point is below the freezing-point.
**hoary** (Bot.): Covered with short greyish-white down.
**hod** (Build.): A three-sided container used for carrying bricks and mortar on the site.
**hoggin** (Build.): A mixture of gravel and clay, used for paving garden paths, etc.
**hoisting**: The process of lifting materials by mechanical means.
**hole** (Civ. Eng.): (1) A bore hole. (2) A depression for accommodating a blasting charge.
**holohe'dral** (Crystal.): Crystal forms exhibiting the highest possible symmetry in their respective systems.
**ho'lotype** (Zool.): The original type specimen, from which the description of a new species is established.
**holozo'ic** (Zool.): Devouring other organisms.
**homo**: A prefix meaning the same.
**homoblas'tic** (Zool.): Showing direct development.
**homoch'romy** (Zool.): The resemblance of the color of the animal to the color of its surroundings.
**homocy'clic** (Chem.): Containing a ring composed entirely of atoms of the same kind.
**homog'amy** (Zool.): Inbreeding, usually due to isolation.
**homoge'neous** (Chem.): Said of a system consisting of only one phase.
**homogen'esis** (Zool.): The reproductive cycle in which the offspring resemble the parents.
**homogeny** (Zool.): Similarity of individuals or of parts, due to common descent.
**homol'ogous** (Bot., Zool.): Of the same essential nature and of common descent.
**homomor'phic** (Cyt.): Said of chromosome pairs which have the same form and size.
**homomor'phous** (Bot., Zool.): Alike in form.
**homophyl'lous** (Bot.): Having foliage leaves all of the same kind.
**homoplas'tic** (Bot.): Of the same structure and manner of development but not descended from a common source.
**ho'moplas'ty** (Zool.): Similarity between two different organs or organisms, due to convergent evolution.
**homop'terous** (Zool.): Having both pairs of wings similar.
**homosexual'ity** (Psycho-path.): A general term denoting sexual attraction for the same sex.
**homosynap'sis** (Cyt.): Pairing of two similar chromosomes.
**homotyp'ic** (Zool.): Conforming to the normal condition.
**honey dew** (Zool.): A sweet substance secreted by certain Aphididae.
**honing** (Eng.): The process of finishing cylinder bores etc., to a very high degree of accuracy.
**hoof** (Zool.): In certain mammals, a horny proliferation of the epidermis, enclosing the toes.
**horizon** (Astron.): That great circle of which the Zenith and the nadir are the poles, in which the plane tangent to the earth's surface, considered spherical, at the point where the observer stands, cuts the celestial sphere. (Surv.): A plane perpendicular to the direction of gravity at the point of observation.
**horizontal** (Bot.): Spreading at a right-angle to a support.
**horizontal component** (Elec. Eng.): The component of the earth's magnetic field which acts in a horizontal direction.
**hormone** (Physiol.): An internal secretion produced by the endocrine or ductless glands of the body and exercising a specific stimulatory physiological action on other organs to which it is carried by the blood.
**horn** (Zool.): One of the pointed or branched hard projections borne on the head in many mammals.
**hornblende** (Min.): An important rock-forming mineral of complex composition.
**horological** (Bot.): Said of a flower which opens and shuts at a definite time of day.
**horology**: The science of time-measurement, or of the construction of timepieces.
**horse** (Carp.): A trestle for supporting a board while it is being sawn.
**horse-power** (Eng.): The engineering unit of power equal to a rate of working 33,000 foot pounds per minute.
**horseshoe curve** (Surv.): A curve whose arc subtends an angle of more than 180' at the center, so that the intersection point lies on the same side of the curve as the center.
**host** (Biol.): An organism which supports another organism (parasite) at its own expense.
**hot** (Elec.): Charged to a dangerously high potential.
**hot-air heater** (Build.): One which supplies warm air through gratings in the floor or openings in the walls.
**hot plate** (Elec. Eng.): An electrically heated plate maintained at a moderate temperature so that dishes placed on it may be kept warm.
**hot-wire** (Elec. Eng.): Said of an electrical indicating instrument whose operation depends on the thermal expansion of, or change in resistance of, a wire when it carries a current.
**hour angle** (Astron.): The angle which the declination circle of a heavenly body makes with the observer's meridian at the celestial pole.
**hour circle** (Astron.): The great circle passing through the celestial poles and a heavenly body, cutting the celestial equator at 90°.
**hull** (Aero.): The main boat of a boat amphibian.

**hum** (Acous.): A single note emitted from a sound reproducer.

**hu'meral** (Zool.): In vertebrates, pertaining to the region of the shoulder.

**humid'ifier:** An apparatus for maintaining desired humidity conditions in the air supplied to a building.

**humidity** (Meteor.): The quantity of water vapor present per unit volume.

**hu'mus** (Bot.): Organic matter present in the soil, and so far decomposed that it has lost all signs of its original structure.

**hurricane** (Meteor.): A wind of force with a velocity of 75 miles per hour.

**hy'aline** (Zool.): Clear, transparent.

**hy'alite** (Min.): A colorless transparent variety of opal.

**hy'alogen'esis** (Cyt.): The secretory process in a cell.

**hyalop'terous** (Zool.): Having transparent wings.

**hybrid** (Gen.): An organism which is the offspring of a union between two different races, species or genera.

**hyd, hydro:** A prefix meaning water.

**hy'drates** (Chem.): Salts which contain water of crystallization.

**hydraulics:** The science relating to the flow of fluids.

**hydraulic lift** (Eng.): A lift or elevator operated by a ram, working in a cylinder to which water is admitted under pressure.

**hydrocarbons** (Chem.): A general term for organic compounds which contain only carbon and hydrogen in the molecule.

**hydrochlor'ic acid** (Chem.): An aqueous solution of hydrogen chloride gas.

**hydro-electric generating set** (Elec. Eng.): An electric generator driven by a water turbine.

**hy'drogen** (Chem.): The lightest element known, having both metallic and non-metallic properties.

**hydrogen ion** (Chem.): An atom of hydrogen carrying a positive charge.

**hydrographical surveying** (Surv.): A branch of surveying dealing with bodies of water at the coast-line and in harbors, estuaries and rivers.

**hydrog'raphy:** The study, determination and publication of the conditions of navigable water.

**hydrol** (Chem.): A name given to the simple water molecule $H_2O$.

**hydrol'ysis** (Chem.): (1) The formation of an acid and a base from a salt by interaction with water. (2) The decomposition of organic compounds by interaction with water.

**hydrome'teor** (Meteor.): Any weather phenomenon which depends on the moisture content of the atmosphere.

**hy'drophi'lous** (Bot.): (1) Living in water. (2) Pollinated by water.

**hydropho'bia** (Med.): Rabies in man.

**hy'drophyte** (Bot.): A plant which lives on the surface or submerged in water

**hydroplane:** (1) A motor-boat which skins the surface of water. (2) A planing surface which enables a submarine to submerge.

**hy'drosol** (Chem.): A colloidal solution in water.

**hydrosphere:** The water on the surface of the earth.

**hydrostatics** (Phys.): The mechanics of fluids at rest.

**hydrotax'is** (Biol.): Response of an organism to the stimulus of moisture.

**hy'etograph** (Meteor.): An instrument which collects, measures and records the fall of rain.

**hygro-:** A prefix meaning moist or wet.

**hygrom'eter** (Meteor.): An instrument for measuring the amount of moisture in the atmosphere.

**hy'grophile** (Bot.): Living where moisture is abundant.

**hy'grophobe** (Bot.): Living best in dry situations.

**hygroscopic** (Chem.): Tending to absorb moisture.

**hygrostat** (Chem.): Apparatus which produces constant humidity.

**hyloph'agous** (Zool.): Wood-eating.

**hy'lophyte** (Bot.): A plant characteristic of damp woods.

**hylot'omous** (Zool.): Wood-cutting.

**hyper:** Prefix meaning above.

**hyperacid'ity** (Med.): Excessive acidity.

**hyperchromato'sis** (Cyt.): Excess of chromotin in a cell.

**hypermnesia** (Med.): Exceptional power of memory.

**hyperon** (Nucleonics): Particles whose mass is between that of neutron and deutron.

**hypertension** (Med.): Increase in tension; a blood pressure higher than normal.

**hy'pha** (Bot.): One of the branched or simple filaments of the thallus of a fungus.

**hyp'nody** (Zool.): The resting period in larval forms.

**hypno'sis** (Psychol.): A condition, induced in a person by suggestion, in which conscious control is discouraged.

**hypo:** A prefix meaning under.

**hypochondri'asis** (Med.): Morbid preoccupation with bodily sensations and functions, with the false belief that bodily diseases are indicated.

**hypoder'mis** (Bot.): A layer of strongly constructed cells, lying immediately beneath the epidermis and reinforcing it.

**hypoder'mic** (Med.): Under the skin.

**hypogene** (Geol.): Said of rocks formed under the earth's surface.

**hypopla'sia** (Zool.): Under-development.

**hyposthe'nic** (Med.): Having diminished strength.

**hy'postyle hall** (Arch.): A hall having columns to support the roof.

**hypotension** (Med.): Low blood pressure.

**hypso:** Prefix meaning height.

**hypsom'eter** (Phys.): An instrument used for determining the boiling point of water.

**hysterec'tomy** (Surg.): Removal of the uterus.

**hysteria** (Psycho-an.): A psychoneurosis in which repressed complexes become dissociated from the personality, forming independent units, partially or completely unrecognized by consciousness.

## I

**iatrochemistry** (Chem.): The study of chemical phenomena in order to obtain results of medical value.

**ice** (Meteor.): Ice is formed when water is cooled below its freezing point.

**ice action** (Geol.): The work and effects of ice on the earth's surface.

**ice apon, ice breaker** (Civ. Eng.): A construction serving to break floating ice or to afford protection against the thrust of the ice upon the pier.

**iceberg** (Meteor.): A large mass of ice, floating in the sea, which has broken away from a glacier or ice barrier.

**iceblink** (Meteor.): A whitish glare in the sky over ice which is too distant to be visible.

**Iceland spar** (Min.): A very pure transparent and crystalline form of calcium carbonate, first brought from Iceland.

**ichthy:** A prefix meaning fish.

**id** (Psycho-an.): A term used to denote the sum total of the primitive instinctual forces in an individual.

**idealism or mentalism:** The conception of natural phenomena as arising within the mind, the external world being ultimately unknowable to the human mind.

**idio:** A prefix meaning distinct or peculiar.

**idioblast** (Min.): A crystal which developed in metamorphic rocks and is bounded by crystal contours.

**idiochro'matin** (Cyt.): A substance within the nucleus which controls the reproduction of the cell.

**idiot** (Med.): One afflicted with the severest grade of feeble-mindedness.

**id'iozome** (Zool.): The attraction sphere or region of char protoplasm surrounding the centrosome.

**idling** (Eng.): The slow rate of revolution of an automobile or aero engine, when the throttle pedal or lever is in the closed position.

**ignite** (Chem.): To heat a gaseous mixture to the temperature at which combustion takes place.

**igni'ter** (Civ. Eng.): A blasting fuse or other contrivance used to fire an explosive charge.

**ignition** (Elec. Eng.): The firing of an explosive mixture of gases, vapors or other substances, by means of an electric spark.

**ignition laz** (Eng.): Of a combustible mixture in an engine cylinder, the time interval between the passage of the spark and the resulting pressure rise due to combustion.

**ileitis** (Med.): Inflammation of the ileum.

**i'leum** (Zool.): In vertebrates, the posterior part of the small intestine.

**il'ium** (Zool.): In vertebrates, a dorsal cartilage bone of the pelvic girdle.

**illusion** (Psychol.): A false interpretation of something perceived through the special senses.

**imagination** (Psychol.): The faculty of forming images in the mind.

**imag'o** (Zool.): Final instar of an insect.

**im'becile** (Med.): A person whose defective mental state does not amount to idiocy, but who is incapable of managing his own affairs.

**imbibition** (Chem.): The absorption or adsorption of a liquid by a solid or a gel, accompanied by swelling of the latter.

**im'bricate** (Bot., Zool.): Said of leaves, scales, etc., which overlap.

**immar'ginate** (Bot.): Lacking a distinct edge.

**immersed** (Bot.): (1) Embedded in the tissues of the plant. (2) Arising beneath the surface of the substratum.

**immersion** (Astron.): The entry of the moon, or other body, into the shadow which causes its eclipse.

**immiscibility** (Chem.): The property of two or more liquids of not mixing and of forming more than one phase when brought together.

**immune** (Med.): Protected against any particular infection.

**immune bodies** (Bacteriol.): Antibodies.

**impacted** (Med.): Firmly fixed; pressed closely in.

**imperforate** (Med.): Not perforated; closed abnormally. (Zool.): Lacking apertures, especially of shells.

**imperial** (Build.): A domed roof shaped to a point at the top.
**impermeable** (Chem., Geol.): Not permitting the passage of gas or liquids.
**impervious** (Build., etc.): Said of materials which have the property of satisfactorily resisting the passage of water.
**impeti'go** (Med.): A contagious skin disease, chiefly of the hands and face, due to infection with pus-forming bacteria.
**impiller** (Eng.): The rotating member of a centrifugal pump or blower, which imparts kinetic energy to the fluid.
**impressed** (Bot.): Having the surface marked by slight depressions.
**impulse** (Elec. Comm.): An unidirectional flow of current of non-repeated wave-form.
**in vitro** (Med.): In a test-tube; in a glass.
**in vivo** (Med.): In the living body.
**inactivation** (Chem.): The destruction of the activity of a serum, catalyst, etc.
**inarticulate** (Bot.): Not jointed.
**inbreeding** (Zool.): Breeding within the descendants of a foundation stock of related animals.
**incandes'cence**: The emission of light by a substance because of its high temperature.
**incendiary**: Tending to cause combustion.
**in'cept** (Bot.): The rudiment of an organ.
**incise** (Arch.): To carve.
**incision** (Surg.). The act of cutting into something; made by a surgical knife.
**inci'sors** (Zool.): The front teeth of mammals.
**inclinom'eter** (Surv.): An instrument for measuring ground and embankment slopes.
**included** (Bot.): Not projecting beyond the surrounding members.
**included angle** (Surv.): Either of the two angles between two survey lines meeting at a station.
**inclusion**: A particle or lump of foreign matter embedded in a solid.
**incompatibility** (Bot.): Any difference in the physiological properties of the protoplasts of a host and a parasite which limits or stops the development of the latter.
**incompetence** (Med.): Inability to perform proper function.
**incubation** (Zool.): The process of causing eggs to hatch by the application of natural or artificial heat.
**indehis'cent** (Bot.): Not opening naturally when ripe.
**indeterminate** (Bot.): Indefinite.
**index** (Surv.): A simple plane table alidade, having sighting vanes at the ends.
**indicator** (Chem.): A substance whose color depends on the alkalinity or acidity of the solution in which it is dissolved. (Elec. Eng.): A signalling device.
**indigenous** (Zool.): Native; not imported.
**indigestion** (Med.): A condition, marked by discomfort and pain, in which the normal digestive functions are impeded.
**indirect heating** (Build.): A system of heating by convection.
**indium** (Met.): A metallic element.
**individual** (Zool.): A single member of a species; a single unit or specimen.
**individuation** (Zool.): The formation of separation functional units which are mutually interdependent.
**indolent** (Med.): Causing little or no pain.
**induced charge** (Elec. Eng.): An electric charge produced as a result of a charge on a neighboring conductor.
**induced reaction** (Chem.): A chemical reaction which is accelerated by the simultaneous occurrence in the same system of a second, rapid reaction.
**induction** (Elec. Eng.): A term sometimes used to denote the density of an electric or magnetic field. (Zool.): The production of a definite condition by the action of an external factor.
**induction furnace** (Elec. Eng.): An electric furnace for melting metals.
**induction period** (Chem.): The interval of time between the initiation of a chemical reaction and its actual occurrence.
**inductor** (Chem.): A substance which accelerates a slow reaction between two or more substances by reacting rapidly with one of the reactants.
**indurated**: Hardened.
**inequality** (Astron.): The term used to signify any departure from uniformity in orbital motion.
**inequi**: Prefix meaning not equal.
**inert** (Chem.): Not readily changed by chemical means.
**inertia** (Mech., Phys.): Reluctance of a body to change its state of rest.
**infection** (Med.): The invasion of body tissue by living micro-organisms causing a diseased condition.
**inferior** (Zool.): Lower, under.
**inferiority complex** (Psychol.): Generally a persisting state of feelings of inferiority.
**infirmary** (Med.): An institution for the surgical and/or medical treatment of disease.
**inflation** (Aero.): The process of filling an airship or balloon with gas.
**inflores'cence** (Bot.): In flowering plants, the part of the shoot which bears flowers.
**infra**: A prefix meaning below.
**ingestion** (Zool.): The act of swallowing food material so that it passes into the body.
**ingot** (Met.): A metal casting of a shape suitable for subsequent rolling or forging.
**inhalation** (Med.): The act of breathing in into the lungs.
**inhibitor** (Bot.): A substance which limits or destroys the catalytic activity of an enzyme.
**initiator** (Chem.): The substance or molecule which starts a chain reaction.
**injected** (Bot.): Having the intercellular spaces filled with water.
**innings** (Civ. Eng.): Lands reclaimed from the sea.
**inoculation** (Bot.): The conveyance of infection to a host plant by any means of transmission. (Chem.): The introduction of a small crystal into a supersaturated solution or supercooled liquid in order to initiate crystallization.
**inop'erable** (Med.): Not suitable for operation.
**inorganic chemistry** (Chem.): The study of the chemical elements and their compounds.
**inscribe**: To draw one plane figure so that it is enclosed within another.
**insecticide** (Chem.): The product used to destroy insects.
**insemination** (Zool.): The approach and entry of the spermatozoon to the ovum.
**insesso'rial** (Zool.): Adapted for perching.
**insolation** (Med.): Sunstroke. (Meteor.): The radiation received from the sun.
**instability** (Aero.): Said of an aircraft when any disturbance of its steady motion tends to increase.
**instinct** (Psychol.): An innate force in an organism attaching to certain biological ends, such as self-preservation and reproduction.
**integ'ument** (Bot.): The seed coat or testa.
**intelligence quotient** (Psychol.): The ratio, expressed as a percentage, of an individual's mental age to his actual age.
**inter-**: A prefix meaning between.
**interbreeding** (Gen.): Experimental hybridization of different species.
**intercel'lular** (Zool.): Between cells.
**interchange** (Cyt.): The mutual transfer of portions between two chromosomes.
**interference** (Aero.): The aerodynamic influence of one body upon another. (Phys.): The effect of superposing two or more trains of waves of equal wavelength.
**intern** (Med.): An assistant physician in a hospital.
**interspecif'ic** (Cyt.): Said of a cross between two separate species.
**inter-vari'etal (Gen.): Said of a cross between two varieties of the same species.**
**intestine (Zool.): In vertebrates, that part of the alimentary canal leading from the stomach to the anus.**
**intracel'lular** (Biol.): Within the cell.
**intracra'nial** (Anat.): Situated within the skull.
**intrader'mal** (Anat.): Situated in the skin.
**intrave'nous** (Anat.): Within a vein.
**intra-vi'tam Staining** (Biol.): The artificial staining of living cells.
**intricate** (Bot.): Intertwined.
**intrinsic system** (Chem.): The store of energy possessed by a material system.
**introspection** (Psychol.): The habit, which may become pathological, of "looking within" one's self.
**in'trovert** (Psychol.): An individual interested mainly in his own mental processes and attitudes; shy and retiring in manner.
**intrusions** (Geol.): Bodies of igneous rocks which, in the condition of magma, were intruded into the pre-existing rocks of the earth's crust.
**in'volucre** (Bot.): A crowded group of bracts around the base of a dense inflorescence.
**involuntary** (Zool.): Outside the control of the will.
**in'volute** (Bot.): Having the margins rolled inwards. (Zool.): Tightly coiled.
**iodine** (Chem.): A non-metallic element.
**ion** (Chem.): A charged atom, molecules or radical.
**ionization**: The production of ions from an electrically neutral substance.
**i'rid, i'rido-**: Prefix meaning rainbow.
**irides'cence** (Phys.): The production of fine colors on a surface.
**irid'ium** (Met.): A brittle, steel-gray metallic element.
**i'ris** (Anat.): In the vertebrate eye, that part of the choroid, lying in front of the lens, which takes the form of a circular curtain with a central opening.
**iron** (Met.): A metallic element.
**iron ores** (Geol.): Rocks or deposits containing iron-rich compounds in workable amounts.
**ironwork** (Build.): A term applied to essentially ornamental work in iron as gates, hinges, etc.
**irrigation** (Civ. Eng.): The storage of flood waters by means of dams.

**irritant** (Biol.): Any external stimulus which produces an active response to a living organism.
**i'singlass** (Chem.): Fish glue.
**iso:** (Chem.): A prefix indicating: (1) The presence of a branched carbon chain in the molecule. (2) An isomeric compound. Also a prefix meaning equal.
**i'sobar** (Chem.): A curve relating quantities measured at the same pressure. (Meteor.): A line drawn on a map through places having the same atmospheric pressure at a given time.
**i'sobilat'eral** (Bot.): Divisible into symmetrical halves by two distinct planes.
**isoch'ronism** (Phys.): Regular periodicity, as the swinging of a pendulum.
**isometric system** (Crystal.): The cubic system.
**isomorphism** (Biol.): Apparent likeness between individuals belonging to different species or races.
**i'soneph** (Meteor.): A line drawn on a map through places having equal amounts of cloudiness.
**isoster'ic** (Chem.): Consisting of molecules possessing similar electronic structures.
**i'sotherm** (Meteor.): A line drawn on a map through places having equal temperatures.
**isothermal** (Chem.): Occurring at constant temperature.
**i'sotopes (Phys.): Atoms of the same element having different nuclear masses but identical chemical properties and atomic numbers.**
**isotrop'ic (Phys.): Said of a substance which possesses the same properties in all directions.**

## J

**jack** (Eng.): A portable lifting machine for raising heavy weights through a short distance.
**jacket** (Eng.): An outer casing constructed around a cylinder or pipe, the space being filled with a fluid for either heating, cooling or maintaining the cylinder contents at constant temperature.
**jalousies** (Build.): Hanging or sliding sun-shutters giving external protection to a window, and allowing for ventilation through louvres cut in the shutters themselves.
**jamb** (Build.): The side of an aperture.
**jaundice** (Med.): Yellow coloration of the skin and and other body tissues.
**jaw** (Eng.): One of a pair of members between which an object is held, crushed or cut as the jaws of a vice.
**jet:** A fluid stream issuing from an orifice or nozzle.
**jet propulsion** (Eng. and Aero.): Propulsion by reaction from the expulsion of a high velocity jet of the fluid in which the machine is moving.
**jet** (Min.): A hard coal-block variety of lignite.
**jettison, fuel** (Aero.): Apparatus for the rapid emergency discharge of fuel.
**jib** (Eng.): The boom of a crane or derrick.
**jig** (Eng.): An appliance used in a machine shop for accurately guiding and locating tools during the operations involved in producing interchangeable parts.
**jimmy** (Build.): A small crowbar.
**joggle** (Eng.): A small projection on a piece of metal fitting into a corresponding recess in another piece, to prevent lateral movement.
**joint:** A connection made between two pieces.
**joints** (Geol.): Vertical, inclined or horizontal divisional planes, found in almost all rocks.
**joist** (Build.): A horizontal beam of steel or timber used with others as a support for a floor or a ceiling.
**joystick** (Aero.): Colloquialism for control column.
**jug'ular** (Zool.): Pertaining to the throat or neck region.
**jumper-cable** (Elec. Eng.): A cable for making electrical connection between two sections of conductor-rail in an electric traction system.
**junket** (Chem.): A product obtained from milk by the action of rennin.
**Jupiter** (Astron.): The largest planet in the solar system, the fifth in order of distance from the sun.
**jutty** (Build.): A projecting part of a building.

## K

**karyas'ter** (Cyt.): A group of chromosomes arranged like the spokes of a wheel.
**karyogamy** (Biol.): The union of two nuclei, especially gametic nuclei.
**karyolysis** (Cyt.): Dissolution of the nucleus by disintegration of the chromatin.
**kar'yosome** (Cyt.): A nucleus; a chromosome.
**kar'yotin** (Cyt.): The substance which makes up the nuclear reticulum.
**katabat'ic** (Meteor.): Said of a wind which is caused by the downward motion of air due to convection.
**katab'olism** (Biol.): The sum-total of the disruptive metabolic processes in an organism, organ or cell.
**katagen'esis** (Zool.): Retrogressive evolution.
**katakinet'ic** (Biol.): Tending to the discharge of energy.
**kataklastic structures** (Geol.): Structures produced in a rock by the action of severe mechanical stress, during dynamic metamorphism.
**katharom'eter** (Chem.): An instrument for the analysis of gases by means of measurements of thermal conductivity.
**keel** (Aero.): The longitudinal member along the under side of the hull of a rigid airship.
**kelp** (Bot.): A general name for large seaweeds.
**keratogenous** (Zool.): Horn-producing.
**kernel** (Bot.): The seed inside the stony endocarp of a drupe.
**kevel** (Build.): A hammer, edged at one end and pointed at the other, used for breaking and rough-hewing stone.
**kham'sin** (Meteor.): A hot dry wind from the south, which blows over Egypt in front of depressions moving eastward along the Mediterranean.
**kilowatt** (Elec. Eng.): A unit of power equal to 1000 watts.
**kilowatt-hour** (Elec. Eng.): The commonly used unit of electrical energy, equal to 1000 watt-hours.
**kinaesthet'ic** (Zool.): Pertaining to the perception of muscular effort.
**kineso'dic** (Zool.): Conveying motor impulses.
**kinetic body** (Cyt.): A tiny granular body lying where a chromosome is attached to the spindle.
**kinetic energy** (Phys.): The energy possessed by a moving body in virtue of its motion.
**kip** (Eng.): A unit of force equivalent to 1,000 lbs.
**knee** (Eng.): An elbow pipe.
**knot** (Bot.): A hard and often resinous inclusion in timber.

## L

**la'bia** (Zool.): Any structures resembling lips.
**la'bile** (Chem.): Unstable.
**lab'oratory:** A place where specific scientific research or testing is done.
**lac:** A resinous substance, an excretion product of certain Coccid insects.
**laccate** (Bot.): Having a shining surface.
**lac'erate** (Bot.): Irregularly cut, as if torn.
**lac'quer** (Chem.): A solution of film-forming substances in volatile solvents.
**lac'rimal** (Zool.): Pertaining to the tear gland.
**lactation** (Zool.): The formation of milk by the mammary glands.
**lacte'ous** (Bot.): Milky.
**lacu'na** (Bot.): (1) Any depression in a surface of a plant. (2) A large intercellular space.
**lacustrine** (Ecol.): Pertaining to a lake or lakes.
**lagging** (Eng.): The process of covering a vessel or pipe with a non-conducting material.
**lake** (Geol.): A body of water lying on the surface of a continent, and unconnected with the ocean.
**lamel'la** (Bot.): A plate of cells.
**lam'ellose** (Bot.): Stratified.
**lam'ina** (Bot.): The flattened blade of a leaf. (Elec. Eng.): Thin sheet steel. (Zool.): A flat plate-like structure.
**laminated magnet** (Elec. Eng.): A permanent magnet built up of magnetized strips.
**lamination** (Geol.): Stratification on a fine scale.
**lan'ate** (Bot., Zool.): Covered with long and loosely tangled hairs.
**lan'ceolate (Bot.): Flattened, two or three times as long as broad, widest in the middle and tapering to a pointed apex.**
**landslip** (Geol.): The sudden sliding of masses of rock, soil or other superficial deposits from higher to lower levels, on steep slopes.
**landing** (Build.): A flat platform at the head of a series of steps. (Civ. Eng.): A space on a pier intended to provide access for passengers alighting.
**landing beam** (Aero.): The beam of radiation from a transmitter along which an aircraft approaches a landing field during blind landing.
**lan'iary** (Zool.): Adapted for tearing, as a canine tooth.
**lan'thanum** (Chem.): A metallic element.
**lap** (Met.): A surface defect on rolled or forged steel.
**lapidic'olous** (Zool.): Living under stones.
**lapil'li** (Geol.): Small rounded pieces of lava whirled from a volcanic vent during explosive eruptions.
**la'pis laz'uli** (Min.): The original sapphire.
**lapse** (Meteor.): The temperature gradient of the atmosphere taken vertically.
**larva** (Zool.): In insects, an immature stage intervening between the egg and the adult.
**lar'ynx** (Anat.): The vocal organ in all land vertebrates except birds.
**la'tent** (Zool.): In a resting condition or state of arrested development, but capable of becoming active when conditions become suitable.
**latent heat** (Phys.): The heat which is required to change the state of a substance from solid to liquid, or from liquid to gas, without change of temperature.
**later-latero-lateri:** A prefix meaning sides.
**lateral:** Situated on or at a side.
**later'igrade** (Zool.): Moving sideways, as some crabs.
**laterit'ious** (Bot.): Brick-red.
**la'tex** (Bot.): A milky fluid, present in many plants.

**lathe** (Eng.): A machine tool for producing cylindrical work, facing, boring and screw cutting.
**latitude, terrestrial**: Angular distance measured on a meridian; now distance measured in degrees north and south from the equator.
**lava** (Geol.): The molten rock material that issues from a volcanic vent or fissure.
**law**: A scientific law is a rule or generalization which describes specified natural phenomena within the limits of experimental observation.
**lax** (Bot.): Arranged loosely.
**layer** (Bot.): A stratum of vegetation, as the shrubs in a wood.
**leaching** (Bot.): The removal, by percolating water, of mineral salts from the soil. (Met.): The extraction of a soluble metallic compound from an ore.
**lead** (Met.): A metallic element.
**lead** (Elec. Eng.): A term often used to denote an electric wire or cable.
**leader** (Bot.): One of the main shoots of a tree.
**leaf** (Bot.): An outgrowth from the stem of a plant, usually green, and largely concerned with transpiration and photosynthesis.
**leaf base** (Bot.): The base of the leaf stalk, where it joins the stem.
**leaf bud** (Bot.): A bud containing vegetative leaves only.
**leaf scar** (Bot.): The scar left on a stem at the point where a leaf has fallen off.
**leaflet** (Bot.): One separate portion of the lamina of a compound leaf.
**leap year** (Astron.): Those years in which an extra day, February 29, is added to the civil calendar to allow for the fractional part of a year of 365 days.
**leg'ume** (Bot.): A fruit formed from a single carpel.
**len'ticel** (Bot.): Structure of the bark of plants which permits passage of gas between internal tissues and atmosphere.
**lenticle** (Geol.): A mass of lens-like form.
**Leo** (Astron.): Lion; the fifth sign of the Zodiac.
**lep'idote** (Bot.): Said of a surface which bears scale-like hairs. (Zool.): Having a coating of minute scales, as butterfly wings.
**lesion** (Med.): Any wound or morbid change anywhere in the body.
**leste** (Meteor.): A dry south wind blowing in Madeira and North Africa in front of a depression.
**le'thal** (Biol.): Causing death.
**leuco**: A prefix meaning white.
**leu'cocyte** (Zool.): A white blood-corpuscle.
**level** (Civ. Eng.): To reduce a cut or fill surface to an approximately horizontal plane. (Surv.): An instrument used by the surveyors for determining the difference in height between two points.
**level line** (Surv.): A line lying wholly on a level surface, and therefore perpendicular at all points to the direction of gravity.
**level man** (Surv.): The operator of a surveyor's level.
**level surface** (Surv.): A surface which is everywhere perpendicular to the direction of gravity.
**levelling** (Surv.): The operation of finding the difference of elevation between two points.
**lever** (Mech.): One of the simplest machines; a rigid beam pivoted at the fulcrum, with a load being applied at one point in the beam and an effort, sufficient to balance the load at another.
**Leyden jar** (Elec. Eng.): A capacitor consisting of a glass jar having its inner and outer surfaces coated with a conducting material.
**libido** (Psycho-an.): A term used to denote the energy attached to the sexual impulse; subsequently used to cover vital energy in general.
**Libra** (Astron.): Balance. Seventh sign of the Zodiac.
**librations** (Astron.): Apparent oscillations of the moon or other body.
**Liche'nes** (Bot.): A large group of composite plants, consisting of an alga and a fungus in intimate association.
**life-cycle** (Biol.): The various stages through which an organism passes, from fertilized ovum to the fertilized ovum of the next generation.
**lig'ament** (Zool.): A bundle of fibrous tissue joining two or more bones or cartilages.
**light**: Electromagnetic radiation capable of inducing visual sensation through the eye. Light is the product of the visibility and the radiant power.
**light valve**: Any device whereby the passage of light is controlled electrically.
**light-year** (Astron.): A spatial unit used to express distances in the stellar universe.
**lightning** (Meteor.): The very large spark which marks the discharge of an electrified thunder cloud, either to another cloud or to earth.
**lig-neous** (Bot.): Woody.
**lig'nite** (Geol.): Brown, compact, fossil wood, representing one stage in the conversion of plant remains into coal.
**lig'ulate** (Bot.): Strap-shaped, flattened, long and narrow.
**limb** (Astron.): The term applied to the rim of a heavenly body having a visible disc. (Bot.): (1) The lamina of a leaf. (2) The widened upper part of a petal. (Zool.): A jointed appendage, as a leg.
**limbous** (Zool.): Overlapping.
**lime** (Build.): A substance produced by heating limestone to 825° C or more.
**limestone** (Geol.): Sedimentary rock containing 50% carbonate of lime or magnesia.
**limic'olous** (Zool.): Living in mud.
**lim'nobiot'ic** (Zool.): Living in fresh water.
**limnoph'ilous** (Zool.): Living in marshes.
**limon'iform** (Bot.): Lemon-shaped.
**line** (Carp.): To mark a straight line on timber as a guide for erection or working. (Elec. Comm.): That part of a communication circuit which has uniformly distributed constants. (Elec. Eng.): A power transmission circuit. (Surv.): The cord to which the lead of a lead-line is secured.
**line** (Maths.): In a plane: the shortest distance between two points. On a sphere: a portion of a great circle.
**line of action** (Mech.): The line along which a force acts.
**lineage** (Gen.): In evolution, a time-character concept representing a racial complex of lines of descent.
**lin'qua** (Zool.): Any tongue-like structure.
**link** (Eng.): Any connecting piece in a machine. (Surv.): The one-hundredth part of a chain.
**linkage** (Gen.): The tendency shown by certain genetical characteristics to be inherited together.
**Linnean System** (Bot., Zool.): The system of classification established by the Swedish naturalist Linnaeus.
**linseed oil** (Chem.): An oil obtained from the seeds of flax.
**lintel** (Build.) A beam across the top of an aperture.
**lip** (Bot.): A large projecting lobe of a corolla.
**lipids, lipoids** (Chem.): Generic terms for fats, waxes and related products found in living tissue.
**lipogenous** (Zool.): Fat-producing.
**lip'oplast** (Bot.): A fatty globule.
**liquefaction**: The change of a gas or solid into a liquid state.
**lithium** (Min.): The lightest metallic element.
**lithod'omous** (Zool.): Living in rocks.
**lithol'ogy** (Geol.): The character of a rock expressed in terms of its structure, its mineral composition, the grain-size and arrangement of its component parts.
**lithoph'agous** (Zool.): Stone-eating
**lith'osphere** (Geol.): The crust of the earth.
**litmus** (Chem.): A material of organic origin used as indicator for acids and alkalines.
**litt'oral** (Bot., Zool.): Pertaining to the shore; sea-shore.
**live** (Acous.): Said of an enclosure in which the reverberation is normal. (Elec. Eng.): Said of an electric circuit or conductor in which there is a difference between it and earth.
**load**: (1) The weight supported by a structure. (2) The power output of an engine or motor under given circumstances.
**loam** (Build.): A brick earth composed of clay and sand.
**lobe** (Bot.): One of the parts into which a flattened plant member is cut, when the parts are too large to be called teeth, but not completely separated from one another. (Zool.): A rounded projection.
**locomotive** (Eng.): A vehicle driven by oil, steam or electricity for hauling on a railway.
**locus** (Cyt.): The position of a gene in a chromosome.
**lode** (Civ. Eng.): An artificial dyke.
**lodestone** (Min.): A form of magnetite, behaving, when freely suspended, as a magnet.
**loess** (Geol.): An aeolian clay originating in arid regions and transported by wind.
**log**: The stem of a felled tree when deprived of its limbs and ready for conversion.
**longi-**: A prefix meaning long.
**longitude, terrestrial**: The portion of the equator intersected between the meridian of a given place and the prime meridian, as from Greenwich, England.
**looming** (Meteor.): The vague enlarged appearance of objects seen through a fog or mist, particularly at sea.
**lopho**: A prefix meaning crest.
**loss** (Elec. Comm.): The negative of gain in a transmission system.
**lo'tic fauna** (Ecol.): Animals living in running waters, as streams and rivers.
**loudness** (Acous.): The subjective measure of the intensity of a sound.
**louver** (Build.): A window space across which are sloping slats fixed horizontally, with spaces between for ventilation.
**low** (meteor.): A region of low pressure.
**lubricant**: A substance capable of reducing friction between bearing surfaces in relative motion; oil or graphite.
**lu'bricous** (Bot.): Having a slippery surface.
**lucif'erin** (Zool.): A protein like substance which occurs in the luminous organs of certain animals.
**lucifu'gous** (Ecol.): Shunning light.
**luciph'ilous** (Ecol.): Seeking light.
**lumbago** (Med.): A rheumatic affection of the muscles

and ligaments in the lower part of the back.
**lumines'cence** (Chem.): The emission of light as a result of causes other than high temperatures.
**lu'minophore** (Chem.): A substance which emits light at room temperature.
**luminosity** (Astron.): The measure of the amount of light actually emitted by a star, irrespective of its distance.
**lunar bows** (Meteor.): Bows of a similar nature to rainbows but produced by moonlight.
**lu'nate**: Crescent-shaped.
**lune** (Maths.): The portion of the surface of a sphere intercepted by two great circles.
**lung** (Zool.): The respiratory organ in air-breathing vertebrates.
**luster** (Min.): This depends upon the quality and amount of light that is reflected from the surface of a mineral.
**lute'cium** (Chem.): A metallic element.
**lutein** (Chem.): A yellow unsaturated compound occurring in leaves and petals of various plants.
**lymph-**: A prefix meaning water.
**lymph** (Zool.): A colorless circulating fluid occurring in the lympathic vessels of vertebrates and closely resembling blood plasma in composition.
**ly'sin** (Zool.): A substance which will cause dissolution of cells.

## M

**macad'amized road** (Civ. Eng.): A road whose surface is formed with broken stones rolled into a 6-10 in. layer.
**machine** (Mech.): A device for overcoming a resistance at one point by the application of a force at some other point.
**macr-, macro-**: A prefix meaning large.
**macrochem'istry** (Chem.): The study of the composition and chemical properties of matter in bulk.
**macroscop'ic**: Visible to the naked eye.
**macrosmat'ic** (Zool.): Having a highly developed sense of smell.
**mac'rosome** (Zool.): A large protoplasmic globule.
**mac'rostructure** (Met.): The general arrangement of crystals in a solid metal as seen by the naked eye or at low magnification.
**maestro** (Meteor.): A fine-weather, non-autumn north-west wind in the Adriatic.
**Mae West** (Aero.): Personal lifejacket designed for airmen.
**magma** (Geol.): A term given to the molten fluids and gaseous fractions which have been generated within the earth, and from which igneous rocks are considered to have been derived.
**mag'nesite** (Met.): Carbonate of magnesium.
**magne'sium** (Chem.): A metallic element.
**magnet**: A mass of iron or other material which possesses the property of attracting or repelling other masses of iron.
**magnet core**: The iron core within the coil of an electromagnet.
**magnetic axis**: A line through the effective centers of the poles of a magnet.
**magnetic bearing** (Surv.): The horizontal angle between any survey line and the direction of magnetic north.
**magnetic circuit** (Elec. Eng.): The closed path taken by the magnetic flux in an electric machine or other apparatus.
**magnetic compass**: A compass consisting of a magnetic needle which sets itself along the lines of the earth's magnetic field.
**magnetic field**: The region in the neighborhood of a permanent magnet or a current-carrying conductor in which magnetic forces can be detected.
**Magnetic North**: The direction in which the north pole of a pivoted magnet will point.
**magnetic polarization** (Chem.): The production of optical activity by placing an inactive substance in a magnetic field.
**Magnetic South**: The direction in which the South pole of a pivoted magnet will point.
**magnetizing coil** (Elec. Eng.): A current-carrying coil used to magnetize an electromagnet.
**magnetism**: A general term used to denote either a magnetic field or the whole science associated with the behavior of such fields.
**magnetite** (Min.): An oxide of iron.
**magne'to** (Elec. Eng.): A small permanent-magnet electric generator capable of producing periodic high-voltage impulses.
**magnetochemistry** (Chem.): The study of the magnetic changes accompanying chemical reactions.
**magnetom'eter**: A pivoted magnetic needle used for measuring the strength of magnetic fields.
**magnetomotive force**: The force which produces a magnetic flux in a magnetic circuit.
**magneto-striction**: The change in dimensions produced in a magnetic material when it is magnetized.
**magnitudes** (Astron.): The scale by which the brightness of stars is measured.
**main** (Civ. Eng.): A principal water or gas pipe, having branch pipes leading supplies to consumers.
**male** (Zool.): An individual of which the gonads produce spermatozoa or some corresponding form of gamete.
**malignant** (Med.): Tending to go from bad to worse; especially, cancerous.
**malleabil'ity** (Met.): The property of being able to be mechanically deformed by rolling, forging, extrusion etc., applied to metals.
**mal'leate** (Zool.): Hammer-shaped.
**mamil'la** (Zool.): A nipple.
**Man** (Zool.): The human race, all varieties of which are included in the single species Homo sapiens, belonging to the order Primates.
**manganese** (Met.): A hard, brittle, metallic element.
**mania** (Psychiatry): The elated phase of manic depressive psychosis.
**manic-depressive psychosis** (Psychiatry): A type of insanity characterized by disorders of affect, either of elation or of depression, with intermediate mixed states.
**manom'eter** (Phys.): An instrument used to measure the pressure of a gas.
**mantel** (Build.): An ornamental front and shelf to a fireplace.
**marble** (Geol.): The term applies to a granular crystalline limestone.
**marbled** (Bot.): Marked by irregular streaks of color.
**marginate** (Bot.): Having a well-marked border.
**mar'igraph** (Surv.): A guage registering the height of the tide at a given place.
**maritime** (Bot., Zool.): Living by the sea.
**mark** (Surv.): Any of the distinguishing tags attached at intervals to a lead-line to denote feet or fathoms.
**marl** (Geol.): A general term for a very fine-grained rock, either clay or loam, with a variable admixture of calcium carbonate.
**marquise** (Build.): A projecting canopy over the entrance to a building.
**marrow** (Zool.): The vascular connective tissue which occupies the central cavities of the long bones in most vertebrates.
**Mars** (Astron.): The fourth planet from the sun in order of distance.
**marsu'pium** (Zool.): A pouch-like structure occupied by the immature young of an animal during the later stages of development.
**ma'sochism** (Psycho-path.): Gratification obtained from the suffering of physical or mental pain.
**mass** (Phys.): The quantity of matter in a body.
**mass number** (Chem.): The atomic weight of an isotope.
**mastication** (Zool.): The act of reducing solid food to a fine state of subdivision or to a pulp.
**mas'ticatory** (Zool.): Pertaining to the chewing of food prior to swallowing.
**ma'trix** (Biol.): An outer layer of stainable material in a chromosome. (Zool.): The inter-cellular ground-substance of connective tissues.
**matromor'phic** (Biol.): Resembling the mother.
**matter** (Phys.): The substances of which the physical universe is composed.
**maturation** (Bot., Zool.): The final stages in the development of the germ cells.
**mean solar time** (Astron.): Time as measured by the hour angle of the mean sun.
**mechanical advantage** (Mech.): The ratio of the resistance to the applied force in a machine.
**mechanical engineering**: That branch of engineering concerned primarily with the design and production of all purely mechanical contrivances.
**mechanics**: The study of the action of forces on bodies and of the motions they produce.
**medi-, medio-**: A prefix meaning middle.
**medium** (Bot., Zool.): A nutritive substance on or in which tissues or culture of micro-organisms may be reared.
**medulla** (Zool.): The central portion of an organ or tissue.
**medul'lary** (Bot.): Relating to the pith.
**mega-, meg-**: A prefix denoting a million.
**mega-, megal, megalo**: A prefix meaning large.
**meg'acycle** (Elec. Comm.): One million cycles.
**megaloma'nia** (Psychiatry): Delusion of grandeur.
**megascopic**: Visible to the naked eye.
**megaton** (Nuclear Warfare): Explosive force equivalent to 1,000,000 tons of T.N.T.
**meg'ohm** (Elec. Eng.): A unit of resistance used for very high resistance values.
**mei'ocyte** (Cyt.): Any cell in which meiosis is begun.
**meiomer'ous** (Bot., Zool.): Having a small number of parts.
**meio'sis** (Cyt.): The type of nuclear division by which the chromosomes are reduced from the diploid to the haploid number.
**melan-, mel'ans-**: A prefix meaning black.
**melancho'lia** (Psychiatry): A condition seen in the depressive state of manic depressive psychosis.
**mel'anin** (Chem.): A black or dark brown pigment occurring in hair and skin.
**melliphagous** (Zool.): Honey-eating.
**melting-point** (Chem.): The temperature at which a solid begins to liquify.

**member** (Bot.): Any part of a plant considered from the standpoint of morphology. (Zool.): An organ of the body, especially an appendage.
**membrane** (Bot., Zool.): A thin sheet-like structure, usually fibrous, connecting other structures or covering or lining a part or organ.
**menis'cus** (Chem.): The surface of a liquid in a tube.
**men'opause** (Med.): The natural cessation of menstruation in women.
**mensa** (Zool.): The biting surface of a tooth.
**menstrua'tion** (Zool.): The periodical discharge from the uterus.
**Mercury** (Astron.): The first planet from the sun in order of distance.
**mercury** (Met.): A white metallic element which is liquid at atmospheric temperature.
**mercury barometer** (Meteor., Phys.): An instrument used for measuring the pressure of the atmosphere in terms of the height of a column of mercury which exerts an equal pressure.
**mer'icarp** (Bot.): A one-seeded portion of a fruit which splits up at maturity.
**meridian** (Astron.): That great circle passing through the poles of the celestial sphere which cuts the observer's horizon in the north and south point, and also passes through his Zenith.
**meris'tic** (Zool.): Segmented.
**mero-**: A prefix meaning part.
**merog'amy** (Bot.): The union of two individual gametes.
**merosthen'ic** (Zool.): Having the hind legs exceptionally well developed, as kangaroos.
**mer'ycism** (Med.): Rumination.
**mes-, meso-**: A prefix meaning middle.
**mesons** (Nucleonics): Short-lived sub-atomic particles arising in cosmic rays.
**mesh** (Civ. Eng.): Expanded metal used as a reinforcement for concrete.
**mesomor'phous** (Chem.): Existing in a state of aggregation midway between the true crystalline state and the completely irregular amorphous state.
**me'sophyte** (Bot.): A plant occurring in places where the water-supply is neither scanty nor excessive.
**me'sostate** (Zool.): An intermediate stage in metabolism.
**meta-**: A prefix meaning after.
**metabol'ic nucleus** (Cyt.): A nucleus when it is not dividing, and when the chromation is in the form of a network.
**metab'olism** (Biol.): The sum-total of the chemical and physical changes constantly taking place in living matter.
**metab'olite** (Zool.): A product of metabolism.
**metab'oly** (Bot.): The power possessed by some cells of altering their external form.
**metachemistry**: The study of atomic and sub-atomic phenomena.
**metachromat'ic** (Micros.): Showing other than the basic color constituent after staining.
**metachro'sis** (Zool.): The ability of an animal to change color by contraction and expansion of chromatophores, as a chameleon.
**metal**: An element which readily forms positive ions.
**metallif'erous veins** (Geol.): Cracks and fissures in rocks which are found to contain the ore of metals.
**metallization** (Chem.): The conversion of a substance into a metallic form.
**metal'lochrome** (Chem.): The tinting produced on a metal surface by means of metallic salts.
**metallog'raphy**: The branch of metallurgy which deals with the study of the structure and constitution of solid metals and alloys, and the relation of this to properties on the one hand and manufacture and treatment on the other.
**met'alloid** (Chem.): (1) A non-metal. (2) An element having both metallic and non-metallic properties.
**metallurgy**: Art and science applied to metals.
**metamorphic rocks** (Geol.): Rocks derived from pre-existing rocks by chemical, mineralogical and structural alterations.
**metamor'phism** (Geol.): The sum of the processes which can operate within the earth's crust and transform a rock into a well characterized new type.
**metamorpho'sis** (Zool.): Pronounced change of form and structure taking place within a short time, as an animal changing from the larval to the adult stage.
**metapla'sia** (Zool.): Tissue transformation.
**metapla'sis** (Zool.): The period of maturity in the life-cycle of an individual.
**metaplasm** (Biol.): Any substance within the body of a cell which is not protoplasm.
**metasitism** (Zool.): Cannibalism.
**met'astable** (Chem.): In a state which is apparently stable.
**metasta'sic electron** (Chem.): An electron which is transferred from one atom to another, or from one shell to another in the same atom.
**metas'tasis** (Med.): The transfer of deseased tissue from one part of the body to another.
**me'teor** (Astron.): A "shooting star".
**meteorites** (Astron.): Mineral aggregates of cosmic origin which reach the earth from interplanetary space.
**meteorograph** (Meteor.): A collection of meteorological recording instruments which are attached to small balloons and sent up to record conditions in the upper atmosphere.
**meteorology**: The study of the earth's atmosphere in its relation to climate and weather.
**meter**: A unit of length in the metric system; 1 meter equals 39.37 inches.
**metric system**: A system of weights and measures depending upon the meter.
**metromor'phic** (Bot.): Resembling the mother.
**metu'liform** (Bot.): Resembling a pyramid.
**mez'zanine** (Build.): An intermediate floor constructed between two other floors in a building.
**mica** (Min.): A group of minerals which crystallize in the monoclinic system.
**mica-schist** (Geol.): A schist composed essentially of micas and quartz.
**micelle** (Chem.): A particle of colloidal size.
**micro-**: A prefix meaning small.
**microanal'ysis** (Chem.): A special technique of both quantitative and qualitative analysis, by means of which very small amounts of substance may be analyzed.
**mi'crobe** (Bacteriol.): A bacterium which can be seen with the aid of a microscope.
**microcrystalline texture** (Geol.): A term applied to a rock in which the individual crystals can be seen as such only under the microscope.
**mi'crolite** (Geol.): A general term for minute crystals of tabular or prismatic habit found in microcrystalline rocks.
**microm'eter**: An instrument used primarily for measuring small angular separations visually.
**mi'cron**: A unit of length equal to $10^{-3}$ mm., used for expressing wave-lengths of light and small distances.
**mi'crophone** (Acous.): An acousti-electrical convertor of sound wave-forms, essential in sound-reproducing systems.
**microphyl'line** (Bot.): Composed of small scales or lobes.
**mi'croscope**: An instrument used for obtaining magnified images in small objects.
**mi'crosome** (Cyt.): A granular or bladder-like inclusion in the cytoplasm, of very small size.
**microspe'cies** (Bot.): A variety of species.
**microstructure** (Met.): A term referring to the size, shape and arrangement with respect to each other of the crystals of the constituents present in a metal or alloy.
**mi'crotome** (Bot., Zool.): An instrument for cutting thin sections of specimens.
**midrib** (Bot.): The largest vein of a leaf, running longitudinally through the middle of the lamella.
**midwater zone** (Ocean.): The depths of the ocean between the surface waters and the abyss.
**migraine** (Med.): Paroxysmal headache.
**migration** (Chem.): The steady motion of particles, ions, etc., in a given direction under the influence of a force. (Zool.): Removal from one habitat to another.
**mil** (Eng.): Measurement unit, $10^{-3}$ inch.
**mile**: A unit of length; 1 statute mile = 1760 yds.
**mill** (Eng.): (1) A machine for grinding. (2) A factory fitted with machinery for manufacturing.
**mil'limeter**: The thousandth part of a meter.
**mil'limicron** (Phys.): A unit of length, equal to $10^{-6}$ millimeter.
**mim'icry** (Zool.): The adoption by one species of the color, habits or structure of another species.
**min'aret** (Arch.): A lofty slender tower rising from a mosque and surrounded by galleries.
**mind** (Psycho-an.): According to Freud, mind consists of a relatively small conscious part and a larger unconscious part, each of which consist of the processes of feeling, thinking and wishing.
**mineral** (Min.): A body produced by processes of inorganic nature; usually with a definite chemical composition, a certain characteristic atomic structure, which is expressed in its crystalline form.
**mineral'ogy**: The scientific study of minerals.
**minute**: (1) A sixtieth part of an hour of time. (2) A sixtieth part of a degree. (3) A sixtieth part of the lower diameter of a column.
**mio'sis** (Med.): Contraction of the pupil of the eye.
**mirage** (Meteor.): An effect caused by total reflection of light at the upper surface of shallow layers of hot air in contact with the ground, the appearance being that of pools of water in which are seen inverted images of more distant objects.
**mirror** (Phys.): A high polished reflecting surface capable of reflecting light-rays without appreciable diffusion.
**miscarriage** (Med.): Expulsion of the foetus before the twenty-eighth week of pregnancy.
**miscilibility** (Chem.): The property enabling two or

more liquids to mix when brought together and thus form one phase.
**mist** (Chem.): A suspension of a liquid in a gas. (Meteor.): A term applied to cloud in contact with the ground.
**mis'tral** (Meteor.): A cold, dry northerly wind occurring along the Mediterranean coast of France during fine clear weather.
**mito'sis** (Cyt.): The series of changes through which the nucleus passes during ordinary cell division, and by which each of the daughter cells is provided with a set of chromosomes similar to that possessed by the parent cell.
**mito'tic index** (Cyt.): The proportion in any tissue of dividing cells.
**miter** (Build.): A joint between two pieces at an angle to one another.
**mixed** (Zool.): Said of nerve trunks containing motor and sensory fibers.
**mixer** (Met.): A large furnace used as a reservoir for molten pig-iron coming from the blast-furnace.
**mode** (Geol.): The actual mineral composition of a rock expressed quantitatively in percentages by weight.
**modification** (Bot.): A change in a plant brought about by environmental conditions and lasting only as long as the operative conditions last.
**modules** (Arch.): The radius of the lower end of the shaft of a column.
**molars** (Zool.): The posterior grinding teeth of mammals.
**mold** (Bot.): A popular name for any of numerous small fungi.
**molding** (Build.): An ornamental band projecting from the surface of a wall or other surface.
**molecular compound** (Chem.): A compound formed by the combination of two or more molecules capable of independent existence.
**molecular heat** (Chem.): The product of the specific heat of a substance and its molecular weight.
**molecular structure** (Chem.): The way in which atoms are linked together in a molecule.
**molecular weight** (Chem.): The weight of a molecule of a substance referred to that of an atom of oxygen as 16.000.
**molecule** (Chem.): The smallest particle of a substance that is capable of independent existence while still retaining its chemical properties.
**momentum** (Mech.): The product of the mass of a body and its velocity.
**mon-, mono-**: A prefix meaning alone.
**mongrel** (Bot., Zool.): The offspring of a cross between varieties of races of a species.
**monitor** (Elec. Comm.): An arrangement for reproducing and checking any transmission without interfering with the regular transmission.
**monkey** (Civ. Eng.): The falling weighting of a pile-driver.
**Monocotyle'dones** (Bot.): One of the two main groups included in the Angiospermae. The embryo has one cotyledon.
**monoe'cious** (Bot.): Having separate staminate and pistillate flowers on the same individual plant.
**monog'ony** (Zool.): Asexual reproduction.
**monokar'yon** (Cyt.): A nucleus with only one centriole.
**mon'olith** (Build.): A single detached column or block of stone.
**monolith'ic** (Build., Civ. Eng.): A structure made of a continuous mass of material.
**monomolec'ular layer** (Chem.): A film of a substance one molecule thick.
**monomor'phic** (Zool.): Showing little change of form during the life history.
**monomor'phous** (Cryst.): Existing in only one crystalline form.
**mononucleo'sis** (Med.): Glandular fever.
**monophylet'ic** (Gen.): Descended from a single parent form.
**mon'oplane** (Aero.): A heavier-than-air aircraft, having one main supporting surface.
**monova'lent** (Chem.): Capable of combining with one atom of hydrogen or its equivalent.
**monsoon** (Meteor.): A wind which blows in opposite directions at different seasons of the year.
**montic'olous** (Zool.): Living in mountainous regions.
**moon** (Astron.): (1) The satellite which revolves about the earth in a variable orbit at a mean distance of 239,000 miles in a period of one month. (2) Any satellite of a planet.
**mo'ron** (Psychiatry): A feeble-minded person whose mentality is that of a child between 8 and 12 years of age.
**morph-, morpho-**: A prefix meaning form.
**morphol'ogy** (Bot., Zool.): The study of the structure and form of organisms, as opposed to the study of their functions. (Geol.): The study of the shapes and contours of objects, especially of the surface of the earth.
**morpho'sis** (Zool.: The development of structural characteristics; tissue formation.
**mortar** (Chem.): A bowl, made of porcelain, glass or agate, in which solids are ground up with a pestle.
**mother cell** (Bot., Zool.): A cell which divides to give daughter cells.
**motor** (Bot., Zool.): Pertaining to movement.
**mound** (Civ. Eng.): An undisturbed hillock left on an excavated site as an indication of the depth of the excavation.
**mu'cins** (Chem.): A group of glucoproteins occurring in saliva and mucus and widely distributed in nature.
**mu'cus** (Zool.): The viscous slimy fluid secreted by the mucous glands.
**multi-**: A prefix meaning many.
**multicel'lular** (Bot., Zool.): Consisting of a number of cells.
**mul'tiform** (Bot.): Diverse in shape.
**multinu'cleate** (Bot., Zool.): With many nuclei.
**mul'tiplet** (Bot.): One of several individuals derived by the segmentation of an ovum.
**multiplication** (Bot.): Increase by vegetative means.
**muscle** (Zool.): Tissue possessing the power of rapidly and forcibly changing shape.
**mus'culature** (Zool.): The disposition and arrangement of the muscles in the body of an animal.
**mutation** (Gen.): The inception of a heritable variation.
**mycol'ogy** (Bot.): The study of fungi.
**myol'ogy** (Zool.): The study of muscles.
**myo'pia** (Med.): Near-sightedness.

## N

**na'cre** (Zool.): Mother-of-pearl.
**nacreous** (Min.): A term applied to the luster of certain minerals.
**narcot'ic** (Med.): Tending to induce sleep or unconsciousness.
**na'dir** (Astron.): The point on the celestial sphere diametrically opposite the zenith.
**nar'cissism** (Psycho-path.): A state of self-love.
**na'sal** (Zool): Pertaining to the nose.
**nas'cent** (Chem.): Just formed by a chemical reaction, and therefore very reactive.
**na'tal** (Med., Zool.): Pertaining to birth.
**nata'tory** (Zool.): Adapted for swimming.
**native** (Min.): Said of naturally occurring metal.
**natural frequency** (Phys.): The frequency of free vibrations of a body.
**neap tides** (Astron.): High tides occurring at the moon's first or third quarter.
**nebula** (Astron.): Any first luminous patch seen among the stars.
**nebule** (Arch.): An ornamental molding characterized by a wavy lower edge.
**neb'ulous** (Bot.): Clouded, dark.
**necro-**: A prefix meaning a dead body.
**necrog'enous** (Biol.): Living or developing in the bodies of dead animals.
**ne'cron** (Bot.): Dead plant material not rotted into humus.
**nec'ropsy** (Med.): Autopsy.
**necro'sis** (Biol): Death of a cell or cells while still part of the living body.
**nectar** (Bot.): A sugary fluid exuded by plants.
**nectary** (Bot.): A glandular organ or surface from which nectar is secreted.
**necto-**: A prefix meaning swimming.
**nectopod** (Zool.): An appendage adopted for swimming.
**needle** (Elec. Eng.): The moving magnet of a compass or galvanometer of the moving-magnet type.
**negative** (Elec.): A particular point or electrode is negative with respect to another point when it is at a lower electric potential.
**negative catalysis** (Chem.): The retardation of a chemical reaction by a substance which itself undergoes no permanent chemical change.
**negative group** (Chem.): An acid radical.
**nemato-**: A prefix meaning thread.
**neo-**: A prefix meaning young.
**Neo-Darwinian** (Zool.): Pertaining to the modern version of the natural selection theory of Darwin.
**Neolithic Period** (Geol.): The later portion of the Stone Age.
**ne'on** (Chem.): A zero-valent element, one of the rare gases.
**ne'oplasm** (Med.): A new formation of tissue in the body.
**nephr-, nephro-**: A prefix meaning kidney.
**neph'ric** (Anat., Zool.): Pertaining to the kidney.
**nephrite** (Min.): One of the minerals grouped under the name of jade.
**neph'ros** (Zool.): A kidney.
**Neptune** (Astron.): Eighth major planet of the solar system, in order of distance from the sun.
**neritic zone** (Geol., Ocean.): That portion of the sea floor lying between low-water mark and the edge of the continental shelf, at a depth of about 100 fathoms.
**nerve** (Anat., Zool.): One of the branches of the central nervous system passing to an organ or part of the body. (Bot.): A general name for the midrib and the larger veins of a leaf.

**nerve center** (Zool.): An aggregation of nerve cells associated with a particular function or sense.
**nerve ending** (Zool.): The free distal end of a nerve or nerve fiber.
**nerve fiber** (Zool.): An axon.
**nerve impulse** (Zool.): The disturbance which passes along a nerve when it is stimulated.
**nerve plexus** (Zool.): A network of interlacing nerve fibers.
**nerve root** (Zool.): The origin of a nerve in the central nervous system.
**nerve trunk** (Zool.): A bundle of nerve fibers united within a connective-tissue coat.
**nervous system** (Zool.): The whole system of nerves, ganglia and nerve endings of the body of an animal, considered collectively.
**net knot** (Cyt.): A small accumulation of chromatin.
**network** (Elec. Comm., Elec. Eng.): A group of electrical elements connected together for the purpose of satisfying specified requirements.
**net'rum** (Cyt.): A minute spindle which arises within the centrosome during the division of the centriole.
**neur-, neuro-**: A prefix meaning nerves.
**neurogen'ic** (Zool.): Activity of a muscle or gland which is dependent on continued nervous stimuli.
**neurogen'esis** (Zool.): The development and formation or nerves.
**neurol'ogy**: The study of the nervous system.
**neuro'sis** (Med.): Any one of a group of diseases thought to be due to disordered function of the involuntary nervous system, shown by instability of the circulatory system. (Psycho-path.): A psychological disorder resulting from a conflict of repressed infantile instinctive demands with those of adult society.
**neurosurgery** (Surg.): That part of surgical science which deals with the nervous system.
**neus'ton** (Ecol.): Aquatic animals associated with the surface film.
**neuter** (Bot., Zool.): (1) Sexless.
**neutral solution** (Chem.): An aqueous solution which is neither alkaline nor acidic.
**neutralization** (Chem.): The interaction of an acid and a base with the formation of a salt.
**neutron** (Phys.): Uncharged sub-atomic particle, mass approximately equal to that of a proton, which enters into the structure of atomic nuclei.
**neu'trophil** (Physiol.): Stainable by neutral dyes.
**new moon** (Astron.): The instant when sun and moon have the same celestial longitude.
**niche** (Build.): A recess in a wall surface. (Ecol.): A term used to describe the status of an animal in its community.
**nickel** (Met.): A silver-white metallic element.
**ni'dus** (Zool.): A nest.
**nimbus** (Meteor.): A dense layer of dark shapeless cloud with ragged edges, from which steady rain or snow falls.
**ni'trates** (Chem.): Salts formed by the action of nitric acid on metallic oxides, hydroxides and carbonates.
**nitrides** (Chem.): Compounds of metals with nitrogen.
**ni'trogen** (Chem.): A non-metallic element.
**nitrogen cycle** (Bacteriol.): The sum total of the transformations undergone by nitrogen and nitrogenous compounds in nature in relation to living organisms.
**noctilu'cent** (Zool.): Light-producing.
**nocturnal** (Zool., etc.): Active at night.
**nodalizer** (Elec. Comm.): An arrangement for adjusting a minimum effect in an electrical circuit.
**node** (Bot.): The place where a leaf is attached to a stem. (Phys.): A point of minimum displacement in a system of stationary waves. (Astron.): The two points, diametrically opposite each other, in which the orbit of a heavenly body cuts some great circle.
**nod'ular** (Bot.): Bearing local thickenings.
**noise** (Acous.): Sounds which are objectionable to some people and which may or may not have significance. That class of sounds which do not exhibit clearly defined frequency components.
**non-conjunction** (Cyt.): The complete failure of synopsis.
**non-disjunction** (Cyt.): Failure of two chromosomes to disjoin in meiosis.
**non-metal** (Chem.): An element which readily forms negative ions and are generally poor conductors of electricity.
**noon** (Astron.): The instant of the sun's upper culmination at any place.
**norm**: The value of a quantity or of a state which is statistically most frequent.
**normal** (Bot., etc.): Quite ordinary in structure and in all other respects. (Math.): The normal to a line or surface is a line drawn perpendicular to it. (Psychol.): Said of one who is well adjusted to himself and to the outside world.
**normalizing** (Met.): A heat-treatment applied to steel.
**northing** (Surv.): A north latitude.
**nosol'ogy** (Med.): Systematic classification of diseases.
**nostrils** (Anat., Zool.): The external nares.
**notching** (Carp.): The process of joining timbers together by fitting one or both into a notch cut in the other. (Civ. Eng.): The method of excavating cuttings for roads or railways in a series of steps marked at the same time.
**nova** (Astron.): A star which makes a sudden appearance in the sky, generally decreasing rapidly in brightness.
**nozzle**: An outlet tube through which a discharge of fluid finally passes.
**nu'clear budding** (Cyt.): Production of two daughter nuclei of unequal size by constriction of the parent nucleus.
**nuclear chemistry** (Chem.): The study of reactions in which new elements are produced.
**nuclear energy** (Phys.): Energy released or absorbed during reactions taking place in atomic nuclei.
**nuclear isomers** (Phys.): Atomic nuclei having the same mass and charge but different radio-active properties.
**nuclear membrane** (Cyt.): The delicate membrane of the nucleus.
**nuclear reactor** (Eng.): Device in which chain reaction of neutrons can be sustained and regulated for the production of heat-energy, synthetic elements and radioisotopes.
**nuclear spindle** (Cyt.): The fusiform structure which appears in the cytoplasm of a cell surrounding the nucleus during mitosis and meiosis.
**nuclei** (Met.): Points at which crystals begin to grow during solidification.
**nucleide** (Nucleonics): The atom of a specific isotope.
**nucleon** (Nucleonics): Component of an atomic nucleus as the proton or neutron.
**nucleonics**: Science of the nucleus of the atom, its components and energies.
**nu'cleoplasm** (Cyt.): The dense protoplasm composing the nucleus of a cell.
**nucleus** (Biol.): The chief organ of the cell.
**nut** (Bot.): A hard, dry, indehiscent fruit and usually containing one seed. (Eng). A metal collar, screwed internally, to fit a bolt.
**nutation** (Astron.): An oscillation of the earth's pole about the mean position.
**nutlet** (Bot.): A one-seeded portion of a fruit which fragments when it matures.
**nutrient** (Med.): Providing nourishment.
**nutrition** (Zool.): The process of feeding and the subsequent digestion and assimilation of food-material.
**nyc'tanthous** (Bot.): Said of flowers which open at night.
**nymph** (Zool.): In insects, a young stage intervening between the egg and the adult.

## O

**obelisk** (Arch.): A slender stone shaft and tapering towards the top, which is surmounted by a small pyramid.
**oblong** (Bot.): Elliptical, blunt at each end, having almost parallel sides, and two to four times as long as broad.
**o'bovate'** (Bot.): Having the general shape of the longitudinal section of an egg.
**ob'ovoid'** (Bot.): Solid, egg-shaped and attached by the narrower end.
**obscure** (Bot.): Said of venation which is very little developed.
**obsession** (Psycho-path.): The morbid persistence of an idea in the mind, against the wish of the obsessed person.
**obsid'ian** (Geol.): A volcanic glass of granitic composition.
**obstetrician**: A medically qualified person who practices obstetrics.
**obstetrics**: That branch of medical science which deals with the problems and management of pregnancy and labor.
**obvol'vent** (Zool.): Folded downwards and inwards, as some insect wings.
**occlusion** (Zool.): Closure of a duct or aperture. (Chem.): The retention of a gas or a liquid in a solid mass or on the surface of solid particles.
**occultation** (Astron.): The hiding of one celestial body by another interposed between it and the observer.
**ocean**: Any of the major expanses of salt water on the face of the globe.
**ocel'lus** (Bot.): An enlarged discolored cell in a leaf.
**ochlopho'bia** (Med.): Morbid fear of crowds.
**o'chery** (Bot.): Yellowish-brown.
**ochroleu'cous** (Bot.): Yellowish-white.
**octa-** (Chem.): Containing eight atoms, groups, etc.
**octant division** (Bot.): The division of an embryonic cell by walls at right-angles, giving eight cells.
**octastyle** (Arch.): A building have a colonnade of eight columns in front.
**octava'lent** (Chem.): Capable of combining with eight atoms of hydrogen or their equivalent.
**octet** (Chem.): An extremely stable group of eight electrons.
**octopod** (Zool.): Having eight feet, tentacles or arms.

**octospo-rous** (Bot.): Containing eight spores.
**ocul-, oculo-**: A prefix meaning eye.
**ocular** (Zool.): Pertaining to the eye.
**o'culate** (Zool.): Possessing eyes.
**oculist** (Med.): One skilled in the knowledge and treatment of diseases of the eye.
**o'culomo'tor** (Zool.): Pertaining to eye movements.
**oculus** (Build.): A round window.
**odom'eter** (Ocean.): A recording sheave used with other machines when it is necessary to know how much warp or wire has been paid out.
**odontal'gia** (Med.): Toothache.
**odon'tic** (Anat.): Pertaining to the teeth.
**odontogeny** (Zool.): The origin and development of teeth.
**odorim'etry** (Chem.): The measurement of the intensity and permanency of odors.
**Oedipus complex** (Psycho-an.): A Freudian name for a complex, present in all boys at an early age characterized by an unconscious rivalry for the mother's love, resulting in hostility to the father.
**oesoph'agus** (Zool.): The section of the alimentary canal leading from the pharynx to the stomach, in vertebrates.
**oestrogen** (Physiol.): The generic term for female sex hormones.
**offset** (Build.): A ledge formed at a place where part of a wall is set back from the face.
**o'gee arch** (Arch.): A pointed arch of which each side consists of a reverse curve.
**ohm** (Elec. Eng.): The practical unit of resistance of an electrical circuit.
**ohm'meter** (Elec. Eng): An indicating instrument for giving a direct reading of the resistance of an electric circuit.
**oils** (Chem.): A group of neutral liquids; fixed oils from animal, vegetable and marine sources, mineral oils from petroleum, coal, etc., and essential oils, volatile products derived from certain plants.
**olfac'tory** (Zool.): Pertaining to the sense of smell.
**olig-, oligo-**: A prefix meaning few, small.
**oligotro'phic** (Ecol.): Said of a type of lake habitat having steep and rocky shores and scanty vegetation.
**oliva'ceous, olive** (Bot.): Greyish-green with a touch of orange.
**ombrom'eter** (Meteor.): A rain-gauge.
**om'brophyte** (Bot.): A plant inhabiting rainy places.
**omniv'orous** (Zool.): Eating both animal and vegetable tissue.
**oncol'ogy** (Med.): The part of medical science that deals with tumors of body-tissue.
**oni'ric** (Med.): Pertaining to dreams.
**onyx** (Min.): A cryptochrystalline variety of silica.
**oö**: A prefix meaning egg.
**oöblas'tema** (Zool.): A fertilized egg.
**ooze** (Geol.): A fine-grained, soft, deep-sea deposit composed of shells and fragments of other organisms.
**opal** (Min.): An amorphous variety of silica with a varying amount of water.
**opales'cence** (Chem.): The milky, iridescent appearance of a mineral or solution, due to the reflection of light from very fine, suspended particles.
**opaque**: Totally absorbent of rays of a specified wavelength. (Bot.): Not shining.
**open circuit** (Elec. Eng.): A break in an electrical circuit along which current can normally pass.
**open floor** (Build.): A floor which is not covered by a ceiling.
**open-hearth process** (Met.): A process for making steel from varying proportions of pig-iron and scrap.
**oper'culate** (Bot., Zool.): Possessing a lid.
**ophthalmo-**: A prefix meaning eye.
**ophthal'mic** (Zool.): Pertaining to the eye.
**ophthalmol'ogy** (Med.): That part of medical science which deals with the eye and its diseases.
**ophthal'moscope** (Med.): An instrument for inspecting the interior of the eye by means of light reflected from a mirror.
**opposite** (Bot.): Said of leaves inserted in pairs at each node, with one on each side of the stem.
**optics**: The study of light. (Zool.): Pertaining to the sense of sight.
**optimism**: Most favorable.
**oral** (Zool.): Pertaining to the mouth.
**orbit** (Astron.): The path of a heavenly body moving about another under gravitational attraction. (Aero): An aircraft circling a given point is said to orbit that point.
**ordinal number** (Maths.): Number derived from the notion of counting and possessing the fundamental property of position in an aggregate.
**ore** (Min.): A term applied to any metalliferous mineral from which the metal may be profitably extracted.
**organic chemistry** (Chem.): The study of the compounds of carbon.
**organism** (Biol.): A living animal or plant.
**organ'osol** (Chem.): A colloidal solution in an organic liquid.
**orientation** (Biol.): The position or change of position, of a part or organ with relation to the whole. (Chem.): The ordering of molecule particles or crystals so that they point in a definite direction. (Met.): The position of important sets of planes in a crystal in relation to any fixed system of planes.
**or'nithoph'ily** (Bot.): Pollination by birds.
**o'ro**: Prefix meaning mouth.
**ortho-**: A prefix meaning straight.
**orthodi'agraph** (Med.): An X-ray apparatus for recording exactly the size and form of organs and structures inside the body.
**orthograph**: A view showing an elevation of a building or of part of a building.
**orthokinet'ic** (Chem.): Migrating in the same direction.
**orthope'dics**: That branch of surgery which deals with deformities arising from injury or disease of bones or of joints.
**orthop'terous** (Zool.): Having the posterior pair of wings straight folded.
**or'thostyle** (Arch.): A colonnade formed of columns arranged in a straight line.
**os'cillograph** (Elec. Eng.): An instrument for producing a curve representing the wave-form of an alternating quantity.
**osmom'eter** (Chem.): An apparatus for the measurement of osmotic pressures.
**osmo'sis** (Chem.): The diffusion of a solvent through a semi-permeable membrane into a more concentrated solution in order to equalize the concentrations on both sides of the membrane.
**os'seous** (Zool.): Bony.
**ossifica'tion** (Zool.): The formation of bone.
**oste-, osteo-**: Prefix meaning bone.
**os'teoblast** (Zool.): A bone-forming cell.
**osteol'ogy** (Zool.): The study of bones.
**osteop'athy**: A system of therapeutics based on the theory that diseases arise chiefly from displacement of bones, with resultant pressure on blood vessels and nerves, and can be remedied by manipulation of the parts.
**osteot'omy** (Surg.): The surgical cutting of a bone.
**os'tiolate** (Bot.): Having an opening.
**ot-, oto-**: A prefix meaning ear.
**otal'gia** (Med.): Earache.
**o'tic** (Zool.): Pertaining to the ear.
**otol'ogy** (Med.): That part of surgical science dealing with the organ of hearing and its diseases.
**o'toscope** (Med.): An instrument for inspecting the ear drum and the external canal of the ear.
**outlet** (Build.): An opening serving to direct the discharge of a liquid.
**outrigger** (Build.): A projecting beam carrying a suspended scaffold.
**o'vary** (Anat., Zool.): A reproductive gland producing ova.
**ovate** (Bot.): Flat and thin, shaped like the longitudinal section of an egg, widest below the middle.
**overall efficiency** (Elec. Eng.): When power is passed through a number of times of plant in succession.
**overcast** (Meteor.): Said of sky when more than eight-tenths of it is covered by cloud.
**overfold** (Geol.): A fold with both limbs dipping in the same direction, but one more steeply inclined than the other.
**overhang** (Aero.): In a wing structure, the distance from the outermost supporting point to the extremity of the wing tip.
**overhead railway** (Civ. Eng.): An elevated railway carried above ground-level on arches or viaducts.
**overhead transmission line** (Elec. Eng.): A transmission line in which the conductors are supported on towels or poles at a considerable height above the ground.
**overlap test** (Elec. Eng.): A test used for locating a fault in a cable.
**overload**: A load on a machine, etc., greater than that which it is designed to withstand continuously.
**overshoot** (Aero.): Failure to land within the intended area due to excessive speed or height.
**overstrain** (Eng.): The result of stressing an elastic material beyond its yield point.
**ovi-**: A prefix meaning egg.
**o'viduct** (Zool.): The tube which leads from the ovary to the exterior and by which the ova are discharged.
**ovip'arous** (Zool.): Egg-laying.
**oviposition** (Zool.): The act of depositing eggs.
**ovipos'itor** (Zool.): In female insects, the egg laying organ.
**o'visac** (Zool.): An egg receptacle.
**o'void** (Bot.): Solid, like an egg in form, and attached by the broader end.
**o'volo** (Arch.): A quarter-round convex molding.
**o'vovivip'arous** (Zool.): Producing eggs which hatch out within the uterus of the mother.
**ovula'tion** (Zool.): The formation of ova.
**ov'ule** (Bot.): A young seed in course of development.

**o'vum** (Bot., Zool.): A non-motile, female gamete.
**oxalates** (Chem.): The salts and esters of oxalic acid.
**oxidase** (Bot., Zool.): One of a group of enzymes occurring in plant and animal cells and promoting oxidation.
**oxidation** (Chem.): The addition of oxygen to a compound.
**oxides** (Chem.): Compounds of oxygen with another element.
**oxidizing agent** (Chem.): A substance which is capable of bringing about the chemical change known as oxidation.
**oxy-**: A prefix meaning sharp.
**oxy-acetylene welding** (Eng.): Welding with a flame resulting from the combustion of oxygen to acetylene.
**oxycelluloses** (Chem.): Products formed by the action of oxidizing agents on cellulose.
**oxychro'matin** (Cyt.): A form of chromatic which stains lightly and contains little nucleic acid.
**oxydac'tylons** (Zool.): Having narrow-pointed digits.
**oxygen** (Chem.): A non-metallic element.
**oxy-hydrogen welding** (Eng.): A method of welding in which the heat is produced by the combustion of a mixture of oxygen and hydrogen.
**oxyn'tic** (Zool.): Acid-secreting.
**ozone** (Chem.): Produced by the action of ultra-violet rays and radium emanation on oxygen; and when oxygen or air is exposed to a silent discharge of electricity.

## P

**pachy-**: A prefix meaning thick.
**pachyder'matous** (Zool.): Thick-skinned.
**pachyphyl'lous** (Bot.): Having thick leaves.
**padder** (Elec. Comm.): A small adjustable condenser for fine adjustment of capacity.
**pediat'ric** (Med.): That branch of medical science that deals with the study of children's diseases.
**pediatric'ian** (Med.): A doctor who specializes in children's diseases.
**palaeo-**: A prefix meaning ancient.
**palaeobot'any**: The study of fossil plants.
**Palaeolith'ic Period** (Geol.): The older stone age.
**palaeontol'ogy** (Geol.): The study of animal life in past geological periods.
**Palaeozo'ic** (Geol.): A major division of geological time.
**pal'ama** (Zool.): The webbing of the feet in birds of aquatic habits.
**palate** (Zool.): The roof of the mouth in vertebrates.
**paling** (Build): One of the upright boards of a fence.
**palisade** (Build.): Fencing formed of pointed wooden poles or iron railings.
**palla'dium** (Met.): A metallic element.
**palles'cent** (Bot.): Becoming lighter in color with age.
**pal'liative** (Med.): A medicinal remedy affording temporary relief from pain or discomfort.
**pal'mate** (Bot.): Having several lobes or leaflets spreading from the same point, like the fingers from the palm.
**palmat'isect** (Bot.): Having the leaf blade cut nearly to the base.
**palpe'bra** (Anat.): An eyelid.
**palpitation** (Med.): Increased frequency of the heart beat.
**paludic'olous** (Ecol.): Living in marshes, ponds and streams.
**pancaking** (Aero.): The alighting of an aircraft at a steep angle with low forward speed.
**pan'creas** (Zool.): A large racemose gland discharging into the intestine, in vertebrates.
**pandem'ic** (Med.): An epidemic very widespread.
**pane** (Build.): (1) A panel; (2) A sheet of glass cut to fit as a window light.
**panel** (Elec. Eng.): A sheet of material upon which switches, instruments, etc., are mounted.
**pangam'ic** (Zool.): Of indiscriminate mating.
**pannose** (Bot.): Felted.
**pantoph'agous** (Zool.): Omnivorous.
**pap** (Build.): An outlet nozzle fitted to an eaves gutter.
**papyra'ceous** (Bot.): Papery in texture.
**parabio'sis** (Embryol.): The union of similar embryos between which a connection exists, as Siamese Twins.
**parab'ola** (Maths.): (1) The section of a right circular cone by a plane parallel to a generator of the cone. (2) The locus of a point equi-distant from a fixed point and a fixed line.
**parabol'ic** (Bot.): Having a broad base and gradually narrowing by curved sides to a blunt apex.
**parachute** (Aero.): An umbrella-shaped fabric device of high drag to retard the descent of a falling body.
**parac'me** (Zool.): The period in the history of a race or an individual when vigor is decreasing.
**par'allax** (Astron.): The apparent displacement of a heavenly body on the celestial sphere due to a change of position of the observer.
**parallel** (Elec. Eng.): When two circuits are connected so that any current flowing divides between the two.
**parallel motion** (Eng.): A system of links by which the reciprocating motion of one point is copied to an enlarged scale by another.
**par'allelism** (Bot.): Evolution along similar lines in unrelated groups of plants.
**paral'ysis** (Med.): The loss in any part of the body of the power of movement, or of the capacity to respond to sensory stimuli.
**paraly'zer** (Chem.): A catalytic poison.
**param'eter** (Maths.): A line or figure that serves to determine a point, figure, line or quantity in a class of such things.
**parametric equations** (Maths.): Equations in which coordinates of points on the surface or curve are given in terms of one or more variables of the surface or curve.
**par'amorph** (Min.): The name given to a mineral species which can change its molecular constitution without any change of chemical substance.
**paramy'osin'ogen** (Chem.): One of the chief proteins contained in living muscle.
**paranoi'a** (Psychiatry): A psychosis characterized by the development of a permanent delusional system and accompanied by the preservation of clear thought, action and will.
**parapet** (Build., Civ. Eng.): A low wall built along the edge of a quay, bridge or roof.
**par'aplasm** (Cyt.): The inactive vegetative portion of the cytoplasm.
**paraple'gia** (Med.): Paralysis of the lower part of the body and legs.
**parasite** (Bot., Zool.): An organism which lives in or on another organism and derives subsistence from it without rendering service in return.
**parasymbio'sis** (Biol.): The condition when two organisms grow together but neither assist nor harm each other.
**parasynop'sis** (Cyt.): Side-by-side union of the elements of a pair of chromosomes.
**paraton'ic movements** (Bot.): Plant movements in relation to an external stimulus.
**par'esis** (Med.): Incomplete paralysis.
**pari'etes** (Anat.): The walls of an organ or a cavity.
**parity** (Med.): The fact of having borne children.
**parquet** (Build.): A floor-covering of hardwood blocks glued to the ordinary floor boarding.
**pars** (Zool.): A part of an organ.
**parsec** (Astron.): The chief unit used in measuring stellar distances.
**parted** (Bot.): Cleft nearly to the base.
**parthenogenet'ic** (Bot., Zool.): Reproducing by the production of ova capable of development with male fertilization.
**partial** (Bot.): Secondary.
**particulate inheritance** (Gen.): Inheritance, in one individual, of distinctive characteristics of both parents.
**parting** (Met.): The process of removing silver from gold-silver bullion.
**partition** (Build.): A dividing wall between rooms.
**parturition** (Zool): The act of bringing forth young.
**pas'cual** (Bot.): Inhabiting pastures.
**passage beds** (Geol.): The general name given to strata laid down during a period of transition from one set of geographical conditions to another.
**passive electrode** (Elec. Eng.): The earthed electrode of an electrical precipitation apparatus.
**pasteurization** (Med.): Reduction of the number of micro-organisms in milk by maintaining it at a temperature of 131°-158° F. for thirty minutes.
**patel'late** (Bot.): Shaped like a saucer.
**path'ogen** (Med.): Any disease-producing micro-organism or substance.
**parthogen'esis** (Med.): The development or production of a disease-process.
**pathological**: Diseased, morbid.
**pathol'ogy**: Medical science that deals with the causes and nature of disease, and with the bodily changes caused by disease.
**pat'ina** (Chem.): The thin film of oxide formed on the surface of a metal.
**patroclin'ic** (Bot., Zool.): Exhibiting the characteristics of the male parent more than those of the female parent.
**pat'ulous** (Bot.): Spreading widely.
**pavement** (Civ. Eng.): The hard surfacing of a road or side-walk.
**paving flags** (Civ. Eng.): Thin flat stones used for surfacing pavements.
**peacock ore** (Min.): Bornite.
**peak arch** (Arch.): A pointed arch.
**peak load** (Elec. Eng.): The maximum load of a generating station or power distribution system.
**peak value** (Elec. Eng.): The maximum positive or negative value of an alternating quality.
**pearl**: An abnormal concretion of nacre formed inside a mollusc shell around a foreign body, as a sand particle.
**pearlite** (Met.): A microconstituent of steel and cast-iron.

**peat** (Geol.): Name given to layers of dead vegetation.
**pecten** (Zool.): Any comb-like structure.
**pectization** (Chem.): The formation of a jelly.
**pec'toral fins** (Zool.): The anterior pair of fins, in fish.
**pedal**: Pertaining to the feet.
**pedestal** (Build.): A base for the support of a column, a statue, etc.
**ped'icel** (Bot.): The stalk which bears a single flower or a single fruit.
**pediculo'sis** (Med.): Infestation of the body with lice.
**pe'dion** (Crystal.): A crystal form consisting of a single plane.
**pedology**: The study of soil.
**pedom'eter** (Surv.): An instrument recording distances travelled by foot.
**ped'uncle** (Bot.): The main stalk or stalks of an inflorescence.
**peg'matite** (Geol.): Applied to igneous rocks of coarse grain occurring in veins of larger intrusive rock bodies.
**pela'gic** (Geol.): A term applied to any accumulation of sediments under deep water.
**pellu'cid** (Bot., Zool.): Transparent.
**pelvic fins** (Zool.): The posterior pair of fins, in fish.
**pelvis** (Zool.): The pelvic girdle or posterior limb girdle of vertebrates; in mammals the funnel-shaped expansion of the upper end of the ureter.
**pen'icillate** (Bot.): Tufted.
**penicillin** (Med.): A filtrate of a broth culture of Penicillium notatum, which tends to inhibit the growth of gram-positive bacteria.
**penis** (Zool.): The male copulatory organ in mammals.
**pennate**: Winged.
**pent-, penta-**: A prefix meaning five.
**pentad**: The period of five days; used for meteorological records.
**pentadac'tyl** (Zool.): Having five digits.
**pen'tastyle** (Arch.): A row of five columns.
**pentava'lent** (Chem.): Capable of combining with five atoms of hydrogen or their equivalent.
**pep'sin** (Zool.): A protein-digesting ferment of the alimentary canal of vertebrates.
**peptization** (Chem.): The production of a colloidal solution of a substance; especially the formation of a sol from a gel.
**peptones** (Chem.): Products obtained by the action of enzymes on albuminous matter.
**perambulator** (Surv.): An instrument for distance measurement.
**peren'nial** (Bot.): A plant which lives for three or more years.
**perfect** (Bot., Zool.): Having all organs in a functional condition.
**per'forate** (Bot.): Pierced by holes. (Zool.): Having apertures.
**peri-**: A prefix meaning round.
**per'ianth** (Bot.): A general term for calyx and corolla together.
**periartic'ular** (Anat.): Said of the tissues around a joint.
**perias'tron** (Astron.): That point in an orbit about a star in which the body describing the orbit is nearest to the star.
**pericar'dium** (Zool.): The space surrounding the heart.
**peri'carp** (Bot.): The wall of a fruit, if derived from the wall of the ovary.
**per'iclase** (Min.): **Native magnesia.**
**periodo'tite** (Geol.): **A coarse-grained igneous rock consisting primarily of olivine.**
**per'igee** (Astron.): The point nearest to the earth on the apse line of a central orbit having the earth as a focus.
**perihe'lion** (Astron.): That point in the orbit of any heavenly body moving about the sun at which it is nearest to the sun.
**period** (Phys.): The time for one complete cycle of any periodic phenomenon.
**periodic system** (Chem.): A classification of the chemical elements.
**periodicity** (Biol.): Rhythmic activity.
**per'istyle** (Arch.): A colonnade encircling a building.
**perlite** (Geol.): An acid and glassy igneous rock which exhibits perlitic structure.
**permeability** (Phys.): The rate of diffusion of gas or liquid under a pressure gradient through a porous material.
**person** (Zool.): An individual organism.
**personality** (Psychol.): The integrated organization of all the psychological, emotional, physical and intellectual characteristics of an individual.
**persorption** (Chem.): The effective absorption of a gas by a solid.
**pertus'sis** (Med.): Whooping cough.
**perversion** (Psycho-path.): Any pathological state in which there is a deviation from the normal method of sexual gratification.
**pestle** (Chem.): An instrument for grinding and pounding solids in a mortar.
**petal** (Bot.): One of the leaves composing the corolla.
**pe'tiole** (Bot.): The stalk of a leaf.
**petri-, petro-**: A prefix meaning stone.
**petrifaction** (Geol.): The term applied to any organic remains which have been changed in composition by molecular replacement but whose original structure is nearly retained.
**petrog'raphy** (Geol.): Systematic description of rocks.
**petroleum** (Chem.): Crude mineral hydrocarbon oils obtained from natural oil wells.
**petrology**: The study of rocks.
**pewter** (Met.): An alloy of tin and lead.
**phantasy** (Psychol.): A mental state of preoccupation with thought which are associated with certain desires unobtainable in reality.
**pharmacology** (Med.): The scientific study of drugs.
**pharynx** (Zool.): In vertebrates, that portion of the alimentary canal which intervenes between the mouth cavity and the oesophagus and serves for the passage of food and also respiratory functions.
**phase** (Astron.): The name given to the changing shape of the visible illuminated surface of the moon. (Chem.): The sum of all those portions of a material system which are identical in chemical composition and physical state.
**phenology** (Biol.): The study of organisms in relation to climate.
**phe'notype** (Gen.): **One of a group of individuals all of which have a similar appearance regardless of their factorial constitution.**
**phenotyp'ic** (Biol.): Caused or produced by environmental factors.
**-philous** (Bot., Zool.): **Suffix meaning preferring, inhabiting.**
**phleb-, phlebo-**: A prefix meaning vein.
**phlo'em** (Bot.): The conducting tissue present in vascular plants, concerned with the transport of food materials.
**phobia** (Psycho-path.): Fear of an internal danger which has been projected on to an external object.
**phon-, phono-**: A prefix meaning voice.
**phon** (Acous.): The unit of the objective loudness.
**phonation** (Zool.): Sound production.
**phonochemistry** (Chem.): The study of the effect of sound and ultrasonic waves on chemical reactions.
**phoresis** (Med.): Electrical passage of ions through a membrane.
**phosphates** (Chem.): Salts of phosphoric acid.
**phosphores'cence** (Chem.): The greenish glow observed during the oxidation of white phosphorous in the air. (Phys.): A glow emitted by certain substances after having been illuminated by visible or ultra-violet rays.
**phos'phorous** (Chem.): A non-metallic element.
**photo-**: A prefix meaning light.
**photo-catalysis** (Chem.): The acceleration or retardation of the rate of a chemical reaction by light.
**photochemistry** (Chem.): The study of the chemical effects of radiation.
**photochron'ograph** (Astron.): An instrument for recording time photographically.
**photo-dissociation** (Chem.): Dissociation produced by the absorption of radiant energy.
**photo-electric cell**: Generally, any device in which the incidence of light causes an alteration in the electrical state.
**photo-electricity**: Electricity produced by the action of light.
**photo-electronic**: The science dealing with the interactions of electricity and light.
**photo-electrons**: Electrons ejected from the surface of a body by the action of incident light.
**pho'togene** (Zool.): A light-producing organ.
**photographic telescope** (Astron.): An astronomical telescope in which a camera replaces the eye-piece.
**photol'ysis** (Bot.): The grouping of the chloroplasts in relation to the amount of light falling on the plant. (Chem.): The decomposition of a molecule as the result of the absorption of light.
**pho'ton** (Phys.): A light quantum.
**photoph'ilous** (Biol.): Light-seeking.
**pho'tophore** (Zool.): A luminous organ of fish.
**photophy'gous** (Zool.): Shunning strong light.
**photorecep'tor** (Zool.): A sensory nerve-ending receiving light stimuli.
**photo-sensitive** (Phys.): The property of being sensitive to the action of visible or invisible light.
**pho'tosphere** (Astron.): The name given to the visible surface of the sun on which sun-spots and other markings appear.
**photosyn'thesis** (Bot.): The building up, in the green cell of a plant, of simple carbohydrates from carbon dioxide and water, with the liberation of oxygen.
**phototax'is** (Biol.): Response of an organism to the stimulus of light.
**photo-therapy** (Med.): Light treatment for therapeutic reasons.
**phreni**: A prefix meaning diaphragm.
**phycol'ogy** (Bot.): The study of algae.

**phylet'ic classification** (Biol.): A scheme of plant classification based on the presumed evolutionary descent of organisms.

**phyllome** (Bot.): A general term for all leaves and leaf-like organs.

**phy'logeny** (Bot., Zool.): The history of the development of a race.

**phy'lon** (Biol.): A line of descent.

**phy'lum** (Zool.): One of the major subdivisions of the animal kingdom.

**physical chemistry** (Chem.): The study of the dependence of physical properties on chemical composition, and of the physical changes accompanying chemical reactions.

**physiological** (Bot., Zool.): Relating to the functions of plant or animal as a living organism.

**physiological anatomy** (Biol.): The study of the relation between structure and function.

**physiological zero** (Biol.): The threshold temperature below which the metabolism of a cell, organ or organism ceases.

**physiology** (Bot., Zool.): The study of the manner in which organisms carry on their life processes.

**phy'topathology** (Bot.): The study of plant diseases.

**phytoph'agous** (Zool.): Plant-feeding.

**piazza** (Arch.): (1) An enclosed court in a building. (2) An arcade.

**picket** (Build.): A narrow upright board in a fence. (Surv.): A short ranging rod about 6 ft. long.

**pickling** (Eng.): The process of removing a coating of scale, tarnish, oxide, etc., from metal objects by immersing in an acid bath.

**pier** (Civ. Eng.): (1) A breakwater adapted for service as a landing. (2) A support for a bridge, an arch, etc.

**pig** (Met.): A mass of metal cast in a simple shape for storage or transportation and subsequently remelted for casting into final shapes.

**pig iron** (Met.): The crude iron produced in the blast furnace and cast into pigs.

**pilas'ter** (Build.): A square tier projecting from a wall, having both a cap and a base.

**pile** (Civ. Eng.): A column sunk into the ground to support vertical loading or to resist lateral pressures.

**pile bridge** (Civ. Eng.): A bridge whose superstructure is carried on piles.

**pile'um** (Zool.): The top of the head, in birds.

**pillar** (Build.): A detached column for the support of a superstructure.

**pillow structure** (Geol.): A term applied to lavas consisting of ellipsoidal and pillow-like masses which have cooled under submarine conditions.

**pi'lomo'tor** (Anat.): Causing movements of hair.

**pi'lose** (Bot.): Bearing a scattering of simple, fairly stiff hairs.

**pilot** (Aero.): The person who operates the flying controls of an aircraft. ((Elec. Eng.): In power systems, a conductor used for auxiliary purposes, not for the transmission of energy.

**pin** (Carp.): A small wooden peg.

**pin'acoid** (Crystal.): An open crystal form which consists of two parallel faces.

**pincers** (Zool.): Claws adapted for grasping.

**pinna** (Bot.): A leaflet, when part of a pinnate compound leaf. (Zool.): In fish, a fin; in mammals, the outer ear; in birds, a wing or feather.

**pinn'iped** (Zool.): Having the digits of the feet united by a membrane or flesh.

**pintle** (Eng.): (1) The pin of a hinge. (2) An iron bolt on which a chassis turns.

**pi'oscope** (Chem.): An instrument in which the fat content of milk is estimated colorimetrically.

**pipe**: A tube for the conveyance of fluids.

**pipette'** (Chem.): Laboratory apparatus consisting of a glass tube which is calibrated to deliver a measured amount of a liquid.

**Pisces** (Astron.): Fishes. Twelfth sign of the Zodiac.

**pisciv'orous** (Zool.): Fish-eating.

**pis'tillate** (Bot.): Said of a flower which has a carpel, but the stamens are lacking or non-functional.

**piston**: A cylindrical metal piece which moves in a cylinder, either under fluid pressure, as in engines, or to displace or compress a fluid, as in pumps.

**pit** (Eng.): A small opening formed in a floor, either to accommodate the moving parts of a large engine or to facilitate inspection of the underside of a machine.

**pitch**: A dark-colored, fusible, more or less solid material, containing bituminous or resinous substances. (Build.): The ratio between the rise and span of a roof.

**pitchblende** (Min.): Uraninite.

**pitching**: The angular motion of a ship or aircraft in a vertical plane about a lateral axis.

**pithed** (Zool.): Having the central nervous system destroyed.

**pitted**: Having the surface marked by small excavations.

**pitting** (Eng.): (1) Corrosion of metal surfaces due to chemical action. (2) A form of failure of gear teeth.

**placen'ta** (Bot.): The portion of the carpel wall to which the ovules are attached. (Zool.): A flattened cake-like structure within the uterine wall of the mother; it serves for the respiration and nutrition of the growing young.

**placers** (Geol.): Superficial deposits, rich in heavy ore minerals, which have become concentrated in the course of time by long-continued disintegration and removed from the lighter associated minerals.

**plane** (Carp.): A wood-working tool used for smoothing surfaces.

**plane of symmetry** (Crystal.): When one half of a crystal is a mirror image of the other.

**plane surveying** (Surv.): Surveying applied to areas of small extent and the curvature of the earth's surface is negligible.

**plane table** (Surv.): A drawing board mounted on a tripod so that the board can be levelled and also rotated about a vertical axis and clamped in position.

**plane tabling** (Surv.): A method of surveying in which the fieldwork and platting are executed simultaneously.

**planet** (Astron.): The name given in antiquity to the seven heavenly bodies, including the sun and moon, which were thought to travel among the fixed stars.

**planetarium** (Astron.): A building in which an optical device displays the apparent motions of the heavenly bodies on the interior of a dome which forms the ceiling of the auditorium.

**planing machine** (Eng.): A machine for producing large flat surfaces.

**plankton** (Ecol.): Plants and animals floating in waters as distinct from those which are attached to or crawl upon, the bottom.

**plan'osome** (Cyt.): An odd chromosome resulting from non-disjunction of a pair during meiosis.

**plant** (Bot.): An organism which has little or no power of dealing with solid food, and which takes in most or all of the material used in nutrition in solution in water.

**plan'tigrade** (Zool.): Walking on the soles of the feet.

**plasma-, plasmo-**: A prefix meaning anything molded.

**plasma** (Physiol.): The watery fluid containing protein, salts and other organic compounds, in which the cells of the blood are suspended.

**plasmol'ysis** (Biol.): Removal of water from a cell by osmotic methods, with resultant shrinking.

**plaster**: A general name for plastic substances which are used for coating wall surfaces and which set hard after application.

**plaster board** (Build.): A building-board made of plaster with paper facings.

**plaster of Paris** (Chem.): Dehydrated gypsum; used for making casts.

**plastics**: A generic name for certain organic substances, mainly synthetic condensation products, capable of being molded.

**plastic surgery** (Surg.): That branch of surgery which deals with the repair and restoration of damaged or lost parts of the body.

**plastid** (Cyt.): Any small dense photoplasmic inclusion in a cell.

**plastin** (Cyt.): An acidophil substance occurring in masses in the nuclei of cells.

**plate** (Elec. Eng.): (1) The electrode of an accumulator cell. (2) One of the conducting surfaces of a condenser.

**plat'en** (Eng.): The work table of a machine tool.

**platform** (Carp.): An area of floor raised above the general floor-level.

**plat'inum** (Met.): A metallic element.

**platinum thermometer** (Phys.): A means of measuring temperature up to 1200° C.

**plat'y-**: A prefix meaning broad, flat.

**plat'yphyl'lons** (Bot.): Having wide leaves.

**plax** (Zool.): A flat plate-like structure, as a scale.

**pleasure** (Psychol.): The feeling-tone which accompanies the emotional satisfaction of any one instinct.

**plei-, pleo-, plio-**: A prefix meaning more.

**Pleiades** (Astron.): The name given to the open cluster of 7 principal stars in the constellation Taurus.

**plei'omer'ous** (Bot.): Having a large number of organs or parts.

**pleion** (Meteor.): An area over which some weather element is above the normal average.

**Pleis'tocene Period** (Geol.): The Great Ice Age.

**pleur-, pleuro-**: A prefix meaning side.

**plexus** (Zool.): A mass of interwoven fibers.

**pli'cate** (Bot.): Folded in longitudinal plaits.

**plinth** (Build.): The projecting course at the base of a building.

**Pli'ocene Period** (Geol.): The period of geological time which followed the Miocene and preceded the Pleistocene.

**plot** (Build.): A ground plan.

**plotting** (Surv.): The operation of drawing on paper from the field notes of a surveyor.

**plough** (Carp.): To cut a groove.

**plug** (Build.): A wooden piece driven into a hole cut in surface brickwork and finished off flush, so as to provide a material to which fittings may be nailed. (Elec. Eng.): A device containing two metal contacts arranged for inserting into a socket-outlet in order to provide a connection to portable electrical apparatus. (Geol.): A roughly cylindrical orifice through which igneous rock is injected.

**plumb:** (Build., Civ. Eng.): Vertical.

**plumb-bob** (Surv.): A small weight hanging at the end of a cord, which under the action of the weight takes up a vertical direction.

**plumba'go** (Chem.): Graphite.

**plume** (Bot.): A light feathery or hairy appendage on a fruit or seed, serving in wind dispersal. (Meteor.): Snow blown over the ridge of a mountain. (Zool.): A feather.

**plu'miped** (Zool.): A bird having feathered feet.

**plummet** (Surv.): A plumb-bob.

**plu'mose** (Bot., Zool.): Hairy, feathered.

**plunger** (Eng.): The ram or solid piston of a force pump.

**plur-, pluri-:** A prefix meaning several, more.

**plural gel** (Chem.): A gel formed from two or more sols.

**pluricel'lular** (Biol.): Composed of two or more cells.

**Pluto** (Astron.): The ninth major planet in the solar system in order of distance from the sun.

**pluton'ic intrusions** (Geol.): A term applied to large intrusions which have cooled at great depth beneath the surface of the earth.

**pluto'nium:** An element.

**pneumo-, pneumat-, pneumato-:** A prefix meaning breath.

**pneumatic** (Eng., etc.): Operated by, or relying on, air pressure.

**pneumatic** (Zool.): Containing air.

**pneumatic brake** (Eng.): A continuous braking system in which air pressure is applied simultaneously to brake cylinders throughout the train.

**pneumatic drill** (Eng.): A hard rock drill operated by the use of compressed air.

**pneumatic trough** (Chem.): A vessel used for the collection of gases.

**pneumaticity** (Zool.): The condition of containing air spaces, as the bones of birds.

**pneumatocyst** (Zool.): Any air cavity used as a float, as the air bladder in fish.

**pneumon-, pneu'mono-:** A prefix meaning lung.

**pneumonia** (Med.): A term generally applied to any inflammatory condition of the lung accompanied by consolidation of the lung tissue.

**pocu'liform** (Bot.): Cup-shaped.

**pod** (Bot.): A dry fruit formed from a single carpel, usually splitting open when mature and containing several seeds.

**pod-, podo-:** A prefix meaning foot.

**po'dal** (Zool.): Pedal.

**po'dium** (Arch.): A continuous low wall under a row of columns.

**poikilother'mal** (Zool.): Cold-blooded.

**point** (Elec. Eng.): In electric wiring installations a termination of the wiring for attachment to a lighting fitting socket-outlet.

**Pointers** (Astron.): The name used for the two stars of the Great Bear.

**pointing** (Build., Civ. Eng.): The process of raking out the exposed jointing of brickwork and refilling with cement mortar.

**point of no return** (Aero.): The point in a flight which it is impossible to return to the departure base with a practical margin of fuel.

**poise** (Chem.): To maintain the oxidation-reduction potential of a solution constant by the addition of a suitable compound.

**poison:** Any substance which, introduced into the body, is capable of destroying life.

**pol** (Cyt.): The pole of a resting nucleus which lies nearest to the centrosome.

**polar** (Maths.): Of a point with respect to a curve or surface.

**Polaroid:** Transparent plastic sheet containing oriented doubly-refracting crystals of an organic iodine compound; transmits plane-polarized light.

**polar axis** (Astron.): That diameter of a sphere which passes through the poles. (Crystal.): A crystal to which no two- or four-fold axes are normal.

**polar body** (Biol.): One of two small cells detached from the ovum during the maturation divisions.

**polar caps** (Astron.): The two white regions around the poles of the planet Mars.

**polar fusion nucleus** (Bot.): The nucleus formed in the embryo sac by the union of the two polar nuclei; later it unites with a male nucleus and gives the first endosperm nucleus.

**polar sequence** (Astron.): The name given to the adopted scale for determining photographic stellar magnitudes.

**polarim'etry** (Chem.): The measurement of optical activity.

**Polar'is** (Astron.): The name given to the star a Ursae Minoris.

**polarization** (Chem.): The separation of the positive and negative charges of a molecule.

**polar'ity** (Elec.): The distinction between the north and south poles of a magnet, or between the north and south poles of a circuit. (Zool.): Existence of a definite axis.

**polder** (Civ. Eng.): A piece of low-lying land reclaimed from the water.

**pole:** Generally, the pivot or axis on which anything turns. (Zool.): Point, apex. (Bot.): One end of an elongated spore. (Carp.): A long piece of timber of circular section and small in diameter. (Elec. Eng.): A wooden, concrete or steel column for supporting the conductors of an overhead transmission or telephone lines.

**pole** (Elec.): The part of a magnet towards which the lines of magnetic flux converge or from which they diverge.

**po'lioplasm** (Biol.): Granular protoplasm.

**poll** (Carp.): The blunt end of an axe or hammer.

**pollen** (Bot.): The sticky or dusty material produced in anthers, each grain ultimately contains two male nuclei equivalent to male gametes.

**pollen sac** (Bot.): A cavity in an anther in which pollen is formed.

**pollination** (Bot.): The transfer of pollen from an anther to a stigma.

**polo'nium** (Chem.): A radioactive element.

**poly-:** A prefix meaning many.

**polybasic acids** (Chem.): Acids with two or more replaceable hydrogen atoms in the molecule.

**polycyclic** (Chem.): Containing more than one ring of atoms in the molecule. (Zool.): Said of shells having numerous whorls.

**polyg'amous** (Bot.): Having staminate, pistillate and hermaphrodite flowers on the same and on distinct individual plants. (Zool.): Mating with more than one of the opposite sex during the same breeding season.

**polymor'phic** (Zool.): Showing a tendency to division of labor among the members of a colony.

**polyp** (Zool.): An individual of a colonial animal.

**polyphylet'ic** (Gen.): Descended from diverse ancestors.

**pome** (Bot.): A term for a fleshy fruit containing seeds inside a papery core formed from the inner walls of the united carpels.

**pom'iform** (Bot.): Apple-shaped.

**pomol'ogy** (Bot.): The study of cultivated fruits and fruit trees.

**pons** (Zool.): A bridge-like or connecting structure.

**pontoon** (Civ. Eng.): A floating vessel for the support of materials and men.

**pore** (Bot.): The aperture of a stoma. (Zool.): A small aperture.

**porom'eter** (Bot.): An instrument for measuring the rate at which air can be drawn through a portion of a leaf.

**porosity** (Build.): The percentage of pore space in a material.

**por'phyry** (Geol.): A general term used for igneous rocks which contain large isolated crystals set in a fine-grained ground mass.

**portico** (Build.): A colonnade at one side of a building.

**positional astronomy** (Astron.): The branch that is concerned with the position of the heavenly bodies regarded as points on the observer's celestial sphere.

**positive** (Elec.): A particular point or electrode is positive with respect to another point when it is at a higher electric potential than the other point.

**positive rays** (Phys.): Streams of positively charged atoms or molecules which take part in the electrical discharge in a rarefied gas.

**positivism:** The conception which regards natural phenomena as being the only reality demonstrable by experiment, without reference to the human mind.

**positron** (Phys.): A sub-atomic particle of mass and charge equal to those of the electron, but having its charge positive.

**post** (Build.): (1) An upright member in a frame. (2) A column or pillar.

**post-:** A prefix meaning after.

**posterior** (Bot.): The rear. (Zool.): Further away from the head region.

**postern** (Build.): A private door or gate.

**po'table:** Suitable for drinking purposes.

**pot'amous** (Ecol.): Living in rivers and streams.

**potas'sium** (Chem.): A very reactive alkali metal.

**potential** (Zool.): Latent. (Elec.): When a point is said to be "at a certain potential" it means there is a potential difference of that amount between the point and earth.

**potential energy** (Phys.): Energy possessed by a body in virtue of its position.

**potom'eter** (Bot.): An instrument for measuring the rate a plant takes in water.
**pouch** (Zool.): Any sac-like structure.
**pound**: A unit of mass.
**power** (Mech.): Rate of doing work.
**pre-**: A prefix meaning before.
**Pre-Cambrian** (Geol.): The oldest era of geological time.
**precipitation** (Chem.): The formation of an insoluble solid by a reaction which takes place in solution. (Meteor.): Moisture falling on the earth's surface from clouds; rain, snow or hail.
**precision instrument** (Elec Eng.): An instrument having a high degree of accuracy.
**pregnancy** (Med.): Gestation.
**prehensile** (Zool.): Adapted for grasping.
**pressure, barometric** (Meteor.): The pressure of the atmosphere as read by a barometer.
**pressure cabin** (Aero.): An airtight cabin which is maintained at greater than atmospheric pressure for the comfort and safety of the occupants.
**pressure suit** (Aero.): An airtight fabric suit for very high altitude flying.
**prickle** (Bot.): A hard epidermal appendage resembling a thorn but not containing woody tissue.
**primary** (Bot., Zool.): Original, first-formed. (Chem.): A substance which is obtained directly from natural raw material.
**primary cell** (Elec.): A voltaic cell in which the chemical energy of the constituents is changed to electrical energy, when current flows.
**Primates** (Zool.): The highest order of mammals.
**primitive** (Bot., Zool.): Of early origin.
**primor'dial** (Bot., Zool.): Primitive.
**prism** (Crystal.): A hollow (open) crystal form consisting of three or more faces parallel to a crystal axis.
**pro-**: A prefix meaning before in time or place.
**profile** (Surv.): A longitudinal section.
**progno'sis** (Med.): The forecast of the probable course of an illness.
**projection** (Psycho-an.): The process whereby we ascribe to other people and to the outside world mental factors and attributes really in ourselves.
**prolopse** (Med.): The sinking of an organ or part of of the body.
**proliferation** (Bot.): A renewal of growth in a mature organ after a period of inactivity. (Med.): Growth by the multiplication of cells.
**promontory** (Zool.): A projecting structure.
**promotor** (Chem.): A substance which increases the activity of catalyst.
**pronu'cleus** (Zool.): The nucleus of a germ cell after the maturation divisions.
**propagation** (Bot.): Increase in the number of plants by vegetative means.
**pro'pane** (Chem.): A colorless gas found in crude petroleum.
**pro'phase** (Cyt.): The preliminary stages of mitosic or meiosis leading up to the formation of the astroid.
**prophylac'tic** (Med.): Tending to prevent or protect against disease.
**prophylax'is** (Med.): The preventive treatment of disease.
**prosce'nium** (Build.): The stage frame in a theatre.
**pros'thesis** (Surg.): The supplying of an artificial bodily part in place of one which is deficient or absent.
**pro'tamines** (Chem.): The simplest proteins.
**protease** (Chem.): A term for any protein-spliting enzyme.
**pro'teins** (Chem.): Any of a class of naturally occurring complex combinations of amino acids which are essential constituents of all living cells and also of the diet of the animal organism.
**proter-, protero-**: A prefix meaning former, before.
**proto-**: A prefix meaning first.
**protoactinium** (Chem.): A radio-active element.
**pro'togam'y** (Biol.): Union of gametes without fusion of their nuclei.
**protogen'ic** (Chem.): Capable of supplying a hydrogen ion.
**pro'toly'sis** (Bot.): The decomposition of chlorophyll by light.
**pro'ton** (Phys.): A positively charged particle of mass.
**pro'tophyte** (Bot.): A simple unicellular plant.
**pro'toplasm** (Biol.): The material basis of all living matter, a grayish semitransparent semi-fluid substance, of complex chemical composition.
**pro'tosome** (Gen.): A hypothetical central body in a gene.
**pro'totype** (Zool.): An ancestral form.
**Protozo'a** (Zool.): A subkingdom of the animal kingdom.
**pseud-, pseudo-**: A prefix meaning false.
**psych-, psycho-**: A prefix meaning mind.
**psyche** (Psychol.): The principle of mental and emotional life, consisting of conscious and unconscious processes.
**psychiatry**: That branch of medical science that deals with disorders and diseases of the mind.
**psycho-analysis**: The method of treatment of functional nervous disorder by bringing unconscious conflicts into consciousness, by the methods of free association, dream analysis and the use of the transference situation.
**psychogen'ic** (Med.): Having a mental orgin.
**psychology**: The science of the mind.
**psy'chopath** (Psychol.): An individual who shows a pathological degree of congenital emotional instability, but not suffering from a true organic mental disorder.
**psychopathology**: That brand of psychology which deals with the abnormal working of the mind.
**psycho'sis** (Med.): A disorder of the mind, characterized by illusions, delusions, hallucinations, etc.
**psychother'apist**: An individual who practices psychotherapy.
**psychother'apy**: The treatment of functional psychic disorder.
**psychophi'lic** (Bot.): Growing best at a low temperature.
**pteropae'des** (Zool.): Young birds which are able to fly as soon as they are hatched.
**pu'berty**: Sexual maturity.
**pubes'cense** (Zool.): A covering of fine hairs or down.
**pull-out** (Aero.): The transition from a dive or spin to normal flight.
**pulley** (Eng.): A wheel on a shaft having a crowned rim for carrying an endless belt, or grooved for carrying a rope or chain.
**pulmo-**: A prefix meaning lung.
**pul'monate** (Zool.): Air-breathing.
**pulp** (Zool.): A mass of soft spongy tissue situated in the interior of an organ.
**pulsating current** (Elec. Eng.): An electric current which periodically changes in magnitude but not in direction.
**pulse** (Med.): The periodic expansion and elongation of the arterial walls which follows each contraction of the heart.
**pump**: A machine driven by some prime mover, and used for raising fluids from a lower to a higher level, or for imparting energy to fluids.
**pu'pa** (Zool.): An inactive stage in the life-history of an insect during which it does not feed and re-organization is taking place to transform the larval body into that of the imago.
**pupil** (Zool.): The central opening of the iris of the eye.
**pure culture** (Bot.): A culture containing a pure stock of one species of plant.
**pure line** (Zool.): A population consisting of individuals whose descent can be traced to a single ancestor.
**pure tone** (Acous.): A sound-wave of a single frequency.
**purposiveness** (Zool.): Correlation of individual reactions to a definite end.
**pus** (Med.): The yellowish fluid consisting of serum, pus cells bacteria, and the debris of tissue destruction.
**pyk'nic type** (Psychol.): One of Kretschmer's three types of individual, characterized by short squat stature, small feet and feet, domed abdomen, round face, the limbs being short in relation to the trunk.
**pyknom'eter** (Chem.): A small graduated glass vessel, of defined volume, used for determining the specific gravity of liquids.
**pyramid** (Crystal.): A crystal form with three or more inclined faces which cut all three axes of a crystal. (Zool.): A conical structure.
**py'retother'apy** (Med.): The treatment of disease by artificially increasing body temperature.
**pyrhe'liom'eter** (Meteor.): An instrument for measuring the rate at which heat energy is received from the sun.
**pyro-, pr-**: A prefix meaning fire.
**pyroclas'tic rocks** (Geol.): A name given to fragmental deposits of volcanic origin.
**pyrocondensation** (Chem.): A molecular condensation caused by heating to a high temperature.
**pyrogen'ic** (Chem.): Resulting from the application of a high temperature.
**pyrol'ysis** (Chem.): The decomposition of a substance by heat.
**pyroxene group** (Min.): A number of mineral species which, although falling into different systems are closely related in form, composition and structure.

## Q

**quadra** (Arch.): A plinth at the base of a podium.
**quadrant** (Surv.): An angle-measuring instrument.
**quadrat** (Bot.): A square area of vegetation marked off for study.
**quadratic system** (Crystal.): The tetragonal system.

**quadra'tus** (Zool.): A muscle of rectangular appearance.
**quad'rimolec'ular** (Chem): Associated with four molecules.
**quadripartition** (Bot.): The division of a spore mother cell to yield four spores.
**quadriplex** (Gen.): Containing four dominant genes.
**quadripole** (Elec. Comm.): A network with two input and two output terminals.
**quadrivalent** (Cyt.): A nucleus having two pairs of homologous chromosomes.
**quadru'manous** (Zool.): Having all four podia constructed like hands, as apes.
**quadruped** (Zool.): Having all four podia constructed like feet, as cattle.
**qualitative analysis** (Chem.): The identification of the constituents of a material irrespective of their amount.
**qu.lity** (Acous.): The sound reproduction, the degree to which a sample of reproduced sound resembles a sample of the original sound.
**quantitative analysis** (Chem.): The determination of the amounts in which the various constituents of a material are present.
**quantum theory** (Phys.): The conception of energy as being atomic in nature, meaning not variable continuously, but only in multiples of a minimum indivisible quantity called a quantum; a basic unit of discrete values of certain quantities.
**quantum statistics** (Phys.): Statistics of the distribution of particles of a specified type in relation to their energies.
**quarry**: An open pit for granite, slate or other rock.
**quarry sap** (Civ. Eng.): The moisture naturally contained in building-stone freshly cut from the quarry.
**quarter** (Astron.): The term applied to the phase of the moon at quadrature.
**quarter** (Bot.): The group of four related cells or nuclei formed as a result of meiosis. (Zool.): A set of four related cells in a segmented ovum.
**quartz** (Min.): Crystalline silica distributed in igneous, metamorphic and sedimentary rocks.
**quartzite** (Geol.): The characteristic product of the metamorphism of a siliceous sandstone.
**quater'nate** (Bot.): In groups of four.
**quay** (Civ. Eng.): A place on the seacoast for the loading and unloading of vessels.
**queen** (Zool.): In social insects, a sexually perfect female.
**quencher** (Phys.): That which is introduced into a luminescent material to reduce the duration of phosphorescence.
**quenching** (Met.): Generally means cooling steel or the rapid cooling of other alloys.
**quicksand**: Loose sand mixed with such a high proportion of water that its bearing-pressure is very low.
**quicking** (Elec. Eng.): Electro-deposition of mercury on a surface before regular plating.
**quill** (Eng.): A hollow shaft revolving on a solid spindle.
**quinine** (Chem.): An alkaloid of the quinoline group, present in Cinchona bark.
**quinquefo'liate** (Bot.): Having five leaflets.
**quinquemolec'ular** (Chem.): Associated with five molecules.

## R

**rabies** (Med.): Hydrophobia.
**race** (Zool.): A category of variant individuals occurring within a species and differing slightly in characteristics from the typical members of the species.
**raceme** (Bot.): A type of simple indeterminate or centripetal inflorescence in which the elongated axis bears flowers on short pedicils in succession toward the apex.
**ra'chis** (Bot.): The main axis of an inflorescence. (Zool.): The shaft of a feather.
**radial**: Radiating out from a common center.
**radian** (Maths.): A unit of circular measure.
**radiant** (Astron.): The point on the celestial sphere from which a series of parallel tracks in space appear to originate.
**radiant heat** (Phys.): Heat communicated to a body by radiation.
**radiation** (Phys.): Energy emitted in the form of electromagnetic waves.
**radiation chemistry**: That which deals with chemical effects arising from the impact of high energy rays and particles on other materials.
**radiation pressure** (Phys.): The mechanical pressure exerted by light and other forms of radiation on surfaces on which they are incident.
**radical** (Bot.): Appearing as if springing from the root at soil-level. (Chem.): A group of atoms which passes unchanged through a series of reactions, but is normally incapable of separate existence.
**rad'icate** (Bot.): Rooted.
**radicle** (Bot.): The root of the embryo of a flowering plant.
**radioactivity** (Chem., Phys.): The emission of radiant energy; the property possessed by certain elements, of spontaneously emitting alpha, beta, or gamma rays, by the disintegration of the nuclei of atoms.
**radiochemistry** (Chem.): The chemistry of the radioactive elements.
**radio-element** (Phys.): A radioactive atom produced by an artificially induced nuclear transformation.
**radiogen'ic** (Chem.): Produced by radioactive disintegration.
**radiology**: That branch of medical science which deals with the examination of the body by means of X-rays, and with the treatment of disease by the use of radiant energy.
**radium** (Chem): A radioactive metallic element.
**ra'dix** (Zool.): The root of a structure.
**ra'don** (Chem.): A radioactive element.
**rafter** (Build., Civ. Eng.): A member in a roof framework extending from the ridge to the eaves.
**rain** (Meteor.): Rain is due to the condensation of excess water vapor when moist air is cooled below its dew-point.
**rainbow** (Meteor., Phys.): Formed by sunlight which is refracted and internally reflected by raindrops.
**rain gauge** (Meteor.): An instrument for measuring the amount of rainfall over a given period.
**rake** (Eng., etc.): An angle of inclination.
**ram** (Civ. Eng.): The monkey of a pile-driver.
**ramification** (Bot., Zool.): Branching.
**ramp** (Civ. Eng.): An inclined surface provided instead of steps.
**ra'mus** (Zool.): The barb of a feather.
**range** (Aero.): The distance that an aircraft can travel without refuelling. (Bot., Zool.): The area over which a species grows or feeds, and breeds in the wild state. (Surv.): To fix points to be in the same straight line.
**ranging rod** (Surv.): A wooden pole used to mark stations conspicuously.
**rapport** (Psychol.): The emotional bond existing between analyst and patient.
**rapto'rial** (Zool.): Adapted for snatching, as birds of prey.
**rarefaction** (Phys.): Diminution of air-pressure below normal.
**raso'rial** (Zool.): Adapted for scratching.
**rate of climb** (Aero.): The rate of ascent from the earth.
**rating** (Elec. Eng.): The maximum output or input of a piece of electrical apparatus as specified by the maker.
**rationalization** (Psychol.): The attempt to substitute conscious reasoning for unconscious motivations in explaining behavior.
**rattle** (Zool.): The series of horny rings representing the modified tail-tip scale in rattlesnakes.
**rays** (Phys.): A line which represents the direction in which light is travelling. (Zool.): A skeletal element supporting a fin.
**raze** (Build., Eiv. Eng.): To demolish.
**reactants** (Chem.): The substances taking part in a chemical reaction.
**reaction** (Bot., Zool.): Any change in behavior in an organism in response to a stimulus. (Chem.): The acidity or alkalinity of a solution.
**reaction chamber** (Aero.): The chamber in which the combustion of a rocket's fuel and oxidant take place.
**regional metamorphism** (Geol.): All those changes in the mineral composition and texture of rocks due to compressional stresses and to the rise of temperature.
**register** (Build.): A metal damper to close a chimney.
**reglette** (Surv.): The short graduated scale attached to each end of the special measuring tape used in base-line measurement.
**regression** (Biol.): A tendency to return from an extreme to an average condition. (Psycho-an.): A return to an earlier stage of development.
**regulating switch** (Elec. Eng.): A switch used for switching the regulating cells of a battery in and out of circuit.
**regurgitation** (Med.): The bringing back into the mouth of undigested food.
**rejuvenes'cense** (Biol.): Renewal of growth from old or injured parts.
**relapse** (Med.): The falling back into an illness after an apparent or partial recovery.
**relative density** (Chem.): The ratio of the density of a gas to that of hydrogen under similar conditions of pressure and temperature.
**relative humidity** (Meteor.): The ratio of the amount of water vapor in the air to the amount which would saturate it at the same temperature.
**relay** (Elec. Comm.): Any piece of apparatus in which a small electrical power is used to control larger electrical power. (Elec. Eng.): A device which, when operated, by the current in one circuit, causes contacts to close or open to control the current in another circuit.

**relict** (Ecol.): A species which occurs at the present time in circumstances different from those in which it originated.

**reluctance** (Elec. Eng.): The ratio which the magnetomotive force acting around a magnetic circuit bears to the flux which it produces.

**rem'iped** (Zool.): Having the feet adapted for paddling.

**remission** (Med.): An abatement of the severity of a disease.

**remote control** (Elec. Eng.): The control of apparatus by means of a switch situated at some distance from the apparatus.

**re'nal** (Zool.): Pertaining to the kidneys.

**rennin** (Chem.): An enzyme found in the gastric juice, causing the clotting of milk.

**replaceable hydrogen** (Chem.): Those hydrogen atoms in the molecule of an acid which can be replaced by atoms of a metal on neutralization of a base.

**repression** (Psycho-an.): The unconscious mental mechanism by which complexes are kept out of consciousness.

**reproduction** (Biol.): The process of generation of new individuals whereby the species is perpetuated.

**repulsion** (Gen., Cyt.): The tendency shown by dominant characters to separate.

**reservoir** (Civ. Eng.): A basin for the storage of water, which is later to be used for irrigation or as a supply for cities.

**residual affinity** (Chem.): The chemical attractive forces which remain after saturation of the normal valencies of the atoms in a molecule.

**resilience** (Eng.): The stored energy of a strained material.

**resin** (Chem.): The product from the secretion of the sap of certain trees and plants.

**regional metamorphism** (Geol.): All those changes in the mineral composition and texture of rocks due to compressional stresses and to the rise of temperature.

**register** (Build.): A metal damper to close a chimney.

**reglette** (Surv.): The short graduated scale attached to each end of the special measuring tape used in base-line measurement.

**regression** (Biol.): A tendency to return from an extreme to an average condition. (Psycho-an.): A return to an earlier stage of development.

**regulating switch** (Elec. Eng.): A switch used for switching the regulating cells of a battery in and out of circuit.

**regurgitation** (Med.): The bringing back into the mouth of undigested food.

**rejuvenes'cense** (Biol.): Renewal of growth from old or injured parts.

**relapse** (Med.): The falling back into an illness after an apparent or partial recovery.

**relative density** (Chem.): The ratio of the density of a gas to that of hydrogen under similar conditions of pressure and temperature.

**relative humidity** (Meteor.): The ratio of the amount of water vapor in the air to the amount which would saturate it at the same temperature.

**relay** (Elec. Comm.): Any piece of apparatus in which a small electrical power is used to control larger electrical power. (Elec. Eng.): A device which, when operated, by the current in one circuit, causes contacts to close or open to control the current in another circuit.

**relict** (Ecol.): A species which occurs at the present time in circumstances different from those in which it originated.

**reluctance** (Elec. Eng.): The ratio which the magnetomotive force acting around a magnetic circuit bears to the flux which it produces.

**rem'iped** (Zool.): Having the feet adapted for paddling.

**remission** (Med.): An abatement of the severity of a disease.

**remote control** (Elec. Eng.): The control of apparatus by means of a switch situated at some distance from the apparatus.

**re'nal** (Zool.): Pertaining to the kidneys.

**rennin** (Chem.): An enzyme found in the gastric juice, causing the clotting of milk.

**replaceable hydrogen** (Chem.): Those hydrogen atoms in the molecule of an acid which can be replaced by atoms of a metal on neutralization of a base.

**repression** (Psycho-an.): The unconscious mental mechanism by which complexes are kept out of consciousness.

**reproduction** (Biol.): The process of generation of new individuals whereby the species is perpetuated.

**repulsion** (Gen., Cyt.): The tendency shown by dominant characters to separate.

**reservoir** (Civ. Eng.): A basin for the storage of water, which is later to be used for irrigation or as a supply for cities.

**residual affinity** (Chem.): The chemical attractive forces which remain after saturation of the normal valencies of the atoms in a molecule.

**resilience** (Eng.): The stored energy of a strained material.

**resin** (Chem.): The product from the secretion of the sap of certain trees and plants.

**resistance** (Biol., Med.): The whole of the characters of an organism which enable it to resist the attacks of a disease. (Elec.): The property of a substance by virtue of which it resists the flow of an electric current through it. (Psycho-an.): An unconscious barrier in the mind against making unconscious processes conscious.

**resistor** (Elec. Eng.): A piece of apparatus used on account of its possessing resistance.

**resolution** (Chem.): The separation of an optically inactive mixture or compound into its optically active components.

**resonance** (Phys.): A vibration of large amplitude resulting on application of a forced vibration to a system, when the period of the force equals that of a natural vibration of the system.

**respiration** (Bot., Zool.): The interchange of oxygen and carbon dioxide associated with katabolic processes.

**resting nucleus** (Cyt.): A nucleus which is not dividing.

**restorative** (Med.): Capable of restoring to health.

**resuscitation** (Med.): Restoration to consciousness or to life one who is unconscious.

**retaining wall** (Civ. Eng.): A wall built to support earth at a higher level on the one side than on the other.

**retardation** (Med.): Arrest of mental development.

**retarder** (Chem.): A negative catalyst which is added to a reacting system to prevent the reaction from being too vigorous.

**rete** (Zool.): A net-like structure.

**ret'icule** (Surv.): A cell carrying cross-hairs and fitting into the diaphragm of a surveying telescope.

**ret'ina** (Anat., Zool.): The light-sensitive layer of the eye of all animals.

**ret'inerved** (Bot.): Net-veined.

**retort**: A vessel used in distillation.

**retrac'tile** (Zool.): Capable of being withdrawn.

**retro-**: A prefix meaning behind, backwards.

**retrogression** (Zool.): Degeneration.

**retrorse** (Bot., Zool.): Pointing backwards; retroverse.

**reversible reaction** (Chem.): A chemical reaction which can take place in both directions, and is therefore incomplete.

**revet'ment** (Civ. Eng.): A retaining wall.

**rev'olute** (Bot.): Rolled backwards and usually downwards.

**revolution** (Astron.): The term for orbital motion, as the earth about the sun. (Geol.): A period of intense change in the disposition of sea and land and of the surface configuration.

**rhe'nium** (Chem.): A metallic element.

**rheology** (Phys.): The science of flow of matter.

**rhemor'phism** (Geol.): Process by which a pre-existing rock is converted into magma.

**rhe-ostat** (Elec. Eng.): A resistor in which the value of the resistance in circuit may be varied.

**rhin-, rhino-**: A prefix meaning nose.

**rhi'nal** (Zool.): Pertaining to the nose.

**rhiz-, rhizo-**: A prefix meaning root.

**rhi'zome** (Bot.): An underground stem, having a superficial resemblance to a root, but bearing scale leaves and one or more buds.

**rhi'zophi'lous** (Bot.): Growing on roots.

**rhodium** (Met.): A metallic element.

**rhombohedron** (Crystal.): A crystal form of the trigonal system.

**rhomboi'dal** (Bot.): Quadrangular, but not square, and attached by one acute angle.

**rhynchoph'orous** (Zool.): Having a beak.

**ria** (Geol.): A normal valley drowned by a rise of sea-level relative to the land.

**rib** (Bot.): One of the larger veins of a leaf. (Build., Civ. Eng.): A curved member of a center or ribbed arch. (Zool.): In vertebrates, an element of the skeleton in the form of a curved rod connected at one end with a vertebra.

**ribbed arch** (Civ. Eng.): An arch composed of side-by-side ribs spanning the distance between the springings.

**rickets** (Med.): A nutritional childhood disease characterized by defective ossification and softening of bones.

**ric'tal** (Zool.): In birds, of the mouth aperture.

**rider** (Chem.): A small piece of platinum wire used on a chemical balance as a final adjustment.

**ridge** (Build., Civ. Eng.): The summit-line of a roof.

**riffler** (Eng.): A file bent so as to be capable of operating in a shallow depression.

**rigging** (Aero.): The operation of adjusting and aligning the various components of an aircraft.

**rigid arch** (Civ. Eng.): A continuous arch without joints or hinges.

**rigor** (Bot.): An inert condition assumed by a plant

when growing conditions are unfavorable. (Zool.): A state of rigidity when subjected to sudden shock.
**rigor mortis** (Med.): The stiffening of the body following death.
**rim** (Bot.): The overhanging part of a wall about a bordered pit.
**ri'ma** (Zool.): A narrow cleft.
**rime** (Build.): A rung of a ladder.
**ri'mose** (Bot.): Having the surface marked by a network of intersecting cracks.
**rind** (Bot.): The outer layers of the fruit body.
**rip** (Carp.): To saw timber along the direction of the grain.
**ripcord** (Aero.): A cable used for opening the pack of a parachute.
**rip-saw** (Carp.): A saw for cutting timber along the grain.
**ripa'rean, riparious** (Bot., Zool.): Living or growing on the banks of streams and rivers.
**ripples** (Phys.): Small waves on the surface of a liquid.
**rise** (Build., Civ. Eng.): (1) The vertical height from end supports to ridge of a roof. (2) The height of a step in a staircase.
**riser** (Build.): The vertical part of a step.
**rising and setting** (Astron.): The positions of a heavenly body when it is exactly on the great circle of the observer's horizon, east or west of the meridian respectively.
**rising arch** (Civ. Eng.): An arch whose springing line is not horizontal.
**river wall** (Civ. Eng.): A wall built as a side boundary to the flow of a river, thereby confining it to a definite path.
**rivet** (Eng.): A headed shank for making a permanent joint between two pieces.
**riv'ulose** (Bot.): Marked with lines, appearing as rivers on a map.
**roasting** (Met.): The operation of heating sulphide ores in air to convert to oxide.
**roasting furnace** (Met.): A furnace in which finely ground ores and concentrates are roasted to eliminate sulphur.
**rock** (Geol.): An aggregate of mineral particles forming part of the earth's crust.
**rock drill** (Civ. Eng.): A tool especially adapted to the boring of holes through rock.
**rocket propulsion** (Aero.): Reaction propulsion using internally stored oxygen for combustion.
**rod-cell** (Zool.): One of the photosensitive cells of the retina of which the percipient structure is rod-shaped.
**rods and cones** (Zool.): The photosensitive cells of the retina.
**Roden'tia** (Zool.): An order of small mammals, as squirrels, beavers, rats, rabbits, etc.
**rodman** (Surv.): A staffman.
**rolling** (Aero.): The angular motion of an aircraft tending to set up a rotation about a longitudinal axis.
**Röntgen rays** (Phys.): X-rays.
**roof truss** (Build., Civ. Eng.): The structural framework built to support the roof covering of a building.
**root** (Bot.): The branching lower portion of the axis of a higher plant. (Civ. Eng.): The part of a dam which runs into the natural ground surface at each end.
**root tuber** (Bot.): A swollen root containing reserve food material.
**rosa'ceous** (Bot.): Having the character of a rose.
**Rose crucible** (Chem.): A crucible used for igniting substances in a current of gas.
**rose'ola** (Med.): Any rose-colored rash.
**rosin** (Chem.): The residue from the distillation of turpentine.
**ros'trate** (Bot.): Ending in a long hard point.
**rostrum** (Build.): A raised platform for speakers.
**rotation** (Astron.): The term generally confined to the turning of a body about an axis passing through itself. (Bot.): The movement of the protoplasm in a cell in a constant direction.
**rotator** (Zool.): A muscle which turns a limb on its axis.
**rotor** (Aero.): A system of revolving aerofoils producing life. (Elec. Eng.): The rotating part of an electric machine.
**rotund** (Bot.): Approximately circular.
**rotunda** (Build.): A building or room which is circular and covered by a dome.
**rough arch** (Build.): An arch built of uncut bricks with wedge-shaped joints.
**roughness integrator** (Civ. Eng.): An instrument for measuring the roughness of a road surface.
**round** (Build.): A rung of a ladder.
**rowlock** (Build.): A term applied to a course of bricks laid on edge.
**rubes'cent** (Bot.): Turning red or pink.
**rubid'ium** (Chem.): A metallic element; one of the alkali metals.
**rudiment** (Bot., Zool.): The earliest recognizable stage of an organ or member.
**rudimentary** (Bot., Zool.): Incompletely developed.
**ru'fous** (Bot.): Red-brown.
**ru'gose** (Biol.): Having a wrinkled surface.
**ru'men** (Zool.): The first division of the stomach in ruminants.
**rumination** (Med.): The regurgitation of swallowed food and its further mastication before reswallowing.
**run** (Build.): A gangway. (Surv.): In a level tube, the movement of a bubble with change of inclination.
**runway** (Aero.): A hard path to facilitate landing and taking-off of aircraft.
**rung** (Build.): A bar connecting the two side posts of a ladder and serving as a step.
**runner** (Bot.): A prostrate shoot which roots at the end and there gives rise to a new plant.
**rupic'olous** (Bot., Zool.): Living or growing on or among rocks.
**rupture** (Med.): Forcible breaking or tearing of a bodily organ or structure.
**rut** (Zool.): To be sexually excited.
**ruthe'nium** (Chem.): A metallic element.
**ru'tilant** (Bot.): Brightly colored in orange, yellow or red.

## S

**sab'ulose** (Bot.): Growing in sandy places.
**sac** (Bot., Zool.): Any pouch-like structure.
**saccharim'eter** (Chem.): A special type of polarimeter adapted for use with white light.
**saccarim'etry** (Chem.): The estimation of the percentage of sugar present in solutions of unknown strength.
**sac'charin** (Chem.): A white crystalline powder used where sugar is harmful.
**saccharolyt'ic** (Bacteriol.): Said of bacteria which use starches and simple carbohydrates as sources of energy.
**saccharom'eter** (Chem.): A hydrometer which is used to determine the concentration of sugar in solution.
**sac'rum** (Zool.): The vertebrae to which the pelvic girdle is attached.
**saddle** (Civ. Eng.): A block surmounting one of the towers of a suspension bridge. (Elec. Eng.): A U-shaped cleat for securing lighting conduits to a flat surface.
**safety fuse** (Elec. Eng.): A protective fuse in part of an electric circuit.
**sag**: To bulge downwards under load.
**Sagitta'rius** (Astron.): Archer. Ninth sign of the Zodiac.
**salient** (Surv.): (1) A jutting-out piece of land. (2) A term applied to an external angle.
**salinom'eter** (Phys.): A hydrometer for measuring the density of sea water.
**sali'va** (Zool.): The secretion, produced by the salivary glands, which facilitates the swallowing of food.
**sali'vary glands** (Zool.): Glands present in many land animals, the ducts of which open into or near the mouth.
**salt** (Chem.): A compound which results from the replacement of one or more hydrogen atoms of an acid by metal atoms or electropositive radicals.
**saltant** (Biol.): A changed form of a species, developed suddenly, and differing from the original in morphology or in physiological properties.
**saltato'rial** (Zool.): Used for jumping.
**samar'a** (Bot.): A single-seeded, dry, indehiscent fruit, bearing a wing-like extension of the pericarp.
**sama'rium** (Chem.): A metallic element.
**sand** (Geol.): Applied to loose, unconsolidated accumulations of detrital sediment consisting primarily of rounded grains of quartz.
**sand-blasting**: A method of cleaning metal surfaces by means of sand or grit directed from a nozzle at high velocity.
**sand culture** (Bot.): An experimental method of determining the mineral requirements of plants.
**sand dunes** (Geol.): Rounded mounds of loose sand piled up by wind action.
**sandpaper** (Carp.): Stout paper with a thin coating of fine sand glued on to one side, for use as an abrading material.
**sandstones** (Geol.): Compacted and cemented sedimentary rocks, which consist essentially of rounded grains of quartz.
**sanding** (Carp., etc.): The operation of cleaning up wood surfaces by rubbing with sandpaper.
**sanguic'olous** (Zool.): Living in blood.
**sanguin'eous** (Bot.): Blood-red.
**sanguiv'orous** (Zool.): Blood-feeding.
**sap** (Bot.): An aqueous solution of mineral salts, sugars and other organic substances, present in the xylem of plants.
**saywood** (Bot.): The layer of recently formed secondary wood.
**sapling** (Bot.): A young tree.
**sapona'ceous** (Bot.): Slippery.
**saprobiot'ic** (Biol.): Feeding on dead animals or plants.
**sap'rophyte** (Biol.): An organism which obtains its food from dead organic material.
**sarcod'ic** (Zool.): Pertaining to flesh.

**sar'cody** (Bot.): Conversion into something of fleshy texture.
**sarco'ma** (Med.): A malignant tumor.
**sarcoph'agous** (Zool.): Flesh-eating.
**sar'cous** (Zool.): Pertaining to flesh; to muscle tissue.
**sash** (Carp.): A framing for window panes.
**sat'ellite** (Astron.): The name given to a small body revolving around another, generally a planet. (Bot.): A small part of a chromosome.
**saturated solution** (Chem.): A solution which can exist in equilibrium with excess of the dissolved substance.
**saturated vapor** (Phys.): A vapor which is sufficiently concentrated to exist in equilibrium with the liquid form of the same substance.
**saturation of the air** (Meteor.): The air, at a given temperature, can contain water vapor up to a limit known as the saturation point.
**Saturn** (Astron.): The sixth planet of the solar system in order of distance from the sun.
**saur'ian** (Zool.): Lizard-like.
**saxica'vous** (Zool.): Rock-boring.
**sax'icale** (Bot.): Growing on rocks or stones.
**scaffold** (Build.): A temporary erection of timber or steelwork, used in the construction, alteration or demolition of a building.
**scala** (Zool.): A ladder-like structure.
**scale** (Bot.): A thin, flat, semi-transparent plant member. (Zool.): A small exoskeletal outgrowth of chitin, bone or some horny material, usually flat and platelike.
**scale leaf** (Bot.): A leaf, usually reduced in size, membranous, of rough texture and protective in function.
**scalloped** (Bot.): Said of a margin bearing rounded teeth.
**scandium** (Chem.): A metallic element.
**scanso'rial** (Zool.): Adapted for climbing trees.
**scape** (Bot.): A peduncle arising from the middle of a rosette of leaves and bearing a flower. (Zool.): The basal joint of the antenna in insects.
**sca'phoid** (Bot., Zool.): Boat-shaped.
**scheelite** (Min.): An ore of tungsten.
**schist** (Geol.): The name given to a group of metamorphic rocks which have a tendency to split, as mica, talc.
**schistos'ity** (Geol.): The tendency in certain rocks to split easily.
**schizogen'esis** (Zool.): Reproduction by fission.
**schizoid** (Psychiatry): Showing qualities of a schizophrenic personality but without definite mental disorder.
**sciat'ic** (Zool.): Pertaining the the hip region.
**science**: The ordered arrangement of ascertained knowledge.
**scintillation** (Astron.): The twinkling of stars.
**sci'ograph** (Build.): A drawing showing a sectional view of a building.
**sci'on** (Bot.): (1) A portion of a plant which is inserted into a root stock in grafting. (2) A stolon.
**sci'ophyte** (Bot.): A plant which grows in shady situations.
**scis'sile** (Bot.): Capable of being split.
**scler-, sclero-**: A prefix meaning hard.
**scleratogenous** (Zool.): Skeleton-forming.
**sclere** (Zool.): A skeletal structure.
**scler'eide** (Bot.): A general term for a cell with a thick, lignified wall.
**sco'pa** (Zool.): The pollen brush of bees.
**scop'ula** (Zool.): A small tuft of hairs.
**sco'ria** (Geol.): A cavernous mass of volcanic rock.
**scorification** (Chem.): The separation of gold or silver from an ore.
**Scorpio** (Astron.): Scorpion. Eighth sign of the Zodiac.
**screen** (Build., Cirv. Eng.): A large sieve used for grading coarse or fine aggregates.
**screenings** (Build., Civ. Eng.): The residue from a sieving operation.
**scum** (Build.): A surface formation of lime crystals on new cement work.
**sea**: An expanse of salt water on the face of the globe.
**seaplane** (Aero.): An aeroplane fitted with means for taking off and alighting on water.
**sealing** (Build.): The operation of closing a joint by means of cement, lead, etc.
**season** (Astron.): One of the four divisions of the tropical year taken from the passage of the sun through the equinoctial and solstitial points.
**seba'ceous** (Zool.): Producing or containing fatty material.
**sec'odont** (Zool.): **Having teeth adapted for cutting.**
**second**: 1/60 of a minute of time.
**secondary** (Zool.): Arising later; of subsidiary importance.
**secre'tion** (Physiol.): A substance discharged by a gland or gland cell.
**section** (Bot.): A division of a genus. (Surv.): The representation to scale of the variations in level of the ground surface along any particular line.
**sector**: A plane figure enclosed by two radii of a circle and the arm cut off by them.
**secto'rial** (Zool.): Adapted for cutting.
**sectroid** (Arch.): The curved surface between adjacent groins on a vault surface.
**secular changes** (Geol., etc.): Changes which take many centuries to accomplish.
**sedentary** (Zool.): Said of animals which remain attached to a substratum.
**sedimentary rocks** (Geol.): All those rocks which result from the wastage of pre-existing rocks.
**sedimentation** (Chem.): The settling of solid particles from a liquid as a result of either gravity or centrifuging.
**seed** (Bot.): A multicellular structure containing the embryo of a higher plant.
**seed crystal** (Chem.): A crystal introduced into a supersaturated solution or a supercooled liquid in order to initiate crystallization.
**seedling** (Bot.): The young plant from a germinated seed.
**segment** (Bot.): (1) A multinucleate portion of a filament. (2) A daughter cell cut off by the division of a single apical cell. (Elec. Eng.): One of many elements, insulated from one another, which collectively form a commutator. (Geom.): A plane figure enclosed by the chord of a circle and the arc cut off by it. (Zool.): One of the joints of an articulate appendage; a cell or group of cells produced by cleavage of an ovum.
**segregation** (Gen.): The separation of hereditary factors from one another during spore formation. (Met.): non-uniform distribution of impurities, inclusions and alloying constituents in metals.
**seis'mograph**: An instrument by means of which earthquake shocks are registered.
**seismology**: The study of earthquake phenomena.
**seistan** (Meteor.): The 120 day summer north wind in East Persia.
**sele'nium** (Chem.): A non-metallic element.
**selenog'raphy** (Astron.): The description and delineation of the moon's surface.
**self-pollination** (Bot.): The transfer of pollen from the anthers to the stigmas of the same flower, or to the stigmas of another flower on the same plant.
**semat'ic** (Zool.): Warning.
**semeiol'ogy** (Med.): The branch of medical science dealing with the symptoms of disease.
**se'men** (Zool.): The fluid formed by the male reproductive organ in which the spermatozoa are suspended.
**semi-**: A prefix meaning half.
**semi-automatic** (Elec. Eng.): Said of an electric control in which the initiation of an operating sequence is manually performed and then proceeds automatically.
**semicircular arch** (Civ. Eng.): An arch describing half a circle.
**semi-diameter** (Astron.): **Half the angular diameter of a celestial body.**
**sender** (Elec. Comm.): A radio transmitting station for broadcasting.
**sending end** (Elec. Eng.): The end of a transmission line from which electrical energy is sent out.
**senes'cent** (Biol.): Said of that period in the life-history of an individual when its powers are declining prior to death.
**senil'ity** (Biol.): Condition of degeneration due to old age.
**sensation** (Psychol.): An awareness in consciousness of a physical experience.
**sense organ** (Bot., Zool.): A structure especially adapted for the reception of stimuli.
**sensibility** (Bot.): The condition of a plant of being liable to parasitic attack.
**sensif'erous** (Zool.): Sensitive.
**sensil'la** (Zool.): A small sensory structure.
**sensitizer** (Chem.): A substance, other than the catalyst, whose presence facilitates the start of a catalytic reaction.
**sensitive** (Zool.): Capable of receiving stimuli.
**sensitive flame** (Phys.): A gas flame which changes its shape or height when sound-waves fall on it.
**sensitivity** (Elec. Eng.): The change in deflection of an instrument per unit torque applied.
**senso'rium** (Zool.): The nervous system.
**sensory** (Zool.): Pertaining to the senses.
**sentiment** (Psycho-an.): A psychological constellation formed when instinctive emotions become attached to persons, ideas, objects, etc.
**sepal** (Bot.): One of the leaf-like members forming the calyx of a flower.
**separation** (Bot.): The liberation of a reproductive body from the parent plant.
**separator** (Elec. Eng.): A thin sheet of wood or perforated celluloid separating the plates of a secondary cell.

**sepsis** (Med.): The invasion of bodily tissue by nonspecific pathogenic bacteria.

**sep'tate** (Bot.): Divided into cells by walls; or into two or more chambers by partitions.

**sep'tenate** (Bot.): Having parts in sevens.

**septum** (Bot.): A wall between one cell and another. (Zool.): A partition separating two cavities.

**sere** (Bot.): A series of plant communities making up a succession.

**serein** (Meteor.): The rare phenomenon of rainfall out of an apparently clear sky.

**ser'eate** (Bot.): Arranged in a row.

**series** (Elec. Eng.): A series connection of two or more electric circuits is one in which the same current traverses all the circuits.

**seroti'nous** (Bot.): Appearing late in the year.

**serous** (Zool.): Watery.

**serpentine** (Min.): A hydrated silicate of magnesium.

**serrate** (Bot.): Said of a toothed margin. (Zool.): Saw-like, notched.

**se'rum** (Med., Zool.): A watery secretion.

**service mains** (Elec. Eng.): Cables of small conductor cross-section which lead the current from a distributor to the consumer's premises.

**ses'sile** (Bot.): Having no stalk.

**set of chromosomes** (Cyt.): A group of chromosomes consisting of one each of the various kinds of chromosomes contained in the nucleus of a gamete.

**se'ta** (Bot.): A bristle.

**setting** (Build.): The name given to the hardening of lime, mortar, plaster or cement.

**sex-**: A prefix meaning six.

**sex** (Biol.): The sum-total of the characteristics which distinguish female organisms, especially with regard to the part played in reproduction.

**sex chromosome** (Cyt.): The chromosome which is responsible for the initial determination of sex.

**sex-linked** (Gen.): Said of hereditary characteristics borne by the sex chromosome.

**sex ratio** (Zool.): The ratio of males to females.

**sexfa'rious** (Bot.): In six rows.

**sexpar'tite** (Bot.): Divided deeply into six segments.

**sextant** (Surv.): A reflecting instrument in the form of a quadrant, for measuring angles up to about 120°.

**sexual cell** (Biol.): A male or female germ-cell.

**sexual organs** (Zool.): Reproductive system.

**sexual reproduction** (Bot., Zool.): The union of gametes, preceding the formation of a new individual.

**sexual selection** (Zool.): A phase of natural selection, based on the struggle for mating.

**shaft** (Arch.): The principal portion of a column, between the base and the capital. (Civ. Eng.): A passage, usually vertical, leading from ground level into an underground excavation. (Zool.): The part of a hair distal to the root.

**shaggy** (Bot.): Covered with long weak hairs.

**shale** (Geol.): A consolidated clay-rock which possesses definite lamination.

**shank** (Build.): (1) The shaft of a column, pillar, etc. (2) The shaft of a tool, connecting the handle and the head.

**shaping machine** (Eng.): A machine tool for producing small flat surfaces, slots, etc.

**sharp** (Build., Civ. Eng.): Said of sand, the grains of which are angular.

**sheath** (Zool.): An enclosing or protective structure.

**sheathing** (Carp.): Close boarding nailed to the framework of a building to form the walls or the roof.

**shed** (Build.): A small outhouse.

**sheeting** (Civ. Eng.): Rough horizontal boards used to support the sides of narrow trenches during excavation in very loose soils.

**shell** (Chem.): A group of electrons in an atom, all of which have the same principal quantum number. (Zool.): A hard outer case of inorganic material.

**shellac'** (Chem.): The purified product of lac.

**shingle** (Build.): A thin, flat rectangular piece of wood laid like a tile, as a roof covering or for the sides of a building.

**shock** (Eng., etc.): The sudden application of load to a member.

**shoe** (Build.): The short bent part at the foot of a downpipe, directing the water away from the wall.

**short-circuit** (Elec. Eng.): The electrical condition created when the terminals of a generator or any other conveyor or source of electrical energy are connected by a conducting path of negligible resistance.

**short waves**: Electromagnetic waves whose wavelength is of the order of 50 meters or less.

**shrinkage** (Civ. Eng.): The difference in the spaces occupied by material before excavation and after settlement in embankment.

**shrub** (Bot.): A woody plant in which most of the side shoots survive, so that there is no main trunk as a tree.

**shutter** (Build.): A removable protective covering to the outside of a window.

**sid'erite** (Geol.): A general term for meteoric iron.

**sidereal time** (Astron.): A method of reckoning intervals based on the rotation of the earth on its axis as the fundamental period.

**sieve** (Build.): An open container fitted with a mesh bottom.

**sight**: The sensation produced when light waves impinge on the photosensitive cells of the eye.

**sig'moid** (Bot., Zool., etc.): Curved like the letter S.

**sign** (Med.): Any objective evidence of disease or bodily disorder.

**signal** (Elec Comm.): The modification of an electrical effect having a variation wave-form or coding which represents the intelligence transmitted. (Surv.): A device used to mark a survey station, as a ranging rod, etc.

**sil'ica** (Met., Min.): Dioxide of silicon; used in the manufacture of glass.

**sil'icates** (Min.): The salts of the silicic acids, the large group among minerals.

**sil'icon** (Chem.): A non-metallic element.

**silk** (Zool.): A fluid substance secreted by various anthropoda; used for spinning cocoons, webs, etc.

**sill** (Geol.): A concordant minor intrusion of igneous rock injected as a tabular sheet between the bedding planes of rocks.

**silt** (Eng.): Material of an earthy character deposited in a finely divided form by flowing water.

**silver** (Met., Min.): A pure-white metallic element.

**silver amalgam** (Min.): A solid solution of mercury and silver.

**sim'ian** (Zool.): Pertaining to the anthropoid apes.

**simoom'** (Meteor.): A hot dry wind of brief duration, occurring in the Arabian and African deserts.

**simple** (Bot.): Consisting of one piece.

**simple curve** (Surv.): A curve composed of a single arc connecting two straights.

**simple fruit** (Bot.): A fruit formed from one pistil.

**simple harmonic motion** (Phys.): A type of vibration represented by projecting into a diameter the uniform motion of a point around a circle.

**simple tissue** (Bot.): A tissue made up of cells all of the same kind.

**simplex channel** (Elec. Comm.): A channel of communication which transmits signals in one direction only at a time.

**simplex group** (Cyt.): The haploid complement of chromosomes and factors.

**simulation** (Zool.): Mimicry.

**sine galvanometer** (Elec. Eng.): A galvanometer in which the coil and scale are rotated to keep the needle at zero.

**sine wave** (Phys.): A wave in which the particles execute transverse vibrations of a simple harmonic type.

**singlet** (Chem.): A chemical bond which consists of a single shared electron.

**sinking** (Civ. Eng.): The operation of excavating for a shaft, well or pit.

**sinter** (Chem.): To coalesce into a single mass under the influence of heat, without actually liquefying.

**sin'uose** (Bot.): Waved from side to side.

**si'nus** (Bot.): A depression in a margin between two lobes. (Zool.): A cavity of irregular shape.

**sipho-**: A prefix meaning tube.

**siphon** (Civ. Eng.): A pipeline full of water connecting two reservoirs, with the flow taking place under the action of atmospheric pressure. (Zool.): A tubular organ serving for the intake and output of fluid.

**sipho'neous** (Bot.): Tubular.

**siroc'co** (Meteor.): A warm moist wind from the south or south-east, which blows before the eastward passage of a depression in Mediterranean regions.

**sisal hemp** (Bot.): A fibrous material used for cordage.

**site** (Build., Civ. Eng.): An area of ground which is to be the location of building works.

**sitotro'pism** (Zool.): Reaction to the stimulus of food.

**skein** (Cyt.): The nuclear reticulum.

**skeleton** (Anat., Zool.): The rigid or elastic, internal or external framework of a body.

**skew**: Irregular, unsymmetrical, oblique.

**skin**: The protective tissue layers of the body-wall of an animal. (Bot.): Epidermis. (Eng.): The hard surface layer found on iron castings.

**skip** (Civ. Eng.): A bucket used for the transport of materials and hung on a crane.

**skirt** (Elec. Comm.): The lower side portions of a resonance curve.

**skull** (Zool.): In vertebrates, the brain case and sense-capsules with the jaws and the bronchial arches.

**skylight** (Build.): A glazed opening in a roof.

**skyscraper** (Build.): A very tall, multistoryed building.

**slab** (Civ. Eng.): A thin flat piece of stone or concrete.

**slag** (Met.): The top layer of the two-layer melt formed during smelting and refining operations.

**slaking** (Build.): The process of combining quicklime with water.
**slashed** (Bot.): Deeply cut by tapering incisions.
**slate** (Geol.): A sedimentary rock of the clay or silt grade which has developed a slaty cleavage.
**slaty cleavage** (Geol.): The property of splitting easily with the cleavage planes lying in the directions of maximum elongation of the mass.
**sledge-hammer** (Eng.): A heavy hammer weighing up to 100 lb. or over, swung by both hands.
**sleet** (Meteor.): A mixture of rain and snow.
**sleeve** (Eng.): A tubular piece.
**slide rule**: A device for performing mechanically arithmetical processes.
**slide valve** (Eng.): A steam-engine inlet and exhaust valve shaped like a rectangular lid.
**slimes** (Met.): Particles of crushed ore which settle very slowly in water.
**slip** (Civ. Eng.): A sloping concrete surface for the support of a vessel in the process of being built or repaired.
**slope** (Civ. Eng.): The inclined side of an embankment.
**slough** (Med.): To form dead tissue. (Zool.): The cast-off outer skin of a snake.
**sluice** (Civ. Eng.): A water channel equipped with means of controlling the flow.
**smell**: The sensation produced by stimulation of the mucous membrane of the olfactory organs.
**smelting** (Met.): Fusion of an ore to produce a melt of two layers.
**smoke** (Chem.): A suspension of a solid in a gas.
**smooth** (Bot.): Said of a surface that is neither hairy nor rough.
**snow** (Meteor.): Precipitation in the form of small ice crystals.
**soaking** (Met.): A phrase of a heating operation during which metal is maintained at the requisite temperature until the temperature is uniform throughout the mass.
**soaps** (Chem.): The alkaline salts of palmitic, oleic or stearic acid.
**social** (Zool.): Living together.
**socket** (Elec. Eng.): The female portion of a plug-**and-socket** connection in an electric circuit.
**sodium** (Chem.): A metallic element.
**softness** (Met.): Tendency to deform easily.
**sol** (Chem.): A colloidal solution.
**solar** (Zool.): Having branches radially arranged.
**solar plexus** (Zool.): In higher mammals, a ganglionic center of the autonomic nervous system.
**solar apex** (Astron.): The point on the celestial sphere towards which the solar system is moving at the rate of 20 kilometers a second.
**solar constant** (Phys.): The quantity of energy received normally per sq. cm. per second by the earth.
**Solar System** (Astron.): The term designating the sun and the attendant bodies moving about it under gravitational attraction.
**solation** (Chem.): The liquefaction of a gel.
**solder** (Met.): A general term for alloys used for joining metals by soldering.
**soldered** (Bot.): United.
**soldier** (Zool.): In some social insects, a form with a large head and mandibles, adapted for defending the community.
**sole** (Carp.): The lower surface of the body of a plane.
**solid** (Chem.): A state of matter, with a definite shape, in which the constituent molecules or ions possess no translational motion, but can only vibrate about fixed mean positions.
**solitary** (Bot., Zool.): Occurring singly. (Zool.): Living alone.
**solstices** (Astron.): The two moments in the year when the sun in its apparent motion attains its maximum distance from the celestial equator.
**solubility** (Chem.): The weight of a dissolved substance which will saturate 100 grams of a solvent.
**sol'ute** (Chem.): A substance which is dissolved in another.
**solution** (Bot.): The abnormal separation of parts normally united. (Chem.): An extremely intimate mixture, of variable composition, of two or more substances, one of which is usually a liquid, which may be separated by simple physical processes.
**solvent** (Chem.): That component of a solution which is present in excess, or whose physical state is the same as that of the solution.
**so'ma** (Zool.): The body of an animal, as distinct from the germ-cells.
**somatic cell** (Zool.): One of the non-reproductive cells of the parent body.
**somatic mitosis** (Cyt.): Division of the metabolic nucleus.
**somatic mutation** (Gen.): A mutation arising in a somatic cell and not in a reproductive structure.
**somatic segregation** (Bot., Gen.): A change in nuclear or hereditary constitution during vegetative growth.
**somatogen'ic** (Zool.): Arising as the result of external stimuli. Developing from somatic cells.
**so'matoids** (Chem.): Small particles of definite shape and possessing a definite arrangement of matter but not homogeneous.
**sonims** (Met.): Solid non-metallic inclusions in metal.
**sough** (Civ. Eng.): A drain at the foot of a slope.
**sound** (Acous.): The perception of external stimuli accepted through the ear and sense of hearing.
**sounder** (Ocean.): Any instrument used for determining the depth of the sea.
**sounding** (Surv.): The depth of an under-water point below some chosen reference datum.
**space**: Continuous and boundless extension considered as a vacuous entity in which things may exist and move.
**spa'dix** (Bot.): A spike with a swollen fleshy axis, enclosed in a spathe.
**span** (Civ. Eng., etc.): The horizontal distance between the supports of an arch, bridge, etc. (Elec. Eng.): The distance between two transmission-line towers.
**spark** (Elec. Eng.): An electric discharge taking place in air or other insulating material.
**spasm** (Zool.): Involuntary contraction of muscle fibers.
**spathe** (Bot.): A large foliar organ which subtends and more or less encloses a spadix.
**spawn** (Zool.): To deposit eggs or discharge spermatozoa.
**spay** (Zool.): To remove the ovaries.
**species** (Bot., Zool.): A classification term used to denote a group of closely allied, mutually fertile individuals, showing differences from allied groups.
**specific gravity** (Phys.): The ratio of the mass of a given volume of a substance to the mass of an equal volume of water at a temperature of 4° C.
**specific heat** (Phys.): The quantity of heat necessary to raise the temperature of unit mass one degree.
**specific volume** (Phys.): The volume of unit mass.
**spectrum** (Phys.): An arrangement of radiated frequencies in order of their frequencies.
**speed**: The ratio of the distance covered by a moving body to the time taken. (Elec. Eng.): The angular velocity of an electrical machine, expressed in revolutions per minute.
**speed of rotation**: In a rotating body, the number of rotations about the axis of rotation divided by the time.
**speleology** (Zool.): The study of the flora and fauna of caves.
**sperm** (Zool.): A male germ-cell.
**Spermatophy'ta** (Bot.): Seed-bearing plants.
**sphe'noid** (Bot., Zool.): Wedge-shaped. (Crystal.): A wedge-shaped crystal-form consisting of four triangular faces.
**sphincter** (Zool.): A muscle which by its contraction narrows or closes an orifice.
**sphyg'mus** (Zool.): The pulse.
**spi'cate** (Bot.): Spike-like.
**spike** (Carp.): A large stout nail. (Bot.): An indefinite inflorescence with sessile flowers.
**spile** (Civ. Eng.): A timber pile.
**spin** (Aero.): The movement of an aircraft in a continuous spiral dive.
**spinal** (Zool.): Pertaining to the vertebral column.
**spindle** (Cyt., Zool.): Any spindle-shaped structure.
**spine** (Zool.): The vertebral column.
**spinif'erous** (Bot.): Thorn-bearing.
**spin'neret** (Zool.): One of the spinning organs in spiders.
**spin'nerule** (Zool.): A duct by which the fluid silk is discharged in spiders.
**spi'nose** (Bot.): Bearing sharp spiny teeth.
**spira** (Arch.): The base of a column.
**spire** (Build.): A slender tower tapering to a point.
**spi'reme** (Cyt.): A stage in which the nuclear chromatin takes the form of a long thread.
**spiril'lum** (Bacteriol.): A curved spiral organism.
**spirit** (Chem.): An aqueous solution of ethyl alcohol.
**spi'rochetes** (Bacteriol.): Filamentous bacteria showing indulations or spirals.
**spirom'eter** (Med.): An instrument for measuring the air inhaled and exhaled during respiration.
**splint** (Med.): Any appliance used for the fixation of displaced or movable parts, especially dislocated or fractured bones.
**spontaneous generation** (Biol.): The production of living matter or organisms from non-living matter.
**spool** (Elec.): The support of a coil.
**sporad'ic** (Bot.): Scattered over a wide area. (Med.): Of disease, occurring here and there.
**spore** (Bot.): A reproductive body characteristic of plants. Consists of one or a few cells, never contains an embryo, and when set free may give rise to a new plant. (Zool.): In protozoa, a minute body formed by multiple fission.
**spori-, sporo-**: A prefix meaning seed.
**sporogen'esis** (Bot., Zood.): Spore formation.
**spo'rophyte** (Bot.): The spore-bearing plant.
**sport** (Gen.): Any individual differing markedly from

the normal by reason of genetical factors.

**spot level** (Surv.): The reduced level of a point chosen at random.

**sprain** (Med.): A wrenching of a joint.

**spray-gun** (Civ. Eng.): An apparatus for forming by pneumatic pressure a fine spray.

**spread** (Biol.): The establishment of a species in a new area.

**sprocket** (Eng.): A toothed wheel used for chain drives.

**spur** (Bot.): A tubular prolongation at the base of a petal. (Geol.): A hilly projection extending from the flanks of a valley.

**squam'a** (Bot., Zool.): A scale.

**stabilizer** (Chem.): (1) A negative catalyst. (2) A substance which makes a solution stable.

**stability**: A general property of mechanical, electrical or aerodynamical systems whereby the system returns to a state of equilibrium after disturbance.

**stable** (Chem., etc.): Possessing no tendency to change.

**stage** (Build., Civ. Eng.): A platform. (Geol.): A succession of rocks which were deposited during an age of geological time.

**stainless steel** (Met.): Corrosion-resistant steel with a high percentage of chromium.

**stair** (Build.): A series of steps.

**stair-head** (Build.): The top of a flight of stairs.

**stake** (Carp.): A piece of timber pointed at one end for driving into the ground.

**stalac'tite** (Geol.): A concretionary deposit of calcium carbonate which hangs icicle-like from the roofs of limestone caverns.

**stalag'mite** (Geol.): A concretionary deposit of calcium carbonate, precipitated from dripping solutions on the floors and walls of limestone caverns.

**stalagmom'etry** (Chem.): The analysis of solutions by means of surface tension measurements.

**stall** (Eng.): Of an engine, to stop owing to the too sudden application of a brake.

**stalling speed** (Aero.): The airspeed of an aeroplane at which it experiences its maximum lift.

**sta'men** (Bot.): One of the members of the flower which produces pollen.

**stanchion** (Civ. Eng.): A pillar for the support of a superstructure.

**sta'sis** (Bot.): Stoppage of growth.

**star** (Astron.): A term for any body that is self-luminous and of the same general nature as the sun though differing in size, distance, etc.

**sta'sis** (Bot.): Stoppage of growth.

**sta'tor** (Elec. Eng.): The fixed part of an electrical machine.

**steam** (Phys.): Water in the vapor state.

**steel** (Met.): Essentially an alloy of iron and carbon.

**steeple** (Build.): A structure surmounted with a spire.

**stellate** (Bot., Zool.): Radiating from a center, like a star.

**stem** (Bot.): The ascending axis of plant.

**steno-**: A prefix meaning narrow.

**stenother'my** (Ecol.): Tolerance of only a very narrow range of temperature.

**step-down transformer** (Elec. Eng.): A transformer for changing a high-voltage supply into a low-voltage supply.

**stepping** (Civ. Eng.): Laying foundations in horizontal steps on sloping ground.

**stereo-**: A prefix meaning solid, stiff.

**stereochemistry** (Chem.): The study of the spatial arrangement of the atoms in a molecule.

**stereophon'ic** (Acous.): Said of reproduced sound in which the illusion of auditory perspective is realized.

**stereotax'is** (Biol.): Response of an organism to the stimulus of contact with a solid body.

**sterile**: Unable to breed.

**sterilization** (Bot., Zool.): (1) Loss of sexual function. (2) The preparation, usually by heating, of a substratum free from any living organism, on which fungi or bacteria may subsequently be grown in pure culture.

**steth'oscope** (Med.): A tube adapted for listening to the sounds produced in the body.

**stigma** (Bot.): The distal end of the style on which pollen alights and germinates.

**stimulus** (Bot., Zool.): An agent which will provoke active reaction in a living organism.

**sting** (Zool.): A sharp-pointed organ by means of which a poison can be injected into a victim.

**sti'pate** (Bot.): Crowded.

**stip'ule** (Bot.): One of the two appendages, usually leaf-like, present at the base of the petiole of a leaf.

**sto'a** (Arch.): A covered portico or collonade.

**stock** (Bot.): A race. (Gen., Zood.): A direct line of descent.

**stoke** (Eng.): To supply fuel to a boiler furnace by mechanical means.

**sto'lon** (Bot.): A weak stem, growing horizontally from the main stem of the plant.

**sto'ma**: A small aperture.

**stomach** (Zool.): In vertebrates, the sac-like portion of the alimentary canal between the oesophagus and the intestines.

**stone** (Bot.): The hard endocarp of a drupe.

**story** (Build.): The part of a building included between two adjacent floors.

**straight** (Surv.): A straight or tangent length connecting curves in a highway or railway.

**strain** (Bot., Zool.): A variety of a species, with distinct physiological and/or morphological characters.

**stratification** (Geol.): The layering in sedimentary rocks due to changes in the rate of deposition, or in the nature of the sediment.

**strat'osphere** (Meteor.): A layer of the earth's atmosphere.

**stratum** (Geol.): A single bed of rock bounded above and below by divisional planes.

**streak** (Min.): The name given to the color of the powder obtained by scratching a mineral with a knife or file.

**streptococ'cus** (Bateriol.): A gram-positive coccus of which the individuals tend to be grouped in chains.

**stri'a**: A streak, a faint ridge.

**strict** (Bot.): Stiff and rigid.

**strike** (Geol.): The horizontal direction which is at right-angles to the dip of a rock.

**striped** (Bot.): Bearing longitudinal stripes of color.

**stripping**: Removal of an electro-deposit by any means.

**stud** (Carp.): An upright scantling in a timber framework. (Eng.): A shank, or headless bolt.

**stu'por** (Med.): A state of mental and physical inertia.

**style** (Bot.): The portion of the carpel between the stigma and the ovary.

**sty'lobate** (Arch.): A continuous pedestal supporting a row of columns.

**styp'tic** (Med.): Astringent.

**sub**: A prefix meaning under.

**suc'culent** (Bot.): Juicy, thick and soft.

**sucker** (Bot.): A strongly growing shoot arising from the base of a stem or a root.

**sullage** (Civ. Eng.): The mud deposited by flowing waters.

**sulphates** (Chem.): Salts of sulphuric acid.

**sulphides** (Chem.): Salts of hydrosulphuric acid.

**sulphur** (Chem.): A non-metallic element.

**summation** (Physiol.): The production of an effect by repetition of causal factor which would be insufficient in a single application.

**Sun** (Astron.): The central body of the solar system, an incandescent gaseous sphere.

**supercooled** (Chem.): Cooled below the normal freezing-point without solidification.

**superficial**: Pertaining to the surface.

**supplementary** (Zool.): Additional.

**supply**: A source of energy.

**suppression** (Bot.): Failure to develop.

**surveying**: The art of making such measurements of the relative positions of points on the surface of the earth that will enable the features to be depicted in their true relationship by drawing them to scale on paper.

**suspension** (Chem.): A system in which denser particles are distributed throughout a less dense liquid or gas.

**suspension bridge** (Civ. Eng.): A bridge suspended from a flexible connection between the two sides.

**swab** (Med.): Any small mass of cotton or gauze used for mopping up blood, or discharges, or for cleansing surfaces.

**swarm** (Zool.): A large number of small animals in movement together.

**switch** (Eng.): A mechanical device for opening and closing an electric circuit.

**switching-off** (Elec. Eng., etc.): The opening of an electric circuit.

**switching-on** (Elec. Eng., etc.): The closing of an electric circuit.

**sylves'tral** (Bot.): Growing in woods.

**symbio'sis** (Biol.): An internal, mutually beneficial partnership between two organisms.

**symptom** (Med.): Evidence of disease as experienced by the patient.

**syn-, sym-**: A prefix meaning with.

**synapse** (Zool.): The mode of connection of one nerve-cell with another.

**syn'desis** (Cyt.): In meiotic nuclear division, fusion of homologous chromosomes.

**syn'ecology** (Bot.): The study of plant communities.

**syn'gamy** (Bot., Zool.): Fusion of gametes.

**synodic month** (Astron.): The interval between two successive passages of the moon.

**synthetic**: Artificial.

**system** (Biol.): A method or scheme of classification. (Chem.): Any portion of matter which is isolated from other matter. (Elec. Eng.): A general term covering the entire complex of apparatus involved in the transmission and distribution of electric power. (Geol.): The name given to the succession of rocks which were formed during a certain period of geological time.

**systems of crystals** (Crystal.): The seven large divisions into which all crystallizing substance can be placed.
**systematics** (Biol.): The branch of biology which deals with nomenclature and classification.

## T

**tabular** (Bot., Geol., Min.): Horizontally flattened.
**tacheom'eter** (Surv.): An instrument which measures distance from any given point by telescopic observation.
**tachom'eter** (Eng.): An instrument for indicating the revolutions per minute of a revolving shaft.
**tack** (Build.): A small clout nail.
**tactile** (Zool.): Pertaining to the sense of touch.
**tail** (Aero.): The hindmost horizontal unit of an aeroplane.
**talc** (Min.): An acid metasilicate of magnesium.
**tally** (Surv.): A brass tag attached to a chain at every tenth link.
**talon** (Arch.): An ogee molding. (Zool.): A sharp-hooked claw.
**tan'talum** (Met., Min.): A metallic element.
**tape** (Build., Surv.): A long flexible measuring scale.
**tapering** (Bot.): Said of a leaf base which becomes gradually narrowed towards the petiole.
**tapping** (Elec. Eng.): A connection taken to an intermediate joint on a winding.
**tarnish** (Chem.): The discoloration produced on the surface of an exposed metal.
**tars-, tarso-**: A prefix meaning the sole of the foot.
**tarsus** (Zool.): The ankle, in vertebrates.
**Taurus** (Astron.): Bull. Second sign of the Zodiac.
**tawny** (Bot.): Dark brownish-yellow.
**taxi** (Aero.): Said of an aircraft that travels under its own power, while in contact with the earth.
**taxis** (Bot., Zool.): A movement of a whole organism towards or away from a stimulus.
**taxon'omy** (Biol.): The science of classification as applied to living organisms.
**technology**: The practice, description and terminology of the applied sciences which have commercial value.
**tela** (Zool.): A web-like tissue.
**telecommunication** (Elec. Comm.): Any communication of information by electrical means.
**telegraph** (Elec. Comm.): A combination of apparatus for conveying messages over a distance by means of electrical impulses.
**telegraphy**: The electrical communication system whereby messages are transmitted in coded signals by trained operators.
**teleme'ter** (Elec. Eng.): An instrument for the remote indication of electrical quantities. (Surv.): The general name for an instrument which acts as a distance measurer without the use of a chain.
**teleol'ogy** (Biol.): The interpretation of animal or plant structures in terms of purpose and utility.
**teleph'ony**: The transmission of speech-currents over wires.
**telescope** (Astron.): An optical instrument for making distant objects appear nearer.
**television**: The electrical transmission of visual scenes and images by wire or radio.
**tellu'rium** (Met.): A metallic element.
**telo-**: A prefix meaning end.
**telomit'ic** (Cyt.): In cell-division, having the chromosomes attached to the fibers of the spindle by their ends.
**tel'ophase** (Cyt.): The period of reconstruction of nuclei which follows the separation of the daughter chromosomes in mitosis.
**temperament** (Psychol.): The quantity and quality of the general affective nature of an individual.
**temperamental** (Psychol.): Displaying alternation of moods.
**temperature** (Phys.): The degree of heat or cold measured with respect to an arbitrary zero.
**tempering** (Met.): The reheating of hardened steel at any temperature below the critical range, in order to decrease the hardness.
**template** (Build.): A long flat stone supporting the end of a beam.
**tendon** (Zool.): A card or sheet of fibrous tissue by which a muscle is attached to another muscle or to a skeletal structure.
**tentacle** (Zool.): An elongate, slender, flexible organ having a variety of functions as grasping, feeling, holding, exploring, etc.
**ter'bium** (Chem.): A metallic element.
**terebrate** (Zool.): Possessing a sting.
**terminal** (Bot.): Situated at the tip of anything. (Elec. Eng.): A point of connection in an electrical circuit.
**ternary** (Chem.): Consisting of three components, etc.
**terrestrial**: Pertaining to the earth.
**terrestrial poles**: The two diametrically opposite points in which the earth's axis cuts the earth's surface.
**Tertiary** (Geol.): the era of geological time during which the strata ranging from the Eocene to the Pilocene were deposited.
**test**: Any routine or special procedure for ascertaining that apparatus is functioning correctly.
**testa** (Bot.): The seed coat.
**tet'anus** (Med.): Lockjaw.
**tetra-**: A prefix meaning four.
**tet'racyte** (Bot.): One of the four cells formed after a meiotic division.
**tetrad** (Cyt.): A bivalent chromosome which shows signs of division into four longitudinal threads.
**tetrag'onal system** (Crystal.): The crystallographic system in which all the forms are referred to three axes at right-angles.
**tetramor'phous** (Chem.): Existing in four different crystalline forms.
**tet'rapod** (Zool.): Having four feet.
**tetrap'terous** (Zool.): Having four wings.
**tetrava'lent** (Chem.): Capable of combining with four atoms of hydrogen or their equivalent.
**thal'amus** (Bot.): The receptacle of a flower.
**thallium** (Chem.): A metallic element.
**than'atoid** (Zool.): Deadly.
**theod'olite** (Surv.): An instrument for measuring horizontal and vertical angles.
**theory**: A scientific theory is a co-ordinated set of hypotheses which are found to be consistent with one another and with specially observed phenomena.
**therapeu'tic** (Med.): Curative.
**ther'apy** (Med.): The curative and preventive medical treatment of disease.
**therm-, thermo-**: A prefix meaning heat.
**thermal** (Aero., Meteor.): An ascending current due to local heating of air.
**thermal analysis** (Met.): The use of cooling or heating curves in the study of changes in metals and alloys.
**thermal dissociation** (Chem.): The dissociation of certain molecules under the influence of heat.
**thermal resistance** (Elec. Eng.): Resistance to the flow of heat.
**thermion'ics**: The science dealing with the emission of electrons from hot bodies.
**thermochemistry** (Chem.): The study of the heat changes accompanying chemical reactions.
**thermoduric** (Phys.): Resistant to heat.
**thermodynam'ics** (Phys.): The mathematical treatment of the relation of heat to mechanical and other forms of energy.
**thermogen'esis** (Zool.): Production of heat within the body.
**thermo'graph** (Meteor.): A continuously recording thermometer.
**thermol'ysis** (Chem.): The dissociation of a molecule by heat. (Zool.): Loss of body heat.
**thermometer**: An instrument for measuring temperature.
**thermonuclear reaction** (Phys.): Nuclear reaction induced by heat.
**ther'mophyte** (Bot.): A plant growing in warm situations.
**thermoplastic** (Chem.): Becoming plastic on being heated.
**thermoscop'ic**: Perceptive of change of temperature.
**ther'mostat**: A device for maintaining an inclosure at a constant temperature.
**thor'ium** (Chem.): A radio-active metallic element.
**thorn** (Bot.): A leaf or shoot which contains vascular tissue and ends in a hard sharp point.
**three-point landing** (Aero.): The normal perfect landing of an aeroplane.
**thrombo'sis** (Med.): The formation of a clot in a blood vessel. (Zool.): Coagulation.
**thrust**: Propulsive force developed by a jet-propelled motor.
**thu'lium** (Chem.): A metallic element.
**thunder** (Meteor.): The noise which accompanies a flash of lightning; its origin is in the violent thermal changes accompanying the discharge, which causes non-periodic wave disturbances in the air.
**tide** (Astron.): The effect of the gravitational attraction of the moon on the waters of the earth.
**tide gauge** (Surv.): An apparatus for determining the variation of sea-level with time.
**tie** (Eng.): A frame member sustaining a tensile load.
**tile** (Build): A thin slab of baked clay, cement, glass or terra-cotta used for roofing or for covering floors or walls.
**timber**: Felled logs or trees suitable for sawing.
**time**: (Astron.): In its astronomical sense of a measured quantity, essentially a measure of angle; the fundamental unit of time measurement is supplied by the earth's rotation on its axis.
**tin** (Met.): A metallic element.
**tissue** (Biol.): An aggregate of similar cells forming a definite and continuous fabric.
**tissue culture** (Bot., Zool.): The growth of detached pieces of tissue in nutritive fluids under conditions which exclude fungi and bacteria.
**tita'nium** (Met.): A metallic element.
**tolerance** (Bot.): The ability of a plant to endure adverse environmental conditions, and also to withstand

the development of a parasite within it without showing signs of a serious disease.

**ton**: A unit of weight for large quantities; 1 ton = 2,000 lbs.

**tone**: (Acous.): Strictly, a sound-wave of one frequency. (Zool.): The condition of elasticity or tension to the living tissues of the animal body, especially muscles.

**tongue** (Zool.): In vertebrates, the moval muscular organ lying on, and attached to, the floor of the buccal cavity; used in connection with tasting, mastication and swallowing.

**tonsils** (Zool.): In vertebrates, lymphoid bodies situated at the junction of the buccal cavity and the pharynx.

**tooth** (Bot.): Any small irregularity on the margin of a leaf. (Zool.): A hard projecting body with a masticatory function.

**topochem'istry** (Chem.): The study of reactions which occur only at certain definite regions in a system.

**topog'raphy** (Surv.): The delineation of the natural and artificial features of an area.

**torna'do** (Meteor.): An intensely destructive, advancing whirlwind formed from strongly ascending currents.

**torque** (Mech.): The fluctuating or uniform turning moment exerted by a tangential force acting at a distance from the axis of rotation or twist.

**torrent'icolis** (Ecol.): Animals living in swiftly running waters.

**Torrid Zone** (Astron.): The region of the earth bounded by the two tropics and bisected by the equator.

**torsion**: The state of strain set up in a part by twisting. (Bot.): Twisting without marked displacement.

**torsion balance** (Phys.): A delicate device for measuring small forces such as those due to gravitation, magnetism or electric charges.

**tor'ticone** (Zool.): A spirally twisted shell.

**tor'us** (Bot.): The receptacle of a flower. (Zool.): A fold or ridge.

**totipo'tent** (Zool.): Capable of development into a complete embryo or organ.

**toughness** (Met.): A term denoting a condition intermediate between softness and brittleness.

**tourniquet** (Surg.): Any appliance, which by means of a constricting band, a pad to lie over the artery, and a device for tightening it, exerts pressure on the artery and controls the bleeding from it.

**tower** (Elec. Eng.): The lattice-type steel structure used to carry the several conductors of a transmission line at a considerable height above the ground.

**toxicol'ogy** (Med.): That branch of medical science which deals with the nature and effects of poisons.

**trache'a** (Bot.): The windpipe leading from the glottis to the lungs, in air breathing vertebrates.

**tracho'ma** (Med.): A highly contagious infection of the conjunctiva covering the eyelids.

**tract** (Zool.): The extent of an organ or system.

**tractile fiber** (Cyt.): A spindle fiber which begins to develop from an attachment to a chromosome and extends to the pole of the spindle.

**traction**: The propulsion of vehicles.

**tractor**: A vehicle capable of propelling itself along a track or road, or for drawing other vehicles.

**trade-winds** (Meteor.): A drying wind blowing almost continually in the same course toward the equator but from an easterly direction. The trade wind blows from n.e. to s.w. on the north side of the equator, and from s.e. to n.w. on the south side of the equator.

**traffic lights** (Elec Eng.): Red, amber and green signal-lights installed at street intersections, etc., for controlling the flow of traffic.

**trails** (Astron.): Long flashes of brightness seen in the wake of some large meteors in the sky.

**tramontan'a** (Meteor.): A northerly mountain wind blowing over Italy.

**transcription** (Elec. Comm.): The recording of a broadcast performance for subsequent re-broadcast.

**tran'sect** (Bot.): A line of vegetation marked off for study.

**transference** (Psycho-an.): The displacement of affect, positive or negative, from the person to whom it was originally directed, on to another.

**transformer** (Elec. Comm.): An electromagnetic device for separating electrical circuits while permitting the flow of electrical power from one to the other.

**transforming station** (Elec. Eng.): A point on an electricity supply system where a change of supply voltage occurs.

**transfusion** (Med.): The operation of transferring the blood of one person into the veins of another.

**translocation** (Bot.): The movement of material in solution inside the body of the plant. (Cyt.): The transfer of a portion of a chromosome, either to another part of the same chromosome, or to a different chromosome.

**translucent** (Bot., Min., etc.): More or less transparent.

**transmission** (Elec. Comm., Elec. Eng.): The conveying of electrical energy over a distance.

**transmission line** (Elec. Eng.): The overhead conductor system by which electric power is transmitted at high voltage from one place to another.

**transmitter** (Elec. Comm.): A generic term for the device which transmits electrical power under the control of some signal, conveyed mechanically.

**transmutation** (Chem.): The conversion of one element into another.

**transpiration** (Aero.): The flow of gas along relatively long passages. (Bot.): The loss of water vapor from a plant.

**transplantation** (Surg., Zool.): Grafting.

**transuranic** (Phys.): Pertaining to an element of atomic weight greater than that of uranium.

**transverse** (Bot., Zool., etc.): Broader than long.

**trapez'ioid**: Shaped like a triangle with one corner cut off.

**trau'ma** (Med.): (1) A wound or bodily injury. (2) Emotional shock.

**trav'erse** (Surv.): A survey consisting of a set of connected lines whose lengths and directions are measured.

**tread** (Build.): The horizontal part of a step.

**tree** (Bot.): A tall woody perennial plant having a well-marked trunk and few branches persisting from the basal parts.

**trench** (Civ. Eng.): A long narrow excavation for drains, pipes, etc.

**tri-**: A prefix meaning three.

**triangular**: Having three angles.

**triax'on** (Zool.): Having three axes.

**triba'sic** (Chem.): Containing three replaceable hydrogen atoms in a molecule.

**tribe** (Bot.): A section of a family consisting of a number of related genera.

**tri'choid** (Zool.): Hair-like.

**triclin'ic system** (Crystal.): The crystallographic system which includes all the forms referred to three unequal axes which are not at right-angles.

**trigger** (Chem.): The agent which causes the initial decomposition of a chain reaction.

**triplet** (Chem.): A chemical bond which consists of three electrons shared between two atoms. (Bot.): Individuals resulting from the division of the ovum into three parts, each then developing.

**troph-, tro'pho-**: A prefix meaning nourishment.

**Tropics** (Astron.): The name given to those two parallels of celestial latitude which pass through the solstices, and which therefore represent the limits of the sun's extreme north and south declinations.

**tro'pism** (Physiol.): A reflex response to an external stimulus, involving movements of the whole body rather than a part.

**tro'posphere** (Meteor.): The lower part of the earth's atmosphere, in which the temperature decreases with height.

**trunk** (Anat., Zool.): The body, apart from the limbs. (Arch.): The shaft of a column. (Bot.): The upright, massive main stem of a tree.

**tuber** (Bot.): A swollen underground stem.

**tu'bercle** (Bot.): A general name for a small swelling. (Zool.): A small rounded projection.

**tufa** (Geol.): A porous form of calcium carbonate, which is deposited from solution around springs.

**tumor** (Med.): Any swelling or enlargement.

**tung'sten** (Met.): A metallic element.

**tu'nicate** (Bot.): Having a coat or covering.

**tunnel** (Civ. Eng.): An underground horizontal passage through which passes a road, canal, railway, etc.

**turbojet** (Aero.): An internal-combustion aero-engine comprising compressors and turbines, of which the net gas energy is used for reaction propulsion through a propelling nozzle.

**tur'gid** (Bot.): Said of a cell which is distended and tense, well supplied with water.

**tur'pentine** (Chem.): An oil obtained by the steam distillation of rosin.

**twin**: One of a pair of two. (Biol.): (1) Individuals arising from the division into two of the fertilized egg, each part proceeding to develop. (2) In mammals, two individuals produced at the same birth.

**type** (Biol.): The individual specimen on which the description of a new species or genus is based.

**typhoon** (Meteor.): A cyclone.

## U

**ulcer** (Med.): A localized destruction of an epithelial surface of the skin or of the gastric mucous membrane, forming an open sore.

**uliginous** (Bot.): Growing in wet places.

**ulno-**: A prefix meaning elbow.

**ulot'richous** (Zool.): Having wooly or curly hair.

**ultra-centrifuge** (Chem.): A high-speed centrifuge for the separation of submicroscope particles.

**ultra-filtration** (Chem.): The separation of colloidal particles by filtration, under suction or pressure, through a colloidal filter or semi-permeable membrane.
**ultramicrobe** (Biol.): An agent of obscure nature, able to cause disease in organisms, but too small to be visible with the microscope.
**ultrasonics** (Acous.): The science of mechanical vibrations and radiations in solids, gas and fluids, which have frequencies in excess of those which, in a sound-wave, are normally perceivable by the ear.
**ultra-violet radiation** (Phys.): Invisible radiations of wave-length less than 3900 A.U.—the limit of visibility at the violet end of the spectrum.
**umbel** (Bot.): An inflorescence consisting of numerous small flowers in flat-topped groups, borne on stalks all arising from about the same point on the main stem.
**umbil'ical cord** (Anat., Zool.): In eutherian mammals, the bascular cord connecting the foetus with the placenta.
**umbil'icate** (Bot.): Having a small central depression.
**umbra** (Astron.): The dark central portion of the shadow of a large body such as the earth or moon.
**umbrella** (Zool.): A flat cone-shaped structure.
**um'brine** (Bot.): Dull darkish-brown.
**unarmed** (Bot.): Without prickles or thorns.
**u'nary** (Chem.): Consisting of one component.
**un'cate, un'ciform, un'cinate** (Bot., Zool.): Hook-like.
**unconformity** (Geol.): A geological structure involving two sets of rocks of different ages.
**unconscious** (Psychol.): A general term used to include all processes which cannot be made conscious by direct effort of will.
**underpinning** (Build., Civ. Eng.): The operation of rebuilding the lower part of a building without damaging or weakening the superstructure.
**undershoot** (Aero.): Failure to reach the intended landing area.
**un'dulate** (Bot.): Having a wavy margin.
**undulated** (Bot.): With gentle depressions and elevations.
**unequal** (Bot.): Having the two sides not symmetrical.
**unguiculate** (Bot., Zool.): Provided with claws.
**un'gula** (Zool.): A hoof.
**Ungula'ta** (Zool.): An order of terrestrial mammals.
**uni-**: A prefix meaning one.
**uniaxial** (Min.): A term for all the crystalline minerals in which there is only one direction of single refraction.
**unicel'lular** (Biol.): Consisting of one cell.
**unidac'tyl** (Zool.): Having one digit.
**unilat'eral** (Bot.): Said of members which are all inserted on one side of the axis; of a raceme with all flowers turned to one side; of a stimulus falling on the plant from one side.
**unilateral conductivity** (Elec. Eng.): The property of unipolarity by which current can flow in one direction only.
**unilateral impedance** (Elec. Comm.): Any device in which power can be transmitted in one direction only.
**uniloc'ular** (Bot.): Consisting of a single compartment.
**uninu'cleate** (Biol.): Containing one nucleus.
**union** (Med.): In the process of healing, the growing together of parts separated by injury.
**unionized** (Chem.): Not ionized.
**unip'arous** (Zool.): Giving birth to one offspring at a time.
**unipo'lar** (Zool.): Said of nerve cells having only one process.
**unise'riate** (Bot.): Arranged in a single series, layer or row.
**unisex'ual** (Bot., Zool.): Distinctly male or female.
**unit cell** (Crystal.): The smallest group of atoms, molecules or ions, whose repetition at regular intervals, in three dimensions, produces the lattice of a given crystal.
**unit characters** (Gen.): Independent characteristics, which act as units, are traceable in each generation.
**univa'lent** (Cyt.): One of the single chromosomes which separate in the first meiotic division. (Chem.): Monovalent.
**u'nivalve** (Zool.): In one piece.
**universal time** (Astron.): A system of time reckoning adopted by international agreement.
**unsaturated** (Chem.): Less concentrated than a saturated vapor or solution.
**unstable** (Chem.): Subject to spontaneous change.
**uran'inite** (Min.): When massive, known as pitchblende.
**ura'nium** (Chem.): A metallic, radioactive element.
**U'ranus** (Astron.): The seventh planet in the solar system in order of distance from the sun.
**ured-, uredo-**: A prefix meaning a blight.
**urine** (Zool.): In vertebrates, the excretory product elaborated by the kidneys, usually of a fluid nature.
**urinogen'ital** (Zool.): Pertaining to the urinary and genital systems.
**urn** (Bot.): The capsule of a moss.
**urol'ogy** (Med.): That part of medical science which deals with diseases and abnormalities of the urinary tract and their treatment.
**uros'copy** (Med.): The scientific examination of urine for diagnostic purposes.
**utero-**: A prefix meaning womb.
**uterus** (Zool.): In female mammals, the muscular posterior part of the oviduct in which the foetus is lodged during the prenatal period.
**u'va** (Bot.): A berry formed from a superior ovary.
**u'vea** (Zool.): In vertebrates, the posterior pigment-bearing layer of the iris of the eye.

## V

**vacancy** (Crystal.): Absence of an atom in a crystal pattern.
**vaccination** (Med.): (1) Inoculation into the skin of the virus of vaccinia in order to immunize the person against smallpox. (2) The therapeutic application of a vaccine made from any micro-organism.
**vac'cine** (Med.): A preparation of any micro-organism or virus, treated so as to lose its virulence, for introduction into the body in order to stimulate antibodies to the micro-organisms introduced, so as to confer immunity against any subsequent infection by the same type of micro-organism.
**vac'uole** (Biol.): A small cavity in cytoplasm, generally containing fluid.
**vacuum** (Phys.): A region in which the gas pressure is considerably lower than atmospheric pressure.
**vagina** (Zool.): Any sheath-like structure.
**valency** (Chem.): The combining power of an atom or group in terms of hydrogen atoms. (Zool.): The numerical arrangement of the chromosomes in a nucleus.
**valley** (Geol.): Any hollow tract of ground between hills or mountains.
**valve** (Zool.): Any structure which controls the passage of material through a tube or aperture.
**vane** (Build.): A weathercock. (Surv.): A disc attachment to a levelling staff.
**vaporization** (Chem.): The conversion of a liquid or a solid into a vapor.
**vapor** (Phys.): A gas which is at a temperature below its critical temperature and therefore can be liquefied by a suitable increase in pressure.
**vapor pressure** (Phys.): The pressure exerted by a vapor.
**variable stars** (Astron.): Those stars whose apparent magnitudes are not constant but vary over a range.
**variance** (Maths.): The square of the standard deviation.
**variant** (Biol.): A specimen differing slightly in its characteristics from the type.
**variation** (Biol.): The difference between the offspring of a single mating; the difference between the individuals of a race, species, etc.
**var'icose** (Bot.): Dilated.
**variegated** (Bot., etc.): Marked irregularly with diverse color.
**variety** (Biol.): A race; a breed; a stock; a subspecie.
**vas** (Zool.): A vessel or tube carrying fluid.
**vascular** (Bot., Zool.): Pertaining to vessels which convey fluids or provide for the circulation of fluids.
**vascular system** (Zool.): The organs responsible for the circulation of blood and lymph, collectively.
**vasofor'mative** (Zool.): Pertaining to the formation of blood vessels or blood.
**vault** (Build.): (1) An arched ceiling or roof. (2) An underground room.
**vector** (Maths.): A vector is one which has magnitude and which is related to a given direction in space. (Biol.): Any agent which transmits a virus disease from one host to another.
**vector ratio** (Elec. Comm., Elec. Eng.): The ratio between two alternating quantities.
**veering** (Meteor.): A change in the direction of the arrival of the wind in a clockwise direction.
**vegetation** (Bot.): The whole of the plants in a given area.
**vegetative functions** (Zool.): The autonomic or involuntary functions, as circulation, digestion.
**vegetative reproduction** (Zool.): Propagation by budding.
**vein** (Bot.): One of the smaller strands of conducting tissues in a leaf. (Geol.): An irregular minor intrusion in rocks. (Zool.): A vessel conveying blood back to the heart from the various organs of the body.
**velocity** (Mech.): Rate of change of position or rate of displacement, expressed in feet per second.
**velum** (Zool.): A veil-like structure.
**velu'tinous** (Bot.): Having a velvety surface.
**velvet** (Zool.): The tissue layers covering a growing antler.
**venation** (Bot., Zool.): The arrangement of the veins.
**venomous** (Zool.): Provided with poison-secreting glands.
**vent** (Aero.): The opening in a parachute canopy which stabilizes it by allowing the air to escape at a controlled rate.

**ventilating fan** (Elec. Eng.): An electrically driven fan whose function is to force cooling air through the ventilating ducts of an electrical machine.
**ventilating tissue** (Bot.): The sum total of the intercellular spaces in a plant, through which air circulates.
**ventilation** (Build., etc.): The process of replacement of vitiated air by fresh air.
**ventilator** (Build.): A device employed in order to promote and maintain ventilation.
**ventral** (Bot.): (1) In front. (23) Uppermost. (3) Nearest to the axis.
**ven'tricle** (Zool.): A chamber, especially the cavities of the vertebrate brain and the main contractile chamber of the heart.
**ventro-, ventri-**: A prefix meaning belly.
**Venus** (Astron.): The second planet in the solar system in order of distance from the sun.
**veranda** (Build.): A covered external balcony along the outside of a building.
**veranil'lo** (Meteor.): The short period of fine weather which ends the rainy season in the tropical countries of America.
**veran'o** (Meteor.): The dry season in the tropical countries of America.
**vermic'ular** (Bot.): Shaped like a worm.
**vermic'ulites** (Min.): A group of hydrous silicates.
**ver'miform** (Zool.): Worm-like.
**vernal** (Bot.): Of spring.
**vernation** (Bot.): The manner in which the leaves are packed in a bud.
**vertebra** (Zool.): One of the bony skeletal elements which compose the backbone.
**vertex** (Zool.): In higher vertebrates, the highest point in the skull.
**vertigo** (Med.): Dizziness.
**vesic'ular** (Bot., Zool.): Like a bladder.
**vespoid** (Zool.): Wasp-like.
**vessel** (Bot.): A long water-conducting tube in the xylem. (Zool.): A duct with definitive walls.
**vestibule** (Build.): A small antechamber just inside the entrance of a building.
**vestigial** (Zool.): A small or reduced structure.
**ves'titure** (Bot., Zool.): A covering as hairs, fur, scales, feathers.
**vet'erinary**: Relating to the science which treats of the diseases of domestic animals.
**viable** (Bot., Zool.): Capable of living and developing normally.
**viaduct** (Civ. Eng.): A structure which carries a road across a wide and deep valley.
**vinegar** (Chem.): The product of the alcoholic and acetic fermentation of fruit juices.
**Virgo** (Astron.): Virgin; the sixth sign of the Zodiac.
**virology**: The study of viruses.
**vir'ulence** (Bot.): The capacity of a parasite to cause disease.
**virus** (Med., Bot.): A particulate infective agent, smaller than accepted bacterial forms, that causes many diseases in man.
**viscid** (Bot.). Said of a surface which is glutinous and covered by a sticky secretion.
**viscosity** (Phys.). Internal friction due to molecular cohesion in fluids.
**vis'cus** (Med.): Any one of the organs situated within the chest and the abdomen.
**vise** (Eng.): A clamping device used for holding work that is to be operated on.
**visibility** (Meteor.) Ability to observe distant objects through suspended water-droplets in the atmosphere.
**vital stain** (Bot., Zool.). A stain which can be used on living cells without killing them.
**vi'tamins** (Chem., Med.): Organic substances required, in relatively small amounts, for the proper functioning of the animal organism.
**vitelline** (Bot., Zool.): Pertaining to yolk; egg-yellow.
**vivip'arous** (Bot.): Producing young plants in place of flowers. (Zool.): Giving birth to living young which have already reached an advanced stage of development.
**vocal cords** (Zool.): In air-breathing vertebrates, folds of the lining membrane of the larynx which vibrate under the influence of breath and thereby the voice is produced.
**voids** (Civ. Eng.): The spaces between the separate particles in a mass of granular material.
**volant** (Zool.): Flying.
**volcanic ash** (Geol.): The typical product of explosive volcanic eruptions, consisting of rock and lava.
**volca'no** (Geol.): A center of volcanic eruption, having the form of a mountain, built of ashes and lava-flows with a central crater from which a pipe leads down to the source of magma beneath.
**volt** (Elec.): The unit of electromotive force.
**volt-ampere** (Elec.): Unit of apparent power.
**voltage** (Elec.): The value of an electromotive force, expressed in volts.
**voltaic current** (Elec.): Current produced by chemical action.
**voltam'eter** (Elec. Eng.): An instrument for measuring a current.
**voltmeter** (Elec.): An instrument, calibrated in volts, for measuring potential differences directly.
**volume** (Acous.): The general loudness of sounds.
**volumetric analysis** (Chem.): A form of chemical analysis using standard solutions for the estimation of the particular constituent present in solution.
**voluntary** (Zool.): Under control of the will.
**vortex** (Aero.): An eddy, or intense spiral motion in a limited region.
**vulcanites** (Geol.): A general name for igneous rocks of fine grain-size.

## W

**wad** (Min.): Bog manganese.
**waist**: A narrowed-down, constricted part of an object.
**wale** (Civ. Eng.): A horizontal timber used to bind together piles driven in a row.
**wall plug** (Elec. Eng.): A plug-in device for connecting a flexible conductor to a circuit terminal in the form of a wall socket.
**walling** (Civ. Eng.): A general term for masonry walls.
**warm-blooded** (Zool.): Said of animals which have the bodily temperature constantly maintained at a point usually above the environmental temperature, of which it is independent.
**warm front** (Meteor.): The leading edge of a mass of advancing warm air as it rises over colder air.
**wart** (Bot.): A small blunt-topped rounded upgrowth. (Med.): A tumor of the skin formed by overgrowth of the prickle-cell layer.
**washer** (Build., Eng.): An annular piece used under a nut to distribute pressure, or between jointing surfaces to make a tight joint.
**water** (Chem., Phys.): A colorless, odorless, tasteless fluid formed when hydrogen burns in oxygen.
**water balance** (Bot.): The ratio between the water taken in by a plant and the water lost by it.
**water culture** (Bot.): An experimental means of determining the mineral requirements of a plant.
**water-gauge** (Eng.): A vertical or inclined protected glass tube connected to the steam and water spaces of a boiler, for showing the height of the water level.
**water-level** (Surv.): An instrument for establishing a horizontal line of sight.
**waterlogged** (Civ. Eng.): A term applied to ground when it is saturated with water.
**waterproofing**: The process of rendering materials impervious to water.
**water-table** (Geol.): The surface below which fissures and pores in the strata are saturated with water.
**watt** (Elec. Eng.): A unit of electric power.
**watt-hour** (Elec. Eng.): The unit of electrical energy, being the work done by 1 watt acting for 1 hour.
**wattmeter** (Elec. Eng.): An instrument that measures the circuit power in watts.
**wave** (Phys.): A single pulse in a vibrational disturbance advanced through a body or an elastic medium.
**wavelength** (Elec. Eng.): The distance between two similar and successive points on an alternating wave.
**wax pocket** (Zool.): In bees, a ventral abdominal pouch which secretes wax.
**weathering** (Build.): The deliberate slope at which an approximately horizontal surface is built or laid so that it be able to throw off the rain. (Geol.): The processes of disintegration and decomposition effected in minerals and rocks as a consequence of exposure to the elements.
**web** (Zool.): The mesh of silk threads produced by some insects and spiders. Also the membrane connecting the toes in aquatic vertebrates.
**weed** (Bot.): A plant growing where it is not wanted by man.
**weight**: The gravitational force acting on a body.
**weir** (Civ. Eng.): A dam placed across a river to raise its level in dry weather.
**welding** (Eng.): The joining of two iron or steel pieces by heat.
**well** (Civ. Eng.): A shaft sunk in the ground for procuring a supply of underground waters.
**wet steam** (Eng.): A steam-water mixture.
**wettability** (Chem.): The extent to which a solid is wetted by a liquid.
**whalebone** (Zool.): Baleen.
**wheel base** (Eng.): The distance between the leading and trailing axles of a vehicle.
**whirlwind** (Meteor.): A small rotating wind-storm which may extend upwards to a height of many hundred feet.
**white light** (Phys.): Light containing all wavelengths in the visible range at the same intensity.
**whorl** (Bot.): A group of similar members arising from the same level on a stem, and forming a circular group around it. (Zool.): A single turn of a spirally coiled shell or other spiral structure.
**wilting** (Bot.): The loss of rigidity in leaves and young stems following the loss of water from the plant.

**winch** (Eng.): A hand power hoisting machine attached to a crane.
**wind** (Meteor.): Air in motion naturally.
**wind pollination** (Bot.): The conveyance of pollen by the wind.
**wind pump** (Civ. Eng.): A pump which is operated by the force of the wind rotating a multi-bladed propeller.
**wind tunnel** (Aero.): Apparatus for producing a steady airstream past a model for aerodynamic investigations.
**winding** (Elec. Eng.): The system of insulated conductors forming the current-carrying element of a dynamo-electric machine.
**window** (Elec. Eng.): The winding space of a transformer. (Geol.): A closed outcrop of strata lying beneath a thrust plane and exposed by denudation.
**wing** (Bot.): A flattened outgrowth from a seed or a fruit, serving in wind dispersal. (Build.): A section of a building projecting from the principal part of it. (Zool.): Any broad flat expansion; an organ used for flight.
**wing nut** (Eng.): A nut with wings similar to those of a butterfly to enable it to be turned by thumb and fingers.
**wire gauge** (Eng.): Any system of designating the size of wires by means of numbers.
**wirephoto** (Elec. Comm.): A photograph transmitted over a wire circuit by electrical means.
**wolf'ramite** (Min.): An important ore of tungsten.
**woody tissues** (Bot.): Tissues which are hard because of the presence of lignin in the cell walls.
**wool** (Bot.): A tangled mass of long, soft, whitish hairs on a plant. (Zool.): A modification of hair.
**work** (Mech.): Work is done when the point of application of a force moves along the line of action of the force.
**working chamber** (Civ. Eng.): The compressed-air chamber at the base of a hollow caisson.
**worm** (Zool.): A term loosely used to indicate any elongate invertebrate without appendages.
**wow** (Acous.): Rhythmic or arrhythmic change in reproduced sound, arising from fluctuation in speed, of either recorder or reproducer.

## X

**x-body** (Bot.): An inclusion in a plant cell suffering from a virus disease.
**x-chromosome** (Cyt.): A heterochromosome associated with sex determination.
**x-generation** (Bot.): The gametes.
**X-rays** (Phys.): Electromagnetic waves of short wavelength which are produced when cathode rays impinge on matter.
**xanth-, xantho-**: A prefix meaning yellow.
**xanthoch'roism** (Zool.): A condition in which all skin pigments other than yellow and golden ones disappear, as in goldfish.
**xanth'ophyll** (Bot., Zool.): One of the two yellow pigments present in the normal chlorophyll mixture of green plants.
**xe'mia** (Bot.): The effect of the pollen upon the characters of the young plant resulting from pollination.
**xe'nogamy** (Bot.): Pollination of a flower from a flower of the same species but on another plant.
**xe'nolith** (Geol.): A fragment of rock of extraneous origin which has been incorporated in magma, and occurs as an inclusion.
**xe'non** (Chem.): A zero-valent element; one of the rare gases.
**xerophyt'ic** (Bot.): Able to withstand drought.
**xiphoid** (Zool.): Sword-shaped.
**xy'lem** (Bot.): Wood.
**xylogenous, xylophilous** (Bot., Zool.): Growing on wood; living in or on wood.
**xylophagous** (Zool.): Wood-eating.
**xylotomous** (Zool.): Wood-cutting; wood-boring.

## Y

**yaw** (Aero.): The angular motion of an aircraft in a horizontal plane about its normal axis.
**year** (Astron.): The calendar year consisting of 365 days in ordinary years and 366 days in leap years, and beginning with January 1.
**yeast** (Bot.): Micro-organisms producing zymase, which induces the alcoholic fermentation of carbohydrates.
**yield point** (Met.): The stress at which a substantial amount of plastic deformation takes place under constant or reduced load.
**yoke** (Civ. Eng.): Stout timbers around the shuttering for a column to secure the part during the process of pouring and setting. (Elec. Eng.): The field poles of an electrical machine.
**yolk** (Zool.): The nutritive non-living material contained by an ovum.
**yolk sac** (Zool.): The yolk-containing sac which is attached to the embryo by the yolk stalk.
**yolk stalk** (Zool.): A short stalk by which the yolk sac is attached to the embryo and by which the yolk substance may pass into the alimentary canal of the embryo.
**ytter'bium** (Chem.): A metallic element.
**ytt'rium** (Chem.): A metallic element.

## Z

**zenith** (Astron.): The point on the celestial sphere vertically above the observer's head; one of the two poles of the horizon, the other being the nadir.
**zenith distance** (Astron.): The angular distance from the zenith of a heavenly body.
**zenith telescope** (Astron.): An instrument used to determine latitude.
**ze'olites** (Min.): A group of amino-silicates.
**zeph'yr** (Meteor.): A warm westerly wind blowing in the Mediterranean.
**zero-potential** (Elec. Eng.): Earth potential in electric circuits.
**zero-valent** (Chem.): Incapable of combining with other atoms.
**zeu'gite** (Bot.): A cell in which nuclear fusion occurs.
**zinc** (Met.): A white metallic element.
**zircon** (Min.): A tetragonal mineral distributed in igneous and sedimentary rocks.
**Zo'diac** (Astron.): A Greek name given to the belt of stars through which the ecliptic passes centrally.
**zo'id** (Bot.): A zoospore.
**zoid'ioph'lous** (Bot.): Pollinated by animals.
**zona** (Zool.): A zone.
**zonation** (Bot.): (1) The formation of bands of different colors on the surface of a plant. (2) The occurrence of vegetation in well-marked bands, each band having its characteristic dominant species.
**zone** (Bot.): A band of color, or of hairs or other surface feature. (Chem.): A region of oriented molecules. (Geol.): A subdivision of a stratigraphical series.
**zoning** (Aero.): The specification of areas in which there is a known clearance for the safe landing and taking-off of airplanes.
**zo'o**: A prefix meaning animal.
**zo'obiot'ic** (Biol.): Parasitic on, or living in association with, an animal.
**zo'ochor'ous** (Bot.): Said of seeds or spores dispersed by animals.
**zo'ogam'ete** (Zool.): A motile gamete.
**zoogamy** (Zool.): Sexual reproduction of animals.
**zo'ogeog'raphy** (Zool.): The study of animal distribution.
**zooming** (Aero.): Utilizing the kinetic energy of an aircraft in order to gain height.
**zo'oplank'ton** (Zool.): Floating and drifting animal life.
**zo'ospore** (Bot.): An asexual reproductive cell which can swim by means of flagella.
**zyg-, zy'go-**: A prefix meaning yoke.
**zygobran'chiate** (Zool.): Having paired, symmetrically placed gills.
**zy'gophase** (Biol.): The diploid portion of the life-history.
**zy'gopleur'y** (Zool.): Bilateral symmetry.
**zy'gote** (Bot., Zool.): The product of the union of two gametes.
**zy'gotene** (Cyt.): The second stage of meiotic prophase, in which the chromatin threads approximate in pairs and become loops.
**zy'mase** (Chem.): An enzyme inducing the alcoholic fermentation of carbohydrates.
**zymot'ic** (Med.): Pertaining to or causing an infectious disease.

# Bible Dictionary

# Bible Dictionary

## KEY TO PRONUNCIATION

The hyphen (-) separates unaccented syllables. The double hyphen (=) separates compound words. (′) marks the primary accent and (″) the secondary accent.

ā as in fāte; â in courâge; ă in hăt; â in câre; ä in fär; ȧ in lȧst; ạ in fạll; a̤ obscure as in lia̤r.

ē as in mēte; ê in rêdeem; ĕ in mĕt; ẽ obtuse as in tẽrm; e̤ obscure as in fue̤l.

ī as in pīne; î in cîtation; ĭ in pĭn; ĩ obtuse in fĩrm; i̤ in famili̤ar; i̤ obscure in rui̤n.

ō as in nōte; ô in annôtate; ŏ in nŏt; ô in fôr; o̤ obscure as in valo̤r.

ū as in mūte; û in tûb; û obtuse as in hûrl; u̇ in ru̇de; u in push.

ȳ as in stȳle; ỹ in nỹmph.

ç soft as in çent; c hard not marked; ġ soft as in ġender; g̃ hard before e, i, and y, as g̃et, G̃ideon; g hard otherwise not marked; ş as z in muşe; ҳ as *gz* in example.

## A

**Ā.** See ALPHA.

**Aâr′o̤n** (*mountaineer or enlightener*). Son of Amram and Jochebed, and elder brother of Moses and Miriam, Num. xxvi. 59. Direct descendant of Levi by both parents. Called "the Levite," Ex. iv. 14, when chosen as the "spokesman" of Moses. Married Elisheba, daughter of the prince of Judah, and had four sons, Nadab, Abihu, Eleazar, and Ithamar, Ex. vi. 23. Eighty-three years old when introduced in the Bible. Mouthpiece and encourager of Moses before the Lord and the people of Israel, and in the Court of the Pharaoh, Ex. iv. 30; vii. 2. Miracle worker of the Exodus, Ex. vii. 19. Helped Hur to stay the weary hands of Moses in the battle with Amalek, Ex. xvii. 9-12. In a weak moment yielded to idolatry among his people and incurred the wrath of Moses, Ex. xxxii. Consecrated to the priesthood by Moses, Ex. xxix. Anointed and sanctified, with his sons, to minister in the priest's office, Ex. xl. Murmured against Moses at the instance of Miriam, but repented and joined Moses in prayer for Miriam's recovery, Num. xii. His authority in Israel vindicated by the miracle of the rod, Num. xvii. Died on Mt. Hor, at age of one hundred and twenty-three years, and was succeeded in the priesthood by his son Eleazar, Num. xx. 22-29. Office continued in his line till time of Eli. Restored to house of Eleazar by Solomon, 1 Kgs. ii. 27.

**Aâr′o̤n-ītes.** Priests of the line of Aaron, 1 Chr. xii. 27, of whom Jehoiada was "chief," or "leader," in the time of King Saul, 1 Chr. xxvii. 5.

**Ăb** (*father*). (1) A syllable of frequent occurrence in the composition of Hebrew proper names, and signifies possession or endowment. Appears in Chaldaic form of Abba in N. T., Mark xiv. 36; Rom. viii. 15; Gal. iv. 6. (2) Eleventh month of the Jewish civil, and fifth of the sacred, year; corresponding to parts of July and August. [MONTH.]

**Ăb′ă-cŭc,** 2 Esdr. i. 40. [HABAKKUK.]

**Ȧ-băd′don** (*destroyer*). King of the locusts, and angel of the bottomless pit. The Greek equivalent is Apollyon, Rev. ix. 11.

**Ăb″ă-dī′as.** 1 Esdr. viii. 35. [OBADIAH.]

**Ȧ-băg′thȧ** (*God-given*). One of the seven chamberlains in the court of King Ahasuerus, Esth. i. 10.

**Ăb′ă-nȧ** (*stony*). A river of Damascus, preferred by Naaman to the Jordan for healing purposes, 2 Kgs. v. 12. Believed to be identical with the present Barada, which rises in the Anti-Libanus range, twenty-three miles N. W. of Damascus, runs by several streams through the city, and thence across a plain into the "Meadow Lakes," where it is comparatively lost.

**Ăb′ă-rĭm** (*mountains beyond*). A range of mountains or highlands of Moab, east of and facing Jordan opposite Jericho, Num. xxvii. 12; xxxiii. 47; Deut. xxxii. 49. Ije-abarim, in Num. xxi. 11, heaps or ruins of Abarim. Nebo, Peor, and Pisgah belong to this range. "Passages," in Jer. xxii. 20.

**Ăb′bȧ** (*father*). Chaldaic form of Hebrew Ab. Applied to God in Mark xiv. 36; Rom. viii. 15; Gal. iv. 6.

**Ăb′dȧ** (*servant*). (1) Father of Adoniram, 1 Kgs. iv. 6. (2) Son of Shammua, Neh. xi. 17. Called Obadiah in 1 Chr. ix. 16.

**Ăb′de̤-el** (*servant of God*). Father of Shelemiah, Jer. xxxvi. 26.

**Ăb′dī** (*my servant*). (1) A Merarite, grandfather of Ethan the Singer, and father of Kishi, 1 Chr. vi. 44. (2) Father of Kish, of Levitical descent, 2 Chr. xxix. 12. (3) Son of Elam, who had married a foreign wife, in time of Ezra, Ez. x. 26.

**Ăb′dī-as,** 2 Esdr. i. 39. [OBADIAH.]

**Ăb′dī-ĕl** (*servant of God*). Father of Ahi and son of Guni. A Gadite chief of Bashan in the time of King Jotham of Judah, 1 Chr. v. 15. Milton uses the name as that of a fallen angel.

**Ab′dŏn** (*servile*). (1) An Ephraimite judge of Israel for eight years, Judg. xii. 13-15. Supposed to be same as Bedan in 1 Sam. xii. 11. (2) Son of Shashak, 1 Chr. viii. 23. (3) A Benjamite, son of Jehiel, of Gibeon, 1 Chr. viii. 30; ix. 36. (4) Son of Micah in Josiah's time, 2 Chr. xxxiv. 20; supposably Achbor in 2 Kgs. xxii. 12. (5) A city in tribe of Asher, assigned to the Levites, Josh. xxi. 30; 1 Chr. vi. 74; associated with modern Abdeh, 10 miles N. E. of Accho, or Acre, the Ptolemais of N. T.

**Ȧ-bĕd′=nē-gō** (*servant of Nego, or Nebo, name of planet Mercury worshipped as scribe and interpreter*). Name given by the prince of Chaldean eunuchs to Azariah, one of the three friends and fellow-captives at Babylon of Daniel, Dan. i. 7. He refused to bow to the golden image of Nebuchadnezzar, and was condemned to the fiery furnace, from which he miraculously escaped, Dan. iii.

**Ā′bĕl** (*breath, vapor*). Second son of Adam and Eve. A keeper of sheep, and murdered by his brother Cain through jealousy, Gen. iv. 2-8. *See* also Heb. xi. 4; 1 John iii. 12; Matt. xxiii. 35.

**Ā′bĕl** (*meadow*). A prefix for several names of towns and places. (1) The "plain of the vineyards" in Judg. xi. 33; *see* marg. (2) A city in the north of Palestine, attacked by Joab, 2 Sam. xx. 14, 15. Probably same as Abel-Beth-Maachah. "Plain of the vineyard," Judg. xi. 33, marg. note. "Great stone of," 1 Sam. vi. 18.

**Ā′bĕl=bĕth=mā′a̤-chah** (*meadow of house of oppression*). A town in N. Palestine, near Damascus, doubtless the same as attacked by Joab, 2 Sam. xx. 14, 15; and attacked by Benhadad, 1 Kgs. xv. 20, and by Tiglath-pileser, 2 Kgs. xv. 29.

**Ā′bĕl=mā′im** (*meadow of waters*). Another name for Abel-beth-maachah, 2 Chr. xvi. 4.

**Ā′bĕl=mē-hō′lah** (*meadow of the dance*). A place in the Jordan valley, 1 Kgs. iv. 12, whither fled the enemy routed by Gideon, Judg. vii. 22. Home of Elisha, 1 Kgs. xix. 16.

**Ā′bĕl=mĭz′rā-ĭm** (*meadow, or mourning, of Egypt*). A name given by the Canaanites to the threshing floor of Atad, where Joseph and his brethren mourned for Jacob, Gen. l. 11. Probably near Hebron.

**Ā'bĕl-shĭt'tim** (*meadow of the acacias*). A spot near Jordan, in Moabite plain, and last halting place of the wandering Israelites, Num. xxxiii. 49. Called Shittim in Num. xxv. 1; Josh. ii. 1.

**Ā'bĕl, Stone of.** Place in the field of Joshua, the Bethshemite, where the ark of the Lord was set down, 1 Sam. vi. 18.

**Ā'bĕz** (*lofty*). A town in the section allotted to the tribe of Issachar, Josh. xix. 20.

**Ā'bī** (*progenitor*). Mother of King Hezekiah and daughter of Zachariah, 2 Kgs. xviii. 2; Isa. viii. 2. Abijah in 2 Chr. xxix. 1.

**Ȧ-bī'ȧ, Ȧ-bī'ah,** and **Ȧ-bī'jah** (*the Lord is my father*), are variants of the same word. Abia in 1 Chr. iii. 10, and Matt. i. 7, is the son of Rehoboam; and in Luke i. 5, is the eighth of the twenty-four courses of priests. For division of priests *see* 1 Chr. xxiv. and particularly vs. 10.

**Ȧ-bī'ah.** (1) A son of Becher, 1 Chr. vii. 8. (2) Wife of Hezron, 1 Chr. ii. 24. (3) Second son of Samuel and associate judge with Joel in Beersheba, 1 Sam. viii. 2; 1 Chr. vi. 28.

**Ā''bī-ăl'bŏn** (*father of strength*). One of David's warriors, 2 Sam. xxiii. 31. Spelled Abiel in other places.

**Ȧ-bī'ă-săph** (*father of gathering*). A Levite, one of the sons of Korah, and head of a Korhite family, Ex. vi. 24. Written Ebiasaph in 1 Chr. vi. 23, 37.

**Ȧ-bī'a-thär** (*father of abundance*). Son of Ahimelech, and fourth high priest in descent from Eli, of the line of Ithamar, younger son of Aaron, 1 Sam. xxiii. 9, only one of Ahimelech's sons who escaped the vengeance of Saul in the slaughter at Nob, 1 Sam. xxii. 19, 20. Fled to David at Keilah, and became a high priest. Deprived of the high priesthood by Solomon. For fuller history read 1 Sam. xxii. to 1 Kgs. iii.

**Ā'bīb** (*green fruits*), called also Nisan. Seventh month of Jewish civil, and first of the sacred year, Ex. xii. 2. [MONTH.]

**Ȧ-bī'dȧ** and **Ȧ-bī'dah** (*father of knowledge*). One of the sons of Midian, 1 Chr. i. 33; Gen. xxv. 4.

**Ăb'i-dăn** (*father of judgment*). Chief of the tribe of Benjamin at exode, Num. i. 11; ii. 22; vii. 60; x. 24.

**Ȧ-bī'el** (*father of strength*). (1) Father of Kish and grandfather of Saul and Abner, 1 Sam. ix. 1. (2) One of David's generals, 1 Chr. xi. 32, called Abialbon in 2 Sam. xxiii. 31.

**Ā''bī-ē'zer** (*father of help*). (1) Eldest son of Gilead and head of a family in tribe of Manasseh, Josh. xvii. 2; 1 Chr. vii. 18. (2) One of David's mighty men, 2 Sam. xxiii. 27; 1 Chr. xi. 28; xxvii. 12.

**Ā''bī-ĕz'rīte** (*father of help*). A family descended from Abiezer, Judg. vi. 11; viii. 32.

**Ăb'ī-gāil** (*father of joy*). (1) Wife of Nabal of Carmel, and afterwards of David. Noted for her beauty and wisdom, 1 Sam. xxv. 3, 14–44. (2) A sister of David, married to Jether the Ishmaelite, and mother of Amasa, 2 Sam. xvii. 25; 1 Chr. ii. 17.

**Ăb''i-hā'il** (*father of strength*). (1) Father of Zuriel, chief of the house of the families of Marari, Num. iii. 35. (2) Wife of Abishur, 1 Chr. ii. 29. (3) Son of Huri of the tribe of Gad, 1 Chr. v. 14. (4) Wife of Rehoboam, 2 Chr. xi. 18. (5) Father of Esther and uncle of Mordecai, Esth. ii. 15; ix. 29.

**Ȧ-bī'hū** (*God is father*). Second son of Aaron and Elisheba, Num. iii. 2; Ex. vi. 23. Ascended Sinai with Moses and the elders, Ex. xxviii. 1. Set apart with his brothers for the priesthood. Consumed, with his brother Nadab, for offering strange fire before the Lord, Lev. x. 1, 2.

**Ȧ-bī'hŭd** (*father of praise*). Son of Bela and grandson of Benjamin, 1 Chr. viii. 3.

**A-bī'jah** and **Ȧ-bī'jam** (*whose father is Jehovah*). (1) A son of King Jeroboam I.; died in early life, 1 Kgs. xiv. (2) Son of Rehoboam, and his successor to the throne. A wicked king. Reign, 959–956 B. C., 2 Chr. xii. 16; xiii. Written Abijam in 1 Kgs. xv. 1. (3) A descendant of the high priest Eleazar, 1 Chr. xxiv. 10; Neh. xii. 17. The priestly course *Abia*, Luke i. 5, belonged to Zacharias, father of John the Baptist. (4) A priest who entered the covenant with Nehemiah, Neh. x. 7.

**Ȧ-bī'jam.** *See* ABIJAH (2).

**Ăb-ĭ-le'nē** (from Abila, *land of meadows*). A Syrian tetrarchy whose capital was Abila, situated on the eastern slopes of the Anti-Libanus range. The district was watered by the Abana River. Governed by Lysanias in the time of John the Baptist, Luke iii. 1.

**Ȧ-bĭm'ă-el** (*father of Mael*). A descendant of Joktan, and supposable father of the Arabic tribe of Mali, Gen. x. 28.

**Ȧ-bĭm'ĕ-lech** (*father of a king*). (1) A line of Philistine kings, like the Pharaohs and Cæsars. Kings of Gerar, Gen. xx., xxi., xxvi. 1. (2) Son of Gideon by his concubine of Shechem, Judg. viii. 31; 2 Sam. xi. 21. (3) Son of Abiathar, in David's time, 1 Chr. xviii. 16. (4) Written for the Achish of 1 Sam. xxi. 10, in title to Ps. 34.

**Ȧ-bĭn'ă-dăb** (*father of nobility*). (1) A Levite of Kirjath-jearim to whose house the ark was brought, and where it stayed for twenty years, 1 Sam. vii. 1, 2; 1 Chr. xiii. 7. (2) Second son of Jesse, and one of the three who followed Saul to battle, 1 Sam. xvi. 8; xvii. 13. (3) Son of Saul slain at Gilboa, 1 Sam. xxxi. 2. (4) Father of one of the twelve chief officers of Solomon, 1 Kgs. iv. 11.

**Ăb'ĭ-nēr,** Hebrew form of Abner, 1 Sam. xiv. 50, marg.

**Ȧ-bĭn'ŏ-ăm** (*gracious father*). Father of Barak, Judg. iv. 6, 12; v. 1, 12.

**Ȧ-bī'răm** (*high father*). (1) A Reubenite conspirator with Korah, Num. xvi. (2) Eldest son of Hiel, 1 Kgs. xvi. 34; written Abiron in Ecclus. xlv. 18.

**Ăb-ĭ-sē'ĭ,** or **Ăb'ĭ-shū,** son of Phinehas, 2 Esdr. i. 2. Abisum in 1 Esdr. viii. 2.

**Ăb'ĭ-shag** (*ignorance of the father*). The fair Shunamite, of tribe of Issachar, whom David, in his old age, introduced into his harem, 1 Kgs. i. 1-4. After David's death, Adonijah desired to marry her, but Solomon put him to death, 1 Kgs. ii. 13, etc.

**Ȧ-bĭsh'ă-ī** (*father of gift*). (1) Eldest son of David's sister Zeruiah and brother of Joab, 1 Chr. ii. 16; one of the chiefs of David's mighty men, 2 Sam. ii. 18. Counselled David to take Saul's life, 1 Sam. xxvi. 5-12. Associated with Joab in assassination of Abner, 2 Sam. iii. 30. A co-general of David's army, 2 Sam. x. 14; xviii. 2. Rescued David from the giant Ishbi-benob, 2 Sam. xxi. 16, 17.

**Ȧ-bĭsh'a-lŏm** (*father of peace*). Father-in-law of King Jeroboam, 1 Kgs. xv. 2, 10. Called Absalom in 2 Chr. xi. 20, 21.

**Ȧ-bĭsh'ū-ȧ** (*father of deliverance*). (1) Son of Bela, 1 Chr. viii. 4. (2) Son of Phinehas, 1 Chr. vi. 4, 5, 50; Ez. vii. 5.

**Ăb'ĭ-shur** (*father of the wall*). Son of Shammai, 1 Chr. ii. 28, 29.

**Ăb'ĭ-tal** (*father of dew*). One of David's wives, 2 Sam. iii. 4; 1 Chr. iii. 3.

**Ăb'ĭ-tŭb** (*father of goodness*). A Benjamite, 1 Chr. viii. 11.

**A-bi'ud** (*father of praise*). An ancestor of Christ, Matt. i. 13.

**Ăb-lū'tion.** [PURIFICATION.]

**Ăb'nēr** (*father of light*). (1) Son of Ner, and commander-in-chief of Saul's armies, 1 Sam. xiv. 50, 51; xvii. 57; xxvi. 5-14. Proclaimed Ishbosheth King of Israel, and went to war with David, by whom he was defeated, 2 Sam. ii. Quarrelled with Ishbosheth and espoused the cause of David, 2 Sam. iii. 7, etc. Murdered by Joab, 2 Sam. iii. 27-39. (2) Father of a Benjamite chief, 1 Chr. xxvii. 21.

**Ȧ-bŏm-ĭ-nā'tion** (*bad omen*). A hateful or detestable thing, Gen. xlvi. 34. Used as to animals and acts in Lev. xi. 13; Deut. xxiii. 18. As to idolatry in 2 Kgs. xxiii. 13; Jer. xliv. 4. As to sins in general, Isa. lxvi. 3. The "abomination of desolation" in Dan. ix. 27; xii. 11; Matt. xxiv 15, doubtless refers to the standards and banners of the conquering Roman armies with their idolatrous images and legends.

**Ā'bră-hăm** and **Ā'brăm** (*father of a multitude*). Son of Terah, a dweller in Ur of the Chaldees, Gen. xi. 25-31. Founder of the Jewish nation. Migrated from Chaldea to Haran. Moved thence to Canaan, to Egypt and back to Canaan, where he settled amid the oak-groves of Mamre. There confirmed in the thrice repeated promise that his seed should become a mighty nation, and his name changed from Abram to Abraham. Died, aged 175 years, and was buried in the tomb of Machpelah, Gen. xii.-xxvi.

**Ăb'sa-lŏm** (*father of peace*). (1) A son of David, 2 Sam. iii. 3. Killed his brother Amnon, 2 Sam. xiii. Fled to Geshur, 2 Sam. xiii. 37, 38. Returned and conspired to usurp his father's throne, 2 Sam. xiv.-xvii. Defeated at Gilead and slain by Joab, 2 Sam. xviii. (2) Father of Mattathias, 1 Macc. xi. 70.

**Ăb'sa-lŏm's Pĭl'lar,** built by Absalom in the "King's dale," or valley of Kedron, 2 Sam. xviii. 18.

**Ăb'sa-lŏn.** An ambassador of John to Lysias, 2 Macc. xi. 17.

**Ā-bū'bŭs.** Son-in-law of Simon, 1 Macc. xvi. 11-15.

**Ā-cā'çĭ-à** (*point*). The *Acacia seyal* of Arabia, a large tree, highly prized for its wood, is supposed to be the Shittim wood of the Bible. A smaller species (*Acacia Arabica*) yielded an aromatic gum.

**Ăc'ă-tăn.** 1 Esdr. viii. 38. [HAKKATAN.]

**Ăc'căd** (*fortress*). A city built by Nimrod in Shinar, Gen. x. 10.

**Ăc'ca-rŏn.** [EKRON.]

**Ăc'chō** (*heated sand*). The Ptolemais of N. T.; now Acre, on Mediterranean coast, Judg. i. 31; Acts xxi. 7.

**Ăc'cŏs.** Grandfather of Eupolemus, 1 Macc. viii. 17

**Ā-çĕl'da-mà** (*field of blood*). A field near Jerusalem purchased with Judas' betrayal money, and in which he violently died, Acts i. 19. But bought by the priests as a potters' field in Matt. xxvii. 7.

**Ā-chā'ịà** (*trouble*). Originally a narrow strip of country on north coast of Peloponnesus, but Achaia and Macedonia came to designate all Greece, Acts xviii. 12, 27; xix. 21; Rom. xv. 26; 2 Cor. i. 1; ix. 2; xi. 10; 1 Thess. i. 7, 8.

**Ā-chā'i-cus** (*of Achaia*). An Achaian friend of Paul, 1 Cor. xvi. 17.

**Ā'chăn** and **Ā'char** (*troubler*). The Judahite who was stoned to death for concealing the spoils of Jericho, Josh. vii. 16–26. Written ACHAR in 1 Chr. ii. 7.

**Ā'chăz** (*one that takes*). In Matt. i. 9 for AHAZ, King of Judah.

**Ăch'bôr** (*mouse*). (1) Father of Baal-hanan king of Edom, Gen. xxxvi. 38, 39. (2) A contemporary of Josiah, 2 Kgs. xxii. 12-14; Jer. xxvi. 22; xxxvi. 12. Written ABDON in 2 Chr. xxxiv. 20.

**Ā''chĭ-ăch'ă-rŭs.** Chief minister of Esarhaddon in Nineveh, Tobit i. 21.

**Ā-chī'ăs.** A progenitor of Esdras, 2 Esdr. i. 2.

**Ā'chĭm.** Son of Sadoc, in Christ's genealogy, Matt. i. 14.

**Ā'chĭ-ôr.** A general in army of Holofernes, Judith v., vii., xiii., xiv.

**Ā'chĭsh** (ā'kĭsh) (*serpent-charmer*). A Philistine king of Gath to whom David twice fled for safety, 1 Sam. xxi. 10–13; xxvii.–xxix.; 1 Kgs. ii. 39, 40. Called Abimelech in title to Ps. xxxiv.

**Ăch'ĭ-tôb** and **Ăch'ĭ-tŭb.** A priest in genealogy of Esdras, 1 Esdr. viii. 2.

**Ăch'me-thà.** The Median city of Ecbatana, Ez. vi. 2.

**Ā'chôr**, valley of. [ACHAN.]

**Ăch'sà** and **Ăch'sah** (*anklet*). Daughter of Caleb. Given in marriage to her uncle Othniel. Josh. xv. 15-18; Judg. i. 12–15. Achsa in 1 Chr. ii. 49.

**Ăch'shăph** (*fascination*). A city of Asher, Josh. xi. 1; xii. 20; xix. 25.

**Ăch'zĭb** (*false*). (1) A town of Judah, Josh. xv. 44. (2) A town of Asher, Josh. xix. 29.

**Ăc'i-phă.** [HAKUPHA.] 1 Esdr. v. 31.

**Ăc'i-thō.** A progenitor of Judith, Judith viii. 1.

**Ā-crăb'bim.** [MAALEH-ACRABBIM.] Josh. xv. 3.

**Acts of the Apostles.** Fifth Book of N. T. Supposably compiled by Luke, shortly after A. D. 63. It carries on the Christian narrative from the ascension of Christ to first imprisonment of Paul, a period of about thirty-three years.

**Ā-cū'ă.** [AKKUB.] 1 Esdr. v. 30.

**Ā'cŭb.** [BAKBUK.] 1 Esdr. v. 31.

**Ăd'ă-dah** (*boundary*). A town in southern Judah, Josh. xv. 22.

**Ā'dah** (*beauty*). (1) One of Lamech's wives, Gen. iv. 19. (2) One of Esau's wives, Gen. xxxvi. 2, 4. Called Bashemath in Gen. xxvi. 34.

**Ăd''a-ī'ah** (*adorned by Jehovah*). (1) Maternal grandfather of King Josiah, 2 Kgs. xxii. 1. (2) A Levite, 1 Chr. vi. 41; called Iddo in vs. 21. (3) A Benjamite, 1 Chr. viii. 21. (4) A son of Jehoram, 1 Chr. ix. 12; Neh. xi. 12. (5) Ancestor of Maaseiah, 2 Chr. xxiii. 1. (6) A descendant of Bani, Ez. x. 29, 39. (7) A Judahite, Neh. xi. 5.

**Ăd''a-lī'à** (*fire-god*). Fifth son of Haman, Esth. ix. 8.

**Ăd'ăm** (*red earth*). A city of Reuben, on Jordan, Josh. iii. 16.

**Ăd'ăm** (*red earth*). Used generically for man and woman, and translated *man* in Gen. i. 26, 27; v. 1; Job xx. 29; xxi. 33; Ps. lxviii. 18; lxxvi. 10.

**Ăd'ăm** (*red earth*). The first man. Creative work of the sixth day. Placed in the "Garden of Eden." Tempted to eat of the forbidden fruit, fell under God's disfavor, and driven out of the Garden subject to the curse of sorrow and toil. Died at age of 930 years. Gen. i. 26, etc.; ii.–v.

**Ăd'a-mah** (*earth*). A fenced city of Naphtali, Josh. xix. 36.

**Ăd'a-mănt** (*diamond*). The original is translated "adamant" in Ezek. iii. 9; Zech. vii. 12; and "diamond" in Jer. xvii. 1. Used metaphorically. [DIAMOND.]

**Ăd'a-mī** (*earth*). A place on the border of Naphtali, Josh. xix. 33.

**Ā'där** (*height*). A boundary town of Edom and Judah, Josh. xv. 3.

**Ā'där.** Sixth month of Jewish civil, and twelfth of sacred, year; corresponding to parts of February and March, Esth. iii. 7.

**Ăd'a-să.** A place in Judea, 1 Macc. vii. 40, 45.

**Ăd'bē-ĕl** (*breath of God*). A son of Ishmael, Gen. xxv. 13; 1 Chr. i. 29.

**Ăd'dăn** (*stony*). One of the places from which Jewish captives returned, Ez. ii. 59. Addon in Neh. vii. 61.

**Ăd'där** (*mighty*). Son of Bela, 1 Chron. viii. 3.

**Ăd'dĕr** (*viper*). Used in the Bible for any poisonous snake known to the Jews, of which there were several species in Palestine. In Gen. xlix. 17, the cerastes, or horned snake, is, from its habits, supposed to be alluded to. The cockatrice of Isa. xi. 8; xiv. 29; lix. 5; Jer. viii. 17, is adder and asp in Prov. xxiii. 32; Ps. lviii. 4. In Ps. cxl. 3 and Prov. xxiii. 32, a species of viper is thought to be meant.

**Ăd'dī** (*adorned*). Son of Cosam in Christ's genealogy, Luke iii. 28.

**Ăd'dŏn.** [ADDAN.]

**Ăd'dŭs.** (1) Son of the servant of Solomon, 1 Esdr. v. 34. (2) A priest in time of Ezra, 1 Esdr. v. 38.

**Ā'der** (*flock*). A Benjamite, 1 Chr. viii. 15. Properly EDER.

**Ăd'ĭ-dà.** A town of lower Judah, 1 Macc. xii. 38.

**Ā-dī'el** (*ornament of God*). (1) A prince of Simeon, 1 Chr. iv. 36. (2) A priest, 1 Chr. ix. 12. (3) An ancestor of David's treasurer, Azmaveth, 1 Chr. xxvii. 25.

**Ā-dĭn** (*dainty*). Head of a returned family, Ez. ii. 15; viii. 6; Neh. vii. 20; x. 16.

**Ăd'ĭ-nà** (*slender*). One of David's captains, 1 Chr. xi. 42.

**Ăd'ĭ-nō.** One of David's mighty men, 2 Sam. xxiii. 8. [JASHOBEAM.]

**Ăd'ị-nŭs**, 1 Esdr. ix. 48. [JAMIN.]

**Ăd''ị-thā'im** (*double ornament*). A town of Judah, Josh. xv. 36.

**Ăd-jūre'.** To bind under a curse, Josh. vi. 26; 1 Sam. xiv. 24. To require a declaration of truth at the peril of God's displeasure, Matt. xxvi. 63.

**Ăd'la-ī** (*Jehovah's justice*). Ancestor of Shaphat, 1 Chr. xxvii. 29.

**Ăd'mah** (*fort*). One of the cities of the plain of Siddim, Gen. x. 19; xiv. 2. Destroyed with Sodom, Deut. xxix. 23; Hos. xi. 8.

**Ăd'mă-thà** (*earthy*). One of the seven Persian princes, in Esth. i. 14.

**Ăd'nà** (*pleasure*). (1) Father of a returned family, Ez. x. 30. (2) A priest in days of Joiakim, Neh. xii. 15.

**Ăd'nah** (*pleasure*). (1) One of Saul's captains who deserted to David, 1 Chr. xii. 20. (2) A captain in Jehoshaphat's army, 2 Chr. xvii. 14.

**Ăd''ō-nā'ī** (*Lord*). The Hebrews spoke this word where the word Jehovah occurred.

**Ā-dŏn'ī=bē'zek** (*lord of Bezek*). King of Bezek, vanquished by Judah, Judg. i. 3–7.

**Ăd''ŏ-nī'jah** (*the Lord is Jehovah*). (1) Fourth son of David, by Haggith, and rival of Solomon for the throne. Afterwards put to death by Solomon, 2 Sam. iii. 4; 1 Kgs. i., ii. (2) A Levite, 2 Chr. xvii. 8. (3) Same as Adonikam, Neh. x. 16.

**Ā-dŏn'ĭ-kăm** (*the Lord is raised*). He returned from captivity with Zerubbabel, Ezr. ii. 13; Neh. vii. 18; 1 Esdr. v. 14. Called Adonijah in Neh. x. 16.

**Ăd''ŏ-nī'ram** (*lord of heights*). Chief receiver of tribute under David, Solomon, and Rehoboam, 1 Kgs. iv. 6. Written Adoram in 2 Sam. xx. 24; 1 Kgs.

xii. 18; and Hadoram in 2 Chr. x. 18.

**A-dŏn'ī=zē'dec** (*lord of justice*). The Amorite king of Jerusalem who formed a league against Joshua, and was slain, Josh. x. 1-27.

**A-dŏp'tion** (*a choosing to*). Receiving a stranger into one's family as an own child thereof, Ex. ii. 10; Esth. ii. 7. Figuratively, reception into the family of God, Rom. viii. 15-17; Gal. iv. 5; Eph. i. 5.

**A-dō'rȧ**, or **Ā'dŏr**, 1 Macc. xiii. 20. [ADORAIM.]

**Ăd″ŏ-rā'ĭm** (*double mound*). A city of Judah, 2 Chr. xi. 9.

**A-dō'răm.** [ADONIRAM and HADORAM.]

**Ăd″ŏ-rā'tion** (*address*). The act of paying homage to God; as in bending the knee, raising hands, inclining head, prostrating the body, etc., Gen. xvii. 3; Ps. xcv. 6; Matt. xxviii. 9.

**A-drăm'mē-lech** (*fire king*). (1) An idol introduced into Samaria and worshipped with the cruel rites of Molech, 2 Kgs. xvii. 31. (2) Son and murderer of Sennacherib, king of Assyria, 2 Kgs. xix. 37; 2 Chr. xxxii. 21; Isa. xxxvii. 38.

**Ăd″ra-mўt'tĭ-ŭm** (*from Adramys, brother of Crœsus*). A seaport town of Mysia in Asia, Acts xvi. 7; xxvii. 2. Now Adramyti.

**Ā'drĭ-ȧ.** The Adriatic Sea, Acts xxvii. 27.

**Ā'drĭ-el** (*flock of God*). Son-in-law of Saul, 1 Sam. xviii. 19; 2 Sam. xxi. 8.

**A-dū'el.** An ancestor of Tobit, Tob. i. 1.

**A-dŭl'lăm** (*justice of the people*). (1) A city of Canaan allotted to Judah, Gen. xxxviii. 1; Josh. xii. 15; xv. 35; 2 Chr. xi. 7. Repeopled after the captivity, Neh. xi. 30; Mich. i. 15. (2) The cave Adullam was David's hiding-place, where his friends gathered, 1 Sam. xxii. 1; 2 Sam. xxiii. 13; 1 Chr. xi. 15.

**A-dŭl'lăm-īte.** A native of Adullam.

**A-dŭl'ter-y** (*ad* = to and *alter*, other). Under Hebrew law the crime of unchastity, wherein a man, married or single, had illicit intercourse with a married or betrothed woman, not his wife. Punished with fire, Gen. xxxviii. 24; by stoning, Deut. xxii. 22-24. In a spiritual sense, apostasy.

**A-dŭm'mĭm** (*a going up*). A steep pass on the road from Jericho to Jerusalem, Josh. xv. 7; xviii. 17; Luke x. 30-37.

**Ăd'vō-cāte** (*calling to*). In N. T., helper, intercessor, or comforter. Jews did not have advocates, or attorneys, till after the Roman conquest, John xiv. 16; xv. 26; xvi. 17; Acts xxiv. 1.

**Æ-dī'as**, Probably Eliah, 1 Esdr. ix. 27.

**Æ'ne-ăs**, or **Æ-nē'ăs** (*laudable*). The paralytic at Lydda, healed by Peter, Acts ix. 33, 34.

**Æ'nŏn** (*springs*). A place, west of Jordan, where John baptized, John iii. 23.

**Af-fĭn'ĭ-ty.** Relation by marriage and not by blood or birth, 1 Kgs. iii. 1. For preventive degrees *see* Lev. xviii. 6-17, and MARRIAGE.

**Ăg'ă-bȧ**, 1 Esdr. v. 30. [HAGAB.]

**Ăg'ă-bŭs** (*locust*). A prophet of Antioch, Acts xi. 28; xxi. 10.

**Ā'găg** (*flame*). General title of the kings of Amelek, Ex. xvii. 14; Num. xxiv. 7; Deut. xxv. 17; 1 Sam. xv. 8-32.

**A-găg'īte.** Subject of Agag, Esth. iii. 1-10.

**A-găr.** [HAGAR, HAGARENES, HAGARITES.]

**Ăg'āte** (from *river Achates*). A species of precious quartz. Second stone in third row of high-priest's breastplate, Ex. xxviii. 19; xxxix. 12; Isa. liv. 12; Ezek. xxvii. 16. Original sometimes translated amethyst.

**Ăg'ĕ-ē** (*fugitive*). Father of one of David's mighty men, 2 Sam. xxiii. 11.

**Ăg'rĭ-cul″ture** (*field culture*). Patriarchal life was pastoral. After the conquest of Canaan, lands were meted and bounded, and landmarks held sacred, Deut. xix. 14. The valley soils of Palestine were fertile; natural waters abundant, Deut. viii. 7; rain plentiful, Deut. xi. 14; Jer. v. 24; James v. 7. The grains grown were wheat, barley, rye, and millet. Orchards produced the vine, olive, and fig. Gardens grew beans, fitches, pease, lettuce, endive, leeks, garlic, onions, melons, cucumbers, cabbage, etc. The implements were the plough, harrow, and hoe, but these were crude. Grains were cut with the sickle, and the sheaves were threshed by treading with oxen, usually drawing sleds; while winnowing was done in sheets before the wind. Lands rested once in seven years, Lev. xxv. 1-7. The poor were allowed to glean, Lev. xix. 9, 10; Deut. xxiv. 19.

**A-grĭp'pȧ.** [HEROD.]

**Ā'gŭr** (*gatherer of wisdom*). An unknown sage who compiled Prov. xxx.

**Ā'hăb** (*uncle*). (1) Seventh king of Israel. Reigned B. C. 919-896, 1 Kgs. xvi. 29. Married Jezebel of Tyre, who introduced the worship of Baal and Astarte. One of the most notorious of O. T. characters. Slain by a chance arrow, and the "dogs licked his blood" according to prophecy, 1 Kgs. xviii.-xxii.; 2 Chr. xviii. (2) A false prophet at Babylon, Jer. xxix. 22.

**A-hăr'ah** (*after the brother*). Third son of Benjamin, 1 Chr. viii. 1. [AHER and AHIRAM.]

**A-hăr'hĕl** (*behind the fort*). A name in the genealogy of Judah, 1 Chr. iv. 8.

**A-hăs'ā-ī** (*whom Jehovah upholds*). A priest, Neh. xi. 13. Called Jahzerah in 1 Chr. ix. 12.

**A-hăs'ba-ī** (*trusting*). Father of one of David's thirty-seven captains, 2 Sam. xxiii. 34.

**A-hăs″ū-ē'rus** (*prince*). (1) King of Media, supposably Cyaxares, whose son Astyages was Darius, Dan. ix. 1. (2) A Persian king, supposed to be Cambyses, Ez. iv. 6. (3) Another Persian king, probably Xerxes. History in Esther.

**A-hā'vȧ** (*water*). The place on the Euphrates whence the captives started, on their second return, Ez. viii. 15-21.

**Ā'hăz** (*who takes*). (1) Son of Jotham, whom he succeeded, and eleventh king of Israel. Reign 742-726 B. C. Weak-minded and idolatrous, 2 Kgs. xvi.: 2 Chr. xxviii. Literally sold out his kingdom. Died dishonored, 2 Kgs. xxiii. 12; 2 Chr. xxviii. 16-27. (2) A son of Micah, 1 Chr. viii. 35, 36; ix. 42.

**Ā″ha-zī'ah** (*Jehovah sustains*). Son of Ahab, and his successor on the throne of Israel, as the eighth king. Reign 896-895 B. C. A weak and foolish idolater, 1 Kgs. xxii. 49-53. (2) Fifth king of Judah. Reign, B. C. 884, 2 Kgs. viii. 25-29. Killed in the rebellion of Jehu, 2 Kgs. ix. Called Azariah in 2 Chr. xxii. 6; and Jehoahaz in 2 Chr. xxi. 17.

**Ah'băn** (*discreet*). Son of Abishur, 1 Chr. ii. 29.

**Ā'hĕr** (*follower*). A title in genealogy of Benjamin, 1 Chr. vii. 12.

**Ā'hī** (*my brother*). (1) A Gadite chief, 1 Chr. v. 15. (2) An Asherite, 1 Chr. vii. 34.

**A-hī'ah** and **A-hī'jah** (*Jehovah's friend*). (1) A priest in Shiloh, 1 Sam. xiv. 3-18. (2) One of Solomon's princes, 1 Kgs. iv. 3. (3) A prophet of Shiloh, 1 Kgs. xiv. 2. His prophecies are in 1 Kgs. xi. 30-39 and 1 Kgs. xiv. 6-16. (4) Father of Baasha, 1 Kgs. xv. 27-34. (5) Name of several other Bible characters, 1 Chr. ii. 25; viii. 7; xi. 36; xxvi. 20; Neh. x. 26.

**A-hī'am** (*uncle*). One of David's thirty captains, 2 Sam. xxiii. 33; 1 Chr. xi. 35.

**A-hī'an** (*brotherly*). A Manassite, 1 Chr. vii. 19.

**Ā″hi-ē'zĕr** (*brother of help*). (1) A chieftain of Dan, Num. i. 12. (2) A chief of archers under David, 1 Chr. xii. 3.

**A-hī'hud** (*renown*). (1) A prince of Asher, Num. xxxiv. 27. (2) A chieftain of Benjamin, 1 Chr. viii. 7.

**A-hī'jah.** [AHIAH.]

**A-hī'kam** (*brother who raises*). An important court officer in reigns of Josiah and Jehoiakim, 2 Kgs. xxii. 12-14; Jer. xxvi. 24.

**A-hī'lud** (*brother born*). (1) Father of Jehoshaphat, the recorder of David's and Solomon's reigns, 2 Sam. viii. 16. (2) Father of Baana, 1 Kgs. iv. 12.

**A-hĭm'a-ăz** (*brother of wrath*). (1) Father-in-law of Saul, 1 Sam. xiv. 50. (2) Son of Zadok the high priest. Played a conspicuous part in the rebellion of Absalom, 2 Sam. xv. 24-37; xvii. 15-22; xviii. 19-33. (3) Solomon's son-in-law, 1 Kgs. iv. 15.

**A-hī'măn** (*brother of the right hand*). (1) One of the giant Anakim of Hebron, Num. xiii. 22, 23; Josh. xi. 21; Judg. i. 10. (2) A gate-keeper of Levi, 1 Chr. ix. 17.

**A-hĭm'e-lech** (*my brother is king*). (1) High priest at Nob, 1 Sam. xxi. 1. Priests of Nob slain by order of Saul, 1 Sam. xxii. 11-20. (2) A Hittite friend of David, 1 Sam. xxvi. 6.

**A-hī'mŏth** (*brother of death*). A Levite, 1 Chr. vi. 25. Mahath in vs. 35, and Maath in Luke iii. 26.

**Ā'hĭn-a-dăb** (*noble brother*). Royal purveyor to Solomon, 1 Kgs. iv. 14.

**A-hĭn'ō-am** (*gracious*). (1) Wife of Saul, 1 Sam. xiv. 50. (2) A wife of David, 1 Sam. xxv. 43; xxvii. 3; xxx. 5, 18.

**A-hī'ō** (*brotherly*). (1) He accompanied the Ark when taken from his father's house, 2 Sam. vi. 3, 4.

(2) A Benjamite, 1 Chr. viii. 14. (3) Son of Jehiel, 1 Chr. viii. 31; ix. 37.

**Ā-hī'rȧ** (*unlucky*). A chief of Naphtali, Num. i. 15.

**Ā-hī'ram** (*lofty*). Founder of the Ahiramites, Num. xxvi. 38.

**Ā-hĭs'a-mach** (*helper*). One of the Tabernacle architects, Ex. xxxi. 6; xxxv. 34; xxxviii. 23.

**Ā-hĭsh'a-här** (*brother of dawn*). A grandson of Benjamin, 1 Chr. vii. 10.

**Ā-hī'shär** (*singer's brother*). A controller of Solomon's household, 1 Kgs. iv. 6.

**Ā-hĭth'o-phel** (*brother of folly*). A privy councillor of David, 2 Sam. xv. 12; xvi. 23; xxiii. 34. Joined Absalom's conspiracy, 2 Sam. xvii. Hanged himself in despair, 2 Sam. xvii. 23.

**Ā-hī'tub** (*brother of goodness*). (1) Grandson of Eli, 1 Sam. xiv. 3; xxii. 9–11. (2) Father of Zadok the high priest, 1 Chr. vi. 7, 8, 11, 12; 2 Sam. viii. 17.

**Ah'lăb** (*fertile*). A city of Canaan, Judg. i. 31.

**Ah'lāi** (*ornamental*). Daughter of Sheshan, and wife of his slave, Jarha, 1 Chr. ii. 31–35.

**Ā-hō'ah** (*brotherly*). Grandson of Benjamin, 1 Chr. viii. 4. Called Ahiah in 1 Chr. viii. 7.

**Ā-hō'hīte.** From Ahoah, a patronymic of some of David's mighty men, 2 Sam. xxiii. 9, 28; 1 Chr. xi. 12; xxvii. 4.

**Ā-hō'lah** (*her tent*). The harlot used by Ezekiel to type Samaria, Ezek. xxiii. 4, 5, 36, 44.

**Ā-hō'lĭ-ab** (*tent of the father*). One of the Tabernacle architects, Ex. xxxv. 31–35.

**Ā-hŏl'ĭ-bah** (*my tent*). The harlot used by Ezekiel to type Jerusalem, Ezek. xxiii. 4, 11, 22, 36, 44.

**Ā''hō-lĭb'a-mah** (*tent of the height*). (1) Wife of Esau, Gen. xxxvi. 2, 25. Called Judith in Gen. xxvi. 34. (2) A title or district in Arabia Petrea, Gen. xxxvi. 41; 1 Chr. i. 52.

**Ā-hū'mȃ-ī** (*cowardly*). A descendant of Judah, 1 Chr. iv. 2.

**Ā-hū'zam** or **Ā-hŭz'zam** (*possession*). A son of Asher, 1 Chr. iv. 6.

**Ā-hŭz'zath** (*possessions*). A friend of King Abimelech, Gen. xxvi. 26.

**Ā'ī** (*heap of ruins*). (1) An ancient city of Canaan, Gen. xii. 8, where it is spelled HA'I. Captured and destroyed by Joshua, Josh. vii. 3-5; ix. 3; x. 1; xii. 9. Written Aiath in Isa. x. 28; and Aija in Neh. xi. 31; Ez. ii. 28. (2) A city of Heshbon, Jer. xlix. 3.

**Ā-ī'ah** (*vulture*). (1) Father of Saul's concubine, 2 Sam. iii. 7; xxi. 8–11. (2) Father of one of Esau's wives, 1 Chr. i. 40. Written Ajah in Gen. xxxvi. 24.

**Āij'a-lŏn.** [AJALON.]

**Āij'e-lĕth Shā'här** (*hind of the dawn*). In title to Ps. xxii. May mean a musical instrument, the argument of the Psalm, the melody, or tune name.

**Ā'in** (*eye*). (1) A landmark on eastern boundary of Canaan, Num. xxxiv. 11. (2) A Levitical city in south Judah and then in Simeon, Josh. xv. 32; xix. 7; xxi. 16. Ashan in 1 Chr. vi. 59.

**Ā-ī'rus.** A temple servant, 1 Esdr. v. 31.

**Ā'jah.** [AIAH.]

**Āj'a-lŏn** (*place of gazelles*). (1) A Levitical city of Dan, Josh. xix. 42. Became a city of refuge, Josh. xxi. 24, where it is written Aijalon; also in 1 Sam. xiv. 31. Prominent in Philistine wars, 2 Chr. xxviii. 18. Fortified as Aijalon by Rehoboam, 2 Chr. xi. 10. Now *Yalo*, 14 miles west of Jerusalem. (2) The valley in which Joshua commanded the moon to stand still, Josh. x. 12. (3) Burial place of the Judge, Elon, Judg. xii. 12.

**Ā'kan** (*keen of vision*). A Horite chieftain, Gen. xxxvi. 27. Jakan in 1 Chr. i. 42.

**Ā-kĕl'da-mȧ.** Spelling of Aceldama in Revised Version, Acts i. 19.

**Ăk'kŭb** (*insidious*). (1) A descendant of Zerubbabel, 1 Chr. iii. 24. (2) A gate-keeper of the temple, 1 Chr. ix. 17. (3) A Levite who assisted Ezra, Neh. viii. 7.

**Ā-krăb'bim** (*scorpion*). A range forming a south boundary of Judah, Num. xxxiv. 4. Maaleh-acrabbim in Josh. xv. 3. An Amorite boundary in Judg. i. 36.

**Ăl'a-băs''tẽr** (*white stone*). A whitish mineral susceptible of easy carving and fine polish, much used by ancients for vases, ointment boxes, sculptures, etc., Matt. xxvi. 7; Mark xiv. 3; Luke vii. 37.

**Ā-lăm'ĕ-lech** (*king's oak*). A border place of Asher, Josh. xix. 26.

**Ăl'a-mĕth** (*covering*). A grandson of Benjamin, 1 Chr. vii. 8.

**Ăl'a-mŏth.** Perhaps a musical instrument or melody, 1 Chr. xv. 20; Ps. xlvi. title.

**Ăl'çi-mŭs** (*valiant*). A high priest, 1 Macc. vii. 9–25.

**Ăl'e-mȧ.** A city of Gilead, 1 Macc. v. 26.

**Ăl'e-mĕth** (*covering*). (1) A city of the priests in Benjamin, 1 Chr. vi. 60. Written Almon in Josh. xxi. 18. (2) A descendant of Jonathan, 1 Chr. viii. 36; ix. 42.

**Ăl''ĕx-ăn'dẽr** (*defender of men*). (1) King of Macedon; surnamed "The Great." Born B. C. 356. Succeeded his father Philip, B. C. 336. Subjugated Asia Minor, Syria, and Palestine. Overthrew the Persian Empire, B. C. 333. Conquered Egypt, B. C. 332. Founded Alexandria, B. C. 332. Consolidated his Persian conquests, with Babylon as capital, B. C. 324. Died, perhaps in Babylon, B. C. 323. Prefigured in Dan. ii. 39; vii. 6; viii. 5–7; xi. 3. (2) Alexander Balas, son of Antiochus IV. Usurped Syrian throne, B. C. 152. His coins are still preserved, 1 Macc. x., xi. (3) Son of Simon, Mark xv. 21. (4) A kinsman of Annas the high priest, Acts iv. 6. (5) A Jewish convert at Ephesus, Acts xix. 33. (6) An Ephesian Christian reprobated by Paul, 1 Tim. i. 20, and perhaps the coppersmith in 2 Tim. iv. 14.

**Ăl''ĕx-ăn'drĭ-ȧ** (*from Alexander*). The Grecian, Roman, and Christian capital of Egypt. Founded by Alexander the Great, B. C. 332. Situated on the Mediterranean Sea, 12 miles W. of Canopic mouth of the Nile. Noted for its libraries, architecture, and commerce. Conspicuous in early church history as a Christian centre, Acts xviii. 24; xxvii. 6; xxviii. 11.

**Ăl''ĕx-ăn'drĭ-anș.** Inhabitants of Alexandria; but in Acts vi. 9, Jewish colonists from Alexandria, admitted to the privilege of citizenship and worship at Jerusalem.

**Ăl'gŭm** or **Ăl'mŭg.** Former in 2 Chr. ii. 8; ix. 10, 11; latter in 1 Kgs. x. 11, 12. Supposed to be the red sandal-wood of India. Used in temple furniture.

**Ā-lī'ah.** [ALVAH.]

**Ā-lī'an.** [ALVAN.]

**Ăl'lē-gō''ry** (*other speech*). That figure of speech by which a subject is set forth under the guise of some other subject, Gal. iv. 24.

**Ăl''le-lū'jȧ** (*Praise ye Jehovah*). Written thus in Rev. xix. 1; but HALLELUJAH, in margin of Ps. cvi., cxi., cxii., cxiii., cxvii., cxviii., cxxxv., etc. A common exclamation of joy and praise in Jewish worship.

**Ăl-lī'ance** (*ans*) (*binding to*). Hebrews forbidden to make alliances with surrounding nations but finally driven to them. Alliances solemnized by presents, oaths, feasts, monuments, offerings, and other pious ceremonies, Gen. xv. 10; xxvi. 30; xxxi. 51–53; Josh. ix. 15; 1 Kgs. xv. 18; v. 2-12; ix. 27. Breach of covenant severely punished, 2 Sam. xxi. 1; Ezek. xvii. 16.

**Ăl'lŏm,** 1 Esdr. v. 34. [AMI and AMON.]

**Ăl'lŏn** (*oak*). (1) Ancestor of Ziza, 1 Chr. iv. 37. (2) A boundary place of Naphtali, Josh. xix. 33.

**Ăl'lŏn-băch'uth** (*oak of weeping*). The tree under which Deborah was buried, Gen. xxxv. 8.

**Ăl-mō'dăd** (*immeasurable*). Progenitor of an Arab tribe, Gen. x. 26; 1 Chr. i. 20.

**Ăl'mŏn.** Josh. xxi. 18. [ALEMETH.]

**Äl'mond** (*hasten*). Tree resembles the peach in form, height, blossom, and fruit. Covering of fruit downy and succulent. Chiefly valuable for its nut. Gen. xliii. 11; Ex. xxv. 33, 34; xxxvii 19, 20; Num. xvii. 8; Eccles. xii. 5; Jer. i. 11.

**Ăl'mŏn-dĭb''la-thā'im** (*hiding of two fig cakes*). One of the last stopping places of the wandering Israelites, Num. xxxiii. 46.

**Älmș** (*pity*). Almsgiving enjoined by Mosaic law, Lev. xix. 9; Ruth ii. 2. Every third year the tithes of increase were shared with the Levite, the stranger, the fatherless and widow, Deut. xiv. 28. Receptacles for taking of alms placed in the Temple, Mark xii. 41. Almsgiving exhorted, Acts xi. 30; Rom. xv. 25-27; 1 Cor. xvi. 1–4.

**Ăl'mŭg.** [ALGUM.]

**Ăl'oes** (*ōz*). Written "Lign (*wood*) Aloes" in Num. xxiv. 6. A costly and sweet smelling wood of India, much prized in the East. Ps. xlv. 8; Prov. vii. 17; S of Sol. iv. 14; John xix. 39.

**Ā'lŏth.** Solomon's ninth commissary district, 1 Kgs. iv. 16.

**Ăl'phȧ.** First letter of the Greek alphabet. Used with omega, the last letter, to express beginning and end, Isa. xli. 4; xliv. 6; Rev. i. 8, 11; xxi. 6; xxii. 13.

**Ăl'pha-bĕt.** *Alpha* and *beta*, first and second letters of Greek alphabet. Hebrew alphabet comprised twenty-two letters.

**Ăl-phæ'us** (*changing*). (1) Father of the apostle James the Less, Matt. x. 3; Mark iii. 18; Luke vi. 15; Acts i. 13. Called Clopas or Cleophas, in John xix. 25. (2) Father of Levi or Matthew, Mark ii. 14.

**Ăl''-ta-nē'us**, 1 Esdr. ix. 33. [MATTENAI.]

**Äl'tar** (*high*). First altars were simple memorial piles, Gen. viii. 20; xii. 7; xxvi. 25; xxxv. 1. Afterwards to lay sacrifices upon, Ex. xvii. 15, 16, xxvii. 1-8. Usually built of earth or stone, Ex. xx. 24-26; but sacrificial altars quite elaborate, Ex. xl. 26-33. Still more elaborate in Solomon's Temple, 1 Kgs. viii. 64; 2 Chr. vii. 7. Altar fires to burn perpetually, Lev. vi. 12, 13. *Altar of Incense*, called "golden" to distinguish it from *Altar of Sacrifice*, called "brazen," Ex. xxx. 1-10; xl. 5, 1 Kgs. vii. 48; 1 Chr. xxviii. 18.

**Al-tăs'chith** (*destroy not*). In title to Ps. lvii., lviii., lix., and lxxv. Probably the tune is meant.

**Ā'lush** (*crowd*). Last halting-place of Israelites before Rephidim, Num. xxxiii. 13, 14.

**Ăl'vah** (*wickedness*). A duke of Edom, Gen. xxxvi. 40. Called Aliah in 1 Chr. i. 51.

**Ăl'văn** (*tall*). A Horite, Gen. xxxvi. 23. Alian in 1 Chr. i. 40.

**Ā'măd** (*enduring*). An unknown place in Asher, Josh. xix. 26.

**Ā-măd'a-thá**, Esth. xvi. 10, and Amadathus, Esth. xii. 7; Apoch. [HAMMEDATHA.]

**Ā'măl** (*labor*). An Asherite, 1 Chr. vii. 35.

**Ăm'a-lĕk** (*valley dweller*). An Edomite chieftain, Gen. xxxvi. 12; 1 Chr. i. 36.

**Ăm'a-lĕk-ītes''.** A nomad tribe of the Sinai wilderness, Gen. xiv. 7. Called the first of all nations in Num. xxiv. 20. Dwelt to the South, Num. xiii. 29. Smitten by Gideon, Judg. vii. 12-23; by Saul, 1 Sam. xv. 3-9; and David, 1 Sam. xxx. 18; 1 Chr. iv. 43. "Mount of Amalekites" was in Ephraim, Judg. xii. 15.

**Ā'măm** (*gathering place*). A city in south Judah, Josh. xv. 26.

**Ā'măn** (*mother*), Esther x. 7; Apoch. [HAMAN.]

**Ăm'a-ná** (*covenant*). Probably a mount of Anti-Libanus range, S. of Sol. iv. 8.

**Ăm''a-rī'ah** (*the Lord says*). (1) Father of Ahitub, 1 Chr. vi. 7. (2) A high priest, 2 Chr. xix. 11. (3) Head of a Kohathite family, 1 Chron. xxiii. 19; xxiv. 23. (4) Head of one of the twenty-four courses of priests, 2 Chr. xxxi. 15; Neh. x. 3. (5) A priest in Ezra's time, Ez. x. 42. (6) A priest who returned with Zerubbabel, Neh. x. 3; xii. 2, 13. (1) An ancestor of Zephaniah the prophet, Zeph. i. 1.

**Ăm'-a-sá** (*burden*). (1) Nephew of David, 2 Sam. xvii. 25. Rebelled with Absalom, and defeated by Joab, 2 Sam. xviii. 6. Reconciled to David, 2 Sam. xix. 13, and killed by Joab, 2 Sam. xx. 10. (2) A prince of Ephraim, 2 Chr. xxviii. 12.

**Ā-măs'a-ī** (*burdensome*). (1) A Levite, 1 Chr. vi. 25, 35. (2) A chief of captains who deserted to David, 1 Chr. xii. 18. (3) A priest who blew the trumpet before the Ark, 1 Chr. xv. 24. (4) A Kohathite, 2 Chr. xxix. 12.

**Ā-măsh'a-ī** (*burdensome*). A priest, Neh. xi. 13.

**Ăm-a-sī' äh** (*whom Jehovah bears*). Captain of 200,000 men in Judah, 2 Chr. xvii. 16.

**Ăm''a-thē'is**, 1 Esdr. ix. 29. [ATHLAI.]

**Ăm'a-this.** A country north of Palestine, 1 Macc. xii. 25.

**Ăm''a-zī'ah** (*strength of Jehovah*). (1) Eighth king of Judah. Reign B. C. 837-809, 2 Kgs. xiv. 1-20. Rebuked by God for idolatry, 2 Chr. xxv. 1-16. Defeated by Joash and murdered at Lachish, 2 Chr. xxv. 17-28. (2) A descendant of Simeon, 1 Chr. iv. 34. (3) A Levite, 1 Chr. vi. 45. (4) An idolatrous priest of Bethel, Amos vii. 10-17.

**Ăm-băs'sa-dŏr** (*servant*). A person chosen by one government to represent it at the seat of another Earliest mention in Num. xx. 14; Josh. ix. 4; Judg. xi. 17-19. Injury to them an insult to their king, 2 Sam. x. 3-6. The term includes both messenger and message, Luke xiv. 32. Ministers called ambassadors of Christ, 2 Cor. v. 20.

**Ăm'bĕr.** Hardly the fossil vegetable gum of commerce, Ezek. i. 4, 27; viii. 2; but rather the yellow composition of gold and silver known as *electrum*.

**Ā-mĕn'** (*true*). A final word used to fix the stamp of truth upon an assertion, Num. v. 22, Deut. xxvii. 15; Matt. vi. 13; 1 Cor. xiv. 16. Promises of God are amen, 2 Cor. i. 20. A title of Christ, Rev. iii. 14.

**Ăm'ē-thyst** (*not wine*). A purplish quartz, ranking among the precious stones, and forming the third stone in the third row of the high priest's breastplate, Ex. xxviii. 19; xxxix. 12. A stone in the foundations of the New Jerusalem, Rev. xxi. 20.

**Ā'mī** (*builder*). A returned captive, Ez. ii. 57. Amon in Neh. vii. 59.

**Ā-mĭn'a-dab**, Matt. i. 4; Luke iii. 33; for AMMINADAB.

**Ā-mĭt'ta-ī** (*true*). The father of Jonah, 2 Kgs. xiv. 25; Jon. i. 1.

**Ăm'mah** (*head*). A hill near Gibeon to which Joab pursued Abner, 2 Sam. ii. 24.

**Ăm'mī** (*my people*). Applied figuratively to the Israelites, Hos. ii. i. marg.

**Ăm-mĭd'ĭ-oi.** A family of returned captives, 1 Esdr. v. 20.

**Ăm'mĭ-el** (*people of God*). (1) The spy of Dan who perished for his evil report, Num. xiii. 12. (2) Father of Machir, 2 Sam. ix. 4, 5. (3) Father of Bathsheba, 1 Chr. iii. 5; called Eliam in 2 Sam. xi. 3. (4) A door-keeper of the Temple, 1 Chr. xxvi. 5.

**Ăm-mī'hŭd** (*people of praise*). (1) Father of the chief of Ephraim at time of Exode, Num. i. 10; ii. 18; vii. 48, 53; x. 22; 1 Chr. vii. 26. (2) A Simeonite, Num. xxxiv. 20. (3) A Naphtalite, Num. xxxiv. 28. (4) Father of Talmai, king of Geshur, 2 Sam. xiii. 37. (5) A descendant of Pharez, 1 Chr. ix. 4.

**Ăm-mĭn'a-dăb** (*one of the prince's people*). (1) A prince of Judah, Num. i. 7; ii. 3; Ruth iv. 19, 20; 1 Chr. ii. 10. (2) Chief of the sons of Uzziel, 1 Chr. xv. 10-12. (3) Written Amminadib in S. of Sol vi. 12.

**Ăm''mĭ-shăd'da-ī''** (*people of the Almighty*). Father of the prince of Dan at time of the Exode, Num. i. 12; ii. 25; vii. 66; x. 25.

**Ăm-mĭz'a-băd** (*people of the giver*). Commander in David's army, 1 Chr. xxvii. 6.

**Ăm'mŏn, Ăm'mŏn-ītes'', Chĭl'drĕn of Ăm'mŏn.** Land of the Ammonites was east of the Dead Sea between the Arnon on the south to the Jabbok on the north, Num. xxi. 24; Deut. ii. 19, 20. People called Ammonites from their ancestor Ben-Ammi; Gen. xix. 38. Nomadic, idolatrous, incursive and cruel, 1 Sam. xi. 1-3; Amos i. 13; Judg. x. 6. Reduced to servitude by David, 2 Sam. xii. 26-31. Denounced by Jeremiah and Ezekiel, Jer. xlix. 1-6; Ezek. xxv. 2-10.

**Ăm''mŏn-īt'ess.** A woman of Ammon.

**Ăm'mŏn=nō'.** [No.]

**Ăm'nŏn** (*faithful*). (1) Eldest son of David, killed by his brother Absalom, 2 Sam. xiii. 1-29. (2) Son of Shimon, 1 Chr. iv. 20.

**Ā'mok** (*deep*). A returned priest, Neh. xii. 7, 20.

**Ā'mon** or **Ā'mĕn** (*mystery*). An Egyptian god worshipped at Thebes as "Amen the Sun." Written No, in Nah. iii. 8.

**Ā'mon** (*builder*). (1) A governor of Samaria under Ahab, 1 Kgs. xxii. 26; 2 Chr. xviii. 25. (2) Fourteenth king of Judah, B. C. 642-640. A shameless idolater, and killed in a conspiracy, 2 Kgs. xxi. 19-26. Reign pictured in Zeph. i. 4; iii. 3, 4, 11.

**Ăm'ŏr-ītes** (*highlanders*). One of the nations of Canaan before the Hebrew conquest, Gen. x. 16; xiv. 7; Num. xiii. 29; Deut. i. 20; Josh. v. 1; x. 6; xi. 3; 1 Sam. xxiii. 29. Occupied both sides of the Jordan, Josh. xiii. 15-27; Num. xxi. 21.

**Ā'mos** (*weighty*). One of the lesser prophets. Lived during reigns of Uzziah and Jeroboam II., Amos i. 1-7; vii. 14-15. His book is 30th of O. T. It rebukes the sins of Israel and closes with God's promise. Book abounds in rural allusions.

**Ā'moz** (*strong*). Father of Isaiah, Isa. i. 1; 2 Kgs. xix. 2.

**Ăm-phĭp'o-lis** (*surrounded city*). A city of Macedonia, 33 miles S. W. of Philippi, Acts xvii. 1.

**Ăm'plī-as** (*large*). A Roman friend of Paul, Rom. xvi. 8.

**Ăm'răm** (*exalted*). (1) Father of Moses and Aaron, Ex. vi. 18-20. (2) A descendant of Seir, 1 Chr. i. 41; Hemdan in Gen. xxxvi. 26. (3) A son of Bani, Ez. x. 34.

**Ăm'răm-ītes.** Descendants of Amram, Num. iii. 27; 1 Chr. xxvi. 23.

**Ăm'ra-phel** (*keeper of gods*). A Hamite king who joined the expedition against Sodom, Gen. xiv.

**Ăm'ū-lĕts** (*charms*). Belts, rings, necklaces, ornaments, mystically inscribed or not, worn for protection against evil enchantment. Referred to in Gen. xxxv. 4; Judg. viii. 24; Isa. iii. 20; Hos. ii. 13.

**Ăm'zi** (*strong*). (1) A Levite, 1 Chr. vi. 46. (2) A priest, Neh. xi. 12.

**Ā'nab** (*grape*). Place in south Judah, **Josh. xi. 21.**

**Ăn'a-ĕl.** Tobit's brother, Tob. i. 21.

**Ā'nah** (*answering*). Father-in-law of Esau, Gen. xxxvi. 2-25.

**Ăn"ă-hā'rath** (*gorge*). A border place of Issachar and Manasseh, Josh. xix. 19.

**Ăn"a-ī'ah** (*whom God answers*). (1) A priest who assisted Ezra, Neh. viii. 4. (2) A co-covenanter with Nehemiah, Neh. x. 22.

**Ā'năk** (*collar*), Children of, Num. xiii. 22. [Anakim.]

**Ăn'a-kim** or **-kims.** A race of giants in southern Canaan, Deut. i. 28. Defeated by Joshua, and land given to Caleb, Josh. xi. 21-22; xiv. 12-15.

**Ăn'a-mim.** A Mizraite people, not located, Gen. x. 13.

**Ă-năm'mĕ-lech** (*kingly image*). Companion god of Adrammelech, worshipped in Samaria, and representing the female power of the sun, 2 Kgs. xvii. 31.

**Ā'nan** (*cloud*). A co-covenanter with Nehemiah, Neh. x. 26.

**An-ā'nī** (*covered by Jehovah*). A descendant of Judah, 1 Chr. iii. 24.

**Ăn-a-nī'ah** (*covered by Jehovah*). (1) A priestly assistant of Nehemiah, Neh. iii. 23. (2) A city of Benjamin, Neh. xi. 32.

**Ăn"a-nī'as** (*whom Jehovah has given*). (1) Five persons mentioned in 1 Esdr. ix. (2) The doubtful convert, whose tragic ending is narrated in Acts v. 1-11. (3) A Jewish disciple at Damascus, Acts ix. 10-27; xxii. 12. (4) A high priest, A. D. 48, Acts xxiii. 2-5; xxiv. 1.

**Ă-năn'i-ĕl.** A progenitor of Tobit, Tob. i. 1.

**Ā'năth** (*answer*). Father of Shamgar, Judg. iii. 31.

**An-ăth'e-mà** (*devoted*). The devoted thing, if inanimate, fell to the priests, Num. xviii. 18; if animate, it was to be slain, Lev. xxvii. 28, 29. In N. T. a curse, Rom. ix. 3; 1 Cor. xii. 3; xvi. 22. In the latter instance Maranatha is added, the meaning being "Let him be accursed."

**Ăn'a-thŏth** (*answers*). (1) A descendant of Benjamin, 1 Chr. vii. 8. (2) A co-covenanter with Nehemiah, Neh. x. 19. (3) A Levitical city of Benjamin, Josh. xxi. 18; 1 Chr. vi. 60; Isa. x. 30.

**Ăn'chŏr** (*hook*). Anchors for holding ships to one spot were formerly cast from the stern. Acts xxvii. 29.

**Ăn'drew** (*manly*). An Apostle of Christ, John i. 35-40; Matt. iv. 18. Brother of Simon Peter, native of Bethsaida, and fisherman. Original disciple of John the Baptist, Mark xiii. 3; John vi. 6-13; xii. 22.

**Ăn"drŏ-nī'cus** (*man conqueror*). (1) A viceroy of Antiochus at Antioch, 2 Macc. iv. 31-38. (2) Another officer of Antiochus at Garizim, 2 Macc. v. 23. (3) A Christian friend of Paul's at Rome, Rom. xvi. 7

**Ā'nem** (*two springs*). A Levitical city of Issachar, 1 Chr. vi. 73.

**Ā'nēr** (*boy*). (1) A Levitical city in Manasseh, 1 Chr. vi. 70. (2) An Amorite chief of Hebron, Gen. xiv. 13-24.

**Ăn'ĕ-thŏth-īte"**, 2 Sam. xxiii. 27; **Ăn'tŏth-īte**, 1 Chr. xi. 28; xii. 3; **Ăn"ĕ-tŏth'īte**, 1 Chr. xxvii. 12. An inhabitant of Anathoth.

**Ăn'gĕl** (*messenger*). A messenger, 2 Sam. ii. 5; Luke vii. 24. In a spiritual sense, a messenger of God, Gen. xxiv. 7; Heb. i. 14. Nature, Matt. xviii. 10. Number, 1 Kgs. xxii. 19; Matt. xxvi. 53; Heb. xii. 22. Strength, Ps. ciii. 20; Rev. v. 2. Activity, Isa. vi. 2-6. Appearance, Matt. xxviii. 2-4; Rev. x. 1, 2. Office, Isa. vi. 1-3; Rev. vi. 11; Matt. xiii. 49; xvi. 27; xxiv. 31.

**Ā'nī-am** (*sighing of the people*). A Manassite, 1 Chr. vii. 19.

**Ā'nīm** (*fountains*). A city in mountains of Judah, Josh. xv. 50.

**Ăn'īse.** A plant of the parsley family, producing aromatic seeds used in medicine and cookery, and with which tithes were paid, Matt. xxiii. 23.

**Ănk'lĕt.** Much worn in the East as ornaments for the ankles, sometimes with bells, Isa. iii. 16-20. [Bells.]

**Ăn'nà** (*gracious*). (1) Wife of Tobit, Tob. i. 9. (2) A prophetess at Jerusalem, Luke ii. 36.

**Ăn'na-as**, 1 Esdr. v. 23. [Senaah.]

**Ăn'nas** (*humble*). (1) 1 Esdr. ix. 32. Same as Harim in Ez. x. 31. (2) A Jewish high priest, A. D. 7-23. Succeeded by his son-in-law, Caiaphas, A. D. 25, John xviii. 13; Luke iii. 2.

**Ă-noint'** (*to smear on*). Anointing with oil or ointment, a common practice in East, Gen. xxviii. 18; xxxi. 13; Deut. xxviii. 40; Ruth iii. 3. A mark of respect, Luke vii. 46, Ps. xxiii. 5; or of induction to priestly office, Ex. xl. 15; Num. iii. 3; or to kingly office, 1 Sam. ix. 16; x. 1; or as an act of consecration, Ex. xxviii. 41; or as an act of healing, Mark vi. 13. Christ was anointed with the Holy Ghost, Luke iv. 18; Acts iv. 27; x. 38; Isa. lxi. 1; Ps. xlv. 7.

**Ănt** (*emmet*). Twice referred to in O. T.; first as to its diligence, and second as to its wisdom. Prov. vi. 6; xxx. 25.

**Ăn'te-lōpe** (*animal*). The word translated "fallow deer" in Deut. xiv. 5, as well as "pygarg," implies a species of antelope.

**Ăn'tī-chrīst** (*against Christ*). In 1 John ii. 18, 22; iv. 3; 2 John 7, applied to those who hold heretical opinions of the incarnation.

**Ăn'tī-ŏch** (*after Antiochus*). (1) Capital of the Greek kings of Syria, on the Orontes. First Gentile church founded there, and disciples first called Christians there; Acts xi. 19-21, 26. (2) A city of Pisidia, Acts xiii. 14. Starting point of the persecutions which followed Paul all through Asia Minor, Acts xiv.

**Ăn-tī'o-chŭs** (*opponent*). (1) A messenger of Jonathan to the Romans, 1 Macc. xii. 16. (2) King of Syria, B. C. 261. Prefigured as "King of the North" in Dan. xi. 6, etc. (3) Antiochus III., called "The Great," B. C. 223, Dan. xi. 14-19. (4) Antiochus IV., called Epiphanes, 1 Macc. i. (5) Antiochus V., Eupator, B. C. 164; 1 Macc. vi. 10. (6) Antiochus VI. and VII., 1 Macc. xii.-xvi.

**Ăn'tī-păs** (*like the father*). A martyr of Pergamos, Rev. ii. 13.

**Ăn-tĭp'a-tēr** (*for the father*). An ambassador to Lacedemon, 1 Macc. xii. 16.

**Ăn-tĭp'a-trĭs** (*for his father*). Ancient Capharsaba, rebuilt and renamed by Herod; 34 miles N. W of Jerusalem, Acts xxiii. 31.

**Ăn-tō'nī-à.** A fortress on N. W. side of Temple at Jerusalem, Acts xxi. 31-40.

**Ăn"to-thī'jah** (*answers of Jehovah*). A son of Jehoram, 1 Chr. viii. 24.

**Ăn'tŏth-īte.** A native of Anathoth, 1 Chr. xi. 28; xii. 3.

**Ā'nub** (*confederate*). A descendant of Judah, 1 Chr. iv. 8.

**Ā'nus**, 1 Esdr. ix. 48. [Bani.]

**Ăp-ā'me.** Daughter of Bartacus, 1 Esdr. iv. 29.

**Ă-pĕl'lēs** (*called*). Friend of Paul, Rom. xvi. 10.

**Āpes.** Were brought from the same countries which supplied ivory and peacocks, 1 Kgs. x. 22; 2 Chr. ix. 21.

**Ă-phär'săch-ītes, Ă-phär'săth-chītes, Ă-phär'sītes** (*rending*). Assyrian nomads settled in Samaria, Ez. iv. 9; v. 6.

**Ā'phĕk** (*strength*). (1) A royal city of the Canaanites, near Hebron, Josh. xii. 18. Probably Aphekah, Josh. xv. 53. (2) A city in the extreme north of Asher, Josh. xix. 30. Probably Aphik, Judg. i. 31. (3) A place N. W. of Jerusalem, 1 Sam. iv. 1. (4) A Philistine encampment near Jezreel, 1 Sam. xxix. 1. (5) A walled city of Syria, 1 Kgs. xx. 26.

**Ă-phē'kah**, Josh. xv. 53. [Aphek.]

**Ă-phĕr'e-ma.** Governor of Judea, 1 Macc. xi. 34.

**Ă-phĕr'ra.** Son of one of Solomon's servants, 1 Esdr. v. 34.

**Ă-phī'ah** (*refreshed*). A progenitor of Saul. 1 Sam. ix. i.

**Ā'phĭk**, Judg. i. 31. [Aphek.]

**Ăph'rah** (*dust.*) An uncertain place, Micah i. 10.

**Ăph'sēs** (*dispersion*). Chief of the 18th course of the temple service, 1 Chr. xxiv. 15.

**Ă-pŏc'ă-lypse** (*uncovered*). The Greek name for Revelation.

**Ă-pŏc'ry̆-pha** (*hidden*). That collection of 14 O. T. books not regarded as canonical. Also the rejected N. T. books

**Ăp"ŏl-lō'nĭ-à** (*belonging to Apollo*). A city of Macedonia, Acts xvii. 1.

**Ăp"ŏl-lō'nĭ-us.** (1) A governor of Celo-Syria, 2 Macc. iv. 4. (2) A general under Antiochus, 1 Macc. iii. 10-12. (2) Several other Syrian generals of same name, 1 and 2 Macc.

**Ăp"ŏl-lŏph'a-nēs.** A Syrian general, 2 Macc. x. 37.

**Ă-pŏl'lŏs** (*belonging to Apollo*). A learned Jew and Christian convert of Alexandria, who became a preacher and friend of Paul, Acts xviii. 24-28; 1 Cor. iii. 6-9; Tit. iii. 13.

**Ă-pŏll'yon** (*destroyer*). Greek name of Abaddon, "angel of the bottomless pit," Rev. ix. 11. [ABADDON.]

**Ăp'pa-im** (*nostrils*). Son of Nadab. 1 Chr. ii. 30, 31.

**Ă-pŏth'ē-cā"ry** (*to place away*). The apothecary's art was called for in the mixing of perfume. Ex. xxx. 35.

**Ă-pŏs'tle** (*one sent forth*). Official name of the twelve disciples. As to power and names *see* Matt. x. 1-42; John xvi. 13; Mark xvi. 20. In a broad sense, any one commissioned to preach the gospel, 2 Cor. viii. 23; Phil. ii. 25. Term applied to Christ, Heb. iii. 1.

**Ăp-păr'ĕl.** [CLOTHES.]

**Ăp-peal'** (*drive to*). This right acknowledged by Jewish law, Deut. xvii. 8, 9. It lay to the judges, Judg. iv. 5; then to the kings; later to a special tribunal, 2 Chr. xix. 8-10; Ez. vii. 25; finally to the Sanhedrim. Paul appealed to the Roman Emperor, Acts xxv. 11.

**Ăp'phī-ȧ** (*productive*). A Christian woman addressed by Paul, Phile. 2.

**Ăp'phŭs** (*wary*). Surname of Jonathan Maccabeus, 1 Macc. ii. 5.

**Ăp"pĭ-ī fō'rŭm** (*market-place of Appius*). A town, 43 miles S. E. of Rome, on the Appian Way, Acts xxviii. 15.

**Ăp'ple, Ăp'ple-tree** (*bursting forth, in Hebrew*). The fruit is alluded to in Prov. xxv. 11; S. of Sol. ii. 5; vii. 8. Tree mentioned in S. of Sol. ii. 3; viii. 5; Joel i. 12. For figurative use *see* Prov. vii. 2; Zech. ii. 8; Ps. xvii. 8; Lam. ii. 18.

**Ăq'uĭ-lȧ** (*eagle*). A Jewish convert of Pontus, and valuable assistant of Paul, Acts xviii. 2; 1 Cor. xvi. 19; Rom. xvi. 3, etc.

**Ār, Ār of Mō'ab** (*city*). A chief place of Moab, Num. xxi. 28; Isa. xv. 1. Aroer in Deut. ii. 36. Used to type the Moabite people or land, Deut. ii. 9, 18, 29.

**Ā'rȧ** (*lion*). Head of a family of Asher, 1 Chr. vii. 38.

**Ā'rab** (*ambush*). A city of Hebron, Josh. xv. 52.

**Ăr'a-bah** (*burnt up*). A Hebrew word, Josh. xviii. 18, designating the valley of Jordan and the Dead Sea, and the depression through Arabia to the Gulf of Akabah.

**Ă-rā'bĭ-ȧ** (*desert*). Known in O. T. as "East Country," Gen. x. 30; xxv. 6; and "Land of the Sons of the East," Gen. xxix.; Judg. vi. 3; vii. 12. Arabia, from *Arâb* the people, in 2 Chr. ix. 14; Isa. xxi. 13; Jer. xxv. 24; Ezek. xxvii. 21. That extensive peninsula lying south of Palestine and between the Red Sea, Indian Ocean, and Persian Gulf. Home of many nomadic races, and in close commerce and even kinship, through Ishmael, with the Hebrews, 1 Kgs. x 15; 2 Chr. ix 14. Paul visited it, Gal. i. 17. Often referred to by prophets, Isa. xlii. 11; Jer xxv. 24.

**Ā'răd** (*wild ass*). (1) A valorous Benjamite, 1 Chr. viii. 15. (2) A royal city of the Canaanites, Num. xxi. 1; Josh. xii. 14.

**Ăr'a-dus**, 1 Macc. xv. 23. [ARVAD.]

**Ā'rah** (*wandering*). (1) An Asherite, 1 Chr. vii. 39. (2) Head of a returned family, Ez. ii. 5; Neh. vii. 10.

**Ā'ram** (*high*). (1) Translated Mesopotamia in Gen. xxiv. 10. The high part of Syria to the N. E. of Palestine. Absorbed by Syria, with capital at Damascus, 1 Kgs. xx. 1; Isa. vii. 8; 1 Kgs. xi. 24. (2) A descendant of Nahor, Gen. xxii. 21. (3) An Asherite, 1 Chr. vii. 34. (4) An ancestor of Christ, Matt. i. 4; Luke iii. 33.

**Ā'ram-nā-ha-rā'im** (*highlands of two rivers*), Ps. lx. title.

**Ā'ram-zō'bah** [Ā'ram]. Ps. xl. title.

**Ā'ram-it"ess.** A female inhabitant of Aram, 1 Chr. vii. 14.

**Ā'răn** (*wild goat*). A Horite, Gen. xxxvi. 28.

**Ăr'ȧ-rat** (*high land*). A high mountain of Armenia, and resting place of Noah's ark, Gen. viii. 4.

**Ă-rau'nah** (*ark*). A Jebusite prince who sold his threshing-floor to David, 2 Sam. xxiv. 18-24; 1 Chr. xxi. 25.

**Ăr'bȧ** (*one of four*). A forefather of Anak, Josh. xiv. 15; xv. 13; xxi. 11.

**Ăr'bah.** Hebron, or Kirjath-arba, Gen. xxxv. 27.

**Ăr'băth-ite.** An inhabitant of the Arabah, 2 Sam. xxiii. 31; 1 Chr. xi. 32.

**Ăr-băt'tis.** A district in Palestine, 1 Macc. v. 23.

**Ăr'bel.** Hos. x. 14. [BETH-ARBEL.]

**Ăr-bē'la.** A town in Galilee, 1 Macc. ix. 2.

**Ăr'bīte.** A native of Arab, 2 Sam. xxiii. 35.

**Ărch-an'gel** (ărk-ān'jel) (*chief angel*). 1 Thess. iv. 16; Jude 9.

**Ăr"chĕ-lā'us** (*prince of the people*). A son of Herod the Great, and ethnarch (B. C. 4-A. D. 9) of Idumea, Judea, and Samaria, Matt. ii. 22.

**Ărch'e-ry** (*use of the arcus, or bow*). Use of the bow and arrow, an important art in Biblical times, Gen. xxvii. 3; Isa. xxii. 6; xlix.; 2 Ps. cxxvii. 4, 5. Benjamites noted archers, Judg. xix.-xxi.

**Ăr'chĕ-vītes.** Probably inhabitants of Erech, Ez. iv. 9.

**Ăr'chī.** A place or clan in Joseph, Josh. xvi. 2. [ARCHITE.]

**Ăr'chĭp'pus** (*chief of stables*). A Christian teacher at Colossæ, Col. iv. 17; Phil. 2.

**Ăr'chīte.** Supposed to refer to a clan of Erech, 2 Sam. xv. 32; xvi. 16; xvii. 5-14. 1 Chr. xxvii. 33.

**Ăr'chĭ-tec"ture** (*builder's art*). Descendants of Shem were city builders, Gen. iv. 17; x. 11, 12. Hebrew ideas of architecture ripened in Egypt, and by contact with Tyre. David enlarged Jerusalem. Solomon built a palace and temple, 2 Sam. v. 11; 1 Kgs. vii. The returned captives were great builders, Ez. iii. 8-10; Neh. iii.; vi. 15.

**Ărc-tū'rus** (*the bear*). The constellation Ursa Major, commonly called the "Great Bear" or "Charles's Wain," Job ix. 9; xxxviii. 32.

**Ărd** (*fugitive*). A grandson of Benjamin, Gen. xlvi. 21; Num. xxvi. 40.

**Ăr'dăth.** A field, 2 Esdr. ix. 26.

**Ărd'ites.** Descendants of Ard or Addar, Num. xxvi. 40.

**Ăr'dŏn** (*fugitive*). A son of Caleb, 1 Chr. ii. 18.

**Ă-rē'lī** (*heroic*). A son of Gad. Children called Arelites, Num. xxvi. 17; Gen. xlvi. 16.

**Ăr"ĕ-op'a-gīte.** A member of the court of Areopagus, Acts xvii. 34.

**Ăr"ĕ-op'a-gus** (*hill of Mars*). A rocky hill near the centre of Athens, where the court of justice sat, Acts xvii. 19-34.

**Ā'rēs**, 1 Esdr. v. 10. [ARAH 2.]

**Ăr'e-tas** (*excellence*). (1) An Arab chief, 2 Macc. v. 8. (2) Father-in-law of Herod Antipas, 2 Cor. xi. 32.

**Ă-rē'us.** A Lacedæmonian king, 1 Macc. xii. 20-23.

**Ăr'gŏb** (*stony*). A country of Bashan, and one of Solomon's commissary districts, Deut. iii. 4; 1 Kgs. iv. 13.

**Ă"rĭ-ȧ-rā'thes.** Mithridates IV., king of Cappadocia, B. C. 163-130, 1 Macc. xv. 22.

**Ă-rĭd'a-ī** (*strong*). Ninth son of Haman, Esth. ix. 9.

**Ă-rĭd'a-thȧ.** Sixth son of Haman, Esth. ix. 8.

**Ă-rī'eh** (*lion*). A prince of Israel, killed by Pekah, 2 Kgs. xv. 25.

**Ā'rĭ-el** (*lion of God*). (1) A leader of returning captives, Ez. viii. 16. (2) The city of Jebus-Salem, Jerusalem, Isa. xxix. 1, 2.

**Ăr"ĭ-mȧ-thæ'ȧ** (*heights*). Home of Joseph in Judea, Matt. xxvii. 57; Mark xv. 43; Luke xxiii. 51; John xix. 38.

**Ā'rĭ-ŏch** (*venerable*). (1) A King of Elassar, Gen. xiv. 1-9. (2) Captain under Nebuchadnezzar, Dan. ii. 14, etc. (3) A king of the Elymeans, Judith i. 6.

**Ă-rĭs'a-ī** (*lion like*). Eighth son of Haman, Esth. ix. 9.

**Ăr"ĭs-tăr'chus** (*best ruler*). A Thessalonian companion of Paul on his third missionary tour, Acts xix. 29; xx. 4; xxvii. 2; Col. iv. 10; Phil. 24.

**Ăr-ĭs"tŏ-bū'lus** (*best counselor*). (1) A Christian and resident at Rome, Rom. xvi. 10. (2) A priest of the Egyptian Jews, 2 Macc. i. 10.

**Ărk** (*chest*). The vessel in which Noah and his family were saved, Gen. vi., vii., viii. Also a little boat of rushes, Ex. ii. 3.

**Ărk of the Cŏv'ĕ-nănt.** Built by direction, Ex. xxv. A chest of Shittim wood for tabernacle use, 3 ft. 9 in. long, by 2 ft. 3 in. wide and high, lined and covered with gold, whose lid was the mercy-seat, on either end of which were cherubs. Golden rings were on the sides, through which poles passed for carrying. Captured by Philistines, 1 Sam. iv. 10, 11; returned to Kirjath-Jearim; brought thence by David to Jerusalem, 2 Sam. vi. 1; 1 Chr. xv. 25, 28, etc.; placed in temple by Solomon, 2 Chr. v. 2-10.

**Ärk'īte.** A descendant of Arka, Gen. x. 17; 1 Chr. i. 15.

**Är-ma-ḡĕd'don** (*hill of Megiddo*). A typical battlefield between the hosts of good and evil, Rev. xvi. 16.

**Är-mē'nĭ-ȧ** (*Land of Aram*). The plateau of Western Asia, whence flow its great rivers Euphrates, Tigris, Araxes, etc., 2 Kgs. xix. 37; Isa. xxxvii. 38.

**Ärm'-let** (*for the arms*). An arm ornament in general use in the East. "Bracelet," 2 Sam. i. 10.

**Är-mō'nĭ.** A son of Saul, 2 Sam. xxi. 8.

**Ärms, Är'mor.** Hebrew offensive weapons were the sword, 1 Sam. xvii. 51; xxv. 13; 2 Sam. xx. 8; Judg. iii. 16; spear, 1 Sam. xvii. 7; 2 Sam. ii. 23; xxiii. 8; bow and arrow [ARCHERY]; sling, 2 Kgs. iii. 25; battle-axe, Jer. li. 20. Among defensive armor were breastplates, cuirasses, coats of mail, helmets, greaves, habergeons, shields, bucklers, 1 Sam. xvii. 5-7; 2 Chr. xxvi. 14.

**Är'my.** Hebrew males twenty years old and upward subject to military duty, Num. i. 2, 3. Tribes formed army divisions. Numerated by hundreds and thousands, each with captains, Num. xxxi. 14. Kings had body-guards, 1 Sam. xiii. 2; xxv. 13. Later, a standing army formed, 2 Chr. xxv. 6. No cavalry till Solomon's time. War declared and exempts used as in Deut. xx. 1-14; xxiv. 5. In N. T. Roman army composed of legions, with chief captains, Acts xxi. 31; tents of legions, or cohorts, and bands, Acts x. 1; maniples, or thirds of legions; centuries, 100 men each and two to a maniple. Captain of a 100 called a Centurion, Matt. viii. 5; xxvii. 54.

**Är'na.** A forefather of Ezra, 2 Esdr. i. 2.

**Är'nan.** Head of a returned family, 1 Chr. iii. 21.

**Är'nŏn** (*noisy*). A stream emptying into Dead Sea from the East, and boundary between the Amorites and Moabites, Num. xxi. 13; Judg. xi. 18. Afterwards between Moab and Israel, Deut. ii. 24; Josh. xii. 1; xiii. 9; Judg. xi. 13.

**Ā'rŏd** (*wild ass*). Gadite founder of the **Ā'rŏd-ītes**, Num. xxvi. 17. Called **Är'ŏ-dī** in Gen. xlvi. 16.

**Ā'rŏd-ītes.** [AROD.]

**Är'ŏ-ēr** (*ruins*). (1) A Reubenite city on the Arnon, Deut. ii. 36; Josh. xii. 1, 2; Judg. xi. 26. Later fell back to Moab, Jer. xlviii. 19, 20. (2) A town of Gad, Num. xxxii. 34; Josh. xiii. 25; 2 Sam. xxiv. 5. (3) An unidentified place, Isa. xvii. 2. (4) A town in South Judah, 1 Sam. xxx. 28.

**Är'ŏ-ēr-īte''.** Designation of Hothan, 1 Chr. xi. 44.

**A'rom.** A returned family, 1 Esdr. v. 16.

**Är'pad** or **Är'phad** (*strong*). A city, or district, in Syria, dependent on Damascus, Isa. xxxvi. 19; xxxvii. 13; Jer. xlix. 23; 2 Kgs. xviii. 34; xix. 13.

**Är-phax'ăd** (*Chaldean fortress*). (1) A son of Shem, Gen. x. 22, 24; xi. 10-13; 1 Chr. i. 17, 18, 24. (2) A king of the Medes, Judith i. 1-4.

**Är'rows.** [ARMS.]

**Är''tăx-ērx'es** (*brave warrior*). (1) A Persian king who stopped the rebuilding of the temple at Jerusalem, Ez. iv. 7, 23, 24. (2) Another Persian king, friendly to Nehemiah, Neh. ii. 1.

**Är'te-măs** (*gift of Artemis*). A friend of Paul, Tit. iii. 12.

**Är-tĭl'lĕ-ry.** The missile equipment of a Jewish soldier, lance, arrows, etc., 1 Sam. xx. 40. [ARMS.]

**Ärts.** The tricks of magic and astrology, Acts xix. 19. [ASTROLOGERS.]

**Är'u-bŏth** (*windows*). The third commissary district of King Solomon, 1 Kgs. iv. 10.

**Ā-ru'-mah** (*height*). Residence of Abimelech, near Shechem, Judg. ix. 41.

**Är'văd** (*wandering*). An island, now Ruad, lying three miles off Tyre, Ezek. xxvii. 8-11.

**Är'vad-īte.** A native of Arvad, Gen. x. 18; 1 Chr. i. 16.

**Är'zȧ.** Keeper of King Elah's palace at Tirzah, 1 Kgs. xvi. 9.

**Ā'sȧ** (*physician*). (1) Third king of Judah, 1 Kgs. xv. 8-34; reigned B. C. 955-914; abolished idolatry; battled victoriously with Ethiopia, 2 Chr. xiv.; involved with Israel; buried with pomp, 2 Chr. xvi. (2) A Levite, 1 Chr. ix. 16.

**Ăs''ā-dī'as.** An ancestor of Baruch, Bar. i. 1.

**Ăs'ā-el.** An ancestor of Tobit, Tob. i. 1.

**Ā'sa-hĕl** (*creature of God*). (1) The fleet-footed nephew of David, killed by Abner, 2 Sam. ii. 18-23. (2) A Levitical legal instructor, 2 Chr. xvii. 8. (3) A Levite and tithing-man, 2 Chr. xxxi. 13. (4) A priest, Ez. x. 15.

**Ā''sa-hī'ah** (*the Lord made*). A learned servant of King Josiah, 2 Kgs. xxii. 12-14. Asaiah in 2 Chr. xxxiv. 20.

**Ā''sa-ī'ah** (*whom the Lord made*). (1) Prince of a Simeonite family, 1 Chr. iv. 36. (2) A Levite chief, 1 Chr. vi. 30; xv. 6-11. (3) A Shilonite, 1 Chr. ix. 5. Maaseiah in Neh. xi. 5. (4) Asaiah, 2 Chr. xxxiv. 20.

**Ăs'a-nȧ,** 1 Esdr. v. 31. [ASNAH].

**Ā'saph** (*gatherer*). (1) Levitical leader of David's choir, 1 Chr. vi. 39; 2 Chr. xxix. 30; Neh. xii. 46. Twelve of the Psalms are attributed to him; to wit, Ps. l. and lxxiii. to lxxxiii. (2) Ancestor of Joah the chronicler, 2 Kgs. xviii. 18; Isa. xxxvi. 3, 22. (3) Keeper of royal forests under Artaxerxes, Neh. ii. 8. (4) Another conductor of the Temple choir, 1 Chr. ix. 15; Neh. xi. 17.

**Ā'saph,** SONS OF. A school of poets and musicians founded by Asaph.

**Ā-sā'rē-el** (*oath bound*). A descendant of Judah, 1 Chr. iv. 16.

**Ăs''ā-rē'lah** (*upright*). A minstrel prophet under David, 1 Chr. xxv. 2. Jesharelah in vs. 14.

**Ăs'ca-lŏn.** [ASHKELON.]

**Ăs-çen'sion,** *see* CHRIST.

**Ăs'e-năth** (*devotee of Neith*, the Egyptian Minerva), Egyptian wife of Joseph, Gen. xli. 45-50; xlvi. 20.

**Ā'sēr,** Luke ii. 36; Rev. vii. 6. [ASHER.]

**Ăsh.** Ash was not indigenous to Palestine; perhaps pine or cedar is meant, Isa. xliv. 14.

**Ā'shan** (*smoke*). A city in Judah, Josh. xv. 42; and Simeon, Josh. xix. 7; 1 Chr. iv. 32.

**Ăsh-bē'ȧ** (*I adjure*). A doubtful genealogical name, 1 Chr. iv. 21.

**Ăsh'bel** (*reproof*). Second son of Benjamin, Gen. xlvi. 21; Num. xxvi. 38; 1 Chr. viii. 1.

**Ăsh'chĕ-naz.** 1 Chr. i. 6; Jer. li. 27. [ASHKENAZ.]

**Ăsh'dŏd** or **Ăz-ō'tus** (*stronghold*). A Philistine city between Gaza and Joppa; assigned to Judah, Josh. xv. 47; 1 Sam. v. 1. Azotus, Acts viii. 40.

**Ăsh'dŏd-ītes''.** Dwellers in Ashdod, Neh. iv. 7.

**Ăsh'dŏth-ītes.** Dwellers in Ashdod, Josh. xiii. 3.

**Ăsh'dŏth=pĭs'gah** (*Springs of Pisgah*). Probably the "slopes of Pisgah," to the east, Deut. iii. 17; iv. 49; Josh. xii. 3; xiii. 20.

**Ăsh'ĕr** (*happiness*). (1) Eighth son of Jacob, Gen. xxx. 13. Aser in Apochrypha and N. T. For boundaries of his allotment *see* Josh. xix. 24-31; xvii. 10, 11; Judg. i. 31, 32. (2) A boundary town of Manasseh, Josh. xvii. 7.

**Ăsh'ĕ-rah** (*straight*). [ASHTAROTH.]

**Ăsh'ĕr-ītes.** Members of the tribe of Asher. Judg. i. 32.

**Ăsh'es.** To sprinkle with or sit in ashes, marked humiliation, grief, and penitence, Gen. xviii. 27; 2 Sam. xiii. 19; Esth. iv. 3; Job ii. 8; Jer. vi. 26; Lam. iii. 16; Matt. xi. 21. The altar ashes, when a red heifer was sacrificed, were watered and used for purifying the unclean, Num. xix. 17-22.

**Ăsh'ĭ-mȧ** (*offence*). A Syrian god worshipped in Samaria, 2 Kgs. xvii. 30.

**Ăsh'ke-lŏn, Ăs'ke-lŏn** (*migration*). A Philistine city and seaport on the Mediterranean, 10 miles N. of Gaza, Josh. (Eshkalon) xiii. 3; Judg. (Askelon) i. 18; Judg. (Ashkelon) xiv. 19; 1 Sam. vi. 17. Its destruction predicted in Jer. xlvii. 5-7; Am. i. 8; Zech. ix. 5; Zeph. ii. 7.

**Ăsh'ke-năz** (*fire that spreads*). A grandson of Japhet, Gen. x. 3. Ashchenaz in 1 Chr. i. 6; Jer. li. 27.

**Ăsh'nah** (*change*). Two towns of Judah, one N. W. the other S.W. of Jerusalem, 16 miles distant, Josh. xv. 33, 43.

**Ăsh'pe-naz** (*horse-nose*). Master of eunuchs under Nebuchadnezzar, Dan. i. 3.

**Ăsh'rĭ-el,** 1 Chr. vii. 14. [ASRIEL.]

**Ăsh'ta-rŏth** and **Ăs'ta-rŏth** (*star*). A city of Bashan, noted for its worship of Ashtoreth, Deut. i. 4; Josh. ix. 10; xii. 4; xiii. 12.

**Ăsh'tĕ-răth-īte″.** An inhabitant of Ashtaroth, 1 Chr. xi. 44.

**Ăsh'tĕ-rŏth Kăr-nā'im** (*Ashteroth of two peaks*). A city of the giant Rephaim in Bashan, Gen. xiv. 5.

**Ăsh'tŏ-rĕth** (*star*). The principal female deity of the Phœnicians; the Ishtar of the Assyrians, and Astarte of the Greeks and Romans. Solomon introduced her worship into his kingdom, Judg. ii. 13; 1 Kgs. xi. 5, 33; 2 Kgs. xxiii. 13.

**Ăsh'ŭr** (*black*). Founder of Tekoa, 1 Chr. ii. 24; iv. 5.

**Ăsh'ŭr-ītes.** Asherites, 2 Sam. ii. 9.

**Ăsh'vath.** A son of Japhlet, 1 Chr. vii. 33.

**Ā'ṣĭȧ** (*eastern*). Only in N. T., and then with reference to Asia Minor, or even to western Asia Minor, with the capital at Ephesus, Acts ii. 9; vi. 9; xvi. 6; 1 Cor. xvi. 19.

**Ā'ṣĭȧ-arch** (*-ark*). Chief of the religious rites and public games of the Roman province of Asia, Acts xix. 31.

**Ăs″ĭ-bī'as,** 1 Esdr. ix. 26. [MALCHIJAH.]

**Ā-sī-el** (*made by God*). (1) A progenitor of Jehu, 1 Chr. iv. 35. (2) A scribe under Esdras, 2 Esdr. xiv. 24.

**Ăs'ke-lŏn.** [ASHKELON.]

**Ăs″mō-dē'us.** An evil spirit, classed with Abaddon and Apollyon, Tob. iii. 8–17.

**Ăs'nah** (*thorn-bush*). Father of a returned family, Ez. ii. 50.

**Ăs-năp'pĕr** (*swift*). Leader of Cuthæan colonists into Samaria, Ez. iv. 10.

**Ăsp** (*viper*). The hooded venomous serpent known as the African cobra. Adder in Ps. lviii. 4; xci. 13, answers the description of asp, Deut. xxxii 33; Job xx. 14–16; Isa. xi. 8; Rom. iii. 13.

**Ăs-pal'ā-thus.** A perfume, or ointment, product of Rhodian wood, Ecclus. xxiv. 15.

**Ăs'pă-thȧ.** Third son of Haman, Esth. ix. 7.

**Ăs'phar.** A pool in the wilderness of Thecoe, 1 Macc. ix. 33.

**Ăs'rī-el** (*help of God*). Founder of the Asrielites, Num. xxvi. 31; Josh. xvii. 2; Ashriel, 1 Chr. vii. 14.

**Ăss.** Five different Hebrew words give it name in the Bible. A patient beast of burden, and palfrey for even kings, Gen. xxii. 3; xii. 16; xxxvi. 24; 1 Chr. xxvii. 30; Job i. 3; Zech. ix. 9, which last is the prophecy of Christ's entry into Jerusalem, Matt. xxi. 1–9.

**Ăs'shur.** Second son of Shem, Gen. x. 22. Also Hebrew form for Assyria, Ezek. xxvii. 23.

**Ăs-shu'rīm** (*steps*). A tribe descended from Abraham, Gen. xxv. 3.

**Ăs″si-dē'ans** (*pious*). A sect of orthodox Jews, bound to the external observance of the law, 1 Macc. ii. 42.

**Ăs'sīr** (*prisoner*). (1) A Levite, Ex. vi. 24; 1 Chr. vi. 22. (2) A forefather of Samuel, 1 Chr. vi. 23, 37. (3) Son of Jeconiah, 1 Chr. iii. 17.

**Ăs'sŏs** or **Ăs'sus** (*approaching*). A Roman seaport on northern shore of Gulf of Adramyttium, Acts xx. 13, 14.

**Ăs'sur,** Ez. iv. 2; Ps. lxxxiii. 8. [ASSHUR; ASSYRIA.]

**Ăs-sўr'ī-ȧ** (*country of Asshur*). That ancient empire on the Tigris whose capital was Nineveh, Gen. ii. 14; x. 11–22. In its splendor it embraced Susiana, Chaldea, Babylon, Media, Armenia, Assyria proper, Mesopotamia, Syria, Phœnicia, Palestine, and Idumea. Assyrian kings frequently invaded Israel, 2 Kgs. xv. 19; xvi. 7–9; xv. 29; 2 Chr. xxviii. 20. Shalmaneser destroyed Samaria, B. C. 721, and carried the people captive. Assyria was overthrown by the Medes and Babylonians, 625 B. C., after an existence of 1200 years.

**Ăs'ta-rŏth,** Deut. i. 4. [ASHTAROTH.]

**Ăs-tăr'te.** [ASHTORETH.]

**Ā-sty'ă-gēs.** Last king of the Medes, B. C. 500. Bel and Drag. 1.

**Ā-sŭp'pīm, HOUSE OF** (*gatherings*). Probably store-rooms in the Temple, 1 Chr. xxvi. 15, 17. "Thresholds" in Neh. xii. 25.

**Ā-sўn'crĭ-tus** (*incomparable*). A Christian friend of Paul, at Rome, Rom. xvi. 14.

**Ā'tad, THRESHING FLOOR OF.** Name changed to Abel-mizraim, which *see*, Gen. l. 10, 11.

**Ăt'a-rah** (*crown*). Mother of Onam, 1 Chr. ii. 26.

**Ā-tăr'ga-tis** (*opening*). A Syrian goddess with a woman's body and fish's tail, 2 Macc. xii. 26.

**Ăt'a-rŏth** (*crowns*). (1) A town of Gilead, Num. xxxii. 3, 34. (2) A place on the southern boundary of Ephraim, Josh. xvi. 2, 7. (3) Perhaps same as above, 1 Chr. ii. 54.

**Ā'tĕr** (*shut up*). Heads of two different returned families, Ez. ii. 42; Neh. vii. 21.

**Ā'thăch** (*stopping place*). A town in southern Judah, 1 Sam. xxx. 30.

**Ăth″a-ī'ah** (*whom God made*). A descendant of Pharez, Neh. xi. 4. Uthai in 1 Chr. ix. 4.

**Ăth″a-lī'ah** (*afflicted by God*). (1) Wicked wife of Jehoram, king of Judah, who introduced the worship of Baal and was slain by her own guards, 2 Kgs. xi.; 2 Chr. xxii.–xxiv. (2) A Benjamite, 1 Chr. viii. 26. (3) Head of a returned Jewish family, Ez. viii. 7.

**A-thē'nĭ-anṣ.** Inhabitants of Athens, Acts xvii. 21.

**Ath″ĕ-nō'bĭ-us.** An envoy of King Antiochus, 1 Macc. xv. 28.

**Ath'ĕnṣ** (*city of Athena, or Minerva*). Capital of Attica and chief seat of Grecian learning and civilization. Situate in S. E. part of the Grecian Peninsula, five miles from its seaport, the Piræus. Paul preached on its Areopagus or Mars' Hill, Acts xvii. 19–22, and founded a church there.

**Ăth'lāi** (*whom God afflicts*). A son of Bebai, Ez. x. 28.

**Ā-tōne'mĕnt** (*reconciliation*). The expiation of sin and propitiation of God by the incarnation, life, suffering, and death of Christ. Day of Atonement, an annual day of Hebrew fasting and humiliation, Ex. xxx. 16; Lev. xvi.; xxiii. 27–32.

**Ăt'rŏth** (*crowns*). A city of Gad, Num. xxxii. 35.

**Ăt'tāī** (*ready*). (1) A grandson of Sheshan, 1 Chr. ii. 35, 36. (2) A lion-faced warrior of Gad, 1 Chr. xii. 11. (3) A son of King Rehoboam, 2 Chr. xi. 20.

**Ăt-tā'lī-ȧ.** A coast town of Pamphylia, Acts xiv. 25.

**Ăt'tă-lus** (*increased*). Names of three kings of Pergamos, 1 Macc. xv. 22.

**Au-gŭs'tus** (*venerable*). Caius Julius Cæsar Octavianus, grand-nephew of, and heir to, Julius Cæsar. Made first emperor of Rome B. C. 27, with title of Augustus. During his reign Christ was born, Luke ii. 1. Died A. D. 14, aged 76 years.

**Au-gŭs'tus' Band,** Acts xxvii. 1. [ARMY.]

**Au-rā'nus.** A riotous fellow at Jerusalem, 2 Macc. iv. 40.

**Ā'vȧ** (*ruin*). A place in Assyria, 2 Kgs. xvii. 24.

**Ăv'ă-răn.** Surname of Eleazer, 1 Macc. ii. 5.

**Ā'ven** (*nothingness*). (1) An unidentified plain, Amos i. 5. (2) Beth-aven, or Bethel, Hosea x. 8. (3) Heliopolis or city of On, Ezek. xxx. 17.

**Ā-vĕnge', Ā-vĕn'ger.** Exaction of just satisfaction, Luke xviii. 8; 1 Thess. iv. 6. "Avenger of Blood" was the pursuer of a slayer to avenge the blood of the slain. He must be a relative of the dead one, Deut. xix. 6.

**Ā'vīm, Ā'vīms, Ā'vītes** (*ruins*). (1) A primitive people who pushed into Palestine from the desert of Arabia, Deut. ii. 23. (2) Colonists from Ava sent to people Israel, 2 Kgs. xvii. 31.

**Ā'vĭth** (*ruins*). The king's city of Edom, Gen. xxxvi. 35; 1 Chr. i. 46.

**Awl.** Shape not known, but use expressed in Ex. xxi. 6; Deut. xv. 17.

**Ăxe.** Seven Hebrew words so translated. It was of stone or iron, crudely fastened to a handle of wood, Deut. xix. 5; 2 Kgs. vi. 5–7.

**Ā'zăl.** Probably a common noun, Zech. xiv. 5.

**Ăz″a-lī'ah** (*near Jehovah*). Father of Shaphan the scribe, 2 Kgs. xxii. 3.

**Ăz″a-nī'ah** (*whom God hears*). Father of Jeshua, Neh. x. 9.

**Ā-zā'phĭ-on.** Probably Sophereth, 1 Esdr. v. 33.

**Ăz'a-rȧ.** A servant of the temple, 1 Esdr. v. 35.

**Ā-zăr'a-el** (*whom God helps*). A Levite musician, Neh. xii. 36.

**Ā-zăr'e-el** (*whom God helps*). (1) A companion of David at Ziklag, 1 Chr. xii. 6. (2) A Levite musician, 1 Chr. xxv. 18. (3) A prince of Dan, 1 Chr. xxvii. 22. (4) Son of Bani, Ezra x. 41. (5) A priest, Neh. xi. 13.

**Ăz″a-rī′ah** (*whom God helps*). (1) Grandson of Zadok, 1 Kgs. iv. 2; 1 Chr. vi. 9. (2) A chief officer under Solomon, 1 Kgs. iv. 5. (3) Tenth king of Judah, commonly called Uzziah, 2 Kgs. xiv. 21; xv. 1-27; 1 Chr. iii. 12. (4) A son of Ethan, 1 Chr. ii. 8. (5) A son of Jehu, 1 Chr. ii. 38, 39. (6) A high priest under Abijah and Asa, 1 Chr. vi. 10. (7) A wrongly inserted name, 1 Chr. vi. 13. (8) An ancestor of Samuel, vi. 36. (9) A prophet in Asa's reign, 2 Chr. xv. 1. (10) Son of King Jehoshaphat, 2 Chr. xxi. 2. (11) Another son of Jehoshaphat, 2 Chr. xxi. 2. (12) For Ahaziah, 2 Chr. xxii. 6. (13) A captain of Judah, 2 Chr. xxiii. 1. (14) High priest in reign of Uzziah, 2 Chr. xxvi. 17-20. (15) A captain of Ephraim in reign of Ahaz, 2 Chr. xxviii. 12. (16) A Levite, 2 Chr. xxix. 12. (17) Another Levite, 2 Chr. xxix. 12. (18) High priest in time of Hezekiah, 2 Chr. xxxi. 10-13. (19) One who helped to rebuild the walls of Jerusalem, Neh. iii. 23, 24. (20) Leader of a returned family, Neh. vii. 7. (21) A Levite who helped Ezra, Neh. viii. 7. (22) A co-covenanter with Nehemiah, Neh. x. 2. (23) Jer. xliii. 2, for Jezaniah. (24) Hebrew name of Abed-nego, Dan. i. 6.

**Ăz″a-rī′as.** A frequent name in Esdras.

**Ā′zaz** (*strong*). A Reubenite, 1 Chr. v. 8.

**Ăz″a-zī′ah** (*whom God strengthens*). (1) A Levite musician, 1 Chr. xv. 21. (2) A chief of Ephraim, 1 Chr. xxvii. 20. (3) Custodian of tithes and offerings under Hezekiah, 2 Chr. xxxi. 13.

**Ăz-băz′a-rĕth.** Probably Esarhaddon, 1 Esdr. v. 69.

**Ăz′bŭk** (*devastation*). Father of Nehemiah, Neh. iii. 16.

**Ā-zē′kah** (*dug over*). A town of Judah, Josh. x. 10, 11.

**Ā′zel** (*noble*). A descendant of Saul, 1 Chr. viii. 37, 38; ix. 43, 44.

**Ā′zem** (*bone*) A city of Judah and Simeon, Josh. xv. 29; xix. 3. Ezem, elsewhere.

**Ā-zē′tas.** A returned Hebrew family, 1 Esdr. v. 15.

**Ăz′gad** (*strength of fortune*). (1) Head of a large returned family, Ez. ii. 12; viii. 12; Neh. vii. 17. (2) A co-covenanter with Nehemiah, Neh. x. 15.

**Ā′zī-el** (*whom God comforts*). A Levite, 1 Chr. xv. 20; Jaaziel in vs. 18.

**Ā-zī′zȧ** (*strong*). A returned captive, Ez. x. 27.

**Ăz′ma-vĕth** (*strong unto death*). (1) One of David's mighty men, 2 Sam. xxiii. 31; 1 Chr. xi. 33. (2) A descendant of Mephibosheth, 1 Chr. viii. 36; ix. 42. (3) A Benjamite, 1 Chr. xii. 3. (4) David's treasurer, 1 Chr. xxvii. 25. (5) A place in Benjamin, Ez. ii. 24; Neh. xii. 29. The Beth-azmaveth of Neh. vii. 28.

**Ăz′mŏn** (*strong*). A place in southern Palestine, Num. xxxiv. 4, 5; Josh. xv. 4.

**Ăz′nŏth=tā′bôr** (*summits of Tabor*). A boundary of Naphtali, Josh. xix. 34.

**Ā′zôr** (*helper*). One of Christ's ancestors, Matt. i. 13, 14.

**Ā-zō′tus.** Greek form of Ashdod in Acts viii. 40. [Ashdod.]

**Ăz′rī-el** (*help of God*). (1) Head of Manassite family, 1 Chr. v. 24. (2) A Naphtalite, 1 Chr. xxvii. 19. (3) Father of Seraiah, Jer. xxxvi. 26.

**Ăz′rī-kam** (*avenging help*). (1) A descendant of Zerubbabel, 1 Chr. iii. 23. (2) A descendant of Saul, 1 Chr. viii. 38; ix. 44. (3) A Levite, 1 Chr. ix. 14; Neh. xi. 15. (4) Prefect of King Ahaz's palace, 2 Chr. xxviii. 7.

**Ā-zū′bah** (*forsaken*). (1) Wife of Caleb, 1 Chr. ii. 18, 19. (2) Mother of Jehoshaphat, 1 Kgs. xxii. 42; 2 Chr. xx. 31.

**Ā′zur** (*helper*). (1) Father of the false prophet Hananiah, Jer. xxviii. 1. (2) Father of one of the princes against whom Ezekiel prophesied, Ezek. xi. 1.

**Ăz′zah** (*strong*). In Deut. ii. 23; 1 Kgs. iv. 24; Jer. xxv. 20, for Gaza.

**Ăz′zan** (*very strong*). A chief of Issachar, Num. xxxiv. 26.

**Ăz′zur** (*helper*). A co-covenanter with Nehemiah, Neh. x. 17. Azur, elsewhere.

## B

**Bā′al** (*lord*). (1) Baal, Bel, or Belus, supreme male god of Phœnicians and Canaanites, worshipped with self-torture and human offerings, Jer. xix. 5. Even house-tops were temples, 2 Kgs. xxiii. 12, Jer. xxxii. 29. Hebrews infected with the worship, Num. xxii. 41; xxv. 3-18; Deut. iv. 16. Became the court religion, 1 Kgs. xvi. 31-33. xviii. 19-28; 2 Kgs. x. 22; xvii. 16. Bel in Isa. xlvi. 1. Baalim, plural form, in Judg. ii. 11; x. 10, and elsewhere. (2) A Reubenite, 1 Chr. v. 5. (3) Grandson of Saul, 1 Chr. viii. 30; ix. 36. (4) A town of Simeon; Bealoth and Baalath-beer, 1 Chr. iv. 33.

**Bā′al-ah** (*mistress*). (1) For Kirjath-jearim in Josh. xv. 9, 10; Baale, 2 Sam. vi. 2; Kirjath-baal, Josh. xv. 60; xviii. 14. (2) A town in south Judah, Josh. xv. 29. Balah in Josh. xix. 3; and Bilhah in 1 Chr. iv. 29.

**Bā′al-ath** (*mistress*). A town in Dan, Josh. xix. 44; 1 Kgs. ix. 18; 2 Chr. viii. 6.

**Bā′al-ath=bē′ēr** (*lord of the well*). [Baal.] (4) [Bealoth.]

**Bā′al=bē′rith** (*Baal of the covenant*). Form of Baal worshipped by the Shechemites, Judg. viii. 33; ix. 4.

**Bā′ā-lē of Jū′dah.** Name for Kirjath-jearim. [Baalah.]

**Bā′al=gad** (*troop of Baal*). Northern limit of Joshua's conquest, Josh. xi. 17; xii. 7; xiii. 5.

**Bā′al=hā′mŏn** (*lord of a multitude*). Solomon had a vineyard there, S. of Sol. viii. 11.

**Bā′al=hā′nan** (*lord of Hanan*). (1) A king of Edom, Gen. xxxvi. 38, 39; 1 Chr. i. 49, 50. (2) Superintendent of David's groves, 1 Chr. xxvii. 28.

**Bā′al=hā′zôr** (*village of Baal*). The shearing-place where Absalom killed Amnon, 2 Sam. xiii. 23.

**Bā′al=hĕr′mŏn** (*lord of Hermon*). A peak of Hermon, Judg. iii. 3; 1 Chr. v. 23.

**Bā′al-ī** (*my lord*). My idol! A repudiated word of endearment, Hos. ii. 16.

**Bā′al-ĭm.** [Baal.]

**Bā′a-lĭs** (*son of exultation*). A king of the Ammonites, Jer. xl. 14.

**Bā′al=mē′on** (*lord of the house*). A Reubenite town, Num. xxxii. 38; 1 Chr. v. 8; Ezek. xxv. 9.

**Bā′al=pē′or** (*lord of the opening*). The form of Baal worship in Peor, Num. xxv. 3-5, 18. Israelites shared in it, Deut. iv. 3; Josh. xxii. 17; Ps. cvi. 28; Hos. ix. 10.

**Bā′al=pĕr′a-zĭm** (*lord of divisions*). Scene of David's victory over the Philistines, 2 Sam. v. 20; 1 Chr. xiv. 11. Mount Perazim in Isa. xxviii. 21.

**Bā′al=shal′ĭ-shȧ.** An unknown place, 2 Kgs. iv. 42.

**Bā′al=tā′mär** (*lord of palms*). A place in Benjamin, Judg. xx. 33.

**Bā′al=zē′bŭb** (*god of the fly*). The form of Baal worshipped at Ekron, 2 Kgs. i. 16.

**Bā′al=zē′phon** (*lord of the north*). A place on western coast of Red Sea near where the Israelites crossed, Ex. xiv. 2; Num. xxxiii. 7.

**Bā′a-nȧ** (*son of affliction*). (1) Son of Solomon's commissary in Jezreel, 1 Kgs. iv. 12. (2) Father of Zadok, Neh. iii. 4.

**Bā′a-nah** (*son of affliction*). (1) Co-murderer of Ish-bosheth, killed by David, 2 Sam. iv. 2-9. (2) Father of one of David's mighty men, 2 Sam. xxiii. 29; 1 Chr. xi. 30. (3) 1 Kgs. iv. 16; Baana in vs. 12. (4) One of the returned, Ez. ii. 2; Neh. vii. 7.

**Bā′a-rah** (*brutish*). Wife of Shaharaim, 1 Chr. viii. 8.

**Bā″a-sē′iah** (*work of Jehovah*). A Levite, 1 Chr. vi. 40.

**Bā′a-shȧ (*bravery*). Third king of Israel, 1 Kgs. xv. 27-34; xvi. Warred continually with King Asa, 1 Kgs. xv. 33, and ruled wickedly for 24 years, B. C. 953 to 931. Family cut off according to prophecy, 1 Kgs. xvi. 3-11.**

**Bā′bel (*confusion*). One of Nimrod's cities in the plain of Shinar, Gen. x. 10. [Babylon.]**

**Bā′bel, Tower of. That brick structure, built in the plain of Shinar, and intended to prevent the very confusion and dispersion it brought about, Gen. xi. 4-9.**

**Băb′ȳ-lon** (*Greek form of Babel*). **Capital city Babylonian empires. Situate on both sides of the Euphrates, 200 miles above its junction with the Tigris, Gen. x. 10; xi. 4-9; Jer. li. 58; Isa. xlv. 1-3. Once the capital of Assyria, 2 Chr. xxxiii. 11. Reached height of its splendor and strength under Nebuchadnezzar, Isa. xiii. 19; xiv. 4; xlvii. 5; Jer. li. 41. Chief home of the captive Jews. Captured by Cyrus the Persian, through his leader Darius, B. C. 539, as prophesied in Jer. li. 31, 39, and narrated in Dan. v. Its decay dates from that date. The Babylon of 1 Pet. v. 13 is conjectural. In Rev. xiv. 8; xvii. 18, Babylon types the power of Rome.**

**Băb″ȳ-lō′nĭ-anș.** Inhabitants of Babylon, Ez. iv. 9.

**Băb″ȳ-lō′nish Gär′mĕnt** (*robe of Shinar*). A richly embroidered robe worn in Babylon and prized by other peoples, Josh. vii. 21.

**Bā′cȧ** (*weeping*). Perhaps a figurative "valley;" but if real, probably Gehenna, Ps. lxxxiv. 6.

**Băc′chĭ-dēs.** A noted Syrian general, 1 Macc. vii. 8.

**Băc-chū′rus.** One of the "holy singers," 1 Esdr. ix. 24.

**Băc′chus.** [DIONYSUS.]

**Bă-çē′nor.** A Jewish captain, 2 Macc. xii. 35.

**Băch′rites.** Becherites, Num. xxvi. 35.

**Bădg′ers' Skins** (*striped skins*). The badger not found in Palestine. Seal, porpoise, or sheep skins may be meant, Ex. xxv. 5; xxxv. 7.

**Băg** (*swelling*). The bag of 2 Kgs. v. 23; xii. 10, was for holding money; that of Deut. xxv. 13–15 for carrying weights. Sack was the Hebrew grain-bag, Gen. xlii. 25. The shepherd's bag was for carrying feeble lambs, Zech. xi. 15–17. The bag of Judas was probably a small chest, John xii. 6; xiii. 29.

**Bā-gō′as** (*eunuch*). An attendant of Holofernes, Judith xii. 1–3.

**Bă-hū′rim** (*low grounds*). A village between the Jordan and Jerusalem, 2 Sam. iii. 16; xvi. 5; xvii. 18; 1 Kgs. ii. 8.

**Bā′jith** (*house*). Temple of the gods of Moab, Isa. xv. 2.

**Băk-băk′kar** (*pleasing*). A descendant of Asaph, 1 Chr. ix. 15.

**Băk′bŭk** (*bottle*). His children returned, Ez. ii. 51.

**Băk″bŭk-ī′ah** (*destruction by Jehovah*). A Levite porter, Neh. xi. 17; xii. 9, 25.

**Bāke.** Baking done at home and by the women, Lev. xxvi. 26; 1 Sam. viii. 13; 2 Sam. xiii. 8; Jer. vii. 18. Perhaps public bakeries in Hos. vii. 4–7.

**Bā′la̤am** (*glutton*). Son of Beor, or Bosor, Deut. xxiii. 4. A man of note and given to prophecy. Slain in battle by the Hebrews, Num. xxii.–xxiv., xxxi.; Rev. ii. 14.

**Bā′lăc,** Rev. ii. 14. [BALAK.]

**Băl′a̤-dăn.** [MERODACH-BALADAN.]

**Bā′lah,** Josh. xix. 3. Short form of Baalah.

**Bā′lăk** (*destroyer*). The king of Moab who hired Balaam to curse Israel, Num. xxii.–xxiv.; Josh. xxiv. 9; Judg. xi. 25. Balac in Rev. ii. 14.

**Băl′ăn-çes** (*two scales*). Were in general use among the ancients for weighing gold and silver, and in traffic, Lev. xix. 36; Mic. vi. 11; Hos. xii. 7.

**Băld′ness** (*ball-like*). Priests forbidden to make themselves bald, Lev. xxi. 5; Deut. xiv. 1; Ezek. xliv. 20. "Bald-head" a cry of contempt, 2 Kgs. ii. 23; as indicating leprosy, Lev. xiii. 40–43. Voluntary baldness a sign of misery, Isa. iii. 24; Ezek. vii. 18; or else the conclusion of the Nazarite vow, Num. vi. 9.

**Bälm** (*balsam*). The Balm of Gilead, or Mecca balsam, exudes an agreeable balsamic resin, highly prized in the East as an unguent and cosmetic, as the crushed leaves were for their odor, Gen. xxxvii. 25; xliii. 11; Jer. viii. 22; xlvi. 11; Ezek. xxvii. 17.

**Băl-thā′sar,** Bar. i. 11, 12. [BELSHAZZAR.]

**Bā′mah** (*high place*). Applied to places of idolatrous worship, Ezek. xx. 29.

**Bā′mŏth,** Num. xxi. 19. [BAMOTH-BAAL.]

**Bā′mŏth=bā′al** (*heights of Baal*). A sanctuary of Baal in Moab, Josh. xiii. 17. Bamoth in Num. xxi. 19.

**Bănd.** Tenth part of a Roman legion; called also "cohort," Matt. xxvii. 27; Acts xxi. 31.

**Bā′nī** (*built*). (1) One of David's captains, 2 Sam. xxiii. 36. (2) A forefather of Ethan, 1 Chr. vi. 46. (3) A Judahite, 1 Chr. ix. 4. (4) "Children of Bani" returned, Ez. ii. 10; x. 29–34; Neh. x. 14. (5) A son of Bani, Ez. x. 38. (6) Three others, Levites, Neh. iii. 17; viii. 7; xi. 22.

**Băn′ner.** [ENSIGN.]

**Băn′quet** (*sitting*). A favorite part of social enjoyment and religious festivity among Hebrews. The posture was usually sitting, Gen. xxi. 8; xl. 20. Morning banquets a mark of excess, Eccles. x. 16; Isa. v. 11. Banquet incidents were foods, wines, flowers, fine robes, music vocal and instrumental, dancing, jests, riddles and merriment, Prov. ix. 2; 2 Sam. xix. 35; Neh. viii. 10; Eccl. x. 19; Isa. v. 12; xxv. 6; Matt. xxii. 11; Luke xv. 25. [FEASTS.]

**Băp′tism** (*dipping, bathing*). The sacrament ordinance or rite commanded by Christ, Matt. xxviii. 19, in which water is used to initiate the recipient into the Christian Church. Christ did not baptize, John iv. 2. John's baptism with water, Christ's "with the Holy Ghost and with fire," Matt. iii. 1–12; Luke iii. 16. Jesus baptized by John, Matt. iii. 13–17. Outpouring of the Holy Spirit, Acts ii. John's baptized persons re-baptized, Acts xix. 1–6; xviii. 25, 26.

**Bȧ-răb′bas** (*son of Abba*). The prisoner at Jerusalem when Christ was condemned, Matt. xxvii. 16–28; Mark xv. 7; Luke xxiii. 18; John xviii. 40.

**Băr′ă-chel** (*blessed of God*). Father of Elihu, Job xxxii. 2–6.

**Băr″a̤-chī′as,** Matt. xxiii. 35. [ZECHARIAS.]

**Bā′rak** (*lightning*). A Hebrew chieftain, Judg. iv.

**Bär-bā′rĭ-an** (*bearded*). In N. T. sense one not a Greek, Acts xxviii. 2; Rom. i. 14; 1 Cor. xiv. 11.

**Bär-hū′mīte,** 2 Sam. xxiii. 31; of BAHURIM.

**Bȧ-rī′ah** (*fugitive*). Son of Shemaiah, 1 Chr. iii. 22.

**Bär″=jē′șus** (*son of Jesus*), Acts xiii. 6. [ELYMAS.]

**Bär″=jō′nȧ** (*son of Jonah*), Matt. xvi. 17. [PETER.]

**Bär′kŏs** (*painter*). "Children of Barkos" returned, Ez. ii. 53; Neh. vii. 55.

**Bär′lēy.** Much cultivated by the Hebrews, Ex. ix. 31; Lev. xxvii. 16; Deut. viii. 8; Ruth ii. 7. Used for bread chiefly among the poor, Judg. vii. 13; 2 Kgs. iv. 42; John vi. 9–13; and for fodder, 1 Kgs. iv. 28. Barley harvest preceded wheat harvest, Ruth i. 22; ii. 23; 2 Sam. xxi. 9, 10.

**Bär′na̤-băs** (*son of comfort*). Joseph or Joses, a convert of Cyprus, and companion of Paul, Acts iv. 36; ix. 27; xi. 25, 26; xv. 22–39.

**Bȧ-rō′dis.** Servant of Solomon, 1 Esdr. v. 34.

**Bär′sa̤-băs.** [JOSEPH, JUDAS.]

**Bär′ta̤-cŭs.** Soldier of Darius, 1 Esdr. iv. 29.

**Bär-thŏl′ŏ-mew** (*son of Tolmai*). One of the twelve apostles, Matt. x. 3; Mark iii. 18; Luke vi. 14; Acts i. 13; perhaps Nathanael in John i. 45.

**Bär″tĭ-mæ′us** (*son of Timæus*). A blind beggar of Jericho, Mark x. 46–52.

**Bā′rṳch** (*blessed*). (1) Jeremiah's friend, amanuensis and fellow prisoner, Jer. xxxvi. 4–32; xxxii. 12; xliii. 3–7. (2) Nehemiah's assistant, Neh. iii. 20. (3) A co-covenanter, Neh. x. 6. (4) A Judahite, Neh. xi. 5. (5) Eighth Apocryphal book.

**Bär-zĭl′la̤-ī** (*strong*). (1) A Gileadite, 2 Sam. xvii. 27; xix. 32–39. (2) Father-in-law of Michal, 2 Sam. xxi. 8. (3) Son-in-law of Barzillai, Ez. ii. 61; Neh. vii. 63.

**Băs′cȧ-mȧ.** A place in Gilead, 1 Macc. xiii. 23.

**Bā′shăn** (*thin soil*). A country east of Jordan between Gilead on the south and Hermon on the north, Deut. iii. 10–13; Josh. xii. 4, 5; xiii. 12–30. Conquered by the Israelites, Num. xxi. 33, and allotted to the half tribe of Manasseh, Josh. xiii. 29, 30

**Bā′shăn=hă′voth=jā′ĭr** (*Bashan of the villages of Jair*). Name given to Argob in Bashan, Deut. iii. 14. Havoth-Jair, Num. xxxii. 41.

**Băsh′ĕ-măth** (*pleasing*). Wife of Esau, Gen. xxvi. 34; xxxvi. 3, 4, 13. Mahalath, Gen. xxviii. 9.

**Bā′sin.** One of the smaller vessels of the tabernacle, for holding the blood of the sacrificial victims. A larger vessel in John xiii. 5.

**Băs′ket.** Mostly of wicker, and variously used for bread, Gen. xl. 16–19; Ex. xxix. 2, 3, 23; Lev. viii. 2; Matt. xiv. 20; xv. 37; first fruits, Deut. xxvi. 2–4; fruits, Jer. xxiv. 1, 2; bulky articles, 2 Kgs. x. 7; Ps. lxxxi. 6.

**Băs′măth** (*pleasing*). Daughter of Solomon, 1 Kgs. iv. 15.

**Băs′tărd.** Not applied to one born out of wedlock, but to issue within the prohibited degrees, Deut. xxiii. 2.

**Băt.** An unclean beast. Same as our bat, Lev. xi. 19; Deut. xiv. 18; Isa. ii. 20.

**Băth.** A Jewish liquid measure, varying from $4\frac{1}{2}$ to $6\frac{1}{2}$ gallons.

**Băth, Bā′thing.** Part of the Jewish ritual of purification, Lev. xiv. 8; xv. 5, 16; xvii 15; xxii. 6; Num. xix. 7; 2 Sam. xi. 2–4; 2 Kgs. v. 10. Customary after mourning, Ruth iii. 3; 2 Sam. xii. 20. Public bathing pools usually sheltered by porticos, 2 Kgs. xx. 20; Neh. iii. 15; Isa. xxii. 11; John v. 2; ix. 7.

**Băth=răb′bim** (*daughter of many*). A gate of ancient Heshbon, S. of Sol. vii. 4.

**Băth′=shĕ-bȧ″** (*daughter of the oath*). Wife of David, and mother of Solomon, 2 Sam. xi; 1 Kgs. i. 15; ii. 13-22. Bathshua in 1 Chr. iii. 5

**Băth′=shụ-ȧ″.** [BATHSHEBA.]

**Băt′tĕr-ing=ram.** A heavy beam of hard wood, with the end sometimes shaped like a ram, used for battering down the gates and walls of a city, Ezek. iv. 2; xxi. 22.

**Băt′tle=axe.** [ARMS.]

**Băt′tle-ment.** The barrier around the flat-roofed houses of the East, Deut. xxii. 8; Jer. v. 10.

**Băv′ă-ī.** A builder, Neh. iii. 18.

**Bāy=tree,** Ps. xxxvii. 35. The laurel, or sweet-bay (*Laurus nobilis*).

**Băz′lith** (*stripping*). His descendants returned, Neh. vii. 54; Ez. ii. 52.

**Băz′lŭth.** [BAZLITH.]

**Bdĕl′li-um** (*del′i-um*) (*a plant and its gum*). A fragrant gum resin. But in Gen. ii. 12 and Num. xi. 7, a precious stone.

**Bea′con** (*signal*). A lighted signal for warning, Isa. xxx. 17.

**Bē″ą-lī′ah** (*Jehovah is Baal*). A friend of David, 1 Chr. xii. 5.

**Bē′ă-lŏth** (*mistresses*). A town of south Judah, Josh. xv. 24.

**Bē′an.** A Bedouin tribe, 1 Macc. v. 4.

**Beans,** Much cultivated in Palestine, as food for man and beast, 2 Sam. xvii. 28; Ezek. iv. 9.

**Bear,** Found in Syria and the mountains of Lebanon, 2 Sam. xvii. 8; 2 Kgs. ii. 24; Prov. xvii. 12.

**Beard** (*barbed*). Badge of manhood. Tearing, cutting, or neglecting, a sign of mourning, Ez. ix. 3; Isa. xv. 2; l. 6; Jer. xli. 5; xlviii. 37. To insult it a gross outrage, 2 Sam. x. 4. Taken hold of in salutation, 2 Sam. xx. 9. Removed in leprosy, Lev. xiv. 9.

**Bĕb′ă-ī** (*fatherly*). (1) Head of a returned family, Ez. ii. 11; Neh. vii. 16; x. 15. (2) Father of Zechariah, Ez. viii. 11.

**Bē′chĕr** (*first born*). (1) Second son of Benjamin, Gen. xlvi. 21; 1 Chr. vii. 6. (2) An Ephraimite, Num. xxvi. 35. Bered in 1 Chr. vii. 20.

**Bĕ-chō′răth** (*first fruits*). An ancestor of Saul, 1 Sam. ix. 1.

**Bĕc′tĭ-leth.** A plain, Judith ii. 21.

**Bed.** The Jewish bed consisted of a mattress and coverings, Gen. xlvii. 31; 1 Sam. xix. 13; Matt. ix. 6. Placed on the floor, or on a bench, 2 Kgs. i. 4; xx. 2; Ps. cxxxii. 3; Am. iii. 12; and later became ornamental and canopied, Am. vi. 4; Esth. i. 6. For bed-chamber furnishings *see* 2 Kgs. iv. 10.

**Bē′dăd** (*alone*). Father of Hadad, king of Edom, Gen. xxxvi. 35; 1 Chr. i. 46.

**Bē′dăn** (*according to judgment*). (1) A judge of Israel, 1 Sam. xii. 11. (2) A son of Gilead, 1 Chr. vii. 17.

**Bĕ-dē′iah.** A son of Bani, Ez. x. 35.

**Bee.** Honey bees and honey abounded in Palestine, Deut. i. 44; 1 Kgs. xiv. 3; Ps. lxxxi. 16; Isa. vii. 15, 18.

**Bē″ĕl-ī′ą-dȧ** (*Baal knows*). A son of David, 1 Chr. xiv. 7; Eliada in 2 Sam. v. 16 and 1 Chr. iii. 8.

**Bē-ĕl=tĕth′mus.** An officer of Artaxerxes, 1 Esdr. ii. 16.

**Bĕ-ĕl′zę-bŭb,** properly **Bĕ-ĕl′zę-bŭl** (*lord of the house*). N. T. form of Baalzebub, "lord of the fly." It personified Satan, and the general sovereignty of evil spirits, Matt. x. 25, xii. 24; Mark iii. 22, Luke xi. 15.

**Bē′er** (*a well*). (1) A halting place of the Israelites, Num. xxi. 16-18. (2) Place to which Jotham fled, Judg. ix. 21.

**Bĕ-ē′rȧ** (*a well*). Son of Zophar, 1 Chr. vii. 37.

**Bĕ-ē′rah** (*well*). A Reubenite, 1 Chr. v. 6.

**Bē-er=ē′lim** (*well of Elim*), Isa. xv. 8. [BEER.]

**Bĕ-ē′rī** (*my well*). (1) Father-in-law of Esau, Gen. xxvi. 34. (2) Father of Hosea, Hos. i. 1.

**Bē′er=Lă-hăi′=roi** (*well of the living*). Hagar's well, Gen. xvi. 6-14; xxiv. 62; xxv. 11.

**Bĕ-ē′rŏth** (*wells*). (1) A Hivite city, Josh. ix. 17. (2) A halting place of the Israelites, Deut. x. 6. Bene-jaakan in Num. xxxiii. 31.

**Bē′er=shē′bȧ** (*well of the oath*). An old place in southern Palestine; so named by Abraham, Gen. xxi. 31-33; or Isaac, Gen. xxvi. 32, 33.

**Bĕ-ĕsh′=tę-rah″** (*house of Ashterah*). A city of Manasseh, Josh. xxi. 27.

**Bee′tle** (*biting animal*). A species of locust is evidently meant in Lev. xi. 21, 22.

**Beeves.** Same as cattle, when limited to the bovine species, Lev. xxii. 19.

**Bĕg′gar** (*asker*). Pauperism was discouraged, Lev. xix. 10; xxv. 5, 6; Deut. xxiv. 19. Poor invited to feasts, Deut. xiv. 29; xxvi. 12. Beggars abhorred, Ps. cix, 10. In N. T. times beggars had a fixed place to beg, Mark x. 46; Acts iii. 2; Luke xvi. 20.

**Bē-hē′mŏth** (*water-ox*). From the poet's description a hippopotamus is meant, Job xl. 15-24.

**Bē′kah.** A half shekel, valued at about thirty-three cents.

**Bĕl.** [BAAL.]

**Bē′lȧ** (*destroying*). (1) A city of the plain; afterwards called Zoar, Gen. xiv. 2; xix. 22. (2) A king of Edom, Gen. xxxvi. 31-33; 1 Chr. i. 43. (3) Eldest son of Benjamin, Gen. xlvi. 21; and founder of the Belaites, Num. xxvi. 38; 1 Chr. vii. 6; viii. 1. (4) Son of Azaz, 1 Chr. v. 8.

**Bē′lah.** [BELA, 3.]

**Bē′la-ītes,** Num. xxvi. 38. [BELA, 3.]

**Bē′lī-al** (*lawlessness*). A vile, worthless person, reckless of God and man, Deut. xiii. 13; Judg. xix. 22; 1 Sam. ii. 12. Hence, Satan, 2 Cor. vi. 15.

**Bĕl′lows** (*bag, blow-skin*), though crude, did not differ in principle and use from ours, Jer. vi. 29.

**Bĕlls** (*bellowers*). Bells of gold were appended to priestly robes, Ex. xxviii. 33-35. Attached to anklets, Isa. iii. 16-18. Horses ornamented with bells, Zech. xiv. 20.

**Bĕl-mā′im, Bĕl′men.** A town of Samaria, Judith iv. 5.

**Bĕl-shăz′zar** (*prince of Bel*). Last king of Babylon; ruling at time of the great feast and handwriting on the wall, B. C. 539, Dan. v.

**Bĕl″tę=shăz′zar** (*protected by Bel*). Name given to Daniel by Nebuchadnezzar, Dan. i. 7.

**Bĕn** (*son*). A Levite, and porter, appointed to carry the ark, 1 Chr. xv. 18.

**Bĕ-nā′iah** (*son of the Lord*). (1) Son of Jehoiada, 1 Chr. xxvii. 5; captain in David's bodyguard, 2 Sam. viii. 18; and commander-in-chief of Solomon's army, 1 Kgs. i. 36; ii. 34-46. (2) One of David's mighty men, 2 Sam. xxiii. 30; 1 Chr. xi. 31; and chief of eleventh monthly course, 1 Chr. xxvii. 14. (3) A priest and trumpeter, 1 Chr. xv. 18, 20; xvi. 5. (4) A priest, 1 Chr. xv. 24; xvi. 6. (5) A Levite, 2 Chr. xx. 14. (6) A Levite, 2 Chr. xxxi. 13. (7) Prince of a family of Simeon, 1 Chr. iv. 36. (8) Four of the returned, Ez. x. 25, 30, 35, 43. (9) Father of Pelatiah, Ezek. xi. 1, 13.

**Bĕn″=am′mī** (*son of my people*). Grandson of Lot, and progenitor of the Ammonites, Gen. xix. 38.

**Bĕn′ę=bē′răk** (*sons of lightning*). A city of Dan, Josh. xix. 45.

**Bĕn′ę=jā′a-kăn** (*sons of Jaakan*). A desert tribe, Num. xxxiii. 31, 32. [BEEROTH.] Akan in Gen. xxxvi. 27.

**Bĕn′ę=kē′dem.** "People of the East," Gen. xxix. 1; Judg. vi. 3, 33; vii. 12; viii. 10; Job i. 3.

**Bĕn=hā′dăd** (*son of Hadad*). (1) King of Syria, B. C. 950, called Benhadad I. Conqueror of northern Israel, 1 Kgs. xv. 18. (2) Benhadad II., son and successor of former, 1 Kgs. xx. 1. Defeated by Jehoram, 2 Kgs. vi. 8-33. Murdered by his servants, 2 Kgs. viii. 1-15; B. C. 890. (3) Benhadad III., son and successor of Hazael on Syrian throne, about B. C. 840. Defeated by King Joash, 2 Kgs. xiii. 3-24.

**Bĕn=hā′il** (*son of strength*). A prince in Judah, 2 Chr. xvii. 7.

**Bĕn=hā′năn** (*son of grace*). Son of Shimon, 1 Chr. iv. 20.

**Bĕn′ī-nū** (*our son*). A co-covenanter, Neh. x. 13.

**Bĕn′ja-min** (*son of the right hand*). (1) Youngest of Jacob's children. First named Benoni, afterwards Benjamin, Gen. xxxv. 16-18. Beloved by Jacob, Gen. xlii.; visited Egypt, Gen. xliii.; tribe distinguished as Jacob prophesied, Gen. xlix. 27; 1 Sam. xx. 20, 36; 2 Sam. i. 22; Judg. xx. 16; 1 Chr. viii. 40. Their allotment described in Josh. xviii. 11-28. Tribe awfully visited, Judg. xx., xxi. (2) Head of a Benjamite family, 1 Chr. vii. 10. (3) A returned captive, Ez. x. 32.

**Bē′nō** (*his son*). A Levite, 1 Chr. xxiv. 26, 27.

**Bĕn=ō′nī** (*son of my sorrow*), Gen. xxxv. 18. [BENJAMIN.]

**Bĕn=zō′heth** (*son of Zoheth*). A descendant of Judah, 1 Chr. iv. 20.

**Bē′ŏn,** Num. xxxii. 3. [BAAL-MEON.]

**Bē′or** (*burning*). (1) Father of Bela, an early king of Edom, Gen. xxxvi. 32. (2) Father of Balaam,

Num. xxii. 5; xxiv. 3, 15; xxxi. 8; Deut. xxiii. 4; Josh. xiii. 22; xxiv. 9; Micah vi. 5. Bosor in N. T.

**Bē'rȧ** (*son of evil*). A king of Sodom, Gen. xiv. 2-22.

**Bĕr'ă-chah** (*blessing*). (1) A Benjamite, 1 Chr. xii. 3. (2) The valley in which Jehoshaphat celebrated his victory, 2 Chr. xx. 26.

**Bĕr''ą-chī'ah** (*God has blessed*). Father of Asaph, 1 Chr. vi. 39.

**Bĕr''ą-ī'ah** (*created by God*). A Benjamite, 1 Chr. viii. 21.

**Bē-rē'ȧ** (*watered*). (1) A city of Macedonia, Acts xvii. 1-15. (2) A Syrian city, now Aleppo, 2 Macc. xiii. 4. (3) A place in Judea, 1 Macc. ix. 4.

**Bĕr''ę-chī'ah** (*blessed of Jehovah*). (1) A descendant of David, 1 Chr. iii. 20. (2) A Levite, 1 Chr. ix. 16. (3) Father of Asaph, 1 Chr. xv. 17. (4) A door-keeper for the Ark, 1 Chr. xv. 23. (5) An Ephraimite, 2 Chr. xxviii. 12. (6) Father of a builder, Neh. iii. 4, 30; vi. 18. (7) Father of Zechariah, Zech. i. 1-7.

**Bē'red** (*hail*). (1) A place in south Palestine, Gen. xvi. 14. (2) An Ephraimite, 1 Chr. vii. 20.

**Bĕr''ĕ-nī'çe.** [Bernice.]

**Bē'rī** (*well*). An Asherite, 1 Chr. vii. 36.

**Bē-rī'ah** (*evil*) (1) A descendant of Asher, Gen. xlvi. 17; Num. xxvi. 44, 45; 1 Chr. vii. 30, 31. (2) An Ephraimite, 1 Chr. vii. 23. (3) A chief of Benjamin, 1 Chr. viii. 13, 16. (4) A Levite, 1 Chr. xxiii. 10, 11.

**Bē-rī'ītes,** Num. xxvi. 44. Descendants of Beriah (1).

**Bē'rītes.** A people in north Palestine, 2 Sam. xx. 14.

**Bē'rīth** (*covenant*), Judg. ix. 46. [Baal-berith.]

**Bĕr-nī'çe** (*bringing victory*). Eldest daughter of Herod Agrippa, Acts xii. 1, and sister of the younger Agrippi, Acts xxv. 13-23; xxvi. 30.

**Bē-rō'dăch-băl'ą-dăn,** 2 Kgs. xx. 12. [Merodach-baladan.]

**Bē-rō'thah** (*of a well*). A boundary town of north Palestine, Ezek. xlvii. 16.

**Bĕr'ǫ-thāi** (*my wells*). A city of north Palestine, 2 Sam. viii. 8.

**Bē'rŏth-ite,** 1 Chr. xi. 39, of Beeroth.

**Bĕr'yl** (*beril*) (*jewel*). The first stone in fourth row of a high priest's breastplate, Ex. xxviii. 20.

**Bē'sāi** (*sword*). His children returned, Ez. ii. 49; Neh. vii. 52.

**Bĕs''ŏ-dē'įah** (*in the Lord's secret*). Father of an architect, Neh. iii. 6.

**Bē'sŏm** (*broom*). Twig broom for sweeping, Isa. xiv. 23.

**Bē'sôr** (*cool*). A brook in south Judah, 1 Sam. xxx. 9-21.

**Bē'tah** (*confidence*). A city of Zoba, 2 Sam. viii. 8. Tibhath in 1 Chr. xviii. 8.

**Bĕt'ą-nȧ.** A place close to oak of Abraham, Judith i. 9.

**Bē'ten** (*raised*). Border city of Asher, Josh. xix. 25.

**Bĕth** (*house*). Used in combinations.

**Beth''=ab'ă-rȧ** (*house at the ford*). A place beyond, or at, Jordan where John baptized Christ, John i. 28.

**Bĕth''=ā'năth** (*house of reply*). City of Naphtali, Judg. i. 33.

**Bĕth''=ā'nŏth** (*house of reply*). A mountain town of Judah, Josh. xv. 59.

**Bĕth'ă-ny̆** (*house of affliction*). A village on the slope of Olivet close to Bethphage, Matt. xxi. 17; Mark xi.; Luke xix. 29; John xi. 18. Now *Lazarieh*.

**Bĕth''=ăr'ă-bah** (*house of the desert*). A city of Judah and Benjamin, Josh. xv. 61; xviii. 22.

**Bĕth''=ā'răm,** properly Bethharan (*house of height*). A town of Gad, Josh. xiii. 27.

**Bĕth''=är'bel** (*house of ambush*). Scene of the massacre by Shalman, Hos x. 14.

**Bĕth''=ā'ven** (*house of idols*). A place in Benjamin, Josh. vii. 2; xviii. 12; 1 Sam. xiii. 5; xiv. 23. Stands for Bethel in Hos. iv. 15; v. 8; x. 5.

**Bĕth''=ăz'mą-veth** (*house of Azmaveth*). A town of Benjamin, Neh. vii. 28; Azmaveth and Beth-samos, elsewhere.

**Bĕth''=bā'al=mē'on** (*house of Baal-meon*). A place in Reuben, Josh. xiii. 17. Beon in Num. xxxii. 3; Baal-meon in xxxii. 38.

**Bĕth''=bā'rah** (*house of the ford*), Judg. vii. 24. [Beth-abara.]

**Bĕth''=bā'sī.** A town near Jericho, 1 Macc. ix. 62-64.

**Bĕth''=bĭr'ę-ī** (*house of my creation*). A town in south Simeon, 1 Chr. iv. 31. Beth-lebaoth in Josh. xix. 6.

**Bĕth'=cär** (*house of the lamb*) A place where the Israelites' pursuit ended, 1 Sam. vii. 11.

**Bĕth''=dā'gon** (*house of Dagon*). (1) Town in Judah, Josh. xv. 41. (2) Town in Asher, Josh. xix. 27.

**Bĕth''=dĭb''lą-thā'ĭm** (*house of dried figs*). A town of Moab, Jer. xlviii. 22. [Almon-diblathaim.]

**Bĕth'=el** (*house of God*). (1) City of Palestine, 12 mls. N. of Jerusalem, Gen. xii. 8; xiii. 3, 4; scene of Jacob's vision, then called Luz, Gen. xxviii. 11-19; xxxi. 13; xxxv. 1-8; Judg. i. 23; residence of "sons of the prophets" and priests, 2 Kgs. ii. 2, 3; xvii. 27, 28. Now *Beitin*. (2) A town in south Judah, Josh. xii. 16; 1 Sam. xxx. 27; Chesil in Josh. xv. 30; Bethul in xix. 4; and Bethuel in 1 Chr. iv. 30. (3) Mount Bethel, near Bethel, Josh. xvi. 1; 1 Sam. xiii. 2.

**Bĕth''=ē'mĕk** (*house of the valley*). A boundary of Asher, Josh. xix. 27.

**Bē'thĕr.** Figurative mountains, S. of Sol. ii. 17.

**Bē-thĕş'dȧ** (*house of mercy*). A pool near the sheep-gate, Jerusalem, John v. 2.

**Bĕth''=ē'zĕl** (*neighbor's house*). A place in Philistia, Mic. i. 11.

**Bĕth''=gā'dĕr** (*house of a wall*). A doubtful place or person, 1 Chr. ii. 51.

**Bĕth''=gā'mŭl** (*camel-house*). A town of Moab, Jer. xlviii. 23.

**Bĕth''=gil'gal,** Neh. xii. 29. [Gilgal.]

**Bĕth''=hăc'çĕ-rĕm** (*house of the vine*). A beacon station near Tekoa, Neh. iii. 14; Jer. vi. 1.

**Bĕth''=hā'ran,** Num. xxxii. 36. [Beth-aram.]

**Bĕth''=hŏg'la,** and **Hŏg'lah** (*partridge-house*). A place in boundary of Judah and Benjamin, Josh. xv. 6; xviii. 19-21.

**Bĕth''=hō'rŏn** (*cave-house*). A town of Benjamin, Josh. xvi. 3, 5; 1 Kgs. ix. 17; 1 Chr. vii. 24.

**Bĕth''=jĕsh'ī-mŏth** and **Jĕs'ī-mŏth** (*house of deserts*). A town of Moab, allotted to Reuben, Num. xxxiii. 49; Josh. xii. 3; xiii. 20.

**Bĕth''=lĕb'ą-ŏth** (*house of lionesses*), Josh. xix. 6. [Beth-birei.]

**Bĕth'=lĕ-hĕm, Beth'lĕ-hĕm** (*house of bread*). (1) A town of Palestine, six miles S. of Jerusalem. First called Ephrath or Ephratah, Gen. xxxv. 16-19; xlviii. 7. Called Bethlehem-judah after the conquest, Judg. xvii. 7. Home of Ruth, Ruth i. 19. Birthplace of David, 1 Sam. xvii. 12. Here Christ was born, Matt. ii. 1, 2; Luke ii. 15-18. (2) A town in Zebulun, Josh. xix. 15.

**Bĕth''=lō'mŏn,** 1 Esdr. v. 17. [Bethlehem.]

**Bĕth''mā'a-chah,** 2 Sam. xx. 14, 15. Same as Abel, Abel-maim, and Abel-beth-maachah.

**Bĕth''=mär'că-bŏth** (*house of chariots*). A town of Simeon, Josh. xix. 5; 1 Chr. iv. 31. Madmannah in Josh. xv. 31.

**Bĕth''=mē'on,** Jer. xlviii. 23. Contraction of Beth-baal-meon.

**Bĕth''=nĭm'rah** (*house of leopards*). A fenced city of Gad, Num. xxxii. 36. Nimrah in vs. 3.

**Bĕth''=pā'let** (*house of expulsion*). A town in south Judah, Josh. xv. 27. Bethphelet in Neh. xi. 26.

**Bĕth''=păz'zez** (*house of dispersion*). A town of Issachar, Josh. xix. 21.

**Bĕth=pę'or** (*house of Peor*). A spot opposite Jericho, dedicated to Baal-peor, Deut. iii. 29; iv. 46; Josh. xiii. 20.

**Bĕth'phą-ġē** (*house of figs*). A place on Olivet, close to Bethany, Matt. xxi. 1; Luke xix. 29; Mark xi. 1.

**Bĕth''=phē'let,** Neh. xi. 26. [Beth-palet.]

**Bĕth''=rā'phȧ** (*house of health*). Son of Eshton, 1 Chr. iv. 12.

**Bĕth''=rē'hŏb** (*house of Rehob*). A province of Aram, or Syria, 2 Sam. x. 6. Rehob in vs. 8.

**Bĕth-sā'ī-dȧ** (*fishing-house*). A fishing-village on Sea of Galilee, and west of Jordan. Birthplace of Andrew, Peter and Philip, Matt. xi. 21; John i. 44; xii. 21. Bethsaida, where the five thousand were fed, Mark vi. 31-53; Luke ix. 10-17, appears to have been on eastward side of Jordan.

**Bĕth''=sā'mos,** 1 Esdr. v. 18. [Beth-azmaveth.]

**Bĕth=shăn',** 1 Macc. v. 52. [Beth-shean.]

**Bĕth''=shē'ăn, Bĕth'=săn, Bĕth'=shăn**

(*house of rest*). A city of Manasseh, Josh. xvii. 11; Judg. i. 27; 1 Chr. vii. 29; Bethshan in 1 Sam. xxxi. 10–12. A commissary district of Solomon, 1 Kgs. iv. 12. Now Beisan.

**Bĕth″-shē′mĕsh** (*house of the sun*). (1) A Levitical town of N. Judah, Josh. xv. 10; xxi. 16. Now Ainshems. (2) A border city of Issachar, Josh. xix. 22. (3) A fenced city of Naphtali, Josh. xix. 38; Judg. i. 33. (4) Probably Heliopolis, Egypt, Jer. xliii. 13.

**Bĕth″-shĭt′tah** (*house of the acacia*). The place where Gideon's pursuit ended, Judg. vii. 22.

**Bĕth″-sū′rȧ**, 1 Macc. iv. 29. [Beth-zur.]

**Bĕth″-tăp′pu-ah** (*house of apples*). A town of Judah, near Hebron. Now Teffuh, Josh. xv. 53.

**Bĕth-u′el** (*filiation of God*). (1) Father of Laban and Rebekah, Gen. xxii. 22, 23; xxiv 15, 24, 47; xxviii. 2-5. (2) [Bethul.]

**Bē′thŭl** (*dweller in God*). A town of Simeon, Josh. xix. 4; Chesil in Josh. xv. 30; Bethuel in 1 Chr. iv. 30.

**Bē-thu′lĭ-ȧ.** Scene of Judith's exploits, Judith iv. 6; vi. 11–14.

**Bĕth′-zûr** (*house of rock*). Now Beit Sûr, 4 mls. N. of Hebron, Josh. xv. 58; 2 Chr. xi. 7.

**Bē-tō′lĭ-us**, 1 Esdr. v. 21. [Bethel.]

**Bĕt″ō-mĕs′them.** A town near Esdraelon, Judith iv. 6.

**Bĕt′ō-nĭm** (*bellies*). A town of Gad, Josh. xiii. 26.

**Bē-trōth′** (*in promise*). To pledge troth, *i. e.*, engage to marry. A betrothed woman was regarded as the lawful wife of her spouse, and he could not break off the match without a divorce, while she, if unfaithful, would be considered an adulteress.

**Beū′lah** (*married*). The land of Israel when the Jewish Church is again in its true relation to God, Isa. lxii. 4.

**Bē′zāi** (*conqueror*). His children returned, Ez. ii. 17; Neh. vii. 23.

**Bē-zăl′ē-el** (*in the shadow of God*). (1) A Tabernacle architect, Ex. xxxi. 1–6. (2) A returned Jew, Ez. x. 30.

**Bē′zek** (*lightning*). (1) A place in Judah, Judg. i. 1–5. (2) Where Saul numbered Israel, 1 Sam. xi. 8.

**Bē′zēr** (*ore*). (1) A city of refuge east of Jordan, Deut. iv. 43; Josh. xx. 8. (2) An Asherite, 1 Chr. vii. 37.

**Bē′zeth.** Encampment of Bacchides, 1 Macc. vii. 19.

**Bī′ble** (*the book*). The term applied, not further back than the fifth century, to that collection of *biblia*, or holy books, which comprises the Old and New Testaments.

**Bĭch′rī** (*first-born*). A Benjamite, 2 Sam. xx. 1.

**Bĭd′kär** (*stabber*). One of Jehu's captains, 2 Kgs. ix. 25.

**Bier** (*that bears*). The frame on which a dead body was carried to the grave, Luke vii. 14; 2 Chr. xvi. 14.

**Bĭg′thȧ, Bĭg′thăn, Bĭg′than-ȧ** (*gift of God*). A chamberlain of King Ahasuerus, Esth. i. 10. Bigthan in ii. 21; Bigthana in vi. 2.

**Bĭg′va-ī** (*happy*). (1) His children returned, Ez. ii. 14; viii. 14; Neh. vii. 19. (2) A chief under Zerubbabel, Ezra ii. 2; Neh. vii. 7; x. 16.

**Bĭl′dăd** (*son of strife*). The Shuhite friend of Job ii. 11; viii., xviii., xxv.

**Bĭl′ē-ăm** (*foreigners*). A town of Manasseh, 1 Chr vi. 70.

**Bĭl′gah** (*first-born*). (1) Head of the fifteenth temple course, 1 Chr. xxiv. 14. (2) A returned priest, Neh. xii. 5, 18. Bilgai in x. 8.

**Bĭl′ga-ī**, Neh. x. 8. [Bilgah.]

**Bĭl′hah** (*timid*). (1) Mother of Dan and Naphtali, Gen. xxix. 29; xxx. 3–8; xxxv. 25; xlvi. 25; 1 Chr. vii. 13. (2) A town of Simeon, 1 Chr. iv. 29.

**Bĭl′hăn** (*modest*). (1) A Horite chief, Gen. xxxvi. 27. (2) A Benjamite, 1 Chr. vii. 10.

**Bĭl′shăn** (*eloquent*). A returned captive, Ez. ii. 2; Neh. vii. 7.

**Bĭm′hăl** (*circumcised*). A son of Japhlet, 1 Chr. vii. 33.

**Bĭn′e-ȧ** (*fountain*). A descendant of Saul, 1 Chr. viii. 37.

**Bĭn′nu-ī** (*building*). Name of five returned captives, Ez. viii. 33; x. 30, 38; Neh. vii. 15; x. 9.

**Bĭrds.** Many birds of Palestine similar to our own. The "speckled bird" of Jer. xii. 9 means a vulture. Birds were snared, Ps. cxxiv. 7; Prov. vii. 23; Am. iii. 5. Used for curing leprosy, Lev. xiv. 2–7. List of birds not to be eaten, Lev. xi. 13–19; Deut. xiv. 11–19.

**Bĭr′shȧ** (*son of godliness*). A king of Gomorrah, Gen. xiv. 2.

**Bĭrth′days.** Observed among ancients by feasts, Gen. xl. 20; Job i. 4; Hos. vii. 5; Matt. xiv. 6–10.

**Bĭrth′right.** Among Jews the first-born son enjoyed the right of consecration, Ex. xxii. 29; great dignity, Gen. xlix. 3; a double portion of the paternal estate, Deut. xxi. 17; right to royal succession, 2 Chr. xxi. 3.

**Bĭr′za-vĭth.** An Asherite, 1 Chr. vii. 31.

**Bĭsh′ŏp** (*looking upon, or over*). Greek *episkopos*, overseer. An officer of the Apostolic church, identical with presbyter, or elder, Acts xx. 17, 18; 1 Tim. iii. 1–13; v. 17; Tit. i. 5–8; 1 Pet. v; 1 Thess. v. 12; James v. 14.

**Bĭsh′ŏp-ric.** The jurisdiction and charge of a bishop, Acts i. 20; 1 Tim. iii. 1.

**Bĭth′ĭ-ah** (*daughter of the Lord*). Daughter of a Pharaoh, 1 Chr. iv. 18.

**Bĭth′rŏn** (*ravine*). A place east of Jordan, 2 Sam. ii. 29.

**Bī-thy̆n′ĭ-ȧ.** A province of Asia Minor, bordering on the Euxine (Black) sea and west of Pontus, Acts xvi. 7; 1 Pet. i. 1. Capital, Nice or Nicæa.

**Bĭt′ter Herbs.** A part of the passover feast, Ex. xii. 8.

**Bĭt′tern.** A bird of the heron family, solitary in its habits, and noted for its melancholy night booming, Isa. xiv. 23; xxxiv. 11; Zeph. ii 14.

**Bĭz-jŏth′jah** (*contempt*). A town of south Judah, Josh. xv. 28.

**Bĭz′thȧ** (*eunuch*) A eunuch, Esth. i. 10.

**Blains** (*boils*). The ulcerous inflammations which constituted the sixth Egyptian plague, Ex. ix. 9–11; Deut. xxviii. 27, 35.

**Blăs′phē-my̆** (*injurious speaking*). Speaking evil of God, Lev. xxiv. 11; Ps. lxxiv. 18; Isa. lii. 5; Matt. xii. 32; Acts xviii. 6; Rom. ii. 24; Col. iii. 8. Royalty could be blasphemed, 1 Kgs. xxi. 10. Punished by stoning, Lev. xxiv. 11–14.

**Blăs′tus** (*that buds*). Chamberlain of Herod Agrippa, Acts xii. 20.

**Blĕm′ĭsh** (*wound, stain*). For ceremonial blemishes *see* Lev. xxi. 18–20; xxii. 20–24.

**Blĭnd′ness.** Blind treated with compassion, Lev. xix. 14; Deut. xxvii. 18. A punishment, Judg. xvi. 21; 1 Sam. xi. 2; 2 Kgs. xxv. 7.

**Blood.** The vital fluid, Gen. ix. 4. Forbidden as food, Ex. xxix. 12; Lev. vii. 26; xvii. 11–13. For N. T. atoning blood *see* Heb. ix, x.; Acts xx. 28; Rom. v. 9; Eph. i. 7; Col. i. 14; Heb. vii. 27; 1 John i. 7.

**Bō′ăn-ēr′ges** (*sons of thunder*). A name given by Christ to James and John, sons of Zebedee, Mark iii. 17.

**Boar.** Found wild in the thickets of Jordan and on the Lebanon ranges, Ps. lxxx. 13.

**Bō′ăz** (*lovely*). (1) The Bethlehemite who married Ruth. *See* Book of Ruth; Matt. i. 5. (2) A brazen pillar in the porch of Solomon's temple, 1 Kgs. vii. 21; 2 Chr. iii. 17; Jer. lii. 21.

**Bŏch′e-ru** (*young*). Son of Azel, 1 Chr. viii. 38.

**Bō′chĭm** (*weepers*). A place near Gilgal, Judg. ii. 1–5.

**Booth** (*hut*). Temporary structures, usually of boughs, Gen. xxxiii. 17; Lev. xxiii. 42.

**Boot′y** (*dealt out*). Spoils of war, regulated as in Num. xxxi. 26–47; 1 Sam. xxx. 24, 25.

**Bō′oz**, Matt. i. 5; Luke iii. 32. [Boaz.]

**Bŏs′căth**, 2 Kgs. xxii. 1. [Bozkath.]

**Bos′om** (*buz′um*). To lean on, implied great intimacy, John xiii. 23. Figuratively, Paradise, Luke xvi. 23; xxiii. 43.

**Bō′sŏr.** Greek form of Beor, 2 Pet. ii. 15.

**Bŏs′ō-rȧ.** Bozrah, 1 Macc. v. 26, 28.

**Bŏs′ses** (*humps*). Knobs on shields and bucklers, Job xv. 26.

**Bŏtch.** [Blain.]

**Bŏt′tle** (*little boot*). Primitive bottles, either of skin or earthenware, Gen. xxi. 14; Jer. xix. 1; Matt. ix. 17; of different sizes and shapes. Tear bottles used, Ps. lvi. 8.

**Bō′han** (*thumb*). A Reubenite, Josh. xv. 6; xviii. 17.

**Boil.** Burning inflammation, Lev. xiii. 23.

**Bŏnd′age.** [Slave.]

**Bŏll′ed** (*budded*). Podded, as flax, Ex. ix. 31.

**Book** (*beech*). Letters were at first engraved on stone, brick, or metal, Deut. xxvii. 2, 3; Job xix. 24; later, on papyrus, bark of trees, tablets of wax, cloth of linen or cotton; the latter in long rolls, or "scrolls," which were the books of the Hebrews.

**Bow**. Besides the bow and arrow the bow-gun was used by the ancients as an offensive weapon, 1 Macc. vi. 20. [ARCHERY.] [ARMS.]

**Bŏw**. The Eastern mode of salutation by kneeling on one knee and bending the head forward, Gen. xxxvii. 10; 1 Kgs. i. 53; ii. 19.

**Bŏw'els**. Used figuratively for the emotions, Col. iii. 12; 1 John iii. 17.

**Box=tree**. The evergreen, whose wood is so prized by engravers, Isa. xli. 19; lx. 13.

**Bō'zēz** (*height*). Sharp rocks mentioned in 1 Sam. xiv. 4, 5.

**Bŏz'kăth** (*craggy*). A lowland city of Judah, Josh. xv. 39; 2 Kgs. xxii. 1.

**Bŏz'rah** (*strong-hold*). (1) Ancient capital of Edom, Gen. xxxvi. 33; Isa. xxxiv. 6; lxiii. 1; Jer. xlix. 13, 22. (2) A city of Moab, Jer. xlviii. 24.

**Brāce'let**. A wrist and arm ornament worn by both sexes, Gen. xxiv. 30; Ezek. xvi. 11. A badge of royalty, and worn above elbow, 2 Sam. i. 10.

**Brăm'ble** (*blackberry*). [THORNS.]

**Brass**. An alloy of copper and zinc, not known to the Jews. The brass of Scripture was probably copper, or a copper alloy, Gen. iv. 22; Deut. viii. 9; Judg. xvi. 21; 2 Kgs. xxv. 7; 1 Sam. xvii. 5; Job xxviii. 2; 1 Cor. xiii. 1.

**Brā'zen Serpent**. [SERPENT.]

**Breach'es** (*broken*). Creeks, bays, and river-mouths; havens in case of storm, Judg. v. 17; Josh. xix. 29.

**Bread** (*brewed, baked*). Early used, Gen. xviii. 5, 6; Ex. xii. 34; Jer. vii. 18. Made of wheat, barley, rye, fitches, and spelt, in loaves or rolls, leavened or unleavened; the kneading being in troughs, bowls, or on flat plates, and the baking in portable ovens of earthenware, or upon heated stones, or on the coals.

**Breast'plate**. The breastplate of the high priest, Ex. xxviii. 15, was of embroidered stuff, some 10 inches square; its upper corners fastened with gold or lace to the ephod, its lower to the girdle, Ex. xxviii. 28. Adorned with 12 precious stones, Ex. xxviii. 12-29.

**Breech'es** (*broken, i. e. crotched*). Drawers or light trousers worn by priests, reaching from loins to thighs, Ex. xxviii. 42.

**Brick** (*fragment*). Bricks were made of clay, mixed with straw, usually larger than our bricks, and burned in a kiln or dried in the sun, Gen. xi. 3; Ex. i. 14; v. 7; 2 Sam. xii. 31; Jer. xliii. 9.

**Bride, Bridegroom**. [MARRIAGE.]

**Brĭg'an-dine** (*brawl*), Jer. xlvi. 4; elsewhere as habergeon.

**Brĭm'stone** (*burn-stone*). Sulphur, Gen. xix. 24; of frequent figurative use, Job xviii. 15; Ps. xi. 6; Isa. xxxiv. 9, Rev. xxi. 8.

**Bŭck'ler** (*cheek*). The small round shield used to catch blows. [ARMOR.]

**Bŭk'kī** (*void*). (1) A prince of Dan, Num. xxxiv. 22. (2) Fifth from Aaron in line of high priests, 1 Chr. vi. 5, 51.

**Bŭk-kī'ah** (*wasting*). A Temple musician, 1 Chr. xxv. 4, 13.

**Bŭl** (*rain*). Marchesvan or Bul, the second month of the Hebrew civil and eighth of the sacred year, corresponding to parts of October and November, 1 Kgs. vi. 38.

**Bŭl'bŭl**. The Persian nightingale, common in the Jordan valley; also the titmouse, in the Latin version.

**Bull, Bullock** (*bellow*). A term used generically for ox, cattle, etc., Ps. xxii. 12. Bullock in Isa. lxv. 25; cow in Ezek. iv. 15; oxen in Gen. xii. 16. The "wild bull" of Isa. li. 20, and the "wild ox" of Deut. xiv. 5, mean probably the oryx.

**Bul'rush** (*large rush*). The bulrush of Ex. ii. 3-5 is supposed to be the papyrus, from which paper was made, Job viii. 11.

**Bū'nah** (*discretion*). A descendant of Judah, 1 Chr. ii. 25.

**Bŭn'nī** (*built*). (1) A Levite, Neh. ix 4. (2) A co-covenanter with Nehemiah, Neh. x. 15. (3) A Levite, Neh. xi. 15.

**Bŭr'ī-al, Bŭr-ȳ** (*mounding*). Place, a cave or hewn rock, Gen. xxiii. 4; xxv. 9; l. 5-13; Matt. xxvii. 60. Body washed, Acts ix. 37; swathed and spiced, Matt. xxvii. 59; Mark xv. 46; xvi. 1. Head covered separately, 2 Chr. xvi. 14; John xix. 40; pall-bearers and mourners, relatives and friends, 2 Sam. iii. 31; Luke vii. 12; sometimes hired mourners, Jer. ix. 17; Ezek. xxiv. 17; Matt. ix. 23.

**Burnt offering**. The offering which was wholly consumed by fire. For ceremonies *see* Lev. viii., ix., xiv., xxix.

**Bush**. Supposably the dwarf acacia, Ex. iii. 2-6. In Deut. xxxiii. 16, Mark xii. 26, Luke xx. 37, the reference is to the locality.

**Bush'el** (*little box*). Hebrew *seah*, twenty pints.

**Bŭt'ler** (*bottler*). Officer of a royal household in charge of the wines and drinking vessels, Gen. xl. 1-13; xli. 9; "cup-bearer," Neh. i. 11; 1 Kgs. x. 5.

**Bŭt'ter** (*cow-cheese*). A curd, or curded milk, evidently meant, Gen. xviii. 8; Job xxix. 6, Judg. v. 25.

**Bŭt'ter-fly**. Nine Hebrew words confusedly translated locust and associated insects. Butterfly a natural incident to caterpillar life.

**Bŭz** (*despised*). (1) Progenitor of Elihu, Gen. xxii. 21. (2) A Gadite, 1 Chr. v. 14. (3) Land of Buz, Jer. xxv. 23.

**Bŭz'īte**. Elihu so called, Job xxxii. 2, 6. [ELIHU, 1.]

**Bū'zī** (*despised*). Father of Ezekiel, Ezek. i. 3.

## C

**Căb**. A Jewish dry measure, about a quart, 2 Kgs. vi. 25.

**Căb'bon** (*understanding*). A town in lowlands of Judah, Josh. xv. 40.

**Căb'ins**. Cells in a dungeon, Jer. xxxvii. 16.

**Cā'bŭl** (*displeasing*). (1) A boundary of Asher, Josh. xix. 27. (2) The district given to Hiram by Solomon, 1 Kgs. ix. 10-14.

**Căd'dis**. Joannan, 1 Macc. ii. 2.

**Cā'des**, 1 Macc. xi. 63. [KEDESH.]

**Căd'mĭ-el**, 1 Esdr. v. 26. [KADMIEL.]

**Çæ'şar** (*hairy, or elephant*). With Julius Cæsar and Augustus Cæsar a surname, but with the latter it became official and remained so till the death of Nero. In Luke ii. 1, Augustus Cæsar is meant; in Luke iii. 1, Tiberius Cæsar; in Acts xi. 28, Claudius Cæsar; in Acts xxv. 8, Phil. iv. 22, Nero.

**Çæs''a-rē'à** (*for Cæsar*). Political capital of Palestine, on Mediterranean, and official residence of Herodian kings and Roman procurators; home of Philip and Cornelius, Acts viii. 40; x., xi. 1-18.

**Çæs''a-rē'à Phĭ-lĭp'pī**. A city of Galilee marking the northern limit of Christ's pilgrimage, and probable scene of the configuration, Matt. xvi. 13-20; xvii. 1-10; Mark viii. 27.

**Cāge** (*hollow*). Bird-trap in Jer. v. 27; prison in Rev. xviii. 2.

**Cā'ia-phās** (*depression*). Appointed high priest by Valerius, and reappointed by Pontius Pilate; A. D. 27-36. Deposed by Vitellius, Matt. xxvi. 3-57; John xi. 49-51; xviii. 13-28; Acts iv. 6.

**Cāin** (*possession*). (1) Eldest son of Adam, Gen. iv. (2) A city in lowlands of Judah, Josh. xv. 57.

**Cā-ī'nan** (*possessor*). (1) Son of Enos, Gen. v. 9; Luke iii. 36. Kenan in 1 Chr. i. 2. (2) Son of Arphaxad, Luke iii. 36.

**Cāke**. [BREAD.]

**Cā'lah** (*old age*). City of Assyria, Gen. x. 11.

**Căl''ă-mŏl'ă-lus**. A compound of Elam, Lod, and Hadidad, 1 Esdr. v. 22.

**Căl'a-mus** (*reed*). Ex. xxx. 23, S. of Sol. iv. 14, Ezek. xxvii. 19, identified with the lemon-grass, or sweet-flag. "Sweet cane" in Isa. xliii. 24, Jer. vi. 20.

**Căl'cŏl** (*nourishment*). A Judahite, 1 Chr. ii. 6.

**Căl'drŏn** (*hot*). A vessel for boiling meats, 1 Sam. ii. 14; 2 Chr. xxxv. 13; Job xli. 20; Micah iii. 3.

**Cā'leb** (*capable*). (1) Son of Hezron, 1 Chr. ii. 18, 19, 42, 50. Chelubai in ii. 9. (2) The spy of Judah, Num. xiii. 6; Josh. xiv., xv.; 1 Sam. xxx. 14. (3) Son of Hur, 1 Chr. ii. 50. (4) Caleb's district, 1 Sam. xxx. 14.

**Călf**. Fatted calf a luxury, Gen. xviii. 7; 1 Sam. xxviii. 24; Am. vi. 4; Luke xv. 23. Molten calf, Ex. xxxii. 4; 1 Kgs. xii. 28, gilded structures. Calf worship denounced, Hos. viii., x., xiii. 2. "Calves of our lips," Hos. xiv. 2, fruits of our lips.

**Căl-lis'thĕ-nēs**. Friend of Nicanor, 2 Macc. viii. 33.

**Căl'neh, Căl'nō** (*fortress*). A city of Nimrod,

Gen. x. 10; Am. vi. 2; Isa. x. 9. Canneh in Ezek. xxvii. 23.

**Căl'phi.** A general, 1 Macc. xi. 70.

**Căl'vă-rў** (*skull*). Latin for Greek *Kranion*, "skull" (referring to shape), and Hebrew "Golgotha." Spot of crucifixion. Calvary, only in Luke xxiii. 33.

**Căm'el** (*carrier*). The Arabian, or one-humped camel, generally meant. Used for carriage, and source of wealth, Gen. xii. 16; Judg. vii. 12; 2 Chr. xiv. 15; Job ' 3; xlii. 12; Isa. xxx. 6. An unclean beast, Lev. xi. 4. Hair used for clothing, 2 Kgs. i. 8; Zech. xiii. 4; Matt. iii. 4. Figuratively for something beyond human power, Matt. xix. 24; xxiii. 24.

**Cā'mŏn** (*straw*). Burial place of Jair, Judg. x. 5.

**Cămp.** [ENCAMPMENT.]

**Căm'phīre.** The gum of the camphor-tree. But in S. of Sol. i. 14; iv. 13; the cyprus flower or henna.

**Cā'nȧ** (*reedy*). A town of Galilee, 7 mls. N. of Nazareth, John ii. 1-11; iv. 46; xxi. 2.

**Cā'năan** (*low*). (1) Fourth son of Ham, Gen. x. 6-19; 1 Chr. i. 8-13. (2) The country between the Mediterranean and Jordan, given by God to the Israelites, Ex. vi. 4; Lev. xxv. 38. "Holy Land," after the captivity, Zech. ii. 13. Palestine, from Philistia.

**Cā'năan-īte.** Dwellers in Canaan, and all tribes known to the Israelites at time of conquest, Gen. x. 18-20; xiii. 7; xiv. 7; xv. 20; Num. xiii. 29; Josh. xi. 3; xxiv. 11.

**Căn'dā-çē** (*queen of servants*). The Ethiopian queen whose servant was converted, Acts viii. 27.

**Căn'dle-stĭck.** The golden candlestick rather a lamp, Ex. xxv. 31-37; xxxvii. 17-24. Ten candelabra used instead, in Solomon's temple, 1 Kgs. vii. 49.

**Cāne.** [CALAMUS.]

**Cănk'er-worm** (*cancer-worm*). A variety of caterpillar. But in Joel i. 4; ii. 25; Nah. iii. 15, 16, probably an undeveloped locust.

**Căn'neh.** Ezek. xxvii. 23. [CALNEH.]

**Căn'on** (*cane, rule*). Word first applied to the Scriptures by Amphilochius about A. D. 380, Gal. vi. 16; Phil. iii. 16. O. T. canon fixed by the Jews, and accepted by Christ and his times. N. T. canon ratified by third council of Carthage, A. D. 397.

**Căn'ō-pў** (*bed with mosquito curtains*). Judith x. 21; xiii. 9; xvi. 19.

**Căn'tĭ-cles** (*song of songs*). The Latinized title of "The Song of Solomon."

**Cȧ-pĕr'na-ŭm** (*hamlet of Nahum*). A city on N. W. shore of Sea of Galilee. Chief residence of Christ and his apostles, Matt. iv. 12-16; viii. 5; ix. 1; xvii. 24; Mark ii. 1; Luke vii. 1-5; John vi. 17.

**Căph'ar** (*hamlet*). Common Hebrew prefix.

**Căph''ăr-săl'a-ma.** A battlefield, 1 Macc. vii. 31.

**Cȧ-phĕn'a-tha.** A suburb of Jerusalem, 1 Macc. xii. 37.

**Căph'tôr, Căph'tŏ-rĭm.** Either Philistines or Copts of Egypt, Gen. x. 14; Deut. ii. 23; Jer. xlvii. 4; Am. ix. 7.

**Căp''pa-dō'çĭ-ȧ** (*fine horses*). Largest Roman province in Asia Minor, with Cæsarea as metropolis, Acts ii. 9; 1 Pet. i. 1.

**Căp'tain** (*head*). Title for a leader of a band of ten, fifty, hundred or thousand, Deut. i. 15; Josh. x. 24; Judg. xi. 6, 11. Also a civic meaning, Isa. i. 10; iii. 3. "Captain of the Guard," Acts xxviii. 16, was commander of the Prætorian troop of Rome. "Captain of the Temple," Acts iv. 1, was chief of the Temple watchmen.

**Căp'tĭve** (*taken*). Captives in war treated with great cruelty in early times, Gen. xiv. 14; Judg. i. 7; 1 Sam. xi. 2; 2 Sam. viii. 2; 2 Kgs. xxv. 7. Later, treated as servants and slaves, 1 Kgs. xx. 31-34.

**Căp-tĭv'ĭ-ty.** Six partial captivities mentioned in Judges. Israel had several, 2 Kgs. xv. 29; 1 Chr. v. 26, the final one being that by Shalmaneser, B. C. 721, 2 Kgs. xvii. 6. Judah was captive to Assyria B. C. 713, and finally to Nebuchadnezzar B. C. 606-562. This captivity broken, Ez. i. 11. Last captivity was to Rome, A. D. 71.

**Cär'bŭn-cle** (*little coal*). A gem of deep red color, Isa. liv. 12. A stone in the high-priest's breastplate, Ex. xxviii. 17; xxxix. 10

**Cär'cas.** A eunuch, Esth. i. 10.

**Cär'chĕ-mĭsh** (*fortress of Chemosh*). A city on the Euphrates, Isa. x. 5-9; 2 Chr. xxxv. 20-23; Jer. xlvi. 2.

**Cȧ-rē'ah** (*bald*). Father of Johannan, 2 Kgs. xxv. 23. Kareah, elsewhere.

**Cā'rĭ-ȧ.** Southwest province of Asia Minor. Cnidus and Miletus were in it, Acts xx. 15; xxvii. 7.

**Cär'mel** (*fruitful*). (1) The promontory which forms the bay of Acre, 1 Kgs. xviii.; 2 Kgs. ii. 25; iv. 25; Isa. xxxiii. 9; xxxv. 2. (2) A city of Judah, 1 Sam. xv. 12; xxv. 2-44; 2 Chr. xxvi. 10.

**Cär'mi** (*vine dresser*). (1) Progenitor of the Carmites, Gen. xlvi. 9; Ex. vi. 14; Num. xxvi. 6; 1 Chr. v. 3. (2) Father of Achan, Josh. vii. 1, 18; 1 Chr. ii. 7.

**Cär'nă-ĭm.** City in Manasseh, 1 Macc. v. 26-44.

**Cär'pĕn-tēr** (*cart-wright*). Carpentry an early art, Gen. vi. 14-16; Ex. xxv. 23; xxvii. 1-15. David and Solomon employed foreign wood-workers, 2 Sam. v. 11; 1 Kgs. v. 6. Joseph a carpenter, Matt. xiii. 55; and Christ, Mark vi. 3.

**Cär'pus** (*fruit*). Paul's friend, 2 Tim. iv. 13.

**Căr'rĭage** (*car*). Baggage, Judg. xviii. 21; Isa. x. 28; xlvi. 1; Acts xxi. 15.

**Cär-shē'nȧ** (*distinguished*). A Persian, Esth. i. 14.

**Cärt** (*carry*). A two-wheeled vehicle usually drawn by oxen, 1 Sam. vi 7-15; Amos ii. 13.

**Cär'vĭng** (*cutting*). Carving and engraving in much request, Ex. xxxi. 5; xxxv. 33; 1 Kgs. vi. 18; 2 Chr. ii. 7-14; Ps. lxxiv. 6; Zech. iii. 9.

**Cāse'ment** (*house-frame*). The latticed opening of the Kiosk, or summer house, of the East, Prov. vii. 6; S. of Sol. ii. 9; Judg. v. 28.

**Cȧ-sĭph'ĭ-ȧ** (*white*). An unknown place, Ez. viii. 17.

**Căs'leu,** 1 Macc. i. 54. [CHISLEU.]

**Căs-lu'hĭm** (*fortified*) A Mizraite people, Gen. x. 14; 1 Chr. i. 12.

**Căs'phor.** City of Gilead, 1 Macc. v. 26.

**Căs'pis,** 2 Macc. xii. 13. [CASPHOR.]

**Căs'sia** (*that peels*). The cinnamon cassia in Ex. xxx. 24; Ezek. xxvii. 19. In Ps. xlv. 8, the shrub is unidentified.

**Căs'tle** (*fort*). The "Tower of Antonia," N. W. corner of the Temple at Jerusalem, Acts xxi. 34, 37; xxii. 24; xxiii. 10, 16, 32.

**Căs'tŏr** and **Pŏl'lux.** Two mythologic heroes; figurehead and name of Paul's ship, Acts xxviii. 11.

**Căt'ĕr-pĭl''lar** (*hairy consumer*). The larva of the butterfly, 1 Kgs. viii. 37; 2 Chr. vi. 28; Ps. lxxviii. 46; Isa. xxxiii. 4; Joel i. 4.

**Căts.** Only in Baruch vi. 22.

**Căt'tle** (*capital*). Domestic bovine animals, as oxen, cows, bulls, and calves; also any live-stock, Gen. xiii. 2; Ex. xii. 29; xxxiv. 19; Num. xx. 19; xxxii. 16; Ps. l. 10; Job. i. 3. [BULL.]

**Cau'dȧ,** Clauda in R. V.

**Caul** (*kŏl*) (*cap*). A net for a woman's hair, Isa. iii. 18. In Hos. xiii. 8, the membrane around the heart.

**Cāve** (*hollow*). Used for storage houses, dwellings, hiding and burial places, Gen. xix. 30; Josh. x. 16; Judg. vi. 2; 1 Sam. xiii. 6; xxii. 1; xxiv. 3; 2 Sam. xxiii. 13; 1 Kgs. xviii. 4; Heb. xi. 38.

**Çē'dăr** (*resinous*). A cone-bearing tree whose reddish fragrant wood was much prized, 1 Kgs. vii. 2; Ps. xcii. 12; S. of Sol. v. 15; Isa. ii. 13; Ezek. xxxi. 6.

**Cē'drŏn** (*turbid*). (1) A brook, Kedron or Kidron, below the eastern wall of Jerusalem, John xviii. 1.

**Çeĭ'lăn.** His sons returned, 1 Esdr. v. 15.

**Çeil'ing** (*heavens*). Hebrew temple ceilings were generally of cedar, richly carved, 1 Kgs. vi. 9-15; vii. 3; 2 Chr. iii. 5-9.

**Çĕn'chrĕ-ȧ** (*millet*). The eastern harbor of Corinth, Acts xviii. 18. Seat of a Christian church, Rom. xvi. 1.

**Çĕn''dē-bē'us.** A Syrian general, 1 Macc. xv. 38.

**Çĕn'sēr** (*set on fire*). A small portable vessel of copper, Num. xvi. 39; Lev. xvi. 12, or gold, 1 Kgs. vii. 50; Heb. ix. 4, for carrying the coals on which incense was burned.

**Çĕn'sus** (*assess*). Twelve different censuses noted in the O. T., Ex. xxxviii. 26; Num. i. 2; xxvi.; 2 Sam. xxiv. 9; 2 Chr. ii. 17, 18; 1 Kgs. xii. 21; 2 Chr. xiii. 3; xiv. 8; xvii. 14; xxv. 5, 6; xxvi. 13; Ez. ii. 64; viii. 1-14. The census in Luke ii. 1-3, was for taxation.

**Çĕn-tū'rĭ-ŏn** (*hundred*). A Roman officer who had command of a hundred soldiers, Matt. viii. 5; Mark xv. 39; Luke vii. 1-10; Acts x. 1.

**Çē'phas** (*stone*). Name given to Peter, John i. 42.

**Cē'ras,** 1 Esdr. v. 29. [KEROS.]

**Çē'tab.** A doubtful name, 1 Esdr. v. 30.

**Chā'brĭs.** Ruler of Bethulia, Judith vi. 15.

**Chā'dĭ-as.** Her citizens returned, 1 Esdr. v. 20.

**Chaff.** Was separated from the grain by throwing all into the air from sheets, or forks, the wind carrying away the chaff, Ps. i. 4; Isa. xvii. 13; Hos. xiii. 3; Zeph. ii. 2.

**Chains** (*links*). Used for ornament on man and beast, and for fetters, Gen. xli. 42; Judg. viii. 21; xvi. 21; 2 Sam. iii. 34; 2 Kgs. xxv. 7; Isa. iii. 19; Acts xii. 6; xxi. 33; xxviii. 20.

**Chăl''çē-dō'ný** (*from Chalcedon*). A many-colored precious stone of the agate variety, Rev. xxi. 19.

**Chăl'cŏl**, 1 Kgs. iv. 31. [CALCOL.]

**Chăl-dē'ȧ, Chăl-dæ'ȧ** (*as demons*). The country lying along the Euphrates on both sides, and between it and the Tigris, for three or four hundred miles back from their mouths, Gen. x. 10; xi. 31; Job i. 17.

**Chăl-dē'ăns, Chăl'deeş.** The people of that country having Babylon for its capital, Dan. i. 4; v. 15; ix. 1.

**Chalk=stōnes.** Possibly burnt lime, Isa. xxvii. 9.

**Chām'bẽr** (*vault, arched*). Sleeping apartment, Gen. xliii. 30; 2 Sam. xviii. 33; Ps. xix. 5; Dan. vi. 10; Acts ix. 37. Dining room, Mark xiv. 14; Luke xxii. 12.

**Chām'bẽr-ing.** Amorous intrigue, Rom. xiii. 13.

**Chām'bẽr-lain** (*man of the chamber*). Officer in charge of the king's chamber, 2 Kgs. xxiii. 11; Esth. i. 10, 12, 15; Dan. i. 8–11. A more dignified office, in Acts xii. 20; Rom. xvi. 23.

**Chȧ-mē'lē-ŏn** (*ground lion*). A species of lizard, arboreal in habit. But the word thus translated implies a frog, Lev. xi. 30.

**Chăm'ois** (*sham-my*) (*buck*). The chamois not known in Palestine. A wild sheep, or goat, may be meant, Deut. xiv. 5.

**Chā'năan.** Greek spelling of Canaan, Acts vii. 11; xiii. 19; Judith v. 3.

**Chăn'çel-lŏr** (*usher of a law-court*). A keeper of the king's seal, Ez. iv. 8.

**Chăp'ĭ-ter** (*head*). The ornamental head of a pillar, Ex. xxxvi. 38; xxxviii. 17; 1 Kgs. vii. 31, 38.

**Chăp'man** (*cheap-man*). A trader, 1 Kgs. x. 15; 2 Chr. ix. 14.

**Chär''ą-ăth'ă-lar**, 1 Esdr. v. 36. [CHERUB.]

**Chăr'ą-cȧ.** An obscure place, 2 Macc. xii. 17.

**Chăr'ą-shim, Valley of** (*ravine of craftsmen*). Where Joab's ancestors lived, 1 Chr. iv. 14.

**Chär'chĕ-mish**, 2 Chr. xxxv. 20; **Chär'chă-mis**, 1 Esdr. i. 25. [CARCHEMISH.]

**Chär'cus**, 1 Esdr. v. 32. [BARKOS.]

**Chär'ġer** (*car*). A dish for receiving water and blood, and for presenting offerings of flour and oil, Num. vii. 13, 79; later, a large service plate, Matt. xiv. 8.

**Chăr'ĭ-ot** (*car*). A two-wheeled vehicle, used for travel and war, Gen. xli. 43; xlvi. 29; 1 Kgs. xviii. 44; 2 Kgs. v. 9. In use by enemies of Israel, Josh. xi. 4; Judg. iv. 3; 1 Sam. xiii. 5. Adopted for war by David and Solomon, 2 Sam. viii. 4; 1 Kgs. ix. 19; x. 26; xxii. 34; 2 Kgs. ix. 16; Isa. xxxi. 1.

**Chăr'mis.** Ruler of Bethulia, Judith vi. 15.

**Chăr'ran**, Acts vii. 2–4. [HARAN.]

**Chăs'ĕ-ba**, 1 Esdr. v. 31. [GAZERA.]

**Chē'bär** (*strength*). A river of Chaldea; seat of Ezekiel's visions, Ezek. i. 3; iii. 15, 23.

**Chĕd''ŏr-lā'o-mẽr** (*handful of sheaves*). King of Elam, Gen. xiv. 1–24.

**Cheese.** The Hebrew words imply curds, or curdled milk, 1 Sam. xvii. 18; Job x. 10; 2 Sam. xvii. 29.

**Chē'lăl** (*perfect*). A returned captive, Ez. x. 30.

**Chĕl'çĭ-as.** Hilkiah, Bar i. 7.

**Chĕl'lụh** (*perfection*). A returned captive, Ez. x. 35.

**Chĕl'lus.** A place west of Jordan, Judith i. 9.

**Chē'lŭb** (*basket*). (1) A Judahite, 1 Chr. iv. 11. (2) Father of one of David's overseers, 1 Chr. xxvii. 26.

**Chĕ-lū'bāi** (*capable*). Caleb, 1 Chr. ii. 9.

**Chĕm'ą-rims** (*black ones*). Sun-worshippers, Zeph. i. 4.

**Chē'mosh** (*subduer*). National god of Moab, and Ammon, Num. xxi. 29; Judg. xi. 23, 24; 1 Kgs. xi. 7; 2 Kgs. xxiii. 13.

**Chĕ-nā'ă-nah** (*merchant*). (1) Father of Zedekiah, 1 Kgs. xxii. 11. (2) A Benjamite, 1 Chr. vii. 10.

**Chĕn'ą-nī** (*contraction of Chenaniah*). A Levite, Neh. ix. 4.

**Chĕn''ą-nī'ah** (*made by God*). A Levite, 1 Chr. xv. 22.

**Chē'phăr=hā-ăm'mo-nāi.** "Hamlet of the Ammonites," in Benjamin, 2 Chr. xviii. 24.

**Chĕ-phī'rah** (*hamlet*). A Gibeonite city, Josh. ix. 17; Ez. ii. 25; Neh. vii. 29.

**Chē'ran** (*lyre*). A Horite, Gen. xxxvi. 26; 1 Chr. i. 41.

**Chē'rē-as.** A general, 2 Macc. x. 32–37.

**Chĕr'ĕth-ims**, Ezek. xxv. 16. [CHERETHITES.]

**Chĕr'ĕth-ītes** (*executioners*). A portion of David's body guard, 2 Sam. viii. 18; xv. 18; xx. 7, 23; 1 Kgs. i. 38, 44; 1 Chr. xviii. 17.

**Chē'rith** (*cutting*). The place where Elijah was fed by ravens, 1 Kgs. xvii. 3–5.

**Chē'rub.** A place in Babylonia, Ez. ii. 59; Neh. vii. 61.

**Chĕr'ub, Chĕr'u-bim** (*terrible*). Guards of Paradise, Gen. iii. 24; and the mercy seat, Ex. xxv. 18. Wrought in gold or wood, Ex. xxxvi. 35; xxxvii. 7–9. Of immense size in Solomon's Temple, 1 Kgs. vi. 27. Four-winged and four-faced, Ezek. i. 6; x. 14; Rev. iv. 8.

**Chĕs'ă-lon** (*hopes*). A landmark of Judah, Josh. xv. 10.

**Chē'sed** (*gain*). Fourth son of Nahor, Gen. xxii. 22.

**Chē'sĭl** (*fool*). A place in south Judah, Josh. xv. 30.

**Chĕst** (*box*). A coffin, Gen. l. 26. Treasure chest, 2 Kgs. xii. 9; 2 Chr. xxiv. 8–11. Trunk or packing-case, Ezek. xxvii. 24. In all other places, "Ark."

**Chĕst'nut=tree**, Gen. xxx. 37; Ezek. xxxi. 8; the plane-tree is meant.

**Chĕ-sŭl'lŏth** (*loins*). Town of Issachar, Josh. xix. 18.

**Chĕt-tī'ĭm**, 1 Macc. i. 1. [CHITTIM.]

**Chē'zĭb** (*lying*), Gen. xxxviii. 5. Probably Achzib.

**Chī'don** (*dart*). Spot where the accident befel the Ark, 1 Chr. xiii. 9–13. Nachon, 2 Sam. vi. 6.

**Chief of Asia**, Acts xix. 31. [ASIAARCH.]

**Chief Priest.** [HIGH PRIEST.]

**Chĭl'dren.** Children an honor, childlessness a misfortune, Gen. xvi. 2; Deut. vii. 14; 1 Sam. i. 6; 2 Sam. vi. 23; 2 Kgs. iv. 14; Ps. cxxvii. 3; Isa. xlvii. 9, Jer. xx. 15. Males circumcised on eighth day, Lev. xii. 3. Weaning an occasion of rejoicing, Gen. xxi. 8.

**Chĭl'e-ăb** (*like the father*). Son of David, 2 Sam. iii. 3.

**Chĭl'ĭ-on** (*sickly*). Husband of Orpah, Ruth 1:2–4.

**Chĭl'măd** (*closed*). A country on the Euphrates, Ezek. xxvii. 23.

**Chĭm'ham** (*longing*). A friend of David, 2 Sam. xix. 37, 38; Jer. xli. 17.

**Chĭn'ne-rĕth, Chĭn'ne-rŏth.** (1) A city on or near coast of Sea of Galilee, Josh. xi. 2. (2) Old name for the inland sea known as Lake Gennesareth, or Sea of Galilee, Num. xxxiv. 11; Deut. iii. 17; Josh. xiii. 27.

**Chī'os** (*open*). The island of Scio, Acts xx. 15.

**Chĭs'lēū.** Ninth month of the Jewish sacred, and third of the civil, year, corresponding to parts of Nov. and Dec., Neh. i. 1.

**Chĭs'lon** (*hope*). A Benjamite, Num. xxxiv. 21.

**Chĭs'lŏth=tā'bôr**, Josh. xix. 12. [CHESULLOTH.]

**Chĭt'tim, Kĭt'tim** (*bruisers*). Descendants of Javan, and their country, supposably Cyprus, Gen. x. 4; Num. xxiv. 24; 1 Chr. i. 7; Isa. xxiii. 1–12.

**Chī'ūn.** An Israelite idol, Am. v. 26. [REMPHAN.]

**Chlō'ē** (*green herb*). A Christian woman of Corinth, 1 Cor. i. 11.

**Chō'bȧ, Chō'bāi.** A place in Bethulia, Judith vi. 4; xv. 4.

**Chôr-ă'shan.** A haunt of David, 1 Sam. xxx. 30.

**Chō-rā'zin** (*secret*). A city on the coast of the Sea of Galilee, Matt. xi. 21; Luke x. 13.

**Chō'ze-bȧ.** Descendants of Judah, 1 Chr. iv. 22.

**Christ.** The Anointed; the Messiah. A title of Jesus, the Saviour: at first with the article, "The Christ;" later, as part of a proper name, "Jesus Christ." [JESUS.]

**Chris'tian.** Follower of Christ. First so called at Antioch, Syria, A. D. 43, Acts xi. 26; xxvi. 28.

**Chrŏn'ĭ-cles** ("*words of days*," *annals*). Thirteenth and fourteenth of O. T. Books. Originally one book called Paraleipomena, "things omitted." A supplement to Kings, compiled, no doubt, by Ezra. The history covers a period of 3500 years.

**Chrȳs'ō-līte** (*gold stone*). Evidently the yellow topaz, Rev. xxi. 20.

**Chrȳs''ō-prā'sus** (*golden leek*). An apple-green variety of chalcedony, Rev. xxi. 20.

**Chŭb.** Allies of Egypt, Ezek. xxx. 5.

**Chŭn** (*ready*). A city that supplied brass to Solomon, 2 Sam. viii. 8.

**Chŭrch** (*assembly*). A congregation of religious worshippers, Acts vii. 38; Matt. xvi. 18. Visible, Acts ii.; Col. i. 24. Invisible, Heb. xii. 23.

**Chŭrn-ing**, Prov. xxx. 33. The milk was enclosed in skin bags, which were shaken or trodden.

**Chū'shan=rĭsh''a-thā'im** (*great conqueror*). A king of Mesopotamia, Judg. iii. 8–10.

**Chū'si.** A place, Judith vii. 18.

**Chū'zȧ** (*seer*). Steward of Herod, Luke viii. 3; xxiv. 10.

**Çi-lĭ'ç!a** (*rolling*). A province of Asia Minor. Chief city, Tarsus, birthplace of Paul, Acts ix. 11, 30; xv. 41.

**Çĭn'nă-mŏn** (*dried*). Inner bark of the cinnamon-tree, Ex. xxx. 23: Rev. xviii. 13. A perfume, Prov. vii. 17.

**Çĭn'ne-rŏth.** A district of Naphtali, 1 Kgs. xv. 20. [CHINNERETH.]

**Çĭr'a-mȧ.** Returned Jews, 1 Esdr. v. 20.

**Çĭr''cŭm-çĭ'sion** (*cutting around*). Cutting off the foreskin. A rite, performed on males on eighth day after birth, Gen. xvii.; Lev. xii. 3; Ex. xii. 44; John vii. 22. Antagonized by Christianity, Acts xv.; 1 Cor. vii. 18; Gal. v. 2.

**Çĭs**, Acts xiii. 21. [KISH.]

**Çĭ'sai**, Esther xi. 12. [KISH.]

**Çĭs'tern** (*chest*). Common and necessary in the East. Sometimes synonymous with "wells," Num. xxi. 22, and "pits," Gen. xxxvii. 22; 2 Sam. xvii 18, Eccl. xii. 6; Jer. xxxviii. 6.

**Çĭt'ims**, 1 Macc. viii. 5. [CHITTIM.]

**Çĭt'i-zĕn-ship.** Roman citizenship exempted from imprisonment or scourging without trial, and gave the right of appeal to the Emperor, Acts xvi. 37; xxii. 28, 29; xxv. 11.

**Çĭt'ȳ** (*place for citizens*). Cain and Nimrod city-builders, Gen. iv. 17; x. 9–11. "Fenced cities," fortified cities, 2 Kgs. x. 2; Isa. xxvi. 1. "City of David," Jerusalem, Bethlehem, 1 Chr. xi. 5; Luke ii. 11. "City of God," Jerusalem, Ps. xlvi. 4; Neh. xi. 1. "Cities of Refuge," six in number, Deut. xix. 7–9; Num. xxxv. 6–15.

**Clau'dȧ** (*lamentable*). A small island near Crete, Acts xxvii. 16.

**Clau'dĭ-ȧ** (*lame*). A female friend of Paul and Timothy, 2 Tim. iv. 21.

**Clau'dĭ-us** (*lame*). Claudius Cæsar. Fifth Roman Emperor. Reign, A. D. 41–54. Banished the Jews from Rome, Acts xviii. 2.

**Clau'dĭ-us Lȳs'ĭ-as.** [LYSIAS.]

**Clāy.** Used variously, Ps. xviii. 42; Isa. lvii. 20; Jer. xxxviii. 6; John ix. 6; for making pottery, Isa. xli. 25; for brick-making, 2 Sam. xii. 31; for sealing, Job xxxviii. 14; for writing tablets.

**Clēan** and **Un'clean.** Words applied to personal and ceremonial conditions, and to edibility of animals, Gen. vii. 2; Lev. xi.–xv.; Num. xix.; Ex. xxii. 31; xxxiv. 15–26.

**Clĕm'ent** (*mild*). A co-worker with Paul, Phil. iv. 3.

**Clē'o-pas** (*renowned father*). One of the two disciples to whom Christ appeared, Luke xxiv. 18.

**Clē'o-phas** (*renowned*). Husband of Mary, John xix. 25. Called also Alphæus.

**Clŏth.** Skins first supplied the place of cloth. Art of weaving cloth early known, Ex. xxxv. 25. Judg. v. 30.

**Clō'thing.** [DRESS.]

**Clôud** (*round mass*). A prominent feature in Oriental imagery, Prov. xvi. 15; Isa. xxv. 5; Job xxx. 15. A token of Divine presence and protection, Ex. xvi. 10; Num. xii. 5.

**Clôut'ed.** Worn out and patched, Josh. ix. 5.

**Cnī'dus** (*nī'dus*) (*age*). The peninsula of Caria, and the city upon it, Acts xxvii. 7; 1 Macc. xv. 23.

**Cōal** (*glow*). The coal of scripture is charcoal, or embers, Prov. xxvi. 21; John xviii. 18; xxi. 9; heated stones, 1 Kgs. xix. 6; Isa. vi. 6; metaphorical, 2 Sam. xxii. 9–13; Ps. xviii. 8, 12, 13; Rom. xii. 20.

**Cōast** (*rib*). Often used as border or boundary, Judg. xi. 20; 1 Sam. v. 6; Matt. viii. 34.

**Cōat** (*coarse mantle*). [DRESS.]

**Cŏck.** The crowing of the cock in Matt. xxvi. 34; Mark xiv. 30; Luke xxii. 34, indicated the third watch of the night, from midnight to daylight.

**Cŏck'a-trīce** (*crocodile like.*) The basilisk, Jer. viii. 17; Isa. xi. 8; xiv. 29; lix. 5; in all which some species of hissing, venomous serpent is meant.

**Cŏck'le** (*stinking*). A weed that grows among grain; doubtless the tare, identified as darnel, Job xxxi. 40.

**Çœl'e=Sȳr'i-ȧ** and **Çĕl'o=Sȳr'i-ȧ** (*hollow Syria*). That part of Syria lying between the Libanus and Anti-Libanus ranges, 1 Macc. x. 69.

**Cŏf'fer** (*basket*). A movable box hanging from the side of a cart, 1 Sam. vi. 8, 11, 15.

**Cŏf'fin** (*basket*). [BURIAL.]

**Cō'hŏrt** (*company*). [ARMY.]

**Cŏl-hō'zeh** (*all-seeing*). A man of Judah, Neh. iii. 15; xi. 5.

**Cō'lĭ-us**, 1 Esdr. ix. 23. [KELAIAH.]

**Cŏl'lar.** "Collars" in Judg. viii. 26, and "chains" in Isa. iii. 19, should be "ear-drops."

**Cŏl'lēge** (*collected*). That part of Jerusalem north of the old city, 2 Kgs. xxii. 14.

**Cŏl'lops** (*tender meat*). Slices of meat, Job xv. 27.

**Cŏl'ō-ny** (*cultivated*). Philippi, colonized by Rome, Acts xvi. 12.

**Côl'ors** (*tints*). Royal colors, purple, Judg. viii. 26; Esth. viii. 15; Luke xvi. 19; Rev. xvii. 4; blue, Ex. xxv. 4; Esth. i. 6. Vermilion used for beams, walls and ceilings, Jer. xxii. 14; Ezek. xxiii. 14.

**Cō-lŏs'sē** (*punishment*). A city of Phrygia. Paul wrote to the church there, Col. i. 2; iv. 13.

**Cō-lŏs'sĭ-ans, Epistle to.** Written by Paul from Rome, A. D. 61 or 62, and delivered by Tychicus, Acts xxviii. 16; Col. iv. 7, 8.

**Cōlt** (*young camel or ass*). The young of camels and asses, Gen. xxxii. 15; xlix. 11; Judg. x. 4; Job xi. 12; Matt. xxi. 2–7.

**Côm'fŏrt-er** (*brave together*). Defender and helper. Applied to the Holy Ghost, and Christ, John xiv. 16.

**Cŏm'merce** (*buying together.*) Limited among Hebrews, Gen. xiii. 2; xxiv. 22, 53. Outside enterprises a failure, 1 Kgs. xxii. 48–9. Used some foreign articles, Ez. iii. 7; Neh. xiii. 16; supplied some, 1 Kgs. v. 11; Acts xii. 20. Temple commerce led to Christ's rebuke, Matt. xxi. 12; John ii. 14.

**Cŏm-mū'nion** (*bound together*). Mutual love, confidence and fellowship, 1 Cor. x. 16; 2 Cor. xiii. 14; 1 John i. 3. The Lord's supper called the "holy communion."

**Côm'pass** (*encircle*). To make a circuit, 2 Sam. v. 23; Acts xxviii. 13.

**Cŏn-a-nī'ah** (*made by Jehovah*). A Levite, 2 Chr. xxxv. 9.

**Cŏn-çĭ'sion** (*cutting off*). A sarcastic use by Paul of the word circumcision, Phil. iii. 2.

**Cŏn'cū-bīne** (*lying with*). In the Jewish economy, a secondary wife, betrothed according to custom, Gen. xxi. 14; xxv. 6; Ex. xxi. 7; Deut. xxi. 10–14. Concubinage repudiated in N. T., Matt. xix. 4–9; 1 Cor. vii. 2–4.

**Cŏn'duit** (*dĭt*) (*conductor*). A water pipe or aqueduct, 2 Kgs. xviii. 17; xx. 20; Isa. vii. 3; xxxvi. 2; ditch, Job xxxviii. 25.

**Cō'ney, Cō'nȳ** (*rabbit*). The small rabbit-like animal known as the *Hyrax Syriacus*, Lev. xi. 5; Deut. xiv. 7; Prov. xxx. 26.

**Cŏn''grē-gā'tion** (*collected together*). Biblically, the Hebrew nationality, Num. xv. 15. Generally, collected Jewry, Ex. xii. 19. A popular assembly, Acts xix. 32, 39, 41. A religious assembly, or church, Acts vii. 38.

**Cō-nī'ah.** [JECONIAH.]

**Cŏn''ŏ-nī'ah** (*the Lord's appointed*). Treasurer of tithes, 2 Chr. xxxi. 12, 13.

**Cŏn'sē-crāte** (*together sacred*). The tribe of Levi consecrated to the priesthood, Ex. xxxii. 28, 29; Lev. vii. 37. Consecrate vessels, Josh. vi. 19; profits, Mic. iv. 13; fields, Lev. xxvii. 28; cattle, 2 Chr. xxix. 33 persons, Num. vi. 9–13; nations, Ex. xix. 6.

**Cŏn''vō-cā'tion** (*called together*). The "congregation," when called in a purely religious capacity, Ex. xii. 16; Lev. xxiii. 2; Num. xxviii. 18.

**Cook'ing.** Done by both sexes, Gen. xviii. 6–8; later by servantage, 1 Sam. viii. 13. Kids, lambs and calves furnished meat for guests, Gen. xviii. 7; Luke xv. 23.

**Cō'ŏs** (*summit*), Acts xxi. 1. [Cos.]

**Cō'ping.** The top and projecting layer of a wall, 1 Kgs. vii. 9.

**Cŏp'per** (*from Cyprus*). The "brass" of the Bible. Known to antediluvians, Gen. iv. 22. Used largely in the temple, 1 Chr. xxii. 3-14; and for vessels, ornaments and mirrors, Ex. xxxviii. 8; helmets and spears, 1 Sam. xvii. 5, 6; 2 Sam. xxi. 16.

**Cŏr.** [HOMER.]

**Cŏr'al.** Used by Hebrews for beads and ornaments. Ranked among precious stones, Job xxviii. 18; Ezek. xxvii. 16.

**Cŏr'ban** (*offering*). The offering in fulfilment of a vow, Lev. xxvii.; Num. xxx. The plea of corban reprehended by Christ, Matt. xv. 3-9.

**Cŏr'be,** 1 Esdr. v. 22. [ZACCAI.]

**Cŏrd** (*string*). Variously made and used, Isa. xix. 9; scourge, John ii. 15; ship-ropes, Acts xxvii. 32.

**Cō'rē,** Ecclus. xlv. 18; Jude 11. [KORAH.]

**Cō"ri-ăn'der** (*smelling like a bed-bug*). A plant of the parsley family producing aromatic seeds. Ex. xvi. 31; Num. xi. 7.

**Cŏr'inth** (*ornament*). Anciently Ephyra; capital of Achaia. Destroyed by Rome, B. C. 146. Rebuilt by Julius Cæsar, B. C. 46, as a Roman colony. Paul founded a church there, Acts xviii. 1; xx. 2, 3.

**Cŏr-ĭn'thĭ-ans, Epistles to.** I. written by Paul at Ephesus, 1 Cor. xvi. 8; treats of church organization, social practices, holy observances, and doctrinal affairs. II. written a few months afterwards, at suggestion of Titus; largely refers to Paul's right to preach and teach, 2 Cor. vii. 5; ix. 2.

**Côr'mō-rant** (*sea raven*). A large, greedy water-bird, pronounced "unclean." Lev. xi. 17; Deut. xiv. 17. Doubtless "pelican" in Isa. xxxiv. 11; Zeph ii. 14.

**Côrn** (*kernel*). In a Bible sense, grain of all kinds except our maize, or Indian corn. Used largely in figurative speech, Gen. xli. 22; Ex. ix. 32; Deut. xi. 14; xviii. 4; xxviii. 51; 2 Chr. ii. 15; Isa. xxviii. 25; Ezek. xxvii. 17; Matt. xii. 1.

**Côr-nē'li̤us** (*of a horn*). A Roman centurion and first Gentile convert, Acts x. 1-33.

**Côr'ner** (*horned*). Grain-field corners not allowed to be wholly reaped, Lev. xix. 9; xxiii. 22. "Legal corner," one sixtieth of the field. "Length and breadth" of a country, Num. xxiv. 17; Jer. xlviii. 45. "Cornerstone," chief stone in a foundation, Job xxxviii. 6. Figuratively in Isa. xxviii. 16; Matt. xxi. 42.

**Côr'net** (*horn*). The curved signal horn of the Jews, usually made of the horn of a ram, ox, chamois, or wild goat, Lev. xxv. 9; Ezek. xxxiii. 4, 5; 1 Chr. xv. 28.

**Cŏs, Cō'ŏs** (*summit*). A small island of the Grecian archipelago, Acts xxi. 1.

**Cō'sam** (*diviner*). One of Christ's ancestors, Luke iii. 28.

**Cōte** (*cot, den*). A sheepfold, 2 Chr. xxxii. 28.

**Cŏt'tage** (*cot*). A rustic tent or shelter, Isa. xxiv. 20.

**Cŏt'ton** (*wool-plant*). Not known to Hebrews. Cotton garments mentioned on the Rosetta stone.

**Cŏuch** (*placed*). [BED.]

**Cŏun'çil** (*called together*). In N. T., (1) The Sanhedrim, Matt. xxvi. 49. (2) Lesser courts, Matt. x. 17; Mark xiii. 9. (3) A jury of councillors, Acts xxv. 12. [SANHEDRIM.]

**Cōur'ses** (*running*). Priests divided into twenty-four classes, courses, or orders, 1 Chr. xxiv. [ABIA.]

**Cōurt** (*enclosure*). The enclosed space within the limits of Oriental houses. The outer area of the tabernacle and temple, Ex. xxvii. 9; Lev. vi. 16; 2 Sam. xvii. 18; 1 Kgs. vi. 36; 2 Kgs. xxiii. 12; 2 Chr. xxxiii. 5.

**Cou̧'tha.** One of the returned, 1 Esdr. v. 32.

**Cŏv'ē-nant** (*coming together*). Ratified by eating together, oaths, witnesses, gifts, pillars, Gen. ix. 15; xxi. 30, 31; xxxi. 50-52. Covenant of the law through Moses, Ex. xx. 24; of the gospel through Christ, Gal. iii.; Heb. viii.

**Cŏv'et** (*desire*). Rightful desire, 1 Cor. xii. 31, good. Wrongful desire, sinful, Ex. xx. 17; xviii. 21; Prov. xxviii. 16; Luke xii. 15-34; 1 Tim. vi. 9, 10.

**Cow.** Cow and calf not to be killed on same day, Lev. xxii. 28. Symbol of plenty, Isa. vii. 21.

**Cŏz** (*thorn*). A Judahite, 1 Chr. iv. 8.

**Cŏz'bī** (*liar*). Daughter of Zur, Num. xxv. 15-18.

**Crăck'nels** (*that cracks*). Hard brittle cakes, 1 Kgs. xiv. 3.

**Crāne.** A large, long-necked, heron-like bird, of gray plumage, noisy on the wing, Isa. xxxviii. 14; Jer. viii. 7.

**Crā'tes.** Governor of Cyprus, 2 Macc. iv. 29.

**Crē-āte', Crē-ā'tion** (*make, made*). To produce out of nothing by Almighty fiat, Gen. i. ii. The universe.

**Crĕs'çens** (*increasing*). Assistant of Paul, 2 Tim. iv. 10.

**Crēte** (*carnal*). Now Candia. One of the largest islands in the Grecian archipelago. Paul founded a church there in charge of Titus, Acts ii. 11; xxvii. 1-12; Tit. i. 5-13.

**Crētes.** Inhabitants of Crete, Acts ii. 11.

**Crĭb.** A stall for cattle, and the manger or rack for hay or straw, Job xxxix. 9; Prov. xiv. 4; Isa. i. 3.

**Crĭm'son** (*carmine*). A deep-red color; or a red tinged with blue, Jer. iv. 30.

**Crĭsp'ing-pins** (*curling pins*). Crimping pins, Isa. iii. 22.

**Crĭs'pus** (*curled*). Chief ruler of the synagogue at Corinth, Acts xviii. 8. Baptized by Paul, 1 Cor. i. 14.

**Crŏss** (*across*). A gibbet of wood of various forms, Deut. xxi. 23; John xix. 17; Gal. iii. 13. Now a sacred emblem.

**Crown** (*curved*). A head-dress, Ezek. xvi. 12. Head-dress of priests, kings, and queens, Ex. xxviii. 36-38; 2 Chr. xxiii. 11; Esth. ii. 17. Symbol of power, honor, and eternal life, Prov. xii. 4; Lam. v. 16; 1 Pet. v. 4.

**Crū"cĭ-fĭx'i̤on** (*fixing to the cross*). A method of death punishment by fixing to a cross, Gen. xl. 19 Esth. vii. 10. Limbs sometimes broken to hasten death, John xix. 31. Sepulture denied, Deut. xxi. 22, 23, but an exception allowed in Christ's case, Matt. xxvii. 58.

**Crū'cĭ-fy.** [CRUCIFIXION.]

**Crūse** (*pot*). A bottle, flask, or jug for holding liquids, 1 Sam. xxvi. 11; 1 Kgs. xvii. 12, xix. 6.

**Crȳs'tal** (*frost*). A disputed original, variously translated crystal, Job xxviii. 17, frost, Gen. xxxi. 40; ice, Job xxxviii. 29.

**Cū'bit** (*elbow*). Distance from the elbow to end of the middle finger, or about 21.8 inches, Gen. vi. 15; 1 Sam. xvii. 4.

**Cu̧ck'oo** (*crower*). A mistranslation; and perhaps the storm-petrel is meant, Lev. xi. 16; Deut. xiv. 15.

**Cū'cŭm-ber** (*cumberer*). Much used for food in the East, Num. xi. 5; Isa. i. 8.

**Cŭm'mĭn.** An annual of the parsley family, producing aromatic seeds, Isa. xxviii. 25; Matt. xxiii. 23.

**Cŭn'ning** (*test*). Skilful, Gen. xxv. 27; 1 Sam. xvi. 16.

**Cŭp** (*coop, tub*). A drinking vessel of various designs, made of horn, clay, or metal, Gen. xliv. 2; 1 Sam. xvi. 13; 1 Kgs. vii. 26. Used figuratively in Ps. xxiii. 5; Isa. li. 17; Rev. xiv. 10; Matt. xx. 22; xxvi. 39.

**Cŭp'beār"er.** [BUTLER.]

**Cūsh** (*black*). (1) Oldest son of Ham, Gen. x. 6, 8; 1 Chr. i. 8-10. (2) That indefinite country translated Ethiopia in Gen. ii. 13. (3) The country settled by Ham's descendants, Gen. x. 6-8; Isa. xviii. 1; Jer. xiii. 23; Dan. xi. 43. (4) A Benjamite, Ps. vii. title.

**Cu̧'shan** (*blackness*), Hab. iii. 7. Some refer it to Cush.

**Cu̧'shī** (*Ethiopian*). (1) A foreigner in David's army, 2 Sam. xviii. 21-32. (2) An ancestor of Jehudi, Jer. xxxvi. 14. (3) Father of Zephaniah, Zeph. i. 1.

**Cŭth** (*burning*). The land in Persia whence colonists came into Samaria, 2 Kgs. xvii. 30. Cuthah in vs. 24.

**Cū'thah, Cŭth-ītes,** 2 Kgs. xvii. 24. [CUTH.]

**Cŭt'tings,** Of the flesh, forbidden by Levitical law, Lev. xix. 28; xxi. 5; Deut. xiv. 1.

**Çȳ'ă-mon.** A place near Carmel, Judith vii. 3.

**Çȳm'bal** (*hollow of a vessel*). Metallic plates, slightly concave, used as musical instruments, by striking them together, 1 Chr. xiii. 8; xvi. 5; Ps. cl. 5; 1 Cor. xiii. 1.

**Çy̆'press** (*from Cyprus*). Not indigenous to Palestine. Juniper may be meant, Isa. xliv. 14.

**Çy̆p'rĭ-an.** Dweller in Cyprus, 2 Macc. iv. 29.

**Çy̆'prus** (*fairness*). A large island in N. E. angle of the Mediterranean. Christianity introduced quite early, Acts xi. 19. Birthplace of Barnabas, Acts iv. 36. Paul visited it, Acts xiii. 4-13.

**Çy̆-rē'nē** (*wall*). Capital of Cyrenaica, in northern Africa, and corresponding to Tripoli. Simon was of Cyrene, Matt. xxvii. 32; Mark xv. 21. Cyreneans present at Pentecost, Acts ii. 10; vi. 9.

**Çy̆-rē'nĭ-us** (*of Cyrene*). Roman governor of Syria, B. C. 4-1, and A. D. 6-11; Luke ii. 2; Acts v. 37.

**Çy̆'rus** (*sun*). Founder of the Persian empire, Dan. vi. 28; xi. 13; 2 Chr. xxxvi. 22. United Media to Persia. Conquered Babylon, B. C. 538, and reigned over the consolidated empire till B. C. 529. A guardian and liberator of captive Jews, Isa. xliv. 28; xlv. 1-7. Daniel was his favorite minister. *See* Dan., also Ez. i. 1-4; iii. 7; iv. 3; v. 13-17; vi. 3.

## D

**Dăb'a-reh,** Josh. xxi. 28. [Daberath.]

**Dăb'ba-shĕth** (*hump*). A boundary of Zebulun, Josh. xix. 11.

**Dăb'e-răth** (*pasture*). A Levitical city, Josh. xix. 12.

**Dăb'rĭ-à.** A swift scribe, 2 Esdr. xiv. 24.

**Dà-cō'bĭ,** 1 Esdr. v. 28. [Akkub.]

**Dăd-dē'us,** or **Săd-dē'us,** 1 Esdr. viii. 45, 46. [Iddo.]

**Dā'gŏn** (*fish*). National male idol of the Philistines, 1 Chr. x. 10. Noted temples at Ashdod, 1 Sam. v. 1-7; Gaza, Judg. xvi. 23; Beth-dagon, Josh. xv. 41; and in Asher, Josh. xix. 27. Represented with human hands and face and a fish's body.

**Dai'san,** 1 Esdr. v. 31. [Rezin.]

**Dăl''a-ī'ah** (*freed by God*). A Judahite, 1 Chr. iii. 24.

**Dāle,** the **King's.** A valley near Jerusalem, Gen. xiv. 17; 2 Sam. xviii. 18.

**Dăl''ma-nū'thà.** A town on Sea of Galilee, Mark viii. 10.

**Dăl-mā'tĭ-à** (*-she-a*) (*deceitful*). A province of Illyricum, 2 Tim. iv. 10; Rom. xv. 19.

**Dăl'phon** (*swift*). Son of Haman, Esth. ix. 7.

**Dăm'a-rĭs** (*heifer*). An Athenian woman converted by Paul, Acts xvii. 34.

**Dà-măs'cus.** A city of Asia, 133 miles N. E. of Jerusalem, Gen. xiv. 15; xv. 2. Adjacent region called "Syria of Damascus," 2 Sam. viii. 5. Taken by David, 2 Sam. viii. 6; and by Jeroboam, 2 Kgs. xiv. 28. Scene of Paul's conversion, Acts ix. 1-27; xxii. 1-16.

**Dăm-nā'tion** (*condemnation*). Consignment to everlasting perdition, Matt. xxiii. 33; Mark iii. 29; John v. 29; 2 Pet. ii. 3.

**Dăn** (*judge*). (1) Fifth son of Jacob, Gen. xxx. 6; xlix. 16. Allotment, Josh. xix. 40-46. Portion of the tribe moved north, Josh. xix. 47, 48; Judg. xviii. (2) Changed name of Laish, or Leshem, Josh. xix. 47; Judg. xviii. 29. (3) A place in Arabia, Ezek. xxvii. 19.

**Dăn'ītes.** Members of the tribe of Dan, Judg. xiii. 2; 1 Chr. xii. 35.

**Dăn-jā'an** (*Danite*). Probably the northern Danites, 2 Sam. xxiv. 6.

**Dănce** (*drag along*). (1) In Hebrew, "leaping for joy." Not a measured step, Ps. xxx. 11. Common on festal occasions, Ex. xv. 20, 21; Judg. xi. 34; 1 Sam. xviii. 6, 7; 2 Sam. vi. 14; Jer. xxxi. 4; Luke vi. 23; xv. 25; Acts iii. 8. (2) A musical instrument, Ps. cl. 3-5. "Pipe," in margin.

**Dăn'iel** (*judgment of God*). (1) Fourth of the greater prophets. Carried captive to Babylon, B. C. 604; and named Belteshazzar, Dan. i., ii. Made a governor under Darius, Dan. vi. 2. Last vision on the Tigris in third year of Cyrus, B. C. 534, x. 1-4. (2) Second son of David, 1 Chr. iii. 1. (3) Son of Ithamar, Ez. viii. 2. (4) A co-covenanter, Neh. x. 6.

**Dăn'iel, Book of** First six chapters historic. Chapters vii.-xii. contain the earliest model of apocalyptic literature. Largely acknowledged in N. T., Matt. xxiv. 15; Luke i. 19, 26; Heb. xi. 33, 34. "The Song of the Three Holy Children," "History of Susanna," and "History of Bel and the Dragon," are apocryphal additions to Daniel's writings.

**Dăn'nah** (*judging*). A city of Judah, Josh. xv. 49.

**Dăph'ne** (*bay-tree*). Sanctuary of Apollo, near Antioch, 2 Macc. iv. 33.

**Dā'rà,** 1 Chr. ii. 6. [Darda.]

**Där'dà** (*pearl of wisdom*). One of four famed for wisdom, 1 Kgs. iv. 31.

**Där'ic** (*kingly*). A Persian coin of gold and silver; former worth about five dollars; latter fifty cents. "Dram," in 1 Chr. xxix. 7; Ez. ii. 69; Neh. vii. 70-72.

**Dà-rī'us** (*Persian "dara," king*). (1) Darius the Mede, Dan. v. 31; vi. 1; ix. 1; xi. 1. Captured Babylon from Belshazzar, B. C. 538. (2) Darius Hystaspes, King of Persia, B. C. 521-486. He restored the captive Jews, Ez. iv. 5, 24; vi. 14, 15; Hag. i. 1, 15; Zech. i. 1, 7; vii. 1. (3) Darius the Persian, Neh. xii. 22. Darius Codomanus, B. C. 336-330, last king of Persia.

**Därk'ness** (*blackness*). Absence of light, Gen. i. 2; 9th plague, Ex. x. 20-23; State of misery, Job xviii. 6; God's dwelling, Ex. xx. 21; 1 Kgs. viii. 12; typical of national convulsion, Acts ii. 19, 20; state of the fallen, Matt. viii. 12; ignorance, John i. 5; sympathetic, Luke xxiii. 44.

**Där'kon** (*scatterer*). His children returned, Ez. ii. 56; Neh. vii. 58.

**Dāte** (*like a finger*). Fruit of the date-palm, 2 Chr. xxxi. 5, marg. [Palm.]

**Dā'than** (*of a spring*). A Reubenite chief and conspirator, Num. xvi.; xxvi. 9; Deut. xi. 6.

**Dăth'ē-ma.** Ramoth-gilead, 1 Macc. v. 9.

**Daugh'ter** (*milk*). Daughter or any female descendant, Gen. xxiv. 48; female inhabitant, Gen. vi. 2; Isa. x. 32; xxiii. 12; Luke xxiii. 28; singing birds, Eccl. xii. 4.

**Dā'vid** (*well-beloved*). Youngest son of Jesse, 1 Sam. xvi. 8-12, born at Bethlehem. Anointed king by Samuel, 1 Sam. xvi. 13. Re-anointed at Hebron, 2 Sam. ii. 4. United his kingdom and raised it to great strength and splendor. Died at the age of 70, B. C. 1015, after a reign of seven and a half years over Judah and thirty-three years over the entire kingdom of Israel. History told in 1 Sam. xvi. to 1 Kgs. ii.

**Dā'vid, City of.** [Jerusalem.]

**Dāy** (*shining*). Natural Hebrew day from sunset to sunset, Gen. i. 5; Ex. xii. 18. Sabbath the only day named; others numbered, Lev. xxiii. 32. Morning, noon, and evening divisions, Ps. lv. 17. Hours introduced, Dan. iii. 6; John xi. 9. Indefinite time, Gen. ii. 4; of birth, Job iii. 1; of ruin, Hos. i. 11; of judgment, Joel i. 15; of Christ's kingdom, John viii. 56.

**Dāys'man.** Umpire or moderator, Job ix. 33.

**Dāy'spring.** Dawn, Job xxxviii. 12; Luke i. 78.

**Dāy'star.** Morning star, 2 Pet. i. 19.

**Dēa'con** (*servant*). A subordinate minister or officer in early Christian Church, Acts vi. 1-6. Qualifications in 1 Tim. iii. 8-12.

**Dēa'cŏn-ess.** A female officer in early Church, Rom. xvi. 1; 1 Tim. v. 10.

**Dĕad Sea.** Not so called until the second century. In O. T. "Salt Sea" and "Sea of the Plain." [Salt Sea.]

**Dēarth.** [Famine.]

**Dē'bĭr** (*oracle*). (1) A Levitical city of Judah, Josh. xxi. 15; Kirjath-sepher, Josh. xv. 15; Kirjath-sannah, xv. 49. (2) A northern boundary of Judah, Josh. xv. 7. (3) A boundary of Gad, Josh. xiii. 26. (4) A king of Eglon, Josh. x. 3-26.

**Dĕb'o-rah** (*bee*). (1) Nurse of Rebekah, Gen. xxxv. 8; xxiv. 59. (2) Prophetess and Judge, Judg. iv. 5-14; v. (3) Grandmother of Tobit, Tob. i. 8.

**Dĕbt'ŏr** (*ower*). Lands or the person might be taken for debt, and held till the year of jubilee, Ex. xxi. 2; Lev. xxv. 29-34; 2 Kgs. iv. 1; Neh. v. 3-5.

**Dē-căp'ŏ-lis** (*ten cities*). A Roman province embracing parts of Syria and Palestine, Matt. iv. 25; Mark v. 20; vii. 31.

**De-çĭ'sion, Valley of.** Joel iii. 14. "Valley of Jehoshaphat," "or judgment," as in verses 2 and 12.

**Dē'dan** (*low*). (1) Grandson of Cush, Gen. x. 7. (2) Son of Jokshan, Gen. xxv. 3. Both founders of Arabian or Idumean tribes, Isa. xxi. 13; Ezek. xxxviii. 13.

**Ded'a-nĭm.** Descendants of Dedan, Isa. xxi. 13.

**Dĕd''ĭ-cā'tion** (*declaration*). Devoting person,

place or thing to holy use, Ex. xl.; Num. vii.; 2 Sam. viii. 11; 1 Kgs. viii.; Ez. vi.; Neh. xii. 27; "Feast of Dedication" commemorated the purging of the temple, John x. 22; 1 Macc. iv. 52–59.

**Dēep.** Abyss, or abode, of lost spirits, Luke viii. 31; Rom. x. 7. "Bottomless pit," Rev. ix. 1, 2, 11; xi. 7.

**Dēer** (*wild*), Deut. xiv. 5; 1 Kgs. iv. 23. [Fallow-Deer.]

**Dē-grēe′** (*step or grade down*). Rank or station, Ps. lxii. 9; 1 Tim. iii. 13. "Song of Degrees," title to Pss. cxx.–cxxxiv.

**Dē-hā′vītes.** Colonists planted in Samaria, Ez. iv. 9.

**Dē′kär** (*lancer*). Father of one of Solomon's commissaries, 1 Kgs. iv. 9.

**Del″a-ī′ah** (*freed by God*). (1) Leader of the 23d priestly course, 1 Chr. xxiv. 18. (2) Returned Jews, Ez. ii. 60; Neh. vii. 62. (3) Father of Shemaiah, Neh. vi. 10. (4) A courtier, Jer. xxxvi. 12.

**Dē-lī′lah** (*longing*). A woman of Sorek, employed to discover the secret of Samson's strength, Judg. xvi. 4–20.

**Dĕl′ūge** (*washing away*). The usual modern word for Noah's flood, Gen. vi.–viii.

**Dē′lus** (*suddenly visible*). Smallest of the Cyclades islands, 1 Macc. xv. 23.

**Dē′mas** (*popular*). A friend of Paul at Rome, Col. iv. 14; 2 Tim. iv. 10.

**Dē-mē′trī-us** (*belonging to Ceres*). (1) A silversmith at Ephesus, Acts xix. 24–30. (2) A disciple, 3 John, 12. (3) Demetrius (I.) Soter, of Syria, 1 Macc. x. 48–50. (4) Demetrius (II.) Nicator, 1 Macc x.

**Dē-nā′rī-us** (*ten asses*). A Roman silver coin worth about 15 cents. The "penny" of N. T., Matt. xx. 2.

**Dĕp′ū-tȳ** (*selected*). In N. T., a proconsul, or governor, Acts xiii. 7, 8, 12.

**Dẽr′bē** (*sting*). A city of Lycaonia in Asia Minor, Acts xiv. 20; xx. 4.

**Dĕs′ert** (*deserted*). An arid sandy plain, or wild mountainous waste, Ex. xxiii. 31; Deut. xi. 24; Ps. lxv. 12.

**Dĕs′să-ū.** A village, 2 Macc. xiv. 16.

**Deū′el** (*knowledge of God*). Father of Eliasaph, Num. i. 14. Reuel in ii. 14.

**Deū″te-rŏn′o-mȳ.** So called because it "repeats the law." Fifth book of O. T. and last of the Pentateuch. Authorship ascribed to Moses, except last chapter. Chapters i.–iv. 40, rehearse the wanderings; v.–xxvi. recapitulate the law; the others deliver the law into keeping of the Levites, and describe the death of Moses.

**Dĕv′il** (*slanderer*). The Hebrew Satan, "adversary," Matt. xvi. 23; Mark viii. 33; Luke xxii. 3; Rev. xx. 2. The devil of bodily possession was rather the polluting power of disease — dumbness, Matt. ix. 32; blindness, xii. 22; epilepsy, Mark ix. 17–27; insanity, Matt. viii. 28; murderous antipathy, John vii. 20.

**Dew.** Source of fertility, Gen. xxvii. 28; Judg. vi 37–40; object of rich imagery, Deut. xxxii. 2; Job xxix. 19; Ps. cxxxiii. 3.

**Dī′al** (*daily*). An instrument for telling the time of day, 2 Kgs. xx. 11; Isa. xxxviii. 8.

**Dī′a-mŏnd** (*adamant*). Pure crystallized carbon. Third stone in second row of high-priest's breastplate, Ex. xxviii. 18; Ezek. xxviii. 13.

**Dī-ăn′ă** (*safety*). A Roman goddess. Artemis of the Greeks. Her temple at Ephesus regarded as one of the seven wonders of the world, Acts xix. 24–28.

**Dĭb′la-ĭm** (*two cakes*). Mother-in-law of Hosea, Hos. i. 3.

**Dĭb′lăth.** Unidentified place, Ezek. vi 14.

**Dī′bŏn** (*wasting*). (1) A town of Gad, Num. xxxii. 3, 34. Dibon-gad, Num. xxxiii. 45, 46. Accounted to Reuben, Josh. xiii. 9, 17. Now Dhiban, within the gateway of which the famous Moabite stone was found in 1868. (2) A town in south Judah, Neh. xi. 25.

**Dī′bon-găd.** [Dibon, 1.]

**Dĭb′rī** (*orator*). A Danite, Lev. xxiv. 11.

**Dĭd′ȳ-mus** (*twin*). Surname of Thomas, John xi. 16; xx. 24; xxi. 2.

**Dĭk′lah** (*palm*). A son of Joktan, Gen x. 27; 1 Chr. i. 21.

**Dĭl′ē-an** (*cucumber*). A lowland city of Judah, Josh. xv. 38.

**Dĭm′nah** (*dung*). A Levitical city, Josh. xxi. 35.

**Dī′mon** (*reddish*). A stream of Moab, Isa. xv. 9.

**Dī-mō′nah** (*dunghill*) A city in south Judah, Josh. xv. 22.

**Dī′nah** (*judged*). First daughter of Jacob and Leah, Gen. xxx. 21; xxxiv.

**Dī′na-ītes.** Cuthean colonists in Samaria, Ez. iv. 9.

**Dĭn′hă-bah.** A capital of Edom, Gen. xxxvi. 32; 1 Chr. i. 43.

**Dī″ō-nȳs′ius** (*devotee of Dionysos, or Bacchus*). A member of the court of Areopagus at Athens, Acts xvii. 34.

**Dī″ō-nȳs′us** (*Bacchus*). Bacchus, 2 Macc. xiv. 33.

**Dī′os=cŏr-ĭn′thi-us** (*Corinthian Jove*). A month in the Cretan calendar, 2 Macc. xi. 21.

**Dī-ot′rē-phēs** (*nourished by Jupiter*). A Christian, 3 John 9.

**Dĭs-çī′ple** (*learner*). Follower of Christ, Matt. x. 24; of John, Matt. ix. 14. Applied specially to the twelve, Matt. x. 1; xi. 1; xx. 17.

**Dĭs′cus** (*round plate*). The quoit, 2 Macc. iv. 14.

**Dĭs-cov′er** (*uncover*). Uncovering, making bare, Ps. xxix. 9; Isa. xxii. 8; Mic. i. 6.

**Dĭs-ēaş′eş** (*uneasy*). Visitations of plagues and pestilences frequent in Bible lands, Gen. vii. viii.; Ex. xii. 21–29; 2 Kgs. xix. 35; 1 Chr. xxi. 12; Acts xii. 23. Principal bodily diseases were, ophthalmia, leprosy, brain and malarial fevers, lung disorders.

**Dī′shan** (*antelope*). Youngest son of Seir, Gen. xxxvi. 21.

**Dī′shon** (*antelope*). Sons of Seir, Gen. xxxvi. 21–30.

**Dĭs″pĕn-să′tion** (*weighing out*), 1 Cor. ix. 17; Eph. i. 10; iii. 2; Col. i. 25. In these instances, authority to preach and teach.

**Dĭs-pẽr′sion** (*scattering*). The breaking up of the Jewish kingdoms and scattering of the tribes by conquest, James i. 1; 1 Pet. i. 1.

**Dĭs′taff** (*flax-staff*). The staff around which flax was wound for spinning, Prov. xxxi. 19.

**Dī′vēş** (*rich*). A popular name for the rich man in Luke xvi. 19–31.

**Dĭv″i-nā′tion** (*belonging to a god*). In Scripture, the false use of means to discover the divine will; by rods, Hos. iv. 12; arrows, Ezek. xxi. 21; cups, Gen. xliv. 5; the liver, Ezek. xxi. 21; dreams, Deut. xiii. 3; Zech. x. 2; consulting oracles, Isa. xli. 21–24; xliv. 7. Faith in divination forbidden, Lev. xix. 26.

**Di-vôrçe′** (*turning asunder*). Allowed by Mosaic law, Deut. xxiv. 1–4, yet forbidden in certain cases, xxii. 19, 29. Christ regarded adultery as an only cause for divorce, Matt. v. 31, 32; xix. 9; Mark x. 11; Luke xvi. 18.

**Dĭz′a-hăb** (*gold region*). Scene of one of Moses' addresses, Deut. i. 1.

**Dŏc′tor** (*teacher*). A teacher of the Law of Moses, Luke ii. 46; v. 17. Teacher of the Christian faith, 1 Cor. xii. 28.

**Dō′cus.** Springs near Jericho, 1 Macc. xvi. 15.

**Dŏd′a-ī** (*loving*). Leader of David's second military course, 1 Chr. xxvii. 4.

**Dŏd′a-nim** (*leaders*). Descendants of Javan, Gen. x. 4; 1 Chr. i. 7.

**Dŏd′a-vah.** Father of Eliezer, 2 Chr. xx. 37.

**Dō′dō** (*loving*). (1) Father of one of David's captains, 2 Sam. xxiii. 24. (2) Father of Eleazar, 2 Sam. xxiii. 9; 1 Chr. xi. 12. (3) Grandfather of Tola Judg. x. 1.

**Dō′eg** (*fearful*). An overseer of Saul's herds, 1 Sam. xxi. 7; xxii. 9–22.

**Dŏg.** An unclean animal, Ex. xi. 7; xxii. 31; Deut. xxiii. 18; regarded with contempt, 1 Sam. xvii. 43; xxiv. 14; 2 Sam. ix. 8; 2 Kgs. viii. 13; Matt. vii. 6; Rev. xxii. 15; guards, Isa. lvi. 10; Job xxx. 1; scavengers, 1 Kgs. xiv. 11; xxi. 19–23; xxii. 38; enemies, Ps. xxii. 16–20.

**Dōor** (*through*). [Gate.]

**Dŏph′kah** (*drover*). A desert station of the Israelites, Num. xxxiii. 12.

**Dôr** (*dwelling*). A city on the coast north of Cæsarea, Josh. xi. 2; xii. 23; xvii. 11; Judg. i. 27; 1 Kgs. iv. 11.

**Dō′ră**, 1 Macc. xv. 11. [Dor.]

**Dŏr′cas** (*gazelle*). The woman of Joppa whom Peter raised from the dead, Acts ix. 36–42. [Tabitha.]

**Dō-rȳm′ē-nēs.** Father of Ptolemy Macron, 1 Macc. iii. 38.

**Dō-sĭth'ē-us.** (1) A Jewish captain, 2 Macc. xii. 19-35. (2) A priest, Esth. xi. 1, 2.

**Dō'tha-ĭm,** Judith iv. 6. [DOTHAN.]

**Dō'than** (*two wells*). The place where Joseph was sold, Gen. xxxvii. 17; 2 Kgs. vi. 13.

**Do You To Wit.** To make known, 2 Cor. viii. 1.

**Dove** (*diver*). Clean by the law and offered as a sacrifice by the poor, Gen. xv. 9; Lev. v. 7; xii. 6-8; Luke ii. 24; symbol of innocence, Matt. x. 16; harbinger of God, Gen. viii.; emblem of Holy Spirit, Matt. iii. 16.

**Dove's Dŭng.** Eaten as a last resort, in time of famine, 2 Kgs. vi. 25.

**Dow'rȳ** (*gift*). The consideration paid the father of the bride by the bridegroom, Gen. xxix. 18; xxxiv. 12; 1 Sam. xviii. 25; Hos. iii. 2.

**Drăch'mȧ, Drăchm** (*handful*). A silver coin of Greece, corresponding to the Roman denarius, and worth about fifteen and a half cents. A piece of silver, Luke xv. 8, 9.

**Drăg'on** (*serpent*). An animal of the lizard species. Evidently a wild beast, as a jackal, in Job xxx. 29; Isa. xxxiv. 13; Ps. xliv. 19; Jer. ix. 11; Mic. i. 8; sea-serpent, Gen. i. 21; land-serpent, Ex. vii. 9-12; Deut. xxxii. 33; devil, Rev. xii. 3-17.

**Drăg'on Well.** Possibly Gihon, Neh. ii. 13.

**Drăm** (*handful*), 1 Chr. xxix. 7; Ez. ii. 69; Neh. vii. 70-72. [DARIC.]

**Draught House.** Cesspool, 2 Kgs. x. 27; Matt. xv. 17.

**Drēam** (*phantom*). Seriously regarded by ancients, Gen. xl. Divine method of approach, Gen. xx. 3-7; 1 Sam. xxviii. 6; Acts xxvii. 22-25. Interpretation of an exceptional gift, Gen. xl. 5-23; xli. 14-45; Dan. iv. 19-27.

**Drĕss** (*keeping straight*). Of leaves, Gen. iii. 7; skins, iii. 21; woolens, xxxviii. 12; Ex. xxv. 4; Lev. xiii. 47; linen, 1 Chr. iv. 21; silk, Rev. xviii. 12; mixed materials forbidden, Lev. xix. 19; colors rich, Ex. xxxv. 25; Luke xvi. 19; no sexual interchanges, Deut. xxii. 5; common inner dresses, armless shirt, second tunic, linen wrapper, Mark xiv. 51; outer, for men, woolen wrap, 2 Sam. xv. 30; Esth. vi. 12; for women, a long shawl, Ruth iii. 15; Isa. iii. 22-24; Jer. xiii. 22; girdled, Matt. xxiv. 18; Acts xii. 8; 1 Kgs. xviii. 46; poor man's bedclothes, Ex. xxii. 26, 27.

**Drink offering.** The pouring of a small quantity of wine on the daily morning and evening sacrificial lamb, Ex. xxix. 40; Lev. xxiii. 18.

**Drink, Strong.** Use of, not uncommon among Hebrews, Gen. ix. 21; xix. 34, 35; Ps. cvii. 27; Isa. xxiv. 20; xlix. 26; li. 17-22; John ii. 1-11; but under prohibitions, Prov. xx. 1; Isa. v. 11.

**Drom'ẹ-dā-ry** (*running*). Post camel of the East, usually the one-humped species, as distinguished from the two-humped, or Bactrian, camel, 1 Kgs. iv. 28; Isa. lx. 6; Jer. ii. 23; Mic. i. 13.

**Drụ-sĭl'lȧ** (*watered by dew*). Daughter of Herod Agrippa I., Acts xii. 1-4, 20-23; xxiv. 24.

**Dụke** (*leader*). Hereditary chief or sheikh of Edom, Gen. xxxvi. 15-43.

**Dŭl'çi-mer** (*sweet song*). The bagpipe and not the stringed dulcimer is meant, Dan. iii. 5-15.

**Dụ'mah** (*silence*). (1) A son of Ishmael, Gen. xxv. 14; 1 Chr. i. 30. (2) A town in Judah, Josh. xv. 52. (3) A region, Isa. xxi. 11.

**Dŭng** (*excrement*). Dung of cattle used for fuel, Ezek. iv. 12. Manure made from straw, Isa. xxv. 10. A fertilizer, Luke xiii. 8.

**Dŭn'geon** (*tower, keep*). [PRISON.]

**Dụ'rȧ** (*circle*). A plain of Babylon, Dan. iii. 1.

**Dŭst** (*storm breath*). Symbol of mourning, Josh. vii. 6; Isa. xlvii. 1; feebleness, Gen. xviii. 27; Job xxx. 19; countless numbers, Gen. xiii. 16; low condition, 1 Sam. ii. 8; rage, 2 Sam. xvi. 13; Acts xxii. 23; renunciation, Matt. x. 14; Mark vi. 11; Acts xiii. 51. A sand storm, Deut. xxviii. 24.

**Dwĕll'ings.** [HOUSES.]

## E

**Ē'a'gle** *dark-colored*). The eagle of Scripture is probably the griffon vulture, Mic. i. 16; Matt. xxiv. 28; Luke xvii. 37; unclean, Lev. xi. 13; Deut. xiv. 12; noted for height and rapidity of flight, Prov. xxiii. 5; 2 Sam. i. 23; Job ix. 26; Deut. xxviii. 49; Jer. iv. 13; great age, Ps. ciii. 5; care of young, Ex. xix. 4; Deut. xxxii. 11, 12; Isa. xl. 31.

**Ē'ạ-nēs.** A returned captive, 1 Esdr. ix. 21.

**Ēar'ing** (*plowing*). Earing time was plowing time, Gen. xlv. 6; Ex. xxxiv. 21; Deut. xxi. 4; 1 Sam. viii. 12.

**Ĕarn'est** (*pledge*). Pledge, Gen. xxxviii. 17; surety, Prov. xvii. 18; hostage, 2 Kgs. xiv. 14; deposit or advance, 2 Cor. i. 22; Eph. i. 14.

**Ēar'rings.** Included "nose-rings;" worn by both sexes; Gen. xxxv. 4; Ex. xxxii. 2; Judg. viii. 24; Job xlii. 11; offerings, Num. xxxi. 50.

**Ĕarth** (*producer*). The world, Gen. i. 1; dry land, i. 10; the soil, ii. 7.

**Ĕarth'en-wâre.** [POTTERY.]

**Ĕarth'quāke** (*earth-shaking*). A natural and historic phenomenon, in Am. i. 1; Zech. xiv. 5; 1 Kgs. xix. 11, 12; Matt. xxvii. 51. Token of God's wrath, Judg. v. 4; 2 Sam. xxii. 8; Ps. lxxvii. 18; xcvii. 4; civ. 32; Am. viii. 8; Hab. iii. 10.

**Ēast** (*dawn*). The Hebrew idea was "before" "in front of," "to the East," Gen. xxix. 1; Num. xxiii. 7; Job i. 3; Ezek. xlvii. 8; Matt. ii. 1.

**Ēast'er** (*Eastre, Saxon goddess*). The day commemorative of Christ's resurrection. Wrongly associated with the Saxon Eastre festival, and the Jewish Passover feast, but corrected in R. V., Acts xii. 4.

**Ēast Sea.** Ezek. xlvii. 18; Joel ii. 20. The Dead Sea.

**Ēat.** Offensive to eat or drink outside of certain limits, Gen. xliii. 32; Matt. ix. 11; John iv. 9.

**Ē'bal** (*stone*). (1) Son of Shobal, Gen. xxxvi. 23. (2) Son of Joktan, 1 Chr. i. 22. Obal, Gen. x. 28.

**Ē'bal, Mount.** The mount of curses in Samaria, Deut. xi. 29; Josh. viii. 30-35.

**Ē'bed** (*servant*). (1) Father of Gaal, Judg. ix. 26-35. (2) One of the returned, Ez. viii. 6.

**Ē'bĕd=mĕ'lĕch** (*king's servant*). An Ethiopian, Jer. xxxviii. 12; xxxix. 15-18.

**Ĕb''en=ē'zēr** (*stone of help*). A memorial stone, 1 Sam. iv. 1-5; vii. 12.

**Ē'bēr** (*beyond*) (1) Great-grandson of Shem, Gen. x. 24; 1 Chr. i. 19. (2) A Benjamite, 1 Chr. viii. 12. (3) A priest, Neh. xii. 20.

**Ē-bi'ạ-săph** (*father that adds*). A Levite, 1 Chr. vi. 23, 37.

**Ĕb'ō-nȳ** (*stone-like*). A hard, heavy, dark wood, used for ornamental work and musical instruments, Ezek. xxvii. 15.

**Ē-brō'nah** (*gateway*). A desert encampment, Num. xxxiii. 34.

**Ē-cā'nus.** A swift scribe, 2 Esdr. xiv. 24.

**Ĕc-băt'ạ-nȧ** (*egress*). Greek for Achmetha, Ez. vi. 2, marg.

**Ĕc-clē''şi-ȧs'tēs** (*preacher*). Twenty-first book of O. T. Authorship ascribed to Solomon. An old man's confession of the vanities of life.

**Ĕc-clē''şi-ȧs'ti-cus** (*of the assembly*). The Latin name of the "Wisdom of Jesus, Son of Sirach," seventh of the Apocryphal books.

**Ĕd** (*witness*). A word, Josh. xxii. 34.

**Ē'där** (*flock*). A tower, Gen. xxxv. 21.

**Ĕd-dī'as,** 1 Esdr. ix. 26. [JEZIAH.]

**Ē'dĕn** (*pleasure*). (1) First residence of man, Gen. ii. 15. Paradise. Site not fixed. (2) A mart of Mesopotamia, 2 Kgs. xix. 12; Isa. xxxvii. 12. (3) Beth-eden, Am. i. 5. (4) A Levite, 2 Chr. xxix. 12. (5) Another Levite, 2 Chr. xxxi. 15.

**Ē'dēr** (*flock*). (1) A town of Judah, Josh. xv. 21. (2) A Levite, 1 Chr. xxiii. 23; xxiv. 30.

**Ē'dēş,** 1 Esdr. ix. 35. [JADDUA.]

**Ĕd'nȧ.** Wife of Raguel, Tob. vii. 2-16.

**Ē'dom** (*red*). Called also Idumea and Mount Seir. Name given to Esau, his country and people, Gen. xxxii. 3-19; xxxiii. 1-16. It lay to the south of Palestine and Moab.

**Ĕd'rẹ-ī** (*fortress*). (1) A capital of Bashan, Num. xxi. 33; Deut. iii. 10; Josh. xii. 4. (2) Town of northern Palestine, Josh. xix. 37.

**Ĕg'lah** (*heifer*). A wife of David, 2 Sam. iii. 5; 1 Chr. iii. 3.

**Ĕg'lạ-ĭm** (*ponds*). A place in Moab, Isa. xv. 8.

**Ĕg'lŏn** (*calf-like*). (1) A King of Moab, Judg. iii. 12-23. (2) A lowland town of Judah, Josh. x. 3-5; xv. 39.

**Ē'ġȳpt** (*Coptic land*). Northeastern country of Africa; the Hebrew "Mizraim," Gen. x. 6, and "Land of Ham," Ps. cv. 23, 27. Bondage place of Israelites, Ex. i.-xiv. Noted for Nile river, rich soil and gigantic ruins. Ancient religion monotheistic, with sun as central object; and attributes of nature in form of trinities. Vast temples and numerous priests. Kings called Pharaohs, who perpetuated their reigns in obelisks, temples, sculptures, sphinxes, pyramids, etc. In intimate commerce with Hebrews, 1 Kgs. iii. 1. Conquered Judea, 1 Kgs. xiv. 25, 26. Frequently mentioned in Scripture.

**Ē'hī**, Gen. xlvi. 21. [AHIRAM.]

**Ē'hŭd** (*united*). (1) Son of Bilhan, 1 Chr. vii. 10. (2) A judge of Israel, Judg. iii. 15–21.

**Ē'kēr** (*tearing up*). A Judahite, 1 Chr. ii. 27.

**Ĕk'rē-bel**. A place in Esdraelon, Judith vii. 18.

**Ĕk'rŏn** (*migration*). One of the five Philistine cities, Josh. xiii. 3; xv. 45; xix. 43; 1 Sam. v. 10.

**Ĕk'rŏn-ītes**. Inhabitants of Ekron, Josh. xiii. 3.

**Ē'lȧ**, 1 Esdr. ix. 27. [ELAM.]

**Ĕl'ă-dah** (*eternity of God*). An Ephraimite, 1 Chr. vii. 20.

**Ē'lah** (*oak*). (1) Son and successor of Baasha on the throne of Israel, B. C. 928–27, 1 Kgs. xvi. 8–10. (2) Father of Hosea, 2 Kgs. xv. 30; xvii. 1. (3) A duke of Edom, Gen. xxxvi. 41. (4) Father of Solomon's commissary, 1 Kgs. iv. 18. (5) Son of Caleb, 1 Chr. iv. 15. (6) A chief of Benjamin, 1 Chr. ix. 8. (7) The valley in which David slew Goliath, 1 Sam. xvii. 2–19.

**Ē'lăm** (*age*). (1) Son of Shem, Gen. x. 22, and his country, xiv. 1–9; Dan. viii. 2, in Mesopotamia. (2) A chief of Benjamin, 1 Chr. viii. 24. (3) A Korhite Levite, 1 Chr. xxvi. 3. (4) Persons whose children returned, Ez. ii. 7, 31; Neh. vii. 12, 34. (5) A priest, Neh. x. 14.

**Ē'lăm-ītes**. Inhabitants of Elam, Ez. iv. 9.

**Ĕl'a-sah** (*whom God made*). (1) A priest, Ez. x. 22. (2) Son of Shaphan, Jer. xxix. 3.

**Ē'lăth, E'lŏth** (*oaks*). A city of Edom, Deut. ii. 8; Seat of Solomon's navy, 1 Kgs. ix. 26; 2 Chr. viii. 17.

**Ĕl-bĕth'-el** (*God of Bethel*). Place where God appeared to Jacob, Gen. xxxv. 7.

**Ĕl'çī-ȧ**. Progenitor of Judith, Judith viii. 1.

**Ĕl'da-ah** (*called of God*). Last son of Midian, Gen. xxv. 4; 1 Chr. i. 33.

**Ĕl'dăd** (*loved of God*). One of the seventy assistants of Moses, Num. xi. 16, 26–29.

**Ĕl'dēr** (*old man*). Highest in tribal authority, Gen. xxiv. 2; l. 7; Ex. iii. 16; iv. 29; Num. xxii. 7. One of the 70 justiciars, Num. xi. 25, or Sanhedrim, Judg. ii. 7; 2 Sam. xvii. 4; Jer. xxix. 1. An official in early Christian church, like presbyter or bishop, Acts xx. 17, 28.

**Ē'le-ăd** (*praised of God*). An Ephraimite, 1 Chr. vii. 21.

**Ē''le-ā'leh** (*ascent of God*). A Moabite town, assigned to Reuben, Num. xxxii. 3, 37; Isa. xv. 4; Jer. xlviii. 34.

**Ē-lē'a-sȧ**. A place near Ashdod, 1 Macc. ix. 5–18.

**Ē-lē'a-sah** (*made by God*). (1) A Judahite, 1 Chr. ii. 39. (2) A descendant of Saul, 1 Chr. viii. 37; ix. 43.

**Ē''le-ā'zar** (*help of God*). (1) Third son of Aaron, Ex. vi. 23. Chief of the Levites, Num. iii. 32; and high priest, Num. xx. 28. (2) Son of Abinadab, 1 Sam. vii. 1. (3) One of David's mighty men, 2 Sam. xxiii. 9; 1 Chr. xi. 12. (4) A Levite, 1 Chr. xxiii. 21. (5) A priest, Neh. xii. 42. (6) Son of Phinehas, Ez. viii. 33. (7) Son of Parosh, Ez. x. 25. (8) Surnamed Avaran, 1 Macc. vi. 43. (9) A scribe, 2 Macc. vi. 18. (10) Father of Jason, 1 Macc. viii. 17. (11) Son of Eliud, Matt. i. 15.

**Ē''le-ā-zū'rus**, 1 Esdr. ix. 24. [ELIASHIB.]

**Ē-lĕct'** (*chosen out*). One called to everlasting life; the saved collectively, Matt. xxiv. 22; Mark xiii. 27; Luke xviii. 7; Rom. viii. 33; Tit. i. 1. The "elect lady," 2 John i. 1, probably refers to the Christian church.

**Ĕl-e-lō'hē-Is'ra-el** (*strength of the God of Israel*). Name of Jacob's altar, Gen. xxxiii. 19, 20.

**Ē'leph** (*ox*). A town of Benjamin, Josh. xviii. 28.

**Ĕl'e-phănt** (*ox*). The Hebrew *eleph* means an ox, 1 Kgs. x. 22; 2 Chr. ix. 21; Job xl. 15, margins.

**Ē-leu'thĕ-rus**. A Syrian river, 1 Macc. xi. 7.

**Ĕl-hā'nan** (*grace of God*). (1) A noted Hebrew warrior, 2 Sam. xxi. 19; 1 Chr. xx. 5. (2) One of David's body-guard, 2 Sam. xxiii. 24.

**Ē'lī** (*going up*). A descendant of Aaron, Lev. x. 12. First of a line of high priests, 1 Sam. i. 9–17; ii. 22–36; iii. 1–14; and Judge of Israel for 40 years, iv. 14–18. Line extinguished, 1 Kgs. ii. 26, 27.

**Ē'lī, Ē'lī, lā'mȧ sā-băch-thā'nī**. The Lord's cry upon the cross, Matt. xxvii. 46; Mark xv. 34, "My God, my God, why hast thou forsaken me?" Ps. xxii. 1.

**Ē-lī'ab** (*God is father*). (1) A Chief of Zebulun, Num. i. 9. (2) A Reubenite, Num. xxvi. 8, 9. (3) A Levite musician, 1 Chr. xv. 18–20. (4) Eldest brother of David, 1 Chr. ii. 13. (5) A Gadite leader, 1 Chr. xii. 9. (6) An ancestor of Samuel, 1 Chr. vi. 27. (7) Son of Nathaniel, Judith viii. 1.

**Ē-lī'a-dȧ** (*known of God*). (1) A younger son of David, 2 Sam. v. 16; 1 Chr. iii. 8. (2) A Benjamite general, 2 Chr. xvii. 17.

**Ē-lī'a-dah**. Father of Rezon, 1 Kgs. xi. 23–25.

**Ē-lī'ah** (*God the Lord*). (1) A Benjamite chief, 1 Chr. viii. 27. (2) One of the returned, Ez. x. 26.

**Ē-lī'ah-bȧ** (*hidden by God*). One of David's guard, 2 Sam. xxiii. 32; 1 Chr. xi. 33.

**Ē-lī'a-kĭm** (*raised of God*). (1) Master of Hezekiah's household, 2 Kgs. xviii. 18–37; Isa. xxxvi. 3. (2) Original name of King Jehoiakim, 2 Kgs. xxiii. 34; 2 Chr. xxxvi. 4. (3) A priest, Neh. xii. 41. (4) Forefather of Joseph, Matt. i. 13. (5) Father of Jonan, Luke iii. 30, 31.

**Ē-lī'a-lī**, 1 Esdr. ix. 34. [BINNUI.]

**Ē-lī'ăm** (*God's people*). (1) Father of Bathsheba, 2 Sam. xi. 3. (2) One of David's warriors, 2 Sam. xxiii. 34.

**Ē-lī'as**. N. T. form of Elijah. [ELIJAH.]

**Ē-lī'a-săph** (*God increaseth*). (1) Chief of Dan, Num. i. 14; ii. 14; vii. 42; x. 20. (2) A Levite chief, Num. iii. 24.

**Ē-lī'a-shib** (*restored of God*). (1) Eleventh priest of "order of governors," 1 Chr. xxiv. 12. (2) A Judahite, 1 Chr. iii. 24. (3) High priest, Neh. iii. 1–21. (4) Three of the returned, Ez. x. 24, 27, 36.

**Ē-lī'a-thah** (*to whom God comes*). Leader of the twentieth temple course, 1 Chr. xxv. 4, 27.

**Ē-lī'dad** (*beloved of God*). A Benjamite, Num. xxxiv. 21.

**Ē-lī'el** (*God, my God*). (1) A chief of Manasseh, 1 Chr. v. 24. (2) A forefather of Samuel, 1 Chr. vi. 34. (3, 4) Two chiefs of Benjamin, 1 Chr. viii. 20, 22. (5, 6) Two heroes of David's guard, 1 Chr. xi. 46, 47. (7) A Gadite, 1 Chr. xii. 11. (8) A Levite, 1 Chr. xv. 9–11. (9) Overseer of Temple offerings, 2 Chr. xxxi. 13.

**Ē''lī-ē'na-ī** (*eyes toward God*). A chief of Benjamin, 1 Chr. viii. 20.

**Ē''lī-ē'zēr** (*help of God*). Servant of Abraham, Gen. xv. 2, 3. (2) Second son of Moses, Ex. xviii. 4; 1 Chr. xxiii. 15–17; xxvi. 25. (3) A chief of Benjamin, 1 Chr. vii. 8. (4) A priest, 1 Chr. xv. 24. (5) A Reubenite chief, 1 Chr. xxvii. 16. (6) A prophet, 2 Chr. xx. 37. (7) Messenger of Ezra, Ez. viii. 16. (8, 9, 10) Returned Jews, Ez. x. 18, 23, 31. (11) Ancestor of Christ, Luke iii. 29.

**Ĕl''ī-hō-ē'nă-ī** (*eyes toward God*). A returned leader, Ez. viii. 4.

**Ĕl''ī-hō'reph** (*God his reward*). A scribe, 1 Kgs. iv. 3.

**Ē-lī'hū** (*God is his*). (1) A forefather of Samuel, 1 Sam. i. 1. (2) Eldest brother of David, 1 Chr. xxvii. 18. (3) A captain of Manasseh, 1 Chr. xii. 20. (4) A Levite door-keeper, 1 Chr. xxvi. 7. (5) One of Job's friends, Job xxxii. 2.

**Ē-lī'jah** (*God is God*). (1) The prophet; Elias in N. T., Matt. xvii. 3. A Tishbite of Gilead; appears suddenly; is fed by ravens; restores the widow's son, 1 Kgs. xvii. 1–24; invokes fire on the prophets of Baal, xviii. 17–40; anoints Hazael, Jehu, and Elisha, xix.; denounces Ahab and Jezebel, xxi. 17–24; is translated in a chariot of fire, 2 Kgs. ii.; reappears on the mount of Transfiguration, Luke ix. 28–35. (2) A son of Harim, Ez. x. 21.

**Ĕl'ī-kȧ** (*rejected of God*). One of David's guard, 2 Sam. xxiii. 25.

**Ē'lĭm** (*oaks*). Second encampment of the Israelites after crossing the Red Sea, Ex. xv. 27; Num. xxxiii. 9.

**Ē-lĭm'ĕ-lech** (*my God is king*). Husband of Naomi, Ruth i. 1–3.

**Ĕl''ī-ō-ē'nă-ī** (*eyes toward God*). (1) A descendant of David, 1 Chr. iii. 23, 24. (2) A Simeonite, 1 Chr. iv. 36. (3) A Levite doorkeeper, 1 Chr. xxvi. 3. (4) A Benjamite, 1 Chr. vii. 8. (5) Two priests, Ez. x. 22, 27.

**Ĕl-ī-ō'nas**, 1 Esdr. ix. 22–32. [ELIOENAI.]

**Ĕl'ī-phal** (*judged of God*). Son of Ur, 1 Chr. xi. 35. Eliphelet, 2 Sam. xxiii. 34.

**Ē-lĭph'a-lĕt** (*God of deliverance*). A son of David, 2 Sam. v. 16; 1 Chr. xiv. 7.

**Ĕl'ĭ-phăz** (*God his strength*). (1) A son of Esau, Gen. xxxvi. 4; 1 Chr. i. 35, 36. (2) One of Job's friends, Job iv., v., xv., xxii.

**Ē'lĭph'e-leh** (*who exalts God*). A harper, 1 Chr. xv. 18–21.

**Ē-lĭph'e-lĕt** (*God of deliverance*). (1) One of David's warriors, 2 Sam. xxiii. 34. (2) Name of two sons of David, 1 Chr. iii. 6, 8. (3) A descendant of Saul, 1 Chr. viii. 39. (4) Two of the returned, Ez. viii. 13; x. 33.

**Ē-lĭs'a-bĕth** (*oath of God*). Wife of Zecharias, Luke i. 36–80.

**Ĕl''ĭ-sē'us.** Greek form of Elisha, Luke iv. 27.

**Ē-lī'shȧ** (*God his salvation*). Anointed prophet by Elijah, 1 Kgs. xix. 16–21. Prophesied in reigns of Jehoram, Jehu, Jehoahaz and Joash, a period of sixty years. Life and works in 2 Kgs. ii.–ix.; xiii. 14-21.

**Ē-lī'shah** (*God saves*). Eldest son of Javan, Gen. x. 4; Ezek. xxvii. 7.

**Ē-lĭsh'a-mȧ** (*whom God hears*). (1) Grandfather of Joshua, Num. i. 10. (2) Two sons of David, 2 Sam. v. 16; 1 Chr. iii. 6, 8. (3) A priest, 2 Chr. xvii. 8. (4) A Judahite, 1 Chr. ii. 41. (5) Grandfather of Ishmael, 2 Kgs. xxv. 25. (6) A scribe, Jer. xxxvi. 12, 20–21. (7) A priest, 2 Chr. xvii. 8.

**Ē-lĭsh'a-phăt** (*whom God judges*). Captain of a hundred, 2 Chr. xxiii. 1.

**Ē-lĭsh'e-bȧ** (*God her oath*). Wife of Aaron, Ex. vi. 23.

**Ĕl''ĭ-shu'ȧ.** A son of David, 2 Sam. v. 15; 1 Chr. xiv. 5. Elishama, 1 Chr. iii. 6–8.

**Ē-lĭs'ĭ-mus,** 1 Esdr. ix. 28. [Eliashib.]

**Ē-lī'ū.** A forefather of Judith, Judith viii. 1.

**Ē-lī'ŭd** (*God my praise*). Ancestor of Joseph, Matt. i. 15.

**Ē-lĭz'a-phan** (*protected of God*). (1) A Levite chief, Num. iii. 30; 1 Chr. xv. 8. Elzaphan, Ex. vi. 22; Lev. x. 4. (2) A chief of Zebulun, Num. xxxiv. 25.

**Ē-lī'zŭr** (*God his rock*). A prince of Reuben, Num. i. 5; ii. 10.

**Ĕl'kă-nah, Ĕl'kŏ-nah** (*provided of God*). (1) Grandson of Korah, Ex. vi. 24; 1 Chr. vi. 23. (2) Another descendant of Korah, 1 Chr. vi. 26, 35. (3) Another Levite, 1 Chr. vi. 27, 34; 1 Sam. i. 1–23; ii. 11, 20. (4) A Levite, 1 Chr. ix. 16. (5) A Korhite, 1 Chr. xii. 6. (6) An officer under Ahaz, 2 Chr. xxviii. 7.

**Ĕl'kosh** (*my bow is of God*). Modern Alkush on the Tigris, Nahum i. 1.

**Ĕl'la-sär** (*oak*). City of King Arioch, Gen. xiv. 1–9.

**Ĕlm,** Hosea iv. 13; elsewhere translated "oak."

**Ĕl-mō'dăm** (*measure*). Son of Er. Elmadam in R. V., Luke iii. 28.

**Ĕl'na-am** (*God his delight*). Father of two of David's guard, 1 Chr. xi. 46.

**Ĕl'na-than** (*gift of God*). (1) Grandfather of Jehoiachin, 2 Kgs. xxiv. 8; Jer. xxvi. 22. (2) Names of three Levites, Ez. viii. 16.

**Ē-lō'ī, Ē-lō'hī, Ĕl'ō-him.** God. Eloi is also Aramaic form of Elias, or Elijah, Mark xv. 34.

**Ē'lon** (*oak*). (1) A Hittite, Gen. xxvi. 34; xxxvi. 2. (2) A son of Zebulun, Gen. xlvi. 14; Num. xxvi. 26. (3) A Zebulunite, Judg. xii. 11, 12. (4) A town of Dan, Josh. xix. 43.

**Ē'lon=bĕth=hā''năn** (*oak of house of grace*). Part of one of Solomon's commissary districts, 1 Kgs. iv. 9.

**Ē'lŏn-ītes,** Num. xxvi. 26. [Elon, 2.]

**Ē'lŏth,** 1 Kgs. ix. 26; 2 Chr. viii. 17; xxvi. 2. [Elath.]

**Ĕl'pȧ-al** (*wages of God*). A Benjamite, 1 Chr. viii. 11, 12.

**Ĕl'pa-let,** 1 Chr. xiv. 5. [Eliphelet, 2.]

**Ĕl-pā'ran.** Oak of Paran, Gen. xiv. 6. [Paran.]

**Ĕl'te-keh** (*fear of God*). A city of Dan, Josh. xix. 44; xxi. 23.

**Ĕl'te-kon** (*founded by God*). A town in Judah, Josh. xv. 59.

**Ĕl'to-lăd** (*kindred of God*). A city of Judah, and Simeon, Josh. xv. 30; xix. 4; Tolad, 1 Chr. iv. 29.

**Ē'lŭl** (*vine*). Twelfth month of Hebrew civil, and sixth of sacred, year, corresponding to parts of September and October, Neh. vi. 15.

**Ē-lū'za-ī** (*God my praise*). A Benjamite warrior, 1 Chr. xii. 5.

**Ĕl''ȳ-mæ'ans,** Judith i. 6. [Elamites.]

**Ĕl'ȳ-măs** (*wise*). Arabic name of Bar-jesus, Acts xiii. 6–12.

**Ĕl'za-băd** (*gift of God*). (1) A Gadite, 1 Chr. xii. 12. (2) A Korhite Levite, 1 Chr. xxvi. 7.

**Ĕl'za-phăn** (*protected by God*). Second son of Uzziel, Ex. vi. 22; Lev. x. 4; 2 Chr. xxix. 13. Elizaphan in Num. iii. 30; 1 Chr. xv. 8.

**Ĕm-bälm'** (*to put in balsam*). Embalming carried to great perfection by the Egyptians, whom the Jews feebly imitated, Gen. l. 2–26.

**Ĕm-broi'der** (*to work a border*). Ex. xxviii. 39; xxxv. 35; xxxviii. 23. Possibly nothing beyond the common weaver's art is meant. "Cunning work," Ex. xxvi. 1, implies embroidery.

**Ĕm'ĕr-ăld.** A bright green variety of beryl. The emerald of Ex. xxviii. 18; xxxix. 11; Ezek. xxvii. 16; xxviii. 13; Rev. iv. 3; xxi. 19, is supposably the carbuncle, a fiery garnet.

**Ĕm'ē-rŏds** (*flowing with blood*). Hemorrhoids or piles, Deut. xxviii. 27; 1 Sam. v. 6–12; vi. 4–11.

**Ē'mĭms** (*terrors*). A race of Anakim east of Dead Sea, Gen. xiv. 5; Deut. ii. 10, 11.

**Ĕm-măn'ū-el,** Matt. i. 23. [Immanuel.]

**Ĕm'ma-us** (*warm springs*). A village of Palestine, 7½ mls. from Jerusalem, Luke xxiv. 13–33.

**Ĕm'mer,** 1 Esdr. ix. 21. [Immer.]

**Ĕm'môr** (*ass*), Acts vii. 16. [Hamor.]

**Ĕn.** A fountain. Used in compounds.

**Ĕn-ā'bled.** Qualified, 1 Tim. i. 12.

**Ē'nam** (*two fountains*). A city of Judah, Josh. xv. 34.

**Ē'nan** (*eyes*). A prince of Naphtali, Num. i. 15; ii. 29; vii. 78, 83; x. 27.

**Ē-năs'i-bus,** 1 Esdr. ix. 34. [Eliashib.]

**Ĕn-cămp'ment** (*field*). Halting place of army or caravan, Ex. xiv. 19; xvi. 13; Num. ii., iii.; Josh. x. 5.

**Ĕn-chȧnt'ment** (*song-spell*). Enchantments unlawful, Lev. xix. 26; Deut. xviii. 10-12; as Egyptian trickery, Ex. vii. 11–22; viii. 7; Balaam's omens, Num. xxiv. 1; muttered spells, 2 Kgs. ix. 22; Mic. v. 12; Nah. iii. 4; serpent charming, Eccl. x. 11; magical spells, Isa. xlvii. 9–12; auguries, Jer. xxvii. 9. [Divination.]

**Ĕn'=dôr** (*fountain of Dor*). A village of Manasseh, Josh. xvii. 11; Ps. lxxxiii. 9, 10; 1 Sam. xxviii.

**Ĕn=eg'la-ĭm** (*fountain of two calves*). An unknown place, Ezek. xlvii. 10.

**Ĕn''ē-mĕs'sär.** Shalmaneser, Tob. i. 2, 15.

**Ē-nē'nĭ-us.** A returned leader, 1 Esdr. v. 8.

**Ĕn-găd'dī,** Ecclus. xxiv. 14. [Engedi.]

**Ĕn=găn'nĭm** (*fount of the garden*). (1) A city of Judah, Josh. xv. 34. (2) A Levitical city, Josh. xix. 21; xxi. 29.

**Ĕn=gē'dī** (*fount of the kid*). A town on west shore of Dead Sea, Josh. xv. 62; Ezek. xlvii. 10; 1 Sam. xxiv. 1–7; S. of Sol. i. 14. Hazezon-tamar, Gen. xiv. 7; 2 Chr. xx. 2.

**Ĕn'gīne** (*skilled product*). The ballista for throwing spears, arrows, stones, 2 Chr. xxvi. 15; the catapult, Ezek. xxvi. 9; battering ram, Ezek. iv. 2; xxi. 22.

**Ĕn-grā'vĕr** (*digger in*). The commandments were engraved, Ex. xxxii. 16; also stones and signets, Ex. xxviii. 11, 21, 36; Job xix. 24; Acts xvii. 29. Graven images were objects of idolatry, Ex. xx 4; xxxii. 4.

**Ĕn=hăd'dah** (*fountain*). A city of Issachar, Josh. xix. 21.

**Ĕn=hak'kō-rē** (*fount of the caller*). Samson's fountain, Judg. xv. 19.

**Ĕn=hā'zôr** (*fount of Hazor*). A fenced city in Naphtali, Josh. xix. 37.

**Ĕn=mish'pat** (*fount of judgment*). Gen. xiv. 7. [Kadesh.]

**Ē'nŏch** (*dedicated*). (1) A son of Cain, Gen. iv. 17. (2) Father of Methuselah, Gen. v. 18–24; Heb. xi. 5–13; Jude 14. (3) "Behemoth," 2 Esdr. vi. 49–51.

**Ē'non** (*springs*). John i. 28; iii. 23. [Ænon.]

**Ē'nos** (*mortal*). Son of Seth, Gen. iv. 26; v. 6–11; Luke iii. 38. Enosh, 1 Chr. i. 1.

**Ē'nosh,** 1 Chr. i. 1. [Enos.]

**Ĕn=rĭm'mon** (*fount of the pomegranate*). A settlement of returned Jews, Neh. xi. 29.

**Ĕn=rō'ḡel** (*fuller's fount*). A celebrated spring, Josh. xv. 7; xviii. 16; 2 Sam. xvii. 17; 1 Kgs. i. 9.

**Ĕn=shē'mesh** (*fount of the sun*). A spring, Josh. xv. 7; xviii. 17.

**Ĕn'sīgn** (*mark upon*). A simple device, elevated on a pole, bearing some emblem to distinguish the tribes and army divisions, Num. i. 52; S. of Sol. ii. 4; Isa. xiii. 2; xviii. 3.

**Ĕn-sūe'.** Pursue, 1 Pet. iii. 11.

**Ĕn=tăp'pu-ah** (*fount of the apple*). Tappuah in Manasseh, Josh. xvii. 7.

**Ĕp'a-phrăs** (*lovely*). A Roman friend of Paul, Col. i. 7; iv. 12.

**Ē-pæn'ē-tus** (*praised*). A Christian at Rome, Rom. xvi. 5.

**Ē-păph"ro-dī'tus** (*lovely*). Probably Epaphras. Phil. ii. 25; iv. 18.

**Ē'phah** (*gloomy*). (1) First son of Midian, Gen. xxv. 4; 1 Chr. i. 33; Isa. lx. 6. (2) Caleb's concubine, 1 Chr. ii. 46. (3) A Judahite, 1 Chr. ii. 47. (4) A Hebrew dry measure, estimated at 2¼ to 3¼ pecks. Ruth ii. 17; Num. v. 15. (5) A Hebrew liquid measure equal to 7½ gallons.

**Ē'phāi** (*gloomy*). His sons were captains left behind in Judah, Jer. xl. 8.

**Ē'pher** (*calf*). (1) A son of Midian, Gen. xxv. 4; 1 Kgs. iv. 10. (2) A son of Ezra, 1 Chr. iv. 17. A chief of Manasseh, 1 Chr. v. 24.

**Ē'phes=dam'mim** (*border of blood*). A Philistine encampment, 1 Sam. xvii. 1. Pasdammim, 1 Chr. xi. 13. [Elah.]

**Ē-phē'sians.** (1) Inhabitants of Ephesus, Acts xix. 28. (2) Epistle to, written by Paul to the Christians at Ephesus, about A. D 61 or 62, and while he was a prisoner at Rome. Forwarded by Tychicus, Eph. vi. 21. Of general import.

**Ĕph'ē-sŭs** (*desirable*). Capital of Ionia, on the Ægean Sea. Noted for its commerce, learning, and architecture. Paul visited it, Acts xviii. 1-20, and founded a church there, to which he addressed one of his best epistles, Acts xix. 1-10; xx. 17-38.

**Ĕph'lăl** (*judgment*). A Judahite, 1 Chr. ii. 37.

**Ĕph'ŏd** (*clothe*). (1) A sleeveless linen garment for priests, covering breast and back, Ex. xxviii. 4-35; 1 Sam. xxii. 18, with onyx clasp at shoulder, and breastplate at breast, crossing. Worn later by other than priests, 1 Chr. xv. 27. [Breastplate.] (2) A Manassite, Num. xxxiv. 23.

**Ĕph'phă-thȧ** (*be opened*). Christ's utterance in Mark vii. 34.

**Ē'phrā-ĭm** (*doubly fruitful*). (1) Second son of Joseph, Gen. xli. 52. Obtained Jacob's blessing, Gen. xlviii. 8-20. Tribe numerous, Num. i. 33; xxvi. 37. Allotment as in Josh. xvi. 1-10. (2) Site of Absalom's sheep-farm, 2 Sam. xiii. 23. (3) Place to which Christ retired, John xi. 54. (4) A gate of Jerusalem, 2 Kgs. xiv. 13; 2 Chr. xxv. 23; Neh. viii. 16; xii. 39. (5) "Mount of," in Ephraim, 1 Sam. i. 1. (6) "The wood of," east of Jordan, 2 Sam. xviii. 6.

**Ē'phrā-ĭm-ītes".** Members of the tribe of Ephraim, Judg. xii. 5. Sometimes Ephrathites.

**Ē'phrā-ĭn** (*doubly fruitful*). A city of Israel, 2 Chr. xiii. 19.

**Ĕph'ra-tah, Ĕph'rath** (*fruitful*). (1) Second wife of Caleb, 1 Chr. ii. 19, 50. (2) Ancient name of Bethlehem-judah, Gen. xxxv. 16, 19; xlviii. 7.

**Ĕph'rath-ītes.** (1) Inhabitants of Bethlehem, or Ephrath, Ruth i. 2. (2) Ephraimites, Judg. xii. 5; 1 Sam. i. 1; 1 Kgs. xi. 26.

**Ĕph'ron** (*fawn-like*). (1) A Hittite who sold Machpelah to Abraham, Gen. xxiii. 8-20; xlix. 29; l. 13. (2) Landmarks of Judah, Josh. xv. 9. (3) A city east of Jordan, 1 Macc. v. 46-52.

**Ĕp"ĭ-cū-rē'ans** (*followers of Epicurus*). A sect of pleasure-loving philosophers at Athens, Acts xvii. 18.

**Ē-pĭph'a-nēs,** 1 Macc. i. 10. [Antiochus, 4.]

**Ē-pĭs'tle** (*sending to*). In O. T. a letter, 2 Sam. xi. 14; 2 Kgs. v. 5, 6; 2 Chr. xxi. 12; Ez. iv. 6-11. In N. T., a formal tract containing Christian doctrine and salutary advice.

**Ĕr** (*watchman*). (1) First-born of Judah, Gen. xxxviii. 3-7; Num. xxvi. 19. (2) A descendant of Shelah, 1 Chr. iv. 21. (3) Son of Jose, Luke iii. 28.

**Ē'răn** (*watchful*). Founder of the Eranites, Num. xxvi. 36.

**Ē-răs'tŭs** (*beloved*). (1) A friend of Paul at Ephesus, Acts xix. 22; 2 Tim. iv. 20. (2) A Corinthian convert, Rom. xvi. 23.

**Ē'rĕch** (*healthy*). A city of Shinar, Gen. x. 10.

**Ē'rī** (*watching*). A son of Gad, Gen. xlvi. 16, and founder of the Erites, Num. xxvi. 16.

**Ē-sā'ias.** N. T. name of Isaiah, Matt. iii. 3.

**Ē"sar-hăd'don** (*conqueror*). A king of Assyria, 2 Kgs. xix. 37; 2 Chr. xxxiii. 11. He united Babylon to Assyria and reigned over both B. C. 680-667.

**Ē'sau** (*hairy*). Eldest son of Isaac and twin brother of Jacob, Gen. xxv. 25. Called also Edom. Sold his birthright to Jacob, Gen. xxv. 26-34; xxxvi. 1-10. Gave his name, Edom, to a country and to his descendants, Gen. xxvi., xxxvi. [Edom.]

**Ē'say,** Ecclus. xlviii. 20-22. [Isaiah.]

**Es"dra-ē'lon.** Greek for Jezreel, Judith iii. 9; iv. 6.

**Ĕs'dras.** (1) A scribe in 1 and 2 Esdras. (2) First and second books of the Apocrypha. First a supplement to Ezra; second a series of visions.

**Ē'sĕk** (*strife*). A well in Gerar, Gen. xxvi. 20.

**Ĕsh=bā'al** (*Baal's man*). Ishbosheth, Saul's fourth son, 1 Chr. viii. 33; ix. 39.

**Ĕsh'băn** (*wise man*). Son of Dishon, Gen. xxxvi. 26; 1 Chr. i. 41.

**Ĕsh'cŏl** (*bunch of grapes*). (1) Brother of Mamre, Gen. xiv. 13-24. (2) A valley or brook near Hebron, Num. xiii. 22-27; xxxii. 9; Deut. i. 24.

**Ē'shē-an** (*slope*). A city of Judah, Josh. xv. 52.

**Ē'shĕk** (*oppression*). A descendant of Saul, 1 Chr. viii. 39.

**Ĕsh'ka-lŏn-ites",** Josh. xiii. 3. [Ashkelon.]

**Ĕsh'tā-ŏl** (*a way*). Town in Judah and Dan, Josh. xv. 33; xix. 41; burial place of Samson, Judg. xiii. 25; xvi. 31; xviii. 2-11.

**Ĕsh'tā-ul-ītes".** Families of Kirjath-jearim, 1 Chr. ii. 53.

**Ĕsh"te-mō'ȧ, Ĕsh'te-mōh** (*bosom of a woman*). A Levitical town of Judah, Josh. xv. 50; xxi. 14; 1 Sam. xxx. 28.

**Ĕsh'ton** (*weak*). A Judahite, 1 Chr. iv. 11, 12.

**Ĕs'lī** (*reserved*). Ancestor of Joseph, Luke iii. 25.

**Ē-sō'rȧ.** Hazor or Zorah, Judith iv. 4.

**Ĕs-pouse'** (*promise*). [Betroth.]

**Ĕs'rom,** Matt. i. 3; Luke iii. 33. [Hezron.]

**Ĕs-sēne'** (*priest*). Member of a Jewish ascetic sect, the Essenes.

**Ĕs-tāte'** (*standing*). In Mark vi. 21, a class or order representing the government. The "estate of the elders," Acts xxii. 5, was a body of advisers cooperating with the Sanhedrim.

**Ĕs'thēr** (*star*). Persian name of Hadassah, Mordecai's cousin, who married King Ahasuerus, and saved the lives of her countrymen. Her book, seventeenth of O. T., tells her story.

**Ē'tam** (*lair*). (1) A village in Simeon, 1 Chr. iv. 32. (2) Favorite resort of Solomon, 2 Chr. xi. 6; Judg. xv. 8-19. (3) A doubtful name, 1 Chr. iv. 3.

**Ē'tham** (*sea bound*). An Israelite encampment, Ex. xiii. 20; Num. xxxiii. 6-8.

**Ē'than** (*strong*). (1) One noted for wisdom, 1 Kgs. iv. 31; 1 Chr. ii. 6; title to Ps. lxxxix. (2) A Levite singer, 1 Chr. vi. 44; xv. 17-19. (3) An ancestor of Asaph, 1 Chr. vi. 42.

**Ĕth'a-nīm** (*flowing*). Seventh month (Tisri) of Jewish sacred, and first of civil, year; corresponding to parts of Sept. and Oct., 1 Kgs. viii. 2.

**Ĕth'bā-al** (*favored of Baal*). King of Sidon, 1 Kgs. xvi. 31.

**Ē'thēr** (*plenty*). Town in Judah and Simeon, Josh. xv. 42; xix. 7.

**Ē"thĭ-ō'pĭ-ȧ** (*burnt faces*). Greek and Roman for Hebrew "Cush." The unbounded country south of Egypt, Ezek. xxix. 10; settled by Hamites, Gen. x. 6; merchants, Isa. xlv. 14; Jer. xiii. 23; Job xxviii. 19; wealthy, Acts viii. 27-37; strongly military, 2 Chr. xii. 3; xiv. 9-12; 2 Kgs. xvii. 4.

**Ē"thĭ-ō'pĭ-ans.** Dwellers in Ethiopia; Cushites, Num. xii. 1; 2 Chr. xiv. 9; Jer. xxxviii. 7; xxxix. 16; Acts viii. 27-37.

**Ĕth'nan** (*hire*). A Judahite, 1 Chr. iv. 5-7.

**Ĕth'nī** (*liberal*). A Levite, 1 Chr. vi. 41.

**Eū-bū'lus** (*prudent*). A Roman Christian, 2 Tim. iv. 21.

**Eū-ēr'gē-tēs** (*benefactor*). A common Grecian surname, and title of honor; applied especially to the Ptolemies.

**Eū'nă-tan**, 1 Esdr. viii. 44. [ELNATHAN.]

**Eū'nīçe** (*good victory*). Mother of Timothy, Acts xvi. 1; 2 Tim. i. 5.

**Eū'nŭch** (*couch guardian*). A castrated male. Eunuchs became court officials, 2 Kgs. ix. 32; Esth. ii. 3; Acts viii. 27; could not enter the congregation, Deut. xxiii. 1. A celibate, Matt. xix. 12.

**Eū-ō'dī-as** (*fragrant*). Euodia in R. V.; a Christian woman of Philippi, Phil. iv. 2.

**Eū-phrā'tēş** (*fructifying*). A great river of western Asia, rising in Armenia and emptying into the Persian Gulf. Boundary of Eden, Gen. ii. 14; "great river," Gen. xv. 18; Deut. i. 7; eastern boundary of the promised land, Deut. xi. 24; Josh. i. 4; 1 Chr. v. 9; and of David's conquests, 2 Sam. viii. 3; 1 Chr. xviii. 3. *See* also, Jer. xiii. 4-7; xlvi. 2-10; li. 63; Ps. cxxxvii. 1; Rev. ix. 14; xvi. 12.

**Eū-pŏl'ę-mus**. An envoy, 1 Macc. viii. 17.

**Eū-rŏc'lȳ-don**. A stormy northeast wind of the Levant, Acts xxvii. 14.

**Eū'tȳ-chus** (*fortunate*). A sleepy youth of Troas, Acts xx. 6-12.

**Ē-văn'ġĕl-ĭst** (*publisher of glad tidings*). One of the four writers of the gospels Matthew, Mark, Luke and John. A preacher of the gospel inferior in authority to the Apostles, Acts viii. 14-19, and apparently to the prophets, Eph. iv. 11, yet superior to the pastor and teacher, Acts xxi. 8; Eph. iv. 11; 2 Tim. iv. 5. A travelling and corresponding missionary, Acts xx. 4, 5.

**Ēve** (*life*). The first woman; made *of* man and *for* him, Gen. ii. 18-25; iii.-iv.

**Ēve'nĭng** (*decline of day*). Two evenings recognized, one before, the other after, sunset, Gen. xxiv. 63; Ex. xii. 6; Num. ix. 3; xxviii. 4.

**Ē'vī** (*desire*). A King of Midian, Num. xxxi. 8; Josh. xiii. 21.

**Ē'vĭl=mē-rō'dach** (*fool of Merodach*). King of Babylon, B. C. 561-559, 2 Kgs. xxv. 27; Jer. lii. 31-34.

**Ĕx″cŏm-mū″nĭ-cā'tion** (*putting out of the community*). Threefold in Jewry. (1) Temporary suspension. (2) Further temporary suspension. (3) Final cutting off. Now rests on Matt. xvi. 19; xviii. 17; 1 Cor. v. 11; 2 Cor. ii. 5-11; 1 Cor. i. 20; Tit. iii. 10.

**Ĕx″ē-cū'tion-ēr** (*a follower out*). In O. T. a position of dignity, Gen. xxxvii. 36, marg.; 1 Kgs. ii. 25, 34. Even in Mark vi. 27, the executioner belonged to the king's body-guard.

**Ĕx'ō-dus** (*going out*). Second Book of the Bible and Pentateuch. Written by Moses. Historic from i. to xviii. 27; legislative from xix. to end. Its history covers the period (about 142 years) of Jewish preparation to leave Egypt, the departure, the desert wanderings and the arrival at Sinai. Its legislation comprises the giving of the law at Sinai, directions for the priesthood, the establishment of the tabernacle and its service.

**Ĕx'ŏr-çĭsts** (*swearers out*). Those who pretended to drive out evil spirits by prayers and conjurations, Matt. xii. 27; Mark ix. 38; Acts xix. 13.

**Ĕx″pĭ-ā'tion**, Feast of. [ATONEMENT.]

**Eȳe**. Putting out the eye a warfare custom, especially with dangerous prisoners. Judg. xvi 21; 1 Sam. xi. 2; 2 Kgs. xxv. 7. Painting the eyelids a fashion, 2 Kgs. ix. 30; Jer. iv. 30; Ezek. xxiii. 40. "Eye-service," reluctant service, Col. iii. 22; Eph. vi. 6.

**Ē'zär**, 1 Chr. i. 38. [EZER, 1.]

**Ĕz'bă-ī** (*shining*). Father of one of David's mighty men, 1 Chr. xi. 37.

**Ĕz'bŏn** (*bright*). (1) A son of Gad, Gen. xlvi. 16; Ozni in Num. xxvi. 16. (2) A Benjamite, 1 Chr. vii. 7.

**Ĕz-ē-chī'as**, 2 Esdr. vii. 40. [HEZEKIAH.]

**Ĕz-ē-çī'as**, 1 Esdr. ix. 43. [HILKIAH.]

**Ĕz-ē-kī'as**, 2 Macc. xv. 22; Matt. i. 9, 10. [HEZEKIAH.]

**Ē-zē'kī-ĕl** (*strength of God*). One of the four greater prophets; carried captive to Babylon B. C. 598; entered the prophetic calling in fifth year of his captivity, Ezek. i. 1-3. Chapters i.-xxiv. of his book contain predictions before the fall of Jerusalem, and xxv.-xlviii. predictions after that event. The visions of the Temple, xl.-xlviii., are a unique feature of the book.

**Ē'zĕl** (*going away*). Scene of the parting of David and Jonathan, 1 Sam. xx. 19.

**Ē'zĕm** (*bone*). A town of Simeon, 1 Chr. iv. 29; Azem in Josh. xix. 3.

**Ē'zēr** (*help*). (1) A Horite duke, Gen. xxxvi. 21, 27, 30; 1 Chr. iv. 4. (2) An Ephraimite, 1 Chr. vii. 21. (3) A Gadite, 1 Chr. xii. 9. (4) A Levite, Neh. iii. 19. (5) A priest, Neh. xii. 42.

**Ĕz″ē-rī'as, Ē-zī'as**, 1 Esdr. viii. 1, 2. [AZARIAH.]

**Ē'zī-on=gā'bēr**, or **gē'bēr** (*backbone of a giant*). An Israelite encampment, Num. xxxiii. 35, 36; Deut. ii. 8. Compare 1 Kgs. ix. 26; 2 Chr. viii. 17; 1 Kgs. xxii. 48.

**Ĕz'nīte**, 2 Sam. xxiii. 8, for Tachmonite in same verse and Hachmonite in 1 Chr. xi. 11.

**Ĕz'rȧ** (*help*). The famous scribe and priest, resident at Babylon, who returned to Jerusalem with his countrymen, B. C. 458, where he began instant reforms. He collected and revised the previous O. T. writings and largely settled the O. T. canon. His book, 15th of O. T., tells the story of the return and the establishment of a new order of things at Jerusalem and in Judea.

**Ĕz'rą-hīte″**. A title applied to Ethan and Heman, 1 Kgs. iv. 31; Ps. lxxxviii. title; lxxxix. title.

**Ĕz'rī** (*my help*). A superintendent of David's farm laborers, 1 Chr. xxvii. 26.

## F

**Fā'ble** (*spoken*). A narrative in which inanimate things are personalized, Judg. ix. 8-15; 2 Kgs. xiv. 9.

**Fair Hā'vens**. A harbor of Crete, Acts xxvii. 8-13.

**Fairs** (*holidays*). Wares, Ezek. xxvii. 12-33.

**Făl'low=deer** (*yellowish brown*). The bubalis or African deer, Deut. xiv. 5; 1 Kgs. iv. 23. Some say the Arabian wild ox.

**Făl'low** (*yellow*). Plowed land left to mellow. Tillage, Prov. xiii. 23. Figurative, Jer. iv. 3; Hos. x. 12. The Sabbatical, or fallow year; year of landrest, Lev. xxv. 1-7; Deut. xxxi. 9-14.

**Făm'īne** (*hunger*). Generally foretold and regarded as a judgment, Gen. xii. 10; xxvi. 1; xli. 54-56, 2 Kgs. vii.

**Făn** (*winnower*). Winnowing shovel or fork used to throw chaff up into the wind, to separate it from the kernels, Isa. xxx. 24; Matt. iii. 12.

**Fąr'thĭng**. Two Roman bronze coins. One, Matt. v. 26; Mark xii. 42, worth ¼ of a cent; the other, Matt. x. 29; Luke xii. 6, worth 1½ cents.

**Făsts** (*keep*). One legal fast, the Atonement, kept by Jews, Lev. xvi. 29-34; Deut. ix. 9; Jonah iii. 5; Zech. vii. 1-7. Special fasts observed, 1 Sam. vii. 6; Jer. xxxvi. 6-10; Esth. iv. 16; Matt. ix. 14; Mark ii. 18; Luke v. 33; Acts x. 30; xiii. 3.

**Făt** (*fed*). Forbidden food, as belonging to God, Lev. iii. 3-17; vii. 3, 23; Neh. viii. 10; yet fatted cattle enjoyed, 1 Kgs. iv. 23; Luke xv. 23. Vat is meant in Joel ii. 24; iii. 13; Hag. ii. 16.

**Fā'ther** (*sire*). Source of authority, Gen. iii. 16; 1 Cor. xi. 3. Disrespect of, condemned, Ex. xxi. 15-17; xxii. 17; Lev. xx. 9; 1 Tim. i. 9. Parental obedience bears a promise, Ex. xx. 12. Father also a priest, Gen. viii. 20. Any ancestor, Deut. i. 11; Matt. xxiii. 30. A title, Judg. xvii. 10; 1 Sam. x. 12; Acts vii. 2. Protector, Ps. lxviii. 5. Author and founder, Gen. iv. 21; Rom. iv. 12. Divine appellation, Deut. xxxii. 6; Matt. vi. 4; Rom. i. 7.

**Făth'om** (*embrace*). Space to which a man can extend his arms; about 6 feet, Acts xxvii. 28.

**Fēasts** (*joyful*). Observed for joyous events, Gen. xxi. 8; xxix. 22; xl. 20; Mark vi. 21, 22. Numerous religious feasts, Ex. xii. 16; Lev. xxiii. 21-24; Jude 12.

**Fēet**. To wash, a sign of hospitality, Gen. xviii. 4; 1 Sam. xxv. 41; John xiii. 5, 6. To remove shoes, a reverence, Ex. iii. 5; sign of mourning, Ezek. xxiv. 17.

**Fē'lix** (*happy*). A procurator of Judea, Acts xxiii. 26.

**Fĕnced Cities** (*defenced*). Walled or palisaded cities. [CITY.]

**Fĕr'ret** (*thief*). A domesticated animal of the weasel family used for catching rats, Lev. xi. 30.

**Fĕs'tŭs**. Procurator, Acts xxiv. 27.

**Fĕt'ters** (*shackles*). Instruments of brass or iron for fastening feet of prisoners, Ps. cv. 18; cxlix. 8.

**Fiēld**. Open area beyond the enclosed gardens or vineyards, Gen. iv. 8; xxiv. 63; Deut. xxii. 25. Landmarks, sacred, Deut. xix. 14; Job xxiv. 2; Prov. xxii. 28.

**Fĭg, Fĭg=tree**. Common in Palestine, Deut. viii. 8; Isa. xxxiv. 4; 1 Kgs. iv. 25. Pressed figs, 1 Sam. xxv. 18. Fruit appears before leaves, Matt. xxi. 19.

**Fir.** A tree of the pine family, 2 Sam. vi. 5; 1 Kgs. v. 8; S. of Sol. i. 17.

**Fire.** Symbol of God's presence, Gen. iv. 4, 5; xv. 17; Ex. iii. 2; Judg. xiii. 19, 20. Worshipped, 2 Kgs. xvii. 17; punishment, Lev. xx. 14; xxi. 9. Christ comes in, 2 Thess. i. 8. World destroyed by, 2 Pet. iii. 7.

**Fire-pan.** The censer and snuff-dish of the temple, Ex. xxv. 38; xxvii. 3; xxxvii. 23; xxxviii. 3; 2 Kgs. xxv. 15.

**Fir'kin** (*fourth*). A Greek measure equal to Hebrew bath, 4 to 6 gals., John ii. 6.

**Firm'a-ment** (*made firm*). Overhead expanse, Gen. i. 17; solid, Ex. xxiv. 10; with windows and doors, Gen. vii. 11. Isa. xxiv. 18; Ps. lxxviii. 23

**First-born.** Consecrated to God, Ex. xiii. 2; received a double portion, Deut. xxi. 17. Paid redemption money after the priesthood started, Num. iii. 12, 13; xviii. 15, 16.

**First-fruits** were offerings and priest's perquisites, Ex. xxii. 29; xxiii. 19; xxxiv. 26; Lev. ii. 12; xxiii. 10-12; Num. xviii. 12; Deut. xviii. 3, 4.

**Fish, Fish-ing.** Grand division of animal kingdom, Gen. i. 21, 22. Without scales, unclean, Lev. xi. 9-12. Plenty in waters of Palestine, Luke v. 5. Worship of, prohibited, Deut. iv. 18. Caught with nets, hooks, and spears, Hab. i. 15; Luke v. 5-7; Job xli. 7.

**Fish-gate.** A Jerusalem gate, 2 Chr. xxxiii. 14.

**Fish-hooks.** [Fish.]

**Fish-pools.** Should read "pools," S. of Sol. vii. 4.

**Fitch'es** (*vetches*). "Spelt," Ezek. iv. 9. "Fennel," or black cummin, Isa. xxviii. 25-27.

**Flag** (*fluttering*). Embraces many water plants, Ex. ii. 3-5; Isa. xix. 6.

**Flag'on** (*flask*). Small vessel for liquids, Isa. xxii. 24; 2 Sam. vi. 19; 1 Chr. xvi. 3; S. of Sol. ii. 5.

**Flax** (*flexible*). Grown and used largely in East, Ex. ix. 31; Josh. ii. 6; Isa. xix. 9. For lamp wicks, Isa. xlii. 3; Matt. xii. 20. Spinning honorable, Prov. xxxi. 13, 19, 24.

**Flēa.** Pests throughout the East, 1 Sam. xxiv. 14; xxvi. 20.

**Flĕsh.** Everything living, Gen. vi. 13-19; mankind, vi. 12; the body, Col. ii. 5; 1 Pet. iv. 6; seat of appetites, Rom. viii. 1, 5, 9; Gal. v. 17-19; Eph. ii. 3. Used much figuratively.

**Flĕsh-hooks.** Three-tined hooks for taking meat from a boiling vessel, Ex. xxxviii. 3; 1 Sam. ii. 13, 14.

**Flint.** Quartz; abounds in Palestine, Ps. cxiv. 8. Types abundance, Deut. xxxii. 13; firmness, Isa. l. 7; Ezek. iii. 9.

**Flōats.** Rafts for floating timber, 1 Kgs. v. 9; 2 Chr. ii. 16.

**Flŏck.** [Sheep.]

**Flood** (*flow*). The Noachian deluge; "the flood," Gen. vi.-viii; Matt. xxiv. 37; 2 Pet. ii. 5; iii. 6. [Noah.]

**Flōor.** [Agriculture.]

**Flŏur.** [Bread.]

**Flūte** (*blow, flow*). Flute or "pipe," made of reeds or copper, and similar to those of to-day, Dan. iii. 5-15; 1 Kgs. i. 40.

**Flŭx** (*flow*). Violent dysentery, Acts xxviii. 8.

**Fly.** Of many varieties in East, and very noisome, Ex. viii. 21-31; Ps. lxxviii. 45; Eccl. x. 1; Isa. vii. 18.

**Food** (*feed*). Vegetable foods, soups, eggs, curds, honey, bread, etc., preferred by Hebrews to animal food, Lev. xxvi. 26; Ps. cv. 16; Ezek. iv. 16. Animal food a feature of entertainments, Gen. xviii. 7; 1 Sam. xvi. 20; Luke xv. 23. Fish used, Num. xi. 5; Matt. xiii. 47, 48; xv. 34.

**Foot.** Used in pumping water from Nile, Deut. xi. 10.

**Foot'men.** Swift runners, couriers, 1 Sam. xxii. 17; 1 Kgs. xiv. 28; 2 Kgs. xi. 4.

**Foot'stool.** Kings used them, 2 Chr. ix. 18. God's footstool, 1 Chr. xxviii. 2; Ps. xcix. 5.

**Fŏre'hĕad.** Unveiled women "hard of forehead," Gen. xxiv. 65; Ezek. iii. 7-9; Jer. iii. 3. Mark of beast on forehead, Rev. xiii. 16; God's name there, Rev. xxii. 4

**Fŏr'eign-er** (*out of doors*). One not of Hebrew stock, Ex. xii. 45; Eph. ii. 12.

**Fōre-knowl'edge.** God's knowledge of the future, Acts ii. 23; xv. 18; 1 Pet. i. 2.

**Fōre-rŭn'ner.** Preparer of the way "within the veil," Heb. vi. 19, 20.

**Fŏr'est.** Woodland and waste land, 1 Sam. xxii. 5. "House of the Forest" was built of cedars thereof, 1 Kgs. vii. 2.

**Fôrks,** 1 Sam. xiii. 21. [Flesh-hooks.]

**Fôr''ni-cā'tion** (*crime under the arch*). Crime of impurity between unmarried persons. Figuratively, infidelity to God, Ezek. xvi. 2; Jer. ii. 20; Matt. v. 32.

**Fôr''tū-nā'tus** (*fortunate*). A Corinthian friend of Paul, 1 Cor. xvi. 17, and postscript.

**Foun'tain** (*font*). Springs of Palestine many but uncertain, Deut. viii. 7. They furnish many figures of speech, Ps. xxxvi. 8, 9; Isa. xlix. 10; Jer. ii. 13; John iv. 10; Rev. vii. 17.

**Fowl** (*flying*). The Hebrew original embraces birds in general, Gen. i. 20; 1 Kgs. iv. 23. The Greek provides the domestic limitation, Luke xii. 24.

**Fŏx** (*hairy*). The jackal meant, as it is gregarious and feeds on carcasses, Judg. xv. 4; Ps. lxiii. 10; S. of Sol. ii. 15; Ezek. xiii. 4; Luke ix. 58.

**Frănk'in-çense** (*free burning*). The yellowish gum used in sacrificial fumigation, Ex. xxx. 7-9; Lev. xvi. 12, 13; Rev. viii. 3. A mixture of gums and spices in Ex. xxx. 34-38.

**Frin'ges** (*fibres*). The ornamental hem of the outer garment. Wearing enjoined, Num. xv. 37-40; Deut. xxii. 12; Matt. ix. 20; xiv. 36.

**Frŏg.** The Egyptian species akin to our own. Source of one of the plagues, Ex. viii. 2-14. Elsewhere only in Ps. lxxviii. 45; cv. 30; Rev. xvi. 13.

**Frŏnt'lets** (*little foreheads*). Phylacteries in Greek. Parchment strips inscribed with texts, Ex. xiii. 2-17; Deut. vi. 4-22; enclosed in calf-skin case, worn at prayers on forehead or left arm, Matt. xxiii. 5; Mark vii. 3, 4; Luke v. 33.

**Fu̧l'ler** (*tramper on*). Fuller's art used for cleaning clothes. They were placed in vessels of water impregnated with natron or soap and trodden with the feet, Prov. xxv. 20; Jer. ii. 22; Mal. iii. 2. Chalk and fuller's earth used for bleaching, 2 Kgs. xviii. 17; Isa. vii. 3; xxxvi. 2.

**Fū'nêr-al.** [Burial.]

**Fûr'long** (*furrow long*). In N. T. for Greek stadium, 600 feet long, Luke xxiv. 13.

**Fûr'nace** (*oven*). Oven in Gen. xv. 17; Neh. iii. 11. Smelting furnace or lime-kiln in Gen. xix. 28; Ex. ix. 8; Isa. xxxiii. 12. Refining furnace in Prov. xvii. 3. Furnace like a brick-kiln in Dan. iii. 15-27.

**Fûr'ni-ture** (*provided*). Oriental furniture scanty, 2 Kgs. iv. 10-13. Camel's trappings in Gen. xxxi. 34. [Bed.]

**Fûr'row** (*ridge*). Usual meaning, except in Hos. x. 10, where it means transgressions.

## G

**Gā'al** (*contempt*). Son of Ebed, Judg. ix. 26-41.

**Gā'ash** (*earthquake*). The hill on which Joshua was buried, Josh. xxiv. 30; 2 Sam. xxiii. 30.

**Gā'bȧ,** Josh. xviii. 24; Ez. ii. 26. [Geba.]

**Găb'ā-el.** Ancestor of Tobit, Tob. i. 1, 14.

**Găb'bą-ī** (*gatherer*). A Benjamite family, Neh. xi. 8.

**Găb'bą-thȧ** (*elevated*). The pavement on which Christ was sentenced, John xix. 13.

**Găb'dēs,** 1 Esdr. v. 20. [Geba.]

**Gā'bri-as.** Brother of Tobit, Tob. i. 14; iv. 20.

**Gā'bri-el** (*man of God*). The announcing angel, Luke i. 11, 19, 26, 38; Dan. viii. 16; ix. 21.

**Găd** (*troop*). (1) Jacob's seventh son, Gen. xxx. 11-13; xlix. 19; Num. i. 24, 25. Tribe settled east of Jordan, and became a fierce, warlike people. Carried captive by Tiglath-pileser, 1 Chr. v. 26. (2) A prophet and David's seer, 1 Sam. xxii. 5; 1 Chr. xxi. 9-19; xxix. 29; 2 Chr. xxix. 25.

**Găd'a-rȧ** (*walled*). A city six miles S. E. of Sea of Galilee. Now Um-keis.

**Găd'a-rēnes, Gĕr'gĕ-sēnes, Gĕr'a-sēnes.** A people east of the Sea of Galilee, Matt. viii. 28-34; Mark v. 1-20; Luke viii. 26-40.

**Găd'dī** (*fortunate*). One of the spies, Num. xiii. 11.

**Găd'di-el** (*fortune of God*). Another of the spies, Num. xiii. 10.

**Gā'dī** (*of God*). Father of King Menahem, 2 Kgs. xv. 15, 17.

**Gā'hăm** (*browned*). Son of Nahor, Gen. xxii. 24.

**Gā'hăr** (*hiding place*). His sons returned, Ez. ii. 47.

**Gā'ius, Cā'ius** (*lord*). (1) Of Macedonia, a friend of Paul, Acts xix. 29. (2) Of Derbe, co-worker with Paul, Acts xx. 4. (3) Of Corinth, baptized by Paul, Rom. xvi. 23; 1 Cor. i. 14. (4) John's third epistle addressed to Gaius.

**Găl'a-ad.** Greek form of Gilead.

**Gā'lăl** (*prominence*). Three Levites, 1 Chr. ix. 15, 16; Neh. xi. 17.

**Gȧ-lā'tià** (*land of the Galli, Gauls*). A central province of Asia Minor, and part of Paul's missionary field, Acts xvi. 6: xviii. 23; 2 Tim. iv. 10.

**Gȧ-lā'tians, Epistle to.** Written by Paul to people of Galatia, A. D. 56 or 57, to strengthen their faith in the divinity of his mission, unfold his doctrine of justification by faith, and urge persistency in Christian work.

**Găl-bā'num** (*fat*). A gum-resin of yellowish color, and pungent, disagreeable odor when burning, Ex. xxx. 34.

**Găl'ē-ed** (*heap of witness*). Memorial heap of Jacob, Gen. xxxi. 47, 48.

**Găl'gă-lȧ**, 1 Macc. ix. 1. [GILGAL.]

**Găl'ĭ-lee** (*circle*). Originally the circuit containing the 20 towns given by Solomon to Hiram, Josh. xx. 7; 1 Kgs. ix. 11; 2 Kgs. xv. 29. In time of Christ, one of the largest provinces of Palestine, in which he spent the greater part of his life and ministry. Luke xiii. 1; xxiii. 6; John i. 43-47; Acts i. 11.

**Gal'ĭ-lee, Sea of.** [GENNESARET.]

**Gall** (*yellow, bitter*). The fluid secreted by the liver. Bitter, Job xvi. 13; poison, xx. 14, 25; Deut. xxxii. 33; "hemlock" in Hos. x. 4; probably myrrh, in Matt. xxvii. 34; as in Mark xv. 23; great troubles, Jer. viii. 14, Acts viii. 23.

**Găl'lēr-ȳ** (*show*). An eastern veranda or portico; but panel work in S. of Sol. i. 17; or pillared walk, Ezek. xli. 15.

**Găl'ley**, Isa. xxxiii. 21. [SHIP.]

**Găl'lĭm** (*heaps*). A village of Benjamin, 1 Sam. xxv. 44; Isa. x. 30.

**Găl'lĭ-ō** (*who lives on milk*). Roman proconsul of Achaia, A. D. 53, Acts xviii. 12-17.

**Găl'lōws.** [PUNISHMENT.]

**Găm'ȧ-el**, 1 Esdr. viii. 29. [DANIEL.]

**Gȧ-mā'lĭ-el** (*recompense of God*). (1) A prince of Manasseh, Num. i. 10; ii. 20; vii. 54; x. 23. (2) A learned president of the Sanhedrim, and Paul's legal preceptor, Acts v. 34; xxii. 3.

**Gāmes** (*sports*). Simple among Hebrews. Falconry, Job xli. 5; foot-racing, Ps. xix. 5; Eccl. ix. 11; bow and sling contests, 1 Sam. xx. 20; Judg. xx. 16; 1 Chr. xii. 2; dancing, Matt. xi. 16, 17; joking, Prov. xxvi. 19; Jer. xv. 17.

**Găm'ma-dĭms** (*dwarfs*). Perhaps watchmen, Ezek. xxvii. 11.

**Gā'mŭl** (*weaned*). Leader of the 22d priestly course, 1 Chr. xxiv. 17.

**Gär.** Sons of, in 1 Esdr. v. 34.

**Gär'den** (*yard*). In Hebrew sense, enclosures for fruits, etc., well watered, Gen. ii. 10; xiii. 10; xxi. 33; Num. xxiv. 6; Job viii. 16; hedged, Isa. v. 5; walled, Prov. xxiv. 31; protected, Isa. i. 8; Job xxvii. 18; Mark xii. i.

**Gā'rĕb** (*scab*). (1) One of David's warriors, 2 Sam. xxiii. 38; 1 Chr. xi. 40. (2) A hill near Jerusalem, Jer. xxxi. 39.

**Găr'ĭ-zĭm**, 2 Macc. v. 23. [GERIZIM.]

**Gär'lic** (*spear leek*). A bulbous plant similar to an onion and leek, Num. xi. 5.

**Gär'ment.** [DRESS.]

**Gär'mīte.** A Judahite, 1 Chr. iv. 19.

**Găr'rĭ-sŏn** (*warning*). In Hebrew sense, a place manned, provisioned, and fortified, 1 Sam. xiii. 23; 2 Sam. xxiii. 14; 1 Chr. xi. 16; guards in 2 Chr. xvii. 2; 1 Chr. xviii. 13.

**Găsh'mŭ**, Neh. vi. 6. [GESHEM.]

**Gā'tam** (*burnt valley*). A duke of Edom, Gen. xxxvi. 11, 16.

**Gāte** (*opening*). Those of walled cities made of wood, iron, or brass, Judg. xvi. 3; Deut. iii. 5; Ps. cvii. 16; Acts xii. 10; flanked by towers, 2 Sam. xviii. 24, 33; market and judgment places near, 2 Sam. xv. 2; 2 Kgs. vii. 1; Job xxix. 7; Deut. xvii. 5; xxv. 7; Am. v. 10; Ruth iv. 1-12; symbol of power, Gen. xxii. 17; Isa. xxiv. 12; Matt. xvi. 18; the city itself, Deut. xii. 12.

**Găth** (*wine press*). A city of Philistia, Josh. xiii. 3; 1 Sam. vi. 17; home of Goliath, 1 Sam. xvii. 4; refuge of David, 1 Sam. xxi. 10.

**Găth-hē'phēr, Gĭt'tah-hē'phēr** (*wine press of Hepher*). A town in Zebulun, now el Meshed, Josh. xix. 13; 2 Kgs. xiv. 25.

**Găth-rĭm'mon** (*high wine press*). (1) A Levitical city of Dan, Josh. xxi. 24; 1 Chr. vi. 69. (2) A Levite town of Manasseh, Josh. xxi. 25. Bileam, 1 Chr. vi. 70.

**Gā'zȧ** (*strong*). Hebrew Azzah, now Ghuzzeh. A city of Philistia, Gen x. 19; assigned to Judah, Josh. x. 41; xv. 47; Judg. i. 18; scene of Samson's exploits, Judg. xvi.; 1 Kgs. iv. 24; Acts viii. 26.

**Găz'a-rȧ**, 1 Macc. ix. 52. [GEZER.]

**Gā'zăth-ītes.** Inhabitants of Gaza, Josh. xiii. 3.

**Gā'zēr**, 2 Sam. v. 25; 1 Chr. xiv. 16. [GEZER.]

**Găz'ē-rȧ.** (1) 1 Macc. iv. 15. [GEZER.] (2) His sons returned, 1 Esdr. v. 31.

**Gā'zĕz** (*shearer*). Son of Caleb, 1 Chr. ii. 46.

**Gā'zītes.** Inhabitants of Gaza, Judg. xvi. 2.

**Găz'zam** (*consuming*). His descendants returned, Ez. ii. 48; Neh. vii. 51.

**Gē'bȧ** (*hill*). Gaba in Josh. xviii. 24; now Jeba, 6 miles N. of Jerusalem. A Levitical city of Benjamin, Josh. xxi. 17; 1 Chr. vi. 60; 1 Sam. xiii. 3; 1 Kgs. xv. 22; 2 Kgs. xxiii. 8; Isa. x. 29.

**Gē'bal** (*mountain*). A maritime town of Phœnicia, near Tyre, Ezek. xxvii. 9. Inhabitants called Giblites, Josh. xiii. 5.

**Gē'bēr** (*man*). Two of Solomon's commissaries, 1 Kgs. iv. 13, 19.

**Gē'bĭm** (*ditches*). A place near Jerusalem, Isa. x. 31.

**Gĕc'ko.** The fan-footed lizard of Palestine. "Ferret," in A. V., Lev. xi. 30; "Gecko" in R. V.

**Gĕd''a-lī'ah** (*God my greatness*). (1) A governor of Judea, 2 Kgs. xxv. 22; and friend of Jeremiah, Jer. xl. 5, 6; xli. 2. (2) A Levite harpist, 1 Chr. xxv. 3. (3) A priest, Ez. x. 18. (4) A persecutor of Jeremiah, Jer. xxxviii. 1. (5) Grandfather of Zephaniah, Zeph. i. 1.

**Gĕd'dur**, 1 Esdr. v. 30. [GAHAR.]

**Gĕd'e-on.** Greek form of Gideon, Heb. xi. 32.

**Gē'dēr** (*wall*). Its king was conquered by Joshua, Josh. xii. 13.

**Gē-dē'rah** (*sheepfold*). A town in lowlands of Judah, Josh. xv. 36.

**Gĕd'ē-răth-īte''.** Inhabitant of Gederah, 1 Chr. xii. 4.

**Gĕd'ē-rīte.** Inhabitant of Geder, 1 Chr. xxvii. 28.

**Gē-dē'rŏth** (*sheepfolds*). A city in lowlands of Judah, Josh. xv. 41; 2 Chr. xxviii. 18.

**Gĕd''ē-rŏth-ā'ĭm** (*two sheepfolds*). A town in lowlands of Judah, Josh. xv. 36.

**Gē'dŏr** (*wall*). (1) A hill town of Judah, Josh. xv. 58. (2) A town of Benjamin, 1 Chr. xii. 7. (3) 1 Chr. iv. 39, probably Gerar. (4) An ancestor of Saul, 1 Chr. viii. 31.

**Gē-hā'zī** (*valley of vision*). Messenger of Elisha, 2 Kgs. iv. 12-37; v. 20-27; viii. 4.

**Gē-hĕn'nȧ.** [HINNOM.]

**Gĕl'ĭ-lŏth** (*circuit*). A landmark of Benjamin, Josh. xviii. 17.

**Gē-măl'lī** (*camel driver*). Father of Ammiel, Num. xiii. 12.

**Gĕm''a-rī'ah** (*perfected by God*). (1) Son of Shaphan, Jer. xxxvi. 10-27. (2) Messenger of King Hezekiah, Jer. xxix. 3, 4.

**Gĕms.** [STONES, PRECIOUS.]

**Gĕn''ē-ăl'ō-gy** (*birth record*). In Hebrew, "book of generations," Gen. v.; x.; 1 Chr. i.-viii.; ix. 1; Matt. i. 1-17; Luke iii. 23-38.

**Gĕn''ēr-ā'tion** (*begotten*). In plural, the genealogical register, Gen. ii. 4; v. 1; Matt. i. 1; family history, Gen. vi. 9; xxv. 12; men of the existing age, Lev. iii. 17; Isa. liii. 8; Matt. xxiv. 34; Acts ii. 40.

**Gĕn'ē-sĭs** (*beginning*). First book of the Bible and Pentateuch. Chapters i.-xi. give history of Creation, Adam, Deluge, Noah, first inhabitants, Babel. Balance devoted to history of the patriarchs Abraham, Isaac, Jacob and Joseph. Covers a period of nearly 2500 years. Authorship attributed to Moses.

**Gĕn-nĕs′a-rĕt** (*garden of the prince*). (1) Land of, the small crescent country N. W. of Sea of Galilee, Matt. xiv. 34; Mark vi. 53. (2) Lake of, "Sea of Chinnereth," in O. T., Num. xxxiv. 11; Josh. xii. 3; and "Sea of Galilee," in N. T.; enlargement of Jordan river; 13 miles long, 6 wide, 700 below bed of ocean. "Lake of Gennesaret," Luke v. 1; "Sea of Tiberias," John vi. 1; "the sea," Matt. iv. 15.

**Gĕn-nĕs′a-rĕth.** [GENNESARET.]

**Gĕn-nē′us.** Father of Apollonius, 2 Macc. xii. 2.

**Gĕn′tīleş** (*nations*). In O. T. sense, all peoples not Jewish, Gen. x. 5; xiv. 1; Neh. v. 8. In N. T., Greeks and Romans seem to type Gentiles, Luke ii. 32; Acts xxvi. 17-20; Rom. i. 14-16; ix. 24. "Isles of the Gentiles," Gen. x. 5, supposed to embrace Asia Minor and Europe.

**Gĕ-nū′băth** (*theft*). An Edomite, 1 Kgs. xi. 20.

**Gē′on,** Ecclus. xxiv. 27. [GIHON.]

**Gē′rȧ** (*grain*). (1) A Benjamite, Gen. xlvi. 21; 1 Chr. viii. 3-7. (2) Father of Ehud, Judg. iii. 15. (3) Father of Shimei, 2 Sam. xvi. 5; xix. 16; 1 Kgs. ii. 8.

**Gē′rah.** One twentieth of a shekel; about 3 cents, Ex. xxx. 13.

**Gē′rär** (*halting place*). A town of Philistia, Gen. x. 19; xx. 1; xxvi. 26; 2 Chr. xiv. 13, 14.

**Gĕr″ȧ-sēneş′.** For Gadarenes in Luke viii. 26, R. V.

**Gĕr′gĕ-sēneş,** Matt. viii. 28. [GADARENES, GERASENES.]

**Gĕr′ĭ-zĭm** (*cutters*). The mountain of blessings in Ephraim, Deut. xi. 29; xxvii. 12-26; xxviii.

**Gĕr-rhē′nĭ-anş.** Of Gerar, 2 Macc. xiii. 24.

**Gĕr′shŏm** (*exile*). (1) Son of Moses, Ex. ii. 22; xviii. 3. (2) A priest, Ez. viii. 2.

**Gĕr′shŏn** (*exile*). Eldest son of Levi, Gen. xlvi. 11; Ex. vi. 16; 1 Chr. vi. 1. Founder of the Gershonites. Given thirteen cities in Canaan, Josh. xxi. 6. Gershom in 1 Chr. vi. 62-71.

**Gĕr′zītes.** Dwellers south of Palestine, 1 Sam. xxvii. 8 marg.

**Gē′sem,** Judith i. 9. [GOSHEN.]

**Gē′shăm** (*filthy*). A descendant of Caleb, 1 Chr. ii. 47.

**Gē′shem, Găsh′mū** (*rain*). A scoffing Arabian, Neh. ii. 19; vi. 1, 2.

**Gē′shŭr** (*bridge*). A province of Syria peopled by Geshuri or Geshurites, Deut. iii. 14; Josh. xiii. 11; 2 Sam. iii. 3; xv. 8; 1 Chr. ii. 23.

**Gĕsh′u-rī,** Deut. iii. 14; Josh. xiii. 2. [GESHUR.]

**Gĕsh′u-rītes.** Besides above, a people of Arabia and Philistia, Josh. xiii. 11; 1 Sam. xxvii. 8.

**Gē′thēr** (*fear*). Son of Aram, Gen. x. 23; 1 Chr. i. 17.

**Gĕth-sĕm′a-nē** (*oil press*). Scene of Christ's agony and betrayal, at the foot of Olivet, near Jerusalem, Matt. xxvi. 36-56; Mark xiv. 26-52; Luke xxii. 39-49; John xviii. 1-13.

**Gĕ-ū′el** (*majesty of God*). The Gadite spy, Num. xiii. 15.

**Gē′zĕr** (*steep*). Gazer, Gazara, Gazera, and Gad. A Levitical city, Josh. x. 33; xii. 12; xvi. 3; xxi. 21; whose native people remained, Judg. i. 29.

**Gĕz′rītes.** [GERZITES.]

**Ghōst** (*that terrifies*). The spirit, Matt. xxvii. 50.

**Gī′ah** (*waterfall*). A hill near Ammah, 2 Sam. ii. 24.

**Gī′ants** (*sons of Gaea*). Huge men — Nephilim, Gibborim, Gen. vi. 4; Rephaim, xiv. 5; Emim, Anakim, Zuzim, etc., Num. xiii. 28-33; Deut. iii. 11; 1 Sam. xvii. 4.

**Gĭb′bar** (*huge*). His children returned, Ez. ii. 20.

**Gĭb′be-thon** (*high*). A Levitical town of Dan, Josh. xix. 44; xxi. 23; 1 Kgs. xv. 27; xvi. 17.

**Gĭb′e-ȧ** (*hill*). A Judahite, 1 Chr. ii. 49.

**Gĭb′e-ah** (*hill*). (1) A town of Judah, Josh. xv. 57. (2) Place where the ark was left, 2 Sam. vi. 3, 4. (3) A place in Benjamin, Judg. xix. 12-15; xx. 19-25; 1 Sam. xiii. 2. (4) Saul's birthplace, 1 Sam. x. 26; xi. 4; xv. 34; xxii. 6; xxiii. 19; Isa. x. 29. (5) Probably Geba, Judg. xx. 31.

**Gĭb′e-ath,** Josh. xviii. 28. [GIBEAH, 3.]

**Gĭb′e-on** (*lofty hill*). A Hivite city of Canaan, given to Levites, Josh. ix. 3-15; x. 12, 13; xxi. 17; 2 Sam. ii. 12-24; xx. 8-10. Tabernacle set up there, 1 Chr. xvi. 39; 1 Kgs. iii. 4, 5; ix. 2; 2 Chr. i. 3, 13; Jer. xli. 12-16.

**Gĭb′e-on-ītes″.** Inhabitants of Gibeon, 2 Sam. xxi. 1-9.

**Gĭb′lītes,** Josh. xiii. 5. [GEBAL.]

**Gĭd-dăl′tī** (*trained up*). Son of Heman, and leader of 22d musical course, 1 Chr. xxv. 4.

**Gĭd′del** (*great*). His children returned, Ez. ii. 47, 56.

**Gĭd′e-on** (*destroyer*). The powerful warrior of Manasseh, and judge of Israel for 40 years, Judges vi.-viii.

**Gĭd″e-ō′nī** (*destroyer*). A Benjamite, Num. i. 11.

**Gī′dom** (*desolation*). A place near Rimmon, Judg. xx. 45.

**Gier** (*jer*) **Eagle** (*sacred eagle*). An unclean bird of prey; probably the Egyptian vulture, Lev. xi. 18; Deut. xiv. 17.

**Gĭft** (*given*). A common way of showing esteem and confidence and securing favors, Gen. xxxii. 13-15; xlv. 22, 23. Kings were donees, 1 Kgs. iv. 21; 2 Chr. xvii. 5. Not to give, a mark of contempt, 1 Sam. x. 27. Cattle given, Gen. xxxii. 13; garments, 2 Kgs. v. 23; money, 2 Sam. xviii. 11; perfumes, Matt. ii. 11.

**Gī′hon** (*stream*). (1) Second river of Paradise, Gen. ii. 13. (2) A spot, or pool, near Jerusalem, 1 Kgs. i. 33-38; 2 Chr. xxxii. 30; xxxiii. 14.

**Gĭl′a-lāi** (*weighty*). A musician, Neh. xii. 36.

**Gĭl-bō′ȧ** (*fountain*). The mountain range east of Esdraelon and overlooking Jezreel, 1 Sam. xxviii. 4; xxxi. 1; 2 Sam. i. 6.

**Gĭl′e-ăd** (*rocky*). (1) Mount and Land of Gilead, east of Jordan, Gen. xxxi. 21-25; Num. xxxii. 1; Josh. xvii. 6. (2) A mountain near Jezreel, Judg. vii. 3. (3) Grandson of Manasseh, Num. xxvi. 29, 30. (4) Father of Jephthah, Judg. xi. 1, 2.

**Gĭl′e-ăd-ītes″.** Manassites of Gilead, Num. xxvi. 29.

**Gĭl′găl** (*rolling*). (1) First encampment of Israelites west of Jordan, Josh. iv. 19, 20; v. 9, 10. Became a city and headquarters, Josh. ix. 6; xv. 7. Saul crowned there, 1 Sam. vii. 16; x. 8; xi. 14, 15. (2) Another Gilgal in Sharon plain, Josh. xii. 23. (3) Another near Bethel, 2 Kgs. iv. 38.

**Gī′loh** (*exile*). A town of Judah, Josh. xv. 51; 2 Sam. xv. 12.

**Gī′lo-nīte.** Inhabitant of Giloh, 2 Sam. xv. 12; xxiii. 34.

**Gĭm′zō** (*producing sycamores*). Now Jimzu, a village 2½ miles from Lydda, 2 Chr. xxviii. 18.

**Gĭn** (*engine*). A bird-trap, Isa. viii. 14; Am. iii. 5.

**Gī′nath** (*protection*). Father of Tibni, 1 Kgs. xvi. 21, 22.

**Gĭn′nĕ-thō** (*gardener*). A priest, Neh. xii. 4.

**Gĭn′nĕ-thon** (*gardener*). A priest, Neh. x. 6; xii. 16.

**Gĭr′dle** (*gird*). Worn by men and women to hold the looser garments. Made of leather, 2 Kgs. i. 8; Matt. iii. 4; of linen, Jer. xiii. 1; Ezek. xvi. 10; embroidered, Dan. x. 5; Rev. i. 13; used for carrying swords and daggers, Judg. iii. 16; 2 Sam. xx. 8.

**Gĭr′ga-site, Gĭr′ga-shītes.** An original tribe of Canaan, Gen. x. 16; xv. 21; Deut. vii. 1.

**Gĭs′pȧ** (*fondle*). An overseer, Neh. xi. 21.

**Gĭt′tah=hē′phēr,** Josh. xix. 13. [GATH-HEPHER.]

**Gĭt′ta-ĭm** (*two wine presses*). An unknown place, 2 Sam. iv. 3.

**Gĭt′tītes.** Gathite followers of David, 2 Sam. xv. 18, 19. [GATH.]

**Gĭt′tith.** A musical instrument or melody, Ps. viii., lxxxi., lxxxiv., titles.

**Gī′zō-nīte.** Hashem, 1 Chr. xi. 34.

**Glȧss.** Only once in O. T. as "crystal," Job xxviii. 17; N. T. "glass" mirrors were metal, 1 Cor. xiii. 12; 2 Cor. iii. 18; James i. 23; Rev. iv. 6.

**Glēan′ing** (*handful*). Field-gleanings were reserved for the poor, Lev. xix. 9, 10; Ruth ii. 2. [CORNER.]

**Glēde** (*glide*). An unclean bird of prey, Deut. xiv. 13. The European kite; but vulture in Lev. xi. 14.

**Gnăt.** A small insect; figuratively mentioned in Matt. xxiii. 24.

**Gōad** (*gad, strike*). A rod spiked at the end for driving oxen, Judg. iii. 31; and iron-shod at the other end for cleaning plows, or even for plowing, 1 Sam. xiii. 21.

**Gōat.** Several varieties in Palestine, both wild and tame. An important source of food, clothing, and wealth, Gen. xxvii. 9; 1 Sam. xxiv. 2; xxv. 2; Job xxxix. 1. "Scape-goat," one of the two offered on Day of Atonement, over which the priest confessed the sins of Israel, and then let it escape to the wilderness, Lev. xvi. 7-26.

**Gō'ath** (*lowing*). An unknown place, Jer. xxxi. 39.

**Gŏb** (*cistern*). A battlefield, 2 Sam. xxi. 18, 19. Gezer in 1 Chr. xx. 4.

**Gŏb'let** (*little cask*). A wine cup.

**God** (*good*). In Hebrew, Jehovah, "the self-existent and eternal," and especially the covenant God. Generally rendered Lord. The ineffable name, not pronounced by the Jews, who substituted for it Adonai, "my Lord;" or Elohim — God, the creator and moral governor — when Adonai was written with Jehovah.

**God'head.** The Supreme Being in all his nature and attributes, Acts xvii. 29; Rom. i. 20; Col. ii. 9.

**Gŏg** (*roof*). (1) A Reubenite, 1 Chr. v. 4. (2) [Magog.]

**Gō'lan** (*circuit*). A refuge city in Bashan, Deut. iv. 43; Josh. xx. 8; xxi. 27.

**Gōld** (*yellow*). Known early to Hebrews, Gen. ii. 11; used for ornaments, Gen. xxiv. 22; money, temple furniture and utensils, Ex. xxxvi. 34-38; 1 Kgs. vii. 48-50; emblem of purity and nobility, Job xxiii. 10; Lam. iv. 1. Obtained chiefly from Ophir, Job xxviii. 16; Parvaim, 2 Chr. iii. 6; Sheba and Raamah, Ezek. xxvii. 22.

**Gŏl'gō-thȧ** (*skull*). Hebrew name of the spot where Christ was crucified, Matt. xxvii. 33; Mark xv. 22; John xix. 17. [Calvary.]

**Gō-lī'ath** (*splendor*). The Philistine giant who defied the army of Israel, 1 Sam. xvii. 4-54. Another Goliath in 2 Sam. xxi. 19-22.

**Gō'mer** (*complete*). (1) Eldest son of Japheth, Gen. x. 2, 3; 1 Chr. i. 5, 6. (2) Wife of Hosea, Hos. i. 3.

**Gō-mŏr'rah** (*submersion*). Gomorrha in N. T. A city of the plain destroyed by fire, Gen. xiv. 1-11; xviii. 20; xix. 24-28; Deut. xxix. 23; xxxii. 32; Matt. x. 15; Mark vi. 11.

**Gō'pher.** The unknown wood of Noah's ark, Gen. vi. 14.

**Gŏr'gĭ-as** (*frightful*). A Syrian general, 1 Macc. iii. 38.

**Gŏr-tȳ'na.** Capital of Crete, 1 Macc. xv. 23.

**Gō'shen** (*drawing near*). (1) The extreme province of Egypt, northward toward Palestine; assigned to the Jews, Gen. xlv. 5-10; xlvi. 28-34; xlvii. 1-6; l. 8. (2) An undefined part of southern Palestine, Josh. x. 41; xi. 16. (3) A city of Judah, Josh. xv. 51.

**Gŏs'pels** (*good tidings*). The four initial books of N. T., containing the biographies of Christ.

**Gŏth''ō-lī'as.** One who returned, 1 Esdr. viii. 33.

**Gō-thŏn'ĭ-el.** Father of Chabris, Judith vi. 15.

**Gōurd** (*encumberer*). A large plant family, covering the melon, pumpkin, squash, calabash, etc., Jonah iv. 6-10. A poisonous apple or cucumber, 2 Kgs. iv. 39-41.

**Gŏv'ẽr-nôr** (*director*). Often captain, chief, or civic official; but generally the political officer in charge of a province, Gen. xlii. 6; 1 Kgs. x. 15; Ez. viii. 36; Neh. ii. 9; Matt. xxvii. 2.

**Gō'zan.** Place or river in Mesopotamia, 2 Kgs. xvii. 6; xviii. 11; 1 Chr. v. 26.

**Grā'bȧ,** 1 Esdr. v. 29. [Hagaba.]

**Grāpe** (*hook, grab*). Grapes of Palestine noted for size and flavor, Gen. xlix. 11; Num. xiii. 24. Used for wine and food, 1 Sam. xxv. 18; xxx. 12; 2 Sam. xvi. 1; 1 Chr. xii. 40.

**Gràss** (*for gnawing*). Large figurative use, Ps. xc. 5, 6; Isa. xl. 6, 8; James i. 10, 11; 1 Pet. i. 24; sometimes herbage in general, Isa. xv. 6; a fuel, Matt. vi. 30; Luke xii. 28.

**Gràss'hop-per.** An insect of the locust species, often translated locust, 2 Chr. vii. 13. A clean animal, Lev. xi. 22; timid, Job xxxix. 20; gregarious and destructive, Judg. vi. 5; vii. 12; Eccl. xii. 5; Jer. xlvi. 23; type of insignificance, Num. xiii. 33; Isa. xl. 22.

**Grāve.** [Burial.] [Engraver.]

**Grēaves** (*shins*). Armor, metallic or leathern, to protect the shins from foot to knee, 1 Sam. xvii. 6.

**Grēēçe, Grēēks, Grē'çians.** The well known country in S. E. of Europe, called also Hellas. Javan in O. T., Gen. x. 2-5; Isa. lxvi. 19; Ezek. xxvii. 13, 19; but direct in Dan. viii. 21; x. 20; xi. 2; Joel iii. 6; Acts xx. 2. Greek the original N. T. language.

**Grey'hound,** Prov. xxx. 31. The original implies a "wrestler," not a quadruped.

**Grīnd'ing.** [Mill.]

**Grōve.** Except in Gen. xxi. 33, the Hebrew original means an idol; primitively set up and worshipped in groves, 1 Kgs. xviii. 19; 2 Kgs. xiii. 6.

**Gŭd'go-dah,** Deut. x. 7. [Hor-Hagidgad.]

**Guĕst.** [Hospitality.]

**Gū'nī** (*painted*). (1) Son of Naphtali and founder of the Gunites, Gen. xlvi. 24; Num. xxvi. 48; 1 Chr. vii. 13. (2) A son of Gad, 1 Chr. v. 15.

**Gûr** (*whelp*). Spot where King Ahaziah was slain, 2 Kgs. ix. 27.

**Gûr-bā'al** (*abode of Baal*). A district south of Palestine, 2 Chr. xxvi. 7.

## H

**Hā''a-hăsh'ta-rī** (*runner*). Son of Ashur, 1 Chr. iv. 6.

**Hȧ-bā'iah** (*God hides*). His children returned, Ez. ii. 61.

**Hȧ-băk'kŭk** (*embrace*). A minor prophet during reigns of Jehoiakim and Josiah. His book, thirteenth of the prophetic, denounces Chaldea, and concludes with a striking poem and prayer.

**Hăb''a-zī-nī'ah** (*God's light*). A Rechabite, Jer. xxxv. 3.

**Hăb'ba-cuc,** B. and D. 33-39. [Habakkuk.]

**Hăb'ẽr-geon** (*neck protector*). Coat of mail for neck and breast, Ex. xxviii. 32.

**Hā'bôr** (*fertile*). A tributary of the Euphrates, 2 Kgs. xvii. 6; 1 Chr. v. 26.

**Hăch''a-lī'ah** (*who waits*). Father of Nehemiah, Neh. i. 1.

**Hăch'ĭ-lah** (*dark hill*). A hill in Ziph, 1 Sam. xxiii. 19.

**Hăch'mō-nī** (*wise*). A Hachmonite, 1 Chr. xi. 11; xxvii. 32.

**Hā'dăd** (*brave*). (1) An Ishmaelite, 1 Chr. i. 30; Hadar, Gen. xxv. 15. (2) A king of Edom, Gen. xxxvi. 35; 1 Chr. i. 46. (3) Another king of Edom, 1 Chr. i. 50; Hadar, Gen. xxxvi. 39. (4) An Edomite, 1 Kgs. xi. 14-25.

**Hăd''ăd-ē'zẽr,** 2 Sam. viii. 3-12. [Hadarezer.]

**Hā'dăd-rĭm'mon.** From two Syrian idols. Spot of mourning for Josiah, Zech. xii. 11.

**Hā'dar,** Gen. xxv. 15; xxxvi. 39. [Hadad.]

**Hăd''ăr-ē'zẽr** (*Hadad's help*). A king of Zoba, 2 Sam. viii. 3; x. 16; 1 Chr. xviii. 7; xix. 16-19.

**Hăd'a-shah** (*new*). Town of Judah, Josh. xv. 37.

**Hȧ-dăs'sah** (*myrtle*). Hebrew name of Esther, Esth. ii. 7.

**Hȧ-dăt'tah** (*new*). Town of Judah, Josh. xv. 25.

**Hā'deș.** Place of departed spirits. Greek equivalent of Hebrew "sheol," unseen world. Hell in A. V.; Hades in R. V., Matt. xi. 23; xvi. 18; Acts ii. 31; Rev. i. 18.

**Hā'dĭd** (*sharp*). Place named in Ez. ii. 33; Neh. vii. 37.

**Hăd'la-ī** (*restful*). An Ephraimite, 2 Chr. xxviii. 12.

**Hȧ-dō'ram** (*power*). (1) Son of Joktan, Gen. x. 27. (2) An ambassador to David, 1 Chr. xviii. 10. (3) 2 Chr. x. 18. [Adoniram.]

**Hā'drăch** (*dwelling*). A Syrian country, Zech. ix. 1.

**Hā'găb** (*locust*). His sons returned, Ez. ii. 46.

**Hăg'a-bȧ,** Neh. vii. 48. Hagabah, Ez. ii. 45. [Hagab.]

**Hā'gar** (*flight*). Abraham's concubine, Gen. xvi. 3; mother of Ishmael, xxi. 9-21. Type of law and bondage, Gal. iv. 24, 25.

**Hā'gar-ītes, Hā'gar-ēneș.** Ishmaelites, 1 Chr. v. 10-20; xxvii. 31; Ps. lxxxiii. 6.

**Hăg'ga-ī** (*festive*). A minor prophet. His book, fifteenth of the prophetic, exhorts the Jews to crown the work of Zerubbabel.

**Hăg-gē'rī** (*wanderer*), 1 Chr. xi. 38. [Bani.]

**Hăg'gī** (*festive*). Son of Gad, Gen. xlvi. 16.

**Hăg-gī'ah** (*Lord's feast*). A Levite, 1 Chr. vi. 30.

**Hăg'gītes.** Of Haggi, Num. xxvi. 15.

**Hăg'gīth** (*dancer*). A wife of David, 2 Sam. iii. 4; 1 Kgs. i. 5.

**Hā'gi-ȧ,** 1 Esdr. v. 34. [Hattil.]

**Hā'ī.** Ancient form of Ai, Gen. xii. 8; xiii. 3.

**Hāil.** The seventh plague, Ex. ix. 18–29. God's weapon, Josh. x. 11; Rev. xvi. 21.

**Hâir.** Worn short with elderly men, long with young men, vowed men and women, Num. vi. 5–9; 2 Sam. xiv. 26; Luke vii. 38. Lepers shorn, Lev. xiv. 8, 9.

**Hăk'ka-tăn** (*little*). Father of Johanan, Ez. viii. 12.

**Hăk'kŏz** (*thorn*). Priest of 7th course, 1 Chr. xxiv. 10.

**Hȧ-kū'phȧ** (*bent*). His children returned, Ez. ii. 51.

**Hā'lah.** Probably Habor, 2 Kgs. xvii. 6.

**Hā'lăk** (*smooth*). An unlocated mountain, Josh. xi. 17; xii. 7.

**Hāle.** Haul, Luke xii. 58; Acts viii. 3.

**Hăl'hŭl** (*trembling*). Town of Judah, Josh. xv. 58.

**Hā'lī** (*necklace*). Border of Asher, Josh. xix. 25.

**Hăl''i-căr-năs'sus.** City of Caria, 1 Macc. xv. 23.

**Häll.** Court of a high priest's house, Luke xxii. 55; Matt. xxvii. 27.

**Hăl''le-lū'jăh** (*ya*). [ALLELUIA.]

**Hăl-lō'hesh** (*enchanter*). Co-covenanter with Nehemiah, Neh. x. 24.

**Hȧ-lō'hesh** (*enchanter*). A builder of the wall, Neh. iii. 12.

**Hăm** (*hot*). Third son of Noah, Gen. v. 32; ix. 22. Father of the Hamitic races, x. 6, etc.

**Hā'man** (*famed*). Prime minister of Ahasuerus, Esth.

**Hā'math** (*fortress*). Chief city of upper Syria, Gen. x. 18; Num. xxxiv. 8. Became part of Solomon's kingdom, 1 Kgs. viii. 65; 2 Chr. viii. 3, 4. Now Hamah.

**Hăm'măth** (*hot springs*). A town near Tiberias, Josh. xix. 35. Hammoth-Dor, Josh. xxi. 32. Hammon, 1 Chr. vi. 76.

**Hăm-mĕd'a-thȧ** (*double*). Father of Haman, Esth. iii. 1.

**Hăm'me-lĕch** (*king*). Hardly a proper name, Jer. xxxvi. 26; xxxviii. 6.

**Hăm'mẽr.** Same as now, Judg. iv. 21; Isa. xliv. 12. Mighty force, Jer. xxiii. 29; l. 23.

**Hăm-mŏl'e-kĕth** (*queen*). Sister of Gilead, 1 Chr. vii. 17, 18.

**Hăm'mŏn** (*warm springs*). (1) City in Asher, Josh. xix. 28. (2) Levitical city in Naphtali, 1 Chr. vi. 76.

**Hăm'moth=dôr**, Josh. xxi. 32. [HAMMATH].

**Hȧ-mō'nah** (*multitude*). Unknown city, Ezek. xxxix. 16.

**Hā'mon=gŏg** (*multitude of Gog*). Unlocated valley, Ezek. xxxix. 11–15.

**Hā'mor** (*ass*). Father of Shechem, Gen. xxxiii. 19; xxxiv. 26. Emmor, Acts vii. 16.

**Hȧ-mū'el** (*wrath*). A Simeonite, 1 Chr. iv. 26.

**Hā'mŭl** (*pity*). Son of Pharez, and founder of Hamulites, Gen. xlvi. 12.

**Hā'mŭl-ītes**, Num. xxvi. 21. [HAMUL.]

**Hȧ-mū'tal** (*like dew*). A wife of Josiah, 2 Kgs. xxiii. 31; Jer. lii. 1.

**Hȧ-năm'e-el** (*given of God*). Jeremiah's cousin, Jer. xxxii. 6–12.

**Hā'nan** (*merciful*). (1) A Benjamite, 1 Chr. viii. 23. (2) Descendant of Saul, 1 Chr. viii. 38. (3) One of David's guard, 1 Chr. xi. 43. (4) His sons returned, Ez. ii. 46. (5, 6, 7) Co-covenanters with Nehemiah, Neh. x. 10, 22, 26. (8) A tithe-keeper, Neh. xiii. 13. (9) One who had temple rooms, Jer. xxxv. 4.

**Hȧ-năn'e-el** (*given of God*). A tower on wall of Jerusalem, Neh. iii. 1; xii. 39; Jer. xxxi. 38.

**Hȧ-nā'nī** (*gracious*). (1) Head of the 18th temple course, 1 Chr. xxv 4, 25. (2) A seer, 2 Chr. xvi. 7-10. (3) A priest, Ez. x. 20. (4) Brother of Nehemiah, Neh. i. 2; vii. 2.

**Hăn''a-nī'ah** (*given of God*). (1) Leader of 16th temple course, 1 Chr. xxv. 4, 5, 23. (2) A general, 2 Chr. xxvi. 11. (3) Father of Zedekiah, Jer. xxxvi. 12. (4) A false prophet, Jer. xxviii. (5) Grandfather of Irijah, Jer. xxxvii. 13. (6) Hebrew name of Shadrach, Dan. i. 3-19. (7) Son of Zerubbabel, 1 Chr. iii. 19. Joanna in Luke. (8) A Benjamite, 1 Chr. viii. 24. (9) One of the returned, Ez. x. 28. (10) Others, Neh. iii. 8; vii. 2, 3; x. 23; xii. 12.

**Hănd.** Conspicuous in Hebrew ceremonial and other customs, Gen. xiv. 22; Deut. xxi. 6, 7; Matt. xxvii. 24; Job xxxi. 27; Isa. lxv. 2.

**Hănd'breadth.** Palm width; about four inches, Ex. xxv. 25.

**Hănd'i-craft.** Though not noted for artisanship, Hebrew boys were taught trades, and reference is made to smiths, Gen. iv. 22; carpenters, Isa. xliv. 14; Matt. xiii. 55; masons, 1 Kgs. v. 18; ship-building, 1 Kgs. ix. 26; apothecaries, Ex. xxx. 25, 35; weavers, Ex. xxxv. 25, 26; dyers, Josh. ii. 18; barbers, Num. vi. 5-19; tent-makers, Acts xviii. 3; potters, Jer. xviii. 2-6; bakers, xxxvii. 21; engravers, Ex. xxviii. 9-11; tanners, Acts ix. 43.

**Hănd'kẽr-chiefs.** These, and napkins and aprons, signify about same as to-day, Luke xix. 20; John xi. 44; Acts xix. 12.

**Hănd'stāves.** Javelins, Ezek. xxxix. 9.

**Hā'nēs.** A city in Egypt, Isa. xxx. iv.

**Hăng'ing, Hăng'ings.** In strict law, culprits were strangled first, then hung, Num. xxv. 4; Deut. xxi. 22, 23. Hangings for doors and tabernacle use, quite the same as modern tapestries, Ex. xxvi. 9, 36; Num. iii. 26.

**Hăn'ī-el** (*grace of God*). An Asherite, 1 Chr. vii. 39.

**Hăn'nah** (*grace*). Mother of Samuel, 1 Sam. i., ii.

**Hăn'na-thon** (*gracious*). A city of Zebulun, Josh. xix. 14.

**Hăn'nī-el** (*grace of God*). A prince of Manasseh, Num. xxxiv. 23.

**Hā'noch** (*dedicated*). (1) Son of Midian, Gen. xxv. 4; Henoch, 1 Chr. i. 33. (2) A son of Reuben, and founder of Hanochites, Gen. xlvi. 9; Num. xxvi. 5.

**Hā'nŭn** (*gracious*). (1) A king of Ammon, 2 Sam. x. 1–6. (2) Two architects, Neh. iii. 13, 30.

**Hăph-rā'im** (*pits*). A city of Issachar, Josh. xix. 19.

**Hā'rȧ** (*hill*). No doubt Haran, 1 Chr. v. 26.

**Hăr'a-dah** (*fear*). An Israelite encampment, Num. xxxiii. 24, 25.

**Hā'ran** (*mountainous*). (1) Brother of Abraham, Gen. xi. 26–31. (2) A Levite, 1 Chr. xxiii. 9. (3) Son of Caleb, 1 Chr. ii. 46. (4) The spot in Mesopotamia where Abraham located after leaving Ur, Gen. xi. 31, 32; xxiv. 10; xxvii. 43. Charran, Acts vii. 2–4.

**Hā'ra-rīte.** Three of David's guard so called, 2 Sam. xxiii. 11, 33.

**Här-bō'nȧ** (*ass driver*). A chamberlain, Esth. i. 10. Harbonah in vii. 9.

**Hâre** (*leaper*). A species of rabbit, wrongly thought to chew the cud, Lev. xi. 6; Deut. xiv. 7.

**Hā'reph** (*plucking*). Son of Caleb, 1 Chr. ii. 51.

**Hā'reth** (*thicket*). A forest of Judah, 1 Sam. xxii. 5.

**Här''hȧ-ī'ah** (*God's anger*). Father of Uzziel, Neh. iii. 8.

**Här'has** (*poor*). Ancestor of Shallum, 2 Kgs. xxii. 14.

**Här'hûr** (*inflamed*). His children returned, Neh. vii. 53.

**Hā'rim** (*flat-nosed*). (1) Priestly head of third course, 1 Chr. xxiv. 8. (2) Name of several who returned, Ez. ii. 32, 39; x. 21; Neh. iii. 11; vii. 35, 42; x. 27; xii. 15.

**Hā'riph** (*plucking*). His children returned, Neh. vii. 24; x. 19.

**Här'lot** (*vagabond*). An abandoned woman, Gen. xxxviii. 15. Harlotry forbidden, Lev. xix. 29. Type of idolatry, Isa. i. 21; Ezek. xvi. Classed with publicans, Matt. xxi. 32.

**Här''ma-gĕd'don.** R. V. for Armageddon.

**Här'ne-phẽr** (*panting*). An Asherite, 1 Chr. vii. 36.

**Hā'rod** (*fear*). A spring near Jezreel, Judg. vii. 1.

**Hā'rod-īte.** Two of David's guard, so called, 2 Sam. xxiii. 25.

**Hăr'ō-eh** (*seer*). Son of Shobal, 1 Chr. ii. 52.

**Hȧ-rō'sheth** (*handicraft*). A city of Naphtali, Judg. iv. 2–16.

**Härp** (*sickle shaped*). Prominent Jewish musical instrument, invented by Jubal, Gen. iv. 21; of various shapes and sizes; different number of strings; played with fingers or plectrum (quill).

**Hăr'row** (*rake*). "Threshing-machine," 2 Sam. xii. 31; 1 Chr. xx. 3. Pulverizer of ground, Isa. xxviii. 24; Job xxxix. 10, and elsewhere.

**Här'shȧ** (*deaf*). His children returned, Ez. ii. 52; Neh. vii. 54.

**Härt.** Male of the red deer, Deut. xii. 15; xiv. 5; 1 Kgs. iv. 23; S. of Sol. ii. 9.

**Hā'rum** (*high*). A Judahite, 1 Chr. iv 8.

**Hȧ-ru̧'maph** (*slit-nosed*). Father of Jedaiah, Neh. iii. 10.

**Hăr'u̧-phīte, The.** A friend of David, 1 Chr. xii. 5.

**Hā'ruz** (*careful*). Amon's grandfather Kgs. xxi. 19.

**Här'vest.** [Agriculture.]

**Hăs''a̧-dī'ah** (*loved of God*). One of David's line, 1 Chr. iii. 20.

**Hăs''ȩ-nū'ah** (*hated*). A Benjamite, 1 Chr. ix. 7.

**Hăsh''a̧-bī'ah** (*regarded*). (1) Two Levites, 1 Chr. vi. 45; ix. 14. (2) Leader of twelfth course, 1 Chr. xxv. 3, 19. (3) A Hebronite, 1 Chr. xxvi. 30. (4) Other Levites, 1 Chr. xxvii. 17; 2 Chr. xxxv. 9; Ez. viii. 19, 24; Neh. iii. 17; x. 11; xi. 15, 22; xii. 24.

**Hȧ-shăb'nah** (*regarded*). A co-covenanter with Nehemiah, Neh. x. 25.

**Hăsh''ăb-nī'ah** (*regarded*). (1) His son repaired the wall, Neh. iii. 10. (2) A Levite, Neh. ix. 5.

**Hăsh-băd'a̧-nȧ** (*judge*). Assistant to Ezra, Neh. viii. 4.

**Hā'shem** (*fat*). His sons were of David's guard, 1 Chr. xi. 34.

**Hăsh-mō'nah** (*fatness*). A desert station, Num. xxxiii. 29.

**Hā'shub** (*informed*). (1) Hasshub, a Levite, 1 Chr. ix. 14. (2) Other Levites and builders, Neh. iii. 11, 23; x. 23.

**Hȧ-shu̧'bah** (*informed*). One of David's line, 1 Chr. iii. 20.

**Hā'shum** (*rich*). (1) His children returned, Ez. ii. 19. (2) Assistant to Ezra, Neh. viii. 4.

**Hȧ-shū'phȧ** (*stripped*). His children returned, Ez. ii. 43; Neh. vii. 46.

**Hăs'rah**, 2 Chr. xxxiv. 22. [Harhas.]

**Hăs''sė-nā'ah** (*thorny*). His sons built the fish-gate, Neh. iii. 3.

**Hăs'shub.** [Hashub.]

**Hȧ-sū'phȧ.** [Hashupha.]

**Hā'tăch.** Chamberlain of Ahasuerus, Esth. iv. 5–10.

**Hā'thăth** (*fear*). Son of Othniel, 1 Chr. iv. 13.

**Hăt'ī-phȧ** (*captive*). His sons returned, Ez. ii. 54.

**Hăt'ī-tȧ** (*searching*). Returned porters, Ez. ii. 42.

**Hăt'til** (*doubtful*). His sons returned, Ez. ii. 57.

**Hăt'tŭsh** (*gathered*). (1) A Judahite, 1 Chr. iii. 22; Ez. viii. 2. (2) Others of the returned, Neh. iii. 10; x. 4; xii. 2.

**Ha̧u'ran** (*caves*). Present Hauran, S. of Syria in Bashan, Ezek. xlvii. 16–18.

**Hăv'ī-lah** (*circle*). (1) Son of Cush, Gen. x. 7. (2) Son of Joktan, x. 29. (3) An unlocated region, Gen. ii. 11; xxv. 18; 1 Sam. xv. 7.

**Hā'voth=jā'ir** (*villages of Jair*). Villages in Gilead or Bashan, Num. xxxii. 41; Deut. iii. 14.

**Häwk** (*havoc*). An unclean bird; species of falcon, Lev. xi. 16; Deut. xiv. 15; Job xxxix. 26.

**Hāy** (*cut*). Grass; but hardly cut and dried grass, Prov. xxvii. 25; Ps. lxxii. 6; Isa. xv. 6.

**Hăz'a-el** (*God sees*). A Syrian king, 1 Kgs. xix. 15; 2 Kgs. viii. 7–16; x. 32; xiii. 24.

**Hȧ-zā'ịah** (*whom God sees*). A Judahite, Neh. xi. 5.

**Hā'zar.** [Hazer.]

**Hā'zar=ăd'dar.** [Hazer.]

**Hā'zar=mā'veth.** Son of Joktan, Gen. x. 26.

**Hā'zel.** The almond doubtless meant, Gen. xxx. 37.

**Hăz''e-lĕl-pō'nī** (*coming shadows*). Sister of Judahites, 1 Chr. iv. 3.

**Hā'zer** (*village*). In composition. (1) Hazar-addar, a landmark of Israel, Num. xxxiv. 4; Adar, Josh. xv. 3. (2) Hazar-enan, a boundary of Israel, Num. xxxiv. 9, 10. (3) Hazar-gaddah, a town of Judah, Josh. xv. 27. (4) Hazar-shual, in southern Judah, Josh. xv. 28. (5) Hazar-susah, in Judah, Josh. xix. 5; Hazar-susim, 1 Chr. iv. 31. (6) Hazar-hatticon, Ezek. xlvii. 16.

**Hȧ-zē'rīm**, Deut. ii. 23. Villagers. [Hazer.]

**Hȧ-zē'roth** (*villages*). An Israelite encampment, Num. xi. 35; Deut. i. 1.

**Hăz'e-zon=tā'mar** (*felling of palms*). Old name of Engedi, Gen. xiv. 7. Hazazon-tamar, 2 Chr. xx. 2.

**Hā'zī-el** (*vision*). A Levite, 1 Chr. xxiii. 9.

**Hā'zō** (*vision*). Son of Nahor, Gen. xxii. 22.

**Hā'zôr** (*court*). (1) City of Naphtali, Josh. xi. 10; 1 Kgs. ix. 15; 2 Kgs. xv. 29. (2) Town of Judah, Josh. xv. 23–25. (3) Place in Benjamin, Neh. xi. 33.

**Hĕad'dress.** Sacerdotal and ornamental, Ex. xxviii. 40. Mantle or veil the usual head-dress.

**Hëarth** (*ground*). Hot stones, Gen. xviii. 6. Pan or brazier, Jer. xxxvi. 23.

**Hēath** (*country*). No heath in Palestine. Evidently a desert scrub, Jer. xvii. 6; xlviii. 6.

**Hēa'then** (*dwellers on the heath*). All except Jews, Ps. ii. 1. Non-believer, Matt. xviii. 17.

**Hĕav'en** (*heaved*). Firmament, Gen. i. 1; Matt. v. 18. Abode of God, 1 Kgs. viii. 30; Dan. ii. 28; Matt. v. 45. Paradise, Luke xxiii. 43.

**Hē'bẽr** (*alliance*). Eber, Luke iii. 35. Others in Gen. xlvi. 17; Num. xxvi. 45; Judg. iv. 17; 1 Chr. iv. 18; v. 13; vii. 31; viii. 17, 22.

**Hē'brews.** "Abram the Hebrew," Gen. xiv. 13, that is, *eber*, the one who had "passed over" the Euphrates, westward. Hence, "seed" or descendants of Abraham. Among themselves, preferably, Israelites, from Gen. xxxii. 28. Jews, *i. e.* Judahites, Judeans, after the captivity.

**He'brews, Epistle to.** Written probably by Paul, from Rome, A. D. 62 or 63, to overcome Hebrew favoritism for the old law.

**Hē'bron** (*friendship*). (1) Son of Kohath, Ex. vi. 18; Num. iii. 19, 27. (2) Person or place, 1 Chr. ii. 42. (3) Ancient city of Judah, 20 mls. S. of Jerusalem, Gen. xiii. 18; Num. xiii. 22; Arba in Josh. xxi. 11; Judg. i. 10.

**Hē'bron-ītes.** Kohathite Levites, Num. iii. 27; xxvi. 58.

**Hĕdge** (*haw*). In Hebrew sense, anything that encloses — wall, fence, or thorn bushes, Num. xxii. 24; Prov. xxiv. 31; Hos. ii. 6.

**Hĕg'a̧-ī, Hē'gē.** Chamberlain of Ahasuerus, Esth. ii. 3, 8, 15.

**Hĕif'ẽr** (*high-bullock*). Red heifers sacrificial, Num. xix. 10. Frequent source of metaphor, Judg. xiv. 18; Isa. xv. 5; Jer. xlvi. 20; Hos. iv. 16.

**Heir** (*inheritor*). Eldest son became head of tribe or family with largest share of paternal estate; sons of concubines given presents; daughters, a marriage portion, Gen. xxi. 10, 14; xxiv. 36; xxv. 6; xxxi. 14; Judg. xi. 2, etc. Real estate apportioned as in Deut. xxi. 17; Num. xxvii. 4–11.

**Hē'lah** (*rust*). Wife of Ashur, 1 Chr. iv. 5.

**Hē'lam** (*fort*). A battlefield, 2 Sam. x. 16, 17.

**Hĕl'bah** (*fertile*). Town of Asher, Judg. i. 31.

**Hĕl'bon** (*fertile*). A Syrian city, Ezek. xxvii. 18.

**Hĕl-chī'ah**, 1 Esdr. viii. 1. [Hilkiah]

**Hĕl'da̧-ī** (*worldly*). (1) Captain of 12th course, 1 Chr. xxvii. 15. (2) One who returned, Zech. vi. 10. Helem in vs. 14.

**Hē'lĕb, Hē'lĕd** (*passing*). One of David's guard, 2 Sam. xxiii. 29; 1 Chr. xi. 30.

**Hē'lek** (*portion*). Founder of Helekites, Num. xxvi. 30.

**Hē'lem** (*strength*). (1) An Asherite, 1 Chr. vii. 35. (2) Probably Heldai, Zech. vi. 14.

**Hē'leph** (*exchange*). Starting point of Naphtali's boundary, Josh. xix. 33.

**Hē'lez** (*strong*). (1) Captain of 7th course and one of David's guard, 2 Sam. xxiii. 26; 1 Chr. xi. 27. (2) A Judahite, 1 Chr. ii. 39.

**Hē'lī** (*climbing*). Eli, father of Joseph, Luke iii. 23.

**Hē''lī-ō-dō'rus.** A Syrian treasurer, 2 Macc. iii.

**Hĕl'ka̧-ī** (*portion*). A priest, Neh. xii. 15.

**Hĕl'kăth** (*part*). (1) Starting point of Asher's boundary, Josh. xix. 25. (2) Hĕl'kăth-hăz'zu-rīm, a battlefield; 2 Sam. ii. 16.

**Hĕl-kī'as**, 1 Esdr. i. 8. [Hilkiah.]

**Hĕll** (*conceal*). Hebrew "sheol;" translated "grave," 1 Sam. ii. 6; "pit," Num. xvi. 30; "hell," Job xi. 8, in O. T. In N. T., Hades and Gehenna are translated hell, Acts ii. 27; Matt. v. 29. Gehenna, or Valley of Hinnom, alone implies a place of burning or torture.

**Hĕl'lĕn-ist.** A Grecian; but limited to Greek-speaking Jews in Acts vi. 1; ix. 29; xi. 20.

**Hĕl'met** (*hide*). Armor, generally metal, for head, 1 Sam. xvii. 5; 2 Chr. xxvi. 14. [ARMOR.]

**Hē'lon** (*strong*). Father of Eliab, Num. i. 9; ii. 7.

**Hĕm** (*field*). Edge, or fringe, of a garment, Num. xv. 38, 39; Matt. xxiii. 5.

**Hē'mam** (*driving out*). Grandson of Seir, Gen. xxxvi. 22.

**Hē'man** (*trusty*). (1) Son of Zerah, 1 Chr. ii. 6. (2) Grandson of Samuel, 1 Chr. vi. 33; xv. 16-22; xxv. 5.

**Hē'măth** (*heat*). Person or place, 1 Chr. ii. 55. Hamath, 1 Chr. xiii. 5; Am. vi. 14.

**Hĕm'dan** (*pleasant*). Son of Dishon, Gen. xxxvi. 26. Amram, 1 Chr. i. 41.

**Hĕm'lock.** Not the bitter, poisonous hemlock as in Hos. x. 4; Am. vi. 12, but "gall," as elsewhere.

**Hĕn** (*rest*). (1) Son of Zephaniah, Zech. vi. 14. (2) The domestic fowl, common in Palestine, but mentioned only in Matt. xxiii. 37; Luke xiii. 34.

**Hē'nȧ** (*troubling*). A city of Mesopotamia, 2 Kgs. xviii. 34; xix. 13; Isa. xxxvii. 13.

**Hĕn'a-dăd** (*favor of Hadad*). His sons returned, Ez. iii. 9; Neh. x. 9.

**Hē'noch.** (1) 1 Chr. i. 3. [ENOCH, 6.] (2) 1 Chr. i. 33. [HANOCH, 1.]

**Hē'phēr** (*pit*). (1) Founder of Hepherites, Num. xxvi. 32; Josh. xii. 17. (2) Son of Ashur, 1 Chr. iv. 6. (3) One of David's guard, 1 Chr. xi. 36. (4) A place W. of Jordan, Josh. xii. 17.

**Hĕph'zĭ-bah** (*my delight in her*). (1) Name of restored Jerusalem, Isa. lxii. 4. (2) Wife of Hezekiah, 2 Kgs. xxi. 1.

**Hĕr'ăld** (*army ruler*). Crier, Dan. iii. 4; preacher, as in 1 Tim. ii. 7; 2 Pet. ii. 5.

**Hĕr'cŭ-lēş.** The god "Melkart," 2 Macc. iv. 19.

**Hĕrd.** A collection of cattle. Herdsmen despised by Egyptians, Gen. xlvi. 34, but honored by Hebrews, 1 Sam. xi. 5; xxi. 7.

**Hē'rēş** (*sun*). A place in Dan, Judg. i. 35.

**Hē'resh** (*carpenter*). A Levite, 1 Chr. ix. 15.

**Hĕr'mas, Hĕr'mēş** (*Mercury*). Two friends of Paul, Rom. xvi. 14.

**Hĕr-mŏg'e-nēş** (*born of Mercury*). One who deserted Paul, 2 Tim. i. 15.

**Hĕr'mŏn** (*lofty*). Highest peak of Anti-Libanus range and northern landmark of Palestine, 10,000 ft. high, Deut. iii. 8; Josh. xi. 17.

**Hĕr'mon-ites.** The three peaks of Hermon, Ps. xlii. 6.

**Hĕr'od** (*heroic*). (1) Herod the Great, tetrarch of Judea, B. C. 41; King of Judea, B. C. 41-4; liberal, yet tyrannical and cruel. Issued murderous edict against children of Bethlehem, Matt. ii. 16. (2) Herod Antipas, son of former; tetrarch of Galilee and Perea, B. C. 4-A. D. 39; murderer of John the Baptist, Matt. xiv. 1; Luke iii. 19; xxiii. 7-15; Acts xiii. 1. (3) Herod Philip, son of Herod the Great. Married Herodias, Matt. xiv. 3; Mark vi. 17; Luke iii. 19. Lived and died in private life. (4) Herod Philip II., son of Herod the Great, and tetrarch of Batanea, Ituræa, etc., B. C. 4-A. D. 34, Luke iii. 1. (5) Herod Agrippa I., grandson of Herod the Great; tetrarch of Galilee; king of his grandfather's realm, A. D., 37-44, Acts xii. 1-19. (6) Herod Agrippa II., son of former, and king of consolidated tetrarchies, A. D. 50-100, Acts xxv. 13-27; xxvi. 1-28.

**Hē-rō'dĭ-anş.** A Jewish political party who favored the Herods and Roman dependence, Matt. xxii. 16; Mark iii. 6; viii. 15.

**Hē-rō'dĭ-as.** Granddaughter of Herod the Great. Wife of her uncle Herod Philip and her step-uncle. She requested the head of John the Baptist, Matt. xiv. 3-6; Mark vi. 17; Luke iii. 19.

**Hē-rō'dĭ-on.** Kinsman of Paul, Rom. xvi. 11.

**Hĕr'on.** A large aquatic bird, pronounced unclean, Lev. xi. 19; Deut. xiv. 18.

**Hē'sed** (*kindness*). Father of one of Solomon's commissaries, 1 Kgs. iv. 10.

**Hĕsh'bŏn** (*device*). An Amorite capital, N. E. of Dead Sea, Num. xxi. 26; Josh. xiii. 17; Isa. xv. 4.

**Hĕsh'mŏn** (*fertile*). Place in south Judah, Josh. xv. 27.

**Hĕs'rŏn.** [HEZRON.]

**Hĕth** (*fear*). Progenitor of the Hittites, Gen. x. 15; xxiii. 3-20; xxv. 10; xxvii. 46.

**Hĕth'lŏn** (*hiding place*). A mountain pass, probably Hamath, Ezek. xlvii. 15; xlviii. 1.

**Hĕz'e-ki** (*strong*). A Benjamite, 1 Chr. viii. 17.

**Hĕz-e-kī'ah** (*strength of God*). (1) Twelfth king of Judah, B. C. 726-698. Noted for abolition of idolatry and powerful resistance to neighboring nations, 2 Kgs. xviii.-xx.; 2 Chr. xxix.-xxxii. (2) Son of Neariah, 1 Chr. iii. 23. (3) [ATER.]

**Hē'zĭ-on** (*sight*). A king of Syria; probably Rezon, 1 Kgs. xv. 18; xi. 23.

**Hē'zīr** (*swine*). (1) Leader of 17th course, 1 Chr. xxiv. 15. (2) A co-covenanter, Neh. x. 20.

**Hĕz'ra-ī** (*enclosure*). One of David's guard, 2 Sam. xxiii. 35. Hezro, 1 Chr. xi. 37.

**Hĕz'ron** (*surrounded*). (1) A Reubenite, Gen. xlvi. 9. (2) Son of Pharez, Gen. xlvi. 12; Ruth iv. 18.

**Hĕz'ron-ites.** Reubenite and Judahite families, Num. xxvi. 6, 21.

**Hĭd'da-ī** (*joyful*). One of David's guard, 2 Sam. xxiii. 30.

**Hĭd'de-kel** (*rapid*). Third river of Eden, no doubt Tigris, Gen. ii. 14; Dan. x. 4.

**Hī'el** (*God lives*). A Bethelite who rebuilt Jericho, 1 Kgs. xvi. 34.

**Hī"e-răp'o-lĭs** (*holy city*). City of Phrygia, on the Meander near Colossæ, Col. iv. 13.

**Hī-er'e-el,** 1 Esdr. ix. 21. [JEHIEL.]

**Hī-er'e-moth.** Jeremoth, Ramoth, in Esdr.

**Hī"e-rŏn'ȳ-mus** (*sacred name*). A Syrian general, 2 Macc. xii. 2.

**Hĭg-gā'ịon** (*meditation*). Musical pause for meditation, Ps. ix. 16; xix. 14, xcii. 3, marg.

**Hīgh Plā'ces.** Altars, temples, and dedicated places originally on high ground, Gen. xii. 8; Judg. vi. 25; Isa. lxv. 7; Jer. iii. 6. When the groves and mounts of idolatry overshadowed true worship, "high places" became a reproach.

**Hīgh Priēst.** Chief priest, Aaron being the first. Originally a life office, limited to a line or family, Ex. xxviii. 1; Lev. xxi. 10; Num. iii. 32; xx. 8; Deut. x. 6.

**Hī'len** (*caves*). A Levitical city in Judah, 1 Chr. vi. 58.

**Hĭl-kī'ah** (*God my portion*). (1) Father of Eliakim, 2 Kgs. xviii. 37. (2) A high priest, 2 Kgs. xxii. 8. (3) Four Levites, 1 Chr. vi. 45; xxvi. 11; Neh. viii. 4; xii. 7, 21. (4) Father of Jeremiah, Jer. i. 1. (5) Father of an ambassador, Jer. xxix. 3.

**Hĭl'lel** (*praise*). Father of Abdon, Judg. xii. 13, 15.

**Hĭn.** A Hebrew liquid measure, about 1¼ gallons, Ex. xxx. 24.

**Hīnd.** Female of the red deer, Gen. xlix. 21; Ps. xxix. 9; Prov. v. 19.

**Hĭnge** (*hanged*). A pivot and socket for swinging doors, 1 Kgs. vii. 50; Prov. xxvi. 14.

**Hĭn'nom** (*wailing*). A narrow valley south and west of Jerusalem, Josh. xv. 8; xviii. 16, where Molech was worshipped, 1 Kgs. xi. 7; 2 Kgs. xvi. 3; hence called Tophet, "drum," noise, Isa. xxx. 33; defiled, 2 Kgs. xxiii. 10, and called ge-Hinnom, gehenna, "place of Hinnom," to type a place of eternal torment. "Hell" in N. T., Matt. v. 22, 29; x. 28; xxiii. 15; Mark ix. 43; Luke xii. 5.

**Hī'rah** (*noble*). An Adullamite, Gen. xxxviii. 1, 12, 20.

**Hī'ram, Hū'ram** (*noble*). (1) King of Tyre who furnished men and material to David and Solomon, 2 Sam. v. 11; 1 Kgs. v.; 1 Chr. xiv. 1. (2) Hiram's chief architect, 1 Kgs. vii. 13, 40.

**Hĭr-cā'nus.** Son of Tobias, 2 Macc. iii. 11.

**Hĭt'tītes.** Descendants of Heth, Gen. x. 15; xxv. 9; Josh. iii. 10; 2 Sam. xi. 3.

**Hī'vītes** (*villagers*). Descendants of Canaan, Gen. x. 17; located at Shechem, xxxiv. 2; noted for craft, Josh. ix.

**Hĭz-kī'ah** (*strength*). Ancestor of Zephaniah, Zeph. i. 1.

**Hĭz-kī'jah** (*strength*). A co-covenanter, Neh. x. 17.

**Hō'băb** (*live*). Brother-in-law of Moses, Num. x. 29-32.

**Hō'bah** (*hiding*). A place beyond Damascus, Gen. xiv. 15.

**Hŏd** (*splendor*). Son of Zophah, 1 Chr. vii. 37.

**Hŏd-a-ī'ah** (*praise ye*). A Judahite, 1 Chr. iii. 24.

**Hŏd-a-vī'ah** (*praise ye*). (1) A Manassite, 1 Chr v. 24. (2) A Benjamite, 1 Chr. ix. 7. (3) A Levite, Ez. ii. 40.

**Hō'desh** (*new moon*). A Benjamite woman, 1 Chr. viii. 9.

**Hō-dē'vah**, Neh. vii. 43. [Hodaviah, 3.]

**Hō-dī'ah** (*splendor*). Wife of Ezra, 1 Chr. iv. 19. Jehudijah in vs. 18.

**Hō'dī-jah** (*splendor*). Three Levites, Neh. viii. 7; x. 13, 18.

**Hŏg'lah** (*quail*). Daughter of Zelophehad, Num. xxvi. 33.

**Hō'ham** (*driven*). A king of Hebron, Josh. x. 3.

**Hōlm-tree**. Holm-oak, Sus. 58.

**Hŏl-ō-fĕr'nēs**. The general slain by Judith, Judith ii. 4, etc.

**Hō'lŏn** (*sandy*). (1) A town of Judah, Josh. xv. 51. (2) A city of Moab Jer. xlviii. 21.

**Hō'mam**, 1 Chr. i. 39. [Hemam.]

**Hō'mēr**. A Hebrew liquid and dry measure, from 47 to 64 gals., according to time, and 6 to 8 bush., Ezek. xlv. 14.

**Hon'ey**. Bees numerous and honey plentiful in Palestine. Much used, Lev. xx. 24; Deut. xxxii. 13; Matt. iii. 4.

**Hooks**. Various kinds. Fishing, Job xli. 2; leading, 2 Kgs. xix. 28; pruning, Isa. ii. 4; hanging meats, Ezek. xl. 43; curtains, Ex. xxvi. 32-37; lifting boiled food, 1 Sam. ii. 13.

**Hŏph'nī** (*fighter*). Impious son of Eli, 1 Sam. i. 3; ii. 12-17; iii. 11-14; iv. 11.

**Hôr** (*hill*). (1) Mount in Edom on which Aaron died, Num. xx. 22-29; xxxiii. 37. (2) A peak of Lebanon range, Num. xxxiv. 7, 8.

**Hō'ram** (*hill*). King of Gezer, Josh. x. 33.

**Hō'reb** (*desert*). [Sinai.]

**Hō'rem** (*offered*). A place in Naphtali, Josh. xix. 38.

**Hôr-hā-gĭd'gad** (*cleft mountain*). A desert station of the Israelites, Num. xxxiii. 32.

**Hō'rī** (*cave-dweller*). (1) Grandson of Seir, Gen. xxxvi. 22. (2) A Simeonite, Num. xiii. 5.

**Hō'rītes, Hōrims**. Original people of Mt. Seir, Gen. xiv. 6.

**Hôr'mah** (*laid waste*). A Canaanite town in southern Judah, Josh. xv. 30; 1 Sam. xxx. 30.

**Hôrn**. Made of horn or metal, and of various shapes, sizes, and uses. Used much figuratively, Deut. xxxiii. 17; 1 Sam. xvi. 1; Job xvi. 15; Jer. xlviii. 25.

**Hôr'net** (*horner*). Plenty in Palestine, Ex. xxiii. 28; Deut. vii. 20; Josh. xxiv. 12.

**Hŏr''o-nā'im** (*two caves*). City of Moab, Isa. xv. 5; Jer. xlviii. 3.

**Hŏrse** (*neigher*). Used chiefly for war, Ex. xiv. 9-23; 2 Chr. i. 14-17; ix. 25; Esth. vi. 8; for threshing, Isa. xxviii. 28.

**Hŏrse'lēech** (*adherer*). Found in stagnant waters of East, and fastens to nostrils of animals when drinking, Prov. xxx. 15.

**Hō'sah** (*refuge*). (1) City of Asher, Josh. xix. 29. (2) A Levite, 1 Chr. xxvi. 10.

**Hō-săn'nȧ**. "Save, we pray," Ps. cxviii. 25, 26. The cry when Christ entered Jerusalem, Matt. xxi. 9-15; Mark xi. 9, 10.

**Hō-sē'ȧ** (*help*). First of minor prophets. Prophetic career, B. C. 784-725, in Israel. Denounces the idolatries of Israel and Samaria. Style obscure.

**Hŏsh''a-ī'ah** (*helped by God*). (1) Nehemiah's assistant, Neh. xii. 32. (2) Jezaniah's father, Jer. xlii. 1.

**Hŏsh-a'mȧ** (*whom God hears*). Son of Jeconiah, 1 Chr. iii. 18.

**Hō-shē'ȧ** (*salvation*). (1) Nineteenth and last king of Israel, B. C. 730-721. Conquered and imprisoned by Shalmaneser, 2 Kgs. xv. 30; xvii. 1-6; Hos. xiii. 16. (2) Son of Nun, Deut. xxxii. 44. (3) An Ephraimite, 1 Chr. xxvii. 20. (4) A co-covenanter, Neh. x. 23.

**Hŏs''pĭ-tăl'ĭ-ty** (*guest treatment*). Regulated in Lev. xix. 33, 34; xxv. 14-17; Deut. xv. 7-11.

**Hō'tham** (*seal*). An Asherite, 1 Chr. vii. 32.

**Hō'than** (*seal*). Father of Shama, 1 Chr. xi. 44.

**Hō'thir** (*fulness*). Son of Heman, 1 Chr. xxv. 4, 28, and leader of 21st course

**Hough** (*hok*) (*hock*). Cutting the sinews of the hind leg, hamstringing, Josh. xi. 6, 9; 2 Sam. viii. 4.

**Hour** (*time*). First division of Jewish day, morning, noon, evening, Ps. lv. 17. Night had three watches, Ex. xiv. 24; Judg. vii. 19; Lam. ii. 19. Later, day was, morning, heat, midday, evening. Hours introduced from Babylon, after captivity, Matt. xx. 1-10. An indefinite time, Dan. iii. 6; Matt. ix. 22.

**House** (*cover*). Prevailing Oriental style, low, flat roofed, with court in centre. A tent, palace, citadel, tomb, family, Gen. xii. 17; property, 1 Kgs. xiii. 8; lineage, Luke ii. 4; place of worship, Judg. xx. 18.

**Hŭk'kŏk** (*cut*). A border of Naphtali, Josh. xix. 34.

**Hū'kŏk**, 1 Chr. vi. 75. [Helkath.]

**Hŭl** (*circle*). Grandson of Shem, Gen. x. 23.

**Hŭl'dah** (*weasel*). A prophetess, 2 Kgs. xxii. 14-20; 2 Chr. xxxiv. 22.

**Hŭm'tah** (*place of lizards*). A city of Judah, Josh. xv. 54.

**Hŭnt'ing**. Hebrews not a hunting people, yet various devices mentioned for capturing wild animals, 2 Sam. xxiii. 20; Job xviii. 9, 10; Prov. xxii. 5; Isa. li. 20; Am. iii. 5.

**Hū'pham** (*coast-man*). Founder of Huphamites, Num. xxvi. 39.

**Hŭp'pah** (*covered*). Leader of 13th priestly course, 1 Chr. xxiv. 13.

**Hŭp'pim** (*covered*). A Benjamite, 1 Chr. vii. 12.

**Hûr** (*hole*). (1) The man who helped stay the hands of Moses, Ex. xvii. 10; xxiv. 14. (2) A Judahite, Ex. xxxi. 2. (3) A king of Midian, Num. xxxi. 8. (4) Father of one of Solomon's commissaries, 1 Kgs. iv. 8. (5) Father of a wall-builder, Neh. iii. 9.

**Hū'raī** (*weaver*). One of David's guard, 1 Chr. xi. 32.

**Hū'ram** (*noble*). (1) A Benjamite, 1 Chr. viii. 5. (2) Hiram, 2 Chr. ii. 3-13; iv. 11-16.

**Hū'rī** (*weaver*). A Gadite, 1 Chr. v. 14.

**Hū'shah** (*haste*). A Judahite, 1 Chr. iv. 4.

**Hū'shāi** (*haste*). A friend of David, 2 Sam. xv. 32; 1 Kgs. iv. 16.

**Hū'sham** (*haste*). A king of Edom, Gen. xxxvi. 34, 35.

**Hū'shath-īte**. Two of David's guard so called. 2 Sam. xxi. 18; xxiii. 27.

**Hū'shim** (*haste*). (1) Son of Dan, Gen. xlvi. 23. Shuham, Num. xxvi. 42. (2) A Benjamite, 1 Chr. vii. 12. (3) Wife of Shaharaim, 1 Chr. viii. 8, 11.

**Hŭsks** (*hulls*). The original means the carob, or locust bean, Luke xv. 16.

**Hŭz** (*strong*). Son of Nahor, Gen. xxii. 21.

**Hŭz'zăb** (*fixed*). A possible queen of Nineveh, Nah. ii. 7.

**Hy-ē'na** (*hog*). A bristled, fierce, carnivorous animal. "Zeboim," in 1 Sam. xiii. 18; Neh. xi. 34, means hyenas. So, it is thought, the original of "speckled bird," Jer. xii. 9, should be rendered.

**Hy-dăs'pēs** (*watery*). A river in India, Judith i. 6.

**Hy''mē-næ'us** (*hymeneal*). A convert and pervert, 1 Tim. i. 20; 2 Tim. ii. 17.

**Hymn** (*praise-song*). Spiritual song, Matt. xxvi. 30; Acts xvi. 25; Eph. v. 19; Col. iii. 16.

**Hys'sop** (*aromatic plant*). A bushy herb, of the mint family, Ex. xii. 22; Lev. xiv. 4, 6, 51; 1 Kgs. iv. 33; John xix. 29.

**Hyp'ō-crīte** (*stage-player*). Who feigns what he is not, Job viii. 13; Luke xii. 1.

## I

**Ĭb'hăr** (*God's choice*). Son of David, 2 Sam. v. 15.

**Ĭb'le-ăm** (*destroying*). City of Manasseh, Josh. xvii. 11; Judg. i. 27.

**Ĭb-nē'iah** (*God builds*). A Benjamite, 1 Chr. ix. 8.

**Ĭb-nī'jah** (*God builds*). A Benjamite, 1 Chr. ix. 8.

**Ĭb'rī** (*Hebrew*). A Levite, 1 Chr. xxiv. 27.

**Ĭb'zăn** (*famous*). A judge of Israel, Judg. xii. 8-10.

**Ī'cha-bŏd** (*inglorious*). Son of Phinehas, 1 Sam. iv. 19-22; xiv. 3.

**Ī-cō'nĭ-um** (*image*). City of Lycaonia, visited twice by Paul, Acts xiii. 51; xiv. 1-22; xvi. 2; 2 Tim. iii. 11.

**Ī-dā'lah** (*memorial*). City of Zebulun, Josh. xix. 15.

**Ĭd'băsh** (*stout*). A Judahite, 1 Chr. iv. 3.

**Ĭd'dō** (*timely*). (1) Father of Ahinadab, 1 Kgs. iv. 14. (2) A Levite, 1 Chr. vi. 21. (3) A Manassite chief, 1 Chr. xxvii. 21. (4) A seer and chronicler, 2 Chr. ix. 29; xiii. 22. (5) Grandfather of Zechariah, Zech. i. 1, 7. (6) One of the returned, Ez. viii. 17.

**Ī'dol, Ī-dŏl'a-try** (*apparent*). An object of worship, other than God, Gen. xxxi. 19; idolatry forbidden, Ex. xx. 3, 4; xxxiv. 13; Deut. iv. 16-19; vii. 25, 26; yet existed largely, especially under the judges and later kings, Ex. xxxii.; Judg. ii. 10-23; 1 Kgs. xi. 33; xii. 27-33; xiv. 22-24; Isa. lvii. 5-8.

**Ī''du-mē'a** (*red*), Isa. xxxiv. 5. Idumæa, Mark iii. 8. Greek name of Edom.

**Ī'găl** (*redeemed*). (1) The spy of Issachar, Num. xiii. 7. (2) One of David's guard, 2 Sam. xxiii. 36.

**Ĭg''da-lī'ah** (*great*). "A man of God," Jer. xxxv. 4.

**Ĭg'e-ăl** (*redeemed*). A Judahite, 1 Chr. iii. 22.

**Ī'ĭm** (*heaps*). (1) Num. xxxiii. 45, Ije-abarim. (2) Town of southern Judah, Josh. xv. 29.

**Ĭj''e-ăb'a-rĭm** (*ruins of Abarim*). An Israelite encampment near Moab, Num. xxi. 11.

**Ī'jon** (*ruin*). Town of Naphtali, 1 Kgs. xv. 20; 2 Kgs. xv. 29.

**Ĭk'kĕsh** (*wicked*). Father of Ira, 2 Sam. xxiii. 26: 1 Chr. xi. 28; xxvii. 9.

**Ī'lāi** (*exalted*). One of David's guard, 1 Chr. xi. 29.

**Ĭl-lўr'ĭ-cŭm** (*joy*). A country on E. shore of Adriatic, N. of Macedonia. Reached by Paul, Rom. xv. 19.

**Ĭm'aġe** (*likeness*). As in Gen. i. 26, 27; Col. i. 15. Also Idol.

**Ĭm'lȧ** (*full*). Father of Micaiah, 2 Chr. xviii. 7, 8. Imlah, 1 Kgs. xxii. 8, 9.

**Ĭm-măn'ū-el** (*God with us*). Name of the prophetic child, Isa. vii. 14. The Messiah, Matt. i, 23.

**Ĭm'mĕr** (*loquacious*). (1) A priestly family in charge of 16th course, 1 Chr. ix. 12; xxiv. 14. (2) Place in Babylonia, Ez. ii. 59; Neh. vii. 61.

**Ĭm'nȧ** (*lagging*). An Asherite, 1 Chr. vii. 35.

**Ĭm'nah** (*lagging*). (1) An Asherite, 1 Chr. vii. 30. (2) A Levite, 2 Chr. xxxi. 14.

**Ĭm'rah** (*stubborn*). An Asherite, 1 Chr. vii. 36.

**Ĭm'rī** (*talkative*). (1) A Judahite, 1 Chr. ix. 4. (2) Father of Zaccur, Neh. iii. 2.

**Ĭn'çense** (*set on fire*). A mixture of gums, spices, etc., Ex. xxx. 34-38, constituted the official incense. Burned morning and evening on the altar of incense, xxx. 1-10. Used also in idolatrous worship, 2 Chr. xxxiv. 25; Jer. xi. 12-17, and by angels, Rev. viii. 3.

**Ĭnd'ia** (*Indus*). The indefinite country which bounded the Persian empire on the east, Esth. i. 1; viii. 9.

**Ĭn-hĕr'ĭ-tance** (*heirship*). [Heir.]

**Ink, Ink'hôrn** (*burnt in*). Ancient ink heavy and thick and carried in an ink-horn, Jer. xxxvi. 18, Ezek. ix. 2.

**Ĭnn** (*in*). In O. T. a halting place for caravans, Gen. xlii. 27; Ex. iv. 24. In N. T. a caravansary afforded food and shelter for man and beast, Luke x. 34, 35.

**Ĭn'stant** (*stand in*). Urgent, Luke vii. 4; xxiii. 23; fervent, Acts xxvi. 7; Rom. xii. 12.

**Ī-ō'nia**. India in 1 Macc. viii. 8.

**Ĭph''e-dē'iah** (*free*). A Benjamite, 1 Chr. viii. 25.

**Ĭr** (*city*). A Benjamite, 1 Chr. vii. 12. Iri, vs. 7.

**Ī'rȧ** (*watchful*). (1) "Chief ruler about David," 2 Sam. xx. 26. (2) Two of David's warriors, 2 Sam. xxiii. 38; 1 Chr. xi. 28.

**Ī'răd** (*fleet*). Son of Enoch, Gen. iv. 18.

**Ī'ram** (*citizen*). A duke of Edom, Gen. xxxvi. 43; 1 Chr. i. 54.

**Ī'rī** (*watchful*). A Benjamite, 1 Chr. vii. 7.

**Ī-rī'jah** (*seen of God*). A ward-keeper, Jer. xxxvii. 13, 14.

**Ĭr-nā'hăsh** (*serpent city*). Unknown person or place, 1 Chr. iv. 12.

**Ī'ron** (*pious*). (1) City of Naphtali, Josh. xix. 38. (2) Iron, the metal, and copper early known, Gen. iv. 22. Prepared in furnaces, 1 Kgs. viii. 51; used for tools, Deut. xxvii. 5; weapons, 1 Sam. xvii. 7; implements, 2 Sam. xii. 31; war-chariots, Josh. xvii. 16, etc.

**Ĭr'pē-el** (*healed*). City of Benjamin, Josh. xviii. 27.

**Ĭr-shē'mĕsh** (*sun city*). A Danite city, Josh. xix. 41.

**Ī'ru** (*watch*). Son of Caleb, 1 Chr. iv. 15.

**Ī'saac** (*laughter*). Son of Abraham, Gen. xvii. 17-22. Second of the patriarchs, and father of Jacob and Esau, Gen. xxi.-xxxv.

**Ī-sā'iah** (*salvation of Jehovah*). Son of Amoz, Isa. i. 1, and first of greater prophets. His book, 23d of O. T., covers sixty years of prophecy, Isa. i. 1, at Jerusalem. It reproves the sins of the Jews and other nations, and foreshadows the coming of Christ. Called "prince of prophets." Poetically for Israel, Am. vii. 9, 16.

**Ĭs'cah** (*who looks*). Sister of Lot, Gen. xi. 29.

**Ĭs-căr'ĭ-ot**. [Judas Iscariot.]

**Ĭs'dȧ-el**, 1 Esdr. v. 33. [Giddel.]

**Ĭsh'bah** (*praising*). A Judahite, 1 Chr. iv. 17.

**Ĭsh'băk** (*leaving*). Son of Abraham, and father of northern Arabians, Gen. xxv. 2; 1 Chr. i. 32.

**Ĭsh-bī=bē'nŏb** (*dweller at Nob*). A Philistine giant, 2 Sam. xxi. 16, 17.

**Ĭsh=bō'sheth** (*man of shame*). Son and successor of Saul. Original name, Esh-baal. Reigned two years, then defeated by David, and assassinated, 2 Sam. ii. 8-11; iii.; iv. 5-12.

**Ĭsh'ī** (*saving*). (1) Two Judahites, 1 Chr. ii. 31; iv. 20. (2) A Simeonite, iv. 42. (3) A Manassite, v. 24.

**Ĭsh-ī'ah** (*loaned*). Chief of Issachar, 1 Chr. vii. 3.

**Ĭsh-ī'jah** (*loaned*). A lay Israelite, Ez. x. 31.

**Ĭsh'mȧ** (*ruin*). A Judahite, 1 Chr. iv. 3.

**Ĭsh'ma-el** (*whom God hears*). (1) Son of Abraham and Hagar, Gen. xvi. 15, 16. Banished to wilderness; became progenitor of Arabian tribes, Gen. xxi.; xxv. 9; xxxvii. 25-28. (2) Descendant of Saul, 1 Chr. viii. 38. (3) A Judahite, 2 Chr. xix. 11. (4) A Judahite captain, 2 Chr. xxiii. 1. (5) A priest, Ez. x. 22. (6) Crafty son of Nethaniah, 2 Kgs. xxv. 23-25; Jer. xli.

**Ĭsh'ma-el-ītes''**. Descendants of Ishmael, Judg. viii. 24. Ishmeelites, Gen. xxxvii. 25; 1 Chr. ii. 17.

**Ĭsh''ma-ī'ah** (*God hears*). Ruler of Zebulun, 1 Chr. xxvii. 19.

**Ĭsh'mē-rāi** (*God keeps*). A Benjamite, 1 Chr. viii. 18.

**Ī'shod** (*famed*). A Manassite, 1 Chr. vii. 18.

**Ĭsh'păn** (*bald*). A Benjamite, 1 Chr. viii. 22.

**Ĭsh'=tŏb** (*men of Tob*). Part of Aram, 2 Sam. x. 6-8. [Tob.]

**Ĭsh'u-ah** (*quiet*). An Asherite, Gen. xlvi. 17; 1 Chr. vii. 30.

**Ĭsh'u-āi** (*quiet*). Son of Asher, 1 Chr. vii. 30.

**Ĭsh'u-ī** (*quiet*). Son of Saul, 1 Sam. xiv. 49.

**Īsle** (*island*). Habitable place, Isa. xlii. 15; island, Gen. x. 5; Isa. xi. 11; coast lands, Isa. xx. 6; xxiii. 2, 6; Ezek. xxvii. 7.

**Ĭs''ma-chī'ah** (*supported*). Overseer of offerings, 2 Chr. xxxi. 13.

**Ĭs'mă-el**, 1 Esdr. ix. 22. [Ishmael.]

**Ĭs''ma-ī'ah** (*God hears*). A chief of Gibeon, 1 Chr. xii. 4.

**Ĭs'pah** (*bald*). A Benjamite, 1 Chr. viii. 16.

**Ĭs'ra-el** (*who prevails with God*). Name given to Jacob, Gen. xxxii. 28; xxxv. 10; became national, Ex. iii. 16; narrowed to northern kingdom after the revolt of the ten tribes from Judah, 1 Sam. xi. 8; 2 Sam. xx. 1; 1 Kgs. xii. 16, with Shechem as capital, 1 Kgs. xii. 25, and Tirzah as royal residence, xiv. 17; afterwards, capital at Samaria, xvi. 24. Kingdom lasted 254 years, with 19 kings, B. C. 975-721, when it fell a prey to the Assyrians. The returned of Israel blended with those of Judah.

**Ĭs'ra-ĕl-ītes''**. "Children of Israel." [Israel.]

**Ĭs'sa-char** (*rewarded*). (1) Fifth son of Jacob by Leah, Gen. xxx. 17, 18. Tribe characteristics foretold, Gen. xlix. 14, 15. Place during march at east of Tabernacle, Num. ii. 5. Allotment N. of Manasseh, from Carmel to Jordan, Josh. xix. 17-23. (2) A temple porter, 1 Chr. xxvi. 5.

**Ĭs'shī-ah** (*loaned*). Descendant of Levi, 1 Chr. xxiv. 21. (2) A Levite, 1 Chr. xxiv. 25.

**Ĭs''tăl-cū'rus**, 1 Esdr. viii. 40. [Zabbud.]

**Ĭs'u-ah**, 1 Chr. vii. 30. [Jesui.]

**Ĭs'ui**, Gen. xlvi. 17. [Jesui.]

**Ĭt'a-lў** (*kingdom of Italus*). In N. T. the whole of Italy between the Alps and sea, Acts xviii. 2; xxvii. 1; Heb. xiii. 24.

**Ĭth'a-ī** (*with God*). A Benjamite, 1 Chr. xi. 31.

**Ĭth'a-mär** (*land of palms*). Son of Aaron, Ex.

vi. 23; xxviii. 1-43; Num. iii. 2-4. Eli was high priest of his line, 1 Chr. xxiv. 6.

**Ĭth′ĭ-el** (*God with me*). (1) Friend of Agur, Prov. xxx. 1. (2) A Benjamite, Neh. xi. 7.

**Ĭth′mah** (*orphan*). One of David's guard, 1 Chr. xi. 46.

**Ĭth′nan** (*given*). Town in south Judah, Josh. xv. 23.

**Ĭth′rȧ** (*plenty*). David's brother-in-law, 2 Sam. xvii. 25.

**Ĭth′ran** (*plenty*). (1) A Horite, Gen. xxxvi. 26. (2) An Asherite, 1 Chr. vii. 37.

**Ĭth′rẹ-ăm** (*populous*). Son of David, 2 Sam. iii. 5.

**Ĭth′rīte.** Two of David's warriors so called, 2 Sam. xxiii. 38; 1 Chr. xi. 40.

**Ĭt′tah-kā′zin** (*hour of a prince*). A landmark of Zebulun, Josh. xix. 13.

**Ĭt′tạ-ī** (*timely*). (1) One of David's generals, 2 Sam. xv. 19; xviii. 2-12. (2) One of David's guard, 2 Sam. xxiii. 29.

**Ĭ″tu-ræ′ȧ.** From Jetur, Gen. xxv. 15; 1 Chr. i 31. A small province N. W. of Palestine, now Jedur, Luke iii. 1.

**Ī′vah, Ā′va.** An Assyrian city, possibly Hit, 2 Kgs. xviii. 34; xix. 13.

**Ī′vŏ-rȳ** (*elephant tooth*). Much used by Hebrews, 1 Kgs. x. 22; 2 Chr. ix. 17-21; Ezek. xxvii. 15.

**Ĭz′ẹ-här**, Num. iii. 19. [Izhar.]

**Ĭz′här** (*oil*). Uncle of Moses, Ex. vi. 18-21; Num. iii. 19. Founder of Izharites, 1 Chr. xxiv. 22.

**Ĭz″ra-hī′ah** (*sparkling*). Descendant of Issachar, 1 Chr. vii. 3.

**Ĭz′ra-hīte.** A captain of David, so called, 1 Chr. xxvii. 8.

**Ĭz′rī** (*created*). Leader of the 4th musical course 1 Chr. xxv. 11.

## J

**Jā′a-kăn**, Deut. x. 6. [Jakan.]

**Jạ̄-ăk′ō-bah** (*supplanter*). Prince of Simeon, 1 Chr. iv. 36.

**Jạ̄-ā′lah** (*wild goat*). His children returned, Ez. ii. 56. Jaala, Neh. vii. 58.

**Jạ̄-ā′lam** (*hidden*). Duke of Edom, Gen. xxxvi. 5, 18.

**Jạ̄-ā′năi** (*answered*). A Gadite, 1 Chr. v. 12.

**Jạ̄-ăr′ĕ-ŏr′e-gĭm** (*weaver's forests*). Father of Elhanan, slayer of Goliath's brother, 2 Sam. xxi. 19.

**Jā′a-sạu** (*created*). Son of Bani, Ez. x. 37.

**Jạ̄-ā′sĭ-el** (*created*). Son of Abner, 1 Chr. xxvii. 21.

**Jạ̄-ăz″ạ-nī′ah** (*heard of God*). (1) A Hebrew captain, 2 Kgs. xxv. 23. (2) A denounced prince, Ezek. xi. 1. (3) Son of Jeremiah, Jer. xxxv. 3. (4) Son of Shaphan, Ezek. viii. 11.

**Jạ̄-ā′zēr, Jā′zēr** (*helped*). City and province of Gilead, Num. xxi. 32; xxxii. 1; Josh. xxi. 39; 1 Chr. xxvi. 31.

**Jā″ạ-zī′ah** (*comforted*). A Levite, 1 Chr. xxiv. 26, 27.

**Jạ̄-ā′zĭ-el** (*comforted*). A temple musician, 1 Chr. xv. 18.

**Jā′băl** (*stream*). Son of Lamech, Gen. iv. 20.

**Jăb′bok** (*flowing*). A tributary of Jordan, on east side; and northern boundary of Ammon, Gen. xxxii. 22; Num. xxi. 24; Deut. ii. 37.

**Jā′besh** (*dry*). (1) King Shallum's father, 2 Kgs. xv. 10, 13. (2) Jabesh-gilead, a city of Gilead, Judg. xxi. 8-14; 1 Sam. xi. 1-11; xxxi. 11-13.

**Jā′bĕz** (*sorrow*). Persons or places, 1 Chr. ii. 55; iv. 9, 10.

**Jā′bin** (*observed*). (1) King of Hazor, Josh. xi. 1-14. (2) Another king of Hazor, defeated by Barak, Judg. iv. 2-24.

**Jăb′nĕ-el** (*building of God*). (1) Stronghold in Judah, Josh. xv. 11; Jabneh, 2 Chr. xxvi. 6. (2) Place in Naphtali, Josh. xix. 33.

**Jăb′neh.** [Jabneel.]

**Jā′chan** (*affliction*). A Gadite, 1 Chr. v. 13.

**Jā′chin** (*established*). (1) A temple pillar, 1 Kgs. vii. 21; 2 Chr. iii. 17. (2) Fourth son of Simeon, Gen. xlvi. 10. (3) Head of 21st priestly course, 1 Chr. ix. 10; xxiv. 17.

**Jā′chin-ites.** Descendants of Jachin, Num. xxvi. 12.

**Jạ̄′cinth** (*hyacinth*). Zircon, a vari-colored gem, Rev. ix. 17; xxi. 20.

**Jā′cob** (*supplanter*). Son of Isaac and second born twin with Esau, Gen. xxv. 24-34. Bought Esau's birthright, fled to Padan-aram, married Rachel and Leah, wandered to Hebron, name changed to Israel, drifted to Egypt, where he died, aged 147 years, Gen. xxv.-l.

**Jạ̄-cŭ′bus**, 1 Esdr. ix. 48. [Akkub, 4.]

**Jā′dȧ** (*knowing*). A Judahite, 1 Chr. ii. 28, 32.

**Jạ̄-dā′ụ** (*loving*). Son of Nebo, Ez. x. 43.

**Jad-dū′ȧ** (*known*). (1) A co-covenanter, Neh. x. 21. (2) High priest, and last mentioned in O. T., Neh. xii. 11, 22.

**Jā′don** (*judge*). Assistant wall builder, Neh. iii. 7.

**Jā′el** (*goat*). Heber's wife; murderess of Sisera, Judg. iv. 17-23; v.

**Jā′gŭr** (*lodging*). Southern town of Judah, Josh. xv. 21.

**Jäh.** Jehovah, in poetry, Ps. lxviii. 4.

**Jā′hăth** (*united*). (1) A Judahite, 1 Chr. iv. 2. (2) Four Levites, 1 Chr. vi. 20; xxiii. 10, 11; xxiv. 22; 2 Chr. xxxiv. 12.

**Jā′hăz** (*trodden*). Place in Moab where Moses conquered the Ammonites, Num. xxi. 23, 24; Deut. ii. 32.

**Jạ̄-hā′zȧ**, Josh. xiii. 18. [Jahaz.]

**Jạ̄-hā′zah**, Josh. xxi. 36. [Jahaz.]

**Jạ̄″hā-zī′ah** (*seen of God*). A priest, Ez. x. 15.

**Jạ̄-hā′zĭ-el** (*seen of God*). (1) A Benjamite, 1 Chr. xii. 4. (2) A trumpeter, 1 Chr. xvi. 6. (3) A Levite, 1 Chr. xxiii. 19; xxiv. 23. (4) A Levite, 2 Chr. xx. 14. (5) His sons returned, Ez. viii. 5.

**Jăh′da-ī** (*directed*). A Judahite, 1 Chr. ii. 47.

**Jăh′dī-el** (*joyful*). A Manassite, 1 Chr. v. 24.

**Jăh′dō** (*united*). A Gadite, 1 Chr. v. 14.

**Jăh′lĕ-el** (*hoping*). Founder of Jahleelites, Gen. xlvi. 14; Num. xxvi. 26.

**Jăh′ma-ī** (*guarded*). Son of Tola, 1 Chr. vii. 2.

**Jăh′zah**, 1 Chr. vi. 78. [Jahaz.]

**Jăh′zĕ-el** (*allotted*). Founder of the Jahzeelites, Gen. xlvi. 24; Num. xxvi. 48.

**Jăh′zĕ-rah** (*led back*). A priest, 1 Chr. ix. 12.

**Jăh′zĭ-el**, 1 Chr. vii. 13. [Jahzeel.]

**Jā′ir** (*enlightened*). (1) Conqueror of Argob and part of Gilead, Num. xxxii. 41; Deut. iii. 14. (2) A judge of Israel, Judg. x. 3-5. (3) A Benjamite, Esth. ii. 5. (4) Father of Elhanan, 1 Chr. xx. 5.

**Jā′ir-ite.** Ira so called, 2 Sam. xx. 26.

**Jạ̄-ī′rus** (*enlightened*). Ruler of a synagogue, Luke viii. 41.

**Jā′kan** (*thoughtful*). A Horite, 1 Chr. i. 42. [Jaakan, Akan.]

**Jā′keh** (*pious*). Father of Agur, Prov. xxx. 1.

**Jā′kim** (*confirmed*). (1) Head of 12th course, 1 Chr. xxiv. 12. (2) A Benjamite, 1 Chr. viii. 19.

**Jā′lon** (*tarrying*). A Judahite, 1 Chr. iv. 17.

**Jăm′brēṣ.** An Egyptian magician, Ex. vii. 9-13; 2 Tim. iii. 8, 9.

**Jăm′brī.** Supposably Ammonites, 1 Macc. ix. 36-41.

**Jāmes** (*Jacob*). (1) "The Greater" or "Elder," son of Zebedee and brother of John, Matt. iv. 21, 22. A fisherman of Galilee, called to the Apostolate about A. D. 28, and styled Boanerges, Matt. x. 2, 3; Mark iii. 14-18; Luke vi. 12-16; Acts i. 13. Labored at Jerusalem. Beheaded by Herod, A. D. 44. (2) "The Less," another Apostle, son of Alphæus, Matt. x. 3; Mark iii. 18; Luke vi. 15. (3) Christ's brother, or more likely cousin, and identical with James the Less, Gal. i. 19. Compare Matt. xiii. 55; Mark vi. 3; Acts xii. 17. Resident at Jerusalem and author of The Epistle of James, written before A. D. 62 to the scattered Jews, urging good works as the groundwork and evidence of faith.

**Jā′min** (*right hand*). (1) Founder of Jaminites, Gen. xlvi. 10; Ex. vi. 15; Num. xxvi. 12. A Judahite, 1 Chr. ii. 27. (3) Ezra's assistant, Neh. viii. 7.

**Jăm′lech** (*reigning*). A Simeonite chief, 1 Chr. iv. 34.

**Jăm′nī-ȧ**, 1 Macc. iv. 15. [Jabneel.]

**Jăn′nȧ** (*God-given*). Ancestor of Christ, Luke iii. 24.

**Jăn′nēṣ.** An Egyptian magician, 2 Tim. iii. 8, 9, Ex. vii. 9-13.

**Jạ̄-nō′ah** (*rest*). Town of Naphtali, 2 Kgs. xv. 29.

**Jā-nō'hah** (*rest*). Border town of Ephraim, Josh. xvi. 6, 7.

**Jā'num** (*sleeping*). Town of Judah, Josh. xv. 53.

**Jā'pheth** (*enlarged*). Son of Noah, Gen. v. 32; vi. 10; ix. 27; x. 21. His generations peopled the "isles of the Gentiles," and type the Indo-European and Caucasian races, Gen. x. 1-5.

**Jā-phī'ā** (*splendor*). (1) A border of Zebulun, Josh. xix. 12. (2) King of Lachish, Josh. x. 3. (3) A son of David, 2 Sam. v. 15; 1 Chr. iii. 7.

**Jăph'let** (*delivered*). An Asherite, 1 Chr. vii. 32, 33.

**Jăph-lē'ti**. Landmark of Ephraim, Josh. xvi. 3.

**Jā'phō**, Josh. xix. 46. [Joppa.]

**Jā'rah** (*honey*). Son of Micah, 1 Chr. ix. 42.

**Jā'reb** (*enemy*). Unknown person or place, Hos. v. 13; x. 6.

**Jā'red** (*descent*). Father of Enoch, Gen. v. 15-20; Luke iii. 37.

**Jăr-ĕ-sī'ah** (*nourished*). A Benjamite, 1 Chr. viii. 27.

**Jär'hā**. An Egyptian servant, 1 Chr. ii. 34, 35.

**Jā'rib** (*enemy*). (1) A Simeonite, 1 Chr. iv. 24. (2) One who returned, Ez. viii. 16. (3) A priest, Ez. x. 18.

**Jär'ī-moth**, 1 Esdr. ix. 28. [Jeremoth.]

**Jär'mŭth** (*high*). (1) Town of lower Judah, Josh. x. 3; xv. 35. (2) A Levitical city of Issachar, Josh. xxi. 29.

**Jā-rō'ah** (*moon*). A Gadite, 1 Chr. v. 14.

**Jā'shen** (*sleeping*). His sons were in David's guard, 2 Sam. xxiii. 32.

**Jā'shēr** (*upright*). Book of, wholly lost, Josh. x. 13; 2 Sam. i. 18.

**Jā-shō'be-ăm** (*turned to*). A chief of David's captains, 1 Chr. xi. 11; xii. 6; xxvii. 2. Adino, 2 Sam. xxiii. 8.

**Jăsh'ŭb** (*he turns*). (1) Founder of Jashubites, Num. xxvi. 24; 1 Chr. vii. 1; Job, Gen. xlvi. 13. (2) Son of Bani, Ez. x. 29.

**Jăsh'u-bī=lē'hĕm** (*turning back for food*). Person or place of Judah, 1 Chr. iv. 22.

**Jā'sī-el** (*created*). One of David's heroes, 1 Chr. xi. 47.

**Jā'son** (*healer*). (1) Son of Eleazar, 1 Macc. viii. 17. (2) Father of Antipater, xii. 16. (3) An historian, 2 Macc. ii. 23. (4) High priest, 2 Macc. iv. 7-26. (5) A friend of Paul, Acts xvii. 5-9.

**Jăs'pēr**. A colored quartz. Last stone in high priest's breastplate, and first in New Jerusalem foundation, Ex. xxviii. 20; Rev. xxi. 19.

**Jăth'nī-el** (*God-given*). A Levite, 1 Chr. xxvi. 2.

**Jăt'tīr** (*prominent*). Town of south Judah, Josh. xv. 48; xxi. 14; 1 Sam. xxx. 27.

**Jā'văn** (*clay*). (1) Fourth son of Japheth, and type of Ionians and Grecians, Gen. x. 2-5; 1 Chr. i. 5-7. (2) An Arabian trading post, Ezek. xxvii. 13, 19.

**Jăve'lĭn**. A short, light spear. [Arms.]

**Jā'zär**, 1 Macc. v. 8. [Jaazer.]

**Jā'zĕr**, Num. xxxii. 1-3; Josh. xxi. 39. [Jaazer.]

**Jā'zīz** (*moved*). Herdsman of David, 1 Chr. xxvii. 31.

**Jĕ'a-rĭm** (*woods*). Border mountain of Judah, Josh. xv. 10.

**Jē-ăt'e-rāi** (*led*). A Levite, 1 Chr. vi. 21.

**Jĕ''bĕr-e-chī'ah** (*blessed*). Father of Zechariah, Isa. viii. 2.

**Jē'bus** (*threshing floor*). Original name of Jerusalem; the "threshing floor" of the Jebushi or Jebusites, Josh. xv. 8; xviii. 16, 28; Judg. xix. 10, 11; 1 Chr. xi. 4, 5.

**Jĕb'u-sīte, Jĕ-bū'si**. Original people of Jebus, Deut. vii. 1; Josh. xi. 3; 2 Sam. v. 6-10; xxiv, 16-25.

**Jĕc''a-mī'ah** (*gathered*). One of David's line, 1 Chr. iii. 18.

**Jĕch''o-lī'ah** (*enabled*). Mother of King Azariah, 2 Kgs. xv. 2. Jecoliah, 2 Chr. xxvi. 3.

**Jĕch''o-nī'as**, Matt. i. 11, 12; Esth. xi. 4. Greek form of Jeconiah and Jehoiachin.

**Jĕc''o-lī'ah**, 2 Chr. xxvi. 3. [Jecholiah.]

**Jĕc''o-nī'ah**, 1 Chr. iii. 16; Jer. xxiv. 1. [Jehoiachin.]

**Jē-dā'iah** (*praise God*). (1) Head of 2d temple course, 1 Chr. xxiv. 7. (2) A priest, Zech. vi. 10-14. (3) A Simeonite, 1 Chr. iv. 37. (4) A wall-repairer, Neh. iii. 10.

**Jē-dī'a-el** (*known of God*). (1) A Benjamite, 1 Chr. vii. 6-11. (2) One of David's guard, 1 Chr. xi. 45. (3) A Manassite chief, 1 Chr. xii. 20. (4) A Levite, 1 Chr. xxvi. 1, 2.

**Jē-dī'dah** (*beloved*). Mother of King Josiah, 2 Kgs. xxii. 1.

**Jĕd''ī-dī'ah** (*beloved of God*). Name given to Solomon by Nathan, 2 Sam. xii. 25.

**Jĕd'u-thŭn** (*praising*). A leader of the temple choir, 1 Chr. xxv. 6; Ps. xxxix., lxii., lxxvii., title.

**Jē-ē'zĕr** (*father of help*). A Manassite, Num. xxvi. 30. Abiezer, elsewhere.

**Jē-ē'zĕr-ītes**. Descendants of above.

**Jē'gar=sā-hā-dū'thā** (*testimonial heap*). Heap of compact between Jacob and Laban, Gen. xxxi. 47.

**Jē''hā-lē'le-el** (*who praises*). A Judahite, 1 Chr. iv. 16.

**Jē-hăl'e-lĕl** (*who praises*). A Levite, 2 Chr. xxix. 12.

**Jēh-dē'iah** (*made joyful*). (1) A Levite, 1 Chr. xxiv. 20. (2) David's herdsman, 1 Chr. xxvii. 30.

**Jē-hĕz'e-kĕl** (*made strong*). Head of the 20th priestly course, 1 Chr. xxiv. 16.

**Jē-hī'ah** (*God lives*). A doorkeeper of the ark, 1 Chr. xv. 24.

**Jē-hī'el** (*God lives*). (1) A Levite, 1 Chr. xv. 18, 20. (2) A treasurer, 1 Chr. xxiii. 8. (3) Son of Jehoshaphat, 2 Chr. xxi. 2. (4) An officer of David, 1 Chr. xxvii. 32. (5) A Levite, 2 Chr. xxix. 14. (6) Ruler of God's house, 2 Chr. xxxv. 8. (7) An overseer, 2 Chr. xxxi. 13. (8) Returned captives, Ez. viii. 9; x. 2, 21, 26.

**Jē-hī'el** (*treasured*). (1) Father of Gibeon, 1 Chr. ix. 35. (2) One of David's guard, 1 Chr. xi. 44.

**Jē-hī'e-lī**. A Levite family, 1 Chr. xxvi. 21, 22.

**Jē''hīz-kī'ah** (*strengthened*). An Ephraimite, 2 Chr. xxviii. 12.

**Jē-hō'a-dah** (*adorned*). A descendant of Saul, 1 Chr. viii. 36.

**Jē''hō-ăd'dan** (*adorned*). Mother of King Amaziah, 2 Kgs. xiv. 2; 2 Chr. xxv. 1.

**Jē-hō'a-hăz** (*possession*). (1) Son and successor of Jehu on throne of Israel, B. C. 856-840, 2 Kgs. xiii. 1-9. Reign disastrous. (2) Son and successor of Josiah on throne of Judah. Reigned 3 months, B. C. 610. Called Shallum. Deposed and died in Egypt, Jer. xxii. 11, 12. (3) Ahaziah, Azariah, 2 Chr. xxi. 17; xxii. 1, 6.

**Jē-hō'ash**. [Joash.]

**Jē''hō-hā'nan** (*God-given*). (1) A temple porter, 1 Chr. xxvi. 3. (2) A general of Judah, 2 Chr. xvii. 15; xxiii. 1. (3) Returned Levites, Ez. x. 28; Neh. xii. 13, 42.

**Jē-hoi'a-chin** (*God-appointed*). Jeconiah, 1 Chr. iii. 17; Coniah, Jer. xxii. 24; Jechonias, Matt. i. 12. Son and successor of Jehoiakim on throne of Judah. Reigned 100 days, B. C. 597; carried prisoner to Babylon; released after 36 years' captivity, 2 Kgs. xxiv. 6-16; Jer. xxix. 2; Ezek. xvii. 12.

**Jē-hoi'a-dā** (*known of God*). (1) Father of Benaiah, 2 Sam. viii. 18; 1 Kgs. i., ii. (2) An Aaronite leader, 1 Chr. xii. 27. (3) No doubt same as (1), 1 Chr. xxvii. 34. (4) High priest and religious reformer under Athaliah and Joash, 2 Kgs. xi. 4-21; xii. 1-16. (5) Second priest, or sagan, Jer. xxix. 25-29. (6) A wall-repairer, Neh. iii. 6.

**Jē-hoi'a-kĭm** (*God-established*) Eliakim, son of Josiah; name changed to Jehoiakim; successor to Jehoahaz, and 19th king of Judah, B. C. 609-598. Nearly entire reign one of vassalage to Egypt or Babylon, 2 Kgs. xxiii. 34-37; xxiv. 1-6; Jer. xxii. 18, 19; xxxvi. 30-32.

**Jē-hoi'a-rīb** (*God-defended*). Head of 1st temple course, 1 Chr. xxiv. 7.

**Jē-hŏn'a-dăb, Jŏn'a-dăb** (*God-impelled*). Son of Rechab, and adherent of Jehu, 2 Kgs. x. 15-23; Jer. xxxv. 6.

**Jē-hŏn'a-than** (*God-given*). (1) David's storehouse keeper, 1 Chr. xxvii. 25. (2) A Levite teacher, 2 Chr. xvii. 8. (3) A priest, Neh. xii. 18.

**Jē-hō'ram, Jō'ram** (*God-exalted*). (1) Son of Ahab and successor to Ahaziah on throne of Israel, B. C. 896-884. Victoriously allied with Judah, but defeated and slain in Jehu's revolt. Last of Ahab's line, 1 Kgs. xxi. 21-29; xxii. 50; 2 Kgs. i. 17, 18; ii.-ix. (2) Son and successor of Jehoshaphat on throne of Judah, B. C. 893-885. Murderer and Baal worshipper. Reign calamitous. Died a terrible death, 2 Chr. xxi.

**Jē″hō-shăb′e-ăth**, 2 Chr. xxii. 11. [Jehosheba.]

**Jē-hŏsh′a-phăt** (*judged of God*). (1) Recorder under David and Solomon, 2 Sam. viii. 16; 1 Kgs. iv. 3. (2) A trumpeter, 1 Chr. xv. 24. (3) Solomon's purveyor, 1 Kgs. iv. 17. (4) Father of Jehu, 2 Kgs. ix. 2-14. (5) Valley of Cedron, or else a visionary spot, Joel iii. 2-12. (6) Son and successor of Asa on throne of Judah, B. C. 914-890. A God-fearing king, in close alliance with Israel, 1 Kgs. xv. 24; 2 Kgs. viii. 16; 2 Chr. xvii.-xxi. 1.

**Jē-hŏsh′e-bȧ** (*oath of God*). Daughter of king Joram and wife of Jehoiada, the high priest, 2 Kgs. xi. 2; 2 Chr. xxii. 11.

**Jē-hŏsh′u-ȧ**. Full form of Joshua, Num. xiii. 16; Jehoshuah, 1 Chr. vii. 27.

**Jē-hō′vah**. "He that is." "I am," Ex. iii. 14. The self-existent and eternal one. Hebrew word for God, generally rendered "Lord." Not pronounced; but Adonai, "Lord," or Elohim, "God," substituted, Ex. vi. 3. [God.]

**Jē-hō′vah=ji′reh** (*God will provide*). Abraham's name for spot where Isaac was offered, Gen. xxii. 14.

**Jē-hō′vah=nĭs′si** (*God my banner*). The altar built in honor of Joshua's victory, Ex. xvii. 15.

**Jē-hō′vah=shā′lom** (*God is peace*). Gideon's altar in Ophrah, Judg. vi. 24.

**Jē-hŏz′a-băd** (*God-given*). (1) A storekeeper and porter, 1 Chr. xxvi. 4. (2) Co-murderer of King Joash, 2 Kgs. xii. 21. (3) A Benjamite captain, 2 Chr. xvii. 18.

**Jē-hŏz′a-dăk** (*God justifies*). Captive father of Jeshua, the high priest, 1 Chr. vi. 14, 15; Ez. iii. 2.

**Jē′hū** (*who exists*). (1) Prophet of Judah, 1 Kgs. xvi. 1-7. (2) Tenth king of Israel, B. C. 884-856. He extirpated Ahab's line according to the prophecies, 1 Kgs. xix. 16, 17; 2 Kgs. ix., x. (3) A Judahite, 1 Chr. ii. 38. (4) A Simeonite, 1 Chr. iv. 35. (5) A Benjamite, 1 Chr. xii. 3.

**Jē-hŭb′bah** (*hidden*). An Asherite, 1 Chr. vii. 34.

**Jē′hū-cal** (*mighty*). Messenger to Jeremiah, Jer. xxxvii. 3.

**Jē′hŭd** (*famed*). Town of Dan, Josh. xix. 45.

**Jē-hū′dī** (*Jew*). A messenger, Jer. xxxvi. 14-23.

**Jē″hū-dī′jah** (*Jewess*). Mother of Jered, 1 Chr. iv. 18.

**Jē′hŭsh** (*collector*). Son of Eshek, 1 Chr. viii. 39.

**Jē-ī′el** (*God's treasure*). (1) Reubenite chief, 1 Chr. v. 7. (2) Levites, 1 Chr. xv. 18; 2 Chr. xx. 14; xxvi. 11; xxix. 13; xxxv. 9; Ez. viii. 13; x. 43.

**Jē-kăb′zẹ-el** (*gathered*). Kabzeel, in south Judah, Neh. xi. 25; Josh. xv. 21; 2 Sam. xxiii. 20.

**Jĕk″a-mē′am** (*who gathers*). A Levite, 1 Chr. xxiii. 19; xxiv. 23.

**Jĕk″a-mī′ah** (*gathered*). A Judahite, 1 Chr ii. 41.

**Jē-kū′thī-el** (*piety*). A Judahite, 1 Chr. iv. 18.

**Jē-mī′mȧ** (*dove*). Job's daughter, Job xlii. 14.

**Jĕm′nā-an**, Judith ii. 28. [Jabneel.]

**Jē-mū′el** (*God's day*). A Simeonite, Gen. xlvi. 10; Ex. vi. 15.

**Jĕph′thā-ē**, Heb. xi. 32. Greek form of Jephthah.

**Jĕph′thah** (*set free*). A judge of Israel, B. C. 1143-1137, Judg. xi., xii.

**Jē-phŭn′neh** (*favorably regarded*). (1) Father of Caleb the spy, Num. xiii. 6. (2) An Asherite, 1 Chr. vii. 38.

**Jē′răh** (*moon*). Son of Joktan, Gen. x. 26; 1 Chr. i. 20.

**Jē-răh′mẹ-el** (*God's mercy*). (1) Son of Hezron, 1 Chr. ii. 9, 42. (2) A Levite, 1 Chr. xxiv. 29. (3) An official of Jehoiakim, Jer. xxxvi. 26.

**Jē-răh′mẹ-el-ītes″**. Descendants of above (1), 1 Sam. xxvii. 10.

**Jĕr′ĕ-cus**, 1 Esdr. v. 22. [Jericho.]

**Jē′rĕd** (*descent*). (1) Father of Enoch, 1 Chr. i. 2. (2) A Judahite, 1 Chr. iv. 18.

**Jĕr′ẹ-māī** (*mountaineer*). A layman, Ez. x. 33.

**Jĕr″ẹ-mī′ah** (*exalted*). (1) Second of greater prophets. His prophecies cover reigns of Josiah, Jehoiakim, and Zedekiah, B. C. 628-586, and constitute the 24th O. T. book. Life one of vicissitude. Prophecies noted for boldness and beauty, and chiefly denunciative of Judah and her policy. Withdrew to Egypt, where he probably died. (2) Seven others in O. T., 2 Kgs. xxiii. 31; 1 Chr. xii. 4-13; v. 24; Neh. x. 2; xii. 1, 12, 34; Jer. xxxv. 3.

**Jĕr″ẹ-mī′as. Jĕr′ẹ-mȳ**. Greek form of Jeremiah, Matt. ii. 17; xvi. 14; xxvii. 9.

**Jĕr′ẹ-mŏth** (*heights*). Persons in 1 Chr. viii. 14; xxiii. 23; xxv. 22; Ez. x. 26, 27.

**Jē-rī′ah** (*founded*). A chief of the house of Hebron, 1 Chr. xxiii. 19; xxiv. 23.

**Jĕr′ī-bāi** (*defended*). One of David's guard, 1 Chr. xi. 46.

**Jĕr′ī-chō** (*fragrance*). Ancient city of Canaan 5 miles W. of Jordan and 18 from Jerusalem. Strongly fortified, and conquered by Joshua. Fell to Benjamin, Deut. xxxiv. 3; Num. xxii. 1; Josh. vi.; xvi. 7; xviii. 21; 1 Kgs. xvi. 34; Matt. xx. 29; Mark x. 46.

**Jē′rī-el** (*founded*). An Issacharite, 1 Chr. vii. 2.

**Jē-rī′jah**, 1 Chr. xxvi. 31. [Jeriah.]

**Jĕr′ĭ-mŏth** (*heights*). Persons in 1 Chr. vii. 8; xii. 5; xxiv. 30; xxv. 4, 22; xxvii. 19; 2 Chr. xi. 18; xxxi. 13.

**Jē′rī-ŏth** (*curtains*). Caleb's wife, 1 Chr. ii. 18.

**Jĕr″o-bō′am** (*many-peopled*). (1) First king of Israel after the division, B. C. 975-954. Plotter for Solomon's throne, 1 Kgs. xi. 26-40; fled to Egypt; returned on death of Solomon; set up kingdom of ten tribes; established idolatry; warred with Judah; defeated by Abijah; soon after died, 1 Kgs. xii.-xiv.; 2 Chr. x.-xiii. (2) Jeroboam II., 13th king of Israel. Successor to Joash. Reigned B. C. 825-784. Idolatrous, but mighty and illustrious. Raised Israel to greatest splendor, 2 Kgs. xiv. 23-29; xv. 8, 9; Am. ; ii. 6-16.

**Jĕr′o-hăm** (*cherished*). (1) Father of Elkanah, 1 Sam. i. 1; 1 Chr. vi. 27. (2) A Benjamite, 1 Chr. viii. 27; ix. 8. (3) Father of Adaiah, 1 Chr. ix. 12. (4) Others in 1 Chr. xii. 7; xxvii. 22; 2 Chr. xxiii. 1.

**Jē-rŭb′ba-ăl** (*contender with Baal*). Surname of Gideon, Judg. vi. 32.

**Jē-rŭb′be-shĕth** (*strife with the idol*). Another surname of Gideon, 2 Sam. xi. 21.

**Jĕr′u-el** (*founded*). Unknown battlefield, 2 Chr xx. 16.

**Jē-rụ′sā-lĕm** (*place of peace*). Capital of Hebrew monarchy and of kingdom of Judah, 24 miles west of Jordan and 37 east of the Mediterranean. "Salem," Ps. lxxvi. 2, and perhaps, Gen. xiv. 18. "Jebus," Judg. xix. 10, 11. "Jebus-salem," Jerusalem, Josh. x. 1. "City of David," Zion, 1 Kgs. viii. 1; 2 Kgs. xiv. 20. "City of Judah," 2 Chr. xxv. 28. "City of God," Ps. xlvi. 4. "City of the great King," Ps. xlviii. 2. "The holy city," Neh. xi. 1. Captured and rebuilt by David, and made his capital, 2 Sam. v. 6-13; 1 Chr. xi. 4-9. Destroyed by Nebuchadnezzar, B. C. 588. Rebuilt by returned captives. Captured by Alexander the Great, B. C. 332; by Antiochus, B. C. 203; by Rome, B. C. 63.

**Jē-rụ′sā-lĕm, New**. Metaphorically, the spiritual church, Rev. iii. 12; xxi.; compare Gal. iv. 26; Heb. xii. 22.

**Jē-rụ′shȧ** (*possessed*). Daughter of Zadok, 2 Kgs. xv. 33. Jerushah, 2 Chr. xxvii. 1.

**Jē-sā′ịah** (*saved*). (1) Grandson of Zerubbabel, 1 Chr. iii. 21. (2) A Benjamite, Neh. xi. 7.

**Jē-shā′ịah** (*God's help*). (1) Head of 8th singing course, 1 Chr. xxv. 3, 15. (2) A Levite, 1 Chr. xxvi. 25. Isshiah, xxiv. 21. (3) Two who returned, Ez. viii. 7, 19.

**Jĕsh′a-nah** (*old*). Unidentified town, 2 Chr. xiii. 19.

**Jē-shăr′e-lah** (*right*). Head of 7th singing course, 1 Chr. xxv. 14. Asarelah, vs. 2.

**Jē-shĕb′e-ăb** (*father's seat*). Head of 14th priestly course, 1 Chr. xxiv. 13.

**Jē′shĕr** (*right*). Son of Caleb, 1 Chr. ii. 18.

**Jĕsh′ī-mŏn** (*waste*). Perhaps desert or plain, Num. xxi. 20; xxiii. 28.

**Jē-shĭsh′a-ī** (*ancient*). A Gadite, 1 Chr. v. 14.

**Jĕsh″ō-ha-ī′ah** (*bowed*). A Simeonite, 1 Chr. iv. 36.

**Jĕsh′u-ȧ** (*saviour*). (1) Joshua, Neh. viii. 17. (2) Priest of 9th course, Ez. ii. 36; Neh. vii. 39. Jeshuah, 1 Chr. xxiv. 11. (3) A Levite, 2 Chr. xxxi. 15. (4) High priest and returned captive, called also Joshua and Jesus, Zech. iii.; vi. 9-15. (5) Other Levites and returned captives, Ez. ii. 6. 40; viii. 33; Neh. iii. 19; viii. 7. (6) A town peopled by returned captives, Neh. xi. 26.

**Jĕsh′u-rŭn** (*blessed*). Symbolically, Israel, Deut. xxxii. 15; xxxiii. 5, 26. Jesurun, Isa. xliv. 2.

**Jē-sī′ah** (*loaned*) (1) One of David's warriors, 1 Chr. xii. 6. (2) Jeshaiah, 1 Chr. xxiii. 20.

**Jē-sim'i-el** (*set up*). A Simeonite, 1 Chr. iv. 36.

**Jĕs'sę** (*strong*). Father of David, 1 Sam. xvi. 1-18.

**Jĕs'su-ē**, 1 Esdr. v. 26. [Jeshua.] Jesu, viii. 63.

**Jes'u-ī** (*level*). Founder of Jesuites, Num. xxvi. 44. Isui, Gen. xlvi. 17. Ishuai, 1 Chr. vii. 30.

**Jē'şus** (*saviour*). (1) Greek form of Joshua, Jeshua, contraction of Jehoshua, Num. xiii. 16; Acts vii. 45. (2) Compiler of the Apocryphal book. Ecclesiasticus. (3) Justus, Paul's friend, Col. iv. 11.

**Jē'şŭs Christ**. Jesus the Saviour; Christ, or Messiah, the anointed. Jesus the Christ. Name given to the long promised prophet and king, Matt. xi. 3; Acts xix. 4. Only begotten of God. Born of Mary at Bethlehem, B. C. 5; reared at Nazareth, baptized at age of 30, Luke iii. 23. • Ministerial career, extending over Galilee, Judea, and Perea, began A. D. 27 and ended with the crucifixion, April 7, A. D. 30. Matthew, Mark, and Luke record his Galilean ministry; John his Judean ministry. The four gospels embrace Christ's biography.

**Jē'thẽr** (*who excels*). (1) Son of Gideon, Judg. viii. 20. (2) Father of Amasa, 1 Chr. ii. 17. (3) Others in 1 Chr. ii. 32; iv. 17; vii. 38.

**Jē'thĕth** (*nail*). A duke of Edom, Gen. xxxvi. 40.

**Jĕth'lah** (*high*). City of Dan, Josh. xix. 42.

**Je'thrō** (*his excellence*). Honorary title, Ex. iii. 1, of Reuel, Ex. ii. 18, or Raguel, Num. x. 29, the father-in-law of Moses, Ex. xviii.

**Jē'tŭr**, Gen. xxv. 15; 1 Chr. i. 31. [Ituræa.]

**Jē-ū'el** (*treasured*). A Judahite, 1 Chr. ix. 6.

**Jē'ŭsh** (*assembler*). (1) Son of Esau, Gen. xxxvi. 5, 14, 18. (2) A Benjamite, 1 Chr. vii. 10. (3) A Levite, 1 Chr. xxiii. 10, 11. (4) Son of Rehoboam, 2 Chr. xi. 18, 19.

**Jē'ŭz** (*assembler*). A Benjamite, 1 Chr. viii. 10.

**Jew**. Contraction of Judah. Man of Judea, 2 Kgs. xvi. 6; xxv. 25. After captivity, Hebrews in general, Ez. iv. 12; Dan. iii. 8-12. Antithesis of Christian in N. T., John; Rom. i. 16.

**Jew'ĕl** (*joy*). Ornament, Gen. xxiv. 22; Num. xxxi. 50.

**Jew'ĕss**. Hebrew woman, Acts xvi. 1.

**Jew'rȳ**. Judah, Judea, Jewish dynasty, Dan. v. 13.

**Jĕz''a-nī'ah** (*heard*). A Jewish captive, Jer. xl. 7-12. Jaazaniah, 2 Kgs. xxv. 23.

**Jĕz'ę-bĕl** (*chaste*). Idolatrous wife of Ahab, 1 Kgs. xvi. 29-33; xvii.-xxi.; 2 Kgs. ix. 30-37.

**Jē-zē'lus**, 1 Esdr. viii. 32-35. [Jahaziel.]

**Jē'zẽr** (*help*). A Naphtalite, Gen. xlvi. 24; founder of Jezerites, Num. xxvi. 49.

**Jē-zi'ah** (*sprinkled*). One with a foreign wife, Ez. x. 25.

**Jē'zī-el** (*sprinkled*). A Benjamite, 1 Chr. xii. 3.

**Jĕz-lī'ah** (*preserved*). A Benjamite, 1 Chr. viii. 18.

**Jĕz'o-ar** (*white*). A Judahite, 1 Chr. iv. 7.

**Jĕz''ra-hī'ah** (*brought forth*). A Levite singer, Neh. xii. 42.

**Jĕz're-el** (*seed of God*). (1) A Judahite, 1 Chr. iv. 3. (2) A city in plain of Jezreel. Ahab's royal residence, Josh. xix. 18; 1 Kgs. xxi. 1; 2 Kgs. ix. 30. (3) Valley of, stretches from Jezreel to Jordan. Greek form, Esdraelon. (4) Town of Judah, Josh. xv. 56; 1 Sam. xxvii. 3. (5) Son of Hosea, Hos. i. 4.

**Jĭb'sam** (*pleasant*). An Issacharite, 1 Chr. vii. 2.

**Jĭd'laph** (*weeping*). Son of Nahor, Gen. xxii. 22.

**Jĭm'nȧ** (*prosperity*). Son of Asher and founder of Jimnites, Num. xxvi. 44. Jimnah, Gen. xlvi. 17. Imnah, 1 Chr. vii. 30.

**Jĭph'tah**. Lowland city of Judah, Josh. xv. 43.

**Jĭph'thah-el** (*God opens*). Valley between Zebulun and Asher, Josh. xix. 14, 27.

**Jō'ăb** (*God his father*). (1) General-in-chief of David's army, 2 Sam. ii. 18-32; iii., xviii., xx., xxiv.; 1 Kgs. ii. (2) Son of Seraiah, 1 Chr. iv. 14. (3) One who returned, Ez. ii. 6.

**Jō'a-chaz**, 1 Esdr. i. 34. [Jehoahaz.]

**Jō'a-chim**, Bar. i. 3. [Jehoiakim.]

**Jō''a-dā'nus**. Son of Jeshua, 1 Esdr. ix. 19.

**Jō'ah** (*God's brother*). (1) Hezekiah's recorder, 2 Kgs. xviii. 18. (2) Josiah's recorder, 2 Chr. xxxiv. 8. (3) Levites, 1 Chr. vi. 21; xxvi. 4; 2 Chr. xxix. 12.

**Jō'ȧ-hăz** (*held of God*). Father of Joah, 2 Chr. xxxiv. 8.

**Jō-ăn'nȧ** (*God-given*). (1) An ancestor of Christ, Luke iii. 27. (2) Wife of Chusa, Luke viii. 3; xxiv. 10.

**Jō'ash** (*God-given*), 2 Kgs. xiii. 1. Jehoash, 2 Kgs. xii. 1. (1) Son of Ahaziah and his successor on throne of Judah, B. C. 878-839. Cruel and idolatrous. Murdered by his servants, 2 Kgs. xi., xii.; 2 Chr. xxiv. (2) Son and successor of Jehoahaz on throne of Israel, B. C. 840-825. Successful warrior, 2 Kgs. xiii. 9-25; xiv. 1-16; 2 Chr. xxv. 17-25. (3) Father of Gideon, Judg. vi. 11-31. (4) Son of Ahab, 2 Chr. xviii. 25. (5) A Judahite, 1 Chr. iv. 22. (6) One of David's heroes, 1 Chr. xii. 3. (7) Son of Becher, 1 Chr. vii. 8. (8) Officer of David, 1 Chr. xxvii. 28.

**Jō'a-thăm**, Matt. i. 9. [Jotham.]

**Jōb** (*persecuted*). (1) The pious and wealthy patriarch of Uz, whose poem constitutes the 18th O. T. book, and first of the poetical. It is a dramatic narrative of his life of vicissitude, the gist being, whether goodness can exist irrespective of reward. Poetry noted for its sublimity, pathos, and beauty. Authorship disputed. Oldest of sacred writings. (2) Son of Issachar, Gen. xlvi. 13. Jashub, 1 Chr. vii. 1.

**Jō'băb** (*desert*). (1) Son of Joktan, Gen. x. 29. (2) King of Edom, Gen. xxxvi. 33. (3) King of Madon, Josh. xi. 1. (4) Two Benjamites, 1 Chr. viii. 9, 18.

**Jŏch'e-bed** (*glorified*). Mother of Moses, Ex. vi. 20; Num. xxvi. 59.

**Jō'dȧ**, 1 Esdr. v. 58. [Judah.]

**Jō'ed** (*witnessed*). A Benjamite, Neh. xi. 7.

**Jō'el** (*Jehovah his God*). (1) Son of Pethuel and second of minor prophets. Probably of Judah and contemporary with Uzziah, B. C. 810-758. His book, 29th of O. T., depicts calamities, rises into exhortation, and foreshadows the Messiah. (2) Son of Samuel, 1 Sam. viii. 2. (3) Others in 1 Chr. iv. 35; v. 4, 8, 12; vi. 36; vii. 3; xi. 38; xv. 7; xxiii. 8; xxvii. 20; 2 Chr. xxix. 12; Ez. x. 43; Neh. xi. 9.

**Jō-ē'lah** (*helped*). A Benjamite chief, 1 Chr. xii. 7.

**Jō-ē'zẽr** (*aided*). A Benjamite, 1 Chr. xii. 6.

**Jŏg'be-hah** (*high*). City of Gad, E. of Jordan, Num. xxxii. 35.

**Jŏg'lī** (*exiled*). A prince of Dan, Num. xxxiv. 22.

**Jō'hȧ** (*given life*). (1) A Benjamite, 1 Chr. viii. 16. (2) One of David's guard, 1 Chr. xi. 45.

**Jō-hā'nan** (*God's mercy*). (1) A Judahite captain who escaped captivity, 2 Kgs. xxv. 23, and carried Jeremiah and other Jews into Egypt, Jer. xl.-xliii. (2) Others in 1 Chr. iii. 15, 24; vi. 9, 10; xii. 4, 12; 2 Chr. xxviii. 12; Ez. viii. 12; x. 6; Neh. vi. 18.

**Jŏhn** (*God's gift*). Johanan, contraction of Jehohanan. (1) Kinsman of the high priest, Acts iv. 6. (2) Hebrew name of Mark, Acts xii. 25; xiii. 5; xv. 37. (3) John the Baptist, son of Zacharias. Birth foretold, Luke i. Born about six months before Christ. Retired to wilderness. Emerged to preach and baptize. Baptized Jesus, Matt. iii. Imprisoned by Herod, Luke iii. 1-22. Beheaded, Matt. xiv. 1-12. (4) John, Apostle and Evangelist; son of Zebedee, Matt. iv. 21; a fisherman of Galilee, Luke v. 1-10; a favorite apostle, noted for zeal and firmness, John xiii. 23; xix. 26; xx. 2; xxi. 7. He remained at Jerusalem till about A. D. 65, when he went to Ephesus. Banished to Patmos, and released A. D. 96. His writings, doubtless done at Ephesus, are the fourth Gospel, giving Christ's ministry in Judea; his three epistles, and Revelation. (5) A frequent name among the Maccabees, 1 Macc.

**Joi'a-dȧ** (*favored*). A high priest, Neh. xii. 10, 11, 22; xiii. 28.

**Joi'a-kim** (*exalted*). A high priest, Neh. xii. 10.

**Joi'a-rib** (*defended*). Two who returned, Ez. viii. 16; Neh. xii. 6, 19.

**Jŏk'de-ăm** (*peopled*). City of Judah, Josh. xv. 56.

**Jō'kim** (*exalted*). A Judahite, 1 Chr. iv. 22.

**Jŏk'me-ăm** (*gathered*). Levitical city in Ephraim, 1 Chr. vi. 68.

**Jŏk'ne-ăm** (*gathered*). Levitical city in Zebulun, Josh. xxi. 34.

**Jŏk'shan** (*fowler*). Son of Abraham, Gen. xxv. 2, 3; 1 Chr. i. 32.

**Jŏk'tan** (*small*). Son of Eber and progenitor of Joktanite Arabs, Gen. x. 25; 1 Chr. i. 19.

**Jŏk'the-el** (*subdued*). (1) City in Judah, Josh. xv. 38. (2) An Edomite stronghold, 2 Kgs. xiv. 7.

**Jō'nȧ** (*dove*). Father of Apostle Peter, Matt. xvi. 17; John i. 42.

**Jŏn'a-dăb** (*God-impelled*). (1) David's subtle

nephew, 2 Sam. xiii. 3, 32-35. (2) Jer. xxxv. 6-19, Jehonadab.

**Jō'nah** (*dove*). Son of Amittai. Commissioned to denounce Nineveh. His book, 32d of O. T. and 5th of minor prophets, narrates his refusal, escape from drowning, final acceptance and successful ministry. Its lesson is God's providence over all nations.

**Jō'nan** (*grace*). Ancestor of Christ, Luke iii. 30.

**Jō'nas**. Greek form of Jonah, Matt. xii. 39-41; Luke xi. 30-32.

**Jŏn'a-than** (*God-given*). (1) A Levite, Judg. xvii. 7-13; xviii. (2) Eldest son of Saul, and friend of David, 1 Sam. xiii. 2, 3; xviii. 1-4; xix. 1-7; xx. Fell in battle of Gilboa. David's lament, 2 Sam. i. 17-27. (3) Others in 2 Sam. xv. 27, 36; xxi. 20, 21; xxiii. 32; 1 Chr. ii. 32, 33; xxvii. 32; Ez. viii. 6; x. 15; Neh. xii. 11, 14, 35; Jer. xxxvii. 15, 20; xl. 8.

**Jŏn'a-thas**, Tob. v. 13. [JONATHAN.]

**Jō'nath-ē''lem-rĕ-chō'kim** (*a dumb dove of distant places*). Title to, and probably melody of, Ps. lvi.

**Jŏp'pȧ** (*beauty*). Mediterranean seaport of Jerusalem; now Jaffa, 1 Kgs. v. 9; 2 Chr. ii. 16; Ez. iii. 7.

**Jŏp'pē**. For Joppa in Apoc.

**Jō'rah** (*rain*). His family returned, Ez. ii. 18.

**Jō'ra-ī** (*taught of God*). A Gadite chief, 1 Chr. v. 13.

**Jō'ram** (*exalted*). (1) Short form of Jehoram, king of Israel, 2 Kgs. viii. 16, etc.; and of Jehoram, king of Judah, 2 Kgs. viii. 21, etc.; Matt. i. 8. (2) Son of Toi, 2 Sam. viii. 10. (3) A Levite, 1 Chr. xxvi. 25.

**Jôr'dan** (*descender*). Chief river of Palestine, rising in the Anti-Libanus range, flowing southward, enlarging into Sea of Galilee, emptying into Dead Sea. A swift, narrow, yet fordable stream, with an entire course of about 200 miles, Gen. xiii. 10; Josh. ii. 7; Judg. iii. 28; 2 Sam. x. 17; Matt. iii. 13.

**Jō'rim** (*exalted*). An ancestor of Christ, Luke iii. 29.

**Jŏr'ko-ăm**. A person or place, 1 Chr. ii. 44.

**Jŏs'a-băd** (*dowered*). (1) One of David's warriors, 1 Chr. xii. 4. (2) Persons in 1 Esdr.

**Jŏs'a-phăt**, Matt. i. 8. [JEHOSHAPHAT.]

**Jō'se**. An ancestor of Christ, Luke iii. 29.

**Jŏs'e-dĕch**, Hag. i. 1. [JEHOZADAK.]

**Jō'seph** (*increase*). (1) Son of Jacob and Rachel, Gen. xxxvii. 3; sold into Egypt; promoted to high office by the Pharoah; rescued his family from famine; settled them in Goshen; died at advanced age; bones carried back to Shechem, Gen. xxxvii.-l. (2) An Issacharite, Num. xiii. 7. (3) Two who returned, Ez. x. 42; Neh. xii. 14. (4) Three of Christ's ancestors, Luke iii. 24, 26, 30. (5) Husband of Mary, and a carpenter at Nazareth, Matt. i. 19; xiii. 55; Luke iii. 23; John i. 45. (6) Of Arimathea, a member of the Sanhedrim, who acknowledged Christ, Matt. xxvii. 57-59; Mark xv. 43; Luke xxiii. 51. (7) The apostle Barsabas, substituted for Judas, Acts i. 23. (8) Frequent name in Apoc.

**Jō'ses** (*helped*). (1) One of Christ's brethren, Matt. xiii. 55; xxvii. 56; Mark vi. 3; xv. 40, 47. (2) Barnabas, Acts iv. 36.

**Jō'shah** (*dwelling*). A Simeonite chief, 1 Chr. iv. 34.

**Jŏsh'a-phăt** (*judged*). One of David's guard, 1 Chr. xi. 43.

**Jŏsh''a-vī'ah** (*dwelling*). One of David's guard, 1 Chr. xi. 46.

**Jŏsh-bĕk'a-shah** (*hard seat*). Head of 17th musical course, 1 Chr. xxv. 4, 24.

**Jŏsh'u-ȧ** (*saviour*). (1) Jehoshuah, 1 Chr. vii. 27. Oshea, Num. xiii. 8. Jesus, Acts vii. 45; Heb. iv. 8. Son of Nun, of tribe of Ephraim. The great warrior of the Israelites during the desert wanderings and conquest and apportionment of Canaan, Ex. xvii. 9-14; 1 Chr. vii. 27; Num. xiii. 8, 16; xxvii. 18-23. His book, 6th of O. T., contains the history of his conquests and governorship, B. C. 1451-1426. (2) A Beth-shemite, 1 Sam. vi. 14. (3) A governor of Jerusalem, 2 Kgs. xxiii. 8. (4) A high priest, Hag. i. 1, 14.

**Jō-sī'ah** (*God-healed*). (1) Son and successor of Amon on throne of Judah, B. C. 641-610. He abolished idolatry, propagated the newly discovered law, aided Assyria against Egypt, and fell in the celebrated battle of Esdraelon, 2 Kgs. xxii.-xxiii. 1-30; 2 Chr. xxxiv.-xxxv. (2) Son of Zephaniah, Zech. vi. 10.

**Jō-sī'as**. (1) Greek form of Josiah, 1 Esdr. i. 1; Matt. i. 10, 11. (2) 1 Esdr. viii. 33. [JESHAIAH.]

**Jŏs''ĭ-bī'ah** (*dwelling*). A chief of Simeon, 1 Chr. iv. 35.

**Jŏs''ĭ-phī'ah** (*increase*). His family returned, Ez. viii. 10.

**Jŏt**. The Greek i, iota. A little thing, Matt. v. 18.

**Jŏt'bah** (*goodness*). Residence of Haruz, 2 Kgs. xxi. 19.

**Jŏt'băth** (*goodness*). Jotbathah, Num. xxxiii. 33. An Israelite encampment, Deut. x. 7.

**Jō'tham** (*God is upright*). (1) Youngest son of Gideon and author of the bramble fable, Judg. ix. 5-21. (2) Son and successor of Uzziah, or Azariah, on throne of Judah, B. C. 758-741. Reign prosperous, 2 Kgs. xv. 5, 6, 32-36; 2 Chr. xxvii. (3) A Judahite, 1 Chr. ii. 47.

**Jour'ney** (*daily*). A day's journey, indefinite. Sabbath day's journey, 2000 paces, or ⅞ of a mile from the walls of a city, Deut. i. 2; Acts i. 12.

**Jŏz'a-băd** (*God-given*). (1) Two Manassite chiefs, 1 Chr. xii. 20. (2) Five Levites, 2 Chr. xxxi. 13, xxxv. 9; Ez. viii. 33; x. 22; Neh. viii. 7; xi. 16.

**Jŏz'a-chär** (*remembered*). Zabad, 2 Chr. xxiv. 26. One of Joash's murderers, 2 Kgs. xii. 21.

**Jŏz'a-dăk**, Ez. iii. 2, 8, etc.; Neh. xii. 26. [JEHOZADAK.]

**Jū'băl** (*music*). Son of Lamech, and inventor of harp and organ, Gen. iv. 19-21.

**Jū'bĭ-lēe** (*blast of trumpets*). Year of, celebrated every fiftieth year; ushered in by blowing of trumpets; land rested; alienated lands reverted; slaves freed; outer circle of seventh or sabbatical system, year, month, and day, Lev. xxv. 8-55.

**Jū'cal**, Jer. xxxviii. 1. [JEHUCAL.]

**Jū'dȧ** (*praised*). (1) Ancestors of Christ, Luke iii. 26, 30. (2) One of Christ's brethren, Mark vi. 3. (3) The patriarch Judah, Luke iii. 33. (4) The tribe of Judah, Heb. vii. 14; Rev. v. 5.

**Jū-dæ'ȧ, Jū-dē'ȧ** (*from Judah*). Vaguely, Joshua's conquest, Matt. xix. 1; Mark x. 1, or Canaanite land. Limitedly, the part occupied by returned captives; the "Jewry" of Dan. v. 13; the "province" of Ez. v. 8; Neh. xi. 3. "Land of Judea" in Apoc. A Roman province jointly with Syria, with a procurator, after A. D. 6.

**Jū'dah** (*praise*). (1) Fourth son of Jacob, Gen. xxix. 35; xxxvii. 26-28; xliii. 3-10; xliv. 14-34. His tribe the largest, Num. i. 26, 27. Allotted the southern section of Canaan, Josh. xv. 1-63. (2) Kingdom of, formed on disruption of Solomon's empire, out of Judah, Benjamin, Simeon, and part of Dan, with Jerusalem as capital, B. C. 975. Had 19 kings, and lasted for 389 years, till reduced by Nebuchadnezzar, B. C. 586. Outlived its rival, Israel, some 135 years. (3) City of Jerusalem, 2 Chr. xxv. 28. (4) A town in Naphtali, Josh. xix. 34. (5) Persons in Ez. iii. 9; x. 23; Neh. xi. 9.

**Jū'das**. Greek form of Judah. (1) Judah, Matt. i. 2, 3. (2) Iscariot, or of Kerioth. Betrayer of Christ, Matt. x. 4; Mark iii. 19; Luke vi. 16; John vi. 71; xii. 6; xiii. 29. (3) Man of Damascus, Acts ix. 11. (4) Barsabas, chief among the brethren, and prophet, Acts xv. 22, 32. (5) A Galilean apostate, Acts v. 37. (6) Frequent name in Apoc.

**Jūde**, Jude i. 1. Judas, brother of James the Less, Luke vi. 16; John xiv. 22; Acts i. 13; Matt. xiii. 55. Thaddæus, Lebbæus, Matt. x. 3; Mark iii. 18. An Apostle and author of the epistle which bears his name, 26th N. T. book. Written about A. D. 65. Place not known.

**Jŭdg'es**. Governors of Israel between Joshua and the kings. They were called of God, elective or usurpative. Qualification, martial or moral prowess. Rule arbitrary. Fifteen are recorded. Period, B. C. 1400-1091, about 310 years. Book of Judges, 7th of O. T., probably compiled by Samuel. Its history is that of a tumultuous period, completing Joshua's conquests and leading to legitimate kingly rule.

**Jŭdg'mĕnt Hall**. Pilate's residence in Jerusalem, John xviii. 28, 33; xix. 9. Prætorium or court, Acts xxiii. 35.

**Jū'dith** (*praised, Jewess*). (1) Wife of Esau, Gen. xxvi. 34. (2) Heroine of the 4th Apocryphal book.

**Jū'el**, Apoc. [JOEL.]

**Jū'li-ȧ** (*feminine of Julius*). A Christian woman at Rome, Rom. xvi. 15.

**Jū'li-us** (*soft-haired*). A Roman centurion, Acts xxvii. 1-3, 43.

**Jū'ni-ȧ** (*youth*). Roman friend of Paul, Rom. xvi. 7.

**Jū'nĭ-pĕr** (*young producer*). Not the evergreen, but the desert broom-shrub, 1 Kgs. xix. 4, 5; Job xxx. 4; Ps. cxx. 4.

**Jū'pĭ-tēr** (*father Jove*). Supreme god of Greeks and Romans, Acts xiv. 12; xix. 35.

**Jū'shăb=hē'sĕd** (*requited love*). Son of Zerubbabel, 1 Chr. iii. 20.

**Jŭs"tĭ-fĭ-cā'tion.** Pardon and acceptance of the just through faith, Rom. iii. 20-31; iv. 25.

**Jŭs'tus** (*just*). (1) Surname of Joseph, or Barsabas, Acts i. 23. (2) A Corinthian convert, Acts xviii. 7. (3) Surname of Jesus, a friend of Paul, Col. iv. 11.

**Jŭt'tah** (*extended*). A Levitical city in mountains of Judah; now Yutta, Josh. xv. 55; xxi. 16.

## K

**Kăb'ze-el** (*gathered*). A city of Judah, Josh. xv. 21. Jekabzeel, Neh. xi. 25.

**Kā'desh** (*holy*). Halting place of Israelites near borders of Canaan, and scene of Miriam's death, Num. xiii. 26; xx. 1. Kadesh-barnea, Deut. ii. 14; Josh. xv. 3. Enmishpat, Gen. xiv. 7.

**Kăd'mĭ-el** (*before God*). One who returned, Ez. iii. 9; Neh. ix. 4.

**Kăd'mŏn-ītes** (*eastern*). Ancient Canaanites, Gen. xv. 19.

**Kăl'la-ī** (*runner*). A priest, Neh. xii. 20.

**Kā'nah** (*reedy*). (1) A boundary of Asher, Josh. xix. 28. (2) Boundary stream between Ephraim and Manasseh, Josh. xvi. 8; xvii. 9.

**Kâ-rē'ah** (*bald*). Father of Johanan, Jer. xl. 8-16.

**Kär'ka-ȧ** (*floor*). A southern boundary of Judah, Josh. xv. 3.

**Kär'kôr** (*foundation*). Scene of Gideon's victory, Judg. viii. 10.

**Kär'tah** (*city*). Levitical city in Zebulun, Josh. xxi. 34.

**Kär'tan,** Josh. xxi. 32. [KIRJATHAIM.]

**Kăt'tath** (*small*). Town of Zebulun, Josh. xix. 15.

**Kē'där** (*dark*). Son of Ishmael and founder of Arabic tribe, Gen. xxv. 13; Isa. xxi. 13-17; Ezek. xxvii. 21.

**Ked'e-mah** (*eastward*). Son of Ishmael, Gen. xxv. 15; 1 Chr. i. 31.

**Kĕd'e-mŏth** (*eastern*). Levitical town of Reuben, Josh. xiii. 18; xxi. 37; 1 Chr. vi. 79.

**Kē'desh** (*sacred*). (1) Josh. xv. 23. [KADESH.] (2) Levitical city in Issachar, Josh. xii. 22; 1 Chr. vi. 72. (3) City of refuge in Naphtali, Josh. xix. 37; Judg. iv. 6; 2 Kgs. xv. 29. Now Kades.

**Kē'dron.** [KIDRON.]

**Kê-hĕl'a-thah** (*assembly*). A desert encampment, Num. xxxiii. 22, 23.

**Kēī'lah** (*fortress*). (1) Lowland town of Judah, Josh. xv. 44; 1 Sam. xxiii. 1-13; Neh. iii. 17, 18. (2) Person or place, 1 Chr. iv. 19.

**Kê-lā'ĭah,** Ez. x. 23. [KELITA.]

**Kĕl'ĭ-tȧ** (*dwarf*). Assistant of Ezra, Neh. viii. 7.

**Kê-mū'el** (*helper*). (1) Son of Nahor, Gen. xxii. 21. (2) A prince of Ephraim, Num. xxxiv. 24. (3) A Levite, 1 Chr. xxvii. 17.

**Kē'nan,** 1 Chr. i. 2. [CAINAN.]

**Kē'nath** (*possession*). A city or section of Gilead, Num. xxxii. 42.

**Kē'năz** (*hunting*). (1) A duke of Edom, Gen. xxxvi. 15, and founder of Kenezites, Josh. xiv. 14. (2) Father of Othniel, Josh. xv. 17. (3) Grandson of Caleb, 1 Chr. iv. 15.

**Kĕn'ez-īte** (*hunter*). Kenizzite, Gen. xv. 19. An ancient Edomite tribe, Num. xxxii. 12; Josh. xiv. 6, 14.

**Kĕn'ītes** (*smiths*). A Midianite tribe allied to Israelites, Gen. xv. 19; Num. xxiv. 21, 22; Judg. iv. 11.

**Kĕr'en=hăp'puch** (*horn of beauty*). Third daughter of Job, Job xlii. 14.

**Kē'rĭ-ŏth** (*cities*). (1) A town of Judah, Josh. xv. 25. (2) A city of Moab, Jer. xlviii. 24.

**Kē'ros** (*crooked*). His children returned, Ez. ii. 44.

**Kĕt'tle** (*deep vessel*). Used for cooking and sacrifices, 1 Sam. ii. 14. Basket, Jer. xxiv. 2; caldron, 2 Chr. xxxv. 13; pot, Job xli. 20.

**Kê-tū'rah** (*incense*). A wife of Abraham, Gen. xxv. 1; 1 Chr. i. 32.

**Kê-zī'ȧ** (*cassia*). Job's second daughter, Job xlii. 14.

**Kē'zĭz** (*end*). A town of Benjamin, Josh. xviii. 21.

**Kĭb'roth=hăt-tā'a-vah** (*graves of lust*). A desert encampment of the Israelites, Num. xi. 31-35.

**Kĭb'za-ĭm** (*heaps*). Levitical city in Ephraim, Josh. xxi. 22. Jokmeam, 1 Chr. vi 68.

**Kĭd.** Young goat. An offering, Num. vii. 12-82. A favorite meat, Gen. xxxviii. 17; 1 Sam. xvi. 20.

**Kĭd'ron** (*turbid*). The brook or ravine between Jerusalem and Olivet, 2 Sam. xv. 23; 2 Kgs. xxiii. 6. Cedron, John xviii. 1.

**Kī'nah** (*dirge*). City of south Judah, Josh. xv. 22.

**Kīne.** Plural of cow, Gen. xli. 17-21.

**King** (*tribe*). Title of Hebrew rulers from Saul to Zedekiah, B. C. 1095-588. Other rulers, Gen. xxxvi. 31; Ex. iii. 19; Num. xxxi. 8. Supreme ruler, 1 Tim. i. 17; vi. 15.

**Kings.** Eleventh and twelfth O. T. books. Originally one. Compilation credited to Ezra or Jeremiah. 1 Kings gives history of Hebrew kingdoms from Solomon, B. C. 1015, to Jehoshaphat, B. C. 890. 2 Kings completes the history, B. C. 890-588.

**Kīr** (*fortress*). An unlocated eastern country, 2 Kgs. xvi. 9; Am. ix. 7.

**Kīr=hăr'a-sĕth** (*brick fortress*). A stronghold of Moab, 2 Kgs. iii. 25. Kirhareseth, Isa. xvi. 7. Kirharesh, Isa. xvi. 11. Kirheres, Jer. xlviii. 31, 36. Kir of Moab, Isa. xv. 1.

**Kĭr"ĭ-a-thā'ĭm,** Jer. xlviii. 1, 23; Ezek. xxv. 9. [KIRJATHAIM.]

**Kĭr"ĭ-ath-ĭ-ā'rĭ-us,** 1 Esdr. v. 19. [KIRJATH-JEARIM.]

**Kĭr'ĭ-ŏth,** Am. ii. 2. [KERIOTH.]

**Kĭr'jath** (*city*). City in Benjamin, Josh. xviii. 28.

**Kĭr"jath-ā'ĭm** (*double city*). (1) A Moabite town, Num. xxxii. 37. (2) Levitical town in Naphtali, Josh. xiii. 19; 1 Chr. vi. 76.

**Kĭr'jath=är'bȧ** (*city of Arba*). Old name of Hebron, Gen. xxiii. 2; Josh. xiv. 15.

**Kĭr'jath=ā'rĭm,** Ez. ii. 25. [KIRJATH-JEARIM.]

**Kĭr'jath=bā'al,** Josh. xv. 60; xviii. 14. [KIRJATH-JEARIM.]

**Kĭr'jath=hū'zoth** (*city of streets*). City in Moab, Num. xxii. 39.

**Kĭr'jath=jē'a-rĭm** (*city of woods*). A Gibeonite city which fell to Judah, Josh. ix. 17; Judg. xviii. 12. Baalah, Josh. xv. 9. Kirjath-baal, xviii. 14.

**Kĭr'jath=săn'nah** (*palm city*). [DEBIR.]

**Kĭr'jath=sē'phĕr** (*city of books*). [DEBIR.]

**Kĭr of Mō'ab.** [KIR-HARASETH.]

**Kĭsh** (*bow*). (1) Father of Saul, 1 Sam. x. 21. (2) A Benjamite, 1 Chr. viii. 30. (3) A Levite, 1 Chr. xxiii. 21. (4) A Levite, 2 Chr. xxix. 12. (5) Ancestor of Mordecai, Esth. ii. 5.

**Kĭsh'ī** (*bow*). A Levite, 1 Chr. vi. 44.

**Kĭsh'ĭ-ŏn** (*hardness*). Levitical city in Issachar, Josh. xix. 20.

**Kī'shŏn** (*crooked*). (1) Josh. xxi. 28. [KISHION.] (2) The brook or wady which drains the valley of Esdraelon, Judg. iv. 7-13; v. 21; 1 Kgs. xviii. 40. Kison, Ps. lxxxiii. 9.

**Kī'son,** Ps. lxxxiii. 9. [KISHON.]

**Kĭss.** Form of salutation, Gen. xxix. 13; token of allegiance, 1 Sam. x. 1; pledge of Christian brotherhood, Rom. xvi. 16; 1 Pet. v. 14.

**Kīte** (*quick of wing*). An unclean bird of the hawk species, Lev. xi. 14; Deut. xiv. 13. Vulture, Job xxviii. 7.

**Kĭth'lish** (*wall*). Lowland town in Judah, Josh. xv. 40.

**Kĭt'rŏn** (*knotty*). Town in Zebulun, Judg. i. 30.

**Kĭt'tĭm,** Gen. x. 4; 1 Chr. i. 7. [CHITTIM.]

**Knēad'ing=troughs.** Were bowls, or leather surfaces, Gen. xviii. 6; Ex. xii. 34.

**Knīfe** (*waster*). Primitively of stone or bone; later of metal. Little used at meals. For killing and cutting, Lev. viii. 20; sharpening pens, Jer. xxxvi. 23; pruning, Isa. xviii. 5; lancing, 1 Kgs. xviii. 28.

**Knŏp** (*knob*). Ornamental knobs, or reliefs, Ex. xxv. 31-36; 1 Kgs. vi. 18.

**Kō'ȧ** (*male camel*). An eastern prince, Ezek. xxiii. 23.

**Kō'hath** (*assembly*). Second son of Levi, and head of the house of Kohathite Levites, Gen. xlvi. 11; Ex. vi. 16, 18; Num. iii. 27; xxvi. 57; Josh. xxi. 4-42.

**Kŏl"a-ī'ah** (*God's voice*). (1) A Benjamite, Neh. xi. 7. (2) Father of the false prophet Ahab, Jer. xxix. 21.

**Kō'rah** (*baldness*). (1) Dukes of Edom, Gen. xxxvi. 5–18. (2) Son of Hebron, 1 Chr. ii. 43. (3) Leader of the rebellion against Moses, Num. xvi.; xxvi. 9-11.

**Kō'rah-ites**. Descendants of Korah, 1 Chr. ix. 19. Korhites, 2 Chr. xx. 19. Korathites, Num. xxvi. 58.

**Kō'rē** (*quail*). (1) A Korahite, 1 Chr. ix. 19. (2) Korhites, 1 Chr. xxvi. 1-19. (3) A Levite, 2 Chr. xxxi. 14.

**Kŏz** (*thorn*). (1) A Judahite, 1 Chr. iv. 8. [Coz.] (2) A priest, 1 Chr. xxiv. 10. [Hakkoz.] (3) Returned captives, Ez. ii. 61; Neh. iii. 4, 21.

**Kŭsh-ā'iah**, 1 Chr. xv. 17. [Kishi.]

# L

**Lā'a-dah** (*order*). A Judahite, 1 Chr. iv. 21.

**Lā'a-dăn** (*ordered*). (1) An Ephraimite, 1 Chr. vii. 26. (2) Son of Gershon, 1 Chr. xxiii. 7-9; xxvi. 21. Libni, elsewhere.

**Lā'ban** (*white*). (1) Father-in-law of Jacob, Gen. xxiv.-xxx. (2) A landmark, Deut. i. 1.

**Lăb'a-nȧ**, 1 Esdr. v. 29. [Lebana.]

**Lăç''e-dē-mō'nĭ-anș**. Inhabitants of Lacedemon. Spartans, 1 Macc. xii. 2-21.

**Lā'chish** (*impregnable*). An Amorite city in southern Judah, Josh. x.; 2 Kgs. xviii. 17; xix. 8; 2 Chr. xi. 9; Neh. xi. 30.

**La-cū'nus**. A returned captive, 1 Esdr. ix. 31.

**Lā'dan**, 1 Esdr. v. 37. [Delaiah.]

**Lā'el** (*of God*). A Gershonite, Num. iii. 24.

**Lā'hăd** (*oppression*). A Judahite, 1 Chr. iv. 2.

**Lȧ-hăi'=roi** (*well of the living God*). Well of Hagar's relief, Gen. xxiv. 62; xxv. 11.

**Lăh'mam** (*bread*). Lowland town of Judah, Josh. xv. 40.

**Lăh'mī** (*warrior*). Brother of Goliath, 1 Chr. xx. 5.

**Lā'ish** (*lion*). (1) A northern Danite city, Judg. xviii. 7-29; Isa. x. 30. (2) Father of Phaltiel, 1 Sam. xxv. 44; 2 Sam. iii. 15. Leshem, Josh. xix. 47.

**Lā'kŭm** (*fortress*). A border of Naphtali, Josh. xix. 33.

**Lămb**. Young of sheep or goat. Favorite sacrifices, Ex. xxix. 38-41; Num. xxviii. 9-29.

**Lā'mech** (*strong*). (1) Father of Noah, Gen. v. 28-32. (2) Father of Jubal, inventor of the harp and organ, Gen. iv. 18-26.

**Lăm''ĕn-tā'tionș** (*weepings*). Twenty-fifth O. T. book. An elegiac poem by Jeremiah, on the destruction of Jerusalem.

**Lămp** (*shine*). The temple candlestick, Ex. xxv. 31-40; 1 Kgs. vii. 49. Torches, Judg. vii. 16. Oriental lamps of many shapes and ornamental. Fed with oil, tallow, wax, etc., Matt. xxv. 1.

**Lăn'çet** (*little lance*). Light spear, 1 Kgs. xviii. 28.

**Lănd'märks**. Were trees, stones, towns, mountains, streams, etc. Removal forbidden, Deut. xix. 14; Prov. xxii. 28.

**Lăn'guāge** (*tongue*). Originally one, Gen. xi. 1. Diversified at Babel, Gen. xi. 7-9.

**Lăn'tĕrn** (*shining*). Covered candle or lamp, John xviii. 3.

**Lȧ-ŏd''ĭ-çē'ȧ** (*just people*). Ancient Diospolis; modern Eski-hissar. A city of Phrygia, and seat of an early Christian church, Col. ii. 1; iv. 15; Rev. i. 11; iii. 14-22.

**Lăp'i-dŏth** (*lamps*). Husband of Deborah, Judg. iv. 4.

**Lăp'wing**. An unclean bird, thought to be the beautiful migratory hoopoe, Lev. xi. 19.

**Lȧ-sē'ȧ**. City in Crete, Acts xxvii. 8.

**Lā'shȧ** (*cleft*). A Canaanite border, Gen. x. 19.

**Lȧ-shăr'on** (*plain*). A Canaanite town, Josh. xii. 18.

**Lăs'thĕ-nēș**. A Cretan, 1 Macc. xi. 31.

**Lătch'et** (*lace*). Sandal lacings, or fastenings, Gen. xiv. 23; Mark i. 7.

**Lăt'in**. Language of Latium, *i. e.* the Romans, Luke xxiii. 38; John xix. 20.

**Lăt'tiçe** (*lath*). Open work of wood or metal; also window, blind, or screen, Judg. v. 28; 2 Kgs. i. 2; Prov. vii. 6.

**Lā'ver** (*wash*). Brazen vessel holding water for priestly washings—hands, feet, and the sacrifices, Ex. xxx. 18-21; xxxviii. 8; 1 Kgs. vii. 38-40; 2 Chr. iv. 6.

**Lạw** (*rule*). In Scripture, reference is nearly always to the Hebrew civil, moral, and ceremonial law, Matt. v. 17; John i. 17; Acts xxv. 8.

**Lạw'yĕr**. Scribe or divine who expounded the Mosaic law in school or synagogue, Matt. xxii. 35; Luke x. 25.

**Lăz'a-rus** (*whom God helps*). Abbreviation of Eleazar. (1) Brother of Mary and Martha, John xi. 1; xii. 1-11. (2) Type of poverty and distress in the parable, Luke xvi. 19-31.

**Lĕad**. Early known, imported and used by Hebrews, Ex. xv. 10; Num. xxxi. 22; Job xix. 24; Ezek. xxvii. 12.

**Lēaf**. Of trees, Gen. viii. 11; Matt. xxi. 19; double doors, 1 Kgs. vi. 34; of books, Jer. xxxvi. 23; prosperity, Jer. xvii. 8; decay, Job xiii. 25.

**Lē'ah** (*weary*). Jacob's wife through deceit of her father, Laban, Gen. xxix., xxx., xlix. 31.

**Lēas'ing** (*lying*). Falsehood, Ps. iv. 2; v. 6.

**Lĕath'er**. Used by Hebrews, 2 Kgs. i. 8; Matt. iii. 4.

**Lĕav'en** (*raise*). Old fermented dough used to lighten new dough, Matt. xiii. 33. Passover bread unleavened, Ex. xii. 15-17. Corrupt doctrines, Matt. xvi. 6; evil passions, 1 Cor. v. 7, 8.

**Lĕb'a-nȧ** (*white*). His children returned, Neh. vii. 48. Lebanah, Ez. ii. 45.

**Lĕb'a-non** (*white*). Two mountain ranges running N. E., between which was Cœlo-Syria. The western is Libanus, or Lebanon proper. The eastern is Anti-Libanus, and skirted Palestine on the north, Deut. i. 7; Josh. i. 4. Many scripture allusions, Isa. x. 34; Jer. xxii. 23.

**Lĕb'a-ŏth** (*lionesses*). Boundary town of southern Judah, Josh. xv. 32.

**Lĕb-bæ'us** (*brave*). Thaddæus, the apostle Jude, Matt. x. 3, Mark iii. 18.

**Lē-bō'nah** (*incense*). Place north of Bethel, Judg. xxi. 19.

**Lē'cah** (*walking*). Person or place, 1 Chr. iv. 21.

**Lēech**. [Horse-leech.]

**Lēek**. Closely allied to the onion, Num. xi. 5.

**Lēes** (*dregs*). Sediment of liquor. Settled, pure wine, Isa. xxv. 6; sloth, Jer. xlviii. 11; extreme suffering, Ps. lxxv. 8.

**Lē'gion** (*gathered*). Division of Roman army; when full, 6200 men and 730 horse. N. T. use indefinite, Matt. xxvi. 53; Mark v. 9.

**Lē'hȧ-bĭm** (*flame*). A Mizraite tribe; Libyans, Gen. x. 13. Lubim, 2 Chr. xii. 3.

**Lē'hī** (*jawbone*). Where Samson slew the Philistines, Judg. xv. 9, 19.

**Lĕm'u-el** (*dedicated*). The unknown king in Prov. xxxi. 1-9.

**Lĕn'tĭl** (*little lens*). A podded food plant, like the pea or bean, Gen. xxv. 34; 2 Sam. xvii. 28.

**Lĕop'ard** (*lion-panther*). This fierce, spotted beast of the cat species once found in Jordan jungles, Jer. xiii. 23; Dan. vii. 6; S. of Sol. iv. 8.

**Lĕp'ĕr** (*peeled*). Who has leprosy; a loathsome, incurable skin disease, common in East, Ex. iv. 6; treatment of, Lev. xiv. 3-32; Luke xvii. 12-19.

**Lē'shem**, Josh. xix. 47. [Laish.]

**Lĕt'tus**, 1 Esdr. viii. 29. [Hattush.]

**Lē-tū'shim** (*hammered*). Son of Dedan, and his Arabian tribe, Gen. xxv. 3.

**Lē-ŭm'mim** (*nations*). Son of Dedan, and his Arabian tribe, Gen. xxv. 3.

**Lē'vī** (*joined*). (1) Third son of Jacob, Gen. xxix. 34; avenged Dinah's wrong, xxxiv. 25-31; cursed, xlix. 5-7; went to Egypt, Ex. vi. 16; blessed, Ex. xxxii. 25-28. (2) Two of Christ's ancestors, Luke iii. 24, 29. (3) Original name of Matthew, Mark ii. 14; Luke v. 27, 29; compare Matt. ix. 9.

**Lē-vī'a-than** (*aquatic monster*). The crocodile is described in Job xli.; and probably meant in Ps. lxxiv. 14; civ. 26.

**Lē'vītes**. Descendants of Levi, Ex. vi. 16-25; Lev. xxv. 32, etc.; Num. xxxv. 2-8; Josh. xxi. 3. In above, the tribe is meant. But Levites came to mean the priestly branch, *i. e.*, descendants of Aaron, Josh. iii. 3; 1 Kgs. viii. 4; Ez. ii. 70; John i. 19. Three Levitical lines, Kohathite, Gershonite, Merarite, Num. iii. 17. Assigned 48 cities among the other tribes, Num. xxxv.

**Lē-vĭt'i-cus** (*for Levites*). Third book of Bible

and Pentateuch, containing the ceremonial law for guidance of Levites. Authorship ascribed to Moses and Aaron.

**Lib'ă-nus.** Greek form of Lebanon. 1 Esdr. iv. 48.

**Lib'ĕr-tines** (*free*). Emancipated Jewish slaves; freedmen, Acts vi. 9.

**Lib'nah** (*white*). (1) An Israelite encampment, Num. xxxiii. 20, 21. (2) Levitical city in Judah, Josh. x. 29-31; 2 Kgs. xix. 8-35; 1 Chr. vi. 57.

**Lib'ni** (*whiteness*). (1) A Levite, founder of Libnites, Ex. vi. 17; Num. iii. 18-21. (2) Probably the above, 1 Chr. vi. 29.

**Lib'y-ȧ,** Ezek. xxx. 5; Acts ii. 10. The African continent west of Egypt and contiguous to Mediterranean. *See* Lubim and Lehabim.

**Liçe** (*destroyers*). Constituted the third Egyptian plague, Ex. viii. 16-18; Ps. cv. 31.

**Lieū-tĕn'ants** (*place-holders*). Satraps or viceroys, Ez. viii. 36. Princes, Dan. iii. 2; vi. 1.

**Life.** Natural, Gen. iii. 17; spiritual, Rom. viii. 6; eternal, John iii. 36; Rom. vi. 23.

**Light.** First gush of creation, Gen. i. 3. Frequent source of imagery, Matt. iv. 16; Luke ii. 32; John i. 7-9.

**Lign-aloes** (*wood-aloes*). [Aloes.]

**Lig'ūre** (*lynx urine*). Possibly amber. First stone in third row of high priest's breastplate, Ex. xxviii. 19; xxxix. 12.

**Lik'hi** (*learned*). A Manassite, 1 Chr. vii. 19.

**Lil'y** (*pale*). Source of rich imagery, 1 Kgs. vii. 19; S. of Sol. ii. 1, 2; v. 13; Matt. vi. 28; Luke xii. 27.

**Lime** (*glue*). Was known and used for plaster and cement work, Deut. xxvii. 2; Isa. xxxiii. 12; Am. ii. 1.

**Lin'en** (*flax*). Used for stately robes, Gen. xli. 42; priestly vestments, Ex. xxviii. 42; Lev. vi. 10; temple veil, 2 Chr. iii. 14; choral gowns, 2 Chr. v. 12, and ordinary dress. Symbol of purity, Rev. xv. 6; of luxury, Luke xvi. 19.

**Lin'tel** (*boundary*). Support over window or door, Ex. xii. 22; 1 Kgs. vi. 31.

**Li'nus** (*net*). Roman friend of Paul, 2 Tim. iv. 21.

**Li'on** (*seeing*). Once found in Palestine, Judg. xiv. 5, 6; 1 Sam. xvii. 34-36; 2 Sam. xxiii. 20. Symbol of strength, Gen. xlix. 9.

**Lit'tĕr** (*bed*). Covered couch or chair, carried by men or animals, Isa. lxvi. 20. "Wagons," Num. vii. 3.

**Liz'ărd** (*muscular*). Abundant in Palestine. Unclean, Lev. xi. 30.

**Lō-ăm'mi** (*not my people*). Figurative name of Hosea's son, Hos. i. 9.

**Lōans.** Allowed by Hebrews, but all debts cancelled in Sabbatical year, Deut. xv. 1-11. Usury not allowed, Ex. xxii. 25; Lev. xxv. 36; Deut. xv. 3-10.

**Lŏck** (*bar*). A bar of wood or metal for outer, and bolt for inner, doors, 1 Kgs. iv. 13; Judg. iii. 24.

**Lō'cust** (*leaping*). Confused original, supposably embracing the destructive insects, — locust, grasshopper, caterpillar, palmer-worm, etc. They constituted the eighth Egyptian plague, Ex. x. 1-15; Joel ii. 3-10.

**Lŏd,** 1 Chr. viii. 12; Ez. ii. 33. [Lydda.]

**Lō-dē'bär** (*barren*). A place east of Jordan, 2 Sam. ix. 4; xvii. 27.

**Lŏg.** Hebrew liquid measure; about five sixths of a pint, Lev. xiv. 10-24.

**Lō'is** (*pleasing*). Timothy's grandmother, 2 Tim. i. 5.

**Looking-glass.** Polished metal plate, Ex xxxviii. 8; Job xxxvii. 18.

**Lôrd** (*loaf-guardian*). Jehovah, LORD, Gen. xv. 4; Ps. vii., c. Adonai, Lord, Christ, The Lord, Our Lord. Supreme ruler, and not the Saxon dignitary.

**Lôrd's Dāy.** First day of the week; resurrection day of Christ, Rev. i. 10. Sunday, after A. D. 321.

**Lôrd's Sŭp'per.** Substitute for the O. T. Paschal feast. Instituted by Christ the night before the crucifixion, as a reminder of his covenant with mankind, Matt. xxvi. 19; Mark xiv. 16; Luke xxii. 13. "Breaking of bread," Acts ii. 42; xx. 7. "Communion," 1 Cor. x. 16. "Lord's Supper," only in 1 Cor. xi. 20.

**Lō-ru'ha-mah** (*unpitied*). Hosea's daughter, Hos. i. 6.

**Lŏt** (*veil*). Abraham's nephew, Gen. xi. 27-31. Settled in Jordan valley, Gen. xiii. 1-13. Escaped to mountains, Gen. xix. Progenitor of Moabites and Ammonites.

**Lō'tan** (*hidden*). A Horite duke, Gen. xxxvi. 20-29.

**Lŏth''a-sū'bus.** 1 Esdr. ix. 44. [Hashum.]

**Lŏts, Feast of.** [Purim.]

**Lŏts.** Casting or drawing of, a usual way of settling questions. Possibly marked pebbles were used, in a bag or box. Canaan was allotted to the tribes of Israel, Num. xxvi. 55; Josh. xv., xix. Scapegoat so chosen, Lev. xvi. 8; priest's courses, 1 Chr. xxiv., xxv.; property divided, Matt. xxvii. 35.

**Lŏve Fēasts.** Feasts of offerings, after the community of goods ceased, Jude 12; 2 Peter ii. 13. Forbidden by Council of Laodicea, A. D. 320.

**Lu-bim,** 2 Chr. xii. 3; xvi. 8. [Libya.]

**Lu'cas.** Luke the evangelist, Phile. 24.

**Lu'çi-fĕr** (*light-giver*). Types the king of Babylon, Isa. xiv. 12. Popularly, Satan.

**Lu'çius** (*morning born*). (1) Paul's kinsman, Rom. xvi. 21. (2) A Cyrenean convert and teacher, Acts xiii. 1.

**Lŭd** (*strife*). Son of Shem, Gen. x. 22.

**Lu'dim** (*strife*). A Mizraite tribe, Gen. x. 13; Isa. lxvi. 19; Ezek. xxvii. 10.

**Lu'hith** (*board-made*). Place in Moab, Isa. xv. 5; Jer. xlviii. 5.

**Luke** (*luminous*). Evangelist and physician, Col. iv. 14; 2 Tim. iv. 11. Author of third gospel and of Acts of the Apostles.

**Lu'nă-tics** (*moon-struck*). Epileptics are probably meant, Matt. iv. 24; xvii. 15.

**Lŭz** (*almond*). Site of Bethel, Gen. xxviii. 19; Josh. xvi. 2; Judg. i. 23.

**Lyc''a-ō'ni-ȧ** (*wolf-land*). Wild district of Asia Minor, containing towns of Derbe, Lystra, and Iconium, Acts xiv. 6-11. Twice visited by Paul.

**Ly'çiȧ.** A southwestern district of Asia Minor, with Myra and Patara as cities, Acts xxi. 2; xxvii. 5.

**Lyd'dȧ** (*strife*). Hebrew Lud or Lod. Now Lidd or Ludd. In Sharon plain, 9 miles east of Joppa, Acts ix. 32.

**Lyd'i-ȧ** (*Lydus land*). (1) A province of Asia Minor, on Mediterranean. Cities, Sardis, Thyatira, Philadelphia, 1 Macc. viii. 8. (2) Woman convert of Thyatira, Acts xvi. 14.

**Ly-să'ni-as** (*that drives away sorrow*). Tetrarch of Abilene, Luke iii. 1.

**Lys'ias** (*dissolving*). Claudius Lysias, captain of the band that rescued Paul, Acts xxi.-xxiv. 1-9. (2) Governor of southern Syria, 1 Macc. iii. 32.

**Ly-sim'a-chus.** (1) Translator of Esther, Esth. xi. 1. (2) Brother of Menelaus, 2 Macc. iv. 29-42.

**Lys'trȧ** (*dissolving*). City of Lycaonia, where Paul was honored, Acts xiv. 6-18; and stoned, 19-21.

# M

**Mā'a-cah** (*oppression*). (1) A wife of David, 2 Sam. iii. 3. Maachah, 1 Chr. iii. 2. (2) A petty kingdom, N. E. of Palestine, 2 Sam. x. 6-8. Syria-maachah, 1 Chr. xix. 6, 7.

**Mā'a-chah** (*oppression*). (1) Daughter of Nahor, Gen. xxii. 24. (2) A Gathite, 1 Kgs. ii. 39. (3) Wife of Rehoboam, 1 Kgs. xv. 2. (4) Concubine of Caleb, 1 Chr. ii. 48. (5) A Benjamitess, 1 Chr. vii. 15; 16. (6) Wife of Jehiel, 1 Chr. viii. 29. (7) Father of Hanan, 1 Chr. xi. 43. (8) A Simeonite, 1 Chr. xxvii. 16.

**Mȧ-ăch'a-thī.** Maachathites. People of Maacah, Deut. iii. 14; Josh. xii. 5.

**Mȧ-ăd'āi** (*ornament*). Son of Bani, Ez. x. 34.

**Mā''a-dī'ah.** A returned priest, Neh. xii. 5. Moadiah, vs. 17.

**Mȧ-ā'i** (*merciful*). A Levite, Neh. xii. 36.

**Mȧ-ăl'eh-ă-crăb'bim,** Josh. xv. 3. Scorpion pass. [Akrabbim.]

**Mȧ-ā'ni,** 1 Esdr. ix. 34. [Baana.]

**Mā'a-răth** (*open*). Town in Judah, Josh. xv. 59.

**Mā''a-sē'iah** (*work of God*). (1) Returned Levites and captive families, Ez. x. 18, 21, 22, 30; Neh. iii. 23; viii. 4, 7; x. 25; xi. 5, 7; xii. 41, 42. (2) Father of Zephaniah, Jer. xxi. 1. (3) Father of Zedekiah, Jer. xxix. 21. (4) A porter, 1 Chr. xv. 18-20. (5) Son of Adaiah, 2 Chr. xxiii. 1. (6) Others in 2 Chr. xxvi. 11; xxviii. 7; xxxiv. 8; Jer. xxxv. 4.

**Mā'ath** (*small*). An ancestor of Christ, Luke iii. 26.

**Mā'ăz** (*wrath*). Son of Ram, 1 Chr. ii. 27.

**Mā''a-zī'ah** (*consolation*). Two priests, 1 Chr. xxiv. 18; Neh. x. 8.

**Măb'dā-ī**, 1 Esdr. ix. 34. [BENAIAH.]

**Măc'a-lon**, 1 Esdr. v. 21. [MICHMASH.]

**Măc'că-bēeş** (*hammer*). The Asmonean princes who upheld the cause of Jewish independence, B. C. 166–40. The two Apocryphal books of Maccabees contain their history.

**Măç''e-dō'nĭ-à** (*extended*). The ancient empire north of Greece proper, whose greatest kings were Philip and Alexander the Great. Often visited by Paul, who made here his first European converts, Acts xvi. 9–12; xvii. 1–15; xx. 1–6.

**Măch'ba-nāi** (*stout*). A Gadite chief, 1 Chr. xii. 13.

**Măch'be-nah** (*cloak*). Person or place, 1 Chr. ii. 49.

**Mā'chī** (*decrease*). Father of the Gadite spy, Num. xiii. 15.

**Mā'chĭr** (*sold*). (1) Eldest son of Manasseh, Num. xxxii. 39; Josh. xvii. 1. (2) Son of Ammiel, 2 Sam. ix. 4; xvii. 27.

**Mā'chĭr-ītes.** Descendants of Machir, Num. xxvi. 29.

**Măch'mas**, 1 Macc. ix. 73. [MICHMASH.]

**Măch''nă-dē'bāi** (*liberal*). Son of Bani, Ez. x. 40.

**Măch-pē'lah** (*double*). Abraham's burial cave at Hebron, Gen. xxiii. 17–19; xxv. 9; xlix. 29–32; l. 13.

**Măd'a-ī** (*middle*). Son of Japheth, and progenitor of the Medes, Gen. x. 2.

**Mā'dĭ-an**, Acts vii. 29. [MIDIAN.]

**Măd-măn'nah** (*dunghill*). Town in southern Judah, near Gaza, Josh. xv. 31.

**Măd'men** (*dunghill*). A place in Moab, Jer. xlviii. 2.

**Măd-mē'nah** (*dunghill*). Town in Benjamin, Isa. x. 31.

**Măd'ness.** Lunacy and passionate outburst, John x. 20.

**Mā'dŏn** (*strife*). Ancient city of Canaan, Josh. xi. 1; xii. 19.

**Măg'bish** (*gathering*). Person or place, Ez. ii. 30.

**Măg'da-là** (*tower*). Village on W. shore of Sea of Galilee, Matt. xv. 39. Magadan in R. V.

**Măg'dĭ-el** (*praise*). A duke of Edom, Gen. xxxvi. 43.

**Mā'ġĕd**, 1 Macc. v. 36. [MAKED.]

**Mā'ġī** (*priests*). Oriental priests and learned men. A Median and Persian caste of royal advisers, Jer. xxxix. 3; Matt. ii. 1–11.

**Măġ'ĭc** (*of Magi*). The magician's art. Acting through occult agencies. Potent in Oriental religions, Ex. vii., viii. Forbidden, Lev. xix. 31; xx. 6.

**Mā'gŏg** (*Gog's region*). (1) Second son of Japheth, and his people, Gen. x. 2. (2) Gog's land; probably Scythia, Ezek. xxxviii. 2; xxxix. 2–6. (3) Symbolical enemies, Rev. xx. 7–9.

**Mā'gôr-mĭs'sa-bĭb** (*fear everywhere*). Pashur, who imprisoned Jeremiah, Jer. xx. 1–3.

**Măg'pĭ-ăsh** (*moth killer*). A co-covenanter, Neh. x. 20.

**Mà-hā'lah** (*sickness*). A Manassite, 1 Chr. vii. 18.

**Mà-hā'la-lē''el** (*God's praise*). (1) Son of Cainan, Gen. v. 12–17. Maleleel, Luke iii. 37. (2) A Judahite, Neh. xi. 4.

**Mā'ha-lath** (*harp*). (1) Wife of Esau, Gen. xxviii. 9. (2) Wife of Rehoboam, 2 Chr. xi. 18. (3) The tune or the instrument, Ps. liii., lxxxviii. titles.

**Mā'ha-lī** (*sick*), Ex. vi. 19. [MAHLI.]

**Mā''hà-nā'im** (*two camps*). Place where Jacob met the angels, Gen. xxxii. 2. Afterwards a Levitical town in Gad, Josh. xxi. 38; 2 Sam. ii. 8–12.

**Mā'hà-neh-dăn** (*camp of Dan*). Located as in Judg. xiii. 25; xviii. 12.

**Mà-hăr'a-ī** (*swift*). One of David's captains, 2 Sam. xxiii. 28; 1 Chr. xi. 30; xxvii. 13.

**Mā'hath** (*grasping*). Two Kohathite Levites, 1 Chr. vi. 35; 2 Chr. xxix. 12.

**Mā'hà-vīte.** Designation of one of David's captains, 1 Chr. xi. 46.

**Mà-hā'zĭ-ŏth** (*visions*). Son of Heman, 1 Chr. xxv. 4, 30.

**Mā'hĕr-shăl''al-hăsh'-băz** (*speeding to the prey*). Name of Isaiah's son, symbolizing the Assyrian conquest of Damascus and Samaria, Isa. viii. 1–4.

**Mäh'lah** (*disease*). Daughter of Zelophehad, Num. xxvii. 1–11.

**Mäh'lī** (*sickly*). (1) A Levite, Num. iii. 20. Mahali, Ex. vi. 19. (2) Another Levite, 1 Chr. vi. 47.

**Mäh'lītes.** Descendants of Mahli, Num. iii. 33.

**Mäh'lon** (*sickly*). Ruth's first husband, Ruth i. 2–5; iv. 9, 10.

**Mā'hol** (*dancing*). Father of the four wise men, 1 Kgs. iv. 31.

**Mā'kăz** (*end*). Unidentified place, 1 Kgs. iv. 9.

**Mā'kĕd.** City of Gilead, 1 Macc. v. 26–36.

**Măk-hē'loth** (*meeting place*). A desert encampment, Num. xxxiii. 25.

**Măk-kē'dah** (*shepherd place*). An ancient Canaanite city, Josh. x. 10–30; xii. 16; xv. 41.

**Măk'tesh** (*mortar*). Denounced quarter of Jerusalem, Zeph. i. 11.

**Măl'a-chī** (*God's messenger*). Last of minor prophets. Nothing known of nativity or lineage. Contemporary with Nehemiah, B. C. 445–433. His book foretells the coming of Christ and John the Baptist.

**Măl'cham** (*their king*). (1) A Benjamite, 1 Chr. viii. 9. (2) The idol Molech, Zeph. i. 5.

**Măl-chī'ah** (*king*). (1) A Levite, 1 Chr. vi. 40. (2) Jeremiah's prison-keeper, Jer. xxxviii. 6. (3) Returned captives, Ez. x. 25, 31; Neh. iii. 14; viii. 4; x. 12.

**Măl'chĭ-el** (*God's king*). An Asherite and founder of Malchielites, or Birzavith, Gen. xlvi. 17; Num. xxvi. 45; 1 Chr. vii. 31.

**Măl-chī'jah** (*king*). Priests and returned captives, 1 Chr. xxiv. 9; Ez. x. 25, 31; Neh. iii. 11; xii. 42.

**Măl-chī'ram** (*king of height*). Son of Jehoiachin, 1 Chr. iii. 18.

**Măl'chĭ-shū'à** (*king of help*). Son of Saul, 1 Chr. ix. 39. Melchishua, 1 Sam. xiv. 49.

**Măl'chus** (*ruling*). The one whose ear Peter cut off, Matt. xxvi. 51; Luke xxii. 50.

**Mà-lē'le-el**, Luke iii. 37. [MAHALALEEL.]

**Măl'lŏs.** City in Cilicia, 2 Macc. iv. 30.

**Măl'lō-thī** (*fulness*). Chief of the 19th musical course, 1 Chr. xxv. 4, 26.

**Măl'lōwş** (*soft*). Jews'-mallows of the East, used for pot-herbs, Job xxx. 4.

**Măl'luch** (*ruling*). Levites, 1 Chr. vi. 44; Ez. x. 29, 32; Neh. x. 4; xii. 2.

**Măm'mon** (*riches*). A Chaldee word used by Christ, Matt. vi. 24; Luke xvi. 9.

**Măm''nĭ-tà-nāi'mus.** 1 Esdr. ix. 34. [MATTANIAH.]

**Măm'rē** (*strength*). The Amorite chief who gave his name to the plain where Abraham dwelt, Gen. xiv. 13–24. Hebron, Gen. xxiii. 19.

**Mà-mū'chus**, 1 Esdr. ix. 30. [MALLUCH.]

**Măn.** Adam, *ruddy*, Gen. i. 26. The human race, Gen. v. 2; viii. 21. As distinguished from woman, Deut. xxii. 5; 1 Sam. xvii. 33. Mortal, Isa. xiii. 14.

**Măn'a-ĕn** (*comforter*). A Christian teacher at Antioch, Acts xiii. 1.

**Măn'a-hăth** (*rest*). (1) A Horite progenitor of the Manahethites, Gen. xxxvi. 23; 1 Chr. ii. 52. (2) Place or person, 1 Chr. viii. 6.

**Mà-năs'seh** (*forgetting*). (1) First son of Joseph, Gen. xli. 51. The tribe divided and occupied both sides of Jordan, Josh. xvi., xvii. (2) Son and successor of Hezekiah on the throne of Judah, B. C. 698–643. Idolatrous, 2 Kgs. xxi. 1–18. Captive in Babylon; repented; restored, 2 Chr. xxxiii. 1–20. (3) Returned captives, Ez. x. 30, 33.

**Mà-năs'sēş.** (1) King Manasseh, Matt. i. 10. (2) Manasseh, Joseph's son, Rev. vii. 6.

**Mà-năs'sītes.** Descendants of Manasseh (1), Deut. iv. 43; Judg. xii. 4.

**Măn'drāke** (*field speaker*). A narcotic plant, resembling rhubarb, bearing a yellow, aromatic fruit, Gen. xxx. 14–16; S. of Sol. vii. 13.

**Mā'neh.** The mina; a variable Hebrew weight, Ezek. xlv. 12.

**Măn'ġer** (*eating place*). Feeding crib or trough for cattle. The stall, and even the cattleyard, Luke ii. 7–16; xiii. 15.

**Mā'nī**, 1 Esdr. ix. 30. [BANI.]

**Măn'nà** (*what is this?*). The bread substitute sent to the wandering Israelites, Ex. xvi. 14–36; Num. xi. 7–9; Deut. viii. 3; Josh. v. 12.

**Mà-nō'ah** (*rest*). Father of Samson, Judg. xiii. 1–23.

**Măn′slāy-er.** The involuntary manslayer found escape in a city of refuge, Num. xxxv. 22, 23; Deut. xix. 5.

**Măn′tle** (*hand-woven*). Blanket, Judg. iv. 18. Garment, 1 Sam. xv. 27. Sleeved wrapper, Isa. iii. 22. Chief outer garment, 1 Kgs. xix. 13–19.

**Mā′och** (*breast-bound*). A Gathite, 1 Sam. xxvii. 2.

**Mā′on** (*dwelling*). Town in Judah, Josh. xv. 55; 1 Sam. xxiii. 24, 25.

**Mā′on-ītes.** Mehunims, Judg. x. 12.

**Mā′rȧ** (*bitter*). Naomi so called herself, Ruth i. 20.

**Mā′rah** (*bitter*). The desert spring whose waters were sweetened, Ex. xv. 22–25; Num. xxxiii. 8, 9.

**Măr′a-lah** (*trembling*). A border of Zebulun, Josh. xix. 11.

**Mär′an=ā′thȧ.** "Our Lord cometh," 1 Cor. xvi. 22.

**Mär′ble** (*shining*). Any white or shining stone is meant, 1 Kgs. vii. 9–12; Esth. i. 6; Rev. xviii. 12.

**Mär-chĕs′van.** [Bul.]

**Mär′cus,** Col. iv. 10; Phile. 24; 1 Pet. v. 13. [Mark.]

**Mär″dô-chē′us.** Mordecai in Apoc.

**Mȧ-rē′shah** (*hill-top*). (1) A Hebronite, 1 Chr. ii. 42. (2) Lowland city of Judah, Josh. xv. 44; 2 Chr. xi. 8; xiv. 9–12.

**Mär′ī-mŏth,** 2 Esdr. i. 2. [Meraioth.]

**Märk** (*polite, shining*). John Mark, Acts xii. 12, 25; xv. 37. John, Acts xiii. 5, 13. Mark, Acts xv. 39. Convert of Peter, 1 Pet. v. 13. Companion of Paul, Col. iv. 10. Author of second Gospel, which was probably written in Rome.

**Mā′roth** (*bitter*). Town in Judah, Micah i. 12.

**Măr′riage** (*husbanding*). Monogamous, Gen. ii. 18–24; vii. 13. Polygamous, Gen. iv. 19; vi. 2. Forbidden within certain degrees, Lev. xviii.; Deut. xxvii.; and with foreigners, Ex. xxxiv. 16. Monogamy re-instituted, Matt. xix. 5, 6; Mark x. 5–10.

**Märs′ Hill,** Acts xvii. 22. [Areopagus.]

**Mär′se-nȧ** (*worthy*). A Persian prince, Esth. i. 14.

**Mär′thȧ** (*lady*). Sister of Mary and Lazarus, Luke x. 38–42; John xi. 5–28.

**Mär′tyr** (*witness*). Matt. xviii. 16; Luke xxiv. 48. Who seals his faith with his blood, Acts xxii. 20; Rev. ii. 13; xvii. 6.

**Mā′rȳ** (*rebellion*). Greek form of Miriam. (1) The betrothed of Joseph and mother of Christ, Matt. i. 18–25; xii. 46; Mark vi. 3; Luke viii. 19; John ii. 1–5; xix. 26; Acts i. 14. (2) Wife of Cleophas, Matt. xxvii. 56, 61; xxviii. 1–9; Mark xvi. 1–8; Luke xxiv. 1–10. (3) Mother of John Mark, Acts xii. 12; Col. iv. 10. (4) Sister of Martha and Lazarus, Luke x. 41, 42; John xi., xii. (5) Mary Magdalene; *i. e.*, of Magdala, Matt. xxviii. 1–10; Mark xvi. 1–10; Luke xxiv. 10; John xx. 1–18. (6) A Roman convert, Rom. xvi. 6.

**Măs′ȧ-lŏth.** Place in Arbela, 1 Macc. ix. 2.

**Măs′chĭl.** "Didactic," or "melody." Title of thirteen Psalms.

**Măsh** (*drawn out*). Son of Aram, Gen. x. 23. Meshech, 1 Chr. i. 17.

**Mā′shal** (*entreaty*). A Levitical city in Asher, 1 Chr. vi. 74. Misheal, Josh. xix. 26. Mishal, Josh. xxi. 30.

**Măs′phȧ,** 1 Macc. iii. 46. [Mizpeh.]

**Măs′re-kah** (*vineyard*). City in Edom, Gen. xxxvi. 36; 1 Chr. i. 47.

**Măs′sȧ** (*gift*). Son of Ishmael, Gen. xxv. 14; 1 Chr. i. 30.

**Măs′sah** (*temptation*). Meribah; spot of temptation, Ex. xvii. 7; Ps. xcv. 8, 9; Heb. iii. 8.

**Mȧ-thu′sa-lȧ,** Luke iii. 37. [Methuselah.]

**Mā′tred** (*shoving*). Mother of Mehetabel, Gen. xxxvi. 39.

**Mā′trī** (*rain*). A Benjamite family, 1 Sam. x. 21.

**Mā′trĭx** (*mother*). The womb, Ex. xiii. 12–15.

**Măt′tan** (*gift*). (1) A priest of Baal, 2 Kgs. xi. 18. (2) Father of Shephatiah, Jer. xxxviii. 1.

**Măt′ta-nah** (*gift*). A desert encampment, Num. xxi. 18, 19.

**Măt″ta-nī′ah** (*God's gift*). (1) Original name of Zedekiah, 2 Kgs. xxiv. 17. (2) Levites, 1 Chr. ix. 15; xxv. 4, 16; 2 Chr. xx. 14; xxix. 13; Ez. x. 26, 27, 30, 37; Neh. xi. 17; xiii. 13.

**Măt′ta-thȧ** (*God's gift*). Grandson of David, Luke iii. 31.

**Măt′ta-thah.** One who returned, Ez. x. 33.

**Măt″ta-thī′as** (*God's gift*). (1) Two of Christ's progenitors, Luke iii. 25, 26. (2) Father of the Maccabees, 1 Macc. ii.

**Măt″te-nā′ī.** Levites, Ez. x. 33, 37; Neh. xii. 19.

**Măt′than.** Grandfather of Joseph, Matt. i. 15.

**Măt″tha-nī′as,** 1 Esdr. ix. 37. [Mattaniah.]

**Măt′that,** Luke iii. 24, 29. [Matthan.]

**Măt′thew** (*gift of God*). Contraction of Mattathias. The Apostle and Evangelist. Levi in Luke, v. 27–29. Son of Alphæus, Mark ii. 14. Tax-collector at Capernaum when called, Matt. ix. 9. His gospel is first of N. T. Its original claimed to be the Hebrew, or Syro-Chaldaic, of Palestine. Time of writing placed at A. D. 60–66. Gist, to establish Jesus as O. T. Messiah.

**Măt-thī′as** (*God's gift*). Apostle allotted to fill the place of Judas, Acts i. 26.

**Măt″tĭ-thī′ah** (*God's gift*). Levites, 1 Chr. ix. 31; xv. 18; xvi. 5; Ez. x. 43; Neh. viii. 4.

**Măt′tŏck** (*hoe*). A crude hoe, Isa. vii. 25.

**Maul** (*hammer*). Heavy wooden hammer, Prov. xxv. 18. Battle axe, Jer. li. 20.

**Măz″i-tī′as,** 1 Esdr. ix. 35. [Mattithiah.]

**Măz′za-rŏth.** The twelve signs of the zodiac, Job xxxviii. 32.

**Mĕad′ōw** (*mead*). Water-plant, flag, Gen. xli. 2. Cave, Judg. xx. 33.

**Mē′ah** (*hundred*). Tower in Jerusalem, Neh. iii. 1; xii. 39.

**Mē-ā′rah** (*cave*). Unknown place, Josh. xiii. 4.

**Mĕas′ures.** Hebrew standard weights and measures provided for, Lev. xix. 35, 36; Deut. xxv. 13–15. Money passed by weight till era of coinage. For various weights and measures, *see* respective titles.

**Mēat.** In Bible sense, food of any kind, Gen. i. 29; Lev. ii.; vi. 14–23; Matt. xv. 37; Luke xxiv. 41.

**Mēat=ŏf′fēr-ing.** Conditions in Lev. ii.; vi. 14–23.

**Mē-bŭn′nāī** (*building*). One of David's warriors, 2 Sam. xxiii. 27. Sibbechai, 2 Sam. xxi. 18. Sibbecai, 1 Chr. xi. 29.

**Mĕch′e-rath-īte″,** 1 Chr. xi. 36. Maacathite. [Maacah.]

**Mē′dăd** (*love*). A camp prophet, Num. xi. 26, 27.

**Mē′dan** (*strife*). A son of Abraham, Gen. xxv. 2; 1 Chr. i. 32.

**Mĕd′e-bȧ** (*quiet waters*). Town in Reuben, east of Dead Sea, Num. xxi. 30; Josh. xiii. 9; 1 Macc. ix. 36.

**Mēdes.** Medians, 2 Kgs. xvii. 6.

**Mē′dĭ-ȧ** (*middle land*). Madai, Gen. x. 2; Media, Esth. i. 3. The country northwest of Persia and south of Caspian Sea. Held early sway in Babylon. Tributary to Assyria, B. C. 880. Independent, and conquered Babylon; next, Assyria. Empire at its height, B. C. 625. Overthrown by Persian Cyrus, B. C. 558. Medo-Persian empire overthrown by Alexander the Great, B. C. 330, Isa. xiii. 17, 18; Esth. i. 19; Dan. vi. 8–12; 1 Chr. v. 26.

**Mĕd′ĭ-çĭne** (*of a physician*). The science, as known in Egypt, was copied by Hebrews, Lev. xiii.–xv.; 2 Kgs. viii. 29; Prov. iii. 8; vi. 15.

**Mē-gĭd′dō** (*crowded*). A city in plain of Esdraelon, Josh. xii. 21; xvii. 11; 2 Kgs. xxiii. 29. Also the plain, or valley, itself and scene of Barak's victory over Sisera, and of Josiah's death, Judg. iv. 6–17; 2 Chr. xxxv. 20–24.

**Mē-gĭd′don,** Zech. xii. 11. [Megiddo.]

**Mē-hĕt′a-beel.** Ancestor of Shemaiah, Neh. vi. 10.

**Mē-hĕt′a-bel** (*God-favored*). Wife of Hadar, king of Edom, Gen. xxxvi. 39.

**Mē-hī′dȧ** (*famed*). His family returned, Ez. ii. 52; Neh. vii. 54.

**Mē′hir** (*price*). A Judahite, 1 Chr. iv. 11.

**Mē-hŏl′ath-īte.** Meholaite, 1 Sam. xviii. 19.

**Mē-hū′ja-el** (*smitten*). Son of Irad, Gen. iv. 18.

**Mē′hū-man** (*true*). Chamberlain of Ahasuerus, Esth. i. 10.

**Mē-hū′nims** (*dwellings*). Maonites, 2 Chr. xxvi. 7; Ez. ii. 50.

**Mē-jär′kŏn** (*yellow waters*). Town in Dan, Josh. xix. 46.

**Mĕk′o-nah** (*pedestal*). Town in Judah, Neh. xi. 28.

**Mĕl″a-tī′ah** (*saved*). Assistant wall-builder, Neh. iii. 7.

**Mĕl′chī** (*king*). Two ancestors of Christ, Luke iii. 24, 28.

**Mĕl-chī′ah** (*royal*). A priest, Jer. xxi. 1.

**Mĕl-chī′el.** Governor of Bethulia, Judith vi. 15.

**Mĕl-chis′e-dĕc.** N. T. form of Melchizedek, Heb. v.-vii.

**Mĕl″chī-shu′ȧ,** 1 Sam. xiv. 49. [MALCHISHUA.]

**Mĕl-chiz′e-dek** (*king of justice*). King of Salem, and priest, Gen. xiv. 18–20. Prototype of Christ, Ps. cx. 4; Heb. v.-vii.

**Mē′le-ȧ** (*full*). Ancestor of Joseph, Luke iii. 31.

**Mē′lech** (*king*). Son of Micah, 1 Chr. ix. 41.

**Mĕl′i-cū,** Neh. xii. 14. [MALLUCH.]

**Mĕl′i-tȧ** (*honey*). The island of Malta, in Mediterranean, south of Sicily, Acts xxvii., xxviii.

**Mĕl′on** (*mellow apple*). Melons of Egypt prized as food, Num. xi. 5.

**Mĕl′zar.** Common noun—steward or tutor, Dan. i. 11, 16.

**Mĕm′phis** (*abode of the good*). Ancient Egyptian city, Hos. ix. 6, on west bank of Nile, near pyramids and sphinx, and 10 miles south of Cairo. Noph, Isa. xix. 13; Jer. ii. 16; Ezek. xxx. 13–16.

**Mē-mū′can.** A Persian prince, Esth. i. 14–21.

**Mĕn′a-hĕm** (*comforter*). Usurper of Israel's throne. Idolatrous and cruel. Reigned B. C. 772–761, 2 Kgs. xv. 14–22.

**Mē′nan.** Ancestor of Joseph, Luke iii. 31.

**Mē′nē.** First word of Belshazzar's warning. Entire, "Mene," he is numbered; "Tekel," he is weighed; "Upharsin," they are divided, Dan. v. 25–28.

**Mĕn″e-lā′us.** High priest, 2 Macc. iv. 23.

**Mē-nĕs′the-us.** Father of Apollonius, 2 Macc. iv. 21.

**Mē-ŏn′e-nim** (*enchanter*). Unlocated plain, Judg. ix. 37.

**Mē-ŏn′o-thāi.** A Judahite, 1 Chr. iv. 14.

**Mĕph′a-ăth** (*height*). Levitical town in Reuben, Josh. xiii. 18.

**Mē-phĭb′o-shĕth** (*idol breaker*). (1) A son of Saul, 2 Sam. xxi. 8. (2) Son of Jonathan, 2 Sam. iv. 4; ix. 6–13; xvi.; xix. 24–30.

**Mē′rab** (*increase*). Daughter of Saul, 1 Sam. xiv. 49; xviii. 17.

**Mĕr″a-ī′ah** (*rebellion*). A priest, Neh. xii. 12.

**Mē-rā′ioth** (*rebellious*). Three priests, 1 Chr. vi. 6; Ez. vii. 3; Neh. xii. 15.

**Mē′ran,** Bar. iii. 23. [MEDAN.]

**Mē-rā′rī** (*bitter*). (1) Third son of Levi, and head of family of Merarites, Gen. xlvi. 11; Ex. vi. 16; Num. iii. 17; iv. 29–33; Josh. xxi. 7–30. (2) Father of Judith, Judith viii. 1.

**Mĕr″a-thā′im** (*double rebellion*). Symbol of Chaldea, Jer. l. 21.

**Mĕr-cū′ri-us** (*Mercury*). Name applied to Paul in Lystra, Acts xiv. 12.

**Mĕr′cy Seat.** Lid of the ark, Ex. xxv. 17–22; hence, covering, or atonement for sin, Heb. ix. 5.

**Mē′rĕd** (*rebellion*). Son of Ezra, 1 Chr. iv. 17.

**Mĕr′e-mŏth** (*heights*). Three priests, Ez. viii. 33; x. 36; Neh. x. 5.

**Mē′rĕs** (*lofty*). One of Ahasuerus' wise men, Esth. i. 14.

**Mĕr′ī-bah** (*strife*). A desert encampment, where the rock was smitten, Ex. xvii. 7. Kadesh, Num. xx. 13–24.

**Mĕr′ib-bā′al,** 1 Chr. viii. 34; ix. 40. [MEPHIBOSHETH, 2.]

**Mē-rō′dăch** (*death*). A Babylonian god, and royal surname, Jer. l. 2.

**Mē-rō′dăch-băl′a-dăn** (*Baal-worshipper*). King of Babylon, B. C. 721, Isa. xxxix. 1. Berodach-baladan, 2 Kgs. xx. 12.

**Mē′rom** (*heights*). The lake on Jordan above Sea of Galilee, Josh. xi. 5–7.

**Mē-rŏn′o-thīte.** Designations in 1 Chr. xxvii. 30; Neh. iii. 7.

**Mē′rŏz** (*refuge*). Unknown place, Judg. v. 23.

**Mē′sech, Mē′shech** (*drawn out*). (1) Son of Japheth, Gen. x. 2; Ezek. xxvii. 13; xxxii. 26; Ps. cxx. 5. (2) 1 Chr. i. 17. [MASH.]

**Mē′shȧ** (*freed*). (1) A Joktanite border, Gen. x. 30. (2) A king of Moab, 2 Kgs. iii. 4. (3) Son of Caleb, 1 Chr. ii. 42. (4) A Benjamite, 1 Chr. viii. 9.

**Mē′shach** (*guest*). Chaldean name of Mishael, Daniel's companion, Dan i. 6, 7; iii.

**Mē-shĕl″e-mī′ah** (*rewarded*). A Levite gatekeeper, 1 Chr. ix. 21; xxvi. 1–9.

**Mē-shĕz′a-be-el** (*delivered*). Returned captives, Neh. iii. 4; x. 21; xi. 24.

**Mē-shil′le-mith** (*repaid*). A priest, 1 Chr. ix. 12.

**Mē-shil′le-mŏth** (*repaid*). (1) A chief of Ephraim, 2 Chr. xxviii. 12. (2) Meshillemith, Neh. xi. 13.

**Mē-shŭl′lam** (*friend*). (1) Ancestor of Shaphan, 2 Kgs. xxii. 3. (2) Son of Zerubbabel, 1 Chr. iii. 19. (3) A Gadite, 1 Chr. v. 13. (4) Three Benjamites, 1 Chr. viii. 17; ix. 7, 8. (5) Eleven Levites, in Ez. and Neh.

**Mē-shŭl′le-mĕth** (*friend*). Mother of King Amon, 2 Kgs. xxi. 19.

**Mĕs′o-bā-īte″.** Designation of Jasiel, 1 Chr. xi. 47.

**Mĕs″o-pō-tā′mī-ȧ** (*between rivers*). The country between the rivers Tigris and Euphrates, Gen. xxiv. 10; Deut. xxiii. 4; Judg. iii. 8–10; Acts ii. 9; vii. 2.

**Mĕs-sī′ah** (*anointed*). Applied to regularly anointed priests or kings, Lev. iv. 3, 5, 16; 1 Sam. ii. 10, 35; xii. 3–5. The Greek *kristos*, "anointed," takes its place in N. T., except in John i. 41; iv. 25.

**Mĕs-sī′as.** Greek form of Messiah, John i. 41; iv. 25.

**Mĕt′als** (*mined*). Precious and useful metals, such as gold, silver, tin, lead, copper, and iron, known to Hebrews and much used, Gen. ii. 11, 12; Num. xxxi. 22.

**Mē-tē′rus.** His family returned, 1 Esdr. v. 17.

**Mē′theg-ăm′mah** (*curb of the city*). A Philistine stronghold, 2 Sam. viii. 1.

**Mē-thu′sa-el** (*man of God*). Father of Lamech, Gen. iv. 18.

**Mē-thu′se-lah** (*dart-man*). Grandfather of Noah; oldest of antediluvians. Lived 969 years, Gen. v. 21–27.

**Mē-ū′nim,** Neh. vii. 52. [MEHUNIMS.]

**Mĕz′a-hăb** (*gilded*). An Edomite, Gen. xxxvi. 39.

**Mī′a-min** (*right hand*). Two who returned, Ez. x. 25; Neh. xii. 5.

**Mĭb′har** (*chosen*). One of David's heroes, 1 Chr. xi. 38.

**Mĭb′sam** (*odorous*). (1) An Ishmaelite, Gen. xxv. 13. (2) A Simeonite, 1 Chr. iv. 25.

**Mĭb′zar** (*fort*). A duke of Edom, Gen. xxxvi. 42.

**Mī′cah** (*God-like*). (1) The erratic Ephraimite whose story is told in Judg. xvii., xviii. (2) Sixth of the minor prophets. Prophesied B. C. 750–698. He foretells the destruction of Samaria and Jerusalem, and prefigures the Messiah. (3) A Reubenite, 1 Chr. v. 5. (4) Grandson of Jonathan, 1 Chr. viii. 34, 35. (5) A Levite, 1 Chr. xxiii. 20. (6) Father of Abdon, 2 Chr. xxxiv. 20.

**Mī-cā′iah** (*God-like*). A Samarian prophet, 1 Kgs. xxii. 8–38; 2 Chr. xviii. 7–27.

**Mī′chȧ.** Persons in 2 Sam. ix. 12; Neh. x. 11; xi. 17, 22.

**Mī′chael** (*God-like*). (1) Prince of angels, Dan. x. 13; xii. 1; Rev. xii. 7. (2) Characters in Num. xiii. 13; 1 Chr. v. 13, 14; vi. 40; vii. 3; viii. 16; xii. 20; xxvii. 18; 2 Chr. xxi. 2; Ez. viii. 8.

**Mī′chah,** 1 Chr. xxiv. 24, 25. [MICAH, 5.]

**Mī-chā′iah** (*God-like*). (1) Full form of Micah in 2 Chr. xxxiv. 20. (2) Same as Micha, 1 Chr. ix. 15; Neh. xii. 35. (3) A priest, Neh. xii. 41. (4) Wife of Rehoboam and mother of Abijah, king of Judah, 2 Chr. xiii. 2. (5) A prince and teacher of the law, 2 Chr. xvii. 7. (6) Son of Gemariah, Jer. xxxvi. 11–14.

**Mī′chal.** Daughter of Saul and wife of David, 1 Sam. xiv. 49; xxv. 44; 2 Sam. iii. 14; vi. 23.

**Mī-chē′as,** 2 Esdr. i. 39. [MICAH.]

**Mĭch′mash** (*hidden*). Noted town in Benjamin, 1 Sam. xiii. 11; Isa. x. 28. Michmas, Ez. ii. 27.

**Mĭch′mē-thah** (*stony*). Border mark of Manasseh, Josh. xvii. 7.

**Mĭch′rī** (*precious*). A Benjamite, 1 Chr. ix. 8.

**Mĭch′tam.** Musical term for six Psalms.

**Mĭd′din** (*measures*). City in Judah, Josh. xv. 61.

**Mĭd′ī-an** (*strife*). Son of Abraham, and founder of Midianites, Gen. xxv. 2; Ex. iii. 1; Num. xxii. 4; Judg. vii. 13.

**Mĭg′dal-ĕl** (*tower of God*). Fenced city of Naphtali, Josh. xix. 38.

**Mig'dal-gad** (*tower of Gad*). Town in Judah, Josh. xv. 37.

**Mig'dol** (*tower*). Place in Egypt, Ex. xiv. 2; Num. xxxiii. 7, 8. Perhaps same in Jer. xliv. 1; xlvi. 14.

**Mig'rŏn** (*pinnacle*). Town near Gibeah, 1 Sam. xiv. 2; Isa. x. 28.

**Mij'a-min** (*right hand*). (1) Chief of the 6th priestly course, 1 Chr. xxiv. 9. (2) Co-covenanters, Neh. x. 7.

**Mik'loth** (*staves*). (1) A Benjamite, 1 Chr. viii. 32; ix. 37, 38. (2) One of David's generals, 1 Chr. xxvii. 4.

**Mik-nē'iah** (*God-possessed*). A temple musician, 1 Chr. xv. 18-21.

**Mil''a-lā'ī** (*eloquent*). A priest, Neh. xii. 36.

**Mil'cah** (*queen*). (1) Wife of Nahor, Gen. xi. 29; xxiv. 15-47. (2) Daughter of Zelophehad, Num. xxvi. 33; Josh. xvii. 3.

**Mil'com.** [MOLECH.]

**Mile.** Roman mile in Matt. v. 41; 1618 yards.

**Mī-lē'tus, Mī-lē'tum** (*red*). City in Ionia, Acts xx. 15-38; 2 Tim. iv. 20.

**Milk**, Of cows, goats, camels, and sheep a favorite Oriental food, Gen. xxxii. 15; Deut. xxxii. 14. Symbol of fertility, Josh. v. 6; Heb. v. 12.

**Mill** (*grind*). A mortar and pestle; or, two stones, upper and nether, the former turned by hand, Job xli. 24; Isa. xlvii. 1, 2; Matt. xxiv. 41. Millstones not pawnable, Deut. xxiv. 6.

**Mil'let.** Here a grass; abroad a cereal, like broom-corn, Ezek. iv. 9.

**Mil'lō** (*mound*). (1) A rampart of Jerusalem, 2 Sam. v. 9; 1 Kgs. ix. 15. (2) Where Joash was murdered, 2 Kgs. xii. 20. (3) A Shechem family, Judg. ix. 6-20.

**Mī'na.** [MANEH.]

**Mī-nī'a-min.** Levites, 2 Chr. xxxi. 15; Neh. xii. 17, 41.

**Min'is-tēr** (*assistant*). Attendant, Ex. xxiv. 13; Josh. i. 1; 1 Kgs. xix. 21; Ez. viii. 17. Magistrate, Rom. xiii. 6. Preacher and teacher, 1 Cor. iv. 1; 2 Cor. iii. 6. Celestial high priest, Heb. viii. 1-3.

**Min'nī.** Part of Armenia, Jer. li. 27.

**Min'nith** (*division*). An Ammonite section east of Jordan, Judg. xi. 33; Ezek. xxvii. 17.

**Min'strel** (*minister*). A musician employed, or strolling, 1 Sam. x. 5; xvi. 16; 2 Kgs. iii. 15. Professional mourners, Matt. ix. 23.

**Mint.** An aromatic herb, varieties numerous, Matt. xxiii. 23; Luke xi. 42.

**Miph'kăd.** A Jerusalem gate, Neh. iii. 31.

**Mir'a-cle** (*wonderful*). In scripture, a supernatural event, Num. xxii. 28; 1 Kgs. xvii. 6; Matt. ix. 18-33; xiv. 25.

**Mir'ī-am** (*rebellion*). (1) Sister of Moses and Aaron. Musician and prophetess, Ex. ii. 4-10; xv. 20, 21; Num. xii. 1-15; xx. 1; 1 Chr. vi. 3. (2) A Judahite, 1 Chr. iv. 17.

**Mir'mȧ** (*fraud*). A Benjamite, 1 Chr. viii. 10.

**Mir'rŏr** (*wonder at*). Egyptian mirrors, which the Hebrew women affected, were highly polished metal plates, chiefly of copper, Ex. xxxviii. 8; Job xxxvii. 18; 1 Cor. xiii. 12.

**Mis'gab** (*high*). Place in Moab, Jer. xlviii. 1.

**Mish'a-el** (*what God is*). (1) Uncle of Moses, Ex. vi. 22; Lev. x. 4. (2) Ezra's assistant, Neh. viii. 4. (3) Daniel's captive companion, Dan. i. 6-19; ii. 17.

**Mī'shal, Mī'she-al** (*entreaty*). Levitical town in Asher, Josh. xix. 26; xxi. 30.

**Mī'sham** (*fleet*). A Benjamite, 1 Chr. viii. 12.

**Mish'mȧ** (*hearing*). (1) An Ishmaelite, Gen. xxv. 14. (2) A Simeonite, 1 Chr. iv. 25.

**Mish-măn'nah** (*fatness*). A Gadite, 1 Chr. xii. 10.

**Mish'ra-ītes.** Colonists from Kirjath-jearim, 1 Chr. ii. 53.

**Mis'pe-rĕth.** A returned captive, Neh. vii. 7.

**Mis're-photh=mā'im** (*burning waters*). Place in northern Palestine, Josh. xi. 8; xiii. 6.

**Mite** (*little*). Half a farthing, or fifth of a cent, Mark xii. 41-44; Luke xxi. 1-4.

**Mith'cah** (*sweetness*) A desert encampment Num. xxxiii. 28

**Mith'nīte.** A designation, 1 Chr. xi. 43.

**Mith're-dăth** (*Mithra-given*). (1) Cyrus' treasurer, Ez. i. 8. (2) Persian governor of Samaria, Ez. iv. 7.

**Mith''rī-dā'tēs**, 1 Esdr. ii. 11. [MITHREDATH.]

**Mī'tre** (*turban*). The priestly head-dress of linen, wrapped round the head, and bearing a frontal inscription, "Holiness to the Lord," Ex. xxviii. 4, 36-39; xxix. 6; xxxix. 28-30; Lev. viii. 9, xvi. 4.

**Mit''y̆-lē'nē** (*curtailed*). Chief town of the island of Lesbos, Acts xx. 14, 15.

**Mixed Multitude.** Camp followers, Ex. xii. 38; Num. xi. 4; Neh. xiii. 3.

**Mī'zar** (*little*). Unlocated hill, Ps. xlii. 6.

**Miz'pah, Miz'peh** (*watch tower*). (1) Jacob's covenant heap, Gen. xxxi. 47-49. (2) Mizpeh-moab, 1 Sam. xxii. 3. (3) Hivite section in northern Palestine, Josh. xi. 3-8. (4) A city in Judah. Josh. xv. 38. (5) A city of Benjamin, Josh. xviii. 26; 1 Sam. x. 17-21; 1 Kgs. xv. 22.

**Miz'par,** Ez. ii. 2. [MISPERETH.]

**Miz'ra-im** (*red soil*). Son of Ham, Gen. x. 6. The O. T. word translated Egypt, Gen. xlv 20; Isa. xi. 11.

**Miz'zah** (*fear*). Grandson of Esau, Gen. xxxvi. 13.

**Mnā'son** (*remembering*). A Cyprian convert. Acts xxi. 16.

**Mō'ab** (*of his father*). Son of Lot by his daughter, and progenitor of the Moabites. The country lay east of the Dead Sea and south of the Arnon, Num. xxi. 13-15; xxii.; Judg. xi. 18. Though idolatrous, worshipping Chemosh, they were a strong, progressive people, holding Israel subject, Judg. iii. 12-14; but finally subdued, 15-30; 2 Sam. viii. 2; Isa. xv., xvi.; Jer. xlviii.; Ruth i., ii.

**Mō'ab-īte Stōne.** The celebrated stone found at Dhiban (Dibon) in Moab, in A. D. 1868, on which is engraved, in Hebrew-Phœnician, the record of Mesha, king of Moab's, rebellion against Israel, 2 Kgs. iii. 4-27.

**Mō''a-dī'ah,** Neh. xii. 17. [MAADIAH.]

**Mŏch'mur.** Brook or wady, Judith vii. 18.

**Mō'din.** Burial ground of the Maccabees, near Lydda, 1 Macc. xiii. 25.

**Mō'eth,** 1 Esdr. viii. 63. [NOADIAH.]

**Mŏl'a-dah** (*birth*). City in south Judah, Josh. xv. 26; xix. 2; Neh. xi. 26.

**Mōle** (*dirt thrower*). No ground-moles in Palestine. Chameleon or lizard in Lev. xi. 30; and rat or weasel in Isa. ii. 20.

**Mō'lech** (*king*). Moloch, Acts vii. 43. Milcom, 1 Kgs. xi. 5. Malcham, Zeph. i. 5. Tutelary divinity (fire-god) of the Ammonites, Lev. xviii. 21; 2 Kgs. xxiii. 10.

**Mō'lī,** 1 Esdr. viii. 47. [MAHLI.]

**Mō'lid** (*begetter*). A Judahite, 1 Chr. ii. 29.

**Mō'lŏch,** Acts vii. 43. [MOLECH.]

**Mŏm'dis,** 1 Esdr. ix. 34. [MAADAI.]

**Mon'ey** (*warning*). Gold and silver passed by weight among Hebrews, Gen. xvii. 13; xxiii. 16; though the ring tokens of Egypt may have been current, Gen. xx. 16; xxxvii. 28. Persian coined money (daric or dram) came into use after the captivity, Ez. ii. 69; Neh. vii. 70-72. The Maccabees first coined Jewish money, B. C. 140, — shekels and half shekels of gold and silver, with minor copper coins. The N. T. coins, Matt. xvii. 27; xxii. 19; x. 29; v. 26; Mark xii 42, were Roman or Grecian.

**Mon'ey Chān'gers.** Those who made a business of supplying the annual half-shekel offering at a premium, Ex. xxx. 13-15; Matt. xxi. 12; Mark xi. 15.

**Month** (*moon*). Hebrew month lunar, from new moon to new moon, Num. x. 10; xxviii. 11-14. Intercalary month every three years. Months named, but usually went by number, Gen. vii. 11; 2 Kgs. xxv. 3. *See* month names in place.

**Moon** (*measurer*). Conjointly with the sun, appointed for signs, seasons, days, months and years. Regulator of religious festivals, Gen. i. 14-18. Worship of, forbidden, Deut. iv. 19. Used largely figuratively, Isa. xiii. 10; Matt. xxiv. 29; Mark xiii. 24.

**Mō'ras-thīte.** Of Moresheth, Jer. xxvi. 18; Mic. i. 1.

**Môr'de-cāi** (*little*). A Benjamite captive at court of Ahasuerus, and deliverer of Jews from plot of Haman, Esth.

**Mō'reh** (*teacher*). (1) First halting place of Abram in Canaan, Gen. xii. 6. (2) Hill in valley of Jezreel, Judg. vii. 1.

**Mōr'esh-eth=găth** (*possession of Gath*). Place named in Mic. i. 14.

**Mō-rī'ah** (*chosen*). (1) The land in which Abraham offered up Isaac, Gen. xxii. 2. (2) Site of Solomon's temple in Jerusalem, 2 Sam. xxiv. 24; 1 Chr. xxi. 24–27; 2 Chr. iii. 1, 2.

**Môr'tar.** (1) Hollow vessel of wood or stone, in which corn was ground with a pestle, Num. xi. 8; Prov. xxvii. 22. (2) Various cementing substances used in building, as bitumen, clay, and ordinary mixture of sand and lime, Gen. xi. 3; Ex. i. 14; Lev. xiv. 42; Isa. xli. 25.

**Mô-sē'rȧ** (*bonds*). A desert encampment, Deut. x. 6.

**Mô-sē'roth**, Num. xxxiii. 30. [MOSERA.]

**Mō'ses** (*drawn out*). The great leader and lawgiver of the Hebrews. Son of Amram, a Levite. Born in Egypt, about B. C. 1571. Adopted by Pharaoh's daughter, liberally educated, fled to Midian, Ex. ii. Called to lead the Exode, Ex. iii.–xix. Promulgated the law, Ex. xx.–xl.; Lev.; Num.; Deut. Died on Nebo, aged 120 years. Reputed author of Pentateuch and Job.

**Mô-sŏl'lam**, 1 Esdr. viii. 44. [MESHULLAM.]

**Mŏth.** Frequent scripture references to the destructiveness of this insect, Job xiii. 28; Ps. xxxix. 11; Isa. l. 9; Matt. vi. 19.

**Moth'er.** Held in high respect by Hebrews, Ex. xx. 12. Often used for grandmother, or remote ancestor, Gen. iii. 20; 1 Kgs. xv. 10.

**Môurn'ing.** Very public and demonstrative, Gen. xxiii. 2; xxxvii. 29–35. Period, seven to seventy days, Gen. l. 3; 1 Sam. xxxi. 13. Hired mourners, Eccl. xii. 5; Matt. ix. 23. Methods, weeping, tearing clothes, wearing sackcloth, sprinkling with ashes or dust, shaving head, plucking beard, fasting, laceration, etc.

**Mouse** (*pilferer*). Many species in Palestine, but Bible word generic, Lev. xi. 29; 1 Sam. vi. 4; Isa. lxvi. 17.

**Mōw'ing.** Reaping with sickle, Ps. cxxix. 7. "King's mowings," perhaps a royal right of pasturage, Am. vii. 1.

**Mō'zȧ** (*departing*). (1) A son of Caleb, 1 Chr. ii. 46. (2) Descendant of Saul, 1 Chr. viii. 36, 37.

**Mō'zah** (*departing*). City in Benjamin, Josh. xviii. 26.

**Mŭl'bĕr-rȳ** (*dark berry*). Translation disputed, 2 Sam. v. 23, 24; 1 Chr. xiv. 14. The bacah or balsam tree is probably meant.

**Mūle.** Mules not bred in Palestine, but imported, 2 Sam. xiii. 29; 1 Kgs. i. 33; 2 Chr. ix. 24. Warm springs meant in Gen. xxxvi. 24.

**Mŭp'pim** (*serpent*). A Benjamite, Gen. xlvi. 21. Shupham, Num. xxvi. 39.

**Mûr'der** (*death*). Punished with death, Ex. xxi. 12; Num. xxxv. 30, 31; but cities of refuge provided for the escape of the involuntary slayer, Ex. xxi. 13; Num. xxxv. 32; Deut. xix. 1–13.

**Mûr'rain** (*die*). The malignant cattle disease which constituted the fifth Egyptian plague, Ex. ix. 1–7.

**Mū'shī** (*deserted*). A son of Merari, Ex. vi. 19; Num. iii. 20.

**Mū'shites.** Descendants of Mushi, Num. iii. 33; xxvi. 58.

**Mū'sic** (*muse*). Anciently known, Gen. iv. 21; xxxi. 27; Job xxi. 12. Vocal and instrumental, reached highest perfection in temple choirs, 2 Sam. vi. 5; 1 Chr. xxv. Usual instruments, harp, timbrel, psalter, trumpet, flute, pipe, etc.

**Mŭs'tard** (*must*). The black mustard of the East grows quite large and strong, Matt. xiii. 31, 32; xvii. 20; Mark iv. 31, 32; Luke xvii. 6.

**Mŭth=lăb'ben.** Enigmatical title to Ps. ix.

**Mȳn'dus.** Town in Caria, 1 Macc. xv. 23.

**Mȳ'rȧ** (*weeping*). Ancient seaport of Lycia, in Asia Minor, Acts xxvii. 5.

**Mȳrrh** (*bitter*). A gum resin much prized and variously used, Ex. xxx. 23; Esth. ii. 12; Ps. xlv. 8; Prov. vii. 17; Mark xv. 23; John xix. 39.

**Mȳr'tle.** A bushy evergreen, whose flowers, leaves, and berries were much used by Hebrews for perfume, ornament, and spicery, Isa. xli. 19; lv. 13; Zech. i. 8–11.

**Mȳs'ia** (*beech land*). Northwestern district of Asia Minor, Acts xvi. 7, 8.

## N

**Nā'am** (*pleasant*). Son of Caleb, 1 Chr. iv. 15.

**Nā'a-mah** (*pleasing*). (1) Sister of Tubal-cain, Gen. iv. 22. (2) A wife of Solomon and mother of King Rehoboam, 1 Kgs. xiv. 21; 2 Chr. xii. 13. (3) Town in Judah, Josh. xv. 41.

**Nā'a-man** (*pleasantness*). (1) The leprous Syrian, cured by Elisha's orders, 2 Kgs. v. (2) Founder of the Naamites, Gen. xlvi. 21; Num. xxvi. 40.

**Nā'a-math-īte''.** Designation of Job's friend Zophar, Job ii. 11.

**Nā'a-mītes**, Num. xxvi. 40. [NAAMAN, 2.]

**Nā'a-rah** (*youth*). Wife of Ashur, 1 Chr. iv. 5, 6.

**Nā'a-rāi** (*youthful*). One of David's warriors, 1 Chr. xi. 37. Paarai, 2 Sam. xxiii. 35.

**Nā'a-răn**, 1 Chr. vii. 28. [NAARATH.]

**Nā'a-răth** (*youthful*). A border of Ephraim, Josh. xvi. 7.

**Nȧ-ăsh'on**, Ex. vi. 23. [NAHSHON.]

**Nȧ-ăs'son.** Greek form of Nahshon, Matt. i. 4; Luke iii. 32.

**Nā'a-thus.** Son of Addi, 1 Esdr. ix. 31.

**Nā'băl** (*fool*). The Carmelite shepherd who refused food to David, 1 Sam. xxv.

**Năb''a-ri'as**, 1 Esdr. ix. 44. [ZECHARIAS.]

**Nā'băth-ītes**, 1 Macc. v. 25. [NEBAIOTH.]

**Nā'bŏth** (*fruits*). The vineyardist of Jezreel whom Jezebel caused to be murdered, 1 Kgs. xxi. 1–16; 2 Kgs. ix. 26.

**Năb''ū-chô-dŏn'ô-sôr.** Apocryphal form of Nebuchadnezzar.

**Nā'chŏn** (*ready*). Owner of the threshing-floor where the over-zealous Uzzah died, 2 Sam. vi. 6, 7.

**Nā'chôr**, Josh. xxiv. 2; Luke iii. 34. [NAHOR.]

**Nā'dăb** (*liberal*). (1) Son of Aaron, Ex. vi. 23; xxiv. 1. Struck dead for offering strange fire, Lev. x. 1–3. (2) Son and successor of Jeroboam on throne of Israel, B. C. 954–953. Slain by Baasha, his successor, 1 Kgs. xv. 25–31. (3) A Judahite, 1 Chr. ii. 28. (4) Uncle of Saul, 1 Chr. viii. 30.

**Nȧ-dăb'a-thȧ.** Place east of Jordan, 1 Macc. ix. 37.

**Năg'ge** (*shining*). Ancestor of Joseph, Luke iii. 25.

**Nā'ha-lăl** (*pasture*). Levitical city in Zebulun, Josh. xxi. 35.

**Nȧ-hā'li-el** (*God's valley*). Israelite encampment in Ammon, Num. xxi. 19.

**Nȧ-hăl'lăl**, Josh. xix. 15. [NAHALAL.]

**Nā'ha-lōl**, Judg. i. 30. [NAHALAL.]

**Nā'ham** (*comforter*). Brother of Hodiah, 1 Chr. iv. 19.

**Nȧ-hăm'a-nī** (*compassionate*). One who returned, Neh. vii. 7.

**Nȧ-hăr'a-ī** (*snorer*). Joab's armor-bearer, 1 Chr. xi. 39.

**Nā'ha-rī**, 2 Sam. xxiii. 37. [NAHARAI.]

**Nā'hăsh** (*serpent*). (1) A king of Ammon, 1 Sam. xi. 1–11; 2 Sam. x. 2. (2) Father of Abigail, 2 Sam. xvii. 25.

**Nā'hăth** (*rest*). (1) A duke of Edom, Gen. xxxvi. 13, 17. (2) Two Levites, 1 Chr. vi. 26; 2 Chr. xxxi. 13.

**Năh'bī** (*secret*). The spy of Naphtali, Num. xiii. 14.

**Nā'hôr** (*snoring*). (1) Abraham's grandfather, Gen. xi. 22–25. (2) Abraham's brother, Gen. xi. 27–29.

**Năh'shon** (*enchanter*). A prince of Judah, Num. i. 7.

**Nā'hum** (*comforter*). Seventh of minor prophets. Probably an exile in Assyria. Approximate time of prophecy, B. C. 726–698. It relates to the fall of Nineveh. Noted for vigor and beauty.

**Nā'ī-dus**, 1 Esdr. ix. 31. [BENAIAH.]

**Nāil** (*hold, claw*). Nails of captives to be pared, Deut. xxi. 12. Ordinary metal nail, 1 Chr. xxii. 3; stylus, Jer. xvii. 1; stake, Isa. xxxiii. 20; tent-peg wood or metal, Ex. xxvii. 19; Judg. iv. 21, 22.

**Nā'in** (*beauty*). A village in Galilee, now Nein, Luke vii. 11.

**Nā'ioth** (*dwellings*). Samuel's dwelling place and school in Ramah, 1 Sam. xix. 18–23; xx. 1.

**Nȧ-nē'ȧ.** A Persian goddess, 1 Macc. vi. 1–4.

**Nȧ-ō'mī** (*my delight*). Mother-in-law of Ruth, Ruth i. 2, etc.

**Nā'phish** (*pleasure*). Son of Ishmael, Gen. xxv. 15; 1 Chr. i. 31.

**Năph'ī-sī**, 1 Esdr. v. 31. [NEPHUSIM.]

**Năph'ta-lī** (*wrestling*). Fifth son of Jacob, Gen. xxx. 8. Large tribe at Sinai and Jordan, Num. i. 43; xxvi. 50. Allotment in northern Canaan, Josh. xix. 32–39. Tribe carried captive in reign of Pekah, 2 Kgs. xv. 29. For "mount Naphtali," Josh. xx. 7, read, mountains of Naphtali.

**Năph'thär** (*cleansing*). Naphtha, 2 Macc. i. 36.

**Năph'tu-hĭm.** A Mizraite (Egyptian) tribe, Gen. x. 13.

**När-çĭs'sus** (*narcotic*). Roman friend of Paul, Rom. xvi. 11.

**Närd** (*smell*). [SPIKENARD.]

**Năs'băs.** Nephew of Tobit, Tob. xi. 18.

**Nā'sith,** 1 Esdr. v. 32. [NEZIAH.]

**Nā'sôr,** 1 Macc. xi. 67. [HAZOR.]

**Nā'than** (*given*). (1) Distinguished prophet, and royal adviser and biographer of David and Solomon, 2 Sam. vii. 2–17; xii. 1–22; 1 Kgs. i. 8–45; 1 Chr. xxix. 29; 2 Chr. ix. 29. (2) A son of David, 1 Chr. iii. 5; Luke iii. 31. (3) Father of one of David's warriors, 2 Sam. xxiii. 36. (4) A returned captive, Ez. viii. 16.

**Nā-thăn'a-el** (*gift of God*). (1) A disciple of Christ, and native of Cana in Galilee, John i. 47–51; xxi. 2. (2) Ancestor of Judith, Judith viii. 1.

**Năth''a-nī'as,** 1 Esdr. ix. 34. [NATHAN.]

**Nā'than-mē'lech.** Chamberlain under King Josiah, 2 Kgs. xxiii. 11.

**Nā'um** (*comfort*). Father of Amos, Luke iii. 25.

**Nāve.** Hub of a wheel, 1 Kgs. vii. 33.

**Nā'vē,** Ecclus. xlvi. 1. [NUN.]

**Năz'a-rēne.** Inhabitant of Nazareth; Jesus so-called, Matt. ii. 23. Nazarenes, followers of Jesus, Acts xxiv. 5.

**Năz'a-rěth** (*separated*). A town of Galilee, now En-nazirah. Home of Jesus, Matt. iv. 13; Mark i. 9; Luke i. 26; iv. 16, 29; John i. 45, 46.

**Năz'a-rite** (*separated*). One bound by a temporary or life vow, Num. vi. 1–21; Am. ii. 11, 12; Acts xxi. 20–26.

**Nē'ah** (*shaking*). A Zebulun boundary mark, Josh. xix. 13.

**Nē-ăp'o-lis** (*new city*). Seaport in northern Greece; now Kavalla, Acts xvi. 11; xx. 1, 6.

**Nē''a-rī'ah** (*child of God*). (1) A Judahite, 1 Chr. iii. 22. (2) A chief of Simeon, 1 Chr. iv. 42.

**Něb'a-ī** (*budding*). A co-covenanter, Neh. x. 19.

**Nē-bā'ĵoth, Nē-bā'joth** (*heights*). Son of Ishmael, Gen. xxv. 13; 1 Chr. i. 29; Isa. lx. 7.

**Nē-băl'lat** (*secret folly*). Re-peopled town of Benjamin, Neh. xi. 34.

**Nē'băt** (*view*). Father of King Jeroboam, 1 Kgs. xi. 26; xii. 2–15.

**Nē'bō** (*prophet*). (1) A mountain of Moab, whence Moses viewed the promised land, Deut. xxxii. 49; xxxiv. 1. (2) A Reubenite city, Num. xxxii. 3, 38; xxxiii. 47. (3) Father of returned captives, Ez. ii. 29. (4) A Chaldean god, presiding over learning. Counterpart of the Greek Hermes, Isa. xlvi. 1; Jer. xlviii. 1.

**Něb''u-chăd-nez'zar** (*may Nebo protect*). King of Babylonish Empire, B. C. 605–561. Brought empire to greatest height of prosperity. Defeated Pharaoh-necho at Carchemish, Jer. xlvi. 2–26. Captured Jerusalem three different times, 2 Kgs. xxiv., xxv.; Dan. i.–iv.

**Něb''u-chăd-rěz'zar.** Jeremiah so writes Nebuchadnezzar.

**Něb''u-shăs'ban** (*Nebo saves*). A chief of eunuchs under Nebuchadnezzar, Jer. xxxix. 13.

**Něb''u-zär'ă-dan** (*whom Nebo favors*). Chief of Nebuchadnezzar's body-guard, 2 Kgs. xxv. 8–21; Jer. xxxix. 11; xl. 1–5.

**Nē'chō,** 2 Chr. xxxv. 20. [PHARAOH-NECHO.]

**Nē-cō'dan,** 1 Esdr. v. 37. [NEKODA.]

**Něd''a-bī'ah** (*driven*). A Judahite, 1 Chr. iii. 18.

**Něg'ĭ-nah.** Singular of Neginoth, Ps. lxi. title.

**Něg'ĭ-nŏth.** Stringed musical instruments. Title to Ps. iv., vi., liv., lv., lxvii., lxxvi.; Hab. iii. 19.

**Nē-hěl'a-mite** (*dreamer*). Designation of Shemaiah, Jer. xxix. 24–32.

**Nē-he-mī'ah** (*consolation*). (1) The Hebrew captive who returned, as leader of his people, to rebuild Jerusalem and administer its affairs. His book, 16th of O. T., B. C. 445–433, tells of his work. (2) Leader of returning captives, Ez. ii. 2; Neh. vii. 7. (3) An assistant wall-builder, Neh. iii. 16.

**Nē''he-mī'as,** 1 Esdr. v. 8, 40. [NEHEMIAH.]

**Nē'hĭ-lŏth** (*perforated*). The flute and similar wind instruments, Ps. v. title.

**Nē'hum** (*comfort*). A returned captive, Neh. vii. 7.

**Nē-hŭsh'tà** (*brazen*). Mother of King Jehoiachin, 2 Kgs. xxiv. 8.

**Nē'hŭsh-tan** (*little brazen thing*). Name of the preserved brazen serpent destroyed by King Hezekiah, 2 Kgs. xviii. 4.

**Nē'ĭ-el** (*God-moved*). An Asherite boundary, Josh. xix. 27.

**Nē'keb** (*cave*). A boundary town of Naphtali, Josh. xix. 33.

**Nē-kō'dà** (*famous*). Two fathers of returned captive families, Ez. ii. 48, 60.

**Nē-mū'el** (*God's day*). (1) A Reubenite, Num. xxvi. 9. (2) A Simeonite, Num. xxvi. 12; Jemuel, Gen. xlvi. 10.

**Nē-mū'el-ītes''.** Descendants of Nemuel (2), Num. xxvi. 12.

**Nē'pheg** (*sprout*). (1) Korah's brother, Ex. vi. 21. (2) Son of David, 2 Sam. v. 15.

**Něph'ew** (*grandson*). Grandchild or descendant, Job xviii. 19; Isa. xiv. 22.

**Nē'phish,** 1 Chr. v. 19. [NAPHISH.]

**Nē-phĭsh'e-sĭm.** His children returned, Neh. vii. 52.

**Něph'ta-lī,** Tob. i. 2–5. [NAPHTALI.]

**Něph'tha-lĭm,** Matt. iv. 13. [NAPHTALI.]

**Něp'tha-lĭm,** Rev. vii. 6. [NAPHTALI.]

**Něph'to-ah** (*opening*). A spring on boundary of Judah and Benjamin, Josh. xv. 9.

**Nē-phū'sim,** Ez. ii. 50. [NEPHISHESIM.]

**Nēr** (*lamp*). Grandfather of Saul, 1 Chr. viii. 33; ix. 39. Appears as an uncle of Saul in 1 Chr. ix. 36.

**Nē're-us.** A Roman Christian, Rom. xvi. 15.

**Něr'gal** (*hero*). A man-lion god of Assyria, corresponding to Mars, 2 Kgs. xvii. 30.

**Něr'gal-shâ-rē'zer** (*fire prince*). A prince of Babylon who released Jeremiah, Jer. xxxix. 3, 13.

**Nē'rī** (*lamp*). Son of Melchi, Luke iii. 27.

**Nē-rī'ah** (*light*). Father of Baruch, Jer. xxxii. 12.

**Nē-rī'as,** Bar. i. 1. [NERIAH.]

**Nět.** Used for hunting and fishing, Isa. xix. 8; Matt. xiii. 47. Style, manufacture, and method borrowed from Egyptians.

**Nē-thăn'e-el** (*gift of God*). Persons of this name in Num. i. 8; 1 Chr. ii. 14; xv. 24; xxiv. 6; xxvi. 4; 2 Chr. xvii. 7; xxxv. 9; Ez. x. 22; Neh. xii. 21, 36.

**Něth''a-nī'ah** (*God-given*). Persons in 2 Kgs. xxv. 23; 1 Chr. xxv. 2, 12; 2 Chr. xvii. 8; Jer. xxxvi. 14; xl. 8.

**Něth'ĭ-nĭm** (*dedicated*). Assistant priests. A class, or order, associated with the temple service and wardship, 1 Chr. ix. 2; Ez. vii. 24; viii. 17–20.

**Nē-tō'phah** (*dropping*). Town near Bethlehem, Ez. ii. 22; Neh. vii. 26.

**Nē-tŏph'a-thī.** Netophathites. Dwellers in Netophah, 1 Chr. ii. 54; Neh. xii. 28.

**Nět'tle** (*sting*). The stinging nettle in Isa. xxxiv. 13; Hos. ix. 6. Supposably the prickly acanthus in Job xxx. 7, Prov. xxiv. 31; Zeph. ii. 9.

**New Moon,** 1 Sam. xx. 5. [MOON.]

**New Těs'tă-ment.** [BIBLE.]

**New Year.** [TRUMPETS, FEAST OF.]

**Nē-zī'ah** (*famed*). Returned Nethinim, Ez. ii. 54; Neh. vii. 56.

**Nē'zib** (*pedestal*). Lowland city of Judah, Josh. xv. 43.

**Nĭb'hăz** (*barker*). The Avite god, in form of a dog-headed man, introduced into Samaria, 2 Kgs. xvii. 31.

**Nĭb'shăn** (*sandy*). Town in wilderness portion of Judah, Josh. xv. 62.

**Nī-cā'nor** (*conqueror*). (1) A governor of Judea, 1 Macc. iii. 38. (2) One of the first seven deacons of the early church, Acts vi. 1–6.

**Nĭc''o-dē'mus** (*people's victor*). The Pharisee ruler and timid convert who assisted at Christ's sepulture, John iii. 1–10; vii. 50; xix. 39.

**Nĭc-o-lā'ĭ-tanes.** An heretical sect condemned in Rev. ii. 6, 15.

**Nĭc'o-lăs** (*people's victor*). Native of Antioch. First a Jewish and then a Christian convert. One of the first seven deacons, Acts vi. 5.

**Nī-cŏp'o-lĭs** (*city of victory*). Many ancient cities of this name. Probably the one in Epirus is meant, Tit. iii. 12.

**Nī'ger** (*black*). Surname of Simeon, Acts xiii. 1.

**Night.** The Hebrew day, from sunset to sunset, embraced the entire night, Gen. i. 5. Death, John ix. 4; sin, 1 Thess. v. 5; sorrow, sin, and death, Rev. xxi. 25; xxii. 5.

**Nīght-hạwk.** An unclean bird, Lev. xi. 16; supposably the owl or night-jar.

**Nīle** (*dark blue*). The great river of Egypt, worshipped as a god, famous for its annual and fertilizing overflows and its many mouths. Name not mentioned in scripture, but alluded to as "the river," Gen. xli. 1; Ex. ii. 3; vii. 21; "the river of Egypt," Gen. xv. 18; "flood of Egypt," Am. viii. 8; Sihor, "black," Josh. xiii. 3; Shihor, "dark blue," 1 Chr. xiii. 5; "Nachal of Egypt," "river of Cush," etc.

**Nĭm′rah** (*clear*). City in Gad, east of Jordan, Num. xxxii. 3.

**Nĭm′rĭm** (*clear*). A stream in Moab, S. E. of Dead Sea, Isa. xv. 6; Jer. xlviii. 34.

**Nĭm′rŏd** (*brave*). Son of Cush. A renowned hunter, city builder, empire founder in Shinar (Babylonia), Gen. x. 8-12; 1 Chr. i. 10.

**Nĭm′shī** (*rescued*). Father of Jehu, 1 Kgs. xix. 16; 2 Kgs. ix. 2, 14.

**Nĭn′ẹ-veh** (*dwelling of Ninus*). Capital of Assyria, on river Tigris. Founded by Asshur, Gen. x. 11. At height of its wealth and splendor during time of Jonah and Nahum, and burden of their prophecies. Taken by Medes about B. C. 750, and destroyed by combined Medes and Babylonians, B. C. 606, Jonah; Nah. i.-iii; Zeph. ii. 13. Among the ruins of Nineveh, which was supposed to embrace Nimrud and other suburbs, have been discovered many palaces and temples, and a richly sculptured obelisk whose references are to Syria and Israel.

**Nĭn′ẹ-vītes.** Dwellers in Nineveh, Luke xi. 30.

**Nī′san** (*standard*). Abib, Ex. xiii. 4. First month of Hebrew sacred and seventh of civil year, corresponding to parts of March and April, Ex. xii. 2.

**Nĭs′rŏch** (*great eagle*). The eagle headed and winged Assyrian god, 2 Kgs. xix. 37; Isa. xxxvii. 38.

**Nī′tre.** The saltpetre of commerce. Evidently natron or washing soda is meant in Prov. xxv. 20; Jer. ii. 22.

**Nō** (*place*). Ancient Thebes and capital of Upper Egypt. The Diospolis of the Greeks. Situate on both banks of the Nile. Populous and splendid from B. C. 1600 to B. C. 800. Site of many imposing ruins. No-amon, "place of Amon," in marg. notes, Ezek. xxx. 14-16; Jer. xlvi. 25; Nah. iii. 8.

**Nō′′a-dī′ah** (*met by God*). (1) A Levite, Ez. viii. 33. (2) A hostile prophetess, Neh. vi. 14.

**Nō′ah** (*rest*). (1) Ninth in descent from Adam, Gen. v. 28-32. Chosen to build the ark, Gen. vi. 8-22. Saved from the flood, with his three sons, Shem, Ham, and Japheth, Gen. vii., viii. Re-peopled the earth, Gen. ix., x. Died at age of 950 years. (2) A daughter of Zelophehad, Num. xxvi. 33.

**Nō-ā′mon** (*place of Amon*). [No.]

**Nŏb** (*height*). Levitical city in Benjamin, noted as scene of the massacre of the priests, 1 Sam. xxi. 1; xxii. 19-23; Neh. xi. 32.

**Nō′bah** (*barking*). Name given by Nobah to Kenath, Num. xxxii. 42; Judg. viii. 11.

**Nŏd** (*fleeing*). The land to which Cain the murderer fled, Gen. iv. 16.

**Nō′dăb** (*noble*). An Arab tribe, 1 Chr. v. 19.

**Nō′e,** N. T. and Apoc. form of Noah, Matt. xxiv. 37; Luke iii. 36.

**Nō-ē′bȧ,** 1 Esdr. v. 31. [NEKODA.]

**Nō′gah** (*bright*). A son of David, 1 Chr. iii. 7.

**Nō′hah** (*rest*). A Benjamite, 1 Chr. viii. 2.

**Nŏn.** Form of Nun, 1 Chr. vii. 27.

**Nŏph,** Isa. xix. 13; Jer. ii. 16; Ezek. xxx. 13. [MEMPHIS.]

**Nō′phah** (*blast*). Town in Moab, Num. xxi. 30.

**Nōṣe-jẹw′elṣ.** Rings worn in the nose. Still affected in the East, Isa. iii. 21.

**Nŏv′ĭçe.** "Newly planted." A recent convert, 1 Tim. iii. 6.

**Nŭm′bẽrṣ** (*distribute*). (1) Hebrews used alphabetic letters for notation. They also had preferential numbers, as "three," "seven," "ten," "seventy," etc., Gen. iv. 24; Ex. xx. 5-17; Num. vii. 13; Rev. xv. 1. (2) Fourth book of Bible and Pentateuch. Authorship ascribed to Moses. Chapters i.-x. 10 describe the departure from Sinai; x. 11-xiv. the marches to borders of Caanan; xv.-xvi. contain laws; xx.-xxxvi. describe events leading to the passage of Jordan and the conquest.

**Nū-mē′nĭ-us.** Jonathan's ambassador to Greece and Rome, 1 Macc. xii. 16.

**Nŭn** (*fish*). Father of Joshua, Ex. xxxiii. 11; 1 Chr. vii. 27.

**Nûrse** (*nourish*). Position of importance and honor among Hebrews, Gen. xxiv. 59; xxxv. 8; 2 Sam. iv. 4.

**Nỹm′phas** (*bridegroom*). A Laodicean Christian, Col. iv. 15.

## O

**Ōak** (*strong*). Three varieties in Palestine, usually of great girth and expanse, but not noted for height, Gen. xxxv. 8; Judg. vi. 11, 19; 2 Sam. xviii. 9-14.

**Ōath.** Appeals to God to attest the truth of an assertion in early use, Gen. xxi. 23; xxvi. 3; Heb. vi. 16. Regulated in Ex. xx. 7; Lev. xix. 12. Forms: lifting hands, Gen. xiv. 22; placing hand under thigh, Gen. xxiv. 2; before the altar, 1 Kgs. viii. 31; laying hand on the law.

**Ō′′ba-dī′ah** (*servant of God*). (1) A Judahite, 1 Chr. iii. 21. (2) A chief of Issachar, 1 Chr. vii. 3. (3) Son of Azel, 1 Chr. viii. 38. (4) A Levite, 1 Chr. ix. 16. (5) A Gadite, 1 Chr. xii. 9. (6) A court officer under Ahab, 1 Kgs. xviii. 3-16. (7) A teacher of the law, 2 Chr. xvii. 7. (8) Others, in 1 Chr. xxvii. 19; 2 Chr. xxxiv. 12; Ez. viii. 9; Neh. x. 5; xii. 25. (9) Fourth of minor prophets. Prophesied after capture of Jerusalem. His book, 31st of O. T., is a denunciation of Edom. Nothing known of his history.

**Ō′bal** (*naked*). Son of Joktan, Gen. x. 28. Ebal in 1 Chr. i. 22.

**Ŏb′dĭ-ȧ,** 1 Esdr. v. 38. [HABAIAH.]

**Ō′bed** (*servant*). (1) Son of Boaz and Ruth, Ruth iv. 17; Luke iii. 32. (2) Descendant of Sheshan, 1 Chr. ii. 37, 38. (3) One of David's warriors, 1 Chr. xi. 47. (4) A temple porter, 1 Chr. xxvi. 7. (5) Father of Azariah, 2 Chr. xxiii. 1.

**Ō′bed-ē′dom** (*servant of Edom*). (1) He kept the ark for three months, 2 Sam. vi. 10-12; 1 Chr. xiii. 13, 14. (2) A temple treasurer, 2 Chr. xxv. 24.

**Ō′beth,** 1 Esdr. viii. 32. [EBED.]

**Ō′bil** (*camel-keeper*). David's camel-keeper, 1 Chr. xxvii. 30.

**Ŏb-lā′tion** (*spread out*). Act of offering. The offering itself, Lev. ii. 4.

**Ō′both** (*bottles*). An Israelite encampment, east of Moab, Num. xxi. 10; xxxiii. 43.

**Ō′chĭ-el** 1 Esdr. i. 9. [JEIEL.]

**Ŏc′ran** (*disturber*). An Asherite, Num. i. 13; ii. 27.

**Ŏd′′a-när′kẹṣ.** Chief of a nomad tribe, 1 Macc. ix. 66.

**Ō′ded** (*restoring*). (1) Father of Azariah, 2 Chr. xv. 1. (2) A Samaritan prophet, 2 Chr. xxviii. 9-11.

**Ō-dŏl′lam.** Greek form of Adullam, 2 Macc. xii. 38.

**Ŏf′fẽr-ĭng** (*bearing towards*). Either bloody, as of animals, or bloodless, as of vegetables. They embraced the burnt, sin, trespass, peace, and meat offerings, Lev. i.-ix.

**Ōg** (*giant*). King of Bashan, last of the giant Rephaim, Num. xxi. 33; Deut. i. 4; iii. 3-13; Josh. ii. 10.

**Ō′hăd** (*strength*). Son of Simeon, Gen. xlvi. 10.

**Ō′hel** (*tent*). Son of Zerubbabel, 1 Chr. iii. 20.

**Oil** (*olive*). Used for preparing food, Ex. xxix. 2; anointing, 2 Sam. xiv. 2; illuminating, Matt. xxv. 1-13; in worship, Num. xviii. 12; in consecration, 1 Sam. x. 1; in medicine, Mark vi. 13; in burial, Matt. xxvi. 12. Types gladness, Ps. xcii. 10.

**Oint′ment** (*smear*). Highly prized, and made of perfumes in oil. For uses, *see* Oil.

**Ŏl′ĭve.** A tree resembling the apple in size and shape, bearing a plum-like fruit, prized for its oil, Gen. viii. 11; Deut. vi. 11; Job xxiv. 11. Olive wood used in the temple, 1 Kgs. vi. 23, 31-33.

**Ŏl′ĭveṣ, Ŏl′ị-vĕt.** The mount of Olives, or Olivet, is the ridge east of Jerusalem, beyond the brook Kidron. So named from its olive-trees. On its slopes were Gethsemane, Bethphage and Bethany, 2 Sam. xv. 30; Zech. xiv. 4; Matt. xxi. 1; Mark xi. 1; Luke xxii. 39; John viii. 1; Acts i. 12.

**Ō-lỹm′pas** (*heavenly*). A Roman Christian, Rom. xvi. 15.

**O-lỹm′pĭ-us.** The Grecian Zeus, or Jupiter, dwelling on Olympus, 2 Macc. vi. 2.

**Ŏm′′a-ē′rus,** 1 Esdr. ix. 34. [AMRAM.]

**Ō′mar** (*speaker*). A duke of Edom, Gen. xxxvi. 11, 15.

**Ō-mĕg′ȧ** or **Ō-mē′gȧ** (*great or long O*). Last letter of Greek alphabet, Rev. i. 8.

**Ō′mẽr.** A Hebrew dry measure, equal to tenth part of an ephah, Ex. xvi. 36.

**Ŏm'rī** (*pupil*). (1) A general under Elah, king of Israel, and eventually king, B. C. 929-918. He built Samaria and made it the capital, 1 Kgs. xvi. 16-28. (2) A Benjamite, 1 Chr. vii. 8. (3) A Judahite, 1 Chr. ix. 4. (4) A chief of Issachar, 1 Chr. xxvii. 18.

**Ŏn** (*strength*). (1) Grandson of Reuben, Num. xvi. 1. (2) City of Lower Egypt, Gen. xli. 45, 50. Bethshemesh or "house of the sun," Jer. xliii. 13. In Greek, Heliopolis, "city of the sun," Ezek. xxx. 17 marg. Noted for its learning, opulence, temples, shrines, monuments, sphinxes, and religious schools.

**Ō'nam** (*strong*). (1) Grandson of Seir, Gen. xxxvi. 23. (2) Son of Jerahmeel, 1 Chr. ii. 26.

**Ō'nan** (*strong*). Second son of Judah, slain for wickedness, Gen. xxxviii. 4-10; Num. xxvi. 19.

**Ō-nĕs'ĭ-mus** (*useful*). Slave of Philemon, at Colosse, in whose behalf Paul wrote the epistle to Philemon, Col. iv. 9; Phile. 10, 15.

**Ŏn''e-sĭph'o-rus** (*profit-bearing*). Friend of Paul at Ephesus and Rome, 2 Tim. i. 16-18; iv. 19.

**Ō-nī'a-rēs**. Onias and Areus, 1 Macc. xii. 19.

**Ō-nī'as**. Name of five high priests during time of Maccabees.

**On'ion** (*one*). The single-bulbed plant growing to perfection in the Nile valley, Num. xi. 5.

**Ō'nō** (*strong*). Town in Benjamin, 1 Chr. viii. 12.

**Ō'nus**, 1 Esdr. v. 22. [Ono.]

**Ŏn'y̆-chă** (*nail*). Incense ingredient; probably burnt seashell, Ex. xxx. 34.

**Ō'ny̆x** (*nail*). A cryptocrystalline quartz, veined and shelled, Ex. xxviii. 9-12; 1 Chr. xxix. 2.

**Ō'phel** (*hill*). A fortified hill in Jerusalem, 2 Chr. xxvii. 3; Neh. iii. 26; xi. 21.

**Ō'phīr** (*fruitful*). (1) Son of Joktan, and his country in Arabia, Gen. x. 29. (2) Place whence the Hebrews drew gold, ivory, peacocks, and woods. Variously located, 1 Kgs. ix. 28; x. 11-22; xxii. 48; 1 Chr. xxix. 4; Job xxviii. 16; Ps. xlv. 9.

**Ŏph'nī** (*mouldy*). Town in Benjamin, Josh. xviii. 24.

**Ŏph'rah** (*fawn*). (1) Town in Benjamin, Josh. xviii. 23; 1 Sam. xiii. 17. (2) Native place of Gideon, Judg. vi. 11, 24. (3) Son of Meonothai, 1 Chr. iv. 14.

**Ŏr'a-cle** (*speaking*). In O. T. sense, the holy place whence God declared his will, 1 Kgs. vi. 5; viii. 6. Divine revelation, Acts vii. 38; Rom. iii. 2.

**Ō'reb** (*raven*). (1) A Midianite chief, Judg. vii. 25. (2) The rock, "raven's crag," east of Jordan, where Oreb fell, Judg. vii. 25; Isa. x. 26.

**Ō'ren** (*pine*). Son of Jerahmeel, 1 Chr. ii. 25.

**Ŏr'gan** (*instrument*). The "pipe," or any perforated wind instrument, Gen. iv. 21; Job. xxi. 12; Ps. cl. 4.

**Ō-rī'on** (*hunter, Orion*). The constellation, Job ix. 9; xxxviii. 31; Am. v. 8.

**Ŏr'na-ments** (*adornments*). Of infinite variety among Oriental peoples, Gen. xxiv. 22; Isa. iii. 16-25; Jer. ii. 32; Ezek. xvi. 11-19.

**Ŏr'nan** (*active*). The Jebusite prince from whom David bought the threshing-floor on which he built the altar, 1 Chr. xxi. 15-25. [Araunah.]

**Ŏr'pah** (*fawn*). Daughter-in-law of Naomi, Ruth i. 4-14.

**Or-thō'si-as**. City of northern Phœnicia, 1 Macc. xv. 37.

**Ō-sē'ă**, 2 Esdr. xiii. 40. [Hosea.]

**Ō'see**. Greek form of Hosea, Rom. ix. 25.

**Ō-shē'ă**. Original name of Joshua, Num. xiii. 8.

**Ŏs'prāy** (*ossifrage, bone-breaker*). An unclean bird; probably the osprey or sea-eagle, Lev. xi. 13; Deut. xiv. 12.

**Ŏs'sĭ-frăge** (*bone-breaker*). An unclean bird; the lammergeir, or bearded vulture, Lev. xi. 13; Deut. xiv. 12.

**Ŏs'trĭch** (*bird*). In Hebrew, "daughter of greediness." In Arabic and Greek "camel-bird." Largest of the bird species, Job xxxix. 13-18.

**Ŏth'ni** (*lion*). Son of Shemaiah, 1 Chr. xxvi. 7.

**Ŏth'nĭ-el** (*lion*). A judge of Israel, Josh. xv. 17; Judg. i. 13; iii. 9-11.

**Ou'ches** (*brooches*). Jewel settings, Ex. xxxix. 6.

**Ŏv'en** (*arch*). Fixed ovens, Hos. vii. 4. Portable, consisting of a large clay jar, Ex. viii. 3; Lev. xxvi. 26.

**Owl** (*howl*). An unclean bird and type of desolation. Five species found in Palestine, Lev. xi. 17; Deut. xiv. 16; Ps. cii. 6; Isa. xxxiv. 11-15.

**Ŏx** (*sprinkle*). (1) Ancestor of Judith, Judith viii. 1. (2) The male of the cow kind, and in scripture synonymous with bull. Used for plowing, Deut. xxii. 10; threshing, without muzzle, xxv. 4; draught, Num. vii. 3; burden, 1 Chr. xii. 40; beef, Deut. xiv. 4; sacrifices, 1 Kgs. i. 9.

**Ō'zem** (*strength*). (1) A brother of David, 1 Chr. ii. 15. (2) Son of Jerahmeel, 1 Chr. ii. 25.

**Ō-zī'as**. (1) Governor of Bethulia, Judith vi. 15. (2) Ancestor of Ezra, 2 Esdr. i. 2. (3) N. T. form of Uzziah, Matt. i. 8, 9.

**Ō-zī'el**. Ancestor of Judith, Judith viii. 1.

**Ŏz'nī** (*hearing*). Son of Gad, Num. xxvi. 16; Ezbon, Gen. xlvi. 16.

**Ŏz'nītes**. Descendants of Ozni, Num. xxvi. 16.

**Ō-zō'rā**, 1 Esdr. ix. 24. [Shelamiah.]

## P

**Pā'a-rāi** (*opening*). One of David's warriors, 2 Sam. xxiii. 35; Naarai, 1 Chr. xi. 37.

**Pā'dan** (*table-land*), Gen. xlviii. 7. [Padan-aram.]

**Pā'dan-ā'ram** (*table-land of Aram*). The plain region of Mesopotamia, Gen. xxiv. 10; xxv. 20; xxviii. 2-7; xxxi. 18; xxxiii. 18; xxxv. 9-26; xlvi. 15.

**Pā'don** (*escape*). His children returned, Ez. ii. 44.

**Pā'gi-el** (*God-allotted*). A chief of Asher, Num. i. 13; ii. 27; vii. 72, 77; x. 26.

**Pā'hath-mō'ab** (*ruler of Moab*). His children returned, Ez. ii. 6; viii. 4; Neh. iii. 11.

**Pā'ī**, 1 Chr. i. 50. [Pau.]

**Pāint**. Much used in East as cosmetic and beautifier, 2 Kgs. ix. 30; Jer. iv. 30. Houses, walls, beams, idols, painted, Jer. xxii. 14; Ezek. xxiii. 14. Painting as a fine art not encouraged by Hebrews.

**Păl'açe**. Royal residence, 1 Kgs. vii. 1-12; citadel, 1 Kgs. xvi. 18; fortress, 2 Kgs. xv. 25; entire royal court, Dan. i. 4; capital city, Esth. ix. 12. In N. T. any stately residence, Matt. xxvi. 3; Luke xi. 21.

**Pā'lal** (*judge*). An assistant wall-builder, Neh. iii. 25.

**Păl''es-tī'nă, Păl'es-tīne** (*land of sojourners*). Philistia, land of the Philistines, Ps. lx. 8; lxxxiii. 7. Palestina, Ex. xv. 14; Isa. xiv. 29, 31. Palestine, Joel iii. 4. Canaan, Gen. xii. 5; Ex. xv. 15; Holy Land, Zech. ii. 12. The indefinitely bounded region promised to Abraham, lying between the Mediterranean Sea and Jordan River and Dead Sea. It also embraced the Hebrew settlements beyond Jordan, Gen. xv. 18; xvii. 8; Num. xxiv. 2-12; Deut. i. 7.

**Păl'lu** (*famous*). Son of Reuben, Ex. vi. 14.

**Păl'lu-ītes**. Descendants of Pallu, Num. xxvi. 5.

**Pälm'er-worm** (*pilgrim-worm*). Cankerworm, or caterpillar, Joel i. 4; ii. 25; Amos iv. 9.

**Pälm-tree** (*hand-leaved*). The date-palm. Once grew luxuriantly in Palestine. Evergreen and stately, often rising to 100 feet, Ex. xv. 27; Deut. xxxiv. 3; Judg. i. 16; 1 Kgs. vi. 32; S. of Sol. vii. 7.

**Pal'sy̆** (*paralysis*). Partial or total death of muscle and nerve, 1 Kgs. xiii. 4-6; Matt. iv. 24; Luke vi. 6.

**Păl'tī** (*deliverance*). The Benjamite spy, Num. xiii. 9.

**Păl'tī-el** (*deliverance*). A prince of Issachar, Num. xxxiv. 26.

**Păl'tite**. Designation of one of David's guardsmen, 2 Sam. xxiii. 26.

**Păm-phy̆l'ĭ-ă** (*mixture of nations*). A seacoast province of Asia Minor. Its chief town was Perga, where Paul preached, Acts xiii. 13; xiv. 24; xxvii. 5.

**Păn** (*open*). A flat plate for baking, and a deeper vessel for holding liquids, Lev. ii. 5; vi. 21.

**Păn'năg**. Disputed word. Probably a place, Ezek. xxvii. 17.

**Pā'per**. [Papyrus.]

**Pā'phos** (*hot*). Town on island of Cyprus, visited by Paul, Acts xiii. 6-13.

**Pā-py̆'rus**. The writing-paper of the Egyptians, Greeks, and Romans, made from the papyrus plant, a rush or flag growing in Egypt, Job xl. 21.

**Păr'ă-ble** (*comparison*). Allegorical representation of something real in nature or human affairs, whence a moral is drawn. A favorite method of Oriental teaching, 2 Sam. xii. 1-4; Isa. v. 1-7. Christ spoke over 30 parables, Matt. xiii. 3-8; 24-30, 31, 32, and elsewhere in Gospels.

**Păr'ȧ-dīse** (*pleasure ground*). "Garden of Eden;" and, figuratively, abode of happy souls — heaven, Luke xxiii. 43; 2 Cor. xii. 4; Rev. ii. 7.

**Pā'rah** (*place of heifers*). City in Benjamin, Josh. xviii. 23.

**Pā'ran, El-pā'ran** (*places of caves*). The "desert of wandering," with Canaan on the north, desert of Sinai on the south, Etham on the west, and Arabah on the east, Gen. xxi. 14-21; Num. x. 12, 33; xii. 16; xiii. 3, 26; xxxiii. 17-36.

**Pā'ran, Mount of**. A mount of the Sinaitic range, Deut. xxxiii. 2; Hab. iii. 3.

**Pär'bar** (*suburb*). A spot between the west wall of temple at Jerusalem and the city beyond, 1 Chr. xxvi. 18.

**Pärched Corn**. Roasted grain, Ruth ii. 14.

**Pärched Ground**. Supposably the mirage frequently seen on desert tracts, Isa. xxxv. 7.

**Pärch'ment** (*from Pergamum*). Skin of sheep or goats prepared for writing on, 2 Tim. iv. 13.

**Pär'lor** (*speaking chamber*). King's audience-chamber, Judg. iii. 20-25.

**Pär-măsh'tȧ** (*stronger*). A son of Haman, Esth. ix. 9.

**Pär'me-năs** (*steadfast*). One of the first seven deacons, Acts vi. 5.

**Pär'nach** (*swift*). A Zebulunite, Num. xxxiv. 25.

**Pā'rŏsh** (*flea*). His children returned, Ez. ii. 3; Neh. vii. 8.

**Pär-shăn'da-thȧ** (*prayer-given*). Eldest son of Haman, Esth. ix. 7.

**Pär'thĭ-ans**. Jews settled in Parthia, that undefined country north of Media and Persia, Acts ii. 9.

**Pär'trĭdge** (*squatting*). Three varieties found in Palestine. Their flesh and eggs esteemed as food, 1 Sam. xxvi. 20; Jer. xvii. 11.

**Păr'u-ah** (*blooming*). Father of Solomon's commissary in Issachar, 1 Kgs. iv. 17.

**Pär-vā'im** (*eastern*). Unknown place whence Solomon shipped gold, 2 Chr. iii. 6.

**Pā'sach** (*cut off*). An Asherite, 1 Chr. vii. 33.

**Păs-dăm'mĭm** (*blood-border*). Spot of battles between Israel and Philistia, 1 Chr. xi. 13. Ephes-dammim, 1 Sam. xvii. 1.

**Pȧ-sē'ah** (*lame*). (1) A Judahite, 1 Chr. iv. 12. (2) His sons returned, Ez. ii. 49.

**Păsh'ŭr** (*freedom*). (1) Head of a priestly family, 1 Chr. ix. 12; Neh. xi. 12; Jer. xxi. 1. (2) Priestly governor of the house of the Lord, 1 Chr. xxiv. 14; Jer. xx. i.

**Păs'sion** (*suffering*). Last sufferings of Christ, Acts i. 3. Kindred feelings, Acts xiv. 15; Jas. v. 17.

**Păss'ō-ver** (*passing over*). First of three great Jewish feasts, instituted in honor of the "passing over" of the Hebrew households by the destroying angel, Ex. xii., xiii. 3-10; xxiii. 14-19; Lev. xxiii. 4-14. Called the "feast of unleavened bread." The Christian Passover is "The Lord's Supper," eucharist, Matt. xxvii. 62; Luke xxii. 1-20; John xix. 42.

**Păs'tor** (*shepherd*). Figuratively, one who keeps Christ's flocks, Eph. iv. 11.

**Păt'a-rȧ** (*trodden*). City on southwest coast of Lycia, Acts xxi. 1, 2.

**Pāte** (*flat*). Top of the head, Ps. vii. 16.

**Pȧ-thē'us**, 1 Esdr. ix. 23. [Pethahiah.]

**Păth'ros** (*southern*). An ancient division of Upper Egypt occupied by the Pathrusim, Isa. xi. 11; Jer. xliv. 1-15; Ezek. xxix. 14.

**Păth-ru'sĭm**, Gen. x. 14. [Pathros.]

**Păt'mos**. The rocky island in the Ægean Sea, to which John was banished, Rev. i. 9.

**Pā'trĭ-arch** (*father*). Father of the family and chief of its descendants. The Hebrew form of government till Moses established the theocracy, Acts ii. 29; vii. 8, 9; Heb. vii. 4.

**Păt'ro-băs** (*paternal*). A Roman Christian, Rom. xvi. 14.

**Pȧ-trŏ'clus**. Father of Nicanor, 2 Macc. viii. 9.

**Pā'u** (*bleating*). Capital of Hadar, king of Edom, Gen. xxxvi. 39. Pai, 1 Chr. i. 50.

**Paul** (*small*). In Hebrew, Saul. Born at Tarsus in Cilicia, of Benjamite parents, about the beginning of 1st century; a Pharisee in faith; a tent-maker by trade, Phil. iii. 5; Acts xviii. 3; xxi. 39; xxiii. 6. Studied law with Gamaliel at Jerusalem; persecuted early Christians; converted near Damascus, Acts v. 34; vii. 58; ix. 1-22. Commissioned an apostle to the Gentiles, Acts xxvi. 13-20. Carried the gospel to Asia Minor, Greece, and Rome. Author of fourteen epistles, amplifying the Christian faith. Supposably a martyr at Rome, A. D. 68.

**Pāve'ment** (*beaten floor*). [Gabbatha.]

**Pȧ-vĭl'ion** (*butterfly tent*). Movable tent or dwelling. Applied to tabernacle, booth, den, etc., 1 Kgs. xx. 12; Ps. xviii. 11; xxvii. 5; Jer. xliii. 10.

**Pēa'cock** (*eye-feathered cock*). An import from Tarshish, 1 Kgs. x. 22; 2 Chr. ix. 21. The peacock of Job xxxix. 13 should be ostrich.

**Pēarls** (*little pears*). Stony secretions of the pearl-oyster. Reckoned as gems and highly prized as ornaments. Source of frequent metaphor, Matt. xiii. 45; 1 Tim. ii. 9; Rev. xvii. 4; xxi. 21. Pearl, in Job xxviii. 18, should be crystal.

**Pĕd'a-hĕl** (*saved*). A chief of Naphtali, Num. xxxiv. 28.

**Pē-däh'zur** (*rock-saved*). Father of Gamaliel, Num. i. 10.

**Pē'dā'iah** (*God-saved*). (1) Grandfather of King Jehoiakim, 2 Kgs. xxiii. 36. (2) Father of Zerubbabel, 1 Chr. iii. 18, 19. (3) A Manassite, 1 Chr. xxvii. 20. (4) Returned captives, Neh. iii. 25; viii. 4; xi. 7; xiii. 13.

**Pē'kah** (*open-eyed*). Murderer and successor of Pekahiah, king of Israel, B. C. 758-738. Conspired with Damascus against Judah, and perished in a conspiracy, 2 Kgs. xv. 25-31; xvi.; 2 Chr. xxviii.

**Pĕk''a-hī'ah** (*God opens*). Son and successor of Menahem on the throne of Israel, B. C. 760-758. Murdered and succeeded by his general, Pekah, 2 Kgs. xv. 22-26.

**Pē'kŏd**. The Chaldeans are so called in Jer. l. 21; Ezek. xxiii. 23.

**Pĕl''a-ī'ah** (*distinguished*). (1) A Judahite, 1 Chr. iii. 24. (2) A co-covenanter, Neh. viii. 7; x. 10.

**Pĕl''a-lī'ah** (*judged*). A returned priest, Neh. xi. 12.

**Pĕl''a-tī'ah** (*saved*). (1) Grandson of Zerubbabel, 1 Chr. iii. 21. (2) A Simeonite warrior, 1 Chr. iv. 42. (3) A co-covenanter, Neh. x. 22. (4) One struck dead for defying Ezekiel, Ezek. xi. 1-13.

**Pē'leg** (*division*). Son of Eber. His family remained in Mesopotamia, Gen. x. 25; xi. 16-19.

**Pē'let** (*freedom*). (1) A Judahite, 1 Chr. ii. 47. (2) An adherent of David, 1 Chr. xii. 3.

**Pē'leth** (*freedom*). (1) Father of the rebellious On, Num. xvi. 1. (2) Son of Jonathan, 1 Chr. ii. 33.

**Pē'leth-ītes** (*runners*). Retainers and messengers of David, 2 Sam. viii. 18; xv. 18; xx. 7.

**Pē-lī'as**, 1 Esdr. ix. 34. [Bedeiah.]

**Pĕl'ĭ-can** (*axe-bill*). A voracious water-bird, large and strong-billed. The female is supplied with a pouch for supplying itself and young with water and food. Symbol of desolation. Original sometimes translated "cormorant," Lev. xi. 18; Deut. xiv. 17; Ps. cii. 6; Isa. xxxiv. 11.

**Pĕl'o-nīte**. Designation of two of David's warriors, 1 Chr. xi. 27, 36.

**Pĕn** (*feather*). Anciently, a metal graver for tracing on hard substances; the stylus, of pointed metal or bone, for writing in wax; the reed pen and hair pencil for writing on parchment and linen, Judg. v. 14; Job xix. 24; Jer. xvii. 1.

**Pē-nī'el** (*face of God*). Place beyond Jordan where Jacob wrestled with the angel, Gen. xxxii. 30. Penuel in Judg. viii. 17; 1 Kgs. xii. 25.

**Pē-nĭn'nah** (*pearl*). A wife of Elkanah, 1 Sam. i. 1-4.

**Pĕn'nȳ** (*cattle*). The Roman silver denarius, worth 15 to 17 cents. The Greek silver drachma was a corresponding coin, Matt. xx. 2; xxii. 19-21; Mark vi. 37; Luke xx. 24; Rev. vi. 6.

**Pĕn'tȧ-teuch** (*five-fold book*). Greek name for the first five O. T. books, or books of Moses. Called Torah, "the law," by Hebrews.

**Pĕn'te-cŏst** (*fiftieth day*). The Hebrew harvest-home festival, celebrated on fiftieth day from the Passover, or on the date of the giving of the law at Sinai, Ex. xxiii. 16; xxxiv. 22; Lev. xxiii. 15-22; Num. xxviii. In the Christian Church, Pentecost is celebrated seven weeks after Easter, to commemorate the day in Acts ii. 1-14.

**Pē-nū'el**. (1) [Peniel.] (2) A Judahite, 1 Chr. iv. 4. (3) A Benjamite, 1 Chr. viii. 25.

**Pē'or** (*cleft*). (1) The mountain in Moab to which Balak brought Balaam, Num. xxiii. 28; xxv. 18; xxxi. 16. (2) [BAAL-PEOR.]

**Pĕr'a-zĭm** (*breach*). A figurative mountain, Isa. xxviii. 21.

**Pē'resh** (*dung*). Son of Machir, 1 Chr. vii. 16.

**Pē'rez** (*rent*). An important Judahite family, 1 Chr. xxvii. 3; Neh. xi. 4-6.

**Pē'rez-ŭz'zah** (*breaking of Uzzah*). Where Uzzah died, 2 Sam. vi. 6-8. Perez-uzza, 1 Chr. xiii. 9-11.

**Pĕr'fūme** (*thorough-fume*). Perfumes largely used by Hebrews in religious rites and for toilet purposes, Ex. xxx. 35; Prov. xxvii. 9.

**Pĕr'gȧ** (*earthy*). A city of Pamphylia, Acts xiii. 13.

**Pĕr'ga-mŏs** (*heights*). Pergamum in R. V. A city of Mysia, in Asia Minor, celebrated for its library, which was transferred to Alexandria. Seat of one of the "seven churches," Rev. i. 11; ii. 12-17.

**Pē-rī'dȧ** (*kernels*). His children returned, Neh. vii. 57.

**Pĕr'ĭz-zītes** (*villagers*). Original village-dwellers in Canaan, Gen. xiii. 7: Josh. xvii. 15.

**Pĕr-sĕp'ō-lis** (*city of Persia*). Capital of Persia. Ruins very extensive, 2 Macc. ix. 2.

**Pĕr'seụs** (*destroyer*). Last king of Macedonia; defeated by Rome, 1 Macc. viii. 5.

**Pĕr'ṣia** (*land of Perses*). Originally the country around the head of the Persian Gulf; afterwards the great empire, including all western Asia, and parts of Europe and Africa. Reached its height under Cyrus, B. C. 486-485. Conquered by Alexander, B. C. 330, Ezek. xxxviii. 5; 2 Chr. xxxvi. 20-23; Ez. i. 8.

**Pĕr'sis** (*Persian*). A Christian woman at Rome, Rom. xvi. 12.

**Pē-rụ'dȧ**, Ez. ii. 55. [PERIDA.]

**Pĕs'tĭ-lence** (*the plague*). In Hebrew, all distempers and calamities, Ex. ix. 14; xi. 1; 1 Kgs. viii. 37.

**Pē'ter** (*stone, rock*). Simon, or Simeon; son of Jonas, Matt. xvi. 17: Acts xv. 14. A fisherman, resident at Capernaum, Matt. viii. 14; called, Matt. iv. 18-20; name changed to Peter, John i. 42. Founder of Christian Church among the Jews, Acts ii.; spokesman of the apostles, Acts x.; author of two epistles: a probable martyr at Rome. His first epistle is dated from Babylon; his second is his valedictory. Both are advisory and exhortatory.

**Pĕth''a-hī'ah** (*freed*). (1) Head of the 19th priestly course, 1 Chr. xxiv. 16. (2) Returned captives, Ez. x. 23; Neh. ix. 5; xi. 24.

**Pē'thôr** (*prophet*). Balaam's residence in Mesopotamia, Num. xxii. 5; Deut. xxiii. 4.

**Pē-thū'el** (*vision*). Father of Joel, Joel i. 1.

**Pē'trȧ** (*rock*). Edom. Modernly, Arabia Petræa.

**Pē-ŭl'thāi** (*wages*). Eighth son of Obed-edom, 1 Chr. xxvi. 5.

**Phāi'sụr**, 1 Esdr. ix. 22. [PASHUR.]

**Phā'lec**, Luke iii. 35. [PELEG.]

**Phăl'lū**, Gen. xlvi. 9. [PALLU.]

**Phăl'ti** (*deliverance*). The man to whom Saul gave Michal, his daughter and David's wife, 1 Sam. xxv. 44. Phaltiel, 2 Sam. iii. 15, 16.

**Phăl'tĭ-el**, 2 Sam. iii. 15. [PHALTI.]

**Phăn-ū'el** (*face of God*). Father of Anna the prophetess, Luke ii. 36.

**Phăr'a-cĭm**. His sons returned, 1 Esdr. v. 31.

**Phā'raōh** (*sun-king*). General name of Egyptian kings. Only a few are definitely named in the Bible. Different ones alluded to are, Gen. xii. 15: xli.; Ex. i. 8; v. 1; 1 Chr. iv. 18; 1 Kgs. xi. 18-22; ix. 16; 2 Kgs. xviii. 21; Pharaoh-nechoh, 2 Kgs. xxiii. 29; Pharaoh-hophra, Jer. xxxvii. 5-8.

**Phā'raōh's Daugh'ter.** (1) Guardian of Moses, Ex. ii. 5-10. (2) Wife of Mered, 1 Chr. iv. 18. (3) Wife of Solomon, 1 Kgs. iii. 1.

**Phā'rēṣ**, Matt. i. 3; Luke iii. 33. [PHAREZ.]

**Phā'rĕz** (*breach*). A Judahite, Gen. xxxviii. 29; xlvi. 12. Father of Pharzites, Num. xxvi. 20. Perez, Neh. xi. 4, 6. Phares, Matt. i. 3; Luke iii. 33.

**Phăr'ĭ-see** (*set apart*). A Jewish sect, strictly orthodox in religion, and politically opposed to foreign supremacy, Matt. xxiii. 23-33; Luke xviii. 9-14.

**Phā'rŏsh**, Ez. viii. 3. [PAROSH.]

**Phär'par** (*swift*). A river of Damascus, 2 Kgs. 12.

**Phär'zītes**. Descendants of Pharez, Num. xxvi. 20.

**Phȧ-sē'ah**, Neh. vii. 51. [PASEAH.]

**Phȧ-sē'lis**. A town on border of Lycia and Pamphylia, 1 Macc. xv. 23.

**Phăs'ĭ-ron**. An Arab chief, 1 Macc. ix. 66.

**Phăs'sȧ-ron**, 1 Esdr. v. 25. [PASHUR.]

**Phē'bē** (*shining*). A servant of the church at Cenchrea, Rom. xvi. 1, 2.

**Phē-nī'çē**. (1) Acts xi. 19; xv. 3. [PHŒNICIA.] (2) Phœnix in R. V. A seaport of Crete, Acts xxvii. 12.

**Phī'col** (*strong*). Chief of Abimelech's army, Gen. xxi. 22; xxvi. 26.

**Phĭl''a-dĕl'phĭ-ȧ** (*brotherly love*). A city of Lydia in Asia Minor, and seat of one of the seven churches of Asia, Rev. i. 11; iii. 7-13.

**Phĭ-lär'chus**. A cavalry leader, 2 Macc. viii. 32.

**Phī-lē'mon** (*friendship*). A Christian convert at Colosse in Phrygia, to whom Paul wrote an epistle during his captivity at Rome, in favor of Onesimus, Philemon's servant. Eighteenth N. T. book.

**Phī-lē'tus** (*amiable*). The convert whom Paul denounced for error, 2 Tim. ii. 17.

**Phĭl'ĭp** (*lover of horses*). (1) The apostle of Bethsaida, of whom little is known, Matt. x. 3; Mark iii. 18; Luke vi. 14; John vi. 5-9; Acts i. 13. (2) The evangelist and deacon, resident at Cæsarea, and preacher throughout Samaria, Acts vi. 5; viii. 5-13; xxi. 8-10. (3) The tetrarch. [HEROD.] (4) Husband of Herodias, Matt. xiv. 3. [HEROD.] (5) Governor of Jerusalem under Antiochus, and regent of Syria, 2 Macc. v. 22. (6) Philip V., king of Macedonia, 1 Macc. viii. 5. (7) King of Macedonia, B. C. 360-336, and father of Alexander the Great, 1 Macc. i. 1.

**Phĭ-lĭp'pī** (*city of Philip*). City in Macedonia, founded by Philip II., 12 miles from the port of Neapolis. Paul founded a vigorous church there, Acts xvi.; xx. 1-6.

**Phĭ-lĭp'pĭ-anṣ**. Dwellers in Philippi. Paul's epistle to the Christians there was written from Rome, A. D. 62 or 63. In it he sends thanks for gifts, praises their Christian walk and firmness, warns against Judaizing tendencies, and exhorts to steadfast faith.

**Phĭ-lĭs'tịȧ** (*land of sojourners*). The plain and coast country on the southwest of Palestine, which imparted its name to Palestine, Ps. lx. 8; lxxxvii. 4; cviii. 9. [PALESTINE.]

**Phĭ-lĭs'tīneṣ** (*villagers*). Dwellers in Philistia. Origin disputed, but associated with Cretans; also with the Caphtorim of Egypt, Jer. xlvii. 4; Am. ix. 7. Permanent settlers in time of Abraham, Gen. xxi. 32. Wealthy, energetic, and warlike, with many strong cities. Land not conquered by Joshua. Gaza, Ashkelon, Ashdod, Gath, and Ekron, their chief strongholds. Subdued by David, 2 Sam. v. 17-25; but became practically independent under the kings. Disappeared as a distinct people after the time of the Maccabees.

**Phĭ-lŏl'o-gus** (*learned*). A Roman Christian saluted by Paul, Rom. xvi. 15.

**Phĭ-lŏs'o-phȳ** (*loving wisdom*). The prominent Grecian schools of philosophy in N. T. times were the Stoic and Epicurean, Acts xvii. 18. But the most formidable enemy of early Christian thought was the tendency of the learned to engraft the speculations of Eastern Gnosticism and Greek philosophy upon the evolving doctrines of Christianity, 1 Cor. i. 18-27; 1 Tim. vi. 20; Col. ii. 8, etc.

**Phĭn'ẹ-es**. Apocryphal form of Phinehas.

**Phĭn'ẹ-has** (*brazen mouth*). (1) Chief of the Korhite Levites, and high priest, Ex. vi. 25; Num. xxv. 6-15; Josh. xxii. 30-32. (2) Wicked son of Eli, 1 Sam. i. 3; ii. 34; iv. 4-19; xiv. 3. (3) A Levite, Ez. viii. 33.

**Phī'son**. Greek form of Pison, Ecclus. xxiv. 25.

**Phlē'gon** (*burning*). A Roman Christian saluted by Paul, Rom. xvi. 14.

**Phœ'be**. [PHEBE.]

**Phœ-nĭ'çịȧ** (*land of palm-trees*). Phenicia in Acts xxi. 2. Phenice in Acts xi. 19; xv. 3. In O. T. referred to as Tyre and Sidon, or coasts of Tyre and Sidon. The small coast country north of Palestine, noted for its commercial enterprise, learning, and skill in arts. Included in the Land of Promise but never conquered, Josh. xiii. 4-6. David and Solomon employed its sailors and artisans, 2 Sam. v. 11; 1 Kgs. v.

**Phœ-nĭ'çians.** Dwellers in Phœnicia. In intimate commercial, political, and even religious relations with Hebrews, 1 Kgs. xvi. 31-33; xviii. 40; 1 Chr. xiv. 1; Isa. xxiii.; Ezek. xxvii. 2-8.

**Phrȳg'ĭ-ȧ** (*barren*). An undefined section of Asia Minor, out of which several Roman provinces were formed, Acts ii. 10; xvi. 6; xviii. 23.

**Phŭd.** Judith ii. 23. [PHUT.]

**Phū'rah** (*bough*). Armor-bearer of Gideon, Judg. vii. 10, 11.

**Phū'rim,** Esth. xi. 1. [PURIM.]

**Phŭt, Pŭt** (*bow*). Son of Ham, Gen. x. 6; 1 Chr. i. 8. Name is rendered Libya and Libyans, people of north Africa, in Jer. xlvi. 9; Ezek. xxx. 5; xxxviii. 5.

**Phū'vah** (*mouth*). Son of Issachar, Gen. xlvi. 13. Pua, Num. xxvi. 23. Puah, 1 Chr. vii. 1.

**Phȳ-gĕl'lus** (*fugitive*). A Christian pervert of Asia, 2 Tim. i. 15.

**Phȳ-lăc'tę-rȳ** (*safeguard*). [FRONTLET.]

**Pī-bē'seth** (*house of Bast*). City of Lower Egypt, on Pelusiac branch of the Nile. Bubastis of the Greeks, noted for its temple of Bast, goddess of fire, Ezek. xxx. 17.

**Pĭc'tūre** (*painting*), Ezek. xxiii. 14; Prov. xxv. 11. Sculptures, reliefs, or cornices, meant. Movable or hanging pictures not favored by Hebrews.

**Piēce** (*part*). In O. T., "pieces of gold," "pieces of silver," may well be read shekels' weight, or shekels, of gold or silver, Gen. xx. 16; 2 Kgs. v. 5. In N. T., "pieces," Matt. xxvi. 15; xxvii. 3-9, are unknown. In Luke xv. 8, for "pieces" read drachmas.

**Pĭg'eŏn** (*chirping bird*). [DOVE.]

**Pī-ha-hī'roth** (*place of sedges*). Last Israelite encampment before crossing the Red Sea, Ex. xiv. 2, 9; Num. xxxiii. 7, 8.

**Pī'lạte** (*spear-armed*). Pontius Pilate in Matt. xxvii. 2. Sixth Roman procurator of Judea, A. D. 26-36. Official residence at Cæsarea, with judicial visits to other places. Christ was brought before him at Jerusalem for judgment. He found no guilt, but lost his moral courage in the presence of the mob. Eventually banished to Gaul, Luke xxiii. 1-7; John xviii. 27-40; xix.

**Pĭl'dăsh** (*flame*). Son of Nahor, Gen. xxii. 22.

**Pĭl'ę-hȧ** (*worship*). A co-covenanter, Neh. x. 24.

**Pĭl'lar** (*pile*). Prominent in Oriental architecture, monumental evidences, and scripture metaphor, Gen. xxviii. 18; xxxv. 20; Ex. xiii. 21; Josh. xxiv. 26; Judg. xvi. 25-30; 1 Tim. iii. 15; Rev. iii. 12.

**Pĭlled** (*peeled*). Peeled, stripped, plundered, Gen. xxx. 37, 38; Isa. xviii. 2.

**Pĭl'tāi** (*saved*). A priest, Neh. xii. 17.

**Pine** (*pitch*). Disputed rendering. Probably plane-tree is meant, Isa. xli. 19; lx. 13.

**Pĭn'na-cle** (*feather, edge*). Not a pinnacle, or summit, but the pinnacle, or wing, of the temple, Matt. iv. 5; Luke iv. 9.

**Pī'non** (*darkness*). A duke of Edom, Gen. xxxvi. 41.

**Pīpe.** Flute. Type of perforated wind instruments, as the harp was of stringed instruments, 1 Sam. x. 5; 1 Kgs. i. 40; Isa. v. 12.

**Pī'ram** (*fleet*). An Amorite king, Josh. x. 3.

**Pĭr'ạ-thon** (*princely*). Now Ferata, six miles southwest of Shechem, Judg. xii. 15.

**Pĭr'ạ-thon-īte''.** Dweller in Pirathon, Judg. xii. 13, 15; 1 Chr. xxvii. 14.

**Pĭş'gah** (*hill*). The elevation, in Moab, whence Moses viewed the Promised Land, Num. xxi. 20; Deut. iii. 27; iv. 49; xxxiv. 1.

**Pī-sĭd'ĭ-ȧ** (*pitchy*). A province of Asia Minor, with Antioch as its capital. Twice visited by Paul, Acts xiii. 14; xiv. 21-24.

**Pī'son** (*flowing*). One of the four rivers of Eden. Unlocated, Gen. ii. 11.

**Pĭs'pah** (*swelling*). An Asherite, 1 Chr. vii. 38.

**Pĭt** (*well*). Cistern or well, Gen. xxxvii. 20; grave, Ps. xxviii. 1; game-trap, Ezek. xix. 8; device, Ps. cxix. 85; Prov. xxvi. 27.

**Pĭtch** (*pine-resin*). The pitch of scripture was asphalt or bitumen, found in Dead Sea regions. Used for mortar, cement, calk, etc., Gen. vi. 14; xi. 3; Ex. ii. 3; Isa. xxxiv. 9.

**Pĭtch'er** (*goblet, wine-vessel*). A large earthen water-jar with one or two handles, Gen. xxiv. 15-20; Mark xiv. 13; Luke xxii. 10.

**Pī'thom** (*house of Tum*). A store-city of Egypt, built by the Israelites, Ex. i. 11.

**Pī'thon** (*harmless*). A son of Micah, 1 Chr viii. 35.

**Plāgue** (*blow*). Pestilential disease, Lev. xiii. 2-8; xxvi. 25. Any calamitous visitation, Mark v. 29; Luke vii. 21. The judgments of God on Egypt are called plagues. They were (1) Nile changed to blood, Ex. vii. 14-25. (2) Visitation of frogs, Ex. viii. 1-15. (3) Lice, Ex. viii. 16-19. (4) Flies, Ex. viii. 20-32. (5) Murrain, Ex. ix. 1-7. (6) Boils, Ex. ix. 8-12. (7) Hail, Ex. ix. 13-35. (8) Locusts, Ex. x. 1-20. (9) Darkness, Ex. x. 21-28. (10) Smiting of the firstborn, Ex. xii. 29, 30.

**Plāin** (*flat*). Hebrew words so rendered have various significations. Plain, Gen. xi. 2; meadow, Judg. xi. 33; oak-grove, Gen. xiii. 18.

**Plāit'ing** (*folding*). Folding or pleating, as of the hair, 1 Pet. iii. 3.

**Plăn'et** (*wanderer*). The reference is evidently to the signs of the zodiac, as in marg. 2 Kgs. xxiii. 5.

**Plȧs'ter** (*forming on*). Used by Hebrews as wall and stone coating, Lev. xiv. 42; Deut. xxvii. 2, 4; Dan. v. 5.

**Plĕdge** (*holding before*). [EARNEST.] [LOAN.]

**Plē'ia-dēş** or **Plei'ȧ-dēş** (*daughters of Pleione*). The "seven stars." A group of stars in the constellation Taurus, Job ix. 9; xxxviii. 31; Am. v. 8.

**Plọw** (*plowland*). In early times, a crude implement made of a forked stick, one branch of which was shod, or shared, with iron. Drawn by oxen, camels, and asses, Gen. xlv. 6; Deut. xxii. 10; Job i. 14.

**Pŏch'ę-rĕth** (*beguiling*). His children returned, Ez. ii. 57; Neh. vii. 59.

**Pō'ĕt-rȳ** (*made up*). Hebrew literature largely poetical, and of lyrical style. Job, Psalms, Proverbs, Ecclesiastes, and Song of Solomon are distinctively poetical.

**Pōll** (*head*). The head, Num. iii. 47. To cut the hair, 2 Sam. xiv. 26.

**Pŏl'lux.** [CASTOR and POLLUX.]

**Pọme'grăn-āte** (*many-seeded fruit*). A low, straight-stemmed tree, native of Persia, Syria, and Arabia, bearing an orange-like fruit, Num. xiii. 23; Deut. viii. 8; S. of Sol. iv. 3; vi. 7; viii. 2.

**Pŏm'mels** (*knobs*). Globular ornaments on the capitals of pillars, 2 Chr. iv. 12, 13. Called "bowls" in 1 Kgs. vii. 41.

**Pŏnds** (*confined*). Egyptian ponds were pools left by subsidence of the Nile waters, Ex. vii. 19. Fish-ponds in Isa. xix. 10.

**Pŏn'tĭ-us Pī'lạte.** [PILATE.]

**Pŏn'tus** (*the sea*). Northeastern province of Asia Minor, bordering on the Pontus Euxinus, Euxine Sea. Empire of Mithridates, defeated by Pompey, B. C. 66. Many Jews settled there, Acts ii. 9; xviii. 2; 1 Pet. i. 1.

**Pool** (*hole*). Artificial reservoir for water. Very necessary in the East and sometimes built very elaborately and expensively, Eccl. ii. 6; Isa. xlii. 15.

**Poor** (*bare*). Poor especially cared for under Jewish dispensation, Ex. xxiii. 6; Lev. xix. 9, 10; Deut. xv. 7. Spirit continued, Luke iii. 11; xiv. 13; Acts vi. 1.

**Pŏp'lär** (*butterfly-leaf*). The white poplar supposed to be meant, Gen. xxx. 37; Hos. iv. 13.

**Pŏr'a-thȧ** (*favored*). A son of Haman, Esth. ix. 8.

**Pōrch** (*door*). In oriental architecture, veranda, colonnade, vestibule, Judg. iii. 23; 1 Chr. xxviii. 11; John x. 23. Any passage from street to inner hall, Matt. xxvi. 71.

**Pôr'çĭ-us Fĕs'tus,** Acts xxiv. 27. [FESTUS.]

**Pōr'terş** (*gate-keepers*). Keepers of city, temple, palace, and private gates and doors. The temple had 4000 of them, in classified service, 2 Sam. xviii. 26; 2 Kgs. vii. 10; 1 Chr. xxiii. 5; xxvi. 1-19; 2 Chr. xxxi. 14.

**Pŏs''ĭ-dō'nĭ-as.** Nicanor's envoy to Judas, 2 Macc. xiv. 19.

**Pōsts** (*placed*). Runners, messengers, on foot, on horses, or on dromedaries, Esth. viii. 10-14; Job ix. 25; Jer. li. 31.

**Pŏt** (*drinking-vessel*). Pots of various designs, sizes, and uses. Made of clay or metal, Lev. vi. 28; 1 Sam. ii. 14; 2 Kgs. iv. 2; Jer. xxxv. 5; Ezek. iv. 9.

**Pŏt'ĭ-phar** (*belonging to the sun*). Captain of Pharaoh's guard, Gen. xxxvii. 36; xxxix.

**Pō-tī′-phe-rah** (*belonging to the sun*). A priest of On, in Egypt, and father-in-law of Joseph, Gen. xli. 45.

**Pŏt′sherd** (*pot-fragment*). A piece of broken pottery, Prov. xxvi. 23.

**Pŏt′tage** (*pot-cooked*). A thick stew of meat or vegetables, or both, Gen. xxv. 29; 2 Kgs. iv. 39.

**Pŏt′ter's Field**. The burial-ground for strangers, outside of Jerusalem, bought with the betrayal money, Matt. xxvii. 7. [ACELDAMA.]

**Pŏt′ter-y** (*pot-ware*). A very ancient art and carried to great perfection. Vessels variously moulded, and often elaborately decorated. The ceramic art furnishes many valuable contributions to ancient history, Gen. xxiv. 14; 1 Chr. iv. 23; Isa. xli. 25; Jer. xviii. 3.

**Pound** (*weight*). A weight; the maneh, 1 Kgs. x. 17; Ez. ii. 69; Neh. vii. 71. One sixtieth of a Grecian talent, Luke xix. 13–27.

**Præ-tō′rĭ-um** (*governor's headquarters*). The court, hearing-hall, and judgment-hall, of a Roman governor, wherever he might be, Matt. xxvii. 27; Mark xv. 16; John xviii. 28; Acts xxiii. 35; Phil. i. 13.

**Prāy′er** (*seeking favor*). Reverent petition to a divinity a universal custom. The Jews had three daily periods of prayer: 9 A. M., 12 M., 3 P. M., Ps. lv. 17; Dan. vi. 10.

**Prĕs′ent**. [GIFT.]

**Prĭcks**. [GOADS.]

**Priēst** (*presbyter, elder*). Representative of man in things appertaining to God. Assistants of Moses as mediator, Ex. xxiv. 5. Function of priesthood conferred on Levites, Ex. xxviii. Priests divided into regular courses, 1 Chr. xxiv. 1–19; 2 Chr. xxiii. 8; Luke i. 5.

**Prĭnce** (*first*). In Bible sense, patriarch, head of a family or chief of a tribe; governor or magistrate, 1 Kgs. xx. 14; satrap or ruler, Dan. vi. 1.

**Prĭn″çi-păl′ĭ-ty**. Territory of a prince. Seemingly an order of angels in Eph. i. 21; vi. 12; Col. i. 16; ii. 10.

**Prĭs′cȧ** (*ancient*), 2 Tim. iv. 19. [PRISCILLA.]

**Prĭs-çĭl′lȧ** (*little Prisca*). Wife of Aquila, Acts xviii. 2, 18, 26; Rom. xvi. 3.

**Prĭş′on** (*seizing*). Ward or lock-up, Lev. xxiv. 12; Num. xv. 34; well or pit, Gen. xxxvii. 24; Jer. xxxviii. 6–11; part of a palace, 2 Chr. xvi. 10; Jer. xxxii. 2; Acts xxiii. 10, 35.

**Prŏch′o-rus** (*choir leader*). One of the first seven deacons, Acts vi. 5.

**Prō-cŏn′sul** (*for a consul*). A Roman official, beneath a consul, who exercised authority in a province. Appointed by the senate, Acts xiii. 7; xix. 38.

**Prŏc′ū-rȧ″tor** (*caring for*). A Roman provincial officer, governor, or viceroy, appointed by the emperor, Matt. xxvii.: Acts xxiii. 24; xxvi. 30.

**Prŏg-nŏs′tĭ-cȧ″tŏr** (*knowing before*). Conjurer and fortune-teller, aided by the heavenly bodies, Isa. xlvii. 13.

**Prŏph′et** (*speaking beforehand*). Who tells the future under God's inspiration. The prophetic order embraced political, as well as spiritual, advisers and warners. The books of seventeen — four greater and thirteen lesser prophets — are comprised in the O. T. Christ is the preëminent and eternal prophet, Luke xxiv. 27, 44.

**Prŏs′ē-lyte** (*come to*). A convert to the Jewish faith. "Stranger" in O. T., Deut. x. 18, 19; Matt. xxiii. 15; Acts xiii. 43.

**Prŏv′ērb** (*for a word*). Wise utterance; enigma, Num. xxi. 27. The proverbs, collected and poetically arranged by Solomon, or by his authority, constitute the twentieth O. T. book.

**Psālms** (*play a stringed instrument*). In Hebrew, "Praises." The collection of one hundred and fifty lyrics which compose the nineteenth O. T. book. The liturgical hymnbook of the Hebrews, and accepted by early Christians. Authorship of seventy of them ascribed to David. The most perfect specimens of Hebrew poetry extant.

**Psal′tēr-ў** (*play on a stringed instrument*). A stringed instrument to accompany the voice, and supposed to resemble a guitar, 2 Sam. vi. 5; 2 Chr. ix. 11. The original frequently translated "viol," Isa. v. 12; xiv. 11.

**Ptŏl″e-mæ′us, Ptŏl′ĕ-my**. (1) The Ptolemies were a race of Egyptian kings sprung from Ptolemy Soter, who inherited that portion of the conquests of Alexander the Great. They are supposed to be alluded to in the visions of Daniel. Ptolemy I., Soter, B. C. 323–285, Dan. xi. 5. Ptolemy II., Philadelphus, B. C. 285–247, Dan. xi. 6. Ptolemy III., Euergetes, B. C. 247–222, Dan. xi. 7–9. Ptolemy IV., Philopator, B. C. 222–205, Dan. xi. 10–12. Ptolemy V., Epiphanes, B. C. 205–181, Dan. xi. 13–17. Ptolemy VI., Philometor, B. C. 181–146, Dan. xi. 25–30. Their kingdom fell under Rome. (2) Father of Lysimachus, Greek translator of Esther, Esth. xi. 1.

**Ptŏ″le-mā′ĭs**, Acts xxi. 7. [ACCHO.]

**Pū′ȧ**, Num. xxvi. 23. [PHUVAH.]

**Pū′ah** (*mouth*). (1) Father of Tola, a judge of Israel, Judg. x. 1. (2) An Egyptian midwife, Ex. i. 15.

**Pŭb′lĭ-can** (*people's servant*). Gatherer of public revenue; tax-collector, abhorred by Jews, Matt. xviii. 17; Luke iii. 12, 13; xix. 2.

**Pŭb′lĭ-us** (*common*). Governor of the island of Melita, Acts xxviii. 7, 8.

**Pū′denş** (*modest*). A Roman Christian who saluted Timothy, 2 Tim. iv. 21.

**Pū′hītes**. A Judahite family, 1 Chr. ii. 53.

**Pŭl** (*lord*). (1) A possible African region, Isa. lxvi. 19. (2) A king of Assyria, 2 Kgs. xv. 19, 20.

**Pŭlse** (*pottage*). Peas, beans, lentils, etc., and, in a Hebrew sense, perhaps the cereals, Dan. i. 12–16.

**Pŭn′ĭsh-ment** (*pain*). Capital punishment was by hanging, 2 Sam. xxi. 6; stoning, Ex. xvii. 4; John x. 31; burning, Gen. xxxviii. 24; shooting, Ex. xix. 13; the sword, 1 Kgs. ii. 25; drowning, Matt. xviii. 6; sawing, 2 Sam. xii. 31; crucifixion. The death penalty was inflicted for parental reviling, blasphemy, adultery, rape, idolatry, perjury. Secondary punishments were generally those of retaliation, an "eye for an eye," etc., Ex. xxi. 23–25; Deut. xix. 18–21.

**Pū′nītes**. Descendants of Phuvah, or Pua, Num. xxvi. 23.

**Pū′non** (*darkness*). A desert encampment, Num. xxxiii. 42.

**Pū″rĭ-fĭ-cā′tion** (*cleansing*). A ritualistic form and sanitary precaution among Hebrews, Lev. xiv. 4–32; Mark vii. 3, 4; John xi. 55.

**Pū′rĭm** (*lots*). The Jewish festival commemorative of the preservation of the Jews in Persia. Celebrated yearly on 14th and 15th of the month Adar, Esth. iii. 7; ix. 20–32.

**Pŭt**, 1 Chr. i. 8. [PHUT.]

**Pū-tē′o-lī** (*sulphurous wells*). Now Pozzuoli, seaport of Campania, on Bay of Naples, Acts xxviii. 13.

**Pū′tĭ-el** (*afflicted*). Father-in-law of Eleazar, Ex. vi. 25.

**Pȳ′garg** (*white-rumped*). A species of antelope, Deut. xiv. 5.

**Pȳr′rhus**. Father of Sopater, in R. V., Acts xx. 4.

**Pȳ′thon** (*serpent*). Pythian Apollo, Acts xvi. 16 marg.

## Q

**Quāils** (*quackers*). Quails of the Old World species, *Coturnix coturnix*, abound in the Arabian desert, and migrate northward, in spring, in enormous flocks, Ex. xvi. 13; Num. xi. 31, 32; Ps. cv. 40.

**Quär′tus** (*fourth*). A Christian at Corinth, Rom. xvi. 23.

**Quȧ-tēr′nĭ-on** (*file of four*). A Roman guard of four soldiers, two of whom watched prisoners within the door, and two watched the door outside, Acts xii. 4–10.

**Quēen** (*woman*). The three Hebrew words so rendered imply a queen-regnant, queen-consort, and queen-mother, with a dignity very like that of the present day, 1 Kgs. ii. 19; x. 1; xv. 13; Esth. i. 9; ii. 17; Jer. xiii. 18; xxix. 2.

**Quēen of Heaven**. The moon, worshipped as Astoreth or Astarte by idolatrous Hebrews, Jer. vii. 18; xliv. 17–25.

**Quĭck′sănds**. The Syrtis, greater and lesser. Two dangerous sandbanks or shoals off the north coast of Africa between Carthage and Cyrene, Acts xxvii. 17.

**Quĭv′er** (*cover*). Case or cover for arrows, Gen. xxvii. 3; Job xxxix. 23.

## R

**Rā′a-mah** (*shaking*). Son of Cush, and father of a trading tribe on the Persian Gulf, Gen. x. 7; Ezek. xxvii. 22.

**Rā″a-mī′ah** (*God's thunder*). A chief who returned, Neh. vii. 7. Reelaiah, Ez. ii. 2.

**Rȧ-ăm′sēş**, Ex. i. 11. [RAMESES.]

**Răb′bah** (*great*). (1) A strong Ammonite city east of Jordan; rebuilt by Ptolemy Philadelphus, B. C. 285–247, and called Philadelphia, Josh. xiii. 25; 2 Sam. xi. 1; xii. 27-29; 1 Chr. xx. 1. Rabbath-ammon, *i. e.*, Rabbath of the Ammonites, or of the children of Ammon, in Deut. iii. 11; 2 Sam. xii. 26; xvii. 27; Jer. xlix. 2; Ezek. xxi. 20. (2) Town in Judah, Josh. xv. 60.

**Răb′bath=am′mŏn.** [RABBAH.]

**Răb′bath=mō′ab.** [AR.]

**Răb′bī** (*my master*). A title of respect applied to Hebrew doctors and teachers. Applied also to priests, and to Christ, Matt. xxiii. 7; Mark ix. 5; John i. 38. Rabboni in John xx. 16.

**Răb′bĭth** (*many*). Town in Issachar, Josh. xix. 20.

**Răb-bō′nī**, John xx. 16. [RABBI.]

**Răb′=măg** (*chief of magi*). An important office at the court of Babylonia, Jer. xxxix. 3, 13.

**Răb′sa-rĭs** (*chief of eunuchs*). (1) An Assyrian general, 2 Kgs. xviii. 17. (2) A Babylonian prince, Jer. xxxix. 3, 13.

**Răb′sha-keh** (*cup bearer*). An Assyrian general, 2 Kgs. xviii. 17-37; xix.; Isa. xxxvi.

**Rā′cȧ** (*worthless*). A Hebrew term of contempt and reproach, Matt. v. 22.

**Rāce** (*rush*). As a public game, not patronized by Hebrews. A favorite game with Greeks and Romans, 1 Cor. ix. 24; Heb. xii. 1.

**Rā′chăb.** Greek form of Rahab, Matt. i. 5.

**Rā′chăl** (*trade*). A town in southern Judah. 1 Sam. xxx. 29.

**Rā′chel** (*ewe*). Daughter of Laban, wife of Jacob, and mother of Joseph and Benjamin, Gen. xxix.-xxxv.

**Răd′da-ī** (*trampling*). Brother of David, 1 Chr. ii. 14.

**Rā′gau.** (1) Judith i. 5. [RAGES.] (2) Luke iii. 35. [REU.]

**Rā′ġēs.** City in Media, Tob. i. 14.

**Rȧ-gū′el** (*friend of God*). (1) A priest, or prince, of Midian, Num. x. 29. Reuel in Ex. ii. 18. (2) Father-in-law of Tobias, Tob. iii. 7.

**Rā′hăb** (*large*). (1) The harlot of Jericho who received the spies, and married Salmon, Josh. ii. 1-21; vi. 17-25; Ruth iv. 21; Matt. i. 5. (2) Symbolical term for Egypt, implying insolence and violence, Ps. lxxxix. 10; Isa. li. 9.

**Rā′hăm** (*belly*). A descendant of Caleb, 1 Chr. ii. 44.

**Rā′hel**, Jer. xxxi. 15. [RACHEL.]

**Rāin.** The early rains of Palestine fall in October, in time for seeding; the later, in April, in time for fruits. May to October is the dry season, Deut. xi. 14; Hos. vi. 3; Joel ii. 23.

**Rāin′bōw.** A sign of the covenant that the earth should not again be destroyed by water, Gen. ix. 12-17.

**Rā′kem** (*flower culture*). Descendant of Manasseh, 1 Chr. vii. 16.

**Răk′kăth** (*coast*). A fenced city in Naphtali, Josh. xix. 35.

**Răk′kŏn** (*void*). Town in Dan, near Joppa, Josh. xix. 46.

**Răm** (*high*). (1) A Judahite, 1 Chr. ii. 9. Aram, Matt. i. 3, 4; Luke iii. 33. (2) Son of Jerahmeel, 1 Chr. ii. 25. (3) Kinsman of Elihu, Job xxxii. 2.

**Răm** (*strong*). (1) Male of the sheep, or any ovine species, Gen. xxii. 13. (2) Battering-ram for breaking down gates and walls, Ezek. iv. 2; xxi. 22.

**Rā′mȧ**, Matt. ii. 18. [RAMAH.]

**Rā′mah** (*height*). (1) City in Benjamin, near Jerusalem, Josh. xviii. 25; 1 Kgs. xv. 17-22. Point of departure for Jewish captives, Jer. xxxix. 8-12; xl. 1. (2) Birthplace of Samuel, 1 Sam. i. 19; vii. 17. (3) A border place of Asher, Josh. xix. 29. (4) Town in Naphtali, Josh. xix. 36. (5) Ramoth-gilead, 2 Kgs. viii. 28, 29. (6) A place repeopled by returned captives, Neh. xi. 33.

**Rā″math-ā′im=zō′phim** (*two watch-towers*). Full form of the town in which Samuel was born, 1 Sam. i. 1. [RAMAH, 2.]

**Răm′ā-them.** A part of Samaria added to Judea, 1 Macc. xi. 34.

**Rā′math-īte.** Dweller in Ramah, 1 Chr. xxvii. 27.

**Rā′math=lē′hī** (*hill of the jaw bone*). Where Samson slew the Philistines, Judg. xv. 17.

**Rā′math=mĭz′peh** (*watch-tower hill*). A border town of Gad, Josh. xiii. 26.

**Rā′math of the South.** A border place of Simeon, Josh. xix. 8; 1 Sam. xxx. 27.

**Rȧ-mē′sēṣ, Rȧ-ăm′sēṣ** (*sun-born*). Country and city in lower Egypt, associated with Goshen; the city being the capital, and one of the Pharaohs' store-cities, located on the Pelusiac mouth of the Nile, Gen. xlvii. 11; Ex. i. 11; xii. 37; Num. xxxiii. 3, 5.

**Rȧ-mī′ah** (*exaltion*). One who had taken a foreign wife, Ez. x. 25.

**Rā′moth** (*high*). A son of Bani, Ez. x. 29.

**Rā′moth=gĭl′e-ăd** (*heights of Gilead*). An ancient Amorite stronghold east of Jordan, and chief city of Gad. Both a Levitical city and city of refuge. Centre of one of Solomon's commissary districts, Deut. iv. 43; Josh. xx. 8; xxi. 38; 1 Kgs. iv. 13.

**Răm's Hôrns**, Josh. vi. 4-20. [CORNET.]

**Rā′phȧ** (*tall*). (1) A Benjamite, 1 Chr. viii. 2. (2) A descendant of Saul, 1 Chr. viii. 37.

**Rā′phȧ-el** (*God's healer*). One of the seven holy angels, Tob. xii. 15.

**Răph′ā-im.** An ancestor of Judith, Judith viii. 1.

**Rā′phŏn.** A city in Gilead, 1 Macc. v. 37.

**Rā′phu** (*healed*). Father of the Benjamite spy, Num. xiii. 9.

**Răs′seṣ.** A land ravaged by Holofernes, Judith ii. 23.

**Rȧ-thū′mus**, 1 Esdr. ii. 16. [REHUM.]

**Rā′ven** (*seizer*). An unclean bird of the crow (*corvus*) family. Translation much disputed, Lev. xi. 15; 1 Kgs. xvii. 6; S. of Sol. v. 11.

**Rā′zis.** An elder at Jerusalem, 2 Macc. xiv. 37-46.

**Rā′zor** (*scraper*). Known to and much used by Hebrews. Levites shaved the entire body, Lev. xiv. 8; Num. vi. 9, 18; viii. 7; Judg. xiii. 5; Acts xviii. 18.

**Rē″a-ī′ȧ** (*seen of God*). A Reubenite prince, 1 Chr. v. 5.

**Rē″a-ī′ah** (*seen of God*). (1) A Judahite, 1 Chr. iv. 2. (2) His children returned, Ez. ii. 47; Neh. vii. 50.

**Rē′bȧ** (*fourth*). A Midianite king slain by Israel, Num. xxxi. 8; Josh. xiii. 21.

**Rē-bĕc′cȧ.** Greek form of Rebekah, Rom. ix. 10.

**Rē-bĕk′ah** (*snare*). Wife of Isaac and mother of Jacob and Esau, Gen. xxii. 23; xxiv.-xxviii.; xlix. 31.

**Rē′chăb** (*horseman*). (1) Father of Jehonadab, 2 Kgs. x. 15, 23; 1 Chr. ii. 55. (2) A traitorous captain under Ishbosheth, 2 Sam. iv. 2, 5-9. (3) Father of Malchiah, an assistant wall-builder, Neh. iii. 14.

**Rē′chab-ītes.** Kenite or Midianite descendants of Rechab, 1 Chr. ii. 55, who became an order or sect — said to still exist near Mecca — whose tenets were abstinence from wine, tent habitations only, freedom from agricultural labor, Jer. xxxv. 2-19.

**Rē′chah** (*uttermost*). Place unknown, 1 Chr. iv. 12.

**Rē-côr′der** (*record keeper*). The high and responsible office of annalist and royal counselor in the Hebrew state, 2 Sam. viii. 16; xx. 24; 1 Kgs. iv. 3; 1 Chr. xviii. 15.

**Rē-dēem′** (*buying back*). In O. T., buying back a forfeited estate. Metaphorically, freeing from bondage, Ex. vi. 6; Isa. xliii. 1. In N. T., rescuing or ransoming from sin and its consequences, Matt. xx. 28; Gal. iii. 13; 1 Pet. i. 18.

**Rĕd Sēa.** The arm of Gulf of Aden which separates Egypt from Arabia. "The sea," Ex. xiv. 2, 9, 16, 21, 28; xv. 1-19; Josh. xxiv. 6, 7. "Egyptian sea," Isa. xi. 15. "Sea of *Suph*," *weedy* or *reedy sea*, translated "Red Sea," Ex. x. 19; xiii. 18; xv. 4; xxiii. 31; Num. xxi. 4. In N. T., the Greek "Erythrean," or Red Sea, Acts vii. 36. At its head it separates into gulfs of Akaba and Suez, the latter of which the Israelites crossed.

**Rēed** (*rod*). Used generically for the tall grasses, sedges, flags, or rushes which grow in marshy soils. Applied to various uses by Hebrews, and source of frequent metaphor, 2 Kgs. xviii. 21; Job xl. 21; Isa. xix. 6; Ezek. xxix. 6; Matt. xi. 7; xii. 20; xxvii. 29.

**Rē″el-ā′iah**, Ez. ii. 2. [RAAMIAH.]

**Rē-fī′ner** (*who makes fine*). A worker in precious metals, Isa. i. 25; Jer. vi. 29; Mal. iii. 3.

**Rĕf′uge, Cities of.** The six Levitical cities set apart for the temporary escape of involuntary manslayers, Num. xxxv. 6, 11-32; Deut. xix. 7-9; Josh. xx. 2-8. [CITY.]

**Rē′ġem** (*friend*). A descendant of Caleb, 1 Chr. ii. 47.

**Re'gem-me'lech** (*royal friend*). A messenger sent by captive Jews to inquire about the ritual, Zech. vii. 2.

**Re-gen"er-a'tion** (*begetting again*). The renovation of the world at and after the second coming of Christ, Matt. xix. 28. The new birth from the Holy Spirit, Tit. iii. 5.

**Re"ha-bi'ah** (*enlarged*). Only son of Eliezer, 1 Chr. xxiii. 17.

**Re'hob** (*breadth*). (1) Father of Hadadezer, king of Zobah, 2 Sam. viii. 3, 12. (2) A co-covenanter, Neh. x. 11. (3) Spot where the journey of the spies ended, Num. xiii. 21 ; 2 Sam. x. 8. Beth-rehob in 2 Sam. x. 6. (4) Place in Asher, Josh. xix. 28. (5) A Levitical town in Asher, Josh. xix. 30.

**Re"ho-bo'am** (*emancipator*). Son of Solomon, 1 Kgs. xi. 43 ; xiv. 21, and successor to his father's throne, B. C. 975-958. During his reign the ten tribes, under Jeroboam, revolted and set up the kingdom of Israel. Shishak, of Egypt, captured Jerusalem from him, 1 Kgs. xiv. 21-31.

**Re-ho'both** (*places*). (1) A city of Assyria founded by Asher or Nimrod, Gen. x. 11, 12. (2) A city on the Euphrates, home of Shaul or Saul, an early Edomite king, Gen. xxxvi. 37 ; 1 Chr. i. 48. (3) The third well dug by Isaac. It is located south of Beersheba, Gen. xxvi. 22.

**Re'hum** (*merciful*). Levites and returned captives, Ez. ii. 2 ; iv. 8, 9, 17, 23 ; Neh. iii. 17 ; x. 25 ; xii. 3. Nehum in Neh. vii. 7, and Harim in xii. 15.

**Re'i** (*friendly*). A friend of David, 1 Kgs. i. 8.

**Reins** (*kidneys*). Once believed to be the seat of emotions ; hence coupled with the heart, Ps. vii. 9 ; xvi. 7 ; Jer. xvii. 10 ; xx. 12.

**Re'kem** (*flowered*). (1) A Midianite king slain by the Israelites, Num. xxxi. 8 ; Josh. xiii. 21. (2) Son of Hebron, 1 Chr. ii. 43, 44. (3) Town in Benjamin, Josh. xviii. 27.

**Rem"a-li'ah** (*God-exalted*). Father of Pekah, king of Israel, 2 Kgs. xv. 25-37.

**Re'meth** (*height*). Town in Issachar, Josh. xix. 21.

**Rem'mon** (*pomegranate*). Town in Simeon. Properly Rimmon, Josh. xix. 7.

**Rem'mon-meth'o-ar** (*Remmon to Neah*). A landmark of Zebulun, Josh. xix. 13.

**Rem'phan.** An idol worshipped secretly by the Israelites in the wilderness, Acts vii. 43. Rephan in R. V. Chiun, Amos v. 26.

**Re'pha-el** (*God-healed*). A Levite porter, 1 Chr. xxvi. 7.

**Re'phah** (*wealth*). An Ephraimite, 1 Chr. vii. 25.

**Reph"a-i'ah** (*God-healed*). (1) Descendant of David, 1 Chr. iii. 21. (2) A Simeonite chief, 1 Chr. iv. 42. (3) Descendant of Issachar, 1 Chr. vii. 2. (4) Descendant of Saul, 1 Chr. ix. 43. Rapha in viii. 37. (5) A wall-repairer and ruler of half of Jerusalem, Neh. iii. 9.

**Reph'a-im** (*giants*). (1) A giant race east of Jordan, and probably driven to the west side, Gen. xiv. 5 ; xv. 20. (2) "Valley of Rephaim" was a landmark of Judah, and supposably the valley stretching from Jerusalem to Bethlehem, Josh. xv. 8 ; 2 Sam. v. 18 ; Isa. xvii. 5.

**Reph'i-dim** (*rests*). Last Israelite encampment before Sinai, Ex. xvii. 1, 8-16 ; xix. 2.

**Re'sen** (*bridle*). An Assyrian city built by Asher or Nimrod, Gen. x. 12.

**Re'sheph** (*fire*). A descendant of Ephraim, 1 Chr. vii. 25.

**Res"ur-rec'tion** (*rising again*). The rising again from the dead, Ps. xvi. 10, 11 ; Matt. xvi. 21 ; xx. 19 ; Acts ii. 31.

**Re'u** (*friend*). Son of Peleg, Gen. xi. 18-21.

**Reu'ben** (*behold a son!*). Eldest son of Jacob and Leah, Gen. xxix. 32. Lost his birthright through crime, Gen. xxxv. 22 ; xlix. 3, 4. Tribe numerous and pastoral, and settled east of Jordan, Num. i. 20, 21 ; Josh. xiii. 15-23. Idolatrous, averse to war, carried captive by Assyria, Judg. v. 15, 16 ; 1 Chr. v. 26.

**Reu'ben-ites.** Descendants of Reuben, Num. xxvi. 7 ; Josh. i. 12 ; 1 Chr. v. 26.

**Reu'el** (*God's friend*). (1) A son of Esau, Gen. xxxvi. 4, 10, 13, 17. (2) Ex. ii. 18. [RAGUEL.] (3) Father of Eliasaph the Gadite leader, Num. ii. 14. (4) A Benjamite, 1 Chr. ix. 8.

**Reu'mah** (*lofty*). Nahor's concubine, Gen. xxii. 24.

**Rev"e-la'tion** (*veil drawn back*). (1) Scripturally, revealing truth through divine agency or by supernatural means, 2 Cor. xii. 1-7. (2) Book of Revelation, or Apocalypse ; last of N. T. books ; written by the Apostle John, about A. D. 95-97, probably at Ephesus. It is a record of his inspired visions while a prisoner on the island of Patmos. Its aim is much disputed, but it is seemingly a prophetic panorama of church history to the end of time.

**Re'zeph** (*heated stone*). An unknown place, 2 Kgs. xix. 12 ; Isa. xxxvii. 12.

**Re-zi'a** (*delight*). An Asherite, 1 Chr. vii. 39.

**Re'zin** (*firm*). (1) A king of Syria or Damascus, 2 Kgs. xv. 37 ; xvi. 5-9 ; Isa. vii. 1-8 ; viii. 6 ; ix. 11. (2) His descendants returned, Ez. ii. 48 ; Neh. vii. 50.

**Re'zon** (*prince*). A Syrian who set up a petty kingdom at Damascus, 1 Kgs. xi. 23-25.

**Rhe'gi-um** (*breach*). Now Rheggio, port and capital of Calabria, southern Italy, Acts xxviii. 13.

**Rhe'sa** (*head*). One mentioned in Christ's genealogy, Luke iii. 27.

**Rho'da** (*rose*). A maid in the house of Mary, mother of John Mark, Acts xii. 12-15.

**Rhodes** (*roses*). An Ægean island, just off the coast of Asia Minor. Noted for the splendor of its capital city, Rhodes. Paul touched there, Acts xxi. 1.

**Rhod'o-cus.** A traitorous Jew, 2 Macc. xiii. 21.

**Rho'dus**, 1 Macc. xv. 23. [RHODES.]

**Ri'bai** (*pleader*). Father of Ittai, one of David's guard, 2 Sam. xxiii. 29 ; 1 Chr. xi. 31.

**Rib'lah** (*fertile*). An ancient strategic city on N. E. frontier of Canaan, and on military route from Palestine to Babylonia, Num. xxxiv. 11 ; 2 Kgs. xxiii. 33 ; xxv. 6-21 ; Jer. xxxix. 5-7.

**Rid'dle** (*counsel*). Oriental peoples fond of riddles. Hebrew riddles embraced proverbs, Prov. i. 6 ; oracles, Num. xii. 8 ; songs, Ps. xlix. 4 ; parables, Ezek. xvii. 2 ; intricate sentences, questions, and problems, Judg. xiv. 12-14 ; 1 Kgs. x. 1 ; 2 Chr. ix. 1 ; Dan. viii. 23.

**Rim'mon** (*pomegranate*). (1) Father of Ishbosheth's murderers, 2 Sam. iv. 2-9. (2) A Syrian deity worshipped at Damascus, 2 Kgs. v. 18. (3) Levitical city in Zebulun, 1 Chr. vi. 77. Remmon-methoar, Josh. xix. 13. (4) Town in Judah and Simeon, Josh. xv. 32. (5) A rock or fastness, now Rummon, 10 miles north of Jerusalem, to which the defeated Benjamites retreated, Judg. xx. 45, 47 ; xxi. 13.

**Rim'mon-pa'rez** (*pomegranates of the wrath*). A desert encampment, Num. xxxiii. 19.

**Ring** (*around*). Rings were indispensable articles of Jewish ornament. Worn on fingers, wrists, ankles, in ears and nostrils, Isa. iii. 20, 21 ; Luke xv. 22 ; Jas. ii. 2. Symbols of authority, Gen. xli. 42 ; Esth. iii. 10. Used as seals, Esth. iii. 12 ; Dan. vi. 17.

**Rin'nah** (*song*). A Judahite, 1 Chr. iv. 20.

**Ri'phath** (*spoken*). Son of Gomer, and founder of a northern nation, Gen. x. 3 ; 1 Chr. i. 6.

**Ris'sah** (*ruin*). A desert encampment of the Israelites, Num. xxxiii. 21, 22.

**Rith'mah** (*bush*). A desert encampment of the Israelites, Num. xxxiii. 18, 19.

**Riv'er** (*banked*). In Hebrew sense, a large flowing stream, rivulet, ravine, valley, or wady. "River of Egypt" is the Nile, Gen. xv. 18 ; Num. xxxiv. 5 ; Josh. xv. 4, 47 ; 1 Kgs. viii. 65 ; 2 Kgs. xxiv. 7. "The river" is the Euphrates, Gen. xxxi. 21 ; Ex. xxiii. 31.

**Riz'pah.** Concubine of Saul, and the mother who watched over the remains of her slain sons, 2 Sam. iii. 7 ; xxi. 8-11.

**Road** (*ride*). In Bible sense, a path or way. For "road" in 1 Sam. xxvii. 10, read "raid" or "inroad."

**Rob'ber-y** (*breaking, riving*). Oppression, pillage, and thievery formed almost an employment among nomad tribes, Gen. xvi. 12 ; Judg. ii. 14 ; Luke x. 30 ; John xviii. 40.

**Ro-bo'am.** Greek form of Rehoboam, Matt. i. 7.

**Rod.** Shoot or branch. Figuratively, Christ, Isa. xi. 1 ; root, Ps. lxxiv. 2 ; Jer. x. 16 ; support, Ps. xxiii. 4 ; authority, Ps. ii. 9 ; affliction, Job ix. 34 ; tithing-rod, Ezek. xx. 37.

**Roe, Roe'buck** (*animal*). A beautiful fleet animal, probably the roe-deer of Western Asia ; but associated with antelope and gazelle, 2 Sam. ii. 18 ; 1 Chr. xii. 8 ; S. of Sol. ii. 17 ; viii. 14.

**Ro-ge'lim** (*fullers*) Home of Barzillai, in Gilead, 2 Sam. xvii. 27.

**Roh'gah** (*clamor*). A chief of Asher, 1 Chr. vii. 34.

**Rŏll** (*little wheel*). The book of ancient times, consisting of long strips of linen, papyrus, or parchment written upon and wrapped on a stick, Isa. viii. 1; Ezek. ii. 9, 10.

**Rō-măm'tī-ē'zĕr.** One of Heman's fourteen sons, 1 Chr. xxv. 4, 31.

**Rōme, Rō'mans.** First mentioned in Bible in 1 Macc. i. 10, when Rome was pushing her conquests in Palestine and Syria. The capital, Rome, is on the Tiber, about 15 miles from the sea. Founded B. C. 753. Governed by kings till B. C. 509; then by consuls till Augustus Cæsar became emperor, B. C. 30. At the Christian era Rome was virtual mistress of the civilized world. Empire declined rapidly after removal of capital to Constantinople by Constantine, A. D. 328. Gospel early introduced among Romans, but Christians persecuted till time of Constantine. Palestine was ruled from Rome by kings, procurators, governors, or proconsuls. Paul wrote his celebrated epistle to the Romans from Corinth, about A. D. 58, to show that Jew and Gentile were alike subject to sin and in equal need of justification and sanctification.

**Roof.** [HOUSE.]

**Room** (*wide*). Frequently used in N. T. for spot, seat, place, as at table, Matt. xxiii. 6; Mark xii. 39; Luke xiv. 7; xx. 46.

**Rōşe** (*ruddy*). Disputed translation. Some say narcissus is meant; others would simply read "flower" for "rose," S. of Sol. ii. 1; Isa. xxxv. 1.

**Rŏsh** (*head*). A Benjamite, Gen. xlvi. 21.

**Rŏş'in** (*resin*). The resin left after turpentine is distilled. But in Bible naphtha is meant, Ezek. xxvii. 17 marg.; Song of Three Children, 23.

**Ru'bȳ** (*red*). A ruddy, valuable gem; but the original word is thought to mean coral or pearl, Job xxviii. 18; Prov. iii. 15.

**Rue** (*thick-leaved*). A shrubby, medicinal plant, cultivated in the gardens of the east. Tithable, Luke xi. 42.

**Ru'fus** (*red*). Son of Simon of Cyrene, Mark xv. 21. Probably the same in Rom. xvi. 13.

**Ru'ha-mah** (*having received mercy*). A symbolical name used in Hos. ii. 1.

**Ru'mah** (*high*). A place, 2 Kgs. xxiii. 36, associated with Arumah and Dumah.

**Rŭsh** (*reed*). [REED.]

**Ruth** (*beauty*). The Moabite wife of Mahlon and Boaz. The beautiful pastoral of Ruth, 8th of O. T. books, contains her life. It supplements Judges and prefaces Samuel, and traces the lineage of David. Time of writing and authorship are unknown.

**Rȳe.** Not an Egyptian cereal. "Spelt" is doubtless meant, it being a common Egyptian food, Ex. ix. 32; Isa. xxviii. 25. Same Hebrew word is rendered "fitches" in Ezek. iv. 9.

## S

**Sā''băch-thā'nī** (*hast thou forsaken me?*). An Aramaic, or Syro-Chaldaic, word, part of Christ's exclamation on the cross, Matt. xxvii. 46; Mark xv. 34. [ELI.]

**Săb'a-ōth** (*hosts*). Used usually with Jehovah, — Lord of hosts;" — hosts being comprehensive, and signifying the powers of earth and heaven, Isa. i. 9; Rom. ix. 29; Jas. v. 4.

**Sā'bat** (*around*). (1) His sons were returned captives, 1 Esdr. v. 34. (2) 1 Macc. xvi. 14. [SEBAT.]

**Săb'băth** (*rest*). Rest day, or seventh of the week, Gen. ii. 2, 3. Became a Mosaic institution for rest and festal occasions, Ex. xvi. 23-30; xx. 8-11; Lev. xix. 3, 30; xxiii. 3; xxv. 4-9; Deut. v. 12-15. Day for consulting prophets, 2 Kgs. iv. 23. A day of teaching and joy, Neh. viii. 1-12; Hos. ii. 11. A whole week of time is implied in Matt. xxviii. 1; Mark xvi. 1; Luke xxiv. 1; John xx. 1; Acts xx. 7; 1 Cor. xvi. 2. Among Christians, the day after the Hebrew Sabbath, or seventh-day, gradually and till fully established, became the Sabbath, or first-day, in commemoration of the resurrection of Christ. Hence, "The Lord's Day," John xx. 26; Acts xx. 6-11; 1 Cor. xvi. 2; Rev. i. 10.

**Săb'băth Day's Journey.** Travel on the Sabbath was limited, Ex. xvi. 29. Custom seemed to sanction 2000 paces from the walls of a city as sufficient for all needs on the day of rest, Acts i. 12.

**Săb''ba-thē'us**, 1 Esdr. ix. 14. [SHABBETHAI.]

**Săb-băt'ī-cal Year.** By the Mosaic code, each seventh year was sacred. The land rested, the poor were entitled to what grew, and debtors were released, Ex. xxiii. 10, 11; Lev. xxv. 2-7; Deut. xv. 1-18.

**Săb-bē'us**, 1 Esdr. ix. 32. [SHEMAIAH.]

**Sā-bē'ans.** (1) Descendants of Sheba, son of Joktan, Joel iii. 8. (2) Evidently the descendants of Seba, son of Cush, Isa. xlv. 14. (3) Perhaps a third tribe, though it may be one of the two just mentioned. (4) A wrong translation in Ezek. xxiii. 42, "drunkards," in margin.

**Sā'bī**, 1 Esdr. v. 34. [ZEBAIM.]

**Săb'tȧ, Săb'tȧh** (*striking*). Third son of Cush, Gen. x. 7; 1 Chr. i. 9.

**Săb'te-chȧ, Săb'te-chah** (*striking*). Fifth son of Cush, Gen. x. 7; 1 Chr. i. 9.

**Sā'car** (*hire*). (1) Father of one of David's warriors, 1 Chr. xi. 35. Sharar in 2 Sam. xxiii. 33. (2) A Levite porter, 1 Chr. xxvi. 4.

**Săck'bŭt** (*pull and push*). A wind instrument, trombone. But in Dan. iii. 5-15, a stringed instrument of triangular shape with from four to twenty strings.

**Săck'cloth** (*coarse cloth*). A coarse, goat-hair cloth used for making sacks and rough garments. The latter were worn next the skin by mourners and repentants, Gen. xxxvii. 34; xlii. 25; 2 Sam. iii. 31; 1 Kgs. xxi. 27; 2 Kgs. vi. 30; Esth. iv. 1, 2; Job xvi. 15; Rev. vi. 12.

**Săc'rī-fīce** (*making sacred*). Propitiatory, atoning or thanksgiving offering to God. An ordained rite, Lev. xvii. 4-9; Deut. xvi. 5-19. Sacrificial offerings numerous; but chiefly, the "burnt-offering," Lev. i. 1-17; "sin-offering," and "trespass-offering," Lev. vii. 1-10; "peace-offering," Lev. vii. 11-34; the latter also a "free-will" offering. Among Christians all sacrificial offerings merged in the universal offering of Christ's body, Heb. ix., x.

**Săd''a-mī'as**, 2 Esdr. i. 1. [SHALLUM.]

**Sā'das**, 1 Esdr. v. 13. [INDO.]

**Săd'du-çees** (*disciples of Zadok*). A Jewish sect, supposably Zadokites, 1 Kgs. i. 32-45, whose chief tenets were (1) rejection of the divinity of the Mosaic oral law and traditions; (2) rejection of the later O. T. books, but acceptance of the Mosaic teachings; (3) denial of angel and spiritual existence, and consequent immortality of the soul; (4) belief in the absolute moral freedom of man. Their hatred of Christianity was as bitter as that of the Pharisees, Matt. iii. 7; Mark xii. 18; Luke xx. 27; Acts iv. 1; v. 17; xxiii. 6-10. Though composed of men of position, the sect was never very numerous nor influential, and it disappeared from history after the first century of the Christian era.

**Sā'dŏc** (*just*). (1) 2 Esdr. i. 1. [ZADOK.] (2) One in the genealogy of Christ, Matt. i. 14.

**Săf'fron** (*yellow*). The fall crocus, much cultivated in the Orient for its perfume and medicinal properties, S. of Sol. iv. 14.

**Saint** (*sanctified*). In O. T., a pious Jew, Ps. xvi. 3. In N. T., a Christian believer, Rom. i. 7; viii. 27; Heb. vi. 10.

**Sā'lȧ, Sā'lah** (*sprout*). A descendant of Shem, Gen. x. 24; xi. 12-15; Luke iii. 35. Shelah in 1 Chr. i. 18, 24.

**Săl'a-mis** (*shaken*). A city of the island of Cyprus, visited by Paul. It was afterwards called Constantia, Acts xiii. 5. The old city was once the capital of the island and carried on a large trade in fruit, wine, flax, and copper with adjacent continents. The Jewish population was large. Its site is now traced by masses of ruins.

**Sā-lā'thī-el** (*asked of God*). Son of Jechonias, 1 Chr. iii. 17; Matt. i. 12; Luke iii. 27. Shealtiel elsewhere.

**Săl'cah, Săl'chah** (*moving*). A city in Bashan which fell to Manasseh. Now Sulkhad, Deut. iii. 10; Josh. xii. 5; xiii. 11; 1 Chr. v. 11.

**Sā'lem** (*peace*). The place over which Melchizedek was king, supposably Jerusalem, Gen. xiv. 18; Ps. lxxvi. 2; Heb. vii. 1, 2.

**Sā'lim** (*peace*). The place near Ænon, where John baptized, John iii. 23.

**Săl'la-ī** (*basket-maker*). (1) A returned Benjamite, Neh. xi. 8. (2) A returned priest, Neh. xii. 20.

**Săl'lu** (*measured*). (1) A Benjamite, 1 Chr. ix. 7. (2) A priest, Neh. xi. 7; xii. 7.

**Săl-lū'mus**, 1 Esdr. ix. 25. [SHALLUM.]

**Săl'mȧ, Săl'mŏn** (*clothed*). (1) Father of Boaz and husband of Rahab, Ruth iv. 20, 21; 1 Chr. ii. 11; Matt. i. 5; Luke iii. 32. (2) One of the high hills surrounding Shechem, which afforded pasturage for

Jacob's flocks, Ps. lxviii. 14. Zalmon in Judg. ix. 48.

**Săl-mō'nç** (*clothed*). Eastern promontory of Crete, Acts xxvii. 7.

**Să'lŏm.** (1) Bar. i. 7. [SHALLUM.] (2) 1 Macc. ii. 26. [SALLU.]

**Sȧ-lō'mę** (*clothed*). (1) Wife of Zebedee, Mark xv. 40; xvi. 1. Mentioned indirectly in Matt. xx. 20-22; xxvii. 56. (2) The daughter of Herodias, who danced before Herod, Matt. xiv. 6; Mark vi. 22.

**Sąlt** (*sea product*). Abundant in Palestine. Used with food and sacrificial offerings, Job vi. 6; Lev. ii. 13; Num. xviii. 19; Mark ix. 49. Monument of divine displeasure, Gen. xix. 26; token of indissoluble alliance, Lev. ii. 13; Num. xviii. 19; 2 Chr. xiii. 5; used to rub new-born children, Ezek. xvi. 4; type of maintenance, Ez. iv. 14 marg.; emblem of sterility, Judg. ix. 45; Jer. xvii. 6; a manure, Luke xiv. 35; emblem of holy life and conversation, Matt. v. 13; Mark ix. 50; Col. iv. 6.

**Sąlt, City of.** Fifth of the six cities of Judah, situate in the wilderness of Judah, Josh. xv. 62.

**Sąlt Sēa.** The Dead Sea. "Sea of the plain," Deut. iv. 49; 2 Kgs. xiv. 25. "Salt sea," Deut. iii. 17; Josh. iii. 16; xii. 3. "East sea," Ezek. xlvii. 18; Joel ii. 20; Zech. xiv. 8. "The sea," Ezek. xlvii. 8. "Vale of Siddim," Gen. xiv. 3. "Sodomitish sea," 1 Esdr. v. 7. Title "Dead Sea" not found among Hebrew writers, but introduced by Greek authors. Situate 16 miles E. of Jerusalem; 46 miles long by 10 wide; 1300 feet below the level of the Mediterranean; waters intensely salt; receives waters of Jordan from the north; no outlet.

**Sąlt, Văl'ley of.** Supposably the valley, or depression, of Akabah, extending from Dead Sea to Gulf of Akabah, 2 Sam. viii. 13; 2 Kgs. xiv. 7; 1 Chr. xviii. 12; 2 Chr. xxv. 11; Ps. lx. title. But many excellent authorities limit it to a section of Edom near Petra.

**Să'lu** (*weighed*). Father of Zimri, a chief of Simeon, Num. xxv. 14.

**Să'lum,** 1 Esdr. v. 28. [SHALLUM.]

**Săl''ū-tā'tion** (*good health, greeting*). Personal salutation very formal in East. The "peace be with thee," or similar expression, was accompanied by a profound bow, kiss, embrace, or other courtesy, Gen. xix. 1; 1 Sam. xxv. 23; Matt. x. 12; Luke i. 41. Epistolary salutation took the form found in the opening and closing of the epistles, Rom. i. 7; 1 Cor. i. 3; etc.

**Săl-vā'tion** (*deliverance*). Temporal deliverance, Ex. xiv. 13. Spiritual deliverance, 2 Cor. vii. 10; Eph. i. 13; Heb. ii. 3.

**Săm''ą-rā'is.** Son of Ozora, 1 Esdr. ix. 34.

**Sȧ-mā'rĭ-ȧ** (*watch mountain*). (1) The kingdom of Samaria, synonymous with the kingdom of Israel, lay to the north of Judah. It varied in size at different times, but in general embraced the territory of the ten revolting tribes on either side of the Jordan, 1 Kgs. xiii. 32. Named from its capital, Samaria. In N. T. times, Samaria was one of the three subdivisions of Palestine, lying between Judea on the south and Galilee on the north. (2) Capital of the kingdom of Samaria or Israel, and located 30 miles north of Jerusalem. Founded by Omri, king of Israel, about B. C. 925, and called Samaria, after Shemer, from whom he bought the ground, 1 Kgs. xvi. 23, 24. It became a beautiful and strong city and remained the capital till Shalmaneser, the Assyrian, destroyed it and the empire, B. C. 721, 2 Kgs. xviii. 9-12. Herod rebuilt it and restored much of its ancient splendor, naming it Sebaste in honor of Augustus, who gave it to him. Philip preached the gospel there, Acts viii. 5-9. It is now a modest village called Sebastiyeh, which perpetuates the name Sebaste, and is noted for its many ruins, chief of which is the famous colonnade, 3000 feet in length, 100 columns of which are still standing. Respecting the city the prophecy, Mic. i. 6, has been literally fulfilled.

**Sȧ-măr'ĭ-tanș.** Inhabitants of Samaria, 2 Kgs. xvii. 29. The planting of Assyrian colonists in Samaria, 2 Kgs. xvii. 24-34, led to a strange admixture of people, language, laws, religions, and customs, and brought the name Samaritan into reproach with Jews, Matt. x. 5; John iv. 9-26; viii. 48; Acts viii. 1; ix. 31.

**Săm'găr-nē'bō** (*sword of Nebo*). A general of Nebuchadnezzar at the taking of Jerusalem, Jer. xxxix. 3.

**Săm'mus,** 1 Esdr. ix. 43. [SHEMA.]

**Săm'lah** (*raiment*). A king of Edom, Gen. xxxvi. 36, 37; 1 Chr. i. 47, 48.

**Să'mos** (*height*). An island of the Grecian archipelago, off the coast of Lydia. Visited by Paul on his third tour, Acts xx. 15.

**Săm''ọ-thrā'çĭȧ** (*Thracian Samos*). An island in the northern Ægean belonging to Thrace. Visited by Paul on his first tour, Acts xvi. 11.

**Sămp'sȧ-mēș.** Probably Samsun, on Black Sea coast, 1 Macc. xv. 23.

**Săm'son** (*sunlike*). Son of Manoah, of Dan, and judge of Israel for 20 years, Judg. xiii. 3-25. Noted for his great strength, marvellous exploits, and moral weakness. Contrary to the wishes of his parents, and to the law as laid down in Ex. xxxiv. 16, Deut. vii. 3, he married a Philistine woman of Timnath, whom he deserted on account of her treachery, Judg. xiv. Wishing to return to her, and finding her given to another, he wreaked his vengeance on the Philistines by burning their crops and slaughtering great numbers of them, Judg. xv. 1-8. He was surrounded by 3000 of his enemies, while he dwelt on the rock Etam, and surrendered to them, but burst his bands, and routed them with great slaughter, Judg. xv. 9-19. Again he was surrounded by enemies in Gaza, but escaped by carrying away the gates of the city. The secret of his strength was finally detected by Delilah, and he was imprisoned and made blind. He finally killed himself and numerous enemies by pulling down the pillars of the house in which they were feasting, Judg. xvi.

**Săm'u-el** (*God hath heard*). Son of Elkanah and Hannah, celebrated Hebrew prophet and last of the judges, 1 Sam. i. 19-28. Educated under Eli, 1 Sam. iii. 4-14, and became his successor in the prophetic office. His sons proved so recreant that the people demanded a king, and Samuel anointed Saul, and resigned his authority to him, 1 Sam. xii. He also anointed David, Saul's successor, 1 Sam. xvi. 13. He died at Ramah, 1 Sam. xxv. 1. The two books which bear his name, the 9th and 10th of O. T., are called also First and Second Books of Kings. They were originally one book and contain the lives of Samuel, Saul, and David. The authorship is ascribed to a period subsequent to the secession of the ten tribes, and it is clearly an authorship different from Kings, for in Kings there are many references to the law, while in Samuel there are none. In Kings the Exile is alluded to; it is not so in Samuel. The plans of the two works vary; Samuel is biographical, Kings annalistic.

**Săn-băl'lat** (*strong*). A Persian officer in Samaria who opposed Ezra and Nehemiah and persistently misrepresented them at court, Neh. ii. 10; iv. 1-9; xiii. 28.

**Sănc'tĭ-fȳ** (*to make holy*). To prepare or set apart persons or things to holy use, Ex. xiii. 2. It was in allusion to the law that Christ spoke in John xvii. 19. To establish union with Christ by faith, John xvii. 17. To exercise the graces of knowledge, such as faith, love, repentance, humility, etc., toward God and man, 2 Thess. ii. 13; 1 Pet. i. 2.

**Sănc'tų-ar''ȳ** (*made holy*). A holy or sanctified place, Ps. xx. 2. The secret part of the temple in which the ark of the covenant was kept, and which none but the high priest might enter, and he only once a year, on the day of solemn expiation, Lev. iv. 6. Also applied to the furniture of the holy place, Num. x. 21; to the apartment where the altar of incense, table of shewbread and holy candlestick, etc., stood, 2 Chr. xxvi. 18; to the whole tabernacle or temple, Josh. xxiv. 26; 2 Chr. xx. 8. "Sanctuary of strength," because belonging to God, Dan. xi. 31. Any place of public worship of God, Ps. lxxiii. 17. Heaven, Ps. cii. 19. Place of refuge, Isa. viii. 14; Ezek. xi. 16. Land of Israel called God's sanctuary, Ex. xv. 17. "Worldly sanctuary," one of an earthly type, Heb. ix. 1.

**Sănd** (*whirling*). Abundant in the wastes of Palestine, Arabia, and Egypt. Used much figuratively. Innumerable multitudes, Gen. xxxii. 12; abundance, Gen. xli. 49; weight, Job vi. 3; Prov. xxvii. 3; sea boundary, Jer. v. 22; hiding place, Ex. ii. 12; Deut. xxxiii. 19.

**Săn'dal** (*board*). A sole of wood, leather, or plaited material, bound to the foot with straps. The shoe of the Bible. Not worn in the house nor in holy places, Ex. iii. 5; Deut. xxv. 9; Josh. v. 15.

**Săn'hę-drim, Săn'hę-drin** (*seated together*). The supreme council of the Jewish nation, whose germ was in the seventy elders, Num. xi. 16, 17, and further development in Jehoshaphat's tribunal, 2 Chr. xix. 8-11. In full power after the captivity, and lasted till A. D. 425. The "great Sanhedrim" was composed of 71 priests, scribes, and elders, and presided over by the high priest. The "lesser Sanhedrims" were provincial courts in the towns, and composed of 23 members appointed by the "great Sanhedrim." The word usually appears as "council" in N. T., Matt. v. 22; Mark xiv. 55; John xi. 47; Acts iv. 5-7. The members of the Sanhedrim embraced the three classes, priests, elders, and scribes. After the Roman conquest it had no control of the death power, but the confirmation and execution of capital sentences rested with the Roman procurator. Thus it was that while the Sanhedrim condemned Christ for blasphemy, he was not brought under the Roman judgment of death till accused by the Jews of treason, Matt. xxvi. 65, 66; John xviii. 31; xix. 12. The stoning of Stephen, Acts vii. 57-59, was either due to mob excitement, or else illegal.

**Săn-săn'nah** (*branch*). A town in southern Judah, Josh. xv. 31.

**Săph** (*giant*). A Philistine giant, 2 Sam. xxi. 18. Sippai, 1 Chr. xx. 4.

**Sā'phat**, 1 Esdr. v. 9. [SHEPHATIAH.]

**Săph'īr** (*fair*). A village addressed by Micah, Mic. i. 11.

**Săp-phī'rá** (*handsome*). Wife of Ananias, and participator in his crime and punishment, Acts v. 1-10.

**Săp'phīre.** A light blue gem, next to the diamond in hardness, Ex. xxiv. 10. Second stone in second row of high priest's breastplate, Ex. xxviii. 18. A foundation stone of the holy Jerusalem, Rev. xxi. 19.

**Sā'rá.** (1) Daughter of Raguel, Tob. iii. 7. (2) Heb. xi. 11; 1 Pet. iii. 6. [SARAH.]

**Sā'rah** (*princess*). (1) Wife of Abraham and mother of Isaac, Gen. xi. 29; xxi. 2, 3. Name changed from Sarai to Sarah, Gen. xvii. 15, 16. At Abraham's request she passed herself off as his sister during their sojourn in Egypt, Gen. xii. 10-20, which angered the Pharaoh and led to their banishment. Relentless toward Hagar (whom she had given to Abraham as a concubine) when she bore Ishmael, and caused her to be banished to the desert, Gen. xvi. 5-16; deceitful when Isaac was promised, Gen. xviii. 15; cruel again toward Hagar on the occasion of Isaac's weaning, causing her to be banished finally from the household, Gen. xxi. 9-21. Commended for her faith, Heb. xi. 11; and obedience, 1 Pet. iii. 6. Died at age of 127 years and buried at Machpelah, Gen. xxiii. (2) Daughter of Asher, Num. xxvi. 46.

**Sā'rāi**, Gen. xi. 29. [SARAH.]

**Săr'a-mel** (*court*). Meeting place where Simon Maccabeus was made high priest, 1 Macc. xiv. 28.

**Sā'răph** (*burning*). A Judahite, 1 Chr. iv. 22.

**Săr-chĕd'ō-nus**, Tob. i. 21. [ESARHADDON.]

**Săr'dīne, Săr'dĭ-us** (*stone of Sardis*). The sard or carnelian, a blood-red or flesh-colored stone, first in first row of high priest's breastplate, Ex. xxviii. 17; Rev. iv. 3.

**Săr'dis.** Capital of Lydia in Asia Minor. Once noted for beauty and wealth; now the miserable village of Sert-Kalessi, Rev. iii. 1-6. It was the residence of Crœsus, renowned for riches, and Cyrus, when he conquered it, B. C. 548, is said to have captured fabulous treasure there. Alexander captured it from the Persians, and it was again sacked and captured by Antiochus, B. C. 214. It was destroyed by an earthquake, A. D. 17, but was speedily rebuilt. The art of wool-dyeing was discovered there. Seat of one of the seven churches of Asia, Rev. iii. 1.

**Săr'dītes.** Descendants of Sered, Num. xxvi. 26.

**Săr'dō-nyx.** A precious stone combining the sard and onyx varieties, whence its name, Rev. xxi. 20.

**Sā'rē-á.** A swift scribe, 2 Esdr. xiv. 24.

**Sâ-rĕp'tá.** Greek form of Zarephath, Luke iv. 26.

**Săr'gon** (*sun-prince*). An Assyrian king whom recently discovered inscriptions make the successor of Shalmaneser and father of Sennacherib, B. C. 722-705, 2 Kgs. xvii. 6; Isa. xx. 1.

**Sā'rid** (*survivor*). A landmark of Zebulun, Josh. xix. 10-12.

**Sā'ron**, Acts ix. 35. [SHARON.]

**Sâ-rō'thie.** His sons returned, 1 Esdr. v. 34.

**Săr-sē'chim** (*master of wardrobes*). A prince of Babylon at taking of Jerusalem, Jer. xxxix. 3.

**Sā'ruch**, Luke iii. 35. [SERUG.]

**Sā'tăn** (*adversary*). In O. T. a common noun, meaning enemy or adversary in general, 1 Sam. xxix. 4; 2 Sam. xix. 22: except in Job i. 6, 12; ii. 1; Zech. iii. 1, where the word becomes a proper noun, and spiritual representative of evil. In N. T. sense, chief of the evil spirits; great adversary of man; the devil, Matt. iv. 10; xxv. 41; Rev. xx., and elsewhere. Called also "the prince of this world;" "the wicked one;" "the tempter;" and in Rev. xii. 9, the old serpent, the devil, and Satan.

**Săt'ȳr.** A mythical creature, half man, half goat, inhabiting woods and waste places, Isa. xiii. 21; xxxiv. 14.

**Saul** (*wished*). (1) An early king of Edom, Gen. xxxvi. 37, 38. Shaul in 1 Chr. i. 48, 49. (2) A Benjamite, son of Kish, and first king of Israel. Anointed by Samuel; reigned B. C. 1095-1055; slain with his sons at Gilboa. His versatile career is described in 1 Sam. ix.-xxxi. He stands in Bible history for the stature, strength, and ruggedness of character so essential to judges in times of danger or necessary reform, and for the bravery, generalship and self-confidence of one called on to institute a new empire. Of boundless ambition and erratic judgment, he usurped the priestly function, and drew the reproaches of the aged prophet Samuel, who had surrendered his line in anointing him. The announcement that royalty could not be perpetuated in his family drove him to inexcusable follies, yet with the courage of youth he fought his last despairing battle with the Philistines, and finished his course on his own sword. (3) Hebrew name of Paul, Acts xiii. 9.

**Săv'a-ran**, 1 Macc. vi. 43. [AVARAN.]

**Sā'vĭ-as**, 1 Esdr. viii. 2. [UZZI.]

**Saw** (*cutter*). Hebrew saws doubtless patterned after those of Egypt, being single-handled, with teeth inclined toward the handle, so that cutting was done by pulling. Used for sawing wood, Isa. x. 15; stone, 1 Kgs. vii. 9; torture, 2 Sam. xii. 31; 1 Chr. xx. 3; Heb. xi. 37.

**Scāpe'gōat**, Lev. xvi. 7-26. [GOAT.]

**Scär'let** (*orange-red*). A Tyrian color much prized by ancients, Ex. xxv. 4; Prov. xxxi. 21.

**Sçĕp'tre** (*prop*). Any rod or staff. A shepherd's crook or tithing rod, Lev. xxvii. 32; Mic. vii. 14. A symbol of royal power, Gen. xlix. 10; Num. xxiv. 17; overlaid with gold, Esth. iv. 11.

**Sçē'vá** (*fitted*). An Ephesian priest, Acts xix. 14-16.

**Scôr'pĭ-on** (*crawler*). A venomous creature allied to the spider, but resembling the lobster. Its sting is painful and often fatal, Deut. viii. 15; 1 Kgs. xii. 11; Rev. ix. 3-10. A dangerous gift, Luke xi. 12.

**Scoûrġ'ing** (*thonging*). A common Hebrew punishment. The scourge was made of three lashes of leather or cord. Not more than forty stripes could be administered, Deut. xxv. 1-3; Matt. x. 17; xxiii. 34. Rods or twigs were also used, 2 Cor. xi. 25.

**Scrībe** (*writer*). The Hebrew scribe or writer appears to have been at first a court or military official, Ex. v. 6; Judg. v. 14; then secretary or recorder, for kings, priests, and prophets, 2 Sam. viii. 17; xx. 25; finally a secretary of state, doctor, or teacher, Ez. vii. 6. Scribes became a class or guild, copyists and expounders of the law, and through their innovations fell under the same denunciations as priests and Pharisees, Matt. xxiii. 1-33; Mark vii. 5-13; Luke v. 30.

**Scrĭp** (*bag*). A shepherd's bag, 1 Sam. xvii. 40. A wallet for carrying food and traveller's conveniences, Matt. x. 10; Luke x. 4.

**Scrĭp'ture** (*written*). By way of preëminence, the sacred writings contained in the Old and New Testaments. [BIBLE.]

**Sçўth'ĭ-an** (*fierce-looking*). Name applied to the fierce, nomadic nations north of the Black and Caspian seas, Col. iii. 11.

**Sçўth-ŏp'ō-lis** (*Scythian city*). The city of Bethshean in Palestine was for a time so called because captured and held by Scythian nomads, 2 Macc. xii. 29.

**Sēa.** The Hebrews so designated any large body of water, whether lake, river, sea, or ocean, Gen. i. 10; Deut. xxx. 13; Job xiv. 11; Isa. xix. 5; Jer. li. 36; Ezek. xxxii. 2. (1) "Molten sea" was the immense brass laver of Solomon's temple, 1 Kgs. vii. 23-26. (2) "Sea of the Plain," Deut. iv. 49. [SALT SEA.] (3) "Great Sea," Josh. xv. 47, "uttermost sea," Deut. xi. 24, the Mediterranean, between Europe and Africa. (4) "Sea of Tiberias" [GENNESARET.] (5) "Sea of Merom." [MEROM.]

**Sēal** (*little mark*). Much used by ancients to authenticate documents and secure packages and doors, the impression being made in clay or wax. Seals were frequently engraved stones set in rings; Gen. xli. 42; Job xxxviii. 14; Jer. xxxii. 10; Matt. xxvii. 66.

**Sē'bá.** A son of Cush, Gen. x. 7. Mentioned as

a nation or country in Ps. lxxii. 10; Isa. xliii. 3; xlv. 14, and associated with Meroe on the upper Nile.

**Sē'băt, Shē'băt** (*rod*). Fifth month of Jewish civil and eleventh of sacred year, corresponding to parts of February and March, Zech. i. 7.

**Sĕc'a-cah** (*thicket*). A city in Judah, Josh. xv. 61.

**Sē'chu** (*tower*). A place between Gibeah and Ramah, noted for its well, 1 Sam. xix. 22.

**Sĕct** (*way, school*). A party adhering to a doctrine, as the sect of Sadducees, Acts v. 17, or Pharisees, Acts xv. 5; xxvi. 5. Christians in general were for a long time called by the Jews, in a spirit of contempt, "the sect of the Nazarenes," Acts xxiv. 5. The word is also applied to a certain set of doctrines or mode of life, Acts xxiv. 14; 2 Pet. ii. 1; and to heresies proper, or perversions of Christian truth, Gal. v. 20.

**Sē-cŭn'dus** (*second*). A Thessalonian friend of Paul. Acts xx. 4.

**Sĕd"ē-çī'as** (1) Ancestor of Baruch, Bar. i. 1. (2) Son of King Josiah, Bar. i. 8.

**Sēed** (*sowed*). Seed for sowing must not be mingled, Lev. xix. 19. Children, descendants, Gen. xvii. 12; Gal. iii. 16. Pedigree, Ez. ii. 59. The male fertilizing element, Gen. xxxviii. 9.

**Sēer** (*who sees*). 1 Sam. ix. 9. [PROPHET.].

**Sēethe** (*boil*). To boil, Ex. xvi. 23.

**Sē'gub** (*lifted up*). (1) A son of Hiel who rebuilt Jericho, 1 Kgs. xvi. 34. (2) A Judahite, 1 Chr. ii. 21, 22.

**Sē'ir** (*hairy*). (1) A Horite chief, Gen. xxxvi. 21; Deut. ii. 12. (2) Land or country corresponding with valley and mountains of Arabah, stretching from the Dead Sea to the Gulf of Akaba, Gen. xiv. 6; xxxii. 3; xxxiii. 14-16. The region was first occupied by the Horites, and fell into possession of Esau and his posterity, Gen. xxxvi. 8-9. Hence Seir and Edom are sometimes spoken of as identical. The Israelites, when refused permission to march through Edom to Moab, marched round the granite ranges of Seir and entered Moab by the east and north. (3) A boundary mark of Judah, Josh. xv. 10

**Sē'ĭ-răth** (*hairy*). Place to which the murderer Ehud fled, Judg. iii. 26.

**Sē'lȧ, Sē'lah** (*rock*). A rock-founded city of Edom, the Petra of the Greeks, half way between the Dead Sea and Gulf of Akaba. Subdued by King Amaziah and called Joktheel, "subdued of God." Remarkable now for its ruins, among which are a rock-hewn temple and amphitheatre, 2 Kgs. xiv. 7; Isa. xvi. 1. The complete destruction and desolation of the place fulfils the prophecy of Jeremiah, Jer. xlix. 16, 17.

**Sē'lah.** A word of frequent occurrence in Psalms, and supposed to mean an interlude in vocal music, or a pianissimo of all parts, Ps. ix. 16; Hab. iii. 3, 9, 13.

**Sē'lȧ=hăm"mah-lē'koth** (*rock of escapes*). Rocky stronghold in wilderness of Maon, where David escaped from Saul, 1 Sam. xxiii. 28.

**Sē'led** (*lifted up*). A Judahite, 1 Chr. ii. 30.

**Sĕl"ē-mī'ah.** A swift scribe, 2 Esdr. xiv. 24.

**Sē-leū'çĭ-ȧ** (*city of Seleucus*). The seaport of Antioch in Syria, Acts xiii. 4. It was the port whence Paul and Barnabas started on their first missionary journey, and lay sixteen miles to the west of Antioch. The city was founded by Seleucus Nicator about B. C. 300, and to distinguish it from other cities of the same name was frequently called "Seleucia by the sea." The harbor is now choked with sand, and the once beautiful city is but the insignificant village of Elkalusi.

**Sē-leū'cus.** The Seleuci, or Seleucidæ, sprung from Seleucus I., a general of Alexander the Great, were a line of Syrian kings, B. C. 312-65, 2 Macc. iii. 3.

**Sĕm.** Greek form of Shem, Luke iii. 36.

**Sĕm"a-chī'ah** (*God-sustained*). A Levite porter, 1 Chr. xxvi. 7.

**Sĕm'e-ī** (*distinguished*). (1) 1 Esdr. ix. 33. [SHIMEI.] (2) Father of Mattathias, Luke iii. 26. Semein in R. V.

**Sē'mel**, Esth. xi. 2. [SHIMEI.]

**Sē-mĕl'lī-us**, 1 Esdr. ii. 16. [SHIMSHAI.]

**Sē-nā'ah** (*brambly*). His sons were returned captives, Ez. ii. 35.

**Sĕn'āte** (*elders*). First body, or class, of Hebrew Sanhedrim; the other two being priests and scribes, Acts v. 21.

**Sē'neh** (*bramble*). One of two rocks in the pass of Michmash, 1 Sam. xiv. 4, 5.

**Sē'nīr** (*glistening*). Amorite name for Mount Hermon, 1 Chr. v. 23; Ezek. xxvii. 5.

**Sĕn-năch'ẹ-rĭb** (*not the first-born*). Son and successor of Sargon, king of Assyria, B. C. 702-680. He extended his conquests to the Mediterranean and to Egypt, 2 Kgs. xviii. 13-37; xix. Most powerful and magnificent of eastern sovereigns, Isa. xxxvi., xxxvii. He made Nineveh his capital and adorned it with many palaces and public structures. His monuments have been found in many places, and a record of his arrival in Egypt has been unearthed close by an inscription of Rameses the Great.

**Sē-nū'ah** (*bristling*). A Benjamite, second in rule over Jerusalem after the captivity, Neh. xi. 9. Hasenuah, 1 Chr. ix. 7.

**Sē-ō'rim** (*bearded*). Head of fourth priestly course, 1 Chr. xxiv. 8.

**Sē'phar** (*number*). A Joktanite border in Arabia, Gen. x. 30.

**Sĕph'a-răd** (*severed*). Unlocated place whence captive Jews would return to possess the cities of the south, Obad. 20.

**Sĕph"ar-vā'im** (*two Sipperas*). One of the two cities of Sippera in Syria, whence colonists were sent to Samaria, 2 Kgs. xvii. 24-34; xix. 13; Isa. xxxvii. 13.

**Sĕph'ar-vītes.** Inhabitants of Sepharvaim, 2 Kgs. xvii. 31.

**Sĕp-tū'a-ġint** (*seventy*). The traditional 70 or 72 translators of the Hebrew Scriptures into Greek; but especially, the Greek version of the O. T. made by 72 learned Jews at Alexandria, at command of Ptolemy Philadelphus, about B. C. 270. The beginning of active work on this, the best known of ancient Bible translations, is fixed for the years B. C. 280-285, and it covered a long period of time, the translation of the Apocryphal books having been gradually added. It was made from Egyptian Hebrew manuscripts, and in its completed form is designated by the Roman numerals LXX. It was the version used by Hebrews in Christ's time and by the Greek Fathers and early N. T. writers, and the Latin version was made from it.

**Sĕp'ŭl-chre** (*ker*) (*bury*), 2 Kgs. xxiii. 16; Isa. xxii. 16; Matt. xxvii. 60; Mark xvi. 2; Luke xxiii. 53. Though the Egyptians and nearly all peoples adjacent to the Hebrews have made the name of sarcophagus familiar as a stone coffin, a chest-like tomb, often ornamented and inscribed, there seems to have been nothing akin to it in all the mention of funeral customs and burial rites in the Scriptures, if we except certain titles and inscriptions over tombs such as are mentioned in 2 Kgs. xxiii. 17. [BURIAL.] [TOMB.]

**Sē'rah** (*lady*). A daughter of Asher, Gen. xlvi. 17; 1 Chr. vii. 30. Sarah, Num. xxvi. 46.

**Sĕr"a-ī'ah** (*warrior of God*). (1) David's scribe, 2 Sam. viii. 17. Sheva, 2 Sam. xx. 25. Shisha, 1 Kgs. iv. 3. Shavsha, 1 Chr. xviii. 16. (2) A high priest, slain at Riblah, 2 Kgs. xxv. 18-21. (3) One who submitted to Gedaliah, 2 Kgs. xxv. 23. (4) A Judahite, 1 Chr. iv. 13, 14. (5) A Simeonite, 1 Chr. iv. 35. (6) A returned priest, Ez. ii. 2; Neh. x. 2. (7) Ancestor of Ezra, Ez. vii. 1. (8) One of the officers who arrested Jeremiah, Jer. xxxvi. 26. (9) Jeremiah's messenger to Babylon, Jer. li. 59-64.

**Sĕr'a-phim** (*burning*). An order of celestial beings, pictured in Isaiah's vision as around the throne of God, Isa. vi. 2-7.

**Sē'red** (*fear*). First-born of Zebulun, Gen. xlvi. 14; Num. xxvi. 26.

**Sĕr'gĭ-us Pau'lus** (*little net*). Proconsul of Cyprus at time of Paul's visit, Acts xiii. 7, 12.

**Sē'ron.** A Syrian general, 1 Macc. iii. 13, 23.

**Sĕr'pent** (*creeper*). The Hebrew original embraces the entire serpent genus. Serpents numerous and venomous in Bible lands. The word appears in Scripture under various names; adder, supposably the cerastes, Gen. xlix. 17; asp, or cobra, Deut. xxxii. 33; cockatrice, Jer. viii. 17; viper, Job xx. 16. Subtile, Gen. iii. 1; wise, Matt. x. 16; poisonous, Prov. xxiii. 32; sharp-tongued, Ps. cxl. 3; charmed, Ps. lviii. 5; emblem of wickedness, Matt. xxiii. 33; cruelty, Ps. lviii. 4; treachery, Gen. xlix. 17; the devil, Rev. xii. 9-15; fiery serpents sent as a punishment, Num. xxi. 6; sight of "brazen serpent," an antidote for poison of bite, Num. xxi. 8, 9; "fiery flying serpent," a probable allusion to dragon, Isa. xiv. 29.

**Sē'rug** (*branch*). Son of Reu and great-grandfather of Abraham, Gen. xi. 20-23. Saruch, Luke iii. 35.

**Sĕr'vant** (*server*). In a broad Bible sense, subject, assistant, person under tribute; in special sense, bondman or slave, by right of purchase, pledge for indebtedness, or indenture; which relationship was carefully guarded by Mosaic law, Lev. xxv. 39-55; Deut. xv. 12-18. [SLAVE.]

**Sêrv'i-tôr** (*server*). A servant, 2 Kgs. iv. 43.

**Sĕth** (*pay*). Third son of Adam, Gen. iv. 25; v. 3-8.

**Sē'thur** (*hidden*). An Asherite spy, Num. xiii. 13.

**Sĕv'en.** A favorite, and often symbolic, number among Hebrews, Gen. ii. 2; vii. 2; xli. 2, 3. Used as a round number, 1 Sam. ii. 5; Matt. xii. 45. Type of abundance and completeness, Gen. iv. 15, 24; Matt. xviii. 21, 22. These references, and other places, show a seventh day and seventh year sabbath and a seven times seventh year of Jubilee; also sacrificial animals limited to seven, and the golden candlesticks. Seven priests with seven trumpets surrounded Jericho for seven days, and seven times on the seventh day. In the Apocalypse we find seven churches, seven candlesticks, seven stars, seven seals, seven trumpets, seven vials, seven plagues, seven angels.

**Shā''al-ăb'bin** (*place of foxes*). A boundary place of Dan, Josh. xix. 42. Shaalbim, Judg. i. 35; 1 Kgs. iv. 9.

**Shā-ăl'bim.** [SHAALABBIN.]

**Shā-ăl'bo-nīte.** One of David's heroes, so called. Place unknown, 2 Sam. xxiii. 32; 1 Chr. xi. 33.

**Shā'aph** (*division*). (1) A Judahite, 1 Chr. ii. 47. (2) Son of Caleb, 1 Chr. ii. 49.

**Shā''a-rā'im** (*two gates*). (1) Town in Judah, 1 Sam. xvii. 52. Sharaim, Josh. xv. 36. (2) Town in Simeon, 1 Chr. iv. 31.

**Shā-ăsh'găz** (*lover of beauty*). Keeper of concubines in palace of Xerxes, Esth. ii. 14.

**Shăb-bĕth'a-ī** (*my rest*). An assistant to Ezra, Ez. x. 15; Neh. viii. 7; xi. 16.

**Shăch-ī'ā** (*God-protected*). A Benjamite, 1 Chr. viii. 10.

**Shăd'da-ī** (*mighty*). *El-Shaddai*, "God Almighty." The name used by Hebrews for God, before "Jehovah" acquired its full significance, Gen. xvii. 1; Ex. vi. 3.

**Shā'drach** (*royal*). Chaldean name given to Hananiah, Dan. i. 7-21; ii.; iii.

**Shā'gē** (*erring*). Father of one of David's guard, 1 Chr. xi. 34.

**Shā''ha-rā'im** (*double morning*). A Benjamite, 1 Chr. viii. 8.

**Shā-hăz'i-mah** (*heights*). Town in Issachar, Josh. xix. 22.

**Shā'lem** (*peaceful*). For "to Shalem," Gen. xxxiii. 18, read "in peace to."

**Shā'lim, Land of** (*land of foxes*). The wild place through which Saul passed when searching for his father's asses, 1 Sam. ix. 4.

**Shăl'i-shā, Land of** (*triangular*). A wild district near Mt. Ephraim through which Saul passed, in search of his father's asses, 1 Sam. ix. 4.

**Shăl'le-chĕth** (*thrown down*). A westward gate of the temple at Jerusalem, 1 Chr. xxvi. 16.

**Shăl'lum** (*revenge*). (1) Fifteenth king of Israel, B. C. 771; slew King Zachariah, and usurped his throne; reigned one month; slain and succeeded by Menahem, 2 Kgs. xv. 10-15. (2) Husband of Huldah the prophetess, 2 Kgs. xxii. 14; 2 Chr. xxxiv. 22. (3) A descendant of Sheshan, 1 Chr. ii. 40, 41. (4) Fourth son of Josiah king of Judah, who became King Jehoahaz, B. C. 610, and reigned for three months, 1 Chr. iii. 15; Jer. xxii. 11, 12; 2 Kgs. xxiii. 30, 31; 2 Chr. xxxvi. 1-4. (5) A Simeonite, 1 Chr. iv. 25. (6) A high priest, 1 Chr. vi. 12; Ez. vii. 2. (7) Shillem, a Naphtalite, 1 Chr. vii. 13. (8) A chief of porters, 1 Chr. ix. 17; Ez. ii. 42. (9) A porter, 1 Chr. ix. 19, 31. (10) An Ephraimite, 2 Chr. xxviii. 12. (11) Uncle of Jeremiah, Jer. xxxii. 7. (12) Four Levites, Ez. x. 24, 42; Neh. iii. 12; Jer. xxxv. 4.

**Shăl'lun** (*revenge*). A wall-repairer and governor of part of Mizpah, Neh. iii. 15.

**Shăl'ma-ī** (*thanks*). His children were returned captives, Ez. ii. 46.

**Shăl'man**, Hos. x. 14. [SHALMANESER.]

**Shăl''man-ē'ser** (*Shalman is lenient*). An Assyrian king, B. C. 727-722, who twice conquered Hoshea, king of Israel, the last time capturing his capital, Samaria, 2 Kgs. xvii. 3-6; xviii. 9-12.

**Shā'mā** (*dutiful*). One of David's guard, 1 Chr. xi. 44.

**Shăm''a-rī'ah** (*God-kept*). Son of King Rehoboam, 2 Chr. xi. 19.

**Shăm'bles** (*little benches*). In general, slaughter-houses, but meat-market in 1 Cor. x. 25.

**Shā'med** (*destroyer*). A Benjamite, 1 Chr. viii. 12.

**Shāme'fāçed-ness.** Wrong writing of shamefastness, modesty. Corrected in R. V., 1 Tim. ii. 9.

**Shā'mer** (*keeper*). (1) A Levite, 1 Chr. vi. 46. (2) An Asherite, 1 Chr. vii. 34. Shomer in vs. 32.

**Shăm'găr** (*sword*). A judge of Israel who slew 600 Philistines with an ox-goad, Judg. iii. 31; v. 6.

**Shăm'huth** (*destruction*). One of David's captains, 1 Chr. xxvii. 8.

**Shā'mīr** (*thorn*). (1) A town in the mountains of Judah, Josh. xv. 48. (2) Residence of Tola, the judge, in Mount Ephraim, Judg. x. 1, 2. (3) Son of Michah, 1 Chr. xxiv. 24.

**Shăm'mā** (*desolation*). A chief of Asher, 1 Chr. vii. 37.

**Shăm'mah** (*desolation*). (1) A duke of Edom, Gen. xxxvi. 13, 17; 1 Chr. i. 37. (2) Third son of Jesse, 1 Sam. xvi. 9; xvii. 13. Called also, Shimea, Shimeah, and Shimma. (3) One of the three greatest of David's mighty men, 2 Sam. xxiii. 11-17, 33. (4) Another of David's mighty men, 2 Sam. xxiii. 25. Shammoth, 1 Chr. xi. 27. Shamhuth, 1 Chr. xxvii. 8.

**Shăm'ma-ī** (*desolated*). Three Judahites, 1 Chr. ii. 28, 32, 44, 45; iv. 17.

**Shăm'moth**, 1 Chr. xi. 27. [SHAMMAH, 4.]

**Shăm-mū'ā, Shăm'mū-ah** (*heard*). (1) The Reubenite spy, Num. xiii. 4. (2) A son of David, born in Jerusalem, 2 Sam. v. 14; 1 Chr. xiv. 4. Shimea, 1 Chr. iii. 5. (3) A Levite, Neh. xi. 17. (4) A priest representing the family of Bilgah, Neh. xii. 18.

**Shăm''she-rā'ī** (*hero*). A Benjamite, 1 Chr. viii. 26.

**Shā'pham** (*bare*). A Gadite, 1 Chr. v. 12.

**Shā'phan** (*rabbit*). Scribe or secretary of King Josiah, 2 Kgs. xxii. 3-14; 2 Chr. xxxiv. 8-20.

**Shā'phat** (*judge*). (1) The Simeonite spy, Num xiii. 5. (2) Father of the prophet Elisha, 1 Kgs. xix. 16, 19; 2 Kgs. iii. 11; vi. 31. (3) One in the royal line of Judah, 1 Chr. iii. 22. (4) A Gadite chief, 1 Chr. v. 12. (5) A herdsman of David, 1 Chr. xxvii. 29.

**Shā'pher** (*bright*). A desert encampment of the Israelites, Num. xxxiii. 23.

**Shăr'a-ī** (*set free*). A descendant of Bani, who had married a foreign wife, Ez. x. 40.

**Shăr-ā'im**, Josh. xv. 36. [SHAARAIM.]

**Shā'rär** (*navel*). Father of one of David's warriors, 2 Sam. xxiii. 33. Sacar, 1 Chr. xi. 35.

**Shā-re'zer** (*prince*). Son of Sennacherib, who helped to murder his father, 2 Kgs. xix. 37.

**Shâr'on** (*plain*). (1) The plain skirting the Mediterranean coast from Judah to Cæsarea. It is an extension of the "shefelah" or lowlands of Judah, and was renowned for its fertility. Called Saron in Acts ix. 35. First mentioned as Lasharon, Josh. xii. 18. David's flocks fed there, 1 Chr. xxvii. 29. Celebrated in S. of Sol. ii. 1; Isa. xxxv. 2; lxv. 10. (2) A town or district east of Jordan, and perhaps in Gilead, 1 Chr. v. 16.

**Shâr'on-īte.** Designation of Shitrai, one of David's herdsmen, 1 Chr. xxvii. 29.

**Shā-ru'hen** (*gracious house*). A town first allotted to Judah and then to Simeon, Josh. xix. 6.

**Shăsh'a-ī** (*noble*). A son of Bani, who had taken a foreign wife, Ez. x. 40.

**Shā'shak** (*eager*). A Benjamite, 1 Chr. viii. 14, 25.

**Shā'ul** (*asked*). (1) A son of Simeon and founder of the Shaulites, Gen. xlvi. 10; Num. xxvi. 13. (2) A king of Edom, 1 Chr. i. 48, 49. Saul in Gen. xxxvi. 37.

**Shā'ul-ītes.** Descendants of Shaul, Num. xxvi. 13.

**Shā'veh** (*plain*). The unidentified place in Palestine mentioned as the "king's dale," Gen. xiv. 17; 2 Sam. xviii. 18.

**Shā'veh Kĭr''ī-a-thā'im** (*plain of Kiriathaim*). Spot where the Emims dwelt when smitten by Chedorlaomer, Gen. xiv. 5. It is supposably the place that afterwards belonged to Reuben, under the name of Kirjathaim, Num. xxxii. 37; Josh. xiii. 19.

**Shăv'shā** (*God's warrior*). Royal secretary or scribe in time of King David, 1 Chr. xviii. 16. Seraiah, 2 Sam. viii. 17. Sheva, 2 Sam. xx. 25. Shisha, 1 Kgs. iv. 3.

**Shā'ving.** [RAZOR.]

**Shawm** (*pipe*). A cornet or clarionet. Only in Prayer-book version of Ps. xcviii. 6.

**Shē'al** (*asking*). One who had a foreign wife, Ez. x. 29.

**Shē-ăl'tī-el** (*asked of God*). Father of Zerubbabel, Ez. iii. 2, 8; v. 2; Neh. xii. 1; Hag. i. 1, 12, 14; ii. 2, 23.

**Shĕ″a-rī′ah** (*prized of God*). A descendant of Saul, 1 Chr. viii. 38; ix. 44.

**Shēar′ing-house.** A spot between Jezreel and Samaria where Jehu slaughtered the royal family of Judah, 2 Kgs. x. 12-14.

**Shē′är-jā′shŭb** (*a remnant shall return*). Symbolical name given by Isaiah to his son, Isa. vii. 3.

**Shē′bȧ** (*oath*). (1) Son of Bichri, a Benjamite, who revolted from David and was beheaded, 2 Sam. xx. 1-22. (2) A Gadite chief, 1 Chr. v. 13. (3) A descendant of Ham, Gen. x. 7; 1 Chr. i. 9. (4) Son of Joktan, Gen. x. 28. (5) Son of Jokshan, Gen. xxv. 3; 1 Chr. i. 32. (6) The kingdom of Sheba, whose queen visited Solomon, 1 Kgs. x. 1-13; 2 Chr. ix. 1-12. This country has been variously located in Africa, in Arabia, on the Persian Gulf, and in Arabia, on the Red Sea. The burden of authority identifies it with Yemen or Arabia Felix, on the Red Sea, and peopled by descendants of Sheba, son of Joktan. (7) A town in Simeon, Josh. xix. 2. Probably the Shema of Josh. xv. 26.

**Shē′bah** (*oath*). The famous well, or series of wells, dug by the servants of Isaac, in accordance with his compact with the Philistines. It gave name to Beersheba, Gen. xxvi. 31-33.

**Shē′bam** (*odor*). A town east of Jordan, given to Reuben and Gad, Num. xxxii. 3. [SIBMAH.]

**Shĕb″a-nī′ah** (*grown by God*). (1) A priestly trumpeter at the bringing up of the ark, 1 Chr. xv. 24. (2) Three co-covenanters with Nehemiah, Neh. ix. 5; x. 4, 10, 12; xii. 14.

**Shĕb′a-rīm** (*ruins*). Place near Ai to which the defeated Israelites were pursued, Josh. vii. 5.

**Shē′băt.** [SEBAT.]

**Shē′ber** (*breaking*). A son of Caleb, 1 Chr. ii. 48.

**Shĕb′nȧ** (*strength*). (1) Prefect of the palace under King Hezekiah, Isa. xxii. 15-25. (2) Scribe under King Hezekiah, 2 Kgs. xviii. 18, 37; xix. 2; Isa. xxxvi. 3.

**Shĕb′u-el** (*captive of God*). (1) A descendant of Moses, 1 Chr. xxiii. 16; xxvi. 24. Shubael, 1 Chr. xxiv. 20. (2) A Levite minstrel, son of Heman, 1 Chr. xxv. 4. Shubael, 1 Chr. xxv. 20.

**Shĕc″a-nī′ah** (*dweller with God*). (1) A priest in time of David, 1 Chr. xxiv. 11. (2) A Levite, 2 Chr. xxxi. 15.

**Shĕch″a-nī′ah** (*dweller with God*). (1) A descendant of the royal line, 1 Chr. iii. 21, 22. (2) Levites and returned captives, in Ez. viii. 3, 5; x. 2; Neh. iii. 29; vi. 18; xii. 3.

**Shē′chem** (*shoulder*). (1) The Canaanite who abducted Dinah and was slain by Simeon and Levi, Gen. xxxiv. (2) An ancient and highly historic city, between mounts Ebal and Gerizim, 34 miles N. of Jerusalem. Called also Sichem, Sychem, Sychar, later Neapolis, now Nablus. Halting place of Abraham, Gen. xii. 6. A Hivite city in time of Jacob, Gen. xxxiii. 18-20; Josh. xxiv. 32. Captured by Simeon and Levi, Gen. xxxiv. Joseph buried there, Josh. xxiv. 32. Destroyed by Abimelech, Judg. ix. Rebuilt by Rehoboam, and fortified and made capital of Israel by Jeroboam, 1 Kgs. xii. 1-19, 25; 2 Chr. x. A centre of Samaritan worship after the captivity, John iv. 5, 39-42. (3) A Manassite, of Gilead, Num. xxvi. 31. (4) A Gileadite, nephew of former, 1 Chr. vii. 19.

**Shē′chem-ītes.** The family of Shechem of Gilead, Num. xxvi. 31.

**Shē-chī′nah** (*dwelling-place*). The visible majesty of God, as in the "pillar of cloud" and the "glory" which covered the tabernacle and filled Solomon's temple. A word found only in the targums, Chaldaic version of Bible, and among early Christian writers. Alluded to in Luke ii. 9; John i. 14; Rom. ix. 4.

**Shĕd′ē-ur** (*light-sender*). Father of Elizur, chief of Reuben at time of exode, Num. i. 5; ii. 10; vii. 30, 35; x. 18.

**Shēep.** An important animal among Hebrews, and a main source of wealth. Shepherd's occupation highly respectable, Gen. iv. 2; Ex. iii. 1; 1 Sam. xvi. 11; Job xlii. 12, though odious to Egyptians. Used for sacrifices, Ex. xx. 24; xxix. 38; Lev. iii. 3; for food, 1 Sam. xxv. 18. Wool used for clothing, Lev. xiii. 47. Skins used for tabernacle coverings, Ex. xxv. 5. Paid as tribute, 2 Kgs. iii. 4. Sheep and shepherd employed much figuratively, 2 Chr. xviii. 16; Ps. cxix. 176; Matt. ix. 36; John x. 11; Heb. xiii. 20. The common sheep of Syria and Palestine was the broad-tailed variety.

**Shēep′fōld.** Place for herding sheep, especially at night. Usually built strong to keep out wild animals, Num. xxxii. 16; 2 Sam. vii. 8; John x. 16. The fold, cote, or enclosure was also the place where the sheep were collected at shearing time, Jer. xxiii. 3; Zeph. ii. 6, which was a season of festivity, 1 Sam. xxv. 7-11; 2 Sam. xiii. 23. Hence "shearing-house," 2 Kgs. x. 12-14.

**Shēep-gate.** One of the gates of Jerusalem as rebuilt by Nehemiah, Neh. iii. 1, 32; xii. 39.

**Shēep-mär′ket.** Should read "sheep-gate" as above, John v. 2.

**Shē″ha-rī′ah** (*Jehovah dawns*). Son of Jeroham of Benjamin, 1 Chr. viii. 26.

**Shĕk′el** (*weight*). A weight for weighing uncoined money, of Assyrian and Babylonian origin. There seem to have been two standards, that of the sanctuary and the king, Ex. xxx. 13; 2 Sam. xiv. 26. Both approximated half an ounce, valued in silver at about 64 cents. Later, a Hebrew silver coin, with bronze half and quarter shekels. Probably the "pieces of silver" in Matt. xxvi. 15, though the "pieces of silver" in Luke xv. 8 are clearly the Greek drachmas. The first Jewish coins were struck by Simon Maccabeus, who obtained permission to coin money from Antiochus, King of Syria. His shekel showed a vase on one side, representing a pot of manna, and on the other an almond branch with flowers, representative supposably of Aaron's rod.

**Shē′lah** (*prayer*). (1) Youngest son of Judah and founder of Shelanites, Gen. xxxviii. 5-26; Num. xxvi. 20. (2) 1 Chr. i. 18, 24. [SALAH.]

**Shē′lan-ītes.** Descendants of Shelah, Num. xxvi. 20.

**Shĕl″e-mī′ah** (*God repays*). (1) 1 Chr. xxvi. 14. [MESHELEMIAH.] (2) Two who married foreign wives, Ez. x. 39, 41. (3) Father of Hananiah, Neh. iii. 30. (4) A priest appointed treasurer, Neh. xiii. 13. (5) Father of Jehucal, Jer. xxxvii. 3. (6) Father of one of Jeremiah's accusers, Jer. xxxviii. 1. (7) Father of the officer who arrested Jeremiah, Jer. xxxvii. 13.

**Shē′leph** (*drawn out*). Son of Joktan, Gen. x. 26.

**Shē′lesh** (*strength*). An Asherite chief, 1 Chr. vii. 35.

**Shĕl′o-mī** (*my peace*). An Asherite, Num. xxxiv. 27.

**Shĕl′o-mīth** (*my peace*). (1) Daughter of Dibri, of Dan, Lev. xxiv. 11. (2) Daughter of Zerubbabel, 1 Chr. iii. 19. (3) Two Levites, 1 Chr. xxiii. 9, 18. (4) A descendant of Eliezer, 1 Chr. xxvi. 25-28. (5) A returned captive, Ez. viii. 10.

**Shĕl′o-mŏth,** 1 Chr. xxiv. 22. [SHELOMITH, 3.]

**Shē-lū′mi-el** (*God's peace*). A prince of Simeon, Num. i. 6; ii. 12; vii. 36, 41; x. 19.

**Shĕm** (*name*). Oldest son of Noah, preserved with his father in the ark, Gen. v. 32. Blessed by Noah for his conduct, Gen. ix. 18-27. His descendants are the Hebrews, Arameans, Persians, Assyrians, and Arabians, whose languages are called Shemitic.

**Shē′mȧ** (*hearing*). (1) A Judahite, 1 Chr. ii. 43, 44. (2) A Reubenite, 1 Chr. v. 8. (3) A Benjamite chief, 1 Chr. viii. 13. (4) An assistant of Ezra, Neh. viii. 4. (5) Josh. xv. 26. [SHEBA, 7.]

**Shē-mā′ah** (*God hears*). A Benjamite whose sons joined David at Ziklag, 1 Chr. xii. 3.

**Shĕm″a-ī′ah** (*God hears*). (1) Prophet and chronicler in reign of Rehoboam, 1 Kgs. xii. 22; 2 Chr. xi. 2. (2) Twenty-four others, mostly priests, Levites, and returned captives, 1 Chr. iii. 22; iv. 37; v. 4; ix. 14; ix. 16; xv. 8, 11; xxiv. 6; xxvi. 4-7; 2 Chr. xxix. 14; xvii. 8; xxxi. 15; xxxv. 9; Ez. viii. 13, 16; x. 21, 31; Neh. vi. 10; x. 8; xii. 6, 18, 34, 36, 42; Jer. xxvi. 20; xxix. 24-32; xxxvi. 12.

**Shĕm″a-rī′ah** (*God keeps*). (1) An adherent of David at Ziklag, 1 Chr. xii. 5. (2) Two who took foreign wives, Ez. x. 32, 41.

**Shĕm′e-ber** (*high flight*). King of Zeboiim, Gen. xiv. 2.

**Shē′mĕr** (*guarded*). Owner of the hill which King Omri bought, and on which he built Samaria, giving it the former owner's name, 1 Kgs. xvi. 24.

**Shē-mī′dȧ** (*wise*). A son of Gilead and founder of the Shemidaites, Num. xxvi. 32; Josh. xvii. 2. Shemidah, 1 Chr. vii. 19.

**Shē-mī′dah,** 1 Chr. vii. 19. [SHEMIDA.]

**Shē-mī′dȧ-ītes.** Descendants of Shemida, Num. xxvi. 32.

**Shĕm′i-nīth** (*eighth*). A musical term, variously surmised to mean the instrument, one of eight strings, the octave, the time of the piece, the part, air, pitch, or key, 1 Chr. xv. 21; Ps. vi; xii. titles.

**Shĕ-mĭr'a-mŏth''** (*heights of heaven*). (1) A musical Levite in time of David, 1 Chr. xv. 18, 20; xvi. 5. (2) A Levite in reign of Jehoshaphat, 2 Chr. xvii. 8.

**Shĕ-mĭt'ic.** The family of languages spoken by the descendants of Shem. [SHEM.]

**Shĕ-mū'el** (*heard of God*). (1) Representative of Simeon during the apportionment of Canaan, Num. xxxiv. 20. (2) Samuel the prophet, 1 Chr. vi. 33. (3) A chief of Issachar, 1 Chr. vii. 2.

**Shĕn** (*tooth*). An unknown place, 1 Sam. vii. 12.

**Shĕ-nā'zar** (*ivory keeper*). A descendant of David, 1 Chr. iii. 18.

**Shē'nir**, Deut. iii. 9; S. of Sol. iv. 8. [SENIR.]

**Shē'pham** (*wild*). A landmark on eastern boundary of Promised Land, Num. xxxiv. 10.

**Shĕph''a-thī'ah** (*God judges*). A Benjamite, 1 Chr. ix. 8.

**Shĕph''a-tī'ah** (*God judges*). (1) Fifth son of David, 2 Sam. iii. 4; 1 Chr. iii. 3. (2) A Benjamite warrior, 1 Chr. xii. 5. (3) A chief of Simeon, 1 Chr. xxvii. 16. (4) Son of Jehoshaphat, 2 Chr. xxi. 2. (5) Four others in Ez. ii. 4, 57; Neh. vii. 9, 59; xi. 4; Jer. xxxviii. 1-4.

**Shĕp'hĕrd** (*herder of sheep*). A highly honorable occupation among pastoral Hebrews, engaged in by both sexes, Gen. xxix. 6; xxx. 29-35; Ex. ii. 16-22. Often arduous and dangerous employment, Gen. xxxi. 40; 1 Sam. xvii. 34. Equipment consisted of a sheepskin mantle, a scrip or wallet, a sling and crook. He led the flock to pasture in the morning, tended them by day and folded and watched them at night, Job xxx. 1; Luke ii. 8; John x. 4. The office of sheep-master or chief shepherd was one of great trust as well as honor, 2 Kgs. iii. 4; Heb. xiii. 20; 1 Pet. v. 4. It was the shepherd's duty to count the sheep daily and to tithe them, and he was held responsible for lost ones, Gen. xxxi. 38, 39; Ex. xxii. 12, 13; Lev. xxvii. 32; Jer. xxxiii. 13. Shepherd is used figuratively for Jehovah in Ps. lxxx. 1; Jer. xxxi. 10; for kings, Ezek. xxxiv. 10; in N. T. for Christ, John x. 11; Heb. xiii. 20; 1 Pet. v. 4. It is applied also to teachers in the synagogue and to those who preside over it. Hence pastor and minister of the gospel.

**Shē'phī** (*barren*). A descendant of Seir, 1 Chr. i. 40. Shepho, Gen. xxxvi. 23.

**Shē'phō**, Gen. xxxvi. 23. [SHEPHI.]

**Shĕ-phū'phan** (*serpent*). A grandson of Benjamin, 1 Chr. viii. 5. Shupham, Num. xxvi. 39. Shuppim, 1 Chr. vii. 12, 15. Muppim, Gen. xlvi. 21.

**Shē'rah** (*relation*). A daughter of Ephraim, 1 Chr. vii. 24.

**Shĕr''e-bī'ah** (*heat of God*). A co-covenanter with Nehemiah, and assistant to Ezra, Ez. viii. 18, 24; Neh. viii. 7; ix. 4; x. 12.

**Shē'resh** (*root*). Son of Machir, of Manasseh, 1 Chr. vii. 16.

**Shĕ-rē'zer** (*fire prince*). A messenger of the people, Zech. vii. 2.

**Shĕr'iff** (*shire officer*). A Babylonian official, Dan. iii. 2.

**Shē'shăch** (*from the goddess Shach*). Symbolical name for Babylon, Jer. xxv. 26.

**Shē'shāi** (*princely*). A son of Anak, slain by Caleb, Num. xiii. 22; Josh. xv. 14; Judg. i. 10.

**Shē'shan** (*princely*). A Judahite, 1 Chr. ii. 31-35.

**Shĕsh-băz'zar** (*fire-worshipper*). Zerubbabel's name at the Persian court, Ez. i. 8-11.

**Shĕth** (*tumult*). (1) 1 Chr. i 1. [SETH.] (2) For Sheth in Num. xxiv. 17, read "tumult," as in Jer. xlviii. 45.

**Shē'thär** (*star*). A Persian prince, Esth. i. 14.

**Shē'thär-bŏz'na-ī** (*star of splendor*). A Persian officer in Syria, Ez. v. 3, 6; vi. 6, 13.

**Shē'vȧ.** Corruption of Seraiah. (1) A son of Caleb, 1 Chr. ii. 49. (2) The scribe of David, 2 Sam. xx. 25. Shavsha, 1 Chr. xviii. 16. Shisha, 1 Kgs. iv. 3. Seraiah, 2 Sam. viii. 17.

**Shew'brĕad** (*showbread*). Unleavened bread baked in twelve loaves corresponding to the twelve tribes, and placed fresh every Sabbath on the golden table of the sanctuary. Eaten only by the priests, Ex. xxv. 30; Lev. xxiv. 8; 1 Sam. xxi. 1-6; Matt. xii. 3, 4. The arrangement of loaves on the table was in two rows of six loaves each. Salt and frankincense were put on each row. It was called "shewbread," "bread of the face," or "bread of the setting before," because it stood continually before the Lord. In later times it was called the "bread of ordering," 1 Chr ix. 32 marg.; Neh. x. 33.

**Shĭb'bo-lĕth** (*ear of corn, stream*). Pronounced *sib'bo-leth* by Ephraimites, and *shib'bo-leth* by Gileadites. When the latter conquered the former, and held the fords of Jordan, they exacted the pronunciation of this word in order to distinguish friend from foe. Any other word beginning with *sh* would have answered the same purpose, Judg. xii. 6.

**Shĭb'mah** (*fragrant*). A town in Reuben, east of Jordan, Num. xxxii. 38. Shebam, Num. xxxii. 3. Sibmah, Josh. xiii. 19.

**Shĭ'crŏn** (*drunkenness*). A boundary mark of northern Judah, Josh. xv. 11.

**Shiēld** (*cover*). A defensive piece of armor, varying in size and shape, and made of skin or metal. Worn on left arm. Metaphorically, divine protection, Judg. v. 8; 1 Kgs. x. 17; Ps. iii. 3.

**Shĭg-gā'ion** (*mournful*). A word which probably designates the character of the ode, Ps. vii. title.

**Shĭ-gĭ'o-noth.** Plural of Shiggaion, Hab. iii. 1.

**Shī'hŏn** (*ruin*). A town in Issachar, Josh. xix. 19.

**Shī'hôr** (*blackness*). (1) Southern boundary of David's empire, 1 Chr. xiii. 5. [SIHOR.] (2) Shihor-libnath, a boundary of Asher, and probably identical with the stream called "Blue River," which empties into the Mediterranean eight miles south of Dor, Josh. xix. 26.

**Shĭl'hī** (*armed*). Grandfather of King Jehoshaphat, 1 Kgs. xxii. 42; 2 Chr. xx. 31.

**Shĭl'him** (*armed*). A city in southern Judah, Josh. xv. 32.

**Shĭl'lem** (*retribution*). Son of Naphtali and founder of Shillemites, Gen. xlvi. 24; Num. xxvi. 49.

**Shĭl'lem-ītes.** Descendants of Shillem, Num. xxvi. 49.

**Shi-lō'ah.** The softly flowing waters of Siloam, Isa viii. 6.

**Shī'lōh** (*peace*). (1) A disputed rendering; referred to a town and to the Messiah, Gen. xlix. 10; Isa. ix. 6. (2) A city in Ephraim, midway between Bethel and Shechem. Now Seilun. Joshua's capital and site where he apportioned his conquests. The ark remained there for three hundred years, till captured by the Philistines, Josh. xviii. 1, 8-10; Judg. xxi. 19-23. Residence of Eli and Samuel, 1 Sam. iii., and it was there that Eli received word of the capture of the ark, and died, 1 Sam. iv. The ark was not returned to Shiloh after its capture, and the tabernacle was removed to Nob and thence to Jerusalem, but the odor of sanctity clung about the venerable city for generations, and it was long a place for annual pilgrimages and religious festivals. The prophet Ahijah dwelt at Shiloh, 1 Kgs. xiv. 1-18. Jeremiah pictures Shiloh as desolate in his day, Jer. vii. 12-14; xxvi. 6-9.

**Shi-lō'nī.** A descendant of Shelah, Neh. xi. 5.

**Shī'lo-nīte.** Dweller in Shiloh, 1 Kgs. xi. 29.

**Shī'lo-nītes.** Members of the family of Shelah, 1 Chr. ix. 5.

**Shĭl'shah** (*third*). An Asherite chief, 1 Chr. vii. 37.

**Shĭm'e-ȧ** (*hearing*). (1) A son of David born in Jerusalem, 1 Chr. iii. 5. (2) A Levite, 1 Chr. vi. 30. (3) Another Levite, 1 Chr. vi. 39. (4) A brother of David, called also Shammah, Shimeah, and Shimma, 1 Chr. xx. 7.

**Shĭm'e-ah** (*hearing*). (1) Brother of David, called also Shammah, Shimma and Shimea, 2 Sam. xxi. 21. (2) A descendant of Jehiel, founder of Gibeon, 1 Chr. viii. 32.

**Shĭm'e-ăm** (*hearing*), 1 Chr. ix. 38. [SHIMEAH, 2.]

**Shĭm'e-ăth** (*hearing*). Mother of one of the murderers of King Joash, 2 Kgs. xii. 21; 2 Chr. xxiv. 26.

**Shĭm'e-ath-ītes''.** A family of scribes, 1 Chr. ii. 55.

**Shĭm'e-ī** (*famed*). (1) A son of Gershon, Num. iii. 18. Shimi, Ex. vi. 17. (2) A Benjamite who cursed David, 2 Sam. xvi. 5-13; 1 Kgs. ii. 44-46. (3) One of David's warriors, 1 Kgs. i. 8. (4) A commissary of Solomon, 1 Kgs. iv. 18. (5) Brother of Zerubbabel, 1 Chr. iii. 19. (6) A Simeonite, 1 Chr. iv. 26, 27. (7) A Reubenite, 1 Chr. v. 4. (8) A Levite, 1 Chr. vi. 42. (9) Leader of 10th musical course, 1 Chr. xxv. 17. (10) David's vineyardist, 1 Chr. xxvii. 27. (11) Ancestor of Mordecai, Esth. ii. 5. (12) Levites in 2 Chr. xxix. 14; xxxi. 12, 13; Ez. x. 23, 33, 38.

**Shĭm'e-on** (*hearing*). One who married a foreign wife, Ez. x. 31.

**Shĭm'hī** (*famed*). A Benjamite, 1 Chr. viii. 21.

**Shĭ'mī**, Ex. vi. 17. [SHIMEI, 1.]

**Shĭm'ītes**. Descendants of Shimei (1), Num. iii. 21.

**Shĭm'mȧ** (*hearing*). Third son of Jesse, 1 Chr. ii. 13.

**Shī'mon** (*waste*). A Judahite, 1 Chr. iv. 20.

**Shĭm'rath** (*watcher*). A Benjamite, 1 Chr. viii. 21.

**Shĭm'rī** (*vigilant*). (1) A Simeonite, 1 Chr. iv. 37. (2) Father of one of David's guard, 1 Chr. xi. 45. (3) A Levite, 2 Chr. xxix. 13.

**Shĭm'rith** (*vigilant*). A Moabitess, mother of Jehozabad, one of the murderers of King Joash, 2 Chr. xxiv. 26. Called Shomer in 2 Kgs. xii. 21.

**Shĭm'rŏm**, 1 Chr. vii. 1. [SHIMRON, 2.]

**Shĭm'rŏn** (*watch-place*). (1) An ancient Canaanite city allotted to Zebulun, Josh. xi. 1; xix. 15. (2) Fourth son of Issachar and founder of Shimronites, Gen. xlvi. 13; Num. xxvi. 24.

**Shĭm'ron-ītes**. Descendants of Shimron (2), Num. xxvi. 24.

**Shĭm'ron-mē'ron**, Josh. xii. 20. Probably complete name of Shimron (1).

**Shĭm'shāi** (*bright*). A scribe and Persian satrap in Judea. He, together with the chancellor, Rehum, wrote a letter to King Artaxerxes in opposition to the rebuilding of the temple by Zerubbabel, Ez. iv. 8, 9, 17, 23.

**Shĭ'nāb** (*splendor*). A king of Admah in time of Abraham, Gen. xiv. 2.

**Shī'när** (*two rivers*). The alluvial plain through which the Tigris and Euphrates pass, and probably inclusive of Babylon and Mesopotamia, Gen. x. 10; xi. 1-9; Isa. xi. 11; Dan. i. 2. It was the seat of the kingdom founded by Nimrod, and which reckoned among its cities, as beginnings, Babel, Erech, Accad, and Calneh, Gen. x. 9, 10. Asshur went forth from Shinar to found Nineveh, Gen. x. 11. It was in the plain in the land of Shinar that the migrating nations undertook to build the tower of Babel, and where the confusion of tongues occurred, Gen. xi. 1-9.

**Ship**. Ships of Scripture dependent on oars and sails for propulsion. Hebrews not sailors. The ships of Acts, xxi. 1-6; xxvii. 6-44; xxviii. 11-13, were capable of carrying many people and much freight. Primitive ships were generally coasters. They were mounted with figure-heads and had figures painted on the sides of the bow. These composed the ship's "sign," Acts xxviii. 11. Among their furnishings were under-girders, anchors shaped like those of modern times, but without flukes, sounding-lines, rudder-bands, Acts xxvii. 40. Ancient ships, being wholly or in part propelled by oars, were properly called galleys.

**Shī'phī** (*many*). A prince of Simeon, in time of Hezekiah, 1 Chr. iv. 37.

**Shĭph'mite**. Probably a native of Shepham, and a designation of Zabdi, David's overseer of vineyard increase and wine cellars, 1 Chr. xxvii. 27.

**Shĭph'rah** (*handsome*). A Hebrew midwife in Egypt, Ex. i. 15.

**Shĭph'tan** (*judging*). Father of a prince of Ephraim, Num. xxxiv. 24.

**Shī'shȧ** (*God's strife*). Father of Solomon's scribes, 1 Kgs. iv. 3.

**Shī'shāk**. The king of Egypt to whom Jeroboam fled, 1 Kgs. xi. 40. He invaded Judea, B. C. 969, defeated Rehoboam, and spoiled the temple, 1 Kgs. xiv. 25, 26; 2 Chr. xii. 2-9. Inscriptions, reliefs, and statuary at Karnak, on the Nile, record his invasion of Palestine.

**Shĭt'ra-ī** (*scribe*). Keeper of David's herds in Sharon, 1 Chr. xxvii. 29.

**Shĭt'tah, Shĭt'tĭm** (*thorny*). (1) An Asiatic tree, a species of acacia, producing a close-grained, yellowish wood used in making the sacred furniture of the tabernacle, Ex. xxv. 10-13; xxvi. 15, 26; xxvii. 1; Isa. xli. 19. (2) Last encampment of the Israelites before crossing the Jordan. Scene of the completion of the law and farewell of Moses, Num. xxv.; xxxi. 1-12; Josh. ii. 1; iii. 1. The spies were sent out from Shittim to Jericho, and there the final preparations were made for crossing the Jordan. It was also called Abel-shittim, "meadow of acacias," and was the well-watered, fertile plain stretching from the foot of the mountains of Moab to the banks of the Jordan. (3) "Valley of Shittim," Joel iii. 18, is doubtless same as Shittim (2), which was also known as Abel-shittim.

**Shī'zȧ** (*loving*). Father of a Reubenite captain, 1 Chr. xi. 42.

**Shō'ȧ** (*fruitful*). An undetermined name or place, Ezek. xxiii. 23.

**Shō'băb** (*hostile*). (1) A son of David, 2 Sam. v. 14; 1 Chr. iii. 5; xiv. 4. (2) A son of Caleb, 1 Chr. ii. 18.

**Shō'băch** (*enlarging*). A Syrian general whom David defeated, 2 Sam. x. 15-18. Shophach, 1 Chr. xix. 16-18.

**Shō'ba-ī** (*captive*). A family of temple doorkeepers who returned from captivity, Ez. ii. 42; Neh. vii. 45.

**Shō'bal** (*current*). (1) Second son of Seir, and a Horite duke, Gen. xxxvi. 20; 1 Chr. i. 38. (2) A son of Caleb, 1 Chr. ii. 50, 52. (3) 1 Chr. iv. 1, 2, probably same as above.

**Shō'bek** (*forsaken*). A co-covenanter with Nehemiah, Neh. x. 24.

**Shō'bī** (*captive*). An Ammonite who succored David during Absalom's rebellion, 2 Sam. xvii. 27-29.

**Shō'cō, Shō'chō, Shō'choh**, 2 Chr. xi. 7, xxviii. 18; 1 Sam. xvii. 1. [SOCOH.]

**Shoe**. [SANDAL.]

**Shō'hăm** (*onyx*). A Levite, 1 Chr. xxiv. 27.

**Shō'mer** (*keeper*) (1) An Asherite, 1 Chr. vii. 32. Shamer in vs. 34. (2) Mother of Jehozabad, a co-murderer of King Joash, 2 Kgs. xii. 21. Called Shimrith in 2 Chr. xxiv. 26.

**Shō'phăch**, 1 Chr. xix. 16-18. [SHOBACH.]

**Shō'phan** (*burrow*). A fenced city east of Jordan, which fell to Gad, Num. xxxii. 35.

**Shō-shăn'nim** (*lilies*). Variously construed as a melody, bridal-song, and musical instrument, Ps. xlv., lxix., lxxx., titles. In the latter, *eduth*, "testimony," is added.

**Shoul'der**. Baring of, signified servitude, Gen. xlix. 15; withdrawing of, denoted rebellion, Neh. ix. 29; bearing upon, meant to sustain, Isa. ix. 6; xxii. 22.

**Shov'el** (*shove*). [FAN.] [WINNOW.]

**Shu'ȧ** (*wealth*). Father-in-law of Judah, 1 Chr. ii. 3. Shuah in Gen. xxxviii. 2, 12.

**Shu'ah** (*pit*). (1) A son of Abraham, Gen. xxv. 2; 1 Chr. i. 32. (2) Brother of Chelub, 1 Chr. iv. 11. (3) Gen. xxxviii. 2, 12. [SHUA.]

**Shu'al** (*fox*). (1) An Asherite, 1 Chr. vii. 36. (2) An unlocated land, 1 Sam. xiii. 17.

**Shu'ba-el** (*God's captive*). (1) Shebuel, son of Gershon, 1 Chr. xxiv. 20. (2) Shebuel, son of Heman the singer, and leader of the thirteenth musical course, 1 Chr. xxv. 20.

**Shu'ham** (*well-digger*). A son of Dan, Num. xxvi. 42. Hushim, Gen. xlvi. 23.

**Shu'ham-ītes**. Descendants of Shuham, Num. xxvi. 42.

**Shu'hīte**. Designation of Bildad, one of Job's friends; associated with *Tsukhi*, an Arabic tribe, Job ii. 11.

**Shu'lam-īte**. One belonging to Shulem or Shunem, S. of Sol. vi. 13.

**Shu'math-ītes**. One of the four families of Kirjath-jearim, 1 Chr. ii. 53.

**Shu'nam-īte**. A native of Shunem. The nurse of David and hostess of Elisha were so called, 1 Kgs. i. 3; 2 Kgs. iv. 12.

**Shu'nem** (*double sleeping-place*). A city of Issachar, near Jezreel. Place where the Philistines encamped before the great battle of Gilboa; home of David's nurse and wife, Abishag; residence of the woman who entertained Elisha. Now Solam, Josh. xix. 18; 1 Sam. xxviii. 4; 2 Kgs. iv. 8.

**Shu'nī** (*resting*). A son of Gad, Gen. xlvi. 16.

**Shu'nītes**. Descendants of Shuni, Num. xxvi. 15.

**Shu'pham**, Num. xxvi. 39. [SHUPPIM.]

**Shu'pham-ītes**. Descendants of Shupham, Num. xxvi. 39.

**Shŭp'pĭm** (*serpents*). (1) Great-grandson of Benjamin, 1 Chr. vii. 12. Shupham, Num. xxvi. 39. (2) A Levite gate-keeper, 1 Chr. xxvi. 16.

**Shûr** (*wall*). A desert region of Arabia, and its town, bordering on Egypt, Gen. xvi. 7; xxv. 18. "Wilderness of Etham," Num. xxxiii. 8. Inhabited by Amalekites, 1 Sam. xv. 7; xxvii. 8.

**Shu'shan** (*lily*). The Greek Susa, ancient capital of Elam, a province in Mesopotamia. A seat of wealth and power after the Persian conquest of Babylon. The events of Esther's history occurred there. Spot of Daniel's visions. Nehemiah commissioned there, Gen. x. 22; xiv. 1; Neh. i. 1; Esth.; Isa. xxi. 2; Jer. xlix. 34; Dan. viii. 2. The decline of this ancient city dates from its capture by Alexander the Great, or from its later conquest by Antigonus, B. C. 315. The site, nearly due east from Babylon and north of the Persian Gulf, is marked by ruins, some three miles in circumference, in the midst of which have been found the remains of the great palace of Darius, scene of the events narrated in the book of Esther.

**Shu'shan-ē'duth.** Abbreviated form of Shoshannim-eduth, which *see*, Ps. lx. title.

**Shu'thal-hītes.** Descendants of Shuthelah, Num. xxvi. 35.

**Shu'the-lah** (*discord*). Head of the Ephraimite family of Shuthalhites, Num. xxvi. 35; 1 Chr. vii. 20, 21.

**Shŭt'tle** (*shooter*). This weaver's device for throwing the filling thread between the warp threads is figurative of fleeting time in Job vii. 6.

**Sī'à** (*assembly*). His children returned from captivity, Neh. vii. 47. Siaha, Ez. ii. 44.

**Sī'a-hà**, Ez. ii. 44. [SIA.]

**Sĭb'be-cāi**, 1 Chr. xi. 29; xxvii. 11. [SIBBECHAI.]

**Sĭb'be-chāi** (*weaver*). One of David's guard, and eighth captain of eighth month, 2 Sam. xxi. 18; 1 Chr. xx. 4. Sibbecai, 1 Chr. xi. 29; xxvii. 11. Mebunnai, 2 Sam. xxiii. 27

**Sĭb'bo-lĕth**, Judg. xii. 6. [SHIBBOLETH.]

**Sĭb'mah** (*fragrant*). A fortified city of Reuben, east of Jordan, Josh. xiii. 19. Shebam, Num. xxxii. 3. Shibmah, Num. xxxii. 38. Noted for its grapes, Isa. xvi. 8, 9; Jer. xlviii. 32.

**Sĭb'ra-ĭm** (*twice hopeful*). A boundary mark of northern Palestine, Ezek. xlvii. 16.

**Sī'chem**, Gen. xii. 6. [SHECHEM.]

**Sĭck'le** (*cutter*). The reaping and mowing implement of the ancients. In its size and curvature, as represented on Egyptian monuments, it resembled the implement as known to us, Deut. xvi. 9.

**Sĭç'ȳ-ŏn.** A city of the Peloponnesus near the Isthmus, 1 Macc. xv. 23.

**Sĭd'dim** (*pitted vale*). A vale, full of slime-pits, supposably near the Dead Sea, in which the kings of the plain cities met their invaders, Gen. xiv. 1-10.

**Sī'de** (*trading*). A trading city in Pamphylia, 1 Macc. xv. 23.

**Sī'dŏn**, Gen. x. 15, 19. [ZIDON.]

**Si-dō'nĭ-ans.** Zidonians, Deut. iii. 9; Josh. xiii. 4, 6; Judg. iii. 3; 1 Kgs. v. 6.

**Siēge** (*sit*), Deut. xx. 19. [WAR.]

**Sieve.** Ancient sieves, or sifters, were crudely made of rushes, though the Gauls are credited with their manufacture from horsehair. They were used for separating the flour from the bran, or broken kernels, and what was left in the sieve was thrown back into the mill to be reground, Isa. xxx. 28.

**Sī'hŏn** (*rooting out*). An Amorite king, defeated by the Israelites, who occupied his country between the Arnon and Jabbok, Num. xxi. 21-31; Deut. i. 4; ii. 24-37; Josh. xiii. 15-28.

**Sī'hôr** (*blackness*). The Sihor, or Shihor, of Egypt, 1 Chr. xiii. 5; Isa. xxiii. 3; Jer. ii. 18, has ever been construed as "the Nile." But when unqualified, some Arabian ravine or wady may be meant.

**Sī'las** (*Silvanus, woody*). An eminent member of the early Christian church. Written Silvanus in Paul's epistles. Resided at Jerusalem as teacher, but accompanied Paul on his tours, and was his fellow-prisoner at Philippi. Said to have been bishop of Corinth, Acts xv. 22, 32-34, 40; xvii. 14; xviii. 5; 2 Cor i. 19; 1 Thess. i. 1.

**Sĭlk** (*Seric stuff*). Silk hardly known to ancient Hebrews. In Prov. xxxi. 22; Ezek. xvi. 10, 13, some fine linen fabric is supposed to be meant. Undoubtedly known in N. T. times, Rev. xviii. 12.

**Sĭl'là** (*branch*). The place near which King Joash was slain, 2 Kgs. xii. 20.

**Sĭ-lō'ah**, Neh. iii. 15. [SILOAM.]

**Sĭ-lō'am** (*sent*). (1) The celebrated pool, or tank, at Jerusalem, on the south side, near the opening of the Tyropheau valley into the Kidron valley. Originally a part of the water supply of the city, Neh. iii. 15; Isa. viii. 6, John ix. 7-11. (2) An unlocated tower whose fall killed eighteen men, Luke xiii. 4. Siloam still retains its ancient name under the form of the Arabic *Silwân* It is partly hewn from rock and partly built with masonry. A flight of steps leads down to it. It is no longer a natural spring of fresh, limpid water, but is fed from the Fountain of the Virgin through a rock tunnel over 1700 feet in length. The waters are brackish and colored, and the walls and steps in ruins.

**Sĭl-vā'nus** (*woody*). [SILAS.]

**Sĭl'ver** (*white*). Used by Hebrews from earliest times for money, vessels, and ornaments, but not in form of coins till after the captivity, Gen. xiii. 2; xxiv. 53; xliv. 2; Job xxviii. 1; Matt. xxvi. 15; Acts xix. 24. Silver supplied to Jerusalem from Arabia and Tarshish, 2 Chr. ix. 14, 21.

**Sĭl'vĕr-lings** (*little silvers*). Evidently bits of silver money, but whether by weight or coinage is not known, Isa. vii. 23.

**Sī''măl-cū'e.** An Arabian chief, guardian of Antiochus, son of Balas, 1 Macc. xi. 39.

**Sĭm'e-on** (*who hears*). (1) Son of Jacob and Leah, Gen. xxix. 33. For the crime in Gen. xxxiv. 25-30 his father denounced him, Gen. xlix. 5-7. His tribe was small, Num. i. 22, 23; xxvi. 14, and their inheritance a scattered portion of Canaan, Josh. xix. 1-9. (2) Son of Judah in genealogy of Christ, Luke iii. 30. (3) Simon Peter, Acts xv. 14. (4) A venerable and pious Jew who blessed the child Jesus in the temple, Luke ii. 25-35. (5) Simeon Niger, Acts xiii. 1. [NIGER.]

**Sī'mon** (*Simeon*). (1) Several distinguished Jews bore this name during the Maccabean period. (2) A native of Samaria and famous sorcerer, who professed Christ for mercenary purposes, Acts viii. 9-24. (3) Simon Peter, Matt. iv. 18. [PETER.] (4) Simon the Canaanite, or Simon Zelotes. was a member of the party of Zealots who advocated the Jewish ritual, and an apostle, Matt. x. 4. (5) Simon the brother of Jesus, Matt. xiii. 55; Mark vi. 3. (6) Simon the Pharisee, in whose house a woman anointed the feet of Jesus, Luke vii. 36-50. (7) Simon, the leper of Bethany, Matt. xxvi. 6. (8) Simon of Cyrene, who was compelled to bear Christ's cross, Matt. xxvii. 32; Mark xv. 21; Luke xxiii. 26. (9) The tanner of Joppa with whom Peter lodged, Acts ix. 43. (10) Simon the father of Judas Iscariot, John vi. 71; xiii. 2, 26.

**Sĭm'rī** (*alert*). A Merarite Levite in David's time, 1 Chr. xxvi. 10.

**Sĭn** (*clay*). (1) A city of Egypt identified with Pelusium, "town of clay or mud," on eastern mouth of Nile near the sea, Ezek. xxx. 15, 16. (2) A desert portion of Arabia between Gulf of Suez and Sinai, Ex. xvi. 1; xvii. 1; Num. xxxiii. 11, 12. It was in this wilderness that the Israelites were first fed with manna and quails. It skirts the eastern coast of the gulf for a distance of 25 miles.

**Sĭn-mon'ey.** Money sent from a distance to buy offerings. The surplus, if any, became a perquisite of the priest, and was called sin-money, 2 Kgs. xii. 16.

**Sĭn-ŏf'fĕr-ĭng.** Like the trespass-offering, the sin-offering was expiatory, but seemingly of general sins. It was presented on the great day of atonement, when one confessed the sins of the nation with his hand on the head of the scapegoat, Lev. xvi. 1-34; Num. xviii. 9.

**Sī'nà.** Greek form of Sinai, Acts vii. 30, 38.

**Sī'nāi** (*bushy*). The peninsula of Sinai lies between the two great arms of the Red Sea, Gulf of Akaba on the east, and Gulf of Suez on the west. This region contains the mountain system of Horeb or Sinai, on one of whose mounts, or peaks, God appeared to Moses in the burning bush, Ex. iii. 1-5, amid whose surrounding wilderness the wandering Israelites encamped, Ex. xix. 1, 2, and from whose cloud-obscured heights the law was delivered to Moses, Ex. xix. 3-25; xx.-xl.; Lev. The numbering also took place there, Num. i.-x. 1-12. The peninsula is a triangle whose base extends from the head of Suez to Akaba. This base is pierced by the plateau of Tih, the "desert of wandering," south of which are those tumultuous mountain clusters above mentioned, central among which is Mount Sinai. The coast ranges along Akaba and Suez are systematic and elevated. The region was a dependency of Egypt from earliest times, but became subject to Rome.

**Sī'nim.** An unidentified land mentioned in Isa. xlix. 12. Referred by some to China.

**Sĭn'īte.** A tribe descended from Canaan, Gen. x. 17; 1 Chr. i. 15.

**Sī'ŏn** (*lofty*). (1) An ancient name of Mount Hermon, Deut. iv. 48. (2) Greek form of Zion, Matt. xxi. 5; John xii. 15; Heb. xii. 22; Rev. xiv. 1.

**Sĭph'moth** (*fertile*). A haunt of David, while an outlaw, in South Judah, 1 Sam. xxx. 28.

**Sĭp'pāi** (*threshold*). Saph. the Philistine giant slain at Gezer, 1 Chr. xx. 4.

**Sī'rach.** Father of Jesus, writer of the Apocryphal book of Ecclesiasticus.

**Sī'rah** (*retreat*). The well, now *Ain Sarah*, from which Abner was called by Joab. It was near Hebron, 2 Sam. iii. 26.

**Sĭr'ĭ-ŏn.** Zidonian name of Mount Hermon, Deut. iii. 9; Ps. xxix. 6.

**Sĭ-săm'a-ī** (*famed*). A descendant of Sheshan, of Judah, 1 Chr. ii. 40.

**Sĭs'e-rȧ** (*ready for war*). (1) Captain of King Jabin's forces when defeated by Barak. Slain by Jael, Judg. iv.; v. (2) His children returned, Ez. ii. 53; Neh. vii. 55.

**Sĭ-sĭn'ēs.** Governor of Syria and Phœnicia under Darius, 1 Esdr. vi. 3.

**Sĭt'nah** (*strife*). Second of the two wells dug by Isaac in valley of Gerar, over which the herdsmen disputed, Gen. xxvi. 21.

**Sī'van.** Third month of Jewish sacred and ninth of civil year, beginning with the new moon of June, Esth. viii. 9.

**Slāve** (*Sclavonian*). Slavery came about under Hebrew institutions. (1) By poverty, when a man sold himself to cancel debt, Lev. xxv. 39; (2) by theft, when restitution could not be made, Ex. xxii. 3; (3) by parents selling their daughters as concubines, Ex. xxi. 7-11. It ended (1) when the debt was paid; (2) on the year of Jubilee, Lev. xxv. 40; (3) at the end of six years of service, Ex. xxi. 2; Deut. xv. 12. This as to Hebrews. As to non-Hebrew slaves, by far the most numerous class, they were purchased, Lev. xxv. 45; or captured in war, Num. xxxi. 26, 40. They were freed if ill treated, Ex. xxi. 26, 27; to slay one was murder, Lev. xxiv. 17, 22; they were circumcised and had religious privileges, Gen. xvii. 12, 13.

**Slīme.** The slime of Babel, and that of the pits of Siddim, and the ark of Moses, was mineral pitch or bitumen, Gen. xi. 3; xiv. 10; Ex. ii. 3.

**Slĭng.** The weapons of shepherds and light troops. It consisted of leather or sinew strings with a pouch at the end for the missile, Judg. xx. 16; 1 Sam. xvii. 40.

**Smĭth** (*smiter*). An artificer in iron, brass, or other metals, Gen. iv. 22; 1 Sam. xiii. 19-22.

**Smȳr'nȧ** (*myrrh*). A coast city of Ionia, Asia Minor, 40 miles north of Ephesus. Mentioned in Rev. ii. 8-11 as site of one of the seven churches of Asia. The old city of Smyrna dates back to Theseus, 1300 years B. C. Alexander the Great built the new city B. C. 320. It became subject to Rome and was noted for its beauty. Christianity got an early foothold there and the city sent a bishop to the council of Nice, A. D. 325. It is still a large city of mixed nationalities and creeds, and of considerable commercial importance.

**Snāil** (*snake*). In Lev. xi. 30 a lizard is meant. In Ps. lviii. 8, the common snail, slug, or slime-snake is meant. Snails abound in the Orient and are not eschewed as a food.

**Snōw.** Only mentioned once as actually falling, 2 Sam. xxiii. 20; but of frequent poetic and metaphoric use, Ex. iv. 6; Num. xii. 10; 2 Kgs. v. 27; Ps. li. 7; Isa. i. 18.

**Snŭff=dĭsh'es.** Small dishes, made of gold, for receiving the snuff from the tabernacle lamps, Ex. xxv. 38.

**Snŭf'fērs.** Scissor-like instruments, made of gold, for snuffing the wicks of the tabernacle lamps, Ex. xxxvii. 23.

**Sō.** A king of Egypt with whom Hoshea formed an alliance against Assyria. The discovery of this led to the imprisonment of Hoshea, the siege and capture of Samaria, and the captivity of the ten tribes of Israel, 2 Kgs. xvii. 4, 6.

**Sōap** (*sap, resin*). The Hebrew word for soap implies any alkaline substance used for cleansing, Jer. ii. 22; Mal. iii. 2.

**Sō'chō,** 1 Chr. iv. 18. [Socoh.]

**Sō'choh,** 1 Kgs. iv. 10. [Socoh.]

**Sō'coh** (*brambly*). (1) A town in lowlands of Judah, Josh. xv. 35. Shocho, 2 Chr. xxviii. 18. Shoco, 2 Chr. xi. 7. Shochoh, 1 Sam. xvii. 1. (2) A town in the mountains of Judah, Josh. xv. 48.

**Sō'dī** (*secret*). Father of the spy from Zebulun, Num. xiii. 10.

**Sŏd'om** (*consuming*). Most prominent of the cities in the plain of Siddim. Destroyed by fire from heaven, Gen. x. 19; xiii. 10-13; xix. 1-29. Site of "the cities of the plain" is not known, but variously referred to the southern end, the northern end, and bottom of the Dead Sea. Sodom is often referred to in Scripture as a symbol of wickedness and warning to sinners, Deut. xxix. 23; Isa. i. 9, 10; xiii. 19; Jer. xxiii. 14; xlix. 18; Ezek. xvi. 49, 50 Matt. x. 15; xi. 23; Rev. xi. 8.

**Sŏd'om-ȧ.** Greek and Vulgate form of Sodom, Rom. ix. 29.

**Sŏd'om-ītes.** Dwellers in Sodom, or, by figure, those who practise the abominations of Sodom, Deut. xxiii. 17; 1 Kgs. xiv. 24; xv. 12.

**Sŏl'o-mon** (*peaceful*). Last of David's sons by Bathsheba. Named Jedidiah, "beloved of God," by Nathan, 1 Chr. iii. 5; 2 Sam. xii. 25. Placed in Nathan's care. Secured the throne according to David's pledge, 1 Kgs. i. 13-53, and much to the consternation of Adonijah, the legal successor. Reigned forty years, B. C. 1015-975. Confirmed his father's conquests, built the palace and temple, extended commerce, contracted favorable alliances, grew famous for wisdom, raised his kingdom to great wealth, splendor, and power, mingled justice with cruelty, endorsed true and false worship, encouraged literature, and wrote largely himself, fell a prey to the sensualities of his time and position, died leaving his kingdom under the eclipse of faction and on the edge of decay, 1 Kgs. ii.-xi.; 2 Chr. i.-ix.

**Sŏl'o-mon's Pools.** Reservoirs erected by Solomon near Bethlehem, whence water was conveyed to the distributing pools at Jerusalem. They are still in partial use, Eccl. ii. 6.

**Sŏl'o-mon's Porch.** The colonnade on east side of the temple, John x. 23; Acts iii. 11; v. 12.

**Sŏl'o-mon's Sēr'vants.** Returned captives, and probable descendants of a class of servants favored by Solomon, Ez. ii. 55, 58; Neh. vii. 57, 60.

**Sŏl'o-mon's Sŏng.** [Song of Solomon.]

**Son.** In Hebrew sense, any descendant however remote, Gen. xxix. 5; 2 Sam. xix. 24. Applied also to pupils, adopted persons, those of kindred faith, etc., Gen. xlviii. 5; 1 Sam. iii. 6; Acts xiii. 6.

**Son of God.** A term applied to the angels, Job xxxviii. 7; to Adam, Luke iii. 38; to believers, Rom. viii. 14; 2 Cor. vi. 18; but preëminently to Christ, signifying his divine origin and nature, Dan. iii. 25; Matt. xi. 27; xvi. 16; John i. 18; v. 19-26; ix. 35.

**Son of Man.** In a limited sense, "man," Num. xxiii. 19; Job xxv. 6; Ps. viii. 4. In a broader, higher, and perhaps more generally received Hebrew sense, "the Messiah." In the N. T. sense, where the term is used some eighty times, it means Christ in incarnate form and relation, Dan. vii. 13; Matt. ix. 6; xii. 8; xviii. 11; Mark ii. 10; John i. 51; iii. 13; vi. 53.

**Sŏng of Sŏl'o-mon.** "Song of Songs," or "Canticles," in Latin. Twenty-second O. T. book and last of poetic. Authorship and meaning much disputed. Some make it type conjugal love; others regard it as purely allegorical; still others as literal and descriptive of Solomon's marriage to some beautiful woman.

**Sooth'say-er** (*truth-sayer*). One who pretends to foretell future events, Dan. ii. 27. [Divination.]

**Sŏp** (*sip*). Bread dipped in soup, milk, wine, sauce, or other liquid, Ruth ii. 14; John xiii. 26.

**Sŏp'a-tēr** (*father saved*). A Berean companion of Paul, Acts xx. 4.

**Sŏph'e-rĕth** (*scribe*). His children were returned captives, Ez. ii. 55.

**Sŏph"ŏ-nī'as.** The prophet Zephaniah, 2 Esdr. i. 40.

**Sôr'çēr-er** (*fate-worker*). [Divination.]

**Sō'rek** (*vine*). A valley of Philistia, where Delilah lived, Judg. xvi. 4.

**Sō-sĭp'a-tēr** (*Sopater*). (1) A general of Judas Maccabeus, 2 Macc. xii. 19-24. (2) A friend of Paul; probably Sopater, Rom. xvi. 21.

**Sŏs'the-nēs** (*saviour*). (1) A ruler of the synagogue at Corinth, who was beaten by the Greeks, Acts xviii. 17. (2) Perhaps the former, after conversion, 1 Cor. i. 1.

**Sŏs'tra-tus.** A Syrian general commanding in Jerusalem, 2 Macc. iv. 27.

**Sō'ta-ī** (*fickle*). His children were returned captives, Ez. ii. 55; Neh. vii. 57.

**Sōul.** The Hebrew ideal of man was threefold: (1) The body, or material part. (2) The vital part, seat of sensations, passions, etc. (3) The sentient, thinking, or spiritual part, Gen. i. 20; ii. 7; Num. xvi. 22; 1 Thess. v. 23; Heb. iv. 12.

**South Rā'moth.** A place in southern Judah, bordering on the desert, and one of the resorts of David during the period of his outlawry by Saul, 1 Sam. xxx. 27.

**Sow.** [SWINE.]

**Sōw'er, Sōw'ing.** Cereal seeds were sown by hand, Ps. cxxvi. 6; Am. ix. 13; Mark iv. 3-29. In moist ground seeds were tramped in by cattle, Isa. xxxii. 20. Mixed seeds prohibited, Lev. xix. 19; Deut. xxii. 9.

**Spāin.** Anciently the whole peninsula of southwestern Europe, embracing Spain and Portugal; known to Greeks as Iberia and to Romans as Hispania. If identical with Tarshish, then known to Hebrews in Solomon's time; certainly to Phœnicians. Known to Paul, who contemplated a visit to it, Rom. xv. 24-28. Christianity early introduced there.

**Spăn** (*bind*). Distance from tip of thumb to that of little finger, when stretched apart; about nine inches. Also any small interval of space or time, 1 Sam. xvii. 4; Isa. xl. 12; Lam. ii. 20.

**Spăr'row** (*spurrer*). The Hebrew word signifies "twitterer" and is mostly rendered "bird" or "fowl." Though tree-sparrows abounded in Palestine, any small bird meets the sense in Ps. lxxxiv. 3; cii. 7. In N. T. the reference is directly to the sparrow species, used as a cheap food, Matt. x. 29; Luke xii. 6, 7.

**Spēar** (*spar*). In general, a wooden staff with a sharp metallic head. Some were light for throwing, others long and heavy for attack either by footmen or horsemen, 1 Sam. xiii. 22; xvii. 7; xxvi. 7; 2 Sam. ii. 23.

**Spēar'men.** Light-armed troops are evidently meant, Acts xxiii. 23.

**Spĕck'led Bird,** Jer. xii. 9. [HYENA.]

**Spīce, Spī'çeş** (*species*). Hardly, as with us, the entire list of aromatic vegetable substances, but rather the fragrant gums, barks, etc., of ceremonial, medicinal, and toilet value, and for embalming, Gen. xxxvii. 25; xliii. 11; S. of Sol. iv. 14; Mark xvi. 1; John xix. 39, 40.

**Spī'der** (*spinner*). The common spider is meant in Job viii. 14; Isa. lix. 5; but the gecko, or lizard, is probably intended in Prov. xxx. 28. The lightness and frailty of the spider's web are made emblematic of visionary hopes and wicked schemes.

**Spīke'närd** (*pointed leaf yielding perfume*). An ancient fragrant and costly ointment made from the spikenard plant of India, S. of Sol. i. 12; iv. 13, 14; Mark xiv. 3; John xii. 3.

**Spĭn'ning** (*spanning, drawing*). A well-known and necessary female occupation among Hebrews. The instrument — distaff and spindle — permitted of much the same drawing and twisting process as is now employed in the East, in the absence of the more modern spinning-wheel, Ex. xxxv. 25; Prov. xxxi. 19; Matt. vi. 28.

**Spĭr'it** (*breath*). The breath, 2 Thess. ii. 8. The vital principle, Eccl. viii. 8. Elsewhere, the soul. [SOUL.] Holy Spirit, or Ghost, is the third person in the Trinity, 2 Cor. xiii. 14; Acts xv. 28. Though Holy Spirit and Holy Ghost are synonymous in meaning, preference is given to the latter form in the Scriptures, Matt. i. 18; John i. 33; Acts ii. 4; Rom. v. 5, and elsewhere, the former being used only four times.

**Spŏil.** Plunder seized by violence, as the spoils of an army or of bandits, 1 Sam. xxx. 19-22; but in Ex. iii. 22, the sense is that of recovery without violence of unjustly taken property. David instituted very strict regulations for the division of spoils of war among his soldiers, 1 Sam. xxx. 20-25.

**Spŏnge.** Only mentioned in N. T., though probably known to ancient Hebrews, Matt. xxvii. 48; Mark xv. 36; John xix. 29.

**Spouşe.** [MARRIAGE.]

**Sprĭn'kling** (*springing*). The blood of the sin-offering was sprinkled with the finger of the priest upon the mercy-seat of the inner sanctuary as an atonement for the holy place because of national uncleanness, Lev. xvi. 14-16. The "blood of sprinkling" or mediatorial blood of the new covenant, Heb. xii. 24, is made antithetical with the blood of vengeance, Gen. iv. 10.

**Stā'chȳs** (*ear of corn*). A Roman Christian saluted by Paul, Rom. xvi. 9.

**Stăc'tē** (*drop*). An oriental gum or spice, one of the components of the holy incense, Ex. xxx. 34.

**Stănd'ard.** [ENSIGN.]

**Stär** (*strew*). All the heavenly bodies, except sun and moon, called stars by Hebrews, Gen. xv. 5; Ps. cxlvii. 4. The "star in the east," seen and followed by the "wise men," and designed to announce the birth of the Messiah, was, according to some, wholly phenomenal, and to others, natural. Stars symbolize rulers and princes, Dan. viii. 10; angels, Job xxxviii. 7; ministers, Rev. i. 16-20. Christ is "the bright and morning star," Rev. xxii. 16.

**Stā'ter** (*standard*). The standard gold coin of ancient Greece, worth about $4.00. Later, the silver stater, containing four drachmæ, or about sixty cents. This is thought to be the "piece of money" of Matt. xvii. 27.

**Stēel.** Hebrews were not acquainted with carbonized iron, or steel. Wherever the word is found in Scripture, copper is meant, Ps. xviii. 34.

**Stĕph'a-năs** (*crown*). One of Paul's earliest converts at Corinth, 1 Cor. i. 16; xvi. 15.

**Stē'phen** (*crown*). Chief of the first seven deacons, and first Christian martyr. A Greek convert of strong faith and great eloquence. Arrested and tried before the Sanhedrim, but stoned to death by an angry mob, before he had time to finish his defence. The date of his martyrdom is fixed at about A. D. 37. It was followed by the conversion of Saul, who was present at the stoning, and a bitter persecutor of early Christians at the time, Acts vi. 5-15, vii., viii. 1-3.

**Stŏcks** (*sticks*). Tree-trunks, Job xiv. 8; idols, Jer. ii. 27; instruments of punishment made of beams of wood which closed over the arms or ankles, Job xiii. 27; xxxiii. 11; Jer. xx. 2; Acts xvi. 24.

**Stō'ĭcs** (*porch scholars*). Members of a Grecian philosophical school, or sect, founded by Zeno, 308 B. C., who taught in the *stoa*, or porch, of the Agora at Athens. They held to a high morality, proud independence of spirit, fateful, in place of providential, superintendence, wisdom as the source of happiness, Acts xvii. 18. Paul encountered both Stoics and Epicureans at Athens, and, on being taken into Areopagus by them, delivered to them the oration in Acts xvii. 22-31.

**Stom'ach-er.** An article of dress worn over breast and stomach. Much affected in the 17th century; but whether that of Isa. iii. 24 was similar is not known.

**Stōneş.** Used for building, 1 Kgs. v. 17; Am. v. 11; memorial marks, Gen. xxviii. 18; xxxv. 14; knives, Ex. iv. 25; ballots, Rev. ii. 17. Symbols of hardness, 1 Sam. xxv. 37; of firmness, Gen. xlix. 24; Christian aggregation, 1 Pet. ii. 4-6. Precious stones highly prized by Hebrews and much used on priestly vestments and as ornaments. Twenty gems are mentioned in the Bible, Gen. ii. 12; Ex. xxviii. 9-21. India, Arabia, and Syria were the sources of gems used by Hebrews, Ezek. xxvii. 16-22.

**Stō'ning.** [PUNISHMENT.]

**Stôrk** (*vulture*). A large wading bird, plentiful in Palestine, gregarious, migratory, nesting in trees and noted for tenderness to its young. Unclean under the law, Lev. xi. 19; Deut. xiv. 18; Ps. civ. 17; Jer. viii. 7.

**Strāin at a,** Matt. xxiii. 24. "Strain out the," in R. V.

**Strān'ger** (*without*). One away from his country, Gen. xxiii. 4. One not a Jew, Ex. xx. 10. One not of Aaron's family, Num. iii. 10. One not of royal blood, Matt. xvii. 25, 26. One alienated or neglected, Ps. lxix. 8. But, in general, any naturalized foreigner in the Jewish State, Deut. xvii. 15. Strangers, in Hebrew acceptation, were numerous in Israel, owing to the mixed multitudes which were permitted to follow the wanderers in the wilderness, to the fact that very many Canaanites remained in the land, and to the liberal regulations respecting captives taken in war.

**Strąw.** Straw used for cattle fodder and litter, Gen. xxiv. 25; 1 Kgs. iv. 28; Isa. xi. 7; lxv. 25; in making bricks, Ex. v. 7, 16.

**Sū'ah** (*sweeping*). An Asherite, 1 Chr. vii. 36.

**Sū'bā.** His sons returned, 1 Esdr. v. 34.

**Sŭc'coth** (*tents*). (1) The place east of Jordan where Jacob built a house and booths, Gen. xxxiii. 17; Josh. xiii. 27; Judg. viii. 5-16. Between Succoth and Zarthan, in the plain of Jordan, lay the clay ground in which were cast the brazen utensils for the temple, 1 Kgs. vii. 46; 2 Chr. iv. 17. (2) First station of the Israelites after starting from Egypt, a day's journey from Rameses, Ex. xii. 37; xiii. 20; Num. xxxiii. 5, 6.

**Sŭc'coth-bē'noth** (*tents of daughters*). Some refer it to a Babylonian idol set up by colonists in Samaria, others to booths or tents in which the daughters of Babylon prostituted themselves in honor of their goddess, 2 Kgs. xvii. 30.

**Sū'chath-ītes.** A family of scribes at Jabez, 1 Chr. ii. 55.

**Sŭd.** River of Sura, probably Euphrates, Bar. i. 4.

**Sŭk'kĭ-ĭms.** An African people who supported Shishak when he invaded Judah, 2 Chr. xii. 3.

**Sŭn.** The greater light, Gen. i. 15-18. Worshipped by idolatrous Hebrews, 2 Kgs. xxi. 3, 5; xxiii. 5; and by other nations, Job xxxi. 26, 27; Gen. xli. 45; furnishes many metaphors, Ps. lxxxiv. 11; John i. 9; Rev. i. 16.

**Sûr.** A place on sea-coast of Palestine, Judith ii. 28.

**Sure'tȳ** (*security*). Suretyship in the older sense of pledge was regulated by the Mosaic law, Gen. xliv. 32; Ex. xxii. 25, 26; Deut. xxiv. 6-17. When Solomon opened Palestine to commerce, suretyship took the forms of general law and trade, Prov. vi. 1; xi. 15; xvii. 18; xx. 16; xxii. 26. [LOANS.] [PLEDGE.]

**Su'să**, Esth. xi. 3. [SHUSHAN.]

**Su'san-chītes.** Dwellers in Shushan or Susa, Ez. iv. 9.

**Su-săn'nă** (*lily*). (1) Heroine of the story of the Judgment of Daniel, as found in "The History of Susanna," one of the Apocryphal books. (2) One of the women who ministered to Christ, Luke viii. 3.

**Sū'sī** (*horseman*). Father of the Manassite spy, Num. xiii. 11.

**Swal'low** (*throat sweller*). The common swift or swallow abounds in Palestine, and its habits, according to Bible mention, are such as we observe: building under the eaves of houses, beneath temple cornices and porticos, and in the sides of cliffs, and rapidly circling above their homes in search of their aerial food, Ps. lxxxiv. 3; Prov. xxvi. 2; Isa. xxxviii. 14; Jer. viii. 7.

**Swan.** Swans rare in Palestine. Unclean, Lev. xi. 18; Deut. xiv. 16. The original seems to imply some other bird, as the ibis or water-hen.

**Swear'ing.** [OATH.]

**Sweat.** The bloody sweat of the agony is known to medical science, and ascribed to violent mental emotion, Luke xxii. 44.

**Swīne.** The hog was pronounced unclean, Lev. xi. 7; Deut. xiv. 8. Priests and Arabians abstained from the meat for dietetic reasons. Swine-keeping a degrading business, Luke xv. 15; yet swine were kept, Matt. viii. 32. To cast "pearls before swine" was to waste truth on those who despised it, Matt. vii. 6.

**Swôrd.** A short, two-edged, dagger-like weapon, carried in a sheath or scabbard, and suspended to the girdle or belt, Gen. xxvii. 40; Judg. iii. 16; 2 Sam. xx. 8; Jer. xlvii. 6; Ezek. xxi. 9, 30.

**Sȳc'a-mine**, Luke xvii. 6. [SYCAMORE.]

**Sȳc'a-mōre** (*fig-mulberry*). Not our sycamore or plane-tree, but a tree of the fig species growing in Egypt and Palestine and valued for its fruit and light, soft, durable wood, 1 Kgs. x. 27; 1 Chr. xxvii. 28; Ps. lxxviii. 47; Luke xix. 4. Sycamine in Luke xvii. 6. Sycamore fruit grows singly or in clusters and in almost direct contact with the branches. It resembles the fig in shape, and though of acrid taste when first pulled soon becomes sweetish. Egyptian mummy-cases were made of the wood of the sycamore tree.

**Sȳ'char**, John iv. 5. [SHECHEM.]

**Sȳ'chem**, Acts vii. 16. [SHECHEM.]

**Sȳ-ē'ne** (*key*). A city of Egypt bordering on Ethiopia. Situated on the Nile below the first cataract, and noted for its quarries of syenite stone, Ezek. xxix. 10; xxx. 6. Syene was an important city during the reigns of the Hyksos, or Shepherd Kings, in Egypt. It is now represented by the Arab village of Aswan.

**Sȳn'a-gōgue** (*led together*). The Jewish assembly for social and religious purposes seems to have had its origin during the captivity, or to have been an outgrowth of it, Ez. viii. 15; Neh. viii. 2; ix. 1. The casual, or house, assemblages soon ran into regular congregations, with suitable buildings and stated meetings, at requisite points. These were the synagogues, often elaborate and costly, presided over by a chief, or rabbi, assisted by a council of elders, Mark v. 22, 35; Luke iv. 20; John xvi. 2; Acts xviii. 8.

**Sȳn'tȳ-chē** (*fate*). A woman of the church at Philippi, Phil. iv. 2.

**Sȳr'a-cūse.** A noted city on eastern coast of Sicily, where Paul spent three days on his voyage to Rome, Acts xxviii. 12.

**Sȳr'i-ă.** The Hebrew Aram. So indefinitely bounded at different times as to have been associated with Assyria (whence its name) and Babylon. More definitely the country to the north of Canaan, extending from the Tigris to the Mediterranean, and northward to the Taurus ranges. Damascus was the capital, and centre of wealth, learning, and power. Joshua subdued its petty kings, Josh. xi. 2-18; David reduced it to submission, 2 Sam. viii., x. During Solomon's reign it became independent, 1 Kgs xi. 23-25. The earliest recorded settlers in Syria were Hittites and other Hamitic races. The Shemitic element entered it from the southeast under Abraham and Chedorlaomer. After Syria became independent it was a persistent enemy of the Jews 1 Kgs. xv. 18-20; xx., xxii.; 2 Kgs. vi. 8-33; vii., ix 14, 15; x. 32, 33; xiii. 3, 14-25. The attempt of the Syrian king to ally Israel with him for the overthrow of Judah led Ahaz to call in the help of Assyria, and Syria was soon merged into the great Assyrian empire. It was conquered by Alexander the Great, B. C. 333, and finally fell to the lot of Seleucus Nicator, who made it the central province of his empire, with the capital at Antioch. The Syriac language was closely allied to the Hebrew.

**Sȳr'i-ac.** The ancient language of Syria, an Aramean dialect. In Dan. ii. 4, the word "Syriac" should read "Aramaic," the court language of Babylon at the time.

**Sȳr'i-ă-mā'a-chah**, 1 Chr. xix. 6. [SYRIA and MAACHAH.]

**Sȳr'i-an.** Inhabitant of Syria, Gen. xxv. 20, and elsewhere.

**Sȳ'rō-phē-nĭ'çian.** A Phœnician at the time Phœnicia was part of the Roman province of Syria; or it may mean one of half Syrian and half Phœnician blood, Mark vii. 26.

**Syr'tis**, in Acts xxvii. 17, R. V. The dangerous quicksands or shallows on the African coast, southwest of Crete.

## T

**Tā'a-năch** (*sandy*). A Canaanite city conquered by Joshua and assigned to Levites, Josh. xii. 21; xvii. 11-18; Judg. i. 27; 1 Kgs. iv. 12. Now Taanak, 4 miles from Megiddo. Tanach, Josh. xxi. 25.

**Tā'a-năth-shī'lōh** (*pass to Shiloh*). A border mark of Ephraim, Josh. xvi. 6.

**Tăb'ba-ōth** (*rings*). Father of returned Nethinim, Ez. ii. 43; Neh. vii. 46.

**Tăb'bath** (*famous*). Where the fleeing Midianites stopped after Gideon's night attack, Judg. vii. 22.

**Tā'be-al** (*good God*). Father of a general under Pekah, or in Rezin's Syrian army, whom it was proposed to make king of Judah, Isa. vii. 6.

**Tā'be-el** (*good God*). A Persian officer in Samaria under King Artaxerxes, Ez. iv. 7.

**Tā-bĕl'li-us**, 1 Esdr. ii. 15. [TABEEL.]

**Tăb'e-rah** (*burning*). A place in the wilderness of Paran, where the Israelites encamped. It was so called because God there consumed the murmurers. The encampment remained there for a month, and the excessive eating of quail led to a pestilence, for which reason the place was called Kibroth-hattavah, or "graves of lust," Num. xi. 3, 34; Deut. ix. 22.

**Tā'bĕr-ing.** Beating upon the taber, tabret, or small drum. Word now obsolete, Nah. ii. 7.

**Tăb'ĕr-nă-cle** (*little shed or tent*). Tent of Jehovah, or movable sanctuary, which Moses was directed to erect in the wilderness, Ex. xxv. 8. Its plan, materials, and furnishings are described in Ex. xxv. 9-40; xxvi., xxvii. It could be readily taken down and set up and accompanied the Israelites during their wanderings, Ex. xl. 38. During the conquest it was stationed at Gilgal, Josh. iv. 19; ix. 6; x. 15; and at Ebal, Josh. viii. 30-35. After the conquest it was set up at Shiloh, Josh. xviii. 1, where it remained during the time of the Judges and where the ark was captured by the Philistines, 1 Sam. iv. 17, 22. Sometime after the return of the ark it was taken to Jerusalem and placed in a new tabernacle, and finally in the temple, 2 Sam. vi. 17; 1 Chr. xv. 1, but the old structure was still venerated, as long as it remained at Shiloh. It was afterwards removed to Nob, 1 Sam. xxi. 1-9, and in the reign of David to Gibeon, 1 Chr. xvi. 39; xxi. 29, where it was at the beginning of Solomon's reign. Some suppose that the tabernacle and its furniture were moved into Solomon's temple when it was completed.

**Tăb'ĕr-nă-cle of Tĕs'tĭ-mō-ny̆.** As the stone tables of the Ten Commandments were called the "tables of testimony," Ex. xxxi. 18; xxxii. 15; xxxiv. 29; and the ark which contained them was called the "ark of testimony," Ex. xxv. 22, so the tabernacle in which the ark was placed was called the "tabernacle of testimony," Ex. xxxviii. 21; Num. i. 50. Called also "the tabernacle of witness," in Num. xvii. 7, 8.

**Tăb'ĕr-nă-cleş, Feast of.** Third of the three great Hebrew feasts, celebrated from the 15th to 22d of Tisri. It commemorated the long tent life of the Israelites, and during its celebration the people dwelt in booths. Called also "feast of ingathering," Ex. xxiii. 16, because it came at end of harvest. It was closed with a holy convocation, Lev. xxiii. 36; and on Sabbatical years was similarly opened and closed, when the law was read anew, Deut. xxxi. 11–13. For law as to solemnization *see* Lev. xxiii. 34–43; Num. xxix. 12–40. Its observance is referred to in Neh. viii. 13–18; Hos. xii. 9; Zech. xiv. 16–19; John vii. 2, 37, 38.

**Tăb'ĭ-thȧ** (*gazelle*). The Christian woman of Joppa whom Peter raised from the dead, Acts ix. 36–42. [DORCAS.]

**Tā'ble** (*board*). Primitive tables were merely leather or skins spread on the floor. After the captivity they were slightly raised. Beds or couches are meant in Mark vii. 4; writing tablet of wax in Luke i. 63. The "tables" of Matt. xxi. 12; John ii. 15, were doubtless sufficiently raised to answer the purposes of a counter for money-changing purposes. The meaning of "serve tables" in Acts vi. 2, is that duty which fell to the early Christian ministry of attending to the gathering and distributing of food to the poor, or of collecting and distributing the church funds. This duty was transferred to the deacons, Acts vi. 5, 6.

**Tā'bôr** (*mound*). (1) A high mountain on north side of plain of Esdraelon; landmark between Issachar and Zebulun, Josh. xix. 22; gathering place of Barak's forces, Judg. iv. 6–14; scene of murder of Gideon's brothers, Judg. viii. 18–21. (2) Levitical town in Zebulun, 1 Chr. vi. 77. (3) "Plain of Tabor," 1 Sam. x. 3, should read "oak of Tabor."

**Tăb'ret** (*little tabor*). A small drum or tambourine, without jingles; used to accompany pipes, 1 Sam. xviii. 6. [TIMBREL.]

**Tăb'rĭ-mŏn** (*Rimmon is good*). Father of Benhadad I., King of Syria in time of Asa, 1 Kgs. xv. 18.

**Tăche** (*tack*). Taches were hooks or clasps of gold or copper for connecting the tabernacle curtains, Ex. xxvi. 6, 11.

**Tăch'mo-nīte,** 2 Sam. xxiii. 8. Hachmonite, or "son of Hachmoni."

**Tăd'môr** (*Tamar, palms*). The Palmyra of the Greeks and Romans. A city built by Solomon in Syria, toward the Euphrates, for the purpose of facilitating trade with the east. Its ruins are numerous and suggestive, 1 Kgs. ix. 18; 2 Chr. viii. 4. Tadmor, or Palmyra, reached the height of its splendor, wealth, and power under the celebrated Zenobia, "Queen of the East," who made it the capital of her empire. It fell a prey to the victorious Romans. Among its notable ruins are the Temple of the Sun. dedicated to Baal, a Street of Columns, of which 150 are still standing, and a series of magnificent tombs intended for both burial places and places of worship. The old name still exists in the form of Thadmor.

**Tā'hăn** (*camp*). An Ephraimite, Num. xxvi. 35; 1 Chr. vii. 25.

**Tā'hăn-ītes.** Descendants of Tahan, Num. xxvi. 35.

**Tȧ-hăp'a-nēş,** Jer. ii. 16. [TAHPANHES.]

**Tā'hăth** (*station*). (1) A desert station of the Israelites, Num. xxxiii. 26, 27. (2) A Levite, 1 Chr. vi. 24, 37. (3) Two Ephraimites, 1 Chr. vii. 20.

**Tăh'pan-hēş.** An ancient city of Egypt on the Tanitic mouth of the Nile. Identical with the Daphne of the Greeks. A favorite resort of exiled Jews, Jer. xliii. 7–9; xliv. 1; xlvi. 14. Jeremiah was taken thither, after the murder of Gedaliah, and the Pharaoh erected a brick palace there. The children of Noph and Tahpanhes are made to type the entire population of Egypt, Jer. ii. 16.

**Tăh'pen-ēş.** An Egyptian queen, wife of the Pharaoh who received Hadad, king of Edom, 1 Kgs. xi. 18–20.

**Tăh-rē'ȧ** (*cunning*). A descendant of Saul, 1 Chr. ix. 41. Tarea, 1 Chr. viii. 35.

**Tăh'tim-hŏd'shī.** An unknown land visited by Joab during his census tour, 2 Sam. xxiv. 6.

**Tāle** (*number*). A reckoning by number and not by weight, Ex. v. 8.

**Tăl'ent** (*weight*). A Hebrew weight and denomination for money, equal to 3,000 shekels, or 93¾ pounds of silver, and varying in value from $1,550 to $2,000, Ex. xxxviii. 25; Matt. xviii. 24. The Attic, or Greek talent, was worth about $1,200; the Roman great talent, $500; the Roman small talent, $375.

**Tăl'ĭ-thȧ cū'mī.** Two Syro-Chaldaic words spoken by Christ, and meaning "Damsel, arise," Mark v. 41.

**Tăl'māi** (*brave*). (1) A son of Anak, Num. xiii. 22; Josh. xv. 14; Judg. i. 10. (2) King of Geshur and father-in-law of David, 2 Sam. iii. 3.

**Tăl'mon** (*captive*). A temple porter, 1 Chr. ix. 17, and father of a family of returned captives, Ez. ii. 42; Neh. vii. 45; xi. 19; xii. 25.

**Tăl'mŭd** (*instruction*). The body of Jewish civil and canonical law not comprised in the Pentateuch, and commonly including the *Mishna* (traditions and decisions) and *Gemara* (expositions).

**Tā'mah** (*mirth*). Ancestor of returned Nethinim, Neh. vii. 55. Thamah, Ez. ii. 53.

**Tā'mar** (*palm-tree*). (1) Widow of Er and Onan, of Judah, and mother of Pharez and Zarah, by Judah, Gen. xxxviii. (2) Daughter of David and sister of Absalom, 2 Sam. xiii. 1–32. (3) Daughter of Absalom, wife of Uriel and mother of Maachah, queen of Abijah, 2 Sam. xiv. 27; 2 Chr. xiii. 2. (4) A frontier place in south Judah, a day's journey from Hebron, Ezek. xlvii. 19; xlviii. 28.

**Tăm'mŭz** (*sprout*). A Syrian idol corresponding to the Greek Adonis, Ezek. viii. 14.

**Tā'năch,** Josh. xxi. 25. [TAANACH.]

**Tăn'hu-mĕth** (*comfort*). Father of one of Gedaliah's captains, 2 Kgs. xxv. 23; Jer. xl. 8.

**Tā'nis,** Ezek. xxx. 14 marg. [ZOAN.]

**Tăn'nĕr** (*oaker*). Tanning not a reputable occupation among Hebrews. It was carried on outside of cities and towns. Peter stopped with Simon, a tanner of Joppa, Acts ix. 43.

**Tā'phath** (*drop*). A daughter of Solomon, 1 Kgs. iv. 11.

**Tā'phŏn,** 1 Macc. ix. 50. [BETH-TAPPUAH.]

**Tăp'pu-ah** (*apple*). (1) A descendant of Judah, 1 Chr. ii. 43. (2) A city in the plain-country of Judah, four miles N. W of Hebron, Josh. xv. 34. (3) A border place between Ephraim and Manasseh, Josh. xvi. 8; xvii. 8.

**Tā'rah** (*station*). A desert encampment of the Israelites, Num. xxxiii. 27.

**Tăr'a-lah** (*winding*). A town in Benjamin, Josh. xviii. 27.

**Tā're-ȧ,** 1 Chr. viii. 35. [TAHREA.]

**Târeş** (*tears*). The darnel is supposed to be meant. It grows somewhat like wheat till near ripening time, and chokes the growth of cereals, Matt. xiii. 25–30.

**Tär'gĕt** (*shield*). A small shield is meant, and not a target or mark in a modern sense, 1 Sam. xvii. 6. In the margin it is called "gorget," which was a defensive piece of armor, in the days of chivalry, used to protect the joint or opening between the helmet and cuirass.

**Tär'pel-ites.** Assyrian colonists in Samaria after the captivity, Ez iv. 9.

**Tär'shish. Thär'shish** (*solid, rocky*). (1) Second son of Javan, Gen. x. 4. (2) The city with which the Phœnicians traded. Associated with Tartessus in Spain, Jer. x. 9; Ezek. xxxviii. 13. (3) Another Tarshish is inferable from the statement that Solomon's ships at Ezion-geber on the Red Sea traded with Tarshish or Tharshish, 1 Kgs. ix. 26; xxii. 48; 2 Chr. ix. 21; 2 Chr. xx. 36. But many suppose that a class of ships — "ships of Tarshish," like "East India merchantmen" — is referred to rather than a port.

**Tär'sus** (*wing*). Chief city of Cilicia, Asia Minor, on river Cydnus, six miles from the Mediterranean. Birthplace of Paul and rival of Athens and Alexandria in literature and fine arts, Acts ix. 11, 30; xi. 25; xxi. 39; xxii. 3. At the mouth of the Cydnus were fine docks, and Tarsus had, at one time, considerable commercial importance. Some would identify it with Tarshish. It was founded by the Assyrian, Sardanapalus, and was captured by the Romans and made a free city. It is now represented by Tersons, a mean Turkish city with a fluctuating population.

**Tär'tăk** (*prince of darkness*). An idol introduced into Samaria by Avite colonists, and worshipped under the form of an ass, symbolizing darkness, 2 Kgs. xvii. 31.

**Tär'tan.** Not a proper name, but an army official, like general or commander-in-chief, 2 Kgs. xviii. 17; Isa. xx. 1.

**Tăt'na-ī** (*gift*). A Persian governor in Palestine, Ez. v. 3, 6; vi. 6, 13.

**Tăv'ẽrns** (*huts*). "Three Taverns" was a place on the Appian Way, 33 miles south of Rome, where Paul met some of his Roman brethren, Acts xxviii. 15.

**Tăx'es** (*touches*). First Hebrew taxes were tithes, first-fruits, redemption money, for use of the priests. Taxes amplified under the kings and became burdensome, 1 Kgs. x. 28, 29; xii. 4. Jews under heavy tribute while subject to foreign rulers, Neh. v. The tithe-tax became a poll-tax, Neh. x. 32, 33; and continued, Matt. xvii. 24. The enrollment, or census, of Luke ii. 2, and Acts v. 37, was for the purpose of Roman taxation, which was onerous, being on the head, the field-hand, the ground and the products thereof, the harbors, city-gates, and city houses.

**Tears.** In Ps. lvi. 8, allusion is supposed, by some, to be made to a custom of preserving the tears of mourners in a bottle and placing it in the sepulchre. Others regard the words as a bold metaphor, expressive of David's wish that God would keep in memory his many penitential tears, as the traveller stores his water, milk, or wine in leather bottles for a journey.

**Tē'bah** (*slaughter*). A son of Nahor, Gen. xxii. 24.

**Tĕb''a-lī'ah** (*purged*). Third son of Hosah the Merarite, 1 Chr. xxvi. 11.

**Tē'beth** (*goodness*). Tenth month of Hebrew sacred, and fourth of civil, year; commencing with new moon in January, Esth. ii. 16.

**Tĕ-hăph'ne-hes**, Ezek. xxx. 18. [TAHPANHES.]

**Tĕ-hĭn'nah** (*entreaty*). Son of Eshton and founder of Ir-nahash, city of Nahash, 1 Chr. iv. 12.

**Tēil=trēe** (*lime-tree*). Terebinth, or oak of Palestine, Isa. vi. 13.

**Tĕ-kō'ȧ, Tĕ-kō'ah** (*fort*). A town of Judah on the Hebron ridge, six miles from Bethlehem, and on the border of the wilderness, 2 Chr. xx. 20; Jer. vi. 1. Colonized by Ashur, 1 Chr. ii. 24; iv. 5; fortified by Rehoboam, 2 Chr. xi. 6. Home of the "wise woman" who interceded for Absalom, 2 Sam. xiv. 2-9. Birthplace and residence of the prophet Amos, Am. i. 1. Now Tekua.

**Tĕ-kō'īte.** Dweller in Tekoa, 2 Sam. xxiii. 26; 1 Chr. xi. 28; xxvii. 9; Neh. iii. 5, 27.

**Tĕl=ā'bĭb** (*grain-heap*). A city in Chaldea or Babylonia where captive Jews resided, Ezek. iii. 15.

**Tē'lah** (*strength*). An Ephraimite ancestor of Joshua, 1 Chr. vii. 25.

**Tĕl'a-im** (*lambs*). Place where Saul collected his forces before attacking the Amalekites, 1 Sam. xv. 4.

**Te-lăs'sar, Thē-lā'sar** (*Assyrian hill*). Place in western Mesopotamia, near Haran and Orfa, 2 Kgs. xix. 12; Isa. xxxvii. 12.

**Tē'lem** (*oppression*). (1) A city in extreme southern Judah, Josh. xv. 24. (2) A temple doorkeeper in time of Ezra, Ez. x. 24.

**Tĕl=här'sȧ, Tĕl=ha-rē'shȧ** (*uncultivated hill*). A place in Babylonia whence captive Jews returned, Ez. ii. 59; Neh. vii. 61.

**Tĕl=mē'lah** (*salt hill*). A city mentioned with the above. Identified by some with the Thelme of Ptolemy, near the Persian Gulf, Ez. ii. 59; Neh. vii. 61.

**Tē'mȧ** (*desert*). Ninth son of Ishmael, and name of his tribe and country. Referred to Teyma in Syria, on the caravan route from Damascus to Mecca, Gen. xxv. 15; 1 Chr. i. 30; Job vi. 19; Isa. xxi. 14; Jer. xxv. 23.

**Tē'man** (*desert*). Oldest son of Eliphaz, and grandson of Esau, Gen. xxxvi. 11. Also the tribe and country of Temani or Temanites, in Edom, Jer. xlix. 7; Ezek. xxv. 13; Am. i. 12; Obadiah 9; Hab. iii. 3.

**Tĕm'a-nī, Tē'man-īte**, Gen. xxxvi. 34; Job ii. 11. [TEMAN.]

**Tĕm'e-nī.** A son of Ashur, father of Tekoa, 1 Chr. iv. 6.

**Tĕm'ple.** (1) Solomon's temple erected at Jerusalem on Mount Moriah. David proposed to transform the tabernacle into a permanent temple at Jerusalem, and collected much material, but its construction was forbidden by the prophet Nathan, 1 Chr. xvii.; 2 Sam. vii. 7-29. Solomon completed the work after David's plans and with the assistance of Hiram, king of Tyre. He began to build in the fourth year of his reign, B. C. 1012, and finished and dedicated it B. C. 1005, 1 Chr. xxi., xxii., xxviii., 11-19; xxix. 4-7; 1 Kgs. vi.-viii.; 2 Chr. iii.-vii. This costly and imposing structure, for the age, was pillaged several times during the Eastern invasions, and was finally destroyed during the last siege of Jerusalem by Nebuchadnezzar, B. C. 588. (2) The temple of Zerubbabel was begun in B. C. 534, by the returned captives under the lead of Zerubbabel and the patronage of King Cyrus of Persia. Owing to discords and direct opposition it was not completed till B. C. 515. It was much inferior to the first in cost and beauty, though one third larger in dimensions. It was partially destroyed by Antiochus Epiphanes, B. C. 163, and restored by Judas Maccabeus, Ex. iii.-vi.; 2 Macc. x. 1-9. (3) Herod the Great removed the decayed temple of Zerubbabel and began the erection of a new one B. C. 17. This gorgeous and costly structure was not completed till the time of Herod Agrippa II., A. D. 64. It was of marble, after Græco-Roman designs, and was destroyed by the Romans under Titus, A. D. 70, thus verifying Mark xiii. 2.

**Tĕmpt** (*hold*). Ordinarily, the offering of an inducement to do wrong, Matt. iv. 1-11; Luke iv. 13; but in Gen. xxii. 1; James i. 2, 3, a trial of one's faith; trial of God's patience, Ex. xvii. 2; 1 Cor. x. 9; an effort to ensnare, Matt. xvi. 1; xix. 3; xxii. 18; Mark x. 2; Luke x. 25.

**Tĕnt** (*stretched*). The house of nomad and pastoral peoples. It was made of strong cloth, chiefly of goat's hair, stretched on poles, and firmly pegged to the ground, Gen. iv. 20; xviii. 1; Judg. iv. 21; Isa. xxxviii. 12.

**Tē'rah** (*laggard*). Father of Abraham. He was of Ur in Chaldea, started west with his family, stopped in Haran, and died there, aged 205 years. Through his sons, Abraham, Nahor, and Haran, he was the ancestor of the Israelites, Ishmaelites, Midianites, Moabites, and Ammonites, Gen. xi. 27-32.

**Tĕr'a-phim** (*images*). Little images kept in Eastern households for private consultation and worship. This species of idolatry or superstition was in favor with Hebrews, though often denounced, Gen. xxxi. 19, 34, 35; Judg. xviii. 17; 1 Sam. xv. 23; xix. 13, 16; 2 Kgs. xxiii. 24; Hos. iii. 4; Zech. x. 2.

**Tĕr'e-bĭnth.** [TEIL-TREE.]

**Tē'resh** (*strict*). A eunuch of Ahasuerus, whose plot to murder his master was discovered by Mordecai, Esth. ii. 21-23.

**Tĕr'tius** (*third*). Paul's scribe in writing his Epistle to the Romans, Rom. xvi. 22.

**Tĕr-tŭl'lus** (*little third*). A Roman lawyer or orator hired by the high priest and Sanhedrim to prosecute Paul before the procurator Felix, Acts xxiv. 1-9.

**Tĕs'tȧ-ment** (*witness*). One of the two volumes of the Sacred Scriptures, which treat of the old and new dispensations; distinguished as the Old Testament, treating of revelation before the Advent of Christ, and the New Testament, containing that made after the Advent, 2 Cor. iii. 6; Heb. ix. 15.

**Tĕs'ti-mō-nȳ** (*witness*). The entire revelation of God, Ps. cxix. 88, 99; the tables of stone, Ex. xxv. 16; the ark in which the tables were deposited, Ex. xxv. 22; the gospel of Christ, 1 Cor. i. 6; Rev. i. 2.

**Tĕt'rärch** (*fourth ruler*). Originally, one governing the fourth part of a country. Under Roman rule, any ruler or petty prince of the republic and empire, especially in Syria, Matt. xiv. 1; Luke iii. 1; ix. 7; Acts xiii. 1. Sometimes called king, Matt. xiv. 9; Mark vi. 14, 22.

**Thăd-dæ'us** (*wise*). Surname of the apostle Jude, and another form of Lebbæus, Matt. x. 3; Mark iii. 18. [JUDE.]

**Thā'hăsh** (*badger*). Son of Nahor, Gen. xxii. 24.

**Thā'mah**, Ez. ii. 53. [TAMAH.]

**Thā'mar**, Matt. i. 3. [TAMAR, 1.]

**Thăm'mŭz.** [TAMMUZ.]

**Thăm'na-thȧ**, 1 Macc. ix. 50. [TIMNATH.]

**Thănk Ŏf'fẽr-ing.** The peace offering of Lev. iii., as offered with thanksgiving in Lev. vii. 11-15.

**Thā'rȧ**, Luke iii. 34. [TERAH.]

**Thär'rȧ**, Esth. xii. 1. [TERESH.]

**Thär'shish** (*rocky*). (1) 1 Kgs. x. 22; xxii. 48. [TARSHISH.] (2) A Benjamite, 1 Chr. vii. 10.

**Thăs'sī.** Surname of Simon, son of Mattathias, 1 Macc. ii. 3.

**Thē'a-trē** (*sight*). A place where dramatic performances are exhibited, as in Acts xix. 29; but the spectacle or performance itself in 1 Cor. iv. 9. The introduction of the theatre by Herod the Great greatly offended the Jews.

**Thēbes** (*life of the god*). Classical name of No or No-amon, Jer. xlvi. 25; Nah. iii. 8; Ezek. xxx. 14, 16. [No.]

**Thē'bez** (*prominent*). Now Tubas, a village near Shechem, and scene of Abimelech's tragic death, Judg. ix. 50–55; 2 Sam. xi. 21.

**Thē-cō'ē**, 1 Macc. ix. 33. [Tekoa.]

**Theft, Thief.** Punishment of theft was severe under the Mosaic law, as in all pastoral countries where the property was chiefly in flocks, more or less exposed to persons of felonious intent. The thief was compelled to make restitution, five-fold for a stolen ox and four-fold for a sheep. To kill a thief, caught in the act, was not a capital offence. If restitution was impossible a thief could be sold, Ex. xxii. 1–4.

**Thē-lā'sar**, 2 Kgs. xix. 12. [Telassar.]

**Thē-lĕr'sas**, 1 Esdr. v. 36. [Telharsa.]

**Thē'man**, Bar. iii. 22. [Teman.]

**Thē-ŏd'ō-tŭs** (*God-given*). Envoy of Nicanor to Judas Maccabeus, 2 Macc. xiv. 19.

**Thē-ŏph'ĭ-lŭs** (*lover of God*). The unknown person, probably an official, to whom Luke addressed his Gospel and his history of the Acts of the Apostles, Luke i. 3; Acts i. 1.

**Thē'ras**, 1 Esdr. viii. 41. [Ahava.]

**Thĕs"sa-lō'nĭ-ans.** People of Thessalonica, to whom Paul addressed two epistles, 13th and 14th N. T. books. The first was written at Corinth, A. D. 52 or 53, soon after the author had founded a church at Thessalonica, and upon the strength of favorable reports from Timothy. Its design was to confirm the new converts in the faith, strengthen them against persecution, correct their errors of doctrine and work, and inculcate purity of life. The second was also written from Corinth, soon after the first, and designed to correct false impressions concerning Christ's advent, and especially to place the author right before the world as an authorized apostle and teacher.

**Thĕs"sa-lō-nī'cȧ.** Ancient Thermæ, "hot springs;" now Salonika. Enlarged by Cassander and called Thessalonica after his wife, daughter of Alexander the Great. An important city of Macedonia, at the head of the Gulf of Thessalonica, or Thermæ. Paul visited it during his second tour and founded a strong church there, to whose members he wrote two epistles, Acts xvii. 1–9.

**Theū'das** (*God's gift*). An insurgent Jew mentioned in Gamaliel's speech before the council, Acts v. 34–39.

**Thigh.** Placing the hand under the thigh was a form of adjuration mentioned in Gen. xxiv. 2; xlvii. 29, and supposedly prevalent in patriarchal times, but only taken by inferiors, as by servants or sons, and as significant of subjection and the purpose of obedience.

**Thĭm'na-thah**, Josh. xix. 43. [Timnah.]

**Thĭs'bē.** A city in Bœotia, Tob. i. 2.

**Thĭs'tle, Thôrn.** No less than eighteen Hebrew words embrace the thistle, thorn, brier, and bramble species, which is prolific in Palestine, Gen. iii. 18. Figurative for desolation, Prov. xxiv. 31; Isa. v. 6; Hos. ii. 6; providential visitation, Num. xxxiii. 55; Judg. ii. 3; 2 Cor. xii. 7; hindrance, Prov. xv. 19; troubles, Prov. xxii. 5. "Crown of thorns," both punishment and derision, Matt. xxvii. 29.

**Thŏm'as** (*twin*). The cautious, susceptible, even doubtful, apostle, whose name, in Greek, was Didymus, "twin," Matt. x. 3; Mark iii. 18; Luke vi. 15; John xi. 16; xiv. 5, 6; xx. 24–29; Acts i. 13.

**Thôrn.** [Thistle.]

**Thrā'çĭȧ.** Classic name for the country now embraced in the northern part of Turkey in Europe, 2 Macc. xii. 35.

**Thrā-sē'us.** Father of Apollonius, 2 Macc. iii. 5.

**Three Tăv'ērns.** [Taverns.]

**Thrĕsh'ing** (*thrashing*). Done anciently by treading with oxen or horses, or by drawn sleds, sometimes spiked, on earthen floors, usually on high spots of ground, Deut. xxv. 4; 1 Chr. xxi. 15–28; Isa. xxviii. 27, 28; xli. 15, 16. The flail or stick is mentioned in Ruth ii. 17.

**Thrōne** (*seat*). The seat of one in authority, as high priest, 1 Sam. i. 9; military chief, Jer. i. 15; but especially of a king, 2 Sam. iii. 10; 1 Kgs. ii. 12; vii. 7; x. 18–20; xxii. 10; Acts xii. 21.

**Thŭm'mim**, Ex. xxviii. 30. [Urim.]

**Thŭn'der** (*sound*). Rare in Palestine, hence regarded as God's displeasure, 1 Sam. xii. 17; Jehovah's voice, Job xxxvii. 2; Ps. xviii. 13; Isa. xxx. 30, 31; John xii. 29; symbol of divine power, Ex. xix. 16; 1 Sam. ii. 10; 2 Sam. xxii. 14; Isa. xxix. 6; Rev. viii. 5.

**Thȳ"a-tī'rȧ** (*burning incense*). A city of northern Lydia in Asia Minor, founded by Seleucus Nicator, much inhabited by Jews, seat of one of the seven churches of Asia, Acts xvi. 14; Rev. ii. 18–29.

**Thȳ'ine-wood.** Wood of the thyia, sandarac, or pine variety, yielding a choice gum and hard, dark colored, fragrant wood. Indigenous to northern Africa, Rev. xviii. 12.

**Tī-bē'rĭ-as.** (1) Sea of, John vi. 1; xxi. 1. [Gennesaret.] (2) A town of Galilee on the west shore of Lake Gennesaret or Sea of Galilee, founded by Herod Antipas, A. D. 16–22, and named in honor of the emperor Tiberius. It seems to have imparted its name to the lake or sea. Once noted for its learning and architectural beauty, but now the miserable village of Tabariyeh, John vi. 1, 23; xxi. 1.

**Tī-bē'rĭ-us.** Tiberius Claudius Nero, second emperor of Rome, A. D. 14–37. Stepson of Augustus, a vigorous warrior, eloquent orator, and able statesman, but an indolent, despotic ruler. He is the Cæsar of Luke iii. 1; xx. 22–25; xxiii. 2; John xix. 12.

**Tĭb'hath** (*killing*). Capital of Hadadezer, king of Zobah, 1 Chr. xviii. 8. Betah, 2 Sam. viii. 8.

**Tĭb'nī** (*knowing*). Competitor of Omri for the throne of Israel, 1 Kgs. xvi. 21, 22.

**Tī'dal** (*great chief*). A chief of nomadic tribes, who joined Chedorlaomer in his attack on the cities of the plain, Gen. xiv. 1–16.

**Tĭg'lath-pĭ-lē'ser** (*Adar's son my help*). Second of the Assyrian kings in contact with Israel. He invaded Samaria, 2 Kgs. xv. 29, and a few years afterwards returned, taking many captives, 1 Chr. v. 26. King Ahaz, of Judah, became his vassal, 2 Kgs. xvi. 7–10. He reigned B. C. 747–739.

**Tī'grĭs** (*arrow*). Great eastern tributary of the Euphrates, rising in the Armenian mountains and flowing southeastwardly 1146 miles. Between it and the Euphrates lay Mesopotamia. In the Septuagint version it stands for Hiddekel, one of the rivers of Eden, Gen. ii. 14; Tob. vi. 1; Judith i. 6; Ecclus xxiv. 25.

**Tĭk'vah, Tĭk'vath** (*hope*). (1) Father-in-law of Huldah the prophetess, 2 Kgs. xxii. 14; 2 Chr. xxxiv. 22. (2) Father of Jahaziah, Ez. x. 15.

**Tīle** (*cover*). A broad, thin slab of burnt clay, used as a shingle on Oriental houses, Ezek. iv. 1.

**Tĭl'găth-pĭl-nē'ser**, 1 Chr. v. 6; 2 Chr. xxviii. 20. [Tiglath-pileser.]

**Tī'lon** (*gift*). A Judahite, 1 Chr. iv. 20.

**Tī-mæ'us** (*honored*). Father of the blind Bartimæus, Mark x. 46.

**Tĭm'brel** (*bell, drum*). A Hebrew musical instrument somewhat resembling the tambourine, Ex. xv. 20; Judg. xi. 34; Ps. lxviii. 25. [Tabret.]

**Tĭm'nȧ, Tĭm'nah** (*portion*). (1) Mother of Amalek, Gen. xxxvi. 12. (2) A duke of Edom, Gen. xxxvi. 40, who gave his name to a boundary of Judah, Josh. xv. 10. (3) A mountain town of Judah, Josh. xv. 57. Thimnathah, Josh. xix. 43.

**Tĭm'năth.** (1) Gen. xxxviii. 14. [Timna, 2.] (2) Home of Samson's wife, Judg. xiv. 1–5.

**Tĭm'năth-hē'rēs**, Judg. ii. 9. [Timnath-serah].

**Tĭm'năth-sē'rah** (*fruitful portion*). A city in Ephraim given to Joshua, and his home and burial place, Josh. xix. 50; xxiv. 30. Written Timnath-heres in Judg. ii. 9.

**Tĭm'nīte.** Designation of Samson's father-in-law, the Timnathite, Judg. xv. 6.

**Tī'mon** (*honorable*). One of the first seven deacons, Acts vi. 1–6.

**Tī-mō'the-ŭs** (*honoring God*). (1) An Ammonite leader defeated by Judas Maccabeus, 1 Macc. v. 6–44. (2) Acts xvi. 1; xvii. 14, etc. [Timothy.]

**Tĭm'o-thȳ** (*honoring God*). Son of Eunice, a Jewess, by a Gentile father. Born in Derbe or Lystra, Lycaonia, Acts xvi. 1; 2 Tim. i. 5. Converted by Paul and became a close friend and valuable assistant, Rom. xvi. 21; Heb. xiii. 23. Recipient of two of Paul's epistles, 15th and 16th N. T. books. The first was written to him while at Ephesus, probably from Macedonia, and about A. D. 65. The second seems to have been written from Rome some three years later. They are called pastoral epistles, because devoted to description of church work and earnest exhortation to faithfulness.

**Tin.** A metal well known to ancients, Num. xxxi. 22; evidently dross in Isa. i. 25. Imported from Tarshish, Ezek. xxvii. 12.

**Tiph'sah** (*ford*). The Greek and Roman Thapsacus, a crossing point of the Euphrates, and eastern limit of Solomon's empire, 1 Kgs. iv. 24. Smitten by Menahem, 2 Kgs. xv. 16.

**Ti'ras** (*longing*). Youngest son of Japheth, and supposable progenitor of the Thracians, Gen. x. 2.

**Ti'rath-ites.** Designation of a family of scribes at Jabez, 1 Chr. ii. 55.

**Tire** (*attire*). A head-dress, Isa. iii. 18; Ezek. xxiv. 17, 23; but the original implies any round ornament, as a necklace, worn by persons or animals, Judg. viii. 21, 26.

**Tir'ha-kah** (*exalted*). A king of Ethiopia and Upper Egypt who became King Hezekiah's ally against Sennacherib, about B. C. 695, 2 Kgs. xix.; Isa. xxxvii. 9.

**Tir'ha-nah** (*favor*). A son of Caleb, son of Hezron, 1 Chr. ii. 48.

**Tir'i-à** (*dread*). A Judahite, 1 Chr. iv. 16.

**Tir'sha-thà** (*governor*). Title of the governors of Judea under Persian rule, Ez. ii. 63; Neh. vii. 65, 70; viii. 9; Neh. x. 1.

**Tir'zah** (*pleasing*). (1) Youngest of the five daughters of Zelophehad, Num. xxvi. 33. (2) An ancient Canaanite city captured by Joshua, and which afterwards became the capital of the kingdom of Samaria, till Samaria, the new capital, was founded by King Omri. It was some 30 miles north of Jerusalem, and 5 miles east of Samaria, Josh. xii. 24; 1 Kgs. xiv. 17; xv. 21, 33; xvi. 6; 2 Kgs. xv. 14, 16; S. of Sol. vi. 4.

**Tish'bite.** Elijah is so designated, 1 Kgs. xvii. 1; xxi. 17, 28; 2 Kgs. i. 3, 8; ix. 36. The place is generally referred to Thisbe in Naphtali, where Tobit lived, Tob. i. 2.

**Tis'ri.** Seventh month of the Jewish sacred, and first of the civil, year, corresponding to parts of September and October. Called also Ethanim, 1 Kgs. viii. 2; 2 Chr. v. 3.

**Tithe** (*tenth*). One tenth of all produce of lands and herds was set apart, under the Levitical law, for the support of the Levites, and a tenth of their tenth went to the priests. There were tithe regulations among other nations, Gen. xiv. 20; xxviii. 22; Lev. xxvii. 30-33; Num. xviii. 21-32; Deut. xii. 17, 18; xiv. 22-27. The Pharisees tithed their mint, anise, cummin, and rue, Matt. xxiii. 23.

**Tit'tle** (*title*). Jot; iota; any minute quantity, Matt. v. 18; Luke xvi. 17.

**Ti'tus** (*pleasant*). A distinguished Grecian who became a Christian convert and a companion of Paul in his trials and on his missionary tours, Tit. i. 4; Gal. ii. 3-5; 2 Cor. viii. 6, 16, 23. Entrusted with many important commissions, 2 Cor. xii. 18; 2 Tim. iv. 10; Tit. i. 5. Paul wrote an epistle to Titus, the 17th N. T. book, about A. D. 65, designed to instruct him in his ministerial duties in Crete, which were arduous, on account of the immorality of the people.

**Ti'zite.** Designation of Joha, one of David's guardsmen. Place unknown, 1 Chr. xi. 45.

**Tō'ah** (*bent*). A Levite ancestor of Samuel, 1 Chr. vi. 34. Tohu, 1 Sam. i. 1.

**Tŏb** (*good*). A place or district beyond Jordan and between Gilead and the desert, to which Jephthah fled when banished from Gilead, Judg. xi. 3-5. Ish-tob, 2 Sam. x. 6, 8.

**Tŏb=ad''o-ni'jah** (*my good God*). A Levite sent out by King Jehoshaphat to teach the law, 2 Chr. xvii. 8.

**Tō-bi'ah** (*God's goodness*). (1) His children returned with Zerubbabel, Ez. ii. 60; Neh. vii. 62. (2) An Ammonite servant of Sanballat who joined his master in opposing Nehemiah, Neh. ii. 10-20.

**Tō-bi'as.** Greek form of Tobiah and Tobijah. (1) Son of Tobit, and hero in his book, Tob. (2) Father of Hyrcanus, and a man of great prominence at Jerusalem, B. C. 187.

**Tō'bie,** 1 Macc. v. 13. [TOB.]

**Tō-bi'jah** (*God's goodness*). (1) A Levite sent out by King Jehoshaphat to teach the law, 2 Chr. xvii. 8. (2) One of the captivity in whose presence Joshua was crowned high priest, Zech. vi. 10-14.

**Tō'bit** (*goodness*). Father of Tobias, and author of Tobit, the fifth Apocryphal book. It was written in Greek, with the scene in Assyria, and is a didactic narrative of Jewish social life after the captivity.

**Tō'chen** (*task*). An unidentified place in Simeon, 1 Chr. iv. 32.

**Tō-gär'mah** (*bony*). Son of Gomer, of the family of Japheth, Gen. x. 3. His descendants became horse and mule merchants, and have been associated with the ancient Armenians, Ezek. xxvii. 14.

**Tō'hu,** 1 Sam. i. 1. [TOAH.]

**Tō'i** (*wandering*). A king of Hamath, who sent his son to congratulate David on his victory over Hadadezer, 2 Sam. viii. 9, 10. Tou, 1 Chr. xviii. 9, 10.

**Tō'là** (*worm*). (1) First-born of Issachar, and progenitor of the Tolaites, Gen. xlvi. 13; Num. xxvi. 23; 1 Chr. vii. 1, 2. (2) Successor of Abimelech as judge of Israel for twenty-three years, Judg. x. 1, 2.

**Tō'lăd** (*generation*). A city in South Judah, called also El-tolad, 1 Chr. iv. 29.

**Tō'là-ites.** Descendants of Tola, Num. xxvi. 23.

**Tŏl'ba-nēs,** 1 Esdr. ix. 25. [TELEM.]

**Toll** (*tell*). The Persian taxation of conquered Judea consisted of "tribute" levied on each province and collected by the authorities thereof; "custom," which could be paid in kind; "toll," which was a cash exaction for the use of bridges, fords, and highways, Ez. iv. 13; vii. 24.

**Tomb.** Burial places among Hebrews were caves, recesses in rocks, natural or artificial, and walled sepulchres. [SEPULCHRE.]

**Tongues.** "And the whole earth was of one language, and of one speech," Gen. xi. 1. Confusion of tongues and dispersion of peoples coincident, Gen. xi. 7-9. "New tongues," Mark xvi. 17, is the first notice of a gift specially characteristic of the first outpouring of the Spirit. Ten days afterward the promise was fulfilled in the Pentecostal phenomenon, Acts ii. 1-13.

**Tooth.** The Jewish law of retaliation permitted the deprivation of "eye for eye, tooth for tooth," Ex. xxi. 24. The principle of this law was condemned by Christ, Matt. v. 38-42. Teeth used figuratively for the inheritable quality of sin, Ezek. xviii. 2; "cleanness of teeth" a figure for famine, Am. iv. 6; "gnashing of teeth" indicative of rage and despair, Matt. viii. 12.

**Tō'păz.** A variously hued gem, corresponding to the modern chrysolite, which the Hebrews obtained from Ethiopia, Job xxviii. 19, and which constituted the second stone in first row of the high priest's breastplate, Ex. xxviii. 17, and a foundation stone of the New Jerusalem, Rev. xxi. 20.

**Tō'phel** (*mortar*). A place east of the Dead Sea near Bozrah, Deut. i. 1.

**Tō'phet, Tō'pheth** (*drum, noise, place of burning*). Part of the valley of Hinnom east or south of Jerusalem. Perhaps once a pleasure garden, but afterward polluted by the abominations incident to the worship of Baal and Molech, 2 Kgs. xxiii. 10; Jer. vii. 31; xix. 13, and then turned into a dumping and burning place of the city's refuse. Hence a place of judgment, Jer. xix. 6-14. [HINNOM.]

**Tôr'mah,** Judg. ix. 31 marg. [ARUMAH.]

**Tôr'toise** (*twisted-foot*). A faulty rendering. The Septuagint has "land-crocodile," and doubtless one of the large lizard species is meant, Lev. xi. 29.

**Tō'u,** 1 Chr. xviii. i. 10. [TOI.]

**Tōw.** The coarser part of flax, Judg. xvi. 9.

**Tow'er** (*shot up*). Watch-towers, or fortified posts, were frequent on frontiers and exposed places, Gen. xxxv. 21; 2 Chr. xxvi. 10; around vineyards, Isa. xxi. 5, 8, 11; Matt. xxi. 33, and for the use of shepherds, Mic. iv. 8. "Tower of Shechem," Judg. ix. 47, evidently a citadel or stronghold. Tower of Babel [BABEL]. "Tower of Siloam," possibly an observatory, Luke xiii. 4.

**Town Clĕrk.** An official in Ephesus, who recorded the laws and decisions and read them in public, Acts xix. 35-41.

**Trăch''o-ni'tis** (*stony*). One of the Roman provinces into which the country north of the Jordan was divided, and generally associated with Argob, south of Damascus, Luke iii. 1.

**Trănce** (*going over*). The word in Num. xxiv. 4, 16, is an interjection, without a Hebrew equivalent. In Acts x. 10, xi. 5, xxii. 17, an ecstasy is implied, which carried the subject beyond the usual limits of consciousness and volition.

**Trăns-fig''ū-rā'tion** (*formed over*). The supernatural change in the appearance of Christ upon the mount — Hermon or Tabor. It served as an attestation of his Messiahship and an emblem of glorified humanity, Matt. xvii. 1-13; Mark ix. 2-13; Luke ix. 28-36.

**Trĕaş'ûre Cĭ'tiēş.** The kings of Judah, and of other nations, kept their treasures in designated cities, called treasure-cities, and in special buildings called treasure-houses, Ex. i. 11; 1 Chr. xxvii. 25; Ez. v. 17.

**Trĕas'ûr-ȳ** (*place*). The place in the temple where gifts were received, 1 Chr. ix. 26; Mark xii. 41; Luke xxi. 1; John viii. 20.

**Trĕnch** (*cut*). In military usage, a ditch for protection, but in 1 Sam. xxvi. 5, the place where the wagons were grouped or packed.

**Trĕs'păss** (*passing over*). To violate the personal or property rights of another, Lev. v. 6. To violate a positive law of God, Matt. vi. 15.

**Trĕs'păss Ŏf'fĕr-ing.** This offering was closely allied to the sin offering, and in some cases offered with it as a distinct part of the same sacrifice, Lev. v. 15; xiv. 13-32.

**Trībe** (*division*). In a Roman sense, the third part of the empire, but with Hebrews any division of the people, especially that division which sprung from the twelve sons of Jacob, and was perpetuated in their descendants, Gen. xlviii. 5; Num. xxvi. 5-51; Josh. xiii. 7-33; xv.-xix. Of these tribes two, Ephraim and Manasseh, sprang from Joseph. Still there were only twelve partitions of conquered Canaan, for the tribe of Levi received no allotment of lands, but was diffused in cities among the other tribes and supported by them. Each tribe was headed by a prince, and each possessed considerable independence even under the monarchy. They waged war separately and among themselves, Judg. i. 2-4; 1 Chr. v. 18-22; 2 Sam. ii. 4-9; and finally ten of the tribes revolted and set up the separate kingdom of Israel, xix. 41-43; 1 Kgs. xii. For history of each tribe *see* its title.

**Trĭb'ūte** (*gift*). A payment made as a token of submission, or for sake of peace, or in pursuance of treaty, Gen. xlix. 15. The head-tax of half a shekel paid annually by Jews for the support of the temple service, Ex. xxx. 13.

**Trĭp'ō-lis** (*three cities*). The commercially linked cities of Aradus, Sidon, and Tyre, in Phœnicia, 2 Macc. xiv. 1.

**Trō'ăs** (*Troad*). Alexandria Troas, or in the Troad, was an important city in Mysia, Asia Minor, 6 miles south of the entrance to the Hellespont and 4 from the site of Ancient Troy. It was founded by Alexander the Great and was for many centuries the key of commerce between Europe and Asia. Paul visited it more than once, Acts xvi. 8-11; xx. 5-10; 2 Tim. iv. 13.

**Trō-ġȳl'lĭ-um** (*fruit-port*). Town and promontory on the western coast of Asia Minor, opposite Samos. Paul visited it on his third missionary tour, Acts xx. 15.

**Troop, Band.** These words imply small bodies of marauders in Gen. xlix. 19; 2 Sam. xxii. 30; Jer. xviii. 22; Mic. v. 1.

**Trŏph'ĭ-mŭs** (*fostered*). A Christian convert residing at Ephesus, and co-worker with Paul, Acts xx. 4; xxi. 29; 2 Tim. iv. 20.

**Trōw** (*trust*). Signifies to think or believe in, Luke xvii. 9.

**Trŭm'pet** (*pipe*). A wind instrument with a flaring mouth, made of horn or metal and differing but little in form and use from the cornet, Ex. xix. 16. [Cornet.]

**Trŭm'pets, Feast of.** The feast of the new moon which fell on the first of Tisri, Num. xxix. 1-6; Lev. xxiii. 24, 25. It was the New Year's day of the Jewish civil year, and was ushered in by the blowing of trumpets and observed by offerings.

**Trȳ-phē'nă** (*shining*). A Christian woman of Rome, saluted by Paul, Rom. xvi. 12.

**Trȳ'phŏn** (*effeminate*). Surname of Diodotus, who usurped the Syrian throne, 1 Macc. xii. 39.

**Trȳ-phō'să** (*shining*). A Christian woman of Rome, saluted by Paul, Rom. xvi. 12.

**Tụ'bal** (*tumult*). Fifth son of Japheth, Gen. x. 2; 1 Chr. i. 5. His descendants supposably inhabited the country between the Caspian and Euxine seas, Isa. lxvi. 19; Ezek. xxvii. 13, xxxii. 26.

**Tụ'bal=cāin.** Son of Lamech the Cainite, by Zillah. He was instructor of artificers in brass and iron, Gen. iv. 22.

**Tụ''bị-ē'nī.** Inhabitants of Tubion, the O. T. Tob, 2 Macc. xii. 17.

**Tûr'pĕn-tīne=trēe.** The terebinth, or teil-tree, Ecclus. xxiv. 16.

**Tûr'tle, Tûr'tle-dọve** (*cooer*). The turtle embraces several species of plaintive-noted doves, Gen. xv. 9; Ps. lxxiv. 19; Isa. lix. 11. Those who could not afford the costlier sacrifices could offer two doves or pigeons, Lev. xii. 6-8; Luke ii. 24. They were migratory, S. of Sol. ii. 12; Jer. viii. 7.

**Tȳch'ĭ-cŭs** (*fate*). A disciple of Paul, Acts xx. 4, and his messenger and spokesman, Eph. vi. 21, 22; Col. iv. 7, 8.

**Tȳ-răn'nus** (*tyrant*). A Greek rhetorician at Ephesus in whose school Paul taught for two years, Acts xix. 9.

**Tȳre** (*rock*). The celebrated commercial city of Phœnicia on the Mediterranean coast. It fell to the lot of Asher, but was never conquered, Josh. xix. 29. In intimate commercial relation with Hebrews, and King Hiram furnished the artificers and material for the temple and royal houses at Jerusalem, 2 Sam. v. 11; 1 Kgs. v. 1; vii. 13; ix. 11-14; 1 Chr. xiv. 1; 2 Chr. ii. 2-18. The city was denounced by the prophets, Isa. xxiii. 1-17; Jer. xxvii. 3; Ezek. xxvi. 3-21. It resisted the five-year siege of Shalmaneser and the thirteen-year siege of Nebuchadnezzar, but fell before that of Alexander. Referred to in N.T., Matt. xi. 21, 22; xv. 21; Mark vii. 24. Paul visited it, Acts xxi. 3, 4.

**Tȳ'rus.** Name for Tyre in O. T. prophecies and in Apocrypha.

## U

**Ū'cal** (*power*). The prophecy of Agur is addressed to Ithiel and Ucal, Prov. xxx. 1. Some regard the names as symbolical, while others treat them as real.

**Ū'el** (*God's will*). One of the sons of Bani, Ez. x. 34. Juel in 1 Esdr. ix. 34.

**Ŭk'năz.** The name is made to stand for Kenaz in margin of 1 Chr. iv. 15.

**Ū'lạ-ī** (*pure water*). A river in the province of Elam, where the palace of Shushan stood, on whose banks Daniel saw the vision of the ram and the he-goat, Dan. viii. 2-16.

**Ū'lam** (*porch*). (1) A descendant of Manasseh, 1 Chr. vii. 16, 17. (2) Son of Eshek, a Benjamite, of the line of Saul, 1 Chr. viii. 39, 40.

**Ŭl'lă** (*yoke*). Head of an Asherite family, 1 Chr. vii. 39.

**Ŭm'mah** (*community*). A city in Asher, associated with modern Alma, five miles from the Mediterranean coast, Josh. xix. 30.

**Ŭn''çĭr-cŭm-çĭ'şion** (*not cut around*). In a Scriptural sense, Gentiles, Rom. ii. 25-29.

**Ŭn-clēan'.** A word which, with clean, was applied to personal and ceremonial conditions, as well as to the edibility of animals. The division of animals into clean and unclean existed before the Flood, Gen. vii. 2. Uncleanness and the processes of purification are particularly described in Lev. xi.-xv.; Num. xix. Unclean animals are specially mentioned in Lev. xi. 9-31; Deut. xiv. 3-20.

**Ŭn''dĕr-gird'ing.** A primitive way of keeping the hull of a ship from opening by passing a cable tightly around it. The ship in which Paul sailed from Crete to Italy was undergirded, Acts xxvii. 17.

**Ŭn''dĕr-sĕt'tĕrş.** The molten projections which ornamented and supported the brazen laver in Solomon's temple, 1 Kgs. vii. 30.

**Ū'nị-côrn** (*one-horned*). A fabulous animal pictured as having one horn on its forehead and the body of a horse. The Hebrew word *re'em*, which is translated "unicorn," Num. xxiii. 22; xxiv. 8; Deut. xxxiii. 17; Job xxxix. 9; Ps. xxii. 21; xxix. 6; Isa. xxxiv. 7, does not refer to the one-horned creature of fable, but evidently to a two-horned animal, Deut. xxxiii. 17, possibly the now nearly extinct wild ox, auroch or urus of naturalists.

**Ŭn'nī** (*afflicted*). (1) A Levite appointed to play upon the psaltery, in the time of David, 1 Chr. xv. 18, 20. (2) Another Levite, who acted as watchman after the return from captivity, Neh. xii. 9.

**U-phär'sin,** Dan. v. 25-28. [Mene.]

**Ū'phăz.** Only in Jer. x. 9; Dan. x. 5, where it has been generally treated as an error for Ophir.

**Ŭr** (*light, region*). (1) Place where Abraham lived with his father Terah and his wife Sarah, before they started for the land of Canaan, Gen. xi. 28, 31. Mentioned in Gen. xv. 7, as of the Chaldees, and Acts vii. 2, as in Mesopotamia. (2) Father of Eliphal, one of David's guard, 1 Chr. xi. 35. Called Ahasbai in 2 Sam. xxiii. 34.

**Ŭr'bane** (*of a city, polite*). Greek form of the Latin Urbanus, a Christian disciple of Paul at Rome whom he salutes in Rom. xvi. 9. Urbanus in R. V.

**Ū'rī** (*fire*). (1) Father of Bezaleel, one of the architects of the tabernacle, Ex. xxxi. 2; xxxv. 30; xxxviii. 22; 1 Chr. ii. 20; 2 Chr. i. 5. (2) Father of Geber, Solomon's commissary officer in the land of Gilead, 1 Kgs. iv. 19. (3) A gate-keeper of the temple in the time of Ezra, Ez. x. 24.

**U-rī'ah** (*light*). (1) A Hittite, 2 Sam. xi. 3, and commander of one of the thirty divisions of David's army, 2 Sam. xxiii. 39; 1 Chr. xi. 41. He was husband of the beautiful Bathsheba whom David coveted, and with whom he had committed the crime of adultery, 2 Sam. xi. 4, 5. In order to conceal his crime and procure her for a wife, he ordered Joab, commander-in-chief, to place Uriah and his forces in the hottest part of the battle with Ammon, and then to desert him, leaving him to be overwhelmed and slain by superior numbers, 2 Sam. xi. 15-17. (2) A high priest in the reign of Ahaz, Isa. viii. 2, and probably the same as Urijah in 2 Kgs. xvi. 10-16. (3) A priest of the family of Hakkoz, in time of Ezra, and head of the seventh priestly course, Ez. viii. 33; written Urijah in Neh. iii. 4, 21.

**U-rī'as.** (1) Matt. i. 6. [Uriah, 1.] (2) 1 Esdr. ix. 43. [Urijah, 3.]

**Ū'rī-el** (*fire of God*). (1) One of the angels, 2 Esdr. iv. 1, 36. (2) A chief of the Kohathite Levites in the time of David, 1 Chr. xv. 5, 11. (3) A Kohathite Levite, son of Tahath, 1 Chr. vi. 24. (4) Father of Michaiah, or Maacha, wife of Rehoboam and mother of Abijah, 2 Chr. xiii. 2.

**U-rī'jah** (*light of God*). (1) A priest in the reign of Ahaz, and probably the same as Uriah (2), 2 Kgs. xvi. 10-16. (2) A priest of the family of Hakkoz or Koz, and probably same as Uriah (3), Neh. iii. 4, 21; viii. 4. (4) A prophet of Kirjath-jearim, and son of Shemaiah, who prophesied in the days of King Jehoiakim against Jerusalem and Judah according to the words of Jeremiah, and whom Jehoiakim sought to put to death. He fled to Egypt, but was pursued, caught, brought back and slain, Jer. xxvi. 20-23.

**Ū'rim and Thŭm'mim** (*light and perfection*). From the way these mysterious words are spoken of in Ex. xxviii. 30, and in Lev. viii. 8, compared with Ex. xxviii. 15-21, they appear to denote some material things, separate from the high priest's breastplate and its gems, and previously well known. Their purpose seems to be indicated in Num. xxvii. 21; 1 Sam. xxviii. 6, and, since they were connected with the ephod, in 1 Sam. xxii. 14, 15; xxiii. 9-12; xxx. 7, 8, it may be inferred they were consulted to ascertain the will of Jehovah, and that they were preserved in the bag of the high priest's breastplate to be borne "upon his heart before the Lord continually," Ex. xxviii. 30. Not in use after the captivity, Ez. ii. 63; Neh. vii. 65; Hos. iii. 4.

**Ū'su-ry̆** (*use*). Exorbitant or unlawful interest for money loaned; but in a Bible sense the taking of any interest at all. The law of Moses prohibited Hebrews from exacting interest of one another on loans, though not of foreigners, Lev. xxv. 36, 37; Deut. xxiii. 19, 20. Usury is severely denounced, Neh. v. 7, 10; Ps. xv. 5; Prov. xxviii. 8; Ezek. xxii. 12.

**Ū'tȧ**, 1 Esdr. v. 30. [Akkub.]

**Ū'tha-ī** (*helpful*). (1) The son of Ammihud, of Judah, 1 Chr. ix. 4. Athaiah in Neh. xi. 4. (2) Son of Bigvai, who returned from captivity, Ez. viii. 14.

**Ū'thī**, 1 Esdr. viii. 40. [Uthai, 2.]

**Ŭz** (*fertile*). (1) The land of Uz was Job's country, Job i. 1. It was located east or southeast of Palestine, Job i. 3; adjacent to the Sabeans or Chaldeans, Job i. 15, and to the Edomites, who once occupied it as conquerors, Lam. iv. 21. It is grouped with Egypt, Philistia, and Moab, Jer. xxv. 19-21. (2) The first son of Aram, son of Shem, Gen. x. 23; 1 Chr. i. 17. (3) Son of Nahor by Milcah, Gen. xxii. 21. Huz in A. V. and probably correct name for Uz. (4) Son of Dishan and grandson of Seir, Gen. xxxvi. 28.

**Ū'za-ī** (*strong*). Father of Palal, who assisted in rebuilding the walls of Jerusalem, Neh. iii. 25.

**Ū'zal** (*wanderer*). Sixth son of Joktan, Gen. x. 27; 1 Chr. i. 21. His descendants occupied the district of Yemen in Arabia and built the city of Uzal, since changed to Sana, and still the capital.

**Ŭz'zȧ** (*strength*). (1) The garden attached to the house of Manasseh, king of Judah. It evidently contained the family sepulchre, 2 Kgs. xxi. 18, 26. (2) A Benjamite descendant of Ehud, 1 Chr. viii. 7. (3) One of the drivers of the cart which bore the ark from Kirjath-jearim to Jerusalem, and who was slain by the Lord for putting his hand to the cart when the oxen stumbled, 1 Chr. xiii. 7-11. Uzzah elsewhere. (4) A Merarite Levite, 1 Chr. vi. 29.

**Ŭz'zah** (*strength*). 2 Sam. vi. 3-8. [Uzza, 3.]

**Ŭz'zen-shē'rah** (*ear of Sherah*). A town built by Sherah, a daughter of Ephraim, 1 Chr. vii. 24.

**Ŭz'zī** (*mighty*). (1) A son of Bukki and father of Zerahiah, in the line of high priests, but never a high priest, 1 Chr. vi. 5, 6; Ez. vii. 4. (2) A son of Tola and grandson of Issachar, 1 Chr. vii. 2, 3. (3) A son of Bela, of the tribe of Benjamin, 1 Chr. vii. 7. (4) A Benjamite progenitor of several families settled in Jerusalem after the captivity, 1 Chr. ix. 8, 9. (5) A Levite, son of Bani, and overseer of the Levites at Jerusalem after the captivity, Neh. xi. 22. (6) A priest, and chief of the house of Jedaiah, in the time of the high priest Joiakim, Neh. xii. 19. (7) A priest who assisted Ezra at the dedication of the walls of Jerusalem, Neh. xii. 42.

**Ŭz-zī'ȧ** (*God's strength*). Designated as the Ashterathite, one of David's guard, 1 Chr. xi. 44.

**Ŭz-zī'ah** (*God's strength*). (1) Son and successor of Amaziah on the throne of Judah, B. C. 810-758, 2 Chr. xxvi. 1-3. He is called Azariah in 2 Kgs. xiv. 21 and elsewhere. He was a godly king, an excellent general, and renowned city builder. But for daring to enter the temple and burn incense in violation of the law, Num. xvi. 40, xviii. 7, he was stricken with leprosy and forced to live in a separate house till he died, 2 Kgs. xv. 1-7; 2 Chr. xxvi. (2) A Kohathite Levite, son of Uriel and ancestor of Samuel, 1 Chr. vi. 24. (3) Father of Jehonathan, superintendent of David's storehouses in fields, cities, villages and castles, 1 Chr. xxvii. 25. (4) A priest of the sons of Harim, Ez. x. 21. (5) A Judahite, Neh. xi. 4.

**Ŭz'zī-el** (*God's might*). (1) Fourth son of Kohath, son of Levi, Ex. vi. 18, 22; ancestor of the Uzzielites, Lev. x. 4; and also, through Elizaphan, of the Kohathites, Num. iii. 19, 27, 30; 1 Chr. xv. 10. (2) A captain of the sons of Simeon, 1 Chr. iv. 42, 43. (3) A son of Bela and grandson of Benjamin, 1 Chr. vii. 7. (4) A son of Heman and one of the temple musicians in time of David, 1 Chr. xxv. 4. Azareel in 1 Chr. xxv. 18. (5) A descendant of Heman, 2 Chr. xxix. 14-19. (6) An assistant wall-builder, Neh. iii. 8.

**Ŭz'zī-el-ītes''.** Descendants of Uzziel (1), Num. iii. 27; 1 Chr. xxvi. 23.

## V

**Văg'a-bŏnd** (*wanderer*). In the Bible vagabond has the original meaning of fugitive or wanderer, Gen. iv. 12; Ps. cix. 10; Acts xix. 13.

**Vā-jĕz'a-thȧ** (*strong as the wind*). One of the ten sons of Haman, Esth. ix. 9.

**Vāle, Văl'ley.** Five Hebrew words are rendered vale or valley in the Bible, only one of which seems to imply that broad sweep of land between mountains or hills generally understood by valley. The others imply (1) a narrow ravine, gorge, or glen, Deut. xxxiv. 3, 6; (2) a wady, dry in summer but a torrent in rainy weather; (3) a plain, Josh. xi. 8, 17; xiii. 17; 2 Chr. xxxv. 22; Zech. xii. 11; (4) a stretch of sloping ground, Deut. i. 7; Josh. x. 40; 1 Kgs. x. 27, 2 Chr. i. 15; Jer. xxxiii. 13.

**Vā-nī'ah** (*praise of God*). A son of Bani, who had married a foreign wife, Ez. x. 36.

**Văsh'nī** (*second*). Name of Samuel's oldest son, 1 Chr. vi. 28. In 1 Sam. viii. 2, Joel appears as his firstborn son.

**Văsh'tī** (*beautiful*). Wife of King Ahasuerus and queen of Persia, Esth. i. 9-22.

**Văt.** A large vessel for holding liquids. "Fat" in Joel ii. 24; iii. 13. [Wine-fat.]

**Veil** (*carry*). The veil of Gen. xxiv. 65; xxxviii. 14; Ruth iii. 15; S. of Sol. v. 7; Isa. iii. 23, was a shawl or mantle. The veil proper was worn by Hebrew women only on special occasions, as in marriage, Gen. xxiv. 65; for ornament, S. of Sol. iv. 1, 3; for concealment as in harlotry, Gen. xxxviii. 14.

**Vĕr-mĭl'ion** (*little worm*). A bright red color much affected by Hebrews in the painting of beams, ceilings, and conspicuous objects, Jer. xxii. 14; Ezek. xxiii. 14.

**Vĕtch'es.** A plant of the bean family. [Fitches.]

**Vī'al** (*shallow cup*). In a general sense any bottle or vessel, 1 Sam. x. 1.

**Vĭl'lage.** In addition to the ordinary meaning,

the unwalled suburbs of a walled town, Lev. xxv. 31.

**Vine** (*wine*). A favorite Oriental plant of many varieties and cultivated from the earliest times, Gen. ix. 20; Num. xiii. 23. Subject of frequent metaphor, Deut. xxxii. 32; emblem of felicity and contentment, 1 Kgs. iv. 25; Ps. cxxviii. 3; Mic. iv. 4; rebellious Israel compared to "wild grapes," Isa. v. 2, "strange vine," Jer. ii. 21, "empty vine," Hos. x. 1; symbol of spiritual union, John xv. 1-5.

**Vĭn'e-gär** (*sharp wine*). A thin wine, Num. vi. 3; Ruth ii. 14; acid, Prov. x. 26; unpalatable, Ps. lxix. 21. The thin sour wine of the Roman soldiers was the beverage in Matt. xxvii. 48; Mark xv. 36; John xix. 29, 30.

**Vĭne'yärd.** Vineyards were generally on hills, Isa. v. 1; Jer. xxxi. 5; Am. ix. 13; surrounded by walls or hedges to keep out boars, Ps. lxxx. 13; jackals and foxes, Num. xxii. 24; Neh. iv. 3; S. of Sol. ii. 15; Ezek. xiii. 4; Matt. xxi. 33. Towers were erected within the vineyard for watch-houses and dwellings for the vine-keeper, Isa. i. 8; v. 2; Matt. xxi. 33.

**Vĭnt'āge** (*taking wine away*). The vintage season a time of joy. Town people went out and lived among the vineyards in lodges and tents, Judg. ix. 27; Isa. xvi. 10; Jer. xxv. 30. Grapes were gathered in baskets, Jer. vi. 9. [WINE-PRESS.]

**Vīne of Sŏd'om,** Deut. xxxii. 32. A phrase used to describe the character of Israel.

**Vīne'yärds, Plain of.** A place east of Jordan, beyond Aroer, Judg. xi. 33. [ABEL.]

**Vī'ol** (*keep holiday, sacrifice*). A stringed instrument like the psaltery, Am. vi. 5. [PSALTERY.]

**Vī'per** (*bringing forth its young alive*). The Hebrew word implies a hissing and venomous serpent, as the common European viper or adder, the horned vipers of the *cerastes* genus, and the Indian vipers, Job xx. 16; Isa. xxx. 6; Acts xxviii. 1-6. A symbol of deceit and destruction, Matt. iii. 7; xii. 34; xxiii. 33; Luke iii. 7.

**Vĭs'ion** (*seeing*). An inspired dream, phantasy, or apparition, Num. xxiv. 4; Isa. vi.; Ezek. i. viii.-x.; Dan. vii., viii.; Acts xxvi. 13-19.

**Vŏph'sī** (*gain*). Father of Nahbi, the spy selected to represent the tribe of Naphtali, Num. xiii. 14.

**Vow** (*wish*). Vows were threefold, vows of devotion, abstinence, and destruction, and respecting them certain laws were laid down, Deut. xxiii. 21-23. The law in Lev. xxvii. regulated the vow of Corban, and that in Num. vi. 1-21 the Nazarite vow.

**Vŭl'ture** (*tearer*). A large falconoid bird, with naked head and neck, feeding mostly on carrion. The bird is pronounced unclean in Lev. xi. 14; Deut. xiv. 13; but the original implies the kite, as also in Isa. xxxiv. 15.

## W

**Wā'fer** (*waffle*). Among Hebrews a thin cake of fine flour used in offerings. The flour was wheaten and the wafers were unleavened and anointed with oil, Ex. xvi. 31; xxix. 2, 23; Lev. ii. 4; vii. 12; viii. 26; Num. vi. 15, 19.

**Wā'ġes** (*pledges*). The earliest O. T. mention of wages shows that they were paid in kind and not in money, Gen. xxix. 15, 20; xxx. 28; xxxi. 7, 8, 41. Wages paid in money are mentioned in N. T., Matt. xx. 2. The Mosaic law was very strict in requiring daily payment of wages, Lev. xix. 13; Deut. xxiv. 14, 15.

**Wăg'on** (*mover*). Wagons of the Hebrews, like those of the ancient Egyptians, were carts, consisting of planks or at most of crude box-like bodies, supported upon axles which connected two solid wooden wheels. They were mostly drawn by oxen or kine, Num. vii. 3, 8; 1 Sam. vi. 3-14.

**Walk** (*move*). Walk has figurative use in the Bible to denote the behavior and spiritual character of a person, Ezek. xi. 20; Rom. viii. 1.

**Wall of Pär-tĭ'tion.** The allusion in Eph. ii. 14 is to the "wall of partition" which separated the holy of holies from the holy place in Solomon's temple, 1 Kgs. vi. 31, 35.

**Walls** (*palisades*). Solid walls limitedly used in Oriental countries for ordinary dwellings, but at times solidly laid and strongly built for palaces and temples, and as a protection to cities. They were of various materials, palisades, clay, cemented pebbles, brick, and stone. Houses were frequently erected on the walls of cities, and towers for archers and slingers, Josh. ii. 15; Ps. lxii. 3; Isa. xxx. 13; Luke vi. 48.

**Wan'dēr-ings** (*windings*). The wilderness wanderings of the Israelites began at Rameses, the place of rendezvous, west of the Red Sea. The time as fixed by modern Egyptologists was during the reign of the Pharaoh Menephthah, B. C. 1317, though another date, B. C. 1491, was for a long time received. After crossing into Arabia, the line of march was southerly to the wilderness of Sinai, where a long halt was made, the law given, the tabernacle built, and the people were numbered, Ex. xv. 23, 27; xvi.-xl.; Lev.; Num. i.-x. 12. From Sinai the route was northward to Kadesh near the southern border of Canaan, the time thus far consumed being two years, Num. xiii. 26. Here they were condemned to further wilderness wanderings for a period of thirty-eight years. This period was seemingly one devoted to nomadic existence like that of other Arabian tribes. When the time came for another move on Canaan, the route lay around the head of the Gulf of Akaba and thence eastward and northward to Moab and the Jordan crossing, Num. xxxiii. 48, 49.

**War** (*embroil*). Primitive Hebrew weapons were clubs, arrows, slings, swords, and spears. No army divisions except those indicated by the tribes. The contests of this period often hand-to-hand and brutal, 2 Sam. i. 23; ii. 18; 1 Chr. xii. 8; 2 Chr. xiii. 17. Many of the modern stratagems employed, as the double attack, Gen. xiv. 15; ambush, Josh. viii. 12; false retreat, Judg. xx. 37; night attack, 2 Kgs. vii. 12. Sometimes battles were settled by single-handed combats, 1 Sam. xvii.; 2 Sam. ii. 15, 16; 1 Chr. xi. 6. King David's army was divided into regularly disciplined and officered bands under a general-in-chief, 2 Sam. xviii. 1, 2; xxiii. 8-39; 1 Chr. xi. 25-47; xii., xxvii. He introduced the heavier weapons, such as catapults and battering-rams for siege-work and chariots for field-work, 2 Sam. viii. 4. Soldiers killed in action were plundered, 1 Sam. xxxi. 8; survivors were mutilated or killed, Judg. i. 6; ix. 45; 2 Sam. xii. 31; 2 Chr. xxv. 12; or carried into captivity, Num. xxxi. 26.

**Ward** (*watch*). A guard-room or lock-up, Gen. xl. 3; Acts xii. 10. A garrison or military post, Neh. xii. 25. A detachment of persons, guard, for any purpose, 1 Chr. ix. 23; Neh. xiii. 30.

**Ward'rōbe** (*watch-robe*). Place where the royal robes and priest's vestments were kept under watch or care, 2 Kgs. xxii. 14.

**Wāres.** [COMMERCE.]

**Wash'ing.** The custom of washing hands before meals or of feet after a journey or on entering a stranger's house was not only a polite ceremony but a religious observance, Matt. xv. 2; Mark vii. 3; Luke xi. 38. After the salutation the first act of hospitality was to proffer a basin of water to the guest for washing the feet, Gen. xviii. 4; Ex. xxx. 19, 21; Judg. xix. 21; 1 Sam. xxv. 41; Luke vii. 37, 38, 44; John xiii. 5-14.

**Watch** (*wake*). The Hebrew night was divided into three watches, instead of hours. The first was called "the beginning of watches," beginning at sunset and lasting till ten o'clock, Lam. ii. 19: the second, the "middle watch," from ten P. M. till two A. M., Judg. vii. 19; the "morning watch," from two A. M. till sunrise, Ex. xiv. 24; 1 Sam xi. 11. After the captivity the Jews gradually adopted the Greek and Roman division of the night into twelve hours of four watches; "evening," 6 to 9; "midnight," 9 to 12; "cock-crowing," 12 to 3; "morning," 3 to 6, Matt. xiv. 25; Mark xiii. 35; Luke xii. 38.

**Wa'ter of Jēal'oŭs-y.** The jealous husband brought his suspected wife before the priest, with her offering of barley meal, without oil or frankincense, in her hand. The priest took holy water in an earthen vessel in his hand and sprinkled it with the dust of the floor. Then the priest administered the oath to her. If she confessed to guilt she was compelled to drink the water, and stood accursed. If otherwise, she was allowed to go free, Num. v. 12-31.

**Wa'ter of Sĕp"a-rā'tion.** The preparation and use of the water of separation are described in Num. xix.

**Wa'ter-spouts.** The word translated "waterspouts" in Ps. xlii. 7 is rendered "gutter" in 2 Sam. v. 8.

**Wāve-ŏf'fēr-ing.** The wave-offering, together with the heave-offering, was a part of the peace-offering. The right shoulder of the victim, which was considered the choicest part, was "heaved" or held up in the sight of the Lord, and was, therefore, to be eaten only by the priests. The breast portion was "waved" before the Lord and eaten by the worshippers. On the second day of the passover feast, a sheaf of wheat and an unblemished lamb of the first year were waved, Ex. xxix. 24–27; Lev. vii. 30–34; viii. 27; ix. 21; x. 14, 15; xxiii. 10–20; Num. vi. 20; xviii. 11–18, 26–29.

**Wăx.** Wax in its original sense, an animal product as of bees, is frequently used in Scripture as a means of illustration, Ps. lxviii. 2; xcvii. 5; Mic. i. 4.

**Wēan** (*accustom*). Weaning-time a festal occasion, and probably late, Gen. xxi. 8; 2 Chr. xxxi. 16.

**Wĕap′ons.** [Arms.] [War.]

**Wēa′sel.** It is thought that "mole" would be a better translation, Lev. xi. 29.

**Wēave.** Most ancient nations knew the art of weaving. The Egyptians were skilled weavers, Gen. xli. 42. That the Hebrews brought the art along with them from bondage is clear from the fabrics manufactured in the wilderness: goat-hair covers, linen curtains, Ex. xxvi. 1–13; embroidered raiment, Ex. xxviii. 4, 39; woolen garments, Lev. xiii. 47. Though the loom is not mentioned, its various parts are, as the shuttle, beam, etc., 1 Sam. xvii. 7; 2 Kgs. xxiii. 7; 1 Chr. iv. 21; Job vii. 6; Prov. xxxi. 13, 24; Isa. xxxviii. 12.

**Wĕd′ding.** [Marriage.]

**Wĕd′ding-gär′ment.** A special garment, required to be worn at marriage-suppers, seems to have been furnished by the hôst, Matt. xxii. 11.

**Wēek.** The division of time into weeks of seven days each dates from the earliest historic times among many and wide-apart nations. The Hebrew week began on our Sunday, their Sabbath being the seventh day or Saturday. The only day of their week they named was the Sabbath. The rest ran by numbers, as first, second, third, etc. Besides their week of days, Hebrews had their week of years, every seven years, and their week of seven times seven years, or year of jubilee, every fiftieth year, Gen. viii. 10; xxix. 27. The "feast of weeks" corresponded with Pentecost, Ex. xxiii. 15; xxxiv. 22; Lev. xxiii. 15–22; Num. xxviii.

**Weights and Meas′ures.** The standard of Hebrew weights and measures was kept in the sanctuary, Lev. xix. 35, 36. A copy of said standard was kept in the household, Deut. xxv. 13–15. The destruction of the ancient standard with the tabernacle led to the adoption of the various weights and measures of such countries as the Hebrews happened to be subject to or in commercial intercourse with. Hence the subject of Hebrew weights and measures is full of perplexity and uncertainty. *See* various weights and measures under their respective headings.

**Wĕll** (*boil*). Wells were of great importance in Palestine, Gen. xxiv. 11; Num. xx. 17–19; Judg. vii. 1. They were sometimes deep, John iv. 11; frequently owned in common, Gen. xxix. 2, 3; covered at times with a stone and surrounded by a low wall to protect them from drifting sand, Gen. xxix. 2–8; to stop them up an act of hostility, Gen. xxvi. 15, 16; to invade them a cause for contention, Gen. xxi. 25; water sometimes drawn by sweeps or windlasses, but generally by a bucket attached to a rope, and in some cases steps led down to them, Gen. xxi. 25–31; Judg. i. 13–15; 1 Sam. xxix. 1; emblem of blessings, Jer. ii. 13; xvii. 13.

**Whāle.** The Hebrew original translated "great whales" in Gen. i. 21 is used of "serpents" in Ex. vii. 9; Deut. xxxii. 33, and of the "crocodile" in Ezek. xxix. 3; xxxii. 2. In Job vii. 12; Isa. xxvii. 1, the name belongs to sea monsters. It is thought that the shark of the Mediterranean is meant in Jonah i. 17; Matt. xii. 40.

**Whēat.** This well-known cereal was cultivated in the East from the earliest times, Gen. xxx. 14, and grew luxuriantly and of many varieties in Egypt, Gen. xli. 22. Syria and Palestine were both fine wheat-growing countries, Ps. lxxxi. 16; cxlvii. 14; Matt. xiii. 8. Wheat-harvest denoted a well-known season, Gen. xxx. 14.

**Whirl′wind.** Whirlwinds of great violence and frequency were well-known desert visitations and gave rise to many Scripture metaphors, Job xxxvii. 9; Isa. xvii. 13.

**Whit′ed Sĕp′ŭl-chres.** Inasmuch as contact with the burial place was a cause of ceremonial defilement, Num. xix. 16, sepulchres were whitewashed that they might be seen and avoided, Matt. xxiii. 27.

**Wĭd′ōw** (*lack*). When a married man died without children, his brother, if still living with the family, had a right under the law to marry the widow in order to preserve the family name and inheritance, Deut. xxv. 5, 6; Matt. xxii. 23–30. Other provisions of the Mosaic law show great consideration for widows, Ex. xxii. 22; Deut. xiv. 29; xvi. 11, 14; xxiv. 19–21; xxvi. 12; xxvii. 19.

**Wīfe.** [Marriage.]

**Wĭl′dēr-ness** (*place of wild beasts*). Like the word desert, wilderness does not necessarily imply an absolutely arid, sandy, and uninhabitable place, but an uncultivated waste, which it was possible for pastoral tribes to occupy, and with stretches of pasturage, Josh. xv. 61; Isa. xlii. 11. The wilderness of wandering in which the Israelites spent forty years, Deut. i. 1; Josh. v. 6; Neh. ix. 19, 21; Ps. lxxviii. 40–52; cvii. 4; Jer. ii. 2, was practically the great peninsula of Sinai lying between Seir, Edom, and Gulf of Akaba on the east, and Gulf of Suez and Egypt on the west. It embraced many minor divisions or wildernesses, as those of Sin or Zin, Paran, Shur, Etham, and Sinai. [Wanderings.]

**Wĭll.** The laws respecting realty rendered wills useless, but nuncupative disposition of personalty seems to be implied in 2 Sam. xvii. 23; 2 Kgs. xx. 1; Isa. xxxviii. 1.

**Wĭl′lōw.** Before the captivity the willow was an emblem of joy, Lev. xxiii. 40; Job xl. 22; Isa. xliv. 4; but in allusion to the captivity, the weeping willow of Babylonia became the poetical type of sorrow, Ps. cxxxvii. 2. The "brook of willows," Isa. xv. 7, was in the land of Moab, and is called "valley of Arabians" in margin.

**Wĭm′ple.** In a Bible sense, a hood or veil as in Isa. iii. 22, or a mantle or shawl as in Ruth iii. 15.

**Wĭnd** (*blow*). Hebrews recognized the cardinal winds in their "four winds," north, south, east, west, Ezek. xxxvii. 9; Dan. viii. 8; Zech. ii. 6; Matt. xxiv. 31. The east wind injured vegetation, Gen. xli. 6; Job i. 19; Isa. xxvii. 8. The south wind brought heat, Luke xii. 55. The southwest and north winds brought clear cool weather, Job xxxvii. 9, 22; Prov. xxv. 23. The west wind, coming from the Mediterranean, brought rain.

**Wĭn′dōw** (*wind-eye*). In primitive Oriental houses the windows were simply openings upon the inner or court side of houses. But on the street or public side there were frequently latticed projections both for ventilation and sitting purposes, 2 Kgs. ix. 30; Judg. v. 28; probably the casements of Prov. vii. 6; S. of Sol. ii. 9.

**Wīne** (*drink*). The Hebrews manufactured and used wine from earliest times, Gen. ix. 20, 21; xix. 32; xxvii. 25; xlix. 12; Job i. 18; Prov. xxiii. 30, 31; Isa. v. 11. A usual drink-offering at the daily sacrifices, Ex. xxix. 40; at the presentation of first fruits, Lev. xxiii. 13; and at other offerings, Num. xv. 5. It was tithable, Deut. xviii. 4. Nazarites could not drink it during their vow, Num. vi. 3, nor priests before service, Lev. x. 9.

**Wīne-făt, Wīne-prĕss.** The Hebrew winefat, vat, or press, consisted of an upper and lower receptacle, the former for treading the grapes, the latter for catching the juice, Isa. lxiii. 3; Joel iii. 13; Hag. ii. 16.

**Wĭn′nōw** (*wind*). The process of winnowing or winding grain was that of tossing the mixed chaff and kernels into the air, on a high, windy spot, with a fork or shovel, so that the wind could carry the chaff away. The floor on which the kernels fell was usually clean and solid, and when not so, a sheet was used to catch the grains, Isa. xxx. 24; xli. 16; Matt. iii. 12. Evening was the favorite winnowing time because the breezes were then steadiest, Ruth iii. 2.

**Wĭn′ter.** Winters in Palestine are short, lasting from December till February, S. of Sol. ii. 11.

**Wĭs′dom of Jē′sŭs.** [Ecclesiasticus.]

**Wĭs′dom of Sŏl′o-mon.** Fifth of the Apocryphal books, devoted to an exposition of wisdom in its moral, philosophic, and historic aspects.

**Wīse Mĕn,** Matt. ii. 1. [Magi.]

**Wĭst.** Same as "knew," Ex. xvi. 15; Acts xii. 9; xxiii. 5.

**Wĭt** (*know*). To become aware, learn, know, Gen. xxiv. 21; Ex. ii. 4.

**Wĭtch** (*wizard*). One who pretends to deal with evil spirits in order to work a spell on persons or their belongings; conjurer, fortune-teller, exorcist, supernatural curer of diseases, Deut. xviii. 10; 1 Sam. xxviii. 3–25. The word formerly embraced both sexes, but is now applied to women. Witches were not allowed to live, Ex. xxii. 18.

**Wĭtch′craft.** The occult practices of witches and wizards, 1 Sam. xv. 23. The art, the pretender, and the person deceived were alike denounced, Lev. xx. 6; Nah. iii. 4; Gal. v. 20.

**Wĭt′ness** (*see*). Under the Mosaic law at least two witnesses were required to establish a capital charge, Num. xxxv. 30; Deut. xvii. 6, 7. False swearing forbidden, Ex. xx. 16; Lev. vi. 1–7.

**Wiz'ärd** (*cunning*). A male witch, Lev. xx. 27.

**Wolf.** Wolves of Palestine were numerous and the dread of shepherds, as they were a terrible enemy to sheep, Matt. vii. 15; x. 16; John x. 12; Acts xx. 29. A wolf typed the rapacity of Benjamin, Gen. xlix. 27; and the cruelty of Israel's oppression, Ezek. xxii. 27; and the destruction of the wicked, Jer. v. 6.

**Wom'an** (*wife-man*). Hebrew women cared for the household, Gen. xviii. 6; carried water, Gen. xxiv. 15; tended flocks, Gen. xxix. 6; spun, Ex. xxxv. 26; made clothes, 1 Sam. ii. 19; acted as hostess and guest on social occasions, Job i. 4; John ii. 3; xii. 2; prophesied, composed, sang, and danced, Ex. xv. 20, 21; Judg. xi. 34; xxi. 21; fêted, 1 Sam. xviii. 6, 7; held public positions, Judg. iv., v.; 2 Kgs. xxii. 14; Neh. vi. 14; Luke ii. 36; acted as workers and officials in the early Christian church, Acts xviii. 18, 26; Rom. xvi. 1.

**Wool.** A highly prized material for clothing among Hebrews, Lev. xiii. 47; Job xxxi. 20; Prov. xxxi. 13; Ezek. xxvii. 18; xxxiv. 3. Mixed woolen and linen fabrics forbidden, Lev. xix. 19; Deut. xxii. 11.

**Word.** The *lŏgos*, or Word, in John i. 1-14; 1 John i. 1; Rev. xix. 13, stands for the Son of God, the Word incarnate.

**Worm.** Many Hebrew words are translated worm, all indicative of something loathsome, destructive, helpless, or insignificant, as the moth, Isa. li. 8; maggot, Job xix. 26; possibly the serpent, Mic. vii. 17. The allusion in Isa. lxvi. 24; Mark ix. 44-48, is thought to be to the valley near Jerusalem where the refuse of the city constantly bred worms and where fires were kept burning to consume the collections. The helplessness of the worm affords the figures in Job xxv. 6; Ps. xxii. 6; Isa. xli. 14.

**Worm'wood.** A bitter plant found in Palestine, and often mentioned in Scripture in connection with gall to denote what is offensive and nauseous, Deut. xxix. 18; Prov. v. 4; Jer. ix. 15; xxiii. 15; Lam. iii. 15, 19; Am. v. 7.

**Wor'ship-per,** Acts xix. 35. The word should be temple-keeper as in marg. and in R. V.

**Wŏt.** "Wotteth not," Gen. xxxix. 8, means "knows not."

**Wri'ting.** The first mention of writing in the Bible is in Ex. xvii. 14. The art among Hebrews was limited to persons of learning and position and to the class of scribes, Isa. xxix. 11, 12. [SCRIBE.] The oldest Semitic writings are the bricks and tablets of Nineveh and Babylon. The Hebrew alphabet was a development of the Phœnician, and it underwent many changes in the course of time. The record of Sinai was written on stone with the finger of God, Ex. xxxi. 18; xxxii. 15-19; xxxiv. 1-29. Later materials were wax, wood, metal, or plaster, Deut. xxvii. 2; Josh. viii. 32; Luke i. 63; and perhaps vellum, or fine parchment from skins, and linen were in early use for other than monumental writings, as they surely were at a later day, 2 Tim. iv. 13. Pliable substances, when written upon, were rolled on sticks, sealed and preserved as books, Ps. xl. 7; Isa. xxix. 11; Dan. xii. 4; Rev. v. 1. Hebrews doubtless knew the use of papyrus, 2 John 12. Rolls were generally written upon one side only, except in Ezek. ii. 9, 10; Rev. v. 1. Hebrew instruments of writing were the stylus and graver for hard materials, Ex. xxxii. 4; Job xix. 24; Ps. xlv. 1; Isa. viii. 1; Jer. viii. 8; xvii. 1; and for pliable materials, a reed pen, 2 Cor. iii. 3; 2 John 12; 3 John 13. Paul used an amanuensis, but authenticated his letters in a few lines with his own pen, 1 Cor. xvi. 21; Col. iv. 18; 2 Thess. iii. 17. Ancient ink was made of pulverized charcoal or burnt ivory in water to which gum had been added. It was carried in an ink-horn suspended to the girdle, Ezek. ix. 3, 4.

## Y

**Yärn.** Though the art of spinning was well known to Hebrews, Ex. xxxv. 25; Prov. xxxi. 19; Matt. vi. 28, the spun product is only mentioned in 1 Kgs. x. 28; 2 Chr. i. 16, and in both these instances the word is rather significant of "band" as applied to a troop or drove of horses than to yarn.

**Yēar.** The Hebrew year was sacred and civil, with two beginnings. The sacred year began with the month Abib, April, the civil with the month Tisri, October. The months were lunar, twelve in number, with, of course, the necessary intercalary month *ve-adar* at the proper time, about every three years. As divided by seasons, the year was solar. There were two seasons, summer and winter, Ps. lxxiv. 17; Jer. xxxvi. 22; Am. iii. 15; Zech. xiv. 8.

**Yēar of Jū'bi-lēe.** [JUBILEE.]

**Yēar, Săb-băt'ĭ-cal.** [SABBATICAL.]

**Yōke** (*join*). This well-known means of coupling oxen for agricultural purposes was primitively laid upon the necks of the cattle, and held there by thongs which passed around their necks. A thong served also as an attachment to the cart-tongue or plow-beam. A pair of oxen yoked together were called a yoke, as to-day, 1 Sam. xi. 7; 1 Kgs. xix. 21. It would seem as if asses and mules went by pairs like oxen, Judg. xix. 10; 2 Kgs. v. 17, and even horses, camels, and chariots, Isa. xxi. 7. The word, like the Latin *jugum*, gave rise to a measurement of land, 1 Sam. xiv. 14, the amount a yoke of oxen could plow in a day. Yoke is used metaphorically for subjection, 1 Kgs xii. 4, 9-11; Isa. ix. 4; Jer. v. 5. An unusually heavy bondage was typed by "iron yoke," Deut. xxviii. 48; Jer. xxviii. 13. Removal of the yoke implied deliverance, Gen. xxvii. 40; Jer. ii. 20; Matt. xi. 29, 30. Breaking of the yoke meant repudiation of authority, Nah. i. 13.

## Z

**Zā''a-nā'im** (*changing*). The plain, or rather the oak, where Heber the Kenite was encamped when Sisera sought refuge in his tent, Judg. iv. 11, 17-22. It is mentioned as near Kedesh.

**Zā'a-năn** (*flocking-place*). A place in the lowlands of Judah, Mic. i. 11.

**Zā''a-năn'nim.** A border place of Naphtali, near Kedesh, and supposed to be same as Zaanaim, Josh. xix. 33.

**Zā'a-văn** (*disturbed*). Son of Ezer and descendant of Seir the Horite, Gen. xxxvi. 27. Zavan in 1 Chr. i. 42.

**Zā'băd** (*gift*). (1) A son of Nathan, 1 Chr. ii. 36, 37, and one of David's mighty men, 1 Chr. xi. 41. (2) An Ephraimite whom the Gathites slew while on a thieving expedition, 1 Chr. vii. 21. (3) Son of Shimeath, an Ammonitess, and one of the murderers of King Joash, 2 Chr. xxiv. 25, 26. Jozachar in 2 Kgs. xii. 21. (4) Three returned captives, Ez. x. 27, 33, 43.

**Zăb''a-dā'ias,** 1 Esdr. ix. 35. [ZABAD, 4.]

**Zăb''a-dē'ans.** An Arab tribe smitten by Jonathan Maccabeus, 1 Macc. xii. 31.

**Zăb'bāi** (*limpid*). (1) One who had taken a foreign wife, Ez. x. 28. (2) Father of Baruch, one of the repairers of the walls of Jerusalem, Neh. iii. 20.

**Zăb'bud** (*given*). One who returned from captivity with Ezra, Ez. viii. 14.

**Zăb'dī** (*gift*). (1) Son of Zerah of the tribe of Judah, and ancestor of Achan, who concealed the spoils of Jericho, Josh. vii. 1, 17, 18. (2) One of the sons of Shimhi, a Benjamite, 1 Chr. viii. 19. (3) An officer who had the care of King David's wine cellars, 1 Chr. xxvii. 27. (4) Son of Asaph the minstrel, and leader of thanksgiving in prayer, Neh. xi. 17. Zaccur, Neh. xii. 35. Zichri, 1 Chr. ix. 15.

**Zăb'dĭ-el** (*gift of God*). (1) Father of Jashobeam, captain of first course for the first month of David's guard, 1 Chr. xxvii. 2. (2) Overseer of a returned troop of captives, Neh. xi. 14. (3) An Arabian chieftain who put Alexander Balas to death, 1 Macc. xi. 17.

**Zā'bud** (*given*). A friend of Solomon and his principal officer, 1 Kgs. iv. 5.

**Zăb'u-lon.** Greek form of Zebulun, Matt. iv. 13; Rev. vii. 8.

**Zăc'ca-ī** (*pure*). His descendants, 760 in number, returned with Zerubbabel, Ez. ii. 9; Neh. vii. 14.

**Zăc-chæ'us** (*just*). The rich chief among publicans, resident at Jericho, who climbed a tree to see Jesus pass, was invited down, became the host of Jesus, and was converted, Luke xix. 1-10.

**Zăc-chē'us.** An officer under Judas Maccabeus, 2 Macc. x. 19.

**Zăc'chur** (*mindful*). A Simeonite of the family of Mishma, 1 Chr. iv. 26.

**Zăc'cur** (*mindful*). (1) Father of Shammua, the spy sent out by the tribe of Reuben, Num. xiii. 4. (2) A Merarite Levite, 1 Chr. xxiv. 27. (3) A son of Asaph the minstrel, and leader of the third musical course, 1 Chr. xxv. 2, 10; Neh. xii. 35. (4) One who assisted in rebuilding the walls of Jerusalem, Neh. iii. 2. (5) One who signed the covenant with Nehemiah, Neh. x. 12. (6) Father of Hanan, whom Nehemiah made one of his treasurers, Neh. xiii. 13.

**Zăch″a-rī′ah** (*remembered by Jehovah*). In better Hebrew, Zechariah. (1) Son of Jeroboam II., and his successor on the throne of Israel, 2 Kgs. xiv. 29; B. C. 773-72. He reigned only six months, 2 Kgs. xv. 8-11. (2) Father of Abi, mother of Hezekiah king of Judah, 2 Kgs. xviii. 2. Written Zechariah in 2 Chr. xxix. 1.

**Zăch″a-rī′as** (*remembered by Jehovah*). Greek form of Zachariah. (1) The name is borne by many priests and laymen in the books of Esdras. (2) Father of John the Baptist and husband of Elizabeth. He was a priest of the course of Abia, or Abijah, 1 Chr. xxiv. 10, and probably lived at Hebron, Luke i. 5-25, 57-80. (3) Son of Barachias, who was slain between the temple and the altar, Matt. xxiii. 35; Luke xi. 51.

**Zăch′a-rȳ**. 2 Esdr. i. 40. [ZECHARIAH, THE PROPHET.]

**Zā′cher** (*testimony*). A Benjamite, one of the sons of Jehiel by Maachah, 1 Chr. viii. 29, 31.

**Zā′dŏk** (*just*). (1) Son of Ahitub, of the line of Eleazar. He was one of the high priests in the time of David, the other being Abiathar, 2 Sam. viii. 17. He joined David at Hebron, as a chieftain of his father's house, 1 Chr. xii. 28, remained faithful to him and subsequently anointed Solomon, 1 Kgs. i. 39. (2) A priest in the reign of King Ahaziah, 1 Chr. vi. 12. (3) Father of Jerusha, wife of Uzziah and mother of Jotham king of Judah, 2 Kgs. xv. 33. (4) Son of Baana, who helped Nehemiah to repair the walls of Jerusalem, Neh. iii. 4. (5) Another assistant wall-builder, Neh. iii. 29. (6) A co-covenanter with Nehemiah, Neh. x. 21. (7) A scribe and treasurer under Nehemiah, Neh. xiii. 13.

**Zā′ham** (*hateful*). A son of King Rehoboam by his wife Abihail, 2 Chr. xi. 19.

**Zā′ir** (*little*). A vague spot or place, where King Joram overcame the Edomites, 2 Kgs. viii. 21.

**Zā′laph** (*hurt*). Father of Hanun who helped to repair the walls of Jerusalem, Neh. iii. 30.

**Zăl′mŏn** (*shade*). (1) The Ahohite who was one of David's guard, 2 Sam. xxiii. 28. Ilai in 1 Chr. xi. 29. (2) A wooded eminence near Shechem, Judg. ix. 47-49.

**Zal-mō′nah** (*shady*). A desert encampment of the wandering Israelites, Num. xxxiii. 41, 42.

**Zal-mŭn′nȧ** (*shadow*). One of two kings of Midian captured and slain by Gideon, Judg. viii. 5-21; Ps. lxxxiii. 11.

**Zăm′bĭs**, 1 Esdr. ix. 34. [AMARIAH.]

**Zăm′brī**, 1 Macc. ii. 26. [ZIMRI.]

**Zā′moth**, 1 Esdr. ix. 28. [ZATTU.]

**Zăm-zŭm′mimș**. An Ammonite name for a race of Rephaim or giants, Deut. ii. 20.

**Zā-nō′ah** (*swamp*). (1) A town in the lowlands of Judah, ten miles southwest of Jerusalem, Josh. xv. 34; 1 Chr. iv. 18. Its inhabitants helped Nehemiah to repair the walls of Jerusalem, Neh. iii. 13; xi. 30. (2) Another town of Judah in the mountains, about ten miles southwest of Hebron, Josh. xv. 56.

**Zăph′nath=pā″a-nē′ah** (*revealer of secrets*). A name given by the Pharaoh to Joseph upon his promotion to a high place in the royal service, Gen. xli. 45.

**Zā′phŏn** (*north*). An unidentified place in Gad, Josh. xiii. 27.

**Zā′rȧ** (*dawn*). Zarah, a son of Judah, in genealogy of Christ, Matt. i. 3.

**Zăr′a-çēș**. A brother of Jehoiakim, King of Judah, 1 Esdr. i. 38.

**Zā′rah** (*dawn*). A son of Judah by Tamar, Gen. xxxviii. 30; xlvi. 12. Called Zerah in Num. xxvi. 20, and founder of the family of Zarhites; also Zerah in Josh. vii. 1, 18; xxii. 20; 1 Chr. ii. 4, 6; ix. 6; Neh. xi. 24. Zara in Matt. i. 3.

**Zăr″a-ī′as**. The name stands for Zerahiah and Zebadiah in the Apocrypha, 1 Esdr. viii.

**Zā′re-ah** (*hornet*). Neh. xi. 29. [ZORAH, ZOREAH.]

**Zā′re-ath-ītes″**. Dwellers in Zareah or Zorah, 1 Chr. ii. 53.

**Zā′red**, Num. xxi. 12. [ZERED.]

**Zăr′e-phăth** (*smelting-place*). The Sarepta of Luke iv. 26. A town in Phœnicia on the Mediterranean coast between Tyre and Sidon, and about seven miles from the latter. Residence of the prophet Elijah during the great drought, 1 Kgs. xvii. 8-24.

**Zăr′e-tăn**, Josh. iii. 16. [ZARTHAN, 2.]

**Zā′reth=shā′har** (*beauty of dawn*). A town in Reuben, Josh. xiii. 19.

**Zär′hītes**. A branch of the tribe of Judah descended from Zerah the son of Judah, Num. xxvi. 13, 20; Josh. vii. 17; 1 Chr. xxvii. 11, 13.

**Zär′ta-nah** (*cooling*). A place usually identified with Zarthan, 1 Kgs. iv. 12.

**Zär′than** (*cooling*). (1) A town in the Jordan valley. Between it and Succoth was the clay-ground in which Solomon cast the utensils for the temple service. Now the mound called *Tell-sa-rem*, 1 Kgs. vii. 46. (2) The same place is doubtless meant by Zaretan, Josh. iii. 16, and by Zererath in Judg. vii. 22. (3) Supposably another name for the Zartanah of 1 Kgs. iv. 12. (4) Doubtless Zarthan (1) is meant by the Zeredathah of 2 Chr. iv. 17.

**Zăth′o-ē**, 1 Esdr. viii. 32. [ZATTU.]

**Zăt′thu** (*branch*). One who sealed the covenant with Nehemiah, Neh. x. 14.

**Zăt′tu** (*branch*). The children of Zattu returned from the captivity, Ez. ii. 8; x. 27; Neh. vii. 13.

**Zā′van**, 1 Chr. i. 42. [ZAAVAN.]

**Zā′zȧ** (*for all*). A son of Jonathan, and descendant of Judah, 1 Chr. ii. 33.

**Zĕal′ŏts** (*zealous*). Name of a fanatical Jewish party, strongest from A. D. 6 to 70. It was political, having for its aim the overthrow of Roman authority; and religious, seeking a Jewish theocracy over the whole earth. In Acts v. 37 it seems to have been headed by one Judas of Galilee.

**Zĕb″a-dī′ah** (*portion of God*). (1) A son of Beriah, of Benjamin, 1 Chr. viii. 15. (2) A son of Elpaal of Benjamin, 1 Chr. viii. 17. (3) A son of Jeroham of Gedor, a Benjamite, 1 Chr. xii. 7. (4) A Korhite Levite, son of Meshelemiah, and one of the temple porters, 1 Chr. xxvi. 2. (5) A son of Asahel, brother of Joab, who succeeded his father as captain of the military course of the fourth month, 1 Chr. xxvii. 7. (6) A Levite sent out by King Jehoshaphat to teach the law to the people, 2 Chr. xvii. 8. (7) A son of Ishmael and ruler of the house of Judah in reign of King Jehoshaphat, 2 Chr. xix. 11. (8) One who returned with Ezra from the captivity, Ez. viii. 8. (9) A priest who had married a foreign wife, Ez. x. 20.

**Zā′bah** (*sacrifice*). One of the two Midianite kings slain by Gideon, Judg. viii. 5-21; Ps. lxxxiii. 11.

**Ze-bā′im** (*gazelles*). A disputed word, regarded as identical with Zeboim, Ez. ii. 57; Neh. vii. 59.

**Zĕb′e-dee** (*God's portion*). A fisherman of Galilee, husband of Salome, and father of the apostles James the Great and John, Matt. iv. 21; xxvii. 56; Mark i. 19, 20; xv. 40. His home is located at or near Bethsaida, and he appears to have been able to employ help in his occupation, Mark i. 20.

**Ze-bī′nȧ** (*buying*). A son of Nebo who had taken a foreign wife after the captivity, Ez. x. 43.

**Ze-bō′im** (*deer*). (1) One of the five cities of the plain, or circle, of Jordan, Gen. x. 19; Deut. xxix. 23; Hos. xi. 8. It is called Zeboiim in Gen. xiv. 2, 8. (2) A valley, or mountain gorge, contiguous to Michmash, 1 Sam. xiii. 18. (3) A place inhabited by Benjamites after the return from captivity, Neh. xi. 34.

**Ze-boi′im**, Gen. xiv. 2, 8. [ZEBOIM, 1.]

**Ze-bŭ′dah** (*given*). Wife of King Josiah and mother of King Jehoiakim, 2 Kgs. xxiii. 36.

**Zē′bul** (*habitation*). Ruler of the city of Shechem at the time of the contest between Abimelech and the native Canaanites, Judg. ix. 28-41.

**Zĕb′u-lon-īte″**, Judg. xii. 11. [ZEBULUNITES.]

**Zĕb′u-lun** (*dwelling*). (1) Tenth son of Jacob, and sixth and last by Leah, Gen. xxx. 20; xxxv. 23. Three sons are ascribed to him at the time of the migration to Egypt, Gen. xlvi. 14. Zebulun was one of the six tribes stationed on Ebal to pronounce the curse, Deut. xxvii. 13. The allotment of the tribe was bounded as in Josh. xix. 10-16, and in general stretched from Acre to Jordan, taking in the plain of Esdraelon. The tribe did not expel the natives in its allotment, but associated with them and fell into easy commercial intercourse with Phœnicia on the west, Judg. i. 30. It became an idolatrous tribe, 2 Chr. xxx. 10-18, and its territory was depopulated in the captivity of Israel by Tiglath-pileser, 2 Kgs. xv. 29. (2) A boundary place of Asher, Josh. xix. 27.

**Zĕb′u-lun-ītes″**. Descendants of Zebulun, Num. xxvi. 27.

**Zĕch″a-rī′ah** (*memory of God*). Son of Berechiah, Zech. i. 1; of Iddo, Ez. v. 1. Eleventh of the minor prophets and contemporary of Haggai, born in Babylon during the captivity, returned with Zerubbabel, Ez. v. 1; vi. 14. The time of his prophecies is reckoned as between B. C. 520 and 518, during the period of building the second temple, whose completion was largely due to his energies as priest and prophet. His book, 38th of O. T., is divided into two parts. Chapters i.-viii. contain hopeful visions of the restored Hebrew state, exhortations to turn to Jehovah, warnings against God's enemies. Chapters ix.-xiv. are prophetic of the future fortunes of the theocracy, the conversion of Israel, the glorification of God's kingdom and of the coming of the Messiah. The style of the book is obscure. Many critics attribute the authorship of the second division of the book to Jeremiah. (2) A Reubenite chief, at time of the captivity by Tiglath-pileser, 1 Chr. v. 7. (3) A Korhite Levite, keeper of one of the doors of the tabernacle, 1 Chr. ix. 21. (4) A son of Jehiel, 1 Chr. ix. 37. (5) A Levite of the second order, one of the temple musicians, 1 Chr. xv. 18, 20. (6) A priest who blew the trumpet before the ark on its return, 1 Chr. xv. 24. (7) A Kohathite Levite, 1 Chr. xxiv. 25. (8) A Merarite Levite, 1 Chr. xxvi. 11. (9) A Manassite, 1 Chr. xxvii. 21. (10) A prince of Judah in reign of Jehoshaphat, 2 Chr. xvii. 7. (11) Father of Jahaziel, 2 Chr. xx. 14. (12) A son of Jehoshaphat, 2 Chr. xxi. 2. (13) Son of the high priest Jehoiada, in reign of Joash king of Judah, 2 Chr. xxiv. 20, and probably same as the Zacharias of Matt. xxiii. 35. (14) A prophet and royal counsellor in reign of Uzziah, 2 Chr. xxvi. 5. (15) Father of Abijah, mother of King Hezekiah, 2 Chr. xxix. 1. (16) A member of the family of Asaph in time of Hezekiah, 2 Chr. xxix. 13. (17) A Kohathite Levite in the reign of Josiah, 2 Chr. xxxiv. 12. (18) One of the temple rulers in reign of Josiah, 2 Chr. xxxv. 8. (19) Nine priests, Levites and returned captives in Ez. viii. 3, 11, 16; x. 26; Neh. viii. 4; xi. 4, 5, 12; xii. 16, 35, 41. (20) A witness for Isaiah, Isa. viii. 2.

**Zē′dăd** (*hillside*). A landmark on the northern border of Canaan, Num. xxxiv. 8; Ezek. xlvii. 15.

**Zĕd″e-chī′as**, 1 Esdr. i. 46. [ZEDEKIAH.]

**Zĕd″e-kī′ah** (*justice of God*). (1) Last king of Judah, son of Josiah, and brother of Jehoahaz. He reigned eleven years, B. C. 598–588, 2 Kgs. xxiv. 18; 2 Chr. xxxvi. 11. He was raised to the throne by Nebuchadnezzar, who changed his name from Mattaniah to Zedekiah, 2 Kgs. xxiv. 17. In the ninth year of his reign, he revolted against Nebuchadnezzar, who thereupon completed the captivity of Judah and ended the kingdom, 2 Kgs. xxv. 1-21; 2 Chr. xxxvi. 11-21; Jer. xxi.-xxxviii.; Ezek. xvii. 15-21. (2) Son of Chenaanah, a prophet and head of the prophetic school in reign of Jehoshaphat, 1 Kgs. xxii.; 2 Chr. xviii. 10-24. (3) Son of Hananiah, and a court officer under Jehoiakim, Jer. xxxvi. 12. (4) A false prophet burnt to death by Nebuchadnezzar, Jer. xxix. 21, 22.

**Zē′eb** (*wolf*). A prince of Midian, slain by the Ephraimites, Judg. vii. 25; Ps. lxxxiii. 11.

**Zē′eb, Wine-press of.** The place where Zeeb was slain by the Ephraimites, Judg. vii. 25.

**Zē′lah** (*rib*). A city in Benjamin in which was located the family tomb of Kish, father of Saul, Josh. xviii. 28; 2 Sam. xxi. 14.

**Zē′lek** (*chasm*). An Ammonite and one of David's guard, 2 Sam. xxiii. 37; 1 Chr. xi. 39.

**Zē-lō′phe-hăd** (*firstborn*). A son of Hepher, descendant of Manasseh. The law of female inheritance was changed in favor of his daughters, Num. xxvi. 33; xxvii. 1-11; Josh. xvii. 3, 4; 1 Chr. vii. 15.

**Zē-lō′tes** (*zealous*). A name added to that of the apostle Simon to distinguish him from Simon Peter, and to emphasize his membership of the party of Zealots, Luke vi. 15. [SIMON, 4.]

**Zĕl′zah** (*shade*). A place in the border of Benjamin, near which was Rachel's tomb, 1 Sam. x. 2.

**Zĕm″a-rā′im** (*two fleeces*). (1) A town in Benjamin, four miles north of Jericho, Josh. xviii. 22. (2) Mount Zemaraim in the mountains of Ephraim, 2 Chr. xiii. 4.

**Zĕm′a-rīte.** An Hamitic tribe or family descended from Canaan, Gen. x. 18; 1 Chr. i. 16.

**Zē-mī′rȧ** (*song*). Son of Becher, a descendant of Benjamin, 1 Chr. vii. 8.

**Zē′nan** (*target*). A town in the lowlands of Judah, Josh. xv. 37.

**Zē′nas.** A Christian lawyer whom Paul wished Titus to bring along with him, Tit. iii. 13.

**Zĕph″a-nī′ah** (*God's secret*). (1) Ninth in order of the twelve minor prophets. Son of Cushi and a descendant of Hezekiah. He flourished during the reign of King Josiah, B. C. 641-610. His prophecy constitutes the 36th O. T. book, and denounces Judah, Nineveh, and surrounding nations, and records many cheerful promises of gospel blessings. The style is characterized by grace, strength, and dignity. (2) Son of Maaseiah and priest in the reign of Zedekiah; Jer. xxi. 1; xxix. 25-29; xxxvii. 3; lii. 24-27. (3) A Kohathite Levite, 1 Chr. vi. 36. (4) Father of Josiah and Hen, Zech. vi. 10, 14.

**Zē′phath** (*watchtower*). An Amorite town in the mountains near Kadesh. Called Hormah after it was conquered by the Israelites, Judg. i. 17. [HORMAH.]

**Zĕph′a-thah** (*watchtower*). The valley near Mareshah in which King Asa marshalled his forces for battle against Zerah, 2 Chr. xiv. 9, 10.

**Zē′phī**, 1 Chr. i. 36. [ZEPHO.]

**Zē′phō** (*watchtower*). Zephi, 1 Chr. i. 36. One of the dukes of Edom, Gen. xxxvi. 11, 15.

**Zē′phon** (*watchman*). A son of Gad, Num. xxvi. 15. Called Ziphion in Gen. xlvi. 16.

**Zē′phon-ītes.** Descendants of Zephon, Num. xxvi. 15.

**Zēr** (*flint*). A city in Naphtali, Josh. xix. 35.

**Zē′rah** (*eastern*). (1) A grandson of Esau and one of the dukes of Edom, Gen. xxxvi. 13, 17, 33; 1 Chr. i. 37, 44. (2) Num. xxvi. 20; Josh. vii. 1, 18; xxii. 20; 1 Chr. ii. 4, 6; ix. 6; Neh. xi. 24. [ZARAH.] (3) A son of Simeon and ancestor of a family of Zarhites, Num. xxvi. 13; 1 Chr. iv. 24. Called Zohar in Gen. xlvi. 10. (4) A Gershonite Levite, 1 Chr. vi. 21, 41. (5) An Ethiopian king whom Asa, king of Judah, defeated, 2 Chr. xiv. 9.

**Zĕr″a-hī′ah** (*rising of God*). (1) Son of Uzzi and priest of the line of Eleazar, 1 Chr. vi. 6, 51; Ez. vii. 4. (2) One whose descendants returned from captivity with Ezra, Ez. viii. 4.

**Zē′red** (*growth of reeds*). A brook or wady separating Moab from Edom, Deut. ii. 13, 14. Called Zared in Num. xxi. 12.

**Zĕr′e-dȧ** (*ambush*). Native place of Jeroboam, in the mountains of Ephraim, 1 Kgs. xi. 26.

**Zē-rĕd′a-thah**, 2 Chr. iv. 17. [ZARTHAN.]

**Zĕr′e-răth**, Judg. vii. 22. [ZARTHAN.]

**Zē′resh.** Wife of Haman, and his adviser in the conspiracy against Mordecai, Esth. v. 10-14.

**Zē′reth** (*bright*). A son of Ashur, founder of Tekoa, 1 Chr. iv. 7.

**Zē′rī** (*built*). A son of Jeduthun, a musician in the time of David, 1 Chr. xxv. 3.

**Zē′rôr** (*tied*). An ancestor of Kish, the father of Saul, 1 Sam. ix. 1.

**Zē-ru′ah** (*leprous*). Mother of King Jeroboam I., 1 Kgs. xi. 26.

**Zē-rŭb′ba-bĕl** (*born in Babylon*). He was of the family of David, and son of Shealtiel, Hag. i. 1, or Salathiel, Matt. i. 12, or Pedaiah, 1 Chr. iii. 19. Born at Babylon, commissioned governor of Judea by the Persian king, Cyrus, Neh. xii. 47; leader of the first colony of captives back to Jerusalem, B. C. 536, Ez. ii. 2; Neh. vii. 7; laid the foundation of the new temple, Zech. iv. 6-10; began the work of reconstruction, in which he was greatly hindered by Samaritan opposition, and petty Persian intrigue; finally succeeded in completing the structure, restored the order of priests according to the institution of David, Ez. vi. 14-22; Hag. i. 12, 15; ii. 2-4. Zorobabel in N. T., Matt. i. 12.

**Zĕr″u-ī′ah** (*bruised*). Sister of David and mother of the three leading heroes of David's army, 1 Sam. xxvi. 6; 1 Chr. ii. 16.

**Zē′tham** (*olive*). A Levite, son of Laadan, 1 Chr. xxiii. 8; xxvi. 22.

**Zē′than** (*olive*). A son of Bilhan, of Benjamin, 1 Chr. vii. 10.

**Zē′thär** (*star*). One of the seven chamberlains of King Ahasuerus, Esth. i. 10.

**Zī′ȧ** (*moving*). A Gadite, Chr. v. 13.

**Zī′bȧ** (*statue*). A steward of Saul, and tiller of the lands of Saul which David restored to Mephibosheth, 2 Sam. ix. 2-13; xvi. 1-4; xix. 17-29.

**Zĭb′e-on** (*robber*). A Horite and son of Seir, Gen. xxxvi. 2, 24, 29; 1 Chr. i. 38, 40.

**Zĭb′ĭ-ȧ** (*deer*). A Benjamite, 1 Chr. viii. 9.

**Zĭb′ĭ-ah** (*deer*). Mother of King Jehoash or Joash, 2 Kgs. xii. 1; 2 Chr. xxiv. 1.

**Zĭch′rī** (*remembered*). (1) A son of Izhar, son of Kohath, Ex. vi. 21. (2) A Benjamite of the sons of Shimhi, 1 Chr. viii. 19. (3) A Benjamite of the sons of Shashak, 1 Chr. viii. 23. (4) A Benjamite of the sons of Jeroham, 1 Chr. viii. 27. (5) A son of Asaph the musician, 1 Chr. ix. 15. Zabdi, Neh. xi. 17; Zaccur, Neh. xii. 35. (6) Son of Eliezer, a descendant of Moses, 1 Chr. xxvi. 25. (7) Father of Eliezer, a ruler of Reuben in reign of David, 1 Chr. xxvii. 16. (8) Father of Amasiah, a captain of 200,000 men of valor under King Jehoshaphat, 2 Chr. xvii. 16. (9) Father of Elishaphat, a captain of hundreds under Jehoiada, 2 Chr. xxiii. 1. (10) A mighty man of Ephraim in the army of Pekah, 2 Chr. xxviii. 7. (11) A Benjamite, father of Joel, overseer of Jerusalem after the captivity, Neh. xi. 9. (12) Priest of the family of Abijah, Neh. xii. 17.

**Zĭd'dim** (*steeps*). A fenced city of Naphtali, Josh. xix. 35.

**Zī'dŏn** (*fishing*). The Sidon of Gen. x. 15, 19, the N. T., and Apocrypha. An ancient and wealthy commercial city of Phœnicia on the Mediterranean coast, twenty miles north of Tyre. It was a limit of the allotment of Asher, but was never conquered, Judg. i. 31; x. 12; xviii. 7, 28. The Zidonians assisted in building the temple, 1 Kgs. v. 6; 1 Chr. xxii. 4; Ezek. xxvii. 8. Israel imported her idolatries, 1 Kgs. xi. 5, 33; 2 Kgs. xxiii. 13. Paul's ship touched at Sidon, Acts xxvii. 3.

**Zī-dō'nĭ-ans.** Dwellers in Zidon, Judg. x. 12.

**Zĭf** (*bloom*). Second month of Hebrew sacred and eighth of the civil year, corresponding to parts of April and May, 1 Kgs. vi. 1.

**Zī'hȧ** (*dried*). (1) His children returned from captivity, Ez. ii. 43; Neh. vii. 46. (2) A ruler of the Nethinims in Ophel, Neh. xi. 21.

**Zĭk'lăg** (*flowing, winding*). A city in southern Judah, Josh. xv. 31, afterwards assigned to Simeon, Josh. xix. 5. It became of great historic importance as the rendezvous of David when outlawed by Saul, and was then, or had just been, in the hands of the Philistines, 1 Sam. xxx. 1, 14, 26; 2 Sam. i. 1; iv. 10; 1 Chr. iv. 30; xii. 1-20.

**Zĭl'lah** (*shadow*). One of the wives of Lamech and mother of Tubal-cain, Gen. iv. 19, 22, 23.

**Zĭl'pah** (*dropping*). A Syrian woman who became Jacob's concubine and the mother of Gad and Asher, Gen. xxix. 24; xxx. 9-13; xxxv. 26; xxxvii. 2; xlvi. 18.

**Zĭl'thāi** (*shadow*). (1) A Benjamite of the sons of Shimhi, 1 Chr. viii. 20. (2) A Manassite captain who deserted to David at Ziklag, 1 Chr. xii. 20.

**Zĭm'mah** (*wickedness*). (1) A Gershonite Levite, son of Jahath, 1 Chr. vi. 20. (2) Another Gershonite Levite, 1 Chr. vi. 42. (3) A Levite and father of Joah, 2 Chr. xxix. 12.

**Zĭm'răn** (*sung*). A son of Abraham by Keturah, Gen. xxv. 2; 1 Chr. i. 32.

**Zĭm'rī** (*sung*). (1) Son of Salu, a prince of Simeon slain by Phinehas, Num. xxv. 6-15. (2) Captain of half the chariots under Elah king of Israel. He smote his master in Tirsah, and reigned in his stead for a period of seven days, B. C. 929, 1 Kgs. xvi. 8-18. (3) A son of Zerah, of Judah, 1 Chr. ii. 6. Zabdi in Josh. vii. 1, 17, 18. (4) Son of Jehoadah and a descendant of Saul, 1 Chr. viii. 36; ix. 42. (5) An obscure name mentioned in Jer. xxv. 25.

**Zĭn** (*shrub*). That part of the Arabian wilderness or desert lying south of Palestine, adjacent to Judah, and bounded on the east by the Dead Sea and valley of Arabah; Num. xiii. 21, 26; xx. 1; xxvii. 14; xxxiii. 36; xxxiv. 3; Josh. xv. 1-3.

**Zī'nȧ** (*fruitful*). The second son of Shimei the Gershonite, 1 Chr. xxiii. 10. Zizah in vs. 11.

**Zī'ŏn** (*mount, sunny*). Zion or Sion in its literal and restricted sense was the celebrated mount in Jerusalem, the highest and southernmost or southwesternmost of the city. It was the original hill of the Jebusites, Josh. xv. 63. After David became king, he captured it, "the stronghold of Zion," from the Jebusites, dwelt in the fort there, and greatly enlarged and strengthened its fortifications, calling it "the city of David," 2 Sam. v. 6-9; 1 Chr. xi. 5-8. Despite David's prestige the name of Zion still clung to it, 1 Kgs. viii. 1; 2 Kgs. xix. 21, 31; 2 Chr. v. 2. The O. T. poets and prophets exalted the word Zion by frequent use and gave it a sacred turn, so that in time it came to type a sacred capital, Ps. ii. 6; holy place, Ps. lxxxvii. 2; cxlix. 2; Isa. xxx. 19; God's chosen people, Ps. li. 18; lxxxvii. 5; the Christian church, Heb. xii. 22; the heavenly city, Rev. xiv. 1.

**Zī'or** (*little*). A town in the mountains of Judah, Josh. xv. 54.

**Zīph** (*that flows*). (1) An unidentified place in South Judah, Josh. xv. 24. (2) A town in the mountains of Judah, Josh. xv. 55. It was in the wilderness, or wastes, of Ziph that David hid himself when pursued by Saul, 1 Sam. xxiii. 14, 15, 24; xxvi. 2. (3) Son of Jehaleleel, of Judah, 1 Chr. iv. 16.

**Zī'phah.** A brother of the above, 1 Chr. iv. 16.

**Zīph'ims.** Dwellers in Ziph, Ps. liv. title.

**Zīph'ītes.** Dwellers in Ziph, 1 Sam. xxiii. 19.

**Zīph'ī-on,** Gen. xlvi. 16. [Zephon.]

**Zīph'rŏn** (*perfume*). A northern boundary of the promised land, Num. xxxiv. 9.

**Zĭp'por** (*little bird*). Father of Balak, king of Moab, Num. xxii. 2, 4, 10, 16; xxiii. 18.

**Zĭp-pō'rah.** A daughter of Reuel or Jethro, whom Moses married, Ex. ii. 16-22; iv. 25; xviii. 2-4.

**Zĭth'rī** (*protected*). A Kohathite Levite, son of Uzziel, Ex. vi. 22.

**Zīz** (*cliff*). The cliff or pass of Ziz was that by which the Moabites and Ammonites came up from the shores of the Dead Sea to give battle to King Jehoshaphat's forces, 2 Chr. xx. 16.

**Zī'zȧ** (*plenty*). (1) A son of Shiphi and a prince of Simeon in the reign of Hezekiah, 1 Chr. iv. 37. (2) A son of King Rehoboam, 2 Chr. xi. 20.

**Zī'zah** (*plenty*), 1 Chr. xxiii. 11. [Zina.]

**Zō'an** (*departure*). An ancient city of Lower Egypt, the Tanis of the Greeks and the San of modern times. It occupied a highly strategic position on the east side of the Tanitic branch of the Nile, and was built seven years before the very ancient city of Hebron, Num. xiii. 22. Isaiah mentions the "princes of Zoan," Isa. xix. 11-13; xxx. 4, and Ezekiel foretells its fate by fire, Ezek. xxx. 14.

**Zō'ar** (*little*). One of the most ancient cities of Canaan, mentioned as in the "plain of Jordan" and in connection with Sodom and Gomorrah, Gen. xiii. 10. It was originally called Bela, Gen. xiv. 2, 8. It was spared from the fiery destruction which came upon Sodom and the other cities of the plain, Gen. xix. 20-23. Isaiah and Jeremiah speak of Zoar as in the land of Moab, Isa. xv. 5; Jer. xlviii. 34.

**Zō'bȧ, Zō'bah** (*encampment*). That portion of Syria which formed a separate empire in the time of Saul, David, and Solomon. It lay to the northeast of Palestine and probably extended to the Euphrates. Though ruled by petty kings at first, it became united and strong and engaged in frequent wars with Israel, 1 Sam. xiv. 47; 2 Sam. viii. 3-8; x. 6-19; 1 Chr. xviii. 3-8; xix. 6. Hamath became the capital of Zobah, and it was captured by Solomon, 2 Chr. viii. 3.

**Zō-bē'bah** (*slothful*). A Judahite, 1 Chr. iv. 8.

**Zō'har** (*white*). (1) Father of Ephron, from whom Abraham bought the field of Machpelah, Gen. xxiii. 8; xxv. 9. (2) A son of Simeon, Gen. xlvi. 10; Ex. vi. 15. Zerah in 1 Chr. iv. 24.

**Zō'he-lĕth** (*serpent*). A stone or rock by En-rogel, where Adonijah slew "sheep, oxen, and fat cattle," 1 Kgs. i. 9.

**Zō'heth.** A Judahite, 1 Chr. iv. 20.

**Zō'phah** (*viol*). An Asherite, 1 Chr. vii. 35, 36.

**Zō'phāi** (*honeycomb*). A Kohathite Levite, 1 Chr. vi. 26. Written Zuph in vs. 35.

**Zō'phar** (*little bird*). A Naamathite, and one of the three friends of Job, Job ii. 11.

**Zō'phim** (*watchmen*). The field on the top of Pisgah to which Balak conducted Balaam for sacrifices, Num. xxiii. 14.

**Zō'rah** (*hornet*). A town in the lowlands of Judah, afterwards assigned to Dan, Josh. xix. 41. Written Zoreah in Josh. xv. 33, and Zareah in Neh. xi. 29. Residence of Manoah and burial place of his son Samson, Judg. xiii. 2, 24, 25; xvi. 31.

**Zō'rath-ītes.** Inhabitants of Zorah; but the designation seems to be limited to the family of Judah descended from Shobal, 1 Chr. iv. 2.

**Zō're-ah,** Josh. xv. 33. [Zorah.]

**Zō'rītes.** Descendants of Salma of Judah, and probably dwellers in Zorah, 1 Chr. ii. 54.

**Zō-rŏb'a-bĕl.** Greek form of Zerubbabel, which *see*, Matt. i. 12, 13; Luke iii. 27.

**Zū'ar** (*little*). Father of Nethaneel, chief of Issachar, Num. i. 8; ii. 5; vii. 18, 23; x. 15.

**Zŭph** (*honeycomb*). (1) The land reached by Saul while in search of his father's asses, 1 Sam. ix. 5. It was there he met Samuel the prophet, 1 Sam. ix. 6-15. (2) A Kohathite Levite, and ancestor of Elkanah and Samuel, 1 Sam. i. 1; 1 Chr. vi. 35. Called Zophai in 1 Chr. vi. 26.

**Zûr** (*rock*). (1) A Midianite king slain by the Israelites, Num. xxv. 15; xxxi. 8. (2) Son of Jehiel, founder of Gibeon, 1 Chr. viii. 30 ; ix. 36.

**Zū'rĭ-el.** (*God my rock*). Son of Abihail, and a chief of the Merarite Levites, Num. iii. 35.

**Zū"rĭ-shăd'da-ī** (*the Almighty my rock*). Father of Shelumiel, chief of the tribe of Simeon at the exodus, Num. i. 6 ; ii. 12 ; vii. 36 ; x. 19.

**Zū'zimş.** An Ammonite name for one of the races of giants, Gen. xiv. 5.

## LITTLE KNOWN BIBLICAL FACTS

## OLD TESTAMENT MIRACLES.

### Miracles in Egypt.

|  |  |
|---|---|
| Aaron's rod turned into a serpent. | Exodus vii, 10-12. |
| The ten plagues: | |
| 1. Water made blood, | Exodus vii, 20-25. |
| 2. Frogs, | Exodus viii, 5-14. |
| 3. Lice. | Exodus viii, 16-18. |
| 4. Flies, | Exodus viii, 20-24. |
| 5. Murrain, | Exodus ix, 3-6. |
| 6. Boils and blains, | Exodus ix, 8-11. |
| 7. Thunder and hail, | Exodus ix, 22-26. |
| 8. Locusts, | Exodus x, 12-19. |
| 9. Darkness, | Exodus x, 21-23. |
| 10. First-born slain, | Exodus xii, 29, 30. |
| Parting of the Red Sea, | Exodus xiv, 6, 21-31. |

### Miracles in the Wilderness.

|  |  |
|---|---|
| The curing of the waters of Marah, | Exodus xv, 23-25. |
| Feeding with manna, | Exodus xvi, 14-35. |
| Water from the rock, at Rephidim, | Exodus xvii, 5-7. |
| Death of Nadab and Abihu, | Leviticus x, 1, 2. |
| Burning of the congregation at Taberah, | Numbers xi, 1-3. |
| Death of Korah, Dathan and Abiram, etc., | Numbers xvi, 31-35. |
| Budding of Aaron's rod at Kadesh, | Numbers xvii, 8. |
| Water from the rock, at Meribah, | Numbers xx, 7-11. |
| The brazen serpent, | Numbers xxi, 8, 9. |
| Stoppage of the Jordan stream, | Joshua iii, 14-17. |

### Miracles in Canaan—Under Joshua.

|  |  |
|---|---|
| Fall of Jericho, | Joshua vi, 6-25. |
| Staying of sun and moon, | Joshua x, 12-14. |

### Miracles Under the Kings.

|  |  |
|---|---|
| Death of Uzzah, | II Samuel vi, 7. |
| Withering of Jeroboam's hand and destruction of the altar at Bethel, | I Kings xiii, 4-6. |

### Miracles by Elijah.

|  |  |
|---|---|
| Staying of the cruse of oil and meal at Zarephath, | I Kings xvii, 14-16. |
| Raising of the widow's son at Zarephath, | I Kings xvii, 17-24. |
| Burning of the sacrifice on Mount Carmel, | I Kings xviii, 30-38. |
| Burning of the captains and their companies, | II Kings i, 10-12. |
| Dividing of Jordan, | II Kings ii, 7, 8. |

### Miracles by Elisha.

|  |  |
|---|---|
| Dividing of Jordan, | II Kings ii, 14. |
| Curing of the waters of Jericho, | Kings ii, 21, 22. |
| Destruction of mocking children of Bethel, | II Kings ii, 24. |
| Supply of water to the allied armies in Moab, | II Kings iii, 16-20. |
| Multiplication of the widow's oil, | II Kings iv, 2-7. |
| Raising the Shunammite's son, | II Kings iv, 32-37. |
| Healing the deadly pottage, | II Kings iv, 38-41. |
| Feeding 100 men with 20 loaves, | II Kings iv, 42-44. |
| Cure of Naaman's leprosy; its transfer to Gehazi, | II Kings v, 10-14, 27 |
| Making an iron axe swim, | II Kings vi, 5-7. |
| Smiting the Syrian army, | II Kings vi, 18-20. |
| Raising of dead man by touching Elisha's bones, | II Kings xiii, 21. |

### Miracles Recorded by Isaiah.

|  |  |
|---|---|
| Destruction of Sennacherib's army, | II Kings xix, 35. |
| Return of sun by the dial of Ahaz, | II Kings xx, 9-11. |

### Miracles During Captivity.

|  |  |
|---|---|
| Deliverance of the three children from the fiery furnace, | Daniel iii, 19-27. |
| Deliverance of Daniel from the lions, | Daniel vi, 16-23. |

### Miscellaneous Miracles.

|  |  |
|---|---|
| Smiting of Philistines and fall of Dagon, | I Samuel v, 4-6. |
| Smiting of Uzziah with leprosy, | II Chron. xxvi, 16-21 |
| Deliverance of Jonah from the great fish, | Jonah ii, 1-10. |

## NEW TESTAMENT MIRACLES.

### Miracles Performed by Christ.

|  |  |
|---|---|
| Turns water into wine, Canaan, | John ii, 1-11. |
| Cures the nobleman's son of Capernaum, Capernaum, | John iv, 46-64. |
| Causes the miraculous draught of fishes, Sea of Galilee, | Luke v, 1-11. |
| Cures a demoniac, Capernaum, | Mark i, 22-28. |
| Heals Peter's wife's mother of a fever, Capernaum, | Mark i, 30, 31. |
| Heals a leper, Capernaum, | Mark i, 40-45. |
| Heals the centurion's servant, Capernaum, | Matt. viii, 5-13. |
| Raises the widow's son, Nain, | Luke vii, 11-17. |
| Calms the tempest, Sea of Galilee, | Matt. viii, 23-27. |
| Cures the demoniacs of Gadara, Gadara, | Matt. viii, 28-34. |
| Cures a man of the palsy, Capernaum, | Matt. ix, 1-8. |
| Restores to life the daughter of Jairus, Capernaum, | Matt. ix, 18-26. |
| Cures a woman of a bloody flux, Capernaum, | Luke viii, 43-48. |
| Restores to sight two blind men, Capernaum, | Matt. ix, 27-31. |
| Heals one possessed of a dumb spirit, Capernaum, | Matt. ix, 32, 33. |
| Cures an infirm man at Bethesda, Jerusalem, | John v, 1-9. |
| Cures a man with a withered hand, Judea, | Matt. xii, 10-13. |
| Cures a demoniac, Capernaum, | Matt. xii, 22, 23. |
| Feeds miraculously 5,000, Decapolis, | Matt. xiv, xv, 21. |
| Heals woman of Canaan's daughter, near Tyre, | Matt. xv, 22-28. |
| Heals a man who was deaf and dumb. Decapolis, | Mark vii, 31-37. |
| Feeds miraculously 4,000, Decapolis, | Matt. xv, 32-39. |
| Gives sight to a blind man, Bethsaida, | Mark xiii, 22-26. |
| Cures a boy possessed of a devil, Tabor, | Matt. xvii, 14-21. |
| Restores to sight a man born blind, Jerusalem, | John ix, 1-7. |
| Heals a woman under an infirmity eighteen years, Galilee, | Luke xiii, 11-17. |
| Cures a man of dropsy, Galilee, | Luke xiv, 1-6. |
| Cleanses ten lepers, Samaria, | Luke xvii, 11-19. |
| Raises Lazarus from the dead, Bethany, | John xi, 43-44. |
| Restores to sight two blind men, Jericho, | Matt. xx, 30-34. |
| Blasts the fig-tree, Olivet, | Matt. xxi, 18-22. |
| Heals the ear of Malchus, Gethsemane, | Luke xxii, 50, 51. |
| Causes the miraculous draught of fishes, Sea of Galilee, | John xxi, 1-14. |

### Miracles Recorded in the Acts of the Apostles.

| | |
|---|---|
| Peter heals a lame man, Jerusalem, | Acts iii, 1-11. |
| Ananias and Saphira struck dead, Jerusalem, | Acts v, 1-10. |
| Apostles perform many wonders, Jerusalem, | Acts v, 12-16. |
| Peter and John communicate the Holy Ghost, Samaria, | Acts viii, 14-17. |
| Peter heals Eneas of a palsy, Lydda, | Acts ix, 33, 34. |
| Peter raises Tabitha, or Dorcas, to life, Joppa, | Acts ix, 37-41. |
| Peter delivered out of prison by an angel, Jerusalem, | Acts xii, 7-17. |
| God smites Herod so that he dies, Jerusalem, | Acts xii, 23. |
| Elymas, the sorcerer, smitten with blindness, Paphos, | Acts xiii, 7-11. |
| Paul converted, Road to Damascus, | Acts ix, 1-9. |
| Paul heals a cripple, Lystra, | Acts xiv, 8-10. |
| Paul casts out a spirit of divination, Phillippi, | Acts xvi, 17-18. |
| Paul and Silas' prison doors opened by an earthquake, Phillippi, | Acts xvi, 25, 27. |
| Paul communicates the Holy Ghost, Corinth, | Acts xix, 1-7. |
| Paul heals the multitudes, Corinth, | Acts xix, 11-12. |
| Paul restores Eutychus to life, Troas, | Acts xx, 9-12. |
| Paul shakes off the viper, Melita, | Acts xxviii, 3-7. |
| Paul heals the father of Publius and others, Melita, | Acts xxviii, 7-9. |

## OLD TESTAMENT PARABLES.

| | |
|---|---|
| The ewe lamb, Nathan to David, | II Samuel xii, 1-4. |
| The two brethren and avengers of blood, Widow of Tekoah, | II Samuel, xiv, 1-11. |
| Escaped captive, Son of the prophets to Ahab, | I Kings xx, 35-40. |
| Vineyard and grapes, Isaiah to Judah, | Isaiah v, 1-7. |
| Eagles and vine, Ezekiel to Israel, | Ezekiel xvii, 3-10. |
| Lion's whelps, Ezekiel to Israel, | Ezekiel xix, 2-9. |
| The boiling pot, Ezekiel to Israel, | Ezekiel xxiv, 3-5. |

### Parabolic Fables.

| | |
|---|---|
| Trees choosing a king, Jotham to Shechemites, | Judges ix, 7-15. |
| Micaiah's vision, | I Kings xxii, 19-23. |
| Thistle and cedar, Jehoash to Amaziah, | II Kings xiv, 9. |

## THE PARABLES OF JESUS.

### Arranged in Chronological Order.

| | |
|---|---|
| Sower, Capernaum, | Matt. xiii, 1-23. |
| Tares, Capernaum, | Matt. xiii, 24-30, 36-43. |
| Seed springing up imperfectly, Capernaum, | Mark iv, 26-29. |
| Grain of mustard seed, Capernaum, | Matt. xii, 31-32. |
| Leaven, Capernaum, | Matt. xiii, 33. |
| Found treasure, Capernaum, | Matt. xiii, 44. |
| Precious pearl, Capernaum, | Matt. xiii, 45, 46. |
| Net, Capernaum, | Matt. xiii, 47-50. |
| Two debtors, Capernaum, | Luke vii, 36-50. |
| Unmerciful servant, Capernaum, | Matt. xviii, 23-35. |
| Samaritan, Near Jericho, | Luke x, 25-37. |
| Rich fool, Galilee, | Luke xii, 16-21. |
| Servants who waited for their Lord, Galilee, | Luke xii, 35-48. |
| Barren fig-tree, Galilee, | Luke xiii, 6-9. |
| Lost sheep, Galilee, | Luke xv, 3-7. |
| Lost piece of money, Galilee, | Luke xv, 8-10. |
| Prodigal son, Galilee, | Luke xv, 11-32. |
| Dishonest steward, Galilee, | Luke xvi, 1-12. |
| Rich man and Lazarus, Galilee, | Luke xvi, 19-31. |
| Unjust judge, Paraea, | Luke xviii, 1-8. |
| Pharisee and publican, Paraea, | Luke xviii, 9-14. |
| Laborers in the vineyard, Paraea, | Matt. xx, 1-16. |
| Pounds, Jericho, | Luke xix, 12-27. |
| Two sons, Jerusalem, | Matt. xxi, 28-32. |
| Vineyard, Jerusalem, | Matt. xxi, 33-46. |
| Marriage feast, Jerusalem, | Matt. xxii, 1-14. |
| Virgins, | Matt. xxv, 1-13. |
| Talents, Jerusalem, | Matt. xxv, 14-30. |
| Sheep and the goats, Jerusalem, | Matt. xxv, 31-46. |

## THE DISCOURSES OF JESUS.

### Arranged in Chronological Order.

| | |
|---|---|
| Conversation with Nicodemus, Jerusalem, | John iii, 1-21. |
| Conversation with woman of Samaria, Sychar, | John iv, 1-42. |
| Discourse in synagogue of Nazareth, Nazareth, | Luke iv, 16-31. |
| Sermon on the mount, Nazareth, | Matt. v, vii. |
| Instruction to the apostles, Galilee, | Matt. x. |
| Denunciations against Chorazin, etc., Galilee, | Matt. xi, 20-24. |
| Discourse on healing of infirm man in Jerusalem, | John v. |
| Discourse concerning disciples plucking corn on the Sabbath, Judea, | Matt. xii, 1-8. |
| Reputation of his working miracles by the agency of Beelzebub, Capernaum, | Matt. xii, 22-37. |
| Discourse on the bread of life, Capernaum, | John vii. |
| Discourse about internal purity, Capernaum, | Matt. xv, 1-20. |
| Discourse against giving or taking offense, and concerning forgiveness of injuries, Capernaum, | Matt. xviii. |
| Discourse at the feast of the tabernacles, Jerusalem, | John vii. |
| Discourse on women taken in adultery, Jerusalem, | John viii, i, ii. |
| Discourse concerning the sheep, Jerusalem, | John x. |
| Denunciations against the Scribes and Pharisees, Paraea, | Luke xi, 29-36. |
| Discourse concerning humility and prudence, Galilee, | Luke xiv, 7-14. |
| Directions how to attain heaven, Paraea, | Matt. xix, 16-30. |
| Discourse concerning his sufferings, Jerusalem, | Matt. xx, 17-19. |
| Denunciation against the Pharisees, Jerusalem, | Matt. xxiii. |
| Prediction of the destruction of Jerusalem, Jerusalem, | Matt. xxiv. |
| The consolatory discourse, Jerusalem, | John xv, xvii. |
| Discourse as he went to Gethsemane, Jerusalem, | Matt. xxvi, 31-36. |
| Discourse to the disciples before his ascension, Jerusalem, | Matt. xxviii, 16-23. |

## THE SEVEN REMARKS MADE BY CHRIST WHEN ON THE CROSS AND THE ATTENDANT INCIDENTS.

1. "Father, forgive them." Luke xxiii, 34.
   His garments parted, and vesture allotted. Matt. xxvii, 35. Mark xv, 24. Luke xxiii, 23-34. John xix, 23.
   Passers-by rail, the two thieves revile. Matt. xxvii, 39-44. Mark xv, 29-32. Luke xxiii, 35. The penitent thief. Luke xxiii, 40.
2. "To-day shalt thou be with me in Paradise." Luke xxiii, 43.
3. "Woman, behold thy Son," &c. John xix, 26, 27. The darkness. Matt. xxvii, 45; Mark xv, 33; Luke xxiii, 44.
4. "My God, my God, why hast thou forsaken me?" Matt. xxvii, 46. Mark xv, 34.
5. "I thirst." John xix, 28.
   The vinegar. Matt. xxvii, 48. Mark xv, 36.

John xix, 29.
6. "It is finished." John xix, 30.
7. "Father, into thy hands I commend my spirit." Luke xxiii, 46.

## APPEARANCES OF CHRIST AFTER HIS RESURRECTION.

1. To Mary Magdalene. Mark xvi, 9-10. John xx, 14.
   "All hail! Fear not. Touch me not."
2. To the women returning home. Matt. xxviii, 9. "Go, tell my brethren that they go into Galilee; there shall they see me."
3. To two disciples going to Emmaus. Mark xvi, 12. Luke xxiv, 13.
   (Exposition of prophecies on the Passion.)
4. To Peter. I Cor. xv, 5. Luke xxiv, 34.
5. To ten apostles in the upper room. Luke xxiv, 36. John xx, 19.
   "Peace be unto you. As my Father hath sent me, even so send I you."
   "Receive ye the Holy Ghost. Whose soever sins ye remit," &c.
6. To the eleven apostles in the upper room. Mark xvi, 14. John xx, 26.
   "Peace be unto you."
   To Thomas:
   "Reach hither thy finger," &c.
   "Blessed are they that have not seen, and yet have believed."
7. To the disciples at the Sea of Tiberias. John xxi, 1-24.
   To Peter:
   "Feed my sheep. Feed my lambs."
8. To eleven apostles on a mountain in Galilee. I Cor. xv, 5. Matt. xxviii, 16.
   "All power is given unto me in heaven and in earth."
   "Go ye and teach all nations, baptizing them," &c.
   "Lo, I am with you alway, even unto the end of the world. Amen."
9. To five hundred brethren at once. I Cor. xv, 6.
10. To James. I Cor. xv, 7.
11. Ascension. Mark xvi, 19. Luke xxiv, 50, 51.
12. To Paul at his conversion. I Cor. xv.
13. To the Apostle John. Rev. i, 13.

## OLD TESTAMENT PROPHECIES RELATING TO CHRIST.

Adoration by Magi. Ps. lxxii, 10, 15; Isa, lx, 3, 6.
Advent. Gen. iii, 15; Deut. xviii, 15; Ps. lxxxix, 20; Isa, ii, 2; ix, 6; xxviii, 16; xxxii, 1; xxxv, 4; xlii, 6; xlix, 1; lv, 4; Ezek. xxxiv, 24; Dan. ii, 44; Mic. iv, 1; Zech. iii, 8.
Advent, time of. Gen. xlix, 10; Num. xxiv, 17; Dan. ix, 24; Hag. ii, 7; Mal. iii, 1.
Ascension and exaltation. Ps. xvi, 11; xxiv, 7; lxviii, 18; cx, 1; cxviii, 19.
Betrayal by own friend. Ps. xli, 9; lv, 13.
Betrayal for thirty pieces. Zech. xi, 12.
Betrayer's death. Ps. lv, 15, 23; cix, 17.
Bone not to be broken. Ps. xxxiv, 20.
Burial with the rich. Isa. liii, 9.
Casting lots for vesture. Ps. xxii, 18.
Conversion of Gentiles. Isa. xi, 10; xlii, 1.
Crucifixion. Ps. xxii, 14, 17.
Death in prime of life. Ps. lxxxix, 45; cii, 24.
Death with malefactors. Isa. lii, 9, 12.
Death attested by convulsions of nature. Amos v, 20; viii, 9; Zech. xiv, 4, 6.
Descent into Egypt. Hos. xi, 1.
Desertion by disciples. Zech. xiii, 7.
Divinity. Ps. ii, 11; xlv, 7; lxxii, 8; cx, 1; Isa. ix, 6; xxv, 9; xl, 10; Jer. xxiii, 6; Mic. v, 2; Mal. iii, 1.
Dominion universal and everlasting. Ps. lxxii, 8; Isa. ix, 7; Dan. vii, 14.
False accusation Ps. xxvii, 12; xxxv, 11; cix, 2.
Forerunner of Christ. Isa. xl, 3; Mal. iii, 1; iv, 5.
Galilee, ministry in. Isa. ix, 1, 2.
Gall and vinegar, offer of. Ps. lxix, 21.
Generation, human. Gen. xii, 3; xviii, 18; xxi, 12; xxii, 18; xxvi, 4; xxviii, 14; xlix, 10; Ps. xviii, 50 lxxxix, 4, 29, 36; cxxxii, 11; Isa. xi, 1; Jer. xxiii, 5; xxxiii, 15.
Insult, buffeting, spitting, scourging. Ps. xxxv, 15, 21; Isa. 1, 6.
Massacre of Innocents. Jer. xxxi, 15.
Miraculous power. Isa. xxxv, 5.
Mission. Gen. xii, 3; xlix, 10; Num. xxiv, 19; Deut. xviii, 18; Ps. xxi, 1; Isa. lix, 20; Jer. xxxiii, 16.
Mocking. Ps. xxii, 16; cix, 25.
Nativity from virgin. Gen. iii, 15; Isa. vii, 14; Jer. xxxi, 22.
Nativity, place of. Num. xxiv, 17, 19; Mic. v, 2.
Patience under suffering. Isa. liii, 7, 9.
Persecution. Ps. xxii, 6; xxxv, 7, 12; cix, 2; Isa. xlix, 7; liii, 3.
Piercing. Ps. xxii, 16; Zech. xii, 10; xiii, 6.
Prayer for enemies. Ps. cix, 4.
Preacher. Ps. ii, 7; Isa. ii, 3; lxi, 1; Mic. iv, 2.
Priest like Melchizedek. Ps. cx, 4.
Prophet like Moses. Deut. xviii, 15.
Purchase of potter's field. Zech. xi, 13.
Purification of temple. Ps. lxix, 9.
Rejection by Jews and Gentiles. Ps. ii, 1; xxii, 12; xli, 5.
Resurrection. Ps. xvi, 10; xxx, 3; xli, 10; cxviii, 17; Hos. vi, 2.
Silence under accusation. Ps. xxxviii, 13; Isa. liii, 7.
Spiritual graces. Ps. xlv, 7; Isa. xi, 2; xlii, 1; lxi, 1.
Triumphal entry into Jerusalem. Ps. viii, 2; Zech. ix, 9.
Vicarious suffering. Isa. liii, 4-6, 12; Dan. ix, 26.

## THE SIZE OF HEAVEN.

### Biblical Assurance That There Will Be Room Enough.

Take a verse from the Revelation as the basis of computation. The text is in xxi, 15, and reads as follows: "And he measured the city with the reed, 12,000 furlongs. The length and the breadth and the height of it are equal." This represents a space of 469,783,088,000,000,000,000 cubic feet. It sets aside one-half of this space for the Throne and the Court of Heaven, and one-half of the balance for streets, which would leave a remainder of 124,198,272,000,000,000,000 cubic feet. Then divide this by 4,096, the number of cubical feet in a room sixteen feet square, and this process gives 30,321,843,750,000,000 rooms of the size indicated. Then upon the hypothesis that the world now contains, always has contained, and will always contain 990,000,000 inhabitants, and that a generation lasts for thirty-three and one-third years, which gives a total number of inhabitants every century of 2,297,000,000, assume that the world will stand 1,000 centuries or 100,000 years, which would give a total of 2,970,000,000,000 inhabitants for this period of time. We then reach the conclusion that if 100 worlds of the same size and duration, and containing the same number of inhabitants, there would be more than 100 rooms of the size indicated for each person.

## HOLY LAND DISTANCES.

From Jerusalem to Jericho is 15 miles.

From Dan to Beersheba, by an air line, is 125 miles.

The River Jordan is 180 yards wide and 3 feet deep at its mouth.

The Sea of Galilee is 13 miles long and 6 miles broad at its greatest width.

## WHERE THE APOSTLES WERE BURIED.

According to Catholic legend, seven of the Apostles are buried at Rome. These seven are distinguished by a star (*).

Andrew lies buried at Amalfi (Naples).

Bartholomew*, at Rome in the Church of Bartholomew Island, on the Tiber.

James the Greater was buried at St. Jago de Compostella, in Spain.

James the Less*, at Rome, in the Church of the Holy Apostles.

John, at Ephesus.

Jude*, at Rome.

Matthew, at Salerno (Naples).

Matthias*, at Rome under the altar of the Basilica.

Paul, somewhere in Italy.

Peter*, at Rome, in the Church of St. Peter.

Philip*, at Rome.

Simon or Simeon*, at Rome.

Thomas, at Ortona (Naples). (? Madras.)

Mark the Evangelist is said to have been buried at Venice.

Luke the Evangelist is said to have been buried at Padua.

N. B.—Italy claims thirteen of these apostles or evangelists—Rome seven, Naples three; Paul somewhere in Italy, Mark at Venice, Luke at Padua.

## PASSAGES FROM THE OLD TESTAMENT QUOTED IN THE FOUR GOSPELS.

### MATTHEW.

| | |
|---|---|
| Behold, a virgin shall be with child. | 1. 23.—Is. 7. 14. |
| Thou Bethlehem, in the land of Juda. | 2. 6.—Micah 5. 2. |
| Out of Egypt have I called my son. | 2. 15.—Hos. 11. 1. |
| In Rama was there a voice heard. | 2. 18.—Jer. 31. 15. |
| The voice of one crying in the wilderness. | 3. 3.—Is. 40. 3. |
| Man shall not live by bread alone. | 4. 4.—Deut. 8. 3. |
| He shall give his angels charge. | 4. 6.—Ps. 91. 11. 12. |
| Thou shall not tempt the Lord. | 4. 7.—Deut. 6. 16. |
| Thou shalt worship the Lord thy God. | 4. 10.—Deut. 6. 13. |
| The land of Zabulon, and the land of Nephthalim. | 4. 15, 16.—Is. 9. 1, 2; 42. 7. |
| Thou shalt not kill. | 5. 21.—Ex. 20. 13. |
| Thou shalt not commit adultery. | 5. 27.—Ex. 20. 14. |
| Whosoever shall put away his wife. | 5. 31.—Deut. 24. 1. |
| Thou shalt not forswear thyself. | 5. 33.—Lev. 19. 12. |
| An eye for an eye, and a tooth for a tooth. | 5. 38.—Exod. 21. 24. |
| Thou shalt love thy neighbour. | 5. 43.—Lev. 19. 18. |
| Be ye therefore perfect. | 5. 48.—Gen. 17. 1. |
| Depart. ye that work iniquity. | 7. 23.—Ps. 6. 8. |
| Himself took our infirmities. | 8. 17.—Is. 53. 4. |
| I will have mercy, and not sacrifice. | 9. 13; 12.7. Hos. 6. 6. |
| Behold, I send my messenger. | 11. 10.—Mal. 3. 1. |
| Behold my servant, whom I have chosen. | 12. 18-21.—Is. 42. 1-4. |
| By hearing ye shall hear, and shall not understand. | 13. 14, 15.—Is. 6. 9. 10. |
| I will open my mouth in parables. | 13. 35.—Ps. 78. 2. |
| Honour thy father and mother. | 15. 4.—Ex. 20. 12. |
| He that curseth father or mother. | 15. 4.—Ex. 21. 17. |
| This people draweth nigh unto me. | 15. 8, 9.—Is. 29. 13. |
| He. . made them male and female. | 19. 4.—Gen. 1. 27. |
| For this cause shall a man leave father and mother. | 19. 5.—Gen. 2. 24. |
| Thou shalt do no murder. | 19. 18.—Ex. 20. 13. |
| Honour thy father and thy mother. | 19. 19.—Ex. 20. 12. |
| Thou shalt love thy neighbour as thyself. | 19. 19.—Lev. 19. 18. |
| Tell ye the daughter of Sion, Behold, thy King cometh. | 21. 5.—Is. 62. 11; Zec. 9. 9. |
| Blessed is he that cometh in the name of the Lord. | 21. 9.—Ps. 118. 26. |
| My house shall be called the house of prayer. | 21. 13.—Is. 56. 7. |
| Ye have made it a den of thieves. | 21. 13.—Jer. 7. 11. |
| Out of the mouth of babes. | 21. 16.—Ps. 8. 2. |
| The stone which the builders rejected. | 21. 42.—Ps. 118. 22. 23. |
| If a man die, having no children. | 22. 24.—Deut. 25. 5. |
| I am the God of Abraham. | 22. 32.—Ex. 3. 6. |
| Thou shalt love the Lord thy God. | 22. 37.—Deut. 6. 5. |
| Thou shalt love thy neighbour as thyself. | 22. 39.—Lev. 19. 18. |
| The Lord said. . Sit thou on my right hand. | 22. 44.—Ps. 110. 1. |
| Blessed is he that cometh in the name of the Lord. | 23. 39.—Ps. 118. 26. |
| I will smite the shepherd. | 26. 31.—Zech. 13. 7. |
| And they took the thirty pieces of silver. | 27. 9. 10.—Zech. 11. 12, 13. |
| They parted my garments. | 27. 35.—Ps. 22. 18. |
| My God, My God, why hast thou forsaken me? | 27. 46.—Ps. 22. 1. |

### MARK.

| | |
|---|---|
| Behold, I send my messenger. | 1. 2.—Mal. 3. 1. |
| Prepare ye the way of the Lord. | 1. 3.—Is. 40. 3. |
| Seeing they may see, and not perceive. | 4. 12.—Is. 6. 9, 10. |
| This people honoureth me with their lips. | 7. 6, 7.—Is. 29. 13. |
| Honour thy father and mother. | 7. 10.—Ex. 20. 12. |
| Whoso curseth father or mother. | 7. 10.—Ex. 21. 17. |
| Where their worm dieth not. | 9. 44.—Is. 66. 24. |
| God made them male and female. | 10. 6.—Gen. 1, 27. |
| They twain shall be one flesh. | 10. 7, 8.—Gen. 2. 24. |
| Do not commit adultery, Do not kill. | 10. 19.—Ex. 20. 13, |
| Hosanna; blessed is he that cometh. | 11. 9.—Ps. 118. 26. |
| My house shall be called the house of prayer. | 11. 17.—Is. 56. 7. |
| Ye have made it a den of thieves. | 11. 17.—Jer. 7. 11. |
| The stone which the builders rejected. | 12. 10, 11.—Ps. 118. 22, 33. |
| If a man's brother die, and leave no children. | 12. 19.—Deut. 25. 5. |
| I am the God of Abraham. | 12. 26.—Ex. 3. 6. |
| The Lord our God is one Lord. | 12. 29.—Deut. 6. 4. |
| Thou shalt love the Lord thy God. | 12. 30.—Deut. 6. 5. |
| Thou shalt love thy neighbour. | 12. 31.—Lev. 19. 18. |
| The Lord said to my Lord, Sit thou on my right hand. | 12. 36.—Ps. 110. 1. |
| I will smite the shepherd. | 14. 27.—Zech. 13. 7. |
| He was numbered with the transgressors. | 15. 28.—Is. 53. 12. |
| My God, My God, why hast thou forsaken me. | 15. 34.—Ps. 22. 1. |

### LUKE.

| | |
|---|---|
| To turn the hearts of the fathers. | 1. 17.—Mal. 4. 6. |
| Every male that openeth the womb. | 2. 23.—Ex. 13. 2, 12. |
| A pair of turtledoves, &c. | 2. 24.—Lev. 12. 8. |
| The voice of one crying in the wilderness. | 3. 4-6.—Is. 40. 3-5. |
| Man shall not live by bread alone. | 4. 4.—Deut. 8. 3. |
| Thou shalt worship the Lord thy God. | 4. 8.—Deut. 6. 13. |
| He shall give his angels charge over thee. | 4. 10, 11.—Ps. 91, [11, 12. |
| Thou shalt not tempt the Lord thy God. | 4. 12.—Deut. 6. 16. |
| The Spirit of the Lord is upon me. | 4. 18, 19.—Is. 61. 1, [2; 58. 6. |
| Behold, I send my messenger. | 7. 27.—Mal. 3. 1. |
| That seeing they might not see. | 8. 10.—Is. 6. 9. |
| Thou shalt love the Lord thy God. | 10. 27.—Deut. 6. 5. [Lev. 19, 18. |
| And thy neighbour as thyself. | 10. 27.—Lev. 19. 18. |

| | |
|---|---|
| Blessed is he that cometh in the name of the Lord. | 13. 35.—Ps. 118. 26. |
| Do not commit adultery, Do not kill. | 18. 20.—Ex. 20. 12-16. |
| My house is the house of prayer. | 19. 46.—Is. 56. 7. |
| Ye have made it a den of thieves. | 19, 46.—Jer. 7. 11. |
| The stone which the builders rejected. | 20. 17.—Ps. 118. 22, 23. |
| If a man's brother die having a wife. | 20. 28.—Deut. 25. 5, 6. |
| The Lord said unto my Lord, Sit thou on my right hand. | 20. 42, 43.—Ps. 110. 1. |
| He was reckoned among the transgressors. | 22. 37.—Is. 53. 12. |
| Say to the mountains, Fall on us. | 23. 30.—Hos. 10. 8. |
| Into thy hands I commend my spirit. | 23. 46.—Ps. 31. 5. |

JOHN.

| | |
|---|---|
| The voice of one crying in the wilderness. | 1. 23.—Is. 40. 3. |
| The zeal of thine house hath eaten me up. | 2. 17.—Ps. 69. 9. |
| He gave them bread from heaven. | 6. 31.—Ps. 78. 24. |
| They shall be all taught of God. | 6. 45.—Is. 54. 13. |
| I said, Ye are gods. | 10. 34.—Ps. 82. 6. |
| Hosanna: Blessed is the King of Israel. | 12. 13.—Ps. 118. 26. |
| Fear not, daughter of Zion; Behold thy King. | 12. 15.—Zech. 9. 9. |
| Lord, who hath believed our report? | 12. 38.—Is. 53. 1. |
| He hath blinded their eyes. | 12. 40.—Is. 6. 9, 10. |
| He that eateth bread with me. | 13. 18.—Ps. 41. 9. |
| They hated me without a cause. | 15. 25.—Ps. 35. 19, 69. 4. |
| They parted my raiment among them. | 19. 24.—Ps. 22. 18. |
| A bone of him shall not be broken. | 19. 36.—Ex. 12. 46; Ps. 34. 20. |
| They shall look on him whom they pierced. | 19. 37.—Zech. 12. 10 |

# Legal Dictionary

# Legal Dictionary

## ABBREVIATIONS

**Abb.** Abbreviation.
**Coll.** Colloquial.
**E., Eng.** England.
**f.** female.
**m.** male
**pl.** plural.
**sing.** singular.
**U.S.** United States.

### A

**A.A.C.** (Abb.) Anno ante Christum (year before Christ).
**A Aver et Tener.** To have and to hold.
**Ab., Abr.** (Abb.). Abridgment.
**A.B.A.** (Abb.). American Bar Association.
**A.C.** (Abb.). Anno Christi (year of Christ).
**A/C.** Account.
**Abactor.** One who steals cattle in large numbers.
**Ab Agendo.** Unable to act.
**Abandon.** To relinquish rights to an object; to desert, forsake or surrender.
**Abandum.** That which is proscribed or abandoned.
**Ab Ante, Ab Antecedented.** In advance.
**Ab Antiquo.** From antiquity.
**Abarnare.** Exposure of a secret crime.
**Abatare.** To abate, put an end to, reduce.
**Abate.** Quash, beat down, destroy; to nullify, lessen or diminish.
**Abatement.** Reduction, decrease or diminution.
**Abatement of Taxes.** Reduction of a tax either before or after payment.
**Abatement, Plea in.** Dilatory plea in procedural law asking for abatement of the action for reasons not connected with the controversy.
**Abator.** One who occupies property without right of title, before the heir.
**Ab Auctoritate.** From authority.
**Abatuda.** Anything diminished.
**Abbettator.** One who abets.
**Abbey.** Monastery or convent.
**Abbot.** Spiritual superior of a monastery.
**Abbreviate.** An abstract.
**Abbreviate of Adjudication.** An abstract of judgment.
**Abbrochment.** Forestalling the market by buying up commodities wholesale for selling at retail.
**Abdication.** Voluntary surrender of rights to the throne by a reigning monarch.
**Abdicatio Tutelae.** Resignation of a guardian.
**Abditorium.** Hiding place for valuables.
**Abduction.** Taking away of wife, child or ward by fraud, persuasion or violence.
**Abearance.** Behavior.
**Aberemurder.** Intentional murder.
**Abet.** To aid or assist.
**Abettare.** To aid or abet.
**Abettor.** One who instigates a crime; one who incites another to commit a crime, thus becoming a principal.
**Ab Extra.** From without.
**Abeyance.** In expectation, remembrance and contemplation of law.
**Abiactus, Aviactus.** Grandson.
**Abide.** To obey, comply with, execute, conform to.
**Abide by.** To stand by the consequences of one's actions.
**Abiding Conviction.** A definite conviction of the guilt of the accused.
**Abiding Faith.** Belief in the guilt of the accused which remains in the minds of the jury.
**Abigeat.** Crime of stealing cattle.
**Abigeatore.** Cattle thief.
**Ability.** In legal terminology, usually refers to pecuniary ability.
**Ab Inconvenienti.** From hardship.
**Ab Initio.** From the beginning.
**Ab Intestate.** From a decedent who dies without leaving a will.
**Ab Invito.** Against one's will.
**Ab Irato.** Done in anger.
**Abishering.** Freedom and exemptions from forfeitures and amercements.
**Abjudicate.** To deprive by a judgment of the court.
**Abjuration.** Renunciation or abandonment by oath.
**Abjuration of Allegiance.** Declaration by a naturalized citizen of U.S., whereby he renounces and abjures all fidelities and allegiances which he owes to any foreign power.
**Abjure.** Renounce.
**Able.** Legally qualified.
**Able-Bodied.** Absence of visible defects which incapacitate a person from performing ordinary duties.
**Able Buyer.** One who has actual cash to meet payment.
**Able Customer.** One has the actual cash to make required payment and who can meet deferred payments.
**Able Seaman.** Grade of merchant seaman.
**Ablocate.** To lease.
**Ablocatio.** Leasing for money.
**Abnegation.** Renunciation; self-denial; abjuration.
**Abode.** Place of residence.
**Ab Olim.** Formerly.
**Abolish.** To annul.
**Abolitio Legis.** Repeal of a law.
**Abolition.** Leave to stop a prosecution; annihilation or extinguishment of anything.
**Abomination.** Anything wicked.
**Aborage.** Collision of vessels.
**Aborticide.** Killing of the fetus in the uterus.
**Abortifacient.** Any drug used to produce an abortion.
**Abortion.** Expulsion of a human fetus before time of viability.
**Abortionist.** One who practices the crime of producing abortions.
**Abortive Trial.** A trial in which no verdict is reached due to no fault of the parties.
**Abortus.** An aborted fetus.
**About.** Near in time, quality, quantity or degree.
**Above Cited.** Quoted before.
**Abridge.** Reduce or cut down.
**Abridgment.** Condensation of the work of another.
**Abridgment of Damages.** Reduction of damages by order of court.
**Abrogate.** Annul.
**Abrogatio Legis.** Repeal of a law.
**Abrogation.** Repeal of a law; an annulment.
**Abscond.** Clandestine withdrawal of one's self in order to avoid legal proceedings.
**Absent.** Being away from.
**Absentee.** One who is not present at his usual place of residence.
**Absente Reo.** In the absence of the defendant.
**Absolute.** Free from condition or qualification; perfect.
**Absolute Assignment.** Outright transfer of title.
**Absolute Contraband.** Munitions and primary material of war.

**Absolute Control.** Freedom to act without hindrance or direction by others.
**Absolute Law.** Immutable law of nature.
**Absolute Majority.** More than half of those entitled to vote on an issue.
**Absolutely.** Wholly; completely.
**Absolution.** A judgment of the court declaring a defendant innocent.
**Absolutism.** Principle of absolute power in the sovereign.
**Absolve.** To free or release from obligation, debt or responsibility.
**Absolvitor.** Acquittal.
**Absque.** Without.
**Abstract.** An abridgment; a complete history in abbreviated form of the case as found in the record.
**Abstract Instruction.** Instructions to the jury amounting to an abstract statement of the law.
**Abstract of Title.** An historical summary to the title of land covering all conveyances, transfers and other facts of title, together with all such facts appearing of record as may impair the title.
**Abstract Question.** Moot question.
**Absurdity.** That which is physically and morally impossible.
**Abuse.** To injure, misuse; excessive or improper use of a legal right.
**Abut.** To reach, to touch.
**Abutments.** Parts of a bridge which support the extremes.
**Abuttals.** Boundaries at which lands touch neighboring lands.
**Abutting Owners.** Owners whose lands touch a highway or other public place.
**Accede.** To attain an office or dignity.
**Acceleration.** Shortening of the time within which a future estate is to vest.
**Accept.** To agree by some overt act to the terms of a contract.
**Acceptance.** The actual or implied taking and receiving of that which is offered.
**Acceptance of Bill of Exchange.** A promise to pay the bill when due.
**Acceptare.** To accept.
**Access.** The power of approaching; (sometimes used in reference to the right of sexual intercourse between husband and wife).
**Accessary.** See Accessory.
**Accession.** The addition by natural or artificial means of new matter to one's property.
**Accessorial.** Pertaining to a principal thing.
**Accessory.** One who encourages or incites another to commit a crime.
**Accessory after the Fact.** One who, knowing a crime to have been committed, aids or assists the felon in any way.
**Accessory before the Fact.** One who contributes to the commission of a crime by will, although not present at the time of the act.
**Accident.** An unforseen, unplanned, unexpected event.
**Accidental.** Happening by chance.
**Accommodation.** Acceptance of an obligation without consideration.
**Accommodation Paper.** A loan without restriction as to its use.
**Accommodation Party.** One who has signed a negotiable instrument as maker, drawer, acceptor or indorser, without receiving value therefor, and for the purpose of lending his name to some other party.
**Accomplice.** One who knowingly and willingly participates in the planning or carrying out of a crime.
**Accord.** Mutual agreement.
**Account.** To render a detailed statement of a transaction; the statement so rendered.
**Accountable.** Liable; responsible.
**Accountable Receipt.** Acknowledgment of the receipt of money or property by a person who is under obligation to account therefor.
**Accountant.** One skilled in keeping books or accounts.
**Account Book.** Ledger in which is kept the record of commercial transactions.
**Account Current.** A running account.
**Accounts Receivable.** Amounts owing to a person on an open account.
**Accouple.** To unite or marry.
**Accredit.** To acknowledge a diplomatic agent and give him credentials and rank accordingly.
**Accredulitare.** To clear a person of an offense by oath.
**Accrescere.** To increase or grow.
**Accretion.** Addition to land by natural causes, such as deposits.
**Accroach.** The exercising of power without due authority.
**Accrocher.** To delay.
**Accrual of Cause of Action.** The coming into existence of the right to sue.
**Accrue.** To increase or augment.
**Accumulated Surplus.** Funds which a corporation has in excess of its capital and liabilities.
**Accumulations.** Requirement that profits from a fund or trust be invested for a definite period.
**Accumulative.** Additional; one thing added to another.
**Accumulative Judgment.** A judgment which is to take effect upon the expiration of a prior judgment.
**Accusation.** A complaint; formal charge.
**Accuse.** To formally charge one of being guilty of a punishable offense.
**Accused.** The defendant in a criminal case.
**Accustomed.** Habitual; used.
**Acknowledge.** To own, avow or admit; to confess.
**Acknowledgment.** Admission or confirmation.
**A Consiliis.** Of counsel.
**Acquaintance.** Familiar knowledge.
**Acquest.** Property acquired other than by inheritance.
**Acquiesce.** Consent implied by silence.
**Acquit.** To set free; to discharge from an accusation.
**Acquittal.** Verdict of not guilty; release from pecuniary liability.
**Acquittance.** Written confirmation of payment of money due.
**Acre.** 160 square rods of land.
**Ac si.** As if.
**Act.** That which is done; a statute.
**Acting.** Substituting; taking the place of temporarily.
**Actio.** An action or suit; a right or cause of action.
**Act of God.** An act caused solely by violence of nature.
**Actionize.** To use.
**Acts of Congress.** Statutes passed by the Congress of the U.S. as opposed to resolutions or other Congressional acts.
**Actual.** Real; substantial.
**Actum.** A deed; something done.
**A.D.** (Abb.). Anno Domini (from the Year of our Lord).
**A Dato.** From the date.
**Ad Colligendum.** Of an administrator or trustee, for collecting.
**Ad Culpam.** Until misbehavior.
**Ad Damnum.** To the damage.
**Ad Exitum.** At issue.
**Addicere.** To condemn.
**Addict.** One who is in the habit of using alcohol or narcotics to the point of losing self-control.
**Addiction.** Formal commission of a prisoner by judicial sentence.
**Ad Diem.** At the day.
**Addition.** That which is added to another thing; extension; increase.
**Adduce.** To bring forward; to present.
**Adeem.** To revoke.
**Ademption.** Revocation of a legacy by act of the testator.
**Adeo.** So far.
**Adeprimes.** In the first place.
**Adequate.** Sufficient.
**Aderere.** In arrears.
**Adesse.** To be present.
**Adeu.** Without day, implying dismissal of a matter from court.
**Adevant.** Before.
**Ad Exitum.** At the end.
**Ad Extremum.** Finally.
**Ad Faciendum.** To make or do.
**Ad Fidem.** An allegiance.
**Adhibere.** To apply, employ or use.
**Adhibere Diligentiam.** To employ care.
**Adhibere Vim.** To use force.
**Ad Hoc.** To this.
**Ad Hominem.** To the man; personal.
**Ad Idem.** To the same thing (agreement).
**Adieu.** See Adeu.

**Ad Illud.** To that.
**Adimere.** To remove.
**Ad Infinitum.** Without end.
**Ad Inquirendum.** To inquire.
**Ad Instantiam.** At the instance.
**Ad Interim.** Meanwhile.
**Adiratus.** Lost.
**Aditus.** An approach; right of entrance.
**Adjacent.** Lying near but not necessarily touching.
**Adjectire.** To summon to court.
**Adjective Law.** Rules of procedure and court organization.
**Adjoining.** Contiguous as opposed to adjacent.
**Adjourn.** To postpone or defer.
**Adjourned Term.** A term of court continued at a later date.
**Adjudge.** To make a judicial decision.
**Adjudicare.** To deprive by judgment of a court.
**Adjudication.** A judgment or decree in a cause.
**Adjunct.** Something added to another.
**Adjunction.** Uniting of a thing belonging to one person to that of another.
**Adjuration.** Placing under oath.
**Adjurnare.** To adjourn.
**Adjust.** To settle.
**Adjuster.** One who ascertains the extent of a claim.
**Adjustment.** Arrangement or settlement, usually applied to insurance.
**Adjutor.** Helper or assistant.
**Ad Largum.** At large.
**Ad Libitum.** At pleasure.
**Ad Litem.** During the interim of an action or proceeding, e.g. appointment of a guardian for a minor.
**Ad Majus.** For the greater.
**Ad Manum.** At hand.
**Admeasurement.** Assignment or apportionment of one's share; a division.
**Ad Melius Inquirendum.** Writ of further inquiry.
**Adminicular.** Corroborative.
**Administer.** To take charge, manage or conduct.
**Administration.** The managing or conduct of anything.
**Administration of Estates.** Supervision by an executor or administrator.
**Administrative Law.** That branch of law which deals with the activities of executive or administrative agencies.
**Administrator** (m.) **Administratrix** (f.). One given the authority by court to settle the estate of a decedent.
**Administrator ad Colligendum.** One appointed to temporarily preserve the estate of a decedent.
**Admiralty.** Court having jurisdiction in civil and criminal maritime cases.
**Admissable Evidence.** Evidence which, in the opinion of the court, may properly be introduced.
**Admission.** Acknowledgment made by a party of the existence of certain facts; recognition of attorneys and counsellors as officers of the court.
**Ad Modum.** In such a way.
**Asmonition.** Cautionary statement by judge in his advice to the accused or his charge to the jury.
**Admr.** (Abb.). Administrator.
**Adnihilare.** To annul.
**Adolescence.** Period between childhood and maturity (f. 12–21; m. 14–25).
**Adopt.** To accept as one's own that which was not so originally.
**Adoptivus.** Adopted child or parent.
**Adpromissor.** A surety.
**Adquieto.** Payment.
**Adquirere.** To acquire.
**Adrectare.** To corrent.
**Ad Respondendum.** To respond.
**Adrogation.** Adoption of a child who has not reached the age of puberty.
**Adscendentes.** Ancestors.
**Adscriptus.** Annexed by writing.
**Ad Sectam.** At the suit of.
**Adsecurare.** To assure; to insure.
**Adsessores.** Judges appointed as substitutes or advisors to the regular magistrates.
**Adsignare.** To seal.
**Ad Testari.** To attest.
**Adult.** One who has attained the legal age, usually twenty-one years.
**Adulter.** One who corrupts.
**Adultera.** Adulteress.
**Adulterated.** Impure.
**Adulteration.** Mixing of a foreign substance with something pure, usually applied to food and beverage sold to the public.
**Adulterine.** Issue of adulterous intercourse.
**Adultery.** Voluntary sexual intercourse of a married person with one other than his or her spouse.
**Ad Valorem.** According to the value.
**Advance.** Rendering before due.
**Advancement.** Money or property given by a parent to child. not required by law, which represents part of the whole of the recipient's share of the donor's estate.
**Advances.** Payments made before they are due.
**Advena.** Unnaturalized alien.
**Adverse.** Opposed.
**Adverse Possession.** Open occupation of real property without title or permission of the person holding title.
**Advertise.** To give public notice.
**Advertisement.** Publication of information designed to attract public attention.
**Advice.** Counsel.
**Advise.** To give an opinion.
**Advisedly.** With deliberation.
**Advisement.** Consideration.
**Advisory.** By way of suggestion; not imperative.
**Advisory Opinion.** Opinion rendered by a court to a lower court or legislature, being neither binding nor decisive.
**Advocare.** To defend.
**Advocate.** One who pleads the cause of another in court.
**Aequitas.** Equity.
**Aequum et Bonum.** Fair and good.
**Aequus.** Equal.
**Aeronautics.** The science of flying in the air.
**Aes Alienum.** Debt.
**Aesnecia.** See Esnecy.
**Aesthetic.** Relating to that which is beautiful or in good taste.
**Aetas.** Age.
**Affect.** To act upon.
**Affected with a Public Interest.** Phrase applied to a business whose activities are deemed vital to the public and, therefore, its use in effect granted to the public.
**Affectus.** Intention.
**Affere.** To appraise.
**Affiance.** To engage to marry.
**Affiant.** One who makes an affidavit.
**Affidare.** To swear.
**Affidavit.** Voluntary oath in writing sworn to before one authorized to administer oaths or affirmations.
**Affilare.** To put on record.
**Affile.** To file.
**Affiliate.** The state of being close to, allied with or united.
**Affines.** Relatives by marriage.
**Affinity.** Relationship of a husband to the blood relatives of his wife and vice versa.
**Affirm.** To ratify; confirm; reassert.
**Affirmation.** A solemn and formal declaration, substituted for a sworn statement by one whose beliefs will not permit him to swear.
**Affirmative.** That which declares as a fact.
**Affirmative Defense.** One which, assuming the complaint to be true, sets up new matter constituting a defense outside the ordinary scope of denial, e.g. Act of God.
**Affirmative Statute.** Mandatory rather than prohibitive.
**Affix.** Fasten or attack physically.
**Affliction.** Distriss of mind or body.
**Afforare.** To set a price.
**Afforce.** To add to; to increase.
**Afforer.** To assess.
**Afforest.** To make into a forest, in a legal sense.
**Affranchir, Affranchise.** To free.
**Affray.** Fighting of two or more persons in a public place.
**Affreightment.** Contract for the hiring of a ship.
**Affront.** Insult.
**Aforesaid.** Already said or mentioned.
**Aforethought.** Premeditated.
**A Fortiori.** With greater reason.
**After.** Later; succeeding.

**After-Acquired.** Acquired after a certain date or event.
**After-Born Child.** Child born after the testator has made his will.
**Against.** Adverse to.
**Age.** Number of years which a person has lived.
**Agency.** Contract by which one person acts for or represents another by the latter's authority.
**Agenda.** Things to be done.
**Agenesia.** Sexual impotence.
**Agens.** Manager; plaintiff.
**Agent.** One intrusted with another's business and given the authority to act for him.
**Age of Consent.** Age at which a statue presumes a girl capable of agreeing to the sexual act.
**Aggravated Assault.** Malicious assault.
**Aggrevation.** Any circumstance which increases the gravity of an offense.
**Aggregate.** Entire number.
**Aggressor.** One who initiates hostile force.
**Aggrieved.** Injured.
**Aggrieved Party.** Party whose rights have been damaged by a judgement.
**Agiser.** To lie.
**Agist.** To feed or pasture another's cattle for a fee.
**Agitator.** One who stirs up.
**Agnates, Agnation.** Relationship by the father's side.
**Agnise.** To acknowledge, admit.
**Agnomen.** Nickname.
**Agony.** Violent physical or mental distress.
**Agrarian.** Pertaining to land.
**A Gratia.** By gratuity.
**Agree.** To give mutual assent.
**Agricultural.** Pertaining to agriculture.
**Agriculture.** Science of cultivating the ground.
**Aid.** Support; help; assist.
**Aid and Abet.** To assist in the commission of a crime.
**Ail.** Grandfather.
**Ailment.** Indisposition of body or mind.
**Air.** Atmosphere. See Easement of Light and Air.
**Aisne, Eigne.** Eldest or first born.
**A Latere.** Collaterally.
**Alcholic Liquor.** Beverage, which when drunk excessively, will produce intoxication.
**Alcoholism.** Addiction to the excessive use of intoxicating beverages.
**Alderman.** Judicial or administrative magistrate.
**Ale.** An intoxicating liquor made from an infusion of malt by fermentation.
**Alea.** Game of chance.
**Aleator.** Gambler.
**Aleatory.** Uncertain.
**Aleager.** To redress.
**Alia.** Other things.
**Aliamenta.** Freedom of passage.
**Alias.** Otherwise or also known as.
**Alias Writ.** A second writ.
**Alibi.** Usually a defense plea stating at the time of the crime the accused was elsewhere or in another place.
**Alien.** Foreigner; one who is not a citizen.
**Alien.** To transfer.
**Alienable.** Lawfully transferable.
**Alien and Sedition Laws.** Four acts of Federalist Congress in July, 1798 imposing penalties on conspirators against government measures.
**Alienate.** To transfer title to property; to cause one to lose affection for a spouse.
**Alienation of Affections.** Causing a spouse to lose the society, affections and assistance of his marital partner.
**Alien Enemy.** One owing allegiance to an enemy state.
**Alieni Generis.** Of another kind.
**Alieni Juris.** Subject to the authority of another person.
**Alimenta.** Necessities of Life.
**Alimony.** The support of a wife by her husband required by order of the court on divorce or separation.
**Alimony in Gross.** Alimony awarded in a gross sum rather than periodically.
**Aliquid.** Something; somewhat.
**Aliquis.** Anyone.
**Aliquot.** Fraction of the whole.
**Aliter.** Otherwise.
**Aliud Examen.** Another trial.
**Aliunde.** From another source.
**All and Singular.** Without exception.
**Allegation.** An assertion, declaration or statement of fact in a pleading.
**Allege.** To assert or charge; to make an allegation.
**Alleged.** Claimed; asserted; charged.
**Allegiare.** To defend one's self.
**Alliance.** Banding together.
**Allocate.** To allot.
**Allocatur.** It is allowed.
**Allocution.** The inquiry made of a defendent after a verdict of guilty as to whether he has anything to say as to why the court should not pronounce sentence against him.
**Alloidal.** Free.
**Allot.** To distribute.
**Allotment.** Share, portion.
**Allow.** To approve.
**Allowance.** Authorization of payments in legal proceedings; a deduction; average payment; portion allowed.
**Alloy.** In coining, a cheaper metal mixed with gold or silver the amount being fixed by law.
**Alms.** Charitable donations.
**Also.** Besides; in addition; likewise.
**Alter.** To change.
**Alteration.** Making different.
**Altercation.** Angry dispute.
**Alter Ego.** Second self.
**Alternatim.** Interchangeably.
**Alternative.** Choice between two things or acts.
**Alteruter.** One of two; either.
**A.M.** (Abb). Ante meridem; before noon.
**Amalgemation.** Consolidation.
**Ambassador.** Diplomatic agent of a country representing that country in a foreign state.
**Ambulance Chaser.** Lawyer who makes a practice of following up accidents, inducing injured persons to sue for damages.
**Ambiguity.** Doubleness of meaning; doubtful.
**Ambit.** Boundary line.
**Amblotic.** Anything used to produce an abortion.
**Ambulatory.** Revocable; movable.
**Ameliorations.** Improvements.
**Amenable.** Subject to answer to the law.
**Amend.** To change for the better.
**Amendment.** Addition or change.
**Amends.** Satisfaction for an injury.
**Amentia.** Insanity.
**Amercement.** Pecuniary fine assessed by a court.
**American.** Pertaining to the Western Hemisphere.
**Ami.** Friend.
**Amicable.** Friendly.
**Amicable Action.** Action brought to court with the agreement of all parties to obtain a decision on doubtful questions of law.
**Amicus Curiae.** Friend of the court.
**Amittere.** To lose.
**Amnesia.** Loss of memory.
**Amnesty.** An act of government granting general pardon to certain classes of people for past, usually political, crimes.
**Amortize.** To provide for the paying off of a liability; to transfer lands in mortmain.
**Amotion.** Eviction.
**Ampliare.** To enlarge.
**Anaesthetic.** Any drug producing insensibility to pain.
**Anagraph.** Inventory.
**Analytical Jurisprudence.** A system of jurisprudence based upon analysis of existing legal theories and institutions rather than principles of right and equity.
**Anarchy.** Absence of government.
**A Nativitate.** From birth.
**Anatocism.** Compound interest.
**Ancestor.** One from whom a person is lineally descended.
**Ancient Deeds.** Deeds more than 30 years old.
**Ancillary.** Auxiliary; aiding.
**Androgyne.** Hermaphrodite.
**Andromania.** Nymphomania.
**Androphonomania.** Homicidal insanity.
**Anew.** Over again.
**Anguish.** Extreme pain of body or mind.
**Aniens.** Null; void.
**Animal.** Irrational, sentient being.
**Animo.** With intent.
**Annex.** To attach to.

**Anni Nubiles.** The age of marriage for a girl.
**Anno Domini.** In the year of our Lord.
**Annoyance.** Nuisance; vexation.
**Annual.** Of or pertaining to a year.
**Annuity.** Yearly payment of money to another in fee for life or years.
**Annul.** To make void.
**Annus.** A year.
**Annuum.** Yearly pension.
**Anomalous.** Deviating from the common rule.
**Anonymous.** Nameless.
**Answer.** A plea by which a defendent resists an allegation of facts.
**Ante.** Before.
**Ante Bellum.** Before the war.
**Antecedent.** Prior in point of time.
**Antedate.** To date an instrument prior to the date of actual execution.
**Ante Litem.** Before suit.
**Antestari.** To subpoena a witness.
**Antichresis.** A contract pledging real property as security for a debt.
**Anticipation.** The performance of an act before its proper time.
**Antigraphy.** A copy of a document.
**Antinomy.** Real or apparent inconsistency in a statute.
**Antitrust Act.** Statute forbidding the formation of monopolies.
**Apertus.** Open; unsealed.
**Apex.** Highest point.
**Apex Juris.** Legal subtlety.
**Apocal, Apocha.** Receipt for payment.
**Apograph.** Copy of a document.
**Apographa, Apographia.** An inventory.
**A Posteriori.** Reasoning from the effect to the cause.
**App.** (Abb.). Appellate.
**App. Ct.** (Abb.). Appellate Court.
**Apparent.** Obvious, e.g. apparent danger or obvious danger.
**Apparent Authority.** Authority which a principal permits his agent to exercise or which he holds the agent out as possessing.
**Appeal.** Complaint to a superior court of an injustice or error committed by an inferior court.
**Appearance.** To be before a court as a party to a suit.
**Appellant.** One who files an appeal.
**Appellate Court.** Court which reviews appeals from inferior courts.
**Appellee.** One against whom a cause is appealed.
**Appellor.** One who prosecutes an appeal.
**Append.** To add or attach.
**Appendant.** Any right or thing of a subordinate nature which is permanently connected to a more worthy right or thing.
**Appertaining.** Belonging to.
**Applicant.** Petitioner.
**Application.** Request; petition.
**Appoint.** Designate; name; assign.
**Appointee.** One appointed for a particular office or duties.
**Apportion.** To divide proportionally.
**Appraise, Appraisal.** Estimation of value of property.
**Appreciate.** To increase in value.
**Apprehend.** To place in legal custody.
**Approbate and Reprobate.** To accept one part and reject another.
**Appropriate.** To make a thing one's own; to set apart for a particular use.
**Approval.** Sanction of a thing or an act of another.
**Appurtenances.** That which belongs to another thing, but which has not always belonged to it, e.g. addition of a barn to a piece of land.
**A Priori.** Reasoning from the cause to the effect.
**Apt.** Fit.
**Apud.** With; at; among.
**Aqua.** Water.
**Aqua Ductus.** Right to run water through the land of another.
**A Quo.** From which.
**Arable Land.** Land suitable for plowing.
**Arbiter.** Arbitrator; one chosen to settle a controversy.
**Arbitrarily, Arbitrary.** Unreasonably.
**Arbitration.** Submission of a disputed matter to private, unofficial persons.
**Arbitrator.** One chosen to settle disputes.
**Archetype.** Original document.
**Archives.** Repository of public records; the records themselves.
**A Retro.** In arrears.
**Argument.** A course of reasoning intended to establish belief.
**Aristocracy.** A government ruled by a class of men.
**Arma.** Arms; weapons.
**Arraign.** To summon a person to court to answer charges made against him in an indictment.
**Array.** The whole body of persons summoned for jury duty at the same time.
**Arrears.** Money past due in payment.
**Arrest.** To detain one by legal authority.
**Arret.** Decree of a court.
**Arson.** The felony of wilfully and maliciously burning the house of another.
**Article.** One of a series of clauses.
**Articles.** System of rules; a statute; written contract containing terms of agreement.
**Articles of Agreement.** A written contract.
**Articulately.** Article by article.
**Artifice.** Fraud; trick.
**Artificial.** See Artificial Person.
**Artificial Boundary.** Boundary erected by man.
**Artificial Person.** An entity created by law and given the attributes of a natural person, e.g. a corporation.
**Ascendants.** Ancestors.
**Ascertain.** To make certain; to fix.
**Asexualization.** Sterilization.
**Ask.** To petition.
**Aspersion.** Defamation; criticism.
**Asportation.** Carrying away of personal property from one place to another.
**Assailant.** An aggressor.
**Assassination.** Murder committed for hire alone; murder committed by stealth or surprise.
**Assault.** An intentional, unlawful attempt to inflict immediate injury on another.
**Assault and Battery.** Assault is the attempt to strike; battery is the actual striking.
**Assay.** A test by chemical analysis of the purity of metals.
**Assecurare.** To give security.
**Assembly.** A meeting of a group of persons at the same place: persons so gathered.
**Assent.** Compliance.
**Assess.** To estimate the value of.
**Assessed Value.** Value of property as estimated for taxation.
**Assets.** Property which can be made available for the payment of debts.
**Assign.** To make over to another.
**Assignation House.** Brothel.
**Assignment.** The transfer of property or right from one person to another.
**Assignor.** Maker of an assignment.
**Assist.** To help or aid.
**Assize.** A jury or inquest; a court; a statute; a tax.
**Association.** A group of persons who have joined together to act for a common end.
**Assume.** To undertake; engage; promise.
**Assumpsit.** An agreement of service or payment to another, not under seal.
**Assurance.** Pledge, guaranty, surety; insurance.
**Assurer.** Insurer or underwriter.
**Astipulate.** To agree.
**Asylum.** A sanctuary.
**At Arms Length.** Careful to avoid being imposed upon.
**At Bar.** Before the court.
**Atheist.** One who denies the existence of a Supreme Being.
**At Maturity.** At the due date.
**Atrocity.** Conduct outrageously criminal or cruel.
**Attach.** To take, bind or fasten.
**Attaché.** One attached to a foreign legation or embassy.
**Attachment.** The taking of persons or property into legal custody by virtue of a writ, summons or other judicial order.
**Attainder.** The forfeiture of civil rights which occurs when a person is convicted of a capital offense.
**Attendant Term.** A mortgage or lease, the

term of which has extended beyond the date of expiration.
**Attest.** To witness.
**Attested Copy.** A copy of a document which has been witnessed.
**Attorn.** To turn over a transfer to another.
**Attorney.** One authorized to act in the place of another to manage his matters of law.
**Attorney General.** Head of the Department of Justice.
**Attorney at Large.** Formerly an attorney who practiced in all courts.
**Auction.** Public sale of land or goods to the highest bidder.
**Audience.** A hearing.
**Audit.** To examine and verify figures and computations.
**Auditor.** Public agent who examines and verifys the accounts of those who have received and expended public money by lawful authority.
**Aunt.** Sister of one's father or mother.
**Authentic.** Properly attested.
**Author.** One who originates a literary work.
**Authorize.** To empower.
**Autocracy.** Self-government.
**Autograph.** One's handwriting.
**Autopsy.** The dissection of a dead body in order to ascertain cause of death.
**Autre.** Other.
**Autrefois.** Formerly.
**Auxiliary.** Collateral; incidental; aiding.
**Avails.** The proceeds or profits of a sale.
**Aviation.** The art of flying.
**A Vinculo Matrimonii.** From the bonds of matrimony.
**Avoid.** To annul.
**Avoucher.** To call upon a warrantor of lands to fulfill his undertaking.
**Avow.** To acknowledge and justify an act which has been committed.
**Award.** The decision of an arbitrator.
**Award.** To grant.
**Axiom.** Self-evident truth.

## B

**Baby Act.** Plea of infancy as a defense.
**Bachelor of Laws.** Degree granted to one graduating from law school.
**Back-Bond.** Indemnity bond.
**Backing.** Indorsement.
**Bad.** Evil.
**Bad Debt.** One which is uncollectable.
**Bail.** Release of a person from legal custody after security has been given for his appearance to answer the charge against him at the designated time; the security thus given.
**Bail Bond.** Bond issued on behalf of a person who has been arrested in connection with a civil suit.
**Bailiff.** Keeper; protector; guardian; sheriff's deputy.
**Bailiwick.** District under jurisdiction of a bailiff.
**Ban.** Public edict or proclamation.
**Bandit.** Outlaw.
**Bane.** Malefactor.
**Banishment.** A penalty which consists of compelling a citizen to leave a city, place or country for a specific period of time or life.
**Bank.** An institution empowered to receive deposits of money, to discount negotiable paper and to lend money.
**Bank Note.** A promissory note issued by a bank payable to bearer on demand.
**Bankruptcy.** The state or condition of one who is unable to pay a debt without respect to time.
**Bannitus.** One who has been banished.
**Banns of Marriage.** Public announcement of an intended marriage.
**Bar.** Collective term for those persons licensed to practice law; obstruction to a suit or action.
**Bar Association.** Society composed of members of the bar.
**Bargain.** A contract or agreement between two parties, the one to sell goods or lands, the other to purchase them.
**Barratry.** Frequently stirring up quarrels and suits.
**Barrenness.** Sterility.
**Barrister.** An advocate learned in the law who is permitted to plead at the bar of England.
**Barter.** A contact whereby one commodity is exchanged for another.
**Base Coin.** Adulterated or alloyed coin.
**Bastard.** An illegitimate child.
**Battery.** Any unlawful touching or physical violence inflected on the person of another without his consent.
**Bawd.** One who procures opportunities for persons of opposite sexes to cohabit in an illicit manner.
**Bawdy House.** House of prostitution.
**Beach.** The area of land between ordinary high and low water marks.
**Bearer.** One in actual possession of a negotiable paper payable to bearer.
**Beast.** An animal.
**Beat.** To strike with successive blows; a subdivision of a county; a voting precinct.
**Beaupleader.** Fair pleading; a writ to prohibit exacting a fine for bad pleading.
**Beget.** To procreate.
**Beggar.** One who solicits alms.
**Begin.** To originate.
**Behalf.** Benefit; defense; in the name of.
**Behavior.** Manner of conducting one's self.
**Belief.** Conviction of the truth of a proposition existing in the mind and based on argument, persuasion or proof.
**Belligerent.** A nation, power or state engaged in war.
**Belong.** To be the property of.
**Bench.** A court; judges of the court.
**Bench Warrant.** Process issued by the court for the apprehension of a person either for contempt of court or a criminal offense.
**Bene.** Well; properly.
**Beneficiary.** One entitled to profit, benefit or advantage from a contract or estate; one to whom a policy of insurance is payable.
**Benevolent Associations.** Charitable societies.
**Bequeath.** To devise; to give personal property to another by last will and testament.
**Bequest.** Legacy.
**Beseech.** To implore.
**Besot.** To stupefy.
**Best Evidence.** Primary evidence.
**Bestiality.** Sexual relations between man and beast.
**Bestow.** To give or confer.
**Betrayal.** Wrongful disclosure of a professional secret, e.g. a doctor violating a patient's trust.
**Betroth(al).** To enter into an agreement of marriage.
**Betterment.** Improvement to real property.
**Bias.** Preconceived opinion.
**Bicameral.** Two-house legislature.
**Biennium.** Period of two years.
**Bigamy.** The crime of wilfully and knowingly contracting a second marriage when already legally married to another.
**Big with Child.** Pregnant.
**Bilan.** Balance sheet.
**Bilateral Contract.** A contract in which both parties involve l are bound to fill reciprocal obligations.
**Bilinguis.** Of two languages.
**Bill.** A proposed statute; first pleading in an equity case; an itemized statement.
**Bill of Exchange.** A draft.
**Bill of Indictment.** That paper which contains a criminal charge and which is submitted to the grand jury to be acted upon by them.
**Bill of Lading.** A document evidencing a contract for the carriage and delivery of the listed goods.
**Bill of Rights.** First ten amendments to the Constitution of the U.S. and that part of each state constitution which guarantees certain rights of the citizen.
**Bill of Sale.** A written instrument professing to pass title to personal property.
**Bind.** To obligate.
**Binder.** A memorandum of an agreement issued by an insurer to give temporary protection pending the investigation and issuance of a formal policy.
**Bind Over.** To hold on bail for trial.
**Bipartite.** In two parts; in duplicate; a document involving two parties.
**B.L.** (Abb). Bachelor of Laws.
**Blackleg.** Swindler; strike breaker.
**Blacklist.** A list of persons who are to be

refused employment circulated among various employers.
**Blackmail.** Extortion of money by threat.
**Blanc.** White; having no marks or writing.
**Blank.** Having no marks or writing.
**Blank Indorsement.** Indorsement of a negotiable instrument by merely writing the name of the indorsee on the back.
**Blasarius.** An incendiary; arsonist.
**Blasphemy.** Malicious revilement of God or religion.
**Blind Tiger.** Place where intoxicants are sold contrary to the law.
**Blockade.** The prevention by a belligerent of access to enemy territory.
**Blood.** Kindred; family relationship.
**Blood Money.** The price paid for causing a person's death.
**Blue Laws.** Laws restricting Sunday sports, entertainment or trade.
**Blue Sky Law.** Popular name for statutes regulating investment companies.
**Board.** An official or representative body entrusted with executive duties and acting for and in the interest of others.
**Bodily.** Pertaining to or concerning the body.
**Bodily Injury.** Any physical or corporeal injury intentionally inflicted by another.
**Body.** Person; corporation; board.
**Body Corporate.** Corporation.
**Body Snatching.** Secret and unlawful disinterment of corpses.
**Bogus.** Spurious.
**Bona.** Goods; chattels.
**Bona Fide.** In good faith.
**Bond.** Long-term promissory note with stipulated interest issued by a corporation or the government; and obligation under seal.
**Bondage.** Slavery or serfdom.
**Bondsman.** A surety.
**Bonus.** Additional payment beyond the stipulated compensation.
**Boodle.** Money paid as a bribe for corrupt official action.
**Bookmaker.** Professional betting man.
**Bookmaking.** The registering of bets on any contest.
**Bootlegger.** One who sells liquor unlawfully.
**Booty.** Goods captured on land from the enemy during war.
**Born.** Brought forth.
**Borrow.** To take or receive any article of value from another with the intention of returning it or its equivalent.
**Bottom.** National registry of a vessel.
**Bottomry.** A mortgage made by the owner of a ship as security for a loan given, to make a voyage possible.
**Bought and Sold Notes.** Memoranda made by brokers employed to buy and sell goods.
**Boundary.** Markings which divide two contiguous estates.
**Bounty.** A gratuity given by the government to encourage the doing of a special act.
**Boy.** Male child from birth to the age of puberty.
**Boycott.** To combine against a named person or business in a policy of nonintercourse.
**Brand.** A mark made with a hot iron.
**Breach.** A break; a violation.
**Breach of Close.** Trespassing.
**Breach of Promise of Marriage.** Violation of an agreement to marry each other made between a man and woman.
**Break.** To separate; to violate.
**Breve.** A writ or brief.
**Bribe.** A reward or gift offered with a view to pervert the judgement of a person in a position of trust.
**Brief.** A written document; a written statement of the points of law made by the parties upon an appeal.
**Bring Suit.** Initiation of legal proceedings.
**Broker.** A person employed in the purchase and sale of goods or other commodities for a principal.
**Brokerage.** Broker's commission.
**Brothel.** House of prostitution.
**Bruise.** Temporary contusion.
**Bubble.** Dishonest investment scheme.
**Budget.** Statement of estimated receipts and expenditures.
**Buggery.** Carnal copulation against nature.
**Bull.** Papal edict.
**Bulla.** Seals used by the Roman emperors.
**Bulletin.** An official notice concerning public affairs.
**Bullion.** Uncoined gold or silver.
**Burden of Proof.** The necessity of affirmatively proving a fact in dispute by a quantum of evidence as the law demands.
**Burglary.** Breaking into and entering a dwelling by night with the intention of committing a felony.
**Burkism.** Murder committed by smothering the victim for the purpose of selling the body to be used for dissection.
**Burn.** To destroy by fire.
**Bursar.** College treasurer.
**Business Month.** A month of 30 days.
**Buttals.** End boundary lines.
**By-Laws.** Rules and regulations adopted by a corporation for its government.
**By-Product.** A secondary product of value.
**Bystander.** One who is present, but not taking part.

## C

**©.** A designation accompanied by the mark of a copywrite proprietor to give notice to the public of the existence of the copyright.
**Cabal.** An intrigue.
**Cabinet.** Advisory board or council.
**Cadavar.** Corpse.
**Cadit.** Ends.
**Cadit Qusestio.** No further dispute.
**Caesarian Operation.** The delivery of a fetus by cutting above the pelvis.
**Caeterus.** Other.
**Cahoots.** Partnership.
**Calaboose.** A city jail.
**Calcea, Calcetum.** Causeway.
**Calculated.** Adapted by design.
**Calendar.** List of cases to be tried before a court during each term.
**Calends.** First day of the month.
**Call.** A notice of a meeting to be held by the board of directors or stockholders of a corporation; demand for payment.
**Calling.** Vocation.
**Calumnia.** Calumny or false charge.
**Calumniatrix.** Female slanderer.
**Calumny.** Libel.
**Camarage.** Rent paid for storage.
**Cambio.** Exchange.
**Campus.** A field.
**Cancellaria.** Chancery.
**Cancellation.** Abandonment of contract.
**Candidate.** One who seeks election to an office.
**Cannot.** Not able to.
**Canon.** A law; church officer.
**Canonic.** Pertaining to a canon or church law.
**Canon Law.** Roman ecclesiastical law.
**Canvass.** Examination of election returns.
**Capable.** Competent.
**Capacity.** The ability to understand the nature and effect of one's acts.
**Capax.** Capable.
**Capita.** Heads.
**Capital.** Assets of a corporation used to conduct corporate business and derive profits.
**Capital Gains Tax.** A tax on gains from the exchange or sale of capital assets.
**Capital Punishment.** Punishment by death.
**Capital Stock.** Money which a corporation regards as the basis for prosecution of business, such funds raised by subscription, divided into shares.
**Capitation.** Poll tax.
**Capitulate.** Conditional surrender.
**Caption.** Heading or title of a document.
**Captives.** Prisoners.
**Capture.** The seizing of property from one of two belligerents by the other.
**Caput.** Head; chief.
**Carat.** Weight of four grains.
**Carcelage.** Prison fee.
**Care.** Freedom from negligence.
**Careless.** Negligent.
**Cargo.** The load of a vessel.
**Carnal Knowledge.** Sexual intercourse.
**Carrier.** One who transports persons or merchandise.

**Carte Blanche.** Unrestricted authority to act.
**Case.** Law suit.
**Case Law.** Law as laid down in the decisions of the courts.
**Case System.** Study of law by analysis of cases and decisions.
**Cash.** Ready money.
**Cash and Carry.** Payment of goods and immediate transportation thereof by the purchaser.
**Cassare.** To make void.
**Cast.** To defeat at law.
**Castigation.** Chastisement.
**Casting Vote.** The deciding vote cast by the presiding officer of a legislative body, who ordinarily does not vote.
**Casual.** Occasional; incidental.
**Casualty.** An unavoidable accident.
**Casus.** Case.
**Casus Major.** Extraordinary casualty.
**Catalla.** Chattels.
**Caucus.** Political meeting, usually secret.
**Causa.** Cause; reason.
**Causa Proxima.** The proximate cause.
**Causa Sine Qua Non.** A cause without which the effect in question could not have happened.
**Cause.** To be the cause of; an action or suit.
**Cause Celebre.** Celebrated case or cause.
**Cautio.** Caution; care; security.
**Caveat.** Let him beware.
**Caveat Emptor.** Let the buyer beware, maxim of common law that the buyer purchases at his own risk.
**Caveat to Will.** Demand that the will be produced and probated in open court.
**C.C.P.** (Abb.). Court of Common Pleas.
**Cease.** Stop.
**Cede.** To yield.
**Celation.** Concealment of pregnancy.
**Celebrate.** To solemnize.
**Celibacy.** State of being unmarried.
**Censorship.** Governmental restrictions over publications and public performances.
**Census.** The official counting of people of a state, nation or district.
**Cent** (Abb.). One hundred.
**Centum.** One hundred.
**Cepi.** I have taken.
**Certain.** Free from doubt.
**Certificate.** A signed statement testifying to the truth of the facts therein stated.
**Certified Check.** A check which is recognized and accepted by the bank drawn upon.
**Certified Copy.** A copy certified as authentic by the officer to whose custody the original is entrusted.
**Certified Public Accountant.** One who has received a certificate qualifying him to practice as a public accountant.
**Cessare.** To cease or stop.
**Cession.** A yielding or giving up.
**Cessionary.** Assignee.
**Cessment.** Assessment or tax.
**Cf.** (Abb.). Compare.
**C.H.** (Abb.). Courthouse.
**Chairman.** Presiding officer of a deliberative body.
**Challenge.** To object.
**Chamberlain.** Treasurer.
**Chambers.** Private office of a judge.
**Champerty and Maintenance.** The act of inducing another party to bring a civil action with or without an agreement to receive part of the resultant profits.
**Chancellor.** Judge of a court of chancery.
**Chancellor, Lord High.** Head of the judicial system of Great Britain.
**Chancery.** Equity.
**Character.** Qualities of an individual.
**Charge.** To impose a duty, obligation or lien; to accuse; to instruct a jury; the duty, obligation, lien, or accusation itself.
**Chargé d'Affaires.** Diplomatic representative of inferior rank.
**Charitable Institution.** An institution supported by public expense or charity.
**Charitable Trust.** One established for the public and intended to carry out benevolent, educational or similar purposes.
**Charity.** Anything done to relieve poverty, advance religion or education or any activity beneficial to the community at large.
**Charlatan.** Cheat.
**Charta.** Charter or deed.
**Charter.** An instrument emanating from the sovereign power which grants certain rights and privileges.
**Chastity.** Virtuous abstinence from sexual intercourse.
**Chattels.** Articles or personal property.
**Chauvinism.** Excessive nationalism.
**Cheat.** Defraud.
**Check.** A negotiable instrument drawn on a bank by a depositor, which is payed by the bank to the payee in the check.
**Checkoff.** A method of paying union dues whereby the employer deducts the dues from wages.
**Cheque.** Check.
**Chicane.** Fraud.
**Chief.** Head.
**Chief Justice.** Presiding justice of the court.
**Chief Magistrate.** Head of the executive department of government of a nation, state or municipal corporation.
**Children.** Progeny; between infancy and youth.
**Chirograph.** An indenture.
**Chit.** A promissory note.
**Chose in Action.** Any claim that can be pleaded in law or equity.
**Chronic.** Of long duration.
**Cicatrix.** Scar.
**C.I.F.** (Add.). Cost, freight and insurance.
**Cipher.** Secret, disguised message.
**Circa.** About; around.
**Circuit.** Division of territory where justice is usually administered by a travelling judge.
**Circuit Courts.** Courts presided over by a judge or judges at different places in the same district.
**Circuity of Action.** Indirect method of adjustment by unnecessary litigation.
**Circular Notes.** Letters of credit.
**Circumduction.** Annulment; cancellation.
**Circumstantial Evidence.** Indirect proof.
**Circumstantibus.** Bystanders in the court.
**Circumvention.** Fraud.
**Cite.** To summon to appear.
**Citizen.** In the U. S., one born therein or naturalized as such; a member of the political community, sharing in its rights, privileges and duties.
**City.** A large community, organized as a chartered municipal corporation.
**Civil.** Pertaining to a city or state.
**Civil Action.** A legal proceeding brought to enforce a civil right.
**Civilian.** One versed in civil law; a private citizen.
**Civil Death.** The state of one who loses all civil rights.
**Civil Law.** The system of law derived from the Roman Law as codified by Justinian.
**Civil Rights.** Rights which an individual possesses and which may not be impaired by the government.
**Civil Service.** The system providing for government employment on the basis of competitive examinations.
**Civil Year.** Solar year.
**C.J.** (Abb.). Chief Justice.
**Claim.** Assertion of a right to have money paid.
**Claimant.** One who makes a claim.
**Clamor.** Outcry.
**Clandestine.** Secret.
**Classify.** Group, by similar character.
**Clause.** Single paragraph or subdivision of a written instrument.
**Clausum.** Land enclosed by a boundary.
**Clean.** Irreproachable; innocent of fraud.
**Clear.** To acquit.
**Clear.** Obvious.
**Clergy.** Ministers of religion.
**Clericus.** Clergyman; clerk.
**Clerk.** Clergyman; one employed to keep accounts or records; shop or store assistant.
**Client.** One who engages an attorney to represent him or give legal advice.
**Close.** An enclosed piece of land; closed.
**Closed Shop.** One which employs only union members.
**Closed Seasons.** Periods in which certain game and fish may not be taken.

**Cloth.** Clergy.
**Co.** (Abb.). Company; county.
**Coagent.** Accomplice.
**Coalition.** Alliance.
**Coast.** Seaboard of a country.
**C.O.D.** (Abb.). Cash on delivery.
**Code.** System of law.
**Codicil.** Amendment of or addition to a will.
**Coercion.** Compulsion; compel by force.
**Coexecutors.** Persons appointed to act jointly in the administration of a testator's estate.
**Cognati.** Blood relations on the mother's side.
**Cognizance.** Recognition.
**Cognomen.** Family name.
**Cognosce.** To adjudge.
**Cohabit.** To live together as man and wife.
**Coitus.** Sexual intercourse.
**Cojudices.** Associate judges.
**Collateral.** Blood relationship other than lineal; additional security besides principal.
**Collateral Attack.** Attack on a prior judicial act in an independent action.
**Collateral Facts.** Facts not directly connected with the facts in issue.
**Collateral Security.** See Collateral.
**Collect.** To gather together.
**Collection Agency.** An agency which collects claims for others.
**Collegium.** An assembly or society; corporation.
**Collide.** To strike against.
**Collision.** A striking against.
**Colloquium.** Term used in an action for slander which alleges the words used were spoken of the plaintiff.
**Collusion.** An agreement to defraud another of his rights by forms of law or to secure an object forbidden by law.
**Color.** Deceptive appearance.
**Combat.** To fight.
**Combustible.** Inflammable.
**Come.** To appear in court.
**Comfort.** To give security from want.
**Comitas.** Courtesy.
**Comitatus.** County.
**Comity.** Courtesy; respect; recognition by states and nations of each other's laws.
**Comme.** As.
**Commerce.** Exchange of goods.
**Commerce Clause.** Article 1, Section 8, Clause 3 of the U.S. Constitution giving Congress power to regulate commerce with foreign powers, the states and the Indians.
**Commercial Law.** Law which relates to commercial enterprise.
**Commercial Paper.** Negotiable instruments.
**Commission.** Authority; writ; authorization.
**Commissioner.** A subordinate administrative Federal, State or Municipal official.
**Commitment.** The order of a court sending a person to an institution.
**Committee.** A group of persons appointed by a court to perform some public service or duty.
**Committitur.** An order naming the committed.
**Commodate.** Gratuitous loan.
**Commodity.** Any movable or tangible thing that is ordinarily used in trade.
**Common.** A right of incorporeal hereditament which one man may have in the land of another.
**Common Assurances.** Title deeds.
**Common Barratry.** Habitual instigation of quarrels and suits.
**Common Carrier.** One engaged in the transportation of freight or passengers for hire.
**Common Highway.** Public highway.
**Common Intent.** Concerted action or intention of several persons to commit a crime.
**Common Law.** General and ordinary law of a country or community; unwritten law founded on immemorial usage and natural justice and reason.
**Common-Law Action.** A civil suit.
**Common-Law Marriage.** Marriage by contract without religious or other ceremony.
**Common Nuisance.** Public danger.
**Common Recovery.** Fictitious suit used to break entails.
**Common Seal.** Corporation seal.
**Commons.** Public grounds.
**Common Schools.** Public schools.
**Commonwealth.** Public; state; body politic.
**Commorancy.** Temporary residence.
**Commorant.** Staying or dwelling.
**Commotion.** Disturbance.
**Commune.** Small town.
**Communia.** Common or ordinary.
**Communism.** A system of social organization in which goods are held in common.
**Community.** Neighborhood.
**Community Property.** Property owned jointly by husband and wife.
**Commutation of Sentence.** Reduction of a punishment of a person to a lesser one.
**Compact.** Agreement or contract.
**Compact.** Closely united.
**Company.** A union of two or more persons for the purpose of carrying on a business.
**Compass.** To plot.
**Compel.** To force.
**Compensation.** Indemnification.
**Competency.** Admissibility of evidence.
**Competent.** Legally qualified; capable.
**Complainant.** One who brings suit.
**Complaint.** Formal allegation or charge.
**Complete.** Full; entire.
**Complete Jurisdiction.** Power to hear and determine the cause, as well as to enforce judgment.
**Complice.** Accomplice.
**Complot.** To conspire.
**Comply.** To accomodate.
**Composition.** A settlement between a debtor and his creditors.
**Compos Mentis.** Sound of mind.
**Compound.** To compromise.
**Compound Interest.** Interest upon interest.
**Compromise.** To settle a controversy, usually out of court.
**Compulsion.** Duress.
**Compulsory.** Involuntary.
**Compurgator.** Character witness.
**Conceal.** To keep secret.
**Conception.** The beginning of pregnancy.
**Concession.** A grant, ordinarily that of specific privileges by a government.
**Concessor.** Grantor.
**Concisely.** Briefly.
**Conclude.** To make a final statement.
**Conclusion.** Termination.
**Conclusive.** Decisive.
**Concord.** Settlement.
**Concordant.** Agreement.
**Concubine.** A woman who cohabits with a man to whom she is not married.
**Concur.** To agree.
**Concurrent.** Running together.
**Concussion.** Extortion; a jolt to the brain.
**Condemn.** To find guilty; to appropriate private property for public use legally.
**Condition.** A provision in a written instrument which is to take effect upon the occurence of an uncertain contingency.
**Conduct Money.** Expense money paid to a witness.
**Confederacy.** Conspiracy.
**Confederation.** An agreement between two or more governments.
**Confession.** An admission by a person charged with a crime.
**Confidence.** Trust.
**Confidence Game.** Obtaining of money or property by means of fraud.
**Confidence Man.** Swindler.
**Confidential Relation.** Fiduciary relation.
**Confirmation.** Affirmation.
**Confiscation.** Seizure of property by the government.
**Confrontation.** Bringing a witness face to face with the accused in a criminal action.
**Confusion.** Blending, mingling; merger.
**Congé.** Permission to depart.
**Congeable.** Lawful.
**Congress.** The legislature of the U.S., consisting of the Senate and House of Representatives.
**Conjecture.** Guess.
**Conjoints.** Husband and wife.
**Conjugal.** Pertaining to the marital state.
**Conjunct.** Concurrent; joint.
**Conjurator.** Conspirator.
**Connubium.** Marriage.
**Consanguinity.** Blood relationship.
**Conscience.** Faculty of discriminating between right and wrong.
**Conscionable.** According to the principles of honesty.
**Conseil.** Counsel; advice.

**Consent.** An agreement.
**Conserve.** To save from loss.
**Consider.** To examine.
**Consign.** To entrust goods for care or sale.
**Consignee.** One to whom goods are consigned.
**Consignor.** One who sends goods to another by consignment.
**Consolidate.** To unit into one.
**Consolidation.** Merger of two or more corporations.
**Consortium.** Right of conjugal fellowship of husband and wife.
**Conspiracy.** An agreement between two or more persons to do an unlawful deed.
**Constate.** To prove.
**Constituent.** The principal of an agent.
**Constituere.** To appoint.
**Constitution.** Fundamental law of a state or nation.
**Constitutional Law.** In the U.S., the body of law created by applying and interpreting the the Constitution of the U.S. and its amendments.
**Constitutional Right.** Any right guaranteed under the constitution.
**Constraint.** Duress.
**Construction.** Interpretation.
**Constructive.** Presumed.
**Construe.** To put together.
**Constuprate.** To violate or rape.
**Consuetudinary.** Customary.
**Consuetudo.** Custom.
**Consul.** A government official, residing in a foreign country, who watches over the interests of his countrymen.
**Consultation.** A writ which returns an action from a temporal to an ecclesiastical court; conference between the counsels.
**Consummate.** To complete.
**Consummation of Marriage.** Sexual intercourse between two parties after marriage.
**Contango.** Broker's charge.
**Contemner.** One who commits a contempt.
**Contempt.** Disregard or disobedience of a public authority.
**Contempt of Court.** Disobedience of a lawful order of a court or any act which hinders the proper functioning of a court or impairs its standing in the community.
**Conterminous.** Adjoining.
**Contested.** Opposed.
**Contiguous.** In close proximity.
**Continens.** Joined together.
**Contingent.** Dependent upon an uncertainty.
**Continuing.** Enduring.
**Continuous.** Uninterrupted.
**Contra.** Against.
**Contraband.** Goods brought in or out of a country against its laws.
**Contracausator.** Criminal.
**Contract.** A promissory agreement by which two or more legally competent persons to do or not to do a particular thing.
**Contract Clause.** Article 1, Section 10, of the U.S. Constitution prohibiting a State from imparing the obligation of contracts.
**Contradict.** To disprove.
**Contradiction in Terms.** An expression which contradicts itself.
**Contrafactio.** Counterfeiting.
**Contrary.** Against.
**Contrary to Law.** Illegal.
**Contravention.** Violation of a law.
**Contribute.** To give assistance or aid.
**Contributory.** Additional.
**Contrivance.** Disguise.
**Control.** To restrain or regulate.
**Controller.** One who has charge of the financial affairs of a public or private corporation.
**Controvert.** To dispute.
**Contumacy.** Contemptuous disobedience of a court order.
**Contumax.** Outlaw.
**Contusion.** Bruise.
**Contutor.** Joint guardian.
**Conus.** Known.
**Convenable.** Suitable.
**Convene.** To file suit.
**Conventio.** Agreement.
**Conventional.** Based upon agreement.
**Conventus.** Contract.
**Conveyance.** The transfer of title to property from one person to another.
**Convicium.** An insult; slander.
**Convict.** To condemn after judicial investigation.
**Convict.** One found guilty of a crime.
**Convocation.** Assembly.
**Copia.** Copy; opportunity.
**Copia Vera.** True copy.
**Copr.** (Abb). Copyright.
**Copula.** Sexual intercourse.
**Copulative Condition.** A condition, the happening of which, depends on several events.
**Copy.** Transcript of an original.
**Copyright.** The exclusive right to print, multiply, publish and sell a literary, artistic or technical work.
**Coram.** Before.
**Coram Judice.** Within the court's jurisdiction.
**Coram Nobis.** Before us.
**Coram Non Judice.** Before one who is not a judge.
**Co-Respondent.** One accused in a divorce suit of having committed adultery with the defendent.
**Corner.** A plan to gain control of the available supply of a commodity.
**Corona.** The crown.
**Coronor.** An officer whose duty it is to make inquiry into the cause and circumstances of any death occurring within his territory caused by violence or marks of suspicion.
**Corporal.** Bodily.
**Corporal Punishment.** Physical punishment.
**Corporate.** Belonging to a corporation.
**Corporate Franchise.** Right to conduct business and exist as a corporation.
**Corporation.** An artifical being or institution created under the law consisting of a group of members associated in a common enterprise, and having a personality distinct from those men who compose it.
**Corporator.** A member of a corporation.
**Corporeal.** Tangible.
**Corpse.** Dead body of a human being.
**Corpus.** Body; an aggregate or mass.
**Corpus Delicti.** Remains of a committed crime.
**Corpus Juris.** Body of law.
**Corpus Juris Civilis.** Body of civil law.
**Correi.** Co-stipulators.
**Corroborate.** To add credibility by evidence.
**Corrupt.** Tainted; debased; depraved.
**Cosmus.** Clean.
**Cost.** Expense.
**Cost Price.** Price actually paid for goods.
**Co-Stipulator.** Joint promisor.
**Costs.** Expenses incurred in a lawsuit.
**Council.** Legislative department of a city or other municipal corporation.
**Counsel.** Attorney.
**Counselor at Law.** An attorney who has been admitted to the bar.
**Count.** Statement of a cause of action.
**Countenance.** Credit; credibility.
**Counter.** Against.
**Counterfeit.** To copy or imitate without authority, with the intent to deceive or to defraud by passing the imitation for the genuine.
**Countermand.** To revoke on order given.
**Counterpart.** Corresponding part of an instrument; a copy.
**Countersign.** To verify by an additional signature.
**County.** An administrative unit of the state created and organized by statute for judicial and political purposes.
**County Court.** A court whose jurisdiction is limited to a specific county.
**Coupons.** Interest and dividend certificates.
**Court.** Persons appointed under law and vested with the power of rendering judgments, issuing writs and hearing appeals.
**Court Martial.** A military court for the enforcement of military regulations.
**Court of Admiralty.** A court having jurisdiction in maritime cases.
**Court of Appeals.** A court in which appeals from a lower court are heard.
**Court of Conscience.** Court of equity.
**Court of Convocation.** Ecclesiastical Court.
**Court of First Instance.** Court of Primary Jurisdiction.
**Court of General Jurisdiction.** Court of record.
**Court of Inquiry.** A military court which conducts preliminary investigations of charges.
**Court of Law.** A duly constituted tribunal administering the laws of the state or nation.
**Cousin German.** First Cousin.
**Coustom.** Duty; toll.

**Covenant.** In the wide sense, a contract in general.
**Covenant, Action of.** Common law action for breach of contract under seal; a written agreement executed by a sealing and delivery.
**Covert.** Covered; protected.
**Coverture.** Status of a married woman.
**Covin.** Fraud.
**Cozen.** To cheat.
**C.P.A.** (Abb.). Certified Public Accountant.
**Crassus.** Gross; large.
**Crave.** To demand.
**Crazy.** Deranged.
**Creance.** Collateral security.
**Creancer.** Creditor.
**Create.** To bring into existence.
**Credibility.** Worthiness of belief.
**Credible Witness.** Competent witness.
**Credit.** Capacity of being trusted.
**Creditor.** One to whom a debt is owing.
**Creed.** Formal declaration of religious belief.
**Cremation.** Reduction of a corpse to ashes.
**Crepusculum.** Twilight.
**Crime.** An act in violation of penal law.
**Crime Against Nature.** Unnatural sexual relations.
**Crimen.** Crime.
**Crimen Furti.** Larceny.
**Crimen Incendii.** Arson.
**Crimen Majestatis.** Treason.
**Criminal.** Pertaining to a crime; one who commits a crime.
**Criminal Homicide.** Unlawful taking of another's life in such a manner that he dies within a year and one day from the time the mortal wound is inflicted.
**Cross Action; Cross Bill.** An action or bill against the plaintiff or codefendent, set up in the defendent's plea or answer.
**Cross Examination.** Examination of a witness by an adverse party.
**Crude.** Raw or unfinished.
**Cruelty.** Abusive treatment.
**Ct.** (Abb.). Cent; cents.
**C.T.A.** (Abb). Cum Testamento Annexo, with the will annexed.
**Cts.** (Abb.). Cents.
**Cui Bono.** For whose good.
**Cul.** Guilty.
**Cul de Sac.** A street open at only one end.
**Culpa.** Fault, guilt.
**Culpable.** Guilty.
**Culprit.** One indicted for a criminal offense.
**Cum.** With.
**Cum Grano Salis.** With a grain of salt.
**Cum Testamento Annexo.** With the will annexed.
**Cumulative.** Additional; two things which are to be added together.
**Cura.** Care.
**Curator.** Guardian.
**Curatrix.** Female guardian.
**Curia.** A court.
**Curia Admiralitatis.** Court of Admiralty.
**Curia Comitatus.** County court.
**Currency.** Money.
**Current.** Running; now in transit.
**Currere.** To run.
**Cursing.** Profane swearing.
**Curtis.** A yard.
**Custa.** Costs.
**Custodes Pacis.** Justices of the Peace.
**Custody.** Control without ownership of personal property.
**Custom.** A rule of conduct which has been followed for an appreciable time and which has become compulsory.
**Customs.** Tariffs and duties on imported and exported merchandise.
**Custum.** Cost.
**Cut.** A wound inflicted by a sharp instrument.
**Cwt.** (Abb.). Hundredweight.

## D

**Dactylography.** Scientific study of fingerprints.
**Daily.** Every day.
**Damage.** Injury; loss.
**Damages.** Compensation from an injury.
**Damn.** To condemn.
**Damnify.** To injure.
**Danger.** Jeopardy; peril.
**Danism.** Usurious loan.
**Dans.** In.
**Day.** Time between two successive midnights.
**Daysman.** An arbiter.
**D.C.** (Abb.). District Court.
**De.** From; of.
**Dead.** Without life.
**Dead body.** Corpse.
**Death.** Cessation of life.
**Death, Civil.** Loss of all legal personality.
**Debase.** To adulterate.
**Debauchery.** Excessive indulgence in sensual pleasures.
**De Bene Esse.** Done conditionally.
**Debenture.** Various kinds of evidence of debt issued by a corporation.
**Debit.** That which is due and owing.
**Debita Fundi.** A debt secured by real estate.
**Debt.** An obligation to pay money.
**Debt, National.** The total sum of obligations owing by the government.
**Debtor.** One who owes money.
**Decalogue.** The Ten Commandments.
**Decapitation.** Beheading.
**Deceased.** A dead person.
**Decedent.** A deceased person who has left property.
**Deceit.** Fraud.
**Decency.** Propriety of action.
**Decision.** Judgment of a court.
**Declaration.** First pleading of a plaintiff in which the cause of action is set out; an admission or statement subsequently used as evidence in the trial of an action.
**Darbies.** Handcuffs.
**Darrein.** Last.
**Darrein Continuance.** The last continuance.
**Date.** The calendar designation of the date on which an instrument is issued or signed.
**Dation.** A giving or transfer in the fulfillment of a duty.
**Daughter.** An immediate female descendant.
**Daughter-in-Law.** The wife of one's son.
**Declaration of Intention.** A declaration by an alien of his intention to become a citizen.
**Declaratory.** Explanatory.
**Declare.** To make known, manifest or clear.
**Decline.** To object.
**Decollation.** Decapitation.
**Decoy.** To entice or lure.
**Decree.** The judgment of a court of equity.
**Decree Absolvitor.** A decree acquitting.
**Decree Nisi.** A provisional decree to be made absolute on motion unless cause be shown against it.
**Decretal Order.** Order of a court of chancery.
**Decry.** To discredit.
**Dedbaba.** Homicide.
**Dedicate.** To set private property aside for public use.
**Deed.** An instrument conveying real property.
**Deeded.** Transferred by deed.
**Deed Poll.** A deed made by one party only.
**Deem.** To judge.
**De Facto.** In fact, as opposed to "by right."
**De Facto Government.** One which maintains itself by force.
**Defalcation.** Misappropriation of moneys.
**Defamation.** Libel, slander and any wilful injury to the reputation of another.
**Default.** Fault; neglect.
**Defeasance, Defeasible.** Subject to be revoked upon the happening of a future event or a conditional limitation.
**Defect.** Deficiency.
**Defend.** To oppose a claim or action.
**Defendant.** One being sued in a civil action or prosecuted in a criminal action.
**Defeneration.** Usurious rate of interest when lending money.
**Defense.** Facts in answer to a complaint.
**Defiance.** Open contempt.
**Defile.** To debauch.
**Definitive.** Final; final determination of an issue in controversy.
**Defloration.** Seduction.
**Deforce.** To withhold wrongfully, particularly land.
**Defraud.** To cheat.
**Degradation.** A deprivation of dignity.
**Degree.** Grade of crime according to its gravity; one's rank in life.
**Dehors.** Outside of; unconnected with.
**Dejeration.** An oath.
**De Jure.** By right or lawful authority.
**Delate.** To accuse.
**Delay.** To retard.

**Delegate.** A representative; to transfer a power to another.
**Delete.** To erase.
**Deleterious.** Morally or physically harmful.
**Deliberate.** Carefully considered; willful.
**Delict.** Wrong; injury; tort.
**Delinquency.** Failure of duty.
**Delinquent Taxes.** Taxes which are owing.
**Delivery.** Transfer of movable and personal property or deed to another.
**De Lunatico Inquirendo.** A writ issued for an inquisition of lunacy.
**De Malo.** Of sickness.
**Demand.** To claim as on's due.
**Demand Instrument or Note.** Note payable on demand.
**Demens.** One who is demented.
**Demented, Dementia.** Of unsound mind.
**Demesne.** Domain; held in one's own right.
**Demi.** One-half.
**Demi-Sangue.** Half-blood.
**Demise.** To convey an estate for years or life.
**Demise and Redemise.** Mutual leasing of the same land, the owner paying a nominal rental.
**Democracy.** A form of government which is directed according to the will of the people.
**Demonstration.** Description or designation.
**Demonstrative Legacy.** A legacy which designates a particular source out of which it is to be paid.
**Demurrage.** Monetary allowance; a compensation for the detention of a vessel by the freighter beyond the time allowed.
**Demurrer.** A denial by the defendant that the allegations of the declaration, even if true, would legally constitute a cause for action.
**Denial.** A refusal.
**Denumeration.** Act of present payment.
**Department.** Division of public administration.
**Departure.** A deviation in the course of pleading, except by a formal amendment.
**Depeculation.** Embezzlement of public moneys.
**Dependent.** One who relies on another.
**De Pone.** A writ to remove a cause to a superior court.
**Depone.** To give a deposition.
**Deponent.** Witness.
**Deport.** To arrest and remove an alien.
**Depose.** To testify under oath.
**Deposit.** To commit to custody; the goods or money received by the bank.
**Depositary.** An person or institution receiving a deposit.
**Deposition.** An affidavit.
**Depreciation.** Reduction in value.
**Depredation.** Plundering.
**Deprive.** To take.
**Deputy.** The subordinate of a public officer.
**Deranged.** Insane.
**Derelict.** Abandoned.
**Derivative.** Subordinate; secondary.
**Derogation.** Substantial change.
**Descend.** To pass by succession.
**Descent.** Hereditary succession.
**Description.** An account of a particular subject by the narration of its characteristics.
**Desert.** To forsake or abandon.
**De Son Tort.** By his own wrong.
**Desperate.** Hopeless.
**Despite.** Contempt.
**Desponsation.** Betrothal.
**Despot.** Tyrant.
**Destitute.** Impoverished.
**Detachiare.** To seize.
**Detainer.** Wrongful withholding of another's property; restraint without consent.
**Deter.** To discourage or stop by fear.
**Determinable.** Liable to come to an end upon the happening of a future event.
**Determinate.** Ascertained.
**Determine.** To bring to an end.
**Detinue.** A common law action used to recover personal chattels wrongfully held by a person whose original holding was lawful.
**Deternicari.** To discover.
**Deuterogamy.** A valid second marriage after the death of one's former spouse.
**Devest.** Deprive.
**Devisa.** Boundary.
**Devise.** To leave real property by will.
**Devisee.** One to whom real property is willed.
**Devolution.** Legal transfer of property from one person to another.
**Diatim.** Daily.
**Dictator.** An absolute ruler.
**Dictum.** A remark or observation made by a judge in pronouncing an opinion which does not embody the resolution of the court.
**Dies.** Day.
**Dies Datus.** A continuance.
**Dies Dominicus.** The Lord's day.
**Dies Juridicus.** A court day.
**Diet.** A legislative assembly.
**Diffacere.** To multilate.
**Differential Duty.** A duty placed on imported goods in addition to ordinary duty.
**Digamy.** A valid second marraige.
**Digests.** Pandects of Justinian.
**Dilation.** A delay.
**Dilatory Plea.** Any plea which tends to delay.
**Diligence.** Prudence.
**Diligiatus.** An outlaw.
**Dimidia.** Half.
**Diminution.** A lessening.
**Dimittere.** To dismiss.
**Diocese.** The district subject to a bishop.
**Dipsomania.** An uncontrollable desire for intoxicating drinks.
**Direct.** To instruct, advise or request.
**Direct.** Immediate.
**Direct Examination.** The interrogation of a witness by the party who called him.
**Direction.** Command; court's instruction to a jury; the complainant's address to the court.
**Directive.** An order issued by an administrative agency.
**Directly.** Without deviation.
**Director.** A member of the governing board.
**Directory.** That which is advisory or instructive as opposed to obligatory.
**Diriment Impediments.** In canon law, absolute bars to lawful matrimony.
**Disability.** Legal or physical incapacity.
**Disable.** To render incapable of proper and effective action.
**Disabling Statute.** One which limits rights.
**Disadvocare.** To deny.
**Disaffirm.** To repudiate.
**Disagreement.** Difference of opinion.
**Disallow.** To overrule.
**Disalt.** To disable a person.
**Disavow.** To repudiate.
**Disbar.** To deprive a lawyer from practice.
**Discharge.** To release.
**Disclaimer.** Renunciation of any claim or power vested in a person.
**Disclose.** To make known.
**Discontinuance.** Termination of an action on the part of the plaintiff before a decision.
**Disconvenable.** Improper.
**Discount.** A deduction made from a gross sum on any account whatever.
**Discovert.** Not married.
**Discovery.** The ascertainment of that which was previously unknown; the right to demand examination under oath of an adverse party or to have documents produced which will aid the litigant in the presentation.
**Discredit.** To injure a person's credit or reputation.
**Discreetly.** Prudently.
**Discrepancy.** A variance.
**Discretely.** Separately.
**Discretion.** Individual judgment.
**Discrimination.** A failure to treat all equally.
**Discussion.** The right of a surety to demand that the creditor resort to the principal before holding the surety liable.
**Disfranchise.** To deprive of the right to vote.
**Disgrace.** Shame.
**Disguise.** To change the appearance of.
**Dishersion.** Disinheritance.
**Disheritor.** One who disinherits.
**Dishonesty.** Lack of integrity.
**Dishonor.** To refuse to honor a negotiable instrument when duly represented.
**Disincarcerate.** To free from prison.
**Disinhersion.** Disinheriting an heir.
**Disinherit.** The act by which a testator passes over a person who would be his heir.
**Disinter.** To take a body out of the grave.
**Disinterested.** Unprejudiced.
**Disjunctim.** Separately.
**Disjunctive Allegation.** An allegation which expresses a thing alternatively.
**Disloyal.** Unfaithful.
**Dismiss.** To order a discontinuance.
**Disorderly.** In violation of good behavior.
**Disorderly Conduct.** Conduct which constitutes a breach of public peace or morality.

**Disorderly House.** House of prostitution.
**Disparage.** To match unsuitably.
**Dispensation.** An exemption from some laws.
**Dispersonare.** To scandalize.
**Displace.** To remove.
**Dispone.** To grant or convey.
**Dispossess.** To legally exclude from realty.
**Dispossession.** Ouster.
**Disprove.** To refute.
**Disputable.** Refutable.
**Dispute.** Controversy.
**Disqualify.** To incapacitate.
**Disrationare.** To clear one's self.
**Disrepute.** Of bad reputation.
**Disseise.** To deprive of the possession of land.
**Desseisin.** Dispossession.
**Dissent.** To disagree.
**Dissignare.** To break a seal.
**Dissolution.** A breaking up; a termination.
**Dissolve.** To terminate.
**Dissuade.** To persuade one not to perform a positive legal duty.
**Distinct.** Clear.
**Distinctively.** Characteristically.
**Distraited.** Insane.
**Distrahere.** To sell.
**Distrain.** To seize goods and chattels as security for the payment of any obligation.
**Distraint.** Seizure.
**Distress.** The act of distraining.
**Distribute.** To divide in proportion.
**Distributee.** An heir.
**District.** Geographical division.
**District Attorney.** Public prosecutor of the U.S. Government in each of the federal judicial districts; state prosecuting office.
**District Courts.** Courts of limited jurisdiction.
**Districtio.** A distress.
**Disturb.** To throw into confusion.
**Divers.** Various.
**Diverse.** Different.
**Diversion.** Alteration of the natural cause of a thing.
**Diversity.** The plea of a prisoner in a criminal action that he is not the man.
**Divest.** To deprive of a right or title.
**Dividend.** That share of the net profits of a corporation to be distributed to stockholders.
**Dividenda.** An indenture.
**Divinare.** To guess.
**Divine Law.** Law of God.
**Divisional Opinion.** The opinion of a divided court with regard to the matter before it.
**Divorce.** The legal dissolution of a marriage.
**Divorcee.** A women who has been divorced.
**Divulge.** To disclose.
**Do.** I give. Apt word of feoffment and gift.
**Dock.** The space enclosed between two wharves; the place reserved in a court-room for the prisoner.
**Docket.** A formal record of court proceedings.
**Doctrine.** A rule, principle or theory.
**Document.** A written instrument in which is recorded matter which may be used as evidence in court.
**Doe, John.** The fictitious plaintiff in the action of ejectment.
**Doer.** One who performs an act.
**Dole.** A part, share or portion; money or commodities distributed to the public in times of disaster.
**Doli Capax.** Capable of evil intent.
**Dollar.** Legal currency in the U.S.
**Dolus.** Malicious fraud.
**Domain.** The absolute ownership of land.
**Dome.** Sentence.
**Domestic.** Pertaining to the family and household; the internal affairs of a country.
**Domestic Corporation.** One which does business in the state it was organized.
**Domestic Relations Court.** One which settles controversies between members of the family.
**Domicile, Domicil.** A place where a person has his permanent residence.
**Dominant.** Principal.
**Dominate.** To rule.
**Dominion.** Ownership.
**Dominium.** Dominion.
**Dominium Directum.** Direct ownership.
**Dominus.** Lord or master.
**Dominus Litis.** The person in control of any litigation.
**Domitae.** Domesticated.
**Domus.** House.
**Dona.** Gifts.
**Donare.** To give.
**Donate.** To give.
**Donation.** Gift.
**Donor.** One who gives.
**Dormant.** Sleeping; inactive; in abeyance.
**Dormant Claim.** One which is in abeyance.
**Dormant Partner.** Silent partner.
**Dos.** Dowry.
**Dot.** Dowry.
**Dotage.** Mental feebleness due to old age.
**Dote.** To be silly, delirious or insane.
**Double.** Twofold.
**Double Bond.** Bond which carries a penalty for its non-fulfillment.
**Double Damages.** Twice the amount of actual damages, provided for by statute in some cases of injuries due to negligence etc.
**Double Entry.** Bookkeeping system which provides a credit and debit entry.
**Double Jeopardy.** The defense in a criminal action that the defendant has previously been tried for the same offense as now charged.
**Doubt.** Uncertainty of mind.
**Dowager.** A widow assigned her dower.
**Dower.** The legal right of a widow to the real estate of her husband.
**Dowry.** The property which a woman brings to her husband upon marriage.
**Draft.** Bill of exchange.
**Draftsman.** One who prepares a legal document.
**Drawback.** Money collected by customs officials on imported merchandise and remitted if the goods are re-exported.
**Drawee.** One on whom a bill of exchange is drawn.
**Drawer.** One who issues a bill of exchange.
**Droit.** Right; justice.
**Droit Commun.** Common law.
**Droit-Droit.** Double right; title and possession.
**Droit Écrit.** Written law.
**Drunkenness.** The condition of one whose rational actions are affected by alcohol.
**Dry.** In the legal sense, formal or nominal; without profit.
**Dry Law.** A statute prohibiting the manufacture and sale of alcoholic beverages.
**Dry Rent.** A rent reserved without a clause of distress.
**Duarchy.** A government with two rulers.
**Dubitans, Dubitante.** Doubting.
**Due.** Just; proper; owing.
**Due Bill.** A written acknowledgment that a debt is owing.
**Due Care.** Care which a reasonably prudent man would exercise under similar conditions.
**Due Process of Law.** The regular procedure in the administration of the law.
**Duellum.** Trial by battle.
**Dues.** Payments to retain membership.
**Duly.** In due course; according to the law.
**Dumb.** Unable to speak.
**Dumb-Bid.** A previously arranged price below which no bid is accepted by an auctioneer.
**Dummage.** Loose material placed around a ship's cargo to prevent chafing or injury.
**Dummodo.** Provided.
**Dummy.** One who legally acts for another, while posing as acting for himself.
**Duodena.** Jury of twelve men.
**Duplex Querela.** Double complaint.
**Duplicate.** The copy of a document, being equal to the original.
**Duplicity.** The technical fault of using more than one cause of action in a declaration or more than one defense in any subsequent pleading; fraud.
**Durante.** During.
**Durante Absentia.** During absence.
**Durante Vita.** During life.
**Duration.** Limit of time.
**Duress.** Unlawful use of force or fear to compel another to act against his will.
**During.** Throughout the course of.
**Duties.** Customs.
**Duty.** Obligation.
**Dwell.** To inhabit.
**Dwelling-House.** Residence.
**Dying Without Issue.** Dying without a child being born to one.
**Dysnomy.** Bad legislation.
**Dyvour.** A bankrupt.

E

**E, Ex.** From.
**Eagle.** Gold coin of the U.S. worth ten dollars.
**Earmark.** Any mark of identification.
**Earn.** To obtain by labor.
**Earned Income.** Income as a result of labor.
**Earnest.** Something given by a buyer to a seller as a part of the purchase price.
**Earnest Money.** Money paid in anticipation of the fulfillment of some agreement.
**Earnings.** Compensation for services.
**Ear Witness.** One who testifies to what he has heard.
**Ease.** Comfort.
**Easement.** The right to use the realty of another for a specific purpose or to limit the use of someone else's realty.
**Easement of Light and Air.** Right to free enjoyment of unobstructed light and air.
**Easterly.** Due east.
**Eau.** Water.
**Ebb.** The going out of the tides of the sea.
**Ebriety.** Drunkenness.
**Eccentricity.** Personal peculiarity of mind and disposition.
**Ecchymosis.** Bruise.
**Ecclesia.** Assembly.
**Ecclesiastical.** Pertaining to an organized church.
**Ecclesiastical Corporation.** A private corporation organized for religious purposes.
**Economy.** Frugality.
**E Contra.** On the contrary.
**E Converso.** On the other hand.
**Ecumenical.** Universal.
**Edict.** Any proclamation or announcement promulgated by a sovereign of a country and having the force of law.
**Editus.** Issued.
**Education.** Proper moral, physical and intellectual instruction.
**E.E.** (Abb.). Errors excepted.
**Effect.** To do; to produce.
**Effect.** Result.
**Effects.** Personal property.
**Effectus Sequitus Causam.** The effect follows the cause.
**Efficient Cause.** That cause which produces results; primary cause.
**Effigy.** A corporeal representation of a person.
**Efflux.** The flow of time.
**Effort.** An attempt.
**Effractor.** Burgular.
**E.G.** (Abb.). For example.
**Egality.** Equality.
**Ego.** I; myself.
**Egress and Regress.** The right to enter and leave land without hindrance.
**Eighteenth Amendment.** Prohibition.
**Eigne.** The eldest son.
**Eignesse.** The share of the eldest son.
**Eisna.** The eldest son.
**Either.** Each of two.
**Eject.** To throw out.
**Ejection.** A compulsory turning out.
**Ejectment.** An action in which the right of corporeal hereditaments may be tried.
**Ejectum.** That which is tossed up by the sea.
**Ejurare.** To abjure or renounce.
**Ejusdem Generis.** Of the same kind.
**Election.** The selection by popular vote of a public representative.
**Election, Right of.** The right of a widow to choose between the will or the statute.
**Elective.** Subject to choice.
**Elector.** One who has the right to vote.
**Electoral College.** The body that elects the President and Vice-President of the U.S.
**Electrocution.** The infliction of the death penalty by passing through the body a current of electricity of high power.
**Eleemosynary.** Charitable.
**Eleganter.** Accurately.
**Elements.** Forces of nature.
**Eligible.** Qualified.
**Ell.** A lineal measure equal to one yard.
**Eloign.** To remove from jurisdiction.
**Eloin.** See Eloign.
**Elopement.** The act of a wife who abandons her husband and subsequently cohabits with another man.
**Elsewhere.** In another place.
**Emancipate.** To set free.
**Emasculate.** To castrate.
**Embargo.** A proclamation of state forbidding vessels to enter or leave without permission.
**Embezzle.** To misappropriate funds.
**Embody.** To include in a written instrument.
**Embracery.** The offense of attempting to bribe or corruptly influence a jury.
**Emendatio.** An amendment.
**Emergency.** A pressing situation.
**Emigrant.** One who departs from his native land and settles in another country.
**Eminent Domain.** The right of the government to take private property for public use after just compensation.
**Emit.** To send forth.
**Emolument.** Compensation of a public servant.
**Emplead.** To indict.
**Employ.** To engage; hire.
**Employee.** One who works for another.
**Empower.** To authorize.
**Emption.** Buying.
**Emptor.** Buyer.
**En.** In.
**Enact.** To establish by law.
**Enacting Clause.** The introductory clause of a statute declaring the authority of the body.
**En Autre Droit.** In the right of another.
**En Bloc.** In mass.
**Enceinte.** Pregnant.
**En Coste.** Collateral.
**Encroachment.** An unlawful extension of rights over another's.
**Encumbrance.** A burden; charge or lien resting on property which limits its use.
**En Demeure.** In default.
**Endorse.** See Indorse.
**Endorsement.** See Indorsement.
**Endow.** To bestow money or property for maintaining a person or institution.
**Enforce.** To put into execution.
**Enfranchise.** To make free; to grant a person the right to vote.
**Engage.** To employ; to take part in.
**Engagement.** Contract; an agreement between a man and woman to marry.
**Engross.** To copy a document.
**Enhanced.** Increased in value.
**Enitia Pars.** The share of the elder.
**Enjoin.** To issue an injunction.
**Enjoyment.** Dominion over or possession of.
**Enlarge.** To increase; to extend.
**Enlargement.** A conveyance from a reversioner or remainderman to the holder of the particular limited estate.
**Enlist.** To volunteer for military service.
**Enormia.** Crimes.
**Enroll.** To register.
**Enroute.** On the way.
**Ensemble.** Together.
**Ensue.** To follow after.
**Entail.** To settle the succession to property.
**Entail.** An estate in fee limited to certain heirs.
**Entendment.** Understanding.
**Enter.** To take part in; to record or make entry; to place anything before a court formally.
**Enterlesse.** Omitted.
**Enterprise.** A hazardous undertaking.
**Entice.** To wrongfully persuade.
**Entire.** Whole.
**Entire Contract.** An indivisible contract.
**Entire Tenancy.** Sole ownership.
**Entirety.** Joint tenancy by husband and wife whereby either is the owner of the whole.
**Entitle.** To give a right or title.
**Entity.** Being.
**Entrebat.** Intruder.
**Entrepot.** Warehouse.
**Entry.** The making of a record; going upon land to make claim; in burglary, the actual going into a place after breaking.
**Entry, Writ of.** A real action brought to recover possession of lands by one from whom the lands are wrongfully withheld.
**Enumerate.** To mention specifically.
**Enumerators.** Persons appointed to take census.
**En Vie.** In life.
**Eo Intuitu.** With that intention.
**Eo Nominee.** By that name.
**Epistola.** Letter.
**E Pluribus Unum.** The motto of the U.S. Government, "One out of many".
**Equal.** Alike; unbiased.
**Equality.** Possessing the same rights.
**Equip.** To furnish for service against a need.
**Equitable.** Fair; just; in accordance with the special rules enforceable in a Court of Equity.

**Equity.** Body of law which aids and supplements the common law; justice; fairness; a mortgagor's interest; a right of any sort.
**Equity of Statute.** The reason or meaning underlying a statute.
**Equity of Redemption.** The right of a mortgagor to redeem his land after it has been forfeited at law by paying the mortgage debt.
**Equivalent.** In patent law, a device by which an inventor reaches the same result as that achieved by the patent which he is charged.
**Equivocal.** Having more than one meaning.
**Erasure.** The obliteration of any words of a document.
**Ergo.** Therefore.
**Ergot.** A drug sometimes used for abortions.
**Erosion.** The gradual wearing away of soil.
**Errant.** Wandering.
**Error.** A mistake of law or fact.
**Error Apparent.** A defect on the face of the proceedings, pleadings or decree.
**Error, Writ of.** A writ to review a judgment of an inferior court in a higher court for errors.
**Errors, Court of.** Common law court of appeals.
**Escape.** The voluntary departure of a prisoner from lawful custody before he is released.
**Escheat.** The right of the state to succeed to property either real or personal where there is no heir.
**Escrier.** To proclaim.
**Escrow.** A written instrument for a transfer of property or interest in property which is deposited with a third person and is not to be delivered to the grantee until some condition is fulfilled.
**Esne.** One in a position of servitude.
**Esnecy.** The privilege of the eldest to have first choice in the division of an inheritance.
**Espera.** The period of time which a court has fixed for the performance of an act.
**Esplees.** The products and profits of the land.
**Espousal.** Mutual promise to marry.
**Espouse.** To engage to marry.
**Espurio.** Bastard.
**Esq.** (Abb.). Esquire.
**Esquire.** Attorney-at-law; title of respect.
**Esse.** To be.
**Essence.** The substance of a thing.
**Essoin, Essoign.** An excuse for non-appearance when a defendant was summoned.
**Establish.** To make or form; to found.
**Estate.** An interest in land; the assets and liabilities, real and personal property left by a decedent when taken together.
**Estate in Fee Simple.** An estate free of any restriction, limitation or condition.
**Estate Tail.** An estate wherein lands and tenements are given to the donee's issue.
**Estate Tax.** Inheritance tax; probate duty.
**Estop.** To prevent.
**Estoppel.** The equitable rule that when anyone executes some deed, or is connected with or does some act either of deed or record, he is precluded from stating anything to the contrary.
**Estreat.** To extract.
**Estrepe.** Waste.
**Estrepement, Writ of.** The common law writ to prevent waste on the part of a defendant in a writ of right pending the outcome of any real action.
**Et.** And; also.
**Et Al.** And another.
**Et Alii.** And others.
**Et Als.** And others.
**Etc.** (Abb.). Et cetera (and other things).
**Et Non.** And not.
**Et Seq.** (Abb.). Et sequitur (and as follows).
**Et Sic.** And so.
**Eugenics Law.** A statute requiring a medical certificate of good physical condition, as a condition for receiving a marriage license.
**Every.** Each.
**Evict.** To turn out of possession of land.
**Evidence.** Any species of proof that may legally be admitted to court in settlement of an issue.
**Evident.** Obvious.
**Evidentiary.** Being used as evidence.
**Ewage.** Toll paid for water passage.
**Ewbrice.** Adultery.
**Ewe.** Water.
**Ex.** From; out of.
**Exaction.** Unauthorized demanding of fees or taxes by an officer or one impersonating.
**Ex Aequitate.** According to equity.
**Examen.** A trial.
**Examination.** An investigation.
**Examination in Chief.** The first examination of a witness by the party who has called him.
**Examiner.** One authorized to examine.
**Excambium.** An exchange.
**Ex Causa.** From or with cause.
**Exception.** An objection; reservation.
**Excerpta.** Excerpts.
**Excerpts.** Extracts.
**Excess.** Extreme force.
**Excessive Force.** Undue or unnecessary force.
**Excess Profits Tax.** A tax levied in profits beyond a specified amount.
**Exchange.** To barter.
**Exchange Broker.** One who handles bargains for others in money or merchandise.
**Exchequer.** The English department of revenue.
**Excise.** A duty levied upon the manufacture, sale or consumption of commodities within a country.
**Exclusion Laws.** Federal statutes which exclude certain specified foreigners.
**Exclusive.** Undivided; sole.
**Ex Concessis.** From what has been conceded.
**Ex Continenti.** At once.
**Ex Contractu.** From contract.
**Ex Culpa Levissima.** From the least negligence.
**Ex Curia.** Out of court.
**Excusable.** That which can be forgiven.
**Excusable Homicide.** Justifiable homicide is accidental, or in self-defense.
**Excuse.** To pardon.
**Excuss.** To seize goods under court process.
**Ex Debito Justitiae.** As a debt of justice.
**Ex Defectu Sanguinis.** From want of issue.
**Ex Delicto.** From the wrongdoing.
**Ex Demissione.** On the demise of.
**Ex Directo.** Directly; immediately.
**Ex Dolo Malo.** From fraud.
**Execute.** To complete; to do; to carry out.
**Executed.** Completed.
**Executed Consideration.** A past consideration.
**Executed Gift.** A gift which has been delivered.
**Executed Remainder.** A remainder whereby a present interest passes to the tenant, although the enjoyment is postponed.
**Executed Use.** An equitable estate which, under the Statute of Uses, is a legal estate.
**Execution.** The term for the process by which judgments are enforced; the final act necessary to make legal a document effective; the enforcement of capital punishment.
**Executor.** One designated n a will to administer the estate of the testator.
**Executory.** Not yet completed.
**Executory Consideration.** A promise to do something in the future.
**Executory Contract.** A contract in which the obligation lies in a future act.
**Executory Instrument.** One which has not been fully executed by the parties.
**Executory Trust.** One in which the directions to the trustee are general and to be determined by some future deed or declaration.
**Executrix.** Female executor.
**Exemplary Damages.** Punitive damages.
**Exemplification.** Certified copy of a document or legal proceeding under the seal of a court or public office.
**Exempli Gratia.** For example; (Abb.) e.g.
**Exemplum.** An example; a copy.
**Exempt.** Free from obligation or liability.
**Exemption.** Freedom from taxation on certain property or a certain amount of one's income; freedom from military service; property which may not be legally levied upon or sold to satisfy a debt after judgment.
**Ex Empto.** From purchase.
**Exequatur.** Permission issued by any government authorizing some person to act within the jurisdiction of that government, as the consul of a foreign government.
**Exercise.** To carry out; to execute.
**Ex Facie.** On the face.
**Exfrediare.** To break the peace.
**Ex Gratia.** Out of grace.
**Ex Gravi Querela.** As a ground of complaint.
**Exhaeridatio.** A disinheritance.
**Exhibere.** To produce in a court of justice.

**Exhibit.** Something offered in evidence.
**Exhibition.** A suit to compel a person to produce writings.
**Exhumation.** Disinterment.
**Exigence, Exigency.** Urgency, need, demand.
**Exigency of a Bond.** The condition upon which the enforcement of the bond depends.
**Exigent.** A writ forming part of the process of outlawry, ordering the sheriff to bring the person summoned before court.
**Exile.** Banishment.
**Exilium.** Exile.
**Ex Improviso.** Without preparation.
**Ex Industria.** Intentionally.
**Ex Intervallo.** After an interval.
**Exist.** To be.
**Existing Person.** A child conceived; not born.
**Existing Rights.** Rights as they exist under general laws.
**Exit.** The process of issuance is complete.
**Exitus.** Issues of land and tenements; offspring.
**Ex Jurae Natural.** By the law of nature.
**Ex Justa Causa.** From a just cause.
**Exlegalitas.** Outlawry.
**Ex Lege.** According to law.
**Ex Maleficio.** From wrong or tortious conduct.
**Ex Malitia.** Out of malice.
**Ex Mero Motu.** Of his own accord.
**Ex Mora.** Because of delay.
**Ex More.** By custom.
**Ex Natura Rei.** From the nature of the thing.
**Ex Necessitate Legis.** By necessity of law.
**Ex Necessitate Rei.** From the necessity of the case.
**Ex Officio.** By virtue of the office.
**Exonerate.** To relieve from liability; clear.
**Exorbitant.** Beyond the rule of established.
**Exordium.** Introduction to a speech.
**Ex Parte.** From one part or side.
**Expatriation.** The voluntary renouncing of one's country and becoming the citizen of another.
**Expectancy.** That which is hoped.
**Expectant.** Dependent upon a contingency.
**Expeditio.** Service; execution.
**Expel.** To eject; to put out.
**Expensae.** Expenses.
**Expensae Litis.** Costs of suit.
**Expert.** Term applied to a witness qualified to speak authoritatively by virtue of the special training, skill or familiarity with the subject.
**Expilare.** To plunder.
**Expiration.** Termination due to lapse of time.
**Expire.** To terminate; to die.
**Explicatio.** In civil law, the fourth pleading; equivalent to the surrejoinder.
**Export.** To send goods from one country to another.
**Export Tax.** Tax on goods shipped out of the country.
**Expose.** To disclose.
**Exposé.** A statement, account or explanation.
**Expositio, Exposition.** Explanation.
**Ex Post Facto.** After the act is done.
**Exposure.** Openness to danger.
**Express.** Explicit; definite; clear.
**Express Acceptance.** Complete acceptance.
**Express Business.** The carrying of goods for hire.
**Express Consideration.** A consideration which is stated in the contract.
**Express Warranty.** In the law of sales, a statement in regard to the nature, quality or use.
**Expropriation.** The taking of private property for public use under the right of eminent domain, upon payment of compensation.
**Ex Proprio Motu.** Of his own accord.
**Ex Proprio Vigore.** Of its own force.
**Ex Provisione Viri.** By provision of the husband.
**Expulsion.** A putting out; ejectment.
**Expunge.** To strike from the record.
**Expurgation.** A cleansing; a purification.
**Ex Relatione.** On the relation or information of.
**Exscript.** Copy.
**Ex Tempore.** Temporarily.
**Extend.** To prolong.
**Extension.** A grant of further time.
**Extenuate.** To lessen.
**Extenuating Circumstances.** Circumstances to be considered when imposing punishment.
**Exterritoriality.** The privilege enjoyed by diplomats of not being subject to the laws of the country in which they are residents.
**Ex Testamento.** By will or testament.
**Extinct.** Extinguished.
**Extinguish.** To destroy, terminate.
**Extinguishment of Debt.** Cancellation of debt.
**Extortion.** Unlawful obtaining (usually by force) of money or property from another.
**Extra.** Outside of.
**Extradition.** The surrender by one nation to another of an individual accused of committing a crime in the latter country.
**Extrajudicial.** That which is done outside the course of regular judicial proceedings.
**Extra-Jus.** Beyond the law.
**Extra Legal.** Outside the law.
**Extra Legem.** Outside the law.
**Extraneus.** Alien; foreigner.
**Extraneus Evidence.** Evidence derived not from the document in question.
**Extraordinary.** Exceeding the normal measure or degree of care; extreme diligence.
**Extraordinary Legislative Session.** A session of a legislative body held between normal sessions to consider special measures.
**Extraparochial.** Out of the parish.
**Extraterritorial.** Outside the boundaries of the state or country.
**Extraterritoriality.** Any place or building in a country which is treated as a part of another country; the privilege of not being subject to the laws of the country in which one is a resident; the effect of a statute or legal rule beyond the jurisdiction in which the statute or legal rule was instituted.
**Extra Viam.** Off the highway.
**Extra Viris.** In excess of power or authority.
**Extreme.** At the utmost point; excessive.
**Extremity.** The furthest point.
**Extrinsic.** Outside; foreign.
**Extrinsic Evidence.** External evidence or evidence in regard to the meaning of a document which is derived from a source other than the document itself.
**Extum.** Thence.
**Exulare.** To exile.
**Ex Vi Termini.** By the intrinsic meaning.
**Ex Voluntate.** Voluntarily.
**Eye Witness.** One who testifies as to what he has seen.

## F

**F.A.A.** (Abb.). Free of all average; in marine insurance, denotes that the insurance is against total loss only.
**Fabricate.** To deceive a court by giving false evidence; to forge or falsify.
**Fabula.** Contract; agreement.
**Face.** The matter which appears on a written instrument.
**Facere.** To make or do.
**Facias.** That you make or cause.
**Face of a Judgment.** The sum for which the judgment was rendered, exclusive of interest.
**Face of Record.** Entire record in a case.
**Face Value.** Par value.
**Faciendo.** In doing or making.
**Facilitate.** To make less difficult.
**Facio Ut Des.** I do that you may give; an agreement to pay money in return for the performance of an act.
**Facsimile.** An exact copy.
**Fact.** A thing done; that which is real or true.
**Facta.** Facts; deeds.
**Facto.** In fact or deed.
**Factor.** A commercial agent engaged in the sale and purchase of goods for a principal.
**Factorage.** Commission paid to a factor for his services.
**Factum.** Deed; a thing done.
**Factum Probans.** A proving fact.
**Faculties of Husband.** The ability of the husband to render support to his wife in the form of alimony.
**Faggot Votes.** Sham or illegal votes.
**Faida.** Malice.
**Failure.** Bankruptcy; insolvency.
**Failure of Consideration.** Absence of consideration necessary to make a valid contract; failure to perform what was agreed.
**Failure of Issue.** To die without lineal descendants.
**Failure to Provide.** Failure of a husband to provide his wife and children with the necessities of life.

**Faint Pleading.** A fraudulent or collusive manner of pleading with the intent of deceiving a third party.
**Fair.** A market.
**Fair.** Reasonable; equitable.
**Fair Comment.** In a suit of libel, the defense that the defamatory words were a fair comment on a matter of public interest.
**Fair Consideration.** Adequate consideration.
**Fair Knowledge.** Ordinary knowledge.
**Fairly.** Impartially.
**Fair Pleader.** See Beaupleader.
**Fair Trial.** Legal trial.
**Fact.** Deed or act.
**Fact Enrolle.** An enrolled deed.
**Faith.** Confidence.
**Fall of Land.** A quantity of land equal to 160th of an acre.
**Fallow.** Barren or unproductive.
**Fallow Land.** Land ploughed but not sown in order that it may recuperate its fertility.
**Falsa Demonstratio.** False description.
**Falsa Moneta.** Counterfeit money.
**Falsare.** To falsify or forge.
**False.** Untrue.
**False Appeal.** An unsuccessful appeal of felony.
**False Arrest.** Illegal restraint by one person of the liberty of another.
**False Character.** Fradulent letter of recommendation used to aid a person seeking employment.
**Falsedad.** Deception.
**Fasehood.** Lie.
**False Imprisonment.** Illegal arrest or detention of a person.
**False Instrument.** Forged instrument.
**False Personation.** Criminal offense of pretending to be another person in order to deceive others.
**False Pretense.** An intentional false statement about a oresent or past fact.
**False Representation.** A representation which is untrue as to matter of fact.
**False Swearing.** A common law misdemeanor not amounting to perjury since the testimony need not be as to a fact material to the issue or point of inquiry and in perjury it must.
**False Verdict.** A verdict which is not the proper verdict of the jury, i.e. arrived at by some improper means such as drawing lots.
**Falsi Crimen.** Concealment of the truth for fraudulent purposes.
**Falsify.** To fraudulently alter a record or document; to prove false.
**Fama.** Character; reputation.
**Famacide.** Slanderer.
**Familia.** Family.
**Family.** Usually refers to parents and children, but can be extended to many relationships.
**Family Bible.** Bible containing family records which may be used as evidence or to prove age or place of birth.
**Family Settlement.** An agreement between the members of a family settling the distribution of family property among them.
**Famosus Libellus.** A libelous writing.
**Fanatic.** A religious enthusiast.
**Fardel.** A fourth part.
**Farding Deal.** One-fourth of an acre of land.
**Fare.** Charge for transportation.
**Farlingarii.** Panderers.
**Farm.** A body of land used for agricultural purposes.
**Farm Let.** In a lease, formal words signifying a letting on a certain rent payable in produce.
**Farthing.** The fourth part of an English penny.
**Farthing Damages.** Nominal damages.
**Fatal Injury.** Injury causing death.
**Father.** Male parent.
**Father's Natural Guardianship.** Guardianship over one's children until they have reached the age of twenty-one.
**Farthing of Land.** A great quantity of land.
**Farvand.** Passage by water.
**Fast Writ.** Any matter which is entitled to precedence on the court calendar.
**Fathom.** Nautical measure of six feet in length.
**Fatua Mulier.** Whore.
**Fatuitas.** Idiocy.
**Fatum.** Fate.
**Fatuous Person.** One with no mind; an idiot.
**Fatuus.** Fatuous, foolish.
**Fatuum Judicum.** Foolish judgment or verdict.
**Faubourg.** In Louisiana, a suburb.
**Fauces Terrae.** Narrow headlands enclosing a bay.
**Fault.** Negligence; an error or defect in judgment or conduct.
**Fautor.** An abettor.
**Faux.** False.
**Fauxer.** To falsify or forge.
**Favor.** Bias or prejudice; an act of kindness.
**Feal.** Faithful.
**Feasance.** Performance.
**Feasant.** Performing; making.
**Federal.** Relating to the U.S.
**Federal Courts.** The courts of the U.S.
**Federal Bureau of Investigation.** An agency of the U.S. government, under the Justice Department, which has the duty of enforcing the laws of the U.S.
**Federal Government.** A union of independent sovereignties.
**Federal Question.** A question arising under the U.S. Constitution of or under Federal statute.
**Fee.** An estate of inheritance; compensation for professional services.
**Fee Conditional.** At common law, a fee limited to some particular heirs, exclusive of others.
**Fee Expectant.** One which is limited to a man and his wife and their direct heirs.
**Fee Farm.** An estate in land, subject to rent.
**Fee Simple.** An estate in which the owner is entitled to the entire property without limitations or qualifications.
**Fee Simple Absolute.** See Fee Simple.
**Fee Tail.** An estate in land limited to the grantee and all or certain of his descendants.
**Feigned.** Fictitious.
**Feigned Action.** An action brought to secure the decision of the court on a point of law and not founded on any actual controversy.
**Feigned Issue.** An issue framed to try questions of fact.
**Fello-Heir.** Joint heir.
**Felo.** Felon.
**Felo de Se.** A suicide.
**Felon.** One who commits felony.
**Felonious.** Done with intent to commit crime.
**Felonious Homicide.** An unjustifiable killing.
**Felony.** A capital crime or one of graver nature than those designated as misdemeanors.
**Feme.** Woman.
**Feme Covert.** Married woman.
**Feme Sole.** Unmarried woman.
**Feme Sole Trader.** A married woman who engages in business independently.
**Femicide.** The killing of a woman.
**Femme.** Woman.
**Fender.** A protection against danger.
**Feneration.** The lending of money for interest.
**Feod.** Fee.
**Feoda.** Feudal.
**Feofee.** The grantee of an estate in land.
**Feoffor.** The grantor of an estate in land.
**Feoffment.** The transfer of the title to an estate in freehold.
**Ferriage.** The fare for transportation by ferry; the transportation itself.
**Ferry.** A place where person or goods are carried across a body of water for a toll.
**Festinum Remedium.** A speedy remedy.
**Festum.** Feast.
**Fet.** Done.
**Feticide.** Criminal abortion.
**Fetters.** Chains or shackles.
**Fetus.** Unborn child.
**Feud.** A grant of land to be held by a form of feudal tenure.
**Fiancer.** To pledge or promise.
**Fiat.** Let it be done.
**Fiat Justitia.** Let justice be done.
**Fiat Money.** Currency whose value is decided by the issuing government without regard to its equivalent value in specie.
**Fictio.** Fiction.
**Fiction.** A false statement on the part of the plaintiff which the defendant is not allowed to deny, giving the court jurisdiction.
**Fictitious.** False; feigned.
**Fidei.** In civil law, a species of trust.
**Fidelis.** Faithful.
**Fides.** Trust; faith.

**Fiduciary.** One who is put in control of property in the interests of others.
**Fieri Facias.** That you cause to be made.
**Fight.** Hostile encounter.
**Filare.** To file.
**File.** A record of the court; to put away papers.
**Filiate.** To determine paternity.
**Filiation Proceeding.** A statutory proceeding to establish the paternity of an illegitimate child in order to impose the duty of support.
**Filius.** Son.
**Filius Nullius.** Illegitimate child.
**Fille.** Girl; daughter.
**Fils.** Son.
**Filium.** Thread; edge.
**Fin.** End.
**Final.** Last; the end.
**Final Decree.** A concluding decree.
**Final Judgment.** A judgment which is not subject to appeal because of a statutory determination or because the time for appeal has expired; a judgment of the highest court in any jurisdiction, a judgment which ends the legal proceeding by resolving the controversy.
**Finance.** Public or government funds.
**Finding.** The determination of an issue of fact by judge or jury.
**Fine.** Financial penalty.
**Fine Force.** Necessity, compulsion.
**Finem Facere.** To impose or pay a fine.
**Fines.** Boundaries; limits.
**Finger Prints.** Patterns made by the ends of the fingers used for identification.
**Finire.** To finish; end; fine.
**Finis.** Finish; end; fine; limit; boundary.
**Finitio.** The end.
**Fire.** The effect of combustion.
**Firearm.** Gunpowder weapon.
**Firebug.** Arsonist; pyromaniac.
**Fire Insurance.** Insurance against fire.
**Fire-Proof.** Incombustible.
**Firm.** Partnership; agricultural lease.
**Firma.** Farm.
**Firman.** Passport; permit.
**Firm Name.** Name under which a firm transacts business.
**First.** Preceeding all others; foremost.
**First Class.** Of the most superior grade.
**First Class Mail.** Written matter and all else sealed against inspection.
**First Class Misdemeanant.** One found guilty of a misdemeanor but judged deserving.
**First Degree Burn.** Burn which causes inflammation of the outer layer of skin.
**First Impression.** A case without precedent.
**First Instance, Court of.** Trial court.
**First Mortgage.** One having priority as a lien over the lien of any other mortgage of the same property.
**First Purchaser.** The one who first acquired the state by any method other than descent.
**Fisc, Fiscus.** Treasury.
**Fiscal.** Pertaining to public revenue.
**Fiscal Year.** For accounting purposes, a year beginning other than the first day of January.
**Fishery.** Right to take fish from water.
**Fish Royal.** Whale, porpoise, sturgeon.
**Fisticuffs.** A pre-arranged fist fight.
**Fistula.** Water conduit or pipe.
**Fit.** Proper, suitable.
**Fitz.** Son.
**Fix.** Fasten a thing immovably; to adjust.
**Fixed Liabilities.** Those definite in obligation.
**Fixed Opinion.** Conviction or prejudgment which disqualifies a juror.
**Fixture.** Personal property attached to realty.
**Flag.** National standard, ensign, banner.
**Flagellat.** Whipped.
**Flagging.** Pavement of flat stones.
**Flagrans.** Burning; raging.
**Flagrans Crimen.** As the crime was committed.
**Flagrant Necessity.** An illegal act made lawful due to urgent necessity.
**Flat.** Area covered with shallow water.
**Flattery.** Insincere praise.
**Fleece.** To cheat.
**Fleet.** Where the tide flows; creek; ships.
**Flem.** Outlaw.
**Flet.** House.
**Flight.** Offense of running away.
**Flim-Flam.** Confidence game.
**Float.** Checks in process of collection; a government certificate authorizing the holder to enter a specific amount of public lands.
**Floating Capital.** Funds for general expenses.
**Float Policy.** Insurance policy covering the interest of the insured without describing particular property.
**Flodemark.** Highwater mark.
**Flogging.** Whipping.
**Flood.** Inundation of water.
**Flood-Tide.** Rising tide of the sea.
**Floor.** Section of a building between horizontal boundaries.
**Flotsam.** Wreckage found at sea.
**Flourish.** Brandish; wave.
**Fluctus.** Flood; flood-tide.
**Flume.** Artificial channel; viaduct.
**Fluvius.** River; stream.
**Fluxus.** Flow of tides.
**F.O.B.** (Abb.) **Free on Board.** Transportation term signifying that no price is due until the seller has delivered the goods.
**Fodder.** Feed for cattle.
**Foedus.** Treaty.
**Foenus.** Interest on money.
**Foeticide.** Criminal abortion.
**Foetus.** Unborn child.
**Fog.** In navigation laws, any atmospheric condition.
**Foi.** Fealty, loyalty.
**Fois.** Time.
**Folgarii.** Followers; menial servants.
**Folio.** Page with a certain number of words.
**Folk Right.** Right or law of the people.
**Fontana.** Fountain; spring.
**Food.** Nourishment.
**Fool Natural.** An idiot.
**Foot.** Measurement of 12 inches; terminal part of leg.
**Foot Frontage Rule.** Taxation confined to actual frontage on line of improvement.
**Footman.** Pedestrian.
**Foot of the Fine.** Concluding part of the fine.
**For.** Because of; on account of; by reason of.
**Foraneus.** Foreigner.
**Forbarrer.** To exclude.
**Forbatudus.** An agressor killed.
**Forbear.** To suspend the enforcement of a legal right.
**Force.** Violence.
**Force and Arms.** An act of violence.
**Forced Heir.** One to whom the testator must leave a certain portion of his property.
**Forces.** Military and naval power.
**Forcible Detainer.** Unlawfully held chattels.
**Forcible Entry.** Illegal entry on real property.
**Forda.** A ford.
**Fordanno.** Agressor.
**Fore.** Before.
**Foreclosure.** Legal proceeding to enforce a lien, pledge or mortgage.
**Foreclosure Sale.** Sale of mortgaged property.
**Foregoer.** Ancestor.
**Foregift.** Premium for a lease.
**Forehand Rent.** Rent paid in advance.
**Foreign.** Belonging to another nation.
**Foreign Bill of Exchange.** A bill drawn in one state or country and payable in another.
**Foreign Corporation.** One doing business in a state other than where incorporated.
**Foreigner.** Citizen of another country; alien.
**Foreign Exchange.** Drafts drawn on a foreign state or country.
**Foreign Plea.** One which raises an objection to the jurisdiction of the court.
**Forejudge.** To expel from court; deprive.
**Foreman.** Presiding member of jury.
**Forensic.** Pertaining to the courts.
**Forensic Medicine.** Medical jurisprudence.
**Forensis.** Forensic.
**Foreright.** Right of primogeniture.
**Foresaid.** Aforesaid; previously mentioned.
**Foreshore.** Land lying between the greatest and least high tides.
**Forest.** Large tract of land covered with trees.
**Forestall.** Lie in wait; obstruct a highway.
**Forethought Felony.** Premeditated felony.
**Forefeit.** Loss of a right by default.
**Forfeiture of Bond.** Failure to meet the condition of the bond and imposition of the stipulated penalty.
**Forfeiture of Lease.** Failure to meet conditions of a lease causing its termination.
**Forgery.** The making or altering of a written instrument for fraud or deceit.
**Forinsic.** Foreign, external.

**Foris.** Outside.
**Forisbanitus.** Banished.
**Forisfacere.** Forfeit.
**Forisjurare.** Forswear; abjure; renounce.
**Form.** Model instrument to be used in judicial proceedings; the legal or technical manner to be observed in legal instruments.
**Forma.** Form.
**Forma Dat Esse.** Form imparts existence.
**Formaldehyde.** Preservative.
**Formality.** Adherence to forms and customs.
**Formed Design.** Wilful, malicious act.
**Formedon.** Writ of right to recover property.
**Former Jeopardy.** Plea under which one cannot be tried for the same offense twice.
**Forms of Action.** Classes of personal action at common law.
**Formula.** Set form of words.
**Fornication.** Illicit intercourse between two unmarried persons.
**Fornix.** Brothel.
**Forno.** Oven.
**Foro.** In the court.
**Foro Seculari.** In the secular court.
**Forprise.** An exception.
**Forsque.** Only; but.
**Forswear.** Adjure; swear falsely.
**Forsworn.** Having committed perjury.
**Fort.** Place protected against attack.
**Fortax.** Tax heavily.
**Forthcoming.** Action whereby an arrestment is made effectual.
**Forthwith.** Immediately.
**Fortia.** Force; violence.
**Fortior.** Stronger, more effective.
**Fortis.** Strong, forcible.
**Fortuitous.** Accidental.
**Fortuitous Event.** One depending upon chance.
**Forty.** Quarter section of land; forty acres.
**Forum.** Court; tribunal.
**For Value Received.** Attestation of value.
**Forward.** Transmit.
**Forwarder.** One who transports merchandise.
**Fossa.** Ditch; grave; moat.
**Fosterage.** Rearing of another's child.
**Fosterlean.** Remuneration for rearing a foster child.
**Foundation.** Endowment of an institution.
**Founded.** Based upon.
**Founder.** One who initially endows an educational or charitable institution.
**Founderosa.** In need of repair.
**Foundling.** An abandoned child.
**Four Corners.** Contents of an instrument.
**Four Seas.** Water surrounding England.
**Fractio.** Fraction; fragment.
**Fraction.** Fragment; portion; part of whole.
**Fraction of a Day.** Portion of a day.
**Fractura Navium.** Shipwrecks.
**Frais.** Expenses.
**Frame-Up.** Conspiracy to falsely incriminate.
**Franc.** Free.
**Franchilanus.** Freeman.
**Franchise.** Special privilege conferred on an individual or corporation by the government.
**Francus.** Free.
**Francus Tenens.** Freeholder.
**Frank.** Free; send mail exempt from postage.
**Franking Privilege.** Use of public mails without payment of postage.
**Frassetum.** Tract of wooded land.
**Frater.** Brother.
**Frater Consanguineus.** Brother born of the same father but different mother.
**Frater Nutricius.** Bastard brother.
**Frater Uterinus.** Brother born of the same mother but different father.
**Fraternity.** Group of men associated for common interests.
**Fratriage.** Inheritance by a younger brother.
**Fratricide.** Killing of one who kills a brother or sister.
**Fraud.** Intentional deception to induce another to part with something of value or to surrender a legal right; deceit; trickery.
**Fraudulent.** That which is done with intent to defraud.
**Fraudulent Concealment.** Suppression of a material fact, duty bound to communicate.
**Fraudulent Conveyance.** Transfer of property to defraud or hinder creditors.
**Fraus.** Fraud.
**Fray.** An affray.
**Frectare.** To freight or load.
**Frectum.** Freight.
**Free.** Unconstrained; exonerated; public.
**Free and Clear.** Not encumbered by any liens.
**Free-Bench.** Widow's dower in some copyhold lands.
**Free-Board.** Land claimed outside a fence.
**Free Course.** Sailing with a favorable wind.
**Freedman.** One freed from bondage.
**Freedom.** Liberty.
**Free Enterprise.** Right to conduct a business.
**Free Entry, Egress, Regress.** Right to enter and leave another's land.
**Freehold.** Full ownership or title to land.
**Freeholder.** One having title to realty.
**Free List.** Articles exempted by Congress from import duty.
**Free On Board.** Freight term meaning that the subject of the sale is to be loaded for shipment without expense to the buyer.
**Free Ships.** During war, neutral ships.
**Free Tenure.** Tenure by free service.
**Freight.** Sum paid for transportation of goods; the goods transported.
**French Pool.** System of gambling.
**Freneticus.** Madman.
**Frequent.** To visit often.
**Fresh.** New; recent.
**Fresh Fine.** Fine levied within the past year.
**Freshet.** Flood; inundation.
**Fresh Pursuit.** Immediate pursuit of an offender after the commission of a crime.
**Fret.** Freight.
**Frettum.** Freight.
**Fretum.** Strait.
**Friars.** Members of monastic religious order.
**Friendly Society.** Mutual aid society.
**Friendly Suit.** An action brought by mutual agreement of parties involved in order to clarify a question of legal right.
**Frigidity.** Incapacity for sexual intercourse.
**Frilinger.** Freemen.
**Friscus.** Fresh; recent; new.
**Frisk.** To run hands over another's person.
**Frithman.** Member of a company or fraternity.
**Frivolous.** Lacking in legal sufficiency.
**From.** Starting point; out of.
**Frontage.** Extent of land facing a street.
**Fructuarius.** Lessee.
**Fructus.** Fruit; fruits; increase.
**Fructus Civiles.** Revenues; compensations.
**Fructus Legis.** Fruit of the law, i.e. execution.
**Fructus Naturales.** Products of nature.
**Fructus Separati.** Plucked fruit.
**Fruges.** Fruits; produce.
**Fruit.** Seed or edible pulp of plants.
**Fruits of Crime.** Loot, booty.
**Frusca Terra.** Uncultivated land.
**Frustra.** In vain.
**Frustrum Terrae.** Land lying by itself.
**Frutex.** Bush; shrub.
**Ft.** (Abb.). Foot; feet.
**Fuer.** Flee.
**Fuer en Fait.** Actual flight.
**Fugacia.** Chase; hunt.
**Fugatio.** Hunting privilege.
**Fugie.** Fugitive.
**Fugie-Warrant.** Warrant for a debtor.
**Fugitate.** To outlaw by sentence of court.
**Fugitation.** Outlawry.
**Fugitive.** One who flees to escape arrest.
**Fugitive Slave.** Slave who has fled.
**Fugitivus.** Fugitive.
**Full.** Ample; complete, perfect.
**Full Age.** Age of legal maturity, usually 21.
**Full Court.** Duly organized with judges present.
**Full Faith and Credit.** Article IV, Section I of the U.S. Constitution which provides that full faith and credit shall be given in each state to the public acts of other states.
**Full Hearing.** The right to present evidence and an opportunity to know the claims.
**Full Jurisdiction.** Complete jurisdiction.
**Full Life.** Life in fact and law.
**Full Pardon.** One which releases the punishment and obliterates the guilt.
**Full Right.** Good title with possession.
**Fully.** Amply, sufficiently.
**Function.** Office; duty.
**Functionary.** Public officer.
**Functus.** Dead; void.
**Functus Officio.** Having performed his duty.
**Fund.** Money or securities for a purpose.
**Fundamental.** Basic.
**Fundatio.** Founding or foundation.
**Fundator.** Founder.

**Funded Debt.** A debt for which a specific fund has been appropriated, usually to redeem public obligations.
**Fundi.** Lands.
**Fundi Patrimoniales.** Lands of inheritance.
**Fundi Publici.** Public lands.
**Funditores.** Pioneers.
**Fundus.** Land; soil; farm; estate.
**Fungible.** Consumable by use and returnable in kind.
**Fungible Goods.** Personal property divided into units in such a way that they are considered interchangeable.
**Fur.** Thief.
**Furandi Animo.** With intent to steal.
**Furca.** Gallows.
**Fur Diurnus.** Daytime thief.
**Furiosity.** Raving madness.
**Furiosus.** Madman.
**Furlong.** One-eighth of a mile.
**Furlough.** Leave of absence.
**Furnish.** Provide for use.
**Fur Nocturnus.** Nighttime thief.
**Furor Brevis.** Sudden anger.
**Further Advance.** Additional loan.
**Further Assurance.** Covenant in real property that the vendor will execute any other documents necessary to perfect the vendee's title.
**Furtively.** Stealthily.
**Furtum.** Theft; larceny.
**Furtum Grave.** Aggravated larceny.
**Fustis.** Staff.
**Future Debt.** Existing debt which is not due.
**Futures.** Commodities or stocks on which delivery is not made until some future time.

## G

**Gabel.** Excise; rent.
**Gag.** Something forced into a person's mouth to prevent outcry.
**Gage.** Pledge; challenge.
**Gain.** Profit.
**Gainage Lands.** Lands reclaimed from the sea.
**Gainful.** Profitable.
**Gallon.** Liquid measure of 4 quarts.
**Gallows.** Scaffold.
**Gamacta.** Assault.
**Gamalis.** Legitimate child.
**Gamble.** Play for money or other stake.
**Game.** Animals hunted for sport; sport.
**Game.** Laws for the preservation of game.
**Gaming.** To play a game of chance.
**Ganancial System.** Spanish system of community property.
**Gang.** Group united for criminal purposes.
**Gaol.** Jail.
**Gaoler.** Jailer.
**Garage.** Place to house motor vehicle.
**Garandia.** Warranty.
**Garaunt.** Warranty.
**Garaunter.** To warrant.
**Garauntor.** Warrantor.
**Garbage.** Refuse
**Garble.** Sort good from bad.
**Gard.** Guardianship; care; custody.
**Gardein.** Guardian.
**Garens.** Private game preserve.
**Garnish.** Warn, notify.
**Garnishes.** One owing money to a debtor or on whom a garnishment is levied.
**Garnishment.** Statutory proceeding whereby property, money or credits of a debtor in possession of another, the garnishee, is applied to the payments of the debtor by means of process.
**Garrant.** Warrant; authority.
**Garrantie.** Warranty.
**Garrote.** Capital punishment by strangulation.
**Gast.** Waste.
**Gastaldus.** Bailiff; steward.
**Gaster.** To waste.
**Gastine.** Uncultivated land.
**Geld.** Sum of money, fine, tribute.
**Gemma.** Gem, jewel.
**Genealogy.** Family history.
**Gener.** Son-in-law.
**General.** Extensive; prevalent.
**General Circulation.** Circulation of a newspaper among the public.
**General Credit.** General reputation of a witness for veracity.
**General Estate.** Entire estate held by one in his individual capacity.
**General Exception.** An objection to a pleading or any part thereof for want of substance.
**General Indorsement.** An indorsement of a negotiable instrument without payee named.
**Generalis.** General.
**General Issue.** Denial by the defendant of every material allegation of fact in the plaintiff's complaint.
**Generaliter.** Generally.
**General Law.** Law that applies to the community at large.
**General Legacy.** One which is to be paid to the legatee from the estate's general assets.
**General Lien.** Lien on a chattel not only for an existing debt, but for any other debt.
**General Mortgage.** Blanket mortgage on all the chattels of the mortgagor.
**General Ownership.** Unqualified dominion.
**General Power of Appointment.** Right to appoint any person the donee pleases.
**General Public Law.** Law which binds all members of the community, always.
**General Property Tax.** Tax on real or personal property to obtain revenue.
**General Statute.** Public statute.
**General Strike.** Strike of all or most of the workingmen in a particular area.
**Generation.** Single succession of living beings in natural descent.
**Generosa.** Gentlewoman.
**Generosus.** Gentleman.
**Geniculum.** Degree of consanguinity.
**Gens.** People; race; tribe.
**Gentes.** People.
**Gentiles.** Member of a common tribe or gens.
**Genuine.** Real; original; not counterfeit.
**Genus.** Class comprising many species.
**Gerens.** Bearing.
**Gerens Datum.** Bearing date.
**Gerere.** To act; behave; engage in.
**German.** Fully related; of the same parents.
**German Cousin.** First Cousin.
**Germane.** Closely related; appropriate.
**Germanus.** Of the same stock.
**Gerrymander.** To subdivide or redistrict a political area for political purposes.
**Gestation.** Period of pregnancy.
**Gestio.** Behavior. conduct.
**Gestor.** Agent.
**Gestum.** Deed; transaction; business.
**Gestura.** Behavior.
**Gibbet.** Gallows.
**Gift.** Voluntary transfer of personal property without compensation therefor.
**Gift Deed.** Deed for a nominal sum.
**Gift Note.** Donor's promissory note.
**Gift Tax.** Tax levied on gifts of property, to supplement estate and inheritance tax.
**Gild, Guild.** English fraternal society of artisans or merchants.
**Gilt Edge.** Of best quality.
**Girth.** Linear measure of 36 inches.
**Gisant.** Resting; reclining.
**Giser.** To lie, rest or recline.
**Gist.** Main point of a question.
**Give.** Transfer; grant; bequeath.
**Give Bail.** Furnish security for one's appearance.
**Given Name.** First name; Christian name.
**Giver.** Donor.
**Gladiolus.** Small sword; dagger.
**Gladius.** Sword.
**Glanders.** Contagious disease of horses.
**Glans.** Fruits of trees.
**Gleaning.** Gathering together of reaped crops.
**Gleba.** Turf; sod; soil.
**Glider.** Form of aircraft.
**Glos.** A husband's sister.
**Gloss.** Translation; explanation.
**Glossator.** Translator; commentator.
**Glyn.** Glen; ravine.
**Go.** To be dismissed or issue from court.
**God's Acre.** Cemetery.
**Go Hence.** Depart from court.
**Going Price.** Current price.
**Going Witness.** One about to leave the jurisdiction of the court.
**Golda.** Coin.
**Goldwit.** Fine in gold.

**Goliardus.** Jester.
**Gonorrhea.** Venereal disease.
**Good.** Valid; effective; unobjectionable.
**Good Abearing.** Good behavior.
**Good and Lawful Men.** Those qualified to serve on juries.
**Good and Valid.** Reliable; adequate.
**Good Behavior.** Orderly conduct; conduct of a prisoner warrenting sentence reduction.
**Good Cause.** Substantial reason.
**Good Faith.** Honesty of intention and absence of information causing doubt of validity.
**Good Health.** Sound of body.
**Good Repute.** Good reputation.
**Goods.** Chattels.
**Goods and Chattels.** Personal property.
**Goods Sold and Delivered.** An action for goods sold and delivered is brought by the seller to recover the purchase price.
**Good Time Provision.** Statutory provision by which the prison term of a convict is shortened because of good behavior.
**Go Quit.** Exonerated.
**Gouge.** Cheat; defraud; deceive.
**Govern.** To direct and control.
**Government.** Political agency through which the state or community acts.
**Government de Facto.** Government of fact, i.e. actually exercising power in the state as opposed to the lawful government.
**Government de Jure.** Government of right, i.e. true and lawful government.
**Governor.** Chief executive officer of a state or territory of the U.S.
**Grace.** Indulgence; favor.
**Gradation.** Gradually.
**Grade.** Line of a street's inclination from the horizontal; quality; value; rank.
**Graduate.** One who has received a degree in a college or university.
**Graduated Tax.** Progressive tax.
**Gradus.** Step; grade; status.
**Gradus Parentelae.** Family tree.
**Graf.** Magistrate.
**Graffer.** Notary; copyist.
**Graft.** Dishonest transaction in relation to public or official acts.
**Grafter.** Swindler or dishonest person.
**Gram Stain Test.** Gonorrhea test.
**Grammatophylacium.** Place for keeping written instruments.
**Grand** (Coll.). One thousand dollars.
**Grand-Stand Play.** An act to draw applause.
**Grandchild.** Child of one's child.
**Grand Jury.** A body of citizens of a county organized for the purpose of inquiring into the commission of crimes within the county.
**Grandfather.** Father of either of one's parents.
**Grandmother.** Mother of either parents.
**Grand Larceny.** Larceny or theft of property worth more than the amount fixed in statute.
**Grand Theft.** See Grand Larceny.
**Grange.** Farm and all its buildings.
**Grangiarius.** Keeper of a grange.
**Grant.** Transfer of real property or of some license or authority; bestow; permit; allow.
**Grantee.** One to whom a grant is made.
**Grantor.** One who makes a grant.
**Grasson, Grassum.** Fine paid upon the transfer of a copyhold estate.
**Gratificaion.** Gratuity; recompense; reward.
**Gratis.** As a favor; free.
**Gratuitous.** Without charge, free.
**Gratuity.** Free gift; recompense.
**Gratulance.** Bribe.
**Gravamen.** Substance of a complaint.
**Gravatio.** Charge; accusation.
**Grave.** Excavation in the earth in which a corpse is or is to be buried.
**Gravel.** Mixture of small stones and sand.
**Graveyard.** Cemetery.
**Gravis.** Grave; important; serious.
**Great.** Important; serious.
**Great Seal.** Seal of state.
**Gree.** An agreement.
**Green Bag.** Symbol of the legal profession.
**Green Goods.** American slang for counterfeit paper money.
**Gremium.** Safeguard; protection.
**Grievance.** Injury; injustice.
**Grievance Committee.** A committee, usually of workingmen, which presents complaints connected with their employment.
**Grieved.** Aggrieved.
**Grievous.** Causing sorrow or pain.
**Griff.** Offspring of a Negro and mulatto.
**Gros.** Large, great.
**Grocer.** Merchant.
**Gross.** Twelve dozen.
**Gross.** Great; culpable; general; absolute.
**Gross Average.** General average.
**Grossement.** Greatly.
**Gross, In.** Phrase used to describe a right.
**Gross Income.** Income before deduction.
**Gross Negligence.** Lack of care or attention.
**Gross Weight.** Total weight of goods.
**Ground.** Soil; earth.
**Ground Rent.** Rent reserved by one who conveys land to another in fee simple.
**Groundage.** Port fee.
**Ground Annual.** Annual rent.
**Guadia.** Pledge.
**Guarantee.** One to whom a guaranty is made; to make a contract of guaranty.
**Guarantor.** One who makes a contract of guaranty.
**Guaranty.** Mercantile contract whereby a person undertakes to answer for the debt, default or miscarriage of another.
**Guardage.** Wardship.
**Guardia.** Ward of a guardian.
**Guardian.** One who has been legally intrusted with the custody and control of the person and/or property of an incompetent.
**Guardian ad Litem.** Guardian for the litigation.
**Guarra.** War.
**Gubernator.** Pilot; governor.
**Gubernatorial.** The office of governor.
**Guerpi.** Abandoned.
**Guess.** Conjecture.
**Guest.** One lodged for pay at an inn or hotel.
**Guilde.** See Gild.
**Guilt.** Cupability.
**Guillotine.** French instrument for beheading.
**Gule of August.** August 1st.
**Gun.** Firearm.
**Gynarchy.** Government ruled by a woman.
**Gyves.** Fetters.

## H

**Hab. Corp.** (Abb.). Habeas corpus.
**Habeas Corpora Juratorum.** That you have the bodies of the jurors. Writ formerly used in Common Pleas to secure compulsory attendance of the jury.
**Habeas Corpus.** You are to bring the body. Name given to various writs having as their object to bring a party before a court.
**Habeas Corpus ad Subjiciendum.** Writ requiring a person detaining a prisoner to produce him and submit to the court's order.
**Habendum.** Part of deed beginning with, "To have and to hold".
**Habendum et Tenendum.** To have and to hold.
**Habentia.** Riches.
**Habere.** To have.
**Habere Facias Possessionem.** Old common law writ issued after a successful suit in ejectment, to put the claimant in possession.
**Habere Facias Siesinam.** Writ to put a claimant in possession of a freehold.
**Habere Facias Visum.** Writ directing the sheriff to view the premises in controversy.
**Habere Licere.** To allow possession.
**Habilis.** Suitable; fit.
**Habilis ad Matrimonium.** Fit for marriage.
**Habit.** Disposition or condition of the body acquired by frequent repetition.
**Habitable.** Tenantable.
**Habitancy.** Fixed place of abode.
**Habitant.** Resident tenant.
**Habitatio.** Right of dwelling.
**Habitation.** Temporary or permanent abode.
**Habitual.** Customary; usual; familiar.
**Habitual Offender.** One who consistently violates the law.
**Habitus.** Habit; garb; apparel.
**Hackney.** Let out for hire.
**Hade.** Grassy slope.
**Haec Est Conventio.** This is the agreement.
**Haec Verba.** These words.
**Haeredes.** Heirs.
**Haeredes Proxime.** Nearest heirs.

**Haeredipeta.** One seeking an inheritance.
**Haereditas.** An inheritance.
**Haereditas Jacens.** An inheritance held in abeyance pending possession by the heir.
**Haereditas Paterna.** Paternal inheritance.
**Haeres.** Heir.
**Haeres Ex Asse.** Sole heir.
**Haeres Institutus.** Testamentary heir.
**Haeres Legitimus.** Lawful heir.
**Haeres Natus.** Born heir.
**Hafne.** Haven; port.
**Haga.** House.
**Hagia.** Hedge.
**Hagne.** Small hand-gun.
**Hakh.** Truth; the true God; legal claim.
**Half-Blood.** Having one parent in common.
**Half-Brother.** Brother through a common mother or father.
**Half-Proof.** Testimony of a single witness.
**Half-Sister.** Sister through a common mother or father.
**Half-Tongue.** Jury half speaking one language, the other half another.
**Half Year.** In law, period of 182 days.
**Hall Day.** Court day.
**Hallucination.** Trick of the senses.
**Ham.** Home, house.
**Hamel.** Village.
**Hamlet.** Small village.
**Hand.** Length of 4 inches.
**Handcuffs.** Wrist shackles.
**Handle.** Control; direct.
**Hand Sale.** Shaking hands over a bargain.
**Handwriting.** Chirography of a person.
**Handy Man.** Man of all work.
**Hang.** Remain undetermined.
**Hanging.** Form of capital punishment.
**Hangman.** Executioner.
**Hanse.** German merchants and traders guild.
**Hansgrave.** Head of a corporation.
**Hap.** To catch.
**Happiness.** Comfort; contentment.
**Harbor.** Port.
**Harbor.** To conceal a fugitive from justice.
**Hard Cider.** Fermented cider.
**Hard Labor.** Punishment which includes useful labor as well as imprisonment.
**Hard Money.** Lawful coined money.
**Harlot.** Prostitute.
**Harrow.** Hue and cry.
**Hat Money.** Small duty paid to the captain.
**Haula.** Court.
**Haut.** High.
**Haut Chemin.** Highway.
**Have.** To possess.
**Hawker.** Peddler.
**Hazar-Zamin.** Bail; surety.
**Hazard.** Game of chance; danger; risk.
**Hazardous.** Perilous.
**Head.** Chief; principal.
**Head Money.** Poll tax; money distributed among officers and crew of a ship.
**Head of a Family.** One who supports and maintains a household.
**Head Taxes.** Taxes levied on aliens.
**Headnotes.** Printed synopses of court decisions which appear in most reports.
**Healer.** One who cures disease by prayer.
**Health.** Absence of disease.
**Hearing.** Examination of one accused of a crime and of the witnesses for and against him; session of court to conduct a trial.
**Hearsay Evidence.** Evidence based on something which has been told to a witness rather than on personal knowledge.
**Head of Passion.** Spontaneous anger aroused by some reasonable provocation which will reduce a homicide from the grade of murder.
**Heat Prostration.** Sunstroke.
**Heat Stroke.** Sunstroke.
**Hebdomad.** A week.
**Heda.** Haven; wharf.
**Hedagium.** Toll for landing goods at a wharf.
**Hedging.** Means of making sales contracts in advance at current prices to protect against loss due to fluctuations.
**Hegemony.** Leadership by one of a group of states or nations.
**Heifer.** Young cow.
**Heir.** One who inherits property.
**Heir Apparent.** One who is sure to succeed to the estate if he survives his ancestor.
**Heiress.** Female who inherits an estate.
**Heirloom.** Any personal chattels which go directly to the heir and not to the executor.
**Heirship.** Condition of being an heir.
**Heir Testamentary.** One to whom property is left by will.
**Hemiplegia.** Paralysis of one side of the body, usually due to a lesion in the brain.
**Henchman.** Attendant; servant.
**Henghen.** Prison.
**Heptarchy.** Government by seven rulers.
**Herald.** Messenger.
**Herbage.** Right or easement of pasturing cattle on another's land.
**Herd.** Indefinite number of cattle assembled.
**Hereafter.** At a future time.
**Hereby Granted.** Transfer of interest.
**Hereditaments.** Anything inherited.
**Hereditament, Corporeal.** Any hereditament that can be perceived by the senses.
**Hereditaments, Incorporated.** Any right concerning a corporeal hereditament.
**Hereditary.** Pertaining to inheritance.
**Hereditary Succession.** Title by descent.
**Heredity.** Biological law whereby all beings tend to repeat themselves in their descendants.
**Heres.** Heir.
**Heresy.** False belief.
**Heretofore.** Formerly.
**Heritable.** Inheritable.
**Heritable Rights.** Rights in real property.
**Heritage.** An inheritance.
**Heritor.** Proprietor of an inheritance.
**Hermaphrodite.** One having the sexual organs of both sexes.
**Heroin.** Narcotic drug.
**Hesia.** Easement.
**Hidel.** Sanctuary.
**Hierarchy.** Organization of a governing body in the order of their importance and rank.
**Highbinder.** Member of a Chinese society organized for murder or blackmail.
**High Diligence.** Great diligence.
**High-Jacker.** Robber.
**High Justice.** The right to try all crimes.
**High Seas.** Open and enclosed parts of ocean.
**High Treason.** Treason against the king or the government.
**High-Water Mark.** Line on shore reached at high tide.
**Highway.** A road open to public use and broad enough to permit the passage of vehicles.
**Highwayman.** Robber.
**H.I.H.** (Abb.:. His or Her Imperial Majesty.
**Hiis Testibus.** With these witnesses.
**Hinc Inde.** On each side.
**Hind.** Agricultural servant.
**Hire.** To receive for payment, the temporary use of a thing or to stipulate for services.
**Hire.** Compensation for the use of a thing.
**Hireman.** A subject.
**Hirer.** One who acquires the right to use a thing belonging to another.
**Hissa.** Lot or portion.
**Hoc.** This.
**Hoc Paratus Est Verificare.** This he is ready to verify.
**Hoc Titulo.** Under this title.
**Hoc Voce.** Under this word.
**Hogshead.** Liquid measure equal to 63 gallons.
**Hold.** To possess; to bind under contract; to maintain; to administer.
**Holder.** One who has legal possession of a negotiable instrument.
**Holder in Due Course.** A holder of a negotiable instrument who has paid value for it.
**Holding.** Tenure.
**Holding Company.** Corporation organized to hold the stocks of other corporations.
**Hold Over.** Retention of real property by a tenant after expiration of the lease.
**Hold-Up.** Robbery by threat and use of lethal weapons.
**Holiday.** A day on which public business is suspended by statute.
**Holographic Will.** Will written entirely in the testator's hand.
**Holt.** Grove.
**Holy Orders.** Ecclesiastical orders.
**Home.** House in which one lives.
**Home Office.** Office of the British Government which supervises the internal affairs of the empire; the office of a corporation in the state where it was created.
**Homestead.** The residence of the family.

**Homicide.** Any killing of a human being.
**Homicide Infortunium.** Excusable homicide.
**Homicide Se Defendendo.** Justifiable homicide committed in self-defense.
**Homicide, Excusable.** Killing of a human being by accident or in self-defense.
**Homicide, Felonious.** Killing of a human being without justification or excuse in law.
**Homicide, Justifiable.** Intentional killing of a human being without evil intent.
**Homocidium.** Homocide.
**Hominum Causa Jus Constitutum.** Law is constituted for the benefit of mankind.
**Homiplagium.** Mayhem.
**Homme.** A man.
**Homo.** A man.
**Homo Liber.** A free man.
**Homologation.** Ratification or confirmation.
**Homonymial.** Cases in which the same principles and rules of law as set down in previous cases are repeated.
**Honestus.** Of good character.
**Honesty.** Financial integrity; loyalty.
**Honor.** To accept a negotiable instrument at maturity and according to tenor.
**Honorable.** Title used when addressing certain officials, e.g. judges, congressmen.
**Honorarium.** Compensation for services.
**Honorary Service.** Service rendered gratis.
**Honoris Causa.** As a mark of honor.
**Hony.** Shame, evil.
**Hooch.** (Slang). Intoxicating beverage.
**Hora.** An hour.
**Horae Judiciae.** Hours of the court sessions.
**Hordera.** Treasurer.
**Hornswoggle** (Slang). Triumph over.
**Hors.** Out, out of; without.
**Horse Power.** Unit of power capable of lifting 33,000 pounds a foot a minute.
**Hors Pris.** Taken out; except.
**Hortus.** Garden.
**Hospes.** Guest.
**Hospita.** Inns.
**Hostage.** Person held as security.
**Hostel.** Inn.
**Hosterler.** Host; innkeeper.
**Hostelry.** Inn.
**Hostes.** Enemies.
**Hosticide.** Killing of or one who kills an enemy.
**Hostile.** Adverse; the character of an enemy.
**Hostile Act.** Act of war.
**Hostile Witness.** A witness who is subject to cross-examination by the party who called him because of obvious hostility or prejudice against that party.
**Hot** (Slang). Term applied to recently stolen goods.
**Hotel.** Inn.
**Housage.** Charges for storage of goods.
**House.** Structure intended for human dwelling; one of the bodies of a bicameral legislature; mercantile firm; reigning family.
**Housebreaking.** Forcible entry into a dwelling with intent to commit a felony.
**Household.** The family living together.
**Household Furniture, Goods or Stuff.** Personal chattels used for the house.
**House of Commons.** Lower house of English Parliament.
**House of Correction.** Reformatory.
**House of Ill Fame.** Brothel.
**House of Lords.** Upper house of English Parliament.
**House of Refuge.** Reformatory for juveniles.
**House of Representatives.** Lower house of U.S. Congress and some state legislatures.
**House of Worship.** Building for religious services; church.
**Hovel.** Hut; cottage.
**How.** Hill.
**Hoy.** Small sailboat.
**H.R.M.** (Abb.). His or Her Royal Highness.
**Huckster.** Peddler, particularly of garden produce.
**Humagium.** A humid place.
**Humane.** Kind; benevolent.
**Humbug.** Imposter.
**Hung Jury.** Jury which cannot agree.
**Hunger.** The desire to eat; hunger is not an excuse for larceny.
**Hunting.** Pursuing of wild animals.
**Hurdle.** A sledge in which criminals were formerly dragged to execution.
**Hurricane.** Violent storm with high winds.
**Hurst.** Grove; wood.
**Hurt.** Physical injury or mental discomfort.
**Husband.** Married man.
**Husband and Wife.** Man and woman married.
**Husbandman.** Farmer.
**Husbandry.** Agriculture.
**Hush-Money** (Coll.). Bribe for silence.
**Hustings.** Council; court.
**Hybrid.** Mongrel.
**Hypermetropia.** Farsightedness.
**Hypotism.** Induced somnambulism.
**Hypothecation.** A contract whereby specific property is pledged as security.
**Hypothesis.** Supposition; theory.
**Hypothetical Question.** A supposition creating a specific situation upon which the opinion of an expert is asked.
**Hysterotomy.** Caesarian operation.

## I

**Ibi.** There; then.
**Ibid.** See Ibidem.
**Ibidem.** In the same place; indicate that a phrase appears in a passage already quoted.
**Ibimus.** We will go.
**I.C.** (Abb.). Inspected and condemned.
**Icona.** Image or representation of a thing.
**Ictus.** Blow.
**Ictus Orbis.** A blow causing a bruise.
**Id.** It; that.
**Idem.** The same.
**Idem Sonans.** Sounding the same; names pronounced the same but varied in spelling.
**Identical.** Exactly the same.
**Identification.** Proof that a person or thing is the same as he or it is represented.
**Identity.** Sameness; see Identification.
**Ideo.** Therefore; on that account.
**Ides.** Roman division of time.
**Id Est.** That is.
**Idiochira.** Privately executed instrument.
**Idiocy.** Extreme mental deficiency.
**Idiot.** One who has been mentally deficient from his birth.
**Idiota.** An unlearned man.
**Idoneare.** To prove one's own innocence.
**Idoneus.** Fit, responsible, qualified.
**Idonietas.** Fitness.
**I.E.** (Abb.). Id est; that is.
**If.** Word which implies a condition.
**Ignis Judicium.** Trial by fire.
**Ignitegium.** Curfew.
**Ignominy.** Public disgrace.
**Ignoramus.** We do not know. Formerly the indorsement on a bill of indictment when the Grand Jury thought the charge groundless.
**Ignorance.** Absence of knowledge.
**Ignorantia.** Ignorance.
**Ignorare.** To be ignorant of; to ignore.
**Ignore.** To be unacquainted with.
**Il.** He; it.
**Ilet.** Small island.
**Illegal.** Unlawful.
**Illegal Interest.** Usury.
**Illegitimate.** Begotten and born out of wedlock; contrary to law.
**Illeviable.** Exempt from levy.
**Ill Fame.** Evil repute.
**Illicenciatus.** Unlicensed.
**Illicit.** Unlawful.
**Illiterate.** Unlettered; unlearned.
**Illocable.** Not able to be hired.
**Illud.** That.
**Illusion.** That which a person believes he sees, but really does not.
**Illusory.** Deceiving by false appearances.
**Imbargo.** See Embargo.
**Imbecile.** One who is mentally deficient and incapable of managing his own affairs.
**Immaterial.** Not pertinent.
**Immediate.** At once.
**Immediately.** Without delay.
**Immediate Death.** Instantaneous death.
**Immediate Family.** Members of the same household bound by relationship.
**Immemorial.** Beyond human memory.
**Immemorial Usage.** Custom.
**Immigration.** Coming into a country to take up permanent residence.
**Imminent.** Impending; threatening; perilous.
**Immiscere.** To mingle.

**Immittere.** To put into; admit.
**Immobilis.** Immovable.
**Immoderate.** Exceeding reasonable limits.
**Immoral.** Contrary to accepted standards.
**Immovables.** Property which by its nature cannot be removed.
**Immunity.** Exemption from legal punishment.
**Immunity of Witness.** Constitutional provision protecting witnesses from giving self-incriminating testimony.
**Impair.** To weaken; make worse.
**Impalare,** To impound.
**Impalement.** Inclosure.
**Imparcare.** Impound; imprison.
**Impargamentum.** Right of impounding.
**Imparl.** To discuss a controversy with the opposing party in a suit in order to settle.
**Imparlance.** Discussion between parties of a suit to settle the dispute amicably.
**Impartial.** Disinterested.
**Impeach.** Accuse; censure.
**Impeachment.** Criminal proceeding against a public official.
**Impeachment of Waste.** Liability for waste.
**Impechiare.** To impeach.
**Impede.** To obstruct; hinder.
**Impediens.** One who impedes or hinders.
**Impediments.** Disabilities; bars to marriage.
**Impensae.** Expenses.
**Imperative.** Imposing an obligation.
**Imperator.** Emperor.
**Imperfect.** Defective, incomplete.
**Imperfect Obligation.** One which cannot be enforced but depends on an individual's will.
**Imperfect Trust.** One which has not been executed.
**Imperite.** Without skill.
**Imperium.** Rule, authority.
**Impertinence.** Irrelevancy.
**Impertinent.** Applied to allegations of a bill in equity which do not belong to a pleading.
**Impescare.** Impeach.
**Impetere.** Impeach.
**Impierment.** Impairing.
**Impignorata.** Pledged, mortgaged.
**Implead.** Sue.
**Implements.** Things necessary to perform the work of any trade.
**Implication.** That which is inferred.
**Implied.** Not explicit; not expressed.
**Implied Authority.** Actual authority possessed by an agent.
**Implied in Fact.** Applied to situations when the conduct of individuals is used to prove the existence of a transaction.
**Implied Power.** Powers exercised by a governing body which are proper and necessary.
**Import.** Bring goods into a country.
**Importunity.** Pressing solicitation.
**Impose.** To levy or exact.
**Imposition.** Impost; tax.
**Impossibility.** That which cannot be done.
**Impotence.** Inability to perform the sexual act; any physical incapacity.
**Impotent.** Incapable of the sexual act.
**Impound.** To shut up stray animals in a pound; to place disputed property in the custody of the court.
**Imprescriptible Rights.** Rights not capable of being lost, whether used or not.
**Impression.** Image fixed in the mind; a belief.
**Impressment.** Seizing seamen for compulsory service in the navy.
**Imprest Money.** Money paid on enlisting.
**Impretiabilis.** Invaluable.
**Imprimatur.** Let it be printed.
**Imprimere.** Impress; print.
**Imprimis.** First of all.
**Imprison.** Confine; deprive of liberty.
**Impristi.** Followers.
**Improbable.** Unlikely.
**Improbare.** Disallow; disprove.
**Improbation.** Action to have an instrument declared false and forged.
**Improper.** Not suitable; unfit.
**Improper Influence.** Undue influence.
**Improve.** Disprove; impeach; augment.
**Improved Land.** Land used to good purpose.
**Improvement.** Anything that enhances the value of property.
**Impruiare.** To improve.
**Impubes.** Minor not the age of puberty.
**Impulse.** Act of driving onward with force.
**Impunity.** Exemption from punishment.
**Imputatio.** Legal liability.
**Imputation of Payment.** Application of a payment made by a debtor to his creditor.
**Imputed.** In the legal use, attributed vicariously.
**In Action.** Not in possession; recoverable by action.
**Inadequate.** Insufficient.
**Inadmissible.** Not receivable as evidence.
**In Adversum.** Against a hostile party.
**Inadvertence.** Lack of care or attention.
**Inaedificatio.** Building on another's land with one's own materials or on one's own land with another's material.
**In Aequali.** In equal right.
**Inalienable.** That which cannot be transferred.
**In Alio Loco.** In another place.
**In Ambiquo.** In doubt.
**In and About.** In connection with.
**In Aperta Luce.** In broad daylight.
**In Apicibus Juris.** In the extremes of the law.
**In Articulo.** On the point.
**In Articulo Mortis.** On the point of death.
**In Auditu.** Within the hearing.
**Inauguration.** The installing into office.
**In Autre Droit.** In the right of another.
**In Banco.** On the bench.
**In Being.** Alive.
**In Blank.** Without qualification.
**Inblaura.** Profit or produce from the soil.
**In Bonis.** Among the goods.
**Inc.** (Abb.). Incorporated.
**In Camera.** In chambers.
**Incapacity.** Lack of legal power.
**In Case.** In the event.
**In Casu Consimili.** In a similar case.
**Incarceration.** Imprisonment.
**Incaustum.** Ink.
**Incendiary.** One guilty of arson.
**Inception.** Beginning; commencement.
**Incest.** Sexual intercourse between persons so closely related that marriage is prohibited.
**In Chief.** Primary; applied to direct examination of a witness.
**Inchoate.** Incomplete; imperfect.
**Incident.** A minor characteristic found in connection with a more important or principal quality.
**Incidental.** Depending upon something else.
**cidere.** Happen; occur.
**Incipitur.** It is begun; used at the beginning of a common law pleading or judgment.
**Incineration.** Burning to ashes.
**Incite.** Arouse to action.
**Incivile.** Unjustly; irregular; improper.
**Incivism.** Hostility to one's government.
**Inclose.** To surround.
**Inclose Lands.** Lands surrounded by barriers.
**Include, Inclusive.** Contain; embrace.
**Incola.** Inhabitant.
**Incombustible.** Incapable of being burned.
**Income.** Money which one receives from business, labor or capital invested.
**Income Excise Tax.** Tax on income.
**Income Tax.** A tax levied directly upon incomes of an individual or corporation.
**In Commendam.** In the care of; in trust.
**In Common.** Sharing the use of a thing.
**In Communi.** In common.
**Incompatibility.** Not able to exist together.
**Incompetency.** Lack of ability.
**Incompetent.** One not mentally capable to manage his affairs.
**Inconclusive.** Subject to disproof or rebuttal.
**Inconsistent.** Mutually contradictory.
**Inconsulto.** Unadvisedly; unintentionally.
**Incontinency.** Illicit sexual intercourse.
**Incontinenti.** Immediately.
**Incontrovertible.** Too certain to admit of dispute.
**Inconvenience.** Disquiet, annoyance.
**Incorporamus.** We incorporate.
**Incorporate.** To form a corporation.
**Incorporation.** The formal act of creating a corporation according to statute.
**Incorporator.** One of the persons who institutes the steps to form a corporation.
**In Corpore.** In body.
**Incorporeal.** Without body.
**Incorporeal Property.** Intangible property.
**Incorrigible.** Incapable of being corrected.
**Increase.** Growth; development; profit.
**Increment.** Increase; improvement; addition.
**Incrementum.** Increase.
**Incriminate.** To charge with a crime.

**Inculpate.** To accuse.
**Inculpatory.** Tending to establish guilt.
**Incumbent.** One presently holding office.
**Incumber.** To make land subject to a liability.
**Incumbrancer.** One who has a legal claim upon an estate.
**Incur.** To become liable for.
**In Curia.** In court.
**Incurramentum.** Liability to fine or penalty.
**In Custodia Legis.** In legal custody.
**In Damno.** Doing damage.
**Inde.** Thence.
**Indebitatus.** Indebted.
**Indebitatus Nunquam.** Never indebted.
**Indebitum.** Not due or owing.
**Indebtedness.** Any liability.
**Indecency.** That which is against good behavior.
**Indecent.** Unfit to be seen or heard.
**Indecent Exposure.** Intentional exposure of the private parts of one's body in public.
**Indefeasible.** That which cannot be defeated.
**Indefensus.** Undefended.
**Indefinite.** Not having fixed boundaries or distinguishing characteristics.
**In Delicto.** Guilty; at fault.
**Indemnatus.** Uncondemned.
**Indemnificatus.** Indemnified.
**Indemnify.** To save harmless against loss or damage by another; to make good.
**Indemnis.** Without harm or damage.
**Indemnity.** Contract by which one person promises to make good any loss or damage another has incurred while acting at his request.
**Indemnity Mortgage.** A mortgage executed to indemnify the mortgagee against future loss.
**Indenture.** A written agreement between two..
**In Descendu.** By descent.
**Indeterminate.** Uncertain.
**Indeterminate Sentence.** Criminal sentence imposing a punishment not greater than the maximum nor less than the minimum penalty.
**Indicare.** Show; reveal; declare.
**Indication.** A fact pointing to some inference.
**Indicia** (pl.). Signs or evidence.
**Indicia of Ownership.** Evidence of title.
**Indicium.** Mark; sign; evidence.
**Indictable Offense.** Felony.
**Indictare.** To indict.
**Indicted.** Charged in an indictment with a criminal offense.
**Indictee.** One who has been indicted.
**Indictio.** Indictment; declaration.
**Indictment.** Formal accusation made by a Grand Jury charging a person with a crime.
**Indicator.** One who causes indictment.
**In Diem.** For, on or at a day.
**Indifferent.** Impartial; neutral; unprejudiced.
**Indigent.** Destitute; poor.
**Indigent Person.** Pauper.
**Indignity.** Any act which manifests contempt or incivility toward another.
**Indirect.** Not an immediate relationship.
**Indirect Evidence.** Circumstantial evidence.
**Indispensable.** Vital; essential.
**Indispensable Evidence.** Evidence without which the proof of a given fact is impossible.
**Indisputable.** Undeniable; conclusive.
**Indistanter.** Without delay.
**Individual.** A single person.
**Individually.** Separately and personally.
**Individuum.** Indivisible.
**Indivisible.** Inseparable; whole; entire.
**Indivisum.** Undivided; owned in common.
**Indorsat.** Indorsed.
**Indorse.** To write one's name on the back of a paper or document.
**Indorsee.** One to whom a negotiable instrument is indorsed.
**Indorsement.** Writing on the back of an instrument.
**Indorser.** One who indorses a negotiable instrument.
**In Dorso.** On the back.
**In Dubio.** In doubt.
**Induce.** Request; entice; cause.
**Inducement.** Motive for an act; matter stated in a pleading by way of introduction.
**Induct.** Install; inaugurate.
**Inductio.** Cancellation; obliteration.
**Indulgence.** Remission of punishment due to sin, granted by the R.C. Church; grade; favor.
**In Duplo, in Duplum.** In double the amount.
**Industry.** Habitual diligence; any business conducted for profit.
**Inebriate.** Alcoholic; drunkard.
**Inebriation.** Intoxication.
**In Effect.** In force; in operation.
**Ineligible.** Not qualified to be elected to office.
**In Equity.** In a court of equity.
**In Esse.** In existence or being.
**In Essentialibus.** In the essentials.
**In Evidence.** Before the court after having been introduced and received as evidence.
**Inevitable.** Unavoidable.
**In Excambio.** In exchange.
**In Extenso.** Fully; verbatim.
**In Extremis.** In the last extremity; at the end.
**In Facie Curiae.** In the presence of the court.
**In Faciendo.** In doing or making.
**In Facto.** In fact or deed.
**Infamia.** Infamy; disgrace.
**Infamis.** Of ill repute; disreputable.
**Infamous.** Wicked; criminal.
**Infamy.** Any criminal or vicious conduct which implies bad character as well as violation of law and involves the guilty person in disgrace.
**Infancy.** One under 21 years of age.
**Infans.** A child under the age of 7.
**Infant.** A minor.
**Infantia.** Between birth and 7 years.
**Infanticide.** Killing of a new born child.
**In Favorem Libertatis.** In favor of liberty.
**In Favorem Vitae.** In favor of life.
**In Fee.** In fee simple.
**Inference.** Conclusion derived from the proof of certain facts.
**Inferential.** Deducible from proven facts.
**Inferior Court.** Any court subordinate to the chief appellate tribunal in the particular judicial system.
**Inficiari.** To deny.
**Inficiatio.** Denial; denial of a debt or liability.
**Infidel.** One who does not believe in God.
**Infidelis.** Infidel.
**Infidelitas.** Infidelity.
**Infidelity.** Unfaithfulness in marriage.
**In Fieri.** In the process of being done.
**In Fine.** At the end.
**Infirm.** Weak; feeble.
**Infirmative.** Having the tendency to weaken.
**Infirmity.** A defect in a document which subjects it to attack on the ground of invalidity; ailment of substantial character.
**In Flagrante Delicto.** In the act of the crime.
**Informal.** Deficient in legal form.
**Informality.** Want of legal form.
**Information.** A written accusation made by an official prosecutor, without a presentment by a Grand Jury, charging a person.
**Informer.** One who gives information to public officials concerning criminal offenses.
**In Foro.** In the court.
**In Foro Conscientiae.** In good faith.
**In Foro Conteintioso.** In a court of litigation.
**In Foro Domestico.** In the home.
**In Foro Legis.** In a court of law.
**Infortunium.** Misfortune.
**Infra.** Under; below; within; duiing.
**Infra Aetatem.** Under age.
**Infra Anno Nubiles.** Under marriageable age.
**Infra Annum.** Within a year.
**Infra Civitatem.** Within the state.
**Infra Corpus Comitatus.** With the county body.
**Infraction.** Violation of a law or contract.
**Infra Dignitatem.** Beneath the dignity.
**Infra Furorem.** While insane.
**Infra Sex Annos.** Within 6 years.
**Infra Tridium.** Within 3 days.
**In Fraudem Legis.** In fraud of the law.
**Infraction.** Violation.
**Infringement.** Encroachment upon; violation of a law, contract or right.
**Infugare.** To chase.
**In Full Life.** Alive both civilly and physically.
**In Futuro.** In the future.
**In Genere.** In class or kind.
**Inge.** Meadow; pasture.
**Ingenium.** Trick; fraud.
**In Gremio Legis.** In the bosom of the law; applied to that held in abeyance.
**Ingress.** Entry.
**Ingress, Egress and Regress.** Used in leases to express the right of a lessee to enter, go upon and return from the land in question.
**Ingressu.** Writ of entry.
**Ingressus.** Ingress.

**In Gross.** In large quantity, personal.
**Ingrossing.** Making a clear copy from a rough draft of a document.
**Inguinal.** Term referring to the groin.
**Inhabit.** Dwell; live.
**Inhabitant.** One residing in a particular place.
**In Hac Parte.** On this side; in this behalf.
**In Haec Verba.** In these words.
**Inherent.** Intrinsic; a part of.
**Inherent Power.** Authority possessed.
**Inheretrix.** Heiress.
**Inherit.** To take by descent on the death of another.
**Inheritance.** The right to succeed to the estate of an intestate; the estate itself.
**Inheritance Tax.** Tax on property transfer.
**Inhibition.** Prohibition.
**In His Verbis.** In these words.
**In Hoc.** In this.
**Inhonestus.** Dishonorable.
**Inhuman Treatment.** As a ground for divorce, any cruelty which endangers the life or health of the party concerned.
**In Hunc Modum.** In this manner.
**In Iisdem Terminis.** In the same terms.
**In Infinitum.** Without end.
**In Initialibus.** In the beginning.
**In Initio Litis.** At the beginning of the litigation.
**In Invidium.** With ill will.
**In Invitum.** Against an unwilling person.
**Iniquity.** A judicial error.
**In Issue.** Applied to a matter regularly and properly in controversy before the court.
**Initiate.** Begun, commenced.
**Initiate Curtesy.** The interest of the husband during the lifetime of his wife in her lands after a child is born who may inherit.
**Initiative.** The right of the people to propose bills and laws to be enacted by the legislature on which the people may vote.
**In Itinere.** On a journey or voyage.
**Initium.** Beginning.
**In Judgment.** In a court.
**In Judicio.** In a legal or judicial proceeding.
**Injunction.** A restraining order.
**In Jure.** In law, legally.
**In Jure Alterius.** In the right of another.
**Injuria.** A wrong; violation of a legal right.
**Injury.** Any wrong or damage done to another.
**In Jus Vocare.** To summon to court.
**Inlagare, Inlagation.** To restore to the law.
**Inland.** Within the limits of a state, territorty or country.
**Inland Bill of Exchange.** Bills drawn and payable in the state where made.
**In Law.** Implied by law.
**Inlaw.** To restore an outlaw.
**Inleased.** Trapped.
**In Lecto.** In bed.
**In Lieu of.** In place of.
**In Limine.** At the outset.
**In Linea Recta.** In the direct line.
**In Litem.** In or for a litigation.
**In Loco.** In the place.
**In Loco Parentis.** In place of a parent.
**In Majorem Cautelam.** Of greater caution.
**In Malam Partem.** In an evil sense.
**Inmate.** One who resides in an institution or part of another's house.
**In Medias Res.** In the heart of the matter.
**In Misericordia.** At the mercy.
**In Mitiori Sensu.** In a milder sense.
**In Mora.** In delay.
**Inn.** Public house where transients can receive food, lodging and other accomodations.
**Innamium.** Pledge.
**Innings.** Lands reclaimed from the sea.
**Innkeeper.** One who keeps a house for the lodging of travelers.
**Innocence.** Freedom from guilt.
**Innocent.** Not guilty.
**Innocent Woman.** One who has never had illicit sexual intercourse.
**Innominate.** In civil law, unclassified.
**Innotescimus.** We make known.
**In Notis.** In the notes.
**Innoxiare.** To exculpate.
**In Nubilius.** In the clouds; applied to that held in abeyance.
**Innuendo.** That part of a declaration or complaint in an action for libel or slander in which the alleged libelous words are explained.
**In Nullo Est Erratum.** No error committed.
**In Octavis.** In 8 days.
**In Odium Spoliatoris.** In hatred of one who despoils.
**Inofficiosum.** Contrary to natural duty.
**Inofficiosum Testamentum, Inofficious Will.** A will which violates the natural wish of a dying man to provide for his family.
**In Omnibus.** In everything.
**In Open Court.** Before the court while it is in public session.
**Inopportune.** At the wrong time.
**Inops Consilii.** Without legal counsel.
**Inordinatus.** An intestate; one who dies without leaving a valid will.
**In Ore.** In the mouth.
**In Pacato Solo.** On peaceful soil.
**In Pais.** In the country; outside the court or legal proceeding.
**In Pari Causa.** In a similar case.
**In Pari Delicto.** Equally in the wrong.
**In Pari Materia.** In the same matter.
**In Pari Passu.** On equal footing.
**In Patiendo.** In suffering or permitting.
**In Pendente.** In suspense.
**In Perpetuum Rei Memoriam.** In perpetual memory of the thing.
**In Person.** Appearing in court on one's own behalf without benefit of counsel.
**In Personam.** In the law of procedure, applied to an action which is instituted by giving notice to the party affected, either by personal or by substituted service of process; applied to describe the fact that a court of equity usually enforces its decree by ordering persons to do or not to do certain acts.
**In Plena Vita.** In full life.
**In Pleno Lumine.** In the daytime.
**In Poenam.** By way of punishment.
**In Posse.** In possibility.
**In Posterum.** In the future.
**In Potentia.** In possibility.
**In Potestate Parentis.** Under the control of a parent.
**In Praesenti.** In the present.
**In Praesentia Diversorum.** In the presence of divers persons.
**In Prender.** That which is to be taken.
**In Primis.** In the first place.
**In Prinicipio.** In the beginning.
**In Promptus.** Impromptu; in readiness.
**In Propria Persona.** In one's own behalf.
**Inquest.** A general name for any judicial inquiry; an investigation held by a coronor.
**In Quindena.** In 15 days.
**Inquirendo.** Authorization to institute an inquiry on behalf of the government.
**Inquisitio.** Inquest; investigation.
**Inquisition.** Inquest; inquiry.
**Inquisitor.** An official investigator.
**In Re.** In the matter.
**In Rebus.** In matters; in transactions.
**In Rem.** Action instituted against a thing rather than a person.
**In Rem Suam.** In his own business.
**In Render.** That which is to be paid or given.
**In Rerum Natura.** In the nature of things.
**In Rixa.** In a quarrel.
**Inroll.** Enroll.
**Insane, Insanity.** Of unsound mind.
**Inscribere.** To charge with a crime.
**Inscriptio.** Written accusation of crime.
**Insecure.** Unsafe and dangerous.
**Insensible.** Unintelligible.
**In Separali.** In severalty.
**Insidiator.** One who lies in wait.
**Insignia.** Emblems of rank; distinctive marks.
**Insilium.** Bad counsel.
**In Simile Materia.** In a like matter.
**Insimul.** Together; jointly.
**Insimul Computassent.** They have together calculated; a common law action to recover a balance due in an account stated.
**Insinuare.** To deposit in the records.
**Insinuatio.** Suggestion, information.
**Insinuation.** In Civil Law, copying something into a public record.
**Insinuation of a Will.** In Civil Law, the production of a will of a decedent for probate.
**Insolation.** Sunstroke.
**Insolent.** Rude; abusive.
**In Solido.** In entirety.
**In Solidum.** As a whole.
**In Solutum.** In payment.
**Insolvency.** Inability to pay one's debts.
**Insolvent.** Status of one who is unable to pay.

**In Spe.** In hope.
**In Specie.** In kind; in U.S. currency.
**Inspect.** Examine.
**Inspectator.** Adversary.
**Inspection.** Careful investigation.
**Inspeximus.** We have seen; an official copy.
**Install.** Induct into office.
**Installment.** Partial payment of a debt.
**Instance.** Request; precedent; solicitation.
**Instant.** Present, current.
**Instantaneous.** Applied to a crime, one which is fully consummated in and by a single act.
**Instanter.** At once, immediately.
**Instantly.** Immediately.
**Instar.** Image; likeness; equal.
**Instar Dentium.** Like teeth.
**In Statu Quo.** In the situation in which.
**Instaurum.** Farming equipment.
**Instigate.** Incite to action.
**Instirpare.** To establish.
**Institor.** In Civil Law, a clerk or agent.
**Institute.** To begin or inaugurate an action; one named in a will as heir but directed to transfer the property.
**Institutes.** Elementary treatises on the law.
**Institution.** Inauguration of anything.
**In Stricto Jure.** In strict law.
**Instruct.** Direct; advise; to give instructions.
**Instructions.** Directions of a superior.
**Instrument.** Formal document in writing.
**Instrumenta.** Unsealed writings admitted as evidence.
**Instrumental.** Helpful.
**Insubordination.** Disobedience to authority.
**In Subsidium.** By way of subsidy.
**In Substantialibus.** Substantially.
**Insufficiency.** Failure of an answer to meet the allegations of any pleading.
**Insula.** Island; separated building.
**Insultus.** An assault.
**In Summa.** On the whole.
**In Summo Jure.** In strictest law.
**Insuper.** Moreover.
**In Superficie.** On the surface.
**Insurance.** A contract whereby one party, the insurer, agrees to indemnify another, the insured, against loss, damage or liability.
**Insurance Agent.** One authorized to negotiate policies for an insurance company.
**Insurance Broker.** One who negotiates insurance contracts.
**Insurer.** One who promises to indemnify.
**Insurgent.** One who participates in an insurrection.
**Insurrection.** Rebellion.
**In Suspenso.** In abeyance.
**Intaker.** Receiver of stolen goods.
**In Tantum.** In so much.
**Integer.** Whole; entire; untouched.
**Integral.** Complete.
**Integration.** The act of making whole or entire.
**Integrity.** Sound principles and character.
**Intemperance.** Inclination to drink to excess.
**Intend.** To design; resolve.
**Intendant.** Manager; director; superintendent.
**Intended Wife.** Betrothed.
**Intendment.** Meaning.
**Intendment of Law.** The meaning of the law.
**Intent, Intention.** The purpose with which a person acts.
**Intentio.** In Civil Law, intent, intention.
**Intentional.** Willful.
**Intentional Injury.** Willful, conduct.
**Inter.** Among or between.
**Inter Alia.** Among other things.
**Inter Alios.** Between or among others.
**Inter Amicos.** Among or between friends.
**Inter Apices Juris.** Among the subtleties of the law.
**Inter Caeteros.** Among others.
**Intercedere.** In Civil Law, intervene; to become bound for another's debt.
**Intercommon.** To enjoy mutual rights.
**Inter Conjuges.** Between husband and wife.
**Intercourse.** Communication.
**Interdiction.** In Civil Law, court order depriving a person of the exercise of his civil rights; in International Law, cessation of all trade between two countries.
**Interesse.** Interest.
**Interesse Termini.** Interest of the term; interest a lessee acquires in the lands.
**Interest.** Right or title of any extent in any property or estate; compensation for the use of money which is due.
**Interest Bearing Stock.** Preferred stock.
**Interested Person.** One who has some legal right or who is under some legal liability.
**Interests.** Any rights of property less title.
**Interfere.** Hinder; intervene.
**Interference.** Proceedings in patent law to determine priority of two inventions.
**Interim.** Meanwhile.
**Interim Curator.** Temporary guardian.
**Interlineation.** Writing between the lines.
**Interlocking Directors.** Persons who simultaneously serve as members of the boards of directors of two or more corporations.
**Interlocutory.** Provisional; temporary.
**Interlopers.** Persons operating without the license required by law.
**Intermarriage.** The act of marriage between two persons considered as members of different groups.
**Intermeddle.** To interfere officiously.
**Intermediary.** Broker; one who negotiates.
**Intermediate.** Intervening.
**Inter Minora Crimina.** Among the minor crimes.
**Intermittent Easement.** An easement used only occasionally.
**Intern.** To incarcerate a person as a political prisoner.
**Internal Revenue.** Revenue raised from any source except duties on imports.
**International Copyrights.** Copyrights which are recognized as such by states or countries other than that of the writer.
**International Law.** Law which governs the intercourse of nations.
**Internuncio.** Representative of the Pope.
**Internuncius.** Messenger, go-between.
**Inter Partes.** Between the parties.
**Interpellation.** Summons.
**Interpleader.** Proceeding in equity in which a person in possession of property claimed by two or more persons adversely to each other, surrenders the property to the court to settle.
**Interpolate.** Add words in a written document.
**Interpret.** Construe; discover the meaning of a statute; to translate.
**Interpretation.** The art of discovering the true meaning of any form of words.
**Interregnum.** The period between the death of one sovereign and the election of another.
**Interrogatories.** Written questions prepared as part of a commission to take an oral deposition; written questions propounded by one party and served on an adversary before trial of the action and answered in writing.
**In Terrorem.** As a threat; applied to legacies given upon condition that the legatee shall not dispute the validity of the will.
**Interruptio.** Interruption.
**Interruption.** An arrest in the running of the statute of limitations or the period of prescription by the voluntary act of the party in whose favor the period runs, by an act of the adverse party, or by the advent of some incapacity of the adverse party.
**Inter Se.** Among themselves.
**Intersection.** The space occupied by two streets at the point where they cross.
**Interstate.** Between two or more states.
**Interstate Commerce.** Transactions which involve the movement of persons or goods from one state to another.
**Intervener.** One who voluntarily enters a litigation in which he was not an original party.
**Intervening Cause.** An independent cause which breaks the chain between the original negligent act and ensuing damage or loss.
**Intervention.** Proceeding permitted by statute in a number of states to enable persons to protect their rights when they are in danger of being injuriously affected by attachment proceedings; procedure whereby persons may intervene in litigation though not originally a party in the suit.
**Inter Virum et Uxorem.** Between husband and wife.
**Inter Vivos.** Between living persons.
**Intestabilis.** One disqualified from testifying.
**Intestable.** One not qualified to make a will.

**Intestacy.** State or condition of dying without leaving a valid will.
**Intestate.** One who dies without a will.
**Intestatus.** Intestate.
**In Testimonium.** In testimony.
**Intimacy.** Proper, friendly relation between persons; sometimes improper relation.
**Intimidation.** Unlawful coercion.
**In Totidem Verbis.** In so many words.
**In Toto.** In all; entirely.
**Intoxicated.** Under the influence of alcohol.
**Intoxicating Liquor.** Any alcoholic beverage which will produce intoxication in such quantities as may practically be drunk.
**Intoxication.** Drunkenness.
**Intra.** Inside; within.
**In Transitu.** In transit.
**Intrastate Commerce.** Trade within a state.
**Intra Vires.** Applied to a person or corporation when acting within authority.
**Intrinsic Evidence.** Evidence derived from a document without anything to explain it.
**Intrinsic value.** Inherent value.
**Introduction.** Part of a document which sets forth preliminary matter.
**Intruder.** One who wrongfully enters.
**Intrusion.** Wrongful entry of a stranger on land after a particular estate of freehold in them is determined.
**Intrust.** To confer a trust upon.
**Intuitu Matrimonii.** Contemplation of marriage.
**Intuitus.** View; regard; contemplation.
**In Tuto.** In safety.
**Inundation.** Flood.
**Inure.** To take effect as to benefit a person.
**Invade.** To assault.
**Invadiare.** To mortgage.
**Invadiatio.** Mortgage.
**Invadiatus.** One who has had pledges given for him.
**In Vadio.** In pledge; by way of security.
**Invalid.** Without binding force; null; void.
**Invasion.** Encroachment upon the rights of another; entry of an army for conquest.
**Inveigle.** Entice.
**Inveniendo.** Finding.
**Inventio.** In Civil Law, finding of goods.
**Invention.** A new and original creation upon which a patent may be issued.
**Inventory.** An itemized, detailed list of articles of property in an estate which executors and administrators are required by law to make.
**Inventus.** Found.
**Inveritare.** To verify.
**Invest.** To place money where it will yield an income or revenue.
**Investment.** The placing of capital in a business or for the purchase of secuirities.
**In Vinvulis.** In chains; in bondage.
**Inviolable.** Not to be violated.
**In Vita.** In life; living.
**Invitee.** One who is invited onto the premises.
**Invito Domino.** The owner being unwilling; used in an indictment for larceny to indicate that the act done in regard to property was not permitted.
**Invitus.** Against the wish.
**Invoice.** An itemized account of merchandise shipped from merchants to their correspondents setting forth the quantity, prices and charges.
**Invoice Price.** Prime cost.
**Involuntary.** Unintentional.
**Involuntary Payment.** Made under coercion.
**Iota.** Minutest quantity possible.
**I.O.U.** I owe you; written acknowledgment ot indebtedness.
**Ipse.** Himself; itself.
**Ipse Dixit.** He said it himself; a bare assertion resting on the authority of the individual.
**Ipsissimis Verbis.** In the very words.
**Ipso Facto.** By the fact itself.
**Ipso Jure.** By the law itself.
**Ira Motus.** Excited by anger.
**Ire Ad Largum.** To go at large.
**Iron Safe Clause.** Clause in an insurance policy stipulating that books of account and inventory be kept in an iron safe.
**Irrational.** Unreasonable.
**Irrebuttable Presumption.** One which is indisputable and cannot be changed.
**Irrecusable.** Contractual obligation imposed without one's consent.
**Irregular.** Not according to rule or form.
**Irregular Judgment.** One contrary to the course and practice of the courts.
**Irrelevant.** Not pertinent.
**Irreparable Injury.** One which cannot be adequately compensated by damages.
**Irrepleviable.** Anything which is not subject to an action for replevin.
**Irresistible Impulse.** A mental state amounting to a disease which overpowers the will.
**Irrevocable.** That which cannot be revoked or withdrawn.
**Irritus.** Ineffectual, void.
**Irrogare.** To impose: levy; as a fine.
**Irrotulatio.** An enrollment.
**Island.** Body of land surrounded by water.
**Issint.** Thus.
**Issuable.** Producing or relating to an issue; plea which permits issue of fact.
**Issue.** Lineal descendents; send forth; point in which one pleading contradicts the allegations of another; a question arising which must be determined for one side or the other; to send forth; to promulgate.
**Issues.** The profits of land.
**Ita.** Thus.
**Ita Est.** It is thus.
**Ita Quod.** So that.
**Ita Te Deus Adjuvet.** So help you God.
**Item.** Also; formerly used to mark the beginning of a new paragraph or every addition to a list of articles or of statements.
**Itemize.** To list.
**Iteratio.** Repetition.
**Itinerant.** Wandering; traveling.

## J

**J.** (Abb.). Judge.
**J.A.** (Abb.: Judge Advocate.
**Ja.** Now; yet.
**Jacens.** Lying in abeyance.
**Jactitation.** False boast.
**Jactitation of Marriage.** Wrongful assertion ol any person that he or she is married.
**Jactivus.** Lost by default.
**Jactura.** Jettison; tossing of goods overboard.
**Jail.** Prison.
**Jailer.** Warden of a prison or jail.
**Jake.** Colloquialism applied to a mixture of Jamaica ginger and some other drink.
**Janitor.** Doorkeeper.
**Jay Walking.** Crossing a street intersection diagonally.
**Jeopardy.** Danger, particularly of conviction and punishment for a crime.
**Jetsam.** Goods cast from a ship to lighten it.
**Jettage.** Tax on incoming ships.
**Jettison.** Voluntary throwing overboard of part of a vessel's cargo to lighten the ship.
**Jetty.** A projection devised to serve as protection against waves.
**Jim Crow Car.** Railway car for the exclusive accomodation of colored passengers.
**Jimmy.** Prying-bar used by burglars.
**J.J.** (Abb.). Judges.
**Jobber.** One who buys and sells goods.
**Jocalia.** Jewels.
**Jocelet.** Small farm.
**Jocus.** Game of chance.
**John Doe.** Fictitious name frequently used to indicate a party in an action or proceeding.
**Join.** Unite; act together.
**Joinder.** Uniting of several causes of action in one suit; uniting of different persons as parties plaintiff or defendent.
**Joint.** United; combined; coupled together.
**Joint Account.** An account in two or more names.
**Joint Action.** An action prosecuted or defended by two or more persons.
**Joint Adventure.** A community of interests among several persons.
**Joint and Several.** A liability in which the creditor may sue one or more of the obligors separately or together.
**Joint Creditors.** Creditors who can only enforce their claim by acting together.
**Joint Executor.** Co-executor.
**Jointist.** One who sells intoxicating liquors where such sales are prohibited by law.
**Jointly.** Unitedly; sharing in interest.
**Joint Resolution.** Resolution adopted concurrently by both houses of legislature.
**Joint Stock Company.** A company engaged in

business for profit, possessing a common capital divided into shares, of which each member possesses one or more.
**Joint Tenancy.** A holding of property by several persons in such a way that any one of them can act as owner of the whole.
**Jour.** Day.
**Jour in Court.** Day in court.
**Journal.** Book in which daily entries are made.
**Journée.** A court day.
**Journey.** Travel from place to place.
**Journeyman.** A laborer hired by the day.
**Journey-Work.** Work by the day.
**J.P.** (Abb.). Justice of the Peace.
**Jr.** (Abb.). Junior.
**Jubere.** To order, command, direct.
**Judaism.** Religion of the Jews.
**Judex.** Judge.
**Judge.** One appointed or elected to preside.
**Judge Advocate.** An officer of a court martial whose duty it is to advise the court and to act as prosecuting attorney.
**Judge Made Law.** Applied to decisions made by the courts as distinct from statute laws.
**Judge pro Tem.** A substitute judge.
**Judge's Chambers.** A judge's private office.
**Judge's Minutes or Notes.** Memoranda jotted down by the judge in the trial of an action.
**Judgement.** An opinion; the court decision.
**Judgment Book.** An official record of court judgments.
**Judgment by Default.** A judgment rendered in consequence of non-appearance.
**Judgment Creditor.** One in whose favor a judgment is rendered.
**Judgment Debtor.** One against whom a judgment has been rendered.
**Judgment Docket.** An official record of court judgments and their satisfaction.
**Judgment in Error.** Judgment of the higher court rendered on a writ of error.
**Judgment Lien.** A lien on real property arising from the filing of a judgment.
**Judgment Nihil.** A judgment against a party due to his failure to plead.
**Judgment Nisi.** A judgment which will become final unless cause is shown.
**Judgment Note.** A promissory note with the provision that upon default the holder may have judgment for the principal with interest.
**Judgment of His Peers.** Trial by jury.
**Judgment Paper.** The paper on which the final judgment of the court is written.
**Judicial Writ.** A writ subsequent to the original writ with which the litigation began.
**Judicare.** To judge, decide.
**Judicatio.** The passing of a sentence.
**Judicatories.** That department of government intended to interpret and administer the laws.
**Judicatory.** Court of justice.
**Judicature.** Court of justice; jurisdiction.
**Judicial.** Any act done under direction of a court; involving the exercise of judgment.
**Judicial Admission.** Statements made by a party in a legal proceeding, such a statement being admissable in evidence.
**Judicial Cognizance.** Knowledge upon which a judge is bound to act without having it proved in evidence.
**Judicial Confession.** A confession made by a party, such a confession being admissable in evidence against the party.
**Judicial Divorce.** One granted by the sentence of a court of justice.
**Judicial Function.** An act performed by virtue of judicial powers.
**Judicially.** Belonging to a judge.
**Judicial Mortgage.** A lien on real property arising from the filing of a judgment.
**Judicial Notice.** The power of a court to accept as proved certain notorious facts.
**Judicial Power.** The power granted to a court or judicial tribunal.
**Judicial Proceedings.** Any proceeding before a judge or court of justice.
**Judicial Review.** The power of the courts to review statutes or administrative acts and to determine their constitutionality.
**Judicial Separation.** Separation of man and wife by court decree, without divorce.
**Judiciary.** That branch of government which interprets and applies the laws; a judge.
**Judiciously.** Directed by good judgment.
**Judicium.** Judicial authority; trial; verdict.
**Judicium Capitale.** Death sentence.
**Judicium Dei.** The judgment of God; name for trial by ordeal or battle.
**Jugulator.** Cutthroat; murderer.
**Jumenta.** Beasts of burden.
**Jump Bail.** To flee in violation of a bail bond.
**Junior.** Younger; of secondary standing.
**Junk.** Rubbish.
**Junk Shop.** Place where odds and ends are bought and sold.
**Junty, Junto.** Political faction; secret council.
**Jura** (sing. Jus). Rights.
**Jura in Re.** Rights in a thing.
**Jural.** Relating to law or right.
**Juramentum.** An oath.
**Juramentum Calumniae.** Oath of calumny.
**Juramentum Corporalis.** Corporal oath; oath taken on the Bible.
**Juramentum Necessarium.** Necessary oath.
**Juramentum Voluntarium.** Voluntary oath.
**Jura Personam.** Rights of persons.
**Jura Praediorum.** The rights of landed estates.
**Jura Publica.** Public rights.
**Jurare.** To swear or take an oath.
**Jurat.** Certificate stating the time and place of an affidavit and the person before whom it was sworn.
**Jurata.** Jury.
**Juration.** The administration of an oath.
**Jurator.** One who swears; member of a jury.
**Jure.** By right; by the law.
**Jure Civili.** By the Civil Law.
**Jure Divino.** By divine right.
**Jure Gentium.** By the law of nations.
**Jure Mariti.** By the right of a husband.
**Jure Naturae.** By the law of nature.
**Jure Propinquitatis.** By right of nearness.
**Jure Representationes.** By right of representation.
**Jure Uxoris.** In the right of the wife.
**Juridical.** Pertaining to the law and the administration of justice.
**Juridical Day.** Day court is in session.
**Juris.** Of right; of law.
**Juris Consultus.** Learned in the law.
**Jurisdiction.** The authority whereby a court can render a valid judgment.
**Jurisdictional Dispute.** A dispute between rival labor organizations affecting their right to control workingmen.
**Juris et de Jure.** Of law and from law.
**Juris et Seisinae Conjunctio.** The union of right and possession forming a complete title.
**Juris Gentium.** Of the law of nations.
**Jurisperitus.** Learned in the law.
**Juris Positivi.** Of positive law.
**Juris Privati.** Of private right.
**Jurisprudence.** The science of law.
**Juris Publici.** Of common right or public use.
**Jurist.** One learned in the law.
**Juristic Act.** One to have a legal effect.
**Juristic Person.** Any legal entity other than a natural person.
**Juror.** Member of a jury.
**Juror's Book.** List of those qualified to serve on juries.
**Jury.** A body of men, usually 12, selected according to law and sworn to hear and determine issues of fact in a trial at law.
**Jury Box.** Enclosed area in a courtroom.
**Jury List.** List of those eligible for jury duty.
**Juryman.** Member of a jury.
**Jury Process.** Process or writ to summon jurors.
**Jury Wheel.** Contrivance by means of which the names of those to serve are selected.
**Jus.** Right; justice; law.
**Jus Abutendi.** The right to abuse, i.e. the right of full ownership.
**Jus Accrescendi.** Right of survivorship.
**Jus ad Rem.** The right to a thing, which has its foundation in an obligation incurred by another person.
**Jus Anglorum.** The law of the Anglo-Saxons.
**Jus Belli.** The law of war.
**Jus Bellum Dicendi.** The right to declare war.
**Jus Canonicum.** The canon law.
**Jus Civile.** The Civil Law.
**Jus Civitatis.** The right of citizenship.
**Jus Cloacae.** The right of sewage or drainage.
**Jus Coronae.** The right of succession to the throne.
**Jus Dare.** To make or enact the law.
**Jus Dicere.** To declare or state the law.

**Jus Disponendi.** The right of disposing of one's property.
**Jus Dividendi.** The right of disposing of realty by will.
**Jus Duplicatum.** A double right; right of possession united with right of property.
**Jus Edicere.** Right to issue edicts.
**Jus Est Ars Boni et Aequi.** Law is the science of that which is good and just.
**Jus Fiduciarium.** A right in trust.
**Jus Fluminum.** The right of using rivers.
**Jus Futurum.** A future right.
**Jus Gentium.** Law of nations.
**Jus Gladii.** The right of the sword; the executory power of the law.
**Jus Habendi.** The right to have a thing.
**Jus Haereditatis.** The right of inheritance.
**Jus Immunitatis.** Exemption from service in public office.
**Jus Incognitum.** An unknown law.
**Jus Individuum.** An indivisible right; an individual right.
**Jus In Personam.** A right against a person, the right arising out of a personal obligation.
**Jus In Re.** A right in a thing; ownership.
**Jus in Re Propria.** Complete ownership.
**Jusjurandum.** An oath.
**Jus Legitimum.** A legal right.
**Jus Mariti.** The right of the husband.
**Jus Naturae.** The law of nature.
**Jus Naturalis aut Divini.** Natural or divine law.
**Jus Navigandi.** The right of navigation.
**Jus Non Scriptum.** The unwritten law.
**Jus Pascendi.** The right to pasture cattle.
**Jus Personarum.** Rights of persons.
**Jus Possessionis.** The right of possession.
**Jus Postliminii.** The right, after war, of the restoration to former state.
**Jus Praescens.** A present or existing right.
**Jus Presentationis.** The right of presentation.
**Jus Privatum.** A private right.
**Jus Proprietatis.** The right of property only.
**Jus Publicum.** Public law.
**Jus Quaesitum.** The right to recover a thing.
**Jus Representationis.** The right of representing or of being represented by another.
**Jus Respicit Aequitatem.** Law regards equity.
**Jus Sanguinis.** The principle that the nationality of a person is the same as his parents.
**Jus Scriptum.** The written law.
**Jus Soli.** The principle that nationality is determined by the place of birth.
**Jus Strictum.** Strict law.
**Just.** Conforming to what is legally right.
**Just Cause.** Legitimate cause.
**Just Claim.** A claim which can be enforced.
**Just Compensation.** Compensation paid to one whose property has been taken in condemnation proceedings.
**Jus Tertii.** The right of a third party.
**Justice.** Judge; a standard of action on the part of public officials in accordance with the entire body of law.
**Justice of the Peace.** A public official having minor judicial power.
**Justices' Courts.** Courts presided over by justices of the peace.
**Justiceship.** Rank or office of a justice.
**Justice's Judgment.** A judgment rendered by a justice of the peace.
**Justiciable.** Subject to court action.
**Justiciar(y).** Justice; judge.
**Justiciatus.** Judicature; perogative.
**Justifiable.** Rightful; lawful.
**Justifiable Homicide.** Excusable homicide.
**Justification.** Valid defense for the performance or non-performance of an act.
**Justify.** Quality as a surety or as bail.
**Justinianist.** Civilian; one studying civil law.
**Justitia.** Justice.
**Justitia Piepoudrous.** Speedy justice.
**Justitium.** Suspension of the court business.
**Juvenile Courts.** Court having special jurisdiction over delinquent or neglected children.
**Jus Tripertitum.** The law of wills.
**Jus Utendi.** The right to use a thing.
**Juxta.** Near; following; according to.
**Juxta Formam Statuti.** According to the form of the statute.
**Juxtaposition.** Being placed in nearness; side by side.

## K

**Kaiser.** Emperor.
**Kalendae.** First day of the Roman month.
**Kalendar.** Calendar.
**Kalends.** See Kalendae.
**Kangaroo Court.** Mock court held in prison whereby prisoners judge another inmate.
**Karat.** Weight of four grains, in weighing gems.
**Kay.** Quay; key.
**Keelage.** Duty for anchoring in a harbor.
**Kadi.** Turkish civil magistrate.
**Kaia.** Key; quay.
**Kaiagium.** Quayage; wharfage-due.
**Keehaul.** To punish a sailor by dragging him under the ship's keel with a rope.
**Keels.** Coal barges.
**Keep.** To continue; maintain; conduct.
**Keep Down Interest.** Payment of interest periodically as it becomes due.
**Keeper.** Custodian; superintendent.
**Keep the Peace.** Prevent a public disturbance.
**Keno.** Gambling game.
**Kern.** Vagrant.
**Kerosene.** Rock or earth oil.
**Key.** Wharf for the loading and unloading of goods from vessels.
**Khedive.** Governor of Egypt.
**Kidnapping.** Forcible abduction of anyone.
**Kilderkin.** Measure of 18 gallons.
**Kill.** To deprive of life, slay; stream.
**Kin, Kindred, Kinship.** Related by blood.
**Kind.** Class; grade; sort.
**Kind, In.** Payment by means of property or service and not in specie.
**King.** Ruler or sovereign of a kingdom.
**Kingdom** Dominion of a king or queen.
**Kings Evidence.** State's evidence.
**Kinsfolk.** Relations.
**Kip.** Brothel
**Kirk.** Church.
**Kleptomania.** An irresistible impulse to steal.
**Knave.** Swindler; cheat.
**Knight.** Lowest order of nobility.
**Knight's of the Garter.** The highest order of knighthood.
**Knock Down.** At an auction, to indicate property is going to the last bidder.
**Knot.** A marine mile of 6086.7 feet.
**Know.** To have information.
**Knowingly.** Intentionally.
**Koran.** Mohammedan book of faith.
**Koshuba.** Jewish marriage contract or settlement.
**Kyn.** Kin.

## L

**La.** There.
**Label.** A slip of paper attached to a written instrument in order to hold the appending seal; identification tag.
**Labor.** Work; toil; name for all workmen.
**Labor Agitator.** One actively engaged in promoting the interest of laboring men.
**Labor a Jury.** To tamper with a jury.
**Labor Arbitration.** Arbitration of controversies arising out of the relationship between management and labor.
**Labor Dispute.** Controversy regarding terms or conditions of employment.
**Laborer.** One engaged in manual labor.
**Labor Union.** An organization of workmen formed to promote common interests.
**Laches.** Term used in equity to indicate unreasonable delay to claim a right.
**Lacta.** Defect in weight.
**Lacuna.** Blank space in a written instrument.
**Lacus.** Lake.
**Laden in Bulk.** In maritime law, loaded with a loose, unboxed cargo.
**Lady Day.** March 25, Feast of the Annunciation of the Blessed Virgin Mary.
**Laesa Majestas.** Injured majesty; high treason.
**Laga.** Law.
**Laicus.** Layman.
**Lais Gents.** Laymen; a jury.
**Laity.** Laymen, secular persons.
**Lake.** Large body of fresh water surrounded by land.
**Laissez Faire.** Non-governmental interference in business or economic affairs.

**Land.** Ground, soil, earth; realty, real estate.
**Landed Estate.** An interest in lands.
**Landed Property.** Real estate.
**Land Gabel.** Tax or rent for the use of land.
**Landing.** A place on navigable water for loading and unloading.
**Landlord.** One who leases land to a tenant.
**Landmark.** Boundary marker.
**Land Patent.** Document whereby the government title to portions of the public domain passes to private ownership.
**Land Poor.** To be in possession of a large amount of unproductive land.
**Land Offices.** Government offices in which titles to public lands and sales of such land are registered, and other business dealing with public land is transacted.
**Lands, Tenements and Hereditaments.** Inheritable lands or interests therein.
**Land-Tax.** Tax laid upon the legal or beneficial owner of land.
**Land-Tenant.** One in possession of land.
**Language.** Any way of communicating ideas.
**Languidas.** Sick; ill.
**Lapidation.** Stoning to death.
**Lapidicina.** Stone quarry.
**Lapilli.** Precious stones.
**Lapse.** To end, cease or fail; forfeiture.
**Lapsed Policy.** Policy on which there has been default in payment of premiums.
**Lapsus Lingual.** Slip of the tongue.
**Larceny.** Theft.
**Larcyn.** Larceny.
**Laron.** Thief.
**Lascivious.** Wanton; lustful.
**Last.** Latest; ultimate.
**Lastage.** Ballast or lading of a ship.
**Last Clear Chance.** Doctrine that the one who has last clear chance is liable.
**Last Illness.** Illness which immediately precedes and results in one's death.
**Last Resort.** Applied to courts from which there is no appeal to a higher court.
**Last Will and Testament.** An instrument whereby one makes a disposition of his property to take effect after his death.
**Lata Culpa.** Gross negligence.
**Latching.** Underground survey.
**Late.** Last; defunct; dead; formerly.
**Latent.** Hidden; concealed.
**Latent Deed.** A deed kept hidden for 20 years or more.
**Latent Defect.** Defect not apparent but which becomes evident in use.
**Lateral.** Proceeding from the side.
**Lateral Support.** Support which adjoining land or the soil beneath gives one's own land.
**Laterare.** To lie sideways.
**Latifundium.** Great or large possessions.
**Latin.** Language of the ancient Romans.
**Latitare.** To lie hidden.
**Latitatio.** Concealment of one's person.
**Latori Praesentium.** To the bearer of these presents.
**Lato Sensu.** Broadly speaking.
**Latro.** Thief; bandit.
**Latrocination.** Pillage.
**Latrociny.** Larceny.
**Laudare.** To name, cite or quote; advise.
**Laudatio.** Testimony favorable to the accused's character.
**Laudator.** Favorable witness; arbitrator.
**Laus Deo.** Praise be to God.
**Law.** Statute; legislative enactment.
**Law Charges.** Court costs.
**Law Day.** The day specified in a contract upon which money was to be paid.
**Lawful.** Legal.
**Lawful Age.** Legal Age; majority.
**Lawful Heirs.** Those designated by law to take by descent.
**Lawful Interest.** Lawful rate fixed by statute.
**Lawful Issue.** Descendents.
**Lawful Money.** Legal tender.
**Lawless.** Not subject to or controlled by law.
**Lawless Man.** Outlaw.
**Law of a General Nature.** One which relates to a subject that may exist everywhere.
**Law of Nations.** International law.
**Law of Nature.** Scientifically determined law of natural phenomena; binding all mankind.
**Law of the Land.** Due process of law.
**Law Spiritual.** Ecclesiastical law.
**Lawsuit.** A suit, action or proceeding in a civil court; a suit at law or in equity.
**Law Worthy.** Entitled to legal protection.
**Lawyer.** One licensed to practice law.
**Lay.** Pertaining to person or things not clerical.
**Lay Corporation.** A corporation of lay persons.
**Lay Damages.** Damages claimed by plaintiff.
**Lay Gents.** Laymen.
**Laying Out.** Expression for locating and establishing a new highway.
**Laying the Venue.** In pleading, stating the county in which the plaintiff proposes that the trial of the action shall take place.
**Layman.** One not of the clergy.
**Lay People.** Jurymen.
**Layoff.** Termination of work by the employer.
**Lazaret.** Quarantine station.
**Le.** The.
**Leading Case.** A case frequently cited.
**Leading Counsel.** Counsel who is in charge of the conduct of a lawsuit.
**Leading Question.** One which suggests answer.
**League.** Treaty of alliance among states.
**Leakage.** Loss in a vessel's cargo by leaking or breaking in transit.
**Lean.** To include in opinion or preference.
**Leap Year.** Year having 366 days and occuring every 4 years.
**Learn.** To gain knowledge or information of.
**Lease.** Grant by one person, the lessor, to another, the lessee, of the used and possession of land for a limited time.
**Leasehold.** Tenancy under a lease.
**Leave.** Give by will; to put, place, deposit.
**Leave and License.** A defense in an action of trespass that the plaintiff consented to the act complained of.
**Leave of Court.** Permission granted by court.
**Leccator.** Lecherous person.
**Lecit.** It is legal.
**L. Ed.** (Abb.). Lawyer's edition.
**Ledger.** Account book.
**Lega.** An alloy once used in making coins.
**Legacy.** Bequest; property left by will.
**Legacy Tax.** Inheritance tax.
**Legal.** Lawful.
**Legal Age.** The age (usually 21) at which one acquires the full capacity to enter into contracts and transact business.
**Legal Aid Society.** An organization for the purpose of giving legal advice and assistance to the indigent.
**Legal Cause.** Substantial factor that caused harm.
**Legal Conclusion.** Legal inference.
**Legal Duty.** An obligation arising from a contract or operation of the law.
**Legal Entity.** Legal existence.
**Legal Ethics.** The usages and customs among members of the legal profession involving their moral and professional duties.
**Legal Evidence.** All admissable evidence.
**Legal Heirs.** Next of kin.
**Legal Holiday.** A day on which juridical proceedings cannot be held.
**Legal Injury.** Violation of legal right.
**Legal Interest.** Rate of interest.
**Legal Liability.** Liability which the courts recognize and enforce.
**Legalis Homo.** A lawful man.
**Legalize.** To make lawful.
**Legally.** According to law.
**Legally Determined.** Determined by process of law.
**Legally Proved.** Established by evidence.
**Legally Reside.** Domicile.
**Legal Malice.** Constructive malice, arising from the circumstances.
**Legal Name.** Christian name and surname.
**Legal Negligence.** Negligence per se.
**Legal Notice.** Notice complying with the requirements of law.
**Legal Obligation.** An obligation to do and perform what the law requires.
**Legal Rate of Interest.** A rate which is not in excess of the maximum rate allowed by law.
**Legal Representative.** Usually applied to the executor or administrator of a decedent.
**Legal Right.** A claim recognizable and enforceable at law.
**Legal Tender.** That which may be legally offered to a creditor by his debtor in payment.
**Legal Voter.** One authorized by law to cast his ballot at an election.

**Legal Wilfulness.** Intentional negligence.
**Legare.** Bequeath.
**Legatee.** One to whom property is left by will.
**Legation.** An embassy; a diplomatic minister.
**Legator.** One who makes a will and leaves legacies.
**Legatum.** Legacy; bequest.
**Legem.** Law.
**Legem Facere.** To make an oath.
**Legem Habere.** To give evidence under oath.
**Legem Pone.** To lay down the law.
**Leges.** Law.
**Leges Scriptae.** Written or statute laws.
**Legislate.** To enact laws or pass resolutions.
**Legislation.** Preparation and enactment of laws.
**Legislative.** Pertaining to the statute-making branch of the government or legislature.
**Legislative Courts.** Courts created by Legislature not named by the Constitution.
**Legislative Power.** Lawmaking power.
**Legislator.** One who makes laws; member of a legislative body.
**Legislature.** That branch of government which makes laws for a state or nation.
**Legisperitus.** One learned in the law.
**Legitimacy.** Status of being born in wedlock.
**Legitimation.** Making lawful.
**Legitimate.** Lawful; born in wedlock.
**Legitimize.** To make lawful.
**Legitimus.** Lawful.
**Lego.** I bequeath.
**Leguleius.** One learned in the law.
**Lend.** Give, grant; put out for hire.
**Lender.** He from whom a thing is borrowed.
**Leod.** The people; country; nation.
**Les.** The.
**Lésé Majesté.** High treason.
**Lesion.** Damage; injury.
**Lessa.** Legacy.
**Lessee.** One to whom property is leased.
**Lessor.** One who gives a lease.
**Let.** To make a lease of real property; to award a contract.
**Let In.** To admit a party as a matter of favor.
**Lethal.** Deadly; mortal.
**Letter.** Character of the alphabet; a written message inclosed, sealed, stamped and sent.
**Letter of Administration.** Written authority by a court giving permission to administer.
**Letter of Advice.** A written notice of an act performed by the writer.
**Letter of Attorney.** Power of attorney.
**Letter of Credit.** An instrument ordering money to be paid to the bearer.
**Letter of License.** An agreement between creditors and their debtor extending time.
**Letter of Recall.** A notice sent to a foreign government by another government of the recall of its representative.
**Letter of Recredentials.** The reply of a foreign government to a letter of recall.
**Letter of Safe Conduct.** Passports issued by a government in time of war.
**Letters Patent.** A governmental grant of property, status, title, authority or privilege.
**Letters Testamentary.** Letters issued by a court empowering an executor of a will to act.
**Letting Out.** The award of a contract.
**Lettre de Change.** A bill of exchange.
**Levee.** An embankment constructed along the bank of a river to prevent overflow.
**Leviable.** That which may be levied.
**Levis.** Light; slight.
**Levissima Deligentia.** Slight diligence.
**Levitical Degrees.** Degrees of kindred within which marriage is prohibited.
**Levy.** To assess, raise, exact, collect, seize.
**Lewd.** Obscene.
**Lewdness.** Open and public indecency.
**Lex.** Law.
**Lex Amissa.** Infamous or outlawed person.
**Lex Angliae.** The law of England.
**Lex Apparens.** Apparent law.
**Lex Domicilii.** Law of the domicile.
**Lex Est ab Aeterno.** Law is from eternity.
**Lex et Consuetudo Regni.** The law and custom of the nation.
**Lex Fori.** The law of the court; the law of the jurisdiction in which the litigation occurs.
**Lex Ligeantiae.** The law of the country of one's allegince.
**Lex Loci.** The law of the place in which the circumstance arose.
**Lex Loci Actus.** The law of the place of the act.
**Lex Loci Commissi.** The law of the place where the act was committed.
**Lex Loci Contractus.** The law of the place of making of the contract.
**Lex Loci Delictus.** The law of the place of the crime.
**Lex Mercatoria.** The law merchant.
**Lex Nil Frustra Facit.** The law does nothing in vain.
**Lex Non Scripta.** The unwritten law.
**Lex Patriae.** National law.
**Lex Reprobat Moram.** The law disapproves of delay.
**Lex Respicit Acquitatem.** The law regards equity.
**Lex Scripta.** The written law.
**Lex Spectat Naturae Ordinem.** The law regards the order of nature.
**Lex Succurrit Minoribus.** Law aids minors.
**Lex Talionis.** The law of retaliation.
**Lex Terrae.** The law of the land.
**Ley.** Law; an oath.
**Ley Civile.** The civil law.
**Le Gager.** To wage one's law.
**Leze Majesty.** High treason.
**Liability.** The condition of one who is under obligation to pay; an obligation to pay money.
**Liability Insurance.** Indemnity against liability.
**Liable.** Bound in law or equity; responsible.
**Libel.** To defame a person's reputation.
**Libellus Conventionis.** A bill or complaint.
**Libellus Famosus.** A defamatory publication.
**Libelous.** Defamatory.
**Liber.** Book; volume; free or open.
**Libera.** Free; exempt.
**Liberal.** Generous, open-minded, not literal.
**Liberam Legem Amittere.** To lose one's status as a free man.
**Liberare.** To free.
**Liberation.** The extinguishment of a contract, by which he who was bound becomes free.
**Liber et Legalis Homo.** A free and lawful man; juryman.
**Libertas.** Liberty; freedom; privilege.
**Libertas Inaestimabilis Res Est.** Liberty is a thing of inestimable value.
**Liberticide.** Destroyer of liberty.
**Liberties.** Privileged communities or districts.
**Liberty.** Freedom; all the rights, privileges and immunities of the Constitution.
**Liberty of the Press.** Freedom from censorship.
**License.** A certificate which gives permission.
**Licensee.** One who holds a license.
**Licensor.** One who gives a license.
**Licentia.** License; leave; permission.
**Licentia Concordandi.** Permission to come to an agreement, a step in levying a fine.
**Licentia Loquendi.** Permission to speak.
**Licentiate.** One who has license to practice.
**Licentious.** Unrestrained; dissolute.
**Licentiously.** Freely; loosely; dissolutely.
**Licentiousness.** Disregard the rights of others.
**Licere.** To be allowed by law.
**Licet.** It is allowed by law.
**Licitare.** To bid.
**Licitation.** An offering for sale to the highest bidder or to the one who will give the most.
**Lie.** To be admissable, as an action or an appeal; to be appropriate as a remedy; an untruth deliberately told.
**Liege.** One bound in fealty to a superior.
**Liegeman.** A feudal vassal.
**Lie in Franchise.** Property is said to lie in franchise when it may be seized by those entitled to it without the aid of a court.
**Lie In Grant.** Property which can be transferred from one person to another.
**Lien.** A charge, security or incumbrance upon property for the payment of a debt.
**Lien Creditor.** One whose claim is secured by a lein on particular property.
**Lienee.** One whose property has a lien.
**Lienor.** One who has a lien.
**Lien for Improvements.** Lien sometimes decreed in equity to one who claims compensation for improvements made on the land of another.
**Lieu.** Place or stead well-known.
**Lieu Conus.** A well known place.

**Lieutenant.** Deputy, substitute, agent; lowest rank commissioned officer in the U.S. Army.
**Life Annuity.** An annual payment made to a person during his lifetime.
**Life Estate.** An estate whose duration is limited to the lifetime of the possessor.
**Life Insurance.** Insurance on the life of a particular individual on whose death payment of a specified amount is made.
**Life Interest.** An interest in property which is to terminate upon the death of the holder of the interest or some other designated person.
**Life-Land.** Land held on a lease for lives.
**Life Policy.** A written contract of life insurance.
**Life-Tables.** Statistical tables showing the length of expectancy of survival of persons at certain ages.
**Life Tenant.** One who has the right to enjoy certain property for the period of his own life or that of another certain person.
**Lift.** To raise or take up; as applied to a promissory note, to cause its cancellation.
**Liga.** League; association.
**Ligan.** Goods cast into the sea to lighten a ship but attached to a buoy so they may be recovered.
**Ligare.** Bind together, unite.
**Ligealty.** Allegiance.
**Ligeantia.** Allegiance.
**Light.** An easement to have natural light unobstructed by buildings, etc.
**Lighter.** Vessel used in assisting to load and unload other vessels.
**Lignum.** Firewood.
**Like.** Equal; exactly corresponding.
**Like Effect.** With like results.
**Like a Shot.** Quickly.
**Likelihood.** Probability.
**Likely.** Probable.
**Limb.** Member of the human body.
**Limit.** To confine, restrict; boundary.
**Limitatio.** Limitation.
**Limitation.** Restriction; settling an estate.
**Limitation of Actions.** See Limitations, Statute of.
**Limitations, Statute of.** A statute establishing fixed periods of time within which various actions or proceedings in law or equity must be brought, after a cause of action has arisen.
**Limited.** Restricted.
**Limited Guaranty.** Usually a guaranty restricted in its application to a single act.
**Limited Jurisdiction.** Jurisdiction which does not extend to the general administration.
**Limited Owner.** One whose ownership is less than full.
**Limited Partnership.** A partnership in which one or more of the partners are not personally liable for partnership debts, beyond the amount they have invested.
**Line.** Course of descent; lineal measure containing one-twelfth of an inch; a boundary between two estates.
**Linea.** Line of descent.
**Lineage.** Progeny.
**Lineal.** In direct line.
**Lineal Consanguinity.** Relationship through some common ancestor.
**Linea Recta.** Direct descent.
**Liquere.** To be clear, evident, apparent.
**Liquet Satis.** It is clear enough.
**Liqueur.** An alcoholic cordial.
**Liquidate.** To settle a debt or an obligation in the form of money; to reduce all the assets and liabilities of a business or estate to a precise sum in money in order to settle the business or estate.
**Liquidated Damages.** Damages which are agreed upon in advance between two parties should either of them breach their contract.
**Liquidation.** The act of settling or winding up business affairs; payment of due amount.
**Liquor.** Alcoholic beverage.
**Lis.** Law suit; dispute.
**Lis Mota.** A controversy which has begun.
**Lis Pendens.** A pending suit; jurisdiction which courts acquire over property in suit pending action and until final judgment.
**List.** Court docket; to enter in an official list.
**Listed.** Included in a list.
**Lister.** One who makes lists of taxables.
**Listing Contract.** An agreement whereby an owner of real property employs a broker to procure a purchaser without right to sell.
**Lite Pendente.** While the action is pending.
**Liter.** A liquid containing 1.056 quarts.
**Litera.** A letter.
**Litera Acquietantia.** A letter of acquittance.
**Literacy Test.** A test in reading and writing required by some states as a qualification to vote.
**Literae.** Letters, written documents, words.
**Literae Mortuae.** Dead letters; superflous words.
**Literae Patentes.** Letters patent.
**Literae Procuratoriae.** Power of attorney.
**Literal.** Closely following the exact words.
**Literal Proof.** Proof by writings in evidence.
**Litera Scripta Manet.** The written word endures.
**Literatura.** Education.
**Litigant.** A party to a lawsuit.
**Litigare.** To carry on a suit.
**Litigate.** To carry on a suit.
**Litigated.** Applied to questions about which there has been a legal hearing.
**Litigation.** A law suit.
**Litigiosity.** The pendency of a suit.
**Litigious.** Contested suit; fond of litigation.
**Litis.** Of a litigation, suit or action.
**Litis Aestimatio.** The measure of damages.
**Litis Contestatis.** A defense to an action.
**Litis Dominum.** Control or direction of a suit.
**Litis Dominus.** One who controls a suit.
**Litis Magister.** One who directs a suit.
**Litispendence.** Pendency of a suit or action.
**Litre.** See Liter.
**Littoral.** Relating to the shore.
**Litura.** Erasure; correction.
**Litus Maris.** Sea-shore.
**Live.** To reside.
**Livelode.** Maintenance; support.
**Livery.** The act of transferring physical possession of property to some person; particular dress appropriate to certain persons.
**Livery Stable.** Building for horses or vehicles.
**Live Oil.** Oil that has gas in it.
**Live Stock.** Domestic animals used on a farm.
**Live Trust.** An active or operative trust.
**Live Wire.** A wire charged with current.
**Living.** Existing; surviving.
**Living Apart.** To live in a separate abode.
**Living Together.** Cohabitation.
**Lloyd's.** London insurance association.
**Loadman.** Pilot.
**Loadmanage.** Pay to loadsmen.
**Loaf.** Loiter.
**Loan.** Borrowing with a promise to repay.
**Loan for Consumption.** Lending of goods for consumption to be repayed in kind.
**Lobby.** To try to influence the passage or rejection of legislative measures; group of persons engaged in this activity.
**Lobbyist.** Member of a lobby.
**Local.** Pertaining to a particular place.
**Local Action.** Action which must be brought in a particular place.
**Local Agent.** Agent of a definite district.
**Local Assessment.** Property charges levied.
**Local Chattel.** Fixture.
**Local Courts.** Courts whose jurisdiction is confined to particular area.
**Local Government.** Government of county, city, town.
**Local Improvement.** Public improvement conferring a benefit on a particular property.
**Locality.** Place; vicinity; neighborhood.
**Local Law.** Law directed to a particular place.
**Local Nature.** Pertaining to an action situated wholly within the district in which filed.
**Local Option.** Local choice whether or not to have prohibition of alcoholic beverages.
**Local Prejudice.** Prejudice or influence warranting the removal of a case from state to federal courts.
**Local Statute.** Local law.
**Local Taxes.** Taxes levied for the benefit of a district or town.
**Locare.** To let for hire; bestow in marriage.
**Locatarius.** Depositee.
**Locate.** Discovery by survey.
**Locatio.** Hiring out of property.
**Locatio Custodiae.** Placing in custody or safe-keeping for hire.
**Location.** Site; place; a mining claim.
**Locatio Operis.** Contract to make repairs and to supply materials.

**Locatio Operis Faciendi.** Hiring of work or services upon a thing.
**Locatio Rei.** Hire of a thing.
**Locative Calls.** Landmarks and physical objects whereby land can be identified.
**Lockout.** A cut-off from work by the employer in an effort to bring the matter to terms.
**Lockup.** Prison; jail.
**Loco Citato.** In the place cited.
**Loco Parentis.** In the place of the parent, e.g. the school teacher.
**Locum Tenens.** Holding the place, e.g. a deputy.
**Locuples.** Wealthy.
**Locus.** Place.
**Locus Contractus.** Place contracted.
**Locus Criminis.** Place where the crime was committed.
**Locus Delicti.** Place where the crime tort was committed.
**Locus in Quo.** The place in which or where.
**Locus Poenitentiae.** A place for repentence; an opportunity to change one's mind.
**Locus Publicus.** Public place.
**Locus Regit Actum.** Place governs the act.
**Locus Rei Sitae.** Place where a thing is located.
**Locus Sigilli.** Place of the seal, (Abb. "l.s."), indicating the document as sealed.
**Locus Solutionis.** Place of payment or performance.
**Locus Standi.** Place of standing, i.e. right to appear in court.
**Lode.** In mining law, a vein.
**Lodeman.** Pilot.
**Lodge.** Fraternal order; meeting place.
**Lodger.** One who has the use but not possession of a dwelling.
**Logbook.** Ship's daily journal.
**Logia.** Lodge.
**Log Rolling.** Legislative practice of combining several unrelated bills into one in order to combine various minorities into a majority.
**Logic.** Science of reasoning.
**Loiter.** To idle or linger.
**Lond.** Land.
**Long.** An order is given to a stockbroker to buy or credit the account with stocks.
**Long and Short Haul.** Practice of some railroad companies of charging lower rates in the face of competition, regardless of distance.
**Loose Waman.** An unchaste woman.
**Loquella.** Speech; talk; discourse.
**Loss.** Damage.
**Losses.** Tax deductible items, if incurred in trade or business or by casualty.
**Lost or Not Lost.** In marine insurance, coverage for past and future losses.
**Lost Papers.** Papers which cannot be found.
**Lost Property.** Property involuntarily parted with through neglect or carelessness.
**Lot.** Group of persons or things; a share; a portion of land.
**Lottery.** A gamble for a prize at a price.
**Low.** Lacking in dignity or character; mean.
**Lower House.** House of Representatives of the U.S. Congress.
**Low Water Mark.** Line on the shore made by receding water at low tide.
**Loyal.** Faithful; lawful.
**Loyalty.** Faithfulness.
**L.S.** (Abb.). Locus sigilli.
**Ltd.** (Abb.). Limited.
**Lucid.** Temporary period of sanity, any affairs conducted at this time being valid.
**Lucre.** Gain; profit.
**Lucri Causa.** In criminal law, for the sake of gain, in regard to larceny.
**Lumen.** Light; window; right to light.
**Lump Sum Payment.** Payment before due.
**Lunacy.** Madness.
**Lunatic.** One who is insane.
**Lupanatrix.** Prostitute.
**Lustful.** Lewd.
**Lying by.** Acquiescing.
**Lying in Wait.** Lying in ambush.
**Lynching.** Punishment by a mob without trial.
**Lynch Law.** Mob law.

## M

**Mace Proof.** Safe from arrest.
**Machination.** Artful contrivance formed with deliberation.
**Machine.** Mechanical device.
**Mactater.** Murderer.
**Maculare.** To wound.
**Mad Point.** Central idea of a monomania.
**Magis.** More; more fully; in a higher degree.
**Magister.** Master; ruler; chief; head.
**Magisterial.** Pertaining to a magistrate.
**Magister Litis.** One in charge of a suit.
**Magister Navis.** Captain of a ship.
**Magister Rerum Usus.** Use is the master.
**Magister Societas.** Manager of a partnership.
**Magistra.** Mistress; directress.
**Magistralia Brevia.** Magisterial writs.
**Magistrate.** One vested with power.
**Magistrate's Certificate.** Certificate of proof of loss without fraud obtained from a magistrate required by some fire insurance.
**Magistratus.** Magistrate.
**Magna Carta (Charta).** The great charter issued by King John of Eng. in 1215, considered basis of Eng. constitutional liberty.
**Magna Culpa.** Gross negligence.
**Magna Culpa Dolus Est.** Gross negligence is the equivalent of fraud.
**Magnum Concilium.** Eng. Parliament.
**Maiden.** Young, unmarried woman.
**Maihematus.** Maimed; wounded.
**Mail.** Letters; correspondence.
**Mailable Matter.** Matter which may legally handled through U.S. mails.
**Maile.** Rent money.
**Maim.** Cripple; mutilate; disable.
**Main-a-Main.** Immediately.
**Mainovre.** Manual labor.
**Mainpernable.** Bailable.
**Mainpernor.** One who provides bail.
**Mainsworn.** Perjured.
**Maintain.** Sustain; support.
**Maintainor.** One guilty of maintenance.
**Maintenance.** To aid someone with the means of prosecuting a suit; supporting someone.
**Maintenance Curialis.** Maintenance in a court of justice.
**Maintenant.** Now.
**Mais.** But; however.
**Major.** Greater, more important.
**Major Annus.** Leap year.
**Majority.** Full age; the greater number.
**Majus Jus.** Greater or better right.
**Make.** To execute, do or perform.
**Maker.** One who makes, executes or signs.
**Mal.** Prefix meaning bad or evil.
**Mala.** Bad or evil things.
**Maladministration.** Mismanagement.
**Mala Fides.** Bad faith.
**Mala in Se.** Evil in themselves.
**Mala Mens.** Bad intention.
**Malandrinus.** Thief.
**Mala Praxis.** Malpractice.
**Mala Prohibita.** Acts forbidden by law.
**Male.** Badly; improperly.
**Male.** Belonging to the masculine sex.
**Malefaction.** Crime.
**Malefactor.** Criminal.
**Maleficium.** Crime.
**Malfeasance.** Commission of a wrongful act.
**Malformation.** Deformity.
**Malice.** State of mind of one who deliberately commits a wrongful act.
**Malice Aforethought.** Intention to kill existing some time before the actual deed is done.
**Malice in Fact.** Express with intent to injure.
**Malice in Law.** Deliberate commission of a wrongful act without just cause.
**Malice Prepense.** Malice aforethought.
**Malicious.** Committed with evil intentions.
**Malicious Arrest.** Arrest of a person without probable cause during the proceeding.
**Malicious Injury.** Wrongful and wilful infliction of injury upon another.
**Maliciously.** Wilfully.
**Malicious Mischief.** Wilful injury to the personal property of another.
**Malicious Prosecution.** Instigation of legal proceedings without probable cause.
**Malignare.** To malign, defame or maim.
**Malinger.** To pretend sickness.
**Malingerer.** One who pretends sickness to avoid some duty.
**Malitia.** Malice.
**Malitia Implicita.** Implied malice.
**Malitia Praecogitata.** Malice aforethought.
**Malo Animo.** With evil intent.
**Malo Grato.** In spite of.
**Malpractice.** Professional misconduct.

**Malum in Se.** A wrong in itself.
**Malum Prohibitum.** A prohibited wrong.
**Malus, Mala, Malum.** Evil; bad wrong.
**Malus Animus.** Evil intent.
**Malversation.** Misconduct in office.
**Man.** A human being; one of the male sex.
**Manacles.** Hand shackles.
**Manage.** To control; direct; govern.
**Management.** Government, control.
**Manager.** One who directs anything.
**Manas Mediae.** Inferior persons.
**Mancipate.** To enslave.
**Mandamus.** We command; a writ issuing from a court of higher jurisdiction commanding the performance of a public duty.
**Mandans.** Commanding; entrusting.
**Mandatary.** An agent or bailee who receives instructions to act by another person; one to whom a charge is given.
**Mandate.** An order of the court; writ of mandamus; gratuitous bailment for work.
**Mandator.** One who employs a mandatary.
**Mandatory.** Imperative; peremptory.
**Mandatum.** In civil law, contract involving the bailment of property.
**Manens.** Remaining.
**Mania.** Type of mental disorder characterized by obsession with particular subjects.
**Mania a Potu.** Type of temporary insanity caused by excessive use of intoxicating drinks.
**Mania Transitoria.** Emotional insanity.
**Manifest.** Evident; declaration of ship's cargo.
**Manifesto.** Public declaration authorized by the government of a nation.
**Manifest Theft.** Open theft.
**Mann Act.** White Slave Traffic Act.
**Manner.** Method; mode of operation.
**Mannire.** To cite an adverse party into court.
**Mannus.** Horse.
**Man of Straw.** A non-existent bondsman.
**Manor.** House; dwelling; residence.
**Manser.** An illegitimate child.
**Manslaughter.** Unlawful or negligent killing of a human being, without malice.
**Manstealing.** Kidnapping.
**Manticulate.** To pick pockets.
**Man Trap.** Device to catch trespassers.
**Manual.** Pertaining to the hand or hands.
**Manu Brevi.** Briefly; directed.
**Manu Longa.** Indirectly; circuitously.
**Manufacture.** Process of making products.
**Manumission.** Act of freeing a slave.
**Manus.** Hand; oath; compurgator.
**Manuscript.** A writing; a handwritten book.
**Many.** Numerous.
**Mar.** Damage greatly; to do serious injury.
**Marauder.** Soldier who plunders and steals.
**Mare.** The sea.
**Mare.** Female horse.
**Mare Altum.** Open sea.
**Mare Apertum.** High sea.
**Maretum.** Overflowed marsh land.
**Margin.** Edge; border.
**Margin.** Money given a stockbroker by one on whose account a purchase or sale is to be made as security against loss.
**Marginal Transactions.** Dealing in stocks on margin.
**Margin of Profit.** Difference between purchase price and selling price of merchandise.
**Marine.** Naval; pertaining to the sea.
**Marine Contract.** One for chartering a vessel or shipping goods for transportation over sea.
**Marine Insurance.** Insurance against loss in maritime transactions.
**Marine League.** Distance equal to three geographical miles.
**Marine Risk.** Perils of the sea.
**Mariner,** Seaman; sailor.
**Marital.** Pertaining to marriage.
**Marital Portion.** In Louisiana, the share of the widow in her husband's estate.
**Marital Rights, Duties and Obligations.** Arising from the marriage contract and constituting its object.
**Maritime.** Pertaining to the sea.
**Maritime Belt.** Part of the sea under control of the riparian states.
**Maritime Blockade.** Blockade by sea.
**Maritime Causes.** All causes of action arising in connection with acts done at sea.
**Maritime Contract.** One relating to commerce and navigation.
**Maritime Law.** Law dealing with cases arising on the high seas.
**Maritime Lien.** Claim on a vessel for work done in relation to maritime employment.
**Maritime Tort.** Civil wrongs committed on navigable waters.
**Maritus.** Married man.
**Mark.** Character used by one unable to write.
**Market.** Place of commercial activity where wares are bought and sold; the demand there is for a particular article; collective name for a group of buyers and sellers of a commodity.
**Market Overt.** Open market.
**Market Price.** Price which a commodity would command if sold at public sale.
**Market Value.** Price which property or a commodity would command in the market.
**Marriage.** A legal contract between a man and a woman to unit for life to the exclusion of all.
**Marriageable Age.** Age of consent.
**Marriage Articles.** Written agreement between parties comtemplating marriage.
**Marriage Ceremony.** Form for the soleminization of a marriage.
**Marriage Certificate.** Document certifying a marriage and executed by person officiating.
**Marriage License.** License issued by public authority, often an essential prerequisite.
**Marriage Portion.** Property a woman brings with her upon marriage; dowry.
**Marriage Promise.** Betrothal, engagement.
**Marriage Settlement.** Written agreement by which title to certain property is settled in the event of the husband's death.
**Marshal.** Ministerial officer in each Federal district whose duties are similar to a sheriff.
**Marshaling of Assets.** In equity, the arrangements of assest in due order of administration.
**Marshaling Securities.** In equity, the ranking of classes of creditors, with respect to the assets of the common debtor, to provide for the satisfaction of the greatest number of claims.
**Mart.** Public market.
**Martial Law.** Law dealing with military affairs; state existing when military authorities carry on government or exercise control over civilians in domestic territory.
**Masochism.** Sexual perversion in which one enjoys infliction of pain by another.
**Massa.** Mass; raw material.
**Massachusetts Trust.** Business trust; trust in which property is conveyed to trustees to manage and deal with.
**Master.** Head of a college or school; employer in relation of master and servant; captain of a merchant ship; a subordinate judge in equity appointed to hear testimony and report his findings to the court.
**Master and Servant.** Relation between two people in which the former may determine what work is to be done and how to do it.
**Master Builder.** Contractor who employs men to build.
**Mate.** Officer second in command on a merchant vessel.
**Mater Familias.** Mother of the family.
**Materia.** Material; subject matter.
**Material.** Physical matter or substance; important; having influence or effect.
**Material Allegation.** One which forms a substantive part of the case presented by the pleading.
**Material Alteration.** One which changes the legal effect of the instrument.
**Material Evidence.** Evidence that might determine a decision on the facts of a case.
**Material Fact.** One which influences a person to enter into a contract; an essential fact.
**Material Injury.** One resulting in damages of a substantial nature.
**Materiality.** Bearing which facts may have on a controversy; importance.
**Materials.** Matter of which a thing is made.
**Materia Prima.** Primary matter.
**Maternal.** Pertaining to a mother.
**Maternal Property.** Property which comes from the mother's side of the family.
**Maternity.** Motherhood.
**Matima.** Godmother.
**Matricide.** Killing of one's mother.
**Matriculate.** Enroll.
**Matrimonial.** Pertaining to matrimony.
**Matrimonial Causes.** Cases involving actions for divorce, annulment, and separation.

**Matrimonial Cohabitation.** The living together of a man and woman.
**Matrimonial Domicile.** Place where parties live together as husband and wife.
**Matrimonial Res.** Marriage state.
**Matrimony.** State of being married.
**Matrix.** An original document.
**Matron.** Married woman; female head of an institution, e.g. prison or nursing home.
**Matter.** Substantial facts constituting the basis of claim or defense.
**Matter in Controversy or in Dispute.** Subject of the litigation.
**Matter in Pais.** Matter of fact.
**Matter of Fact.** Issues of fact to be determined by the jury.
**Matter of Form.** Established mode.
**Matter of Law.** Issues of law to be determined by the court.
**Matter of Record.** Matter in the court records.
**Matter of Substance.** See Matter of Form.
**Maturity.** Time at which payment is due.
**Maxim.** Tradtionally and generally accepted.
**Maximum.** Greatest amount, quality or value.
**Mayhem.** Wrongful act resulting in the loss or damage of some part of the body of the person.
**Mayor.** Governor or chief magistrate of a city.
**Mayor's Court.** Municipal court presided over by the mayor.
**M.D.** (Abb.). Doctor of Medicine.
**Mean, Mesne.** Middle between two extremes.
**Meander Line.** Line used in surveying to indicate the end of a plot of ground that has unsurveyable real boundaries.
**Meaning.** Signification; sense.
**Means.** Intermediate agent, instrument.
**Means of Support.** Resources from which the necessities and comforts of life are supplied.
**Measure.** A definite, specific act or resolution.
**Measure of Damages.** Means of determining the amount of the plaintiff's damages sustained by a breach of contract or tort.
**Mechanic.** One skilled in the use of tools.
**Mechanic's Lien.** Claim created by law in order to secure a priority of payment for the price or value of work performed and materials furnished in erecting or repairing a building or structure.
**Media Concludendi.** Steps of an argument.
**Mediae et Infirmae Manus Homines.** Men of mean and lowly condition.
**Media Nox.** Midnight.
**Mediate.** Intervening; indirect; arbitrate.
**Mediately.** That which is derived by inference from facts known or proved.
**Mediate Testimony.** Secondary evidence.
**Mediation.** Intervention; the act of a third party attempting to reconcile a dispute between two parties.
**Mediator.** One who attempts to reconcile.
**Medical.** Pertaining to the science, practice or study of medicine.
**Medical Evidence.** Testimony given by medical men.
**Medical Jurisprudence.** Branch of the science of medicine concerned with the law.
**Medicine.** Science and art of dealing with the prevention, cure and relief of diseases.
**Medico-Legal.** Law concerning medical questions.
**Medio Tempore.** In the meantime.
**Medium Concludendi.** Means of reaching a conclusion.
**Medley.** Affray; sudden fight.
**Meet.** To come together.
**Meeting.** Coming together of persons.
**Meeting of the Minds.** Concurrence of intention between two parties to make a contract.
**Melancholia.** Type of mental illness characterized by depression and grief.
**Melior.** Better.
**Meliorations.** Betterments; improvements.
**Member.** Part or organ of the body; one of the persons constituting a family.
**Member of Congress.** Member of the Senate or House of Representatives of the U.S. Congress.
**Membrana.** Membrane; parchment.
**Memoranda.** Notes used by a witness.
**Memorandum.** Notes or record of fact.
**Memorandum Decision.** Decision of an appellate court usually a brief paragraph.
**Memorial.** Memorandum or note.
**Memoriter.** From memory.
**Memory.** Recollection of past events.
**Menace.** Threats of bodily violence.
**Menial.** Household servants.
**Mens.** Mind; intention.
**Mensis.** A month.
**Mensa et Thora.** From bed and board.
**Mensor.** Surveyor.
**Mens Rea.** A guilty mind.
**Mensura.** A measure.
**Mental.** Pertaining to the mind.
**Mental Alienation.** Descriptive of insanity.
**Mental Anguish.** Mental grief, suffering.
**Mental Capacity or Competence.** Ability to understand the nature of a transaction.
**Mental Cruelty.** Cruelty on the part of one spouse toward another of such a nature that it may endanger the health of the spouse.
**Mental Imbecility.** Childishness; dotage.
**Mental Reservation.** An exception in mind only to a term or terms of a promise.
**Mentiri.** To lie.
**Mentition.** A lie.
**Mera Noctis.** Midnight.
**Mercantile.** Pertaining to merchants.
**Mercantile Law.** Law of commercial transactions.
**Mercantile Paper.** Commercial paper.
**Mercat.** Market.
**Mercative.** Pertaining to trade.
**Merces.** Wages for labor.
**Merchandise.** Commodities which merchants usually buy and sell.
**Merchantable.** Of good and salable quality.
**Merchant Seamen.** Seamen employed on private vessels.
**Merciament.** Amerciament; penalty; fine.
**Mercy, In.** In criminal law, discretion of a judge within the limits prescribed by positive law to remit punishment.
**Mere.** Mother.
**Mere Motion.** A voluntary act.
**Mere Right.** Mere right of property without either possession or right of possession.
**Meretricious.** Lewd; of unlawful sexual connection.
**Merger.** The absorption of one thing by another.
**Meritorious Consideration.** Consideration consisting in moral obligations.
**Merits.** Strict legal rights of parties.
**Merit System.** System of appointing employees to office in the civil service.
**Mere Motu.** See Mere Motion.
**Merscum.** Lake.
**Merx.** Merchandise.
**Mese.** House.
**Mesen.** Intermediate; intervening.
**Mesne Conveyance.** Any conveyance or transfer of property executed prior to the last one.
**Mesne Encumbrance.** An intermediate charge, burden or liability.
**Mesne Process.** Those writs intervening between the first and the judgment.
**Mesque.** Unless; except.
**Message.** Any communication sent from one person to another.
**Messenger.** The bearer of messages or one who performs errands.
**Messuage.** House.
**Mestizo.** One of mixed blood.
**Meter.** Instrument of measurement.
**Metes and Bounds.** Boundary lines of land with determination of terminal points and angles.
**Metropolis.** A mother city.
**Metus.** Fear; dread.
**Meum et Teum.** Mine and thine.
**Middleman.** An agent who brings persons together to make their own contracts.
**Midwife.** Woman who assists at childbirth.
**Mile.** Distance of 1,760 yards or 5,280 feet.
**Mileage.** Allowance for traveling expense at a certain sum per mile.
**Military.** Pertaining to war or the army.
**Military Courts.** Courts of military jurisdiction.
**Military Law.** System of law for governing the armed forces.
**Military Testament.** Verbal or nuncupative will by which a soldier engaged in actual military operation may make his will by either word of mouth or informal writing.

**Militia.** Body of citizens trained to military duty, but not engaged in actual service.
**Milled Money.** Coined money.
**Mind.** Ability to will, direct, permit or assent.
**Mind and Memory.** Applied to the ability of a testator to make a will.
**Mine.** Excavation in the earth from which minerals are removed.
**Mineral.** Any mined inorganic substance.
**Minerator.** Miner.
**Minimus.** The least; the smallest.
**Mining Claim.** Portion of land containing precious metal appropriated by an individual.
**Mining Partnership.** Partnership created for the purpose of operating a mine but differing in many respects from ordinary partnership.
**Minister.** Clergyman; diplomat.
**Ministerial.** That which is performed by a subordinate official under the directions of a superior.
**Ministerial Duty.** A simple, definite duty.
**Minor.** One under the legal age of competence.
**Minor Aetas.** Under age.
**Minor Fact.** A relative, collateral or subordinate fact in giving evidence.
**Minority.** Under age; lesser of two factions.
**Mint.** Place where money is legally coined.
**Mintage.** Charge made for coining money.
**Minus.** Less; smaller; not.
**Minute.** Small portion; 1/60 of an hour.
**Minute Book.** Book kept by the court clerk for entering memoranda of the court.
**Minutes.** Notes of a transaction or proceeding.
**Minutio.** A reduction; subtraction.
**Misadventure.** An accident.
**Misae.** Costs of a suit; expenses.
**Misallege.** To state or cite falsely.
**Misappropriate.** To use funds or property entrusted to an agent for other purposes.
**Misbehavior.** Misconduct; improper or unlawful conduct.
**Misbranding.** False labeling.
**Miscarriage.** Failure of a judicial proceeding to observe the ends of justice while observing legal forms; expulsion of a human fetus before maturity.
**Miscasting.** An error in an account audit.
**Miscegenation.** Intermarriage of a person of the white race with one of a colored race.
**Miscognizant.** Without knowledge of.
**Misconduct.** A transgression of some established and definite rule of action.
**Misconduct in Office.** Any willful, unlawful behavior of a public official in relation to the duties of his office.
**Misdemeanant.** One who has committed a misdemeanor.
**Misdate.** A false date on a document.
**Misdemeanor.** Any crime punishable by fine or imprisonment other than in a penitentiary.
**Misdirection.** An error made by the judge.
**Mise.** The issue on a writ of right.
**Miserecordia.** Mercy; a fine.
**Misfeasance.** Wrongful doing of an act which might be done lawfully.
**Misfortune.** Ill luck; calamity.
**Mishering.** A freedom from amercement.
**Misjoinder.** Joining together of different causes of action which under rules of procedure may not be litigated together; the adding of a litigant in a pleading as a party plaintiff or defendant in an action or suit in which he is not a proper plaintiff or defendant.
**Misnomer.** A mistake in a name.
**Mispleading.** Essential errors in defense.
**Misprision.** Applied to a misdemeanor which does not have a specific name; misapprehension; applied to a clerical error; applied to offenses involving concealment of crime.
**Misprision of Felony.** Offense of concealing a felony that has been committed.
**Misreading.** The false reading of a written instrument to one who cannot read.
**Misrecital.** Misstatement of facts.
**Misrepresentation.** A false statement or other conduct by one person to another which amounts to a false assertion.
**Missio.** Discharging.
**Mistake.** An unintentional act, omission or error due to ignorance, surprise, imposition or misplaced confidence.
**Mistake of Fact.** Mistake consisting of unconscious ignorance or forgetfulness of a fact material to the transaction.
**Mistake of Law.** A mistake of a party who having full knowledge of the facts.
**Mistery.** Trade; calling.
**Mistrial.** Erroneous or invalid trial.
**Misuser.** Unlawful use of a right.
**Mitigate.** To reduce or lessen.
**Mitigation.** Reduction of damages or punishment by reason of extenuating facts.
**Mitigation of Damages.** Reduction of the amount of damages.
**Mitior Sensus.** More favorable interpretation.
**Mittimus.** Warrant to remove records from one place to another; a warrant to the prison official to receive or keep a prisoner.
**Mixed Action.** Action both real and personal.
**Mixed Contract.** Contract in which parties exchange things of different value.
**Mixed Gift.** One in which there is included both real and personal property.
**Mixed Insurance Company.** One which is both a mutual and a stock company.
**Mixed Larceny.** Larceny which is complicated by the presence of aggravating factors.
**Mixed Marriage.** Marriage between a white and colored person.
**Mixed Personalty.** Personal property which is associated with real property.
**Mixed Property.** Property which has the characteristics of realty and personalty.
**Mixed Questions of Law and Fact.** Questions which cannot be decided by the judge or jury.
**Mob.** An assemblage of people acting violent.
**Mobilia.** Movables.
**Mock.** To deride or ridicule.
**Mode.** Manner; method.
**Moderata Misericordia.** Writ to prevent an excessive fine.
**Moderator.** Presiding officer of an assembly.
**Modification.** Change; alteration; variance.
**Modo et Forma.** In the manner and form.
**Modus.** Mode; manner; method; form.
**Modus Hiabilis.** A proper manner.
**Modus Injuriae.** The means of injury.
**Modus Operandi.** The method of operation.
**Modus Transferrendi.** Manner of transfer.
**Modus Vivendi.** The mode of living.
**Moiety.** One half.
**Molest.** To annoy a person to the extent of a criminal offense.
**Molliter.** Gently.
**Momentum.** An instant.
**Monarchy.** Government controlled by one.
**Money.** Coin or that which is lawfully and actually current in buying and selling.
**Money Bill.** Bill for raising money.
**Money Demand.** Claim for a fixed and liquidated amount of money.
**Moneyed Capital.** Capital of a corporation used for investing and reinvesting.
**Moneyed Corporation.** One engaged in investing money for profit.
**Money Judgment.** A judgment which can be fully satisfied by a monetary payment.
**Monition.** In admiralty, an order to appear.
**Monogamy.** The state of being married to only one person at a time.
**Monomachy.** Single combat.
**Monomania.** Mental derangement on some particular subject, apparently sane on others.
**Monopoly.** The exclusive control of a particular business or trade, manufacture of a particular article, sale of the whole supply.
**Monster.** Human being abnormal at birth.
**Month.** In statutes and contracts, a calendar month of the ordinary year.
**Monument.** Something erected in memory.
**Moonshine.** Whiskey illicitly distilled or produced.
**Moot.** A subject for argument; unsettled.
**Moot Case.** Case which seeks to determine an abstract question.
**Moot Court.** Practice court for law students.
**Moot Question.** Undecided point of law.
**Mora.** Delay; hindrance.
**Moral.** Pertaining to character and right conduct.
**Moral Certainty.** Certainty beyond a reasonable doubt.
**Moral Consideration.** A consideration good only in conscience.
**Moral Insanity.** Mental disease which destroys the ability to distinguish between right and wrong as to a particular act.

**Moral Law.** Law of conscience.
**Moral Turpitude.** Applied to an act which is dishonest, and contrary to good morals.
**Morari.** To delay or hinder.
**Moratorium.** The temporary suspension by statute of the enforcement of liability for debt because of an existing emergency.
**Moratory Interest.** Interest by way of damages.
**Moratur in Lege.** Plaintiff demurs in favor of a judgement of the court.
**Morbus Sonticus.** An illness which prevents one from attending to business.
**More Colonico.** In a husbandlike manner.
**More or Less.** An uncertain amount.
**Moreover.** In addition to; furthermore.
**Morgue.** Place where unidentified dead are temporarily kept.
**Moron.** One with the mentality of a child between 7 and 12 years of age.
**Morphine.** A narcotic drug.
**Mors.** Death.
**Mort.** Death.
**Mortal.** Deadly.
**Mortality Tables.** Life expectency tables.
**Mort Civile.** Cessation of one's legal rights.
**Mortgage.** A conditional conveyance of property to a creditor as security for a debt.
**Mortgage, Chattel.** Mortgage in the form of personalty.
**Mortgage, Conventional.** Contact by which a person binds the whole part of his property in favor of another to secure the execution of some engagement.
**Mortgage, Equitable.** Specific lien upon real property to secure the performance of an obligation by a court of equity.
**Mortgage, First.** The first in a series of two or more mortages covering the same property.
**Mortgage, General.** One which binds all property, present and future, of the debtor.
**Mortgage of Goods.** Mortgage of personal property.
**Mortgage, Second.** One which ranks immediately after a first mortgage on the same property, without any intervening liens.
**Mortgage Pools.** Groups of mortgages.
**Mortgagee.** Holder of mortgage.
**Mortgagor.** Debtor under a mortgage.
**Mortis Causa.** By reason of death; in contemplation of death.
**Mortmain.** Inalienable ownership; the holding of land by a corporation beyond the period of time or in violation of the law.
**Mortmain Statute.** One which restricts the granting of lands to corporations by will or limits the amount that any testator leaving a wife and children may donate to charity or restricts the period before death in which a charitable bequest may be made.
**Mortuary.** Undertaking establishment.
**Mortuary Tables.** See Mortality Table.
**Mortuus.** Dead.
**Mortuus Sine Prole.** Dead without issue.
**Mos Pro Lege.** Custom instead of law.
**Mother.** Woman who has given birth to a child.
**Motion.** An application to the court for some rule or order granting some type of relief.
**Motive.** That which induces one to indulge in a criminal act, admissable as evidence in order to arrive at the truth of the matter.
**Mourant.** Dying.
**Movables.** Movable objects.
**Move.** To make a motion.
**Movent.** One who makes a motion.
**Mugging.** Photographing of persons arrested.
**Muggle.** Marihuana.
**Mulatto.** Child of Negro and white parents.
**Mulct.** Fine. penalty.
**Mulier.** Woman; wife; legitimate child.
**Mulierty.** Legitimacy.
**Multifariousness.** The misjoinder of causes of action in a bill.
**Multipartite.** Having several parts.
**Multiple Taxation.** Taxation of the same property by several states.
**Multiplicity of Actions or Suits.** A large number of unnecessary attempts to litigate.
**Multitude.** In legal parlance, an assembly of 10 or more persons.
**Multi Will.** Will executed by more than one.
**Municipal.** Belonging to a city or town.
**Municipal Affairs.** Internal business activities of a city or town.
**Municipal Corporation.** An organized town, generally established by the legislature.
**Municipal Law.** Law dealing with municipalities or municipal corporations.
**Municipal Securities.** Bonds issued by cities and towns.
**Municipality.** A legally incorporated association of inhabitants of a prescribed area for local governmental or other public purposes.
**Muniments.** Documents which prove title.
**Muniments of Title.** Original title deeds.
**Murder.** The intentional and unlawful killing.
**Murder in the First Degree.** Murder committed after deliberation.
**Murder in the Second Degree.** Murder committed in the heat of passion.
**Muster.** To assemble troops.
**Mustizo.** Child of an Indian and Negro.
**Mutato Nominis.** Change of name.
**Mutation.** Change; transfer; conveyance.
**Mutilate.** To deprive of an essential part.
**Mutilation.** Rendering a document imperfect.
**Muting.** Insurrection.
**Mutual.** Reciprocal.
**Mutual Insurance.** Type of insurance in which the insured becomes a company member.
**Mutuality.** Reciprocation; that element of every contract making it binding.
**Mutual Promises.** Promises reciprocally exchanged a bilateral contract is formed.
**Mutual Wills.** Similar wills made by two parties giving the property to each other.
**Mutuari.** To borrow.
**Mutuatis.** A loan of money.
**Mutus.** Dumb; mute.
**Mutus et Surdus.** Dumb and deaf.
**Mutuum.** A loan of personal property for consumption, the loan to be returned in kind.
**Myelitis.** Chronic inflammation of the spine.
**Myself Note.** Promissory note with the word "myself" inserted as the name of the payee.
**Mystery.** Trade; art; occupation.

## N

**Naked.** Nude; lacking in power.
**Naked Authority.** Authority granted by a principal to an agent without obligations.
**Naked Confession.** One not corroborated.
**Naked Contract.** Promise without consideration, therefore not really a contract.
**Naked Title.** One which gives the holder no rights in relation to the property.
**Naked Trust.** One which requires no action on the part of the trustee other than turning over money or property to the beneficiary.
**Name.** Word used to identify.
**Narrare.** To allege in a declaration.
**Narratio.** A declaration or complaint.
**Nasciturus.** One conceived but not yet born.
**Nastre.** To be born.
**Natale.** The state of a man at birth.
**Natio.** Nation; birthplace.
**Nation.** A political group of persons having a government, associated with a particular territory and organized for the purpose of obtaining mutual interests.
**National.** Of a nation as a whole.
**National Bank.** Bank incorporated and doing business under the laws of the U.S.
**National Corporations.** Corporations organized under the authority of acts of Congress.
**National Currency.** Notes issued by national banks and the U.S. government.
**National Emergency.** State of national crisis.
**Nationality.** A person's natural political allegiance with all its duties and obligations.
**Native.** A citizen by reason of birth.
**Naturae Vis Maxima.** The force of nature is greatest.
**Natural.** Normal; in accordance with nature.
**Natural Affection.** Presumed affection between two close relatives.
**Natural Allegiance.** Allegiance by birth.
**Natural Child.** Illegitimate child.
**Natural Consequences.** Those consequences which flow from an act.
**Natural Fool.** Idiot.
**Natural Guardian.** Parent of a minor child.
**Natural Infancy.** Child under seven years.
**Naturalization.** The act of giving a foreigner the privilege of citizenship.
**Natural Citizen.** Person made a citizen of the U.S. by act of Congress.

**Natural Law.** Rules of conduct founded in nature and man, discoverable by reason, which act as a guide to civil conduct.
**Naturally.** In the normal course of events.
**Natural Monopoly.** One based on control of a natural resource.
**Natural Obligation.** One which rests wholly in the conscience.
**Natural Person.** An individual.
**Natural Presumption.** Presumption based upon proof of a fact from which other facts may be naturally presumed.
**Natural Year.** 365¼ days.
**Naulage.** The freight of a ship's passengers.
**Naulum.** Freight; fare.
**Nauta.** Sailor.
**Ne.** Not; lest.
**Nearest Kin.** Next of kin.
**Nearest of Blood.** Next of kin.
**Neat Cattle.** Bulls, cows or oxen.
**Ne Baila Pas.** Denial of defendent's suit.
**Necation.** The act of killing.
**Necessaries.** Those things which one actually needs; those things indispensable to maintain human life.
**Necessary.** Applied to that which is indispensable or an obsolute physical necessity.
**Necessary Domicile.** One established by law.
**Necessitas.** Necessity; need; poverty.
**Necessitas Vincit Legem.** Necessity supersedes the law.
**Necessity.** Controlling force.
**Nee.** Born.
**Needs.** Requirements.
**Needy.** Indigent.
**Nee Vife.** Born alive.
**Ne Exeat.** Writ forbidding a person to leave.
**Nefas.** Unlawful act.
**Negare.** To deny.
**Negative.** A denial.
**Negative Condition.** One which provides against the occurrence of some event.
**Negative Evidence.** Testimony that an alleged fact did not exist.
**Negative Pregnant.** Negative statement which contains an affirmative statement.
**Negative Statute.** Statute which prohibits.
**Negative Testimony.** See Negative Evidence.
**Negatum.** Denied.
**Neglect.** To omit or fail to do an act; lack of care or attention.
**Negligence.** Failure to use the amount of care a reasonable man would exercise.
**Negligent Escape.** Escape occurring through the negligence of the officer.
**Negligently.** Without due caution.
**Negotiability.** Transferable quality.
**Negotiable.** Any written security which can be negotiated, transferred or assigned.
**Negotiable Bonds.** Bonds of railroad, industrial and municipal corporations.
**Negotiable Instrument.** Any written securities which may be transferred by endorsement and/or delivery.
**Negotiate.** To transfer a negotiable instrument in due course of business; to bargain or trade.
**Negotiorum Gestor.** On who without authority to do so acts as agent for another.
**Negro.** One of African descent.
**Neighborhood.** A surrounding district.
**Ne Luminibus Officiatur.** An easement preventing a person from obstructing light to another's dwelling.
**Nemine Contradicente.** No one saying the contrary; indicates a unanimous vote.
**Nemo.** No man.
**Nemo Debit Bis Puniri pro Uno Delicto.** No one ought to be punished twice for one offense.
**Nemy.** Not.
**Nephew.** Male child of a brother or sister.
**Nepos.** Grandson.
**Neptis.** Granddaughter.
**Ne Recipiatur.** A warning given to a law officer, by a defendant, not to receive the next proceedings of his opponent.
**Net.** That which remains after all deductions.
**Net Cash.** As applied to a payment, payment in cash without the allowance of any discount.
**Net Earnings.** The gross receipts of a business less the expenses of operating.
**Net Gains.** Profits.
**Net Income.** Income remaining after the subtraction of allowable deductions and exemptions from gross income.
**Net Loss.** Any operational deficit, plus any reduction in value of plant investment.
**Net Premium.** In life insurance, that portion of the premium intended to meet the cost.
**Net Price.** Price after all discounts.
**Net Profits.** Investment gain after deductions.
**Net Weight.** The weight of the commodity shipped exclusive of all crating, etc.
**Ne Unques Accouple.** Never married.
**Ne Varietur.** Not to be altered; a notary's endorsement upon a negotiable instrument.
**Never Indebted.** General issue of debt.
**New and Useful.** Two qualities essential to a product to make it patentable.
**New Assignment.** A restatement in detail.
**Newly Discovered Evidence.** As a basis for a new trial, it must be likely to change the result if a new trial is granted, must have been discovered after the trial.
**New Matter.** Statements of facts made during the course of a litigation.
**New Trial.** A complete retrial of a case in the same court before another jury.
**Next.** Nearest; closest.
**Next Friend.** One who appears without official appointment or designation on behalf of an infant or other person who cannot appear.
**Next of Kin.** Those persons who stand in the closest degree of blood relationship.
**Nickname.** Short name.
**Niece.** Female child of a brother or sister.
**Nient.** Not.
**Nient Comprise.** Not included.
**Nient Culpable.** Not guilty.
**Nient Dedire.** To say or deny nothing.
**Night.** Period between sunset and sunrise.
**Nightwalker.** Prostitute.
**Nihil, Nil.** Nothing.
**Nihil ad Rem.** Nothing to the point.
**Nihil Dicit.** He says nothing; failure of the defendant to plead.
**Nil.** Contracted form of nihil.
**Nil Debet.** He owes nothing; form of the general issue in all actions of debt.
**Nimmer.** Thief.
**Nisi.** Unless.
**Nisi Prius.** Civil causes before a jury and judge.
**No Award.** Plea which denied that the award sued upon was made.
**Nocent.** Guilty.
**Nocere.** To harm or injure.
**Nocumentum.** Nuisance; annoyance.
**Nolens Volens.** Willing, unwilling.
**Nolle.** To be unwilling.
**Nolle Proseque.** To refuse to prosecute, the power to enter a nolles proseque.
**Nolo Contendere.** A plea in a criminal prosecution by which the defendant announces his intention not to contest the action.
**Nol. Pros.** (Abb.). Nolle Proseque.
**Nomen.** Name.
**Nomen Collectivum.** Collective name.
**Nomen Generale.** General name.
**Nomen Juris.** Legal term.
**Nominal.** Titular; not substantial.
**Nominal Damages.** Trifling sum awarded to a plaintiff in an action where no serious loss or damage has been sustained.
**Nominal Partner.** One who allows his name to be used in a business although he has no interest in it.
**Nominal Plaintiff.** One who appears as a plaintiff in an action, although not the real party in interest.
**Nominate.** To name, designate or appoint; to choose for election to office.
**Nomination.** By name; the act of nominating.
**Nominee.** One chosen as a candidate.
**Nomini Poenae.** Under the name of a penalty.
**Non.** Not; by no means.
**Nonability.** Legal incapacity.
**Non Acceptavit.** Denial of agreement.
**Nonaccess.** Absence of sexual intercourse between husband and wife.
**Nonage.** Under age.
**Non Assumpsit.** Plea in an action of special assumpsit which denies a promise was made.
**Non Assumpsit infra Sex Anno.** Plea assumsit is null if not within six year limitation.
**Non Claim.** Failure to assert a claim or right.
**Non Compos Mentis.** Not in possession of his full mental faculties; totally incompetent.
**Non Constant.** It is not certain.
**Non Culpabilis.** Not guilty.
**Non Damnifactus.** Not injured.

**Non Demisit.** Not granted, leased.
**Non Est Factum.** It was not made.
**Non Est Inventus.** He has not been found.
**None Effect.** Void.
**Nonfeasance.** Failure to perform a duty.
**Non Fecit.** He did not make it.
**Non Infregit Conventionem.** He has not broken the agreement; denial of breach of contract.
**Nonissuable Plea.** No issue of fact plea.
**Nonjoinder.** Failure of the plaintiff to include in his declaration all of the necessary parties.
**Non Juridicus.** Not legal.
**Non Liquet.** It is not clear.
**Nonmailable Matter.** Material which cannot legally be sent through the U.S. mails.
**Non Memini.** Not remembered.
**Non Obstante.** Notwithstanding.
**Non Obstante Veredicto.** Notwithstanding the verdict of the jury.
**Nonpar Value Stock.** Corporation stock having no face or par value.
**Nonpayment.** Failure of payment of a debt.
**Non Pros.** (Abb.). Non Prosequitur.
**Non Prosequitur.** He has not proceeded.
**Non-Residence.** Residence beyond the limits of a particular jurisdiction.
**Non Sanae Mentis.** Not of sound mind.
**Nonsane Memory.** Unsound mind.
**Nonsense.** Unintelligible written matter.
**Non Sequitur.** It does not follow.
**Non Sui Juris.** Not in his own right.
**Nonsuit.** Judgement against a plaintiff for technical failure to prove his case.
**Nonsupport.** Failure of a husband to provide.
**Non Tenuit.** He did not hold.
**Non-Term.** Court vacation.
**Non-User.** Neglect to use.
**Non Vult Contendere.** At common law, a plea in a criminal prosecution that the defendant will not contest.
**Noon.** The middle of the day.
**Nota.** A note; a distinguishing mark.
**Nota Bene.** Note well.
**Notarial.** Pertaining to a notary.
**Notary Public.** A public official authorized to attest to the authenticity.
**Note.** A written instrument containing a promise of signer to pay another.
**Note of Hand.** Promissory note.
**Not Found.** Indorsement by a grand jury on a bill of indictment upon failure to indict.
**Not Guilty.** Plea of the general issue in trespass and certain other civil actions; verdict in favor of a defendant.
**Notice.** Information; knowledge.
**Notice, Averment of.** Allegation in a pleading that required notice has been given.
**Notice of Dishonor.** Notice given by the holder to the drawer of a bill, that the person primarily liable has failed to honor it.
**Notice of Motion.** Written notice advising the defendant when and where he is to appear and states cause of complaint.
**Notice of Protest.** Notice given by the holder of a bill to the drawer that the bill has been protested for refusal of payment.
**Notice to Plead.** Written notice served upon the defendant by the plaintiff.
**Notice to Produce.** Written notice requiring the adverse party to produce a certain described document at the trial.
**Notice to Quit.** Written notice given by a landlord to a tenant according to the terms of the lease, requiring him to leave the premises.
**Notify.** To inform in words or writing.
**Noting Protest.** The notation by a notary on a bill exchange showing it was dishonored.
**Notitia.** Notice; knowledge.
**Notoriety.** State of being well-known.
**Notorious.** Applied to things universally known and recognized; flagrant.
**Notorious Possession.** Conspicuous possession of real property which may lead to the acquisition of title by adverse possession.
**Nova Customa.** New duties or customs.
**Novation.** Substitution of new contract.
**Novel.** New; recent.
**Noverint Universi per Praesentes.** Know all men by these presents.
**Novi Operis Nunciato.** Protest a new work.
**Novitas.** Novelty.
**Novum Opus.** A new work.
**Novus Homo.** A new man; a man pardoned.
**Now.** At this time.
**Noxious.** Harmful; offensive.
**Nubilis.** Marriageable.
**Nuda.** Nude, naked; mere.
**Nuda Pactio Obligationem Non Parit.** A naked agreement does not beget an obligation.
**Nuda Patientia.** Mere sufferance.
**Nuda Possessio.** Mere possession.
**Nude.** Naked, unclothed; mere.
**Nude Contract.** One without consideration.
**Nudum Pactum.** Promise with no consideration.
**Nuisance.** Anything which interferes with the enjoyment of property or common right.
**Nuisance Per Se.** That which is a nuisance at all times and under all circumstances.
**Nul.** No; no one; none.
**Nul Agard.** No award.
**Nul Disseisin.** Name given to a plea of the general issue in a writ of entry.
**Null.** Void.
**Null and Void.** Binding on no one.
**Nullity.** That which has no legal effect.
**Nullity of Marriage.** Defect in the marriage state which renders it void.
**Nullus, Nulla.** No.
**Nullius Juris.** Without legal effect.
**Nul Tiel Corporation.** No such corporation.
**Nul Waste.** Plea in a common law action of waste denying waste has been committed.
**Nunciato.** Protest; declaration.
**Nuncius.** Messenger.
**Nuncupate.** To make a verbal will.
**Nuncupative Will.** An oral or verbal will.
**Nunquam.** Nowhere; never.
**Nuquam Indebitatus.** Never indebted.
**Nuptial.** Pertaining to or concerning marriage.
**Nuture.** To rear or educate a child.
**Nutander.** By right.
**Nute.** Night.
**Nymphomania.** A woman with a morbid, uncontrollable desire for sexual intercourse.

## O

**Oath.** Statement by a witness at a trial, with God as his witness, that he will tell the truth.
**Oath in Litem.** An oath respecting the value of the property which is the subject.
**Oath of Office.** Oath by one assuming office.
**Oathworthy.** Credible.
**Ob.** On account of.
**Obedient.** Submissive to authority.
**Obiter.** On the way; in passing.
**Obiter Dictum.** That which is said in passing.
**Obit Sine Prole.** He died without issue.
**Objection.** Argument against a statement.
**Object of Statute.** Purpose of the statute.
**Oblatio.** An offer of payment of debt.
**Obligatio.** Obligation.
**Obligation.** A legal and/or moral duty.
**Obligee.** One to whom another is bound.
**Obligor.** One bound by some obligation.
**Obliquus.** Oblique; collateral; indirect.
**Obliteration.** Erasure of written words.
**Oblivion.** Forgetfulness.
**Obloquy.** Disgrace; reproach.
**Obreption.** Obtaining a thing by fraud.
**Obrogation.** The annulling of a law.
**Obscene.** Words, actions or representation which shock the public ideas of sexual purity.
**Observe.** To perform that which is prescribed.
**Obsignare.** To sign and seal an instrument.
**Obsolete.** Term applied to a law which is not enforced although it has not been repealed.
**Obstante.** Obstructing.
**Obstetrics.** Branch of medicine for the care of women during pregnancy and birth.
**Obstriction.** A bond; an obligation.
**Obstruct.** To hinder, prevent from progress.
**Obstruction of Justice.** An act or acts hindering or tending to hinder justice.
**Obtain.** To get possession of, procure.
**Obtest.** To protest.
**Obventio.** Rent; revenue; income.
**Obvious.** Easily seen or understood.
**Obvious Risk.** One apparent to a reasonable man.
**Occasion.** An incident as opposed to a cause.
**Occasional.** Not regularly; casual.
**Occision.** A killing.
**Occult.** Hidden; secret.
**Occultatio.** Concealment.
**Occupancy.** Mode of acquiring property, which before belonged to nobody.
**Occupant.** One in actual possession.

**Occupare.** To occupy.
**Occupation.** An occupation; a seizure.
**Occupation.** Taking possession; trade.
**Occupational Disease.** Disease resulting as a natural consequence of one's occupation.
**Occupy.** To hold in possession.
**Of Course.** As a matter of right.
**Occur.** To happen.
**Odium.** Hatred; dislike.
**Oeconomicus.** An executor of the estate.
**Oeconomus.** Administrator.
**Oeps.** Use.
**Of Age.** Over 21 years of age.
**Of Counsel.** An associate counsel in an action.
**Offend.** To commit a public offense.
**Offender.** Person implicated in a crime.
**Offense.** Violation of law or established rules.
**Offer.** Proposal by one person to another.
**Office.** A public position in any branch of government.
**Office Copy.** Transcript of legal proceedings.
**Officer.** One entrusted with the duties of either a public or private office.
**Official.** Pertaining to a public office; officer.
**Officious Will.** Will in which the testator leaves his property to his family.
**Offset.** A deduction; counterclaim.
**Offspring.** Issue.
**Of New.** Anew a second time.
**O.K.** (Abb.). All right.
**Olographic Will.** One which is hand written in entirety by the testator.
**Omissio.** An omission.
**Omission.** Failure to do that which is required.
**Omme.** Man; anyone.
**Omnibus Bill.** A statute which contains a number of bills.
**Omnium.** The aggregate value of the different stock in which a loan is usually funded.
**On.** Upon; as soon as; near to.
**On Account.** In partial payment.
**On Account of Whom It May Concern.** An insurance term used to include all persons having an insurable interest in the subject matter for whose benefit the policy is intended.
**On Call.** On demand.
**On Demand.** A promissory note payable on demand.
**Onerari Non.** Not chargeable with the debt.
**Onerous.** Burdensome; difficult.
**Onerous Gift.** Gift which imposes some obligation upon the donee by the donor.
**Only.** Solely; alone.
**Onomastic.** Applied to the signature of an instrument which is different than the writing.
**On or About.** An approximation of date.
**Onus Probandi.** The burden of proof.
**Ope Consilio.** By aid and counsel.
**Open.** To begin a trial; to be first to present argument during a trial.
**Open and Current Account.** One in which there is a series of financial transactions in which debits and credits are balanced.
**Open and Notorious.** Flagrant misconduct.
**Open Court.** Public session of court.
**Opening.** Beginning; first statement of counsel.
**Open Policy.** An insurance policy in which the value is determined after loss.
**Open Season.** Part of the year when the laws for the preservation of game and fish permit the unlimited killing or taking of a particular species of game or fish.
**Open Shop.** Business or industry in which both union and non-union labor is employed.
**Open Theft.** A larceny wherein the thief is caught in the act.
**Operation of Law.** Manner in which rights and liabilities pass to a person with no act done by the party.
**Operative.** Workmen.
**Operative Words.** Words in a deed or lease which effect the transaction intended to be consummated by the instrument.
**Operis Novi Nuntiato.** A protest or warning against a new work.
**Opiates.** Drugs, sedatives.
**Opinion.** Expression of a conclusion or inferences based upon observation.
**Opinion Evidence.** Evidence based upon what the witness thinks or believes.
**Opium.** Drug made from poppy.
**Oportet.** It is necessary, fitting or proper.
**Oppignerare.** To pledge.
**Opposition.** Act of resisting; antagonism.
**Opposite Party.** One whose interests are antagonistic to the protected party.
**Oppression.** An act of cruelty.
**Opprobrium.** Infamy; shame.
**Optimacy.** Nobility.
**Option.** Choice; contract to keep an offer open.
**Optional.** Left to choice.
**Optionee.** One who has secured by contract the right to keep an offer open.
**Optioner.** One bound by contract to keep an offer open.
**Opus.** Work.
**Opus Locatum.** Work let out to another.
**Opus Manificium.** Manual labor.
**Opus Novum.** New work.
**Oral.** Spoken.
**Oral Defamation.** Slander.
**Orator.** (m.), **Oratrix** (f.). Petitioner in an action in equity
**Ordain.** To decree or enact.
**Order.** Command; direction; written direction.
**Order of Business.** Order in which legislative business is conducted.
**Order of Filiation.** Court order determining the paternity of a bastard child.
**Order of the Coif.** Legal fraternity.
**Ordnance.** A rule established by authority.
**Ordinandi Lex.** Law of procedure.
**Ordinary.** Common; usual.
**Ordinary Care.** Care exercised by a reasonable man under the particular conditions.
**Ordinary Conveyances.** Deed of transfer entered into without an assurance.
**Ore Tenus.** By word of mouth.
**Organic Act.** Federal statute conferring powers of government upon a territory.
**Organic Law.** Constitutional law.
**Original.** First in time or importance.
**Original Bill.** Bill filed at the beginning of a suit in equity.
**Original Conveyance.** Conveyance which creates an estate.
**Original Evidence.** Original document.
**Original Jurisdiction.** Jurisdiction of a court to hear a case at its beginning.
**Orphan.** A minor child who has lost one or both of his parents.
**Orphans' Court.** Courts of probate jurisdiction in a number of states.
**Ostensible.** Applied to that which claims to be what it is not.
**Ostensible Partner.** One who although not a member of a firm, allows the use of his name as a general partner in transactions with third persons.
**Ostentum.** Monster.
**Osteopath.** One who treats disease by manipulation.
**Oust.** To put out.
**Ouster.** A wrongful dispossession.
**Outer Door.** The door of each separate apartment where there are different apartments having a common outer door.
**Outlaw.** One violating the law.
**Outlawed.** As applied to debt, to have become invalid by lapse of time.
**Out of Benefit.** Term applied to insurance policy holders who have been suspended for nonpayment of premiums.
**Out of Term.** Between terms of court.
**Output.** Amount of material produced within a certain time.
**Outrage.** A grave wrong; violation of a right.
**Outre.** Outside; beyond.
**Outroper.** Licensed auctioneer.
**Outstanding.** Unpaid; uncollected.
**Over.** In conveyance, used to describe a gift or limitation that comes into existence on the termination of a previous estate.
**Overcharge.** A charge in excess of that permitted by law.
**Overcyted.** Found guilty.
**Overdraft.** Taking out more than deposited.
**Overdraw.** To write checks on a bank for a larger amount than one has deposited.
**Overdue.** Delayed or unpaid.
**Overlive.** Survive.
**Overload.** To burden too heavily.
**Overplus.** Remaining balance.
**Overrule.** To deny; to annul or make void.
**Overseer.** Superintendent; supervisor.
**Overt.** Open; manifest, public.
**Owe.** To be bound to pay a debt.
**Owing.** Unpaid.

**Own.** To have title.
**Ownership.** Group of rights to use and enjoy property, including the right to transmit it to others.
**Owner's Risk.** The risk, assumed by the owner of merchandise, in transit that the goods may be damaged.
**Oyer and Terminer.** Name of a court in several states with general jurisdiction.
**Oyez.** Hear ye.

## P

**Pace.** 2½ feet.
**Paceatur.** Let him be freed or discharged.
**Package.** A parcel made up of smaller parcels.
**Packing a Jury.** Use of improper means in selecting a jury.
**Pact.** Agreement.
**Pactio.** Pact.
**Pactitious.** Settled by a pact or contract.
**Pagus.** A county.
**Paid-Up Insurance.** Insurance upon which no further premiums are due.
**Pais.** The country; the jury; outside of court.
**Palam.** Openly.
**Palm Off.** To impose by fraud.
**Palpable.** Obvious.
**Pander.** Procurer; pimp.
**Panel.** Persons available each month for Federal and State jury duty.
**Paper.** A document or pleading.
**Paper Title.** Title shown only by deeds.
**Par.** Equal.
**Paragraph.** An entire statement of action.
**Paramount.** Above; upwards.
**Paramount Title.** Superior title to property.
**Paranoia.** Type of insanity.
**Paraphernalia.** Property of a married woman other than that included in her dowry.
**Parcel.** In regard to land, a lot or tract.
**Parcenary.** The holding of an inheritable estate jointly by parceners.
**Parcener.** Joint heir.
**Parchment.** A document on parchment.
**Par Delictum.** Equal wrong or fault.
**Pardon.** The release from the legal consequenses of a specific crime.
**Parens Patriae.** Father of his country.
**Parent.** The natural father or mother.
**Parenticide.** One who kills or the killing of a parent.
**Pari.** With equal or in equal.
**Pari Causa.** With equal right.
**Pari Delicto.** In equal guilt.
**Pari Materia, In.** On the same subject.
**Pari Passu.** Of the same degree.
**Pari Ratione.** By the same reasoning.
**Parish.** In Louisiana, a district corresponding to a county in other states.
**Parity.** Equality.
**Park.** A public ground for recreation.
**Parking.** The stationing of automobiles.
**Parking on the Highway.** The voluntary act of leaving an automobile on the highway.
**Parliament.** The legislative branch of the English government.
**Parliamentary Law.** The body of regulations of procedure governing legislative assemblies.
**Parliamentary Procedure.** The procedure and rules governing the conduct of business.
**Par of Exchange.** The value of the money of one country in that of another.
**Parol.** Oral; verbal.
**Parol Contract.** A contract not under seal.
**Parole.** A conditional release from prison.
**Parol Evidence.** Oral testimony of a witness.
**Parol Evidence, Rule of.** A rule which prohibits the receipt of oral agreements to contradict or modify a written agreement.
**Parricide.** One who murders or the murder of one's parent.
**Pars.** A part; a party to a deed or action.
**Pars Gravata.** The party aggrieved.
**Pars Rationabilis.** A reasonable part or share.
**Pars Rea.** A party defendant.
**Part.** Portion, share.
**Parte Inaudia.** One side being unheard.
**Parte Non Comparente.** The party not having appeared; a party in default.
**Particips Criminis.** A party to the crime.
**Particeps Doli.** A party to the fraud.
**Participate.** To take part in.
**Particular Averment.** An allegation or pleading a particular fact.
**Particular Malice.** Grudge.
**Particulars.** The items of an account.
**Parties.** Those persons who take part in any act or directly interested in the action.
**Partition.** Any division of real or personal property by co-owners.
**Partitione Facienda.** Concerned with making a division.
**Partner.** Member of a partnership or firm.
**Partnership.** An association of two or more persons sharing profits and losses.
**Part Owners.** Owners in common property.
**Part Payment.** Partial payment of a debt due.
**Part Performance.** Partial completion.
**Parturition.** Giving birth to a child.
**Partus.** A child.
**Party.** One who takes part in a legal transaction; a litigant; a political group.
**Party Aggrieved.** One who has been directly and injuriously affected by the act or omission.
**Party in Interest.** One who has a beneficial interest in the result of an action or who might be injured as the result thereof.
**Party To Be Charged.** In the statute of frauds, the party against whom the contract is sought.
**Par Value.** As applied to bonds, a value equal to the face of the bonds.
**Parum.** Little.
**Parvise.** Moot.
**Pas.** Precedence.
**Pass.** To utter or pronounce; to transfer.
**Passage.** Voyage over water or the money paid for such a voyage; enactment.
**Passagium.** A voyage.
**Pass Book.** Bank book in which deposits made by a customer are entered.
**Passenger.** One who uses a public conveyance.
**Passim.** Scattered; indiscriminately.
**Passion.** Any emotion which renders the mind incapable of cool reflection.
**Passive.** Inactive; permissive.
**Passive Bond.** One which bears no interest.
**Passive Trust.** One in which the trustee no longer has any active duty to perform.
**Passport.** A document issued to a citizen by his country, certifying his status.
**Past Consideration.** In the law of contracts, a consideration which was furnished or rendered in the absence of any previous request.
**Patent.** A document by which a state or government grants public lands to an individual; the exclusive right granted to an inventor to make, use and sell his invention.
**Patent Ambiguity.** An apparent error on the face of an instrument.
**Patentee.** One to whom letters patent are granted by the government.
**Patent Medicine.** Medicine made by secret formula.
**Patent Writ.** An open or unsealed writ.
**Pater.** Father.
**Paterfamilia.** The father of a family.
**Parternal.** Pertaining to the father.
**Paternal Power.** Paternal authority of a father over his children.
**Paternity.** Fatherhood.
**Pathology.** That branch of medicine which deals with the nature, causes and symptoms.
**Patiens.** A patient.
**Patria.** A country; a jury.
**Patria Potestas.** Paternal power.
**Patricide.** One who kills or the killing of one's own father.
**Patrimonial.** Paternal.
**Patrimony.** An inherited estate; property inherited from the paternal side.
**Patrinus.** A godfather.
**Patronymic.** Surname.
**Patruelis.** Paternal first cousin.
**Pauper.** One who is destitute.
**Pawn.** A bailment of goods to a creditor as security for some debt.
**Pawnbroker.** One licensed to lend money on the security of personal property.
**Pawnee.** One to whom goods are pledged.
**Pax.** Peace.
**Pay.** To discharge a debt.
**Payable.** To be paid.
**Payable on Demand.** Indicates a bill is payable on its date.
**Payee.** One to whom a payment is made.
**Payment.** The discharge of a debt.

**Payment into Court.** The placing of money in the custody of the court by a person who is actually sued for it or is so threatened.
**Peace.** State of public order, tranquility.
**Peace, Justice of the.** A public official having minor judicial power.
**Peace Offfcers.** Those charged with the enforcement of the law.
**Peccatum.** A sin; a crime.
**Peculation, Peculatus.** The embezzlement of public funds.
**Peculiar.** Particular; special.
**Pecunia.** Money; property.
**Pecunia Non Numerata.** Money not paid.
**Pecuniary.** Financial.
**Pecuniary Injury.** One estimated financially.
**Peddler.** An itinerant trader.
**Pederasty.** Copulation between two men.
**Pedestrian.** Person traveling on foot.
**Pedigree.** Genealogy.
**Peeping Tom.** One who peers in windows on the sly in the hope of seeing nude women.
**Peine.** Punishment.
**Penal.** Pertaining to punishment.
**Penal Action.** An action to recover.
**Penal Statute.** Statute which forbids an act and imposes a penalty for it.
**Penalty.** Punishment for a crime.
**Pendency.** Suspense; undecided; pending.
**Pendente Lite.** While the suit is pending.
**Pending.** During; before the conclusion of.
**Penses Me.** In my possession.
**Penetration.** In a case of rape, the insertion of the male sex organ into the female sex organ.
**Penitentiary.** Prison.
**Pensa.** A weight.
**Pensio.** A payment; a rent.
**Pension.** A regular allowance paid to a public or private employee, retired from the service.
**Pensioner.** One who receives a pension.
**Pentways.** Byways; private roads.
**Per.** By, through, by means of.
**Per and Cui.** By and to whom.
**Per Annum.** Yearly.
**Per Autre Vie.** For the lifetime of another.
**Per Bouche.** Orally.
**Per Capita.** As applied to descent and distribution of estates, equally.
**Perception.** Taking into possession.
**Per Consequences.** In consequence.
**Per Contra.** On the other hand.
**Per Curiam.** By the court.
**Per Defaltam.** By default.
**Per Diem.** Daily.
**Perduellio.** Treason.
**Perdurable.** Lasting forever.
**Peregrini.** Foreigner; alien.
**Peremptory.** Imperative; positive; conclusive.
**Peremptory Defense.** A defense denying suit.
**Peremptory Mandamus.** A writ of obedience.
**Per Equipollens.** By an equivalent.
**Perfect.** Free from error; to complete.
**Perfect Trust.** Executed trust.
**Perfidy.** Treachery, faithlessness.
**Perform.** To execute or fulfill according to terms.
**Performance.** Fulfillment of a duty.
**Per Fraudem.** By fraud.
**Periculum.** Danger; hazard.
**Periel.** Risk; hazard.
**Per Incuriam.** Through inadvertence.
**Per Industriam.** By industry.
**Per Infortunium.** Accidentally.
**Period.** Any point, space or division of time.
**Period of Gestation.** Time between a child's conception and birth.
**Peripharasis.** Verbosity.
**Perjury.** Lying under oath.
**Per Legem Terrae.** By the law of the land.
**Permanent.** Lasting; fixed; stable.
**Permenent Abode.** Fixed residence.
**Permanent Disability.** One which is more than temporary and presumably permanent.
**Per Minas.** By threats or duress.
**Permission.** Leave; license; authority to do.
**Permissive.** Allowed.
**Permissive Waste.** Negligent waste.
**Permit.** A license.
**Per Omnes.** By all persons.
**Perpetrator.** One who commits a crime.
**Perpetual.** Everlasting; eternal; continuous.
**Perpetual Injunction.** Injunction which is final.
**Perpetual Lease.** One which the tenant has the option of renewing as soon as it expires.
**Perpetuating Testimony.** Procedure for taking and preserving testimony.
**Perpetuity.** An interest under which property is less than completely alienable for longer than allowed by law.
**Per Plegium.** By a security or pledge.
**Per Procuration.** By an agent.
**Perquisites.** Anything lawfully acquired by an officer beyond the salary or regular fees.
**Perquisitio.** A purchase.
**Per Quod.** By which.
**Per Se.** In itself.
**Persecutio.** A suit or prosecution.
**Person.** A human being (natural person) or a corporation (artificial person).
**Persona.** Person.
**Persona Designata.** Person pointed out as an individual.
**Persona Grata.** An acceptable person.
**Personal.** Pertaining to an individual person.
**Personal Action.** Action to recover damages due to breach of contract or injury.
**Personal Chattels.** Movable property.
**Personal Contract.** Contract involving personal property.
**Personal Effects.** Items having an intimate relation to the possessor; movable or chattel
**Personal Injury.** An invasion of a personal right; bodily injury.
**Personality.** The law dealing with persons.
**Personal Knowledge.** First-hand knowledge.
**Personal Liberty.** Freedom of movement.
**Personal Representative.** Executor or administrator of a deceased person.
**Personality.** Personal property; chattels.
**Persona Non Grata.** A person not acceptable.
**Personate.** To assume another's identity with intent to deceive and defraud.
**Persona Non Compos Mentis.** Persons of unsound mind.
**Per Stirpes.** By representation.
**Persuade.** Induce.
**Per Testes.** By witnesses.
**Pertinens.** Appurtenant.
**Pertinent.** Relevant.
**Perturbation.** A disturbance.
**Perverse Verdict.** Verdict in which the jury does not follow the directions of the judge.
**Petitio.** Petition; demand; claim.
**Petition.** In equity, an application for a court order giving the circumstances.
**Petit Jury.** A trial jury.
**Petitor.** Petitioner; plaintiff.
**Petitory Action.** An action in which the plaintiff seeks to establish right of property or title.
**Petty.** Small; trifling.
**Petty Larceny.** A misdemeanor; larceny or theft of property worth less than the amount fixed by statute.
**Pharmacist.** Druggist.
**Philanthropic.** Charitable.
**Physical.** Relating to the body.
**Physical Force.** Actual violence.
**Physical Incapacity.** Inability to copulate due to an incurable physical imperfection.
**Physical Injury.** Bodily harm.
**Physician.** A doctor of medicine.
**Picaroon.** Robber.
**Picketing.** The posting of men before a business organization to make public protest.
**Pickpocket.** One who secretly steals from the person of another.
**Pierage.** Toll charge for the use of a pier.
**Pignus.** Property pledged as security.
**Pilfer.** Steal.
**Pillage.** Robbery by force or violence.
**Pillory.** A frame erected on a pillar, made with holes through which a man's head, hands or fingers could be fixed and held.
**Pimp.** A procurer; a pander.
**Piracy.** Robbery on the high seas.
**Pirate.** A sea-robber.
**Piscary.** The right of fishing.
**Pistol.** A short, hand firearm.
**P.J.** (Abb.). Presiding judge.
**Placard.** Edict; declaration.
**Place of Abode.** Residence.
**Placit, Placitum.** Decree; determination.
**Placitabile.** Pleadable.
**Placita Communia.** Common pleas.
**Placita Juris.** Rules of law.

**Placitamentum.** Pleading.
**Placitum.** Marginal title.
**Plaga.** Wound; stroke.
**Plagerism.** Copying an author's work.
**Plaint.** Complaint; the introductory pleading.
**Plaintiff.** One who brings an action at law.
**Plat.** A scale map of land.
**Plea.** In common law pleading, the forma answer of the defendant; in criminal law, the answer of "guilty" or "not guilty"; any action.
**Plead.** To deliver the defendant's answer to the plaintiff's declaration.
**Pleader.** One who prepares a pleading.
**Pleadings.** The successive statements delivered alternately by the parties involved.
**Plea in Bar.** Plea which defeats the plaintiff's.
**Plea of Guilty.** Admission of guilt in court.
**Plea of Nolo Contendere.** Implied confession.
**Plea Side.** Civil department of a court.
**Plebian.** One of the common people.
**Plebiscite.** Popular vote.
**Pledge.** Personal property given as security.
**Pledgee.** One to whom goods are pledged.
**Pledgery.** Suretyship; an answering for.
**Pledgor.** One who delivers goods in pledge.
**Plee.** Plea; an action.
**Plenary.** Full; complete; entire.
**Plenary Suit.** A suit on formal pleadings.
**Plene Administravit.** Plea of an administrator when sued for a debt of his decedent.
**Plenipotentiary.** One fully empowered to act for another.
**Plenum Dominum.** Full ownership.
**Plenum Rectum.** Absolute right.
**Plumbism.** Lead poisoning
**Plunder.** To take by open force.
**Plural.** More than one.
**Plurality.** The largest number of votes cast.
**Pluries.** Often; frequently.
**Plus.** More.
**Poach.** To steal game from another man.
**Poena.** Punishment.
**Poena Corporalis.** Corporal punishment.
**Point.** A question of law in a particular case.
**Poison.** Any substance which when taken internally can destroy life.
**Police.** Branch of the government which enforces the law.
**Police Court.** Municipal court for the trial of minor criminal offenses.
**Policy of Insurance.** Contract between the insured and the insurer.
**Political Offense.** An offense against the state.
**Politics.** The science of government.
**Poll.** To examine each juror to determine whether they agree with the verdict.
**Polling the Jury.** See Poll.
**Polls.** Place where votes are cast in an election.
**Polyandry.** Marriage of a woman to several men at the same time.
**Polygamy.** Marriage to more than one person at the same time.
**Ponere.** To place or put.
**Pool.** The combined money, property or interests of a group of people.
**Poor.** Needy; destitute.
**Poor Person.** Pauper.
**Populus.** The people.
**Port.** Place where vessels load and unload.
**Portatica.** Port duties.
**Portion.** Part; share; division.
**Port of Entry.** Port where there is a customhouse.
**Portorium.** Customs duty.
**Positive.** Certain; absolute.
**Positive Evidence.** Direct proof.
**Positive Juris.** Of positive law.
**Positive Law.** Law established by members of a society to govern their actions.
**Posse.** Possible.
**Posse Comitatus.** The force of the county.
**Possess.** To occupy, control.
**Possessed.** A temporary interest in lands.
**Possessio.** To have full right and control.
**Possessio Bonorum.** The possession of goods.
**Possessio Malae Fidei.** Possession in bad faith.
**Possession.** Exclusive ownership and control.
**Possession in Fact.** Actual possession.
**Possession in Law.** Possession which the law annexes to the title.
**Possession, Writ of.** In an action of ejectment, a writ used to put a plaintiff in possession of real property.
**Possessor.** One who possesses.
**Possessory.** Pertaining to possession.
**Post Entry.** An entry of goods at a custom house to correct an original entry.
**Posthumous Child.** Born after father's death.
**Possibilities.** A possibility.
**Possibility.** An uncertain future event.
**Possibility of Reverter.** Possibility of estate.
**Post.** After.
**Post-Act.** An act done afterwards.
**Postage.** Charge for the delivery of mail.
**Post-Date.** To put a future date on.
**Post Diem.** After the day.
**Postea.** Afterwards.
**Posterity.** Direct descendants.
**Post Facto.** After the commission of a crime.
**Post Litem Motam.** After the start of suit.
**Post Mortem.** After death; autopsy.
**Post Notes.** Bank notes payable at a future date.
**Post-Nuptial.** After the marriage has taken place.
**Post Obit.** After death; an agreement to pay a sum of money after the death of a person from whom the promisor hopes to inherit property.
**Postpone.** Delay.
**Post Rem.** After the transaction.
**Post Terminum.** After the term.
**Potable.** Drinkable.
**Potentia.** Power; authority; possibility.
**Potential.** Existing in possibility.
**Potestas.** Power; authority.
**Pound.** Place to confine animals.
**Poverty Affidavit.** An affidavit filed by one of the parties in an action, that he is unable to pay court costs.
**Power.** The authority to do a thing; the authority to dispose of real or personal property.
**Power Coupled with an Interest.** Authority to do some act coupled with an interest in the thing itself.
**Power of Attorney.** Formal instrument by which an agent is appointed.
**Powers that Be.** Duly constituted authorities.
**Practice.** Habit, custom, usage; execution of legal proceedings in all its stages and forms; the exercise of the profession of law.
**Practitioner.** One engaged in the practice of his profession.
**Praecipe.** An original writ; an order; a command.
**Praecognita.** Things which must be known in order to understand that which follows.
**Praedictus.** Aforesaid.
**Praedium.** Land.
**Praefatus.** Aforesaid.
**Praejudicialis.** Prejudged.
**Praejudicium.** Prejudgment; prejudice.
**Praemissa.** The premises.
**Praemium.** Reward; price.
**Praesens in Curia.** Present in court.
**Prayer.** In equity, that part of the bill or complaint which asks for the relief sought by the party.
**Preamble.** A clause at the beginning of a constitution or statute stating the reason and purpose of the legislation.
**Precarious.** Descriptive of anything which may be ended at the will of the person who granted it.
**Precatory.** Having the character of a request.
**Precatory Trust.** A trust created by words of entreaty and request rather than by command.
**Precaution.** Foresight.
**Precedence.** Superiority in rank.
**Precedent.** Previous decision of court relied upon as authority.
**Prece Partium.** By the prayer of the parties.
**Precept.** A written order issued to an officer(s) to give him (them) the authority to perform some act.
**Precinct.** A police district; an election district.
**Preclude.** Estop.
**Preconceived Malice.** Malice aforethought.
**Predecessor.** One who goes before.
**Pre-Emption.** The right to buy property before some other person.
**Pre-Existing Debts.** Debts previously contracted.
**Prefer.** To bring before; to prosecute.
**Preference.** The transfer of property by an insolvent debtor to one or more of his creditors, to the exclusion of the rest.

**Preferred.** Having a priority, advantage or privilege.
**Preferred Stock.** Stock having a priority over other stock in the distribution of dividends.
**Pregnant.** The state of being with child.
**Prejudice.** Bias; preconceived opinion; to injure or damage.
**Preliminary.** Introductory; preceding.
**Premeditation.** The planning of a deed before the doing thereof; plotting.
**Premises.** Foregoing statements; in equity, the stating part of a bill; in estates, the actual property conveyed; in insurance, the subject matter insured.
**Premium.** Reward; compensation; money paid by the insured to the insurer under a policy of insurance.
**Prenomen.** First name.
**Prepense.** Forethought.
**Preponderance of Evidence.** Greater weight of or more credible evidence.
**Prerogative.** An exclusive privilege.
**Prescribe.** To make invalid or to outlaw; to claim title by virtue of long use and enjoyment.
**Prescription.** Mode of acquisition to title of land by long use and enjoyment.
**Presence.** State of being in a certain place.
**Present.** A gift; now existing.
**Presently.** Immediately; now.
**Presentement.** The written statement of a grand jury concerning an offense based on their own knowledge and observation without any bill of indictment being laid before them; the presentation of a negotiable instrument to the maker, drawee or acceptor at the proper time and place.
**Preservation.** To keep safe from harm.
**Preside.** To direct some proceeding.
**President.** One in a position of authority over others.
**Presume.** Assume beforehand.
**Presumed Bias.** Implied bias.
**Presumption.** That which may be taken for granted.
**Presumption of Fact.** Inference drawn from evidence adduced at a trial.
**Presumption of Law.** Legal conclusion derived from the proof of certain facts.
**Presumptive.** Based upon a presumption.
**Presumptive Title.** Titled inferred from possession and use.
**Pretend.** To feign, sham.
**Preterition.** Omission by a testator of a legally entitled heir.
**Preter Legal.** Not legal.
**Pretermission.** See Preterition.
**Pretermit.** To omit.
**Pretext.** Pretense.
**Pretium.** Price; cost; value.
**Pretium Affectionis.** The price of affection.
**Pretium Periculi.** The price of risk, such as an insurance policy premium.
**Prevailing.** Predominant; effectual.
**Prevarication.** Breach of confidence; lie.
**Prevent.** To impede; to obstruct.
**Previous.** Prior; former.
**Price.** Monetary consideration paid for a thing.
**Prima Facie.** At first sight; a fact presumed true unless proven otherwise.
**Prima Facie Case.** Case supported by sufficient evidence to justify a favorable verdict unless contradicted by other evidence.
**Primary.** First in importance or time.
**Primary Cause.** The responsible cause of a legal liability.
**Primary Evidence.** The best evidence to prove a fact.
**Primary Legacy.** A gift of money by will.
**Primer Election.** First choice.
**Primogeniture.** The state of being of the eldest of several children of the same parents.
**Principal.** One who grants authority to an agent to transact business for him; one primarily liable to a creditor, but jointly a third person, the surety; the one who actually commits a crime; the amount of a debt, not including interest.
**Principal Fact.** The main fact at issue in a cause.
**Principalis.** A principal.
**Principium.** The beginning.
**Principle.** A fundamental doctrine of law.
**Prior.** Earlier, preceding; preferable.
**Priority.** Precedence; preference.
**Prison.** Place of confinement.
**Prisoner.** One confined to a prison by due process of law.
**Private.** Pertaining to a private individual as opposed to the public.
**Private Law.** Law concerned with the legal relations between private individuals.
**Private Person.** An individual not holding public office.
**Private Property.** Property belonging to an individual who has the exclusive right of disposition thereof.
**Private Residence.** Residence for one family.
**Private Trust.** Trust created for purposes other than public or charitable.
**Privies.** Persons mutually interested in a thing due to some relation other than actual contract between them.
**Previgna.** Step-daughter.
**Prevignus.** Step-son.
**Privilege.** A benefit or immunity.
**Privileged Communications.** A communication made in professional confidence (client to lawyer, patient to doctor) which may not be divulged.
**Privilege Tax.** Excise tax.
**Priviligium.** Privilege.
**Privity.** A succession of relationship to the same rights of property.
**Privity of Contract.** Relationship among two or more contracting parties.
**Privy.** One who participates in any action, matter or thing; private.
**Privy in Representation.** Executor of a testator; administrator of an intestate.
**Privy Verdict.** Verdict given privately to the judge out of court.
**Prize.** A reward for some feat.
**Pro.** For; before; by way of; in place of.
**Pro and Con.** For and against.
**Probability.** Likelihood.
**Probable.** Appearing to be true.
**Probable Cause.** Reasonable cause.
**Probable Consequence.** One most likely to follow its supposed cause.
**Probate.** The process of proving a will.
**Probate Court.** Court established for the administration of the estates of decedents, and the control of the adoption and guardianship of minors; Orphan's Court.
**Probate Duty.** Estate tax.
**Probatio.** Proof; trial.
**Probation.** Proof; trial; test; suspended sentence during good behavior, usually under supervision of a probation officer.
**Probationer.** One on probation.
**Probation Officer.** An officer who supervises those on probation or suspended sentence.
**Probatio Viva.** Living proof.
**Probe.** An inquiry or investigation.
**Pro Bono et Malo.** For good and evil.
**Procedure.** Method of proceeding by which a legal right is enforced.
**Proceeding.** The form and manner of conducting a legal action before a court; an inquiry before a grand jury.
**Process.** Method, mode or operation producing a result or effect; all the acts of the court from the beginning to the end of a proceeding.
**Prochein.** Next.
**Prochein Ami.** Next friend; the adult representative (not a guardian) of an infant plaintiff.
**Proclamare.** To proclaim, warn.
**Proclamation.** A public notice.
**Pro Concilio.** For advice.
**Pro Confesso.** As confessed; in equity, applied to the decree founded upon a bill where no answer is made to it by the defendant.
**Proctor.** One authorized to act for another; an attorney in a court of probate or admiralty or in an ecclesiastical court.
**Procuracy.** A written instrument empowering a procurator to act.
**Procuration.** Power or authority given in writing.
**Procurator.** Proctor.
**Procure.** To initiate a proceeding; to cause or bring about; to obtain.
**Procurer.** One who brings about a thing.
**Pro Defectu.** Because of the lack of.

**Pro Defectu Exitus.** For failure of issue.
**Pro Defendente.** In favor of the defendant.
**Prodigal.** Spendthrift.
**Prodition.** Treason.
**Proditor.** Treason.
**Produce.** To make, manufacture; to bring forward.
**Producent.** One who produces a person as a witness.
**Pro Emptore.** As a purchaser.
**Pro Facti.** As a fact.
**Pro Falso Clamore Suo.** By reason of his false claim.
**Profanity.** Cursing; swearing.
**Profectitus.** Property which can be inherited.
**Profert.** An offer to produce a written instrument in court.
**Profert in Curia.** He produces in court.
**Profess.** To make a public declaration.
**Profession.** A public declaration; vocation; occupation.
**Proffer.** To offer, propose.
**Profit.** Gain.
**Profiteering.** Acquisition of excessive profits.
**Profits.** Net gain from a business investment.
**Pro Forma.** As a matter of form.
**Pro Hac Vice.** For this occasion.
**Prohibit.** To forbid by law.
**Prohibition.** Writ issued from a superior court forbidding an inferior court to hear a case because of lack of jurisdiction; restraint on the sale of alcoholic beverages.
**Pro Indiviso.** As undivided.
**Pro Legato.** As a legacy.
**Proles.** Offspring; posterity.
**Prolicide.** The killing by a parent of his child.
**Prolixity.** Superfluous statement of facts in pleading.
**Prolongation.** Extension of time.
**Promise.** An agreement or declaration to perform a certain act.
**Promisee.** One to whom a promise is made.
**Promisor.** One who makes a promise.
**Promissory Note.** A negotiable instrument.
**Promote.** Encourage; advance.
**Promoter.** Informer; one who undertakes the organization of a corporation.
**Promulgation.** Publication of the enactment of a law.
**Proof.** Evidence.
**Proper.** Suitable; correct.
**Proper Care.** Care exercised by a prudent man under like circumstances.
**Proper Name.** Christian name.
**Proper Party.** One other than a necessary party who has an interest in the subject matter of the litigation.
**Property.** Means the exclusive and unrestricted right to a thing as well as the physical thing itself.
**Property Insurance.** A contract for the indemnification against loss or damage to certain property named in the policy.
**Propinquity.** Relationship.
**Propinquus.** Next of kin.
**Propone.** To propound; to offer; to make a motion.
**Proponent.** One who offers a will for probate or makes a motion.
**Proportum.** Import.
**Proposal.** Offer; expression of intention.
**Proposition.** An offer to do a thing.
**Pro Posse Suo.** According to his own ability.
**Proprietary.** Pertaining to an owner.
**Proprietas.** Property; ownership.
**Proprietor.** Owner.
**Proprio Vigore.** By its own force; automatically.
**Propter.** Because of; for.
**Propter Adulterium.** By reason of adultery.
**Propter Affectum.** Term applied to the challenge of a juryman for bias.
**Propter Defectum.** Because of the lack of.
**Propter Delictum.** On account of some defect.
**Propter Saevitiam.** Because of cruelty.
**Pro Querente.** For the plaintiff.
**Pro Rata.** Proportional.
**Prorate.** To divide or distribute proportionately.
**Pro Re Nata.** According to the occasion as it arises.
**Proscribed.** Outlawed.
**Pro Se.** On his own behalf.
**Prosecute.** To act against through law.
**Prosecuting Attorney.** Public officer who conducts trial on behalf of the state.
**Prosecution.** Legal proceedings for purpose of determining guilt or innocence.
**Prosecutor.** Witness or public official who instigates a criminal proceeding.
**Prosequi.** Pursue; prosecute.
**Prospective Law.** Law applicable to cases arising after its enactment.
**Prospectus.** Document setting forth nature and objectives of securities; an invitation to purchase stock, bonds, debentures.
**Prostitution.** Practice of a woman who engages in sexual intercourse for pay.
**Protectim Order.** Order protecting wife's property in willful direction by husband.
**Protest.** Expression of dissent or disapproval.
**Pro Tempore.** Temporarily.
**Protestation.** Manner of pleading involving an indirect affirmation or denial of fact that cannot be definitely alleged or denied.
**Prothonotary.** Office of courts having custody of court records and seals.
**Protocol.** A record.
**Prout.** As charged.
**Prove.** To establish; make certain.
**Pro Veritate.** For the truth.
**Proviso.** Part of legal document which provides for certain conditions of the basic instrument.
**Provocation.** Act of inciting to do particular act.
**Provoke.** Arouse; stimulate.
**Proximity.** Relationship; closeness.
**Proxeneta.** One who arranges contract between two parties.
**Proxy.** One who is charged with representing another.
**Pseudo.** False; counterfeit.
**Puberty.** The age of maturity at which person is capable of begetting children (Common Law).
**Public.** The citizens of a community, state or nation.
**Publish.** To make known, circulate.
**Pudendum.** External female sexual organ.
**Pudicity.** Purity; modesty.
**Pierita.** Age from 7 to 14 years.
**Punish.** To impose a penalty for an act.
**Punitive Damages.** Exemplary or vindictive damages.
**Purchaser.** Buyer.
**Pure.** Free of conditions or restrictions; chaste.
**Purge.** To cleanse.
**Purloin.** To steal.
**Purpart.** Part of an estate, after having been held in common, allotted to a single person.
**Purport.** Convey; imply.
**Pusue.** Prosecute.
**Purveyor.** One who purchases or procures for another.
**Purview.** Enacting pact of a statute.
**Put.** Stockbroker's privilege of delivering or not delivering the thing sold.
**Putative.** Assumed; supposed.
**Put in Suit.** To sue upon.
**Pyx.** Receptacle in mint for testing coins.
**Pyromania.** Morbid desire for house burning.

## Q

**Qua.** Considered as; in what manner; how; in the capacity of.
**Quack.** An incompetent physician.
**Quadrans.** A fourth part.
**Quadripartite.** Divided into four parts; having four parties.
**Quadroon.** Offspring of mulatto and white.
**Quaere.** Query.
**Quaerens.** Plaintiff.
**Quaeritus.** It is doubted.
**Quaestio Facti.** A question of fact.
**Quaestio Juris.** A question of law.
**Quaestus.** An estate acquired by purchase as opposed to inheritance.
**Qualification.** A requisite, essential; condition which must be fulfilled in order to attain a certain status; a modification.
**Qualified.** Adapted; entitled; capable; competent; possessing legal power or capacity.
**Qualified Acceptance.** Conditional acceptance.
**Qualified Elector.** One legally qualified to vote.
**Qualified Indorsement.** Indorsement of a negotiable instrument qualifying the liability of the endorser.
**Qualified Interest.** An interest in property which is less than absolute.
**Qualified Privilege.** In the law of libel and

slander, applied to all communications made in good faith upon any subject matter in which the person communicating has an interest, or in reference to which he has a duty to a person having a corresponding interest or duty, although not a legal one, but of moral or social character.
**Qualified Voter.** One who votes.
**Qualify.** To prepare to exercise a right, office or franchise; to limit; modify or restrict.
**Quamdiu.** As long as; until.
**Quando Acciderint.** When they shall come in.
**Quandocumque.** Whenever; as often as.
**Quantes Fois.** How many times.
**Quantum.** How much; the whole; a totality.
**Quantum Indemnificatus.** To what amount he should be indemnified.
**Quantum Meriut.** As much as deserved; in the common counts, which evaluates services rendered.
**Quantum Valebant.** As much as they were worth; in the common counts which evaluate for goods sold and delivered.
**Quarantine.** Isolation of infected persons to prevent spread of serious disease; period during which a ship with infectious disease aboard is isolated.
**Quare.** Wherefore; why; because.
**Quarre!.** Applied to real and personal actions and the causes of actions and suits; controversy; debate.
**Quarry.** An open excavation where marble, stone, etc. are dug.
**Quart.** A liquid measure of one-fourth of a gallon.
**Quarter.** One-fourth.
**Quarter-Dollar.** 25 cents.
**Quarter-Eagle.** U.S. coin worth $2.50.
**Quarterly.** Every 3 months.
**Quarter of a Year.** 91 days.
**Quarter Section.** In U.S. land law, one of the square divisions employed in the survey and designation of public lands, containing 160 acres and measuring ¼ of a mile on each side.
**Quarter Year.** 91 days.
**Quash.** To annul or make void.
**Quasi.** As; as if; as it were.
**Quasi Affinity.** Relationship of an engaged person to the relatives of the person to whom he or she is engaged.
**Quasi-Contractus.** An obligation arising not from an agreement of parties, but from some relationship between them.
**Quasi Corporation.** Name sometimes given to a county.
**Quasi-Delict.** A tort in which there is an absence of malice.
**Quasi Ex-Contractu.** As if from a contract; applied to obligations which are not really contractual but to which the actions of assumpsit have been extended.
**Quasi-Fee.** Estate gained wrongfully.
**Quasi Judicial Act.** Judicial act performed by one other than a judge.
**Quay.** Wharf.
**Querela.** An action preferred in any court.
**Querens.** Plaintiff.
**Querulous.** Fault-finding; fretful; whining.
**Question.** Query; inquiry; problem.
**Quia.** Because; inasmuch as.
**Quibble.** Verbal objection; unnecessary objection.
**Quick.** Alive.
**Quickening.** First motion of the fetus in the womb felt by the mother.
**Quick with Child.** Having conceived.
**Quid Pro Quo.** What for what; something for something.
**Quidam.** Somebody.
**Quiet.** To pacify; to silence; peaceful; free from disturbance.
**Quietare.** To acquit, discharge.
**Quinquepartite.** Divided into 5 parts.
**Quintal.** 100 pounds.
**Quit.** Clear; discharged; free.
**Quitclaim.** To reliuquish a claim; a release or acquittance given to one man by another in respect of any action that he has against him.
**Quitclaim Deed.** Deed of co veyance operating by way of release.
**Quittance.** Acquittance; a release.
**Quoad Hoc.** As to this; with respect to this.
**Quo Animo.** With what intention.
**Quod Computet.** That he account.
**Quod Recuperet.** That he recovbr; the ordinary form of judgments for the plaintiff in actions at law.
**Quod Vide.** Which see.
**Quorum.** A majority.
**Quota.** A proportional part or share.
**Quote.** To copy or repeat a passage from; to cite.
**Quousque.** How long; how far.
**Quovis Modo.** In whatever manner.

## R

**Race.** An ethnical stock; a contest for stakes with judges presiding.
**Rachater.** To redeem or buy back.
**Rachetum.** Redemption; ransom.
**Rack.** Instrument of torture.
**Racketeer.** One who make money in violation of the Penal Law.
**Racketeering.** An organized conspiracy to gain control of a business or commodity through acts of violence.
**Rack-Rent.** A rent amounting to the full value of the tenement or close to it.
**Radiograph.** X-ray.
**Radius.** A straight line drawn from the center of the circle to its periphery.
**Raffle.** Game of chance in the form of a lottery.
**Railroad.** To force through legislation over the objection of a minority; a road or way on which iron rails are laid for purposes of transportation.
**Railroad Commission.** A state board empowered to make and enforce regulations concerning railroad companies.
**Railway.** Railroad.
**Raise.** To create; to infer; to produce; to rear.
**Raise an Issue.** To bring pleadings to an issue.
**Raise a Rate.** Levy a tax.
**Raising a Check.** Forgery of a check in which the amount has been increased, but the signatures are genuine.
**Random.** Without aim, purpose or direction.
**Rank.** Grade; official standing.
**Ransom.** Money paid for the release of a person or property from captivity.
**Rape.** Forcible and unlawful sexual knowledge of a woman without her consent.
**Rapina.** Robbery.
**Raptim et Sparsim.** Hastily and spasmodically.
**Raptor.** One who commits rape.
**Raptus.** Rape.
**Rasure.** Erasure.
**Rasus.** Erased.
**Ratable.** Taxable.
**Ratable Value.** Appraised or assessed value of property for purposes of taxation.
**Ratam Rem Habere.** To consider the matter as ratified.
**Rate.** Tax; assessment; proportional or relative value.
**Rate of Exchange.** The actual value in a foreign country of a negotiable instrument drawn upon a person in that country.
**Ratification.** Confirmation by a principal of an act performed by his agent in his behalf; affirmation.
**Ratify.** To make valid; to confirm.
**Ratihabito.** Ratification.
**Ratio.** Rate; proportion.
**Ratio Decidendi.** The reason for deciding.
**Ratio Legis.** The reason underlying the law.
**Rationabilis.** Reasonable; rational.
**Rational.** Sane.
**Rational Doubt.** Reasonable doubt.
**Ratione Contractus.** By reason of the contract.
**Ratione Loci.** By reason of the place.
**Ratione Materiae.** By reason of the matter involved.
**Ratione Personae.** By reason of the person concerned.
**Rationes.** The pleadings filed in an action.
**Ratione Tenurae.** By reason of one's tenure.
**Ravish.** Forcible and unlawful sexal knowledge of a woman without her consent.
**Ravishment.** A rape.
**Raze.** Erase.
**R.C.L.** (Abb.). Ruling Case Law.
**Re.** In the matter of; in regard to.
**Read.** To make known the contents of a writing or document.

**Ready.** Prepared.
**Ready and Willing.** Not only the capacity, but the disposition to act.
**Ready Money.** Cash.
**Real.** Pertaining to a thing or realty.
**Real Action.** An action brought for the specific recovery of lands, tenements and hereditaments.
**Real Estate.** Right, interest or ownership existing in the land.
**Real Evidence.** Evidence furnished by physical objects brought into court.
**Real Injury.** Physical injury due to an unlawful act.
**Real Law.** Body of laws relating to real property; law relating to specific property, movable or immovable.
**Realize.** To bring into actual possession; to convert property into money; to receive returns on an investment.
**Realm.** State; country.
**Real Party in Interest.** One directly interested in a litigation.
**Real Property.** Lands, tenements and hereditaments and all that makes up the earth in its natural condition.
**Real Security.** Security upon property.
**Real Statute.** Statute regulating property within the state where it is in force.
**Real Things.** Things which are permanent, fixed and immovable.
**Realty.** Real property.
**Real Value.** Market value under normal conditions.
**Reason.** Intellect; sanity; motive or cause for action.
**Reasonable.** Just; proper.
**Reasonable Care.** Prudent action.
**Reason and Probable Cause.** Existing grounds for suspecting one of a crime.
**Reasonable Creature.** A human being.
**Reasonable Doubt.** Such a doubt as will leave the juror's mind uncertain after examination of the evidence.
**Reasonable Prudence.** Ordinary care.
**Reasonable Time.** Length of time fairly and properly allowed for the performance of a duty or obligation.
**Reattachment.** A second attachment of a defendant's person subsequent to his release from a previous attachment in the same action.
**Rebate.** Discount; refund; reduction in consideration of prompt payment.
**Rebel.** One who unjustly and unlawfully acts against the government or duly constituted authority.
**Rebellion.** Insurrection.
**Rebouter.** To rebut; to bar.
**Rebut.** To deny, contradict or avoid.
**Rebuttable Presumption.** A presumption which may be contradicted by evidence.
**Rebuttal.** Showing that a statement of a witness is not true; testimony addressed to evidence of the opposition.
**Rebutter.** A defendant's answer of fact to a plaintiff's surrejoinder.
**Recall.** To set aside; method of removal from office.
**Recall of Pardon.** Cancellation of a pardon before its delivery and acceptance.
**Recapture.** A taking back; a remedy or reprisal.
**Receipt.** Written acknowledgment that an obligation has been discharged.
**Receive.** To get by transfer; accept custody of.
**Receiver.** One appointed to hold in trust, property under litigation.
**Receiver Pendente Lite.** One appointed to take charge of the fund or property to which the receivership extends while the case is still undecided.
**Receptus.** Arbitrator.
**Recess.** A brief cessation or interruption to a meeting or proceeding.
**Recession.** A giving back of property by the grantee to his grantor.
**Recessus.** An exit.
**Rechater.** To ransom.
**Recidivist.** An habitual criminal.
**Reciprocal.** Mutual.
**Reciprocal Contract.** A bilaterial contract.
**Reciprocal Wills.** Wills giving the property of each testator to the other.
**Reciprocity.** Mutuality.
**Recital.** The formal statement in any deed or writing setting forth the reasons upon which the transaction is founded.
**Reck.** To care, mind or heed.
**Reckless.** Negligent.
**Reckless Driving.** Operating a motor vehicle in a negligent manner with disregard of consequences and indifference to the rights of others.
**Recognition.** Ratification; adoption.
**Recognizance.** An obligation of record, entered into before some court of record or a duly authorized magistrate, to do some particular act.
**Recognize.** To try; to examine in order to determine the facts; to ratify.
**Recognizee.** One to whom the promise is made in a recognizance.
**Recognizor.** One who binds himself by a recognizance.
**Recommend.** To advise or counsel.
**Recommendatory.** Precatory; advisory.
**Recompense.** Reward; compensation.
**Reconcile.** To harmonize.
**Reconduction.** Renewal of a lease.
**Recontinuance.** The recovery of an incorporeal hereditament of which one has been wrongfully deprived.
**Reconvenire.** To plead a cross-demand.
**Reconvention.** An action by a defendant against a plaintiff in a former action; a cross-bill or litigation.
**Record.** To write or transcribe for the purpose of preservation; an official memorandum of proceedings, acts, etc.
**Recordare.** A writ to bring up judgments of justices of the peace.
**Recorder.** Public officer who keeps record books required by law.
**Recordum.** Record.
**Recount.** A counting over again of election ballots.
**Recoupment.** A keeping back and stopping of something which is due because there is an equitable reason to withhold it.
**Recourse.** Resort; recur.
**Recover.** To collect; to regain; to acquire by litigation.
**Recovery.** Obtained by process and course of law; payment compelled by action in the revenue laws of the state.
**Recreant.** Coward.
**Recrimination.** Charge by an accused person against the accuser.
**Recte.** Rightly; correctly.
**Rectifier.** A person who purifies spirits in any manner or who makes a mixture of spirits with anything else and sells it under any name.
**Rectify.** To correct; to purify by distillation; to adjust.
**Rectum.** Right.
**Rectum Esse.** To be right in court.
**Recurrent Insanity.** Temporary insanity which returns from time to time.
**Recusation.** A challenge directed against a judge before whom the case is to be tried on the ground of prejudice or some others diqualification.
**Recusatio Testis.** Rejection of a witness on the ground of his incompetency.
**Red.** Communist; anarchist.
**Reddendum.** In conveyancing, rendering; yielding; a clause in which the grantor creates some new thing to himself out of that which he has granted.
**Reddition.** Surrender; restoration.
**Redditus Assisus.** A fixed rent.
**Redeem.** To buy back.
**Redeemable Bonds.** Bonds which are due and payable at a specified time, but redeemable on demand of the issuing body.
**Redelivery.** A yielding back of a thing.
**Redemption.** A buying back.
**Red-Handed.** While committing the crime.
**Redhibition.** Avoidance of a sale because of a defect in the thing sold which renders it useless or undesirable.
**Redirect Examination.** Re-examination of a witness by the party who called him, after the cross examination.
**Reditus.** Revenue; return.
**Reditus Assisus.** A set rent.
**Red Light District.** Area where houses of prostitution are located.

**Redraft.** The drawing of a new bill of exchange which has been protested by the holder of the original draft.
**Redraw.** To make a redraft.
**Redress.** Reparation.
**Red Tape.** Order or system carried to extremes.
**Reduced.** Improverished.
**Reduce to Possession.** To convert a claim in action to a tangible possession.
**Redundancy.** Introduction of superfluous matter into a legal document.
**Re-Entry.** The act of resuming possession pursuant to a right reserved when the party exercising the right quit his possession.
**Refare.** To bereave; to rob.
**Refection.** Redress; reparation.
**Refer.** To call in an auditor or referee in a case which requires special handling.
**Referee.** One appointed by the court to perform certain duties in a cause pending in court.
**Reference.** An agreement to arbitrate; to send a cause pending in court to a referee.
**Referendum.** The determination of legislation by direct vote of the people.
**Reform.** Correct; rectify
**Reformatory.** Penal institution directed toward rehabilitation.
**Refunding Bond.** Bond which replaces an outstanding bond which the holder surrenders in return for the new security.
**Refund.** To repay or return.
**Refuse.** To fail to comply with a demand.
**Regency.** Rule; government; kingship.
**Regent.** Temporary ruler; governor; member of governing board of some colleges.
**Regicide.** Murder of or one who murders a sovereign.
**Régime.** System of rules.
**Regina.** Queen.
**Register.** To record; to enroll; an officer who keeps such a record; the book containing a record.
**Registered.** Entered; recorded.
**Registered Letter.** A letter which is recorded and for which the sender receives a receipt.
**Registered Trade-Mark.** A trade-mark filed in U.S. patent office.
**Registered Voter.** One lawfully registered and who has the right to vote.
**Register of Deeds.** Officer who records instruments affecting realty.
**Registry.** Record book; recording of an instrument in the proper office.
**Regnant.** Regent.
**Regress.** A going back.
**Regula.** Rule.
**Regulae Juris.** Rules of law.
**Regular.** Conforming to law; steady; according to custom.
**Regular Army.** Standing army.
**Regulate.** To control or direct.
**Regulation.** Rule; precept.
**Rehabilitate.** To return to a former state.
**Rehearing.** Second consideration of a cause.
**Reimburse.** To refund; pay back.
**Reinstate.** To restore to a former state.
**Reinstate A Case.** To put a case in the same position as before dismissal.
**Reinsurance.** A contract by which an insurer insures himself with another insurer against loss in the original policy.
**Reissuable Note.** Bank notes, which after having been paid, may be put into circulation again.
**Reject.** To discard, throw away.
**Rejoin.** To answer a plaintiff's replication.
**Rejoinder.** The second pleading on the part of the defendant in answer to the plaintiff's replication.
**Relate.** To pertain to or refer to.
**Related.** Connected; akin.
**Relation.** Relative.
**Relations by Affinity.** Persons related through marriage.
**Relations by Consanguinity.** Persons related by blood.
**Relative.** Kinsman.
**Relative Fact.** One which has bearing on another fact.
**Relative Impediment.** Bar to marriage because of relationship.
**Relative Powers.** Powers which relate to land.
**Relator.** One who brings an action in which he is beneficially interested, but which under existing procedure can only be brought by some state official.
**Relaxare.** To free or discharge.
**Relaxatio.** A release.
**Release.** Relinquishment; liberation; to surrender a claim due at a specified time; the conveyance of the rights of one person to another who is actually in possession.
**Releasee.** One who is released or to whom a release is given.
**Release of a Debt.** Discharge of a debt by writing under seal.
**Releasor.** One who releases or executes a release.
**Relegatio.** Type of exile in which one retains his civil rights.
**Relevancy.** Applicability; connection between two facts.
**Relevant.** In relation to testimony, directly touching upon the issue.
**Relict.** Surviving spouse.
**Relief.** Assistance given to the indigent.
**Religion.** Body of beliefs encompassing man's relationship to the supernatural
**Religious Freedom.** The right to worship God according to the dictates of one's conscience as safeguarded in the First Amendment of the Constitution.
**Relinquish.** To abandon or give up.
**Reliqua.** Balance of an account.
**Relocatio.** Renewal of a lease without change in terms.
**Remainder.** An estate in expectancy, created by the act of the parties, which becomes an estate in possession upon the determination of a particular prior estate, created by the same instrument at the same time.
**Remainderman.** One entitled to the remainder of an estate after a particular estate out of it has expired.
**Remand.** To order or send back.
**Remanet.** A cause, the trial of which must await the next term of court.
**Remedial.** Able to be remedied or redressed.
**Remedial Action.** An action brought to obtain compensation or indemnity.
**Remedy.** Means by which a right is protected or enforced.
**Remise.** To remit or give up; to pass title of property.
**Remission.** Release of a debt; pardon; exoneration.
**Remit.** To send or transmit; to pardon.
**Remittance.** Money sent by one person to another.
**Remittee.** One to whom a remittance is sent.
**Remitter.** One who remits.
**Remittere.** To release.
**Remittitur.** Writ of reversal issued by an appellate court upon reversing the order or judgement appealed.
**Remonstrance.** Giving reasons against a proposal.
**Remote.** Afar; slight.
**Remote Cause.** In negligence, improbable cause.
**Remote Damages.** Result over and beyond which the negligent party has no control.
**Removal of Cause.** Change of venue; transfer of a cause from one court to another.
**Remover.** Trasfer of a suit or cause from one court to another.
**Renant.** Denying.
**Rencounter.** A sudden fight or dispute.
**Render.** To give up, yield.
**Render an Account.** To present an account.
**Rendezvous.** Meeting place.
**Rendition of Judgment.** Oral pronouncing of a judgment which determines the rights of the parties to an action.
**Renegade.** Deserter.
**Renew.** To remake, rebuild, re-establish.
**Renewal.** The act of renewing or reviving; an obligation on which time of payment is extended.
**Renounce.** To relinquish; disclaim; forsake; abandon.
**Rent.** Compensation paid for the use or occupation of property.
**Rentage.** Rent.
**Rental.** Amount paid periodically for the use of property.
**Rental Agent.** One who leases premises and collects rents thereon.

**Rent Sec.** Rent created by a deed without any clause for distress.

**Rents of Assize.** The certain and demanded rents of freeholders and copyholders of ancient manors.

**Renunciation.** A legal act by which a person abandons a right acquired without transferring it to another.

**Repair.** To mend; restore; renovate.

**Reparable Injury.** An injury which can be fully compensated.

**Reparation.** Compensation; redress.

**Repatriation.** Restoration of citizenship.

**Repay.** To return or restore money or goods.

**Repeal.** Recall or revoke; annulment of a law by a subsequent statute.

**Repeaters.** Habitual offenders or criminals.

**Repetition.** A demand or action for the recovery of payment made under mistake on a condition which had not been performed.

**Repleader.** Permission by the court to plead over again.

**Repleviable.** Subject to an action of replevin.

**Replevin.** A personal action whereby the owner recovers possession of his own goods.

**Replevisor.** Plaintiff in an action of replevin.

**Replevy.** To secure the possession of personal property by means of replevin.

**Repliant.** Plaintiff who pleads a replication in answer to a defendant's plea.

**Replication.** Reply; answer; rejoinder; a reply made by the plaintiff in an action to the defendant's plea, or a suit in chancery to the defendant's answer.

**Reply.** Answer of the plaintiff to the defendant' replication.

**Report.** Official statement of facts.

**Represent.** To stand in someone's place; to substitute.

**Representative.** One who stands in place of another.

**Representative Form of Government.** Government conducted by delegates elected by the people.

**Reprieve.** Temporary suspension of a death sentence.

**Reproach.** Censure; rebuke.

**Republic.** Commonwealth; the state.

**Repudiation.** Rejection; disclaimer; denial of responsibility.

**Repudium.** Breach of marriage contract.

**Repugnancy.** Inconsistency between two or more clauses in the same deed, contract or statute or in the same count or plea.

**Reputable.** Worthy; honorable.

**Reputable Citizen.** One of good character.

**Repute.** Esteem with which a man is held by his neighbors.

**Reputed.** Accepted by public opinion.

**Request.** Petition; asking for that which is desired.

**Require.** Need; command; demand; to ask by right and authority.

**Requisition.** Demand in writing.

**Res.** Thing; object; subject matter of a suit; property; transaction.

**Res Accessoria.** An accessory thing.

**Res Aliena.** The property of another.

**Res Caduca.** An escheat.

**Recind.** To terminate a contract as to future transactions; to annul a contract from the beginning.

**Rescissio.** Repeal; abrogation.

**Rescession.** Termination or annulment of a contract.

**Res Communes.** Common property.

**Res Corpales.** Corporeal property.

**Rescript.** Duplicate; copy; written court order to the clerk, giving directions concerning the further disposition of a case.

**Rescue.** Unlawfully and knowingly aiding another to escape from prison without any effort of the prisoner to free himself; unlawful setting free of a distrained animal.

**Rescyt.** Haboring of a felon.

**Res Derelicta.** Abandoned property.

**Reservation.** A clause in a deed or other instrument of conveyance whereby something is created or reserved out of the thing granted which was not in existence before.

**Reserve.** In insurance, the amount of money which insurance companies are legally required to have to mature or liquidate claims made upon them.

**Reserve Fund.** See Reserve.

**Reset.** Harboring of an outlaw.

**Res Fungibles.** Property consumable by use and returnable in kind.

**Res Furtivae.** Stolen things.

**Res Gestae; Res Gesta.** Things done; thing done; circumstances incidental to an act ligitated.

**Resiant.** Residing.

**Reside.** Live, dwell.

**Residence.** Place of abode; dwelling place.

**Resident.** One who lives in a place.

**Resident Freeholder.** One who lives in a particular place, and who owns property amounting to a freehold interest.

**Residual.** Pertaining to the remaining part.

**Residuary.** That which remains of an estate after the legacies have been paid.

**Residuary Clause.** Clause in a will providing for the disposition of property remaining after the legacies have been paid.

**Residuary Device.** The person to whom all the land is given which is not specifically disposed of in a will.

**Residuary Estate.** Property of a testator not disposed of by the will and which may not be legally disposed of.

**Residue.** Surplus.

**Residum.** Residue; balance.

**Resignation.** Formal renouncement of office.

**Resignee.** One in favor of whom a resignation is tendered.

**Res Immobiles.** Immovable corporeal things.

**Res in Re.** In rape, reference to the entering of the male organ into that of the female.

**Resist.** Oppose.

**Resisting an Officer.** Obstructing, opposing or endeavoring to prevent an officer from legally discharging his duty.

**Res Mobiles.** Corporeal movable things.

**Res Nova.** A new matter; something without precedent.

**Res Nullius.** Property of no one.

**Resolution.** A formal decision; determination or expression of an opinion by an official body or any assembly or meeting.

**Resolutory.** Determinative.

**Resolutory Condition.** A condition subsequent; one which, when accomplished, revokes an obligation valid until its happening.

**Reson.** Right; justice; reason.

**Resort.** To go back; to frequent; a place of frequent assembly.

**Resources.** Assets; means; income.

**Respectable.** Decent; proper.

**Res Perit Domino.** The thing is lost for the owner.

**Respite.** Temporary suspension or reprieve; delay.

**Respond.** Answer; to be liable or answerable.

**Respondeat Ouster.** A judgment against a defendant upon an issue of law raised by his dilatory plea.

**Respondent.** Defendant; appellee.

**Responsibility.** Obligation; duty; liability.

**Responsible.** Liable; answerable.

**Responsio.** Answer; reply of a witness.

**Res Private.** Private property.

**Res Publica.** Public property.

**Res Quotidianae.** Common, everyday mat-

**Rest.** Repose; to announce that no more testimony will be presented because the plaintiff or defendant considers his case completed.

**Restitution.** Act of restoring; to return a thing to its rightful owner; remedy for breach of contract whereby the aggrieved party occupies as good a position as he occupied before the contract.

**Restitutor.** Restorer.

**Restore.** To bring back or return.

**Restrain.** Prohibit; limit; confine or abridge a thing.

**Restraining Order.** Order similar to an injuction; court order to prevent the doing of some act.

**Restraint of Marriage.** A condition in a gift or will which prohibits the free choice of husband or wife of the donee or grantee.

**Rest, Residue and Remainder.** Phrase used in will to device and bequeath all of the property of the testator not specifically bequeathed.

**Restrictive Covenant.** A covenant in a lease or

deed limiting the way in which the land may be used.
**Restrictive Indorsement.** Indorsement restricting the use of a negotiable instrument, e.g. "for deposit."
**Resulting Trust.** Trust which arises by implication of law or through equity, and which is established as consonant to the presumed intentions of the parties as inferred from the nature of the transaction.
**Res Universitatis.** Things in common.
**Retail.** To sell in small quantities, directly to the consumer.
**Retain.** To keep possession; to engage the services of an attorney.
**Retainer.** Fee which a client pays an attorney.
**Retaining Fee.** See Retainer.
**Retaliation.** Reprisal.
**Retorna Brevum.** Return of Writs with an indorsement of an officer as to what he has done in execution of the writ.
**Retorsion, Retortion.** Retaliation; in international law, the treatment by one State of citizens of another State in a similar way as that State treats the first State's citizens.
**Retraction.** Withdrawal of a renunciation.
**Retraxit.** He has withdrawn; the formal withdrawal of a suit by a plaintiff.
**Retreat to the Wall.** In self-defense, to avail oneself of all means of escape.
**Retroactive.** Retrospective; acting on things past.
**Rette.** Accusation.
**Return.** To bring back; an official statement by an officer in respect to a writ which he has executed; filing of a tax form or other form required by authority.
**Return-Day.** The day on which a writ or process must be returned.
**Returns.** Number of ballots cast in an election.
**Reus.** Defendant; one accused of a crime; party to a suit.
**Reus Stipulandi.** Promise.
**Revendication.** To reclaim or to demand the restoration of.
**Revenge.** To inflict malicious injury in return for harm done.
**Revenue.** Return; yield; income.
**Revenue Law.** Law authorizing taxation.
**Reversal.** Annulment; making void of a judgment.
**Reve Se.** To set aside; make void; annul.
**Reversion.** This residue of an estate which the grantor has not disposed of in a grant, which commences in possession after the determination of some particular estate.
**Reversionary.** Relating or pertaining to a reversion.
**Reversionary Lease.** Lease the term of which begins at a future time.
**Reversioner.** One entitled to a reversion.
**Revert.** To turn back; to return to.
**Reverter.** Reversion.
**Revest.** To come into possession again; to restore an interest in property to one who has been divested of that property.
**Review.** Judicial re-examination, reconsideration, revision; the power, by a bill in equity, to correct errors in a court record.
**Revise.** To review for correction.
**Revival.** Agreement to maintain as valid a rescinded contract; restoration of power to levy execution on a judgment, which while still valid, has been dormant for a specified time.
**Revivor.** Bill in equity to reestablish and continue proceedings which have been abated.
**Revocation.** Withdrawal; recall; annulment; repudiation.
**Revocation of a Will.** Annulment of a will by some subsequent act of the testator.
**Revoke.** To annul or make void by calling back.
**Revolution.** The overthrow of an established government.
**Reward.** Recompense for some service or attainment.
**Rex.** King.
**Ribaldu.** A vagrant.
**Ribaud.** Rogue; vagrant.
**Rider.** An additional clause or provision annexed to a bill while in the course of passage in order to "slip" it through.
**Rien.** Nothing.
**Rien Culp.** Not guilty.
**Right.** Legally enforceable claim; privilege; power of appointment or choice.
**Rightful.** Lawful; proper.
**Right in Personam.** Right against the person.
**Right of Conscience.** Religious freedom.
**Right of Dower.** Legal interest which a wife acquires by marriage in the property of her husband.
**Right of Eminent Domain.** Right of a community to possess itself of the property of an individual when necessary for public welfare.
**Right of Entry.** Right to take possession of certain land in a peaceful manner.
**Right of Possession.** Right to occupy and enjoy property.
**Right of Privacy.** Right to be let alone.
**Right of Redemption.** Right to redeem real property from judicial sale.
**Right of Sufferage.** Right of qualified citizen to vote.
**Right of Way.** Right to pass over the land of another.
**Rights in Action.** See Chose in Action.
**Right to Counsel.** Right of one accused of a crime to have legal assistance.
**Rigor Juris.** Strict Law.
**Rigor Mortis.** Cadaveric rigidity.
**Ring Fight.** Prize fight.
**Riot.** Tumultuous public disturbance committed by 3 or more persons.
**Riotous.** Violent.
**Riparian.** Of or belonging to the bank of a river.
**Riper.** Mature; ready.
**Risicum.** Insurance risk.
**Rising Of Court.** Final adjournment of court for the term.
**Rite.** Duly and formally; legally.
**Rixa.** Quarrel.
**Road.** Highway; place of public passage.
**Road Tax.** Tax for the maintenance of public roads.
**Robbery.** Felonious taking of something of value from the person of another by forcible means.
**Rod.** 16½ feet.
**Rogo.** I ask, expression used in wills.
**Rogue.** Cheat; rascal.
**Rogues' Gallery.** A collection of photographs of criminals kept for purposes of identification.
**Roll.** Record.
**Roll.** To rob.
**Rondo.** Game of chance.
**Rood.** ¼ acre.
**Root.** Stock of descent.
**Roster.** List of persons; register.
**Rota.** A court.
**Rough Minutes.** Unofficial memoranda made by the court clerk.
**Roup.** Auction sale.
**Rout.** Group of persons assembled with the intention to incite riot.
**Royalty.** Money paid to the holder of a patent or copyright for the right to manufacture, sell or use the patented or copyrighted article.
**Rudely.** Uncivilly; violently.
**Rule.** Regulation; principle set up by authority.
**Rule Absolute.** Court order to be immediately enforced without conditions.
**Rule Nisi.** A rule which shall become imperative or final unless cause be shown why it should not.
**Rules.** Times or seasons when motions are entertained by the court.
**Rule To Show Cause.** Rule summoning an adverse party to appear before court and show cause why a certain thing shall not be done.
**Ruling.** A settlement of a point of law arising during the course of a trial.
**Rumor.** Popular report; current story.
**Running Account.** Current or open account.
**Running at Large.** Applied to domestic animals wandering without restraint.
**Running Policy.** In insurance, a policy which anticipates that the property insured shall be added to or further defined by later additions to the policy.
**Rusticum Jus.** Simple justice.
**Rustler.** Cattle thief.

## S

**Sabbath.** Sunday.
**Sabotage.** Intentional damage to the property of an employer by an employee.
**Sacrilege.** Stealing of things from a churco.
**Sadism.** Type of sexual perversion in which the man enjoys inflecting pain on the woman he desires.
**Safe.** Receptacle for valuables.
**Safe Deposit Company.** Company which rents boxes in vaults for the safe-keeping of valuables.
**Safe-Pledge.** Surety for a person's appearance in court.
**Said.** Aforesaid; mentioned before.
**Salarium.** Salary; wages.
**Salary.** Recompense for services rendered.
**Sale.** Transfer of property from one man to another for recompense.
**Sale at Auction.** Public sale of property to the highest bidder.
**Sale for Payment.** Judicial sale of the property of a decedent to pay his debts.
**Sale in Gross.** Sale by the tract without regard to quantity.
**Sale Notes.** Memorandum with respect to the sale of merchandise usually given to the buyer by the broker.
**Sale on Approval.** Conditional sale which becomes effective only in case the buyer, on trial, is satisfied with the merchandise.
**Sale on Execution.** Public sale conducted by a writ of execution.
**Sale or Return.** Sale, usually by manufacturer to a retailer, with the understanding that he may consider some or all of the goods as a consignment and return them within a certain period of time.
**Sales Guaranteed.** If goods purchased by the buyer cannot be sold, they may be returned to the seller.
**Sales Tax.** Tax upon retail merchandise, usually paid by the buyer.
**Saloon.** Place where alcoholic beverages are sold.
**Salus.** Health; safety.
**Salvage.** Compensation paid to persons by whose voluntary services a ship or her cargo are saved, in whole or in part in time of peril.
**Salvo.** Saving; excepting.
**Salvor.** One who conducts a salvage operation.
**Salvus Plegius.** A safe-pledge.
**Same.** Identical; of a kind or species.
**Same Offense.** Constitutional provision that no person shall be twice put in jeopardy for the same crime.
**Sample.** A part used to show the quality of the whole.
**Sanae Mentis.** Of sound mind.
**Sanction.** To consent, concur, ratify; penalty or punishment for disobedience to the law.
**Sane.** Of sound mind.
**Sanguis.** Blood-relationship; blood.
**Sanipractice.** Method of drugless healing.
**Sanitarium.** Health retreat.
**Sanitary.** That which pertains to health and cleanliness.
**Sanity.** Mental soundness.
**Sans.** Without.
**Sans Ceo Que.** Without this.
**Sans Frais.** With expense.
**Sans Recours.** Without recourse.
**Sanus.** Sane; whole; sound.
**Satisdare.** To guaranty the obligation.
**Satisdatio.** Security given by a party to an action.
**Satisfaction.** Fulfilling of a legal obligation
**Satisfaction Contract.** Contract whereby one party agrees to perform his obligation to the satisfaction of the other.
**Satisfaction of the Jury.** To prove to the jury that a thing existed.
**Satisfaction Piece.** A written instrument stating that satisfaction is acknowledged between the parties, plaintiff and defendant.
**Satisfactory.** To meet with one's approval or expectation.
**Satisfactory Evidence.** Evidence or proof which ordinarily satisfies an unprejudiced mind.
**Satisfy.** To answer or discharge a claim or obligation; to convince a jury.
**Save.** To except, reserve or exempt; to suspend the running or operation of.
**Saving Clause.** In a statute, an exception of a special thing out of general things mentioned in the statute.
**Savings Bank.** An institution for the deposit and safekeeping of money.
**Savings Bank Check.** A receipt for the money withdrawn from a savings account.
**S.C.** (Abb.). Same Case.
**Scab.** Working man who works contrary to union rules.
**Scale.** To cut down; to proportion.
**Scale Tolerance.** Nominal weight variation between different scales in weighing the same goods.
**Scaling Laws.** Laws which formerly regulated the relation between depreciated currency and specie.
**Scalped Ticket.** Ticket purchased from a ticket broker.
**Scandal.** Defamatory rumors; scandalous talk.
**Scandalous Matter.** Allegations of fact in a pleading which are immaterial and impertinent and unbecoming the court's dignity.
**Schedule.** List; inventory.
**Schedule in Bankruptcy.** An inventory filed by the bankrupt listing all his property and credits.
**Scheme.** Plan; plot.
**School.** Educational institution.
**School Taxes.** Taxes levied for the support and maintenance of the public schools.
**School Trustees.** School direetors.
**Sciagraph.** X-ray, admissible as evidence.
**Sciant Praesentes et Futuri.** Know all men present and in future.
**Scienter.** Knowingly; in torts, an allegation that the defendant knew a fact which was essential to create liability.
**Scit.** (Abb.) Scilicet.
**Scilicet.** To wit.
**Scintilla of Evidence.** Spark of evidence; any material evidence, which if true, might create interest in a reasonable juror.
**Scintilla Rule.** Rule that if there is any evidence supporting a claim it must be submitted to jury.
**Scire Facia.** A judicial writ, founded upon some matter of record, requiring the person against whom it is brought to show cause why the plaintiff should not have advantage of such a record, or why the record should not be annulled.
**Scire Facias ad Audiendum Errores.** To hear the errors.
**Scire Facias ad Disporbandum.** To disprove the debts.
**Scire Facias Quare Restitutionem Habere Non Debet.** Make it known why he ought not to have restitution.
**Scire Feci.** I have made known or notified.
**Scite.** Site; location.
**Scold.** Troublesome woman.
**Scolding.** Personal reproof.
**Scope.** Design; aim; intention.
**Scope of Authority.** Actual and implied authorization conferred upon an agent by his principal.
**Scoundral.** Villian; rascal.
**Scrambling Possession.** Situation where two or more persons are struggling for the possession of land.
**Scrawl.** Scroll.
**Screwball.** Eccentric person.
**Scribere Est Agers.** Writing is the doing of an act..
**Script** Certificates of ownership.
**Script.** An original written instrument.
**Scriptum.** A written instrument.
**Scrivener.** Draftsman; copyist; clerk; conveyancer.
**Scroll.** A writing designed to be rolled up; a scrawl intended as a seal; an escrow.
**Se.** Himself; themselves; itself.
**Seal.** Wax impression giving authenticity to a document; a written or printed circle or scroll with the initials "l.s." (locus sigilli, place of seal).
**Sealed.** Under seal.
**Sealed Instrument.** An instrument to which the party to be bound has affixed both his name and seal.
**Sealed Verdict.** The verdict of the jury placed in a sealed envelope.
**Seaman.** Sailor.

**Search.** Examination by an officer of the law.
**Searchers and Seizures.** The power possessed by public authority to inspect private premises for the purpose of arresting a man or obtaining evidence of his guilt of a crime.
**Search of Title.** Examination of public records to ascertain a person's title to real estate.
**Search Warrent.** A written order issued by legal authority for the examination or inspection of one's premises or person in the search for stolen goods or evidence to be used in prosecution of a criminal.
**Seasonable Appearance.** A defendant's appearance within the time allowed by law, after receiving a summons.
**Seated Land.** Land used for residence or farming; productive land.
**Seat of Justice.** A county seat.
**Seat On Exchange.** Membership in a stock exchange.
**Seaworthy.** Applied to a ship reasonably fit to transport cargo.
**Sebastomania.** Religious mania.
**Secession of State.** An attempt of a state to withdraw from the Union.
**Seck.** Without the right or remedy of distraining.
**Secondary.** Of a subsequent or subordinate class.
**Secondary Boycott.** A boycott directed against relations with those against whom there is a primary boycott.
**Secondary Conveyance.** One which alters or modifies an interest already granted by a conveyance.
**Secondary Easement.** Evidence which is admissible after proof is offered of the excused absence of primary evidence.
**Second Degree Murder.** Statutory degree of murder usually punishable by life imprisonment.
**Second-Hand Evidence.** Hearsay.
**Second Mortgage.** Mortgage on previously mortgaged property.
**Secret.** Hidden; not public.
**Secretary.** Corporate officer in charge of records; correspondence, etc.; one who acts as the agent of a person in matters of communication; title given to several Cabinet officers of U.S. government.
**Secretary of State.** Member of Cabinet of U.S. government charged with the general administration of the international and diplomatic affairs of the government.
**Secret Service.** Agency of the Department of Treasury charged with the protection of the president and his family, and the suppression of counterfeiting.
**Sect.** Religious denomination.
**Sectarian.** Pertaining to a religious sect.
**Sectarian School.** Denominational school.
**Section.** Division; part; portion; division of land consisting of 640 acres and equal to one square mile.
**Secular.** Temporal; worldly.
**Secundum.** According to; in favor of.
**Secundum Aequum et Bonum.** According to justice and right.
**Secundum Allegata.** According to the allegations contained in the pleadings.
**Secundum Allegata et Probata.** According to what has been alleged and proved.
**Secundum Formam Statuti.** According to the form of the statutes.
**Secundum Naturam.** According to nature.
**Secundum Regulam.** According to rule.
**Secure.** To give security; to guaranty; safe; free from danger.
**Securities.** Negotiable instruments; evidences of debt or of property.
**Security.** Protection; assurance; indemnification; a negotiable instrument; one who becomes a guarantor for another.
**Security for Costs.** A bond required of a party to an action to ensure the fact that the costs of the action will be paid if he loses.
**Securus.** Safe; secure; sure.
**Secus.** Otherwise; not so.
**Sed.** But; however.
**Sedato Animo.** With settled intent.
**Sed Contra.** But otherwise.
**Se Defendendo.** In self-defense.
**Sedente Curia.** During a session of the court.
**Sedition.** Insurrection; acts which disturb the peace and imperil the government.
**Se Non Allocatur.** But it is not allowed.
**Sed per Curiam.** But by the court.
**Seduce.** To corrupt.
**Seduction.** To persuade a chaste woman to have illicit sexual intercourse.
**Sed Vide.** But see.
**See.** The area of a bishop's jurisdiction.
**Seen.** Used to denote acceptance of a bill of exchange.
**Segration Laws.** Laws authorizing separate accommodations for people of different races.
**Seigneur.** Lord.
**Seised.** State of ownership coupled with right of possession.
**Seised in His Demesne as of Fee.** Seised in fee simple.
**Seized.** See Seised.
**Seizin.** Possession of premises after full investiture, coupled with a claim to the right of exclusive possession.
**Seizin in Fact.** Seizin in deed; actual seizin; possession with intent to claim a freehold interest.
**Seizin in Fee.** Person's actual possession of land, with a fee-simple estate therein.
**Seizin in Law.** Right of immediate possession according to the nature of the estate.
**Seizure.** Taking possession of goods by public authority.
**Select.** To pick out.
**Selectmen.** Officers constituting a local council.
**Self-Defense.** Protection of one's person or property from injury by another; the right to such protection.
**Self-Destruction.** Suicide.
**Self-Disserving Evidence.** Evidence unfavorable to the person offering it.
**Self-Executing Constitutional Provision.** Effective immediately without additional legislation.
**Self-Incrimination.** Subjecting of one's self to criminal prosecution by the disclosure of certain facts during the course of a trial.
**Self-Serving Evidence.** Evidence favorable to the party offering it.
**Sell.** To dispose of for profit.
**Seller.** One who sells anything.
**Seller's Option.** Transaction wherein stock is sold to be delivered at a future time.
**Semble.** It seems; a dictum holds.
**Semblement.** Similarly.
**Semi-Matrimonium.** Concubinage.
**Seminary.** Ministerial school.
**Semi-Plena Probatio.** Half proof.
**Semper.** Always; at all times.
**Semper Paratus.** Always ready.
**Senate.** Upper house of Congress.
**Senator.** Member of the senate.
**Senatus Consultum Ultimae Necessitatis.** The act of the senate in an emergency.
**Senile Dementia.** Imbecility due to old age.
**Senility.** Mental state of an aged person.
**Senior.** Higher in rank; older.
**Senior Mortgage.** One which has priority over another incumbrance.
**Sentence.** Judgment passed by the court on a convicted criminal.
**Sentence of Nullity.** Legal annulment of a marriage.
**Sententia.** An opinion; decision; judgment.
**Separable.** Severable.
**Separaliter.** Separately.
**Separate.** Disconnected; independent; distinct.
**Separate Action.** An action brought by each of several complainants for himself although all are concerned in the same transaction, but cannot legally join in suit.
**Separate Estate.** Individual property of one of two persons who have a social or business relationship; the property of a married woman over which her husband has no right in equity.
**Separate Examination.** Questioning of a married woman by a notary, apart from her husband, to determine if she acts on her own will.
**Separate Maintenance.** Support granted to a wife and her children by the husband upon their voluntary separation; alimony.
**Separate Property.** Property owned by a husband or wife in his or her own right during marriage.

**Separatin.** Separately.
**Separatim.** Cessation of cohabitation by man and wife by mutual consent.
**Sepulchre.** Grave; tomb.
**Sequela.** Suit; prosecution.
**Sequela Curiae.** Suit of court.
**Sequester.** To renounce or disclaim; to seize property under a writ of sequestration.
**Sequestration.** The setting apart of something in controversy to await final disposition; a form of seizure of property to be held as a means of enforcing a decree from the payment of money.
**Sergeant-at-Arms.** An officer of a legislative body charged with keeping order.
**Serial Bonds.** Bonds issued in a series, different parts being redeemable at different specified dates.
**Seriatim.** Successively.
**Serious.** Important; weighty.
**Serious and Wilful Misconduct.** Intentionally doing something likely to have serious consequences.
**Servant.** One who gives domestic help.
**Servato Juris Ordine.** In keeping with the order of the court.
**Serve.** To deliver legal papers.
**Service.** Employment; performance of labor; the delivery of an order, a summons or a writ; the furnishing of public utilities.
**Service by Publication.** Publication of a summons or other process in the newspaper in order to reach an absent or nonresident defendant.
**Service of Process.** The delivering of writs, summonses, rules, etc. to the party to whom they are directed.
**Serviens ad Legem.** A sergeant-at-law.
**Servient Tenement.** An estate in land burdened with an easement for the benefit of some other estate or tenement.
**Servitium.** Service.
**Servitude.** An easement; a right or interest which one proprietor has in the estate of another proprietor.
**Servitus.** Slavery; servitude.
**Servitus Luminum.** Easement of having unobstructed light come into one's premises.
**Servitus Viae.** Right of way over the land of a neighbor.
**Servus.** Slave; servant.
**Sess.** Assessment; tax.
**Sessio.** Session; meeting.
**Session.** Period of time during which a legislative body transacts business.
**Session Laws.** All of the enactments passed by a legislative body at a single session.
**Sessions.** A meeting of the justices.
**Set.** Lease.
**Set Aside.** Annulled; made void; cancelled.
**Set of Exchange.** A set of bills of exchange in duplicate or triplicate, the honoring of any one of them voiding the others.
**Set-Off.** The discharge of one demand by an opposite one; a counter-demand.
**Set Out.** In pleading, to state the facts; to allege; to set out a deed or contract.
**Settle.** To come to an agreement in a legal dispute; to pay; to compromise.
**Settlement.** An arrangement by which property is to be held by several persons in succession; establishment of a permanent residence in a place, entitling the settlor to the privileges of such residence; a compromise by the parties in a litigation to settle the dispute.
**Settlement, Deed of.** Deed settling a controversy or property.
**Settling Day.** Day in the month when transactions on the stock exchange are accounted for and settled.
**Settlement in Paris.** Settlement out of court.
**Settlor.** Grantor or donor in a deed of settlement; a person who creates a trust.
**Sever.** To separate; to divide; to disjoin; to separate one cause of action from another and plead them separately; to try persons separately who were jointly indicted.
**Severable Contract.** Contract in which consideration may be apportioned or divided.
**Several Actions.** Actions which are separate.
**Several Inheritance.** An inheritance in which the heirs take severally in equally parts.
**Severally.** Separately.
**Several Ownership.** Ownership by one person.
**Severalty.** An estate held by one person alone.
**Severance.** Act of separating; partition; separation.
**Severance of Actions.** Entering of separate pleas by several defendants, instead of joining in the same plea.
**Severe Illness.** An illness having a permanent, detrimental effect.
**Sexual Commerce.** Sexual intercourse.
**Sexual Intercourse.** Copulation.
**Shackles.** Chains used to bind a prisoner.
**Shakedown.** Extortion.
**Sham.** False; counterfeit.
**Sham Pleading.** A pleading which is false.
**Share.** To have a portion of; a part or portion; a stock certificate.
**Share and Share Alike.** To take in equal shares or portions.
**Shareholder.** Stockholder.
**Share of Stock.** The right which a stockholder has in the management, profits and assets of a corporation.
**Share Tenant.** Tenant who leases land with the provision that crops produced be shared with his landlord.
**Shave.** To lend money on usury; to extort; the buying of notes and securities at a discount.
**Sheriff.** The chief executive officer of a county, elected by the people.
**Sheriff's Sale.** Sale by a sheriff under a writ of execution of property of the judgment debtor.
**Shifting.** Changing; varying.
**Shifting Use.** A use limited to take effect and arise in derogation of another use.
**Ship.** To place on board a ship; to transport; any vessel used in navigation.
**Shipmaster.** Commander of a merchant vessel.
**Shipment.** Transport of goods on a ship or other carrier; delivery of goods to a carrier and his issuance of a bill of lading therefore; the property transported.
**Shipper.** One who makes a contract with a carrier for the transportation of goods.
**Shipping.** General term of the use of ships or vessels for any public or private purposes; collective term for ships.
**Ship's Bill.** Ship's bill of lading, kept by the master.
**Ship's Husband.** General agent of the owner of a ship who manages the concerns of the ship.
**Ship's Papers.** Papers which every ship must carry, showing the nationality of her registry and cargo and compliance with the navigational laws of her country.
**Shire.** County.
**Shock.** Sudden physical or mental agitation.
**Shoot.** To injure someone with a bullet; to kill.
**Shop.** Place where merchandise is retailed.
**Shopbook Rule.** Introduction of a party's account books of original entry as evidence in his favor, this being an exception to the hearsay rule.
**Shop-Right.** Right of an employer to the invention of an employee without payment of royalties.
**Shore.** Land lying between the lines of high water and low water, over which the tides ebb and flow; beach; shore line.
**Shore of Watercourse.** The spaces between high and low water marks.
**Short Cause.** A suit the trial of which is estimated to be brief.
**Short Haul.** Transportation of merchandise for a short distance.
**Short Sale.** Sale of stock before purchase in hope to acquire at a lower price than that of the delivery price; sales upon margin.
**Show.** To prove; to make clear.
**Show Cause.** Court order to a party in a law suit to show good reason why a certain action should not be taken.
**Shut Down.** To stop work.
**Shyster.** A dishonest and unethical attorney; a pettifogger.
**Si.** If; although; as if.
**Sic.** So; such; in this manner.
**Sic Hic.** So here.
**Sic. Jubeo.** I so order.
**Sick.** Ill.

**Sickness.** Illness.
**Si Contingat.** If it happens.
**Sicut Alias.** As on another occasion.
**Sicut Me Deus Adjuvet.** So help me God.
**Sic Volo.** I so will it.
**Side Judge.** An associate judge.
**Sidewalk.** Part of the street reserved for pedestrians.
**Siens.** Scions; descendants.
**Sight.** In regard to negotiable instruments, presentment.
**Sight Draft.** A bill of exchange payable on presentment.
**Sigillare.** To affix a seal.
**Sigillum.** A seal.
**Sigla.** Abbreviations.
**Sign.** To place one's signature on; to ratify by hand or seal.
**Signa.** Evidence addressed to the senses.
**Signare.** To sign or seal.
**Signature.** The affixing of one's name at the end of an instrument intended to authenticate the instrument; the name itself.
**Signed, Sealed and Delivered.** Executed.
**Signum.** Sign; signature; mark.
**Si Ita Est.** If it be so.
**Silent Partner.** Dormant partner.
**Silver.** Base metal used in coins.
**Similar.** Resembling; nearly corresponding.
**Similiter.** Likewise; a short formula in pleading expressive of the acceptance of an issue tendered by the adversary.
**Simony.** The buying or selling of religious favor.
**Simple.** Pure; unadulterated; not aggravated.
**Simple Assault.** Futile attempt to do bodily injury to another.
**Simple Confession.** Plea of guilty.
**Simple Contract.** Oral contract; one which is not sealed.
**Simple Interest.** Interest paid for the principal, at a certain rate or allowance, made by law or mutual agreement.
**Simple Trust.** A conveyance of property in trust without further specifications or directions.
**Simplex.** Simple.
**Simplex Dictum.** Mere allegation.
**Simplex Justitiarius.** Simple justice.
**Simplex Loquela.** A mere allegation.
**Simpliciter.** Simply.
**Simulated.** Counterfeited; pretended.
**Simul cum.** Together with.
**Simul et Simul.** Together and at the same time.
**Simultaneously.** At the same time.
**Sine.** Without.
**Sine Animo Revertendi.** Without intention of returning.
**Sine Consideratione Curiae.** Without having been considered by the court.
**Sine Cura.** Without care.
**Sinecure.** An office which yields a revenue, but imposing little responsibility.
**Sine Decreto.** Without a decree.
**Sine Die.** Without day; final adjournment; final dismissal of a cause.
**Sine Hoc Quod.** Without this, that.
**Sine Liberis.** Without children.
**Sine Prole.** Without issue.
**Sine Qua Non.** Without which not; an indispensable requisite or condition.
**Sine Vi aut Dolo.** Without force or fraud.
**Single.** One; alone; detached; unmarried.
**Single Adultery.** Adultry between two persons, only one of whom is married.
**Single Bill.** Written promise to pay a certain person a certain amount on a certain date.
**Single Bond.** Single Bill.
**Singulariter.** Singly.
**Sinking Fund.** A fund put aside for the extinguishment of a debt, expecially of a government or corporation, by the accumulation of interest.
**Si Prius.** If before.
**Si Quis.** If anyone.
**Sit.** To preside.
**Sit Down Strike.** Strike in which the employees occupy the property of the employer until agreement is reached.
**Site.** Land suitable or set apart for special use.
**Sit in Bank.** To hold a session of court with all judges present.
**Sit in Camera.** To hold a session of court in chambers or privately.
**Sitting In Bank.** Session of the court with all judges present.
**Sitting of Court.** Term of court.
**Situated.** Located.
**Situs.** Location; location of a concrete object, particularly land.
**Skeleton Bill.** Bill drawn, indorsed or accepted in blank.
**Skill.** Slip; failure of automobile tires to grip the road.
**Skilled Witness.** Expert witness.
**Slacker.** One derlict in his duty or responsibility; one who shirks military duty.
**Slander.** False statements made orally which bring another into disrepute.
**Slander of Title.** A false and malicious statement made in regard to a person's title to property.
**Slave.** One subject to the will of another.
**Slavery.** State of bondage.
**Slay.** To kill.
**Sleep.** To delay action in securing one's right.
**Sleeping Partner.** Dormant partner.
**Sleeping Rent.** Fixed rent.
**Slight.** Inconsiderable; unimportant; remote.
**Slot Machine.** An automated gambling machine into which one deposits coins, hoping to win a prize or money.
**Slum.** Dirty, impoverished area.
**Slush Fund.** Money used for corrupt purposes, e.g. lobbying.
**Slut.** Careless, sloppy woman; female dog; a bitch.
**Small Claims Courts.** Courts with jurisdiction over very small amounts.
**Smart Money.** Punitive damages in addition to actual damages.
**Smuggling.** Unlawful bringing in of goods into the U.S., such importation being prohibited without payment of duty.
**Snap Judgement.** Judgement by default.
**So.** In this way.
**Sober.** Moderate in use of alcoholic beverages.
**Socer.** A father-in-law.
**Social Security Acts.** Acts designed for the economic security of the individual.
**Societas.** Partnership.
**Societe Anonyme.** Stock corporation; an association in which the liability of the members is limited.
**Society.** An association of people united in a common purpose; the capacity of usefulness, aid and comfort which a wife possesses in regard to her husband in her normal state.
**Sodomy.** Sexual relations between two men.
**Soit.** Let it be.
**Soit Droit Fait al Partie.** Let right be done to the party.
**Solar Day.** Period from sunrise to sunset.
**Solar Month.** Calendar month.
**Solatium.** Compensation for injury to feelings.
**Sold Note.** Note given by a broker to a buyer indicating the sale of certain goods.
**Sole.** Single; only; separate.
**Sole and Unconditional Ownership.** In insurance, the insured is the only one having any interest in the property as owner, that property not being limited to or affected by any condition.
**Sole Corporation.** A corporation consisting of a single person in which there is a succession of interest.
**Solemnitas.** Solemnity.
**Solemn.** Following certain set forms.
**Solemnity.** Rite or ceremony.
**Solicit.** To ask for something; to entreat or implore.
**Solicitation.** Asking; enticing; inciting another to commit a crime, particularly one which affects society.
**Solicitation of Chastity.** To entice a woman to give up her chastity.
**Solicitor.** In E. a lawyer licensed as a legal representative; in U.S., a lawyer in the Court of Bankruptcy.
**Solidum.** The whole.
**Solitary Confinement.** Complete isolation of a prisoner from human contacts.
**Solum.** Soil; ground.
**Solutio.** Payment of a debt.
**Solutio Indebite.** Payment of a debt which does not exist.
**Solutus.** Free; released from debt or mortgage.
**Solvency.** Ability to pay one's debts.

**Solvendum in Futuro.** To be paid in the future.
**Solvent.** Able to pay one's debts.
**Solvere.** To pay; to release.
**Solviet ad Diem.** He paid at the day; plea made that the money was paid on the day mentioned in the condition.
**Somnambulism.** Sleep-walking.
**Son.** An immediate male descendant.
**Son Assault Demesne.** His own assault; a plea of self-defense.
**Son-in-Law.** The husband of one's daugher.
**Sonticus.** That which delays; injurious; hindering.
**Soon.** Within a reasonable time.
**Sortitio.** Drawing of lots.
**Sound Health.** Good health.
**Sounding in Damages.** Applied to an action seeking satisfaction only in money damages.
**Sound Mind.** Sane.
**Sound Physical Condition.** Good health.
**Souvent.** Often.
**Sovereign.** Ruler; supreme power in government.
**Sovereign.** Right reserved to the state or its agencies.
**S.P.** (Abb.). Sine Prole.
**Spado.** Impotent person.
**Sparsim.** Sparsely; rarely.
**Spay.** To remove the ovaries of a female animal to prevent propagation.
**Speak.** In practice, to argue.
**Speaking Demurrer.** A demurrer which alleges and relies on new matter as well as the ground of the demurrer.
**Special.** Pertaining to a particular thing or person.
**Special Acceptance.** Qualified acceptance of a bill of exchange.
**Special Act.** Private statute.
**Special Action.** Statutory action.
**Special Agent.** An agent authorized to act in a specific transaction but not employed in continuous service.
**Special Assessment.** A tax on property to finance public improvements.
**Special Assumpsit.** An action brought on an express promise.
**Special Bastard.** One born before marriage of his parents.
**Special Count.** A statement of the facts ot a particular cause of action.
**Special Damages.** Damages which are the actual, but not the necessary result of the injury complained of.
**Special Demurrer.** One which states the exact ground on which the complaint or pleading is alleged to be inadequate.
**Special Deposit.** Deposit of something to be returned in kind.
**Special Finding.** Answer of a jury to a particular question of fact submitted to them.
**Special Imparlance.** An imparlance reserving exceptions and objections.
**Special Indorsement.** Indorsement of a negotiable instrument naming the payee to whom or to whose order the instrument is to be paid.
**Special Issue.** A plea denying a particular material and traversable allegation of the preceding pleading.
**Specialist.** One skilled in a particular field.
**Special Legislation.** Legislation which applies to particular persons and things.
**Special Letter of Credit.** One addressed to a particular person.
**Special Lien.** Lien upon particular property.
**Special Matter.** Matter of a certain nature which upon notice may be raised at a hearing after a plea of the general issue.
**Special Partner.** Limited partner.
**Special Pleading.** A pleading which avoids an allegation without expressly denying it.
**Special Property.** Property in which a person's interest is less than that of ownership, existing only to carry out a specific legal right or interest.
**Special Sessions, Court of.** Court of limited jurisdiction in criminal cases.
**Special Statute.** One applying to particular persons and things.
**Special Tail.** An estate tail which is limited to the issue of named persons.
**Special Tax.** A tax levied for a particular public person.
**Special Trust.** An operative trust in which the trustee performs certain specified acts.
**Specialty.** An instrument or document under seal.
**Special Verdict.** Verdict whereby a jury finds facts only, submitting the decision of the case to the court.
**Specie.** Gold or silver coins.
**Species.** Kind; class.
**Specifically.** Explicitly.
**Specification.** In Patent Law, a particular or detailed statement of the various elements involved; detailed statement of the acts constituting a military offense charged against the defendant in a court martial.
**Specific Denial.** A denial of each material allegation of the declaration or complaint.
**Specific Legacy.** A legacy consisting of a definitely described article or thing which is not a sum of money.
**Specific Performance.** Accomplishment of a contract according to the precise terms agreed upon.
**Speculate.** To risk loss in view of possible gain.
**Speculative Damages.** Damages awarded in excess of the actual loss suffered by the plaintiff.
**Speedy Trial.** The constitutional guaranty that a trial be conducted according to fixed rules, regulations and proceedings of law, free from unreasonable delay.
**Spendthrift.** One who spends money foolishly; prodigal.
**Spendthrift Trust.** A trust created to provide for the maintenance of the beneficiary at the same time guarding against his improvidence or incapacity.
**Spermatozoa.** Seminal fluid.
**Spes.** Hope.
**Spex Accrescendi.** The hope of surviving.
**Spes Recuperandi.** Hope of recovering.
**Spinster.** A woman who has never married.
**Spiritual.** Relating to the religious or ecclesiastical.
**Speritual Courts.** Ecclesiastical courts.
**Spirituous Liquor.** Liquor produced by distillation.
**Spite Fence.** Fence erected solely to annoy an adjoining neighbor.
**Spoliation.** A material change or alteration in a written document by a stranger, this not changing the legality of such a document.
**Spondeo.** I promise.
**Sponsalia.** Mutal promises to marry.
**Sponsor.** A surety; one who voluntarily intervenes for another.
**Sporting Woman.** Prostitute.
**Spot Cash.** Cash on delivery.
**Spotter.** Paid informer.
**Spouse.** A husband or wife.
**Spouse-Breach.** Adultery.
**S.P.Q.R.** (Abb.). The senate and people of Rome.
**Spring Gun.** Device used against trespassers.
**Springing Use.** A use limited to arise on a future event either absolutely or contingently.
**Spur.** A railroad siding.
**Spurius.** Illegitimate child.
**Squatter.** One who takes possession of the land of another without authority.
**SS.** (Abb.). Scilicet; that is to say.
**Stab.** A wound inflicted with a pointed weapon.
**Stabilize.** To keep steady.
**Stabilize Prices.** To hold prices steady against increases.
**Stagiarius.** A resident.
**Stake.** Deposite made as coverage for a wager.
**Stakeholder.** One who holds money or property pending the outcome of a wager or claim.
**Stale Claim or Demand.** A claim which has not been asserted for an unreasonable period of time, whether or not barred by the statute of limitations.
**Stamp.** Instrument for making imprinted mark; mark imprinted; die; piece of gummed paper used as postage.
**Stand.** To pause or remain stationary; to submit to; to remain as is; to appear in court.
**Standard.** General recognition of and con-

formity to established practice; flag; type; model.

**Stand By.** In the equitable principle of estoppel, to make no effort to change a situation, when the situation will cause a false impression on some other person.

**Stand Mute.** To refuse to plead.

**Staple.** Principle commodity of a region.

**Stare ad Rectum.** To stand trial.

**Stare Decisus.** To abide by; the decisions of the court should stand as precedents for future guidance.

**Stare in Judicio.** To stand in judgement; the right to appear in court.

**State.** Politically organized community; civil powers of such.

**State Aid.** Support or help given by the state to institutions or individuals for a public purpose.

**Stated Account.** An action for money admitted to be due, after both parties have computed their claims against each other.

**State-Lands.** Lands belonging to the Government which may be acquired by private citizens under general land laws.

**Statement.** An allegation; a declaration of matters of fact.

**State's Attorney.** Public prosecutor; district attorney.

**State's Evidence.** Evidence of an accomplice who testifies for the prosecution, usually in expectancy of a lighter punishment or pardon.

**State Tax.** Any tax levied for general state purposes.

**Statim.** Immediately.

**Stating Part.** Part of a bill in equity in which the plaintiff states the facts of his case.

**Statu Liber.** A free person.

**Status.** Standing; state; condition.

**Status Quo.** Existing state of things at any given date.

**Statute.** Law passed by legislature.

**Statute of Amendment.** Statute which provides for the correction of certain omissions and imperfections in pleadings.

**Statute of Limitations.** A statute establishing fixed periods of time within which actions must be brought after cause for such an action has arisen.

**Statutes of Repose.** See Statute of Limitations.

**Statutory.** Created or existing by statute.

**Statutory Interpretation.** The sum total of methods used in aiding the court to apply law derived from statutes.

**Statutory Pardon.** Pardon effected by act of legislature.

**Statutory Rape.** Felony of sexual intercourse with a girl under the aged fixed by statute, whether with or without her consent.

**Stay.** Temporarily stop further proceedings; restraining order.

**Stay of Execution.** The stopping or arresting of an execution on a judgment for a limited period.

**Stay Laws or Statutes.** An act of legislature which provides a temporary suspension of the enforcement of an obligation or liability for a debt.

**Steal.** To commit larceny; to take property feloniously.

**Stellionate.** Fraud of contracting for the sale of property which the vendor has previously sold.

**Step-Child.** Child of one of the spouces by former marriage.

**Sterility.** Barrenness; inability to have children.

**Sterilize.** To make incapable of reproduction.

**Stet Processus.** An entry of the dismissal of an action voluntarily made by the plaintiff.

**Stick Up.** Rob at gun point.

**Stiletto.** Dagger.

**Still.** Apparatus for the distillation of alcholic beverages.

**Still-Born.** Born dead.

**Stillicidium.** The drip of water from the eves of a house.

**Stipend.** Salary.

**Stipulate.** To enter into an agreement.

**Stipulated Damages.** Liquidated damages; damages designated to be paid in the event of breach of contract.

**Stipulation.** A material article in an agreement; an agreement between the parties in a litigation, as to the proceeding or part of it.

**Stirps, Stirpes.** Descent; lines of descent.

**Stock.** Commodity which a merchant sells; the capital or principal fund of a corporation, usually divided in equal shares held by members of the corporation.

**Stock, Common.** Ordinary stock of a corporation.

**Stock, Preferred.** Stock given a preference or priority in respect to dividends, over the remainder of the stock of the corporation, the common stock.

**Stockbroker.** One who buys and sells stock for others.

**Stock Certificate.** A certificate issued by a corporation stating that a specified person owns a certain number of shares of the capital stock of the corporation.

**Stock Dividend.** Dividend payable to stockholders of a corporation in shares of stock of that corporation.

**Stock Exchange.** Place where stock is bought and sold.

**Stockholder.** Member of a corporation who owns one or more shares of stock in the company.

**Stock in Trade.** The goods or chattels which a merchant holds for sale.

**Stock of Descent.** An ancestor in whom a succession of inheritance begins.

**Stock of Merchandise.** See Stock in Trade.

**Stocks.** Formerly, a device used to publicly punish criminals.

**Stop, Look and Listen** Rule that anyone who fails to stop at a railroad crossing, look both ways and listen for an oncoming train is guilty of contributory negligence.

**Stop Order.** Direction to a stock broker that if a commodity touches a certain price, the broker shall close trade at the best available price.

**Stoppage.** Hindrance to doing a certain thing.

**Stowage.** Storage; payment for storage.

**Stowaway.** One who conceals himself on board ship.

**Stramineus Homo.** Man of Straw.

**Stramonium.** Narcotic poison.

**Stranding.** Causing a ship to run on the shore.

**Stranger.** One not a party to an instrument or legal proceeding.

**Straw Bail.** Nominal or worthless bail.

**Straw-Bond.** An undertaking sgined by irresponsible or fictitious sureties.

**Straw Man.** Fictitious person used in a number of transactions.

**Street.** An urban way or throughfare.

**Street Intersection.** A street or highway, common to two or more streets or highways.

**Streetwalker.** Prostitute.

**Strict.** Exact; precise; undeviating.

**Strict Construction.** Interpretation of a statute confined to the actual language used rather than the intentions of the legislators.

**Stricti Juris.** According to strick law.

**Strictissimi Juris.** Of the strictest right or law.

**Strictly.** Closely; precisely; stringently.

**Stricto Jure.** In strict law.

**Strictum Jus.** The strict law; the letter of the law.

**Strike.** The cessation of work by a group of workmen in order to force their employer to accede to some demand.

**Strikebreaker.** One who takes the place of a striking workman.

**Strike Out.** To expunge from a court record or pleading.

**Strip.** The spoiling or unlawful taking away of anything from the land.

**Struck Jury.** A jury of 12 men selected from names remaining after each side has exercised his right of striking out a certain number of those eligible for jury duty.

**Structure.** Any construction; an edifice for any use.

**Strumpet.** Prostitute.

**Stub Line.** Small branch line of a railroad.

**Stuffing Ballot Box.** Fraudulent placing in ballot boxes of ballots which have not been voted.

**Stultify.** To plead one's self mentally incapacitated for the performance of an act.

**Stumpage.** Fee paid for permission to enter on another man's land and cut standing timber.

**Stuprum.** Rape of a virgin.
**Style.** To call, name or entitle one; a title or official name.
**Strong.** Cogent; powerful; forceful.
**Suable.** Liable to be sued.
**Suapte Natura.** In its own nature.
**Sua Sponte.** Upon his own responsibility; of his own motion.
**Sub.** Under.
**Sub Colore Officii.** Under color of right or office
**Sub Conditions.** Upon condition.
**Subcontractor.** One who takes a portion of a contract from the principal contractor or another subcontractor.
**Sub Cura Mariti.** Under the care of the husband.
**Sub Curia.** Under law
**Subdivision.** Division into smaller parts of the same thing or subject matter.
**Sub Disjunctione.** In the alternative.
**Subhastatio.** Sale at public auction.
**Subject.** One subject to and who owes allegiance to the government of a state; matter of public or private concern for which law is enacted.
**Subject-Matter.** That which is under consideration or in dispute.
**Subject to.** Liable; subordinate; governed by; provided; answerab e for.
**Sub Judice.** Before the court; in litigation.
**Subalta Causa Tollitur Effectus.** By removing the cause, the effect is removed.
**Sublease.** A lease executed by the lessee of an estate to a third person; to enter into a sublease; to sublet.
**Subletting.** See Sublease.
**Submission.** Yielding to authority; agreement to abide by a decision of an arbiter.
**Submit.** To commit to the discretion of another.
**Sub Modo.** Subject to a modification or qualification; on condition.
**Subordinate.** To place in a lower class, order or rank; accessory.
**Subornation.** Procuring another to commit a crime.
**Subpoena.** Under penalty; writ, process or mandate requiring a person to appear in court to testify in a certain case.
**Subpoena ad Testificandum.** See Subpoena.
**Sub Potestate.** Under the protection.
**Sub Potestate Parentis.** Under the protection of a parent.
**Sub Potestate Viri.** Under control of her husband.
**Subreption.** Obtaining property by concealment of the truth.
**Subrogation.** The substitution of one person in place of another with reference to a lawful claim, demand or right.
**Subrogee.** One who by subrogation acquires the rights of another, the subrogor.
**Subrogor.** See Subrogee.
**Subscribe.** To sign one's name; to agree to pay.
**Subscribing Witness.** One who attests the signature of a party to an instrument by signing the instrument himself.
**Subscription.** A written signature; an agreement to give or pay some amount to a designated purpose.
**Subsequent.** Coming after.
**Subsidiary Corporation.** A corporation controlled by a parent corporation.
**Subsidy.** Aid given or appropriated by the government through its proper agencies.
**Sub Sigillo.** Under seal.
**Sub Silento.** Silently.
**Subsistence.** Support.
**Sub Spe Reconcilliationis.** In the hope of reconciliation.
**Substance.** Essence; that which is essential.
**Substantial.** Of real worth and importance; valuable.
**Substantial Claim.** One which is real and actual.
**Substantiate.** To establish the existance or truth of by competent evidence.
**Substantive Law.** Law concerned with the determination of rights and legal powers.
**Substitute.** To put in the place of another person or thing; the thing or person so put.
**Substitution.** In the law of wills, to bequeath property to one or more persons, to be succeeded in the enjoyment thereof by others designated by the testator.
**Sub Suo Periculo.** At his own risk.
**Subtenant.** A sub-lessee; an undertenant.
**Sub Voce.** Under the word or title.
**Succession.** The taking of property by inheritance or will or by operation of law.
**Succession Tax.** Probate or estate tax levied on the transfer of the decedent's estate; a legacy tax levied on the right to receive such property.
**Successor.** One who succeeds to the place of another.
**Sudden.** Happening without notice; unforseen.
**Sue.** To bring an action in a court of law or equity.
**Sue Out.** To obtain by application; to petition for certain relief.
**Suffer.** To permit or authorize.
**Sufferance.** Toleration; passive consent.
**Sufficent.** Adequate; competent.
**Sufficient Cause.** Indicates the presence of facts which will justify an action, especially by a court.
**Sufficient Evidence.** Adequate evidence; satisfactory evidence.
**Suffocate.** To kill by stopping respiration, e.g. strangling.
**Suffrage.** The right to vote at public elections.
**Suggest.** To hint; to intimate.
**Suggestio Falsi.** A false suggestion; a misrepresentation.
**Suicide.** Taking of one's own life.
**Sui Generis.** Of its own kind.
**Sui Juris.** In his own right; capable of making a contract.
**Suit.** An action of any kind, in law or equity; prosecution of a claim or right in a court of law.
**Suit Money.** An allowance granted the wife in divorce cases to cover court costs and provide temporary alimony.
**Suitable.** Fit; appropriate.
**Suitor.** Party to a suit or action in court.
**Sum.** Money.
**Summa Injuria.** The greatest injury.
**Summa Providentia.** The greatest prudence.
**Summary.** Short, brief; without formal trial or proceeding.
**Summary Abatement.** Abatement of a nuisance by physical means.
**Summary Conviction.** Conviction of a person without a formal trial.
**Summary Judgment.** A judgment in an action which is entered without plenary trial, based upon the affidavits of the parties.
**Summary Jurisdiction.** Power of a court to give a judgment or make an order itself forthwith.
**Summary Proceedings.** Proceeding which dispenses with many formalitites.
**Summary Trial.** Trial on a criminal charge without jury.
**Summation.** Closing address to the jury.
**Summing Up.** See Summation.
**Summon.** To notify a defendant that an action has been instituted against him; to notify to appear in court.
**Summonea.** A summons.
**Summons.** A writ or process by which a defendant is notified to appear in court. See Summon.
**Summum Jus.** A strict insistence on a legal right.
**Sunday.** The first day of the week.
**Suo Nomine.** In his own name.
**Suo Periculo.** At his own risk.
**Super.** Above, over; on; during; concerning.
**Supercargo.** One employed by the owner of a vessel to take charge of the cargo.
**Superficies.** The surface; anything erected upon the land so as to become a part of it.
**Superhuman Cause.** Act of God.
**Superintend.** To direct; to manage; to take care of with authority.
**Superintendence.** Direction; guidance.
**Superintendent.** Manager; director; employer's representative who directs work of employees.

**Superior Court.** Court of general jurisdiction in the first instance.
**Superior Lien.** A prior lien.
**Supersede.** Set aside; annul.
**Supersedeas.** In practice, a writ that stays the proceedings at law.
**Supersedere.** To supersede; to stay.
**Supervise.** To superintend or inspect.
**Supervision.** Inspection.
**Supervisor.** One who has authority over and directs others.
**Supervisor of Elections.** One appointed to supervise the registration of voters.
**Super Visum Corporis.** On view of the body (at a coroner's inquest).
**Supplemental.** Additional.
**Supplemental Bill.** In equity practice, a new bill filed to supply a defect in the original bill or add something to it.
**Supplemental Pleading.** A pleading consisting of facts arising since the institution of the suit.
**Supplementary Proceedings.** Proceedings by which a judgment debtor, against whom execution has been returned unsatisfied, may be examined under oath about his property.
**Suppletory Oath.** Oath taken by a party to an action who testified in his own behalf.
**Suppliant.** Petitioner.
**Supplicium.** Death penalty.
**Support.** Source or means of living; maintenance; subsistence; sustenance.
**Supposition.** Conjecture based on probability or possibility.
**Suppress.** To prevent, subdue or prohibit.
**Suppressio Veri.** Concealment of the truth, known to be relevant to a transaction.
**Supra.** Above; upon; in addition to.
**Supra Dictus.** As stated above.
**Suprema Voluntas.** The last will.
**Supremacy.** Paramount authority; sovereignty.
**Supreme Court.** Highest court of U.S. government; highest court in many states; in New York, the court of general jurisdiction in the first instance.
**Supreme Law of the Land.** The Constitution of the U.S. and all laws and treaties enacted thereunder.
**Sur.** On; upon.
**Surcharge.** In equity, to place an item in an account to the debit of a trustee or other holder of property, which in the account has not been so debited.
**Sur Disclaimer.** On disclaimer.
**Surety.** One legally liable for another.
**Surgeon.** One who cures disease by manual operation.
**Surname.** One's name; family name.
**Surplus.** Remainder; residue; undistributed profits of a business.
**Surplusage.** Unnecessary, extraneous matter.
**Surplus Earnings.** Amount owned by a corporation over and above its capital and liabilities.
**Surprise.** Taken unawares; sudden confusion and perplexity.
**Surrebutter.** Plaintiff's answer to the defendant's rebutter.
**Surrejoinder.** Plaintiff's answer to the defendant's rejoinder.
**Surrender.** To give back; yield; restore; to relinquish patent rights; to yield up an estate for life or for years so that the reversioner or remainderman may enter into possession at once.
**Surreptitious.** Stealthily; fraudulently.
**Surrogate Court.** Court with jurisdiction in guardianship and probate matters.
**Sursise.** Negligence; default.
**Surtax.** Tax levied in addition to the normal tax.
**Survey.** To ascertain boundaries, corners, diversions, etc. of land; process by which land is measured; an examination.
**Survival.** Living longer than another.
**Survive.** To outlive another; to remain alive.
**Survivor.** One who outlives others.
**Suspect.** To have a vague idea concerning.
**Suspend.** To interrupt; to hold in abeyance; to delay or hinder.
**Suspendatur per Collum.** Let him be hanged by the neck.
**Suspended Sentence.** A sentence which is delayed by the trial court after the defendant has been found guilty.
**Suspension.** Temporary delay; temporary extinguishment of a right of an estate.
**Suspension of Sentence.** Postponement of the execution of a sentence for an indefinite period.
**Sus. Per. Co.,** (Abb.). Suspendature per Collum.
**Suspicion.** Imagination of something wrong without proof.
**Sustain.** To carry on; to maintain.
**Sustenance.** Food; that which maintains life.
**Suus.** His own.
**Swear.** To take an oath; to use profane language.
**Swear in.** To administer an oath.
**Swearing.** Cursing.
**Sweating.** Abusing prisoners under interrogation.
**Sweat Shop.** A plant whose employees work under extremely unfavorable conditions.
**Sweepstakes.** In a public race, the sum of the stakes for which the subscribers agree to pay for each horse nominated.
**Swindle.** To cheat and defraud; to obtain property by false pretenses.
**Swindler.** A cheat; one who defrauds others.
**Sworn.** Verified.
**Sworn Evidence.** Testimony given under oath.
**Syllabi.** The headnotes which precede the decisions in the printed reports.
**Syllabus.** An abstract; a headnote.
**Sympathetic Strike.** A boycott.
**Synallagmatic Contract.** In civil law, a contract in which both parties are bound.
**Syndic.** Business agent or representative of a corporation.
**Syndicate.** An association of individuals formed to carry out some special financial transaction or group of transactions.
**Synonymous.** Expressing the same ideas.
**Syphilis.** A venereal disease.

## T

**Table.** A condensed, tabulated statement; synopsis.
**Tabularius.** Notary.
**Tacit.** Silent; implied.
**Tacite.** Tacitly.
**Tacit Law.** Law deriving its authority from the common consent of the people.
**Tail.** An estate tail or in fee tail is an estate of inheritance limited to the heirs of the body of the grantee.
**Taini.** Freeholders.
**Take.** To acquire, obtain or procure.
**Take Back.** Revoke; retract.
**Take by Stealth.** Steal.
**Take Effect.** To become operative.
**Take Testimony.** To receive evidence.
**Take Up.** To pay or discharge a note.
**Taking.** To seize or grasp.
**Tales. Talesman.** Jurors called to fill vacancies in the regular panel of jurors.
**Tales de Circumstantibus.** Jurors from the bystanders.
**Tacit Hypothecation.** Type of lien or mortgage which is created by operation of the law without any express agreement of the parties.
**Taking per Capita.** In the distribution of estates, equally.
**Tales Jurors.** See Tales.
**Talesmen.** See Tales.
**Talio.** Punishment in the same kind.
**Talis Qualis.** As much as; such as.
**Taliter.** Thus; so.
**Tallagium.** A term including all taxes.
**Tallia.** Tax.
**Tam.** So; to such extent.
**Tamen.** However; nevertheless.
**Tamper.** To interfere with a thing for some improper purpose; to meddle.
**Tam Quam.** As much as; as well as.
**Tangible.** Capable of being touched; tactile; real; substantial; evidence.
**Tangible Property.** Property which may be felt or touched.
**Tanquam Testamentum Inofficiosum.** An improvident will; one which overlooks the nearest relatives.

**Tantus.** So much; so great.
**Tarde.** Return of an officer stating that he received the process too late to execute it.
**Tare.** An allowance for the weight of a container made by customs officers in computing duties on imports.
**Tariff.** Duty on imports; tabulated list of rates.
**Tavern.** Place where alcoholic beverages are sold to be drunk on the premises.
**Tax.** To assess, particularly money for the support of the government; to demand; to lay a burden upon; financial burden levied upon persons or property by the government for public purposes.
**Taxable.** Subject or liable to taxation.
**Taxable Costs.** Expenses of the prevailing party in an action which may be included in the judgment of a court.
**Taxable Credit.** Any obligation or contract which creates an enforceable indebtedness on the part of the promisor.
**Taxable Property.** Property liable to or subject to taxation.
**Taxable Value.** The bonded indebtedness together with the stock of a corporation.
**Taxation.** The act of levying or imposing a tax.
**Taxation of Costs.** The fixing of the costs which are to be paid by the party losing the suit.
**Tax Avoidance.** The legal attempt to minimize one's taxes.
**Tax Certificate.** A certificate of the scale of real estate for delinquent taxes.
**Tax Collector.** One authorized to collect and to enforce payment of taxes.
**Tax Deed.** The conveyance given upon a sale of property upon which taxes have not been paid.
**Tax Ferrets.** Persons who search for property omitted from taxation.
**Taxi, Taxicab.** Vehicle for public hire.
**Taxing Power.** Power of a government to levy taxes.
**Tax Levy.** Establishment of a rate of taxation by a duly authorized government.
**Tax Lien.** A lien existing in favor of state or municipality upon the property of a delinquent taxpayer on which unpaid taxes are due, or on all his property.
**Tax List.** Official listing of the descriptions of property and the names of those liable to assessment.
**Taxpayer.** One subject to and chargeable with a tax.
**Tax Roll.** List of persons and property subject to the payment of a particular tax, with the amounts severally due.
**Tax Sale.** Sale of property for unpaid delinquent taxcs.
**Tax Title.** Title acquired by purchase of land land at a tax sale.
**Teacher.** One who instructs.
**Teamster.** One engaged in the hauling of freight for others.
**Teazer.** Railroad operated at a loss.
**Technical.** Pertaining or peculiar to an art or science; immaterial.
**Technical Error.** An error during the course of a trial which is not serious.
**Technical Mortgage.** A true and formal mortgage.
**Tegula.** A title.
**Teller.** Bank employee who takes in and pays out money; one who keeps tallies, e.g. of votes.
**Temere.** Rashly; accidentally.
**Temperance.** Moderation; restrained indulgence.
**Temperate Damages.** Reasonable damages.
**Temporalis.** Temporary.
**Temporalis Actio.** An action which had to be brought within a certain time.
**Temporary.** For a limited time.
**Temporary Alimony.** Allowance paid a wife pending court action.
**Temporary Damages.** In real estate, recovery made from time to time as damages accrue.
**Temporary Disability.** One which is not permanent, lasting for a limited time.
**Temporary Injunction.** Restraining Order; an injunction to maintain the status quo until the action is finally determined.
**Temporary Loan.** A loan which is to be paid with and by the taxes of a current fiscal year.
**Temporary Statute.** Statute limited in duration from the time of its inception.
**Tempore et Loco.** In time and place.
**Temporis Exceptio.** A plea of lapse of time, in bar of an action.
**Tempus.** Time.
**Tempus Continuum.** A continuous time.
**Tempus Semestrae.** The six-months period.
**Tempus Utile.** The period to be used; indicates how a period of time for procedure or limitations is to be reckoned.
**Tenancy.** The estate of a tenant; a mode of holding an estate; temporary possession of another's property.
**Tenancy at Sufferance.** Possession of land by lawful title but holding thereof after title has expired.
**Tenancy by the Entirety.** Joint tenenacy by husband and wife, each being seized and possessed of the entire estate, after the death of one, the survivor taking the whole.
**Tenancy for Life.** One which continues for the period of a designated life or lives.
**Tenancy for Years.** One which terminated after a fixed time.
**Tenancy from Year to Year.** Tenancy which can be terminated after a year, usually by giving six months' notice.
**Tenancy in Common.** Tenancy in lands by more than one person in such a way that each owns an undivided share.
**Tenant.** One who holds land in return for service or rent.
**Tenant at Sufferance.** See Tenancy at Sufferance.
**Tenant by Entirety.** See Tenancy by Entirety.
**Tenant for Life.** See Tenancy for life.
**Tenant for Years.** See Tenancy for Years.
**Tenant from Year to Year.** See Tenancy from Year to Year.
**Tenant in Common.** See Tenancy in Common.
**Tenant in Fee Simple.** One who holds land or tenements for himself and his heirs forever.
**Tenant in Severalty.** A sole tenant.
**Tenants by the Entireties.** Tenants who hold by one title, e.g. joint tenancy.
**Tenants in Common.** Tenants who hold in unity of possession.
**Tender.** Offer to perform an obligation which is due.
**Tender of Issue.** In pleading, an offer to submit the question to the court or jury.
**Tenement.** Landed property held by one person of another; a large building for the occupation of three or more persons, usually of the poorer class.
**Tenements.** Corporeal hereditaments, and incorporeal hereditaments issuing out of corporeal ones or which are annexed thereto.
**Tenementum.** A tenement; an estate held by a tenant.
**Tenens.** A tenant.
**Tener.** To hold or keep.
**Tenere.** To hold or keep; to understand.
**Tenet.** He holds.
**Tenor.** The actual wording of a document; an exact copy.
**Tenor Praesentium.** By tenor of these presents.
**Tenor of Bill of Exchange.** Refers to the time and manner of payment of the bill.
**Tenure.** The nature of the holding or tenancy of lands; term of office.
**Terce.** Dower.
**Tercerone.** Mulatto.
**Term.** A word; a phrase; a fixed period of time; the limit of time in a leasehold; a session of court; time for which one holds an office.
**Terminare.** To terminate; to decide finally.
**Terminating Building and Loan Association.** One in which all of the stock matures at the same time.
**Terminus.** Limit; term; boundary; an estate for years.
**Terminus ad Quem.** Limit to which.
**Term of Court.** Sesson of court.
**Terra.** Land.
**Terra Affirmata.** Farmed land.
**Terra Debilis.** Barren land.
**Terra Firma.** Dry land.
**Terra Frisca.** Uncultivated land.
**Terra Lucrabilis.** Reclaimed land.
**Terra Testamentalis.** Land transferrable by will.

**Terre.** Land.
**Terre-Tenant.** One actually in occupation or possession of land.
**Terrible.** Frightful; dreadful.
**Territorial Waters.** Waters contiguous to the coast of a country.
**Territory.** A part of the national domain of the U.S.
**Terror.** Fright; dread.
**Tertia.** The third part; dower.
**Tertius Interveniens.** A third party who intervenes in an action.
**Test.** Examination; trial; a criterion; standard; norm.
**Testacy.** The state or condition of leaving a valid will at one's death.
**Testament.** The disposition of personal property according to the decedent's will and desire.
**Testamentary.** Pertaining to a will.
**Testamentary Capacity.** The mental ability recognized by law as sufficient for making a will.
**Testamentary Disposition.** The disposition of property not to take effect until after the grantor dies.
**Testamentary Guardian.** The guardian of a decedent's child appointed by his will.
**Testamentary Instrument.** Any instrument intended as a will; an unprobated will.
**Testamentary Power.** Power to dispose of one's property by will.
**Testamentum.** Testament; will.
**Testari.** To testify; to attest; to make a will.
**Testate.** One who has made a will or dies leaving a will.
**Testation.** Witness; evidence.
**Testator.** A man who dies leaving a valid will.
**Testatrix.** Woman who dies leaving a valid will.
**Testatum.** Testified.
**Testatus.** Testate; a testator.
**Test Case.** Case seeking to answer an abstract question.
**Teste.** Bear witness.
**Tested.** Witnessed; attested.
**Teste of Writ.** The concluding clause, showing date of issuance.
**Testify.** To bear witness; to give evidence under oath.
**Testimonia.** Testimony; evidence.
**Testimonium, Testimonium Clause.** See Teste of Writ.
**Testimony.** Evidence given by a witness under oath.
**Testis.** Witness.
**Test Oath.** Oath required as a criterion of the fitness of a person to hold a public or political office; an oath of past and present fidelity to an established government.
**Thalweg.** Middle of the main channel of a river.
**Theft.** Larceny; the unlawful taking of the personal property of another.
**Then.** At that time; a specific time; also used to denote a contingency.
**Theocracy.** Government which recognizes God as its ruler.
**Theolonium.** Toll.
**Theory of a Case.** Facts or basis on which a right of action is claimed.
**Thearapy.** Treatment of a disease.
**There.** In or at that place.
**Thereafter.** After that time; afterward.
**Thereby.** Because of; by reason of.
**Therefor.** For that thing.
**Therein.** In that place.
**Thereupon.** Without delay.
**Thesaurus Inventus.** Treasure-trove.
**Thief.** One who commits larceny.
**Things.** Objects of ownership or property.
**Things in Action.** A right to recover money or personal property by court proceedings.
**Things of Value.** Tangible objects recognized by the law as personal property.
**Things Personal.** Goods, money and all other movables which a person may move about with him.
**Things Real.** Permanent, fixed, immovable things which cannot be moved about, e.g. land.
**Think.** To believe; to conclude; to recollect.
**Third Degree.** Method used to force a prisoner to confess or give information.
**Third House.** An organized and generally unscrupulous lobby.
**Third Party.** One who has an interest in a legal transaction but not actually a party to it.
**Third Party Beneficiary.** One not a party to a contract, who receives a benefit thereunder and who may bring suit to protect his interest.
**Third Possessor.** One who buys mortgaged property without assuming the mortgage.
**Thoroughfare.** A passage through.
**Thread.** A middle line; center line of the main channel of a stream or river.
**Threat.** Declaration of an intention to harm another by the doing of some unlawful act; a menace.
**Three Mile Limit.** Territorial waters which mark the limit of jurisdiction of national control.
**Throw Out.** To ignore a bill.
**Thus.** In the way indicated.
**Tick.** (Coll.). Credit or trust.
**Ticket.** A certificate entitling the holder to some right or privilege; list of candidates running for office; a ballot.
**Ticket Speculator.** One who sells tickets at an advance over the price charged by the management.
**Tide.** The ebb and flow of the ocean.
**Tide Lands.** Lands which are covered and uncovered by the daily ebb and flow of the tides.
**Tie.** To bind; the failure of either of two candidates to obtain a majority.
**Tiel.** Such.
**Tignum.** Building material.
**Timber.** Trees which can be used for building purposes.
**Time.** The measure of duration.
**Time Bargain.** An agreement to buy or sell stock at a future time at a fixed price.
**Time Immemorial.** Time beyond the memory of man.
**Tipstaff.** A court bailiff.
**Tithes.** Tenths.
**Title.** Ownership; means whereby the owner has just possession of his property; certificate of ownership; a claim or right; a distinctive appellation; the caption describing a statute or legal proceeding.
**Title Bond.** Bond given to the purchaser of real property as security in the transfer of title to property.
**Title by Descent.** Title by hereditary succession.
**Title by Prescription.** Title acquired by use and time.
**Title, Chain of.** Record of the succession of conveyances of real property, giving the origin and history to the title of property.
**Title Deeds.** Deeds which give evidence of title to lands.
**Title in Fee Simple.** Full and unconditional ownership in fact.
**Title Insurance.** Insurance against loss or damage resulting from defects or failure of title or from the enforcement of liens existing at the time of the insurance.
**Through.** By means of; within; from one side to the other; by agency of.
**Title of a Cause.** Manner of designating a suit at law, e.g. Brown vs. Jones.
**Title of an Act or Statute.** The name of a statute, usually the first part.
**Title Search.** A search of public record to ascertain the state of a person's title to real estate.
**Title Theory.** The theory that the mortage passes legal title to the property.
**Titulus.** Title.
**Toft.** Vacant site on which a building formerly stood.
**To Have and To Hold.** Clause in an instrument which defines and limits the extent of the estate granted.
**Token.** A sign or mark; symbol of the existence of a fact.
**Tolerate.** To permit, although not wholly approved of.
**Toll.** To bar, defeat or take away; to interrupt the statute of limitations; a tax for the use of something.
**Tollage.** Toll; the payment of or exaction of a toll.
**Toll Bridge.** A bridge built and maintained under public authority, the use of which is subject to a reasonable toll.

**Tollere.** To raise, lift up or elevate; to take away; to defeat.
**Toll Gate.** Gate erected on private or public property allowing passage only upon payment of toll.
**Toll Road.** Turnpike.
**Toll the Statute.** To stop the running of the statute of limitations.
**Toll-Traverse.** A toll on passage over private property.
**Tonnage.** The capacity of a vessel for carrying freight, etc., calculated in tons.
**Tontine.** Insurance whereby perpetual or life annuities and benefits are enjoyed by several persons with the agreement that on the death of any one of them, his share goes to the survivors.
**Tort.** An act or omission which causes injury and which creates a claim for damage in the injured party; a private or civil wrong or injury.
**Tort-Feasor.** One who commits a tort.
**Tortious.** Wrongful; injurious.
**Torture.** The use of instruments to inflict pain in order to extort confessions or information.
**Tota Curia.** The whole court.
**Total.** Whole; complete; full.
**Total Loss.** Complete loss of insured property.
**Totidem Verbis.** In so many words.
**Toties Quoties.** As often as.
**Toujours et Uncore Prist.** Now and always ready.
**Tout.** All; whole.
**Towage.** The towing of ships and vessels; the fee therefor.
**Toward.** In the direction of.
**To Wit.** That is to say; namely.
**Town.** A civil and political division of a state larger than a village, but not incorporated as a city.
**Town-Clerk.** An officer of a municipality who acts as a recorder and general secretary.
**Town-Meeting.** A legal assembly of the qualified voters of an incorporated town.
**Town-Plat.** A map or chart showing the arrangement of streets and the division of lots of a town.
**Township.** A division of land, six miles square.
**Townsite.** Portion of public domain set apart to be the site for a town.
**Toxic.** Poisonous.
**Toxicant.** A poison.
**Toxicology.** The science of poisons.
**Tp** (Abb.). Township.
**Tracing.** A mechanical copy or facsimile of an original document.
**Tract** (of Land). Lot; parcel.
**Tradas in Bailium.** To deliver for bail.
**Trade.** Commerce; barter; any bargain or sale; the business of buying and selling for money.
**Trade Acceptance.** A draft or bill of exchange drawn by the seller of goods on the buyer and accepted by him.
**Trademark** A distinguishing mark or charac-f teristic,. through which the products o particular manufacturers are identified.
**Trade-Name.** Name under which a person, firm or corporation does business.
**Trader.** One who deals in the purchase and sale of goods for profit.
**Trade-Union.** A labor organization formed to protect the rights and interests of the workingman through collective bargaining with the employer.
**Tradition.** Delivery of real or personal property.
**Traffic.** Commerce; trade; sale or exchange of merchandise; the transportation of passengers, goods and merchandise.
**Trahere.** To draw.
**Traitor.** One who betrays; one who commits treason.
**Tramp.** A vagrant.
**Tramp Corporation.** A corporation which does not intend to do business in the state of incorporation.
**Transact.** To conduct, manage or carry out.
**Transactio.** A voluntary compromise or settlement of a litigation.
**Transaction.** The conducting of any business; negotiation; proceeding; a compromise.
**Transcript.** A copy of a writing.
**Transcript of Judgment.** A certificate that a judgment has been entered.
**Transcript of Record.** Printed copy of the record of an entire case.
**Transfer.** To convey from one person or place to another.
**Transfer by Indorsement.** The indorsement and delivery of a negotiable instrument.
**Transferee.** One to whom a transfer is made.
**Transferor.** One who makes a transfer.
**Transgressio.** Trespass.
**Transient.** Passing across; not lasting or permanent.
**Transient Foreigner.** A foreigner who comes to a country without intending to remain.
**Transient Person.** One who has no fixed address in the state in which he is.
**Transire.** To go or pass over.
**Transit.** Carriage and delivery of goods in accordance with the terms of a contract.
**Transitory.** Passing from one place to another.
**Transitus.** Transit; a conveyance.
**Translation.** Reproduction of a document, paper, etc. in another language; a testamentary provision in the same will or in a codicil, by which a legacy previously given is transferred to another person.
**Transport.** To carry; to convey.
**Transportation.** The removal of goods or persons from one place to another.
**Transhipment.** Transfer of cargo from one ship to another before reaching the ultimate destination.
**Trassans.** Drawing; the drawer of a bill of exchange.
**Trassitus.** The drawee of a bill of exchange.
**Trauma.** A wound; bodily injury.
**Traumatic Disease.** Disease caused by physical injury.
**Travail.** Childbearing; suffering.
**Travel.** To go from one place to another; journey.
**Traveler.** One who goes from one place to another.
**Travel Pay.** Allowance given to military officers upon their honorable discharge to return to their place of enlistment.
**Traverse.** To deny an allegation in a pleading.
**Traverse Jury.** Trial jury.
**Traverser.** Party to an action who pleads by way of denial.
**Treason.** The attempt to overthrow by overt acts the state to which one owes allegiance.
**Treasurer.** Officer of the state, a corporation or organization entrusted with the custody and disbursement of money.
**Treasure-Trove.** Money or other precious metals hidden away by an unknown owner and accidentally found by another.
**Treasury.** Place where public funds are kept.
**Treasury Note.** Bill issued by the U.S. Treasury and circulating as legal tender.
**Treaty.** Formal agreement between two or more sovereign states.
**Treble Damages.** Three times the actual damages sustained.
**Tres.** Three.
**Trespass.** Any violation of law; unlawful and intentional injury to another's person or property.
**Trespass Quare Clausum Fregit.** "Trespass wherefore he broke the close;" common-law action for trespass upon the plaintiff's land.
**Trespasser.** One who enters upon the property of another without permission.
**Tret.** An allowance made for water or dust in weighing certain commodities.
**Trial.** Judicial examination, according to the law of the land, of issues presented in due course of procedure.
**Trial by Jury.** Trial by a body of 12 men duly selected, impaneled and sworn.
**Trial by Court.** Trial by one or more judges without a jury.
**Trial de Novo.** A re-trial in a superior court on an appeal of the case from an inferior court.
**Trial Judge.** Judge who presides at a court case.
**Trial per Testes.** Trial by witnesses; a trial without the intervention of a jury.
**Triare.** To try.
**Triatio.** A trial.
**Tribunal.** Court; the place where a judge administers justice.
**Tribute.** A tax levied by a sovereign on his subjects or by one nation on another.
**Triens.** The third part; dower.

**Trigamus.** One who has been lawfully married three separate times.
**Trinkets.** Small, decorative ornaments.
**Triors.** Persons appointed by the court to determine whether a juror challenged for favor is or is not qualified to serve.
**Trip.** Journey from one place to another.
**Tripartite.** Having three parts or parties.
**Trithing.** The third of a country.
**Trivial.** Trifling; of small importance.
**Trove.** Found.
**Troy Weight.** A weight of 12 oz. to the pound.
**Truce.** A suspension of hostilities between belligerents.
**True.** Correct; actual; genuine; honest.
**True Bill.** Indorsement on an indictment when the jury finds that the accused should be prosecuted.
**Trust.** Reliance upon another; confidence; credit given; that committed to another for management or safekeeping; a right of property, real or personal, held by one party for the benefit of another; a confidence reposed in one person, the trustee, for the benefit of another, the cestui que-trust, respecting arrangements of rights over property which is held by the trustee for the benefit of the cestui que trust; term used for combinations of large industrial corporations or individuals which control or tend to control an industry or groups of industries.
**Trust Company.** A bank organized under general statutes for the purpose of accepting, and executing trusts and managing the various financial matters of corporations organized as trusts.
**Trust Deed.** A species of mortgage given to a creditor to secure a loan.
**Trustee.** One in whom property is vested in trust for others; one appointed to execute a trust.
**Trustee in Bankruptcy.** An officer of the court appointed to collect and reduce to money the estate of a bankrupt.
**Trustee Process.** In New England States, the process of garnishment.
**Trustee Estate.** Either the estate of the trustee, i.e. legal title, or the estate of the beneficiary.
**Trust Fund Doctrine.** The doctrine that the capital stock of a corporation is held by the corporation in trust for its creditors and stockholders.
**Trust in Invitum.** A trust imposed by operation of law without consent of the trustee.
**Trustor.** One who settles or creates a trust; the grantor.
**Try.** To examine judicially.
**Tug.** Tow-boat.
**Tulit.** He brought.
**Tumult.** Noisy quarrel; brawl.
**Tunc.** Then; at that time.
**Turn-Over.** Repeated use of the same invested capital in the buying and selling of goods.
**Turnpike.** Toll gate; road having toll gates.
**Turpis.** Bad; wicked; immoral.
**Turpis Contractus.** Dishonorable contract.
**Turpitude.** Inherent baseness; depravity; everything contrary to justice, honesty or good morals.
**Tuta.** Safe; secure.
**Tutela.** Guardianship; tutelage.
**Tutor.** Guardian of a minor.
**Twelve Mile Limit.** Provision in an agreement between Britian and U.S. allowing the latter to search British ships within 12 miles of shore.
**Tyrant.** Despot.

## U

**Uberrima Fides.** The most complete good faith.
**Ubi Re Vera.** Where, in truth.
**Ulterior.** Beyond what is apparent.
**Ulterior Estate.** An estate in remainder.
**Ulterius Concilium.** Further consideration or argument.
**Ultimo Ratio.** The last reason or resort.
**Ultimate.** The last in a sequence; final.
**Ultimate Facts.** The facts that are in issue in a case; facts necessary and essential for decision by the court.
**Ultimatum.** The last proposition.
**Ultima Voluntas.** A last will.
**Ultimum Supplicium.** The extreme punishment; punishment of death.
**Ultimus Haeres.** Ultimate heir.
**Ultra.** Beyond; outside of; in excess of.
**Ultra Mare.** Beyond the sea.
**Ultra Reprises.** After deductions.
**Ultra Vires Act.** An act beyond the scope of the power of a corporation.
**Umpirage.** The decision of the umpire.
**Umpire.** Arbitrator.
**Una cum.** Together with.
**Una cum Omnibus Aliis.** Together with all the others.
**Unalienable.** Inalienable.
**Unanimous.** Agreeing.
**Una Voce.** With one voice; unanimously.
**Unavoidable Accident.** An inevitable, unforseeable accident.
**Unavoidable Cause.** Accidental cause.
**Uncertain.** Vague; indefinite.
**Unchaste Woman.** Woman who is not sexually pure.
**Unchasity.** Impurity in mind and conduct.
**Uncle.** The brother of one's father or mother.
**Unclean Hands.** Principle which will prevent a court of equity from giving equitable relief to a person whose conduct is unconscionable.
**Unconditional.** Without conditions or reservations; not limited.
**Unconscionable.** Morally reprehensible.
**Unconstitutional.** That which is contrary or irreconcilable to the constitution.
**Uncontrollable.** Ungovernable; irresistible.
**Uncontrollable Impulse.** Irresistible impulse.
**Uncore.** Again; now.
**Unde.** Whence; from what.
**Undefended.** Without defense; applied to one who must make his own defense when on trial.
**Unde Petit Judicium.** Whereof he demands judgment.
**Under-Lease.** Where lessee lets premises for a part only of his unexpired terms.
**Under Seal.** Applied to any document to which a seal has been attached.
**Undertake.** To take on oneself; set about; attempt; to perform or execute; to contract; to accept responsibility for.
**Undertaker.** One who contracts to do something, ordinarily in the public service; one who prepares the dead for burial.
**Undertaking.** A guaranty; a bond.
**Under-Tenant.** Sub-tenant.
**Under the Law.** In conformity with the law.
**Underwriter.** Insurer; investment banker who underwrites corporate bonds and stocks.
**Underwriting Contract.** Contract to insure the sale of bonds.
**Undique.** In all directions.
**Undisclosed Principal.** A principal in an agency relationship whose identity is not known to the persons with whom the agent transacts business.
**Undisputed.** Uncontested.
**Undivided Profits.** Profits which have not been distributed or set aside as surplus.
**Undres.** Minors.
**Undue.** More than necessary or proper; illegal.
**Undue Influence.** Pressure brought to bear upon a person so as to interfere with the exercise of freedom of will.
**Unearned Income.** Income received from property.
**Unequal.** Not uniform.
**Unequivocal.** Clear; capable of being interpreted in only one way.
**Unerring.** Sure; infallible.
**Unethical.** Not according to business or professional standards.
**Unexpected.** Sudden.
**Unfair.** In regard to labor, unfriendly to organized labor.
**Unfair Competition.** All dishonest or fradulent rivalry in trade and commerce; the endeavor to drive a competitor out of business by fraud, intimidation, counterfeiting, etc.
**Unfit.** Unsuitable; incompetent.
**Unforseen.** Not expected.
**Unforseen Event.** An uncontrollable force.
**Unified.** Made one.
**Uniform.** Unvarying; equable; as applied to statutes, one which treats alike all persons similarly situated.

**Uniform Operation of Laws.** In constitutional law, the requirement that laws of a general nature have uniform application to all persons within a legitimate class.
**Unilateral.** One-sided.
**Unilateral Contract.** Contract in which one party undertakes the performance of an act without receiving in return any express promise of performance from the other party, the promise becoming binding only when the act is performed.
**Unilateral Mistake.** A mistake on the part of only one of the parties to a contract.
**Unintelligible.** That which cannot be understood.
**Union.** League; federation; an unincorporated association of workingmen. See Trade Union.
**Union Labels.** Certain labels attached to goods made by union members.
**Union Shop.** One in which only union members may work.
**Unitas Personarum.** Merger of two legal persons into one.
**Unite.** To join in an act.
**United Kingdom.** Great Britain and Ireland.
**United Nations.** An international organization chartered in 1945 with the objective of maintaining peace and friendly relations among nations.
**United States.** Collective name of the states united by and under the Constitution; territory under the sovereignty of the U.S.
**United States Bond.** Obligations for payment of money issued by the U.S. government at various times.
**United States Commissioners.** Subordinate judicial officers appointed by the Federal District Court for a term of four years.
**United States Courts.** Under the Constitution, the judicial power of the U.S. is vested in a supreme court and other inferior courts as established by Congress.
**United States Notes.** Promissory notes issued by the U.S. government intended to circulate as money and with the national bank notes to constitute the credit currency of the country.
**Unity of Interest.** The identity of the interest of joint tenants with respect to the property which is subject to the tenancy.
**Unity of Possession.** Joint possession of two rights in the same property, one dependent upon the other.
**Unity of Time.** That essential aspect of joint tenancy, that the estates of the joint tenants be vested at one and the same time.
**Unity of Title.** That essential aspect of joint tenancy, that the estates of the joint tenants be created by one and the same act.
**Universal.** That which pertains to all without exception.
**Universal Agent.** One authorized to transact all of his principal's business.
**Universal Legacy.** A legacy which beqneaths all of the decedent's property.
**Universal Partnership.** Partnership in which each partner contributes all of his property.
**Universites.** Corporation.
**Universitas Bonorum.** All of a person's goods or estate.
**Universitas Juris.** A quantity of things which for legal purposes may be treated as a whole.
**Universum Jus.** Sole ownership.
**Universus.** Whole; entire.
**Unjust.** Contrary to right and justice.
**Unjust Enrichment.** Principle that one should not profit inequitably at another's expense.
**Unkerjay.** Morphine addict.
**Unlawful** That which is contrary to the law; wrong.
**Unlawful ab Inirio.** Unlawful from the beginning.
**Unlawful Act.** Act contrary to law.
**Unlawful Assembly.** Meeting of three or more persons for an unlawful purpose by force or violence.
**Unlawful Cohabitation.** The living together as husband and wife of two persons not married to each other.
**Unlawful Combination.** Agreement with tendency to restrain trade, inhibit competition, or create a monopoly.
**Unlawful Conspiracy.** Two or more persons acting together in a criminal transaction.
**Unlawful Contract.** Agreement calling for performance of acts prohibited by law.
**Unlawful Detainer.** Refusal to grant possession to property being unlawfully held.
**Unlawful Entry.** Peaceful entry upon lands by means of fraud or willful wrong.
**Unlimited.** Unrestricted.
**Unliquidated.** Unsettled or unassessed.
**Unmarried.** Not having husband or wife; single; never married.
**Unnatural Offense.** Crime against nature, i.e. sodomy.
**Uno Actu.** By a single act.
**Uno Flatu.** In one breath.
**Unprecedented.** New; no prior example.
**Unques.** Always; ever; still.
**Unques Prist.** Always ready.
**Unrestricted.** Absolute; without limits or conditions.
**Unsafe.** Dangerous; applied to a bank, insolvent.
**Unseated.** Unsettled; uncultivated.
**Unseaworthy.** Vessel incapable of withstanding dangers of sea.
**Unsolemn War.** War without formal declaration.
**Unsound Mind** Person incapable of handling own affairs due to infirmity of mind.
**Untenantable.** Unfit for occupacy.
**Unthrift.** A spendthrift.
**Unwritten Law.** Customs, mores; principles accepted without enactment; common law.
**Uplands.** Lands bordering on waters.
**Urban.** Referring to city or town.
**Ure.** Practice; effect.
**User.** Exercise or enjoyment of a right or property.
**Uso.** Usage.
**Usque.** Until; up to.
**Usufruct.** Enjoying property not belonging to user as long as nature of property is not altered.
**Usura.** Interest on money borrowed.
**Usura Manifesta.** Open usury.
**Usurare.** To pay interest.
**Usura Velata.** Concealed usury.
**Usurp.** To unlawfully seize and hold by force.
**Usurpation.** To unlawfully assume possession of the property of another.
**Usury.** Illegal rate of interest.
**Usus.** Use.
**Usus Fori.** The practice of the court.
**Ut.** That; so that; as.
**Ut Audivi.** As I have heard.
**Ut Credo.** As I believe.
**Uterine.** Applied to children born of the same mother.
**Utero Gestation.** Pregnancy.
**Utilis.** Useful; profitable.
**Utility.** Industrial value; capable of use.
**Utmost Care.** Highest or greatest care.
**Ut Supra.** As above.
**Utter.** To publish or put in circulation; entrice; complete.
**Uxor.** Wife.
**Uxorcide.** Killing of one's own wife.

## V

**V.** (Abb.). Versus.
**Vacant.** Empty; without inanimate objects.
**Vacantia Bona.** Goods without an owner or claimant and which may be held by the first occupant or finder.
**Vacate.** To leave empty; to annul or cancel.
**Vacatio.** An immunity; an exemption.
**Vacation.** Time between court terms.
**Vacation of Judgment.** Setting aside of a judgment.
**Vacatur.** Let it be vacated.
**Vaccination.** Innoculation with vaccine for purposes of immunization.
**Vacuity.** Vacancy.
**Vacuus.** Empty; void.
**Vadari.** To give bail.
**Vades.** Pledges; sureties; bail.
**Vadiari.** To wage; to give security.
**Vadiare Legem.** To wage law.
**Vadium.** A pledge.
**Vadium Mortuum.** A mortgage or "dead pledge".
**Vagabond.** Vagrant; tramp.

**Vagrant.** Person without visible means of support or of fixed residence.
**Vague.** Indefinite.
**Vale.** A promissory note.
**Valentia.** Value or price of a thing.
**Valid.** Having legal effect; operative; not void.
**Validate.** To make valid; to confirm.
**Validating Statute.** Statute which cures or makes valid past transactions.
**Validity.** Legal effectiveness.
**Valuable.** Of financial value; estimable.
**Valuable Consideration.** A class of consideration in which some right, interest or profit may accrue to one party, or some detriment or loss to the other party.
**Valuation.** Estimated worth of a thing.
**Value.** The utility or worth of a thing.
**Valued Policy.** Insurance policy which states the value of the thing insured.
**Valuer.** Appraiser.
**Value Received.** Phrase used in negotiable instruments to indicate that a lawful consideration has been given for it.
**Variance.** A material difference; any substantial difference between the allegations of a pleading and the evidence addressed to sustain it.
**Various.** Separate.
**Vary.** To change to something else.
**Vas.** A surety or pledge.
**Vasectomy.** Surgical operation for the purpose of sterilization.
**Vastitas.** Wasteland.
**Vauderie.** Witchcraft.
**Vectura.** Freight.
**Vehicle.** That which is used for transportation.
**Vel.** Whether; or.
**Velle.** To consent.
**Vel Non.** Or not.
**Vend.** To transfer title for a monetary consideration.
**Vendee.** Purchaser.
**Vender.** To sell; vendor.
**Vendetta.** Private blood feud.
**Vendition.** A sale.
**Venditor.** A seller or vendor.
**Vendor.** One who transfers property by sale.
**Vendor's Lien.** Right of the vendor to retain possession of goods until their price has been paid.
**Vendue.** Sale; auction.
**Veneral.** Sexual.
**Venereal Disease.** Disease associated with sexual intercourse.
**Venire.** To come; to appear in court.
**Venireman.** One summoned as a juror.
**Venit et Dicit.** Comes and says.
**Venture.** To take chances; a risky undertaking.
**Venue.** Neighborhood; area in which an injury is claimed to have occurred; geographical unit in which a trial court has jurisdiction.
**Veracity.** Truth; honesty.
**Vera Copula.** True and natural intercourse.
**Veray.** True.
**Verba.** Words.
**Verbal.** In words; by word of mouth.
**Verbal Act.** That which a person says or writes.
**Verba Precaria.** Precatory words.
**Verba Sunt Indices Animi.** Words are the indexes of the mind.
**Verdict.** Decision of the jury.
**Verdict Against Evidence.** Verdict contrary to the evidence.
**Verdicto Non Obstante.** Notwithstanding the verdict.
**Verification.** Confirmation.
**Verify.** To confirm by oath.
**Verily.** Beyond doubt; really.
**Veritas.** Truth; correctness.
**Veritatem Dicere.** To speak the truth.
**Versari.** To be employed; to be conversant with.
**Versus.** Against; vs. (Abb.).
**Verus.** Genuine.
**Vessel.** Ship..
**Vest.** To give immediate right of present or future enjoyment; to give possession; to give power or authority.
**Vested.** An unconditional right to property.
**Vested Interest.** A fixed, present right or title to a thing which carries an existing right of alienation.
**Vested Legacy.** A legacy which is given to be paid at a future time.
**Vested Remainder.** An interest in real property to be enjoyed at a future time, with no other condition imposed other than the determination of the precedent estate.
**Vestigium.** A vestage or trace.
**Vestimentum.** Investitute; seisin.
**Vestire.** To vest.
**Veteran's Preference.** Preference given to honorably discharged veterans by the civil service.
**Vetitio Principii.** A begging of the question.
**Veto.** I forbid; refusal of assent by an executive officer.
**Veto Power.** Constitutional power of the President and most Governors to prevent acts of Legislature from becoming law.
**Vetustas.** Antiquity.
**Vexatae Quaestiones.** Moot questions.
**Vi.** By force or violence.
**Via.** Way; road.
**Via Alta.** Highway.
**Via Amicabili.** In a friendly way.
**Viability.** Ability of the newborn to live.
**Viaggio, Viagium.** A voyage.
**Via Publica.** A public road.
**Vi aut Clam.** By force or fraud.
**Vicarious.** Through an agent or representative.
**Vice.** Fault; defect; imperfection; in place of; as a substitute for, e.g. vice-president.
**Vice Versa.** On the contrary; the other way around.
**Vicinage.** Vicinity; neighborhood.
**Vicious.** Wicked; harmful.
**Vi Clam aut Precario.** Forcible, secretly or by sufferance.
**Victuals.** Food prepared to eat.
**Victus.** Means of support; the vanquished.
**Vicus.** Village.
**Vide.** See; refer to.
**Videlicet.** That is to say; to wit; namely.
**Vidimus.** We have seen.
**Vidua.** A widow.
**Viduity.** Widowhood.
**Vi et Armis.** Force and arms.
**View.** The taking of the jury to the place where an event is alleged to have happened.
**Vigilia.** Vigil; watch.
**Vigilance.** Watchfulness; precaution.
**Vigore Cujus.** By the force of which.
**Vill.** Village.
**Village.** A community of limited area and population, smaller than a city or town.
**Villein.** Serf attached to the soil.
**Vinculum.** Chain; bond.
**Vinculum Matrimonii.** Bond of marriage.
**Vindex.** A defender.
**Vindicare.** To claim or challenge.
**Vindictive Damages.** Punitive or exemplary damages.
**Vinous.** Alcoholic.
**Vintner.** Wine seller.
**Vinum.** Wine.
**Violate.** To disobey a law; to force; to rape.
**Violence.** Force.
**Virtue.** Effect; chastity.
**Virtuous.** Pure.
**Virilia.** The testicles.
**Viripotens.** Capable of sexual intercourse.
**Virtuate Cujus.** By virtue of which.
**Virtute Officii.** By virtue of his office.
**Vis.** Force; violence.
**Visa.** Indorsement on a passport allowing the holder to enter a foreign state.
**Vis Armata.** An armed force.
**Vis Divina.** Divine force.
**Vise.** To certify that a document has been examined and found to be correct.
**Vis et Metus.** Force and fear.
**Visible.** Noticeable; apparent.
**Vis Impressa.** Force directly applied.
**Visitation.** Inspection; superintendence.
**Vis Laica.** A lay force.
**Vis Major.** An act of God.
**Visores.** Viewers.
**Visus.** A view.
**Vita.** Life.
**Vital Statistics.** Statistics relating primarily to the subject of health, usually including the registration of births, deaths and marriages.
**Vitium.** Vice; error.
**Vitium Clerici.** Clerical mistake.
**Viva Voce.** The living voice; by word of mouth.

**Vix.** Scarcely; with difficulty.
**Viz.** (Abb.). Videlicet; that is to say; to wit; namely.
**Vocabula Artis.** Technical terms.
**Vocans.** A voucher.
**Vocare.** To call or summon.
**Vocation.** Calling; occupation.
**Vociferatio.** Hue and cry.
**Vociferous.** Noisy; clamerous.
**Void.** Wholly without effect.
**Voidable.** Able to be nullified.
**Voidance.** A vacancy.
**Void Tax.** Tax which never had any effect.
**Voir Dire.** To speak the truth.
**Volo.** I will.
**Volstead Act.** National Prohibition Act of 1919.
**Voluntarily.** Willingly.
**Voluntary.** Intentional.
**Voluntary Association.** An organization not constituted as a legal entity.
**Voluntary Bankruptcy.** Bankruptcy proceeding brought by the bankrupt.
**Voluntary Deed.** Deed executed without consideration.
**Voluntary Manslaughter.** Intentional killing of a person under the influence of sudden passion, but without malice.
**Voluntary Waste.** Intentional and deliberate waste committed by a tenant.
**Voluntas.** Volition, purpose or intention.
**Volunteer.** One who freely gives of his services.
**Vote.** Suffrage; choice.
**Voter.** An elector; one possessing the legal qualifications to vote.
**Voting Trust.** A trust in which the shares of stock belonging to various stockholders are transferred to a trustee who has the power to cast votes for the stockholders in the various corporations which have issued the stock.
**Votum.** Vow; promise.
**Vouch.** To call upon; to call in to warranty; to quote as an authority; to request a warrantor to defend a grantee's title.
**Vouchee.** Person called or summoned; one for whom another vouches.
**Voucher.** A receipt or release discharging a person or giving evidence of payment of a debt.
**Vouch to Warranty.** To call a person, under a warranty title, to defend a suit in which the voucher's title is attacked.
**Vox Dei.** Voice of God.
**Voyage Policy.** Policy insuring a ship's voyage on a specific course.
**Vs.** (Abb.). Versus.
**Vulgo Concepti.** Bastards.

## W

**Wager.** Bet.
**Wagering Contract.** Gambling contract.
**Wager of Law of Nonsummons.** A form of plea in real action.
**Wager Policy.** An insurance policy wherein the person insured has no interest in the subject matter.
**Wages.** Compensation for manual labor.
**Waifs.** Goods found, but claimed by nobody.
**Waive.** To abandon or throw away; to surrender a claim or privilege voluntarily.
**Waiver.** Intentional relinquishment of a right or privilege.
**Want of Issue.** Having no children.
**Wanton.** Wilful; reckless; unrestrained; wicked.
**Wanton Act.** An act performed with reckless disregard for the rights of others.
**Wanton Injury.** Injury inflicted by conscious and intentional wrongful act or omission of duty with flagrant disregard for consequences.
**War.** Mutual hostility between two nations carried on by armed forces.
**Warantia.** Warranty; guaranty.
**Warantus.** Warrantor.
**Ward.** A minor under care of a guardian municipal district.
**Warda.** A ward; guard.
**Warden.** Guardian; prison superintendent.
**Warehouse.** Place for storage of goods.
**Warentare.** To warrant; to guarantee.
**Wares.** Goods and merchandise.
**Warrant.** Judicial writ authorizing the arrest of a person or the seizure of property; authorization for a policeman to search the premises of a private citizen; to defend; to guarantee.
**Warantee.** One to whom a warranty is made.
**Warrant in Deed.** A written warrant under seal.
**Warrant in Law.** Authority of law.
**Warrant Officer.** Noncommissioned officer of U.S. Navy.
**Warrantor.** Maker of a warranty.
**Warranty.** A promise or guaranty that a proposition of fact is true; a collateral undertaking in the sale of real or personal property whereby one party promises another to indemnify or make good any defect in the contemplation of the parties; a provision in an insurance policy making certain statements about the person or thing insured or about the risk insured.
**Warranty of Goods.** Warranty that goods are of a specified quality.
**Warranty of Title.** A warranty that title to property sold is good.
**Warren.** Game preserve.
**Wash Sale.** The operation of simultaneously buying and selling the same stock.
**Wasserman Test.** Test for syphilis.
**Waste.** Destruction or abuse of property.
**Wastors.** Thieves.
**Water Company.** A public utility to supply water to the inhabitants of a municipality.
**Watered Stock.** Stock of a corporation issued as paid in full, whereas the cash or property value of the stock has not in fact been received by the corporation in exchange.
**Water Right.** Right to the use of water from a running stream.
**Waterscape.** Aqueduct.
**Way.** Right of passage.
**Way-Bill.** List of passengers or freight transported by a common carrier.
**Wayfarer.** Traveler.
**Ways and Means Committee.** Committee of a legislative body which determines how necessary revenues are to be raised.
**Weapon.** Combat instrument.
**Wedlock.** Matrimoney.
**Week.** Period of seven days.
**Weight.** Measure of heaviness.
**Weight of Evidence.** Valuation made of the credibility of evidence based on its quality; the preponderance of evidence.
**Welfare.** State or condition of well-being.
**Welsh Mortgage.** Mortgage whereby the rents and profits of the mortgaged property go to the creditor until the debt is paid.
**Wharf.** Place for the loading and unloading of ships.
**Wharfage.** Charge for use of a wharf.
**When.** At the time that; at what time.
**Whereby.** By or through which.
**Whiteacre.** Term used to distinguish one parcel of land from another, particularly in moot cases.
**White Person.** Caucasian.
**White Slavery.** The procurement and transportation of women across state lines for immoral purposes.
**Whole.** Hearty; strong.
**Whole Blood.** Relationship of children who have the same parents.
**Wholesale.** Selling to retailers rather than consumers.
**Wholesale Price.** Price paid by the retailer.
**Wholly.** Entirely.
**Whore.** Woman who practices illicit sexual intercourse; prostitute.
**Wick.** Town; village.
**Widow.** Woman who survives her husband.
**Widower.** Man who survives his wife.
**Wife.** Woman who has a living husband.
**Wild Land.** Land in its natural state.
**Wilful.** Intentional; deliberate.
**Wilful Desertion.** In divorce, unjustifiable refusal to maintain the family relationship.
**Will.** Directions for the disposal of one's property after death.
**Winding Up.** Dissolution of a corporation or partnership.
**Wire Tapping.** Unauthorized interception of telephone conversations.
**Wit.** To know.

**Wit.** (Abb.). Witness.
**With Child.** Pregnant.
**Withdrawal.** Removal of money or securities from a bank.
**Withold.** To keep in one's possession that which is sought or claimed by another; to conceal.
**Without Day.** Without naming a special day.
**Without Impeachment of Waste.** Without liability for the commission of waste.
**Without Notice.** In good faith.
**With Strong Hand.** With force.
**Witness.** One called to give testimony under oath; one present at a transaction; one who attests the genuineness of a document by offering his signature thereto.
**Wittingly.** With knowledge and by design.
**Wolf's Head.** Outlaw.
**Woman Suffrage.** Right of women to vote and participate in government.
**Woods.** Forest; land covered by trees.
**Words, Act for.** An action of slander.
**Words Actionable in Themselves.** Language from which the law would presume damage.
**Words of Art.** Words having a special or technical meaning.
**Words of Limitation.** Words used to define the character of an interest granted.
**Words of Procreation.** Words necessary to create an estate-tail.
**Work.** To put forth effort for a particular purpose.
**Workhouse.** Place where prisoners convicted of minor offenses are confined and kept at labor.
**Working Capital.** Cash or quick assets.
**Workman.** One who labors.
**Workmen's Compensation Acts.** Statutes which protect the working man and give security against injury and death occurring during the course of employment.
**Works.** An establishment for performing industrial labor.
**World.** All those who have an interest in the subject matter.
**Worship.** Paying respect to the Divine Being.
**Worth.** The quality of a thing, giving it value.
**Worthless.** Having no value.
**Worthy.** Having merit or value.
**Wound.** A physical injury which breaks the skin.
**Wreck.** To destroy or damage; unclaimed goods cast upon the shore by the sea; ship damaged so that it cannot be navigated.
**Writ.** Mandatory precept issued by a court of justice; a court order directing a party to do a specific act, usually to appear in or report to court.
**Writing.** Expression of ideas in visible form.
**Writing Obligatory.** A bond.
**Writ of Attachment.** A writ used to enforce a court order or judgment.
**Writ of Covenant.** Writ to recover damages for breach of a covenant.
**Writ of Debt.** Writ for recovery of a debt.
**Writ of Delivery.** A writ of execution to enforce a judgment for the delivery of chattels.
**Writ of Entry.** A real property possessory action to recover possession of property of which the claimant was wrongfully dispossessed.
**Writ of Error.** A writ used to review the judgment of an inferior court.
**Writ of Error Coram Nobis.** Writ of error used to correct errors of fact.
**Writ of Execution.** Writ to enforce the judgment of a court.
**Writ of Injunction.** A restraining or preventive court order.
**Writ of Mandamus.** A writ to compel the performance of an act.
**Writ of Mandate.** See Writ of Mandamus.
**Writ of Possession.** Writ of execution for the recovery of possession of land.
**Writ of Prevention.** Writ to prohibit filing of a suit.
**Writ of Review.** Writ to bring up for review the record or decision of an inferior court.
**Writ of Right.** Writ to recover real property.
**Written Contract.** A contract in writing signed by the parties involved.
**Written Law.** Statute law.
**Wrong.** Violation of a legal right; a legal injury; a tort.
**Wrongful.** Injurious; reckless; unfair.

## X

**X.** Symbol of the word "by"; symbol used by those who cannot write.
**X-Ray Photographs.** Photographs of the interior body which may be submitted as evidence.

## Y

**Yacht.** Pleasure boat.
**Yard.** Measure of three feet or thirty-six inches.
**Yea or Nay.** Yes and No.
**Year.** 365 days; leap year, 366 days.
**Year and a Day.** Period of limitation in which the right to seize and sell land under a judgment must be exercised.
**Year of Our Lord.** The beginning of the Christian era.
**Yeas and Nays.** The affirmative and negative votes on a bill or proposal.
**Yellow Dog Contract.** Contract between an employer and employee whereby the employee promises not to join a labor union.
**Yen Pock.** Opium pill.
**Yield.** Proceeds or returns from an investment; to produce; to earn; to perform; to resign or surrender.
**Yielding and Paying.** In conveyancing, the words which create the agreement to pay rent.

## Z

**Zealous Witness.** One who shows partiality for the side calling him.
**Zetetick.** Proceeding by inquiry.
**Zone.** An area restricted by municipal regulation to certain purposes, i.e. residental, industrial or commercial.

# Medical Dictionary

# Medical Dictionary

## — A —

**Abacterial,** sterile, free of bacteria.

**Abalienation,** mental derangement.

**Abarognosis,** loss of sense of weight

**Abarticular,** not affecting a joint.

**Abarticulation,** dislocation.

**Abasia,** unable to walk because of loss of motor coordination.

**Abatement,** lessening of pain.

**A.B.C. Process,** purifying water or sewage by use of alum, blood and charcoal.

**Abdomen,** area of body between diaphragm and pelvic bones.

**Abdominal,** pertaining to the abdomen.

**Abduce,** abduct.

**Abduct,** movement of an extremity away from the body or of a part from the middle of the whole.

**Aberration,** different from normal action.

**Abevacuation,** incomplete evacuation.

**Abeyance,** condition of suspended activity.

**Abiology,** study of nonliving things.

**Abionarce,** insanity due to infirmity.

**Abiosis,** absence of life.

**Abirritant,** soothing.

**Ablactation,** weaning.

**Ablation,** removal.

**Ablepsia,** blindness.

**Ablucent,** detergent.

**Ablution,** a washing.

**Abnormal,** not normal.

**Aborad,** away from the mouth.

**Abortion,** termination of pregnancy before the child is able to exist outside the womb.

**Abrachia,** congenital absence of arms.

**Abrade,** chafe, roughen.

**Abrasion,** any injury which rubs off the surface skin.

**Abscess,** collection of pus enclosed anywhere in the body.

**Abscission,** surgical removal of a growth.

**Absorb,** to seep in.

**Abstract,** to take away from.

**Abtorsion,** turning outward of both eyes.

**Abutment,** anchorage tooth for a bridge.

**Acampsia,** rigidity of a part or limb.

**Acapnia,** decrease in carbon dioxide in the blood.

**Acarbia,** decrease of bicarbonate in the blood.

**Acarid,** tick, mite.

**Acathexia,** inability to retain bodily secretions.

**Acceleration,** increase the motion or speed.

**Accident,** unpleasant, unexpected happening.

**Acclimatize,** to get used to a climate.

**Accommodation,** adjustment.

**Accouchement,** act of being delivered.

**Accretion,** accumulation of matter at a part.

**Acedia,** mental depression.

**Acephalous,** headless.

**Acescence,** sour.

**Acetabulum,** hollow area in the hip bone in which thigh bone fits.

**Acetate,** salt of acetic acid.

**Acetic,** sour like vinegar.

**Acetone,** a colorless, inflammable solvent.

**Acetychlorine,** hormone secreted by the nervous system.

**Achalasia,** inability of certain hollow, muscular organs to contract.

**Achilles Tendon,** the tendon at the back of the heel.

**Achlorhydria,** inability of the stomach wall to manufacture hydrochloric acid.

**Achondroplasia,** form of dwarfism in which the trunk is of normal size, the limbs are too short.

**Achor,** small skin elevation on hairy parts of body.

**Achromyan,** antibiotic.

**Achoresis,** diminution of the capacity of an organ.

**Achroma,** absence of color.

**Achylia,** absence of chyle, an emulsion of fat globules formed in the intestine.

**Acicular,** needle-shaped.

**Acid,** a sour substance that combines with metals, releasing hydrogen.

**Acid-forming,** applied to foods, which when digested, leave a residue that is acid.

**Acidosis,** condition in some diseases which causes more acid in the blood than normal.

**Acidity,** excess of the hydrochloric acid normally found in the stomach.

**Acme,** crisis

**Acne,** skin condition found usually in adolescents in which glands of skin become infected.

**Acneform,** resembling acne.

**Acoria,** insatiable appetite.

**Acousma**, hearing imaginary sounds.
**Acoustic**, relating to sound or hearing.
**Acquired**, obtained after birth.
**Acral**, affecting the extremities.
**Acrid**, irritating.
**Acroarthritis**, arthritis of the extremities.
**Acromegaly**, gigantism; state of excessive growth of the body caused by overactivity of the pituitary gland.
**Acronyx**, ingrowing nail.
**Acropathy**, disease of the extremities.
**Acrophobia**, fear of great heights.
**Acrosphacelus**, gangrene of the fingers or toes.
**Acrotism**, pulse defect.
**A. C. T. H.**, Adreno-Cortico-Tropic-Hormone; hormone that stimulates one part of the adrenal gland.
**Actinic**, applies to those rays of sunlight beyond the violet end of the spectrum, which produce chemical change.
**Actinomycosis**, disease of cattle that can be transmitted to man.
**Acuity**, sharpness, clearness.
**Acute**, illness which had a sudden beginning, a short course and severe symptoms.
**Acyesis**, female sterility.
**Addiment**, complement.
**Addison's Disease**, condition in which adrenal glands are underactive.
**Adduct**, movement of an extremity toward the body or parts toward the midline of the body.
**Adenalgia**, pain in a gland.
**Adenase**, enzyme.
**Adenitis**, inflammation of a gland.
**Adenoidectomy**, surgical removal of the adenoids.
**Adenoids**, lymph glands in back of nasal passage which function to trap germs and debris.
**Adenoma**, tumor consisting of glandular material.
**Adenopathy**, any disease of the glands.
**Adhesions**, abnormal growing together of tissue following injury or operation.
**Adiaphanous**, opaque.
**Adicity**, valance.
**Adipose**, fatty.
**Adiposity**, obesity.
**Adjuvant**, an auxiliary agent or medication.
**Adneural**, toward a nerve.
**Adnexa**, appendages or accessory parts of an organ.
**Adrenal Gland**, small gland immediately above each of the two kidneys.
**Adrenalin**, hormone secreted by the adrenal gland, with many properties.
**Adtorsion**, turning inward of both eyes.
**Adult**, fully developed.
**Adventitious**, accidental or acquired; pertaining to the tough outer coat of an organ or blood vessel; occurring in unusual places.
**Aeriform**, gaseous.
**Aeropathy**, decompression sickness.
**Afebrile**, without fever.
**Affect**, feeling, mood.
**Afferent**, conducting toward a center.
**Affinity**, attraction.
**Afterbirth**, material from womb after childbirth.
**Agalactia**, absence of milk secretion.
**Agar**, form of seaweed used in treating constipation.
**Agenesia**, sterility; imperfect development.
**Ageusia**, lack of sense of taste.
**Agitation**, restlessness; mental illness.
**Aglutition**, inability to swallow.
**Aglycemia**, lack of sugar in the blood.
**Agnogenic**, of unknown origin.
**Agnosia**, inability to perceive things.
**Agonad**, person having no sex glands.
**Agony**, extreme pain.
**Agorophobia**, extreme fear of open places.
**Ague**, an old-fashioned name for malaria or other fevers.
**Ahypnia**, insomnia.
**Air**, the gaseous mixture which constitutes the atmosphere.
**Air-sickness**, sickness caused by high altitudes and motion during air travel.
**Airway**, instrument used to keep breathing passages open.
**Akalamathesia**, inability to understand.
**Alae Nasi**, nostril openings.
**Alalia**, speech impairment.
**Alba**, white.
**Albinism**, absence of pigmentation.
**Albino**, lack of pigment in the skin.
**Albumen**, protein.
**Albuminuria**, albumin in urine.
**Alcoholism**, drunkenness.
**Alexia**, unable to read.
**Algesia**, sensitivity to pain.
**Algid**, cold.
**Algogenic**, causing pain; lowering temperature.
**Algophobia**, extreme fear of pain.
**Alienist**, psychiatrist.
**Alimentary**, pertaining to nutrition.
**Alimentation**, act of nutrition.
**Alkalosis**, an excess of alkaline in the body and blood stream.
**Allergen**, that which produces an allergic reaction.
**Allergist**, specialist in allergies.

**Allergy,** abnormal sensitivity to any substance.
**Allochroism,** variation in color.
**Allodromy,** irregular heart rhythm.
**Aloe,** vegetable used as a laxative.
**Alogia,** inability to form words; senseless behavior.
**Alopecia,** baldness.
**Alvine,** pertaining to the belly.
**Amaurosis,** blindness.
**Ambidextrous,** proficient with each hand.
**Amblyacusia,** dullness of hearing.
**Amblyopia,** dimness of vision due to errors of refraction.
**Ambulatory,** able to walk.
**Ambustion,** burn, scald.
**Amenia,** amenorrhea.
**Amenorrhea,** stoppage of normal menstrual periods.
**Amentia,** mental impairment.
**Amino Acids,** a chemical radical in all proteins.
**Amnesia,** loss of memory.
**Amorphous,** shapeless.
**Ampule,** container for hypodermic solutions.
**Ampulla,** widened end of a small passageway.
**Amputation,** removal of a limb or appendage.
**Amyasthenic,** muscular weakness.
**Amyloid,** starchlike.
**Amylophagia,** Eating of starch.
**Amylum,** starch.
**Amyotonia,** flaccidity of muscles.
**Amyotrophic Lateral Sclerosis,** a disease causing paralysis because of degeneration of spinal cord.
**Amyxia,** absence of mucus.
**Ana,** of each.
**Anadipsia,** intense thirst.
**Anal,** pertaining to the anus.
**Analygesia,** lack of feeling any pain. [pain.
**Analgesic,** drug used to relieve
**Analysand,** one undergoing psychoanalysis.
**Anamnesis,** patient's history.
**Anandria,** absence of male characteristics.
**Anemic,** pertaining to anemia.
**Anmeophobia,** extreme fear of winds and draughts.
**Anepia,** inability to speak.
**Anesthesia,** loss of sensation.
**Anesthesiology,** study and administration of anesthetics.
**Anesthetic,** drug or gas used to abolish pain.
**Aneuria,** deficiency of nervous energy.
**Anaphia,** lack of sense of touch.
**Anaphrodisia,** loss of sexual desire.
**Anastattis,** highly astringent.
**Anastole,** retraction.
**Anatomy,** science which deals with the structure of the body.
**Ancipital,** two-edged.
**Anconal,** pertaining to the elbow.
**Androcyte,** spermatid.
**Androphobia,** fear of men.
**Anemia,** condition in which the normal amount of red blood cells is reduced.
**Aneurysm,** swelling in a blood-vessel arising from the stretching of a weak place in the wall.
**Anfractuous,** convoluted.
**Angina Pectoris,** severe attacks of pain over the heart.
**Angitis,** inflammation of a vessel.
**Anhelation,** shortness of breath.
**Anhematosis,** defective blood formation.
**Anhydrous,** containing no water.
**Anhypnosis,** insomnia.
**Anility,** like an old woman.
**Animation,** liveliness.
**Anisomastia,** inequality of the breasts.
**Ankle,** region between the foot and lower leg.
**Ankylosis,** partial or complete rigidity of a joint produced either by disease, such as arthritis, or deliberately, by surgical operation.
**Ankyroid,** hooklike.
**Annectent,** connecting.
**Annular,** ring-shaped.
**Annulus,** circular opening.
**Anodyne,** pain reliever.
**Anoia,** idiocy.
**Anomaly,** abnormality.
**Anopsia,** defective vision.
**Anorchism,** absence of testes.
**Anorexia,** loss of appetite.
**Anoscope,** instrument used for rectal examination.
**Anoscopy,** examination of the anus.
**Anosmia,** lack of sense of smell.
**Anostosis,** defective formation of bone.
**Anoxemia,** reduction in the normal amount of oxygen in the blood.
**Anoxia,** insufficient supply of oxygen.
**Ansa,** looplike structure.
**Antabuse,** proprietary drug used in the treatment of alcoholism.
**Antacid,** substance that neutralizes acids.
**Antebrachium,** forearm.
**Antemortem,** before death.
**Antenatal,** before birth.
**Ante-Partum,** before maternal delivery.
**Anterior,** before.
**Anteversion,** forward displacement of part of the body, particularly the womb.
**Anthelmintic,** drugs used to rid the body of worms.
**Anthophobia,** extreme dislike of flowers.
**Anthorisma,** swelling.
**Anthracosis,** inflammation of the

lungs due to inhalation of carbon dust.

**Anthrax,** disease of man from animals; two forms exist, one on skin and other in lungs.

**Antianemic Principle,** substance which counteracts anemia.

**Antiarthritic,** that which relieves or cures arthritis.

**Antibechic,** relieving cough.

**Antibiotics,** the group of drugs usually prepared from molds or mold-like organisms, which are used in treatment of specific infections.

**Antibody,** a protein produced by body which reacts specificially with a foreign substance in the body.

**Antibromic,** deodorant.

**Anticoagulants,** a group of drugs which reduce the clotting tendencies of the blood.

**Anticus,** anterior.

**Antidote,** remedy given to counteract a poison.

**Antiemetic,** remedy to prevent vomiting.

**Antigen,** any protein not normally present in the body and which stimulates the body to produce antibodies.

**Antihistamine Drugs,** a series of drugs used in the treatment of allergy.

**Antilemic,** counteracting plague.

**Antipathic,** opposite in nature.

**Antipathy,** dislike.

**Antipyretic,** anything that reduces fever.

**Antirabic,** counteracting rabies.

**Antiseptic,** substance used to inhibit growth or destroy germs.

**Anti-Toxin,** substance manufactured by the blood, which specifically neutralizes the poison (toxin) given off by a particular germ.

**Antixerotic,** preventing dryness.

**Antrum,** space within a bone, usually that in the maxilla or upper jaw.

**Anuria,** absence of urine flow.

**Anus,** outlet of the bowel.

**Anxietas,** anxiety, worry.

**Aorta,** main artery leaving the heart.

**Aortitis,** inflammation of the aorta.

**Aortits,** inflammation of the aorta.

**Apandria,** dislike of men.

**Apanthropy,** dislike of human society.

**Apathic,** not having sensation.

**Aperient,** mild laxative.

**Aperture,** .opening.

**Aphagia,** inability to swallow.

**Aphakia,** absence of a lens behind the pupil of the eye.

**Aphasia,** inability to form words.

**Aphephobia,** fear of being touched.

**Aphonia,** inability to speak.

**Aphrodisiac,** drug which produces sexual excitement.

**Aphtha,** white spot.

**Apogee,** state of greatest severity of a disease.

**Apoplexy,** condition which is the result of decreased blood flow to part of brain, also called stroke.

**Apostasis,** abscess.

**Apothecary,** druggist.

**Appendage,** outgrowth.

**Appendectomy,** surgical removal of the appendix.

**Appendicitis,** inflammation of the appendix.

**Appendix,** fingerlike projection from the large intestine with no known function.

**Appetite,** desire for food.

**Applicator,** instrument used to make local application of medicine.

**Approximal,** close.

**Apsychia,** unconsciousness.

**Aptyalism,** lack of saliva

**Aqua,** water.

**Aqueous,** watery.

**Arachnephobia,** extreme fear of spiders.

**Arachnidism,** condition resulting from spider bite.

**Arachnoid,** fine, thin tissue.

**Arcate,** curved

**Archepyon,** very thick pus.

**Arenoid,** like sand.

**Areola,** ring of color around a particular point, e.g., the nipple.

**Argentic,** containing silver.

**Ariboflavinosis,** deficiency of riboflavin.

**Arm,** region from shoulder to elbow.

**Armamentarium,** doctor's entire equipment.

**Arrest,** stopping; restraining.

**Arrhenic,** pertaining to arsenic.

**Arrhythmia,** disturbance of normal rhythm.

**Arrowroot,** nutrient starch.

**Arsenic,** poisonous chemical element.

**Arteria,** artery.

**Arteriole,** smallest sized artery.

**Arterioplasty,** operation in which the artery is reconstructed.

**Arteriosclerosis,** condition in which arteries of body become thickened and inelastic.

**Arteriostenosis,** constiction of an artery.

**Arteristis, inflammation of an artery.**

**Artery,** vessel which carries blood away from the heart.

**Arthralgia,** pain in a joint.

**Arthrifuge,** remedy for gout.

**Arthritis,** inflammation of one or more joints.

**Arthrocace,** ulceration of a joint.

**Arthronosos,** any joint disease.

**Arthropathy,** any joint disease.

**Arthrophyma,** joint swelling.

**Arthroplasty,** an operation upon a joint to make it function.

**Arthrosclerosis,** stiffening of the joints.

**Articulation,** enunciation of speech; a joint.
**Artificial,** not natural.
**Artificial Respiration,** the act of restoring breathing, the best method being mouth to mouth respiration.
**Asbestosis,** lung disease occurring in those who inhale asbestos or asbestos-like material.
**Ascariasis,** invasion of the body by roundworms.
**Ascites** (Dropsy), an accumulation of body fluid in the abdomen.
**Asepsis,** absence of infected material or infection.
**Asexual,** without sex.
**Asexualization,** castration.
**Asiderosis,** iron deficiency.
**Asitia,** dislike of food.
**Aspermatism,** nonformation of sperm.
**Asphyxia,** stoppage of breathing due to obstruction of the air passages.
**Aspirator,** instrument for withdrawing fluids by suction.
**Aspirin,** Acetylsalicylic acid, commonly used to relieve headache.
**Assay,** examine.
**Asteroid,** shaped like a star.
**Asthenia,** lack or loss of strength.
**Asthma,** condition of lungs characterized by decrease in diameter of some air passages.
**Astigmatism,** a defect of eyesight caused by uneven curvature of the outside membrane of the eye.
**Astringent,** that which causes contraction and stops discharges.
**Asynergy,** lack of coordination.
**Atactitia,** loss of the sense of touch.
**Ataxia,** loss of co-ordinated movement caused by disease of the nervous system.
**Atheroma,** hardening of the arteries.
**Atherosclerosis,** form of hardening of the arteries.
**Athetosis,** repetitive, involuntary, slow movements.
**Athlete's Foot,** fungus infection of the foot.
**Athrombia,** defective blood clotting.
**Atlas,** topmost vertebra in the spinal column.
**Atocia,** sterility in the female.
**Atomization,** breaking up of a liquid into a fine spray.
**Atony,** lack of normal tone.
**Atopy,** allergy.
**Atoxic,** not poisonous.
**Atresia,** absence of a normal body opening.
**Atrophy,** decrease in size of a normally developed organ or tissue.
**Atrichia,** absence of hair.
**Attack,** the onset of illness.
**Attenuation,** weakening, thinning.
**Audiograph,** graph showing acuteness of hearing.
**Audiology,** science of hearing.
**Audiometer,** instrument for measuring acuteness of hearing.
**Audiphone,** hearing aid.
**Aura,** sensations experienced before the onset of a disease or convulsion.
**Aural,** pertaining to the ear or hearing.
**Aureomycin,** antibiotic.
**Auris,** ear.
**Aurotherapy,** treatment with gold salts.
**Auscultation,** part of physical examination which uses detection of sounds in body by use of stethescope to aid diagnosis.
**Autism,** morbid concentration.
**Autoclave,** sterilizer.
**Autodigestion,** self-digestion.
**Autoerotism,** sexual stimulation of self.
**Autogenous,** self, generated.
**Autointoxication,** poisoning by toxins formed within the body.
**Autokinesis,** voluntary motion.
**Automatic,** involuntary motion.
**Autonomic,** independent in action or function. [tude.
**Autophobia,** extreme fear of soli-
**Autopsy,** examination of a body after death to discover the cause of death.
**Autonomic Nervous System,** part of the central nervous system which supplies the internal organs. It is divided into two parts: the sympathetic and the parasympathetic nervous systems.
**Avitamic Acid,** vitamin C; ascorbic acid. [body.
**Autotoxin,** toxin formed in the
**Auxesis,** increase in size.
**Avitaminosis,** disease resulting from a vitamin deficiency.
**Avulsion,** tearing away of a part.
**Axilla,** armpit.
**Axillary,** pertaining to the armpit.
**Azoospermia,** absence of sperm in the semen.
**Azote,** nitrogen.

## — B —

**Bacca,** berry.
**Baccate,** berry-shaped.
**Bacillary,** pertaining to bacillus bacteria.
**Bacillemia,** presence of bacilli in the blood.
**Baccilliform,** similar to a bacillus in shape.
**Bacilluria,** presence of bacilli in the urine.
**Bacillus,** pl., Bacilli, one of the major forms of bacteria.
**Bacitracin,** an antibiotic drug.
**Back,** posterior part of the body from the neck to the pelvic girdle.
**Backache,** pain in spine or adjacent areas.
**Bacteremia,** bacteria in the blood
**Bacteria,** microscopic organisms.

**Bactericide,** that which destroys bacteria.

**Bacteriuria,** bacteria in the urine.

**Bagassosis,** Lung disease.

**Balanitis,** inflammation of the tip of the penis or clitoris.

**Balanus,** tip of the penis or clitoris.

**Balbuties,** stammering.

**Baldness,** lack of hair.

**Ballistophobia,** extreme fear of missiles.

**Ballooning,** distention of a cavity.

**Ballottement,** rebound of a part when pressure is released.

**Balm,** soothing ointment.

**Balsam,** an aromatic resin.

**Bandage,** piece of gauze or other material for wrapping any part of the body.

**Barber's Itch,** infection of the beard area, also known as sycosis.

**Barbiturates,** drugs used as a hypnotic or sleep producer.

**Barium Sulfate,** powder used in an emulsion which a patient drinks prior to X-rays of the stomach and intestines.

**Barren,** sterile.

**Baryecois,** deafness.

**Basal Metabolism,** the processes and/or measurement of vital cellular activity in the fasting and resting state based on oxygen usage.

**Baseplate,** plastic material for making dental trial plates.

**Basic,** opposite of an acid; fundamental.

**Basilic Vein,** large vein on the inner side of the upper arm.

**Bastard,** one born of an unwed mother.

**Bath,** method of cleansing; therapeutic treatment.

**Bathophoia,** extreme fear of high objects.

**Battarism,** stuttering.

**Beaker,** glass with a wide mouth.

**Behavior,** the observable activity of an individual.

**Bearing Down,** the expulsive effort of a woman in the second stage of labor.

**Beat,** throb due to the contraction of the heart or passage of blood through a vessel.

**Bedsores,** lesions over pressure areas on body of a bedridden patient.

**Begma,** cough.

**Belch,** escape of gas from the stomach through the mouth.

**Belladonna,** drug used to help spasmodic disorders.

**Bell's Palsy,** paralysis of the facial nerve; shown in weakness of one side of the face. The eye on the affected side will not close properly, and it becomes impossible to blow out the cheeks or whistle.

**Belly,** stomach.

**Bends,** decompression sickness.

**Benign,** non-repeating when referring to a disease.

**Benignant,** not recurrent.

**Benzedrine,** the proprietary name of a nervous stimulant.

**Beriberi,** disease, uncommon in this country, caused by eating food deficient in vitamin B.

**Beryllosis,** inflammation of the lungs due to beryllium oxide dust.

**Bestiality,** intercourse with an animal.

**Beta Rays,** negatively charged particles emitted by radium.

**Betalin S,** synthetic vitamin B.

**Bex,** cough.

**Bicameral,** having two cavities.

**Biceps,** major muscle of the upper arm.

**Bicarbonate,** salt containing two parts carbonic acid and one part basic substance.

**Bicellular,** composed of two cells.

**Bicuspid,** premolar tooth.

**Bifurcate,** forked.

**Bile,** liver secretion.

**Biliation,** excretion of bile.

**Biliousness,** mild upset of the liver caused by dietary indiscretion.

**Biliuria,** bile in the urine.

**Binder,** broad bandage used to encircle and support.

**Biochemistry,** chemistry of living things.

**Biologicals,** medical preparations used in the treatment or prevention of disease.

**Biology,** science of life and living things.

**Biolytic,** able to destroy life.

**Bion,** any living organism.

**Bionomy,** science dealing with vital functions.

**Biopsy,** tissue taken from a living living person for study.

**Biostatics,** vital statistics.

**Biotics,** pertaining to the laws of living organisms.

**Biotomy,** vivisection.

**Bipara,** woman who has had two labors.

**Birth,** process of being born.

**Birth Control,** measures used to prevent pregnancy.

**Birth Injury,** any injury to an infant during the birth process.

**Birth-Mark,** blemish on skin of new born child, which is usually permanent.

**Bisexual,** both sexes in one person.

**Bismuthosis,** poisoning due to use of bismuth, a drug formerly used in the treatment of syphilis.

**Bistoury,** surgical knife.

**Bite,** cut with teeth; puncture by an insect.

**Bitter,** of disagreeable taste.

**Black**, absence of light; of dark pigmentation.
**Blackblood**, impure blood.
**Black Death**, bubonic plague.
**Blackout**, sudden temporary loss of sight and even consciousness.
**Blackwater Fever**, form of malaria.
**Black Widow**, poisonous spider.
**Bladder**, collecting pouch for urine from kidneys.
**Bland**, soothing; mild.
**Blastoma**, tumor.
**Blear-eye**, chronic inflammation of margins of eyelids.
**Bleb**, blister.
**Bleeder**, One suffering from hemophilia; an inborn incurable disease in which severe bleeding follows even a slight cut.
**Bleeding**, emitting blood.
**Bleeding Time**, time necessary for the natural stoppage of bleeding from a cut, about 3 minutes or less.
**Blenna**, mucus.
**Blennagenic**, producing mucus.
**Blepharitis**, inflammation of the eyelids shown by redness, crusting, swelling and infection of the eyelashes.
**Blepharon**, eyelid.
**Blindness**, inability to see.
**Blister**, collection of fluid under the skin.
**Bloated**, swollen beyond normal [size.
**Blood**, fluid contained in arteries and veins of body that carries nutrients to and waste away from all tissues. Made up of cells and plasma.
**Blood Bank**, storing place for reserve blood.
**Blood Clot**, coagulated mass of blood.
**Blood Count**, a procedure that determines the number and type of red and white blood cells per cubic millimeter of blood.
**Blood Groups**, categories under which all human blood can be classified.
**Bloodshot**, locally congested with [blood.
**Blood-Pressure**, this term refers to two different pressures in the blood system; the systolic pressure, which is that existing when the heart contracts and the diastolic pressure when the heart is in full relaxation.
**Blood Type**, classification of blood into different groups.
**Bloody Flux**, dysentery.
**Blue Baby**, child born with a blue color due usually to a heart defect.
**Blue Ointment**, mercurial ointment.
**Blushing**, rush of blood to the face.
**Body**, the physical man; trunk.
**Body Cavities**, thorax, abdomen, pelvis.
**Bolus**, round mass; pill; food prepared for swallowing by mastication.
**Boil**, infection of the skin.
**Bone Grafting**, transplanting a healthy bone to replace missing or defective bone.
**Bonelet**, small bone.
**Bone Onlay**, portion of transplanted bone placed across a break in a bone.
**Bones**, framework of body, composed of calcium and elastic tissue.
**Bone Wax**, material used to pack bone in order to stop bone bleeding.
**Boric Acid**, an antiseptic used on skin to help infections.
**Boss**, protuberance at one side of a bone.
**Botulism**, the most dangerous form of food poisoning.
**Bowel**, intestine.
**Box Splint**, used for fractures below the knee.
**Brachium**, arm.
**Bradycardia**, slow heart rate.
**Braidism**, hypnotism.
**Brain**, the primary nervous structure which sends out and receives stimulations to and from the rest of the body.
**Brain Fever**, meningitis.
**Breakbone Fever**, acute epidemic febrile disease.
**Breast**, front of the chest; mammary gland.
**Breath**, air inhaled and exhaled in the respiratory process.
**Breathe**, to inhale and exhale air.
**Breathing**, act of taking in air to the body and exhaling carbon dioxide.
**Bright's Disease**, kidney disease.
**Bromides**, salts of bromine.
**Bromidrosis**, offensive body odor.
**Bromide**, any salt containing bromine.
**Bronchiectasis**, state in which the lung tissue around the end of the breathing tubes becomes infected with the formation of sac-like cavities which fill with infectious material.
**Bronchiole**, smallest subdivision of the breathing tubes within the lung.
**Bronchitis**, inflammation of the windpipe which divides and subdivides into narrower tubes making up the network of air passages within the lungs.
**Brown Mixture**, cough syrup containing opium and licorice.
**Brucella**, type of bacillus.
**Bruise**, any injury to the surface of the body in which the skin is discolored but not broken.
**Bruit**, abnormal sound or murmur.
**Buerger's Disease**, disease of the

blood vessels, usually in the arms and legs, in which spasm of the arteries leads to numbness, coldness, pain in the muscles and change of color.
**Bubonic Plague,** fatal infectious disease.
**Bucca,** mouth.
**Bug,** small insect.
**Buggery,** sexual relations through the anus.
**Bulimia,** an insatiable appetite.
**Bulla,** large blister.
**Bunion,** thickened area of skin on skin on lateral side of big toe.
**Bundle,** group of fibers.
**Burn,** an injury to the body caused by high temperature.
**Bursa,** a sac like cavity usually found in or near joints.
**Bursitis,** inflammation of a bursa.
**Buttonhole,** straight cut through the wall of a cavity.
**Bysma,** plug; tampon.
**Bythus,** lower abdominal region.
**Byssinosis,** irritation of the air passages in the lung due to inhalation of cotton dust.

— C —

**Cacation,** defecation.
**Cachet,** capsule.
**Cachexia,** extreme wasting and weakness found in the later stages of a severe illness or starvation.
**Cachinnation,** hysterical laughter.
**Cadaver,** corpse.
**Caduceus,** symbol of the medical, i.e., the wand of Hermes.
**Caffeine,** stimulant found mainly in coffee.
**Cainotophobia,** extreme fear of anything new.
**Caisson Disease,** occurs in workers, such as divers, who work under high atmospheric pressure, occurs when the pressure is reduced too rapidly, and the nitrogen in the blood escapes in the form of bubbles.
**Calamine,** pink substance composed of zinc and iron oxides, used in the form of lotion to soothe the skin.
**Calcaneus,** heel bone.
**Calcareous,** chalky; containing calcium.
**Calcicosis,** inflammation of the lungs due to marble dust.
**Calcification,** calcium deposits within the tissues of the body.
**Calcinosis,** calcium deposit in the skin and its underlying tissue.
**Calcium,** element which is the basis of limestone, important in body skeleton and function.
**Calculus,** stone-like mass which may form in the body under abnormal conditions.
**Calf,** the fleshy part of the back of the leg.
**Calibrator,** instrument for measuring openings.
**Callous,** any thickening of the skin formed on the site of continual irritation, unusually on the feet or hands.
**Callus,** the new tissue formed at the site of fracture when a bone heals.
**Calmant, Calmative,** sedative.
**Calomel,** mercurous chloride; formerly used in the treatment of syphilis.
**Calorie,** measure of energy intake and output in the body.
**Calvities,** baldness.
**Campbor,** drug obtained from the camphor tree and used to stimulate the skin.
**Camphorated,** containing camphor.
**Canal,** passage, duct.
**Cancer,** any malignant tumor.
**Cancroid,** like cancer; a tumor; type of skin cancer.
**Canine Teeth,** four teeth (upper and lower) between the incisors and molars.
**Canker,** type of mouth ulceration.
**Capillary,** smallest blood vessel.
**Capsule,** tissue covering a part; soluble coating surrounding medication.
**Caput,** head.
**Carbo,** carbon, charcoal.
**Carbohydrates,** the scientific name for sugars, starches and cellulose.
**Carbolic Acid,** coal tar derivative used as an antiseptic and disinfectant.
**Carbon,** element which is the characteristic constituent of organic compounds.
**Carbon Dioxide** ($CO_2$), colorless, odorless gas used with oxygen to promote respiration.
**Carbuncle,** large boil.
**Carcinogenic,** causing cancer.
**Carcinoma,** particular type of cancer.
**Cardiac,** concerning the heart.
**Cardiac Failure,** heart failure.
**Cardiogram,** record of changes in electrical energy of hèart cycle.
**Cardiograph,** apparatus for making a graph of heart cycle.
**Cardiology,** medical specialty dealing with the heart.
**Cardiophobia,** extreme fear of heart disease.
**Cardiospasm,** contraction of the muscles controlling the inlet to the stomach.
**Cardiovascular,** pertaining to the heart and blood vessels.
**Caries,** condition of decay, usually applied to decay of the teeth.
**Carminative,** drug to aid digestion and relieve flatulence, e.g., ginger, peppermint.
**Carnal,** pertaining to the flesh.

**Carnal Knowledge,** sexual knowledge.

**Carnivorous,** flesh-eating.

**Carotid,** major artery leading to the brain.

**Carpal,** relating to the wrist.

**Carpus,** wrist.

**Carrier,** one who harbors disease germs without suffering from the disease himself.

**Car Sickness,** illness due to motion of a car.

**Cartilage,** gristle.

**Cascara,** a laxative.

**Case,** particular example.

**Caseation,** conversion of tissue into a cheese-like substance by certain diseases.

**Casebook,** Physician's record book.

**Casein,** protein product of milk.

**Cast,** mold to hold bone rigid and straight.

**Castor Oil,** old-fashioned purgative.

**Castrate,** to remove the testicles or ovaries.

**Castration Complex,** extreme fear of injury to the sex organs.

**Casualty,** accidental injury.

**Catabolism,** the breaking down of complex compounds into simpler ones.

**Catalepsy,** general name to describe various states marked by loss of power to move the muscles.

**Catalyst,** agent which influences a chemical reaction without taking part in it. [period.

**Catemenia,** onset of first menstrual

**Cataract,** clouding of the lens of the eye which prevents clear vision.

**Catarrh,** any illness which causes inflammation of membranes with a discharge of mucus.

**Catatonia,** type of schizophenia characterized by immobility.

**Catgut,** Sheep's intestine twisted for use as surgical thread.

**Catharsis,** purging.

**Cathartic,** purgative.

**Catheter,** tube for passage through body channels, usually to evacuate fluids.

**Cathexis,** emotional energy attached to an object.

**Caustic,** irritating, burning.

**Cautery,** application of a burning agent to destroy tissue.

**Cauterization,** application of heat or burning chemicals to the surface of the body.

**Cavernous,** having hollow spaces.

**Cavity,** hollow space.

**Cecostomy,** establishing an artificial opening into the large intestine near the appendix for evacuation.

**Cecum,** first part of the large intestine. [egion.

**Celiac,** pertaining to the abdominal

**Cell,** small cavity; a mass of protoplasm containing a nucleus.

**Cellular,** composed of cells.

**Cellulitis,** deep inflammation of the tissues just under the skin caused by infection with germs.

**Centrifugal,** moving away from a center.

**Cephalalgia,** headache.

**Cephalic,** pertaining to the head.

**Cerebellum,** small part of the nervous system, situated at the back of the brain, which is concerned with co-ordination of movements and bodily functions such as respiration.

**Cerebration,** mental activity.

**Cerebro-Spinal Fluid,** the clear fluid which surrounds the brain and spinal cord as they lie inside the skull and in the canal of the spinal column; acts mainly as a shock absorber.

**Cerebrum,** the brain, especially the large frontal portion, as distinct from the cerebellum and the spinal cord.

**Cerumen,** Ear wax.

**Cervix,** the neck or that part of an organ resembling the neck.

**Cervical,** pertaining to the neck or mouth of womb.

**Cesarean Operation,** abdominal operation to remove a child from the womb of a pregnant woman.

**Cestoid,** resembling a tapeworm.

**Chafing,** irritation caused by the rubbing together.

**Chalazion,** tumor of the eyelid.

**Chancre,** the name given to the sore that appears on the body when infected with certain types of venereal disease organisms.

**Change of Life,** the menopause, usually occurring in women between the ages of forty and fifty-five, and about ten years later in men.

**Chapped Skin,** skin becomes dry and cracks due to decreased activity of glands in the area.

**Charley Horse,** bruised or torn muscle associated with cramping pain in the muscle.

**Charting,** recording the progress of a disease.

**Check,** slow down; stop, verify.

**Cheek,** side of the face below the eye.

**Cheilitis,** inflammation of the lips.

**Cheilosis,** lip disorder due to vitamin deficiency. [sternum.

**Chest,** area enclosed by the ribs and

**Chigger,** mite whose bite causes severe inflammation.

**Chilblains,** painful swelling of fingers, toes and ears caused by exposure to cold.

**Child,** one in the period between infancy and youth.

**Chill,** symptoms that occur when one first becomes infected with any germs which cause fever; result of nervous stimulation.

**Chin,** area below lower lip.

**Chirology,** means of communicating with deaf mute by sign-language.

**Chiropractic,** system of treatment based on the belief that all disease is caused by pressure on the nerves as they leave the spinal column.

**Chiropractor,** one who specializes in bone manipulation.

**Chloasma,** brownish discoloration of the skin found in patches on any part of the body; particularly apparent in some pregnant women.

**Chloremia,** decrease of hemoglobin and red corpuscles of the blood.

**Chloroform,** heavy, clear, colorless liquid used as an anesthetic.

**Chloromycetin,** antibiotic.

**Chlorosis,** form of anemia.

**Choke,** obstruction of the pharynx or esophagus.

**Cholecystectomy,** removal of the gall bladder.

**Cholecystitis,** inflammation of the gall bladder.

**Cholelith,** gallstone.

**Cholemia,** presence of bile in the blood.

**Cholera,** tropical intestinal disease.

**Cholesteral,** substance found in fats and oils.

**Choleric,** irritable.

**Cholinesterase,** an enzyme.

**Chondral,** pertaining to cartilage.

**Chondroma,** tumor of a resembling cartilage.

**Chorda,** string, tendon.

**Chorea,** also known as St. Vitus' dance or Sydenham's chorea; disease of the nervous system, usually considered to be related to rheumatism or rheumatic fever.

**Choriomeningitis,** inflammation of the coverings of the brain.

**Chorion,** outermost of the fetal membranes.

**Chromatelopsia,** color blindness.

**Chromatic,** pertaining to color.

**Chromatosis,** pigmentation.

**Chromocyte,** colored cell.

**Chronic,** of long duration.

**Chronological,** according to time sequence.

**Chyme,** food after digestion in the stomach.

**Cicatrix,** scar.

**Circulation,** flowing in a circular course.

**Circulation Time,** rate of blood flow.

**Circumcision,** operation of cutting off the foreskin of male penis.

**Cirrhosis,** hardening of any tissue, but particularly of the liver.

**Cirsectomy,** removal of a part of a varicose vein.

**Clamp,** surgical device for compressing a part or structure.

**Claudication,** lameness due to decreased blood flow.

**Claustrophobia,** extreme fear of enclosed spaces.

**Clavicle,** collar bone.

**Clavus,** corn.

**Cleavage,** division into distinct parts.

**Cleft,** fissure.

**Cleft Palate,** congenital fissure of the palate forming one cavity for the nose and throat.

**Climacteric,** change of life.

**Clinic,** bedside examination; center where patients are treated by a group of physicians practicing together.

**Climax,** period of greatest intensity.

**Clinical,** pertaining to bedside treatment.

**Clitoris,** small erectile organ of the femal genitalia.

**Clot,** to coagulate.

**Club-Foot,** congenital deformity of the feet of unknown cause.

**Clunis,** buttock.

**Clyster,** enema.

**Coagulation,** formation of a blood clot.

**Coalescence,** fusion of parts.

**Cocaine,** a local anesthetic.

**Coccygodynia,** pain in the area of the tail bone.

**Coccyx,** small bones at the end of the spine.

**Cochlea,** cavity in the internal ear.

**Codeine,** sedative.

**Cod-Liver Oil,** the chief outside source of vitamins A and D, obtained from oil of cod fish.

**Cognition,** processes involved in knowing.

**Coitus,** sexual intercourse.

**Colchicine,** drug which helps to relieve symptoms of gout.

**Colds,** common viral infection of man causing symptoms of nasal fullness, cough and fever.

**Cold Sores,** lesions particularly in and around mouth caused by herpes simplex virus.

**Colectomy,** removal of part of the large intestine.

**Colic,** severe abdominal pain caused by spasm of one of the internal organs, usually the intestines; pertaining to the colon or large intestine.

**Collapse,** to flatten; breakdown; prostration.

**Colitis,** inflammation of the large intestine.

**Collodion,** drug which, when painted on the skin, forms a thin transparent protective film.

**Collyrium,** local eye medication, e.g., eye wash.

**Colon,** large intestine.
**Color Blindness,** an inborn condition in which, while ordinary vision remains normal the individual is unable to distinguish between particular colors.
**Colostrum,** first milk from a mother's breast after childbirth.
**Colpalgia,** vaginal pain.
**Colpatitis,** vaginal inflammation.
**Column,** supporting part.
**Coma,** complete loss of consciousness, which may be the result of various causes.
**Comatose,** state of being in a coma.
**Comedo,** blackheads in glands of skin.
**Comminution,** breaking into small fragments.
**Comminute,** a bone shattered in several pieces.
**Commitment,** placing a patient in an institution.
**Comparative Anatomy,** human anatomy compared to that of animals.
**Complication,** added difficulty.
**Compound,** substance composed of different elements.
**Compress,** a pad for application of pressure or medication to a specific area.
**Conception,** fertilization.
**Concha,** shell-like organ.
**Concussion,** stunning; condition of dizziness, mental confusion and sometimes unconsciousness, due to a blow on the head.
**Condom,** rubber covering worn over the penis to prevent conception.
**Conduction,** conveyance of energy.
**Condyloma,** wartlike growth near the anus or genitals.
**Congenital,** existing at or before birth.
**Congestion,** excess accumulation of blood or mucus in any part of the body.
**Conjunctivitis,** inflammation of the transparent membrane which covers the eyeball.
**Connective,** that which binds together.
**Connective Tissue,** one of the four main tissues of the body which support bodily structures, bind parts together and take part in other bodily functions.
**Consciousness,** awareness.
**Constipation,** failure of bowels to excrete residue at proper intervals.
**Consumption,** tuberculosis.
**Contagion,** (see infection.)
**Contagious,** easily transmitted by contact.
**Contagium,** agent causing infection.
**Continence,** ability to control natural impulses.
**Contraception,** use of mechanical devices or medicines to prevent conception.
**Contraction,** a drawing together.
**Contracture,** a shortening of tissue, causing deformity or distortion, e.g., scar.
**Contusion,** bruise.
**Convex,** rounded and somewhat elevated.
**Convulsant,** medicine which causes convulsions.
**Convolution,** coil of tissue on the brain surface, separated by fissures.
**Convulsion,** temporary loss of consciousness with severe muscle contractions due to many causes; fit or generalized spasm.
**Co-ordination,** working together of various muscles.
**Copulation,** sexual intercourse.
**Cord, Spinal,** that portion of the central nervous system contained in the spinal canal.
**Cord, Umbilical,** cord which connects the umbilicus of the fetus to the placenta.
**Cordate,** heart-shaped.
**Corium,** layer of skin under the epidermis.
**Corn,** thickening of the skin, hard or soft, according to location on the foot.
**Cornea,** transparent membrane covering the eye and lying beneath the conjunctiva.
**Corneum,** outmost layer of skin.
**Coronary Thrombosis,** clotting of blood in the blood vessels which supply the heart.
**Coroner,** one who holds inquests over those dead from violent or unknown causes.
**Corpus,** principal part of an organ; mass.
**Corpuscle,** blood cell.
**Corrosive,** destructive; disintegrating.
**Cortex,** outer layer of the brain and other organs.
**Cortisone,** a hormone produced by the adrenal glands.
**Corsucation,** sensation of flashes of light before the eyes.
**Coryza,** nasal catarrh or common cold.
**Costalgia,** rib pains.
**Costive,** constipated.
**Cough,** an attempt on the part of the body to expel something causing irritation in the respiratory tract.
**Coxa,** hip; hip joint.
**Cramp,** painful, spasmodic contraction.
**Cranium,** skull.
**Crapulent,** characterized by excessive eating and drinking.
**Cremaster,** muscle which draws up the testis.
**Crest,** ridge on a bone.
**Cretinism,** condition caused by the lack of or decreased secretion of

the thyroid gland in a child.
**Crevice**, small fissure.
**Crisis**, the turning point of a disease.
**Critical**, dangerous; severe.
**Cross-eyes**, condition in which eyes do not move together.
**Cross-Knee**, knock knee.
**Croup**, a disease of children characterized by coughing and difficult breathing.
**Cryptogenic**, of unknown or obscure origin.
**-cule, -cle** (suffix), little.
**Culture**, propagation of an organism.
**Cumulative**, increasing.
**Cure**, system of treatment; restoration to health.
**Curettage**, scraping the interior of a cavity with a curette.
**Curette**, a spoon-shaped instrument used for scraping away dead tissue.
**Cusp**, point of the crown of a tooth; pointed projection on a segment of a cardiac valve.
**Cuspid**, canine tooth.
**Cutaneous**, pertaining to the skin.
**Cuticle**, outermost layer of the skin.
**Cyanosis**, term used to describe blueness of the skin, generally caused by lack of oxygen.
**Cycle**, sequence.
**Cyesis**, pregnancy.
**Cyst**, any sac in the body filled with liquid or semi-liquid substance.
**Cystitis**, inflammation of the bladder.
**Cystoscopy**, process of examining the inside of the bladder with an instrument.

— D —

**Dacryorrhea**, excessive flow of tears.
**Dactyl**, digit.
**Dactylion**, webbing of the fingers and toes.
**Dactylitis**, inflammation of a finger or toe.
**Dactylology**. communication with the fingers, i.e., sign language.
**Dactylus**, finger; toe.
**Daltonism**, color blindness.
**D. & C.**, dilation and curettage of uterus.
**Dandruff**, condition of the scalp characterized by dry scaling.
**Dartos**, fibrous layer under the skin of the scrotum.
**Deaf-mutism**, inability to hear or speak.
**Deafness**, complete or partial loss of hearing.
**Dealbation**, bleaching.
**Dearterialization**, conversion of arterial into venous blood.
**Death Rate**, number of people who die each year, compared with the total number of population.
**Death Rattle**, gurgling noise caused by passage of air through accumulated fluid in the windpipe.
**Debility**, weakness.
**Decalcification**, decrease in the normal mineral salts content of bone.
**Decalvant**, making bald.
**Decerebration**, removal of the brain.
**Decidua**, membranous lining of the uterus shed after childbirth or at menstruation.
**Decompensation**, failure of an organ to adjust itself to changing condition.
**Decompression**, removal of pressure.
**Decripitude**, senile feebleness.
**Decubitus**, lying down posture.
**Decubation**, period of convalescence from an infectious disease.
**Defecation**, evacuation of the bowels.
**Defective**, imperfect.
**Defemination**, loss of female and assumption of male sex characteristics.
**Deficiency Disease**, any disease caused by the lack of some essential part of the diet.
**Defloration**, loss in a woman of virginal characteristics, i.e., rupture of the hymen.
**Defluvium**, falling out of hair.
**Deformity**, distortion, malformation.
**Degeneration**, deterioration or breaking down of a part of the body.
**Deglutition**, act of swallowing.
**Dehydration**, loss of water.
**Dejecta**, excrement.
**Dejection**, meloncholy.
**Delactation**, weaning, stopping of lactation.
**Deliquesence**, liquefaction of a salt by absorption of moisture from the air.
**Delirium**, mental disturbance, usually occuring in the course of some infectious disease, or under the influence of poisonous drugs.
**Deliver**, to aid in birth.
**Deltoid**, triangular.
**Delusion**, false belief.
**Demented**, insane.
**Dementia**, deterioration of intelligence.
**Demorphinization**, treatment of morphine addiction by gradual withdrawal.
**Demulcent**, reducing irritation; a soothing substance.
**Dengue**, tropical disease carried by mosquitoes, causing fever and joint pain.
**Denigration**, process of becoming black.
**Dens**, tooth.
**Dentagra**, toothache; forceps for pulling teeth.

**Dentalgia,** toothache.
**Dentifrice,** any substance used for cleaning teeth.
**Dentin,** chief substance of teeth.
**Dentistry,** branch of medicine deal-with teeth.
**Denture,** complete unit of teeth.
**Deodorant,** that which destroys odors.
**Deontology,** medical ethics.
**Deorsum,** downward.
**Depersonalization,** loss of the sense of one's own reality.
**Depilate,** to remove hair.
**Depilatory,** substance used to remove hairs.
**Deplete,** to empty.
**Depraved,** perverted.
**Depressant,** that which retards any function.
**Derangement,** disorder.
**Dermad,** toward the skin.
**Dermatitis,** inflammation of the skin, eczema.
**Dermatologist,** skin specialist.
**Dermatology,** branch of medicine which deals with the skin and its diseases.
**Dermatosis,** any skin disease.
**Dermoid,** resembling skin.
**Desiccant,** a drying medicine; tendency to cause drying.
**Desiccate,** to dry.
**Desmalgia,** pain in a ligament.
**Detergent,** cleansing.
**Deviation,** variation from the normal condition.
**Dexter,** right.
**Dextrocardia,** position of the heart in the right side of the chest.
**Dextrophobia,** extreme fear of objects on the right side of the body.
**Dextrose,** form of sugar.
**Diabetes,** a disease which shows itself in an inability of the body to handle glucose.
**Diagnosis,** determination of a patient's disease.
**Diagnostician,** one skilled in determining the nature of a disease.
**Di-** (prefix), two.
**Diaphragm,** large muscle which separates the inside of the chest from the inside of the abdomen; contraceptive device.
**Diaphysis,** shaft of a long bone.
**Diarrhea,** watery, loose bowel movements.
**Diarticular,** pertaining to two joints.
**Diastole,** period of relaxation of the heart during which it fills with blood.
**Diastalsis,** forward movement of the bowel contents.
**Diastema,** space, cleft.
**Diathermy,** treatment of disease or injury by use of heat.
**Diathesis,** type of constitution which makes one liable to a particular disease.
**Dichotomy,** division into two separate parts.
**Dick Test,** test to discover whether a patient is liable to or immune from scarlet fever.
**Didymalgia,** pain in a testis.
**Diet,** nutritional intake; prescription of food permitted to be eaten by a patient.
**Dietetics,** science of diet and nutrition.
**Dietitian,** specialist of diet in health and disease.
**Dietotherapy,** use of a diet regimen for cure.
**Diffuse,** widely spread.
**Digestant,** that which aids digestion.
**Digestion,** assimilation of food by the body.
**Digit,** finger; toe.
**Digitalis,** drug used in the treatment of heart diseases.
**Dilatation,** stretching; increase in diameter.
**Dionism,** homosexuality.
**Diphasic,** having two phases.
**Diphtheria,** disease causing the development of membrane in nose and throat.
**Diploplia,** double vision.
**Dipsomania,** excessive desire for drink.
**Disarticulation,** separation of bones at a joint.
**Disc, Disk,** platelike structure or organ.
**Discharge,** setting free; excretion.
**Discrete,** separate.
**Disease,** sickness; ailment.
**Disengagement,** liberation of the fetus from the vaginal canal.
**Disinfection,** killing germs by antiseptics or other methods.
**Disinfectation,** extermination of pests.
**Dislocation,** displacement of the bones in a joint.
**Disseminated Schlerosis,** disease of the nervous system in which small patches of hard tissue (sclerosis) develop throughout the spinal cord and brain.
**Distention,** widening; enlargement.
**Dismemberment,** amputation.
**Dispensary,** place which gives free or low cost medical treatment.
**Dissection,** cutting up.
**Distillation,** purification of a liquid by vaporizing it and then condensing it.
**Distrix,** the splitting of the hairs at the end.
**Diuresis,** frequent urination.
**Dieuretic,** medicine which increases the flow of urine.
**Divagation,** unintelligible speech.
**Diverticulitis,** inflammation of

small pouches or diverticuli in large intestine.

**Dizziness,** sensation of spinning or off balance.

**Dolorific,** causing pain.

**Domatophobia,** extreme fear of being in a house.

**Donor,** one who gives blood or body tissue for the use of others.

**Doraphobia,** extreme fear of fur.

**Dorsal,** pertaining to the back or hind part of an organ.

**Dorsalgia,** pain in the back.

**Dorsum,** back.

**Dose,** amount of medication to be given at one time.

**Dose, Lethal,** dose large enough to to cause death.

**Dossier,** file containing a patient's case history.

**Douche,** stream of water directed into a body cavity or against the body itself.

**Dowel,** pin used to hold an artificial crown to a natural tooth root.

**D.P.H.,** Department of Public Health.

**Dragee,** large, sugar-coated pill.

**Drain,** channel of exit for discharge from a wound.

**Dramamine,** drug commonly used for seasickness.

**Dressing,** protective covering placed over a wound to aid the healing process.

**Drive,** basic urge.

**Drop Foot,** state of inability to raise the foot upwards due to paralysis of the leg muscles.

**Dropper,** tube for giving liquid in drops.

**Dropsy,** generalized accumulation of fluid in body, edema.

**Drowning,** suffocation and death due to filling the lungs with liquid.

**Drug,** any medicinal substance.

**Duct,** tube or channel that conducts fluid, especially the secretion of a gland.

**Duipara,** woman who has had two children.

**Dumb,** unable to speak.

**Duodenum,** first eight to ten inches of the small intestine.

**Dura Mater,** outermost covering of the brain and spinal cord.

**Dwarf,** an undersized person.

**Dynamia,** energy.

**Dys-** (prefix), bad; difficult.

**Dysarthria,** stammering.

**Dysarthrosis,** dislocation; disease or deformity of a joint.

**Dysbasia,** difficulty in walking.

**Dyschiza,** painful bowel movement.

**Dysemesia,** painful vomiting.

**Dysentery,** name given to a group of disorders in which there is diarrhea, produced by irritation of the bowels.

**Dysfunction,** impairment of function.

**Dysgenesis,** malformation.

**Dysgraphia,** inability to write.

**Dyskinesia,** impairment of the ability to make any physical motion.

**Dysmenorrhea,** painful menstruation.

**Dyspepsia,** indigestion.

**Dysphagia,** difficulty in swallowing.

**Dyspnea,** labored breathing.

**Dysomia,** sleep disorder.

**Dyspareunia,** pain felt by the woman during sexual intercourse.

**Dystithia,** difficulty in breast feeding.

**Dystocia,** difficult childbirth.

**Dystrophy,** weakening of muscle due to abnormal development.

**Dysuria,** painful urination.

## — E —

**Ear,** organ of hearing.

**Earache,** pain in ear usually due to inflammation.

**Eat,** to take solid food.

**Ebullition,** boiling.

**Eburnation,** hardening of teeth or bone.

**Ecbolic,** that which speeds up child birth or produces abortion.

**Eccentric,** peripheral, peculiar in ideas.

**Ecchymosis,** a discoloring of the skin caused by the seepage of blood beneath skin.

**Eccysesis,** extrauterine pregnancy.

**Ecdemic,** pertains to disease brought into a region from without.

**Echinococcosis,** infestation with a type of tapeworm.

**Echo,** reverbrating sound.

**Echolalia,** senseless repetition of words spoken by others.

**Eclampsia,** form of internal poisoning and convulsions which may occur in late pregnancy.

**Ecouvillonage,** cleansing of a wound or cavity.

**Ecphuma,** outgrowth.

**Ecstasy,** exaltation.

**Ectal,** external.

**Ectasia,** widening in diameter of a tubular vessel.

**Ecthyma,** inflammation of the skin, characterized by large pimples that rupture and become crusted.

**Ectocardia,** displacement of the heart.

**Ectoderm,** outermost layer of cells in a developing embryo.

**-ectomy** (suffix), excision.

**Ectopic,** abnormal position of an organ, part of a body; pregnancy outside the uterus.

**Ectropion,** the turning out of a part, particularly an eyelid.

**Eczema,** an itching disease of the skin.

**Edema,** an excessive accumulation of tissue fluid.

**Edentate,** without teeth.

**Edeology**, study of the genitalia.

**Edible**, suitable to be eaten.

**Effemination**, assumption of feminine qualities in a man.

**Efferent**, conducting away from a center.

**Effluvium**, foul exhalation.

**Effusion**, accumulation of fluid, or the fluid itself, in various spaces of the body, e.g., joints.

**Egesta**, body excretions or discharges.

**Egg**, ovum.

**Ego**, that part of the mind which possesses reality and attempts to bring harmony between the instincts and reality.

**Egocentric**, self-centered.

**Egomania**, morbid self-esteem.

**Egotism**, exaggerated evaluation of one's self.

**Eiloid**, coiled.

**Ejaculation**, ejection of semen.

**Ejection**, the act of expelling.

**Elastic**, able to return to normal shape after distortion.

**Elation**, joyful emotion.

**Elbow**, juncture at which the arm and forearm meet.

**Electric Shock**, burns with loss of consciousness.

**Electricity**, form of energy having magnetic, chemical and thermal effects.

**Electrocardiography**, a machine which records the electrical activity of the heart muscles.

**Electrocogulation**, the deterioration or hardening of tissues by high-frequency currents.

**Electrode**, an electric conductor through which current enters or leaves a cell, an apparatus or body.

**Electroencepalogram**, record of the electrical changes of the brain.

**Electron**, an elementary unit of electricity; negatively charged particle of the atom.

**Electroshock**, shock produced by electric current.

**Electrotherapy**, treatment of disease by use of electricity.

**Electuary**, soft, medicated confection.

**Elephantiasis**, tropical disease in which blocking of the lymph vessels by a parasite leads to great swelling of the tissues, especially in the lower part of the body.

**Elimination**, discharge of indigestible materials and waste products from the body.

**Elixer**, a sweetened, alcoholic liquid used to disguise unpleasant tasting medicines.

**Emaciated**, excessively thin.

**Emasculation**, castration.

**Embalming**, preservation of a corpse against decomposition.

**Embolism**, small clot or foreign substance detached from the inside of a blood vessel and floating free in the blood stream.

**Embryo**, earliest stage of development of a young organism; the human young through the third month of pregnancy.

**Emedullate**, to deprive of marrow.

**Emesis**, vomiting.

**Emetic**, drug that causes vomiting.

**Emetine**, drug that causes sweating and expectoration.

**Emiction**, urination.

**Emission**, sending forth; discharge of semen.

**Emmenia**, the menses.

**Emmenology**, that which is known about menstruation.

**Emmenagogue**, that which stimulates the menstrual flow.

**Emollient**, relaxing, soothing agent used to soften the skin or internally to soothe an irritated surface.

**Emotion**, mental attitude.

**Empathy**, understanding, sympathy.

**Emphysema**, lung disease characterized by the thinning and loss of elasticity of lung tissue.

**Emphiric**, based on experience.

**Empyema**, collection of pus in the lung.

**Emulgent**, draining out.

**Emulsion**, product made up of tiny globules of one liquid suspended in another liquid.

**Enamel**, the hard, white substance which covers and protects the tooth.

**Encelialgia**, pain in abdominal region.

**Encephalic**, pertaining to the brain.

**Encephalitis**, inflammation of the brain.

**Encephalogram**, brain x-ray.

**Encephalomalacia**, softening of the brain due to deficient blood supply.

**Encephalon**, the brain.

**Encranial**, located within the cranium.

**Endomoeba**, a single-celled parasite that lives in humans.

**Endeictic**, symptomatic.

**Endemic**, disease prevalent in a particular area.

**Endangium**, membrance which lines blood vessels.

**Endermic**, administered through the skin.

**Endoblast**, cell nucleus.

**Endocardial**, pertaining to the interior of the heart.

**Endocarditis**, inflammation of the inner lining of the heart, especially the heart valves.

**Endocardium**, tissue lining the inside of the heart.

**Endochrome**, coloring matter of a cell.

**Endocranial**, within the cranium.

**Endocrine Glands**, ductless glands

that secrete directly into the blood stream.

**Endocrinology,** study of ductless glands and their secretions.

**Endoderm,** inner layer of cells of an embryo.

**Endodontitis,** inflammation of the dental pulp.

**Endometritis,** inflammation of the lining of the womb.

**Endometrium,** tissue that lines the interior wall of the womb.

**Endoplast,** nucleus of a cell.

**End-Organ,** any terminal structure of a nerve.

**End Pleasure,** pleasure enjoyed at the height of the sexual act.

**End Product,** the final excretory product that passes from the system.

**Endothermic,** characterized by heat absorption.

**Enema,** an injection of liquid into the rectum, usually intended for the treatment of constipation.

**Energy,** ability to work.

**Enervation,** weakness.

**Engorgement,** excessive fulness.

**Engram,** the indelible impression which experience makes upon nerve cells.

**Enomania,** craving for alcoholic drink, delerium tremens.

**Enstrophe,** turning inward.

**Ental,** inner.

**Enteralgia,** pain in the intestine.

**Enteric,** pertaining to the intestines.

**Enteritis,** inflammation of the intestinal tract by infection or irritating food.

**Enterocolitus,** inflammation of the small and large intestines.

**Enteron,** the intestine.

**Enthetic,** introduced from without.

**Entopic,** located in the proper place.

**Entropian,** turning in of the edge of the eyelid so that the lashes rub against the eyeball.

**Enucleate,** to remove a tumor or an organ in its entirety.

**Enuresis,** bed wetting.

**Environment,** external surroundings.

**Enzyme,** a substance produced by living cells which, although not participating in a chemical reaction, promotes its speed.

**Ephebic,** pertaining to puberty.

**Ephedrine,** drug used to shrink the lining of the nose in colds and in the treatment of asthma.

**Ephelis,** freckle.

**Ephidrosis,** profuse sweating.

**Epibular,** upon the eyeball.

**Epicutaneous,** on the surface of the skin.

**Epicyte,** wall of a cell.

**Epidemic,** disease that affects many people at one time in the same area.

**Epidemiology,** study of the occurrence and distribution of disease.

**Epidermis,** outermost layer of the skin.

**Epididymitis,** inflammation of the epididymis, a structure which covers the upper end of the testicle.

**Epiglottis,** a lid which covers the opening to the windpipe and prevents food from getting into the voice box or lungs.

**Epilation,** removal of hair by the root.

**Epilepsy,** convulsive disorder.

**Epinephrine,** the active principle of one of the secretions of the adrenal gland.

**Epiotic,** located on or above the ear.

**Epiphora,** continuous overflow of tears.

**Episiotomy,** cutting of the wall of the vagina during childbirth to avoid tearing.

**Epistasis,** substance which rises to the surface instead of sinking.

**Epistaxis,** nose bleeding.

**Epithelioma,** cancer of the skin.

**Epithelium,** cellular substance of skin and mucous membrane.

**Eponym,** using the name of a person to designate a disease, organ, syndrome, etc.

**Equilibrium,** balance.

**Equivalent,** of equal value.

**Erasion,** abrasion.

**Erection,** becoming upright and rigid.

**Eremophobia,** extreme fear of being alone.

**Erepsin,** intestinal enzyme.

**Erg,** unit of work.

**Ergasiatrics,** psychiatry.

**Ergophobia,** extreme fear of work.

**Ergosterole,** substance found in the skin and elsewhere which, when exposed to sunlight, becomes converted to vitamin D.

**Ergot,** drug used to cause contraction of the uterus and control bleeding after childbirth.

**Ergotamine,** an alkaloid substance used in treatment of migraine and can produce contractions of the uterus.

**Erode,** wear away.

**Erogenous,** producing sexual excitement.

**Erosion,** wearing away of a substance.

**Erotic,** pertaining to sex.

**Erotogenic,** originating from sexual desire.

**Erotogenic Zones,** areas of the body, stimulation of which promote sexual feelings.

**Erotophobia,** extreme fear of sexual love.

**Errhine,** causing sneezing and nasal discharge.

**Eructation,** belching.

**Eruption,** rash; cutting of a tooth.
**Erysipelas,** infection of the skin with streptococci.
**Erythema,** rednes of the skin.
**Erythrocytes,** red blood cells.
**Erythroderma,** skin disturbance characterized by abnormal redness.
**Esbach's Method,** a method of estimating quantity of albumin in urine.
**Eschar,** sloughed tissue due to a burn.
**Esophagus,** the tube that connects the stomach to the throat, about nine inches long.
**Ester,** compound formed by the combination of an organic acid with an alcohol.
**Estrogens,** the female sex hormone.
**Estrus,** female sexual cycle.
**Estuarium,** vapor bath.
**Ether,** organic liquid used as an anesthetic.
**Ethics, Medical,** system of moral principles governing medical conduct.
**Ethnic,** pertaining to the races of mankind.
**Etiology,** study of the causes of disease.
**Eucalyptus,** an oil used as an antiseptic in nasal solutions and mouth washes.
**Eugenics,** study of inheritance.
**Eunuch,** castrated male.
**Eupepsia,** normal digestion.
**Euphonia,** normal clear condition of the voice.
**Euphoria,** exaggerated sense of well-being.
**Eupnea,** normal respiration.
**Eusitia,** normal appetite.
**Euthanasia,** mercy killing.
**Evacuant,** medicine which empties an organ; laxative.
**Evagination,** protusion of a part or organ.
**Eversion,** turning outward.
**Evisceration,** removal of inner parts.
**Evolution,** gradual transition from one state to another.
**Ex-** (previx), out; away from.
**Exacerbation,** increase in the degree of sickness.
**Examination,** scrutiny of a patient's state of health.
**Exanthema,** any fever accompanied by a rash.
**Excerebration,** removal of the brain.
**Excise,** surgical removal.
**Excitability,** susceptible to stimulation.
**Excitation,** stimulation; irritation.
**Excoriation,** rubbing away of part of the skin by disease or injury.
**Excrement,** feces.
**Ergrescence,** abnormal out-growth upon the body.
**Exenteration,** evisceration.
**Exercise,** physical exertion.
**Exhalation,** expulsion of air from the lungs.
**Exhaustion,** extreme fatigue.
**Exhibitionist,** abnormal impulse to show one's genitals to a member of the opposite sex.
**Exhilarant,** cheering.
**Exo-** (prefix), outside; outward.
**Exocardia,** abnormal position of the heart.
**Exodontia,** tooth extraction.
**Exophthalmos,** bulging of the eyes, usually caused by over-activity of the thyroid gland.
**Exostosis,** outgrowth from the surface of a bone.
**Expansion,** increase in size.
**Expectorant,** drug supposed to have the effect of liquefying the sputum.
**Expectoration,** spittle.
**Expire,** exhale; die
**Exploration,** investigation.
**Expression,** the act of squeezing out; facial disclosure of feeling or emotion.
**Exterior,** outside.
**Extern,** medical student who works in a hospital but lives elsewhere.
**Extima,** outermost covering of a blood vessel.
**Extirpation,** complete surgical removal or destruction of a part.
**Extra-** (prefix), outside of; in addition.
**Extract,** to pull out; remove the active portion of a drug.
**Extremity,** terminal part of anything; a limb of the body.
**Extrinsic,** of external origin.
**Extrovert,** one interested in external objects and actions.
**Eye,** the organ of vision.
**Eyebrow,** hair ridge above the eye.
**Eyelash,** hair growing on the edge of an eyelid.
**Eyestrain,** eye fatigue.
**Eyetooth,** a cuspid or upper canine tooth.

## — F —

**F.,** Fahrenheit, one gauge of measuring temperature.
**Face,** anterior part of the head.
**Facial,** pertaining to the face.
**Facies,** appearance of the face.
**Facilitation,** hastening of a natural process.
**Facioplegia,** facial paralysis.
**Factitious,** artificial.
**Faculty,** normal power or function; mental attribute.
**Farenheit Scale,** boiling point of water 212 degrees, freezing point, 32 degrees.
**Fahr.,** Fahrenheit.
**Fainting,** temporary loss of consciousness due to insufficient blood reaching the brain.
**Fallopian Tubes,** tubes which connect the ovaries with the womb.

**Fallout,** settling of radioactive dust from the atmosphere after a nuclear explosion.

**False,** not true.

**False Ribs,** lower five pairs of ribs.

**Familial,** pertaining to the same family.

**Family,** group descended from a common ancestor.

**Fang,** root of a tooth.

**Farina,** meal; flour.

**Far Point,** farthest point which an eye can see distinctly when completely relaxed.

**Fastigium,** acme; highest point.

**Fat,** obese; greasy deposits in body tissue.

**Fatigue,** exhaustion; weariness.

**Fauces,** space in the back part of the mouth, surrounded by the soft palate, the tonsil arches and the base of the tongue.

**Favus,** contagious skin disease.

**F. D.,** fatal disease.

**Fear,** emotional response to danger.

**Fear Reaction,** emotional illness in which anxiety is shown by the conscious fear of a particular event or object.

**Febricide,** that which destroys fever.

**Febrifacient,** producing fever.

**Febrile,** pertaining to fever.

**Febris,** fever.

**Fecal,** pertaining to feces.

**Feces,** waste matter excreted by the bowels.

**Fecundity,** fertility.

**Feeble-mindedness,** state of low development of the intelligence.

**Feeding,** taking of food.

**Fee Splitting,** unethical practice of dividing the patient's charges between the referring physician and the consultant.

**Feet,** the extremities of the legs on which humans stand.

**Fellatio,** type of sexual perversion in which the male sex organ is placed in the mouth of another.

**Felon,** deep skin, infection on the far end and inner surface of a finger.

**Female,** woman; girl; pertaining to a woman.

**Feminism,** possession of female characteristics by a male.

**Femur,** thighbone.

**Fenestration,** surgical operation designed for the treatment of certain types of deafness.

**Fermentation,** decomposition of complex substances under the influence of enzymes.

**Ferrule,** metal band applied to a tooth to strengthen it.

**Fertile,** capable of reproduction.

**Fester,** to produce pus.

**Fetal,** pertaining to a fetus.

**Fetation,** pregnancy.

**Feticide,** killing of an unborn child.

**Fetid,** having a disagreeable odor.

**Fetish,** that which becomes attractive because of its association with sexual pleasure.

**Fetus,** an unborn child from the third month until birth.

**Fever,** elevation of the body temperature.

**Fiber,** threadlike structure.

**Fibrillation,** state of tremor in the muscles found in certain nervous, muscular and heart diseases.

**Fibrin,** protein substance produced by elements of the blood and tissues which forms a network as the base of clots.

**Fibroid,** benign tumor of the womb consisting of tough, fibrous tissue.

**Fibroidectomy,** surgical removal of a fibroid tumor.

**Fibroma,** benign tumor composed of fibrous tissue.

**Fibula,** bone of lower leg.

**Filament,** small, threadlike structure.

**Field,** limited area.

**Figure,** body; shape; outline.

**Filament,** delicate fiber or thread.

**Filariasis,** tropical disease due to infection of the body with tiny worms which block the lymph vessels, causing swelling of the limbs, elephantiasis.

**Filling,** material inserted in the cavity of a tooth.

**Filter,** to pass a liquid through a porous substance to eliminate solid particles; device used in this process.

**Filtrate,** fluid which has passed through a filter.

**Finger,** digit of the hand.

**First Aid,** emergency, temporary medical care and treatment of an injured person.

**Fission,** division into parts.

**Fissure,** groove, cleft.

**Fistula,** abnormal passage leading from the surface of the body to an internal cavity.

**Fit,** convulsion; sudden attack.

**Flaccid,** flabby; weak; soft.

**Flagellation,** to beat or whip; beating as a means of satisfying sexual desires.

**Flap,** mass of partly detached tissue.

**Flat, Foot,** not having the normal arch of the sole of the foot.

**Flatulence,** gas in the stomach or intestines.

**Flatus,** stomach or intestinal gas.

**Flaxseed,** linseed.

**Flesh,** soft tissue and muscles of the animal body.

**Fletcherism,** thorough mastication of food.

**Flex,** to bend.

**Flexion,** bending.

**Flexor**, muscle that bends or flexes.
**Floating**, moving around; out of normal position.
**Flora**, plant life.
**Florid**, having a bright color.
**Fl. Oz.**, fluid ounce.
**Fluid**, a non-solid, liquid or gaseous substance.
**Fluoroscope**, an X-ray instrument used to examine the interior of the body.
**Flush**, to blush; to clean with a stream of water.
**Flutter**, irregular, rapid motion; agitation, especially of the heart.
**Flux**, a large flow of any body excretion, particularly the bowel contents.
**Fold**, ridge; a doubling back.
**Folie**, mania; psychosis.
**Follicle**, small secretory sac or gland.
**Folliculitis**, inflammation of the follicles of the hair.
**Fomentation**, treatment of inflammation by applying heat and moisture to the affected part.
**Fontanel**, the soft spot of a baby's head that later is closed by the growth of bone.
**Food**, that which nourishes.
**Food Poisoning**, digestive disorder due to eating foods containing poisonous substances.
**Foot**, terminal part of the leg.
**Foot Print**; impuression of the foot.
**Foramen**, any opening or perforation.
**Forceps**, two-pronged instrument for extracting.
**Forearm**, portion of the arm between the elbow and wrist.
**Forefinger**, first finger.
**Forehead**, portion of the head above the eyes; brow.
**Forensic Medicine**, aspects of medicine related to law.
**Formation**, structure; shape; figure.
**Formula**, rule prescribing the kind and quantity of ingredients in a preparation.
**Fornication**, sexual intercourse of persons not married to each other.
**Fossa**, pit; depression.
**Fracture**, breaking of a bone.
**Fragilitas**, brittleness.
**Fragility**, characteristic of being easily broken.
**Frenum**, fold of skin or lining tissue that limits the movement of an organ, e.g., tissue under the tongue.
**Freckles**, small patches of pigmented skin more commonly found in blonde or red-headed people.
**Freezing**, frigidity of a limb due to severe cold.
**Frenzy**, maniacal excitement.
**Friable**, easily broken into small pieces.
**Friction**, rubbing.
**Fright**, extreme, sudden fear.
**Frigidity**, absence of sexual desire in women, coldness.
**Frons**, forehead.
**Frontal**, relating to the front of the body or an organ; pertaining to the forehead.
**Frost Bite**, condition caused by long exposure to severe cold; freezing of a part of the body, usually nose, fingers, toes.
**Frottage**, rubbing, massage.
**Frustration**, the feeling aroused when physical or personal desides are thwarted.
**Fugitive**, wandering.
**Fulguration**, therapeutic destruction of tissue by means of electric sparks.
**Fulling**, kneading.
**Full Term**, normal end of pregnancy.
**Fumes**, vapors.
**Fumigation**, disinfecting.
**Function**, normal and specific action of a part.
**Fundament**, base; foundation.
**Fundus**, base of an organ.
**Fungicide**, an agent that destroys fungi.
**Fungus**, mold.
**Funny Bone**, outer part of the elbow which is crossed by part of the ulnar nerve.
**Fur**, deposit forming on the tongue.
**Furfur**, dandruff.
**Furibund**, maniacal.
**Furor**, rage.
**Furuncle**, boil.
**Furunculosis**, boils on skin.
**Fusiform**, spindle-shaped.
**Fusion**, uniting.

— G —

**Gait**, manner of walking.
**Galactic**, pertaining to milk.
**Galactischia**, suppression of the secretion of milk.
**Galactorrhea**, excessive flow of milk.
**Galeophobia**, extreme fear of cats.
**Gall**, secretion stored in the liver which helps in emulsifying fats.
**Gall Bladder**, sac beneath the liver which stores bile and secretes mucus.
**Gall Stones**, stone-like objects found in gall bladder and its drainage system, composed primarily of calcium.
**Galvanism**, uninterrupted electric current.
**Gammacism**, imperfect pronunciation of g and k sounds.
**Gamogenesis**, sexual reproduction.
**Gamophobia**, extreme fear of marriage.
**Ganglion**, cyst-like swelling found in the region of a joint or the sheath of a tendon; area between two nerve fibers.
**Gangrene**, death and deterioration

of a part of the body, caused by interference with the blood supply.
**Gapes**, disease of fowls caused by a worm.
**Gargle**, mouth wash.
**Gastralgia**, stomach pain.
**Gastric**, pertaining to the stomach.
**Gastritis**, inflammation of the stomach walls.
**Gastrobrosis**, perforation of the stomach.
**Gastrocnemius**, calf muscle.
**Gastroenteritis**, inflammation of the stomach and intestine.
**Gastroptosis**, abnormal relaxation of stomach musculature.
**Gastrorrhagia**, stomach hemorrhage.
**Gastrosis**, any stomach disease.
**Gatophilia**, abnormal fondness for cats.
**Gatophobia**, extreme fear of cats.
**Gauntlet**, hand bandage.
**Gavagi**, liquid nourishment supplied through a tube inserted into the mouth, down the gullet and into the stomach.
**Gelatin**, body protein in a solid state, used in manufacture of drug capsules.
**Gelatinous**, like jelly.
**Gelosis**, hard, swollen mass.
**Gelotolepsy**, spontaneous loss of normal muscle tension.
**Geminate**, in pairs.
**Gen.**, gene.
**Genal**, pertaining to the cheek.
**Gender**, sexual category; male or female.
**Gene**, biological unit which transmits hereditary characteristics.
**Generation**, reproduction; period of family history.
**Generative**, pertaining to reproduction.
**Generic**, pertaining to genus; distinctive.
**Genesis**, origin and development.
**Genetics**, the science of natural differences and similarities in successive generations of living organisms.
**Genetous**, dating from fetal life.
**Genial**, pertaining to the chin.
**Genicular**, pertaining to the knee
**Genital**, pertaining to the sex organs.
**Genitalia**, reproductive organs.
**Genocide**, race destruction.
**Genu**, knee; knee-like structure.
**Genus**, biological classification.
**Geophagy**, eating of soil.
**Geratic**, pertaining to old age.
**Geriatrics**, medical study of old age.
**Germ**, organism that infects man; primitive beginning of a developing embryo.
**German Measles**, a viral infection characterized by high fever and skin rash.
**Germicide**, agent that destroys germs.
**Geroderma**, wrinking of the skin.
**Gestation**, pregnancy.
**Gestosis**, toxemia in pregnancy.
**Gibbous**, humpbacked.
**Gigantism**, abnormal height and size.
**Gingiva**, the gum that surrounds the tooth.
**Gingivitis**, inflamation of the gums.
**Girdle**, encircling structure.
**Glabella**, space between the eyebrows.
**Glabrous**, smooth.
**Gladiolus**, main portion of the sternum.
**Glanders**, contagious horse disease.
**Glandilemma**, outer covering of a gland.
**Glandula**, smal gland.
**Glands**, there are three main types of glands: the lymph glands, which are found mainly at various junctions in the body, such as the armpit and the groin, and also within the body and around the base of the neck, their function being to trap germs and prevent them from reaching vital areas; larger glands, such as the pancreas and liver which produce digestive agents such as bile, enzymes, etc. and which empty their products into the intestines through a duct or tube; the endocrine glands, which are also called ductless glands because they empty their products directly into the blood stream.
**Glandular**, pertaining to a gland.
**Glandule**, small gland.
**Glans**, cone-shaped body that forms the tip of the penis or clitoris.
**Glasses**, lenses to aid vision.
**Glaucoma**, disease of the eyes in which the pressure of the fluid in the eye increases.
**Gleet**, discharge from the urethra found in chronic gonorrhea.
**Glioma**, tumor of the nerve cells.
**Globular**, spherical.
**Globule**, small droplet.
**Globulicidal**, destroying red corpuscles.
**Globulin**, the name of a group of proteins.
**Globus**, ball, sphere.
**Globus Hystericus**, imaginary lump in the throat.
**Glomerulonephritis**, Kidney disease.
**Glomerulus**, small, round mass; important element of the kidney.
**Glossa**, tongue.
**Glossalgia**, tongue pain.
**Glossitis**, inflammation of the tongue.
**Glottis**, the space between the vocal cords.
**Glucohemia**, sugar in the blood.

**Glucose,** liquid which is sweet and important to body chemistry; sugar.
**Gluteal,** pertaining to the buttocks.
**Gluten,** protein, found in cereals.
**Glutinous,** sticky.
**Glycemia,** sugar in the blood.
**Glycerin,** clear, syrupy liquid used for medicinal purposes.
**Glycolysis,** digestion of sugar.
**Glycosuria,** sugar in the urine.
**Glycyrrhyza,** licorice.
**Gnathic,** pertaining to the jaw.
**Gnosia,** faculty of perception and recognition.
**Goiter,** an enlargement of the thyroid gland.
**Goitrogenic,** causing goiter.
**Gomphiasis,** looseness of teeth.
**Gonad,** ovary or testes.
**Gonadotrophin,** hormone which stimulates the ovary or testes.
**Gonagra,** gout in the knee.
**Gonalgia,** pain in the knee.
**Gonococcus,** germ which causes gonorrhea.
**Gonorrhea,** veneral disease.
**Gouge,** instrument for cutting bone.
**Gout,** disease in which there is an upset in the metabolism of uric acid, causing symptoms of joint pain.
**Gouty,** pertaining to gout.
**G.P.,** general practitioner.
**Gracile,** slender.
**Gradatim,** gradually.
**Graft,** piece of tissue for transplantation.
**Grand Mal,** epileptic attack.
**Granulation,** process of wound healing.
**Granulocytopenia,** disease which reduces the defensive cells in the blood, the white blood cells.
**Granum,** grain.
**Grave's Disease,** increased activity of thyroid gland with bulging of the eyes.
**Gravid,** pregnant.
**Gravida,** pregnant woman.
**Gravity,** weight.
**Grip,** influenza; grasp.
**Groin,** depression between the thigh and abdomen.
**Grumous,** lumpy; clotted.
**G. U.,** genitourinary.
**Gumboil,** a swelling in the mouth due to an abscess at the root of a tooth.
**Guilt,** feeling of having committed an offense.
**Gullet,** passage to the stomach.
**Gustation,** sense of taste.
**Gustatory,** pertaining to the sense of taste.
**Gut,** bowel; intestine.
**Gutta,** a drop.
**Guttate,** like a drop.
**Guttur,** throat.
**Guttural,** pertaining to the throat.
**Gymnastics,** physical exercise.
**Gymnophobia,** extreme fear of the naked body.
**Gymandromorphism,** condition in which one has male and female characteristics.
**Gynatrisia,** condition in which there is no passageway in the vagina.
**Gynecic,** pertaining to women.
**Gynecoid,** like a woman.
**Gynecologist,** specialist in female diseases.
**Gynecology,** study of the diseases of women.
**Gynecomastia,** enlargement of male breasts.
**Gynoplasty,** plastic surgery of the female genitals.

## — H —

**Habit,** automatic action; bodily temperament.
**Habituation,** becoming accustomed to a thing.
**Hachement,** hacking.
**Hacking,** chopping stroke in massage.
**Hair,** threadlike outgrowth from the skin.
**Halazone,** white powder used as drinking water disinfectant.
**Halitosis,** offensive breath.
**Halitous,** covered with moisture.
**Hallucination,** mistaken sense impression.
**Hallucinosis,** condition of persistent hallucinations.
**Hallux,** big toe.
**Ham,** back part of the thigh above the knee and below the buttock; hip, thigh; buttock.
**Hamarthritis,** arthritis in all the joints.
**Hammer,** instrument for striking blows; middle ear bone.
**Hammer Toe,** claw-like deformity of the toe.
**Hamster,** rodent frequently used in laboratory tests.
**Hamular,** hook-shaped.
**Hand,** terminal part of an arm.
**Handedness,** tendency to use a particular hand.
**Hangnail,** partly detached piece of skin at the root of a fingernail.
**Haphiphobia,** extreme fear of contact.
**Haptics,** science of the sense of touch.
**Hare Lip,** cleft lip.
**Haunch,** hips and buttocks.
**Haut-Mal,** epileptic attack at its peak.
**Hay Fever,** an allergic disease caused by abnormal sensitivity to certain air borne pollens.
**HB.,** hemoglobin.
**Head,** uppermost part of the body; top of anything.
**Headache,** pain in the head.
**Heal,** cure.

**Healing,** process of making well.
**Health,** state of having a normally active body and mind.
**Hearing,** perceiving sound.
**Hearing Aid,** device used by one who is deaf to amplify sound waves.
**Heart,** the powerful, muscular, contractile organ, the center of the circulatory system.
**Heart Block,** disease of the heart in which the impulse of contraction is unable to pass from the auricles to the ventricles, with the result that both beat independently of each other.
**Heartburn,** burning sensation, either in the back of the throat or in the left side of the chest, usually occurs after eating.
**Heart Failure,** inability of the heart to maintain adequate body circulation.
**Heart Murmur,** abnormal heart sound.
**Heart Rate,** number of heart beats per minute.
**Heat,** warmth; high temperature; form of energy; sexual excitement in certain animals; to make hot.
**Heatstroke,** state of dizziness, nausea and spots before the eyes due to direct exposure to high temperatures.
**Hebetic,** pertaining to puberty.
**Hebetude,** mental slowness.
**Hectic,** habitual; constitutional.
**Hedonism,** devotion to pleasure.
**Heel,** hind extremity of the foot.
**Helcoid,** resembling an ulcer.
**Helcosis,** formation of an ulcer.
**Helicine,** spiral.
**Heliophobia,** extreme fear of sunlight.
**Heliosis,** sunstroke.
**Heliotherapy,** treatment of disease by the rays of the sun or by the use of an ultra violet-lamp.
**Heliotropism,** tendency of an organism to turn toward sunlight.
**Helix,** margin of the external ear.
**Helminthiasis,** presence of parasitic worms in the body.
**Helminthology,** study of parasitic worms.
**Heloma,** callosity, corn.
**Helotomy,** surgical removal of a corn.
**Hemafacient,** blood producing agent.
**Hemagogue,** agent which promotes the flow of blood.
**Hemal,** pertaining to blood or blood vessels.
**Hemangiectasis,** enlargement of blood vessels.
**Hemarthrosis,** accumulation of blood in a joint.
**Hemase,** blood enzyme.
**Hematemesis,** vomiting of blood.
**Hemathermous,** warm-blooded.
**Hematic,** pertaining to blood.
**Hematischesis,** stopping of bleeding.
**Hematocolpos,** collection of blood in the vagina.
**Hematocryal,** cold-blooded.
**Hematoid,** resembling blood.
**Hematologist,** one who specializes in the study of blood and its diseases.
**Hematology,** science of the blood.
**Hematoma,** swelling containing clotted blood, usually caused by direct violence, e.g., a black eye.
**Hematometachysis,** blood transfusion.
**Hematonosis,** blood disease.
**Hematuria,** the passing of blood in the urine.
**Hemeralopia,** day blindness.
**Hemi-** (prefix), half.
**Hemianopsia,** blindness in half of the visual field of each eye.
**Hemic,** pertaining to blood.
**Hemicrania,** headache on one side of the head only; migraine.
**Hemifacial,** affecting one side of the face.
**Hemiplezia,** paralysis of one side of the body.
**Hemocidal,** destructive of blood cells.
**Hemocyte,** blood corpuscle.
**Hemofuscin,** brown coloring matter of blood.
**Hemoglobin,** red pigment in the blood.
**Hemoid,** resembling blood.
**Hemolysis,** destruction of elements of the blood.
**Hemopathy,** blood disease.
**Hemopericardium,** blood in the heart sac.
**Hemopexin,** blood coagulating enzyme.
**Hemopexis,** coagulation of blood.
**Hemophilia,** blood disease characterized by defective coagulation of the blood and a strong tendency to bleed.
**Hemophiliac,** one afflicted with hemophilia.
**Hemophobia,** aversion to blood.
**Hemophoris,** conveying blood.
**Hemoptysis,** spitting up of blood.
**Hemorrhage,** bleeding.
**Hemorrhagenic,** causing hemorrhage.
**Hemorrhoids,** varicose vein condition of the lower rectum and anus.
**Hemopasia,** withdrawal of blood.
**Hemostasis,** stopping of hemmorhage.
**Hemostat,** instrument which stops bleeding, clamp.
**Hemotherapy,** using blood to treat disease.
**Hemothorax,** accumulation of blood between the lungs and chest wall.

**Hepar,** liver.
**Heparin,** substance which prevents clotting of blood.
**Hepatic,** concerning the liver.
**Hepatitis,** inflammation of the liver.
**Hepatogenic,** produced in the liver.
**Hepatoma,** tumor with its origin in the liver.
**Hepatomegaly,** enlargement of the liver.
**Hepatopathy,** liver disease.
**Hereditary,** transmitted from one's forefathers.
**Heredity,** traits and characteristics transmitted from parents and other ancestors to offspring.
**Heredosyphilis,** congenital syphilis.
**Hermaphodite,** one having both male and female sex characteristics.
**Hermetic, Hermetical,** airtight.
**Hernia,** rupture; the bulging out of a part of any of the internal organs through a weak area in the muscular wall.
**Herpes,** skin disease characterized by clusters of small blisters.
**Heroin,** narcotic.
**Heroinism,** addiction to the use of heroin.
**Herpes Simplex,** fever blisters, mouth blisters.
**Herpes Zoster,** acute, infectious, inflammatory skin disease; shingles.
**Herpetiform,** resembling herpes.
**Heterogeneous,** of unlike natures.
**Heterosexuality,** sexual desire for one of the opposite sex.
**Hexavaccine,** vaccine having six different organisms.
**Hiatus,** fissure, gap.
**Hiccups,** sharp, inspiratory sound caused by contractions of the diaphragm.
**Hidrosis,** sweating.
**Hip,** upper part of the thigh where it joins with the pelvis.
**Hipprocrates,** Greek physician, the Father of Medicine.
**Hippocratic Oath,** oath taken by the graduating physician on which he bases his medical ethics.
**Hirsute,** hairy.
**Histamine,** bodily substance found in most tissues, released when tissue is damaged.
**Histoblast,** tissue cell.
**Histology,** science of the microscopic structure of tissues.
**Histoma,** any tissue tumor.
**History,** patient's record of past illness, present illness and symptoms.
**Hitch,** knot.
**Hives,** skin rash characterized by large wheals.
**Hoarseness,** difficulty in speaking.
**Hodegetics,** medical etiquette.
**Hodgkin's Disease,** disease in which, the lymph glands and spleen become enlarged.
**Holarthritis,** inflammation of all joints.
**Homicide,** murder.
**Homogeneous,** of uniform structure
**Homosexuality,** psychological disorder which causes one to be attracted to people of same sex.
**Hook,** curved instrument used for traction or holding.
**Hooping Cough,** acute, infectious disease marked by a paroxysmal cough ending in a crowing or whooping inspiration.
**Hordeolum,** sty.
**Hormone,** a chemical that originates in the glands and is carried to all parts of the body by the blood.
**Horror,** fear, dread.
**Hosp.,** hospital.
**Hospital,** institution for the care of those in need of medical attention.
**Hospitalization,** placing of a person in a hospital for treatment.
**Host,** organism on which a parasite lives.
**Hot,** having a high temperature.
**Hottentotism,** abnormal form of stuttering.
**House Physician,** doctor who lives in the hospital and is available for help at all times.
**House Staff,** residents, interns and certain doctors of a hospital.
**Humerus,** arm bone.
**Humidifier,** device used to increase moisture in the air of a room.
**Humidity,** amount of moisture in the air.
**Humor,** body fluid.
**Humpback,** curvature of the spine.
**Hunger,** desire, especially for food.
**Hyaline,** glassy.
**Hybrid,** product of parents of different species.
**Hydatid,** cyst formed in the tissues.
**Hydragogue,** strong laxative.
**Hydrarthrosis,** accumulation of fluid in a joint.
**Hydraulics,** science of liquids in motion.
**Hydroa,** skin disease with blister-like patches.
**Hydrocarbon,** compound of hydrogen and carbon.
**Hydrocephalus,** abnormal enlargement of the head due to interference with the drainage of cerebral fluid.
**Hydrocyst,** cyst with watery contents.
**Hydrogenate,** combine with water.
**Hydrophilia,** absorbing water.
**Hydrophobia,** rabies.
**Hydrops,** dropsy.
**Hydrotherapy,** treatment of disease by means of water.
**Hygiene,** science of health and observance of its rules.

**Hygienic,** pertaining to health.
**Hygiene, Mental,** development and preservation of mental health.
**Hygiene, Oral,** proper care of the mouth and teeth.
**Hygienist,** specialist in hygiene.
**Hymen,** membrane fold located at the entrance to the female sex organs.
**Hymenectomy,** surgical removal of the hymen.
**Hymenotomy,** surgical opening of the hymen.
**Hypacusia,** faulty hearing.
**Hypalgesia,** reduced sensitivity to pain.
**Hyperacidity,** excess of stomach acid.
**Hyperacuity,** sharp vision.
**Hyperacusia,** acute hearing.
**Hyperbulia,** excessive willfulness.
**Hyperemesis,** abnormal amount of vomiting.
**Hyperglycemia,** excess blood sugar.
**Hyperhydrosis,** excessive sweating.
**Hypermastia,** unusually large breasts; having more than two breasts.
**Hypermotility,** increased activity.
**Hyperpresia,** unusually high blood pressure.
**Hyperpnea,** hard breathing with an increase in the depth of inhalation.
**Hyperrhinolalia,** marked nasal quality of the voice.
**Hypersensitivity,** allergy.
**Hypersthenia,** unusual strength or tone of body.
**Hypertension,** high blood pressure.
**Hyperthermia,** abnormally high temperature.
**Hyperthymia,** excessive emotionalism.
**Hyperthyroidism,** condition caused by excessive secretion of the thyroid gland.
**Hypertrichosis,** excessive hairiness.
**Hypnagogic,** causing sleep.
**Hypnagia,** pain while asleep.
**Hypnogenetic,** causing sleep.
**Hypnosis,** trance induced through verbal suggestion or concentration upon an object.
**Hypnotherapy,** treatment by hypnotism.
**Hypnotize,** to put in a state of hypnosis.
**Hypobaropathy,** decompression sickness.
**Hypocalcia,** calcium deficiency.
**Hypochrondria,** undue concern about one's health; suffering with imaginary illnesses.
**Hypochondriac,** one who suffers from imaginary illness.
**Hypodermic,** beneath the skin; injection under the skin; needle used for injections.
**Hypogastrium,** lowest middle abdominal region.
**Hypoglobulia,** decrease of red blood cells.
**Hypoglossal,** under the tongue.
**Hypogonadism,** deficient activity of testis or ovary.
**Hypomastia,** unusual smallness of the breast.
**Hypomenorrhea,** deficient menstruation.
**Hyponoia,** mental sluggishness.
**Hypophrenia,** feeblemindedness.
**Hypopraxia,** deficient activity.
**Hypophysis,** pituitary gland.
**Hypoplasia,** incomplete tissue development.
**Hyposensitization,** treatment of allergy by giving small doses of the material to which the person is allergic and gradually increasing the doses until the allergic reaction is reduced.
**Hypotension,** low blood pressure.
**Hypothesis,** supposition.
**Hypotonia,** abnormally low strength or tension.
**Hysterectomy,** surgical removal of whole or part of the womb.
**Hysteria,** psychological state or neurosis resulting from failure to face reality.
**Hysterosalpingectomy,** surgical removal of the womb and fallopian tubes.

## — I —

**Iateria,** therapeutics.
**Iatric,** medical.
**Iatrogenic Disease,** condition caused by a doctor's statements or procedure.
**Iatrology,** medical science.
**Ice,** frozen water.
**Ichnogram,** footprint.
**Ichor,** watery discharge from a sore.
**Iconologny,** sexual desire aroused by pictures or statues.
**Ichthyol,** coal tar product used in the treatment of skin diseases.
**Icthyophobia,** extreme fear of fish.
**Ichthyosis,** condition in which babies have dry and scaly skin.
**Icterpatitis,** jaundice.
**Icteric,** relating to or characterized by jaundice.
**Icterus,** jaundice.
**Ictus,** beat; stroke; attack.
**Id,** psychological term for the unconscious.
**Idea,** concept.
**Idea, Flight of,** rapid, disconnected speech characteristic of certain mental diseases.
**Ideal,** concept of perfection.
**Ideation,** thinking.
**Idée Fixe,** obsession.
**Identical,** exactly the same.
**Identical Twins,** twins developed from one fertilized cell.
**Idiosyncrasy,** peculiar characteristics whereby one person differs from another.
**Idiocrasy,** peculiarity.

**Idiocy,** mental deficiency with an I.Q. under 25.
**Idiogamist,** man capable of having sexual relations only with his wife, or only with a few women.
**Idiot,** person suffering from congenital feeblemindedness.
**Idiotic,** like an idiot.
**Idiotypic,** relating to heredity.
**Idrosis,** excessive sweating.
**Ignis,** cautery.
**Ileitis,** inflammation of the lower small intestine.
**Ileocolitis,** inflammation of the lower small intestine and the large intestine.
**Ileum,** lower part of the small intestine.
**Ileus,** intestinal obstruction.
**Ilium,** flank, upper wide part of the hipbone.
**Ill,** not healthy; diseased.
**Illegal,** not lawful.
**Illegitimate,** not according to law; born out of wedlock.
**Illness,** ailment.
**Illusion,** misinterpretation of a real sensation.
**Imagery,** imagination.
**Imago,** memory of a loved person formed in childhood.
**Imbalance,** lack of balance.
**Imbecility,** mental deficiency with the mental age between three and seven years and an I.Q. between 25 and 49.
**Imbibation,** absorption of a liquid.
**Imbrication,** surgical procedure for closing wounds.
**Immature,** not fully developed.
**Immedicable,** incurable.
**Immersion,** placing a body under a liquid.
**Immiscible,** not able to be mixed.
**Immobilization,** making immovable.
**Immune,** protected against disease.
**Immunity,** ability to resist infectious disease.
**Immunologist,** one who specializes in the science of immunity.
**Immunology,** science dealing with the study of the processes by which the body fights infection.
**Impaction,** firmly wedged in.
**Impalpable,** too weak or fine to be felt.
**Impar,** unequal.
**Imperative,** obligatory, involuntary.
**Impermeable,** not allowing to pass through.
**Impervious,** unable to be penetrated.
**Impetigo,** infectious disease of the skin characterized by isolated pustules.
**Implant,** graft, insert.
**Impotence,** sexual weakness in the male.
**Impotent,** unable to copulate; sterile.
**Impregnation,** fertilization; saturation.
**Impulse,** instinctual urge.
**Inanimate,** lifeless.
**Inanition,** starvation.
**Inarticulate,** without joints; not given to clear expression.
**Inborn,** innate; inherent.
**Inbreeding,** mating between close relatives.
**Incest,** sexual relations between those of close relationship.
**Incipient,** beginning; about to appear.
**Incision,** cut.
**Incisor,** any one of the four front teeth of either jaw.
**Inclination,** tendency.
**Incompetent,** not functioning properly.
**Incontinency,** inability to control evacuation.
**Increment,** increase.
**Incretion,** internal secretion.
**Incrustation,** scab.
**Incubate,** to provide favorable conditions for growth and development.
**Incubation,** stage of an infectious disease from the time the germ enters the body until the appear- of the first symptoms.
**Incubus,** nightmare.
**Incurable,** not able to be cured.
**Index,** forefinger.
**Indication,** any aspect of a disease that points out its treatment.
**Indigenous,** native to a particular place.
**Indigestion,** failure of digestive function.
**Indolent,** inactive.
**Induced,** brought about by indirect stimulation.
**Indurated,** hardened.
**Inebriation,** intoxication.
**Inert,** inactive.
**Inertia,** inactivity.
**In Extremis,** at the point of death.
**Infant,** baby.
**Infanticide,** killing of an infant.
**Infantile,** pertaining to infancy; possessing characteristics of early childhood.
**Infantile Paralysis,** infection of central nervous system; poliomyelitis.
**Infantilism,** failure of development.
**Infarction,** blockage of a vessel.
**Infection,** implantation of a germ; spread of a disease.
**Infectious,** liable to be transmitted by infection.
**Inferior,** of a lower position or situation.
**Infertility,** sterility.
**Infiltration,** process by which substances pass into cells or into the spaces around cells.
**Infirm,** weak, feeble.
**Infirmary,** place for the care of the sick.

**Infirmity,** weakness, sickness.
**Inflammation,** changes that occur in living tissues when they are invaded by germs, e.g. redness, swelling, pain and heat.
**Inflation,** distention.
**Inflection,** bending inward.
**Influenza,** virus infection characterized by fever, inflammation of the nose, larynx and bronchi, neuralgic and muscular pains and gastrointestinal disorder.
**Infracostal,** below a rib.
**Infracture,** incomplete bone fracture.
**Inframaxillary,** below the jaw.
**Infrared,** beyond the red portion of the visible spectrum.
**Ingestion,** taking by mouth; eating; drinking.
**Ingravescent,** gradually becoming worse.
**Inguinal,** referring to the groin.
**Inhalant,** that which is inhaled.
**Inhalation,** taking of air into the lungs.
**Inherent,** intrinsic, innate.
**Inherited,** received from one's ancestors.
**Inhibition,** restraint.
**Initial,** beginning; first; commencing.
**Initis,** inflammation of muscular substance.
**Injection,** forcing a liquid into body tissue or a cavity.
**Injury,** hurt; damage.
**Inlay,** filling for a dental cavity.
**Inlet,** means of entrance.
**Innate,** hereditary; congenital.
**Innervation,** distribution of nerves to a part; amount of nervous stimulation received by a part.
**Innocent,** harmless; benign.
**Innocuous,** harmless.
**Innominate,** nameless.
**Inoculation,** immunization against disease by introducing one form of the germ or its products into the body.
**Inoculum,** material used in inoculation.
**Inoperable,** not surgically curable.
**Inorganic,** without organs; not of organic origin.
**Inquest,** medical examination of a corpse to determine cause of death.
**Insanity,** mental disorder.
**Insatiable,** not able to be satisfied.
**Inscription,** part of a prescription which states the names and amounts of ingredients.
**Insecticide,** agent which kills insects.
**Insemination,** fertilization of the female by introduction of male sperm.
**Insensible,** not perceived by the senses; unconscious.
**Insheathed,** enclosed.
**Insidious,** stealthy; applied to a disease that does not show early symptoms of its advent.
**Insipid,** without taste; without animation.
**In Situ,** in the normal place.
**Insoluble,** not capable of being dissolved.
**Insomnia,** sleeplessness.
**Inspection,** visual examination.
**Inspersion,** sprinkle with powder or fluid.
**Inspiration,** breathing in.
**Inspissated,** thickened.
**Instillation,** pouring a liquid by drops.
**Instinct,** inherent behaviour pattern.
**Insulin,** internal secretion of the pancreas concerned with metabolism of glucose in the body.
**Integration,** assimilation.
**Integument,** skin.
**Intellect,** mind.
**Intelligence,** ability to see the relationship between things.
**Intercellular,** between the cells.
**Intercostal,** between two ribs.
**Intercourse,** communication between persons.
**Intercourse, Sexual,** coitus.
**Intermittent Claudication,** pain in legs after brief exercise caused by a defect in blood circulation.
**Intern,** an assistant physician of a hospital staff who is in training prior to receiving a license to practice medicine.
**Internist,** doctor who specializes in diseases of the internal organs.
**Internship,** term of service of an intern.
**Internus,** internal.
**Interstice,** space or gap in a tissue or structure.
**Intervascular,** between blood vessels.
**Intestinal,** pertaining to the intestines.
**Intestine,** the digestive tract beginning at the mouth and ending at the anus.
**Intima,** innermost covering of a blood vessel.
**Intolerance,** not able to endure.
**Intoxication,** drunkenness.
**Intra-Abdominal,** within the abdomen.
**Intracapsular,** within a capsule.
**Intrad,** inwardly.
**Intramuscular;** within the muscular substance.
**Intravenous,** within a vein.
**Intravital,** during life.
**Intrinsic,** innate.
**Introvert,** one whose thoughts and interests are turned inward upon himself.
**Intuition,** instinctual knowledge.
**Inunction,** massaging the skin with an ointment.

**Invagination,** becoming insheathed.
**Invalid,** one who is sickly.
**Inversion,** turning inside out.
**Inversion, Sexual,** homosexuality.
**Invertebrate,** having no backbone.
**Invest,** enclose.
**Inveterate,** hard to cure.
**In Vitro,** process or reaction that is carried out in laboratory test tube.
**In Vivo,** within the living organism.
**Involution,** return to normal that certain organs undergo after fulfilling their function, e.g., the breast after breast feeding; period of decline after middle age.
**Iodine,** chemical element used as an antiseptic and therapeutic agent in medicine.
**Iophobia,** extreme fear of poisons.
**Ipecac,** died plant root used against dysentery and as an emetic; expectorant and diaphoretic.
**Ipsilateral,** situated on the same side.
**I.Q.,** intelligence quotient.
**Iridial,** pertaining to the iris.
**Iridectomy,** surgical removal of the iris, the colored portion of the eye.
**Iris,** colored portion of the eye.
**Iritis,** inflammation of the iris.
**Iron,** chemical element found mainly in the hemoglobin of the red blood cell.
**Iron Lung,** respirator; apparatus to aid breathing.
**Irritable,** capable of reacting to a stimulus; sensitive to stimuli.
**Ischium,** bone upon which body rests when sitting.
**Ischuria,** retention of urine.
**ism** (suffix), condition; theory; method.
**Isocellular,** composed of identical cells.
**Isolation,** separation of persons having a contagious disease.
**Issue,** offspring; suppurating sore kept open by a foreign body in the tissue.
**Isthmus,** neck or narrow part of an organ.
**Itching,** annoying skin sensation relieved by scatching.
**Iter,** tubular passage.
**-itis** (suffix), inflammation.
**I. V.,** intravenously.
**Ixodic,** pertaining to or caused by ticks.

## — J —

**Jacket,** covering for the thorax; plaster of Paris or leather bandage used to immobilize spine or correct deformities.
**Jactitation,** convulsive movements; restless tossing.
**Jail Fever,** typhus fever.
**Jargon,** incoherent speech.
**Jaundice,** increase in bile pigment in blood causing yellow tinge to skin, membranes and eyes; can be caused by disease of liver, gallbladder, bile system or blood.
**Jaw,** applied to one of two bones that form the skeleton of the mouth.
**Jecur,** the liver.
**Jejunitis,** inflammation of the jejunium.
**Jejunum,** middle section of the small intestine.
**Jelly,** thick, homogeneous mass.
**Jerk,** abrupt muscular movement.
**Jockey Strap,** suspensory, scrotum support.
**Joint,** area where two different bones meet.
**Jugal,** pertaining to the cheek or bone.
**Jugular Vein,** large vein at front of throat.
**Juice,** body secretions.
**Junction,** point of meeting or coming together.
**June Cold,** rose fever.
**Jungle Rot,** tropical fungus infection.
**Justo Major,** larger than normal.
**Justo Minor,** smaller than normal.
**Juvenile,** pertaining to youth; young; immature.
**Juxtaposition,** placed side by side; close together.
**Juxtaspinal,** near the spinal column.

## — K —

**Kaif,** tranquil state caused by drugs.
**Kainophobia,** extreme fear of new things.
**Kakosmia,** foul odor.
**Kakotrophy,** malnutrition.
**Kala-Azar,** disease which occurs in tropical countries and shows itself in fever, anemia, dropsy and swelling of the liver and spleen.
**Kali,** potash.
**Kaolin,** powdered aluminum silicate used for ulcerations, wounds that discharge freely or internally for inflammation of the intestines.
**Karezza,** prolonged sexual intercourse without ejaculation.
**Karyogenesis,** formation and development of a cell nucleus.
**Karyomorphism,** the form of a cell nucleus.
**Karyon,** cell nucleus.
**Kata-** (prefix), down.
**Katabolism,** breaking down process in metabolism.
**Keloid,** large scar formation.
**Kelotomy,** relief of hernia strangulation by incision.
**Kenophobia,** extreme fear of empty spaces.
**Kephalin,** commercial remedy for headache.

**Kephyr**, type of fermented milk.
**Keratalgia**, pain in the cornea.
**Keratectomy**, surgical removal of part of the cornea. [nea.
**Keratitis**, inflammation of the cor-
**Keratoiritis**, inflammation of both the cornea and iris.
**Keratolytic**, agent that causes skin to shed.
**Keratoma**, horny growth.
**Keratosis**, any skin disease that causes an overgrowth of a horny material, e.g., multiple warts.
**Kelosteroid**, group of chemical substances produced by the body of primary importance to normal development, body functioning and life.
**Kidney**, organ which secretes urine and aids in maintaing the body's chemical equilibrium.
**Kidney, Floating**, one loosely attached and displaced.
**Kilo**, one thousand.
**Kilogram**, one thousand grams.
**Kinemia**, blood output of the heart.
**Kinematics**, science of motion.
**Kinesia**, motion sickness.
**Kinesis**, motion.
**Kinesthesia**, the muscle sense.
**Kinetic**, pertaining to motion.
**Kink**, bend; twist.
**K. J.**, knee jerk.
**Kleptomania**, obsessive stealing.
**Kleptophobia**, fear of stealing.
**Kneading**, type of massage.
**Knee**, the point of juncture of the femur and tibia.
**Knife**, surgical instrument.
**Kneecap**, patella.
**Knife**, surgical instrument.
**Knock Knee**, condition when legs are turned in at knees.
**Knot**, knoblike structure; small nodule.
**Kolp-** (prefix), vagina.
**Kolpitis**, inflammation of the vagina.
**Kopiopia**, eyestrain.
**Kraurosis**, dryness and hardening of skin.
**Kreotoxism**, meat poisoning.
**Kresol**, germicide.
**Kyllosis**, clubfoot.
**Kymoscope**, apparatus for measuring blood pressure variations.
**Kyogenic**, causing pregnancy.
**Kyphosis**, curvature of the spine.

## — L —

**Labial**, pertaining to a lip.
**Labialism**, speech defect with the use of labial sounds.
**Labile**, changeable; unsteady.
**Lability**, instability.
**Labiology**, study of lip movements.
**Labiomancy**, lipreading.
**Labium**, lip.
**Labor**, period of giving birth to a child.
**Labor, Artificial**, induced labor.
**Labor, Induced**, labor brought on by extraneous means.
**Labor Pains**, pains produced by the contractions of the womb during labor.
**Laboratory**, place for testing and experimental work.
**Labrum**, edge; lip.
**Labyrinth**, internal ear.
**Lac**, milk.
**Lacerate**, to tear.
**Laceration**, tear; wound. [arm.
**Lacertus**, muscular portion of the
**Lacrimal**, pertaining to tears.
**Lacrimation**, secretion of tears from the eye.
**Lactation**, secretion of milk by the breasts.
**Lacteal**, relating to milk.
**Lactescence**, resembling milk.
**Lactic Acid**, an acid normal to the blood and connected with muscle fatigue.
**Lactiferous**, conveying milk.
**Lactifuge**, agent which stops milk secretion.
**Lactigenous**, producing milk.
**Lactin**, lactose; a sugar.
**Lactinated**, containing milk sugar.
**Lactoglobulin**, protein found in milk.
**Lactolin**, condensed milk.
**Lactose**, milk sugar.
**Lactotherapy**, treatment by milk diet.
**Lacuna**, small space; pit.
**Lag**, time between application of a stimulus and the response.
**La Grippe**, influenza.
**Laity**, non professional public.
**Lake**, small fluid cavity.
**Labiatry**, study of speech disorders.
**Laliatry**, babbling.
**Lalopathy**, any speech disorder.
**Lambdacism**, inability to pronounce the l sound.
**Lameness**, limping or abnormal walk.
**Lamina**, thin layer or membrane.
**Laminated**, in layers.
**Lancet**, short, double-edged, puncturing knife.
**Languor**, weariness; exhaustion.
**Lanolin**, wool fat used in ointments and cosmetics.
**Lanugo**, fine hair which covers a baby before birth.
**Lapactic**, purgative.
**Laparotomy**, surgical incision into the abdominal cavity.
**Lapis**, stone.
**Larva**, first stage of an insect from the egg.
**Larvate**, hidden.
**Larvicide**, agent which kills larvae.
**Laryngectomy**, surgical removal of part or all the voice box.
**Laryngismus**, muscular spasm of the voice box.
**Laryngitic**, due to laryngitis.
**Laryngitis**, inflammation of the vocal cords. [box.

**Laryngology**, study of the voice
**Larynx**, voice box.
**Latent**, hidden.
**Lateral**, pertaining to the side.
**Latrine**, public toilet.
**Lattissimus**, widest.
**Lattissimus Dorsi**, back muscle.
**Latus, Lata, Latum**, broad.
**Laudable**, healthy, normal.
**Laughing Gas**, nitrous oxide.
**Laudanum**, tincture of opium.
**Lavage**, cleansing out an organ.
**Lax**, without tension.
**Laxative**, substance when taken helps to evacuate the bowels.
**Lazaretto**, quarantine station, place for treatment of contagious diseases.
**Lean**, emaciated; thin.
**Lechery**, lewdness.
**Lechopyra**, puerperal fever; child birth fever.
**Leech**, blood sucking water worm.
**Left-Handedness**, tendency to use the left hand.
**Leg**, lower extremity; part of the body from the knee to the ankle.
**Leiphemia**, thinness of the blood.
**Leitrichous**, having smooth straight hair.
**Lemic**, pertaining to any epidemic disease.
**Lemology**, study of epidemic diseases.
**Lemostenosis**, stricture of the esophagus.
**Lens**, magnifying glass; transparent, egg-shaped body behind the pupil of the eye.
**Lenticular**, lens-shaped.
**Lenti-form**, lens-shaped.
**Lentigo**, freckle.
**Lentitis**, inflammation of the eye lens.
**Leper**, one afflcted with leprosy.
**Lepra**, leprosy.
**Leprology**, study of leprosy.
**Leprosarium**, place for the care of lepers.
**Leprosy**, chronic disease affecting the skin and nerves, caused by a germ similar to that of tuberculosis.
**Leprous**, afflicted with leprosy.
**Leptodermic**, having a thin skin.
**Leptophonia**, having a feeble voice.
**Leresis**, talkativeness in old age.
**Lesbianism**, homosexuality between women.
**Lesion**, wound; injury; tumor.
**Lethal**, fatal; morbid.
**Lethargy**, marked lack of energy; stupor.
**Leucotomy**, brain operation used in treatment of some mental disorders.
**Leukemia**, fatal disease characterized by excessive production of white blood cells.
**Leukoblast**, immature white blood cell.
**Leukocytes**, white blood cells.
**Leukocythemia**, leukemia.
**Leukocytolysis**, destruction of white blood cells.
**Leukocytosis**, increase in the number of white blood cells.
**Leukopenia**, decreased number of white blood cells.
**Leukoplakia**, white, thickened patches which appear on the skin following chronic irritation.
**Leukorrhea**, whitish discharge from the womb.
**Leukosis**, abnormal pallor.
**Leukous**, white.
**Levoduction**, movement of an eye toward the left.
**Levorotation**, turning to the left.
**Libidinous**, characterized by lewdness.
**Libido**, the instinctual energy of life, usually sexual energy.
**Lichen**, any form of skin disease.
**Lichenification**, thickening and hardening of the skin.
**Licorice**, dried root used in medication.
**Lid**, eyelid.
**Lien**, spleen.
**Lienal**, pertaining to the spleen.
**Lienectomy**, surgical removal of the spleen.
**Lienitis**, inflammation of the spleen.
**Lientery**, diarrhea with evacuation of undigested food.
**Life**, state of being alive.
**Ligaments**, fibrous bands that hold bones together in the region of a joint.
**Ligamentous**, pertaining to a ligament.
**Ligature**, thread for tying off vessels; binding or tying.
**lightening**, dropping of the head of the developing infant into the mother's pelvis in the first stage of labor.
**Limb**, arm or leg.
**Limbus**, rim; border.
**Liminal**, barely noticeable.
**Limitans**, limiting.
**Lingism**, treatment by exercise.
**Limp**, impediment in walking.
**Linctus**, thick syrupy medicine.
**Lingua**, tongue.
**Lingual**, pertaining to the tongue.
**Liniment**, an oily substance rubbed into the skin to relieve pain and muscle cramps.
**Lip**, external soft structure around the mouth.
**Liparous**, fat
**Lipemia**, fat in the blood.
**Lipocyte**, fat cell
**Lipogenic**, producting fat.
**Lipoma**, fatty tumor, usually benign.
**Liposarcoma**, cancerous tumor composed of undeveloped fat cells.
**Lip-Reading**, understanding speech by watching the movements of the lips.
**Listerism**, principles and practice

of antiseptic and asceptic surgical procedures.
**Liquefacient,** converting into a liquid.
**Liquescent,** becoming liquid.
**Lisping,** substitution of sounds due to a speech defect, e.g., **th** for **s.**
**Lithiasis,** formation of stone in the body, e.g., gallstones.
**Litter,** stretcher.
**Livedo,** discolored patch of skin.
**Liver,** important organ of body vitally concerned with metabolism, blood clotting and protein manufacture.
**Livid,** pale, ashen.
**Lividity,** discoloration.
**Lobar,** pertaining to a lobe.
**Lobe,** globular portion of an organ separated by boundaries.
**Lobectomy,** surgical removal of a lobe of an organ.
**Lobites,** inflammation of a lobe.
**Lobatomy,** cutting across of brain tissue.
**Lobule,** small lobe; part of a lobe.
**Lobus,** lobe.
**Localization,** limited to a definite area; determination of the place of infection.
**Lochia,** postnatal vaginal discharge.
**Lochiopyra,** puerperal fever.
**Lock Jaw,** tetanus.
**Locomotion,** movement from place to place.
**Loculpus,** small space; cavity.
**Locus,** place; site.
**Logamnesia,** inability to recall words.
**Logokophosis,** word deafness.
**Logopathy,** any speech disorder of central origin.
**Logopedia,** study and treatment of speech defects.
**Loin,** portion of back between thorax and pelvis.
**Longevity,** long life.
**Longsightedness,** farsightedness.
**Lordosis,** an abnormal curvature of the spine with the convexity towards the front.
**Lotio,** lotion.
**Lotion,** liquid substance for washing a part.
**Loupe,** convex lens. [eases.
**Louse,** parasite that transmits dis-
**Loxia,** wry neck.
**Loxotic,** slanting.
**Loxotomy,** oblique amputation.
**Lozenge,** soothing, medicated solid to be held in the mouth until it it dissolves.
**Lubb-Dupp,** vocal interpretation of heart sounds.
**Lubricant,** an agent which makes smooth.
**Lucid,** clear.
**Lucipetal,** attracted by bright light.
**Lues,** syphilis.
**Lumbago,** backache in the loin region.
**Lumbar,** pertaining to the loin.
**Lumbodynia,** lumbago.
**Lumen,** space within a tube.
**Luminal,** sedative; phenobarbital.
**Lunacy,** mental illness.
**Lunatic,** insane person.
**Lungs,** organs of breathing.
**Lunula,** pale crescent at root of nail.
**Lupiform,** resembling lupus.
**Lupous,** pertaining to lupus.
**Lupus,** disease of unknown origin affecting skin and vital organs.
**Lusus Natural,** freak of nature.
**Luxation,** dislocation.
**Luxus,** excess.
**Lying-in,** puerperal state; child-bed.
**Lymph,** special functioning fluid that flows through specific vessels, passing through the filter of the lymph glands before entering the blood stream.
**Lymphadentis,** inflammation of a lymph gland.
**Lymphatic,** relating to lymph or a vessel through which it flows.
**Lysemia,** disintegration of the blood.
**Lysis,** gradual disappearance of a disease.
**Lyssa,** rabies.
**Lyssoid,** resembling rabies.

## — M —

**Maceration,** soften in a fluid.
**Machonnement,** chewing motion.
**Macies,** wasting.
**Macrobiosis,** longevity.
**Macrocephalus,** having an unusually large head.
**Macrocyte,** large red blood cell.
**Macrodont,** having large teeth.
**Macropodia,** unusually large feet.
**Macroscopic,** visible to the naked eye.
**Macrosonia,** gigantism.
**Macula,** pigmented spot on the skin, spot in the retina.
**Maculate,** spotted.
**Mad,** insane; angry.
**Madarosis,** lose of eyelashes or eyebrows.
**Madescent,** damp.
**Madura Foot,** disease of the foot caused by a fungus infection.
**Maggot,** worm.
**Maidenhead,** hymen.
**Maidism,** pellagra.
**Maieutics,** obstetrics.
**Maim,** injure, disable.
**Main,** hand. [hands.
**Main Succulente,** edema of the
**Mal,** sickness; pain; disease.
**Mala,** cheek; cheekbone.
**Malacosarcosis,** softness of muscle tissue.
**Malacosteon,** softening of the bones.
**Malacostic,** soft.
**Malady,** illness.
**Malaise,** uneasiness, indisposition.
**Malar,** pertaining to the cheek or cheek bone.

**Malaria**, acute, febrile, infectious disease caused by the presence of parasitic organisms in the red blood cells.
**Malariologist**, specialist in malaria.
**Malassimilation**, defective assimilation.
**Malaxation**, kneading motion in massage.
**Male**, masculine; fertilizing member of the sex.
**Malformation**, deformity, an abnormal development. [life.
**Malignant**, poisonous, threatening
**Malingerer**, one who fakes illness and pretends to be suffering.
**Malleolus**, an extension of bone having the shape of a hammerhead on either side of the ankle joint.
**Malnutrition**, improper nutrition.
**Malposition**, abnormal position of any organ or part.
**Malpractice**, improper medical care due to carelessness or ignorance of the doctor.
**Malpresentation**, faulty fetal presentation.
**Malum**, disease.
**Mamma**, breast, mammary gland.
**Mammalgia**, breast pain.
**Mammary Glands**, the breasts.
**Mamma Virilis**, male breast.
**Mammilla**, nipple.
**Mammillary**, resembling a nipple.
**Mammose**, having unusually large breasts.
**Man**, male of the species.
**Mancinism**, left-handedness.
**Mandible**, lower jawbone.
**Mandibular**, pertaining to the mandible or lower jaw bone.
**Manducation**, chewing.
**Maneuver**, skillful procedure.
**Mania**, violent passion or desire; extreme excitement.
**Maniac**, one obsessed by a violent passion or desire.
**Manic-Depressive**, characterized by alternate excitement and depression.
**Manipulation**, skillful use of the hands.
**Mantle**, brain cortex.
**Manual**, pertaining to the hands.
**Manubrium**, handle; top part of the breastbone.
**Manus**, hand.
**Marantic**, marasmic.
**Marasmic**, pertaining to marasmus.
**Marasmus**, progressive wasting in infants without an obvious cause.
**Mareo**, seasickness.
**Margo**, pl., **Margines**, border, margin.
**Mark**, spot; blemish.
**Marrow**, soft tissue in center of bone.
**Marsh Fever**, malarial fever.
**Marsupium**, pouch.
**Masculation**, having male characteristics.
**Masculine**, pertaining to the male.
**Masculinization**, acquisition of male secondary sex characteristics by the female.
**Masochism**, sexual pleasure derived from pain.
**Masochist**, one who derives pleasure from pain.
**Massage**, treatment of disease of the tissues.
**Masseur**, man who massages.
**Masseuse**, woman who massages.
**Mastadenitis**, mammary gland inflammation.
**Mastadenoma**, breast tumor.
**Mastalgia**, pain in the breast.
**Mastauxe**, breast enlargement.
**Mastectomy**, surgical removal of the breast.
**Mastication**, chewing.
**Mastitis**, inflammation of the breasts.
**Mastodynia**, pain in the breast.
**Mastoid**, bone situated behind the ear; nipple-shaped.
**Mastoidectomy**, surgical destruction of the cells in the mastoid.
**Mastology**, study of the breasts.
**Mastoncus**, breast tumor, swelling.
**Mastoncus**, breast tumor, swelling.
**Masturbation**, self-stimulation of the sex organs.
**Materia**, material; substance.
**Materia Medica**, pharmacology.
**Maternal**, pertaining to the mother.
**Matrix**, pl., **Matrices**, uterus, generative structure.
**Maturation**, achieving maturity.
**Mature**, fully developed.
**Maxilla**, bone of the upper jaw.
**Maxillofacial**, pertaining to the lower half of the face.
**M. B.**, Bachelor of Medicine.
**M.D.**, Doctor of Medicine.
**Mean**, average.
**Measles**, an infectious viral disease marked by fever, a rash of pink spots, redness of the eyes and mild bronchitis.
**Measles-German**, an acute viral fever which is like a mild attack of measles, running a shorter course.
**Meatus**, opening; passage.
**Meconium**, opium; first feces of the newborn.
**Medi-** (prefix), middle.
**Medial**, pertaining to the middle.
**Median**, located in the middle.
**Medicable**, receptive to cure.
**Medical**, pertaining to medicine.
**Medical Examiner**, an official whose duty it is to determine cause of death in questionable cases.
**Medical Jurisprudence**, medicine and its relation to law.
**Medicament**, medicinal substance.
**Medication**, giving of remedies; medicinal agent.
**Medicinal**, of a curative nature.

**Medicine,** art and science of healing.

**Medicolegal,** pertaining to medical jurisprudence.

**Medicus,** doctor.

**Medulla,** marrow.

**Medulla Oblongata,** cone-shaped part of the nervous system which is at the junction between the spinal cord and the brain.

**Medullary,** pertaining to a medulla.

**Medullispinal,** pertaining to the spinal cord. [row.

**Medullitis,** inflammation of mar-

**Megacephalic,** having an usually large head.

**Megalgia,** acute pain.

**Megalocornea,** bulging of the cornea.

**Megalogastria,** enlargement of the stomach.

**Megalohepatia,** enlargement of the liver.

**Megalomania,** delusions of personal grandeur.

**Megalomelia,** unusual largeness of the limbs.

**Megarectum,** enlargement of the rectum.

**Megrim,** migraine.

**Mel,** honey.

**Melaena,** black vomit.

**Melalgia,** pain in the extremities.

**Melancholia,** depression and self pity.

**Melanin,** black or dark-brown pigment.

**Melanoglossia,** black tongue.

**Melanoma,** tumor arising from a pigmented mole.

**Melanopathy,** excessive skin pigmentation.

**Melanosis,** deposits of black pigment found in various parts of the body.

**Melasma,** dark pigmentation.

**Melitemia,** excess blood sugar.

**Melitis,** inflammation of cheek.

**Mellite,** honey preparation.

**Membrana,** membrane.

**Membrane,** thin layer of tissue covering or dividing an organ.

**Membranoid,** resembling a membrane.

**Membrum,** body; part; organ.

**Memory,** recall of past experience.

**Menacme,** years of menstrual activity in a woman's life.

**Menarche,** onset of the menstrual period.

**Meniere's Disease,** a disease of the organs of balance in the inner ear in which there is deafness and sudden attacks of extreme giddiness, vomiting and loss of balance.

**Meninges,** thin covering of the brain and spinal cord.

**Meningioma,** tumor arising from membranes covering the brain.

**Meningitides,** inflammation of the lining membrane of the brain or spinal cord.

**Meningitis,** inflammation of the lining of the brain and spinal cord with both mental and motor systems usually involved.

**Meningomalacia,** softening of a membrane.

**Meningopathy,** any disease of the meninges.

**Meninx,** see meninges.

**Meniscus,** crescent-shaped piece of gristle usually found in the knee joint.

**Menolipsis,** temporary absence of menstruation.

**Menopause,** age at which normal cessation of the monthly period occurs, usually between 45 and 50.

**Menorrhagia,** excessive bleeding during the monthly period.

**Menorrhea,** normal menstruation; profuse menstruation.

**Menoschesis,** suppression of menstruation.

**Menostaxis,** prolonged menstruation.

**Menses,** menstruation.

**Menstruation,** monthly bleeding of the womb occurring between puberty and menopause.

**Mensuration,** measuring.

**Mental,** pertaining to the mind; pertaining to the chin.

**Mentum,** chin.

**Mephitic,** noxious; foul.

**Meralgia,** thigh pain.

**Meropia,** partial blindness.

**Merotomy,** cutting into sections.

**Mesiad,** toward the center.

**Mesial,** located in the middle.

**Mesmerism,** hypnotism.

**Metabolism,** the building-up and breaking-down processes of the body as a whole.

**Metabolism, Basal,** minimum amount of energy necessary to maintain life when the body is at complete rest.

**Metacarpus,** five bones in the palm of the hand.

**Metachrosis,** change of color.

**Metachysis,** blood transfusion.

**Metacyesis,** extrauterine pregnancy

**Metallophobia,** extreme fear of metallic objects.

**Metamorphosis,** change of shape or structure.

**Metastasis,** movement of bacteria or a disease from one part of the body to another.

**Metatarsus,** part of the foot between the ankle and the beginning of the toes.

**Metopagus,** twins joined at the forehead.

**Metopic,** pertaining to the forehead.

**Metra,** the uterus.

**Metralgia,** pain in the uterus.

**Metrectasia,** dilatation of the uterus
**Metritis,** inflammation of the uterus
**Metrocarcinoma,** cancer of the uterus.
**Metrocyte,** mother cell.
**Metrodynia,** pain in the uterus.
**Metrology,** science of measurements.
**Metropathy,** any uterine disorder.
**Metrorrhagia,** vaginal bleeding unrelated to monthly bleeding.
**M.F.D.,** minimum fatal dose.
**Miasm, Miasma,** foul odor.
**Mication,** involuntary, rapid winking; fast motion.
**Microbe,** small, living organism discernible only through a microscope.
**Microbicidal,** destroying microbes.
**Microbiologist,** specialist in microbiology.
**Microbiology,** science dealing with microscopic organisms.
**Microcardia,** abnormal smallness of the heart.
**Microcoria,** smallness of the pupil.
**Microcyst,** tiny cyst.
**Microcyte,** small red blood corpuscle.
**Microglossia,** abnormal smallness of the tongue.
**Microlesion,** very small lesion.
**Micromastia,** unusual smallness of the breast.
**Micronize,** reduce to very small particles.
**Microorganism,** microscopic organism.
**Microphallus,** abnormal smallness of the penis.
**Micropsia,** defective vision; seeing things smaller than they are.
**Microscope,** instrument which enlarges objects for visual examination.
**Microscopic,** able to be seen only under a microscope.
**Microscopy,** observation with the microscope.
**Micturition,** urination.
**Midget,** one who does not attain full growth; very small person.
**Midriff,** diaphragm.
**Midwife,** woman who helps at childbirth.
**Midwifery,** obstetrics.
**Midriasis,** enlargement of the pupil of the eye.
**Migraine,** severe, periodic, one-sided headache, usually accompanied by abdominal distress.
**Miliaria,** heat rash.
**Milieu,** environment.
**Milphosis,** loss of eyebrows or eyelashes.
**Miocardia,** heart contraction.
**Miscarriage,** loss of product of conception before age of viability; abortion.
**Miscegenation,** people of two different races that are married.
**Miscible,** able to be mixed.
**Misogamy,** hatred of marriage.
**Misopedia,** hatred of children.
**Mite,** tiny insect.
**Mitral valve,** the heart valve on left side of heart between upper and lower chambers.
**Mittelschmerz,** pain at time of ovulation.
**M.M.,** mucous membrane.
**Mnemonics,** improvement of the memory.
**Mobile,** movable.
**Moccasin,** poisonous snake.
**Modus,** method.
**Modus Operandi,** method of performing an act.
**Mogigraphia,** writers' cramp.
**Mogilalia,** speech defect.
**Mogitocia,** difficult birth.
**Moist,** damp.
**Molar,** grinder tooth.
**Mold,** fungus.
**Molding,** shaping of the fetal head at birth.
**Mole,** skin growth usually colored and sprouting hair.
**Molecule,** tiny mass of matter.
**Molimen,** effort to establish the monthly period.
**Mollities,** abnormal softening.
**Molluscum,** chronic skin disease with pulpy bumps.
**Monarticular,** pertaining to a single joint.
**Mongolism,** arrest of physical and mental development, with features similar to the Asiatic race.
**Moniliasis,** fungus infection of various areas of the body, especially mouth, throat, vagina.
**Moniliform,** beaded.
**Monocular,** pertaining to or affecting one eye; having a single lens.
**Monocyesis,** pregnancy with one fetus.
**Monocyte,** type of white blood cell.
**Monodiplopia,** double vision in one eye.
**Monogenesis,** nonsexual reproduction.
**Monogenous,** a sexual reproduction.
**Monohemerous,** lasting only one day.
**Monomania,** obsession with one subject or idea.
**Monomelic,** affecting one limb.
**Mononucleosis,** glandular fever; virus disease in which monocytes are increased beyond normal number, lymph nodes enlarged, sore throat.
**Monopathy,** disease affecting a single part.
**Monoplegia,** paralysis of a single group of muscles or one limb.
**Monosexual,** having characteristics of only one sex.
**Mood,** attitude; state of mind.
**Mons,** elevated area.

**Mons Pubis, Mons Veneris,** area over the symphysis pubis in the female.
**Monster,** abnormally formed fetus.
**Monstrosity,** state of being a monster.
**Monthlies,** menses.
**Monticulus,** probuterance.
**Morbid,** pertaining to disease; the disease itself.
**Morbid Condition,** condition of disease.
**Morbific,** causing disease.
**Morbilli,** measles.
**Morbilliform,** like measles.
**Morbus,** disease.
**Morbus Caducus,** epilepsy.
**Mores,** customs.
**Morgue,** public mortuary.
**Moria,** foolishness.
**Moribund,** dying.
**Morning Sickness,** nausea and vomiting during the early stages of pregnancy.
**Moron,** one whose mental age is from seven to twelve years.
**Morosis,** feeblemindedness.
**Morphine,** drug used as an analgesic and sedative.
**Morphinism,** addiction to morphine.
**Mors,** death.
**Morsus,** bite.
**Morsus Humanus,** human bite
**Mortal,** deadly.
**Mortise Joint,** ankle joint.
**Mosquito,** blood sucking insect.
**Mosquitocide,** agent which kills mosquitoes.
**Mother,** female parent.
**Mother's Mark,** birthmark.
**Motile,** able to move.
**Mottling,** discoloration in various areas.
**Mounding,** lumping.
**Mountain Sickness,** condition caused by low air pressure.
**Mouth,** oral cavity.
**M.S.,** Master of Surgery.
**M.T.,** Medical Technologist.
**Muciferous,** secreting mucus.
**Mucilage,** paste.
**Mucilaginous,** adhesive.
**Mucin,** main substance of mucus.
**Mucopus,** mucus mixed with pus.
**Mucosa,** mucous membrane; lining tissue that produces mucus
**Mucous,** pertaining to mucus.
**Mucus,** a thick, white liquid secreted by mucous glands.
**Mulatto,** anyone of both Negro and White blood.
**Muliebria,** female genitalia.
**Muliebrity,** femininity.
**Multi-** (prefix), many; much.
**Multigravida,** pregnant woman who had more than two past pregnancies.
**Multipara,** woman who has had more than two live children.
**Mumps,** infectious disease marked by swelling of the large salivary glands in front of the ears.
**Murmur,** abnormal heart sound with a blowing or rasping quality.
**Musca,** fly.
**Muscae Volitantes,** spots before the eyes.
**Muscle,** bundle of contractile fibers which produce movement.
**Muscle Cramp,** involuntary contraction of muscles.
**Muscular,** pertaining to muscle.
**Musculus,** muscle.
**Musophobia,** extreme fear of mice.
**Mussitation,** delirious muttering.
**Mustard Plaster,** home remedy no longer commonly used.
**Mutation,** change.
**Mute,** unable to speak; one who cannot speak.
**Mutism,** speechlessness; dumbness.
**Myalgia,** muscle pain.
**Myasthenia,** muscle weakness.
**Myatonia,** muscle limpness.
**Mycetismus,** mushroom poisoning.
**Mycology,** science of fungi.
**Mycosis,** infection caused by fungi.
**Mydriasis,** abnormal pupil dilation.
**Myectomy,** surgical removal of a piece of muscle.
**Myectopia,** muscle displacement.
**Myelauxe,** bone marrow increase.
**Myelin,** nerve covering.
**Myelon,** spinal cord.
**Myelopathy,** disease of the spinal cord.
**Myeloplegia,** spinal paralysis.
**Myelitis,** spinal cord inflammation.
**Myeloma,** bone marrow tumor that may be cancerous.
**Myenteron,** muscular layer of the intestine.
**Myiasia,** condition when larvae of flies enter eyes, ears or intestines.
**Myitis,** muscle inflammation.
**Myocarditis,** inflammation of the heart muscle.
**Myocardium,** muscle that makes up the heart.
**Myoclonus,** muscle spasm.
**Myocyte,** cell of muscular tissue.
**Myoid,** resembling muscle.
**Myology,** study of muscles.
**Myoma,** tumor from muscle tissue.
**Myomectomy,** surgical removal of a myoma.
**Myopathy,** any muscle disease.
**Myope,** one who is nearsighted.
**Myopia,** nearsightedness.
**Myosis,** construction of the eye pupil.
**Myositis,** muscle inflammation, usually a voluntary muscle.
**Myospasm,** muscle spasm.
**Myotasis,** stretching of muscle.
**Myotonia,** continuous muscle spasm not relieved by relaxation.
**Myringitis,** inflammation of the eardrum.
**Myringotomy,** incision into the eardrum.
**Mythomania,** habitual lying or exaggeration.

**Myxedema,** a disease due to failure of the thyroid gland.
**Myxoma,** tumor of mucous tissue.
**Myxorrhea,** flow of mucus.
**Myzesis,** sucking.

— N —

**Nail,** horny structure covering the ends of the fingers and toes.
**Nail Bed,** part of a finger or toe covered by a nail.
**Nail Biting,** nervous tendency to bite or or chew the fingernails.
**Naked,** exposed to view.
**Nanism,** dwarfishness.
**Nanus,** dwarf; stunted.
**Nap,** short sleep.
**Nape,** back of the neck.
**Narcissism,** self love.
**Narcolepsy,** disease of unknown origin in which there are periodic episodes of sleep any time of day or night.
**Narcomania,** morbid desire for narcotics.
**Narcosis,** state of unconsciousness.
**Narcotic,** producing a state of unconsciousness; any sleep inducing drug; one addicted to the use of narcotics.
**Narcotize,** to make unconscious.
**Naris,** nostril.
**Nasal,** pertaining to the nose; bone forming the bridge of the nose.
**Nasus,** nose.
**Natal,** pertaining to birth; pertain- to the buttocks.
**Natality,** birth rate.
**Natant,** floating.
**Natis,** buttocks.
**Native,** inherent; indigenous.
**Natural,** not artificial.
**Natural Childbirth,** childbirth without anesthesia.
**Naturopathy,** curing without drugs.
**Nature Cure,** any system of treatment which is based upon the belief that disease may best be cured and health maintained by the use of "natural remedies", as opposed to artificial and man-made drugs.
**Naupathia,** seasickness.
**Nausea,** stomach discomfort with the feeling of a need to vomit.
**Nauseant,** causing nausea.
**Navel,** remnant on outside of body where umbilical cord was attached at birth.
**Near Point,** point closest to the eye at which an object can be seen distinctly.
**Nearsighted,** able to see clearly only a short distance.
**Nebula,** haziness; cloudy urine.
**Necator,** hookworm.
**Neck,** part of the body connecting the head and trunk; narrow part near the extremity of any organ.
**Necromania,** obsession with death.
**Necrophilism,** intercourse with a corpse.
**Necropneumonia,** gangrene of lung.
**Necropsy,** autopsy.
**Necrosis,** death of a part of the body due to absence of blood supply.
**Needle,** pointed instrument for sewing or puncturing.
**Negativism,** a symptom in mental diseases in which the patient resists or is against everything.
**Neogala,** first milk after childbirth.
**Neogenesis,** new formation.
**Neonatal,** concerning the newborn.
**Neonatorum,** pertaining to the newborn.
**Neonatus,** a newborn infant.
**Neopathy,** new disease or complication.
**Negativism,** a symptom in mental diseases in which the patient resists or is against everything.
**Neogala,** first milk after childbirth.
**Neogenesis,** new formation.
**Neonatal,** concerning the newborn.
**Neonatorum,** pertaining to the new born.
**Neonatus,** a newborn infant.
**Neopathy,** new disease or complication.
**Neophilism,** excessive love of new things. [things.
**Neophobia,** extreme fear of new
**Neoplasm,** an abnormal growth.
**Nephralgia,** pain in a kidney.
**Nephrectomy,** surgical removal of a kidney.
**Nephrelcus,** renal ulcer.
**Nephric,** pertaining to the kidney.
**Nephritis,** inflammation of the kidneys.
**Nephrolithiases,** formation of kidney stones.
**Nephrology,** study of the kidney.
**Nephroma,** tumor of the outer portion of the kidney.
**Nephropexy,** sewing a floating kidney into place.
**Nephros,** the kidney.
**Nephrosis,** disintegration of the kidney without signs of inflammation.
**Nepiology,** study of newborn.
**Nerve,** bundle of nerve fibers existing outside the central nervous system.
**Nervous,** highly excitable.
**Nervous,** a condition of being easily disturbed or distressed.
**Nervous System,** entire nervous structure of the body.
**Nervus,** pl., **Nervi,** nerve.
**Network,** structure composed of interlacing fibers.
**Neural,** pertaining to nerves or nervous tissue.
**Neuralgia,** pain along course of nerve.
**Neurasthenia,** exhaustion of the nerves.

**Neure,** neuron.
**Neurectasia,** stretching of a nerve to relieve pain.
**Neuritis,** inflammation of a nerve.
**Neurocranium,** portion of the cranium enclosing the brain.
**Neurocyte,** any nerve cell.
**Neurodynamic,** pertaining to nervous energy.
**Neuroid,** resembling a nerve.
**Neuro-induction,** mental suggestion.
**Neurologist,** specialist in disorders of the nervous system.
**Neuroma,** tumor composed of nerve substance.
**Neuromuscular,** pertaining to the nerves and muscles.
**Neuron,** nerve cell.
**Neuronitis,** inflammation of a neuron.
**Neuropathy,** any disease of the nervous system.
**Neurophthisis,** degeneration or wasting of nerve tissue.
**Neuroplasm,** protoplasm of a nerve cell.
**Neuropsychiatry,** branch of medicine dealing with nervous and mental disorders.
**Neurosis,** minor mental disorder.
**Neurospasm,** muscular twitching.
**Neurosurgeon,** specialist in surgery of the brain and nervous system.
**Neurosyphilis,** syphilis of the nervous system.
**Neurothlipsis,** nerve pressure.
**Neurotrauma,** nerve lesion.
**Nevus,** birthmark; mole.
**Nexus,** a binding together.
**Niche,** depression; recess.
**Nicotine,** poisonous alkaloid of tobacco.
**Nictitation,** excessive winking.
**Nidus,** cluster, focus of infection; nerve nucleus.
**Night Cry,** cry of a child during sleep.
**Nightmare,** bad dream.
**Nightwalking,** sleepwalking.
**Nigra,** black.
**Negrities Linguae,** black tongue.
**N.I.H.,** National Institutes of Health.
**Niphablepsia,** snow blindenss.
**Nipple,** protuberance in each breast from which the female secretes milk.
**Nit,** egg of a louse.
**N.L.N.,** National League for Nursing
**Noctophobia,** extreme fear of night.
**Nocturia,** bed wetting; frequent urination at night.
**Nocuity,** harmfulness.
**Node,** small rounded protuberance; point of constriction.
**Nodule,** small node; small group of cells.
**Nodus,** node.
**Noma,** form of gangrene of the mouth found in ill-nourished or weak children.
**Non compos mentis,** not of sound mind.
**Non Repetat,** do not repeat.
**Nonsexual,** without sex, asexual.
**Nontoxic,** not poisonous.
**Nonunion,** failure of bone fragments to knit together.
**Nonviable,** incapable.
**Noopsyche,** intellectual processes.
**Norm,** standard.
**Normal,** usual.
**Normocyte,** normal sized red blood cell.
**Normoptopic,** normally located.
**Nose,** organ of the sense of smell.
**Nosebleed,** hemorrhage from the nose.
**Nosema,** sickness; disease.
**Nosology,** science of disease classification.
**Nosophilia,** extreme desire to be sick.
**Nosophobia,** extreme fear of illness.
**Nosopoietic,** causing disease.
**Nostalgia,** homesickness; feeling for past experiences and things.
**Nostomania,** extreme homesickness.
**Nostril,** nasal aperture.
**Nostrum,** patent medicine.
**Notal,** dorsal.
**Notalgia,** back pain.
**Notifiable,** pertaining to any disease which must be reported to health authorities.
**Noxious,** harmful; deadly; poisonous.
**Nubile,** of childbearing age.
**Nucha,** nape of the neck.
**Nucleus,** pl., **Neuclei,** center of a cell.
**Nudomania,** extreme desire to be nude.
**Nudophobia,** extreme fear of being nude.
**Nullipara,** woman who has not given birth to a child.
**Numb,** insensible.
**Numbness,** lack of sensation.
**Nurse,** one who is trained to care for the sick; to care for the sick; to breast feed.
**Nutation,** nodding.
**Nutrient,** nourishing.
**Nutrition,** food; nourishment of its assimilation.
**Nutritious,** giving nourishment.
**Nux,** nut.
**Nyctalgia,** pain during the night.
**Nycterine,** occurring at night.
**Nyctalopia,** night blindness due to lack of vitamin A.
**Nyctophobia,** extreme fear of darkness.
**Nyctotyphlosis,** night blindness.
**Nygma,** puncture wound.
**Nymphectomy,** surgical removal of the small lips of the vagina.
**Nymphomania,** excessive sexual desire in the female.
**Nystagmus,** jerking movement of

the eyes which may be inborn or a sign of disease of the nervous system.
**Nyxis,** puncture; pricking.

— O —

**Oaric,** concerning the ovary.
**Oaritis,** ovarian inflammation.
**Ordormition,** numbness and tingling in an arm or leg.
**Obduction,** autopsy.
**Obesity,** excessive stoutness.
**Obfuscation,** confusion.
**Oblique,** diagonal.
**Obliteration,** complete surgical removal of a part; total memory loss.
**Obmutescence,** loss of power to speak.
**Obnubilation,** confused state.
**Obsession,** all consuming emotion or idea.
**Obstetrical,** pertaining to obstetrics.
**Obstetrician,** physician who specializes in pregnant women.
**Obstetrics,** branch of medicine dealing with pregnancy and delivery of infants.
**Obstipation,** constipation due to obstruction.
**Obstruction,** blockage of structure; usually intestine.
**Obtund,** to dull sensation.
**Obturation,** closing of an opening.
**Occipital,** pertaining to the bone that constitutes the back part of the skull.
**Occiput,** back part of skull.
**Occlude,** to block or obstruct.
**Occlusion,** shutting; the full meeting of the chewing surfaces of the upper and lower teeth.
**Occult,** hidden; obscure.
**Occupational Disease,** disease caused by one's work.
**Occupational Therapy,** use of an activity as treatment. [ing.
**Ochlesis,** disease due to overcrowding.
**Ochlophobia,** extreme fear of crowds. [skin.
**Ochrodermia,** yellowness of the
**Octoroon,** one who is 1/8 Negro and 7/8 Caucasian.
**Ocular,** pertaining to the eye or vision.
**Oculist,** specialist in eye diseases.
**Oculus,** eye.
**Odaxesmus,** biting of tongue or skin of mouth during a fit.
**Odaxitic,** stinging or itching.
**Odontalgia,** toothache.
**Odontexesis,** cleaning of teeth.
**Odontiasis,** teething.
**Odontic,** pertaining to the teeth.
**Odonitis,** tooth inflammation
**Odontogeny,** development of teeth.
**Odontology,** study of the teeth.
**Odontechtomy,** tooth extraction.
**Odonterism,** chattering of teeth.
**Odontoclasis,** breaking a tooth.
**Odontodynia,** toothache.
**Odontoma,** tumor arising from the same tissue from which teeth are formed.
**Odontoprisis,** grinding teeth.
**Odontotomy,** incision of a tooth.
**Odontotrypy,** drilling of a tooth.
**Odynophagia,** pain with swallowing.
**Odynophobia,** extreme fear of pain.
**Oedipus Complex,** abnormal love of a child for a parent of the opposite sex, usually a boy for his mother.
**Oikophobia,** extreme hatred of the home.
**Ointment,** soft fat substance spread on skin as therapy.
**Oleaginous,** oily.
**Olecranon,** bony inner portion of elbow.
**Oleum,** oil.
**Olfaction,** smelling; sense of smell.
**Olfactory,** pertaining to the sense of smell.
**Oligemia,** deficiency of blood.
**Oligocholia,** bile deficiency.
**Oligogalactia,** deficient milk secretion.
**Oligoposy,** insufficient liquid intake.
**Oligotrichia,** lack of hair.
**Oligotrophy,** insufficient nutrition.
**Oliguria,** decreased amount of urine production.
**Omagra,** shoulder gout.
**Omalgia,** neuralgia of the shoulder.
**Omentum,** large fatty membrane which acts as a cover for the bowels.
**Omitis,** shoulder, inflammation.
**Omnivorous,** eating all types of food.
**Omodynia,** shoulder pain.
**Omphalic,** pertaining to the umbilicus.
**Omphalitis,** inflammation of the navel.
**Omphalocele,** hernia around navel.
**Omphalos,** navel.
**Onanism,** complete sexual intercourse with ejaculation outside, the vagina; masturbation.
**Oncosis,** multiple tumors.
**Onocyte,** tumor cell.
**Oncogenous,** causing tumors.
**Oncoma,** tumor.
Oncosis, **multiple tumors.**
**Oncotic,** pertaining to swelling.
**Oneiric,** pertaining to dreams.
**Oniomania,** excessive desire to buy things.
**Onomatomania,** compulsion to repeat words.
**Onychia,** infection and inflammation around fingernails.
**Onychophagia,** nail biting.
**Onychosis,** disease of the nails.
**Onyx,** fingernail; toenail.
**Onyxis,** ingrown nails.
**Oncyesis,** pregnancy in the ovary.
**Oophoralgia,** ovarian pain.

**Oophorectomy,** surgical removal of an ovary.
**Oophoritis,** inflammation of an ovary. [mor.
**Oophoroma,** malignant ovarian tu-
**Oophoron,** ovary.
**Oosperm,** fertilized ovum.
**Ootheca,** ovary.
**Opaque,** dark; not transparent; mentally dull.
**Operable,** capable of being relieved by an operation.
**Operation,** surgical procedure.
**Operation Major,** one in which there is considerable risk to life.
**Operation, Minor,** one in which there is little or no danger to life.
**Ophidism,** snake poisoning.
**Ophthalmia,** inflammation of the eye.
**Ophthalic,** pertaining to the eyes.
**Ophthalmologist,** specialist in the eye and its diseases.
**Ophthalmology,** study of eye and its diseases.
**Ophthalmoplegia,** paralysis of the eye muscles.
**Ophthalmoscope,** instrument for ex-examining the eyes.
**Opiate,** any opium derivative.
**Opisthotonis,** arched-back position with head and heel on the horizontal.
**Opsialgia,** pain in region of face.
**Opsomania,** extreme craving for a particular food.
**Optic,** concerning sight or eye.
**Optical,** pertaining to vision.
**Optician,** one who makes lenses or optical instruments.
**O.R.,** operating room.
**Ora,** border; margin.
**Orad,** toward the mouth.
**Oral,** pertaining to the mouth.
**Oralogy,** oral hygiene; study of mouth diseases.
**Orbicular,** circular.
**Orbit,** eyesocket.
**Orchic,** pertaining to the testes.
**Orchiectomy,** surgical removal of a testes.
**Orchiodynia,** testicle pain.
**Orchioncus,** tumor of a testes.
**Orchis,** testicle. [ticle.
**Orchitis,** inflammation of the tes-
**Orderly,** male hospital attendant.
**Orexigenic,** appetite stimulant.
**Oreximania,** abnormal desire for food.
**Organ,** group of tissue with specific function.
**Organism,** individual animal or plant.
**Orgasm,** sexual climax.
**Orifice,** opening, entrance.
**Oropharynx,** first part of throat starting at mouth.
**Orotherapy,** treatment with serums.
**Orrhorrhea,** watery discharge; flow of serum.
**Orrhology,** study of blood serum.
**Orthogenics,** eugenics.
**Orthopedics,** branch of medicine dealing with the surgery of bones and joints. [dics.
**Orthopedist,** specialist in orthope-
**Orthosis,** correction of a deformity.
**Orthostatic,** concerning standing position.
**Orthopnea,** condition in which difficult breathing is aided by propping up head and shoulders.
**Orthopschiatry,** branch of psychiatry dealing mainly with adolescents.
**Orthuria,** normal frequency of urination.
**Os,** pl., **Ora,** mouth, opening.
**Os,** pl., **Ossa,** bone.
**Oscedo,** yawning; white spots in the mouth. [tum.
**Oscheitis,** inflammation of the scro-
**Oscitation,** yawning.
**Osculum,** aperature.
**Osculation,** kissing; joining of two structures by their mouths.
**Osmatic,** having an acute sense of smell.
**Osmesis,** smelling.
**Osmics,** science of odors.
**Osmosis,** passage of fluid from lower to higher area of concentration.
**Osphresis,** sense of smell.
**Osphus,** loin.
**Ossa,** bones.
**Osseous,** bonelike.
**Ossicle,** small bone of ear.
**Ossiferous,** producing bone
**Ossofication,** bone formation; change of tissue to bone.
**Ossify,** to turn into bone.
**Ostectomy,** surgical removal of a bone.
**Osteitis,** bone inflammation.
**Osteocarcinoma,** bone cancer.
**Osteochrondritis,** inflammation of both bone and cartilage from which bone is formed.
**Osteochrondroma,** tumor arising from bone cartilage.
**Osteology,** study of bones.
**Osteoma,** tumor composed of various parts of bone.
**Osteomalacia,** softening of bone.
**Osteomyelitis,** an inflammatory disease of bone caused usually by infection with streptococcus or staphylococcus.
**Osteopathy,** system of treatment based on the idea that diseases are caused by minor dislocations of the spine, and, therefore,curable by bone manipulation.
**Osteosis,** formation of bony tissue.
**Ostum,** vaginal, outer opening of the vagina.
**Ostium,** small opening.
**O.T.,** occupational therapy.
**Otalgia,** earache.

**Otic,** pertaining to the ear.
**Otitis,** inflammation of the ear.
**Otolaryngology,** medical specialty concerned with ear, nose and throat.
**Otologist,** ear specialist.
**Otology,** branch of medicine dealing with the ear.
**Otopathy,** any ear disease.
**Otosclerosis,** type of deafness caused by hardening of the tissues and bones in the inner ear.
**Otoscope,** instrument used to examine ear.
**Oula,** the gums.
**Ouloid,** scar-like.
**Outlay,** graft.
**Outpatient,** one who received treatment at a hospital without being admitted.
**Oval,** egg-shaped.
**Ovarian,** pertaining to the ovaries.
**Ovariectomy,** surgical removal of an ovary.
**Ovary,** the sex glands in women.
**Ovate,** oval.
**Overgrowth,** excessive growth.
**Overweight,** exceeding desired weight by more than 10%.
**Oviduct,** tube from ovary to uterus.
**Ovulation,** process of discharge of egg from ovary.
**Ovum,** pl., **Ova,** egg cell.
**Oxyblepsia,** very acute vision.
**Oxycinesia,** pain on motion.
**Oxygen,** an element needed for life which is brought into the body by the process of breathing.
**Oxygeusia,** acute sense of taste.
**Oxylalia,** rapid speech.
**Oxyopia,** acute sight.
**Oxytocic,** agent used to stimulate uterus to contract.
**Ozostomia,** offensive breath.
**Ozena,** disease of nasal passage leading to the production of a foul-smelling discharge.

## — P —

**Pabulum,** food, nourishment.
**Pacemaker,** area of heart where rhythm of heart beat starts.
**Pachyblepharon,** thickening of the eyelid.
**Pachycephalous,** thick wall.
**Pachychilla,** thick lips.
**Pachyderma,** thick skin.
**Pachyglossia,** thick tongue.
**Pachyhemia,** thickening of the blood.
**Pachymeningitis,** inflammation of the outer covering of the brain and spinal cord.
**Pachymeter,** instrument for measuring thickness.
**Pachynsis,** thickening.
**Pachyonychia,** thickening of the nails.
**Pachypodous,** big feet.
**Pack,** a dry or wet, hot or cold blanket wrapped around the patient.
**Packing,** material used to fill wound or cavity.
**Pad,** soft cushion.
**Paget's Disease; Osteitis Deformans,** thickening of bones, mainly skull and shin; rash of nipple connected with breast tumor.
**Pain,** distress; agony, suffering.
**Pain, False,** false labor pains.
**Palate,** roof of the mouth divided into hard and soft portions.
**Palantine,** pertaining to the palate.
**Palatitis,** inflammation of the palate.
**Paleontology,** study of early man.
**Palliate,** to reduce or allay discomfort. [ing.
**Palliative,** relieving pain or suffer-
**Pallid,** lacking.
**Pallor,** paleness of skin.
**Palm,** inside portion of hand.
**Palma,** palm.
**Palmar,** pertaining to the palm.
**Palpable,** able to be touched.
**Palpate,** to examine by feeling.
**Palpebra,** eyelid.
**Palpebra Inferior,** lower eyelid.
**Palpebra Superior,** upper eyelid.
**Palpitation,** rapid pulsation in an organ, usually refers to the heart. [sis.
**Palsy,** impaired function or paraly-
**Paludism,** malaria.
**Panacea,** cure for all ills.
**Panarthritis,** inflammation of the entire joint.
**Pancarditis,** infection of all parts of heart.
**Panchrest,** panacea.
**Pancreas,** gland lying behind and below the stomach which produces ferments which are passed into the intestinal tract to help in digestion; site of insulin production.
**Pancreatitis,** inflammation of the pancreas.
**Pancreectomy,** removal of pancreas in part or whole.
**Pandemic,** widely-spread epidemic.
**Pandiculation,** stretching and yawning.
**Panesthesia,** all of the sensations experienced.
**Pang,** spontaneous, sudden emotion or pain.
**Panhidrosis,** perspiration over entire body.
**Panhysterectomy,** complete removal of the womb.
**Panic,** extreme anxiety, with temporary loss of reason.
**Panniculitis,** inflammation of abdominal wall fat. [layer.
**Panniculus,** layer of tissue, fatty
**Pannus,** abnormal membrane on the cornea.
**Panophobia,** extreme fear of everything in general.

**Pansinusitis**, inflammation of all the sinuses.
**Pant**, breathe fast and hard.
**Pap**, nipple; soft food.
**Pappilla**, nipple-like protuberance.
**Papilla, Mammary**, breast nipple.
**Papilledema**, swelling of optic nerve where nerve enters eye.
**Papilloma**, benign tumor of skin or inner membranes.
**Papule**, small red raised area on skin.
**Par**, pair.
**Para-** (prefix), beside.
**Paracentesis**, puncture.
**Paracusia**, any hearing defect.
**Parachroma**, skin discoloration.
**Paracyesis**, pregnancy outside uterus.
**Paralalia**, speech disorder.
**Paralgesia**, painful sensation.
**Paralysis**, loss of the power of movement or sensation in one or more parts of the body.
**Paralytic**, pertaining to paralysis.
**Paralyze**, to cause loss of muscle control and/or feeling.
**Paramenia**, irregular or abnormal menstrual period.
**Parametrium**, tissue surrounding and supporting the womb.
**Paranoia**, chronic psychosis characterized by fears, suspicion and well organized imaginery thoughts.
**Paraphemia**, distorted speech.
**Paraphobia**, mild phobia.
**Paraplegia**, paralysis of the legs or lower part of the body.
**Parapoplexy**, slight apoplexy.
**Parasite**, any animal or plant which lives inside or on the body of of another animal or plant.
**Parateresiomania**, compulsion to see new sights.
**Parathymia**, disordered emotion.
**Parathyroid Glands**, group of six small glands situated around the thyroid gland concerned with calcium and phosporus in body.
**Paregoric**, derivative of opium used to help relieve pain or diarrhea.
**Parenchyma**, productive part of an organ.
**Parent**, one who begets offspring.
**Parenchyma**, functional tissue of an organ.
**Parenteral**, outside of digestive tract.
**Paresis**, paralysis due to disease of brain, usually syphilis.
**Paries**, wall of a cavity.
**Pareunia**, sexual intercourse.
**Parity**, capable of bearing children.
**Parkinson's Disease**, nervous system disorder causing tremor and odd gait.
**Paronychia**, infection of the tissues at the base of a nail.
**Paroniria**, frightful dreams.
**Paropsis**, disorder of vision.
**Parorexia**, craving for special foods.
**Parosmia**, smelling imaginary odors.
**Parotid**, located near the ear.
**Parotid gland**, large salivary gland located over the jaw in front of the ear.
**Parotitis**, inflammation of the parotid gland, a large salivary gland.
**Parous**, having given birth to one or more children.
**Parovarian**, beside the ovary.
**Paroxysm**, sudden attack or recurrency of symptoms.
**Pars**, pl., **Partes**, a part.
**Particulate**, composed of minute particles.
**Parturient**, giving birth; labor.
**Parturifacient**, medicine which speeds up birth.
**Parturition**, childbirth.
**Paruria**, any abnormality in excretion of urine.
**Passion**, strong emotion.
**Pasteurization**, method of sterilizing foods.
**Patch Test**, test carried out to determine sensitivity.
**Patella**, knee-cap.
**Patency**, state of being open, e.g., ducts, hollow tubes.
**Patent Medicine**, remedy for public use obtained without prescription.
**Patent**, open.
**Pathetic**, pertaining to the feelings.
**Pathic**, pertaining to disease.
**Pathogens**, anything capable of producing disease.
**Pathogenic**, pertaining to the ability to produce disease.
**Pathology**, study of diseases for their own interest, rather than directly with an immediate view to curing them.
**Pathomania**, abnormal wish to commit crime.
**Pathophobia**, extreme fear of disease.
**Pathophoresis**, communication of disease.
**Patient**, one under medical care.
**Patulous**, open; exposed.
**Paunch**, protruding abdomen.
**Pavor**, fear; fright.
**Peccant**, unhealthy.
**Pectinate**, like teeth of comb.
**Pectoral**, pertaining to the chest.
**Pectus**, chest; breast.
**Pectus Carination**, "Chicken breast"
**Pedal**, pertaining to the foot.
**Pederasty**, sexual intercourse through the anus.
**Pediatrician**, specialist in diseases of children.
**Pediatrics**, branch of medicine dealing with the diseases of children and their cure.
**Pediatrist**, pediatrician.
**Pedicular**, infested with lice.
**Pediculicide**, agent which kills lice.

**Pediculosis**, infestation with lice.
**Pediculosis Capititis**, head lice.
**Pediophobia**, extreme fear of children or dolls.
**Pedodontics**, branch of dentistry dealing with children.
**Pedophila**, abnormal fondness for children.
**Peduncle**, stalk or stem.
**Pelada**, patchy baldness.
**Pelage**, hair covering the body.
**Pelagism**, seasickness.
**Pellagra**, disease due to lack of vitamin B.
**Pellet**, small pill.
**Pellicle**, thin tissue; scum on a liquid.
**Pellucid**, translucent.
**Pelvis**, bony part of the body lying between the thighs and the abdomen.
**Pemphigus**, skin disease characterized by large blisters and pigmented spots.
**Pendulous**, heavy and loosely hanging.
**Penicillin**, an antibiotic discovered in 1928 by Sir Alexander Fleming.
**Penis**, male sex organ.
**Penitis**, inflammation of the penis.
**Pepo**, pumpkin seed used in removal of tapeworm.
**Pepsic**, peptic.
**Pepsin**, ferment found in the gastric juice which helps in the breakdown of protein.
**Peptic**, pertaining to the digestive tract.
**Peracidity**, excessive acidity.
**Per Anum**, by anus.
**Perception**, awareness.
**Percussion**, striking body as an aid to physical examination and diagnosis.
**Percutanteous**, through the skin.
**Perforating**, piercing.
**Perforation**, opening or hole in any area of body.
**Peri-** (prefix), around; near.
**Periorticular**, surrounding a joint.
**Perianal**, situated around the anus.
**Pericardiac**, around the heart.
**Pericarditis**, inflammation of sac surrounding the heart.
**Pericardium**, sac surrounding the heart.
**Pericolic**, around the colon.
**Pericytial**, around a cell.
**Perimetrium**, covering tissue of the womb.
**Perinephric**, situated around the kidneys.
**Perineum**, area between the sex organs and the anus.
**Periodicity**, occurring at regular intervals.
**Period of Gestation**, period from conception to childbirth.
**Periodontal**, around a tooth.
**Perionchyia**, inflammation of area around a fingernail or toenail.
**Periosteum**, tissue around bone through which bone is nourished.
**Periostitis**, inflammation of the membrane surrounding a bone.
**Periotic**, located around the ear.
**Peripatetic**, changing from place to place.
**Periphery**, away from center or midline of body.
**Perirenal**, around the kidney.
**Perirhinal**, around the nose.
**Perish**, die; disintegrate.
**Peristalsis**, the normal movements of the intestines which move the food along the digestive tract.
**Peritonitis**, inflammation of the lining tissue of the abdominal cavity.
**Peritonsillar**, around the tonsil.
**Perivascular**, around a vessel.
**Pernicious**, severe; fatal.
**Pernicious Anemia**, disease of unknown origin affecting many systems of body.
**Pernio**, chillblain.
**Per Os**, by mouth.
**Per Rectum**, by rectum.
**Perseveration**, repetitive statements or answers to questions.
**Perspiration**, fluid produced by body at surface of the skin which helps to control body temperature.
**Pertussis**, whooping cough.
**Pervert**, one who practices abnormal behavior.
**Pervigilium**, abnormal wakefulness.
**Pes**, foot or footlike structure.
**Pes Contortis**, clubfoot.
**Pes Planus**, flatfoot.
**Pessary**, device used to hold uterus in proper position.
**Pestiferous**, causing pestilence.
**Pestilence**, epidemic of contagious disease.
**Pestle**, device used to break up drugs in pharmacy.
**Petit Mal**, type of epilepsy in which the attacks are relatively slight.
**pH**, concentration of hydrogen ion or acidity; Neutral =pH 7.
**Phactis**, inflammation of the eye lens.
**Phacomatacia**, soft cataract.
**Phagocyte**, absorbing cell.
**Phalanges**, bones of fingers.
**Phalanx**, one of the bones of the fingers or toes.
**Phallectomy**, amputation of the penis.
**Phallic**, concerning male sex organ.
**Phallus**, male sex organ.
**Phanic**, visible.
**Pharm.**, pharmaceutical; pharmacy.
**Pharmaceutical**, pertaining to drugs.
**Pharmacist**, druggist.
**Pharmacy**, drug store.

**Pharyngitis,** inflammation of the pharynx.
**Pharyngoscope,** instrument for examining the throat.
**Pharynx,** membraneous tube extending from oral cavity to level of first part of esophagus.
**Phatne,** tooth socket.
**Phenobarbital,** barbiturate used to sedate or produce sleep.
**Phenolphthalein,** purgative.
**Phimosis,** excessive tightness of the foreskin of the penis.
**Phlebitis,** inflammation of a vein.
**Phlebosclerosis,** hardening of a vein.
**Phlebothrombosis,** formation of a clot in a vein.
**Phlebotomy,** opening of a vein.
**Phlegm,** thick mucus from respiratory tract.
**Phlegmatic,** sluggish.
**Phlogistic,** inducing inflammation.
**Phobia,** an extreme fear.
**Phonal,** pertaining to the voice.
**Phonetics,** science of vocal sounds.
**Photodynia,** pain in the eyes due to intense light.
**Photophobia,** extreme fear of light.
**Photosensitive,** sensitive to light.
**Phrenetic,** maniacal.
**Phrenic,** pertaining to the diaphragm or mind.
**Phrenitis,** delirium.
**Phrenologfy,** study of the mind through the shape of the skull.
**Phrenoplegia,** paralysis of the diaphragm.
**Phthisology,** study of tuberculosis.
**Phthisis,** tuberculosis.
**Phylctenuls,** small blister, usually occurring with an eye inflammation.
**Phylaxis,** bodily defense against infection.
**Phyma,** skin tumor.
**Physic,** cathartic; art of medicine.
**Physician,** licensed medical doctor.
**Physics,** study of natural forces and phenomena.
**Physiogonomy,** face.
**Physiology,** science which deals with the functions of the body.
**Physique,** body build.
**Phytin,** material from plants used as stimulants.
**Phytotoxin,** plant poison.
**Pia,** one of membranous coverings of brain and spinal cord.
**Pica,** an abnormal craving to eat odd things.
**Piedra,** hair disease.
**Pigment,** coloring substance.
**Pilary,** pertaining to the hair.
**Pileous,** hairy.
**Piles,** enlarged, painful veins in the rectum or around the anus.
**Pill.** capsule containing medication.
**Pillion,** temporary artificial leg.
**Pilonidal,** cyst containing hairs, frequently found at the base of the spine.
**Pilose,** hairy.
**Pilus,** hair.
**Pimple,** small pointed area on skin, at times filled with infectious material.
**Pineal Gland,** small gland about the size of a pea in the lower part of the brain.
**Pinquecula,** thickened area on edge of cornea of eye.
**Pinkeye,** contagious eye inflammation; conjunctivitis.
**Pinna,** projecting part of external ear.
**Pinworm,** parasite found in intestine and around anus.
**Pit,** depression.
**Pithecoid,** apelike.
**Pituita,** phlegm.
**Pituitarism,** disorder of pituitary function.
**Pituitary Gland,** small gland at the base of the brain which affects all the other glands of the body.
**Pityriasis,** group of diseases in which the main symptom is a scaly skin.
**Placebo,** inactive substance.
**Placenta,** organ by which the unborn infant is attached to the inside of the womb and through which infants' body needs are supplied.
**Plague,** epidemic disease transmitted by fleas of rats.
**Planocyte,** wandering cell.
**Planta,** sole of the foot.
**Plantar,** pertaining to the sole of the foot.
**Plantar Wart,** painful wart occurring on the bottom of the foot.
**Plasma,** colorless fluid part of the blood as distinct from blood cells.
**Plastic,** pertaining to plastic surgery; moldable; any material that can be molded.
**Platelet,** small disc in blood stream used for blood coagulation.
**Platycrania,** flattening of the skull.
**Platypodia,** flat foot.
**Pledget,** small piece of gauze soaked in antiseptic.
**Pleonemia,** increased amount of blood in a part.
**Pleonexia,** extreme greediness.
**Plethora,** abnormal amount of blood.
**Pleonexia,** a psychic condition characterized by selfishness.
**Pleura,** thin tissue covering the lungs and lining the interior walls of the chest cavity.
**Pleurisy,** inflammation of the Pleura.
**Pleurodynia,** pain in the muscles between the ribs.
**Plexor,** percussion hammer.
**Plexus,** groups of nerves, lymphatic glands or blood vessels in the body.
**Plica,** fold.

**Plombage,** filling a cavity with paraffin.
**Plug,** obstruction.
**Plumbism,** lead poisoning.
**Pneoscope,** the instrument that records breathing.
**Pneumatic,** pertaining to respiration.
**Pneumococcus,** germ which can attack the body, usually the lungs.
**Pneumonectomy,** surgical removal of a lung.
**Pneumonia,** inflammation of the lungs.
**Pneumonopathy,** any lung disease.
**Pneumorrhagia,** lung hemorrhage.
**Pneumothorax,** abnormal entrance of air or gas into lung sacs, causing an imbalance of pressures and difficult respiration.
**Pock,** pustule.
**Podagra,** gout affecting foot.
**Podalgia,** pain in the feet.
**Podiatrist,** specialist in foot ailments.
**Pogoniasis,** excessive beard growth.
**Point,** tiny spot or area.
**Pointillage,** massage with the finger tips.
**Poisoning,** ingestion of substance toxic to body.
**Poison Ivy,** vine causing severe skin irritation.
**Poitrinaire,** one having a chronic chest disease.
**Poliomyelitis (Infantile Paralysis),** inflammation of the grey matter of the spinal cord.
**Poliosis,** absence of hair coloring.
**Pollen,** male sex cells of plants.
**Pollinosis,** hay fever
**Pollex,** thumb or big toe.
**Pollution,** making impure; discharge of semen without sexual intercourse.
**Polyarthritis,** inflammation of several joints.
**Polycholia,** excessive bile secretion.
**Polyclinic,** medical center treating many diseases.
**Polycyesis,** pregnancy with more than one fetus.
**Polycythemia,** condition in which there is an excess of red blood cells.
**Polycytosis,** excess of blood cells.
**Polydactylism,** having more than five fingers or five toes.
**Polydipsia,** excessive desire to drink.
**Polyemia,** excessive blood in the body.
**Polyglandular,** affecting many glands.
**Polygny,** marriage to more than one woman at one time.
**Polyhedral,** many sides.
**Polymenorrhea,** unusual frequency of menstruation.
**Polymyositis,** inflammation of many muscles.
**Polyneural,** pertaining to many nerves.
**Polyneuritis,** inflammation of more than one group of nerves.
**Polyp,** outgrowths in the nose, intestines or bladder.
**Polypathia,** having more than one disease at a time.
**Polyphagia,** excessive eating.
**Polyplegia,** paralysis of several muscles.
**Polypus,** polyp.
**Polyuria,** excessive urination.
**Ponophobia,** extreme fear of pain or fatigue.
**Pons,** a part of the brain which bridges several other sections of the nervous system.
**Pontic,** false tooth.
**Popliteal,** pertaining to the back of the leg and the bend of the knee.
**Pore,** small opening in skin or tissue.
**Pornerastic,** excessive fondness for prostitutes.
**Porous,** having many pores.
**Porrigo,** ringworm.
**Portio,** part.
**Portio Dura,** facial nerve.
**Porus,** pore.
**Position,** placement of the body.
**Positive,** affirmative; indicating the presence of a disorder.
**Posology,** system of dosage.
**Postcibal,** after eating.
**Postcoital,** after sexual intercourse.
**Postepileptic,** after an epileptic attack.
**Posterior,** behind; at the back part.
**Posthetomy,** circumsion.
**Posthumous,** after death.
**Postmortem,** autopsy; after death.
**Postnasal,** situated behind the nose.
**Postnatal,** immediately after birth.
**Postoperative,** happening after an operation.
**Postoral,** in the back of the mouth.
**Postpartum,** after childbirth.
**Postprandial,** after a meal.
**Postpubescent,** after puberty.
**Posture,** body position.
**Postuterine,** behind the uterus.
**Potable,** adequate for drinking.
**Potamophobia,** extreme fear of large bodies of water.
**Potency,** strength; ability to perform coitus.
**Potion,** dose of liquid medicine.
**Pouch,** pocket-like cavity.
**Poultice,** hot, moist mass to be placed on the skin.
**Pox,** blisters and scars on the skin caused by certain diseases.
**Practice,** professional diagnosis and treatment of disease.
**Practitioner,** physician.
**Pragmatagnosia,** inability to recognize objects.
**Prandial,** pertaining to a meal.
**Precordia,** area overlying heart.

**Pregnancy**, state of being with child.
**Pregravidic**, preceeding pregnancy.
**Prehensile**, able to grasp.
**Prehension**, grasping. [tack.
**Preictal**, preceeding a stroke or at-
**Premature**, born before maturity.
**Premature Infant**, one weighing less than 5.5 pounds at birth.
**Premenstrual**, preceeding menstruation.
**Premonitary**, warning.
**Premunition**, immunization by vaccination.
**Prenatal**, before birth.
**Preoral**, in front of the mouth.
**Prepuce**, foreskin of penis.
**Presbyatry**, treatment of diseases of the aged.
**Presbyacusia**, partial loss of hearing in old age.
**Presbyopia**, loss of elasticity in eyes which occurs in old age.
**Prescription**, written order for drug authorized by a physician.
**Pressure**, stress; strain.
**Preventive**, prophylactic.
**Priapism**, continued erection of the penis without sexual desire.
**Primary**, principal.
**Prickly Heat**, irritations of the skin in which blisters form due to increased temperature.
**Primigravida**, woman in her first pregnancy.
**Primipara**, woman who has given birth once.
**Primitive**, original.
**Primordial**, Primitive.
**Princeps**, primary artery.
**Principal**, most important.
**Probe**, instrument for exploring the interior of the body.
**Proconceptive**, aiding conception.
**Procreate**, to beget children.
**Proctalgia**, pain in the rectum.
**Proctitis**, inflamation of the rectum or anus.
**Proctology**, branch of medicine concerned with the rectum.
**Proctoscopy**, examination of the rectum.
**Procumbent**, prone.
**Prodrome**, early symptoms of impending illness.
**Progeny**, offspring.
**Progeria**, condition causing early aging. [jaws.
**Prognathism**, having projecting
**Prognosis**, medical name for the outlook of a disease.
**Proiota**, sexual precocity.
**Prolapse**, abnormal position of internal organ.
**Proliferation**, muplication of cells.
**Prominence**, projection; elevation.
**Prone**, lying face downward.
**Prootic**, in front of the ear.
**Propagation**, reproduction.
**Prophylactic**, preventing disease.
**Prophylaxis**, prevention of disease.
**Pro Re Nata**, according to circumstances.
**Prorrhaphy**, advancement.
**Prosodemic**, spread from one person to another.
**Prosopospasm**, facial spasm.
**Prostate**, small gland in the male situated at the base of the bladder, concerned with preparation of the semen.
**Prostatitis**, inflamation of the prostate gland. [part.
**Prosthesis**, substitute for missing
**Prosthetics**, branch of surgery dealing with artifical parts.
**Prostitution**, having sexual relations for profit or gain.
**Prostration**, exhaustion.
**Prothrombin**, chemical substance important in blood coagulation.
**Protistology**, microbiology.
**Protoplasm**, prime material in living organism.
**Protozoa**, microscopic, one-celled organisms.
**Protuberance**, projection.
**Provisional**, of temporary use.
**Proximate**, nearest.
**Pruritus**, itching.
**Prussiate**, cyanide.
**Psellism**, stuttering.
**Pseudocrisis**, false crisis.
**Pseudocyesis**, imaginary pregnancy with some physical findings of the condition.
**Psittacosis**, disease spread by parrots, love-birds, canaries and other birds kept as pets.
**Psoriasis**, chronic skin disease in which red scaly patches develop.
**Psychanalysis**, psychoanalysis.
**Psyche**, mind.
**Psychectampsia**, acute mania.
**Psychiatrist**, one who specializes in psychiatry.
**Psychiatry**, study and treatment of mental disorders.
**Psychic**, pertaining to the mind.
**Psychics**, psychology.
**Psychoanalysis**, method of obtain-a patient's past emotional history.
**Psychocoma**, mental stupor.
**Psychogenesis**, mental development.
**Psychognosis**, study of mental and emotional activity.
**Psychology**, science dealing with mental functions.
**Psychopath**, one who has no sense of moral obligation.
**Psychopathy**, any mental disorder.
**Psychophylaxis**, mental hygiene.
**Psychosis**, type of insanity in which one loses almost complete touch with reality.
**Psychosomatic Disease**, physical ailments due to emotional causes.
**Psychotherapy**, treatment of mental and emotional disorders.
**Ptarmic**, causing sneezing.
**Ptarmus**, sneezing.

**Ptomaine**, specific poisoning caused by putrified food.

**Ptosis**, drooping of the upper eye-[lid.

**Ptyalism**, excess secretion of saliva.

**Ptyalorrhea**, excessive secretion of saliva.

**Ptysis**, spitting.

**Puberal**, pertaining to puberty.

**Puberty**, period of rapid growth and development between childhood and adult life.

**Pubes**, hairy area above the geni-[tals.

**Pubis**, bone at front of pelvis.

**Pudenda**, the external sex organ.

**Pudic**, pudendal.

**Puerile**, pertaining to a child.

**Puerilism**, childishness.

**Puerpera**, woman who has had a child.

**Puerperium**, period immediately following childbirth.

**Pulmonary**, pertaining to the lungs.

**Pulmonic**, pulmonary.

**Pulpalgia**, pain in the pulp of a tooth.

**Pulpy**, soft

**Pulsation**, rhythmic throb.

**Pulso**, pressure variation in arteries due to action of heart; can be felt where arteries are close to skin.

**Pulsus**, pulse.

**Pulverulent**, powdery.

**Punctum**, point.

**Punctum Caecum**, blind spot.

**Puncture**, pierce.

**Pupil**, part of eye which opens or closes to adjust to light or object.

**Pupillary**, pertaining to the pupil.

**Purgative**, drug to relieve constipation.

**Purge**, to evacuate the bowels by medicine.

**Purpura**, purple areas or bruises on body due to abnormal blood clotting.

**Purulent**, forming or containing pus.

**Pus**, product of infection containing dead cell and cell debris.

**Pustule**, pimple.

**Pyarthrosis**, pus in a joint cavity.

**Pyelitis**, inflammation of the pelvis of the kidney, that is, the area where the kidney is connected to the ureter, the tube leading down to the bladder.

**Pyemia**, form of blood poisoning in which the germs are carried in the blood and produce abscesses.

**Pygal**, pertaining to the buttocks.

**Pyknemia**, thickening of the blood.

**Pylorus**, valve which lies at one end of the stomach and controls the entry of food into the small intestine.

**Pyocele**, pus around the testis.

**Pyocolpos**, pus in the vagina.

**Pyocyst**, sac of pus in body.

**Pyoderma**, any skin inflammation that produces pus.

**Pyogenesis**, formation of pus.

**Pyorrhea**, infection of the gums which causes the edges of the tooth sockets to bleed easily when teeth are being brushed.

**Pyretic**, pertaining to fever.

**Pyretolysis**, lowering of fever.

**Pyrexia**, increased body temperature, high fever.

**Pyrogenic**, causing fever.

**Pyromania**, obsessive compulsion to start fires.

**Pyrophobia**, extreme fear of fire.

**Pyrosis**, burning pain in stomach; acid taste in mouth.

**Pyrotic**, burning.

**Pyuria**, pus in urine.

## — Q —

**Quack**, a faker in medical science.

**Quadripara**, woman giving birth to her fourth child.

**Quadriplegia**, paralysis of arms and [legs.

**Quarantine**, enforced isolation of people suffering from an infectious disease.

**Quassation**, shattering.

**Quickening**, the feeling of life of a baby by a pregnant woman.

**Quinsy**, formation of an abscess around one of the tonsils.

**Quinine**, drug used in the treatment of malaria.

**Quintan**, every fifth day.

**Quintipara**, woman giving birth to her fifth child.

## — R —

**Rabbeting**, interlocking of the splintered edges of a fractured bone.

**Rabbit Fever**, virus disease transmitted by eating or handling infected animals; tularemia.

**Rabiate**, one who has rabies.

**Rabic**, pertaining to rabies

**Rabid**, pertaining to rabies.

**Rabies**, a fatal disease of man affecting the brain and spinal cord if untreated.

**Race**, class of people of similar inheritance and ethnic qualities.

**Rachialgia**, pain in spine.

**Rachianalgesia**, spinal anesthesia.

**Rachicentesis**, puncture into spinal canal.

**Rachidian**, pertaining to the spine.

**Rachiocampsis**, curvature of the spine.

**Rachiodynia**, painful condition of spinal column.

**Rachis**, spinal column.

**Rachisschisis**, spinal column fissure; congenital opening.

**Rachitec**, pertaining to rickets.

**Radiation**, rays that in proper dosage can be used to treat certain diseases.

**Radicular**, pertaining to a root.

**Radiculitis**, inflammation of a nerve root.

**Radiectomy**, removal of the root of a tooth.

**Radioactivity**, emitting of penetrating rays or small particles.

**Radiograph**, an x-ray film.

**Radiography**, taking of x-rays.

**Radiologist**, medical specialist who uses radiation for diagnosis and treatment.

**Radiology**, branch of medicine using radiant energy in diagnosis and treatment of disease.

**Radiolus**, sound; probe.

**Radiotherapeutic**, use of x-ray or radium for treatment.

**Radius**, short arm bone extending from elbow to wrist.

**Radix**, root.

**Rale**, abnormal sound coming from air passages of lungs.

**Rami**, branch.

**Ramify**, to branch.

**Ramitis**, inflammation of a nerve root.

**Ramollissement**, morbid softening of some organ or tissue.

**Ramus**, branch of an artery, vein or nerve; branchlike part.

**Rancid**, offensive; sour.

**Range of Accommodation**, difference between the least and greattest distance of clear vision.

**Ranula**, swelling under the tongue due to the blocking of a salivary gland.

**Rape**, sexual intercourse without consent of female.

**Rash**, skin eruption.

**Raspatory**, surgical file.

**Rasura, Rasure**, scraping; shaving.

**Rat**, rodent frequently used in experiments.

**Rat Bite Fever**, an infectious disease passed to human beings by bite of an infected animal.

**Ratio**, proportion.

**Ration**, fixed portion of food and drink for a certain period.

**Rational**, according to reason.

**Rationalization**, making an irrational thing appear reasonable.

**Rattle**, rale.

**Rattle, Death**, gurgling sound heard in the trachea of the dying.

**Rave**, talk irrationally.

**Ravish**, rape.

**Raynaud's Disease**, circulatory disturbance affecting extremities.

**R.C.P.**, Royal College of Physicians.

**R.C.S.**, Royal College of Surgeons.

**Rauwolfia**, drug which lowers blood pressure and causes relaxation in mind and body.

**Re-** (prefix), back; again.

**Reaction**, response.

**Recall**, memory.

**Receptaculum**, vessel or cavity which contains fluid.

**Recessus**, small hollow or recess.

**Recidivation**, recurrence of a disease.

**Recipe**, prescription; formula.

**Recipient**, one who receives a thing.

**Recline**, lie down.

**Reconstituent**, an agent which strengthens a part of the body by replacing lost material.

**Recrement**, secretion which is reabsorbed into the body after performing its function.

**Recrudescence**, reappearance of symptoms of a disease.

**Rectal**, pertaining to the rectum.

**Rectal Reflex**, normal desire to evacuate feces.

**Rectalgia**, rectal pain.

**Rectectomy**, surgical removal of the rectum or anus.

**Rectified**, made pure or straight.

**Rectitis**, inflammation of the rectum.

**Rectoclysis**, gradual introduction of fluid into rectum.

**Rectocolitis**, inflammation of the rectum and colon.

**Rectostenosis**, stricture of the rectum.

**Rectostomy**, making an artificial opening into the rectum to relieve stricture.

**Rectum**, lowest six inches of the intestinal tract adjoining the anus.

**Rectus**, straight; any straight muscle.

**Recumbent**, lying down.

**Recuperation**, restoration to health.

**Recurrent**, reappearing.

**Recurve**, bend backward.

**Red Blood Cell**, blood corpuscle containing hemoglobin.

**Red Softening**, hemorrhagic soften- of brain and spinal cord.

**Redressment**, correction of a deformity; dressing a wound a second time or more.

**Reduce**, decrease.

**Reduction**, restoration to normal position.

**Reduction Diet**, diet which eliminates fat producing foods.

**Reduplicated**, folded back on itself.

**Referred Pain**, pain felt in part of the body other than its source.

**Refine**, purify.

**Reflex**, an involuntary action caused by a stimulus to the nerves.

**Reflexogenic**, causing a reflex action.

**Reflux**, backward flow.

**Refracta Dosi**, in divided doses.

**Refraction**, eye testing to determine amount of vision.

**Refractory**, not easily treated.

**Refracture**, break again.

**Refrangible**, capable of refraction.

**Refresh**, renew, revive.

**Refrigerant**, medicine which relieves thirst and reduces fever.

**Refusion**, return flow of blood to the vessels.

**Regeneration**, regrowth or repair of part of body.

**Regimen**, course of therapy to improve health.

**Region**, particular body area.
**Registry**, placement bureau for nurses.
**Regression**, process of going back to a prior status in physical or mental illness.
**Regressive**, subsiding, reverting.
**Regular**, normal.
**Regurgitant**, backward flow.
**Regurgitate**, to vomit.
**Rehabilitation**, restoration to activity of a handicapped person.
**Rehalation**, rebreathing.
**Reichman's Disease**, constant excessive gastric secretion.
**Reinfection**, return of infection.
**Reimplantation**, replacement of a part to its original location.
**Rejuvenation**, return to a youthful or normal state.
**Relapse**, recurrence of an illness.
**Relapsing Fever**, an infectious disease in which periods of fever alternate with periods of normal temperature.
**Relaxant**, agent which lessens tension or loosens bowels.
**Relaxation**, reduction of tension.
**Remak's Axis Cylinder**, conducting part of a nerve.
**Remedial**, curative.
**Remedy**, substance that is used in treatment of disease.
**Remission**, abatement.
**Ren**, the kidney.
**Renal**, pertaining to the kidney.
**Renifleur**, one who is sexually stimulated by certain odors, especially that of urine.
**Reniform**, kidney-shaped.
**Repair**, replace; heal.
**Repellent**, reducing swelling; that which repels insects.
**Repletion**, full; satisfied; fullness of blood; plethora.
**Reportable Diseases**, diseases which must be reported to public health authorities.
**Reposition**, act of replacing a part.
**Repositor**, instrument for replacing a part.
**Repression**, suppression into unconsciousness of unacceptable ideas and emotion.
**Reproduction**, begetting of offspring.
**Resection**, excision of part of body tissue.
**Reserpine**, drug used to lower blood pressure.
**Residue**, that which remains after removal of a part.
**Residuum**, residue.
**Resilience**, elasticity.
**Resilient**, elastic
**Resistance**, ability to protect self from disease.
**Resolution**, subsiding of an inflammation.
**Respirable**, suitable for respiration.
**Respiration**, breathing.
**Respirator**, mechanical device used to aid breathing.
**Respiratory**, pertaining to respiration.
**Rest**, period of inactivity.
**Restiform**, ropelike; rope-shaped.
**Restitution**, restoring.
**Restorative**, promoting health; remedy.
**Restraint**, forcible control.
**Resuscitation**, artificial respiration which is used to restore breathing after drowning, electric shock or other conditions interfering with breathing.
**Resuscitator**, mechanical device used for artificial respiration.
**Retardation**, delay.
**Retarded Depression**, depressed state of manic depressive psychosis.
**Retching**, unsatisfactory attempt to vomit.
**Rete**, network.
**Retention**, holding back.
**Retention Cyst**, cyst caused by retention of a secretion in a gland.
**Retention of Urine**, failure to urinate.
**Reticular**, netlike.
**Reticulation**, formation of a network mass.
**Reticulum**, network in cells.
**Retina**, part of the eye that receives the image and which is connected to the brain by the optic nerve.
**Retinal**, pertaining to the retina.
**Retinitis**, inflammation of the retina, the innermost coat of the eye.
**Retinosis**, degeneration of the retina.
**Retractile**, able to be drawn back.
**Retraction**, drawing back.
**Retractor**, surgical instrument used to hold back the edges of an incision.
**Retro-** (prefix), behind or in back of.
**Retrocedent**, going backward.
**Retrocolic**, behind the colon.
**Retrocollic**, pertaining to the back of the neck.
**Retrograde**, going backward.
**Retroinfection**, infection transmitted by the fetus to the mother.
**Retrolingual**, behind the tongue.
**Retronasal**, behind the nose.
**Retropharynx**, back wall of the throat.
**Retroposed**, displaced backward.
**Retroversion**, state of turning back.
**Revivification**, attempt to restore to life.
**Revulsant**, causing transfer of disease or blood from one part of body to another; agent which draws blood to inflamed site.
**Rhabdophobia**, extreme fear of being corrected.
**Rhachis**, spinal column.
**Rhagades**, skin cracks.
**-rhagia**, (suffix), bleeding.

**Rhaphe**, seam, ridge.
**Rhegma**, rupture, fracture, tear.
**Rheum**, watery discharge.
**Rheumatalgia**, rheumatic pain.
**Rheumatic Fever**, disease affecting joints, skin and sometimes the heart; believed due to an allergic reaction to specific bacteria.
**Rheumatism**, pain, swelling and deformity of joints of unknown cause.
**Rheumatoid**, of the nature of rheumatism.
**Rhexis**, rupture of a blood vessel or organ.
**Rh. Factor**, a substance found in the red blood cells; about 15% of people do not have this factor and are therefore called RH negative.
**Rhinal**, pertaining to the nose.
**Rhinalgia**, nasal pain.
**Rhinesthesia**, sense of smell.
**Rhinitis**, inflammation of the lining of the nose.
**Rhinobyon**, nasal plug.
**Rhinocleisis**, nasal obstruction.
**Rhinodynia**, nasal pain.
**Rhinolalia**, nasal voice quality.
**Rhinologist**, nose specialist.
**Rhinology**, branch of medicine dealing with the nose.
**Rhinopathy**, any nasal disease.
**Rhinophonia**, nasal speaking tone.
**Rhinophyma**, disease of the nose in which it becomes greatly enlarged.
**Rhinorrhagia**, nosebleed.
**Rhinotomy**, surgical incision of the nose.
**Rhodocyte**, red blood cell.
**Rhoncus**, rale; rattling sound in chest.
**Rhypophagy**, eating of filth.
**Rhypophobia**, extreme fear of filth.
**Rhythm**, measured time or movement; noting the periods of fertility and sterility in the female during the menstrual cycle.
**Rhytidosis**, wrinkling of skin or cornea.
**Rib**, bone and cartilage that form the chest cavity and protects its contents.
**Ribs, False**, five ribs on each side not directly attached to sternum.
**Ribs, Floating**, two lower ribs not attached to sternum.
**Rickets**, this is a disease caused by lack of vitamin D.
**Ridge**, narrow, elevated border.
**Rigidity**, stiffness. [idity
**Rigor**, chill preceding a fever; rig-
**Rigor Mortis**, stiffening of muscles after death.
**Rima**, crack.
**Rimula**, minute crack.
**Rind**, skin or cortex of an organ or person.
**Ringworm**, fungus infection.
**Risus**, laugh; grin.
**Ritter's Disease**, severe skin inflammation seen in infants.
**R.N.**, registered nurse.
**Roborant**, tonic; strengthening.
**Rock Mountain Spotted Fever**, infectious disease characterized by fever, pains in bone and muscle and reddish eruptions.
**Rodent Ulcer**, small, hard skin ulcer on the face in region of the inner corner of the eye or around the nose.
**Roentgen**, measure of radiation.
**Roentgenogram**, x-ray.
**Rongeur**, gouge forceps used to remove bone fragments.
**Root**, proximal end of a nerve; portion of an organ implanted in tissues.
**Root Canal**, pulp cavity of tooth root.
**Rosacea**, skin disease of the face in which there is permanent redness over the nose and cheeks.
**Rose Fever**, hay fever.
**Roseola**, red rash from various causes. [tion.
**Rose Rash**, any red colored erup-
**Rossbach's Disease**, excessive secretion of gastric juice.
**Rot**, decay.
**Rotate**, twist; revolve.
**Rotular**, pertaining to the kneecap.
**Roughage**, coarse material.
**Rotula**, kneecap or patella.
**Roust**, delivery room nurse who carries out unsterile tasks.
**Rubedo**, temporary redness of skin.
**Rubella**, German measles.
**Rubeola**, measles.
**Rubor**, redness of skin due to infection.
**Rubrum**, red.
**Ructus**, belching.
**Rudimentary**, elementary; undeveloped.
**Ruga**, fold or crease.
**Rugose**, wrinkled.
**Rumination**, regurgitation.
**Rump**, buttocks.
**Run**, to exude pus or mucus.
**Runaround**, infection extending around a finger or toenail.
**Rupophobia**, extreme dislike for dirt or filth.
**Rupture**, tearing apart; hernia.
**Rutilizm**, red-headedness.
**Rx**, symbol for "take" or "recipe"

— S —

**Saburra**, foulness of stomach or mouth.
**Sac**, pouch. [ener.
**Saccharin**, sugar substitute; sweet-
**Saccharum**, sugar.
**Sacculation**, grouping of sacs.
**Saccule**, small sac.
**Sacrificial Operation**, removal of an organ for the patient's good.
**Sacroiliac**, relating to the juncture of the hipbone and lower part of the spine.

**Sacroiliac Strain,** type of backache.
**Sacrum,** part of vertebral column or spine.
**Sadism,** perversion in which sexual pleasure is obtained by inflicting pain on someone.
**Sadist,** one who enjoys inflicting pain on others.
**St. Vitus' Dance,** involuntary muscular action.
**Sal,** salt.
**Salacious,** lustful.
**Salicylate,** main component of aspirin.
**Saline,** pertaining to salt.
**Saline Solution,** salt water.
**Saliva,** fluid secreted by the glands of the mouth.
**Salivant,** stimulating secretion of saliva.
**Salivary,** pertaining to saliva.
**Salivation,** excess secretion of saliva.
**Sallow,** having a pale, yellowish complexion.
**Sal Mirabile,** purgative salt.
**Salmonella,** bacteria causing intestinal disorder.
**Salmonellosis,** infestation with Salmonella bacteria.
**Salpingectomy,** surgical removal of Fallopian tube.
**Salpingitis,** inflammation of the Fallopian tubes.
**Salpinx,** uterine tube; eustachian tube.
**Salt,** sodium chloride.
**Saltation,** dancing.
**Saltatory,** characterized by leaping or dancing.
**Salt Free Diet,** diet which allows no more than two grams of salt.
**Saltpeter,** postassium nitrate.
**Salubrious,** promoting good health.
**Salutary,** healthful; curative.
**Salve,** ointment.
**Sanative,** healing.
**Sanatorium,** place for preserving health or caring for a long term illness.
**Sanatory,** promoting health.
**Sane,** of sound mind.
**Sanger's Operation,** type of Cesarean section.
**Sangucolous,** inhabiting the blood.
**Sanguifacient,** forming blood.
**Sanguiferous,** conducting blood.
**Sanguine,** bloody.
**Sanguineous,** bloody; having a plethora of blood.
**Sanguis,** blood.
**Sanitarium,** place for the care and cure of those suffering from mental or physical illness.
**Sanitary,** pertaining to health.
**Sanity,** soundness of mind.
**Saphena,** large vein of leg.
**Sapid,** possessing flavor.
**Sapo,** soap.
**Saponatus,** mixed with soap.
**Sapphism,** Lesbianism.
**Saphemia,** blood poisoning.
**Saprodontis,** tooth decay.
**Sacritis,** inflammation of muscle tissue.
**Sarcocele,** tumor of testicle.
**Sarcode,** protoplasm.
**Sarcogenic,** forming flesh.
**Sarcology,** study of soft body tissues.
**Sarcolytic,** decomposing flesh.
**Sarcoma,** one of the two main types of cancer, the other being carcinoma.
**Sarcophagy,** practice of eating flesh.
**Sarcopoietic,** forming flesh or muscle.
**Sarcous,** pertaining to flesh or muscle.
**Sartorius,** muscle of thigh.
**Satiety,** satisfying fullness.
**Saturnine,** pertaining to lead.
**Saturnism,** lead poisoning.
**Satyriasis,** abnormal sex drive associated with mental excitement in male.
**Satyromania,** excessive sexual desire in the male.
**Savory,** appetizing.
**Saw,** cutting instrument.
**Scab,** crust formation over wound.
**Scabies,** disease of the skin caused by a mite which burrows under the skin surface and causes extreme discomfort and itching.
**Scald,** burn of skin.
**Scale,** small, thin, dry particle.
**Scalenus,** three muscles located in the vertebrae of the neck and attached to the first two ribs.
**Scall,** scalp disease.
**Scalp,** hairy component of head.
**Scalpel,** surgical knife.
**Scanty,** insufficient.
**Scapula,** shoulder blade.
**Scapular,** pertaining to the shoulder blade.
**Scapulectomy,** surgical removal of scapula.
**Scar,** end product of healed wound.
**Scarfskin,** epidermis.
**Scarlatina,** scarlet fever.
**Scarlet Fever,** contagious disease causing chills, high fever, sore throat, skin rash, discolored tongue.
**Scatacratia,** fecal incontinence.
**Scatemia,** intestinal toxemia.
**Scatology,** study and analysis of waste product of body.
**Scelalgia,** pain in leg.
**Schick Test,** test for susceptability to diphtheria
**Schistasis,** any congenital fissure.
**Schizophrenia,** psychiatric disorder of many and varied manifestations in which person loses contact or misinterprets reality.
**Schizotrichia,** splitting of hair.
**Schwelle,** threshold.
**Sciage,** sawing massage movement.

**Sciatic Nerve,** largest nerve in body located in back of leg.
**Sciatica,** inflammation of or injury to the sciatic nerve in back of thigh.
**Scirrhoma,** scirrhus.
**Scirrhus,** hard cancer.
**Schlera,** white of eye.
**Schlerectomy,** surgical removal of part of the sclera.

**Schleritis,** inflammation of the white of the eye.
**Schleroderma,** skin disease of unknown origin in which patches of skin become thickened, hard and white or yellowish.
**Scleroma,** sclerosis.
**Sclerose,** to become hardened.
**Sclerosis,** hardening of a tissue.
**Schlerothrix,** abnormal hardness and dryness of hair.
**Scoliosis,** curvature of the spine to one side or the other.
**Scopophobia,** extreme fear of being seen.
**Scorbutus,** scurvy.
**Scordinemia,** yawning and stretching.
**Scotoma,** blind spot.
**Scotophobia,** extreme fear of darkness.
**Scoptopia,** adjustment of eyes to darkness.
**Scours,** diarrhea.
**Scratch,** superficial injury.
**Scrobiculate,** pitted.
**Scrobiculus,** pit.
**Scrobiculus Cordis,** pit of the stomach.
**Scrofula,** condition of tuberculous gland of the neck.
**Scrotal,** pertaining to the scrotum.
**Scrotum,** pouch of male containing testicles.
**Scrub Nurse,** operating room nurse.
**Scurf,** dandruff.
**Scurvy,** disease due to lack of vitamin C, causing bleeding, weakness and swelling of skin.
**Scutum,** thyroid cartilage.
**Scytitis,** dermatitis.
**Sea Sickness,** nausea, vomiting and unsteadiness due to unusual motion.
**Sebaceous,** pertaining to sebum.
**Sebaceous Cyst,** a wen; a swelling caused by the blocking of a duct of a sebaceous gland.
**Sebastomania,** religious insanity.
**Seborrhagia,** excessive secretion of sebaceous glands.
**Seborrhea,** condition of excessive oiliness of the skin caused by glandular upset.
**Sebum,** oily secretion of the oil glands of the skin.
**Secondary,** not of primary importance.
**Secreta,** waste material expelled by a gland or organ.
**Secretion,** fluid discharged from gland or organ.
**Secretomotory,** stimulating secretion.
**Section,** divide by cutting.
**Sectorial,** cutting.
**Secundigravida,** woman in her second pregnancy.
**Secundines,** afterbirth material.
**Sedative,** agent used to quiet patient.
**Sediment,** material which settles at the bottom of a fluid.
**Seed,** semen.
**Segment,** part of a whole.
**Seizure,** sudden attack.
**Sella,** saddle-shaped depression; area within skull.
**Semantic,** pertaining to the meaning of words.
**Semeiosis,** approach to disease according to symptoms.
**Semel,** once.
**Semen,** male secretion containing sperm.
**Semenuria,** presence of semen in urine.
**Semi-** (prefix), half.
**Semilunar,** wrist bone.
**Semination,** introduction of semen into the vagina.
**Seminiferous,** producing or carrying semen.
**Seminology,** study of semen.
**Semis,** half.
**Senescence,** process of growing old.
**Senile,** old.
**Senilism,** premature old age.
**Sensation,** awareness of stimulus to nervous system.
**Sense,** perceive through nervous system; perceiving faculty.
**Sensibility,** sensitivity.
**Sensitive,** responsive; unusually receptive to stimuli.
**Sensorium,** any sensory nerve center.
**Sensory,** pertaining to sensation.
**Sentient,** sensitive.
**Sepsis,** poisoning of body by products of bacteria.
**Septicemia,** blood poisoning.
**Septum,** tissue dividing cavities.
**Sequela,** after affects of a disease.
**Sequestrum,** piece of dead bone.
**Serial,** arranged in sequence.
**Seriate,** saw-toothed.
**Serology,** study of serum.
**Serosa,** layer of tissue.
**Serous,** thin and watery.
**Serrate,** notched.
**Serrulate,** minutely notched.
**Serum,** clear fluid which separates from blood when it clots.
**Sex,** distinctive feature between male and female; Freud-pleasure.
**Sexual,** pertaining to sex.
**Shakes,** shivering due to chill.
**Shank,** leg from knee to ankle.
**Sheath,** tubular case.
**Shift,** change.
**Shigella,** organism causing dysentery.

**Shin**, front part of lower leg.
**Shingles**, herpes zoster, viral infection of nerve path.
**Ship-Fever**, typhus fever.
**Shiver**, chill.
**Shock**, decreased effective circulating fluid volume.
**Shortsighted**, not able to see very far.
**Shoulder**, joint between arm and body.
**Show**, vaginal discharge prior to start of labor.
**Shunumitism**, belief that proximity to young person rejuvenates elders.
**Sialaden**, salivary gland.
**Sialadenitis**, inflammation of a salivary gland.
**Silagogue**, causing the secretion of saliva.
**Sialaporia**, deficiency in saliva secretion.
**Sialine**, pertaining to saliva.
**Sialism**, increased production of saliva.
**Sialoporia**, deficient saliva secretion.
**Sialorrhea**, flowing of saliva.
**Sibilant**, whistling; hissing.
**Sibling**, brother or sister.
**Siccative**, drying.
**Sick**, not in normal health.
**Sickness**, illness.
**Siderodromophobia**, extreme fear of train travel.
**Sigh**, involuntary inspiration of emotional origin.
**Sight**, act of seeing.
**Sigmatism**, faulty pronunciation of s sound.
**Sign**, symptom, evidence.
**Signature**, directions for taking medicine on a prescription.
**Silicosis**, condition of the lungs found in those who work among stone dust.
**Sinapism**, mustard plaster.
**Sinciput**, upper part of head.
**Sinew**, tendon or fibrous tissue.
**Singultus**, hiccough.
**Sinister**, left.
**Sinistrad**, toward the left.
**Sinistral**, pertaining to the left side.
**Sinuous**, winding.
**Sinus**, hollow area of a bone.
**Sinusitis**, inflammation of the nasal sinuses.
**Sinusotomy**, incision of a sinus.
**Sippy Diet**, diets used to decrease acid or stomach juice.
**Siriasis**, sunstroke.
**Sitology**, study of food and its use.
**Sitophobia**, extreme dislike of food.
**Situs**, position.
**Sitz-Bath**, a therapeutic bath in sitting position.
**Skelalgia**, leg pain.
**Skeleton**, bones of body.
**Skin**, outer covering of body.
**Skull**, bones of head, 22 in all.
**Sleep**, normal loss of consciousness.
**Sleeping Sickness**, an infection of brain causing increased drowsiness; encephalitis.
**Sling**, support of arm or leg.
**Slough**, dead tissue which separates from living tissue.
**Smallpox**, serious infectious disease with fever, pain, vomiting and an eruption of red spots which later become blisters and afterwards are filled with pus.
**Smear**, preparation of body secretions spread on a glass slide for microscopic study.
**Smegma**, thick, odorous secretion of certain glands.
**Smog**, mixture of smoke and fog.
**Smell**, odor; to stimulate olfactory cells.
**Sneezing**, a nose irritation which causes sudden expulsion of air from mouth and nose.
**Snoring**, a nose or throat obstruction causing a noise when breathing during sleep.
**Snowblindness**, temporary loss of sight due to glare on snow.
**Snuffles**, yellow discharges from nose of infants.
**Soak**, immerse in a solution.
**Sociology**, study of social relationships.
**Socket**, hollow into which another part fits.
**Sodokosis**, rat-bite fever.
**Sodomy**, unusual sexual relations, bestiality.
**Soft**, not hard or firm.
**Soft Palate**, posterior part of palate.
**Solar**, pertaining to the sun.
**Solar Fever**, infectious febrile disease.
**Solar Plexus**, anatomical area in upper part of abdomen.
**Sole**, bottom of foot.
**Soleus**, soft, broad muscle of calf or leg.
**Solid**, not hollow, gaseous or liquid.
**Soluble**, able to be dissolved.
**Solute**, substance which is dissolved in a solution.
**Solution**, homogeneous mixture of a solid in a liquid.
**Solvent**, solution used to dissolve material.
**Soma**, the body.
**Somal**, pertaining to the body.
**Somatalgia**, bodily pain.
**Somatesthesia**, bodily sensation.
**Somatic**, pertaining to the body.
**Somnambulism**, sleepwalking.
**Somnifacient**, causing sleep.
**Somniferous**, causing sleep.
**Somniloquism**, talking while asleep.
**Somnolent**, sleepy.
**Soor**, thrush.
**Sophistication**, adulteration of a product.
**Sopor**, coma.
**Soporific**, producing sleep.

**Sore**, an ulcer or wound.
**Sore Throat**, inflammation of pharynx, tonsils or larynx.
**Sororiation**, growth of breasts at puberty.
**Soterocyte**, blood platelet.
**Sound**, noise; auditory sensations caused by vibrations.
**Space**, area; region, segment.
**Span**, distance from fingertip to fingertip with arms outstretched.
**Spanogyny**, decrease in female births.
**Spargosis**, swelling of female breasts with milk; thickening of skin.
**Spasm**, contraction of any muscle that is sudden and involuntary.
**Spasmodic**, occuring in spasms.
**Spasmophemia**, stuttering.
**Spasmophilia**, tendency to spasms.
**Spasmus**, spasm.
**Spastic**, rigid; flexed; pertaining to spasms.
**Spasticity**, sustained increased muscle tension.
**Spay**, to remove femile sex gland.
**Specialists**, one skilled in a particular field.
**Species**, category; classification.
**Specimen**, part of tissue or material used for analysis.
**Spectacles**, eye glasses.
**Speculum**, instrument which widens the opening of body cavities for examination.
**Speech**, thought expressed in words.
**Sperm**, male fertilizing cell.
**Spermatocidal**, killing sperm.
**Sphacelate**, to become gangrenous.
**Sphacelation**, gangrene.
**Spheroma**, spherelike tumor.
**Sphincter**, muscle that surrounds and closes an opening.
**Sphincterismus**, spasm of sphincter.
**Sphygmic**, pertaining to the pulse.
**Sphygmomonometer**, blood pressure gauge.
**Spica**, figure-of-8 bandage.
**Spina**, sharp protuberance; spine.
**Spina Bifida**, condition in which there is a defect in the development of the spinal column.
**Spinal**, pertaining to a spine.
**Spinal Cord**, part of nervous system enclosed within the backbone; part of the nervous system which transmits impulses to and from the brain.
**Spinal Curvature**, condition where spine is abnormally bent forward or backward.
**Spinal Fracture**, broken back.
**Spine**, sharp piece of bone; backbone.
**Spinthecism**, seeing sparks before the eyes. [guid.
**Spirit**, volatile liquid; alcoholic li-
**Splanchnic**, concerning abdominal organs.
**Spleen**, organ situated in the left upper part of the abdomen which manufactures, stores and destroys blood cells.
**Splenalgia**, pain in the spleen.
**Splenauxe**, enlargement of the spleen.
**Splenectomy**, surgical removal of spleen.
**Splenic**, pertaining to the spleen.
**Splenitis**, inflammation of the spleen.
**Splenoma**, splenic tumor. [spleen.
**Splenomegaly**, enlargement of the
**Splint**, appliance to protect or stabilize injured part.
**Spondyle**, vertebra.
**Spondylitis**, inflammation of spine.
**Sporadic**, intermittent; occurring at different times and places.
**Spot**, blemish.
**Sprain**, injury of a joint caused by over-stretching of the ligaments.
**Sprue**, disease in which the patient is unable to absorb necessary nutrients.
**Spur**, pointed outgrowth. [of mouth
**Sputum**, material that is spat out
**Squama**, scale.
**Squatting**, sitting on the heels.
**Stab**, puncture with sharp object.
**Stabilization**, making firm and steady.
**Stable**, immobile. [drops.
**Stactometer**, device for measuring
**Staff**, hospital personnel.
**Stalagmometer**, instrument for measuring drops.
**Stamina**, endurance.
**Stammering**, hesitant speech.
**Stanch**, to stop a flow of blood.
**Stapes**, small bone of middle ear.
**Staphylococcus**, bacteria causing body infection.
**Staphyloma**, budging of the white of the eye. [of food.
**Starvation**, continued deprivation
**Stasis**, stoppage of flow of blood or urine. [ing up.
**Stasophobia**, extreme fear of stand-
**Stat.**, at once.
**State**, condition.
**Statim**, at once.
**Status**, condition; state. [tissue.
**Steatitis**, inflammation of fatty
**Steatopygia**, having large buttocks.
**Stillate**, star-like shape.
**Stenochoria**, stenosis.
**Stenosed**, narrowed; constricted.
**Stenosis**, constricted; decrease in diameter.
**Stercus**, excrement. [idea.
**Stereotypy**, persistence of a single
**Sterile**, barren; aseptic.
**Sterility**, inability to have children.
**Sterilize**, to make bacteria free; remove ability to reproduce.
**Sterilizer**, device for eliminating bacteria on instruments.
**Sternal**, pertaining to the sternum.
**Sternalgia**, pain in the sternum.
**Sternodynia**, pain in breastbone

**Sternum**, breastbone.
**Sternutation**, sneezing.
**Stertor**, snoring.
**Stethalgia**, chest pain.
**Stethoscope**, instrument used to listen to sounds of body.
**Sthenia**, force; strength.
**Stigma**, mark or spot on tissue.
**Stigmatosis**, skin disease characterized by ulcerated spots.
**Stillbirth**, birth of a dead baby.
**Stillborn**, born dead. [activity.
**Stimulant**, anything that increases
**Stimulus**, exciting agent. [loop.
**Stitch**, localized sharp pain; sewing
**Stoma**, mouth. [digestion begins.
**Stomach**, large pouch where food
**Stomach Ulcers**, sores or ulcer in stomach wall usually due to increased secretion of acid.
**Stomachalgia**, pain in the stomach.
**Stomachic**, gastric stimulant.
**Stomatalgia**, pain in mouth.

**Stomatitis**, inflammation of the mouth.
**Stomatodynia**, pain in mouth.
**Stomatopathy**, any mouth disorder.
**Stool**, feces.
**Strabismus**, squint, cross-eye. [ing.
**Strain**, overexertion; overstretch-
**Strait**, narrow passage.
**Strangulation**, choking; stopping of blood supply.
**Strangury**, painful urination.
**Strap**, bind with bandages.
**Stratified**, layered.
**Stratum**, layer of tissue nearly uniform in thickness.
**Streak**, line; stripe.
**Streptococcus**, any organism infecting man. [sick.
**Stretcher**, device for carrying the
**Stria**, linear mark or line on body.
**Striate**, having streaks.
**Stricture**, narrowing of any tube in in the body. [sound.
**Stridor**, harsh, rasping breath
**Stroke**, apoplexy; seizure; fit.
**Stroma**, framework of an organ.
**Struma**, goiter.
**Strumitis**, thyroiditis.
**Strumectomy**, thryoidectomy.
**Strychnism**, strychnine poisoning.
**Stump**, remaining part of limb after amputation. [ness.
**Stun**, momentary loss of conscious-
**Stupefacient**, narcotic.
**Stupemania**, manic stupor.
**Stupor**, state of decreased feeling.
**Stuprum**, rape.
**Stuttering**, speech impediment characterized by repeating syllables.
**Sty**, infection of gland of eyelid.
**Styloid**, long and pointed.
**Stype**, tampon.
**Sub-** (prefix), under.
**Subacute**, mildly acute. [ishment.
**Subalimentation**, inadequate nour-
**Subaural**, below the ear.
**Subclavian**, below collar bone.
**Subconscious**, out of awareness.
**Subcostal**, below a rib.
**Subcutaneous**, under the skin.
**Subdelirium**, mild delirium.

**Sublatio**, detachment of a part.

**Sublimation**, process of passing from solid to vapor state without liquifying. [ness.
**Subliminal**, below conscious aware-
**Sublingual Gland**, salivary gland beneath tongue.

**Subluxation**, minor dislocation.
**Submaxilla**, mandible. [along jaw.
**Submixillary Gland**, salivary gland
**Submental**, beneath the chin.
**Subphrenic**, beneath the diaphragm.
**Subscription**, part of a prescription giving directions for compounding the ingredients.

**Substance**, material of which a thing is composed.
**Substantia**, substance.
**Subtotal**, incomplete.
**Sububeres**, unweaned infants.
**Subungual**, beneath a nail.
**Subvirile**, lacking in virility.
**Succorrhea**, excessive secretion.
**Succus**, fluid secretion.
**Sudation**, perspiring.
**Sudatorium**, sweat bath.
**Sudor**, sweat.
**Sudoresis**, excessive sweating.
**Suffocation**, blockage of air ways.
**Suffusion**, spreading; diffusion.
**Sugar**, carbohydrate.
**Suicide**, self-destruction.
**Sulcus**, groove or furrow.
**Sulfa Drugs**, name referring to the group of drugs used in the treatment of various bacterial diseases [sun's rays.
**Sunburn**, skin inflammation from
**Sunstroke**, stroke due to excessive exposure to the sun. [ing.
**Superalimentation**, excessive feed-
**Superciliary**, concerning eyebrow.
**Supercilium**, eyebrow.
**Superego**, conscience.
**Superficial**, near the surface. [milk.
**Superlactation**, oversecretion of
**Supernumeray**, more than usual.
**Superscription**, Rx before a prescription.
**Supinate**, turn hand upward
**Supine**, lying flat on back.
**Suppository**, solid medication for insertion into a cavity other than the mouth.
**Suppurate**, form infection.
**Sura**, calf of the leg.
**Sural**, pertaining to the calf.
**Suralimentation**, overfeeding.
**Surditas**, deafness.
**Surdomute**, deaf and dumb.
**Surgeon**, medical specialist performing surgery.
**Surgery**, specialty of medicine that deals with disease and trauma by operative means.
**Surgical**, pertaining to surgery.
**Surrogate**, a substitute.

**Susceptible**, having little resistance, easily influenced.
**Suspiration**, sigh.
**Suspirious**, breathing heavily.
**Susurration**, murmur.
**Suture**, to stitch together.
**Swab**, gauze wrapped around a stick for application of medicine.
**Swallow**, voluntary act of passing food from mouth to stomach.
**Sweat**, perspiration. [licles.
**Sycosis**, inflammation of hair fol-
**Syllepsis**, pregnancy. [ite sides.
**Symmetry**, similar parts on oppos-
**Symphysis**, immovable joint.
**Symphysis Pubis**, pubic bones above the midline of the external genital.
**Symptom**, perceptible change from normal function.
**Synalgia**, referred pain.
**Synchronous**, occurring simultaneously. [cranium.
**Synciput**, anterior upper half of the
**Syncope**, fainting. [fingers.
**Syndactylus**, one having webbed
**Syndrome**, any group of symptoms commonly occurring together.
**Synechia**, abnormal joining of parts.
**Synergy**, cooperation.
**Syngamy**, sexual reproduction.
**Synizesis**, contraction of the eye pupil.
**Synovitis**, inflammation of the lining of a joint.
**Syntaxis**, junction of two bones.
**Syphilid**, skin eruption due to syphilis.
**Syphilis**, serious venereal disease.
**Syringe**, instrument used to inject fluids into body.
**Syrinx**, cavity or tube. [ing organs.
**System**, group of similar function-
**Systole**, period during which contraction of heart takes place.

— T —

**Tobacosis**, tobacco poisoning.
**Tobagism**, tobacco poisoning.
**Tabefacation**, emaciation.
**Tabes**, gradual deterioration in a chronic illness.
**Tabes Dorsalis**, a disease of the nervous system leading to paralysis and caused by syphilis.
**Tablet**, pill.
**Tabule**, pill.
**Tache**, spot; blemish.
**Tachycardia**, rapid beating of the heart coming on in sudden attacks.
**Tachylalia**, rapid speech.
**Tachyphagia**, rapid eating.
**Tachyphasia**, rapid speech.
**Tachypnea**, unusually fast rate of breathing.
**Tachyrhythmia**, rapid heart action.
**Tactile**, pertaining to sense of touch.
**Tactual**, pertaining to touch.
**Tactus**, touch. [tapeworm.
**Taenia**, band-like muscle or tissue;
**Tagma**, protoplasm.
**Talalgia**, pain in the heel.
**Talc**, a powder.
**Talipes**, club foot.
**Talipes Planus**, flatfoot.
**Tallus**, ankle.
**Tampon**, round cotton plug used to close wound or cavity.
**Tamponade**, act of plugging.
**Tap**, puncture of body cavity.
**Tapeworm**, type of intestinal worm.
**Taphephobia**, extreme fear of live burial. [the instep.
**Tarsal**, pertaining to the eyelid or
**Tarsus**, arch of foot.
**Tartar**, dental calculus. [tongue.
**Taste**, sensation through nerves on
**T.A.T.**, toxin-antoxin.
**Taxonomy**, science of classification of plants and animals.
**Tear**, saline fluid secreted by lacrimal glands.
**Teat**, nipple.
**Technic**, technique.
**Technique**, method; procedure.
**Tectonic**, pertaining to plastic surgery.
**Tectum**, roof-like structure.
**Teeth**, bony growths in jaw used for chewing.
**Teeth, Milk**, first set of teeth.
**Teething**, appearance of teeth.
**Tegmen**, covering.
**Tegument**, skin.
**Teinodynia**, pain in the tendons.
**Tela**, weblike structure.
**Telalgia**, referred pain. [laries.
**Telangitis**, inflammation of capil-
**Telangiosis**, disease of capillary vessels.
**Teleorganic**, vital.
**Telepathist**, mind reader.
**Telepathy**, communication of two minds at a distance through means undetectable by science.
**Telergy**, automatism. [tion.
**Telesthesia**, extrasensory percep-
**Temperament**, physical and mental characteristics of an individual.
**Temperature**, degree of heat and cold; body temperature is normally 98.6.
**Temple**, area in front of ear.
**Temporal**, pertaining to the temple or time.
**Temulence**, drunkenness.
**Tenacious**, adhesive.
**Tenalgia**, pain in a tendon.
**Tenderness**, soreness. [don.
**Tendinitis**, inflammation of a ten-
**Tendinous**, pertaining to or composed of tendons.
**Tendo**, tendon.
**Tendon**, fibrous tissue that connects muscles to other structures.
**Tenectomy**, surgical removal of a tendon. [der.
**Tenesmus**, spasm of anus or blad-

**Tenia**, tapeworm; band.

**Teniacide**, medication which destroys tapeworms.

**Tennis Elbow**, pain in the arm, particularly on twisting inwards, caused by excessive strain.

**Tenodynia**, pain in a tendon.

**Tenonitis**, inflammation of tendon.

**Tenoplasty**, surgical repair of a tendon.

**Tenorrhaphy**, suture of a tendon.

**Tenosynovitis**, inflammation of a tendon and its sheath.

**Tension**, condition of being strained or stretched.

**Tentative**, subject to change.

**Tentigo**, unusual sex desires.

**Tephrosis**, cremation.

**Tepid**, warm.

**Tepidorium**, warm bath.

**Teras**, fetal monster.

**Teratism**, fetal monster.

**Teratoid**, monster.

**Teratology**, science dealing with monstrosities and malformations.

**Tere**, to rub.

**Terebration**, boring.

**Teres**, round; smooth. [time.

**Term**, boundary; definite period of

**Terminal**, end.

**Terracing**, suturing in several rows.

**Terror**, extreme fear. [glands.

**Testicles**, the male reproductive

**Testis**, male reproductive gland.

**Tetanus**, infectious disease characterized by painful spasms of voluntary muscles.

**Tetany**, disease characterized by painful muscle spasms with convulsive movements, usually due to inability to utilize calcium.

**Tetraplegia**, paralysis of all four extremities.

**Tetter**, blister; pimple.

**Textural**, pertaining to the constitution of tissues.

**Thalamus**, area in the brain concerned with many bodily functions, often called the seat of the emotions. [sea.

**Thalassophobia**, extreme fear of

**Thanatobiologic**, pertaining to life and death.

**Thanatoid**, resembling death.

**Thanatomania**, suicidal obsession.

**Thebaism**, opium poisoning.

**Theca**, case; sheath. [of tea

**Theism**, poisoning from overdose

**Thelalgia**, pain in nipples.

**Thelerethism**, erection of the nipple.

**Thelitis**, inflammation of nipple.

**Thelium**, nipple.

**Thenal**, pertaining to the palm.

**Thenar**, area beneath thumb; palm.

**Theomania**, delusion that one is a deity.

**Theory**, hypothesis.

**Therapeutic**, pertaining to healing.

**Therapeutics**, scientific treatment of disease.

**Therapy**, treatment of disease.

**Thermal**, pertaining to heat.

**Thermanalgesia**, inability to react to heat. [or cold.

**Thermesthesia**, perception of heat

**Thermic**, pertaining to heat.

**Thermofuge**, reducing fever.

**Thermometer**, instrument to meassure heat.

**Thermoplegia**, heatstroke; sunstroke [heat.

**Thermostat**, device for controlling

**Thigh**, part of leg above knee.

**Thirst**, desire for liquid.

**Thoracalgia**, chest pain.

**Thoracic**, pertaining to the chest.

**Thoracectomy**, surgical removal of a rib.

**Thoracodynia**, pain in thorax.

**Thoracomyodynia**, pain in chest muscles.

**Thoracoschisis**, fissure of chest wall.

**Thoracotomy**, surgical opening of chest.

**Thorax**, chest.

**Threadworm**, parasitic worm.

**Threpsology**, study of nutrition.

**Threshold**, point at which an effect is produced.

**Thrill**, heart murmur or abnormal blood vessel tremor that can be felt.

**Thrix**, hair. [esophagus.

**Throat**, area between mouth and

**Throb**, pulsation.

**Throe**, sharp pain.

**Thrombin**, substance in blood which aids clotting. [ting.

**Thrombopathy**, defective blood clot-

**Thrombophlebitis**, inflammation of a vein.

**Thrombosin**, thrombin.

**Thrombosis**, formation of a clot within a blood vessel.

**Thrombus**, blood clot.

**Thrush**, disease of the mouth and throat caused by a fungus.

**Thumb**, first digit of hand. [thymus.

**Thymectomy**, surgical removal of

**Thymona**, tumor of thyroid.

**Thymion**, wart. [gland.

**Thymitis**, inflammation of thryroid

**Thymona**, tumor of thymus.

**Thymus**, glandular structure in the chest having an unknown function. [thyroid.

**Thyroadenitis**, inflammation of

**Thyrocele**, goiter.

**Thyrogenic**, originating in thyroid.

**Thyroid**, glandular structure in the neck secreting thyroxin, a substance vital to life.

**Thyroidectomy**, surgical removal of all or part of the thyroid gland.

**Thyroiditis**, inflammation of the thyroid gland. [thyroid gland.

**Thyroxin**, hormone secreted by the

**Tibia**, shin bone.

**Tibial**, pertaining to the tibia.

**Tic**, muscular twitch, usually of the face.
**Tick**, blood sucking parasite.
**Tigroid**, striped.
**Tilmus**, pulling out of hair.
**Tinea**, ringworm.
**Tinnitus**, noises in the ear which may take the form of buzzing, clicking or thudding.
**Tiqueur**, one afflicted with a tic.
**Tire**, exhaust, fatigue.
**Tissue**, structure of body made up of similar cells.
**Tocalogy**, obstetrical science. [birth.
**Tocophobia**, extreme fear of child-
**Tocus**, childbirth.
**Toe**, digit of the foot.
**Tolerance**, endurance.
**Tongue**, organ of speech and taste.
**Tongue-Tie**, congenital shortening of frenuum below tongue.
**Tonic**, muscular tightness. [sue.
**Tonsil**, mass of special lymph tis-
**Tonsilla**, tonsil.
**Tonsillectomy**, removal of tonsils.
**Tonsillitis**, infection of the tonsils.
**Tooth**, hard structure in the jaws used for chewing.
**Tophaceous**, gritty, sandy. [spot.
**Topical**, pertaining to a particular
**Topoalgia**, localized pain.
**Toponarcosis**, local anesthesia.
**Torpidity**, sluggishness.
**Torpor**, inactivity; apathy.
**Torsion**, twisting.
**Torso**, trunk of body.
**Torticollis**, wryneck; abnormal twisting of the neck caused by injury or infection to the muscle or nerve.
**Torulus**, small elevation.
**Touch**, tactile sense. [bleeding.
**Tourniquet**, band used to control
**Toxemia**, any illness due to poisons absorbed from organisms in the system.
**Toxenzyme**, any poisonous enzyme.
**Toxic**, poisonous.
**Toxicant**, poisonous; a poison.
**Toxicity**, poisonous.
**Toxicohemia**, toxemia.
**Toxicology**, science dealing with poisons. [sons.
**Toxicophobia**, extreme fear of poi-
**Toxipathy**, disease caused by poisoning. [tion.
**T.P.R.**, temperature, pulse, respira-
**Trachea**, the windpipe.
**Tracheal**, pertaining to trachea.
**Tracheitis**, inflammation of the windpipe.
**Trachelagra**, gout in the neck.
**Trachelismus**, spasm of neck muscles.
**Tracheofissure**, incision of trachea.
**Tracheotomy**, cutting into windpipe to relieve obstruction.
**Trachitis**, inflammation of trachea.
**Trachoma**, infectious disease of the eyes.
**Trachyphonia**, roughness of voice.
**Traction**, pulling or drawing.
**Tragopodia**, knock-knee.
**Trait**, distinguishing characteristic.
**Trance**, sleeplike state.
**Tranquilizer**, calming agent.
**Transcalent**, able to be penetrated by heat rays.
**Transfix**, pierce.
**Transforation**, perforation of the skull of a fetus. [to another.
**Transfusion**, giving of one's blood
**Transmissable**, communicable.
**Transmission**, communication of a disease from one person to another. [perspiration.
**Transpirable**, allowing passage of
**Transplant**, remove tissue from one part of the body to another. [side.
**Transverse**, extending from side to
**Transvestitism**, uncontrollable urge to dress in the clothing of the opposite sex.
**Trapizius**, muscle of back.
**Trauma**, injury; wound.
**Trauma, Psychic**, injury to subconscious due to emotional shock.
**Treatment**, medical care of a patient.
**Tremor**, shake or quiver.
**Tremulous**, quivering.
**Trench Mouth**, mouth infection caused by organism; also called Vincent's angina.
**Trend**, course.
**Trepan**, to make a hole in skull to relieve pressure on brain.
**Tresis**, perforation. [laries.
**Trichangiectasis**, dilation of capil-
**Trichauxe**, excessive hair growth.
**Trichinosis**, disease caused by the trichina organism found in raw pork.
**Trichitis**, inflammation of the hair roots. [testinal tract.
**Trichobezar**, hair-ball found in in-
**Trichocardia**, hairy heart.
**Trichoclasia**, brittleness of hair.
**Trichocryptosis**, brittleness of hair.
**Trichology**, science of hair care.
**Trichoptilosis**, hair splitting.
**Trichosis**, any hair disease.
**Trifid**, divided into three parts.
**Trigonid**, first three cusps of a lower molar tooth.
**Trilobate**, having three lobes.
**Triorchid**, having three testes.
**Triphasic**, having three phases.
**Triplegia**, paralysis of three extremities.
**Triquetrum**, wrist bone.
**Trismus**, spasm of jaw muscles.
**Tristimania**, melancholia.
**Troche**, lozenge. [on its axis.
**Trochocardia**, rotation of the heart
**Trochoides**, pivot joint.
**Trophic**, pertaining to nutrition.
**Trophology**, science of body nutrition. [ease.
**Trophonosis**, any nutritional dis-
**Truncal**, pertaining to the trunk.
**Truncate**, cut off limbs or branches.

**Truncus,** trunk.
**Trunk,** torso.
**Truss,** device to hold hernia in place. [ture.
**Tube,** long, hollow cylindrical struc-
**Tuber,** enlargement; swelling.
**Tubercle,** small swelling; rounded elevation on a bone; change in tissue caused by the tuberculosis germ. [cles.
**Tuberculated,** covered with tuber-
**Tuberculophobia,** extreme fear of tuberculosis.
**Tuberculosis,** infectious disease of man and animals caused by tubercle bacilli having many and varied manifestations in lungs, brain, bone, etc. [tuberculosis.
**Tuberculous,** caused by or having
**Tuberosity,** bone projection.
**Tubule,** small tube.
**Tuborrhea,** discharge from eustachian tube.
**Tularemia,** an infectious disease transmitted by insects or small animals caused by the pasteurella organism.
**Tumefaction,** swelling.
**Tumesence,** swelling.
**Tumor,** a swelling or growth.
**Tunic,** lining membrane.
**Tunnel,** enclosed passage.
**Turbidity,** cloudiness.
**Turgesence,** distention; swelling.
**Turgescent,** becoming swollen.
**Turgid,** congested and swollen.
**Turgor,** swelling.
**Tussis,** cough.
**Tutamen,** a protection.
**Twin,** one of two persons of the same birth. [tion.
**Twitch,** slight muscular contrac-
**Tyloma,** callus.
**Tylosis,** formation of callosities.
**Tympanal,** pertaining to the tympanum. [due to gas or air.
**Tympanites,** abdominal distention
**Tympanous,** distended with gas.
**Tympanum,** ear drum.
**Typhlosis,** blindness.
**Typhoid Fever,** an infectious fever caused by the typhoid bacillus, characterized by diarrhea and other symptoms. [typhoid fever.
**Typhomania,** delirium found with
**Typhous,** pertaining to typhus.

## — U —

**Uberous,** prolific.
**Uberty,** fertility.
**Ulalgia,** pain in the gums.
**Ulatrophia,** shrinkage of gums.
**Ulcer,** sores on skin or internal parts of body caused by various things.
**Ulceration,** formation of an ulcer.
**Ulcus,** ulcer.
**Ulectomy,** surgical removal of part of gums; removal of scar tissue.

**Ulemorrhagia,** bleeding from the gums.
**Uletic,** pertaining to the gums.
**Ulitis,** gum inflammation.
**Ulna,** bone of forearm.
**Ulnar,** pertaining to the ulna.
**Ulocace,** ulcer and infection of gums.
**Uloid,** scarlike
**Ulorrhagia,** bleeding from gums.
**Ulosis,** scar formation.
**Ultimate,** final; highest.
**Ululation,** hysterical crying.
**Umbilicus,** site on abdomen of attachment of umbilical cord.
**Umbo,** funnel-shaped area of ear drum.
**Uncia,** ounce; inch. [wrist.
**Unciform,** hook-shaped; bone of
**Unconscious,** state in which person is unaware of both his external and internal environment as in a faint.
**Unction,** ointment.
**Unctuus,** oily.
**Undulant Fever,** an infectious disease caused by the Brucella organism; found in animals and transmitted to man.
**Undulation,** wave.
**Ungual,** pertaining to the nails.
**Unguent,** ointment.
**Unguis,** fingernail or toenail.
**Unilateral,** pertaining to one side.
**Unigravida,** woman in her first pregnancy.
**Union,** juncture. [one live child.
**Unipara,** woman who has borne
**Uracratia,** inability to retain urine.
**Uraniscus,** palate.
**Uranium,** radioactive element. [skin.
**Uredo,** sensation of burning on
**Uremia,** poisoning from urinary substances in the blood.
**Ureter,** the tube leading from the kidneys to the bladder.
**Ureterolith,** stone in the ureter.
**Uretha,** tube which carries the urine from the bladder to the outside. [thra.
**Urethritis,** inflammation of the ure-
**Uretic,** promoting urination.
**Urinary,** pertaining to urine.
**Urinate,** discharge urine. [activity.
**Urine,** fluid end product of kidney
**Urologist,** medical specialist who deals with organs producing and transporting urine. [tem.
**Urology,** study of the urinary sys-
**Uroschesis,** to retain urine.
**Urous,** urine-like.
**Urticaria,** hives.
**Ustion,** incinerate, burn.
**Ustus,** burned.
**Uterine,** pertaining to the womb.
**Uterus,** womb.
**Uvea,** tissue layer of eye.
**Uvula,** small tissue projecting in the middle of palate in throat.

## — V —

**Vaccin,** substance used for inoculation.
**Vaccination,** injection with a germ

or germ product to produce immunity and protect against disease.

**Vaccinia,** contagious disease as a result of inoculation with cowpox virus.

**Vagina,** the passage connecting the outer and inner female sex organs. [vagina.

**Vaginismus,** painful spasm of the

**Vaginitis,** inflammation of vagina.

**Vagus,** tenth cranial nerve.

**Valence,** ability of a chemical agent to combine in a reaction.

**Valetudinarian,** person afflicted with frequent illness.

**Valgus,** bowlegged; knock-kneed.

**Valve,** structure which prevents backward flow in a passage.

**Valvulitis,** inflammation of a valve.

**Valvulotomy,** incision of a heart valve.

**Varicella,** chickenpox.

**Varices,** enlarged, tortuoris vein.

**Varicocle,** varicose veins in the area of scrotum.

**Varicose Veins,** swollen veins caused by improper valve function.

**Variola,** smallpox.

**Vas,** vessel, passageway.

**Vascular,** pertaining to blood vessels.

**Vas Deferens,** duct in testis which transports semen.

**Vasectomy,** excision of vas deferens; operation to stérilize male.

**Vasoconstrictor,** causing a narrowing of blood vessels.

**Vasodepressor,** agent which relaxes the blood vessels, thus increasing diameter and lowering blood pressure. [ber of blood vessel.

**Vasospasm,** sudden decrease in cali-

**Vein,** blood vessels carrying blood to heart. [tercourse.

**Venereal,** pertaining to sexual in-

**Venery,** sexual intercourse.

**Venesection,** puncture of a vein to remove blood. [a vein.

**Venipuncture,** surgical puncture of

**Venom,** poison from an animal.

**Ventricle,** small cavity; pouch.

**Vermis,** worm.

**Verruca,** wart.

**Version,** turning; changing the position of the fetus in the womb to facilitate birth.

**Vertebra,** bone of the spinal column.

**Vertex,** crown of the head.

**Vertical,** pertaining to the vertex.

**Vertigo,** dizziness.

**Vesica,** bladder.

**Vesicant,** blistering.

**Vesicle,** blister; small bladder.

**Vessel,** tube; passageway

**Vestigial,** non-functioning part in body more highly developed in embryo or lower animal.

**Viable,** alive. [to hemorrhage.

**Vibex,** linear spots beneath skin due

**Vibrissal,** stiff hairs in nose.

**Vicious,** faulty.

**Vigil,** wakefullness.

**Vincent's Angina,** mouth infection; also called trench mouth.

**Vinum,** wine.

**Virgin,** one who has not experienced sexual relations.

**Virile,** masculine, mature.

**Virilism,** maleness. [diseases.

**Virology,** study of virus and viral

**Virose,** poisonous.

**Virulence,** poisonousness; infectiousness; endangering life.

**Viruses,** minute organisms which cause certain diseases among which are the common cold, measles, mumps, poliomyelitis, chickenpox, smallpox.

**Vis,** energy, power.

**Viscera,** organs within body.

**Viscid,** thick; adherent.

**Vision,** sight; seeing.

**Vitals,** important body organs.

**Vitamins,** chemical substances found in foods that are necessary for proper bodily function.

**Vitiligo,** lack of pigment in certain areas of the skin.

**Vitium,** a defect.

**Vitiation,** injury; decrease in function of a part. [animal.

**Vivisect,** to cut or dissect living

**Vocal Cords,** tissue bands whose vibration causes speech.

**Voice,** sounds produced by the vibration of the vocal cords.

**Void,** to empty bladder or rectum.

**Volce,** palm or sole of foot.

**Volition,** act of selecting.

**Volvulus,** twisting of the bowel causing obstruction.

**Vomer,** bone of nose.

**Vomicose,** containing ulcers.

**Vomiting,** dislodging the food in stomach through mouth.

**Vomitus,** vomited material.

**Vox,** voice.

**Voyeur,** person receiving sexual pleasure from watching activities of others. [ing to maturity.

**Vril,** inborn energy from birth lead-

**Vulva,** female genital.

**Vulvitis,** inflammation of the female external genitalia.

**Vulnus,** wound.

## — W —

**Waist,** area between chest and hip encircling body.

**Wart,** growth on the skin that may be caused by viruses.

**Wash,** lotion.

**Wasserman Test,** test of the blood to determine if syphilis is present.

**Weak,** lacking strength.

**Wean,** substitution of other substances for breast milk.

**Webbed,** connected by a thin membrane.

**Weeping,** crying; seeping of a fluid.

**Wen,** a sebaceous cyst.

**Wheal,** a red, round elevation on skin.

**Wheeze,** sound in chest due to abnormalities in lungs.

**White Leg,** swelling and blanching of the leg produced by thrombosis of the veins.

**Whitlow,** infected finger.

**Whooping Cough,** infectious disease characterized by episodes of coughing punctuated by whooping noises between episodes during periods of gasping for breath, pertussis.

**Wisdom Tooth,** the most posterior teeth or molar on each side of jaw.

**Woman,** mature female.

**Womb,** uterus; organ in which developing fetus resides.

**Wound,** an injury or break in the skin.

**Wrist,** joint between forearm and hand.

**Wryneck,** torticollis.

## — X —

**Xanthic,** yellow.

**Xanthoma,** yellow tumor or growth.

**Xanthopsia,** yellow vision.

**Xanthosis,** jaundice.

**Xenogenous,** disease caused by foreign body or toxin.

**Xenomenia,** bleeding from other than normal site at time of menstrual period.

**Xenophobia,** extreme fear of strangers.

**Xenopthalmia,** inflammation of eye due to foreign body.

**Xerocheilia,** dry lips.

**Xeroderma,** a skin disease characterized by dryness.

**Xeransis,** condition of dryness.

**Xerasia,** dryness of hair leading to baldness.

**Xerophthalmia,** eye condition in which the lining membrane of the lid and eyeball is dry and thickened.

**Xerosis,** condition of dryness.

**Xiphoid,** sword-shaped cartilage at lowest part of breast bone.

**X-Ray,** device used to photograph interior parts of body; also used as therapeutic tool.

**Xysma,** membranous like material in some diarrhea stools.

**Xyster,** surgical instrument used to scrape bone.

## — Y —

**Yawn,** involuntary opening mouth when fatigued.

**Yaws,** tropical disease.

**Yeast,** a rich source of vitamin B.

**Yellow Fever,** infectious fever found in tropical lands.

**Youth,** period of adolescence between childhood and adult life.

## — Z —

**Zein,** protein from corn.

**Zestocausis,** to burn with steam.

**Zinc,** a metal used in medicines.

**Zoanthropy,** belief that one is an animal.

**Zoetic,** pertaining to life.

**Zondal-Aschheim Test,** test to determine pregnancy.

**Zonesthesia,** sensation of tightness around the waist.

**Zooerastea,** coitus with an animal.

**Zooid,** animal-like.

**Zoopsia,** hallucinations involving animals.

**Zoosis,** disease in man carried by animals.

**Zygoma,** a part of the cheek bone.

**Zyme,** fermenting substance.

# Crossword Puzzle Dictionary

# Crossword Puzzle Dictionary

## ABBREVIATIONS

ab.—abbreviation
alch.—alchemy
Amer.—American
anat.—anatomical
arch.—archaic
bacteriol.—bacteriological
bldg.—building
Calif.—California
co.—company
colloq.—colloquial
comb. form—combined form
contr.—contraction
Dep.—Deputies
dept.—department
dial.—dialectic
E.—East
Eng.—English
Fr.—French
gram.—grammatically
her.—heraldry
imp.—imperial
internat.—international
isl.—island
Jan.—January
Jap.—Japanese
L.—Latin
lang.—language
Mass.—Massachusetts
math.—mathematical
med.—medical
Mex.—Mexican
mt.—mountain
mus.—musical
N.—North
naut.—nautical
obs.—obsolete
Pa.—Pennsylvania
pert. to—pertaining to
Phil.—Philippine
Phoen.—Phoenician
poet.—poetical
rel.—reluctance
rep.—republic
rev.—reverential
S.—South
Scand.—Scandinavian
Scot.—Scotch
Shosh.—Shoshone
ter.—territorial
Test.—Testament
trig.—trigonomical
Tues.—Tuesday
var.—variant
vest.—vestment
W.—West

### A

abaft: aft, astern, behind
abandon: despair, forsake, leave, desolate, desert
abase: lower, discredit, humble, degrade, dishonor
abash: shame, disconcert, humiliate, chagrin, ashame, contuse
abate: lessen, diminish, subside, moderate
abbess: amma
abbey superior: abbot
abbot: abbe [quish
abdicate: demit, relin-
Abraham's birthplace: Ur
" nephew: Lot
" wife: Sarah
abet: aid assist, urge, instigate, egg, incite, encourage, promote, foment, help, sanction, uphold, second
abhor: hate, detest, loath
abide: wait, remain, sojourn, dwell, tarry
ability: competence, talent, power
abjure: disavow, renounce, recant
able: competent, could, clever, capable
" to pay: solvent
abnormal: aberrant
abode: residence, lodge, home, habitat, habitation, lodging
" of ancient harp: tara
" of the dead: aralu, aaru
abolish: repeal
abominate: hate, execrate, loathe
aborigine: native [ate
abound: teem, exuber-
abounding: replete, rife
about: of, on, anent, around, at
above: over, up, atop
" (poet.) oer [ra
" (prefix): super, sup-
" & touching: onto, on, upon
abrade: wear, grate, rasp, excoriate
abrasive material: emery, bort
abridgement: epitome
abridge (var.): rasee
abroad: overseas, afar
abrogate: repeal, rescind, annul, cancel
abrupt: steep, sudden, hasty, unexpected, short [eloin
abscond: elope, desert,
absent minded: distrait, away
absolute: utter, sheer, stark, implicit, mere, total, pure
" monarch: despot
" superlative: elative
absolve: free, remit, pardon
absorb: merge, imbib
absorbed: rapt
abstain from: avoids, eschew, refrain
" " food: fast
" being: ens [condite
abstruse: complex, re-
absurd: inept
abundance: plenitude, plenty, galore, store flow
abundant: ample, galore, plentiful, copious
abuse: revile, maltreat, maul, outrage, mistreat [project
abut: border, adjoin,
abyss: pit, chasm, deep, gulf
Abyssinian: Ethiop
" herb: ramtil
" title or governor: ras, negus [comply
accede: consent, agree,
accent: stress, emphasize, tone
accept: take
" as one's own: adopt
" as true: credits, believe [entry, adit
access: entree, door,
accessible: open [hap
accident: chance, mis-
acclaim: praise, clap, ovation, applause
accommodate: adapt, suit, please, oblige
accompany: escort, attend
accomplice: tool, pal
accomplish: do, realize, execute [deed
accomplishment: feat,
accost: hail, greet, assail, address [tab
account: report, recital,
" entry: item
accountable: liable
accumulate: store, pile, amass, collect [true
accurate: exact, correct,
accuse: censure, blame, charge, arraign
accustom (var.): enure, inure [ured
accustomed: used, in-
ace: top, unit, expert, jot, particle
" of clubs: basto
acerb: bitter, harsh, sour, tart
acetic: sour
ache: ail, pain, pang
achieve: win, earn, do, gain, attain
achievement: deed, act, record, feat, gest
acid: sour, biting
" of apples: malic
" chemical: amide
" condiment: vinegar
" neutralizer: alkali
acidity: acor
acknowledge: own, admit, avow, confess, concede
acknowledgement of a wrong: apology
acme: apex, top
aconite: atis
acquaint: apprise
acquiesce: assent, consent, agreement, agree
acquire: gain, learn, secure, win, get, attain, earn
" with difficulty: eke
acquit: exonerate, clear, free
acre (¼): rood
acrid: sour, bitter, pungent, tart [beyond
across: astride, over,
" (poet.): oer
act: deed, feat, behave, do, feign, simulate, law
" out of sorts: mope
" wildly; rave
action: deed, act
" in law: res, re
active: spry, alive, astir, nimble, brisk, quick
actor: player, thespian, doer
actual: real
" being: esse
actuality: fact
actuate: incite, move, arouse, impel, urge, impell [gacity
acumen: sharpness, sa-
acute: keen, intense, pointed, tart, shrewd, poignant, critical
adage: saw, proverb, saying, maxim, motto
adamant: hard, firm, immovable [form, fit
adapt: adjust, suit, con-
add: append, increase, total, augment, attach, annex, affix
addicted: prone
addition: also, besides, aside, plus, yet, more, too, else, and
" to a bill: rider
" " " building: ell
" " " document: rider
additional: extra, other, more, plus
" allowance: bonus
address: sermon, direct, oration, talk, apply, accost, greet
adduce: cite, allege
adept: expert, proficient, skilled [equal
adequate: sufficient, fit,
adhere: stick, persist, cling
adherent of the crown: Tory
" (suffix): ite
adhesive: glue, paste, mucilage, gum
adipose: fatty, fat
adit: entrance, access approach
adjective (suffix): ile, ent, ian, ive, ic

**adjoin**: abut, touch
**adjudge**: opine, deem, award, decree
**adjudged unfit for use**: condemned
**adjunct**: accessory
**adjust**: adapt, set, arrange, deem, regulate, fix, range, frame, settle, align
**administer**: manage
**admirable**: good, fine
**admire**: revere, approve
**admission**: entree, access
**admit**: concede, allow, confess, own [mand
**admonish**: warn, reprimand
**ado**: fuss, bustle [sume
**adopt**: pass, take, assume
**adore**: venerate, worship [nament
**adorn**: crest, trim, deck, grace, drape, ornate, bedeck, decorate, ornament
**Adriatic island**: Eso, Lido
" **seaport**: Trieste
" **winter wind**: bora
**adrift**: afloat [deft
**adroit**: skillful, neat, deft
**adulate**: flatter
**adulation**: praise
**adult**: grown [imago
" **form of insect**: imago
" **steer**: beeve
**advance**: gain, progress, promote
" **guard**: van
" **notice**: warning
**advantage**: stead, behoof, profit [enemy
**adversary**: foe, rival, enemy
" **of man**: satan
**adversity**: ill
**advocate**: proponent, plead, pleader [dea
**Aetes's daughter**: Medea
**Aegean Island**: Psara, Nio, Ios, Samos, Delos
**aerial**: airy [los
**aeriform matter**: gas
**aeronaut**: aviator
**aery**: lofty
**affairs**: matters
" **of chance**: lottery
**affect**: rasp, influence
" **deeply**: penetrate, impress
**affection**: love, ardor, pretension, pretence
**affidavit**: oath
**affirm**: allege, assert, asseverate, aver, declare
**affirmative**: yes, aye, yep, yea
**affix**: append, add
**affliction**: ill, sore, distress, pain, woe, sorrow
**affluence**: wealth [row
**afford**: supply, lend, furnish, provide
" **aid**: help
**affray**: melee, feud
**affront**: insult, displease
**Afghan coin**: amania
" **prince**: amir, ameer
**afire**: eager, blazing, flaming [awash
**afloat**: buoyed, adrift, awash
**afraid**: timorous, fearful, fear
**afresh**: anew
**African**: Negro, Taal
" **animals**: ayeayes, okapi, giraffes
" **antelope**: gnu, eland, addax, peele, bongo
" **city**: Tripoli
" **cony**: dassie, das
" **desert**: Gobi
" **fly**: tsetse
" **gazel**: ariel, cora
" **giraffe**: okapi
" **hartebeest**: tora
" **hemp**: ife
" **hottentot**: nama
" **hunting expedition**: safari
" **lake**: Chad, Tana
" **monkey (small)**: grivet
" **mountain**: Cameroon
" **native**: Zulu, ibo
" **tribe**: Kabonga, Krepi, Nuba
" **Portuguese territory**: Angola
" **region**: Sudan
" **republic**: Liberia
" **river**: Nile, Congo, Niger, Bia, Calabar, Nun, Senegal
" **seaport**: Tunis
" **scup ingredient**: lalo
" **tree**: shea, cola, tarfa, baobab
" **tribesman**: bantu
" **village**: stad
" **wild hog**: wart
" **wildcat**: serval
" **wood**: ebony
" **worm**: loa
**aft**: astern, stern
**after**: behind, later
" **awhile**: anon, later
**aftersong**: epode
**again**: anew, over, encore, moreover
" **(Latin)**: iterum
" **(prefix)**: ob, anti, re
**against**: con, versus
" **(prefix)**: anti
**agalloch**: agar, aloes
**agape**: open, staring
**agave**: aloe
**age**: seniority, era, eon, epoch, century, lifetime
**aged**: senile, old [time
**agent**: consignee, doer, broker, factor, deputy, promoter, representative
**aggravate**: tease, nag, intensify
**aggregate**: sum
**aggregation**: tribe, mass
**agile**: spry, nimble, alert, lithe, lively
**agitate**: stir, roil, rile, fret, disturb, vex perturb, flurry, move
**ago**: past, since
" **(poet.)** agone
**agog**: eager [tering
**agony**: pain, pang, suffering
**agree**: consent, accede assent, accept, coincide, concur, comport, gibe, homologate, conform [ant
**agreeable**: nice, pleasant
**agreement**: covenant, yes, pact, consent, unity, assent, treaty, unison, contract, coincidence, unity
**agriculturist**: farmer, gardener
**ahead**: on forward
**aid**: abet, assist, befriend, sustain, succor
**ail**: suffer, bother
**ailment**: malady
**aim**: point, goal, ambition, purpose, end, intent, ideal, objective, aspiration, target, direct, object
" **high**: aspire
**air**: tone, aria, breeze, tune, carriage, manner, mien, display, atmosphere, song, melody, vapor
" **(comb. form)**: aeri, aero, aer
" **(pert. to)**: aural, ariel
" **hero**: ace
**aircraft**: aeri, aero, blimp
" **shelter**: hangar, nacelle
**airy**: ethereal, light, sprightly, aerial
**aisle**: passage
**akin**: related, alike, sib, similar, allied
**alackaday**: alas
**alarm**: alert, frighten, arouse, startle, scare
" **whistle**: siren
**alas**: ay
**Alaska auks**: arries
" **cape**: Nome
" **capital**: Juneau
" **city & town**: Nome
" **district**: Sitka
" **garment**: parkas
" **Mt.**: Ada,
" **native**: Aleut
" **river**: Yukon
**Albanian coin**: lek
**alcohol**: spirits
**alcoholic beverage**: gin, mead, posset, wine, rum
**alder tree (Scot.)**: arn
**alert**: ready, agile, vigilant, prepared, nimble, awake, aware
**alfalfa**: lucerne
**alga**: seaweed
**Algerian cavalryman**: spahs, spahee
" **city**: Oran
" **governor**: Dey
" **seaport**: Oran, Bone
**Algonquin Indian**: Cree, Sac, Lenape
**alienate**: separate, disaffect, estrange, wean
**alike**: equally, similar, akin, analogous, same
**aliment**: food
**alive**: rank, active, animate, swarming
**alkaline compound**: soda
" **solution**: lye
**alkaloid in bean**: eserin
" **in tea plant**: theine
**all**: entire, wholly, totally, total, every, individually, solely, quite
" **(comb. form)**: pan
**allay**: ease, relieve, mitigate, assuage, mollify, calm, quell, slake
**allege**: adduce, affirm, maintain, cite, assert, aver, quote [elod
**alleged electric force**: elod
**alleviate**: allay, ease, mitigate, relieve
**alliance**: treaty, union
**allied**: cognate, agnate, akin
**alligator pear**: avocado
**allot**: mete, destine, assign, ration
**allow**: let, permit, grant, admit
" **to remain**: leave
" **free use of**: lend
**allowance**: ration
" **for past services**: pension
" " **waste**: tret, stet, tare
" " **weight or wt. of container**: tare
**alloy of copper & zinc**: brass
" **for domestic utensils**: pewter
" **of gold & silver**: asem
" " **iron**: steel
" " **tin & zinc**: oroide [tion
**allude to**: refer, mention
**allure**: tempt, win, entice, lead, decoy
**ally**: helper, unite
**almanac**: yearbook, calendar
**almost**: nearly
" **(arch.)**: anear
**alms**: dole, doles, charity
" **box**: arca [ity
**almsgiving**: charity
**alone**: solo, singly, unique, solitary, only
**along**: ever, on, forward, onward
**aloud**: oral, audibly
**alphabetic character**: letter, rune
**alps**: alpine, mountains
**also**: and, too, withal
" **(arch.)**: eke
" **called**: alias
" **(poet.)**: eke
**altar screen**: reredos
" **slab**: mensa
**alter**: change, modify, amend, vary, mutate, emend
**alternate**: other, rotate
**alternative**: or
**always**: ever, evermore, aye
" **(contr. or poet.)**: eer
**amalgamate**: fuse, unite
**amaryllis plant**: agave
**amass**: heap, collect
**amateur**: dabbler, dilettante
**amaze**: surprise, astound, astonish
**Amazon estuary**: Para
**ambary**: da
**ambassador**: legate
**ambiguous**: delphic, indefinite, oracular
**ambition**: aim, goal, target, aspiration
**ambrosia**: nectar
**ambush**: trap
**amend**: alter, rectify, repeal, revise, improve, better
**amerces**: fines, mulcts, deprives [dian
**American aborigine**: Indian
" **actor**: Drew
" **admiral**: Evans, Sims, Dewey
" **artist**: Pyle, Peale
" **author**: Harte, Reo, Grey, Paine, Alden, Roe
" **canal**: Panama
" **capitalist**: Astor, Rascob
" **caricaturist**: Nast
" **cartoonist**: Arno, Dorgan
" **cataract**: Niagara
" **clergyman**: Olin
" **composer**: Paine, Nevin, Speaks
" **critic**: Ayres [Grew
" **diplomat**: Reid, Grew
" **divine**: Olin
" **editor**: Bok [Fisk
" **educator**: Hume, Fisk
" **engineer**: Eads
" **essayist**: Mabie
" **explorer**: Peary, Lewis, Byrd
" **feminist**: Catt
" **financier**: Biddle
" **general**: Otis, Lee, Ord
" **geologist**: Dana
" **herb**: sego, leafcup
" **humorist**: Ade, Nye, Twain, Lardner, Artemus, Cobb, Day
" **illustrator**: Newell
" **inventor**: Morse, Hoe, Howe
" **isthmus**: Panama
" **journalist**: Bigelow, Holt, Reid
" **jurist**: Moore, Paine
" **lawyer**: Paine, Ellery

" **machinist**: Howe
" **monetary unit**: dollar
" **novelist**: Steele, Roe, Harte
" **operatic singer**: Farrar
" **painter**: Peters
" **pathologist**: Ewing
" **patriot**: Paine, Otis, Ross
" **philanthropist**: Riis
" **pioneer**: Boone
" **pirate**: Kidd
" **poet**: Riley, Lanier, Tate, Poe
" **statesman**: Blaine, Logan, Dawes, Jay
" **writer**: Bok, Pyle
**amical**: friendly
**amid**: among, amist
**amiss**: awry, faultily, wrong, faulty, astray improper
**ammonia derivative**: amine, amide, amin, anilide [son
**ammunition wagon**: caisson
**among**: in, amid, mid, amidst
" **(poet.)**: mid, amid
**amorous look**: leer, ogle
**amort**: lifeless, spiritless
**amount**: sum, quantity
" **offered**: bid
**amphibia order**: anura
**amphibian**: toad, frog
**amphibole**: edenite
**ample**: plenty, abundant, full, plenteous
" **(poet.)**: enow
**amplify**: add, widen, enlarge
**amulet**: charm, talisman
**amuse**: entertain, divert [game
**amusement**: sport,
**anaconda**: boa
**analyze gram.**: parse
**anarchist**: red [ban
**anathematize**: curse,
**Anatolian goddess**: Ma
**ancestor**: sire, elder, forbear, forefather, forebear
**ancestral**: avital
**anchor**: moor, cat, kedge
" **bill**: pee
" **(small)**: grapnel
" **tackle**: cat
**ancient**: early, olden, old, aged, archean—*see also early, olden*
" **alloy**: asem
" **Arabian measure**: saa
" **ascetic people**: essene
" **Caucasian race**: Aryans
" **chariot**: essed
" **Chinese**: Seres
" **city**: Nineveh, Tyre
" **country**: Media,
" **court**: eyre [Aram
" **Danish legal code**: danelaw
" **drink**: morat
" **Egyptian City**: No, Thebes
" " **scroll**: papyri
" " **title**: Soter
" " **wt.**: kat
" **English court**: Leet
" " **king**: Canute
" **fine for homicide**: cro
" **firearm**: dag
" **form for shaping objects**: ame [Erin
" **Gaelic capital**: Tara,
" **galley**: trireme, bi-
" **game**: mora [reme
" **Genoa coin**: jane
" **tribesmen**: Teuton
" **gold coin**: rial
" **Greek**: Ionian
" " **city**: Argos, Corinth, Elis
" " **contest**: agon
" " **country**: Epirus, Elis, Aeolia
" " **invader**: Dorian
" " **judge**: dicast
" " **kingdom**: Attica
" " **marker**: stela
" " **milestone**: stele
" " **platform**: bema
" " **warship**: trireme
" **hammering form**: ame
" **headdress**: mite
" **Hebrew measure**: bath
" " **notes on old Test.**: masora [far
" " **ram's horn**: shofar
" **Hindu scripture**: veda
" **implement of war**: onager, celt
" **instrument of torture**: cross, rack
" **Irish chieftain**: Tanist
" " **clan**: Sept
" " **fort**: Lis, Liss
" " **party**: sept
" " **priest**: Druid
" **Jap race**: Ainu
" **Jewish cabalistic book**: Zohar
" " **measure**: homer
" " **sacred objects**: urim
" " **title**: abba
" **lang.**: pali, sanskrit, Latin
" **Latin grammar**: Donat
" **manuscript**: codex
" **Media people**: Medes
" **Mexican**: Aztec
" **military machine**: onager, catapult
" **money**: aes
" " **unit**: talent
" **musical character**: neume
" **Norse minstrel**: Scald
" **Norwegian king**: Olaf
" **Palestinian city**: Gilead
" " **cry**: jericho
" " **lang.**: aramaic
" " **town**: Bire
" " **village**: Endor
" **persecutor of Christians**: Nero
" **Persian coin**: daric
" " **priests**: magi
" **Peruvian title**: inca
" **Phoenicia capital**: Tyre
" **Pilgrim's protector**: Templar
" **pillarlike monument**: stela
" **playing card**: tarot
" **race**: Medes, Goth
" **Roman citadel**: Arx
" " **coin**: sesterce
" " **diety**: Ianus
" " **festivals**: cerealia
" " **measure**: wina
" " **port**: Ostia
" " **priestess**: vestal
" " **seats**: sellae
" " **shield**: clypeus
" " **wall**: spina
" **Sc. minstrel**: scald
" **Scottish fine**: cro
" " **name**: Alba
" " **tax**: cro
" **Semitic god**: Baal
" **sepulchral slab**: stela
" **spice**: stacte
" **story teller**: Aesop
" **stringed instrument**: lute, nebel, asor, rebec
" **Syrian country**: Aram
" **tax**: cro
" **temple**: naos
" **Toltec capital**: Tula
" **tracing vessel**: nef
" **Troy**: Iliac, Troas, Ilion
" **region**: Troad
" **Turkish title**: Dey
" **vehicle**: chariot
" **war machine**: onager
" **warship**: galleon
" **weapon**: dag, celt, lance, sling, spear, pike, mace
" **weight**: talent
" **wicked city**: Sodom
" **wine pitcher**: olpe
" " **receptacle**: ama
**and**: also
**andiron**: firedog
**anecdotes**: ana, tales
**anesthetic**: ether, gas
**anet**: dill, dillseed
**anew**: again, afresh
**angel**: seraph
" **of light**: cherub [ly
**angelic**: cherubic, saint-
**anger**: enrage, ire, wrath, rage, irritate, fury, choler, exasperate, animosity
" **(colloq.)**: rile
**angle**: corner, fish, nook
" **iron**: lath
" **of leaf & stem**: axil
**angler**: fisher
" **'s basket**: creel
" **'s hope**: bite
**Anglo-Indian monetary unit & coin**: anna
" " **number**: crore
" " **nurse**: amah
" " **title of address**: babu
" " **weight**: tola, ser
" **Saxon coin & money of account**: ora
" " **consonant**: eth
" " **free servant**: thane [tul, mad
**angry**: irate, sore, ire
**anguish**: pain, travail, remorse, dolor
**animal**: brute, beast, sloth, genet, creature, boar
" **'s backbone**: chine
" **body**: soma [lage
" **coat**: hair, fur, pe-
" **disease**: mange
" **fat**: adeps, suet, wax, ester, lard, tallow, grease
" **food**: flesh, meat
" **inclosure**: corral, cage, pen
" **neck hair**: mane
" **skin**: hide, fur
" **stomach**: maw, craw
" " **part**: tripe
" **thigh**: ham
" **track**: trail, spoor
" **trail**: run, track
**animate**: liven, alive, invigorate, enliven
**animation**: life, pep, vivacity, spirit
**animosity**: anger, spite,
**ankle**: talus [rancor
" **(of the)**: tarsal
**Annamese measure**: sao, quo, tao
**anneal**: temper, fuse
**annex**: add, attach, subjoin, extension, join
**announcement**: notice
**annoy**: pester, irk, nag, harass, bless, vex, disturb, harry, irritate, exasperate, tease, rile, molest, peeve, nettle
**annoyance**: bore, pest, peeve
**annul**: revoke, rescind, elide, repeal, abolish, nullify, cancel, undo, abrogate
**anoint**: oil, anele
**anon**: later, soon
**anonymous**: nameless
**another time**: again
**answer**: reply, retort, respond, response, solution [do
" **the purpose**: serve,
**antagonist**: enemy
**Antarctic bird**: penguin
" **sea**: Ross
**ante**: stake [prior
**antecedent**: precedent,
" **period**: past
**antelope (female)**: doe
" **(kind)**: screw, gnu, addax, eland, bongo
" **(male)**: buck
**antenna**: feeler, aerial
**anterior**: forward, previous, prior, before
**anthem**: motet
**anthropoid**: ape
" **ape**: orang
**antic**: caper, dido
**anticipate**: antedate, expect, hope, devance
**antipathy**: aversion, distaste, dislike [ish, old
**antiquated**: passe, old-
**antiquity (arch. & poet.)**: eld [sera (pl.)
**antitoxin**: serum (sg.),
**antlered animal**: stag, deer, moose
**antrum**: cavern
**anvil**: teest
**anxiety**: care, concern
**anxious**: eager, concerned
**apace**: swiftly, fast, rapidly, quick
**apart**: aside, separate, borders, asunder, separately
" **(prefix)**: dis
**apartment**: suite, flat
**ape**: lar, mimic, simian, simulate, copy, imitator, gorilla, monkey, imitate
**apelike**: simian
**aperture**: slot, gap, leak, mouth, hole, vent
**apex**: point, acme, summit, top, vertex
**aphorism**: adage, saw
**apogee**: climax
**Apollo's mother**: Leto
" **oracle**: delos [mis
" **sister**: Diana, Arte-
" **son**: Iamus
**apostate**: renegade
**apostle**: Paul, Peter, disciple, Mark
**apothecaries wt.**: dram, grain
**appal**: awe, astonish, horrify, shock, dismay, overcome
**appall**: dismay
**apparatus for heating liquids**: etna
**apparel**: raiment, gear, attire, garb
**apparent**: evident, patent, plain
**apparition**: shape, specter, ghost, idolon

**appeal**: plead, request, entreaty, refer
**appear**: seem, arise, look
" **again**: recur
**appearance**: aspect, mien, guise, phase, look
**appearing gnawed**: erose
**appease**: placate, atone, propitiate, conciliate, pacify
**appellation**: title, name, epithet
**Appellation of Athena**: Alea, Palea
**append**: add, attach, affix
**appendages**: tails, addenda, tabs, arista, tags
**appertain**: relate, belong
**appetite**: stomach, longing, craving
**appetizer**: canape, aperitif
**applaud**: clap, cheer
**apple**: pome, pippin, crab, winesap, russet,
" **acid**: malic [esopus
" **juice**: cider
" **seed**: pit, pip
**application**: use, term
**apply**: devote, address, treat
**appoint**: ordain, detail, commission, nominate, assign,
" **as agent**: depute
**appointment**: tryst date,
**apportion**: mete, dele, ration, deal, allot, dole, lot, allocate
**apposite**: relative, relevant
**appraise**: rate, evaluate, price, estimate, value, gauge
**appreciate**: value
**apprehend**: nab, arrest, grasp, perceive
" **clearly**: realize
" **thru the senses**: sensate
**apprehension**: fear
**apprise**: inform
**approach**: verge, come, near, adit
**appropriate**: fit, proper, suit, apt, suitable, becoming
**approval**: endorsement, consent, sanction
**approve**: admire, pass, O. K. [aptly
**approximate**: approach,
**apron**: pinafore
" **(dial.)**: brat
" **top**: bib
**apt**: fit, pat, liable talented, clever, fitting, timely, skilled, dextrous
**aptitude**: art, talent, bent
**aquatic animal**: otter, fish, polyp, newt
" **bird**: dabchick, flamingo, goose, gull, coot, swan, duck, smew
" **mammal**: sirenian, whale, otter, seal
" **worm**: cadew
**Arab**: Saracen, tad, gamin, bedouin, semite, urchin
**Arabia (poet.)**: Araby
**Arabian capital**: Sana
" **chieftain**: Emir,
" **city**: Aden [emeer
" **cloth**: aba
" **commander**: Emir, Emeer, ameer, amir
" **country**: Yemen
" **garment**: aba
" **gazelle**: ariel
" **gulf**: Aden
" **jasmine**: bela
" **judge**: cadi
" **kingdom**: Irak, Iraq
" **language**: arabic
" **Moslem**: Wahabi
" **Night bird**: roc
" **peninsula**: Aden, Sinai
" **prince**: sherif
" **river bed**: wadi
" **seaport**: Aden
" **shrub**: kat
" **state**: Oman
" **sultanate**: Oman
" **tambourine**: taar,
" **title**: emir [daira
" **wind**: simoon
**arachnid**: spider, mite, acarus, tick
**arbiter**: judge, umpire, referee [cide
**arbitrate**: mediate, de-
**arbor**: bower, pergola
**arboreal mammal**: lemur, opossum, rac-
**arc**: bow, arch [coon
**arch**: curve, chief, arc, bend, sly, bow, span, waggish, roguish
" **over**: cove, span
**archaic pronoun**: ye, thy, thine
**archer**: bowman
**archetype**: ideal
**architectural column**: pilaster
" **design**: spandrel
" **ornament**: dentil,
" **pier**: anta [corbeil
" **screen**: spier
**Arctic**: Polar, frigid
" **exploration base**: Etah
" **explorer**: Kane
" **lawyer**: Hyde
" **native**: Eskimo
**ardent**: intense, zealous, fervid, eager, flery, fiery
" **partison**: devotee
**ardor**: elan, fervor, affection, zeal
**area**: space, extent, site, tract, section, range, scope, region
" **(small)**: areola, plot
**arena**: oval, stadium, field, ring
**arenaceous**: sandy
**Ares's sister**: Eris
**argent**: silvery, silver
**Argonaut's leader**: Jason [jargon, cant
**argot**: slang, dialect,
**argue**: debate, reason, dispute, discuss
**argument**: debate, spat, row, add
" **against**: con
" **in favor of**: pro
**aria**: tune, song, solo
**arid**: barren, waterless, dry, parched
" **region**: Sahara
**Aries**: ram
**arise**: emanate, ascend originate, mount, issue, spring
**arista**: beard, awn
**Arius's follower**: Arian
**ark's builder (var.)**: Noe
" **landing place**: Ararat
**arm**: fortify, might, branch
" **covering**: sleeve
" **of sea**: inlet, bay, firth, gulf
**armadillo**: apara, apar, peba, tatou
**armed band**: posse
" **conflict**: war, battle
" **fleet**: navy [ment
" **force**: army, regi-
" **galley of Northmen**: Aesc [nel
" **guard**: sentry, senti-
" **merchantman**: raider
" **power**: armament
**armistice**: truce
**armor**: mail [quire
" **bearer**: squire, es-
" **splint**: tace
" **for the thigh**: taslet,
**armpit**: ala tace
**army**: host, horde
" **follower**: sutler
" **section**: corps
" **unit**: brigade
**aroma**: fragrance, odor, scent, flavor [rant,
**aromatic**: spicy, frag-
" **condiment**: spice
" **gum resin**: myrrh
" **herb**: anise, mint, thyme, spearmint, caraway
" **plant**: mint, nard, basil, herb, tansy, angelica
" **principal of violet root**: irone
" **seasoning**: spice
" **seed**: anise
" **smoke**: fume
" **spice**: mace
" **tree gum**: balsam
" **wood**: cedar
**arouse**: actuate, excite, stir, alarm
" **to action**: rally
**arraign**: indict, denounce
**arrange**: prepare, adjust, plan, fettle, dispose, place
" **for exhibition**: stage
" **in folds**: drape
" **in layers**: tier, laminate
" **side by side**: appose
" **in succession**: seriate
" " **thin layers**: laminal
**arrangement**: plan, system, setup, order, disposal
" **of interwoven parts**: web
" " **sails**: rig
**array**: dress, garb, clothe, deck, robe, attire, restrain, capture, stop, apprehend
**arrest**: halt, stem, check, rein, hinder, seizure, detain
**arrive**: come, reach
**arrogant**: haughty, proud
**arrow**: dart, barb
" **body**: stele
" **case**: quiver [rare
" **poisoning**: inee, cu-
**art**: knack, aptitude, science, wile, facility
**Artemis's mother**: Leto
**Artemus's twin**: Apollo
**artery (large)**: aorta
**artful**: sly, wily [a, the
**article**: thing, item, an,
" **of apparel**: gaiter
" **(arch.)**: ye [creed
" **of belief**: tenet,
" " **commerce**. staple
" **in a document**: clause
**artifice**: guile, trickery, ruse, finesse, wile, dodge, stratagem, art
**artificial**: unreal, paste,
" **butter**: oleo [sham
" **as jewels**: paste
" **lang.**: ide, ido, ro, esperanto
" **light**: lamp
" **manners**: airs
" **teeth**: denture
**artificial waterway**: canal, sluice
**artists medium**: oil
" **mixing board**: palette
**artless**: naive, naif
" **woman**: ingenue
**artlessness**: naivete
**arum plant**: arad, aroid, lily
**Aryan**: Slav, Mede
**as before**: ditto
" **compared with**: than
" **far as**: unto, to
" **it stands (mus.)**: sta
" **long as**: while
" **well**: also, and
**ascend**: arise, mount up, climb, scale
**ascertain**: learn, see
" **the bearings of**: orient [sene
**ascetic**: stoic, yogi, es-
**ascribable**: due
**ascribe**: refer, impute, attribute
**ashes (Scot.)**: ase
**ashy**: pale, wan, white, ashen, livid, grey
**Asia Minor Island**: Samos
" " **Mt.**: Ida
" " **republic**: Syria
**Asiatic**: Asian, Tatar, Hun, Korean, Turk
" **animal**: rasse, tiger.
" **bean**: soy [serow
serow
" **bird**: minivet, myna
" **coast wind**: monsoon
" **country**: Siam, India, Tibet, Korea, Nepal, Irak, Arabia, Russia, Anam, Syria, Burma, China
" " **(ancient)**: Medea, Elam, Eolis
" **domestic cattle**: zobo
" **gazelle**: Cora, ahu
" **isthmus**: kra
" **kingdom**: Nepal, Irak, Annam, Iraq, Anam, Siam
" **lemur**: loris
" **mountains**: Altai
" **native**: arab
" **nomad**: arab
" **palm**: areca, nipa, betel [Arabia
" **peninsula**: Korea,
" **perennial**: ramie
" **plant**: odal
" **river**: Amur, Indus, Ob, Tigris, Lena
" **ruminant**: camel,
" **sea**: Aral [yak
" **tea**: cha
" **tree**: siris, dita
" **tribeman**: tatar
" **vine**: betel
" **weight**: catty, tael
" **wild ass**: onager
" " **sheep**: rasse, argali [arate
**aside**: apart, away, sep-
**ask**: inquire, invite, bid, solicit, request, beg
" **payment**: dun
" **(Scot.)**: spere
**askew**: wry, atilt, awry, crooked
**asleep**: abed, dormant
**asp**: viper, reptile, snake
**aspect**: phase, guise, appearance, side, mien
**aspen**: poplar, shaking
**asperation**: slur
**asperse**: slander, vilify,

villify, traduce, calumniate
**aspiration:** aim, desire, ambition
**aspire:** pretend, desire, seek, reach
**assail:** beset, attack, scathe, assault, ac- [cost
**Assam silk:** eri
**Assamese tribe:** Ao
**assault:** assail, onset, attack, raid, on- [slaught
**assay:** test
**assaying vessel:** cupel
**assemblage:** meeting, host
**assemble:** meet, convene, mass, convoke, congregate, muster
**assembly:** diet, agora
**assent:** agree, agreement, consent, concur, sanction
**assert:** state, aver, allege, attest, avow, predicate, affirm, maintain, avouch, declare, contend, pronounce
" **as fact:** posit [mate
**assess:** tax, levy, esti-
**asset:** estate [aver
**asseverate:** affirm, vow,
**assign:** relegate, award, designate, label, appoint, allot
" **parts:** cast
" **to:** refer, class
**assignment:** task
**assimilate:** digest
**assist:** befriend, aid, help, abet
**assistance:** help, succor
**associate:** partner, fellow, ally, mix, herd,
**assort:** classify [consort
**assuage:** relieve, slake, mitigate, allay
**assume:** don, wear, suppose, adopt, pretend
" **an attitude:** pose
" **as fact:** posit
**assumed character:** role
**assurance:** aplomb
**assure:** convince, confirm, vouch
**Assyrian deity:** Ashur, Ira
**asterisk:** stars, star
**astern:** aft, abaft, backward, behind
**astir:** agog, active
**astonish:** awe, appal, amaze, surprise
**astound:** amaze, awe, stun
**astraddle:** astride
**astral:** starry, stellar
**astray:** amiss
**astride:** astraddle [nin
**astringent:** alum, tan-
**astronomical:** uranian
**astute:** shrewd, crafty, sly, cunning
**asunder:** apart
**at:** near, by, about, during, in [studio
**atelier:** workshop,
**Athama's wife:** Ino
**Athena lawgiver:** solon
" **statesman:** Pericles
" **title:** alea
**atilt:** askew, aslant, slanting
**atmosphere:** aura, air, ether [airy
**atmospheric:** aerial,
" **conditions:** climate
" **disturbance:** storm, fog
**atom:** particle, iota, ion, jot, proton
**atomic:** tiny
**atone:** expiate, appease, reparation, redeem, reconcile
**atop:** above, upon
**attach:** annex, append, add, fasten, link
**attachment:** adherence, devotion, adhesion
**attack:** assail, assault, onset, onslaught, raid
**attain:** gain, achieve, reach, earn, compass, acquire
" **success:** arrive, win
**attempt:** trial, effort, essay, strive, try, endeavor, stab
" **(colloq.):** go, stab
" **(Scot.):** ettle
**attend:** await, escort, wait, minister
" **to:** heed, listen, nurse
**attendant:** aide, helper, ministering, clerk, server
**attention:** ear, diligence, observance, heed
**attenuated:** rarefied, thin, diluted, weakened
**attest:** assert, witness, confirm, testify, cer- [tify
**attic:** garret, loft
**attire:** garb, dress, raiment, equip, rig, robe, habit, array
**attitude:** pose, mien, posture [charm, lure
**attract:** draw, allure,
**attractive:** taking, engaging
" **(colloq.):** cute
**attribute:** refer, ascribe
**auction:** sale
**audacious:** bold
**audacity:** nerve, cheek
**audibly:** aloud
**audience:** ear
**audition:** hearing
**auditor:** listener, hearer
**auditory:** otic
**augment:** eke, add
**augur:** bode, portend, forebode
**augury:** omen
**auk:** murre
**aural:** aricular, otic
**aureola:** halo
**aureole:** halo
**auricle:** ear, pinna
**auricular:** otic, aural
**auriferous:** golden
**aurora:** dawn, eos
**auroral:** eoan
**austere:** severe, granitic, stern, hard, frosty
**Australian aborigine:** mara
" **badger:** wombat
" **bear:** koala
" **bird:** emu
" **boomerang:** kylie
" **brushwood:** mallee
" **cape:** Howe
" **city:** Perth, Sydney
" **clover fern:** nardoo
" **insect:** lerp
" **lake:** Eyre [tait
" **marsupial:** koala,
" **ostrich:** emu
" **resin:** damar
" **soldier:** anzac
" **tree:** billa
" **tribe:** Mara
" **wild dog:** dingo
**Austrian botanist:** Mendel
" **capital:** Vienna
" **coin:** florin
" **composer:** Mozart
" **province:** Tyrol,
" **wt.:** saum [Tirol
**authentic:** real, true
**author:** writer, creator
**authoritative:** assertive, official
" **answer:** oracle
" **requirement:** mandate
**authority:** expert, dominance, dominion
**authorize:** accredit, delegate, license
**autocrat:** despot, mogul
**automaton:** robot, golem
**auxiliary:** ancillary, ally, alar, helping, assistant
**avail:** stead, benefit, profit, use, boot
**avalanche:** slide
**avarice:** greed, cupidity, grasping [etous
**avaricious:** greedy, cov-
**avenaceous:** oaten
**avenge:** revenge, retaliate, requite
**aver:** state, varify, assert, allege, affirm, avouch, say, declare, vouch
**average:** mean, ordinary, usual, medium, medial
**averse:** reluctant, loath, opposed, inimical, unwilling
**aversion:** dislike, distaste, hate, hatred
**avert:** prevent, avoid
**aviator:** ace, pilot, flier, flyer, aeronaut
**avid:** eager, greedy
**avoid:** shun shirk, evade, avert, elude, sidestep, escape, eschew, beware
**avouch:** aver, assert
**avow:** aver, acknowledge, a sert, testify, own, confess, profess
**await:** expect, attend, bide
" **settlement:** pend
**awake:** vigilant, alert
**awaken:** rouse, arouse
**award:** mete, assign bestow, prize
" **of valor:** medal
**aware** cognizant, informed, alert, know, knowing, vigilant
**away:** off, fro, begone, out, removed, far, aside, absent
" **from:** off, fro
" **(prefix):** apo
" **(Scot.):** awa
**awe:** appal, dread, fear
**awful:** dire terrible
**awkward:** clumsy, ungainly [arista
**awn:** beard, bristle,
**awry:** amiss, askew, crooded, askance oi- [lique
**ax handle:** helve
**axillary:** alar
**axiom:** maxim
**aye:** yes, ever, always
**Azores town:** Horta

**B**

**Babylonian abode of the dead:** aralu
" **chief priest:** En
" **god:** el, ea, bel, anu, adad, hea, baal
" **hero:** Etana
" **numeral:** sar
" **storm god:** Adad
**babble:** prattle, prate, jabber, blather
**baby:** infant, humor
" **carriage:** stroller, pram, gocart [A.B.
**Baccal. degree:** B.A.,
**Bacchan cry:** evoe
**back:** rear, fro, support, uphold
" **of animal:** dorsum
" **gate:** postern
" **of neck:** nape
" **payment:** arrear
" **(prefix):** un, ana
**backbone:** spine
" **of animal:** chine
**backer:** sponsor
**backward:** astern, arear
**bacon cut:** rasher
**bacteriol. culture:** agar
" **wire:** oese
**bad:** spoiled, harmful, baleful, inferior, ill, poor, faulty
" **habits:** vice
**badge:** pin, token
" **of honor:** medal
**badgerlike mammal:** ratel
**badinage:** banter
**badly:** illy
" **(prefix):** mal
**baffle:** pose, elude, poise, evade
**baffling question:** poser
**bag:** sack, pouch, satchel, valise, entrap, cap- [ture
**bagpipe:** drone
**Bahama Isl. Capital:** Nassau
**bail:** lade, security, replevin, hoop
**bait:** lure, harass, torment, worry
**baked clay:** tile
**baker's implement:** peel
**baking dish:** ramekin
" **soda:** saleratus
**balance:** scales, poise, remainder, par, even
**baleful:** bad [let
**ball:** dance, globe, pel-
" **of thread or yarn:** clew
**ballad:** song, lay, derry
**balloon basket:** car
**ballot:** vote [balm
**balsam (kind of):** tolu,
**balustrade:** railing
**bamboo shoot:** achar
**ban:** forbid, curse, exclude
**banal:** trite, trivial
**band:** belt, company, group, strip, troop, strap, girdle, crew, fetter, unite, stripe
" **across an escutcheon:** fess
" **for hair:** fillet
**bandage:** ligate
**bandit:** brigand
**bandy:** exchange, cart
**bane:** harm, poison, ruin, mischief, woe
**baneful:** ill, bad
**bang:** slam, thump
**banish:** exile, deport, oust, evict, expel, expatriate
**banister:** baluster
**bank:** tier, brink
**bankrupt:** ruin [pennon
**banner:** flag, ensign,
**banquet:** feast
**banteng:** tsine
**banter:** badinage, raillery, chaff, wit, pleasantry
**Bantu lang.:** ila, ronga
" **tribesman:** zulu
**baptismal vessel:** font
" **water:** laver
**bar:** exclude, cake, except, rail, stripe, estop
" **of balance:** beam
" **" cast metal:** ingot
" **legally:** estop
" **in a loom:** easer
" **of a soap frame:** sess

" **to transmit force**: lever
**barb**: dart, arrow
**barbarian**: Hun, Goth
**barbarity**: savagery, ferity
**bard**: poet, minstrel
**bare**: open, plain, exposed, expose, mere, meager, stark, denude, nude, strip, bald, blank, naked
**bargain**: deal, sale
**barge**: tow, scow
**bark**: yap, yelp, bay, clamor, rind
" **cloth**: tapa
" **exterior**: ross
" **of paper mulberry**: tapa
**baronet's title**: sir
**barracks**: etape, casern
**barracuda**: spet
**barrel**: cask, keg, tun
" **hook side piece & slat**: stave
" **maker**: cooper
**barren**: sterile, fallow, arid, effete
**barrier**: dam, hedge, barricade, hurdle
**barrister**: lawyer
**barter**: sell, trade, exchange, truck
**base**: low, mean, sordid, station, bed, pedestal, ignoble, abject, vile, establish, snide
" **forming element**: metal
" **for a statue**: plinth
**bashful**: shy, coy
**basin**: vessel, laver
**basis**: root
" **of assessment**: ratal
" " **a conclusion**: premise
" " **fruit jellies**: pectin
" " **quartz**: silica
**basket**: hamper
**basque cap**: beret
**bass horn**: tuba
**basswood**: linden
**bast**: fiber
**bat**: cudgel, club
**bate**: restrain, reduce, lower, lessen
**bathe**: lave
**batter**: hitter, bombard, ram, bruise
**battle**: fight, conflict, war [gaw
**bauble**: trinket, gew-
**bawl out**: berate, scold
**bay**: cove, sinus, inlet,
" **(scot.)**: loch [bark
" **tree**: laurel [ador
" **window**: oriel, mir-
**bazaar**: fair
**be enough**: do
" **expected**: natural
" **in harmony**: agree, chord
" **of the opinion**: feel
" **situated**: lie [rue
" **sorry for**: repent,
" **in store for**: await
" **undecided**: doubt,
" **of use**: avail [pend
**beach**: strand, sand, shore
**bead**: globule, drop
**beak**: neb, nib, bill
**beam**: ray, shine, rafter, radiate [goa, legume
**bean**: soya, lima, soy,
**bear**: endure, stand, carry, bruin
" **(the)**: Ursa
" " **(female)**: ursa
" **weapons**: arm
" **witness to**: attest, depone [awn
**beard**: arista, goatee,
" **of grains & grasses**: awns, avels, aristae
**bearded**: aristate
**bearer**: carrier
**bearing**: air, mien, orle, carriage
" **(her.)**: ente
" **spines**: spinate
**bearlike**: ursine
**beast**: animal
" **of burden**: onager, ass, camel, yak, donkey, mule, llama
**beat**: thrash, hammer, defeat, lash, drub, flay, lam, best, flog, pulsate, swinge, pulsation, pummel, conquer, flail, drum, surpass
" **back**: repel, repulse
" **hard**: hammer
**beater**: dasher, rab
**beatify** bless
**beau**: dandy, suitor
**because**: since, for, as, that
**beck**: nod, command
**becloud**: bedim, darken
**become**: grow, wax, get, suit, befit
" **buoyant**: levitate
" **exhausted**: peter
" **less severe**: relent
" **operative**: inure, enure
" **visible**: appear
" **void**: lapse
**bed**: stratum, matrix, couch, base
" **canopy & drapery**: tester [spread
" **coverlet**: quilt,
" **of straw**: pallet
**bedaub**: smear
**bedeck**: adorn
**bedim**: becloud, mist
**bee (male)**: drone
**beef on hoof**: steer,
**beer**: lager, ale [cattle
" **ingredient**: malt
" **mug**: stein, seidel
**bees**: apian, drones
**Beethoven's birthplace**: Bonn
**beetle**: dor, overhang, elater, scarab [tide
**befall**: happen, hap,
**befit**: become, suit
**befitting**: proper, suit-
**befog**: confuse [able
**befool**: delude, deceive
**before**: pre, ere, ante, di, anterior, prior, previously
" **all others**: first
" **long**: presently, soon, anon
" **(naut.)**: afore
" **(prefix)**: pro, pre, ante
" **this**: erenow
**befriend**: aid, help
**befuddle**: addle
**beg**: plead, implore, beseech, entreat, petition
**beget**: sire, father, engender [cant
**beggar**: rogue, mendi-
**begin**: open, start, commence, initiate, lead
**beginner**: novice, entrant, neophyte, tyro
**beginning**: onset, opening, first, origin, inceptive, genesis, start, outset, dawn
**begone**: avaunt, out, off, scat
**begrudge**: envy [tain
**beguile**: delude, enter-
**behalf**: sake [react
**behave**: act, demean,
**behavior**: manners, treatment, demeanor
**behead**: decapitate
**behind**: rear, after, abaft, astern
" **(naut.)**: abaft, aft
" **a vessel**: astern, aft
**behold**: lo, see [ence
**being**: esse, ens, exist-
**belabor**: drub, flog,
**belate**: delay [thrash
**beldam**: hag [seige
**beleaguerment**: siege,
**Belgian canal**: Yser
" **city**: Ans, Schent, Ghent, Arlon, Ypres,
" **coin**: belga [Spa
" **commune**: Ans
" **Congo river**: Uele
" **marble**: rance
" **province**: Namur
" **resort**: spa
" **river**: Yser, Lys
" **seaport**: Ostend
" **town**: Spa, Ypres
" **violinist**: Ysaye
**belie**: slander, calumniate
**belief**: ism, faith, creed, tenet, creedence, credence, credo, idea, trust, doctrine
**believe**: credit, opine, think suppose
**believer in God**: Deist
**belittled**: derided, decried, disparaged
**bell**: gong
" **clapper**: tongue
" **tower**: belfry [tain
**belong**: appertain, per-
**belonging to**: of
" " **neither** neuter
" " **spring**: vernal
**belongings**: traps, gear
**below**: infra, under, beneath
" **(poet.)**: neath
**belt**: girdle, sash, band, encircle, zonic, strap, zone, surround
**bemoan**: lament, bewail, wail
**bend**: stoop, trend, lean, crook, curve, flex, nod, bow arch, sag
" **in timber**: sny
**benediction**: blessing
**beneath**: below, under
**benefactor**: patron, donor, giver
**beneficent gift**: blessing, boon [good
**beneficial**: salutary,
**benefit**: avail, profit, interest [charity
**benevolence**: mercy,
**benevolent**: kind
**bent**: trend, proneness, inclination, aptitude, tendency
**bequeathed**: demised, left, willed
**berate**: scold, rail, lash
**bereave**: deprive
**bereft**: lorn, forlorn
**beseech**: pray, plead, entreat, beg [siege
**beset**: harass, assail,
**beside (prefix)**: par, para [moreover, and
**besides**: also, yet, else,
**besiege**: beleaguer, storm [mar
**besmirch**: soil, smear,
**besom**: broom
**bespangle**: star [dy
**bespatter**: splash, mud-
**best**: finest, overcome, defeat, cream
" **of its kind**: ace
**bestial**: brutish, depraved
**bestow**: grant, give, confer, render, award, impart
" **approval**: smile
" **as due**: award
" **income upon**: endow
**bet**: wager, stake, gamble
" **in roulette**: bas
**betel**: siri
" **palm**: areca
**betide**: happen, befall
**betimes**: early
**betoken**: foreshow, indicate, bode, augur
**betrayer**: traitor
**between**: amid, betwixt [meta
" **(prefix)**: dia, inter,
" **two extremes**: mesne
**bevel**: slope, slant
**beverage**: lager, porter, drink, cocoa, lemonade, tea, ale
**bevy**: group, flock, galaxy [bemoan
**bewail**: lament, weep,
**bewilder**: daze, stun, fog, dazzle
**bewitch**: enchant, hex
**beyond**: over, across, farther, past [sur
" **(prefix)**: eg, para,
**bias**: influence, slant, diagonal, ply [sided
**biased**: partial, one-
**Biblical city**: Aven, Tyre, Nain, Ivah, Sidon, Nob, Sodon, Sodom, Ono
" **country**: Edam, Edom, Elam, Ophir, Sodom, Seba, Moab
" " **native**: Elamite, Edomite
" **expression**: selah
" **food**: manna
" **giant**: Goliath
" **hunter**: Nimrod
" **judge**: elon
" **king**: Asa, Evi, Amon, Agag, Reba, Herod
" **kingdom**: Sheba
" **land**: Tob, Nod
" **Mt.**: Horeb, Ararat, Olivet, Peor
" **name**: Caleb, Eri, Ater, Adah, Leah, Pelleg, Ari, Iri
" **passage**: text
" **patriarch**: Abraham, Israel, Noah
" **people**: Moabite
" **plain**: Sharon
" **pool**: Siloam
" **priest**: Eli, Aaron
" **prophet**: Elisha, Elias [enon
" **region**: Enom,
" " **of darkness**: Rahab
" **sign**: selah
" **site**: Ophir
" **spice**: stacte
" **tower**: Edar, Babel
" **town**: Cana, Nain, Bethel, Endor
" **tribe**: Amon
" **vessel**: ark
" **weed**: tare
" **wise men**: magi
" **word**: selah, mene
**bid**: offer, summon, order, invite, obey, enjoin, command
**bide**: tarry, tolerate, await [narrow

**bigoted:** intolerant,
**bilk:** cheat
**bill:** beak, poster
" **of fare:** carte, menu
**billiard cue:** mace
" **player & writer:** Hoppe
" **shot:** carom, masse
" **stick:** cue
**billow:** wave, surge, sea
**bin:** crib
**binary:** double
**bind:** tape, truss, tie, restrain, fasten, obligate
**biographical fragment:** anecdote
**biography:** memoir, life
**biological factor:** id, genes (pl.)
" **group:** species
**bird dog:** setter
" **food:** seed
" **of gull family:** tern
" **house:** aviary, nest, sea [can
" **(large):** emu, peli-
" **of peace:** dove
" **(pert. to):** avine, avian
" **plumage:** heron
" **of prey:** eagl , kite, vulture, erne, owl, elanet, hawk, ern
" " **a region:** ornis
" **(small):** tody, serin, tit, wren, pewee, finch, tontit, virec
" **wing part:** alula
**birdling:** nestling
**birth (pert. to):** natal
**birthright:** heritage
**biscuit:** roll, bun, rusk, cracker [tei, mitre
**Bishop's headress:** mi-
" **jurisdiction:** dio-
" **office:** see [cese
**bit:** scrap, morsel, piece
**bite:** sting, chop, morsel, corrode, snap, nip [champ
" **noisily:** gnaw,
**biting:** sharp, acid, sarcastic
**bitter:** virulent, poignant, gall, acerb, acrid, painful
" **cynic:** timon
" **flavoring agent:** asarum
" **herb:** rue, aloe
" **nut:** cola
" **vetch:** ers
**bivalve:** oyster, clam
**bivouac:** camp, encamp
**bizarre:** odd, outre
**Bizet's opera:** Carmen
**black:** ebon, melanic, inky, sooty, sable, jet
" **& blue:** livid
" **covering:** pall
" **gum:** tupelo
" **magic:** witchcraft
" **mineral:** jet
" **nightshade:** morel
" **pipe of Otago:** Miro
" **powdery substance:** soot
" **rock:** basalt
" **Sea peninsula:** Crimea
" **Seaport:** Odessa
" **substance:** tar, soot
" **swan:** trumpeter
" **& white mixture:** gray, grey
" **wood:** ebony, jackdaw
**blackbird:** 'law, crow, ani, raven, merl, starling, jackdaw
**blacken:** sooty, ink, denigrate
**blackfish:** tautog [work
**blacksmith's art:** smith-
" **tool:** anvil [er
**blacksnake (kind):** rac-
**blackthorn fruit:** sloe
**blade of grass:** spear
**blame:** censure, accuse, reproach
**blameless:** innocent
**blanch:** pale, whiten
**bland:** mild, balmy, open, gentle
**blandish:** flatter [tara
**blare of trumpet:** tan-
**blarney:** flattery
**blase:** bored, sated
**blaspheme:** swear
**blast:** sere, sear, blight, shrivel
" **furnace:** smelter
**blatant:** noisy
**blaze:** flame, flare
**bleach:** whiten, etiolate
**bleak:** drear, raw, dismal
**bleat:** baa
**blemish:** stain, mar, spot, speck, fault, scar, taint, blot
**blend:** mix, mingle, merge
**bless:** anele, glorify, hallow, protect, beatify, concentrate
**blessing:** benison, boon
**blight:** nip, blast
**blind:** seel, sightless, shutter
" **fear:** panic
**blissful:** edenic, paradisiac
**blister:** scorch
**blithe:** gay, riant, cheerful, joyful
**block:** dam, bar, prevent, chump, stoppage
**blockade:** siege [lout
**blockhead:** dolt, oaf,
" **(arch.):** mome
**blood:** gore
" **(comb. form):** hem
" **of the gods:** ichor
" **kindred:** gens
" **sucking animal:** leech
" **vessel:** artery, vein
**bloody:** gory [glow
**bloom:** flower, blossom,
**blossom:** bud, flower, bloom, flourish
**blot:** spot, sully blemish, stain [cancel
" **out:** erase, delete,
**blotch:** mess, stain, mottle, blob
**blow:** rap, stroke, slap, thump, inflate
" **air forcibly thru nose:** snort
" **on head:** nob
" **up:** inflate
**blowgun missile:** dart
**blue:** azure, perse, depressed
" **bird:** jay
" **grass:** poa
**bluish gray:** merle, pearl, slate [take
**blunder:** err, error, mis-
**blunt:** dull, outspoken, obtuse, deaden, heb-
" **end:** stub [etate
**blur:** blear, dull
**blushing:** rosy, red
**bluster:** roister
**board:** plank
" **a ship:** embark
**boast:** vaunt, brag, praise, extol
**boat:** barge, scow, tug, punt, vessel, dory freighter, canoe, coracle, skiff
" **marker:** buoy
" **part:** prow, aft
**bobbin:** reel, spool
**bode:** indicat , portend, augur, presage
**bodice:** waist
" **posy:** corsage
**bodily appetite:** lust
**body of advisers:** cabinet
" " **armed men:** posse
" **bones:** ribs
" **of church:** nave
" **(comb. form):** soma
" " **Jewish law** Talmud, Tora, Torah
" " **laws:** code
" " **learning:** lore
" **organ:** lung, liver, gland
" **(pert. to):** somal
" **of printed matter:** text [maid
" **servant:** valet,
" **of solar system:** planet
" " **soldiers:** platoon, corps, militia, troop, regiment
" " **tree:** bole
**bog:** fen, moor, mire, morass, syrt, muskeg, marsh, swamp
" **substance:** peat
**bogus:** spurious
**Bohemia city:** Pilsen
" **dance:** redowa
" **religious reformer:** Huss
" **river:** Iser [mer
**boil:** stew, seethe, sim-
" **on eyelid:** stye
**boisterous play:** romp
**bolar:** clayey
**bold:** pert, daring, keep
**Bolivian Indian:** Uro, Uru, Iten
" **product:** tin
**bolster:** support, crop
**bolt:** rivet, lock, dart, pin, fasten, fastener, sift
**bomb (kind):** petard, grenade, atom, shell
**bombard:** batter, shell
" **fiercely:** strafe
**bombast:** rant, rave
**bombastic:** stilted
" **talk:** rant
**bombproof chamber:** casemate [eggers
**bombycid moths:** ios,
**bond:** tie, security, covenant, ligament [ery
**bondage:** serfage, slav-
**bondman:** slave, thrall, vassal, serf
**bone:** os, rib, ilia, talus
" **of arm:** ulna
" **cavity:** antrum
" **(comb. form):** osteo [ulnar
" **of forearm:** ulna,
" " **hard palate:** palatine [one, fibula
" " **leg:** tibia, per-
" **(prefix):** oste [mur
" **of thigh:** tibia, fe-
**bones:** ossa
**bony:** osteal, thin
**book:** mo
" **of accounts:** ledger
" " **Bible:** Jonah, Kings, Amos, Genesis, Lev, Titus, Romans, Micah, Luke, Psalms, Hosea, Ezra, Exodus, Acts, Mark
" " **devotions:** missal
" " **gospel:** Mark
" **(large):** tome
" **of Jewish law:** Talmud
" " **Old Testament:** Hosea, Isaiah, Daniel, Amos, Ezra
" **palm:** tara
" **of psalms:** psalter
" " **runrics:** ordo
**boon:** blessing
**boor:** churl, kern, rustic
**boost:** hoist, raise
**booth:** stall, loge, stand
**booty:** prey, swag, spoils, spoil, loot
**border:** abut, skirt, fringe, hem, margin, side, edge, brink, verge
" **for a picture:** mat
**bore:** pall, drill, weary
" **into:** eat
**boredom:** ennui
**boring:** dull, tiresome
" **tool:** awl, drill, bit, auger, wimble, gimlet
**born:** natural, nee
**boron with another element:** bo ide
**bother:** molest, pester, harass, trouble, ado, bore, fuss, a l, perplex
**bottle for liquids:** car-
" **(small):** vial [boy
" **stopper:** cork
**bottom:** root
" **of ship** :keel
**bottomless:** abysmal
**bough:** limb, branch
" **of tree:** ramage
**bound:** dart, obligated, tied, base, leap, limit, ambit
**boundary:** terminus, limit, mete, line, side,
" **line:** mete [margin
" **(outer):** perimeter
**bounder:** cad [profuse
**bountiful:** generous,
**bouquet:** corsage, aroma bunch, spray, posy
**bout:** setto, contest
**bovine animal:** cow, ox, cattle (pl.)
" **(male):** steer, bull
**bow:** nod, arc, bend, prow, submit, stoop, yield, curve, arch
" **of vessel:** prow
**bower:** arbor
**bowfin:** amia
**bowman:** archer
**box:** crate, spar, case, chest, stow, loge
" **for live fish:** car
" " **packing:** kit
**boy atendant:** page
" **(small):** tad
**brace:** pair, prop, support, strut
**braced framework:** trestle
**bracing:** tonic
**brad:** nail
**brag:** cite, crow, boast
**braid:** plait, lacet, cue, tress, interlace, pat
**brain:** thwart, intellect, mind
" **passage:** iter [ly
**brambly:** thorny, prick-
**branch:** bough, limb, arm [art
" **of learning:** arts,
" " **math.:** calculus
" **off:** diverge, fork
" **(small):** sprig, twig
**branched:** ramose
**brand:** stamp, mark
**brandish:** swing, flourish
**brash:** bold, brittle, impudent, saucy
**brave:** valiant, intrepid,

dare, spartan, daring, defy, stout, gallant, heroic
" & enduring person: spartan
bravery: valor [fracas
brawl: riot melee, row,
braying instrument: pestle
Brazilian bird: agami, ara, seriema
" city: Para, Rio
" coin: rei
" drink: assai
" estuary: para
" money: rei
" palm: jupati
" parrot: ara
" river: Ica, Apa
" rubber tree: para
" seaport: Para, Natal, Santos
" state: Bahia, Para
" tapir: anta, antae
" tree: araroba [gap
breach: strand, rent,
bread basket: pannier
" & milk: panada
break: snap, fracture, destroy, rent, rift, sever, rend
" away: escape
" in continuity: gap
" a hole in: stave
" off: end
" one'sword: renig
" into pieces: shatter, crumble
" suddenly: pop
" up: disband
" violently: burst
" without warning: snap [tive
breaking forth: erup-
breakwater: pier, mole,
breastplate: armor [cob
breastwork: parapet
breathe: respire
" convulsively: gasp
" in: inhale
" noisily: snort
" quickly: pant
breathing: rale
" orifice: spiracle
breed: progeny, ilk, originate, propagate
" of cattle: devon
" " chickens: shanghai, bantam
" " pigeons: nun
" " Scottish terriers: skye [zephyr
breeze: aura, air,
breezy: airy, windy
brew: ale, gather
brewing agent: malt
bribe: sop, grease
bric a brac stand: etagere, whatnot
brick: tile
" carrier: hod
brickbat: missile
bridge: span
" over gorge: viaduct
bridle: restrain, repress
" bit without curb: snaffle
" part: bit
" strap: rein
brief: short, curt, curtal, transitory, terse
" extract: scrap
" notice: mention
" period: spurt
" remark: word
brier: thorn, pipe
brigand: pirate
bright: garnish, smart, sunny, rosy, nitid,
" saying: mot [riant
" star: nova
brighten: light [lucida
brightest star: cor, sun,
brightness sunniness, sheen, sunshine

brilliancy of achievement: eclat
brilliant: refulgent
brim: lip, edge, margin
brimless cap: tam, fez
bring: fetch
" back: restore
" charge against: accuse, delate
" down: lower
" forth (Scot.): ean
" forward: adduce
" into being: create
" " conflict: engage
" " court: arraign
" " harmony: attune [align
" " row: aline,
" on: induce, incur
" to life again: revive
" " light: unearth, elicit
" " memory: remind, recall
" " standstill: stall
" together: compile
" up: rear
bringer of misfortune: jonah, jinx
brink: edge, verge, border, rim, bank
briny: salty
brisk: lively, live, spry, snappy, fresh, active, brightly
bristle: seta, tela, awn
" like appendage: arista
bristly: setose, seta
British bar: pub
" colony in Arabia: Aden
" gasoline: petrol
" Indian coin: anna
" " district: Banda, Bengal
" " monetary unit: anna rupee
" legislature: parliament
" mining truck: corf
" oak: robur
" parliament members: commons
" territorial division: shire
" territory in Africa: Nigeria
brittle: crisp, brash, fragile [liberal
broad: wide, spacious,
" thick piece: slab
" thin piece: sheet
" topped hill: loma
brokerage: agio
bronze: tan
" money: aes
brood: incubate, sit, set, team, ponder
" of pheasants: nyes, nide, nye, ni
" " young fishes: fry
brook: run, stomach
" (small): rill, rillet, rivulet
broom: besom, barsom
brother: fra
brown: toast
" apple: russet
" color: sepia, pablo, umber, tenne
brownie: nis
bruise: pommel, batter, contuse, contusion
brush: sweep, skirmish
brute: animal
brutish: coarse, bestial, stolid, gross
bryophictic plant: moss
bubble: bleb, bead
" up: boil
buccaneer: pirate
bucket: pail

" used in mining: tub
buckwheat tree: titi, teetee
bucolic: rustic, rural
bud: sprout, scion, burgeon, blossom, cion
Buddhist church in Japan: Tera
" column: lat
" mound: stupa
" pillar: lat
" priest: lama, bo
" scripture lang.: pali
" temple approach: toran
buddy: crony, pal
buffoon: mime, clown, mimer, droll
build: erect, create, construct [fice
building: erection, edi-
" lot: site
" material: mortar, concrete, laterite
" part: wing, apse
Bulgarian coin: lev
bulging pot: olla
bulk: mass, size
bulky: big, large
bull toro, taurus
bullet: shot, slugs
bullfighter: toreador, matador, torero, picador
bullfinch: olp
bully: hector
bulrush: tule
bulwark: rampart, defense, fence
bunch: wad, tuft, wisp
bundle: parcel, bale, package
" of grain: sheaf
" " sticks: fagot
bundling machine: baler
bungle: botch
bunting: etamine
buoy: float
buoyant: elastic, levitate, sprightly
burden: lade, load, laden, saddle, onus
burdensome: grievous, heavy, onerous
bureau: dresser
burglar: thief
" (slang): yegg
" 's tool: jimmy [ire
burlesque: parody, sat-
Burmese city: Rangoon
" demon: nat
" native: wa, lai
" town: Mandalay
" tribe: Tai, Lai
" umbrella finial: tee
burn: scald, sear, char, smart, singe
" to ashes: cremate, incinerate
" brightly: flame
" slowly: smoulder
" unsteadily: flicker, flare [torrid
burning: afire, ablaze,
" pile: pyre
burr in wood: knar
burrow: dig, mine
burrowing animal: mole, gopher, marmot, rabbit [plode
burst: spurt, rend, ex-
" asunder: disrupt
" of cheers: salvo
" forth: pop, sally,
bury: inter [erupted
bush: shrub, tod
bushy: shaggy
" clump: tod
" herb: rue
business getter: ad
" house: firm

bustle: ado, tod, stir, bother, fuss
busy: engaged, diligent, occupied
" place: hive
busybody: meddler
but: yet, save, merely,
butt: ram, target [mere
butter: oleo
butterfly: io
" (kind): diana, skipper, ursula
button: stud
buttress: prop
buy: purchase
" back: redeem
buzz: drone, hum
by: per, at, past, alongside, near, via
" means of: per
" oneself (comb. form): aut
" passes: tunnels
" side of: beside, along
" way of: via, per
bypath: lane

## C

caama: asse [taxi
cab: hack, hansom,
cabal: plot
cabbage: kale
" like plant: cole
" (var.): cale, kale
cabin: hut, lodge
cache: hide
cachet: seal
cactus (small): mescal
caddis worm: cadew
cadillo: burdock
cadis worm: cadew
Cadmus's daughter: Temple, Ino, Semele
cadre: framework
cage: confine, imprison
cajole: flatter, wheedle,
cake: scone, bar [coax
" (small): bun
calabash: gourd
calamitous: dire, evil, tragic, fatal
calculate: rate, estimate, figure, reckon
" means of: average
calculating instrument: abacus
Caledonian: Scot
calendar: almanac
calf flesh: veal
" of leg (of the): sural
caliber: bore
Calif. bulrush: Tule
" holly: toyon
" lake: Tahoe
" laurel: myrtle
" mt.: Sierras
" " peak: Shasta
" volcano: Shasta
call: dub, term, name, page, entitle, style, summon, denominate, visit
" for aid: appeal
" boy: page
" forth: evoke, elicit
" loudly: cry, hail
" together: convoke
caller: visitor, guest
calloused: horny
calm: serene, mild, allay, soothe, composed, cool, peace
calorie: therm
calumniate: asperse, slur, belie, slander
calyx leaf: sepal, petal
came to rest: lit, alit, sat
camel driver: sarwan
" hair cloth: aba
camelopard: giraffe
camera stand: tripod

**Cameron native**: Sara, Abo
**can**: able, tin, preserve
**Canadian city**: Saskat, Levis, Banff
" **emblem**: maple
" **lake**: Reindeer
" **national park**: Yoho
" **peninsula**: Gaspe
" **province**: N.S., Ontario, Manitoba, Alta
" **river**: Yukon
**canal**: passage, duct, Suez, Panama
**canard**: hoax
**cancel**: delete, dele, revoke, rescind, remit, erase, annul
**candid**: frank
**candidate**: aspirant, nominee
" **list**: slate
**candle**: taper, luminary, dip
**candlenut tree**: ama
**candy**: sweets, caramel
**cane**: flog, rattan, flay
**canine disease**: rabies, [mange
**canoe**: proa
**canon**: law
**canonize**: saint [dais
**canopy**: finial, tester,
**cant**: slant, tip, tilt, slope, heel, argot
**canter**: lope
**canticle**: song [py
**canvas covering**: cano-
**canyon**: valley, ravine
**Caoutchouc tree**: ule
**cap**: beret, fez, tam crown, cover, excel, top, coif, complete
**capable**: able, competent, efficient
" **of being extended**: tensile
" " " **maintained**: tenable
**capacious**: ample, large
**cape**: ness, ras
**Cape Verde Island**: Fogo, Sal
**caper**: prank, antic, prance, dido, gambol, frisk [nent
**capital**: chief, preemi-
**caprices**: whimsies, vagaries, fancies, whims
**captain's boat**: gig
**captivate**: enamor, charm, enthrall
**capture**: bag, take, arrest, catch
**Capuchin monkey**: sai
**caravansary**: serai, ho-
**carbon**: soot [tel
**carborundum**: emery
**card in faro**: soda
" **game**: skat, whist, monte, bezique, pam, ecarte, faro, vint, stuss, lu, hearts, pedro, casino, brag, cassino, fantan, pinochle, nullo
" " **(old)**: pam, loo
" **holding**: tenace
" **(as wool)**: tease, rove
**care**: concern, desire, vigilance, worry, heed, mind, caution, anxiety, tend
" **for**: tend, attend, mind, nurse
**careen**: list, lurch
**career**: course, vocation
**careful**: provident, discreet
**careless**: heedless, remiss, neglectful, slack
**caress**: fondle, pet
**cargo**: load, lading, freight
" **cast overboard**: jetsam
**caribou**: reindeer
**caricature**: cartoon
**carnelian**: sard
**carvivore**: civet, genet, ratel, cat, lion
**carnivorous insect**: mantis
**carol**: sing, warble
**Caroline Island**: Yap
**carom**: rebound [orgy
**carousal**: spree, revel,
**carouse**: revel
**carp fish**: dace
**carpenter's tool**: saw, plane
**carpet**: mat
**carriage**: phaeton, mien, poise, shay, rig, gig, air, clarence, chariot, bearing
**carried**: borne
**carry**: sustain, tote, convey, bear
" **across water**: ferry
" **away as property**: eloin [prosecute
" **on**: wage, transact,
" **out**: execute
" " **again**: reenact
" **too far**: overdo
**carrying charge**: cartage [van
**cart**: wagon, haul, dray,
**cartridge**: shot, shell
**carve**: cut, slice
**carved gem & stone**: cameo [statues
" **images**: statuary,
**carving tool**: chisel
**cascade**: waterfall
**case**: instance, crate, chest, encase, box, container, example, plight
" **for small toiletries**: etui
**cash**: specie, money
" **box**: till
**cask**: tun, barrel, keg, tierce, tub, vat, bareca
**casket for valuables**: coffer
**cast**: shade, throw, heave, hove
" **down**: abase
" **forth**: heave, hove
" **metal mass**: pig, ingot
" **off**: shed, molt
" **out**: expel [leer
" **sidelong glances**:
**castaway**: waif
**caste**: class
**caster**: cruet
**castigate**: punish
**castle**: fort, palace, fortress
**Castor & Pollux's mother**: Leda
**cat**: feline, felid, grimalkin, puss, manx, anchor
" **cry**: mew, pur, purr
" **(kind)**: angora, maltese, ocelot
**catalogue**: list
**catapult (kind)**: onager
**catch**: nab, snare, seize, detent, hasp, overtake, trap
" **the breath**: gasp
" **of game**: bag
" **for a hook**: eye
" **sight of**: espy
" **(slang)**: cop, nab
**catching device**: net
**catchword**: cue, slogan
**category**: genre
**catena**: chain
**cater**: purvey
" **to base desires**: pander
**catkin**: ament
**catlike**: feline
**catnip**: nep
**cattle**: kine, cows
" **dealers**: drovers
**caudal appendage**: tail
**cause**: reason, produce, motive, provoke
" **to adhere**: cement, unite
" **to branch**: ramify
" **to coalesce**: merge
" **emotion**: emote
" **exhaustion of**: drain
" **to float gently**: waft
" **to go**: send [mind
" **to remember**: re-
" **to revolve**: trundle
" **of ruin**: bane
" **(Scot.)**: gar
" **sudden surprise & fear**: startle
**caustic**: acrid, erodent, lye, tart
" **compound**: lye, erodent, lime
**cauterize**: scar, sere, sear, burn
**caution**: warn, care, wariness
" **in advance**: forewarn
**cautious**: careful, wary, canny
**cavalier**: knight
**cavalry soldier**: lancer
**cave**: grotto, cavern, den, lair
" **(arch.)**: antre
**cavil**: carp
**cavities**: atria, antra
**cavity**: sinue, sac, orater, pit, hole
**cavort**: play, prance
**cease**: desist, cessate, pause, stop, quit
" **(naut.)**: avast
**cebine monkey**: sai
**cede**: yield, grant
**celebration**: gala, festivity, fete
**celestial**: uranic
" **beings**: angles, seraphs, seraphim
" **body**: comet, star, sun, moon [ula
" **phenomenon**: neb-
" **region**: sky
" **sphere**: orb
**celibate**: unmarried
**cellulose fiber**: rayon
**Celtic**: Irish
" **lang.**: Gael, Erse, Welsh, Irish
**cement**: paste, lime, mastic, solder, lute, unite
**censure**: asperse, slate, accuse, taunt, blame, reprove, condemn
**center**: core, middle
**centerpiece**: epergne
**central**: eboe, mid, chief, hub
**Central Amer. Indian**: Ona, Carib, Inca, Nahua
" " **republic**: Panama
" " **rodent**: paca
" " **tree**: ule, Eboe, Ebo
" **cylinder of plants**: stela, stele
" **part**: core
" **point**: focus, hub
" " **(pert. to)**: focal
**century**: age [pita
" **plant**: aloe, agave,
**ceratoid**: horny
**cere**: wax
**cereal**: rice, grain
" **grass**: oat
" **husk**: bran
" **spike**: ear
**ceremonial dance**: pavane, pavan [pomp
**ceremony**: rite, fete,
**certain**: sure, positive
**certificate in lieu of cash**: scrip
**certify**: attest
**cess**: tax
**cessation**: pause, failure, stop, lull
" **of being**: desition
**cetacean**: inia
**chafe**: fret, grate, rub, gall, irk
**chaff**: banter, guy
**chaffy part of grain**: brain, bran
**chagrin**: abash, shame, vexation
**chain**: catenae, catena, fetter, restrain
" **part & ring**: link
**chainlike**: catenate
**chair**: seat
" **back piece**: splat
**chalcedony (var.)**: sard, agate
**Chaldea city**: Ur
**chalice**: grail, grill, ama, goblet
" **cover**: pall
**chalk**: crayon, whiten
**challenge**: dare, cartel, stump, defy
**chamber**: room
**champagne (kind)**: ay
**chance**: odd, hap, random, fortune, risk, happen, accident, luck
**chancel part**: bema
**change**: revise, alter, shift, mutation, mutate, convert, transmute, transfer, emend, amend, vary, revision
" **color of**: dye
" **course**: reverse
" **direction**: veer, turn
" **form**: remodel
" **the title**: rename
**changeless**: constant
**changeling**: oaf
**channel**: chute, flume, vale, strait, gat, way, passage
**chant**: intone, chortle, sing
**chap**: fellow, split, crack
**chaplet**: anadem
**char**: scorch, burn
**character**: role, nature, quality, tone, stamp
" **of a people**: ethos
**characteristic**: mark, trait, typical, feature
" **form of expression**: idiom
" **mark**: stamp
" **taste**: smack
**characterization**: role
**characterless**: inane
**charge**: cost, rate, load, debit, fee, accusation, fare, rush, price, ac-
" **per unit**: rate [cuse
" **on property**: lien,
" **a sum**: debit [tax
" **for using a road**: toll
" **with crime**: indict
" " **gas**: aerate
" **with electricity**: alive, live
**charger**: steed
**chariot**: essed, carriage
**charioteer**: Hur
**charity**: alms, love, benevolence

**charlatan**: quack
**Charles Dickens**: Boz
**charm**: grace, attract, captivate, amulet, talisman, spell, entrance, entice, enchant
**chart**: plan, map, plot, graph, plat
**chary**: frugal, sparing, prudent [hunt
**chase**: pursue, follow,
**chasm**: abyss, gulf, cleft
**chaste**: pure, modest
**chasten**: smite, train, chastize [reprove
**chastise**: berate, swinge,
**chat**: talk, converse
**chatter**: prate, gab, gabble
**cheat**: dupe, cozen, fraud, hocus, fleece, defraud, mulct, fob, bilk, swindler
" **(colloq.)**: stick
" **(slang)**: welsh, bam
**check**: repress, stem, rein, arrest, test, curb, inhibit, restrain
" **growth**: stunt, nip
**checkered cloth**: tartan, [plaid
**cheek**: gena
" **bone**: malar
" **(of the)**: molar, malar, genal
**cheer**: gladden, elation, rah, encourage, hearten, applaud, inspirit
**cheerful**: genial, blithe, joyful, sunny
" **tune**: lilt
**cheerless**: dreary
**cheese dish**: rarebit
" **(kind)**: edam, brie, gruyere, parmesan, cheddar, stilton
**chemical compound**: ester, amine, water, amide, sucrate
" **suffix**: ine, yl, al, ol, ite, ose, olid
" **vessel**: udell, aludel
**cherish**: bosom, nurse, foster
**cherry color**: cerise
**chess opening**: gambit
" **pieces**: men, pawns, rooks, knights, castles, queens
**chest**: safe, thorax, case, coffer
" **bone**: rib
" **noise**: rale
**chestnut & grey**: roan
**chevrotain**: napu
**chew**: manducate, masticate
" **audibly**: crunch
**chic**: modish, smart
**chick pea**: gram [tam
**chicken (small)**: bantam
**chickory like herb**: endive [rebuke
**chide**: scold, berate,
**chief**: headman, head, principal, staple, primal, arch, main, prime, capital, paramount, first, central
" **of clan**: Thane
" **commodity of region**: staple
**child (comb. form)**: ped
" **(small)**: tot, tad
**childish**: puerile, anile
**Chile city**: Talca, Arica
" **timber tree**: muermo, rauli [frost
**chill**: ice, cool, ague,
" **'s & fever**: ague, malaria
**chimes**: bells
**chimney**: flue, stack
" **passage**: flue
**Chinese animal**: rasse
" **antelope**: tserin
" **boat**: sampan
" **building**: pagoda
" **bushy plant**: udo
" **card game**: lu, loo
" **city**: Amoy, Ude, Nom, Pekin
" **civet cat**: rasse
" **coin**: tael, tsien, pu
" **(comb. form)**: sino
" **dependency**: Tibet
" **dialect**: wu
" **dynasty**: Ming, Han Yin, Tang
" **herb**: ginseng, tea
" **laborer**: coolie
" **measure**: tua, li, tael, tu, ri
" **medium of exchange**: sycee
" **mile**: li
" **monetary unit**: tael
" **money**: sycee
" " **of account**: tiao
" **obeisance (var.)**: salam
" **official**: Mandarin
" **pagoda**: taa, ta
" **philosopher**: Confucius
" **plant**: tea
" **pound**: catty
" **puzzle**: tangram
" **religion**: taoism
" **river**: Peh, Gan, Tung
" **secret society**: tong
" **shrub**: tea
" **skiff**: sampan
" **statesman**: Koo
" **tea**: tsia
" **temple**: pagoda
" **treaty port**: Amoy, Wenchow
" **unit of value**: tael
" **wax**: pela [li
" **weight**: liang, tsien,
**chip**: fragment, flake
**chirp**: peep, twitter, tweet
**chisel to break ore**: gad
**chloroform substance**: acetone [best, option
**choice**: elite, prime,
" **morsel**: titbit
**choicest**: best
" **part**: marrow
**choose**: select, prefer, elect, opt
" **for office**: slate
**chop**: hew, mince, lop, bite, hack
**chord of 3 tones**: triad
**chore**: stint, task
**Christmas**: Yule, Noel
**chronicle**: record, annal
**chrysalis**: pupa, pupae
**chum**: friend, crony, pal
**church**: chapel, basilica
" **body**: nave
" **caretaker**: sexton
" **chancel**: bema
" **congregation**: synaxis
" **council**: synod
" **dignitary**: canon, prelate, pope
" **land**: glebe
" **officer**: trustee, bishop, elder, sexton
" **official**: elder, pope, deacon, beadle, pastor, priest
" **part**: apse, nave, chancel, steeple, altar, transept
" **service**: mass
" **sitting**: pew
" **vault**: crypt
**churl**: boor, thane
**cicada**: locust
**cicatrix**: scar
**cigar**: panetela, cheroot, stogie, stogy
" **fish**: scad
" **(long)**: corona
**cigarette (slang)**: fag
**cinder**: ash
**cion**: sprout, twig, bud
**cipher**: zero, code, null, naught,
**Circe's sister**: Medea
**circle**: arc, ring, orb, loop
" **around the moon**: corona
" **of light**: halo
" **part**: sector
**circlet**: ring, wreath
**circuit**: tour, cycle, lap, ambit
" **court**: Eyre
**circular**: round
" **band**: hoop
" **disc**: plate
" **indicator**: dial
" **plate**: disc, disk
**circumscribed**: narrow, limited [event
**circumstance**: fact
**cistern**: bac, tank, vat
**citadel**: tower, stronghold [lin
" **of Moscow**: Kremlin
**cite**: adduce, allege, quote, summon
**citizen**: resident
**citron**: cedrat
**city official**: mayor, alderman
" **(pert. to)**: civic, urban, municipal
**civet**: rasse
" **like animal**: genet
**civil injury & wrong**: tort
" **law term**: aval
**clad**: garbed, dressed, drest
**claim**: maintain, require, title, demand, lien
" **on property**: lien
**claimant**: pretender
**clamor**: din, noise, outcry, bark
**clamorous**: loud, noisy
**clamp**: nip, fastener
**clamping device**: vise
**clan**: sept, tribe, sect, gens, clique
**clandestine**: secret
**clarify**: define, clear
**clash**: jar, conflict
**clasp**: grasp, fastener, hold, hook, seize
" **pin**: broach
**class**: sect, grade, caste, genus, group, sort, rank, genus
**class jargon**: argot
**classify**: rate, sort, arrange, assort, label, grade [din
**clatter**: rattle, clack,
**claw**: talon, scratch
**clay**: loam, laterite, marl, pug, earth
" **(pert. to)**: bolar
**clayey**: bolar, loamy
" **earth**: loess, loam, marl
**clean**: pure, neat, spotless, purify, fair, wipe
**cleanse**: bathe, rinse, scrub, scour, deterge
" **wool**: card
**clear**: pure, exonerate, net, serene, rid, clarify, plain, evident, crystal, lucid
" **sky**: ether [glade
**cleared woods**: grove,
**cleave**: cut, rend, tear, rive, split, hew
**cleft**: divided, riven, chasm, fissure, cut, rift, gap [niency
**clemency**: mercy, le-
**clement**: mild, lenient
**Cleopatra's attendant**: Iras
" **pet**: asp [tor
**clergyman**: vicar, priest, cleric, rector, parson, minister, curate, pas-
**clerical collar**: rabat
" **dress**: vestment
" **title**: reverend, abba, abbe
" **vestment**: alb
**clever**: astute, smart, talented, cute, apt, able, dexterous, shrewd, slick
**cleverness**: wit, art
**click beetle**: elater, dor
**cliff**: crag, precipice
**climax**: apogee, top, end [rise, shin
**climb**: scale, ascend,
**climbing herb**: hop, pea
" **palm**: rattan
" **pepper**: betel [ivy
" **plant**: vine, liane, liana, bine, creeper,
" **stem**: bine
**clime**: region
**clinch**: nail, grapple
**cling**: cohere, adhere
**clinging fish**: remora
**clip**: shear, snap, curtail, snip, nip, mow
**cloak**: robe, wrap, mantle, disguise, hide
**clock**: time
" **face**: dial
" **part**: pendulum
" **in shape of ship**: nef
**clog**: impede [ory
**cloister**: hermitage, pri-
**close**: end, near, shut, dense, finale, seal
" **bond**: tie
" **by**: nigh [sunset
" **of day**: eventide,
" " " **(Poet.)**: een, eve [cloche
" **fitting cap**: coif,
" **mouthed**: clam
" **(poet.)**: anear
" **ties**: bonds
" **to**: near, at
**closing chord**: cadence
**cloth**: denim, serge, marl, baize, satinet, rep, satin, melton, tweed, worsted, leno
" **fibers**: nap
" **measure**: ell
" **strainer**: tamis
**clothed**: clad, garbed, attired, dressed, arrayed [toggery
**clothes**: togs, apparel,
" **basket**: hamper
" **brush**: whisk [er
" **dryer**: airer, wring-
" **moth**: tinea
" **rack**: tree, airer
**cloud**: cumulus, cirrus
**cloudless**: clear
**cloudlike mass**: nebula
**cloudy**: nebulous, dim, nebular
**cloverlike plant**: melitot
**clown**: loon, mime, buffoon, bumpkin
**cloy**: sate, pall, surfeit
**club**: mace, bat
" **shaped**: claviform clavate,
**clue**: hint, tip
**clump**: tuft
" **of earth**: clod
**clumsy**: inept, awkward
" **boat**: ark
" **fellow**: lout, lubber, oaf, gawk
" **work**: botch
**cluster of spore cases**: sori, sorus [grove
" " **trees**: thicket,
**clutch**: grasp, hold, grab, seize, grip

coach: trainer, train
coachman: driver [gel
coagulate: clot, curdle,
coal box: hod
" fragment: ember
" lifter: shovel
" mine shaft: pit
" miner: collier
" product: tar
" shuttle: hod
" wagon: tram
coalesce: unite
coalition: fusion, union
coarse: brutish, ribald,
thick, crass
" cloth: manta, burlap, leno, scrim
" fiber: tow, adad
" hominy: samp,
grits [ecru
" linen fabric: crash,
" matted wool: shag
" of procedure: process [bristle
" rigid hair: seta,
coast: shore, slide
coat: cover, layer
" of animal: fur, pelage [heraldic
" " arms: crest,
" " certain alloy:
tern, terne
" " gold: gild
" with icing: glace
" " metal: plate
coax: tease, cajole
cocoanut fiber: coir
code: cipher, law
coffee bean: nib
" cake: stollen [java
" (kind): mocha,
coffer: chest, ark
coffin: bier
cog: tooth, pawl, gear
cogent: valid, conclusive, convincing
cogitate: think, ponder,
muse, mull
cognizance: ken
cognizant: aware
cogwheel: gear [wind
coil: twist, twine, curl,
" into a ball: clew
coin: mint, money, originate, pence [spond
coincide: agree, corre-
cold: icy, frigid, gelid,
chilly, frosty
" dish: salad
collarbone: clavicle
colleague: ally, partner, confrere
collect: gather, levy,
amass, garner, pool,
accumulate, compact
" & keep: hoard
" to a point: center
collection: set
" of cattle: drove
" " facts: ana
" " implements: kit
collector's item: curio
college dance: prom
" officer: proctor
" official: regent
" session: seminar
" song: glee
collide with: ram, bump
colonist: settler, planter
" greeting to Indian:
netop [sepia, red
color: tint, dye, roan,
paint, stain, puce,
tinge, bice, hue, olive,
" lightly: tinge
" matter: dye
" quality: tone, hue
Colorado Indian: Ute
" Mt.: Owen, Oso
coloring agent: dye,
paint [pallid
colorless: wan, pale,
" liquid: olein
Columbus's birthplace:
Genoa
" ship: Nina, Pinta
column: pillar, pilaster
coma: stupor, lethargy
comb wool: card, tease
combat: duel, struggle
fight
" place: arena
combine: unite merge
" resources: pool
combustible heap: pyre
combustion: fire
" product: smoke,
soot, ash [approach
come: arrive, reach,
" ashore: land
" before: precede
" forth: emerge, issue
" " operation:
enure [emerge, loom
" " view: appear,
" to pass: transpire,
befall, happen
" " rest: lodge,
light [meet
" together: clash,
comedy: farce
comely: fair, pretty
comestible: edible
comfort: wry, ease, rest,
solace, console
comical: funny, ludicrous [join, edict
command: order, bade,
behest, bid, fiat, beck,
mandate, dictate, en-
" to a horse: gee, wo
commander: leader,
chief [orial
commemorative: mem-
" disc: medal
commence: open, start
commend: praise, order
commerce: trade, start
commission (honorary):
brevet
commit: intrust, entrust, consign
" to memory: con
common: usual
" fund: pool
" level: par [demos
" people: populace,
" sayings: dicta
" talk: rumor
commonplace: banal,
trite, stale, usual,
prosaic [state
commonwealth: demos,
commotion: stir, todo,
noise, welter, ado,
fray [sage, word
communication: mes-
communion cup: ama
" plate: paten
" table: altar
compact: tight, solid
terse, condense
" mass: wad [friend
companion: mate, playmate, comrade, pal,
companionship: society
company: band, troop
" of players: team,
troupe
" " seamen: crew
comparative: relative
" suffix: er [trast
compare: liken, con-
" critically: collate
" with fixed standard: measure [alogy
comparison: simile, an-
compass: attain
compassion: pity
compel: oblige, force,
impel, coerce, drive
compendium: digest
compensate: redeem,
requite, pay, remunerate [ment
compensation: fee, pay-
compete: vie, race
competent: able, capable, fit
compile: edit
complacement: smug
complain: repine, moan,
grunt, grumble, kick,
whine, beef
complement of bolt: nut
" " a hook: eye
complete: plenary, entire, finish, end, utter,
perfect, fulfill, total,
entire, cap, intact
" disorder: chaos
completed: over
" (poet): oer
completely: all, quite
" developed: mature
complex: abstruse, intricate [node
complication: nodus,
comply: adapt, obey,
accede, conform
component: element,
material, ingredient
" of molecule: atom
comport: agree [repose
compose: write, frame,
composed: calm
" of: consist
" " different parts:
compound [lar
" " grains: granu-
" " hackled flax:
towy, toury
" " two elements:
binary [say, opus
composition: theme, es-
" for nine: nonet
" " two: duet
" in verse: poem
composure: poise [ken
comprehension: grasp,
comprehensive: wide,
compress: squeeze,
wring, stupe [ess
compulsion: stress, dur-
compunction: penitence,
remorse
compute: add, reckon
conceal: hide, mask,
veil, mew, secrete,
palliate [yield, admit
concede: grant, hide,
conceited: vain, prided,
opinioned, egotistic
" nature: ego [tist
" person: snob, ego-
conceive: ideate, realize
concentrate: bless, center, focus, mass
concept: notion, idea,
opinion
concern: pertain, care,
matter, anxiety, interest [about, on, of
concerning: anent, re,
conciliate: propitiate,
appease, mollify
conciliatory: irenic
concise: terse, curt
conclude: end, determine, infer, terminate
concluding passage:
coda, epilogue
conclusion: end, finis,
upshot
concoct: brew, hatch
concord: peace, unison
concrete: beton, specific, real
concur: agree, assent
condemn: doom, censure, denounce, sentence
condense: compact
condensed moisture:
dew
" vapor: fog
condescend: deign
condiment: vinegar,
curry, spice, mustard,
salt, pepper
" cruet: caster
condition: state, status,
if, estate, term, situation, fettle
" barley: malt
" of payment: terms
conduct: lead, wage,
direct, run, preside,
transact, deportment,
demean, escort
conduct oneself: behave, demean
conductor: maestro,
leader, guider
" of electricity: metal
conduit: main
cone: pina
" bearing trees: firs,
pines, coniferae
" shaped: conic
confectionary: candy,
sweets
confederacy: league
confederate: ally, band
confer upon: endow,
dub, grant, bestow
conference: powwow,
parley [avow
confess: admit, own,
confession of faith: credo, creed [entrust
confide: intrust, trust,
confidence: secret,
trust, faith
confident: sure, reliant
confine: stint, pend,
seal, pen, coop, mew,
cage, restrict, tether,
limit, imprison, intern [ratify, attest
confirm: assure, seal,
conflict: war, clash, contest, battle [ply
conform to: adapt, com-
" to the shape: fit
confuse: befog, fluster,
bemuddle, muddle,
distract, abash
confused: chaotic
" lang.: jargon
" murmur: bizz, buzz
confusion: bother, mess,
turmoil
congeal: freeze, set
congenial: boon
congregate: mass, meet,
swarm, assemble
conic section: parabola,
ellipse
coniferous tree: yew,
cedar, fir, pine [ween
conjecture: opine, guess,
imagine, speculate,
conjurer: mage
" 's rod: wand
connect: unite, join
connected: coherent
" sequence: series
connecting body of water: strait
" link: liaison, bond
" pipe: tee [relation
connection: link, nexus,
connective: and, that
connoisseur: judge
" of food: epicure
connubial: marital
conquer: master, defeat,
overcome, tame, beat
conqueror: victor, hero
conquest: victory
consecrate: bless, devote, dedicate
consent: agree, assent,
approval, permission
consequence: end, result [thus
consequently: so, hence,
conservative: Tory
conserve: save
consider: rate, ponder,
deem, regard, opine,
esteem, judge, think
consideration: reason,
price, attention, regard [mit

**consign**: relegate, com-
**console**: solace, com- fort, condole
**consolidate**: unite, knit
**conspiracy**: plot, cabal
**conspire**: plot, scheme, collude
**constant**: invariant
" **desire**: itch
**constantly**: ever
**constellation**: aries, leo, bootes, ara, ram, orion, ursa, gemina, argo, lyra, dipper, mensa, draco, sirius
**consternation**: terror, dismay [part
**constituent**: element,
**constrain**: astrict, manacle, force tie, oblige, impel
**constrict**: cramp [rear
**construct**: build, erect,
**construe**: translate, interpret [fect
**consummate**: end, per-
**contact**: touch
**contain**: hold, embrace
**container**: case, pail, basket, crate, pot, box, holder, urn, can, crate, sack, tub, vat,
**containing iron**: ferric
" **lumps**: nodular
" **maxims**: gnomic
" **salt**: saline [file
**contaminate**: taint, de-
**contemn**: scorn
**contemplate**: meditate, ponder [able
**contemptible**: cheap, mean, base, despic-
**contend**: vie, cope, strive, maintain, militate, assert
**content**: fain, satisfy
**contention**: strife
**contest**: game, dispute, race, conflict, vie, argue, strife, bout, struggle [gate
" **law**: deraign, liti-
**contiguous**: near
**continent**: mainland
**contingency**: event, case
**contingent**: dependent
**continual**: endless, incessant [ceed
**continue**: last, resume, remain, persist, pro-
**continued knocking**: ratatat [twist
**contorted**: wry, warped,
**contour**: shape, line, outline
**contract**: narrow, incur, shrink, agreement, knit, lease, covenant,
**contradict**: negate, belie, rebut, deny
**contradictory statement**: paradox
**contrary**: reverse
" **to rules**: foul
**contrast**: compare
**contribute**: redound, render, tend
**contribution**: scot
**contrite**: penitent, sorry, repentant, sorrowful
**contrivance**: device, engine [weave
**contrive**: devise, invent, manage, plan,
**control**: rein, dominate, govern, steer, manage, demean
**controversial**: polemic, polemical, eristical
**contuse**: bruise
**conundrum**: riddle
**convene**: meet, sit
**convenient**: handy
**conversation**: speech, talk, chat
**convert**: change, proselyte, transmute
**convex molding**: ovolo boltel, torus, reed
**convey**: sell, impart, remove, bring, ride, bear, carry, move, transfer, transport
" **beyond jurisdiction** (law): eloin [vehicle
**conveyance**: transit, car,
" **charge**: fare
" **for dead**: hearse
**convince**: assure
**convincing**: cogent
**convoke**: assemble
**convulsion**: spasm, fit
**convulsive cry**: sob
**cooking term**: rissole
" **pot**: olla
**cooky**: snap
**cool**: ice, sober, calm, fan [frigerant
**cooling device**: fan, re-
**coop up**: pent, pen, corral, confine
**copious**: abundant
**copper**: CU, cent, penny
" **money**: aes
**copy**: imitate, ape, mimic, replica, image, transcribe
**copyright**: patent
**coquettish**: coy
Coral Islands: Atolls, Keys, Atoll [rope
**cord**: line, twine, string,
**corded cloth**: rep, poplin [ame
**core**: heart, gist, pith,
**cork**: stopper, suberic
**corn**: pickle, callus
" **bread**: pone
" **lily**: ixia
" **meal mush**: atole
**corner**: angle, nook, tree, niche, coign, in
" **of a sail**: clew
**cornucopia**: horn
**corolla leaf**: petal
**coronet**: tiara, crown
**corpulent**: fat, obese
**correct**: amend, emend, right, accurate, fit, OK
**correlative**: nor
**correspond**: tally, coincide [rust
**corrode**: bite, eat, gnaw,
**corrosion**: erosion, rust
**corrupt**: taint, degrade, poison, deprave, pervert, evil, attaint
**corsair**: pirate, privateer
**corundum**: emery
**corvine bird**: crow, raven, rook
**cosmetic**: paint, rouge
**Cossack chief**: Ataman
**cosset**: fondle, pamper, pet [price, rate
**cost**: expense, charge,
**costly**: dear, expensive, high, valuable
**costume**: attire, getup
**cote**: shed
**coterie**: clique, set
**cotton fabric**: percale, denim, leno, pima, surat, silesia, muslin, satinet, calico, khaki
" **seed capsule**: boll
" " **machine**: gin
**couch**: bed, divan, sofa
**cougar**: puma
**counsel**: advice
" (**arch.**): rede
**count**: number [visage
**countenance**: abet, face,
**counterfeit**: pretend, base, sham, simulate, fake, forge [twin
**counterpart**: parallel,
**countrified**: rural [soil
**country**: land, nation,
" **gallant**: swain
**county**: shire, parish
**coup**: upset [link
**couple**: pair, yoke, two,
**courage**: valor, nerve, mettle, dares, heart, grit, sand
**courageous**: bold, brave
**course**: way, trail, route, career, path, direction, tenor, road
" **of action**: trend, routine, habit
" " **eating**: diet
" " **operation**: run
" " **travel**: route
**court**: woo, solicit, patio
" **crier**: beadle
" " **'s call**: oyes
" **hearings**: oyers
" **of justice**: bar
" **officer**: crier
" **order**: writ, mem-
**courtly**: aulic [damus
**courtyard**: patio [bond
**covenant**: promise, testament, contract,
**cover**: sheathe, lid, screen, cap, coat, tree, pretext, envelop, shelter, hide
" **for the face**: mask
" **the inside**: line
" **the top**: cap
" **with asphalt**: pave
" " **cloth**: drape
" " **dots**: bedot, stipple
" " **first plain coat**: prime [gild, engild
" " **gold**: plate,
" " **jewels**: begem
**covered cloister**: stoa
" **colonade**: stoa
" **walk**: arcade
" **with hair**: pilar
" " **vine**: ivied
" " **water**: awash
**covering of head**: scalp
**covert**: thicket, sheltered, secret, hidden
**covet**: desire, envy, crave, wish
**covetousness**: avarice
**cow**: daunt, overawe
" **barn**: byre
" **headed deity**: Isis
**coward**: recreant, craven, dastard, sneak, poltroon [tardly
**cowardly**: craven, das-
" **carnivore**: hyena
**cower**: cringe, shrink, quail
**cowfish**: toro
**coy**: shy, demure, reserved, bashful
**cozenage**: deceit
**cozy**: snug
" **retreat**: nest
**crackle**: snap, crepitate
**crack**: snap, fissure, chap
**craft**: art, trade, vessel
**crafty**: sly, astute
**crag**: cliff, tor
**cram**: wad, stuff, crowd
**cramp**: restrain, constrict, hinder
**cranium**: skull
**cranny**: fissure
**crash**: smash
**cravat**: tie, ascot
**carve**: seek, covet, desire, long, entreat
**craven**: coward, cowardly [imia
**craving**: yen, desiring, appetite, thirst, bul-
**craw**: crop, maw
**crawl along**: slither, creep [worm
**crawling animal**: reptile,
**crayon**: chalk, pencil
" **picture**: pastel
**craze**: mania, fad, derange, furor, madden
**crazy**: daft, loco, loony, demented, daffy
**cream** (**the**): elite [ruga
**crease**: wrinkle, fold,
**create**: originate, generate, make, form, produce, devise
" **force**: nature
**creator**: author
**credence**: belief
**credible**: likely [honor
**credit**: trust, believe,
**credo**: creed, belief
**creed**: credo, tenet
**creek**: rivulet, stream, bayou, ria, cove
**creep away**: slink [liana
" **plant**: ipecac, vine,
**crepitate**: crackle
**cresent shaped**: moony, lunate [nate, lunette
" " **figure**: lune, lu-
**crest**: peak, top, crown, plume, tuft, summit
" **of a wave**: comb
**Crete Mt.** Ada, Ida
**crew**: gang, band
**crib for storage**: bin
**cribbage pin**: peg
" **score**: peg
" **term**: nob
**cricket play**: twister
" **position**: slip
" **side**: eleven
" **sound**: chirp
**crime**: felony, iniquity
**Crimea river**: Alma [ado
**criminal**: felon, desper-
**crimp**: wrinkle, crinkle
**cringe**: cower, grovel, fawn [wrinkle
**crinkle**: crumple, crimp,
**cripple**: maim, lame
**crisp**: brittle, curt
" **cookie**: snap
**criterion**: test, standard
**critic**: censor, caviler
**critical**: acute
" **moment**: crisis [sor
**criticize officially**: cen-
" **severely** (**colloq.**): roast, pan, rap
**Croatian**: Croat [loop
**crochet stitch**: tricot,
**crocodile**: mugger, goa
**crone**: hag [pal, chum
**crony**: friend, buddy,
**crook**: curve, bend
**crooked**: awry, wry, bent, askew
" (**Scot.**): agee [duce
**crop**: sprout, craw, pro-
**cross**: traverse, rood, angry, span, intersect, surly, peevish
" **rib**: lierne
" **shaped**: cruciate
" **stroke**: serif
" **timber**: spale
" **by wading**: ford
**crossbeam**: trave
**crossbreed**: hybrid
**crow**: brag, rook, raven
**crowbar**: lever
**crowd**: mob, gathering, horde, serry, press, throng, cram, jam, pack, herd
**crowfoot flower**: anemone, peony [raven
**crowlike bird**: oriole, rook, daw, jackdaw,
**crown**: tiara, crest, diadem, coronet, cap
**crucifix**: rood
**crude**: raw, crass
" **dwelling**: hut
" **metal**: ore [mean
**cruel**: pitiless, ogrish,
**cruet**: caster
**crus**: shank, leg
**crush**: mash, grind
" (**colloq.**): scrunch
**crustacean**: crab, lobster, prawn, isopod
**cry**: weep, moan, snivel,

sob, hue, shout, wail
**cryptic:** occult
**cryptogamous plant:** moss
**crystal:** clear
" **gazer:** seer
**crystalline compound:** elaterin, alanine, parillin [spar
" **mineral:** spinelle,
" **salt:** borax, niter
**Cuban measure:** tarea
" **tobacco:** capa
**cube:** die, dice
**cubic content:** volume
" **decimeter:** liter
" **measure:** cord
" **meter:** stere
**cuckoo:** ani
**cuckoopint:** arum
**cud:** rumen
**cuddle:** nestle, snuggle
**cudgel:** bat, staff, drub
**cue:** hint, braid
**cuirass:** lorica
**cull:** sift, sort, assort
**culmination:** acme, end, climax, zenith
**culpable:** guilty
**culprit:** criminal
**cultivate:** till, farm, hoe, garden, foster, [do
**cultivated ground:** ara-
**culture:** refinement
**culture media:** agar
**cunning:** astute, cute, craft, sly, foxy
**Cupid:** Eros, Amor
" **'s love:** Psyche
**cupidity:** avarice, greed
**cupola:** dome, turret
**curate:** clergyman
**curb:** repress, restrain, rein, check
**cure:** heal, vulcanize, remedy, preserve
" **all:** panacea, elixir
**curl:** tress, ringlet, coil, twine [rife, torrent
**current:** tide, stream,
" **of air:** draft
" **(comb. form):** rheo
**curse:** oath, ban, anathema [cise, brusk, crisp
**curt:** short, brief, con-
**curtail:** shorten, clip
**curtain:** drape, veil
**curve:** arc, bend, wind, arch, loop, bow
**curved structure:** arch
" **support:** rib
**cushion:** pad, mat
**custom:** usage, habit, wont, use, manner
**customary:** habitual, wonted, usual [cleft
**cut:** clip, bob, snip, hew, slash, gash, nip, incision, shear, sunder, mow, lop, slit, saw, carve, cleave, lance, fell, incise, shorten, slice, sever, reap, snee, sawed,
" **after terms with snick:** snee [slit
" **lengthwise:** slitted,
" **of meat:** loin, rump, steak
" **out:** elide, excide
" **roughly:** hack
" **in small pieces:** mince, dice, hash
" **in thin slices:** shave
" **through:** intersect
" **in two:** sever, bisect
**cute:** clever
**cutting implement:** razor, knife, jackknife, scissors, shears, mower, slicer, ax, adz
" **off of a vowel:** elision
" **wit:** satire
**cuttlefish:** sepia, spirula

**Cyclades Isl.:** Samos, Delos, Syra, Nio
**cylinder:** spool, roller, roll, tube
" **disk:** piston
**cylindral:** terete
**cylindrical & hollow:** tubular
**Cymric:** Welsh
" **sun god:** Lleu
**cyprinoid fish:** id, ide
**cyst:** wen

## D

**dabble:** mess
**daft:** idiotic
**dagger:** snee, dirk, stiletto, poniard
**daily:** diurnal, aday
" **fare:** diet
" **food & drink:** fare
" **record:** diary
**dairymaid (Scot.):** dey
**daisy (kind):** oxeye
" **(Scot.):** gowan
**dale:** glen, vale
**dally:** trifle, toy
**dam:** obstacle, millpond, barrier, restrain
**damage:** loss, hurt, mar, scathe, harm, injure, impair
**damp:** moist, humid
" **& cold:** dank, raw
**dampen:** wet, depress, moisten [ball, frisk
**dance:** ballet, dandle,
" **(kind):** galop, jig, reel, redowa, polka, pavan, adagio, minuet
" **step:** pas
**dancing shoes:** pumps
**dandy:** dude, fop
**danger:** peril, harm, hazard, risk [ous
**dangerous:** risky, peril-
**Danish coin:** ore, krone
" **composer:** Gade
" **divisions:** amt
" **fiord:** ise [Faroe
" **island:** Aero, Als,
" **king:** Canute
" **measure:** alen, rode
" **money:** ora
" **wt.:** eser, lod
**dap:** dib, dip, dibble
**dapple:** spot, spotting
**dared:** durst, defied, risked, ventured, braved [brave
**daring:** fearless, bold,
**dark:** deep, gloomy, unlighted, dusky, ebon
**darkened:** clouded, deepened, shadowed, murk, obscured
**darkness:** murk, gloom
**dart:** flit, arrow, bolt, spear, bound, darb, barb, javelin, shoot
" **(colloq.):** scoot
" **forth:** spurt
" **suddenly:** dash
**dash:** spirit, elan, dart, shatter, sprint
**dastardly:** cowardly
**data:** facts
**dating from birth:** natal
**daub:** smear, plaster
**David's son:** Solomon
**dawdle:** poke, linger
**dawn:** daybreak, aurora
" **(comb. form):** eo
" **(pert. to):** eoan
" **(poet.):** morn
**day before:** eve
**daydream:** reverie
**days march:** etape [muse
**daze:** trance, stun, bedazzle: glare
**dead:** adead, extinct lifeless [mute
**deaden:** stun, blunt,
**deadly:** lethal, fatal

**deal:** bargain, trade
" **in:** sell
" **out:** dole [cope
" **with:** handle, trade,
**dealer in cloth:** draper
**dear:** beloved, darling, costly, precious, loved
**dearth:** lack, famine
**death:** decrease
" **notice:** obit
" " **(var.):** obet
" **rattle:** rale [clude
**debar:** preclude, ex-
**debark:** land
**debase:** demean, traduce, degrade, sink, reduce, lower, defile
**debatable:** moot
**debate:** reason, argue, discuss, discussion, moot, palaver
**debit:** charge [trash
**debris:** ruins, rubbish,
**decade:** ten
**decay:** rot, decompose
**deceit:** fraud, guile, imposture [hoodwink
**deceive:** betray, delude, dupe, entrap, mislead, fool, befool,
**decent:** modest, proper
**deceptive:** illusive
**decide:** determine, resolve, settle, opt
**decide upon:** elect
**decimal unit:** ten
**decipher:** decode
**deck out:** tog, array
**declaim:** orate, rant
**declare:** aver, assert, state, proclaim, avow, affirm, pronounce
**decline:** fall, droop, deteriorate, die, refuse, ebb, dip, wane
**decompose:** rot, decay
**decorate:** deck, embellish, adorn, festoon, ornate, trim, paper
**decoration for valor:** medal [mure
**decorous:** decent, de-
**decoy:** entrap, lure, entice, allure [ebb
**decrease:** lower, wane,
**decree:** tenet, ordain, law, ukase, enact, fiat, adjudge, rescript, edict, arret
**dedicate:** devote, inscribe, consecrate
**deduce:** infer, derive, evolve [subtract
**deduct:** bate, rebate,
**deduction:** rebate, inference [exploit
**deed:** act, feat, action, event, remise, escrow,
**deem:** consider, regard, think, judge
**deep:** dark, profound, obscure, hidden
**deepen:** thicken, intensify, dredge
**deer:** stag, doe, hart, hind, elk, moose
" **flesh:** venison
**defamation:** libel
**defame:** slander, malign
**default:** failure, neglect
**defeat:** beat, best, foil, rout, overcome, conquer, frustrate, frustration, loss, vanquish, worst
" **at chess:** mate
**defect:** flaw, fault
**defective:** bad
" **explosive:** dud
**defense:** protection, bulwark [mail
**defensive armor:** egis,
" **bastions:** forts
" **enclosure:** boma
" **head covering:** helmet

" **plating:** armor
**defer:** postpone, prolong, adjourn [spect
**deference:** homage, re
**deficiency:** want, short age, lack, scarcity
**defile:** moil, pollute, soil, pass, ubra, abra, taint, debase
**deflect:** divert [rob
**defraud:** trick, cheat,
**defy:** dare, beard, brave, handy
" **(colloq.):** stump
**degrade:** corrupt, debase, lower, abase depose, demean
**degree:** extent, stage, step, rank, grade
**dehydrate:** dry
**deity:** God, divinity
**dejected:** low, spiritless, sad, glum, depressed
**Delaware town:** Lewes
**delay:** stall, retard, demur, belate, wait, linger, lag, remora, hinder, loiter, demurral, detain
" **(law):** mora
**delegate:** depute, deputize, authorize
**delete:** dele, remove, erase [sider, ponder
**deliberate:** slow, con-
**delicacy:** cate, caviar tact [fragile, frail
**delicate:** tender, fine,
" **fabric:** lace
" **perception:** tact
**delight:** regale, elate, please, entrance, revel, delectate
**delineate:** limn, draw, picture, depict, portray, describe
**delirium:** frenzy
**deliver:** rid, send, free, render, rescue, release, redeem
**dell:** dene, ravine, glen
**delude:** mislead, trick, beguile,
**deluge:** flood, inundate
**delve:** dig, fathom
**demand:** exact, insist, require, claim, need
" **as due:** claim
**demean:** degrade, lower, conduct, control, behave [behavior
**demeanor:** mien, air,
**demented:** mad, insane, crazy [die
**demise:** death, decease
**demit:** abdicate, dismiss, oust, resign
**demolish:** rase, destroy, raze, ruin
**demon:** imp, ogre, fiend, devil, rahu [evince
**demonstrate:** prove,
**demur:** protest, delay, object, hesitate
**demure:** serious, sober, prim, coy, staid, sedate, grave, decorous
**den:** lair, dive, nest, hunt, cave, sanctum, cavern [rejection
**denial:** negative, negation, refusal, nay, no,
**Denmark:** see under "Danish" [title
**denominate:** call, en-
**denomination:** sect
**denote:** indicate, signify, show, mean, mark
" **a final purpose:** telic [arraign
**denounce:** condemn,
**dense:** crass, close, obtuse, thick
" **growth of trees:** forest, jungle

" **smoke:** smudge

**dent:** hollow, dint, indent, notch, tooth

**dentine:** ivory

**dentist's drill:** burr

**denude:** bare, strip, scalp [ban

**denunciation:** threat,

**deny:** negate, gainsay, disown, refuse, disavow, renege, abnegate, renounce

**depart:** go, leave [mose

" **quickly (slang):** va-

" **secretly:** decamp, abscond [drawal

**departure:** exit, with-

**depend:** rely, hinge, lean, trust

**depict:** picture, delineate, draw, portray

**deplete:** drain, lessen, exhaust, empty

**depone:** testify

**deport:** banish, exile

**deportment:** conduct

" **(arch.):** geste, gest

**depose:** degrade, dethrone [set

**deposit:** lay, leave, put,

**depot:** station, entrepot, storehouse

**depraved:** bad, corrupted, bestial [sen

**depreciate:** belittle, les-

**depress:** sadden, lower, discourage, dispirit, dampen, deject

**depression:** dent, pit, dip, dint

" **between mt. peak:** col, dip

" **in golf green:** cup

" **worn by running water:** ravine, gully

**deprive:** bereave, divest, dispossess

" **of:** lose

" " **moisture:** drain

" " **reason:** dement

**depute:** delegate, send

**deputy:** agent, surrogate

**deride:** taunt, sneer, ridicule, mock, scoff, scorn, gibe, belittle

" **(slang):** rag

**derisive cry:** hoot, hiss

**derive:** deduce, evolve, obtain, infer, get, trace [sebacic

**derived from fat:** adipic,

" " **oil:** oleic

**dervish's cap:** taj

**descend:** sink

" **abruptly:** plunge

**descendant:** scion, son

" **of Jacob:** Levite

" " **Shem:** Semite

**describe:** relate, delineate

" **gram.:** parse

**descry:** espy, see

**desert:** abandon, abscond, forsake, ice, wasteland [Arab

" **dweller:** bedouin,

" **plant:** cactus

" **train:** caravan

" **wind:** simoom, sirocco

**deserter:** turncoat, renegade, absconder, rat

**deserve:** merit, mete, earn [pose

**design:** intention, plan, pattern, model, pur-

" **of scattered objects:** seme [name

**designate:** signate, assign, label, dub, term, distinguish, connote, appoint, entitle,

**desire:** crave, lust, want, yen, wish, care, longing, hope, thirst, covet, aspire, yearn

" **(colloq.):** yen

" **wrongfully:** covet

**desirous:** eager

**desist:** cease, forbear, stop, spare, rest, end

**despairing:** hopeless

**desperado:** ruffian

**despicable:** vile, sordid

**despise:** hate, disdain, contemn, detest

**despoil:** spoil, plunder, fleece

**despoiled (arch.):** reft

**despondent:** blue, sad

**despot:** tyrant, satrap

**despotism:** tyranny

**destine:** allot

**destiny:** fate, lot, doom

**destitude:** devoid [raze

**destroyed:** rase, ruined, extirpated, broke, demolished, perish,

**destruction:** loss, demolition, ruin, death

**desultory:** aimless

**detach:** disengage, isolate, disunite [tion

**detached state:** isola-

**detail:** item, appoint

**detain:** halt, hinder, retard, harass, delay, deter, arrest, withhold, intern [spy, nose

**detect:** discover, espy,

**detective:** sleuth

" **(slang):** tec, dick

**detent:** pawl, catch

**deter:** restrain, hinder, prevent, retard

**deterge:** cleanse

**detergent:** soap

**deteriorate:** fail, degenerate, decline, wear

**determine:** conclude, destine, settle, will, decide, resolve

**detest:** despise, loathe

**detonate:** explode [draw

**detract:** derogate, with-

**devastate:** rase

**devastation:** havoc

**develop:** volve, grow

**deviate:** stray, lapse, err, digress, swerve

**device to hoist large stones:** lewis

**device for raising chicks:** brooder

" **to spread lamp flame:** cric [mon, imp

**devil:** satan, fiend, de-

**devilfish:** manta

**devilish:** infernal

**devise:** plan, contrive, invent, frame, create

**devote:** apply, dedicate

**devoted:** liege, faithful

**devotee:** fan, partisan

**devoutness:** piety

**dewy:** roric, wet, moist

**dexterity:** art, ease

**dexterous:** clever, deft

**diabolical:** infernal

**diadem:** tiara, crown

**diagonal:** bias

**dialect:** patois, argot, speech, patois, idiom

**diameter:** caliper

**diamond cutter:** dop

**dibble:** dap, dib

**dice:** cube

**Dicken's pen name:** Boz [prank

**dido:** antic, caper,

**die:** perish, demise, decline, expire, mold, stamp, print

" **to make pipe:** dod

**diet:** fast, fare

**different:** diverse, another, other, variant, novel [rub

**difficult:** hard, knotty,

" **(prefix):** dys

" **question:** poser

**difficulty:** snag, strait

**diffident:** coy, shy

**diffuse:** radiate, strew, disperse, spread

**dig:** mine, delve, burrow, spade

" **up:** unearth

**digit:** toe, figure, number, finger

**dignify:** ennoble

**digress:** deviate

**dike:** levee, causeway

**dilate:** swell, enlarge, expand, distend

**dilatory:** remiss, slow

**diligent:** busy, sedulous

**dillseed:** anet, anise

**dilute:** water, weaken, thin [faint, faded, pale

**dim:** obscure, blear,

**diminish:** fade, lessen, wave, bate, abate, decrease, wane, lower, moderate, taper, ebb

" **strength of:** dilute

**diminutive:** small, petite, dwarf

" **ending:** ie, ette

" **suffix:** ile, ot, ole, ie, et, ule

**din:** noise, clamor

**dine:** eat, sup

**dingy:** dull, soiled [grill

**dining room:** cenacle,

**dinner course:** entree

**dip:** immerse, decline, sink, incline, lade, plunge, dap

**dip out:** bail

**diplomacy:** tact

**dipthong:** ae, ea

**dire:** fatal, dreadful

**direct:** lead, drive, steer, manage, aim, address, refer, immediate, guide, manage, straight, govern

" **course:** pilot

" **one's way:** wend

" **proceedings:** preside

**direction:** trend, course

**director:** stager, manager, head, leader

**dirk:** poniard, dagger, snee

**dirt:** grime, sod, trash, refuse, soil, loam

**dirty:** soil, grimy, foul

**disagree:** dissent, differ

**disagreeable:** nasty, mean, vile

**disappoint:** fail

**disaster:** woe, calamity, misfortune [abjure

**disavow:** retract, deny,

**disburden:** ease, rid

**disburse:** pay, spend

**discard:** shed, scrap

**discern:** espy, see, look, spy [sagacious

**discerning:** astute, nice,

**discharge:** shoot, emit, exude, pay, payment

**disciple:** apostle

**discipline:** train, chasten, ferule

**disclaim:** disavow, repudiate, deny

**disclose:** reveal, bare, open, unearth, unveil, tell

**discolor:** stain, spot

**discompose:** upset

**disconcert:** abash, rattle, upset, jar, faze

**disconnect:** sever, separate [desist, quit

**discontinue:** suspend,

**discordant:** harsh

**discount:** rebate, agio

**discourage:** appal, depress, deter

**discover:** spy, espy, detect, invent, find, locate [dent

**discreet:** careful, pru-

**discretion:** tact

**discriminating:** astute, nice, judicial

**discrimination:** acumen

**discuss:** debate, argue

**disdain:** pooh, scorn, despise, spurn [pox

**disease:** malady, gout,

" **of animals:** mange

" " **cattle & horses:** hoove [ergot

" " **cereals:** smut,

" " **fowl:** pip

**disembark:** land

**disencumber:** rid

**disengage:** ravel, free, detach [evolve

**disentangle:** ravel,

" **wool:** card

**disfigure:** mar, deface

**disgrace:** sham, humble, shame, ignominy

**disguise:** veil, mash, cloak, incognito

**disgust (Scot.):** ug

**dish:** tureen, platter, plate, bowl

" **of crackers & water:** panada

" " **eggs & milk:** custard [averse

**disincline:** indispose,

**disjoin:** sever, separate

**dislike:** aversion, hatred, antipathy, mind

**dismal:** bleak, drear, gray, triste, mournful, dreary, lurid

**dismay:** dread, appall, fear, appal, terrify

**dismiss:** oust, demit

" **from office (law):** amove

**dismounted:** alit

**disorder:** chaos, mess

**disown:** repudiate, deny

**disparage:** belittle, slur

**dispatch:** send, message, haste

" **boat:** aviso [pate

**dispel:** disperse, dissi-

**disperse:** scatter, dispel, spread, diffuse

**dispirit:** depress, mope

**display:** pomp, parade, show, wear, evince, manifest, air, expose

**displease:** offend

**displeasure:** anger

**dispose:** divest, settle, arrange [ture, mood

**disposition:** mien, na-

**dispossess:** deprive, divest [rebuttal

**disprove:** refute, rebut,

**dispute:** contest, argue, chaffer, wrangle

" **(colloq.):** spat

**disregard:** waive, override, ignore, neglect

**disrupt:** split

**disseminate:** sow, propagate, scatter, strew, spread [test

**dissent:** disagree, pro-

**dissenter:** heretic

**dissipate:** waste, squander, dispel

**distance:** space

**distant:** formal, remote, yon, far, afar, aloof

" **(prefix):** tel, tele

**distaste:** aversion, dislike [expand, swell

**distend:** inflate, dilate,

**distilling vessel:** retort

**distinctive mark:** badge

**distinguish:** discern

**distinguished:** eminent

**distort:** warp, screw

**distress:** pain, grief

**distributed:** dole, dealt,

meted, allotted, dole, assort, dispensed
**disturb:** roil, rile, unsettle, agitate, ail, molest, annoy, ruffle, heckle, stir, vi late
" **the peace:** riot
**disunite:** detach, sever
**ditch:** trench, moat, rut
**diurnal:** daily [sofa
**divan:** couch, canape,
**dive:** plunge [various
**divers:** several, sundry,
**diverse:** unlike, different
**diversify:** vary
**diversion:** sport, game
**divert:** entertain, amuse, deflect, sport, recreate, distract
**divest:** dispossess, disposes, deprive [cleft
**divide:** share, sunder, apportion, separate, fork, halve, bisect,
**dividing wall:** septum
**diving bird:** loon, tern, smew, auk, grebe
**divinity:** deity
**division:** share, class, squadron, partition, schism, game, section, part
" **of Ancient Greece:** Demes, Deme [cinct
" " **city:** ward, pre-
" " **Greece:** Nomes
" " **Israelites:** tribe
" " **mankind:** race
" " **music:** bar
" " **opera:** scena
" " **poem:** canto, verse, stanza
" " **stock:** shares
**do:** perform, act, fare, achieve,
" **again:** iterate
" **without:** spare
**docile:** tractable, gentle, tame
**dock:** pier
**doctrine:** dogma, tenet, creed, ism, belief, gospel, hedonism
**document:** paper, script
**dodge:** elude, evade
**doer:** actor, agent
**doff:** remove
**dog:** canine, pug, terrier hound, beagle,
" (**large**): alan, dane
" **of mixed breed:** mongrel [sept
**dogfish:** rosset, tope,
**dogma:** tenet, doctrine
**doily:** mat
**dole:** alms, gratuity, mete, share, grief
" **out:** ration
**doleful:** sad [sorrow
**dolor:** grief, mourning,
**dolphin:** porpoise, inia
**dolt:** ass, clod, dunce, oaf, simpleton, fool
**domain:** realm, empire
**dome:** edifice, cupola
**domestic:** maid, menial
**domesticate:** tame
**domicile:** house, menage
**dominate:** control, rule
" (**colloq.**): boss
**domineer:** lord [empire
**dominion:** sway, reign,
**domino:** tile
**DonJuan's mother:** Inez
**donate:** present, give, bestow
" (**Scot.**): gie [ass
**donkey:** onager, burro,
" **call:** bray
**doom:** fate, condemn, lot, sentence, destiny
**door:** portal, access, stoa [latch
" **fastening:** hasp,
" **knocker:** rapper
**doorkeeper:** porter, ostiarius, tiler [asleep
**dormant:** latent, torpid,
**dormouse:** lerot, loir
**dose of medicine:** potion [stipple
**dot:** dowry, period, iota, speck, scatter, point,
**double:** dual, twin, binary, duplex, twain
" (**prefix**): di, dis
**doubly:** twice
**doubt:** mistrust
**doubter:** skeptic
**doughy:** pasty
**dove:** pigeon, cushat
" **'s home:** cote
**dower:** dos, endowment
" (**pert. to**): dotal
**down** (**prefix**): de
**downcast:** sad [spill
**downpour:** rainstorm,
**downright:** stark
**downy surface:** nap
**dowry:** dos, dot
" (**pert. to**): dotal
**doze:** nap, sleep
**draft:** potion, sketch, conscript [ox
" **animal:** mule, oxen,
**drag:** lug, haul, trail
**drain:** sewer, deplete, milk, sump
**dramatic piece:** skit, monodram
" **portrayal:** acting
**drape:** curtain, adorn
**draw:** extract, attract, portray, haul, drag, delineate, tie, tow, pull, lure, limn, depict, stipple [rive
" **as conclusion:** de-
" **forth:** educe, elicit, extract, evoke
" **off:** drain
" " **thru a bent tube:** siphon
" **out:** lengthen, extract, educe, lade
" **sap:** bleed
" **tight:** taut, frap
" **to:** attract
" " **a point:** taper
" **up shoulders:** shrug [ror, terror
**dread:** fear, awe, hor-
**dreadful:** dire, horrid, terrible, frightful
**dream:** reverie, imagine, vision, romance, fancy
**drear:** bleak, dismal, gloomy [remnant
**dreg:** lee, lea, settling,
**drench:** saturate, souse, douse, soak, hose
**dress:** attire, garb, tog, frock, gown, align, rig, clothe, array
" **ornament:** sash
" **stone:** nig
" **trimming:** ruche, ruching, piping, gimp
" **up:** tog, rig, primp
" **with beak:** preen
**dresser:** bureau
**dressing gown:** kimono
**dressmaker:** modiste
**dried:** sere
" **brick:** adobe
" **grape:** raisin
" **grass:** hay
**drift:** tenor, trend, sag
**drill:** bore, train, practice, perforate, anet
" **hall:** armory
**drink:** beverage, gin, potation, nectar, imbibe, swig
" **anothers health:** pledge, toast
" **heavily:** tope
" **made from molasses:** rum [nip
" (**small**): dram, sip,
**drinker:** toper [ard
" **vessel:** gourd, cup, beaker, stein, mug, goblet, tumbler, tank-
**drip:** drop, trickle [urge
**drive:** impell, impel, ride, propel, force,
" **away:** repel, banish, dispel, scat, shoo
" **back:** repulse
" **nail at angle:** toe
**drivel:** dote, slaver
**droll:** whimsical, comic
**dromedary:** camel
**drone:** idler, hum, snail
**drool:** slaver
**droop:** sag, wilt, decline, languish, lop, loll, flag, slouch
**drooping:** nutant [bead
**drop:** drip, fall, plummet, trapdoor, sink,
" **gently:** dap
**dropsy:** edema
**dross:** scum, waste
" **of a metal:** slag
**drove:** herd, horde
**drowse:** nod, nap
**drudge:** moil, slave, plod, fag [ural
**drug:** heroin, stupefy, dope, opium, aloes,
" **plant:** aloe [bour
**drum:** beat, snare, tam-
" (**small**): tabor
**drunkard:** sot
**dry:** sec, arid, ted, sere, thirsty, parch, dull
" (**poet.**): sere
" **by rubbing:** wipe
" **as wine:** sep, brut
**drying cloth:** towel
**duck** (**kind**): pintail, tern, eider, teal, mallard, goldeneye, smew
" (**male**): drake
**duct:** vas, passage, canal
**ductile:** tensile
**dude:** dandy, fop
**due:** payable, toll, owing
**duel:** combat
**duet:** duo [glassy
**dull:** dim, blunt, slow, sluggish, mope, stolid, stodgy, vapid, drab, dry, blur, tarnish dingy, stupid, leaden,
" **color:** drab, dun
" **finish:** matte, mat
" **sound:** thud
" **& tedious:** prosy
**Dumas character:** Athos [pid
**dumb:** mute, still, stu-
**dunce:** dolt, fool, ninny
**dupe:** tool, victim, deceive, gull, fool
**duplicate:** bis, replica
" (**colloq.**): ditto
**duarble:** lasting
**duration:** time, space, term, eternity
**dusk:** gloom
**Dutch admiral: Tramp**
" **cheese:** edam
" **city:** Ede
" **coin:** doit
" **commune: Ede**
" **E. Indies Isl.: Java** Timor, Moena,
" **food:** eel
" **geographer: Aa**
" **island:** Aruba [kop
" **measure:** vat, aam,
" " **of length:** roede
" **meter:** el [Steen
" **painter:** Dow, Hals,
" **S. African:** Boer
" **village:** Doorn
" **weight:** aam
**duty:** task, chore, tariff, devoir, impost, tax
**dwarf:** stunt, pygmy, troll, runt
" **negrito of Mindaneo:** aeta [side
**dwell:** live, abide, re-
" **on:** harp
" **upon:** brood [dent
**dweller:** tenant, resi-
**dwelling:** home, hovel, tenement, mansion, abode [anil
**dye:** color, stain, henna,
" **indigo:** anil
**dynamite inventor:** Nobel
**dynamo:** generator
" **part:** armature
**dynasty:** realm

## E

**eager:** anxious, avid, keen, earnest, agog, intent, desirous, afire, ardent, athirst
**eagerness for action:** elan
**eagle:** ern, erne [aery
" **'s nest:** aerie, eyrie,
**eaglestone:** etite [lug
**ear:** auricle, harken, pinna, heed, spike,
" **covering:** earlap
" **lobe:** lug, earlop
" **part:** pinna, lobe
" (**pert. to**): aural, otic
**earache:** otalgia
**early:** betimes, soon
" **alphabetic character:** rune
" " " (**pert. to**): runic
" **Briton:** Pict
" **Christian champion:** Cid
" **Eng. money:** ora
" **Irish tenant:** Saer
" **Norse gods:** Vanir
" **physician:** Galen
" (**poet.**): rath
" **prohibitionist:** Dow
" **Scots:** Picts
" **theologian:** Arius
" " (**pert. to**): Arian
" **Venetian coin** (**var.**): betso
**earn:** gain, merit, deserve, attain, achieve
" **profit:** net
" **with difficulty:** eke
**earnest:** serious, eager, pledge, zealous
**earnings:** salary
**earth:** terra, soil, geal, dirt, loam, world, sod, globe, clay, land
" (**comb. form**): geo, ge, gea
" (**dial.**): erd
" (**latin**): terra
" **mound:** rideau
" (**poet.**): marl [jug
**earthenware:** crockery, faience, crock, pot,
**earthnut:** peanut
**earthquake:** seism [rene
**earthy:** temporal, ter-
" **deposit:** marl
" **iron ore:** ocher
" **material:** mold, clay, marl
**ease:** comfort, allay, relieve, repose, rest, facility, lighten, relief
**easily:** readily, smoothly [irascible
" **angered:** iracund,
" **bent:** limp [frail
" **broken:** crumbly,
" **frightened:** timid
" **moved:** mobile
" **tempted:** frail
" **vaporized:** volatile
**East:** occident, orient, levant
**E. African ascetic:** fakir
" " **cart:** tonga

" " **caste**: dom
" " **cavalryman**: Sowar
" " **cedar**: deodar
" " **cereal grass**: ragee, ragi
" " **chief of police**: daroga, darogah
" " **coin**: anna, pesa, rupee
" " **cymbals**: tal
" " **fiber plant**: da
" " **food staple**: ragi
" " **gateway**: Toran
" " **granary**: gola
" " **grass**: glagah, kasa, rice
" " **hartebeest**: tora
" " **harvest**: rabi
" " **hat plant**: sola
" " **helmet**: topee
" " **herb**: pia, sola, sesame, rea
" " **language**: tamil
" " **litter**: doolie
" " **money**: anna
" " **palm**: nipa [ang
" " " **civet**: mus-
" " **peasant**: ryot
" " **perennial**: ramie [al
" " **pheasant**: mon-
" " **plant**: ramie, benne, sola
" " **poet**: Tagore
" " **sailor**: lascar
" " **soldier**: sepoy
" " **sword**: pata
" " **temple**: pagoda
" " **tent**: pawl
" " **timbertree**: sal, dar, salai, teak
" " **title**: aya, sahib, mian
" " **tree**: banyan, ach, niepa, sal, salai palay, khair, teak
" " **vehicle**: tonga
" " **vine**: odal
" " **water vessel**: lota [ser tola
" " **weight**: bahar,
" " " **sheep**: urial
" " **wood**: eng, aloe
**Eastern inhabitant**: Asian
" **Mediterranean**: Levant [emir
" **potentate**: ameer,
**easy**: comfortable, gentle, facile, simple
" **chair**: rocker
" **to do**: facile
" **job**: sinecure
" **to manage**: docile
" **task (slang)**: snap
**eat**: dine, corrode, devour, sup, gnaw, rust, feed [gnaw
" **away**: erode, erose,
" **sparingly**: diet [ed
**eaten away**: erose, erod-
**eating (pert. to)**: dietary
" **regimen**: diet
**ebb**: recede, decline, subside, reflux, wane, decrease, sink
" **tide**: neap
**ebbing & flowing**: tidal
**eccentric wheel portion**: cam
**Ecclesiast**: fra
**Ecclesiastical council**: synod
" **court**: rota
" **headdress**: miter
" **linen cloth**: fanon
" **plate**: paten
" **residence**: manse
" **scarf & vest**: orale
" **service**: matin
" **unit**: parish
" **vest**: amice, orale, alb, stole [gal
**economical**: sparing, fru-
**economize**: scrimp
**ecstasy**: rapture, bliss
**Ecuador province**: Oro
**eddy**: swirl, whirlpool, pool, vortex
**edge**: lip, brim, rim, brink, sharpen, margin, verge, border, sharpness, sidle, hem
" **of crater**: lip
" **(poet.)**: marge
**edged tool**: axe, edger, ax, sword
**edible**: esculent
" **bulb**: onion
" **fruit portion**: pulp
" **fungus**: morel
" **grain**: cereal
" **mollusk**: asi, clam,
" **root**: garlic, carrot, beet, parsnip, yam, radish, potato
" " **stock**: taro
" **seaweed**: agar laver, dulse [pea
" **seed**: lentil, bean,
" **tuber**: oca, taro
**edict**: decree, arret
**edify**: construct
**edit**: revise, redact, compile publish, issue,
**educated**: liberate, literate, trained, taught instructed, lettered,
**educe**: elicit, evolve evoke [ger, siren
**eel (kind)**: moray, con-
" **trap**: eelpot
**eerie**: uncanny, weird, macabre, scary
**efface**: erase, sponge
**effect**: result, do
**effective as an agent**: causal [womanish
**effeminate**: epicene,
**efficacy**: dint
**efficient**: able, capable
**effigy**: image, doll
**effort**: attempt, exertion, struggle, nisus, essay
**effortless**: easy
**eft**: newt
**egest**: excrete
**egg**: ovum, urge, incite, ova (pl) [lette
**egg dish**: omelet, ome-
" **shaped**: ovate, ovoid, ovated, ooidal,
**egis**: shield
**ego**: self, past
**egress**: exit
**Egyptian**: Copt
" **city**: Cairo
" **cotton**: pima
" **crown**: atef
" **dancing girl**: Alme
" **deity**: Bes, Amon, Min, Ptah, Isis, Ra, Dera, Osiris, Apet Thoth, Serapis, Maat, Sati, Geb
" **gold or silver alloy**: asem
" **king**: Rameses
" **lizard**: adda
" **measure**: dera, ket
" **monarch**: Rameses Tut
" **month**: Apap
" **queen of the gods**: Sati
" **religious body**: ka
" " **heart**: Ab
" " **soul**: Ba
" **river**: Nile
" **sacred bull**: apis
" **singing girl**: Alme, Alma
" **snake**: asp
" **structure**: pyramid
" **sun disk**: aten
" " **God**: Ra, Tem, Ammon, Amon
" **symbolic eye**: uta
**eidolon**: icon, image
**eight**: octet, octave, octa
**eire**: erin
**ejaculation**: alas
**eject**: emit, oust, evict eliminate, expel, out
" **in a jet**: spout
**elan**: dash, zeal, ardor impulse, spirit
**elapse**: pass, expire
**elastic**: resilient, springy
**elate**: gladden excite, exalt
**elation**: joy
**elbow**: ancon
**elder**: senior, prior
**elect**: choose, chosen, prefer, decide
**electric catfish**: raad
" **circuit**: loop
" **current**: A.C., D.C.
" **generator**: dynamo
" **light (kind)**: arc
" **od**: elod
**electrical degree**: ee
" **devise**: coder, reverser, generator
" **particle**: ion, ian
" **transmission**: radio
" **unit**: farad, watt, volt, ampere, ohm, rel
**electricity (kind)**: static
" **(pert. to)**: voltaic
**elegance**: grace, polish, refined [ponent
**element**: neon, factor, arsenic, silver, constituent, barium, com-
" **of borax**: boron
" " **the earth's crust**: silicon
**elemental**: primal, primary, simple
**elementary substance**: metal
**elephant's ear**: taro
" **goad**: ankus,
" **jockey**: mahout
**elevate**: heighten, rear, lift, raise, exalt
**elevated**: lofty, high
" **line**: el [mountain
**elevation of land**: hill,
**elevator carriage**: car
**elf**: gnome, sprite, fay, peri, fairy
**elflike creature**: peri
**elicit**: educe, evoke
**elide**: dele, ignore, annul, suppress, omit
**eliminate**: remove, exclude, eradicate, eject
**elite**: pick
**elk**: eland, moose, stag, wapiti
**elliptical**: oval, ovate
**elocutionist**: reader
**elongate**: lengthen, stretch
**elope**: abscond
**eloquence**: oratory
**else**: other, besides
**elude**: evade, avoid, dodge, escape, baffle
**elusive**: evasive
**elysium**: eden, paradise
**emanation**: aura
**emancipate**: deliver
**embankment**: levee
**embellish**: adorn
**ember**: coal, cinder
**embezzle**: steal [ard
**emblem**: badge, image-symbol, type, stand-
" **of authority**: baton, mace [dent
" " **Neptune**: Tri-
**embrace**: clasp, adopt, hug, comprise, fold, contain [taboret
**embroidery frame**:
**emend**: reform, amend. rectify, revise
**Emerald Isle**: Erin
**emery**: corundum
**eminence**: fame, height, hill [nent, great
**eminent**: noted, promi-
**emissary**: agent
**emit**: eject, erupt, exude, discharge, voice, issue, shed, radiate
" **light & heat**: glow
" **ray**: eradiate, radiate, beam
**emmet**: ant [ary
**emolument**: profit sal-
**emotion**: feeling
**emperor (former)**: tsar
**emphasis**: salience stress, accent [use
**employ**: hire engage,
**emporium**: mart
**empty**: void, inane, bare, vain, deplete
" **form**: blank
**emulate**: vie, rival
**enact**: decree, perform, play, pass
" **law**: legislate
**enamored**: captivated, smit, fond
**encamp**: bivouac, tent
**encase**: case, ensheath, wrap, surround
**enchanted**: bewitched, charmed, rapt
**enchantress**: Medea, siren, Circe [environ
**encircle**: ring, enclasp, surround, belt, hoop,
**encircled**: girt
**enclose**: case, surround, hem, pen, insert
**enclosed**: internal
**enclosure**: pen, yard, cage, coop [corral
" **for cattle**: kraal,
**encore**: bis, again
**encourage**: abet, hearten, egg, cheer, impel
**encroach**: trespass, invade, intrude [per
**encumber**: load, ham-
**end**: terminate, finis, omega, cease, outcome, tip, close, purpose, terminal, finale, climax, limit, desist
" **aimed at**: goal
**endeavored**: striven, tried, aimed, essayed, assayed, attempted
**endings**: finales, finises
**endless**: eternal, everlasting, continual, infinite, perpetual
" **time**: eternity
**endorse**: sanction, OK, ratify, back
**endow**: dower, invest, furnish, vest, gift
**endowment**: fund, dos
**endue**: invest
**endure**: bear, tolerate, abide, stand, sustain, last, withstand
**endure (Scot.)**: dree
**enemy**: foe [vim, force
**energy**: vigor, power,
" **(colloq.)**: pep
**enervate**: weaken, sap
**enfold**: wrap, lap
**enforce**: compel
**engage**: hire, employ, retain, betroth
" **in**: wage
**engender**: breed, produce, exite, occasion, beget, gender [tive
**engine**: motor, locomo-
**engineer**: manage
" **'s shelter**: cab [CE
**engineering degree**: EE,
" **unit**: bel
**engirdle**: zone
**English**: Saxon — see also British
" **actor & manager**: Tree
" **architect**: Wren
" **author**: Dickens,

Milne, Roget, Ramee, Sterne, Reade, Caine, Bronte, Hardy, Opie
" **baby carriage:** pram [ers
" **banker poet:** Rog-
" **bishop:** Ken
" **borough:** Leeds
" **cathedral:** Ely
" " **city:** Truro
" " **passage:** Slype
" **cheese:** stilton
" **chemist & psysicist:** Faraday
" **city:** Leeds, Chester, Wallsend
" **clergyman:** Sterne
" **coins:** pence, shillings, farthings, guineas [Elgar
" **composer:** Arne,
" **country:** Shire, Doset, Kent, Essex
" **dance:** morris
" **dean:** Inge
" **diarist:** Pepys
" **divine:** Inge, Donne
" **dramatist:** Pinero, Udal, Marlowe, Peele, Kyd, Lyly
" **essayist:** Lamb
" **forest tract:** Arden
" **hedgerow:** rew
" **historian:** Grote
" **humorist:** Sterne
" **hymn writer:** Lyte
" **journalist:** Henty
" **law court:** Leet
" **monk:** Bede, Beda
" **murderer:** Aram
" **musician:** Arne
" **nat. emblem:** rose
" **painter:** Turner
" **philologist:** Aram
" **philosopher:** Bacon
" **physician:** Ross
" **poet:** Keats, Spenser, Donne, Blake
" **policeman:** bobby
" **political party:** Tory
" **port:** Preston
" **quaker:** Penn
" **race course & race horse:** Ascot
" **river:** Ure, Avon, Exe, Dee, Thames, Tee, Usk, Aire, Ouse, Tyne, Wye, Tees, Trent, Mersey, Severn [dor, Stuart
" **royal family:** Tu-
" " **stables:** Mews
" **sandy tract of land:** dene [Eton, Rugby
" **school:** Harrow,
" **schoolmaster:** Aram [Deal
" **seaport:** Dover,
" **spy:** Andre
" **stage:** plateau
" **statesman:** Grey, Pitt [tram
" **streetcar:** tramcar,
" **surgeon:** Lister
" **title:** baronet [Ely
" **town:** Eton, Leeds,
" **weight:** stone [ver
" **wood pigeon:** cul-
**engrave by dots:** stipple
" " **a nee lle:** etch
**engraving:** cut [rapt
**engrossed:** engaged,
**enigma:** mystery, riddle, charade, puzzle,
**enjoin:** command, bid, press, forbid [ure
**enjoyment:** fun, pleas-
**enlarge:** spread, magnify, dilate, increase, expand, amplify, grow
**enlist:** enroll, recruit
**enliven:** animate, exhilarate, quicken
**enmesh:** tangle, entangle, enlace,
**enmity:** hatred, rancor
**ennead:** nine
**ennoble:** elevate, honor
**ennui:** boredom
**enormous:** huge, large
**Enos's father:** Seth
**enough (poet.):** enow
**enrage:** madden, anger, inflame
**enrich:** fatten, lard
**enroll:** enlist, record, poll, enter, join
**ensconce:** hide
**ensemble:** whole, decor
**ensign:** banner
**ensnare:** tangle, trap, entrap, net [result
**ensue:** succeed, follow,
**entangle:** mat, embroil, snare, ravel, mesh, ensnarl, knot, web
**enter:** pierce, record, penetrate, register, enroll, insert, join
**enterprise:** venture
**entertain:** amuse, treat, regale, beguile, fete, divert, harbor
" **royally:** regale, fete
**enthusiasm:** pep, spirit, elan, ardor, verve
**enthusiast:** zealot
**enthusiastic:** eager, ardor, keen
**entice:** inveigle, attract, tempt, allure, charm, invite, lure, decoy, win
" **(var.):** tole
**enticement:** lure, bait
**entire:** total, complete, whole, integral, all
" **man:** egos, ego
**entitle:** name, dominate, designate, qualify, dub
**entity:** ens, unit
**entomb:** inter
**entrance:** charm, adit, entry, portal, ingress, doorway, gate, inlet, gateway, door, transport, delight
" **halls:** atria, foyers
**entranced:** rapt
**entrap:** noose, deceive, decoy, trepan, ensnare, bag
**entreat:** pray, beseech, supplicate, crave, implore, plead, request, adjure, woo, beg
**entrepot:** depot
**entrust:** consign, confide, commit
**entry:** entrance, access engress, passage, item
" **in an account:** item, debit
**entwined:** wove, laced
**environ:** surround, encircle [medium
**environment:** setting,
**envoy:** legate
**envy:** covet, jealousy
**enwrap:** roll
**enzyme:** ase
**eon:** age [noble, grand
**epic:** heroic, poem,
" **poem:** epos, epo, epopee [gourmet
**epicure:** gourmand,
**epidemic:** pest
**Episcopal pastor:** rector
**episode:** event, scene, incident
**epistle:** letter, missive
**epithet:** name [mary
**epitome:** synopsis, sum-
**epoch:** age, era, event
**epochal:** eral
**equal:** peer, iso, even, equitable, compeer, coordinate, tie, same, adequate, par [iso
" **(comb. form):** pari,
**equality:** par, parity
**equalize:** even
**equally:** alike, as
**equilibrium:** poise
**equine:** horse, mare, ass
**equip:** rig, attire, gear
" **with crew:** man
**equipment:** tackle, rig, gear [fair
**equitable:** even, equal,
" **part:** share
**era:** age, period, time, epoch, date
" **(pert. to):** eral
**eradicate:** eliminate, uproot, remove, erase
**erase:** delete, dele, efface expunge, cancel
**eraser:** rubber
**ere:** soon, anon
**erect:** rear, construct, raise, upright, build
**eremite:** hermit, recluse
**Erin:** Eire
**ermine:** stoat
**eroded:** eat, corroded
**err:** blunder, sin, slip, stray
**errand:** mission
**errant:** arrant, erratic
**erroneous:** mistaken, false
**error:** misstep, mistake, blunder, slip, fallacy
" **in printing:** erratum, errata (pl.)
**Erse:** Gaelic
**erudite critic:** pundit
**erudition:** lore, wisdom, learning
**escape:** evade, leakage, flee, elude, avoid
" **(slang):** lam
**eschew:** avoid, shun
**escort:** convoy, usher, accompany, squire, conduct, attend
**esker:** asar, osar, os
**Eskimo canoe:** kayak, umiak
" **hut:** iglu, igloo
" **settlement:** Etah
**esne:** serf
**esoteric:** inner
**espy:** detect, descry
**essays:** theses, tries, tests, efforts, papers, attempts, themes
**essence:** attar, substance, pith, perfume, yolk, nature, soul
**essential:** vital, virtual, necessary, needful
" **part:** element, factor, vital, pith
**establish:** settle, rear, base, instate, set, institute, plant
" **ownership:** claim
**estate:** manor, property
**esteem:** regard, revere, estimate, value, honor, prize, respect, consider [judge, appraise
**estimate:** rate, calculate, measure gage, rank, esteem, assess,
**estimation:** repute
**estop:** plug, bar, impede, hinder, obstruct
**estrange:** alienate
**eternal:** deathless, endless, everlasting, timeless, ceaseless, infinite
**ether:** ester
**ethereal:** airy, aerial
**ethereal salt:** ester
**ethical:** moral [ras
**Ethiopian title:** negus,
**ethnic:** pagan [lars
**Etruscan gods:** lares,
**eulogy:** eloge, praise
**euphony:** meter
**European:** Pole, Dane, Finn, Swede, Slav, Lapp, Lett, Serb, Slovak, Croat
" **bass:** brasse
" **bird:** serin, motacil, ortolan, pie
" **bison:** aurochs
" **blackbird:** merle, ousel
" **capital city:** Riga
" **cavalryman:** Hussar [ant, peasandry
" **countryman:** peas-
" **deer:** roe
" **dormouse:** lerot
" **finch:** serin, terin, citril, tarin
" **fish:** id
" **gulf:** Riga, Aden
" **gull:** mew
" **herring:** sprat
" **juniper:** cade
" **kite:** glede
" **lime:** teil [Alps
" **mts.:** alpine, ural,
" **native:** Serb, Croat
" **oriole:** loriot
" **rabbit:** cony
" **river:** Saar, Bug
" **thrush:** mavis, ousel
" **tree:** sorb, lentisk
**Eva's friend:** Topsy
**evade:** elude, dodge, shun, escape, baffle, shirk, avoid, gee
**evanescent:** fleety
**evangel:** gospel
**evasive:** shifty, deceitful, elusive
**even:** unvaried, smooth, equalize, flush, qual, balance, level
" **(poet.):** een
**evening party:** soiree
" **(poet.):** een, eve
" **song:** serenade
" **star:** vesper
**event:** episode, incident, deed, epoch, fact
**ever:** once, aye
" **(poet.):** eer [myrtle
**evergreen shrub:** box, furze, holly, oleander,
" **tree:** pine, cedar, fir carob, spruce, olive, yew, holly, balsam
**everlasting:** eternal, endless, agelong, unending [etern
" **(poet.):** eterne,
**every:** each, complete
**everyone:** each, all
**evict:** object, banish, expel, eject, oust
**evidence:** proof, show
**evident:** patent apparent, clear, plain, manifest, obvious
**evil:** bad, bane, sin, ill, iniquity, sinful, harm, corrupt, vice
" **act:** crime
" **intent:** malice
" **(prefix):** mal
" **spirit:** demon, devil, satan, fiend
**evince:** show, manifest, display, exhibit
**evoke:** educe, elicit
**evolve:** educe, develop, derive
**ewer:** jug [literal
**exact:** demand, accurate, precise, wreak,
" **counterpart:** match
" **likeness:** image
" **reasoning:** logic
" **satisfaction:** avenge, revenge
**exaggerate:** overtell, overstate, overdo
**exalt:** laud, raise, elevate, honor
" **the spirits of:** elate
**examination:** test
" **of accounts:** audit
**examine:** test, scrutinize, inspect, scan, overhaul [sift, probe
" **critically:** censor,

**example:** norm, case
**exasperate:** anger, irritate [anger
**exasperation:** ire, heat,
**excavation:** pit, hole, cut, mine
" **for extracting ore:** stope [pass
**exceed:** surpass, better, transcend, overstep,
**exceedingly:** extremely, greatly, very
**excel:** top, surpass, cap, outdo [tue
**excellence:** merit, vir-
**excellent:** fine, capital
" **(slang):** super [bar
**except:** but, save, exclude, unless, omit,
**excess of solar over lunar year.:** epact
**exchange:** trade, swap, barter
" **for money:** sell
" **premium or discount:** agio
**excite:** elate, arouse, stir, startle
**excited:** agog, nervous
**exclamation:** ahem, ah, ho, alas, fie, tut, wow, rats, expletive, ouch
" **of contempt:** pah, foh [bah, tush, ugh
" " **disgust:** aw, fie,
" " **pity:** ay
**exclude:** debar, eliminate, bar, ban, except
**exclusive:** select
" **person:** snob [only
**exclusively:** solely, all,
**excrete:** egest [jaunt
**excursion:** tour, tramp,
**excuse:** apology, plea, alibi, pardon, pretext, extenuate
" **for not appearing in court:** essoin
**exercise:** lesson, use
" **control:** dominate, preside
" **sovereign power:** reign [steam
**exhalation:** breathe,
**exhale:** emit
**exhaust:** deplete, spend, sap, fag, waste
**exhibit:** evince, display, show, stage, wear
" **malign satisfaction:** gloat [cant
**exhibition:** show, pag-
**exigency:** need, demand
**exile:** deport, banish
**exist:** live
**existence:** esse, alive, ens, life, being, entity
**existing in name only:** titular
**exit:** egress, door
**exonerate:** clear, acquit
**exorbitant interest:** usury
**exotic:** foreign
**expand:** dilate stretch, grow, distend, open, enlarge, [tract
**expanse:** room, area,
**expansive:** wide
**expatriate:** banish
**expect:** hope, await, anticipate
**expectation:** hope
**expectorate:** spit
**expedient:** politic
**expedition:** trek, safari
**expel:** oust, eject, evict, banish, deport [bar
" **from the bar:** dis-
**expend:** spend, pay
**expense:** cost, outlay
**expensive:** dear, costly
**experience:** feel, undergo, live
**experiences regret:** repent
**experiment:** test [ace
**expert:** skilled, adept,
**expiate:** atone
**expiration:** end [die
**expire:** perish, elapse,
**explain:** interpret, define, solve [gosh, gee
**expletive (mild):** egad,
**explode:** blast, detonate, burst [bolide
**exploding meteor:** bolis,
**exploit:** feat, deed, gest, act, geste (var.)
**explosion:** blast, pop
" **devise:** cap, petard, torpedo
**explosive:** TNT, tonite
**expose:** bare, detect, open, display, reveal
" **to moisture:** ret
" " **ridicule:** pillory
**exposition:** fair
**expostulate:** protest
**express:** voice
" **disapproval:** deprecate, rebuke
" **displeasure:** resent
" **gratitude:** thank
" **official disapproval:** veto [term
**expression:** phrase,
" **of approval:** smile
" " **contempt:** pish, sneer, hiss
" " **inquiry:** eh
" **peculiar to a lang.:** idiom
" **of pity:** ay
" " **sorrow:** alas
**expressive action:** gesture [erase, sponge
**expunge:** delete, dele,
**exquisite:** fine, elegant, lovely [prolong
**extend:** spread, lie, stretch, run, reach,
" **the depth:** deepen
" **over:** lap, span, cover [spread, ran
**extended:** long, lengthy,
" **view:** panorama
**extent:** area, ambit, degree, scope, span, length, size, limit, range [igate, excuse
**extenuate:** palliate, mit-
**exterior:** surface, out, outer
" **of bark:** ross
" **(anat.):** ectal
**external:** outer, cortical, out, outside
" **appearance:** face, mien, guise
" **(comb. form):** ecto
**extinct:** dead
" **bird:** moa, dodo
" **reptile:** dinosaur
**extinguish:** quench
**extirpate:** root, destroy
**extol:** praise, laud, boast
**extra:** spare, more, over
" **payment:** bonus
" **supply:** relay, reservoir [wring, educt
**extract:** draw, excerpt,
" **fat:** render
**extravagant:** wasteful, prodigal, outre
**extreme:** limit, dire, radical, intense, ultra, rank [ing, end, very
**extremely:** so, exceed-
**exude:** emit, discharge, ooze, seep [elate
**exult:** rejoice, crow,
**eye:** ogle, orb, observe, watch, view, optic, vision, regard, sight
" **of bean:** hilum
" **coat:** retina
" **part:** retina, uvea, irian, pupil, lens, iris, cornea, eyeball
" **(pert. to):** optic
" **(Scot.):** ee, een (pl.)
" **(slang):** glim
" **socket (anat.):** orbit
**eyeglass:** monocle, lens
**eyelashes:** cilia
**eyelid infection:** sty
**eyes:** peepers

## F

**fable:** story, myth
" **maker:** Aesop
**fabric:** material, voile, moire, rayon, terry, web, leno, etoile
" **filling:** welt, weft
" **(glossy):** satin
**fabricate:** make
**fabulous bird:** roc [front
**face:** confront, prestige,
" **of a coin:** head
" **downward:** prone
" **of a gem:** facet
" **hair:** beard
" **on hewn stone:** panel
" **up a glacier:** stoss
" **value:** par
" **with stone:** revet
**facetious:** witty, jocose
**facial bone:** jaw [grin
" **expression:** pout,
**facility:** ease, art
**facing direction of glacier's move:** stoss
**fact:** reality, datum, truth [clique
**faction:** side, sect, party,
**factor:** manager, agent, gene, element
**factory:** mill, plant
**facts:** data [hobby
**fad:** whim, fancy, craze,
**fade:** wane, vanish, pale
**Faerie Queen:** Una
" " **author:** Spenser [Amoret, Alma
" " **character:** Ate,
**fag:** tire, fatigue, weary
**fail:** peter, miss, disappoint, default
" **in duty:** lapse
" **to follow suit:** reneg [get
" " **remember:** for-
" **(slang):** flunk
**failure (slang):** dud, flop [weak
**faint:** dim, swoon, pale,
**fainting spell:** syncope
**fair:** blond, decent, just, impartial, comely, bazaar
**fairy:** elf, sprite, fay
" **chief:** Puck
" **queen:** Titania, Una, Mab
**fairylike:** elfin
**faith:** troth, belief, credit, confidence, trust
**faithful:** liege, true, leal, loyal, devoted
" **(poet.):** leal [falsify
**fake:** fraud, feign, sham
**fakir:** yogi
**falcon:** lanneret, peregrine, eagle, hawk
**fall:** drop, tumble, subside, plummet, slip
" **back:** retreat
" " **in former state:** relapse [drip
" **in drops:** patter,
" " " **(obs.):** drib
" **forward:** topple
" **from power:** wane
" **headlong:** pitch
" **into disuse:** lapse
" **profusely:** pour
" **short:** lack, fail
" **suddenly:** plop
" **upon:** assail
**falling:** cadent
" **star:** meteor
**false:** erroneous, lie, untrue, sham, spurious, fake
" **gods:** idols
" **idea:** fallacy
" **jewelry:** paste
" **move:** misstep
" **report:** canard
**falsehood:** tale, lie, fib
**falsify:** forge, fake
**falter:** waver, fail, hesitate, lag [household
**family:** genus, kindred,
**famous:** noble, noted, renowned, eminent
" **murder & murderer:** Aram
" **soprano:** Patti, Lind
" **uncle:** Sam
**fan:** winnow, devotee, rooter, cool
**fanatical:** rabid
" **partisan:** zealot
**fanciful:** unreal, dreamy
**fancy:** fad, whim, idea, dream, caprice, vagary, ideate
" **(poet.):** ween
**fane:** temple, sanctuary
**fanon:** orale
**fantasy:** dream
**far:** remote, away, advanced, widely
" **across:** wide
" **down:** deep, low
" **off:** remote, distant
" " **(comb. form):** tele
" **reaching:** long
**farce:** comedy, mockery [do, prosper
**fare:** passenger, diet,
**farewell:** ave, adieu, tata, adios
**farinaceous:** mealy
" **food:** sago
**farm:** till, plow [shed
" **bldg.:** silo, barn,
**farmer:** planter, cultivator
**Faroe Isl. Windstorm:** Oe
**farther than:** beyond
**farthest:** endmost
" **in:** inmost
**fascinating woman:** siren, charmer
**fascination:** spell
**fashion:** style, mode, shape, mold, vogue, fad, frame
" **follower:** modist
**fast:** rapid, fleet, firm, speedy, securely, secure, diet, apace, firmly [brace
**fasten:** nail, lace, tie, pin, seal, glue, tether, bolt, secure, rivet, bind, paste, moor, attach, lock, clamp
**fastener:** hasp, snapper, snap, pin, lock, bolt, dowel, strap, clamp, clasp, rivet, cleat
**fastidious:** finical, elegant, refined, nice, dainty
**fat:** obese, obesity, suet, plane, fleshy, plump, portly, oily, lard
**fatal:** lethal, dire, mortal, deadly
**fate:** doom, lot, destiny, kismet
**father:** sire, papa, abbe, abba, parent, dad, pa, padre, beget,
" **(Arabic):** abu
" **of engraving:** Pye
**fathom:** delve
**fatigue:** overdo, harass, tire, weary, irk, fag
**fatty:** adipose
" **fruit:** olive

**fatuous:** inane, insensate, silly
**faucet:** tap, spigot
**fault:** defect, foible, slip, blemish, offense
" **finding:** captious
**faultless:** ideal [bad
**faulty:** wrong, amiss
**faun:** satyr
**favor:** boon, prefer
**favorable:** good
**favorite:** pet, dear
**fawn:** cringe
**fawning:** servile
**fay:** elf, sprite
**fear:** awe, terror, dread, panic [timid, afraid
**fearful:** dire, nervous,
**fearless:** daring
**feast:** regale, fete, banquet, repast, fiesta
**feat:** deed, act, exploit, stunt
**feather:** pennas, plumage, plume, pinna
" **shaft:** scape
**featherlike:** pinnate
**federation:** league, union
**fee:** hire, charge, payment, price
**feeble:** anile, lame, infirm, weak
**feebleminded:** anile
**feed:** nourish, nurture, eat, graze, subsist
" **to the full:** sate
**feeding box:** manger
**feel:** sense, touch, grope
" **discontent:** repine
" **indignant at:** resent [regret
" **sorryfor:** repent,
" **sympathy or pity:** yearn
" **want of:** miss
**feeler:** tentacle, antenna, palp
**feet (having):** pedate
" **(of the):** pedal
**feign:** pretend, sham, simulate, act, fake
" **sickness:** malinger
**felicity:** bliss, happiness
**felony:** crime
**female demon:** ogress
" **elephant:** cow
" **ruff:** ree, reeve
" **saint:** ste
" **sandpiper:** ree
" **singer:** diva
" **warrior:** amazon
**fen:** swamp, moor, bog, marsh, morass
**fence:** rail, bulwark
" **barrier:** bars
" **picket:** pale, paling
" **steps:** stiles
**fencer cry:** sasa, touche
" **dummy:** pel
**fencing leaping movement:** volt [tierce
" **position:** carte,
" **term:** touche, riposte
" **weapon:** rapier, foil, epee, sword
**fend:** guard, parry
**feral:** savage, wild
**ferine:** wild [wine
**fermented drink:** mead,
" **liquor:** ale, beer
**fern leaf:** frond [wild
**ferocious:** grim, savage,
**fertile spot:** oasis, oases
**fertilizer:** marl
**fervent:** warm, eager
**fervid:** ardent, intense
**fervor:** ardor, zeal
**fester:** rankle
**festival:** fete, gala, fair, carnival, fiesta
**festive:** joyous, gala
**festivity:** gala
**fetch:** bring
**fetid:** olid
**fetish:** obi
**fetter:** bind, iron, band, shackle, chain
**feudal estate:** feod, fief
**fiat:** decree [thread
**fiber:** hemp, bast, ramie,
" **of Amer. aloe:** pita
" " **peacock feathers:** marl
" **plant:** aloe, ramie, sisal, cotton, flax, istle, hemp [fealty
**fidelity:** constancy,
**fidgety:** restive
**field:** lea, arena
" **of activity:** terrain
" **(arch.):** glebi
" **of granular snow:** neve
**fiend:** satan, devil [wild
**fierce:** grim, savage,
**fiery:** hot, intense
**fiesta:** holiday, festival
**fig (kind):** eleme, elemi
**fight:** scrap, battle, fray, melee, strive, combat
" **against:** resist
" **(general):** melee
**fighter:** warrior
**figure:** digit, calculate
" **out (slang):** dope
" **of speech:** trope, metaphor, simile,
**filament:** hair, thread
**file:** rasp, row
**fill:** sate, saturate
" **with air:** aerate
" " **mud:** silt
" " **rev. fear:** awe
**filled pastry shell:** dariole, eclair
**fillet for hair:** snood
" **at top of column:** orle
**filly:** foal
**film:** negative
" **on copper:** patina
" " **liquid:** scum
**filter:** purify, strain, sieve [timate
**final:** last, decisive, ul-
**finale:** end, termination, finish, close, ending, coda
**financial:** monetary
" **instrument:** mortgage [terin
**finch:** serin, linnet,
**find:** locate, discover
" **fault:** nag, carp
" **out:** detect, learn, see
**fine:** dainty, thin, nice, mulct, amerce, keen,
" **for murder:** cro
" **& delicate:** lacy
" **dirt:** dust
" **ravelings:** lint
**finger game:** mora
**finger or toe:** digit
**finial:** epi, canopy
" **on pagoda:** tee
**finical:** fussy, nice
**finis:** nding, end
**finished:** over, done, closed, completed
" **(poet.):** oer
**Finnish city:** Abo
**fire:** shoot, ignite, kindle, inflame
" **basket:** cresset
" **(comb. form):** .yr, Igni
" **feeder:** stoker
" **particle:** spark
" **worshipper:** parsee
**firearm:** pistol, weapon, gun, piece, shotgun, repeater, rifle
**firecracker:** petard, retard
**fired clay:** tile
**firedog:** ardiron
**fireman:** stoker [grate
**fireplace:** ingle (Scot),
" **facing:** mantel [hob
" **part:** spit, grate,
**fireside:** hearth
**firm:** stable, solid, immutable, steady, iron, adamant, secure, fast
**firmament:** sky, heaven
**first:** erst, prime, foremost, original, initial, primary, chief, primal, preeminent
" **high priest:** Aaron
" **king of Israel:** Saul
" **letter:** initial
" **magnitude star:** altair, vega
" **man (pert. to):** adamic, adamical
" **name:** forename
" **Pope:** Peter [seed
" **principle:** arche,
" **team (colloq.):** varsity [snapper, ide
**fish:** perch, gar, shad, par, scrod, hake, ray, id, carp, dace, bass, sprat, ray, sturgeon, darter, opah, wrasse, tarpon, ling, eelpout, chub, sennet, angle,
" **basket:** creel
" **eggs:** roe
" **like vertebrate:** ray
" **hawk:** osprey
" **from moving boat:** troll
" **net:** trawl, seine
" **part:** fin, scale
" **sauce:** alec
" **(small):** sparat, id, sardine, shiner, dace, minnow, smelt darter, fry, ide
" **spear:** gig, gaff
" **trap:** eelpot
" **which clings to another fish:** remora
**fisherman:** seiner, angler
**fishhook:** angle
**fishline:** snell
" **(part):** barb
**fishing device:** net
**fissile rock:** shale
**fissure:** rime, rent, cleft, rima, seam, cranny rift, crack,
**fit:** adapt, proper, prepared, correct, adapted, apt, suit, ready
" **of anger:** rage
" **one inside another:** nest
" **of passion:** tantrum
" **for plowing:** arable
" **together:** mesh, piece, nest
**five sided figure:** pentagon [tad, lustrum
" **year period:** pen-
**fix:** repair, mend, correct, set, adjust, settle [anchor
" **firmly:** brace, root,
" **grade of:** rate [dow
" **income upon:** en-
**fixed:** stationary, stable, steady
" **allowance:** ration
" **charge:** rate, fee
" **course:** rote
" **ratio:** rate
" **time:** term
" **value on:** assess
**flaccid:** limp
**flag:** standard, banneret banner, sag, streamer, iris, pennon, pennant, lanquish, droop
**flail:** beat
**flaky:** scaly, laminar
" **mineral:** mica
**flambeau:** torch
**flamboyant:** ornate
**flame:** blaze, flare
**flaming:** aglow, afire
**flap:** tab, fold [glint
**flash:** spark, sparkle
**flashy:** sporty, gaudy
**flat:** level, tenement, plane, insipid, tame, vapid, apartment
" **bodied fish:** skate
" **bottle:** flask
" **bottom boat:** bateau, scow, punt, barge, keel, ark
" **disc:** plate
" **piece:** slab, fin
" **stick:** ferule
" **stone:** flag, slab
" **surface:** area, plane
**flatfish:** dab, sole, skate, ray, turbot
**flatter:** adulate
**flattery:** blarney
**flaunt:** parade
**flavor:** salt, sapor, aroma, savor, taste, anise
**flawless:** perfect
**flax (dial):** lin
**flax fiber:** tow
**flaxen fabric:** linen
**flaxseed:** linseed
**flay:** beat, skin, cane, reprove [escape, shun
**flee:** vanish, hasten,
" **(slang):** lam
**fleece:** despoil, swindle, shear, cheat
**fleer:** mock, scoff
**flesh:** meat
" **of calf:** veal
**fleshy:** fat [date, drupe
" **fruit:** pome, pear,
**fleur delis:** lis, iris
**flexible:** lithe, elastic, limber, pliable, willowy, pliant
" **branch:** withe
" **pipe:** hose
" **shoot:** bine
" **& tough:** withy
**flicker:** flare, waver
**flight:** aviation
**flightless bird:** moa
**flinch:** wince [hurl
**fling:** sling, throw, toss,
**flip:** toss, snap, fillip
**flippant:** glib
**flit:** dart, skim, flutter
**float:** raft, drift, waft, swim, ride, buoy, sail
**floating fish box:** car
" **in water:** natant
**flock:** herd, troop, bevy
" **of seals:** pod
**flog:** lash, tan, beat, cane, trounce
**flood:** deluge, torrent, inundate, overflow, spate
**floor:** story, down
**floral leaf:** petal, sepal
" **organs:** stamens
**florid:** ruddy, ornate
**Florida bird:** ani [do
" **city:** Tampa, Orlan-
" **Indian:** Seminole
**floss silk:** sleave
**flounder:** dab, grovel
**flour receptacle:** bin
**flourish:** wield, prosper, blossom, brandish
**flout:** deride, sneer, mock, gibe, jeer
**flow:** run, stream, pour, abundance, recover
" **against:** lap
" **back:** ebb
" **(comb. form):** rheo
" **forth:** emanate
" **off:** drain
" **out:** emit
" **through:** seep
" **of water:** flood
**flower:** blossom, bloom
" **border:** platband
" **cluster:** corymb, raceme, cyme
" **part:** stamen, petal,

sepal, corolla, spadix, anther, pericarp
**flowering plant:** arum, lupin, canna, fern, yucca, lupine, spirea, geranium
" **shrub:** lilac, waratah, japonica, sumac, oleander, azalea, oleaster, spirea
" **water plant:** lotus
**flowerless plant:** fern, lichen, moss
**fluctuate:** waver, veer, vary, sway
**flue:** chimney, pipe
**fluent:** glib
**fluid:** liquid
" **rock:** lava [agitate
**flurry:** ado, agitation,
**flush:** even, redden
" **success:** elate
**flutter:** wave, flit [flit
**fly:** tsetse, bot, gnat, soar, hasten, aviate,
**flying Dutchman heroine:** Senta
" **water:** spray
**foal:** filly [er, spume
**foam:** froth, suds, lath-
**fob:** pendent, cheat
**focus:** center, concentrate [grass, silage
**fodder:** hay, ensilage,
" **pit & tank:** silo
**fog:** vapor, mist, obscure, haze
**foible:** fault, weakness
**foil:** frustrate, outwit
**fold:** plait, ply, plicate, flap, ruga, rimple, lap, crease, loop, embrace, pleat, seam
" **on animal's throat:** dewlap
" **of coat:** lapel
" **over & stitch:** hem
" **of sail:** reef
**foliage:** leaves
**follow:** ensue, trace, result, trail, chase, tail
" **closely:** dog, heel, tag
**follower:** adherent, fan
" **of (suffix):** ite [next
**following:** after, sect,
**foment:** incite, abet
**fond:** attached, loving, doting, dote
**fondle:** caress, nestle, pet cosset
**food:** aliment, meat
" **fish:** salema, tuna, ling, cero, mackerel, pompane, trout, shad, smelt, mullet, alewife, salmon, robalo, spot cod
" **of the gods:** ambrosia [na
" **from heaven:** man-
" **medium for bacteria:** agar [grub
" **(slang):** eats, chow,
**fool:** ninny, dolt, deceive, dupe, dunce, jester, ass
**foolish:** daft, mad, unwise, daffy [tard
" **person:** simp, do-
**foolishness:** folly
**foot:** iamb
" **(comb. form):** podo
" **like part:** pes [step
" **part:** toe, sole, in-
" **pedal:** treadle, lever
" **(pert. to):** pedal
" **traveler:** tramp
**footless:** apod, apodal
" **animal:** apod, apoda (pl.) [track
**footprint:** step, trace,
**fop:** dude, dandy
**for:** pro, since, per, to
" **example:** as
" " **(abbr.):** eg, ec
" **fear that:** lest
**foray:** raid, pillage
**forbear:** parent, ancestor, desist
**forbearing:** patient
**forbid:** ban, tabu, prohibit, veto, vote, enjoin [banned
**forbidden:** taboo, tabu,
**forbidding:** grim
**forbode:** portend, omen
**force:** vis, power, dint, pressure, compel, impel, constrain, drive, vim, urge, violence, energy
" **air thru nose:** snort
" **back:** repel
" **of a blow:** brunt
" **down:** ram
" **(Latin):** vis
" **of men:** posse
**forceful:** dynamic, energetic [lent, emphatic
**forcible:** cogent, vio-
**forcibly:** amain
**ford:** wade
**fore:** front
" **limbs:** wings, arms
**forebear:** spare, parent, ancestor
**forebode:** augur
**foreboding:** omen, dire
**forefather:** elder, ancestor
**forego:** waive, remit
**forehead:** brow [strange
**foreign:** alien, exotic,
" **(comb. form):** xeno
**foreman:** boss
**foremost:** first, front, prime, main [ing,
**forenoon:** morn morn-
**forerun:** precede, usher
**forerunner:** herald
**forest:** trees, woods, woodland, wood
" **divinity:** nymph
" **warden:** ranger
" **(pert. to):** sylvan
**forestless tract:** steppe
**foretell:** predict, presage, prophesy
" **(Scot.):** spae
**foretoken:** omen [aye
**forever:** eternally, ay,
**forewarning:** portent
**forfeit:** lose
**forge:** falsify, frame
**forgive:** pardon, remit
**fork:** divide
**forlorn:** bereft, lorn
**form:** shape, ceremony, mold, create, frame, make, variety, style
" **of architect.:** ionic
" " **croquet:** roque
" " **Esperanto:** ido
" **into groove:** channel
" **hollows in:** pit
" **into jelly:** gel [ate
" " **league:** feder-
" **in the mind:** ideate
" **(pert. to):** modal
" **in small grains:** pearl [bank
" **into a terrace:** em-
" **of worship:** ritual, liturgy [precise
**formal:** distant, stiff,
" **address:** lecture
" **choice:** election
" **dance:** ball, hop, prom
**formative:** plastic
**former:** erst, quondam, sometime, previous, whilim, old, ex
" **autocrat:** tsar
" **czar:** Ivan
" **days:** pasts, past
" **English coin:** groat, ryal
" **European coin:** ecu
" **German monetary unit:** taler
" **public conveyance:** stage
" **Roman emperor:** Otto, Nero
" **Russian ruler:** tsar, Lenin, Paul
" **Span. coin:** real, peseta, pistole
" **times:** yore
" " **(poet.):** eld
**formerly:** erst, once, erewhile, onetime, ago
" **(prefix):** ex
**forsaken:** lorn
**fort:** castle
**fortification:** redan, ravelin, abatis, redoubt
**fortify:** arm, strengthen, man
**fortress:** castle, citadel, rampart, stronghold
**fortune:** lot, fate, hap, chance [ist, sibyl
" **teller:** seer, palm-
**forward:** ahead, on, anterior, to, along, send, front, transmit
" **part:** front, fore
**foster:** nurse, cultivate, cherish, rear, promote
**foul:** dirty, unfair, rank
**foundation:** base, basis, root, bottom, bed
" **timber:** sill
**fountain:** well
**four (comb. form):** tetra
**fourscore & ten:** ninety
**fourth calif:** ali, uli
**fowl:** hen, goose, bird
**fox:** tod
" **(female):** vixen
" **(Scot.):** tod
" **(var.):** renard
**foxy:** sly, wily [brawl
**fracas:** melee, quarrel,
**fracture:** break [brittle
**fragile:** frail, delicate,
**fragment:** shread, bit, scarp, tatter, crumb, relic, shard, chip, snip
" **of cloth:** rag
" **left at a meal:** ort
" **ointment:** spikenard
" **of pottery:** sherd
**fragrance:** aroma [ous
**fragrant:** olent, redolent, sweet, aromatic, odor-
" **oil:** attar
" **seed:** anise [tiara
" **shrub:** rosemary,
**frail:** fragile, slender, puny, weak, delicate
**frame:** forge, compose, adjust, fashion, devise, shape, form
" **of bed:** bedstead
" " **a car:** chassis
" " **mind:** mood
" " **vessel:** hull
" " **bars:** grate
" " **crossing laths:** lattice
" " **slats:** crate
" " **a window:** casing [trestle
**framework:** cadre, rack,
**frank:** candid, honest, open
**frankness:** candor
**frantic:** desperate, frenzied, mad, furious
**fraternal:** brotherly
**fraud:** cheat, swindle, faker, fake, trickery, humbug, deceit, jape
**fray:** melee, fight, setto
**free:** rid, clear, release, gratis, deliver, independent, unchecked loose, rescue, liberate
" **of impurities:** refine, cleanse, clean
" **from restraint:** loosen, unbend
**freedom:** liberty
" **of access:** entree
**freeholder:** yeoman
**freeze:** ice, refrigerate, congeal, gelate
**freight:** lade, cargo
" **boat:** barge, ark, flatboat [boose
" **car:** gondola, ca-
**French:** Gallic
" **African capital city:** Tunis
" **annuity & security:** rente
" **article:** le, un, la
" **artist:** Dore
" **astronomer:** Pons
" **author:** Loti, Gide, Dumas, Verne. Hugo, Renan
" **bond:** rente
" **brandy:** cognac
" **cheese:** Sens
" **city:** Nantes, Arles, Nancy, Rennes, Sens, Caen, Lyons, Ariens, Ay, Sevres, Cannes, Amiens, Lille, Nice, Limoges, Aix, Reims
" **clergyman:** abbe
" **coin:** centime, sou, franc, ecu, obole
" **composer:** Widor, Lalo, Ravel
" **dept.:** Orne, Nord, Somme, Eure, Isere, Oise, Ain
" **dugout:** abri
" **emperor:** Napoleon
" **illustrator:** Dore
" **income:** rente
" **Indo China capital:** Hanoi [Ney
" **marshall:** Murat,
" **painter:** Tissot, Dore, Corot, Degas, Manet, Gelee, Monet
" **parliament:** senat
" **poet:** Verlaine,
" **porcelain:** limoges
" **priest:** abbe [at
" **revolutionist:** Mar-
" **river:** Isere, Oise, Marne, Lys, Meuse, Saar, Saone, Ain, Rhone, Loire, Seine, Vesle, Scarpe, Yser, Somme, Orne
" **scientist:** Curie
" **sculptor:** Rodin
" **shooting match:** tir
" **soldier:** poilu, chasseur
" **symbol:** lily
" **theologian:** Calvin
" **town:** Valence, Nerac, Bareges, Lens, Ay, Laon
" **village:** Ham
**Frenchman:** Gaul
**frenzied:** frantic, berserk, frenetic [amok
" **manner:** amuck,
**frenzy:** furor, delirium, rage
**frequent:** haunt [sort
**frequented place:** re-
**frequently:** oft, often
**fresh:** modern, new, brisk, recent
" **supply:** relay
" **water fish:** dace, bass, id, ide, roach, ellpout, burbot
" " **porpoise:** inia
**freshet:** flood, spate
**fret:** stew, nag, worry, chafe, agitate, repine, irritate, fuss, annoy,

vex [pettish, petulant
**fretful:** peevish, testy,
**friar:** monk, fra
**fried meatball:** rissole
**friend:** ally, crony, ami, chum, companion
" **(greeting to Indian):** netop
**friendly:** amicable, kind
" **associate:** ally
**friendship:** amity
**fright:** terror, panic, awe
**frighten:** alarm, startle, scare [stiff
**frigid:** cold, icy, arctic,
**frisk:** gambol, sport, caper, frolic, romp
**frivolous:** inane, gay
**frog:** rana, rama, anuran, anura
**froglike:** ranine
**frolic:** caper, spree, fun, romp, play, gambol, prank, sport, frisk, lark [sportive
**frolicsome:** gay, merry,
**from (prefix):** de
" **that place or there:** thence, since
" **what place:** whence
" **within:** out [formost
**front:** fore, van, face,
" **of bldg.:** facade
" " **hoof:** toe
" " **mouth:** preoral
" **part of helmet:** visor
" **of ship:** bow, prow
**frost:** ice, chill, cold, rime, foam [cold
**frosty:** rimy, austere,
**froth:** yeast, spume, foam
**frowning:** glum, scowling
**frozen:** icy, gelid, glace
" **desserts:** mousses
" **dew:** rime
**frugal:** sparing, economical, provident, thrifty, chary [ade
**fruit drink:** ade lemon-
" **of fir:** cone
" " **gourd:** pepo
" " **hawthorn:** haw
" **kernel:** pit
" **of nut:** kernel
" " **palm:** date
" **part:** core, rind
" **pulp:** pap
" **seed:** pip [tive
**fruitless:** useless, abor-
**frustrate:** foil, defeat, balk, thwart
**fry quickly:** saute [der
**frying pan:** skillet, spi-
**fuddled:** tipsy, flustered
**fuel:** peat, stoke, charcoal, gas, coke
**fulfill:** complete
**full:** plenary, ample, replete, laden [ted
" **of depressions:** pit-
" **dress:** tails
" **of fissures:** rimose
" **force:** amain
" **grown:** adult
**fume:** rave, smoke, reek, incense, rage
**fun:** sport, play
**fundamental:** essential, basic, basal, organic
" **mass of life tendencies:** id
**funeral announcement:** obit
" **car:** hearse
" **hymn:** dirge
" **oration:** eloge
" **pile:** pyre
**fungi (kind):** rust
" **(pert. to):** agaric
**fungus:** agaric, yeast
" **disease:** ergot
" **growth:** mildew, mold [ous, comic
**funny:** comical, humor-
**fur:** pelt
" **animal:** otter, sable, seal, genet, mink, marten, calabar
" **of coypu:** nu ria
" **scarf:** tippet
**furious:** rabid, raving, frantic [kiln
**furnace:** heater, oven,
" **tender:** stoker [rig
**furnish:** provide, lend, indue, afford, equip, endow, render, cater
" **a crew:** man
" **with authority:** vest
" " **feathers:** fledge
" " **money:** endow
**furniture wheel:** caster
**furor:** rage, frenzy, craze [groove, plow
**furrow:** line, stria, rut,
**further:** promote, abet, yet, remote
**furthersome:** also
**furtive:** sly, stealthy, sneaky [anger, wrath
**fury:** rage, ire, violence,
**fuse:** melt, anneal
**fused metal & refuse:** slag
**fusible alloy:** solder
" **substance:** metal
**fuss:** ado, bother, todo, fret, bustle
**futile:** useless, idle

## G

**Gael:** Celt, Scot
**Gaelic:** Erse
" **sea god:** Ler
**gag:** joke, silence
**gaiety:** mirth, glee
**gaily:** merrily [gress
**gain:** net, win, profit, attain, advance, improve, acquire, obtain, lucre, earn, pro-
" **advantage over:** worst [tort
" **by compulsion:** ex-
" **control over:** master
" **success:** prosper
" **superiority:** master
**gainsay:** deny [gallop
**gait:** lope, step, pace, stride, trot, amble
**gaiter:** spat
**gala:** festive, festivity
**Galatea's lover:** Acis
**gale:** wind, gust [chafe
**gall:** harass, irritate,
**gallant:** cavalier, spark, brave, knight
**Gallic:** French [game
**gamble:** frolic, bet, dice,
**gambler's capital:** stake
**gambling:** gaming
" **house:** casino
**gambol:** frisk, caper, romp, frolic
**game:** sport, contest, plucky, jest, mockery, diversion, gamble
" **bird:** grouse, snipe
" **of chance:** loo, bingo, keno, lotto
" **fish:** tarpon, bass, cero, trout, marlin
" **like Napoleon:** Pam
" **of skill:** chess
**gamin:** arab, tad, urchin
**gaming cube:** dice, die
**gamut:** scale
**gang:** crew, squad
**gannet:** solan
**ganoid fish:** amia
**gap:** breach, hiatus, notch, opening, cleft
" **in mt. ridge** col
**garb:** attire, dress, clothe, array, apparel
**garden:** cultivate, hoe
" **bed:** plot
" **implement:** trowel, hoe, weeder, rake
**garish:** gaudy, showy
**garland:** lei, anadem, wreath [aba, stole
**garment:** robe, vesture,
**garner:** reap, glean, gather, collect [loft
**garret:** attic, mansard,
**gaseous (comb. form):** aeri
" **compound:** ethane
" **element:** neon, oxygen
" **mixture:** air
**gash:** slit, cut, slash
**gastropod:** snail, slug
**gate:** entrance, portal, passageway
**gather:** amass, assemble, mass, shirr, brew, congregate, collect, reap, collect, garner, glean, muster
" **after a reaper:** glean
**gathering:** bee, crowd, harvest, reunion
" **implement:** rake
**gaudy:** tawdry, garnish, garish, flashy
" **ornament:** tinsel
**gaunt:** rawboned, lean, lank, thin, spare
**gauntlet:** glove
**gauzy fabric:** tulle, chiffon, tissue
**gay:** merry, blithe, riant, sportive [glare
**gaze:** stare, look, peer,
" **askance:** leer
" **with close attention:** pore
" " **satisfaction:** gloat, admire
**gazelle:** cora, goa
**gazing:** astare
**gear:** harness, outfit, clothing, rig, tackle, trappings
" **tooth:** cog
**gelatinous matter:** agar
**gelid:** frozen, icy, cold
**gem:** muffin, stone
" **carved in relief:** cameo
" **weight:** carat
**gemel:** coupled, twin
**gender:** sex, engender
**genealogicial record:** tree
**general character:** tenor, nature
" **course of action:** career, trend
" **fight:** melee
" **type:** average
**generate:** gender, produce, create, develop
**generation:** age
**generator:** dynamo
**genteel:** nice, polite
**gentle:** soft, docile, tame, kind, mild, tender, meek, easy
" **blow:** dab, pat
**gentleman:** sir
**genuflect:** kneel
**genuine:** sincere, sterling, real, true
**genus:** kind, class, variety [weed
" **of ambrosia:** rag-
" " **auks:** alle, alca
" " **beet:** beta
" " **birds:** otis
" " **burbots:** lota
" " **cabbage:** brassica, cos, kale [ris
" " **candytuft:** ibe-
" " **cattle:** bos
" " **cetaceans:** inia
" " **cow:** bos
" " **dogs:** canis
" " **ducks:** anas, anser
" " **flowering shrubs:** acacia [rana
" " **frog:** anura,
" " **garter:** elaps
" " **gastropods:** triton [solar
" " **geese:** anser,
" " **goose barnacles:** lepas [poa
" " **grasses:** avena,
" " **herbs:** ruta, arum, liatria
" " **honey bee:** apis
" " **insect:** nepa
" " **kites:** elanus
" " **lily:** aloe
" " **lindens:** tilia
" " **lizards:** iguana, uta
" " **man:** homo
" " **maples:** acer
" " **mollusks:** eolis
" " **moose:** alces
" " **moth:** tinea
" " **mouse:** mus
" " **myrtle trees:** pimenta [ta
" " **nuthatches:** sit-
" " **oak:** quercus
" " **oat:** avena
" " **olive tree:** olea
" " **orchids:** laelia
" " **palms:** areca
" " **peacock:** pavo
" **(pertaining to):** generic
" **of pickerel:** esox
" " **pig:** sus
" " **pineapple:** ananas
" " **plants:** aloe
" " **rails:** sora
" " **rye:** secale
" " **S. Amer. & S. African garter snakes:** elaps [pa
" " **sac fungi:** ver-
" " **sea birds:** sula
" " **shad:** alosa
" " **sheep:** ovis
" " **shrubs:** itea, rosa, olea, erica
" " **spider monkeys:** ateles
" " **sticklike insects:** emesa
" " **succulent plants:** aloe
" " **sumac:** rhus
" " **swan:** olor
" " **toad:** anura
" " **trees & shrubs:** acer
" " **turtle:** emy
" " **vipers:** echis
" " **Virginia willow:** ites, itea
" " **wasp:** vespa
**geological age:** era
" **direction:** stoss
" **formation:** lias
" **period:** eocene
**geometrical curve:** parabola, spiral, polar
" **figure:** cone, prism, ellipse, circle, rhomb, rhombus, lune [rem
" **proportion:** theo-
" **ratio:** pi
**Geraint's wife:** Enid
**germ:** seed, spore, microbe
" **cells:** ova, eggs
**German:** Teuton, Hegel
" **admiral:** Spee
" **article:** der
" **author:** Mann
" **beer:** mum
" **city:** Ulm, Essen, Emden, Ems, Trier
" **coin:** taler, mark
" **composer:** Abt, Bach
" **district:** Saar, Ruhr

" doctor: Kant
" E. African coin: pesa
" emperor's title: kaiser
" engraver: Stoss
" hall: sala
" inventor: Otto
" kobold: nis
" mathematician: Klien [Marc
" painter: Durer,
" philosopher: Hegel, Kant
" physicist: Ohm
" poet: Heine
" port: Stettin
" religious reformer: Luther [Ruhr, Saar
" river: Eser, Oder, Eder, Elbe, Weser, Ems, Rhine, Isar,
" ruler: kaiser
" sculptor: Stoss
" socialist: Marx
" soldier: uhlan [ony
" state: Hesse, Saxtitle: herr, von
" watering place: Ems
germinate: sprout
germinated grain: malt
gest: exploit, gesture
gesture: motion, gest
" of affection: caress
get: obtain, receive, secure, procure, win, become, acquire, derive
" along: fare
" away: scat, escape
" back: recover, regain
" out (colloq.): scram
" ready: prepare
" to in time: catch
" up: gee, arise
ghastly: lurid, wan
ghost: specter, shade, spook, apparition, phantom, spirit
giant: titan, huge, ogre
" killer: David
gibbon: lar
gibe: sneer, quip, deride, agree, jape, taunt, flout
gift: grant, present, endow, donation, talent
" to bride: dower
" to employe: bonus
gigantic: mammoth, titan, immense, huge
giggle: snicker, tehee, snickerer, titter
gilded bronze: ormolu
gin: snare, trap
" (kind): sloe
giraffelike animal: okapi
girdle: sash, belt, cest, band, cincture, zone
girl: maid, lassie, damsel, maiden, damosel
" (dial.): gal [point
gist: pith, core, pitch,
give: donate, render, contribute, present, proffer, hand, bestow, impart
" an account of: report [power
" authority to: em-
" away: betray [turn
" back: restore, re-
" bevel to: cant [sure
" confidence to: as-
" courage to: nerve
" ear to: heed
" expression to: voice
" forth: emit, utter
" a grant: charter
" high value to: idealize [date
" legal force to: vali-
" the meaning: define
" nourishment: feed
" off: emit
" " fumes: reek
" one's word: promise [emit
" out: mete, issue,
" permission: consent
" pleasure: delight
" reluctantly: begrudge, grudge
" right to: entitle
" rise to: gender
" (Scot.): gie
" sloping edge to: bevel
" up: resign, cede, yield, despair [sify
" variety to: diver-
" way: yield
" zest to: sauce
given to jesting: jocular, jocose [moraines
glacial deposits: eskers,
" direction: stoss
" fissure: crevass
" ice pinnacle: serac
" ridges: osar, eskers, eskars
" snowfields: neves
glad: elated, happy, joyful, gratified, delighted, pleased
gladden: cheer, elate, please
glaring light: flare
glass: tumbler, mirror
" for artificial gems: strass
" container: phial, jar, cruet, ampule
" " (small): vial
" tube for blowpipe: matrass
glassy: smooth, dull
glaze: enamel
gleam: shine, glow, radiate, light, glint, glimmer, sparkle
glean: garner, gather
glee: mirth, joy, gaiety
glib: smooth, fluent, flippant [slither
glide: slide, sail, slip,
" hurriedly: skitter
" over: skim
" smoothly: flow [ter
glint: gleam, flash, glitglisten: sparkle, shine
glitter: shine, glint, spangle, sparkle
globe: orb, ball, sphere, earth, steer
globule: bead, drop
gloom: melancholy, murk, dusk
gloomy: dreary, lurid, glum, drear, sad, morose, saturnine, stygian, dark, tenebrous
glorify: bless, exalt, laud [pride, renown
glory: splendor, eclat,
gloss: luster, palliate, sheen, lustre
glossy: sleek, silken, nitid, lustrous, shiny
" fabric: silk, sateen, satin, rayon, satinet
" paint: enamel
glove: mit, gauntlet, mitt [bloom
glow: gleam, shine
glowing: radiant
glue: paste, fasten
glut: sate, satiate
glutinous: viscid
gnar: snarl, growl
gnarl: twist distort
gnat: midge [corrode
gnaw: eat, nibble, peck,
" away: erose
gnawing animal: rodent
gnome: elf, goblin
go: proceed, precede, depart, leave, went, wend, betake [embark
" abroad: entrain,
" against: oppose
" ahead: lead
" aloft: ascend
" around: bypass
" astray: err
" away: scat, shoo, depart, begone, leave
" back: retreat, revert, ebb [lead
" before: precede,
" by: pass [sink, set
" down: descend,
" easily: amble, lope
" frequently: resort
" furtively: sneak, steal
" and get: fetch
" heavily: lumber
" hunting: gun [tire
" into seclusion: re-
" on: gee, proceed
" " with: resume
" (poet.): wend
" quickly: scoot, dart
" rapidly: race, tear
" the rounds: patrol
" (Scot.): gae
" silently: steal
" to: attend
" " law: sue
" too far: overstep
" up in rank: rise
" without food: fast
" wrong: err [sting
goad: spur, prod, incite,
goal: end, aim, target, ambition, mecca
goat cry: maa, bleat
" (kind): alpaca, ibex
" (wild): ibex
gob: mass
goblet: chalice, hanap
goblin: sprite, gnome
god: idol, deity
God of altar fire: Agni
" " Ancient Memphis: Ptah
" " Fields & Herds: Faun
" " Flocks & pastures: Pan
" " Gates: Janus
" " Love: Amor, Eros, Cupid
" " manly youth: Apollo
" " metal working: Vulcan
" " mirth: Comus
" " mischief: Loki
" " pastures: Pan
" " revelry (class myth): Comus
" " Sea: Poseidon, Neptune, Ler
" " Shepherds: Pales [Thor
" " Thunder: Dis,
" " Underworld: Dis
" for whom Jan. is named: Janus
" " " " Tues. is named: Tyr
" of War: Ares, Tyr, Mars, Ira, Odin, Thor
" wearing the solar disk: Ra
" of Winds: Aeolus
goddess: dea, ge
Goddess of Agriculture: Ops, Demeter, Ceres
" " Arts & Sciences: Athena
" banished from Olympus: Ate
" of Dawn: Eos
" " Destiny: Fate
" " Discord: Eris, Ate [Ge
" " Earth: Erda,
" " Fertility: Ma, Ops
" " Grain: Ceres
" " Harvest: Ops Ceres
" " Healing: Eir
" " Hearth: Vesta
" " Hope: Spes
" " Horses: Epons
" " Hunt: Diana
" " Infatuation: Ate [traea
" " Justice: As-
" " Love: Venus, Eros
" " Marriage: Hera
" " Mischief: Eris, Ate [Selene Selena
" " Moon: Luna.
" " Morning: Aurora [Irine
" " Peace: Irene,
" " Plenty: Ops
" " Rainbow: Iris
" " Retribution: Ara
" " sea: Ran
" " seasons: Horae
" " sorrow: Mara
" " vegetation: Ceres
" " vengeance: Ara
" " victory: Nike
" " war: Alea
" " wisdom: Minerva [ana, nymph
" " the wood: Di-
" " youth: Hebe
godlike: deific, divine
godly person: saint
gold (alchem.): sol
" bar: ingot
" (heraldry): or
" in Latin Amer. countries: oro
" paint: gilt
" symbol: A.U.
golden: precious, aureate [mashie
golf club: cleek, spoon, putter, brassy, driver, midiron, iron, brassie,
" " nose: toe
" course: links
" " depression: cup
" " parts: greens, fairways, tees
" hazard: trap
" holes unplayed: bye
" mound: tee:
" position: stance
" score: par, bogey, stroke [chip
" stroke: putt, drive,
" turf: divot
golfer's target: cup
" warning cry: fore
Goliath's home: Gath
gone: past, lost [past
" by: ago, agone,
goober: peanut
goodbye: adieu, tata
good fortune: hap
" luck charm: mascot
" manners: breeding
" name: honor
" (prefix): eu
" promise: hope
" turn: favor [ness
" will: amity, kind-
goods cast adrift: ligan, lagan
" on hand: stock
" for sale: wares
" as shipped: invoice
" shipped by public carrier: freight
" thrown overboard. jetsam [brant
goose (kind): solan,

" (male): gander
gore: stab, blood
gorge: ravine, chasm, glut, abides, stuff
gorse: furze [trine
gospel: evangel, doc-
gossip: tattle, rumor
" (dial.): norate
Gounod opera: Faust
gourd plant: squash, melon, pepo
gourmand: epicure
govern: rule, control, regulate, direct, reign
government duty: tariff
" grant: patent
" levy: tax
" rep.: consul
governor: regent
grab: seize, collar, trap, snatch, clutch
grace: charm, adorn
graceful: elegant
" woman: sylph [fa r
gracious: polite, benign,
grade: incline, standing, rank, degree, sort, rate, rating, class
grafted: ente [nel, cereal
grain: granulate, ker-
" (artificial): malt
" beating instrument: flail
" of a cereal: oat
" fungus: ergot
" grinder: miller
" for gringing: grist
" (pert. to): oaten
" stalk: straw [tor
" warehouse: eleva-
grampus: orc, orca
grand: august, great, epic
" slam at cards: vole
grandchild (Scot.): oe
grandeur: eclat
grandparents: aval
grant: concede, cede, bestow, allow, confer, yield gift, lend
grape: uva, rasp, ao ni, acinus
" (dried): raisin
" drink: wine
" (kind): malaga, tokay, niagara
" pomace: rape
" preserve: uvate
" refuse: marc
graphic: vivid
" symbol: character
grasp: apprehend, seize, clutch, take, clasp
grass: graze, pasture
" covered earth: sod
" flower part: palea
" (kind of): rie, reed, sedge, fodder, poa, sward, grama
" like herb: sedge
" mowed & cured: hay
" stem: reed
grassland: lea, meadow
grassy land surface: sward
grate: rub, rasp, grill, abrade, irritate. grit grind, scrape,
gratified: glad
gratify: please, humor, sate, wreak
grating: grid, grille, raspy, grate, grill
gratitude: thanks
gratuity: tip, dole, fee
grave: solemn, sober, demure, somber
" robber: ghoul
gravel: grit, sand
gravy: sauce
" dish: boat [dismal
gray: ashen, leaden, ashy, hoary, taupe,
" cloth: Irab
" with age: hoar
grayish-green: reseda
" -white: ashen
graze: pasture, grass, browse, feed
grazing tract: range, pasture, pasturage
grease: lard, oil, fat, lubricate, lubricant, bribe
great: vast, immense, eminent, large, grand
" age: ancient
" Britain: Albion
" deal: lots,lot, much
" desert: Sahara
" Lake: Erie, Huron, Ontario, Superior
" number: multitude
" personage: mogul
greatest: largest, most, supreme
" age: oldest
Greece: Hellas
" (division of):Deme
" (pert. to): Greco
greed: avarice, cupidity
greedy: avid
" person: Midas, pig
Greek: Argive
" assembly: agora
" capital: Athens
" city: Arta
" coin: obol, obolo, lepton [ter
" " (ancient): sta-
" communes: demes
" country: Elis
" deity: Eos
" dialect: eolic, ionic
" district: Argolis
" enchantress: Medea / [odyssey
" epic poem: iliad,
" festival: delia
" fury: erinys, alecto
" garment: tunic
" ghost: Ker
" god: Leto, Apollo, Eros, Ares
" goddess: Athena
" gravestone: stela, stele
" hall: saal
" hero: Ajax [phon
" historian: Xeno-
" Island: Melos, Ios, Samos, Nio, Rhodes, Crete, Milo Delos
" legendary hero: Idas
" market place: agore, agora
" measure: stadium
" " of length: bema
" mountain: Ossa
" nome: elis
" patron: Pan
" peninsula: Morea
" philosopher: Plato, Galen, stoic, Aristotle, Zeno
" " school: Ionian
" physician: Galen
" poet: Homer, Pindar, Arion, Hesiod
" portico: stoa
" priestess: Hero
" province: Nome
" room: saal
" sea: Ionian
" seaport: Enos, Volo
" sylvan deity: satyr
" tense: aorist
" theater: odeon
" warrior: Ajax
green: verdant, wreath
" film on copper: patina
" mineral: erinite
" Mt. Boys leader: Allen
" pigment: bice
" plum: gage
" tea: hyson
greenish yellow: olive
Greenland Eskimos: Ita
" settlement: Etah
greet: salute, hail, welcome, address
greeting: hi, salutation, bow, hello, salute
gregarious: social
griddle cake: scone
gridiron: grill
grief: dolor, woe, distress, dole, sorrow
" (poet.): dolor
grieve: sigh, lament, mourn, pine, sorrow
grievously afflicted: smitten [broil
grill: gridiron, grate,
" with pepper: devil
grim: fierce, stern, terrible, gaunt
grime: dirt, sully [bray
grind: grate, crush,
" together: gnash, crunch, grit [ting
grinding: molar, grit-
grip: valise, seize, grasp, handbag, clutch
gripping device: clamp, vise [pluck, courage
grit: sand, grind, gravel,
groove: rut, slot, score, stria
" part of joint: rabbet
grope: fumble, feel
grotto: cave [land
ground: soil, terrain,
" grain: grist, meal
groundless: baseless
groundwork: base, basis
group: band, set, class, bevy, squad, team
" of animals or plants: genus
" " bees: swarm
" " horses: dorp
grow: wax, increase, become, expand, mature, raise, enlarge, develop, thrive [mose
" in clusters: race-
" dim: fade, blear
" less: wane
" " severe: relent
" out: enate
" rich: fatten
" uninteresting: pall
growl: snarl, gnarl, gnar
growth: tumor, stature
grub: larva [plain
grumble: mutter, com-
Guam capital: Agana
guarantee: insure, avouch, bail, assure, pledge, endorse
guaranty: pledge, warranty, security
guard: protect, keeper, fend, tend, sentinel
guardian: patron, warden
" deities: genii
" spirit: angel
Gudrun's husband: Atli
guerdon: reward
guest: visitor, caller, patron, visitant, lodger
guide: steer, pilot, direct, lead, clue, leader
guiding light: beacon
Guido's high note: ela
" low note: ut
" note: alamire
" second note: are
guile: deceit
guileless: naive
guinea pig: cavy
gulch: canyon, ravine
gulf: chasm, abyss
Gulf in Baltic Sea: Riga
" of New Guinea: Huon
gull: dupe, cob [ternes
" like bird: tern,
gully: ravine
gum resin: elemi, copal, damar, sandarac, ava
gumbo: okra
" (var.): ocra
gun: rifle, cannon
" dog: setter, pointer
" (slang): gat, rod
gush: pour, jet, spurt, spout
gust: gale, waft, wind
guy: chaff, josh
gymnastic bar: trapeze
gypsum: selenite
gypsy: rom, romany
" book: lil

## H

habit: usage, custom, routine, attire, wont
habitation: abode, lair
habitual: customary
habituate: inure
" (var.): enure
hackle: comb
hackneyed: trite, banal
Hades river: Lethe, Styx
haft: handle, hilt
haggard: gaunt
hail: ave, greet, call, salute. accost
hair braid: pigtail
" cloth: aba
" (comb. form): pil
" disease: xerasia, mange
" dye: henna
" fellet, covering & ribbon: snood
" line (var.): cerif
" ointment: pomade
" ornament: comb
" roll: rat
hairy: pilary, hirsute, pilar, comate
hale: strong, robust, hearty, vigorous, pull
half boot: pac [tee
" breed: metis, mes-
" diameters: radii
" an em: en
" a farthing: mite
" man, half goat: faun [taur
" " " horse: cen-
" mask: domino
" note: minim
" penny: mag [demi
" (prefix): semi, hemi,
" score: ten
" sole: tap
" tone: semitone
" woman, half bird: siren
hall: aula, corridor
hallow: holy, bless
hallowed place: shrine
halo: areola, nimbus, aureole, aureola
halt: stem, pause, lame, arrest, hesitate
halting place: etape
hammer: sledge, maul, pound, beat, mallet, oliver [poll
" head (end): peen,
" out: anvil
hamper: trammel, crate, cramp, basket, hinder, hanaper, encumber [proffer
hand: give, pointer,
" (arch.): nieve
" propellor: oar
" pump: syringe
" (slang): fin
handbag: grip, reticule, satchel, valise
handful: wisp [wield
handle: ansa, hilt, haft, treat, manage, helve,
" of a pail: bail
" roughly: paw, maul
hands on hips: akimbo

**handsome (Scot.):** braw
**handwriting:** script
**handy:** convenient, deft
**hang:** pend, drape, suspend, hover, cling
" **about:** hover
" **down:** sag, droop, lop, slouch [dangle
" **loosely:** drape, loll,
**hanger on:** parasite
**hanging:** drape, pensile, pendent [dossal
" **for back of altar:**
" **mass of ice:** icicle
" **ornament:** tassel, pendant
**hangman's loop:** noose
**hanker:** long
**hap:** luck, chance, befall, fortune [casual
**haphazard:** random,
**happen:** occur, betide, befall, chance
" **again:** recur
**happenings:** events, news, incidents
**happiness:** bliss, joy, felicity [blest
**happy:** glad, elate,
**harangue:** nag, tirade, orate, screed, spiel
**harass:** nag, beset, fret, bother, gall, perplex, plague, vex, annoy, gripe, pester, bait, irk, tease, distract
" **with clamor:** din
**harbor:** cove, port, hold
" **boat:** tug [severe
**hard:** austere, renitent, callous, set, adamant, arduous, solid, iron,
" **drawn:** taut, tense
" **finish:** enamel
" **to manage:** ornery
" **metal:** steel [spinel
" **mineral:** emery,
" **(prefix):** dys
" **question:** poser
" **rock:** flint
" **rubber:** ebonite
" **substance:** adamant
" **tissue:** bone
" **wood:** ash, teak, oak, lana, ebony, elm
**harden:** gel, set, enure, ossify, steel, inure
" **sails:** tan
**hardness:** adamant
**hardship:** trial, rigor
**hardwood tree:** ash, oak, hickory
**hardy:** hale, spartan, robust, well
**Hardy heroine:** Tess
**harem:** seraglio
" **room:** oda
**harken:** listen, hear, ear
**harm:** bane, damage, injure, evil, hurt
**harmonious:** musical
**harmonize:** attune, agree, tone, blend, tune, chime
" **(colloq.):** gee
**harmony:** peace, union, unison
**harness:** gear [halter
" **part:** hame, reins, trace, bridle, rein,
**harsh:** stern, severe, acerb, rasping, raucous, rigorous
" **cry:** bray [acerb
" **tasting:** bitter,
**hart:** stag [caama
**hartebeest:** lecama,
**harvest:** reap, crop, gathering
**haste:** speed, hurry, dispatch, quickness
**hasten:** hie, run, hurry, fly, scurry, race
" **away:** scamper
**hasty:** rash, sudden, impatient, brash, abrupt, impulsive
" **(colloq.):** brash
" **pudding:** hash, mush [fedora, cap
**hat:** bonnet, headgear,
" **crown:** poll [loathe
**hate:** detest, abhor,
**hateful:** crused, odious
**hatred:** rancor, dislike, odium, aversion, enmity
**haughty:** arrogant, proud, lofty [tug
**haul:** tow, lug, pull, cart draw, drag, hale,
" **(naut.):** hea e [dive
**haunt:** den, resort, visit, lair, frequent, nest,
**hautboy:** oboe
**have:** own, possess
" **ambitions:** aspire
" **confidence:** hope, trust [ate
" **impression of:** ide-
" **life:** be
" **meter:** scan
" **recourse to:** betake, refer, resort
" **weight or effect:** militate [shelter
**haven:** port, refuge,
**having ability:** able
" **branches:** ramose, ramulose
" **feeling:** sentient
" **a handle:** ansate
" **hoofs:** ungulate
" **a large nose:** nasute
" **limits:** finite
" **made & left a will:** testate
" **no feet:** apodal
" " **interest or care:** supine [free
" " **worries:** care-
" **offensive smell:** olid
" **raised strips:** ridgy
" **retired:** abed
" **ribs:** costate
" **risen:** up
" **spikes:** tined
" **supports:** piered
" **toothed margin:** erose
" **two horns:** bicorn
" **wings:** alated, alate
**Hawaiian bird:** oo, io, ooaa
" **cloth:** tapa
" **dance:** hula
" **district:** Puna
" **farewell:** aloha
" **fish:** lania, ahi
" **food:** poi
" **goose:** nene
" **hawk:** io
" **herb:** hola [aloha
" **salutation:** aloaa,
" **taro paste:** poi
" **town:** Hilo
" **tree:** koa, aalii
" **valley:** Manoa
" **wreath:** lei
**hawk's cage:** mew
" **headed deity:** Ra
" **(kind):** kestrel, elanet, falcon, io, harrier
" **leash:** lune
" **like bird:** kite
" **nest:** aerie
" **parrot:** hia
**hawser:** rope
**hay storage compartment:** mow, loft
**haying machine:** tedder
**haystack:** rick
**hazard:** risk, peril, lot, stake, danger, dare
**hazardous:** unsafe
**haze:** fog, mist
**head:** pate, lead, poll, director, leader, cop
" **of convent:** abess
" **covering:** hood, hair
" **part:** scalp
**headdress:** tiara, hat
**heading:** caption, title
**headland:** cape, ness, ras, hook
**headliner:** star
**heal:** cure
**healthy:** hale, well, sane
**heap:** pile, mass, stack, amass
" **adulation on:** praise [cairn
" **of stones:** scree,
**hear:** harken, regard, heed, listen [hear
" **by accident:** over-
" **ye:** oyez
**hearing:** audition, mien
" **(pért. to):** otic
**hearsay:** rumor
**heart:** cor, core, spirit
" **chamber:** camera, [illegible]le
[illegible]rt. to): cardiac
" **shaped:** cordate
**hearty:** hale, sincere
**heat:** warmth
" **excessively:** toast
" **(pert. to):** caloric
" **producer:** fuel
**heated:** hot
**heath:** erica, moor
**Heathen:** pagan
" **diety:** idol
**heather:** gorse, erica
**heating implement:** stove, etna, radiator, boiler [lift, hoist
**heave:** cast, surge, raise, strain, throw,
**heaven:** firmament, sky
**heavenly:** celestial, supernal
" **being:** angel planet
" **body:** star, sun, comet, meteor, luminary, moon, lamp,
" **bread:** manna
" **food:** manna
**heavy:** leaden, stolid
" **blow (slang):** oner
" **impact:** slam
" **& sweet:** sirupy
**Heb**[illegible] Jewish
" **deity:** Baal, El
" **judge:** Elon, Eli
" **king:** Saul, David
" **kingdom:** Israel
" **letter:** tav, ab, pe daleth, mem, ayin, resh, teth
" **lyre:** asor
" **measure:** omer, cab, hin, kab
" **musical instrument:** Asor
" **name for God:** El
" **plural ending:** im
" **prophet:** Jeremiah, Amos, Hosea, Elias, Daniel, Isaiah, Elisha
" **proselyte:** Ger
" **vowel point:** tsere
**Hebrides Isl.:** Iona
**hector:** tease, bully
**heed:** notice, note, attention, mind, ear, care, hear
**heedless:** careless, rash
**heel:** cant [reen
" **over:** tip, tilt, careen
**height:** altitude, stature, elevation
**heir:** legatee, scion
**Helen of Troy's mother:** Leda
**helical:** spiral
**helix:** spiral
**hell:** inferno
**helm:** steer, tiller
**helmet shaped organ:** galea [man
**helmsman:** pilot, steersman
**help:** aidance, benefit, stead, attend, abet, aid, assist, succor
**helper:** ally, aide [border
**hem:** restrict, margin,
" **in:** beset
**hematite:** ore
**hemp fiber:** tow, sisal
**hence:** ergo, so, therefore
**Hengist's brother:** Horsa
**heraldic bearing:** orle
" **cross:** patee, patte
" **grafted:** ente [dill
**herb:** sage, sedum, catnip, anise, moly, rue,
" **of aster family:** arnica
" **(cloverlike):** medic
" **dill:** anet
" **eve:** iva
**herbage:** grass
**herd:** drove, flock
**hereditary:** lineal
" **factor:** gene
**heretic:** dissenter [cluse
**hermit:** eremite, re-
**Herod's granddaughter:** Salome
**heroic:** epic, brave, epical, valiant, issustrate [saga
" **tale:** sage, gest,
**heroism:** valor
**heron:** egret, crane, aigret, bittern, rail
**herring like fish:** sprat, lile, shad, alewives
**hesitate:** haw, demur, falter, halt, pause, waver [mer
" **in speech:** stam-
**hew:** chop, cut, cleave
**hewing tool:** axe, ax
**hiatus:** gap, opening
**hibernian:** Irish
**hickory:** pecan [covert
**hidden:** inner, secret, latent, perdu, deep,
" **obstacle:** snag
**hide:** stow, pelt, secrete, conceal, skin, cache, cover, veil, concede, ensconce, cloak, screen
**hideous:** ugly, horrible [niche
**hiding place:** cache,
**high:** tall, up, lofty, costly, elevated
" **(comb. form):** alti
" **hill:** tor
" **honor:** homage
" **mts.:** Andes
" **note:** ela, ala
" **priest:** Eli
" **temperature:** heat
" **volley:** lob
" **waters:** floods
**higher:** up, above
**highest:** upmost, supreme
" **Mt.:** Everest, peak
" **note of gamut:** ela pinnacle, noon, apex
**highlander:** Scot
" **costume:** kilt
" **purse:** sporran
" **seasoned dish:** olla, ragout
**highway:** pike, avenue
" **division:** lane
**highwayman:** bandit, ladrone, footpad
**hill (flat):** mesa
**hilt:** handle, haft
**Himalayan animal:** panda [goral
" **antelope:** serow,
" **monkshood:** atis
" **peak:** Everest
" **wild sheep:** nahoor

**hinder:** impede, obstruct, arrest, let, delay, hamper, estop, deter, bar, retard, harass, detain, cramp
**hindrance:** bar, rub, restraint, let, balk
**Hindu acrobat:** nat
" **army man:** Sepoy
" **ascetic:** Yogi
" **avatar:** rama
" **charitable gift:** enam
" **cymbals:** dal, tal
" **deity:** siva, rama, uma, deva, varuna
" " **with 7 arms:** Agni
" **demon:** asura, rahu
" **game:** rance
" **garment:** sari
" **god:** siva
" " **(unknown):** ka
" **goddess:** devi
" **gods abode:** meru
" **guitar:** sitar [abar
" **handkerchief:** mal-
" **hero:** rama
" **holy city:** Benares
" **measure:** ryots
" **merchant:** banian
" **month:** pus, asin
" **peasant:** ryot
" **pillar:** lat [thana
" **police station:**
" **policeman:** sepoy
" **political leader:** Gandhi
" **prayer rug:** asan
" **prince:** raja, rajah, rana [ranee
" **princess:** rani,
" **progenitor:** Manu
" **proprietor:** malik
" **queen:** ranee, rani
" **red dye:** alta
" **sacred literature:** veda
" **social class:** caste
" **symbals:** tal [rajah
" **title:** mir, sahib,
" " " **respect:** swami
" **trinity:** siva
" **weight:** tola, ser
" **word (sacred):** om
**Hindustan:** India
" **hill dweller:** toda
" **(poet.):** Ind. [pivot
**hinge:** joint, depend,
**hint:** clue, cue, trace, clew, suggest, intimate, tip, imply, allusion, intimation
**hire:** charter, engage, rent, fee, employ, let, contract, lease
**hireling:** slave, esne
**hirsute:** hairy [hair
" **adornment:** beard,
**hiss:** siss, boo
**hissing:** sibilant, sis
**historical period (pert. to):** erol, eral
**history:** annals
**hit:** swat, batted, strike, bat, smite
" **aloft:** lob
" **gently:** tap
" **(slang):** swat, lam
**hoar:** white
" **frost:** rime
**hoarder:** miser
**hoax:** canard
" **(slang):** kid, spoof
**hobby:** fad, avocation
**hocus:** cheat
**hod:** scuttle
**hodgpodge:** olio
**hoist:** boost, cat, raise, winch, heave [davit
**hoisting apparatus:** gin, derrick, cage, crane, elevator, capstan,
**hold:** have, retain, clutch, harbor, keep
" **in affection:** endear
" **attention:** interest
" **back:** dam, retard, deter, restrain, stem, hinder, delay, resist, detain, refrain
" **balance:** poise
" **in common:** joint
" **dear:** love, cherish
" **fast:** cling, anchor, pin
" **firmly:** grip
" **in greater favor:** prefer
" **ones ground:** stand
" **in respect:** awe
" **a session:** sit
" **in suspense:** hang
" **together:** cohere, clamp
" **under spell:** charm
**holder:** container, owner
" **of a lease:** lessee
**holding:** tenure, property
" **at bridge:** tenace
" **device:** vise
**hole:** orifice, aperture, opening, cavity, perforation, eyelet
" **in one (slang):** ace
" **repairer:** darner
**holidays:** fiestos, vacations, feria
**Holland city:** Ede
" **seaport:** Edam
**hollow:** depression, concave, cavernous, dent
**holly:** ilex
**holy:** sacred, blessed, hallow
" **person:** saint
" **picture:** icon
" **scriptures:** Bible
**home:** abode
" **coming:** return
**homeless child:** waif
" **outcast:** arab
**Homer's epic:** Iliad, Odyssey
**homicide:** murder
**homily:** sermon
**hominy:** samp [upright
**honest:** se, true, frank,
**honey:** mel
" **badger:** ratel
" **buzzard:** pern
" **container:** comb
**honeyed:** sugary
**honor:** venerate, revere, credit, esteem, reputation, renown, exalt, ennoble, respect
**hooded cloak:** capote
**hoo wink:** deceive
**hooligan:** ruffian
**hoop:** encircle, ring, bail
**Hoosier humorist:** Ade
" **poet:** Riley
" **state (abbr.):** Ind.
**hop:** leap, spring, vine
" **kiln:** oast
**hop stem:** bine
**hope:** desire, reliance, anticipate, trust, wish, expectation
**hopelessness:** despair
**horde:** crowd, drove, swarm, throng, army, host
**horizontal:** flat, level
" **beam over door:** lintel
**horned horse:** unicorn
" **quadruped:** ibex
**horrify:** appal
**horror:** dread, terror
**horse:** nag, steed, hunter, miler, arab, pacer
" **blanket:** manta
" **color:** roan, pinto
" **disease:** glander
" **fodder:** oats
" **'s foot part:** pastern
" **of a gait:** gaiter, pacer, trotter
" **'s gait:** rack
" **headstall flap:** blinder [nag, pacer
" **(kind):** roan, pad-
" **leg:** fetlock
" **in a race:** entry
" **(small):** tit, pony, bidet, cob
" **tender:** groom
" **'s working gear:** harness [horde
**host:** army, throng,
**hostelry:** inn
**hostile feeling:** animus
**hostler:** groom
**hot:** torrid, peppery, fiery, heated
" **wind:** sirocco
**hotel:** inn [pursus
**hound:** dog, basset,
**hourly:** horal
**house:** lodge, domicile
" **(pert. to):** domal
" **plant:** calla [tage
" **(small):** cabin, cot-
**houseboat:** barge
**household:** menage family [lars
" **gods:** penates, di,
**hover:** poise, linger
**however:** yet, but
**howl:** ululate, wail, roar
**hoyden:** tomboy
**hub:** nave
**hubbub:** clamor, tumult, noise, uproar
**hue:** color, tint, cry, shade, tinge [vast
**huge:** giant, enormous, massive, gigantic,
" **(poet.):** enorm
**hulled corn:** samp
**hum:** croon, drone, boom, buzz [mortal
**human:** man, adamite,
" **affairs:** lives
" **trunk:** torso
**humble:** abase, low, disgrace, lower
**humbug:** fraud, imposture [moist
**humid:** damp, wet,
**humiliate:** shame, mortify, abase, debase, abash [ava
**hummingbird:** colibri,
**humor:** wit, mood, indulge, baby, whim, comicality, gratify
**humorist (colloq.):** wag
**humorous:** funny, droll
" **play:** farce, bigwig
**Hun:** Asiatic, vandal
**hunt:** en, chase, trail, search, pursue, seek
**hunter:** nimrod [basset
**hunting dog:** setter, hound, aland, beagle,
" " **(arch.):** alan
" **expedition:** safari
**hurl:** cast, sling, toss, throw, fling, pelt
" **(poet.):** evance
**hurry:** speed, rush, haste, hasten, hie
**hurt:** pain, pained, damage, dere, injury, harm, injure
**hurtful:** malefic, sore
**husband or wife:** spouse
**husk:** shell, shuck
**husks of fruit:** lemma, hulls [straw, bran
" " **grain:** chaff,
**hut:** hovel, cabin, shack, shanty
**hydraulic pump:** ram
**hydrophobia:** rabies
**hymn:** psalm
" **of praise:** paean
" **tune:** choral
**hynotic state:** trance
**hypocritical talk:** cant
**hypothetical force:** od
" **maiden:** io
" **structural unit:** id

## I

**Ibsen character:** Ase, Nora, Hedda
**ice:** sleet, chill, dessert, frost, frosting, sherbet [cone
" **cream container:**
" **creeper:** crampon
" **crystals:** snow
" **(floating mass):** floe, berg, iceberg
" **runner:** skate
" **sheet:** glacier
**Icelandic giant:** Atli
" **lang.:** Norse
" **literary work:** edda
" **measure of length:** lina
" **story:** saga
**icy:** frigid, gelid
**Idaho capital:** Boise
" **county:** Ada
**idea:** opinion, concept, notion, theory, impression, belief, fancy, thought, intention
**ideal:** aim, pattern, standard, faultless, perfect, mental
" **place:** Utopia [same
**identical:** same, self-
**identification mark:** tag, marker [pleton
**idiot:** moron, oaf, sim-
**idiotic:** daft [otiose, laze
**idle:** inactive, loiter, loaf, useless, lazy, indolent, vacant, sluggish, vain, futile,
" **(colloq.):** laze
" **fancy:** dream
" **talk:** patter, gab, gossip, prate, palaver
**idler:** rounder, drone, dawdler, lazer, loafer
**idol:** image [porphyry
**igneous rock:** basalt,
**ignite:** fire, kindle, light
**ignoble:** mean, base
**ignorant:** nescient, unaware, unlearned
**Igorot town division:** Ato
**Iliad character:** Ajax
**i.k:** sort, breed, kind
**ill:** baneful, evil, bad, harmful, unkind, woe, poorly, ailing
" **boding:** dire
" **bred person:** boor, cad, churl
" **gotten gain:** pelf
" **humored:** morose
" **natured:** nasty
" **(prefix):** mal
" **tempered woman:** virago, shrew
" **will:** rancor, malice, animus
**illness:** malady
**illuminant:** gas
**illusion:** mirage [liant
**illustrious:** noble, bril-
**image:** idol, emblem, likeness, statue, icon, copy, picture, effigy
**imaginative:** poetic
**imagine:** ideate, dream, fancy, conjecture
**imbecile:** cretin, anile
**imbibed:** drank, absorbed
**imbue:** ingrain, leaven, steep, infuse, tincture, pervade, permeate, saturate
" **with vigor:** nerve
**imitate:** ape, emulate, simulate, min, copy, echo, mock, mimic
**imitation:** paste, sham
" **gold:** oroide
" **pearl:** olivet
**immature:** unripe
**immediate:** direct

immediately: anon, presto, now [vasty
immense: vast, enormous, gigantic, great,
immerse: souse, dip, submerge, douse
immigration center: Ellis [still
immovable: adamant,
immutable: firm
imp: sprite, demon
impair: mar, wear, damage, sap, ruin
" by time: rust
impart: instil, tell, convey, inspire, give
impartial: unbiased, fair, just
impassive: stolid
impatient: restive, hasty, tolerant
impede: obstruct, hinder, estop, clog [bar
impediment: remora,
impel: urge, send, induce, constrain, force, drive, compel, incite, spur
imperative: urgent
imperfection: blemish
imperfect (prefix): mal
imperial: regal, majestic
" domains: emperies, empires [saucy, sassy
impertinent: officious,
" (colloq.): sass
impetuous: rash, eager, abrupt, fiery [lodged
implanted: rooted, inculcated, infixed,
implement: tool, spade, utensil, fulfill
" for bruising: pestle
implicate: involve
implied: tacit
implore: beg, entreat, plead, pray
imply: mean, hint
import: interest, sense, matter
importance: stress
importune: solicit, pray, tease, dun
impose: obtrude, lay
" as necessary result: entail
impost: duty, toll, tax
imposture: deception, sham, humbug, deceit [curse
imprecation: oath,
impress: print, stamp, mark, awe [affect
" deeply: engrave,
impression: dent, idea
" of type: print
imprint: stamp, dint
imprison: cage, inter, sconce, incarcerate, jail, confine
imprisonment: durance
improve: better, amend, emend, gain, revise
impudent: saucy, rude, brash, pert, sassy
impure from ore: ocher
impute: ascribe
in: at, among, into
" advance: ahead, before
" any degree: ever
" behalf of: pro, for
" the capacity of: as, qua [with
" company: along,
" direction of: to, axial, toward, on
" existence: extant
" fact: indeed, truly
" favor of: pro, for
" front: ahead, aface
" high spirits: elated, exulted
" the lead: ahead
" like manner: so
" a line: arow
" the main: generally
" name only: nominal [noways
" no matter: not,
" order that: lest
" passing: obiter
" the past: ago
" place of: for, else, stead, instead
" (prefix): en
" progress: afoot
" pursuit of: after
" quick time: presto
" reality: indeed
" a row: alinement
" same degree: so
" " place: ibidem, ibid, ib
" " state: so
" so far as: qua
" store for: await
" such a manner: so
" that case: so, then
" this: herein
" " matter: so
" " place: here
" " way: thus
" time of: during
" " (mus.): train
" a trice: anon
" truth: verily
" what place: where
" " way: how
inactive: inert, indolent, idle, inanimate, otiose, passive, resting, retired [stupid
inane: empty, silly, fatuous, vaculity,
inappropriate: inept
inaugurate: open
inborn: innate, inbred, natural, native
inbred: inborn, innate
incantation: spell
incarnation: avator
incase: case, surround
incendiarism: arson
incensed: irate, enraged, wroth
incentive: motive, spur
ncident: episode, event, happening, act
incidental: bye, stray
incinerate: cremate
incipient: initial
" laugh: smile
incision: cut
incite: egg, exhort, edge, urge, abet, goad, spur, forment, stimulate, impel
" to activity: prod
inclination: trend, bent, penchant, slant, rake, grade, tilt, will, bevel
" of the head: bow
incline: lean, grade, dip, slope, slant, tend, tilt, trend
inclined: prone
" (arch.): fain
" (poet.): leant
" railway: ramp
" trough: chute [yard
inclosure: cage, pen,
income: revenue
incomparable: rare
incomplete: broken, partial
incongruous: alien
incorporate: blend, mix, embody
increase: grow, enhance, raise, enlarge, deepen, add, spread, rise, wax [rich
" knowledge of: en-
incrustation: scar
" on teeth: tartar
inculcate: implant, instil, instill
incursion: raid [truly
indeed: really, yea,
indefinite: vague [one
" pronoun: one, any-
" quantity: some, many, any
indemnify: pay [dent
indent: depress, notch,
independent: free
India (poet.): Ind.
Indian: Amerind, Delaware, Erie, Ute, Otee, Kaw, Mohave, Oto, Otoe, Osage, Keres, Ewers, Cree, Hopi, Mohawk, Seminole, Sac, Oneida, Redskin, Apache, Serrano, Aht
" antelope: nilgai
" arrow poison: curare
" boat: canoe
" building material: laterite
" carpet: agra
" city: Agra, Benares, Lahore, Madira
" class society: caste
" coin: anda, rupee, anna, paisa, spare, annas
" (comb. form): indo
" corn: samp, maize
" currency: wampum
" divisions: tribal, tribals, agras
" festival: mela
" fetish: totem
" god: manitou
" groom: sice, syce
" harvest: rabi
" hemp: ramie, kef
" hut: lodge
" jungle: Soola
" landing place: Ghat
" lodge: teepee, tepee
" madder: el, aal
" measure: kos
" memorial post: Xat
" moccasin: pac
" monetary unit: anna
" mountain pass: Ghat [ash, ach
" mulberry: al, aal,
" noble title: Raia
" nurse: amah [bian
" Ocean Sea: Ara-
" " vessel: dhow
" peace pipe: calumet
" peasant: ryot
" poll: totem
" pony: cayuse
" prince: ameer
" province: Assam
" race: Jat, Tamil
" river: Ul, Ganges, Deo
" robber: dacoit
" seaport: Surat
" silk: eri
" snake: krait
" soldier: sepoy
" song bird: shama
" sovereign: raj
" spirit: manitou
" spring crop: rabi
" symbol: totem
" tent: tepee
" thorny tree: bel
" title of address: sahib
" town: Patan, Arcot
" tree: dar
" tribe: Ao
" utterance: ugh
" village: Pueblo
" war cry: whoop
" " trophy: scalp
" warrior: brave
" weight: tola, ser
" woman: squaw
indicate: dominate, denote, connote, bode, betoken, read, signify
indicating succession: ordinal [dence, note
indication: sign, evi-
indicator: pointer, dial
indifference: apathy
indifferent: supine, cool, apathetic [stoic
" to pain or pleasure:
indigence: want, poverty [natural
indigenous: native,
indigent: poor, needy
indignation: wrath
indigo dye & plant: anil
indisposed: ails, ail, ill
indisposition: ailment
" to motion: inertia
indistinct: dim, blur, obscure
indite: write, pen
individual: one, person, self, ego, sole
" (comb. form): idio
" performance: solo
Indo Chinese city: Hanoi
" " kingdom: Anam
" " language: bama, tai [Tai
" " race: Naga,
indolence: sloth
indolent: inert, otiose, lazy, idle
Indonesian: Ata
induce: urge, prevail, lead, make, persuade
indulge: humor, pamper, please
indulgent: easy
industrialist: magnate
ineffectual: weak, futile
inequality: odd, odds
inert: inactive, lifeless, sluggish, torpid, indolent [lay
inexperienced: callow,
infatuation: ate
infect: taint [derive,
infer: deduce, conclude
inferior: worse, low, bad
" cloth: surat, shoddy
" horse: tit, plater
" (prefix): sub
" wares: seconds
infernal: devilish
inferno: hell
infinite: endless, boundless, eternal
infinitive part: to [lame
infirm: anile, feeble,
inflame: rankle, fire, enrage [den
" with passion: mad-
inflexible: rigid, iron
inflict: wreak, deal
influence: interest, affect, prestige
" corruptly: bribe
influx: inflow, inset
infold: lap, wrap
inform: apprise, tell
informal conversation: chat
" gathering: social
information: data, word
informed: aware, hep
informer: spy [dom
infrequent: rare, sel-
infuriate: madden, enrage
infuse: imbue, instill
ingenuity: art, wit
ingenuous: naive
ingrained: innate
ingredient: materials, component, element
ingress: entry, entrance
inhabitant: inmate, denizen
" of city: cit [otes
" 's of (suffix): ites,
inhibit: check
inhume: inter
inimical: hostile, averse
iniquity: crime, sin, evil, vice [begin
initiate: institute, start,

**injunction**: order, precept, mandate
**injure**: harm, damage, maim, hurt, mar, wrong [damage, hurt
**injury**: lesion, harm,
**inky**: black
**inland body of water**: river, pond, brook
**inlay**: insert, inset
**inlet**: ria, bay, cove, slew, entrance or'fice
" **from sea**: arm, bayou
**inn**: hotel, tavern, hostel, hostelry
**innate**: hidden, natural, inherent, ingrained, inborn [scure
**inner**: hidden, internal, within inside, ob-
" **bark**: bast [heart
" **part**: inside, core,
" **point**: into [gestion
**innuendo**: slur, sug-
**inorganic**: mineral
**inquiry**: search
" **for lost goods**: tracer [ing
**inquisitive**: nosy, pry-
" **(colloq.)**: snoopy, nosey [luny
**insane**: demented, mad,
**inscribe**: write, dedicate, letter
**insect**: mantis, flea, fly, termite, gnat, ant, aphis, bee, bug, moth, wasp, mite, midge, aphid, nit, earwig, dor, cricket, beetle
" **egg**: nit
" **exudation**: lac
" **feeler**: antenna
**insectivorous mammal**: tenrec
**insecure**: risky, unsafe, perilous [put
**insert**: enter, enclose,
**inset**: inlay, influx
**inside**: into, interior, within, inner, internal
**insight**: ken
**insignia**: regalia, badge
**insignificant**: trivial, null, tiny
" **par.**: iota
" **person**: snip
**insipid**: vapid, flat, stale
**insist**: persist, demand, urge
**inspect**: pry, examine
**inspector of electric lamps**: ager
" " **wts. & measures**: sealer [stir
**inspire**: uplift, impart,
**inspirit**: cheer, liven
**install**: seat, invest
**instance**: case
**instant**: moment, trice
**instead**: else [egg
**instigate**: abet, foment,
**instill**: infuse [tiate
**institute**: establish, ini-
" **suit**: sue
**instruct**: train, teach, educate, school, edify
**instrument**: tool, organ
" **board**: panel
" **to record time**: dater [cy, mean
**instrumentality**: agen-
**insufficient**: scanty
**insulate**: isle, isolate
**insult**: affront, offend, slap
**insurgent**: rebel [tire
**integral**: composite, en-
**integrity**: honor
**intellect**: mind, brain
" **(pert. to)**: noetic
**intellectual**: mental
**intelligence**: sense, wit, mind, wants, reason
**intend**: mean, purpose, propose, aim
**intense**: ardent, extreme, acute, fierce, fervid, deep [rapt
**intent**: purpose, eager,
**intention**: aim, purpose, idea
**inter**: inhume, entomb
**intercede**: mediate
**interdict**: ban, bar
**interdiction**: veto, ban
**interfere**: meddle
**interim**: meantime
**interior**: inside, inner
" **(comb. form)**: ento
**interjection**: ha, ho, oh, ah, ahem
**interlace**: braid, weave
**interlock**: knit [between
**intermediate**: mesne,
**intermix**: mingle
**internal**: inner, enclosed, inside
" **fruit decay**: blet
**internat. agreement**: treaty, cartel
" **lang.**: ro [tente
" **understanding**: en-
**interprets**: decodes, renders, construes, redc, reads
**interrogate**: ask, inquire
**interruption**: hiatus, gap, break [join
**intersect**: meet, cross,
**intersecting**: secant [ola
**interstice**: crevice, are-
**intertwine**: lace
**interval**: space, time, respite, span, gap
**intervening**: between
" **(law)**: mesne
**interweave**: braid, mat, plait, lace, raddle
**intimate**: hint, near, suggest [homey
" **(colloq.)**: homy,
**intimation**: cue, hint
**intimidate**: cow, awe, deter, daunt, overawe
[illegible] within, inside, in
**intolerant**: bigoted
**intone**: chant, sing
**intransitive**: neuter
**intrepid**: bold, dreadless, brave, dauntless
**intrepidity**: nerve
**intricate**: dedal, gordian, complex
**intrigue**: cabal, plot
**intrinsic nature**: essence
**introduce**: herald, insert, present, usher
**introduction**: entree, prelude, preamble, debut, prologue, preface, insertion
**inundate**: flood, deluge
**inure**: harden, season, accustom, use
**inutile**: useless
**invade**: raid, encroach
**invalid**: null
**invaluable**: priceless
**invariable**: steady
**invariant**: constant
**invent**: create, feign, coin, originate, devise, discover
**inventor of sewing machine**: Howe
" " **telegraph**: Morse [verse
**invert**: transpose, re-
**invest**: instate, install, envelop, endue, vest, endow [quire
**investigate**: probe, in-
**invigorate**: renew, strengthen
**invisible emanation**: aura
**invite**: bid, ask, entice
**involve**: tangle, entail, implicate, engage
**inward**: secret [dot
**iota**: jot, atom, whit,
**Iowa college**: Coe
" **town**: Ames
**Ipecac plant**: evea
**Iranian**: Persian
**Iraq capital**: Bagdad
**irascible**: touchy, testy
**irate**: wroth, wrath, angry, mad
**ire**: rage, anger, wrath, fury, passion
**Ireland**: Eire, Erin
**irenic**: peaceful, serene
**iridescent**: opaline, irised
" **gem**: opal
**iris**: flag
" **of the eye (pert. to)**: irian
" **(heraldry)**: lis
" **(kind)**: orris
" **layer**: uvea
" " **(pert. to)**: uveal [flag
" **plant**: irid, ixia,
**Irish**: celtic
" **ancient capital**: Tara
" **author**: Shaw
" **battle cry**: abu
" **bay**: Sligo
" **Chamber of Dep.**: Dail
" **city**: Cork
" **coin**: rap
" **cudgel**: alpeen
" **dramatist**: Steele Shaw
" **epic tale**: tana [rah
" **expletive**: arra, ar-
" **fish**: pollan
" **floral emblem**: shamrock
" **lassie**: colleen
" **Neptune**: Ler
" **peasant**: kern
" **poet**: Wilde, Moore, Yeats
" **river**: Nore, Lagan
" **sea god**: Ler
**irk**: annoy, chafe
**irksome**: tedious
**iron**: F.E., fetter, ferrum, firmness, hard, smooth, manacle, firm, press
" **alloy**: steel
**ironic**: sarcastic, satirical, satiric
**Iroquois tribe**: Oneida
**irredescent jewels**: opals [erose
**irregular**: abnormal,
**irrigate**: water
**irritable**: testy, edgy
**irritate**: gall, fret, rile, peeve, grate, nettle, tease, provoke, vex, anger, exasperate
**irritation**: itch, pique
**isinglass**: mica
**island**: ait, alt
" **(Fr.)**: ile [moa
" **group**: Faroe, Sa-
" **off Ireland**: Aran
" " **Tuscany coast**: Elba
" **(poet.)**: isle
" **of Saints**: Erin
" **(small)**: isle, islet
**islet**: cay, bay, ait, alt
**isolated**: singular, alone, detached
**Israelite**: see "Hebrew" & "Jewish"
" **tribe**: Gad, Dan, Asher, Levi, Aser
**issue**: print, outcome, emerge, emit, arise
" **forth**: emanate
**Italian**: Roman, Latin
" **actress**: Duse
" **anatomist**: Aselli
" **article**: il
" **astronomer**: Secchi, Galileo
" **building**: Casa
" **chief magistrate**: doge
" **city**: Taranto, Pisa, Asti, Milan, Nola, Venice, Trieste, Alba, Ferrara, Bra, Teano, Rome, Trent, Turin, Este, Genoa, Sassari
" **coins**: lire, lira, soldos
" **(comb. form)**: Italo
" **composer**: Verdi
" **condiment**: tamara
" **dept.**: Calabria
" **family**: Este
" " " **health**: Salus
" **house**: casa
" **island**: Cos, Lido, Elba, Capri
" **lake**: Como
" **legislative chamber**: camera
" **measure**: stero
" **millet**: tenai
" **music reformer**: Guido
" **novelist**: Serao [ma
" **opera**: Aida, Nor-
" **painter**: Reni, Titian, Raphael
" **physicist**: Volta
" **poet.**: Dante, Tasso
" **princely house**: este
" **province**: Mantua, Parma, Este, Como, Pisa [Tiber, Piave
" **river**: Po, Arno,
" **saint**: Neri
" **seaport**: Pola, Trieste, Genoa
" **seaside resort**: Lido
" **soprano**: Patti [dra
" **statesman**: Salan-
" **tenor**: Caruso
" **title**: donna
" **violin**: amati
" **wine**: asti
" **woodwork**: tarsia
" **writer**: Cellini
" **for yes**: si [maxim
**item**: detail, entry,
" **of property**: asset
**itemize**: list
**iterate**: repeat
**ivory**: dentine

## J

**jab**: poke
**jabber**: babble, sputter
**jackdaw**: daw
**jacket**: reefer, eton
**Jacob's brother**: Esau, Edom [ban
" **father-in-law**: La-
" **son**: Dan, Levi, Reuben, Gad
" **wife**: Leah [lockup
**jail**: prison, imprison,
**Jap**: Nip [aino, aeta
" **aborigine**: ainu,
" **admiral**: Ito, Togo
" **boxes**: inro
" **church**: tera
" **city**: Osaka, Ujina, Nagasaki, Kobe [rin
" **coin**: sen, yen, ril,
" **dancing girl**: geisha
" **drink**: sake, saki
" **emperor**: Mikado, Hirohito
" **family badge**: mon
" **festival**: bon
" **fortress**: truk [cho
" **measure**: ri, se, rin,
" **money**: sen
" **mt.**: Usu
" **pagoda**: taa
" **peninsula**: Corea
" **plane**: zero
" **plant**: udo
" **porgy**: tai

" **rice paste**: ame
" **sash**: obi
" **statesman**: Ito
" **wt.**: mo, shi [trick
**jape**: gibe, fraud, jest,
**jar**: jolt, shock, disconcert, shake, clash, discord olla, urn
**jargon**: cant, slang, patter, lingo, argot
**Jason's follower**: Argonaut
" **helper**: Medea
" **ship**: Argo, Argonaut
**jaunt**: sally, trip [upas
**Java poisonous tree**:
**javelin**: dart, spear
**jealousy**: envy [taunt
**jeer**: scoff, flout, boo,
**jejune**: dry, arid
**jellyfish**: medusa
**jellylike material**: gel
**jeopardy**: danger, peril
**jerk**: yank, bob
**Jerusalem hill**: Zion
" **mosque**: Omar
" **oak**: ambrose
**jest**: joke, game, jape
**jet**: spout, gush, jut, black
" **black**: raven, ebon
**jewel**: stone, gem, opal
" **mounting**: setting
**jeweler's weight**: carat
**jewelry alloy**: oroide
**Jewish**: see also Hebrew
" **festival**: seder [Eli
" **high priest**: Ezra,
" **law**: torah, talmud
" **leader**: Moses
" **month**: Nisan, Adar, Tisri, Elul, Ab, Sebat, Tebet, Shebat
" **ram's horn**: shofar
" **teacher**: rabbi
" **weight**: gerah, omer
**jib**: gib, balk
**jocularity**: wit
**jog**: nudge, trot
**John (Scot.)**: Ian
**johnnycake**: pone
**join**: unite, meet, team, connect, mortise, ally, enter, intersect, annex, yoke, engage, add, meld, merge
" **closely**: weld, enlink
**joint**: hinge, tenon, seam [wrist
" **of arm**: elbow,
" " **door**: hinge
" " **leg**: knee
" **legatee**: coheir
" **of stem**: node
**joke**: jest, gag
**joker**: wit, wag
**jolly**: jovial, merry
**jolt**: jar, bump
**josh**: guy
**Joshua's father**: Nun
**jostle rudely**: elbow
**jot**: iota, mite, speck, whit, atom, ace, particle [trip, trek, tour
**journey**: fare, travel,
**joust**: tilt
**jovial**: jolly[ness, elation
**joy**: bliss, glee, glad-
**joyful**: cheerful, blithe
**joyous**: glad, happy, riant, festal, festive
**jubilant**: elated
**Judah's son**: Er
**judge**: consider, arbiter, decide, deem, opine, arbitrator, referee, estimate
" **chamber**: camera
" **circuit (arch.)**: iter
" **court bench**: banc
" **gavel**: mace
" **robe**: gown
**judgment**: doom, sense, award, verdict, opinion, sentence
**judicial command**: mandate
" **order**: writ
" **writ**: elegit
**jug**: ewer, cruse
**juice of plant**: sap
**juicy plant**: uva
**Jules Verne character**: Nemo
**jumble**: displace, pie
**jumbled type**: pi
**jump**: leap, hop [per
" **about**: prance, ca-
**jumping stick**: pogo
**junction**: union, meeting
" **lines**: suture, seam
**june bug**: dor
**juniper (kind of)**: Cade
**Jupiter**: Beus, Jove
" **'s son**: Caster
**jurisdiction (law)**: soc
**jurisprudence**: law
**jury**: panel
**just**: fair, impartial
" **clear the ground (naut.)**: atrip, aweigh
**justice**: law, fairness
**jutting rock**: tor, crag
**juvenile**: young, youthful

## K

**Kaffir warriors**: Impi
**kaka**: parrot
**kava**: ava
**keen**: sharp, nice, fine, acute, shrewd, pungent [zest
" **enjoyment**: gusto,
**keeness of mind**: acumen [maintain
**keep**: retain, hold,
" **afloat**: buoy [clude
" **apart**: separate, se-
" **away from**: avoid
" **back**: detain, hinder, stifle, deter
" **close to**: hug
" **company**: consort
" **from action**: deter
" **intact**: preserve
" **order**: police
" **from progressing**: delay
" **from shaking**: steady [warden
**keeper**: custodian,
**keeve**: tub, vat
**keg**: cask, barrel
**Kentucky bluegrass**: poa [barrel
**kernel**: nut, grain,
**kettledrum**: atabal, typani, timbal
**key**: cay, wharf, pitch, solution
" **note in music**: tonic
**Keystone state**: Pa.
**kick a football**: punt
**killer whale**: orc, orca
**kiln**: ost, oven, oast, osier, furnace, stove
**kind**: sort, ilk, genus, humane, gentle, genre, friendly, type
**kindle**: fire, fume, lume, ignite, light
**kindly**: benign
**kindness**: favor, tenderness [family, sib
**kindred**: gens, kinship,
**King Arthur's abode**: Camelot, Avalon
" " **father**: Uther
" " **lance**: ron
" **of Bosham**: Og
" **David's ruler**: Ira
" **of England & Denmark**: Canute, Cnut
" " **fairies**: Oberon
" **fish**: barb
" " **Huns**: Attila
" " **Israel**: Saul, Omri, Ahab, David
" " **Judah**: Asa, Ahaz, Herod
" **(latin)**: rex [das
" " **Phrygia**: Mi-
" " **Troy**: Priam
" " **Tyre**: Hiram
" " **underground**: Satan [ric
" " **Visigoths**: Ala-
**kingdom**: realm, empire
**kingly**: regal [relative
**kinsman**: relation, sib,
**kiss**: buss, osculate
**kite**: elanet
**kittenish**: playful
**kiwi**: roa
**knack**: art [varlet
**knave**: rascal, rogue,
" **of clubs**: pam
" **in cribbage**: nob
**knead**: massage, elt
**kneecap**: patella [vet
" **to cut loops**: tre-
" **(large)**: machete, snee, bolo
**knifelike instrument**: spatula
**knight**: cavalier, gallant
" **'s cloak**: tabard
**knighterrant**: paladin
**knit**: contract, unite
**knob**: node, nub, lump
**knock lightly**: tap [ko
**knockout (slang)**: kayo,
**knot**: node, noose, tie, gnarl, entangle, nodule, mat
" **of hair**: chignon
" **(pert. to)**: nodal
" **in wood**: gnarl, burl, knar, gnar
" **of wool**: noil
" " **yarn**: skein
**knotted lace**: tatting
**knotty**: gnarly, gnarled, nodal, nodose
**know**: ken
" **(arch.)**: wot, wis
" **(Scot.)**: ken [aware
**knowing**: shrewd, wise,
**knowledge**: lore, ken, cognition, wisdom
" **gained**: lesson
" **(pert. to)**: gnostic, gnostical
**known facts**: data
**kobold**: nisse, nis

## L

**Laban's daughter**: Leah
**label**: designate, brand, docket, stamp, mark, classify, tag, tab
**labor**: toil
" **hard**: strive
" **organization**: union
**labored breath**: gasp, pant
**laborer**: peon, serf
**Labrador tea**: ledum [tie
**lace**: thread, embroider,
" **collar**: bertha
" **edging**: frill
" **pattern**: toile
**lacelike**: lacy [mangle
**lacerate**: rend, tear,
**lacet**: braid
**lachrymal drop**: tear
**lack**: need, dearth
" **of good qualities**: badness [cord
" " **harmony**: dis
" " **vigor**: atony
**lackadaisical**: blah
**lacking**: destitute, shy
**Laconia capital**: Sparta
**laconic**: terse
**lacquer**: lac
**lacteal fluid**: milk
**lad**: stripling, boy
**ladderlike**: scalar
**lade**: load, bail, burden, freight, dip
**ladle**: scoop, dipper
**lag**: trail, linger, falter, loiter, delay, tarry
**laggard**: loiterer, remiss
**lair**: den, tier, row, haunt, amass, cave
**laity**: people
" **(pert. to)**: laic
**lake (small)**: mere
**lamb**: tag
**Lamb's mother**: Ewe
" **pen name**: Elia
**lame**: halt, infirm, feeble [cry
**lament**: deplore, bemoan, sigh, grieve, bewail, regret, wail, beweep, pine, moan,
**lamentation**: moan
**lamia**: witch
**lamina**: leaf
**laminar**: scaly, flaky
**laminated**: slaty
" **rock**: shale [tern
**lamp**: torch, light, lan-
" **cord**: wick
" **fuel**: kerosene
" **iron frame**: cresset
" **part**: burner
" **(slang)**: glim
**lampoon**: satire, ridicule, squib, skit
**lamprey**: eel
**lanate**: wooly
**lance**: spear, open, pierce, dart
**land**: terra, soil, ground, shore, earth, country, debark, alight
" **conveyance**: deed
" **held absolutely**: alod [decare
" **measure**: are, rod, acre, ar, meter, rood,
**landed**: alit
" **estate**: manor
" **property**: estate
**landing place**: quay, wharf [ery
**landscape**: scene, scen-
**lane**: path
**language**: tongue, ro
" **peculiar to a people**: idiom
**languid**: wan, listless
**languish**: pine, droop, flag [slander
**lank**: lean, gaunt,
**lanneret**: falcon
**lap**: circuit, fold, unfold, enfold, truncate
**lapped joint**: scarf
**lapse**: slip
**lapwing**: pewit
**lard**: adeps, fat
**larded**: enriched
**larder**: pantry [bulky
**large**: huge, great, big,
" **amount**: plenty
" **animal**: behemoth
" **body of land**: continent [cro
" **(comb. form)**: ma-
" **fish**: shark, tuna, skate, snapper
" **number**: score, host, billion, myriad
" " **(colloq.)**: raft
" " **(slang)**: slew
**lariat**: riata, lasso
**larva**: grub, loa
" **of fly**: maggot
**lash**: flog, tie, whip, satirize, berate [girl
**lass**: maid, maiden,
**lassitude**: inertia, languor, debility [lariat
**lasso**: riata, reata, rope,
**last**: final, endure, con-

tinue, omega, ultimate
" act: finale
" (arch.): dure
" month: ultimo
" state of insect: imago
" traces: ashes
late: recent, tardy, delayed
" afternoon service: vespers
" (comb. form): neo
" information: news
latent: hidden, dormant, potential quiescent [newer
later: after, tardier,
lateral boundry: side
lath: slat
lather: suds, soap, foam
Latin: Roman, Italian
" greeting: ave
" poet: Ovid
latite: lava
lattice structure: trellis
Latvian: Lett, Lettic
" capital: Riga
" coin: lat
" river: Aa [glorify
laud: praise, extol, exalt,
laugh: chorlte
" loudly: snort [fleer
" to scorn: deride,
laughing: riant
laurel tree: bay
lava: latite
" (cooled): aa
lave: bathe, wash
lavender: aspic [ta
Lavinia's mother: Amalavish: profuse
" fondness on : dote
law: canon, code, justice, statute, rule, act
" (delay): mora
" (intervening): mesne
" (Latin): ius, lex
" note: ut
lawful: legal, licit
lawless: unruly, disorderly
lawmaker: solon
lawn (fine): batiste [ter
lawyer: legalist, barrislax: slack, loose, remiss
lay: put, song, ballad
" away: store, reposit
" hidden: lurked
" siege to: invest
" waste: ravage, desolate, devastate
layers: coats, strata, beds, rows, tiers, thickness, plies
" of clay in coal: sloam
" " metal: seam
" " mineral: vein
laymen: laics, seculars
leaf: tendril, spathe, petal, lamina, page
" part: blade
" vein: rib
leafy shelter: bower
" stemmed herb: aster [union
league: federation,
leak: drip, seep [trust
lean: lank, gaunt, tip, incline, tilt, rest, spare, slant, depend,
" on one side: heel
" to: shed
Leander's love: Hero
leap: spring, hop, bound, vault, jump
" (dial.:) lep
" over: skip
" playfully: gambol
learn: acquire, memorize, ascertain, con
learned: erudite, wise, erudition, scholarly
" man: pundit
learning: lore
lease: charter, let, hire, rent, contract, tenure
least: minimum, slightest, fewest [nery
leather factory: tan-
" on football shoe: cleat
" (kind): napa, oxhide, levant, kid, calf, roan, cowhide
" (long piece): strap
" (soft): suede, napa, roan [quit
leave: depart, vacate, retire, permission, go,
" country: emigrate
" helpless: strand, maroon [miss
" out: omit, elide
leaven: yeast
leaves: foliage
leaving: ort
" a will: testate
ledge: shelf
ledger entry: item
leer: ogle, mock, entice
left after expenses: net
" hand page: V.O.
" " side of an account: debtor
" side: aport
leg: crus, support
" joint: ankle, knee
" part: shin, shank
legacy recipient: legatee
legal: lawful, dominate, valid, licit [levin
" action: res, rep-
" charge: due, fee
" claim: lien
" defense: alibi
" hearing: trial
" offense: crime
" official: notary
" order: writ
" paper: deed
" profession: bar
" records: acta
" suffix: ee [lars
" tender notes: dol-
" wrong: tort
legate: envoy [recipient
legatee: heir, heiress,
legend: saga, myth
legendary bird: roc
" founder of Rome: Remus
legislate: enact
legislative body division: house [tor
legislator: solon, sena-
legume: pod, bean, uva, lentil, pea, loment
leguminous plant: lentil, peas, pulse, pea
lei: wreath
leisure: time
lemur: loris, lori [nish
lend: loan, afford, fur-
lengthen: extend, elongate, prolong
lengthwise of: along
lengthy: long, extended
lenient: clement, merciful
lens (type of:) toric
leonine: lionlike
leopard: panther, chetah
leper: lazar, outcast
"Les Miserables" author: Hugo
less: minus, minor, fewer, smaller [rarer
" common: rare,
" (musical): meno
" (prefix): mis
" ripe: greener
" severe: relent
lessee: tenant, renter
lessen: bate, abate, reduce, wane, ease, lower, taper, diminish, shrink, deplete [hire
lesser: smaller, minor
let: lease, rent, hinder,
" air out of: deflate
" the bait bob: dib
" down: lower
" " tension: relax
" go: release
" in: admit
" slip by: lapse
" stand: stet
" " (mus.): sta
lethal: fatal, deadly
lethargic: dull, sleepy
" sleep: sopor
" state: coma
lethargy: stupor, torpor, apathy, coma
letter: epistle, missive, inscribe
" of defiance: cartel
lettered: literate, educated
lettuce: cos, romaine
Levantine: oriental
" ketch: saic, proa
levee: dike, quay [aim
level: even, flat, plane,
lever: pry, crowbar
" in a loom: lam
levy: tax, assess, collect
liable: apt
" to punishment: guilty [malign
libel: slander, calumny,
liberal: generous, broad
" gift: largess
liberate: redeem, release, free
Libyan seaport: Derna
license: permit, authority
lichen: moss [legal
licit: lawful, permitted,
lick up: lap
lid: cover, top
lie: fib, falsehood
" in ambush: lurk
" at anchor: moor
" dormant: sleep
" at ease: bask, loll
" in warmth: bask
liege: devoted, loyal, faithful, vassal
lien: claim, mortgage
lieu: place, stead
life: vitality, existence
" of business: sales
" fluid: blood
" insurance tontine
lifeboat crane: davit
lifeless: inert, amort, dead [exalt
lift: hoist, raise, elevate, heave, elevator, pry,
" price: up
" in spirits: elate
lifting implement: tongs
light: lamp, gleam, pale, ignite, airy, leger
" brushing sound: swish
" carriage: gig, shay, phaeton, surrey
" colored: claro
" of day: sun
" " evening: star
" & fine: leger
" hasty lunch: snack
" helmet: sallet
" (kind): arc [tion
" meal: tea, colla-
" material: gauze
" rain: shower
" repast: tea
" sketch: pastel
" substance: cork
" tan: almond
" up: illume
lightheaded: gay
lighthouse: pharos
like: admire, as, similar, enjoy, relish, prefer
likelihood: chance
likely: probable, verisimilar, credible
likewise: too, also
" (poet.): eke
lilac color: mauve
lily, the: lis
" (day): niobe
" (kind): calla, sego, aloe, onion, yucca, tulip, arum
limb: bough, branch
limber: limp, pliant
lime tree: teil, linden
limit: term, solstice, end, restrict, boundary, confine, extent
limited: finite, few
" to small area: local
limn: paint, sketch, draw
limp: limber, clop
linden tree: lin, teil
line: row, streak, rein, cord, boundry, mark, course, string, rule
" of descent: strain
" " juncture: seam
" " persons: cue
" " poetry: verse
" " revolution: axis
" the roof of: ceil
" with ridges: rib
lineage: race, pedigree
lineament: feature, line
linen clothes: napery
" fabric: crash
" (fine): damask, lawn, cambric
" fluff: lint
" plant: flax
" (sheer): toile
" vestment: alb [er
liner: steamship, steam-
linger: hover, lag, loiter, tarry, dawdle, stay, delay, wait
lingo: jargon
lining of a well: steen
link: yoke, nexus, couple, unite, tie, attach
" together: catenate, couple
linseed: flaxseed
lionlike: leonine
lip: labium, edge, brim
lips (pert. to): labial
liqueur: creme
liquid: fluid
" compound: oleir.
" container: pail, tank
" dose: potion
" fat (var.): elaine, elain, olein
" measure: gallon, minim, pint
" particle: drop
liquify by heat: melt
liquor: rum, noyau, anisette, ale, grog, tipple, hydromel
lissome: lithe, supple, nimble
list: rota, roll, roster, itemize, agendum, careen, register, catalog, catalogue
" of electors: poll
" " errors: errata
" " things to be done: agenda
listen: harken, hark, attend, hear
listless: languid
literal: exact
literary: literate [thesis
" composition: paper, tragedy, essay,
" fragments: ana
" supervisor: editor
" " (abbr.): ed
literate: educated, literary, lettered
lithe: supple, pliant, lissome, agile, flexible
litter: bier, clutter

little: bit, small, petty
live: reside, are, be, brisk, subsist, quick
" coal: ember
" in a tent: camp
lively: brisk, nimble, animated, pert, agile
" dance: reel
" song: lilt
liven: animate, activate, inspirit
liver secretion: bile, gall
livid: ashen
living: alive
lixivium: lye [monitor
lizard: agama, gila, iguana, lacerta, eft, adda, skink, seps
" like amphibian: salamander, newt
llama (kind): alpaca
load: lade, burden, cargo, saddle
loadstone: magnet
loaf: idle, loiter, lounge
loam: soil, earth, marl, dirt, clay
" deposit: loess
loath: abhor, hate, averse, detest, reluctant, abominate
loathsome: foul
lobby: foyer, vestibule
lobster chela: pincer
" claw: chela
" row: coral
local ordinance: bylaw
locale: position, place
localities: loci, sites, spots, regions, places
located: situate, stands
location: site, seat, spot, place
lock: bolt, hasp, fasten
" of hair: tress, ringlet
lockup: jail
locomotive: engine
" part: cab
" service car: tender
locus: place
locust: cicada, acacia
lodge: room, cabin, lie, house, implant, lay
" doorkeeper: tiler
lodger: guest
lodging: abode
loft: attic
lofty: elevated, aerial, tall, eminent, haughty, aery, high
" in style: epic
log: record
" float: raft
" from which shingles are cut: spalt
loge: booth, box
logger's boot: pac
logogriph: anagram
Lohengrin's wife: Elsa
loiter: linger, lag, idle, tarry, saunter, delay
loll: recline, droop, sprawl, laze
London district: Soho
lone: solo, solitary, sole
long: tall, hanker, lengthy, crave, yearn
" distance runner: miler
" fish: eel
" for: pine, crave, desire, yearn, hanker
" handled implement: hoe, poleax
" hill: ridge
" intently: pant
" leg bird: steve, stilt, wader, egret, stork, avocet, curlew, crane, rail, heron
" low seat: settee
" since: yore [reedy
" & slender: spindle,
" space of time: eon
" standing: old
longing: yen, appetite, desire [leer
look: gaze, search, see, discern, peer, eye, seem, appearance, appear, glance, lo,
" after: tend, attend
" aimlessly: grope
" angrily: glare
" approvingly: smile
" askance: leer, ogle
" at: view
" attentively: pore
" of contempt: sneer
" despondent: gloom
" for: crave, seek
" at intently: stare
" into: pry
" joyous: smile
" on with contempt: despise
" out: beware [ogle
" slyly: peek, peep,
" sullen: pout, lower
" upon: regard
" well on: become
loom part: reed
loop: noose, curve, circle, fold, tab, picot
" on edge of lace or ribbon: picot
loophole: eyelet
loose: free, slack, release, unbound, lax
" end: tag, dag
" fragments of rock: gravel
loosen: relax, slacken, untie, release, free
loot: sack, rob, plunder, booty, pillage, spoil
lop: pendent, chop, trim, droop
" off: prune
lope: canter
lopsided: alop
loquacity (colloq.): gab
lord's chief manor place: demesne
lore: learning
lose: waste, stray, misplace, miss, spill
" color: pale, fade
" freshness: wilt, stale, fade
" heat: cool [spond
" hope: despair, de-
" luster: fade, tarnish
" vigor: flag [damage
loss: defeat, failure,
" of hope: despair
lot: fate, destiny, portion, hazard, share, fortune
lottery (form of): raffle
lotto (form of): keno
loud: noisy, clamorous
" call: cry
" cry: howl, yawp
" lamentation: wail
" noise: bang, din, roar, clang
" sound: noise [tor
" voice person: sten-
Louisiana court decree: arret
lounge: loll, sofa, loaf
louse egg: nit
lout: boor, yahoo, oaf, bumpkin, blockhead
love: fondness, charity, affection, gra
" apple: tomato
" greatly: dote
" missive: valentine
" (pert. to): erotic, amatory
" potion: philter
" story: romance
lover: swain, ami
" of one's country: patriot [ly, bellow
low: moo, base, soft, humble, inferior, soft-
" bow: salaam
" cloud: nebula
" deck of ship: orlop
" form of animal life: amoeba
" island: key
" necked: decollete
" noise: hum
" note: ut
" sound: hum, murmur, drone, rumble
" spirits: dumps, blues
" tree: shrub
" tufted plant: moss
lower: reduce, lessen, abase, nether, frown, diminish, sink, debase, humble, demean, depress, degrade, bate
" the bottom: deepen
" end of mast: heel
" region: Hades
" in value: debase
lowest: see also "low"
" ebb: neap
" form of wit: pun
" of high tides: neap
" limit: minimum
" part: bottom
" " in music: bass
" point: nadir
lowing sound: moo
loyal: leal, true, liege, faithful
loyalist: Tory
lozenge: pastil [graphite
lubricate: oil, grease,
lucent: shining
lucerne: alfalfa
lucid: clear, sane
luck: hap, chance
lucre: gain [comic
ludicrous: comical,
lug: drag, haul, ear
lukewarm: tepid
lull: quiet, respite
lumber: timber
luminous body: star
lump: mass, nodule, nub, piece, knob, gob
" of earth: clod
lunar creator: linne
" months: moons
lure: bait, entice, decoy, tempt, draw, attract
lurk: prowl [shine
luster: sheen, gloss,
lustrous mineral: spar
lusty: robust
luxuriant: lush
luxuriate: bask [Igorot
Luzon native & savage: Atta, Ata, Aeta,
Lyra star: Vega
lyrelike instrument: asor
lyric: poem, musical

## M

macabre: eerie [parrot
macaw: ara, arara, arar,
macebearer: beadle
macerate: steep
machine: engine, motor
" bar: rod
" to compress: baler
" " cut hay: mower
" " grind grain: mill
" " move heavy wts.: gin
" " notch girders: coper [et
" part (slang): gadg-
" to raise pile on cloth: napper
" " spread hay: tedder
" tool: lathe [irate
mad: insane, frantic,
madagascar animals: ayeayes, tenrecs
madden: enrage, craze
made of cereal: oaten
" " grain: cereal
" " flowers: floral
" " tile: tegular
" " wood: treen
madness: mania
magazine: arsenal, store
mage: wizard
maggot: larva
magic: rune, sorcery
magician: Houdini
" 's word: presto
magnesia: talc
magnet: loadstone
" end: pole
magnificence: pomp, splendor, grandeur
magnificent: splendid, grand, palatial, superb
magnitude: size
mahognany pine: totara
maid: lass, nymph, girl, domestic
mail: post, armor
maim: cripple, lame, injure, disable
main: ocean, principal, chief, foremost
" blood stream: aorta
" body: trunk, mass
" course: entree
" idea: gist
Maine capital: Augusta
" lake: Sebago
" town: Orono, Milo, Bangor, Hiram [tend
maintain: keep, preserve, claim, assert, vindicate, allege, con-
" order: police
maize: corn
majestic: leonine, stately, imperial, superb, glorious [render
make: fabricate, construct, create, form, manufacture, induce,
" additions to: eke
" allegations against: accuse [tion
" allusion to: men-
" amends: atone, redress, redeem
" angry: rile
" ashamed: abash
" believe: sham, pretend, feign
" beloved: endear
" a botch of: flub
" certain: assure, insure
" choice: opt [cus
" clear: explain, fo-
" cloth: weave
" complicated: snarl
" dejected: mope
" designs by lines: etch [bereave
" destitute: bereft,
" dizzy: stun
" an edging: tat
" an end of: destroy
" enduring: anneal
" equal: equate
" ethereal: aerate
" evident: evince
" excuses: stall
" explanation: atone
" faint: bedim [belay
" fast: secure, gird,
" finer: strain
" firm: fix
" first move: lead
" fleshy: fatten
" fun of: guy
" glossy: sleek
" of goods: brand
" a hedge: plash
" " hole: bore

" **ill:** ail
" **an imitation of:** pattern [knit
" **into fabric:** weave,
" " **law:** enact [taw
" " **leather:** tan,
" " **thread:** spin
" **knotted lace:** tat
" **known:** notify, impart
" **late:** belate
" **laws:** legislate
" **lean:** emaciate
" **dense:** rarefy
" **lustrous:** gild
" **muddy:** roil
" **necessary:** entail
" **note of:** jot
" **obeisance:** kneel
" **out:** discern [vate
" **over:** remodel, reform, remake, reno-
" **petulant:** peeve
" **possible:** enable
" **precious:** endear
" **proud:** elate
" **public:** delate, air
" **quiet:** hush
" **quilt:** piece [atone
" **reparation:** expiate,
" **requital for:** repay
" **resolute:** steel
" **(Scot.):** gar
" **sleek:** preen [pall
" **spiritless:** mope,
" **suitable:** adapt, fit
" **too small:** scrimp
" **turbid:** roil, mud
" **untidy:** litter
" **unyielding:** steel
" **up:** compromise
" " **for:** atone
" **vapid:** pall [liven
" **vigorous:** energize,
" **well:** cure, heal
" **wine:** vint
**maker of roofing material:** tiler
" " **wills:** testator
**malady:** disease
**malaria & malarial fever:** ague
**Malay animal:** napu
" **ape:** lar
" **canoe:** proa
" **coin:** tra, ora
" **dagger:** kris
" **disease:** amok
" **fan palm:** gebang
" **garment:** sarong
" **gibbon:** lar [Java
" **island:** Sumatra, Timor, Borneo, Oma,
" **isthmus:** kra
" **vessel:** proa
**male:** mas, man
" **ancestry:** paternity
" **attendant:** page
" **figure for supporting column:** telamon
" **forbears:** sires
**malediction:** curse
**malevolent:** evil, ill
**malice:** spite
**malicious:** spiteful, leer, carry, felonious, evil
" **damage:** sabotage
**malign:** evil, defame, libel, revile
**malignity:** rancor, hate
**malleable:** soft
" **metal:** tin
**mallet:** gravel, maul, gavel, hammer
**malodorous:** fetid
**malt hop drink:** beer
" **liquor:** alt, porter, stout, ale [ery
" " **factory:** brew-
**man of courage:** lion
" **of great strength:** Samson [bob
" " " **wealth:** Na-
" " **learning:** savant, pundit
" **leaving a will:** testator
" **'s arch enemy:** satan [fetter
**manacle:** iron, shackle,
**manage:** contrive, regulate, handle, wield, direct, manipulate, administer, control, operate, engineer
**manager:** steward, director, factor, boss
**mandate:** order, command, injuction
**mandatory precept:** writ
**manducate:** chew
**manger:** stall
**mangle:** 1 cerate, mutilate, ironer
**mania:** craze, madness
**manifest:** patent, signify, plain, display, evident, evince, clear, overt, palpable
**manifesto:** edict
**Manila hemp:** abaca
**manipulate:** handle, use, treat, manage, wield
**mankind:** world
**manly:** virile, resolute
**manner:** mien, air, custom, style, sort, way, mode, means
**mannerly:** polite
**manor:** estate, mansion
" **court (kind):** leet
**mansion:** palace, manor
**mantle:** cloak, robe
**manual art:** craft
" **digit:** finger, thumb
" **vocation:** trade
**manufacture:** make
**many:** several, multiple, numerous, various
**map:** plat, chart, sketch
" **(kind):** relief
" **out:** plan
" **of solar system:** orrery
**maples:** acer
**mar:** deface, damage, spoil, impair, tarnish, injure [agate, mib
**marble:** taw, mig, alley,
**march:** parade
" **king:** Sousa
" **on:** troop
**marching cry:** hep
**margin:** lip, border, edge, hem, verge, scope, brim
**marginal note:** apostil
**marinate:** pickle
**marine:** maritime, oceanic, nautical
" **animal:** coral
" **carnivore:** otter
" **fish:** opah, scaroid, ling, eelpout
" **gastropod:** trition, yet, limpet, nerite
" **mammal:** seal
" **plant:** moss, seaweed, enalid
**mariner:** sailor, seaman, navigator
**maritime:** marine, naval, nautical
**mark:** trace, track, lane, target, label, brand, note, tab
" **aimed at in curling:** tee [dint
" **of a blow:** dent,
" " **infamy:** stigma
" " **injury:** scar
" **the limits:** define
" **of omission:** caret, dele, apostrophe
" **paid:** receipt
" **of pronunciation:** tilde
" **to retain:** stet
" **the skin:** tattoo
" **with asterisk:** star
" " **cuts:** score
" " **ridges:** rib
" " **spots:** dapple, notate, mottle [er
" " **squares:** check-
" " **streaks:** line
" **of wrinkle:** crease
**marker:** peg
**market:** store, sell, mart
" **place:** mart, agora
" **town:** bourg
**marksman:** shot
**marl:** loam
**marriage:** marital, connubial, matrimony, union, wedlock
" **(comb. form):** gamo
" **dot:** dower
**marry:** mate, espouse, wed
**marsh:** swamp, morass, swale, bog, fen [sora
" **bird:** snipe, rail,
" **crocodile:** goa
" **elder:** iva [sedge
" **grass (tall):** reed,
" **marigold:** cowslip
" **plant:** cattail
" **(soft):** salina
**marshy:** paludic
" **place:** slew
**martial:** warlike
**Martinique volcano:** Pelee [igy, miracle
**marvel:** wonder, prod-
**masculine:** male, luis
**mash:** crush
" **down:** stomp, rice
**mask:** visor, disguise, veil, conceal
**mason's hammer point:** peen
**Masonic doorkeeper:** tiler [gob, heap
**mass:** wad, bulk, lump, throng, pat, assemble,
" **book:** missal
" **of bread:** loaf
" " **butter:** pat
" **(comb. form):** mas
" **of floating ice:** floe, berg
" " " **logs:** drive
" " **hay:** mow
" " **ice:** berg, serac
" **meeting:** rally
" **of untidy hair:** mop
" " **water:** eddy
" " **yarn:** cop
**Mass. cape:** Ann, Cod
" **city:** Salem
" **mt.:** Tom
" **town:** Lee
**massage:** kneed, rub
**mast:** spar [due
**master:** conquer, sub
" **stroke:** coup
**masticate:** chew
**mat:** carpet, knot, cushion, doily, entangle
**match:** mate, pair, twin, cope, peer, tally, team [stance
**material:** real, data, corporeal, fabric, sub-
**math. arc:** radian
" **function & ratio:** sine, pi, cosine
" **instrument:** sector
" **line in space:** vector
" **quantity:** surd
**matrix:** mold, bed
**matron:** dame [import
**matter:** substance, affair, concern, signify,
" **(arch.):** reck
" **of fact:** literal
**mattress covering:** tick
**mature:** age, ripen, mellow, ripe, season, grow [mallet
**maul:** abuse, gavel,
**mauser:** rifle
**maw:** craw
**maxim:** adage, moral, motto, tenet, item, precept, axiom, saw, proverb, principle
**May apple:** mandrake
**meadow:** lea, grassland
" **mouse:** vole
" **(poet.):** mead [bare
**meager:** scant, scanty,
**meal:** repast
" **(fine):** farina
" **to be ground:** grist
**mean:** intend, brutal, average, signify, base, cruel, stingy, shabby, snide, imply, denote
**meaning:** sense, intending [poses, wealth
**means:** resources, pur-
" " **crossing fence:** stile [ment, abatis
" " **defense:** muni-
" " **education** travel [hole
" " **escape:** loop-
" " **livelihood:** trade
" " **transmitting force:** lever
" " " **power:** belt
**meantime:** interim
**measure:** mete, gage, estimate, are, acre, meter, ton
" **of capacity:** pint, liter, bushel, peck, gill, litre, stere, quart,
" " **extent:** acre
" " **length:** ell meter, mile, metre, rod, cubit, pik, dra, foot, yard
" **(pert. to):** metric
" **thickness of:** caliper
" **(var.):** gazer
" **of wire:** mil
" " **weight:** carat, ounce, grain
" **for wood:** cord
" **of yarn:** lea
**measurement:** metric, dimension
**measuring instrument:** altimeter, meter, caliper [yardwand
" **stick:** ellwand, pole,
**meat:** flesh
" **ball:** rissole
" **in dough shells:** ravioli
" **jelly:** aspic
" **paste:** pate
" **pie:** pasty
" **pin:** skewer
" **& vegetable dish:** ragout
**meaty:** pithy
**mecca shrine:** Caaba
**mechanical device:** lever, wheel, machine, pump, robot
**mechanism:** action
**meddle:** tamper, mess
**medial:** average
**mediate:** arbitrate, intercede, muse
**medical fluids:** sera
**medicinal herb:** senna aloe, arnica
" **nut:** cola [na, tansy
" **plant:** herb, aconite, ephedra, aloe, ipecac, camomile, sen-
" **root:** jalap
**medicine:** drug, tonic
**medieval:** see also under ancient, old, etc.
" **dagger:** anlace
" **fabric:** samite [tle
" **fortified bldg.:** cas-

" **French kingdom:** Arles
" **hat:** abacot
" **knight:** pennon
" **romantic island:** Avalon
" **shield:** ecu
" **ship:** nef
" **silk fabric:** samite
" **sport:** tilt
" **sword:** estoc
" **tale:** lai [templ te
**meditate:** muse, ponder, study, brood, mull, ruminate, con-
**Mediterranean island:** Malta, Crete, Capri, Elba, Sardinia, Sicily
" **sailing vessel:** saic, setee, mistic, tartan, xebec polacre, felucca
**medium:** average
**medley:** olio, melange
**meek:** tame, gentle
**meet:** confer, assemble, encounter, join, convene, intersect, proper, confront
**meeting:** trysting, tryst, assemblage, conclave, parley, junction
" **room for students:** seminar
" **of spiritualists:** seance
**mel:** honey
**melancholy:** sad, gloom, rueful, blue
**melange:** mixture
**melee:** skirmish, battle, feud, affray, fray, brawl [soft
**mellow:** age, mature, ripe, ripen, soften,
**melodious:** ariose, tuneful, dulcet, musical
**melody:** tune, aria, air, strain, lay song, music [solve, liquify
**melt:** fuse, thaw, dis-
" **down:** render
**member of governing board:** regent [laic
" " **laity:** layman,
" " **religious order:** monk
**membership:** seat
" **charges:** dues
**membrane:** tela
**memento:** relic
**memoir:** eloge
**memorandum:** notes, note, memo
**memorial post:** Xat
" **stones:** cairn
**memorize:** learn, rote
**Memphis divinity:** Ptah
**menace:** threat, threaten, imperil [domicile
**menage:** household,
**menagerie:** zoo
**mend:** repair, darn, fix heal, patch, sew
**mendicant:** beggar
**menial:** servile, domestic, varlet servant
**mental:** ideal, intellectua
" **concept:** idea
" **confusion:** fog
" **function:** power
" **perception:** tact
" **power:** wit [rale
" **state:** mood, mo-
**menthyl ketol:** acetol
**mention:** name, cite
**menu card:** carte
**mephistopheles:** Satan, devil [ling
**mercenary:** venal, hire-
**merchandise:** ware, goods
**merchant:** dealer, trader seller, vender
" **of Bagdad:** Sindbad
" **ship:** argosy
" **of Venice:** Portia
**mercurous chloride:** calomel [duceus
**Mercury's wand:** ca-
" **winged shoes:** talaria [pond
**mere:** bare, simple, only, absolute, pool,
**merely:** only, but
**merganser:** smew
**merge:** fuse, sink, join, combine, unite, absorb, blend
**meridian:** noonday
**merit:** earn, warrant, worth, deserve, rate
**mermaid:** siren
**merriment:** glee, fun, hilarity, gayety
**merry:** gay, sunny, hilarious, jolly
" **go round:** carousel
" **makings:** revel
" **song:** lilt
" **Widow" composer:** Lehar
**mesa:** plateau
**meshed fabric:** lace, net, netting, web, tulle [er
" **instrument:** strain-
**Mesopotamia:** Iraq
**mess:** botch, meddle
**message:** word, note
**messenger:** carrier, page, herald
" **of the gods:** Hermes
**metal:** steel, lead, ore, silver, tin
" **bar:** rivet, rod, rail
" **bearing vein:** lode
" **disk:** paten, sequin, medal, gong [nail
" **fastener:** rivet, nut,
" **flask:** canteen
" **mass:** pig, ingot
" **plate:** disc, paten, platen
" **tag of a lace:** aglet
" **thread:** wire [eter
" **worker:** smith, riv-
" **working tool:** swage
**metallic alloy:** brass
" **bracelet:** bangle
" **cloth:** tinsel
" **element:** zinc, iridium, silver, iron, lead
" **mixture:** alloy
**metamere:** somite
**mete:** allot, dole, distribute [ure
**meter:** rhythm, meas-
**method:** system, plan, way, order, technique, process, rule
" **(pert. to):** modal
**metric measure:** liter, stere, decare, are, gram
**metrical beat:** ictus
" **composition:** verse, poem [pest, anapaest
" **foot:** iambs, ana-
" **land measure:** ar, are, meter
" **units of verses:** feet [rape
**Mexican blanket:** se-
" **cake:** tortilla
" **city:** Tampico
" **coin:** peso, rei
" **conquerer:** Cortes
" **corn mush:** atole
" **cotton cloth:** manta
" **cottonwood:** alamo
" **dish:** tamale [cal
" **drink:** pulque, mes-
" **fiber:** istle
" **guardian spirit:** Nagual
" **hero:** Jaurez
" **hut:** jacal [Maya
" **Indian:** Tlascalan, Alais, Aztec, Cora,
" " **(var.):** xova
" **mammal:** ocelot
" **peasant:** peon
" **president:** Aleman
" **race (early):** Toltec
" **ranch:** hacienda
" **stirrup hood:** tapadero
" **tea:** apasote
" **town:** Tula
" **wt.:** arroba
**microbe:** germ
**microscopic:** little
" **animal:** amoeba
" **fungi:** yeast
**middle:** mesne, center, mid, median
" **ages (pert. to):** mediaeval, medieval
" **(law):** mesne
**midshipman:** plebe, reefer
**midst of:** among [pect
**mien:** bearing, air, as-
**might:** power, arm
**mighty:** strong, potent
**mignonette color:** reseda
**migration:** trek
**migratory worker:** hobo
**mild:** tame, gentle soft, bland
" **& easy:** facile
**military artifice (use of):** strategy
" **assistant:** aide
" **barrier:** abattis
" **chaplain (slang):** padre [vet
" **commission:** bre-
" **front:** sector
" **group:** corps, troop
" **hat:** shako, kepi
" **inspection:** review
" **post:** station, base
" **signal:** taps
" **spectacles:** parades
" **storehouse:** arsenal
" **truck:** camion
" **vehicle:** caisson
" **warehouse:** etape
**milk (comb. form):** lacto, lact
" **curdler:** rennet
" **farm:** dairy
" **(pert. to):** lactic
" **(pharm.):** lac
" **protein:** casein
**milkfish:** awa
**Milky Way:** Galaxy
**mill:** factory
**millstone support:** rynd
**milt:** spleen
**mime:** clown, buffoon
**mimic:** ape, aper, imitate, mime
**mince:** chop
**minced dish:** hash
" **oath:** ecod, egad
**mind:** care, obey, tend, heed, mentality, dislike, brain, sentient
" **(of the):** mental
**Mindanao Indonesian:** Ata
" **lake:** lanao
" **language:** ata
**mine:** burrow
" **division:** panel
" **entrance:** adit
" **vein:** lode
**mineral:** metal, iolite, ore, erinite, spinel
" **bed:** seam [er
" **deposit:** lode plac-
" **(kind of):** edenite, egeran, epidote, irite, uralite, galactite, cal, rutile, aragonite
" **pitch:** asphalt
" **salt:** alkali, alum
" **(soft):** talc
" **spring:** spa
**mingle:** mix, blend
**minister:** pastor, cleric priest, divine, preacher, parson, attend, serve, tend
" **'s home:** parsonage, manse
**Minnesota city:** Ely
" **inhabitant:** gopher
**minor:** lesser, smaller,
**minority:** nonage
**minstrel:** bard, harper
" **show (part):** olio
**mint:** coin
" **plant:** basil, catnip
**minus:** less [mite
**minute:** wee, small,
" **difference:** shade
" **distinction:** nicety
" **groove or channel:** stria
" **organism:** spore
" **orifice:** stoma, pore
" **particle:** molecule, mote, atom [der
**miracle:** marvel, won-
" **man:** fakir
**mirage:** illusion, serab
**mire:** mud, muck, stall, bog, muddy, ooze
**mirror:** glass, reflect
**mirth:** glee, gaiety, jollity
**miry:** muddy, boggy
**miscellany:** ana
**mischievous:** evil, elfish, elfin, sly, arch, devilish
" **spirit:** imp, pixie, elf [trip
" **trick:** prank, can-
**miscreant:** villain
**misdeed:** crime, sin
**miser:** niggard, hoarder
**miserable:** wretched
**miserly:** stingy, pain
**misery:** woe
**misfortune:** ill, disaster blow, evil, woe
**misgiving:** fear, qualm
**misjudge:** err
**mislead:** delude, misdirect, deceive
**misleading argument:** fallacy
**misrepresent:** belie
**miss:** omit, fail, lose, overlook, skip, err
**missile:** dart, bullet, brickbat, arrow, bolas, spear, shaft
**mission:** errand, purpose, delegation
**missive:** note, letter
**misstep:** trip
**mist:** fog, haze, bedim
**mistake:** err, boner, blunder
**mistakes in published work:** errato, errata
**misuse:** abuse [acarus
**mite:** tick, acarid,
**mix:** stir, blend, mingle
" **up:** melee
" **when wet:** pug
**mixed dish:** salad
" **drink:** nog
" **type:** pi
**mixture:** olio, melange, hash, blend
" **of spirits & water:** grog, toddy
**moan:** complain, wail, lament
**moat:** ditch, fosse, foss
**mob:** rabble, populace, crowd
**moccasin:** pac, larrigan
**mock:** taunt, deride, sneer, gibe, mow, leer, fleer, imitate, flout
" **orange:** syringa
**mockery:** farce, game, crony [style
**mode:** fashion, manner,
**model:** norm, type, pattern, shape, paragon, paradigm, design

" **of perfection**: paragon, standard
**moderate**: bate, abate, restrain, cool, some, temperate, diminish
**modern**: new, recent
**modest**: retiring, demure, decent, prim
**modish**: chic
**Mohammedan**: also see Moslem: Islam
" **adopted son**: ali
" **Ali's son**: Ahmed
" **ascetic**: fakir
" **caravan.**: imaret
" **chieftan**: emir
" **cleric**: imam, iman
" **daughter**: Fatima
" **decree**: irade
" **descendant**: Emir
" **festival**: bairam
" **Filipino**: Moro
" **God**: Allah
" **judge**: cadi, mollah
" **leader**: aga, ata
" **month**: Safar, ramadan
" **name**: ali
" **nature spirit**: genie
" **noble**: amir, ameer
" **nymph**: houri
" **prayer**: salat
" " **call**: azan
" **priest**: imam
" " **'s (body of)**: ulema [sultan
" **prince**: amir, emir, ameer, amee, emeer,
" **princess**: emir
" **religion**: islam
" " **teacher**: Alim
" **ruler**: aga, calif
" **saint**: Pir
" " **tomb**: pir
" **scholars**: ulema
" **scriptures**: Koran
" **son**: ali
" **state head**: kalif
" **title**: ali, aga, calif
" **tribe**: arain
" **uncle**: Abbas
**moil**: toil, soil, drudge, drudgery
**moist**: damp, humid, wet, dewy, dank
**moisture**: dew
**molar**: tooth, grinding
**molasses**: treacle
**mold**: matrix, shape, form, fashion, die, must [torus listed
**molding**: ogee, ovolo,
**mole**: pier
**moleskin color**: taupe
**molest**: disturb, tease, annoy, trouble
**mollify**: sleek, allay, smooth, conciliate
**mollusk**: snail, clam, abalone, mussel, scallop shellfish,
**molt**: shed
**molten glass**: metal
" **lava**: aa
" **rock**: lava
**moment**: instant, trice, jiff [important
**momentous**: weighty,
**monarch**: king, emperor, ruler, sovereign
**monastery**: abbey
" **room**: cell
**monastic house**: priory
**monetary**: financial
**money**: coin, cash, coinage, specie [ment
" **on account**: pay-
" **box**: till
" **due but not paid**: arrears
" **matters**: economic
" **owed**: debt
" **paid**: scot
" **(slang)**: moss, tin
**Mongolian**: tatar
" **desert region**: Gobi
**mongoose**: urva [mutt
**mongrel**: cur, mut,
**monk**: friar, fra
" **'s hood**: cowl, aconite, atis
**monkey**: stentor, tamarin, mono, ape, titi, sai, marmoset
" **like animals**: lemurs, ayeayes
**monopoly**: trust
**monotonous**: dreary, humdrum
**monster**: ogre, giant, centaur, sphinx
" **(med.)**: tarata, teras [Butte
**Montana city**: Helena,
**month preceding**: ultimo
**moo**: low
**mood**: tune, humor
**moody**: morose, peevish [ana, lune
**moon**: luna, lunar, Di-
" **'s age at beginning of year**: epact
" **cresent point**: cusp, horn
" **in her first quarter**: crescent [fen, heath
**moor**: anchor, fasten,
**moorish drum**: tabor
" **tabor**: atabal
**moose**: elk
**mop**: swap, swab, wipe
**mope**: sulk, pine
**moral**: ethical, teaching, maxim
" **teachings**: precepts
**morass**: bog, swamp, marsh, fen
**moray**: eel
**more**: extra, greater
" **than**: over
" " **enough**: too
**moreover**: besides
**morindin dye**: al [noon
**morning**: morn, fore-
" **prayer**: matin
" **(relat. to)**: matinal
" **star**: daystar, venus
**Moro chief**: Dato
" **high priest**: sarip
**Morocco cape**: nun
" **coin**: okia, rial
" **native**: Moor
" **seaport**: Rabat
" **tree**: sandarac
**morose**: gloomy, glum, sullen, moody, sour
**morsel**: bite, bit, ort, tidbit, piece, crumb
**mortal**: fatal, human
**mortar**: cement, petard
" **tray**: hod
**mortification**: chagrin
" **of tissue**: gangrene
**mortify**: abash, spite, shame, humiliate
**mortise (part of)**: tenon
**Moslem**: (also Moham.)
" **gold coin**: dinar
" **javelin**: jereed
" **official**: aga
" **ruler**: Nawab
**Mosque tower**: minaret
**moss**: rag, lichen
**moth (kind)**: regal, lappet, egger, tinea
**mother**: matron, mama
" **(Latin)**: mater
" **of mankind**: Eve
" " **Pearl**: nacre
" **(Phil. Isl.)**: Ina
**motion**: gesture, movement
**motion of horse in rearing**: pesade
" **of sea**: tidal, tide
**motionless**: still, stagnant [incentive
**motive** reason, cause,
**motor**: engine, machine
" **car (colloq.)**: auto
" **coach**: bus
" **part**: cam [aviette
**motorless plane**: glider,
**mottled**: pinto, pied
" **appearances in mahogany**: roes
**motto**: saw, maxim, adage, slogan [dune
**mound**: hill, knoll, tee,
**mt. aborigines**: atis
" **ash**: rowan
" **chain**: range, sierra
" **in Colorado**: Owen
" **(comb form)**: oro
" **crest**: arete
" **gap**: col
" **lake**: tarn [ad
" **nymph**: oread, dry-
" **pass**: ghat, col
" **passage**: tunnel
" **pasture land**: alp
" **pool**: tarn
" **range**: ridge, sierra, andes, alps, ural
" **ridge**: range, arete
" " **(flat top)**: loma
" **(Scot.)**: ben
" **spinach**: orach
" **spur**: arete
" **near Troy**: Ida
**mourn**: sorrow, grieve
**mournful**: plaintive, sad, sorrowful, funereal, dismal
" **cry**: wail [ting
**mourning**: dolor, regret-
" **hymn**: dirge
" **poem**: elegy
" **sumbal**: crepe
**mouth**: os
" **(comb. form)**: oro
" **(of the)**: oral
" **organ**: harmonica, lip, tongue
" **of river**: delta
" " **volcano**: crater
**mouthlike opening**: stoma [door
**movable barrier**: gate,
" **frame**: sley
" **part**: rotor [tate
**move**: stir, budge, agi-
" **ahead steadily**: forge [treat, retire
" **back**: recede, re-
" " **& forth**: way, saw, wave, wag
" **forward**: progress
" " **with difficulty**: wade [sneak, prowl
" **furtively**: steal,
" **heavily**: lug
" **on**: onrush, go
" **rapidly**: hurtle, fly, career, flit, dart
" **sideways**: sidle, slue
" **slowly**: lag, inch
" **smoothly**: glide, slide, sail
" **vigorously**: bestir
" **on wheels**: roll
**movement**: trend, motion
" **of the feet**: gait
" " " **sea**: tide
**moving**: astir, transient
" **force**: agent
" **part**: rotor
" **power**: motor
**mud**: mire, slime, slosh, sludge
" **eel**: siren
" **volcano**: salse
**muddle**: addle, mess, confuse [mire
**muddled**: asea
**muddy**: bespatter, roil, sludgy, miry, roily,
**muddy ground**: sog
**mudworm**: ipo
**muffin**: gem
**muffle**: deaden, mute
**muffler**: scarf, silencer
**mug**: stein, noggin
**mulberry**: al, ach, aal
**mulct**: bilk, amerce, cheat, fine
**mule**: ass
" **cry**: bray
**multiform**: diverse
**multitude**: host, legion
**municipality**: city
" **(pert. to)**: civic
**murder**: homocide, slay
**murk**: gloom, darkness
**murmur**: repine, mutter
" **softly**: purl, coo, hum, purr
**muscle**: sinew, thew
**muscle in arm**: biceps, triceps
" **band**: tendon
" **of mouth**: lip [sor
" **for stretching** : ten-
**muscular**: torose, sinewed
**muse**: meditate, reve, cogitate, ponder
" **of history**: clio
" " **music**: euterpe
" " **poetry**: erato
**mushroom**: agaric, morel
**music**: melody
" **(as it stands)**: sta
" **(concluding passage)**: coda
" **(high)**: alt
" **(increase in volume)**: crescendo
" **(melodious)**: arioso
" **(moderately slow)**: andante
" **(silent)**: tacet
" **(slow)**: lento, adagio, largo
" **(smooth & connected)**: legato
" **(soft)**: piano
" **(stately)**: largo
**musical**: melic, lyric, harmonious, melodious, lyrical [song
" **air**: tune, melody,
" **aria**: solo
" **bells**: chimes
" **character**: rest, clef, sharp, note
" **comedy**: revue
" **composition**: song, rondo, oratorio, serenade, nocturne, cantata, sonata, ballade, opus, trio, glee, sextet, serenata, arioso, opera
" **direction**: tacet
" **drama**: cantata
" **exercise**: etude
" **group**: band
" **half step**: semitone
" **instrument**: rebec, gora, oboe, saxhorn, tuba, bugle, spinet, cornet, ocarina, marimba, uke, fife, lute, guitar, cello, lyre, viol, concertina, reed
" **interval**: rest, octave, tritone, second
" **key**: minor
" **line**: tie [tal, concert
" **performance**: reci-
" **pipe**: reed
" **pitch**: tone
" **reed**: pipe [molo
" **shake**: trill, tre-
" **show**: revue [note
" **sound**: tone, tonal,
" " **(pert. to)**: tonal
" **study**: etude
" **sylable**: si, tra, re
" **tone**: chord
" **triplet**: tercet
" **up beat**: arsis
" **wave**: tremolo
" **work**: opus
" " **(abbr.)**: O.P.
**muss**: rumple, crumple
**mustang**: bronco
**mustard**: sinapis
" **plant**: cress, radish
**muster**: assemble, gather
**musty**: moldy

**mutation:** change
**mute:** dumb, muffle, silent, speechless
" **consonant:** lene
**mutilate:** mangle
**mutiny:** revolt [ble
**mutter:** murmur, grumble
**mysterious:** sphinxine, occult, runic [enigma
**mystery:** cabala, secret,
**mystic:** epoptic
" **ejaculation:** om
**myth:** legend, saga, fable
**mythical:** imaginary
" **being:** giant
" **bird:** ro, roc
" **character:** Pandora
" **hero:** Leander
" **hunter:** Orion
" **king:** Atli, Midas
" " **of Britain:** Lud, Lear, Bran
" " **of Crete:** Minos
" **kingdom:** Oz
" **maiden:** Io, Danae
" **monster:** ogree, giant, dragon
" **mountain:** Ossa
" **swimmer:** Leander
" **Titan:** Atlas
" **world:** Limbo

## N

**nab:** catch, seize, trap, snatch,
**nacre:** pearl
**nag:** tease, horse, scold, pester, henpeck
**nahoor sheep:** sna
**nail:** brad, hob, stud, spike, spad, fasten, secure, tack, clinch
" **driven obliquely:** toed
" **marker:** spad
**naive:** artless, guileless
**name:** term, mention, entitle, call, title, dub
**namesake:** homonyon
**nap:** pile, siesta, doze, sleep, slumber
**nape:** scruff, nucha
**napkin:** bib, doily
**Napoleonic marshall:** Ney
**Napoleon's exile:** Elba
**nappy:** shaggy [opium
**narcotic:** opiate, dope,
" **drug:** hemp
" **shrub:** kat [tell
**narrate:** relate, recite,
**narrow:** strait, contract
" **bar:** stripe
" **board:** lath, slat
" **(comb. form):** sten
" **fabric:** braid [listle
" **fillet (arch):** orle,
" **inlet:** ria
" **minded:** bigoted
" **opening:** rima, slit, slot
" **pass:** abra
" **passage:** gut, alley, strait, gorge, lane
" **piece:** strip
" **strip:** ribbon, strap
" **track:** lane
" **waterway:** inlet, ria
**nasal:** rhinal, narine
" **noise:** snort, whine
" **tone:** twang
**nation:** empire, country, people, realm
**national emblem:** eagle
" **guard:** militia
" **hymn:** anthem
" **park:** Estes
**native:** natal, son, inborn, indigenous
" **borax:** tincal
" **garment:** sarong
**natty:** dapper, neat, spruce

**natural:** normal, inborn, innate, lifelike
" **abode:** habitat
" **capacity:** talent
**naturalness:** ease
**nature:** creation, type, essence, character, sort [cipher
**naught:** zero, nothing,
**nautical:** marine, naval, maritime
" **command:** avast
" **fly:** burgee
**nautical hazard:** fog
" **instrument:** sextant
" **mile:** knot
" **term to cease:** avast [ahoy
" " **in hailing:** aloe,
**Navajo Indian hut:** hogan [maritime
**naval:** marine, nautical,
" **officer:** yeoman
" " **(var.):** bosun
" **weapons:** torpedo
**nave:** hub
**navigate:** sail
" **the air:** fly, aviate
**near:** at, close, nigh, by
" **the back:** dorsal
" **by:** beside
" **the center:** inner
" " **cheek:** malar
" " **ear:** otic
" **(poet.):** anear
" **(prefix):** be
" **(Scot.):** nar
" **the stern:** aft
**nearer (dial.):** nar
**nearly:** almost
**nearsighted person:** myope
**neat:** tidy, trim, trig, orderly, adroit, prim, natty, spruce, precise
**neb:** beak [Omaha
**Nebraska city:** Ord,
" **county:** Otoe
**nebris:** fawnskin
**nebulous:** misty
**necessity:** want, need
**neckband:** collar, scarf
**neckpiece:** boa, boas, stole, collar [scarf
**necktie:** cravat, ascot.
**necromancy:** magic, sorcery, conjuration
**need:** necessitate, lack, want, require, poverty, demand
" **(urgent):** exigency
**needle shaped:** acerose, acerate
**needlefish:** gar
**needless:** useless
**needy:** poor, indigent
**negate:** deny, nullify
**negation:** not, no, denial, blankness
**negative:** nay, not, film
" **particle:** non, anion
**neglect:** omit, disregard
**neglected:** untended undone, forgot, defaulted [careless
**negligent:** remiss, lax,
**negotiate:** treat, transact
**negrito:** ita
**Negro of Fr. W. Africa:** Habe
" " **Niger Delta:** Ibo [Edo, Vai, Ibo
" " **Negeria:** Aro,
**neighborly gathering:** bee [dent
**Neptune's spear:** trinerve: pluck [neuro
" **(comb. form):** neur,
" **of leaf:** vein
" **network (sg.):** rete, arete, plexus
" **substance:** alba
**nervous:** uneasy [tic

" **disorder:** chorea,
" **system (pert. to):** neural
" **twitching:** tic
**nest:** den, aerie, retreat, haunt, nide
**nestle:** cuddle, snuggle
**nestling:** bird, birdling, eyas [trap
**net:** clear, seine, mesh, gain, yield, snare,
**nether:** lower, under
**Netherlands measure:** roede [tate, annoy
**nettle:** provoke, irri-
" **rash:** uredo
**network:** mesh, web, rete, plexus [tice
" **of thin strips:** lat-
" " **threads:** lace
**networks:** retia [tatic
**neutral equilibrium:** as-
**Nevada city:** Reno, Elko
" **lake:** Tahoe
**new:** recent, neoteric, fresh, late, unused, modern, untried
" **(comb. form):** neo
" **Guinea seaport:** Lae [ron
" " **tribesman:** Ka-
**New Hampshire city:** Keene
" " **river:** Saco,
" **Mex. co.:** Otero
" " **dollar:** sia [Sia
" " **Indian:** Taos,
" " **river:** Gila
" " **state flower:** yucca
" **(prefix):** neo, nea
" **star:** nova
" **start:** redeal
" **Test. part:** Gospel
" **World Rep.:** Haiti
" **York Canal:** Erie
" " **capital:** Albany
" " **Indian tribe:** Oneida
" " **island:** Ellis
" " **river:** Mohawk Niagara
" " **state city:** Troy, Utica, Olean, Elmira
" " " **county:** Yates, Tioga
" " " **flower:** rose
" " " **lake:** Seneca, Oneida, George
" " " **village:** Avon
" **Zealand aborigine:** maori [pork, moa
" " **bird:** kea, more-
" " **clan:** ati
" " **demon:** taipo
" " **district:** Otago
" " **food fish:** ihi
" " **hedge laurel:** Tarata
" " **mahogany pine:** Totara
" " **native:** maori
" " " **fort:** Pa
" " **parrot:** kea
" " **parson bird:** koko, poe
" " **plant:** karo
" " **soldier:** anzac
" " **tree:** ake, taro, rata, tawa, tarata
" " **woody vine:** aka
**newcomer:** entrant
**newest:** neo
**news:** tidings
" **monger:** gossip
" **stand:** kiosk [tion
**newspaper issue:** edi-
**newspapers:** press, sheets, news
**newt:** triton, eft
**nexus:** link
**nib:** point, beak, prong

**nibble:** peck, gnaw
**nice:** finical, pleasant, genteel, agreeable, sociable, fine
**niche:** corner, recess
**nick:** notch
**nickname:** agname
**nictitate:** wink
**niggard:** miser
**nigh:** near, close
**nightfall (poet.):** eve, een, eventide
**nimble:** agile, active, spry, lissome, alert
**nimbus:** halo
**nimrod:** hunter
**nine:** nonet, ennead
" **(comb. form):** ennea [vena
" **days devotion:** no-
" **headed monster:** hydra
" **inches:** span
**ninefold:** nenary
**ninny:** fool, dunce
**nip:** bite, pincer, pinch, blight, peck, clamp, clip
**nitid:** glossy, bright
**nitrogenous compound:** kenatin, protein
**no extent:** not
**Noah (N. Test. Spell.):** Noe [Ahab
" **son:** Shem, Ham,
**noble:** epic, peer, sublime, epical, baron
**nobleman:** baron, peer, earl, prince, lord, grandee, marquis
**nocturnal animal:** coon
" **bird:** owl, bat
" **mammal:** weasel, lemur [beck, sway
**nod:** bow, drowse, bend,
**nodding:** nutant [by
**nodose:** knotty, knob-
**nodule:** knot
" **of stone:** geode
**nog:** pin
**noise:** din, sound, roar, hubbub, clamor, rattle, racket
**noisy:** loud, blatant, clamorous
" **bird:** pie [crial
" **condemnation:** de-
" **laugh:** guffaw
**nom de plume:** alias
**nomad:** bedouin, rover, wanderer
**nominal stock value:** par [point
**nominate:** name, ap-
**non-professional:** lay, laic, amateur
" **Semetic:** Aryan
**none (dial.):** nin
**nonentity:** nobody
**nonmetallic element:** boron, silicon, iodine
**nonsense:** bah, bosh, fudge, falderal
**nook:** corner, in, angle, recess
**noose:** loop, entrap, snare [ard
**norm:** pattern, stand-
**normal:** sane, natural, same, standard, regular
" **state:** order
" **value:** par
**Norse deities home:** Asgard
" **fate:** Norn, Norm
" **fire demon:** Surtr
" **galley:** aesc [Eir
" **god:** Odin, Tyr, Thor, Aesir (pl), Ve,
" " **of dead:** Hel
" **goddess:** Eir, Norn
" **gods:** Aesir
" **literary work:** edda
" **myth. giant:** Atli

" saint: Olaf
" sea deity: Van
" tale: saga
" ter. division: amt
North African: see also African
" " native: eritrean, hamite
" " plant: anise
" " seaport: Oran, Derna
" " wt.: rotl [gan
" American mt.: Lo-
" " Island: Iceland
" Carolina county: Ashe
" " river: Tar
" Pole discoverer: Peary [star, polaris
" star: polestar, lode-
" Syrian diety: El
" wind: boreas
northern: boreal
" bird: loon, auk
" European: Finn, Slav, Lapp, Lett
Norwegian: Norseman, Norse
" capital: Oslo [sund
" city: Narvik, Ale-
" county: Amt
" dramatist: Ibsen
" land division: amt
" measure: alen
" name: Olaf, Olav
" painter: Dahl
" river: Oi, Nea, Ena
nose: sniff, scent, detect
" (comb. form): rhin
" (pert. to): rhinal, nasal
nostril: nare, nose
" (pert. to): narine
notable act: feat
notch: nick, gap, dent, serrate, indent
notched bar: ratch
" wheel: ratchet
note: observe, heed, remark
" of chromatic scale: ri, di, li
" the speed: time
noted: famed, eminent, marked, famous
notes: memoranda, memo [hil, nought
nothing: nil, zero, ni-
" (colloq.): nix
" more than or nothing but: mere
notice: heed, observe, see, sign, spot
notion: idea, fad, whim
" (dial.): idee
notoriety: eclat [rant
notorious: infamous, ar-
notwithstanding: despite, however, yet
nought: nothing, zero
noun suffix: ier, ac, ist, ite [alible, meaty
nourishing: alimental,
Nova Scotia: Acadia
" " seaport: Truro
novel: new, unusual, strange, romance, different [acolyte, tiro
novice: tyro, beginner,
now: here, forthwith
noxious: ill, miasmic
" substance: poison
nuance: shade
nub: pith, lump, knot
nucha: nape
nucleus of atom: proton
nudge: jog [valid
null: void, cipher, in-
nullify: negate
number: count, enumerate, digit
" to be added to another: addend
" of Muses: nine
numbness: torpor
numeral style: arabic
numerical: ten [tiful
numerous: many, plen-
nurse: nurture, foster, nana, tend
" shark: gat
nurture: breed, cherish, nurse, feed
nut: problem [nougats
" confection: praline,
" (kind): kola, cola, almond [ing
nutant: nodding, droop-
nutriment: food, meat
nutritious: alimentary
Nyx's daughter: Eris

## O

oaf: dolt, lout, idiot
oak: blackjack, alder
oar: paddle, row, rower
" blade: palm
" fulcrum: thole
" part: loom
oarsman: rower
oath: vow, curse
" (mild): drat, egad
" (old): ecod, egad
obedient: dutiful
obeisance: homage
obese: fat
obey: mind, comply, submit, yield
object: intention, demur, thing, aim, evict, protest, target
" of alm: butt
" " bric a brac: curio
" " devotion: idol
objective: goal, target, aim
objurgate: scold
obligation: debt, bond, duty, due, tie
oblique: lateral, slant, bevel, awry, skew, sidelong
obliterate: erase, efface, raze, rase, blot
oblivion: annesty, lethe
obscure: dim, shade, fog, deep, indistinct, see, darken, inner, blur [tion
observance: rite, atten-
observe: notice, note, regard, remark, eye, lo [hitch
obstacle: dam, snag, bar,
obstinate: stubborn, set
obstruct: dam, bar, deter, impede, clog, hinder, occlude, estop
obtain: derive, gain, get, procure, secure, win
" control of: take
" aboriously: eke
obtuse: crass, dense, blunt [evident
obvious: overt, patent,
" facts: truisms
occasion: once, nonce, time, breed, engender
" (Scot): sele
occasional (Scot.): orra
occident: west
occlude: obstruct, close
occult: cryptic
occultism: cabala [dent
occupant: tenant, resi-
occupation: career, tenure, business, metier, work, trade
occupied: rapt, busy
occupy: interest, use, engage, fill
" a seat: sit, preside
occur: happen, pass, betide
" every year: annual
" at irregular intervals: sporadic
" " stated intervals: regular [incident
occurrence: event, hap,
ocean: main, sea
" (pert. to): pelagic
" route: lane
" vessel: liner
oceanic: marine, pelagic
Octavia's husband: Nero
ocular: visual [unique
odd: strange, eccentric, queer, singular, uneven, quaint, rare,
" (Scot.): orra
odds: chances
Odin's brother: Ve
" son: Tyr
odious: hateful [smell
odor: aroma, scent,
" (offensive): olid
odorous: fragrant, redolent
odylic force: od
Odysseus's dog: Argos
of: about
" (Dutch): van
" each (Med.): ana
" the matter: re
" " past: yore
" (prefix): de
" the side: lateral
" that kind: such
" " thing: its
off: away, begone, mistaken [insult
" hand: impromptu
offend: pique, displease,
offense: crime, fault
" against the law: delict
offensiveness: odium
offer: bid, tender, proffer, propose, proposal
" objections: demur
" to pay: bid
" for sale: vend
" solemnly: pledge
" to verify: aver
offering: tribute
office head: manager
" holders: ins
official: magnate
" decree: ukase [ture
" document: inden-
" endorsement: visa
" examiner: censor
" message: brevet
" paper: document
" proof of a will: probate [roll, actum
" record: protocol,
" sitting: session
" stamp: seal
" transactions: acta
officiate: act [son
offspring: descendant,
often (poet.): oft
ogle: leer, eye, gaze
ogrish: cruel, monstrous
Ohio city: Xenia, Lima
" county: Ross, Erie
" town: Ada
oil: oleic, oleo, grease, lubricate, anoint, petroleum
" based ointment: ecrate
" bottle: cruet
" can: oiler
" of orange: neroli
" of orris root: irone
" of roses (var.): atar, otto, attar, ottar
" ship: tanker
" (suffix): ol
" tree: eboe
" well: gusher [nut
" yielding herb: pea-
oilstone: hone
oily: fat, sebaceous
" ketone: irone
" substance: fat
ointment: cerate, salve, pomade, unguent, balsam, balm, nard
" of the ancients: nard
Okinawa capital: Naha
Oklahoma city: Enid, Tulsa, Ada
" nickname of natives: Sooners
okra: gumbo
old: stale, aged, ancient, former
" age: senile
" Dominion State (abbr.): Va
" Dutch measure: aam [groat
" English coin: ora,
" English rent: tac
" " tax: tallage, prisage [archaic
" fashioned: passe,
" " fellow: fogy
" love song: amoret
" maid: spinster
" military device: petard [it
" moneyer's wt.: per-
" Moslem coin: dinar
" musical instrument: rebec, lyre, citole, rota, asor, cithern, spinet [are
" " note: ela, fe, ut,
" Norse work: edda
" piano: spinet
" pronoun: thee
" rifle part: tige
" Roman chest: cyst
" salt: tar
" saying: saw [baubee
" Scot. coin: demy,
" " wt.: trone
" time beverage: posset
" " dance: carole
" times: yore
" vessel: galleon, frigate
" woman: crone, hag
" womanish: anile, senile
" World bird: starling, terek [genet
" " carnivore:
" " crow: rook
" " finch: serin
" " fish: loach
" " genus of herbs: paris
" " lizard: seps
" " plant: aloe
" " sandpiper: terek [der
" " shrub: olean-
olden: ancient [yore
" times (poet.): eld,
older: elder, senior, staler, sr
oldest member: dean
oldtimer: veteran
oleaginous: oily
olent: fragrant
oleo esin: elemi, anime
olfactory organ: nose
olive: relish, tawny, olea
" tree: ash
Oliver Twist character: Fagin
olla: pot, jug [temis
Olympian goddess: Ar-
omen: sign, presage, portent, forbode [ful
ominous: sinister, fate-
omission: elision
" of end of a word: afocope
" " letter from word: syncope
" mark: caret
omit: delete, skip, cut, miss, spare, except, neglect, elide [elide
" from pronouncing:

**on:** above, along, about, upon, forward
" **all sides:** around, about
" **board ship:** asea
" **condition that:** so, if
" **fire:** ablaze
" **the line of:** along
" **that account:** thereat
" **this:** hereupon
" **top of:** atop, upon
" **the way:** enroute
**onager:** donkey, catapult
**once:** formerly, occasion, ever, singly
" **again:** over
" " (poet.): oer
" **more:** anew, encore
**one:** unit, unity, same, anybody, united, person, an, single
" **before another:** tandem [mono
" **(comb. form):** uni,
" **devoted to monastic life:** oblate
" **of gigantic size:** Titan
" **given to a habit:** addict
" **horse carriage:** shay
" **impervious to pain or pleasure:** stoic
" **lately arrived:** newcomer [maker
" **in the lead:** pacе-
" **less than par:** birdie
" **masted vessel:** sloop
" **of mixed breed:** metis
" **named after another:** namesake [inee
" " **for office:** nom-
" **omitted:** out
" **(prefix):** mono, uni
" **(Scot.):** ane, ae
" **skilled in colors:** colorist [guist
" " **in lang.:** lin-
" **spot:** ace, pip
" " " **Musketeers:** Aramis
" **of two:** either
" " " **equal parts:** half, moiety [er
" **unclean (bib.):** lep-
**oneness:** unity
**onion (variety):** rareripe, leek, cibol
**only:** sole, mere, solely, alone [outset, dash
**onset:** attack, start,
**onslaught:** onset, attack, assault
**onus:** burden, weight
**onward:** along
**ooze:** exude, seep, mire, slime, spew
**open:** overt, accessible, unfold, unlock, bare, exposed, frank, start, unfurl, bland, agape, unstopped, expanded, lance, unclose, disclose, expand [patio
" **court:** area, hiatus,
" **to general use:** public [moor
" **land:** field, heath,
" **shelved cabinet:** etagere
" **space in forest:** glade
" **to view:** bare, overt
" **wide:** gape, yawn
**opening:** gap, fissure, aperture, vent, eyelet, hole, pore, rima, hiatus, rift [som
" **above door:** tran-
" **in net:** mesh
" " **nose:** nare
" **wide:** agape
**openwork fabric:** lace
**opera:** Aida [run
**operate:** work, manage,
" **on a skull:** trepan
**operatic soprano:** Eames, Melba
**operative:** artisan
**ophidian:** snake
**opine:** think, judge, suppose, consider
**opinion:** view, concept, credo, thought, idea, judgment, repute
**opium:** narcotic, drug
" **paste:** dope
" **poppy seed:** maw
**opponent:** foe, rival
**opportune:** apropos, pat, timely
**opportunity:** opening
**oppose:** face, withstand, repel, resist
**opposed:** averse, anti
" " **stoss:** lee
**opposite:** inverse, reverse [subtend
" **to:** against, reverse,
" **of aweather:** alee-
" " **liabilities:** assets [persecute
**oppress:** aggrieve, lade,
**Op's daughter:** Ceres
**opt:** choose, decide
**optic:** eye
" **(comb. form):** opto
**optical glass:** lens
" **illusion & phenomenon:** mirage
" **instrument:** prism, periscope, telescope
" " **part:** alidade
**optimistic:** roseate, rosy, sanguine
**option:** choice
**optional:** elective
**opulent:** rich, profuse, wealthy
**opus:** work, burden
**oracle:** mentor [vatic
**oracular:** ambiguous,
**orage:** tempest, storm
**oral:** spoken, parol, verbal, aloud, vocal
" **utterance:** parol
**orange dye:** mandarin, henna, chica
**orangutan:** mias, satyr
**orate:** declaim, speak, talk, harangue, say
**oration:** address, prayer, speech [globe
**orb:** circle, sphere, eye,
" **of day:** sun
**orbed:** round, lunar
**orbit:** path
**orc:** grampus, whale
**orchid (kind):** arethusa, pogonia, faham
" **meal or root:** salep
**ordain:** decree
**ordeal:** trial
**order:** command, mandate, method, bade, regulate, bid, system
" **of aquatic mammals:** cete, cetacea
" " **architecture:** doric, ionic
" **back:** remand [da
" **of business:** agen-
" " **mammals:** primate, cete
" " **reptiles:** sauria
" " **whales:** ceta
**orderly:** trim, neat, shipshape [tem, series
" **arrangement:** sys-
**ordinary:** usual, average, mediocre
**ore:** metal [nanza, bed
" **deposit:** lode, bo-
" **of lead:** galen
" **refiner:** smelter
" **vein:** lode
**Oregon capital:** Salem
**organ bass note:** pedal
" **desk:** console
" **pipe:** reed, flue
" **shrub:** salal
" **of speech:** lip, voice, throat, tongue
" **stop:** celeste, gamba, tremolo
**organic unit:** monad
**organism living on another:** parasite
" **(minute):** spore
" **(simple):** monad
**organization:** setup
**orgy:** carousal, frolic, lark [tine
**oriental:** Asian, eastern, asiatic, levan-
" **animal:** rasse
" **bird:** mino, mina
" **bow:** salaam
" **building:** pagoda
" **captain:** ras
" **caravansary:** serai
" **cart:** araba
" **case:** inro
" **coin:** rin, yen, sen
" **commander:** Ras
" **country:** India
" **dish:** pilaw, pilau
" **drums:** tomtoms
" **dwelling:** dar
" **food fish:** tai
" **garment:** aba
" **governor:** dey
" **greeting:** salam
" **guitar:** sitar, samisen
" **inn:** serai
" **laborer:** coolie
" **measure:** parah
" " **of capacity:** ardeb [Asian
" **native:** Korean,
" **nature spirits:** genii
" **nurse:** amah, ayah
" **obeisance:** salaam, salam
" **plant:** sesame
" **prince:** amir
" **receptacle:** inro
" **ruler:** ameer [goda
" **sacred tower:** pa-
" **sail:** lateen [salam
" **salutation:** salaam,
" **shrub:** tea, henna, oleander
" **tea:** cha
" **wagon:** araba
" **weight:** mo, cantar, tael, catty, rotl [let
**orifice:** hole, pore, in-
**origin:** root, source, parentage, genesis, beginning [emanate
**originate:** arise, invent, create, breed, coin,
**originator of atomic theory:** Dalton
**Orion meteor:** orionid
" **star:** rigel
**orison:** prayer
**orle:** bearing [ette
**ornament:** pin, trinket, amulet, adorn, ros-
**ornamental:** decorative, bow, bead, fancy
" **ball:** bead, pompon
" **device:** pin
" **ensemble:** decor
" **grass:** neti [tain
" **jet of water:** foun-
" **part of wall:** dodo, dado
" **tree:** almond, palm
**ornamented leather:** tooled [elaborate
**ornate:** florid, decorated, showy, adorn,
**ort:** morsel, scrap, bit
**orthographer:** speller
**os:** bone, mouth
**oscilate:** wag, rock, swing, vibrate, sway
**osculate:** kiss
**osier:** willow, wand, rod
**Osiris's brother:** Set
" **crown:** atef
" **wife:** Isis
**ossified tissue:** bone
**ostentatious:** pretentious, showy, gaudy
" **display:** pomp, parade, splurge
**ostiole:** stoma, pore
**ostrich:** rhea, emu
**otalgia:** earache
**Othello's false friend:** Iago [alternate
**other:** else, different,
**otherwise:** else, or, alias
**otiose:** indolent, inactive, idle [ish
**Ottoman:** Turk, Turk-
" **court:** Porte
" **standard:** alem
**oust:** remove, evict, expel, eject
**out:** ex, forth, eject, outside, external
**out of:** from [agasp
" **of breath:** winded,
" " **date:** passe, old
" **& out:** arrant
" " **(prefix):** ec, de
" " " **way:** remote, afield, aside
**outbreak:** riot, eruption [steria
" **of enthusiasm:** hy-
**outbuilding:** shed, barn
**outcast:** leper, pariah
**outclass:** surpass, excel
**outcome:** issue, result, end, sequel
**outcry:** clamor [exceed
**outdo:** cap, excel, trump,
**outer:** external, exterior
" **boundary of plane figure:** perimeter
" **covering:** rind, hull, skin, shell, wrap, coat, husk, crust
" " **of tire:** shoe
" **grain husk:** bran
**outfit:** rig, equipment, gear, kit, tog [cost
**outlay:** price, expense,
**outlet:** vent [sis, sketch
**outline:** contour, synop-
" **of play:** scenario
**outlook:** aspect, prospect, vista
**outmoded:** passe, dated
**outpouring:** tirade, torrential, emitting, flood
**outrage:** abuse
**outside:** out
" **(comb. form):** ecto
" **(prefix):** ect
**outspoken:** blunt, candid, frank [salient
**outstanding:** notable,
**outward:** ectad, outer
**oven:** kiln, baker
**over:** above, again, past, across, finished, extra, completed, beyond, ended, done
" **again:** anew
" **(poet.):** oer
**overcoat:** ulster, topcoat, paletot
**overcome:** rout, best, surmount, conquer, appal, defeat
**overflow:** flood, teem
**overhang:** beetle, jut
**overhead:** above, aloft
**overlook:** miss, skip
**overly:** too, careless
**overpower:** awe, master, repress, subdue
" **with sudden emotion:** stun
**overseer:** boss, censor, curator, taskmaster

**overt:** open, public, manifest, obvious
**overtop:** surpass, transcend
**overture:** prelude
**overturn:** upset, tip
**overwhelm:** swamp
**ovule:** seed, egg
**ovum:** egg, seed, spore
**own:** possess, confess, avow, have
" **(Scot.):** ain
**ownership:** title
**ox:** bos, steer, yak
" **of Celebes:** Anoa, goa, noa
**oxidize:** rust
**oxlike quadruped:** yak, bison [ide
**oxygen compound:** ox-
" **(form of):** ozone
**oxygenate:** aerate
**oyster:** bivalve, reefer
" **bed:** layer

## P

**pace:** gait, stride, rate, amble, step, trot
**Pacific:** Irenic [salal
" **coast shrub:** salad,
" **Isl. aroid:** taro
" " **group:** Samoa, Saipan, Hawaii
" " **pine:** ei, ie
" " **tree:** ipio, ipil
**pacify:** pacate, placate, soothe, appease
**pack:** stow, cram
" **of cards:** deck
" **down:** tamp
**package:** carton, parcel, bundle
**packing box:** crate
" **ring:** gasket
**pact:** treaty, agreement
**pad:** cushion, tablet
**paddle:** oar, row
**pagan:** heathen, ethnic, idolater
**page:** folio, leaf
**pageant:** pomp
**pagoda ornament & final:** tee
" **top:** finial
**pain:** ache, pang, sting, throe, disquiet, misery, hurt, distress
**painful:** bitter, sore
**paint:** color, pigment, rouge, decorate, limn
**painter:** artist, limner
" **'s tablet:** palette
**painting of Madonna:** Sistine
" **on plaster:** fresco, secco, frescoing
" **style:** genre [dyad
**pair:** duo, team, brace, twain, match, two,
" **(var.):** diad
**paired (her.):** gemel
**palatable:** savory, sapid
**palate:** taste
" **(soft):** uvula
**palatial:** palatine, velar
**pale:** wan, stake, pallid, blanch, ashy, dim, white, picket, ashen, faint, fade
**Palestine animal:** daman [ia
" **city:** Haifa, Samar-
" **coin:** mil
" **mountain:** Carmel, Gilead, Sinai
" **plain:** Sharon
" **town:** Cana
**paletot:** overcoat
**palliate:** extenuate, mitigate, conceal, gloss, salve
**palm:** areca
" **cockatoo:** arara
" **of hand:** vola thenar
" **(kind):** coco, assai
" **leaf:** ola, ole, frond
" **lily:** ti, titree
" **off:** foist
" **stem:** rattan
" **wine:** taree [ola
**Palmyra palm:** tal, ole,
**palp:** feeler [ifest
**palpable:** tangible, man-
**pamper:** coddle, spoil, pet, cosset
**pamphlet:** tract
**panacea:** elixir, cure
**Panama Canal dam:** Gatun
**panel:** jury [throe
**pang:** agony, pain, ache,
**pant:** gasp, throb, beat, puff, yearn [leopard
**panther:** puma, pard,
**pantry:** larder
**pants:** trousers, slacks
**papal:** apostolic
" **veil:** orale [quire
**paper measure:** ream,
**parade:** spectacle, display, flaunt, march, review
**Paradise:** Eden
**paragon:** model, pattern, type
**paragraph:** item
**Paraguay city:** Ita
**parallel:** even
**parallelogram (kind):** rhomb [preme
**paramount:** chief, su-
**parasite:** sponge
**parasitic insect:** flee, louse, lice (pl.)
**parcel:** package, packet
" **of land:** lot, let
" **out:** allot, mete
**parched:** thirsty, arid, seared
**pard:** panther
**pardon:** condone, forgive, reprieve, remit, remission, excuse, absolve, amnesty
**pardonable:** venial
**pare:** peel, remove, reduce, cut, shave
**parget:** coat, whitewash, plaster
**Paris's father:** Priam
" **wife:** Oenone
**Park in Rockies:** Estes
**parlance:** diction
**parley:** conference, confer, discuss
**parliament:** diet [satire
**parody:** skit, travesty,
**parol:** unwritten, oral
**paronomasia:** pun
**paroxysm:** spasm, fit
**parrot:** macaw, kea
" **fish:** lania, cotoro
" **(kind):** lory, ara, macaw, kaka
**parry:** fend, avoid
**parsimonious:** stingy
**parsley plant:** dill
**parson:** pastor, minister
" **bird:** tui, tue, poe
**parsonage:** manse, rectory
**part:** section, sever, portion, piece, side, sunder, role, bit
**partake:** share, use
**partial:** half, biased, favorable [shadow
" **darkness:** shade,
" **to:** favor
**participator:** party
**particle:** iota, mite, jot, shred, atom, grain, speck, mote, ace
" " **fire:** spark, arc
**particolored:** pied
**particular:** special, especial, fussy [tion
**partition:** severance, division, cell, wall, sec-
**partly open:** ajar
" **(prefix):** semi [ally
**partner:** mate, sharer,
**party:** sect, faction
**pasquinade:** lampoon
**pass:** elapse, fare, approve, circulate, occur, defile, adopt, devolve, enact
" **around:** skirt
" **away:** elapse, perish, die [file
" **between hills:** de-
" " **peaks:** col
" **into use:** enure
**pass on:** relay [omit
" **over:** elide, cross,
" " **lightly:** skim
" **a rope thru:** reeve
" **slowly:** drag, lapse
" **swiftly:** sweep
" **through:** penetrate, cross
" " **cautiously:** reeve
" " **a sieve:** sift
" **as time:** spend
" **without touching:** clear
**passage:** transit, aisle, aperture, alley, way, entry, alee, canal, channel, voyage
" **out:** exit, egress
" **of Scripture:** text
" **from shore inland:** gat
**passageway:** arcade, ramp, aisle, gate
**passe:** obsolete
**passenger:** fare, rider, traveler, passer
**passerine bird:** starling, finch [lust
**passion:** ire, feeling,
**passive:** inert, inactive
**passport indorsement:** visa, vise [gone, over
**past:** by, agone, ago,
" **(poet.):** agone
" **tense:** preterit
**paste:** cream, glue, artificial, imitation, cement, fasten, adhesive, dough, stick
**pastime:** sport, diversion [keeper
**pastor:** rector, parson, minister, clergyman,
**pastoral:** rustic, rural, idyl, drama, poem
" **poem:** idyll, idyl, eclogue
**pastry:** pie, tart
**pasture:** lea, grass, graze
" **grass:** grama
" **for hire:** agist
" **plant:** clover
**pasty cement:** mastic
**pat:** apt, timely, trap, tap, stroke [bos
**Patagonian deity:** sete-
**patch:** piece, mend
**paten:** disc [right
**patent:** manifest, copy-
**path:** trail, lane, route, way, footway, track, course, orbit
**patio:** court
**patriotic:** national
**patrol:** scout, watch
**patron:** protector factor, guest
" " **of cripples:** Giles
" " " **Ireland:** Patrick
" " " **lawyers:** Ives
" " " **Norway:** Olaf
" " " **sailors:** Elmo
" " " **Wales:** David [digm
**pattern:** norm, model, ideal, design, para-
**pause:** rest, selah, respite, hesitate, stop
**paving block:** paver
**pawl:** detent, cog
**pay:** remunerate, defray, disburse, discharge, wages, stipend, compensate, expend, wage
" **attention:** heed
" **back:** retaliate, remit, render, reimburse
" **homage to:** honor
" **one's part:** antes
" **out:** spend
**payable:** due
**payment:** fee
**peace:** serenity, repose, concord, calm
" **(Latin):** pax
" **pipe:** calumet
**peacock:** moa, pawn
" **butterfly:** io
**peak:** acme, crest, summit, cusp
**peal:** ring, respond, toll
**peanut:** earthpea, earthnut, mani, goober
**pear:** pome
" **shaped vessel:** aludel
**peart:** frisky [serf
**peasant:** ryot, rustic,
**peat bog:** moss, cess
**pebbles (sand):** gravel
**pecan:** hickory
**peck:** dot, dab, nip
**peculiar:** strange, singular, queer, odd
" **saying:** idiom
**pedagogue:** tutor
**pedal digit:** toe
" **extremity:** foot
**peddler:** hawker [anta
**pedestal:** support, base,
" **face:** dado
**pedigree:** race, lineage
**peduncle:** pedicel, stem, scape
**peek:** peep, peer [rind
**peel:** ring, bark, pare, remove, skin, strip,
**peep:** chirp, peek
" **show:** raree
**peepers:** eyes
**peer:** pry, nobleman, look, match, noble, gaze, peek
**Peer Gynt's author:** Ibsen
" " **mother:** Ase
**peeve:** vex, annoyance, irritate, annoy, nettle
**peevish:** pettish, fretful, cross, testy, moody, techy
**peg:** dowel, pin, marker, nob
**pegu ironwood:** acle
**pelagic:** oceanic
**pellet:** pill
**pelt:** fur, skin, hide, hurl, throw, pepper
**pen:** sty, quill, coop, indite, write, cage, confine, enclose
" **point:** nib, neb
**penalty:** fine, loss
**pend:** hang
**pendant:** tassel, earring
**pendent:** lop fob, bob, hanging [bore
**penetrate:** enter, pierce,
**penetrating:** acute, raw
**penitent:** repent, contrite, repentant [rere
**penitential chant:** mise-
" **period:** Lent
**pennant:** streamer, flag
**pennon:** flag, banner
**Penn. borough:** Sayre, Etan

" **city & lake port:** Erie, Easton
" **town:** Ono, Avoca
**penurious:** poor, stingy, miserly, mean
**people:** demos, nation, populate, laity, folks, race, inhabit, ones
**pepper:** betel ava, kava
**per:** by, for
**perceive:** see, sense, realize, apprehend
" **by senses:** sensate
**perch:** roost, seat, sit
**percolate:** seer, seep, filter
**percussion instrument:** gong, triangle, drum, trap [eign
**peregrine:** falcon, for-
**perennial herb:** madder, pia, sedum [plete
**perfect:** ideal, flawless, consummate, com-
" **(comb. form):** teleo
**perforate:** punch, terebrate, drill, bore
" **design:** stencil
" **ornament:** bead
**perforation:** hole
**perform:** do, act, play, enact [tion
**performance:** act, rendi-
**performer:** doer
**perfume:** essence, attar, scent, cense
" **bag:** sachet
" **of flowers:** attar
" **(kind):** civet
" " **(var.):** atar
" **with odors:** cense
**pergola:** arbor
**perhaps (arch.):** mayhap, belike
**peril:** menace, danger, hazard, risk, jeopardy [time
**period:** age, dot, era,
" **of denial:** lent
" **just before:** eve
" " **time:** eral, eon, term, decade, epoch
**perish:** expire, die, ruin
**permanent:** durable, enduring
**permeable by liquids:** porous [bue
**permeate:** pervade, im-
**permission:** leave, consent, license
" **to travel:** passport
**permit:** let, allow, license
**pernicious:** bane, evil, bad [sine
**perpendicular:** sheer,
**perpetual:** endless, constant, unceasing,
**perpetually:** ever
**perplex:** harass, bother
**persecute:** harry, badger, oppress
**perserverance:** grit
**persevere:** persist
**Persia:** Iran [Perse
**Persian:** Iranian, Mede,
" **angel:** mah
" **coin:** rial, kran
" **(ancient):** daric
" **fairy & elf:** peri
" **gazelle:** cora
" **governor:** satrap
" **judge:** cadi
" **king:** Xerxes
" **money:** dinar
" **poet:** Omar
" **race:** Lur
" **ruler:** Shah
" **title:** shah, mir
" **town:** Fao
" **water wheel:** noria
" **weight:** abbas, sang
**persiflage:** banter
**persist:** last, persevere, remain, insist, endure, continue
**person:** one, soul, being
" **a dressed:** you, ye
" **appointed to act as sheriff:** elisor
" **of foresight:** sage
" **named for office:** nominee
" **not in office:** out
" **of rank:** magnate
" **with loud voice:** stentor [ions
**personal beliefs:** opin-
" **belongings:** traps, gear
" **consideration & interest:** self
**personality:** ego, self
**personification of rumor:** fama
" **of truth:** una
**perspicacity:** acumen
**perspiration:** sudor
**persuade:** urge, influence, induce, coax, reason, convince
**pert:** lively, bold, impudent, short
" **girl:** minx [belong
**pertain:** relate, concern,
**pertaining to:** anent
" **to (suffix):** ar, ac, ile, ic [relevant
**pertinent:** relative, apt,
**perturb:** agitate
**peruke:** wig
**perusal:** reading
**peruse:** read, con, scan
**Peruvian capital:** Lima
" **chieftan:** Inca
" **coin:** diner, dinero
" **dance:** cueca
" **Indian:** Cana, Inca
" **plant:** oca
" **race:** Inca
" **seaport:** Calloa
" **tinamou:** yutu
" **volcano:** Misti
**pervade:** permeate, imbue, fill
**perverse:** froward
**pest:** bore, epidemic
**pester:** harry, harass, annoy, nag
**pet:** fondle, cosset
" **lamb:** cosset
**petal:** leaf
**petiole:** leafstalk, stem
**petit:** small
**petition:** sue, beg, plea, ask, solicit, suit
**petty:** small, trifle, little [satrap
**petty officer:** yeoman,
" " **(colloq.):** bosun
**petulant:** short, cross, fretful [eidolon
**phantom:** idolon, ghost,
**phase:** aspect, side, appearance, stage
**phial:** vial, bottle
**philippic:** screed, tirade
**Philippine aborigine:** aeta, ata, ita
" **archipelago:** sulu
" **dagger:** itac
" **dwarf race:** aeta
" **foe:** Samson
" **garment:** saya
" **group:** igorot
" **Island:** Mindanso, Leyte, Panay, Cebu, Samar [vite
" " **province:** Ca-
" **knife:** bolo
" **Moham.:** Moro
" **mountain:** Apo, Iba
" **native:** Ati, Ata, Tagalog, Aeta, Moro
" **negrito:** iti, ita, ati
" **peasant:** tao
" **rice:** macan
" **termite:** anay, anai
" **tree:** tua, ipil, dita, dao, amaga
" " **(poisonous):** ligas
" **tribe:** Atas, Moros
" **weapon:** bolo
" **god:** Baal [tarte
**Phoen. goddess:** As-
**phosphorous compound source:** apatite [mug
**photograph:** print, snap,
" **bath:** reducer, developer, toner, fixer
**physiognomy:** face
**piano keyboard:** clavier
**piazza:** veranda
**pick:** pluck, select, elite
**icket:** pale, stake
**pickle:** marinate, corn, souse
**pickpocket (slang):** dip
**picnic:** outing
**picture:** depict, portrayal, photo, image, icon, pastel
" **frame:** easel
" **puzzle:** rebus [llic
**picturesque:** scenic, idy-
**piece:** patch, portion, fragment, section, chip, missel, part, bit, lump, stab, morsel, scrap
" " **log:** slab
" " **money:** coin
" **put in:** inset
" **of timber:** plank
" " **turf:** divot, sod, peat
" " **wastesilk:** noil
" " **work:** job
**pieces out:** eke
**pier:** anta, dock, mole, wharf, jetty
**pierce:** stab, penetrate, enter, gore, lance, puncture
" **with a stake:** impale, empale
**pigeon:** dove, pouter, barb, nun
" **food:** saltcat, pea
**house:** dovecot
" **pea:** tur, dal
**pigment:** paint
" **from plants:** etiolin
" **used in water color:** bistre
**pigtail:** queue
**pike:** highway, luce
" **like fish:** gara, gar, robalo
**piker:** tightwad
**pilaster:** anta, column
**pile:** heap, mass, stack, load, nap, spile
" **to be burnt:** pyre
" **of earth:** hill
" " **hay or straw:** rick, mow
" **up:** amass, stack
**pilfer:** rob, steal, plunder
**pilgrim Father:** Alden
" **from Holy Land:** Palmer
" **leader:** Standish
**pill:** pellet, bolus
" **bug:** slater
**pillage:** loot, ravage, rapine, plunder, sack, ransack, rifle, foray
**pillar:** obelisk, lat, post, shaft, stela
**pillow:** cover: sham
**pilot:** steer, steersman, guide, guider, steerer, aviator
" **fish:** romero
**pin:** fasten, bolt, peg, nog, badge, skittle
" **to fasten meat:** skewer
**pinch:** nip [grieve
**pine:** languish, mope, sulk, yearn, lament,
**pineapple:** pina, anana, nana, ananas
**pink**, rose, rosy
**pinnacle:** top, apex
" **of ice in a glacier:** serac
" **ornament:** finial
" **of rock:** needle
**pinochle score & term:** meld
**pintail duck:** smee
**pipe:** tube, flagolet, flue, hose, cinch, brier
" **to discharge liquid:** spout [zesty
**piquant:** racy, salty,
**pique:** offend, spite, resent, dudgeon, stir
**piquet term:** capot
**pirate:** corsair, rover, buccaneer, privateer
" **flag:** roger
**pistol (old):** dag
**pit:** hole, grave, excavate, abyss, cavity, gravity
**pitch:** tar, tone, key, toss, throw, gist
**pitcher:** ewer, toby, tosser
" **'s area:** box
**pitfall:** snare, trap
**pith:** core, gist, nub, essence
" **helmet:** topee
**pithy:** meaty, terse
" **saying:** mot
**pitiable:** forlorn, sorry
**pitiless:** cruel
**pivot:** turn, hinge, slue
" **pin:** pintle
**placard:** sign, poster
**placate:** appease
**place:** see also put
" stead, station, put, set, locality, lay, spot, seat, locale, deposit, situate, locus, rank, lieu, arrange, position
" **of activity:** hive
" **alone:** isolate [sort
" **of amusement:** re-
" **to anchor:** moorage
" **at an angle:** skew
" **of barter:** mart
" " **bliss:** paradise, Eden
" **in charge:** entrust
" **(comb. form):** gea
" **in common fund:** pool
" " **confinement:** prison [bus
" " **darkness:** ere-
" **in different order:** transpose, rearrange
" **elsewhere:** relocate
" **end for end:** reverse
" **of entry:** port
" **at intervals:** spaces
" **of justice:** bar
" **levy on:** tax
" **on a mound:** tee
" **in office:** seat
" **one inside another:** nestle, nest
" **opposite:** appose
" **(pl.):** loci
" **of refuge:** ark, harbor [cess
" " **retirement:** re-
" **in rows (var.):** aline
" **of safety:** haven
" **for storing corn:** crib
" " " **fodder:** silo
" " " **hay:** mow
" **of trade:** mart
" **trust in:** repose
" **of worship:** chapel, altar [law
" **under a ban:** out-
" " " **promise:** obligate [tern
" " **restraint:** in-
" " **water:** sub-

merge [lam
" **of uproar:** bed-
" " **wealth exists:** Indies
**placid:** calm, serene
**plague:** tease, taunt, torment, harass
**plaid:** tartan [dent
**plain:** bare, clear, apparent, simple, evi-
**plaintive:** mournful, sad
**plait:** braid [method
**plan:** plot, intend, design, arrange, devise, contrive, diagram, plat, scheme, project,
" **of action:** idea
" " **future procedure:** program
**plane:** level
" **handle:** tote [giro
" **(kind):** router, jet,
" **maneuver:** loop
" **surface:** flat, level, area
**planet:** Mars, Saturn, Asteroid, Neptune, Uranus, Venus, Pluto
**planetarium:** orrery
**plank:** board
**plant:** seed, endogen, embed, factory, sow sapling, shrub
" **of abnormal development:** ecad
" **axis:** stalk
" **bearing aromatic seeds:** cumin, anise
" **disease:** scab, rot
" **embryo:** seed
" **exudation:** resin
" " **(var.):** rosin
" **of gourd family:** melon
" **life:** flora
" **of mustard family:** cress
" **not having woodey stem:** herb
" **organ:** leaf, tendril, soma
" **stem:** bine
" **substance:** resin
**plants of a region:** flora
**plash:** puddle, pool
**plaster:** stucco, smear, daub, parget
" **support:** lath
**plat:** plot, plan, map, chart, braid
**plate:** dish, saucer
**plateau:** tableland, mesa [estrade
**platform:** stage, dais,
**platinum loop:** oese
**play:** sport, enact, perform, drama, toy, disport, cavort, frolic, romp [lick, romp
" **boisterously:** rol-
" **carelessly:** strum
" **first card:** lead
" **the lead:** star
" **at love:** flirt
" **on words:** pun
**player:** actor, gambler
**playing card spot:** pip
**playlet:** skit
**plead:** entreat, appeal, implore, solicit, beg, advocate, argue
**pleasant:** sweet, agreeable, nice, amiable
**please:** suit, gratify, delight, indulge
**pledge:** vow, truce, commit, earnest, seal, promise, token, guaranty, guarantee
**plentiful:** abound, numerous, abundant
**plexus:** rete, retia, network
**pliable:** soft, supple, flexible, plastic
**pliant:** lithe, limber, supple, flexible
**plicate:** fold, pleat
**plot:** plan, plat, scheme, conspire, chart, intrigue, cabal, conspiracy, bed
" **of land:** lot, parcel
**plow:** till, furrow
**pluck:** spunk, grit, nerve, pick
" **or pull off: avulse**
**plucky:** game
**plug:** estop, **stopper**
**plum: gage, sloe**
" **kernel:** pit
**plume:** preen, feather, crest, egret
**plummet:** fall, drop
**plunder:** despoil, loot, rob, raid, prey, gut, spoil, sack, steal, pillage, pilfer rapine, spoliate, maraud
" **(Arch.):** reave
**plundered (arch.):** reft
**plunge:** dive, dip
**ply:** bias, fold, layer, thickness, wield
**poach:** trespass
**pocket case:** etui
" **in trousers:** fob
**pocketbook:** purse, reticule, bag
**Poe's heroine:** Lenore
" **poem:** Lenore
**poem:** epic, sonnet, lay, epode, verse, epepee, lyric, elegy, ballade, ballad, epos
**poet:** lyrist, bard, rimer
**poetical measure & rhythm:** meter
**poetry (arch.):** poesy
**poignant:** acute
**point:** peak, neb, tip, apex, indicate, aim, cusp, sharpen, apice, gist, nib, dot, focus
" **between extremes:** mesne [rhumb, airth
" **of compass:** airt,
" " **crescent moon:** cusp [men
" " **difference:** li-
" " **land:** spit
" " **magnet:** pole
" **opposite the zenith:** nadir
" **under discussion:** issue
" **where leaf branches:** axil
**pointed:** cultrat acute
" **arch:** ogive
" **end:** cusp
" **instrument:** needle, awl, prod
" **part:** nib
" **process;** awn
" **stick:** stake [row
" **weapon:** spear, ar-
**pointer:** hand, tip
**pointless:** inane
**poise:** balance, hover, carriage, equipoise
**poison:** venom, bane, corrupt, virus, taint
**poisonous:** venomous, toxic
" **element:** arsenic
" **tree:** upas
" **weed:** loco [dle
**poke:** prod, jab, daw-
" **around:** root, probe
" **fun at:** josh
**poker chip:** dib
" **stake:** ante
**polar:** arctic
**pole:** rod, staff, stick, pike, stake
" **(pert. to):** nodal
" **(Scot.):** caber
**polecat:** skunk [sheen
**polish:** gloss, scour, elegance, rub, shine,
**Polish cake:** baba
" **river:** San, Narew, Bug, Seret
**polishing material:** rabat, emery
**polite:** courteous, gracious, mannerly, urbane, genteel, civil
**political group:** bloc, party [roll, head
**poll:** election, vote, en-
**polliwog:** tadpole
**pollute:** taint, defile
**Pollux's twin:** Castor
**polo mount:** pony
**poltroon:** coward
**Polynesian apple:** hevi
" **baking pit:** umu
" **chestnut:** rata
" **cloth:** tapa
" **herb:** pia
" **island group:** Samoa
" **yam:** uve, ube, ubi
**pome:** apple, pear
**pompous:** stilted
**ponder:** pore, cogitate, meditate, consider, brood, contemplate, ruminate, muse, reflect, deliberate
**pony:** nag, pinto
**pool:** puddle, mere
" **(Scot.).** dib
**poor:** indigent, needy, bad, scanty, penurious, inopulent
**poorhouse:** almshouse
**poorly:** ill, illy, badly
**Pope (relating to):** papal
" **scarf,collar or veil:** orale
" **triple crown:** tiara
**poplar:** alamo, aspen
" **(white):** abele
**populace:** mob, demos
**popular:** demotic
**porch:** plaza, veranda, stoop, portico [hog
**porcine animal:** pig,
**pore:** ponder, study, stoma, opening
**porgy:** scup
" **(red):** tai
**porridge:** gruel, atole
**port:** haven, harbor
**portal:** gate
**portend:** bode, augur, presage, forbode
**portent:** omen, sign
**portentous:** dire [redcap
**porter:** carrier, suisse,
**Portia's maid:** Nerissa
**portico:** stoa, porch
**portion:** piece, some, share, part, dole, bit whit, dab, lot, half, sample, taste
**portly:** fat
**portray:** paint, draw, picture, limn, depict, delineate [bon
**Portuguese capital:** Lis-
" **city:** Ovar
" **coin:** rei
" **money of account:** rei, escudo
" **poet & historian:** Melo
" **province:** Azores
" **river:** Soa, Sado
" **territory in India:** Goa
" **title:** dom [ture
**pose:** sit, attitude, pos-
**Poseidon's son:** Triton
**position:** locale, job, station, stand, post, stance, place
**positive:** sure, certain
" **terminal:** anode
**possess:** own, have [sin
**possession (Law):** sei-
**post:** mail, station, office, stake, mall, pillar, bitt
" **to secure haw-**
**poster:** bill, placard, ad
**postpone:** defer, delay
**posture:** stance, attitude, pose
**pot:** kettle, olla
**potato:** tuber, spud
" **masher:** ricer
**potency:** vis [mighty
**potent:** powerful, strong,
**potential:** latent
" **energy:** ergal
**pother:** bustle, ado
**potpourri:** olio [pallet
**potter's wheel:** lathe,
**pottery fragment:** shard
" **(kind):** delft
" **(pert. to):** ceramic
**pouch:** sac, bag
**pound:** beat, hammer, thump, ram
" **down:** tamp [cant
**pour:** stream, flow, de-
" **forth:** emit, gush
" **off liquid:** drain
" **oil upon:** anoint
**pout:** sulk, mope
**poverty:** penury, need, want, indigence
**powder:** talc, dust, pulverize
**power:** energy; force, strength, ability, vis, might, steam, vigor
**powerful:** strong, potent
" **jokes:** pranks, hoaxes [use
**practice:** drill, rehearse,
**prairie wolf:** coyote
**praise:** laud, bless, commend, flatter, extol, acclaim, adulation, tribute
**praiseworthy:** laudable
**prance:** caper, cavort
**prank:** antic, escapade, trick, dido frolic,
**prate:** babble, prattle, gab [seech
**pray:** entreat, importune, implore, be-
**prayer:** orison, ave, litany, plea, entreaty
" **(arch.):** bene, orison
**precarious:** dubious
**precede:** lead, forerun
" **in time:** predate, antedate
**precedence:** priority
**precpt:** maxim [rare
**precious:** dear, golden,
" **stone:** garnet sard, opal, zircon, gem, lazuli, beryl, **asteria,**
**precipice:** cliff
**precipitation:** rainfall rain, mist
**precipitous:** steep
**precis:** summary
**precise:** exact, **formal,** neat, prim, nice
**preclude:** debar, bar
**predetermine:** destine
**predicament:** dilemma, scrape, plight, pickle, fix, scrape [sert, base
**predicate:** connote, as-
**predict:** foretell, bode, prophesy [first, star
**preeminent:** capital,
**preen:** plume, trim
**prefer:** favor, choose
**prejudiced:** partial, biased [ture
**prelude:** proem, over-
**premature development:** precocity
**premier:** principal
**premium:** bonus, agio
**prepare:** arrange, set, ready, prime
" **for action:** alert

" leather: taw, tan
" for publication: edit
presage: omen, bode, portend
prescribe: define, set
present: boon, gift here, attend, proffer, give, introduce, donate
" occasion: nonce, now
presently: anon
preserve: can, save, maintain, protect, cure, spare [cate
" by drying: desic-
press: iron, urge, impel, squeeze, crowd, enjoin [press
" down: tamp, de-
" for payment: dun
" forward: drive
" into dough: knead
pressure: stress, force, weight, urgency
presto: quickly, speedily [pose, impose
presume: venture, sup-
pretend: feign, sham, simulate [terfuge
pretense: sham, plea, pretext, feint, sub-
pretentious: arty, elaborate, showy
pretext: pretense, peg, cover, excuse
pretty: comely [win
prevail: triumph, reign,
" upon: lead, induce
prevalent: refe, spread, dominant, rife
prevent: stop, preclude, avert, deter, block, forestall
previous: anterior, prior, former, preceding
previously: erst, before, supra [quarry
prey: victim, booty,
" upon: raven
Priam's kingdom: Troy
" son: Paris
price: rate, cost, value, charge, outlay, fee
prickly envelope of fruit: bur, burr
" herb: teasel
" pear: nopal, tuna
" plant: thistle, acanthus, nettle [briar
" shrub: rose, gorse,
pride: vanity, conceit, arrogance, vainglory, glory [mure
prim: neat, modest, de-
prima donna: diva
primal: elemental, first, chief
prime: first, chief, foremost, prepare, choice
" minister: premier
primer: reader, textbook [can, pristine
primitive: early, pris-
prince of apostate angels: Eblis
" " darkness & evil: Satan
principal: main, premier, chief, cardinal
" element: staple
principle: reason, ideal, tenet, credo, maxim
print: publish, impress, die, stamp
printed defamation: libel
printer's apprentice: devil
" (colloq.): typo [tum
" error: errato, erra-
" mark: stet [pica
" measure: em, en,
" spacing block: quad
printing: edition
" form: mat, type
" need: ink
" press part: platen
prior: anterior, before, elder, previous
" to: ere
priory: abbey, cloister
priscan: primitive
prison: gaol [tive
prisoner: captor, cap-
pristine: primitive, primeval, original
privacy: seclusion [rate
privateer: corsair, pi-
privately: aside
privation: loss
prize: treasure, esteem, value, award
" in lottery: tern
pro: for
probabilities: odds
probe: search [nut
problem: poser, task,
proboscis: nose, snout
proceed: go, continue
proceeds: starts, income, goes
process of decision: pend
procession: parade
proclaim: herald
proclamation: edict
proclivity: talent
procrastination: delay
procurator of Judea: Pilate [obtain
procure: get, provide,
prod: goad, punch, slog, poke, thrust, nudge
prodigal: lavish, wasteful, extravagant
prodigious: marvelous
prodigy: marvel
produce: cause, generate, engender, stage, yield, create, crop
produced by a river: fluvial
" by the wind: eolian
product: fruit
productive: rich, fertile, creative
proem: preface, prelude
profane: desecrate
profess: avow
profession: metier, vocation, trade
professional mourner: weeper, wailer [hand
proffer: bid, tender, offer, give, present,
proficient: adept, skilled, versed
profit: avail, gain, benefit, advantage
profound: deep, recondite, [ful, opulent
profuse: lavish, bounti-
" talk: palaver
progenitor: parent, sire
progeny: seed, breed, strain, issue
progress: gain, advance
" with difficulty: wade [bid
prohibit: bar, ban, debar, estop, veto, for-
prohibitionist: dry
project: scheme, plan
projecting crane arm: gib
" member: tenon
" nose: snout
" part: nob, apse
" piece: fin, shelf
" " of a cap: visor
" point: peak, jag
" rim: flange
" rock: crag
" tooth: snag
" window: dormer
prolong: lengthen, extend, defer, protract
prominence: salience
prominent: eminent, important, star
promise: pledge, vow, swear, word
promising: favonian
promontory: cape, ness
" (var.): nase [vance
promote: abet, foster, serve, further, ad-
promoter: agent
prone: apt, prostrate
prong: tine, nib, fork
pronounce: assert, utter, declare
" holy: bless
pronto: quickly
pronunciation mark: diacritic, tilde
proofreader: reviser
" 's mark: caret, stet
prop: stay, brace, shore, strengthen [row, urge
propel: drive, impel,
propeller: driver, fan
proper: decent, meet, prim, fit, right
property: estate, realty, asset, holdings
" charge: lien
" of a matter: inertia, mass [tell
prophesy: predict, fore-
prophet: seer, Amos, oracle, sage, seeress
prophetical: vatical, vatic [pease, conciliate
propitiate: atone, ap-
proportion: ratio, rate
proposal: suggest, intend, offer
proposed act: bill
" international lang.: ro, ido, od
propound: premise, pose
propped up: shored
prorogue: adjourn
proscribe: ban
proselyte: convert, ger
prospect: outlook, vista
prosper: thrive, flourish, fare
prosperity: welfare, weal
prosperous times: ups, boom
prostrate: prone
prosy: dull, tedious
protect: shelter, shield, defend, armor, preserve, bless
" against loss: insure
protection: armor, egis, defense, aegis, lee
protective covering: armor, raincoat, paint
" ditch: moat, foss
" garment: apron, duster, coverall [met
" head covering: hel-
" influence: aegis
" railing: parapet
protector: patron
protest: demur, complaint, dissent
proton: atom
protract: eke, prolong
proturberance: snag, wen, node, nub, lobe, bulge, wart
" (pert. to): lobar
" of skull: inion
prove: test [fute
" false: betray, con-
proverb: adage, saw, maxim
provide: store, purvey, furnish, afford
" food: cater, purvey
" quarters for: lodge
provided: if
" that: so
provident: careful, frugal thrifty, [tois
provincial speech: pa-
provision: grist, store, ration [cause, irritate
provoke: nettle, ire,
prow: stem, bow
prowl about: lurk
proximity: nearness, presence [creet, chary
prudent: wise, sage, dis-
prune: trim [Anklam
Prussian city: Essen,
" river: Ruhr, Lena
" seaport: Emden, Stettin, Kiel
" town: Ems, Ems
" watering place: Ems
pry: lever, snoop, peep
pseudonym: alias
ptarmigan: ripa
public: universal, overt exoteric, national
" announcement: ad
" announcer: crier
" estimation: repute
" guardian: police
" house: tavern, inn, hotel
" life: career
" meeting: forum
" notice: edict
" officer: notary
" performer: artiste
" recreation ground: park
" regard: repute
" room: hall
" storehouse: etape
" vehicle: cab, bus
" walk: promenade, mall [print
publish: edit, issue,
" without authority: piratic, pirate
pucker: purse
puddle: pool, plash
Pueblo Indian: Hopi
puerile: childish
Puerto Rican city: Lares, Ponce
puff: pant, waft [elate
" up: bloat, swell,
pugilist: pug, boxer
pule: whimper
pull: tug, tow, draw, lug, yank, hale, haul
" apart: tear, rend
" off: avulse
pulley wheel: sheave
pulpy fruit: uva, grape
pulsate: beat, throb
pulverize: grind, stamp powder, pestle, fine
pummel: beat
pump handle: swipe
punch: prod, perforate
" (colloq.): pep
puncture: pierce, stab
pungent: bitter, acrid, keen, sharp, racy
punish: chastize, castigate, aveng
" by fine: amerce
punishing rod: ferule
" (law): peine
punitive: penal
puny: weak, frail
pupil: student, scholar
puppet: doll, marionette
puppy: whelp
purchasable: venal
pure: chaste, clean, clear, absolute, vestal
purify: refine, cleanse, aerate, clean, filter, lustrate, purge
purple: tyrian, mauve
purplish brown: puce
purport: tenor
purpose: end, aim, design, intend, mission, mean, intention, intent, goal
purposive: telic
purse: wallet, pucker
pursue: bound, ply, con, trace, chase, steer, hunt
pursuit: chase

**purvey:** supply, provide, cater
**push:** jostle, shove, urge
" **gently:** nudge
**put:** see also place
**put:** deposit, place, set, lay, insert, laid
" **in action:** exert, bestir
" **aside:** fob, table
" **away:** store
" **back:** replace, restore [lade
" **burden on:** strain,
" **in circulation:** publish [case
" " **container:** en-
" **in disordered condition:** litter [press
" **down:** deposit, lay, laid, deposited, de-
" **on file:** filed [rout
" **to flight:** routed,
" **in forgotten place:** mislaid
" **forth:** exert, issue
" " **effort:** strive
" **on guard:** warn
" **in:** insert, inserted
" **off:** postpone, defer
" **in order:** regulate, arrange, file [evict
" **out:** expel, oust,
" **to shame:** abash
" " **a strain:** tax
" **together:** frame, add
" **in type:** print, set
" **up:** can, post, erect
" " **with:** add, tolerated, tolerate [ply
" **to use:** applied, ap-
" **with:** add, tolerate
**puzzle (kind):** acrostic, riddle, enigma, rebus, charade
**pygmy:** dwarf
**pylon:** tower
**pyramid builder:** Cheops [dorra
**Pyrenees republic:** An-
**Pythias's friend:** Damon

## Q

**quack:** charlatan
" **medicine:** nostrum
**quadruped:** horse, deer, sheep, goat, beast
**quagmire:** bog, fen, lair
**quail:** cower, colin
**quake:** tremble, tremor
**Quaker:** friend
**quaking:** aspen
**qualified:** fit, able, apt
**qualify:** temper, entitle
**quality of sound:** tone
**quantity:** amount
" **of matter:** mass
" **of medicine:** dosage [hank
" **of yarn:** skein,
**quarrel:** affray, row, tiff, feud, spat, fracas
**quarry:** game, prey
**quartz (kind of):** prase ogate, flint, onyx
**quaver:** trill, shake
**quay:** levee, wharf
**queen of beasts:** Lioness [Titania, Una
" " **Fairies:** Mab,
" " **Gods:** Hera
**queer:** erratic, odd, singular, peculiar
**quell:** repress, allay, suppress
**quench:** slake
**queue:** pigtail [apace
**quick:** fast, rapid, active, speedy, sudden,
" **blow:** rap
" **to learn:** apt
" **movement:** dart
**quicken:** animate, urge, enliven [pronto
**quickly:** apace, presto,
**quickness:** haste
**quid of tobacco:** cud
**quiescent:** dormant, latent, static
**quiet:** still, serene, silence, static, allay, inert, silent, lull, stilly, soothe, peace
**quill:** pen, cop
**quip:** gibe
**quirk:** twist
**quit:** retire, cease, leave, vacate, stop [pletely
**quite:** entirely, all, com-
**quiver:** tremble, tremor
**quivering:** aspen
**quoit:** discus
**quota:** share
**quote:** cite, allege

## R

**Ra's wife:** Mut [dent
**rabbit:** hare, cony, ro-
" **(female):** doe
" **fur:** lapin
" **home:** hutch
" **tail:** scut
**rabble:** raff, mob
**rabid:** mad, furious
**raccoon:** coon, coati
" **like carnivore:** panda
**race:** speed, contest, lineage, hasten, subspecies, people, run
" **of animals:** breed
" **horse:** trotter, arabian, mantis, plater
" **(kind):** relay [dash
" **(short):** sprint,
" **track tipster:** tout
**Rachael's father:** Laban
**racing boat:** shell
**racket:** noise
**radiant:** beaming, glowing [glow
**radiate:** shine, emit,
**radical:** red, organic, surd, extreme
**radicel:** rootlet
**radio:** wireless
" **chain:** network
" **wire:** aerial
**radium emanation:** niton, radon
**radix:** root
**raft:** float
**rafter:** beam [nant
**rag:** tatter, shred, rem-
**rage:** storm, rant, furor, ire, fury, wrath fume, violence, frenzy
**ragout of lamb:** haricot
**raid:** forage, maraud, foray, invade, incursion, attack
**rail:** fence, scold, heron, bar, scoff, sora, revile, scoff, berate, rant
**railbird:** crake, sora
**railing:** parapet
**raillery:** banter
**railroad tie:** sleeper
**raiment:** dress, attire
**rain:** shower
" **cloud:** nimbus
**rainbow:** iris
**rainspout (Scot.):** rone
**rainstorm:** downpour
**rainy:** wet [heft
**raise:** elevate, lift, exalt, rear, breed, hoist, emboss, boost, erect, grow, uplift, increase
" **a nap:** teasel, teasle
" **spirits of:** elate
" **to third power:** cube
**raised lawns:** terrace
" **strip:** ridge
" **stripe:** welt, rib
**Rajah's wife:** ranee, rani
**rake:** roue [batter
**ram:** butt, stuff, aries, tup, strike, tamp,
" **down:** tamp
" **(the):** Aries [roam
**ramble:** meander, gad, rove, range, stroll,
**rampart:** wall, redan, parapet bulwark
**rancid:** rank
**rancor:** enmity, spite,
**range:** scope, stove, sweep, ramble, rank, adjust, roam, area, gamut, extent
" **of hills:** ridge
" " **knowledge:** ken
**rank:** degree, caste, grade, rate, tier, row, foul, estimate, class, extreme, range, rancid, status, flagrant
**rankle:** inflame, fester
**ransack:** rake, pillage
**ransom:** redeem [bast
**rant:** rage, rail, bom-
**rapier:** sword
**rapid:** fleet, quick, fast, swift, speedy
**rapine:** pillage, plunder
**rapt:** absorbed, intent
**rapture:** bliss, ecstasy
**rare:** unique, odd, scarce, infrequent, unusual, tenuous
**rascal:** scamp, knave, rogue, scoundrel
**rash:** hasty, headstrong
**rasp:** grate, scrape, file, affect, abrade
**rasping:** harsh
**rasse:** civet [percent
**rate:** pace, value, grade, calculate, scold, degree, regard, price, charge, merit, cost
" **of movement:** pace, tempo
**rather (Scot.):** gey
" **than:** ere [dorse
**ratify:** seal, confirm, en-
**ration:** allowance, allot, share, apportion
**rational:** sane, sensible
**rattan:** reed, sega, cane
**rattle:** clatter, noise
**raucous:** hoarse, harsh
**ravage:** ruin [bast
**rave:** rant, fume, bom-
**ravel:** unknit, entangle
**ravine:** dell, gulch, dale, gorge, canyon
**raw:** crude, bleak,
**ray:** shine, beam
**raze:** obliterate, destroy, cut, demolish
**razor billed auk:** murre
" **sharpener:** strop
**reach:** attain, arrive, extend, aspire, span, come [minate
" **highest point:** cul-
**react:** respond, behave
**read:** peruse, pore
" **metrically:** scan
**reading:** perusal
**ready:** alert, prepared, willing, fit, ripe, apt
**real:** true, concrete, actual, factual, genuine [realty
" **estate:** property,
" " **absolutely owned:** alod
" " **contract:** lease
**realize:** sense, accomplish, conceive, perceive, see [empire
**realm:** domain, nation,
**reap:** gather, garner
**rear:** hind, posterior, elevate, behind, raise, erect, construct, back
" **(in the):** astern
" **of vessel:** aft
**reason:** cause, motive
**reasoning:** logic
**rebel:** rise, insurgent
**rebellion:** revolt
**rebound:** dap, carom
**rebuff:** slap, repell, snub, scorn, repulse
**rebuke:** snub, reprimand, chide
**rebut:** disprove, refute
**recall:** remember, retract, remind [revoke
**recant:** retract, abjure,
**recede:** ebb
**receipt:** recipe, stub
**receive:** get, accept, take [dern, fresh
**recent:** new, late, mo-
**receptacle:** bin, receiver, tray, box, tank
**reception:** tea
" **room:** parlor, salon
**recess:** niche, nook
" **in seashore:** bay, inlet
**recipe:** receipt
**recipient:** receiver, legatee [donee
" **of gift:** presentee,
**reciprocal:** mutual
**recite:** relate, narrate, report
" **metrically:** scan
" **in musical monotone:** intone, chant
**reckless:** rash, bold, mad, desperate
**reckon:** rate, date, tally, compute, calculate [deem, rescue
**reclaim:** recover, re-
**recline:** repose, lie, loll, rest [mite
**recluse:** hermit, ere-
**recoil:** shrink, shy
**recollect:** recall
**recollection:** mind
**recommence:** resume
**recommit:** remand
**recompense:** pay, reward, meed, renew, fee [sign
**reconcile:** atone, re-
**recondite:** abstract, abstruse [scout
**reconnoiter:** pickeer,
**record:** annal, log, enter, enroll, pen
" **book:** ledger
" **of proceedings:** acta, actum
**recount:** tell, relate
**recourse:** resort
**recover:** restore, regain, reclaim, rally, retrieve, flow
**recreation:** play, sport
" **area:** park
**rectangular:** oblong
" **inserts:** panels
**rectify:** correct, amend, emend
**rectory:** parsonage
**red:** ruddy, vermilion, roset, crimson, rosy, carmen, flushed, roseate, scarlet, cerise
" **cedar:** savin
" **dye:** alta
" **pepper:** cayenne
" **planet:** Mars
" **purple:** claret
**redact:** edit
**redcap:** porter [flush
**redden:** blush, ruddle,
**reddish:** roseate
" **brown:** auburn, bay, henna, sepia, sorrel, chestnut

" color: peony, coral
" orange dye: henna
" yellow: orange, amber, totem, titian
**redeem**: reclaim, ransom [liverer
**redeemer**: savior, de-
**redolent**: fragrant, odorous [pare
**reduce**: lessen, abate, bate, lower, debase,
" to ashes: cremate
" in density: thin
" to fine state: refine
" " fluid state: liquefy [age
" " a means: aver-
" " a pulp: mash, crush
" in rank: demote
" " size: shrink
" to soft mass: macerate [ize
" " a spray: atom-
**reducing medium**: diet
**reef**: shoal, lode
**reek**: smoke, fume
**reel**: spin, stagger, spool, waver, sway, falter, bobbin, troll
**refer**: appeal, allude, ascribe, relegate, direct, cite, mention
**referee**: umpire, judge
**reference**: allusion
" table: index
**refine**: pure, nice, neat
**refinement**: polish, culture, elegance
**reflect**: mirror, ponder, ruminate
**reflux of the tide**: ebb
**reform**: amend, regenerate, correct
**Reformation leader**: Lutheran
**refractory**: unruly
**refrain**: chorus, abstain, forgo, ditty
**refrigerate**: ice, freeze
**refuge**: haven, retreat
**refulgent**: brilliant
**refund**: repay, rebate
**refuse**: deny, veto, marc, scum, reject, decline, waste, trash
" approval: veto
**refute**: deny, disprove, rebut
**regain**: recover, restore
**regal**: imperial, royal, kingly, stately
**regale**: treat, entertain
**regard**: observe, consider, eye, estimation, hear, care, rate
" favorably: approve
" highly: admire, esteem, honor, deem
" reverently: adore
" studiously: con
" with honor: venerate, respect [form
**regenerate**: renew, re-
**regent**: ruler
**region**: clime, zone, tract, area, district, realm, territory, locality, terrain
" beyond Jordan: Perea, Enon [bus
" of darkness: Ere-
" in general: demesne [areal
**regional**: local, zonal,
**register**: enlist, slate, tally, roll, list, enter
**regret**: rue, repent, resent, mourn, lament, deplore, spurn
**regretful**: sorry
**regular**: stated, normal, canonic, periodic
**regulate**: settle, manage, order, adjust, govern, direct
**regulation**: rule, law
**reign**: rule, prevail, govern
**reigning beauty**: belle
**reimbue with courage**: reman
**reimburse**: pay, repay
**rein**: restrain, line, curb, check
**reindeer**: caribou
**reject**: repel, deny, spurn, refuse
**rejoinder**: answer, repartee, retort, response
**relate**: recite, tell, pertain, appertain, narrate, recount, detail
**related**: kin, akin
" by blood: akin, sib
" on father's side: agnate
" by marriage: inlaw
" on mother's side: enate, enatic, enation
**relative**: pertinent, kin, kinsman, relation
**relax**: ease, loosen, unbend, slacken, remit
**relaxation**: rest
**release**: loose, free, deliver, relet, undo, unbind, loosen, liberate
" on honor: parole
**relent**: yield, soften
**relevant**: pertinent, germane [confidence
**reliance**: trust, hope,
**relict**: widow
**relieve**: lessen, ease, allay, mitigate, aid, spell, vent
**religious awakening**: revival
" belief: creed
" ceremony: mass
" class: sect
" composition: motet, anthem [ish
" congregation: par-
" discipline: penance
" faith: religion [rim
" festival: Easter, Pu-
" hermit: monk
" holiday: fiesta
" image: icons, ikon
" observance: rite
" pamphlet: tract
" poem: psalm
" song: chant, psalm
" talk: cant
" woman: nun
**relinquish**: cede, go, waive, resign, abdicate, leave
**reliquary**: arca, apsis
**relish**: flavor, zest, canape, savor, taste, olive, gusto, like
**reluctant**: averse, loath
**rely**: depend, trust, rest
**remain**: stay, abide tarry, continue [rest
**remainder**: balance, recall, relic, monitor,
**remaining**: remanent, other, residual, left
**remark**: say, note, comment, observe, word
**remedy**: cure, repair
**remind oneself**: bethink, recall
**remiss**: negligent, laggard, lax
**remit**: send, forgive, absolve, forego, relax
**remnant**: rag, ort, dreg
" of fire: ash
**remonstrate**: protest
**remote**: far, distant, old, secluded
**remove**: elide, eliminate, dele, delete, rid, oust, peel, eradicate, doff, pare, convey
" afar off: eloin, eloign
" air: deflate
" beyond jurisdiction (law): eloin
" a cargo: unload
" cream: skim
" error: correct
" from high position: depose, unseat
" hair: epilate
" impurities: refine
" by light rubbing: wipe [rate, dry
" moisture: evapo-
" pits from: stone
" in printing: dele
" utterly: raze
**remunerate**: compensate, pay [break
**rend**: split, rive, tear, cleave, rupture, rip,
**render**: translate, contribute, transmit, deliver, give, bestow, sunder, make furnish
" accesible: open
" active: activate
" asunder: split, rive
" desolate: destroy
" enduring: anneal
" fat: lard [enervate
" ineffective: negate,
" muddy: roil
" senseless: stun
" suitable: adapt
" turbid: roil
" unconscious: stun
" useless: null
**rendezvous**: tryst
**renegade**: deserter, apostate, traitor
**renege**: revoke, deny, renounce
**renew**: restore, resale, resume, regenerate, renovate, revive
" wine: stum
**renounce**: repudiate, disown, deny, abjure, renege, waive
**renovate**: repair, restore, alter, cleanse, renew, clean, furnish
**renown**: glory, honor, fame [schism
**rent**: lease, hire, riven, let, breach, break,
**renter**: lessee, tenant
**repair**: mend, renovate, fix, redress, resort, remedy [atonement
**reparation**: amends, redress, amend, atone,
" for injury: damages [retort
**repartee**: riposte, reply,
**repast**: meal, feast, reflection, dinner, lunch
**repay**: refund, requite
**repeal**: abrogate, annul, rescind, revoke, abolish [echo
**repeat**: iterate, parrot,
" mechanically: parrot [tatat
**repeated knocking**: ra-
**repel**: repulse, ward, reject, oppose
**repent**: atone, rue
**repentant**: penitent, contrite
**repetition**: encore, echo, rote, reiterate, iteration, iterance
**repine**: complain, fret
**replaced**: reset, restored
**replenish**: refill, fill
**replete**: rife, full
**replica**: copy, duplicate, facsimile [answer
**reply**: retort, respond,
**report**: rumor, recite, account [rest, peace
**repose**: compose, ease,
**repository**: safe, vault
**representative**: agent, delegate, legate
" example: type
**repress**: restrain, bridle
**reprimand**: admonish, rebuke, slate, lesson
" (Scot.): ston
**reproach**: blame, slur, upbraid, taunt
" abusively: revile
**reprove**: rebuke, censure, flay [asp
**reptile**: snake, turtle,
**repudiate**: renounce, disown, disclaim, recant, deny
**repulse**: repel, rejection, rebuff [prestige
**reputation**: repute, credit, stamp, honor
**request**: ask, entreaty, solicit, entreat, appeal [tition
**request formally**: peti-
" for payment: dun
**require**: need, demand claim
**requisition**: order
**requite**: repay, revenge, avenge, retaliate, reward [gate
**rescind**: repeal, retract, revoke, cancel, abro-
**rescue**: save, deliver, succor, free, reclaim
**reserve**: spare, reticence, retain
**reserved**: taken, aloof, offish, coy, shy, cold
" in speech: reticent [live
**reside**: abide, dwell,
**resident**: citizen, inherent, dweller, occupant [maining
**residual**: remanent, re-
**residue**: ash, rest
**resign**: demit, relinquish, reconcile,
**resilient**: elastic
**resin**: lac, anime, copal, elemin
" (fragrant): aloe, elemi, nard
**resist**: rebel, oppose, repel, withstand
**resistance to attack**: defense [nitent
**resisting pressure**: re-
**resolute**: determined, manly [mine, rotate
**resolve**: decide, deter-
**resonant**: ringing
**resort**: spa, haunt, recourse, repair
**resound**: ring, peal, echo, reverberate, clang, toll [sets
**resources**: means, as-
**respect**: esteem, awe, reverence, homage, deference, honor
**respectable**: decent
**respiratory organ**: lung
" sound: rale
**respire**: breathe
**respite**: rest, reprieve, pause, truce, interval, lull [golden
**resplendent**: aureate,
**respond**: react, answer, peal, reply
**response**: answer, reaction, rejoinder
**rest**: pause, repose, lean, sit, respite, ease, lair, desist, recline, rely, support
**restless**: uneasy, tossing, restive
**restore**: renew, replace, renovate, reinstate, return, revive

" to normal position: right
restrain: dam, stint, moderate, curb, bate, chain, check, repress, tether, bridle, cramp, bind, deter, confine, arrest, rule, rein
" thru fear: deter
restrict: limit, hem, resew, dam, stint
result: eventuate, outcome, ensue, follow, upshot, effect
" of an inquiry: findings [continue
resume: renew, reopen,
resuscitate: revive
ret: soak, steep
retain: save, hold, keep, engage, reserve
retaliate: avenge, requite, repay
retaliation: reprisal, revenge [hinder
retard: delay, slow,
reticence: reserve
reticent: secretive,
reticule: handbag
retinue: suite, train
" of wives: harem
retire: retreat, quit, leave, resign, withdraw
retired: inactive, abed
" from the world: recluse [tus
" with honor: emeri-
retiring: shy
retract: recant, disavow, recall [nest
retreat: recess, retire, withdraw, refuge
retribution: revenge, avenge, nemesis, pay
retrieve: recover [recur
return: restore, revert,
" evil for evil: retaliate
" to office: reelect
" thrust: riposte
reveal: bare, disclose, show, unveil, expose
revel: feast, spree, delight, riot
revelry: riot, joy
revenge: requite, retaliate avenge,
revenue: income
reverberate: resound, echo, roll, ring
revere: adore, venerate, admire [honor
reverence: awe, revere,
reverie: dream, daydream
revert: reverse, recur, return
review: survey, consider, revise, parade, critique [scoff, vilify
revile: malign, abuse,
revise: amend, proofread, edit, review, change, emend
revive: freshen, resuscitate, rally, reanimate, renew [scind
revoke: repeal, cancel, renig, adeem, renege, reverse, recant, re-
" a legacy: adeem
revolt: rebel, mutiny, rise, rebellion, uprising
revolution: rotation
" hero: Hale, Revere, Allen
" traitor: Arnold
revolve: rotate, gyrate, spin, roll, turn, whirl,
revolving arrow: vire
" part: rotor [guerdon
reward: mend, prize, meed, medal, requite,
rhea: emu
rhetorical: oratorical
" device: aporia
Rhine affluent: Ruhr
rhythm: cadence, meter, tempo [rical
rhythmic: cadent, met-
" beat: pulse
" silence: rest
" swing: lilt
ria: inlet [gay blithe
riant: bright, smiling,
rib: vein, vertebra, purl
ribald: coarse
ribbed fabric: rep, twill, dimity [sette
ribbon decoration: ro-
rice in the husk: paddy
" liquor: sake
" paste: ame
rich: affluent, opulent
" man: nabob
" source: mine [om
richochet: glance, car-
rid: clear, free [bus
riddle: enigma, sift, re-
" in cloth: rib
" (colloq.): welt
" 's of drift: osar, eskar, esker
" of earth: rideau
" of rock: reed, reef
ridicule: deride, satire, satirize, lampoon, snort, banter, roast, scout, twit
" (Colloq.): roast, pan
ridiculous failure: fiasco [nege
riding academy: ma-
" whip: quirt, crop
rife: replete, current, abounding, widespread
rifle: garand, gun, pillage, ransack, mauser
rift: fissure, cleft, break
rig: attire, gear
Riga Island gulf: Oesel
right: proper, just, correct
" away: pronto
" hand page: recto
" " (Pert. to): dexter [ure
" to hold office: ten-
" of suffrage: vote
" of using another's property: easement
rigid: set, tense, stark, severe, stiff, strict
rigor: asperity
rigorous: severe, drastic, spartan, strait, inclement, stern
rile: vex, annoy, irritate
rill: streamlet, rillet
rim: border, edge, brink, edging
rima: fissure
rimple: fold, wrinkle
rind: peel, skin
ring: peal, circle, toll, knell, arena, hoop, encircle, ringlet [rona
" around moon: co-
" of chain: link
" to hold reins: terret
" shaped: annular
ringed boa: aboma
ringlet: trees, curl
ringworm: tinea [revel
riot: uproar, brawl, unsew, revelry, orgy,
rip: tear, rend [ready
ripe: mellow, mature,
riposte: repartee
ripple: wavelet
" against: lap [climb
rise: elevate, levitate, mount, soar, lift, ascent, rebel, revolt,
" & fall of sea: tide
" high: tower
" threateningly: loom
risible: funny
risk: dare, venture, hazard, stake, danger, chance, peril
rite: ceremony
rival: foe, emulate, competitor, emulator, competing [rent
rive: rend, cleave, split,
river: stream, run
" bank: ripa
" " (pert. to): riparian, riverain
" bed: wady, wadi
" boat: barge, ark
" bottom: bed
" dam: weir
" deposit: silt
" descent: rapids
" duck: teal
" embankment: dam
" of forgetfulness: Lethe
" god's daughter: Io
" of ice: glacier
" island: ait
" lowland: flat
" mouth: delta
" mussel: unio
" nymph: naiad, nais
" shore: bank
" tract: flat
" of underworld: Styx
rivet: bolt, fasten
rivulet: rill, streamlet, creek
road: course, way
roam: range
" about idly: gad
roar: bellow, scream, yell, boom, din, howl
" of surf: rote
roasting iron & stick: spit [burgle
rob: steal, loot, plunder, defraud, pilfer,
robbed: reft
robbery on high seas: piracy [ray, talar
robe: mantle, attire, ar-
Robinson Crusoe's author: Defoe
robust: strong, hardy, vigorous hale, rugged
rock: vibrate, totter, stone, ore, shake
" (kind): slate, spar, agate, stone, trap, besalt, prase, shale, gneiss, basalt
" (sharp): crag
rockfish: rena, reina
Rocky Mt. Park: Estes
" " Range: Teton
" pinnacle: tor
rod: staff, pole, wand, twig, ferule, baton, spindle, axle
" used in basketry: osier [bit, gnawer
rodent: paca, hare, marmot, mouse, rab-
rodeo: roundup
rogue: beggar, knave, rascal, scamp, picaroon, scoundrel
roguish: sly, arch
roil: muddy [ter
roister: swagger, blus-
role: part
roll: rota, list, bun, revolve, register, roster
" of cloth: bolt
" (dial): whelve
" " parchment: pell
" " thread: cop
" up: furl
romaine lettuce: cos
Roman: Latin
" bascilica: lateran
" boxing glove: ceestus
" bronze: aes
" chariot: essed
" church cathedral: Lateran
" clan: gens
" coin: as, ae
" cuirass: lorica
" date: nones, ides
" emperor (old): Caesar, Otho, Nero, Otto
" fate: nona
" garment: stola, tunic, stolae, toga
" god: di, lare
" " of underworld: Dis, Pluto
" goddess: Luna, Lua
" " of horses: Epona [Ceres
" " " vegetation:
" greeting: ave
" highway: iter
" hill: Viminal, Palatine [Livy
" historian: Nepos,
" house god: Lar, Lare, Penate
" magistrate: pretor, edile, tribune
" meal: cena
" monetary unit: ley
" money: aes
" naturalist: Pliny
" official: prefect, edile, tribune
" orator: Pliny
" palace: lateran
" patriot: Cato [eca
" philosopher: Sen-
" poet: Ovid, Horace
" priest: flamen
" room: atria (pl.)
" sock (ancient): udo
" statesman: Cato
" tribune: rienzi
" tyrant: Nero
" weight: as
" writer: Terence
romance: novel, dream
romp: frolic, gambol
romping girl: tomboy
rood: cross, crucifix
roof: slate, summit
" edge: eave [tile
" material: tile, pan-
" of mouth: palate
rook: chessman
" cry: caw
room: space, lodge, chamber, aula
" for pitchers & linens: ewery
" (small): cell
roost: set, sit, perch
root: radix, bottom, origin, basis, source
" of certain plant: bulb [tirpate, stub
" out: eradicate, ex-
" word: etymon
rootlet: radicel [cable
rope: hawser, riata,
" fiber: sisal
" for hoisting a ships yard: tye
" to moor a boat: painter
rose (dial.): ris
" essence: attar
" fruit: hip
" red dye: eosin, eosine [rosette
" shaped ornament:
roseate: rosy, reddish
roster: list, rota, roll
rosy: blushing, roseate, red, blooming, pink
rot: decay, rubbish
rota: roll, list
rotary motor: turbine
rotate: turn, spin, revolve, resolve, alternate, swirl [cam
rotating part: rotor,
" pin: spindle
roue: rake [aspirate
rough breathing: asper,
" house: shack

" **with bristles**: hispid
**roughen**: shag, nurl
**roulade**: run
**roulette bet**: bas
**round**: circular, orbed, spherical
" **about way**: detour
" **& hollow**: concave
" **muscle**: teres
" **projection**: lob, nob
" **room**: rotunda
**rounded appendage**: lobe
" **hill**: knoll, knob
" **molding**: ovolo
**roundup**: rodeo
**rouse**: stir, bestir, waken, spur, awaken
" **to vigilance**: alarm
**rout**: defeat
**route**: way, course, line, trail, path
**rove**: prowl, wander, stroll
" **about**: gad, range
**rover**: pirate, nomad
**roving**: errant, errantry, migrant
**row**: tier, line, oar, layer, spat, quarrel, brawl, rank, argument
**rowan tree**: sorb
**rowboat**: gig, caique
**rower**: oarsman, oar
**royal**: regal
**rub**: abrade, scrape, polish, chafe, scour
" **gently**: stroke, wipe
" **hard**: scrub
" **out**: erase, expunge
" **with rough file**: rasp
**rubber**: para, eraser, gum
" **jar ring**: lute
" **tree**: ule
**rubbish**: trash, refuse, debris, rot
" **(mining)**: attle
**rude**: borish, uncivil uncouth, impolite
" **house**: shack, hut, cabin, shed
" **person**: boor, cad
**rue**: regret, repent, herb
**ruffian**: desperado, thug
**ruffle**: roil, frill, disturb
**rug (small)**: mat, runner
**ruga**: wrinkle, crease
**rugged**: robust
" **crest**: tor
" **rock**: crag
**ruin**: wreck, undoing, impair, bankrupt, doom, destroy, devastate, ravage, rase, demolish, undo, bane
**rule**: preside, reign, restrain, dominate, formula, law, govern, regime, line
**ruler**: dynast, gerent, regent, monarch, ferule, oligarch, emperor, sovereign
" **in place of a king**: viceroy
**Rumanian coin**: leu, ley
**rumen**: cud
**ruminant**: sheep, camel, goat, llama
" **stomach**: rumen, tripe
**ruminate**: ponder, muse, meditate, reflect
**rumor**: report, gossip hearsay
" **personified**: fama
**rumple**: tousle, muss
**run**: flow, race, operate, extend, speed, sprint, conduct, brook
" **after**: chase
" **aground**: strand, sand
" **away**: decamp
" **between ports**: ply
" **(dial.)**: rin
" **down**: decry
" **easily**: lope, trot
" **off**: elope, bolt
" " **(colloq.)**: peter
" **over**: spill
" **rapidly**: scud
" **(Scot.)**: rin
" **slowly**: trickle
" **on wheels**: roll
**runagate**: fugitive
**rung of ladder**: ratline, spoke
fugitive
**runner**: miler, speeder, operator, racer, ski,
**rural**: pastoral, arcadian, rustic, bucolic
" **deity**: faun
" **poem**: georgic
" **residence**: villa
**ruse**: trick, artifice
**rush**: hurry, cattail, charge, speed, surge
" **headlong**: bolt
" **suddenly**: hurtle sally, tear
**rusk**: bun, biscuit
**Russian**: Slav, Soviet, Red
" **antelope**: saiga
" **bay**: Luga
" **cavalryman**: cossack
" **city**: Tula, Grosny, Orel, Dno, Minsk, Osa, Samara, Ufa
" **coin**: kopeck, kopek, altin, rupee
" " **(old)**: altin
" **composer**: Cui
" **council**: Duma, Soviet
" **czar**: Ivan
" **emperor**: Nicholas
" **empress's title**: Tsarina
" **gulf**: Ob
" **hemp**: rive, rine
" **leader**: Lenin
" **measure**: verst
" **monarch**: tsar
" **money**: ruble
" **mountain**: Ural
" **name**: Igor, Ivan
" **news agency**: Tass
" **novelist**: Gorki
" **peninsula**: Kola
" **plain**: steppe
" **river**: Ural, Neva, Don, Lena, Ros, Ob, Ner, Amur, Duna, Kara, Irtish, Volga, Ik, Ilet, Ai
" **ruler**: Ivan, Tsar
" **sea & lake**: Aral, Azof, Azov
" **stockade**: etah, etape
" **storehouse**: etape
" **sturgeon**: sterlet
" **tea urn**: samovar
" **town**: Elista
" **trade commune**: artel
" **union**: artel
" **village**: Mir
" **wagon**: telega
**rustic**: rural, yokel, peasant, pastoral, bucolic, sylvan, boor
" **(colloq.)**: hodge
" **dance**: hay
" **gallant**: swain
" **workman**: peasant
**rut**: groove, ditch,
**Ruth's husband**: Boaz
" **mother in law**: Naomi
**rye disease**: ergot
" **drink**: gin

## S

**S shaped curve**: ess
" " **molding**: ogee
**sable**: black
**sacshaped**: saccate
**saccharine**: sweet, sugary
**sack**: loot, pouch, bag, pillage
**sacrament**: rete, rite
**sacred**: holy, hallowed
" **beetle**: scarab
" **bull**: apis
" **city of Islam**: Medina
" **image**: icon, idol
" " **(var.)**: ikon
" **musical composition**: motet
" **picture**: icon, ikon
" **poem**: hymn, psalm
" **tune**: chorale, choral
" **vessel**: ark
" **work**: om
" **writing**: scripture
**sad**: plaintive, mournful, doleful, gloomy, downcast, dejected, despondent, woeful
**saddle loop**: stirrup
" **pad**: panel
**sadness**: sorrow
**safe**: secure
" **keeping**: storage
**sag**: droop, sink
**saga**: tale, myth, legend
**sagacious**: wise, discerning
**sagacity**: acumen
**sage**: wise, seer, sapient, prophet, prudent, solon
**said to be**: reputed
**sail**: navigate, voyage, cruise, jib, lateen
" **upward**: soar
" **yard (Scot.)**: Ra, Rae
**sailing race**: regatta
" **vessel**: sloop, saic, ketch, yawl
**sailor**: tar, salt, mariner, gob, seaman
" **'s outfit**: kit
**saintly**: pious, angelical, holy
**salad plant**: cress, endive
**salamander**: newt, eft, triton
**salary**: wages, stipend, earnings, emolument
**sale**: auction, bargain
**saline**: salty
" **solution**: brine
**sally**: sortie, start
" **forth**: issue
**salt**: sal, season, marinate, alum
" **of acetic acid**: acetate
" " **anisic acid**: anisate
" " **boric acid**: borate
" **marsh**: salina
" **of nitric acid**: nitrate, nitrite
" " **oleic acid**: oleate
" **solution**: brine
" **water**: brine
**salted (Phil. Isl.)**: alat
**saltpeter**: niter, nitre
**salty**: saline, briny
**salutation**: ave, bow, greeting, hello
**salute**: greet, hail
**salve**: ointment, palliate
**salver**: tray
**Sambar deer**: maha
**same**: similar, identical, equal, ditto, alike, one
" **(of) kind**: akin
" **(Lat. abbr.)**: id
**sameness**: monotony
**Samoan bird**: iao
" **city**: Apia
" **mollusk**: asi
" **mudworm**: ipo
" **seaport**: Apia
" **warrior**: toa
**sample**: taste, specimen
" **of fabric**: swatch
**Samuel's mentor**: Eli
**sanctify**: bless
**sanction**: approve, approval, fiat, abet, ratify, endorse, assent
**sanctuary**: fane, bema
**sanctum**: den
**sand**: grit, beach, gravel
" **bank**: shoal
" **bird**: snipe
" **clay mixture**: loam
" **hill**: dune, dene
" **ridge**: dune, reef
" **on sea bottom**: paar
**sandal**: slipper
**sandarac tree**: arar, adar
" **wood**: alerce
**sandpaper**: stib
**sandpiper**: ree, stint, reeve, ruff
**sandy**: arenose
**sane**: lucid, rational, sound
**sap**: vitality, enervate, weaken, exhaust
**sapidity**: savor, taste
**sarcasm**: irony
**sarcastic**: satiric, ironic, sardonic, biting, mordant
**sash**: scarf, belt, girdle
**sartor**: tailor
**satan**: devil, tempter, lucifer
**satchel**: handbag, bag, valise
**sate**: glut, satiate, fill, surfeit
**sated with pleasure**: blase
**satellite**: moon
" **of the sun**: planet
" " **Uranus**: Ariel
**satire**: lampoon, irony
**satisfy**: sate, suit, satiate, content, serve
**saturate**: soak, imbue, steep, drench, souse
**satyr**: faun
**sauce**: gravy, pertness
**saucy**: malapert, pert, insolent, brash
" **girl**: minx
**saunter**: stroll, loiter
**savage**: feral, fierce
**savant**: scientist, sage
**save**: rescue, but, spare, except, hoard, preserve, conserve
**savior**: redeemer
**savor**: sapidity, relish, smack, taste
**savory**: sapid, tasty
" **meat jelly**: aspic
**sawlike edge**: serrate
" **part**: serra
**saxifrage**: seseli
**Saxon**: English
**say**: utter, aver, state, voice
" **further**: add
**saying**: adage
**scabbard**: sheath
**scalawag**: scamp
**scale**: climb, gamut, flake
" **(comb. form)**: lepis
**scalloped**: crenate
**scaly**: laminar
**scamp**: rascal, scalawag, rogue
**scan**: study
**Scand.**: Dane, Norse, Finn, Swede, Lapp
" **division**: amt
" **giant**: Troll
" **goddess**: Hel
" **lang.**: Norse
" **literary work**: edda
" **measure**: alen
" **mongoloid**: Lapp
" **myth**: saga
" **mythical monarch**: Atli
" **navigator**: Eric
" **(pert. to)**: Norse, Nordic
" **poet**: Scald
**scanty**: meager, sparse, scarce, bare, poor, spare
**scar**: blemish
**scarce**: sparse, rare, scanty, deficient
**scarcely**: hardly
**scarcity**: dearth, fam-

ine, want [alarm
**scare**: frighten, startle,
**scarf**: ascot, necktie, sash, tippet, tie
" **of feathers**: boa
**scarflike vestment**: orale
**scarlet**: red
**scathe**: damage
**scatter**: dispel, radiate, sow, disperse, strew, spread, disseminate, disband, bestrew, dot
" **carelessly**: litter
**scene**: view, vista, outlook, episode, landscape [stage
" **of action**: arena,
**scenic view**: scape
" **word enigma**: charade [aroma, smell
**scent**: perfume, nose,
" **bag**: sachet
" **of cooking**: nidor
**scepter**: wand, mace
**scheme**: plot, plan, conspire, project
**schism**: rent, division
**scholar**: student, pupil, pedant, savant
**scholarly**: learned
**school**: train, tutor
" **of seals**: pod [inar
" **session**: term, sem-
" **of whales**: gam
**schoolmaster**: pedant, pedagogue
**science**: art
" " **government** politics
" " **life**: biology
" " **plants**: botany
" " **reasoning**: logic [spark, sparkle
**scintillate**: twinkle,
**scion**: bud, sprout, heir, descendant, son
**scoff**: sneer, scorn, rail, deride, mock, fleer, revile, jeer
**scold**: berate, rate, nag, rant, chide, rail, objurate
**sconce**: shelter
**scoop**: shovel [gin
**scope**: range, extent, latitude, area, mar-
**scorch**: blister, char, singe, sear, toast
**score**: tally, groove, twenty, scratch, goal
**scoria**: slag
**scorn**: scoff, spurn, disdain, rebuff, mock, deride, derision, contemn [donian
**Scot**: Gael, tax, Cale-
**Scotch author**: Milne
" **cake**: scone
" **child**: bairn [Perth
" **city & town**: Ayr,
" **dairymaid**: dey
" **dance**: reel
" **explorer**: Rae
" **girl**: lassie
" **highlander**: Gael
" " **lang.**: erse
" **hillside**: brae
" **island**: Iona
" **jurist**: Erskine
" **king**: Robert
" **landowner**: laird
" **mountain**: Nevis
" **music instrument**: bagpipe
" **musician**: piper
" **negative**: nae
" **petticoat**: kilt
" **plaid**: tartan
" **poet**: Burns, Hogg
" **river**: Dee, Tay, Afton, Clyde, Devon
" **weighing machine**: trone [Scot
**Scotchman**: Bluecap,
**scoundrel**: knave, cad, varlet, rogue, rascal
**scour**: scrub, rub
**scourge**: bane
**scowl**: frown, glower
**scrap**: bit, shred, fragment, fight, ort
**scrape**: grate, rasp
" **off**: abrade
" **together**: rake
" **with something sharp**: scratch, paw
**scraped linen**: lint
**scratch**: scrape, claw, rist, score
**screed**: tirade [cover
**screen**: sift, shade, hide,
**screw**: distort, twist
**scribe**: write, writer
**scrimp**: stint [son
**scripture reading**: les-
**scrub**: mop, scour
**scruff**: nape
**scrutinize**: scan, examine, eye, peruse, pry
**scuffle**: tussle
**scull**: oar, shoal
**scum**: dross, silt, refuse
**scurrilous**: abusive
**scurry**: run, scamper
**scuttle**: hod
**scythe handle**: snead, snath, snathe
**sea**: wave, ocean, main
" **anemones**: polyps
" **animal**: coral, orc
" **bird**: petrel, erne, tern, gull, solan, auk, ern, gannet
" **cow**: manatee
" **cucumber**: trepang
" **demigod**: triton
" **duck**: eider, coot
" **eagle**: erne, tern
" **ear**: abalone
" **god**: Ler, Neptune
" **gull**: cob, mew
" **kale beet**: chard
" **mile**: naut, knot
" **nymph**: nereid, naiad, siren [naval
" **(pert. to)**: marine,
" **robbery**: piracy
" **shell**: conch [ton
" **swallow**: tern, tri-
**seal**: stamp, cere, signet, ratify, confirm, sigil, pledge, cachet
**seam**: suture, stratum, juncture
" **of ore**: vein
**seaman**: sailor, mariner
**sear**: blast, scorch, burn, parch
**search**: ransack, hunt, seek, grope, ferret, inquiry, quest, probe
" **for food**: forage
**seashore**: coast
**season**: tide, weather, winter, inure, mature, autumn
" **for use**: age
**seasoned**: ripe [spice
**seasoning**: spice, all-
" **herb**: sage, thyme, basil, parsley
**seat**: install, perch, chair, bench, settee
**seaweed**: alga, ore, laver, kelp, algae (pl.)
" **ashes**: varec, kelp
" **derivative**: agar
**secluded**: private, remote, lonely
**seclusion**: privacy
**second**: abet
" **childhood**: dotage
" **growth crop**: rowen
**secondary**: bye
" **school**: prep
**secondhand**: used
**secret**: private, hidden, covert, concealed
" **agent**: spy
" **procedure**: stealth
" **writing**: code
**secretary**: desk
**secreting organ**: gland
**secretive**: reticent
**sect**: cult, faction, party
**section**: division, part, piece, partition, area
**secular**: laic, layman
**secure**: safe, obtain, get, acquire, fast, nail, firm, fasten
**security**: pawn, guaranty, bond, tie, bail, warranty
" **for payment**: lien
**sedate**: staid, sober, settled, tranquil, matronly [lees
**sediment**: silt, dreg,
**seductive woman**: siren, vampire
**sedulous**: diligent
**see**: lo, behold, witness, notice, descry [corn
**seed**: germ, ovule, pip, plant, progeny, spore, source, sow, seedlet,
" **of cereal**: kernel
" **coat (hard)**: testa
" **container**: pod, bur, loment
" **covering**: aril, testae, testa, pod
" **of flowerless plant**: spore
" **integument**: testa
" **of leguminous plants**: pulse
" " **opium poppy**: maw
" **plant**: herb [meg
" **used as spice**: nut-
" **vessel**: pod, legume
**seedlike fruit**: bean
**seek**: crave, search, aspire, hunt, court
" **after**: sue
**seem**: appear, look
**seep**: percolate, transude, ooze, leak
**seer**: prophet, sage
**seesaw**: teeter
**seethe**: boil, stew
**segment of curve**: arc
**seine**: net, trap
**seize**: grasp, grab, nab, catch, take, arrest, clasp, clutch, grip
**seizure**: arrest
**select**: choose, pick
" **body**: quorum
" **group**: elite
**self**: ego
" **centered person**: egoist, egotist
" **(comb. form)**: auto
" **conceit**: egotism
" **esteem**: pride
" **evident truth**: axiom, truism
" **exaltation**: pride
" **interested**: egoist
" **(pert. to)**: personal
" **possessed**: cool
" **reproach**: remorse
" **satisfied**: smug
" **(Scot.)**: sel
" **sufficient person**, prig [pose
**sell**: vend, trade, dis-
" **to customer**: retail
**semi circular recess**: apse [dius
" **diameter**: radii, ra-
**semiprecious stone**: agate, olivin, onyx, garnet, sards
**semite**: arab
" **language**: arabic
**send**: dispatch, deliver, transmit, forward
" **along**: relay [mand
" **back**: remit, re-
" **down**: demit
" **forth**: emit
" **out**: emit, radiate
**senile**: aged [doter
" **person**: dotard,
**senior**: eldest, elder
**sensational**: lurid
**sense**: feel, meaning, comprehend, wit
" **of dignity**: pride
" " **guilt**: shame
" " **smell**: olfactory, nose
" " **taste**: palate
**senseless**: inane, folly, unideaed, mad
**sensible**: rational
**sensitive**: sore, tender
**sentence**: doom, judgment, condemn
**sentimental**: romantic
**sentinel**: guard
**sentry's greeting**: halt
**separate**: divorce, part, apart, partitive, alienate, sever, divide, aside, disjoin, sort
" **& classify**: assort
" **& divide**: sleave
" **entry**: item
**sepulcher**: tomb
**sepulchral**: charnel
**sequel**: outcome, upshot
**seraglio**: harem
**seraphic**: angelic
**Serbian**: Serb, Slav
**sere**: dry, wither
**serene**: calm, placid, tranquil, irenic
**serf**: esne, slave, vassal, bondman, thrall, helot, villein, peasant
**serfage**: bondage
**series**: sets
" **of ancestors**: line
" " **links**: chains
" " **meetings**: session
" " **names**: list
" " **rings**: coil
" " **stairs**: flight
**serious**: sober, solemn, severe, grim, earnest, grave, demure, rapt
" **attention**: care
" **discourse**: sermon
**sermon**: address, oration, homily
" **subject**: text [sera
**serous fluid**: serum,
**serpent**: aboma, asp, snake, adder, cobra, boa, python
**serpentine**: snaky
" **fish**: eel
**serrate**: notch [ial
**servant**: servitor, men-
" **'s garb**: livery
**serve**: bestead, satisfy, minister, attend
" **food**: cater
" **the purpose**: do
**server**: tray, attendant
**service**: use [abject
**servile**: menial, slavish,
" **dependent**: minion
**sesame**: til, semsem
**session**: seance
**set**: fix, coterie, series, clique, group, hard, adjust, rigid, appoint, mount, congeal, put
" **apart**: isolate, allocate, devote
" **back**: recess
" **of boxes**: nest
" **fire to**: burn, ignite, lit
" **forth**: sail
" **of four**: tetrad
" **in from margin**: indent
" **of instruments**: kit
" **of jeweled ornaments**: parure
" **in motion**: stir

" **of nested boxes:** inro
" **of organ pipes:** stop [rure
" " **ornaments:** pa-
" **out:** embark, start, sail
" **of players:** team
" **right:** correct
" **to rights:** settled
" **of signals:** code
" **solidly:** embed
" **the speed:** pace
" **of three:** tierce
" **to:** bout
" **of type:** font
" **up:** rear
" **upright:** erect, rear
" **value on:** appraise, rate
**Seth's brother:** Abel
" **mother:** Eve
" **son:** Enos
**settle money on:** endow
**settled:** sedate, sedentary, lit, determined, agreed, decided, adjusted, regulated, colonized, disposed
" **habit:** rut
**settler:** colonist
**settling:** dreg, lee
**setto:** bout, fray
**seven (comb. form):** hepta
" **part composition:** septet
**sever:** cut, disunite, part, disjoin, rend, separate, break
**several:** divers, many
**severe:** stern, strict, spartan, drastic, austere, crucial, rigid, hard, rigorous, disjoin, harsh [ness
**severity:** rigor, stern-
**sew:** plant, stitch, mend
" **loosely:** baste
**sewer:** ditch, drain
**sex:** gender
**shack:** hut [manacle
**shackle:** fetter, pinion,
**shad:** alose, alosa
**shade:** tone, shadow, hue, tint, screen, cast, ghost, nuance, tinge
" **of the dead:** mane
" **tree:** elm, lin, ash
**shaded walk:** mall
**shadow:** shade, darken
**shaft:** pole, missile
" " **vehicle:** thill
**shaggy:** bushy, nappy
**shake:** tremor, wag, jar, tremble, shiver, bob, dodder, convulse, rattle
" **up fire:** stoke
**Shakesperian character:** Salerio, Falstaff, Othello, Iras, Iago, Oberon [sius
" **conspirator:** Cas-
" **forest:** Arden
" **heroine:** Portia
" **king:** Lear
" **lord:** Bigot
" **river:** Avon
" **villain:** Iago
**shaking:** tremor, aspen
" **box:** tray
" **dish:** plate, saucer
" **vessel:** basin
**sham:** pretend, feign, false, imposture, artificial, fake
**shame:** mortify, abash, disgrace, chagrin, humiliate, abasement
**shameless:** arrant
**shank:** shin, crus [tour
**shape:** form, model, mold, frame, con-
" **conically:** cone
**shaped like pine cone:** pineal [hewn
" **with an ax:** hewed,
**share:** impart, portion, partake, quota, divide, bit, lot, dole
**shark:** gata, tope
**sharp:** tart, acute, keen, ration, pungent, edgy, edged, stern, nippy, biting, incisive, acerb
" **answer:** retort
" **cornered:** angular
" **cry:** yelp, yell
" **end:** point [twinge
" **pain:** pang, sting,
" **point:** barb, cusp
" **pointed:** acute, aculeate [ness
" **taste:** tang, tart-
" **to taste:** acid, tart
" **tempered:** edgy
**sharpen:** strop, whet, hone, point, edge
**sharpening machine:** grinder
" **stone:** hone
**sharpshooter:** sniper
**shatter:** smash, break
**shave:** shear, pare
" **head of:** tonsure
**shawl:** paisley, wrap
**Shawnee's chief:** Tecumseh [fleece, strip
**shear:** poll, clip, shave,
**sheath:** case, encase, scabbard
" **internally:** ceil
**shed:** leanto, spill, cote, molt, emit [molt
" **feathers:** moult,
**sheen:** luster, polish, gloss, brightness
**sheep:** ewe, ram, sna
" **(breed):** merino
" **coat:** fleece, wool
" **cry:** bleat
" **disease:** coe
" **dog:** collie
" **(female):** ewe
" **killing parrots:** keas
" **(male):** ram
" **two years old:** teg
" **shelter:** cote, fold
**sheeplike:** ovine
**sheet of floating ice:** floe [plate
" **of glass:** pane,
**shelf:** ledge
**shell:** shot, bomb
" **not exploding:** dud
**shellac:** varnish, lac
**shellfish:** clam, crab, abalones, mollusk
**shelter:** lee, haven, protect, shed, abri, tent, roof, sconce, cover, asylum [covert
**sheltered:** shady, lee,
" **side:** lee [ite
**Shem descendant:** sem-
**sherbet:** ice
**sheriff's deputy:** bailiff
" **group:** posse [ecus
**shield:** egis, protect, buckler, targe, ecu,
" **division (her.):** ente
**shift:** veer, tour, change
**shine:** gleam, radiate, beam, glitter, ray, polish, glisten, glow, luster, gloss
**shining:** radiant, lucent, aglow
**Shinto temple:** Sha
" **gateway:** Torii
**ship:** boat vessel
" **body:** hull
" **bow:** stem, prow
" **cabin:** saloon
" **channel:** gat
" **crane:** davit
" **cubical content:** tonnage
" **deck:** poop
" **employe:** steward
" **guns:** teeth
" **kitchen:** galley
" **line:** lanyard
" **load:** cargo
" **officer:** mate, purser, navigator
" **part:** keel, mast, rudder
" **personnel:** crew
" **(pert. to):** naval
" **(poet.):** keel, prow
" **prison:** brig
" **rear:** aft [spar
" **timber:** keel, bitt,
**shipboard:** asea
**shipbuliding to bend upward:** sny [shun
**shirk:** evade, avoid,
**shirt (arch.):** sark
" **button:** stud
**shiver:** shudder, shake, splinter, tremor
**shoal:** flat, shallow, reef
**shock:** appal, strike, jar, startle, brunt
**shoe:** boot, brogan
" **fastener:** latchet
" **form:** last, tree [per
" **(kind):** sandal, slip-
" **part:** rand, welt, insole, upper, vamp
" **store:** bootery
**shoemaker tool:** awl
**shoestring:** lace, lacet
**shoot:** cion, fire, sprout, discharge, dart, sprig
" **out:** dart [leonid
**shooting star:** meteor,
**shore:** coast, strand, land, beach, prop, support [ree
" **bird:** snipe, rail, stilt, avocet, plover,
**short:** curt, brief, succinct, pert, abrupt
" **contest:** setto
" **distance:** step, pace
" **letter:** billet, line
" **napped fabric:** ras
" **piece of pipe:** tee,
" **& to the point:** terse
" **race:** dash, sprint
" **rest:** siesta, nap
" **sentence:** clause
" **skirt:** kilt
" **stop:** pause
" **story:** anecdote
" **& thick:** stocky, dumpy
" **time:** spell
**shortage:** deficit
**shorten:** cut, curtail
**shortening:** lard
**Shosh. Indian:** Ute, Paiute, Piute
**shoulder (comb. form):** omo
" **ornament:** epaulet
" **pack:** knapsack
" **of road:** berm
**shout:** yell, hoot, cry, hooy, bawl, root
" **applause:** cheer
**shove:** push, thrust
**shovel:** spade, scoop
**show:** array, parade, evince, display, exhibit denote, reveal
" **approval:** smile
" **contempt:** sneer, hiss, boo [trast
" **difference:** con-
" **to be false:** belie, disprove
" **fondness:** dote
" **mercy:** spare
" **off:** parade
" **sorrow for:** pity
" **to be true:** prove
**shower:** rain
**showy:** ornate, garish
" **clothes:** regalia, finery [sy
" **(colloq.):** loud, dres-
" **display:** splurge
" **ornament:** tinsel
**shred:** rag, particle, scrap, tatter, wisp, fragment, snip
**shrew:** virago, vixen, termagant [clever
**shrewd:** canny, keen, astute, politic, smart, knowing, sly, acute,
" **(slang):** cagy
" **woman:** virago
**shrewdness:** acumen
**shrill bark:** yap, yelp
" **cry:** shriek, scream
**shrink:** wane, contract, cower, recoil, lessen, cringe, shrivel
**shrivel:** wither, wizen, blast, shrink
**shroud:** sheet
**shrub:** spirea, elder, alder, lilac, baretta, bush, laurel, sumac, plant, senna, bush
" **fence:** hedge
**shudder:** tremble, shiver [eschew, flee
**shun:** avoid, evade,
" **(archaic):** evite
**shunt:** switch
**shut:** close, closed
" **close:** seal
" **in:** hem
" **up:** pent
**shutter:** blind [orous
**shy:** timid, demure, coy, recoil, bashful, swerve, wary, reserved, retiring, tim-
" **(colloq.):** mim
**Siamese:** Thai
" **coin:** at, att, tical
" **Island group:** Tai
" **measure:** niu, rai, sen
" **race:** tai
" **river:** Si
" **twin:** Eng, Chang
" **wt.:** pai
**Siberian antelope:** saiga
" **Mongoloid:** Tatar
" **mountain:** Altai
" **natives:** Sagai, Tatars
" **plains:** Steppes
" **river:** Ob, Lena, Amur, Onon, Om, Tom, Opus
" **squirrel:** miniver
" **sound:** hiss
**Sicilian city:** Palermo
" **mt.:** Etna [sala
" **seaport:** Aci, Mar-
" **volcano:** Etna
**sick:** ail, abed
**sickness:** disease
**side:** party, lateral, faction, support, aspect, border, slope, part, flank, phase
" **away from the wind:** alee
" **of book leaf:** page
" " **bldg.:** wall
" **dish:** entree
" **(of the):** lateral
" **order:** rasher
" **piece:** rib
" " **of window or door:** jamb
" **portion:** rasher
" **road:** byway
" **shoots:** laterals
" **by side:** abreast, parallel
" **tracked:** shunted
" **of triangle:** leg
" **view:** profile
**sidelong:** oblique
" **glance:** leer, ogle
**sideslip:** skid
**sidestep:** avoid, duck
**sidetrack:** shunt
**sidle:** edge
**siege:** beset, blockade

**siesta**: nap [strainer
**sieve**: sift, screen, filter,
**sigh**: groan, sob, lament, suspire [otic
**sight (pert. to)**: visual,
**sigil**: seal
**sign**: shingle, symbol, token, portent, trace, signal, notice, omen
" **of addition**: plus
" " **assent**: nod
" " **infinitive mood**: to
" " **omission**: caret
**signal**: sign, noticeable, warning, alarm
" **bell**: gong, curfew
**signature of approval**: visa, vise
**signet**: seal [import
**significance**: meaning,
**signification**: sense
**signify**: denote, mean, matter, indicate
**silence**: gag, quiet, still, hush [tacit, muted
**silent**: still, mum, mute, noiseless, taciturn,
**silicate**: wellsite
**silk fabric**: alamode, pongee, satin, surah, samite
" **fibers**: floss
" **filling**: tram
" **(kind)**: eria, moire
" **net**: tulle
" **thread**: tram, floss
**silken**: seric, glossy
**silkworm**: eri, eria
" **'s envelope**: cocoon
**silly**: inane, asinine, fatuous
**silver**: splinter, argent
" **(symbol)**: A. G.
**silverweed**: tansy
**silvery**: argent
**simian**: ape, apelike
**similar**: alike, same, like, akin, such
**simper**: smirk
**simple**: mere, elementary, plain, easy
" **animal**: amoeba, monad
" **song**: ballad, lay
**simpleton**: idiot, oaf, fool, ass, daw, dolt, goose, sap, ninny
**simulate**: pretend, imitate, ape, act, feign
**sin**: err, evil, iniquity, transgress [cause
**since**: ago, as, for, be-
" **(arch.)**: sith
" **(prefix)**: cis
" **(Scot.)**: syne
**sincere**: honest, genuine, gearty [thew
**sinew**: muscle, tendon,
**sinewy**: wiry
**sinful**: evil, wicked
**sing**: chant, lilt, carol, warble, intone, croon, hum [del, yodle
" **in Swiss style**: yo-
**singe**: burn
**singers**: choir, divas, vocalists, tenors
**singing bird**: robinet, wren, shama, lark, vireo, linnet, pipit, veery, redstart, bobolink, oriole
**single**: sporadic, lone, one, solo [uni
" **(comb. form)**: mon,
" **note**: monotone
" **thing**: unit
**singly**: alone, once
**singular**: odd, queer
**sink**: drain, settle, sag, merge, descend, dip, drop, debase, lower, ebb [otoe
**Siouan Indian**: Osage,
**sip**: sup, taste

**sister**: nun [pose, perch
**sit**: roost, rest, brood,
**site**: locality, area, situs
**sitting**: session, sedent, seated [place, lie
**situate**: locate, located,
**situated at the back**: postern [dial
" **in the middle**: me-
**situation**: site, condition, seat [sestet
**six (group of)**: senary,
" **line stanza**: sestet
**sixty sixties**: sar, saros
**size**: area, extent, bulk
" **of book**: quarto
" " **coal**: pea, egg
" " **paper**: atlas, demy, cap
" " **shot**: T. T.
" " **type**: pica, gem, agate, diamond
**skeleton**: frame, remains
" **part**: bone, rib
**skeptic**: doubter
**sketch**: trace, draft, paint, drawing, limn, skit, map, outline
**ski (var.)**: skee
**skid**: slide, slip, slue, sideslip
**skiing race and term**: slalom
**skill**: art, craft [tor
**skilled person**: opera-
" **shot**: marksman
**skillful**: adept, deft, clever, adroit, apt
**skin**: peel, rind, pelt, flay, hide
" **(comb. form)**: derm, derma
" **covering**: fur
" **disease**: psora, acne, tinea, rupia, hives
" " **of dogs**: mange
" **inflammation**: papula
" **layer**: enderon
" **(of the)**: dermal
" **opening and orifice**: pore
" **protuberance**: wen, mole, wart, blister
" **of seal**: sculp
**skink**: lizard
**skip**: omit, trip, miss
" **about**: caper
" **over water**: dap
**skirmish**: feud, melee, battle, brush
**skirt**: border
" **of a suit of armor**: tasse
**skit**: parody, playlet, sketch, lampoon
**skittle**: pin
**skoal**: toast
**skulk**: hedge
**skull**: cranium
" **(pert. to)**: cranial
**skunk**: conepate, polecat [less
**slack**: loose, lax, care-
**slacken**: relax, loosen
**slag**: dross, scoria
**slam**: bang
" **at cards**: vole
**slander**: aperse, libel, defame, asperse, belie, caluminiate, aspersion, calumniate
**slang**: argot, jargon
**slant**: bias, slope, cant, incline, tilt, lean, bevel, incline [askew
**slanting**: alist, atilt,
**slap**: hit, cuff, rebuff, blow, strike, insult
**slash**: slit, cut, gash
**slate cutter's tool**: sax
**slattern**: trollop
**slaughter**: massacre
" **house**: abattoir

**slave**: esne, serf, bondman, vassal, minion, thrall, helot, drudge
**Slavic tribe**: Serb
**slay**: murder, kill
**sled**: sleigh, sledge, tode
**sleep**: rest, nap, doze, slumber
**sleeveless garment**: aba, cape
**slender**: slim, thin, svelte, lank, frail
" **fish**: gar
" **graceful woman**: selph, sylph
" **prickle**: seta
**slice**: split, carve, cut, shave, slab
**slid**: slipped [coast
**slide**: skid, slip, slither,
**slight**: snub, scant, trivial, ignore
" **amount**: trace
" **breeze**: breath
" **coloring**: tint
" **sound**: peep
**slighting remark**: **slur**
**slightly opened**: **ajar**
**slim**: svelte, slender, spare, thin
**slime**: ooze, muck, mud
**sling**: fling, hurl, slue
**slip**: slide, lapse, skid, err, fault, glide, error
" **away**: elapse, elope
**slipper**: mule, sandal
**slippery**: eely, elusive
**slit**: gash, slash
**slogan**: motto
**slop over**: spill [ramp
**slope**: slant, incline, declivity, side, cant, bevel, gradient, dip,
" **upward**: climb, rise
**slot**: groove [mal, unau
**sloth**: ai, indolence, ani-
**slothfully**: idly
**slough off**: moult, molt
**slovenly woman**: trollop, slob, slattern
**slow**: deliberate, sluggish, dilatory, poky, gradual, retard
" **leak**: drip
" **moving person**: snail [largo, ritard
" **(musical)**: lento,
" " **(abbr.)**: rit
**slowed**: retarded
**slue**: twist, swamp, veer, pivot, skid
**sluggard**: drone
**sluggish**: inert, leaden, slow, supine, dull, idle
**slumber**: nap, sleep
" **music**: snore
**slur**: aspersion, traduce, soil, reproach
" **over**: elide [shrewd
**sly**: foxy, cunning, furtive, rougish, crafty, artful, arch, wily,
" **artifice**: wile
" **look**: leer
" **(Scot.)**: slee
**smack**: strike, savor
**small**: petty, atomic, trivial, paltry, miniature, petite, wee, tiny, minute, little, few, petit, less
" **amount**: trace, bit, mite, hair
" **animal**: insect, genet, organism
" **(colloq.)**: teeny, weeny [cro, lepto
" **(comb. form)**: mi-
" **(prefix)**: micro
" **(Scot.)**: sma
**smallest**: least
" **integer**: one
" **particle**: whit
" **planet**: Mercury
**smart**: trig, chic, clever,

sting, shrewd, dashing, bright
**smarten**: spruce
**smash**: crash, shatter
**smear**: daub, bedaub, smudge, smirch, plaster, stain, soil
**smell**: olid, odor, scent
**smile**: grin, smirk
" **foolishly**: simper
**smiling**: riant [stain
**smirch**: soil, smear,
**smirk**: simper, grin
**smoke**: smudge, reek
" **flue**: funnel, stack
**smooth**: sleek, lene, sand, level, glib, even, plane, iron, glassy, greasy, pave, ease
" **as with beak**: preen
" **and glossy**: sleek
" **over**: plaster
" **and shining**: waxen
" **spoken**: glib
**smoothing implement**: sadiron, planer, scraper, plane
**smoothly polite**: suave
**smother**: stifle [smear
**smudge**: blot, smoke,
**Smyrna figs**: eleme
**snail (soft)**: slug, drone
**snake**: asp, reptile, boa, adder, serpent, viper
" **bird**: darter
" **(black)**: racer
" **in the grass**: enemy
**snakelike fish**: eel
**snap**: crack, clip, wafer, bite, fastener, cooky, crackle, flip, sneck
" **with fingers**: fillip
**snapper**: fastener, turtle
**snare**: net, entrap, trap, entangle, pitfall, web, springe, noose, benet, drum, gin [growl
**snarl**: tangle, gnar,
**snatch**: nab, grab, wrest
" **(slang)**: swipe
**sneaky**: furtive
**sneer**: gibe, scoff, mock, taunt, deride
**snide**: mean, base
**sniff**: nose [ment
**snip**: clip, shred, frag-
**snood**: fillet
**snoop**: pry, prowl, peer
**snow**: neve, whiten
" **runner**: ski, skee
**snub**: slight, rebuff, rebuke
**snug**: cosy, cozy
" **retreat**: den, nest
**snuggle**: nestle, cuddle
**so**: thus, ergo, hence
" **be it**: amen
" **(Scot.)**: sic, sae
**soak**: ret, sop, sog, saturate, drench, steep
" **flax**: ret
**soap ingredient**: lye
" **frame part**: sess
" **plant**: amole
**soapstone**: talc
**soar**: tower, rise, fly
**sober**: sedate, serious, staid, grave, solemn, abstinent, demure
**social affair**: tea, reception, dance, party
" **class**: caste
" **error**: boner
" **group**: tribe [riah
" **outcast**: leper, pa-
" **unit**: clan, sept, tribe, caste
**society bud (colloq.)**: deb [tippe
**Socrates wife**: Xan-
**sod**: sward, dirt, turf, earth, soil, glebe
**soda**: pop
" **ash**: alkali
**sodium**: N. A., sal

" **carbonate**: trona
" **chloride**: salt, sal
" **nitrate**: niter
**sofa**: divan, settee, lounge
**soft**: tender, malleable, pliable, mild, mellow, low, yielding
" **candy**: fudg
" **cheese**: brie
" **drink**: soda, pop
" **fabric**: velvet, plush
" **feathers**: down
" **food**: pap
" **fruit part**: pulp
" **hematite**: ore
" **limestone**: chalk
" **mass**: pulp
" **metal**: tin
" **palate**: uvula
" **shoe**: moccasin
" **substance**: pap
**soften**: relent, mellow, mitigate, relent [ate
" **by soaking**: macer-
" " **tone**: mute
**softly**: low
**soggy**: sodden
" **mass**: sop
**soil**: mess, dirt, earth, begrime, smirch, sod, dirty, country, land, defile, moil, sully, slur, tarnish, mire
" **(kind of)**: marl, loam, clay
" **(poet.)**: glebe
**sojourn**: abide, stay
**solace**: comfort, console
**solan**: gannet
**solar disc**: aten, aton
" **year excess**: epact
**solder**: cement
**soldering flux**: rosin
**soldier**: warrior
" **cap**: baret, shako
" **cloak**: capote
**soldiers**: troops
**sole**: one, only, lone
" **of foot**: plantar
" " **plow**: slade
**solemn**: sober, grave, serious, somber [vow
" **assertion**: oath,
**solicit**: beg, ask, canvass, canvas, urge, court, woo, petition, request, plead
" **(colloq.)**: tout
**solicitude**: care
**solid**: hard, firm, compact, rigid, prism
" **(C. form)**: stereo
**solidified mass**: cake
**solidify**: set, harden, gel
**solitary**: lone, alone
" **(form)**: eremo
**solo**: aria, lone, single
**solution**: answer, key
**somber**: solemn, grave, lenten
**some**: one, any, few
**something added**: insert
" **attached**: tag
" **found**: trove
" **new**: novelty
" **owed**: debit
**sometime**: former, once
**somewhat**: rather
**son**: scion
**sonance**: sound
**song**: melody, ballad, ditty, air, lay, canticle, carol, lilt
" **bird**: wren, robin
" **of joy or praise**: paean, paeon
" " " **(var.)**: pean
" **thrush**: mavis
" **verse**: lyric
**soon**: anon, early, ere, shortly, promptly
**sooner than**: ere
**soot**: carbon, smut
**soothe**: ease, allay, pacify, calm, quiet
**soothing**: balmy
" **ointment**: balsam, balm [diviner
**soothsayer**: seer, augur,
**sora**: rail
**sorcerer**: magi
" **(plural)**: mages
**sorceress**: witch
**sorcery**: magic
**sordid**: base [tender
**sore**: painful, angry,
**sorrow**: dolor, woe, repine, mourn,, pine, sadness, grieve, grief
**sorrowful**: sadden, contrite, mournful
" **sinner**: penitent
" **state**: woe [gretful
**sorry**: regret, pitiable, grieved, contrite, re-
**sort**: sift, kind, ilk, variety, manner, seggregate, cull, class, classify, type, grade
**sortie**: sally [son
**soul**: spirit, esprit, essence, pneuma, per-
**sound**: valid, sonance, sane, noise, tone
" **accompanying breathing**: rale
" **of or as a bell**: ding, toll
" " **distress**: moan
" **to frighten**: boo
" **loudly**: blare
" **(relating to)**: tonal
" **resonantly**: ring
" **of surf**: rote
**soup**: pottage, broth, puree, bisque
" **basis**: okra
" **dish, ladle, & vessel**: tureen [acetose
**sour**: acid, acerb, tart, acetic, acrid, morose,
**source**: origin, font, fount, root, seed, rise
" " **heat**: steam
" " " **& light**: gas
" " **help**: recourse
" " **iodine**: kelp
" " **light**: sun, lamp
" " **oil**: olive
" " **ore**: mine
" " **perfume**: musk
" " **power**: motor
" " **sugar**: cane
" " **water**: well
**S. African**: Boer
" " **animal**: suricate, ratel [eland
" " **antelope**: gnu,
" " **Dutch**: taal, Boer
" " **farmer**: Boer
" " **fox**: asse, caama
" " **grassland**: veld, veldt
" " **legislative assembly**: raad [bantu
" " **native**: kafir,
" " **plateau**: Karoo
" " **province**: Transvaal
" " **thong**: riem
" " **tribesman**: Bantu, Zulu
" " **underground stream**: Aar
" " **village**: Kraal
" **American animal**: tapir, llama, tayra
" " **arrow poison**: curare
" " **bird**: screamer, seriema, rara, ara, tinamou, agami
" " **cape**: Horn
" " **hare**: tapeti
" " **Indian**: Ona, Carib, Ge, Caril, Mayan, Inca
" " **laborer**: peon
" " **linguistic family**: Onan [Andean
" " **mts.**: Andes,
" " **ostrich**: rhea
" " **plain**: Llano, Pampa
" " **wind**: Pampero
" " **rabbit**: tapeti
" " **republic**: Peru
" " **river**: Apa, Plata, Amazon, Orinoco, Acre, Para
" " **rodent**: paca, ratel, tapir [ma, boas
" " **serpents**: abo-
" " **tree**: Mora, Balsa, Carob
" " **snake**: lora [lu
" " **tribesman**: Zu-
" " **tuber**: oca [bolo
" " **weapon**: bolas,
" " **wood sorrel**: oca [erre
" **Dakota capital**: Pi-
" **Sea canoe**: proa
" " **island**: Bali, Samoa
" " **islander**: Kanaka, Samoan
**southeast wind**: eurus
**southwest wind**: aner, afer [lic
**souvenir**: memento, re-
**sovereign**: ruler, monarch [strew
**sow**: plant, seed, swine,
**space**: room, area, time, void, distance [ment
" **above door**: pedi-
" **surrounding castle**: ambit
" **theory**: plenism
**spacious**: roomy, broad, large [bridge, arch
**span**: cross, reach, extent, interval, team,
**spangle**: glitter
**Spanish article**: el, las
" **channel**: Cano
" **city**: Irun, Cadiz, Toledo
" **cloth**: leno
" **coin**: peseta, peso, centavo, real
" **commune**: irun
" **conquerer of Mexico**: Cortez [olla
" **cooking pot**: alla,
" **dance**: bolero, jota, tango
" **farewell**: adios
" **feast days**: fiestas
" **gentleman**: caballero, don
" **griddle cake**: arepa
" **head covering**: mantilla
" **hero**: Cid
" " **(var.)**: Sid
" **horse**: genet
" **house**: casa
" **larait**: reata, riata
" **legislature chamber**: camera
" **mackerel**: bonita
" **measure**: cantara, vara
" **painter**: Goya
" **peninsula**: Iberia
" **priest**: cura, padre
" **river**: Ebro, Oro
" **room**: sala [manta
" **shawl**: serape,
" **title of address**: don, senor, senora
" **weapon**: bolas
" **wt.**: arroba [yard
**spar**: mast, sprit, box,
" **end**: arm
" **to stow**: steeve
**spare**: lean, disposable, save, desist, reserve, stint, omit, slim, extra, tire, gaunt
**sparing**: chary
**sparkle**: glisten, flash, glitter, gleam [tai
**sparoid fish**: gar, sar,
**sparse**: scanty, scarce, thin, scant [hardy
**Spartan**: Stoic, brave,
" **army**: Mora
" **bondsman**: helot
" **serf & slave**: helot
**spasmodic breaths**: gasps
" **exhalation**: sneeze
" **twitch**: tic
**spat**: gaiter, tiff, row
**spate**: freshet, flood
**spatter**: sprinkle, splash
**speak**: orate, utter
" **in defense**: plead
" **haltingly**: stammer
" **imperfectly**: lisp, stutter [cite
" **from memory**: re-
" **of**: mention
" **rhetorically**: declaim [parage
" **slightingly of**: dis-
" **in slow tone**: drawl
" **softly**: whisper
" **in surly manner**: snarl [arrow
**spear**: dart, harpoon, javelin, lance, pike,
**special**: particular
**specify**: mention, name
**specimen**: sample
**speck**: dot, spot, mote, jot, blemish, nit [play
**spectacle**: parade, dis-
**spectator**: observer
**specter**: ghost, spirit
**speech**: dialect, voice, oration [rade
" **(long, abusive)**: ti-
" **(pert. to)**: vocal
" **(slang)**: lingo
**speechless**: mute [rush
**speed**: race, haste, hie, pace, rapidity, run,
**speedily**: apace, presto
**speedy**: fast, fleet, rapid
**spell**: trance, relieve, charm [Enid
**Spencer character**: Una,
**spend**: exhaust, disburse [laze
" **time idly**: loiter,
**spendthrift**: wastrel
**sphere**: orb, globe, ball, arena [ate
**spherical**: round, globular, orbicular, glob-
" **body**: orb, ball
**spice**: mace, ginger, seasoning, zest
**spicy**: aromatic
**spider**: arachnid, tarantula, spinner
**spigot**: tap
**spike**: nail
" **of cereal**: ear
" " **flowers**: ament
" " **fork**: prong, tine
**spikenard**: na, nard
**spill**: shed, tumble, slop, downpour [revolve
**spin**: reel, turn, whirl, rotate, twirl, weave,
**spindle**: axle
**spinner**: spider, top
**spiral**: coil, helical, coiled, helix [mit
**spire**: epi, steeple, sum-
**spirit**: elan, demon, elf, vim, soul, mettle, dash, heart, ghost, animation, specter
" **of air**: ariel
" " **the dead**: mane
" " **evil**: satan, mara, mora
" **lamp**: etna
" **of nature**: genie
" " **the people**: ethos
" **in Tempest**: Ariel
**spirited**: fiery, lively

" **horse:** steed, arab, courser
**spiritless:** amort, dull, dejected, vapid
**spiritual beings:** essences, angel
" **nourishment:** manna
" **session:** seance
**spite:** pique, venom, thwart, rancor
**splash:** splatter, spatter
**splatter:** splash, dab
**splay:** expand
**spendid:** superb
" **(Scot.):** braw
**splendor:** eclat, glory
**splinter:** sliver, shiver
**split:** rive, rivet, rend, riven, slice, tear, disrupt, chap, cleave
" **asunder:** riven
" **pulse:** dal
**splotch:** blot [pamper
**spoil:** addle, impair, rot, mar, taint, vitiate, plunder, loot, booty,
**spoiled:** bad
**spoils:** booty
**spoken:** oral, parol
**spoliation:** rapine
**sponge:** expunge, efface
**spongy:** porous
**sponsor:** backer
**spook:** ghost [inder
**spool:** bobbin, reel, cyl-
**spoon (deep):** ladle
**spore:** seed [divert
**sport:** game, play, fun, frisk, frolic, pastime,
" **group:** team
**sportive:** playful, gay
**spot:** stain, blemish, notice, blot, tarnish, locality, speck, dapple
" **on playing card or domino:** pip [ocelot
**spotted cat:** cheetah,
**spout:** gush, jet
" **to draw sap:** spile
**sprawl lazily:** loll
**spread:** scatter, unfurl, disseminate, ted, disperse, broaden, unfold, diffuse, extend
" **by rumor:** noise
" **out:** deploy
" **outward:** flare
**spree:** frolic
**sprig:** twig [per, pert
**sprightly:** alive, nimble, buoyant, airy, chip-
" **tune:** lilt
**spring:** leap, vault, spa, bolt, ramp, arise
" **back:** rebound [let
" **flower:** crocus, vio-
" **from:** derive
" **(old word):** ver
" **(pert. to):** vernal
" **up:** arise, rise
**springe:** snare
**springy:** elastic [zle, wet
**sprinkle:** spatter, driz-
" **with flour:** dredge
**sprint:** run, dash, race
**sprite:** elf, imp, goblin, fairy, fay [ate
**sprout:** bud, crop, cion, shoot, scion, germin-
**spruce:** dapper, neat, smarten, trim, trig, natty [ble, brisk
**spry:** agile, active, nim-
**spud:** potato
**spume:** froth, foam
**spur:** incite, goad, impel, urge, stimulus, rouse [false, fake
**spurious:** snide, bogus,
**spurn:** scorn, reject
**spurt:** dart, spout, gush, burst, squirt
**spy:** scout, discoverer, informer, detect, dissern [gang
**squad:** team, group,
**squall:** gust
**squander:** waste, spend, dissipate, misspend
**squatter:** nester
**squeeze:** press, crush, pinch, compress, hug
**squelch:** suppress
**squib:** lampoon
**squire:** escort
**squirm:** wring, wriggle
**squirrel:** gopher
" **shrew:** tana [ture
**stab:** gore, pierce, attempt, pink, punc-
**stable:** barn, stall, fixed
**stableman:** ostler, hostler [ney
**stack:** pile, heap, chim-
" **of corn:** shock
" " **hay or grain:** rick
**stadium:** arena [wand
**staff:** pole, rod, cudgel,
" **of life:** bread
" " **office:** mace
" **officer:** aide
**stag:** pollard, elk, hart
**stage:** produce, degree, dais, platform, phase
" **extra:** super
" **hangings:** scenery
" **part:** role
" **(pert. to):** scenic
" **show:** revue
" **speech & whisper:** aside [ter, waver
**stagger:** reel, stun, tot-
**staid:** sedate, demure
**stain:** dye, tax, discolor, color, spot, tinge, blemish, smirch, soil, stigma, smear, blot
**stair:** step
**stair part:** riser, tread
" **post:** newel
**stake:** post, wager, bet, picket, ante, hazard, risk, pole [insipid
**stale:** trite, vapid, old,
**stalk:** stem, stipe
" **of grain:** straw
**stall:** stable, booth, manger
**stalwart:** strong
**stammer:** stutter
**stamp:** postage, brand, impress, print
**stamping form:** die
**stance:** position
**stanch:** stem
**stand:** bear, endure, position, booth, tolerate
" **against:** oppose
" **for:** represent
" **opposite:** face
" **up:** rise
**standard:** flag, norm, ideal, normal, test, classic, criterion, emblem, streamer [norm
" **of conduct:** moral,
" " **excellence:** ideal
" **quality & quantity:** unit
**standing:** status, grade
" **as grain:** uncut
**stannum:** tin
**stanza:** verse, strophe
**star:** asterisk, feature, nova, celebrity, sun, vega, bespangle, giansar, mirak
" **(comb. form):** aster, astero [etamin
" **in Dragon:** adib,
" **flower:** aster
" **in heraldry:** etoile
" " **Orion:** rigel
" " **virgo:** spica
**starch:** sago, arrowroot, cassava, farina
**stare:** gaze, agape, gape, glare [absolute
**stark:** stiff, rigid, bare,
**starry:** astral, sparkling, stellar
**start:** initiate, begin, onset, open, commense
**starting line:** scratch
**startle:** surprise, shock, frighten, scare, alarm
**starve:** famish
**state:** declare, say, assert, aver, condition, nation, republic, assert [situation
" **of affairs:** pass,
" " **being equal:** par
" **of bliss:** eden
" **(comb. form):** stato
" **differently:** reword
" **house:** capitol
" **by items:** itemize
" **of lost soul:** perdition [spirits, mood
" **of mind:** morale,
" **on oath:** depose
" **policeman:** trooper
" **of relief:** easiness
" **treasury:** fisc
" **troops:** militia [lege
" **without proof:** al-
" **wrongly:** misstate
**stately:** majestic, regal
**statement:** assertion, fact [credo
" **of belief:** creed,
**station:** post, base, depot, degree
**stationary part:** stator
**statue:** image
**statute:** law, edict
**stay:** remain, wait, stop, linger
**stead:** avail, place, lieu
**steadfast:** staid, true
**steady:** firm, fixed, invariable [fer, filch
**steal:** rob, purloin, pil-
" **(arch.):** nim
" **as cattle:** rustle
**stealthy:** furtive
**steam:** vapor, power
**steamer:** liner
**steed:** horse, charger
**steel:** harden
**steep:** ret, brew, sop, imbue, hilly, soak, abrupt, macerate, sheer
" **descent:** escarp, scarp, bank
" **as flax:** ret
" **hill:** butte
" **in oil & vinegar:** marinate
**steeple:** spire, epi
**steer:** pilot, guide, ox, pursue, control, helm
" **wild:** yak, yaw
**steering apparatus:** rudder, helm, wheel
" **lever:** tiller
**steeve:** stow
**stein:** mug
**stellar:** astral, starry
**stem:** prow, arrest, stalk, check, peduncle, petiole, stanch
" **of an arrow:** shaft
" **from:** derive
**step:** pace, stride, race, stair, gait, tread, degree, walk [rime
" **of ladder:** rung,
**sterotyped:** trite
**sterile:** barren
**stern:** grim, harsh, severe, rigorous
" **of vessel:** aft [er
**stevedore:** loader, stow-
**stew:** ragout, worry, boil, seethe, simmer
**stick:** rod, stall, adhere, cohere, transfix, pole, paste, wand
**stickler for perfect English:** purist
**sticky stuff:** goo, glue, tar [formal, stilted
**stiff:** rigid, stark, frigid,
**stifle:** smother, strangle
**stigma:** brand, stain
**still:** yet, silent, quiet, dumb, silence, immobile, immovable
**stimulate:** fan, stir, incite, joy, sting, whet, exhilarate, innervate
**stimulus:** spur, incentive [ulate, goad
**sting:** bite, smart, stim-
**stinging fish:** ray [net
" **insect:** wasp, hor-
" **plant:** nettle
**stingy:** miserly, mean
**stint:** scrimp, task, chore, spare, restrict
**stipend:** salary, wages, pay [excitement
**stir:** mix, move, arouse, rouse, inspire, excite, stimulate, disturb, agitate, urge, bustle,
" **the air:** fan [foment
" **up:** agitate, rouse, roust, roil, provoke,
**stitch:** sew
" **bird:** ihi
**stoat:** ermine, weasel
**stock:** store
" **certificates:** scrip
**stogie:** cigar
**stoker:** fireman [ment
**stole:** garment, vest-
**stolen goods:** mainor
" **property:** pelf
**stolid:** dull, impassive, wooden, heavy
**stomach of mammal:** maw
**stone:** gem, lapis, agate, rock, flint, lapidate, jewel, pebble, marble
" **fruit:** drupe, plum
" **jar:** crock
" **(L.):** lapis
" **nodule:** geode
" **tablet:** stele
" " **(var.):** stela
" **writing tablet:** slate
**stoneworker:** mason
**stony:** rocky [bow
**stoop:** bend, submit,
**stop:** cease, prevent, rest, desist, ho, cessation, stay, pause, suspend, bar, arrest, avast, deter, quit
" **(naut.):** avast
" **seams of a boat:** calk
" **unintentionally:** stall
" **up:** dam, clog, plug
" **watch:** timer
**stoppage:** block
**stopper:** plug, cork
**storage box:** bin
" **place for arms:** arsenal
" " " **grain:** silo
**store:** mart, fund, shop, stock, provide, stow, supply, accumulate
" **attendant:** clerk
" **fodder:** ensile
" **for safety:** reposit, deposit
" **in a silo:** ensile
**storehouse:** depot, etape
**storekeeper:** merchant
**storm:** rave, rampage, tempest, wester, rain, orage, rage, besiege
**story:** tale, yarn, novel, floor, fable
**stout:** strong, brave
**stove:** range, etna, kiln, heater
" **part:** oven, grate
**stow:** store, pack, box, steeve, stuff
**straddle:** astride, bestride [gut
**straight:** direct, arow,

" **batted ball**: liner
**straighten**: aline, align
**straightforward**: candid, direct [exert
**strain**: tension, tax, sprain, strive, sift, stretch, filter, melody, progeny, trace,
" (**comb. form**): tono
" **forward**: press
**strainer**: sieve, sifter
**strait**: channel, narrow
**strand**: string, breach
**strange**: odd, alien, novel
" **C. (form)**: xeno
**stranger**: odder, alien, foreigner
**strangle**: stifle
**strap**: belt, thong, strop
" **to lead**: halter leash
" **shaped**: lorate
**strategem**: ruse, wile, artifice [seam
**stratum**: layer, bed,
**straw hat**: panama
**stray**: divagate, wander, deviate, lose, err
**streak**: stripe, line, vein, trace, brindle
**stream**: freshet, torrent, river, creek, pour, run, rill, flow
**streamer**: pennant, flag, standard [waif, arab
**street urchin**: gamin,
**strength**: vigor, power, soundness, stamina
**strengthen**: brace, fortify, invigorate, prop
**stress**: strain, accent, pressure, tension, emphasis [span
**stretch out**: eke, prolate, sprawl, expand, lie,
" " **one's neck**: cran, crane
**stretched**: taut, extended, strained, reached
" **tight**: tense
**stretcher**: litter [sor
**stretching muscle**: ten-
**strew**: scatter, diffuse, sow [rigid
**strict**: stern, rigorous,
**strictness**: rigor
**stride**: pace, gait
**strident**: shrill [test
**strife**: feud, war, con-
**strike**: slap, beat, rap, smite, carome, swat, hit, ram, smack, bang
" (**arch.**): smite
" **as a bell**: chime
" **breaker**: scab
" (**colloq.**): lam [dab
" **gently**: pat, tap,
" **out**: dele, elide, fan, cancel, delete
" **& rebound**: carom
" **together**: collide
" **violently**: ram
**striking effect**: eclat
**string**: cord, rope, line, twine, strand
**stringed instrument**: viol, viola, rebec, lute, harp, lyre, piano, cello
**stringent**: strict, alum
**strip**: stripe, divest, band, denude, peel, shear, bare
" **of cloth**: tape
" **of leather**: welt, strop, thong, cleat
**stripe**: bar, streak
**stripling**: lad
**strive**: strain, struggle, attempt, vie, try, contend, endeavor, toil
" **after**: seek
" **to equal**: emulate
**stroke**: blow, pat
**stroll**: meander, saunter, ramble, rove
**strong**: potent, stout, hale, robust, sturdy, powerful, stalwart
" **box**: chest, safe
" **point**: forte
" **rope**: cable
" **scented**: redolent
" **smelling**: olid, sisal
" **tackle (naut.)**: cat
" **voiced person**: stentor [ress, citadel
**stronghold**: fort, fort-
**strop**: hone, strap
**structure**: edifice, shed, frame [test, strive
**struggle**: cope, tussle, combat, wrestle, con-
**stub**: stump, receipt
**stuck in the mud**: mired, bemired
**student**: scholar, pupil
**studio**: atelier
**study**: con, pore, peruse, pon, scan, meditate
**stuff**: pad, sate, cram, fill, wad, ram, gorge
**stulm**: adit
**stumble**: trip
**stump**: stub, challenge
**stun**: daze, astound
**stunt**: feat, dwarf, trick
**stupefy**: stun, daze, drug, besot
**stupid**: crass, insipient, asinine, dumb, dull, inane, doltish
" **person**: dolt, ass, dunce, log, moron
" " (**colloq.**): ass
" **play (slang)**: boner
**stupor**: coma, trance
**sturdy**: strong
**stutter**: stammer
**sty**: pen
**style**: see also "type"
**style**: manner, mode, fashion
" **of architecture**: doric, ionic
" " **painting**: genre
" " **penmanship**: hand
" " **poetry**: epic
" " **sewing**: shirr
" **type**: italic, pica, italica, roman, gothic
**stylish**: chic, alamode, dressy [nifty, tony
" (**slang**): classy,
**suave**: bland
**subdue**: master, overpower, tame
**subject**: topic, theme, vassal, text
**subjoin**: annex
**subjugate**: conquer
**sublime**: exalted, noble [immerse
**submerge**: sink, drown,
**submissive**: passive, meek, servile
**submit**: stoop, bow, yield, obey
" **to**: endure [minor
**subordinate**: secondary,
" **bldg.**: annex [ter
**subsequently**: later, af-
**subside**: abate, ebb, fall
**subsist**: live, feed [pith
**substance**: material, matter, gist, essence,
**substantial**: solid, real
**substitute**: alternate, ersatz, vicar, agent
**subtle emanation**: aura
**success**: go, hit, victory [dinal
**succession**: series, or-
" **of family sovereigns**: dynasty
**succinct**: terse, short
**succor**: aid, relief, rescue, help
**succulent**: juice
" **fruit**: uva
" " **part**: pulp
" **plant**: herb, aloe
**succumb**: yield
**sudden**: quick, abrupt
" **attack**: raid
" **blast of wind**: gust
" **effort**: spurt, spasm
" **impulse**: start
" **sensation**: thrill
" **thrust**: lunge, jab
**sue**: woo, urge
**suet**: tallow, fat
**suffer**: ail, agonize, let, tolerate, ache
" (**Scot.**): dree
**suffering**: agony, pain
**suffice**: do, avail [quate
**sufficient**: ample, ade-
" (**be:**) do
" (**poet.**): enow
**sugar (kind of)**: tetrose, ose, dextrose
" **plum**: bonbon
" **solution**: syrup
**sugary**: sweet, honeyed
**suggest**: intimate, hint, propose
**suit**: please, satisfy, adapt, become, fit, petition, befit
" (**colloq.**): gee
" **at law**: case
**suitable**: pat, befitting, adapted, apt, fit, meet
**suite**: retinue
**suited for song**: lyric
**suitor**: beau, wooer
**sulk**: mope, pout [glum
**sullen**: morose, dour,
**sully**: defile, tarnish, soil, blot, grime
**sulphur alloy**: niello
**sum**: total, amount [cis
**summary**: epitome, pre-
" **pf principles**: credo
**summer (of the)**: estival
" (**Fr.**): ete
**summit**: tip, apical, apex, crest, roof, top, spire, peak [cite
**summon**: bid, call, page,
" **forth**: evoke
" **publicly**: page
" **together**: muster
" **up**: rally
**sun**: star, sol
" (**of the**): solar [lio
" (**comb. form**): he-
" **disk**: aton
" **dried brick**: adobe
" **god**: ra, Apollo
" **part**: corona
**sunburnt**: adust, tanned
**sunder**: part, rend, cut, rive, divide
**sundry**: divers
**sung by a choir**: choral
**sunk fence**: haha, aha
**sunny**: clear, bright, merry, cheerful
**sunset**: sundown
**sunshade**: parasol
**sup**: sip, eat
**supercilious person**: snob [shallow
**superficial**: outward,
**superintendent**: manager, overseer, boss
**superior**: finer, upper, above
" **mental endowment**: talent [niority
**superiority in office**: se-
**supernatural being**: fairy
" **event**: miracle
**supersede**: replace
**supine**: sluggish [vert
**supplant**: replace, sub-
**supple**: pliable, lithe, lissome, compliant, pliant
**supplement**: eke, add
**supplicate**: appeal, beg, plead, entreat, pray, implore
**supply**: afford, store, purvey, fund, cater
" **with fuel**: stoke
**support**: prop, behalf, abet, shore, second pedestal, stay, rest, brace, leg, aid, bear, side, guy, back, bolster, hinge
" **for plaster**: lath
" " **rails**: tie
" " **sail**: topmast, mast [tal
" " **statue**: pedes-
" **by timbers**: shore
" **for a vine**: trellis
**supporter**: booster, rooter [tron
" **of institution**: pa-
**supporting beam**: sleeper [easel
" **framework**: trestle,
" **member**: leg
" **rod** rib
" **wires**: guys [deem
**suppose**: presume, believe, opine, assume,
" (**arch.**): trow, wis
**supposition**: if [quell
**suppress**: elide, squelch,
**suppression of a part**: elision [est
**supreme**: highest, great-
**surcease**: balm, end
**sure**: certain, confident, positive
**surety**: bail, backer
**surf duck**: coot
**surface of gem**: facet
**surfeit**: sate, cloy, glut, satiate
**surfeited with enjoyment** : blase
**surge**: swell, heave, tide, billow
**surgical compress**: stupe
" **sewing**: suture
" **thread**: seton
**surly**: cross, gruff
**surmise**: guess
**surmount**: overcome, tide, hurdle, top
**surmounting**: above, atop [doe
**surname**: cognomen,
**surpass**: beat, exceed, best, transcend, top, cap, excel, outclass
**surplice (short)**: cotta
**surprise**: startle, amaze
**surrender**: cede, cession [case
**surround**: beset, hem, encircle, envelop, environ, enclose, incase, belay, mew, belt, en-
**surrounded**: girt [mid
" **by**: amid, among,
**survey**: review
**surveying instrument**: aliner, transit
**survival**: relic
**survive**: outlive, live
**suspend**: hang, stop
**suspicious (slang)**: leery
**Sussex land**: Laine
**sustain**: stand, prop, endure, aid [bread
**sustenance**: aliment,
**suture**: seam [thin
**svelte**: slender, slim,
**swab**: mop, wipe
**swag**: booty
**swagger**: strut, roister
**swain**: lover
**swallow hurriedly**: bolt, engorge, gulp, engulf, absorb [tern
" (**kind**): martin,
**swamp**: bog, fin, marsh, everglade, morass, slue, overwhelm
**swan**: leda, trumpeter

" (male): cob
**swap**: trade
**sward**: sod, turf, grass
**swarm**: teem, horde
" **of bees**: hive
" " " **(Scot)**: byke, bike
**swarming**: alive
**swarthy**: dun
**swat**: hit
**swathe**: wrap [nod, wag
**sway**: totter, rock, reel, teeter, fluctuate,
" **from side to side**: careen, waddle
**swear**: vow
" **falsely**: perjure
**sweat**: perspire
**Swedish chemist**: Nobel [krona
" **coin**: ore, krone,
" **nightingale**: Lind
" **province**: Laen, Lan
" **river**: Klar
**sweet**: sugary
" **cake**: cruller
" **clover**: melilot
" **drink**: nectar [cet
" **to the ears**: dul-
" **potato**: yam [rup
" **solution**: sirup, sy-
" **sound**: music
**sweetbrier**: eglantine
**sweeten**: sugar, candy
**sweetheart**: lover, inamorata, leman, amoret
" **(Anglo. Ir.)**: gra
" **(Scot.)**: jo ]gat
**sweetmeat**: candy, nou-
**sweetsop**: ates, atta
**swell**: dilate, bulb, surge, expand, distend [sea
" **of water**: surge,
**swerve**: veer, sheer, careen, shy, deviate
**swift**: rapid, fleet, fast
**swiftly**: apace [ity
**swiftness**: speed, celer-
**swimming**: natant [auk
" **bird**: loon, grebe,
" **organ**: fins, fin
**swindle**: wangle, dupe, fraud, bilk, fleece, cheat, gip, gyp [hog
**swine**: porcine, tapir,
" **(female)**: sow
" **(male)**: boar
**swing**: sway
**swirl**: eddy, whirl [gau
**Swiss canton**: Uri, Aar-
" **capital**: Bern, Berne
" **city**: Basle, Sion, Basel, Aarau
" **commune**: Sion
" **cottage**: chalet
" **dialect**: ladin
" **lake**: Uri, Lucerne
" **measure**: staab, elle
" **mountain**: rigi
" **patriot**: Tell
" **poet**: Amiel
" **river**: Aar
" **song**: yodel
**switch**: shunt
**switchboard section**: panel
**swollen**: tumid
**swoon**: faint, trance
**sword**: saber, epee, rapier, sabre, toledo
" **handle**: hilt, haft
" **shaped**: ensate, ensiform
**swordsmen's dummy stake**: pels, pel
**sycophant**: parasite, toady
**syllable of hesitation**: er
" **stress**: tone
**sylvan**: wooded, rustic
" **deity**: satyr
**symbol**: sign, emblem
" **of bondage**: yoke
" " **dead**: orant
" " **office**: mace
" " **peace**: dove
" " **power**: sword
" " **victory**: palm
" " **wedlock**: ring
**symetrical**: regular
**synopsis**: outline, table, epitome
**Syrian antelope**: addax
" **city**: Aleppo
" **deity**: el
" **garment**: aba
**system**: order, method
" **of management**: regime [laws
" " **rules**: code,
" " **signals**: code
" " **weights**: Troy
" " **worship**: cult

## T

**tab**: flap, label, tally, account, mark
**table linen**: napery
" **(small)**: stand
" **vessel**: tureen [teau
**tableland**: mesa, pla-
**tablet**: pad, troche
**tabulation**: calendar
**tacit**: implied, silent
**taciturn**: reticent
**tack**: brad, baste, gear
**tadpole**: polliwog
**Tai race (branch)**: Lao
**tailor**: sartor
" **'s iron**: goose
**taint**: pollute, poison, infect, defile, blemish, corrupt, vitiate
**Taj Mahal city**: Agra
**take**: seize, accept, receive, capture, grasp
" **as one's own**: adopt
" **away**: adeem, deduct, detract, remove
" **(law)**: adeem
" **back**: rescind, retract, recant [mind
" **care**: beward, tend,
" " **(arch.)**: reck
" " **horse**: groom
" **on cargo**: lade
" **charge**: preside, attend [tice
" **cognizance of**: no-
" **credit**: pride
" **delight**: revel
" **ease**: rest [dine
" **evening meal**: sup,
" **exception**: demur
" **from**: wrest
" **for granted**: assume, presume
" **illegally**: steal, poach
" **the initiative**: lead
" **into custody**- arrest [gest
" **into stomach**: in-
" **liberties**: presume
" **medicine**: dose
" **oath**: swear
" **off**: doff, depart
" **offense at**: resent
" **one's way**: wend
" **out**: dele, delete
" **place**- happen
" " **again**: recur
" " **of**: supplant
" **pleasure in**: enjoy
" **position**: stand
" **precedence**: rank
" **in sail**: reef [rotate
" **turns**: alternate,
" **umbrage**: resent
" **unawares**: surprise
" **up again**: resume
**tale**: story, anecdote, legend
**talebearer**: tattler
**talent**: gift, aptitude, flair
**talented**: apt, clever
**talisman**: amulet
**talk**: chat, converse, orate, address
" **childlessly**: prattle [ture
" **dogmatically**: lec-
" **effusively**: gush
" **foolishly**: drivel, prate [ter
" **glibly**: prate, pat-
" **hypocritically**: cant
" **idly**: prate, gab, chatter, tattle
" **imperfectly**: lisp
" **informally**: chat
" **(slang)**: spiel, gab, chatter, jabber
" **tediously**: prose
" **vainly**: prate [ter
" **volubly**: chin, pat-
" **wildly or with enthusiasm**: rave, rant
**tall**: long, high, lofty
" **bldg**: tower
" **& thin**: lane, lank
" **timber**: teak
**tallow**: suet
**tally**: score, count, reckon, register
" **(colloq.)**: tab
**talon**: claw
**tamarisk salt tree**: atlee, atle, atli [subdued
**tame**: subdue, docile, gentle, flat, tractable, mild, conquer, meek,
**tamper**: meddle, tinker
**tan**: ecru, sunburn, bronze
**tang**: taste, trace [able
**tangible**: tactile, palp-
**tangle**: snarl, mat, ravel, enmesh ensnare [shag, ravel
**tangled mass**: mop,
**tank**: cistern
**tanned**: tawny
" **hide**: leather [mac
**tanning material**: su-
**tantalize**: taunt, tease
**Tantalus's daughter**: Niobe
**tantrum**: rage
**tap**: pat, spigot
**taper**: candle, diminish
" **a timber in shipbldg.**: snape
**tapering**: terete [gusset
" **piece**: shim, gore,
" **solid**: cone
**tapestry**: arras, tapis
**Tapuyan Indian**: Ges
**tar**: sailor [late
**tardy**: belated, slow,
**target**: aim, mark, goal, object, ambition, butt
**tariff**: duty [spot
**tarnish**: mar, dull, soil,
**Taro paste**: poi
" **roots**: eddoes, eddo
**tarry**: wait, remain, lag, bide, linger, loiter, abide
**tart**: acute, acid, sour, acrid, sharp, caustic
**tartan**: plaid
**Tartar**: Turk
**task**: chore, stint, stent, job, duty, tax
**taste**: relish, penchant, savor, sip, flavor, palate, sapor, tang
**tasteless**: pall, sapid, vapid
**tasty**: savory, sapid
" **(Scot)**: taver
**tattle**: gossip, blab
**taunt**: sneer, plague, censure, twit, gibe, reproach, mock, jibe
**taut**: tense, tight
**tavern**: inn, cabaret
" **(slang)**: pub [gaudy
**tawdry**: cheap, tinsel,
**tax**: stent, assess, levy, toll, duty, scot, tribute, tariff, strain, assessment, exaction, cess, excise, impost, task
" **(kind)**: poll
**tea**: cha
" **(kind)**: oolong
" **tester**: taster
" **urn**: samovar
**teacake**: scone
**teach**: instruct, train
**team**: crew, overflow, squad, yoke, group
" **drivers**: teamsters
" **of horses**: span
**teamster**: carter [gee
" **'s command**: haw,
**tear**: rip, rend, lacerate, cleave, sever split
" **apart**: tatter, rend, rip [molish, raze
" **down**: rase, de-
**tease**: plague, annoy, molest, tantalize, pester, coax, nag
" **(slang)**: rag
**tedious**: prose, irksome tiresome, fatiguing
**tedium**: ennui
**teem**: abound [sway
**teeter**: seesaw, jiggle,
**teeth**: fangs
" **coating**: enamel
" **incrustation**: tartar
" **(pert to)**: dental
**tela**: web, tissue
**telegraph**: wire
" **code**: morse
**tell**: relate, narrate, impart, recount, inform, disclose
" **tales**: blab, tattle
**teller's office**: cage
**temper**: anneal, meddle, tone, qualify, tantrum, mitigate
**temperate**: moderate,
**tempest**: storm, tumult
**"The Tempest's" character**: Caliban
**"The Tempest's" spirit** Ariel [violent
**tempestuous**: stormy,
**temple**: fane [rhythm
**tempo**: time, meter,
**temporarily**: nonce [tice
**tempt**: allure, lure, en-
**ten**: decade, denary
" **(comb. form)**: deca
" **thousand**: myriad
**tenant**: lessee, renter
**tend**: care, mind, trend, contribute, conduce, guard, incline, treat
" **to wear away**: abrasive, erosive
**tendency**: trend, bent
**tender**: sore, soft, gentle, proffer, offer, sensitive, kind
" **feeling**: sentiment
**tendon**: sinew
" **(comb. form)**: teno
**tenement**: flat, dwelling ]trine, dogma
**tenet**: belief, maxim, principle, creed, doc-
**tenfold**: denary
**tennis point**: ace [deuce
" **score**: set, all, love,
" **stroke**: lob, chop
**Tennyson hero**: Arden
" **heroine**: Enid, Elaine
**tenor**: trend, course, purport, drift [taut,
**tense**: rigid, strained
**tensile**: ductile
**tension**: strain, stress
**tent**: encamp, tepee
**tentacle**: feeler
**tenth**: tithe
**tenuous**: rare [term
**tenure**: lease, holding,

**tepid**: warm [duration
**term**: word, call, limit,
" **of holding**: tenure
" **in tag**: it
**termagant**: shrew
**termination**: ending, limit, finale
**terpsichoreans**: dancers
**Terra del Fuego Indian**: Ona
**terrace**: balcony
**terrain**: region
**terrapin**: turtle [earthy
**terrestrial**: terrene,
**terrible**: dire, awful, tragic, dreadful, grim
**terrier( kind)**: skye
**terrified**: agast, aghast
**terrify**: dismay [ton
**territorial division**: can-
**terror**: dread, fright, fear, horror
**terse**: laconic, concise pithy, compact, brief
**test**: trial, try, tryout, essay,check, examine, prove, standard, assay, criterion
" **ore**: assay
**testify**: aver, depone, avow, attest [pone
" **under oath**: de-
**testimony**: evidence
**testy**: peevish, touchy
**tether**: fasten, restrain confine, try, tie
**Teutonic alphabet character**: rune
" **goddess**: Norm
" **god**: Aesirf Odin, Tyr, Er
**Texas mission**: Alamo
**text**: topic, subject
**textbook**: manual, primer
**texture**: wale, web
**that**: **(arch.)**: yon
" **is (abbr.)**: ie, eg
" " **to say**: namely
" " **is kept**: retent
" " **is left**: remnant
**the (Scot.)**: ta
**theatrical**: stagy
" **profession**: stage
**theme**: topic, subject, motif, essay
**theoretical force**: od
**therefore**: ergo, hense, so, thus, hence
**thespian**: actor
**Thessaly mt.**:Ossa
**thick**: dense, fat, coarse
**thicken**: deepen, gel
**thicket**: bush brake, hedge, covert, copse
**thickness**: ply, layer
**thief**: robber, looter
**thin**: slender, rarefied, lean, sparse, fine, sheer, dilute, watery, slim, bony, svelte, diluted, gaunt, lank
" **cake**: wafer [neer
" **coating**: film, ve-
" **layer**: lamella
" **& light**: papery
" **out**: peter
" **paper**: tissue
" **piece of stone**: slab
" **plate**: lamina, lamella, disc
" **scale**: lamina
" **strip of wood**: lath, splint, sliver
" **& vibrant**: reedy
**thing**: matter
" **in law**: res, les, re
" **lost**: losses
**things to be added**: addenda
" **be done**: agenda
" **done**: acta, actum
" **owned**: property
**think**: opine, ponder, cogitate, believe, deem, cerebrate, consider [ween
" **(arch.)**: wis, trow,
" **logically**: reason
**thinly scattered**: sparse
**third in degree**: tertiary
" **(mus.)**:tierce
" **power**: cube
**thirsty**: dry, parched
**this place**: here
" **springs eternal**: hope [amenta
**thong**: strap, lasso,
**thorn**: briar, brier, spine, seta [brambly
**thorny**: spinose, spinate,
" **shrub**: acacia, brier
**thorough**: arrant
**those against**: antis
" " **office**: ins
" **who ask alms**: beggars [opined
**thought**: opinion, idea,
**thoughtful**: pensive considerate
**thousand**: chiliad [mille
" **(comb. form)**: kilo.
**thrall**: bondman, slave, serf [drub, whiplash
**thrash**: beat, belabor,
" **(slang)**: lam
**thread**: lace, twine, lisle, fiber, reeve, filament
" **(kind)**: linen, lisle, cotton, silk
" **of a story**: clue
**threadlike**: filose, filar
" **tissue**: fiber
**threat**: menace
**threatening**: lowery
**three**: triad, trio [teen
" **cornered sail**: la-
" **dimensional**: cubic
" **joints**: trinodal
" **legged chair**: stool
" " **stand**: tripod, trivet, teapoy
" **(mus.)**: ter
" **in one**: triune
" **(prefix)**: tri
" **pronged weapon**: trident [enty
" **score & ten**: sev-
" **toed sloth**: ai
" **toned chord**: triad
**threefold**: trine, treble trinal, triple
**threshing tool**: flail
**threshold**: sill [tro
**thrice (prefix)**: ter, tri,
**thrifty**: provident, frugal [grow
**thrive**: prosper, batten,
**throat part**: tonsil,
" **(pert. to)**: gular
" **swelling**: goiter
**throb**: beat, pant, pulse
**throe**: pang [crowd
**throng**: mass, horde,
**through**: per, dia, by
**throw**: hurl, toss, cast, heave, fling, pitch
" **away**: discard
" **back**: repel [turb
" **into confusion**: dis-
" **of dice**: main
" **into disorder**: derange, pie, clutter
" **light on**: illume
" **lightly**: toss
" **off**: shed, emit
" " **track**: derail
" **out**: eject
" **over**: jilt
" **(poet.)**: elance
" **of six at dice**: sise
" **up**: retch
**thrush**: mavis, missel, robin, veery
**thrust**: poke, lunge, stab, prod, shove
**thrusting weapon**: lance
**thump**: bang, bump, blow, pound
**thurible**: censer [hence
**thus**: sic, therefore, so,
" **far**: yet
" **(Scot.)**: sae
**thwart**: spite, frustrate, brain [frontlet
**tiara**: coronet, diadem,
**Tibetian capital**: Lassa
" **gazel**: goa
" **monk**: lama
" **ox**: yak
" **priest**: lama
**tick**: mite: acarid
**tidal wave**: eagre
**tide**: current, season, surge, befall, neap
**tidings**: news, word
**tidy**: trim, neat, trig
**tie**: draw, knot, bond, cravat, lace, bind, equal, tether, unite, link, scarf, fasten
" **game**: draw
**Tierra del Friego Indian**: Ona
**tiff**: spat
**tight**: taut, tense, snug
**til**: sesame
**tile**: domino, slate
**till**: plow, farm, cultivate, hoe
**tillable**: arable
**tilled land**: arada, arado
**tilt**: tip, lean, incline, cant, slant, name, joust [cedar, lumber
**timber**: wood, ash, oak,
" **bend**: sny
" **piece**: tenon
**timberwolf**: lobo
**timbrel**: tabor
**time**: tempo, era, schedule, leisure, period, duration, occasion
" **long ago**: yore
" **before event**: eve
" **(Scot.)**: tid
**timeless**: ageless, eternal [apt
**timely**: opportune, pat,
**timepiece**: clock
**times ten (suffix)**: ty
**timid**: shy
**Timor coin**: avo [trepid
**timorous**: afraid, shy,
**tin**: stannum, can, Sn
" **container**: canister
" **foil for mirrors**: tain [bue, tint
**tincture**: modicum, im-
**tine**: prong, spike
**tinge**: tint, imbue, hue, stain, trace, shade
**tinkle**: dingle, clink
**tint**: hue, tinge, dye, shade, tincture
**tiny**: small, atomic
**tip**: point, apical, cue, careen, overturn, top, tilt, lean, cant, hint
" **of fox's tail**: tag
" **to one side**: careen, tilt, list
" **over**: overset, cant
" **of a pen**: neb
**tippet**: fur, scarf
**tipping**: atilt [sot
**tippler**: toper, drinker,
**tipster**: tout
**tirade**: screed, philippic
**tire**: exhaust, weary, fag [bored, weary
**tired**: jaded, fatigued,
**tiresome**: dreary, boring, tedious
" **person**: bore, pill
**tissue**: telo, tela, teca
**Titania's husband**: Oberon
**tithe**: tenth
**title**: name, sir, claim, ownership, heading
" **of Athena**: Alea
**titmouse**: tomtit
**titter**: giggle
**to**: unto, forward, into, toward, until, for
" **lee side**: alee
" **the left**: aport
" **other side**: over
" **a point on**: onto
" **(prefix)**: ac
" **same degree**: as
" **(Scot.)**: tae [even
" **such degree**: so,
" **this**: hereto [until
" **the time that**: till,
" **your health**: prosit
**toad (Scot.)**: tade
**toads**: agua, anurans, anura
**toady**: truckle
**toast**: scorch, warm, prosit, brown, skoal
**tobacco box**: humidor
" **(kind of)**: capa, caporal, snuff, latakia
" **roll**: cigar
" " **(var.)**: segar
**together**: along
" **(prefix)**: co
" **with**: and
**toggery**: clothes
**toil**: labor, ring, moil
**token**: relic, pledge, sign, badge
**tolerable**: soso, passable
**tolerate**: endure, stand, bide, digest [knell
**toll**: due, tax, impost, strive, resound, ring,
**tomato sauce**: catsup
**tomboy**: hoyden
**tomcat**: gib
**tone**: sound, accent, air
" **color**: timbre
" **down**: soften
**tongue**: language
**tonic**: bracer
**too**: overly
" **bad**: alas
" **late**: belated
**tool**: utensil, chaser, dupe, implement
" **to enlarge**: reamer
" " **flesh hides**: slater
**tooth**: molar, cog, fang
" **(comb. form)**: denti
" **decay**: caries [dent
" **of gear wheel**: cog,
" **point**: cusp
" **substance**: dentine
" **wheel**: sprocket, gear, cog
**toothed**: serrate, dentate, cerose [comb
" **instrument**: saw,
", **irregular**: erose
**top**:crest, ace, surmount, apex, head, cap, excel, surpass, tip, lid, acma, summit
" **of altar**: mensa
" **of doorway**: lint l
**topaz hum. bird**: ava
**toper**: sot, drinker [ject
**topic**: text, theme, sub-
**topple**: upset
**Topsy's friend**: Eva
**torch**: lamp, flambeau
**torment**: bait, torture, plague, tease, rack
**tornado**: twister
**torpid**: inert, dormant
**torpor**: coma, numbness
**torrent**: flood
**torrid**: tropical, hot
**torture**: torment [buffet
**toss**: hurl, pitch, flip,
**total**: add, sum, whole, entire, complete, tot, utter, absolute, all
**totter**: stagger, waver, toddle, rock
**touch**: contact, feel, adjoin, finger, nudge
" **at boundary line**: abut
" **lightly**: pat, dab
" **at one point**: tangent
**touchwood**: punk

**tough**: wiry
**toupee**: wig
**tourist**: traveler
**tousle**: rumple, dishevel
**tout**: tipster [barge
**tow**: drag, draw, pull,
**toward**: to, at, facing
" **the center**: entad, orad [ward
" **the inside**: into, in-
" " **left side**: aport
" " **mouth**: orad, entad [tern, aft
" " **rear of ship**: as-
" **(Scot.)**: tae
" **the stern**: aft, abaft
**tower**: turret, soar, pylon, citadel
**town (colloq.)**: burg
**toy**: dally, trifle, play
**trace**: track, sign, footprint, tinge, vestige, tail, mark, streak, follow, tang, derive
**track**: trail, rail, trace, path, mark, footprint
" **worn by a wheel**: rut [expanse, area
**tract**: treatise, region,
" **drained by river**: basin [easy
**tractable**: docile, tame,
**trade**: barter, sell, exchange, craft, deal, swap, traffic, strain
" **agreement**: cartel
**trader**: dealer, merchant [legend, folklore
**traditional tale**: saga,
**traduce**: debase, slur, revile, asperse
**traffic**: trade, barter
**trail**: path, track, route, way, course, lag, follow, drag, hunt
" **(slang)**: tail
" **of wild animal**: spoor
**train**: educate, school, tame, instruct, drill, teach, retinue, coach
" **of wives**: harem
**tramp**: hike, slog, hobo, vagrant, tread
**trample**: tread, crush
**trance**: spell, stupor, daze, swoon [calm
**tranquil**: serene, sedate,
**tranquility**: peace
**transact**: conduct, negotiate [act, deed
**transaction**: deal, sale,
**transcend**: overtop, surpass, overpass
**transcribe**: copy, write
**transfer**: transmit, convey, transpose
**transfix**: pin, stick
**transgress**: violate, err, sin [poral
**transitory**: brief, tem-
**translate**: render, decode, construe
**translation**: rendition, version
**transmit**: render, send, transfer, forward
**transmute**: transform, convert [crystal
**transparent**: laky, clear,
" **mineral**: mica
**transport**: convey, cart, ferry
**transported**: rapt
**transpose**: reverse, invert, transfer [nab
**trap**: gin, snare, tree, ensnare, pitfall, web, net, ambush, grab,
**trap door**: drop
**trappings**: gear [use
**trash**: rubbish, dirt, ref-
**trashy**: worthless

**travel**: tour, wend, ride, journey
" **by wagon**: trek
**traveler**: tourist, viator, passenger, wayfarer
**traveling co.**: caravan
**traverse**: cross, scour, run [parody
**travesty**: mime, satire,
**tray**: server, salver
**treachery**: treason
**treacle**: molasses
**tread**: step, trample, walk, tramp [value
**treasure**: wealth, prize,
**treasurer**: bursar
**treat**: use, regale, tend, handle, negotiate
" **indulgently**: pamper
" **maliciously**: spite
" **unkindly**: mistreat
**treatise**: tract, discourse
**treaty**: pact, alliance
**tree**: catalpa, yew, ule, tamarack, rack, aspen, corner, myrtle
" **of antiquity**: olive
" **covering**: bark
" **exudation**: rosin, resin, gum
" **frog (young)**: peeper
" **snake**: lora, lerot
" **trunk**: bole, log
" **yielding caucho**: ule
**treeless plains**: pampas, tundras
**trees**: forest
" **(pert. to)**: arboreal
**trellis**: lattice, espalier
**tremble**: quiver, quake, dodder, shake, shiver,
**tremulous**: aspen
**trench**: ditch, moat
**trend**: tendency, movement, tend, tenor, incline, drift, bent
**trepan**: entrap
**trespass**: encroach, intrude, poach, venture
**tress**: braid, lock, ringlet, curl [ternary
**triad**: trine, trivalent,
**trial**: test, ordeal, attempt, hardship
**triangle with unequal sides**: scalene
" **piece**: gore, gusset
**tribal sign**: totem
**tribe**: clan, gens
**tribulation**: trial, woe
**tribunal**: bar
**tributary**: feeder
" **of the Amazon**: Napo
" " " **Colo.**: Gila
" " " **Elbe**: Iser
" " " **Missouri**: Osage, Platte
" " " **Ohio River**: Wabash [fering
**tribute**: tax, praise, of-
**tricar**: tricycle
**trice**: moment, instant
**trick**: stunt, jape, feint, prank, delude, ruse, antic, defraud, palter, wile, deceit, fraud
**trickle**: drip
**tricky (slang)**: snide
**trifle**: dally, toy, petty, straw [spruce, smart
**trig**: trim, neat, tidy,
**trig. function, ratio or figure**: sine, secant, cosine
**trill**: warble, roll
**trim**: decorate, adoren, prune, trig, spruce, neat, preen, lop
" **& simple**: tailored
" **with the beak**: preen [ing
**trimming**: ruche, edg-
**trip**: stumble, misstep, jaunt, tour

**triple**: trine, threefold
**triste**: dismal [stale
**trite**: banal, threadbare,
**triton**: newt, salamander [prevail, victory
**triumph**: pervail, win,
**trivial**: small, slight, banal
**Trojan hero & defender**: Eneas, Aeneas
" **warrior**: agenor
**troop**: band, company
**tropical**: torrid, sultry, warm [parrot
" **bird**: ani, toucan,
" **carnivore**: ratel
" **fruit**: papaw, date, bana, guava, mango
" **herb**: sida [taro
" **plant**: aloe, ipecac,
" **tree**: palm, tamarind, mabi, zorro
**trot**: jog [sore, woe
**trouble**: bother, aid, ail, agitate, molest, ado,
**trough to cool**: bosh
**trousers**: slacks, pants
**truck**: barter, van, lorry
**truckle**: toady
**trudge**: plod
**true**: honest, loyal, accurate, faithful
" **to fact**: literal
" **hearted**: leal
**truly**: indeed, yes, yea, verily, veritably
**trump**: ruff, outdo [oma
**trumpet creeper**: tec-
" **(small)**: clarion
" **sound**: blare, blast
**trumpeter bird**: agami
**trunk of statue**: torso
**trunkfish**: toro
**truss**: bind
**trust**: monopoly, rely, credit, confide, believe, hope, lean, reliance, merger, faith, depend, belief
**trustworthy**: safe, honest, reliable [fact
**truth**: verity, veracity,
" **(arch.)**: sooth
**truthful**: honest
**try**: test, sample, endeavor, essay, strive, attempt, teth r, undertake, trial
**tub**: keeve, cask, vat
**tube**: pipe
" **on which silk is wound**: cop [crest
**tuft**: bunch, clump,
**tug**: haul
**tumble**: spill, wilter
**tumbler**: glass
**tumeric**: rea
**tumor**: wen
**tumult**: bedlam, riot, din, tempest, hubbub
**tun**: cask [adapt
**tune**: aria, air, melody,
**Tungsten ore**: cal
**Tunisia capital**: Tunis
" **city**: Sfax
" **measure**: saa, saah
" **pasha**: dey
" **ruler**: Bey, dey
**turban hat**: moab
**turbid**: roily
**turf**: sod, sward
" **in golf**: divot
" **(poet.)**: glebe
**Turk**: Tatar, Ottoman, Tartar
**turkey buzzard**: aura
" **(male)**: tom
**Turkish**: Ottoman
" **bath**: hammam
" **capital**: Ankara
" **city**: Adana, Aintab
" **coin**: asper, para
" **commander**: aga
" **decree**: Irade
" **flag**: alem

" **government**: Porte
" **governor**: Pasha, Bey
" **hat**: fez
" **imp. standard**: alem
" **inn**: imaret
" **judge**: cadi, aga
" **measure of length**: arshin
" **mon. unit**: asper
" **money**: asper
" **mt. range**: Alai
" **name**: ala, ali
" **officer**: emir, aga, pasha
" **official (var.)**: emeer
" **prince**: ameer
" **province**: Angora
" **regiment**: alai
" **ruler**: sultan
" **sailing vessel**: saic
" **soldier**: nizam
" **sultan**: Selim
" **title**: aga, emir, pasha, bey
" " **(var.)**: amir
" **town**: Bir [tatar
" **tribesman**: tatir,
" **vilayet**: Adana
" **weight**: oka
**turmeric**: rea [whirl
**turn**: twist, rotate, revolve, bend, pivot,
" **aside**: shunt, deviate, wry, deter, divert, swerve, avert
" **away**: shy
" **back**: repel, revert
" **down**: reject, veto
" **the front wheels**: cramp
" **for help**: resort
" **inside out**: evert
" **into money**: cash
" **inward**: introvert
" **to left**: haw
" **out to be**: prove
" **outward**: extrovert, evert
" **over**: keel [form
" " **new leaf**: re-
" **pages of**: leaf [slue
" **on pivot**: swivel,
" **to right**: gee
" **the soil**: spade
" **white**: pale
**turner**: gymnast
**turning**: rotary
" **joint**: hinge
" **point**: pivot, crisis
**turret**: tower, cupola
**turtle**: terrapin, snapper, tortoise
" **shell**: carapace
**tussle**: struggle
**Tutelary gods**: lares
**tutor**: school
**twelve dozen**: gross
**twice**: bis, doubly
" **(prefix)**: di, bi
**twig**: sprig, rod, cion
**twilight**: dusk, eve
**twilled fabric**: serge, silesia, denim, covert, surah [gemel
**twin**: match, double,
" **crystal**: macle
**twine**: wind, twist, coil, meander, string, encurl, cord, wreath
**twining plant**: smilax, winder, vine
" " **part**: tendril
**twinkle**: wink
**The Twins**: Gemini
**twirl**: turn, spin [screw
**twist**: contort, writh, warp, bend, turn, coil, twine, slue, wry, spiral, wrench, quirk, gnarl, skew, wring,
" **around**: slue, slew
" **out of shape**: contort, warp, distort

twisted: wry
" cotton thread: lisle
" roll of wool: slub
" silk: sleave
" (var.): slewed
twit: taunt, upbraid, ridicule
twitching: tic
two: pair, both, couple
" edged: ancipital
" feet (having): bipedal, dipode [ped
" footed animal: bi-
" headed deity: Janus
" (prefix): di, bi
" pronged instrument: bident
" (Scot.): twa
" toed sloth: unau
" wheeled cab: hansom [essede
" " chariot: essed,
" " conveyance: bike, gig, cart
" winged fly: gnat
twofold: dual, twin
" (prefix): di
type: see also "style"
type: variety, sort, nature, kind, model, norm, emblem, genre
" (kind): italic
" of lens: toric
" measure: em, en
" of molding: torus
" " perfection: paragon
" square: em [en
typewriter roller: plat-
typical example: norm
typographer: printer
tyrant: despot
tyro: novice [final

## U

ultimate: eventual, last
ululant: howling
umbrella (colloq.): gamp
" part: rib
umpire: referee, arbiter
unaccompanied: alone, sole, lone [bald
unadorned: bare, stark,
unadulterated: pure
unaspirated: lene
unassumed: natural
unassuming: modest
unattached: loose, free
unbalanced: deranged, onesided
unbend: thaw, relax
unbiased: impartial
unbind: untie, release
unbleached: ecru
unbound: loose
unbounded: limitless
unbroken: intact [eerie
uncanny (var.): eery,
unceremonious: abrupt
uncertainty: doubt
unchanging: uniform
unchecked: rampant, free
uncivil: rude
uncivilized: savage
Uncle Remus creator: Harris
uncle (Scot.): eme
unclose: open, ope
uncommon: unusual, rare, odd
uncompromising: stern
unconcealed: open
unconfined: free
unconscious: unaware
uncouth: rude [lidless
uncovered: bare, open,
unctuous: oily [low
uncultivated: wild, fal-
uncultured: unrefined
undecided: pend
under: beneath, below
" obligation: indebted
" part of auto: chasis
" (poet.): neath
" (prefix): sub
underground bud: bulb
" chamber: cavern, cave [nel
" passageway: tun-
" room: cellar
" stem: tuber
underhanded: sly
" person: sneak
underlings: slave, serfs
undermine: sap
underneath: below
understand: see, realize, know, comprehend
understanding: reason, entente, sense
understood: tacit [try
undertake: endeavor,
undertaking: venture
underwater ridge: reef
" worker: diver
underworld: Hades
undisclosed: ulterior
undivided: one, entire, whole, total [unclasp
undo: release, neglect, offset, annul, ruin,
undoing: ruin [wild
undomesticated: feral,
undressed calfskin: kip
" kid: suede
undulate: wave, roll
undulation: crimp, wave [close
unearth: uncover, dis-
unearthy: eerie
uneasy: restive, restless, nervous
unemployed: idle
unenclosed: fenceless
unencumbered: free
uneven: erose, odd
unexciting: tame
unexpected: abrupt
" pleasure: treat
" result: upset
unexplosive shell: dud
unfair: foul[known, new
unfamiliar: strange, un-
unfastened: ripped, loose, undid, untied, untethered [bad
unfavorable: averse, ill,
unfeeling: stony, insensate, marble, numb
unfeigned: sincere
unfettered: free
unfledged: callow
unfold: open, spread
" gradually: develop
unfounded: idle
unfriendly: inimical
unfruitful: sterile
unfurl: spread, open
ungainly: awkward
ungrateful person: ingrate [an, tapir
ungulate animal: dam-
unheeding: deaf
uniform: even, unchanging, consistent
unimaginative: literal
unimpaired: intact
uninhabited: deserted, desolate
uninteresting: dry, dull
union: junction, coalition, fusion, league, merger, marriage, juncture, alliance
unique: odd, rare, alone
unison: harmony, agreement, accord, concord
unit: see "measure"
unit: ace, one, item
" of acoustics: Bel
" " conduct.: mho
" " dis.: word
" " drymeas.: peck
" " electric capacity: farad [ere
" " " int.: amp-
" " " pow.: watt
" " " reluct.: rel
" " " resist.: ohm
" " elect.: volt
" " electrol.: ion
" " energy: erg
" " force: dene, dyne
" " germ plasm: ids, id [therm
" " heat: calory,
" " illum.: phot
" " inductance (elect.): henry
" " light: lumen
" " " intensity: pyr
" " power: watt [ad
" " pressure: bar-
" " resist.: ohm
" " square measure: acre, rod [day
" " time: month,
" " velocity: kine, kin [gram, ton, grain
" " weight: carat,
" " wire measure: mil [erg
" " work: erg, kil-
" " " (pert. to): ergal
unite: coalesce, link, tie, undo, merge, cement, add, band, connect, ally, knit, consolidate, combine, splice [fay
" closely: ally, weld,
" by weaving: splice
unity: one, oneness, agreement [acea
universal remedy: pan-
unkind: ill, cruel
unknit: ravel, unravel
unless (Latin): nisi
unlike: diverse
unmannerly person: cad
unmarried: celibate
unmarried girl: maid, spinster [sheer
unmitigated: arrant,
unmixed: pure
unnecessary: needless
unoccupied: idle, vacant
unpaid debt: arrear
unparalleled: alone
unprepared: raw
unproductive: barren, sterile
unreal: visionary
unrefined: crude, wild, uncultivated, inelegant, uncultured, raw
unrelenting: iron
unrestrained: free [cool
unruffled: serene, calm,
unruly: restive, lawless, disorderly [lick
" lock of hair: cow-
" person: rebel
unsafe: insecure
unsatisfactory: lame
unseal: open
unsettle: disturb
unshackled: free
unsightly: ugly
unskilled: inept
unsoiled: clean
unspoken: tacit [lish
unstable: erratic, tick-
unstitched glove: trank
unsubstantial: airy, aery, flimsy
unsuitable: inept, inapt
untamed: wild, feral
untidy: messy, mussy
" person: sloven, slattern
untie: loosen, unfasten
until: unto, to, til
unto: until, to
untrammeled: free
untried: new
unused: untried, new
unusual: rare, odd, novel, uncommon
unvarying: even
unwilling: averse
unwritten: oral, parol
unyielding: grim, set stern, obdurate, hard adamant, rigid
up: aloft, above, higher, upon, atop
up (prefix): ana
" to: until
upbraid: reproach, twit
uphold: sustain, abet, back [erect
uplift: raise, inspire,
upon: atop, onto, on, up, above
" (poet.): oer
" (prefix): epi, ep
upper: high, higher, superior, top
" air: ether
" house: senate
" room: loft
upright: erect, honest, vertical
" doorway piece: jamb
uprightness: virtue, honesty [din, hubbub
uproar: tumult, riot,
upset: topple, keel, overthrow, coup, disconcert, discompose
upshot: result, sequel
upstart: parvenu, snob
upward movement of ship: scend
Uranus's daughter: Rhea
" mother: Ge
urbane: suave, polite
urchin: tad, elfin, arab, gamin [push, goad
urge: egg, press, spur, insist, prod, stir, incite, flagitate, impel, drive, actuate, sue, solicit, persuade, dun,
" on: abet, hurry, incite, spur, egg
urial: sha
urn: vase [custom
usage: habit, manners,
use: exercise, worth, practice, avail, employ, utility, custom, treat, service, manipulate, occupy, inure
" diligently: ply
" frugally: spare
" a lever: pry, prise
" of new word: neology
" trickery: palter
" up: consume
used: secondhand
" in flight: volar
" to be: was
useful: utile [needless
useless: idle, inutile, futile, vain, fruitless,
usher: escort, introduce, forerun, forearm [age, customary
usual: common, aver-
Utah state flower: sego
utensil: tool, implement
utility: use
utmost: best
" degrees: tops
" limit: extreme
utopian: ideal [say
utter: state, speak, absolute, stark, pronounce, total, voice,

## V

vacant: hollow, idle, empty
vacate: evacuate, quit
vacillate: waver, teeter
vagabond: bum, vagrant, tramp, hobo
vagary: fancy, caprice
vagrant: bum, tramp, vagabond [indefinite
vague: sketchy, hazy,

**vain**: empty, idle, useless, conceited
**vale**: glen, dale, channel
**valiant**: brave, heroic
**valid**: sound, cogent, legal [bag, satchel
**valise**: grip, bag, hand-
**valley**: dale, vale, glen, dell, dingle, canyon
**valor**: courage, heroism
**valorous person**: hero
**value**: prize, price, worth, rate, esteem, appraise, treasure
" **highly**: endear
**valve**: piston
**Vandal**: Hun [appear
**vanish**: flee, fade dis-
**vanity**: pride
**vanquish**: defeat, conquer, worst, beat
**vapid**: stale, spiritless, insipid, dull, tasteless, flat [mist
**vapor**: gas, steam, air,
" **in the air**: haze
" (dense): fog [nova
**variable star**: mira,
" " **in Perseus**: algol
**variegated**: pied, tissued, dappled, striped
**variety**: specie, sort, class, form, diversity, type, genus
**various**: many, diverse
**varnish**: lac, shellac
" **ingredient**: resin, lac [diverge
**vary**: change, alter,
**vas**: duct, vessel
**vase**: urn
**vassal**: subject, slave, serf, bondman, liege
**vast**: immense, huge, great
" **age**: eon
" **horde**: legion
" **number**: billion
" (poet.): enorm
**vat**: tub, keeve, bac, cistern
**vault**: leap, crypt
**vaunt**: boast
**Vedic fire god**: Agni
**veer**: shift, slue, fickle, fluctuate, turn
**vegetable exudation**: resin [tree
" **organism**: plant,
**vehemence**: fury, rage, ardor, heat [dent
**vehement**: fervent, ar-
**vehemently**: amain
**vehicle carrying a display**: float
" **for heavy loads**: lorry, dray [sledge
" **on runner**: cutter,
**veil**: curtain, disguise, conceal, hide
" (silk): orale
**vein**: rib, vena, streak
**velocity**: speed
**velvetlike fabric**: panne, velure
**vend**: sell
**venerable**: august, aged
**venerate**: revere, honor, adore, worship, reverse, reverence [ence
**veneration**: awe, rever-
**Venetian bridge**: Rialto
" **magistrate**: doge
" **painter**: Titian
" **red**: siena
**Venezeula capital**: Caracas
" **coin**: bolivar
" **tree snake**: lora
**venom**: spite, virus
**vent**: outlet, opening, aperture
" **in earth's crust**: volcano
**venture**: dare, presume, risk, enterprise
**ventured**: durst [bold
**venturesome**: daring,
**Venus's love**: Adonis
" **son**: Cupid
**veracity**: truth
**veranda**: porch, piazza
**verb form**: tense
**verbal**: oral
**verdant**: green
**Verdi's opera**: Aida
**verge**: brink, border, edge, margin, approach [prove
**verify**: aver, collate,
**verily**: indeed, amen, yea, truly
**veritable**: real
**verity**: truth
**vermilion**: red [stave
**verse**: rime, poem, poetry, canto, stanza,
" **form**: tercet, poem, triolet, sonnet
" **pattern**: meter
" **of two feet**: dimeter
**verso (ab.)**: vo
**vertebral**: spinal
**vertical**: upright
" (naut.): apeak
" **pipe**: stack
" **support**: pillar
" **timber**: bitt, mast
**verve**: elan, ardor, pep
**very (comb. form)**: eri
" **large** (poet.): enorm
" **loud** (Mus.): ff
" (Scot.): vera
**vessel**: basin, craft, liner, settee, pot, vas, ship, sloop, tug, setee, can, yawl, boat, urn, barque, pan, tub
" (abbr.): S. S.
" **curved planking**: sny
" **to heat liquid**: etna
" **to hold liquid**: cruse, teapot, vial
" (large): tureen, vat, tankard [flask
" **for liquors**: flagon,
" (poet): bark [hall
**vestibule**: entry, lobby,
**vestige**: trace, relic
**vestment**: cope, alb, stole
**vetch**: tare
**veto**: prohibit, forbid
**vex**: roil, irk, irritate, tease, harass, peeve, agitate, fret, annoy
" (colloq.): rile
**vexation**: pest, pique, chagrin
**viaduct**: trestle
**vial**: phial
**viator**: traveler
**vibration**: tremor
**vicarage**: manse
**vice**: evil, sin, iniquity
**vicious**: cruel, mean
**victim**: prey, dupe
**victor**: winner, conqueror [cess, conquest
**victory**: triumph, suc-
**victual**: meat
**vie**: contend, emulate, contest, strive
**view**: scene, vista, eye
**vigilance**: care
**vigilant**: alert, aware, awake, watchful
**vigor**: pep, vim, energy, strength, power, vis
**vigorous**: energetic, sturdy, robust, hale, forcible, animated, virile, lusty
**vile**: filthy, vulgar, unclean, base
**vilify**: asperse, revile
**village**: hamlet, town, dorp [force
**vim**: pep, vigor, energy,
**vindicate**: justify, maintain, exculpate
**vine**: ivy, wistaria pea, creeper, hop
**vinegar bottle**: cruet
" **made from ale**: alegar
" (pert. to): acetic
**vineyard**: cru [force
**violence**: fury, rage,
**violent**: rabid
" **woman**: virago
**violently**: hard, amain
**violin** (colloq.): strad
" **maker**: amati
" (old): cremona, amati, rebec
" (small): kit
**viper**: adder, snake, asp
**Virgil's hero**: Eneas
" **poem**: Aeneid
**virile**: vigorous, manly
**virtuous**: moral
**viscous substance**: tar, glue, grease
**vise part**: jaw
**Vishnu's incarnation**: rama
**vision**: dream eye
**visionary**: dreamer, idealist, ideal, aery, Utopian, unreal
**visit**: see, haunt, call
**visitor**: guest, caller
**vista**: view, outlook, scene, prospect
**visual**: ocular [pep
**vitality**: sap, tamina,
**vitiate**: deprave, taint, spoil [mated, airy
**vivacious**: gay, ani-
**vivid**: graphic
**vixen**: shrew
**vocal**: oral
" **inflection**: tone
**vocation**: calling, profession, career, trade
**vociferated**: clamored, roared, yelled
**vociferous**: blatant
**vogue**: fashion
**voice**: emit, divulge, say, speech, express, utter [phonetic
" (pert. to): vocal,
**voiceless**: spirate, surd
**void**: space, annul, empty, null
" **space**: inanity
**voided escutcheon**: orle
**volatile liquid**: alcohol, ether, ligroin
**volcanic cinder**: scoria
" **deposit**: trass
" **glass froth**: pumice
" **matter**: lava
" **rock**: basalt, trass, tephrite, obsidian
**volcano**: Etna, Pelee
" **mouth**: crater, lava
**volumn**: mo
" (large): tome
**volunteer**: offer
**vortex**: eddy, gyre,
**vote**: ballot, poll, elect
**vouch for**: sponsor, attest, assure, aver
**vouchsafe**: deign
**vow**: oath, pledge
**vowel mutation**: umlaut
**vulcanize**: cure
**vulgar**: vile
" **fellow**: cad
**vulture (large)**: condor

## W

**wad**: stuff, cram
**wade**: ford
**wader**: snipe [sora, rail
**wading bird**: stilt, heron, flamingo, crane, jabiru, stork, ibis,
**wafer**: snap [sway
**wag**: wit, joker, shake,
**wager**: ante, bet, stake, parlay, wit [stipend
**wages**: salary, pay,
**Wagnerian character**: Hagen, Erda [Senta
" **heroine**: Elsa,
**wagon**: wain, cart, dray, lorry, tram truck
" **track**: rut
**wail**: howl, lament, moan, bemoan
**wainscot**: ceil
**wais'**: bodice
**waistcoat**: vest [delay
**wait**: stay, linger, tarry,
" **for**: bide
" **on**: attend, serve, tend, clerk, cater
**walk**: step, tread, stride, pace, hike, ambulate, tramp, plod
" **feebly**: totter
" **lamely**: limp
" **leisurely**: stroll
" **on**: tread [stalk
" **pompously**: strut,
" **proudly**: prance
" **unsteadily**: stagger, toddle, totter
" **wearily**: trudge, plod, trail [pogo
**walking stick**: cane, rattan, staff, stilt,
**wall border**: ogee, dado
" **coating**: plaster
" (pert. to): mural,
" **section**: panel
**Wallaba**: apa
**walrus collection**: pod
**wampum**: peag
**wan**: pale, pole, pallid, colorless, ashy, languid [osier, staff
**wand**: rod, scepter,
**wander**: err, roam, stray, rove, stroll, traipse, ramble, disgress, gad, meander, divagate
**wandering**: errant, vagrant, astray, aberrant, nomadic, erring
" **race**: gypsy
**wane**: ebb, fade, decrease, shrink
**wangle**: wriggle
**want**: need, lack, poverty, desire, wish, scarcity, deficiency
**Wapiti**: elk [battle
**war**: conflict, strire,
" **fleet**: armada
" **horse**: steed
" (pert. to): martial
**warble**: yodel, sing, trill, carol
**ward off**: avert, fend, prevent, parry, repel, stave [ian
**warden**: keeper, guard-
**wariness**: caution
**warm**: thermal, toasty, tepid, tropical, toast
**warmth**: heat, ardor
**warn**: caution
**warning**: notice, alert, caveat, signal [alarm
" **signal**: tocsin, siren, alarum, alert,
**warp yarn**: abb
**warriors**: cohort, soldiers, fighters
**wary**: shy, cautious, watchful
" (colloq.): leery
**wash**: lave, launder, bathe, rinse
**wasp**: hornet
**waste**: emaciate, refuse, squander, lose, fritter, exhaust, dross
" **allowance**: tare
" **away**: repine
" **land (Eng.)**: moor
" **matter**: dross
" **pipe**: sewer
" **silk (piece)**: noil
" **time**: dally, idle

**wasteland:** desert, heath [vigil, tend
**watch:** patrol, eye,
" **dog:** mastiff
" **pocket:** fob
" **secretly:** spy
**watchful:** alert, vigilant, wary
**watchman:** sentinel
**water:** irrigate, aqua, eau, dilute
" **barrier:** dam
" **bird:** coot, swan
" **bottle:** carafe
" **excursion:** sail
" **(flying):** spray
" **fowl:** brant, egret
" **(Fr.):** eau
" **jar:** hydria
" **jug:** ewer, olla
" **lily:** lotus [strait
" **passage:** sound,
" **pipe (large):** main
" **plant:** lotus
" **of the sea:** brine
" **spirit:** Undine, Ariel
" **wheel:** noria
**watercresses (dial.):** ekers
**watered appearance:** moire [linn, cascade
**waterfall:** cataract, lin,
" **(Scot.):** lin [oasis
**watering place:** spa,
**waterless:** arid, dry
**waterway:** channel, stream, canal
**watery:** wet, thin
**wave:** sea, comber, surf, breaker, flutter, waft, crimp, roller, surge, undulate
" **to & fro:** flap, wag
**wavelet:** ripple
**waver:** falter, stagger, fluctuate, totter, reel, hesitate, flicker
**wavy (heraldry):** onde
**wax:** cere, grow, increase, cerate
" **(obs.):** cere
" **(pert. to):** ceral
**way:** manner, route, method, path, passage, course, road, lane [ble, faint
**weak:** puny, frail, fee-
" **(arch.):** seely
**weaken:** sap, enervate, dilute, unnerve, debiliate, attenuate
**weakness:** foible
**wealthy:** rich, affluent
**wealthy person:** nabob, midas
**weapon:** bomber, gun, spear, sword, pistol, arms, dagger, firearm
**wear:** exhibit, display
" **away:** erode, fray abrade, eat, rub
" **at the edge:** fray
**wearisomeness:** tedium
**weary:** tire, irk fatigue, fag, bore [marten
**weasel:** ermine, stoat, otter, ferret, sable,
**weather:** season
" **cock:** vane
" **conditions:** climate
**weave:** spin, interlace
**weaver's reed:** sley
**weaving machine:** loom
**web:** network, fabric, trap, texture, snare, ply, tela
" **footed bird:** swan, goose, avocet, penguin, gannet
" **like:** telar [tela
" " " **membrane:**
" " " **(pl.):** telae
**wedge:** cleat
" **in:** jam
" **shaped:** cuneated
**weed:** tare
**weekly:** aweek [boohoo
**weep:** moan, sob, cry,
**weeping:** tearful
**weight:** dram, ton, pressure, heft, onus, troy, carat, pound, mite
" **allowance:** tare
" **on fishlines:** sinkers
" **for wool:** tod
**weighty:** momentous
**weir:** dam [in
**welcome:** greet, pleas-
**welkin:** sky, air
**well:** hardy, fit, healthy
" **assured:** confident
" **bred:** genteel
" " **woman:** lady
" **grounded:** valid
" **known:** familiar
" **lining:** steen
**Welsh onion:** cibol
**West African baboon:** mandrill, mandril
" " **seaport:** Dakar
" **Indian bird:** tody
" " **fish:** pelon, pega
" " **fruit:** genipap
" " **Isl.:** Bahamas, Antilles, Haiti, Cuba
" " **lizard:** arbalo
" " **plant:** anil
" " **rodent:** hutia
" " **shark:** gata
" " **shrub:** anil
" " **sorcery:** obi
" " **tree:** genip
" " **vessel:** droger
" **Point freshman:** pleb, plebe
" **Saxon king:** Ine
**wet:** moist, watery, rainy, humid, damp, dampen
" **(Scot.):** wat [soak
" **thoroughly:** souse,
**whale:** cete, sperm, orc
" **(pert. to):** cetic
" **school:** gam
" **skin:** rind
**whalebone:** baleen
**wharf:** pier, key, quay
**whatnot:** etagere
**wheedle:** cajole
**wheel bar:** axle
" **braker:** sprad
" **of caster:** roller
" **groove:** rut
" **hub:** nave [rim, tire
" **part:** cam, spoke,
" **(pert. to):** rotal
" **(small):** caster
" **of spur:** rowel
" **tooth:** cog [en
**whet:** stimulate, sharp-
**whether:** if
**whetstone:** hone
**whey of milk:** serum
**while:** yet, as [fad
**whim:** notion, caprice,
**whimper:** mewl, pule
**whimsy:** caprice
**whine & cry:** snivel
**whinny:** neigh
**whip:** beat, flay, defeat, scourge, cane, lash, flog, knout
" **handle:** crop
**whirl:** spu, spin, swirl, twirl, reel, eddy, revolve
**whirlpool:** eddy, vortex
**whistle:** pipe, siren
**whit:** doit, jot, iota
**white:** pale, hoar, ashy, snowy [glair
" **animal:** albino
" **of egg:** albumen,
" **man:** paleface
" **substance:** ivory
" **vestment:** amice, alb [bleach
**whiten:** blanch, snow,
**whither:** where
**whitish:** chalky
**whittle:** cut
**whole:** all, entire, complete, aggregate, total
" **number:** integer
**wicked:** evil, sinful
**wide:** broad
" **awake:** alert
" **mouth jar or jug:** olla, ewer
" " " **(var.):** ola
**widespread:** prevalent, rife
**widgeon:** smee
**widow:** relict
" **'s coin:** mite
" " **dower (law):** terce
" " **income:** dower
**wield:** manage, ply, handle
**wife:** spouse
**wig:** toupee, peruke, tete
**wigwam:** tepee, teepee
**wild:** ferocious, feral, ferine, fierce
" **animal:** beast, polecat, elk, fox, tiger, lion, lynx, moose
" **ass of Asia:** onager
" **buffalo of India:** arna, arnee [ocelot
" **cat:** eyra, lynx,
" **cherry:** gean
" **cry:** evoe
" **duck:** mallard
" **ox:** anoa, urus
" **plant:** weed [urial
" **sheep:** sha, argali,
" **swine:** boar
" **tract of land:** heath
**wile:** trick, art
**will:** bequeath, decree
" **leaver:** testator
" **left & made:** testate
**willing:** lieve, ready
**willow:** osier, itea, salix
**wilt:** droop
**wily:** sly, foxy, artful
**win:** gain, acquire, entice, prevail, earn, triumph, get, obtain
" **over:** defeat, persuade
**wince:** flinch
**wind:** gale, breath, coil
" **blast:** gust
" **indicator:** vane
" **instrument:** reed, horn, clarinet, tuba, organ, bagpipe, flute, bugle, accordion
**windflower:** anemone
**winding:** spiral, sinuous
**windlass:** winch
**windmill arm:** vane
**window cover:** shutter
**wing:** ala, pinion, alea
" **of bldg.:** annex
" **footed:** aliped
" **of house:** ell
" **shaped:** alary, alar, alate [alated
**winged:** alate, flew,
" **insect:** wasp, moth
" **serpent:** dragon
" **steed:** Pegasus
**wingless:** apteral
**wink:** nictate, nictitate
**winner:** victor
**winnow:** fan
**winter (pert.to):** hiemal
**wipe:** mop, clean, swab
**wire:** telegraph
" **coil:** spring
" **rope:** cable
**wireman:** wirer
**wiry:** sinewy
**wisdom:** lore, gnosis, erudition, knowledge
**wise:** sage, learned, erudite, prudent, knowing [mentor
" **counselor:** nestor,
" **men:** sage, magi, solomons, solons, nestors [acle
" **saying:** adage, or-
**wisely:** sagely
**wiser:** sager [covet
**wish:** hope, desire, want,
**wisp of smoke:** floc
**wit:** wag, humor, sense, satire, banter, waggery, cleverness, as
**witch:** hex, lamia, hag
**witchcraft:** sorcery
**with might:** amain [con.
" **(prefix):** syn, con,
" **(Scot.):** wi [tract
**withdraw:** retreat, retract, retire, secede, seclude, recede, de-
**wither:** sere, sear, dry, shrink, droop, wilt, shrivel [detain
**withhold:** keep, deny,
**within:** into, inside, inner, in [endo
" **(comb. form):** eso,
" **(prefix):** intra
**without elevations:** flat
" **feet:** apod
" **(Fr.):** sans
" **friends:** lorn
" **life:** amort
" **luster:** mat
" **mate:** odd
" **purpose:** aimless
" **reserve:** freely
" **teeth:** edentate
" **title:** nameless
**withstand:** resist, oppose, endure
" **use:** wears, wear
**witness:** attest, see
**witnessing clause of a writ:** teste [sally
**witticism:** mot, joke,
**witty:** facetious [ster
" **person:** wag, pun-
" **reply:** repartee
" **saying:** mot, quip
**woe:** ill, disaster, bane
**woeful:** sad
**wolfhound:** alan
**wolframite:** cal
**woman's cloak:** dolman
" **club:** sorosis
" **marriage (pert. to) or portion:** dotal
**wonder:** marvel, awe
**wont:** custom, habit
**woo:** sue, court, solicit
**wood:** ebony, teak, grove, timber, walnut, oak, fir, balsa
" **ash substance:** potash
" **deity:** faun [mite
" **eating insect:** ter-
" **(light):** balsa
" **louse:** slater
" **nymph:** sprite, dryas, dryad
" **(small):** grove
" **sorrel:** oca, oxalis
**woodchuck:** marmot
**woodcutter:** sawyer
**wooded hill:** holt
**wooden bench:** settee
" **container:** crate, box, barrel, case
" **cup:** noggin
" **joint:** tenon [nog
" **pin:** peg, dowel, fid,
" **shoe:** sabot
**woods:** trees, forest
**woody corn spike:** cob
" **fiber:** bast
**wool colored:** beige
" **(kind):** merino, challis, alpaca
**woolen cluster:** nep
" **fabric:** tamis, serge, beige, ratine, tamine, moreen, delaine, challis, tweed
" **surface:** nap
**wooly:** lanate, fleecy

**word:** message, term, tidings, promise
" **of assent:** amen
" " **honor:** parole
" " **lamentation:** alas
" " **mouth:** parol
" **for word:** literal
**work:** operate, opus, remark, toil
" **for:** serve [drudge
" **hard:** moil, ply,
" **hard (Scot.):** tew
" **out:** solve, elaborate [vamp, rework
" **over:** rehash, re-
" **party:** bee
" **at steadily:** ply
" **too hard:** overdo
" **with hands:** knead
**workman:** laborer
**workshop:** atelier, studio, lab
**world wide:** global
**worm:** asp, cadew, ess, eis, loa, annelid
**worn out:** effete, passe, spent, old [harass
**worry:** fret, stew, care,
**worship:** idolize, revere, venerate, adoration
**worstedcloth:** serge
**worth:** value, merit, use, deserving
**worthless:** bad, trashy
" **(Biblical):** raca
" **(colloq.):** N G.
" **leaving:** ort
" **scrap:** ort
**wound mark:** scar, stab
**woven cloth:** fabric
" **fabric:** tissue, texture, blanket, web
**wrangle:** bicker, dispute, spar [infold
**wrap:** envelop, swathe, cere, enswathe, shawl,
" **round & round:** roll [rage
**wrath:** anger, ire, fury,
**wrathful:** irate [green
**wreath:** twine, anadem, garland, lei, circlet,
" **bearing a knight's crest:** orle
**wreck:** ruin [wrest
**wrench:** spanner, twist,
" **out of shape:** distort [snatch
**wrest:** wrench, wring,
" **illegally:** extort
**wretched:** miserable, ill, forlorn
**wriggle:** squirm, wangle
**wriggling:** eely [twist
**wring:** extract, wrest,
**wrinkled:** rugate
**wrinkles:** creases, rugas, rugae, crimp, rimples, crinkles, crimps, fold
**wrist:** carpus
**write:** transcribe, pen, indite, compose, inscribe, scribe
" **carelessly:** scrawl
**writer:** author, scribe, penman [songster
" **of verse:** poet,
**writing instrument:** stylus
**written agreement:** cartel
" **instrument:** deed
" **promise to pay:** note [injure, err
**wrong:** amiss, faulty,
" **(prefix):** mal, mis
**wrongdoing:** sin, evil, crime
**wrongful act:** tort
**wrongs:** mala
**wroth:** irate [Teton
**Wyoming Mt.:** Moran.

## Y

**Yale:** Eli
**yam:** uve, ube
**yank:** jerk
**yap:** yelp
**yarn:** tale, clew, crewel
**yawn:** gape
**year:** annum
" **'s record:** annal
**yearbook:** almanac
**yearn:** long, desire, pant, pine [ferment
**yeast:** leaven, froth,
" **(brewing):** barm
**yell:** shout, roar
**yellow bugle:** iva
" **gray color:** drab
" **ocher:** sil
**yelp:** yap, yip
**yeoman:** freeholder
**yes:** yea, ay, aye [still
**yet:** besides, though, but, while, however,
**yield:** obey, cede, return, bow, succumb, net, concede, relent, submit, produce, give
**yielding:** soft
**yogi:** fakir, ascetic
**yoke:** servitude, link, team, couple, join
" **of beasts:** span
**yonder (poet.):** yon [ye
**you (arch.):** thee, thou,
**young:** juvenile
" **of animals:** brood
" **antelope:** kid
" **bird:** nestling
" " **of prey:** eaglet
" **bluefish:** snapper
" **branch:** shoot
" **cat:** kitten, kit
" **chicken:** fryer
" **child:** tad
" **cod:** scrod
" **deer:** fawn
" **dog:** pup
" **eel:** elver
" **fish:** fry
" **fowl:** bird
" **fox:** cub
" **frog:** tadpole
" **goat:** kid
" **hare:** leveret
" **hawk:** eyas [en
" **hen:** pullet, chick-
" **herring:** brit
" **hog:** shoat, shote
" **horse:** colt, foal
" **lady:** belle
" **lion:** lionet
" **man (Scot.):** laddy
" **onion:** scallion
" **owl:** owlet
" **oyster:** spat
" **pig:** shote, shoat
" **plant:** seedling
" **rowdy:** hoodlum
" **salmon:** parr
" **screen star:** starlet
" **seal:** pup
" **sheep:** lamb
" **swan:** cygnet
" **swine:** pig
**younger:** tot, junior
**youngster:** lad, tot, tad, shaver
**your (arch.):** thy
**yours (arch.):** thine
**youth:** lad, stripling, boyhood [nile
**youthful:** young, juve-
**Yugoslav:** Serb
" **coin:** dinar
" **leader:** Tito

## Z

**Z (English form):** zed
**zeal:** ardor, elan, fervor, interest [siast
**zealot:** fanatic, enthu-
**zealous:** ardent, earnest
**zenith:** top, meridian, acme [cipher, nought
**zero:** nothing, naught,
**zest:** spice
**zesty:** piquant
**Zeus brother:** Hades
" **first wife:** Metis
" **love:** Io
" **mother:** Rhea
" **sister:** Hera [Argus
" **son:** Ares, Hermes,
" **'s wife:** Hera
**Zodiac's sign:** Aries, Leo, Libra, Virgo
" **2nd sign:** Taurus
" **3rd sign:** Gemini
" **5th sign:** Leo
**Zola's novel:** Nana
**zone:** belt, area, region, engirdle, girdle
**zoroastrian bible:** avesta

## Miscellaneous

**1/6 drachma:** obol
**1/8 mile:** furlong [meter
**1/10 of a meter:** deci-
**1/12 inch:** en
**1/16 of an ounce:** dram
" " **a yard:** nail
**.025 acre:** are
**1 kiloliter:** stere
**2:** twain
" **ens:** em
" **quarts:** flagon
**3 miles:** league
**4 inches:** hand
" **rods:** acre
**5 centimes:** sou [pent
" **(comb. form):** tent,
**6 (prefix):** hex
**9 inches:** span
**10:** X
**12:** dozen
" **dozen:** gross
**16 annas:** rupee
**16-1/2 feet:** rod
**20:** score
" **cwt.:** ton
" **quires:** ream
" **year sleeper:** rip
**39.37 inches:** meter
**40:** XL
**49:** IL
**50:** L
**51:** LI
**55:** LV
**60 grains:** dram
**90:** XC
**99:** IC
**100:** C
" **cubic feet:** ton
" **make a yen:** sen
" **sen:** yen [are
" **square meters:** ar,
**110:** CX
**120 yards of silk:** lea
**144 units:** gross
**150:** CL
**160 Square rods:** acre
**200 milligrams:** carat
**220 yards:** furlong
**300 yards of linen:** lea
**320 rods:** mile
**433d asteroid:** Eros
**451:** LDI
**480 sheets:** ream
**501:** DI
**550:** DL
**600:** DC
**900:** CM
**1000:** M
" **sq. meters:** decare
**1001:** MI
**1050:** ML
**1100:** MC
**1196 sq. yds.:** are, ar
**1760 yds:** mile
**2000:** MM
" **lbs.:** ton
**4047 sq. meters:** acre
**4840 sq. yds.:** acre
**3.1416:** pi
**1,000,000 rupees:** lac

# NOTES

# NOTES

# NOTES

# NOTES

# NOTES

# NOTES

# NOTES

# NOTES

# NOTES

# NOTES